The Best Books for Academic Libraries

The Best Books for Academic Libraries
10 Volumes (ISBN 0-7222-0014-5)

Volume 1 — Science, Technology, and Agriculture
(ISBN 0-7222-0011-0)
Q   Science
S   Agriculture
T   Technology, Engineering

Volume 2 — Medicine
(ISBN 0-7222-0012-9)
BF   Psychology
R   Medicine
RM-RS   Therapeutics
RT   Nursing

Volume 3 — Language and Literature
(ISBN 0-7222-0013-7)
P   Language and Literature
PA   Classical Language and Literature
PB-PH   Modern European Languages and Slavic
           Languages and Literature
PJ-PL   Oriental Language and Literature
PN   Literature: General and Comparative
PQ   Romance Literatures
PR   English Literature
PS   American Literature
PT   German, Dutch and Scandinavian Literature
PZ   Juvenile Literature

Volume 4 — History of the Americas
(ISBN 0-7222-0014-5)
E   America
E151-E970   United States
F1-975   US Local History
F1001-3799 Canada, Latin America

Volume 5 — World History
(ISBN 0-7222-0015-3)
C   Auxiliary Sciences of History
D   History

Volume 6 — Social Sciences
(ISBN 0-7222-0016-1)
G-GF   Geography, Oceanography, Human Ecology
GN   Anthropology, Ethnology, Archaeology
GR-GT   Folklore, Customs, Costumes
GV   Recreation, Physical Training, Sports
H-HA   Social Sciences. General Statistics
HB-HJ   Economics, Population
HM-HV   Sociology, Social History, Social Pathology
HX   Socialism, Communism, Anarchism

Volume 7 — Political Science, Law, Education
(ISBN 0-7222-0017-X)
J   Political Science
L   Education
K   Law

Volume 8 — Religion and Philosophy
(ISBN 0-7222-0018-8)
B-BJ   Philosophy
BL-BX   Religion

Volume 9 — Music & Fine Arts
(ISBN 0-7222-0019-6)
ML, MT Music
N-NX   Fine Arts

Volume 10 — General Works, Military & Naval,
Library Science Author Index, Title Index,
Subject Guide
(ISBN 0-7222-0020-X)
A   General Works
U   Military Science
V   Naval Science
Z   Bibliography, Library Science
           Author and Title Indexes
           Subject Guide

The Best Books for Academic Libraries

Social Sciences

Volume 6

First Edition

The Best Books, Inc.
P. O. Box 893520
Temecula, CA. 92589-3520

Copyright © 2003
by
The Best Books, Inc.

Printed in the United States of America

ISBN 0-7222-0010-2 (10 Volume Set)
ISBN 0-7222-0016-1 (Volume 6)

```
Library of Congress Cataloging-in-Publication Data

The best books for academic libraries.-- 1st ed.
     v. cm.
Includes indexes.
Contents: v. 1. Science, technology, and agriculture -- v. 2. Medicine
-- v. 3. Language and literature -- v. 4. History of the Americas -- v.
5. World history -- v. 6. Social sciences -- v. 7. Political science,
law, education - v. 8. Religion and philosophy -- v. 9. Music & fine
arts -- v. 10. General works, military & naval, library science.
    ISBN 0-7222-0020-21-0.(set : alk. paper) -- ISBN 0-7222-0011-0 (v. 1 :
alk. paper. ISBN 0-7222-0012-9 (v. 2 : alk. paper) -- ISBN 0-7222-
0013-7 (v.3 : alk. paper) -- ISBN 0-7222-0014-5 (v. 4 : alk.
paper) -- ISBN 0-7222-0015-3 (v. 5 : alk. paper) ISBN 0-7222-0016-1
(v. 6 : alk. paper) -- ISBN 0-7222-0017-X (v. 7 : alk. paper) -- ISBN
0-7222-0018-8 (v. 8 : alk. paper) -- ISBN 0-7222-0019-6 (v. 9 : alk.
paper) -- ISBN 0-7222-0020-X (v. 10 : alk. paper).
    1.  Academic libraries--United States--Book lists.  I.  Best Books,
Inc.

Z1035 .B545 2002
011'.67—dc21   2002013790
```

For further information, contact:

The Best Books, Inc.
P.O. Box 893520
Temecula, CA 92589-3520
(Voice) 888-265-3531
(Fax) 888-265-3540

For product information/customer service, e-mail: customerservice@thebbooks.net

Visit our Web site: www.bestbooksfor.com

Table of Contents

vii

xi

Introduction

ABOUT THE PROJECT:

The Best Books for Academic Libraries was created to fill a need that has been growing in collection development for undergraduate and college libraries since the late 1980's. Our editorial department organized *The Best Books Database* (designed as a resource for university libraries) by consulting the leading book review journals, bibliographies, and reference books with subject bibliographies. It was compiled based upon the bibliographic standard from the Library of Congress (LC) MARC records. Each section was arranged by Library of Congress Classification Numbers.

PROCESSES FOR SUBJECT SELECTION AND COMPILATION:

To create *The Best Books for Academic Libraries,* the Editor conducted a comprehensive search of prominent Subject Librarians and Subject Specialists, experts in their area(s), to participate as Subject Advisors. The editorial processes utilized by The Best Books editorial staff are as follows:

1. Subject Advisors were asked to select the best books recommended for undergraduate and college libraries. Those who volunteered selected approximately one-third from over 170,000 books in *The Best Books Database* that they felt were essential to undergraduate work in their area(s) of expertise. Each Subject Advisor made their selections from subject surveys that were arranged by LC Classification Number. They added their choices of titles that were omitted from the surveys, and updated titles to the latest editions.

2. The Best Books editorial staff tabulated the returned surveys, and added the omissions into the database, following the LC MARC record standard, to arrive at a consensus of approximately the best 80,000 books.

3. Senior Subject Advisors were selected to conduct a final review of the surveys. They added any other titles they felt were essential to undergraduate work in their area(s) of expertise.

4. The final results were tabulated to create the First Edition of the 10 Volume set – *The Best Books for Academic Libraries.*

The actual title selection was left to the Subject Advisors. Each Advisor used the bibliographic resources available to them in their subject areas to make the best possible recommendations for undergraduate and college libraries. In order to achieve results that were well rounded, two to three Subject Advisors reviewed each section.

When there were discrepancies in the LC sorting and/or the description of any titles, The Best Books editorial staff defaulted to the information available on the LC MARC records.

The intention of this project, and The Best Books editorial staff, was to include only books in this listing. However, other titles may have been included, based upon recommendations by Subject Advisors and Senior Subject Advisors. In some cases, the Advisors did select annual reviews and multi-volume sets for inclusion in this work.

The editorial department has made every attempt to list the most recent publications for each title in this work. In the interest of maintaining a current core-collection bibliographic list, our Advisors were asked to note the most recent publications available, especially with regards to series and publishers that regularly produce new editions. Books were listed as the original edition (or latest reprint) when no information of a recent publication was available.

ARRANGEMENT BY LC CLASSIFICATION SCHEDULE:

Each section of this work was arranged by Library of Congress Classification Numbers (LCCN), using the Library of Congress Classification Schedule for ready reference. For the purposes of this project, we have organized a system of varying font sizes and the incorporation of Em-dashes (—) to identify whether the subject headings herein are **primary** (Main Class), **secondary** (Sub-Class), or **tertiary** (Sub-Sub-Class) in the LC Classification Schedule outline. The primary heading is presented in 14 point Times New Roman, the secondary in 12 point, and the tertiary in 10 point. This distinction can be viewed in the examples that follow:

Primary Classification:
(14 Point Times New Roman)

P49 Addresses, essays, lectures

P49.J35 1985
Jakobson, Roman,
Verbal art, verbal sign, verbal time / Roman Jakobson ; Krystyna Pomorska and Stephen Rudy, editors ; with the assistance of Brent Vine. Minneapolis : University of Minnesota Press, c1985. xiv, 208 p. :
84-007268 808/.00141 0816613583
Philology. Semiotics. Space and time in language.

Secondary Classification:
(12 Point Times New Roman)

P51 Study and teaching. Research — General

P51.L39 1998
Learning foreign and second languages : perspectives in research and scholarship / edited by Heidi Byrnes. New York : Modern Language Association of America, 1998. viii, 322 p.
98-039497 418/.007 087352800X
Language and languages -- Study and teaching. Second language acquisition.

Tertiary Classification:
(10 Point Times New Roman)

P92 Communication. Mass media — By region or country — Individual regions or countries, A-Z

P92.C5.C52 2000
Chinese perspectives in rhetoric and communication / edited by D. Ray Heisey. Stamford, Conn. : Ablex Pub. Corp., 2000. xx, 297 p. ;
99-053426 302.2/0951 1567504949
Communication and culture -- China. Rhetoric -- Political aspects -- China.

ERRORS, LACUNAE, AND OMISSIONS:

The Subject Advisors and Senior Subject Advisors were the sole source for recommending titles to include in the completed work, and no titles were intentionally added or omitted other than those that the Subject Advisors and Senior Subject Advisors recommended. There is no expressed or implied warranty or guarantee on this product.

The Best Books editorial department requests that any suggestions or errors be sent, via e-mail or regular mail, to be corrected in future editions of this project.

BEST BOOKS EDITORIAL STAFF:

This work is the ongoing product and group effort of a number of enthusiastic individuals: The Best Books editorial staff includes: Assistant Editor, Annette Wiles; Database Administrator, Richelle Tague; and Editor, Ashley Ludwig.

CONTRIBUTING ADVISORS:

This volume would not be possible without the dedicated work of our Subject Advisors and Senior Subject Advisors who donated their time, resources and knowledge towards creating this Best Books list. To them, we are truly grateful. *(Denotes Senior Subject Advisors for *Volume 6 – Social Sciences*).

SUBJECT ADVISORS:

Chris Africa, *History and Social Sciences Bibliographer, University of Iowa Libraries*
Subject Advisor for: G-GF – Geography, Oceanography, Human Ecology, GN – Anthropology, Ethnology, Archaeology, H – Sociology, HM, HN – Sociology, Social History, Social Pathology, HX – Socialism, Communism, Anarchism.

Kelly Blessinger, *Geographic Information Systems Librarian, Louisiana State University Libraries*
Subject Advisor for: H-HA – Social Sciences, General Statistics, HB-HJ – Economics, Population.

Peggy Chalaron, *Head, Education Resources Library, Louisiana State University Libraries*
Subject Advisor for: GV – Recreation, Physical Training, Sports

Susan Hurst, *Business Librarian, King Library, University of Ohio*
Subject Advisor for: HB-HJ – Economics, Population.

Donald C. Johnson, *South Asia Bibliographer, University of Minnesota Libraries - Twin Cities, Ames Library*
Subject Advisor for: HC – Economic Development, HQ – Women's Studies.

Deborah Lee, *Reference Librarian/Outreach liaison for Business, Mississippi State University Libraries*
Subject Advisor for: G-GF – Geography, Oceanography, Human Ecology, GN – Anthropology, Ethnology, Archaeology, HB-HJ – Economics, Population.

Nancy Noe, *Women's Studies Liaison, Auburn University Library, Auburn University*
Subject Advisor for: HQ – Women's Studies.

Jenny Presnell, *Information Services Librarian, Women's Studies Bibliographer, Miami University, Ohio*
Subject Advisor for: HC – Economic Development, HQ – Women's Studies.

Karen Reiman-Sendi, *Head, Reference Department, Central Connecticut State University*
Subject Advisor for: HV – Social Work, Social Welfare.

Fred Stoss, *Sciences Librarian, Arts & Sciences Library, University at Buffalo, SUNY*
Subject Advisor for: GE – Environment, GF – Ecology.

Suzanne Wise, *Bibliographer for Health, Leisure & Exercise, Carol G. Belk Library, Appalachian State University*
Subject Advisor for: GV – Recreation, Physical Training, Sports.

SENIOR SUBJECT ADVISORS:

Chris Africa,* *History and Social Sciences Bibliographer, University of Iowa Libraries.* Chris Africa earned her Bachelor of Arts degree in history at Smith College, and her Ph.D. in History at the State University of New York at Binghamton. She subsequently earned her Masters of Library Science from the State University of New York at Albany. She was previously employed as a Reference Librarian at Miami University at Oxford, Ohio. Africa is currently serving as the History and Social Sciences Bibliographer at the University of Iowa Libraries in Iowa City.

Deborah Lee,*Reference Librarian/Outreach liaison for Business, Mississippi State University Libraries.* Deborah Lee earned her Masters in Library and Information Science from the University of North Carolina, Chapel Hill, where she also earned her Bachelors & Masters Degrees in Political Science. Her professional career includes serving as the Acquisitions Librarian and Coordinator of Serials at Mississippi State University Libraries, and Collection Development Librarian at Millsaps College Library. Her other professional duties have included teaching courses in Economics, Library Science, and Political Science. Lee's areas of research include both Economics and Library Science. She has completed over 30 book reviews for *Choice, Journal of Business & Finance Librarianship, Journal of Academic Librarianship,* and *Mississippi Libraries.* Lee has refereed research in Economics and Library Science; she has also contributed to professional articles for such publications as *Mississippi Libraries* and the *LITA Newsletter.* In 2001, her presentations included the Southern Economic Association Annual Meeting, Academy of Economics and Finance Meeting, and the Society of Business, Industry and Economics. She has also made many presentations in the area of Library Science, including the Mississippi Library Association, the American Library Association, and the Going Global: Teaching International Relations for the 21st Century Conference.

Karen Reiman-Sendi,* *Social Work Librarian and Manager, Harlan Hatcher Graduate Library, University of Michigan.* Karen received her B.A. degree in German Language and Literature from the University of Toledo. Following completion of her Master's degree in Library and Information Studies at the University of Michigan, she returned to the University of Toledo where she held various positions, from CD-ROM Coordinator and reference librarian to Head of Reference Services to Acting Coordinator of Library Automation and Associate Professor. Currently, she serves as the Social Work Librarian and Manager for the Harlan Hatcher Graduate Library. Ms. Sendi has contributed to her profession through many publications including *Choice, CD-ROM Librarian, Collection Building, Library Hi-Tech, & Library Journal.* She has given presentations for the American Library Association, ALA-Ohio, ACRL, University of Ohio – Toledo, the Ohio Genealogical Society, and Michigan State University.

G1-875 Geography (General)

G1 Serials

G1.N27 Suppl. 2
National geographic index, 1888-1988. [Washington, D.C.]: National Geographic Society, 1989. 1215 p.
88-033086   910/.5   0870447645
Geography -- Periodicals -- Indexes.

G3 Societies — United States

G3.A56.W7
Wright, John Kirtland, 1891-1969.
Geography in the making; the American Geographical Society, 1851-1951. Foreword by Richard Upjohn Light. New York, Published by the Society, 1952. xxi, 437 p.
52-011527   910.6273
American Geographical Society of New York.

G63 Dictionaries. Encyclopedias

G63.E5213 1995
World geographical encyclopedia/ [Sybil P. Parker, editor]. New York: McGraw-Hill, c1995. 5 v.
94-029086   910/.3   0079114962
Geography -- Encyclopedias.

G63.H68 1997
The Houghton Mifflin dictionary of geography: places and peoples of the world. Boston; New York: 1997. 458 p.
97-010624   910/.3 21   0395864488
Geography -- Dictionaries.

G63.M39 1997
Mayhew, Susan.
A dictionary of geography/ Susan Mayhew. Oxford [England]; Oxford University Press, 1997. 460 p.
96-052361   910/.3   0192800345
Geography -- Dictionaries.

G63.M57 1991
Modern geography: an encyclopedic survey/ edited by Gary S. Dunbar. New York: Garland, 1991. xx, 219 p.
90-003742   910/.3   0824053435
Geography -- Dictionaries.

G63.W67 2001
Worldmark encyclopedia of the nations. Detroit: Gale Group, c2001. 6 v.
2001-276540   0787605115
History -- Encyclopedias. Economics -- Encyclopedias. Political science -- Encyclopedias.

G67 Geographers — Biography — Collective

G67.L37 1993
Larkin, Robert P.
Biographical dictionary of geography/ Robert P. Larkin and Gary L. Peters. Westport, Conn.: Greenwood Press, 1993. xii, 361 p.
92-018364   910.922   0313276226
Geographers -- Biography -- Dictionaries.

G69 Geographers — Biography — Individual, A-Z

G69.S49.L58 1987
Livingstone, David N., 1953-
Nathaniel Southgate Shaler and the culture of American science/ David N. Livingstone. Tuscaloosa: University of Alabama Press, c1987. xiv, 395 p.
85-028982   910/.924   0817303057
Shaler, Nathaniel Southgate, -- 1841-1906. Geographers -- United States -- Biography.

G70 Philosophy. Relation to other topics. Methodology — General works

G70.D75 2001
Driver, Felix.
Geography militant: cultures of exploration and empire/ Felix Driver. Oxford, UK; Blackwell Publishers, 2001. viii, 258 p.
00-025855   910/.941/09034   0631201114
Geography -- Philosophy. Geography -- Great Britain -- History -- 19th century. Explorers -- Great Britain -- History -- 19th century.

G70.G446 1992
Geography's inner worlds: pervasive themes in contemporary American geography/ edited by Ronald F. Abler, Melvin G. Marcus, and Judy M. Olson. New Brunswick, N.J.: Rutgers University Press, c1992. xxiii, 412 p.
91-043478   910/.01   0813518296
Geography -- philosophy. Geography -- United States.

G70.G72 1994
Gregory, Derek, 1951-
Geographical imaginations/ Derek Gregory. Cambridge, MA: Blackwell, c1994. xii, 442 p.
93-009601   910/.01   0631183299
Geography -- Philosophy.

G70.H22 1990
Haggett, Peter.
The geographer's art/ Peter Haggett. Oxford, OX, UK; B. Blackwell, 1990. xviii, 219 p.
89-028937   910/.01   0631171444
Geography -- Philosophy.

G70.H32
Hartshorne, Richard, 1899-
Perspective on the nature of geography/ Richard Hartshorne. Chicago, Ill.: Published for the Association of American Geogra c1959. 201 p.
59-007032   910   0892910801
Geography.

G70.S62 1989
Soja, Edward W.
Postmodern geographies: the reassertion of space in critical social theory/ Edward W. Soja. London; Verso, 1989. 266 p.
88-020578   910/.01   0860912256
Geography -- Philosophy.

G70.2 Philosophy. Relation to other topics. Methodology — Special methods — Data processing

G70.2.B66 1994
Bonham-Carter, Graeme.
Geographic information systems for geoscientists: modelling with GIS/ Graeme F. Bonham-Carter. Oxford; Pergamon, 1994. xvii, 398 p.
94-028315   910/.285   0080418678
Geographic information systems.

G70.2.G432 2000
GeoComputation/ edited by Stan Openshaw and Robert J. Abrahart. London; Taylor & Francis, 2000. xii, 413 p.
99-029605   910/.285   0748409009
Information storage and retrieval systems -- Geography. Geographic information systems.

G70.2.G45 1990
Geographic information systems: developments & applications/ edited by Les Worrall London; Belhaven Press, 1990. 251 p.
90-044434   910/.285   185293140X
Geographic information systems.

G70.2.M354 1991
Geographical information systems: principles and applications/ edited by David J. Maguire, Michael F. Goodchild, and David W. Rhind. Harlow, Essex, England: Longman Scientific & Technical; 1991. 2 v.
91-003724   910/.285   0582056616
Geographic information systems.

G70.212 Philosophy. Relation to other topics. Methodology — Special methods — Geographic information systems

G70.212.D45 1999
Delaney, Julie, 1970-
Geographical information systems: an introduction/ Julie Delaney. Melbourne; Oxford University Press, c1999. xxii, 194 p.
00-711153   910/.285 21   0195507894
Geographic information systems. Geographic information systems -- Computer programs. Geographic information systems -- Computer programs.

G70.212.I57 1997
Integration of geographic information systems and remote sensing/ edited by Jeffrey L. Star, John E. Estes, Kenneth C. McGwire. Cambridge; Cambridge University Press, 1997. xvii, 225 p.
96-014027   910/.28   0521440327
Geographic information systems. Remote sensing.

G70.212.K67 2001
Korte, George.
The GIS book/ George B. Korte. 5th ed., updated and expanded. Australia; Onword Press c2001. xi, 387 p.
00-061154   910/.285 21   0766828204
Geographic information systems.

G70.3 Philosophy.
Relation to other topics.
Methodology — Special methods
— Statistical methods

G70.3.H35 1978
Hammond, Robert.
Quantitative techniques in geography: an introduction/ by Robert Hammond and Patrick McCullagh. Oxford: Clarendon Press; 1978. xx, 364 p.
79-308406   910/.01/82   0198740662
Geography -- Statistical methods.

G70.3.P73 1996
Practical handbook of spatial statistics/ editor-in-chief, Sandra Lach Arlinghaus; specialist associate editor, Daniel A. Griffith; associate editors, William C. Arlinghaus, William D. Drake, John D. Nystuen. Boca Raton: CRC Press, c1996. xv, 307 p.
95-024710   910/.021 20   0849301327
Geography -- Statistical methods. Spatial analysis (Statistics)

G70.4-70.6 Philosophy.
Relation to other topics.
Methodology — Special methods
— Remote sensing

G70.4.C23 1996
Campbell, James B., 1944-
Introduction to remote sensing/ James B. Campell [sic]. New York: Guilford Press, c1996. xxvii, 622 p.
96-015196   621.36/78 20   1572300418
Remote sensing.

G70.4.D78 1990
Drury, S. A. 1946-
A guide to remote sensing: interpreting images of the earth/ S.A. Drury. Oxford [England]; Oxford University Press, 1990. viii, 199 p.
89-037597   621.36/78   0198544944
Remote sensing.

G70.4.G52 2000
Gibson, Paul J. 1954-
Introductory remote sensing: principles and concepts/ Paul J. Gibson; with contributions to the text by Clare H. Power; and [companion] Website development by John Keating. London; Routledge, 2000. xix, 184 p.
2001-274294   621.36/78   0415170249
Remote sensing.

G70.4.R435 1999
Rees, Gareth 1959-
The remote sensing data book/ Gareth Rees. Cambridge; Cambridge University Press, c1999. xii, 262 p.
98-030283   621.36/78 21   052148040X
Remote sensing -- Handbooks, manuals, etc. Remote sensing -- Dictionaries.

G70.4.R44 1990
Rees, Gareth 1959-
Physical principles of remote sensing/ W.G. Rees. Cambridge [England]; Cambridge University Press, 1990. xiv, 247 p.
90-001455   621.36/78   0521352134
Remote sensing.

G70.4.S36 1997
Schott, John R. 1951-
Remote sensing: the image chain approach/ John R. Schott. New York: Oxford University Press, 1997. xiv, 394 p.
95-047216   621.36/78   0195087267
Remote sensing.

G70.4.S87 1985
The surveillant science: remote sensing of the environment/ [edited by] Robert K. Holz. New York: Wiley, c1985. xvi, 413 p.
84-007508   621.36/7   047108638X
Geography -- Remote sensing. Astronautics in geographical research. Aerial photography in geography.

G70.4.T47 1989
Theory and applications of optical remote sensing/ edited by Ghassem Asrar. New York: Wiley, c1989. xiv, 734 p.
88-035182   621.36/78   0471628956
Remote sensing.

G70.4.W438 1996
Wilkie, David S., 1955-
Remote sensing imagery for natural resources monitoring: a guide for first-time users/ David S. Wilkie and John T. Finn. New York: Columbia University Press, c1996. xvii, 295 p.
95-022750   621.36/78 20   0231079281
Remote sensing.

G70.6.S93 1988
Szekielda, Karl-Heinz.
Satellite monitoring of the earth/ Karl-Heinz Szekielda. New York: Wiley, c1988. xiv, 326 p.
88-021978   621.36/78   0471613304
Remote sensing -- Equipment and supplies.

G71.5 Geographical
perception

G71.5.C68 2001
Cosgrove, Denis E.
Apollo's eye: a cartographic genealogy of the earth in the western imagination/ Denis Cosgrove. Baltimore: Johns Hopkins University Press, c2001. xiii, 331 p.
00-009623   910/.9 21   0801864917
Geographical perception. Globes.

G71.5.L48 1997
Lewis, Martin W.
The myth of continents: a critique of metageography/ Martin W. Lewis, Karen E. Wigen. Berkeley: University of California Press, c1997. xv, 344 p.
96-030294   304.2 20   0520207424
Geographical perception.

G73 Study and teaching.
Research — General works

G73.M62
Morris, John Wesley.
Methods of geographic instruction. John W. Morris, editor. Waltham, Mass., Blaisdell Pub. Co. [1968] 342 p.
68-020560   910.007
Geography -- Study and teaching.

G74 Study and teaching.
Research — General special

G74.K47
King, Leslie J.
Statistical analysis in geography [by] Leslie J. King. Englewood Cliffs, N.J., Prentice-Hall [1969] xii, 288 p.
69-015045   910/.001/82
Geography -- Statistical methods.

G80 History of geography —
General works

G80.B3 1967
Baker, John Norman Leonard.
A history of geographical discovery and exploration, by J. N. L. Baker. New York, Cooper Square Publishers, 1967. 552 p.
66-030785   910.09
Discoveries in geography.

G80.J34 1981
James, Preston Everett, 1899-
All possible worlds: a history of geographical ideas/ Preston E. James and Geoffrey J. Martin; maps and ill. by Eileen W. James. New York: Wiley, c1981. xvii, 508 p.
80-025021   910/.9   0471061212
Geography -- History.

G80.L54 1993
Livingstone, David N., 1953-
The geographical tradition: episodes in the history of a contested enterprise/ David N. Livingstone. Oxford, UK; Blackwell, 1993. viii, 434 p.
92-015681   910/.9   0631185356
Geography -- History.

G80.N43 1975
Newby, Eric.
The Rand McNally world atlas of exploration/ by Eric Newby; introd. by Sir Vivian Fuchs. Chicago: Rand McNally, c1975. 288 p.
74-027897   910/.9   0528830155
Discoveries in geography -- History. Explorers.

G80.P36 1981
Parry, J. H. 1914-
The age of reconnaissance/ J.H. Parry. Berkeley: University of California Press, c1981. vii, 365 p.
81-051175   910/.94   0520042344
Discoveries in geography. Colonization -- History.

G80.S35
Sauer, Carl Ortwin, 1889-
Northern mists [by] Carl O. Sauer. Berkeley, University of California Press [1968] 204 p.
68-016757   973.1
Discoveries in geography.

G80.S63
A Source book in geography/ edited by George
Kish. Cambridge: Harvard University Press, 1978.
xvi, 453 p.
77-025972   910/.9   0674822706
Geography -- History -- Sources.

G81 History of geography — General special

G81.W47 1998
Whitfield, Peter,
New found lands: maps in the history of
exploration/ Peter Whitfield. New York:
Routledge, c1998. viii, 200 p.
97-047767   910/.9 21   0415920264
*Discoveries in geography. Cartography --
History.*

G86 History of geography — Ancient — Modern authors

G86.N5313 1990
Nicolet, Claude, 1930-
Space, geography, and politics in the early Roman
empire/ Claude Nicolet. Ann Arbor: University of
Michigan Press, c1991. viii, 230 p.
90-048168   913.7   0472100963
*Geography -- Rome. Geography, Ancient. Rome
-- Politics and government -- 30 B.C.-68 A.D.*

G89 History of geography — Medieval to 1600/1650 — Modern writers

G89.B38
Beazley, Charles Raymond, 1868-
The dawn of modern geography. New York, P.
Smith, 1949. 3 v.
51-008933
*Discoveries (in geography) Geography --
History.*

G89.L68 2000
Lozovsky, Natalia.
The earth is our book: geographical knowledge in
the Latin West ca. 400-1000/ Natalia Lozovsky.
Ann Arbor: University of Michigan Press, c2000.
viii, 182 p.
99-050981   910 21   0472111329
Geography, Medieval.

G89.P48 1988
Phillips, J. R. S.
The medieval expansion of Europe/ J.R.S. Phillips.
Oxford, OX; Oxford University Press, 1988. x,
303 p.
87-031360   910/.9   0192192329
*Discoveries in geography. Geography, Medieval.
Europe -- Civilization.*

G89.W7 1965
Wright, John Kirtland, 1891-1969.
The geographical lore of the time of the Crusades;
a study in the history of medieval science and
tradition in Western Europe. With a new introd. by
Clarence J. Glacken. New York, Dover
Publications [1965] xxxii, 563 p.
65-012262   910.902
Geography -- History. Geography, Medieval.

G95 History of geography — Medieval to 1600/1650 — 15th-16th centuries (1420/1492 to 1600/1650)

G95.D38 1994
Dathorne, O. R., 1934-
Imagining the world: mythical belief versus reality
in global encounters/ O.R. Dathorne. Westport,
Conn.: Bergin & Garvey, 1994. x, 241 p.
93-009016   910.4   0897893646
*Discoveries in geography. Voyages and travels.
Geographical myths.*

G96 History of geography — Modern, 1600/1650- — General works

G96.S36 2001
Schulten, Susan.
The geographical imagination in America, 1880-
1950/ Susan Schulten. Chicago: University of
Chicago Press, 2001. x, 319 p.
00-010159   917   0226740552
*Geography -- History. Geography -- United
States -- History. Geography -- Social aspects --
United States. United States -- History.*

G97 History of geography — Modern, 1600/1650- — 17th-18th centuries

G97.H4
Heawood, Edward, 1863-1949.
A history of geographical discovery in the
seventeenth and eighteenth centuries, by Edward
Heawood. Cambridge [Eng.] University Press,
1912. xii, 475 p.
13-007788
Discoveries in geography.

G103 Toponymy — Gazetteers — 1871-1974

G103.L7 1962
The Columbia Lippincott gazetteer of the world.
Edited by Leon E. Seltzer with the geographical
research staff of Columbia University Press and
with the cooperation of the American Geographical
Society. With 1961 supplement. Morningside
Heights, New York, Columbia University Press
[1962] x, 2148 p.
62-004711   910.3
Geography -- Dictionaries.

G103.5 Toponymy — Gazetteers — 1975-

G103.5.C44 1990
Cambridge world gazetteer: a geographical
dictionary/ edited by David Munro. Cambridge
[England]; Cambridge University Press, [1990]
xviii, 733 p.
90-001515   910/.3 20   0521394384
Gazetteers.

G103.5.C645 1998
The Columbia gazetteer of the world/ edited by
Saul B. Cohen. New York: Columbia University
Press, c1998. 3 v.
98-071262   910/.3 21   0231110405
Gazetteers.

G103.5.O92 1999
The Oxford desk dictionary of people and places/
edited by Frank Abate. New York: Oxford
University Press, 1999. xv, 879 p.
00-041649   920.02   0195138724
Gazetteers. Biography -- Dictionaries.

G105 Toponymy — Geographic names (Universal) — By language

G105.R66 1997
Room, Adrian.
Placenames of the world: origins and meanings of
the names for over 5000 natural features, countries,
capitals, territories, cities, and historic sites/ by
Adrian Room. Jefferson, NC: McFarland, c1997.
441 p.
96-038011   910/.01/4 21   0786401729
Names, Geographical.

G116 General works, treatises, and advanced textbooks — General systematic works — 1975-

G116.C645 1996
Companion encyclopedia of geography: the
environment and humankind/ edited by Ian
Douglas, Richard Huggett, and Mike Robinson.
New York: Routledge, 1996. 1021 p.
96-006097   910   0415074177
Geography.

G116.R43 1997
Rediscovering geography: new relevance for
science and society/ Rediscovering Geography
Committee, Board on Earth Sciences and
Resources, Commission on Geosciences,
Environment, and Resources, National Research
Council. Washington, D.C.: National Academy
Press, 1997. xiv, 234 p.
97-004630   910   0309051991
Geography.

G116.U44
Ullman, Edward Louis, 1912-1976.
Geography as spatial interaction/ Edward L.
Ullman; ed. by Ronald R. Boyce; foreword by
Chauncy D. Harris. Seattle: University of
Washington Press, c1980. xix, 231 p.
79-006759   910   0295957115
Geography.

G122 General works, treatises, and advanced textbooks — Compends — 1871-1974

G122.W67
The world factbook. Detroit, Mich.: Grand River
Books, [1981-]
86-644009   910
*Political science -- Handbooks, manuals, etc.
Economic history -- 1971-1990 -- Handbooks,
manuals, etc. Economic history -- 1990- --
Handbooks, manuals, etc.*

G126 General works, treatises, and advanced textbooks — Textbooks — 1871-1970 Octavos

G126.R85 1961
Russell, Richard Joel, 1895-
Culture worlds [by] Richard Joel Russell, Fred Bowerman Kniffen [and] Evelyn Lord Pruitt. New York, Macmillan [1961] 476 p.
61-005508   910
Geography.

G128 General works, treatises, and advanced textbooks — Textbooks — 1971-

G128.G474 1995
Geographies of global change: remapping the world in the late twentieth century/ edited by R.J. Johnston, Peter J. Taylor, and Michael J. Watts. Oxford; Blackwell, 1995.
94-026900   910   063119326X
Geography.

G128.G57 1991
Global change and challenge: geography for the 1990s/ edited by Robert Bennett and Robert Estall. London; Routledge, 1991. xii, 264 p.
90-027303   910   0415001420
Geography.

G140 Great cities of the world

G140.E59 1998
Envisioning the city: six studies in urban cartography/ edited by David Buisseret. Chicago: University of Chicago Press, c1998. xiii, 181 p.
97-037158   912/.19732 21   0226079937
Cities and towns -- Maps.

G141 Historical geography

G141.P43 1997
Penn, James R.
Encyclopedia of geographical features in world history: Europe and the Americas/ James R. Penn. Santa Barbara: ABC-CLIO, c1997. xxi, 317 p.
97-024437   911 21   0874367603
Historical geography.

G141.P6
Pounds, Norman John Greville.
Political geography.   New York, McGraw-Hill [c1963] 422 p.
62-014863   911   0070505667
Political geography.

G151 Travel. Voyages and travels (General) — Traveling instructions — 1975-

G151.F75 1998
Fritze, Ronald H., 1951-
Travel legend and lore: an encyclopedia/ Ronald H. Fritze. Santa Barbara, Calif.: ABC-CLIO, c1998. xiv, 443 p.
98-045613   910.4 21   087436759X
Travel -- Encyclopedias. Travel -- Foklore -- Encyclopedias.

G151.L44 1991
Leed, Eric J.
The mind of the traveler: from Gilgamesh to global tourism/ Eric J. Leed. New York, N.Y.: Basic Books, c1991. xiii, 328 p.
90-055590   910   0465001122
Travel.

G155 Travel. Voyages and travels (General) — Travel and the state. Tourism — By region or country, A-Z

G155.A1.A75 1990
Ashworth, G. J.
The tourist-historic city/ G.J. Ashworth and J.E. Tunbridge. London; Belhaven Press, c1990. 283 p.
90-037103   338.4/791091732   1852930225
Tourism. Historic sites. Heritage tourism.

G155.A1.G49 1994
Global tourism: the next decade/ edited by William F. Theobald. Oxford [England]; Butterworth-Heinemann, 1994. xix, 406 p.
93-032527   338.4/791   0750615680
Tourism.

G155.A1.H64 2000
Holden, Andrew.
Environment and tourism/ Andrew Holden. London; Routledge , 2000.
00-038250   338.4/791   0415207177
Tourism -- Environmental aspects. Tourism -- Economic aspects. Tourism -- Social aspects.

G155.A1.H67 1989
Hosts and guests: the anthropology of tourism/ Valene L. Smith, editor. Philadelphia: University of Pennsylvania Press, c1989. xi, 341 p.
88-027795   380.1/4591   0812212800
Tourism.

G155.A1.L377 1993
Law, Christopher M.
Urban tourism: attracting visitors to large cities/ Christopher M. Law. New York, NY, USA: Mansell, 1993. xii, 189 p.
93-017220   338.4/791   0720121299
Tourist trade. Cities and towns.

G155.A1.L434 2000
Lennon, J. John.
Dark tourism/ John Lennon and Malcolm Foley. London; Continuum, 2000. vii, 184 p.
2001-270509   0826450644
Tourism. War memorials. Historic sites.

G155.A1.M388 1998
McLaren, Deborah, 1959-
Rethinking tourism and ecotravel: the paving of paradise and what you can do to stop it/ Deborah McLaren. West Hartford, Conn., USA: Kumarian Press, c1998. viii, 181 p.
97-015016   338.4/791 21   1565490665
Ecotourism.

G155.A1.M397 1993
Medlik, S.
Dictionary of travel, tourism, and hospitality/ S. Medlik. Oxford [England]; Butterworth-Heinemann, 1993. xii, 360 p.
93-231001   338.4/791   0750609532
Tourism -- Dictionaries.

G155.A1.M399 2001
Meethan, Kevin.
Tourism in global society: place, culture, consumption/ Kevin Meethan. Basingstoke, Hampshire [UK]; Palgrave, 2001. x, 214 p.
00-068214   338.4/791   0333760573
Tourism. Tourism -- Social aspects.

G155.A1.M4753 1998
Middleton, Victor T. C.
Sustainable tourism: a marketing perspective/ Victor T.C. Middleton with Rebecca Hawkins. Oxford; Butterworth-Heinemann, 1998. xiv, 266 p.
97-038506   338.4/791   0750623853
Ecotourism.

G155.A1.N37 1996
Nash, Dennison.
Anthropology of tourism/ Dennison Nash. Kidlington, Oxford: Pergamon; 1996. ix, 205 p.
96-218409   338.4/791   0080423981
Tourism.

G155.A1.N39 1991
Nature tourism: managing for the environment/ edited by Tensie Whelan; foreword by Peter A.A. Berle. Washington, D.C.: Island Press, c1991. xii, 223 p.
91-002646   338.4/791   155963037X
Ecotourism.

G155.A1.O65 1999
Orams, Mark, 1963-
Marine tourism: development, impacts and management/ Mark Orams. London; Routledge, 1999. xvi, 115 p.
98-018191   333.78   0415195721
Tourism -- Environmental aspects. Tourism -- Environmental aspects -- Case studies. Coastal zone management -- Environmental aspects.

G155.A1.T5893 1992
Tourism alternatives: potentials and problems in the development of tourism/ edited by Valene L. Smith and William R. Eadington. Philadelphia, PA: University of Pennsylvania Press, 1992. xv, 253 p.
92-010657   338.4/791   0812231481
Tourism.

G155.A1.V453 1995
Vellas, Francois.
International tourism: an economic perspective/ Francois Vellas and Lionel Becherel; foreword by Eduardo Fayor-Sola. New York: St. Martin's Press, 1995. xxv, 359 p.
95-008230   338.4/791   0312127235
Tourism.

G155.C35.W5 1997
Wilkinson, Paul F., 1948-
Tourism policy and planning: case studies from the Commonwealth Caribbean/ Paul F. Wilkinson. Elmsford, NY: Cognizant Communication Corp., c1997. x, 250 p.
97-018753   338.4/791729 21   1882345126
Tourist trade and state -- Caribbean Area.

G155.C35.W65 2001
Women at sea: travel writing and the margins of Caribbean discourse/ edited by Lizabeth Paravisini-Gebert and Ivette Romero-Cesareo. New York: Pelgrave, 2001. x, 301 p.
99-037439   917.2904/082   0312219962
Women travelers -- Caribbean Area. Travelers writings -- Caribbean Area.

G155.C96W56 2000
Williams, Allan M.
Tourism in transition: economic change in Central Europe/ Allan M. Williams and Vladimir Balaz. London; I.B. Tauris, 2000. xi, 256 p.
2001-268414   186064578X
Tourism -- Czech Republic. Tourism -- Slovakia. Tourism -- Europe, Eastern.

G155.E8.T675 1988
Tourism and economic development: Western European experiences/ edited by Allan M. Williams and Gareth Shaw. London; Belhaven Press, 1988. xi, 257 p.
88-006156   380.1/459140455   1852930098
Tourist trade -- Europe.

G155.U6.B76 1995
Brown, Dona.
Inventing New England: regional tourism in the nineteenth century/ Dona Brown. Washington: Smithsonian Institution Press, c1995. ix, 253 p.
94-023220   338.4/791740443   1560984732
Tourist trade -- New England -- History.

G155.U6.R66 1998
Rothman, Hal, 1958-
Devil's bargains: tourism in the twentieth-century American West/ Hal K. Rothman. Lawrence, Kan.: University Press of Kansas, c1998. xi, 434 p.
98-018520   338.4/791780433 21   0700609105
Tourism -- West (U.S.)

G156.5 Travel.
Voyages and travels
(General) —
Special topics, A-Z

G156.5.E26.H66 1999
Honey, Martha, 1945-
Ecotourism and sustainable development: who owns paradise?/ Martha Honey. Washington, D.C.: Island Press, c1999. x, 405 p.
98-048342   338.4/791 21   1559635819
Ecotourism. Ecotourism -- Latin America. Ecotourism -- Africa.

G161 Travel.
Voyages and travels
(General) —
Collected works (nonserial)

G161.H2 2d ser., no. 104
Quinn, David B.
The Roanoke voyages, 1584-1590; documents to illustrate the English voyages to North America under the patent granted to Walter Raleigh in 1584. London, Hakluyt Society, 1955. 2 v.
56-002460   973.17
Raleigh's Roanoke Colonies, 1584-1590. America -- Discovery and exploration -- English.

G161.H2 2nd ser., no. 174
Prutky, Remedius, 1717-1770.
Prutky's travels in Ethiopia and other countries/ translated and edited by J.H. Arrowsmith-Brown and annotated by Richard Pankhurst. London: Hakluyt Society, 1991. xxviii, 546 p.
91-220663   0904180301
Prutky, Remedius, -- 1717-1770 -- Journeys -- Ethiopia. Ethiopia -- Description and travel -- Early works to 1800.

G200 History of discoveries,
explorations, and travel —
Collective biography

G200.E88 1993
Explorers and discoverers of the world/ edited by Daniel B. Baker. Detroit: Gale Research, c1993. xli, 637 p.
92-055094   910/.92/2   0810354217
Explorers -- Biography.

G200.T55 1989
Tinling, Marion, 1904-
Women into the unknown: a sourcebook on women explorers and travelers/ Marion Tinling. New York: Greenwood Press, 1989. xxvi, 356 p.
88-018677   910/.88042   0313253285
Women explorers -- Biography.

G200.W67 1992
World explorers and discoverers/ editor, Richard E. Bohlander; consultants, John L. Allen ... [et al.]. New York: Macmillan; c1992. xi, 531 p.
91-023156   910/.922   002897445X
Explorers -- Biography -- Dictionaries.

G246 History of discoveries,
explorations, and travel —
By nationality — English

G246.B8.B7
Brodie, Fawn McKay, 1915-
The devil drives; a life of Sir Richard Burton, by Fawn M. Brodie. New York, W. W. Norton [1967] 390 p.
66-018069   910.0942
Burton, Richard Francis, -- Sir, -- 1821-1890. Explorers -- Great Britain -- Biography. Scholars -- Great Britain -- Biography.

G246.B8.C37 1990
Casada, James A.
Sir Richard F. Burton: a biobibliographical study/ James A. Casada. Boston, Mass.: G.K. Hall, 1990. xi, 187 p.
89-015340   910/.92   0816190828
Burton, Richard Francis, -- Sir, -- 1821-1890. Burton, Richard Francis, -- Sir, -- 1821-1890 -- Bibliography. Explorers -- Great Britain -- Biography. Scholars -- Great Britain -- Biography.

G246.B8.L68 1998
Lovell, Mary S.
A rage to live: a biography of Richard and Isabel Burton/ Mary S. Lovell. New York: W.W. Norton, 1998. 910 p.
98-029886   910/.92/241   0393046729
Burton, Richard Francis, -- Sir, -- 1821-1890. Burton, Richard Francis, -- Sir, -- 1821-1890 -- Marriage. Burton, Isabel, -- Lady, -- 1831-1896. Explorers -- Great Britain -- Biography. Scholars -- Great Britain -- Biography. Explorers' spouses -- Great Britain -- Biography.

G246.B8.R46 1990
Rice, Edward.
Captain Sir Richard Francis Burton: the secret agent who made the pilgrimage to Mecca, discovered the Kama Sutra, and brought the Arabian nights to the West/ Edward Rice. New York: Scribner's, c1990. xix, 522 p.
89-010898   910/.92   0684191377
Burton, Richard Francis, -- Sir, -- 1821-1890. Explorers -- Great Britain -- Biography. Scholars -- Great Britain -- Biography.

G246.C7.B38
Beaglehole, J. C.
The life of Captain James Cook. Stanford, Calif., Stanford University Press [1974] xi, 760 p.
73-087124   910/.92/4   0804708487
Cook, James, -- 1728-1779.

G246.C7.C33
Captain James Cook and his times/ edited by Robin Fisher & Hugh Johnston. Seattle: University of Washington Press, 1979. 278 p.
78-073989   910/.92/4   0295956542
Cook, James, -- 1728-1779 -- Congresses. Explorers -- England -- Biography -- Congresses.

G246.C7.M6 1966a
Moorehead, Alan, 1910-
The fatal impact; an account of the invasion of the South Pacific, 1767-1840. New York, Harper & Row [1966] xiv, 230 p.
66-011888   910.0916654
Cook, James, -- 1728-1779. Tahiti -- Discovery and exploration. Australia -- Discovery and exploration. Antarctica.

G246.V3.A7 1960
Anderson, Bern.
Surveyor of the sea; the life and voyages of Captain George Vancouver. Seattle, University of Washington Press [1960] xii, 274 p.
60-005654   923.942
Vancouver, George, -- 1757-1798.

G286 History of discoveries, explorations, and travel — By nationality — Portuguese and Spanish

G286.H5 R879 2000
Russell, P. E. 1913-
Prince Henry "the Navigator": a life/ Peter Russell. New Haven: Yale University Press, c2000. xvi, 448 p.
99-049569 946.9/02/092 B 21 0300082339
Henry, -- Infante of Portugal, -- 1394-1460. Explorers -- Portugal -- Biography. Princes -- Portugal -- Biography. Discoveries in geography.

G286.M2.N6
Nowell, Charles E.
Magellan's voyage around the world; three contemporary accounts [by] Antonio Pigafetta, Maximilian of Transylvania [and] Gaspar Correa. Evanston [Ill.] Northwestern University Press, 1962. 351 p.
62-014936 910.41
Magalhaes, Fernao de, -- d. 1521.

G296 History of discoveries, explorations, and travel — By nationality — Russian

G296.B4.F57
Fisher, Raymond Henry, 1907-
Bering's voyages: whither and why/ Raymond H. Fisher. Seattle: University of Washington Press, c1977. xiii, 217 p.
77-073307 910/.92/4 0295955627
Bering, Vitus Jonassen, -- 1681-1741.

G370 Special voyages and travels — Medieval — By explorer or traveler, or if better known, by name of ship, A-Z

G370.M2.H3634 1997
Higgins, Iain Macleod.
Writing East: the "travels" of Sir John Mandeville/ Iain Macleod Higgins. Philadelphia: University of Pennsylvania Press, c1997. ix, 335 p.
96-045601 910.4 21 0812233433
Mandeville, John, -- Sir. -- Itinerarium. Geography, Medieval. Travel, Medieval.

G400 Special voyages and travels — 1400-1520 — General works

G400.G58 1995
The global opportunity/ edited by Felipe Fernandez-Armesto. Aldershot, Great Britain; Variorum, 1995. xxiv, 326 p.
95-003136 910/.95 0860785009
Discoveries in geography -- Asian.

G420 Special voyages and travels — Modern, 1521- — Circumnavigations (Expeditions)

G420.C62.J66 1985
Joppien, Rudiger, 1946-
The art of Captain Cook's voyages/ Rudiger Joppien and Bernard Smith. New Haven: Published for the Paul Mellon Centre for Studies 1985-1988. 3 v. in 4
84-052812 910/.92/4 0300034504
Cook, James, -- 1728-1779.   Voyages around the world. Oceania in art.

G420.D7A3 1969
Drake, Francis,
The world encompassed and analogous contemporary documents concerning Sir Francis Drake's circumnavigation of the world, with an appreciation of the achievement by Richard Carnac Temple. [Editor: N. M. Penzer] New York, Cooper Square, 1969. lxv, 235 p.
78-075030 910
Voyages around the world.

G420.D7.W53 1977b
Wilson, Derek A.
The world encompassed: Francis Drake and his great voyage/ by Derek Wilson. New York: Harper & Row, c1977. xiii, 240 p.
77-003782 910/.41/0924 0060146796
Drake, Francis, -- Sir, -- 1540?-1596.   Voyages around the world.

G420.M2.J69 1992
Joyner, Tim.
Magellan/ Tim Joyner. Camden, Me.: International Marine, c1992. xviii, 365 p.
91-042835 910/.92 087742263X
Magalhaes, Fernao de, -- d. 1521.   Voyages around the world.

G420.U55.M34 1985
Magnificent voyagers: the U.S. exploring expedition, 1838-1842/ Herman J. Viola and Carolyn Margolis, editors; with the assistance of Jan S. Danis and Sharon D. Galperin. Washington, D.C.: Smithsonian Institution Press, 1985. 303 p.
85-040192 973.5/7 0874749468
United States Exploring Expedition (1838-1842)

G440 Special voyages and travels — Modern, 1521- — Tours around the world

G440.G672 1958
Cocteau, Jean, 1889-1963.
My journey round the world. Translated from the French by W.J. Strachan. London, P. Owen [1958] 175 p.
62-003012
Voyages around the world.

G463-490 Special voyages and travels — Modern, 1521- — Travels in several parts of the world

G463.B423 1953
Bell, Gertrude Lowthian, 1868-1926.
The letters of Gertrude Bell/ selected by Lady Richmond from Lady Bell's standard edition. London, Penguin Books [1953] 377 p.
54-001110
Iraq. Iraq -- Politics and government. Middle East -- Description and travel.

G463.D66
Dos Passos, John Roderigo, 1896-1970.
--Journeys between wars. New York, Harcourt, Brace and company [c1938] 394 p.
38-027270 910.4
Voyages and travels.

G464.K62
Knowles, John, 1926-
Double vision; American thoughts abroad. New York, Macmillan [1964] 210 p.
64-017600 910.4
Travel

G465.B765 2000
Brown, Christopher K. 1967-
Encyclopedia of travel literature/ Christopher K. Brown. Santa Barbara, Calif.: ABC-CLIO, c2000. x, 257 p.
00-009591 910/.2 21 0874369401
Travelers' writings -- Encyclopedias. Travel in literature -- Encyclopedias.

G465.N47 2001
Netzley, Patricia D.
Encyclopedia of women's travel and exploration/ by Patricia D. Netzley. Phoenix, Ariz.: Oryx Press, 2000. x, 259 p.
00-010720 910/.82 1573562386
Voyages and travels -- Encyclopedias. Women travelers -- Encyclopedias.

G468.S73 1984
Stafford, Barbara Maria, 1941-
Voyage into substance: art, science, nature, and the illustrated travel account, 1760-1840/ Barbara Maria Stafford. Cambridge, Mass.: MIT Press, c1984. xxiii, 645 p.
83-018802 910/.9/033 0262192233
Voyages and travels -- Pictorial works. Landscape in art. Illustration of books.

G469.W55
Wilson, Edmund, 1895-1972.
Red, black, blond, and olive; studies in four civilizations: Zu~ni, Haiti, Soviet Russia, Israel. New York, Oxford University Press, 1956. 500 p.
56-005162 910.4
Zuni Indians. Ethnic Groups Soviet Union -- Social life and customs. Israel -- Social life and customs. Haiti -- Social life and customs.

G490.I2 1929
Ibn Batuta, 1304-1377.
Travels in Asia and Africa, 1325-1354, translated and selected by H.A.R. Gibb, with an introduction and notes. London, G. Routledge & sons [1929] vii, 398 p.
29-017061
Ibn Batuta, -- 1304-1377.   Travelers -- Islamic Empire -- Biography. Voyages and travels. Africa -- Description and travel. Asia -- Description and travel.

G510 Mountaineering

G510.S69
Spectorsky, A. C. 1910-1972,
The book of the mountains, being a collection of writings about the mountains in all their aspects; with 64 pages of illus. in halftone and gravure, and many line drawings. New York, Appleton-Century-Crofts [1955] x, 492 p.
55-010908
Mountains. Mountaineering.

G515 Tropics

G515.B3
Bates, Marston, 1906-1974.
Where winter never comes: a study of man and nature in the tropics. Scribner, 1952. 1 v.
52-006464   910
Man -- Influence of environment. Tropics.

G525 Adventures, shipwrecks, buried treasures, etc. — General works

G525.D38 1996
Delgado, James P.
Ghost fleet: the sunken ships of Bikini Atoll/ James P. Delgado. Honolulu: University of Hawai'i Press, c1996. x, 204 p.
96-022635   996.8/3 20   0824818644
Shipwrecks -- Marshall Islands -- Bikini Atoll. Operation Crossroads, 1946.

G525.H827 1999
Howard, Roger, 1966-
Great escapes and rescues: an encyclopedia/ Roger Howard. Santa Barbara, Calif.: ABC-CLIO, c1999. xvii, 256 p.
99-030992   904/.7 21   1576070328
Escapes. Adventure and adventurers. Rescues.

G530 Adventures, shipwrecks, buried treasures, etc. — Individual narratives. By explorer or traveler, or if better known, by name of ship, A-Z

G530.E18.H55 1995
Hilton, George Woodman.
Eastland: legacy of the Titanic/ George W. Hilton. Stanford, Calif.: Stanford University Press, 1995. xvii, 364 p.
93-033883   977.3/11   0804722919
Shipwrecks -- Illinois -- Chicago River. Shipwrecks -- North Atlantic Ocean.

G530.G599713 1972
Graham, Robin Lee.
Dove [by] Robin Lee Graham, with Derek L. T. Gill. New York, Harper & Row [1972] 199 p.
73-181623   910/.410   006011603X
Graham, Robin Lee. Voyages around the world.

G530.H46.H463 1950
Heyerdahl, Thor.
Kon-Tiki: across the Pacific by raft. Translated by F. H. Lyon. Chicago, Rand McNally [1950] 304 p.
50-009489   910.4
Polynesians. Pacific Ocean.

G530.T6.H49 1995
Heyer, Paul, 1946-
Titanic legacy: disaster as media event and myth/ Paul Heyer. Westport, CT: Praeger, 1995. xi, 175 p.
95-022016   363.12/3/09631   0275953521
Shipwrecks -- North Atlantic Ocean. Disasters -- Press coverage.

G530.T6.L6
Lord, Walter, 1917-
A night to remember. Illustrated with photos. New York, Holt [1955] 209 p.
55-010643   910.45*
Titanic (Steamship)

G535 Adventures, shipwrecks, buried treasures, etc. — Pirates, buccaneers, etc. — Collective

G535.G28 1999
Galvin, Peter R., 1958-
Patterns of pillage: a geography of Caribbean-based piracy in Spanish America, 1536-1718/ Peter R. Galvin. New York: Peter Lang, c1999. xiv, 271 p.
97-042002   972.9 21   0820437719
Pirates -- Caribbean Area -- History.

G540 Seafaring life, ocean travel, etc. — General works

G540.A43 1999
Albee, Parker Bishop.
Letters from sea, 1882-1901: Joanna and Lincoln Colcord's seafaring childhood/ Parker Bishop Albee, Jr. Gardiner, Me.: Tilbury House Publishers/Penobscot Marine Museum c1999. xxiii, 168 p.
99-043369   910.4/5 21   0884482146
Colcord, Joanna Carver, -- 1882-1960. Colcord, Lincoln, -- 1883-1947. Seafaring life. Voyages around the world.

G540.B272 1972
Bass, George Fletcher.
A history of seafaring; based on underwater archaeology. Edited by George F. Bass. Contributors: George F. Bass [and others] New York, Walker [1972] 320 p.
72-081455   910/.45/09   0802703909
Voyages and travels -- History. Seafaring life -- History. Underwater archaeology.

G540.C685 2001
Cordingly, David.
Women sailors and sailors' women: an untold maritime history/ David Cordingly. New York: Random House, c2001. xv, 286 p.
00-062762   910.4/5 21   0375500413
Women and the sea.

G540.D2 2001
Dana, Richard Henry,
Two years before the mast: a personal narrative of life at sea/ Richard Henry Dana; introduction by Gary Kinder; notes by Duncan Hasell. 1st ed. New York: Modern Library, 2001.
2001-031243   910.4/52   0375757945
Dana, Richard Henry, 1815-1882. Voyages and travels. Seafaring life.

G540.V646
Villiers, Alan John, 1903-
Men, ships, and the sea, by Alan Villiers and other adventures on the sea. Foreword by Melville Bell Grosvenor. Washington, National Geographic Society [1962] 436 p.
62-020190   910/.45
Seafaring life. Ships -- History. Navigation -- History.

G545 Seafaring life, ocean travel, etc. — Whaling voyages

G545.F44 1979
Ferguson, Robert,
Arctic harpooner: a voyage on the schooner Abbie Bradford, 1878-1879 / by Robert Ferguson; edited by Leslie Dalrymple Stair; illustrated by Paul Quinn. Stanfordville, N.Y.: E. M. Coleman, 1979. x, 216 p.
79-022529   910/.09/16327   0930576292
Whaling -- Arctic regions.

G545.L27
Lawrence, Mary Chipman, 1827-1916.
The captain's best mate: the journal of Mary Chipman Lawrence on the whaler Addison, 1856-1860. edited by Stanton Garner. Providence, Brown University Press, 1966. 311 p.
66-019585
Whaling.

G560 Imaginary voyages

G560.F25 1993
Fausett, David.
Writing the new world: imaginary voyages and utopias of the great southern land/ David Fausett. Syracuse, N.Y.: Syracuse University Press, 1993. x, 237 p.
93-028555   809.3/9372   0815625855
Voyages, Imaginary

G580 Arctic and Antarctic regions — Polar regions — History

G580.M85 2001
Mulvaney, Kieran.
At the ends of the earth: a history of the polar regions/ Kieran Mulvaney. Washington, DC: Island Press/Shearwater Books, 2001. 286 p.
2001-001599   998   1559639083
Polar regions -- History.

G585 Arctic and Antarctic regions — Polar regions — Biography

G585.A6.A3 1987
Amundsen, Roald, 1872-1928.
The Amundsen photographs/ edited and introduced by Roland Huntford. New York: Atlantic Monthly Press, c1987. 199 p.
87-018743　919.8/04/0924　0871131714
Amundsen, Roald, -- 1872-1928.　Polar regions - - Discovery and exploration -- Slides.

G585.B3.G58 1999
Glines, Carroll V., 1920-
Bernt Balchen: polar aviator/ Carroll V. Glines. Washington, DC: Smithsonian Institution Press, c1999. x, 310 p.
99-020698　919.8/04/092 B 21　1560989068
Balchen, Bernt, -- 1899-1973.　Air pilots -- United States -- Biography. Explorers -- United States -- Biography. Arctic regions. Antarctica.

G585.B8.A33 1938
Byrd, Richard Evelyn, 1888-1957.
Alone [by] Richard E. Byrd; decorations by Richard E. Harrison. New York, G. P. Putnam's sons, 1938. ix, 296 p.
38-027911　919.9
Solitude.　Antarctica.

G587 Arctic and Antarctic regions — Polar regions — General works

G587.C48 1996
Chaturvedi, Sanjay.
The polar regions: a political geography/ Sanjay Chaturvedi. Chichester; Published in association with the Scott Polar Re 1996. xviii, 306 p.
95-044829　919.8　0471948985
Polar regions.

G587.S93 1982
Sugden, David E.
Arctic and Antarctic: a modern geographical synthesis/ David Sugden. Totowa, N.J.: Barnes & Noble, 1982. viii, 472 p.
82-013788　919.8　0389202983
Polar regions.

G606 Arctic and Antarctic regions — Arctic regions. Arctic exploration — General works

G606.H35 1987
Hall, Sam.
The fourth world: the heritage of the Arctic and its destruction/ Sam Hall. New York: Knopf, 1987. x, 240 p.
86-046121　919.8　0394559428
Arctic regions.

G606.H66 1994
Holland, Clive.
Arctic exploration and development, c. 500 B.C. to 1915: an encyclopedia/ by Clive Holland. New York: Garland Pub., 1994. xvi, 704 p.
92-042340　919.9804　0824076486
Arctic regions -- Discovery and exploration -- History -- Encyclopedias.

G608 Arctic and Antarctic regions — Arctic regions. Arctic exploration — Popular works

G608.O33 2001
Officer, Charles B.
A fabulous kingdom: the exploration of the Arctic/ Charles Officer, Jake Page. Oxford; Oxford University Press, 2001. xii, 222 p.
00-038538　919.8　0195123824
Arctic regions -- Discovery and exploration.

G626-670 Arctic and Antarctic regions — Arctic regions. Arctic exploration — History of exploration

G626.F65 1992
Fogelson, Nancy.
Arctic exploration & international relations, 1900-1932/ Nancy Fogelson. Fairbanks: University of Alaska Press, 1992. xiv, 220 p.
92-007321　919.8　0912006617
International relations.　Arctic regions -- Discovery and exploration

G630.G7
David, Robert G.
The Arctic in the British imagination, 1818-1914/ Robert G. David. Manchester; Manchester University Press; 2000. xx, 278 p.
998　0719059437
Arctic regions -- Discovery and exploration. Great Britain -- Civilization -- 19th century. Arctic regions -- Civilization -- 19th century.

G635.R6.R67 1994
Ross, M. J. 1908-
Polar pioneers: John Ross and James Clark Ross/ M.J. Ross. Montreal; McGill-Queen's University Press, c1994. xvi, 435 p.
95-170373　919.8/904　0773512349
Ross, John, -- Sir, -- 1777-1856. Ross, James Clark, -- Sir, -- 1800-1862. Explorers -- Great Britain -- Biography. Explorers -- Canada -- Biography.　Polar regions -- Discovery and exploration -- British. Northwest Passage.

G640.B47 1988
Berton, Pierre, 1920-
The Arctic grail: the quest for the North West Passage and the North Pole, 1818-1909/ by Pierre Berton. New York, NY: Viking, 1988. 672 p.
88-040063　910/.091632　0670824917
Northwest Passage -- Juvenile literature. Northwest Passage. North Pole.

G640.D45 1999
Delgado, James P.
Across the top of the world: the quest for the Northwest Passage/ James P. Delgado. New York, NY: Checkmark Books, c1999. xii, 228 p.
99-033408　910/.916327 21　0816041245
Northwest Passage -- Discovery and exploration.

G640.G7 1992
Graf, Miller, 1931-
Arctic journeys: a history of exploration for the Northwest Passage/ Miller Graf. New York: P. Lang, c1992. viii, 377 p.
91-030738　910/.91632　0820417459
Northwest Passage. Arctic regions -- Discovery and exploration.

G640.S75
Stefansson, Vilhjalmur, 1879-1962.
Northwest to fortune; the search of Western man for a commercially practical route to the Far East. Maps designed by James MacDonald. New York, Duell, Sloan and Pearce [1958] 356 p.
58-012267　919.8
Transportation -- North America.　Northwest Passage.

G665 1850 .C36 1998
Carter, Robert Randolph, 1826-
Searching for the Franklin expedition: the Arctic journal of Robert Randolph Carter/ edited by Harold B. Gill, Jr. and Joanne Young. Annapolis, Md.: Naval Institute Press, c1998. 201 p.
98-005219　919.804 21　1557503214
Carter, Robert Randolph, -- 1826- -- Diaries. Franklin, John, -- Sir, -- 1786-1847.　Northwest Passage. Arctic regions -- Discovery and exploration. Canada, Northern -- Discovery and exploration.

G670.1908.A52
Stefansson, Vilhjalmur,
The friendly Arctic; the story of five years in polar regions, by Vilhjalmur Stefansson. New ed.,with new material. New York, Macmillan, 1943. xxxvii, 812 p.
43-005284　919.8
Eskimos.

G743 Arctic and Antarctic regions — Arctic regions. Arctic exploration — Special regions

G743.F67
Freuchen, Peter, 1886-1957.
Adventures in the Arctic. Edited by Dagmar Freuchen. New York, J. Messner [1960] 383 p.
60-013801　919.8
Greenland -- Description and travel. Arctic regions.

G850 Arctic and Antarctic regions — Antarctic regions. Antarctic exploration — Voyages, By date

G850.B44 1998
Behrendt, John C., 1932-
Innocents on the ice: a memoir of Antarctic exploration, 1957/ by John C. Behrendt. Niwot, Colo: University Press of Colorado, 1998. xviii, 428 p.
98-026379　919.8/904　0870814931
Behrendt, John C., -- 1932- -- Diaries. Antarctica -- Discovery and exploration -- History. Antarctica -- Discovery and exploration -- United States -- History.

G850 1901.D68.B38 1999
Baughman, T. H., 1947-
Pilgrims on the ice: Robert Falcon Scott's first Antarctic expedition/ T.H. Baughman. Lincoln: University of Nebraska Press, c1999. xv, 334 p.
99-020685　919.8/9 21　0803212895
Scott, Robert Falcon, -- 1868-1912.　Antarctica - - Discovery and exploration.

G850 1910.A5213 1976
Amundsen, Roald, 1872-1928.
The South Pole: an account of the Norwegian Antarctic expedition in the "Fram", 1910-1912/ by Roald Amundsen; translated from the Norwegian by A. G. Chater. New York: Barnes & Noble, 1976. xxxv, 392 p.
75-041594   919.8/9   0064910661
South Pole. Antarctica.

G850.1914.S52
Shackleton, Ernst Henry, 1874-1922.
South; the story of Shackleton's last expedition, 1914-1917: by Sir Ernest Shackleton, c. v. o.: with eighty-eight illustrations and diagrams. New York, The Macmillan company, 1920. xvi, 380 p.
20-001604
Imperial trans-Antarctic expedition, 1914-1917. Antarctica.

G850 1914 .S53.A58 1998
Alexander, Caroline, 1956-
The Endurance: Shackleton's legendary Antarctic expedition/ Caroline Alexander. New York: Knopf, c1998. 211 p.
98-087214   919.8/904 21   0375404031
Shackleton, Ernest Henry, -- Sir, -- 1874-1922 -- Journeys.

G850 1916.B43 2000
Bickel, Lennard.
Shackleton's forgotten men: the untold tragedy of the endurance epic/ Lennard Bickel. New York: Thunder's Mouth Press: 2000. xi, 241 p.
99-045483   919.804   1560252561
Mackintosh, A. L. A. -- (Aeneas Lionel Acton), -- 1879-1916 -- Journeys. Shackleton, Ernest Henry, -- Sir, -- 1874-1922.   Antarctica -- Discovery and exploration.

G850 1928.B95.R63 1990
Rodgers, Eugene.
Beyond the barrier: the story of Byrd's first expedition to Antarctica/ Eugene Rodgers. Annapolis, Md.: Naval Institute Press, c1990. xiv, 354 p.
89-028450   919.8904   087021022X
Byrd, Richard Evelyn, -- 1888-1957.

G855 Arctic and Antarctic regions — Antarctic regions. Antarctic exploration — Dictionaries. Encyclopedias. Gazetteers. Geographic names

G855.S74 1990
Stewart, John, 1952-
Antarctica: an encyclopedia/ John Stewart; foreword by Edmund Hillary. Jefferson, N.C.: McFarland, c1990. 2 v.
89-043631   919.8/9   0899504701
Antarctica -- Dictionaries.

G860 Arctic and Antarctic regions — Antarctic regions. Antarctic exploration — General works

G860.F64 1992
Fogg, G. E. 1919-
A history of Antarctic science/ G.E. Fogg. Cambridge [England]; Cambridge University Press, 1992. xxi, 483 p.
91-048063   919.8/904   0521361133
Scientific expeditions -- Antarctica. Antarctica -- Discovery and exploration.

G860.H36 1989
Headland, Robert, 1944-
Chronological list of Antarctic expeditions and related historical events/ R.K. Headland. Cambridge [England]; Cambridge University Press, 1989. vii, 730 p.
88-037622   998.9/002/02   0521309034
Antarctica -- Discovery and exploration -- Chronology.

G860.L9
Lewis, Richard S., 1916-
A continent for science; the Antarctic adventure [by] Richard S. Lewis. New York, Viking Press [1965] xx, 300 p.
65-013204   919.9
Antarctica.

G860.W48 1998
Wheeler, Sara.
Terra incognita: travels in Antarctica/ Sara Wheeler. New York: Random House, 1998.
97-034528   919.8/904   067944078X
Antarctica -- Description and travel.

G870 Arctic and Antarctic regions — Antarctic regions. Antarctic exploration — History

G870.B26 1994
Baughman, T. H., 1947-
Before the heroes came: Antarctica in the 1890s/ T.H. Baughman. Lincoln: University of Nebraska Press, c1994. xi, 160 p.
93-001056   919.8/9   0803212283
Antarctica -- Discovery and exploration -- History.

G875 Arctic and Antarctic regions — Antarctic regions. Antarctic exploration — Biography

G875.D49.A3 1989
Dewart, Gilbert, 1932-
Antarctic comrades: an American with the Russians in Antarctica/ Gilbert Dewart. Columbus: Ohio State University Press, c1989. xi, 194 p.
89-003354   919.8/904   0814204902
Dewart, Gilbert, -- 1932-   Explorers -- United States -- Biography.

G875.M33.B53 2000
Bickel, Lennard.
Mawson's will: the greatest polar survival story ever written/ Lennard Bickel; foreword by Sir Edmund Hillary. South Royalton, Vt.: Steerforth Press, 2000. x, 261 p.
99-059210   919.89   1586420003
Mawson, Douglas, -- Sir, -- 1882-1958 -- Journeys. Antarctica -- Discovery and exloration -- Australian.

G875.S95.A3 1997
Swithinbank, Charles.
An alien in Antarctica: reflections upon forty years of exploration and research on the frozen continent/ Charles Swithinbank. Blacksburg, Va.: McDonald & Woodward Pub. Co., 1997. xviii, 214 p.
96-026746   919.8/904   0939923432
Swithinbank, Charles.   Explorers -- Great Britain -- Biography.   Antarctica -- Discovery and exploration.

G1000.2-2800 Atlases

G1000.2 Atlases of the moon, planets, etc. — Celestial atlases

G1000.2.S8 2000
Strong, Robert A., 1951-
Sky atlas 2000.0 companion/ Robert A. Strong and Roger W. Sinnott. Cambridge, Mass.: Sky Pub. Corp.; c2000. xix, 281 p.
00-030011   523.8/022/3 21   0933346956
Stars -- Atlases. Astronomy -- Charts, diagrams, etc.

G1000.2.T4 2001
Tirion, Wil.
The Cambridge star atlas/ Wil Tirion. Cambridge, UK; Cambridge University Press, 2001. vi, 90 p.
2001-622030   523.8/022/3   0521800846
Stars -- Charts, diagrams, etc. Astronomy -- Charts, diagrams, etc. Stars -- Atlases. Southern Hemisphere -- Charts, diagrams, etc. Northern Hemisphere -- Charts, diagrams, etc.

G1019-1021 World atlases — By period — Modern, 1570-

G1019.D863 2000
Duncan, Andrew.
Trouble spots: the world atlas of strategic information/ Andrew Duncan & Michael Opatowski; foreword by Francois Heisbourg. Stroud: Sutton, 2000. xii, 324 p.
2001-326088   912   0750921714
Strategy. Low-intensity conflicts (Military science)

G1019.R22
Rand McNally and Company.
Rand McNally commercial atlas and marketing guide. New York: Rand McNally, 1936-1968.
06-000009
Atlases. Transportation -- United States -- Maps. Communication -- United States -- Maps. United States -- Maps. United States -- Economic conditions -- Statistics -- Periodicals. United States -- Economic conditions -- Maps.

G1021.A7545 2000
Atlas of the world/ [cartography by Philip's]. New York: Oxford University Press c2000. xxiv, 304 p.
2001-622005   912 21   0195216849
Atlases.

G1021.G417 2000
George Philip & Son.
Encyclopedic world atlas/ [cartography by Philip's]. New York: Oxford University Press, c2000. 280 p.
2001-622013   912 21   0195215893
Atlases. Encyclopedias and dictionaries.

G1021 .H2662 1996
Hammond Incorporated.
Hammond atlas of the 20th century. [Maplewood, NJ]: Hammond Incorporated, c1996. 239 p.
97-675540   912 20   0843711485
Atlases.

G1021 .H2665 1997
Hammond Incorporated.
Hammond atlas of the world. Maplewood, N.J.: Hammond Incorporated, 1997. 303 p.
96-027533   912   0843711752
Atlases.

G1021.M213 1999
Macmillan centennial atlas of the world. Rev. ed. New York: Macmillan Library Reference USA, 1999.
99-034651   912 21   002865370X
Atlases.

G1021.M2382 1996
The Macmillan world atlas.   New York: Macmillan, c1996. xv, 415 p.
95-034908   912 20   0028608127
Atlases.

G1021 .R15 1996
Rand McNally and Company
Rand McNally atlas: passport edition. [Skokie, Ill.]: Rand McNally, c1996. 126 p.
96-069991   912 20   0528838830
Atlases.

G1021.T55 1999
The Times atlas of the world. 2000 mini ed., 2nd ed. London: Times Books, 1999. 1 atlas (253 p.)
00-560647   912 21   0723009929
Atlases, British.

G1025 World atlases — Atlases of facsimiles — Compilation from various sources

G1025.S8 1960
Sterling Publishing Company.
Antique maps of the world in color. New York [1960]
60-000491   911
Early maps.

G1030-1038 World atlases — By subject — Historical atlases

G1030.C66 1997
The complete atlas of world history/ John Haywood ... [et. al.]. Armonk, N.Y.: Sharpe Reference, c1997. 3 v.
97-014309   911 21   1563248549
Historical geography -- Maps. World history. Atlases.

G1030.F6513 1990
Friesel, Evyatar.
Atlas of modern Jewish history/ Evyatar Friesel. New York: Oxford University Press, 1990. 159 p.
88-675689   0195053931
Jews -- Civilization -- Maps. Jews -- Migrations -- Maps. Jews -- History.

G1030.G48 1990
Gilbert, Martin, 1936-
The illustrated atlas of Jewish civilization: 4,000 years of Jewish history/ consulting editor, Martin Gilbert. New York: Macmillan, c1990. 224 p.
90-675150   909/.04924/00223   0025434152
Jews -- History. Jews -- Civilization -- Maps.

G1030.G68513 1992
The Harper atlas of world history. Rev. ed. New York: HarperCollins, 1992. xi, 355 p.
92-052538   911 20   0062700677
Historical geography -- Maps. Civilization -- History. Chronology, Historical -- Charts, diagrams, etc.

G1033.A84 1981
Atlas of the Greek and Roman world in antiquity/ Nicholas G.L. Hammond, editor-in-chief. Park Ridge, N.J.: Noyes Press, 1981. viii, 56 p.
81-675203   912/.38   081555060X
Classical geography -- Maps. Geography, Ancient -- Maps. History, Ancient. Greece -- Antiquities -- Maps. Rome -- Antiquities -- Maps. Rome -- History.

G1033.B3 2000
Barrington atlas of the Greek and Roman world/ edited by Richard J.A. Talbert, in collaboration with Roger S. Bagnall ... [et al.]; and map editors, Mary E. Downs, M. Joann McDaniel; cartographic managers, Janet E. Kelly, Jeannine M. Schonta, David F. Stong. Princeton, N.J.: Princeton University Press, 2000. xxviii, 102 maps
00-030044   912.38   069103169X
Civilization, Greco-Roman -- Maps. History, Ancient -- Maps. Greece -- Antiquities -- Maps. Greece -- History. Rome -- Antiquities -- Maps.

G1034.B413 1992
Beinart, Haim.
Atlas of medieval Jewish history/ Haim Beinart; [cartography, design, and production, Carta, Jerusalem; English translation, Moshe Shalvi]. New York: Simon & Schuster, c1992. 144 p.
92-000995   909/.04924/00223   0130506915
Jews -- History -- 70-1789 -- Maps.

G1034.R5 1990
Riley-Smith, Jonathan Simon Christopher, 1938-
The atlas of the Crusades/ Jonathan Riley-Smith. New York: Facts on File, 1991, c1990. 192 p.
90-033846   911   0816021864
Crusades -- Maps. Geography, Medieval -- Maps.

G1035 .B6 1998
Boyd, Andrew, 1920-
An atlas of world affairs/ Andrew Boyd. London; New York: 1998. 252 p.
97-022867   911   0415106702
World politics -- 1945- -- Maps. Historical geography -- Maps.

G1036.N4 1990
Nebenzahl, Kenneth, 1927-
Atlas of Columbus and the great discoveries/ by Kenneth Nebenzahl. Chicago: Rand McNally, c1990. viii, 168 p.
90-052620   970.01/5/0223   052883407X
Columbus, Christopher -- Journeys -- Maps. Discoveries in geography -- Maps. Explorers -- Maps. Voyages and travels -- Maps. North America -- Discovery and exploration -- Maps.

G1037.L55 1994
Livesey, Anthony.
The historical atlas of World War I/ Anthony Livesey; H.P. Willmott, consultant. New York: H. Holt, c1994. 192 p.
93-047649   940.4/1/0223   0805026517
World War, 1914-1918 -- Maps. World War, 1914-1918 -- Campaigns.

G1038.M37 1989
Messenger, Charles, 1941-
The chronological atlas of World War Two/ text by Charles Messenger. New York: Macmillan, c1989. 255 p.
89-002567   940.53/02/02   0025843915
World War, 1939-1945 -- Chronology. Historical geography -- Maps. World War, 1939-1945 -- Maps.

G1038.P55 1995
Pimlott, John, 1948-
The historical atlas of World War II/ John Pimlott; foreword by Alan Bullock. New York: H. Holt, 1995. 224 p.
94-039820   940.54/2/022/3   0805039295
World War, 1939-1945 -- Campaigns. World War, 1939-1945 -- Maps.

G1038.T6 1989
The Times atlas of the Second World War/ edited by John Keegan. New York: Harper & Row, c1989. 254 p.
89-045070   911   0060161787
Historical geography -- Maps. World War, 1939-1945 -- Maps.

G1046 World atlases — By subject — Other subject atlases

G1046.C2.S6 1980
Snead, Rodman E.
World atlas of geomorphic features/ Rodman E. Snead. Huntington, N.Y.: R.E. Krieger Pub. Co., c1980. ix, 301 p.
77-028009   912/1/5514   0882752723
Landforms -- Maps. Geomorphology -- Maps.

G1046.E1.P7 1989
Price, David H., 1960-
Atlas of world cultures: a geographical guide to ethnographic literature/ David H. Price. Newbury Park, Calif.: Sage Publications, c1989. 156 p.
88-675683   912/.13058   0803932405
Human geography -- Maps. Ethnic groups -- Maps. Archaeology -- Maps.

G1046.E15.P3 1988
Past worlds: the Times atlas of archaeology. Maplewood, N.J.: Hammond Incorporated, 1988. 319 p.
88-675201   912   0723003068
Archaeology -- Maps.

G1046.E27.S4 1993
Segal, Aaron.
An atlas of international migration/ Aaron Segal; cartography by Patricia M. Chalk and J. Gordon Shields. London; Hans Zell Publishers, 1993. vii, 233 p.
93-019502 304.8/022/3 1873836309
Emigration and immigration -- Maps. Forced migration -- Maps.

G1046.E4.L5 1976
Littell, Franklin Hamlin.
The Macmillan atlas history of Christianity/ by Franklin H. Littell; cartography by E. Hausman; prepared by Carta, Jerusalem. New York: Macmillan, c1976. 176 p.
75-022113 912/.1/2 0025731408
Church history. Civilization, Christian. Ecclesiastical geography -- Maps.

G1046.E51.C5 1988
Cliff, A. D.
Atlas of disease distributions: analytic approaches to epidemiological data/ Andrew D. Cliff and Peter Haggett. Oxford, UK; Basil Blackwell, 1988. xv, 300 p.
88-675321 912/.16144/2 0631131493
Cartography -- Statistical methods. Epidemiology -- Statistical methods. Epidemiology -- Mathematical models.

G1046.F1 .A5 1993
Anderson, Ewan W.
An atlas of world political flashpoints: a sourcebook of geopolitical crisis/ by Ewan W. Anderson; maps produced by Gareth Owen under the direction of Don Shewan. New York, NY: Facts on File, 1993. xiv, 243 p.
92-030193 327.1/01/0223 0816028850
Geopolitics -- Maps. Boundary disputes -- Maps. World politics -- 1985-1995 -- Maps.

G1046.J1.W6 1969
World atlas of agriculture; under the aegis of the International Association of Agricultural Economists. Monographs edited by the Committee for the World Atlas of Agriculture. Novara, Istituto Geografico De Agostini [1969-]
77-653907 912.16/3
Agriculture -- Maps. Land use -- Classification -- Maps. Agriculture.

G1046.J4 .M5 1997
United Nations Environment Programme.
World atlas of desertification/ UNEP; co-ordinating editors, Nick Middleton and David Thomas. London; Arnold; c1997. x, 182 p.
98-676256 333.73/6/0223 21 0340691662
Desertification -- Maps. Soil degradation -- Maps. Soil degradation -- Africa -- Maps.

G1046.P57.P5 1994
Pickford, Nigel.
The atlas of shipwrecks & treasure: the history, location, and treasures of ships lost at sea/ by Nigel Pickford. London; Dorling Kindersley; 1994. 200 p.
93-048856 910.4/5/03 1564585999
Shipwrecks -- Maps. Treasure-trove -- Maps.

G1106-1545 By region or country — America. Western Hemisphere — North America

G1106.E627.G8 1994
Guiley, Rosemary.
Atlas of the mysterious in North America/ Rosemary Ellen Guiley. [New York: Facts On File, [c1994] xiii, 178 p.
93-041985 398.2/097/022 0816028761
Folklore -- North America -- Maps. Folklore -- United States -- Maps.

G1115.C6313 1980
Canada gazetteer atlas. [Montreal?]: Macmillan of Canada, 1980. 164 p.
81-675339 912/.71 0770518737
Canada -- Maps.

G1116.S1.K4 1975
Kerr, Donald Gordon Grady, 1913-
A historical atlas of Canada/ D. G. G. Kerr; [cartography preparation by C. C. J. Bond; drawing by Ewan Walsh ... [et al.]. Don Mills, Ont.: T. Nelson & Sons (Canada), 1975. iii, 100 p.
77-356671 911/.71 0176004092
Atlases. Canada -- Historical geography -- Maps.

G1200.D6 1994
Doyle, Rodger Pirnie.
The atlas of contemporary America: portrait of a nation--politics, economy, environment, ethnic and religious diversity, health issues, demographic patterns, quality of life, crime, personal freedo Rodger Doyle. New York: Facts on File, c1994. 254 p.
90-675147 912.73 0816025452
United States -- Maps. United States -- Economic conditions -- 1981- United States -- Social conditions -- 1980-

G1200.M355 1990
Mattson, Catherine M.
Contemporary atlas of the United States/ Catherine M. Mattson, Mark T. Mattson; organization and editing, Yvonne Keck Holman; photography, Stephen B. Shore; text contributor, Chester Zimolzak. New York: Macmillan; c1990. vii, 118 p.
90-675182 912.73 0028972813
United States -- Social conditions -- 1980- -- Maps. United States -- Maps. United States -- Economic conditions -- 1981- -- Maps.

G1200.M4 1996
Mattson, Mark T.
Macmillan color atlas of the states/ Mark T. Mattson. New York: Macmillan Library Reference USA; c1996. 377 p.
96-010494 912.73 20 0028646592
United States -- Social conditions -- Maps. United States -- Statistics -- Maps. United States -- Maps.

G1201.C8.U55 1975
United States.
Weather atlas of the United States = originally titled Climatic atlas of the United States/ U.S. Dept. of Commerce, Environmental Science Services Administration, Environmental Data Service. Detroit: Gale Research Co., 1975. 262 p.
74-011931 912/.1/5516973 0810310481
United States -- Climate -- Maps.

G1201.E1.A4 1988
Allen, James Paul, 1936-
We the people: an atlas of America's ethnic diversity/ James Paul Allen, Eugene James Turner. New York: Macmillan, c1988. xii, 315 p.
87-028194 305.8/00973 0029014204
Ethnologie -- Etats-Unis -- Statistiques demographiques. -- ram Ethnology -- United States. Ethnology -- United States -- Maps. United States -- Population. United States -- Census, 20th, 1980. Etats-Unis -- Population. -- ram

G1201.E1.G5 1995
Fast, Timothy.
The women's atlas of the United States/ Timothy H. Fast & Cathy Carroll Fast. New York: Facts on File, c1995. 246 p.
94-029084 305.4/0973/022 0816029709
Women -- United States -- Social conditions -- Maps. Sex distribution (Demography) -- United States -- Maps. Women -- United States -- Statistics.

G1201.E1.P7 1990
Prucha, Francis Paul.
Atlas of American Indian affairs/ Francis Paul Prucha. Lincoln: University of Nebraska Press, c1990. 191 p.
90-675000 912.7 0803236891
Indians of North America -- History -- Maps. Indians of North America -- Maps. Indians of North America -- Population -- Maps.

G1201.E2.I5 1982
Infomap, Inc.
Atlas of demographics: U.S. by county: from the 1980 census. Boulder, Colo.: Infomap, c1982. 60 p.
82-083101 912/.13173 0910471002
United States -- Statistics, Vital. United States -- Population -- Maps.

G1201.E2.M3 1992
Mattson, Mark T.
Atlas of the 1990 census/ Mark T. Mattson. New York: Macmillan Publishing, c1992. 168 p.
92-024006 304.6/0973/09049 002897302X
United States -- Population -- Maps. United States -- Census, 21st, 1990 -- Maps.

G1201.E2.U45 1953 (Map Div.)
United States.
Portfolio of United States census maps, 1950. A selection of maps used in the publications of the 1950 censuses of population and agriculture. Washington, U. S. Govt. Print. Off., 1953. iv, 28 p.
53-001317
Agriculture -- United States -- Maps. United States -- Population -- Maps. United States -- Census, 17th, 1950.

G1201.E4.C3 2000
Carroll, Bret E., 1961-
The Routledge historical atlas of religion in America/ Bret E. Carroll. New York: Routledge, 2000. 144 p.
00-030007 200/.973/022 0415921317
Ecclesiastical geography -- United States -- Maps. United States -- Church history -- Maps. United States -- Religion -- Maps.

G1201.E4.N4 2001
New historical atlas of religion in America/ Edwin Scott Gaustad and Philip L. Barlow; with the special assistance of Richard W. Dishno. New York: Oxford University Press, c2001. xxiii, 435 p.
00-030001 200.973/022 21 019509168X
Ecclesiastical geography -- United States -- Maps. United States -- Church history.

G1201.E68.F6 1993
Fonseca, James W.
The atlas of American higher education/ James W. Fonseca and Alice C. Andrews; computer cartography by Peter J. LaPlaca New York: New York University Press, c1993. ix, 257 p.
93-000522 378.73/022/3 0814726100
Education, Higher -- United States -- Statistics. Education, Higher -- United States -- Maps.

G1201.F7 .A8 1993 N.C.
Atlas of historical county boundaries. John H. Long, editor; compiled by Gordon DenBoer. New York: Charles Scribner's Sons; c1998. xxii, 434 p.
98-012581 911/.756 21 0133664694
North Carolina -- Administrative and political divisions -- Maps. North Carolina -- Historical geography -- Maps. North Carolina -- History.

G1201.F7 .L5 1998
Lilley, William.
The almanac of state legislatures: changing patterns 1990-1997/ William Lilley III, Laurence J. DeFranco, Mark F. Bernstein. Washington, D.C.: Congressional Quarterly, 1998. xvii, 387 p.
98-047468 912.73 1568024347
Election districts -- United States -- Maps. Election districts -- United States -- Statistics. United States -- Statistics, Vital -- Maps. United States -- Economic conditions -- 1981- -- Maps. United States -- Social conditions -- 1980- -- Maps.

G1201.F7.M3 1993
Martis, Kenneth C.
The historical atlas of state power in Congress, 1790-1990/ Kenneth C. Martis, Gregory A. Elmes. Washington, D.C.: Congressional Quarterly, c1993. xv, 190 p.
92-046583 0871877422
Apportionment (Election law) -- United States -- Maps. Election districts -- United States -- History -- Maps. United States -- Census.

G1201.F7.P3 1978
Parsons, Stanley B.
United States congressional districts, 1788-1841/ Stanley B. Parsons, William W. Beach, Dan Hermann. Westport, Conn.: Greenwood Press, 1978. xvi, 416 p.
77-083897 328.73/07/345 0837198283
United States. Congress. House -- Election districts -- History.

G1201.F7.P353 1990
Parsons, Stanley B.
United States congressional districts, 1883-1913/ Stanley B. Parsons, Michael J. Dubin, Karen Toombs Parsons. New York: Greenwood Press, 1990. xxv, 439 p.
89-675315 328.73/07345/0223 0313264821
United States. Congress. House -- Election districts -- Maps. United States. Congress. House -- Election districts -- History. United States. Congress. House -- Election districts -- Statistics.

G1201.F9.M26 1989
Martis, Kenneth C.
The historical atlas of political parties in the United States Congress, 1789-1989/ Kenneth C. Martis, author and editor; Ruth Anderson Rowles, cartographer; Gyula Pauer, production cartographer. New York: Macmillan Pub. Co.; c1989. x, 518 p.
88-675270 912/.1324273/09 0029201705
Political parties -- United States -- History -- Maps. Election districts -- United States -- Maps. Local elections -- United States -- Maps. United States -- Politics and government. United States -- History.

G1201.F9.M3 1982
Martis, Kenneth C.
The historical atlas of United States Congressional districts, 1789-1983/ author and editor, Kenneth C. Martis; cartographer and assistant editor, Ruth Anderson Rowles; compilation draftsmen, David Durham, Brian Raber, Thomas Kokernak; research assistants, Rowland Dent ... [et al.]. New York: Free Press; c1982. xiii, 302 p.
82-070583 912/.132873/0775 0029201500
Legislation -- United States

G1201.G3.M3 1990
Mason, Robert J., 1955-
Atlas of United States environmental issues/ Robert J. Mason and Mark T. Mattson. New York: Macmillan; c1990. xi, 252 p.
90-043707 333.7/0973/022 0028972619
Nature -- Effect of human beings on -- United States -- Maps. Natural resources -- United States -- Maps. Nature conservation -- United States -- Maps.

G1201.J1 .P5 1996
Pillsbury, Richard.
Atlas of American agriculture: the American cornucopia/ Richard Pillsbury, John Florin. New York: Macmillan Pub. USA, c1996. 278 p.
95-046039 338.1/0973/022 20 002897333X
Agriculture -- United States -- Statistics -- Maps.

G1201.P2 R35
Road atlas: United States, Canada, and Mexico. [Boston, etc.] Rand McNally.
26-000019 629.281
Roads -- United States -- Maps. Roads -- Canada -- Maps. Roads -- Mexico -- Maps.

G1201.S1 .C3 1996
Carnes, Mark C. 1950-
Mapping America's past: a historical atlas/ Mark C. Carnes and John A. Garraty with Patrick Williams. New York: H. Holt, c1996. 288 p.
96-034030 911/73 20 0805049274
United States -- Historical geography -- Maps.

G1201.S1 .U5 1995
United States Military Academy.
The West Point atlas of American wars/ compiled by the Department of Military Art and Engineering, the United States Military Academy; chief editor Vincent J. Esposito; with prefactory letter by Dwight D. Eisenhower; forward by John R. Galvin. New York: Henry Holt, [1995-]
95-006753 0805033912
United States -- History, Military -- Maps.

G1201.S3.A8 1976
Atlas of early American history: the Revolutionary era, 1760-1790/ Lester J. Cappon, editor-in-chief; Barbara Bartz Petchenik, cartographic editor; John Hamilton Long, assistant editor; William B. Bedford ... [et al.], research associates; Nancy K. Morbeck, cartographic assistant; Gretchen M. Oberfranc, editorial [Princeton, N.J.]: Published for the Newberry Library and the Insti 1976. 157 p.
75-002982 911/.73
United States -- history -- maps United States -- History -- Revolution, 1775-1783. United States -- History -- Revolution, 1775-1783 -- Maps.

G1201.S3.N4 1974
Nebenzahl, Kenneth, 1927-
Atlas of the American Revolution/ map selection and commentary by Kenneth Nebenzahl; narrative text by Don Higginbotham. Chicago: Rand McNally, 1974. 218 p.
74-006976 911/.73
United States -- History -- Revolution, 1775-1783 -- Maps.

G1201.S5.A85 1994
The atlas of the Civil War/ edited by James M. McPherson. [New York]: Macmillan, c1994. 223 p.
94-016962 973.7/3/0223 0025790501
United States -- History -- Civil War, 1861-1865 -- Campaigns -- Maps.

G1254.N4E1.M6 1993
Mollenkopf, John H., 1946-
New York City in the 1980's: a social, economic, and political atlas. Simon & Schuster, [1993] 108 p.
93-025096 912.747/1 0136162932
New York (N.Y.) -- Politics and government -- Maps. New York (N.Y.) -- Social conditions -- Maps. New York (N.Y.) -- Economic conditions -- Maps.

G1281.F8.M3 1994
Martis, Kenneth C.
The historical atlas of the Congresses of the Confederate States of America, 1861-1865/ Kenneth C. Martis; Gyula Pauer, cartographer. New York: Simon & Schuster, 1994. xii, 157 p.
93-046478 973.7/022/3 0133891151
Confederate States of America -- Politics and government -- Maps. United States -- Politics and government -- Civil War, 1861-1865 -- Maps. United States -- Historical geography -- Maps.

G1281.J1.H5 1984
Hilliard, Sam Bowers.
Atlas of antebellum southern agriculture/ Sam Bowers Hilliard; cartography by Clifford P. Duplechin, Mary Lee Eggart. Baton Rouge: Louisiana State University Press, c1984. 77 p.
84-675089 912/.13381/0975 080711202X
Slavery -- Southern States -- Maps. Agriculture -- Southern States -- Maps. Southern States -- Population -- Maps.

G1380.R35 1956
Rand McNally and Company.
Pioneer atlas of the American West; containing facsimile reproductions of maps and indexes from the 1876 first edition of Rand, McNally & Co.,s business atlas of the great Mississippi Valley and Pacific slope; together with contemporary railroad maps and travel literature. Historical text Chicago [1956] 51 p.
57-000005
Railroads -- West (U.S.) -- Maps. -- cm. West (U.S.) -- Maps. -- cn.

G1381.S1.B4 1989
Beck, Warren A.
Historical atlas of the American West/ by Warren A. Beck and Ynez D. Haase. Norman: University of Oklahoma Press, c1989. xlii, 78 p.
88-040540 0806121939
West (U.S.) -- History. West (U.S.) -- Historical geography -- Maps.

G1417.L4P5 2000
Plamondon, Martin.
Lewis and Clark trail maps, a cartographic reconstruction/ Martin Plamondon II. Pullman, Wash.: Washington State University Press, [2000-] v. <1,2>
00-042857 912.78 0874222443
Cartography -- Northwestern States -- History-- Maps.

G1466.G3.O7 1985
Oregon State University.
Atlas of the Pacific Northwest/ edited by A. Jon Kimmerling and Philip L. Jackson; contributing authors, Robert E. Frenkel ... [et al.]. Corvalis, Or.: Oregon State University Press, c1985. 136 p.
86-107258 912/.13337/09795 0870714147
Natural resources -- Northwest, Pacific -- Maps. Northwest, Pacific -- Economic conditions -- Maps.

G1525.D8 1972
Durrenberger, Robert W.
Patterns on the land; geographical, historical, and political maps of California [by] Robert W. Durrenberger. 4th ed. Palo Alto, Calif., National Press Books [1972] vi, 102 p.
73-161455 912/.794 0874842077
California -- Maps. California -- Economic conditions -- Maps. California -- Historical geography -- Maps.

G1540.U5 1955 (Map Div.)
United States.
Census atlas maps of Latin America. Washington, U. S. Dept. of Commerce, 1955-
56-000310
Latin America -- Maps.

G1545.P5 1989
Pick, James B.
Atlas of Mexico/ James B. Pick, Edgar W. Butler, Elizabeth L. Lanzer. Boulder [Colo.]: Westview Press, 1989. xxi, 367 p.
88-675255 912/.72 0813376955
Mexico -- Economic conditions -- 1970- -- Maps. Mexico -- Social conditions -- 1970- -- Maps. Mexico -- Population -- Maps.

G1785-1786 By region or country — Eastern Hemisphere. Eurasia. Africa, etc. — Islamic Empire. Islamic countries

G1785.F3 1990
Boustani, Rafic.
The atlas of the Arab world: geopolitics and society/ Rafic Boustani, Philippe Fargues. New York; Facts on File, 1991. 144 p.
89-675447   0816023468
Arab countries -- Social conditions -- Maps. Arab countries -- Economic conditions -- Maps. Arab countries -- Maps.

G1786.S1.H6 1981
An historical atlas of Islam/ edited by William C. Brice under the patronage of the Encyclopaedia of Islam. Leiden: Brill, 1981. viii, 71 p.
81-212100   9004061169
Islamic countries -- Civilization -- Maps. Islamic countries -- Historical geography -- Maps.

G1786.S1R6 1957
Roolvink, Roelof.
Historical atlas of the Muslim peoples. [Compiled by R. Roolvink, with the collaboration of Saleh A. El Ali, Hussain Mones, and Mohd. Salim. With a foreword by H.A.R. Gibb] Cambridge, Harvard University Press, 1957. 81 p.
59-004149
Muslims -- History -- Maps. Muslims -- Maps. Middle East -- Maps.

G1797.2-2111 By region or country — Eastern Hemisphere. Eurasia. Africa, etc. — Europe

G1797.2.E2 1992
The Economist atlas of the new Europe. New York: H. Holt, 1992. 288 p.
92-010565 912.4 0805019820
Human geography -- Europe -- Maps. Human ecology -- Europe -- Maps. Europe -- Maps. Europe -- Economic conditions -- Maps. Europe -- Environmental conditions -- Maps.

G1797.21.E29.G58 1982
Gilbert, Martin, 1936-
The Macmillan atlas of the Holocaust/ Martin Gilbert. New York: Macmillan Pub. Co., c1982. 256 p.
81-675599 912/.1940531503924 0025433806
Holocaust, Jewish (1939-1945) -- Maps.

G1797.21.E65.M6 1999
Moretti, Franco, 1950-
Atlas of the European novel, 1800-1900/ Franco Moretti. London; Verso, 1999. xi, 206 p.
00-553474 809.3/0022/3 1859842240
European fiction -- 19th century -- Maps. Literary landmarks -- England -- London -- Maps. Literary landmarks -- France -- Paris -- Maps.

G1805.A8 1991
Atlas of British overseas expansion/ edited by A.N. Porter. New York: Simon & Schuster, c1991. x, 279 p.
91-017405 911./41 013051988X
Imperialism -- History -- Maps. Great Britain -- Historical geography -- Maps. Great Britain -- Colonies -- Maps.

G1812.21.E1.D6 1995
Dorling, Daniel.
A new social atlas of Britain/ Daniel Dorling. Chichester; J. Wiley, c1995. xxxvii, 247 p.
94-036042 912.41 0471948683
Great Britain -- Economic conditions -- Statistics -- Maps. Great Britain -- Social conditions -- Statistics -- Maps. Great Britain -- Population -- Statistics -- Maps.

G1812.21.E2.C4 1996
Champion, A. G.
The population of Britain in the 1990s: a social and economic atlas/ Tony Champion ... [et al.]. Oxford, England: Clarendon Press; 1996. ix, 155 p.
96-001647 304.6/0941/022 019874174X
Great Britain -- Social conditions -- Maps. Great Britain -- Economic conditions -- Maps. Great Britain -- Population.

G1812.21.S1.H5 1981
Historical atlas of Britain/ Malcolm Falkus, John Gillingham [general editors]. New York, N.Y.: Continuum, 1981. 223 p.
81-675330 911/.41 0826401791
Great Britain -- Historical geography -- Maps. Great Britain -- History.

G1812.21.S2.J6 1990
Jones, Barri.
An atlas of Roman Britain/ Barri Jones and David Mattingly. Cambridge, Mass.: Basil Blackwell, Inc., 1990. x, 341 p.
90-675155 912.361 0631137912
Great Britain -- History -- Roman period, 55 A.D.-449 A.D. -- Maps. Great Britain -- Antiquities, Roman -- Maps.

G1815.H36 1993
Harvey, P. D. A.
Maps in Tudor England/ P.D.A. Harvey. Chicago: University of Chicago Press, 1993. 120 p.
93-011710 526/.0942/0903 0226318788
Cartography -- England -- History. England -- Maps -- Early works to 1800 -- Facsimiles. England -- Civilization -- 16th century.

G2081.S1 .H8 1996
Hupchick, Dennis P.
A concise historical atlas of Eastern Europe/ Dennis P. Hupchick and Harold E. Cox. New York: St. Martin's Press, 1996.
96-035560 911/.47 0312158939
Europe, Eastern -- Historical geography -- Maps. Europe, Eastern -- History.

G2081.S1.M3 1993
Magocsi, Paul R.
Historical atlas of East Central Europe/ Paul Robert Magocsi; cartographic design by Geoffrey J. Matthews. Seattle; University of Washington Press, 1993. xiii, 218 p.
93-013783 911.47 0295972483
Europe, Eastern -- Historical geography -- Maps. Europe, Eastern -- History. Europe de l'Est -- Geographie historique -- Atlas.

G2110.B7 1994
Brawer, Moshe, 1919-
Atlas of Russia and the independent republics/ Moshe Brawer. New York: Simon & Schuster, c1994. 144 p.
94-021023 912.47 0130519960
Former Soviet republics -- Maps. Baltic States -- Maps.

G2111.S1.C5 1970
Chew, Allen F.
An atlas of Russian history; eleven centuries of changing borders, by Allen F. Chew. New Haven, Yale University Press, 1970. xi, 127 p.
78-653611 911.47 0300014457
Soviet Union -- Historical geography -- Maps.

G2111.S1.G52 1993
Gilbert, Martin, 1936-
Atlas of Russian history/ Martin Gilbert. New York: Oxford University Press, 1993.
93-021920 911/.47 0195210417
Soviet Union -- Historical geography -- Maps. Soviet Union -- Historical geography -- Maps.

G2201-2401 By region or country — Eastern Hemisphere. Eurasia. Africa, etc. — Asia

G2201.K3.C6 1991
The Conservation atlas of tropical forests: Asia and the Pacific/ the World Conservation Union; editors, N. Mark Collins, Jeffrey A. Sayer, Timothy C. Whitmore. New York; Simon & Schuster, c1991. 256 p.
90-675139 333.75/16/095022 013179227X
Nature -- Effect of human beings on -- Asia -- Maps. Nature -- Effect of human beings on -- Pacific Area -- Maps. Conservation of natural resources -- Asia -- Maps.

G2205.C3 1987
The Cambridge atlas of the Middle East and North Africa/ [edited by] Gerald Blake, John Dewdney, Jonathan Mitchell. Cambridge [Cambridgeshire]; Cambridge University Press, 1987. vii, 124 p.
87-006548 912/.56 0521242436
Middle East -- Economic conditions -- Maps. Middle East -- Social conditions -- Maps. Middle East -- Maps.

G2205.K33 1988
Karta (Firm)
Atlas of the Middle East/ edited by Moshe Braver; prepared by Carta, Jerusalem. New York: Macmillan Publishing Co.; c1988. 140 p.
88-675435 912/.56 0029052718
Middle East -- Maps.

G2230.A2 1993
Aharoni, Yohanan, 1919-1976.
The Macmillan Bible atlas/ Yohanan Aharoni and Michael Avi-Yonah; designed and prepared by Carta, Jerusalem. New York: Macmillan; c1993. 215 p.
92-027895 220.9/1/0223 0025006053
Bible -- Geography -- Maps.

G2230.H47 1987
The Harper atlas of the Bible/ edited by James B. Pritchard. New York: Harper & Row, c1987. 254 p.
86-675550 912/.122 0061818836
Bible -- Geography -- Maps.

G2236.S1.G52 1993
Gilbert, Martin, 1936-
Atlas of the Arab-Israeli conflict/ Martin Gilbert. New York: Oxford University Press, 1993. 1 v.
93-021921 911/.56 0195210425
Israel-Arab conflicts -- Maps. Jewish-Arab relations -- Maps. Palestine -- Historical geography -- Maps.

G2239.J4.B34 1990
Bahat, Dan.
The illustrated atlas of Jerusalem/ Dan Bahat; with Chaim T. Rubinstein; translated by Shlomo Ketko. New York: Simon & Schuster, 1990. 152 p.
90-675114 912.5694/42 0134516427
Jerusalem -- Maps.

G2261.S1.H5 1992
A Historical atlas of South Asia/ edited by Joseph E. Schwartzberg; with the collaboration of Shiva G. Bajpai ... [et al.]; final map drafts by the American Geographical Society of New York; principal sponsors, Charles Lesley Ames ... [et al.]. New York: Oxford University Press, 1992. xxxix, 376 p.
91-039119 0195068696
South Asia -- Historical geography -- Maps. South Asia -- History.

G2305.H84 1995
Hsieh, Chiao-min, 1921-
China: a provincial atlas/ Chiao-min Hsieh, Jean Kan Hsieh. New York: Macmillan Publishing Co., c1995. 303 p.
93-025436 912.51 0028971841
China -- Social conditions -- Maps. China -- Administrative and political divisions -- Maps. China -- Maps.

G2306.E2.P6 1987
The Population atlas of China/ compiled and edited by the Population Census Office of the State Council of the People's Republic of China and the Institute of Geography of the Chinese Academy of Sciences. Hong Kong; Oxford University Press, 1987. xxiv, 217 p.
87-675262 912/.13046/0951 0195840925
China -- Economic conditions -- 1976- -- Maps. China -- Social conditions -- 1976- -- Maps. China -- Population -- Statistics.

G2306.G1 .K813 1994
Kuo chia ti tu chi pien tsuan wei yuan hui (China).
The national economic atlas of China/ supported by the State Planning Committee, the Chinese Academy of Sciences, the State Statistical Bureau, and the National Bureau of Surveying and Mapping; compiled and edited by Institute of Geography, Chinese Academy of Sciences and State Planning Co Hong Kong; Oxford University Press, 1994. xvi, 314 p.
93-031441 912.43 0195857364
China -- Economic conditions -- 1976- -- Maps. China -- Social conditions -- 1976- -- Maps.

G2360.U4 1989
Ulack, Richard, 1942-
Atlas of Southeast Asia/ Richard Ulack, Gyula Pauer, with the assistance of Jane Johnshoy Domier & Julsun D. Pacheco. New York: Macmillan Pub. Co., c1989. xvii, 171 p.
88-017543 912/.59 0029332001
Asia, Southeastern -- Economic conditions -- Maps. Asia, Southeastern -- Social conditions -- Maps. Asia, Southeastern -- Maps.

G2361.S1.H5 1995
Pluvier, Jan M.
Historical atlas of South-East Asia/ by Jan M. Pluvier. Leiden; E.J. Brill, 1995. 64 p.
95-030385 911/.59 9004102388
Asia, Southeastern -- Historical geography -- Maps. Asia, Southeastern -- Maps.

G2401.S1
Cribb, R. B.
Historical atlas of Indonesia/ Robert Cribb. Honolulu: University of Hawai'i Press, 1999. x, 256 p.
99-012717 911.598 0824821114
Indonesia -- Historical geography -- Maps. Indonesia -- Maps.

G2446-2566 By region or country — Eastern Hemisphere. Eurasia. Africa, etc. — Africa

G2446.G1.A3 1965
Ady, Peter H.
Africa, prepared by P.H. Ady and the Cartographic Department of the Clarendon Press, with the assistance of A.H. Hazlewood. Oxford, Clarendon Press, 1965. 164 p.
65-000304
Africa -- Economic conditions -- 1918- -- Maps.

G2446.K3.C6 1992b
The conservation atlas of tropical forests: Africa/ editors, Jeffrey A. Sayer, Caroline S. Harcourt, N. Mark Collins; editorial assistant, Clare Billington; map editor, Mike Adam. New York; Simon & Schuster, c1992. 288 p.
91-039120 333.75/096022 0131753320
Nature -- Effect of human beings on -- Africa. Conservation of natural resources -- Africa -- Maps. Conservation of natural resources -- Africa.

G2446.S1.F73 1991
Freeman-Grenville, G. S. P.
The new atlas of African history/ G.S.P. Freeman-Grenville. New York: Simon & Schuster, c1991. 144 p.
90-047195 911/6 0136121519
Africa -- Historical geography -- Maps.

G2446.S1.H5 1985
Historical atlas of Africa/ general editors, J.F. Ade Ajayi & Michael Crowder; geographical editor, Paul Richards; linguistic editor, Elizabeth Dunstan, cartographic designer, Alick Newman. Cambridge; Cambridge University Press, 1985. 167 p.
83-675975 911/.6 0521253535
Africa -- Maps. Africa -- Historical geography -- Maps.

G2566.E625.C5 1994
Christopher, A. J.
The atlas of apartheid/ A.J. Christopher. New York; Routledge; c1994. xi, 212 p.
93-024510 305.8/00968/022 0415048095
Apartheid -- South Africa -- Maps. Anti-apartheid movements -- South Africa -- Maps. Apartheid -- South Africa.

G2800 By region or country — Oceans (General) — General

G2800.R3 1977
The Rand McNally atlas of the oceans/ [editor, Martyn Bramwell]. New York: Rand McNally, c1977. 208 p.
77-073772 912/.1/55146 0528830821
Oceanography -- Charts, diagrams, etc.

G2800.T5 1989
The Times atlas and encyclopedia of the sea/ edited by Alastair Couper. New York: Harper & Row, 1989.
89-675164 551.46/00223 0060162872
Marine resources. Shipping. Oceanography -- Charts, diagrams, etc.

G3701-9250 Maps

G3701-4361 By region or country — America. Western Hemisphere — North America

G3701.K2 1974 .U5
United States.
Forest and range ecosystems of the United States: 1974/ United States Department of Agriculture, Forest Service. [Washington]: The Service, [1974] 1 map
90-681410
Forest ecology -- United States -- Maps. Range ecology -- United States -- Maps.

G4262.Y4 1998 .U5
Yellowstone National Park, Wyoming, Idaho, Montana/ National Park Service, U.S. Department of the Interior. [Washington, D.C.]: The Service, [1998] 1 map
98-680885
Yellowstone National Park -- Maps.

G4361.C5250.R41
Regional geologic map series/ California Division of Mines and Geology. [Sacramento]: The Division,
91-001391
Geology -- California -- Maps.

G9250 By region or country — Oceans (General) — Pacific Ocean

G9250 1976.N4
New Zealand.
Islands of the South Pacific. [Wellington] 1976.
78-691553
Oceania -- Maps.

GA Mathematical Geography. Cartography

GA9 Mathematical geography — General works, treatises, and textbooks — 1801-1974

GA9.B53
Berry, Brian Joe Lobley, 1934-
Spatial analysis; a reader in statistical geography [by] Brian J. L. Berry [and] Duane F. Marble. Englewood Cliffs, N.J., Prentice-Hall [1968] xi, 512 p.
68-010856   910/.001/82
Mathematical geography. Spatial analysis (Statistics)

GA9.B56 1964
Birch, Thomas William.
Maps, topographical and statistical, by T.W. Birch. Oxford, Clarendon Press, 1964. xiv, 240 p.
65-003116   526.8
Cartography.

GA9.F85 1992
Fuller, R. Buckminster 1895-
Cosmography: a posthumous scenario for the future of humanity/ R. Buckminster Fuller; adjuvant, Kiyoshi Kuromiya. New York: Macmillan; c1992. viii, 277 p.
91-033459   113   0025418505
Cosmography.

GA9.L8 no. 1 1966
Bunge, William, 1928-
Theoretical geography, by William Bunge. Lund, Royal University of Lund, Dept. of Geography; Gl [1966] xvii, 289 p.
67-097303
Geography -- Methodology.

GA13 Mathematical geography — General works, treatises, and textbooks — 1975-

GA13.L4713 1994
Lestringant, Frank.
Mapping the Renaissance world: the geographical imagination in the age of discovery/ Frank Lestringant; translated by David Fausett; with a foreword by Stephen Greenblatt. Berkeley: University of California Press, 1994. xvii, 197 p.
93-040812   909/.5   0520088719
Thevet, Andre, -- 1502-1590.   Cosmography.

GA23 Mathematical geography — General special (Special aspects of the subject as a whole)

GA23.C46 1967
Chorley, Richard J.
Models in geography; edited by Richard J. Chorley [and] Peter Haggett. London, Methuen; distributed in the U.S.A. by Barnes & N 1967. 816 p.
68-071825   910/.001/82
Geography -- Mathematical models.

GA102.4 Cartography — Philosophy. Relation to other topics. Methodology — Special methods, A-Z

GA102.4.E4.C377 1990
Clarke, Keith C., 1955-
Analytical and computer cartography/ Keith C. Clarke. Englewood Cliffs, N.J.: Prentice Hall, c1990. xiii, 290 p.
89-071104   526/.0285   0130334812
Cartography -- Data processing.

GA102.4.R44.W55 1995
Williams, Jonathan, 1960-
Geographic information from space: processing and applications of geocoded satellite images/ Jonathan Williams. Chichester; Wiley; 1995. xii, 210 p.
95-200107   526   0471958336
Cartography -- Remote sensing. Geographic information systems.

GA105.3 Cartography — General works, treatises, and advanced textbooks — 1975-

GA105.3.M32 1995
MacEachren, Alan M., 1952-
How maps work: representation, visualization, and design/ Alan M. MacEachren. New York: Guilford Press, c1995. xiii, 513 p.
94-031138   526   0898625890
Cartography.

GA105.3.M83 1986
Muehrcke, Phillip.
Map use: reading, analysis, and interpretation/ Phillip C. Muehrcke; with Juliana O. Muehrcke. Madison, WI: JP Publications, c1986. xi, 512 p.
85-082616   912   0960297820
Maps.

GA105.3.W49 2000
Wilford, John Noble.
The mapmakers/ by John Noble Wilford. New York: A.A. Knopf, 2000. xi, 507 p.
99-049957   912/.09   0375409297
Cartography -- History.

GA105.3.W67 1987
World mapping today/ [edited by] R.B. Parry, C.R. Perkins; graphic indexes prepared by Cartographic Unit, Department of Geography, Portsmouth Polytechnic, UK. London; Butterworths, 1987. 583 p.
87-025604   025.2/86   0408028505
Maps. Maps -- Bibliography -- Catalogs.

GA108.7 Cartography — General special (Special aspects of the subject as a whole)

GA108.7.B58 1997
Black, Jeremy.
Maps and politics/ Jeremy Black. Chicago: University of Chicago Press, 1997. 188 p.
97-028355   912   0226054934
Cartography.

GA108.7.M66 1993
Monmonier, Mark S.
Mapping it out: expository cartography for the humanities and social sciences/ Mark Monmonier. Chicago: University of Chicago Press, 1993. xiii, 301 p.
92-039894   912   0226534162
Cartography. Humanities -- Graphic methods. Social sciences -- Graphic methods.

GA109.5 Cartography — Cadastral mapping

GA109.5.K35 1992
Kain, R. J. P.
The cadastral map in the service of the state: a history of property mapping/ Roger J.P. Kain and Elizabeth Baigent. Chicago: University of Chicago Press, 1992. xix, 423 p.
92-010661   333.3/022/3   0226422615
Real property -- Maps -- History.

GA110 Cartography — Projection — General works

GA110.S576 1993
Snyder, John Parr, 1926-
Flattening the earth: two thousand years of map projections/ John P. Snyder. Chicago: University of Chicago Press, c1993. xviii, 365 p.
92-036750   526/.8   0226767469
Map projection -- History.

GA125 Cartography — Topographic drawing

GA125.L37 1984
Larsgaard, Mary Lynette, 1946-
Topographic mapping of the Americas, Australia, and New Zealand/ Mary Lynette Larsgaard. Littleton, Colo.: Libraries Unlimited, 1984. xii, 180 p.
84-003874   912   0872872769
Topographic maps.   North America -- Maps, Topographic. Latin America -- Maps, Topographic. Australia -- Maps, Topographic.

GA130 Cartography — Elementary map drawing and reading

GA130.S6 1998
Sobel, David, 1949-
Mapmaking with children: sense-of-place education for the elementary years/ David Sobel. Portsmouth, NH: Heinemann, c1998. x, 164 p.
98-014641   372.89/1 21   0325000425
Map drawing.

GA193 Cartography — Collections of maps, globes, etc. Map libraries — By region or country, A-Z

GA193.G7.H58 1994
Historians' guide to early British maps: a guide to the location of pre-1900 maps of the British Isles preserved in the United Kingdom and Ireland/ general editor, Helen Wallis, assisted by Anita McConnell. London: Offices of the Royal Historical Society, 1994. ix, 465 p.
95-118489   912.41/074/41   0861931416
Map collections -- Great Britain -- Directories. Map collections -- Ireland -- Directories. Early maps.

GA193.U5.C62 1986
Cobb, David A., 1945-
Guide to U.S. map resources/ David A. Cobb, compiler. Chicago, Ill.: American Library Association, 1986. xvi, 196 p.
85-022958   026/.912/0973   0838904394
Map collections -- United States -- Directories.

GA193.U5.E37 1987
Ehrenberg, Ralph E., 1937-
Scholars' guide to Washington, D.C. for cartography and remote sensing imagery: (maps, charts, aerial photographs, satellite images, cartographic literature, and geographic information systems)/ Ralph E. Ehrenberg; preface by Alan K. Henrikson; consultants, Joseph W. Wiedel, John A. Wolter; editor, Zdenek V. David. Washington, D.C.: Smithsonian Institution Press, 1987. xx, 385 p.
86-600371   026/.912/025753   0874744067
Map collections -- Washington (D.C.) -- Directories.

GA193.U5.M36 1985
Map collections in the United States and Canada: a directory/ David K. Carrington and Richard W. Stephenson, editors. New York: Special Libraries Association, c1985. 178 p.
84-027571   026/.912/02573   0871113066
Map collections -- United States -- Directories. Map collections -- Canada -- Directories.

GA198 Cartography — Cartographers — Biography (General)

GA198.T66
Tooley, R. V. 1898-
Tooley's Dictionary of mapmakers/ compiled by Ronald Vere Tooley; with a pref. by Helen Wallis. New York: A. R. Liss,; c1979. xii, 684 p.
79-001936   526/.092/2   0845117017
Cartographers -- Biography -- Encyclopedias.

GA201 Cartography — History — General

GA201.B313 1985
Bagrow, Leo.
History of cartography/ Leo Bagrow. Chicago, Ill.: Precedent Pub.; 1985. 312 p.
85-016958   526/.09
Cartography -- History. Maps.

GA201.B47 1991
Berthon, Simon.
The Shape of the world/ [Simon Berthon, Andrew Robinson]. Chicago: Rand McNally, 1991. 192 p.
90-053291   526/.09   0528834193
Cartography -- History. Surveying -- History.

GA201.B75 1998
Brotton, Jerry.
Trading territories: mapping the early modern world/ Jerry Brotton. Ithaca, N.Y.: Cornell University Press, 1998, c1997. 208 p.
97-037603   526/.09   0801434998
Cartography -- History.

GA201.H53 1987
The History of cartography/ edited by J.B. Harley and David Woodward. Chicago: University of Chicago Press, 1987-c1994. v. 1-2; in 3.
86-006995   526/.09   0226316335
Cartography -- History.

GA201.H53 1987 vol. 2., bk. 3
Cartography in the traditional African, American, Arctic, Australian, and Pacific societies/ edited by David Woodward and G. Malcolm Lewis. Chicago: University of Chicago Press, c1998. xxi, 639 p.
98-021504   912.6 21   0226907287
Cartography -- Africa -- History. Cartography -- America -- History. Cartography -- Arctic regions - - History.

GA201.R63 1982
Robinson, Arthur Howard, 1915-
Early thematic mapping in the history of cartography/ Arthur H. Robinson. Chicago: University of Chicago Press, c1982. xiv, 266 p.
81-011516   912   0226722856
Cartography -- History.

GA201.T47 1996
Thrower, Norman Joseph William.
Maps & civilization: cartography in culture and society/ Norman J.W. Thrower. Chicago: University of Chicago Press, 1996. xiii, 326 p.
95-024656   526/.09   0226799719
Cartography -- History.

GA221-231 Cartography — History — By period

GA221.H37 1991
Harvey, P. D. A.
Medieval maps/ P.D.A. Harvey. Toronto; University of Toronto Press, 1991. 96 p.
92-165038   912/.09/02   0802028063
Early maps. Geography, Medieval -- Maps.

GA231.C36 1987
Campbell, Tony.
The earliest printed maps, 1472-1500/ by Tony Campbell. Berkeley: University of California Press, c1987. xi, 244 p.
87-038099   016.912   0520062701
Destombes, Marcel, -- 1905- -- Catalogue des cartes gravees au XVe siecle. Early maps.

GA304 Cartography — World maps, general atlases, etc. — Ancient and medieval to 1400

GA304.R5.H37 1996
Harvey, P. D. A.
Mappa mundi: the Hereford world map/ P.D.A. Harvey. Toronto; University of Toronto Press, 1996. 58 p.
96-185742   912   0802009859
Ricardus, -- de Bello, -- fl. 1276-1312. Geography, Medieval. Cartography -- History. Early maps.

GA359 Cartography — Maps. By region or country — Oceans. Seas. Marine cartography

GA359.L36 1984
Langeraar, W., 1915-
Surveying and charting of the seas/ W. Langeraar. Amsterdam; Elsevier, 1984. xvii, 612 p.
83-025286   623.89/2/0222   0444422781
Nautical charts. Cartography.

GA401 Cartography — Maps. By region or country — America. Western Hemisphere

GA401.P67 1987
Portinaro, Pierluigi.
The cartography of North America, 1500-1800/ Pierluigi Portinaro and Franco Knirsch. New York, N.Y.: Facts on File, 1987. 319 p.
87-020028   912/.7   0816015864
Cartography -- North America -- History.

GA405-408.5 Cartography — Maps. By region or country — United States

GA405.C8
Cumming, William Patterson, 1900-
The Southeast in early maps, with an annotated check list of printed and manuscript regional and local maps of southeastern North America during the colonial period. Chapel Hill, University of North Carolina Press [1962] ix, 284 p.
62-005390   526.80975
Cartography -- Southern States. Southern States -- Maps.

GA405.W5
Wheat, Carl I. 1892-1966.
Mapping the transmississippi West, 1540-1861. San Francisco, Institute of Historical Cartography, 1957-1963. 5 v. in 6.
57-059400   912.78
Cartography -- West (U.S.)

GA405.5.H37
Harley, John Brian.
Mapping the American Revolutionary War/ J. B. Harley, Barbara Bartz Petchenik, and Lawrence W. Towner. Chicago: University of Chicago Press, 1978. viii, 187 p.
77-008023   911/.73   0226316319
United States -- History -- Revolution, 1775-1783 -- Cartography -- Addresses, essays, lectures.

GA408.5.S68.M37 1987
The Mapping of the American Southwest/ edited by Dennis Reinhartz and Charles C. Colley. College Station: Texas A&M University Press, c1987. xv, 83 p.
86-022992   912/.76   0890962375
Cartography -- Southwestern States -- History -- Congresses. Southwestern States -- Maps -- Congresses. Southwestern States -- Discovery and exploration -- Congresses.

GA481-1131.3 Cartography — Maps. By region or country — Other regions or countries

GA481.M86 1996
Mundy, Barbara E.
The mapping of New Spain: indigenous cartography and the maps of the relaciones geograficas/ Barbara E. Mundy. Chicago: University of Chicago Press, c1996. xxiii, 281 p.
96-015824   912.72 20   0226550966
Cartography -- Mexico -- History. Cartography -- New Spain -- History. Indian cartography -- New Spain -- History.

GA793.5.K57 2001
Klein, Bernhard, 1963-
Maps and the writing of space in early modern England and Ireland/ Bernhard Klein. New York: St. Martin's Press, c2001. xii, 235 p.
00-033348   526/.0942/09031 21   0333779339
Cartography -- England -- History -- 16th century. Cartography -- England -- History -- 17th century. Cartography -- Ireland -- History -- 16th century.

GA863.5.A1.C66 1996
Conley, Tom.
The self-made map: cartographic writing in early modern France/ Tom Conley. Minneapolis, Minn.: University of Minnesota Press, c1996. xiii, 372 p.
96-020302   840.9/003 20   0816627002
Cartography -- France -- History -- 16th century. Maps in literature.

GA1131.E36 1997
Edney, Matthew H.
Mapping an empire: the geographical construction of British India, 1765-1843/ Matthew H. Edney. Chicago: University of Chicago Press, 1997. xv, 458 p.
96-039703   912/.54   0226184870
Cartography -- India -- History.

GA1131.3.M34 1997
Madan, P. L.
Indian cartography: a historical perspective/ P.L. Madan. New Delhi: Manohar Publishers & Distributors, 1997. 144 p.
97-904245   912.54   8173041776
Cartography -- India -- History. India -- Historical geography -- Maps. India -- Early maps -- History.

GB Physical Geography

GB3 Congresses

GB3.E54 1987
Energetics of physical environment: energetic approaches to physical geography/ edited by K.J. Gregory. Chichester; Wiley, c1987. xi, 172 p.
86-026801   910/.02   0471913588
Physical geography -- Congresses. Energy budget (Geophysics) -- Congresses. Erosion -- Congresses.

GB10 Dictionaries. Encyclopedias

GB10.D53 2000
The dictionary of physical geography/ edited by David S.G. Thomas and Andrew Goudie. Malden, MA: Blackwell Publishers, 2000. xiv, 610 p.
99-049818   910./02/03   0631204725
Physical geography -- Dictionaries.

GB10.F3
Fairbridge, Rhodes Whitmore, 1914-
The encyclopedia of geomorphology, edited by Rhodes W. Fairbridge. New York, Reinhold Book Corp. [c1968] xvi, 1295 p.
68-058342   551.4/03
Geomorphology -- Dictionaries.

GB10.H82 1988
Huber, Thomas Patrick.
Dictionary of concepts in physical geography/ Thomas P. Huber, Robert P. Larkin, and Gary L. Peters. New York: Greenwood Press, 1988. x, 291 p.
87-029582   910/.02/0321   0313253692
Physical geography -- Dictionaries.

GB11 History

GB11.E88 1993
The Evolution of geomorphology: a nation-by-nation summary of development/ edited by H.J. Walker and W.E. Grabau. Chichester; Wiley, c1993. xvi, 539 p.
92-037336   551.4/1/09   0471938580
Geomorphology -- History.

GB11.G739 2000
Gregory, K. J.
The changing nature of physical geography/ K.J. Gregory. London: Arnold; 2000. x, 368 p.
00-711764   910/.02/09   034074118X
Physical geography -- History.

GB21.5 Philosophy. Relation to other topics. Methodology — Special methods, A-Z

GB21.5.M33.C65 1987
Computer simulation in physical geography/ M.J. Kirkby ... [et al.]. Chichester [West Sussex]; J. Wiley, c1987. viii, 227 p.
87-008125   910/.02/0724   0471906042
Physical geography -- Mathematical models. Physical geography -- Data processing.

GB23 Study and teaching. Research — General works

GB23.G6813 1997
Grano, J. G. 1882-1956.
Pure geography/ Johannes Gabriel Grano; edited by Olavi Grano and Anssi Paasi; translated by Malcolm Hicks. Baltimore: The Johns Hopkins University Press, 1997. xxxvii, 191 p.
97-007649   910/.02   0801855918
Physical geography -- Study and teaching. Physical geography -- Estonia. Physical geography -- Finland.

GB54.5 General works, treatises, and advanced textbooks — 1975-

GB54.5.H67 1987
Horizons in physical geography/ edited by Michael J. Clark, Kenneth J. Gregory, and Angela M. Gurnell. Totowa, N.J.: Barnes & Noble, 1987. xiv, 395 p.
87-011427   910/.02   0389207527
Physical geography.

GB54.5.S8 1987
Strahler, Arthur Newell, 1918-
Modern physical geography/ Arthur N. Strahler, Alan H. Strahler. New York: J. Wiley, c1987. xii, 544 p.
86-024662   551   0471850640
Physical geography.

GB55 Elementary textbooks

GB55.L4
Leopold, Luna Bergere, 1915-
Fluvial processes in geomorphology [by] Luna B. Leopold, M. Gordon Wolman [and] John P. Miller. San Francisco, W. H. Freeman [1964] xiii, 522 p.
64-010919   551.4
Rivers. Physical geography.

GB59 Popular works

GB59.W9
Wyckoff, Jerome.
Rock, time, and landforms. New York, Harper & Row [1966] 372 p.
66-010662   910.02
Physical geography.

GB70 General special (Special aspects of the subject as a whole)

GB70.W45
White, Gilbert F.
Natural hazards, local, national, global/ edited by Gilbert F. White. New York: Oxford University Press, 1974. xvi, 288 p.
73-090368   363.3/4   0195017579
Natural disasters. Disaster relief.

GB121 By region or country — America — North America

GB121.H79
Hunt, Charles Butler, 1906-
Natural regions of the United States and Canada [by] Charles B. Hunt. San Francisco, W. H. Freeman [1973, c1974] xii, 725 p.
73-012030   917./02   071670255X
Physical geography -- United States.

GB121.H8
Hunt, Charles Butler, 1906-
Physiography of the United States [by] Charles B. Hunt. San Francisco, W. H. Freeman [1967] 480 p.
66-024952   917.3/02
Physical geography -- United States. Natural resources -- United States.

GB178 By region or country — Europe — Mediterranean Basin

GB178.H6 1967
Houston, J. M. 1922-
The western Mediterranean world; an introduction to its regional landscapes [by] J. M. Houston. With contributions by J. Roglic and J. I. Clarke. New York, Praeger [1967] xxxii, 800 p.
67-025037   910.09/18/22
Physical geography -- Western Mediterranean. Landscape -- Western Mediterranean.

GB400.2 Geomorphology. Landforms. Terrain — Congresses

GB400.2.G439 1995
Geomorphology and land management in a changing environment/ edited by Duncan F.M. McGregor and Donald A. Thompson. Chichester; Wiley, c1995. xiv, 339 p.
94-024604   333.73/15   0471955116
Geomorphology -- Congresses. Land use -- Management -- Congresses.

GB400.4 Geomorphology. Landforms. Terrain — Methodology — General works

GB400.4.T46 1977
Thornes, John B.
Geomorphology and time/ J. B. Thornes and D. Brunsden. New York: Wiley, 1977. xvi, 208 p.
76-030862   551.4   0470990708
Geomorphology -- Methodology. Geological time.

GB400.5 Geomorphology. Landforms. Terrain — Study and teaching. Research — General works

GB400.5.C45
Chorley, Richard J.
The history of the study of landforms; or, The development of geomorphology, by Richard J. Chorley, Antony J. Dunn [and] Robert P. Beckinsale. [London] Methuen; 1964-1991 v. 1-3.
64-006231   551.4
Geomorphology -- History.

GB401.5 Geomorphology. Landforms. Terrain — General works, treatises, and advanced textbooks — 1975-

GB401.5.B55
Bloom, Arthur L. 1928-
Geomorphology: a systematic analysis of Late Cenozoic landforms/ Arthur L. Bloom. Englewood Cliffs, N.J.: Prentice-Hall, c1978. xvii, 510 p.
77-025816   551.4   0133530868
Geomorphology. Geology, Stratigraphic -- Quaternary.

GB401.5.B75 1990
Bridges, E. M.
World geomorphology/ E.M. Bridges. Cambridge [England]; Cambridge University Press, 1990. x, 260 p.
90-031050   551.4/1   0521383439
Geomorphology.

GB401.5.C5 1985
Chorley, Richard J.
Geomorphology/ Richard J. Chorley, Stanley A. Schumm, David E. Sugden. London; Methuen, 1985, c1984. xxiii, 605 p.
84-014709   551.4   0416325904
Geomorphology.

GB401.5.H37 1986
Hart, M. G.
Geomorphology, pure and applied/ M.G. Hart. London; Allen & Unwin, 1986. xviii, 228 p.
85-018539   551.4   0045510873
Geomorphology.

GB401.5.S82 1991
Summerfield, M. A.
Global geomorphology: an introduction to the study of landforms/ Michael A. Summerfield. [Harlow, Essex, England]: Longman Scientific & Technical; 1991. xiv, 537 p.
89-013805   551.4/1   0470216662
Geomorphology.

GB401.5.T47 1988
Thorn, Colin E.
An introduction to theoretical geomorphology/ Colin E. Thorn. Boston: Unwin Hyman, 1988. xiv, 247 p.
88-006236   551.4   0045511179
Geomorphology.

GB402 Geomorphology. Landforms. Terrain — Elementary textbooks

GB402.A4613 1998
Ahnert, Frank O., 1927-
Introduction to geomorphology/ Frank Ahnert. London: Arnold; 1998. viii, 352 p.
98-175542   551.41   034069260X
Geomorphology.

GB406 Geomorphology. Landforms. Terrain — General special

GB406.D26 1992
Daniels, Raymond Bryant, 1925-
Soil geomorphology/ Raymond B. Daniels, Richard D. Hammer. New York: Wiley, c1992. xvi, 236 p.
92-003789   551.4/1   0471511536
Geomorphology. Soils.

GB406.G498 1992
Gerrard, John, 1944-
Soil geomorphology: an integration of pedology and geomorphology/ John Gerrard. London; Chapman & Hall, 1992. ix, 269 p.
92-026461   551.3/05   0412441705
Geomorphology. Soils.

GB406.O44
Ollier, Cliff.
Tectonics and landforms/ Cliff Ollier; edited by K. M. Clayton. London; Longman, 1981. 324 p.
79-041722   551.4   0582300320
Geomorphology. Plate tectonics. Geology, Structural.

GB406.T47 1974
Thomas, Michael Frederic.
Tropical geomorphology; a study of weathering and landform development in warm climates [by] Michael F. Thomas. New York, Wiley [1974] xii, 332 p.
73-013428   551.4/0913   0470858974
Geomorphology -- Tropics.

GB406.W39 1978
Way, Douglas S.
Terrain analysis: a guide to site selection using aerial photographic interpretation/ Douglas S. Way. Stroudsburg, Pa.: Dowden, Hutchinson & Ross, 1978. x, 438 p.
77-020240   551.4/028   0070686416
Landforms. Petrology. Building sites.

GB436 Geomorphology. Landforms. Terrain — By region or country — Europe

GB436.G7.G69 1990
Goudie, Andrew.
The landforms of England and Wales/ Andrew Goudie. Cambridge, Mass.: B. Blackwell, 1990. xi, 394 p.
89-038718   551.4/1/0942   0631173064
Geomorphology -- England. Geomorphology -- Wales.

GB446 Geomorphology. Landforms. Terrain — By region or country — Tropics

GB446.T46 1994
Thomas, Michael Frederic.
Geomorphology in the tropics: a study of weathering and denudation in low latitudes/ Michael F. Thomas. Chichester [England]; Wiley, c1994. xix, 460 p.
93-006094   551.4/1/0913   0471930350
Geomorphology -- Tropics.

GB446.W5713 2000
Wirthmann, Alfred, 1927-
Geomorphology of the Tropics/ Alfred Wirthmann; translated by Detlef Busche. Berlin; Springer, c2000. ix, 314 p.
99-044585   551.41/0913 21   3540635831
Geomorphology -- Tropics.

GB447 Geomorphology. Landforms. Terrain — Climatic geomorphology

GB447.B85 1991
Bull, William B., 1930-
Geomorphic responses to climatic change/ William B. Bull. New York: Oxford University Press, 1991. xviii, 326 p.
90-032977   551.4/1   0195055705
Climatic geomorphology.

GB450.4 Geomorphology. Landforms. Terrain — Coasts — Dictionaries. Encyclopedias

GB450.4.E53 1982
The Encyclopedia of beaches and coastal environments/ edited by Maurice L. Schwartz. Stroudsburg, Pa.: Hutchinson Ross Pub. Co., c1982. xx, 940 p.
81-007250   551.4/57/0321   0879332131
Coasts -- Dictionaries. Beaches -- Dictionaries. Coastal ecology -- Dictionaries.

GB451-451.2 Geomorphology. Landforms. Terrain — Coasts — General works, treatises, and textbooks

GB451.Z4213 1967b
Zenkovich, V. P. 1910-
Processes of coastal development [by] V. P. Zenkovich. Edited by J. A. Steers, assisted by Cuchlaine A. M. King. Translated by D. G. Fry. New York, Interscience Publishers, 1967. xv, 738 p.
68-003065   551.3/6
Coasts.

GB451.2.B55 2000
Bird, E. C. F. 1930-
Coastal geomorphology: an introduction/ by Eric Bird. Chichester; Wiley, c2000. xv, 322 p.
00-032095   551.45/7 21   0471899763
Coasts.

GB451.2.B58 1993
Bird, Eric C. F. 1930-
Submerging coasts: the effects of a rising sea level on coastal environments/ Eric C.F. Bird. Chichester; New York: c1993. viii, 184 p.
92-030175   551.4/58   0471938076
Coast changes. Sea level.

GB451.2.D39 1994
Davis, Richard A. 1937-
The evolving coast/ Richard A. Davis, Jr. New York: Scientific American Library: c1994. x, 231 p.
93-025452   551.4/57   0716750422
Coast changes.

GB451.2.K65 1998
Komar, Paul D., 1939-
Beach processes and sedimentation/ Paul D. Komar. Upper Saddle River, N.J.: Prentice Hall, c1998. x, 544 p.
97-022893   551.45/7 21   0137549385
Coast changes. Marine sediments. Ocean waves.

GB451.2.K6813 2000
Kosian, R. D.
Coastal processes in tideless seas/ R.D. Kosian, N.V. Pykhov, B.L. Edge. Reston, Va.: American Society of Civil Engineers, c2000. xii, 316 p.
00-023204   551.45/7 21   0784400180
Coast changes. Water waves. Sediment transport.

GB451.2.S86 1992
Sunamura, Tsuguo, 1941-
Geomorphology of rocky coasts/ Tsuguo Sunamura. Chichester; J. Wiley, c1992. xii, 302 p.
91-047199   551.4/57   0471917753
Coasts.

GB451.2.T735 1997
Trenhaile, Alan S.
Coastal dynamics and landforms/ A.S. Trenhaile. Oxford: Clarendon Press; 1997. xvi, 366 p.
96-038341   551.4/57   0198233531
Coast changes.

GB452 Geomorphology. Landforms. Terrain — Coasts — Pictorial works

GB452.S64
Snead, Rodman E.
Coastal landforms and surface features: a photographic atlas and glossary/ Rodman E. Snead. Stroudsburg, Pa.: Hutchinson Ross, c1982. xx, 247 p.
81-002949   551.4/57   087933052X
Coasts -- Pictorial works. Coasts -- Dictionaries.

GB461 Geomorphology. Landforms. Terrain — Reefs — General works

GB461.G85 1988
Guilcher, Andre.
Coral reef geomorphology/ Andre Guilcher. Chichester; Wiley, c1988. xiii, 228 p.
87-025422   551.4/24   0471917559
Coral reefs and islands.

GB478.58 Geomorphology. Landforms. Terrain — Islands — Other countries

GB478.58.S513 1967
Porarinsson, Sigurdur, 1912-
Surtsey, the new island in the North Atlantic [by] Sigurdur Thorarinsson. Translated by Solvi Eysteinsson. New York: Viking Press, 1967, c1966. 47 p.
67-010220   551.4/2/094912
Surtsey.

GB501.2 Geomorphology. Landforms. Terrain — Mountains. Orography — General works

GB501.2.B46 2000
Beniston, Martin.
Environmental change in mountains and uplands/ Martin Beniston. London: Arnold; 2000. x, 172 p.
00-703213   551.43/2   0340706384
Mountains -- Environmental aspects. Global environmental change. Geomorphology.

GB581-591 Geomorphology. Landforms. Terrain — Other natural landforms — Glacial landforms

GB581.E75 1996
Erickson, Jon, 1948-
Glacial geology: how ice shapes the land/ Jon Erickson. New York: Facts on File, Inc., c1996. viii, 248 p.
95-035271   551.3/15 20   0816033552
Glacial landforms. Glacial epoch.

GB591.A45 1990
Alluvial fans: a field approach/ edited by Andrzej H. Rachocki and Michael Church. Chichester, West Sussex, England; Wiley, c1990. x, 391 p.
89-022435   551.4/56 20   0471916943
Alluvial fans.

GB600-601 Geomorphology. Landforms. Terrain — Other natural landforms — Karst landforms

GB600.D75 1988
Dreybrodt, Wolfgang.
Processes in Karst systems: physics, chemistry, and geology/ Wolfgang Dreybrodt. Berlin; Springer-Verlag, c1988. xii, 288 p.
88-015982   551.4/47   0387188398
Karst.

GB600.F66 1989
Ford, Derek
Karst geomorphology and hydrology/ D.C. Ford, P.W. Williams. London; Unwin Hyman, 1989. xv, 601 p.
88-039654   551.4/47   0045511055
Karst. Hydrology, Karst.

GB600.W47 1988
White, William B. 1934-
Geomorphology and hydrology of karst terrains/ William B. White. New York: Oxford University Press, 1988. ix, 464 p.
87-023996   551.4/47   0195044444
Karst. Hydrology, Karst.

GB601.A8813 1989
Atlas of the great caves of the world/ Paul Courbon ... [et al.]. St. Louis: Cave Books, 1989. 368 p.
89-015722   551.4/47/0223   0939748215
Caves -- Maps.

GB601.G5 1996
Gillieson, David S.
Caves: processes, development, and management/ David Gillieson. Oxford; Blackwell Publishers, 1996. xi, 324 p.
96-012123   551.4/47   0631178198
Caves.

GB601.M58 1997
Moore, George William, 1928-
Speleology: caves and the cave environment/ George W. Moore, Nicholas Sullivan; prepared in cooperation with the National Speleological Society; illustrated by John C. Schoenherr. St. Louis: Cave Books, c1997. xiv, 176 p.
96-085614   551.44/7 21   0939748460
Speleology.

GB611 Geomorphology. Landforms. Terrain — Other natural landforms — Deserts. Arid regions

GB611.C66 1993
Cooke, Ronald U.
Desert geomorphology/ Ron Cooke, Andrew Warren, Andrew Goudie. London: UCL Press, 1993. viii, 526 p.
93-142064   551.4/15   1857280164
Deserts. Geomorphology.

GB611.D48 1993
Deserts: the encroaching wilderness: a world conservation atlas/ edited by Tony Allan and Andrew Warren; introduction by Mostafa Tolba. New York: Oxford University Press, 1993. 176 p.
92-031992   508.315/4   0195209419
Deserts.

GB611.E65 1999
Encyclopedia of deserts/ edited by Michael A. Mares. Norman: University of Oklahoma Press, c1999. xxxvii, 654 p.
98-044437   910/.02154/03 21   0806131462
Deserts -- Encyclopedias. Arid regions -- Encyclopedias.

GB611.T48 1994
Thomas, David S. G.
Desertification: exploding the myth/ David S. G. Thomas and Nicholas J. Middleton. Chichester; Wiley, c1994. xii, 194 p.
94-159189   333.73/6   0471948152
Desertification

GB621 Geomorphology. Landforms. Terrain — Other natural landforms — Wetlands

GB621.M66
Moore, Peter D.
Peatlands [by] P. D. Moore [and] D. J. Bellamy. London, Elek Science [1974] vi, 221 p.
74-165364   574.5/2632   0236154737
Peatlands. Peat industry.

GB621.S34 1991
Saltmarshes: morphodynamics, conservation, and engineering significance/ edited by J.R.L. Allen and K. Pye. Cambridge [England]; Cambridge University Press, 1992. viii, 184 p.
91-039962   551.4/57   0521418410
Salt marshes.

GB621.W47 1996
Wetlands: environmental gradients, boundaries, and buffers/ edited by George Mulamoottil, Barry G. Warner, Edward A. McBean. Boca Raton: CRC, Lewis Publishers, c1996. 298 p.
95-046404   551.4/57 20   1566701473
Wetlands -- Congresses.

GB632 Geomorphology. Landforms. Terrain — Other natural landforms — Dunes

GB632.L36 1995
Lancaster, Nicholas, 1948-
Geomorphology of desert dunes/ Nicholas Lancaster. London; Routledge, 1995. xix, 290 p.
94-047289   551.3/75   0415060931
Sand dunes. Deserts.

GB641 Geomorphology. Landforms. Terrain — Other natural landforms — Frozen ground. Cold regions

GB641.D39 2001
Davis, T. Neil.
Permafrost: a guide to frozen ground in transition/ by Neil Davis. Fairbanks, Alaska: University of Alaska Press, c2001. xvi, 351 p.
00-057719   551.3/84 21   1889963194
Frozen ground.

GB641.W37 1980
Washburn, A. L. 1911-
Geocryology: a survey of periglacial processes and environments/ A. L. Washburn. New York: Wiley, c1980. vi, 406 p.
78-022026   551.3/8   0470265825
Frozen ground. Erosion.

GB641.W55 1989
Williams, Peter J. 1932-
The frozen earth: fundamentals of geocryology/ Peter J. Williams and Michael W. Smith. Cambridge; Cambridge University Press, 1989. xvi, 306 p.
88-030458   551.3/84   0521365341
Frozen ground.

GB656.2 Hydrology. Water — Methodology — Special methods, A-Z

GB656.2.E43.H64 1989
Hoggan, Daniel H.
Computer-assisted floodplain hydrology and hydraulics/ Daniel H. Hoggan. New York: McGraw-Hill, c1989. xxii, 518 p.
88-029028   551.48/9/0285   0070293503
Hydrology -- Data processing.

GB656.2.H9.S558 1997
Singh, V. P.
Kinematic wave modeling in water resources: environmental hydrology/ Vijay P. Singh. New York: Wiley, c1997. xvii, 830 p.
96-034534   551.48/01/1 20   0471109487
Hydrologic models. Water waves -- Mathematical models. Hydrology -- Environmental aspects.

GB656.2.M33.P56
Pinder, George Francis, 1942-
Finite element simulation in surface and subsurface hydrology/ George F. Pinder, William G. Gray. New York: Academic Press, 1977. xii, 295 p.
76-042977   551.4/8/018   0125569505
Hydrology -- Mathematical models. Hydrology -- Data processing. Finite element method.

GB656.2.S7.H3
Haan, C. T. 1941-
Statistical methods in hydrology/ Charles T. Haan. Ames: Iowa State University Press, 1977. xv, 378 p.
77-011734   551.4/8/0182   081381510X
Hydrology -- Statistical methods.

GB661.2 Hydrology. Water — General works, treatises, and advanced textbooks — 1975-

GB661.2.B35 2000
Ball, Philip, 1962-
Life's matrix: a biography of water/ Philip Ball. New York: Farrar, Straus, and Giroux, 2000. xii, 417 p.
99-059110   553.7   0374186286
Water.

GB661.2.B42 1988
Bedient, Philip B., 1948-
Hydrology and floodplain analysis/ Philip B. Bedient, Wayne C. Huber. Reading, Mass.: Addison-Wesley, c1988. xix, 650 p.
87-014308   551.48   0201120569
Hydrology.

GB661.2.B7 1990
Bras, Rafael L.
Hydrology: an introduction to hydrologic science/ Rafael L. Bras. Reading, Mass.: Addison-Wesley, c1990. xvii, 643 p.
88-016793 551.48 0201059223
Hydrology.

GB661.2.E44 1998
Elements of physical hydrology/ George M. Hornberger ... [et al.]. Baltimore: Johns Hopkins University Press, c1998. viii, 302 p.
97-042533 551.48 21 0801858569
Hydrology.

GB661.2.P54 1998
Pielou, E. C., 1924-
Fresh water/ E.C. Pielou. Chicago: University of Chicago Press, 1998. x, 275 p.
97-051562 551.48 0226668150
Hydrology.

GB662.5 Hydrology. Water — Handbooks, tables, etc.

GB662.5.M35 1993
Handbook of hydrology/ David R. Maidment, editor in chief. New York: McGraw-Hill, c1993. 1 v.
92-018193 551.48 0070397325
Hydrology -- Handbooks, manuals, etc.

GB665 Hydrology. Water — General special

GB665.S64 1998
Spellman, Frank R.
The science of water: concepts & applications/ Frank R. Spellman. Lancaster, PA: Technomic Pub., c1998. xiii, 235 p.
97-062221 553.9 21 1566766125
Water. Water -- Industrial applications. Water -- Pollution.

GB671 Hydrology. Water — Popular works

GB671.L43 1997
Leopold, Luna Bergere, 1915-
Water, rivers, and creeks/ Luna B. Leopold. Sausalito, Calif.: University Science Books, c1997. xi, 185 p.
97-009507 551.48 21 0935702989
Water.

GB701-705 Hydrology. Water — By region or country — North America

GB701.O88 1996
Outwater, Alice B.
Water: a natural history/ Alice Outwater; illustrations by Billy Brauer. New York, NY: BasicBooks, c1996. xii, 212 p.
96-024182 551.48 20 0465037798
Hydrology -- United States. Hydraulic engineering -- United States.

GB705.K4.K37 1989
Karst hydrology: concepts from the Mammoth Cave area/ edited by William B. White, Elizabeth L. White. New York: Van Nostrand Reinhold, c1989. xiii, 346 p.
88-020971 551.49 0442226756
Hydrology, Karst -- Kentucky -- Mammoth Cave Region.

GB843 Hydrology. Water — Karst hydrology

GB843.M5413 1981
Milanovic, Petar T.
Karst hydrogeology/ by Petar T. Milanovic; [translated by J.J. Buhac]. Littleton, Colo.: Water Resources Publications, c1981. x, 434 p.
80-054287 551.4/47 0918334365
Karst hydrology.

GB845 Hydrology. Water — Hydrological forecasting

GB845.H93 1985
Hydrological forecasting/ edited by M.G. Anderson and T.P. Burt. Chichester [West Sussex]; Wiley, c1985. xii, 604 p.
84-017364 551.48 047190614X
Hydrological forecasting.

GB848 Hydrology. Water — Hydrologic cycle

GB848.G89 1994
Guymon, Gary L.
Unsaturated zone hydrology/ Gary L. Guymon. Englewood Cliffs, N.J.: Prentice Hall, c1994. xiv, 210 p.
94-001212 551.48 0133690830
Hydrologic cycle. Zone of aeration.

GB855 Hydrology. Water — Natural water chemistry

GB855.B74 1994
Brezonik, Patrick L.
Chemical kinetics and process dynamics in aquatic systems/ Patrick L. Brezonik. Boca Raton: Lewis, c1994. 754 p.
92-042114 551.48 0873714318
Water chemistry. Chemical kinetics.

GB855.D48 1997
Deutsch, W. J.
Groundwater geochemistry: fundamentals and applications to contamination/ William J. Deutsch. Boca Raton, Fla.: Lewis Publishers, c1997. 221 p.
97-011261 551.49 21 0873713087
Water chemistry. Groundwater. Groundwater -- Pollution.

GB855.M67 1993
Morel, Francois, 1944-
Principles and applications of aquatic chemistry/ Francois M.M. Morel, Janet G. Hering. New York: Wiley, c1993. xv, 588 p.
92-018608 551.48 0471548960
Water chemistry.

GB855.S78 1995
Stumm, Werner, 1924-
Aquatic chemistry: chemical equilibria and rates in natural waters/ Werner Stumm, James J. Morgan. New York: Wiley, c1996. xvi, 1022 p.
94-048319 359.9 20 0471511846
Water chemistry.

GB855.S79 1992
Stumm, Werner, 1924-
Chemistry of the solid-water interface: processes at the mineral-water and particle-water interface in natural systems/ Werner Stumm; with contributions by Laura Sigg (chapter 11), Barbara Sulzberger (chapter 10). New York: Wiley, c1992. x, 428 p.
92-009701 551.46 0471576727
Water chemistry. Surface chemistry.

GB855.T72 1995
Trace elements in natural waters/ edited by Brit Salbu, Eiliv Steinnes. Boca Raton: CRC Press, c1995. 302 p.
94-013929 628.1/61 0849363047
Water chemistry. Trace elements.

GB980 Hydrology. Water — Ground and surface waters — General works

GB980.B57 1996
Black, Peter E.
Watershed hydrology/ Peter E. Black. Chelsea, Mich.: Ann Arbor Press, c1996. xxx, 449 p.
95-045360 551.48 20 1575040271
Watersheds.

GB1001.7-1198 Hydrology. Water — Ground and surface waters — Groundwater. Hydrogeology

GB1001.7.F57 1997
Fletcher, Frank W.
Basic hydrogeologic methods: a field and laboratory manual with microcomputer applications/ Frank W. Fletcher. Lancaster, Pa.: Technomic Pub. Co., c1997. xii, 310 p.
96-061337 551.49 21 1566764009
Hydrogeology -- Methodology.

GB1001.72.R34.C57 1997
Clark, Ian D. 1954-
Environmental isotopes in hydrogeology/ Ian D. Clark and Peter Fritz. Boca Raton, FL: CRC Press/Lewis Publishers, c1997. 328 p.
97-021889 551.49/028 21 1566702496
Radioactive tracers in hydrogeology.

GB1001.72.R42.R46 2000
Remote sensing in hydrology and water management/ G.A. Schultz, E.T. Engman (eds.). Berlin; Springer, c2000. xx, 483 p.
00-026397 551.48/028 21 3540640754
Hydrology -- Remote sensing. Water resources development -- Remote sensing.

GB1003.2.C425 1997
Chapelle, Frank.
The hidden sea: ground water, springs, and wells/ Francis H. Chapelle; illustrated by James E. Landmeyer. Tuscon, Ariz.: Geoscience Press, c1997. x, 238 p.
97-005640 553.79 21 0945005261
Groundwater.

GB1003.2.F47 2001
Fetter, C. W.
Applied hydrogeology/ C.W. Fetter. 4th ed. Upper Saddle River, N.J.: Prentice Hall, c2001. xvii, 598 p.
00-048329   551.49 21   0130882399
Hydrogeology. Water supply.

GB1003.2.S76 1999
Stone, William J. 1941-
Hydrogeology in practice: a guide to characterizing ground-water systems/ William J. Stone. Upper Saddle River, NJ: Prentice Hall, 1999. viii, 248 p.
98-041441   551.49   0138991545
Hydrogeology.

GB1003.2.T6 1980
Todd, David Keith, 1923-
Groundwater hydrology/ David Keith Todd. New York: Wiley, c1980. xiii, 535 p.
80-011831   551.49   047187616X
Groundwater.

GB1004.C47 1983
Chemical hydrogeology/ edited by William Back and R. Allan Freeze. Stroudsburg, Pa.: Hutchinson Ross Pub. Co.: c1983. xiii, 416 p.
82-011853   551.49   0879334401
Hydrogeology. Geochemistry.

GB1005.E58 1998
Environmental hydrogeology/ Mostafa M. Soliman ... [et al.]. Boca Raton: Lewis Publishers, c1998. 386 p.
97-005718   628.1/68 21   0873719492
Hydrogeology. Environmental geology.

GB1019.S68 1989
Smith, Zachary A. 1953-
Groundwater in the West/ Zachary A. Smith. San Diego: Academic Press, c1989 xi, 308 p.
88-003476   553.7/978   0126529957
Groundwater -- West (U.S.)

GB1197.7.S74 1995
Stephens, Daniel B.
Vadose zone hydrology/ Daniel B. Stephens; cover illustration by Andrea J. Kron; cartography by Andrea Kron, Los Alamos, New Mexico. Baca Raton, Fla.: CRC, Lewis Publishers, c1996. 339 p.
95-013527   551.49 20   0873714326
Groundwater flow. Zone of aeration.

GB1197.7.T56 1999
Tindall, James A., 1953-
Unsaturated zone hydrology for scientists and engineers/ James A. Tindall, James R. Kunkel with Dean E. Anderson. Upper Saddle River, N.J.: Prentice Hall, 1999. xv, 624 p.
98-036758   551.49   0136607136
Groundwater flow. Zone of aeration. Soil chemistry.

GB1197.7.V365 1999
Vadose zone hydrology: cutting across disciplines/ edited by Marc B. Parlange, Jan W. Hopmans. New York: Oxford University Press, 1999. xvii, 454 p.
98-003468   551.49   0195109902
Groundwater flow. Zone of aeration.

GB1198.C66 1991
Cone, Joseph.
Fire under the sea: the discovery extroaordinary environment o earth--volcanic hot springs on the ocean floor/ Joseph Cone. New York: Morrow, c1991. 285 p.
90-015574   551.2/3   0688098347
Hydrothermal vents.

GB1203.2-1399.4 Hydrology. Water — Ground and surface waters — Rivers. Stream measurements

GB1203.2.M67 1985
Morisawa, Marie.
Rivers: form and process/ Marie Morisawa; edited by K.M. Clayton. London; Longman, 1985. 222 p.
83-007931   551.48/3   0582489822
Rivers.

GB1205.G65 1992
Gordon, Nancy D.
Stream hydrology: an introduction for ecologists/ Nancy D. Gordon, Thomas A. McMahon, Brian L. Finlayson; software author, Rory J. Nathan. Chichester, West Sussex, England; Wiley, c1992. xvi, 529 p.
91-026728   551.48/3   0471930849
Rivers. Hydrology.

GB1205.R5 1982
Richards, K. S.
Rivers: form and process in alluvial channels/ Keith Richards. London; Methuen, 1982. xi, 358 p.
82-008133   551.4/4   0416749003
Rivers. Channels (Hydraulic engineering)

GB1205.R57 1992
The Rivers handbook: hydrological and ecological principles: in two volumes/ edited by Peter Calow and Geoffrey E. Petts. Oxford; Blackwell Scientific Publications, 1992-1994. 2 v.
91-041421   551.48/3   0632028327
Rivers. Stream ecology.

GB1215.L42 1994
Leopold, Luna Bergere, 1915-
A view of the river/ Luna B. Leopold. Cambridge, Mass.: Harvard University Press, 1994. xi, 298 p.
93-034698   551.48/3   0674937325
River channels. Rivers -- United States.

GB1225.C3.M68 1995
Mount, Jeffrey F., 1954-
California rivers and streams: the conflict between fluvial process and land use/ Jeffrey F. Mount; illustrations by Janice C. Fong. Berkeley: University of California Press, c1995. xvi, 359 p.
95-010822   333.91/62/09794   0520201922
Rivers -- California. Land use -- California.

GB1227.G85.S48 1999
Shelton, Napier.
Huron: the seasons of a Great Lake/ Napier Shelton. Detroit, Mich.: Wayne State University Press, c1999. 268 p.
98-035662   508.774 21   0814328342
Limnology -- Huron, Lake (Mich. and Ont.) Natural history -- Huron, Lake (Mich. and Ont.)

GB1227.S67
Wohl, Ellen E., 1962-
Virtual rivers: lessons from the mountain rivers of the Colorado front range/ Ellen E. Wohl. New Haven: Yale University Press, c2001. x, 210 p.
00-043771   333.91/6214/097887   21   0300084846
Water use -- South Platte River Watershed (Colo. and Neb.) -- History. Rivers -- Colorado -- History. South Platte River Watershed (Colo. and Neb.) -- History.

GB1361.S25 1993
Said, Rushdi.
The river Nile: geology, hydrology, and utilization/ Rushdi Said. Oxford [England]; Pergamon, 1993. xii, 320 p.
93-028862   551.48/3/0962   0080418864
Nile River.

GB1399.F55 1988
Flood geomorphology/ edited by Victor R. Baker, R. Craig Kochel, Peter C. Patton. New York: Wiley, c1988. xvi, 503 p.
87-027920   551.48/9   0471625582
Floods. Geomorphology.

GB1399.I54 2000
Inland flood hazards: human, riparian, and aquatic communities/ edited by Ellen E. Wohl. Cambridge; Cambridge University Press, 2000. xiii, 498 p.
99-052944   363.34/93   0521624193
Floods. Flood control.

GB1399.4.M72.G74 1996
The Great flood of 1993: causes, impacts, and responses/ edited by Stanley A. Changnon. Boulder, CO: Westview Press, c1996. xii, 321 p.
95-050340   363.3/493/097709049   20   0813326192
Floods -- Mississippi River.

GB1603.2 Hydrology. Water — Ground and surface waters — Lakes. Limnology

GB1603.2.L34
Lakes--chemistry, geology, physics/ edited by Abraham Lerman; with contributions by P. Baccini ... [et al.]. New York: Springer-Verlag, c1978. x, 363 p.
78-017842   551.4/82   0387903224
Lakes. Limnology.

GB2403.2-2425 Hydrology. Water — Ground and surface waters — Ice. Glaciers. Ice sheets. Sea ice

GB2403.2.H35 1994
Hambrey, M. J.
Glacial environments/ Michael J. Hambrey. London: UCL Press, 1994. viii, 296 p.
94-229308   551.3/12   1857280059
Glaciers.

GB2403.2.H36 1992
Hambrey, M. J.
Glaciers/ Michael Hambrey, Jurg Alean. Cambridge; Cambridge University Press, 1992. 207 p.
91-041974   551.3/12   0521419158
Glaciers.

GB2403.2.L63 1990
Lock, G. S. H.
The growth and decay of ice/ G.S.H. Lock. Cambridge [England]; Cambridge University Press, 1990. xvii, 434 p.
89-025441   551.3/1   0521331331
Ice. Freezing points.

GB2403.2.M632 2001
Modern and past glacial environments/ editor, John Menzies. Rev. student ed. Boston: Butterworth-Heinemann, 2001.
2001-052844   551.31 21   0750642262
Glaciers. Glacial epoch.

GB2403.2.S5 1988
Sharp, Robert P.
Living ice: understanding glaciers and glaciation/ Robert P. Sharp. Cambridge; Cambridge University Press, 1988. x, 225 p.
88-003800   551.3/1   0521330092
Glaciers. Glacial landforms.

GB2425.C2.G89 1998
Guyton, Bill, 1932-
Glaciers of California: modern glaciers, ice age glaciers, origin of Yosemite Valley, and a glacier tour in the Sierra Nevada/ Bill Guyton. Berkeley: University of California Press, c1998. xvi, 197 p.
97-044790   551.31/2/09794 21   0520212959
Glaciers -- California.

GB5010 Natural disasters — By region or country — United States

GB5010.M37 1997
Mason, Owen K.
Living with the coast of Alaska/ Owen Mason, William J. Neal, and Orrin H. Pilkey; with chapters by Jane Bullock ... [et al.] . Durham: Duke University Press, 1997. xix, 348 p.
97-015156   363.34/09798   0822320096
Natural disasters -- Alaska -- Pacific Coast. Natural disaster hazards assessment -- Alaska -- Pacific Coast. Coastal zone management -- Alaska -- Pacific Coast.

GB5014 Natural disasters — General works

GB5014.B79 1991
Bryant, Edward, 1948-
Natural hazards/ Edward Bryant. Cambridge [England]; Cambridge University Press, 1991. xviii, 294 p.
90-045981   363.3/4   052137295X
Natural disasters.

GB5014.C63 1995
Coch, Nicholas K.
Geohazards: natural and human/ Nicholas K. Coch. Englewood Cliffs, N.J.: Prentice Hall, c1995. xix, 481 p.
94-023581   363.3/4   0023229926
Natural disasters. Disasters.

GB5014.K68 1995
Kovach, Robert L.
Earth's fury: an introduction to natural hazards and disasters/ Robert L. Kovach. Englewood Cliffs, N.J.: Prentice-Hall, c1995. x, 214 p.
94-032127   363.3/4   0130424331
Natural disasters.

GB5014.R63 1993
Robinson, Andrew, 1957-
Earth shock: hurricanes, volcanoes, earthquakes, tornadoes and other forces of nature/ Andrew Robinson. New York: Thames and Hudson, 1993. 304 p.
93-060201   363.3/49   0500277389
Natural disasters. Hurricanes. Volcanoes.

GB5014.S6 1992
Smith, Keith, 1938-
Environmental hazards: assessing risk and reducing disaster/ Keith Smith. London; Routledge, 1992. xx, 324 p.
91-014713   363.3/4   0415012163
Natural disasters.

GB5014.T63 1997
Tobin, Graham A.
Natural hazards: explanation and integration/ Graham A. Tobin and Burrell E. Montz. New York: Guilford Press, c1997. xi, 388 p.
97-001191   363.34 21   1572300612
Natural disasters.

GB5014.U53 1992
Understanding catastrophe/ edited by Janine Bourriau. Cambridge; Cambridge University Press, 1992. 213 p.
92-196016   574.5/222   0521413249
Natural disasters.

GB5014.Z43 1997
Zebrowski, Ernest.
Perils of a restless planet: scientific perspectives on natural disasters/ Ernest Zebrowski, Jr. Cambridge, UK; Cambridge University Press, 1997. xi, 306 p.
96-037794   363.34   0521573742
Natural disasters.

GC Oceanography

GC9 Dictionaries. Encyclopedias

GC9.E38 2000
Ellis, Richard, 1938-
Encyclopedia of the sea/ written and illustrated by Richard Ellis. New York: Alfred A. Knopf, 2000. vii, 380 p.
99-042401   551.46/003   0375403744
Ocean -- Encyclopedias. Oceanography -- Encyclopedias. Marine organisms -- Encyclopedias.

GC9.E56 1992
Encyclopedia of marine sciences/ J.G. Baretta-Bekker, E.K. Duursma, B.R. Kuipers, eds. Berlin; Springer-Verlag, c1992. 311 p.
92-002877   551.46   3540545018
Marine sciences -- Encyclopedias.

GC9.F28 2001
The Facts on File dictionary of marine science/ [edited by] Barbara Charton. Rev. ed. New York: Facts on File, c2001. viii, 373 p.
00-052817   551.46/003 21   0816042934
Marine sciences -- Dictionaries.

GC9.G76
Groves, Donald G.
Ocean world encyclopedia/ Donald G. Groves and Lee M. Hunt. New York: McGraw-Hill, c1980. xv, 443 p.
79-021093   551.4/6/003   0070250103
Oceanography -- Encyclopedias.

GC9.T86
Tver, David F.
Ocean and marine dictionary/ David F. Tver. Centreville, Md.: Cornell Maritime Press, 1979. ix, 358 p.
79-001529   551.4/6/003   0870332465
Oceanography -- Dictionaries. Marine engineering -- Dictionaries. Marine biology -- Dictionaries.

GC9.U5 1966
Glossary of oceanographic terms. Edited by B.B. Baker, Jr., W.R. Deebel [and] R.D. Geisenderfer. 2d ed. Washington, U.S. Naval Oceanographic Office, 1966. vi, 204 p.
66-062513   551.4/6/003
Oceanography -- Dictionaries.

GC10.4 Philosophy. Relation to other topics. Methodology — Special methods, A-Z

GC10.4.R4.M38 1985
Maul, George A.
Introduction to satellite oceanography/ by G.A. Maul. Dordrecht; Martinus Nijhoff; 1985. x, 606 p.
84-022693   551.46/0028   9024730961
Oceanography -- Remote sensing.

GC10.4.R4.R39 1998
Cherny, Igor V.
Passive microwave remote sensing of oceans/ Igor V. Chreny, Victor Yu. Raizer. Chichester; Wiley, 1998. viii, 195 p.
97-028549   551.46/0028   0471971707
Oceanography -- Remote sensing. Microwave remote sensing.

GC11.2 General works, treatises, and advanced textbooks — 1975-

GC11.2.P73 1994
Practical handbook of marine science/ edited by Michael J. Kennish. Boca Raton, Fla.: CRC Press, c1994. 566 p.
93-003715   551.46   0849337127
Oceanography. Marine biology.

GC11.2.T66 1994
Tomczak, M., 1941-
Regional oceanography: an introduction/ Matthias Tomczak and J. Stuart Godfrey. Oxford, England; Pergamon, 1994. vii, 422 p.
93-030118   551.46   0080410219
Oceanography.

GC11.2.W55 1998
Wilder, Robert Jay.
Listening to the sea: the politics of improving environmental protection/ Robert Jay Wilder. Pittsburgh: University of Pittsburgh Press, c1998. xv, 269 p.
98-008947   333.91/6415 21   0822940590
Oceanography. Marine resources. Ocean engineering.

GC16 Elementary textbooks

GC16.G7 1987
Gross, M. Grant 1933-
Oceanography, a view of the earth/ M. Grant Gross. Englewood Cliffs, N.J.: Prentice-Hall, c1987. ix, 406 p.
86-020506   551.46   0136296920
Oceanography.

GC21 Popular works

GC21.C3 1961
Carson, Rachel, 1907-1964.
The sea around us. New York, Oxford University Press, 1961. 237 p.
61-006295   551.46
Oceanography.

GC24 Handbooks, tables, etc.

GC24.S64
Smith, F. G. Walton
Handbook of marine science/ editor, F. G. Walton Smith. Cleveland: CRC Press, [1974-]
74-190653   551.4/6/00212   087819388X
Oceanography -- Handbooks, manuals, etc. Ocean engineering -- Handbooks, manuals, etc. Marine biology -- Handbooks, manuals, etc.

GC28 General special (Special aspects of the subject as a whole)

GC28.O23 1990
The Ocean in human affairs/ edited by S. Fred Singer. New York: Paragon House, c1990. vii, 374 p.
87-030840   551.46   0892260378
Oceanography. Human beings -- Effect of environment on.

GC57 Oceanographic research — General works

GC57.O23 1992
Ocean frontiers: explorations by oceanographers on five continents/ edited by Elisabeth Mann Borgese. New York: Abrams, 1992. 288 p.
91-032711   551.46   0810936658
Oceanography -- Research.

GC63 Oceanographic expeditions

GC63.C47.V47 1996
Verdon, Frank P.
The other way around/ Frank P. Verdon. London; Radcliffe Press; 1996. xxii, 182 p.
95-062330   551.46/0072   1860640303
Oceanography -- Research. Voyages around the world.

GC65 Underwater exploration — General works

GC65.B275 2000
Ballard, Robert D.
The eternal darkness: a personal history of deep-sea exploration/ Robert D. Ballard, with Will Hively. Princeton, N.J.: Princeton University Press, c2000. xii, 388 p.
99-043072   551.46/07/09 21   0691027404
Underwater exploration -- History.

GC87.2 Submarine topography — Ocean bottom. Ocean basin

GC87.2.A86.E45 1996
Ellis, Richard, 1938-
Deep Atlantic: life, death, and exploration in the abyss/ Richard Ellis. New York: Alfred A. Knopf, 1996. ix, 395 p.
95-046523   508.3163   0679433244
Abyssal zone -- Atlantic Ocean.

GC89 Sea level — General works

GC89.E54 1991
Emery, K. O. 1914-
Sea levels, land levels, and tide gauges/ K.O Emery, David G. Aubrey. New York: Springer-Verlag, c1991. xiv, 237 p.
90-049743   551.4/58   0387974490
Sea level. Subsidences (Earth movements) Tide-gages.

GC89.S413 1990
Sea-level change/ Geophysics Study Committee, Commission on Physical Sciences, Mathematics, and Resources, National Research Council. Washington, D.C.: National Academy Press, 1990. xii, 234 p.
90-005839   551.4/58   0309040396
Sea level.

GC89.S429 2000
Sea level rise: history and consequences/ [edited by] Bruce C. Douglas, Michael S. Kearney, Stephen P.Leatherman. San Diego: Academic Press, 2000. xix, 232 p.
00-104280   551.45/8 21   0122213459
Sea level.

GC96.5 Estuarine oceanography — Congresses

GC96.5.W67 1979
Estuarine and wetland processes, with emphasis on modeling/ edited by Peter Hamilton and Keith B. Macdonald. New York: Plenum Press, c1980. xi, 653 p.
80-014721   551.46/09   0306404524
Estuarine oceanography -- Mathematical models -- Congresses. Estuarine oceanography -- United States -- Congresses. Wetlands -- Mathematical models -- Congresses.

GC97 Estuarine oceanography — General works

GC97.E79 1996
Estuarine shores: evolution, environments, and human alterations/ edited by Karl F. Nordstrom and Charles T. Roman. Chichester; Wiley, c1996. xxiv, 486 p.
96-012984   551.46/09 20   0471965960
Estuaries. Coast changes.

GC97.7 Estuarine oceanography — Estuarine sediments — General works

GC97.7.A7813 1996
Artemev, V. E.
Geochemistry of organic matter in river-sea systems/ by V.E. Artemyev. Dordrecht; Kluwer Academic Publishers, c1996. xiii, 190 p.
96-011978   551.46/09 20   0792340302
Estuarine sediments. River sediments. Organic geochemistry.

GC111.2 Chemical oceanography — General works — 1975-

GC111.2.M38 2000
Marine geochemistry/ [edited by] Horst D. Schulz, Matthias Zabel. New York: Springer, c2000. xx, 455 p.
99-050190   551.46/083 21   354066453X
Chemical oceanography. Marine sediments. Geochemistry.

GC111.2.M55 1991
Millero, Frank J.
Chemical oceanography/ Frank J. Millero, Mary L. Sohn. Boca Raton: CRC Press, c1992. 531 p.
91-015798   551.46/01   0849388406
Chemical oceanography.

GC150.5 Physical oceanography — General works — 1975-

GC150.5.B69 1983
Bowden, K. F. 1916-
Physical oceanography of coastal waters/ K.F. Bowden. Chichester [West Sussex]: E. Horwood; 1983. 302 p.
83-018444   551.46   0853126860
Oceanography. Coasts.

GC150.5.M45 1996
Mellor, G. L.
Introduction to physical oceanography/ George L. Mellor. Woodbury, N.Y.: American Institute of Physics, c1996. xiii, 260 p.
96-008478   551.46 20   1563962101
Oceanography.

GC190.5 Ocean-atmosphere interaction — Methodology

GC190.5.K34 1995
Kagan, B. A.
Ocean-atmosphere interaction and climate modelling/ Boris A. Kagan; translated by Mikhail Hazin. Cambridge [England]; Cambridge University Press, 1995. xiii, 377 p.
94-014977   551.25   0521444454
Ocean-atmosphere interaction -- Mathematical models. Climatology -- Mathematical models.

GC201 Dynamics of the ocean — General works — 1801-1974

GC201.E8
Estuary and coastline hydrodynamics [by P. S. Eagleson and others. Arthur T. Ippen, editor. New York, McGraw-Hill Book Co., [1966] xvii, 744 p.
65-027677   551.36
Coast changes. Ocean waves. Tides.

GC201.W5
Wiegel, Robert L.
Oceanographical engineering [by] Robert L. Wiegel. Englewood Cliffs, N.J., Prentice-Hall [1964] xi, 532 p.
64-023185   551.47
Oceanography. Ocean waves. Hydraulic structures.

GC211-211.2 Dynamics of the ocean — Waves — General works

GC211.K5
Kinsman, Blair.
Wind waves, their generation and propagation on the ocean surface.   Englewood Cliffs, N.J., Prentice-Hall [1965] xxiii, 676 p.
64-010136   551.47
Ocean waves.

GC211.2.B37 1980
Bascom, Willard.
Waves and beaches: the dynamics of the ocean surface/ Willard Bascom; ill. by the author. Garden City, N.Y.: Anchor Press, 1980. xvii, 366 p.
79-007038   551.4/7022   0385184445
Ocean waves. Beaches.

GC221.2 Dynamics of the ocean — Waves — Tsunamis. Tidal waves

GC221.2.B78 2001
Bryant, Edward, 1948-
Tsunami: the underrated hazard/ Edward Bryant. New York: Cambridge University Press, 2001. xxx, 320 p.
00-046761   551.47/024   0521772443
Tsunamis.

GC228.5 Dynamics of the ocean — Ocean circulation — General works

GC228.5.O26 2001
Ocean circulation and climate: observing and modelling the global ocean/ edited by Gerold Siedler, John Church, John Gould. San Diego: Academic Press, c2001. xix, 715 p.
00-106870   551.47 21   0126413517
Ocean-atmosphere interaction. Ocean circulation.

GC296-296.8 Dynamics of the ocean — Currents — By individual current

GC296.G9.S7 1965
Stommel, Henry M., 1920-
The Gulf Stream; a physical and dynamical description.   Berkeley, University of California Press, 1965. xiii, 248 p.
64-023710   551.471
Gulf Stream.

GC296.8.E4.F34 1999
Fagan, Brian M.
Floods, famines, and emperors: El Nino and the fate of civilizations/ Brian Fagan. New York: Basic Books, c1999. xix, 284 p.
99-215189   363.34/92 21   0465011209
Climatic changes -- Social aspects -- History. Human beings -- Effect of climate on -- History. El Nino Current.

GC296.8.E4.G53 2001
Glantz, Michael H.
Currents of change: impacts of El Nino and La Nina on climate and society/ Michael H. Glantz. Cambridge; Cambridge University Press, 2001. xiii, 252 p.
00-036291   551.47/6   052178672X
El Nino Current. Climatic changes.

GC301.2 Dynamics of the ocean — Tides — General works

GC301.2.C37 1999
Cartwright, David Edgar, 1926-
Tides: a scientific history/ David Edgar Cartwright. New York: Cambridge University Press, 1999. xii, 292 p.
98-004660   551.47/08   0521621453
Tides. Tides -- History.

GC1015.2 Marine resources. Applied oceanography — General works — 1975-

GC1015.2.W43 1995
Weber, Michael
The wealth of oceans/ Michael Weber and Judith Gradwohl. New York: W.W. Norton & Co., c1995. 256 p.
94-035997   333.91/64   0393037649
Marine resources.

GC1020 Marine resources. Applied oceanography — By region or country — United States

GC1020.H45 2001
Helvarg, David, 1951-
Blue frontier: saving America's living seas/ David Helvard. New York: W.H. Freeman, 2001. 299 p.
00-010956   333.91/6416/0973   0716737159
Marine resources conservation -- United States.

GC1023.15 Marine resources. Applied oceanography — By region or country — Other regions or countries

GC1023.15.S43 1994
The sea has many voices: oceans policy for a complex world/ edited by Cynthia Lamson. Montreal: McGill-Queen's University Press, 1994. x, 327 p.
94-227055   333.91/64/0971   0773511121
Marine resources -- Government policy -- Canada. Law of the sea -- Canada.

GC1081 Marine pollution. Sea water pollution — Congresses

GC1081.I48 1982
Impact of marine pollution on society/ Virginia K. Tippie, Dana R. Kester, editors. New York, N.Y.: Praeger; 1982. vi, 313 p.
81-012270   363.7/394   0030597323
Marine pollution -- Social aspects -- Congresses.

GC1085 Marine pollution. Sea water pollution — General works

GC1085.F75 1995
Frankel, Ernst G.
Ocean environmental management: a primer on the role of the oceans and how to maintain their contributions to life on Earth/ Ernst G. Frankel. Englewood Cliffs, N.J.: Prentice Hall PTR, c1995. xvi, 381 p.
94-033448   333.91/6415   0131845578
Marine pollution.

GC1085.G67 1993
Gorman, Martha, 1952-
Environmental hazards: marine pollution/ Martha Gorman. Santa Barbara, Calif.: ABC-CLIO, c1993. xiii, 252 p.
93-039789   363.73/94/09162   0874366410
Marine pollution.

GC1212-1311 Marine pollution. Sea water pollution — By region — Atlantic Ocean

GC1212.N5.S33 1998
Scanlan, Phillip M.
The dolphins are back: a successful quality model for healing the environment/ Phillip M. Scanlan. Portland, Or.: Productivity Press, c1998. xxiv, 308 p.
97-048648   363.739/45/09749 21   1563271834
Marine pollution -- New Jersey -- Atlantic Coast.

GC1311.M37
Marine Biological Association of the United Kingdom.
"Torrey Canyon" pollution and marine life: a report by the Plymouth Laboratory of the Marine Biological Association of the United Kingdom, under the general editorship of J. E. Smith. London, published for the Marine Biological Association 1968. xiv, 196 p.
68-021400   628/.1686   0521071445
Marine pollution -- English Channel. Oil pollution of rivers, harbors, etc. Detergent pollution of the sea.

GE Environmental Sciences

GE1 Societies. Serials

GE1.K38 1993
Katz, Linda Sobel.
Environmental profiles: a global guide to projects and people/ Linda Sobel Katz, Sarah Orrick, and Robert Honig; foreword by Al Gore; illustrations by Jane Svoboda. New York: Garland Pub., 1993. xxvi, 1083 p.
92-041800   363.7/0601 20   0815300638
Environmental sciences -- Societies, etc. -- Directories. Environmentalists -- Directories. Environmental sciences -- Information services -- Directories.

GE1.R64 1993
Rogers, Adam.
The Earth Summit: a planetary reckoning/ Adam Rogers. Los Angeles, CA: Global View Press, c1993. 351 p.
93-138486   363.7/0526   1881294935
Environmental policy -- International cooperation -- Congresses. Environmental law, International -- Congresses.

GE10 Dictionaries. Encyclopedias

GE10.C68 1995
Conservation and environmentalism: an encyclopedia/ editor, Robert Paehlke. New York: Garland Pub., 1995. xxxiii, 771 p.
94-049708   363.7/003 20   0824061012
Environmental sciences -- Encyclopedias. Environmental protection -- Encyclopedias. Environmentalism -- Encyclopedias.

GE10.C78 1993
Crump, Andy.
Dictionary of environment and development: people, places, ideas, and organizations/ Andy Crump. 1st MIT Press ed. Cambridge, Mass.: MIT Press, 1993. 272 p.
92-036484   363.7/003 20   0262531178
Environmental sciences -- Encyclopedias. Economic development -- Encyclopedias.

GE10.D37 1993
Dashefsky, H. Steve.
Environmental literacy: everything you need to know about saving our planet/ H. Steven Dashefsky. New York: Random House, c1993. xix, 298 p.
92-056808   363.7/003   0679412808
Environmental sciences -- Dictionaries.

GE10.D53 1993
The Dictionary of ecology and environmental science/ Henry W. Art, general editor; foreword by F. Herbert Bormann; contributing editors, Daniel Botkin ... [et al.]. New York: H. Holt, 1993. viii, 632 p.
92-038526   363.7/003   0805020799
Environmental sciences -- Dictionaries. Ecology -- Dictionaries.

GE10.E49 1998
Encyclopedia of environmental analysis and remediation/ Robert A. Meyers, editor. New York: Wiley, c1998. 8 v.
97-041586   628 21   0471117080
Environmental sciences -- Encyclopedias. Pollution -- Analysis -- Encyclopedias. Environmental protection -- Encyclopedias.

GE10.E52 2000
Encyclopedia of environmental issues/ editor, Craig W. Allin; project editor, Robert McClenaghan. Pasadena, Calif.: Salem Press, c2000. 3 v.
99-046373   363.7/003 21   0893569941
Environmental sciences -- Encyclopedias. Pollution -- Encyclopedias.

GE10.E53 1994
The encyclopedia of the environment/ Ruth A. Eblen and William R. Eblen, editors. Boston: Houghton Mifflin Co., c1994. xvii, 846 p.
94-013669   363.7/003   0395550416
Environmental sciences -- Encyclopedias.

GE10.E58 1994
Environmental encyclopedia/ William P. Cunningham ... [et al.], editors. Detroit: Gale Research, c1994. xxi, 981 p.
94-177482   363.7/003   0810349868
Environmental sciences -- Encyclopedias. Ecology -- Encyclopedias. Earth sciences -- Encyclopedias.

GE10.K45 1998
Kemp, David D.,
The environment dictionary/ David D. Kemp. London; Routledge, 1998. xvi, 464 p.
97-038997   363.7/003 21   041512753X
Environmental sciences -- Dictionaries. Pollution -- Dictionaries.

GE10.M33 1997
Macmillan encyclopedia of the environment/ general editor, Stephen R. Kellert; associate editors, Matthew Black, Richard Haley. New York: Macmillan Library Reference USA; 6 v.
96-029045   333.7 20   0028973879
Environmental sciences -- Dictionaries, Juvenile. Environmental protection -- Dictionaries. Ecology -- Dictionaries.

GE10.M66 2000
Mongillo, John F.
Encyclopedia of environmental science/ by John Mongillo and Linda Zierdt-Warshaw. Phoenix, Ariz.: Oryx Press, 2000. v, 450 p.
00-032657   363.7/003   1573561479
Environmental sciences -- Encyclopedias.

GE10.P67 1996
Porteous, Andrew.
Dictionary of environmental science and technology/ Andrew Porteous. 2nd ed. Chichester; J. Wiley, c1996. xvi, 635 p.
95-046374   628/.03 20   0471960756
Environmental sciences -- Dictionaries. Sanitary engineering -- Dictionaries.

GE10.U54 1997
United Nations.
Glossary of environment statistics/ Department for Economic and Social Information and Policy Analysis. New York: United Nations, 1997. vi, 83 p.
97-168765   363.7/003   9211613868
Environmental sciences -- Dictionaries. Environmental sciences -- Statistics -- Dictionaries.

GE10.W45 1997
Wells, Edward R. 1964-
Historical dictionary of North American environmentalism/ Edward R. Wells and Alan M. Schwartz. Lanham, Md.: Scarecrow Press, 1997. xxix, 226 p.
97-011258   363.7/003   081083331X
Environmental sciences -- Dictionaries. Environmentalism -- Dictionaries. Environmentalism -- North America -- History -- Dictionaries.

GE30 Communication in environmental sciences — General works

GE30.I56 1997
Information sources in environmental protection/ edited by Selwyn Eagle and Judith Deschamps. London; Bowker-Saur, c1997. xviii, 280 p.
96-024228   363.7 20   1857390628
Environmental sciences -- Information services. Environmental literature.

GE35 Communication in environmental sciences — Environmental literature

GE35.E58 1999
Environmental literature: an encyclopedia of works, authors, and themes/ [compiled by] Patricia D. Netzley. Santa Barbara, Calif.: ABC-CLIO, c1999. xiv, 337 p.
99-035271   333.7/2 21   157607000X
Environmental literature -- Encyclopedias. Environmental literature -- Bibliography.

GE40 Philosophy. Relation to other topics. Methodology — General works

GE40.M94 1994
Myers, Norman.
Scarcity or abundance?: a debate on the environment/ Norman Myers & Julian L. Simon. New York: W.W. Norton, c1994. xix, 254 p.
93-027995   363.7   0393035905
Environmental sciences -- Philosophy. Environmental degradation. Nature -- Effect of human beings on.

GE40.S55 1999
Simon, Julian Lincoln, 1932-
Hoodwinking the nation/ Julian Simon. New Brunswick, N.J.: Transaction, c1999. xiv, 140 p.
99-017327   363.7 21   1560004347
Environmental sciences -- Philosophy. Environmental degradation. Nature -- Effect of human beings on.

GE42 Philosophy. Relation to other topics. Methodology — Environmental ethics

GE42.C87 1999
Curtin, Deane W.
Chinnagounder's challenge: the question of ecological citizenship/ Deane Curtin. Bloomington: Indiana University Press, c1999. xviii, 218 p.
99-025161   179/.1 21   0253335760
Environmental ethics. Postcolonialism.

GE42.E25 1996
Earth summit ethics: toward a reconstructive postmodern philosophy of environmental education/ edited by J. Baird Callicott and Fernando J.R. da Rocha. New York: State University of New York Press, c1996. xiii, 247 p.
95-042277   179/.1 20   0791430537
Environmental ethics. Environmental education -- Philosophy.

GE42.K64813 2000
Kohak, Erazim V.
The green halo: a bird's-eye view of ecological ethics/ Erazim Kohak; with a foreword by Holmes Rolston III. Chicago, Ill.: Open Court; c2000. xxvi, 209 p.
99-038665   179/.1 21   0812694112
Environmental ethics.

GE42.L364 2002
Lappé, Frances Moore.
Hope's edge: the next diet for a small planet/ Frances Moore Lappé and Anna Lappé. New York: Jeremy P. Tarcher/Putnam, 2002. 448 p.
2001-048256   179/.1 21   1585421499
Environmental ethics. Globalization -- Social aspects. Capitalism -- Social aspects.

GE42.P35 1997
Palmer, Clare, 1967-
Environmental ethics/ Clare Palmer. Santa Barbara, Calif.: ABC-CLIO, c1997. xiv, 192 p.
97-025966   179/.1 21   0874368405
Environmental ethics.

GE42.S58 1997
Smith, Pamela.
What are they saying about environmental ethics?/ Pamela Smith. New York: Paulist Press, c1997. iii, 122 p.
97-036615   179/.1 21   0809137542
Environmental ethics. Human ecology -- Religious aspects. Religion and science.

GE42.W458 2001
Wenz, Peter S.
Environmental ethics today/ Peter S. Wenz. New York: Oxford University Press, 2001. xv, 351 p.
00-058895   179/.1   0195133846
Environmental ethics.

GE45 Philosophy. Relation to other topics. Methodology — Special methods, A-Z

GE45.S73 E53 2002
Encyclopedia of environmetrics/ editors-in-chief, Abdel H. El-Shaarawi, Walter W. Piegorsch. Chichester; Wiley, c2002. 4 v.
2001-046817   363.7/007/27 21   0471899976
Environmental sciences -- Statistical methods -- Encyclopedias. Environmental sciences -- Methodology -- Encyclopedias.

GE45.S73.S83 1992
Statistics for the environment/ edited by Vic Barnett and K. Feridun Turkman. Chichester, West Sussex, England; Wiley, c1993. xix, 427 p.
92-021239   0471934674
Environmental sciences -- Statistical methods -- Congresses.

GE45.U6 A44 1997
ASTM standards on environmental sampling. 2nd ed. West Conshohocken, PA: ASTM, 1997. xii, 1010 p.
97-015930   628 21   080311835X
Environmental sampling -- Standards -- United States. Atmospheric chemistry -- Standards -- United States. Chemistry, Analytic -- Standards -- United States.

GE50 Philosophy. Relation to other topics. Methodology — History

GE50.B68 1993
Bowler, Peter J.
The Norton history of the environmental sciences/ Peter J. Bowler. New York: W.W. Norton, 1993. xvii, 634 p.
93-019049   363.7/009   0393035352
Environmental sciences -- History.

GE55 Biography — Collective

GE55.B43 2000
Becher, Anne.
American environmental leaders: from colonial times to the present/ Anne Becher with Kyle McClure, Rachel White Scheuering, and Julia Willis. Santa Barbara, Calif.: ABC-CLIO, c2000. 2 v.
00-011296   363.7/0092/273 21   1576071626
Environmentalists -- United States -- Biography.

GE55.G54 1998
Glazer, Penina Migdal.
The environmental crusaders: confronting disaster and mobilizing community/ Penina Migdal Glazer and Myron Peretz Glazer. University Park, Pa.: Pennsylvania State University Press, c1998. xxvi, 218 p.
97-049828   363.7/0092/2 21   0271017759
Environmentalists -- United States. Environmentalists -- Israel. Environmentalists -- Czechoslovakia.

GE55.L485 2000
Life stories: world-renowned scientists reflect on their lives and on the future of life on earth/ edited by Heather Newbold. Berkeley: University of California Press, 2000. xii, 234 p.
99-054133   363.7/0092/2   0520211146
Environmentalists -- Biography. Environmental sciences.

GE60 Vocational guidance

GE60.D69 1999
Doyle, Kevin.
The complete guide to environmental careers in the 21st century/ the Environmental Careers Organization; Kevin Doyle, Sam Heizmann, Tanya Stubbs, writers. Washington, D.C.: Island Press, c1999. xvi, 447 p.
98-039091   363.7/0023 21   155963586X
Environmental sciences -- Vocational guidance.

GE60.E38
Education for the earth: a guide to top environmental studies programs. Princeton, NJ: Peterson's Guides, <c1993- >
96-652811   363.7/0023/73 20
Environmental sciences -- Vocational guidance -- United States -- Handbooks, manuals. etc. Environmental sciences -- Vocational guidance -- Canada -- Handbooks, Ecological engineering -- Vocational guidance -- United States -- Handbooks,

GE60.E58
Environmental career directory: practical, one-stop guide to getting a job preserving the environment. Detroit: Gale Research Inc., <c1993- >
94-648089   363.7/0023/73 20
Environmental sciences -- Vocational guidance -- United States

GE60.S4713 1995
Serres, Michel.
The natural contract/ Michel Serres; translated by Elizabeth MacArthur and William Paulson. Ann Arbor: University of Michigan Press, c1995. 124 p.
95-002685   363.7   0472095498
Environmental sciences -- Philosophy. Environmental responsibility.

GE70 Environmental education. Study and teaching. Research — General works

GE70.H8 1998
Hutchison, David
Growing up green: education for ecological renewal/ David Hutchison; foreword by Thomas Berry. New York: Teachers College Press, c1998. xiv, 177 p.
97-043995   363.7/0071/2 21   0807737259
Environmental education -- Philosophy. Green movement.

GE80 Environmental education. Study and teaching. Research — By region or country — United States

GE80.E58
Environmental grantmaking foundations: directory. Rochester, NY: Environmental Data Research Institute, [c1992-]
93-640543   363.7/0576/0257
Environmental sciences -- United States -- Endowments -- Directories. Environmental sciences -- Canada -- Endowments -- Directories. Environmental sciences -- Endowments -- Directories.

GE80.H69 1993
Hoyle, Russ.
Gale environmental almanac/ Russ Hoyle. Detroit: Gale Research, 1993. xx, 684 p.
93-037699   363.7/0097   0810388774
Sustainable development -- United States. Environmental education -- United States. Environmental policy -- United States.

GE105 General works

GE105.C54 1995
Climate change: impact on coastal habitation/ edited by Doeke Eisma. Boca Raton: Lewis Publishers, c1995. 260 p.
94-035116   333.91/7   087371301X
Environmental sciences. Coastal ecology. Marine ecology.

GE105.S68 1996
Southwick, Charles H.
Global ecology in human perspective/ Charles H. Southwick. New York: Oxford University Press, 1996. xxi, 392 p.
95-030198   304.2   0195098676
Environmental sciences. Nature -- Effect of human beings on. Pollution.

GE123 Handbooks, manuals, etc.

GE123.C64 1996
Cooper, Andre R.
Cooper's comprehensive environmental desk reference/ compiled and edited by Andre R. Cooper, Sr. New York: Van Nostrand Reinhold, c1996. ix, 1039 p.
95-038571   363.7 20   0442021593
Environmental sciences -- Handbooks, manuals, etc. Environmental sciences -- Dictionaries. Environmental protection -- Handbooks, manuals, etc.

GE123.S73 2000
Standard handbook of environmental science, health, and technology/ Jay H. Lehr, editor; Janet K. Lehr, associate editor. New York: McGraw-Hill, c2000. 1 v.
00-036172   363.7 21   007038309X
Environmental sciences -- Handbooks, manuals, etc. Environmental protection -- Handbooks, manuals, etc. Environmental health -- Handbooks, manuals, etc.

GE140 Environmental conditions. Environmental quality. Environmental indicators. Environmental degradation — General works

GE140.E18 1999
Earth, air, fire, water: humanistic studies of the environment/ edited by Jill Ker Conway, Kenneth Keniston, and Leo Marx. Amherst: University of Massachusetts Press, c1999. ix, 349 p.
99-016970   304.2/8 21   1558492208
Environmental degradation -- Social aspects. Nature -- Effect of human beings on.

GE140.J64 1995
Johnson, Douglas L.
Land degradation: creation and destruction/ Douglas L. Johnson and Laurence A. Lewis. Oxford, UK; Blackwell, 1995. xx, 335 p.
94-027799   333.73/137   0631179976
Land degradation -- Environmental aspects. Nature -- Effect of human beings on.

GE140.K47 1997
Kellert, Stephen R.
Kinship to mastery: biophilia in human evolution and development/ Stephen R. Kellert. Washington, D.C.: Island Press, c1997. xvi, 256 p.
96-029893   304.2/8 21   1559633727
Environmental degradation. Human evolution. Human ecology.

GE140.R46 1996
Renner, Michael, 1957-
Fighting for survival: environmental decline, social conflict, and the new age of insecurity/ Michael Renner. New York: Norton, c1996. 239 p.
96-232410   304.2/8 20   039303996X
Environmental degradation -- Social aspects. Violence -- Environmental aspects. Social ecology.

GE145 Environmental conditions. Environmental quality. Environmental indicators. Environmental degradation — Environmental risk assessment — General works

GE145.C68 1995
Cothern, C. Richard.
Handbook for environmental risk decision making: values, perceptions, and ethics/ C. Richard Cothern. Boca Raton, FL: Lewis Publishers, 1995, c1996. 408 p.
95-016857   363.7/0068/4   1566701317
Environmental ethics -- Congresses. Values -- Congresses. Environmental risk assessment -- Congresses.

GE149 Environmental conditions. Environmental quality. Environmental indicators. Environmental degradation — Global environmental change

GE149.E443 2002
Encyclopedia of global environmental change/ editor-in-chief, Ted Munn. Chichester; Wiley, c2002. 5 v.
2001-046740   363.7/003 21   0471977969
Global environmental change -- Encyclopedias.

GE149.E47 2002
Encyclopedia of global change: environmental change and human society / Andrew S. Goudie, editor in chief; David J. Cuff, associate editor. Oxford; Oxford University Press, 2002. 2 v.
00-058918   363.7 21   0195145194
Global environmental change -- Encyclopedias. Nature -- Effect of human beings on -- Encyclopedias. Global environmental change -- Social aspects -- Encyclopedias.

GE149.L65 2001
Lomborg, Bjørn,
The skeptical environmentalist: measuring the real state of the world / Bjørn Lomborg. Cambridge; Cambridge University Press, c2001. xxiii, 515 p.
00-068915   363.7 21   0521010683
Global environmental change. Pollution. Human ecology.

GE149.M37 1999
Mannion, Antoinette M.
Natural environmental change: the last 3 million years/ A.M. Mannion. London; Routledge, 1999. xiii, 198 p.
98-025877   363.7   0415139325
Global environmental change. Climatic changes.

GE149.S36 1997
Schneider, Stephen Henry.
Laboratory earth: the planetary gamble we can't afford to lose/ Stephen H. Schneider. New York: BasicBooks, c1997. xvii, 174 p.
96-042987   304.2/8 20   0465072798
Global environmental change. Climatic changes. Nature -- Effect of human beings on.

GE150-155 Environmental conditions. Environmental quality. Environmental indicators. Environmental degradation — By region or country — United States

GE150.G72 1995
Great events from history II. edited by Frank N. Magill. Pasadena, CA: Salem Press, c1995. 5 v.
95-005035 363.7 0893567515
United States -- Environmental conditions -- History -- 20th century.

GE150.K46 1995
Kempton, Willett, 1948-
Environmental values in American culture/ Willett Kempton, James S. Boster, and Jennifer A. Hartley. Cambridge, Mass.: MIT Press, c1995. xiii, 320 p.
94-027765 363.7/00973 0262111918
Public interest -- United States. Values -- United States. United States -- Environmental conditions.

GE150.L47 1997
Lerner, Steve.
Eco-pioneers: practical visionaries solving today's environmental problems/ Steve Lerner. Cambridge, Mass.: MIT Press, c1997. xii, 462 p.
97-008333 363.7/0092/273 B 21 0262122073
Environmental degradation -- United States -- Case studies. Sustainable development -- United States -- Case studies. Environmental engineers -- United States -- Biography.

GE155.E84.M34 1999
McCally, David, 1949-
The Everglades: an environmental history/ David McCally; foreword by Raymond Arsenault and Gary R. Mormino. Gainesville: University Press of Florida, 1999. xxii, 215 p.
99-018766 333.91/8/0975939 0813016487
Drainage -- Florida -- Everglades -- History. Everglades (Fla.) -- Environmental conditions -- History.

GE155.M85.S36 1999
Schneiders, Robert Kelley, 1965-
Unruly river: two centuries of change along the Missouri/ by Robert Kelley Schneiders. Lawrence: University Press of Kansas, 1999. xi, 314 p.
98-033976 333.91/15/0978 0700609377
Water resources development -- Missouri River Watershed. Missouri River Watershed -- Environmental conditions. Missouri River Watershed -- Description and travel.

GE155.W47.R43 1998
Reclaiming the native home of hope: community, ecology, and the American West/ edited by Robert B. Keiter; foreword by Page Stegner. Salt Lake City: University of Utah Press, c1998. xviii, 178 p.
97-049564 333.7/15/0978 21 0874805589
Environmental management -- West (U.S.) West (U.S.) -- Environmental conditions.

GE160 Environmental conditions. Environmental quality. Environmental indicators. Environmental degradation — By region or country — Other regions or countries, A-Z

GE160.D44.I43 1994
Imber, Mark.
Environment, security, and UN reform/ Mark F. Imber. New York, N.Y.: St. Martin's Press, 1994. xi, 180 p.
94-005974 363.7/009172/4 0312121687
Environmental responsibility -- Developing countries. Environmental policy -- Developing countries. Environmental degradation -- Developing countries.

GE160.E83.B76 1995
Brownson, J. M. Jamil, 1941-
In cold margins: sustainable development in Northern bioregions/ J.M. Jamil Brownson. Missoula, Mont.: Northern Rim Press, 1995.
94-003141 363.7/009181/3 096400867X
Environmental policy. Human ecology. Sustainable development. North America -- Environmental conditions. Eurasia -- Environmental conditions.

GE160.F6.P79 1995
Environmental resources and constraints in the former Soviet Republics/ edited by Philip R. Pryde. Boulder: Westview Press, 1995. ix, 366 p.
94-033120 363.7/00947 0813317428
Environmental policy -- Former Soviet republics. Former Soviet republics -- Environmental conditions.

GE160.G75.D87 1995
Durnil, Gordon K., 1936-
The making of a conservative environmentalist: with reflections on government, industry, scientists, the media, education, economic growth, the public, the Great Lakes, activists, and the sunsettin Gordon K. Durnil. Bloomington: Indiana University Press, c1995. xii, 200 p.
94-024989 363.7/0092 025332873X
Durnil, Gordon K., -- 1936- Environmental policy -- Canada. Environmental policy -- United States. Environmentalists -- United States -- Biography. Great Lakes Region -- Environmental conditions.

GE170 Environmental policy — General works

GE170.A53 1996
Anderson, Eugene N. 1941-
Ecologies of the heart: emotion, belief, and the environment/ E.N. Anderson. New York: Oxford University Press, 1996. ix, 256 p.
95-013747 363.7 0195090101
Environmental policy. Environmental protection. Human ecology.

GE170.B83 1998
Buck, Susan J.
The global commons: an introduction/ Susan J. Buck. Washington, D.C.: Island Press, 1998. xiv, 225 p.
97-049587 363.7 1559635509
Environmental policy. Commons. Natural resources, Communal.

GE170.D465 2000
De-Shalit, Avner.
The environment: between theory and practice/ Avner de-Shalit. Oxford; Oxford University Press, 2000. vii, 238 p.
99-057190 363.7 0198297696
Environmental policy. Environmental protection. Environmentalism.

GE170.E47 1998
Elliott, Lorraine M.
The global politics of the environment/ Lorraine Elliott. New York, N.Y.: New York University Press, 1998. xvi, 311 p.
97-022763 363.7/0526 081472163X
Environmental policy -- International cooperation. Environmental degradation. Nature -- Effect of human beings on.

GE170.E5763 1998
Environmental injustices, political struggles: race, class, and the environment/ David E. Camacho, editor. Durham, NC: Duke University Press, 1998. viii, 232 p.
98-016749 363.7/03 0822322250
Environmental justice. Environmental justice -- Case studies. Environmental policy.

GE170.F57 1995
Forman, Richard T. T.
Land mosaics: the ecology of landscapes and regions/ Richard T.T. Forman. Cambridge; Cambridge University Press, 1995. xx, 632 p.
94-039092 304.2/3 0521474620
Environmental policy. Landscape ecology. Human ecology.

GE170.G5625
Global environment outlook. New York: Oxford University Press, <c1997- >
98-658027 363.7 21
Environmental policy -- Periodicals. Environmental responsibility -- Periodicals.

GE170.G67 1992
Gore, Albert, 1948-
Earth in balance: ecology and the human spirit/ Al Gore. Boston: Houghton Mifflin, c1992. 407 p.
91-042676 363.7 0395578213
Environmental policy. Environmental protection. Human ecology.

GE170.I55 2001
International encyclopedia of environmental politics/ edited by John Barry and E. Gene Frankland. London; Routledge, 2001.
2001-019754 363.7/056 21 041520285X
Environmental policy -- Encyclopedias.

GE170.M35 1995
Malnes, Raino.
Valuing the environment/ Raino Malnes. Manchester; Manchester University Press; 1995. xiv, 136 p.
95-033687 363.7 0719044855
Environmental policy. Environmental responsibility.

GE170.P38 2000
Paterson, Matthew, 1967-
Understanding global environmental politics: domination, accumulation, resistance/ Matthew Paterson. Houndmills, Basingstoke, Hampshire: Macmillan Press; c2000. x, 199 p.
99-053110 363.7 21 0312230907
Environmental policy.

GE170.P45 1999
People, plants, and justice: the politics of nature conservation/ Charles Zerner, editor. New York: Columbia University Press, c2000. xvii, 449 p.
99-053777   333.7 21   0231108117
   Environmental justice. Natural resources -- Management. Environmental management.

GE170.S68 1997
Soroos, Marvin S.
The endangered atmosphere: preserving a global commons/ Marvin S. Soroos. Columbia, S.C.: University of South Carolina Press, c1997. xv, 339 p.
96-051243   363.739/2 21   1570031606
   Environmental policy. Pollution -- Environmental aspects. Climatic changes -- Environmental aspects.

GE170.W4513 1994
Weizsacker, Ernst U. von 1939-
Earth politics/ Ernst U. von Weizsacker; foreword by the president of the Club of Rome. London; Zed Books, 1994. xii, 234 p.
93-037606   363.7   1856491730
   Environmental policy. Environmental protection.

GE180-185 Environmental policy — By region or country — United States

GE180.B57 2001
Bliese, John Ross Edward, 1943-
The greening of conservative America/ John R.E. Bliese. Boulder, Colo.: Westview Press, 2001. x, 339 p.
00-065430   363.7/0525/0973   0813338026
   Environmental policy -- United States. Conservatism -- United States.

GE180.C34 1995
Cahn, Matthew Alan, 1961-
Environmental deceptions: the tension between liberalism and environmental policymaking in the United States/ Matthew Alan Cahn. Albany: State University of New York Press, c1995. xi, 179 p.
94-006017   363.7/00973   0791422631
   Environmental policy -- United States. Liberalism -- United States. United States -- Politics and government -- 1945-1989. United States -- Politics and government -- 1989-

GE180.E546 2003
Environmental policy: new directions for the twenty-first century/ edited by Norman J. Vig, Michael E. Kraft. 5th ed. Washington, D.C.: CQ Press, c2003. xii, 436 p.
2002-008811   363.7/056/0973 21   1568026986
   Environmental policy -- United States.

GE180.F54 1994
Fleagle, Robert Guthrie, 1918-
Global environmental change: interactions of science, policy, and politics in the United States/ Robert G. Fleagle. Westport, Conn.: Praeger, 1994. xiv, 243 p.
93-044500   363.7/00973   0275944778
   Environmental policy -- United States. Global environmental change.

GE180.G68 1993
Gottlieb, Robert, 1944-
Forcing the spring: the transformation of the American environmental movement/ Robert Gottlieb. Washington, D.C.: Island Press, c1993. xi, 413 p.
93-003513   363.7/0525/0973   1559631236
   Environmental policy -- United States -- History. Green movement -- United States -- History.

GE180.H392 2000
Hays, Samuel P.
A history of environmental politics since 1945/ Samuel P. Hays. Pittsburgh: University of Pittsburgh Press, c2000. ix, 256 p.
00-009651   363.7/05/0973 21   0822941287
   Environmental policy -- United States -- History -- 20th century. Environmentalism -- United States -- History -- 20th century.

GE180.L47 2001
Lester, James P., 1944-
Environmental injustice in the United States: myths and realities/ James P. Lester, David W. Allen, Kelly M. Hill. Boulder, Colo.: Westview Press, c2001. xv, 216 p.
00-043787   363.7/05/793 21   0813338182
   Environmental justice -- United States. Environmental justice -- Political aspects -- United States. Social justice.

GE180.M38 1999
Matystik, Walter F.
State environmental agencies on the Internet/ Walter F. Matystik, Louis Theodore, Roberto Diaz. Rockville, Md.: Government Institutes, c1999. xxxvii, 344 p.
99-053924   025.06/3543/280973   21
0865876851
   Environmental policy -- United States -- States -- Directories. Administrative agencies -- United States -- States -- Directories. Internet.

GE180.M56 1995
Mintz, Joel A., 1949-
Enforcement at the EPA: high stakes and hard choices/ by Joel A. Mintz. Austin: University of Texas Press, 1995. x, 200 p.
95-013922   363.7/56/0973   0292751877
   Environmental policy -- United States.

GE180.S42 1999
Shaiko, Ronald G., 1959-
Voices and echoes for the environment: public interest representation in the 1990s and beyond/ Ronald G. Shaiko. New York: Columbia University Press, c1999. xvi, 300 p.
98-052088   363.7/0525/0973 21   0231113544
   Environmental policy -- United States -- Societies, etc. Environmental policy -- United States -- Citizen participation. Public interest -- United States.

GE180.W43 1998
Weber, Edward P.
Pluralism by the rules: conflict and cooperation in environmental regulation/ Edward P. Weber. Washington, D.C.: Georgetown University Press, c1998. xx, 308 p.
97-037976   363.7/00973 21   0878406719
   Environmental policy -- United States. Environmental management -- United States. Pluralism.

GE180.W55 1998
Wilkinson, Todd.
Science under siege: the politicians' war on nature and truth/ Todd Wilkinson; foreword by David Brower; introduction by Jim Baca. Boulder, Colo.: Johnson Books, c1998. xix, 364 p.
98-012458   363.7 21   1555662102
   Environmental responsibility -- United States -- Case studies. Environmental degradation -- United States -- Case studies.

GE185.U6 W47 2001
Western public lands and environmental politics/ edited by Charles Davis. 2nd ed. Boulder, CO: Westview Press, 2001. xii, 276 p.
00-048472   333.73/15/0978 21   0813337682
   Environmental policy -- West (U.S.) Public lands -- Government policy -- West (U.S) Land use -- Government policy -- West (U.S.)

GE190 Environmental policy — By region or country — Other regions or countries

GE190.C6.S56 1995
Sinkule, Barbara J.
Implementing environmental policy in China/ Barbara J. Sinkule and Leonard Ortolano. Westport, Conn.: Praeger, 1995. xvi, 226 p.
95-007346   363.7/00951   027594980X
   Environmental policy -- China. Environmental protection -- China. China -- Environmental conditions.

GE190.E95.E855 1997
European environmental policy: the pioneers/ edited by Mikael Skou Anderson and Duncan Liefferink. Manchester, [Eng.]; Manchester University Press, 1997. xi, 340 p.
96-040303   363.7/0094   071905043X
   Environmental policy -- Europe.

GE195 Environmentalism. Green movement — General works

GE195.C65 1994
Coleman, Daniel A., 1952-
Ecopolitics: building a green society/ Daniel A. Coleman. New Brunswick, N.J.: Rutgers University Press, c1994. 236 p.
93-006029   363.7/05   0813520541
   Green movement. Environmental policy -- Social aspects.

GE195.D437 2001
Deep ecology and world religions: new essays on sacred grounds/ edited by David Landis Barnhill and Roger S. Gottlieb. Albany: State University of New York Press, c2001. xiii, 291 p.
00-030081   179.1 21   0791448835
   Deep ecology -- Religious aspects.

GE195.D45 1999
DeLuca, Kevin Michael.
Image politics: the new rhetoric of environmental activism/ Kevin Michael DeLuca. New York: Guilford Press, 1999. xvi, 203 p.
99-019839   363.7/0525   1572304618
   Environmentalism. Mass media and the environment. Rhetoric.

GE195.E18 1995
Easterbrook, Gregg.
A moment on the Earth: the coming age of environmental optimism/ Gregg Easterbrook. New York: Viking, 1995. xxi, 745 p.
94-023411   363.7/005   0670839833
Environmentalism. Green movement. Environmental protection.

GE195.E37 1996
Ehrlich, Paul R.
Betrayal of science and reason: how anti-environmental rhetoric threatens our future/ Paul R. Ehrlich, Anne H. Ehrlich. Washington, D.C.: Island Press, 1996. xiii, 335 p.
96-034249   363.7   1559634839
Anti-environmentalism. Environmental degradation.

GE195.J64 1995
Johnson, Huey D.
Green plans: greenprint for sustainability/ Huey D. Johnson. Lincoln: University of Nebraska Press, c1995. xiv, 206 p.
94-037336   363.7   0803225792
Environmental policy. Sustainable development. Green movement.

GE195.K38 1994
Kaufman, Wallace.
No turning back: dismantling the fantasies of environmental thinking/ Wallace Kaufman. New York: Basic Books, c1994. 212 p.
93-049618   363.7   0465051189
Environmentalism. Green movement. Environmental policy -- United States.

GE195.L57 1996
Lipschutz, Ronnie D.
Global civil society and global environmental governance: the politics of nature from place to planet/ Ronnie D. Lipschutz with Judith Mayer. Albany: State University of New York Press, c1996. xiv, 365 p.
95-052245   363.7/00523 20   0791431177
Environmentalism -- International cooperation. Community power -- International cooperation. World politics.

GE195.M47 1992
Merrow, Susan D.
One for the earth: journal of a Sierra Club president/ Susan D. Merrow and Wanda A. Rickerby. Champaign, Ill.: Sagamore Pub. Co., c1992. xv, 244 p.
91-098423   333.9516/06073   091561152X
Merrow, Susan D. -- Diaries. Environmental policy -- United States. Nature -- Effect of human beings on. Environmentalism.

GE195.P36 1998
Papadakis, Elim.
Historical dictionary of the green movement/ Elim Papadakis. Lanham, Md.: Scarecrow Press, 1998. xx, 223 p.
98-007912   363.7/052 21   0810835029
Green movement -- Dictionaries. Green movement -- History -- Dictionaries.

GE195.S43 1996
Shabecoff, Philip.
A new name for peace: international environmentalism, sustainable development, and democracy/ Philip Shabecoff. Hanover: University Press of New England, c1996. xiii, 271 p.
96-002235   363.7 20   0874516889
Environmentalism. Sustainable development. Geopolitics.

GE195.S97 1996
The symbolic earth: discourse and our creation of the environment/ James G. Cantrill & Christine L. Oravec, editors. Lexington, Ky.: University Press of Kentucky, c1996. 284 p.
96-005956   363.7 20   0813119731
Environmentalism. Environmental policy -- United States.

GE197-198 Environmentalism. Green movement — By region or country — United States

GE197.E7 1999
The environmental debate: a documentary history/ edited by Peninah Neimark and Peter Rhoades Mott. Westport, Conn.: Greenwood Press, 1999. xxviii, 319 p.
99-017844   363.7/05/0973   0313300208
Environmentalism -- United States -- History.

GE197.F55 1998
Flattau, Edward.
Tracking the charlatans: an environmental columnist's refutational handbook for the propaganda wars/ Edward Flattau. Washington, D.C.: Global Horizons Press, 1998. xi, 296 p.
97-094082   363.7   0965916200
Anti-environmentalism. Environmental degradation. Environmentalists -- Attitudes.

GE197.G33 1998
Gaard, Greta Claire.
Ecological politics: ecofeminists and the Greens/ Greta Gaard. Philadelphia: Temple University Press, 1998. x, 337 p.
97-012413   363.7/0525   1566395690
Green movement -- United States. Ecofeminism -- United States. Environmental policy -- United States.

GE197.G67 2001
Gottlieb, Robert, 1944-
Environmentalism unbound: exploring new pathways for change/ Robert Gottlieb. Cambridge, Mass.: MIT Press, c2001. xvii, 396 p.
00-060932   363.7 21   0262072106
Environmentalism -- United States. Environmental justice -- United States. Pollution prevention -- United States.

GE197.G76 1994
Grossman, Mark.
The ABC-CLIO companion to the environmental movement/ Mark Grossman. Santa Barbara, Calif.: ABC-CLIO, c1994. xiii, 445 p.
94-036186   363.7/00525/0973   0874367328
Environmentalism -- United States. Environmental policy -- United States.

GE197.R69 2000
Rothman, Hal K.
Saving the planet: the American response to the environment in the twentieth century/ Hal K. Rothman. Chicago: Ivan R. Dee, c2000. 215 p.
99-049372   333.7/2/09730904 21   1566632889
Environmentalism -- United States -- Public opinion -- History -- 20th century. Conservation of natural resources -- United States -- Public opinion -- History -- 20th century. Public opinion -- United States.

GE197.S3 1994
Schwab, James.
Deeper shades of green: the rise of blue-collar and minority environmentalism in America/ Jim Schwab. San Francisco: Sierra Club Books, c1994. xxii, 490 p.
93-029848   363.7/00973   0871564629
Green movement -- United States. Environmentalism -- United States. Environmental protection -- United States -- Case studies.

GE197.S95 1997
Switzer, Jacqueline Vaughn.
Green backlash: the history and politics of the environmental opposition in the U.S./ Jacqueline Vaughn Switzer. Boulder: Lynne Rienner Publishers, 1997. xviii, 323 p.
96-043237   363.7/00973   155587651X
Anti-environmentalism -- United States -- History. Anti-environmentalism -- Political aspects -- United States.

GE198.W6.H84 1994
Huffman, Thomas R.
Protectors of the land and water: environmentalism in Wisconsin, 1961-1968/ Thomas R. Huffman. Chapel Hill: University of North Carolina Press, c1994. viii, 252 p.
93-032479   363.7/05/09775   0807821381
Environmentalism -- Wisconsin -- History. Environmental policy -- Wisconsin -- History.

GE199 Environmentalism. Green movement — By region or country — Other regions or countries, A-Z

GE199.G3.B47 1998
Berglund, Eeva K.
Knowing nature, knowing science: an ethnography of environmental activism/ Eeva K. Berglund. Cambridge, UK: White Horse Press, c1998. viii, 225 p.
98-159996   363.7/05/0943 21   1874267340
Environmentalism -- Germany. Ethnology -- Germany.

GE199.R8.W45 1999
Weiner, Douglas R., 1951-
A little corner of freedom: Russian nature protection from Stalin to Gorbachev/ Douglas R. Weiner. Berkeley, Calif.: University of California Press, c1999. xiv, 556 p.
97-040206   363.7/056/0947 21   0520213971
Environmentalism -- Soviet Union -- History. Environmentalism -- Former Soviet republics -- History.

GE300 Environmental management — General works

GE300.C66 1999
Cortner, H.
The politics of ecosystem management/ Hanna J. Cortner, Margaret A. Moote. Washington, D.C.: Island Press, c1999. xii, 179 p.
98-034883   363.7/056 21   1559636718
Environmental management -- Political aspects.

GE300.E53 1998
The encyclopedia of ecology & environmental management/ editor-in-chief, Peter Calow; editorial board, D.A. Falk ... [et al.]. Osney Mead, Oxford; Blackwell Science, 1998. xv, 805 p.
97-043092 363.7/003 21 0865428387
Environmental management -- Encyclopedias. Ecology -- Encyclopedias.

GE310 Environmental management — By region or country — United States

GE310.C74 1998
Creighton, Sarah Hammond.
Greening the ivory tower: improving the environmental track record of universities, colleges and other institutions/ Sarah Hammond Creighton. Cambridge, Mass: MIT Press, c1998. xvii, 337 p.
97-039382 363.7/0576 21 0262531518
Environmental management -- United States. Universities and colleges -- Environmental aspects -- United States. Green movement -- United States.

GE320 Environmental management — By region or country — Other regions or countries, A-Z

GE320.N7.E58 1998
Environmental management on North America's borders/ edited by Richard Kiy and John D. Wirth. College Station, Tex.: Texas A&M University Press, c1998. xvi, 306 p.
98-008291 363.7/056/097 21 0890968322
Environmental management -- North America.

GF Human Ecology. Anthropogeography

GF3 Congresses

GF3.C37 1985
The Cassandra Conference: resources and the human predicament/ edited by Paul R. Ehrlich and John P. Holdren. College Station, Tex.: Texas A&M University Press, c1988. xi, 330 p.
86-023070 304.2 0890962952
Human ecology -- Congresses.

GF3.E17 1990
The Earth in transition: patterns and processes of biotic impoverishment/ edited by George M. Woodwell. Cambridge [England]; Cambridge University Press, 1990. xiv, 530 p.
90-001471 304.2 0521391377
Human ecology -- Congresses. Biotic communities -- Congresses.

GF4 Dictionaries. Encyclopedias

GF4.D52 1994
The Dictionary of human geography/ edited by R.J. Johnston, Derek Gregory, and David M. Smith. Oxford, UK; Blackwell Reference, 1994. xx, 724 p.
92-044285 304.2/03 0631181415
Human geography -- Dictionaries.

GF13 History

GF13.H58 2001
The historical ecology handbook: a restorationist's guide to reference ecosystems/ edited by Dave Egan and Evelyn A. Howell. Washington, D.C.: Island Press, c2001. xix, 457 p.
00-011160 577.27 21 1559637455
Human ecology -- History. Biotic communities -- History. Conservation of natural resources -- History.

GF13.M39 2000
McNeill, John Robert.
Something new under the sun: an environmental history of the twentieth-century world/ J.R. McNeill. New York: W.W. Norton & Company, c2000. xxvi, 421 p.
99-054900 304.2/8/0904 21 0393049175
Human ecology -- History -- 20th century. Nature -- Effect of human beings on -- History -- 20th century.

GF13.R6 1998
Roberts, Neil, 1953-
The Holocene: an environmental history/ Neil Roberts. Malden, MA: Blackwell Publishers, 1998.
97-043339 930.1 0631186379
Human ecology -- History. Paleoecology -- Holocene. Environmental archaeology.

GF21 Philosophy. Relation to other topics. Methodology — General works

GF21.B87 1993
Buttimer, Anne.
Geography and the human spirit/ Anne Buttimer; with a foreword by Yi-Fu Tuan. Baltimore: Johns Hopkins University Press, c1993. xiv, 285 p.
92-025972 304.2 0801843383
Human geography -- Philosophy.

GF21.E47 1993
Ehrenfeld, David.
Beginning again: people and nature in the new millennium/ David Ehrenfeld. New York: Oxford University Press, 1993. xiv, 216 p.
92-014538 304.2/8 0195078128
Human ecology -- Philosophy. Environmental protection. Environmental policy.

GF21.F47 1993
Ferkiss, Victor C.
Nature, technology, and society: cultural roots of the current environmental crisis/ Victor Ferkiss. New York: New York University Press, c1993. viii, 341 p.
92-027184 304.2 0814726119
Human ecology -- Philosophy -- History. Human ecology -- Religious aspects -- History. Technology and civilization.

GF21.F4813 1995
Ferry, Luc.
The new ecological order/ Luc Ferry; translated by Carol Volk. Chicago: University of Chicago Press, c1995. xxix, 159 p.
94-049333 304.2 0226244822
Human ecology -- Political aspects. Human ecology -- Philosophy. Deep ecology -- Philosophy.

GF21.G8313 2000
Guattari, Felix.
The three ecologies/ Felix Guattari; translated by Ian Pindar and Paul Sutton. London; Athlone Press, 2000.
99-086086 304.2 0485004089
Human ecology -- Philosophy.

GF21.K47 1996
Kellert, Stephen R.
The value of life: biological diversity and human society/ Stephen R. Kellert. Washington, D.C.: Island Press/Shearwater Books, c1996. xix, 263 p.
95-032210 179/.1 20 1559633174
Human ecology -- Philosophy. Philosophy of nature. Environmental degradation -- Moral and ethical aspects.

GF21.O34 1991
Oelschlaeger, Max.
The idea of wilderness: from prehistory to the age of ecology/ Max Oelschlaeger. New Haven: Yale University Press, c1991. xii, 477 p.
90-046016 333.78/2 0300048513
Human ecology -- Philosophy. Wilderness areas. Nature -- Effect of human beings on.

GF21.S33 1997
Sack, Robert David.
Homo geographicus: a framework for action, awareness, and moral concern/ Robert David Sack. Baltimore: Johns Hopkins University Press, c1997. 292 p.
96-047994 304.2/3 21 0801855527
Human geography -- Philosophy. Human territoriality. Geographical perception.

GF21.S53 1995
Sibley, David.
Geographies of exclusion: society and difference in the West/ David Sibley. London; New York: 1995. xviii, 206 p.
94-047516 305 0415119243
Human geography -- Philosophy. Marginality, Social. Minorities.

GF21.W75 1992
Wright, Will.
Wild knowledge: science, language, and social life in a fragile environment/ Will Wright. Minneapolis: University of Minnesota Press, c1992. xiv, 236 p.
91-037574 304.2 0816620504
Human ecology -- Philosophy. Knowledge, Sociology of. Language and languages.

GF23 Philosophy. Relation to other topics. Methodology — Special methods, A-Z

GF23.M35.H85 1993
Huggett, Richard J.
Modelling the human impact on nature: systems analysis of environmental problems/ Richard John Huggett. Oxford; Oxford University Press, 1993. xi, 202 p.
93-012093   304.2/01/5118   0198741707
Human ecology -- Mathematical models. Nature - - Effect of human beings on -- Mathematical models. Environmental degradation -- Mathematical models.

GF26 Study and teaching. Research — General works

GF26.R47 1988
Research in human geography: introductions and investigations/ edited by John Eyles. Oxford, UK; B. Blackwell, 1988. x, 210 p.
87-029390   307   0631150099
Human geography -- Research.

GF27 Study and teaching. Research — By region or country — United States

GF27.B69 1993
Bowers, C. A.
Education, cultural myths, and the ecological crisis: toward deep changes/ C.A. Bowers. -- Albany, N.Y.: State University of New York Press, c1993. 232 p.
91-013356   304.2/071/073   0791412555
Environmental protection -- Study and teaching - - United States. Environmental ethics -- United States. Educational anthropology -- United States.

GF31 General works, treatises, and textbooks — Early through 1969 — Comprehensive works

GF31.M35 1965
Marsh, George Perkins, 1801-1882.
Man and nature. Edited by David Lowenthal. Cambridge. Belknap Press of Harvard University Press, 1965. xxix, 472 p.
65-011591   910
Nature -- Effect of human beings on. Conservation of natural resources.

GF37 General works, treatises, and textbooks — Early through 1969 — Popular works

GF37.S3 1963
Sauer, Carl Ortwin, 1889-
Land and life; a selection from the writings of Carl Ortwin Sauer. Edited by John Leighly. Berkeley, University of California Press, 1963. vi, 435 p.
63-021069
Human geography.

GF41 General works, treatises, and textbooks — 1970- — Comprehensive works

GF41.J3
Jackson, Barbara Ward 1914-
Only one earth; the care and maintenance of a small planet, by Barbara Ward and Rene Dubos. New York, Norton [1972] xxv, 225 p.
72-000447   301.31   0393063917
Human ecology.

GF41.J67 1982
Jordan-Bychkov, Terry G., 1938-
The human mosaic: a thematic introduction to cultural geography/ Terry G. Jordan, Lester Rowntree. New York: Harper & Row, c1982. xv, 444 p.
81-006968   900   0060434619
Human geography. Ethnology.

GF41.S17 1990
Santos, Miguel A.
Managing planet earth: perspectives on population, ecology, and the law/ Miguel A. Santos. New York: Bergin & Garvey Publishers, 1990. xi, 172 p.
89-049264   344/.046   089789216X
Human ecology. Environmental protection. Environmental policy.

GF41.T57 2000
Townsend, Patricia K., 1941-
Environmental anthropology: from pigs to policies/ Patricia K. Townsend. Prospect Heights, Ill. Waveland Press, c2000. vii, 119 p.
2001-270535   304.2 21   1577661265
Human ecology. Biotic communities. Ecosystem management.

GF49 Addresses, essays, lectures

GF49.E59 1999
Environments and historical change/ edited by Paul Slack. Oxford; Oxford University Press, 1999. x, 196 p.
99-037562   304.2   0198233884
Human ecology -- History. Human geography -- History. Landscape changes -- History.

GF50 General special (Special aspects of the subject as a whole)

GF50.B67 1992
Boyden, Stephen Vickers.
Biohistory: the interplay between human society and the biosphere/ S. Boyden; illustrations by Jorge Bontes. Paris: UNESCO; 1992. xiv, 265 p.
91-046009   304.2   185070371X
Human ecology. Biosphere. Human evolution.

GF50.B68 1987
Boyden, Stephen Vickers.
Western civilization in biological perspective: patterns in biohistory/ Stephen Boyden. Oxford: Clarendon Press; 1987. xi, 370 p.
86-023575   304.5   0198576722
Human ecology. Social evolution. Human evolution.

GF50.H33 1977
Haggett, Peter.
Locational analysis in human geography/ Peter Haggett, Andrew D. Cliff, Allan Frey. New York: Wiley, 1977. xiv, 605 p.
77-008967   301.3   0470992077
Human geography. Economic geography.

GF50.P68 1989
The Power of geography: how territory shapes social life/ edited by Jennifer Wolch, Michael Dear. Boston: Unwin Hyman, 1989. xvi, 393 p.
88-011103   304.2   0044450567
Human geography. Social history. Human territoriality.

GF50.R68 1993
Rose, Gillian.
Feminism and geography: the limits of geographical knowledge/ Gillian Rose. Minneapolis: University of Minnesota Press, 1993. 205 p.
93-010411   304.2/082   0816624178
Human geography. Feminist criticism. Geography -- Philosophy.

GF50.S33 1995
Schama, Simon.
Landscape and memory/ Simon Schama. New York: A.A. Knopf; c1995. xi, 652 p.
93-048546   304.2/3   0679402551
Landscape -- History. Landscape assessment -- History. Human ecology -- History.

GF51 Environmental influences on humans

GF51.M58 1982
Moran, Emilio F.
Human adaptability: an introduction to ecological anthropology/ Emilio F. Moran. Boulder, Colo.: Westview Press, 1982. xii, 404 p.
82-008605   304.2   0865314306
Human beings -- Effect of environment on. Adaptation (Physiology)

GF51.V35
Vayda, Andrew Peter,
Environment and cultural behavior; ecological studies in cultural anthropology. Edited by Andrew P. Vayda. Garden City, N.Y., Published for American Museum of Natural History 1969. xvi, 485 p.
69-010994   301.31
Human ecology. Human beings -- Effect of environment on. Ethnology.

GF54.5 Humans and specific environments — Forests

GF54.5.P46 1988
People of the tropical rain forest/ edited by Julie Sloan Denslow and Christine Padoch. Berkeley: University of California Press; [c1988] 231 p.
87-030173   304.2/0915/2   0520062957
Human ecology -- Tropics. Ethnology -- Tropics. Rain forests. Tropics -- Social conditions. Tropics - - Economic conditions.

GF57 Humans and specific environments — Mountains

GF57.H85 1987
Human impact on mountains/ edited by Nigel J.R. Allan, Gregory W. Knapp, Christoph Stadel. Totowa, N.J.: Rowman & Littlefield, 1988. xii, 308 p.
86-031471   910/.0943
Nature -- Effect of human beings on. Mountains. Mountain people.

GF71 Climatic influences on humans

GF71.R47 2000
Resnick, Abraham.
Due to the weather: ways the elements affect our lives/ Abraham Resnick. Westport, Conn.: Greenwood Press, 2000. xi, 220 p.
99-088484   304.2/5   031331344X
Human beings -- Effect of climate on. Weather.

GF75 Human influences on the environment

GF75.B37 1991
Barrow, Christopher J.
Land degradation: development and breakdown of terrestrial environments/ C.J. Barrow. Cambridge [England]; Cambridge University Press, 1991. xvii, 295 p.
90-002534   628.5/5   0521353335
Nature -- Effect of human beings on. Land degradation. Pollution -- Environmental aspects.

GF75.D88 1992
Durning, Alan Thein.
How much is enough?: the consumer society and the future of the earth/ Alan Thein Durning. New York: Norton, c1992. 200 p.
92-015410   333.7/13   039303383X
Nature -- Effect of human beings on -- Forecasting. Consumer behavior -- Forecasting. Consumption (Economics) -- Forecasting.

GF75.E15 1990
The Earth as transformed by human action: global and regional changes in the biosphere over the past 300 years/ edited by B.L. Turner II ... [et al.]; with computer graphics by Montine Jordan. Cambridge; Cambridge University Press with Clark University 1990. xvi, 713 p.
89-022362   304.2   0521363578
Nature -- Effect of human beings on -- Congresses. Human ecology -- Congresses. Global environmental change.

GF75.E25 1995
Ecological relations in historical times: human impact and adaptation/ edited by Robin A. Butlin and Neil Roberts. Oxford; Blackwell, 1995.
94-038784   304.2   0631195068
Nature -- Effect of human beings on. Biotic communities -- History. Landscape changes -- History.

GF75.E4 1991
Ehrlich, Paul R.
Healing the planet: strategies for resolving the environmental crisis/ Paul R. Ehrlich and Anne H. Ehrlich. Reading, Mass.: Addison-Wesley, c1991. xv, 366 p.
91-002734   363.7 20   0201550466
Nature -- Effect of human beings on. Environmental protection. Environmental policy.

GF75.G68 1982
Goudie, Andrew.
The human impact: man's role in environmental change/ Andrew Goudie. Cambridge, Mass.: MIT Press, 1982, c1981. x, 316 p.
81-015643   304.2   0262070863
Nature -- Effect of human beings on.

GF75.L59 1994
Livingston, John A.
Rogue primate: an exploration of human domestication/ John A. Livingston. Toronto: Key Porter Books, c1994. ix, 229 p.
94-156385   304.2 20   1550135082
Nature -- Effect of human beings on. Human ecology -- Philosophy. Technology -- Moral and ethical aspects.

GF75.N566 1991
Nisbet, E. G.
Leaving Eden: to protect and manage the earth/ E.G. Nisbet. Cambridge [England]; Cambridge University Press, 1991. xviii, 358 p.
90-021823   363.7   0521393116
Nature -- Effect of human beings on. Pollution. Global warming.

GF75.S68 1994
Solbrig, Otto Thomas.
So shall you reap: farming and crops in human affairs/ Otto T. Solbrig & Dorothy J. Solbrig. Washington, D.C.: Island Press, c1994. xx, 284 p.
93-043330   306.3/49   1559633085
Nature -- Effect of human beings on. Agriculture -- History. Agriculture -- Environmental aspects.

GF80 Ethical, moral and religious aspects

GF80.E57 1991
The Environment in question: ethics and global issues/ edited by David E. Cooper and Joy A. Palmer. London; Routledge, 1992. xii, 256 p.
91-016823   179/.1   0415049679
Environmental ethics.

GF80.J64 1991
Johnson, Lawrence E.
A morally deep world: an essay on moral significance and environmental ethics/ Lawrence E. Johnson. Cambridge [England]; Cambridge University Press, 1991. ix, 301 p.
90-043042   179/.1   0521393108
Ecology -- Moral and ethical aspects. Environmental ethics. Animal rights.

GF80.M53 1990
Miller, Alan S.
Gaia connections: an introduction to ecology, ecoethics, and economics/ Alan S. Miller. Savage, Md.: Rowman & Littlefield, c1991. xvi, 301 p.
90-020632   179/.1   0847676552
Environmental ethics. Environmental policy. Economic development -- Environmental aspects.

GF80.N36 1989
Nash, Roderick.
The rights of nature: a history of environmental ethics/ Roderick Frazier Nash. Madison, Wis.: University of Wisconsin Press, c1989. xiii, 290 p.
88-017169   179/.1   0299118401
Environmental ethics -- History. Human ecology -- Philosophy.

GF80.R64 1988
Rolston, Holmes, 1932-
Environmental ethics: duties to and values in the natural world/ Holmes Rolston III. Philadelphia: Temple University Press, 1988. xiii, 391 p.
87-006499   179/.1   087722501X
Environmental ethics.

GF85 Hazardous aspects of the environment

GF85.W67 1993
The World at risk: natural hazards and climate change, Cambridge, MA 1992/ editor, Rafael Bras. New York: American Institute of Physics, c1993. xiii, 352 p.
93-071333   363.3/42   1563960664
Hazardous geographic environments -- Congresses. Climatic changes -- Congresses. Natural disasters -- Congresses.

GF90 Landscape assessment — General works

GF90.A58 1995
The anthropology of landscape: perspectives on place and space/ edited by Eric Hirsch and Michael O'Hanlon. Oxford: Clarendon Press; 1995. xi, 268 p.
95-009157   304.2   0198278802
Landscape assessment. Human geography. Geographical perception.

GF90.H68 1990
Hough, Michael.
Out of place: restoring identity to the regional landscape/ Michael Hough. New Haven: Yale University Press, c1990. 230 p.
89-035127   712   0300045107
Landscape assessment. Geographical perception. Landscape architecture.

GF90.I57
The Interpretation of ordinary landscapes: geographical essays/ D. W. Meinig, editor; J. B. Jackson ... [et al.]. New York: Oxford University Press, 1979. viii, 255 p.
78-023182   301.31   0195025369
Landscape assessment -- Addresses, essays, lectures.

GF90.S83 2001
Suchantke, Andreas.
Eco-geography/ by Andreas Suchantke; translated by Norman Skillen. Great Barrington, Mass.: Lindisfarne Books, c2001. xix, 250 p.
00-067172   304.2 21   0940262991
Landscape assessment. Landscape ecology. Human geography.

GF90.U53 1997
Understanding ordinary landscapes/ edited by Paul Groth and Todd W. Bressi. New Haven: Yale University Press, c1997. ix, 272 p.
97-005776   333.73/15 21   0300063717
Landscape assessment. Human geography.

GF91 Landscape assessment — By region or country, A-Z

GF91.N7.W55 1992
Wilson, Alexander.
The culture of nature: North American landscape from Disney to the Exxon Valdez/ Alexander Wilson. Cambridge, MA: Blackwell, 1992. 335 p.
91-042250   304.2/097   1557863369
Landscape assessment -- North America. Nature -- Effect of human beings on -- North America. Human ecology -- North America -- Philosophy.

GF95 Spatial studies

GF95.M67 1988
Morrill, Richard L.
Spatial diffusion/ Richard Morrill, Gary L. Gaile, Grant Ian Thrall. Newbury Park: Sage Publications, c1988. 86 p.
87-062683   306   0803928521
Human geography. Culture diffusion.

GF95.S55 1992
Shields, Rob, 1961-
Places on the margin: alternative geographies of modernity/ Rob Shields. London; Routledge, 1991 xiii, 334 p.
90-008264   304.2/3   0415080223
Human geography. Spatial behavior. Geographical perception.

GF125 Settlements — Cities. Urban sociology

GF125.C85 1993
The Cultural meaning of urban space/ edited by Robert Rotenberg and Gary McDonogh. Westport, Conn.: Bergin & Garvey, 1993. xix, 226 p.
92-032179   307.76   0897893190
Urban geography. Urban anthropology.

GF127 Settlements — Rural settlements. Rural geography

GF127.H38 1998
Hart, John Fraser.
The rural landscape/ John Fraser Hart. Baltimore, Md.: Johns Hopkins University Press, 1998. viii, 401 p.
97-028553   333.76   0801857171
Rural geography. Rural geography -- United States. Agricultural geography. United States -- Geography.

GF503-504 By region or country — America — United States

GF503.E46
Ekirch, Arthur Alphonse, 1915-
Man and nature in America/ Arthur A. Ekirch. Lincoln: University of Nebraska Press, 1973. xii, 231 p.
63-014925   572.9
Human geography -- United States. Natural resources -- United States. Man -- Influence on nature.

GF503.U57 1988
The United States--a contemporary human geography/ P.L. Knox ... [et al.]. Harlow, Essex, England: Longman Scientific & Technical; 1988. x, 287 p.
87-003166   973   0470208457
Human geography -- United States. United States -- Economic conditions. United States -- Social conditions.

GF503.W35 1991
Wallach, Bret, 1943-
At odds with progress: Americans and conservation/ Bret Wallach; [maps by Allan Yokisaari]. Tucson: University of Arizona Press, c1991. xiv, 255 p.
90-011296   333.7/2/0973   0816509174
Human geography -- United States -- Philosophy. Nature -- Effect of human beings on -- United States. Conservation of natural resources -- United States.

GF503.W53 1994
Whitney, Gordon Graham.
From coastal wilderness to fruited plain: a history of environmental change in temperate North America, 1500 to the present/ Gordon G. Whitney. Cambridge; Cambridge University Press, 1994. xxxiv, 451 p.
93-029701   333.73/13/0973   052139452X
Landscape changes -- United States -- History. Nature -- Effect of human beings on -- United States. Biotic communities -- United States -- History.

GF504.A6.M67 1996
Morehouse, Barbara J. 1945-
A place called Grand Canyon: contested geographies/ Barbara J. Morehouse. Tucson: University of Arizona Press, c1996. viii, 202 p.
95-032495   333.73/09791/32 20   0816516030
Human geography -- Arizona -- Grand Canyon Region -- History. Land use -- Arizona -- Grand Canyon Region -- History. Landscape changes -- Arizona -- Grand Canyon Region -- History. Grand Canyon National Park (Ariz.) -- History. Grand Canyon Region (Ariz.) -- History. Grand Canyon Region (Ariz.) -- Environmental conditions.

GF504.L8
Transforming New Orleans and its environs: centuries of change/ Craig E. Colten, editor. Pittsburgh: University of Pittsburgh Press, c2000. x, 272 p.
00-011648   304.2/8/0976335 21   0822941341
Nature -- Effect of human beings on -- Louisiana -- New Orleans Region. Human ecology -- Louisiana -- New Orleans Region -- History.

GF504.M53.F58 1993
Fitzpatrick, Tony, 1958-
Signals from the heartland/ Tony Fitzpatrick. New York: Walker, 1993. xx, 230 p.
92-015732   333.7/2/0978   0802712606
Human ecology -- Middle West. Environmentalists -- Middle West. Natural history -- Middle West.

GF504.N45.M47 1989
Merchant, Carolyn.
Ecological revolutions: nature, gender, and science in New England/ Carolyn Merchant. Chapel Hill: University of North Carolina Press, c1989. xv, 379 p.
89-030945   304.2/0974   0807818585
Human ecology -- New England -- History. Indians of North America -- New England -- Economic conditions. Human ecology -- Philosophy -- History. New England -- Economic conditions.

GF504.S67.S55 1990
Silver, Timothy, 1955-
A new face on the countryside: Indians, colonists, and slaves in South Atlantic forests, 1500-1800/ Timothy Silver. Cambridge; Cambridge University Press, 1990. xii, 204 p.
89-027263   304.2/0975   0521343747
Nature -- Effect of human beings on -- South Atlantic States -- History. Forest ecology -- South Atlantic States. Indians of North America -- South Atlantic States -- History. South Atlantic States -- History.

GF504.W35.M34 1984
Malin, James Claude, 1893-
History & ecology: studies of the Grassland/ James C. Malin; edited by Robert P. Swierenga. Lincoln: University of Nebraska Press, c1984. xxix, 376 p.
83-016951   333.74/0978   0803241445
Human beings -- Effect of environment on -- West (U.S.) Grasslands -- West (U.S.) Agriculture -- Kansas -- History. West (U.S.) -- History. Kansas -- Rural conditions. West (U.S.) -- Description and travel.

GF511 By region or country — America — Canada

GF511.D43 1998
Dearden, Philip.
Environmental change and challenge: a Canadian perspective/ Philip Dearden and Bruce Mitchell. Toronto Oxford University Press, 1998 565 p.
98-131570   333.7/0971   0195410149
Human ecology -- Canada. Environmental protection -- Canada. Nature -- Effect of human beings on -- Canada.

GF514 By region or country — America — Latin America

GF514.S63
Social fabric and spatial structure in colonial Latin America/ edited by David J. Robinson. Ann Arbor, MI: Published for Dept. of Geography, Syracuse Unive 1979. xviii, 478 p.
79-015744   309.1/8/01   083570419X
Human geography -- Latin America. Land settlement patterns -- Latin America. Latin America -- Social conditions. Latin America -- Economic conditions.

GF517 By region or country — America — Mexico

GF517.C87.S54 1988
Sheridan, Thomas E.
Where the dove calls: the political ecology of a peasant corporate community in northwestern Mexico/ Thomas E. Sheridan. Tucson: University of Arizona Press, c1988. xxiv, 237 p.
87-030139   304.2/0972/17   0816510555
Human ecology -- Mexico -- Cucurpe. Natural resources -- Mexico -- Cucurpe -- Management. Economic anthropology -- Mexico -- Cucurpe. Cucurpe (Mexico) -- Economic conditions.

GF532 By region or country — America — South America

GF532.A4.M6713 1993
Moran, Emilio F.
Through Amazonian eyes: the human ecology of Amazonian populations/ Emilio F. Moran. Iowa City: University of Iowa Press, c1993. xix, 230 p.
93-001148   304.2/0981/1   0877454175
Human ecology -- Amazon River Region. Indians of South America -- Amazon River Region. Human ecology -- Brazil.

GF532.A4.S36 1992
Schmink, Marianne.
Contested frontiers in Amazonia/ Marianne Schmink and Charles H. Wood. New York: Columbia University Press, c1992. xxxii, 387 p.
91-044979   333.73/0981/1   0231076606
Nature -- Effect of human beings on -- Amazon River Region. Economic development -- Environmental aspects -- Amazon River Region. Land settlement -- Environmental aspects -- Amazon River Region. Para (Brazil: State) -- Social conditions. Para (Brazil: State) -- Economic conditions.

GF551 By region or country — Europe — Great Britain. England (General)

GF551.T39 1983
Taylor, Christopher, 1935-
Village and farmstead: a history of rural settlement in England/ Christopher Taylor. London: G. Philip, 1983. 254 p.
83-157398   307.7/2/0942   0540010715
Land settlement patterns -- England -- History. Villages -- England -- History. England -- Rural conditions.

GF551.W56 1999
Winter, James H., 1925-
Secure from rash assault: sustaining the Victorian environment/ James Winter. Berkeley: University of California Press, c1999. xi, 342 p.
98-043970   333.7/13/094109034   21 0520216091
Human ecology -- Great Britain -- History -- 19th century. Nature -- Effect of human beings on -- Great Britain.

GF645 By region or country — Europe — Other regions or countries of Europe, A-Z

GF645.E92.T87 1989
Turnock, David.
The human geography of Eastern Europe/ David Turnock. London; Routledge, 1989. xii, 345 p.
88-031679   304.2/0947   0415004691
Human geography -- Europe, Eastern. Europe, Eastern -- Economic conditions -- 1945-1989.

GF651 By region or country — Asia

GF651.C85 1997
Culture and the city in East Asia/ edited by Won Bae Kim ... [et al.]. Oxford: Clarendon Press; 1997. xvii, 262 p.
96-024109   307.76/095   0198233582
Urban geography -- East Asia. Human geography -- East Asia. Cities and towns -- East Asia -- Growth. East Asia -- Social policy. East Asia -- Economic policy.

GF669.4 By region or country — Asia — Southeast Asia

GF669.4.B75 1993
Broad, Robin.
Plundering paradise: the struggle for the environment in the Philippines/ Robin Broad with John Cavanagh. Berkeley: University of California Press, c1993. xvi, 197 p.
92-027742   363.7/009599   0520080815
Human ecology -- Philippines. Environmental policy -- Philippines. Environmental protection -- Philippines. Philippines -- Social conditions. Philippines -- Economic conditions.

GF696 By region or country — Asia — Other regions or countries of Asia, A-Z

GF696.N35.S74 1993
Stevens, Stanley F.
Claiming the high ground: Sherpas, subsistence, and environmental change in the highest Himalaya/ Stanley F. Stevens. Berkeley: University of California Press, c1993. xx, 537 p.
92-004808   304.2/095496   0520076990
Human ecology -- Nepal -- Khumbu Valley. Sherpa (Nepalese people) -- Economic conditions. Landscape changes -- Nepal -- Khumbu Valley. Khumbu Valley (Nepal) -- Economic conditions.

GF701 By region or country — Africa — General works

GF701.N48 1995
Newman, James L.
The peopling of Africa: a geographic interpretation/ James L. Newman. New Haven: Yale University Press, c1995. xiv, 235 p.
94-038259   960/.1   0300060033
Human geography -- Africa. Prehistoric peoples -- Africa. Africa -- History. Africa -- Antiquities.

GF746.2 By region or country — Africa — West Africa

GF746.2.F35 1996
Fairhead, James, 1962-
Misreading the African landscape: society and ecology in a forest-savanna mosaic/ James Fairhead and Melissa Leach with the research collaboration of Dominique Millimouno and Marie Kamano. Cambridge; Cambridge University Press, 1996. xviii, 354 p.
95-052318   304.2/096652   0521563534
Human ecology -- Guinea -- Kissidougou (Region) Landscape assessment -- Guinea -- Kissidougou (Region) Forest ecology -- Guinea -- Kissidougou (Region) Kissidougou (Guinea: Region) -- Environmental conditions.

GF801 By region or country — Pacific area — Australia

GF801.H36 2000
Head, Lesley.
Second nature: the history and implications of Australia as Aboriginal landscape/ Lesley Head. Syracuse, N.Y.: Syracuse University Press, 2000. xiii, 272 p.
99-024394   306/.0899/915   0815605870
Human ecology -- Australia. Australian aborigines -- Land tenure. Landscape assessment -- Australia.

GF801.K65 1995
Kohen, J. L.
Aboriginal environmental impacts/ James L. Kohen. Sydney, Australia: UNSW Press; 1995. ix, 160 p.
95-199954   304.2/8/0994   0868403016
Nature -- Effect of human beings on -- Australia -- History. Australian aborigines -- Social life and customs.

GF801.L55 1991
Lines, William J.
Taming the great south land: a history of the conquest of nature in Australia/ William J. Lines. Berkeley: University of California Press, 1991. xx, 337 p.
92-126817   0520078306
Nature -- Effect of human beings on -- Australia -- History. Ecology -- Australia -- History. Landscape changes -- Australia -- History.

GF801.S77 1997
Strang, Veronica.
Uncommon ground: cultural landscapes and environmental values/ Veronica Strang. Oxford; Berg, 1997. xiv, 309 p.
97-202745   1859739466
Human ecology -- Australia. Landscape assessment -- Australia. Landscape changes -- Australia.

GF852 By region or country — Pacific area — Pacific islands

GF852.P6.L48 1992
Lewis, Martin W.
Wagering the land: ritual, capital, and environmental degradation in the Cordillera of northern Luzon, 1900-1986/ Martin W. Lewis. Berkeley: University of California Press, c1992. xii, 280 p.
91-012307   333.76/09599/1   0520072723
Nature -- Effect of human beings on -- Philippines -- Buguias. Agricultural ecology -- Philippines -- Buguias. Tropical vegetable industry -- Philippines -- Buguias. Buguias (Philippines) -- Religious life and customs. Buguias (Philippines) -- Politics and government.

GF891 By region or country — Arctic regions

GF891.C66 1997
Contested Arctic: indigenous peoples, industrial states, and the circumpolar environment/ edited by Eric Alden Smith, Joan McCarter; preface by Kurt E. Engelmann. Seattle: Russian, East European, and Central Asian Studie c1997. xix, 156 p.
97-013803   304.2/0911 21   0295976551
Human ecology -- Arctic regions -- Congresses. Environmental policy -- Arctic regions -- Congresses. Arctic peoples -- Congresses. Arctic regions -- Environmental conditions -- Congresses.

GF891.K7813 1993
Krupnik, I. I.
Arctic adaptations: native whalers and reindeer herders of northern Eurasia/ Igor Krupnik; translated and edited by Marcia Levenson. Hanover, NH: University Press of New England [for] Dartmouth c1993. xvii, 355 p.
93-010996   304.2/0911   0874516323
Human ecology -- Arctic regions. Arctic peoples -- Social life and customs.

GF895 By region or country — Tropic

GF895.P37 1992
Park, Chris C.
Tropical rainforests/ Chris C. Park. London; Routledge, 1992. xiii, 188 p.
92-005659   304.2/0915/2   0415062381
Human ecology -- Tropics. Deforestation -- Tropics. Rain forest conservation.

GF900 Developing countries

GF900.N37 1998
Nature's geography: new lessons for conservation in developing countries/ edited by Karl S. Zimmerer and Kenneth R. Young. Madison, Wis.: The University of Wisconsin Press, 1998. xvi, 351 p.
98-025743   333.7/2/091724   0299159108
Landscape changes -- Developing countries. Biological diversity conservation -- Developing countries. Conservation of natural resources -- Developing countries.

GN Anthropology

GN2 Societies

GN2.A27 vol. 71
Averkieva, IUliia Pavlovna.
Kwakiutl string figures/ Julia Averkieva and Mark A. Sherman; foreword by Bill Holm. Seattle: University of Washington Press; c1992. xxxi, 199 p.
92-002728   306 s   029597172X
Kwakiutl Indians -- Games. String figures -- British Columbia.

GN2.S9243 no. 16
Bilingualism, social issues and policy implications/ Andrew W. Miracle, Jr., editor. Athens, Ga.: University of Georgia Press, c1983. x, 188 p.
82-013447   301 s   0820306460
Bilingualism -- Congresses. Language policy -- Congresses. Education, Bilingual -- Congresses.

GN2.S9243 no. 20
Visions and revisions: ethnohistoric perspectives on southern cultures/ George Sabo III and William M. Schneider, editors. Athens: University of Georgia Press, c1987. vi, 154 p.
86-016043   306/.0975   0820309117
Ethnology -- Southern States -- Congresses. Indians of North America -- Southern States -- Congresses. Southern States -- Antiquities -- Congresses. Southern States -- Social life and customs -- Congresses.

GN2.S9243 no. 25
African Americans in the South: issues of race, class, and gender/ Hans A. Baer and Yvonne Jones, editors. Athens: University of Georgia Press, c1992. xii, 181 p.
91-017728   305.896/073075   0820313769
Afro-Americans -- Southern States -- Social conditions. Southern States -- Social conditions. Southern States -- Race relations.

GN3 Congresses

GN3.S9 1959
Man, race, and Darwin; papers read at a joint conference of the Royal Anthropological Institute of Great Britain and Ireland and the Institute of Race Relations. With an introd. and epilogue by Philip Mason. London, Oxford University Press, 1960. vi, 151 p.
60-051836   572
Darwin, Charles, -- 1809-1882.   Race -- Congresses. Race relations -- Congresses.

GN6-8 Collected works (nonserial) — Individual authors

GN6.B4
Benedict, Ruth, 1887-1948.
An anthropologist at work; writings of Ruth Benedict, by Margaret Mead. Boston, Houghton Mifflin, 1959. xxii, 583 p.
58-009071   572.081
Anthropology.

GN6.B57 1974
Boas, Franz, 1858-1942.
The shaping of American anthropology, 1883-1911; a Franz Boas reader. Edited by George W. Stocking, Jr. New York, Basic Books [1974] xi, 354 p.
73-081727   301.2   0465077676
Boas, Franz, -- 1858-1942. Anthropology.

GN6.K7
Kroeber, A. L. 1876-1960.
The nature of culture. [Chicago] University of Chicago Press [1952] 437 p.
52-012545   572.04
Anthropology. Culture.

GN8.B68
Boas, Franz, 1858-1942.
Race, language and culture. New York: The Maxmillan company, 1940. xx, 647 p.
40-004051   572/.08/1   002904490
Race. Indians of North America -- Languages. Anthropology.

GN8.M286
Malinowski, Bronislaw, 1884-1942.
Magic, science and religion, and other essays; selected and with an introd. by Robert Redfield. Boston, Beacon Press, 1948. xii, 327 p.
48-006987   572.04
Anthropology.

GN11 Dictionaries. Encyclopedias

GN11.E52
Encyclopedia of anthropology/ edited by David E. Hunter, Phillip Whitten. New York: Harper & Row, c1976. 411 p.
75-041386   301.2/03   0060470941
Anthropology -- Dictionaries.

GN14 Communication of information — Anthropological archives

GN14.A77 1999
Anthropological resources: a guide to archival, library, and museum collections/ compiled by Library-Anthropology Resource Group (LARG); Lee S. Dutton, editor. New York: Garland, 1999. xxxii, 517 p.
98-037660   026/.301/025   0815311885
Anthropological archives -- Directories. Anthropological museums and collections -- Directories. Anthropology -- Library resources -- Directories.

GN17 History

GN17.A57 1973b
Anthropology & the colonial encounter. Edited by Talal Asad. [London] Ithaca Press [1973] 281 p.
73-180718   301.2   0903729008
Ethnology -- History. Applied anthropology. Great Britain -- Colonies.

GN17.S75
Stanton, William Ragan.
The leopard's spots: scientific attitudes toward race in America, 1815-59. [Chicago] University of Chicago Press [1960] 244 p.
59-011625   572.973
Anthropology -- United States -- History. Race.

GN17.T69
Totems and teachers: perspectives on the history of anthropology/ Sydel Silverman, editor. New York: Columbia University Press, 1981. xv, 322 p.
80-018457   301/.092/2   0231050860
Anthropology -- History. Anthropologists.

GN17.3 By region or country, A-Z

GN17.3.A8.F57 1993
First in their field: women and Australian anthropology/ edited by Julie Marcus. Carlton, Vic.: Melbourne University Press; 1993. xvi, 189 p.
92-176390   306/.092/294   0522844669
Women anthropologists -- Australia. Ethnology -- Australia. Australian aborigines.

GN17.3.N7
Darnell, Regna.
Invisible genealogies: a history of Americanist anthropology/ Regna Darnell. Lincoln: University of Nebraska Press, c2001. xxvi, 373 p.
00-055956   301/.097 21   0803217102
Anthropology -- North America -- History. Ethnology -- Philosophy. Indianists -- North America.

GN17.3.S67F68 2000
Fowler, Don D., 1936-
A laboratory for anthropology: science and romanticism in the American Southwest, 1846-1930/ Don Fowler. Albuquerque: University of New Mexico Press, c2000. xiii, 497 p.
00-009359   301/.0979 21   0826303068
Anthropology -- Southwest, New -- History. Ethnological expeditions -- Southwest, New -- History. Indians of North America -- Southwest, New -- Public opinion. Public opinion -- Southwest, New. Southwest, New -- Discovery and exploration. Southwest, New -- Description and travel.

GN17.3.U6.A37 1999
African-American pioneers in anthropology/ edited by Ira E. Harrison and Faye V. Harrison. Urbana: University of Illinois Press, c1999. 296 p.
98-019724   301/.089/96073 21   0252024303
Afro-American anthropologists. Anthropology -- United States -- History. Ethnology -- United States -- History.

GN17.3.U6.B35 1998
Baker, Lee D., 1966-
From savage to Negro: anthropology and the construction of race, 1896-1954/ Lee D. Baker. Berkeley: University of California Press, c1998. xii, 325 p.
97-031602   305.8 21   0520211677
Racism in anthropology -- United States -- History. Anthropology -- United States -- History. Racism in popular culture -- United States -- History. United States -- Race relations.

GN20 Biography — Collective

GN20.I5 1991
International dictionary of anthropologists/ compiled by Library-Anthropology Resource Group (LARG); Christopher Winters, general editor; editorial board: Michele Calhoun ... [et al.]. New York: Garland Pub., 1991. xl, 823 p.
91-004782   016.301/03   0824050940
Anthropology -- Bio-bibliography -- Dictionaries.

GN21 Biography — Individual, A-Z

GN21.B45.C34 1989
Caffrey, Margaret M. 1947-
Ruth Benedict: stranger in this land/ by Margaret M. Caffrey. Austin: University of Texas Press, 1989. xi, 432 p.
88-020589   306/.092/4   0292746555
Benedict, Ruth, -- 1887-1948. Anthropologists -- United States -- Biography. Ethnology.

GN21.B45.M63 1983
Modell, Judith Schachter, 1941-
Ruth Benedict, patterns of a life/ Judith Schachter Modell. Philadelphia: University of Pennsylvania Press, 1983. x, 355 p.
82-021989   306/.092/4   0812278747
Benedict, Ruth, -- 1887-1948. Anthropologists -- United States -- Biography.

GN21.B56.C65 1999
Cole, Douglas, 1938-
Franz Boas: the early years, 1859-1906/ Douglas Cole. Vancouver: Douglas & McIntyre; c1999. 360 p.
99-042589   301/.092 B 21   0295979038
Boas, Franz, -- 1858-1942. Anthropologists -- United States -- Biography. Anthropologists -- Germany -- Biography.

GN21.B56.W55 1996
Williams, Vernon J.
Rethinking race: Franz Boas and his contemporaries/ Vernon J. Williams, Jr. Lexington, Ky.: University Press of Kentucky, c1996. ix, 152 p.
95-034914   305.8/96073 20   0813119634
Boas, Franz, -- 1858-1942. Anthropologists -- United States -- Biography. Anthropologists -- United States -- Attitudes. Physical anthropology -- United States -- History. United States -- Race relations.

GN21.D68.F37 1999
Fardon, Richard.
Mary Douglas: an intellectual biography/ Richard Fardon. London; Routledge, 1999. xx, 315 p.
98-025907   305.8/0092   0415040922
Douglas, Mary. Ethnologists -- Great Britain -- Biography.

GN21.F65.A27 1987
Ackerman, Robert, 1935-
J.G. Frazer: his life and work/ Robert Ackerman. Cambridge [Cambridgeshire]; Cambridge University Press, 1987. x, 348 p.
87-009343   301/.092/4   0521340934
Frazer, James George, -- Sir, -- 1854-1941. Anthropologists -- England -- Biography.

GN21.H24.A3 1992
Hall, Edward Twitchell, 1914-
An anthropology of everyday life: an autobiography/ Edward T. Hall. New York: Doubleday, c1992. xv, 269 p.
91-018989   301/.092   0385237448
Hall, Edward Twitchell, -- 1914- Ethnologists -- United States -- Biography. Intercultural communication. Personality and culture.

GN21.K5.G58 1992
Givens, Douglas R.
Alfred Vincent Kidder and the development of Americanist archaeology/ Douglas R. Givens. Albuquerque: University of New Mexico Press, c1992. xiii, 216 p.
91-043853   973.9/092   0826313515
Kidder, Alfred Vincent, -- 1885-1963. Anthropologists -- United States -- Biography. Archaeology -- United States -- History. Indians of Mexico -- Antiquities. Pecos National Monument (N.M.) America -- Antiquities.

GN21.K86.A3 1992
Kumar, Nita, 1951-
Friends, brothers, and informants: fieldwork memoirs of Banaras/ Nita Kumar. Berkeley: University of California Press, c1992. xi, 260 p.
91-033815   305.8/00954/2   0520071387
Kumar, Nita, -- 1951- -- Diaries. Ethnologists -- India -- Varanasi -- Diaries. Ethnology -- India -- Varanasi -- Field work. Varanasi (India) -- Social life and customs.

GN21.L372.A33 1984
Leakey, Mary D. 1913-
Disclosing the past/ Mary Leakey. Garden City, N.Y.: Doubleday, 1984. 224 p.
84-010189   306/.092/4   0385189613
Leakey, Mary D. -- (Mary Douglas), -- 1913- Women physical anthropologists -- Tanzania -- Biography. Women archaeologists -- Tanzania -- Biography. Fossil hominids -- Tanzania -- Olduvai Gorge.

GN21.L4.A513 1991
Levi-Strauss, Claude.
Conversations with Claude Levi-Strauss/ Claude Levi-Strauss, Didier Eribon; translated by Paula Wissing. Chicago: University of Chicago Press, c1991. viii, 184 p.
90-011052   301/.092   0226474755
Lévi-Strauss, Claude -- Interviews. Anthropologists -- France -- Interviews. Structural anthropology. Ethnology -- Philosophy.

GN21.L4.H4613 1998
Henaff, Marcel.
Claude Levi-Strauss and the making of structural anthropology/ Marcel Henaff; translated by Mary Baker. Minneapolis, MN: University of Minnesota Press, 1998. x, 292 p.
97-041271   306   0816627606
Levi-Strauss, Claude -- Philosophy. Structural anthropology. Kinship.

GN21.M25.M34 1988
Malinowski between two worlds: the Polish roots of an anthropological tradition/ edited by Roy Ellen ... [et al.]. Cambridge; Cambridge University Press, 1988. xxv, 261 p.
87-026551   306/.09438   0521345669
Malinowski, Bronislaw, -- 1884-1942. Anthropology -- Poland -- History. Anthropology -- History -- 20th century.

GN21.M36.A35 1979
Mead, Margaret, 1901-1978.
Margaret Mead, some personal views/ edited by
Rhoda Metraux. New York: Walker, 1979. 286 p.
79-063636   301.2/092/4   0802706266
Mead, Margaret, -- 1901-1978.

GN21.M36.A4 1977
Mead, Margaret, 1901-1978.
Letters from the field, 1925-1975/ Margaret Mead.
New York: Harper & Row, c1977. xxii, 343 p.
73-004110   301.2/092/4   0060129611
*Mead, Margaret, -- 1901-1978. Anthropologists --
United States -- Correspondence. Ethnology --
Oceania. Ethnology -- Field work.*

GN21.M36.B38 1984
Bateson, Mary Catherine.
With a daughter's eye: a memoir of Margaret Mead
and Gregory Bateson/ Mary Catherine Bateson.
New York: W. Morrow, c1984. 242 p.
84-060564   306/.092/2   0688039626
*Mead, Margaret, -- 1901-1978. Bateson, Gregory.
Bateson, Mary Catherine. Anthropologists --
United States -- Biography.*

GN21.M36 L36 1999
Lapsley, Hilary.
Margaret Mead and Ruth Benedict: the kinship of
women/ Hilary Lapsley. Amherst, Mass.:
University of Massachusetts Press, c1999. viii,
351 p.
98-054185   301/.092/2 21   1558491813
*Mead, Margaret, 1901-1978. Benedict, Ruth,
1887-1948. Anthropologists -- Biography. Female
friendship. Lesbian anthropologists -- Biography.*

GN21.P37.Z86 1992
Zumwalt, Rosemary Levy, 1944-
Wealth and rebellion: Elsie Clews Parsons,
anthropologist and folklorist/ Rosemary Levy
Zumwalt; foreword by Roger D. Abrahams.
Urbana: University of Illinois Press, c1992. xxi,
360 p.
91-036288   301/.092   0252019091
*Parsons, Elsie Worthington Clews, -- 1874-1941.
Women anthropologists -- United States --
Biography. Women folklorists -- United States --
Biography. Indians -- Folklore.*

GN21.S27.D37 1990
Darnell, Regna.
Edward Sapir: linguist, anthropologist, humanist/
Regna Darnell. Berkeley: University of California
Press, c1990. xix, 480 p.
89-005016   306/.092   0520066782
*Sapir, Edward, -- 1884-1939. Anthropologists --
United States -- Biography. Linguists -- United
States -- Biography. Anthropological linguistics --
United States.*

GN21.W43.W48 1990
Wetherell, David.
Camilla: C.H. Wedgwood, 1901-1955, a life/ D.
Wetherell, C. Carr-Gregg. Kensington, N.S.W.:
New South Wales University Press, 1990. xiii,
242 p.
92-209599   0868403873
*Wedgwood, Camilla H. -- (Camilla Hildegarde), --
1901-1955. Women anthropologists -- Biography.
College teachers -- New South Wales -- Sydney --
Biography. Women college teachers -- New South
Wales -- Sydney -- Biography.*

GN24 General works, treatises, and textbooks — 1871-1974

GN24.B4 1971
Beals, Ralph Leon, 1901-
An introduction to anthropology [by] Ralph L.
Beals [and] Harry Hoijer. New York, Macmillan
[1971] xix, 711 p.
71-126513   301.2
Anthropology.

GN24.B6
Boas, Franz, 1858-1942.
General anthropology, edited by Franz Boas, with
contributions by Ruth Benedict, Franz Boas, Ruth
Bunzel [and others] ... Boston, D.C. Heath and
Company, 1938. xi, 718 p.
38-032351   572.982
Anthropology.

GN24.F5 1956
Firth, Raymond William, 1901-
Human types, an introduction to social
anthropology. London, T. Nelson [1956] 224 p.
57-004417   301.2
Race. Ethnology. Primitive societies.

GN24.H7
Hooton, Earnest Albert, 1887-1954.
Apes, men, and morons, by Earnest Albert Hooton
... New York, G.P. Putnam's Sons, 1937. viii,
307 p.
37-028753   572
Primates. Anthropology. Evolution.

GN24.K7 1948
Kroeber, A. L. 1876-1960.
Anthropology: race, language, culture, psychology,
pre-history. New York, Harcourt, Brace [1948]
xii, 856 p.
48-006956   572
Anthropology.

GN24.M58 1969
Montagu, Ashley 1905-
Man: his first two million years; a brief
introduction to anthropology. New York,
Columbia University Press, 1969. vi, 262 p.
69-016956   573
Anthropology.

GN25 General works, treatises, and textbooks — 1975-

GN25.K87 1994
Kuper, Adam.
The chosen primate: human nature and cultural
diversity/ Adam Kuper. Cambridge, Mass.:
Harvard University Press, c1994. xiv, 269 p.
93-031770   301   0674128257
Anthropology. Human beings. Culture.

GN27 General special (Special aspects of the subject as a whole)

GN27.B6
Boas, Franz, 1858-1942.
Anthropology and modern life, by Franz Boas.
New York, W.W. Norton & company, inc. [c1928]
vii, 246 p.
28-029158   301.2
*Anthropology. Anthropology -- popular works.
Social problems.*

GN27.M34
Malinowski, Bronislaw 1884-1942.
A scientific theory of culture, and other essays by
Bronislaw Malinowski; with a preface by
Huntington Cairns. Chapel Hill, The University of
North Carolina press, 1944. ix, 228 p.
44-008385
*Frazer, James George, -- Sir, -- 1854-1941.
Culture. Anthropology.*

GN27.W66 1995
Women writing culture/ edited by Ruth Behar and
Deborah A. Gordon. Berkeley: University of
California Press, c1995. xiii, 457 p.
95-036791   305.42   0520202074
*Women anthropologists -- Attitudes. Ethnology --
Authorship. Ethnology -- Philosophy.*

GN29 Addresses, essays, lectures

GN29.W6
Wolf, Eric R., 1923-
Anthropology [by] Eric R. Wolf. Englewood
Cliffs, N.J., Prentice-Hall [1964] xiii, 113 p.
64-016039   572
Anthropology.

GN33 Philosophy. Relation to other topics. Methodology — General works

GN33.C695 1995
Counterworks: managing the diversity of
knowledge/ edited by Richard Fardon. London;
Routledge, 1995. vi, 233 p.
94-048385   306/.01   041510792X
*Anthropology -- Philosophy. Culture --
Philosophy. Knowledge, Theory of.*

GN33.C74 1998
Critical anthropology now: unexpected
contexts,shifting constituencies, changing agendas/
edited by George E. Marcus. Santa Fe, NM: School
of American Research Press, 1998. viii, 440 p.
98-041001   301/.07/2   0933452500
*Anthropology -- Research. Anthropolog -- Field
work. Anthropology -- Methodology.*

GN33.D5 1998
Di Leonardo, Micaela 1949-
Exotics at home: anthropologies, others, American
modernity/ Micaela di Leonardo. Chicago, Ill.:
University of Chicago Press, 1998. xvi, 445 p.
97-048475   305.8/001   0226472639
*Ethnology -- Philosophy. Ethnology --
Authorship. Ethnology -- United States. United
States -- Social life and customs.*

GN33.D563 1991
Digging into popular culture: theories and methodologies in archeology, anthropology, and other fields/ edited by Ray B. Browne and Pat Browne. Bowling Green, Ohio: Bowling Green State University Popular Press, c1991. 184 p.
91-073878　306　0879725214
Anthropology -- Methodology. Archaeology -- Methodology. Popular culture.

GN33.E44 2001
Ellingson, Terry Jay.
The myth of the noble savage/ Ter Ellingson. Berkeley: University of California Press, c2001. xxii, 445 p.
99-059341　301/.01 21　0520222687
Anthropology -- Philosophy. Noble savage. Noble savage in literature.

GN33.G64 1991
Golden ages, dark ages: imagining the past in anthropology and history/ edited by Jay O'Brien and William Roseberry. Berkeley: University of California Press, c1991. x, 288 p.
90-024806　301　0520070186
Anthropology -- Methodology. Ethnohistory. Economic anthropology.

GN33.H34 1995
Hastrup, Kirsten.
A passage to anthropology: between experience and theory/ Kirsten Hastrup. New York: Routledge, 1995. xiii, 217 p.
95-008619　301/.01　0415129222
Anthropology -- Philosophy. Anthropology -- Methodology. Anthropology -- Field work.

GN33.M4
Mead, Margaret, 1901-1978.
The study of culture at a distance, edited by Margaret Mead and Rhoda Metraux. [Chicago] University of Chicago Press [1953] x, 480 p.
53-013135　572.07
Anthropology -- Methodology. Civilization -- Study and teaching. Civilization

GN33.R43 1991
Recapturing anthropology: working in the present/ edited by Richard G. Fox. Santa Fe, N.M.: School of American Research Press: 1991. viii, 248 p.
91-026724　301/.01　0933452772
Anthropology -- Methodology -- Congresses. Anthropology -- Philosophy -- Congresses. Ethnology -- Methodology -- Congresses.

GN33.W46 1988
Wengle, John L., 1956-
Ethnographers in the field: the psychology of research/ John L. Wengle. Tuscaloosa: University of Alabama Press, c1988. xxii, 197 p.
87-019218　301/.0723　0817303898
Anthropology -- Field work -- Psychological aspects.

GN33.8 Philosophy. Relation to other topics. Methodology — Feminist anthropology

GN33.8.B53 2001
Black feminist anthropology: theory, politics, praxis, and poetics/ edited by Irma McClaurin. New Brunswick, NJ: Rutgers University Press, c2001. xiv, 277 p.
00-045686　305.42 21　0813529263
Feminist anthropology. African American anthropologists. Ethnology -- Philosophy.

GN34.3 Philosophy. Relation to other topics. Methodology — Other special methods, A-Z

GN34.3.F53.B45 1999
Being there: six anthropological accounts of fieldwork/ edited by C.W. Watson. London; Pluto Press, 1999. vii, 169 p.
98-037448　301/.07/23　074531497X
Anthropology -- Field work. Anthropology -- Philosophy.

GN34.3.F53.H68 1990
Howell, Nancy.
Surviving fieldwork: a report of the Advisory Panel on Health and Safety in Fieldwork, American Anthropological Association/ by Nancy Howell. Washington, D.C.: American Anthropological Association, 1990. xii, 217 p.
90-000246　306/.072　091316738X
Anthropology -- Field work. Anthropology -- Safety measures. Anthropologists -- Health risk assessment.

GN50.3 Physical anthropology. Somatology — Dictionaries. Encyclopedias

GN50.3.H57 1997
History of physical anthropology/ edited by Frank Spencer. New York: Garland Pub., 1997. 2 v.
96-034389　573/.03　0815304900
Physical anthropology -- Encyclopedias.

GN50.3.S74 1991
Stevenson, Joan C.
Dictionary of concepts in physical anthropology/ Joan C. Stevenson. New York: Greenwood Press, 1991. xiv, 432 p.
90-022815　573/.03　0313247560
Physical anthropology -- Dictionaries.

GN50.4 Physical anthropology. Somatology — History

GN50.4.B66 1988
Bones, bodies, behavior: essays on biological anthropology/ edited by George W. Stocking, Jr. Madison, Wis.: University of Wisconsin Press, c1988. viii, 272 p.
87-040377　573/.09　0299112500
Physical anthropology -- History. Ethnology -- History.

GN50.6 Physical anthropology. Somatology — Biography — Individual, A-Z

GN50.6.J64.A3 1989
Johanson, Donald C.
Lucy's child: the discovery of a human ancestor/ Donald Johanson and James Shreeve. New York: Morrow, c1989. 318 p.
89-009461　569/.9　0688064922
Johanson, Donald C. Physical anthropologists -- United States -- Biography. Australopithecus afarensis. Fossil hominids -- Africa, East.

GN51-58 Physical anthropology. Somatology — Philosophy. Relation to other topics. Methodology — Anthropometry

GN51.S63 1994
Stature, living standards, and economic development: essays in anthropometric history/ edited by John Komlos. Chicago: University of Chicago Press, 1994. xv, 247 p.
94-008700　573/.6　0226450929
Anthropometry -- History. Anthropometry -- Cross-cultural studies. Human growth -- Economic aspects.

GN57.A73.S54 1996
Shephard, Roy J.
The health consequences of "modernization": evidence from circumpolar peoples/ Roy J. Shephard, Andris Rode. Cambridge; Cambridge University Press, 1996. xiii, 306 p.
95-009112　306.4/61/0911　0521474019
Arctic peoples -- Anthropometry. Arctic peoples -- Health and hygiene. Arctic peoples -- Social conditions. Arctic regions -- Social conditions.

GN58.O34.C65 1989
The Colonization of the Pacific: a genetic trail/ edited by Adrian V.S. Hill and Susan W. Serjeantson. Oxford [England]: Clarendon Press; 1989. ix, 298 p.
89-033095　304.5/0995　0198576951
Human population genetics -- Oceania. Land settlement -- Oceania. Anthropometry -- Oceania.

GN58.S64.K46 2000
Kennedy, Kenneth A. R.
God-apes and fossil men: paleoanthropology of South Asia/ Kenneth A. R. Kennedy. Ann Arbor: University of Michigan Press, c2000. xvii, 480 p.
00-022837　599.9 21　0472010136
Physical anthropology -- South Asia. Human evolution. Fossil hominids -- South Asia. South Asia -- Antiquities.

GN60 Physical anthropology. Somatology — General works

GN60.A67 1991
Applications of biological anthropology to human affairs/ edited by C.G.N. Mascie-Taylor and G.W. Lasker. Cambridge [England]; Cambridge University Press, 1991. ix, 252 p.
90-025499　573　0521381126
Physical anthropology. Human biology.

GN60.B57
Bleibtreu, Hermann K.,
Human variation; readings in physical anthropology [by] Hermann K. Bleibtreu and James F. Downs. Beverly Hills, Calif., Glencoe Press [1971] x, 380 p.
76-146942   573/.08
Physical anthropology. Human evolution.

GN62 Physical anthropology. Somatology — General special

GN62.B85 1998
Building a new biocultural synthesis: political-economic perspectives on human biology/ edited by Alan H. Goodman and Thomas L. Leatherman. Ann Arbor: University of Michigan Press, c1998. xxi, 486 p.
98-025385   306 21   0472096060
Physical anthropology. Social history. Human remains (Archaeology)

GN62.8 Physical anthropology. Somatology — Human variation — General works

GN62.8.M37 1995
Marks, Jonathan
Human biodiversity: genes, race, and history/ Jonathan Marks. New York: Aldine de Gruyter, c1995. xiv, 321 p.
94-019450   573   0202020320
Physical anthropology. Human population genetics. Biological diversity.

GN66-66.5 Physical anthropology. Somatology — Human variation — Physical form and dimensions

GN66.S46 1990
Shephard, Roy F.
Body composition in biological anthropology/ Roy J. Shephard. Cambridge [England]; Cambridge University Press, 1991. x, 345 p.
90-036079   573   0521362679
Body composition. Physical anthropology.

GN66.5.C37 1990
Carter, J. E. L.
Somatotyping-development and applications/ J.E. Lindsay Carter and Barbara Honeyman Heath. Cambridge [England]; Cambridge University Press, 1990. xiv, 503 p.
89-035775   573/.6   0521359511
Somatotypes. Physical anthropology. Human beings -- Constitution.

GN69.8-74 Physical anthropology. Somatology — Human variation — The skeleton. Osteology

GN69.8.D43 1987
Death, decay, and reconstruction: approaches to archaeology and forensic science/ edited by A. Boddington, A.N. Garland, and R.C. Janaway. Manchester, UK; Manchester University Press, c1987. viii, 249 p.
87-001538   616.07/8   0719023033
Forensic anthropology. Paleopathology. Demographic archaeology.

GN69.8.N33 2000
Nafte, Myriam.
Flesh and bone: an introduction to forensic anthropology/ Myriam Nafte. Durham, N.C.: Carolina Academic Press, c2000. xvi, 173 p.
00-108364   363.25 21   0890896380
Forensic anthropology. Facial reconstruction (Anthropology)

GN70.S57 1992
Skeletal biology of past peoples: research methods/ editors, Shelley R. Saunders, M. Anne Katzenberg. New York: Wiley-Liss, c1992. xvii, 265 p.
91-026243   573/.6/072   047156138X
Anthropometry -- Research. Anthropometry -- Methodology. Human skeleton.

GN70.S78 1988
Steele, D. Gentry.
The anatomy and biology of the human skeleton/ D. Gentry Steele, Claud A. Bramblett; photographs by Virginia K. Massey, Jean M. Christiansen, and D. Gentry Steele. College Station: Texas A&M University Press, c1988. viii, 291 p.
86-014394   611/.71   0890963002
Human skeleton. Forensic anthropology. Bone and Bones -- anatomy & histology.

GN70.W45 2000
White, T. D.
Human osteology/ text by Tim D. White; images by Pieter Arend Folkens. San Diego: Academic Press, c2000. xxiii, 563 p.
99-061961   611/.71 21   0127466126
Physical anthropology. Bones. Skeleton.

GN74.P73 1997
Prag, John.
Making faces: using forensic and archaeological evidence/ John Prag and Richard Neave. College Station: Texas A & M University Press, 1997. 256 p.
97-018786   930.1/01   0890967849
Facial reconstruction (Anthropology) Archaeology -- Methodology.

GN197 Physical anthropology. Somatology — Human variation — Skin

GN197.R6 1991
Robins, Ashley H.
Biological perspectives on human pigmentation/ Ashley H. Robins. Cambridge [England]; Cambridge University Press, 1991. xiii, 253 p.
90-015121   573/.5   0521365147
Human skin color. Human skin color -- Physiological aspects. Melanins.

GN209 Physical anthropology. Somatology — Human variation — Teeth. Dental anthropology

GN209.D48 1998
Dental anthropology: fundamentals, limits, and prospects/ Kurt W. Alt, Friedrich W. Rosing, Maria Teschler-Nicola (eds.). Wien; Springer, 1998.
98-037799   599.9/43   3211829741
Dental anthropology.

GN209.S33 1997
Scott, George Richard.
The anthropology of modern human teeth: dental morphology and its variation in recent human populations/ G. Richard Scott and Christy G. Turner II. Cambridge; Cambridge University Press, 1997. xxiii, 382 p.
96-046112   573/.6314   0521455081
Dental anthropology.

GN269 Physical anthropology. Somatology — Race (General) — General works

GN269.B368 1992
Barkan, Elazar.
The retreat of scientific racism: changing concepts of race in Britain and the United States between the world wars/ Elazar Barkan. Cambridge; Cambridge University Press, 1992. xiv, 381 p.
90-020129   305.8   0521391938
Race. Physical anthropology. Eugenics -- Great Britain -- History. Great Britain -- Race relations. United States -- Race relations.

GN269.G73 2001
Graves, Joseph L., 1955-
The Emperor's new clothes: biological theories of race at the millennium/ Joseph L. Graves, Jr. New Brunswick, N.J.: Rutgers University Press, c2001. viii, 252 p.
00-034205   599.97 21   081352847X
Race. Physical anthropology. Sociobiology.

GN269.L49 1997
Levin, Michael E.
Why race matters: race differences and what they mean/ Michael Levin. Westport, Conn.: Praeger, 1997. x, 415 p.
96-036361   305.8   0275957896
Race. Nature and nurture. Blacks -- Intelligence levels. United States -- Race relations.

GN269.S63 1993
Smedley, Audrey.
Race in North America: origin and evolution of a worldview/ Audrey Smedley. Boulder: Westview Press, 1993. xii, 340 p.
92-025269   305.8/009   0813306213
Race -- Origin. Racism -- History. Black race.

GN281 Physical anthropology. Somatology — Human evolution — General works

GN281.B618 1997
Boaz, Noel Thomas.
Eco homo: how the human being emerged from the cataclysmic history of the earth/ Noel T. Boaz. New York: BasicBooks, c1997. ix, 278 p.
97-014604   599.93/8 21   0465018033
Human evolution.

GN281.C345 1992
The Cambridge encyclopedia of human evolution/ edited by Steve Jones, Robert Martin, and David Pilbeam; executive editor, Sarah Bunney; foreword by Richard Dawkins. Cambridge [England]; Cambridge University Press, xiii, 506 p.
92-018037   573.2 20   0521323703
Human evolution -- Encyclopedias.

GN281.C385 2000
Cavalli-Sforza, L. L. 1922-
Genes, peoples, and languages/ Luigi Luca Cavalli-Sforza; translated from the Italian by Mark Seielstad. New York: North Point Press, 2000. xii, 227 p.
98-026360   599.93/8   0865475296
Human evolution. Human population genetics. Fossil hominids.

GN281.E4 1982
Eldredge, Niles.
The myths of human evolution/ Niles Eldredge, Ian Tattersall. New York: Columbia University Press, 1982. 197 p.
82-001118   573   0231051441
Human evolution. Social evolution. Progress.

GN281.E53 1999
Encyclopedia of human evolution and prehistory. 2nd ed./ editors, Eric Delson ... [et al.]. New York: Garland Pub., 1999.
99-045824   599.93/8 21   0815316968
Human evolution -- Encyclopedias. Prehistoric peoples -- Encyclopedias.

GN281.E93 1997
The evolving female: a life-history perspective/ Mary Ellen Morbeck, Alison Galloway, and Adrienne L. Zihlman, editors. Princeton, N.J.: Princeton University Press, c1997. xix, 332 p.
96-020402   573.2 20   069102748X
Human evolution. Women -- Evolution. Females -- Physiology.

GN281.F64 1987
Foley, Robert.
Another unique species: patterns in human evolutionary ecology/ Robert Foley. Harlow, Essex, England: Longman Scientific & Technical; 1987. xxii, 313 p.
86-023442   573.2   0470207280
Human evolution. Human ecology.

GN281.F66 1995
Foley, Robert.
Humans before humanity: an evolutionary perspective/ Robert Foley. Cambridge, MA: Blackwell Publishers, 1995 ix, 238 p.
95-021626   573.2   0631170871
Human evolution.

GN281.H848 1989
Human origins/ edited by John R. Durant. Oxford [Oxfordshire]: Clarendon Press; 1989. viii, 147 p.
88-012037   573.2   0198576129
Human evolution.

GN281.H849 1989
The Human revolution: behavioural and biological perspectives on the origins of modern humans/ Paul Mellars and Chris Stringer, editors. Princeton, N.J.: Princeton University Press, c1989. xiii, 800 p.
89-010330   573.2   0691085390
Human beings -- Origin. Human evolution.

GN281.J57 1996
Johanson, Donald C.
From Lucy to language/ Donald Johanson & Blake Edgar; principal photography, David Brill. New York, N.Y.: Simon & Schuster Editions, c1996. 272 p.
96-031576   573.2 20   0684810239
Human evolution. Fossil hominids. Australopithecines.

GN281.J6 1999
Jolly, Alison.
Lucy's legacy: sex and intelligence in human evolution/ Alison Jolly. Cambridge, Mass.: Harvard University Press, 1999. 518 p.
99-032252   599.93/8   0674000692
Human evolution. Social evolution. Women -- Evolution.

GN281.K55 1989
Klein, Richard G.
The human career: human biological and cultural origins/ Richard G. Klein. Chicago: University of Chicago Press, c1989. xxi, 524 p.
88-036259   573.2   0226439623
Human beings -- Origin. Fossil hominids. Human evolution.

GN281.L487 1987
Lewin, Roger.
Bones of contention: controversies in the search for human origins/ Roger Lewin. New York: Simon and Schuster, c1987. 348 p.
87-009541   573.2   067152688X
Human evolution. Human beings -- Origin.

GN281.M396 2000
McKee, Jeffrey Kevin.
The riddled chain: chance, coincidence, and chaos in human evolution/ Jeffrey K. McKee. New Brunswick, N.J. Rutgers University Press, c2000. x, 280 p.
99-045720   599.93/8 21   081352783X
Human evolution. Chance.

GN281.M444 1995
Megarry, Tim, 1941-
Society in prehistory: the origins of human culture/ Tim Megarry. New York: New York University Press, 1995. ix, 400 p.
95-037355   573.2   0814755372
Human evolution. Evolution (Biology) Human behavior.

GN281.M53 1990
Milner, Richard, 1941-
The encyclopedia of evolution: humanity's search for its origins/ Richard Milner; foreword by Stephen Jay Gould. New York: Facts on File, c1990. xii, 481 p.
90-003344   573.2/03   0816014728
Human evolution -- Dictionaries.

GN281.T357 1995
Tattersall, Ian.
The fossil trail: how we know what we think we know about human evolution/ Ian Tattersall. New York: Oxford University Press, 1995. xi, 276 p.
94-031633   573.2   0195061012
Human evolution. Fossil hominids. Anthropology, Prehistoric.

GN281.T36 1993
Tattersall, Ian.
The human odyssey: four million years of human evolution/ Ian Tattersall; foreword by Donald C. Johanson. New York: Prentice Hall General Reference, c1993. xiii, 191 p.
92-021341   573.2   0671850059
Human evolution.

GN281.T84 1996
Tudge, Colin.
The time before history: 5 million years of human impact/ Colin Tudge. New York: Scribner, c1996. 366 p.
95-042026   573.2 20   0684807262
Human evolution. Evolution (Biology) Mammals -- Evolution.

GN281.4 Physical anthropology. Somatology — Human evolution — General special

GN281.4.B76 1990
Brown, Michael Harold, 1952-
The search for Eve/ Michael H. Brown; [text illustrations by Diana Coe]. New York: Harper & Row, c1990. x, 357 p.
89-045632   573.2   0060160551
Human evolution. Genetic psychology.

GN281.4.E374 2000
Ehrlich, Paul R.
Human natures: genes, cultures, and the human prospect/ Paul R. Ehrlich. Washington, D.C.: Island Press [for] Shearwater Books, c2000. xii, 531 p.
00-010436   599.93/8 21   155963779X
Human evolution. Social evolution. Human behavior.

GN281.4.K48 1994
King, Barbara J., 1956-
The information continuum: evolution of social information transfer in monkeys, apes, and hominids/ Barbara J. King. Santa Fe: SAR Press; c1994. xii, 166 p.
94-001690   302.2   093345239X
Human evolution. Communication. Animal communication.

GN281.4.L68 2000
Low, Bobbi S.
Why sex matters: a Darwinian look at human behavior/ Bobbi S. Low. Princeton, N.J.: Princeton University Press, c2000. xviii, 412 p.
99-024612   305.3 21   0691028958
Human evolution. Sex role. Nature and nurture.

GN281.4.M57 1996
Mithen, Steven J.
The prehistory of the mind: a search for the origins of art, religion, and science/ [Steven Mithen]. London: Thames and Hudson, c1996. 288 p.
96-060367   0500050813
Genetic psychology. Cognition. Brain -- Evolution.

GN281.4.N63 1996
Noble, William, 1944-
Human evolution, language, and mind: a psychological and archaeological inquiry/ William Noble, Iain Davidson; illustration, D. Hobbs. Cambridge; Cambridge University Press, 1996. xiii, 272 p.
95-053827   573.2   0521445027
Human evolution. Language and languages -- Origin. Signs and symbols.

GN281.4.P65 1996
Potts, Richard, 1953-
Humanity's descent: the consequences of ecological instability/ Rick Potts; illustrations by Jennifer Clark. New York: Morrow, c1996. 325 p.
96-001699   573.2 20   0688104703
Human evolution. Human ecology. Natural selection.

GN281.4.S72 2001
Stanford, Craig B. 1956-
Significant others: the ape-human continuum and the quest for human nature/ Craig Stanford. New York: Basic Books, 2001.
2001-025158   304.5   0465081711
Human evolution. Apes -- Behavior. Human behavior.

GN281.4.T36
Tanner, Nancy Makepeace.
On becoming human/ Nancy Makepeace Tanner. Cambridge; Cambridge University Press, 1981. xviii, 373 p.
80-021526   573.2   0521235545
Human evolution. Social evolution.

GN281.4.T39 2000
Tattersall, Ian.
Extinct humans/ by Ian Tattersall and Jeffrey H. Schwartz; principal photography by Jeffrey H. Schwartz. 1st ed. Boulder, Colo.: Westview Press, c2000. 256 p.
00-022088   599.93/8 21   0813334829
Human evolution. Fossil hominids.

GN282-285 Physical anthropology. Somatology — Human evolution — Fossil man. Human paleontology

GN282.F85 1997
Function, phylogeny, and fossils: Miocene hominoid evolution and adaptations/ edited by David R. Begun, Carol V. Ward, and Michael D. Rose. New York: Plenum Press, c1997. xii, 424 p.
96-040485   599.93/8 21   0306454572
Fossil hominids. Human evolution. Paleontology -- Miocene.

GN282.5.S63 1990
Spencer, Frank.
Piltdown: a scientific forgery/ Frank Spencer. London; Oxford University Press, 1990. xxvi, 272 p.
90-007688   573.3 20   0198585225
Piltdown forgery.

GN282.5.S64 1990
Spencer, Frank, 1941-
The Piltdown papers, 1908-1955: the correspondence and other documents relating to the Piltdown forgery/ Frank Spencer. London [England]; Natural History Museum Publications: 1990. xii, 282 p.
90-032881   573.3   0198585233
Piltdown forgery.

GN282.5.W35 1996
Walsh, John Evangelist, 1927-
Unraveling Piltdown: the science fraud of the century and its solution/ John Evangelist Walsh. New York: Random House, c1996. xx, 279 p.
95-009399   573.3 20   0679444440
Piltdown forgery -- History.

GN282.6.C56 1990
Ciochon, Russell L.
Other origins: the search for the giant ape in human prehistory/ Russell Ciochon, John Olsen, and Jamie James. New York: Bantam Books, c1990. xix, 262 p.
90-038913   569/.8   0553070819
Gigantopithecus.

GN284.R54 1990
Rightmire, G. Philip.
The evolution of Homo Erectus: comparative anatomical studies of an extinct human species/ G. Philip Rightmire. Cambridge; Cambridge University Press, 1990. xii, 260 p.
89-070814   573.3   0521308801
Homo erectus.

GN284.W35 1996
Walker, Alan, 1938-
The wisdom of the bones: in search of human origins/ Alan Walker and Pat Shipman. New York: Knopf: 1996. x, 338 p.
95-037525   573.3   0679426248
Homo erectus -- Kenya.

GN284.6.S55 2001
Shipman, Pat, 1949-
The man who found the missing link: Eugene Dubois and his lifelong quest to prove Darwin right/ Pat Shipman. New York: Simon & Schuster, c2001. 514 p.
00-044049   569.9 21   068485581X
Dubois, Eugene, -- 1858-1940.   Java man. Physical anthropologists -- Netherlands -- Biography. Physical anthropologists -- Indonesia - - Java -- Biography.

GN285.M45 1996
Mellars, Paul.
The Neanderthal legacy: an archaeological perspective from western Europe/ Paul Mellars. Princeton, N.J.: Princeton University Press, c1996. xix, 471 p.
95-004300   936 20   0691034931
Neanderthals -- Europe. Paleolithic period -- Europe. Human evolution -- Europe -- Philosophy. Europe -- Antiquities.

GN285.T37 1999
Tattersall, Ian.
The last Neanderthal: the rise, success, and mysterious extinction of our closest human relatives/ Ian Tattersall. Rev. ed. Boulder, Colo.: Westview Press, c1999. 208 p.
99-040327   569.9 21   0813336759
Neanderthals.

GN285.T73 1993
Trinkaus, Erik.
The Neandertals: changing the image of mankind/ Erik Trinkaus and Pat Shipman. New York: Knopf, 1993. xxii, 454 p.
91-047553   573.3   0394589009
Neanderthals. Fossil hominids -- History.

GN289 Physical anthropology. Somatology — Human evolution — Population genetics

GN289.B55 1988
Biological aspects of human migration/ edited by C.G.N. Mascie-Taylor and G.W. Lasker. Cambridge [Cambridgeshire]; Cambridge University Press, 1988. viii, 263 p.
87-008055   304.8   0521331099
Human population genetics. Human beings -- Migrations. Emigration and immigration.

GN289.S94 2001
Sykes, Bryan.
The seven daughters of Eve/ Bryan Sykes. New York: Norton, 2001. x, 306 p.
2001-030820   599.93/5   0393020185
Human population genetics. Human evolution. Women -- Anthropometry.

GN293 Physical anthropology. Somatology — Mummies

GN293.M34 2000
Mallory, J. P.
The Tarim mummies: ancient China and the mystery of the earliest peoples from the West, with 190 illustrations, 13 in color/ J.P. Mallory, Victor H. Mair. New York, N.Y.: Thames & Hudson, 2000. 352 p.
99-066166   0500051011
Mummies -- China -- Xinjiang Uygur Zizhiqu. Tarim Basin (China) -- Antiquities. Xingjiang Uygur Zizhiqu (China) -- Antiquities.

GN296 Physical anthropology. Somatology — Medical anthropology — General works

GN296.A628 1993
The Anthropology of disease/ edited by C.G.N. Mascie-Taylor. Oxford; Oxford University Press, 1993. ix, 169 p.
93-003221   306.4/61   0198522878
Medical anthropology. Diseases -- Social aspects. Environmentally induced diseases.

GN296.C83 1979
Culture and curing: anthropological perspectives on traditional medical beliefs and practices/ edited by Peter Morley and Roy Wallis. [Pittsburgh]: University of Pittsburgh Press, 1979, c1978. vii, 190 p.
78-062194   362.1   0822911361
Medical anthropology. Traditional medicine.

GN296.E53 1987
Encounters with biomedicine: case studies in medical anthropology/ edited by Hans A. Baer. New York: Gordon and Breach Science Publishers, c1987. xxiii, 349 p.
87-011988   306/.4   2881241956
Medical anthropology -- Case studies. Social medicine -- Case studies. Anthropology.

GN296.K566 1995
Kleinman, Arthur.
Writing at the margin: discourse between anthropology and medicine/ Arthur Kleinman. Berkeley: University of California Press, c1995. xiii, 314 p.
95-035194   306.4/61/01   0520200993
Medical anthropology -- Philosophy. Medical anthropology -- Methodology.

GN296.L68 1997
Loustaunau, Martha O., 1938-
The cultural context of health, illness, and medicine/ Martha O. Loustaunau and Elisa J. Sobo. Westport, Conn.: Bergin & Garvey, 1997. 221 p.
97-016136   306.4/61   0897894871
Medical anthropology. Social medicine.

GN296.P65 1989
Polednak, Anthony P.
Racial and ethnic differences in disease/ Anthony P. Polednak. New York: Oxford University Press, 1989. ix, 364 p.
89-003121   616.07/1   0195059700
Medical anthropology. Health and race. Ethnic groups -- Diseases.

GN296.W65 1989
Women as healers: cross-cultural perspectives/ edited by Carol Shepherd McClain. New Brunswick: Rutgers University Press, c1989. xiv, 274 p.
88-016896   610/.88042   0813513707
Women healers -- Cross-cultural studies. Medical anthropology. Traditional medicine -- Cross-cultural studies.

GN296.5 Physical anthropology. Somatology — Medical anthropology — By region or country, A-Z

GN296.5.U6.M37 1994
Martin, Emily.
Flexible bodies: tracking immunity in American culture from the days of polio to the age of AIDS/ Emily Martin. Boston: Beacon Press, c1994. xxiii, 320 p.
93-039065   306.4/61   0807046264
Medical anthropology -- United States. Immunity -- Social aspects. Immune system -- Social aspects.

GN298 Physical anthropology. Somatology — Social aspects of the human body

GN298.B63 1993
Bodylore/ edited by Katharine Young. Knoxville: University of Tennessee Press, c1993. xxiv, 261 p.
93-015390   306.4   0870497995
Body, Human -- Social aspects. Body, Human -- Symbolic aspects. Body, Human -- Folklore.

GN298.M36 1994
Many mirrors: body image and social relations/ edited by Nicole Sault. New Brunswick, N.J.: Rutgers University Press, c1994. xiv, 346 p.
93-037997   306.4   0813520797
Body, Human -- Social aspects -- Cross-cultural studies. Body image -- Cross-cultural studies. Feminine beauty (Aesthetics) -- Cross-cultural studies.

GN298.Y68 1997
Young, Katharine Galloway.
Presence in the flesh: the body in medicine/ Katharine Young. Cambridge, Mass.: Harvard University Press, 1997. xiii, 199 p.
96-039721   306.4   067470181X
Body, Human -- Social aspects. Body, Human -- Symbolic aspects. Medicine -- Practice.

GN307 Ethnology. Social and cultural anthropology — Dictionaries. Encyclopedias

GN307.D485 1997
The dictionary of anthropology/ edited by Thomas Barfield. Cambridge, Mass: Blackwell, 1997. xiii, 626 p.
96-037337   306/.03   1557862826
Ethnology -- Dictionaries.

GN307.E52 1996
Encyclopedia of cultural anthropology/ editors, David Levinson, Melvin Ember. New York: Henry Holt and Co., 1996. 4 v.
95-037237   305.8/03   0805028773
Ethnology -- Encyclopedias.

GN307.E525 1996
Encyclopedia of social and cultural anthropology/ edited by Alan Barnard, Jonathan Spencer. London; Routledge, 1996. xxiv, 658 p.
97-177211   306/.03   041509996X
Ethnology -- Encyclopedias.

GN307.E53 1991
Encyclopedia of world cultures/ David Levinson, editor in chief. Boston, Mass.: G.K. Hall, 1991-1996. 10 v.
90-049123   306/.03   081688840X
Ethnology -- Encyclopedias.

GN307.I44 1989
The Illustrated encyclopedia of mankind/ editor-in-chief, Richard Carlisle; foreword, C. von Furer-Haimendorf; consultant anthropologist, Michael Sallnow; preface, Robert Canfield. New York: M. Cavendish, [1989-] 22 v.
88-022903   306/.03/21   1854350323
Ethnology -- Dictionaries. Human beings -- Dictionaries.

GN307.W56 1991
Winthrop, Robert H.
Dictionary of concepts in cultural anthropology/ Robert H. Winthrop. New York: Greenwood Press, 1991. xiv, 347 p.
91-006283   306/.03   0313242801
Ethnology -- Dictionaries.

GN307.7 Ethnology. Social and cultural anthropology — Communication of information — Writing of ethnographies

GN307.7.A85 1990
Atkinson, Paul, 1947-
The ethnographic imagination: textual constructions of reality/ Paul Atkinson. London; Routledge, 1990. vii, 195 p.
89-049330   305.8   0415050251
Ethnology -- Authorship.

GN307.7.G44 1988
Geertz, Clifford.
Works and lives: the anthropologist as author/ Clifford Geertz. Stanford, Calif.: Stanford University Press, 1988. vi, 157 p.
87-020310   306   0804714282
Ethnology -- Authorship.

GN307.7.J33 1991
Jacobson, David, 1940-
Reading ethnography/ David Jacobson. Albany: State University of New York Press, c1991. ix, 138 p.
90-035230   305.8   079140546X
Ethnology -- Authorship. Ethnology -- Methodology.

GN307.7.V36 1988
Van Maanen, John.
Tales of the field: on writing ethnography/ John van Maanen. Chicago: University of Chicago Press, 1988. xvi, 173 p.
87-025502   306   0226849619
Ethnology -- Authorship. Sociology -- Authorship.

GN308 Ethnology. Social and cultural anthropology — History — General works

GN308.K87 1988
Kuper, Adam.
The invention of primitive society: transformations of an illusion/ Adam Kuper. London; Routledge, 1988. 264 p.
88-012201   306/.09   0415009022
Ethnology -- History. Primitive societies.

GN308.3 Ethnology. Social and cultural anthropology — History — By region or country, A-Z

GN308.3.A35.M66 1994
Moore, Sally Falk, 1924-
Anthropology and Africa: changing perspectives on a changing scene/ by Sally Falk Moore. Charlottesville: University Press of Virginia, 1994. vii, 165 p.
93-040047   301/.096   081391504X
Ethnology -- Africa -- History.

GN308.3.G7.K85 1991
Kuklick, Henrika.
The savage within: the social history of British anthropology, 1885-1945/ Henrika Kuklick. Cambridge; Cambridge University Press, 1991. ix, 325 p.
91-020109   301/.0941/09034   0521411211
Ethnology -- Great Britain -- History -- 19th century. Ethnology -- Great Britain -- History -- 20th century.

GN308.3.G7.S74 1995
Stocking, George W., 1928-
After Tylor: British social anthropology, 1888-1951/ George W. Stocking, Jr. Madison: University of Wisconsin Press, c1995. xx, 570 p.
95-006365   306/.0941   0299145808
Ethnology -- Great Britain -- History -- 19th century. Ethnology -- Great Britain -- History -- 20th century. Social evolution -- Great Britain -- History.

GN315 Ethnology. Social and cultural anthropology — General works, treatises, and textbooks — 1871-1974

GN315.B4 1945
Benedict, Ruth, 1887-1948.
Race: science and politics, by Ruth Benedict. New York, The Viking press, 1945. xi, 206 p.
45-010060   572
Race. Race relations.

GN315.G36
Geertz, Clifford.
The interpretation of cultures; selected essays. New York, Basic Books [1973] ix, 470 p.
73-081196   301.2   046503425X
Ethnology. Culture.

GN316 Ethnology. Social and cultural anthropology — General works, treatises, and textbooks — 1975-

GN316.B377 1984
Barrett, Richard A.
Culture and conduct: an excursion in anthropology/ Richard A. Barrett. Belmont, Calif.: Wadsworth Pub. Co., c1984. viii, 240 p.
83-014836 306 0534030343
Ethnology. Culture.

GN316.L4 1982
Leach, Edmund Ronald.
Social anthropology/ Edmund Leach. New York: Oxford University Press, 1982. 254 p.
81-085134 306 0195203712
Ethnology.

GN316.R37 2000
Rapport, Nigel, 1956-
Social and cultural anthropology: the key concepts/ Nigel Rapport and Joanna Overing. London; Routledge, 2000. xii, 464 p.
00-710863 306 0415181550
Ethnology.

GN320 Ethnology. Social and cultural anthropology — General special (Special aspects of the subject as a whole)

GN320.G56 2000
Global ethnography: forces, connections, and imaginations in a postmodern world/ Michael Burawoy ... [et al.]. Berkeley: University of California Press, c2000. xv, 392 p.
99-053114 305.8 21 0520222156
Ethnology.

GN320.H328
Harris, Marvin, 1927-
Cows, pigs, wars & witches; the riddles of culture. New York, Random House [1974] viii, 276 p.
73-020268 392 0394483383
Ethnology -- Miscellanea. Witchcraft.

GN320.H33
Harris, Marvin, 1927-
The rise of anthropological theory; a history of theories of culture. New York, Crowell [1968] 806 p.
68-017392 572/.09
Ethnology -- History.

GN320.P44 1993
Perilous states: conversations on culture, politics, and nation/ George E. Marcus, editor. Chicago: University of Chicago Press, 1993. viii, 381 p.
94-229710 306 0226504468
Ethnology. Anthropologists -- Interviews.

GN325 Ethnology. Social and cultural anthropology — Addresses, essays, lectures

GN325.F7
Freilich, Morris, 1928-
Marginal natives; anthropologists at work. Contributors: Morris Freilich [and others] Morris Freilich, editor. New York, Harper & Row [c1970] xi, 624 p.
76-091252 527/.07/2
Ethnology -- Field work.

GN325.K89 1999
Kuper, Adam.
Among the anthropologists: history and context in anthropology/ Adam Kuper. New Brunswick, NJ: Athlone Press, 1999.
99-014802 306/.0968 21 0485115360
Ethnology. Ethnology -- Africa, Southern.

GN325.L46 1998
Levinson, David, 1947-
Ethnic groups worldwide: a ready reference handbook/ by David Levinson. Phoenix, Ariz.: Oryx Press, 1998. x, 436 p.
98-013274 305.8 1573560197
Ethnology -- Handbooks, manuals, etc. Ethnic groups -- Handbooks, manuals, etc.

GN333 Ethnology. Social and cultural anthropology — Juvenile works

GN333.W67 1998
Worldmark encyclopedia of cultures and daily life/ Timothy L. Gall, editor. Detroit: Gale, c1998. 4 v.
97-003278 305.8/003 21 0787605522
Ethnology -- Encyclopedias, Juvenile. Manners and customs -- Encyclopedias, Juvenile. Ethnology -- Encyclopedias.

GN345 Ethnology. Social and cultural anthropology — Philosophy. Relation to other topics. Methodology — General works

GN345.B37 1988
Bernard, H. Russell 1940-
Research methods in cultural anthropology/ H. Russell Bernard. Newbury Park, Calif.: Sage Publications, c1988. 520 p.
87-023735 306/.072 0803929773
Ethnology -- Methodology.

GN345.C65 1987
Comparative anthropology/ edited by Ladislav Holy. Oxford, UK; Blackwell, 1987. viii, 252 p.
86-026380 306 0631151559
Ethnology -- Comparative method -- Congresses. Cross-cultural studies -- Congresses.

GN345.C657 1991
Constructing knowledge: authority and critique in social science/ edited by Lorraine Nencel and Peter Pels. London; Sage Publications, 1991. xvi, 224 p.
91-052866 0803984014
Ethnology -- Philosophy. Ethnology -- Methodology. Knowledge, Sociology of.

GN345.E73 2000
Ethnographic artifacts: challenges to a reflexive anthropology/ edited by Sjoerd R. Jaarsma and Marta A. Rohatynskyj. Honolulu: University of Hawaii Press, c2000. viii, 255 p.
99-058503 305.8/001 21 0824822250
Ethnology -- Philosophy. Ethnology -- Authorship. Ethnology -- Methodology.

GN345.F87 1995
The future of anthropology: its relevance to the contemporary world/ edited by Akbar S. Ahmed and Cris N. Shore. London; Athlone, 1995. ix, 291 p.
95-034567 305.8/001 0485114453
Ethnology -- Philosophy. Ethnology -- Methodology.

GN345.H36 1991
Hammersley, Martyn.
What's wrong with ethnography?: methodological explorations/ Martyn Hammersley. London; Routledge, 1992. ix, 230 p.
91-010212 305.8 0415054761
Ethnology -- Methodology. Ethnology -- Research. Ethnology -- Philosophy.

GN345.H37 1998
Handbook of methods in cultural anthropology/ H. Russell Bernard, editor. Walnut Creek, Calif.: AltaMira Press, c1998. 816 p.
98-025423 305.8/001 21 0761991514
Ethnology -- Methodology.

GN345.H47 2001
Herzfeld, Michael, 1947-
Anthropology: theoretical practice in culture and society/ Michael Herzfeld. Malden, Mass.: Blackwell Publishers, 2001. xvi, 368 p.
00-057915 301 0631206582
Ethnology -- Philosophy. Ethnology -- Methodology.

GN345.M67 1991
Morris, Brian, 1936-
Western conceptions of the individual/ Brian Morris. New York: Berg: 1991. ix, 505 p.
91-013878 301/.01 0854966986
Anthropology -- Philosophy. Anthropology -- Methodology. Ethnopsychology.

GN345.R667 1989
Rosaldo, Renato.
Culture & truth: the remaking of social analysis/ Renato Rosaldo. Boston: Beacon Press, c1989. xii, 253 p.
88-047659 306/.01 0807046086
Ethnology -- Philosophy. Subjectivity. Discourse analysis, Narrative.

GN345.S24
Sahlins, Marshall David, 1930-
Culture and practical reason/ Marshall Sahlins. Chicago: University of Chicago Press, 1976. xi, 252 p.
75-027899 301.2 0226733599
Ethnology. Dialectical materialism. Structural anthropology.

GN345.S74 2002
Wolf, Eric R., 1923-
Pathways of power: building an anthropology of the modern world/ Eric R. Wolf with Sydel Silverman; foreword by Aram A. Yengoyan. Berkeley: University of California Press, c2001. xx, 463 p.
00-055969 306 21 0520223330
Ethnology -- Philosophy. Ethnology -- Comparative method. Political anthropology.

GN345.T36 1990
Tambiah, Stanley Jeyaraja, 1929-
Magic, science, religion, and the scope of rationality/ Stanley Jeyaraja Tambiah. Cambridge [England]; Cambridge University Press, 1990. xi, 187 p.
89-031436   305.8/001   0521374863
Ethnology -- Philosophy -- History. Rationalism.

GN345.W52 2001
Willis, Paul E.
The ethnographic imagination/ Paul Willis. Malden, Mass.: Polity Press, 2001. xx, 153 p.
00-037502   305.8/001   0745601731
Ethnology -- Philosophy. Ethnology -- Methodology.

GN345.W65 1992
Wolf, Margery.
A thrice-told tale: feminism, postmodernism, and ethnographic responsibility/ Margery Wolf. Stanford, Calif.: Stanford University Press, 1992. viii, 153 p.
91-024593   301   0804719799
Ethnology -- Methodology. Ethnology -- Philosophy. Feminist criticism. Taiwan -- Social life and customs.

GN345.5 Ethnology.
Social and cultural anthropology
— Philosophy.
Relation to other topics.
Methodology —
Cultural relativism

GN345.5.C85 1991
Cultural relativism and philosophy: North and Latin American perspectives/ edited by Marcelo Dascal. Leiden; E.J. Brill, 1991. xii, 316 p.
91-023928   306   9004094334
Cultural relativism -- Philosophy. Ethnocentrism -- Latin America. Ethnocentrism -- North America.

GN345.6 Ethnology.
Social and cultural anthropology
— Philosophy.
Relation to other topics.
Methodology —
Intercultural communication

GN345.6.B46 1993
Bentley, Jerry H., 1949-
Old world encounters: cross-cultural contacts and exchanges in pre-modern times/ Jerry H. Bentley. New York: Oxford University Press, 1993. viii, 220 p.
92-016378   303.48/2   0195076397
Intercultural communication -- History. World history.

GN345.7-347 Ethnology.
Social and cultural anthropology
— Philosophy.
Relation to other topics.
Methodology —
Special methods

GN345.7.E53 2001
Ember, Carol R.
Cross-cultural research methods/ Carol R. Ember and Melvin Ember. Lanham, MD: AltaMira Press, 2001. viii, 164 p.
00-059346   306/.072   0742504263
Cross-cultural studies.

GN346.A42
Agar, Michael.
The professional stranger: an informal introduction to ethnography/ Michael H. Agar. New York: Academic Press, c1980. xi, 227 p.
79-008870   301/.01/8   012043850X
Ethnology -- Field work. Ethnology -- Methodology.

GN346.A7 1988
Arab women in the field: studying your own society/ edited by Soraya Altorki and Camillia Fawzi El-Solh. Syracuse, N.Y.: Syracuse University Press, 1988. xii, 184 p.
88-020018   306/.0917/4927   081562445X
Ethnology -- Arab countries -- Field work. Women anthropologists -- Arab countries. Women -- Research -- Arab countries.

GN346.F52 1990
Fieldnotes: the makings of anthropology/ edited by Roger Sanjek. Ithaca: Cornell University Press, 1990. xviii, 429 p.
89-046169   306/.072   0801424364
Ethnology -- Field work -- Congresses. Ethnology -- Authorship -- Congresses.

GN346.F536 1995
Fieldwork under fire: contemporary studies of violence and survival/ edited by Carolyn Nordstrom, Antonius C.G.M. Robben. Berkeley: University of California Press, c1995. vii, 300 p.
95-006235   303.6/072   0520089936
Ethnology -- Field work. Violence -- Research. Violence -- Moral and ethical aspects.

GN346.O27 1983
Observers observed: essays on ethnographic fieldwork/ edited by George W. Stocking, Jr. Madison, Wis.: University of Wisconsin Press, 1983. vi, 242 p.
83-047771   306/.0723   0299094502
Ethnology -- Field work. Participant observation. Ethnology -- History.

GN346.R3
Rabinow, Paul.
Reflections on fieldwork in Morocco/ Paul Rabinow; with a foreword by Robert N. Bellah. Berkeley: University of California Press, c1977. xiii, 164 p.
77-071066   301.29/64   0520034503
Rabinow, Paul. Ethnology -- Morocco -- Field work.

GN346.4.B44 1996
Behar, Ruth, 1956-
The vulnerable observer: anthropology that breaks your heart/ Ruth Behar. Boston: Beacon Press, c1996. xii, 195 p.
96-011409   301/.0723 20   0807046302
Participant observation -- Psychological aspects. Anthropologists -- Attitudes. Anthropologists -- Psychology.

GN347.A59 1992
Anthropology and photography, 1860-1920/ edited by Elizabeth Edwards. New Haven: Yale University Press in association with the Ro 1992. xi, 275 p.
91-041482   301/.028   0300051689
Photography in ethnology -- Great Britain -- History. Ethnology -- Great Britain -- History.

GN347.C64 1986
Collier, John, 1913-
Visual anthropology: photography as a research method/ John Collier, Jr., and Malcolm Collier. Albuquerque: University of New Mexico Press, c1986. xvii, 248 p.
86-006926   306/.0208   0826308988
Photography in ethnology. Motion pictures in ethnology.

GN347.M33 1998
MacDougall, David.
Transcultural cinema/ David MacDougall; edited and with an introduction by Lucien Taylor. Princeton, N.J.: Princeton University Press, c1998. x, 318 p.
98-021197   305.8 21   0691012342
Motion pictures in ethnology. Documentary films.

GN347.P66 1997
Poole, Deborah.
Vision, race, and modernity: a visual economy of the Andean image world/ Deborah Poole. Princeton, N.J.: Princeton University Press, c1997. xiv, 263 p.
96-045561   305.8/0098 21   0691006466
Visual anthropology -- Andes Region. Photography in ethnology -- Andes Region -- History. Indians of South America -- Andes Region -- Pictorial works -- History.

GN347.R83 2000
Ruby, Jay.
Picturing culture: explorations of film & anthropology/ Jay Ruby. Chicago: University of Chicago Press, 2000. xiii, 339 p.
99-089536   301   0226730980
Motion pictures in ethnology. Visual anthropology.

GN357 Ethnology.
Social and cultural anthropology
— Culture and cultural processes
— General works

GN357.H39 1999
Harris, Marvin, 1927-
Theories of culture in postmodern times/ Marvin Harris. Walnut Creek, CA: AltaMira Press, c1999. 224 p.
98-040132   306 21   0761990208
Culture. Ethnology -- Philosophy. Anthropology -- Philosophy.

GN357.K87 1999
Kuper, Adam.
Culture: the anthropologists' account/ Adam Kuper. Cambridge, Mass: Harvard University Press, c1999. xv, 299 p.
98-046126   306 21   0674179579
Culture. Ethnology -- Philosophy.

GN357.R45 1989
The Relevance of culture/ edited by Morris Freilich. New York: Bergin & Garvey Publishers, 1989. vi, 250 p.
89-017729   306   0897891813
Culture. Anthropology -- Philosophy.

GN357.S68 1987
Spiro, Melford E.
Culture and human nature: theoretical papers of Melford E. Spiro/ edited by Benjamin Kilborne and L.L. Langness. Chicago: University of Chicago Press, 1987. xv, 309 p.
87-005089   306   0226769941
Culture. Anthropology -- Philosophy. Ethnopsychology.

GN357.S85 1991
Swiderski, Richard M.
Lives between cultures: a study of human nature, identity, and culture/ Richard M. Swiderski. Juneau, Alaska: Denali Press, c1991. 273 p.
90-049515   306   0938737244
Culture. Acculturation. Socialization.

GN357.W47
White, Leslie A., 1900-1975.
The concept of cultural systems: a key to understanding tribes and nations/ Leslie A. White. New York: Columbia University Press, 1975. xiii, 192 p.
75-033003   301.2   0231039611
Culture. Ethnology.

GN358 Ethnology.
Social and cultural anthropology
— Culture and cultural processes
— Culture change. Social change

GN358.H37
Harris, Marvin, 1927-
Cannibals and kings: the origins of cultures/ Marvin Harris. New York: Random House, c1977. xii, 239 p.
77-005977   301.2   0394407652
Social evolution. Culture -- Origin. Human beings -- Effect of environment on.

GN360-360.4 Ethnology.
Social and cultural anthropology
— Culture and cultural processes
— Cultural evolution.
Evolutionism

GN360.D87 1991
Durham, William H.
Coevolution: genes, culture, and human diversity/ William H. Durham. Stanford, Calif.: Stanford University Press, 1991. xxii, 629 p.
90-043867   304.5   0804715378
Culture. Social evolution. Human population genetics -- Social aspects.

GN360.S25 1990
Sanderson, Stephen K.
Social evolutionism: a critical history/ Stephen K. Sanderson. Cambridge, Mass. USA: Blackwell, 1990. xviii, 251 p.
89-018385   303.4   1557860734
Social evolution.

GN360.W55 1988
Wilson, Peter J., 1933-
The domestication of the human species/ Peter J. Wilson. New Haven: Yale University Press, c1988. xvi, 201 p.
88-005516   306   0300042434
Social evolution. Architecture and society. Dwellings, Prehistoric.

GN360.4.S73 1977
Steward, Julian Haynes, 1902-1972.
Evolution and ecology: essays on social transformation/ by Julian H. Steward; edited by Jane C. Steward and Robert F. Murphy. Urbana: University of Illinois Press, c1977. 406 p.
76-046341   301.24   0252006127
Steward, Julian Haynes, -- 1902-1972. Social evolution. Social change. Indians.

GN362 Ethnology.
Social and cultural anthropology
— Culture and cultural processes
— Structuralism.
Structural anthropology

GN362.L42
Leach, Edmund Ronald.
Culture & communication: the logic by which symbols are connected: an introduction to the use of structuralist analysis in social anthropology/ by Edmund Leach. Cambridge [Eng.]; Cambridge University Press, 1976. 105 p.
75-030439   301.2   052121131X
Structural anthropology. Semiotics.

GN362.L4813
Levi-Strauss, Claude.
Structural anthropology/ Claude Levi-Strauss; translated from the French by Claire Jacobson and Brooke Grundfest Schoepf. New York: Basic Books, c1963-76. 2 v.
63-017344   301.2   0465082300
Structural anthropology.

GN365 Ethnology.
Social and cultural anthropology
— Culture and cultural processes
— Culture diffusion

GN365.T73 1988
The Transfer and transformation of ideas and material culture/ edited by Peter J. Hugill and D. Bruce Dickson. College Station: Texas A&M University Press, c1988. xxii, 281 p.
87-007115   303.4   0890963649
Culture diffusion. Social change.

GN365.9 Ethnology.
Social and cultural anthropology
— Culture and cultural processes
— Biological determination.
Sociobiology

GN365.9.B67 1990
The Boundaries of humanity: humans, animals, machines/ edited by James J. Sheehan and Morton Sosna. Berkeley: University of California Press, c1991. x, 274 p.
90-022378   304.5   0520071530
Sociobiology. Artificial intelligence. Culture.

GN365.9.E96
Evolutionary biology and human social behavior: an anthropological perspective/ edited by Napoleon A. Chagnon, William Irons. North Scituate, Mass.: Duxbury Press, c1979. xvi, 623 p.
78-014564   301.2   0878721932
Sociobiology -- Congresses. Social structure -- Congresses.

GN365.9.H37 1991
Haraway, Donna Jeanne.
Simians, cyborgs, and women: the reinvention of nature/ Donna J. Haraway. New York: Routledge, 1991. x, 287 p.
90-008762   304.5   0415903866
Sociobiology. Feminist criticism. Primates -- Behavior.

GN365.9.K58 1985
Kitcher, Philip, 1947-
Vaulting ambition: sociobiology and the quest for human nature/ Philip Kitcher. Cambridge, Mass.: MIT Press, c1985. xi, 456 p.
85-007229   0262111098
Sociobiology.

GN365.9.L47 1992
Lerner, Richard M.
Final solutions: biology, prejudice, and genocide/ Richard M. Lerner; with forewords by R.C. Lewontin and Benno Muller-Hill. University Park, Pa.: Pennsylvania State University Press, c1992. xxii, 238 p.
91-019711   304.5   0271007931
Lorenz, Konrad, -- 1903- Biology -- Social aspects. Social policy. Nature and nurture.

GN365.9.P68 1991
Power, Margaret, 1920-
The egalitarians, human and chimpanzee: an anthropological view of social organization/ Margaret Power. Cambridge [England]; Cambridge University Press, 1991. xviii, 290 p.
90-048014   304.5   0521400163
Sociobiology. Human behavior. Primates -- Behavior.

GN365.9.S38 1986
Schwartz, Barry, 1946-
The battle for human nature: science, morality, and modern life/ Barry Schwartz. New York: Norton, c1986. 348 p.
85-032057   304.5   0393023192
Sociobiology. Economics. Human behavior.

GN365.9.W54
Wilson, Edward Osborne, 1929-
On human nature/ Edward O. Wilson. Cambridge: Harvard University Press, 1978. xii, 260 p.
78-017675   301.2   0674634411
Sociobiology. Social Darwinism.

GN366 Ethnology. Social and cultural anthropology — Culture and cultural processes — Acculturation. Culture contact

GN366.H44 1988
Helms, Mary W.
Ulysses' sail: an ethnographic odyssey of power, knowledge, and geographical distance/ Mary W. Helms. Princeton, N.J.: Princeton University Press, c1988. xii, 297 p.
87-014038 304.2 0691094357
Acculturation. Intercultural communication. Voyages and travels -- Religious aspects.

GN370 Ethnology. Social and cultural anthropology — Migrations of peoples (General)

GN370.C43 1995
Chaliand, Gerard, 1934-
Penguin atlas of the diasporas/ by Gerard Chaliand and Jean-Pierre Rageau; maps by Catherine Petit; translated from the French by A.M. Berrett. New York: Viking, 1995. xxi, 182 p.
94-020640 304.8 0670854395
Human beings -- Migrations -- Atlases. Migrations of nations -- Atlases.

GN380-395 Ethnology. Social and cultural anthropology — Collected ethnographies — Ethnographys of special categories of peoples

GN380.B87 1987
Burger, Julian.
Report from the frontier: the state of the world's indigenous peoples/ Julian Burger. London; Zed Books, 1987. viii, 310 p.
88-005522 305.8 0862323916
Indigenous peoples. Minorities. Acculturation.

GN380.I52 2000b
Indigenous cultures in an interconnected world/ edited by Clair Smith and Graeme K. Ward. Vancouver: UBC Press, 2000. xvii, 230 p.
2001-430709 0774808063
Indigenous peoples. Globalization -- Social aspects. Autochtones.

GN380.W55 1993
Wilmer, Franke.
The indigenous voice in world politics: since time immemorial/ Franke Wilmer. Newbury Park, Calif.: Sage, c1993 xiv, 249 p.
93-026648 306/.08 0803953348
Indigenous peoples. Acculturation. Economic development -- Social aspects.

GN388.C35 1999
The Cambridge encyclopedia of hunters and gatherers/ edited by Richard B. Lee and Richard Daly. Cambridge, U.K.; Cambridge University Press, 1999. xx, 511 p.
98-038671 306.3/64/03 052157109X
Hunting and gathering societies -- Encyclopedias.

GN388.C37 1993
Cartmill, Matt.
A view to a death in the morning: hunting and nature through history/ Matt Cartmill. Cambridge, Mass.: Harvard University Press, 1993. xiii, 331 p.
92-044960 304.5 067493735X
Hunting and gathering societies. Hunting -- History. Human-animal relationships.

GN388.C85 1996
Cultural diversity among twentieth-century foragers: an African perspective/ edited by Susan Kent. Cambridge; Cambridge University Press, 1996. xiv, 344 p.
95-017648 306.3/64 0521482372
Hunting and gathering societies. Pluralism (Social sciences) Subculture.

GN388.H87 1988
Hunters and gatherers/ edited by Tim Ingold, David Riches, James Woodburn. Oxford [Oxfordshire]; Berg; 1988. 2 v.
87-021216 306/.3 0854961534
Hunting and gathering societies -- Congresses.

GN388.K44 1995
Kelly, Robert L.
The foraging spectrum: diversity in hunter-gatherer lifeways/ Robert L. Kelly. Washington: Smithsonian Institution Press, c1995. xvi, 446 p.
94-021100 306.3/49 1560984651
Hunting and gathering societies.

GN395.U72
Urban anthropology; cross-cultural studies of urbanization. Edited by Aidan Southall. New York, Oxford University Press, 1973. vi, 489 p.
73-076911 301.36/1 0195016912
Urban anthropology -- Congresses. Urbanization -- Congresses.

GN397.5 Ethnology. Social and cultural anthropology — Applied anthropology — General works

GN397.5.M35 1989
Making our research useful: case studies in the utilization of anthropological knowledge/ edited by John van Willigen, Barbara Rylko-Bauer, and Ann McElroy. goulder: Westview Press, 1989. xiv, 370 p.
88-027804 306 0813377188
Applied anthropology -- Case studies.

GN397.5.S67 1990
Social change and applied anthropology: essays in honor of David W. Brokensha/ edited by Miriam S. Chaiken and Anne K. Fleuret. Boulder: Westview Press, 1990. xi, 308 p.
90-012092 303.4 081337734X
Brokensha, David. Social change. Human geography. Applied anthropology.

GN397.7 Ethnology. Social and cultural anthropology — Applied anthropology — By region or country, A-Z

GN397.7.S73.F78 1990
Fruzzetti, Lina.
Culture and change along the Blue Nile: courts, markets, and strategies for development/ Lina Fruzzetti, Akos Ostor. Boulder: Westview Press, 1990. xxi, 230 p.
89-014658 307.1/4/09624 0813377889
Applied anthropology -- Sudan. Rural development -- Sudan. Social change. Sudan -- Economic conditions. Blue Nile River Valley (Ethiopia and Sudan) -- Economic conditions.

GN400-405 Ethnology. Social and cultural anthropology — Cultural traits, customs, and institutions

GN400.B4 1961
Benedict, Ruth, 1887-1948.
Patterns of culture. With a new pref. by Margaret Mead. Boston, Houghton Mifflin, 1961 [c1959] 290 p.
61-019375 572
Culture. Ethnopsychology. Zuni Indians. Dobu Island (Papua New Guinea) -- Social life and customs.

GN400.F53 1969
Firth, Raymond William, 1901-
Essays on social organization and values by Raymond Firth. London, Athlone Press; [1969] vi, 326 p.
74-449416 301 048519628X
Ethnology. Social structure. Sociology.

GN400.M78
Murdock, George Peter, 1897-
Culture and society, twenty-four essays. Foreword by Alexander Spoehr. [Pittsburgh] University of Pittsburgh Press [1965] xii, 376 p.
65-018206 301.2
Anthropology. Ethnology.

GN405.M4 1961
Mead, Margaret, 1901-1978,
Cooperation and competition among primitive peoples. Boston, Beacon Press [1961] 544 p.
61-014390 572
Ethnology. Cooperation. Competition.

GN406-440 Ethnology. Social and cultural anthropology — Cultural traits, customs, and institutions — Technology. Material culture

GN406.G53 1999
Glassie, Henry H.
Material culture/ Henry Glassie; photographs, drawings, and design by the author. Bloomington: Indiana University Press, 1999. 413 p.
99-036047 306 0253335744
Material culture.

GN406.G73 2000
Graves-Brown, P. 1960-
Matter, materiality, and modern culture/ edited by P.M. Graves-Brown. London; Routledge, 2000. xii, 171 p.
99-056410   306   0415167043
Material culture. Civilization, Modern.

GN406.L43 1996
Learning from things: method and theory of material culture studies/ edited by W. David Kingery. Washington, D.C.: Smithsonian Institution Press, c1996. x, 262 p.
95-011673   306 20   1560986077
Material culture. Technology and civilization. Archaeology and history.

GN406.M349 1987
Material anthropology: contemporary approaches to material culture/ edited by Barrie Reynolds, Margaret A. Stott. Lanham, MD: University Press of America, c1987. ix, 232 p.
87-015927   306   0819165433
Material culture -- Congresses.

GN406.M57 1987
Mirror and metaphor: material and social constructions of reality/ edited by Daniel W. Ingersoll, Jr., and Gordon Bronitsky. Lanham, MD: University Press of America, c1987. xii, 420 p.
87-025065   306   0819166855
Material culture. Symbolism. Ethnoarchaeology.

GN407.P67 1999
Pottier, Johan.
Anthropology of food: the social dynamics of food security/ Johan Pottier. Cambridge, UK; Polity Press; 1999. ix, 230 p.
98-052197   306.3/49   0745615333
Food -- Social aspects. Food supply -- Government policy. Food supply -- Economic aspects.

GN407.3.B48 1991
Bettinger, Robert L.
Hunter-gatherers: archaeological and evolutionary theory/ Robert L. Bettinger. New York: Plenum Press, c1991. xv, 257 p.
90-025228   303.4   0306436507
Hunting and gathering societies. Social evolution. Prehistoric peoples.

GN407.4.N48 1993
Netting, Robert McC.
Smallholders, householders: farm families and the ecology of intensive, sustainable agriculture/ Robert McC. Netting. Stanford, Calif.: Stanford University Press, 1993. xxi, 389 p.
92-020376   630   0804720614
Traditional farming. Agricultural ecology. Agriculture -- Economic aspects.

GN407.4.S38 1989
Schusky, Ernest Lester, 1931-
Culture and agriculture: an ecological introduction to traditional and modern farming systems/ Ernest L. Schusky; foreword by John W. Bennett. New York: Bergin & Garvey, 1989. xiii, 210 p.
89-017676   306.3/49   0897891856
Agriculture -- Social aspects. Agriculture -- Economic aspects. Agriculture, Prehistoric.

GN414.D65 1990
Domestic architecture and the use of space: an interdisciplinary cross-cultural study/ edited by Susan Kent. Cambridge [England]; Cambridge University Press, 1990. 192 p.
89-035778   728/.01/03   0521381606
Dwellings -- Cross-cultural studies. Space (Architecture) -- Cross-cultural studies. Architecture -- Social aspects -- Cross-cultural studies.

GN419.5.N85 1999
Nunley, John W. 1945-
Masks: faces of culture/ John W. Nunley, Cara McCarty. New York: Abrams in association with the Saint Louis Art M 1999. 344 p.
98-053973   391.4/34   0810943794
Masks. Masks -- Exhibitions.

GN422.S9 1966
Man the hunter. Edited by Richard B. Lee and Irven DeVore, with the assistance of Jill Nash. Chicago, Aldine Pub. Co. [1969, c1968] xvi, 415 p.
67-017603   390
Hunting and gathering societies -- Congresses.

GN433.P68 1999
Pottery and people: a dynamic interaction/ edited by James M. Skibo and Gary M. Feinman. Salt Lake City: University of Utah Press, c1999. xiii, 260 p.
98-038075   306.4/7 21   0874805767
Pottery -- Themes, motives. Pottery -- Analysis. Indian pottery.

GN433.5.B43 1998
Beads and bead makers: gender, material culture, and meaning/ edited by Lidia D. Sciama and Joanne B. Eicher. Oxford [England]; Berg, 1998. xvi, 317 p.
98-188414   1859739954
Beadwork -- Cross-cultural studies. Sex role -- Cross-cultural studies.

GN440.I53 1992
Goetzfridt, Nicholas J.
Indigenous navigation and voyaging in the Pacific: a reference guide/ compiled by Nicholas J. Goetzfridt. New York: Greenwood Press, 1992. xix, 294 p.
91-034621   623.89/099   0313277397
Navigation -- Polynesia -- History -- Sources. Navigation -- Melanesia -- History -- Sources. Navigation -- Micronesia -- History -- Sources.

GN448 Ethnology. Social and cultural anthropology — Cultural traits, customs, and institutions — Economic organization. Economic anthropology

GN448.D68 1982
Douglas, Mary.
In the active voice/ Mary Douglas. London; Routledge & K. Paul, 1982. xi, 306 p.
81-018263   306/.3   071009065X
Economic anthropology. Food habits. Ethnology.

GN448.R48 1989
Roseberry, William, 1950-
Anthropologies and histories: essays in culture, history, and political economy/ William Roseberry. New Brunswick: Rutgers University Press, c1989. xiii, 278 p.
89-030378   306   0813514452
Economic anthropology. Political anthropology. Ethnology -- Philosophy.

GN451-476.73 Ethnology. Social and cultural anthropology — Cultural traits, customs, and institutions — Intellectual life

GN451.B7 1938
Boas, Franz, 1858-1942.
The mind of primitive man. New York, Macmillan, 1938. x, 285 p.
38-008023   136.4
Man, Primitive. Ethnopsychology. Race relations. United States -- Race relations.

GN451.L3813
Levi-Strauss, Claude
The savage mind. [Chicago] University of Chicago Press [1966] xii, 290 p.
66-028197   155.81
Ethnopsychology.

GN451.T87
Turner, Victor Witter.
Dramas, fields, and metaphors; symbolic action in human society [by] Victor Turner. Ithaca [N.Y.] Cornell University Press [1974] 309 p.
73-016968   301.2/1   0801408164
Symbolism -- Addresses, essays, lectures. Rites and ceremonies -- Addresses, essays, lectures. Metaphor -- Addresses, essays, lectures.

GN452.5.N37 1992
Napier, A. David.
Foreign bodies: performance, art, and symbolic anthropology/ A. David Napier. Berkeley: University of California Press, c1992. xxix, 223 p.
90-034530   306.4   0520065832
Symbolic anthropology -- Cross-cultural studies. Symbolism in art -- Cross-cultural studies. Mythology -- Comparative studies.

GN454.B56 1985
Blanchard, Kendall, 1942-
The anthropology of sport: an introduction/ Kendall Blanchard and Alyce Taylor Cheska; introduction by Edward Norbeck. S. Hadley, Mass.: Bergin & Garvey, 1985. xii, 306 p.
84-012395   306/.483   089789040X
Games -- History. Sports -- History.

GN468.2.C48 1988
Choice and morality in anthropological perspective: essays in honor of Derek Freeman/ edited by G.N. Appell and T.N. Madan. Albany, N.Y.: State University of New York Press, c1988. xv, 248 p.
87-006534   174/.9301   0887066062
Freeman, Derek. Choice (Psychology) -- Cross-cultural studies. Ethics -- Cross-cultural studies. Ethnology -- Psychology.

GN468.4.A87 1990
Atran, Scott, 1952-
Cognitive foundations of natural history: towards an anthropology of science/ Scott Atran. Cambridge [England]; Cambridge University Press; 1990. xii, 360 p.
89-036129   303.4/5   0521372933
Folk classification. Cognition and culture. Natural history -- Classification.

GN470.A55 1997
Anthropology of religion: a handbook/ edited by Stephen D. Glazier. Westport, Conn.: Greenwood Press, 1997. viii, 542 p.
96-010742   306.6   0313283516
Religion.

GN470.G5
Gill, Sam D., 1943-
Beyond the primitive: the religions of nonliterate peoples/ Sam D. Gill. Englewood Cliffs, N.J.: Prentice-Hall, c1982. xvii, 120 p.
81-005913   306/.6   013076034X
Religion.

GN470.H35 1996
Firth, Raymond William, 1901-
Religion: a humanist interpretation/ Raymond Firth. London; Routledge, 1996. 243 p.
95-009180   306.6   041512896X
Religion. Religion and culture. Ethnology -- Religious aspects.

GN471.4.H65 2000
Holden, Lynn.
Encyclopedia of taboos/ Lynn Holden. Oxford; ABC-CLIO, c2000. xii, 302 p.
390.03 21   1576070697
Taboo -- Encyclopedias.

GN472.4.D625 1984
Dobkin de Rios, Marlene.
Hallucinogens, cross-cultural perspectives/ Marlene Dobkin de Rios. Albuquerque: University of New Mexico Press, 1984. x, 255 p.
84-007244   394   082630737X
Hallucinogenic plants -- Cross-cultural studies. Hallucinogenic drugs and religious experience -- Cross-cultural studies.

GN473.F5 1967
Firth, Raymond William, 1901-
The work of the gods in Tikopia, by Raymond Firth. London, Athlone P.; 1967 viii, 492 p.
67-010515   299/.9
Tikopia (Solomon Islands people) Rites and ceremonies -- Polynesia.

GN473.F68 1980
Fried, Martha Nemes.
Transitions: four rituals in eight cultures/ Martha Nemes Fried and Morton H. Fried. New York: Norton, c1980. 306 p.
79-024473   301.2/1   0393013502
Rites and ceremonies. Initiation rites. Ethnology.

GN473.G513 1960a
Gennep, Arnold van, 1873-1957.
The rites of passage. Translated by Monika B. Vizedom and Gabrielle L. Caffee. Introd. by Solon T. Kimball. [Chicago] University of Chicago Press [1960] 198 p.
59-014321   392
Rites and ceremonies.

GN475.8.E9 1963
Evans-Pritchard, Edward Evan, 1962-
Witchcraft, oracles and magic among the Azande, by E. E. Evans-Pritchard ... with a foreword by professor C. G. Seligman. Oxford, The Clarendon Press [1963] xxv, 558 p.
38-005545   572.96755
Witchcraft -- Africa, Central. Zande (African people) Magic.

GN476.I53 2000
Indigenous knowledges in global contexts: multiple readings of our world/ edited by George J. Sefa Dei, Budd L. Hall, and Dorothy Goldin Rosenberg. Toronto; Buffalo: c2000. xvi, 282 p.
2001-274018   0802042007
Ethnoscience. Ethnophilosophy. Ethnosciences.

GN476.15.A83 1991
Ascher, Marcia, 1935-
Ethnomathematics: a multicultural view of mathematical ideas/ Marcia Ascher. Pacific Grove, Calif.: Brooks/Cole Pub. Co., c1991. ix, 203 p.
90-048677   510   0534148808
Ethnomathematics.

GN476.73.B35 1996
Balick, Michael J., 1952-
Plants, people, and culture: the science of ethnobotany/ Michael J. Balick, Paul Alan Cox. New York: Scientific American Library, c1996. ix, 228 p.
96-006493   581.6 20   0716750619
Ethnobotany.

GN476.73.E84 1995
Ethnobotany: evolution of a discipline/ edited by Richard Evans Schultes and Siri von Reis. Portland, Or.: Dioscorides Press, c1995. 414 p.
94-015515   581.6/1   0931146283
Ethnobotany.

GN476.73.G66 1993
Goody, Jack.
The culture of flowers/ Jack Goody. Cambridge; Cambridge University Press, 1993. xvii, 462 p.
92-037740   302.2/22   0521414415
Ethnobotany. Ethnobotany -- Africa. Flowers -- History.

GN476.73.J64 1990
Johns, Timothy, 1950-
With bitter herbs they shall eat it: chemical ecology and the origins of human diet and medicine/ Timothy Johns. Tucson: University of Arizona Press, c1990. xviii, 356 p.
90-031694   613.2   0816510237
Ethnobotany. Food, Prehistoric. Plant toxins.

GN476.73.M37 1995
Martin, Gary J.
Ethnobotany: a methods manual/ Gary. J. Martin. London; Chapman & Hall, 1995. xxiv, 268 p.
94-072447   306.6/5   041248370X
Ethnobotany -- Methodology.

GN478-491.7 Ethnology. Social and cultural anthropology — Cultural traits, customs, and institutions — Social organization

GN478.H4713 1981
Heusch, Luc de.
Why marry her?: society and symbolic structures/ Luc de Heusch; translated by Janet Lloyd. Cambridge; Cambridge University Press, 1981. vi, 218 p.
80-041710   305   0521224608
Social structure. Religion. Structural anthropology.

GN479.L56 1989
Lincoln, Bruce.
Discourse and the construction of society: comparative studies of myth, ritual, and classification/ Bruce Lincoln. New York: Oxford University Press, 1989. ix, 238 p.
89-002874   306/.6   0195057570
Social structure. Myth. Ritual.

GN479.65.S49
Sexual meanings, the cultural construction of gender and sexuality/ edited by Sherry B. Ortner and Harriet Whitehead. Cambridge; Cambridge University Press, 1981. x, 435 p.
80-026655   305.3   0521239656
Sex role -- Addresses, essays, lectures. Sex symbolism -- Addresses, essays, lectures.

GN479.7.B48 1990
Beyond the second sex: new directions in the anthropology of gender/ edited by Peggy Reeves Sanday and Ruth Gallagher Goodenough. Philadelphia: University of Pennsylvania Press, c1990. viii, 350 p.
90-030497   305.3   0812282574
Women -- Cross-cultural studies -- Congresses. Sex role -- Cross-cultural studies -- Congresses.

GN479.7.F57 1999
Fisher, Helen E.
The first sex: the natural talents of women and how they are changing the world/ Helen Fisher. New York: Random House, c1999. xx, 378 p.
99-012545   305.4 21   0679449094
Women. Women -- Psychology. Women -- Physiology.

GN479.7.M66 1988
Moore, Henrietta L.
Feminism and anthropology/ Henrietta L. Moore. Minneapolis: University of Minnesota Press, c1988. ix, 246 p.
88-022032   305.4/2   0816617481
Sex role. Women. Ethnology -- Philosophy.

GN479.7.T68 1975
Toward an anthropology of women/ edited by Rayna R. Reiter. New York: Monthly Review Press, [1975] 416 p.
74-021476   301.41/2   0853453721
Women. Sex role.

GN480.B67 1998
Bossler, Beverly Jo.
Powerful relations: kinship, status, & the state in Sung China (960-1279)/ Beverly J. Bossler. Cambridge, Mass.: Council on East Asian Studies, Harvard Universit 1998. x, 370 p.
97-027130   306/.0951/09021   0674695925
Kinship -- China. Social classes -- China. Elite (Social sciences) -- China. China -- Social life and customs -- 960-1644. China -- History -- Sung dynasty, 960-1279.

GN480.B76 1994
Broude, Gwen J.
Marriage, family, and relationships: a cross-cultural encyclopedia/ Gwen J. Broude. Santa Barbara, Calif.: ABC-CLIO, c1994. xiv, 372 p.
94-038979   306.8/03   0874367360
Marriage -- Cross-cultural studies -- Encyclopedias. Family -- Cross-cultural studies -- Encyclopedias. Kinship -- Cross-cultural studies -- Encyclopedias.

GN480.D843 1963
Durkheim, Emile, 1858-1917.
Incest; the nature and origin of the taboo, by Emile Durkheim. Translated, with an introd., by Edward Sagarin. Together with The origins and the development of the incest taboo, by Albert Ellis. New York, L. Stuart [1963] 186 p.
63-007913   392.6
Incest. Clans

GN480.2.F56 2000
Finkler, Kaja.
Experiencing the new genetics: family and kinship on the medical frontier/ Kaja Finkler. Philadelphia: University of Pennsylvania Press, c2000. xiv, 276 p.
99-056639   306.4/61 21   081223538X
Family. Heredity, Human -- Social aspects. Kinship.

GN484.D64 1994
Dorkenoo, Efua.
Cutting the rose: female genital mutilation: the practice and its prevention/ by Efua Dorkenoo. London, UK: Minority Rights Group, 1994. xi, 196 p.
95-174522   392/.1   1873194609
Clitoridectomy -- Cross-cultural studies. Female circumcision -- Cross-cultural studies. Infibulation -- Cross-cultural studies.

GN484.F443 2000
Female "circumcision" in Africa: culture, controversy, and change/ edited by Bettina Shell-Duncan, Ylva Hernlund. Boulder: Lynne Rienner Publishers, 2000. viii, 349 p.
00-023511   392.1/4/096   1555878717
Female circumcision -- Africa.

GN484.G78 2001
Gruenbaum, Ellen.
The female circumcision controversy: an anthropological perspective/ Ellen Gruenbaum. Philadelphia: University of Pennsylvania Press, c2001. 242 p.
00-041803   392.1 21   0812235738
Female circumcision.

GN484.3.F73 1985
Frayser, Suzanne G.
Varieties of sexual experience: an anthropological perspective on human sexuality/ Suzanne G. Frayser. New Haven, Conn.: HRAF Press, 1985. xii, 546 p.
85-060217   0875363423
Sex customs -- Cross-cultural studies. Sex (Biology)

GN484.3.M38 1990
Mating and marriage/ edited by Vernon Reynolds and John Kellett. Oxford; Oxford University Press, 1990. xii, 164 p.
90-038943   306.7   0198584067
Sex customs. Marriage. Sexual behavior in animals.

GN484.35.H47 1997
Herdt, Gilbert H., 1949-
Same sex, different cultures: gays and lesbians across cultures/ Gilbert Herdt. Boulder, Colo.: Westview Press, 1997. xix, 204 p.
97-001839   306.76/6   0813331633
Homosexuality. Lesbianism. Gay men -- Cross-cultural studies.

GN484.38.B56 1988
Blood magic: the anthropology of menstruation/ edited, with an introduction by Thomas Buckley and Alma Gottlieb. Berkeley: University of California Press, c1988. x, 326 p.
87-012529   305.4   0520060857
Menstruation -- Cross-cultural studies. Menstruation -- Folklore. Menstruation -- Social aspects.

GN484.38.G73 1993
Grahn, Judy, 1940-
Blood, bread, and roses: how menstruation created the world/ Judy Grahn. Boston: Beacon Press, c1993. xxiii, 323 p.
93-007701   392/.14   0807075043
Menstruation -- Social aspects. Menstruation -- Cross-cultural studies.

GN484.38.K58 1991
Knight, Chris, 1942-
Blood relations: menstruation and the origins of culture/ Chris Knight. New Haven: Yale University Press, 1991. x, 581 p.
90-071194   392/.6   0300049110
Menstruation -- Social aspects.

GN485.C64 1998
Cohen, Lawrence, 1961-
No aging in India: Alzheimer's, the bad family, and other modern things/ Lawrence Cohen. Berkeley: University of California Press, c1998. xxv, 367 p.
97-038659   305.26 21   0520083962
Aging -- Anthropological aspects. Ethnology -- India -- Varanasi. Aging -- Anthropological aspects -- India -- Varanasi. Varanasi (India) -- Social life and customs.

GN486.M48 1991
Metcalf, Peter.
Celebrations of death: the anthropology of mortuary ritual/ Peter Metcalf, Richard Huntington. Cambridge [England]; Cambridge University Press, 1991. xiii, 236 p.
91-019464   393   0521413125
Funeral rites and ceremonies. Death.

GN487.F7 1993
Fox, Robin, 1934-
Reproduction and succession: studies in anthropology, law, and society/ Robin Fox. New Brunswick, U.S.A.: Transaction Publishers, c1993. xi, 269 p.
92-013207   306.83   1560000678
Kinship. Kinship (Law) Human reproduction.

GN490.D813 1963
Durkheim, Emile, 1858-1917.
Primitive classification, by Emile Durkheim and Marcel Mauss. Translated from the French and edited with an introd. by Rodney Needham. [Chicago] University of Chicago Press [1963] xlviii, 96 p.
63-009737   572.012
Folk classification.

GN490.R3
Radcliffe-Brown, A. R. 1881-1955.
Structure and function in primitive society, essays and addresses; with a foreword by E.E. Evans-Pritchard and Fred Eggan. Glencoe, Ill., The Free Press, 1952. vii, 219 p.
54-003649
Social Behavior Primitive societies. Anthropology, Cultural

GN491.4.Q54 1993
Quigley, Declan.
The interpretation of caste/ Declan Quigley. Oxford: Clarendon Press; 1993. viii, 184 p.
92-027757   305.5/122   0198278829
Caste. Caste -- India.

GN491.7.D66 1999
Donnan, Hastings.
Borders: frontiers of identity, nation and state/ Hastings Donnan and Thomas M. Wilson. Oxford; Berg, 1999. xiv, 182 p.
1859732410
Boundaries -- Social aspects. Boundaries.

GN492-494.5 Ethnology. Social and cultural anthropology — Cultural traits, customs, and institutions — Political organization. Political anthropology

GN492.C5613 1987
Clastres, Pierre, 1934-
Society against the state: essays in political anthropology/ Pierre Clastres; translated by Robert Hurley in collaboration with Abe Stein. New York: Zone Books; 1987. 218 p.
87-050396   306/.2   0942299000
Political anthropology. Indians of South America.

GN492.E96 1990
The Evolution of political systems: sociopolitics in small-scale sedentary societies/ edited by Steadman Upham. Cambridge [England]; Cambridge University Press, 1990. xxi, 310 p.
89-035789   306.2   0521382521
Political anthropology -- Congresses. Marxist anthropology -- Congresses.

GN492.G55 1994
Gledhill, John.
Power & its disguises: anthropological perspectives on politics/ by John Gledhill. London; Pluto Press, 1994. vii, 248 p.
93-036729   306.2   0745307396
Political anthropology. Power (Social sciences)

GN492.3.K47 1988
Kertzer, David I., 1948-
Ritual, politics, and power/ David I. Kertzer. New Haven: Yale University Press, c1988. xi, 235 p.
87-016122   306/.2   0300040075
Political customs and rites -- Cross-cultural studies. Power (Social sciences) -- Cross-cultural studies. Symbolism in politics -- Cross-cultural studies.

GN492.6.O7
Origins of the state: the anthropology of political evolution/ edited by Ronald Cohen and Elman R. Service. Philadelphia: Institute for the Study of Human Issues, c1978. 233 p.
77-019091   320.1/1   0915980681
Political anthropology. State, The -- Origin.

GN492.6.S53 1991
Sicker, Martin.
The genesis of the state/ Martin Sicker. New York: Praeger, 1991. x, 161 p.
90-007375   320.1   0275937046
State, The -- Origin. Authority.

GN493.3.S68 1996
Social rules: origin, character, logic, change/ edited by David Braybrooke. Boulder, Colo.: Westview Press, 1996. xiii, 290 p.
95-047094   306   0813328675
Social norms. Social interaction. Social change.

GN494.D6 1966a
Douglas, Mary Tev.
Purity and danger; an analysis of concepts of pollution and taboo [by] Mary Douglas. New York, Praeger [1966] viii, 188 p.
66-023887 390
Purity, Ritual. Taboo.

GN494.R3
Radcliffe-Brown, A. R. 1881-1955.
Taboo, by A. R. Radcliffe-Brown. Cambridge [Eng.] University press, 1939. 47 p.
40-032203
Tabou. -- ram Taboo.

GN494.5.R67 1993
Ross, Marc Howard.
The management of conflict: interpretations and interests in comparative perspective/ Marc Howard Ross. New Haven: Yale University Press, c1993. xvi, 226 p.
92-047397 303.6/9 0300053983
Political anthropology. Conflict management -- Cross-cultural studies. Conflict (Psychology) -- Cross-cultural studies.

GN495.4-497 Ethnology. Social and cultural anthropology — Cultural traits, customs, and institutions — Societal groups. Ethnic groups

GN495.4.E53 1993
The Encyclopedia of the peoples of the world/ edited by Amiram Gonen. New York: H. Holt, 1993. 703 p.
93-022942 305.8/003 0805022562
Ethnic groups -- Encyclopedias. Indigenous peoples -- Encyclopedias.

GN495.4.P37 1997
Parker, Philip M., 1960-
Ethnic cultures of the world: a statistical reference/ Philip M. Parker. Westport, Conn.: Greenwood Press, 1997. viii, 408 p.
96-043832 305.8 0313297673
Ethnic groups -- Statistics. Demographic surveys.

GN495.6.B57 2000
Blum, Susan Debra.
Portraits of "primitives": ordering human kinds in the Chinese nation/ Susan D. Blum. Lanham: Rowman & Littlefield Publishers, c2001. xx, 235 p.
00-036923 305.8/00951 21 0742500918
Ethnicity -- China. China -- Ethnic relations.

GN495.6.B65 1998
Borders, exiles, diasporas/ edited by Elazar Barkan and Marie-Denise Shelton. Stanford, Calif.: Stanford University Press, 1998. xiv, 340 p.
97-016108 305.8 0804329050
Ethnicity. Identity (Psychology) Ethnic relations.

GN495.6.E67
Epstein, A. L.
Ethos and identity: three studies in ethnicity/ A. L. Epstein. London: Tavistock Publications; 1978. xvi, 181 p.
78-314380 301.45/1 0202011658
Ethnicity -- Addresses, essays, lectures.

GN495.6.E86
Ethnic change/ edited by Charles F. Keyes. Seattle: University of Washington Press, c1981. xii, 331 p.
80-054426 305.8 029595812X
Ethnicity. Ethnology. Cross-cultural studies.

GN495.6.M35 1998
Making majorities: constituting the nation in Japan, Korea, China, Malaysia, Fiji, Turkey, and the United States/ edited by Dru C. Gladney. Stanford: Stanford University Press, 1998. xv, 350 p.
97-042928 305.8 0804730474
Ethnicity -- Case studies. Majorities -- Case studies. Minorities -- Case studies.

GN495.6.R66 1989
Roosens, Eugeen, 1934-
Creating ethnicity: the process of ethnogenesis/ Eugeen E. Roosens. Newbury Park, Calif.: Sage Publications, c1989. 168 p.
89-010549 305.8 080393422X
Ethnicity. Ethnic groups.

GN495.8.J34 1999
Jahoda, Gustav.
Images of savages: ancients [sic] roots of modern prejudice in Western culture/ Gustav Jahoda. London; Routledge, 1999. xx, 297 p.
98-011795 305.8 0415179521
Ethnocentricism. Prejudices. Racism.

GN496.C8 1999
Cultural divides: understanding and overcoming group conflict/ Deborah A. Prentice and Dale T. Miller, editors. New York: Russell Sage Foundation, c1999. xvi, 507 p.
99-019380 305.8 21 0871546906
Ethnic relations. Culture conflict -- United States. Intergroup relations -- United States. United States -- Ethnic relations.

GN496.F67 1997
Forbes, H. D.
Ethnic conflict: commerce, culture, and the contact hypothesis/ H.D. Forbes. New Haven: Yale University Press, c1997. xi, 291 p.
96-050343 303.48/2 21 0300068190
Ethnic relations. Culture conflict. Ethnocentrism.

GN496.H363 1998
The handbook of interethnic coexistence/ edited by Eugene Weiner; foreword by Alan B. Slifka. New York: Continuum, 1998. 653 p.
97-031303 305.8 0826410561
Ethnic relations. International relations. Culture conflict.

GN496.L48 1994
Levinson, David, 1947-
Ethnic relations: a cross-cultural encyclopedia/ David Levinson. Santa Barbara, Calif.: ABC-CLIO, c1994. ix, 293 p.
94-040253 305.8 0874367352
Ethnic relations -- Cross-cultural studies -- Encyclopedias.

GN496.S7 1996
Stavenhagen, Rodolfo.
Ethnic conflicts and the nation-state/ Rodolfo Stavenhagen. New York: St. Martin's Press, 1996. xii, 324 p.
96-010553 305.8 0312159714
Ethnic relations -- Political aspects. International relations. Culture conflict.

GN497.K45 2000
Kelly, Raymond C. 1942-
Warless societies and the origin of war/ Raymond C. Kelly. Ann Arbor: University of Michigan Press, c2000. x, 192 p.
00-009898 303.6/6 21 0472097385
War and society -- History. Warfare, Prehistoric.

GN502-512 Ethnology. Social and cultural anthropology — Cultural traits, customs, and institutions — Psychological anthropology

GN502.C76 1992
Cross-cultural psychology: research and applications/ John W. Berry ...[et al.]. Cambridge [England]; Cambridge University Press, 1992. xiv, 459 p.
91-018275 155.8 0521373875
Ethnopsychology.

GN502.C85 1990
Cultural psychology: essays on comparative human development/ edited by James W. Stigler, Richard A. Shweder, Gilbert Herdt. Cambridge; Cambridge University Press, 1990. ix, 625 p.
88-037008 155.8 0521371546
Ethnopsychology -- Congresses. Cognition and culture -- Congresses.

GN502.D36 1995
D'Andrade, Roy G.
The development of cognitive anthropology/ Roy D'Andrade. Cambridge; Cambridge University Press, 1995. xiv, 272 p.
94-004749 155.8 0521453704
Ethnopsychology. Cognition and culture.

GN502.H34 1990
Hamill, James F. 1942-
Ethno-logic: the anthropology of human reasoning/ James F. Hamill. Urbana: University of Illinois Press, c1990. xiii, 124 p.
89-048194 155.8 0252017145
Ethnopsychology. Logic -- Cross-cultural studies. Cognition and culture.

GN502.J325 1993
Jahoda, Gustav.
Crossroads between culture and mind: continuities and change in theories of human nature/ Gustav Jahoda. Cambridge, Mass.: Harvard University Press, 1993. x, 221 p.
92-019501 155.8 0674177754
Ethnopsychology. Ethnopsychology -- History.

GN502.P47
Perspectives on cross-cultural psychology/ edited by Anthony J. Marsella, Roland G. Tharp, Thomas J. Ciborowski. New York: Academic Press, 1979. xv, 413 p.
79-006950 155.8 0124735509
Ethnopsychology. Personality and culture -- Cross-cultural studies.

GN502.S49 1996
Shore, Bradd, 1945-
Culture in mind: cognition, culture, and the problem of meaning/ Bradd Shore. New York: Oxford University Press, 1996. xvii, 428 p.
95-011828 155.8 0195095979
Ethnopsychology. Cognition and culture. Social perception.

GN512.F57 1993
Fitzgerald, Thomas K.
Metaphors of identity: a culture-communication dialogue/ Thomas K. Fitzgerald; foreword by George and Louise Spindler. Albany: State University of New York Press, c1993. xii, 264 p.
92-027080   155.2   0791415953
Identity   (Psychology)   Intercultural communication. Interpersonal relations.

GN512.S63 1989
Societies at peace: anthropological perspectives/ edited by Signe Howell and Roy Willis. London; Routledge, 1989. ix, 250 p.
88-030271   303.6   0415018242
Ethnopsychology -- Congresses. Self-perception - - Cross-cultural studies -- Congresses. Ethnophilosophy -- Congresses.

GN547-549 Ethnology. Social and cultural anthropology — Ethnic groups and races — Groups not limited to particular regions

GN547.E34 1994
Efron, John M.
Defenders of the race: Jewish doctors and race science in fin-de-siecle Europe/ John M. Efron. New Haven: Yale University Press, c1994. xii, 255 p.
94-010413   572   0300054408
Jews -- Identity. Race. Physical anthropology -- History.

GN549.B3.E86 1989
Essays in Basque social anthropology and history/ edited by William A. Douglass. Reno, Nev.: Basque Studies Program, c1989. 327 p.
89-015013   306/.0899992   1877802026
Basques -- Social life and customs. Basques -- Folklore. Basques -- History.

GN549.B3.V3413 1994
Valle, Teresa del.
Korrika: Basque ritual for ethnic identity/ Teresa del Valle; translated by Linda White. Reno: University of Nevada Press, c1994. xxxi, 223 p.
93-019034   796.42/7/09466   0874172152
Basques -- Rites and ceremonies. Basques -- Games. Basques -- Ethnic identity.

GN549.C3.C48 1992
Chapman, Malcolm
The Celts: the construction of a myth/ Malcolm Chapman. New York: St. Martin's Press, 1992. xv, 342 p.
91-044261   940/.04916   0312079389
Celts -- History. Celts -- Social life and customs. Ethnology -- France -- Plouhinec -- Field work. Plouhinec (France) -- Social life and customs.

GN560-673 Ethnology. Social and cultural anthropology — Ethnic groups and races — By region or country

GN560.M6.R33 1997
Radding Murrieta, Cynthia.
Wandering peoples: colonialism, ethnic spaces, and ecological frontiers in northwestern Mexico, 1700-1850/ Cynthia Radding. Durham: Duke University Press, 1997. xx, 404 p.
96-035147   305.8/0097217   0822319071
Ethnicity -- Mexico -- Sonora (State) Social ecology -- Mexico -- Sonora (State) Social change - - Mexico -- Sonora (State) Indians of Mexico -- Mexico -- Sonora (State) -- History. Sonora (Mexico: State) -- History. Sonora (Mexico: State) -- Social conditions.

GN562.S74 1999
Stephens, Thomas M.
Dictionary of Latin American racial and ethnic terminology/ Thomas M. Stephens. Gainesville: University Press of Florida, c1999. xxviii, 863 p.
99-012817   305.8/0098/03 21   081301705X
Ethnology -- Latin America -- Dictionaries -- Spanish. Ethnology -- Latin America -- Dictionaries -- Portuguese.

GN564.P4.D85 1994
Duke, James A., 1929-
Amazonian ethnobotanical dictionary/ James Alan Duke, Rodolfo Vasquez. Boca Raton, Fla.: CRC Press, c1994. 215 p.
94-000390   581.6/1/098543   0849336643
Ethnobotany -- Peru -- Dictionaries. Ethnobotany -- Amazon River Valley -- Dictionaries. Botany, Economic -- Peru -- Dictionaries.

GN564.T7.B57 1999
Birth, Kevin K., 1963-
Any time is Trinidad time: social meanings and temporal consciousness/ Kevin K. Birth. Gainesville, Fla.: University Press of Florida, c1999. xiv, 190 p.
99-020574   304.2/3 21   0813017130
Ethnology -- Trinidad. Time -- Social aspects -- Trinidad. Time perception -- Trinidad. Trinidad -- Social life and customs.

GN575.N15 2001
Naimark, Norman M.
Fires of hatred: ethnic cleansing in twentieth-century Europe/ Norman M. Naimark. Cambridge, Mass.: Harvard University Press, 2001. 248 p.
00-057500   305.8/0094   0674003136
Racism -- Europe -- History -- 20th century. Population transfers. Political atrocities -- Europe. Europe -- Ethnic relations.

GN575.R83 2000
Rubies, Joan-Pau.
Travel and ethnology in the Renaissance: South India through European eyes, 1250-1625/ Joan-Pau Rubies. Cambridge; Cambridge University Press, 2000. xxii, 443 p.
2001-267152   915.4042   0521770556
Ethnology -- Europe. Travel literature -- India. Travel literature -- Europe. India, South -- Description and travel.

GN585.F8.A2413 1991
Abeles, Marc.
Quiet days in Burgundy: a study of local politics/ Marc Abeles; translated from the French by Annella McDermott. Cambridge; Cambridge University Press; 1991. xxvii, 279 p.
90-046666   306.2/0944/41   0521383021
Political anthropology -- France -- Yonne. Yonne (France) -- Politics and government. Yonne (France) -- Social conditions.

GN585.G4.B67 1992
Borneman, John, 1952-
Belonging in the two Berlins: kin, state, nation/ John Borneman. Cambridge; Cambridge University Press, 1992. xiv, 386 p.
91-034054   305.8/009431/55   0521415896
Ethnology -- Germany -- Berlin. Kinship -- Germany -- Berlin. National characteristics, West German. Berlin (Germany) -- Social conditions. Berlin (Germany) -- Economic conditions. Berlin (Germany) -- Social life and customs.

GN585.G85.C66 1991
Contested identities: gender and kinship in modern Greece/ edited by Peter Loizos and Evthymios Papataxiarchis.   Princeton,   N.J.:   Princeton University Press, c1991. viii, 259 p.
90-047780   306.83/09495   0691094608
Kinship -- Greece. Marriage -- Greece. Friendship -- Greece. Greece -- Social life and customs.

GN585.G85.P35 1995
Panourgia, E. Neni K. 1958-
Fragments of death, fables of identity: an Athenian anthropography/ Neni Panourgia. Madison, Wis.: University of Wisconsin Press, c1995. xxiii, 242 p.
95-006196   306/.09495/12   0299145603
Ethnology -- Greece -- Athens. Ethnology -- Greece -- Athens -- Methodology. Death -- Social aspects -- Greece -- Athens. Athens (Greece) -- Social life and customs.

GN585.S65.K56 1984
Kinship and marriage in the Soviet Union: field studies/ edited by Tamara Dragadze. London; Routledge & Kegan Paul, 1984. xiii, 269 p.
83-024607   306.8/3/0947   071000995X
Kinship -- Soviet Union. Family -- Soviet Union. Ethnology -- Soviet Union. Soviet Union -- Social life and customs.

GN585.S7.B47 1990
Bestard-Camps, Joan.
What's in a relative?: household and family in Formentera/ Joan Bestard-Camps; translated by Robert Pitt. New York: Berg; 1991. xvii, 213 p.
90-000394   306.85/0946/756   0854965866
Kinship -- Spain -- Formentera. Family -- Spain - - Formentera. Formentera (Spain) -- Social life and customs.

GN588.P37 1996
Patton, Mark.
Islands in time: island sociogeography and Mediterranean prehistory/ Mark Patton. London; Routledge, 1996. x, 213 p.
95-044147   304.2/09182/2   0415126592
Prehistoric peoples -- Islands of the Mediterranean. Human geography -- Islands of the Mediterranean. Social evolution -- Islands of the Mediterranean. Islands of the Mediterranean -- Antiquities.

GN635.B6.F46 1991
Female and male in Borneo: contributions and challenges to gender studies/ edited by Vinson H. Sutlive, Jr. Williamston, VA, USA: Borneo Research Council, [1991] xlvi, 528 p.
91-072229 305.3/09595/3 0962956805
Ethnology -- Borneo. Sex role -- Borneo. Borneo -- Social life and customs.

GN635.B8.S63 1997
Spiro, Melford E.
Gender ideology and psychological reality: an essay on cultural reproduction/ Melford E. Spiro. New Haven, Conn.: Yale University Press, c1997. xx, 220 p.
97-003919 305.3/09591 21 0300070071
Sex role -- Burma. Gender identity -- Burma. Ethnopsychology -- Burma. Burma -- Social life and customs.

GN635.C5.C4813 1991
Chu, Hsi, 1130-1200.
Chu Hsi's family rituals: a twelfth-century Chinese manual for the performance of cappings, weddings, funerals, and ancestral rites/ translated, with annotation and introduction by Patricia Buckley Ebrey. Princeton, N.J.: Princeton University Press, c1991. xxxi, 234 p.
90-044943 392/.0951 0691031495
Rites and ceremonies -- China. Manners and customs -- China. China -- Social life and customs -- 960-1644.

GN635.C5.G65 1990
Goldstein, Melvyn C.
Nomads of western Tibet: the survival of a way of life/ photography and text by Melvyn C. Goldstein and Cynthia M. Beall. Berkeley: University of California Press, [c1990] 191 p.
90-010892 305.9/0693 0520072103
Nomads -- China -- Tibet -- Social life and customs. Nomads -- China -- Tibet -- Economic conditions. Nomads -- Government policy -- China -- Tibet. Tibet (China) -- Social life and customs.

GN635.C5.H67 2001
Hostetler, Laura.
Qing colonial enterprise: ethnography and cartography in early modern China/ Laura Hostetler. Chicago: University of Chicago Press, c2001. xx, 257 p.
00-010974 951/.03 21 0226354202
Ethnology -- China. Cartography -- China. China -- Colonization. China -- Social life and customs. China -- History -- Ching dynasty, 1644-1912.

GN635.I4.B345 1996
Bailey, F. G.
The civility of indifference: on domesticating ethnicity/ F.G. Bailey. Ithaca: Cornell University Press, 1996. xvi, 184 p.
95-037324 305.8/00954/13 0801432170
Ethnicity -- India -- Bisipara. Racism -- India -- Bisipara. Apathy -- India -- Bisipara. Bisipara (India) -- History. Bisipara (India) -- Ethnic relations. Bisipara (India) -- Social conditions.

GN635.I4.B35 1994
Bailey, F. G.
The witch-hunt, or, The triumph of morality/ F.G. Bailey. Ithaca: Cornell University Press, 1994. ix, 221 p.
94-003193 306/.0954/13 0801430216
Ethnology -- India -- Bisipara. Witchcraft -- India -- Bisipara. Caste -- India -- Bisipara. Bisipara (India) -- History. Bisipara (India) -- Social conditions. Bisipara (India) -- Religious life and customs.

GN635.I4.B6 1989
Blue mountains, the ethnography and biogeography of a south Indian region/ edited by Paul Hockings. Delhi; Oxford University Press, 1989. vii, 406 p.
90-900145 305.8/0954/13 0195621778
Ethnology -- India -- Nilgiri (District) Nilgiri (India: District) -- History. Nilgiri (India: District) -- Antiquities. Nilgiri (India: District) -- Social life and customs.

GN635.I4.D58 1990
Divine passions: the social construction of emotion in India/ edited by Owen M. Lynch. Berkeley: University of California Press, c1990. x, 312 p.
89-004975 152.4 0520066472
Ethnology -- India -- Congresses. Emotions -- Congresses. Love -- Religious aspects -- Hinduism -- Congresses. India -- Social life and customs -- Congresses.

GN635.I65.B38 1993
Barth, Fredrik, 1928-
Balinese worlds/ Fredrik Barth. Chicago: University of Chicago Press, c1993. x, 370 p.
92-018043 306/.09598/6 0226038335
Ethnology -- Indonesia -- Bali (Province) Religion and culture -- Indonesia -- Bali (Province). Bali (Indonesia: Province) -- Social life and customs.

GN635.I65.B69 1998
Brenner, Suzanne April, 1960-
The domestication of desire: women, wealth, and modernity in Java/ Suzanne April Brenner. Princeton, N.J.: Princeton University Press, c1998. xiii, 301 p.
97-046124 306/.09598/2 21 0691016933
Ethnology -- Indonesia -- Surakarta. Social change -- Indonesia -- Surakarta. Women -- Indonesia -- Surakarta. Surakarta (Indonesia) -- Social conditions.

GN635.I65.E76 1989
Errington, Shelly, 1944-
Meaning and power in a Southeast Asian realm/ Shelly Errington. Princeton, N.J.: Princeton University Press, c1989. xiv, 322 p.
88-039412 306/.09598/4 0691094454
Ethnology -- Indonesia -- Luwu. Spatial behavior -- Indonesia -- Luwu. Luwu (Indonesia) -- Social life and customs.

GN635.I65.L35 1991
Lansing, John Stephen.
Priests and programmers: technologies of power in the engineered landscape of Bali/ J. Stephen Lansing. Princeton, N.J.: Princeton University Press, c1991. xvi, 183 p.
91-009993 306.3/49 0691094667
Rites and ceremonies -- Indonesia -- Bali (Province) Irrigation -- Indonesia -- Bali (Province) -- Management. Irrigation -- Indonesia -- Bali (Province) -- Religious aspects. Bali (Indonesia: Province) -- Politics and government.

GN635.I65 S948 1999
Sullivan, Gerald.
Margaret Mead, Gregory Bateson, and highland Bali: fieldwork photographs of Bayung Gedé, 1936-1939/ Gerald Sullivan. Chicago: University of Chicago Press, 1999. ix, 213 p.
98-055903 306/.09598/6 21 0226384349
Mead, Margaret, 1901-1978 -- Photograph collections. Bateson, Gregory -- Photograph collections. Photography in ethnology -- Indonesia -- Bayung Gedé (Bali) Ethnology -- Indonesia -- Bayung Gedé (Bali) -- Field work.

GN635.J2.H35 1997
Hanley, Susan B., 1939-
Everyday things in premodern Japan: the hidden legacy of material culture/ Susan B. Hanley. Berkeley, Calif.: University of California Press, c1997. xiv, 213 p.
96-033421 306/.0952 20 0520204700
Material culture -- Japan. Japan -- Social life and customs. Japan -- History -- Tokugawa period, 1600-1868. Japan -- History -- Meiji period, 1868-1912.

GN635.J2.R62 1998
Robertson, Jennifer Ellen.
Takarazuka: sexual politics and popular culture in modern Japan/ Jennifer Robertson. Berkeley: University of California Press, c1998. xvi, 278 p.
97-038671 306/.0952 21 0520211502
Ethnology -- Japan. Theater -- Japan. Musicals -- Japan. Japan -- Social life and customs.

GN635.M4.C39 1997
Carsten, Janet.
The heat of the hearth: the process of kinship in a Malay fishing community/ Janet Carsten. Oxford: Clarendon Press; 1997. ix, 314 p.
96-035165 306.83/09595/1 0198280459
Kinship -- Malaysia -- Langkawi Island (Kedah) Fishing villages -- Malaysia -- Langkawi Island (Kedah) Langkawi Island (Kedah) -- Social life and customs. Malaysia -- Social life and customs.

GN635.M4.P45 1988
Peletz, Michael G.
A share of the harvest: kinship, property, and social history among the Malays of Rembau/ Michael Gates Peletz. Berkeley: University of California Press, c1988. xxv, 383 p.
88-002466 306/.089992/05951 0520061535
Malays (Asian people) -- Kinship. Malays (Asian people) -- Land tenure. Clans -- Malaysia -- Rembau (Negeri Sembilan) Rembau (Negeri Sembilan) -- Economic conditions. Rembau (Negeri Sembilan) -- Social conditions.

GN635.O43.C48 1996
Chatty, Dawn.
Mobile pastoralists: development planning and social change in Oman/ Dawn Chatty. New York: Columbia University Press, c1996. xiv, 230 p.
95-045923 305.8/0095353 20 0231105487
Nomads -- Oman. Pastoral systems -- Oman. Rural development projects -- Oman. Oman -- Ethnic relations. Oman -- Politics and government.

GN635.P27.A38 1998
Ahmed, Feroz.
Ethnicity and politics in Pakistan/ Feroz Ahmed. Karachi; Oxford University Press, 1998. xxii, 294 p.
98-202437 305.8/0095491 0195779061
Ethnicity -- Pakistan. Pakistan -- Politics and government. Pakistan -- Ethnic relations.

GN635.S5.C75 1988
Crossroads of continents: cultures of Siberia and Alaska/ [edited by] William W. Fitzhugh and Aron Crowell. Washington, D.C.: Smithsonian Institution Press, 1988. 360 p.
88-042630 306/.0957 0874744423
Ethnology -- Russia (Federation) -- Siberia -- Exhibitions. Indians of North America -- Alaska -- Exhibitions. Eskimos -- Alaska -- Exhibitions. Siberia (Russia) -- Social life and customs -- Exhibitions. Alaska -- Social life and customs -- Exhibitions.

GN635.S58.R57 1989
Ritual, power, and economy: upland-lowland contrasts in mainland Southeast Asia/ Susan D. Russell, editor. [DeKalb, IL]: Northern Illinois University, Center for Southea 1989. v, 143 p.
90-182057   306/.0959   1877979147
Rites and ceremonies -- Asia, Southeastern. Power (Social sciences) Asia, Southeastern -- Politics and government. Asia, Southeastern -- Religious life and customs. Asia, Southeastern -- Economic conditions.

GN635.S72.B76 1996
Brow, James.
Demons and development: the struggle for community in a Sri Lankan village/ James Brow. Tucson: University of Arizona Press, c1996. xviii, 218 p.
96-009982   305.8/0095493 20   0816516383
Ethnology -- Sri Lanka -- Anuradhapura (District) Vedda (Sri Lankan people) -- Social conditions. Community. Anuradhapura (Sri Lanka: District) -- Religious life and customs. Anuradhapura (Sri Lanka: District) -- Social conditions.

GN635.T28.C63
Cohen, Myron L., 1937-
House united, house divided: the Chinese family in Taiwan/ Myron L. Cohen. New York: Columbia University Press, 1976. xvi, 267 p.
75-028473   301.42/1   0231038496
Ethnology -- Taiwan. Family -- Taiwan. Taiwan -- Social life and customs -- 1945-1975.

GN635.T4.A53 1993
Anderson, Edward F., 1932-
Plants and people of the Golden Triangle: ethnobotany of the hill tribes of northern Thailand/ Edward F. Anderson. Portland, Or.: Dioscorides Press, c1993. 279 p.
92-025857   581.6/1/09593   0931146259
Ethnobotany -- Thailand, Northern. Ethnobotany -- Golden Triangle (Southeastern Asia) Mountain peoples -- Thailand, Northern. Thailand, Northern -- Social life and customs. Golden Triangle (Southeastern Asia) -- Social life and customs.

GN635.V5.H53 1993
Hickey, Gerald Cannon, 1925-
Shattered world: adaptation and survival among Vietnam's highland peoples during the Vietnam War/ Gerald Cannon Hickey. Philadelphia: University of Pennsylvania Press, c1993. xxxiv, 297 p.
92-045143   306/.089/9592   0812231724
Indigenous peoples -- Vietnam -- Central Highlands. Kinship -- Vietnam -- Central Highlands. Material culture -- Vietnam -- Central Highlands. Central Highlands (Vietnam) -- History. Central Highlands (Vietnam) -- Social life and customs.

GN645.A36
The African diaspora: interpretive essays/ edited by Martin L. Kilson, Robert I. Rotberg. Cambridge, Mass.: Harvard University Press, 1976. xiii, 510 p.
75-030643   909/.04/96   0674007794
Blacks. Slave-trade.

GN645.A95 1991
Ayittey, George B. N., 1945-
Indigenous African institutions/ George B.N. Ayittey. Ardsley-on-Hudson, N.Y.: Transnational Publishers, c1991. xlvii, 547 p.
91-019161   960   0941320650
Indigenous peoples -- Africa. Customary law -- Africa -- History. Chiefdoms -- Africa -- History. Africa -- Politics and government. Africa -- History. Africa -- Social life and customs.

GN645.B53 1996
Biebuyck, Daniel P., 1925-
African ethnonyms: index to art-producing peoples of Africa/ Daniel P. Biebuyck, Susan Kelliher, Linda McRae. New York: G.K. Hall, c1996. xxviii, 378 p.
96-019439   305.8/00967 20   0783815328
Names, Ethnological -- Africa, Sub-Saharan -- Dictionaries. Art, Black -- Africa, Sub-Saharan.

GN645.C73 1989
Creativity of power: cosmology and action in African societies/ edited by W. Arens and Ivan Karp. Washington: Smithsonian Institution Press, c1989. xxix, 315 p.
89-032176   303.3   0874746175
Ethnology -- Africa. Power (Social sciences) Political anthropology -- Africa. Africa -- Social life and customs.

GN645.E7613 1981
Erny, Pierre.
The child and his environment in Black Africa: an essay on traditional education/ Pierre Erny; translated, abridged, and adapted by G.J. Wanjohi. Nairobi; Oxford University Press, 1981. xxii, 230 p.
83-122735   303.3/2/0967   0195725093
Education -- Africa, Sub-Saharan. Socialization.

GN645.H45 1991
Herders, warriors, and traders: pastoralism in Africa/ edited by John G. Galaty and Pierre Bonte. Boulder: Westview Press, 1991. xviii, 338 p.
91-025206   306.3   0813380677
Herders -- Africa. Economic anthropology -- Africa. Africa -- Economic conditions.

GN645.J42 1991
Jean, Clinton M.
Behind the Eurocentric veils: the search for African realities/ Clinton M. Jean; foreword by James Jennings. Amherst: University of Massachusetts Press, c1991. xxi, 113 p.
91-022685   305.8/0096   0870237578
Ethnology -- Africa, Sub-Saharan -- Philosophy. Eurocentrism. Africa, Sub-Saharan -- Historiography. Africa, Sub-Saharan -- Civilization.

GN645.M26
Mair, Lucy Philip, 1901-
African kingdoms/ Lucy Mair. Oxford [Eng.]: Clarendon Press, 1977. 151 p.
77-004861   301.5/92   019821698X
Ethnology -- Africa, Sub-Saharan. Africa, Sub-Saharan -- Kings and rulers. Africa, Sub-Saharan -- Politics and government.

GN645.M3 1961
Malinowski, Bronislaw, 1884-1942.
The dynamics of culture change; an inquiry into race relations in Africa. Edited, with a new introd., by Phyllis M. Kaberry. New Haven, Yale University Press [1961] 171 p.
61-011403   572.96
Indigenous peoples -- Africa. Ethnology -- Africa. Acculturation -- Africa.

GN645.M47 1998
Memory and the postcolony: African anthropology and the critique of power/ edited by Richard Werbner. London; Zed Books; 1998. x, 236 p.
98-008150   301/.096   1856495914
Anthropology -- Africa -- Philosophy. Memory. Social psychology -- Africa. Africa -- Social life and customs. Africa -- Politics and government.

GN645.N82 1994
Nuptiality in Sub-Saharan Africa: contemporary anthropological and demographic perspectives/ edited by Caroline Bledsoe and Gilles Pison. Oxford: Clarendon Press; 1994. xii, 326 p.
93-048892   306.81/0967   0198287615
Marriage -- Africa, Sub-Saharan -- Congresses. Marriage customs and rites -- Africa, Sub-Saharan -- Congresses. Sex customs -- Africa, Sub-Saharan -- Congresses. Africa, Sub-Saharan -- Social life and customs -- Congresses.

GN645.O47 1996
Olson, James Stuart, 1946-
The peoples of Africa: an ethnohistorical dictionary/ James S. Olson. Westport, Conn.: Greenwood Press, 1996. viii, 681 p.
95-036433   305.8/0096   0313279187
Ethnology -- Africa -- Dictionaries. Ethnohistory -- Africa -- Dictionaries. Africa -- Social life and customs -- Dictionaries.

GN645.S57 1992
Smith, Andrew B.
Pastoralism in Africa: origins and development ecology/ Andrew B. Smith. London: Hurst & Co.; 1992. xv, 288 p.
92-014788   304.2/096   1850651213
Herders -- Africa -- History. Transhumance -- Africa -- History. Pastoral systems -- Africa -- History.

GN649.M65.E57 1999
Ensel, Remco.
Saints and servants in southern Morocco/ by Remco Ensel. Leiden; Brill, 1999. xv, 279 p.
99-027414   305.8/00964/6   9004114297
Ethnology -- Morocco -- Ktawa Oasis. Marginality, Social -- Morocco -- Ktawa Oasis. Caste -- Morocco -- Ktawa Oasis. Ktawa Oasis (Morocco) -- Ethnic relations.

GN651.E9
Evans-Pritchard, E. E. 1902-1973.
Essays in social anthropology. New York, Free Press of Glencoe [1963, c1962] 233 p.
63-000669   572.9624
Shilluk (African people) Zande (African people) Ethnology.

GN652.M25.A4713 1998
Amselle, Jean-Loup.
Mestizo logics: anthropology of identity in Africa and elsewhere/ Jean-Loup Amselle; translated by Claudia Royal. Stanford, Calif.: Stanford University Press, 1998. xvi, 207 p.
97-020403   305.8/001   0804724296
Ethnology -- Mali. Ethnology -- Guinea. Ethnology -- Philosophy. Mali -- History. Guinea -- History.

GN652.M25.M35 1998
McIntosh, Roderick J.
The peoples of the Middle Niger: the island of gold/ Roderick James McIntosh. Malden, MA: Blackwell Publishers, 1998. xxviii, 346 p.
98-010817   305.8/009662   0631173617
Ethnology -- Mali. Ethnology -- Senegal. Ethnology -- Niger River Valley. Mali -- Social life and customs. Senegal -- Social life and customs. Niger River Valley -- Social life and customs.

GN654.F35 1998
Fabian, Johannes.
Moments of freedom: anthropology and popular culture/ Johannes Fabian. Charlottesville: University Press of Virginia, 1998. xv, 172 p.
97-042296   306/.096751/8   0813917859
Ethnology -- Congo (Democratic Republic) -- Katanga. Popular culture -- Congo (Democratic Republic) -- Katanga. Katanga (Congo) -- Social life and customs.

GN654.T87
Turnbull, Colin M.
Wayward servants; the two worlds of the African pygmies [by] Colin M. Turnbull. Garden City, N.Y., Published for the American Museum of Natural His 1965. xiv, 390 p.
65-017265   309.1675
Mbuti (African people)

GN656.C74 1989
The Creation of tribalism in Southern Africa/ edited by Leroy Vail. London: Currey; 1989. xiv, 422 p.
88-004753   305.8/00968   0520062841
Ethnicity -- Africa, Southern. Tribal government -- Africa, Southern. Nationalism -- Africa, Southern. Africa, Southern -- Politics and government.

GN656.K86 1982
Kuper, Adam.
Wives for cattle: bridewealth and marriage in Southern Africa/ Adam Kuper. London; Routledge & Kegan Paul, 1982. xiii, 202 p.
81-017872   392/.5/0968   0710009895
Bride price -- Africa, Southern. Marriage customs and rites -- Africa, Southern. Africa, Southern -- Social life and customs.

GN657.R4.H36 1996
Hansen, Karen Tranberg.
Keeping house in Lusaka/ Karen Tranberg Hansen. New York: Columbia University Press, c1997. xii, 228 p.
96-021351   307.76/096894 20   0231081421
Urban anthropology -- Zambia -- Mtendere Township (Lusaka). Urbanization -- Zambia -- Mtendere Township (Lusaka) -- History -- 20th century. Public housing -- Zambia -- Mtendere Township (Lusaka) Mtendere Township (Lusaka, Zambia) -- History -- 20th century. Mtendere Township (Lusaka, Zambia) -- Economic conditions. Mtendere Township (Lusaka, Zambia) -- Social life and customs.

GN657.R4.S59 1989
Skjonsberg, Else.
Change in an African village: Kefa speaks/ Else Skjonsberg. West Hartford, Conn.: Kumarian Press, c1989. viii, 271 p.
88-026685   306/.096894   0931816572
Ethnology -- Zambia -- Kefa. Social change. Kefa (Zambia) -- Social conditions.

GN657.Z8.S5 1948
Sibiya, Christina, 1900-
Zulu woman. [Her autobiography, related] by Rebecca Hourwich Reyher. New York, Columbia Univ. Press, 1948. xiv, 281 p.
48-006654   572.9683
Solomon ka Dinuzulu, -- 1893-1933.   Zulu (African people)

GN658.M34 1977
Mair, Lucy Philip, 1901-
Primitive government: a study of traditional political systems in eastern Africa/ Lucy Mair. Bloomington: Indiana University Press, c1977. 244 p.
77-006963   321.1/2   0253346037
Political anthropology -- Africa, East. Africa, East -- Politics and government.

GN658.S64 1998
Spencer, Paul, 1932-
The pastoral continuum: the marginalization of tradition in East Africa/ Paul Spencer. Oxford: Clarendon Press; 1998. xiii, 302 p.
97-023105   306/.09676   0198233752
Pastoral systems -- Africa, Eastern. Herders -- Africa, Eastern. Camels -- Africa, Eastern. Africa, Eastern -- Social conditions. Africa, Eastern -- Economic conditions.

GN659.K4.S35 1989
Schlee, Gunther.
Identities on the move: clanship and pastoralism in northern Kenya/ Gunther Schlee. Manchester, UK; Manchester University Press for the Internationa c1989. ix, 278 p.
89-013230   305/.096762   0719030102
Ethnology -- Kenya. Clans -- Kenya. Kinship -- Kenya. Kenya -- Social life and customs.

GN659.U3.W59 1997
Whyte, Susan Reynolds.
Questioning misfortune: the pragmatics of uncertainty in Eastern Uganda/ Susan Reynolds Whyte. Cambridge; Cambridge University Press, 1997. xiv, 258 p.
97-010235   306/.096761   0521594022
Ethnology -- Uganda -- Bunyole (District) Medical anthropology -- Uganda -- Bunyole (District) Divination -- Uganda -- Bunyole (District) Bunyole (Uganda: District) -- Social conditions. Bunyole (Uganda: District) -- Religious life and customs.

GN662.C57 1990
Clio in Oceania: toward a historical anthropology/ edited by Aletta Biersack. Washington: Smithsonian Institution Press, c1991. vii, 383 p.
90-009765   995   0874743044
Ethnohistory -- Oceania. Ethnology -- Oceania. Oceania -- Historiography. Oceania -- History.

GN662.C64 1992
Confronting the Margaret Mead legacy: scholarship, empire, and the South Pacific/ edited by Lenora Foerstel and Angela Gilliam. Philadelphia: Temple University Press, 1992. xxxv, 298 p.
91-016194   306/.0995   0877228868
Mead, Margaret, -- 1901-1978.   Ethnology -- Oceania. Anthropology -- Government policy -- Oceania.

GN662.C77 1990
Cultural identity and ethnicity in the Pacific/ edited by Jocelyn Linnekin and Lin Poyer. Honolulu: University of Hawaii Press, c1990. vi, 323 p.
89-005228   306/.0995   0824812085
Ethnicity -- Oceania. Oceania -- Social life and customs.

GN662.H85 1990
The Humbled anthropologist: tales from the Pacific/ edited by Philip R. DeVita. Belmont, Calif.: Wadsworth Pub. Co., c1990. xxiv, 184 p.
89-037243   306/.09   0534125700
Ethnology -- Oceania -- Field work. Ethnologist -- United States -- Biography. Oceania -- Social life and customs.

GN662.O46 1989
Oliver, Douglas L.
Oceania: the native cultures of Australia and the Pacific Islands/ Douglas L. Oliver; illustrations by Lois Johnson. Honolulu: University of Hawaii Press, c1989. 2 v.
88-029551   306/.099   0824810198
Ethnology -- Oceania. Oceania -- Social life and customs.

GN662.W45 1992
Weiner, Annette B., 1933-
Inalienable possessions: the paradox of keeping-while-giving/ Annette B. Weiner. Berkeley: University of California Press, c1992. xiii, 232 p.
91-043580   305.42/0995   0520076036
Ceremonial exchange -- Oceania. Women -- Oceania -- Economic conditions. Women -- Oceania -- Social conditions.

GN663.B88 1988
Burbank, Victoria Katherine.
Aboriginal adolescence: maidenhood in an Australian community/ Victoria Katherine Burbank. New Brunswick: Rutgers University Press, c1988. xvii, 153 p.
87-020505   305.2/35/0899915094   0813512867
Australian aborigines -- Social life and customs. Teenage girls -- Australia -- Sexual behavior. Marriage -- Australia.

GN663.F36 1989
Family and gender in the Pacific: domestic contradictions and the colonial impact/ edited by Margaret Jolly and Martha Macintyre. Cambridge; Cambridge University Press, 1989. xi, 296 p.
88-025834   306.8/099   0521346673
Family -- Oceania. Women -- Oceania. Missions -- Oceania. Oceania -- Social life and customs.

GN663.H37 1996
Hage, Per, 1935-
Island networks: communication, kinship, and classification structures in Oceania/ Per Hage, Frank Harary. Cambridge; Cambridge University Press, 1996. xx, 296 p.
95-031639   306/.099   052155232X
Ethnology -- Oceania -- Mathematical models. Structural anthropology -- Oceania. Graph theory. Oceania -- Social life and customs -- Mathematical models.

GN663.J69 2001
Joyce, Barry Alan.
The shaping of American ethnography: the Wilkes Exploring Expedition, 1838-1842/ Barry Alan Joyce. Lincoln: University of Nebraska Press, c2001. xiv, 196 p.
00-059963   305.8/09/034 21   0803225911
Ethnology -- United States -- History -- 19th century. Ethnology -- Oceania. Indians of South America.

GN663.L43 1992
Lebot, Vincent.
Kava: the Pacific drug/ Vincent Lebot, Mark Merlin, and Lamont Lindstrom. New Haven: Yale University Press, c1992. vii, 255 p.
92-013444   615/.782   0300052138
Kava (Beverage) Kava plant. Kava ceremony.

GN665.B76 1982
Broome, Richard, 1948-
Aboriginal Australians: black response to white dominance, 1788-1980/ Richard Broome. Sydney; Allen & Unwin, 1982. 227 p.
81-040687   994/.0049915   0868610437
Australian aborigines -- History. Australian aborigines -- Government relations.

GN666.C653 1995
Contested ground: Australian aborigines under the British Crown/ edited by Ann McGrath. St. Leonards, NSW: Allen & Unwin, 1995. xxxi, 415 p.
95-228999   994/.0049915   1863736468
Australian aborigines -- History. Australian aborigines -- Government relations. Australia -- Race relations.

GN666.C657 1994
Coombs, H. C. 1906-
Aboriginal autonomy: issues and strategies/ H.C. Coombs; edited by Diane Smith. Cambridge; Cambridge University Press, 1994. xvi, 251 p.
94-010309   994/.0049915   0521440971
Australian aborigines -- Government relations. Australian aborigines -- Politics and government. Australian aborigines -- Land tenure. Australia -- Ethnic relations.

GN666.F58 1997
Flood, Josephine.
Rock art of the dreamtime: images of ancient Australia/ Josephine Flood. Pymble, Sydney, NSW, Australia: Angus & Robertson; 1997. xii, 372 p.
97-158536   759.01/13/0994   0207189080
Australian aborigines -- Antiquities. Petroglyphs -- Australia. Rock paintings -- Australia.

GN666.I5 1996
In the age of Mabo: history, Aborigines, and Australia/ edited by Bain Attwood. St Leonards, N.S.W.: Allen & Unwin, 1996. xxxviii, 193 p.
96-118225   186373841X
Australian Aborigines -- Land tenure. Australian Aborigines -- History. Australian Aborigines -- Legal status, laws, etc.

GN666.M58 1974
Montagu, Ashley, 1905-
Coming into being among the Australian Aborigines: a study of the procreative beliefs of the native tribes of Australia/ Ashley Montagu; with a foreword by Bronislaw Malinowski. London; Routledge and Kegan Paul, 1974. x, 426 p.
74-080751   299/.9   0710079338
Australian aborigines -- Social life and customs. Australian aborigines -- Religion. Childbirth -- Religious aspects.

GN666.S93 1993
Swain, Tony.
A place for strangers: towards a history of Australian Aboriginal being/ Tony Swain. Cambridge; Cambridge University Press, 1993. xi, 303 p.
92-030379   305.89/915   0521430054
Australian aborigines. Philosophy, Australian aboriginal. Australian aborigines -- Foreign influences.

GN667.N6.P68 1993
Povinelli, Elizabeth A.
Labor's lot: the power, history, and culture of aboriginal action/ Elizabeth A. Povinelli. Chicago: University of Chicago Press, 1993. xii, 331 p.
93-002511   306/.089/991509429   0226676730
Australian aborigines -- Australia -- Cox Peninsula (N.T.) -- Economic conditions. Australian aborigines -- Land tenure -- Australia -- Cox Peninsula (N.T.) Australian aborigines -- Australia -- Cox Peninsula (N.T.) -- Ethnic identity. Belyuen (Australia) -- Economic conditions.

GN667.Q4.T75 1991
Trigger, David S. 1953-
Whitefella comin': aboriginal responses to colonialism in northern Australia/ David S. Trigger. Cambridge [England]; Cambridge University Press, 1992. xiv, 250 p.
91-021376   305.8/991509437   052140181X
Australian aborigines -- Australia -- Queensland -- Government relations. Australian aborigines -- Australia -- Queensland -- History. Queensland -- Race relations.

GN668.B54 1991
Big men and great men: personifications of power in Melanesia/ edited by Maurice Godelier and Marilyn Strathern. Cambridge [England]; Cambridge University Press; 1991. xviii, 328 p.
90-001312   306.2/0995   0521390184
Political anthropology -- Melanesia. Big man (Melanesia) Political leadership -- Melanesia.

GN668.R54 1984
Ritualized homosexuality in Melanesia/ edited by Gilbert H. Herdt. Berkeley: University of California Press, c1984. xvii, 409 p.
83-018015   306.7/662/0993   0520050371
Melanesians -- Rites and ceremonies. Melanesians -- Social life and customs. Homosexuality, Male -- Melanesia.

GN668.S55 1998
Sillitoe, Paul.
An introduction to the anthropology of Melanesia: culture and tradition/ Paul Sillitoe. Cambridge; Cambridge University Press, 1998. xxiii, 254 p.
97-035251   306/.0995   0521581869
Melanesians -- Social life and customs. Ethnology -- Melanesia.

GN669.W37 1989
Ward, Martha Coonfield.
Nest in the wind: adventures in anthropology on a tropical island/ Martha C. Ward; [illustrations by Nancy Zoder Dawes]. Prospect Heights, Ill.: Waveland Press, c1989. vii, 161 p.
89-149206   306/.09965   0881334057
Ethnology -- Micronesia (Federated States) -- Pohnpei Island. Pohnpei Island (Micronesia) -- Social life and customs.

GN670.G35 1993
Gell, Alfred.
Wrapping in images: tattooing in Polynesia/ Alfred Gell. Oxford: Clarendon Press; 1993. xi, 347 p.
93-001780   306.4/7   0198278691
Tattooing -- Polynesia. Body, Human -- Social aspects -- Polynesia. Art and anthropology -- Polynesia. Polynesia -- Social life and customs.

GN670.K43 1980
Keesing, Felix Maxwell, 1902-1961.
Social anthropology in Polynesia: a review of research/ Felix M. Keesing. Westport, Conn.: Greenwood Press, 1980, c1953. x, 126 p.
80-017490   996   0313224986
Ethnology -- Polynesia. Ethnology -- Polynesia -- Bibliography. Polynesia -- Social conditions. Polynesia -- Social conditions -- Bibliography.

GN670.K56 1984
Kirch, Patrick Vinton.
The evolution of the Polynesian chiefdoms/ Patrick Vinton Kirch. Cambridge [Cambridgeshire]; Cambridge University Press, 1984. xii, 314 p.
84-003249   306/.2/0996   0521253322
Political anthropology -- Polynesia. Chiefdoms -- Polynesia. Polynesia -- Politics and government. Polynesia -- Antiquities.

GN670.P59 1992
Pollock, Nancy J. 1934-
These roots remain: food habits in islands of the central and eastern Pacific since western contact/ Nancy J. Pollock. Laie, Hawaii: Institute for Polynesian Studies; c1992. xv, 298 p.
92-012250   394.1/2/0996   093915451X
Nutritional anthropology -- Polynesia. Nutritional anthropology -- Micronesia. Food habits -- Polynesia. Polynesia -- Social life and customs. Micronesia -- Social life and customs.

GN671.C3.L54 1994
Lieber, Michael D.
More than a living: fishing and the social order on a Polynesian atoll/ Michael Lieber. Boulder, Colo.: Westview Press, 1994. xx, 235 p.
93-025451   306.3/64   0813387809
Ethnology -- Micronesia (Federated States) -- Kapingamarangi Atoll. Fishing -- Micronesia (Federated States) -- Kapingamarangi Atoll. Ethnology -- Methodology. Kapingamarangi Atoll (Micronesia) -- Social life and customs.

GN671.C3.L87 1988
Lutz, Catherine.
Unnatural emotions: everyday sentiments on a Micronesian atoll & their challenge to western theory/ Catherine A. Lutz. Chicago: University of Chicago Press, c1988. xii, 273 p.
88-000329   155.8/0996/5   0226497216
Ethnopsychology -- Micronesia (Federated States) -- Ifalik Atoll. Emotions. Micronesians -- Psychology.

GN671.F5.B43 1995
Becker, Anne E.
Body, self, and society: the view from Fiji/ Anne E. Becker. Philadelphia: University of Pennsylvania Press, c1995. xvi, 206 p.
95-022730   155.8/099611   0812231805
Ethnology -- Fiji -- Singatoka (Western Division) Ethnopsychology -- Fiji -- Singatoka (Western Division) Identity (Psychology) -- Fiji -- Singatoka (Western Division) Singatoka (Western Division, Fiji) -- Social life and customs.

GN671.F5.K37 1995
Kaplan, Martha, 1957-
Neither cargo nor cult: ritual politics and the colonial imagination in Fiji/ Martha Kaplan. Durham: Duke University Press, 1995. xviii, 226 p.
94-038508   306/.099611   0822315785
Navosavakadua, -- d. 1897. Cargo cults -- Fiji. Fiji -- Politics and government. Fiji -- Biography.

GN671.M33.C37 1997
Carucci, Laurence Marshall, 1949-
Nuclear nativity: rituals of renewal and empowerment in the Marshall Islands/ Laurence Marshall Carucci. DeKalb: Northern Illinois University Press, 1997. xiii, 217 p.
96-030262   305.8/0099683   0875802176
Ethnology -- Marshall Islands -- Enewetak Atoll. Rites and ceremonies -- Marshall Islands -- Enewetak Atoll. Christmas -- Marshall Islands -- Enewetak Atoll. Enewetak Atoll (Marshall Islands) -- Social life and customs.

GN671.N5.C68 1989
A Continuing trial of treatment: medical pluralism in Papua New Guinea/ edited by Stephen Frankel and Gilbert Lewis. Dordrecht; Kluwer Academic Publishers, c1989. 334 p.
88-012044   362.1/0995/3   155608076X
Medical anthropology -- Papua New Guinea. Traditional medicine -- Papua New Guinea. Medical innovations -- Social aspects -- Papua New Guinea. Papua New Guinea -- Social life and customs.

GN671.N5.F45 1987
Feil, D. K. 1948-
The evolution of highland Papua New Guinea societies/ D.K. Feil. Cambridge [Cambridgeshire]; Cambridge University Press, 1987. xii, 313 p.
86-032681   306/.0995/3   0521334233
Ethnology -- Papua New Guinea. Papua New Guinea -- Social life and customs.

GN671.N5.G66 1996
Goodale, Jane C. 1926-
Two-party line: conversations in the field/ Jane C. Goodale with Ann Chowning. Lanham: Rowman & Littlefield, c1996. ix, 209 p.
96-015066   305.8/009953 20   0847682633
Ethnology -- Papua New Guinea -- West New Britain Province -- Field work. Women ethnologists -- Papua New Guinea -- West New Britain Province -- Correspondence. Women ethnologists -- Papua New Guinea -- West New Britain Province -- Attitudes. West New Britain Province (Papua New Guinea) -- Social life and customs.

GN671.N5.K64 1993
Knauft, Bruce M.
South coast New Guinea cultures: history, comparison, dialectic/ Bruce M. Knauft. Cambridge [England]; Cambridge University Press, 1993. xii, 298 p.
92-012472   306/.0995   0521418828
Ethnology -- New Guinea. Melanesians -- Sexual behavior. Melanesians -- Social life and customs. New Guinea -- Social life and customs.

GN671.N5.K85 1992
Kulick, Don.
Language shift and cultural reproduction: socialization, self, and syncretism in a Papua New Guinean village/ Don Kulick. Cambridge [England]; Cambridge University Press, 1992. xvi, 317 p.
91-031919   305.8/009953   0521414849
Ethnology -- Papua New Guinea -- Gapun. Language and culture -- Papua New Guinea -- Gapun. Tok Pisin language -- Grammar. Gapun (Papua New Guinea) -- Social life and customs.

GN671.N5.L35 1998
Lattas, Andrew, 1956-
Cultures of secrecy: reinventing race in bush Kaliai cargo cults/ Andrew Lattas. Madison: University of Wisconsin Press, c1998. xliv, 360 p.
97-044008   299/.92 21   0299158004
Acculturation -- Papua New Guinea -- West New Britain Province. West New Britain Province (Papua New Guinea) -- Race relations. Cargo cults -- Papua New Guinea -- West New Britain Province. West New Britain Province (Papua New Guinea) -- Religious life and customs.

GN671.N5.M4 1953
Mead, Margaret, 1901-1978.
Growing up in New Guinea; a comparative study of primitive education. With a preface by the author. [New York] New American Library [1953, c1930] 223 p.
53-002526   572.995
Manus (Papua New Guinea people) Children -- New Guinea.

GN671.N5.R55 1982
Rituals of manhood: male initiation in Papua New Guinea/ edited by Gilbert H. Herdt; with an introduction by Roger M. Keesing. Berkeley: University of California Press, c1982. xxvi, 365 p.
81-001807   392/.14   0520044487
Initiation rites -- Papua New Guinea. Sex symbolism -- Papua New Guinea. Papua New Guinea -- Social life and customs.

GN671.N6.V35713 1996
Arts of Vanuatu/ edited by Joel Bonnemaison ... [et al.]. Honolulu: University of Hawai'i Press, c1996. 338 p.
96-053569   700/.99595 20   082481956X
Material culture -- Vanuatu. Art, Vanuatuan. Melanesians -- Industries -- Vanuatu. Vanuatu -- Social life and customs.

GN671.P5.H37
Hart, Donn Vorhis, 1918-
Compadrinazgo: ritual kinship in the Philippines/ by Donn V. Hart. De Kalb: Northern Illinois University Press, c1977. xvi, 256 p.
75-015015   301.42/1/09599   0875800629
Sponsors -- Philippines. Kinship -- Philippines. Philippines -- Social life and customs.

GN671.S2.D87 1994
Duranti, Alessandro.
From grammar to politics: linguistic anthropology in a Western Samoan village/ Alessandro Duranti. Berkeley: University of California Press, c1994. xiii, 208 p.
93-018095   306.2/099614   0520082451
Political anthropology -- Samoa -- Falefa. Linguistic anthropology -- Samoa -- Falefa. Samoans -- Samoa -- Falefa -- Politics and government.

GN671.S2.F73 1983
Freeman, Derek.
Margaret Mead and Samoa: the making and unmaking of an anthropological myth/ Derek Freeman. Cambridge, Mass.: Harvard University Press, 1983. xvii, 379 p.
82-015620   306/.0996   0674548302
Mead, Margaret, -- 1901-1978. Ethnology -- Samoan Islands. Adolescence. Nature and nurture.

GN671.S2.S25 1990
The Samoa reader: anthropologists take stock/ edited by Hiram Caton. Lanham, Md.: University Press of America, c1990. xii, 351 p.
89-070423   306/.09961/3   0819177202
Ethnology -- Samoan Islands. Ethnology -- Philosophy. Nature and nurture. Samoan Islands -- Social life and customs.

GN671.S6.F46 1988
Feinberg, Richard.
Polynesian seafaring and navigation: ocean travel in Anutan culture and society/ Richard Feinberg. Kent, Ohio: Kent State University Press, c1988. xviii, 210 p.
87-022572   993/.5   0873383524
Ethnology -- Solomon Islands -- Anuta Island. Polynesians -- Social life and customs. Navigation -- Solomon Islands -- Anuta Island. Anuta Island (Solomon Islands) -- Social life and customs.

GN671.S6.W45 1992
White, Geoffrey M. 1949-
Identity through history: living stories in a Solomon Islands society/ Geoffrey M. White. Cambridge; Cambridge University Press, 1991. xv, 270 p.
90-025590   306/.099593   0521401720
Ethnology -- Solomon Islands -- Santa Isabel Island. Ethnicity -- Solomon Islands -- Santa Isabel Island. Missions -- Solomon Islands -- Santa Isabel Island -- History. Santa Isabel Island (Solomon Islands) -- Religious life and customs. Santa Isabel Island (Solomon Islands) -- History.

GN671.T46.H86 1996
Huntsman, Judith.
Tokelau: a historical ethnography/ Judith Huntsman & Antony Hooper. Honolulu, Hawaii: University of Hawai'i Press, c1996. xii, 355 p.
96-027748   305.8/009615 20   0824819128
Ethnology -- Tokelau. Villages -- Tokelau. Folklore -- Tokelau. Tokelau -- History. Tokelau -- Social life and customs.

GN671.T5.G35 1987
Gailey, Christine Ward, 1950-
Kinship to kingship: gender hierarchy and state formation in the Tongan Islands/ Christine Ward Gailey. Austin, Tex.: University of Texas Press, 1987. xviii, 326 p.
87-010804   306.8/3/099612   029272456X
Kinship -- Tonga. Sex role -- Tonga. Acculturation -- Tonga. Tonga -- Politics and government. Tonga -- Social conditions.

GN671.T5.M67 1996
Morton, Helen, 1960-
Becoming Tongan: an ethnography of childhood/ Helen Morton. Honolulu: University of Hawai'i Press, c1996. ix, 343 p.
95-041374   305.23/099612 20   0824817583
Ethnology -- Tonga -- Holonga (Tongatapu Island) Children -- Tonga -- Holonga (Tongatapu Island) Child psychology -- Tonga -- Holonga (Tongatapu Island) Holonga (Tongatapu Island, Tonga) -- Social life and customs.

GN673.S64 1994
Slezkine, Yuri, 1956-
Arctic mirrors: Russia and the small peoples of the North/ Yuri Slezkine. Ithaca: Cornell University Press, 1994. xiv, 456 p.
93-048466   947/.004971   0801429765
Arctic peoples. Arctic peoples -- Russia, Northern. Indigenous peoples -- Russia, Northern. Russia, Northern -- History -- 20th century. Russia, Northern -- Ethnic relations. Russia, Northern -- Politics and government.

GN710 Prehistoric archaeology — Dictionaries. Encyclopedias

GN710.E53 2001
Encyclopedia of prehistory/ edited by Peter N. Peregrine and Melvin Ember. New York: Kluwer Academic/Plenum, <c2001- >
99-049489   960/.1/03 21   0306462613
Prehistoric peoples -- Encyclopedias. Antiquities, Prehistoric -- Encyclopedias.

GN720 Prehistoric archaeology — History — General works

GN720.D32 1988
Daniel, Glyn Edmund.
The idea of prehistory/ Glyn Daniel and Colin Renfrew. Edinburgh: Edinburgh University Press, c1988. 221 p.
88-136150   930.1   0852245327
Archaeology -- History.

GN722 Prehistoric archaeology — History — By region or country, A-Z

GN722.G7.C57 1989
Clark, Grahame, 1907-
Prehistory at Cambridge and beyond/ Grahame Clark. Cambridge [England]; Cambridge University Press, 1989. x, 176 p.
87-033393   936.2   052135031X
Anthropology, Prehistoric -- England -- History. Archaeology -- England -- History.

GN739 Prehistoric archaeology — General works, treatises, and textbooks — 1951-1974

GN739.W54
Willey, Gordon Randolph, 1913-
Archaeological researches in retrospect, edited by Gordon R. Willey. Cambridge, Mass., Winthrop Publishers [1974] xix, 296 p.
73-020134   913/.031   087626044X
Antiquities, Prehistoric. Indians -- Antiquities. Archaeology. America -- Antiquities.

GN740 Prehistoric archaeology — General works, treatises, and textbooks — 1975-

GN740.G36 1994
Gamble, Clive.
Timewalkers: the prehistory of global colonization/ Clive Gamble. Cambridge, Mass.: Harvard University Press, 1994. x, 309 p.
93-028825   930.1   067489202X
Prehistoric peoples. Anthropology, Prehistoric. Human beings -- Migrations.

GN740.W46 1996
Wenke, Robert J.
Patterns in prehistory: humankind's first three million years/ Robert J. Wenke. New York: Oxford University Press, 1996.
95-043456   573.3   0195085728
Prehistoric peoples. Archaeology.

GN741 Prehistoric archaeology — General special

GN741.B8 1971
Butzer, Karl W.
Environment and archeology; an ecological approach to prehistory [by] Karl W. Butzer. Chicago, Aldine-Atherton [1971] xxvi, 703 p.
74-115938   551.7/92   0202330231
Prehistoric peoples. Paleoclimatology. Geology, Stratigraphic -- Pleistocene.

GN741.F68 1995
Foundations of social inequality/ edited by T. Douglas Price and Gary M. Feinman. New York: Plenum Press, c1995. xvii, 290 p.
95-031600   930.1   030644979X
Prehistoric peoples. Primitive societies. Equality.

GN741.H85 1996
Humans at the end of the Ice Age: the archaeology of the Pleistocene-Holocene transition/ edited by Lawrence Guy Straus ... [et al.]. New York: Plenum Press, c1996. xiii, 378 p.
96-008914   930.1 20   0306451778
Prehistoric peoples. Human beings -- Effect of climate on. Agriculture -- Origin.

GN746 Prehistoric archaeology — Pictorial works

GN746.M67 1998
Moser, Stephanie.
Ancestral images: the iconography of human origins/ Stephanie Moser; foreword by Clive Gamble. Ithaca, N.Y.: Cornell University Press, 1998. xxiv, 200 p.
98-009890   599.93/8   0801435498
Prehistoric peoples -- Pictorial works -- History. Human evolution -- Pictorial works -- History.

GN751 Prehistoric archaeology — Lost continents — General works

GN751.Z36 1992
Zangger, Eberhard.
The flood from heaven: deciphering the Atlantis legend/ Eberhard Zangger; with a foreword by Anthony Snodgrass. New York: W. Morrow, c1992. xi, 256 p.
92-001304   398.23/4   0688113508
Atlantis.

GN768-776.32 Prehistoric archaeology — By period division — Stone age

GN768.R83 1999
Rudgley, Richard, 1961-
The lost civilizations of the Stone Age/ Richard Rudgley. New York, NY: Free Press, c1999. 310 p.
98-037079   930.1/2 21   0684855801
Stone age. Culture -- Origin. Civilization -- History.

GN771.A73 1996
The archaeology of human ancestry: power, sex, and tradition/ edited by James Steele and Stephen Shennan. London; Routledge, 1996. xxiii, 446 p.
95-019856   573.3   041511862X
Paleolithic period. Prehistoric peoples. Primates.

GN772.A35.L4
Leakey, L. S. B. 1903-1972.
The progress and evolution of man in Africa. London, Oxford University Press, 1961. 50 p.
62-000860   573.096
Man -- Origin. Man, Prehistoric -- Africa.

GN772.2.A1.B44 1993
Before Lascaux: the complex record of the Early Upper Paleolithic/ edited by Heidi Knecht, Anne Pike-Tay, Randall White. Boca Raton: CRC Press, c1993. 304 p.
92-026479   936   084938883X
Paleolithic period -- Europe. Paleolithic period -- Middle East. Europe -- Antiquities. Middle East -- Antiquities.

GN772.2.A1.F76 1993
From Kostenki to Clovis: Upper Paleolithic Paleo-Indian adaptations/ edited by Olga Soffer and N.D. Praslov. New York: Plenum Press, c1993. xx, 334 p.
92-036558   930.1/2   030644271X
Paleolithic period -- Europe. Paleolithic period -- Russia (Federation) Paleo-Indians. Europe -- Antiquities. Russia (Federation) -- Antiquities. North America -- Antiquities.

GN772.2.A1.G38 1999
Gamble, Clive.
The Palaeolithic societies of Europe/ Clive Gamble. Cambridge, U.K.; Cambridge University Press, 1999. xxii, 505 p.
98-038087   936   0521651050
Paleolithic period -- Europe. Tools, Prehistoric -- Europe. Anthropology, Prehistoric -- Europe. Europe -- Antiquities.

GN772.22.E854.D53 1990
Dickson, D. Bruce.
The dawn of belief: religion in the Upper Paleolithic of southwestern Europe/ D. Bruce Dickson. Tucson: University of Arizona Press, c1990. xii, 259 p.
89-038911   291/.042/094   0816510768
Paleolithic period -- Europe, Southern. Religion, Prehistoric -- Europe, Southern. Europe, Southern -- Antiquities.

GN772.22.G7.S65 1992
Smith, Christopher, 1945-
Late Stone Age hunters of the British Isles/ Christopher Smith. London; Routledge, 1992. ix, 206 p.
91-023152   936.1   0415031613
Paleolithic period -- Great Britain. Mesolithic period -- Great Britain. Tools, Prehistoric -- Great Britain. Great Britain -- Antiquities.

GN772.22.S6.B7
Brain, C. K.
The hunters or the hunted?: An introduction to African cave taphonomy/ C. K. Brain. Chicago: University of Chicago Press, 1981. x, 365 p.
79-028104   573   0226070891
Australopithecines. Animal remains (Archaeology) -- Africa, Southern. Caves -- Africa, Southern.

GN772.25.A1.P47 1991
Perspectives on the past: theoretical biases in Mediterranean hunter-gatherer research/ edited by Geoffrey A. Clark. Philadelphia: University of Pennsylvania Press, c1991. xix, 538 p.
91-016444   909/.09822   081228190X
Paleolithic period -- Mediterranean Region. Mesolithic period -- Mediterranean Region. Hunting and gathering societies -- Mediterranean Region. Mediterranean Region -- Antiquities.

GN772.42.T34.P67 1988
Potts, Richard, 1953-
Early hominid activities at Olduvai/ Richard Potts. New York: A. de Gruyter, c1988. xi, 396 p.
88-014791   967.8   0202011763
Paleolithic period, Lower -- Tanzania -- Olduvai Gorge. Animal remains (Archaeology) -- Tanzania -- Olduvai Gorge. Olduvai Gorge (Tanzania) -- Antiquities. Tanzania -- Antiquities.

GN776.2.A1.B37 1990
Barber, E. J. W., 1940-
Prehistoric textiles: the development of cloth in the Neolithic and Bronze Ages with special reference to the Aegean/ by E.J.W. Barber. Princeton, N.J.: Princeton University Press, c1991. xxix, 471 p.
89-010329 746/.09/01 0691035970
Textile fabrics, Prehistoric -- Europe. Textile fabrics, Prehistoric -- Middle East. Neolithic period -- Europe. Europe -- Antiquities. Middle East -- Antiquities.

GN776.2.A1.E87 2000
Europe's first farmers/ edited by T. Douglas Price. New York: Cambridge University press, 2000. xv, 395 p.
99-015477 306.3/49 0521662036
Neolithic period -- Europe. Agriculture -- Origin. Europe -- Antiquities.

GN776.2.A1.H63 1990
Hodder, Ian.
The domestication of Europe: structure and contingency in neolithic societies/ Ian Hodder. Oxford, OX, UK; B. Blackwell, 1990. x, 331 p.
90-001695 936 0631177698
Neolithic period -- Europe. Agriculture, Prehistoric -- Europe. Architecture, Prehistoric -- Europe. Europe -- Antiquities.

GN776.2.A1.W46 1988
Whittle, Alasdair.
Problems in neolithic archaeology/ Alasdair Whittle. Cambridge [Cambridgeshire]; Cambridge University Press, 1988. xiii, 232 p.
87-035915 930.1/4 0521351219
Neolithic period -- Europe. Archaeology -- Methodology. Europe -- Antiquities.

GN776.22.G7.A94 1991
Avebury reconsidered: from the 1660s to the 1990s/ Peter J. Ucko ... [et al.]. London; Unwin Hyman, 1991. xiv, 293 p.
90-044449 936.231 004445919X
Neolithic period -- England -- Avebury. Monolithic monuments -- England -- Avebury. Avebury (Wiltshire) -- Antiquities. England -- Antiquities.

GN776.22.G7.C36 1992
Castleden, Rodney.
Neolithic Britain: new stone age sites of England, Scotland, and Wales/ Rodney Castleden; illustrated by the author. London; Routledge, 1992. xiv, 432 p.
91-016745 936.1 0415058457
Neolithic period -- Great Britain. Great Britain -- Antiquities.

GN776.22.G7.T48 1991
Thomas, Julian.
Rethinking the Neolithic/ Julian Thomas. Cambridge [England]; Cambridge University Press, 1991. xvi, 212 p.
90-024159 936.2 0521403774
Neolithic period -- Great Britain. Neolithic period -- England. Archaeology -- Philosophy. Great Britain -- Antiquities. England -- Antiquities.

GN776.22.G8 P47 2001
Perlès, Catherine.
The early Neolithic in Greece: the first farming communities in Europe/ Catherine Perles; illustrations by Gerard Monthel. Cambridge; Cambridge University Press, 2001. xiv, 356 p.
00-054728 338.1/0938 21 0521000270
Neolithic period -- Greece. Agriculture, Prehistoric -- Greece.

GN776.32.M628.H45 1989
Henry, Donald O.
From foraging to agriculture: the Levant at the end of the Ice Age/ Donald O. Henry. Philadelphia: University of Pennsylvania Press, c1989. xx, 277 p.
88-027848 939.4 0812281373
Neolithic period -- Middle East. Agriculture, Prehistoric -- Middle East. Paleoclimatology -- Middle East. Middle East -- Antiquities.

GN776.32.M628.L54 2000
Life in Neolithic farming communities: social organization, identity, and differentiation/ edited by Ian Kuijt. New York: Kluwer Academic/Plenum Publishers, c2000. xvi, 325 p.
99-052091 306.3/0939/4 21 0306461226
Neolithic period -- Middle East. Agriculture, Prehistoric -- Middle East. Land settlement patterns, Prehistoric -- Middle East. Middle East -- Antiquities.

GN776.32.N4.C38 2000
Cauvin, Jacques.
The birth of the Gods and the origins of agriculture/ Jacques Cauvin; translated by Trevor Watkins. Cambridge , UK; Cambridge University Press, 2000. xvii, 259 p.
99-033530 939.4 0521651352
Neolithic period -- Middle East. Religion, Prehistoric -- Middle East. Agriculture -- Origin. Middle East -- Antiquities.

GN778.2-778.32 Prehistoric archaeology — By period division — Copper and bronze ages

GN778.2.A1.K75 1998
Kristiansen, Kristian, 1948-
Europe before history/ Kristian Kristiansen. Cambridge [England]; Cambridge University Press, 1998. xxix, 505 p.
97-014350 936 0521552273
Bronze age -- Europe. Iron age -- Europe. Europe -- Antiquities.

GN778.22.I8
The Iceman and his natural environment: palaeobotanical results/ Sigmar Bortenschlager, Klaus Oeggl (eds.). Wien; Springer, c2000. x, 166 p.
00-038816 937 21 3211826602
Otzi (Ice mummy) Copper age -- Italy -- Hauslabjoch Pass. Neolithic period -- Italy -- Hauslabjoch Pass. Hauslabjoch Pass (Italy) -- Antiquities.

GN778.22.S72.F45 1995
Fernandez Castro, Maria Cruz.
Iberia in prehistory/ Maria Cruz Fernandez Castro. Oxford, UK; Blackwell, 1995. xvi, 419 p.
94-027629 936.6 0631167943
Copper age -- Spain. Bronze age -- Spain. Iberians -- History. Spain -- Antiquities.

GN778.3.A1.D74 1993
Drews, Robert.
The end of the Bronze Age: changes in warfare and the catastrophe ca. 1200 B.C./ Robert Drews. Princeton, N.J.: Princeton University Press, c1993. xii, 252 p.
92-046511 930/.09822 0691048118
Bronze age -- Mediterranean Region. Warfare, Prehistoric -- Mediterranean Region. Chariot warfare -- Mediterranean Region. Mediterranean Region -- Antiquities.

GN778.32.C5.B37 1999
Barber, E. J. W., 1940-
The mummies of Urumchi/ Elizabeth Wayland Barber. New York: W.W. Norton & Company, c1999. 240 p.
98-018958 393/.3 21 0393045218
Mummies -- China -- Sinkiang Uighur Autonomous Region. Bronze age -- China -- Sinkiang Uighur Autonomous Region. Textile fabrics, Prehistoric -- China -- Sinkiang Autonomous Region. Tarim Basin (China) -- Antiquities. Sinkiang Uighur Autonomous Region (China) -- Antiquities.

GN780-780.4 Prehistoric archaeology — By period division — Iron age

GN780.D4.G53 1969b
Glob, P. V. 1911-
The bog people; Iron Age man preserved [by] P. V. Glob. Translated from the Danish by Rupert Bruce-Mitford. Ithaca, N.Y., Cornell University Press [1969] 200 p.
69-020391 913.3/6
Iron age -- Denmark. Bog bodies -- Denmark. Denmark -- Antiquities.

GN780.22.G7.B76 1987
Brothwell, Don R.
The bog man and the archaeology of people/ Don Brothwell. Cambridge, MA: Harvard University Press, 1987. 128 p.
87-008435 573 0674077326
Lindow Man. Bog bodies. Anthropometry. Great Britain -- Antiquities, Celtic.

GN780.22.G7.C86 1991
Cunliffe, Barry W.
Iron Age communities in Britain: an account of England, Scotland, and Wales from the seventh century BC until the Roman conquest/ Barry Cunliffe. London; Routledge, 1991. xii, 685 p.
90-024328 936.1 0415054168
Iron age -- Great Britain. Britons. Great Britain -- Antiquities, Celtic. Great Britain -- History -- To 55 B.C.

GN780.4.A1.C85 1996
The culture and technology of African iron production/ edited by Peter R. Schmidt. Gainesville: University Press of Florida, c1996. xviii, 338 p.
95-031930 960/.1 20 0813013844
Iron age -- Africa. Iron-works -- Africa -- History. Africa -- Antiquities.

GN780.4.A1.O44
Oliver, Roland Anthony.
Africa in the Iron Age, c500 B.C. to A.D. 1400/ Roland Oliver, Brian M. Fagan. Cambridge; Cambridge University Press, 1975. xi, 228 p.
74-025639 960 0521205980
Iron age -- Africa. Africa -- Antiquities. Africa -- History.

GN784 Prehistoric archaeology — By special topic — Coastal sites. Coastal archaeology

GN784.P35 1992
Paleoshorelines and prehistory: an investigation of method/ edited by Lucille Lewis Johnson; with the assistance of Melanie Stright. Boca Raton: CRC Press, c1992. xii, 243 p.
91-029294 970/.00946 0849388554
Coastal archaeology -- Methodology. Indians -- Antiquities. America -- Antiquities.

GN790 Prehistoric archaeology — By special topic — Megolithic monuments

GN790.M7413 1990
Mohen, Jean-Pierre, 1944-
The world of megaliths/ Jean-Pierre Mohen; [translated by Helen McPhail in association with First Edition]. New York: Facts on File, 1990. 318 p.
89-016972 930.1/4 0816022518
Megalithic monuments. Neolithic period.

GN799 Prehistoric archaeology — By special topic — Other special topics, A-Z

GN799.A4.B46 1975b
Bender, Barbara.
Farming in prehistory: from hunter-gatherer to food-producer/ Barbara Bender; ill. by Annabel Rowe and Jan Farquharson. New York: St. Martin's Press, 1975. xi, 268 p.
75-013899 630/.9/01
Agriculture -- History. Prehistoric peoples. Agriculture, Prehistoric.

GN799.A4.B83 1992
Budiansky, Stephen.
The covenant of the wild: why animals chose domestication/ Stephen Budiansky. New York: W. Morrow, c1992. xi, 190 p.
91-016974 636 0688096107
Domestic animals -- Origin. Domestic animals -- Evolution. Philosophy of nature.

GN799.A4.F67 1989
Foraging and farming: the evolution of plant exploitation/ edited by David R. Harris, Gordon C. Hillman. London; Unwin Hyman, 1989. xxxiii, 733 p.
88-028751 630/.93 0044450257
Agriculture, Prehistoric -- Congresses. Hunting and gathering societies -- Congresses. Plant remains (Archaeology) -- Congresses.

GN799.A4.H37 1995
Harlan, Jack R.
The living fields: our agricultural heritage/ Jack R. Harlan. Cambridge [England]; Cambridge University Press, 1995. xi, 271 p.
94-042948 630/.9 0521401127
Agriculture -- Origin. Plants, Cultivated -- History. Crops -- History.

GN799.A4.M34 1991
MacNeish, Richard S.
The origins of agriculture and settled life/ by Richard S. MacNeish. Norman: University of Oklahoma Press, c1992. xix, 433 p.
91-050304 306.3/64 0806123648
Agriculture -- Origin. Agriculture, Prehistoric. Indians -- Agriculture.

GN799.A4 R56 1984
Rindos, David.
The origins of agriculture: an evolutionary perspective/ David Rindos; with foreword by Robert C. Dunnell. Orlando: Academic Press, 1984. xvii, 325 p.
83-007165 630/.9/01 19 0125892802
Agriculture -- Origin. Social evolution.

GN799.A4.S52 1994
Smith, Bruce D. 1946-
The emergence of agriculture/ Bruce D. Smith. New York: Scientific American Library: c1995. 231 p.
94-022833 630/.9 0716750554
Agriculture -- Origin. Agriculture, Prehistoric. Plants, Cultivated -- Origin.

GN799.A4.T73 1992
Transitions to agriculture in prehistory/ edited by Anne Birgitte Gebauer and T. Douglas Price. Madison, Wis.: Prehistory Press, 1992. vii, 180 p.
91-038392 306.3/49 0962911038
Agriculture -- Origin -- Congresses. Agriculture, Prehistoric -- Congresses.

GN799.A4.Z64 1988
Zohary, Daniel.
Domestication of plants in the old world: the origin and spread of cultivated plants in west Asia, Europe, and the Nile Valley/ Daniel Zohary and Maria Hopf. Oxford, OX: Clarendon Press; 1988. ix, 249 p.
86-033292 631 0198541988
Agriculture, Prehistoric. Plants, Cultivated -- History.

GN799.A8.O94 1986
World archaeoastronomy: selected papers from the 2nd Oxford International Conference on Archaeoastronomy, held at Merida, Yucatan, Mexico, 13-17 January 1986/ edited by A.F. Aveni. Cambridge [Cambridgeshire]; Cambridge University Press, 1989. xiii, 504 p.
87-035400 520/.97 0521341809
Astronomy, Prehistoric -- Congresses. Astronomy, Ancient -- Congresses. Indian astronomy -- Congresses.

GN799.F6.C64
Cohen, Mark Nathan.
The food crisis in prehistory: overpopulation and the origins of agriculture/ Mark Nathan Cohen. New Haven [Conn.]: Yale University Press, 1977. x, 341 p.
76-041858 338.1/9/3 0300020163
Prehistoric peoples -- Food. Prehistoric peoples -- Population. Agriculture -- Origin.

GN799.P4.H333 2001
Handbook of rock art research/ edited by David S. Whitley. Walnut Creek, CA: AltaMira Press, 2000. 863 p.
00-036276 759.01/13 0742502562
Rock paintings -- Handbooks, manuals, etc. Cave paintings -- Handbooks, manuals, etc. Petroglyphs -- Handbooks, manuals, etc.

GN799.P6.E44 1995
The emergence of pottery: technology and innovation in ancient societies/ edited by William K. Barnett and John W. Hoopes. Washington: Smithsonian Institution Press, c1995. xviii, 285 p.
94-044464 930.1/028/5 156098516X
Pottery, Prehistoric -- Themes, motives. Pottery, Prehistoric -- Classification. Industries, Prehistoric.

GN799.T43.B37 1994
Barber, E. J. W., 1940-
Women's work: the first 20,000 years: women, cloth, and society in early times/ Elizabeth Wayland Barber. New York: Norton, c1994. 334 p.
93-047924 305.4/3/09 0393035069
Textile fabrics, Prehistoric. Women, Prehistoric. Textile fabrics, Ancient.

GN799.T6.K66 2000
Kooyman, Brian P. 1953-
Understanding stone tools and archaeological sites/ Brian P. Kooyman. Calgary: University of Calgary Press 2000. vii, 206 p.
00-364112 1552380211
Stone implements. Archaeology -- Methodology. Indians of North America -- Great Plains -- Antiquities. Great Plains -- Antiquities.

GN799.T6.S35 1993
Schick, Kathy Diane.
Making silent stones speak: human evolution and the dawn of technology/ Kathy D. Schick and Nicholas Toth. New York: Simon & Schuster, c1993. 351 p.
92-035337 930.1/2 0671693719
Tools, Prehistoric. Flintknapping. Stone age.

GN799.T6.S83 1996
Stone tools: theoretical insights into human prehistory/ edited by George H. Odell. New York: Plenum Press, c1996. xiv, 401 p.
95-043087 930.1/028/5 20 0306451980
Tools, Prehistoric -- Analysis -- Congresses. Stone implements -- Analysis -- Congresses. Projectile points -- Analysis -- Congresses.

GN799.T6.W445 1994
Whittaker, John C. 1953-
Flintknapping: making and understanding stone tools/ John C. Whittaker. Austin: University of Texas Press, 1994. 341 p.
93-020729 930.1/028/5 0292790821
Flintknapping. Stone implements.

GN799.W66.E47 1989
Ehrenberg, Margaret R.
Women in prehistory/ by Margaret Ehrenberg. Norman: University of Oklahoma Press, 1989. 192 p.
89-040214 305.4/09/01 0806122234
Women, Prehistoric. Women, Prehistoric -- Europe. Europe -- Antiquities.

GN799.W66 E54 1991
Engendering archaeology: women and prehistory/ edited by Joan M. Gero and Margaret W. Conkey. Oxford, UK; B. Blackwell, 1991. xiii, 418 p.
90-035335 305.4/09/01 20
Women, Prehistoric. Feminism. Archaeology -- Philosophy.

GN799.W66.G45 1996
Gender and archaeology/ edited by Rita P. Wright. Philadelphia: University of Pennsylvania Press, c1996. xii, 296 p.
96-025802 305.4/09/01 20 0812233395
Women, Prehistoric. Women -- History. Civilization, Ancient.

GN803-845 Prehistoric archaeology — By region or country — Europe

GN803.C5813 1998
Clottes, Jean.
The Shamans of prehistory: trance and magic in the painted caves/ Jean Clottes and David Lewis-Williams; translated from the French by Sophie Hawkes. New York: Harry N. Abrams, 1998.
98-004151   709/.01/13094   0810941821
Cave paintings -- Europe. Petroglyphs -- Europe. Art, Prehistoric -- Europe.

GN803.G57 1999
Gimbutas, Marija Alseikaite, 1921-
The living goddesses/ Marija Gimbutas; edited and supplemented by Miriam Robbins Dexter. Berkeley: University of California Press, c1999. xx, 286 p.
98-046634   291.1/4 21   0520213939
Religion, Prehistoric -- Europe. Goddesses -- Europe. Neolithic period -- Europe. Europe -- Antiquities.

GN803.O94 1994
The Oxford illustrated prehistory of Europe/ edited by Barry Cunliffe. Oxford; Oxford University Press, 1994. ix, 532 p.
93-049342   936   0198143850
Prehistoric peoples -- Europe. Antiquities, Prehistoric -- Europe. Europe -- Antiquities.

GN803.R46 1973
Renfrew, Colin, 1937-
Before civilization: the radiocarbon revolution and prehistoric Europe. New York, Knopf; [distributed by Random House] 1973. 292 p.
73-006552   913.36/03   0394481933
Man, Prehistoric -- Europe. Megalithic monuments -- Europe. Radiocarbon dating. Europe -- Antiquities.

GN803.S5 1997
Sherratt, Andrew.
Economy and society in prehistoric Europe: changing perspectives/ Andrew Sherratt. Princeton, N.J.: Princeton University Press, c1997. xiii, 561 p.
97-008494   936 21   0691016976
Prehistoric peoples -- Europe. Economics, Prehistoric -- Europe. Antiquities, Prehistoric -- Europe. Europe -- Antiquities.

GN805.B866 1993
Burl, Aubrey.
From Carnac to Callanish: the prehistoric stone rows and avenues of Britain, Ireland, and Brittany/ Aubrey Burl. New Haven: Yale University Press, 1993. xvi, 286 p.
93-019539   936.1   0300055757
Leys -- Great Britain. Leys -- Ireland. Leys -- France -- Brittany. Great Britain -- Antiquities. Ireland -- Antiquities. Brittany (France) -- Antiquities.

GN805.B8665 1999
Burl, Aubrey.
Great stone circles: fables, fictions, facts/ Aubrey Burl. New Haven, CT: Yale University Press, 1999. 199 p.
98-034056   936.2   0300076894
Stone circles -- England. Megalithic monuments -- England. Stonehenge (England) England -- Antiquities.

GN805.D26 1996
Darvill, T. C.
Prehistoric Britain from the air: a study of space, time, and society/ Timothy Darvill. Cambridge; Cambridge University Press, 1996. xxii, 283 p.
95-038565   936.1   0521551323
Antiquities, Prehistoric -- Great Britain. Aerial photography in archaeology -- Great Britain. Great Britain -- Antiquities.

GN805.H39 1997
Hayman, Richard, 1959-
Riddles in stone: myths, archaeology, and the ancient Britons/ Richard Hayman. London: Hambledon Press, 1997. xiv, 332 p.
96-029733   936.1   1852851392
Megalithic monuments -- Great Britain. Prehistoric peoples -- Great Britain. Great Britain -- Antiquities.

GN805.M36 1989
Manley, John.
Atlas of prehistoric Britain/ John Manley; photographs by David Lyons. New York: Oxford University Press, 1989. 160 p.
89-016185   936.1   0195208072
Prehistoric peoples -- Great Britain. Antiquities, Prehistoric -- Great Britain. Great Britain -- Antiquities.

GN806.5.F53 1998
Flanagan, Laurence.
Ancient Ireland: life before the Celts/ Laurence Flanagan. New York: St. Martin's Press, 1998. vii, 264 p.
98-028261   936.1/5   0312218818
Prehistoric peoples -- Ireland. Antiquities, Prehistoric -- Ireland. Ireland -- Antiquities.

GN806.5.O38 1989
O'Kelly, Michael J.
Early Ireland: an introduction to Irish prehistory/ Michael J. O'Kelly; prepared for the press by Claire O'Kelly. Cambridge [England]; Cambridge University Press, 1989. xiii, 375 p.
87-010961   936.1/5   0521334896
Prehistoric peoples -- Ireland. Antiquities, Prehistoric -- Ireland. Ireland -- Antiquities.

GN811.S65 1992
Smith, Noel W.
An analysis of Ice Age art: its psychology and belief system/ Noel W. Smith. New York: P. Lang, c1992. xvi, 242 p.
91-017245   930.1/2   082041557X
Art, Prehistoric -- France. Art, Prehistoric -- Spain. Religion, Prehistoric -- France. France -- Antiquities.

GN836.C33.S77 1992
Straus, Lawrence Guy.
Iberia before the Iberians: the Stone Age prehistory of Cantabrian Spain/ Lawrence Guy Straus. Albuquerque: University of New Mexico Press, c1992. xiii, 336 p.
91-039171   936.6   0826313361
Prehistoric peoples -- Spain -- Cantabria. Stone age -- Spain -- Cantabria -- History. Paleoecology -- Spain -- Cantabria. Cantabria (Spain) -- Antiquities. Spain -- Antiquities.

GN845.B28
Bailey, Douglass W. 1963-
Balkan prehistory: exclusion, incorporation and identity/ Douglass W. Bailey. London; Routledge, 2000. xvi, 350 p.
99-057122   939/.8   0415215978
Antiquities, Prehistoric -- Balkan Peninsula. Prehistoric peoples -- Balkan Peninsula. Balkan Peninsula -- Antiquities.

GN855 Prehistoric archaeology — By region or country — Asia

GN855.C6.C5
Chang, Kwang-chih.
The archaeology of ancient China. New Haven: Yale University Press, 1963. 346 p.
63-007932   913.31
China -- Antiquities. China -- Civilization.

GN855.J2.A36
Aikens, C. Melvin.
Prehistory of Japan/ C. Melvin Aikens, Takayasu Higuchi. New York: Academic Press, c1982. xv, 354 p.
81-012850   952/.01   0120452804
Prehistoric peoples -- Japan. Antiquities, Prehistoric -- Japan. Japan -- Antiquities.

GN855.J67.H46 1995
Henry, Donald O.
Prehistoric cultural ecology and evolution: insights from Southern Jordan/ Donald O. Henry. New York: Plenum Press, c1995. xxiii, 466 p.
95-023639   933   0306450488
Prehistoric peoples -- Jordan. Antiquities, Prehistoric -- Jordan. Human ecology -- Jordan -- History. Jordan -- Antiquities.

GN861-865 Prehistoric archaeology — By region or country — Africa

GN861.A73 1993
The Archaeology of Africa: foods, metals, and towns/ edited by Thurstan Shaw ... [et al.]. London; Routledge, 1993. xxxvi, 857 p.
92-013921   960/.1   041508444X
Prehistoric peoples -- Africa. Agriculture, Prehistoric -- Africa. Commerce, Prehistoric -- Africa. Africa -- Antiquities.

GN861.F73 1984
From hunters to farmers: the causes and consequences of food production in Africa/ edited by J. Desmond Clark and Steven A. Brandt. Berkeley: University of California Press, c1984. xi, 433 p.
82-020004   307.7/2/096   0520045742
Agriculture, Prehistoric -- Africa -- Addresses, essays, lectures. Agriculture -- Origin -- Addresses, essays, lectures. Neolithic period -- Africa -- Addresses, essays, lectures. Africa -- Antiquities -- Addresses, essays, lectures.

GN861.P36 1996
PanAfrican Association for Prehistory and Related Studies. 1995:
Aspects of African archaeology: papers from the 10th Congress of the PanAfrican Association for Prehistory and Related Studies/ edited by Gilbert Pwiti and Robert Soper. Harare: University of Zimbabwe Publications, 1996. xiv, 857 p.
97-980077   960/.1   0908307551
Prehistoric peoples -- Africa -- Congresses. Excavations (Archaeology) -- Africa -- Congresses. Africa -- Antiquities -- Congresses.

GN865.E3.H63 1979
Hoffman, Michael A., 1944-
Egypt before the pharaohs: the prehistoric foundations of Egyptian civilization/ Michael A. Hoffman. New York: Knopf, 1979. xxi, 391 p.
78-020371   932   0394410491
Prehistoric peoples -- Egypt. Egypt -- Antiquities.

GN871-875 Prehistoric archaeology — By region or country — Australia and Pacific islands

GN871.B44 1979
Bellwood, Peter S.
Man's conquest of the Pacific: the prehistory of Southeast Asia and Oceania/ Peter Bellwood. New York: Oxford University Press, 1979, c1978. 462 p.
78-059765   959   0195201035
Prehistoric peoples -- Oceania. Prehistoric peoples -- Asia, Southeastern. Oceania -- Antiquities. Asia, Southeastern -- Antiquities.

GN871.H57 1997
Historical ecology in the Pacific Islands: prehistoric environmental and landscape change/ edited by Patrick V. Kirch and Terry L. Hunt. New Haven: Yale University Press, c1997. xv, 331 p.
96-015733   304.2/0995 20   0300066031
Prehistoric peoples -- Oceania -- Congresses. Land settlement patterns, Prehistoric -- Oceania -- Congresses. Landscape changes -- Oceania -- History -- Congresses.

GN871.I78 1992
Irwin, Geoffrey.
The prehistoric exploration and colonisation of the Pacific/ Geoffrey Irwin. Cambridge; New York: 1992. vii, 240 p.
91-023105   990   0521403715
Navigation, Prehistoric -- Pacific Area. Trade routes -- Pacific Area -- Computer simulation. Pacific Area -- Discovery and exploration. Pacific Area -- Colonization. Pacific Area -- Antiquities.

GN871.K57 1997
Kirch, Patrick Vinton.
The Lapita peoples: ancestors of the oceanic world/ Patrick Vinton Kirch. Cambridge, Mass.: Blackwell Publishers, 1997. xxv, 353 p.
96-008287   995   1557861129
Lapita culture. Prehistoric peoples -- Oceania. Pottery, Prehistoric -- Oceania. Oceania -- Antiquities.

GN871.K575 2000
Kirch, Patrick Vinton.
On the road of the winds: an archaeological history of the Pacific islands before European contact/ Patrick Vinton Kirch. Berkeley, Calif.: University of California Press, c2000. xxii, 424 p.
99-036664   995 21   0520223470
Prehistoric peoples -- Oceania. Oceania -- Antiquities.

GN875.H3.S73 1989
Stannard, David E.
Before the horror: the population of Hawai'i on the eve of Western contact/ David E. Stannard. Honolulu, Hawaii: Social Science Research Institute, University of c1989. xvii, 149 p.
88-032127   304.6/09969   0824812328
Hawaiians -- Population. Hawaii -- Population -- History.

GN885 Prehistoric archaeology — By region or country — Arctic regions (General)

GN885.A44 1996
American beginnings: the prehistory and palaeoecology of Beringia/ edited by Frederick Hadleigh West; with the assistance of Constance F. West ... [et al.]. Chicago: University of Chicago Press, 1996. xxi, 576 p.
96-011719   909/.0964/51   0226893995
Antiquities, Prehistoric -- Bering Land Bridge. Paleo-Indians -- Bering Land Bridge. Excavations (Archaeology) -- Russia (Federation) Bering Land Bridge -- Antiquities.

GR Folklore

GR35 Dictionaries. Encyclopedias

GR35.J664 1995
Jones, Alison, 1969-
Larousse dictionary of world folklore/ Alison Jones. Edinburgh: Larousse, 1995. ix, 493 p.
95-054592   398.03   0752300121
Folklore -- Dictionaries.

GR35.P53 1999
Pickering, David, 1958-
A dictionary of folklore/ David Pickering. New York: Facts on File, c1999. viii, 324 p.
00-703027   398/.03 21   0816042500
Folklore -- Dictionaries. Mythology -- Dictionaries.

GR40 Philosophy. Relation to other topics. Methodology — General works

GR40.B3313 1990
Bausinger, Hermann.
Folk culture in a world of technology/ Hermann Bausinger; translated by Elke Dettmer. Bloomington: Indiana University Press, c1990. xv, 187 p.
89-015492   398   0253311276
Folklore. Popular culture. Civilization, Modern.

GR40.T393 1998
Teaching oral traditions/ edited by John Miles Foley. New York: Modern Language Association, 1998. viii, 540 p.
98-020667   398/.07   0873523709
Oral tradition -- Study and teaching. Oral tradition in literature -- Study and teaching.

GR41.3 Philosophy. Relation to other topics. Methodology — Relation to literature

GR41.3.H39 1997
Hayes, Kevin J.
Folklore and book culture/ Kevin J. Hayes. Knoxville: University of Tennessee Press, c1997. xvi, 167 p.
96-045802   398/.09 21   0870499785
Literature and folklore. Books -- Folklore. Tales -- History and criticism.

GR45.5 Study and teaching. Research — Fieldwork

GR45.5.J33 1987
Jackson, Bruce.
Fieldwork/ Bruce Jackson. Urbana: University of Illinois Press, c1987. xiii, 311 p.
86-016010   390/.072   0252013700
Folklore -- Field work. Social sciences -- Field work.

GR55 Folklorists — Biography — Individual, A-Z

GR55.S53.B76 1996
Bronner, Simon J.
Popularizing Pennsylvania: Henry W. Shoemaker and the progressive uses of folklore and history/ Simon J. Bronner. University Park: Pennsylvania State University Press, c1996. xxii, 277 p.
95-015354   398/.092 B 20   0271014865
Shoemaker, Henry W. -- (Henry Wharton), -- b. 1880. Folklorists -- Pennsylvania -- Biography. Folklore -- Pennsylvania. Pennsylvania -- Social life and customs.

GR67 General special (Special aspects of the subject as a whole)

GR67.R83 1995
Rubin, David C.
Memory in oral traditions: the cognitive psychology of epic, ballads, and counting-out rhymes/ David C. Rubin. New York: Oxford University Press, 1995. xi, 385 p.
94-008997   153.1/33   0195082117
Oral tradition. Memory. Counting-out rhymes -- History and criticism.

GR72 Folk literature (General) — General works

GR72.F62 1991
Foley, John Miles.
Immanent art: from structure to meaning in traditional oral epic/ John Miles Foley. Bloomington: Indiana University Press, c1991. xvi, 278 p.
90-020318   809.1/32 20   0253322162
Oral tradition. Epic literature -- History and criticism. Folk literature -- History and criticism.

GR72.L66 1991
Lord, Albert Bates.
Epic singers and oral tradition/ Albert Bates Lord. Ithaca: Cornell University Press, 1991. xii, 262 p.
90-055888   809.1/32   0801424720
Oral tradition -- History and criticism. Oral-formulaic analysis. Epic poetry -- History and criticism.

GR72.O5613 1992
Olrik, Axel, 1864-1917.
Principles for oral narrative research/ by Axel Olrik; translated by Kirsten Wolf and Jody Jensen. Bloomington: Indiana University Press, c1992. xxviii, 209 p.
88-046034   398.2/072   0253341752
Oral tradition -- Methodology. Folk literature -- History and criticism. Epic literature -- History and criticism.

GR72.S76 1997
Storytelling encyclopedia: historical, cultural, and multiethnic approaches to oral traditions around the world/ general editor, David Adams Leeming; project editor, Marion Sader. Phoenix, Ariz.: Oryx Press, 1997. xi, 543 p.
97-023081   808.5/43   1573560251
Storytelling -- Encyclopedias. Tales -- Encyclopedias. Oral tradition -- Encyclopedias.

GR72.3 Folk literature (General) — Performance

GR72.3.F65 1995
Foley, John Miles.
The singer of tales in performance/ John Miles Foley. Bloomington: Indiana University Press, c1995. xvi, 235 p.
94-017638   398/.01 20   0253322251
Folklore -- Performance. Oral tradition. Oral-formulaic analysis.

GR72.3.N56 1999
Niles, John D.
Homo Narrans: the poetics and anthropology of oral literature/ John D. Niles. Philadelphia: University of Pennsylvania Press, c1999. 280 p.
99-010074   398.2 21   0812235045
Storytelling. Oral tradition. Folk literature.

GR72.3.S62 1999
Sobol, Joseph Daniel.
The storytellers' journey: an American revival/ Joseph Daniel Sobol. Urbana: University of Illinois Press, c1999. xvi, 265 p.
98-019690   808.5/43/0973 21   0252024362
Storytelling -- United States.

GR98 By race or group not limited to special places — Semitic — Jewish

GR98.D93 2000
The dybbuk and the Yiddish imagination: a haunted reader/ edited and translated from the Yiddish by Joachim Neugroschel. Syracuse, NY: Syracuse Press, 2000. xix, 412 p.
00-037016   398.2/089/924   0815628714
Jews -- Folklore. Spirits -- Folklore. Legends, Jewish.

GR98.H225 1992
Haboucha, Reginetta.
Types and motifs of the Judeo-Spanish folktales/ Reginetta Haboucha. New York: Garland, 1992. xxvii, 965 p.
92-008897   398.2/0467   0824097270
Folk literature, Ladino -- Themes, motives. Sephardim -- Folklore. Tales -- Classification.

GR101 By region or country — North America — General works

GR101.A54 1996
American folklore: an encyclopedia/ edited by Jan Harold Brunvand. New York: Garland Pub., 1996. xviii, 794 p.
95-053734   398/.0973/03   0815307519
Folklore -- North America -- Encyclopedias. North America -- Social life and customs -- Encyclopedias.

GR103 By region or country — North America — African American

GR103.L48
Levine, Lawrence W.
Black culture and black consciousness: Afro-American folk thought from slavery to freedom/ Lawrence W. Levine. New York: Oxford University Press, 1977. xx, 522 p.
76-009223   398.2   019502088X
Afro-Americans -- Folklore. Folklore -- United States.

GR105-111 By region or country — North America — United States

GR105.B483 1994
Bluestein, Gene, 1928-
Poplore: folk and pop in American culture/ Gene Bluestein. Amherst: University of Massachusetts Press, c1994. xiii, 167 p.
93-043614   398/.0973   0870239031
Herder, Johann Gottfried, -- 1744-1803 -- Contributions in folklore. Popular culture -- United States. Folklore -- United States -- History and criticism. United States -- Social life and customs.

GR105.B716 2000
Brunvand, Jan Harold.
The truth never stands in the way of a good story/ Jan Harold Brunvand; with a chapter on the heroic hacker by Erik Brunvand. Urbana: University of Illinois Press, c2000. 217 p.
99-006465   398.2/0973/091732 21   0252024249
Urban folklore -- United States. Legends -- United States. United States -- Social life and customs.

GR105.D44 1994
Degh, Linda.
American folklore and the mass media/ Linda Degh. Bloomington: Indiana University Press, c1994. 217 p.
93-007543   398/.0973   0253316774
Popular culture -- United States. Folklore -- United States. Mass media -- United States.

GR105.G74 1993
Green, Archie.
Wobblies, pile butts, and other heroes: laborlore explorations/ Archie Green. Urbana: University of Illinois Press, c1993. xii, 523 p.
92-020168   398/.0973   0252019636
Occupations -- United States -- Folklore. Folklore -- United States.

GR105.L58 2001
Long, Carolyn Morrow.
Spiritual merchants: religion, magic, and commerce/ Carolyn Morrow Long. Knoxville: University of Tennessee Press, c2001. xxix, 314 p.
00-009886   299/.64 21   1572331097
Charms -- United States. Talismans -- United States. Medicine, Magic, mystic, and spagiric -- United States.

GR105.R66 1999
Rooted in America: foodlore of popular fruits and vegetables/ edited by David Scofield Wilson and Angus Kress Gillespie. Knoxville: University of Tennessee Press, c1999. xiii, 239 p.
98-058096   398/.355 21   1572330589
Fruit -- United States -- Folklore. Vegetables -- United States -- Folklore. Food -- Symbolic aspects -- United States. United States -- Social life and customs.

GR105.34.B78 2001
Brunvand, Jan Harold.
Encyclopedia of urban legends/ Jan Harold Brunvand; artwork by Randy Hickman. Santa Barbara, Calif.: ABC-CLIO, 2001. xxxiv, 524 p.
2001-000883   398.2/0973/091732   157607076X
Urban folklore -- United States -- Encyclopedias. Legends -- United States -- Encyclopedias.

GR105.5.S337 1996
Schamschula, Eleonore.
A pioneer of American folklore: Karl Knortz and his collections/ Eleonore Schamschula; foreword by Alan Dundes. Moscow, Idaho: University of Idaho Press, 1996. 326 p.
96-003879   398/.0973   0893011851
Folklore -- United States. Knortz, Karl, -- 1841-1918. Folklorists -- United States.

GR108.M67 1998
Moss, Kay.
Southern folk medicine, 1750-1820/ Kay K. Moss. Columbia, S.C.: University of South Carolina Press, 1998. xv, 259 p.
98-040223   615.8/82/097509032   1570032890
Traditional medicine -- Southern States -- History. Traditional medicine -- Southern States -- Formulae, receipts, prescriptions. Medicine, Popular -- Southern States -- Formulae, receipts, prescriptions. Southern States -- Social life and customs.

GR108.M85 1991
Mullen, Patrick B., 1941-
Listening to old voices: folklore, life stories, and the elderly/ Patrick B. Mullen. Urbana: University of Illinois Press, c1992. xii, 292 p.
90-026694   398/.09755   0252018087
Folklore -- Blue Ridge Mountains. Folklore -- Ohio. Aged -- Blue Ridge Mountains -- Folklore.

GR108.W585 1995
Williams, Michael Ann.
Great Smoky Mountains folklife/ Michael Ann Williams. Jackson: University Press of Mississippi, c1995. xviii, 216 p.
95-013341 398/.09768/89 0878057919
Folklore -- Great Smoky Mountains (N.C. and Tenn.) Great Smoky Mountains (N.C. and Tenn.) -- History. Great Smoky Mountains (N.C. and Tenn.) -- Social life and customs. Great Smoky Mountains National Park (N.C. and Tenn.)

GR110.K4A46 1992
Alvey, R. Gerald,
Kentucky Bluegrass country/ R. Gerald Alvey; with a foreword by Thomas D. Clark. Jackson: University Press of Mississippi, c1992. xxiv, 322 p.
91-048029 976.9/3 0878055444
Folklore -- Kentucky. Material culture -- Kentucky.

GR110.M4H63 2000
Hoberman, Michael.
Yankee moderns: folk regional identity in the Sawmill Valley of western Massachusetts, 1890-1920/ Michael Hoberman. Knoxville: University of Tennessee Press, c2000. liii, 162 p.
00-008138 974.4/22 21 1572330872
Oral tradition -- Massachusetts -- Sawmill River Valley. Folklore -- Massachusetts -- Sawmill River Valley. Group identity -- Massachusetts -- Sawmill River Valley. Sawmill River Valley (Mass.) -- Social life and customs.

GR111.A47.B37 1992
Bascom, William Russell, 1912-
African folktales in the New World/ William Bascom. Bloomington: Indiana University Press, c1992. xxiv, 243 p.
91-046789 398.2/08996073 0253311284
Afro-Americans -- Folklore. Tales -- United States -- History and criticism. Tales -- Africa -- History and criticism.

GR111.A47J69 2000
Jones, Charles Colcock,
Gullah folktales from the Georgia coast/ Charles Colcock Jones; foreword by Susan Millar Williams. Athens: University of Georgia Press, 2000. xxxv, 192 p.
99-089728 398.2/089/960758 0820322164
Gullahs -- Georgia -- Folklore. Tales -- Georgia -- Atlantic Coast. Animals -- Folklore.

GR111.A47.T36 1993
Talley, Thomas Washington.
The Negro traditions/ Thomas W. Talley; edited, with an introduction, by Charles K. Wolfe and Laura C. Jarmon. Knoxville: University of Tennessee Press, c1993. xxvi, 334 p.
92-047011 398.2/089/960730768 0870498037
Afro-Americans -- Tennessee -- Folklore. Tales -- Tennessee.

GR111.A47.T87 1993
Turner, Patricia, 1955-
I heard it through the grapevine: rumor in African-American culture/ Patricia A. Turner. Berkeley: University of California Press, c1993. xvi, 260 p.
93-027463 398/.08996073 0520081854
Afro-Americans -- Folklore. Urban folklore -- United States. Rumor -- United States.

GR111.F73.C35 1994b
Cajun and Creole folktales: the French oral tradition of South Louisiana/ collected and annotated by Barry Jean Ancelet. New York: Garland Pub., 1994. lxxii, 224 p.
93-031848 398.21/089/410763 0815314981
Cajuns -- Folklore. Tales -- Louisiana. Folklore -- Louisiana.

GR111.F73.G85 1992
Gutierrez, C. Paige.
Cajun foodways/ C. Paige Gutierrez. Jackson: University Press of Mississippi, c1992. xv, 149 p.
92-009963 394.1/2/089410763 0878055622
Cajuns -- Folklore. Food habits -- Louisiana. Cookery, Cajun. Louisiana -- Social life and customs.

GR111.P65.S55 2000
Silverman, Deborah Anders, 1954-
Polish-American folklore/ Deborah Anders Silverman. Urbana: University of Illinois Press, c2000. xii, 236 p.
99-006985 398/.089/9185073 21 0252025695
Polish Americans -- Folklore. Polish Americans -- Social life and customs. Polish Americans -- Ethnic identity.

GR113.5 By region or country — North America — Canada

GR113.5.N54.H35 1996
Halpert, Herbert.
Folktales of Newfoundland: the resilience of the oral tradition/ Herbert Halpert and J.D.A. Widdowson; with the assistance of Martin J. Lovelace and Eileen Collins; music transcription and commentary by Julia C. Bishop. New York: Garland Pub., 1996. 2 v.
96-003648 398.2/09718 0815317360
Tales -- Newfoundland.

GR121 By region or country — Latin America — West Indies. Caribbean Area

GR121.J2.S63 1993
Sobo, Elisa Janine, 1963-
One blood: the Jamaican body/ by Elisa Janine Sobo. Albany: State University of New York Press, c1993. vii, 329 p.
92-022887 398/.353 0791414299
Traditional medicine -- Jamaica. Body, Human -- Social aspects -- Jamaica. Jamaicans -- Kinship.

GR133 By region or country — South America — By region or country, A-Z

GR133.B62.A527 1994
Slater, Candace.
Dance of the dolphin: transformation and disenchantment in the Amazonian imagination/ Candace Slater. Chicago: University of Chicago Press, c1994. xi, 314 p.
93-027472 398/.369953 0226761835
Folklore -- Brazil -- Amazonas. Tales -- Brazil -- History and criticism. Folklore -- Brazil -- Para (State)

GR133.T57.S35 1997
Salles-Reese, Veronica, 1950-
From Viracocha to the Virgin of Copacabana: representation of the sacred at Lake Titicaca/ Veronica Salles-Reese. Austin, Tex.: University of Texas Press, 1997. ix, 208 p.
96-021683 200/.984/12 0292777124
Mary, -- Blessed Virgin, Saint -- Cult -- Bolivia -- Copacabana (Manco Kapac) Mary, -- Blessed Virgin, Saint -- In literature. Colla mythology. Incas -- Religion. Inca mythology. Titicaca Lake (Peru and Bolivia) -- In literature.

GR135 By region or country — Europe — General works

GR135.S3613 1998
Schmitt, Jean Claude.
Ghosts in the Middle Ages: the living and the dead in Medieval society/ Jean-Claude Schmitt; translated by Teresa Lavender Fagan. Chicago: University of Chicago Press, c1998. xiii, 290 p.
97-038308 398/.47/094 21 0226738876
Ghosts -- Europe -- History. Ghosts in art. Death -- Religious aspects -- Christianity -- History of Doctrines -- Middle Ages, 600-1500.

GR141 By region or country — Europe — Great Britain. England

GR141.S55 1999
Silver, Carole G.
Strange and secret peoples: fairies and Victorian consciousness/ Carole G. Silver. New York: Oxford University Press, 1999. xiv, 272 p.
98-010318 398.21 0195121996
Fairies. Folklore -- Great Britain. Literature and folklore -- Great Britain. Great Britain -- Social conditions -- 19th century.

GR141.S59 2001
Simpson, Jacqueline.
A dictionary of English folklore/ Jacqueline Simpson & Steve Roud. Oxford; Oxford University Press, 2000. vii, 411 p.
2001-266642 019210019X
Folklore -- England -- Dictionaries. England -- Social life and customs -- Dictionaries.

GR153.5 By region or country — Europe — Ireland

GR153.5.B74 1995
Brenneman, Walter L.
Crossing the circle at the holy wells of Ireland/ Walter L. Brenneman, Jr., Mary G. Brenneman. Charlottesville: University Press of Virginia, 1995. xii, 141 p.
94-018909 291.3/5/09415 0813915481
Holy wells -- Ireland. Folklore -- Ireland. Mythology, Celtic. Ireland -- Religious life and customs. Ireland -- Antiquities.

GR154.7 By region or country — Europe — Hungary

GR154.7.K39.P35 1996
Palko, Zsuzsanna.
Hungarian folktales: the art of Zsuzsanna Palko/ collected, transcribed, annotated, and introduced by Linda Degh; translated by Vera Kalm. Jackson, Miss.: University Press of Mississippi, [1996] xxiv, 382 p.
96-028121   398.2/09439   0878059121
Palko, Zsuzsanna. Tales -- Hungary -- Karkasd -- History and criticism. Storytelling -- Hungary -- Karkasd. Szeklers -- Hungary -- Karkasd -- Folklore.

GR202-203 By region or country — Europe — Russia. Soviet Union. Former Soviet republics

GR202.P7513 1984
Propp, V. IA. 1895-1970.
Theory and history of folklore/ Vladimir Propp; translated by Ariadna Y. Martin and Richard P. Martin and several others; edited, with an introduction and notes, by Anatoly Liberman. Minneapolis: University of Minnesota Press, c1984. lxxxi, 252 p.
83-014840   398.2/0947   0816611807
Folk literature, Russian -- History and criticism. Tales -- Soviet Union -- History and criticism. Tales -- History and criticism.

GR203.R88.P47 1987
Perrie, Maureen, 1946-
The image of Ivan the Terrible in Russian folklore/ Maureen Perrie. Cambridge [Cambridgeshire]; Cambridge University Press, 1987. x, 269 p.
86-026820   398.2/2/0947   0521330750
Ivan -- IV, -- Czar of Russia, -- 1530-1584. Monarchy -- Russia (Federation) -- Folklore. Folklore -- Russia (Federation)

GR205 By region or country — Europe — Scandinavia

GR205.S23 1988
Scandinavian folk belief and legend/ Reimund Kvideland, Henning K. Sehmsdorf, editors. Minneapolis: University of Minnesota Press, c1988. xxii, 429 p.
86-025039   398.2/0948   0816615039
Folklore -- Scandinavia. Legends -- Scandinavia.

GR230 By region or country — Europe — Spain

GR230.G57 1998
Goldberg, Harriet.
Motif-index of medieval Spanish folk narratives/ by Harriet Goldberg. Tempe, Ariz.: Medieval & Renaissance Texts & Studies, 1998. xxviii, 288 p.
97-031019   398.2/0946/0902   0866982035
Folklore -- Spain -- Themes, motives. Folklore -- Spain -- Classification. Tales, Medieval -- Themes, motives.

GR268 By region or country — Asia — By race or group not limited to one country, A-Z

GR268.A73.E4 1995
El-Shamy, Hasan M., 1938-
Folk traditions of the Arab world: a guide to motif classification/ Hasan M. El-Shamy. Bloomington: Indiana University Press, c1995. 2 v.
95-001424   398.2/0956/0012 20   0253352010
Folklore -- Middle East -- Classification. Tales -- Middle East -- Classification. Folk literature, Arabic -- Classification.

GR285 By region or country — Asia — Middle East

GR285.S64 1989
Speak, bird, speak again: Palestinian Arab folktales/ [edited and translated by] Ibrahim Muhawi and Sharif Kanaana. Berkeley: University of California Press, c1989. xix, 420 p.
88-004832   398.2/095694   0520058631
Tales -- Palestine. Palestinian Arabs -- Folklore. Folk literature, Arabic -- Palestine -- Translations into English.

GR302.7-305.5 By region or country — Asia — South Asia

GR302.7.H47.M54 1991
Mills, Margaret Ann.
Rhetorics and politics in Afghan traditional storytelling/ Margaret A. Mills. Philadelphia: University of Pennsylvania Press, c1991. xi, 388 p.
90-022019   398/.09581   0812281993
Tales -- Afghanistan -- Herat (Province) Storytelling -- Afghanistan. Folklore -- Political aspects -- Afghanistan.

GR305.R358 1997
Ramanujan, A. K.,
A flowering tree and other oral tales from India/ A.K. Ramanujan; edited with a preface by Stuart Blackburn and Alan Dundes. Berkeley: University of California Press, c1997. xv, 270 p.
95-043422   398.2/0954/87 20   0520203992
Tales -- India -- Karnataka. Kanarese (Indic people) -- Folklore.

GR305.5.B4.D27 1995
DasGupta, Sayantani.
The demon slayers and other stories: Bengali folk tales/ collected and written by Sayantani DasGupta and Shamita Das Dasgupta. New York: Interlink Books, 1995. viii, 167 p.
94-001706   398.2/0954/14   1566561647
Tales -- India -- Bengal.

GR305.5.C46.F58 1996
Flueckiger, Joyce Burkhalter.
Gender and genre in the folklore of Middle India/ Joyce Burkhalter Flueckiger. Ithaca: Cornell University Press, 1996. xxiii, 351 p.
95-050444   398/.0954/3   0801432065
Folklore -- India -- Chattisagarh (India) Women -- India -- Chattisagarh -- Folklore. Folklore -- Performance. Chattisagarh (India) -- Social life and customs.

GR305.5.R3.G65 1992
Gold, Ann Grodzins, 1946-
A carnival of parting: the tales of King Bharthari and King Gopi Chand as sung and told by Madhu Natisar Nath of Ghatiyali, Rajasthan/ translated with an introduction and afterword by Ann Grodzins Gold. Berkeley: University of California Press, c1992. xx, 369 p.
91-044882   398.22/0954/4   0520075358
Nath, Madhu Natisar. Tales -- India -- Rajasthan. Storytellers -- India -- Rajasthani. Folk singers -- India -- Rajasthani.

GR313 By region or country — Asia — Southeastern Asia

GR313.N4813 1993
Nhat Hanh,
A taste of earth, and other legends of Vietnam/ Thich Nhat Hanh; translated from the Vietnamese by Mobi Warren; drawings by Nguyen Thi Hop and Nguyen Dong. Berkeley, Calif.: Parallax, c1993. ix, 121 p.
93-024083   398.2/09597   093807766X
Legends -- Vietnam.

GR335-336 By region or country — Eastern Asia. Far East — China

GR335.K3313 1996
Kan, Pao, fl. 317-322.
In search of the supernatural: the written record/ translated by Kenneth J. DeWoskin and J.I. Crump, Jr. Stanford, Calif.: Stanford University Press, c1996. xxxvi, 283 p.
95-022091   398.2/0951 20   0804725063
Legends -- China.

GR336.F8.I43 1995
Imagining women: Fujian folk tales/ selected and translated by Karen Gernant. New York: Interlink Books, 1995. viii, 276 p.
94-038505   398.2/0951/245   1566561736
Tales -- China -- Fujian Sheng. Women -- China -- Fujian Sheng -- Folklore.

GR340 By region or country — Eastern Asia. Far East — Japan

GR340.D66
Dorson, Richard Mercer, 1916-
Studies in Japanese folklore/ advisory editors: Toichi Mabuchi [and] Tokihiko Oto.; chief translator: Yasuyo Ishiwara. Bloomington: Indiana University Press, c1963. ix, 347 p.
63-062500
Folklore -- Japan.

GR350 By region or country — Africa — By group not limited to one region or country

GR350.O37 1992
Okpewho, Isidore.
African oral literature: backgrounds, character, and continuity/ Isidore Okpewho. Bloomington: Indiana University Press, c1992. xiii, 392 p.
91-025671   398.2/096   0253341671
Folk literature, African -- History and criticism. Oral tradition -- Africa.

GR350.3-359.2 By region or country — Africa — By region or country

GR350.3.W45 1991
West African folktales/ collected and translated by Jack Berry; edited and with an introduction by Richard Spears. Evanston, Ill.: Northwestern University Press, 1991. xxvi, 229 p.
91-024282   398.2/0966   0810109794
Tales -- Africa, West.

GR350.32.D98.G57 1996
Giray-Saul, Eren, 1953-
Nsiirin! Nsiirin!: Jula folktales from West Africa/ Eren Giray, with the assistance of Awa Outtara & Jean Go. East Lansing: Michigan State University Press, [1996] 271 p.
96-046145   398.2/089/9634   087013454X
Dyula (African people) -- Folklore. Tales -- Africa, West. Oral tradition -- Africa, West.

GR351.32.I34.O56 1998
Okpewho, Isidore.
Once upon a kingdom: myth, hegemony, and identity/ Isidore Okpewho. Bloomington: Indiana University Press, c1998. xiii, 252 p.
98-019792   398.2/089/96332 21   0253333962
Igbo (African people) -- Folklore. Mythology, Igbo. Folklore -- Nigeria -- Delta State -- History and criticism. Benin (Kingdom) -- Legends -- History and criticism.

GR351.32.Y56.O86 1997
Owomoyela, Oyekan.
Yoruba trickster tales/ Oyekan Owomoyela. Lincoln, Neb.: University of Nebraska Press, c1997. xviii, 218 p.
96-037321   398.2/08996333 21   0803235631
Yoruba (African people) -- Folklore. Tales -- Nigeria. Turtles -- Folklore.

GR353.52.Q53.W43 1991
Webber, Sabra Jean.
Romancing the real: folklore and ethnographic representation in North Africa/ Sabra J. Webber. Philadelphia: University of Pennsylvania Press, c1991. xxviii, 293 p.
91-003348   398/.09611   0812282361
Tales -- Tunisia -- Qulaybiyah. Oral tradition -- Tunisia -- Qulaybiyah. Folklore -- Africa, North. Qulaybiyah (Tunisia) -- History. Qulaybiyah (Tunisia) -- Social life and customs.

GR357.H38 1992
Haring, Lee.
Verbal arts in Madagascar: performance in historical perspective/ Lee Haring. Philadelphia: University of Pennsylvania Press, c1992. 242 p.
91-033129   398/.09691   0812231414
Folk literature, Malagasy -- History and criticism. Folklore -- Madagascar -- Performance. Madagascar -- Social life and customs.

GR357.2.M47.I26 1994
Ibonia: epic of Madagascar/ translated and introduced by Lee Haring. Lewisburg: Bucknell University Press; c1994. 169 p.
94-016117   398.2/04993   0838752845
Merina (Malagasy people) -- Folklore. Folk literature, Malagasy -- Madagascar -- Imerina -- History and criticism. Epic literature, Malagasy -- Madagascar -- Imerina -- History and criticism.

GR358.J36 1992
Janzen, John M.
Ngoma: discourses of healing in central and southern Africa/ John M. Janzen. Berkeley: University of California Press, c1992. xv, 241 p.
91-043703   398/.353   0520072650
Traditional medicine -- Africa, Southern. Traditional medicine -- Africa, Central. Healing -- Africa, Southern.

GR358.Q47 2000
The quest for fruition through ngoma: the political aspects of healing in South Africa/ edited by Rijk van Dijk, Ria Reis, and Marja Spierenburg. Athens: Ohio University Press, 2000. 172 p.
99-045652   398/.353/0968   0821413031
Traditional medicine -- Africa, Southern. Rites and ceremonies -- Africa, Southern. Africa, Southern -- Social conditions. Africa, Southern -- Politics and government.

GR358.S34 1998
Scheub, Harold.
Story/ Harold Scheub. Madison, Wis.: University of Wisconsin Press, c1998. xi, 351 p.
98-015478   808.5/43/0968 21   0299159302
Storytelling -- Africa, Southern. Tales -- Africa, Southern.

GR359.O73 1999
Oral literature & performance in southern Africa/ edited by Duncan Brown. Athens: Ohio University Press, 1999. x, 243 p.
99-016622   398.2/0968   0821413082
Folk literature -- South Africa -- History and criticism. Literature and folklore -- South Africa. Oral tradition -- South Africa.

GR359.S34 1996
Scheub, Harold.
The tongue is fire: South African storytellers and apartheid/ Harold Scheub. Madison: University of Wisconsin Press, c1996. xxvii, 448 p.
96-017774   398/.0968 20   0299150909
Storytelling -- South Africa. Oral tradition -- South Africa. Folklore -- Political aspects -- South Africa. South Africa -- Social life and customs.

GR359.2.X64.Z46 1992
Zenani, Nongenile Masithathu.
The world and the word: tales and observations from the Xhosa oral tradition/ Nongenile Masithathu Zenani; collected and edited, with an introduction, commentaries, and annotations by Harold Scheub. Madison, Wis.: University of Wisconsin Press, c1992. xii, 499 p.
92-050261   398.2/089/963985   0299133109
Xhosa (African people) -- Folklore. Tales -- South Africa. Xhosa (African people) -- Social life and customs.

GR366 By region or country — Australia — Local or individual groups, A-Z

GR366.A87.B56 1995
Blows, Johanna M.
Eagle and crow: an exploration of an Australian aboriginal myth/ by Johanna M. Blows. New York: Garland Pub., 1995. xviii, 216 p.
94-036191   398.24/528864   081531258X
Australian aborigines -- Folklore. Mythology, Australian aboriginal.

GR385 By region or country — Pacific islands — By country, island, or island group, A-Z

GR385.P36.G55 1993
Gillison, Gillian.
Between culture and fantasy: a New Guinea highlands mythology/ Gillian Gillison. Chicago: University of Chicago Press, 1993. xxi, 392 p.
92-011319   398/.0899912   0226293807
Gimi (Papua New Guinea people) -- Folklore. Women, Gimi -- Social conditions. Women, Gimi -- Psychology.

GR450 By subject — Folklore relating to private life — Birth, love, marriage, and death, etc.

GR450.D45 1992
Delaney, Carol Lowery, 1940-
The seed and the soil: gender and cosmology in Turkish village society/ Carol Delaney. Berkeley: University of California Press, c1991. xiii, 360 p.
90-028545   302/.12   0520073142
Childbirth -- Turkey -- Folklore. Childbirth -- Religious aspects -- Islam. Human reproduction -- Social aspects -- Turkey.

GR498 By subject — Folklore relating to private life — Eating. Drinking

GR498.A53 2000
Andrews, Tamra, 1959-
Nectar & ambrosia: an encyclopedia of food in world mythology/ Tamra Andrews. Santa Barbara, Calif.: ABC-CLIO, c2000. xv, 287 p.
00-010485   398.27 21   1576070360
Food -- Folklore. Food habits -- Folklore. Food -- Symbolic aspects.

GR524 By subject — Folklore relating to private life — Trickster

GR524.C48 1998
Christen, Kimberly A.
Clowns & tricksters: an encyclopedia of tradition and culture/ Kimberly A. Christen. Denver, Colo.: ABC-CLIO, c1998. xix, 271 p.
98-027562   398.2/09 21   0874369363
Trickster. Clowns -- Mythology.

GR530 By subject — Demonology

GR530.S53 1997
Sidky, H., 1956-
Witchcraft, lycanthropy, drugs, and disease: an anthropological study of the European witch-hunts/ H. Sidky. New York: Peter Lang, c1997. xiv, 330 p.
96-018078   133.4/3/09409031 20   0820433543
Witchcraft -- Europe -- History. Trials (Witchcraft) -- Europe -- History. Demoniac possession -- Europe -- History.

GR550 By subject — Fairies — Fairy tales

GR550.R613 1992
Rohrich, Lutz.
Folktales and reality/ by Lutz Rohrich; translated by Peter Tokofsky. Bloomington: Indiana University Press, c1991. xxiii, 290 p.
90-026381 398.21 025335028X
Fairy tales -- History and criticism.

GR550.Z56 1994
Zipes, Jack David.
Fairy tale as myth/myth as fairy tale/ Jack Zipes. Lexington: University Press of Kentucky, c1994. xii, 192 p.
94-013777 398.21 0813118905
Fairy tales -- History and criticism. Fairy tales -- Classification.

GR650 By subject — Nature — Geographical topics

GR650.M36 2000
Manguel, Alberto.
The dictionary of imaginary places/ Alberto Manguel & Gianni Guadalupi; illustrated by Graham Greenfield; with additional illustrations by Eric Beddows; maps and charts by James Cook. New York: Harcourt Brace, c2000. xvi, 755 p.
99-046994 809/.93372 21 0151005419
Geographical myths -- Dictionaries. Imaginary places -- Dictionaries.

GR780-830 By subject — Nature — Animals, plants, and minerals

GR780.R3813 1992
Ratsch, Christian, 1957-
Dictionary of Sacred and Magical Plants, The/ Christian Ratsch; with a foreword by Albert Hofmann; translated by John Baker. Santa Barbara, Calif.: ABC-CLIO, 1992. 223 p.
92-029983 398/.368/03 0874367166
Medicinal plants -- Dictionaries. Plants -- Folklore -- Dictionaries. Psychotropic plants -- Dictionaries.

GR830.V3.A92 1995
Auerbach, Nina, 1943-
Our vampires, ourselves/ Nina Auerbach. Chicago: University of Chicago Press, 1995. vii, 231 p.
95-001044 820.9/375 0226032019
Vampires -- History. Vampires -- Psychology. Gays in popular culture.

GR830.V3.B35 1988
Barber, Paul, 1941-
Vampires, burial, and death: folklore and reality/ Paul Barber. New Haven: Yale University Press, c1988. viii, 236 p.
88-000143 398/.45 0300041268
Vampires. Postmortem changes -- Folklore. Dead -- Folklore.

GR880 By subject — Medicine. Folk medicine

GR880.A8 1992
Anthropological approaches to the study of ethnomedicine/ edited by Mark Nichter. Yverdon, Switzerland; Gordon and Breach Science Publishers, 1992. xxii, 259 p.
92-020369 615.8/ 2881245307
Traditional medicine. Medical anthropology.

GR940 By subject — Mythical places — General works

GR940.L67 1999
Lorenz, Albert, 1941-
Buried blueprints: maps and sketches of lost worlds and mysterious places/ Albert Lorenz with Joy Schleh. New York: Harry N. Abrams, 1999. 1 v.
99-023417 398.23/4 0810941104
Geographical myths -- Juvenile literature. Lost continents -- Juvenile literature. Curiosities and wonders -- Juvenile literature.

GT Manners and Customs (General)

GT76 General works, treatises, and textbooks — 1975-

GT76.P67 1989
Pounds, Norman John Greville.
Hearth & home: a history of material culture/ Norman J.G. Pounds. Bloomington: Indiana University Press, c1989. x, 437 p.
87-046367 306/.094 0253327121
Material culture -- Europe. Europe -- Social life and customs.

GT129 By period — Modern — General works

GT129.S68 1991
Spierenburg, Petrus Cornelis.
The broken spell: a cultural and anthropological history of preindustrial Europe/ Pieter Spierenburg. New Brunswick: Rutgers University Press, c1991. x, 313 p.
90-019386 391/.6 0813516757
Family -- Europe -- History. Attitude (Psychology) -- Europe -- History. Body, Human -- Social aspects. Europe -- Social conditions. Europe -- Social life and customs.

GT135 By period — Modern — 16th century

GT135.J66 2000
Jones, Ann Rosalind.
Renaissance clothing and the materials of memory/ Ann Rosalind Jones, Peter Stallybrass. Cambridge [England]; Cambridge University Press, 2000. xiii, 368 p.
99-055694 391/.0094/09031 0521781027
Costume -- History -- 16th century. Fashion -- History -- 16th century. Renaissance.

GT225 Houses. Dwellings — By region or country — North America

GT225.N8.W55 1991
Williams, Michael Ann.
Homeplace: the social use and meaning of the folk dwelling in southwestern North Carolina/ Michael Ann Williams. Athens: University of Georgia Press, c1991. xii, 190 p.
90-021654 392/.36/0097563 0820313467
Dwellings -- North Carolina. Vernacular architecture -- North Carolina -- Social aspects. Dwellings -- Appalachian Region, Southern. North Carolina -- Social life and customs.

GT298 Houses. Dwellings — By region or country — Europe

GT298.P37.P3713 1991
Pardailhe-Galabrun, Annik.
The birth of intimacy: privacy and domestic life in early modern Paris/ Annik Pardailhe-Galabrun; translated by Jocelyn Phelps. Philadelphia: University of Pennsylvania Press, c1991. xiv, 241 p.
91-050607 392/.36/0094436 0812231244
Dwellings -- France -- Paris -- History. House furnishings -- France -- Paris -- History. Interior decoration -- France -- Paris -- History. Paris (France) -- Social life and customs.

GT352.2 Houses. Dwellings — By region or country — Asia. The Orient

GT352.2.H6513 1991
Man and his house in the Himalayas: ecology of Nepal/ edited by Gerard Toffin. New Delhi: Sterling Publishers, c1991. 243 p.
91-909156 392/.36/0095496 8120713648
Dwellings -- Nepal. Dwellings -- Himalaya Mountains Region. Vernacular architecture -- Nepal. Nepal -- Social life and customs. Himalaya Mountains Region -- Social life and customs.

GT425 Houses. Dwellings — Special topics — Heating. Hearths. Fireplaces. Stoves

GT425.U5
Brewer, Priscilla J.
From fireplace to cookstove: technology and the domestic ideal in America/ Priscilla J. Brewer. Syracuse, N.Y.: Syracuse University Press, 2000. xix, 338 p.
00-029705 392.3/7 0815606508
Stoves -- Social aspects -- United States. Stoves -- United States -- History.

GT481 Household arts. Households — By region or country, A-Z

GT481.U6
Crowley, John E., 1943-
The invention of comfort: sensibilities & design in early modern Britain & early America/ John E. Crowley. Baltimore, Md.: Johns Hopkins University Press, c2001. xi, 361 p.
00-008958   306/.0973 21   0801864372
Households -- United States -- History. Households -- Great Britain -- History. House furnishings -- United States -- History. United States -- Social life and customs. Great Britain -- Social life and customs.

GT499 Personal beauty

GT499.S49 2001
Sherrow, Victoria.
For appearance' sake: the historical encyclopedia of good looks, beauty, and grooming/ Victoria Sherrow. Phoenix, Ariz.: Oryx Press, 2001. x, 299 p.
00-010107   646.7/042   1573562041
Beauty, Personal -- Encyclopedias. Beauty, Personal -- Social aspects.

GT507 Costume. Dress. Fashion — Dictionaries. Encyclopedias

GT507.O53 1998
O'Hara, Georgina.
The Thames and Hudson dictionary of fashion and fashion designers/ Georgina O'Hara Callan. New York: Thames and Hudson, 1998. 272 p.
97-061609   391/.003   050020313X
Fashion -- Dictionaries. Costume -- History -- 19th century -- Dictionaries. Costume -- History -- 20th century -- Dictionaries.

GT510 Costume. Dress. Fashion — General works — 1801-1974

GT510.B6713 1987
Boucher, François,
20,000 years of fashion: the history of costume and personal adornment/ by François Boucher; with a new chapter by Yvonne Deslandres. Expanded ed. New York: H.N. Abrams, 1987. 459 p.
86-072852   391/.009 19   0810916932
Costume -- History.

GT511 Costume. Dress. Fashion — General works — 1975-

GT511.B74 1995
Breward, Christopher, 1965-
The culture of fashion: a new history of fashionable dress/ Christopher Breward; picture research, Jane Audas. Manchester; Manchester University Press; c1995. xii, 244 p.
94-005415   391 20   0719041244
Costume -- History. Fashion -- History.

GT525 Costume. Dress. Fashion — Philosophy. Relation to other topics — Relation to sociology. Social aspects

GT525.D74 1991
Dress and gender: making and meaning in cultural contexts/ edited by Ruth Barnes and Joanne B. Eicher. New York: Berg: 1992. viii, 293 p.
91-015885   391   0854967206
Costume -- Sex differences -- Cross-cultural studies. Costume -- Social aspects -- Cross-cultural studies.

GT525.F556 1998
Finkelstein, Joanne.
Fashion: an introduction/ Joanne Finkelstein. New York: New York University Press, 1998. 127 p.
97-038914   391 21   0814726836
Fashion -- Social aspects. Fashion -- Psychological aspects. Fashion -- Economic aspects.

GT525.O6 1994
On fashion/ edited by Shari Benstock and Suzanne Ferriss. New Brunswick, N.J.: Rutgers University Press, c1994. ix, 317 p.
93-013886   391   0813520320
Fashion -- Social aspects. Fashion -- Psychological aspects.

GT596 Costume. Dress. Fashion — By period — Modern

GT596.B56 1999
Blau, Herbert.
Nothing in itself: complexions of fashion/ Herbert Blau. Bloomington, Ind.: Indiana University Press, c1999. xiii, 302 p.
99-019964   391/.009/04 21   0253335876
Costume -- History -- 20th century. Fashion -- History -- 20th century. Costume -- Symbolic aspects.

GT596.D74 1991
Dress and popular culture/ edited by Patricia A. Cunningham and Susan Voso Lab. Bowling Green, Ohio: Bowling Green State University Popular Press, c1991. 165 p.
90-086155   391/.009/04   0879725079
Costume -- History -- 20th century. Popular culture.

GT596.L5713 1994
Lipovetsky, Gilles, 1944-
The empire of fashion: dressing modern democracy/ Gilles Lipovetsky; translated by Catherine Porter; with a foreword by Richard Sennett. Princeton, N.J.: Princeton University Press, c1994. x, 276 p.
94-004830   391/.009/04   0691033730
Costume -- History -- 20th century. Fashion -- History -- 20th century.

GT603-617 Costume. Dress. Fashion — By region or country — North America

GT603.D4 1990
De Marly, Diana.
Dress in North America/ Diana de Marly. New York: Holmes & Meier, [1990-] v. 1.
90-004905   391/.0097   0841911991
Costume -- United States -- History. Costume -- Canada -- History. United States -- Social conditions -- To 1865. Canada -- Social conditions -- To 1763.

GT610.F57 2001
Fischer, Gayle V.
Pantaloons and power: nineteenth-century dress reform in the United States/ Gayle V. Fischer. Kent, Ohio: Kent State University Press, c2001. x, 262 p.
00-010253   391/.2/097309034 21   0873386825
Costume -- United States -- History -- 19th century. Women's rights -- United States -- History.

GT610.S42 1995
Severa, Joan L., 1925-
Dressed for the photographer: ordinary Americans and fashion, 1840-1900/ Joan L. Severa. Kent, Ohio: Kent State University Press, c1995. xxii, 592 p.
95-001155   391/.00973/09034 20   0873385128
Costume -- United States -- History -- 19th century. Fashion -- United States -- History -- 19th century. Portrait photography -- united States -- History -- 19th century.

GT615.C68 1997
Countryman, Ruth S.
Women's wear of the 1920's, with complete patterns/ by Ruth S. Countryman and Elizabeth Weiss Hopper. Studio City, Calif.: Players Press, 1997. vi, 201 p.
97-041614   646.4/78   0887346545
Costume -- United States -- History -- 20th century. Dressmaking -- Patterns.

GT617.H3.K39 1993
Kawakami, Barbara F., 1921-
Japanese immigrant clothing in Hawaii, 1885-1941/ Barbara F. Kawakami. Honolulu: University of Hawaii Press, c1993. xvii, 253 p.
92-042593   391/.0089/9560969   0824813510
Costume -- Hawaii -- History. Japanese Americans -- Hawaii -- Costume.

GT720-871 Costume. Dress. Fashion — By region or country — Europe

GT720.B67 1996
Boscagli, Maurizia.
Eye on the flesh: fashions of masculinity in the early twentieth century/ Maurizia Boscagli. Boulder, Colo.: Westview Press, 1996. xii, 242 p.
95-046430   391/.1/0940909   0813327261
Men's clothing -- Europe -- History -- 20th century. Men's clothing -- Europe -- Psychological aspects. Costume -- Symbolic aspects -- Europe.

GT730.C86 1968
Cunnington, C. Willett 1878-1961.
A dictionary of English costume, by C. Willett Cunnington, Phillis Cunnington and Charles Beard. With colour frontispiece and 303 line illus. by Cecil Everitt and Phillis Cunnington. New York, Barnes & Noble [1968, c1960] vi, 281 p.
72-028853   391/.00942   0389041904
Costume -- Great Britain -- Dictionaries.

GT736.R53 1995
Ribeiro, Aileen, 1944-
The art of dress: fashion in England and France 1750 to 1820/ Aileen Ribeiro. New Haven: Yale University Press, c1995. 257 p.
94-035347   391/.00942/09033 20   0300062877
Costume -- England -- History -- 18th century. Costume -- France -- History -- 18th century. Costume in art.

GT871.P3913 1994
Perrot, Philippe.
Fashioning the bourgeoisie: a history of clothing in the nineteenth century/ by Philippe Perrot; translated by Richard Bienvenu. Princeton, N.J.: Princeton University Press, c1994. xiii, 273 p.
93-040094   391/.024/0944   0691033838
Middle class -- France -- Costume -- History -- 19th century. Costume -- France -- History -- 19th century.

GT1460-1560 Costume. Dress. Fashion — By region or country — Asia

GT1460.T37 1996
Tarlo, Emma.
Clothing matters: dress and identity in India/ Emma Tarlo. Chicago, IL: University of Chicago Press, c1996. xxi, 360 p.
95-031464   391/.00954 20   0226789756
Costume -- India -- History. Costume -- Symbolic aspects -- India. Costume -- India -- Psychological aspects. India -- Social life and customs.

GT1555.G36 1994
Garrett, Valery M., 1942-
Chinese clothing: an illustrated guide/ Valery M. Garrett. Hong Kong; Oxford University Press, 1994. xiv, 224 p.
93-042487   391/.00951   0195864263
Costume -- China -- History. Chinese -- Costume.

GT1560.D35 1993
Dalby, Liza Crihfield.
Kimono: fashioning culture/ Liza Crihfield Dalby. New Haven, Conn.: Yale University Press, c1993. xi, 384 p.
93-004079   391/.00952   0300056397
Kimonos. Costume -- Japan.

GT1580-1589 Costume. Dress. Fashion — By region or country — Africa

GT1580.C56 1996
Clothing and difference: embodied identities in colonial and post-colonial Africa/ edited by Hildi Hendrickson. Durham: Duke University Press, 1996. viii, 268 p.
95-053957   391/.00967   0822317915
Costume -- Africa, Sub-Saharan -- History -- 19th century. Costume -- Africa, Sub-Saharan -- History -- 20th century. Costume -- Africa, Sub-Saharan -- Psychological aspects.

GT1589.Z33
Hansen, Karen Tranberg.
Salaula: the world of secondhand clothing and Zambia/ Karen Tranberg Hansen. Chicago: University of Chicago Press, c2000. xv, 298 p.
99-462387   381/.45687 21   0226315800
Costume -- Zambia. Fashion -- Zambia. Used clothing industry -- Zambia. Zambia -- Social conditions. Zambia -- Economic conditions.

GT2112 Costume. Dress. Fashion — Materials and articles of clothing. Details and accessories — Headgear

GT2112.E5 1999
El Guindi, Fadwa.
Veil: modesty, privacy, and resistance/ Fadwa El Guindi. Oxford, UK; Berg, c1999. xx, 242 p.
00-687589   1859739245
Veils -- Social aspects. Islam -- Customs and practices. Muslim women -- Costume.

GT2130 Costume. Dress. Fashion — Materials and articles of clothing. Details and accessories — Footwear

GT2130.F55 2001
Footnotes: on shoes/ edited by Shari Benstock and Suzanne Ferriss. New Brunswick, N.J.: Rutgers University Press, c2001. ix, 325 p.
00-034204   391.4/13 21   0813528704
Shoes -- Social aspects.

GT2130.R48 2000
Rexford, Nancy E., 1947-
Women's shoes in America, 1795-1930/ written and illustrated by Nancy E. Rexford. Kent, Ohio: Kent State University Press, c2000. xvi, 393 p.
99-055197   391.4/13/0820973 21   0873386566
Shoes -- United States -- History. Shoes -- Collectors and collecting -- United States.

GT2290 Costume. Dress. Fashion — Materials and articles of clothing. Details and accessories — Hair. Hairdressing. Hairstyles

GT2290.T73 1994
Trasko, Mary.
Daring do's: a history of extraordinary hair/ Mary Trasko. Paris; Flammarion, c1994. 142 p.
96-115232   208013549X
Hairstyles -- History. Hairdressing -- History.

GT2420 Customs relating to private life — Family life. Home life

GT2420.W44 1999
When we say we're home: a quartet of place and memory/ W. Scott Olsen ... [et al.]; foreword by Judith Kitchen. Salt Lake City: University of Utah Press, c1999. 308 p.
98-054376   392.3/6 21   0874805910
Home. Family life. Dwellings.

GT2465 Customs relating to private life — Children — Birth customs, baptism, adoption rites, etc.

GT2465.C74.H85 1999
Hunt, Nancy Rose.
A colonial lexicon of birth ritual, medicalization, and mobility in the Congo/ Nancy Rose Hunt. Durham: Duke University Press, 1999. xix, 475 p.
99-026315   392.1/2/096751   0822323311
Birth customs -- Religious aspects. Childbirth -- Religious aspects -- Christianity. Birth customs -- Congo (Democratic Republic) Congo (Democratic Republic) -- Social life and customs.

GT2465.F8.G44 1991
Gelis, Jacques.
History of childbirth: fertility, pregnancy and birth in early modern Europe/ Jacques Gelis; translated by Rosemary Morris. Boston: Northeastern University Press, c1991. xvii, 326 p.
90-024132   392/.12/0944   1555531024
Birth customs -- France -- History. Childbirth -- France -- History. Pregnancy -- France -- History.

GT2465.I8.M87 1999
Musacchio, Jacqueline Marie, 1967-
The art and ritual of childbirth in Renaissance Italy/ Jacqueline Marie Musacchio. New Haven: Yale University Press, c1999. xiv, 212 p.
98-033417   392.1/2/0945 21   0300076290
Birth customs -- Italy -- History. Childbirth -- Italy -- History. Women -- History -- Middle Ages, 500-1500. Italy -- Social life and customs.

GT2713-2783.5 Customs relating to private life — Love. Courtship. Marriage. Sex customs — Marriage customs

GT2713.W37 1990
Ward, W. Peter.
Courtship, love, and marriage in nineteenth-century English Canada/ Peter Ward. Montreal; McGill-Queen's University Press, c1990. x, 219 p.
90-162447   392/.5/0971   0773507493
Courtship -- Canada -- History -- 19th century. Marriage customs and rites -- Canada -- History -- 19th century. Canada -- Social life and customs.

GT2762.A2.M37 1991
Martin Gaite, Carmen.
Love customs in eighteenth-century Spain/ Carmen Martin Gaite; translated by Maria G. Tomsich. Berkeley: University of California Press, c1991. xv, 204 p.
90-024575   391/.5/094609033   0520070437
Marriage customs and rites -- Spain -- History -- 18th century. Courtship -- Spain -- History -- 18th century. Friendship -- Spain -- History -- 18th century. Spain -- Social life and customs.

GT2772.A2.G66 1990
Goody, Jack.
The oriental, the ancient, and the primitive: systems of marriage and the family in the pre-industrial societies of Eurasia/ Jack Goody. Cambridge; Cambridge University Press, 1990. xix, 542 p.
89-007283   392/.5/095   0521365740
Marriage customs and rites -- Asia. Marriage customs and rites -- Europe. Asia -- Social life and customs. Europe -- Social life and customs.

GT2783.5.W65 1995
Wolf, Arthur P.
Sexual attraction and childhood association: a Chinese brief for Edward Westermarck/ Arthur P. Wolf. Stanford, Calif.: Stanford University Press, 1995. xxiii, 561 p.
95-018842   391/.4/0951   0804724261
Westermarck, Edward, -- 1862-1939 -- Philosophy. Sexual attraction -- China. Sex in marriage -- China. Incest -- China. China -- Social life and customs.

GT2850 Customs relating to private life — Eating and drinking customs — General works

GT2850.C68 1999
Counihan, Carole, 1948-
The anthropology of food and body: gender, meaning, and power/ Carole M. Counihan. New York: Routledge, 1999. viii, 256 p.
98-049970   394.1   0415921929
Food habits -- Cross-cultural studies. Food habits -- Italy. Food habits -- United States.

GT2853 Customs relating to private life — Eating and drinking customs — By region or country, A-Z

GT2853.U5.G39 1996
Gay, Kathlyn.
Encyclopedia of North American eating & drinking traditions, customs & rituals/ Kathlyn Gay, Martin K. Gay. Santa Barbara, Calif.: ABC-CLIO, c1996. xii, 289 p.
95-015219   394.1/2/097 20   0874367565
Food habits -- United States -- Encyclopedias. Drinking customs -- United States -- Encyclopedias. United States -- Social life and customs -- Encyclopedias.

GT2853.U5.L47 1993
Levenstein, Harvey A., 1938-
Paradox of plenty: a social history of eating in modern America/ Harvey Levenstein. New York: Oxford University Press, 1993. ix, 337 p.
91-048170   394.1/2/0973   0195055438
Food habits -- United States -- History -- 20th century. Diet -- United States -- History -- 20th century. United States -- Social life and customs.

GT2853.U5.M39 1995
McIntosh, Elaine N.
American food habits in historical perspective/ Elaine N. McIntosh. Westport, Conn.: Praeger, 1995. xii, 251 p.
95-007550   394.1/2/0973   0275946010
Food habits -- United States -- History. Diet -- United States -- History. Nutrition -- United States -- History. United States -- Social life and customs.

GT2855-2884 Customs relating to private life — Eating and drinking customs — Foods and beverages

GT2855.M35 1996
McIntosh, Wm. Alex
Sociologies of food and nutrition/ Wm. Alex McIntosh. New York: Plenum Press, c1996. xi, 314 p.
96-031303   394.1 20   0306453355
Food habits -- Social aspects. Nutrition -- Social aspects.

GT2884.H4 2000
Heath, Dwight B.
Drinking occasions: comparative perspectives on alcohol and culture/ Dwight B. Heath. Philadelphia: Brunner/Mazel, c2000. xv, 240 p.
99-059618   394.1/3 21   1583910476
Drinking customs -- Cross-cultural studies. Drinking of alcoholic beverages -- Cross-cultural studies.

GT2956 Customs relating to private life — Eating and drinking customs — Picnics

GT2956.U6N48 1992
Neustadt, Kathy,
Clambake: a history and celebration of an American tradition/ Kathy Neustadt. Amherst: University of Massachusetts Press, c1992. x, 227 p.
91-045599   394/.3   0870237993
Clambakes -- United States -- History. Clambakes -- Massachusetts -- Allen's Neck -- History. Festivals -- United States.

GT3041 Customs relating to private life — Exchange of gifts. Gift wrapping — By region or country, A-Z

GT3041.F8
Davis, Natalie Zemon, 1928-
The gift in sixteenth-century France/ Natalie Zemon Davis. Madison: University of Wisconsin Press, c2000. x, 185 p.
00-008913   394 21   0299168808
Gifts -- France -- History -- 16th century. Ceremonial exchange -- France -- History -- 16th century. Renaissance -- France. France -- History -- 16th century. France -- Social life and customs -- 16th century.

GT3150 Customs relating to private life — Burial and funeral customs. Treatment of the dead — General works

GT3150.T25 2000
Taylor, Richard P.
Death and the afterlife: a cultural encyclopedia/ Richard P. Taylor. Santa Barbara, Calif.: ABC-CLIO, c2000. x, 438 p.
00-010926   393/.03 21   0874369398
Funeral rites and ceremonies -- Encyclopedias. Death -- Social aspects -- Encyclopedias. Future life -- Encyclopedias.

GT3203-3256.2 Customs relating to private life — Burial and funeral customs. Treatment of the dead — By region or country, A-Z

GT3203.A2.S56 1991
Sloane, David Charles.
The last great necessity: cemeteries in American history/ David Charles Sloane. Baltimore: Johns Hopkins University Press, c1991. xxiii, 293 p.
90-041906   393/.1/0973   0801840686
Funeral rites and ceremonies -- United States. Cemeteries -- Landscape architecture -- United States. United States -- Social life and customs.

GT3210.N8.L57 1998
Little, M. Ruth 1946-
Sticks & stones: three centuries of North Carolina gravemarkers/ M. Ruth Little; photography by Tim Buchman. Chapel Hill: University of North Carolina Press, c1998. xvi, 328 p.
97-032589   736/.5/09756 21   0807824178
Sepulchral monuments -- North Carolina. Epitaphs -- North Carolina. North Carolina -- Social life and customs.

GT3242.P39 1990
Paxton, Frederick S., 1951-
Christianizing death: the creation of a ritual process in early medieval Europe/ Frederick S. Paxton. Ithaca: Cornell University Press, 1990. xiv, 229 p.
90-034072   265/.85/09409021   0801424925
Funeral rites and ceremonies -- Europe -- History. Death -- Religious aspects -- Christianity. Europe -- Religious life and customs.

GT3243.A2.D38 1992
Death in towns: urban responses to the dying and the dead, 100-1600/ edited by Steven Bassett. Leicester; Leicester University Press; 1992. vi, 258 p.
92-042629   393/.0942   0718514181
Funeral rites and ceremonies -- England -- History -- 16th century. Funeral rites and ceremonies -- England -- History -- To 1500. Funeral rites and ceremonies -- Europe -- History. England -- Social life and customs -- To 1066. England -- Social life and customs -- 1066-1485.

GT3243.A2.J35 1996
Jalland, Patricia.
Death in the Victorian family/ Pat Jalland. Oxford; Oxford University Press, 1996. xii, 464 p.
96-002389   306.9/0941/09034   0198201885
Funeral rites and ceremonies -- Great Britain -- History -- 19th century. Funeral rites and ceremonies -- Great Britain -- History -- 20th century. Death -- Social aspects -- Great Britain. Great Britain -- Social life and customs -- 19th century. Great Britain -- Social life and customs -- 20th century.

GT3244.A2.H68 1998
Houlbrooke, Ralph A. 1944-
Death, religion, and the family in England, 1480-1750/ Ralph Houlbrooke. Oxford: Clarendon Press; 1998. xiii, 435 p.
98-003013   393/.0942   0198217617
Funeral rites and ceremonies -- England. Death - Social aspects -- England. Funeral sermons -- England -- History. England -- History -- Sources. England -- Religious life and customs. England -- Social life and customs.

GT3249.A2.K74 1993
Kselman, Thomas A. 1948-
Death and the afterlife in modern France/ Thomas A. Kselman. Princeton, N.J.: Princeton University Press, c1993. xvii, 413 p.
92-014559   393/.9/094409034   0691008892
Funeral rites and ceremonies -- France -- History -- 19th century. Death -- Religious aspects -- Catholic Church. France -- Religious life and customs. France -- Social life and customs. France -- History -- 19th century.

GT3251.A3.M367 1991
Seremetakis, C. Nadia
The last word: women, death, and divination in inner Mani/ C. Nadia Seremetakis. Chicago: University of Chicago Press, c1991. ix, 275 p.
90-040640 393/.9 0226748758
Funeral rites and ceremonies -- Greece -- Mani. Women -- Greece -- Mani -- Social conditions. Social structure -- Greece -- Mani. Mani (Greece) -- Religious life and customs.

GT3252.F56.S76 1992
Strocchia, Sharon T., 1951-
Death and ritual in Renaissance Florence/ Sharon T. Strocchia. Baltimore: Johns Hopkins University Press, c1992. xix, 308 p.
92-000068 393/.0945/5109024 0801843642
Funeral rites and ceremonies -- Italy -- Florence -- History. Renaissance -- Italy -- Florence. Florence (Italy) -- Politics and government. Florence (Italy) -- Social life and customs.

GT3256.2.A2
Merridale, Catherine, 1959-
Night of stone: death and memory in twentieth century Russia/ Catherine Merridale. New York: Viking, 2001. 402 p.
00-043357 393/.0947 0670894745
Funeral rites and ceremonies -- Russia (Federation) -- History -- 20th century. Death -- Social aspects -- Russia (Federation) -- History -- 20th century. Death -- Russia (Federation) -- Psychological aspects -- History -- 20th century. Russia (Federation) -- Religious life and customs -- History -- 20th century.

GT3330 Customs relating to private life — Burial and funeral customs. Treatment of the dead — Incineration. Cremation

GT3330.P76 2001
Prothero, Stephen R.
Purified by fire: a history of cremation in America/ Stephen Prothero. Berkeley: University of California Press, c2001. xiv, 266 p.
00-059005 393/.2 21 0520208161
Cremation -- United States -- History. Cremation -- United States -- Public opinion. Funeral rites and ceremonies -- United States -- History. United States -- Social life and customs.

GT3390 Customs relating to private life — Burial and funeral customs. Treatment of the dead — Mourning customs

GT3390.H65 2000
Holst-Warhaft, Gail, 1941-
The cue for passion: grief and its political uses/ Gail Holst-Warhaft. Cambridge, Mass.: Harvard University Press, 2000. 228 p.
00-021841 393/.9 0674002245
Mourning customs -- Political aspects. Grief -- Political aspects.

GT3415 Customs relating to private life — Entertaining. Hospitality — By region or country

GT3415.J3.A45 1994
Allison, Anne, 1950-
Nightwork: sexuality, pleasure, and corporate masculinity in a Tokyo hostess club/ Anne Allison. Chicago: University of Chicago Press, 1994. xiii, 213 p.
93-034877 394.1/2/0952135 0226014851
Bars (Drinking establishments) -- Japan -- Toyko. Entertaining -- Japan -- Tokyo. Male friendship -- Japan -- Tokyo. Tokyo (Japan) -- Social life and customs.

GT3520 Customs relative to public and social life — Court and castle life — By period

GT3520.S34 1991
Scaglione, Aldo D.
Knights at court: courtliness, chivalry & courtesy from Ottonian Germany to the Italian Renaissance/ Aldo Scaglione. Berkeley: University of California Press, c1991. xi, 489 p.
91-006703 940.1 0520072707
Courts and courtiers. Civilization, Medieval. Courts and courtiers in literature.

GT3670 Customs relative to public and social life — Court and castle life — Court fools. Jesters

GT3670.B45 1984
Billington, Sandra.
A social history of the fool/ Sandra Billington. Brighton, Sussex: Harvester Press; 1984. x, 150 p.
83-040624 306/.48 0312732937
Fools and jesters -- England -- History. Fools and jesters in literature.

GT3670.O77 2001
Otto, Beatrice K.
Fools are everywhere: the court jester around the world/ Beatrice K. Otto. Chicago: University of Chicago Press, c2001. xxiii, 420 p.
00-044706 792.7/028 21 0226640914
Fools and jesters -- History. Fools and jesters -- Cross-cultural studies.

GT3913 Customs relative to public and social life — Graffiti — By region or country

GT3913.C62.D473 1993
Ferrell, Jeff.
Crimes of style: urban graffiti and the politics of criminality/ Jeff Ferrell; photographs by Eugene Stewart-Huidobro. New York: Garland, 1993. xv, 236 p.
92-034668 302.2/22 0815308108
Graffiti -- Colorado -- Denver. Graffiti -- Social aspects -- Colorado -- Denver. Architecture -- Mutilation, defacement, etc. -- Colorado -- Denver.

GT3925 Customs relative to public and social life — Festivals. Holidays — Dictionaries. Encyclopedias

GT3925.H65 1995
Holidays and festivals index: a descriptive guide to information on more than 3,000 holidays .../ edited by Helene Henderson and Barry Puckett. Detroit: Omnigraphics, c1995. cv, 782 p.
94-039351 394.2/6 20 0780800125
Holidays -- Indexes. Festivals -- Indexes. Special days -- Indexes.

GT3930 Customs relative to public and social life — Festivals. Holidays — General works

GT3930.F4 2001
Feasts: archaeological and ethnographic perspectives on food, politics, and power/ edited by Michael Dietler and Brian Hayden. Washington, D.C.: Smithsonian Institution Press, c2001. xi, 432 p.
00-061932 394.26 21 1560988614
Festivals -- Congresses. Fasts and feasts -- Congresses.

GT3930.G74 1983
Gregory, Ruth W. 1910-
Anniversaries and holidays/ by Ruth W. Gregory. Chicago: American Library Association, c1983. xiii, 262 p.
83-003784 394.2/6 0838903894
Holidays. Anniversaries. Fasts and feasts.

GT4211-4262 Customs relative to public and social life — Festivals. Holidays — Public rejoicing. Spectacles. Fetes

GT4211.N4.M57 1995
Mitchell, Reid.
All on a Mardi Gras day: episodes in the history of New Orleans Carnival/ Reid Mitchell. Cambridge, Mass: Harvard University Press, 1995. 243 p.
94-028098 394.2/5 067401622X
Carnival -- Louisiana -- New Orleans -- History. New Orleans (La.) -- History.

GT4211.N4.R63 1996
Roach, Joseph R., 1941-
Cities of the dead: circum-Atlantic performance/ Joseph Roach. New York: Columbia University Press, c1996. xvi, 328 p.
95-033447 791 20 023110460X
Carnival -- Louisiana -- New Orleans -- History. Folklore -- Louisiana -- New Orleans -- Performance. Theater and society -- Louisiana -- New Orleans -- History. New Orleans (La.) -- History. London (England) -- History.

GT4229.T7.C69 1996
Cowley, John.
Carnival, Canboulay, and calypso: traditions in the making/ John Cowley. Cambridge [England]; Cambridge University Press, 1996. xv, 293 p.
96-140867 394.2/5/0972983 0521481384
Carnival -- Trinidad and Tobago -- History. Music -- Trinidad and Tobago -- History and criticism. Trinidad and Tobago -- Social life and customs.

GT4233.A2.M38 1991
Matta, Roberto da.
Carnivals, rogues, and heroes: an interpretation of the Brazilian dilemma/ by Roberto DaMatta; translated by John Drury. Notre Dame, Ind.: University of Notre Dame Press, c1991. xii, 279 p.
90-070861   394.2/5/0981   0268007802
Carnival -- Brazil. National characteristics, Brazilian. Brazil -- Social life and customs.

GT4262.A55.G55 1998
Gilmore, David D., 1943-
Carnival and culture: sex, symbol, and status in Spain/ David D. Gilmore. New Haven: Yale University Press, c1998. xi, 244 p.
98-016185   394.25/0946 21   0300074808
Carnival -- Spain -- Andalusia. Sex role -- Spain -- Andalusia. Andalusia (Spain) -- Social life and customs.

GT4803-4856 Customs relative to public and social life — Festivals. Holidays — By region or country

GT4803.D6
Christianson, Stephen G.
The American book of days. New York: H.W. Wilson, 2000. xxvi, 945 p.
99-086611   394.26973   0824209540
Holidays -- United States. Fasts and feasts -- United States. Festivals -- United States.

GT4856.A2
Petrone, Karen.
Life has become more joyous, comrades: celebrations in the time of Stalin/ Karen Petrone. Bloomington, Ind.: Indiana University Press, c2000. x, 266 p.
00-023201   394.26947 21   0253337682
Holidays -- Soviet Union -- History. Festivals -- Soviet Union -- History. Popular culture -- Soviet Union -- History. Soviet Union -- Social life and customs -- 1917-1970.

GT4985-4986 Customs relative to public and social life — Festivals. Holidays — Special days and periods of time

GT4985.E45 1999
Encyclopedia of Christmas: nearly 200 alphabetically arranged entries covering all aspects of Christmas, including folk customs, religious observances, history, legends, symbols, and related days f edited by Tanya Gulevich. Detroit: Omnigraphics, c1999. xvii, 729 p.
99-052285   394.2663/03 21   0780803876
Christmas -- Encyclopedias.

GT4986.A1.P54 2000
Pleck, Elizabeth Hafkin.
Celebrating the family: ethnicity, consumer culture, and family rituals/ Elizabeth H. Pleck. Cambridge, Mass.: Harvard University Press, 2000. ix, 328 p.
99-045200   394.26973   067400230X
Holidays -- Economic aspects -- United States. Special events -- Economic aspects -- United States. Family -- United States. United States -- Economic conditions. United States -- Social life and customs.

GT4986.A1.R47 1995
Restad, Penne L.
Christmas in America: a history/ Penne L. Restad. New York: Oxford University Press, 1995. x, 219 p.
94-042357   394.2/663/09   0195093003
Christmas -- United States -- History. United States -- Social life and customs.

GT4986.A1.S35 1995
Schmidt, Leigh Eric.
Consumer rites: the buying & selling of American holidays/ Leigh Eric Schmidt. Princeton, N.J.: Princeton University Press, c1995. xvi, 363 p.
95-010604   394.2/6973 20   0691029806
Holidays -- Economic aspects -- United States. United States -- Religious life and customs. United States -- Economic conditions.

GT4986.A1.W35 1993
Waits, William Burnell.
The modern Christmas in America: a cultural history of gift giving/ William B. Waits. New York: New York University Press, c1993. xxii, 267 p.
92-028974   394.2/68282/0973   0814792510
Christmas -- United States -- History. Gifts -- United States -- History. United States -- Social life and customs.

GT5280 Customs relative to transportation and travel — Vehicles. Chariots. Cars — General works

GT5280.P54 1992
Piggott, Stuart.
Wagon, chariot, and carriage: symbol and status in the history of transport/ Stuart Piggott. [London]: Thames and Hudson, c1992. 184 p.
93-135511   388.3/41/09   0500251142
Wagons -- History. Horses -- History. Chariots -- History.

GV Recreation. Leisure

GV11 Dictionaries. Encyclopedias

GV11.S57 1990
Smith, Stephen L. J., 1946-
Dictionary of concepts in recreation and leisure studies/ Stephen L.J. Smith. New York: Greenwood Press, 1990. x, 372 p.
89-078447   790/.03   0313252629
Recreation -- Dictionaries. Leisure -- Dictionaries.

GV14 Philosophy. Relation to other topics — General works

GV14.B46 1991
Benefits of leisure/ edited by B.L. Driver, Perry J. Brown, George L. Peterson. State College, Pa.: Venture Pub., c1991. ix, 483 p.
91-067118   790/.01/35   0910251487
Leisure -- Philosophy. Leisure -- Physiological aspects. Leisure -- Psychological aspects.

GV14.C47
Cheek, Neil H.
The social organization of leisure in human society/ Neil H. Cheek, Jr., William R. Burch, Jr. New York: Harper & Row, c1976. xx, 283 p.
76-020582   301.5/7   006041037X
Leisure. Recreation.

GV14.L394 2002
Leisure and life satisfaction: foundational perspectives/ Christopher R. Edginton ... [et al.]. 3rd ed. New York: McGraw-Hill, c2002. xvi, 474 p.
2001-034513   790/.01/35097 21   007235397X
Leisure -- United States. Leisure -- Canada. Leisure industry -- United States.

GV14.P47 1989
The Philosophy of leisure/ edited by Tom Winnifrith and Cyril Barrett. New York: St. Martin's Press, 1989. ix, 174 p.
88-019756   790/.01/32   0312024029
Leisure.

GV14.45 Philosophy. Relation to other topics — Relation to sociology

GV14.45.C76 1990
Cross, Gary S.
A social history of leisure since 1600/ Gary Cross. State College, PA: Venture Pub., c1990. 297 p.
90-070208   306.4812   0910251355
Leisure -- Social aspects -- History. Leisure -- Social aspects -- United States -- History. Leisure - - Social aspects -- Great Britain -- History.

GV14.45.K447 2000
Kelly, John R.
21st century leisure: current issues/ John R. Kelly, Valeria J. Freysinger. Boston: Allyn & Bacon, c2000. xi, 298 p.
99-036609   306.4/812/0973 21   0205273602
Leisure -- Social aspects -- United States. Debates and debating -- Study and teaching -- United States.

GV14.45.L44 1989
Leisure and life-style: a comparative analysis of free time/ edited by Anna Olszewska and K. Roberts. London; Sage Publications, 1989. 200 p.
89-062875   306.4/812 20
Leisure -- Social aspects -- Cross-cultural studies. Leisure -- Economic aspects -- Cross-cultural studies. Hours of labor -- Cross-cultural studies.

GV14.5 Study and teaching. Research

GV14.5.C55
Clarke, David H.
Research processes in physical education, recreation, and health [by] David H. Clarke and H. Harrison Clarke. Englewood Cliffs, N.J., Prentice-Hall [1970] x, 470 p.
76-095759   613.7/072   0137744633
Physical education and training -- Research. Recreation -- Research.

GV14.5.S79 1994
Stokowski, Patricia A.
Leisure in society: a network structural perspective/ Patricia A. Stokowski. London; Mansell Pub., 1994. xi, 141 p.
93-010901   790/.01/35   0720121418
Leisure -- Research. Leisure -- Social aspects. Social networks.

GV15 History — General works

GV15.S533 1997
Shivers, Jay Sanford, 1930-
The story of leisure: context, concepts, and current controversy/ Jay S. Shivers, Lee J. deLisle. Champaign, IL: Human Kinetics, c1997. v, 217 p.
96-048339   790 21   0873229967
Leisure -- History. Leisure -- Sociological aspects. Leisure -- Political aspects.

GV17 History — Ancient. Classical games, etc. — General works

GV17.C73 2002
Craig, Steve,
Sports and games of the ancients/ Steve Craig. Westport, Conn.: Greenwood Press, 2002. xii, 271 p.
2001-050101   796/.093 21   0313316007
Sports -- History -- To 1500. Games -- History -- To 1500. History, Ancient.

GV17.M38 1991
Matz, David.
Greek and Roman sport: a dictionary of athletes and events from the eighth century B.C. to the third century A.D./ by David Matz. Jefferson, N.C.: McFarland, c1991. v, 169 p.
90-053509   796/.03   0899505589
Sports -- Greece -- Dictionaries. Sports -- Rome -- Dictionaries. Athletes -- Greece -- Biography -- Dictionaries.

GV17.P65 1987
Poliakoff, Michael.
Combat sports in the ancient world: competition, violence, and culture/ Michael B. Poliakoff. New Haven: Yale University Press, c1987. xviii, 202 p.
86-032419   796.8/15   0300037686
Games -- Greece. Games -- Rome. Hand-to-hand fighting -- History.

GV21-23 History — Ancient. Classical games, etc. — Greek

GV21.K95 1993
Kyle, Donald G.
Athletics in ancient Athens/ by Donald G. Kyle. 2nd rev. ed. Leiden: E.J. Brill, 1993. xiv, 240 p.
92-042730   796/.0938/5 20   9004097597
Athletics -- Greece -- Athens -- History. Games -- Greece -- Athens -- History.

GV21.S94 1987
Sweet, Waldo E.
Sport and recreation in ancient Greece: a sourcebook with translations/ Waldo E. Sweet; foreword by Erich Segal. New York: Oxford University Press, 1987. xiv, 281 p.
86-018209   796/.0938   0195041267
Games -- Greece -- History -- Sources. Sports -- Greece -- History -- Sources. Recreation -- Greece -- History -- Sources.

GV23.K5 1977
Kieran, John, 1892-
The story of the Olympic games: 776 B.C. to 1976/ by John Kieran, Arthur Daley, and Pat Jordan. Philadelphia: Lippincott, 1977. 575 p.
76-056106   796.4/8/09   0397011687
Olympics.

GV23.S56 2000
Sinn, Ulrich.
Olympia: cult, sport, and ancient festival/ by Ulrich Sinn; translated from German by Thomas Thornton. Princeton: M. Wiener, 2000.
00-028275   306.4/83/0938   1558762396
Olympic games (Ancient) -- History. Archeology -- Greece.

GV31-35 History — Ancient. Classical games, etc. — Roman

GV31.G53 2000
Gladiators and caesars: the power of spectacle in ancient Rome/ edited by Eckart Köhne and Cornelia Ewigleben. Berkeley: University of California Press, 2000.
00-059004   796/.0937 21   0520227980
Games -- Rome. Gladiators.

GV35.F88 1997
Futrell, Alison, 1962-
Blood in the arena: the spectacle of Roman power/ Alison Futrell. Austin: University of Texas Press, 1997. xii, 338 p.
97-004693   796/.0937   0292725043
Gladiators -- Rome. Games -- Social aspects -- Rome. Amphitheaters -- Rome. Rome -- Civilization.

GV53-75 History — Modern — By region or country

GV53.S47 1986
Shelby, Byron Bruce, 1948-
Carrying capacity in recreation settings/ Bo Shelby and Thomas A. Heberlein. Carvallis, Or.: Oregon State University Press, c1986. viii, 164 p.
86-008428   790/.06/9   0870713477
Recreation areas -- Public use -- United States. Recreation areas -- United States -- Management. Recreational surveys -- United States.

GV75.B33 1978
Bailey, Peter, 1937-
Leisure and class in Victorian England: rational recreation and the contest for control, 1830-1885/ Peter Bailey. London: Routledge & K. Paul; 1978. x, 260 p.
78-040390   301.5/7/0941   0802022588
Recreation -- England -- History -- 19th century. Working class -- Recreation -- History -- 19th century. Middle class -- England -- Recreation -- History -- 19th century. England -- Social life and customs -- 19th century.

GV75.V398 1987
Veal, Anthony James.
Leisure and the future/ A.J. Veal. London; Allen & Unwin, 1987. 201 p.
86-022191   790/.0941   0047900067
Leisure -- Great Britain. Social prediction -- Great Britain.

GV171 General works, treatises, and textbooks — American, through 1975

GV171.M43 1969
Meyer, Harold Diedrich, 1892-
Community recreation; a guide to its organization [by] Harold D. Meyer, Charles K. Brightbill [and] H. Douglas Sessoms. Englewood Cliffs, N.J., Prentice-Hall [1969] viii, 456 p.
74-076297   790   0131531557
Recreation leadership.

GV171.M55
Miller, Norman P.
The leisure age: its challenge to recreation [by] Norman P. Miller [and] Duane M. Robinson. Belmont, Calif., Wadsworth Pub. Co. [1963] xiii, 497 p.
63-008485   790.13
Recreation. Leisure.

GV174 General works, treatises, and textbooks — American and English, 1976-

GV174.R94 1991
Rybczynski, Witold.
Waiting for the weekend/ Witold Rybczynski. New York, N.Y., U.S.A.: Viking, 1991. ix, 260 p.
90-050760   790.01/35   0670830011
Leisure. Recreation.

GV181.3 General special (Special aspects of the subject as a whole)

GV181.3.G73 2000
Gratton, Chris,
Economics of sport and recreation/ Chris Gratton and Peter Taylor. London; E & FN Spon, 2000. 234 p.
99-041898   338.4/7796 21   0419189602
Leisure -- Economic aspects. Recreation -- Economic aspects. Sports -- Economic aspects.

GV181.3.S55 1986
Shivers, Jay Sanford, 1930-
Recreational safety: the standard of care/ Jay S. Shivers. Rutherford [N.J.]: Fairleigh Dickinson University Press; c1986. 324 p.
85-047630   790/.028/9   0838632416
Recreation -- Safety measures. Sports -- Safety measures. Recreation -- Management.

GV181.4 Recreation leadership — General works

GV181.4.N53 1983
Niepoth, E. William, 1928-
Leisure leadership: working with people in recreation and park settings/ E. William Niepoth. Englewood Cliffs, N.J.: Prentice-Hall, c1983. xv, 380 p.
82-018118   790/.023   0135300711
Recreation leadership.

GV181.4.R87 2001
Russell, Ruth V.,
Leadership in recreation/ Ruth V. Russell. 2nd ed. Boston: McGraw-Hill, c2001. xiv, 370 p.
00-022121   790/.06/94 21   0070123306
Recreation leadership.

GV181.4.S54
Shivers, Jay Sanford, 1930-
Recreational leadership: group dynamics and interpersonal behavior/ Jay S. Shivers. Princeton, N.J.: Princeton Book Co., c1980. ix, 268 p.
79-092381   790/.023   0916622177
Recreation leadership.

GV181.5 Recreation leadership — Administration of recreation services. Community recreation — General works

GV181.5.R43 1983
Recreation planning and management/ edited by Stanley R. Lieber and Daniel R. Fesenmaier. State College, Pa.: Venture Pub., c1983. viii, 396 p.
82-050955   333.78/0973   0910251037
Recreation -- Management. Leisure -- Planning. Outdoor recreation.

GV181.55 Recreation leadership — Administration of recreation services. Community recreation — Evaluation of services

GV181.55.H45 2002
Henderson, Karla A.
Evaluating leisure services: making enlightened decisions/ by Karla A. Henderson and M. Deborah Bialeschki. 2nd ed. State College, Pa.: Venture Pub., c2002. xxiii, 393 p.
2001-095417   790/.07 21   1892132265
Leisure -- Evaluation. Leisure -- Research. Leisure -- Management -- Evaluation.

GV182 Recreational areas and facilities. Recreation centers — General works

GV182.H56
Hjelte, George.
Public administration of park and recreational services [by] George Hjelte & Jay S. Shivers. New York, Macmillan [1963] 357 p.
63-008968   790
Recreation areas.

GV182.15 Recreational areas and facilities. Recreation centers — Financial and business aspects

GV182.15.B36
Bannon, Joseph J.
Leisure resources, its comprehensive planning/ Joseph J. Bannon. Englewood Cliffs, N.J.: Prentice-Hall, c1976. xxii, 454 p.
75-030512   711/.4   013528208X
Recreation -- Management. City planning.

GV183 Recreation for special classes of persons — Girls and women

GV183.B57 1996
Both gains and gaps: feminist perspectives on women's leisure/ Karla A. Henderson ... [et al.]. State College, PA: Venture Pub., c1996. xv, 337 p.
95-061907   790.1/94 20   0910251797
Women -- Recreation -- Social aspects. Leisure -- Psychological aspects. Feminism.

GV183.W43 1998
Wearing, Betsy.
Leisure and feminist theory/ Betsy Wearing. London; SAGE, 1998. xvi, 207 p.
98-061180   0803975376
Women -- Recreation -- Social aspects. Leisure. Feminist theory.

GV183.5 Recreation for special classes of persons — Handicapped — General works

GV183.5.D37 2002
Dattilo, John.
Inclusive leisure services: responding to the rights of people with disabilities/ John. Dattilo. 2nd ed. State College, PA: Venture Pub., c2002. xiii, 471 p.
2001-097303   790.1/96 21   1892132273
People with disabilities -- Recreation. Recreation -- Management.

GV183.6 Recreation for special classes of persons — Handicapped — Handicapped children

GV183.6.F56 2000
Fink, Dale Borman, 1949-
Making a place for kids with disabilities/ Dale Borman Fink. Westport, Conn.: Praeger, 2000. xviii, 204 p.
99-037526   790.1/96   0275965651
Handicapped children -- Recreation -- United States. Handicapped youth -- Recreation -- United States. Sports for the handicapped -- United States.

GV188.3 Recreation for special classes of persons — Leisure industry — By region or country, A-Z

GV188.3.U6.F67 1990
For fun and profit: the transformation of leisure into consumption/ edited by Richard Butsch. Philadelphia: Temple University Press, 1990. viii, 239 p.
89-027699   338.4/77900135/0973   0877226768
Leisure industry -- United States -- History. Leisure -- Economic aspects -- United States. Popular culture -- Economic aspects -- United States.

GV191.4 Outdoor life. Outdoor recreation — By region or country — United States

GV191.4.J46 1985
Jensen, Clayne R.
Outdoor recreation in America/ Clayne R. Jensen. Minneapolis, Minn.: Burgess Pub. Co., c1985. vi, 412 p.
84-007709   790/.0973   0808710826
Outdoor recreation -- United States. Outdoor recreation -- United States -- Management. Outdoor recreation -- Government policy -- United States.

GV191.4.O868 1990
Outdoor recreation policy: pleasure and preservation/ edited by John D. Hutcheson, Jr., Francis P. Noe, and Robert E. Snow; foreword by James Carroll. New York: Greenwood Press, 1990. xx, 289 p.
90-036580   790/.0973   031327522X
Outdoor recreation -- Government policy -- United States.

GV191.4.T73 2001
Trails for the twenty-first century: planning, design, and management manual for multi-use trails/ Charles A. Flink, Kristine, Olka, Robert M. Searns; Rails-to-Trails Conservancy. Washington, DC: Island Press, c2001. xviii, 212 p.
00-012958   796.5/0973 21   1559638184
Trails -- United States -- Planning. Trails -- United States -- Design.

GV191.4.W45 1997
Wellner, Alison Stein.
Americans at play: demographics of outdoor recreation & travel/ [by Alison S. Wellner]. Ithaca, N.Y.: New Strategist Publications, c1997. xiii, 367 p.
98-157389   188507011X
Outdoor recreation -- United States -- Statistics. Sports -- United States -- Statistics. Americans -- Travel -- Statistics.

GV191.4.Z56 1995
Zinser, Charles I.
Outdoor recreation: United States national parks, forests, and public lands/ Charles I. Zinser; mapping by Janice Millea. New York: J. Wiley, c1995. xx, 898 p.
94-038100   350.858 20   0471053732
Outdoor recreation -- United States -- Management. Public lands -- United States -- Recreational use -- Management. Natural resources -- United States -- Management.

GV191.6 Outdoor life. Outdoor recreation — General works

GV191.6.E85 1989
Ewert, Alan W., 1949-
Outdoor adventure pursuits: foundations, models, and theories/ Alan W. Ewert. Columbus, Ohio: Pub. Horizons, c1989. xvii, 234 p.
88-023651   370.11/07/11   0942280504
Outdoor recreation. Outward bound schools.

GV191.6.M314 1999
Manning, Robert E.,
Studies in outdoor recreation: search and research for satisfaction/ by Robert E. Manning. 2nd ed. Corvallis: Oregon State University Press, c1999. vii, 374 p.
00-266928   306.4/83 21   0870714635
Outdoor recreation -- Research -- Evaluation.

GV191.67 Outdoor life. Outdoor recreation — Outdoor recreation resources — Special types, A-Z

GV191.67.W5.B76 1979
Brockman, C. Frank 1902-
Recreational use of wild lands/ C. Frank Brockman, Lawrence C. Merriam, Jr., with two specially prepared chapters by William R. Catton, Jr., Barney Dowdle. New York: McGraw-Hill, c1979. xiv, 337 p.
78-015712   333.7/8   007007982X
Wilderness areas -- Recreational use. Recreation areas -- Management. Recreation leadership.

GV199.42 Hiking. Pedestrian tours — By region or country

GV199.42.A42.F676 1996
Potterfield, Peter.
In the zone: epic survival stories from the mountaineering world/ Peter Potterfield. Seattle, WA: Mountaineers, c1996. 270 p.
96-025476   796.5/22 20   0898864828
Mountaineering accidents -- Alaska -- Foraker, Mount. Mountaineering accidents -- Pakistan -- K2 (Mountain) Mountaineering accidents -- Washington (State) -- Chimney Rock (Kittitas County)

GV199.42.W22R345 1979
Molenaar, Dee.
The challenge of Rainier: a record of the explorations and ascents, triumphs and tragedies, on the Northwest's greatest mountain/ Dee Molenaar. 3d ed. Seattle: Mountaineers, 1979. xix, 364 p.
79-014923   917.97/78   0916890708
Mountaineering -- Washington (State) -- Rainier, Mount -- History.

GV199.44 Outdoor life. Outdoor recreation — Hiking. Pedestrian tours — By region or country

GV199.44.E85.B69 1997
Boukreev, Anatoli.
The climb: tragic ambitions on Everest/ Anatoli Boukreev and G. Weston DeWalt. New York: St. Martin's Press, 1997. xi, 255 p.
97-023194   796.52/2/095494   0312168144
Boukreev, Anatoli. Mountaineering accidents -- Everest, Mount (China and Nepal) Mountaineering -- Search and rescue operations -- Everest, Mount (China and Nepal)

GV199.44.E85.K725 1997
Krakauer, Jon.
Into thin air: a personal account of the Mount Everest disaster/ Jon Krakauer. New York: Villard, c1997. xx, 293 p.
96-030031   796.52/2/092 21   0679457526
Krakauer, Jon. Mountaineering expeditions -- Everest, Mount (China and Nepal) Mountaineering accidents -- Everest, Mount (China and Nepal)

GV199.44.E85.M66 2000
Morris, James, 1926-
Coronation Everest/ Jan Morris. Short Hills, NJ: Burford Books, [2000]. viii, 150 p.
99-059691   796.52/2/092   1580800475
Hillary, Edmund, -- Sir. Mountaineers -- New Zealand -- Biography. Reporters and reporting.

GV199.44.E85.O78 1999
Ortner, Sherry B., 1941-
Life and death on Mt. Everest: Sherpas and Himalayan mountaineering/ Sherry B. Ortner. Princeton, N.J.: Princeton University Press, c1999. xii, 376 p.
99-031247   796.52/2/095496 21   069100689X
Mountaineering -- Everest, Mount (China and Nepal) -- History. Sherpa (Nepalese people)

GV199.44.H55.F36 1996
Fanshawe, Andy.
Himalaya alpine-style: the most challenging routes on the highest peaks/ Andy Fanshawe & Stephen Venables. Seattle, WA: The Mountaineers, 1996. 192 p.
95-080516   796.5/22/095496   0898864569
Mountaineering -- Himalaya Mountains. Mountaineering expeditions -- Himalaya Mountains. Himalaya Mountains -- Description and travel.

GV199.44.N67 J66 1997
Jones, Chris,
Climbing in North America/ Chris Jones. Seattle, WA: Mountaineers, c1997. 365 p.
96-049400   796.52/2/097 21   089886481X
Mountaineering -- North America -- History. Rock climbing -- North America -- History.

GV199.44.P18.C87 1995
Curran, Jim.
K2: the story of the savage mountain/ Jim Curran. Seattle, WA: Mountaineers, 1995. 271 p.
95-207051   796.5/22/095491   0898864550
Mountaineering -- Pakistan -- K2 (Mountain) -- History. K2 (Pakistan: Mountain) -- Description and travel.

GV199.6 Outdoor life. Outdoor recreation — Hiking. Pedestrian tours — Backpacking

GV199.6.F532 2002
Fletcher, Colin.
The complete walker IV/ Colin Fletcher & Chip Rawlins; illustrations by Vanna Prince & Hannah Hinchman. Fully updated and rev. New York: Knopf, 2002. xii, 845 p.
2002-103252   796.51 21   0375703233
Backpacking. Hiking.

GV199.6.H37
Hart, John, 1948-
Walking softly in the wilderness: the Sierra Club guide to backpacking/ John Hart. San Francisco: Sierra Club Books, 1977. 436 p.
76-021620   796.5   0871561913
Backpacking.

GV199.89 Outdoor life. Outdoor recreation — Mountaineering — History

GV199.89.U57 1994
Unsworth, Walt, 1928-
Hold the heights: the foundations of mountaineering/ Walt Unsworth. Seattle: The Mountaineers, 1994. 432 p.
93-011770   796.5/22   0898863791
Mountaineering -- History.

GV199.9 Outdoor life. Outdoor recreation — Mountaineering — Biography

GV199.9.R63 1990
Robertson, Janet, 1935-
The magnificent mountain women: adventures in the Colorado Rockies/ Janet Robertson. Lincoln: University of Nebraska Press, c1990. xxi, 220 p.
89-014717   796.5/22/0922   0803238924
Women mountaineers -- Colorado -- Biography. Women -- Colorado -- Biography. Rocky Mountains -- Biography.

GV199.92 Outdoor life. Outdoor recreation — Mountaineering — Biography

GV199.92.H52 A3 2002
Hill, Lynn,
Climbing free: my life in the vertical world/ Lynn Hill with Greg Child; foreword by John Long. 1st ed. New York: W.W. Norton & Co., c2002. xvi, 270 p.
2002-016636   796.52/2/092.B 21   0393049817
Hill, Lynn, 1961- Women mountaineers -- United States -- Biography. Mountaineers -- United States -- Biography.

GV200 Outdoor life. Outdoor recreation — Mountaineering — General works

GV200.C44 1995
Child, Greg.
Climbing: the complete reference/ compiled by Greg Child. New York, NY: Facts on File, c1995. 264 p.
94-033254   796.5/22 20   0816026920
Mountaineering -- Encyclopedias.

GV200.M688 2003
Mountaineering: the freedom of the hills/ editors, Steven M. Cox and Kris Fulsaas. 7th ed. Seattle, WA: Mountaineers Books, 2003.
2002-153642   796.52/2 21   0898868289
Mountaineering. Rock climbing. Snow and ice climbing.

GV200.4 Outdoor life. Outdoor recreation — Orienteering

GV200.4.B87 1999
Burns, Bob,
Wilderness navigation: finding your way using map, compass, altimeter & GPS/ Bob Burns, Mike Burns; [edited by Paul Hughes; illustrations by Gray Mouse Graphics unless otherwise noted]. 1st ed. Seattle, WA: Mountaineers, 1999. 125 p.
98-049711   796.58 21   0898866294
Orienteering -- Equipment and supplies. Navigation -- Equipment and supplies. Outdoor recreation -- Equipment and supplies.

GV200.5 Outdoor life. Outdoor recreation — Wilderness survival — General works

GV200.5.M3513 1994
Maniguet, Xavier.
Survival: how to prevail in hostile environments/ Xavier Maniguet; translated by Ivanka Roberts. New York: Facts on File, c1994. ix, 454 p.
93-016118   613.6/9   0816025185
Wilderness survival.

GV200.5.N486 1996
Newman, Bob, 1958-
Survival in the 90s: a guide for outdoor enthusiasts/ Bob Newman; illustrations by Susan Newman. Birmingham, Ala.: Menasha Ridge Press, c1996. xviii, 204 p.
96-014168   089732191X
Wilderness survival -- Handbooks, manuals, etc.

GV211 Physical education and training — History — General works

GV211.F73 2001
Freeman, William Hardin,
Physical education and sport in a changing society/ William H. Freeman. 6th ed. Boston: Allyn and Bacon, c2001. xii, 371 p.
00-060554   613.7/1 21   0205320392
Physical education and training -- History. Sports -- History.

GV211.M43 2002
Mechikoff, Robert A.,
A history and philosophy of sport and physical education: from ancient civilizations to the modern world/ Robert A. Mechikoff, Steven G. Estes. 3rd ed. Boston: McGraw-Hill, c2002. xviii, 379 p.
2001-032707   796/.09 21   0072354127
Physical education and training -- History. Sports -- History. Physical education and training -- Philosophy.

GV223 Physical education and training — History — By region or country

GV223.H57 1997
The history of exercise and sport science/ John D. Massengale, Richard A. Swanson, editors. Champaign, IL: Human Kinetics, c1997. xiv, 472 p.
96-010555   613.7/1/071173 20   0873225244
Physical education and training -- Study and teaching (Higher) -- United States -- History. Sports -- Study and teaching (Higher) -- United States -- History. Exercise -- Study and teaching (Higher) -- United States -- History.

GV223.P467 1994
Physical education and kinesiology in North America: professional & scholarly foundations/ edited, with introductory and concluding essays by Earle F. Zeigler; with contributions in this order by Laura J. Huelster ... [et al.]. Champaign, Ill.: Stipes Pub. Co., c1994. xii, 415 p.
94-065402   613.7/0973   0875634958
Physical education and training -- United States. Physical education and training -- Canada. Kinesiology.

GV333 Physical education and training — Biography — Individual

GV333.M3.E76 1990
Ernst, Robert, 1915-
Weakness is a crime: the life of Bernarr Macfadden/ Robert Ernst. Syracuse, NY: Syracuse University Press, 1991. xiv, 278 p.
90-038194   613.7/092   081562512X
Macfadden, Bernarr, -- 1868-1955. Physical fitness -- United States.

GV341 Physical education and training — General works, treatises, and textbooks

GV341.B86 1987
Bucher, Charles Augustus, 1912-
Foundations of physical education and sport/ Charles A. Bucher, Deborah A. Wuest. St. Louis: Times Mirror/Mosby College Pub., 1987. xiii, 385 p.
86-012875   613.7   0801608856
Physical education and training. Sports. Physical education and training -- Vocational guidance.

GV341.T65 1998
Training in sport: applying sport science/ edited by Bruce Elliott; consulting editor, J. Mester. Chichester; J. Wiley & Sons, c1998. xx, 426 p.
97-034184   613.7/1 21   0471978701
Physical education and training. Sports sciences.

GV342 Physical education and training — Philosophy. Relation to other topics. Methodology — General works

GV342.D74 2001
Drewe, Sheryle Bergmann.
Socrates, sport, and students: a philosophical inquiry into physical education and sport/ Sheryle Bergmann Drewe. Lanham, Md.: University Press of America, 2001.
2001-041484   613.7/01 21   0761820809
Physical education and training -- Philosophy. Sports -- Philosophy. Physical education and training -- Study and teaching.

GV342.P43 1996
Physical activity in human experience: interdisciplinary perspectives/ Sponsored by the Canadian Fitness and Lifestyle Research Institute with the support of Health Canada; James E. Curtis, Storm J. Russell [editors]. Champaign, IL: Human Kinetics, c1997. xii, 290 p.
96-008065   796 20   0873227654
Physical education and training. Physical education and training -- Social aspects. Physical education and training -- Psychological aspects.

GV342.Z43 1989
Zeigler, Earle F.
An introduction to sport and physical education philosophy/ Earle F. Zeigler. Carmel, Ind.: Benchmark Press, c1989. xxvi, 425 p.
89-042643   613.7/1 20   0936157429
Physical education and training -- Philosophy. Sports -- Philosophy. Philosophy.

GV342.27 Physical education and training — Philosophy. Relation to other topics. Methodology — Relation to sociology. Social aspects

GV342.27.H45 2003
Hellison, Donald R.,
Teaching responsibility through physical activity/ Don Hellison. 2nd ed. Champaign, IL: Human Kinetics, c2003.
2002-152863   306.4/83 21   0736046011
Physical education and training -- Sociological aspects -- Study and Responsibility -- Study and teaching.

GV342.27.L25 2000
Laker, Anthony, 1951-
Beyond the boundaries of physical education: educating young people for citizenship and social responsibility/ Anthony Laker. London; Routledge/Falmer Press, 2000. 133 p.
99-053989   0750709316
Physical education and training -- Social aspects. Sports -- Social aspects. Citizenship -- Study and teaching.

GV342.27.P49 1986
Physical education, sport, and schooling: studies in the sociology of physical education/ edited by John Evans. London; Falmer Press, 1986. vii, 235 p.
86-013372   613.7   1850001162
Physical education and training -- Social aspects.

GV343.5 Physical education and training — Organization and administration

GV343.5.B787 2002
Bucher, Charles Augustus,
Management of physical education and sport/ Charles A. Bucher, March L. Krotee. 12th ed. New York: McGraw-Hill, c2002. xiv, 578 p.
2001-034100   613.7/068 21   0072329041
Physical education and training -- Administration. Sports administration.

GV343.5.V67 1979
The Organization and administration of physical education/ Edward F. Voltmer ... [et al.]. Englewood Cliffs, N.J.: Prentice-Hall, c1979. xii, 480 p.
78-018724   375/.6137   0136411002
Physical education and training -- Administration.

GV344 Physical education and training — Safety measures. Accident prevention

GV344.P75 2002
Principles of safety in physical education and sport/ edited by Neil J. Dougherty; a project of the National Association for Sport and Physical Education. 3rd ed. Reston, VA: The Association, c2002. 281 p.
2002-281062   613.7/1 21   0883147246
Physical education and training -- Safety measures. Sports -- Safety measures.

GV345 Physical education and training — Value of physical training in schools and colleges

GV345.V35 2001
Van Deusen, Kira,
The flying tiger: women shamans and storytellers of the Amur/ Kira Van Deusen. Montreal: McGill-Queen's University Press, c2001. xxii, 260 p.
2002-421637   398.2/089/9410577   21   0773521569
Tales -- Amur River Valley (China and Russia) Woman storytellers -- Amur River Valley (China and Russia). Women shamans -- Amur River Valley (China and Russia)

GV346 Physical education and training — School athletics. Intramural and interscholastic athletics

GV346.F86
Fuoss, Donald E.
Creative management techniques in interscholastic athletics/ Donald E. Fuoss, Robert J. Troppmann. New York: Wiley, c1977. xviii, 494 p.
76-046500   375/.6137   0471288152
School sports -- Management.

GV346.H86 2002
Humphrey, James Harry,
Principles and practices in interscholastic athletics: guidelines for administrators/ James H. Humphrey. Huntington, N.Y.: Nova Science Publishers, c2002. xiv, 133 p.
2001-059041   796/.06/0973 21   1590331591
School sports -- United States -- Management. Sports administration -- United States.

GV346.M36
Mangan, J. A.
Athleticism in the Victorian and Edwardian public school: the emergence and consolidation of an educational ideology/ J. A. Mangan. Cambridge [Eng.]; Cambridge University Press, 1981. xv, 345 p.
80-041516   796/.07/1242   0521233887
School sports -- Great Britain -- History. Endowed public schools (Great Britain) -- History.

GV346.M57 1994
Miracle, Andrew W.
Lessons of the locker room: the myth of school sports/ Andrew W. Miracle, Jr. and C. Roger Rees. Amherst, N.Y.: Prometheus Books, 1994. 243 p.
93-048666   796/.0973   0879758791
School sports -- Moral and ethical aspects -- United States. School sports -- Social aspects -- United States.

GV346.S55 2003
Shepard, Greg,
Bigger, faster, stronger/ Greg Shepard. Champaign, IL: Human Kinetics, c2003.
2003-004604   613.7/11 21   0736048146
High school athletes -- Training of. School sports. Physical education and training -- Study and teaching (Secondary)

GV346.S66 2000
Sports in school: the future of an institution/ John R. Gerdy, editor. New York: Teachers College Press, c2000. xi, 177 p.
00-032559   796/.071/073 21   0807739715
School sports -- United States. College sports -- United States.

GV346.V36 1984
VanderZwaag, Harold J.
Sport management in schools and colleges/ Harold J. VanderZwaag. New York: Wiley, c1984. xviii, 265 p.
83-014763   796/.07/1173   0471871354
School sports -- Management. Sports administration. School sports -- United States -- Management.

GV347 Physical education and training — College athletics. Intramural and interscholastic athletics — General works

GV347.H86 2000
Humphrey, James Harry, 1911-
Stress in college athletics: causes, consequences, coping/ James H. Humphrey, Deborah A. Yow, William W. Bowden. New York: Haworth Press, c2000. xiii, 183 p.
99-056493   796/.01 21   078900934X
College athletes -- Psychology. Stress (Psychology)

GV351 Physical education and training — College athletics. Intramural and interscholastic athletics — By region or country

GV351.B34 1991
Bailey, Wilford S.
Athletics and academe: an anatomy of abuses and a prescription for reform/ Wilford S. Bailey, Taylor D. Littleton. New York: American Council on Education: c1991. xii, 147 p.
90-041860   796.04/3/0973   0028970284
Sports -- Corrupt practices -- United States. College sports -- United States.

GV351.B35 1990
Bale, John.
The brawn drain: foreign student-athletes in American universities/ John Bale. Urbana: University of Illinois Press, c1991. xvii, 226 p.
90-032829   796/.071/173   0252017323
College sports -- United States. Athletics -- Recruiting. Students, Foreign -- United States.

GV351.B94 1995
Byers, Walter, 1922-
Unsportsmanlike conduct: exploiting college athletes/ Walter Byers with Charles Hammer. Ann Arbor: University of Michigan Press, c1995. 413 p.
95-016973   796.04/3 20   047210666X
College sports -- Moral and ethical aspects -- United States.

GV351.D83 2000
Duderstadt, James J., 1942-
Intercollegiate athletics and the American university: a university president's perspective/ James J. Duderstadt. Ann Arbor: University of Michigan Press, c2000. xvi, 331 p.
00-008203   796.04/3/0973 21   0472111566
College sports -- Corrupt practices -- United States. College sports -- United States -- Management. College sports -- Social aspects -- United States.

GV351.G47 1997
Gerdy, John R.
The successful college athletic program: the new standard/ John R. Gerdy. Phoenix, Ariz.: Oryx Press, 1997. ix, 180 p.
97-022605   796.04/3/0973 21   1573561096
College sports -- Standards -- United States. Education, Higher -- Aims and objectives -- United States.

GV351.G52 2000
Clark, Andy, 1958-
Athletic scholarships: thousands of grants--and over Andy Clark and Amy Clark; Karen Breslow, general editor. New York: Facts on File, c2000. xiii, 338 p.
00-022078   796/.079/73 21   0816043094
Sports -- Scholarships, fellowships, etc. -- United States -- Directories. Universities and colleges -- United States -- Directories.

GV351.L38 1987
Lawrence, Paul R.
Unsportsmanlike conduct: the National Collegiate Athletic Association and the business of college football/ Paul R. Lawrence. New York: Praeger, 1987. xvi, 173 p.
87-012496   338.4/7796/071173   0275927253
College sports -- Economic aspects -- United States. College sports -- Moral and ethical aspects -- United States. Football -- Economic aspects -- United States.

GV351.S23 1998
Sack, Allen L.
College athletes for hire: the evolution and legacy of the NCAA's amateur myth/ Allen L. Sack and Ellen J. Staurowsky; foreword by Kent Waldrep. Westport, Conn.: Praeger, 1998. xviii, 184 p.
97-043956   796.04/3/0973   0275961915
College sports -- Moral and ethical aspects -- United States. College sports -- Corrupt practices -- United States.

GV351.S48 2001
Shulman, James Lawrence, 1965-
The game of life: college sports and educational values/ James L. Shulman and William G. Bowen; in collaboration with Lauren A. Meserve and Roger C. Schonfeld. Princeton: Princeton University Press, c2001. xxxvi, 447 p.
00-061146   796.04/3/0973 21   069107075X
College sports -- United States. Education, Higher -- Aims and objectives -- United States.

GV351.S6 1988
Smith, Ronald A. 1936-
Sports and freedom: the rise of big-time college athletics/ Ronald A. Smith. New York: Oxford University Press, 1988. xii, 290 p.
88-017855   796/.07/1173   0195053141
College sports -- United States -- History. College sports -- England -- History.

GV351.S63 2000
Sperber, Murray A.
Beer and circus: how big-time college sports is crippling undergraduate education/ Murray Sperber. 1st ed. New York: H. Holt, 2000. xxii, 322 p.
00-037021   796.04/3/0973 21   0805038647
College sports -- United States -- History. College sports -- Economic aspects -- United States. College sports -- Moral and ethical aspects -- United States.

GV351.S66 1985
Sport and higher education/ Donald Chu, Jeffrey O. Segrave & Beverly J. Becker, editors. Champaign, IL: Human Kinetics Publishers, c1985. xv, 423 p.
85-000143   796/.07/1173   0087322005
College sports -- United States.

GV351.T43 1994
Thelin, John R., 1947-
Games colleges play: scandal and reform in intercollegiate athletics/ John R. Thelin. Baltimore: Johns Hopkins University Press, c1994. xviii, 252 p.
93-026950   796/.071/173   0801847168
College sports -- Corrupt practices -- United States -- History. College sports -- Moral and ethical aspects -- United States. College sports -- United States -- Management.

GV351.Y34 1991
Yaeger, Don.
Undue process: the NCAAs injustice for all/ Don Yaeger; foreword by Dale Brown. Champaign, Ill.: Sagamore Pub., c1991. xiv, 277 p.
90-062973   796/.071/1   0915611341
College sports -- Moral and ethical aspects -- United States. College sports -- United States -- Management.

GV351.Z56 1999
Zimbalist, Andrew S.
Unpaid professionals: commercialism and conflict in big-time college sports/ Andrew Zimbalist. Princeton, N.J.: Princeton University Press, c1999. xii, 252 p.
99-017410   796.04/3/0973 21   0691009554
College sports -- Moral and ethical aspects -- United States. College sports -- Economic aspects -- United States. College sports -- United States -- Management.

GV361 Physical education and training — Study and teaching. Research — General works

GV361.I652 2001
Ingersoll, Christopher D.
Research in athletic training/ Christopher Ingersoll. Thorofare, NJ: SLACK, c2001. vi, 115 p.
2001-031371   796 21   1556424396
Physical education and training -- Research.

GV363 Physical education and training — Study and teaching. Research — Methods of teaching

GV363.A76 1998
Armour, Kathleen M.
Physical education teachers' lives and careers: PE, sport, and educational status/ Kathleen M. Armour and Robyn L. Jones. London; Falmer Press, 1998. vi, 154 p.
98-185973   0750708182
Physical education teachers -- Great Britain -- Case studies. Physical education and training -- Study and teaching (Secondary) -- Great Britain -- Case studies.

GV363.H28 2000
Hanrahan, Stephanie J., 1961-
GameSkills: a fun approach to learning sport skills/ Stephanie J. Hanrahan, Teresa B. Carlson. Champaign, IL: Human Kinetics, c2000. xxi, 175 p.
99-057711   796/.07/7 21   0736002030
Physical education and training -- Curricula.

GV363.M33 2001
McCracken, Bane, 1944-
It's not just gym anymore: teaching secondary school students how to be active for life/ Bane McCracken. Champaign, IL: Human Kinetics, c2001. vii, 247 p.
00-053520   613.7/071/273 21   0736001271
Physical education and training -- Study and teaching (Secondary) Physical education and training -- Curricula.

GV365-365.5 Physical education and training — Study and teaching. Research — By region or country

GV365.M45 1996
Melograno, Vincent.
Designing the physical education curriculum/ Vincent J. Melograno. 3rd ed. Champaign, IL: Human Kinetics, c1996. x, 277 p.
95-020773   375.6137/0973 20   0873225252
Physical education and training -- United States -- Curricula. Curriculum planning -- United States.

GV365.P36 2001
Darst, Paul W.
Dynamic physical education for secondary school students/ Paul W. Darst and Robert P. Pangrazi. 4th ed. Boston, MA: Allyn and Bacon, 2001.
2001-033387   613.7/071/2 21   020534092X
Physical education and training -- United States -- Curricula. Physical education and training -- Study and teaching (Secondary) -- United Physical education and training -- Study and teaching (Secondary)

GV365.S76 1997
Strand, Bradford N., 1955-
Fitness education: teaching concepts-based fitness in the schools/ Bradford N. Strand, Ed Scantling, Martin Johnson. Scottsdale, Ariz.: Gorsuch Scarisbrick, Publishers, c1997. xxii, 378 p.
96-034885   796/.071/2 20   0897876334
Physical education and training -- Study and teaching (Secondary) -- United States. Physical fitness -- Study and teaching (Secondary) -- United States.

GV365.5.G3.H3613 1993
Hanke, Udo.
Beyond dichotomy: an integrative model of teacher education/ by Udo Hanke; with a preface by L.F. Locke. Seattle: Hogrefe & Huber Publishers, c1993. vii, 217 p.
92-034953   613.7/07   0889370567
Physical education teachers -- Training of -- Germany. Physical education and training -- Study and teaching (Higher) -- Germany. Teachers -- Training of -- Germany.

GV416 Physical education and training — Physical education facilities. Sports facilities — Athletic fields. Playing fields

GV416.N48.S85 2000
Sullivan, Neil J., 1948-
The diamond in the Bronx: Yankee Stadium and the politics of New York/ Neil J. Sullivan. Oxford; Oxford University Press, c2001. xv, 225 p.
2001-269770   0195123603
Yankee Stadium (New York, N.Y.) -- History -- 20th century. Baseball -- New York (State) -- New York -- Political aspects. Baseball -- New York (State) -- New York -- History -- 20th century.

GV423-425 Physical education and training — Physical education facilities. Sports facilities — Playgrounds. Play spaces

GV423.B74 1993
Brett, Arlene.
The complete playground book/ Arlene Brett, Robin C. Moore, and Eugene F. Provenzo, Jr.; photographs by Michael Carlebach and Robin C. Moore. 1st ed. Syracuse, N.Y.: Syracuse University Press, 1993. xi, 192 p.
92-043598   796/.06/8 20   0815602715
Playgrounds.

GV425.H46 2001
Hendricks, Barbara E.
Designing for play/ Barbara E. Hendricks. Aldershot, England; Ashgate, c2001. viii, 267 p.
00-111538   0754613208
Playgrounds -- Design and construction.

GV429 Physical education and training — Physical education facilities. Sports facilities — By region or country

GV429.A45 1997
ACSM's health/fitness facility standards and guidelines/ American College of Sports Medicine; Stephen J. Tharrett, James A. Peterson, editors. 2nd ed. Champaign, IL: Human Kinetics, c1997. xi, 211 p.
97-010276   613.7/1 21   0873229576
Physical fitness centers -- Standards -- United States.

GV429.E36 2000
The economics and politics of sports facilities/ edited by Wilbur C. Rich. Westport, Conn.: Quorum Books, 2000. x, 237 p.
99-056365   338.4/7796/06873   1567203175
Sports facilities -- Economic aspects -- United States. Sports facilities -- Political aspects -- United States.

GV429.W44 1996
Welch, Paula D.
History of American physical education and sport/ by Paula D. Welch. 2nd ed. Springfield, Ill.: C.C. Thomas, c1996. ix, 401 p.
95-025845   796/.0973 20   0398065667
Physical education and training -- United States -- History. Sports -- United States -- History.

GV436 Physical education and training — Physical tests, etc. Fitness tests — General works

GV436.F53 2001
Fitness and exercise sourcebook/ edited by Kristen M. Gledhill. 2nd ed. Detroit, MI: Omnigraphics, 2001. xiv, 646 p.
2001-021453   613.7   0780803345
Physical fitness -- Handbooks, manuals, etc. Exercise -- Handbooks, manuals, etc.

GV436.H48 2002
Heyward, Vivian H.
Advanced fitness assessment and exercise prescription/ Vivian H. Heyward. 4th ed. Champaign, IL: Human Kinetics, c2002. xiii, 369 p.
2002-017210   613.7 21   0736040161
Physical fitness -- Testing. Exercise tests. Health.

GV436.M37 1978
Mathews, Donald K.
Measurement in physical education/ Donald K. Mathews; ill. by Nancy Allison Close. Philadelphia: Saunders, 1978. x, 495 p.
77-024002   613.7   0721661785
Physical fitness -- Testing. Physical education and training.

GV436.M42 1989
Measurement concepts in physical education and exercise science/ Margaret J. Safrit, Terry M. Wood [editors]. Champaign, Ill.: Human Kinetics Books, c1989. xvi, 382 p.
88-039286   613.7/1   0873222237
Physical fitness -- Testing. Physical education and training -- Evaluation.

GV436.S45
Sheehan, Thomas J.
An introduction to the evaluation of measurement data in physical education [by] Thomas J. Sheehan. Reading, Mass., Addison-Wesley Pub. Co. [1971] xii, 274 p.
78-137837   613.7/043
Physical education and training -- Statistical methods. Physical fitness -- Testing.

GV436.5 Physical education and training — Physical tests, etc. Fitness tests — Evaluation of performance

GV436.5.S87 1993
Strand, Bradford N.,
Assessing sport skills/ Bradford N. Strand, Rolayne Wilson. Champaign, IL: Human Kinetics Publishers, c1993. ix, 165 p.
92-022433   796/.07 20   0873223772
Athletic ability -- Testing.

GV443 Physical education and training — Physical education and training for special classes of persons — Children

GV443.A27 1998
Sammann, Patricia, 1951-
Active youth: ideas for implementing CDC physical activity promotion guidelines/ Patricia Sammann, writer. Champaign, IL: Human Kinetics, c1998. ix, 156 p.
97-017532   613.7 21   0880116692
Physical education for children -- United States -- Case studies.

GV443.C59 2000
Colvin, A. Vonnie, 1951-
Teaching the nuts and bolts of physical education: building basic movement skills/ A. Vonnie Colvin, Nancy J. Egner Markos, Pam Walker. Champaign, IL: Human Kinetics, c2000. vii, 279 p.
99-038507   372.86 21   0880118830
Physical education for children. Movement education.

GV443.G15 1987
Gabbard, Carl, 1948-
Physical education for children: building the foundation/ Carl Gabbard, Elizabeth LeBlanc, Susan Lowy. Englewood Cliffs, N.J.: Prentice-Hall, c1987. xii, 467 p.
86-025458   613.7/042   0136670237
Physical education for children. Physical education for children -- Study and teaching. Movement education.

GV443.G82 2000
Guidelines for physical education programs, grades K-12: standards, objectives, and assessments/ edited by Steveda Chepko, Ree K. Arnold; Eastern District Association of the American Alliance for Health, Physical Education, Recreation and Dance. Boston: Allyn and Bacon, c2000. vi, 287 p.
00-551332   0205283268
Physical education for children -- Evaluation. Curriculum planning.

GV443.H77 1999
Human Kinetics (Organization)
Physical education methods for classroom teachers/ Human Kinetics with Bonnie Pettifor. Champaign, IL: Human Kinetics, c1999. xv, 343 p.
98-041469   372.86/044 21   0880118423
Physical education for children -- Study and teaching (Elementary) -- United States. Physical education for children -- United States -- Curricula.

GV443.M66 1999
Morris, G. S. Don.
Changing kids' games/ G.S. Don Morris, Jim Stiehl. Champaign, IL: Human Kinetics, c1999. xi, 147 p.
98-027142   372.1/337 21   0880116919
Physical education for children. Games. Movement education.

GV445 Physical education and training — Physical education and training for special classes of persons — Handicapped persons

GV445.A3 2000
Adapted physical education and sport/ Joseph P. Winnick, editor. 3rd ed. Champaign, IL: Human Kinetics, c2000. xii, 492 p.
00-039636   371.9/04486 21   0736033246
Physical education for people with disabilities. Sports for people with disabilities.

GV445.E34 2003
Developmental/adapted physical education: making ability count/ Michael Horvat ... [et al.]. 4th ed. San Francisco, CA: Benjamin Cummings, c2003. x, 422 p.
2002-067678   796.04/56 21   0205313914
Physical education for people with disabilities -- United States. Mainstreaming in education -- United States.

GV445.N38 1995
National Consortium for Physical Education and Recreation
Adapted physical education national standards/ National Consortium for Physical Education and Recreation for Individuals with Disabilities; Luke E. Kelly, project director. Champaign, IL: Human Kinetics, c1995. viii, 216 p.
95-003492   371.9/04486   0873229622
Physical education for handicapped children -- Standards -- United States. Physical education teachers -- Certification -- United States.

GV452 Physical education and training — Movement education

GV452.M56 1989
Minton, Sandra Cerny, 1943-
Body & self: partners in movement/ Sandra Cerny Minton. Champaign, Ill.: Human Kinetics Books, c1989. ix, 186 p.
88-030383   613.7/1   0873222199
Movement education.

GV461 Physical education and training — Gymnastics. Gymnastic exercises — General works

GV461.B63
Boone, William T., 1944-
Better gymnastics: how to spot the performer/ William T. Boone. Mountain View, Calif.: World Publications, c1979. 221 p.
78-000368   796.4/1   089037127X
Gymnastics -- Safety measures. Gymnastics -- Study and teaching.

GV461.U53 1979
United States Gymnastics Safety Association.
Gymnastics safety manual: the official manual of the United States Gymnastics Safety Association/ contributors to text, Norman Barnes ... [et al.]; Eugene Wettstone, editor, with the assistance of Raleigh DeGeer Amyx ... [et al.; drawings in text by C. K. Bingham]. University Park: Pennsylvania State University Press, 1979. 147 p.
80-105595   796.4/1/0289   0271002425
Gymnastics. Gymnastics -- Safety measures.

GV464 Physical education and training — Gymnastics. Gymnastic exercises — Gymnastics for women and girls

GV464.S55 1995
Simons, Minot. Volume 1, 1966-1994
Women's gymnastics: a history/ by Minot Simons II; technical assistance, Joanne Giannini Pasquale; photography, Albrecht Gaebele and other photographers. Carmel, CA: Welwyn Pub. Co., [c1995-] v. 1.
95-090224   796.44/082   0964606208
Gymnastics for women -- History. Gymnasts -- Biography.

GV481-510 Physical education and training — Gymnastics. Gymnastic exercises — Calisthenics. Group exercises

GV481.A322 2002
ACSM fitness book/ American College of Sports Medicine. 3rd ed. Champaign, IL: Human Kinetics, c2002. viii, 175 p.
2002-008864   613.7/1 21   073604406X
Exercise. Physical fitness -- Testing.

GV481.B76 1998
Brooks, Douglas, 1957-
Program design for personal trainers: bridging theory into application/ Douglas Brooks. Champaign, IL: Human Kinetics, c1998. 328 p.
98-025930   613.7/1 21   0736000798
Physical fitness -- Planning -- Handbooks, manuals, etc. Physical fitness -- Planning -- Case studies. Personal trainers -- Handbooks, manuals, etc.

GV481.I58 1988
International Council for Physical Fitness Research. (1988:
Fitness for the aged, disabled, and industrial worker/ edited by Masahiro Kaneko. Champaign, Ill.: Human Kinetics Books, c1990. xi, 290 p.
89-024655   613.7/0446   0873222628
Physical fitness -- Congresses. Physical fitness for the aged -- Congresses. Working class -- Physical training -- Congresses.

GV481.S6443 2001
Smith, Stewart,
Maximum fitness:the complete guide to cross training/ Smith, contributions by M. Laurel Cutlip and James C. Villepigue. Stewart New York: Hatherleigh Press, 2001.
2001-016682   613.7/1   1578260604
Physical fitness -- Handbooks, manuals, etc. Exercise -- Handbooks, manuals, etc. Physical education and training -- Handbooks, manuals, etc.

GV481.W47 2003
Westcott, Wayne L.,
Building strength & stamina/ Wayne Westcott. 2nd ed. Champaign, IL: Human Kinetics, c2003. viii, 223 p.
2002-010890   613.7/1 21   0736045155
Physical fitness. Exercise. Nautilus weight training equipment.

GV481.2.W55 1992
Willis, Joe Don,
Exercise psychology/ Joe D. Willis, Linda Frye Campbell. Champaign, IL: Human Kinetics Publishers, c1992. xi, 258 p.
92-015246   613.7/1 20   0873223667
Exercise -- Psychological aspects. Physical fitness -- Psychological aspects.

GV505.F58 1987
Fleck, Steven J., 1951-
Designing resistance training programs/ Steven J. Fleck, William J. Kraemer. Champaign, Ill.: Human Kinetics Books, c1987. xv, 264 p.
87-002850   613.7/1   0873221133
Isometric exercise.

GV510.U5.F58 1989
Fitness in American culture: images of health, sport, and the body, 1830-1940/ edited by Kathryn Grover. Amherst: University of Massachusetts Press; c1989. viii, 178 p.
89-004772   613.7/1   0870236814
Physical fitness -- United States -- History -- 19th century. Sports -- United States -- History -- 19th century. Physical fitness -- United States -- History -- 20th century.

GV545.52-546 Physical education and training — Gymnastics. Gymnastic exercises — Heavy exercises

GV545.52.S26.C43 1994
Chapman, David L., 1948-
Sandow the Magnificent: Eugen Sandow and the beginnings of bodybuilding/ David L. Chapman. Urbana: University of Illinois Press, c1994. xiii, 229 p.
93-015736   646.7/5/092   0252020332
Sandow, Eugen, -- 1867-1925. Bodybuilders -- United States -- Biography. Bodybuilding -- United States -- History.

GV546.H6
Hoffman, Bob, 1897-1985.
Weight training for athletes. Photography by Robert L. Hasse. New York, Ronald Press Co. [1961] 216 p.
61-017428   796.41
Weight training.

GV558 Sports sciences — General works

GV558.D53 1991
Dictionary of the sport and exercise sciences/ Mark H. Anshel, editor; Patty Freedson ... [et al.]. Champaign, Ill.: Human Kinetics Books, c1991. xii, 163 p.
90-045252   613.7/103   0873223055
Sports sciences -- Dictionaries. Exercise -- Physiological aspects -- Dictionaries.

GV558.E53 1997
Encyclopedia of sports science/ John Zumerchik, editor. New York: Macmillan Library Reference USA, c1997. 2 v.
96-047502   613.7/1 21   0028975065
Sports sciences -- Encyclopedias. Sports -- Physiological aspects -- Encyclopedias.

GV558.H36 2000
Handbook of sports studies/ edited by Jay Coakley and Eric Dunning. London: SAGE, 2000. xxxviii, 570 p.
00-709715   080397552X
Sports sciences -- Handbooks, manuals, etc. Sports -- Sociological aspects -- Handbooks, manuals, etc. Sports -- Study and teaching -- Handbooks, manuals, etc.

GV558.N86 2001
Ntoumanis, Nikos,
A step-by-step guide to SPSS for sport and exercise studies/ Nikos Ntoumanis. London; Routledge, 2001.
00-068433   796/.028/5369 21   0415249783
Sports sciences -- Statistical methods -- Computer programs.

GV558.W55 2001
Williams, Craig A.,
Science for exercise and sport/ James. Craig A. Williams and David V.B. London; Routledge, 2001.
00-042484   502/.4/796   0419251707
Sports sciences -- Study and teaching (Higher) -- Great Britain. Science -- Study and teaching (Higher) -- Great Britain. Physiology -- Study and teaching (Higher) -- Great Britain.

GV567 Sports — Dictionaries. Encyclopedias

GV567.C43 2002
Chandler, Timothy John Lindsay.
Sport and physical education: the key concepts/ Timothy Chandler, Mike Cronin, Wray Vamplew. London; Routledge, 2002.
2002-021324   796/.03 21   0415231426
Sports -- Encyclopedias. Physical education and training -- Encyclopedias.

GV567.E49
Encyclopedia of physical education, fitness, and sports/ Thomas K. Cureton, Jr., series editor; sponsored by the American Alliance for Health, Physical Education, and Recreation. Salt Lake City, Utah: Brighton Pub. Co., c1977-c1985. v. 1, 3-4.
76-046608   796/.03   0201010771
Sports -- Encyclopedias. Physical education and training -- Encyclopedias.

GV567.E56 1996
Encyclopedia of world sport: from ancient times to the present/ David Levinson and Karen Christensen, editors. Santa Barbara, Calif.: ABC-CLIO, c1996. 3 v.
96-045437   796/.03 21   0874368197
Sports -- Encyclopedias.

GV567.H518 2002
Hickok, Ralph.
The encyclopedia of North American sports history/ Ralph Hickok. 2nd ed. New York: Facts on File, c2002. xiv, 594 p.
2001-055646   796/.097 21   0816050716
Sports--North America -- Encyclopedias.

GV567.W37
Webster's sports dictionary. Springfield, Mass.: G. & C. Merriam, c1976. 503 p.
75-042076   796/.03   0877790671
Sports -- Dictionaries.

GV567.W85 2000
Wukovits, John F.,
The encyclopedia of world sports/ by John Wukovits. Danbury, Conn.: F. Watts, c2000. iv, 186 p.
00-038222   796/.03 21   0531117774
Sports -- Encyclopedias, Juvenile. Sports -- Encyclopedias.

GV571 Sports — History — General works

GV571.B25 1988
Baker, William J.
Sports in the Western world/ William J. Baker. Rev. ed., Illini books ed. Urbana: University of Illinois Press, 1988, c1982. viii, 359 p.
88-018838   796/.09 19   0252060423
Sports -- History. Sports -- Europe -- History. Sports -- United States -- History.

GV571.F73 2001
Franck, Irene M.
Famous first facts about sports/ Irene M. Franck & David M. Brownstone. New York: H.W. Wilson, 2001. xii, 903 p.
00-043883   796   0824209737
Sports -- History. Sports records.

GV571.S56 2000
Sport and physical activity in the modern world/ [edited by] J. Richard Polidoro. Boston: Allyn and Bacon, c2000. xvi, 218 p.
99-038056   796 21   0205271588
Sports -- History. Physical education and training -- History. Sports -- Cross-cultural studies.

GV573-575 Sports — History — By period

GV573.D4213 1990
Decker, Wolfgang.
Sports and games of ancient Egypt/ Wolfgang Decker; translated by Allen Guttmann. New Haven: Yale University Press, c1992. xi, 212 p.
90-036482   796/.0962   0300044631
Sports -- Egypt -- History. Games -- Egypt -- History. Egypt -- History -- To 640 A.D.

GV573.G65 1998
Golden, Mark, 1948-
Sport and society in ancient Greece/ Mark Golden. Cambridge; Cambridge University Press, 1998. xiii, 216 p.
98-003004   306.4/83/0938   0521496985
Sports -- Social aspects -- Greece -- History. Olympic games (Ancient) Greece -- Civilization -- To 146 B.C. Greece -- Social conditions -- To 146 B.C.

GV573.H3
Harris, Harold Arthur.
Sport in Greece and Rome [by] H. A. Harris. Ithaca, N.Y., Cornell University Press [1972] 288 p.
77-039824   796/.0938   0801407184
Sports -- Greece. Sports -- Rome.

GV575.C372 1992
Carter, John Marshall.
Medieval games: sports and recreations in feudal society/ John Marshall Carter. New York: Greenwood Press, 1992. xiii, 159 p.
91-000785   796/.094   0313256993
Sports -- Europe -- History. Recreation -- Europe -- History. Sports -- Social aspects -- Europe -- History.

GV581-655 Sports — History — By region or country

GV581.B78 2001
Brucato, Thomas W.
Major leagues/ Thomas W. Brucato. Lanham, Md.: Scarecrow Press, 2001. x, 283 p.
00-063744   796.04/4/097   0810839083
Sports teams -- North America -- History. Sports teams -- North America -- Names -- History. Sports -- North America -- History.

GV581.G37 1997
Gaschnitz, K. Michael.
Professional sports statistics: a North American team-by-team and major non-team events, year-by-year reference, 1876 through 1996/ K. Michael Gaschnitz. Jefferson, N.C.: McFarland & Co., c1997. xiv, 1338 p.
97-013593   796.04/4/097021 21   0786402997
Professional sports -- North America -- History -- Statistics.

GV581.N48 1997
The new American sport history: recent approaches and perspectives/ edited by S.W. Pope. Urbana: University of Illinois Press, c1997. xv, 423 p.
96-006137   796/.0973 20   0252065670
Sports -- United States -- History. Sports -- United States -- Historiography. Sports -- Social aspects -- United States -- History.

GV581.S655 1992
Sports in North America: a documentary history/ edited by Thomas L. Altherr. Gulf Breeze, FL: Academic International Press, 1992-1998. v. 1-6; in 7.
92-171131   796.097   0875691889
Sports -- North America -- History. Sports -- United States -- History.

GV583.A56 1998
African Americans in sport: contemporary themes/ edited by Gary A. Sailes. New Brunswick, N.J.: Transaction Publishers, c1998. xiv, 271 p.
98-010468   796/.089/96073 21   0765804409
African American athletes. African American athletes -- Social conditions. Sports -- Social aspects -- United States.

GV583.A64 1989
American women in sport, 1887-1987: a 100-year chronology/ compiled by Ruth M. Sparhawk ... [et al.]. Metuchen, N.J.: Scarecrow Press, 1989. xvi, 149 p.
89-006150   796/.0194   0810822059
Women athletes -- United States -- History -- Chronology. Sports for women -- United States -- History -- Chronology.

GV583.A74 1993
Ashe, Arthur.
A hard road to glory: a history of the African-American athlete/ Arthur R. Ashe, Jr.; with the assistance of Kip Branch, Oceania Chalk, and Francis Harris. New York, N.Y.: Amistad: 1993. 3 v.
93-007395   796/.089/96073   1567430066
Afro-Americans -- Sports -- History. Afro-American athletes.

GV583.B46 1986
Berry, Robert C.
Labor relations in professional sports/ Robert C. Berry, William B. Gould IV, Paul D. Staudohar. Dover, Mass.: Auburn House Pub. Co., c1986. xii, 289 p.
85-026806   331.88/11796/0973   0865691371
Professional sports -- Economic aspects -- United States. Professional sports contracts -- United States. Professional sports -- Law and legislation -- United States.

GV583.B47
Betts, John Rickards, 1917-1971.
America's sporting heritage, 1850-1950/ John Rickards Betts. Reading, Mass.: Addison-Wesley Pub. Co., [1974] xv, 428 p.
73-010590   796/.0973   0201005573
Sports -- United States -- History.

GV583.E36 2000
The economics of sports/ William S. Kern, editor. Kalamazoo, Mich.: W.E. Upjohn Institute for Employment Research, v, 146 p.
00-040871   338.4/3796044/0973   21
0880992093
Professional sports -- Economic aspects -- United States.

GV583.G68 1974
Government and the sports business; papers prepared for a conference of experts, with an introduction and summary. Roger G. Noll, editor. Washington, D.C., Brookings Institution [1974] xiv, 445 p.
74-004371   338.4/7/7960973   0815761066
Sports and state -- United States -- Congresses. Sports -- United States -- Congresses.

GV583.G87 1988
Guttmann, Allen.
A whole new ball game: an interpretation of American sports/ Allen Guttmann. Chapel Hill: University of North Carolina Press, c1988. x, 233 p.
87-026131   796/.0973   0807817864
Sports -- United States -- History. Sports -- Social aspects -- United States.

GV583.H6 1997
Hoberman, John M. 1944-
Darwin's athletes: how sport has damaged Black America and preserved the myth of race/ John Hoberman. Boston: Houghton Mifflin Co., 1997. xxvi, 341 p.
96-036170   796/.089/96073   0395822912
Afro-American athletes -- Public opinion. Public opinion -- United States. Stereotype (Psychology) in sports. United States -- Race relations.

GV583.L45 1995
Leifer, Eric Matheson.
Making the majors: the transformation of team sports in America/ Eric M. Leifer. Cambridge, Mass.: Harvard University Press, 1995. xiv, 378 p.
95-013469   796/.06/0973   067454322X
Professional sports -- United States -- History. Sports teams -- United States -- History.

GV583.L696 1995
Lowe, Stephen R.
The kid on the sandlot: Congress and professional sports, 1910-1992/ Stephen R. Lowe. Bowling Green, OH: Bowling Green State University Popular Press, c1995. 176 p.
94-079195   796/.0973   087972675X
Professional sports -- United States -- History -- 20th century. Professional sports -- Law and legislation -- United States -- History -- 20th century.

GV583.M76 1983
Mrozek, Donald J.
Sport and American mentality, 1880-1910/ Donald J. Mrozek. Knoxville: University of Tennessee Press, c1983. xx, 284 p.
83-003667   796/.0973   0870493949
Sports -- United States -- History. Sports -- Social aspects -- United States. National characteristics, American -- History.

GV583.P39
Peterson's sports scholarships and college athletic programs.   Princeton, NJ: Peterson's Guides, c1994-
94-660088   796/.079
Sports -- Scholarships, fellowships, etc. -- United States -- Directories.

GV583.P655 1998
Pollak, Mark, 1947-
Sports leagues and teams: an encyclopedia, 1871 through 1996/ by Mark Pollak. Jefferson, N.C.: McFarland & Co., 1998. v, 708 p.
96-050084   796/.06/0973   0786402520
Professional sports -- United States -- History. Sports teams -- United States -- History. Professional sports -- Canada -- History.

GV583.R53 1984
Riess, Steven A.
The American sporting experience: a historical anthology of sport in America/ Steven A. Riess. New York: Leisure Press, c1984. 400 p.
84-007188   796/.0973   0880112107
Sports -- United States -- History.

GV583.R54 1989
Riess, Steven A.
City games: the evolution of American urban society and the rise of sports/ Steven A. Riess. Urbana: University of Illinois Press, c1989. xii, 332 p.
88-017346   796/.0973   0252015738
Sports -- United States -- History -- 19th century. Sports -- United States -- History -- 20th century. Working class -- United States -- Recreation -- History.

GV583.R6 1989
Roberts, Randy, 1951-
Winning is the only thing: sports in America since 1945/ Randy Roberts and James S. Olson. Baltimore: Johns Hopkins University Press, c1989. xii, 258 p.
89-001689   796/.0973   0801838304
Sports -- United States -- History -- 20th century. Sports and state -- United States.

GV583.R66
Rooney, John F.
A geography of American sport: from Cabin Creek to Anaheim [by] John F. Rooney, Jr. Reading, Mass., Addison-Wesley Pub. Co. [1974] 306 p.
73-016555   796/.0973
Sports -- United States. Sports -- Social aspects -- United States.

GV583.W545 1997
Wiggins, David Kenneth, 1951-
Glory bound: Black athletes in a White America/ David K. Wiggins. Syracuse, N.Y.: Syracuse University Press, c1997. xx, 302 p.
96-046218   796/.089/96073   20   0815627335
Afro-American athletes -- History. Sports -- United States -- History. Discrimination in sports -- United States -- History.

GV603.S55 1999
Sport in Europe: politics, class, gender/ edited by J.A. Mangan. London: Frank Cass, 1999. ix, 268 p.
00-265224   306.4/83/094   0714649465
Sports -- Europe -- Philosophy -- History. Sports -- Europe -- Sociological aspects -- History.

GV605.H65 1989
Holt, Richard, 1948-
Sport and the British: a modern history/ Richard Holt. Oxford [England]: Clarendon Press; 1989. 396 p.
88-021675   796/.0941   0198225865
Sports -- Great Britain -- History. Sports -- Social aspects -- Great Britain.

GV605.S73 1989
Sport in Britain: a social history/ edited by Tony Mason.   Cambridge   [England];   Cambridge University Press, 1989. 363 p.
89-007048   796/.0941   0521351197
Sports -- Great Britain -- History.

GV623.E27 1993
Edelman, Robert, 1945-
Serious fun: a history of spectator sports in the USSR/ Robert Edelman. New York: Oxford University Press, 1993. xvi, 286 p.
92-023762   796/.0947   0195079485
Sports -- Soviet Union -- History. Sports and state -- Soviet Union.

GV651.B76 1995
Brownell, Susan.
Training the body for China: sports in the moral order of the People's Republic/ Susan Brownell. Chicago: University of Chicago Press, c1995. xi, 393 p.
94-049561   796/.0951/0*9045   0226076466
Sports -- China. Sports -- China -- Sociological aspects. Sports -- Moral and ethical aspects -- China. China -- Social life and customs -- 1976-

GV651.S655 1999
Sport and physical education in China/ edited by James Riordan and Robin Jones. London; E & FN Spon, 1999. xviii, 278 p.
98-051481   613.7/0951   0419247505
Sports -- China -- History. Physical education and training -- China -- History.

GV655.G88 2001
Guttmann, Allen.
Japanese sports: a history/ Allen Guttmann, Lee Thompson. Honolulu: University of Hawai'i Press, c2001. ix, 307 p.
00-066665   796/.0952 21   0824824644
Sports -- Japan -- History.

GV697 Sports — Biography of sports personalities

GV697.A1.B336 1996
Baldwin, David
Track and field record holders: profiles of the men and women who set World, Olympic, and American marks, 1946 through 1995/ by David Baldwin. Jefferson, N.C.: McFarland & Co., 1996. vi, 338 p.
96-003026   796/.092/2   0786402490
Track and field athletes -- Biography. Track-field athletics -- History.

GV697.A1.C67 1990
Condon, Robert J., 1934-
The fifty finest athletes of the 20th century: a worldwide reference/ Robert J. Condon. Jefferson, N.C.: McFarland & Co., c1990. viii, 152 p.
89-043643   796/.092/2   0899503748
Athletes -- Biography. Athletes -- Rating of. Athletes.

GV697.A1.C68 1991
Condon, Robert J., 1934-
Great women athletes of the 20th century/ by Robert J. Condon. Jefferson, N.C.: McFarland, c1991. ix, 180 p.
91-052633   796.092/2   0899505554
Women athletes -- Biography. Women athletes -- History -- 20th century.

GV697.A1 E28 2002
Edelson, Paula.
A to Z of American women in sports/ Paula Edelson. New York: Facts on File, c2002.
2001-054735   796/.082/092273.B   21   0816045658
Women athletes -- United States -- Biography -- Encyclopedias. Sports for women -- United States.

GV697.A1 F37 1995
African-American sports greats: a biographical dictionary/ edited by David L. Porter. Westport, Conn.: Greenwood Press, 1995. xix, 429 p.
95-007189   796/.092/2.B 20   0313289875
African American athletes -- Biography -- Dictionaries.

GV697.A1.H367 2000
Hawkes, Nena.
Celebrating women coaches: a biographical dictionary/ Nena Rey Hawkes and John F. Seggar; foreword by Russell L. Sturzebecker and Linda J. Carpenter. Westport, Conn.: Greenwood Press, 2000. xxv, 281 p.
99-088485   796/.082/092273   0313309124
Coaches (Athletics) -- United States -- Biography -- Dictionaries. Women coaches (Athletics) -- United States -- Biography -- Dictionaries.

GV697.A1.P576 1993
Porter, David L., 1941-
A cumulative index to the Biographical dictionary of American sports/ compiled by David L. Porter. Westport, Conn.: Greenwood Press, c1993. ix, 325 p.
93-018030   796/.092/2   0313284350
Athletes -- United States -- Biography -- Dictionaries.

GV697.A1 S42 2002
The Scribner encyclopedia of American lives. Arnold Markoe, volume editor. New York: C. Scribner's Sons, c2002. 2 v.
2001-049603   796/.092/2.B 21   0684312255
Athletes -- United States -- Biography -- Dictionaries. Sports -- United States -- Encyclopedias.

GV697.A1 T63 2000
Todhunter, Andrew.
Dangerous games: ice climbing, storm kayaking, and other adventures from the extreme edge of sports/ Andrew Todhunter. 1st ed. New York: Doubleday, 2000. 178 p.
99-087492   796/.092/273.B 21   038548643X
Athletes -- United States -- Biography. Extreme sports -- United States. Risk-taking (Psychology)

GV697.A1.W69 1992
Woolum, Janet, 1955-
Outstanding women athletes: who they are and how they influenced sports in America/ by Janet Woolum; forewords by Billie Jean King, Anita DeFrantz, Deborah Slaner Anderson. Phoenix, AZ: Oryx Press, 1992. xvi, 279 p.
92-000199   796/.0194/0922   0897747135
Women athletes -- United States -- Biography -- Dictionaries. Sports for women -- United States -- History.

GV697.O9.B35 1986
Baker, William J. 1938-
Jesse Owens: an American life/ William J. Baker. New York: Free Press; c1986. xii, 289 p.
86-004671   796.4/2/0924   0029017807
Owens, Jesse, -- 1913-   Track and field athletes -- United States -- Biography.

GV704 Sports — General works — American, and English, 1976-

GV704.D42 2000
Deardorff, Donald L.
Sports: a reference guide and critical commentary, 1980-1999/ Donald L. Deardorff II. Westport, Conn.: Greenwood Press, 2000. xi, 361 p.
00-020466   796/.09/048   0313304459
Sports. Sports -- United States -- History -- 20th century.

GV706 Sports — Philosophy. Relation to other topics — General works

GV706.L59
Lowe, Benjamin.
The beauty of sport: a cross-disciplinary inquiry/ Benjamin Lowe. Englewood Cliffs, N.J.: Prentice-Hall, c1977. xix, 327 p.
76-028308   796/.01   0130665894
Sports -- Philosophy. Sports in art. Physical education and training -- Philosophy.

GV706.M6 1994
Morgan, William John, 1948-
Leftist theories of sport: a critique and reconstruction/ William J. Morgan. Urbana: University of Illinois Press, c1994. xiii, 267 p.
93-024135   796/.01   0252020685
Sports -- Philosophy. Sports -- Sociological aspects.

GV706.P478 1988
Philosophic inquiry in sport/ William J. Morgan, Klaus V. Meier, editors. Champaign, Ill.: Human Kinetics Publishers, c1988. x, 546 p.
87-002767   796/.01   0873221192
Sports -- Philosophy.

GV706.V33
VanderZwaag, Harold J.
Toward a philosophy of sport [by] Harold J. Vander-Zwaag. Reading, Mass., Addison-Wesley Pub. Co. [1972] xxii, 261 p.
71-174337   796/.01
Sports -- Philosophy.

GV706.W44 1991
Wertz, Spencer K.
Talking a good game: inquiries into the principles of sport/ Spencer K. Wertz. Dallas: Southern Methodist University Press, 1991. x, 275 p.
90-053579   796/.01   0870743201
Sports -- Philosophy. Sports -- Moral and ethical aspects. Sports in art.

GV706.2 Sports — Philosophy. Relation to other topics — Relation to anthropology

GV706.2.A58 1999
Anthropology, sport, and culture/ edited by Robert R. Sands; foreword by Kendall Blanchard. Westport, Conn: Bergin & Garvey, 1999. xv, 218 p.
98-020128   306.4/83   0897895991
Sports -- Anthropological aspects.

GV706.2.M55 2001
Miller, Toby.
Sportsex/ Toby Miller. Philadelphia: Temple University Press, 2001. viii, 180 p.
00-049098   306.4/83 21   1566398649
Sports -- Anthropological aspects. Gender identity. Sports -- Social aspects.

GV706.3 Sports — Philosophy. Relation to other topics — Relation to ethics. Fair play. Sportsmanship

GV706.3.B47 1994
Berlow, Lawrence H.,
Sports ethics: a reference handbook/ Lawrence H. Berlow. Santa Barbara, Calif.: ABC-CLIO, c1994. xii, 204 p.
94-034467   796/.01 20   0874367697
Sports -- Moral and ethical aspects -- Handbooks, manuals, etc.

GV706.3.E86 2001
Ethics in sport/ [edited by] William J. Morgan, Klaus V. Meier, Angela Schneider. Champaign, IL: Human Kinetics, c2001. xi, 427 p.
00-046151   175 21   0736036431
Sports -- Moral and ethical aspects -- United States. Sports -- Social aspects -- United States.

GV706.3.S54 1995
Shields, David Lyle, 1950-
Character development and physical activity/ David Lyle Light Shields, Brenda Jo Light Bredemeier. Champaign, IL: Human Kinetics, c1995. xi, 269 p.
94-007514   796/.01   0873227115
Sports -- Moral and ethical aspects. Moral development. Personality development.

GV706.3.S66 2003
Sports ethics: an anthology/ edited by Jan Boxill.
Malden, MA: Blackwell Pub., 2003.
  2002-071229 796/.01 21 0631216979
  Sports -- Moral and ethical aspects. Sports --
  Social aspects.

GV706.32 Sports — Philosophy.
Relation to other topics —
Relation to race and discrimination

GV706.32.E57 2000
Entine, Jon.
Taboo: why Black athletes dominate sports and
why we are afraid to talk about it/ Jon Entine. New
York: PublicAffairs, c2000. ix, 387 p.
  99-041889 796/.089/96073 21 1891620398
  Athletes, Black. Blacks -- Race identity.

GV706.32.M47 2003
Messner, Michael A.
Taking the field: women, men, and sports/ Michael
A. Messner. Minneapolis: University of Minnesota
Press, c2003.
  2001-008548 796/.082 21 0816634491
  Sex discrimination in sports -- United States.
  Sports -- United States -- Sex differences.
  Feminism and sports -- United States.

GV706.32.S48 1996
Shropshire, Kenneth L.
In black and white: race and sports in America/
Kenneth L. Shropshire; foreword by Kellen
Winslow. New York: New York University Press,
c1996. xxvii, 212 p.
  95-050200 305.8/00973 20 0814780164
  Discrimination in sports -- United States. Racism
  -- United States. Afro-Americans -- Sports.

GV706.32.W66 1994
Women, media, and sport: challenging gender
values/ edited by Pamela J. Creedon. Thousand
Oaks, Calif.: Sage Publications, c1994. x, 358 p.
  93-041211 796/.0194 0803952333
  Sex discrimination in sports. Mass media and
  sports.

GV706.34 Sports — Philosophy.
Relation to other topics —
Relation to nationalism

GV706.34.P67 1997
Pope, S. W., 1962-
Patriotic games: sporting traditions in the
American imagination, 1876-1926/ S.W. Pope.
New York: Oxford University Press, 1997. xi,
212 p.
  96-005506 796/.0973 0195091337
  Nationalism and sports -- United States --
  History -- 19th century. Nationalism and sports --
  United States -- History -- 20th century. Sports --
  United States -- Sociological aspects -- History --
  19th century.

GV706.35 Sports — Philosophy.
Relation to other topics —
Relation to politics.
Sports and state

GV706.35.D36 1997
Danielson, Michael N.
Home team: professional sports and the American
metropolis/ Michael N. Danielson. Princeton, N.J.:
Princeton University Press, c1997. xx, 397 p.
  96-035200 796/.06/9 20 0691036500
  Sports and state -- United States. Sports --
  United States -- Sociological aspects. Sports --
  Economic aspects -- United States.

GV706.35.D97 1998
Dyreson, Mark, 1959-
Making the American team: sport, culture, and the
Olympic experience/ Mark Dyreson. Urbana:
University of Illinois Press, c1998. viii, 269 p.
  97-004663 796/.0973 21 0252023498
  Sports -- Political aspects -- United States.
  Nationalism and sports -- United States. Sports --
  Social aspects -- United States.

GV706.35.I57 1999
The international politics of sport in the 20th
century/ edited by James Riodan and Arnd Kruger.
London: E & FN Spon; 1999. x, 253 p.
  98-041234 796/.09/04 0419211608
  Sports -- Political aspects -- History -- 20th
  century. Sport and state -- History -- 20th century.
  Sports -- Social aspects -- History -- 20th century.

GV706.35.N38 1996
National   sports   policies: an   international
handbook/ edited by Laurence Chalip, Arthur
Johnson, and Lisa Stachura. Westport, Ct.:
Greenwood Press, 1996. xiv, 442 p.
  95-025327 796/.06/9 0313284814
  Sports and state.

GV706.35.R56 1991
Riordan, James, 1936-
Sport, politics, and communism/ James Riordan.
Manchester,   England;   Manchester   University
Press; c1991. vi, 169 p.
  90-025265 796/.0947 0719028507
  Sport and state -- Europe, Eastern.

GV706.35.S58 1998
Sport and international politics/ edited by Pierre
Arnaud and James Riordan. London; E & FN
Spon, 1998. x, 227 p.
  98-189017   0419214402
  Sports and state -- History -- 20th century. Sports
  -- Political aspects -- History -- 20th century.
  Sports and state -- Europe -- History -- 20th
  century.

GV706.4 Sports — Philosophy.
Relation to other topics —
Relation to psychology.
Sports psychology

GV706.4.C67 1998
Cooper, Andrew, 1953-
Playing in the zone: exploring the spiritual
dimensions of sports/ Andrew Cooper. Boston:
Shambhala, 1998. 160 p.
  98-005799 796/.01 1570621519
  Sports -- Psychological aspects. Spirituality.
  Sports -- Social aspects.

GV706.4.E459 2000
Emotions in sport/ Yuri L. Hanin, editor.
Champaign, IL: Human Kinetics, c2000. xii, 395 p.
  99-016522 796/.01 21 0880118792
  Sports -- Psychological aspects. Athletes --
  Psychology.

GV706.4.E87 1995
European perspectives on exercise and sport
psychology/ Stuart J.H. Biddle [editor]. Leeds,
U.K.; Human Kinetics, c1995. xviii, 342 p.
  94-032258 796/.01/094 087322826X
  Sports -- Europe -- Psychological aspects.
  Exercise -- Psychological aspects.

GV706.4.E96 2002
Exploring sport and exercise psychology/ edited by
Judy L. Van Raalte, Britton W. Brewer. 2nd ed.
Washington,   DC: American   Psychological
Association, c2002. xxiii, 561 p.
  2002-020856 796/.01 21 1557988862
  Sports -- Psychological aspects. Exercise --
  Psychological aspects. Sports -- psychology.

GV706.4.G55 1986
Gill, Diane L., 1948-
Psychological dynamics of sport/ Diane L. Gill.
Champaign, IL: Human Kinetics Publishers, c1986.
xv, 286 p.
  86-010440 796/.01 0873220706
  Sports -- Psychological aspects. Motivation
  (Psychology)

GV706.4.H37 1993
Handbook of research on sport psychology/
sponsored by the International Society of Sport
Psychology; edited by Robert N. Singer, Milledge
Murphey, L. Keith Tennant. New York:
Macmillan; c1993. xvii, 984 p.
  92-013400 796/.01 0028971957
  Sports -- Psychological aspects. Sports --
  Research.

GV706.4.H373 1996
Hardy, Lew.
Understanding psychological preparation for sport:
theory and practice of elite performers/ Lew Hardy,
Graham Jones, Daniel Gould. Chichester; J. Wiley,
c1996. xvi, 346 p.
  96-021493 796/.01 20 0471950238
  Sports -- Psychological aspects. Physical
  education and training.

GV706.4.J33 1999
Jackson, Susan A., 1963-
Flow in sports/ Susan A. Jackson, Mihaly
Csikszentmihalyi.   Champaign,   IL: Human
Kinetics, c1999. viii, 183 p.
  99-012526 796/.01 21 0880118768
  Sports -- Psychological aspects. Athletes --
  Psychology. Happiness.

GV706.4.J37 1999
Jarvis, Matt, 1966-
Sport psychology/ Matt Jarvis. London; Routledge,
1999. xv, 169 p.
  99-012984 796/.01 0415206413
  Sports -- Psychological aspects. Athletes --
  Psychology.

GV706.4.K74 1994
Kremer, John M. D.
Psychology in sport/ John M.D. Kremer and
Deirdre M. Scully. London; Taylor & Francis,
1994. x, 194 p.
  93-046607 796/.01 0748401814
  Sports -- Psychological aspects.

GV706.4.M47 1992
Messner, Michael A.
Power at play: sports and the problem of masculinity/ Michael A. Messner. Boston: Beacon Press, c1992. xi, 240 p.
91-028600 796/.0194 0807041041
Sports -- Psychological aspects. Sports -- Social aspects. Masculinity.

GV706.4.P673 2002
Psychological foundations of sport/ edited by John M. Silva, Diane E. Stevens. Boston, MA: Allyn and Bacon, c2002. xviii, 558 p.
00-052200 796/.01 21 0205331440
Sports -- Psychological aspects.

GV706.4.W38 2003
Weinberg, Robert S.
Foundations of sport and exercise psychology/ Robert S. Weinberg, Daniel Gould. 3rd ed. Champaign, IL: Human Kinetics, c2003.
2002-013861 796/.01 21 0736044191
Sports -- Psychological aspects. Exercise -- Psychological aspects.

GV706.5 Sports — Philosophy. Relation to other topics — Relation to sociology

GV706.5.B73 1990
Brailsford, Dennis, 1925-
Sport, time, and society: the British at play/ Dennis Brailsford. London; Routledge, 1991. xv, 188 p.
89-049245 306.4/83 0415007666
Sports -- Social aspects -- Great Britain -- History. Play -- Great Britain -- History.

GV706.5.B7613
Brohm, Jean-Marie, 1940-
Sport, a prison of measured time: essays/ by Jean-Marie Brohm; translated [from the French] by Ian Fraser. London: Ink Links Ltd., 1978. ix, 185 p.
78-326614 796 0906133017
Sports -- Social aspects. Sports and state. Olympics.

GV706.5.C383 2000
Cashmore, Ernest.
Sports culture/ Ellis Cashmore. London; Routledge, 2000.
99-016891 306.4/83/03 0415181690
Sports -- Sociological aspects -- Encyclopedias. Sports -- Anthropological aspects -- Encyclopedias.

GV706.5.C63 2001
Coakley, Jay J.
Sport in society: issues & controversies/ Jay Coakley. 7th ed. Boston: McGraw-Hill, c2001. xv, 555 p.
00-060920 306.4/83 21 0072328916
Sports -- Social aspects. Sports -- Psychological aspects.

GV706.5.D85 1999
Dunning, Eric.
Sport matters: sociological studies of sport, violence, and civilization/ Eric Dunning. London; Routledge, 1999. ix, 281 p.
98-047958 306.4/83 0415064139
Sports -- Sociological aspects. Sports -- Cross-cultural studies. Violence in sports.

GV706.5.F7 1986
Fractured focus: sport as a reflection of society/ edited by Richard E. Lapchick. Lexington, Mass.: Lexington Books, c1986. xix, 388 p.
85-045745 306/.483 0669128600
Sports -- Social aspects -- United States. Sports -- Social aspects.

GV706.5.G87
Guttmann, Allen.
From ritual to record: the nature of modern sports/ Allen Guttmann. New York: Columbia University Press, 1978. viii, 198 p.
77-020886 301.5/7 023103993X
Sports -- Social aspects. Sports -- Social aspects -- United States.

GV706.5.I55 1999
Inside sports/ edited by Jay Coakley and Peter Donnelly. London; Routledge, 1999. xviii, 248 p.
98-036508 306.4/83 0415170885
Sports -- Social aspects.

GV706.5.M363 2001
Markovits, Andrei S.
Offside: soccer and American exceptionalism/ Andrei S. Markovits and Steven L. Hellerman. Princeton, N.J.: Princeton University Press, c2001. xiv, 367 p.
00-061115 796.334/0973 21 0691074461
Sports -- United States -- Sociological aspects. Soccer -- Social aspects -- United States.

GV706.5.M365 2000
Masculinities, gender relations, and sport/ edited by Jim McKay, Michael A. Messner, and Don Sabo. Thousand Oaks, Calif.: Sage Publications, c2000. xiv, 330 p.
00-008019 796/.081 21 0761912711
Sports -- Social aspects. Sports -- Psychological aspects. Masculinity.

GV706.5.M37 1989
McPherson, Barry D.
The social significance of sport: an introduction to the sociology of sport/ Barry D. McPherson, James E. Curtis, John W. Loy. Champaign, Ill.: Human Kinetics Books, c1989. xv, 334 p.
89-001975 306/.483 0873222350
Sports -- Social aspects. Sports -- Social aspects -- United States.

GV706.5.M47 1994
Messner, Michael A.
Sex, violence & power in sports: rethinking masculinity/ Michael A. Messner & Donald F. Sabo. Freedom, CA: Crossing Press, c1994. 220 p.
94-018562 306.4/83 0895946890
Sports -- Sociological aspects. Sports -- Psychological aspects. Masculinity.

GV706.5.P88 1999
Putnam, Douglas T., 1953-
Controversies of the sports world/ Douglas T. Putnam. Westport, Conn.: Greenwood Press, 1999. xii, 253 p.
98-038217 796/.0973 0313305587
Sports -- Social aspects -- United States. Sports -- Moral and ethical aspects -- United States.

GV706.5.R42 2000
Reading sport: critical essays on power and representation/ Susan Birrell and Mary G. McDonald. Boston: Northeastern University Press, c2000. 326 p.
99-088217 306.4/83/0973 21 1555534309
Sports -- Social aspects -- United States. Sports -- Anthropological aspects -- United States. Sports -- United States -- Psychological aspects.

GV706.5.R54 1995
Riess, Steven A.
Sport in industrial America, 1850-1920/ Steven A. Riess. Wheeling, Ill.: Harlan Davidson, c1995. viii, 221 p.
94-043286 306.4/83/0973 0882959166
Sports -- United States -- Sociological aspects. Sports -- United States -- History -- 19th century. Sports -- United States -- History -- 20th century.

GV706.5.S228 1998
Sage, George Harvey.
Power and ideology in American sport: a critical perspective/ George H. Sage. Champaign, IL: Human Kinetics, c1998. xiii, 335 p.
98-017002 306.4/83/0973 21 0880116609
Sports -- Social aspects -- United States.

GV706.5.S56 1991
Simon, Robert L., 1941-
Fair play: sports, values, and society/ Robert L. Simon. Boulder: Westview Press, 1991. xi, 229 p.
91-031293 306.4/83/0973 0813379733
Sports -- Social aspects. Sports -- Social aspects -- United States.

GV706.5.S59 1998
Sleap, Mike.
Social issues in sport/ Mike Sleap. New York: St. Martin's Press, 1998. xvii, 214 p.
97-008879 306.4/83 0312176023
Sports -- Sociological aspects.

GV706.5.S645 2001
The sociology of sport and physical education: an introductory reader / [edited by] Anthony Laker. London; RoutledgeFalmer, 2001.
2001-019961 306.4/83 21 0415235944
Sports -- Social aspects. Physical education and training -- Social aspects.

GV706.5.S694 1992
Sport and leisure in the civilizing process: critique and counter-critique/ edited by Eric Dunning and Chris Rojek. Toronto; University of Toronto Press, c1992. xix, 289 p.
92-195982 306.4/83 0802028047
Sports -- Sociological aspects. Leisure -- Sociological aspects.

GV706.5.S6943 1998
Sport and postmodern times/ edited by Genevieve Rail. Albany: State University of New York Press, c1998. xxi, 399 p.
97-050231 306.4/83 21 0791439259
Sports -- Sociological aspects. Physical education and training -- Social aspects.

GV706.5.S696 1988
Sport and society in Latin America: diffusion, dependency, and the rise of mass culture/ edited by Joseph L. Arbena. New York: Greenwood Press, 1988. 162 p.
87-032271 306/.483/098 0313247749
Sports -- Social aspects -- Latin America.

GV706.5.S7326 1994
Sport in Australia: a social history/ edited by Wray Vamplew and Brian Stoddart. Cambridge, UK; Cambridge University Press, 1994. xiv, 346 p.
94-019932 306.4/83 0521435137
Sports -- Social aspects -- Australia. Popular culture -- Australia. Australia -- Social conditions.

GV706.5.S75 1993
The Sports process: a comparative and developmental approach/ Eric G. Dunning, Joseph A. Maguire, Robert E. Pearton, editors. Champaign, IL: Human Kinetics Publishers, c1993. xiii, 321 p.
92-029998   306.4'83   0873224191
Sports -- Sociological aspects. Sports -- Social aspects -- History. Sports and state.

GV706.5.W54 1994
Williams, Peter, 1937 Jan. 30-
The sports immortals: deifying the American athlete/ Peter Williams. Bowling Green, OH: Bowling Green State University Popular Press, c1994. 170 p.
94-078929   0879726695
Hero worship -- United States. Sports -- Sociological aspects -- United States. Athletes -- United States.

GV706.5.W55 1994
Wilson, John, 1942-
Playing by the rules: sport, society, and the state/ John Wilson. Detroit: Wayne State University Press, c1994. 429 p.
93-019671   306.4'83'0973   0814321070
Sports -- Social aspects -- United States. Sports and state -- United States.

GV706.8 Sports — General special (Special aspects of the subject as a whole)

GV706.8.B35 2002
Bale, John.
Sports geography/ John Bale. 2nd ed. New York: Routledge, 2002.
2002-068169   796 21   0419252304
Sports. Sports -- Regional disparities. Human geography.

GV707 Sports — Addresses, essays, lectures

GV707.M25 2000
Sports quotations: maxims, quips, and pronouncements for writers and fans/ Andrew J. Maikovich and Michele D. Brown, editors. 2nd ed. Jefferson, N.C.: McFarland & Co., c2000. vii, 237 p.
99-059281   796 21   0786408170
Sports -- Quotations, maxims, etc.

GV707.U47 2001
The ultimate dictionary of sports quotations/ [compiled by] Carlo De Vito. New York: Facts on File, 2001. xvii, 332 p.
99-059375   796 21   0816039801
Sports -- Quotations, maxims, etc. Sports personnel -- Quotations.

GV708.8 Sports — Sports for special classes of persons — Gay men and Lesbians

GV708.8.G75 1998
Griffin, Pat.
Strong women, deep closets: lesbians and homophobia in sport/ Pat Griffin. Champaign, IL: Human Kinetics, c1998. xvii, 245 p.
97-032363   796/.086/643 21   088011729X
Lesbian athletes. Homophobia in sports.

GV709-709.18 Sports — Sports for special classes of persons — Women

GV709.B66 1983
Boutilier, Mary A.
The sporting woman/ Mary A. Boutilier, Lucinda SanGiovanni. Champaign, IL: Human Kinetics Publishers, c1983. xvii, 289 p.
82-083147   796/.01/94   0931250358
Sports for women. Sports for women -- Social aspects. Sports for women -- United States.

GV709.E53 1998
Encyclopedia of women and sport in America/ edited by Carole A. Oglesby; with [contributions by] Doreen L. Greenberg ... [et al.]. Phoenix: Oryx Press, 1998. xxiii, 360 p.
97-052787   796/.082   0897749936
Women athletes -- United States -- Encyclopedias. Sports for women -- United States -- Encyclopedias.

GV709.F37 1996
Festle, Mary Jo.
Playing nice: politics and apologies in women's sports/ Mary Jo Festle. New York: Columbia University Press, c1996. xxviii, 379 p.
96-004739   796/.0194 20   0231101627
Sports for women -- United States -- History. Sex differences (Psychology) Women athletes -- United States -- History.

GV709.G85 1991
Guttmann, Allen.
Women's sports: a history/ Allen Guttmann. New York: Columbia University Press, c1991. x, 339 p.
90-028692   796/.0194   0231069561
Sports for women -- History.

GV709.I58 2000
International encyclopedia of women and sports/ edited by Karen Christensen, Allen Guttmann, Gertrud Pfister. New York: Macmillan Reference USA, 2001. 3 v.
00-062518   796/.082   0028649540
Sports for women -- Encyclopedias. Women athletes -- Encyclopedias.

GV709.L38 2002
Lawler, Jennifer,
Punch!: why women participate in violent sports/ Jennifer Lawler. Terre Haute, Ind.: Wish Pub.; xxxii, 152 p.
2001-093468   796/.082 21   1930546505
Sports for women -- Social aspects. Violence in sports -- Social aspects.

GV709.N44 1991
Nelson, Mariah Burton.
Are we winning yet?: how women are changing sports and sports are changing women/ by Mariah Burton Nelson. New York: Random House, c1991. xi, 238 p.
90-042698   796/.0194   0394575768
Sports for women. Sports for women -- Social aspects. Femininity.

GV709.S32 1996
Salter, David F.
Crashing the old boys' network: the tragedies and triumphs of girls and women in sports/ David F. Salter. Westport, Conn.: Praeger, 1996. xiii, 163 p.
96-010427   796/.0194   0275955125
Women athletes. Sports for women. Sex discrimination in sports.

GV709.S44 1996
Sherrow, Victoria.
Encyclopedia of women and sports/ Victoria Sherrow. Santa Barbara, Calif.: ABC-CLIO, c1996. xxii, 382 p.
96-019600   796/.082 20   087436826X
Women athletes -- Encyclopedias. Sports -- Encyclopedias. Women athletes -- Biography.

GV709.W52 1999
Whatever it takes: women on women's sport/ edited and with an introduction by Joli Sandoz and Joby Winans. 1st ed. New York: Farrar, Straus and Giroux, 1999. x, 323 p.
98-031855   796/.082 21   0374525978
Sports for women.

GV709.W575 1983
Women, philosophy, and sport: a collection of new essays/ edited by Betsy C. Postow. Metuchen, N.J.: Scarecrow Press, 1983. xv, 315 p.
83-010146   796/.01/94   0810816385
Sports for women -- United States. School sports -- United States. Sex discrimination in sports -- United States.

GV709.W577 1994
Women, sport, and culture/ Susan Birrell, Cheryl L. Cole, editors. Champaign, IL: Human Kinetics, c1994. viii, 408 p.
93-038013   796/.0194   087322650X
Sports for women -- Sociological aspects. Sex discrimination in sports. Feminism.

GV709.W589 1997
The women's sports encyclopedia/ Robert Markel, executive editor; Susan Waggoner, managing editor; Marcella Smith, research and records editor; foreword by Billie Jean King; preface by Donna Lopiano. New York: H. Holt, 1997. x, 340 p.
97-008850   796/.082   0805044949
Sports for women -- History. Sports for women -- Records. Women athletes -- Biography.

GV709.18.C2.S66 1999
Sport and gender in Canada/ edited by Philip White and Kevin Young. Ontario; Oxford University Press, c1999. xix, 324 p.
00-698323   0195413172
Sex discrimination in sports -- Canada. Sports -- Social aspects -- Canada.

GV709.18.U6 G38 2002
Gavora, Jessica.
Tilting the playing field: schools, sports, sex, and Title IX/ Jessica Gavora. 1st ed. San Francisco: Encounter Books, 2002. 181 p.
2001-055597 796/.082 21 189355435X
Sports for women -- United States. Sex discrimination in sports -- United States. Sex discrimination in education -- United States.

GV709.18.U6.N55 1998
Nike is a goddess: the history of women in sports/ edited by Lissa Smith; introduction by Mariah Burton Nelson. New York: Atlantic Monthly Press, c1998. xix, 331 p.
98-027049 796/.082/0973 21 0871137267
Sports for women -- United States -- History. Sports for women -- Social aspects -- United States. Women athletes -- United States -- History.

GV709.18.U6.W65 1993
Women in sport: issues and controversies/ Greta L. Cohen editor; foreword by Jackie Joyner-Kersee. Newbury Park: Sage Publications, c1993. xix, 338 p.
93-006510 796/.0194 0803949790
Sports for women -- United States. Women athletes -- United States.

GV709.2 Sports —
Sports for special classes of persons — Children

GV709.2.G75 1998
Griffin, Robert S.
Sports in the lives of children and adolescents: success on the field and in life/ Robert S. Griffin. Westport, Conn.: Praeger, 1998. 158 p.
97-033711 796/.083 0275961273
Sports for children -- Psychological aspects. Sports for children -- Social aspects. Character.

GV709.2.I58 1993
Intensive participation in children's sports/ American Orthopaedic Society for Sports Medicine; Bernard R. Cahill, Arthur J. Pearl, editors. Champaign, IL: Human Kinetics Publishers, c1993. xiii, 240 p.
92-026253 796/.01922 0873224094
Sports for children -- Psychological aspects. Sports for children -- Physiological aspects. Sports for children -- Social aspects.

GV709.2.W67 1996
Worldwide trends in youth sport/ Paul De Knop ... [et al.], editors. Champaign, IL: Human Kinetics, c1996. xi, 311 p.
95-033994 796/.01922 20 0873227298
Sports for children -- Cross-cultural studies. Sports for children -- Social aspects -- Cross-Cultural studies.

GV709.3 Sports —
Sports for special classes of persons — Handicapped persons

GV709.3.D47 1995
DePauw, Karen P.
Disability and sport/ Karen P. DePauw, Susan J. Gavron. Champaign, IL: Human Kinetics, c1995. xii, 298 p.
94-025215 790.1/96 0873228480
Sports for the handicapped.

GV709.5-709.6 Sports —
Sports for special classes of persons — Minorities

GV709.5.E83 2000
Encyclopedia of ethnicity and sports in the United States/ edited by George B. Kirsch, Othello Harris, and Claire E. Nolte. Westport, Conn.: Greenwood Press, 2000. xv, 530 p.
99-015392 796/.089/00973 0313299110
Minorities in sports -- United States -- History. Sports -- Sociological aspects -- United States -- History.

GV709.5.E84 1994
Ethnicity and sport in North American history and culture/ edited by George Eisen and David K. Wiggins. Westport, Conn.: Greenwood Press, 1994. xvii, 249 p.
93-050538 796.1/9 0313288143
Minorities in sports -- United States -- History. Minorities in sports -- Canada -- History. Popular culture -- United States.

GV709.6.S76 1998
Sports and the American Jew/ edited by Steven A. Riess. Syracuse, N.Y.: Syracuse University Press, 1998. xvi, 337 p.
97-020930 796/.089/924073 0815627610
Jewish athletes -- United States -- History. Jews -- United States -- Social life and customs. Sports -- United States -- Sociological aspects.

GV711 Sports — Coaching

GV711.L96 2001
Lynch, Jerry, 1942-
Creative coaching/ Jerry Lynch. Champaign, IL: Human Kinetics, c2001. xiv, 217 p.
00-053932 796/.07/7 21 0736033270
Coaching (Athletics)

GV711.M355 1997
Martens, Rainer,
Successful coaching/ Rainer Martens. Updated 2nd ed. Champaign, Ill.: Human Kinetics, c1997. x, 219 p.
96-031259 796/.071/273 20 0880116668
School sports -- Coaching -- United States.

GV711.5 Sports —
Training and conditioning

GV711.5.E88 2000
Essentials of strength training and conditioning/ National Strength and Conditioning Association; Thomas R. Baechle, Roger Earle, editors. 2nd ed. Champaign, Ill.: Human Kinetics, c2000. xiii, 658 p.
99-087979 0873226763
Physical education and training. Muscle strength. Physical fitness -- Physiological aspects.

GV711.5.Z38 1995
Zatsiorsky, Vladimir M., 1932-
Science and practice of strength training/ Vladimir M. Zatsiorsky. Champaign, IL: Human Kinetics, c1995. xii, 243 p.
94-040135 613.7/11 0873224744
Physical education and training. Muscle strength. Biomechanics.

GV713-716 Sports —
Athletic contests. Sports events — Organization and administration

GV713.M35 2001
The management of sport: its foundation and application/ Bonnie L. Parkhouse. 3rd ed. Dubuque, IA: McGraw-Hill, c2001. xvi, 416 p.
00-026077 796/.06/9 21 0072300329
Sports administration -- Study and teaching -- United States.

GV713.V35 1998
VanderZwaag, Harold J.
Policy development in sport management/ Harold J. VanderZwaag. Westport, Conn.: Praeger, c1998. xi, 232 p.
98-004973 796/.06/073 21 0275960897
Sports administration -- United States.

GV714.5.K56 2001
Team spirits: the Native American mascots controversy/ edited by C. Richard King and Charles Fruehling Springwood; foreword by Vine Deloria, Jr. Lincoln: University of Nebraska Press, c2001. xv, 356 p.
00-059968 306.4/83 21 0803277989
Indians as mascots. Sports team mascots -- Social aspects -- United States. Indians of North America -- Social conditions -- 20th century.

GV715.G88 1986
Guttmann, Allen.
Sports spectators/ Allen Guttmann. New York: Columbia University Press, 1986. viii, 236 p.
86-008268 363.3/2 0231064004
Sports spectators -- History. Violence in sports -- History.

GV716.Q57 1992
Quirk, James P.
Pay dirt: the business of professional team sports/ James Quirk and Rodney D. Fort. Princeton, N.J.: Princeton University Press, c1992. xviii, 538 p.
92-015349 338.4/3796 0691042551
Professional sports -- Economic aspects -- United States.

GV716.S64 1990
Sportometrics/ edited by Brian L. Goff and Robert D. Tollison. College Station: Texas A & M University Press, c1990. vii, 319 p.
89-049065 338.4/7796 0890964254
Sports -- Economic aspects.

GV716.S647 1997
Sports, jobs, and taxes: the economic impact of sports teams and stadiums/ Roger G. Noll and Andrew Zimbalist, editors. Washington D.C.: Brookings Institution Press, c1997. xii, 525 p.
97-033764 338.4/3796/0973 21 0815761104
Sports franchises -- Economic aspects -- United States. Sports teams -- Economic aspects -- United States. Stadiums -- Economic aspects -- United States. United States -- Economic conditions -- 1981-

GV717 Sports — Athletic contests. Sports events — Betting

GV717.D38 2001
Davies, Richard O.,
Betting the line: sports wagering in American life/ Richard O. Davies and Richard G. Abram. Columbus: Ohio State University Press, c2001. 212 p.
2001-000771 796 21 0814208800
Sports betting -- United States -- History. Sports -- Corrupt practices -- United States -- History.

GV719 Sports — Mass media — Biography of sports writers, broadcasters, promoters, etc. *(See GV742-742.42)*

GV719.C67.A32 1973
Cosell, Howard, 1918-
Cosell, by Howard Cosell, with the editorial assistance of Mickey Herskowitz. Chicago, Playboy Press, 1973 ix, 390 p.
73-084918 070.4/49/7960924
Cosell, Howard, -- 1918- Television broadcasting of sports -- United States.

GV721.2-722 Sports — Athletic contests. Sports events — Special contests and events

GV721.2.C68.K75 1995
Kristy, Davida.
Coubertin's Olympics: how the games began/ Davida Kristy. Minneapolis: Lerner Publications Co., c1995. 128 p.
94-012889 338.4/7796/092 0822533278
Coubertin, Pierre de, -- 1863-1937 -- Juvenile literature. Coubertin, Pierre de, -- 1863-1937. Olympics -- Revival, 1896 -- Juvenile literature. Sports promoters -- France -- Biography -- Juvenile literature. Sports promoters.

GV721.5.C474 1998
Chronicle of the Olympics, 1896-2000. 1st American ed. New York: DK Pub., c1998. 330 p.
97-041746 796.48 21 078942312X
Olympics -- History. Olympics -- Pictorial works. Olympics -- Records.

GV721.5.G85 2002
Guttmann, Allen.
The Olympics, a history of the modern games/ Allen Guttmann. 2nd ed. Urbana: University of Illinois Press, c2002. x, 214 p.
2001-041383 796.48 21 0252070461
Olympics -- History.

GV721.5.H54 1996
Hill, Christopher R.
Olympic politics/ Christopher R. Hill. Manchester, UK; Manchester University Press; c1996. xv, 283 p.
95-036982 796.48 20 0719044502
Olympics -- Political aspects.

GV721.5.J37 1990
Jarrett, William S.
Timetables of sports history. by William S. Jarrett. New York: Facts on File, c1990. vi, 94 p.
89-048159 796.48 0816019215
Olympics -- History. Olympics -- Records. Olympics -- History.

GV721.5.O425 2000
The Olympics at the millennium: power, politics, and the games/ edited by Kay Schaffer and Sidonie Smith. New Brunswick, N.J.: Rutgers University Press, c2000. xi, 318 p.
99-056801 796.48 21 0813528194
Olympics -- Social aspects. Olympics -- History.

GV721.5.Y68 1996
Young, David C.
The modern Olympics: a struggle for revival/ David C. Young. Baltimore: Johns Hopkins University Press, 1996. xv, 252 p.
96-016496 796.48 20 0801853745
Olympics -- History.

GV721.6.L83 1992
Lucas, John A. 1927-
Future of the Olympic Games/ John A. Lucas. Champaign, IL: Human Kinetics Books, c1992. xv, 231 p.
91-046818 796.48 0873223578
Olympics -- Philosophy. Olympics -- Social aspects.

GV722 1932.P54 1996
Pieroth, Doris Hinson.
Their day in the sun: women of the 1932 Olympics/ Doris H. Pieroth. Seattle: University of Washington Press, c1996. xii, 186 p.
96-023104 796.48 20 0295975539
Women athletes -- United States -- Biography.

GV722 1936.M3
Mandell, Richard D.
The Nazi Olympics, by Richard D. Mandell. New York, Macmillan [1971] xvi, 316 p.
74-130949 796.4/8
Sports -- Germany. National socialism and sports. Sports and state -- Germany.

GV722 1972.M35 1991
Mandell, Richard D.
The Olympics of 1972: a Munich diary/ by Richard D. Mandell. Chapel Hill: University of North Carolina Press, c1991. xvi, 207 p.
90-023544 796.48 0807819549
Mandell, Richard D.

GV731 Sports — Rules (Collections)

GV731.B56 1998
The book of rules: a visual guide to the laws of every commonly played sport and game. New York: Facts on File, Inc., 1998. 224 p.
98-024910 796 0816039194
Sports -- Rules. Games -- Rules.

GV731.D52 1995
Rules of the game: the complete illustrated encyclopedia of all the sports of the world/ by the Diagram Group. 1st rev. pbk. ed. New York: St. Martin's Press, 1995. 320 p.
94-036062 796 20 0312119402
Sports -- Rules.

GV731.H85 1998
The sports rules book/ Human Kinetics with Thomas Hanlon. Champaign, IL: Human Kinetics, c1998. ix, 372 p.
97-027774 796 21 0880118075
Sports -- Rules.

GV731.S75 1990
Sports rules encyclopedia/ Jess R. White [editor]. Champaign, Ill.: Leisure Press, c1990. x, 732 p.
89-002280 796 0880113634
Sports -- Rules.

GV734.5 Sports — Professional sports (General) — Sports agents

GV734.5.S57 1990
Shropshire, Kenneth L.
Agents of opportunity: sports agents and corruption in collegiate sports/ Kenneth L. Shropshire. Philadelphia: University of Pennsylvania Press, c1990. viii, 181 p.
90-041858 338.4/7796/0973 0812282124
Sports agents -- United States. Sports -- Corrupt practices -- United States. College sports -- United States.

GV734.5.S58 2003
Shropshire, Kenneth L.
The business of sports agents/ Kenneth L. Shropshire and Timothy Davis. Philadelphia: University of Pennsylvania Press, c2003. viii, 206 p.
2002-072534 796/.06/9 21 0812236823
Sports agents -- United States. Sports -- Corrupt practices -- United States. College sports -- United States.

GV735 Sports — Umpires. Sports officiating

GV735.B8 1968
Bunn, John William, 1898-
The art of officiating sports [by] John W. Bunn. Englewood Cliffs, N.J., Prentice-Hall [1967, c1968] xxiii, 367 p.
67-027958 796
Sports officiating.

GV735.W45 1990
Weinberg, Robert S.
Psychology of officiating/ Robert S. Weinberg, Peggy A. Richardson. Champaign, Ill.: Leisure Press, c1990. viii, 184 p.
90-031893 796 0880114002
Sports officiating -- Psychological aspects.

GV741 Sports — Sports records and statistics. Champions

GV741.R47
Richards, Jack W., 1933-
Complete handbook of sports scoring and record keeping [by] Jack Richards [and] Danny Hill. West Nyack, N.Y., Parker Pub. Co. [1974] 266 p.
73-014815 796/.021/2 0131612573
Sports -- Statistics. Sports records. Sports officiating.

GV742 Sports — Mass media — General works

GV742.M33 1989
Media, sports & society/ edited by Lawrence A. Wenner. Newbury Park, Calif.: Sage Publications, c1989. 315 p.
89-010214   306.4/83   080393243X
Mass media and sports -- United States. Sports -- Social aspects -- United States.

GV742.O88 1997
Out of bounds: sports, media, and the politics of identity/ edited by Aaron Baker and Todd Boyd. Bloomington: Indiana University Press, c1997. xviii, 206 p.
96-019729   070.4/49796 20   0253332281
Mass media and sports -- United States. Sports -- Social aspects -- United States.

GV742.3 Sports — Mass media — Radio and television broadcasting

GV742.3.D33 1998
Daddario, Gina, 1954-
Women's sport and spectacle: gendered television coverage and the Olympic games/ Gina Daddario. Westport, Conn.: Praeger, 1998. ix, 174 p.
97-038544   302.23/45/082   0275958566
Television and sports -- United States. Women on television. Sex role on television.

GV742.3.K53 1988
Klatell, David A.
Sports for sale: television, money, and the fans/ David A. Klatell & Norman Marcus. New York: Oxford University Press, 1988. xi, 253 p.
88-018789   070.4/49796/0973   0195038363
Television broadcasting of sports -- United States. Sports -- Economic aspects -- United States.

GV742.3.R33 1984
Rader, Benjamin G.
In its own image: how television has transformed sports/ Benjamin G. Rader. New York: Free Press; c1984. ix, 228 p.
84-047856   070.4/49796/0973   002925700X
Television broadcasting of sports -- United States -- History. Sports -- United States -- History.

GV742.4-742.42 Sports — Mass media — Biography of sports writers, broadcasters, promoters, etc.

GV742.4.S47 2002
Shannon, Mike.
Baseball: the writer's game/ Mike Shannon. 1st ed. Washington, D.C.: Brassey's, c2002. xi, 271 p.
2002-074471   070.4/49796/0922.B   21
1574884212
Sportswriters -- United States--Biography. Baseball.

GV742.42.B47.A3 1997
Berkow, Ira.
To the hoop: the seasons of a basketball life/ Ira Berkow. New York: BasicBooks, c1997. 295 p.
97-002009   070.4/49796/092 B 21   0465084958
Berkow, Ira. Sportswriters -- United States -- Biography. Basketball players -- United States -- Biography.

GV742.42.R53 F68 1993
Fountain, Charles.
Sportswriter: the life and times of Grantland Rice/ Charles Fountain. New York: Oxford University Press, 1993. 327 p.
92-046146   070.4/49796/092.B 20   0195061764
Rice, Grantland, 1880-1954. Sportswriters -- United States -- Biography.

GV745 Sports — Athletic and sporting goods, supplies, etc. — General works

GV745.W35 1992
Walker, Marcia L.
Sports equipment management/ Marcia L. Walker, Todd L. Seidler. Boston: Jones and Bartlett, c1993. xi, 146 p.
92-013401   796/.028   0867202815
Sporting goods. Physical education and training -- Equipment and supplies.

GV775 Sports — Water sports — Boats and boating (General)

GV775.R68 1998
Rousmaniere, John.
The illustrated dictionary of boating terms: 2,000 essential terms for sailors & powerboaters/ John Rousmaniere. New York: W.W. Norton, c1998. 168 p.
97-045938   797.1/24/03 21   0393046494
Boats and boating -- Dictionaries.

GV784 Sports — Water sports — Canoeing

GV784.B35 1991
Bailey, Donna.
Canoeing/ Donna Bailey. Austin, Tex.: Steck-Vaughn Library, c1991. 32 p.
90-023055   797.1/22   0811429032
Canoes and canoeing -- Juvenile literature. Kayaking -- Juvenile literature. Canoes and canoeing.

GV791 Sports — Water sports — Rowing

GV791.D63 1992
Dodd, Christopher.
The story of world rowing/ Christopher Dodd. London: Stanley Paul, 1992. xi, 468 p.
93-169662   796.1/23   0091746108
Rowing -- History.

GV811 Sports — Water sports — Sailing (General)

GV811.S546 1999
Sleight, Steve.
DK complete sailing manual/ Steve Sleight; editorial consultant Truman Morris. 1st American ed. New York: DK Pub., 1999. 320 p.
99-028974   797.1/24 21   0789446065
Sailing -- Handbooks, manuals, etc.

GV811.W275 1998
Walker, Stuart H.
The sailor's wind/ Stuart H. Walker; illustrated by the author and Thomas C. Price. New York: W.W. Norton, c1998. xviii, 362 p.
97-039322   797.1/24 21   0393045552
Sailing. Winds. Sailboat racing.

GV822 Sports — Water sports — Yachting

GV822.G5.C5 1961a
Chichester, Francis, 1901-1972.
Alone across the Atlantic/ Francis Chichester. New York: D. McKay, c1961. 191 p.
61-009489   794.14
Voyages and travels. Atlantic Ocean.

GV837-838.67 Sports — Water sports — Swimming, diving, lifesaving

GV837.O17 2003
O'Brien, Ronald F.
Springboard & platform diving/ Ron O'Brien. 2nd ed. Champaign, IL: Human Kinetics, c2003. vi, 226 p.
2002-013393   797.2/4 21   0736043780
Diving.

GV837.W55 1994
Whitten, Phillip.
The complete book of swimming/ Phillip Whitten; illustrations by Ethan Berry. New York: Random House, c1994. xviii, 372 p.
92-056805   797.2/1   0679746676
Swimming.

GV837.4.L47 1998
Lepore, Monica, 1956-
Adapted aquatics programming: a professional guide/ Monica Lepore, G. William Gayle, Shawn F. Stevens. Champaign, IL: Human Kinetics, c1998. xiv, 314 p.
98-022953   797.2/1/087 21   0880116951
Swimming for handicapped persons. Aquatic exercises -- Therapeutic use. Physically handicapped -- Rehabilitation.

GV838.67.T73 M33 2003
Maglischo, Ernest W.
Swimming fastest/ Ernest W. Maglischo. Champaign, IL: Human Kinetics, c2003. viii, 791 p.
2002-008867   797.2/1 21   0736031804
Swimming -- Training. Swimming Physiological aspects.

GV838.67.T73.M34 1982
Maglischo, Ernest W.
Swimming faster: a comprehensive guide to the science of swimming/ Ernest W. Maglischo. Palo Alto, Calif.: Mayfield Pub. Co., 1982. xxi, 472 p.
81-081278   797.2/1   0874845483
Swimming -- Training. Swimming Physiological aspects.

GV840 Sports — Water sports — Other water sports, A-Z

GV840.S8 C66 2001
Cralle, Trevor.
The surfin'ary: a dictionary of surfing terms and surfspeak/ compiled and edited by Trevor Cralle. Rev. and updated 2nd ed. Berkeley, CA: Ten Speed Press, c2001. xxi, 362 p.
00-057730   797.3/2/03 21   1580081932
Surfing -- Dictionaries.

GV846.5-848.6 Sports — Winter sports — Ice hockey

GV846.5.W45 1999
Weir, Glenn.
Ultimate hockey/ Glenn Weir, Jeff Chapman, and Travis Weir. Toronto, Canada; Stoddart; 1999. xii, 522 p.
00-268735   796.962/09   0773760571
Hockey -- History. Hockey -- Histoire.

GV847.8.N3 C64 1993
The Complete encyclopedia of hockey/ edited by Zander Hollander. 4th ed. expanded & updated Detroit: Gale Research, c1993. xv, 604 p.
92-029950   796.962/092/2.aB 20   0810388693
Hockey players -- Biography -- Dictionaries. Hockey -- Records.

GV848.3.S7 2001
Stamm, Laura.
Laura Stamm's power skating/ Laura Stamm; [foreword by Herb Brooks]. 3rd ed. Champaign, IL: Human Kinetics, c2001. xiv, 225 p.
2001-024792   796.962/2 21   0736037357
Hockey -- Training. Skating.

GV848.4.C2.R63 1998
Robinson, Laura.
Crossing the line: violence and sexual assault in Canada's national sport/ Laura Robinson. Toronto, Ont.: McClelland & Stewart, c1998. ix, 254 p.
99-161083   077107560X
Hockey players -- Canada -- Sexual behavior. Sexually abused teenagers -- Canada. Violence in sports -- Canada.

GV848.6.W65
Theberge, Nancy.
Higher goals: women's ice hockey and the politics of gender/ Nancy Theberge. Albany: State University of New York Press, c2000. xiii, 182 p.
99-057333   796.962/082/0971 21   0791446417
Hockey for women -- Social aspects -- Canada -- Case studies. Women hockey players -- Canada -- Social conditions -- Case studies. Sex discrimination in sports -- Canada -- Case studies.

GV849-850.4 Sports — Winter sports — Ice skating

GV849.M34 1998
Malone, John Williams.
The encyclopedia of figure skating/ by John Malone. New York: Facts on File, 1998. viii, 264 p.
97-046360   796.91/2/03   0816032262
Skating -- Encyclopedias.

GV850.4.O33 1998
The official book of figure skating/ U.S. Figure Skating Association; introduction by Peggy Fleming. New York: Simon & Schuster Editions, c1998. 266 p.
98-027343   796.91/2 21   068484673X
Skating.

GV854.4-855.3 Sports — Winter sports — Skiing. Downhill skiing

GV854.4.A4 1993
Allen, E. John B., 1933-
From skisport to skiing: one hundred years of an American sport, 1840-1940/ E. John B. Allen. Amherst: University of Massachusetts Press, c1993. xiii, 229 p.
93-009224   796.93/0973   0870238442
Skis and skiing -- United States -- History.

GV855.3.W53 1995
Wicks, David, 1939-
Making tracks: an introduction to cross-country skiing/ David Wicks. Boulder, Colo.: Pruett Pub. Co., c1995. vii, 104 p.
94-043251   796.93/2   0871088495
Cross-country skiing.

GV859 Sports — Roller skating — General works

GV859.L48 1997
Lewis, David H., 1940-
Roller skating for gold/ David H. Lewis. Lanham, Md.: Scarecrow Press, 1997. xii, 195 p.
96-021274   796.2/1   0810830485
Olympics. Roller skating.

GV861 Sports — Ball games — General works

GV861.H4 2001
Henderson, Robert W.
Ball, bat, and bishop: the origin of ball games/ Robert W. Henderson; foreword by Leonard Koppett. Urbana: University of Illinois Press, 2001. xxiv, 220 p.
00-067239   796.3/09 21   0252069927
Ball games -- History. Baseball -- History.

GV862.3-881 Sports — Ball games — Baseball

GV862.3.D53 1999
Dickson, Paul.
The new Dickson baseball dictionary: a cyclopedic reference to more than 7,000 words, names, phrases, and slang expressions that define the game, its heritage, culture, and variations/ Paul Dickson. New York: Harcourt Brace & Co., 1999. xxv, 579 p.
98-040700   796.357/0973/03   0151003807
Baseball -- United States -- Dictionaries.

GV862.3.L54 1997
Light, Jonathan Fraser, 1957-
The cultural encyclopedia of baseball/ Jonathan Fraser Light. Jefferson, N.C.: McFarland, c1997. viii, 888 p.
97-000763   796.357/03 21   078640311X
Baseball -- Social aspects -- Encyclopedias.

GV862.5.B37 1991
The Baseball chronology: the complete history of the most important-events in the game of baseball/ edited by James Charlton. New York: Macmillan; c1991. 707 p.
90-023254   796.357   0025239716
Baseball -- History -- Chronology.

GV863.A1.D53 1994
Dickson, Paul.
The Worth book of softball: a celebration of America's true national pastime/ Paul Dickson; photographs by Russell Mott. New York: Facts on File, c1994. xii, 276 p.
93-019312   796.357/8   0816028974
Softball -- United States. Softball -- United States -- History.

GV863.A1.E27 1995
Early innings: a documentary history of baseball, 1825-1908/ compiled & edited by Dean A. Sullivan; introduction by Benjamin G. Rader. Lincoln: University of Nebraska Press, c1995. xix, 312 p.
94-030847   796.357/0973/09034   0803242379
Baseball -- United States -- History -- 19th century -- Sources. Baseball -- United States -- History -- 20th century -- Sources.

GV863.A1.G66 1989
Goldstein, Warren Jay.
Playing for keeps: a history of early baseball/ Warren Goldstein. Ithaca: Cornell University Press, 1989. 182 p.
89-042876   796.357/0973   0801418291
Baseball -- United States -- History -- 19th century.

GV863.A1 J36 2001
James, Bill,
The new Bill James historical baseball abstract/ Bill James. New York: Free Press, 2001. x, 998 p.
2001-040062   796.357/0973 21   0684806975
Baseball -- United States -- History. Baseball -- Records -- United States.

GV863.A1.K57 1989
Kirsch, George B.
The creation of American team sports: baseball and cricket, 1838-72/ George B. Kirsch. Urbana: University of Illinois Press, c1989. xiv, 277 p.
88-014209   796/.0973   0252015606
Baseball -- United States -- History. Cricket -- United States -- History. Sports -- United States -- History.

GV863.A1.K66 1998
Koppett, Leonard.
Koppett's Concise history of major league baseball/ Leonard Koppett. Philadelphia: Temple University Press, 1998. xiv, 521 p.
98-004932   796.357/64/0973   1566396387
Baseball -- United States -- History.

GV863.A1 L28 2002
Late innings: a documentary history of baseball, 1945-1972/ compiled and edited by Dean A. Sullivan. Lincoln: University of Nebraska Press, c2002. xxi, 299 p.
2001-043063   796.357/0973/09045   21   0803292856
Baseball -- United States -- History -- 20th century -- Sources.

GV863.A1.L5 1977
Lieb, Fred, b. 1888.
Baseball as I have known it/ Fred Lieb. New York:
Coward, McCann & Geoghegan, c1977. 349 p.
77-005309   796.357/0973   0698108159
Lieb, Fred, -- b. 1888.   Baseball -- United States --
History.   Sportswriters -- United States --
Biography.

GV863.A1.M52 1998
Middle innings: a documentary history of baseball,
1900-1948/ compiled & edited by Dean A.
Sullivan. Lincoln: University of Nebraska Press,
c1998. xvii, 238 p.
97-036995   796.357/0973 21   0803242581
Baseball -- United States -- History -- 20th
century -- Sources.

GV863.A1.M87 1991
Murdock, Eugene Converse.
Baseball players and their times: oral histories of
the game, 1920-1940/ Eugene Murdock. Westport,
Conn.: Meckler, c1991. xxi, 352 p.
91-009444   796.357/0973   0887362354
Baseball -- United States -- History -- 20th
century.   Baseball players -- United States --
Biography.

GV863.A1 R33 2002
Rader, Benjamin G.
Baseball: a history of America's game/ Benjamin
G. Rader. 2nd ed. Urbana, IL: University of Illinois
Press, c2002. xiii, 274 p.
2001-002477   796.357/0973 21   0252070135
Baseball -- United States -- History.

GV863.A1.S48 1960
Seymour, Harold, 1910-
Baseball. New York: Oxford University Press,
1960-1990. v. 1-3.
60-005799   796.357/09   0195014080
Baseball -- United States -- History.

GV863.A1.T68 1993
Total baseball/ edited by John Thorn and Pete
Palmer with Michael Gershman. New York, NY:
HarperPerennial, c1993. v, 2362 p.
92-045555   796.357/0973   0062731890
Baseball -- United States -- Statistics. Baseball
players -- United States -- Statistics. Baseball --
United States -- History.

GV863.A1.V65 1983
Voigt, David Quentin.
American   baseball/   David   Quentin   Voigt.
University Park: Pennsylvania State University
Press, c1983. 3 v.
83-002300   796.357/64/0973   0271003316
Baseball -- United States -- History.

GV863.A1.W37 1994
Ward, Geoffrey C.
Baseball: an illustrated history/ narrative by
Geoffrey C. Ward; based on a documentary
filmscript by Geoffrey C. Ward and Ken Burns;
preface by Ken Burns and Lynn Novick; with an
introduction by Roger Angell; contributions by
John Thorn ... [et al.]. New York: A.A. Knopf:
c1994. xxv, 486 p.
93-039809   796.357/0973   0679404597
Baseball -- United States -- History -- Pictorial
works. Baseball -- United States -- History.

GV863.A1.W448 1995
White, Sol, b. 1868.
Sol White's history of colored base ball, with other
documents on the early Black game, 1886-1936/
compiled and introduced by Jerry Malloy. Lincoln:
University of Nebraska Press, c1995. lxv, 187 p.
94-020992   796.357/0973   0803247710
Negro leagues -- History. Baseball -- United
States -- History.

GV863.A1.W752 1996
Wright, Marshall D.
Nineteenth century baseball: year-by-year statistics
for the major league teams, 1871 through 1900/ by
Marshall D. Wright. Jefferson, N.C.: McFarland &
Co., c1996. x, 350 p.
96-019833   796.357/0973/09034021   20
0786401818
Baseball -- United States -- History -- 19th
century -- Statistics. Baseball players -- United
States -- History -- 19th century -- Statistics.

GV863.155.B53 1994
Bjarkman, Peter C.
Baseball with a Latin beat: a history of the Latin
American game/ by Peter C. Bjarkman. Jefferson,
N.C.: McFarland, c1994. x, 460 p.
94-003526   796.357/098   0899509738
Baseball -- Latin America. Baseball players --
Latin America -- Biography. Baseball -- United
States.

GV863.29.A1.D655 1991
Klein, Alan M., 1946-
Sugarball: the American game, the Dominican
dream/ Alan M. Klein. New Haven, Conn.: Yale
University Press, c1991. x, 179 p.
90-045953   796.357/097293   0300048734
Baseball -- Social aspects -- Dominican
Republic. Baseball -- Political aspects --
Dominican Republic.

GV865.A1.B55 2000
Biographical dictionary of American sports. edited
by David L. Porter. Westport, Conn.: Greenwood
Press, 2000. 3 v.
99-014840   796.357/092/273   031329884X
Baseball -- United States -- Biography --
Dictionaries. Baseball -- United States -- History.

GV865.A1.F72 1998
Freedman, William, 1938-
More than a pastime: an oral history of baseball
fans/ by William Freedman. Jefferson, N.C.:
McFarland & Co., c1998. x, 253 p.
98-010297   796.357/0973 21   0786405104
Baseball fans -- United States -- Interviews.
Baseball -- Social aspects -- United States.
Baseball -- United States -- History.

GV865.A1 G56 1992
The glory of their times: the story of the early days
of baseball told by the men who played it/
[compiled by] Lawrence S. Ritter. The enl. ed., 1st
Quill ed. New York: Quill, William Morrow, 1992.
xviii, 360 p.
91-040203   796.357/092/2.B 20   0688112730
Baseball players -- United States -- Biography.
Baseball -- United States -- History.

GV865.A1.R38 1998
Regalado, Samuel O. 1953-
Viva baseball!: Latin major leaguers and their
special hunger/ Samuel O. Regalado. Urbana:
University of Illinois Press, c1998. xvi, 224 p.
97-021066   796.357/64/098 21   0252023722
Hispanic American baseball players --
Biography. Baseball players -- Latin America --
Biography.

GV865.A1.W55 2000
Wilson, Nick, 1947-
Voices from the pastime: oral histories of surviving
major leaguers, Negro leaguers, Cuban leaguers,
and writers, 1920-1934/ by Nick Wilson. Jefferson,
N.C.: McFarland & Co., c2000. viii, 208 p.
00-026695   796.357/092/273 21   0786408243
Baseball players -- Interviews. Baseball --
History -- 20th century.   Sportswriters --
Interviews.

GV865.B69.A3 1970
Bouton, Jim.
Ball four; my life and hard times throwing the
knuckleball in the Big Leagues. Edited by Leonard
Shecter. New York, World Pub. Co. [1970] xiii,
400 p.
78-120125   796.357/0924
Bouton, Jim.   Baseball.

GV865.B75.A3
Brosnan, Jim.
The long season. New York, Harper [1960] 273 p.
60-010398   796.33278
Baseball.

GV865.C3.A3
Campanella, Roy, 1921-
It's good to be alive. Boston, Little, Brown [1959]
306 p.
59-011889   927.96357
Campanella, Roy, -- 1921-

GV865.D5.S45 1988
Seidel, Michael, 1943-
Streak: Joe DiMaggio and the summer of '41/
Michael Seidel. New York: McGraw-Hill, c1988.
xxi, 260 p.
87-033884   796.357/092/4   007055966X
Di Maggio, Joe, -- 1914-   Baseball players --
United States -- Biography.

GV865.D83.A36
Durocher, Leo Ernest, 1906-
Nice guys finish last/ by Leo Durocher, with Ed
Linn. New York: Simon and Schuster, [1975]
448 p.
75-001462   796.357/092/4   0671220578
Durocher, Leo, -- 1906- Baseball.

GV865.F45.A3
Flood, Curt, 1938-
The way it is, by Curt Flood, with Richard Carter.
New York, Trident Press [1971] 236 p.
70-143045   796.357/0924   0671270761
Flood, Curt, -- 1938-

GV865.G53 R53 1996
Ribowsky, Mark.
The power and the darkness: the life of Josh
Gibson in the shadows of   the game/ Mark
Ribowsky. New York: Simon & Schuster, c1996.
319 p.
96-000292   796.357/092.B 20   0684804026
Gibson, Josh, 1911-1947.   Baseball players --
United States -- Biography. Negro leagues --
United States -- History.

GV865.G68.A3 1989
Greenberg, Hank.
Hank Greenberg, the story of my life/ edited and
with an introduction by Ira Berkow. New York:
Times Books, c1989. xxi, 311 p.
88-029555   796.357/092/4   0812917413
Greenberg, Hank.   Baseball players -- United
States -- Biography.

GV865.H6.A32 1995
Alexander, Charles C.
Rogers Hornsby: a biography/ Charles C. Alexander. New York: H. Holt and Co., 1995. xiv, 366 p.
95-003841   796.357/092   0805020020
Hornsby, Rogers, -- 1896-1963. Baseball players -- United States -- Biography.

GV865.J29 G76 1999
Gropman, Donald.
Say it ain't so, Joe!: the true story of Shoeless Joe Jackson/ Donald Gropman. 2nd rev. ed. Secaucus, N.J.: Carol Pub. Group, 1999. xxvi, 357 p.
00-268846   796.357/092.B 21   0806521155
Jackson, Joe, 1888-1951. Baseball players -- United States -- Biography.

GV865.J67.A34
Jordan, Pat.
A false spring/ by Pat Jordan. New York: Dodd, Mead, [1975] 277 p.
74-031082   796.357/092/4   0396070787
Jordan, Pat. Baseball. Pitching (Baseball)

GV865.L37.A33 1978
LeFlore, Ron.
Breakout: from prison to the big leagues/ by Ron LeFlore with Jim Hawkins. New York: Harper & Row, c1978. viii, 180 p.
77-003759   796.357/092/4   0060125527
LeFlore, Ron. Baseball players -- United States -- Biography. Prisoners -- United States -- Biography.

GV865.M325 O94 1998
Overmyer, James.
Queen of the Negro leagues: Effa Manley and the Newark Eagles/ James Overmyer. Lanham, Md.: Scarecrow Press, 1998. x, 297 p.
97-049909   338.7/61796357/092.B   21   1578860016
Manley, Effa, 1900- Baseball team owners -- United States -- Biography. Afro-American business enterprises.

GV865.P3.A3 1992
Paige, Leroy, 1906-
Pitchin' man: Satchel Paige's own story/ by Leroy Satchel Paige as told to Hal Lebovitz; with a new foreword by John B. Holway. Westport, CT: Meckler, c1992. xxv, 96 p.
92-005526   796.357/092   0887368360
Paige, Leroy, -- 1906- Baseball players -- United States -- Biography. Pitchers (Baseball) -- United States -- Biography.

GV865.R58.A32
Robinson, Brooks, 1937-
Third base is my home [by] Brooks Robinson, as told to Jack Tobin. Waco, Tex., Word Books [1974] 202 p.
73-091547   796.357/092/4
Robinson, Brooks, -- 1937- Baseball.

GV865.R59.A3 1975
Robinson, Frank, 1935-
My life is baseball/ by Frank Robinson, with Al Silverman. Garden City, N.Y.: Doubleday, [1975] c1968. 237 p.
74-033224   796.357/092/4   0385057091
Robinson, Frank, -- 1935- Baseball.

GV865.R596.A3 1999
Robinson, Frazier, 1910-1997.
Catching dreams: my life in the Negro baseball leagues/ Frazier "Slow" Robinson with Paul Bauer; foreword by John "Buck" O'Neil; introduction by Gerald Early. Syracuse: Syracuse University Press, 1999. xxiv, 230 p.
98-051650   796.357/092   0815605633
Robinson, Frazier, -- 1910-1997. Baseball players -- United States -- Biography. Afro-American baseball players -- Biography. Negro leagues -- History.

GV865.R6.A29 1972
Robinson, Jackie, 1919-1972.
I never had it made, by Jackie Robinson as told to Alfred Duckett. New York, Putnam [1972] 287 p.
75-175272   796.357/092/4   0399110100
Robinson, Jackie, -- 1919-1972. Afro-Americans.

GV865.R6.R34 1997
Rampersad, Arnold.
Jackie Robinson: a biography/ Arnold Rampersad. New York: Knopf, c1997. x, 512 p.
97-005165   796.357/092 B 21   0679444955
Robinson, Jackie, -- 1919-1972. Baseball players -- United States -- Biography.

GV865.R6 T93 1997
Tygiel, Jules.
Baseball's great experiment: Jackie Robinson and his legacy/ Jules Tygiel. Expanded ed. New York: Oxford University Press, 1997. xii, 413 p.
96-038551   796.357/092.aB 20   0195106202
Robinson, Jackie, 1919-1972. Baseball players -- United States -- Biography. Baseball -- United States -- History.

GV865.R8 C73 1992
Creamer, Robert W.
Babe: the legend comes to life/ Robert W. Creamer. 1st Fireside ed. New York: Simon & Schuster, 1992. 443 p.
91-039086   796.357/092.B 20   067176070X
Ruth, Babe, 1895-1948. Baseball players -- United States -- Biography.

GV865.V4.A3
Veeck, Bill.
Veeck--as in wreck; the autobiography of Bill Veeck with Ed Linn. New York: Putnam, [1962] 380 p.
62-010982   796.357   0345240863175
Veeck, Bill. Baseball.

GV865.W33.D38 1996
DeValeria, Dennis.
Honus Wagner: a biography/ Dennis DeValeria and Jeanne Burke DeValeria. New York: H. Holt, 1996. xiii, 334 p.
95-037706   796.357/092   0805037500
Wagner, Honus, -- 1874-1955. Baseball players -- United States -- Biography.

GV865.W34.Z35 1995
Zang, David.
Fleet Walker's divided heart: the life of baseball's first black major leaguer/ David W. Zang. Lincoln: University of Nebraska Press, c1995. xvi, 157 p.
94-033517   796.357/092   0803249136
Walker, Moses Fleetwood, -- b. 1858. Afro-American baseball players -- United States -- Biography. Baseball -- United States -- History -- 19th century.

GV865.W5.A3
Williams, Theodore Samuel, 1918-
My turn at Bat: the story of my life, by Ted Williams with John Underwood. New York, Simon and Schuster [1969] 288 p.
78-075869   796.357/0924   0671202286
Williams, Ted, -- 1918- Williams, Ted, -- 1918- Baseball players -- United States -- Biography.

GV865.Y58.B76 2000
Browning, Reed.
Cy Young: a baseball life/ Reed Browning. Amherst: University of Massachusetts Press, c2000. xiv, 283 p.
99-088275   796.357/092 B 21   1558492623
Young, Cy, -- 1867-1955. Baseball players -- United States -- Biography. Pitchers (Baseball) -- United States -- Biography.

GV867.3.H69 2000
How to do baseball research/ general editor, Gerald Tomlinson; chapter authors, Gerald Tomlinson ... [et al.]; contributors, A.D. Suehsdorf ... [et al.]. Cleveland, OH: Society for American Baseball Research; c2000. 163 p.
2001-267032   796.357/07/2 21   0910137838
Baseball -- Research -- Handbooks, manuals, etc. Baseball players -- Research -- Handbooks, manuals, etc.

GV867.64.R52 2000
Rielly, Edward J.
Baseball: an encyclopedia of popular culture/ Edward J. Rielly. Santa Barbara, Calif.: ABC-CLIO, c2000. xvii, 371 p.
00-010704   796.357/0973   1576071030
Baseball -- Social aspects -- United States. Popular culture -- United States.

GV867.64.R68 2000
Rossi, John P.
The national game: baseball and American culture/ John P. Rossi. Chicago: I.R. Dee , 2000. ix, 343 p.
99-053674   796.357/0973   1566632870
Baseball -- Social aspects -- United States -- History.

GV875.A1.C47 1992
Chadwick, Bruce.
When the game was black and white: the illustrated history of the Negro leagues/ Bruce Chadwick. New York: Abbeville Press, c1992. 796.357/0973
92-013673   796.357/0973   1558593721
Negro leagues -- History. Baseball -- United States -- History.

GV875.A1.F45 1993
Filichia, Peter.
Professional baseball franchises: from the Abbeville Athletics to the Zanesville Indians/ Peter Filichia. New York: Facts on File Publications, c1993. xiv, 290 p.
92-012766   796.357/64/0973   0816026475
Baseball teams -- United States -- Registers. Baseball teams -- Registers. Baseball teams -- United States -- History.

GV875.A1 O26
Obojski, Robert.
Bush league: a history of minor league baseball. New York, Macmillan [1975] xiv, 418 p.
74-016345   796.357/64/09   002591300X
Minor league baseball -- United States -- History.

GV875.B7.K3 1972
Kahn, Roger.
The boys of summer. New York, Harper & Row [1972] xxii, 442 p.
76-144179   796.357/64/0974723   0060122390
Baseball -- United States -- History.

GV875.C65.G87 1998
Guschov, Stephen D., 1965-
The Red Stockings of Cincinnati: base ball's first all-professional team and its historic 1869 and 1870 seasons/ by Stephen D. Guschov. Jefferson, N.C.: McFarland & Co., c1998. vii, 174 p.
97-050027   796.357/64/0977178   21
0786404671
Cincinnati Red Stockings (Baseball team)

GV875.D6.B35 1991
Bak, Richard, 1954-
Cobb would have caught it: the golden age of baseball in Detroit/ Richard Bak. Detroit: Wayne State University Press, c1991. 383 p.
91-004156   796.357/64/0977434   0814323553
Baseball players -- Michigan -- Detroit -- Interviews.   Detroit (Mich.) -- History -- 20th century.

GV875.N18.R93 1992
Ryczek, William J., 1953-
Blackguards and Red Stockings: a history of baseball's National Association, 1871-1875/ by William J. Ryczek. Jefferson, N.C.: McFarland & Co., 1992. xii, 272 p.
91-045274   796.357/64/0973   0899507107
National Association of Professional Base Ball Players (U.S.) -- History.

GV875.N35.R53 1995
Ribowsky, Mark.
A complete history of the Negro leagues, 1884 to 1955/ Mark Ribowsky. Secaucus, N.J.: Carol Pub. Group, c1995. xix, 332 p.
94-042194   796.357/64/0973   1559722835
Negro leagues -- History.

GV875.N4.S84 1997
Sullivan, George, 1933-
The Yankees: an illustrated history/ George Sullivan and John Powers. Philadelphia, PA: Temple University Press, 1997.
97-006536   796.357/64/097471   1566395534
New York Yankees (Baseball team) History. New York Yankees (Baseball team) -- History -- Pictorial works.

GV875.5.B38 2000
The baseball coaching bible/ Jerry Kindall, John Winkin, editors. Champaign, IL: Human Kinetics, c2000. xii, 369 p.
99-052257   796.357/07/7 21   0736001611
Baseball -- Coaching. Baseball -- Training.

GV877.B27 1993
The Baseball encyclopedia: the complete and definitive record of major league baseball. New York: Macmillan; 1993. x, 2857 p.
92-044145   796.357/0973/021   0025790412
Baseball -- Records -- United States. Baseball -- United States -- Statistics. Baseball players -- United States -- Registers.

GV878.4.H35 1994
Halberstam, David.
October 1964/ David Halberstam. New York: Villard Books, 1994. xiv, 380 p.
94-014323   796.357/646   0679415602
World Series (Baseball)

GV879.5.B46 1989
Benson, Michael.
Ballparks of North America: a comprehensive historical reference to baseball grounds, yards, and stadiums, 1845 to present/ by Michael Benson. Jefferson, N.C.: McFarland, c1989. xxx, 475 p.
89-045007   796.357/06/81812   0899503675
Baseball fields -- America -- History. Baseball fields -- North America -- History. Baseball fields -- Central America -- History.

GV879.5.G47 1993
Gershman, Michael.
Diamonds: the evolution of the ballpark/ Michael Gershman. Boston: Houghton Mifflin, 1993. ix, 259 p.
93-008025   796.357/06/873   0395612128
Baseball fields -- United States -- History. Stadiums -- United States -- History.

GV880.B869 2001
Burk, Robert Fredrick, 1955-
Much more than a game: players, owners, & American baseball since 1921/ Robert F. Burk. Chapel Hill: University of North Carolina Press, c2001. xi, 372 p.
00-041774   796.357/09/04 21   0807825921
Baseball -- Economic aspects -- United States -- History -- 20th century. Baseball players -- United States -- Economic conditions -- 20th century. Baseball team owners -- United States -- Economic conditions -- 20th century.

GV880.B87 1994
Burk, Robert Fredrick, 1955-
Never just a game: players, owners, and American baseball to 1920/ Robert F. Burk. Chapel Hill: University of North Carolina Press, c1994. xv, 284 p.
93-022719   338.4/3796357/0973   0807821225
Baseball -- Economic aspects -- United States -- History -- 19th century. Baseball players -- United States -- Economic conditions. Industrial relations -- United States -- History.

GV880.D56 2000
Diamond mines: baseball and labor/ edited by Paul D. Staudohar; with a foreword by Alvin L. Hall. Syracuse, N.Y.: Syracuse University Press, 2000. xxx, 188 p.
00-046571   331.88/11796357/0973   0815628595
Baseball -- Economic aspects -- United States -- Congresses. Baseball players -- Labor unions -- United States -- Congresses. Collective bargaining -- Baseball -- United States -- Congresses.

GV880.J64 1993
Johnson, Arthur T.
Minor league baseball and local economic development/ Arthur T. Johnson. Urbana: University of Illinois Press, c1993. xiv, 273 p.
92-015713   338.4/7796357/640973   0252018656
Minor league baseball -- Economic aspects -- United States. Urban renewal -- Economic aspects -- United States. Stadiums -- Economic aspects -- United States.

GV880.Z56 1992
Zimbalist, Andrew S.
Baseball and billions: a probing look inside the big business of our national pastime/ by Andrew Zimbalist. New York, NY: BasicBooks, c1992. xviii, 270 p.
91-059016   338.4/7796357   0465006140
Baseball -- United States -- Finance. Baseball -- Economic aspects -- United States. Baseball -- United States -- Management.

GV880.15.J46 1990
Jennings, Kenneth M.
Balls and strikes: the money game in professional baseball/ Kenneth M. Jennings. New York: Praeger, 1990. x, 273 p.
89-038009   331.89/041796357/0973
0275934411
Collective bargaining -- Baseball -- United States -- History.

GV880.7.B47 1994
Berlage, Gai.
Women in baseball: the forgotten history/ Gai Ingham Berlage. Westport, Conn.: Praeger, 1994. xiv, 208 p.
93-025049   796.357/0973   0275947351
Women baseball players -- United States. Baseball -- United States -- History.

GV881.A1.A6
American Association for Health, Physical Education, and Recreation.
Softball guide, with official rules and standards. [Washington] American Association for Health, Physical Education & Recreation.
40-006050
Softball. Volley-ball.

GV884-889.26 Sports — Ball games — Basketball

GV884.A1.T37 1991
Taragano, Martin, 1959-
Basketball biographies: 434 U.S. players, coaches, and contributors to the game, 1891-1990/ by Martin Taragano. Jefferson, N.C.: McFarland & Co., c1991. xvii, 318 p.
91-052761   796.323/092273   0899506259
Basketball players -- United States -- Biography -- Dictionaries. Basketball coaches -- United States -- Biography -- Dictionaries.

GV884.B7.A34 1976
Bradley, Bill, 1943-
Life on the run/ Bill Bradley. New York: Quadrangle/New York Times Book Co., c1976. 229 p.
75-036268   796.32/3/0924   0812906233
Bradley, Bill, -- 1943- Basketball.

GV884.C5.A38
Chamberlain, Wilt, 1936-
Wilt; just like any other 7-foot Black millionaire who lives next door [by] Wilt Chamberlain and David Shaw. New York, Macmillan [1973] vi, 310 p.
73-002124   796.32/3/0924
Chamberlain, Wilt, -- 1936- Basketball.

GV884.J32
Jackson, Phil.
More than a game/ Phil Jackson and Charley Rosen. New York: Seven Stories Press, c2001. 320 p.
00-050957   796.323/092 B 21   1583220607
Jackson, Phil. Rosen, Charles. Basketball coaches -- United States -- Biography.

GV884.J67.H35 2000
Halberstam, David.
Playing for keeps: Michael Jordan and the world he made/ by David Halberstam. New York: Broadway Books, 2000.
99-041931   796.323/092   0767904443
Jordan, Michael, -- 1963- Basketball players -- United States -- Biography. Basketball -- United States -- History.

GV884.K58 F44 1986
Feinstein, John.
A season on the brink: a year with Bob Knight and the Indiana Hoosiers/ John Feinstein. New York: Macmillan, c1986. xv, 311 p.
86-018033   796.32/3/0924.B 19   0025372300
Knight, Bobby.   Basketball coaches -- United States -- Biography.

GV884.R86.A35
Russell, William Felton, 1934-
Second wind: the memoirs of an opinionated man/ Bill Russell and Taylor Branch. New York: Random House, c1979. 265 p.
79-004780   796.32/3/0924   0394503856
Russell, Bill, -- 1934-   Basketball players -- United States -- Biography.

GV885.R82
Russell, William Felton, 1934-
Go up for glory, by Bill Russell, as told to William McSweeny. New York Coward-McCann [1966] 224 p.
66-014593   796.3230924
Russell, William. Russell, Bill, -- 1934- Basketball -- Biography. Negroes -- Biography.

GV885.4.A53 1998
Anderson, Lars.
Pickup artists: street basketball in America/ Lars Anderson and Chad Millman. London; Verso, 1998. x, 203 p.
98-017460   796.323/0973   1859848532
Basketball -- United States. Urban youth -- Recreation -- United States.

GV885.45.B74 1999
Brenner, Morgan G.
College basketball's national championships: the complete record of every tournament ever played/ Morgan G. Brenner. Lanham, Md.: Scarecrow Press, 1999. xv, 1036 p.
98-041568   793.323/63/0973   081083474X
Basketball -- Tournaments -- United States. Basketball -- Records -- United States. College sports -- Records -- United States.

GV885.7.D68 1995
Douchant, Mike, 1951-
Encyclopedia of college basketball/ Mike Douchant; foreword, Hoop heaven, by Dick Vitale. New York: Gale Research, c1995. xv, 615 p.
94-035209   796.323/0973   0810396408
Basketball -- United States -- History. College sports -- United States -- History.

GV885.7.N37 1981
The NBA's official encyclopedia of pro basketball/ edited by Zander Hollander; foreword by Lawrence F. O'Brien. New York: New American Library, c1981. xi, 532 p.
81-082815   796.32/364/0973   0453004075
Basketball -- United States -- History.

GV885.7.T46 2002
Thomas, Ron.
They cleared the lane: the NBA's Black pioneers/ Ron Thomas. Lincoln: University of Nebraska Press, c2002. xvii, 276 p.
2001-052234   796.323/64/08996073   21
0803244371
Basketball -- United States -- History. African American basketball players -- History.

GV886.B53 1995
Blais, Madeleine.
In these girls, hope is a muscle/ Madeleine Blais. New York: Atlantic Monthly Press, c1995. viii, 263 p.
94-030394   796.323/62/09744   0871135728
Basketball for girls -- Massachusetts -- Case studies.

GV889.26.A33 1991
Adler, Patricia A.
Backboards & blackboards: college athletes and role engulfment/ Patricia A. Adler, Peter Adler. New York: Columbia University Press, c1991. xii, 262 p.
90-040396   796/.071/173   0231073062
Basketball -- Social aspects -- United States -- Case studies. College athletes -- United States -- Case studies. Self -- Case studies.

GV903 Sports — Ball games — Bowling

GV903.J69 2002
Jowdy, John,
Bowling execution/ John Jowdy. Champaign, IL: Human Kinetics, c2002. xii, 210 p.
2002-020869   794.6 21   0736042172
Bowling.

GV917-928 Sports — Ball games — Cricket

GV917.M45 1993
Melville, Tom.
Cricket for Americans: playing and understanding the game/ Tom Melville; with a preface by Ian Chappell. Bowling Green, OH: Bowling Green State University Popular Press, c1993. iv, 214 p.
92-074880   796.358   0879726067
Cricket.

GV917.R86 1995
Rundell, Michael.
The dictionary of cricket/ Michael Rundell. Oxford; Oxford University Press, 1995. vi, 218 p.
94-047141   796.358/03   0198661983
Cricket -- Dictionaries.

GV928.U6 M45 1998
Melville, Tom.
The tented field: a history of cricket in America/ Tom Melville. Bowling Green, OH: Bowling Green State University Popular Press, vii, 280 p.
98-004030   796.358/0973 21   0879727705
Cricket -- United States -- History.

GV928.W47.L53 1995
Liberation cricket: West Indies cricket culture/ edited by Hilary McD. Beckles and Brian Stoddart. Manchester [England]; Manchester University Press; c1995. xii, 403 p.
94-011595   796.358/09729   071904314X
Cricket -- Social aspects -- West Indies. West Indies -- Social conditions.

GV939-958.5 Sports — Ball games — Football games

GV939.A1 P63 2001
Pont, Sally.
Fields of honor: the golden age of college football and the men who created it/ Sally Pont. 1st ed. New York: Harcourt, c2001. ix, 228 p.
2001-024364   796.332/63/0973 21   0151006075
Football coaches -- United States -- Biography. Football -- Coaching -- United States -- History. College sports -- United States -- History.

GV939.G7.C37 1999
Carroll, John M. 1943-
Red Grange and the rise of modern football/ John M. Carroll. Urbana: University of Illinois Press, c1999. ix, 265 p.
99-006056   796.332/092 B 21   0252023846
Grange, Red, -- 1903- Football players -- United States -- Biography. Football -- United States -- History.

GV939.H35B76
Brondfield, Jerry,
Woody Hayes and the 100-yard war. [1st ed.] New York, Random House [1974] 309 p.
74-009070   796.33/2/0924   0394490916
Hayes, Woody, 1913-1987. Football -- Coaching.

GV939.H38.U46 1992
Umphlett, Wiley Lee, 1931-
Creating the big game: John W. Heisman and the invention of American football/ Wiley Lee Umphlett. Westport, Conn.: Greenwood Press, 1992. xiv, 269 p.
92-010087   796.332/092   0313284040
Heisman, John W. -- (John William), -- 1869-1936. Football coaches -- United States -- Biography. Football -- United States -- History.

GV939.M4.A3
Meggyesy, Dave, 1941-
Out of their league. Berkeley, Calif., Ramparts Press; [distributed by Simon & Schuster 1970 257 p.
79-132222   796.332/0924   0671207768
Meggyesy, Dave, -- 1941-

GV939.N28.A3
Namath, Joe Willie, 1943-
I can't wait until tomorrow ... 'cause I get better-looking every day, by Joe Willie Namath, with Dick Schaap. New York, Random House [1969] 279 p.
70-089691   796.332/0924
Namath, Joe Willie, -- 1943-

GV939.P66.C37 1991
Carroll, John M. 1943-
Fritz Pollard: pioneer in racial advancement/ John M. Carroll. Urbana: University of Illinois Press, c1992. xiii, 298 p.
90-025556   796.332/092   0252018141
Pollard, Fritz. Football players -- United States -- Biography. Afro-American businesspeople -- Biography.

GV939.R6 R56 1999
Robinson, Ray,
Rockne of Notre Dame: the making of a football legend/ Ray   Robinson. New York: Oxford University Press, 1999. xiv, 290 p.
99-013712   796.332/092.B 21   0195105494
Rockne, Knute, 1888-1931. Football coaches -- United States -- Biography.

GV939.S43.A35
Shaw, Gary.
Meat on the hoof; the hidden world of Texas football. New York, St. Martin's Press [1972] xii, 234 p.
72-091415   796.33/2/0924
Shaw, Gary.

GV942.5.G35 1998
Galeano, Eduardo H., 1940-
Soccer in sun and shadow/ by Eduardo Galeano; translated by Mark Fried. New York: Verso, 1998. viii, 228 p.
98-006769   796.334   1859848486
Soccer -- History. Soccer -- Anecdotes. Soccer -- Social aspects.

GV942.5.M87 1994
Murray, W. J.
Football: a history of the world game/ Bill Murray. Aldershot, Hants, England: Scolar Press; c1994. xvi, 297 p.
94-015190   796.334   1859280919
Soccer -- History.

GV942.5.M88 1996
Murray, W. J.
The world's game: a history of soccer/ Bill Murray. Urbana: University of Illinois Press, c1996. xix, 218 p.
95-013742   796.334/09 20   025201748X
Soccer -- History.

GV943.M475 1993
Merrill, Christopher.
The grass of another country: a journey through the world of soccer/ Christopher Merrill. New York: H. Holt, 1993. xiii, 204 p.
93-004022   796.334   0805027718
Soccer -- United States. Soccer.

GV943.9.F35.T39 1992
Taylor, Rogan P.
Football and its fans: supporters and their relations with the game, 1885-1985/ Rogan Taylor. Leicester; Leicester University Press; 1992. viii, 198 p.
92-005666   796.334/0941   0718514483
Soccer fans -- Great Britain -- Societies, etc.

GV943.9.S64.G576 1999
Giulianotti, Richard, 1966-
Football: a sociology of the global game/ Richard Giulianotti. Oxford, UK: Polity Press; 1999. xvi, 218 p.
99-011069   306.4/83   0745617689
Soccer -- Social aspects. Soccer -- History. Sports -- Sociological aspects.

GV944.S64.M27 1995
Mason, Tony.
Passion of the people?: football in South America/ Tony Mason. London; Verso, 1995. x, 174 p.
95-163189   796.334/098   0860914038
Soccer -- South America. Soccer -- Social aspects -- South America.

GV944.U6 A44 2001
Allaway, Roger.
The encyclopedia of American soccer history/ Roger Allaway, Colin   Jose, David Litterer. Lanham, Md.: Scarecrow Press, c2001. xiv, 454 p.
00-053140   796.334/0973 21   0810839806
Soccer -- United States -- History -- Encyclopedias.

GV945.85.P75.M35 1996
Making men: rugby and masculine identity/ edited by John Nauright and Timothy J.L. Chandler. London; F. Cass, 1996. 260 p.
95-035435   796.333/01/9   0714646377
Rugby football -- Psychological aspects. Masculinity. Men -- Identity.

GV945.9.G7.C65 1998
Collins, Tony, 1960-
Rugby's great split: class, culture, and the origins of Rugby League football/ Tony Collins. London; F. Cass, 1998. xix, 273 p.
97-043920   796.333/8/0941   0714648671
Rugby League football -- Social aspects -- England -- History. Rugby Union football -- Social aspects -- England -- History. Working class -- England -- Recreation -- History.

GV950.O73 2001
Oriard, Michael,
King Football: sport and spectacle in the golden age of radio and   newsreels, movies and magazines, the weekly & the daily press/ Michael Oriard. Chapel Hill: University of North Carolina Press, c2001. xiv, 491 p.
2001-041459   796.332/09/041 21   0807826502
Football -- History -- 20th century. Mass media and sports -- History -- 20th century.

GV950.O75 1993
Oriard, Michael, 1948-
Reading football: how the popular press created an American spectacle/ Michael Oriard. Chapel Hill: University of North Carolina Press, c1993. xxv, 319 p.
92-042840   796.332/0973   0807820830
Football -- Social aspects -- United States -- History. Sports journalism -- United States -- History. Popular culture -- United States -- History.

GV950.W28 2000
Watterson, John Sayle.
College football: history, spectacle, controversy/ John Sayle Watterson. Baltimore: Johns Hopkins University Press, 2000. xiv, 456 p.
00-008247   796.332/63/0973   0801864283
Football -- United States -- History. Football -- Social aspects -- History.

GV951.H45 2000
Heisman, John W.
Principles of football/ by John Heisman. Athens, GA: Hill Street Press, c2000. 373 p.
00-059669   796.332/2 21   1892514990
Football. Football players -- Training of.

GV951.18.D44 2000
Defensive football strategies/ American Football Coaches   Association. Champaign, IL: Human Kinetics, c2000. xii, 307 p.
00-039597   796.332/26 21   0736001425
Football -- Defense. Football -- Coaching.

GV954.M37 1998
McClellan, Keith.
The Sunday game: at the dawn of professional football/ by Keith McClellan. Akron, OH: University of Akron Press, 1998. xi, 503 p.
98-024175   796.332/0973   1884836356
Football -- United States -- History.

GV955.N44 1994
Nelson, David M., 1920-1991.
The anatomy of a game: football, the rules, and the men who made the game/ David M. Nelson; with a foreword   by   Forest Evashevski. Newark: University of Delaware Press; c1994. 599 p.
91-051009   796.332/02/022   0874134552
Football -- United States -- Rules -- History. Football -- United States -- History.

GV955.5.N35.R67 1999
Ross, Charles Kenyatta, 1964-
Outside the lines: African Americans and the integration of the National Football League/ Charles K. Ross. New York: New York University Press, c1999. 201 p.
99-006581   796.332/64/08996073   21   0814774954
Afro-American football players -- Biography. Discrimination in sports -- United States -- History.

GV956.G7.K7
Kramer, Jerry, 1936-
Instant replay; the Green Bay diary of Jerry Kramer. Edited by Dick Schaap. Photos. by John and Vernon J. Biever. New York, World Pub. Co. [1968] xvi, 286 p.
68-031469   796.332/0924
Kramer, Jerry, -- 1936- -- Diaries.   Football players -- United States -- Diaries.

GV956.6.B623 1998
Bobo, Mike.
Principles of coaching football/ Mike Bobo, Spike Dykes. Boston: Allyn and Bacon, c1998. xii, 287 p.
97-029510   796.332/07/7 21   0205262538
Football -- Coaching -- United States. School sports -- Coaching -- United States.

GV956.6.F68 2002
The football coaching bible/ American Football Coaches Association. Champaign, IL: Human Kinetics, c2002. vii, 366 p.
2002-001185   796.332/07/7 21   0736044116
Football -- Coaching.

GV958.5.I9 B47 2001
Bernstein, Mark F.
Football: the Ivy League origins of an American obsession/ Mark F.   Bernstein. Philadelphia: University   of   Pennsylvania   Press,   c2001. xiii,336 p.
2001-027488   796.332/63/0974 21   0812236270
Football -- United States -- History.

GV963-981 Sports — Ball games — Golf

GV963.B7 1990
Browning, Robert
A history of golf: the royal and ancient game/ by Robert Browning. London: A&C Black; 1990. xii, 236 p.
92-188226   796.352   0713632364
Golf -- History. Golf -- Great Britain -- History.

GV964.D94.A3 1995
Dye, Pete.
Bury me in a pot bunker: golf through the eyes of the game's most challenging course designer/ Pete Dye with Mark Shaw. Reading, Mass.: Addison-Wesley Pub. Co., c1995. xiv, 241 p.
94-018252   796.352/06/8092   0201407698
Dye, Pete. Golf course architects -- United States -- Biography.

GV964.H3.L69 2000
Lowe, Stephen R.
Sir Walter and Mr. Jones: Walter Hagen, Bobby Jones, and the rise of American golf/ Stephen R. Lowe. Chelsea, MI: Sleeping Bear Press, c2000. xxvii, 387 p.
00-009875   796.352/0973 21   1585360090
Hagen, Walter, -- 1892-1969. Jones, Bobby, -- 1902-1971. Golfers -- United States -- Biography.

GV964.L67.A33
Lopez, Nancy, 1957-
The education of a woman golfer/ Nancy Lopez, with Peter Schwed. New York: Simon and Schuster, c1979. 191 p.
79-009149   796.352/092/4   0671247565
Lopez, Nancy, -- 1957- Golfers -- United States -- Biography. Golf.

GV964.N5.A3
Nicklaus, Jack.
The greatest game of all; my life in golf, by Jack Nicklaus, with Herbert Warren Wind. Foreword by Robert Tyre Jones, Jr. New York, Simon and Schuster [1969] 416 p.
77-075866   796.352/0924   0671202154
Nicklaus, Jack. Golf.

GV964.W66 O94 2001
Owen, David,
The chosen one: Tiger Woods and the dilemma of greatness/ David Owen. New York: Simon & Schuster, c2001. 201 p.
2001-047407   796.352/092.B 21   0743222342
Woods, Tiger. Golfers -- United States -- Biography.

GV964.Z3.C39 1995
Cayleff, Susan E., 1954-
Babe: the life and legend of Babe Didrikson Zaharias/ Susan E. Cayleff. Urbana: University of Illinois Press, c1995. xiii, 327 p.
94-035584   796.352/092   0252017935
Zaharias, Babe Didrikson, -- 1911-1956. Women golfers -- United States -- Biography.

GV965.C664 1999
Corcoran, Mike.
The PGA Tour complete book of golf/ Michael Corcoran. New York: H. Holt, c1999. xiii, 395 p.
99-010390   796.352 21   0805057684
Golf -- United States.

GV965.H59
Hogan, Ben, 1912-
Five lessons: the modern fundamentals of golf [by] Ben Hogan, with Herbert Warren Wind. Drawings by Anthony Ravielli. New York, Barnes [1957] 127 p.
57-012022   796.352
Golf.

GV965.N494
Nicklaus, Jack.
Golf my way, by Jack Nicklaus with Ken Bowden. Illus. by Jim McQueen. New York, Simon and Schuster [1974] 264 p.
73-014090   796.352/3   067121702X
Golf.

GV965.W743 2001
Woods, Tiger.
How I play golf/ by Tiger Woods with the editors of Golf digest. New York: Warner Books, 2001. 306 p.
2001-026495   796.352/3 21   0446529311
Golf.

GV966.C76 1995
Crosset, Todd W.,
Outsiders in the clubhouse: the world of women's professional golf/ Todd W. Crosset. Albany: State University of New York Press, c1995. viii, 276 p.
94-027916   796.352 20   0791424901
Golf for women -- United States. Women golfers -- United States. Sex discrimination in sports -- United States.

GV966.S385 2000
Saunders, Vivien.
The golf handbook for women: the complete guide to improving your game/ Vivien Saunders. New York: Three Rivers Press, 2000. 224 p.
00-710409   796.352/3/082   0609805118
Golf for women -- Handbooks, manuals, etc. Golf -- Handbooks, manuals, etc. Swing (Golf) -- Handbooks, manuals, etc.

GV970.F45 1995
Feinstein, John.
A good walk spoiled: days and nights on the PGA tour/ John Feinstein. 1st ed. Boston: Little, Brown, c1995. xx, 475 p.
94-049552   796.352/66 20   0316277207
Golf -- Tournaments. Golf -- Psychological aspects.

GV970.3.B75
Sampson, Curt.
Royal and ancient: blood, sweat, and fear at the British Open/ Curt Sampson. New York: Villard, c2000. xxvii, 238 p.
99-087568   796.352/66 21   0375502785
British Open (Golf tournament) -- History.

GV979.P75.C66 1993
Coop, Richard H.
Mind over golf: play your best by thinking smart/ Richard H. Coop with Bill Fields. New York: Macmillan Pub. Co.; c1993. xiii, 194 p.
92-020575   796.352/01   0025278304
Golf -- Psychological aspects.

GV979.S63
Moss, Richard J.
Golf and the American country club/ Richard J. Moss. Urbana: University of Illinois Press, c2001. 214 p.
00-010832   796.352/06/873 21   025202642X
Golf -- Social aspects -- United States. Country clubs -- Social aspects -- United States.

GV981.B39 2000
Barkow, Al.
The golden era of golf: how America rose to dominate the old Scots game/ Al Barkow. 1st ed. New York: St. Martin's Press, 2000. 314 p.
00-031666   796.352/0973 21   0312252382
Golf -- United States -- History.

GV981.D39 2000
Dawkins, Marvin P.
African American golfers during the Jim Crow era/ Marvin P. Dawkins and Graham C. Kinloch. Westport, Conn.: Praeger, 2000. xv, 182 p.
99-034486   796.352/089/96073   0275959406
Afro-American golfers -- History. Discrimination in sports -- United States -- History. Golf -- Social aspects -- United States -- History.

GV981.W5 1956
Wind, Herbert Warren, 1918-
The story of American golf, its champions and its championships. New York, Simon and Schuster, 1956. 564 p.
56-013439   796.352
Golf -- United States -- History.

GV989.F56 2002
Fisher, Donald M.,
Lacrosse: a history of the game/ Donald M. Fisher. Baltimore: Johns Hopkins University Press, c2002. xii, 361 p.
2001-005690   796.34/7/09 21   0801869382
Lacrosse -- North America -- History.

GV990.U5 1972
United States Lawn Tennis Association.
Official encyclopedia of tennis, edited by the staff of the U.S.L.T.A. New York, Harper & Row [1972] viii, 472 p.
71-181644   796.34/2/03   0060144793
Tennis -- Dictionaries.

GV992.B78 1997
Bud Collin's tennis encyclopedia/ edited by Bud Collins and Zander Hollander. 3rd ed. Detroit: Visible Ink Press, c1997. xxxix, 698 p.
97-013215   796.342 21   1578590000
Tennis -- History. Tennis -- Records. Tennis players -- Biography.

GV994.A1 W45 2001
Wertheim, L. Jon.
Venus envy: a sensational season inside the women's tennis tour/ L. Jon Wertheim. 1st ed. New York: HarperCollins, 2001. 225 p.
2001-024314   796.342/082/0922.B 21   0060197749
Williams, Venus, 1980- Women tennis players -- Biography.

GV994.A7.A3 1993
Ashe, Arthur.
Days of grace: a memoir/ by Arthur Ashe and Arnold Rampersad. New York: Alfred A. Knopf: 1993. xii, 317 p.
92-054919   796.342/092   0679423966
Ashe, Arthur. Tennis players -- United States -- Biography. AIDS (Disease) -- Patients -- United States -- Biography.

GV994.D39 K75 1999
Kriplen, Nancy.
Dwight Davis: the man and the cup/ Nancy Kriplen. London: Ebury, 1999. 256 p.
00-421416   0091868505
Davis, Dwight Filley, 1879-1945. Tennis -- United States -- Biography. Cabinet officers -- United States -- Biography.

GV994.G5.A3
Gibson, Althea, 1927-
I always wanted to be somebody. Edited by Ed Fitzgerald. New York, Harper [1958] 176 p.
58-012447   927.9634
Gibson, Althea, -- 1927-

GV994.K7.A34 1979
Kramer, Jack 1921-
The game: my 40 years in tennis/ by Jack Kramer, with Frank Deford. New York: Putnam, c1979. 318 p.
78-031299   796.34/2/0924   0399123369
Kramer, Jack, -- 1921- Tennis players -- United States -- Biography.

GV994.L4.E54 1988
Engelmann, Larry.
The goddess and the American girl: the story of Suzanne Lenglen and Helen Wills/ Larry Engelmann. New York: Oxford University Press, 1988. xiv, 464 p.
87-031556 796.342/092/2 0195043634
Lenglen, Suzanne, -- 1899-1938. Wills, Helen, -- 1905- Tennis players -- France -- Biography. Tennis players -- United States -- Biography.

GV995.B39 2000
Bassett, Glenn.
Tennis today/ Glenn Bassett, William Otta, Christine Shelton. 2nd ed. Belmont, CA: Wadsworth, c2000. xii, 225 p.
99-016332 796.342/2 21 0534358357
Tennis.

GV1002.8.S65 2002
Smith, Stan,
Stan Smith's winning doubles/ Stan Smith. Champaign, IL: Human Kinetics, c2002. xiv, 177 p.
2002-002156 796.342/28 21 0736030077
Tennis -- Doubles.

GV1002.95.E85.G5613 1997
Gillmeister, Heiner, 1939-
Tennis: a cultural history/ Heiner Gillmeister. London; Leicester University Press, 1997. xii, 452 p.
97-011809 796.342/094 0718501470
Tennis -- Europe -- History. Social history.

GV1003.34.T87 1996
Turner, Edward T.
Winning racquetball: skills, drills, and strategies/ Ed Turner, Woody Clouse. Champaign, IL: Human Kinetics, c1996. viii, 277 p.
95-013029 796.34/3 20 0873227212
Racquetball.

GV1015.3-1015.5 Sports — Ball games — Volleyball

GV1015.3.V54 1996
Viera, Barbara L.,
Volleyball: steps to success/ Barbara L. Viera, Bonnie Jill Ferguson. 2nd ed. Champaign, IL: Human Kinetics, c1996. vi, 161 p.
95-042643 796.325 20 0873226461
Volleyball.

GV1015.5.C63 G69 2001
Gozansky, Sue,
Volleyball coach's survival guide: practical techniques and materials for building an effective program and a winning team/ Sue Gozansky. Paramus, N.J.: Parker Pub., c2001. xiii, 344 p.
00-051032 796.325 21 0130207578
Volleyball -- Coaching.

GV1029-1033.5 Sports — Motorsports — Automobile racing

GV1029.J68 1998
Jones, Bruce.
The complete encyclopedia of Formula One: the bible of motorsport/ Bruce Jones. 1st ed. London: Carlton, 1998. 647 p.
99-231534   185868515X
Formula One automobiles -- Encyclopedias. Grand Prix racing -- Encyclopedias. Automobile racing drivers -- Encyclopedias.

GV1029.P675 1994
Post, Robert C.
High performance: the culture and technology of drag racing, 1950-1990/ Robert C. Post. Baltimore: Johns Hopkins University Press, c1994. xxiii, 416 p.
93-004845 796.7/2 0801846544
Drag racing -- United States -- History. Drag racing -- Social aspects -- United States.

GV1029.3.M59 1991
Moorhouse, H. F.
Driving ambitions: an analysis of the American hot rod enthusiasm/ H.F. Moorhouse. Manchester; Manchester University Press: c1991. 231 p.
90-025264 796.7/2/0973 0719029163
Drag racing -- United States -- History. Hot rods -- History. Automobile driving -- Social aspects.

GV1029.9.S74.G65 1993
Golenbock, Peter, 1946-
American zoom: stock car racing--from the dirt tracks to Daytona/ Peter Golenbock. New York: Macmillan Pub.; c1993. xiii, 493 p.
92-038026 796.7/2/0973 0025446150
Stock car racing -- United States.

GV1029.9.S74 H34 1998
Hagstrom, Robert G.,
The NASCAR way: the business that drives the sport/ Robert G. Hagstrom, Jr. New York: Wiley, c1998. xvi, 230 p.
97-037082 796.72/0973 21 0471183164
Stock car racing -- United States. Stock car racing -- Economic aspects -- United States.

GV1029.9.S74.H68 1997
Howell, Mark D.
From moonshine to Madison Avenue: a cultural history of the NASCAR Winston Cup series/ Mark D. Howell; with a foreword by Brett Bodine. Bowling Green, OH: Bowling Green State University Popular Press, c1997. xvi, 266 p.
97-004215 796.72/0973 21 087972739X
Stock car racing -- Economic aspects -- United States. Stock car racing -- United States -- History.

GV1033.5.G65 G68 2002
Gould, Todd,
For gold and glory: Charlie Wiggins and the African-American racing car circuit/ Todd Gould. Bloomington: Indiana University Press, 2002. xx, 212 p.
2002-004211 796.72/092.B 21 0253341337
Wiggins, Charlie.   Automobile racing drivers -- United States -- Biography. African American automobile racing drivers -- Biography.

GV1048 Sports — Cycling. Bicycling — Training for cycling

GV1048.A76 2000
Armstrong, Lance.
The Lance Armstrong performance program: the training, strengthening, and eating plan behind the world's greatest cycling victory/ by Lance Armstrong and Chris Carmichael with Peter Joffre Nye. [Emmaus, Pa.]: Rodale, c2000. xvi, 240 p.
00-009332   1579542700
Bicycle racing -- Training.

GV1049.2 Sports — Cycling. Bicycling — Racing

GV1049.2.T68 F54 2001
Fife, Graeme.
Inside the peloton: riding, winning & losing the Tour de France/ Graeme Fife. Edinburgh: Mainstream Pub., 2001. 220 p.
2001-409579 796.6/092 21 1840184000
Cyclists -- Biography.

GV1051 Sports — Cycling. Bicycling — Biography

GV1051.A76 A3 2000
Armstrong, Lance.
It's not about the bike: my journey back to life/ Lance Armstrong with Sally Jenkins. New York: Putnam, c2000. 275 p.
00-035612 796.6/2/092.B 21 0399146113
Armstrong, Lance.   Cyclists -- United States -- Biography. Cancer -- Patients -- United States -- Biography.

GV1051.T3.R58 1988
Ritchie, Andrew.
Major Taylor: the extraordinary career of a champion bicycle racer/ Andrew Ritchie. San Francisco: Bicycle Books; c1988. 304 p.
87-070730 796.6/092/4 0933201141
Taylor, Major, -- 1878-1932.   Cyclists -- United States -- Biography. Bicycle racing -- History.

GV1060.7-1060.73 Sports — Track and field athletics — All-round athletics

GV1060.7.Z36 1989
Zarnowski, Frank.
The decathlon: a colorful history of track and field's most challenging event/ Frank Zarnowski. Champaign, Ill.: Leisure Press, c1989. xiv, 353 p.
88-027308 796.4/2 19 0880113448
Decathlon -- History. Decathlon -- Records.

GV1060.73.H63 2001
Hobson, Wes,
Swim, bike, run/ Wes Hobson, Clark Campbell and Michael F. Vickers. Champaign, IL: Human Kinetics, c2001. viii, 255 p.
00-054239 796.42/57 21 0736032886
Triathlon -- Training -- Handbooks, manuals, etc.

GV1060.8-1071 Sports — Track and field athletics — Foot racing. Running

GV1060.8.T75 1996
Tricard, Louise Mead, 1936-
American women's track and field: a history, 1895 through 1980/ by Louise Mead Tricard. Jefferson, N.C.: McFarland & Co., c1996. xiv, 746 p.
96-013463 796.4/2/082 20 0786402199
Track-athletics for women -- History. Women athletes -- History.

GV1061.B445 2002
Benyo, Richard.
Running encyclopedia/ Richard Benyo, Joe Henderson. Champaign, IL: Human Kinetics, c2002. xx, 417 p.
2001-039460   796.42 21   0736037349
Running races -- History. Runners (Sports) -- History.

GV1061.15.H49.A3 1998
Heywood, Leslie.
Pretty good for a girl/ Leslie Heywood. New York: Free Press, c1998. viii, 220 p.
98-018532   796.42/092 B 21   0684850702
Heywood, Leslie -- Childhood and youth. Women runners -- United States -- Biography. Sports -- United States -- Sex differences. Femininity.

GV1065.L69 1997
Lovett, Charles C.
Olympic marathon: a centennial history of the games' most storied race/ Charlie Lovett. Westport, Conn.: Praeger, 1997. xiii, 176 p.
96-047618   796.42/52   0275957713
Marathon running -- History. Olympics -- History.

GV1065.17.T73 M37 1997
Martin, David E.,
Better training for distance runners/ David E. Martin, Peter N. Coe. 2nd ed. Champaign, IL: Human Kinetics, c1997. xxvi, 435 p.
96-043851   796.42/5 20   0880115300
Marathon running -- Training. Running races.

GV1065.2.C66 1998
Cooper, Pamela
The American marathon/ Pamela Cooper. Syracuse: Syracuse University Press, c1998. xvi, 217 p.
97-045156   796.42/52/0973 21   081560520X
Marathon running -- United States -- History. Runners (Sports) -- United States -- Biography.

GV1071.L35 2000
Laird, Ron,
Fast walking/ Ron Laird. 1st ed. Mechanicsburg, PA: Stackpole Books, c2000. xii, 83 p.
00-029702   796.51 21   0811727580
Walking (Sports)

GV1107-1108.5 Sports — Fighting sports. Martial arts — Animal fighting

GV1107.H4 1999
Hemingway, Ernest,
Death in the afternoon/ Ernest Hemingway. 1st Scribner Classics ed. New York: Scribner, 1999. 397 p.
99-231717   791.8/2 21   068485922X
Bullfights.

GV1108.A1 S54 2002
Sherwood, Lyn A.,
Yankees in the afternoon: an illustrated history of American bullfighters/ Lyn Sherwood; foreword by Barnaby Conrad. Jefferson, N.C.: McFarland & Company, 2002. vi, 282 p.
2001-044778   791.8/2/092273 21   0786409312
Bullfighters -- United States -- Biography. Bullfighters -- United States -- Pictorial works. Bullfights -- United States -- History.

GV1108.5.M58 1991
Mitchell, Timothy
Blood sport: a social history of Spanish bullfighting/ Timothy Mitchell; with an essay and bibliography by Rosario Cambria. Philadelphia: University of Pennsylvania Press, c1991. xv, 244 p.
91-007231   791.8/2/0946   0812231295
Bullfights -- Spain -- History. Bullfights -- Social aspects -- Spain -- History.

GV1108.5.S58 1999
Shubert, Adrian,
Death and money in the afternoon: a history of the Spanish bullfight / Adrian Shubert. New York: Oxford University Press, 1999. 270 p.
98-028292   791.8/2/0946 21   0195095243
Bullfights -- Social aspects -- Spain -- History -- 18th century. Bullfights -- Social aspects -- Spain -- History -- 19th century.

GV1114.3-1147 Sports — Fighting sports. Martial arts — Human fighting. Hand-to-hand fighting

GV1114.3.B44 2003
Beasley, Jerry,
Mastering karate/ Jerry Beasley. Champaign, IL: Human Kinetics, c2003. xvi, 175 p.
2002-009246   796.815/3 21   0736044108
Karate.

GV1114.35.S765 2001
Stevens, John, 1947-
The philosophy of Aikido/ John Stevens. Tokyo; Kodansha International; 2001. 132 p.
00-047822   796.815/4   4770025343
Ueshiba, Morihei, -- 1883-1969 -- Teachings. Aikido -- Philosophy.

GV1114.9.P36 1997
Park, Yeon Hwan.
Taekwondo techniques & tactics/ Yeon Hwan Park, Tom Seabourne. Champaign, IL: Human Kinetics, c1997. x, 181 p.
96-037724   796.8/153 21   0880116447
Tae kwon do . Tae kwon do -- Training.

GV1125.G67 1986
Gorn, Elliott J., 1951-
The manly art: bare-knuckle prize fighting in America/ Elliott J. Gorn. Ithaca: Cornell University Press, 1986. 316 p.
86-006410   796.8/3/0973   0801419204
Boxing -- United States. Boxing matches -- United States -- History.

GV1125.S26 1988
Sammons, Jeffrey T. 1949-
Beyond the ring: the role of boxing in American society/ Jeffrey T. Sammons. Urbana: University of Illinois Press, c1988. xix, 318 p.
87-019041   796.8/3/0973   0252014731
Boxing -- United States. Boxing -- Social aspects -- United States.

GV1131.H64 2002
Hietala, Thomas R.,
The fight of the century: Jack Johnson, Joe Louis, and the struggle for racial equality/ Thomas R. Hietala. Armonk, N.Y.: M.E. Sharpe, c2002. 375 p.
2001-049165   796.83/092/2 21   0765607220
Johnson, Jack, 1878-1946. Louis, Joe, 1914- African American boxers -- Biography. Boxing -- United States -- History -- 20th century.

GV1132.A44 M35 1997
Mailer, Norman.
The fight/ Norman Mailer. 1st Vintage International ed. New York: Vintage International, 1997. vi, 234 p.
97-011107   796.83 21   0375700382
Ali, Muhammad, 1942- Foreman, George, 1949- Boxing -- United States.

GV1132.A44.M37 1999
Marqusee, Mike.
Redemption song: Muhammad Ali and the spirit of the sixties/ Mike Marqusee. London; Verso, 1999. 310 p.
99-023701   796.83/092 185984717X
Ali, Muhammad, -- 1942- Boxers (Sports) -- United States -- Biography. Nineteen sixties -- United States.

GV1132.A44.R46 1998
Remnick, David.
King of the world: the rise of Muhammad Ali/ David Remnick. New York: Random House, c1998. xvii, 326 p.
98-024539   796.83/092 B 21   0375500650
Ali, Muhammad, -- 1942- Boxers (Sports) -- United States -- Biography.

GV1132.L3 A3 1997
La Motta, Jake.
Raging bull: my story/ by Jake La Motta with Joseph Carter and Peter Savage. 1st Da Cap Press ed. New York: Da Capo Press, 1997. xii, 222 p.
97-015581   796.83/092.B 21   0306808080
La Motta, Jake. Boxers (Sports) -- United States-- Biography.

GV1132.L53 T68 2000
Tosches, Nick.
The Devil and Sonny Liston/ Nick Tosches. 1st ed. Boston: Little, Brown, and Co., c2000. 266 p.
99-042098   796.83/092.B 21   0316897752
Liston, Sonny, 1932-1970. Boxers (Sports) -- United States -- Biography.

GV1132.M3 S85 2002
Sullivan, Russell.
Rocky Marciano: the rock of his times/ Russell Sullivan. Urbana: University of Illinois Press, c2002. xii, 368 p.
2001-008553   796.83/092.B 21   0252027639
Marciano, Rocky, 1923-1969. Boxers (Sports) -- United States -- Biography.

GV1132.S95.I84 1988
Isenberg, Michael T.
John L. Sullivan and his America/ Michael T. Isenberg. Urbana: University of Illinois Press, c1988. xii, 465 p.
87-016183   796.8/3/0924   0252013816
Sullivan, John Lawrence, -- 1858-1918. Boxers (Sports) -- United States -- Biography. Boxing -- United States -- History.

GV1133.H34 2000
Hauser, Thomas.
The black lights: inside the world of professional boxing/ Thomas Hauser. Fayetteville: University of Arkansas Press, 2000.
99-086546   796.83 21   1557285977
Boxing. Professional sports.

GV1133.O2 1987
Oates, Joyce Carol, 1938-
On boxing/ Joyce Carol Oates; with photographs by John Ranard. Garden City, N.Y.: Dolphin/Doubleday, 1987. 118 p.
86-019710   796.8/3/0973   0385239424
Boxing.

GV1136.8.S84 1996
Sugden, John Peter.
Boxing and society: an international analysis/ John Sugden. Manchester, UK; Manchester University Press; 1996. 218 p.
96-029445 796.8/3 0719043204
Boxing -- Social aspects -- Cross-cultural studies. Boxing -- Political aspects -- Cross-cultural studies.

GV1147.G36 1994
Garret, Maxwell R.
Foil, saber, and epee fencing: skills, safety, operations, and responsibilities/ Maxwell R. Garret, Emmanuil G. Kaidanov, Gil A. Pezza. University Park, Pa.: Pennsylvania State University Press, c1994. xii, 227 p.
93-017603 796.8/6 0271010193
Fencing.

GV1157-1185 Sports — Fighting sports. Martial arts — Shooting

GV1157.O3.R55 1994
Riley, Glenda, 1938-
The life and legacy of Annie Oakley/ by Glenda Riley. Norman: University of Oklahoma Press, c1994. xvii, 252 p.
94-010260 796.3/092 0806126566
Oakley, Annie, -- 1860-1926. Shooters of firearms -- United States -- Biography. Frontier and pioneer life -- West (U.S.)

GV1185.F33 1999
Fadala, Sam,
Traditional archery/ Sam Fadala. 1st ed. Mechanicsburg, PA: Stackpole Books, c1999. ix, 246 p.
98-043191 799.3/2 21 0811729435
Archery. Archery -- History.

GV1195-1198.12 Sports — Fighting sports. Martial arts — Wrestling

GV1195.M327 1993
Martell, Bill.
Greco-Roman wrestling/ William A. Martell. Champaign, IL: Human Kinetics Publishers, c1993. x, 166 p.
92-028782 0873224086
Greco-Roman wrestling.

GV1196.A1.L45 1997
Lentz, Harris M.
Biographical dictionary of professional wrestling/ Harris M. Lentz, III. Jefferson, N.C.: McFarland & Company, c1997. x, 373 p.
96-046346 796.812/092/2 B 21 0786403039
Wrestlers -- Biography -- Dictionaries. Wrestling -- Encyclopedias.

GV1198.12.C43 1990
Chapman, Mike, 1943-
Encyclopedia of American wrestling/ Mike Chapman. Champaign, Ill.: Leisure Press, c1990. viii, 533 p.
89-002701 796.8/12/0973 0880113421
Wrestling -- United States -- History.

GV1200 Games and amusements — History

GV1200.W55 2002
Wilkins, Sally
Sports and games of medieval cultures/ Sally Wilkins. Westport, Conn.: Greenwood Press, c2002. viii, 325 p.
2001-040553 790/.09 21 0313317119
Games -- History -- To 1500. Sports -- History -- To 1500.

GV1201 Games and amusements — General works

GV1201.M67 1997
Mohr, Merilyn Simonds.
The new games treasury: more than 500 indoor and outdoor favorites with strategies, rules, and traditions/ by Merilyn Simonds Mohr; illustrations by Roberta Cooke; [photographs by Stephen Mark Needham]. Boston: Houghton Mifflin Co., c1997. 432 p.
97-023216 790.1 21 1576300587
Games.

GV1201.38 Games and amusements — Social aspects. Relation to sociology

GV1201.38.U55 2001
Unique games and sports around the world: a reference guide/ edited by Doris Corbett, John Cheffers, and Eileen Crowley Sullivan. Westport, CT: Greenwood Press, 2001. xiii, 407 p.
00-033125 790.1 0313297789
Games -- Cross-cultural studies. Sports -- Cross-cultural studies.

GV1215 Games and amusements — Children's games and amusements — Singing and dancing games

GV1215.O65 1985
Opie, Iona Archibald.
The singing game/ by Iona and Peter Opie. Oxford; Oxford University Press, 1985. xxii, 521 p.
85-193118 796.1/3 0192115626
Singing games -- Great Britain.

GV1229 Games and amusements — Indoor games and amusements — General works

GV1229.P285 2002
Parlor games: amusements and entertainments for everyone, containing explanations of the most excellent games suited to the family circle, such as- pantomimes, games with pen and pencil, games of thought and memory, riddles and conundrums and enigmas edited by Roy Finamore. 1st ed. New York: Clarkson Potter, c2002. xi, 208 p.
2002-025276 794 21 0609610279
Indoor games. Amusements.

GV1233-1282.3 Games and amusements — Indoor games and amusements — Card games

GV1233.H3 1966
Hargrave, Catherine Perry.
A history of playing cards and a bibliography of cards and gaming/ Compiled and illustrated from the old cards and books in the collection of the United States Playing Card Company in Cincinnati. Dover Publications, 1966. 462 p.
66-015935 795.409
Cards -- History. Cards -- Bibliography. Games -- Bibliography.

GV1233.P37 1991
Parlett, David Sidney.
A history of card games/ David Parlett. Oxford; Oxford University Press, 1991. 361 p.
91-004220 795.4 20 019282905X
Card games -- History. Card games -- Social aspects.

GV1243.F85 1956
Frey, Richard L.
The new complete Hoyle; the official rules of all popular games of skill and chance with the most authoritative advice on winning play, by Albert H. Morehead, Richard L. Frey [and] Geoffrey Mott-Smith. Garden City, N.Y., Garden City Books [1956] 740 p.
55-011330 795
Indoor games. Cards.

GV1243.H88 2001
Hoyle's rules of games: descriptions of indoor games of skill and chance, with advice on skillful play: based on the foundations laid down by Edmond Hoyle, 1672-1769/ edited by Albert H. Morehead and Geoffrey Mott-Smith. 3rd rev. & updated ed./ revised and updated by Philip D. Morehead. New York: Plume, 2001. xvii, 362 p.
2002-278550 795.4 21 0452283132
Hoyle, Edmond, 1672-1769. Card games.

GV1282.3.G6532 1971
Goren, Charles Henry, 1901-
Goren's bridge complete. New York, Doubleday [1971] xiii, 657 p.
71-160881 795.4/15
Contract bridge.

GV1301 Games and amusements — Indoor games and amusements — Gambling. Chance and banking game

GV1301.T47 2001
Thompson, William Norman.
Gambling in America: an encyclopedia of history, issues, and society / William N. Thompson. Santa Barbara: ABC-CLIO, c2001. xxx, 509 p.
2001-003493 795/.0973 21 1576071596
Gambling -- Encyclopedias. Gambling -- United States -- Encyclopedias. Gambling -- Canada -- Encyclopedias.

GV1312-1445 Games and amusements — Indoor games and amusements — Board games. Move games

GV1312.P37 1999
Parlett, David Sidney.
The Oxford history of board games/ David Parlett. Oxford; Oxford University Press, c1999. xiii, 386 p.
99-229056   0192129988
Board games -- History. Board games -- Social aspects.

GV1317.K44 1991
Keene, Raymond D.
Chess: an illustrated history/ Raymond Keene. New York: Simon and Schuster, 1990. 128 p.
89-048570   794.1/09 20   0671708147
Chess -- History.

GV1445.H616 1992
Hooper, David,
The Oxford companion to chess/ David Hooper and Kenneth Whyld. 2nd ed. Oxford [England]; Oxford University Press, 1992. 483 p.
92-009619   794.1/03 20   0198661649
Chess -- Encyclopedias. Chess players -- Biography -- Encyclopedias.

GV1445.P2579 1992
Pandolfini, Bruce.
Pandolfini's chess complete/ Bruce Pandolfini. New York: Simon & Schuster, c1992. 254 p.
92-016152   794.1 20   067170186X
Chess -- Miscellanea.

GV1469.3 Games and amusements — Indoor games and amusements — Video games

GV1469.3.M43 2002
The medium of the video game/ edited by Mark J.P. Wolf. 1st ed. Austin: University of Texas Press, 2002. xvi, 203 p.
2001-037625   794.8/0973 21   029279150X
Video games -- United States. Video games -- History -- United States.

GV1493 Games and amusements — Parties. Party games and stunts — Puzzles

GV1493.D334 1997
Danesi, Marcel, 1946-
Increase your puzzle IQ: tips and tricks for building your logic power/ Marcel Danesi. New York: J. Wiley & Sons, c1997. xv, 201 p.
96-034965   793.73 20   0471157252
Logic puzzles.

GV1493.D337 2002
Danesi, Marcel,
The puzzle instinct: the meaning of puzzles in human life/ Marcel Danesi. Bloomington: Indiana University Press, c2002. x, 269 p.
2001-007492   793.73 21   0253340942
Puzzles -- Psychological aspects. Puzzles -- Social aspects. Games -- Psychological aspects.

GV1525 Games and amusements — Peep shows

GV1525.B35 1998
Balzer, Richard.
Peepshows: a visual history/ Richard Balzer. New York, N.Y.: Harry N. Abrams, [1998] 160 p.
97-033267   791   0810963493
Peep shows -- History.

GV1543 Games and amusements — Parlor magic and tricks — History

GV1543.C45 1996
Christopher, Milbourne.
The illustrated history of magic/ Milbourne and Maurine Christopher; foreword by David Copperfield. Portsmouth, NH: Heinemann, c1996. x, 484 p.
96-032984   793.8 20   0435070169
Magic tricks -- History.

GV1543.D87 2002
During, Simon,
Modern enchantments: the cultural power of secular magic/ Simon During. Cambridge, Mass.: Harvard University Press, 2002. x, 336 p.
2001-059411   793.8 21   0674006070
Magic tricks -- History. Magicians -- History.

GV1545 Games and amusements — Parlor magic and tricks — Biography

GV1545.H8.S55 1996
Silverman, Kenneth.
Houdini!: the career of Ehrich Weiss: American self-liberator, Europe's eclipsing sensation, world's handcuff king & prison breaker/ Kenneth Silverman. New York, NY: HarperCollins Publishers, c1996. xi, 465 p.
96-007163   793.8/092 20   0060169788
Houdini, Harry, -- 1874-1926. Magicians -- United States -- Biography. Escape artists -- United States -- Biography.

GV1585 Dancing — Dictionaries. Encyclopedias

GV1585.B46 1998
International dictionary of modern dance/ with a preface by Don McDonagh; editor, Taryn Benbow-Pfalzgraf; contributing editor, Glynis Benbow-Niemier. Detroit, MI: St. James Press, c1998. xxvi, 891 p.
98-009853   792.8/03 21   1558623590
Modern dance -- Dictionaries.

GV1585.C78 2000
Craine, Debra.
The Oxford dictionary of dance/ Debra Craine, Judith Mackrell. Oxford [England]; Oxford University Press, 2000. vi, 527 p.
2001-274422   792.8/03   0198601069
Dance -- Dictionaries.

GV1585.I57 1993
International dictionary of ballet/ editor, Martha Bremser; assistant editor, Larraine Nicholas; picture editor, Leanda Shrimpton. Detroit: St. James Press, c1993. 2 v.
93-025051   792.8/03   1558620842
Ballet -- Encyclopedias.

GV1585.I586 1998
International encyclopedia of dance: a project of Dance Perspectives Foundation, Inc./ founding editor, Selma Jeanne Cohen; area editors, George Dorris ... [et al.]; consultants, Thomas F. Kelly ... [et al.]. New York: Oxford University Press, 1998. 6 v.
97-036562   792.8/03   019509462X
Dance -- Encyclopedias. Ballet -- Encyclopedias.

GV1585.P74 1995
Preston-Dunlop, Valerie Monthland.
Dance words/ compiled by Valerie Preston-Dunlop. Chur, Switzerland; Harwood Academic Publishers, c1995. xx, 718 p.
99-521798   792.8/03   3718656019
Dance -- Dictionaries.

GV1588 Dancing — Philosophy. Relation to other topics — General works

GV1588.C37 1999
Cass, Joan.
The dance: a handbook for the appreciation of the choreographic experience/ by Joan Cass. Jefferson, NC: McFarland & Co., c1999. vii, 237 p.
99-039737   792.8 21   0786401478
Dance -- Philosophy. Choreography.

GV1588.W38 1990
Watkins, Andrea.
Dancing longer dancing stronger: a dancer's guide to improving technique and preventing injury/ Andrea Watkins, Priscilla M. Clarkson; photography by Vicki Johnson; illustrations by David A. Gabriel. Princeton, N.J.: Princeton Book Co., c1990. xii, 281 p.
89-064300   792.8   0916622983
Dance. Physical fitness. Dance -- Physiological aspects.

GV1588.3 Dancing — Philosophy. Relation to other topics — Relation to aesthetics

GV1588.3.M37 1992
McFee, Graham.
Understanding dance/ Graham McFee. New York: Routledge, 1992. viii, 344 p.
91-044620   792.8   0415078091
Dance -- Philosophy. Aesthetics.

GV1588.3.N34 2001
Nagrin, Daniel.
Choreography and the specific image: nineteen essays and a workbook/ Daniel Nagrin. Pittsburgh, Pa.: University of Pittsburgh Press, c2001. xi, 274 p.
2001-002663   792.8/2 21   0822957507
Dance -- Philosophy. Choreography.

GV1588.45 Dancing — Philosophy. Relation to other topics — Relation to politics. Government policy

GV1588.45.S5 2002
Shay, Anthony,
Choreographic politics: state folk dance companies, representation, and power / Anthony Shay. Middletown, CT: Wesleyan University Press, c2002. xix, 271 p.
2001-008180 793.3/1 21 0819565210
Dance -- Government policy. Dance companies -- Government policy. Folk dancing -- Government policy.

GV1588.5 Dancing — Philosophy. Relation to other topics — Relation to psychology

GV1588.5.T39 1995
Taylor, Jim, 1958-
Psychology of dance/ Jim Taylor, Ceci Taylor. Champaign, IL: Human Kinetics, c1995. viii, 154 p.
94-040398 792.8/01 0873224868
Dance -- Psychological aspects. Dancers -- Psychology.

GV1588.6 Dancing — Philosophy. Relation to other topics — Relation to society

GV1588.6.A43 1997
Albright, Ann Cooper.
Choreographing difference: the body and identity in contemporary dance/ Ann Cooper Albright. [Middletown, Conn.]: Wesleyan University Press; c1997. xxvi, 216 p.
97-017034 792.8 21 0819563153
Modern dance -- Social aspects. Modern dance -- Psychological aspects. Body image.

GV1588.6.D37 1993
Dance, gender, and culture/ edited by Helen Thomas. New York: St. Martin's Press, c1993. xvi, 219 p.
92-027878 306.4/84 0312088817
Dance -- Sociological aspects. Dance -- Sex differences. Feminism.

GV1588.6.T66 1999
Tomko, Linda J.
Dancing class: gender, ethnicity, and social divides in American Dance, 1890-1920/ Linda J. Tomko. Bloomington: Indiana University Press, 1999. 283 p.
99-018556 306.4/84 025333571X
Dance -- Social aspects -- United States -- History -- 20th century. Dance -- Anthropological aspects -- United States -- History -- 20th century. Dance -- Sex differences.

GV1589 Dancing — Study and teaching. Research — General works

GV1589.B63 2002
The body can speak: essays on creative movement education with emphasis on dance and drama/ edited by Annelise Mertz; with a foreword by Joseph Roach. Carbondale: Southern Illinois University Press, 2002. xiv, 148 p.
2001-049021 792.8/071 21 0809324199
Dance -- Study and teaching. Movement education.

GV1589.H35 1999
Hanna, Judith Lynne.
Partnering dance and education: intelligent moves for changing times/ Judith Lynne Hanna. Champaign, IL: Human Kinetics, c1999. xv, 255 p.
98-034340 792.8/071/073 21 0880115114
Dance -- Study and teaching -- United States. Interdisciplinary approach in education -- United States. Dance -- Social aspects -- United States.

GV1589.J65 1999
Jones, Mark W. 1947-
Dancer's resource: the Watson-Guptill guide to academic programs, internships and apprentice programs, residential and artist-in-residence programs, studio schools and private teachers, workshops a Mark W. Jones. New York: Watson-Guptill Publications, c1999. 208 p.
99-050104 792.8/071/073 21 0823076563
Dance -- Study and teaching -- United States -- States -- Directories. Dance -- Vocational guidance -- United States.

GV1589.R47 1999
Researching dance: evolving modes of inquiry/ edited by Sondra Horton Fraleigh and Penelope Hanstein. Pittsburgh, Pa.: University of Pittsburgh Press, c1999. xii, 368 p.
98-040181 792.8/072 21 0822940841
Dance -- Research.

GV1594 Dancing — General works — 1975-

GV1594.J66 1992
Jonas, Gerald, 1935-
Dancing: the pleasure, power, and art of movement/ Gerald Jonas; preface by Rhoda Grauer. New York: Harry N. Abrams in association with Thirteen/WNE 1992. 256 p.
92-008038 792.8 0810932121
Dance. Dance -- Social aspects. Dance -- History.

GV1595 Dancing — General special (Special aspects of the subject as a whole)

GV1595.D342 1998
Dance on camera: a guide to dance films and videos/ edited by Louise Spain; foreword by Jacques dÁmboise. Lanham, Md.: Scarecrow Press; xiv, 238 p.
96-053236 792.8/0216 21 0810833034
Dance -- Film catalogs. Dance -- Video catalogs.

GV1595.H33 1988
Hanna, Judith Lynne.
Dance, sex, and gender: signs of identity, dominance, defiance, and desire/ Judith Lynne Hanna. Chicago: University of Chicago Press, c1988. xx, 311 p.
87-023784 793.3/2 0226315509
Sex in dance. Dance -- Social aspects. Dance -- Anthropological aspects.

GV1595.M6
Moore, Lillian.
Images of the dance; historical treasures of the Dance Collection, 1581-1861. New York, New York Public Library [1965] 86 p.
65-018552 793.30222
Dance -- Pictorial works.

GV1595.N35 1997
Nagrin, Daniel.
The six questions: acting technique for dance performance/ Daniel Nagrin. Pittsburgh, Pa.: University of Pittsburgh Press, c1997. xvii, 221 p.
96-051277 792.7/8 21 0822956241
Dance. Acting.

GV1599 Dancing — Addresses, essays, lectures

GV1599.D393 1998
Denby, Edwin, 1903-
Dance writings & poetry/ Edwin Denby; edited by Robert Cornfield. New Haven [CT]: Yale University Press, c1998. xiv, 320 p.
98-002517 793.3 21 0300076177
Dance -- Reviews.

GV1600 Dancing — Dance criticism. Appreciation

GV1600.M68 1996
Moving words: re-writing dance/ edited by Gay Morris. London; Routledge, 1996. xiv, 343 p.
95-039924 792.8 0415125421
Dance criticism. Dance -- Philosophy. Dance -- History.

GV1601 Dancing — History — General works

GV1601.C34 1993
Cass, Joan.
Dancing through history/ Joan Cass. Englewood Cliffs, N.J.: Prentice Hall, c1993. xiii, 386 p.
93-000106 792.8/09 20 0132043890
Dancing -- History. Folk dancing -- History. Ballet -- History.

GV1601.J68 1988
Jowitt, Deborah.
Time and the dancing image/ Deborah Jowitt. New York: W. Morrow, c1988. 431 p.
87-034171 793.3/2 0688049109
Dance -- History. Dance -- Anthropological aspects. Dance -- Social aspects.

GV1601.R63 1990
Robertson, Allen.
The dance handbook/ Allen Robertson, Donald Hutera. Boston, Mass.: G.K. Hall, [1990], c1988 278 p.
89-077759   792.8   081619095X
Dance -- History. Ballet -- History.

GV1623-1705 Dancing — History — By region or country

GV1623.F68 2002
Foulkes, Julia L.
Modern bodies: dance and American modernism from Martha Graham to Alvin Ailey/ Julia L. Foulkes. Chapel Hill: University of North Carolina Press, c2002. 257 p.
2001-059758   792.8 21   0807853674
Modern dance -- United States -- History.

GV1623.I22 2002
I see America dancing: selected readings, 1685-2000/ edited by Maureen Needham. Urbana: University of Illinois Press, c2002. 248 p.
2001-002651   792.8/0973 21   0252069994
Dance--United States -- History--Sources.

GV1623.M37 1994
Martin, Carol J.
Dance marathons: performing American culture of the 1920sand 1930s/ Carol Martin; foreword by Brooks McNamara. Jackson: University Press of Mississippi, c1994. xxv, 182 p.
94-012157   792.8   0878056734
Dance marathons -- United States -- History. Dance marathons -- Social aspects -- United States. United States -- Social life and customs -- 1918-1945.

GV1623.S54
Siegel, Marcia B.
Watching the dance go by/ Marcia B. Siegel. Boston: Houghton Mifflin, 1977. xvii, 345 p.
76-058029   793.3/2   0395251737
Dance -- United States -- Reviews.

GV1623.S67
Stearns, Marshall Winslow.
Jazz dance; the story of American vernacular dance [by] Marshall and Jean Stearns. New York, Macmillan [1968] xvi, 464 p.
68-023637   793.33
Jazz dance -- United States.

GV1623.W25 1997
Wagner, Ann Louise.
Adversaries of dance: from the Puritans to the present/ Ann Wagner. Urbana: University of Illinois Press, c1997. xvi, 442 p.
96-025187   792.8/0973 20   0252022742
Dance -- Moral and ethical aspects -- United States -- History. Dance -- Social aspects -- United States -- History. United States -- Moral conditions.

GV1624.7.A34.D38 2002
Dancing many drums: excavations in African American dance/ edited by Thomas F. DeFrantz. Madison, Wis.: University of Wisconsin Press, c2002. xiii, 366 p.
2001-001943   793.3/089/96073 21   0299173143
African American dance -- History. African Americans -- Social life and customs.

GV1624.7.A34 E43 1988
Emery, Lynne Fauley.
Black dance: from 1619 to today/ Lynne Fauley Emery. 2nd rev. ed./ new chapter by Brenda Dixon-Stowell; foreword by Princeton, NJ: Princeton Book Co., c1988. xii, 397 p.
88-061031   793.3089/96073 20   0916622614
Afro-American dance -- History.

GV1624.7.A34.L66 1989
Long, Richard A., 1927-
The Black tradition in American dance/ Richard A. Long; photographs selected and annotated by Joe Nash. New York: Rizzoli, 1989. 192 p.
89-031739   793.3/1973   0847810925
Afro-American dance -- History -- 20th century. Modern dance -- United States -- History -- 20th century.

GV1624.7.A34.M35 1996
Malone, Jacqui.
Steppin' on the blues: the visible rhythms of African American dance/ Jacqui Malone. Urbana: University of Illinois Press, c1996. xiii, 272 p.
95-004413   793.3/1973 20   0252022114
Afro-American dance -- History.

GV1624.7.A34 S74 1994
Stearns, Marshall Winslow.
Jazz dance: the story of American vernacular dance/ Marshall and Jean Stearns; [updated with a new foreword & afterword by Brenda Bufalino]. 1st Da Capo Press ed. New York: Da Capo Press, 1994. xviii, 472 p.
93-040957   793.3/089/96073 20   0306805537
Afro-American dance -- History. Dance -- United States -- History. Jazz dance -- History.

GV1624.7.N4.E44 1972
Emery, Lynne Fauley.
Black dance in the United States from 1619 to 1970. With a foreword by Katherine Dunham. Palo Alto, Calif.: National Press Books, [1972] x, 370 p.
79-187213   793.3089/96073   0874842034
Afro-American dance -- History.

GV1626.E84 1997
Everynight life: culture and dance in Latin/o America/ Celeste Fraser Delgado and Jose Esteban Munoz, editors. Durham: Duke University Press, 1997. x, 366 p.
96-043796   792.8/098   0822319268
Dance -- Latin America -- History. Dance -- Latin America -- Sociological aspects. Dance -- Political aspects -- Latin America.

GV1637.B76 1995
Browning, Barbara, 1961-
Samba: resistance in motion/ Barbara Browning. Bloomington: Indiana University Press, c1995. xxv, 189 p.
94-038586   306.4/84   0253328675
Dance -- Social aspects -- Brazil. Dance, Black -- Brazil.

GV1643.E87 2000
Europe dancing: perspectives on theatre dance and cultural identity/ edited by Andree Grau and Stephanie Jordan. London; Routledge, 2000. xi, 235 p.
99-089366   793.3/094   0415171024
Dance -- Europe -- Cross-cultural studies.

GV1643.R48 1997
Rethinking the sylph: new perspectives on the Romantic ballet/ edited by Lynn Garafola. Hanover, NH: University Press of New England, c1997. xi, 287 p.
97-021728   792.8/094/09034 21   0819563250
Ballet -- Europe -- History -- 19th century.

GV1649.C48 1988
Chazin-Bennahum, Judith.
Dance in the shadow of the guillotine/ Judith Chazin-Bennahum; foreword by Selma Jeanne Cohen. Carbondale: Southern Illinois University Press, c1988. xxxiii, 209 p.
88-012199   792.8/0944   0809314878
Ballet -- France -- History -- 18th century. Ballets -- Stories, plots, etc. France -- History -- 1789-1815.

GV1649.F67 1996
Foster, Susan Leigh.
Choreography & narrative: ballet's staging of story and desire/ Susan Leigh Foster. Bloomington: Indiana University Press, c1996. xvii, 371 p.
96-002237   792.8/0944 20   0253330815
Ballet -- France -- History -- 18th century. Ballet -- France -- History -- 19th century. Choreography -- France -- History -- 18th century.

GV1650.P3.G8
Guest, Ivor Forbes.
The romantic ballet in Paris [by] Ivor Guest. With an introd. by Lillian Moore. Middletown, Conn., Wesleyan University Press [1966] xix, 313 p.
66-023922   792.8/0944/36
Ballet -- France -- Paris -- History.

GV1664.R87.C46 1990
A Century of Russian ballet: documents and accounts, 1810-1910/ selected and translated by Roland John Wiley. Oxford [England]: Clarendon Press; 1990. x, 444 p.
89-071063   792.8/0947   0193164167
Ballet -- Russia -- History -- 19th century. Ballet -- Russia -- History -- Sources.

GV1673.M35 1990
Matteo.
The language of Spanish dance/ by Matteo (Matteo Marcellus Vittucci) with Carola Goya; foreword by Richard Cragun; drawings by Louis Gioia; flamenco guitar music by Peter Baime; piano arrangements by Marc Saint-Germain. Norman: University of Oklahoma Press, c1990. xx, 298 p.
89-048953   793.3/1946/014   0806122579
Dance -- Spain -- Terminology.

GV1693.R25 1990
Ragini Devi.
Dance dialects of India/ Ragini Devi. 2nd rev. ed. Delhi: Motilal Banarsidass, 1990. 234 p.
90-904903   8120806743
Dance -- India.

GV1703.C3.P55 1999
Phim, Toni Samantha, 1957-
Dance in Cambodia/ Toni Samantha Phim and Ashley Thompson. Kuala Lampur; Oxford University Press, 1999. xii, 91 p.
99-024608   792.8/09596   9835600597
Dance -- Cambodia. Cambodia -- Social life and customs.

GV1703.I532.B34322 1995
Bandem, I Made.
Balinese dance in transition: kaja and kelod/ I Made Bandem, Fredrik Eugene deBoer. Kuala Lampur; Oxford University Press, 1995. xviii, 162 p.
94-041032   793.3/19598/6   9676530719
Dance -- Indonesia -- Bali (Province)

GV1705.H8313 1995
Huet, Michel,
The dances of Africa/ [photos by] Michel Huet; text by Claude Savary; [translated from the French Danses d'Afrique by Dorothy Blair]. New York: Harry N. Abrams, 1996. 170 p.
95-023201   793.3/196 20   0810932288
Dance -- Africa.

GV1746 Dancing — Social dancing. Ballroom dancing — Balls. Dance parties

GV1746.M28 1992
Malnig, Julie.
Dancing till dawn: a century of exhibition ballroom dance/ Julie Malnig. New York: Greenwood Press, 1992. xi, 174 p.
91-033482   793.3/3   0313276471
Ballroom dancing -- History. Musical theater -- History. Musical films -- History.

GV1751 Dancing — Social dancing. Ballroom dancing — Technique (General)

GV1751.H322 2000
Dance a while: handbook for folk, square, contra, and social dance/ Jane Harris ... [et al.]. 8th ed. Boston: Allyn and Bacon, c2000. xxi, 538 p.
99-049853   793.3 21   0205279368
Dancing.

GV1779 Dancing — Dancing in motion pictures, television, etc.

GV1779.B55 1997
Billman, Larry.
Film choreographers and dance directors: an illustrated biographical encyclopedia, with a history and filmographies, 1893 through 1995/ by Larry Billman. Jefferson, N.C.: McFarland & Co., Publishers, c1997. xi, 652 p.
96-031756   793.82/092/2 B 21   0899508685
Dance in motion pictures, television, etc. -- History. Choreography -- Filmography. Choreographers -- Biography.

GV1779.D63 2001
Dodds, Sherril,
Dance on screen: genres and media from Hollywood to experimental art / Sherril Dodds. Houndmills, Basingstoke, Hampshire; Palgrave, 2001. xv, 196 p.
00-069217   791.43/655 21   0333801458
Dance in motion pictures, television, etc.

GV1781.2 Dancing — Theatrical dancing — Improvisation

GV1781.2.N68 1990
Novack, Cynthia Jean.
Sharing the dance: contact improvisation and American culture/ Cynthia J. Novack. Madison, Wis.: University of Wisconsin Press, c1990. xvii, 258 p.
89-040534   792.8   0299124401
Improvisation in dance -- History. Dance -- Anthropological aspects -- United States.

GV1782.5 Dancing — Theatrical dancing — Choreography

GV1782.5.H85 1978
Humphrey, Doris, 1895-1958.
Doris Humphrey, the collected works. New York: Dance Notation Bureau Press, 1978-1992. v. 1-2.
78-067320   793.3/2   0932582281
Humphrey, Doris, -- 1895-1958. Choreography. Dance notation.

GV1782.5.M56 1997
Minton, Sandra Cerny, 1943-
Choreography: a basic approach using improvisation/ Sandra Cerny Minton. Champaign, IL: Human Kinetics, c1997. ix, 125 p.
96-048348   792.8/2 21   0880115297
Choreography.

GV1782.62 Dancing — Theatrical dancing — Individual dances

GV1782.62.B35.S65 1993
Sokolow, Anna.
Ballade/ choreography, Anna Sokolow; music by Alexander Scriabin; text and labanotation by Ray Cook; edited by Ann Hutchinson Guest. Yverdon, Switzerland; Gordon and Breach, c1993. xiv, 151 p.
93-016973   792.8/2   2881249124
Ballade (Dance) Labanotation.

GV1783-1783.2 Dancing — Theatrical dancing — Modern or expressionistic dancing. Revival of classical dancing

GV1783.A48 1994
Alter, Judith B.
Dancing and mixed media: early twentieth-century modern dance theory in text and photography/ Judith B. Alter. New York: P. Lang, c1994. xiv, 225 p.
93-002968   792.8   0820421677
Modern dance -- Philosophy -- History -- 20th century. Dance -- Social aspects -- History -- 20th century.

GV1783.A53 1997
Anderson, Jack, 1935-
Art without boundaries: the world of modern dance/ by Jack Anderson. Iowa City: University of Iowa Press, c1997. xiii, 346 p.
96-052226   792.8 21   087745583X
Modern dance -- History.

GV1783.C39 2000
Celichowska, Renata.
The Erick Hawkins modern dance technique/ by Renata Celichowska; illustrations by Leon Belokon; labanotation by Ilene Fox. Hightstown, NJ: Princeton Book Co. 2000.
00-044091   792.8   087127213X
Hawkins, Erick -- Philosophy. Modern dance -- Philosophy.

GV1783.H67 1996
Howe, Dianne Shelden.
Individuality and expression: the aesthetics of the new German dance, 1908-1936/ Dianne S. Howe. New York: P. Lang, c1996. xii, 312 p.
94-030669   792.8/0943 20   0820426563
Modern dance -- Germany -- History -- 20th century. Dancers -- Germany -- Biography. Choreographers -- Germany -- Biography.

GV1783.P46 1992
Perces, Marjorie B., 1921-
The dance technique of Lester Horton/ Marjorie B. Perces, Ana Marie Forsythe, Cheryl Bell; illustrated by Libby Yoakum; photographs by Tom Caravaglia. Princeton, NJ: Princeton Book Co., c1992. xiii, 205 p.
92-000241   792.8   0871271648
Horton, Lester, -- 1906-1953   Modern dance -- Study and teaching.

GV1783.S53 1991
Siegel, Marcia B.
The tail of the dragon: new dance, 1976-1982/ Marcia B. Siegel; photographs by Nathaniel Tileston. Durham, N.C.: Duke University Pres, 1991. xvi, 204 p.
91-000522   792.8   0822311569
Modern dance -- History.

GV1783.2.B87.F73 1999
Fraleigh, Sondra Horton, 1939-
Dancing into darkness: Butoh, Zen, and Japan/ Sondra Horton Fraleigh. Pittsburgh, Pa.: University of Pittsburgh Press; c1999. xiii, 272 p.
98-058109   792.8/0952 21   0822940981
Buto. Arts, Zen -- Japan.

GV1785 Dancing — Theatrical dancing — Biography

GV1785.A1.F69 1990
Frank, Rusty E.
Tap!: the greatest tap dance stars and their stories, 1900-1955/ Rusty E. Frank. New York: W. Morrow, c1990. 331 p.
90-036636   792.8/092/2   0688089496
Dancers -- United States -- Biography. Tap dancing -- History.

GV1785.A1.L526 1997
Livingston, Lili Cockerille, 1945-
American Indian ballerinas/ Lili Cockerille Livingston. Norman, Okla.: University of Oklahoma Press, 1997. xx, 328 p.
96-032307   792.8/028/0922   0806128968
Tallchief, Maria. Chouteau, Yvonne. Tallchief, Marjorie. Indian ballerinas -- United States -- Biography.

GV1785.A1 P47 2001
Perpener, John O.
African-American concert dance: the Harlem
Renaissance and beyond/ John O. Perpener III.
Urbana: University of Illinois Press, c2001. xviii,
284 p.
00-013096   792.8/089/96073 21   0252026756
*African American dancers -- Biography. African
American dance -- History. Harlem Renaissance.*

GV1785.A1.S7813 1990
Surits, E. IA.
Soviet choreographers in the 1920s/ Elizabeth
Souritz; translated from the Russian by Lynn
Visson; edited, with additional translation, by Sally
Banes. Durham: Duke University Press, 1990. ix,
356 p.
89-016877   792.8/2/0922   0822309521
*Choreographers -- Russia (Federation) --
Biography. Ballet -- Russia (Federation) -- History
-- 20th century.*

GV1785.A1.V35 2000
Hill, Constance Valis.
Brotherhood in rhythm: the jazz tap dancing of the
Nicholas Brothers/ Constance Valis Hill. New
York: Oxford University Press, 2000. xvi, 320 p.
99-030917   792.7/8   0195131665
*Dancers -- United States -- Biography. Jazz tap -
- United States -- History.*

GV1785.A38.A3 1994
Ailey, Alvin.
Revelations: the autobiography of Alvin Ailey/ by
Alvin Ailey with A. Peter Bailey. Secaucus, N.J.:
Carol Pub. Group, c1995. viii, 183 p.
94-016684   792.8/028/092   155972255X
*Ailey, Alvin.   Dancers -- United States --
Biography. Choreographers -- United States --
Biography.*

GV1785.A38 D85 1996
Dunning, Jennifer.
Alvin Ailey: a life in dance/ Jennifer Dunning.
Reading, Mass.: Addison-Wesley, c1996. xi, 468 p.
96-015167   792.8/028/092.B 20   0201626071
*Ailey, Alvin.   Dancers -- United States --
Biography.*

GV1785.A83.A3 1979
Astaire, Fred.
Steps in time/ Fred Astaire. New York: Da Capo
Press, 1979, c1959. viii, 327 p.
79-009148   793.3/2/0924   0306795752
*Astaire, Fred.   Dancers -- United States --
Biography.*

GV1785.B3.B35 1993
Baker, Jean-Claude.
Josephine: the hungry heart/ by Jean-Claude Baker
and Chris Chase. New York: Random House,
c1993. xxiii, 532 p.
92-056797   792.8/028/092   0679409157
*Baker, Josephine, -- 1906-1975.   Dancers --
France -- Biography. Afro-American entertainers -
- France -- Biography.*

GV1785.B32.B83 1988
Buckle, Richard.
George Balanchine, ballet master: a biography/ by
Richard Buckle in collaboration with John Taras.
New York: Random House, c1988. xi, 409 p.
87-042667   792.8/2/0924   0394539060
*Balanchine, George.   Choreographers -- United
States -- Biography.*

GV1785.B32.T3 1984
Taper, Bernard.
Balanchine, a biography/ Bernard Taper. New
York, N.Y.: Times Books, c1984. x, 438 p.
84-040107   792.8/2/0924   0812911369
*Balanchine, George.   Choreographers -- United
States -- Biography.*

GV1785.C85 M48 1998
Merce Cunningham: dancing in space and time/
edited by Richard Kostelanetz; essays 1944-1992
by Jack Anderson ... [et al.]. 1st Da Capo Press ed.
New York: Da Capo Press, 1998. xiv, 243 p.
98-006776   792.8/028/092.aB 21   0306808773
*Cunningham, Merce.   Dancers -- United States --
Biography. Choreographers -- United States --
Biography. Modern dance -- United States --
History.*

GV1785.D8.D35 1995
Daly, Ann, 1959-
Done into dance: Isadora Duncan in America/ Ann
Daly. Bloomington: Indiana University Press,
c1995. xvi, 266 p.
95-011633   792.8/028/092   0253329248
*Duncan, Isadora, -- 1877-1927 Dancers -- United
States -- Biography.*

GV1785.F8.C87 1997
Current, Richard Nelson.
Loie Fuller, goddess of light/ Richard Nelson
Current & Marcia Ewing Current. Boston:
Northeastern University Press, c1997. xv, 400 p.
96-052659   792.8/028/092 B 21   1555533094
*Fuller, Loie, -- 1862-1928.   Dancers -- United
States -- Biography. Modern dance.*

GV1785.G7.D4 1992
De Mille, Agnes.
Martha: the life and work of Martha Graham/ by
Agnes De Mille. New York: Vintage Books, 1992.
xviii, 509 p.
92-050608   792.8/028/092   0679741763
*Graham, Martha.   Dancers -- United States --
Biography. Modern dance.*

GV1785.G7.T73 1997
Tracy, Robert.
Goddess: Martha Graham's dancers remember/ by
Robert Tracy. New York: Limelight Editions,
1997. 339 p.
96-031310   792.8/028/092   0879100869
*Graham, Martha.   Dancers -- United States --
Biography. Choreographers -- United States --
Biography. Modern dance.*

GV1785.H267.A3 1995
Halprin, Anna.
Moving   toward   life: five   decades   of
transformational dance/ Anna Halprin; edited by
Rachel Kaplan. Hanover: Wesleyan University
Press, c1995. xviii, 274 p.
95-001696   792.8/028   0819552844
*Halprin, Anna.   Dancers -- United States --
Biography. Modern dance. Dance therapy.*

GV1785.H64.W37
Warren, Larry.
Lester Horton, modern dance pioneer/ Larry
Warren. New York: M. Dekker, c1977. xvi, 265 p.
76-023364   793.3/2/0924   0824765036
*Horton, Lester, -- 1906-1953.   Choreographers --
United States -- Biography. Modern dance.*

GV1785.K596.A3 1989
Koner, Pauline.
Solitary song/ Pauline Koner. Durham: Duke
University Press, 1989. xi, 305 p.
89-001546   793.3/2/0924   0822308789
*Koner, Pauline.   Dancers -- United States --
Biography. Modern dance -- United States.*

GV1785.L2 P74 1998
Preston-Dunlop, Valerie Monthland.
Rudolf Laban: an extraordinary life/ Valerie
Preston-Dunlop. London: Dance Books, 1998. xiv,
306 p.
99-214788   792.8/2/092.B 21   1852730609
*Laban, Rudolf von, -- 1879-1958. Laban, Rudolf von,
1879-1958 -- Criticism and interpretation.
Choreographers -- Hungary -- Biography. Modern
dance -- History.*

GV1785.L515.A3 1998
Limon, Jose.
Jose Limon: an unfinished memoir/ edited by Lynn
Garafola; introduction by Deborah Jowitt;
foreword by Carla Maxwell; afterword by Norton
Owen. Hanover, NH: University Press of New
England, [1998?] xx, 207 p.
98-030941   792.8/028/092   0819563749
*Limon, Jose.   Dancers -- United States --
Biography. Choreographers -- United States --
Biography.*

GV1785.L515.P65 1993
Pollack, Barbara.
Dance is a moment: a portrait of Jose Limon in
words and pictures/ Barbara Pollack, Charles
Humphrey Woodford. Pennington, NJ: Princeton
Book Co., c1993. xv, 93 p.
92-038369   792.8/028/092   0871271834
*Limon, Jose.   Dancers -- United States --
Biography. Choreographers -- United States --
Biography.*

GV1785.M35.G37 1995
Garcia-Marquez, Vicente, 1953-
Massine: a biography/ by Vicente Garcia-Marquez.
New York: Knopf, 1995. xiii, 446 p.
93-035666   792.8/2/092   0394510038
*Massine, Leonide, -- 1896-   Choreographers --
Soviet Union -- Biography Dancers -- Soviet Union
-- Biography.*

GV1785.N6.B8 1971b
Buckle, Richard.
Nijinsky. New York, Simon and Schuster [c1971]
xiv, 482 p.
78-180717   792.8/2/0924   0671211692
*Nijinsky, Waslaw, -- 1890-1950.   Dancers --
Biography.*

GV1785.N6.K66 1997
Kopelson, Kevin, 1960-
The queer afterlife of Vaslav Nijinsky/ Kevin
Kopelson. Stanford, Calif.: Stanford University
Press, 1997. xii, 224 p.
97-013449   792.8/2/092   0804729492
*Nijinsky, Waslaw, -- 1890-1950.   Homosexuality.
Gesture in dance -- Psychological aspects.*

GV1785.N6.O88 1990
Ostwald, Peter F.
Vaslav Nijinsky: a leap into madness/ by Peter
Ostwald. New York, NY: Carol Pub. Group,
c1991. xxi, 372 p.
90-020646   792.8/092   081840535X
*Nijinsky, Waslaw, -- 1890-1950.   Ballet dancers --
Russia (Federation) -- Biography.*

GV1785.N8.S66 1998
Solway, Diane.
Nureyev, his life/ Diane Solway. New York:
William Morrow, c1998. x, 625 p.
98-013483   792.8/028/092 B 21   0688128734
*Nureyev, Rudolf, -- 1938- Ballet dancers -- Russia
(Federation) -- Biography.*

GV1785.S3.S53
Shelton, Suzanne.
Divine dancer: a biography of Ruth St. Denis/ by
Suzanne Shelton. Garden City, N.Y.: Doubleday,
1981. xvi, 338 p.
80-002442   793.3/2/0924   0385141599
*St. Denis, Ruth, -- 1880-1968.   Dancers -- United
States -- Biography. Modern dance.*

GV1785.S59.W37 1990
Warren, Larry.
Anna Sokolow: the rebellious spirit/ Larry Warren.
Princeton, NJ: Princeton Book Co., c1991. xiii,
402 p.
90-063072   792.8/2/092   0871271621
*Sokolow, Anna.   Choreographers -- United States
-- Biography.*

GV1785.T39 A3 1999
Taylor, Paul,
Private domain: an autobiography/ Paul Taylor.
Pittsburgh, Pa.: University of Pittsburgh Press,
1999. 371 p.
99-234679   792.8/2/092 21   0822956993
*Taylor, Paul, 1930- Dancers -- United States --
Biography. Choreographers -- United States --
Biography.*

GV1785.T83.C53 1994
Chazin-Bennahum, Judith.
The ballets of Antony Tudor: studies in psyche and
satire/ Judith Chazin-Bennahum. New York:
Oxford University Press, 1994. 311 p.
93-001088   792.8/2/092   0195071867
*Tudor, Antony, -- 1909-1987.   Choreographers --
Great Britain -- Biography.*

GV1785.W5.M36 1993
Manning, Susan.
Ecstasy and the demon: feminism and nationalism
in the dances of Mary Wigman/ Susan A. Manning.
Berkeley: University of California Press, c1993.
xix, 353 p.
92-032232   792.8/028/092   0520081935
*Wigman, Mary, -- 1886-1973.   Dancers --
Germany -- Biography. Choreographers --
Germany -- Biography. Modern dance -- Social
aspects -- Germany -- History.*

GV1786 Dancing —
Theatrical dancing —
Dance groups of companies

GV1786.B315.H3413 1990
Hager, Bengt Nils Richard, 1916-
The Swedish Ballet/ Bengt Hager; additional texts
by Isaac Albeniz ... [et al.]; sets and costumes by
Aleksandr Alekseev ... [et al.]; translated from the
French by Ruth Sharman. New York: H.N.
Abrams, c1990. 303 p.
90-030453   792.8/09485   0810938030
Ballet suédois -- History.

GV1786.B355.G37 1989
Garafola, Lynn.
Diaghilev's Ballets russes/ Lynn Garafola. New
York: Oxford University Press, 1989. xviii, 524 p.
89-009365   792.8/0947   0195057015
*Diaghilev, Serge, -- 1872-1929.   Ballets russes --
History. Impresarios -- Russia (Federation) --
Biography.*

GV1786.N4.D36 1999
Dance for a city: fifty years of the New York City
Ballet/ edited by Lynn Garafola with Eric Foner.
New York: Columbia University Press, c1999. ix,
236 p.
98-039377   792.8/09747/1 21   0231115466
*New York City Ballet -- History. New York City
Ballet -- Anniversaries, etc.*

GV1786.W67 N34 1993
Nagrin, Daniel.
Dance and the specific image: improvisation/
Daniel Nagrin. Pittsburgh: University of Pittsburgh
Press, c1994. xiii, 223 p.
93-027793   792.8 20   0822955202
Improvisation in dance.

GV1787-1790 Dancing —
Theatrical dancing — Ballet

GV1787.A79 2002
Au, Susan.
Ballet and modern dance/ Susan Au; introduction
by Selma Jeanne Cohen. 2nd ed. New York:
Thames & Hudson, c2002. 224 p.
2001-092923   792.8 21   0500203520
*Ballet -- History. Modern dance -- History.
Dance -- History.*

GV1788.W37 1989
Warren, Gretchen Ward.
Classical ballet technique/ Gretchen Ward Warren;
photographs by Susan Cook; foreword by Robert
Joffrey. Tampa: University of South Florida Press,
c1989. xiii, 395 p.
89-031141   792.8/2   0813009456
Ballet dancing. Ballet dancing -- Pictorial works.

GV1788.5.W27 1996
Warren, Gretchen Ward.
The art of teaching ballet: ten twentieth-century
masters/ Gretchen Ward Warren. Gainesville:
University Press of Florida, c1996. xi, 386 p.
96-024408   792.8/07 20   081301459X
*Ballet -- Study and teaching -- History -- 20th
century. Dance teachers -- Biography.*

GV1790.P34.R68 1991
Rothschild, Deborah Menaker.
Picasso's parade: from street to stage: ballet by
Jean Cocteau; score by Erik Satie; choreography by
Leonide Massine/ Deborah Menaker Rothschild.
London: Sotheby's Publications in association with
the D c1991. 280 p.
90-063717   792.8/4   0856673927
*Picasso, Pablo, -- 1881-1973 -- Exhibitions.
Ballet -- Stage-setting and scenery -- Exhibitions.
Ballet -- Costume -- Exhibitions.*

GV1794 Dancing —
Theatrical dancing — Tap dancing

GV1794.K67 2002
Knowles, Mark,
Tap roots: the early history of tap dancing/ by
Mark Knowles. Jefferson, N.C.: McFarland & Co.,
c2002. xiii, 269 p.
2002-000751   792.7/8 21   0786412674
Tap dancing -- History.

GV1796 Dancing —
Special dances, A-Z

GV1796.B4.G38 1996
Gaston, Anne-Marie.
Bharata natyam: from temple to theatre/ Anne-
Marie Gaston. New Delhi: Manohar, 1996. 403 p.
97-904128   8173041466
*Bharata Natyam -- History. Dance -- India,
South -- History.*

GV1796.C145.L48 1992
Lewis, John Lowell.
Ring of liberation: deceptive discourse in Brazilian
capoeira/ J. Lowell Lewis; with a foreword by
Robert Farris Thompson. Chicago: University of
Chicago Press, c1992. xxx, 263 p.
92-003749   793.3/1   0226476820
Capoeira (Dance) Capoeira (Dance) -- History.

GV1796.K38.K68 1989
Kothari, Sunil.
Kathak, Indian classical dance art/ Sunil Kothari.
New Delhi: Abhinav Publications, 1989. 234 p.
90-902562   8170172233
*Kathak (Dance) -- History. Dancers -- India --
Biography.*

GV1796.R8 D36 1995
Daniel, Yvonne,
Rumba: dance and social change in contemporary
Cuba/ Yvonne Daniel. Bloomington: Indiana
University Press, c1995. viii, 196 p.
94-034363   784.18/88 20   025320948X
*Rumba (Dance) -- Cuba. Dance -- Cuba --
Anthropological aspects.*

GV1796.T3.S28 1995
Savigliano, Marta.
Tango and the political economy of passion/ Marta
E. Savigliano. Boulder: Westview Press, 1995.
xvii, 289 p.
94-032610   784.18/885   0813316375
*Tango (Dance) -- Social aspects. Tango (Dance)
-- Social aspects -- Argentina. Sex in dance.*

GV1799.4 Dancing —
Dancing for special classes of
persons — Women

GV1799.4.B35 1998
Banes, Sally.
Dancing women: female bodies on stage/ Sally
Banes. London; Routledge, 1998. xii, 279 p.
97-024496   792.8/082   0415096715
Women dancers. Women -- Identity. Sex in dance.

GV1799.4.D3 1997
Dancing female: lives and issues of women in contemporary dance/ edited by Sharon E. Friedler and Susan B. Glazer. Amsterdam: Harwood Academic Publishers, 1997 xvii, 318 p.
99-526577   9057020262
Women dancers. Choreographers.

GV1803 Circuses, spectacles, etc. — Circuses — History

GV1803.A43 1995
Albrecht, Ernest J., 1937-
The new American circus/ Ernest Albrecht. Gainesville: University Press of Florida, c1995. xiv, 258 p.
95-002792   791.3/0973/09   081301364X
Circus -- United States -- History.

GV1803.C85 1990
Culhane, John.
The American circus: an illustrated history/ John Culhane. New York: Holt, c1990. xxii, 504 p.
89-002182   791.3/0973   0805004246
Circus -- United States -- History.

GV1803.D38 2002
Davis, Janet M.
The circus age: culture & society under the American big top/ Janet M. Davis. Chapel Hill: University of North Carolina Press, c2002. xviii, 329 p.
2002-000863   791.3/0973 21   0807853992
Circus -- Social aspects -- United States. Circus -- United States -- History -- 20th century.

GV1803.H64 1990
Hoh, LaVahn G., 1942-
Step right up!: the adventure of circus in America/ LaVahn G. Hoh and William H. Rough. White Hall, Va.: Betterway Publications, c1990. 272 p.
89-029910   791.3/0973   1558701400
Circus -- United States -- History.

GV1811 Circuses, spectacles, etc. — Circuses — Biography

GV1811.B3 A3 2000
Barnum, P. T.
The life of P.T. Barnum/ written by himself, Phineas T. Barnum;   introduction by Terence Whalen. Urbana: University of Illinois Press, c2000. xxxvii, 404 p.
99-462094   791.3/092.B 21   0252069021
Barnum, P. T.   (Phineas Taylor),   1810-1891. Circus owners -- United States -- Biography.

GV1811.B3.A525 1997
Adams, Bluford.
E pluribus Barnum: the great showman and the making of U.S. popular culture/ Bluford Adams. Minneapolis, Minn.: University of Minnesota Press, c1997. xv, 249 p.
96-031754   338.7/617913/092   B   20
0816626308
Barnum, P. T. -- (Phineas Taylor), -- 1810-1891. Circus owners -- United States -- Biography. Circus -- Social aspects -- United States. Popular culture -- United States.

GV1815 Circuses, spectacles, etc. — Circuses — General works

GV1815.O33 1993
Ogden, Tom.
Two hundred years of the American circus: from Aba-Daba to the Zoppe-Zavatta Troupe/ Tom Ogden; foreword by Albert F. House. New York, NY, USA: Facts on File, c1993. xiv, 402 p.
92-031880   791.3/03   0816026114
Circus -- United States -- Encyclopedias. Circus -- United States -- History.

GV1821 Circuses, spectacles, etc. — Circuses — Individual circuses. Special shows, A-Z

GV1821.B8.K37 2000
Kasson, Joy S.
Buffalo Bill's Wild West: celebrity, memory, and popular history/ Joy S. Kasson. New York: Hill and Wang, 2000. ix, 319 p.
99-056101   791.8/4/0973   0809032430
Buffalo Bill's Wild West Show -- History.

GV1828 Circuses, spectacles, etc. — Circuses — Clowning. Clown acts

GV1828.R46 1997
Remy, Tristan, b. 1897.
Clown scenes/ Tristan Remy; translated from the French, with a foreword by Bernard Sahlins. Chicago: I.R. Dee, c1997. viii, 244 p.
96-038289   791.3/3 20   1566631440
Clowns. Clowning.

GV1833 Circuses, spectacles, etc. — Wild West shows

GV1833.M67 1996
Moses, L. G. 1948-
Wild West shows and the images of American Indians, 1883-1933/ L.G. Moses. Albuquerque: University of New Mexico Press, c1996. xvii, 364 p.
95-032450   791.8/4 20   0826316859
Wild west shows -- History. Dakota Indians -- Public opinion. Public opinion -- United States. United States -- Ethnic relations.

GV1833.R43 1999
Reddin, Paul.
Wild West shows/ Paul Reddin. Urbana: University of Illinois Press, c1999. xvi, 312 p.
98-058008   791.8/4/0973 21   0252024648
Wild west shows -- United States -- History.

GV1834 Circuses, spectacles, etc. — Rodeos — General works

GV1834.A55 1998
Allen, Michael, 1950-
Rodeo cowboys in the North American imagination/ Michael Allen. Reno: University of Nevada Press, c1998. xiii, 270 p.
98-022963   791.8/4/0978 21   0874173159
Rodeos -- West (U.S.) -- History. Cowboys -- West (U.S.) -- History. Popular culture -- United States.

GV1834.5-1834.55 Circuses, spectacles, etc. — Rodeos — By region or country

GV1834.5.W66 1996
Wooden, Wayne S.
Rodeo in America: wranglers, roughstock & paydirt/ Wayne S. Wooden & Gavin Ehringer. Lawrence: University Press of Kansas, c1996. xi, 297 p.
96-016328   791.8/4/0973 20   0700608133
Rodeos -- United States -- History. Cowboys -- United States -- Biography.

GV1834.55.W47.L43 1993
LeCompte, Mary Lou, 1935-
Cowgirls of the rodeo: pioneer professional athletes/ Mary Lou LeCompte. Urbana: University of Illinois Press, c1993. xii, 252 p.
92-042635   791.8/4   0252020294
Cowgirls -- West (U.S.) -- History. Rodeos -- West (U.S.) Cowgirls -- West (U.S.) -- Social conditions.

GV1853.3 Amusement parks, amusement park resorts, etc. — By region or country — United States

GV1853.3.F62.W344 1992
Fjellman, Stephen M.
Vinyl leaves: Walt Disney World and America/ Stephen M. Fjellman. Boulder: Westview Press, 1992. xvii, 492 p.
91-043693   381/.45179106875924   0813314739
Leisure industry -- United States -- Case studies. Leisure -- Economic aspects -- United States -- Case studies. Popular culture -- Economic aspects -- United States -- Case studies.

GV1853.4 Amusement parks, amusement park resorts, etc. — By region or country — Other regions or countries, A-Z

GV1853.4.J3
Hendry, Joy.
The Orient strikes back: a global view of cultural display/ Joy Hendry. Oxford; Berg, 2000. xiii, 257 p.
306.480952   185973328X
Amusement parks -- Japan. Amusement parks -- Social aspects -- Japan.

H Social Sciences (General)

H31-35 Collected works

H31.C2 vol. 17
Kennedy, William Francis.
Humanist versus economist: Berkeley, University of California Press, 1958. 96 p.
58-009235
Coleridge, Samuel Taylor, -- 1772-1834 -- Political and social views.

H31.C514 no. 118
Johnson, Douglas L.
The nature of nomadism; a comparative study of pastoral migrations in southwestern Asia and northern Africa, by Douglas L. Johnson. [Chicago, Dept. of Geography, University of Chicago] 1969. viii, 200 p.
69-018022   301.45
Nomads.

H31.C514 no. 179, etc.
Harris, Chauncy Dennison, 1914-
Bibliography of geography/ by Chauncy D. Harris. Chicago: University of Chicago, Dept. of Geography, 1976-1984 v. 1.
76-001910   910   0890650861
Geography -- Bibliography. Geography -- Bibliography of bibliographies.

H31.C7 no. 380 1968
Cahill, Marion Cotter, 1901-
Shorter hours; a study of the movement since the Civil War. New York, AMS Press [1968] 300 p.
68-054258   331.81/9/73
Hours of labor -- United States. Labor laws and legislation -- United States.

H31.C7 no.405
Benson, Mary Sumner, 1903-
Women in eighteenth-century America; a study of opinion and social usage, by Mary Sumner Benson, Ph.D. New York, Columbia University press; 1935. 343 p.
35-006356   396.0973
Women -- United States -- History. Women -- United States -- Social conditions. Women in literature.

H31.C7 no. 445
Alpert, Harry, 1912-
Emile Durkheim and his sociology.   Russell & Russell, 1961 [c1939] 233 p.
61-013089   301
Durkheim, Emile, -- 1858-1917. Sociology.

H31.C7 no.604
Betts, Raymond F.
Assimilation and association in French colonial theory, 1890-1914.   New York, Columbia University Press, 1961 [c1960] 224 p.
61-013033
France -- Colonies -- Administration. France -- Colonies -- Native races.

H31.J6 ser. 86, no. 1
Cooper, William J.
The conservative regime: South Carolina, 1877-1890, by William J. Cooper. Baltimore, Johns Hopkins Press, 1968. 239 p.
67-026859   975.7/04
Conservatism -- South Carolina.

H31.J6 ser.62, no.1
Lane, Frederic Chapin, 1900-
Andrea Barbarigo, merchant of Venice, 1418-1449, by Frederic C. Lane. Baltimore, The Johns Hopkins press, 1944. 224 p.
45-001041   308.2
Barbarigo, Andrea, -- 1398 or 9-1449   Venice -- Commerce -- History

H31.J6 ser. 77, no. 1
De Santis, Vincent P.
Republicans face the Southern question: the new departure years, 1877-1897.   Baltimore, Johns Hopkins Press, 1959. 275 p.
59-010767   329.6
Political parties -- Southern States. Republican Party. Southern States -- Politics and government -- 1865-

H31.S67 no. 9
Kanter, Rosabeth Moss.
Work and family in the United States: a critical review and agenda for research and policy/ by Rosabeth Moss Kanter. New York: Russell Sage Foundation, 1977. 116 p.
76-046870   300/.8 s   0871544334
Work and family -- United States.

H33.W3613
Weber, Max, 1864-1920.
From Max Weber: Essays in sociology. Translated, edited, and with an introduction, by H. H. Gerth and C. Wright Mills. New York, Oxford university press, 1946. xi, 490 p.
46-005298
Social sciences.

H35.K68 1991
Krieger, Susan.
Social science and the self: personal essays on an art form/ Susan Krieger. New Brunswick, N.J.: Rutgers University Press, c1991. x, 273 p.
90-028754   300   0813517141
Social sciences. Social sciences -- Methodology. Social scientists.

H35.R7 1970
Roosevelt, Theodore, 1858-1919.
American ideals, and other essays, social and political. New York, Putnam, 1897. St. Clair Shores, Mich., Scholarly Press [1970?] viii, 354 p.
77-121312   320.9/73   0403001951
National characteristics, American.   United States -- Politics and government -- Addresses, essays, lectures. United States -- Social conditions -- 1865-1918.

H41 Dictionaries. Encyclopedias — English

H41.B53 2003
The Blackwell dictionary of modern social thought. 2nd ed./ edited by William Outhwaite. Malden, MA: Blackwell Publishers, 2003.
2002-066698   300/.3 21   0631221646
Social sciences -- History -- 20th century -- Encyclopedias. Philosophy -- History -- 20th century -- Dictionaries. Civilization, Modern -- 20th century -- Dictionaries.

H41.I58 2001
International encyclopedia of the social & behavioral sciences/ editors in chief Neil J. Smelser, Paul B. Baltes. 1st ed. Amsterdam; Elsevier, 2001. 26 v.
2001-044791   300/.3 21   0080430767
Social sciences -- Encyclopedias.

H41.R417 2001
Reader's guide to the social sciences/ editor Jonathan Michie. London; Fitzroy Dearborn, c2001. 2 v.
2001-269501   300/.3 21   1579580912
Social sciences -- Encyclopedias. Social sciences -- Bibliography.

H41.S63 1996
The social science encyclopedia/ edited by Adam Kuper and Jessica Kuper. London; Routledge, 1996. xxiv, 923 p.
97-166752   300/.3   0415108292
Social sciences -- Encyclopedias.

H51 History — General works

H51.G67 1991
Gordon, Scott.
The history and philosophy of social science/ Scott Gordon. London: Routledge, 1991. x, 690 p.
90-045920   300
Social sciences -- History. Social sciences -- Philosophy.

H51.O57 1993
Olson, Richard, 1940-
The emergence of the social sciences, 1642-1792/ Richard Olson. New York: Twayne Publishers; c1993. viii, 230 p.
92-036978   300/.9   0805786074
Social sciences -- History.

H51.R86 1987
Rundell, John F.
Origins of modernity: the origins of modern social theory from Kant to Hegel to Marx/ John F. Rundell. Madison, Wis.: University of Wisconsin Press, c1987. 249 p.
87-008152   300/.1   0299114503
Kant, Immanuel, -- 1724-1804 -- Contributions in social sciences. Hegel, Georg Wilhelm Friedrich, -- 1770-1831 -- Contributions in social sciences. Marx, Karl, -- 1818-1883 -- Contributions in social sciences. Social sciences -- History. Philosophical anthropology -- History.

H53 History — By region or country, A-Z

H53.U5.E85 1991
The estate of social knowledge/ edited by JoAnne Brown and David K. van Keuren. Baltimore: Johns Hopkins University Press, c1991. xxvi, 266 p.
90-039696   300/.9   0801840600
Social sciences -- United States -- History -- 19th century. Social sciences -- United States -- History -- 20th century. Social sciences -- Great Britain -- History -- 19th century.

H53.U5.G45 1998
Gender and American social science: the formative years/ edited by Helene Silverberg. Princeton, N.J.: Princeton University Press, c1998. x, 334 p.
97-042951   305.4/0973 21   0691017492
Social sciences -- United States -- History. Women social scientists -- United States -- History. Women -- United States -- History.

H59 Biography — Individual, A-Z

H59.D75.A33 1979
Drucker, Peter Ferdinand, 1909-
Adventures of a bystander/ Peter F. Drucker. New York: Harper & Row, c1979. viii, 344 p.
78-002120   300/.92   0060111011
Drucker, Peter Ferdinand, -- 1909-   Social scientists -- United States -- Biography.

H59.H36.A3 1988
Harrington, Michael, 1928-
The long-distance runner: an autobiography/
Michael Harrington. New York: Holt, c1988.
260 p.
88-010334 300/.92/4 0805007903
Harrington, Michael, -- 1928- Social scientists --
United States -- Biography. Political scientists --
United States -- Biography. Socialists -- United
States -- Biography.

H59.T8.A3
Tugwell, Rexford G. 1891-
The light of other days.   Garden City, N.Y.,
Doubleday, 1962. 404 p.
62-007690 923.273
Tugwell, Rexford G. -- (Rexford Guy), -- 1891-
Economists -- United States -- Biography. Political
scientists -- United States -- Biography.

H59.W4.D54 1996
Diggins, John P.
Max Weber: politics and the spirit of tragedy/ John
Patrick Diggins. New York, NY: Basic Books,
c1996. xvi, 334 p.
96-001616 301/.092 B 20 0465017509
Weber, Max, -- 1864-1920.   Social scientists --
Biography. Social sciences -- Methodology. Social
sciences -- Philosophy.

H59.W4.H65 2000
Honigsheim, Paul, 1885-1963.
The unknown Max Weber/ Paul Honigsheim;
edited and with an introduction by Alan Sica. New
Brunswick, N.J.: Transaction Publishers, c2000.
xxvi, 290 p.
00-034405 300 21 0765800152
Weber, Max, -- 1864-1920 -- Contributions in
social sciences.

H61 Theory. Method. Relation to other subjects — General works

H61.A54 1997
Albrow, Martin.
The global age: state and society beyond
modernity/ Martin Albrow. Stanford, Calif.:
Stanford University Press, 1997, c1996. ix, 246 p.
96-069671 300 0804728690
Social sciences -- Philosophy. International
relations. Sociology.

H61.B26 1982
Bartholomew, David J.
Stochastic models for social processes/ D.J.
Bartholomew. Chichester; Wiley, c1982. xii, 365 p.
82-117228 300/.724 0471280402
Social sciences -- Mathematical models.
Stochastic processes.

H61.B425 2000
Bechhofer, Frank.
Principles of research design in the social sciences/
Frank Bechhofer and Lindsay Paterson. London;
Routledge, 2000. ix, 172 p.
99-044348 300/.7/2 0415214424
Social sciences -- Research. Social sciences --
Methodology.

H61.B472
Bernstein, Richard J.
The restructuring of social and political theory/
Richard J. Bernstein. New York: Harcourt Brace
Jovanovich, c1976. xxiv, 286 p.
76-012054 300/.1 0151769400
Social sciences. Political science.

H61.B613 1991
Bohman, James.
New philosophy of social science: problems of
indeterminacy/ James Bohman. Cambridge, Mass.:
MIT Press, c1991. x, 273 p.
91-062790 300/.1 0262023431
Social sciences -- Philosophy.

H61.B793 1996
Bunge, Mario Augusto.
Finding philosophy in social science/ Mario Bunge.
New Haven, [Conn.]: Yale University Press,
c1996. xii, 432 p.
96-004399 300/.1 20 0300066066
Social sciences -- Philosophy.

H61.D3377 1999
Delanty, Gerard.
Social theory in a changing world: conceptions of
modernity/ Gerard Delanty. Malden, MA: Polity,
1999. vi, 211 p.
99-011068 301 0745619177
Social sciences -- Philosophy. Sociology --
Philosophy.

H61.D882
Dunn, William N.
Public policy analysis: an introduction/ William N.
Dunn. Englewood Cliffs, N.J.: Prentice-Hall,
c1981. xii, 388 p.
80-019571 361.6/1 0137379579
Policy sciences. Political planning -- Evaluation.

H61.F355 1996
Fay, Brian.
Contemporary philosophy of social science: a
multicultural approach/ Brian Fay. Oxford, UK;
Blackwell, 1996. xi, 266 p.
95-042638 300/.1 155786537X
Social sciences -- Philosophy. Multiculturalism.

H61.F6144 2001
Flyvbjerg, Bent.
Making social science matter: why social inquiry
fails and how it can succeed again/ Bent Flyvbjerg;
translated by Steven Sampson. Oxford, UK;
Cambridge University Press, 2001. x, 204 p.
00-023608 300/.1 0521772680
Social sciences -- Philosophy.

H61.H68
Hook, Sidney, 1902-
Reason, social myths and democracy [by] Sidney
Hook. New York, The John Day company [c1940]
xii, 302 p.
40-034126 301
Arnold, Thurman Wesley, -- 1891- -- Folklore of
capitalism. Lerner, Max, -- 1902- -- Ideas are
weapons. Maritain, Jacques, -- 1882-1973 --
Humanisme integral. Social sciences Dialectic.
Science -- Philosophy. Soviet Union -- Politics and
government -- 1917-1936.

H61.K24
Kaplan, Abraham, 1918-
The conduct of inquiry; methodology for
behavioral science. San Francisco, Chandler Pub.
Co. [1964] xix, 428 p.
64-013470 301.018
Social sciences -- Methodology.

H61.K5437 1994
King, Gary.
Designing social inquiry: scientific inference in
qualitative research/ Gary King, Robert O.
Keohane, Sidney Verba. Princeton, N.J.: Princeton
University Press, c1994. xi, 245 p.
93-039283 300/.72 0691034702
Social sciences -- Methodology. Social sciences -
- Research. Inference.

H61.L58 1990
Little, Daniel.
Varieties of social explanation: an introduction to
the philosophy of social science/ Daniel Little.
Boulder: Westview Press, 1991. xiii, 258 p.
90-043602 300/.1 0813305659
Social sciences -- Methodology. Social sciences -
- Philosophy.

H61.O895 1987
Outhwaite, William.
New philosophies of social science: realism,
hermeneutics, and critical theory/ William
Outhwaite. New York: St. Martin's Press, 1987.
viii, 137 p.
87-010083 300/.1 0312003951
Social sciences -- Philosophy. Realism.
Hermeneutics.

H61.O9 1976
Outhwaite, William.
Understanding social life: the method called
Verstehen/ by William Outhwaite. New York:
Holmes & Meier, 1976, c1975. 127 p.
75-028500 300/.1/8 0841902399
Social sciences -- Methodology. Knowledge,
Sociology of. Hermeneutics.

H61.R668 1988
Rosenberg, Alexander, 1946-
Philosophy of social science/ Alexander
Rosenberg. Boulder: Westview Press, 1988. xiv,
218 p.
88-005573 300/.1 0813306175
Social sciences -- Philosophy.

H61.S44
Schutz, Alfred, 1899-1959.
Collected papers. Edited and introduced by
Maurice Natanson. With a pref. by H. L. van
Breda. The Hague, M. Nijhoff, 1962-66. 3 v.
63-039472 300.1
Social sciences -- Methodology. Phenomenology.

H61.S4435 2001
Schwandt, Thomas A.
Dictionary of qualitative inquiry/ Thomas A
Schwandt. Thousand Oaks, Calif.: Sage
Publications, c2001. xxxiv, 281 p.
00-012062 300/.7/2 21 0761921656
Social sciences -- Methodology -- Dictionaries.
Social sciences -- Research -- Dictionaries.

H61.S5885 1989
Smith, John K. 1942-
The nature of social and educational inquiry:
empiricism versus interpretation/ John K. Smith.
Norwood, N.J.: Ablex, c1989. viii, 187 p.
89-006613 300/.1 0893915149
Social sciences -- Philosophy.

H61.S8824 1987
Strauss, Anselm L.
Qualitative analysis for social scientists/ Anselm L.
Strauss. Cambridge [Cambridgeshire]; Cambridge
University Press, 1987. xv, 319 p.
86-021608 300/.72 0521328454
Social sciences -- Methodology. Social sciences -
- Statistical methods.

H61.W4
Weber, Max, 1864-1920.
Max Weber on the methodology of the social sciences; translated and edited by Edward A. Shils and Henry A. Finch. With a foreword by Edward A. Shils. Glencoe, Ill., Free Press, 1949. xvii, 188 p.
49-009843   301.8
Social sciences -- Methodology.

H61.W496 1998
What is social theory?: the philosophical debates/ edited by Alan Sica. Malden, Mass.: Blackwell, 1998. ix, 286 p.
98-013166   300/.1   0631209549
Social sciences -- Philosophy.

H61.W554
Wildavsky, Aaron B.
Speaking truth to power: the art and craft of policy analysis/ Aaron Wildavsky. Boston: Little, Brown, c1979. xiv, 431 p.
78-061738   309.1
Policy sciences.

H61.15 Theory. Method. Relation to other subjects — Relation to philosophy. Social philosophy

H61.15.B46 2001
Benton, Ted,
Philosophy of social science: the philosophical foundations of social thought/ Ted Benton and Ian Craib. Houndmills, Basingstoke, Hampshire; Palgrave, 2001. vii, 203 p.
2001-027372   300/.1 21   033377499X
Social sciences -- Philosophy.

H61.25 Theory. Method. Relation to other subjects — Mathematics. Mathematical models

H61.25.B7 1994
Brams, Steven J.
Theory of moves/ Steven J. Brams. Cambridge [England]; Cambridge University Press, 1994. xii, 248 p.
93-008056   300/.1/5118   0521452260
Social sciences -- Mathematical models. Game theory.

H61.25.B95 1998
Byrne, D. S. 1947-
Complexity theory and the social sciences: an introduction/ David Byrne. London; Routledge, 1998. viii, 206 p.
98-023769   300/.1/5118   0415162955
Social sciences -- Mathematical models. Chaotic behavior in systems. Social sciences -- Research.

H61.25.H4 1995
Heap, Shaun Hargreaves, 1951-
Game theory: a critical introduction/ Shaun P. Hargreaves Heap and Yanis Varoufakis. London; Routledge, 1995. xii, 282 p.
94-022051   519.3   041509402X
Social sciences -- Mathematics. Game theory.

H61.25.S49 1982
Shubik, Martin.
Game theory in the social sciences: concepts and solutions/ Martin Shubik. Cambridge, Mass.: MIT Press, c1982. 514 p.
82-000063   300/.1/5193   0262191954
Social sciences -- Mathematical models. Game theory.

H61.28 Theory. Method. Relation to other subjects — Interviewing. Focused group interviewing

H61.28.H36 2002
Handbook of interview research: context & method/ editors, Jaber F. Gubrium, James A. Holstein. Thousand Oaks, Calif.: Sage Publications, c2002. xiii, 981 p.
00-013201   158/.39 21   0761919511
Interviewing -- Handbooks, manuals, etc.

H61.3 Theory. Method. Relation to other subjects — Data processing

H61.3.C654 2002
Computing in the social sciences and humanities/ edited by Orville Vernon Burton. Urbana: University of Illinois Press, c2002. viii, 194 p.
2001-001491   300/.285 21   0252026853
Social sciences -- Data processing. Humanities -- Data processing.

H61.3.P66 2000
Pool, Ithiel de Sola, 1917-
Humane politics and methods of inquiry/ Ithiel de Sola Pool; Lloyd S. Etheredge, editor. New Brunswick, N.J.: Transaction Publishers, c2000. xviii, 324 p.
00-020761   300 21   1560004010
Social sciences -- Data processing. Social sciences -- Computer simulation. Social sciences -- Forecasting.

H61.4 Theory. Method. Relation to other subjects — Forecasting in the social sciences

H61.4.H828 1993
Hughes, Barry, 1945-
International futures: choices in the creation of a new world order/ Barry B. Hughes. Boulder, Colo.: Westview Press, c1993. xvii, 205 p.
93-007227   003/.2   0813316502
Forecasting. Policy sciences. Forecasting -- Mathematical models.

H61.8 Communication of information — General works

H61.8.W543 2000
Willinsky, John, 1950-
If only we knew: increasing the public value of social science research/ John Willinsky. New York: Routledge , 2000. ix, 252 p.
00-035275   306.4/2   0415926513
Communication in the social sciences -- Technological innovations. Knowledge, Sociology of.

H61.95 Communication of information — Computer networks

H61.95.S45 1998
Selnow, Gary W.
Electronic whistle-stops: the impact of the Internet on American politics/ Gary W. Selnow. Westport, Conn.; Praeger, 1998. xxxiii, 221 p.
97-034745   320.973   027596163X
Internet (Computer network) -- Political aspects. Communication in politics -- United States.

H62-62.5 Study and teaching. Research

H62.A1.F57 1993
Fisher, Donald, 1944-
Fundamental development of the social sciences: Rockefeller philanthropy and the United States Social Science Research Council/ Donald Fisher. Ann Arbor: University of Michigan Press, c1993. xiv, 343 p.
92-036235   300/.72073   0472102702
Social sciences -- Research -- United States -- History.

H62.B785 1988
Bryman, Alan.
Quantity and quality in social research/ Alan Bryman. London; Unwin Hyman, 1988. viii, 198 p.
87-034024   300/.72   0043120393
Social sciences -- Research.

H62.C813 1993
Cunningham, J. Barton.
Action research and organizational development/ J. Barton Cunningham; foreword by A.W. McEachern. Westport, Conn.: Praeger, 1993. xi, 274 p.
92-001744   300/.72   0275942651
Social sciences -- Research. Action research. Organizational change.

H62.D53
Diener, Edward, 1946-
Ethics in social and behavioral research/ Edward Diener and Rick Crandall. Chicago: University of Chicago Press, 1978. x, 266 p.
78-008881   174/.9/301   0226148238
Social sciences -- Research -- United States. Ethical problems. Applied ethics.

H62.E453 1988
Eichler, Margrit.
Nonsexist research methods: a practical guide/ Margrit Eichler. Boston: Allen & Unwin, c1988. x, 183 p.
87-011477   300/.72   0044970447
Social sciences -- Research. Sexism.

H62.G82 1997
Gubrium, Jaber F.
The new language of qualitative method/ Jaber F. Gubrium, James A. Holstein. New York: Oxford University Press, 1997. x, 244 p.
96-023816   300/.72   0195099931
Social sciences -- Research -- Methodology.

H62.H2455 2000
Handbook of qualitative research/ Norman K. Denzin, Yvonna S. Lincoln, editors. 2nd ed. Thousand Oaks, Calif.: Sage Publications, c2000. xx, 1065 p.
00-008104   300/.7/2 21   0761915125
Social sciences -- Research.

H62.H2456 1991
The Handbook of qualitative research in education/ edited by Margaret D. LeCompte, Wendy L. Millroy, Judith Preissle. San Diego: Academic Press, c1992. xxxvi, 881 p.
91-019105   300/.72   0124405703
Social sciences -- Research. Education -- Research.

H62.K416
Kelman, Herbert C.
A time to speak; on human values and social research [by] Herbert C. Kelman. San Francisco, Jossey-Bass, 1968. xvi, 349 p.
68-021319   300/.72
Social sciences -- Research. Social values. Social sciences and ethics.

H62.K515 1996
Kincaid, Harold, 1952-
Philosophical foundations of the social sciences: analyzing controversies in social research/ Harold Kincaid. Cambridge [England]; Cambridge University Press, 1996. xvi, 283 p.
95-013774   300/.1   0521482682
Social sciences -- Research. Social sciences -- Philosophy.

H62.L419 2000
Lee-Treweek, Geraldine, 1969-
Danger in the field: risk and ethics in social research/ Geraldine Lee-Treweek and Stephanie Linkogle. New York: Routledge, 2000.
00-035278   300/.7/2   0415193214
Social scientists -- Vocational guidance. Social scientists -- Professional ethics. Social sciences -- Research -- Moral and ethical aspects.

H62.M277 1989
Marshall, Catherine.
Designing qualitative research/ Catherine Marshall, Gretchen B. Rossman. Newbury Park, Calif.: Sage Publications, c1989. 175 p.
88-030875   300/.72   0803931573
Social sciences -- Research -- Methodology.

H62.T465 2001
Thomson, William, 1949-
A guide for the young economist/ William Thomson. Cambridge, Mass.: MIT Press, c2001. xiv, 118 p.
00-064588   808/.06633 21   026220133X
Economics -- Research. Economics -- Authorship. Academic writing.

H62.W38
Webb, Eugene J., 1933-
Unobtrusive measures; nonreactive research in the social sciences by Eugene J. Webb and others Chicago, Rand McNally 1966. xii, 225 p.
66-010806   301.018
Social science research.

H62.W457 1991
Whyte, William Foote, 1914-
Social theory for action: how individuals and organizations learn to change/ William Foote Whyte. Newbury Park: Sage Publications, c1991. vii, 301 p.
91-006941   302.3/5 20   0803941668
Action research. Social participation. Management -- Employee participation.

H62.5.U5.H45 1991
Heims, Steve J.
The cybernetics group/ Steve Joshua Heims. Cambridge, Mass.: MIT Press, c1991. xii, 334 p.
91-000409   003/.5   0262082004
Social sciences -- United States -- Philosophy. Cybernetics -- United States. Science -- Social aspects -- United States.

H62.5.U5.H96 1991
Hyman, Herbert Hiram, 1918-
Taking society's measure: a personal history of survey research/ Herbert H. Hyman; edited and with an introduction by Hubert J. O'Gorman with the assistance of Eleanor Singer. New York: Russell Sage Foundation, c1991. xxiv, 257 p.
90-046449   300/.72   0871543958
Hyman, Herbert Hiram, -- 1918- Social surveys -- United States -- Case studies. Economic surveys -- United States -- Case studies. Public opinion polls -- Case studies.

H62.5.U5.S76 1991
Stotsky, Sandra.
Connecting civic education & language education: the contemporary challenge/ Sandra Stotsky with Barbara Hardy Beierl ... [et al.]. New York: Teachers College Press, c1991. xxiv, 223 p.
91-002222   320.4/071/073   0807730815
Civics -- Study and teaching (Secondary) -- United States. Civics -- Study and teaching (Higher) -- United States. Language arts (Secondary) -- United States.

H67 Schools. Institutes of social sciences

H67.L9.D33 1995
Dahrendorf, Ralf.
LSE: a history of the London School of Economics and Political Science, 1895-1995/ Ralf Dahrendorf. Oxford; Oxford University Press, 1995. xx, 584 p.
94-042604   330/.071/14212   0198202407
London School of Economics and Political Science -- History.

H83 General works — 1871-1975

H83.B673
Boulding, Kenneth Ewart, 1910-
The impact of the social sciences, by Kenneth E. Boulding. New Brunswick, N.J., Rutgers University Press [1966] vi, 117 p.
66-064653   301.24
Social sciences.

H85 General works — 1976-

H85.M394 1998
Mazlish, Bruce, 1923-
The uncertain sciences/ Bruce Mazlish. New Haven: Yale University Press, c1998. viii, 328 p.
98-009716   300 21   0300074778
Social sciences.

H85.L83 1990
Luard, Evan, 1926-
International society/ Evan Luard. Basingstoke: Macmillan, 1990. vii, 273 p.
89-011569   301   0333487273
Social sciences.

H91 General special

H91.M8
Mullins, Carolyn J.
A guide to writing and publishing in the social and behavioral sciences/ Carolyn J. Mullins. New York: Wiley, c1977. xvi, 431 p.
77-001153   808/.0663021   0471624209
Social sciences -- Authorship -- Vocational guidance. Academic writing -- Vocational guidance.

H91.W56 1988
Wildavsky, Aaron B.
Searching for safety/ Aaron Wildavsky. New Brunswick, USA: Transaction Books, 1988. xii, 253 p.
87-037659   303   0912051175
Risk. Uncertainty. Safety regulations.

H97 Public policy (General). Policy sciences — General works

H97.B6 1987
Bobrow, Davis B.
Policy analysis by design/ Davis B. Bobrow and John S. Dryzek. Pittsburgh, Pa.: University of Pittsburgh Press, c1987. viii, 246 p.
87-005974   361.6/1   0822953927
Policy sciences.

H97.B68 1996
Bovens, M. A. P.
Understanding policy fiascoes/ Mark Bovens, Paul 't Hart. New Brunswick, N.J.: Transaction Publishers, c1996. v, 173 p.
95-009318   320/.6 20   156000214X
Policy sciences.

H97.D45 1988
DeLeon, Peter.
Advice and consent: the development of the policy sciences/ Peter deLeon. New York: Russell Sage Foundation, c1988. xii, 131 p.
88-032140 361.6/1 0871542153
Policy sciences. Political planning -- United States. United States -- Politics and government -- 20th century.

H97.H67 1991
House, Peter William, 1937-
The practice of policy analysis: forty years of art & technology/ by Peter W. House and Roger D. Shull; foreword by Aaron Wildavsky. Washington, D.C.: Compass Press, c1991. xviii, 188 p.
91-024363 320/.6 0929590031
Policy sciences -- Case studies. Energy policy -- United States -- Case studies. Environmental policy -- United States -- Case studies.

H97.H68 1988
House, Peter William, 1937-
Rush to policy: using analytic techniques in public sector decision making/ Peter W. House, Roger D. Shull. New Brunswick, U.S.A.: Transaction Books, c1988. xi, 219 p.
87-032742 361.6/1 0887381340
Policy sciences.

H97.H69 1995
Howlett, Michael, 1955-
Studying public policy: policy cycles and policy subsystems/ Michael Howlett and M. Ramesh. Toronto; Oxford University Press, 1995. vi, 239 p.
96-121480 320/.6 0195409760
Policy sciences.

H97.N335 1988
Nagel, Stuart S., 1934-
Policy studies: integration and evaluation/ Stuart S. Nagel. New York: Greenwood Press, 1988. xvi, 303 p.
88-003122 361.6/1 031326256X
Policy sciences.

H97.P373 1995
Parsons, D. W.
Public policy: an introduction to the theory and practice of policy analysis/ Wayne Parsons. Aldershot, UK; Edward Elgar, c1995. xviii, 675 p.
95-010756 320/.6 1852785535
Policy sciences.

H97.P664 1990
Policy theory and policy evaluation: concepts, knowledge, causes, and norms/ edited by Stuart S. Nagel. New York: Greenwood Press, 1990. xxiv, 227 p.
89-025784 320/.6 0313273561
Policy sciences. Evaluation research (Social action programs)

H97.S33 1997
Schneider, Anne L.
Policy design for democracy/ Anne Larason Schneider and Helen Ingram. Lawrence: University Press of Kansas, c1997. xii, 241 p.
97-020360 320/.6 21 0700608435
Policy sciences. Political planning -- United States. Democracy.

H97.V4313 1997
Vedung, Evert, 1938-
Public policy and program evaluation/ Evert Vedung. New Bruswick, N.J.: Transaction Publishers, c1997. xx, 336 p.
96-052816 320/.6 21 1560002999
Political planning. Political planning -- Evaluation. Policy sciences.

H97.W544 1995
Williams, Bruce Alan.
Democracy, dialogue, and environmental disputes: the contested languages of social regulation/ Bruce A. Williams and Albert R. Matheny. New Haven: Yale University Press, c1995. xii, 256 p.
95-007650 363.7 0300062419
Policy sciences. Communication in politics -- United States. Delegated legislation -- United States.

HA Statistics

HA12.5 Congresses

HA12.5.U63
Statistical yearbook/ Department of Economic and Social Information and Policy Analysis, Statistical Division = Annuaire statistique/ Département de l'information économique et sociale et de l'analyse des politiques, Division de statistique. New York: United Nations, <1993- >
95-641266 310/.5
Statistics -- Periodicals.

HA17 Dictionaries. Encyclopedias

HA17.D45
Demographic yearbook. Annuaire demographique. New York [etc.] Dept. of Economic and Social Affairs 1999
50-000641 312.058
Population -- Statistics -- Periodicals.

HA17.V64 1993
Vogt, W. Paul.
Dictionary of statistics and methodology: a nontechnical guide for the social sciences/ W. Paul Vogt. Newbury Park, Calif.: Sage Publications, c1993. xiv, 253 p.
93-000728 300/.1/5195 0803952767
Social sciences -- Statistical methods -- Dictionaries. Social sciences -- Methodology -- Dictionaries.

HA29 Theory and method of social science statistics — General works

HA29.B59 1972
Blalock, Hubert M.
Social statistics [by] Hubert M. Blalock, Jr. New York, McGraw-Hill [1972] xiv, 583 p.
76-037090 519.5 0070057516
Statistics.

HA29.B732 1989
Bollen, Kenneth A.
Structural equations with latent variables/ Kenneth A. Bollen. New York: Wiley, c1989. xiv, 514 p.
88-027272 300/.28 0471011711
Social sciences -- Statistical methods. Latent variables.

HA29.F4 1971
Ferguson, George Andrew.
Statistical analysis in psychology & education [by] George A. Ferguson. New York, McGraw-Hill [1971] xii, 492 p.
74-150459 519.5 0070205051
Statistics. Psychometrics. Educational tests and measurements.

HA29.S2365 2000
Salkind, Neil J.
Statistics for people who (think they) hate statistics/ Neil J. Salkind. Thousand Oaks, Calif.: Sage Publications, Inc., c2000. xxi, 385 p.
99-050472 519.5 21 0761916210
Statistics.

HA30.6 Theory and method of social science statistics — Spatial analysis

HA30.6.H35 1990
Haining, Robert P.
Spatial data analysis in the social and environmental sciences/ Robert Haining. Cambridge [England]; Cambridge University Press, 1990. xxi, 409 p.
90-001361 300/.1/5192 0521384168
Spatial analysis (Statistics) Population geography -- Statistical methods.

HA31.3 Theory and method of social science statistics — Regression. Correlation

HA31.3.E94 1998
Eye, Alexander von.
Regression analysis for social sciences/ Alexander von Eye, Christof Schuster. San Diego, Calif.: Academic Press, c1998. xv, 386 p.
98-084465 300/.01/519536 21 0127249559
Social sciences -- Statistical methods. Regression analysis.

HA33 Communication of information — General works

HA33.H4
Hendricks, Walter Anton, 1904-
The mathematical theory of sampling. New Brunswick, N.J., Scarecrow Press, 1956. vii, 364 p.
57-003502
Sampling (Statistics)

HA36 Statistical services. Statistical bureaus — International

HA36.K87 1997
Kurian, George Thomas.
Global data locator/ George Thomas Kurian. Lanham, Md.: Bernan Press, c1997. xvii, 375 p.
98-119239   0890590397
Statistical services -- Directories. Statistics -- Databases -- Directories. Information services -- Directories.

HA36.W67
World directory of non-official statistical sources. London: Euromonitor plc, [c1996-]
96-032254
Statistical services -- Directories. Statistics -- Information services -- Directories. Statistics -- directories.

HA37 Statistical services. Statistical bureaus — By region or country, A-Z

HA37.U55.A53 1988
Anderson, Margo J., 1945-
The American census: a social history/ Margo J. Anderson. New Haven: Yale University Press, c1988. xiii, 257 p.
87-029828   304.6/0973   0300040148
United States -- Census -- History. United States -- Population -- History. United States -- Statistical services -- History.

HA37.U55.E53 2000
Encyclopedia of the U.S. Census/ Margo J. Anderson, editor. Washington, DC: CQ Press, c2000. xxiv, 424 p.
00-030522   304.6/07/23 21   1568024282
United States -- Census -- Encyclopedias.

HA154 Statistical data — Universal statistics — Societies. Serials

HA154.S68
Statistical abstract of the world. New York: Gale Research, Inc., [c1994-]
95-640698   310/.5
Statistics -- Periodicals. Economic indicators -- Periodicals. Political indicators -- Periodicals.

HA155 Statistical data — Universal statistics — General works

HA155.M85 1988
Muller, Georg P.
Comparative world data: a statistical handbook for social science/ Georg P. Muller with the collaboration of Volker Bornschier. Baltimore: Johns Hopkins University Press, c1988. viii, 496 p.
88-045391   519.5   0801837340
Statistics.

HA155.P65 1997
Political data handbook: OECD countries/ [edited by] Jan-Erik Lane, David McKay, and Kenneth Newton. 2nd ed. Oxford; Oxford University Press, 1997. ix, 357 p.
97-164375   320/.021 21   019828053X
OECD countries -- Statistics. OECD countries -- Politics and government -- Statistics.

HA201-214 Statistical data — By region or country — America

HA201.1990ar
Lavin, Michael R.
Understanding the census: a guide for marketers, planners, grant writers, and other data users/ Michael R. Lavin. Kenmore, N.Y.: Epoch; c1996. ix, 545 p.
96-146991   304.6/0723 20   0897749952
Census -- Handbooks, manuals, etc. United States -- Census, 21st, 1990 -- Handbooks, manuals, etc.

HA202.A36
County and city data book. [Washington, D.C.]: U.S. Dept. of Commerce, Bureau of the Census: [1952-]
52-004576   317.3
Cities and towns -- United States -- Statistics. United States -- Statistics.

HA203.S7
State and local statistics sources. Detroit, MI: Gale Research, [c1990-]
90-642553   016.3173
Cities and towns -- United States -- Statistics -- Periodicals. United States -- Statistics -- Periodicals.

HA214.H57 1993
Historical statistics of the states of the United States: two centuries of the census, 1790-1990/ compiled by Donald B. Dodd. Westport, Conn.: Greenwood Press, c1993. viii, 478 p.
93-025014   317.3   0313283095
United States -- Statistics. United States -- Population -- History. United States -- Census -- History.

HA214.S84 1998
A Statistical portrait of the United States: social conditions and trends/ edited by Mark S. Littman; [contributors: Mark S. Littman ... [et. al.]]. Lanham, Md.: Bernan Press, c1998. xxi, 404 p.
98-072991   306/.0973/021 21   0890590761
United States -- Statistics. United States -- Social conditions -- Statistics.

HA744-745 Statistical data — By region or country — Canada

HA744.S81
The Canada year book. Ottawa: Census and Statistics Office, 1906-
73-640929   317.1
Canada -- Statistics -- Yearbooks.

HA745.H57 1983
Historical statistics of Canada. [Ottawa]: Statistics Canada, c1983. 900 p.
83-173149   317.1   0660112590
Canada -- Statistics -- History.

HA1107-1444 Statistical data — By region or country — Europe

HA1107.M5 2003
Mitchell, B. R.
International historical statistics: Europe, 1750-2000/ B.R. Mitchell. 5th ed. New York: Palgrave Macmillan, 2003.
2002-035257   314 21   0333994116
Europe -- Statistics -- History.

HA1444.R93 1990
Ryan, Michael, 1937-
Contemporary Soviet society: a statistical handbook/ compiled, with translation, by Michael Ryan. Aldershot, Hants, England; E. Elgar, c1990. ix, 283 p.
90-013847   304.6/0947/021   1852783494
Soviet Union -- Population -- Statistics.

HA4675 Statistical data — By region or country — Asia

HA4675.M552 2003
Mitchell, B. R.
International historical statistics: Africa, Asia & Oceania, 1750-2001/ B.R. Mitchell. 4th ed. New York: Palgrave Macmillan, 2003.
2002-035523   310 21   0333994124
History -- Africa -- Statistics. History -- Asia -- Statistics. History -- Pacific Islands -- Statistics.

HB Economic Theory. Demography

HB1 Economic theory — Societies. Serials

HB1.R435
Review of political economy. London: E. Arnold, c1989-
93-640889   330/.05
Economics -- Periodicals.

HB31-34 Economic theory — Collected works (nonserial)

HB31.H37 v.63
Sweezy, Paul Marlor, 1910-
Monopoly and competition in the English coal trade, 1550-1850, by Paul M. Sweezy. Cambridge [Mass.] Harvard University Press, 1938. xii, 186 p.
39-000309   338.2
Coal trade -- Great Britain.

HB34.A48
American Economic Association.
Surveys of economic theory. Prepared for the American Economic Association and the Royal Economic Society. London, Macmillan; 1965-66. 3 v.
65-026933   330
Economics -- Addresses, essays, lectures.

HB34.C64 1991
Companion to contemporary economic thought/
edited by David Greenaway, Michael Bleaney, and
Ian Stewart. London; Routledge, 1991. xii, 858 p.
91-023817   330.1   0415026121
Economics.

HB34.H25 1972
Harrod, Roy Forbes, 1900-
Economic essays [by] Roy Harrod. London,
Macmillan, 1972. xx, 317 p.
72-197426   330/.08   0333135369
Economics -- Addresses, essays, lectures.

HB34.H3 1972
Hayek, Friedrich A. von 1899-
Individualism and economic order, by Friedrich A.
Hayek. Chicago, H. Regnery Co. [1972, c1948] vi,
271 p.
74-183821   330
Economics.

HB34.V38
Veblen, Thorstein, 1857-1929.
Essays in our changing order, by Thorstein Veblen;
edited by Leon Ardzrooni ... New York, The
Viking Press, 1934. xviii, 472 p.
34-027284   330.4
Economics. World War, 1914-1918

HB34.V4 1990
Veblen, Thorstein, 1857-1929.
The place of science in modern civilization and
other essays/ Thorstein Veblen; with a new
introduction by Warren J. Samuels. New
Brunswick (U.S.A.): Transaction Publishers,
c1990. xxx, 509 p.
89-030458   330   0887388086
Economics. Science.

HB61 Economic theory — Dictionaries. Encyclopedias

HB61.B554 1997
Black, John, 1931-
A dictionary of economics/ John Black. Oxford;
Oxford University Press, 1997. 507 p.
96-052401   330/.03   0192800183
Economics -- Dictionaries.

HB61.E55 1994
The McGraw-Hill encyclopedia of economics/
Douglas Greenwald, editor in chief. New York:
McGraw-Hill, c1994. xl, 1093 p.
93-009805   330/.03   0070244103
Economics -- Encyclopedias.

HB61.N49 1987
The New Palgrave: a dictionary of economics/
edited by John Eatwell, Murray Milgate, Peter
Newman. London: Macmillan; 1987. 4 v.
87-001946   330/.03/21   0333372352
Economics -- Dictionaries.

HB61.R68 1999
The Routledge critical dictionary of global
economics/ edited by Robert Beynon. New York:
Routledge, 1999. xx, 374 p.
98-055077   330/.03   0415923522
Economics -- Dictionaries.

HB61.S466 1995
Shim, Jae K.
Dictionary of economics/ Jae K. Shim and Joel G.
Siegel. New York: J. Wiley & Sons, c1995. x,
373 p.
94-040402   330/.3   047101317X
Economics -- Dictionaries.

HB62 Economic theory — Terminology. Abbreviations. Notation

HB62.K57 2000
Knapp, Peggy Ann.
Time-bound words: semantic and social economies
from Chaucer's England to Shakespeare's/ Peggy
A. Knapp. Houndmills, Basingstoke, Hampshire:
Macmillan Press; 2000. vii, 224 p.
99-042134   330/.01/4   0312224044
*Economics -- Terminology -- History. English
language -- History.*

HB71 Economic theory — Economics as a science. Relation to other subjects — General works

HB71.B3137 1989
Bartlett, Randall, 1945-
Economics and power: an inquiry into human
relations and markets/ Randall Bartlett. Cambridge;
Cambridge University Press, 1989. xi, 209 p.
88-031571   330.1   0521355621
Economics. Power (Social sciences)

HB71.B658
Boulding, Kenneth Ewart, 1910-
Economics as a science [by] Kenneth E. Boulding.
New York, McGraw-Hill [1970] vi, 157 p.
75-105420   330/.08
Economics -- Addresses, essays, lectures.

HB71.B7794 1989
Buchanan, James M.
Essays on the political economy/ James M.
Buchanan. Honolulu: University of Hawaii Press,
c1989. xii, 85 p.
89-004690   338.9   0824812506
Economics. Free enterprise. Social choice.

HB71.C558 1992
Clark, Charles Michael Andres.
Economic theory and natural philosophy: the
search for the natural laws of the economy/ Charles
Michael Andres Clark. Aldershot, Hants, England;
E. Elgar, c1992. x, 198 p.
93-119441   330   1852784458
*Economics. Economics -- Philosophy. Economics
-- Methology.*

HB71.H4 1992
Hausman, Daniel M., 1947-
The inexact and separate science of economics/
Daniel M. Hausman. Cambridge; Cambridge
University Press, 1992. xi, 372 p.
91-018967   330   0521415012
Economics.

HB71.H799 1977
Hutchison, T. W.
Knowledge and ignorance in economics/ T. W.
Hutchison. Chicago: University of Chicago Press,
1977. 186 p.
76-054771   330   0226362361
Economics. Economics -- Methodology.

HB71.K48 1989
Kindleberger, Charles Poor, 1910-
Economic laws and economic history/ Charles P.
Kindleberger. Cambridge [England]; Cambridge
University Press, 1989. xi, 190 p.
84-009595   330   0521267919
*Economics. Economics -- History. Economic
history.*

HB71.M38 1998
McCloskey, Deirdre N.
The rhetoric of economics/ Deirdre N. McCloskey.
Madison, Wis.: University of Wisconsin Press,
c1998. xxi, 223 p.
97-037740   330 21   0299158101
Economics. Rhetoric.

HB71.N44 1982
Nelson, Richard R.
An evolutionary theory of economic change/
Richard R. Nelson and Sidney G. Winter.
Cambridge, Mass.: Belknap Press of Harvard
University Press, 1982. xi, 437 p.
81-013455   338.9/001   0674272277
*Economics. Economic development.
Organizational change.*

HB71.O26 2000
O'Connor, David E.
Basic economic principles: a guide for students/
David E. O'Connor and Christopher Faille.
Westport, Conn.: Greenwood Press, 2000. viii,
255 p.
00-021050   330   031331005X
Economics.

HB71.P654 2000
Political economy and contemporary capitalism:
radical perspectives on economic theory and
policy/ Ron Baiman, Heather Boushey, Dawn
Saunders, editors. Armonk, N.Y.: M.E. Sharpe,
c2000. xv, 352 p.
99-047226   330 21   0765605295
Economics. Capitalism.

HB71.R35 1991
Redman, Deborah A.
Economics and the philosophy of science/ Deborah
A. Redman. New York: Oxford University Press,
1991. xiv, 252 p.
90-032099   330/.01/5   0195064127
Economics -- Philosophy. Science -- Philosophy.

HB71.V64 1969
Von Mises, Ludwig, 1881-1973.
Theory and history; an interpretation of social and
economic evolution. New Rochelle, N.Y.,
Arlington House [1969] ix, 384 p.
77-097129   330/.01   0870000705
Economics. History -- Philosophy.

HB71.W397
Weintraub, E. Roy.
Microfoundations: the compatibility of
microeconomics and macroeconomics/ E. Roy
Weintraub. Cambridge [Eng.]; Cambridge
University Press, 1979. viii, 175 p.
78-016551   330.1   0521223059
*Microeconomics. Macroeconomics. Equilibrium
(Economics)*

HB72 Economic theory — Economics as a science. Relation to other subjects — Relation to philosophy, religion, ethics

HB72.B65 1992
Bonar, James, 1852-1941.
Philosophy and political economy/ James Bonar; with a new introduction by Warren J. Samuels. New Brunswick, N.J., U.S.A.: Transaction Publishers, c1992. xxv, 410 p.
91-008166   330.1   0887384382
Economics -- Moral and ethical aspects. Economics -- Philosophy.

HB72.B833 1994
Buchanan, James M.
Ethics and economic progress/ by James M. Buchanan. Norman: University of Oklahoma, c1994. ix, 156 p.
93-031846   174/.4   0806125969
Economics -- Moral and ethical aspects. Work ethic. Economic development -- Moral and ethical aspects.

HB72.E2664 2001
The economic world view: studies in the ontology of economics/ edited by Uskali Mäki. Cambridge; Cambridge University Press, 2001. xvi, 400 p.
00-045499   330.1 21   0521000203
Economics -- Philosophy. Economics -- Methodology. Economic man.

HB72.E273 1998
Economics, ethics, and public policy/ edited by Charles K. Wilber. Lanham, MD: Rowman & Littlefield, c1998. 416 p.
97-030482   338.9 21   0847687899
Economics -- Moral and ethical aspects. Economic policy -- Moral and ethical aspects. Economic development -- Moral and ethical aspects.

HB72.F637 2001
Folbre, Nancy.
The invisible heart: economics and family values/ Nancy Folbre. New York: New Press, 2001. xx, 267 p.
00-062207   306.3/0973   1565846559
Economics -- Moral and ethical aspects. Feminist economics. Social justice. United States -- Economic policy -- 1993-2001. United States -- Economic conditions -- 1981- United States -- Social policy -- 1993-

HB72.F85 1995
Fukuyama, Francis.
Trust: the social virtues and the creation of prosperity/ Francis Fukuyama. New York: Free Press, c1995. xv, 457 p.
95-019320   306.3   0029109760
Economics -- Moral and ethical aspects. Trust. Virtue.

HB72.H355 1996
Hausman, Daniel M., 1947-
Economic analysis and moral philosophy/ Daniel M. Hausman, Michael S. McPherson. Cambridge [England]; Cambridge University Press, 1996. ix, 249 p.
95-008814   330   0521552028
Economics -- Moral and ethical aspects.

HB72.L364 2000
Lane, Robert Edwards.
The loss of happiness in market democracies/ Robert E. Lane. New Haven: Yale University Press, c2000. x, 465 p.
99-029817   330.1 21   0300078013
Economics -- Moral and ethical aspects. Economics -- Sociological aspects. Quality of life.

HB72.M53 1993
Minowitz, Peter, 1955-
Profits, priests, and princes: Adam Smiths emancipation of economics from politics and religion/ Peter Minowitz. Stanford, Calif.: Stanford University Press, 1993. xv, 345 p.
93-018798   330.15/3   0804721661
Smith, Adam, -- 1723-1790.   Economics -- Philosophy. Economics -- Moral and ethical aspects.

HB72.N45 2001
Nelson, Robert H. 1944-
Economics as religion: from Samuelson to Chicago and beyond/ Robert H. Nelson; foreword by Max Stackhouse. University Park, Pa.: Pennsylvania State University Press, c2001. xxvi, 378 p.
00-052444   330.1 21   0271020954
Economics -- Philosophy. Economics -- Moral and ethical aspects. Religion -- Economic aspects.

HB72.N684 2001
Novak, Michael.
Three in one: essays on democratic capitalism, 1976-2000/ Michael Novak; edited by Edward W. Younkins. Lanham, Md.: Rowman & Littlefield Publishers, c2001. xv, 345 p.
00-053352   330.12/2 21   0742511707
Economics -- Moral and ethical aspects. Capitalism -- Moral and ethical aspects. Democracy -- Moral and ethical aspects.

HB72.P53 1993
Piderit, John J.
The ethical foundations of economics/ John J. Piderit. Washington, D.C: Georgetown University Press, c1993. xxi, 339 p.
92-041288   330/.01   0878405356
Economics -- Moral and ethical aspects. Economics -- Philosophy.

HB72.P65 1998
Powelson, John P., 1920-
The moral economy/ John P. Powelson. Ann Arbor: University of Michigan Press, c1998. xii, 282 p.
98-008146   330/.01 21   0472109251
Economics -- Moral and ethical aspects. Social problems. Social justice.

HB72.R63 1994
Roemer, John E.
Egalitarian perspectives: essays in philosophical economics/ John E. Roemer. Cambridge [England]; Cambridge University Press, 1994. xi, 356 p.
93-024807   330/.01   0521450667
Economics -- Philosophy. Equality. Social justice.

HB72.V498 1997
Vickers, Douglas, 1924-
Economics and ethics: an introduction to theory, institutions, and policy/ Douglas Vickers. Westport, Conn.: Praeger, 1997. ix, 173 p.
97-005594   174/.9339   0275959783
Economics -- Moral and ethical aspects.

HB72.Y43 2001
Yeager, Leland B.
Ethics as social science: the moral philosophy of social cooperation/ Leland B. Yeager. Cheltenham, UK; Edward Elgar, c2001. viii, 334 p.
00-042968   171/.5 21   1840645210
Economics -- Moral and ethical aspects. Utilitarianism.

HB72.Y68 1994
Young, H. Peyton, 1945-
Equity: in theory and practice/ H. Peyton Young. Princeton, N.J.: Princeton University Press, c1994. xiii, 238 p.
93-002273   305   0691043191
Distributive justice. Game theory.

HB73 Economic theory — Economics as a science. Relation to other subjects — Relation to law

HB73.B83 1991
Buchanan, James M.
The economics and the ethics of constitutional order/ James M. Buchanan. Ann Arbor: University of Michigan Press, c1991. viii, 258 p.
90-026666   330 20   0472102222
Economics -- Political aspects. Economics -- Moral and ethical aspects. Free enterprise.

HB73.O78 1987
O'Sullivan, Patrick J., 1951-
Economic methodology and freedom to choose/ Patrick J. O'Sullivan. London; Allen & Unwin, 1987. xvii, 265 p.
86-022247   330.1   0043303757
Economics -- Philosophy. Economics -- Methodology.

HB74 Economic theory — Economics as a science. Relation to other subjects — Relation to other special topics, A-Z

HB74.M3.C653 1960
Cournot, A. A. 1801-1877.
Researches into the mathematical principles of the theory of wealth, 1838. Translated by Nathaniel T. Bacon. With an essay on Cournot and mathematical economics and a bibliography of mathematical economics by Irving Fisher. New York, A. M. Kelley, 1960. xxiv, 213 p.
64-007663
Economics, Mathematical.

HB74.P49.M57 1989
Mirowski, Philip, 1951-
More heat than light: economics as social physics, physics as nature's economics/ Philip Mirowski. Cambridge; Cambridge University Press, 1989. xii, 450 p.
89-009728   330   0521350425
Economics. Physics.

HB74.P65.C37 1992
Caporaso, James A., 1941-
Theories of political economy/ James A. Caporaso and David P. Levine. Cambridge; Cambridge University Press, 1992. viii, 243 p.
92-007793   338.9   0521415616
Economics. Political science.

HB74.P8.N484 1995
The New economics of human behavior/ edited by Mariano Tommasi and Kathryn Ierulli. Cambridge [England]; Cambridge University Press, 1995. xvii, 238 p.
94-019809   330/.01/9   0521474205
Economics -- Psychological aspects. Economics -- Sociological aspects.

HB74.8 Economic theory — Study and teaching. Research — By region or country

HB74.8.K57 1990
Klamer, Arjo.
The making of an economist/ Arjo Klamer and David Colander. Boulder: Westview Press, 1990. xvii, 216 p.
89-037899   330/.071/1073   0813306981
Economics -- Study and teaching (Graduate) -- United States. Economists -- United States. Graduate students -- United States.

HB74.8.T4 1998
Teaching economics to undergraduates: alternatives to chalk and talk/ edited by William E. Becker and Michael Watts. Cheltenham, UK; E. Elgar, c1998. xvi, 274 p.
98-048149   330/.071/173 21   1858989728
Economics -- Study and teaching (Higher) -- United States.

HB74.8.W66 1995
Women of value: feminist essays on the history of women in economics/ edited by Mary Ann Dimand, Robert W. Dimand, Evelyn L. Forget. Aldershot, Hants, UK; E. Elgar, c1995. xii, 228 p.
95-007191   330/.082   185278959X
Women economists -- United States -- History. Economists -- United States -- History. Feminism -- United States -- History.

HB75 Economic theory — History of economics. History of economic theory — General works

HB75.B1363 2001
Backhouse, Roger.
The ordinary business of life: a history of economics from the ancient world to the twenty-first century/ Roger E. Backhouse. Princeton, N.J.: Princeton University Press, c2002. ix, 368 p.
2001-096894   330/.09 21   0691096260
Economics -- History.

HB75.B664 1997
Blaug, Mark.
Economic theory in retrospect/ Mark Blaug. 5th ed. Cambridge; Cambridge University Press, 1997. xxv, 725 p.
95-026743   330.1/09 20   0521577012
Economics -- History.

HB75.G27
Galbraith, John Kenneth, 1908-
The age of uncertainty/ John Kenneth Galbraith. Boston: Houghton Mifflin, 1977. 365 p.
76-026965   330/.09   0395249007
Economics -- History. Economic history.

HB75.G274 1987
Galbraith, John Kenneth, 1908-
Economics in perspective: a critical history/ John Kenneth Galbraith. Boston: Houghton Mifflin, 1987. 324 p.
87-003644   330/.09   0395355729
Economics -- History. Economic history.

HB75.H375 1996
Heilbroner, Robert L.
Teachings from the worldly philosophy/ Robert Heilbroner. New York: W.W. Norton, 1996. xiv, 353 p.
95-037470   330   0393039196
Economics -- History.

HB75.H77 2002
Hunt, E. K.
History of economic thought: a critical perspective/ E.K. Hunt. 2nd, updated ed. Armonk, N.Y.: M.E. Sharpe, c2002. xxii, 543 p.
2002-024023   330/.09 21   0765606070
Economics -- History.

HB75.M953 1953
Myrdal, Gunnar,
The political element in the development of economic theory; translated from the German by Paul Streeten. London, Routledge & Paul [1953] xvii, 248 p.
54-000894   330.1932
Economics -- History. Economic policy.

HB75.N54 1990
Niehans, Jürg.
A history of economic theory: classic contributions, 1720-1980/ Jürg Niehans. Baltimore: Johns Hopkins University Press, c1990. x, 578 p.
89-045489   330/.09 20   0801838347
Economics -- History.

HB75.P453 1998
Perlman, Mark.
The pillars of economic understanding: ideas and traditions/ Mark Perlman and Charles R. McCann Jr. Ann Arbor: University of Michigan Press, c1998. xx, 639 p.
98-008953   330/.09 21   0472109073
Economics -- History.

HB75.R526 1998
Robbins, Lionel Robbins, 1898-1984.
A history of economic thought: the LSE lectures/ Lionel Robbins; edited by Steven G. Medema and Warren J. Samuels. Princeton, N.J.: Princeton University Press, c1998. xxviii, 359 p.
97-051808   330.1 21   069101244X
Economics -- History.

HB75.R6724 1990
Rostow, W. W. 1916-
Theorists of economic growth from David Hume to the present: with a perspective on the next century/ W.W. Rostow; including a mathematical appendix by Michael Kennedy and the author. New York: Oxford University Press, 1990. xx, 712 p.
89-032560   338.9/009   0195058372
Economists -- History. Economic development -- History.

HB75.S686 1989
The Spread of economic ideas/ edited by David C. Colander and A.W. Coats. Cambridge [England]; Cambridge University Press, 1989. xvi, 262 p.
88-035363   330/.09   0521362334
Economics -- History -- Congresses.

HB75.W5
Weber, Max, 1864-1920.
General economic history, by Max Weber, translated by Frank H. Knight. New York, Greenberg [c1927] xviii, 401 p.
27-014337
Economics -- History.

HB76 Economic theory — History of economics. History of economic theory — Collective biography

HB76.B5 2000
Arestis, Philip, 1941-
A biographical dictionary of dissenting economists/ edited by Philip Arestis and Malcolm Sawyer. Cheltenham, UK; E. Elgar, c2000. xiv, 722 p.
00-034824   330/.092/2 21   1858985609
Economists -- Biography -- Dictionaries.

HB76.B535 2000
A biographical dictionary of women economists/ edited by Robert W. Dimand, Mary Ann Dimand, and Evelyn L. Forget. Northampton, Mass: Edward Elgar, 2000. xxviii, 491 p.
00-028842   330/.082/0922   1852789646
Women economists -- Biography.

HB76.B83 1989
Buchholz, Todd G.
New ideas from dead economists: an introduction to modern economic thought/ by Todd G. Buchholz; with a foreword by Martin Feldstein. New York: New American Library, c1989. xi, 321 p.
89-012666   330/.092/2   0453006884
Economists -- Biography. Economics -- History.

HB76.E96 2000
Exemplary economists: introducing economics of the 20th century/ edited by Roger E. Backhouse, Roger Middleton. Cheltenham, UK; Elgar, c2000. 2 v.
00-023771   330/.092/2 21   1840644052
Economists -- Biography. Economics -- History -- 20th century.

HB76.H4 1999
Heilbroner, Robert L.
The worldly philosophers: the lives, times, and ideas of the great economic thinkers/ Robert L. Heilbroner. Rev. 7th ed. New York: Simon & Schuster, c1999. 365 p.
99-014050   330/.092/2 B 21   068486214X
Economists -- Biography. Economics -- History.

HB76.L58 1995
Lives of the laureates: thirteen Nobel economists/ edited by William Breit and Roger W. Spencer. 3rd ed. Cambridge, Mass.: MIT Press, 1995. xiv, 271 p.
95-016632   330/.092/2.aB 20   0262023911
Economists -- Biography. Nobel Prizes -- Biography.

HB76.P37 1998
Passion and craft: economists at work/ Michael Szenberg; foreword by Paul A. Samuelson. Ann Arbor: University of Michigan Press, c1998. xvii, 314 p.
98-027739   330/.092/2 21   0472096850
Economists -- Biography. Economics -- Philosophy.

HB76.P74 1999
Pressman, Steven.
Fifty major economists/ Steven Pressman. London; Routledge, 1999. xi, 207 p.
98-033133 330/.092/2.B 21 0415134811
Economists -- Biography. Economics -- History.

HB77-87 Economic theory — History of economics. History of economic theory — By period

HB77.M45 1995
Meikle, Scott.
Aristotle's economic thought/ Scott Meikle. Oxford: Clarendon Press; 1995. viii, 216 p.
95-010594 330 0198150024
Aristotle -- Contributions in economics. Economics -- History.

HB79.L36 1992
Langholm, Odd Inge, 1928-
Economics in the medieval schools: wealth, exchange, value, money, and usury according to the Paris theological tradition, 1200-1350/ by Odd Langholm. Leiden; E.J. Brill, 1992. viii, 633 p.
91-024347 330/.09/022 9004094229
Economics -- History -- To 1800. Education, Medieval.

HB83.H8 1988
Hutchison, T. W.
Before Adam Smith: the emergence of political economy, 1662-1776/ Terence Hutchison. Oxford, UK; B. Blackwell, 1988. x, 469 p.
87-029368 330/.09/032 0631158987
Economics -- History -- 18th century. Economics -- History -- 17th century.

HB83.R68 2001
Rothschild, Emma, 1948-
Economic sentiments: Adam Smith, Condorcet, and the Enlightenment/ Emma Rothschild. Cambridge, Mass.: Harvard University Press, 2001. ix, 353 p.
00-053943 330.15/3 0674004892
Smith, Adam, -- 1723-1790. Condorcet, Jean-Antoine-Nicolas de Caritat, -- marquis de, -- 1743-1794. Liberalism -- History -- 18th century. Economics -- History -- 18th century. Free enterprise -- History -- 18th century.

HB85.B35 1980
Berg, Maxine, 1950-
The machinery question and the making of political economy, 1815-1848/ Maxine Berg. Cambridge [Eng.]; Cambridge University Press, 1980. 379 p.
79-015271 338/.06/09034 0521227828
Economics -- History -- 19th century. Machinery in the workplace -- History -- 19th century. Technological innovations -- History -- 19th century.

HB87.H35 1995
Heilbroner, Robert L.
The crisis of vision in modern economic thought/ Robert Heilbroner, William Milberg. New York: Cambridge University Press, 1995. ix, 131 p.
95-016469 330/.09 0521497140
Economics -- History -- 20th century.

HB87.L45 1988
Levinson, Marc.
Beyond free markets: the revival of activist economics/ Marc Levinson. Lexington, Mass.: Lexington Books, c1988. xvii, 195 p.
87-045775 338.973 0669169714
Economics. Keynesian economics. Industrial policy -- United States. United States -- Economic policy -- 1981-1993.

HB87.R67 1997
Rosenof, Theodore.
Economics in the long run: New Deal theorists and their legacies, 1933-1993/ Theodore Rosenof. Chapel Hill: University of North Carolina Press, c1997. 223 p.
96-024647 338.973/009/04 20 0807823155
Keynes, John Maynard, -- 1883-1946. Hansen, Alvin Harvey, -- 1887- Means, Gardiner Coit, -- 1896- Economics -- History -- 20th century. New Deal, 1933-1939. United States -- Economic policy.

HB87.W3613 2001
McCarty, Marilu Hurt.
The Nobel laureates: how the world's greatest economic minds shaped modern thought/ by Marilu Hurt McCarty. New York: McGraw-Hill, 2001. xvi, 397 p.
00-024447 330 0071356142
Economics -- History -- 20th century. Economists. Nobel Prizes -- History.

HB90-99.7 Economic theory — History of economics. History of economic theory — Special schools

HB90.A77 1994
Arnold, N. Scott.
The philosophy and economics of market socialism: a critical study/ N. Scott Arnold. New York: Oxford University Press, 1994. xiv, 301 p.
93-031714 335 20 0195088271
Mixed economy. Marxian economics. Socialism.

HB90.B47 1999
Berliner, Joseph S.
The economics of the good society: the variety of economic arrangements/ Joseph S. Berliner. Malden, MA: Blackwell Publishers, 1999. ix, 448 p.
98-052530 330 21 0631208291
Comparative economics -- Case studies. Income distribution -- Case studies. Welfare economics -- Case studies.

HB90.C52 1998
Clark, Barry Stewart, 1948-
Political economy: a comparative approach/ Barry Clark. Westport, Conn.: Praeger, 1998. xiii, 359 p.
98-015657 330 0275958698
Comparative economics.

HB90.M363 1993
Market socialism: the current debate/ edited by Pranab K. Bardhan, John E. Roemer. New York: Oxford University Press, 1993. x, 324 p.
92-043241 338.9 0195080491
Mixed economy. Socialism. Capitalism.

HB90.M54 1989
Miller, David
Market, state, and community: theoretical foundations of market socialism/ David Miller. Oxford, England: Clarendon Press; c1989. ix, 359 p.
89-003365 330.12/6 0198273401
Mixed economy. Socialism. Libertarianism.

HB90.M63 1991
A Modern guide to economic thought: an introduction to comparative schools of thought in economics/ edited by Douglas Mair and Anne G. Miller. Aldershot, Hants, England; E. Elgar, c1991. xi, 281 p.
91-018139 330.1 1852783230
Comparative economics. Economics. Economics -- History.

HB90.O38 1975
Okun, Arthur M.
Equality and efficiency, the big tradeoff/ Arthur M. Okun. Washington: The Brookings Institution, [1975] xi, 124 p.
75-005162 330.12 0815764766
Comparative economics. Equality.

HB90.S379 1993
Schweickart, David.
Against capitalism/ David Schweickart. Cambridge [England]; Cambridge University Press; 1993. xiii, 387 p.
92-047480 330.12/2 0521418518
Comparative economics. Capitalism. Socialism.

HB90.S78 1994
Stiglitz, Joseph E.
Whither socialism?/ Joseph E. Stiglitz. Cambridge, Mass.: MIT Press, c1994. xii, 338 p.
93-043188 330.12/6 026219340X
Mixed economy -- Mathematical models. Capitalism -- Mathematical models. Neoclassical school of economics.

HB90.Z89 2002
Zwass, Adam.
Globalization of unequal national economies: players and controversies/ Adam Zwass. Armonk, N.Y.: M.E. Sharpe, c2002. xix, 265 p.
2001-034197 337 21 076560731X
Comparative economics. Economic history -- 20th century. Post-communism.

HB91.E42 1997
Ekelund, Robert B. 1940-
Politicized economies: monarchy, monopoly, and mercantilism/ by Robert B. Ekelund, Jr. and Robert D. Tollison. College Station, Tex.: Texas A&M University Press, c1997. xi, 300 p.
96-038971 382/.3/0940903 20 0890967458
International trade -- History. Mercantile system -- History. Economic history -- 1600-1750.

HB94.M37 1988
McNally, David.
Political economy and the rise of capitalism: a reinterpretation/ David McNally. Berkeley: University of California Press, c1988. xvi, 329 p.
88-003185 330.12/2 0520061330
Classical school of economics. Capitalism.

HB95.F66 1994
Fones-Wolf, Elizabeth A., 1954-
Selling free enterprise: the business assault on
labor and liberalism, 1945-60/ Elizabeth A. Fones-
Wolf. Urbana: University of Illinois Press, c1994.
xii, 307 p.
94-010785   330.12/2/0973   0252021185
*Free enterprise -- United States -- Public
opinion. Public opinion -- United States. Political
culture -- United States.*

HB95.L39 1991
Lazonick, William.
Business organization and the myth of the market
economy/ William Lazonick.   Cambridge
[England]; Cambridge University Press, 1991. xiv,
372 p.
91-008865   330.12/2   0521394198
*Free enterprise -- History -- 20th century.
Capitalism -- History -- 20th century. Economics --
History -- 20th century.*

HB95.S587 2000
Smith, J. W., 1930-
Economic democracy: the political struggle of the
twenty-first century/ J.W. Smith. Armonk, N.Y.:
M.E.Sharpe, c2000. xii, 380 p.
99-016254   330.12/2 21   076560468X
*Free enterprise -- History. Free trade -- History.
Capitalism -- History.*

HB97.K57 1990
Kindleberger, Charles Poor, 1910-
Historical economics: art or science?/ Charles P.
Kindleberger. Berkeley: University of California
Press, c1990. x, 371 p.
90-011217   330/.09   0520073436
*Historical school of economics. Economics --
History.*

HB97.5.B8513 1972
Bukharin, Nikolai Ivanovich, 1888-1938.
The economic theory of the leisure class. Introd. by
Donald J. Harris. New York, Monthly Review
Press [1972, c1927] xvi, 220 p.
72-081775   335.43   085345261X
*Marxian economics. Marginal utility. Austrian
school of economics.*

HB97.5.H36 1967
Hayek, Friedrich A. von 1899-
Collectivist economic planning; critical studies on
the possibilities of socialism, by N. G. Pierson [and
others] Edited, with an introd. and a concluding
essay by F. A. Hayek. New York, A.M. Kelley
[1967?] v, 293 p.
67-016638   335
Marxian economics. Economic policy. Socialism.

HB97.5.H659 1989
Howard, Michael Charles, 1945-
A history of Marxian economics/ M.C. Howard and
J.E. King. Princeton, N.J.: Princeton University
Press, c1989-c1992. 2 v.
88-039312   335.4   0691042500
Marxian economics -- History.

HB97.5.I823 1988
Ito, Makoto, 1936-
The basic theory of capitalism: the forms and
substance of the capitalist economy/ Makoto Itoh.
Totowa, N.J.: Barnes & Noble Books, 1988. xiii,
432 p.
87-000905   330.12/2   0389207292
Marxian economics. Capitalism. Value.

HB97.5.L318 1989
Lenin, Vladimir Ilich, 1870-1924.
Lenin's economic writings/ edited by Meghnad
Desai. Atlantic Highlands, NJ: Humanities Press
International, 1989. 363 p.
88-022985   335.4/12   0391036092
Marxian economics. Economics.

HB97.5.M2713 1969
Mandel, Ernest.
Marxist economic theory. Translated by Brian
Pearce. New York, M[onthly] R[eview] Press
[1969, c1968] 2 v.
68-013658   335.4/01
Marxian economics.

HB97.5.M3313 1971b
Marx, Karl, 1818-1883.
The Grundrisse. Edited and translated by David
McLellan. New York, Harper & Row [1971] 152 p.
78-138747   335.41   0060128283
Marxian economics.

HB97.5.M334194 1991
Marx and modern economic analysis/ edited by
G.A. Caravale. Aldershot, Hants, England; E.
Elgar, c1991. 2 v.
90-026477   335.4   1852784350
*Marx, Karl, -- 1818-1883. Caravale, Giovanni.
Marxian economics.*

HB97.5.M5525 2000
Milward, Bob.
Marxian political economy: theory, history, and
contemporary relevance/ Bob Milward. New York:
St. Martin's Press, 2000. xii, 219 p.
00-023490   335.4/12   0312234171
Marxian economics.

HB97.5.P335 1991
Peet, Richard.
Global capitalism: theories of societal
development/ Richard Peet. London; Routledge,
1991. xiv, 206 p.
90-045919   330.15/42   0415013143
*Marxian economics. Dependency. Economic
development.*

HB97.5.R6 1967
Robinson, Joan, 1903-
An essay on Marxian economics.   London,
Macmillan; 1966 xxiv, 104 p.
67-086994   335.41
*Marx, Karl, -- 1818-1883. -- Kapital.   Marxian
economics.*

HB97.5.Y864 1997
Yunker, James A.
Economic justice: the market socialist vision/
James A. Yunker. Lanham, Md.: Rowman &
Littlefield Publishers, c1997. xii, 392 p.
96-051869   335.4 21   0847684768
Marxian economics. Mixed economy. Socialism.

HB97.7.R334 1996
Radical political economy: explorations in
alternative economic analysis/ [edited by] Victor
D. Lippit. Armonk, N.Y.: M.E. Sharpe, c1996. xi,
391 p.
95-016934   330 20   0873326067
Radical economics.

HB98.K57
Kirzner, Israel M.
Perception, opportunity, and profit: studies in the
theory of entrepreneurship/ Israel M. Kirzner.
Chicago: University of Chicago Press, 1979. xiv,
274 p.
79-011765   338.5/2/01   0226437736
Entrepreneurship. Austrian school of economics.

HB98.S483 1990
Shand, Alexander H.
Free market morality: the political economy of the
Austrian school/ Alexander H. Shand. London;
Routledge, 1990. x, 228 p.
89-005929   330.15/7   0415040450
*Austrian school of economics -- Moral and
ethical aspects. Capitalism -- Moral and ethical
aspects.*

HB98.2.F47
Ferguson, C. E.
The neoclassical theory of production and
distribution [by] C. E. Ferguson. London,
Cambridge U.P., 1969. xviii, 383 p.
71-092248   330.15/3   521074533
*Economics -- Mathematical models. Neoclassical
school of economics.*

HB98.2.G65 1992
Gondwe, Derrick K.
Political economy, ideology, and the impact of
economics on the Third World/ Derrick K.
Gondwe. New York: Praeger, 1992. viii, 192 p.
91-037624   338.9/009172/4   027594025X
*Neoclassical school of economics. Economics --
Developing countries. Developing countries --
Economic policy.*

HB98.2.G76 1995
Groenewegen, Peter D.
A soaring eagle: Alfred Marshall, 1842-1924/ Peter
Groenewegen. Aldershot; E. Elgar, c1995. xiv,
874 p.
94-037278   330.15/7   1858981514
*Marshall, Alfred, -- 1842-1924.   Neoclassical
school of economics. Economists -- Great Britain -
- Biography.*

HB98.2.H85 1997
Human well-being and economic goals/ edited by
Frank Ackerman ... [et al.]. Washington, D.C.:
Island Press, c1997. xxxii, 427 p.
97-036687   330.15/7 21   1559635606
*Neoclassical school of economics. Economic
man. Values.*

HB98.2.M37
Marshall, Alfred, 1842-1924.
The early economic writings of Alfred Marshall,
1867-1890/ edited and introduced by J. K.
Whitaker. London: Macmillan for the Royal
Economic Society, 1975. 2 v.
75-330141   330.1
Economics.

HB98.2.W44 1989
Weeks, John, 1941-
A critique of neoclassical macroeconomics/ John
Weeks. New York: St. Martin's Press, 1989. xxi,
290 p.
89-010140   339   0312034709
*Neoclassical school of economics. Keynesian
economics. Macroeconomics.*

HB98.3.L435 2000
Leeson, Robert.
The eclipse of Keynesianism: the political economy of the Chicago counter-revolution/ Robert Leeson. Houndmills, Basingstoke, Hampshire; Palgrave, 2000. vii, 182 p.
00-031118 330.15/6 21 0312235755
Chicago school of economics. Keynesian economics.

HB99.3.H6 1968
Hobson, J. A. 1858-1940.
Work and wealth: a human valuation. New York, A. M. Kelley, 1968. xvi, 367 p.
68-030527 330.1
Welfare economics. Industries. Social problems.

HB99.5.A63 2001
Aoki, Masahiko,
Toward a comparative institutional analysis/ Masahiko Aoki. Cambridge, Mass.: MIT Press, c2001. xi, 467 p.
2001-032633 3330 21 0262011875
Institutional economics. Game theory.

HB99.5.N67 1990
North, Douglass Cecil.
Institutions, institutional change, and economic performance/ Douglass C. North. Cambridge; Cambridge University Press, 1990. viii, 152 p.
90-001673 302.3/5 0521394163
Institutional economics. Organizational change. Economic development.

HB99.5.Y66 1998
Yonay, Yuval P., 1958-
The struggle over the soul of economics: institutionalist and neoclassical economists in America between the wars/ Yuval P. Yonay. Princeton, N.J.: Princeton University Press, c1998. xiii, 290 p.
97-042954 330.1 21 0691034192
Institutional economics -- History -- 20th century. Neoclassical school of economics -- History -- 20th century. Economics -- United States -- History -- 20th century.

HB99.7.C38 1992
Carvalho, Fernando J. Cardim de, 1953-
Mr Keynes and the post Keynesians: principles of macroeconomics for a monetary production economy/ Fernando J. Cardim de Carvalho. Brookfield, Vt.: E. Elgar, c1992. xxiv, 236 p.
92-001108 330.15/6 1852786531
Keynes, John Maynard, -- 1883-1946. Keynesian economics. Macroeconomics.

HB99.7.C63
Collins, Robert M.
The business response to Keynes, 1929-1964/ Robert M. Collins. New York: Columbia University Press, 1981. xii, 293 p.
81-003898 338.973 0231044860
Keynesian economics -- History. Industrial policy -- United States -- History. United States -- Economic policy.

HB99.7.E528 1997
An encyclopedia of Keynesian economics/ edited by Thomas Cate; associate editors, Geoff Harcourt, David C. Colander. Cheltenham, UK; Edward Elgar, c1997. xxiv, 638 p.
96-023171 330.15/6/03 20 185898145X
Keynesian economics -- Encyclopedias.

HB99.7.F364 1998
Fanning, Connell.
The general theory of profit equilibrium: Keynes and the entrepreneur economy/ Connell Fanning and David O Mahony; consultant editor, Jo Campling. New York: St. Martin's Press, 1998. xii, 220 p.
97-028026 330.15/6 21 0312210272
Keynesian economics. Profit. Supply and demand.

HB99.7.J64 1978
Johnson, Elizabeth S.
The shadow of Keynes: understanding Keynes, Cambridge, and Keynesian economics/ Elizabeth S. Johnson, Harry G. Johnson. Chicago: University of Chicago Press, 1978. xiv, 253 p.
78-056338 330.15/6 0226401480
Keynes, John Maynard, -- 1883-1946. Keynesian economics.

HB99.7.K38.A85 1991
Asimakopulos, A., 1930-
Keynes's General theory and accumulation/ A. Asimakopulos. Cambridge [England]; Cambridge University Press, 1991. xviii, 207 p.
90-041557 330.15/6 0521362482
Keynes, John Maynard, -- 1883-1946. -- General theory of employment, interest, and money. Keynesian economics.

HB99.7.K38 K485 2002
Keynes, uncertainty and the global economy: beyond Keynes, volume two / edited by Sheila C. Dow and John Hillard. Cheltenham; E. Elgar, c2002. ix, 319 p.
2001-057495 330.1 21 1858987970
Keynes, John Maynard, 1883-1946. Keynesian economics. Macroeconomics. Microeconomics.

HB99.7.K38.P46 1989
Perelman, Michael.
Keynes, investment theory, and the economic slowdown: the role of replacement investment and q-ratios/ Michael Perelman. New York: St. Martin's Press, 1989. x, 298 p.
88-014010 332.6/01 0312020708
Keynes, John Maynard, -- 1883-1946. -- General theory of employment, interest, and money. Keynesian economics. Investments -- United States.

HB99.7.K3815 1988
Keynes and public policy after fifty years/ edited by Omar F. Hamouda, John N. Smithin. New York: New York University Press, c1988. 2 v.
87-020368 330.15/6 0814734448
Keynesian economics -- Congresses. Economic policy -- Congresses.

HB99.7.K77 1994
Krugman, Paul R.
Peddling prosperity: economic sense and nonsense in the age of diminished expectations/ Paul Krugman. New York: W.W. Norton, c1994. xv, 303 p.
93-029965 330.15/6 0393036022
Keynesian economics. Supply-side economics. Economics -- Political aspects.

HB99.7.P67 1989
The Political power of economic ideas: Keynesianism across nations/ edited by Peter A. Hall. Princeton, N.J.: Princeton University Press, c1989. vi, 406 p.
88-032680 330.15/6 0691077991
Keynesian economics. Economic policy.

HB99.7.T63 1987
Tobin, James, 1918-
Policies for prosperity: essays in a Keynesian mode/ James Tobin; edited by P.M. Jackson. Cambridge, Mass.: MIT Press, 1987. xiv, 508 p.
87-002967 330.15/6 026220066X
Keynesian economics. Supply-side economics -- United States. United States -- Economic policy -- 1981-1993.

HB101-126.4 Economic theory — History of economics. History of economic theory — By region or country

HB101.H39 G73 1998
Gray, John,
Hayek on liberty/ John Gray. 3rd ed. London; Routledge, 1998. xi, 187 p.
97-051498 323.44 21 0415173159
Hayek, Friedrich A. von (Friedrich August), 1899- -- Political and government. Liberty. Liberalism.

HB101.H39.S73 1993
Steele, G. R.
The economics of Friedrich Hayek/ G.R. Steele. New York, N.Y.: St. Martin's Press, 1993. x, 262 p.
93-007914 330/.092 031210071X
Hayek, Friedrich A. von -- (Friedrich August), -- 1899- Economics -- History -- 20th century. Austrian school of economics -- History.

HB101.V66.A35
Von Mises, Ludwig, 1881-1973.
Ludwig von Mises, notes and recollections/ foreword by Margit von Mises; translation and postscript by Hans F. Sennholz. South Holland, Ill.: Libertarian Press, c1978. x, 181 p.
76-029877 330/.092/4 0910884048
Von Mises, Ludwig, -- 1881-1973. Economists -- Austria -- Biography. Austrian school of economics.

HB101.V66.G7 1993
Greaves, Bettina Bien.
Mises: an annotated bibliography: a comprehensive listing of books and articles by and about Ludwig von Mises/ compiled by Bettina Bien Greaves and Robert W. McGee. -- Irvington-on-Hudson, N.Y.: Foundation for Economic Education, 1993. xvi, 391 p.
0910614792
Von Mises, Ludwig, -- 1881-1973 -- Bibliography.

HB101.V66 K57 2001
Kirzner, Israel M.
Ludwig von Mises: the man and his economics/ Israel M. Kirzner. Wilmington, Del.: ISI Books, 2001. 226 p.
00-110950 330.15/7 21 1882926684
Von Mises, Ludwig, 1881-1973. Economists -- Austria -- Biography. Austrian school of economics.

HB101.V66.S73 1992
Steele, David Ramsay.
From Marx to Mises: post-capitalist society and the challenge of economic calculation/ David Ramsay Steele. La Salle, Ill.: Open Court, c1992. xviii, 440 p.
92-035738 330.9 0875484492
Von Mises, Ludwig, -- 1881-1973. Marx, Karl, -- 1818-1883. Economics -- History. Capitalism -- History. Post-communism.

HB101.V66.V66
Von Mises, Margit.
My years with Ludwig von Mises/ Margit von Mises. New Rochelle, N.Y.: Arlington House, c1976. 191 p.
76-040265   330/.092/4   0870003682
Von Mises, Ludwig, -- 1881-1973.   Economists -- Biography.

HB103.A2.B4 1967
Beer, Max, 1864-
Early British economics from the XIIIth to the middle of the XVIIIth century, by M. Beer. New York, A.M. Kelley, 1967. 250 p.
67-017840   330/.0942
Economics -- History -- Great Britain.

HB103.A2.K24 1989
Kadish, Alon, 1950-
Historians, economists, and economic history/ Alon Kadish. London; Routledge, 1989. xii, 297 p.
88-022970   330/.0941   0415027705
Economics -- Great Britain -- History. Neoclassical school of economics. Economists -- Great Britain -- History.

HB103.A2.K65 1987
Koot, Gerard M.
English historical economics, 1870-1926: the rise of economic history and neomercantilism/ Gerard M. Koot. Cambridge [Cambridgeshire]; Cambridge University Press, 1987. viii, 277 p.
87-011592   330/.0941   0521328543
Economics -- Great Britain -- History. Economic history.

HB103.A2.M53 1998
Middleton, Roger, 1955-
Charlatans or saviours?: economists and the British economy from Marshall to Meade/ Roger Middleton. Cheltenham, UK; Edward Elgar, c1998. xx, 462 p.
98-021065   330/.094 21   1858989043
Economists -- Great Britain. Economics -- Great Britain -- History. Great Britain -- Economic policy.

HB103.A2.W56 1996
Winch, Donald.
Riches and poverty: an intellectual history of political economy in Britain, 1750-1834/ Donald Winch. Cambridge [England]; Cambridge University Press, 1996. xi, 428 p.
95-009223   330.15/3   0521551056
Economics -- Great Britain -- History -- 18th century. Economics -- Great Britain -- History -- 19th century.

HB103.A3.K485 1988
King, J. E.
Economic exiles/ J.E. King. New York: St. Martin's Press, 1988. x, 286 p.
87-026118   330/.092/2   0312016190
Economists -- Great Britain -- Biography. Economists -- Biography.

HB103.H3.E23 2001
Ebenstein, Alan O.
Friedrich Hayek: a biography/ Alan Ebenstein. New York: Palgrave, 2001. xiii, 403 p.
00-062710   330/.092   0312233442
Hayek, Friedrich A. von -- (Friedrich August), -- 1899- Economists -- Great Britain -- Biography.

HB103.H47.H36 1993
Hamouda, O. F.
John R. Hicks: the economist's economist/ O.F. Hamouda. Oxford, UK; Blackwell, 1993. xviii, 316 p.
92-015426   330/.092   1557860653
Equilibrium (Economics) Capital. Money.

HB103.J5.S33 1990
Schabas, Margaret, 1954-
A world ruled by number: William Stanley Jevons and the rise of mathematical economics/ Margaret Schabas. Princeton, N.J.: Princeton University Press, 1990. xii, 192 p.
89-070245   330.15/7   0691085439
Jevons, William Stanley, -- 1835-1882. Economics, Mathematical.

HB103.J66.O27 1993
O'Brien, D. P. 1939-
Thomas Joplin and classical macroeconomics: a reappraisal of classical monetary thought/ D.P. O'Brien. Aldershot, England; E. Elgar, c1993. xiv, 289 p.
92-027661   332.4/01   1852786760
Joplin, T. (Thomas), -- 1790?-1847. Economists -- Great Britain -- Biography. Economics -- Great Britain -- History -- 19th century. Monetary policy -- Great Britain -- History -- 19th century.

HB103.K47.B333 1996
Bateman, Bradley W., 1956-
Keynes's uncertain revolution/ Bradley W. Bateman. Ann Arbor: University of Michigan Press, c1996. xi, 183 p.
96-014662   330.15/6 20   0472107089
Keynes, John Maynard, -- 1883-1946 -- Views on uncertainty. Keynes, John Maynard, -- 1883-1946 -- Views on probabilities.

HB103.K47.J64 1991
John Maynard Keynes (1883-1946)/ edited by Mark Blaug. Aldershot, Hants, England; E. Elgar, c1991. 2 v.
91-015828   330.15/6   1852785101
Keynes, John Maynard, -- 1883-1946. Economists -- Great Britain -- Biography.

HB103.K47.M563 1992
Moggridge, D. E. 1943-
Maynard Keynes: an economist's biography/ D.E. Moggridge. London; Routledge, 1992. xxxi, 941 p.
91-025882   330.15/6   041505141X
Keynes, John Maynard, -- 1883-1946. Economists -- Great Britain -- Biography. Educators -- Great Britain -- Biography. Bloomsbury group.

HB103.K47.O36 1989
O'Donnell, R. M., 1946-
Keynes: philosophy, economics, and politics: the philosophical foundations of Keynes's thought and their influence on his economics and politics/ R.M. O'Donnell. New York: St. Martin's Press, 1989. xi, 417 p.
89-032732   330.15/6   0312035780
Keynes, John Maynard, -- 1883-1946. Keynesian economics.

HB103.K47.S57 1986
Skidelsky, Robert Jacob Alexander, 1939-
John Maynard Keynes/ Robert Skidelsky. New York: Viking, 1986, c1983. v. 1.
86-001514   330.15/6   0670408107
Keynes, John Maynard, -- 1883-1946. Economists -- Great Britain -- Biography.

HB103.K47.T87 1993
Turner, Marjorie Shepherd, 1921-
Nicholas Kaldor and the real world/ Marjorie S. Turner. Armonk, N.Y.: M.E. Sharpe, c1993. xii, 235 p.
93-021759   330/.092   1563241471
Kaldor, Nicholas, -- 1908-1986. Economists -- Great Britain -- Biography. Keynesian economics. Economic development.

HB103.M3.A67 1990
Alfred Marshall in retrospect/ edited by Rita McWilliams Tullberg. Aldershot, Hants, England; E. Elgar, c1990. vii, 228 p.
90-043353   330.15/5   1852783443
Marshall, Alfred, -- 1842-1924. Neoclassical school of economics.

HB103.R63.T87 1989
Turner, Marjorie Shepherd, 1921-
Joan Robinson and the Americans/ by Marjorie S. Turner. Armonk, N.Y.: M.E. Sharpe, c1989. xv, 315 p.
88-030858   330.1/092/4   0873325338
Robinson, Joan, -- 1903- Economists -- Great Britain -- Biography.

HB103.R8.A87 1991
Austin, Linda Marilyn.
The practical Ruskin: economics and audience in the late work/ Linda M. Austin. Baltimore: Johns Hopkins University Press, c1991. xiii, 233 p.
90-023911   330/.092   0801841623
Ruskin, John, -- 1819-1900. Ruskin, John, -- 1819-1900 -- Political and social views. Ruskin, John, -- 1819-1900 -- Aesthetics. Economics -- Great Britain -- History -- 19th century. Arts -- Economic aspects.

HB103.S6.F58 1995
Fitzgibbons, Athol.
Adam Smith's system of liberty, wealth, and virtue: the moral and political foundations of The wealth of nations/ Athol Fitzgibbons. Oxford: Clarendon Press; 1995. vi, 214 p.
94-042603   330.15/3   0198289235
Smith, Adam, -- 1723-1790. Economics -- History -- 18th century. Economics -- Moral and ethical aspects -- History. Classical school of economics.

HB103.S6 M83 1995
Muller, Jerry Z.,
Adam Smith in his time and ours: designing the decent society/ Jerry Z. Muller. Princeton, N.J.: Princeton University Press, [1995] x, 272 p.
95-013210   330.15/3 20   0691001618
Smith, Adam, 1723-1790. Economics -- Moral and ethical aspects.

HB103.S6.R67 1995
Ross, Ian Simpson.
The life of Adam Smith/ Ian Simpson Ross. Oxford: Clarendon Press; 1995. xxviii, 495 p.
95-012836   330.15/3/092   0198288212
Smith, Adam, -- 1723-1790. Economists -- Great Britain -- Biography.

HB103.S6.W38 1991
Werhane, Patricia Hogue.
Adam Smith and his legacy for modern capitalism/ Patricia H. Werhane. New York: Oxford University Press, 1991. ix, 219 p.
90-020791   330.15/3   0195068289
Smith, Adam, -- 1723-1790. Capitalism. Economics -- Great Britain -- History -- 18th century.

HB103.S6.Y677 1997
Young, Jeffrey T.
Economics as a moral science: the political economy of Adam Smith/ Jeffrey T. Young. Cheltenham, UK; Edward Elgar, c1997. x, 225 p.
97-023203   330.15/3 21   1858982677
Smith, Adam, -- 1723-1790.   Economics -- Moral and ethical aspects.

HB105.S25
Whatmore, Richard.
Republicanism and the French Revolution: an intellectual history of Jean-Baptiste Say's political economy/ Richard Whatmore. Oxford; Oxford University Press, 2000. xiii, 248 p.
00-034009   330.15/3/092   0199241155
Say, Jean Baptiste, -- 1767-1832.   Economists -- France -- Biography. Economics -- France -- History. Republicanism -- France -- History.

HB107.H38.H44 1987
Hegel on economics and freedom/ edited by William Maker. Macon, Ga.: Mercer University Press, c1987. viii, 236 p.
87-007887   330.1   0865542562
Hegel, Georg Wilhelm Friedrich, -- 1770-1831 -- Views on economics. Hegel, Georg Wilhelm Friedrich, -- 1770-1831 -- Views on liberty.

HB107.H55.Z66 1990
Zoninsein, Jonas.
Monopoly capital theory: Hilferding and twentieth-century capitalism/ Jonas Zoninsein. New York: Greenwood Press, 1990. 137 p.
90-037844   330.12/2   0313274029
Hilferding, Rudolf, -- 1877-1941.   Capitalism. Monopolies. Marxian economics.

HB108.A2.L68 1987
Lowry, S. Todd.
The archaeology of economic ideas: the classical Greek tradition/ S. Todd Lowry. Durham: Duke University Press, 1987. xviii, 366 p.
87-015507   330/.0938   082230774X
Economics -- Greece -- History. Public administration -- Greece -- History. Greece -- Economic conditions -- To 146 B.C.

HB109.P3.C57 1979
Cirillo, Renato.
The economics of Vilfredo Pareto/ R. Cirillo; preface by F. Oules. London; Cass, 1979. ix, 148 p.
79-313800   330.15/43   0714631086
Pareto, Vilfredo, -- 1848-1923.

HB116.5.M9.A54 1997
Angresano, James, 1946-
The political economy of Gunnar Myrdal: an institutional basis for the transformation problem/ James Angresano. Cheltenham, UK; Edward Elgar, c1997. xiii, 197 p.
97-012121   330.1 21   1858985307
Myrdal, Gunnar, -- 1898- Economists -- Sweden -- Biography. Economic policy. Social policy.

HB119.A2.W18 1997
Waligorski, Conrad.
Liberal economics and democracy: Keynes, Galbraith, Thurow, and Reich/ Conrad P. Waligorski. Lawrence, Kan.: University Press of Kansas, c1997. xiii, 258 p.
96-042442   330.1 20   0700608036
Economics -- United States -- History -- 20th century. Liberalism -- United States -- History -- 20th century. Democracy -- United States -- History -- 20th century.

HB119.A3.A42 1996
American economists of the late twentieth century/ edited by Warren J. Samuels. Cheltenham, UK; Edward Elgar, c1996. xxi, 409 p.
95-051767   330/.0973/09045 20   1852788763
Economists -- United States -- Biography.

HB119.A3.F75 1998
Friedman, Milton, 1912-
Two lucky people: memoirs/ Milton & Rose D. Friedman. Chicago: The University of Chicago Press, 1998. xii, 660 p.
97-048951   330/.092/273   0226264149
Friedman, Milton, -- 1912- Friedman, Rose D. Economists -- United States -- Biography.

HB119.C5.H46 1995
Henry, John F.
John Bates Clark: the making of a neoclassical economist/ John F. Henry. New York, N.Y.: St. Martin's Press, 1995. xi, 180 p.
94-045745   330.15/7/092   0312126093
Clark, John Bates, -- 1847-1938.   Economists -- United States -- Biography. Economics.

HB119.E5.A3 1977
Ely, Richard Theodore, 1854-1943.
Ground under our feet: an autobiography/ Richard T. Ely. New York: Arno Press, 1977. xi, 330 p.
76-055184   330/.092/4   0405100116
Ely, Richard Theodore, -- 1854-1943.   Economists -- United States -- Biography.

HB119.E5.R3
Rader, Benjamin G.
The academic mind and reform; the influence of Richard T. Ely in American life [by] Benjamin G. Rader. [Lexington] University of Kentucky Press [1966] 276 p.
66-026694   330.0924
Ely, Richard Theodore, -- 1854-1943.

HB119.F5.A74 1993
Allen, Robert Loring.
Irving Fisher: a biography/ Robert Loring Allen. Cambridge, Mass.: Blackwell Publishers, 1993. xv, 324 p.
92-022250   330.15/7/092   1557863059
Fisher, Irving, -- 1887-1947.   Economists -- United States -- Biography.

HB119.F84.H57 1990
Hirsch, Abraham.
Milton Friedman: economics in theory and practice/ Abraham Hirsch and Neil de Marchi. Ann Arbor: University of Michigan Press, 1990. viii, 325 p.
89-020266   330.1   0472101757
Friedman, Milton, -- 1912-   Economics -- Methodology.

HB119.G33 A25 2001
Galbraith, John Kenneth,
The essential Galbraith/ John Kenneth Galbraith; selected and edited   by Andrea D. Williams. Boston: Houghton Mifflin, 2001. x, 316 p.
2001-024986   330 21   0618119639
Galbraith, John Kenneth, 1908- Economists -- United States.

HB119.G33.A34
Galbraith, John Kenneth, 1908-
A life in our times: memoirs/ John Kenneth Galbraith. Boston: Houghton Mifflin, 1981. x, 563 p.
80-027373   330/.092/4   0395305098
Galbraith, John Kenneth, -- 1908- Economists -- United States -- Biography.   United States -- Politics and government -- 1945-1989.

HB119.G74.B43 1996
Beckner, Steven K.
Back from the brink: the Greenspan years/ Steven K. Beckner. New York: Wiley, c1996. xii, 452 p.
96-036171   332.1/1/092 B 20   0471161276
Greenspan, Alan, -- 1926- Government economists -- United States -- Biography. Monetary policy -- United States.

HB119.G74 T83 2002
Tuccille, Jerome.
Alan shrugged: the life and times of Alan Greenspan, the world's most powerful banker/ Jerome Tuccille. Hoboken, N.J.: Wiley, c2002. xvi, 302 p.
2002-005221   332.1/12/092.B 21   047139906X
Greenspan, Alan, 1926- Government economists -- United States--Biography. Monetary policy -- United States.

HB119.H44.C37 1998
Carroll, Michael C., 1958-
A future of capitalism: the economic vision of Robert Heilbroner/ Michael C. Carroll. New York, N.Y.: St. Martin's Press, 1998. ix, 117 p.
97-026473   330.12/2   0312177542
Heilbroner, Robert L.   Economists -- United States. Economics -- United States. Capitalism.

HB119.H57.M45 1995
Meldolesi, Luca, 1939-
Discovering the possible: the surprising world of Albert O. Hirschman/ by Luca Meldolesi. Notre Dame: University of Notre Dame Press, c1995. xiii, 333 p.
94-042834   330/.092   0268008779
Hirschman, Albert O.   Economists -- United States. Economics -- United States.

HB119.P35.F6
Fox, Daniel M.
The discovery of abundance: Simon N. Patten and the transformation of social theory, by Daniel M. Fox. Ithaca, N.Y., Published for the American Historical Associatio [1967] xiii, 259 p.
67-022192   330.1/61/0924
Patten, Simon Nelson, -- 1852-1922.   Wealth. Social problems.

HB119.S25.P38 1983
Paul Samuelson and modern economic theory/ edited by E. Cary Brown, Robert M. Solow. New York: McGraw-Hill, c1983. xiii, 210 p.
82-020343   330   0070596670
Samuelson, Paul Anthony, -- 1915- Addresses, essays, lectures.   Economics -- Addresses, essays, lectures.

HB119.S35.A64 1990
Allen, Robert Loring.
Opening doors: the life and work of Joseph Schumpeter/ Robert Loring Allen; foreword by Walt W. Rostow. New Brunswick, N.J.: Transaction Publishers, c1991. 2 v.
90-034813   330/.092   0887383815
Schumpeter, Joseph Alois, -- 1883-1950. Economists -- United States -- Biography.

HB119.S35.S36 1990
Schumpeter, Joseph Alois, 1883-1950.
The economics and sociology of capitalism/ Joseph A. Schumpeter; edited by Richard Swedberg. Princeton, N.J.: Princeton University Press, c1991. viii, 492 p.
90-035148   330.12/2   0691042535
Schumpeter, Joseph Alois, -- 1883-1950. Capitalism.

HB119.S35.S76 1994
Stolper, Wolfgang F.
Joseph Alois Schumpeter: the public life of a private man/ Wolfgang F. Stolper. Princeton, N.J.: Princeton University Press, c1994. xx, 400 p.
93-050667   330/.092   0691043051
Schumpeter, Joseph Alois, -- 1883-1950. Economists -- United States -- Biography. Economists -- Austria -- Biography. Economics -- History -- 20th century.

HB119.S47.A3 1991
Simon, Herbert Alexander, 1916-
Models of my life/ Herbert A. Simon. [New York]: Basic Books, c1991. xxix, 415 p.
90-055595   330/.092   0465046401
Simon, Herbert Alexander, -- 1916- Economists -- United States -- Biography.

HB119.V4.D65
Dowd, Douglas Fitzgerald, 1919-
Thorstein Veblen [by] Douglas Dowd. New York, Washington Square Press [1964] xvii, 205 p.
64-056158   330.1
Veblen, Thorstein, -- 1857-1929.

HB119.V4.E34 2001
Edgell, Stephen.
Veblen in perspective: his life and thought/ Stephen Edgell. Armonk, N.Y.: M.E. Sharpe, c2001. xiii, 207 p.
00-068767   330/.092 B 21   1563241161
Veblen, Thorstein, -- 1857-1929. Economists -- United States -- Biography. Institutional economics.

HB119.V4.J67 1999
Jorgensen, Elizabeth Watkins.
Thorstein Veblen: Victorian firebrand/ Elizabeth Watkins Jorgensen, Henry Irvin Jorgensen. Armonk, N.Y.: M.E. Sharpe, c1999. viii, 280 p.
98-020416   330/.092 B 21   076560258X
Veblen, Thorstein, -- 1857-1929. Economists -- United States -- Biography. Social reformers -- United States -- Biography. Economics -- United States -- History.

HB126.I4.D365 1993
Dasgupta, Ajit Kumar.
A history of Indian economic thought/ Ajit Dasgupta. London; Routledge, 1993. x, 206 p.
93-018818   330/.0954   0415061954
Economics -- India -- History.

HB126.J2.M67 1989
Morris-Suzuki, Tessa.
A history of Japanese economic thought/ Tessa Morris-Suzuki. London; Routledge; 1989. vii, 213 p.
89-003484   330/.0952   0415012643
Economics -- Japan -- History.

HB126.4.C49 1992
Choudhury, Masudul Alam, 1948-
The foundations of Islamic political economy/ Masudul Alam Choudhury and Uzir Abdul Malik. New York: St. Martin's Press, 1992. xxi, 336 p.
91-023347   330/.0917/671   0312068549
Economics -- Islamic countries. Economics -- Religious aspects -- Islam. Islam -- Economic aspects.

HB131 Economic theory — Methodology — General works

HB131.B56 1992
Blaug, Mark.
The methodology of economics, or, How economists explain/ Mark Blaug. 2nd ed. Cambridge; Cambridge University Press, 1992. xxviii, 286 p.
92-004375   330/.072 20   0521436788
Economics -- Methodology.

HB131.C65 1991
Colander, David C.
Why aren't economists as important as garbagemen?: essays on the state of economics/ David Colander. Armonk, N.Y.: M.E. Sharpe, c1991. x, 177 p.
90-008841   330/.092/2   0873327764
Economics -- Methodology. Economists.

HB131.D69 2002
Dow, Sheila C.
Economic methodology: an inquiry/ Sheila C. Dow. Oxford; Oxford University Press, 2002. xiii, 206 p.
2002-510288   330.01 21   0198776128
Economics -- Methodology.

HB131.E258 1996
Economics and the historian/ Thomas G. Rawski ... [et al.]. Berkeley: University of California Press, c1996. xiv, 297 p.
94-024931   330 20   0520072685
Economics -- Methodology. Historiography.

HB131.F75 1994
Friedman, Daniel, 1947-
Experimental methods: a primer for economists/ Daniel Friedman and Shyam Sunder. Cambridge [England]; Cambridge University Press, 1994. xiv, 229 p.
93-008005   330/.01/1   0521450683
Economics -- Methodology. Economics -- Simulation methods. Economics -- Research.

HB131.H354 1998
The handbook of economic methodology/ edited by John B. Davis, D. Wade Hands, Uskali Maki. Cheltenham, UK; E. Elgar, c1998. xviii, 572 p.
97-029958   330/.01 21   1852787953
Economics -- Methodology -- Handbooks, manuals, etc.

HB131.M39 1993
Mayer, Thomas, 1927-
Truth versus precision in economics/ Thomas Mayer. Aldershot, Hants, England; E. Elgar, 1993. x, 192 p.
92-025821   330   1852785462
Economics -- Methodology.

HB133 Registration of vital events. Vital records — By region or country — Other regions or countries, A-Z

HB133.L6 1999
Loasby, Brian J.
Knowledge, institutions, and evolution in economics/ Brian J. Loasby. London; Routledge, 1999. xv, 168 p.
98-033940   330/.01 21   0415205379
Information theory in economics. Economics -- Methodology. Knowledge, Theory of.

HB135-144 Economic theory — Methodology — Mathematical economics. Quantitative methods

HB135.A62 1996
Anthony, Martin.
Mathematics for economics and finance: methods and modelling/ Martin Anthony and Norman Biggs. Cambridge [England]; Cambridge University Press, 1996. 394 p.
96-001581   330   0521551137
Economics, Mathematical. Finance -- Mathematical models.

HB135.B38 1977
Baumol, William J.
Economic theory and operations analysis/ William J. Baumol. Englewood Cliffs, N.J.: Prentice-Hall, c1977. xxi, 695 p.
76-046591   330/.01/84   013227132X
Microeconomics. Economics, Mathematical. Operations research.

HB135.B87
Burrows, Paul.
Macroeconomic theory: a mathematical introduction/ [by] Paul Burrows and Theodore Hitiris. London; Wiley, 1974. xiii, 210 p.
73-002779   339/.01/82   0471125253
Economics, Mathematical. Macroeconomics -- Mathematical models.

HB135.E27 1984
Eastman, Byron D.
Interpreting mathematical economics and econometrics/ Byron D. Eastman. New York: St. Martin's Press, 1984. ix, 110 p.
84-008303   330/.028   0312424779
Economics, Mathematical. Econometrics. Economics -- Mathematical models.

HB135.H63 1989
Holcombe, Randall G.
Economic models and methodology/ Randall G. Holcombe. New York: Greenwood Press, 1989. x, 201 p.
89-007495   330/.01/5118   0313266794
Economics -- Mathematical models.

HB135.K47 1982
Kennedy, Gavin.
Mathematics for innumerate economists/ Gavin Kennedy. New York: Holmes & Meier, 1982. vii, 134 p.
81-013337   510/.24339   0841907773
Economics, Mathematical. Mathematics.

HB135.L83 2002
Luderer, Bernd.
Mathematical formulas for economists/ Bernd Luderer, Volker Nollau, Klaus Vetters. Berlin; Springer, c2002. x, 186 p.
2001-049831   515 21   3540426167
Economics, Mathematical. Mathematics -- Formulae.

HB135.N52 2000
Nicola, Pier Carlo
Mainstream mathematical economics in the 20th century/ PierCarlo Nicola. Berlin; Springer, c2000. xix, 521 p.
00-035817   330.15/43 21   354067084X
Economics, Mathematical -- History -- 20th century.

HB135.S24 1983
Samuelson, Paul Anthony, 1915-
Foundations of economic analysis/ Paul A. Samuelson. Cambridge, Mass.; Harvard University Press, 1983. xxvi, 604 p.
82-021304   330/.01/51   0674313011
Economics, Mathematical.

HB135.S825 2000
Sutton, John, 1948-
Marshall's tendencies: what can economists know?/ John Sutton. Leuven, Belgium: Leuven University Press; c2000. xvi, 122 p.
00-029196   330 21   0262194422
Marshall, Alfred, -- 1842-1924.   Economics -- Mathematical models.

HB137.F83 2000
Fuente, Angel de la.
Mathematical methods and models for economists/ Angel de la Fuente. Cambridge, UK; Cambridge University Press, 2000. xii, 835 p.
98-052086   330/.01/51 21   0521585295
Economics -- Statistical methods. Mathematical models.

HB139.B69 1984
Bowden, Roger J. 1943-
Instrumental variables/ Roger J. Bowden and Darrell A. Turkington. Cambridge [Cambridgeshire]; Cambridge University Press, 1984. viii, 227 p.
84-007802   519.5/35   0521262410
Instrumental variables (Statistics)

HB139.D358 1994
Darnell, A. C.
A dictionary of econometrics/ Adrian C. Darnell. Aldershot, Hants, England; E. Elgar, c1994. xii, 458 p.
93-039138   330/.01/5195   1852783893
Econometrics -- Dictionaries.

HB139.G74 2003
Greene, William H.,
Econometric analysis/ William H. Greene. 5th ed. Upper Saddle River, N.J.: Prentice Hall, c2003. xxx, 1026 p.
2002-029308   330/.01/5195 21   0130661899
Econometrics.

HB139.H548 2001
Hill, R. Carter.
Undergraduate econometrics/ R. Carter Hill, William E. Griffiths, George G. Judge. 2nd ed. New York: Wiley, c2001. xvi, 402 p.
00-042295   330/.01/5195 21   0471331848
Econometrics.

HB139.I58 1988
Introduction to the theory and practice of econometrics/ George G. Judge ... [et al.]. 2nd ed. New York: Wiley, c1988. xxxvii, 1024 p.
87-028569   330/.028 19   0471624144
Econometrics.

HB139.K45 2003
Kennedy, Peter,
Guide to econometrics/ Peter Kennedy. 5th ed. Malden, MA: Blackwell Publishing Ltd, 2003.
2002-156370   330/.01/5195 21   1405115025
Econometrics.

HB139.M355 1983
Maddala, G. S.
Limited-dependent and qualitative variables in econometrics/ by G.S. Maddala. Cambridge [Cambridgeshire]; Cambridge University Press, 1983. xi, 401 p.
82-009554   330/.028   052124143X
Econometrics.

HB139.P34 1999
Pagan, A. R.
Nonparametric econometrics/ Adrian Pagan, Aman Ullah. Cambridge; Cambridge University Press, 1999. xviii, 424 p.
98-037218   330/.01/5195 21   0521586119
Econometrics.   Mathematical statistics. Economics -- Statistical methods.

HB139.P675 2002
Post Keynesian econometrics, microeconomics and the theory of the firm: beyond Keynes, volume 1/ edited by Sheila C. Dow and John Hillard. Cheltenham; E. Elgar, c2002. ix, 266 p.
2001-054781   338.5 21   1858985846
Keynes, John Maynard, 1883-1946. Econometrics. Microeconomics. Corporations.

HB139.Q3 1993
Qin, Duo.
The formation of econometrics: a historical perspective/ Qin Duo. Oxford, [England]: Clarendon Press; 1993. xii, 212 p.
93-018799   330/.01/5195   0198283881
Econometrics -- History.

HB139.W663 2002
Wooldridge, Jeffrey M.,
Econometric analysis of cross section and panel data/ Jeffrey M. Wooldridge. Cambridge, Mass.: MIT Press, c2002. xxi, 752 p.
2001-044263   330/.01/5195 21   0262232197
Econometrics -- Asymptotic theory.

HB141.C659 1984
Contemporary macroeconomic modelling/ edited by Pierre Malgrange and Pierre-Alain Muet. Oxford [Oxfordshire]; Blackwell, 1984. x, 319 p.
84-016722   339/.0724   0631134719
Economics -- Mathematical models -- Addresses, essays, lectures. Macroeconomics -- Mathematical models -- Addresses, essays, lectures.

HB144.C37
Case, James H., 1940-
Economics and the competitive process/ by James H. Case. New York: New York University Press, 1979. xiii, 295 p.
78-000376   0814713734
Game theory. Competition.

HB144.G3727 2002
Game theory and economic analysis/ [edited by] Christian Schmidt. London; Routledge, 2002.
2001-056890   330/.01/5193 21   0415259878
Game theory. Economics.

HB144.R66 1997
Romp, Graham.
Game theory: introduction and applications/ Graham Romp. Oxford [England]; Oxford University Press, 1997. x, 284 p.
97-000475   330/.01/5193   0198775016
Game theory. Economics, Mathematical.

HB153 Economic theory — General works — Before Adam Smith to 1776/1789

HB153.Q55713
Quesnay, Francois, 1694-1774.
Quesnay's Tableau economique. Edited, with new material, translations and notes by Marguerite Kuczynski & Ronald L. Meek. London, Macmillan; [1972] 1 v.
78-157694   330.15/2   0333111737
Economics. Physiocrats.

HB161-163 Economic theory — General works — Classical period, 1776/1789-1843/1876

HB161.B72 1995
Bonner, John.
Economic efficiency and social justice: the development of utilitarian ideas in economics from Bentham to Edgeworth/ John Bonner. Aldershot, Hants, England; E. Elgar Pub., 1995. vii, 211 p.
95-019606   330.15   1852782951
Economics -- Great Britain -- History. Utilitarianism -- Great Britain -- History.

HB161.C25 1965
Carey, Henry Charles, 1793-1879.
Principles of political economy. New York, A. M. Kelly, Bookseller, 1965. 3 v.
65-016983   330
Economics. Social sciences.

HB161.M6 1965
Mill, John Stuart, 1806-1873.
Principles of political economy, with some of their applications to social philosophy. Edited with an introd. by Sir W. J. Ashley. New York, A. M. Kelley, bookseller, 1965. liii, 1013 p.
65-018329   330
Economics. Classical school of economics.

HB161.M645 1968
Mill, John Stuart, 1806-1873.
Essays on some unsettled questions of political economy. New York, A. M. Kelley, 1968. vi, 164 p.
68-025642   330/.08
Economics -- Addresses, essays, lectures. Classical school of economics.

HB161.R485 1971
Ricardo, David, 1772-1823.
On the principles of political economy, and taxation; edited with an introduction by R. M. Hartwell. Harmondsworth, Penguin, 1971. 427 p.
74-025420   330   0140400192
Economics. Taxation. Classical school of economics.

HB163.S613 1991
Sismondi, J.-C.-L. Simonde de 1773-1842.
New principles of political economy: of wealth in its relation to population/ J.-C.-L. Simonde de Sismondi; translated and annotated by Richard Hyse; with a foreword by Robert L. Heilbroner. New Brunswick, N.J., U.S.A.: Transaction Publishers, c1991. l, 658 p.
90-010824   330   088738336X
Economics.

HB171-177 Economic theory — General works — Recent, 1843/1876-

HB171.B135 1988
Backhouse, Roger.
Economists and the economy: the evolution of economic ideas, 1600 to the present day/ Roger Backhouse. Oxford [Oxfordshire]; B. Blackwell, 1988. 224 p.
88-006045   330   0631155589
Economics. Economic history.

HB171.B535 1987
Blinder, Alan S.
Hard heads, soft hearts: tough-minded economics for a just society/ Alan S. Blinder. Reading, Mass.: Addison-Wesley Pub. Co., c1987. xi, 236 p.
87-014078   330   0201115042
Economics. Economic policy.

HB171.C59 1967
Clark, John Bates, 1847-1938.
The philosophy of wealth; economic principles newly formulated.   New York, A. M. Kelley Publishers, 1967. xv, 236 p.
67-025955   330.15/5
Economics.

HB171.D7 1972
Dobb, Maurice Herbert, 1900-
Political economy and capitalism; some essays in economic tradition, by Maurice Dobb. Westport, Conn., Greenwood Press [1972, c1945] viii, 357 p.
76-108389   330.12/2   0837138124
Economics. Capitalism.

HB171.E2487 1998
Economics and its discontents: twentieth century dissenting economists/ edited by Richard P.F. Holt, Steven Pressman. Cheltenham, UK; Edward Elgar Pub., c1998. xii, 289 p.
97-035417   330 21   1858982723
Economics. Economists.

HB171.F618 1991
Foundations of economic thought/ edited by John Creedy. Oxford, UK; Blackwell, 1991. xiii, 406 p.
90-035175   330   0631156429
Economics.

HB171.F767 1996
Friedman, David D.
Hidden order: the economics of everyday life/ David Friedman. 1st ed. New York, NY: HarperBusiness, c1996. xi, 340 p.
96-011703   330 20   0887307507
Economics. Consumer behavior.

HB171.F768 2000
Friedman, David D.
Law's order: what economics has to do with law and why it matters/ David D. Friedman. Princeton, N.J.: Princeton University Press, c2000. 329 p.
99-058555   330.1 21   0691010161
Economics. Law.

HB171.G43
Georgescu-Roegen, Nicholas.
The entropy law and the economic process. Cambridge, Mass., Harvard University Press, 1971. xv, 457 p.
78-115186   330/.01/53673   0674257804
Economics. Entropy.

HB171.H6343
Hicks, John Richard, 1904-
Economic perspectives: further essays on money and growth/ by John Hicks. Oxford [Eng.]: Clarendon Press, 1977. xviii, 199 p.
77-005770   330   0198284071
Economics. Money. Economic development.

HB171.H646 1965
Hla Myint,
Theories of welfare economics, by Hla Myint. Published for the London School of Economics and Political Science, University of London. New York, A. M. Kelley, bookseller, 1965. xiii, 240 p.
65-016990   330.1
Welfare economics.

HB171.J57 1965
Jevons, William Stanley, 1835-1882.
The theory of political economy. With pref. and notes and an extension of the bibliography of mathematical economic writings by H. Stanley Jevons. New York, A. M. Kelley, 1965. lxiv, 343 p.
65-018334   330.182
Economics. Economics, Mathematical.

HB171.K28 1980
Kaldor, Nicholas, 1908-1986.
Essays on economic stability and growth/ Nicholas Kaldor. New York: Holmes & Meier Publishers, 1980. 312 p.
80-018145   339.5   0841904529
Macroeconomics.   Economic   stabilization. Business cycles.

HB171.K2852 1981
Kaldor, Nicholas, 1908-1986.
Essays on value and distribution/ Nicholas Kaldor. New York: Holmes & Meier Publishers, 1981, c1980. xxxi, 238 p.
81-006523   330   0841904510
Value. Equilibrium (Economics) Competition, Imperfect.

HB171.K286 1989
Kaldor, Nicholas, 1908-1986.
The essential Kaldor/ edited by F. Targetti and A.P. Thirlwall. New York: Holmes & Meier, 1989. vi, 560 p.
89-034890   330   0841912351
Economics. Keynesian economics. Economic development.

HB171.K44
Keynes, John Maynard, 1883-1946.
The collected writings of John Maynard Keynes. [London] Macmillan; [1971-]
74-013349   330.15/6/08   0333107381
Economics.

HB171.K45
Keynes, John Maynard, 1883-1946.
The general theory of employment, interest and money. New York, Harcourt, 1936. 403 p.
48-031064   330.1
Economics. Money. Interest and usury.

HB171.K62 1969
Knight, Frank Hyneman, 1885-
The ethics of competition and other essays. Freeport, N.Y., Books for Libraries Press [1969] 363 p.
70-084316   330/.08   0836910885
Economics. Competition. Value.

HB171.M354
Marshall, Alfred, 1842-1924.
Official papers, by Alfred Marshall ... Published for the Royal economic society. London, Macmillan and Co., limited, 1926. vii, 428 p.
27-015292
Currency question -- Great Britain. Tariff -- Great Britain.   Great Britain -- Economic conditions. Great Britain -- Commercial policy.

HB171.M523 1999
Mennis, Edmund A., 1919-
How the economy works: an investor's guide to tracking the economy/ Edmund A. Mennis. New York: New York Institute of Finance, c1999. xix, 268 p.
98-025274   332.67/8 21   0735200769
Economics.   Investments.   United States -- Economic conditions -- 1981-

HB171.M557
Modigliani, Franco.
The collected papers of Franco Modigliani/ edited by Andrew Abel. Cambridge, Mass.: MIT Press, c1980-c1989 v. 1-5.
78-021041   330   0262131501
Economics -- Addresses, essays, lectures.

HB171.P697 1996
Power, Thomas M.
Environmental protection and economic well-being: the economic pursuit of quality/ Thomas Michael Power. Armonk, N.Y.: M.E. Sharpe, c1996. xv, 251 p.
96-003646   330 20   1563247348
Economics.   Economic   development -- Environmental aspects. Environmental protection.

HB171.R415 1997
Redman, Deborah A.
The rise of political economy as a science: methodology   and   the   classical   economists/ Deborah A. Redman. Cambridge, Mass.: MIT Press, c1997. xviii, 471 p.
97-022275   330/.09 21   0262181797
Economics. Economics -- History. Economics -- Philosophy.

HB171.S384 1999
Schumacher, E. F. 1911-1977.
Small is beautiful: economics as if people mattered: 25 years later ... with commentaries/ E.F. Schumacher. Point Roberts, Wash.: Hartley & Marks Publishers, 1999. xvii, 286 p.
98-028470   330.1   0881791695
Economics.

HB171.S385 1969
Schumpeter, Joseph Alois, 1883-1950.
Essays on economic topics of J. A. Schumpeter. Edited by Richard V. Clemence. Port Washington, N.Y., Kennikat Press [1969] 327 p.
79-086567   330   0804605858
Economics -- Addresses, essays, lectures.

HB171.S73 2000
Sowell, Thomas, 1930-
Basic economics: a citizen's guide to the economy/ Thomas Sowell. New York, NY: Basic Books, c2000. xi, 366 p.
00-044420   330 21   046508138X
Economics.

HB171.T48 1990
Eggertsson, Thrainn.
Economic behavior and institutions/ Thrainn Eggertsson. Cambridge: Cambridge University Press, 1990. 1 v.
90-001798   330.1   052134445X
Economics.

HB171.V4
Veblen, Thorstein, 1857-1929.
The portable Veblen; edited, and with an introd., by Max Lerner. New York, Viking Press, 1948. vii, 632 p.
48-006993   330.1
Economics.

HB171.W22
Wanniski, Jude, 1936-
The way the world works: how economies fail--and succeed/ Jude Wanniski. New York: Basic Books, c1978. xiii, 319 p.
77-020412   330   0465090958
Economics.

HB171.W578 1998
Why economists disagree: an introduction to the alternative schools of thought/ edited by David L. Prychitko. Albany: State University of New York Press, c1998. xi, 415 p.
97-001725   330 21   0791435709
Economics. Economics -- History. Economics -- Philosophy.

HB171.5.B692 1966
Boulding, Kenneth Ewart, 1910-
Economic analysis [by] Kenneth E. Boulding. New York, Harper & Row [1966] 2 v.
66-010054   330.1
Economics.

HB171.5.H3253 1997
Harding, Rebecca.
One semester economics: an introduction for business and management students/ Rebecca Harding. Malden, Mass.: Blackwell Publishers, 1997.
97-014137   330   0631200258
Economics.

HB171.5.H39 1972
Heilbroner, Robert L.
The economic problem [by] Robert L. Heilbroner. Englewood Cliffs, N.J., Prentice-Hall [1972] xx, 747 p.
70-037146   330   0132269104
Economics.

HB171.5.P34 2000
Payson, Steven, 1957-
Economics, science, and technology/ Steven Payson. Cheltenham, UK; Edward Elgar, c2000. xiii, 262 p.
99-086197   330 21   1858986729
Economics. Science and industry. Technological innovations.

HB171.5.P974 2001
Putterman, Louis G.
Dollars and change: economics in context/ Louis Putterman. New Haven, Conn.: Yale Univeristy Press, c2001. xiii, 284 p.
00-044919   330 21   0300087098
Economics. Economic history. Social history.

HB172.L48 1995
Levy, John M.
Essential microeconomics for public policy analysis/ John M. Levy. Westport, Conn.: Praeger, 1995. xi, 234 p.
95-007990   338.5   0275943623
Microeconomics. Neoclassical school of economics. Economic policy.

HB172.5.B43 1982
Begg, David K. H.
The rational expectations revolution in macroeconomics: theories and evidence/ David K.H. Begg. Baltimore, Md.: Johns Hopkins University Press, 1982. xii, 291 p.
82-047785   339/.0724   0801828813
Rational expectations (Economic theory) Macroeconomics.

HB172.5.B63 1991
Bodkin, Ronald G., 1936-
A history of macroeconometric model-building/ Ronald G. Bodkin, Lawrence R. Klein, Kanta Marwah. Aldershot, Hants, England; E. Elgar, c1991. xvii, 573 p.
90-020761   339.3/011   1852783699
Macroeconomics -- Econometric models -- History.

HB172.5.C455 1983
Chick, Victoria.
Macroeconomics after Keynes: a reconsideration of the General theory/ Victoria Chick. Cambridge, Mass.: MIT Press, 1983. x, 374 p.
83-000844   339   0262030950
Keynes, John Maynard, -- 1883-1946. -- General theory of employment, interest and money. Macroeconomics.

HB172.5.D69 1996
Dow, Sheila C.
The methodology of macroeconomic thought: a conceptual analysis of schools of thought in economics/ Sheila C. Dow. Brookfield, VT: E. Elgar, c1996. xiv, 255 p.
96-000922   339 20   1852789808
Macreconomics.

HB172.5.E55 2003
An encyclopedia of macroeconomics/ edited by Brian Snowdon and Howard R. Vane. Cheltenham, UK; Edward Elgar Pub., 2003.
2002-026392   339/.03 21   1840643870
Macroeconomics -- Encyclopedias. Economics -- Encyclopedias.

HB172.5.H66 1988
Hoover, Kevin D., 1955-
The new classical macroeconomics: a sceptical inquiry/ Kevin D. Hoover. Oxford, UK; B. Blackwell, 1988. xiv, 310 p.
88-006056   339   0631146059
Macroeconomics. Neoclassical school of economics.

HB172.5.K457 2000
Kennedy, Peter,
Macroeconomic essentials: understanding economics in the news/ Peter E. Kennedy. 2nd ed. Cambridge, Mass.: MIT Press, c2000. xiii, 418 p.
99-052796   339 21   0262112515
Macroeconomics. Economic policy.

HB172.5.M683 1984
Moss, Scott J.
Markets and macroeconomics: macroeconomic implications of rational individual behaviour/ Scott Moss. Oxford, OX; B. Blackwell, 1984. xi, 344 p.
84-147330   339   0855207566
Macroeconomics.

HB172.5.O38
Okun, Arthur M.
Prices and quantities: a macroeconomic analysis/ Arthur M. Okun. Washington, D.C.: Brookings Institution, c1981. xiii, 367 p.
80-070076   339   0815764804
Macroeconomics. Inflation (Finance)

HB172.5.S365 1992
Schultze, Charles L.
Memos to the president: a guide through macroeconomics for the busy policymaker/ Charles L. Schultze. Washington, D.C.: Brookings Institution, c1992. xiv, 334 p.
92-013098   339   0815777787
Macroeconomics. United States -- Economic policy.

HB172.5.S523 1983
Sheffrin, Steven M.
Rational expectations/ Steven M. Sheffrin. Cambridge [Cambridgeshire]; Cambridge University Press, 1983. x, 203 p.
82-019747   339   0521243106
Rational expectations (Economic theory) Macroeconomics.

HB172.5.S64 1990
Smithin, John N.
Macroeconomics after Thatcher and Reagan: the conservative policy revolution in retrospect/ John N. Smithin. Aldershot, Hants, England; E. Elgar, c1990. ix, 185 p.
90-040016   339.5/0941   1852781092
Macroeconomics. Supply-side economics -- United States. Supply-side economics -- Great Britain. United States -- Economic policy -- 1981-1993. Great Britain -- Economic policy -- 1979-1997.

HB175.S462
Schumpeter, Joseph Alois, 1883-1950.
The theory of economic development; an inquiry into profits, capital, credit, interest, and the business cycle, by Joseph A. Schumpeter ... translated from the German by Redvers Opie ... Cambridge, Mass., Harvard University Press, 1934. xii, 255 p.
34-038868   330.1
Economics. Economic conditions. Economic history.

HB175.V65 1966
Von Mises, Ludwig, 1881-1973.
Human action; a treatise on economics. Chicago, H. Regnery Co. [1966, c1963] xvii, 907 p.
67-003943   330
Economics. Commerce.

HB177.P2913
Pareto, Vilfredo, 1848-1923.
Manual of political economy. Translated by Ann S. Schwier. Edited by Ann S. Schwier and Alfred N. Page. New York, A. M. Kelley, 1971. xii, 504 p.
71-179960   330   0678008817
Economics.

HB195 Economic theory — Economics of war

HB195.M225 1988
Mann, Michael, 1942-
States, war, and capitalism: studies in political sociology/ Michael Mann. Oxford [England]; B. Blackwell, 1988. xiii, 240 p.
87-030914   303.6/6   0631159738
War -- Economic aspects. Militarism -- Economic aspects. Capitalism.

HB195.R6 1968
Robbins, Lionel Robbins, 1898-1984.
The economic causes of war, by Lionel Robbins. New York, H. Fertig, 1968. 124 p.
67-024595
War -- Economic aspects.

HB199 Economic theory — General special

HB199.B33 1970
Baumol, William J.
Economic dynamics; an introduction [by] William J. Baumol. With a contribution by Ralph Turvey. [New York] Macmillan [1970] xix, 472 p.
76-084434   330/.01
Economics. Statics and dynamics (Social sciences)

HB199.B82
Buchanan, James M.
Cost and choice; an inquiry in economic theory, by James M. Buchanan. Chicago, Markham Pub. Co. [1969] xv, 104 p.
70-085975   338/.013
Cost. Economics -- History. Welfare economics.

HB199.B84
Burenstam Linder, Staffan, 1931-
The harried leisure class. New York, Columbia University Press, 1970. viii, 182 p.
73-092909   301.5/7   0231033028
Time allocation. Leisure.

HB199.C45
Chase, Stuart, 1888-
The economy of abundance, by Stuart Chase. New York, The Macmillan Company, 1934. vii, 327 p.
34-027051   330.1
Economic conditions -- 1918-1945. Social history. Social problems. United States -- Economic conditions -- 1918-1945.

HB199.C635 1998
The coming age of scarcity: preventing mass death and genocide in the twenty-first century/ edited by Michael N. Dobkowski and Isidor Wallimann; with a foreword by John K. Roth. Syracuse, N.Y.: Syracuse University Press, 1998. xix, 350 p.
97-018715   333.7   0815627440
Scarcity. Natural resources. Economic development.

HB199.H647 1993
Hout, Wil, 1961-
Capitalism and the Third World: development, dependence and the world system/ Wil Hout. Aldershot, Hants, England; E. Elgar, 1993. ix, 227 p.
93-016075   338.9/009172/4   1852787856
Dependency. International economic relations. Capitalism. Developing countries.

HB199.K75 1996
Krugman, Paul R.
The self-organizing economy/ Paul Krugman. Cambridge, Mass., USA: Blackwell Publishers, 1996. vi, 122 p.
95-031593   338.9   1557866996
Economics. Self-organizing systems.

HB199.L5
Lippmann, Walter, 1889-1974.
The method of freedom, by Walter Lippmann. New York, Macmillan, 1934. xiv, 117 p.
34-015767   330.1
Collectivism. Industry and state. Economic history -- 1918-1945. United States -- Economic history -- 1918-1945.

HB199.R66 1991
Rostow, W. W.
The stages of economic growth: a non-communist manifesto/ W.W. Rostow. 3rd ed. Cambridge [England]; Cambridge University Press, 1990. xlvii, 272 p.
90-038354   338.9 20   0521409284
Economic development. Capitalism -- United States. Marxian economics.

HB199.T35
Tawney, R. H. 1880-1962.
The acquisitive society, by R. H. Tawney ... New York, Harcourt, Brace and Howe, 1920. 188 p.
20-021421
Industries. Social problems. Economics.

HB199.T47 1992
Thaler, Richard H., 1945-
The winner's curse: paradoxes and anomalies of economic life/ Richard H. Thaler. New York: Free Press; c1992. ix, 230 p.
91-026489   330   0029324653
Economics -- Miscellanea. Paradoxes.

HB201 Economic theory — Value. Utility — General works

HB201.D48
Dewey, Donald
The theory of imperfect competition; a radical reconstruction. New York, Columbia University Press, 1969. xii, 205 p.
73-079190   338/.0185
Value. Competition, Imperfect. Prices.

HB201.M2985 1999
Mandler, Michael.
Dilemmas in economic theory: persisting foundational problems of microeconomics/ Michael Mandler. New York: Oxford University Press, 1999. ix, 211 p.
98-005437   338.5 21   0195100875
Value. Microeconomics.

HB201.R6 1969
Robinson, Joan,
The economics of imperfect competition. 2nd ed. London, Macmillan, 1969. xx, 352 p.
77-415316   330.1/62   0333083628
Value. Monopolies. Competition, Imperfect.

HB221 Economic theory — Price — General works

HB221.A76 1998
Asking about prices: a new approach to understanding price stickiness/ Alan S. Blinder ... [et al.]. New York: Russell Sage Foundation, c1998. xiv, 380 p.
97-026536   338.5/2 21   0871541211
Prices -- Mathematical models. Business cycles -- Mathematical models.

HB221.S82 1987
Stigler, George Joseph,
The theory of price/ George J. Stigler. 4th ed. New York: Macmillan; c1987. viii, 371 p.
86-008408   338.5/2 19   0024174009
Prices. Economics.

HB225 Economic theory — Price — Price indexes. Consumer price indexes

HB225.P62 1989
Pollak, Robert A., 1938-
The theory of the cost-of-living index/ Robert A. Pollak. New York: Oxford University Press, 1989. viii, 207 p.
88-023552   338.5/28   0195058704
Consumer price indexes.

HB235 Economic theory — Price — By region or country, A-Z

HB235.G7.B4 1965
Beveridge, William Henry Beveridge, 1879-1963.
Prices and wages in England from the twelfth to the nineteenth century [by] Lord Beveridge, with the collaboration of L. Liepmann and others. New York, A. M. Kelley, [1965-]
66-006227
Prices -- Great Britain -- History. Wages -- Great Britain -- History.

HB235.U6.G46 1998
Getting prices right: the debate over the consumer price index/ Dean Baker, editor. Armonk, N.Y.: M.E. Sharpe, c1998. ix, 190 p.
97-017606   338.5/28/0973 21   0765602210
Consumer price indexes -- United States. Prices -- United States.

HB235.U6.S7
Stigler, George Joseph, 1911-
The behavior of industrial prices [by] George J. Stigler & James K. Kindahl. New York, National Bureau of Economic Research; distribute 1970. xiv, 202 p.
79-121003   338.52/0973   087014216X
Prices -- United States. Price indexes.

HB235.U6 V35 1999
The value of a dollar: prices and incomes in the United States, 1860-1999/ edited by Scott Derks. 2nd ed. Lakeville, CT: Grey House Pub., 1999. xiii, 493 p.
99-214827   338.5/2/0973 21   1891482491
Prices -- United States -- History. Wages -- United States -- History. Purchasing power -- United States -- History.

HB238 Economic theory — Competition. Monopolistic competition

HB238.H46 1990
Henley, Andrew, 1961-
Wages and profits in the capitalist economy: the impact of monopolistic power on macroeconomic performance in the USA and UK/ Andrew Henley. Aldershot, Hants, England; E. Elgar, c1990. ix, 205 p.
90-038070   339.5/0941   1852780908
Competition, Imperfect -- United States. Competition, Imperfect -- Great Britain. Monopolies -- United States.

HB241 Economic theory — Production. Theory of the firm. Supply-side economics

HB241.H83 2001
Hudson, Raymond.
Producing places/ Ray Hudson. New York: Guilford Press, c2001. xiii, 385 p.
00-066341   338.5 21   1572306343
Production (Economic theory) Marxian economics. Capitalism.

HB241.S63 1990
Skousen, Mark.
The structure of production/ Mark Skousen. New York: New York University Press, c1990. xvi, 415 p.
89-013181   338.5   081477895X
Production (Economic theory) Macroeconomics.

HB241.S65 2000
Smith, Tony, 1951-
Technology and capital in the age of lean production: a Marxian critique of the "New economy"/ Tony Smith. Albany: State University of New York Press, c2000. xii, 199 p.
00-028520   335.4/12 21   0791445992
Production (Economic theory) Marxian economics. Capitalism.

HB251 Economic theory — Wealth

HB251.S94 1988
Sweeney, Richard J. 1944-
Wealth effects and monetary theory/ Richard J. Sweeney. New York, NY, USA: B. Blackwell, 1988. xi, 329 p.
87-036077   339.3   0631158464
Wealth. Monetary policy. Macroeconomics.

HB301 Economic theory — Labor economics. Wages

HB301.M4
Marx, Karl, 1818-1883.
Wage-labour and capital. Value, price, and profit, by Karl Marx. New York, International Publishers [c1933-35] 2 v. in 1.
37-013364   331.214
Capital. Value. Wages.

HB301.M57
Microeconomic foundations of employment and inflation theory [by] Edmund S. Phelps [and others. New York, Norton [1970] viii, 434 p.
75-080022   330.1/63
Employment (Economic theory) -- Addresses, essays, lectures. Inflation (Finance) -- Addresses, essays, lectures.

HB301.T22 1968
Taussig, F. W. 1859-1940.
Wages and capital; an examination of the wages fund doctrine. New York, A.M. Kelley, 1968 xviii, 329 p.
67-028293
Wages. Capital.

HB401 Economic theory — Rent

HB401.M19 1969
Malthus, T. R. 1766-1834.
An inquiry into the nature and progress of rent, and the principles by which it is regulated. New York, Greenwood Press [1969] 61 p.
69-013984   333.5   0837123623
Rent.

HB401.T68
Toward a theory of the rent-seeking society/ edited by James M. Buchanan, Robert D. Tollison, and Gordon Tullock. College Station: Texas A & M University, c1980. xi, 367 p.
79-005276   333/.012   0890960909
Rent (Economic theory) Transfer payments. Industrial policy.

HB501-501.5 Economic theory — Capital. Capitalism

HB501.A553 2001
Allman, Paula.
Critical education against global capitalism: Karl Marx and revolutionary critical education/ Paula Allman; foreword by Peter McLaren. Westport, CT: Bergin & Garvey, 2001. xxvi, 275 p.
00-064211   330.12/2   0897897439
Capitalism. Marxian economics.

HB501.A558 1989
Alternatives to capitalism/ edited by Jon Elster and Karl Ove Moene. Cambridge; Cambridge University Press; 1989. viii, 179 p.
88-030182   338.9   0521371783
Capitalism. Socialism. Central planning.

HB501.B49 1990
Beyond the marketplace: rethinking economy and society/ edited by Roger Friedland and A.F. Robertson. New York: Aldine de Gruyter, c1990. vi, 365 p.
89-077722   306.3   0202303705
Capitalism -- Social aspects. Political science -- Economic aspects. Family -- Economic aspects.

HB501.B8453 2000
Bruyn, Severyn Ten Haut, 1927-
A civil economy: transforming the market in the twenty-first century/ Severyn T. Bruyn. Ann Arbor: University of Michigan Press, c2000. xviii, 308 p.
99-046137   338.9 21   0472097067
Capitalism -- Social aspects. Economics -- Moral and ethical aspects. Democracy -- Economic aspects.

HB501.C24226 1994
Capitalism and development/ edited by Leslie Sklair. London; Routledge, 1994. xiii, 372 p.
93-049038   330.12/2   0415075467
Capitalism -- History. Capitalism -- Developing countries. Economic development.

HB501.C63 2000
Coates, David.
Models of capitalism: growth and stagnation in the modern era/ David Coates. Malden, Mass.: Polity Press, 2000. x, 304 p.
99-032965   330.12/2   0745620582
Capitalism.

HB501.D3
Dahlberg, Arthur.
Jobs, machines, and capitalism, by Arthur Dahlberg, Ph.D., foreword by Edward Alsworth Ross. New York, The Macmillan company, 1932. xviii, 298 p.
32-008549
Capitalism. Economics. Machinery in industry. United States -- Economic conditions -- 1918-1945.

HB501.D68 2000
Dowd, Douglas Fitzgerald, 1919-
Capitalism and its economics: a critical history/ Douglas Dowd. London; Pluto Press, 2000. xv, 319 p.
00-020283   330.12/2   0745316433
Capitalism -- History. Economic history.

HB501.G443 1996
Gianaris, Nicholas V.
Modern capitalism: privatization, employee ownership, and industrial democracy/ Nicholas V. Gianaris. Westport, Conn.: Praeger, 1996. xiv, 206 p.
95-030658   330.12/2   027595241X
Capitalism. Privatization. Employee ownership.

HB501.G46
Gilder, George F., 1939-
Wealth and poverty/ George Gilder. New York: Basic Books, c1981. xii, 306 p.
80-050556   330.12/2   0465091059
Capitalism. Wealth. United States -- Economic conditions -- 1945- United States -- Economic policy.

HB501.H3597 1982
Harvey, David, 1935-
The limits to capital/ David Harvey. Chicago: University of Chicago Press, 1982. xviii, 478 p.
82-040322   335.4   0226319520
Capitalism. Marxian economics.

HB501.H395 1993
Heilbroner, Robert L.
21st century capitalism/ Robert Heilbroner. New York: Norton, 1993. 175 p.
93-007662   330.12/2/0973   0393035166
Capitalism -- United States. Twenty-first century.

HB501.H397 1976
Heilbroner, Robert L.
Business civilization in decline/ Robert L. Heilbroner. New York: Norton, c1976. 127 p.
75-033367   330.9/04   039305571X
Capitalism. Industries -- Social aspects. Civilization, Modern -- 1950-

HB501.H398 1985
Heilbroner, Robert L.
The nature and logic of capitalism/ Robert L. Heilbroner. New York: Norton, c1985. 225 p.
85-005656   330.12/2   0393022277
Capitalism.

HB501.I665 2001
Isbister, John, 1942-
Capitalism and justice: envisioning social and economic fairness/ John Isbister. Bloomfield, Conn.: Kumarian Press, 2001. xiii, 255 p.
00-046222   174   156549122X
Capitalism -- Moral and ethical aspects. Social justice. Distributive justice.

HB501.L332 1970
Lenin, Vladimir Ilich, 1870-1924.
Imperialism, the highest stage of capitalism, a popular outline [by] V. I. Lenin. Moscow, Progress Publishers [1970] 128 p.
72-178843   330.12/2
Capitalism. Imperialism.

HB501.L372 1970
Lenin, Vladimir Ilich, 1870-1924.
New data for V. I. Lenin's "Imperialism, the highest stage of capitalism." Edited by E. Varga [and] L. Mendelsohn. New York, AMS Press [1970] vii, 322 p.
71-121288   330.12/2   0404039650
Capitalism. Imperialism. Economic history -- 20th century.

HB501.L512 2001
Lindblom, Charles Edward, 1917-
The market system: what it is, how it works, and what to make of it/ Charles E. Lindblom. New Haven: Yale University Press, c2001. 296 p.
00-043865   330.12/2 21   0300087527
Capitalism.

HB501.L93 1969
Lutz, Friedrich A. 1901-
The theory of investment of the firm, by Friedrich and Vera Lutz. New York, Greenwood Press [1969, c1951] x, 253 p.
69-013978   330.1
Capital. Cost. Corporation -- Finance.

HB501.M3393
Marx, Karl, 1818-1883.
Pre-capitalist economic formations. Translated by Jack Cohen. Edited and with an introd. by E. J. Hobsbawm. New York, International Publishers [1965, c1964] 153 p.
65-016393   335.411
Capital. Economics.

HB501.M367T6 1942
Marx, Karl, 1818-1883.
Karl Marx and Frederick Engels: selected correspondence, 1846-1895. New York: International publishers, [c1942] 551 p.
43-011421

HB501.M37.B73 1984
Brewer, Anthony, 1942-
A guide to Marx's Capital/ Anthony Brewer. Cambridge [Cambridgeshire]; Cambridge University Press, 1984. xiv, 211 p.
83-014329   335.4/1   0521257301
Marx, Karl, -- 1818-1883. -- Kapital.

HB501.M37.L5
Lindsay, A. D. 1879-1952.
Karl Marx's Capital; an introductory essay, by D. A. Lindsay. London, Oxford University Press, 1925. 128 p.
26-026615
Marx, Karl, -- 1818-1883. -- Das Kapital. Value.

HB501.M5.E48
Engels, Freidrich, 1820-1895.
Engels on Capital; synopsis, reviews, letters and supplmentary material. New York, International Publishers [c1937] ix, 147 p.
38-001498   331
Marx, Karl, -- 1818-1883. -- Das kapital. Economics. Capital.

HB501.M5.H6
Hook, Sidney, 1902-
Towards the understanding of Karl Marx, a revolutionary interpretation. New York, The John Day Company [c1933] xiv, 347 p.
33-009547
Marx, Karl, -- 1818-1883.

HB501.M5.L3 1933
Laski, Harold Joseph, 1893-1950.
Karl Marx: an essay/ by Harold J. Laski; with the Communist manifesto by Karl Marx and Friedrich Engels. With introduction by Norman Thomas. [New York]: League for Industrial Democracy, [1933] 94 p.
33-017902
Marx, Karl, -- 1818-1883. Socialism.

HB501.M5.S9
Sweezy, Paul Marlor, 1910-
The theory of capitalist development; principles of Marxian political economy [by] Paul M. Sweezy ... New York, Oxford University Press, 1942. xiv, 398 p.
42-025876   330.15
Marx, Karl, -- 1818-1883. Economics. Capitalism. Socialism.

HB501.M632 1994
Michelman, Irving S.
The moral limitations of capitalism/ Irving S. Michelman. Aldershot; Avebury, c1994. xiii, 168 p.
94-022129   174/.4   1856288773
Capitalism -- Moral and ethical aspects. Distributive justice. Capitalism -- United States -- Case studies.

HB501.M655 1989
Miliband, Ralph.
Divided societies: class struggle in contemporary capitalism/ Ralph Miliband. Oxford: Clarendon Press; 1989. viii, 277 p.
89-015975   305.5   0198275358
Capitalism. Social conflict. Pressure groups.

HB501.O824 2002
Otteson, James R.
Adam Smith's marketplace of life/ James R. Otteson. Cambridge; Cambridge University Press, 2002. xiii, 338 p.
2002-023867   174 21   0521016568
Smith, Adam, 1723-1790. Capitalism -- Moral and ethical aspects. Ethics.

HB501.P125 1991
Pack, Spencer J.
Capitalism as a moral system: Adam Smith's critique of the free market economy/ Spencer J. Pack. Aldershot, Hants, England; E. Elgar, c1991. viii, 199 p.
90-028093   330.12/2 20   1852784423
Smith, Adam, -- 1723-1790. Capitalism -- Moral and ethical aspects.

HB501.P6357 1987
Racism, sexism, and the world-system/ edited by Joan Smith ... [et al.]. New York: Greenwood Press, 1988. xii, 221 p.
88-010248   331.13/3/09   0313263310
Capitalism -- History -- Congresses. Women -- Employment -- History -- Congresses. Minorities -- Employment -- History -- Congresses.

HB501.P638 1990
Pollack, Norman.
The humane economy: populism, capitalism, and democracy/ Norman Pollack. New Brunswick [N.J.]: Rutgers University Press, c1990. xiv, 215 p.
90-031078   330.12/2   0813515998
Capitalism -- Moral and ethical aspects -- United States. Populism -- United States -- History. Democracy -- History.

HB501.R7456 1990
Ross, Robert J. S., 1943-
Global capitalism: the new leviathan/ by Robert J.S. Ross and Kent C. Trachte. Albany: State University of New York Press, c1990. xviii, 300 p.
89-021858   330.12/2   0791403394
Capitalism. Business cycles. Monopolies. Massachusetts -- Economic conditions. Detroit (Mich.) -- Economic conditions. New York (N.Y.) -- Economic conditions.

HB501.S545 1990
Seldon, Arthur.
Capitalism/ Arthur Seldon. Oxford, UK; Basil Blackwell, 1990. xii, 419 p.
89-018200   330.12/2   0631125582
Capitalism. Capitalism -- Social aspects. Socialism.

HB501.S5896 1996
Silk, Leonard Solomon, 1918-
Making capitalism work/ Leonard Silk and Mark Silk; with Robert Heilbroner, Jonas Pontusson, and Bernard Wasow. New York: New York University Press, c1996. xx, 228 p.
96-025257   330.12/2 20   0814780644
Capitalism. Post-communism. Economic policy.

HB501.S778 2000
Soto, Hernando de, 1941-
The mystery of capital: why captitalism triumphs in the West and fails everywhere else/ Hernando de Soto. New York: Basic Books, c2000. 276 p.
00-034301   330.12/2 21   0465016146
Capitalism.

HB501.S9154 1998
Still, Judith, 1958-
Feminine economies: thinking against the marketplace in the enlightenment and the late twentieth century/ Judith Still. New York: Manchester University Press, 1998.
97-012984   330/.082   071904555X
Capitalism -- History -- 18th century. Capitalism -- History -- 20th century. Women -- Economic aspects.

HB501.S98 1976
Sweezy, Paul Marlor, 1910-
The transition from feudalism to capitalism/ Paul Sweezy ... [et al.]; introd. by Rodney Hilton. London: NLB; 1976. 195 p.
76-361182   330.12/2   0902308211
Capitalism -- History -- Addresses, essays, lectures.

HB501.V355 2001
Varieties of capitalism: the institutional foundations of comparative advantage/ edited by Peter A. Hall and David Soskice. Oxford [England]; Oxford University Press, 2001. xvi, 540 p.
2001-033838   330.12/2 21   0199247749
Capitalism. Institutional economics. Comparative economics.

HB501.W495 1999
Whitley, Richard.
Divergent capitalisms: the social structuring and change of business systems/ Richard Whitley. Oxford; Oxford University Press, 1999. vi, 301 p.
98-043685   330.12/2 21   0198293968
Capitalism -- Case studies. Business enterprises -- Case studies. Economic history -- 20th century.

HB501.W615 1999
Wood, Ellen Meiksins.
The origin of capitalism/ Ellen Meiksins Wood. New York: Monthly Review Press, 1999. vii, 138 p.
98-048940   330.12/2/09   1583670009
Capitalism -- History.

HB501.W89 1988
Wolf, Charles, 1924-
Markets or governments: choosing between imperfect alternatives/ Charles Wolf, Jr. Cambridge, Mass.: MIT Press, c1988. xv, 220 p.
87-118516   338.9   0262231344
Capitalism. Economic policy.

HB501.5.S3
Schultz, Theodore William, 1902-
Investment in human capital; the role of education and of research [by] Theodore W. Schultz. New York, Free Press [1970, c1971] xii, 272 p.
77-122273   331
Human capital. Education -- Economic aspects.

HB523 Economic theory — Income. Factor shares — Income distribution. Distributive justice

HB523.E45 1992
Elster, Jon, 1940-
Local justice/ by Jon Elster. New York: Russell Sage Foundation, 1992. ix, 283 p.
91-039717   330   0871542315
Distributive justice. Resource allocation.

HB523.L39 1988
Lazear, Edward P.
Allocation of income within the household/ Edward P. Lazear and Robert T. Michael. Chicago: University of Chicago Press, 1988. vii, 220 p.
87-035837   339.2/2   0226469662
Income distribution. Child support. Households -- Economic aspects.

HB523.M37 1990
McClelland, Peter D.
The American search for economic justice/ Peter D. McClelland. Cambridge, Mass., USA: B. Blackwell, 1990. xiv, 502 p.
89-037707   174
Distributive justice. Income distribution -- United States. Capitalism -- Moral and ethical aspects -- United States.

HB523.M468 2000
Meritocracy and economic inequality/ Kenneth Arrow, Samuel Bowles, and Steven Durlauf, editors. Princeton, N.J.: Princeton University Press, 2000. xv, 348 p.
99-039632   305.5/13   0691004676
Income distribution. Equality. Elite (Social sciences)

HB523.R63 1996
Roemer, John E.
Theories of distributive justice/ John E. Roemer. Cambridge, Mass: Harvard University Press, 1996. ix, 342 p.
95-023768   339.2   0674879198
Income distribution -- Mathematical models. Distributive justice -- Mathematical models. Welfare economics -- Mathematical models.

HB523.W46 1988
Wenz, Peter S.
Environmental justice/ Peter S. Wenz. Albany: State University of New York Press, c1988. xiv, 368 p.
87-013206   363.7/0525   0887066445
Distributive justice. Environmental justice. Environmental law.

HB539 Economic theory — Income. Factor shares — Interest

HB539.L813
Lutz, Friedrich A. 1901-
The theory of interest. [By] Friedrich A. Lutz. [Translated from the German by Claus Wittich] Dordrecht, D. Reidel [1968] ix, 339 p.
68-081397   332.8
Interest.

HB601 Economic theory — Income. Factor shares — Profit

HB601.K53
Kilby, Peter,
Entrepreneurship and economic development. New York, Free Press [1971] viii, 384 p.
79-122279   338/.04
Entrepreneurship. Economic development.

HB601.P8854 1995
Profits and morality/ edited by Robin Cowan and Mario J. Rizzo. Chicago: University of Chicago Press, 1995. vii, 183 p.
94-021331   174/.4   0226116328
Profit -- Moral and ethical aspects.

HB615 Economic theory — Income. Factor shares — Entrepreneurship. Risk and uncertainty

HB615.B617 2000
The Blackwell handbook of entrepreneurship/ edited by Donald L. Sexton, Hans Landström, in conjunction with the School of Business and Entrepreneurship at Nova Southeastern University. Oxford, U.K.; Blackwell Business; [Ft. Lauderdale, xxiv, 468 p.
99-087791   658.4/21 21   0631215735
Entrepreneurship -- Case studies.

HB615.B66 1999
The book of entrepreneurs' wisdom: classic writings by legendary entrepreneurs/ edited by Peter Krass. New York: Wiley, c1999. xiv, 514 p.
99-048274   658.4/21 21   0471345091
Entrepreneurship -- Case studies. Businessmen -- Case studies. Businesswomen -- Case studies.

HB615.E59
Encyclopedia of entrepreneurship/ edited by Calvin A. Kent, Donald L. Sexton, Karl H. Vesper. Englewood Cliffs, NJ: Prentice-Hall, c1982. xxxviii, 425 p.
81-010602   338/.04   0132758261
Entrepreneurship. Small business -- Technological innovations.

HB615.K58 1989
Kirzner, Israel M.
Discovery, capitalism, and distributive justice/ Israel M. Kirzner. Oxford, UK; B. Blackwell, 1989. x, 179 p.
88-033355   330.1   0631161538
Entrepreneurship. Capitalism. Distributive justice.

HB615.K64 2001
Koehn, Nancy F. 1959-
Brand new: how entrepreneurs earned consumers' trust from Wedgwood to Dell/ Nancy F. Koehn. Boston: Harvard Business School Press, c2001. 469 p.
00-063224   658.4/21 21   1578512212
Entrepreneurship. Businesspeople.

HB615.M3732 2002
McDaniel, Bruce A.,
Entrepreneurship and innovation: an economic approach/ Bruce A. McDaniel. Armonk, N.Y.: M.E. Sharpe, c2002. xiii, 269 p.
2001-057687   338/.04 21   0765607085
Entrepreneurship.

HB615.M674 1998
Morris, Michael H.
Entrepreneurial intensity: sustainable advantages for individuals, organizations, and societies/ Michael H. Morris; foreword by Leyland Pitt. Westport, Conn.: Quorum, 1998. xix, 170 p.
97-031518   338/.04 21   0899309755
Entrepreneurship.

HB615.S353 1995
Schneider, Mark, 1946-
Public entrepreneurs: agents for change in American government/ Mark Schneider and Paul Teske with Michael Mintrom. Princeton, N.J.: Princeton University Press, c1995. x, 263 p.
94-021311   306.2   0691037256
Entrepreneurship -- United States. Government business enterprises -- United States. Local government -- United States.

HB615.S55 1987
Simon, Julian Lincoln, 1932-
Effort, opportunity, and wealth/ Julian L. Simon. Oxford [Oxfordshire], UK; B. Blackwell, 1987. x, 198 p.
86-017644   330.1   0631144285
Entrepreneurship. Struggle -- Economic aspects. Competition.

HB701-711 Economic theory — Income. Factor shares — Property

HB701.C54 1994
Christman, John.
The myth of property: toward an egalitarian theory of ownership/ John Christman. New York: Oxford University Press, 1994. ix, 219 p.
93-031713 330.1/7 0195085949
Property.

HB701.E14 1995
Early modern conceptions of property/ edited by John Brewer and Susan Staves. London; Routledge, 1995. xiv, 599 p.
94-016164 330.1/7 20 0415105331
Property -- History.

HB701.G45 1969
Godwin, William, 1756-1836.
Godwin's "Political justice." A reprint of the essay on "Property," from the original edition. Edited by H. S. Salt. London, S. Sonnenschein, 1890. St. Clair Shores, Mich., Scholarly Press [1969?] 155 p.
78-008160 330.1/7
Property.

HB701.R89 1987
Ryan, Alan.
Property/ Alan Ryan. Minneapolis: University of Minnesota Press, c1987. 143 p.
87-025538 330/.17 0816616698
Property.

HB701.R9 1984
Ryan, Alan.
Property and political theory/ Alan Ryan. Oxford, England; B. Blackwell, 1984. 198 p.
84-011126 330/.17/09 0631136916
Property -- History.

HB711.B477 1998
Bethell, Tom.
The noblest triumph: property and prosperity through the ages/ Tom Bethell. New York: St. Martin's Press, 1998. vi, 378 p.
98-006010 330.1/7 0312210833
Property. Right of property -- Economic aspects.

HB801 Economic theory — Consumption. Demand — General works

HB801.B267 2002
Bagozzi, Richard P.
The social psychology of consumer behaviour/ Richard P. Bagozzi, Zeynep Gurhan-Canli, Joseph R. Priester. Philadelphia, Pa.: Open University, 2002.
2001-056007 306.3 21 0335207227
Consumption (Economics) -- Social aspects. Consumer behavior. Consumers -- Psychology.

HB801.F52 2002
Fine, Ben.
The world of consumption: the material and cultural revisited/ Ben Fine. 2nd ed. London; Routledge, 2002.
2001-048675 339.4/7 21 0415279453
Consumption (Economics)

HB801.L233 1991
Lancaster, Kelvin.
Modern consumer theory/ Kelvin Lancaster. Aldershot, Hants, England; E. Elgar, c1991. v, 242 p.
90-020725 339.4/7 1852783842
Consumption (Economics)

HB801.S23 1992
Sack, Robert David.
Place, modernity, and the consumer's world: a relational framework for geographical analysis/ Robert David Sack. Baltimore: Johns Hopkins University Press, c1992. xiv, 256 p.
92-004391 658.8/35 0801843367
Consumption (Economics) Advertising. Space in economics.

HB801.S775 2001
Steedman, Ian.
Consumption takes time: implications for economic theory/ Ian Steedman. New York: Routledge, 2001.
00-062812 339.4/7 21 0415250994
Consumption (Economics) -- Mathematical models. Time -- Economic aspects -- Mathematical models.

HB820-831 Economic theory — Consumption. Demand — Household consumption. Consumer demand

HB820.E26 1991
The Economics of household consumption/ Frances M. Magrabi ... [et al.]. New York: Praeger, 1991. xiv, 278 p.
91-020302 339.4/7 0275934063
Consumption (Economics) Households.

HB822.W37 1999
Warneryd, Karl Erik, 1927-
The psychology of saving: a study on economic psychology/ Karl-Erik Warneryd. Northampton, Mass.: E. Elgar, c1999. ix, 389 p.
98-031080 332/.0415/019 21 1840640162
Saving and investment -- Psychological aspects. Economics -- Psychological aspects.

HB831.V4 2001
Veblen, Thorstein,
The theory of the leisure class/ Thorstein Veblen; introduction by Alan Wolfe; notes by James Danly. Modern library pbk. ed. New York: Modern Library, 2001. xvi, 298 p.
2001-041759 305.5/234 21 0375757872
Leisure class.

HB843 Economic theory — Consumption. Demand — Aggregate demand

HB843.K68 1989
Kotlikoff, Laurence J.
What determines savings?/ Laurence J. Kotlikoff. Cambridge, Mass.: MIT Press, c1989. xvi, 533 p.
88-009091 339.4/3 0262111373
Saving and investment.

HB846 Economic theory — Welfare theory — General works

HB846.B37 1998
Barr, N. A.
The economics of the welfare state/ Nicholas Barr. 3rd ed. Stanford, Calif.: Stanford University Press, 1998. xxvi, 471 p.
98-060890 330.15/56 21 0804735522
Welfare economics.

HB846.E78 1990
Esping-Andersen, Gosta, 1947-
The three worlds of welfare capitalism/ Gosta Esping-Andersen. Princeton, N.J.: Princeton University Press, c1990. xi, 248 p.
89-024254 330.15/56 0691094578
Welfare economics.

HB846.G35 1996
Galbraith, John Kenneth,
The good society: the humane agenda/ John Kenneth Galbraith. Boston: Houghton Mifflin Co., 1996. vii, 152 p.
96-000983 330.12/6 20 0395713285
Welfare economics. Income distribution. Social justice.

HB846.J36 1994
Janoski, Thomas.
The comparative political economy of the welfare state/ Thomas Janoski, Alexander M. Hicks. Cambridge, UK; Cambridge University Press, 1994. xvi, 395 p.
93-017335 330.12/6 0521434734
Welfare economics. Welfare state. Comparative economics.

HB846.R53 1989
Rich, David Z.
The economics of welfare: a contemporary analysis/ David Z. Rich. New York: Praeger, 1989. viii, 212 p.
89-030899 330.15/5 0275933091
Welfare economics.

HB846.T56 1990
Tinbergen, Jan, 1903-
World security and equity/ Jan Tinbergen. Aldershot, Hants, England: E. Elgar Pub.; c1990. x, 106 p.
89-023686 361.6/1 1852781874
Welfare economics -- Mathematical models. Economic security -- Mathematical models. National security -- Mathematical models.

HB846.2 Economic theory — Welfare theory — Cost benefit analysis

HB846.2.M55 1988
Mishan, E. J.
Cost-benefit analysis: an informal introduction/ by E.J. Mishan. 4th ed. London; Unwin Hyman, 1988. xxx, 461 p.
87-037133 658.1/554 19 0044450923
Welfare economics. Cost effectiveness. Expenditures, Public.

HB846.5 Economic theory — Welfare theory — Public goods

HB846.5.B65 2002
Bollier, David.
Silent theft: the private plunder of our common wealth/ David Bollier. New York: Routledge, 2002. x, 260 p.
2001-045727   306.3/2/0973 21   0415932645
Public goods. Commons -- United States. Capitalism -- United States.

HB846.5.C48 1991
Chong, Dennis.
Collective action and the civil rights movement/ Dennis Chong. Chicago: University of Chicago Press, 1991. xiii, 261 p.
90-048848   323.1/196073   0226104400
Public goods. Social choice. Civil rights movements -- United States.

HB846.5.C86 1986
Cummings, Ronald G.
Valuing environmental goods: an assessment of the contingent valuation method/ R.G. Cummings, D.S. Brookshire, W.D. Schulze; contributors, Richard Bishop ... [et al.]; commentators, Kenneth Arrow ... [et al.]. Totowa, N.J.: Rowman & Allanheld, 1986. xiii, 270 p.
85-014298   363   0847674487
Public goods -- Cost effectiveness. Public goods -- Valuation. Contingent valuation.

HB846.5.M58 1989
Mitchell, Robert Cameron.
Using surveys to value public goods: the contingent valuation method/ Robert Cameron Mitchell, Richard T. Carson. Washington, D.C.: Resources for the Future; c1989. xix, 463 p.
87-028633   363   0915707322
Public goods -- Valuation. Public goods -- Cost effectiveness. Contingent valuation.

HB846.5.N68 2000
Not for sale: in defense of public goods/ [edited by] Anatole Anton, Milton Fisk, Nancy Holmstrom. Boulder, Colo.: Westview Press, 2000. xx, 468 p.
00-042864   363 21   0813366186
Public goods.

HB846.5.S36 1991
Schmidtz, David.
The limits of government: an essay on the public goods argument/ David Schmidtz. Boulder: Westview Press, 1991. xviii, 197 p.
90-047486   338.9   0813308704
Public goods.

HB846.5.S56 1991
Shmanske, Stephen.
Public goods, mixed goods, and monopolistic competition/ Stephen Shmanske. College Station: Texas A & M University Press, 1991. 225 p.
90-041465   338.8/2   0890964645
Public goods. Monopolistic competition.

HB846.5.T46 1988
The Theory of market failure: a critical examination/ edited by Tyler Cowen. Fairfax, Va.: George Mason University Press; c1988. 384 p.
88-014743   363   0913969133
Public goods. Externalities (Economics) Welfare economics.

HB846.8 Economic theory — Social choice

HB846.8.B79 1989
Buchanan, James M.
Explorations into constitutional economics/ James M. Buchanan; compiled and with a preface by Robert D. Tollison and Viktor J. Vanberg. College Station: Texas A&M University Press, c1989. x, 437 p.
88-016082   302/.13   0890963258
Social choice.

HB846.8.M57 1994
Mitchell, William C.
Beyond politics: markets, welfare, and the failure of bureaucracy/ William C. Mitchell and Randy T. Simmons. Boulder: Westview Press, 1994. xix, 234 p.
94-012008   350   0813322073
Social choice. Bureaucracy.

HB846.8.P47 1997
Perspectives on public choice: a handbook/ [edited by] Dennis C. Mueller. Cambridge, U.K.; Cambridge University Press, c1997. xiii, 672 p.
95-044023   302/.13 20   0521556546
Social choice. Political science -- Economic aspects.

HB846.8.R55 1988
Riley, Jonathan, 1955-
Liberal utilitarianism: social choice theory and J.S. Mill's philosophy/ Jonathan Riley. Cambridge [England]; Cambridge University Press, 1988. xiv, 398 p.
87-006598   302/.13   0521306922
Mill, John Stuart, -- 1806-1873.   Social choice. Utilitarianism. Liberalism.

HB846.8.W34 1989
Wagner, Richard E.
To promote the general welfare: market processes vs. political transfers/ by Richard E. Wagner. San Francisco, Calif.: Pacific Research Institute for Public Policy, c1989. xv, 239 p.
88-064203   361.6   0936488255
Social choice. Welfare state. Income distribution.

HB849 Demography. Population. Vital events — Congresses

HB849.P63
Political science in population studies [edited by] Richard L. Clinton, William S. Flash [and] R. Kenneth Godwin. Lexington, Mass., Lexington Books [1972] xviii, 156 p.
75-186337   304.6   0669820571
Population -- Congresses. Political science -- Congresses.

HB849.S62
Social demography/ edited by Karl E. Taeuber, Larry L. Bumpass, James A. Sweet; Center for Demography and Ecology, University of Wisconsin--Madison. New York: Academic Press, c1978. xv, 336 p.
78-606153   301.32   0126826501
Fertility, Human -- Congresses. Population density -- Congresses. Social mobility -- Congresses.

HB849.2 Demography. Population. Vital events — Dictionaries. Encyclopedias

HB849.2.I55 1982
International encyclopedia of population/ editor in chief, John A. Ross (Center for Population and Family Health, International Institute for the Study of Human Reproduction, Faculty of Medicine, Columbia University). New York: Free Press, c1982. 2 v.
82-002326   304.6/03/21   0029274303
Population -- Encyclopedias.

HB849.4 Demography. Population. Vital events — Theory. Method. Relation to other subjects — General works

HB849.4.S53 2002
Siegel, Jacob S.
Applied demography: applications to business, government, law and   public policy/ Jacob S. Siegel. San Diego: Academic Press, c2002. xxii, 686 p.
2001-090929   304.6 21   0126418403
Demography.

HB849.4.U55 1991
United Nations Population Fund.
Population policies and programmes: lessons learned from two decades of experience/ edited by Nafis Sadik. New York: Published for United Nations Population Fund by c1991. xxiv, 464 p.
91-012388   363.9   0814785530
Population policy. Population research.

HB849.4.W54 1982
Willigan, J. Dennis.
Sources and methods of historical demography/ J. Dennis Willigan, Katherine A Lynch. New York, N.Y.: Academic Press, c1982. xv, 505 p.
82-008819   304.6/09   0127570225
Population -- History -- Methodology. Demography.

HB849.41 Demography. Population. Vital events — Theory. Method. Relation to other subjects — Relation to economics

HB849.41.F87 1997
Furedi, Frank, 1948-
Population and development: a critical introduction/ Frank Furedi. New York: St. Martin's Press, 1997. 201 p.
97-016710   304.6   0312176562
Population policy. Population -- Economic aspects. Economic development.

HB849.41.P633 1997
Pol, Louis G.
Demography for business decision making/ Louis G. Pol, Richard K. Thomas. Westport, Conn.: Quorum, 1997. x, 270 p.
96-046087   304.6/024/658   1567200141
Demography. Marketing research. Decision making. United States -- Population.

HB849.41.P646 1994
Population and environment: rethinking the debate/ edited by Lourdes Arizpe, M. Priscilla Stone, and David C. Major. Boulder: Westview Press, 1994. viii, 352 p.
94-002805   304.2/8   0813388430
Population -- Economic aspects. Population -- Social aspects. Population -- Environmental aspects.

HB849.41.R4 1998
The reader in population and development/ edited by Paul Demeny and Geoffrey McNicoll. New York: St. Martin's Press, 1998. x, 363 p.
98-013495   338.9   0312215169
Population -- Economic aspects. Economic development.

HB849.41.S548 2000
Simon, Julian Lincoln, 1932-
The great breakthrough and its cause/ Julian L. Simon; edited by Timur Kuran. Ann Arbor: University of Michigan Press, c2000. xxii, 214 p.
00-059983   304.6 21   0472110977
Population -- Economic aspects. Economic development.

HB849.415 Demography. Population. Vital events — Theory. Method. Relation to other subjects — Relation to environment

HB849.415.H374 2000
Harrison, Paul, 1945-
AAAS atlas of population & environment/ Paul Harrison, Fred Pearce; foreword by Peter H. Raven. Berkeley, CA: University of California Press, c2000. xi, 204 p.
00-067228   333.7 21   0520230817
Population -- Environmental aspects.

HB849.49 Demography. Population. Vital events — Theory. Method. Relation to other subjects — Demographic and household survey techniques

HB849.49.M63 1988
Modelling household formation and dissolution/ edited by Nico Keilman, Anton Kuijsten, Ad Vossen. Oxford [England]: Clarendon Press; 1988. xxii, 298 p.
87-018581   306.8/5/0724   0198295006
Households -- Mathematical models -- Congresses. Household surveys -- Congresses.

HB849.49.R875 2000
Russell, Cheryl, 1953-
Demographics of the U.S.: trends and projections/ by Cheryl Russell. Ithaca, N.Y.: New Strategist Publications, c2000. xviii, 570 p.
2001-267410   304.6/2/0973 21   1885070314
Demographic surveys -- United States. Population forecasting -- United States. Economic forecasting -- United States. United States -- Population. United States -- Economic conditions.

HB849.53 Demography. Population. Vital events — Theory. Method. Relation to other subjects — Population forecasting

HB849.53.L44 2002
Leisinger, Klaus M.
Six billion and counting: population growth and food security in the 21st century/ Klaus M. Leisinger, Karin Schmitt, and Rajul Pandya-Lorch. Washington, DC: International Food Policy Research Institute, xiii, 155 p.
2001-039391   363.8 21   0896297055
Population forecasting. Overpopulation. Population -- Environmental aspects.

HB849.53.P66 1982
Population estimates: methods for small area analysis/ edited by Everett S. Lee, Harold F. Goldsmith. Beverly Hills: Sage Publications, c1982. 248 p.
82-000648   304.6/2/028   0803918127
Population forecasting -- Congresses.

HB851 Demography. Population. Vital events — History of demography — General works

HB851.C49 1991
Cigno, Alessandro.
Economics of the family/ Alessandro Cigno. Oxford: Clarendon Press; 1991. vii, 212 p.
91-006319   339.2/2   0198287097
Households -- Economic aspects. Family demography -- Economic aspects.

HB851.H286 2001
Harris, P. M. G.
The history of human populations/ P.M.G. Harris. Westport, Conn.: Praeger, <2001- > v. <1 >
00-061110   304.6/09 21   0275971317
Population -- History.

HB851.M32
McEvedy, Colin.
Atlas of world population history/ Colin McEvedy and Richard Jones. New York: Facts on File, c1978 368 p.
78-016954   301.32/9   0871964023
Population -- History. Population -- Statistics. Population -- Charts, diagrams, etc.

HB851.P46 1975
Petersen, William.
Population. New York, Macmillan [1975] xi, 784 p.
73-018768   301.32   0023948809
Population.

HB853 Demography. Population. Vital events — History of demography — By region or country, A-Z

HB853.R66.P37 1992
Parkin, Tim G.
Demography and Roman society/ Tim G. Parkin. Baltimore, Md.: Johns Hopkins University Press, c1992. xvi, 225 p.
91-045647   304.6/0937/6   0801843774
Demography -- Rome -- History. Rome -- Population -- History.

HB861-863 Demography. Population. Vital events — Biography — Malthus

HB861.E7 1976
Malthus, T. R. 1766-1834.
An essay on the principle of population: text, sources and background, criticism/ Thomas Robert Malthus; edited by Philip Appleman. New York: Norton, c1976. xxvii, 260 p.
75-026853   301.32   039304419X
Population.

HB863.M23.J35 1979
James, Patricia.
Population Malthus, his life and times/ Patricia James. London; Routledge & Kegan Paul, 1979. xv, 524 p.
79-040584   304.6/092/4   0710002661
Malthus, T. R. -- (Thomas Robert), -- 1766-1834. Demographers -- Great Britain -- Biography. Economists -- Great Britain -- Biography.

HB863.M253 1971
Marx, Karl, 1818-1883.
Marx and Engels on the population bomb; selections from the writings of Marx and Engels dealing with the theories of Thomas Robert Malthus. Edited by Ronald L. Meek. Translations from the German by Dorothea L. Meek and Ronald L. Meek. Berkeley, Calif.] Ramparts Press [1971] xxii, 215 p.
71-132220   301.3/1   0878670025
Malthus, T. R. -- (Thomas Robert), -- 1766-1834. Malthusianism.

HB863.P47
Petersen, William.
Malthus/ William Petersen. Cambridge, Mass.: Harvard University Press, 1979. vi, 302 p.
78-031479   301.32/092/4   0674544250
Malthus, T. R. -- (Thomas Robert), -- 1766-1834. Demographers -- Great Britain -- Biography. Economists -- Great Britain -- Biography.

HB863.R67 1998
Ross, Eric B.
The Malthus factor: population, poverty, and politics in capitalist development/ Eric B. Ross. London; Zed Books; 1998. 264 p.
98-029913   338.9   1856495639
Malthus, T. R. -- (Thomas Robert), -- 1766-1834. Overpopulation -- Economic aspects. Poverty. Capitalism.

HB871-875 Demography. Population. Vital events — General works — 1835-

HB871.B587
Boserup, Ester.
Population and technological change: a study of long-term trends/ Ester Boserup. Chicago: University of Chicago Press, 1981. xi, 255 p.
80-021116   304.6/2   0226066738
Population. Technological innovations.

HB871.B738 1994
Brown, Lester Russell, 1934-
Full house: reassessing the earth's population carrying capacity/ Lester R. Brown, Hal Kane. New York: W.W. Norton & Co., c1994. 261 p.
95-112766   363.9   0393037134
Overpopulation. Pollution -- Economic aspects. Food supply.

HB871.B74
Brown, Lester Russell, 1934-
In the human interest; a strategy to stabilize world population [by] Lester R. Brown. New York, Norton [1974] 190 p.
74-006339   301.32   0393055264
Population.

HB871.E35 1972
Ehrlich, Paul R.
Population, resources, environment; issues in human ecology [by] Paul R. Ehrlich [and] Anne H. Ehrlich. San Francisco, W. H. Freeman [1972] xiv, 509 p.
70-179799   301.3   0716706954
Population. Pollution. Human ecology.

HB871.E92 1998
Evans, L. T.
Feeding the ten billion: plants and population growth/ L.T. Evans. Cambridge, UK; Cambridge University Press, 1998. xiv, 247 p.
98-026457   363.9   0521640814
Population. Agriculture -- Economic aspects. Overpopulation.

HB871.L56513 2000
Livi Bacci, Massimo.
A concise history of world population: an introduction to population processes/ Massimo Livi-Bacci; translated by Carl Ipsen. 3rd ed. Malden, MA: Blackwell Publishers, 2001. xv, 251 p.
00-051920   304.6 21   0631223355
Population -- History.

HB871.M57 1994
Moffett, George D., 1943-
Critical masses: the global population challenge/ George D. Moffett. New York: Viking, 1994. ix, 353 p.
94-011798   363.9/1   067085235X
Overpopulation. Population forecasting. Environmental degradation.

HB871.M9
Myrdal, Gunnar, 1898-
Population, a problem for democracy, by Gunnar Myrdal. Cambridge, Mass., Harvard University Press, 1940. xiii, 237 p.
40-007943   312.09485
Population. Sweden -- Population.

HB871.N33 1998
National population policies/ Department of Economic and Social Affairs, Population Division. New York: United Nations, 1998. x, 444 p.
99-194044
Population policy. Population -- Statistics.

HB871.S25213 1970
Sauvy, Alfred, 1898-
General theory of population. With a foreword by E. A. Wrigley. Translated by Christophe Campos. New York, Basic Books [1970, c1969] x, 550 p.
69-016315   301.3/2
Population.

HB871.S57
Simon, Julian Lincoln, 1932-
The economics of population growth/ Julian L. Simon. Princeton, N.J.: Princeton University Press, c1977. xxx, 555 p.
75-015278   301.32   0691100535
Population. Fertility, Human -- Economic aspects. Birth control.

HB871.S573 1996
Simon, Julian Lincoln, 1932-
The ultimate resource 2/ Julian L. Simon. Princton, N.J.: Princeton University Press, c1996. xliii, 734 p.
95-039586   333.7 20   0691042691
Population. Natural resources. Economic policy.

HB871.S6514
Spengler, Joseph John, 1902-
Facing zero population growth: reactions and interpretations, past and present/ Joseph J. Spengler. Durham, N.C.: Duke University Press, 1978. xiv, 288 p.
78-052031   301.32/1   0822304120
Population. Stable population model. Stagnation (Economics) United States -- Population.

HB871.T45 1965
Thompson, Warren Simpson, 1887-
Population problems [by] Warren S. Thompson [and] David T. Lewis. New York, McGraw-Hill [1965] xiv, 593 p.
64-023282   301.32
Population.

HB871.W763 1987
World population policies. New York: United Nations, 1987-1990. 3 v.
88-141080   304.6   9211511658
Population. Population policy.

HB871.Z45
Zelinsky, Wilbur, 1921-
A prologue to population geography. Englewood Cliffs, N.J., Prentice-Hall [1966] ix, 150 p.
66-010948   301.32018
Population.

HB875.E35 1971
Ehrlich, Paul R.
The population bomb [by] Paul R. Ehrlich. New York [Ballantine Books, [1971] xiv, 201 p.
78-022647   301.3/2   0345021711
Population.

HB875.Y35
Yates, Wilson.
Family planning on a crowded planet. Minneapolis, Augsburg Pub. House [1971] 96 p.
78-135221   301.42/6   0806694629
Population. Family size. Birth control.

HB881 Demography. Population. Vital events — Addresses, essays, lectures

HB881.B564
Bogue, Donald Joseph, 1918-
Principles of demography [by] Donald J. Bogue. New York, Wiley [1969] xiii, 917 p.
68-026847   312   0471086207
Demography.

HB881.F76
Freedman, Ronald, 1917-
Population: the vital revolution. Garden City, N.Y., Anchor Books [1964] vi, 274 p.
64-019296   301.32
Population. Demographic transition. United States -- Population.

HB881.H38
Heer, David M.
Readings on population [compiled by] David M. Heer. Englewood Cliffs, N.J., Prentice-Hall [1968] ix, 234 p.
68-020158   312/.08
Demography -- Addresses, essays, lectures.

HB881.H625
Hollingsworth, Thomas Henry.
Historical demography, by T. H. Hollingsworth. Ithaca, N.Y., Cornell University Press [1969] 448 p.
71-079388   312   0801404975
Demography.

HB881.K48
Keyfitz, Nathan, 1913-
World population; an analysis of vital data [by] Nathan Keyfitz and Wilhelm Flieger. Chicago, University of Chicago Press [1968] xi, 672 p.
68-014010   312
Population -- Statistics.

HB881.M2553
McCormack, Arthur.
The population problem. New York, Crowell [1970] 264 p.
74-109908   301.3/2   0690648928
Population. Food supply.

HB881.S526 1976
Shryock, Henry S.
The methods and materials of demography/ Henry S. Shryock, Jacob S. Siegel, and associates. New York: Academic Press, c1976. ix, 577 p.
76-018312   301.32/01/82   0126411506
Demography.

HB881.S68 1968
Spiegelman, Mortimer.
Introduction to demography. Cambridge, Harvard University Press, 1968. xix, 514 p.
68-021984   312
Demography.

HB883-883.5 Demography. Population. Vital events — Population policy

HB883.P67 2000
Population: opposing viewpoints/ Charles F. Hohm, book editor, Lori Justine Jones, book editor, Shoon Lio, book editor. San Diego, Calif.: Greenhaven Press, c2000. 224 p.
99-056750   304.6 21   0737702923
Population. Population.

HB883.5.A23 1993
Abernethy, Virginia.
Population politics: the choices that shape our future/ Virginia D. Abernethy; with a foreword by Garrett Hardin. New York: Insight Books, c1993. xix, 350 p.
92-041791   363.9   0306444615
Population policy. Fertility, Human. Demographic transition.

HB883.5.K37 1988
Kasun, Jacqueline R. 1924-
The war against population: the economics and ideology of world population control/ Jacqueline Kasun. San Francisco: Ignatius Press, c1988. 225 p.
87-083505   304.6/6   0898701910
Population policy. Economic development. Birth control.

HB884 Demography. Population. Vital events — By region or country

HB884.O253 1993
Oberai, A. S.
Population growth, employment, and poverty in Third-World mega-cities: analytical and policy issues/ A.S. Oberai. New York, N.Y.: St. Martin's Press, 1993. xv, 224 p.
93-010561   304.6/09172/4   0312099738
Labor market -- Developing countries. Poor -- Developing countries. Urbanization -- Developing countries. Developing countries -- Population.

HB884.P6624 1994
Population and development: old debates, new conclusions / Robert Cassen ... [et al.]. New Brunswick: Transaction Publishers, 1994. x, 282 p.
94-011399   304.6/09172/6   1560001658
Population -- Economic aspects. Developing countries -- Population -- Economic aspects.

HB884.5 Demography. Population. Vital events — Population assistance

HB884.5.D66 1990
Donaldson, Peter J.
Nature against us: the United States and the world population crisis, 1965-1980/ Peter J. Donaldson. Chapel Hill: University of North Carolina Press, c1990. xi, 207 p.
89-038870   363.9   0807819050
Population assistance, American -- Developing countries.

HB884.5.J64 1987
Johnson, Stanley, 1940-
World population and the United Nations: challenge and response/ Stanley P. Johnson. Cambridge [Cambridgeshire]; Cambridge University Press, 1987. xxxviii, 357 p.
87-005126   363.9   0521322073
Population policy. Population.

HB885 Demography. Population. Vital events — General special

HB885.B333
Bayles, Michael D.
Morality and population policy/ Michael D. Bayles. University: University of Alabama Press, c1980. 143 p.
79-023965   176   0817300333
Population -- Moral and ethical aspects. Population policy -- Moral and ethical aspects.

HB885.F58
Ford, Thomas R.,
Social demography. Edited by Thomas R. Ford [and] Gordon F. De Jong. Englewood Cliffs, N.J., Prentice-Hall [1970] x, 690 p.
69-014426   301.3/2/08   0138155550
Demography -- Addresses, essays, lectures. Sociology -- Addresses, essays, lectures.

HB885.N5 1965
Ng, Larry K. Y.
The population crisis; implications and plans for action. Edited by Larry K. Y. Ng. Stuart Mudd, co-editor. Associate editors: Hugo Boyko [and others] Bloomington, Indiana University Press, 1965. xi, 364 p.
65-011796   301.32082
Natural resources. Population.

HB887 Demography. Population. Vital events — Demographic transition

HB887.C4813 1992
Chesnais, Jean-Claude, 1948-
The demographic transition: stages, patterns, and economic implications: a longitudinal study of sixty-seven countries covering the period 1720-1984/ Jean-Claude Chesnais; translated by Elizabeth and Philip Kreager. Oxford [England]: Clarendon Press; 1992. xii, 633 p.
91-041100   304.6   0198286597
Demographic transition -- History. Economic development -- History.

HB901 Demography. Population. Vital events — Births. Fertility — General works

HB901.D48 1983
Determinants of fertility in developing countries/ Panel on Fertility Determinants, Committee on Population and Demography, Commission on Behavioral and Social Sciences and Education, National Research Council; edited by Rodolfo A. Bulatao, Ronald D. Lee with Paula E. Hollerbach, John Bongaarts. New York: Academic Press, [1983-] v. 1-2.
83-017135   304.6/32/091724   012140501X
Fertility, Human -- Developing countries. Family size -- Developing countries. Birth control -- Developing countries.

HB915-1108 Demography. Population. Vital events — Births. Fertility — By region or country

HB915.L56
Lindert, Peter H.
Fertility and scarcity in America/ Peter H. Lindert. Princeton, N.J.: Princeton University Press, c1978. xi, 395 p.
77-071992   301.32/1/0973   0691042179
Family size -- Economic aspects -- United States. Fertility, Human -- Economic aspects -- United States. Income distribution -- United States.

HB991.W38 1991
Watkins, Susan Cotts, 1938-
From provinces into nations: demographic integration in Western Europe, 1870-1960/ Susan Cotts Watkins. Princeton, N.J.: Princeton University Press, c1991. xvii, 235 p.
90-036900   304.6/32/094   0691094519
Fertility, Human -- Europe -- History. Nationalism -- Europe -- History. Regionalism -- Europe -- History. Europe -- Population -- History.

HB995.G55 1982
Gittins, Diana.
Fair sex, family size and structure in Britain, 1900-39/ Diana Gittins. New York: St. Martin's Press, 1982. 240 p.
81-021248   304.6/3/0941   0312279620
Fertility, Human -- Great Britain -- History -- 20th century. Family size -- Great Britain -- History -- 20th century. Women -- Employment -- Great Britain -- History -- 20th century.

HB1050.D45.B38 1992
Basu, Alaka Malwade.
Culture, the status of women, and demographic behaviour/ Alaka Malwade Basu. Oxford [England]: Clarendon Press; 1992. xvii, 265 p.
91-036547   305.4/0954/56   0198283601
Fertility, Human -- India -- Delhi. Mortality -- India -- Delhi. Rural-urban migration -- India -- Delhi.

HB1108.F46 1985
Fertility in developing countries: an economic perspective on research and policy issues/ edited by Ghazi M. Farooq and George B. Simmons; foreword by Rafael M. Salas. New York: St. Martin's Press, 1985. xxiv, 533 p.
83-040609   304.6/32/091724   0312287526
Fertility, Human -- Developing countries.

HB1108.H48 1988
Hess, Peter N.
Population growth and socioeconomic progress in less developed countries: determinants of fertility transition/ Peter N. Hess. New York: Praeger, 1988. xiv, 166 p.
87-038472   304.6/2/091724   0275929795
Fertility, Human -- Developing countries. Demographic transition -- Developing countries. Developing countries -- Economic conditions. Developing countries -- Social conditions.

HB1125 Demography. Population. Vital events — Marriages. Nuptiality — By region or country

HB1125.C33
Carter, Hugh, 1895-
Marriage and divorce: a social and economic study [by] Hugh Carter and Paul C. Glick. Cambridge, Mass., Harvard University Press, 1970. xxix, 451 p.
79-105369   301.42   0674550757
Marriage -- United States -- Statistics. Divorce -- United States -- Statistics.

HB1323 Demography. Population. Vital events — Deaths. Mortality — Other special subjects, A-Z

HB1323.C5.K46 1990
Kent, George, 1939-
The politics of children's survival/ George Kent. New York: Praeger, 1991. x, 204 p.
90-007578   304.6/4/083   0275937232
Children -- Mortality.

HB1323.C52.U655 1991
Preston, Samuel H.
Fatal years: child mortality in late nineteenth-century America/ Samuel H. Preston and Michael R. Haines. Princeton, N.J.: Princeton University Press, c1991. xxi, 266 p.
90-045129   304.6/4/083   0691042683
Children -- United States -- Mortality -- History -- 19th century.

HB1323.C52.U658 1998
Sanders, Rickie.
Growing up in America: an atlas of youth in the USA/ Rickie Sanders & Mark T. Mattson. New York: Macmillan Library Reference USA; c1998. xii, 291 p.
97-039575 305.23/0973 21 0028972627
Children -- United States -- Statistics.

HB1335-1379 Demography. Population. Vital events — Deaths. Mortality — By region or country

HB1335.Z67 1992
Zopf, Paul E.
Mortality patterns and trends in the United States/ Paul E. Zopf, Jr. Westport, Conn.: Greenwood Press, 1992. xx, 281 p.
92-015488 304.6/4/0973 0313267693
Mortality -- United States.

HB1379.D52 1983
Diaz-Briquets, Sergio.
The health revolution in Cuba/ by Sergio Diaz-Briquets. Austin: University of Texas Press, 1983. xvii, 227 p.
82-010865 304.6/4/097291 0292750714
Mortality -- Cuba -- History. Public health -- Cuba -- History. Cuba -- Statistics, Vital -- History.

HB1831 Demography. Population. Vital events — Sex — By region or country

HB1831.A3
Women and men in Europe and North America, 2000/ [prepared by the Statistical Division of the Economic Commission for Europe]. New York: United Nations, 2000. xx, 252 p.
00-423421 9211167477
Sex distribution (Demography) -- Europe -- Statistics. Sex distribution (Demography) -- North America -- Statistics.

HB1951 Demography. Population. Vital events — Population geography. Migration — General works

HB1951.H84 1978
Human migration: patterns and policies/ edited by William H. McNeill and Ruth S. Adams. Bloomington, Ind.: Indiana University Press, c1978. xviii, 442 p.
77-023685 301.32 0253328756
Migration, Internal -- Congresses. Emigration and immigration -- Congresses.

HB1951.P655 1994
Population migration and the changing world order/ edited by W.T.S. Gould and A.M. Findlay. Chichester, England; J. Wiley, 1994. x, 293 p.
93-049629 304.8 0471949167
Population geography. Emigration and immigration. Economic history -- 1971-1990. Developing countries -- Emigration and immigration.

HB1952 Demography. Population. Vital events — Population geography. Migration — Internal migration

HB1952.I55 1990
International handbook on internal migration/ edited by Charles B. Nam, William J. Serow, and David F. Sly. New York: Greenwood Press, 1990. xv, 438 p.
89-007487 304.8 0313258589
Migration, Internal.

HB1953 Demography. Population. Vital events — Population geography. Migration — Population density

HB1953.C64 1995
Cohen, Joel E.
How many people can the earth support?/ Joel E. Cohen. New York: Norton, c1995. x, 532 p.
95-006133 304.6/1 0393038629
Population density. Population -- Economic aspects. Population forecasting.

HB1971-2126.4 Demography. Population. Vital events — Population geography. Migration — By region or country

HB1971.A3.B47 2000
Berry, Chad, 1963-
Southern migrants, Northern exiles/ Chad Berry. Urbana: University of Illinois Press, c2000. xiii, 236 p.
99-006511 304.8/0975 21 025202429X
Migration, Internal -- Southern States -- History -- 20th century. Migration, Internal -- Middle West -- History -- 20th century. Poor -- Southern States -- History -- 20th century.

HB1985.C2G74 1989
Gregory, James Noble.
American exodus: the Dust Bowl migration and Okie culture in California/ James N. Gregory. New York: Oxford University Press, 1989. xviii, 338 p.
88-036230 304.8/794/0766 0195044231
Migration, Internal -- United States -- History -- 20th century. Agricultural laborers -- California -- Economic conditions. Agricultural laborers -- California -- Social conditions.

HB2041.M53
Migration in post-war Europe: geographical essays/ edited by John Salt and Hugh Clout. London; Oxford University Press, 1976. 228 p.
77-352366 301.32/6/0941 0198740271
Migration, Internal -- Europe. Rural-urban migration -- Europe. Migrant labor -- Europe.

HB2041.P66 1996
Population migration in the European Union/ edited by Philip Rees ... [et al.]. Chichester, England; J. Wiley & Sons, 1996. xvi, 390 p.
95-024756 304.8/2/094 047194968X
Migration, Internal -- European Union countries. European Union countries -- Emigration and immigration.

HB2045.M54 1988
Migration and society in early modern England/ edited by Peter Clark and David Souden. Totowa, N.J.: Barnes & Noble Books, 1988, c1987. 355 p.
87-035088 304.8/0942 0389207780
Migration, Internal -- England -- History. Migration, Internal -- North America -- History.

HB2099.W44
Weiner, Myron.
Sons of the soil: migration and ethnic conflict in India/ Myron Weiner. Princeton, N.J.: Princeton University Press, c1978. xviii, 383 p.
78-051202 301/.32/0954 0691093792
Migration, Internal -- India. Social mobility -- India. Ethnology -- India. India -- Population.

HB2114.A3.C45 1986
Chao, Kang, 1929-
Man and land in Chinese history: an economic analysis/ Kang Chao. Stanford, Calif.: Stanford University Press, 1986. xii, 268 p.
84-051715 304.6/1 0804712719
Population density -- China -- History. Land use -- China -- History.

HB2121.A3.R42 1982
Redistribution of population in Africa/ edited by John I. Clarke and Leszek A. Kosinski. London; Heinemann Educational, 1982. x, 271 p.
81-170774 304.8/096 0435950304
Population density -- Africa. Migration, Internal -- Africa.

HB2126.4.A3.C67 1996
Cordell, Dennis D., 1947-
Hoe and wage: a social history of a circular migration system in West Africa/ Dennis Cordell, Joel W. Gregory, Victor Piche. Boulder, Colo.: Westview Press, 1996. xiv, 384 p.
96-017630 304.8/2/0966 0813381681
Migration, Internal -- Burkina Faso -- History. Migration, Internal -- Africa, West -- History.

HB2385-2516.5 Demography. Population. Vital events — Population geography. Migration — Rural population

HB2385.F836 1989
Fuguitt, Glenn Victor, 1928-
Rural and small town America/ Glenn V. Fuguitt, David L. Brown, Calvin L. Beale; assisted by Max J. Pfeffer ... [et al.] for the National Committee for Research on the 1980 Census. New York: Russell Sage Foundation, c1989. xxvii, 471 p.
89-010067 304.6/0973/091734 0871542722
Rural population -- United States. Rural-urban migration -- United States.

HB2516.5.P67 1989
Population growth and poverty in rural South Asia/ edited by Gerry Rodgers. New Delhi; Sage Publications, 1989. 249 p.
88-035627 304.6/0959 0803996004
Rural poor -- South Asia. South Asia -- Population, Rural.

HB2595 Demography. Population. Vital events — Professions. Occupations — By region or country

HB2595.O16 1998
The O*NET dictionary of occupational titles. 1998 ed. Indianapolis, Ind.: Jist Works, 1998. xxxvi, 625 p.
98-018600   331.7/003 21   1563705109
Occupations -- United States -- Dictionaries. Occupations -- United States -- Classification.

HB2595.U543 1977
Dictionary of occupational titles/ U.S. Department of Labor, Employment and Training Administration, U.S. Employment Service. [Washington]: The Administration: for sale by the Supt. of Do 1977. xli, 1371 p.
78-601723   331.7/003
Occupations -- United States. Occupations -- Dictionaries. Occupations -- Classification.

HB3501-3675 Demography. Population. Vital events — By region or country

HB3501.W45
Wells, Robert V., 1943-
The population of the British colonies in America before 1776: a survey of census data/ Robert V. Wells. Princeton, N.J.: Princeton University Press, [1975] xii, 342 p.
75-004976   301.32/9/73   0691046166
America -- Population -- History. Great Britain -- Colonies -- America.

HB3503.A3.H35 2000
A population history of North America/ edited by Michael R. Haines, Richard H. Steckel. Cambridge, UK; Cambridge University Press, 2000. xix, 736 p.
99-023284   304.6/097   0521496667
North America -- Population -- History.

HB3505.A683 1999
America's demographic tapestry: baseline for the new millennium/ edited by James W. Hughes and Joseph J. Seneca. New Brunswick, N.J.: Rutgers University Press, c1999. vii, 228 p.
98-044986   304.6/0973 21   0813526477
Population forecasting -- United States.

HB3505.B63 1997
Anderton, Douglas L.
The population of the United States/ Douglas L. Anderton , Richard E. Barrett, Donald J. Bogue; with statistical assistance of Alison Kadlec Donta. 3rd ed. New York: Free Press, c1997. viii, 693 p.
96-048990   304.6/2/0973 21   0684827743
United States -- Population. United States -- Census, 21st, 1990.

HB3505.B67 1994
Bouvier, Leon F.
How many Americans?: population, immigration and the environment/ Leon F. Bouvier and Lindsey Grant. San Francisco: Sierra Club Books, c1994. xii, 174 p.
94-006163   304.6/0973 20   0871564963
Population forecasting -- United States.

HB3505.C35
Callahan, Daniel, 1930-
The American population debate. Edited by Daniel Callahan. Garden City, N.Y., Doubleday, 1971. xv, 380 p.
79-144256   301.3/29/73
Birth control -- United States.   United States -- Population.

HB3505.E247
Easterlin, Richard A., 1926-
Birth and fortune: the impact of numbers on personal welfare/ Richard A. Easterlin. New York: Basic Books, c1980. xi, 205 p.
79-056369   304.6   0465006884
Fertility, Human -- United States.   United States -- Population.   United States -- Economic conditions -- 1945- United States -- Social conditions -- 1945-

HB3505.E44 1992
Elephants in the Volkswagen: facing the tough questions about our overcrowded country/ [edited by] Lindsey Grant. New York: W.H. Freeman, c1992. xii, 272 p.
91-037321   304.6/0973   0716722674
Population -- Economic aspects. Population -- Environmental aspects.   United States -- Population.

HB3505.M868 1995
Murdock, Steven H.
An America challenged: population change and the future of the United States/ Steve H. Murdock. Boulder: Westview Press, 1995. xxiii, 253 p.
94-029676   304.6/0973/01   0813318084
Population forecasting -- United States.   United States -- Population.

HB3505.P33 2002
Pack, Janet Rothenberg.
Growth and convergence in metropolitan America/ Janet Rothenberg Pack. Washington, D.C.: Brookings Institution Press, c2002. xvii, 214 p.
2001-006592   330.973/009173/2   21   0815702477
Regional disparities -- United States. Metropolitan areas -- Economic aspects. Cities and towns -- United States -- Growth.

HB3505.R63 1985
Robey, Bryant.
The American people: a timely exploration of a changing America and the important new demographic trends around us/ Bryant Robey. New York: Dutton, c1985. 287 p.
85-001481   304.6/0973   0525242961
United States -- Population.

HB3505.R87 1982
Russell, Louise B.
The baby boom generation and the economy/ Louise B. Russell. Washington, D.C.: Brookings Institution, c1982. xiii, 183 p.
82-070890   330.973/092   0815776284
Fertility, Human -- Economic aspects -- United States. Age distribution (Demography) -- Economic aspects -- United States. Baby boom generation -- United States. United States -- Population -- Economic aspects. United States -- Economic conditions -- 1945-

HB3505.S52 1990
Simon, Julian Lincoln, 1932-
Population matters: people, resources, environment, and immigration/ Julian L. Simon. New Brunswick, N.J., U.S.A.: Transaction Publishers, c1990. xiv, 577 p.
89-020240   304.6/0973   0887383009
Population forecasting -- United States. Natural resources -- United States. Natural resources. United States -- Population. United States -- Emigration and immigration.

HB3527.N7.R66
Rosenwaike, Ira, 1936-
Population history of New York City. [Syracuse, N.Y.] Syracuse University Press, 1972. xvii, 224 p.
75-039829   301.32/9/7471   0815621558
New York (N.Y.) -- Population -- History.

HB3530.5.S2613
Sanchez-Albornoz, Nicolas.
The population of Latin America; a history. Translated by W. A. R. Richardson. Berkeley, University of California Press [1974] xv, 299 p.
77-123621   301.32/9/8   0520017668
Latin America -- Population -- History.

HB3531.C6 1978
Cook, Sherburne Friend, 1896-1974.
The population of central Mexico in the sixteenth century/ by Sherburne F. Cook and Lesley Byrd Simpson. New York: AMS Press, 1978. 241 p.
76-029408   301.32/9/72   040415333X
Mexico -- Population -- History.

HB3539.A83.L87 1994
Lutz, Christopher, 1941-
Santiago de Guatemala, 1541-1773: city, caste, and the colonial experience/ by Christopher H. Lutz. Norman: University of Oklahoma Press, c1994. xx, 346 p.
93-046131   304.6/097281/62   0806125977
Antigua (Guatemala) -- Population -- History. Antigua (Guatemala) -- History.

HB3558.P3 1965a
Population dilemma in Latin America. Washington, Potomac Books, 1966. xiii, 249 p.
66-018575   301.3298
Latin America -- Population.

HB3581.E885 1995
Europe's population: toward the next century/ edited by Ray Hall, Paul White. London; UCL Press, 1995. xiii, 208 p.
95-020794   304.6/094/0904901   1857281780
Population forecasting -- Europe. Fertility, Human -- Europe. Labor market -- Europe. Europe -- Population.

HB3581.F54
Flinn, Michael W. 1917-
The European demographic system, 1500-1820/ Michael W. Flinn. Baltimore, Md.: Johns Hopkins University Press, c1981. 175 p.
80-019574   304.6/094   0801824265
Europe -- Population -- History.

HB3581.L58 1990
Livi Bacci, Massimo.
Population and nutrition: an essay on European demographic history/ Massimo Livi-Bacci; translated by Tania Croft-Murray with the assistance of Carl Ipsen. Cambridge [England]; Cambridge University Press, 1990. xiv, 149 p.
89-013895   304.6/094   052136325X
Nutrition -- Europe -- History. Food supply -- Europe -- History.   Europe -- Population -- History.

HB3581.M37 1983
McIntosh, C. Alison.
Population policy in western Europe: responses to low fertility in France, Sweden, and West Germany/ C. Alison McIntosh. Armonk, N.Y.: M.E. Sharpe, c1983. viii, 286 p.
82-005840 363.9/1/094 0873322266
Fertility, Human -- Europe. Europe -- Population policy.

HB3583.B73 1996
British population history: from the Black Death to the present day/ edited by Michael Anderson. New York, NY: Cambridge University Press, 1996. v, 421 p.
95-043306 304.6/0941 20 0521578841
Great Britain -- Population -- History.

HB3585.H37 1977
Hatcher, John.
Plague, population, and the English economy, 1348-1530/ prepared by John Hatcher. London: Macmillan, 1977. 95 p.
77-364449 301.32/9/42 0333212932
Plague -- Great Britain -- History. Great Britain -- Population -- History. Great Britain -- Economic conditions.

HB3585.M33 1997
Macfarlane, Alan.
The savage wars of peace: England, Japan and the Malthusian trap/ Alan Macfarlane. Oxford, UK; Blackwell Publishers, 1997. xiii, 427 p.
96-028823 304.6/0941 0631181172
Demographic transition -- England. Demographic transition -- Japan. Malthusianism -- Case studies. England -- Population -- History. Japan -- Population -- History.

HB3589.G84 1997
Guinnane, Timothy.
The vanishing Irish: households, migration, and the rural economy in Ireland, 1850-1914/ Timothy W. Guinnane. Princeton, N.J.: Princeton University Press, c1997. xvii, 335 p.
97-005383 304.6/2/09415 21 0691043078
Households -- Ireland -- History. Ireland -- Population -- History. Ireland -- Emigration and immigration -- History. Ireland -- Rural conditions.

HB3593.C614 2000
Cole, Joshua, 1961-
The power of large numbers: population, politics, and gender in nineteenth-century France/ Joshua Cole. Ithaca: Cornell University Press, 2000. ix, 252 p.
99-046229 304.6/0944/09034 0801437016
Statistics -- France -- History -- 19th century. France -- Population -- History -- 19th century. France -- Population policy -- History -- 19th century.

HB3593.D9 1978
Dyer, Colin L.
Population and society in twentieth century France/ Colin Dyer. New York: Holmes & Meier Publishers, 1978. 247 p.
77-002908 301.32/9/44 0841903085
France -- Population. France -- Social conditions -- 20th century.

HB3617.M82 1945
Myrdal, Alva Reimer, 1902-
Nation and family; the Swedish experiment in democratic family and population policy, by Alva Myrdal. London, K. Paul, Trench, Trubner & Co., ltd. [1945] xiv, 441 p.
45-007805
Family. Public welfare -- Sweden. Sweden -- Population.

HB3631.K58 1998
Kligman, Gail.
The politics of duplicity: controlling reproduction in Ceausescu's Romania/ Gail Kligman. Berkeley: University of California Press, c1998. xv, 358 p.
97-049421 363.9/09498 21 0520210743
Birth control -- Moral and ethical aspects -- Romania. Romania -- Population policy. Romania -- Politics and government -- 1944-1989. Romania -- Social conditions.

HB3633.A3.S26 1995
Sanderson, Warren C.
Population in Asia/ Warren C. Sanderson, Jee-Peng Tan. Washington, D.C.: World Bank, c1995. xvii, 243 p.
94-041460 304.6095 0821331310
Birth control -- Asia. Fertility, Human -- Asia. Asia -- Population.

HB3633.3.A3.G55 1997
Gilbar, Gad G.
Population dilemmas in the Middle East: essays in political demography and economy/ Gad G. Gilbar. London: F. Cass, 1997. xix, 141 p.
97-201137 304.6/0956 0714647063
Family policy -- Middle East. Middle East -- Population -- Economic aspects. Middle East -- Population.

HB3654.A3 C4733 2000
The changing population of China/ edited by Peng Xizhe with Zhigang Guo. Oxford, UK; Blackwell, c2000. xvi, 291 p.
00-030470 304.6/0951 21 0631201920
Human geography -- China.

HB3654.A3.C49813 1994
Chu, Ko-ping.
Population and the environment in China/ Qu Geping and Li Jinchang; translated by Jiang Baozhong & Gu Ran; English-language edition edited by Robert B. Boardman. Boulder: L. Rienner Publishers, 1994. xii, 217 p.
93-040821 304.6/0951 1555874355
Environmental policy -- China. China -- Population policy. China -- Population.

HB3661.A3 A35 1994
African population and capitalism: historical perspectives/ edited by Dennis D. Cordell and Joel W. Gregory. 2nd ed. Madison, Wis.: University of Wisconsin Press, c1994. 304 p.
93-039164 304.6/096 20 0299142744
Africa -- Population -- History. Capitalism -- Africa -- History. Africa -- Economic conditions -- To 1918.

HB3661.A3.F365 1997
Family, population and development in Africa/ edited by Aderanti Adepoju. London; Zed Books, 1997. x, 230 p.
96-022286 304.6/096 1856494659
Family -- Economic aspects -- Africa. Households -- Africa. Africa -- Population. Africa -- Economic conditions -- 1960-

HB3661.7.A3.B33 1994
Bagnall, Roger S.
The demography of Roman Egypt/ Roger S. Bagnall and Bruce W. Frier. Cambridge [England]; Cambridge University Press, 1994. xix, 354 p.
93-032406 304.6/0932 0521461235
Egypt -- Population -- History. Egypt -- Census -- History.

HB3662.5.A3.P64 1984
Population and development in Kenya/ edited by S.H. Ominde with Roushdi A. Henin, and David F. Sly. Nairobi: Heinemann Educational Books, 1984. viii, 129 p.
85-230770 304.6/09676/2 0435957619
Land use -- Kenya. Population forecasting -- Kenya. Kenya -- Population. Kenya -- Economic policy.

HB3665.5.A3.S49 1987
Sex roles, population, and development in West Africa: policy-related studies on work and demographic issues/ edited by Christine Oppong. Portsmouth, N.H.: Heinemann; 1987. xiii, 242 p.
87-027386 304.6/0966 0435080229
Women -- Employment -- Africa, West -- Case studies. Women in development -- Africa, West -- Case studies. Manpower policy -- Africa, West -- Case studies. Africa, West -- Population policy -- Case studies.

HB3675.H84 1986
Hugo, Graeme.
Australia's changing population: trends and implications/ Graeme Hugo. Melbourne; Oxford University Press, 1986. x, 354 p.
87-107294 304.6/0994 0195546806
Population forecasting -- Australia. Australia -- Population. Australia -- Population policy.

HB3711 Business cycles. Economic fluctuations — General works

HB3711.B497 1987
Black, Fischer, 1938-
Business cycles and equilibrium/ Fischer Black. Oxford [Oxfordshire] UK; B. Blackwell, 1987. xi, 180 p.
87-006578 338.5/42 0631157549
Business cycles. Equilibrium (Economics)

HB3711.B936 1997
Business cycles and depressions: an encyclopedia/ editor, David Glasner; consulting editors, Thomas F. Cooley ... [et al.]. New York: Garland Pub., 1997. xv, 779 p.
96-018457 338.5/42/03 0824009444
Business cycles -- Encyclopedias. Depressions -- Encyclopedias.

HB3711.D54 1999
Diebold, Francis X.,
Business cycles: durations, dynamics, and forecasting/ Francis X. Diebold and Glenn D. Rudebusch. Princeton, N.J.: Princeton University Press, c1999. xiii, 420 p.
98-034877 338.5/42/0151 21 0691012180
Business cycles -- Statistical methods. Business forecasting -- Statistical methods.

HB3711.H263 1991
Hall, Robert Ernest, 1943-
Booms and recessions in a noisy economy/ Robert
E. Hall. New Haven: Yale University Press, c1991.
xii, 71 p.
90-044179   338.5/42 20   0300048572
*Recessions. Business cycles. Equilibrium
(Economics)*

HB3711.H265 1990
Hall, Thomas E. 1954-
Business cycles: the nature and causes of economic
fluctuations/ Thomas E. Hall. New York: Praeger,
1990. xiv, 238 p.
89-070955   338.5/42   0275930858
Business cycles. Macroeconomics.

HB3711.H32 1965
Harrod, Roy Forbes, 1900-
The trade cycle; an essay, by R. F. Harrod. New
York, A. M. Kelley, 1965. ix, 234 p.
65-025859
Business cycles.

HB3711.H365
Hayek, Friedrich A. von 1899-
Profits, interest, and investment, and other essays
on the theory of industrial fluctuations, by
Friedrich A. von Hayek ... London, G. Routledge
and Sons, ltd. [1939] viii, 266 p.
40-008258   330.4
Business cycles. Economics.

HB3711.L24 2000
Lamfalussy, Alexandre.
Financial crises in emerging markets: an essay on
financial   globalisation and fragility/ Alexandre
Lamfalussy. New Haven, [Conn.]: Yale University
Press, c2000. xx, 199 p.
99-059157   332 21   0300082304
Business cycles. Financial crises.

HB3711.L43 1991
Leading economic indicators: new approaches and
forecasting records/ edited by Kajal Lahiri and
Geoffrey H. Moore. Cambridge [England];
Cambridge University Press, 1991. xiv, 464 p.
90-001757   330/.01/12   0521371554
*Business cycles. Economic forecasting. Economic
indicators.*

HB3711.L83
Lucas, Robert E.
Studies in business-cycle theory/ Robert E. Lucas,
Jr. Cambridge, Mass.: MIT Press, c1981. x, 300 p.
81-000692   338.5/42   0262120895
Business cycles -- Addresses, essays, lectures.

HB3711.M49 1996
Miron, Jeffrey A.
The economics of seasonal cycles/ Jeffrey A.
Miron. Cambridge, Mass.: MIT Press, c1996. xv,
225 p.
95-052634   338.5/4 20   0262133237
Seasonal variations (Economics) Business cycles.

HB3711.M548 1989
Modern business cycle theory/ edited by Robert J.
Barro. Cambridge, Mass.: Harvard University
Press, 1989. 337 p.
88-028303   338.5/42   0674578600
Business cycles.

HB3711.P377 1999
Perelman, Michael.
The natural instability of markets: expectations,
increasing returns, and the collapse of capitalism/
by Michael Perelman. New York: St. Martin's
Press, 1999. xiv, 188 p.
98-048413   338.5/42   0312221215
Business cycles. Capitalism. Competition.

HB3711.R54 1991
The Risk of economic crisis/ edited and with an
introduction by Martin Feldstein. Chicago:
University of Chicago Press, 1991. x, 197 p.
91-011736   338.5/42   0226240908
*Business cycles -- Congresses. Economic
stabilization -- Congresses. Economic policy --
Congresses. United States -- Economic policy --
1981-1993 -- Congresses.*

HB3711.S4722 1991
Sherman, Howard J.
The business cycle: growth and crisis under
capitalism/ Howard J. Sherman. Princeton, N.J.:
Princeton University Press, c1991. xx, 447 p.
90-043440   338.5/42   0691042624
Business cycles. Capitalism.

HB3714 Business cycles.
Economic fluctuations —
History of theories

HB3714.C57 1994
Clarke, Simon.
Marx's theory of crisis/ Simon Clarke. New York:
Scholarly and Reference Division, St. Martin's P
1994. vii, 293 p.
93-037978   338.5/42   0312120354
*Marx, Karl, -- 1818-1883. Depressions. Marxian
economics. Business cycles.*

HB3714.D67 1993
Dore, M. H. I.
The macrodynamics of business cycles: a
comparative evaluation/ Mohammed H.I. Dore.
Cambridge, MA: B. Blackwell, 1993. xi, 242 p.
92-016330   338.5/42   1557860645
Business cycles -- History.

HB3714.T84 1997
Tvede, Lars, 1957-
Business cycles: the business cycle problem from
John Law to chaos theory/ Lars Tvede.
Amsterdam, the Netherlands: Harwood Academic
Publishers, c1997. vi, 275 p.
99-457380   338.5/42 21   9057020653
*Business cycles. Economics -- History.
Economists.*

HB3716 Business cycles.
Economic fluctuations —
History of crises — General works

HB3716.K76 1999
Krugman, Paul R.
The return of depression economics/ Paul
Krugman. New York: W.W. Norton, 1999. xiv,
176 p.
99-012965   338.5/42   039304839X
*Recessions -- History -- 20th century. Business
cycles -- History -- 20th century. Economic history
-- 1990-*

HB3717 Business cycles.
Economic fluctuations —
History of crises —
Particular crises. By date of crises

HB3717 1857.H87 1987
Huston, James L., 1947-
The panic of 1857 and the coming of the Civil
War/ James L. Huston. Baton Rouge: Louisiana
State University Press, c1987. xviii, 315 p.
87-002705   338.5/42   0807113689
*Depressions -- 1857 -- United States. United
States -- Economic conditions -- To 1865. United
States -- Politics and government -- 1857-1861.*

HB3717 1929.B37 1987
Bernstein, Michael A. 1954-
The Great Depression: delayed recovery and
economic change in America, 1929-1939/ Michael
A. Bernstein. Cambridge [Cambridgeshire];
Cambridge University Press, 1987. xvii, 269 p.
87-006403   338.5/42   0521340489
*Depressions -- 1929 -- United States. United
States -- Economic conditions -- 1918-1945.*

HB3717 1929.B388 1998
Bierman, Harold.
The causes of the 1929 stock market crash: a
speculative orgy or a new era?/ Harold Bierman, Jr.
Westport, Conn.: Greenwood Press, 1998. xi,
162 p.
97-032007   338.5/4/097309043   031330629X
*Depressions -- 1929 -- United States. Stock
exchanges -- United States -- History -- 20th
century. Wall Street -- History -- 20th century.*

HB3717 1929.C47
Chandler, Lester Vernon, 1905-
America's greatest depression, 1929-1941 [by]
Lester V. Chandler. New York, Harper & Row
[1970] vii, 260 p.
79-108407   338.54/0973
Depressions -- 1929 -- United States.

HB3717 1929 .H325 1998
Hall, Thomas E. 1954-
The Great Depression: an international disaster of
perverse economic policies/ Thomas E. Hall and J.
David Ferguson. Ann Arbor: University of
Michigan Press, c1998. xvii, 194 p.
97-021196   338.5/42 21   0472096672
*Depressions -- 1929 -- United States.
Depressions -- 1929 -- Europe. International
economic relations. United States -- Economic
conditions -- 1918-1945. Europe -- Economic
conditions -- 1918-1945.*

HB3717 1929.K55 1986
Kindleberger, Charles Poor, 1910-
The world in depression, 1929-1939/ Charles P.
Kindleberger. Berkeley: University of California
Press, c1986. xxiii, 355 p.
85-008662   338.5/42   0520055918
*Depressions -- 1929. Economic history -- 1918-
1945.*

HB3717 1929.R658 1996
Rothermund, Dietmar.
The Global impact of the Great Depression, 1929-
1939/ Dietmar Rothermund. New York: Routledge,
1996.
95-025780   338.5/42   0415118182
*Depressions -- 1929 -- Developing countries.
Economic history -- 1918-1945. Developing
countries -- Economic conditions.*

HB3717 1929.S73 1996
Starr, Kevin.
Endangered dreams: the Great Depression in California/ Kevin Starr. New York: Oxford University Press, 1996. xii, 402 p.
95-002662   979.4/052   0195100808
Depressions -- 1929 -- California. California -- Economic conditions. California -- Politics and government -- 1850-1950.

HB3717 1929.T45 1976
Temin, Peter.
Did monetary forces cause the Great Depression?/ Peter Temin. New York: Norton, c1976. xiii, 201 p.
75-028367   338.5/42   0393055612
Depressions -- 1929 -- United States. Money supply -- United States. Monetary policy -- United States.

HB3717 1929.T45 1989
Temin, Peter.
Lessons from the Great Depression/ Peter Temin. Cambridge, Mass.: MIT Press, c1989. xv, 193 p.
89-034040   330.9/0437   0262200732
Depressions -- 1929 -- Great Britain. Depressions -- 1929 -- France. Depressions -- 1929 -- Germany.

HB3717 1929.K588 2001
Klein, Maury,
Rainbow's end: the crash of 1929/ Maury Klein. Oxford [England]; Oxford University Press, 2001. xx, 345 p.
2001-036069   338.5/4/097309043   21
0195135164
Depressions -- 1929. Depressions -- 1929 -- United States. Stock Market Crash, 1929.

HB3717 1929.S55 2002
Smiley, Gene,
Rethinking the Great Depression/ Gene Smiley. Chicago: I.R. Dee, c2002. xii, 179 p.
2002-023761   330.973/0917 21   1566634717
Depressions -- 1929. Economic history -- 1918-1945. Business cycles -- History -- 20th century.

HB3722 Business cycles. Economic fluctuations — Relation to special topics — Finance and cycles. Financial crises

HB3722.A36 1999
Allen, Roy E.,
Financial crises and recession in the global economy/ Roy E. Allen. 2nd ed. Cheltenham, UK; Edward Elgar, 1999. xvi, 212 p.
99-021908   338.5/42 21   1840646322
Financial crises. Recessions. Economic history -- 1990-

HB3722.K73 1992
Krainer, Robert E.
Finance in a theory of the business cycle: production and distribution in a debt and equity economy/ Robert E. Krainer. Cambridge, MA: Blackwell, 1992. xx, 245 p.
91-039967   338.5/42   1557863288
Business cycles. Finance.

HB3722.S67 2000
Soros, George.
Open society: reforming global capitalism/ George Soros. New York: Public Affairs, c2000. xxix, 369 p.
00-042542   332/.042 21   1586480197
Financial crises. Financial crises -- Social aspects. Capitalism -- Social aspects.

HB3722.W43 2000
Weathering the storm: Taiwan, its neighbors, and the Asian financial crisis/ Peter C.Y. Chow, Bates Gill, editors. Washington D.C.: Brookings Institution Press, c2000. xiii, 234 p.
00-008805   330.95/0429 21   0815713991
Financial crises -- Taiwan. Financial crises -- East Asia. East Asia -- Economic conditions.

HB3729 Business cycles. Economic fluctuations — Long waves. Kondratieff cycles

HB3729.B47 1990
Berry, Brian Joe Lobley, 1934-
Long-wave rhythms in economic development and political behavior/ Brian J.L. Berry. Baltimore: Johns Hopkins University Press, c1991. xiii, 241 p.
90-004586   338.9   080184035X
Long waves (Economics) Business cycles -- Political aspects. Economic development.

HB3730 Business cycles. Economic fluctuations — Economic forecasting — General works

HB3730.B57 1990
Block, Fred L.
Postindustrial possibilities: a critique of economic discourse/ Fred Block. Berkeley: University of California Press, c1990. x, 227 p.
89-029622   330/.01/12   0520068130
Economic forecasting.

HB3730.H54 1992
Hildebrand, George, 1930-
Business cycle indicators and measures: a complete guide to interpreting the key economic indicators/ George Hildebrand. Chicago, Ill.: Probus Pub. Co., c1992. ix, 277 p.
94-112532   155738410X
Business forecasting. Business cycles -- United States.

HB3730.P54 1998
Pindyck, Robert S.
Econometric models and economic forecasts/ Robert S. Pindyck, Daniel L. Rubinfeld. 4th ed. Boston, Mass.: Irwin/McGraw-Hill, c1998. xx, 634 p.
97-010357   330/.01/5195 21   0070502080
Economic forecasting -- Econometric models. Econometrics.

HB3730.T55 1996
Thurow, Lester C.
The future of capitalism: how today's economic forces shape tomorrow's world/ Lester C. Thurow. 1st ed. New York: W. Morrow, c1996. x, 385 p.
95-042443   330.12/2 20   0688129692
Economic forecasting. Capitalism -- Forecasting. Technological innovations -- Economic aspects -- Forecasting.

HB3730.T93 1999
Twenty-first century economics: perspectives of socioeconomics for a changing world/ edited by William E. Halal and Kenneth B. Taylor. New York: St. Martin's Press, 1999. xxvii, 414 p.
98-012393   330.9/001/12   0312161999
Economic forecasting. Twenty-first century -- Forecasts. Social prediction.

HB3730.U49 2001
Understanding economic forecasts/ edited by David F. Hendry and Neil R. Ericsson. Cambridge, Mass.: MIT Press, c2001. xvii, 207 p.
2001-042740   330/.01/12 21   0262083043
Economic forecasting.

HB3730.W66 1995
World index of economic forecasts: including industrial tendency surveys/ edited by Robert Fildes. Aldershot, Hampshire, England; Gower, c1995. viii, 663 p.
94-044989   338.5/443/025   0566074885
Economic forecasting -- Directories.

HB3743-3812 Business cycles. Economic fluctuations — By region or country

HB3743.A45 1995
Alesina, Alberto.
Partisan politics, divided government, and the economy/ Alberto Alesina and Howard Rosenthal. Cambridge [England]; Cambridge University Press, 1995. xiii, 280 p.
93-048512   338.5/42   0521430291
Business cycles -- Political aspects -- United States -- History -- 20th century. Presidents -- United States -- Election -- History -- 20th century. Representative government and representation -- United States -- History -- 20th century. United States -- Economic policy -- Decision making.

HB3743.H52 1987
Hibbs, Douglas A., 1944-
The American political economy: macroeconomics and electoral politics/ Douglas A. Hibbs, Jr. Cambridge, Mass.: Harvard University Press, 1987. xiii, 404 p.
87-000155   338.973   0674027353
Business cycles -- Political aspects -- United States. Elections -- United States. United States -- Economic policy -- 1981-1993. United States -- Economic conditions -- 1981-

HB3743.N53 1994
Niemira, Michael P., 1955-
Forecasting financial and economic cycles/ Michael P. Niemira, Philip A. Klein. New York: Wiley, c1994. xvi, 526 p.
93-027196   338.5/442   0471845442
Business cycles -- United States. Economic forecasting -- United States. Business cycles. United States -- Economic conditions -- 1918-1945. United States -- Economic conditions -- 1945-

HB3743.P67 1988
Political business cycles: the political economy of money, inflation, and unemployment/ edited by Thomas D. Willett. Durham [N.C.]: Duke University Press, 1988. xxii, 521 p.
88-007148   338.5/42/0973   082230824X
Business cycles -- Political aspects -- United States. Unemployment -- Effect of inflation on -- United States. Monetary policy -- United States.

HB3746.C66 1996
Confronting southern poverty in the Great Depression: The report on economic conditions of the South with related documents/ edited with an introduction by David L. Carlton, Peter A. Coclanis. Boston: Bedford Books of St. Martin's Press, 1996. viii, 168 p.
95-080791   0312114974
Depressions -- 1929 -- Southern States. Poverty -- Southern States -- History -- 20th century.

HB3808.A858 2000
The Asian financial crisis and the architecture of global finance/ edited by Gregory W. Noble and John Ravenhill. New York: Cambridge University Press, 2000. xvi, 310 p.
00-031239   332/.095   0521790913
Financial crises -- Asia. International finance. Asia -- Economic conditions -- 1945-

HB3808.A859 2000
The Asian financial crisis: lessons for a resilient Asia/ edited by Wing Thye Woo, Jeffrey D. Sachs, and Klaus Schwab. Cambridge, Mass.: MIT Press, c2000. x, 280 p.
00-033255   330.95 21   026219452X
Financial crises -- Asia -- Case studies. Asia -- Economic policy -- Case studies.

HB3812.T36 2000
Tan, Gerald.
The Asian currency crisis/ Gerald Tan. Singapore: Times Academic Press, 2000. xi, 283 p.
99-506202   332/.042/09509049 9812101578
Financial crises -- Asia, Southeastern. Financial crises -- East Asia.

HC Economic History and Conditions

HC10 Societies. Serials

HC10.E3746
Economic freedom of the world ... annual report. [Vancouver?]: Fraser Institute, <c1997- >
98-641586   330.9/005 21
Economic surveys -- Periodicals. Economic development -- Statistics -- Periodicals. Economic history -- 1990 ---Periodicals.

HC10.E375
Economic handbook of the world. New York: Published for the Center for Social Analysis of c1981-c1982. 2 v.
81-643338   330.9/005
Economic history -- 1971-1990 -- Handbooks, manuals, etc.

HC10.W7975
World business & economic review.   London: Kogan Page, [1994-]
94-033384
World politics -- 1989- -- Periodicals. Economic history -- 1990- -- Periodicals.

HC10.W7978
World economic data. Santa Barbara, Calif.: ABC-CLIO, [c1987-]
88-651959   310 p.
Economic indicators -- Periodicals.

HC12 Addresses, essays, lectures

HC12.C32
Carus-Wilson, Eleanora Mary,
Essays in economic history; reprints, edited for the Economic History Society by E. M. Carus-Wilson. New York, St. Martin's Press, 1966 [c1954-6] 3 v.
67-000220   330.9
Economic history.   Great Britain -- Economic conditions.

HC13 Congresses

HC13.L35 1998
Lal, Deepak.
Unintended consequences: the impact of factor endowments, culture, and politics on long run economic performance/ Deepak Lal. Cambridge, Mass.: MIT Press, c1998. x, 287 p.
98-038290   330.9 21   0262122103
Economic history -- Congresses. Social history -- Congresses. Individualism -- Congresses.

HC15 Dictionaries. Encyclopedias

HC15.D86 1996
Dunster, Julian A. 1954-
Dictionary of natural resource management/ Julian and Katherine Dunster. Vancouver, BC: UBC Press, c1996. xv, 363 p.
96-158111   077480503X
Natural   resources -- Management -- Dictionaries.

HC21 General works

HC21.C33 2003
Cameron, Rondo E.
A concise economic history of the world: from paleolithic times to the present. 4th ed./ Rondo Cameron , Larry Neal. New York: Oxford University Press, 2003. xvi, 463 p.
2001-051380   330.9 21   0195127056
Economic history.

HC21.D5
Dillard, Dudley D.
Economic development of the North Atlantic community; historical introduction to modern economics [by] Dudley Dillard. Englewood Cliffs, N.J., Prentice-Hall [1967] viii, 747 p.
67-015169   330/.0918/21
Europe -- Economic conditions. United States -- Economic conditions.

HC21.H84 1993
Hugill, Peter J.
World trade since 1431: geography, technology, and capitalism/ Peter J. Hugill. Baltimore: Johns Hopkins University Press, c1993. xxiii, 376 p.
92-006765   382/.09 0801842417
Economic history. Capitalism -- History. International trade -- History.

HC21.M285 2001
Maddison, Angus.
The world economy: a millennial perspective/ Angus Maddison Paris, France: Development Centre of the Organi c2001. 383 p.
2001-438142   9264186085
Economic   history. International economic relations -- History Population -- History

HC26 Theory. Method. Relation to other subjects

HC26.H5
Hicks, John Richard, 1904-
A theory of economic history, by John Hicks. Oxford, Clarendon P., 1969. ix, 181 p.
70-437823   330/.09 0198282478
Economic history. Economics -- History.

HC26.K39 1984
Kaye, Harvey J.
The British Marxist historians: an introductory analysis/ Harvey J. Kaye. New York: Polity Press, 1984. xii, 316 p.
84-026304   335.4/072041 0745600158
Economic history -- Historiography. Historical materialism. Marxian historiography -- Great Britain.

HC29 Biography — Collective

HC29.L36 1993
Landrum, Gene N.
Profiles of genius: thirteen creative men who changed the world/ Gene N. Landrum. Buffalo, N.Y.: Prometheus Books, 1993. 263 p.
93-018637   338/.04/0922 0879758325
Businesspeople -- Biography. Creative ability in business -- Case studies. Success in business -- Case studies.

HC29.R66 1992
Room, Adrian.
Corporate eponymy: a biographical dictionary of the persons behind the names of major American, British, European, and Asian businesses/ by Adrian Room. Jefferson, N.C.: McFarland & Co., c1992. xx, 280 p.
92-053502   338.7/4/0922 0899506798
Businesspeople -- Biography -- Dictionaries. Industrialists -- Biography -- Dictionaries. Business names -- Dictionaries.

HC31-39 History — By period — Antiquity

HC31.F5x 1985
Finley, M. I. 1912-
The ancient economy/ by M.I. Finley. Berkeley: University of California Press, 1985, c1973. 262 p.
86-672785   330.938 0520054520
Economic history -- To 500.

HC31.W42213 1976
Weber, Max, 1864-1920.
The agrarian sociology of ancient civilizations/ Max Weber; translated by R. I. Frank. London: NLB; 1976. 421 p.
76-370998   330.9/01   0902308084
Economic history -- To 500. Agriculture -- History. Social history -- To 500. Middle East -- Economic conditions.

HC37.A8813 1977b
Austin, M. M.
Economic and social history of ancient Greece: an introduction/ M. M. Austin and P. Vidal-Naquet; translated and revised by M. M. Austin. Berkeley: University of California Press, 1977. xv, 397 p.
73-090665   309.1/38   0520026586
Greece -- Economic conditions -- To 146 B.C. Greece -- Social conditions -- To 146 B.C. Greece -- Colonies.

HC37.F56
Finley, M. I. 1912-
Economy and society in ancient Greece/ by M.I. Finley; edited with an introduction by Brent D. Shaw and Richard P. Saller. New York: Viking Press, 1982. xxvi, 326 p.
81-051886   330.938   0670288470
Greece -- Economic conditions -- To 146 B.C. -- Addresses, essays, lectures. Greece -- Social conditions -- To 146 B.C. -- Addresses, essays, lectures. Greece -- History -- To 146 B.C. -- Addresses, essays, lectures.

HC37.S7
Starr, Chester G., 1914-
The economic and social growth of early Greece, 800-500 B.C./ Chester G. Starr. New York: Oxford University Press, 1977. 267 p.
76-057265   330.9/38/02   0195022238
Greece -- Economic conditions -- To 146 B.C. Greece -- Social conditions.

HC39.A9 1994
Aubert, Jean-Jacques, 1958-
Business managers in ancient Rome: a social and economic study of Institores, 200 B.C.-A.D. 250/ by Jean-Jacques Aubert. Leiden; E.J. Brill, 1994. xv, 520 p.
94-017201   658/.00937   9004100385
Management -- Rome. Commercial agents -- Rome. Farm management -- Rome. Rome -- Economic conditions.

HC39.C53
Cipolla, Carlo M.,
The economic decline of empires; edited with an introd. by Carlo M. Cipolla. London, Methuen [1970] 280 p.
79-019611   330/.09   0416160905
Economic history -- Addresses, essays, lectures.

HC39.D886 1990
Duncan-Jones, Richard.
Structure and scale in the Roman economy/ Richard Duncan-Jones. Cambridge; Cambridge University Press, 1990. xvi, 245 p.
89-007345   330.937   0521354773
Rome -- Economic conditions.

HC39.J65 1974
Jones, A. H. M. 1904-1970.
The Roman economy; studies in ancient economic and administrative history. Edited by P. A. Brunt. Totowa, N.J., Rowman and Littlefield [1974] xi, 450 p.
73-005960   330.9/37/6   0874711940
Rome -- Economic conditions. Rome -- Politics and government -- 284-476.

HC39.M67 1996
Morley, Neville.
Metropolis and hinterland: the city of Rome and the Italian economy, 200 B.C.-A.D. 200/ Neville Morley. Cambridge [England]; Cambridge University Press, 1996. xi, 211 p.
95-051652   330.937/6   0521560063
Agriculture -- Economic aspects -- Rome. Urbanization -- Rome. Rome -- Economic conditions. Rome -- Social conditions. Italy -- Economic conditions.

HC41 History — By period — Medieval, 500-1500

HC41.A28 1989
Abu-Lughod, Janet L.
Before European hegemony: the world system A.D. 1250-1350/ Janet L. Abu-Lughod. New York: Oxford University Press, 1989. xvi, 443 p.
88-025580   330.94/017   0195058860
Economic history -- Medieval, 500-1500. International trade -- History. Cities and towns, Medieval.

HC41.F6913 1976b
Fourquin, Guy.
Lordship and feudalism in the Middle Ages/ by Guy Fourquin; translated by Iris and A. L. Lytton Sells. New York: Pica Press, 1976. 253 p.
75-011141   330.9/4/01   0876637187
Economic history -- Medieval, 500-1500. Feudalism.

HC51-60.5 History — By period — Modern

HC51.B38313 2001
Beaud, Michel.
A history of capitalism, 1500-2000/ Michel Beaud; translated by Tom Dickman & Anny Lefebvre. New York: Monthly Review Press, 2001.
2001-045221   330.12/2 21   1583670408
Economic history. Capitalism -- History.

HC51.B65 1972
Boulding, Kenneth Ewart, 1910-
Economic imperialism; a book of readings. Edited by Kenneth E. Boulding and Tapan Mukerjee. Ann Arbor, University of Michigan Press [1972] xviii, 338 p.
74-146490   330.9   0472168304
Economic history -- Addresses, essays, lectures. Imperialism -- Addresses, essays, lectures.

HC51.B7
Bruchey, Stuart Weems.
The roots of American economic growth, 1607-1861; an essay in social causation, by Stuart Bruchey. New York, Harper & Row [1965] xiii, 234 p.
64-025110   338.0973
United States -- Economic conditions -- To 1865.

HC51.H44 2001
Heilbroner, Robert L.
The making of economic society/ Robert Heilbroner and William Milberg. 11th ed. Upper Saddle River, N.J.: Prentice Hall, c2002. xviii, 206 p.
2001-021124   330.9 21   0130910503
Economic history.

HC51.K49 1996
Kindleberger, Charles Poor, 1910-
World economic primacy, 1500 to 1990/ Charles P. Kindleberger. New York: Oxford University Press, 1996. xiv, 269 p.
95-010091   330.9   0195099028
Economic history.

HC51.P37 1984
Parker, William Nelson.
Europe, America, and the wider world: essays on the economic history of Western capitalism/ William N. Parker. Cambridge [Cambridgeshire]; Cambridge University Press, 1984-1991. 2 v.
84-003161   330.9181/2   0521254671
Economic history. Capitalism -- History.

HC51.R615 1993
Robinson, Richard, 1924-
Business history of the world: a chronology/ compiled by Richard Robinson. Westport, Conn.: Greenwood Press, 1993. xii, 562 p.
93-025476   330.9   031326094X
Economic history -- Chronology. Business -- History -- Chronology. Industries -- History -- Chronology.

HC51.W28 1974 vol. 1
Wallerstein, Immanuel Maurice, 1930-
Capitalist agriculture and the origins of the European world-economy in the sixteenth century [by] Immanuel Wallerstein. New York, Academic Press [1974] xiv, 410 p.
73-005318   330.9/4/022   0127859209
Economic history -- 16th century. Capitalism. Agriculture -- Economic aspects -- Europe -- History -- 16th century. Europe -- Economic conditions -- 16th century.

HC53.C57
Conrad, Alfred H.
The economics of slavery, and other studies in econometric history, by Alfred H. Conrad and John R. Meyer. Chicago, Aldine Pub. Co. [1964] ix, 241 p.
64-015914   339.2
Slavery. Econometrics -- Case studies. Great Britain -- Industries. United States -- Economic conditions.

HC53.M613 1967
Moraze, Charles, 1913-
The triumph of the middle classes: a study of European values in the nineteenth century/ Charles Moraze. -- Cleveland: World Pub. Co., [1967, c1966] xv, 414 p.
67-013834   901.9/34
Middle class -- Europe. Economic history -- 1750-1918. Social history -- 19th century.

HC53.P6 1957
Polanyi, Karl, 1886-1964.
The Great transformation/ Karl Polanyi; foreword by Robert M. MacIver. Boston: Beacon Press, 1971, 1957. xii, 315 p.
57-009208   330.9
Economic history -- 1750-1918. Social history. Economics -- History.

HC54.F565 1983
Foreman-Peck, James.
A history of the world economy: international economic relations since 1850/ James Foreman-Peck. Totowa, N.J.: Barnes & Noble, 1983. xiii, 394 p.
82-024295   337/.09   0389203378
Economic history -- 20th century. Economic history -- 1750-1918. International economic relations -- History.

HC54.H213 1975
Habermas, Jurgen.
Legitimation crisis/ by Jurgen Habermas; translated by Thomas McCarthy. Boston: Beacon Press, [1975] xxiv, 166 p.
74-017586 301/.045 0807015202
Capitalism. Economic history -- 1971-1990. Social history -- 20th century.

HC54.L85
Lundberg, Erik, 1907-
Instability and economic growth. New Haven, Yale University Press, 1968. xv, 433 p.
68-013917 330.9/04
Economic history -- 20th century. Business cycles. Economic development.

HC54.M255 1995
Maddison, Angus.
Monitoring the world economy, 1820-1992/ by Angus Maddison. Paris: Development Centre of the Organisation for Econo c1995. 255 p.
96-122432 9264145494
Economic history -- 20th century. Economic history -- 19th century.

HC54.M3513 1999
Mazier, Jacques.
When economic crises endure/ Jacques Mazier, Maurice Basle, Jean-Francois Vidal; translated by Myriam Rosen. Armonk, N.Y.: M.E. Sharpe, c1999. xxxiii, 261 p.
98-030972 330.944/08 21 156324568X
Economic history -- 20th century. Depressions. France -- Economic conditions -- 20th century.

HC55.B25
Banks, Ferdinand E.
The economics of natural resources/ Ferdinand E. Banks. New York: Plenum Press, c1976. xiii, 267 p.
76-025583 333.7 0306309262
Natural resources. Raw materials. Economics.

HC56.H3713
Hardach, Gerd, 1941-
The First World War, 1914-1918/ Gerd Hardach. Berkeley: University of California Press, c1977. xvi, 328 p.
75-017142 940.3/113 0520030605
World War, 1914-1918 -- Economic aspects.

HC57.D36 1975
Davis, Joseph Stancliffe, 1885-
The world between the wars, 1919-39: an economist's view/ Joseph S. Davis. Baltimore: Johns Hopkins University Press, [1975] viii, 436 p.
74-006821 330.9/04 0801814502
Economic history -- 1918-1945. Depressions -- 1929. Business cycles.

HC57.K4 1988
Keynes, John Maynard, 1883-1946.
The economic consequences of the peace. Harcourt, Brace, and Howe, c1920. 298 p.
20-002057 940.53/14
Economic history -- 1918-1945. World War, 1914-1918 -- Economic aspects.

HC57.K45
Keynes, John Maynard, 1883-1946.
Essays in persuasion, by John Maynard Keynes ... New York, Harcourt, Brace and Company [1932] xiii, 376 p.
31-028686 330.904
Economic history -- 1918-1945. Economic conditions -- 1918- Currency question.

HC57.R57 1971
Robbins, Lionel Robbins, 1898-1984.
The great depression, by Lionel Robbins. Freeport, N.Y., Books for Libraries Press [1971] xiv, 238 p.
75-150198 330.9/04 0836957113
Economic history -- 1918-1945. Currency question. Depressions -- 1929. United States -- Economic policy -- To 1933.

HC57.S75 1968
Stolper, Gustav, 1888-1947.
This age of fable; the political and economic world we live in. New York, Greenwood Press [1968] xi, 369 p.
68-057641 330
Economics. Political science. Economic history -- 1918-1945.

HC57.Z5413 1990
Ziebura, Gilbert.
World economy and world politics, 1924-1931: from reconstruction to collapse/ Gilbert Ziebura; translated from the German by Bruce Little. Oxford, UK; Berg; 1990. xiv, 190 p.
89-035884 330.9/042 0854966463
Economic history -- 1918-1945. World politics -- 1919-1932. Depressions -- 1929.

HC58.M53 1977
Milward, Alan S.
War, economy, and society, 1939-1945/ Alan S. Milward. Berkeley: University of California Press, c1977. xiv, 395 p.
76-040823 940.53/14 0520033388
World War, 1939-1945 -- Economic aspects.

HC59.A7852513 1994
Amin, Samir.
Re-reading the postwar period: an intellectual itinerary/ Samir Amin; translated by Michael Wolfers. New York: Monthly Review Press, c1994. 256 p.
94-014480 330.9 0853458936
Economic history -- 1945- World politics -- 1945- Marxian economics.

HC59.D69 1969b
Drucker, Peter Ferdinand, 1909-
The age of discontinuity; guidelines to our changing society, by Peter F. Drucker. New York, Harper & Row [1969] xiii, 402 p.
71-007708 309.1/04
Economic history -- 1945-1971. Social history -- 1945-

HC59.L54
The Limits to growth; a report for the Club of Rome's project on the predicament of mankind [by] Donella H. Meadows [and others] New York, Universe Books [1972] 205 p.
73-187907 330.9/04 0876631650
Economic history -- 1971-1990. Economic development. Social history -- 1945-

HC59.M458 1974
Mesarovic, Mihajlo D.
Mankind at the turning point: the second report to the Club of Rome/ Mihajlo Mesarovic and Eduard Pestel. New York: Dutton, 1974. xiii, 210 p.
74-016787 330.9/04 052515230X
Economic history -- 1971-1990. Food supply. Population.

HC59.N415 1993
The New global economy in the information age: reflections on our changing world/ Martin Carnoy ... [et al.]. University Park, Pa.: Pennsylvania State University Press, c1993. 170 p.
92-033652 330.9/04 0271009101
Economic history -- 20th century. World politics -- 20th century. Information society.

HC59.P639 1989
Poverty amidst plenty: world political economy and distributive justice/ edited by Edward Weisband. Boulder, Colo.: Westview Press, 1989. xiv, 270 p.
87-012829 330.9/048 0813305233
Economic history -- 1945- Distributive justice. Poor.

HC59.R626 1968
Roll, Eric, 1907-
The world after Keynes; an examination of the economic order [by] Eric Roll. New York, F. A. Praeger [1968] xiii, 193 p.
67-022295 330.9/04
Economic history -- 1945-1971. Economic policy. International economic relations.

HC59.S494
Shonfield, Andrew, 1917-
Modern capitalism; the changing balance of public and private power. London, Oxford University Press, 1965. xvi, 456 p.
65-028179 330.904
Economic history -- 1945- Economic policy.

HC59.S5375 1987
Singer, Max, 1931-
Passage to a human world/ Max Singer. Indianapolis, Ind.: Hudson Institute, c1987. xv, 390 p.
87-082068 338.5/443 1558130004
Economic history -- 1971-1990. Economic forecasting. Natural resources.

HC59.S564 1999
Solomon, Robert.
The transformation of the world economy/ Robert Solomon. 2nd ed. New York: St. Martin's Press, 1999. xii, 217 p.
98-053537 330.9/048 21 0312221126
Economic history -- 1970-1990. Economic history -- 1990-

HC59.S734
State of the world: a Worldwatch Institute report on progress toward a sustainable society. New York: Norton, [c1984-]
85-643206 330.9/005
Economic history -- 1971-1990 -- Periodicals. Economic history -- 1990- -- Periodicals. Economic policy -- Periodicals.

HC59.T36 2000
Teeple, Gary.
Globalization and the decline of social reform: into the twenty-first century/ Gary Teeple. Aurora, Ontario: Garamond Press; c2000. x, 239 p.
2001-265859 330.12/2 21 1551930269
Economic history -- 1945- Capitalism. Socialism.

HC59.T5157 1992
Thurow, Lester C.
Head to head: the coming economic battle among Japan, Europe, and America/ Lester Thurow. New York: Morrow, c1992. 336 p.
91-033300   337.52   0688111505
Economic history -- 1990- Economic forecasting. International economic relations. European Economic Community countries -- Economic policy. United States -- Economic policy -- 1981-1993. Japan -- Economic policy -- 1989-

HC59.15.A4313 1993
Albert, Michel.
Capitalism vs. capitalism: how America's obsession with individual achievement and short-term profit has led it to the brink of collapse/ Michel Albert; introduction by Felix G. Rohatyn; translated by Paul Haviland. New York: Four Walls Eight Windows, c1993. xix, 260 p.
93-004542   330.973   1568580045
Economic history -- 1990- Capitalism. United States -- Economic conditions -- 1981- European Economic Community countries -- Economic conditions.

HC59.15.D78 1993
Drucker, Peter Ferdinand, 1909-
Post-capitalist society/ Peter F. Drucker. New York, NY: HarperBusiness, c1993. 232 p.
92-054323   330.9/049   0887306209
Economic history -- 1990- Capitalism. World politics -- 1989-

HC59.15.G564 1994
Global trends: the world almanac of development and peace/ edited by Ingomar Hauchler and Paul M. Kennedy; [translated by Diet Simon]. New York: Continuum, 1994. 416 p.
94-020985   909.82/9   0826406742
Economic history -- 1990- Economic forecasting.

HC59.15.H33 1998
Hammond, Allen L.
Which world?: scenarios for the 21st Century/ Allen Hammond. Washington, DC: Island Press, c1998. xiv, 306 p.
98-013589   330.9/051 21   1559635754
Economic forecasting. World politics -- -1989- - Forecasting. Twenty-first century -- Forecasts.

HC59.15.P33 1999
Pahre, Robert.
Leading questions: how hegemony affects the international political economy/ Robert Pahre. Ann Arbor: University of Michigan Press, c1999. xv, 277 p.
98-040162   337 21   0472109707
Economic history -- 1990- International economic relations.

HC59.69.D45 1992
Development and democratization in the Third World: myths, hopes, and realities/ edited by Kenneth E. Bauzon. Washington: Crane Russak, c1992. xix, 344 p.
92-006894   338.9/009172/4   0844817228
Economic development. Democracy Developing countries. Democratization Developing countries. Developing countries. Economic conditions.

HC59.69.S63
Social indicators of development. Washington, D.C.: World Bank, c1996.
88-647378   306/.09172/4 19
Economic indicators -- Developing countries -- Periodicals. Social indicators -- Developing countries -- Periodicals. Developing Countries -- Periodicals.

HC59.7.A714 2001
Adams, W. M.
Green development: environment and sustainability in the South/ W.M. Adams. 2nd ed. London; Routledge, 2001.
2001-016595   338.9/27/091724 21   0415147662
Sustainable development -- Developing countries. Green movement -- Developing countries.

HC59.7.A7777 1990
Amin, Samir.
Maldevelopment: anatomy of a global failure/ Samir Amin; [translation by Michael Wolfers]. Tokyo: United Nations University Press; 1990. 244 p.
89-070607   338.9/009172/4   0862329302
Economic history -- 1971-1990.   Africa -- Economic conditions -- 1960- Developing countries -- Economic policy.

HC59.7.A7784 2001
Amsden, Alice H.
The rise of "the rest": challenges to the west from late-industrializing economies/ Alice H. Amsden. Oxford; Oxford University Press, 2001. vi, 405 p.
00-039947   338.9/009172/4   0195139690
Industrialization -- Developing countries -- History. Competition, International.

HC59.7.A8335 1993
Arnold, Guy.
The end of the Third World/ Guy Arnold. New York: St. Martin's Press, 1993. viii, 232 p.
93-015803   330.9172/4   0312100922
Developing countries -- Economic conditions.

HC59.7.A83358 1997
Arnold, Guy.
The resources of the Third World/ by Guy Arnold. New York: Cassell, 1997.
96-034108   333.7/09172/2   0304332496
Natural resources -- Developing countries. Developing countries -- Population.

HC59.7.A923 1995
Auty, R. M.
Patterns of development: resources, policy and economic growth/ Richard M. Auty. London; Edward Arnold, 1995. xii, 300 p.
95-176209   0340625112
Income distribution -- Developing countries. Economic development. Economic development -- Environmental aspects. Developing countries -- Economic policy. Developing countries -- Economic conditions.

HC59.7.B24 1982
Bagchi, Amiya Kumar.
The political economy of underdevelopment/ Amiya Kumar Bagchi. Cambridge; Cambridge University Press, 1982. viii, 280 p.
81-010237   330.9172/4   0521240247
Developing countries -- Economic conditions.

HC59.7.B3873 1999
Bello, Walden F.
Dark victory: the United States and global poverty/ Walden Bello with Shea Cunningham and Bill Rau; foreword by Susan George. London: Pluto Press; 1999. xii, 162 p.
98-047956   337.73   0935028765
Structural adjustment (Economic policy) -- Developing countries. Poverty -- Developing countries. Supply-side economics -- United States. Developing countries -- Foreign economic relations -- United States. United States -- Economic policy -- 1981-1993. United States -- Foreign economic relations -- Developing countries.

HC59.7.B576 1993
Boom, crisis, and adjustment: the macroeconomic experience of developing countries/ I.M.D. Little ... [et al.]. New York: Published for the World Bank [by] Oxford Univers c1993. x, 455 p.
93-027208   339.5/09172/4   0195208919
Structural adjustment (Economic policy) -- Developing countries -- Case studies. Economic stabilization -- Developing countries -- Case studies. Developing countries -- Economic policy -- Case studies.

HC59.7.B587 1990
Boserup, Ester.
Economic and demographic relationships in development/ Ester Boserup; essays selected and introduced by T. Paul Schultz. Baltimore: Johns Hopkins University Press, c1990. vi, 307 p.
89-035239   338.9/09172/4   0801839297
Economic development. Population. Developing countries -- Economic conditions. Developing countries -- Population.

HC59.7.B6893 1994
Brown, M. Leann.
Developing countries and regional economic cooperation/ M. Leann Brown. Westport, Conn.: Praeger, 1994. ix, 174 p.
94-008314   338.9/09172/4   0275949605
Developing countries -- Economic integration -- Case studies. Developing countries -- Economic policy -- Decision making -- Case studies.

HC59.7.B867 2000
Business Monitor International guide to the world's major emerging economies: country analysis and forecast reports, 2000-2002. Chicago, Ill.: Fitzroy Dearborn, 2000. 2 v.
2001-274592   330.9172/4   1579582834
Economic forecasting -- Developing countries. Developing countries -- Economic conditions.

HC59.7.C337 1990
The Challenge to the South/ the report of the South Commission. Oxford, [England]; Oxford University Press, 1990. xv, 325 p.
90-044041   338.9/0091724   0198773110
Democracy. International cooperation. Developing countries -- Economic policy -- Citizen participation.

HC59.7.C595 1994
Colman, David.
Economics of change in less developed countries/ David Colman and Frederick Nixson. 3rd ed. New York: Harvester Wheatsheaf, 1994. xvii, 469 p.
94-026473   330.9172/4 20   0745013201
Economic development.

HC59.7.D4453 1998
Development and underdevelopment: the political economy of global inequality/ edited by Mitchell A. Seligson and John T. Passe-Smith. Boulder, Colo.: Lynne Rienner Publishers, 1998. xi, 468 p.
98-014864   338.9   155587794X
Economic development. Income distribution. Capitalism. Developing countries -- Economic conditions.

HC59.7.D513 1990
Dictionary of development: Third World economy, environment, society/ edited by Brian W.W. Welsh & Pavel Butorin. New York: Garland Pub., 1990. 2 v.
90-003051   338.9/009172/4   0824014472
Developing countries -- Economic policy. Developing countries -- Social policy.

HC59.7.E277 1994
Economic development/ edited by Enzo Grilli and Dominick Salvatore. Westport, Conn.: Greenwood Press, 1994. xvii, 630 p.
93-030449   338.9/009172/4   0313280479
Economic development. Developing countries -- Economic policy.

HC59.7.E313
Economic stabilization in developing countries/ William R. Cline and Sidney Weintraub, editors; [authors] William R. Cline ... [et al.]. Washington, D.C.: Brookings Institution, c1981. xv, 517 p.
80-026363   338.9/009172/4   0815714661
Economic stabilization -- Developing countries. Developing countries -- Economic policy.

HC59.7.G747 1999
Griffin, Keith B.
Alternative strategies for economic development/ Keith Griffin. 2nd ed. New York: St. Martin's Press, in association with OECD Development xxviii, 269 p.
99-018657   338.9/009172/6 21   0312223404
Economic development.

HC59.7.G749 1987
Griffin, Keith B.
World hunger and the world economy: and other essays in development economics/ Keith Griffin. New York: Holmes & Meier, 1987. xvi, 274 p.
86-033626   330.9172/4   0841911282
Hunger. Debts, External -- Developing countries. Agriculture -- Economic aspects -- Developing countries. Developing countries -- Economic conditions. Developing countries -- Social conditions.

HC59.7.H275 1990
Haggard, Stephan.
Pathways from the periphery: the politics of growth in the newly industrializing countries/ Stephan Haggard. Ithaca, N.Y.: Cornell University Press, 1990. xi, 276 p.
90-032300   338.9/009172/4   0801424992
Industrialization -- Developing countries. Economic development. Developing countries -- Economic policy.

HC59.7.H35
Haq, Mahbub ul, 1934-
The poverty curtain: choices for the third world/ Mahbub ul Haq. New York: Columbia University Press, 1976. xvii, 247 p.
76-007470   330.9/172/4   0231040628
Poverty. Economic development. Developing countries -- Economic conditions.

HC59.7.H353
Harrington, Michael, 1928-
The vast majority: a journey to the world's poor/ Michael Harrington. New York: Simon and Schuster, c1977. 281 p.
77-009525   330.9/172/4   0671225294
Economic assistance, American. Poor. Developing countries -- Economic conditions.

HC59.7.H45 1979
Higgins, Benjamin Howard, 1912-
Economic development of a small planet/ Benjamin Higgins and Jean Downing Higgins. New York: Norton, c1979. x, 292 p.
79-013316   330.9/172/4   039305697X
Economic development. Developing countries -- Economic conditions.

HC59.7.H655 1996
Hope, Kempe R.
Development in the Third World: from policy failure to policy reform/ Kempe Ronald Hope, Sr. Armonk, N.Y.: M.E. Sharpe, c1996. xvii, 201 p.
95-038405   338.9/009172/4 20   1563247321
Economic development. Developing countries -- Economic conditions. Developing countries -- Economic policy.

HC59.7.K386 2000
Kennes, Walter, 1949-
Small developing countries and global markets: competing in the big league/ Walter Kennes. New York: St. Martin's Press, 2000. xii, 201 p.
00-022309   337.1/724   0312233582
States, Small -- Economic integration. Globalization. International economic integration. Developing countries -- Economic integration.

HC59.7.K75 1992
Krueger, Anne O.
Economic policy reform in developing countries: the Kuznets memorial lectures at the Economic Growth Center, Yale University/ Anne O. Krueger. Oxford, UK; B. Blackwell, 1992. xiii, 184 p.
91-025959   338.9/009172/4   1557862745
Developing countries -- Economic policy.

HC59.7.L322 1978
Latham, A. J. H.
The international economy and the undeveloped world 1865-1914/ A. J. H. Latham. London: Croom Helm; 1978. 217 p.
79-303582   330.9/172/4   0847660885
International economic relations. Developing countries -- Economic conditions.

HC59.7.L4172 1995
Lewellen, Ted C., 1940-
Dependency and development: an introduction to the Third World/ Ted C. Lewellen. Westport, Conn.: Bergin & Garvey, c1995. xi, 272 p.
94-039193   337/.09172/4   0897893999
Sustainable development -- Developing countries. Developing countries -- Dependency on foreign countries. Developing countries -- Politics and government.

HC59.7.M326 1997
Martinussen, John.
Society, state, and market: a guide to competing theories of development/ John Martinussen. London; Zed Books; 1997. xiv, 386 p.
96-024005   338.9/009172/4   1856494411
Development economics -- Developing countries. Developing countries -- Economic policy. Developing countries -- Dependency on foreign countries.

HC59.7.M5337 1988
Mittelman, James H.
Out from underdevelopment: prospects for the Third World/ James H. Mittelman. New York: St. Martin's Press, 1988. xix, 204 p.
87-022927   338.9/009172/4   0312011881
Developing countries -- Economic policy. Developing countries -- Economic conditions.

HC59.7.M5338 1997
Mittelman, James H.
Out from underdevelopment revisited: changing global structures and the remaking of the Third World/ James H. Mittelman and Mustapha Kamal Pasha. New York: St. Martin's Press, 1997. xxv, 289 p.
96-028753   330.9172/4   0312164661
International economic relations. Economic development. Developing countries -- Economic conditions. Developing countries -- Economic policy.

HC59.7.M592 1979
Morris, Morris David.
Measuring the condition of the world's poor: the physical quality of life index/ Morris David Morris. New York: Published for the Overseas Development Council [c1979. xiv, 176 p.
79-016613   330.9172/4   0080238904
Poor -- Developing countries. Economic indicators -- Developing countries. Social indicators -- Developing countries.

HC59.7.M926
Myrdal, Gunnar, 1898-
The challenge of world poverty; a world anti-poverty program in outline. With a foreword by Francis O. Wilcox. New York, Pantheon Books [1970] xviii, 518 p.
78-079797   338.91/172/4
Economic assistance -- Developing countries.

HC59.7.N44 1989
Nguyen, Quoc Tri, 1929-
Third-World development: aspects of political legitimacy and viability/ Tri Q. Nguyen. Rutherford: Fairleigh Dickinson University Press; c1989. 221 p.
87-045959   338.9/009172/4   0838633277
Economic assistance -- Developing countries. Legitimacy of governments -- Developing countries. Economic assistance -- Vietnam. Developing countries -- Economic policy. Vietnam -- Economic policy. Korea (South) -- Economic policy.

HC59.7.O835 1992
Osterfeld, David.
Prosperity versus planning: how government stifles economic growth/ David Osterfeld. New York: Oxford University Press, 1992. 273 p.
91-033042   338.9/009172/4   0195073533
Free enterprise -- Developing countries. Economic assistance -- Developing countries. Capitalism -- Developing countries. Developing countries -- Economic policy.

HC59.7.P283 1999
Page, Sheila.
Regionalism among developing countries/ Sheila Page. New York: St. Martin's Press, 1999.
99-033860   337.1/1724   0312226608
Regionalism -- Developing countries. Trade blocs -- Developing countries. Developing countries -- Economic integration. Developing countries -- Commerce.

HC59.7.R268 1991
Ranis, Gustav.
The political economy of development policy change/ Gustav Ranis, Syed Akhtar Mahmood. Cambridge, MA: B. Blackwell, 1992. vii, 248 p.
91-014513   338.9/009172/4   1557862508
Economic development. Developing countries -- Economic policy -- Case studies.

HC59.7.R475 1985
Reynolds, Lloyd George, 1910-
Economic growth in the Third World, 1850-1980/ Lloyd G. Reynolds. New Haven: Yale University Press, c1985. xii, 469 p.
84-019542   338.9/009172/4   0300032552
Economic history -- 1750-1918. Economic history -- 1918- Developing countries -- Economic conditions.

HC59.7.R56
Robinson, Joan, 1903-
Aspects of development and underdevelopment/ Joan Robinson. Cambridge [Eng.]; Cambridge University Press, 1979. x, 146 p.
78-025610   330.9/172/4   0521226376
Economic development. Developing countries -- Economic conditions.

HC59.7.S283 1995
Savitt, William, 1962-
Global development: a reference handbook/ William Savitt and Paula Bottorf. Santa Barbara, Calif.: ABC-CLIO, c1995. x, 369 p.
95-040213   338.9   0874367743
Economic development. International economic relations. Developing countries -- Economic policy.

HC59.7.S4669 1993
Singer, Hans Wolfgang, 1910-
Economic progress and prospects in the Third World: lessons of development experience since 1945/ H.W. Singer and Sumit Roy. Aldershot, England; E. Elgar, c1993. ix, 187 p.
92-019132   338.9/009172/409045   1852786493
Economic forecasting -- Developing countries. Developing countries -- Economic conditions. Developing countries -- Economic policy.

HC59.7.S58913 1990
Sorman, Guy.
The new wealth of nations/ Guy Sorman. Stanford, Calif.: Hoover Institution Press, c1990. xxii, 215 p.
89-029285   330.9172/4   0817989110
Developing countries -- Economic conditions. Developing countries -- Politics and government.

HC59.7.S859 1981
Streeten, Paul.
First things first: meeting basic human needs in the developing countries/ Paul Streeten with Shahid Javed Burki ... [et al.]. New York: Published for the World Bank [by] Oxford Univers c1981. xii, 206 p.
81-016836   338.9/009172/4   0195203682
Economic assistance -- Developing countries. Basic needs -- Developing countries. Developing countries -- Economic policy.

HC59.7.S8736 1992
Structural adjustment and the environment/ edited by David Reed. Boulder: Westview Press, 1992. xvi, 209 p.
92-023516   338.9/009172/4   0813387027
Structural adjustment (Economic policy) -- Developing countries. Economic development -- Environmental aspects. Environmental policy -- Developing countries.

HC59.7.U266 1992
Unequal burden: economic crises, persistent poverty, and women's work/ edited by Lourdes Beneria & Shelley Feldman. Boulder: Westview Press, c1992. ix, 278 p.
92-002873   331.4/09172/4   0813382297
Structural adjustment (Economic policy) -- Developing countries. Poor women -- Developing countries. Women -- Employment -- Developing countries.

HC59.7.U73 1991
Urban and rural development in Third World countries: problems of population in developing nations/ edited by Valentine James; William M. Alexander ... [et al., contributors]. Jefferson, N.C.: McFarland & Co., c1991. xiii, 350 p.
90-053499   338.9/009172/4   0899505848
Agriculture -- Economic aspects -- Developing countries. Appropriate technology -- Developing countries. Technology transfer -- Developing countries. Developing countries. Developing countries -- Population.

HC59.7.W454 1988
Weiss, John, 1948-
Industry in developing countries: theory, policy, and evidence/ John Weiss. London; Croom Helm; c1988. xvii, 347 p.
87-031031   338.09172/4   0709936540
Industries -- Developing countries. Industrial policy -- Developing countries. Developing countries -- Economic policy.

HC59.7.W6592
World development report. Washington, D.C.: The World Bank, [c1997-]
97-038206
Economic development -- Periodicals. Developing countries -- Economic conditions -- Periodicals.

HC59.72.C3.M355 1996
Maitra, Priyatosh.
The globalization of capitalism in Third World countries/ Priyatosh Maitra. Westport, Conn.: Praeger, 1996. ix, 242 p.
95-007549   330.12/2/091724   0275951596
Capitalism -- Developing countries -- Case studies. Capitalism -- India -- Case studies. India -- Economic policy -- 1980- -- Case studies. India -- Economic conditions -- 1947- -- Case studies.

HC59.72.D4.B35 1988
Ball, Nicole.
Security and economy in the Third World/ Nicole Ball. Princeton, N.J.: Princeton University Press, c1988. xxvii, 432 p.
88-009875   338.4/76234/091724   0691077827
Developing countries -- Defenses -- Economic aspects.

HC59.72.E44.S72 1991
Staudt, Kathleen A.
Managing development: state, society, and international contexts/ Kathleen Staudt. Newbury Park, Calif.: Sage Publications, c1991. x, 283 p.
90-026172   338.9/0068   080394005X
Economic development projects -- Developing countries -- Management. Economic assistance -- Developing countries -- Management. Non-governmental organizations -- Developing countries.

HC59.72.E5.P36 1993
Panaiotov, Todor.
Green markets: the economics of sustainable development/ Theodore Panayotou; foreword by Oscar Arias. San Francisco, Calif.: ICS Press, c1993. xvii, 169 p.
92-038901   338.9/009172/4   155815244X
Environmental policy -- Economic aspects -- Developing countries -- Case studies. Sustainable development -- Developing countries -- Case studies.

HC59.72.E5.P46 1995
People and environment/ edited by Stephen Morse, Michael Stocking. London: UCL Press, 1995. viii, 215 p.
96-112923   1857282825
Sustainable development -- Developing countries.

HC59.72.E5.R33 1990
Race to save the tropics: ecology and economics for a sustainable future/ edited by Robert Goodland. Washington, D.C.: Island Press, c1990. xvi, 219 p.
89-071677   333.7/0913   1559630396
Environmental policy -- Economic aspects -- Developing countries. Rain forest ecology -- Economic aspects -- Developing countries. Tropics -- Economic conditions.

HC59.72.P6.D37 1993
Dasgupta, Partha.
An inquiry into well-being and destitution/ Partha Dasgupta. Oxford: Clarendon Press; 1993. xviii, 661 p.
92-043313   330.9172/4   0198287569
Poverty -- Developing countries. Quality of life -- Developing countries. Resource allocation.

HC59.72.P6.E17 2001
Easterly, William Russell.
The elusive quest for growth: economists' adventures and misadventures in the tropics/ William Easterly. Cambridge, Mass.: MIT Press, c2001. xiii, 342 p.
00-068382   338.9/009172/4 21   026205065X
Poor -- Developing countries. Poverty -- Developing countries. Developing countries -- Economic policy.

HC59.72.P6.S73 1999
Statistical handbook on poverty in the developing world/ edited by Chandrika Kaul and Valerie Tomaselli-Moschovitis. Phoenix, AZ: Oryx Press, 1999. xxi, 425 p.
99-029114   339.4/6/091724   1573562491
Poverty -- Developing countries -- Statistics.

HC59.72.T4.F7 1986
Fransman, Martin.
Technology and economic development/ Martin Fransman. Boulder, Colo.: Westview Press, 1986. xi, 161 p.
86-050429   338.9/27/091724   0813304180
Technological innovations -- Developing countries. Developing countries -- Economic policy.

HC60.A738 1996
Arnold, Guy.
Historical dictionary of aid and development organizations/ by Guy Arnold. Lanham, Md.: Scarecrow Press, c1996. xvi, 196 p.
95-012561   338.9/1/091724 20   081083040X
Economic assistance -- Developing countries -- History. Developing countries -- Economic policy -- History. Non-governmental organizations -- Developing countries -- History.

HC60.C345 1996
Caufield, Catherine.
Masters of illusion: the World Bank and the poverty of nations/ Catherine Caufield. New York: Henry Holt, 1996. xii, 432 p.
96-016804   332.1/532   0805028757
Economic assistance -- Developing countries. Developing countries -- Economic conditions.

HC60.C53 1986
Cassen, Robert.
Does aid work?: report to an intergovernmental task force/ Robert Cassen & Associates. Oxford: Clarendon Press; 1986. xv, 381 p.
86-012621   338.91/09172/4   0198772505
Economic assistance -- Developing countries -- Evaluation. Technical assistance -- Developing countries -- Evaluation.

HC60.C6534 1990
Conteh-Morgan, Earl, 1950-
American foreign aid and global power projection: the geopolitics of resource allocation/ Earl Conteh-Morgan. Aldershot, Hants., England: Dartmouth Pub. Co.; c1990. ix, 246 p.
90-003590   338.9/17301724   1855210061
Economic assistance, American -- Developing countries. United States -- Foreign relations -- Developing countries. Developing countries -- Foreign relations -- United States. United States -- Foreign relations -- 1945-1989.

HC60.F35
Feis, Herbert, 1893-1972.
Foreign aid and foreign policy. New York, St. Martin's Press [1964] vii, 246 p.
64-018364   338.9173
Economic assistance, American. United States -- Foreign relations -- 1961-1963.

HC60.G534 1998
The global crisis in foreign aid/ edited by Richard Grant and Jan Nijman; with a foreword by John Rennie Short. Syracuse, N.Y.: Syracuse University Press, 1998. xxiv, 224 p.
97-033567   338.91   0815627718
Economic assistance.

HC60.H69 1998
Hoy, Paula, 1969-
Players and issues in international aid/ Paula Hoy. West Hartford, CT: Kumarian Press, 1998. vi, 181 p.
97-035131   338.91   156549072X
Economic assistance. Economic assistance, American. International agencies.

HC60.L443
Leontief, Wassily W., 1906-
The future of the world economy: a United Nations study/ by Wassily Leontief, et al. New York: Oxford University Press, 1977. vii, 110 p.
77-072024   338/.09   0195022327
Economic assistance. Economic development. Economic forecasting.

HC60.L86 1993
Lumsdaine, David Halloran.
Moral vision in international politics: the foreign aid regime, 1949-1989/ David Halloran Lumsdaine. Princeton, N.J.: Princeton University Press, c1993. xviii, 355 p.
92-018508   338.9/17301724   0691078874
Economic assistance, American -- Developing countries. Economic assistance -- Developing countries.

HC60.O78 1990
Orr, Robert M.
The emergence of Japan's foreign aid power/ Robert M. Orr, Jr. New York: Columbia University Press, c1990. x, 178 p.
90-030301   338.9/152   0231070462
Economic assistance, Japanese. Economic assistance, American.

HC60.S548 1990
Smith, Brian H., 1940-
More than altruism: the politics of private foreign aid/ Brian H. Smith. Princeton, N.J.: Princeton University Press, c1990. xxi, 352 p.
89-038399   338.9/17301724   0691078459
Economic assistance, American -- Moral and ethical aspects -- Developing countries. Economic assistance, Canadian -- Moral and ethical aspects -- Developing countries. Economic assistance, European -- Moral and ethical aspects -- Developing countries. Canada -- Foreign relations. Europe -- Foreign relations. United States -- Foreign relations.

HC60.T677 2000
Transforming development: foreign aid for a changing world/ edited by Jim Freedman. Toronto; University of Toronto Press, c2000. vi, 296 p.
00-703121   0802041930
Economic assistance -- Developing countries. Aide economique -- Pays en voie de developpement.

HC60.Y372 1995
Yasutomo, Dennis T.
The new multilateralism in Japan's foreign policy/ Dennis T. Yasutomo. New York: St. Martin's Press, 1995. x, 230 p.
95-016441   338.9/152   0312047789
Economic assistance, Japanese. Japan -- Foreign economic relations.

HC60.5.F57 1998
Fischer, Fritz.
Making them like us: Peace Corps volunteers in the 1960s/ Fritz Fischer. Washington: Smithsonian Institution Press, c1998. viii, 237 p.
98-016158   361.6 21   1560988894
Peace Corps (U.S.)

HC60.5.R45 1988
Reeves, T. Zane.
The politics of the Peace Corps & VISTA/ T. Zane Reeves. Tuscaloosa, Ala.: University of Alabama Press, c1988. x, 215 p.
86-019194   361.2/6   0817303235
Peace Corps (U.S.) Volunteers in Service to America.

HC60.5.S39 1991
Schwartz, Karen.
What you can do for your country: an oral history of the peace corps/ by Karen Schwartz. New York, N.Y.: W. Morrow, 1991. 316 p.
90-022948   361.6   0688075592
Peace Corps (U.S.) -- History.

HC79.A4 Special topics, A-Z — Air pollution

HC79.A4.C55 1992
Cline, William R.
The economics of global warming/ William R. Cline. Washington, DC: Institute for International Economics, 1992. xi, 399 p.
92-016111   363.73/87   0881321508
Air -- Pollution -- Economic aspects. Global warming. Greenhouse effect, Atmospheric.

HC79.B38 Special topics, A-Z — Basic needs

HC79.B38.W45 1989
Weigel, Van B., 1954-
A unified theory of global development/ Van B. Weigel. New York: Praeger, 1989. xix, 263 p.
88-025211   338.9   027593134X
Basic needs. Economic development.

HC79.C3 Special topics, A-Z — Capital. Capital productivity. Infrastructure

HC79.C3.A45 1998
Allen, Larry.
The ABC-CLIO world history companion to capitalism/ Larry Allen. Santa Barbara, Calif.: ABC-CLIO, c1998. xi, 404 p.
98-003908   330.12/2 21   0874369444
Capitalism -- History.

HC79.C6 Special topics, A-Z — Consumer demand. Consumers. Consumption

HC79.C6.A43 2000
All the world and her husband: women in twentieth-century consumer culture/ edited by Maggie Andrews and Mary M. Talbot. London; Cassell, 2000. ix, 278 p.
99-019273   658.8/34/082   0304701513
Women consumers. Culture -- Economic aspects. Consumption (Economics)

HC79.C6.B34 1989
Bartos, Rena.
Marketing to women around the world/ by Rena Bartos. Boston, Mass.: Harvard Business School Press, c1989. xvii, 320 p.
88-024379   658.8/348   0875842011
Women consumers. Marketing. Women -- Employment.

HC79.C6.C673 1993
Consumption and the world of goods/ edited by John Brewer and Roy Porter. London; Routledge, 1993. xix, 564 p.
93-180136   339.4/7   0415037123
Consumption (Economics) -- History. Consumers -- History. Consumer goods -- History.

HC79.C6.L87 1996
Lury, Celia.
Consumer culture/ Celia Lury. New Brunswick, N.J.: Rutgers University Press, c1996. vii, 273 p.
96-010825   306.3 20   0813523281
Consumption (Economics) -- Social aspects. Consumer behavior. Culture -- Economic aspects.

HC79.C6 R87 2001
Russell, Cheryl,
Best customers: demographics of consumer demand/ by Cheryl Russell. 2nd ed. Ithaca, N.Y.: New Strategist Publications, c2001. 789 p.
2002-511430   1885070373
Consumers -- United States -- Statistics. Consumer behavior -- United States -- Statistics.

HC79.C63 Special topics, A-Z — Consumer protection

HC79.C63.E53 1997
Encyclopedia of the consumer movement/ Stephen Brobeck, editor; Robert N. Mayer, Robert O. Herrmann, associate editors. Santa Barbara, Calif.: ABC-CLIO, c1997. xxxi, 659 p.
97-041345   381.3/2/03 21   0874369878
Consumer protection -- Encyclopedias.

HC79.D4 Special topics, A-Z — Defense and disarmament, Economic impact of

HC79.D4.G33 1996
Gaddy, Clifford G.
The price of the past: Russia's struggle with the legacy of a militarized economy/ Clifford G. Gaddy. Washington, D.C.: Brookings Institution, c1996. xiii, 250 p.
96-009966   338.974 20   0815730160
Economic conversion -- Russia (Federation) Defense industries -- Russia (Federation) Russia (Federation) -- Economic policy -- 1991-

HC79.D4.K37 1992
Kapstein, Ethan B.
The political economy of national security: a global perspective/ Ethan Barnaby Kapstein. New York: McGraw-Hill, c1992. xvii, 232 p.
91-023566   338.4/76233   0070342563
National security -- Economic aspects. Defense industries. Military-industrial complex.

HC79.D4.W37 2001
War and underdevelopment/ Frances Stewart and Valpy FitzGerald and associates. Oxford; New York: Oxford University Press, 2001. 2 v.
00-060668   338.9   0199241872
War -- Economic aspects. Economic development.

HC79.E5 Special topics, A-Z — Environmental policy and economic development. Sustainable development

HC79.E5 B759 2001b
Brown, Lester Russell,
Eco-economy: building an economy for the earth/ Lester R. Brown. London: Earthscan, 2001. xviii, 333 p.
2002-392789   1853838268
Environmental economics.

HC79.E5.C27 1992
Cairncross, Frances.
Costing the earth: the challenge for governments, the opportunities for business/ Frances Cairncross. Boston, Mass.: Harvard Business School Press, c1992. viii, 341 p.
91-033750   363.7/056   0875843158
Environmental policy. Social responsibility of business. Marketing -- Social aspects.

HC79.E5.C333 1995
Caldwell, Lynton Keith, 1913-
Environment as a focus for public policy/ by Lynton K. Caldwell; edited, with an introduction, by Robert V. Bartlett and James N. Gladden. College Station: Texas A&M University Press, c1995. vi, 358 p.
94-037751   363.7
Environmental policy. Policy sciences.

HC79.E5 D345 2000
Davidson, Eric A.
You can't eat GNP: economics as if ecology mattered/ Eric A. Davidson; foreword by George M. Woodwell. Cambridge, Mass.: Perseus, c2000. xvi, 247 p.
00-102282   0738202762
Environmental economics.

HC79.E5.D4637 1997
DeSimone, Livio D.
Eco-efficiency: the business link to sustainable development/ Livio D. DeSimone and Frank Popoff with the World Business Council for Sustainable Development. Cambridge, Mass.: MIT Press, c1997. xxv, 280 p.
96-049857   338.98 21   0262041626
Sustainable development. Economic development -- Environmental aspects. Social responsibility of business.

HC79.E5.D53 2001
Dictionary of environmental economics/ Anil Markandya ... [et al.]. Sterling, VA: Earthscan Publications, 2001. ix, 196 p.
00-067275   333.7/03   1853835293
Environmental economics -- Dictionaries.

HC79.E5.E17 1996
Earthly goods: environmental change and social justice/ edited by Fen Osler Hampson, and Judith Reppy. Ithaca, N.Y.: Cornell University Press, 1996. x, 263 p.
96-019784   333.7   0801432898
Environmental policy -- Economic aspects. Social justice. Conservation of natural resources.

HC79.E5.E2835 1995
The economics of sustainable development/ edited by Ian Goldin and L. Alan Winters. Cambridge; Cambridge University Press, 1995. xx, 314 p.
94-027994   338.9   0521465559
Sustainable development. Environmental policy. Economic policy.

HC79.E5.E578
Environmental improvement through economic incentives/ Frederick R. Anderson ... [et al.]. Baltimore: Published for Resources for the Future by Johns c1977. xi, 195 p.
76-047400   301.31   0801820006
Environmental policy. Pollution -- Costs. Pollution -- Economic aspects.

HC79.E5.F557 1997
Flashpoints in environmental policymaking: controversies in achieving sustainability/ edited by Sheldon Kamieniecki, George A. Gonzalez, and Robert O. Vos. Albany: State University of New York Press, c1997. vi, 367 p.
96-017898   333.7 20   0791433293
Sustainable development. Environmental policy.

HC79.E5.F7
Freeman, A. Myrick, 1936-
The benefits of environmental improvement: theory and practice/ A. Myrick Freeman III. Baltimore: Published for Resources for the Future by Johns c1979. xiv, 272 p.
78-020532   338.4/3   0801821630
Environmental policy -- Cost effectiveness.

HC79.E5.F723 2000
French, Hilary F.
Vanishing borders: protecting the planet in the age of globalization/ Hilary French. New York: W.W. Norton, c2000. 257 p.
00-701646   0393320049
Environmental policy -- International cooperation. Sustainable development -- International cooperation. Conservation of natural resources.

HC79.E5.G57 1995
Glaeser, Bernhard.
Environment, development, agriculture: integrated policy through human ecology/ Bernhard Glaeser. Armonk, N.Y.: M.E. Sharpe, 1995. xii, 174 p.
95-023920   338.1   1563246929
Sustainable development. Sustainable agriculture. Human ecology.

HC79.E5.G5927 2000
The global environment in the twenty-first century: prospects for international cooperation/ edited by Pamela S. Chasek. Tokyo; United Nations University Press, c2000. xi, 465 p.
99-050800   363.7/0526 21   9280810294
Environmental policy -- International cooperation. Environmental protection -- International cooperation. Sustainable development -- International cooperation.

HC79.E5.G6848 1995
Gowdy, John M.
Economic theory for environmentalists/ John Gowdy, Sabine O'Hara. [Ankeny, Iowa]: Soil and Water Conservation Society; c1995. xiv, 192 p.
94-009069   658.7/2   188401500X
Environmental economics.

HC79.E5.H3295 1993
Hanley, Nick.
Cost-benefit analysis and the environment/ Nick Hanley and Clive L. Spash. Aldershot, Hants, England: E. Elgar, c1993. x, 278 p.
93-018898   338.4/33637   1852784555
Environmental policy -- Cost effectiveness. Environmental protection -- Cost effectiveness.

HC79.E5.H457 1996
Hempel, Lamont C.
Environmental governance: the global challenge/ Lamont C. Hempel. Washington, D.C.: Island Press, c1996. xviii, 291 p.
95-039224   333.7 20   1559634472
Environmental policy.

HC79.E5.I513 1983
Incentives for environmental protection/ edited by Thomas C. Schelling. Cambridge, Mass.: MIT Press, c1983. xix, 355 p.
82-004631   363.7   0262192136
Environmental policy -- Case studies. Environmental protection -- Economic aspects -- Case studies.

HC79.E5.K578 1984
Kneese, Allen V.
Measuring the benefits of clean air and water/
Allen V. Kneese. Washington, D.C.: Resources for
the Future; c1984. xii, 159 p.
84-017899   338.4/33637392   0915707098
*Environmental policy -- Cost effectiveness.
Environmental protection -- Cost effectiveness. Air
-- Pollution -- Economic aspects.*

HC79.E5.L48 1992
Lewis, Martin W.
Green delusions: an environmentalist critique of
radical environmentalism/ Martin W. Lewis.
Durham: Duke University Press, 1992. viii, 288 p.
92-005671   363.7/057   0822312573
*Environmental policy -- Citizen participation.
Radicalism.*

HC79.E5.M347 1998
Managing the commons/ edited by John A. Baden
and Douglas S. Noonan; with a foreword by
William D. Ruckelshaus. Bloomington: Indiana
University Press, c1998. xvii, 243 p.
97-020390   304.2 21   025333361X
*Environmental policy. Natural resources --
Management.*

HC79.E5.M353 1990
Manes, Christopher, 1957-
Green rage: radical environmentalism and the
unmaking of civilization/ Christopher Manes.
Boston: Little, Brown, c1990. x, 291 p.
90-005697   363.7/057   0316545139
*Green movement. Environmental policy -- Citizen
participation. Environmental protection.*

HC79.E5.M47 1984
Milbrath, Lester W.
Environmentalists, vanguard for a new society/
Lester W. Milbrath; with the advice and assistance
of Barbara V. Fisher. Albany: State University of
New York Press, c1984. xv, 180 p.
83-024250   363.7   087395887X
*Environmental policy. Social change.
Environmentalists.*

HC79.E5.P669 1991
Porter, Gareth, 1942-
Global environmental politics/ Gareth Porter, Janet
Welsh Brown. Boulder: Westview Press, c1991.
xv, 208 p.
91-024160   363.7/056   0813310342
Environmental policy.

HC79.E5 P748 1999
Prugh, Thomas.
Natural capital and human economic survival/ by
Thomas Prugh; with Robert Costanza ... [et al.].
2nd ed. Solomons, Md: International Society for
Ecological Economics; 180 p.
99-012121   333.7 21   1566703980
*Environmental economics. Environmental policy
-- Economic aspects.*

HC79.E5.S216 1998
Sachs, Wolfgang.
Greening the north: a post-industrial blueprint for
ecology and equity/ Wolfgang Sachs, Reinhard
Loske and Manfred Linz; with Ralf Behrensmeier
... [et al.]; translated by Timothy Nevill. London:
Zed, 1998. xii, 247 p.
99-168110   1856495078
*Environmental economics. Environmental
economics -- Germany. Sustainable development.*

HC79.E5.S29
Schnaiberg, Allan.
The environment, from surplus to scarcity/ Allan
Schaiberg. New York: Oxford University Press,
1980. xiii, 464 p.
79-012439   301.31   0195026101
*Environmental policy. Environmental protection.
Nature -- Effect of human beings on.*

HC79.E5.S36 1993
Seager, Joni.
Earth follies: coming to feminist terms with the
global environmental crisis/ Joni Seager. New
York: Routledge, 1993. xvii, 332 p.
92-045793   363.7   0415907209
*Environmental policy -- Political aspects. Human
ecology -- Political aspects. Feminist theory.*

HC79.E5.S75 1993
Stone, Christopher D.
The gnat is older than man: global environment
and human agenda/ Christopher D. Stone.
Princeton, N.J.: Princeton University Press, c1993.
xxv, 341 p.
92-021139   363.7   0691032505
*Environmental policy. Environmental law.
Human ecology.*

HC79.E5.S8645 2001
A Survey of sustainable development: social and
economic dimensions/ edited by Jonathan M.
Harris ... [et al.]. Washington, D.C.: Island Press,
c2001. xxxvii, 409 p.
00-012957   338.9/27 21   1559638621
Sustainable development.

HC79.E5.T476 1997
Thinking ecologically: the next generation of
environmental policy/ edited by Marian R.
Chertow and Daniel C. Esty. New Haven: Yale
University Press, c1997. xi, 271 p.
97-014996   363.7 21   0300073011
Environmental policy. Environmental protection.

HC79.E5.W36 1997
Warford, Jeremy J.
The greening of economic policy reform/ Jeremy
Warford, Mohan Munasinghe, Wilfrido Cruz.
Washington, D.C.: World Bank, c1997. 2 v.
95-039068   333.7 20   0821334778
*Economic policy -- Case studies. Sustainable
development -- Case studies.*

HC79.E5.W43 1997
Weaver, James H., 1933-
Achieving broad-based sustainable development:
governance, environment, and growth with equity/
James H. Weaver, Michael T. Rock, Kenneth
Kusterer. West Hartford, Conn.: Kumarian Press,
1997. viii, 293 p.
96-004728   363.7   1565490592
*Sustainable development. Democracy. Economic
development -- Environmental aspects.*

HC79.F3 Special topics, A-Z — Famines

HC79.F3.D38 2001
Davis, Mike, 1946-
Late Victorian holocausts: El Nino famines and the
making of the third world/ Mike Davis. London;
Verso, 2001. x, 464 p.
00-054989   363.8/09172/4   1859847390
*Famines -- History -- 19th century. Famines --
India -- History -- 19th century. Famines -- China -
- History -- 19th century.*

HC79.F3.H86 1990
Hunger in history: food shortage, poverty, and
deprivation/ general editor, Lucile F. Newman;
associate editors William Crossgrove ... [et al.].
Cambridge, Mass., USA: B. Blackwell, 1990. xi,
429 p.
89-006981   363.8/09   1557860440
*Famines -- History. Food supply -- History.
Poverty -- History.*

HC79.H53 Special topics, A-Z — High technology industries

HC79.H53.D94 1999
Dyer-Witheford, Nick, 1951-
Cyber-Marx: cycles and circuits of struggle in
high-technology capitalism/ Nick Dyer-Witheford.
Urbana: University of Illinois Press, c1999. x,
344 p.
98-058056   338.4/762 21   0252024796
*High technology industries. Technological
innovations -- Economic aspects Capitalism.*

HC79.H53.N67 1998
Norman, Donald A.
The invisible computer: why good products can
fail, the personal computer is so complex, and
information appliances are the solution/ Donald A.
Norman. Cambridge, Mass.: MIT Press, c1998. xii,
302 p.
98-018841   004.16 21   0262140659
*High technology industries -- Marketing. Human-
computer interaction. Design, Industrial.*

HC79.I5 Special topics, A-Z — Income. Income distribution. National income

HC79.I5.T388 1998
Tilly, Charles.
Durable inequality/ Charles Tilly. Berkeley:
University of California Press, c1998. xi, 299 p.
97-031570   339.2 21   0520211715
Income distribution. Equality.

HC79.I52 Special topics, A-Z — Industrial productivity. Industrial efficiency

HC79.I52.C66 1994
Convergence of productivity: cross-national studies
and historical evidence/ edited by William J.
Baumol, Richard R. Nelson, Edward N. Wolff.
New York: Oxford University Press, c1994. xii,
343 p.
93-011494   338/.06   019508389X
*Industrial productivity -- History -- 20th century
-- Congresses. Income -- History -- 20th century --
Congresses. Technological innovations --
Economic aspects -- History -- 20th century --
Congresses.*

HC79.I55 Special topics, A-Z — Information technology. Information economy

HC79.I55 C373 2000
Castells, Manuel.
The rise of the network society/ Manuel Castells. 2nd ed. Oxford; Blackwell Publishers, 2000. xxix, 594 p.
00-037832   3303.48/33 21   0631221409
Information technology -- Economic aspects. Information technology -- Social aspects. Information society.

HC79.I55.D37 1993
Davenport, Thomas H., 1954-
Process innovation: reengineering work through information technology/ Thomas H. Davenport. Boston, Mass.: Harvard Business School Press, c1993. x, 337 p.
92-021959   338/.064   0875843662
Information technology. Technological innovations. Organizational change.

HC79.I55.K358 2001
Kanter, Rosabeth Moss.
Evolve!: succeeding in the digital culture of tomorrow/ Rosabeth Moss Kanter. Boston, Mass.: Harvard Business School Press, c2001. x, 352 p.
00-047241   658.4/062 21   1578514398
Information technology. Internet -- Economic aspects. Organizational change.

HC79.I55.N34 1994
Naisbitt, John.
Global paradox: the bigger the world economy, the more powerful its smallest players/ John Naisbitt. New York: W. Morrow, 1994. 304 p.
93-033829   330.9/001/12   0688127916
Information society. Economic forecasting. International economic relations.

HC79.I55.O45 2000
Omae, Kenichi, 1943-
The invisible continent: four strategic imperatives of the new economy/ Kenichi Ohmae. New York: HarperBusiness, 2000. 262 p.
00-026313   382/.71   0060197536
Information technology. Free trade. Internet.

HC79.I55 S53 1999
Shapiro, Carl.
Information rules: a strategic guide to the network economy/ Carl Shapiro, Hal R. Varian. Boston, Mass.: Harvard Business School Press, c1999. x, 352 p.
98-024923   658.4/038 21   087584863X
Information technology -- Economic aspects. Information society.

HC79.I55.T368 1996
Tapscott, Don, 1947-
The digital economy: promise and peril in the age of networked intelligence/ Don Tapscott. New York: McGraw-Hill, c1996. xviii, 342 p.
95-037962   004.6 20   0070622000
Information technology.

HC79.P55 Special topics, A-Z — Pollution

HC79.P55.R43 1995
Reducing toxics: a new approach to policy and industrial decisionmaking/ edited by Robert Gottlieb. Washington, D.C.: Island Press, c1995. xiii, 447 p.
94-046257   658.4/08   1559633360
Pollution -- Government policy. Industrial management -- Environmental aspects.

HC79.P6 Special topics, A-Z — Poor. Poverty

HC79.P6.C345 2000
Can anyone hear us?/ Deepa Narayan ... [et al.]. New York: Published by Oxford University Press for the Wor c2000. xi, 343 p.
00-026952   362.5 21   0195216016
Poverty. Poor.

HC79.P6.C44 1996
Cheal, David J.
New poverty: families in postmodern society/ David Cheal. Westport, Conn.: Greenwood Press, 1996. xviii, 209 p.
95-050520   362.5/0973   0313294445
Poverty. Poor. Family. United States -- Economic conditions. Canada -- Economic conditions.

HC79.P6.D47 1998
DeRose, Laurie Fields, 1968-
Who's hungry? And how do we know?: Food shortage, poverty, and deprivation/ Laurie DeRose, Ellen Messer, and Sara Millman. New York: United Nations University, 1998. xi, 201 p.
97-045294   363.8   9280809857
Poverty. Hunger. Starvation.

HC79.P6.G34
Galbraith, John Kenneth, 1908-
The nature of mass poverty/ John Kenneth Galbraith. Cambridge, Mass.: Harvard University Press, 1979. viii, 150 p.
78-011839   339.4/6   0674605330
Poverty. Poor -- Developing countries. Rural poor. Developing countries -- Rural conditions.

HC79.P6.L56 1977b
Lipton, Michael.
Why poor people stay poor: urban bias in world development/ Michael Lipton. Cambridge: Harvard University Press, 1977, c1976. 467 p.
76-023584   301.44/1   0674952383
Poor. Rural poor. Economic assistance, Domestic. Developing countries -- Economic conditions.

HC79.P6.P682 1984
Poverty and economic justice: a philosophical approach/ edited by Robert H. Hartman. New York: Paulist Press, c1984. vii, 261 p.
83-082020   339.4/6   0809125978
Poverty -- Addresses, essays, lectures. Distributive justice -- Addresses, essays, lectures. Economics -- Religious aspects -- Christianity -- Addresses, essays, lectures.

HC79.P6.S335 1993
Schultz, Theodore William, 1902-
The economics of being poor/ Theodore W. Schultz. Oxford, UK; Blackwell, 1993. ix, 340 p.
92-027436   330/.08/6942   1557863202
Poor. Rural poor. Human capital.

HC79.P6 U53 2001
Understanding poverty/ Sheldon H. Danziger, Robert H. Haveman, editors. New York: Russell Sage foundation; ix, 566 p.
2001-040818   362.5 21   0674008766
Poverty.

HC79.S3 Special topics, A-Z — Saving and investment

HC79.S3 I54 1994
International comparisons of household saving/ edited by James M. Poterba. Chicago: University of Chicago, 1994. ix, 276 p.
94-022549   339.4/3 20   0226676218
Saving and investment -- Case studies -- Congresses. Households -- Economic aspects -- Case studies -- Congresses.

HC79.S9 Special topics, A-Z — Subsidies

HC79.S9.V68 2000
Vouchers and the provision of public services/ C. Eugene Steuerle ... [al et.], editors. Washington DC: Brookings Institution Press: c2000. viii, 552 p.
00-009439   361/.05 21   0815781547
Subsidies. Social services. Subsidies -- United States.

HC79.T4 Special topics, A-Z — Technological innovations. Technology transfer

HC79.T4.B74 1981
Brown, Lawrence A., 1935-
Innovation diffusion: a new perspective/ Lawrence A. Brown. London; Methuen, 1981. xx, 345 p.
80-049706   338/.06   041674270X
Technological innovations. Diffusion of innovations. Economic development.

HC79.T4.D53
The Diffusion of new industrial processes; an international study. Edited by L. Nabseth and G. F. Ray. Cambridge [Eng.] University Press [1974] xvii, 324 p.
73-088309   338.4/5   0521204305
Technological innovations. Economic development. Diffusion of innovations.

HC79.T4 E25283 2001
The economic payoff from the internet revolution/ Robert E. Litan and Alice M. Rivlin, editors. Washington, D.C.: Brookings Institution Press, c2001. viii, 292 p.
2001-002503   330.9 21   0815700652
Technological innovations -- Economic aspects. Business enterprises -- Computer network resources. Internet.

HC79.T4.F38 1991
Favorites of fortune: technology, growth, and economic development since the Industrial Revolution/ edited by Patrice Higonnet, David S. Landes, Henry Rosovsky. Cambridge, Mass.: Harvard University Press, 1991. viii, 558 p.
91-012249 338/.064/09 067429520X
Technological innovations -- Economic aspects -- History. Economic history. Industries -- History.

HC79.T4.G67 1988
Government innovation policy: design, implementation, evaluation/ edited by J. David Roessner. New York: St. Martin's Press in association with the Polic c1988. xi, 208 p.
86-021958 338.4/5/0973 0312341342
Technological innovations -- Government policy.

HC79.T4.H56 1988
Hippel, Eric von.
The sources of innovation/ Eric von Hippel. New York: Oxford University Press, c1988. xi, 218 p.
86-028620 338/.06 0195040856
Technological innovations -- Economic aspects.

HC79.T4.K3
Kamien, Morton I.
Market structure and innovation/ Morton I. Kamien and Nancy L. Schwartz. Cambridge; Cambridge University Press, 1982. xi, 241 p.
81-012254 338 0521221900
Technological innovations. Industrial organization (Economic theory)

HC79.T4.M346 1991
Malecki, Edward J., 1949-
Technology and economic development: the dynamics of local, regional, and national change/ Edward J. Malecki. Essex, England: Longman Scientific & Technical: 1991. xvi, 495 p.
90-023690 338.9 0470217235
Technological innovations -- Economic aspects. Economic development. Regional economic disparities.

HC79.T4.M648 1990
Mokyr, Joel.
The lever of riches: technological creativity and economic progress/ Joel Mokyr. New York: Oxford University Press, 1990. ix, 349 p.
89-028298 338/.064 0195061136
Technological innovations -- Economic aspects -- History. Economic development -- History.

HC79.T4.R673 1982
Rosenberg, Nathan, 1927-
Inside the black box: technology and economics/ Nathan Rosenberg. Cambridge [Cambridgeshire]; Cambridge University Press, 1982. xi, 304 p.
82-004563 338/.06 0521248086
Technological innovations. Technology -- Social aspects. Economic development.

HC79.T4.R88 2001
Ruttan, Vernon W.
Technology, growth, and development: an induced innovation perspective/ Vernon W. Ruttan. New York: Oxford University Press, 2001. xvi, 656 p.
00-029124 338/.064 21 0195118715
Technological innovations -- Economic aspects. Economic development.

HC79.T4.T4395 1992
Technology and the wealth of nations/ edited by Nathan Rosenberg, Ralph Landau, and David C. Mowery. Stanford, Calif.: Stanford University Press,c 1992. xiv, 443 p.
92-024181 338/.064 0804720827
Technology -- Economic aspects. Technological innovations -- Economic aspects. Research, Industrial -- Economic aspects.

HC79.W3 Special topics, A-Z — Waste

HC79.W3.D69 1989
Dowd, Douglas Fitzgerald, 1919-
The waste of nations: dysfunction in the world economy/ Douglas Dowd. Boulder: Westview Press, 1989. xii, 138 p.
88-026107 338.9 0813308100
Waste (Economics) Economic policy. Capitalism. United States -- Economic policy.

HC79.W32 Special topics, A-Z — Water pollution

HC79.W32.A37 1990
Agriculture and water quality: international perspectives/ edited by John B. Braden and Stephen B. Lovejoy. Boulder, Colo.: L. Rienner, 1990. xii, 224 p.
89-010811 363.73/1 1555871836
Water quality management -- Government policy. Water -- Pollution -- Prevention -- Government policy. Agricultural pollution -- Prevention -- Government policy.

HC79.W4 Special topics, A-Z — Wealth

HC79.W4.D377 2000
Davis, Stanley M.
Future wealth/ Stan Davis, Christopher Meyer. Boston, Mass.: Harvard Business School Press, c2000. xii, 201 p.
99-059014 330.1/6 21 1578511941
Wealth. Income. Equality.

HC79.W4.E35 2001
Edmunds, John C., 1947-
The wealthy world: the growth and implications of global prosperity/ John C. Edmunds; edited by Karen Maccaro and W. Randolph Thompson. New York: Wiley, c2001. xxi, 262 p.
00-043609 332.63/22 21 0471390771
Wealth. Stock exchanges. International business enterprises.

HC79.W4.J39 2000
Jay, Peter.
The wealth of man/ Peter Jay. New York: Public Affairs, c2000. xxiii, 373 p.
00-037362 330.9 21 1891620673
Wealth -- History. Economic man -- History. Economic development -- History.

HC79.W4.W424 1996
The wealth of nations in the twentieth century: the policies and institutional determinants of economic development/ edited by Ramon H. Myers. Stanford, Calif.: Hoover Institution Press, c1996. xxi, 314 p.
96-035432 330.1/6 20 0817994513
Wealth -- Case studies. Economic development -- Case studies.

HC85 Natural resources

HC85.A83 1999
Ascher, William.
Why governments waste natural resources: policy failures in developing countries/ William Ascher. Baltimore, Md.: Johns Hopkins University Press, 1999. xi, 333 p.
98-051020 333.7/09172/4 0801860954
Natural resources -- Government policy -- Developing countries. Natural resources -- Developing countries -- Management.

HC85.F44 2001
Ffolliott, Peter F.
Natural resources management practices: a primer/ Peter F. Ffolliott, Luis A. Bojorquez-Tapia, Mariano Hernandez-Narvaez. Ames: Iowa State University Press, c2001. xiii, 237 p.
00-063145 333.7 21 0813825415
Natural resources -- Management.

HC85.O63 2002
On the edge of scarcity: environment, resources, population, sustainability, and conflict/ edited by Michael N. Dobkowski and Isidor Wallimann; with a foreword by John K. Roth. [2nd ed.] Syracuse, N.Y.: Syracuse University Press, 2002. xxxi, 204 p.
2002-265899 0815629435
Natural resources. Scarcity. Economic development.

HC94 By region or country — America. Western Hemisphere — General

HC94.R668 1995
Rosenberg, Jerry Martin.
Encyclopedia of the North American Free Trade Agreement, the New American Community, and Latin-American trade/ Jerry M. Rosenberg. Westport, Conn.: Greenwood Press, 1995. x, 562 p.
94-016984 382/.917/03 0313290695
Free trade -- America -- Encyclopedias. Commercial treaties -- Encyclopedias. Tariff -- Law and legislation -- North America -- Encyclopedias. America -- Economic integration -- Encyclopedias. Latin America -- Commerce -- Encyclopedias.

HC95-120 By region or country — America. Western Hemisphere — North America

HC95.P64 2001
Poitras, Guy E., 1942-
Inventing North America: Canada, Mexico, and the United States/ Guy Poitras. Boulder, CO: Lynne Rienner Publishers, 2001. v, 204 p.
2001-018070 337.7 1555879640
North America -- Economic integration. North America -- Economic conditions. North America -- Foreign economic relations.

HC101.A13122
Business statistics of the United States. Lanham, MD: Bernan Press, [1996-]
96-645954 338
Commercial statistics -- Periodicals. United States -- Economic conditions -- 1981- -- Periodicals. United States -- Commerce -- Periodicals.

HC102.D8
D&B million dollar directory: America's leading public & private companies/ Dun & Bradstreet. Bethlehem, PA: Dun & Bradstreet, Inc., <1997- >
97-660611   338.7/4/0973
Industries -- United States -- Directories. Corporations -- United States -- Directories.

HC102.E53 1994
Encyclopedia of American industries/ Kevin Hillstrom, editor; Mary K. Ruby, associate editor. Detroit, Mich.: Gale Research, 1994. 2 v.
94-034720   338.0973   0787601020
Industries -- United States -- Encyclopedias.

HC102.G35 1999
Gale encyclopedia of U.S. economic history/ Thomas Carson, editor, Mary Bonk, associate editor. Detroit: Gale Group, c1999. v. 2.
99-039623   330.973/003 21   0787638889
United States -- Economic conditions -- Encyclopedias.

HC102.O57 1992
Olson, James Stuart, 1946-
Dictionary of United States economic history/ James S. Olson, with Susan Wladaver-Morgan. Westport, Conn.: Greenwood Press, 1992. 667 p.
91-032193   330.973/003   0313265321
United States -- Economic conditions -- Dictionaries.

HC102.5.A2.H36 1999
Hamilton, Neil A., 1949-
American business leaders: a biographical dictionary/ Neil A. Hamilton. Santa Barbara, Calif.: ABC-CLIO, 1999. 2 v.
99-027928   338.092/272   1576070026
Businesspeople -- United States -- Biography -- Dictionaries.

HC102.5.A2.W73 1998
Wren, Daniel A.
Management innovators: the people and ideas that have shaped modern business/ Daniel A. Wren, Ronald G. Greenwood. New York: Oxford University Press, 1998. x, 254 p.
97-030036   658/.0092/273   0195117050
Businesspeople -- United States -- Biography. Executives -- United States -- Biography. Industrial management -- United States -- History.

HC102.5.A76.M33 2001
Madsen, Axel.
John Jacob Astor: America's first multimillionaire/ Axel Madsen. New York: John Wiley, c2001. vii, 312 p.
00-042273   380.1/092 B 21   0471385034
Astor, John Jacob, -- 1763-1848. Businesspeople -- United States -- Biography. United States -- Economic conditions -- To 1865.

HC102.5.B97.A32
Byrd, Harold Eugene.
The Black experience in big business/ Harold Eugene Byrd. Hicksville, N.Y.: Exposition Press, c1977. 143 p.
77-372223   338/.092/4   0682489018
Byrd, Harold Eugene. Afro-American businesspeople -- United States -- Biography. Big business -- United States.

HC102.5.K457.C35 1996
Campbell, Walter E.
Across fortune's tracks: a biography of William Rand Kenan, Jr./ Walter E. Campbell. Chapel Hill: University of North Carolina Press, c1996. xvi, 417 p.
95-034702   338.092 B 20   080782268X
Kenan, William Rand, -- 1872-1965. Businesspeople -- United States -- Biography. Dairy farmers -- United States -- Biography. Philanthropists -- United States -- Biography.

HC102.5.M377.A3 1994
Mellon, Thomas, 1813-1908.
Thomas Mellon and his times/ Thomas Mellon; foreword by David McCullough; preface to the second edition by Paul Mellon; edited by Mary Louise Briscoe. Pittsburgh: University of Pittsburgh Press, c1994. xxxii, 478 p.
94-011892   332/.092   0822937778
Mellon, Thomas, -- 1813-1908. Mellon family. Capitalists and financiers -- United States -- Biography.

HC102.5.R3.A3
Randall, Clarence Belden, 1891-
Over my shoulder, a reminiscence. Boston: Little, Brown, [1956] 248 p.
56-010648   923.373

HC103.A37 1987
Agnew, John A.
The United States in the world-economy: a regional geography/ John Agnew. Cambridge; Cambridge University Press, 1987. xvii, 264 p.
86-032743   337.73   0521304105
Regional economics. United States -- Economic conditions. United States -- Economic conditions -- Regional disparities. United States -- Foreign economic relations.

HC103.B78845 1990
Bruchey, Stuart Weems.
Enterprise: the dynamic economy of a free people/ Stuart Bruchey. Cambridge, Mass.: Harvard University Press, 1990. xiv, 645 p.
89-011102   330.973   0674257456
Capitalism -- United States -- History. Free enterprise -- United States -- History. Industrial laws and legislation -- United States -- History. United States -- Economic conditions.

HC103.C26 1996
The Cambridge economic history of the United States/ edited by Stanley L. Engerman, Robert E. Gallman. Cambridge [England]; Cambridge University Press, 1996-2000. 3 v.
95-000860   330.973   5213944221
United States -- Economic conditions.

HC103.D753 1993
Dowd, Douglas Fitzgerald, 1919-
U.S. capitalist development since 1776: of, by, and for which people?/ Douglas Dowd. Armonk, N.Y.: M.E. Sharpe, c1993. xxvii, 561 p.
93-016219   338.973/009   1563241668
Capitalism -- United States -- History. Income distribution -- United States -- History. Wealth -- United States -- History. United States -- Economic conditions.

HC103.E52
Encyclopedia of American economic history: studies of the principal movements and ideas/ Glenn Porter, editor. New York: Scribner, c1980. 3 v.
79-004946   330.9/73   0684162717
United States -- Economic conditions -- Addresses, essays, lectures.

HC103.F3 1976
Faulkner, Harold Underwood, 1890-1968.
American economic history: a comprehensive revision of the earlier work by Harold Underwood Faulkner/ Harry N. Scheiber, Harold G. Vatter, Harold Underwood Faulkner. New York: Harper & Row, c1976. viii, 514 p.
76-016126   330.9/73   0060420014
United States -- Economic conditions.

HC103.F58
Fogel, Robert William,
The reinterpretation of American economic history. Edited by Robert William Fogel and Stanley L. Engerman. New York, Harper & Row [1971] xxiv, 494 p.
75-141166   330.973   0060421096
United States -- Economic conditions -- Addresses, essays, lectures.

HC103.F9 2000
Frumkin, Norman.
Guide to economic indicators/ Norman Frumkin. 3rd ed. Armonk, N.Y.: M.E. Sharpe, c2000. xviii, 328 p.
99-041506   330.973/0021 21   076560437X
Economic indicators -- United States. Business cycles -- United States -- Statistics.

HC103.H76 1991
Hughes, Jonathan R. T.
The governmental habit redux: economic controls from colonial times to the present/ Jonathan R.T. Hughes. Princeton, N.J.: Princeton University Press, c1991. xv, 265 p.
90-020145   338.973   0691042721
United States -- Economic policy.

HC103.J3
Jaher, Frederic Cople.
The age of industrialism in America; essays in social structure and cultural values. Edited by Frederic Cople Jaher. New York, Free Press [1968] x, 400 p.
68-014107   309.1/73
Industries -- United States. Social structure -- United States. United States -- Economic conditions. United States -- Social conditions.

HC103.M56 1993
Minority group influence: agenda setting, formulation, and public policy/ edited by Paula D. McClain. Westport, Conn.: Greenwood Press, 1993. x, 218 p.
93-007707   338.973   0313290369
Minorities -- United States. United States -- Economic policy -- Decision making. United States -- Social policy -- Citizen participation. United States -- Social policy -- Decision making.

HC103.N63 1968b
North, Douglas Cecil,
The growth of the American economy to 1860, edited by Douglass C. North & Robert Paul Thomas. Columbia, University of South Carolina Press [1968] vii, 251 p.
68-005916   330.973
United States -- Economic conditions -- To 1865.

HC103.P417 2002
Perelman, Michael.
The pathology of the U.S. economy revisited: the intractable contradictions of economic policy/ Michael Perelman. 1st ed. New York, N.Y.: Palgrave, 2002. 247 p.
2001-044659   330.973 21   0312293178
Industrial relations -- United States. Monetary policy -- United States. Finance -- United States.

HC103.S43 1993
Second thoughts: myths and morals of U.S. economic history/ edited by Donald N. McCloskey. New York: Oxford University Press, 1993. x, 208 p.
92-009096   330.973   0195066332
United States -- Economic conditions. United States -- Economic policy.

HC103.7.N278 1998
Natural resources/ editors, Mark S. Coyne, Craig W. Allin; project editor McCrea Adams. Pasadena, Calif.: Salem Press, c1998. 3 v.
97-043364   333.7/03 21   0893569127
Natural resources -- United States -- Encyclopedias.   Natural   resources   -- Encyclopedias.

HC103.7.N296 1990
Natural resources for the 21st century/ edited by R. Neil Sampson and Dwight Hair. Washington, D.C.: Island Press [in cooperation with] American Fore c1990. xiv, 349 p.
89-019946   333.7/0973   1559630035
Renewable natural resources -- United States -- Management -- Congresses. Environmental policy -- United States -- Congresses.

HC103.7.P48 1988
Petulla, Joseph M.
American environmental history/ Joseph M. Petulla. Columbus: Merrill Pub. Co., c1988. xv, 444 p.
87-061585   333.7/0973   0675208858
Natural resources -- United States -- History. Conservation of natural resources -- United States -- History. Human ecology -- United States -- History.

HC103.7.S84 1983
Stroup, Richard.
Natural resources: bureaucratic myths and environmental management/ by Richard L. Stroup and John A. Baden, with the assistance of David T. Fractor; foreword by William A. Niskanen. San Francisco, Calif.: Pacific Institute for Public Policy Research; c1983. xvi, 148 p.
83-002607   333.7/0973   0884103803
Conservation of natural resources -- United States -- Decision making. Conservation of natural resources -- Government policy -- United States. Environmental management -- United States -- Decision making.

HC104.E26 1988
The Economy of early America: the revolutionary period, 1763-1790/ edited by Ronald Hoffman ... [et al.]. Charlottesville: Published for the United States Capitol Historic 1988. xvi, 334 p.
87-006169   330.973/02   0813911397
United States -- Economic conditions -- To 1865 -- Regional disparities. Great Britain -- Colonies -- America -- Economic conditions -- Regional disparities.

HC104.J67
Jones, Alice Hanson, 1904-
Wealth of a nation to be: the American colonies on the eve of the Revolution/ Alice Hanson Jones. New York: Columbia University Press, 1980. xxxvi, 494 p.
79-028543   330.973/027   0231036590
Wealth -- United States -- History.   United States -- Economic conditions -- To 1865.

HC104.K85 2000
Kulikoff, Allan.
From British peasants to colonial American farmers/ by Allan Kulikoff. Chapel Hill, NC: University of North Carolina Press, 2000. xiii, 484 p.
00-029904   338.1/0973 21   0807848824
Agriculture -- Economic aspects -- United States -- History. Agriculture -- Economic aspects -- Great Britain -- History. Agriculture -- Economic aspects -- Europe -- History.

HC104.P47
Perkins, Edwin J.
The economy of colonial America/ Edwin J. Perkins. New York: Columbia University Press, 1980. xii, 177 p.
80-016478   330.973/02   0231049587
United States -- Economic conditions -- To 1865.

HC105.B45 2000
Bensel, Richard Franklin, 1949-
The   political   economy   of   American industrialization, 1877-1900/ Richard Franklin Bensel. Cambridge [England]; Cambridge University Press, 2000. xxiii, 549 p.
00-023677   338.973/009/034   0521772338
Industrialization -- United States -- History -- 19th century. Democracy -- United States -- History -- 19th century. United States -- Economic conditions -- 1865-1918.

HC105.B77 1989
Bourgin, Frank, 1910-
The great challenge: the myth of laissez-faire in the early republic/ Frank Bourgin; foreword by Arthur Schlesinger, Jr. New York: G. Braziller, 1989. 223 p.
88-031184   330.15/3   0807612170
Laissez-faire.   United States -- Economic conditions -- To 1865. United States -- Economic policy -- To 1933.

HC105.C64
Cochran, Thomas Childs, 1902-
Frontiers of change: early industrialism in America/ Thomas C. Cochran. New York: Oxford University Press, 1981. 179 p.
80-020788   338.0973   0195028759
Industries -- United States -- History. Technological innovations -- United States -- History. United States -- Social conditions -- To 1865. United States -- Economic conditions -- To 1865.

HC105.H8 1970
Hoffmann, Charles, 1921-
The depression of the nineties; an economic history. Westport, Conn., Greenwood Pub. Corp. [1970] lvi, 326 p.
78-090790   338.54   0837118557
Depressions -- 1893. United States -- Economic conditions -- 1865-1918.

HC105.K87 1992
Kulikoff, Allan.
The agrarian origins of American capitalism/ Allan Kulikoff. Charlottesville: University Press of Virginia, 1992. xiv, 341 p.
92-011395   338.1/0973 20   0813913888
Agriculture -- Economic aspects -- United States -- History. Capitalism -- United States -- History.

HC105.L26 2001
Larson, John Lauritz, 1950-
Internal improvement: national public works and the promise of popular government in the early United States/ John Lauritz Larson. Chapel Hill: University of North Carolina Press, c2001. xv, 324 p.
00-060721   338.973 21   0807825956
Infrastructure (Economics) -- Government policy -- United States -- History -- 19th century. Public works -- Government policy -- United States -- History -- 19th century. United States -- Economic policy -- To 1933. United States -- Economic conditions -- To 1865.

HC105.L53 1995
Licht, Walter, 1946-
Industrializing America: the nineteenth century/ Walter Licht. Baltimore: Johns Hopkins University Press, 1995. xviii, 219 p.
94-037654   338.0973/09/034   0801850134
Industrialization -- United States -- History -- 19th century. Capitalism -- United States -- History -- 19th century. Industrial policy -- United States -- History -- 19th century. United States -- Economic conditions -- To 1865 -- Regional disparities. United States -- Economic conditions -- 1865-1918 -- Regional disparities.

HC105.P94
Pred, Allan Richard, 1936-
The spatial dynamics of U.S. urban-industrial growth, 1800-1914: interpretive and theoretical essays [by] Allan R. Pred. Cambridge, Mass., M.I.T. Press [1966] x, 225 p.
66-026016   301.364
Cities and towns -- Growth. Cities and towns -- United States. Industries -- United States -- History.

HC105.S38 1991
Sellers, Charles Grier.
The market revolution: Jacksonian America, 1815-1846/ Charles Sellers. New York: Oxford University Press, 1991. 502 p.
90-024188   0195038894
Capitalism -- Social aspects -- United States -- History -- 19th century. Representative government and representation -- United States -- History -- 19th century. Democracy -- History -- 19th century. United States -- Economic conditions -- To 1865.

HC105.T4
Temin, Peter.
The Jacksonian economy.   New York, Norton [1969] 208 p.
69-018099   330.973
Jackson, Andrew, -- 1767-1845. Depressions -- 1836-1837 -- United States.   United States -- Economic conditions -- To 1865.

HC105.W54
Williams, William Appleman.
The roots of the modern American empire; a study of the growth and shaping of social consciousness in a marketplace society.   New York, Random House [1969] xxiv, 547 p.
77-085619   330.973
United States -- Economic conditions -- 1865-1918. United States -- History -- 1865-1898.

HC105.6.G3
Gates, Paul Wallace, 1901-
Agriculture and the Civil War, by Paul W. Gates. New York, Knopf, 1965. x, 383 p.
65-013461   973.71
Agriculture -- Economic aspects -- United States. United States -- History -- Civil War, 1861-1865 -- Economic aspects.

HC105.6.R53 1997
Richardson, Heather Cox.
The greatest nation of the earth: Republican economic policies during the Civil War/ Heather Cox Richardson. Cambridge, Mass.: Harvard University Press, 1997. viii, 342 p.
96-046707 338.973 0674362136
United States -- Economic conditions -- To 1865. United States -- History -- Civil War, 1861-1865 United States -- Economic policy -- To 1933.

HC106.C52 1974
Chamberlain, John, 1903-
The enterprising Americans: a business history of the United States. New York, Harper & Row [1974] xix, 282 p.
73-004069 330.9/73 0060107022
United States -- Economic conditions.

HC106.C6315
Cochran, Thomas Childs, 1902-
American business in the twentieth century [by] Thomas C. Cochran. Cambridge, Harvard University Press, 1972. vi, 259 p.
72-078424 330.9/73/09 0674021010
United States -- Economic conditions.

HC106.P6
Pinchot, Gifford, 1865-1946.
The fight for conservation, by Gifford Pinchot. New York, Doubleday, Page, 1910. vii, 152 p.
10-019948
Natural resources. United States -- Economic conditions.

HC106.S676 1993b
Sobel, Robert, 1931 Feb. 19-
The age of giant corporations: a microeconomic history of American business, 1914-1992/ Robert Sobel. Westport, Conn.: Greenwood Press, 1993. xiii, 315 p.
92-033304 338.7/4/09730904 0313287309
Industries -- United States -- History -- 20th century. Industrial policy -- United States -- History -- 20th century. Corporations -- United States -- History -- 20th century.

HC106.S79 1994
Stein, Herbert,
Presidential economics: the making of economic policy from Roosevelt to Clinton/ Herbert Stein. 3rd rev. ed. Washington, D.C.: American Enterprise Institute for Public Policy 495 p.
93-040697 338.973 20 0844738506
Presidents -- United States -- History -- 20th century.

HC106.S85 2001
The structure of American industry/ Walter Adams, James W. Brock, editors. 10th ed. Upper Saddle River, N.J.: Prentice Hall, c2001. xii, 384 p.
00-035958 338.0973 21 0130179167
Industries -- United States.

HC106.V4 1964
Veblen, Thorstein, 1857-1929.
Absentee ownership and business enterprise in recent times; the case of America. New York, A. M. Kelley, bookseller, 1964 [c1923] 445 p.
63-023516 338.01
Economic history -- 1918-1945. Industries -- United States.

HC106.W15 1997
Walker, John F., 1937-
The rise of big government in the United States/ John F. Walker, Harold G. Vatter. Armonk, N.Y.: M.E. Sharpe, c1997. xiii, 260 p.
96-040286 330.973 21 0765600668
Fiscal policy -- United States -- History -- 20th century. Free enterprise -- United States -- History -- 20th century. Mixed economy -- United States -- History -- 20th century. United States -- Economic policy. United States -- Politics and government -- 20th century. United States -- Foreign relations -- 20th century.

HC106.W515 1980
Weiss, Leonard W.
Case studies in American industry/ Leonard W. Weiss. New York: Wiley, c1980. xix, 396 p.
78-031149 338/.0973 0471031593
Industrial policy -- United States -- Case studies. Agriculture and state -- United States -- Case studies. United States -- Economic policy -- Case studies.

HC106.3.B269 1996
Barber, William J.
Designs within disorder: Franklin D. Roosevelt, the economists, and the shaping of American economic policy, 1933-1945/ William J. Barber. Cambridge; Cambridge University Press, 1996. ix, 178 p.
95-045049 338.9 0521560780
Roosevelt, Franklin D. -- (Franklin Delano), -- 1882-1945. United States -- Economic policy -- 1933-1945. United States -- Politics and government -- 1933-1945. United States -- Economic policy -- To 1933.

HC106.3.B43
Beard, Charles Austin, 1874-1948.
The open door at home: a trial philosophy of national interest/ by Charles A. Beard; with the collaboration of G.H.E. Smith. New York: Macmillan, 1934. viii, 331 p.
34-038709 330.973
Economic policy United States -- Economic policy -- 1933-1945. United States -- Foreign relations. United States -- Commercial policy.

HC106.3.C714 vol. 30
Output, employment, and productivity in the United States after 1800. New York, National Bureau of Economic Research; 1966. xiv, 660 p.
65-015964 330.973
United States -- Economic conditions.

HC106.3.C714 vol. 48
The Measurement of labor cost/ edited by Jack E. Triplett. Chicago: University of Chicago Press, 1983. xi, 539 p.
83-005920 330 s 0226812561
Labor costs -- United States -- Congresses. Employee fringe benefits -- United States -- Congresses.

HC106.3.C748 1998
Couch, Jim F., 1959-
The political economy of the New Deal/ Jim F. Couch, William F. Shughart II. Cheltenham, UK; E. Elgar, c1998. xvi, 247 p.
98-027149 338.973/009/043 21 1858988993
Depressions -- 1929 -- United States. New Deal, 1933-1939. United States -- Economic policy -- 1933-1945. United States -- Politics and government -- 1933-1945.

HC106.3.D3667
Denison, Edward Fulton, 1915-
Accounting for United States economic growth, 1929-1969 [by] Edward F. Denison. Washington, Brookings Institution [1974] xviii, 355 p.
74-001137 330.9/73/09 0815718047
United States -- Economic conditions -- 1918-1945. United States -- Economic conditions -- 1945-

HC106.3.E18 1998
The economics of the great depression/ Mark Wheeler, editor. Kalamazoo, Mich.: W.E. Upjohn Institute for Employment Research, c1998. iii, 213 p.
98-045367 330.973/0916 21 0880991925
Depressions -- 1929 -- United States. United States -- Economic conditions -- 1918-1945.

HC106.3.G625 1994
Gordon, Colin, 1962-
New deals: business, labor, and politics in America, 1920-1935/ Colin Gordon. Cambridge [England]; Cambridge University Press, 1994. xii, 329 p.
93-034538 338.973/009/043 0521451221
New Deal, 1933-1939. Labor policy -- United States -- History -- 20th century. United States -- Economic policy -- To 1933. United States -- Economic policy -- 1933-1945. United States -- Politics and government -- 1933-1945.

HC106.3.H544 1991
Hixson, William F.
A matter of interest: reexamining money, debt, and real economic growth/ William F. Hixson; foreword by John H. Hotson. New York: Praeger, 1991. xxix, 274 p.
91-004628 330.12/6 0275938956
United States -- Economic conditions -- 1918-1945. United States -- Economic conditions -- 1945-

HC106.3.H6149 1972
Hoover, Herbert, 1874-1964.
American ideals versus the New Deal. St. Clair Shores, Mich., Scholarly Press, 1972. 96 p.
78-131746 330.9/73/0917 0403006333
New Deal, 1933-1939. United States -- Economic policy -- 1933-1945. United States -- Politics and government -- 1933-1945.

HC106.3.L398 1988
Levine, Rhonda F.
Class struggle and the New Deal: industrial labor, industrial capital, and the state/ Rhonda F. Levine. Lawrence, Kan.: University Press of Kansas, c1988. xi, 233 p.
88-017183 338.973 0700603735
Social conflict -- United States -- History -- 20th century. New Deal, 1933-1939. United States -- Economic policy -- 1933-1945.

HC106.3.L53
Lippmann, Walter, 1889-1974.
The new imperative, by Walter Lippmann. New York, The Macmillan Company, 1935. 52 p.
35-027319 330.973
Industries -- Organization, control, etc. Industrial policy -- United States. United States -- Economic policy. United States -- Politics and government -- 1929-1933. United States -- Politics and government -- 1933-1945.

HC106.3.L9
Lyon, Leverett S. b. 1885.
Government and economic life; development and current issues of American public policy. Washington, D.C., The Brookings institution, 1939-1940. 2 v.
39-031511   330.973
Industrial policy -- United States. United States -- Economic policy. United States -- Politics and government.

HC106.3.N59 1985
Norton, Hugh Stanton, 1921-
The quest for economic stability: Roosevelt to Reagan/ by Hugh S. Norton. Columbia, S.C.: University of South Carolina Press, c1985. xvii, 329 p.
85-014002   338.973   087249456X
Economic stabilization -- United States -- History -- 20th century. United States -- Economic policy.

HC106.3.R36 1999
Reagan, Patrick D., 1953-
Designing a new America: the origins of New Deal planning, 1890-1943/ Patrick D. Reagan. Amherst: University of Massachusetts Press, c2000. xii, 362 p.
99-030717   338.973/009/043 21   1558492305
New Deal, 1933-1939. United States -- Economic policy -- 1933-1945.

HC106.3.T78 1969
Tugwell, Rexford G. 1891-
The battle for democracy, by Rexford G. Tugwell. New York, Greenwood Press [1969, c1935] vi, 330 p.
69-014124   330.973   083711862X
United States -- Politics and government -- 1933-1945. United States -- Economic conditions -- 1918-1945.

HC106.3.V4 1965
Veblen, Thorstein, 1857-1929.
The engineers and the price system. New York, A. M. Kelley, bookseller, 1965. 169 p.
65-015955   338
Industries. Capitalism. United States -- Economic conditions -- 1918-1945.

HC106.4.C42 1968
Chase, Stuart, 1888-
The road we are traveling, 1914-1942; guide lines to America's future as reported to the Twentieth Century Fund. New York, Greenwood Press, 1968 [c1942] 106 p.
68-008057   330.973
Reconstruction (1939-1951) -- United States. United States -- Economic policy.

HC106.5.A5948
The American economy in transition/ edited by Martin Feldstein. Chicago: University of Chicago Press, 1980. viii, 696 p.
80-017450   330.973/092   0226240819
United States -- Economic conditions -- 1945- - - Addresses, essays, lectures.

HC106.5.B763
The Brookings model: some further results. Edited by James S. Duesenberry [and others] Chicago, Rand McNally, 1969. xxi, 519 p.
69-016034   330/.01/82
United States -- Economic conditions -- Econometric models -- Addresses, essays, lectures.

HC106.5.C29 1995
Carroll, Richard J.
An economic record of presidential performance: from Truman to Bush/ Richard J. Carroll. Westport, Conn.: Praeger, 1995. xv, 268 p.
95-003334   330.973/092   0275948366
Budget -- United States -- History -- 20th century. Government spending policy -- United States -- History -- 20th century. United States -- Economic conditions -- 1945-

HC106.5.C685 1996
Cosgrove, Michael
The cost of winning: global development policies and broken social contracts/ Michael H. Cosgrove. New Brunswick, N.J.: Transaction Publishers, c1996. xvii, 317 p.
95-044246   337.73 20   1560002298
Economic forecasting -- United States. United States -- Economic conditions -- 1945- United States -- Economic policy. United States -- Foreign economic relations.

HC106.5.F727 1997
French, Michael.
U.S. economic history since 1945/ Michael French. New York: Manchester University Press: 1997. 236 p.
96-046267   330.973/091   0719041856
United States -- Economic conditions -- 1945-

HC106.5.G32 1984
Galbraith, John Kenneth, 1908-
The affluent society/ John Kenneth Galbraith. Boston: Houghton Mifflin, 1984. xxxvii, 291 p.
84-012880   330.973   0395366135
Economics -- United States. United States -- Economic conditions -- 1945- United States -- Economic policy.

HC106.5.H516 1996
History of the U.S. economy since World War II/ Harold G. Vatter and John F. Walker, editors. Armonk, N.Y.: M.E. Sharpe, c1996. xx, 499 p.
95-019965   333.973/092 B 20   156324473X
United States -- Economic conditions -- 1945- United States -- Economic policy.

HC106.5.J33 1997
Jacoby, Sanford M., 1953-
Modern manors: welfare capitalism since the New Deal/ Sanford M. Jacoby. Princeton, NJ: Princeton University Press, c1997. xii, 345 p.
97-007835   330.12/2/0973 21   0691015708
Welfare state. Capitalism -- United States. United States -- Economic conditions -- 1945-

HC106.5.P79 1996
Pryor, Frederic L.
Economic evolution and structure: the impact of complexity on the U.S. economic system/ Frederic L. Pryor. Cambridge; Cambridge University Press, 1996. xv, 399 p.
95-013037   330.973   0521550971
Economic forecasting -- United States. Economic indicators -- United States. Organizational change. United States -- Economic conditions -- 1945-

HC106.5.S64 1993
Sommers, Albert T.
The U.S. economy demystified: the meaning of U.S. business statistics and what they portend for the future/ Albert T. Sommers with Lucie R. Blau. 3rd ed. New York: Lexington Books; xiv, 192 p.
92-034701   330.973/0928 20   0029301165
National income -- United States -- Accounting.

HC106.5.S696 1995
Spulber, Nicolas.
The American economy: the struggle for supremacy in the 21st century/ Nicolas Spulber. Cambridge [England]; Cambridge University Press, 1995. xvii, 286 p.
94-031451   330.973   0521480132
Competition, International. United States -- Economic conditions -- 1945-

HC106.5.U42 1994
Understanding American economic decline / edited by Michael A. Bernstein, David E. Adler. Cambridge [England]; Cambridge University Press, 1994. xvii, 403 p.
93-048755   330.973   0521450632
United States -- Economic conditions -- 1945- United States -- Economic policy.

HC106.5.W32
Walton, Scott D.
American business and its environment [by] Scott D. Walton. New York, Macmillan [1966] xvi, 654 p.
66-014694   338.0973
Industries -- Social aspects. Industrial policy -- United States. United States -- Commerce.

HC106.6.C287 1991
Campagna, Anthony S.
The economic consequences of the Vietnam war/ Anthony S. Campagna. New York: Praeger, 1991. xiv, 159 p.
90-045296   973.923   0275933881
Vietnamese Conflict, 1961-1975 -- Economic aspects -- United States. United States -- Economic conditions -- 1961-1971. United States -- Economic conditions -- 1971-1981.

HC106.6.E237 2000
Economic events, ideas, and policies: the 1960s and after/ George L. Perry, James Tobin, editors. Washington, DC: Brookings Institution Press, c2000. xiv, 365 p.
00-009634   338.973/009/046 21   081577012X
United States -- Economic policy -- 1961-1971. United States -- Economic policy. United States -- Economic conditions -- 1961-1971.

HC106.6.G344
Galbraith, John Kenneth, 1908-
Economics and the public purpose. Boston, Houghton Mifflin, 1973. xvi, 334 p.
73-008750   338.973   0395172063
Corporations -- United States. Industrial policy - - United States. United States -- Economic conditions -- 1961-1971. United States -- Economic policy -- 1971-1981.

HC106.6.G35 1978
Galbraith, John Kenneth, 1908-
The new industrial state/ John Kenneth Galbraith. Boston: Houghton Mifflin, 1978. xxiv, 438 p.
78-006310   338/.0973   0395257123
Industries -- United States. Industrial policy -- United States.

HC106.6.H35
Heath, Jim F.
John F. Kennedy and the business community [by] Jim F. Heath. Chicago, University of Chicago Press [1969] ix, 198 p.
75-082114   338.973   0226322319
Industrial policy -- United States. United States -- Economic policy -- 1961-1971.

HC106.6.M383 1998
Matusow, Allen J.
Nixon's economy: booms, busts, dollars, and votes/ Allen J. Matusow. Lawrence, Kan.: University Press of Kansas, c1998. xii, 323 p.
97-049995 338.973/009/047 21 0700608885
Nixon, Richard M. -- (Richard Milhous), -- 1913- United States -- Economic policy -- 1961-1971. United States -- Economic policy -- 1971-1981.

HC106.6.O46
Okun, Arthur M.
The political economy of prosperity [by] Arthur M. Okun. Washington, Brookings Institution [1970] vi, 152 p.
76-108835 338.973 0815764782
Economic stabilization. United States -- Economic policy -- 1961-1971.

HC106.6.R69 1994
Rowen, Hobart.
Self-inflicted wounds: from LBJ's guns and butter to Reagan's voodoo economics/ Hobart Rowen. New York: Times Books, c1994. xvi, 447 p.
94-004081 338.973 0812918649
International economic relations. United States -- Economic policy -- 1971-1981. United States -- Economic policy -- 1981-1993. United States -- Economic policy -- 1961-1971.

HC106.6.T93 1988
Two revolutions in economic policy: the first economic reports of Presidents Kennedy and Reagan/ edited by James Tobin and Murray Weidenbaum; [with introductions by Robert M. Solow ... et al.]. Cambridge, Mass.: MIT Press, c1988. ix, 533 p.
87-035828 338.973 0262700344
Kennedy, John F. -- (John Fitzgerald), -- 1917-1963. Reagan, Ronald. United States -- Economic policy -- 1961-1971. United States -- Economic policy -- 1981-1993.

HC106.6.W56 1988
Winant, Howard.
Stalemate: political economic origins of supply-side policy/ Howard A. Winant. New York: Praeger, 1988. xv, 203 p.
87-015157 338.973
Supply-side economics -- United States -- History -- 20th century. United States -- Economic policy -- 1971-1981. United States -- Economic policy -- 1981-1993. United States -- Economic policy -- 1961-1971.

HC106.7.C34 1995
Campagna, Anthony S.
Economic policy in the Carter administration/ Anthony S. Campagna. Westport, Conn.: Greenwood Press, 1995. xv, 216 p.
95-022981 338.973/009/047 0313295689
Carter, Jimmy, -- 1924- United States -- Politics and government -- 1977-1981. United States -- Economic policy -- 1971-1981.

HC106.7.P67
Porter, Roger B.
Presidential decision making: the Economic Policy Board/ Roger B. Porter. Cambridge; Cambridge University Press, 1980. xii, 265 p.
80-010165 353.0082 0521233372
United States -- Economic policy -- 1971-1981.

HC106.7.R35
The Reindustrialization of America/ by the Business week team, Seymour Zucker ... [et al.]. New York: McGraw-Hill, c1982. v, 200 p.
81-008360 338.0973 0070093245
Industries -- United States. United States -- Economic policy -- 1981-1993.

HC106.8.A42 1984
Alperovitz, Gar.
Rebuilding America/ Gar Alperovitz & Jeff Faux. New York: Pantheon Books, [1984] xi, 319 p.
83-004206 338.973 0394532007
United States -- Economic policy -- 1981-1993.

HC106.8.B345 1993
Baily, Martin Neil.
Growth with equity: economic policymaking for the next century/ Martin Neil Baily, Gary Burtless, Robert E. Litan. Washington, D.C.: Brookings Institution, c1993. xv, 239 p.
92-044225 338.973 0815707665
Income distribution -- United States. Technological innovations -- Economic aspects -- United States. Labor supply -- United States. United States -- Economic policy -- 1981- United States -- Economic conditions -- 1981-

HC106.8.B365 1998
Barnes, William R.
The new regional economies: the U.S. common market and the global economy/ William R. Barnes, Larry C. Ledebur. Thousand Oaks, Calif.: Sage Publications, c1998. xvi, 191 p.
97-004751 330.973 21 0761909389
Intergovernmental fiscal relations -- United States. Regional economics. Competition, International. United States -- Economic conditions -- 1981- -- Regional disparities.

HC106.8.D68 1997
Dowd, Douglas Fitzgerald, 1919-
Against the conventional wisdom: a primer for current economic controversies and proposals/ Douglas Dowd. Boulder, Colo.: Westview Press, 1997. x, 198 p.
97-011797 338.973 0813327954
Free enterprise -- United States. Radical economics. United States -- Economic policy -- 1981-1993. United States -- Economic policy -- 1993-

HC106.8.E45 1994
Eisner, Robert.
The misunderstood economy: what counts and how to count it/ Robert Eisner. Boston, Mass.: Harvard Business School Press, c1994. xv, 222 p.
93-031481 330.973 087584443X
Economics -- United States. United States -- Economic conditions -- 1981-

HC106.8.F78 1998
Frumkin, Norman.
Tracking America's economy/ Norman Frumkin. Armonk, N.Y.: M.E. Sharpe, c1998. xxi, 335 p.
97-038468 338.5/44/0973 21 0765600013
Economic forecasting -- United States. Economic indicators -- United States. United States -- Economic policy -- 1981-1993. United States -- Economic policy -- 1993-

HC106.8.G3394 1992
Galbraith, John Kenneth, 1908-
The culture of contentment/ John Kenneth Galbraith. Boston: Houghton Mifflin Co., 1992. ix, 195 p.
91-047038 306.3/0973/09075 0395572282
Poor -- United States. Free enterprise -- United States. Social values. United States -- Economic policy -- 1981-1993. United States -- Economic conditions -- 1981- United States -- Social conditions -- 1980-

HC106.8.G594 2001
Global warming and the American economy: a regional assessment of climate change impacts/ edited by Robert Mendelsohn. Northampton, MA: Edward Elgar Pub., 2001. xiv, 209 p.
2001-018972 330.973/092 21 1840645938
Climatic changes -- United States.

HC106.8.G73 1982
Greider, William.
The education of David Stockman and other Americans/ William Greider. New York: Dutton, c1982. xxx, 159 p.
82-072489 338.973 0525480102
Stockman, David Alan, -- 1946- Budget -- United States. Government spending policy -- United States. United States -- Economic policy -- 1981-1993.

HC106.8.I53 2002
Industry studies/ edited by Larry L. Duetsch. 3rd ed. Armonk, N.Y.: M.E. Sharpe, c2002. xvii, 394 p.
2002-023102 338.0973 21 0765609630
Industries -- United States -- Case studies. Industrial policy -- United States -- Case studies. Competition -- United States -- Case studies.

HC106.8.K78 1990
Krugman, Paul R.
The age of diminished expectations: U.S. economic policy in the 1990s/ Paul Krugman. Cambridge, Mass.: MIT Press, c1990. xii, 209 p.
90-006310 338.973/001 026211156X
Economic forecasting -- United States. United States -- Economic policy -- 1981-1993.

HC106.8.N453 1995
Nelson, Joel I.
Post-industrial capitalism: exploring economic inequality in America/ Joel I. Nelson. Thousand Oaks: Sage Publications, c1995. 193 p.
95-008957 330.973 0803973322
Capitalism -- United States. Income distribution -- United States. Poverty -- United States. United States -- Economic conditions -- 1981-

HC106.8.O47 2000
O'Hara, Frederick M.
Handbook of United States economic and financial indicators/ F.M. O'Hara, Jr. and F.M. O'Hara III. Westport, Conn.: Greenwood Press, 2000. x, 395 p.
99-054281 330.973 0313274509
Economic indicators -- United States -- Handbooks, manuals, etc.

HC106.8.O78 1990
Ortner, Robert.
Voodoo deficits/ Robert Ortner. Homewood, Ill.: Dow Jones-Irwin, c1990. x, 192 p.
90-030834 339.5/23/0973 1556232802
Supply-side economics -- United States. Budget deficits -- United States. Balance of trade -- United States. United States -- Foreign economic relations. United States -- Economic policy -- 1981-1993.

HC106.8.P345 1998
Palley, Thomas I., 1956-
Plenty of nothing: the downsizing of the American dream and the case for structural Keynesianism/ Thomas I. Palley. Princeton, N.J.: Princeton University Press, c1998. xvi, 238 p.
97-034907 338.973 21 0691048479
Keynesian economics. United States -- Economic policy -- 1993- United States -- Economic conditions -- 1981- United States -- Economic policy -- 1981-1993.

HC106.8.R6 1984
Roberts, Paul Craig, 1939-
The supply-side revolution: an insider's account of policymaking in Washington/ Paul Craig Roberts. Cambridge, Mass.: Harvard University Press, 1984. 327 p.
83-018340   338.973   0674856201
Supply-side economics. United States -- Economic policy -- 1981-1993.

HC106.8.S574 1999
Sloan, John W., 1940-
The Reagan effect: economics and presidential leadership/ John W. Sloan. Lawrence, Kan.: University Press of Kansas, c1999. xi, 311 p.
98-043844   338.973/009/048 21   0700609512
Reagan, Ronald. Conservatism -- United States -- History -- 20th century. Political leadership -- United States -- History -- 20th century. Supply-side economics -- United States. United States -- Politics and government -- 1981-1989. United States -- Economic policy -- 1981-1993.

HC106.8.S7352 1995
State of the union: America in the 1990s/ Reynolds Farley, editor. New York: Russell Sage Foundation, c1995. 2 v.
94-040284   303.4/0973   0871542404
Economic forecasting -- United States. United States -- Economic conditions -- 1981- United States -- Census, 21st, 1990.

HC106.8.S7414 1999
The illustrated guide to the American economy/ by Herbert Stein & Murray Foss; with the assistance of Matthew Clement. Washington, D.C.: AEI Press, 1999. xvi, 285 p.
99-039716   330.973/092 21   0844741035
United States -- Economic conditions -- 1981-

HC106.82.A456 2002
American economic policy in the 1990s/ editors, Jeffrey Frankel, Peter Orszag. Cambridge, Mass.: MIT Press, c2002. xii, 1119 p.
2002-019898   338.973/009/049 21   0262062305
United States -- Economic policy -- 1993-2001. United States -- Economic conditions -- 1981-2001.

HC106.82.B58 1999
Bjork, Gordon C.
The way it worked and why it won't: structural change and the slowdown of U.S. economic growth/ Gordon C. Bjork. Westport, Conn.: Praeger, 1999. xviii, 299 p.
98-053395   338.973 21   0275965317
Structural adjustment (Economic policy) -- United States.

HC106.82.G55 2001
Glazer, Amihai.
Why government succeeds and why it fails/ Amihai Glazer, Lawrence S. Rothenberg. Cambridge, Mass.: Harvard University Press, 2001. xii, 204 p.
00-050027   338.973   0674004663
Political planning -- United States. Policy sciences. Rational expectations (Economic theory) United States -- Social policy -- 1993- United States -- Economic policy -- 1993-2001.

HC106.82.K87 1997
Kuttner, Robert.
Everything for sale: the virtues and limits of markets/ Robert Kuttner. 1st ed. New York: Alfred A. Knopf, 1997. xvi, 410 p.
96-021010   338.973 20   0394583922
Industrial policy -- United States. Environmental policy -- United States. Full employment policies -- United States.

HC106.82.M39 2000
McCraw, Thomas K.
American business, 1920-2000: how it worked/ Thomas K. McCraw. Wheeling, Ill.: Harlan Davidson, c2000. xii, 270 p.
99-086083   338.0973/09/04 21   0882959859
Industries -- United States -- History -- 20th century. Corporations -- United States -- History -- 20th century. Labor -- United States -- History -- 20th century. United States -- Commerce -- History -- 20th century. United States -- Economic conditions.

HC106.82.P79 2002
Pryor, Frederic L.
The future of U.S. capitalism/ Frederic L. Pryor. Cambridge, UK; Cambridge University Press, 2002. xiii, 447 p.
2001-052694   330.12/2/0973 21   0521813581
Capitalism -- United States.

HC106.82.S5 1999
Shaffer, Harry G.
American capitalism and the changing role of government/ Harry G. Shaffer. Westport, Conn.: Praeger, 1999. xiv, 134 p.
98-056638   338.973 21   0275966585
Capitalism -- Moral and ethical aspects -- United States. Free enterprise -- Moral and ethical aspects -- United States.

HC107.A11.M17
McManis, Douglas R.
Colonial New England: a historical geography/ Douglas R. McManis; cartographer, Miklos Pinther. New York: Oxford University Press, 1975. ix, 159 p.
74-021824   330.9/74/02   0195019075
New England -- Economic conditions. New England -- Historical geography.

HC107.A11 N46 1998
Newell, Margaret Ellen,
From dependency to independence: economic revolution in colonial New England/ Margaret Ellen Newell. Ithaca, N.Y.: Cornell University Press, 1998. x, 329 p.
97-050566   330.974/09/032 21   080143405X
New England -- Economic conditions. New England -- History -- Colonial period, ca. 1600-1775.

HC107.A115.E37 1996
Egnal, Marc.
Divergent paths: how culture and institutions have shaped North American growth/ Marc Egnal. New York: Oxford University Press, 1996. xvi, 300 p.
95-031904   330.974   0195098668
Northeastern States -- Economic conditions. Southern States -- Economic conditions. Quebec (Province) -- Economic conditions.

HC107.A12.M26 1991
Mancall, Peter C.
Valley of opportunity: economic culture along the upper Susquehanna, 1700-1800/ Peter C. Mancall. Ithaca: Cornell University Press, 1991. xviii, 253 p.
90-055719   330.974802   0801425034
Entrepreneurship -- Susquehanna River Region -- History -- 18th century. Susquehanna River Region -- Social conditions. Susquehanna River Region -- Economic conditions.

HC107.A127.E4 1982
Eller, Ronald D., 1948-
Miners, millhands, and mountaineers: industrialization of the Appalachian South, 1880-1930/ by Ronald D. Eller. Knoxville: University of Tennessee Press, c1982. xxvi, 272 p.
81-016020   330.975   087049340X
Appalachian Region, Southern -- Economic conditions. Appalachian Region, Southern -- Social conditions. Appalachian Region, Southern -- History.

HC107.A127.S24 1994
Salstrom, Paul, 1940-
Appalachia's path to dependency: rethinking a region's economic history, 1730-1940/ Paul Salstrom. Lexington, Ky.: University Press of Kentucky, c1994. xxxvi, 204 p.
93-039818   330.974   0813118603
Poor -- Appalachian Region, Southern -- History. Appalachian Region, Southern -- Social conditions. Appalachian Region, Southern -- Economic conditions.

HC107.A13.C65 1982
Cobb, James C. 1947-
The selling of the South: the Southern crusade for industrial development, 1936-1980/ James C. Cobb. Baton Rouge: Louisiana State University Press, c1982. xii, 293 p.
81-018594   338.975   0807109940
Industrial promotion -- Southern States. Southern States -- Economic conditions -- 1918-

HC107.A13.F66
Flynt, J. Wayne, 1940-
Dixie's forgotten people: the South's poor whites/ J. Wayne Flynt. Bloomington: Indiana University Press, c1979. xviii, 206 p.
78-020613   301.44/1   0253197651
Poor -- Southern States.

HC107.A13.P48 1992
Persky, Joseph.
The burden of dependency: colonial themes in southern economic thought/ Joseph J. Persky. Baltimore: Johns Hopkins University Press, c1992. xi, 183 p.
92-010844   330/.0975   0801844223
Dependency. Southern States -- Economic conditions.

HC107.A13 R28 2001
Ransom, Roger L.,
One kind of freedom: the economic consequences of emancipation/ Roger L. Ransom, Richard Sutch. 2nd ed. Cambridge [England]; Cambridge University Press, 2001. xxvii, 458 p.
00-063045   330.976/04 21   0521795508
African Americans -- Southern States -- Economic conditions.

HC107.A13.S38 1991
Schulman, Bruce J.
From Cotton Belt to Sunbelt: federal policy, economic development, and the transformation of the South, 1938-1980/ Bruce J. Schulman. New York: Oxford University Press, 1991. xii, 333 p.
90-006836   338.975/009/04   0195057031
Economic assistance, Domestic -- United States -- Southern States. Southern States -- Economic conditions -- 1918- Southern States -- Economic policy. Southern States -- Politics and government -- 1865-

HC107.A13.W68 1978
Wright, Gavin.
The political economy of the cotton South: households, markets, and wealth in the nineteenth century/ Gavin Wright. New York: Norton, c1978. xv, 205 p.
77-026715   330.9/75/04   0393056864
Cotton trade -- Southern States -- History. Southern States -- Economic conditions.

HC107.A14.B553 2000
Blanke, David, 1961-
Sowing the American dream: how consumer culture took root in the rural midwest/ David Blanke. Athens, OH: Ohio University Press, 2000. xiii, 282 p.
00-040672   306.3/0977   0821413473
Consumption (Economics) -- Middle West -- History. Consumer behavior -- Middle West -- History.

HC107.A14.K45 1997
Kehoe, Terence.
Cleaning up the Great Lakes: from cooperation to confrontation/ Terence Kehoe. DeKalb: Northern Illinois University Press, 1997. 250 p.
97-013939   363.739/406   0875802257
Water -- Pollution -- Economic aspects -- Great Lakes Region. Environmental policy -- Great Lakes Region.

HC107.A17.L68 1984
Lowitt, Richard, 1922-
The New Deal and the West/ Richard Lowitt. Bloomington: Indiana University Press, c1984. xviii, 283 p.
83-048188   338.973   0253340055
New Deal, 1933-1939 -- West (U.S.) West (U.S.) -- Economic conditions. West (U.S.) -- Economic policy. United States -- Economic policy -- 1933-1945.

HC107.A17.N37 1985
Nash, Gerald D.
The American West transformed: the impact of the Second World War/ Gerald D. Nash. Bloomington: Indiana University Press, c1985. x, 304 p.
83-049524   330.978/032   0253306493
World War, 1939-1945 -- Economic aspects -- West (U.S.) World War, 1939-1945 -- Social aspects -- West (U.S.)

HC107.A17.W67 1985
Worster, Donald, 1941-
Rivers of empire: water, aridity, and the growth of the American West/ Donald Worster. New York: Pantheon Books, c1985. x, 402 p.
85-042890   333.91/00978   039451680X
Water resources development -- West (U.S.) -- History. Water-supply -- West (U.S.) -- History. Hydrology -- West (U.S.) West (U.S.) -- Economic conditions. West (U.S.) -- History.

HC107.C22.N677 1994
Saxenian, AnnaLee.
Regional advantage: culture and competition in Silicon Valley and Route 128/ AnnaLee Saxenian. Cambridge, Mass.: Harvard University Press, 1994. xi, 226 p.
93-039416   338.4/762/000979473   0674753399
High technology industries -- California, Northern. High technology industries -- Massachusetts. United States -- Economic conditions -- 1981- -- Regional disparities.

HC107.C22.S3965 2000
The Silicon Valley edge: a habitat for innovation and entrepreneurship/ edited by Chong-Moon Lee ... [et al.]. Stanford, Calif.: Stanford University Press, c2000. xxiii, 424 p.
00-056340   330.9794/73 21   0804740623
High technology industries -- California -- Santa Clara Valley (Santa Clara County) New business enterprises -- California -- Santa Clara Valley (Santa Clara County) Entrepreneurship -- California -- Santa Clara Valley (Santa Clara County) Santa Clara Valley (Santa Clara County, Calif.) -- Economic conditions. Santa Clara Valley (Santa Clara County, Calif.) -- Social conditions.

HC107.C22.S3975 2000
Understanding Silicon Valley: the anatomy of an entrepreneurial region/ edited by Martin Kenney. Stanford, Calif.: Stanford University Press, c2000. xvi, 285 p.
00-034523   330.9794/73 21   0804737339
High technology industries -- California -- Santa Clara Valley (Santa Clara County) Business enterprises -- California -- Santa Clara Valley (Santa Clara County) Santa Clara Valley (Santa Clara County, Calif.) -- Economic conditions. Santa Clara Valley (Santa Clara County, Calif.) -- Social conditions.

HC107.C8.C47 2001
Chin, Elizabeth M. Liew Siew, 1944-
Purchasing power: black kids and American consumer culture/ Elizabeth Chin. Minneapolis, MN: University of Minnesota Press, c2001. xiii, 258 p.
00-012081   306.3/089/96073 21   0816635102
Consumption (Economics) -- Connecticut -- New Haven. Purchasing power -- Connecticut -- New Haven. Afro-American children -- Connecticut -- New Haven.

HC107.M3.H63
Hoffman, Ronald, 1941-
A spirit of dissension: economics, politics, and the Revolution in Maryland. Baltimore, Johns Hopkins University Press [1973] xiv, 280 p.
73-008127   975.2/03   0801815215
Maryland -- Economic conditions. Maryland -- Politics and government -- To 1775. Maryland -- Politics and government -- 1775-1783.

HC107.M3.M23 1982
Main, Gloria L. 1933-
Tobacco colony: life in early Maryland, 1650-1720/ Gloria L. Main. Princeton, N.J.: Princeton University Press, c1982. xv, 326 p.
82-047603   338.1/7371/09752   069104693X
Cost and standard of living -- Maryland -- History. Plantation life -- Maryland -- History. Tobacco industry -- Maryland -- History. Maryland -- Economic conditions. Maryland -- History -- Colonial period, ca. 1600-1775.

HC107.M4.H23 1969
Handlin, Oscar, 1915-
Commonwealth; a study of the role of government in the American economy: Massachusetts, 1774-1861 [by] Oscar Handlin & Mary Flug Handlin. Cambridge, Belknap Press of Harvard University Press, 1969. xvii, 314 p.
69-018032   330.9744
Industrial policy -- Massachusetts -- History. Massachusetts -- Economic conditions.

HC107.M4.R67 1992
Rothenberg, Winifred Barr.
From market-places to a market economy: the transformation of rural Massachusetts, 1750-1850/ Winifred Barr Rothenberg. Chicago: University of Chicago Press, c1992. xiv, 275 p.
92-013535   330.9744/03   0226729532
Capitalism -- Massachusetts -- History. Rural industries -- Massachusetts -- History. Markets -- Massachusetts -- History.

HC107.N6.F73 2000
Frank, Ross, 1957-
From settler to citizen: New Mexican economic development and the creation of Vecino society, 1750-1820/ Ross Frank. Berkeley: University of California Press, c2000. xxiv, 329 p.
00-034381   338.9789/009/033 21   0520222067
New Mexico -- Economic conditions. New Mexico -- History.

HC107.N72 C653 2002
Bruegel, Martin,
Farm, shop, landing: the rise of a market society in the Hudson Valley, 1780-1860/ Martin Bruegel. Durham, NC: Duke University Press, 2002. xiii, 305 p.
2001-050107   330.9747/3703 21   0822328496
Industrialization -- New York (State) -- Columbia County. Industrialization -- New York (State) -- Greene County.

HC107.N8.B5
Billings, Dwight B., 1948-
Planters and the making of a "new South": class, politics, and development in North Carolina, 1865-1900/ by Dwight B. Billings, Jr. Chapel Hill: University of North Carolina Press, c1979. xiii, 284 p.
78-025952   330.9/756/04   080781315X
Industries -- North Carolina -- History -- 19th century. North Carolina -- Economic conditions. North Carolina -- Social conditions.

HC107.N8.E37
Ekirch, A. Roger, 1950-
"Poor Carolina": politics and society in colonial North Carolina, 1729-1776/ A. Roger Ekirch. Chapel Hill: University of North Carolina Press, c1981. xix, 305 p.
80-039889   330.9756/02   080781475X
North Carolina -- Economic conditions. North Carolina -- Social conditions. North Carolina -- Politics and government -- To 1775.

HC107.N83.P613 1994
Bolton, Charles C.
Poor whites of the antebellum South: tenants and laborers in central North Carolina and northeast Mississippi/ by Charles C. Bolton. Durham: Duke University Press, 1994. x, 258 p.
93-025978   305.5/69/09756   0822314282
Rural poor -- North Carolina -- History. Rural poor -- Mississippi -- History. Whites -- North Carolina -- Social conditions.

HC107.S7 M56 2001
Money, trade, and power: the evolution of colonial South Carolina's plantation society/ edited by Jack P. Greene, Rosemary Brana-Shute, and Randy J. Sparks. Columbia: University of South Carolina Press, 2001. xiii, 399 p.
00-012601   306.3/49 21   1570033749
Plantation life -- South Carolina.

HC107.V8.R33 1996
Ragsdale, Bruce A.
A planters' republic: the search for economic independence in Revolutionary Virginia/ Bruce A. Ragsdale. Madison, WI: Madison House, c1996. xiv, 305 p.
95-018435   330.9755/01 20   0945612400
Virginia -- Economic conditions. Virginia -- Commerce -- History -- 18th century. Virginia -- Politics and government -- To 1775.

HC107.W5.L39 1998
Lewis, Ronald L., 1940-
Transforming the Appalachian countryside: railroads, deforestation, and social change in West Virginia, 1880-1920/ Ronald L. Lewis. Chapel Hill: University of North Carolina Press, c1998. xv, 348 p.
97-036616   338.9754 21   0807824054
Industrialization -- West Virginia. West Virginia -- Social conditions. West Virginia -- Environmental conditions. West Virginia -- Economic conditions.

HC107.W9 W47 2002
Western, Samuel.
Pushed off the mountain, sold down the river: Wyoming's search for its soul/ Samuel Western. Rev. ed. Moose, Wyo.: Homestead Pub., 2002. 128 p.
2002-106486   330.9787 21   0943972736
Wyoming -- Economic conditions.

HC108.A75.P73
Preston, Howard L. 1944-
Automobile age Atlanta: the making of a southern metropolis, 1900-1935/ Howard L. Preston. Athens: University of Georgia Press, c1979. xix, 203 p.
78-017088   309.1/758/23104   0820304638
Automobiles -- Social aspects -- Georgia -- Atlanta -- History. Transportation -- Georgia -- Atlanta -- History. Atlanta (Ga.) -- Economic conditions.

HC108.B65.R62 1991
Roberts, Edward Baer.
Entrepreneurs in high technology: lessons from M.I.T. and beyond/ Edward B. Roberts. New York: Oxford University Press, 1991. xii, 385 p.
90-026256   338.4/76200097446   0195067045
Entrepreneurship -- Massachusetts -- Boston Metropolitan Area. New business enterprises -- Massachusetts -- Boston Metropolitan Area. High technology industries -- Massachusetts -- Boston Metropolitan Area.

HC108.C4 P47 2000
Persky, Joseph.
When corporations leave town: the costs and benefits of metropolitan job sprawl/ Joseph Persky, Wim Wiewel. Detroit: Wayne State University Press, c2000. 189 p.
00-009540   338.6/042/0977311 21   0814329071
Industrial location -- Illinois -- Chicago Metropolitan Area -- Decision making -- Mathematical models. Land use, Urban -- Environmental aspects -- Illinois -- Chicago Metropolitan Area -- Costs -- Mathematical models. Land use, Rural -- Environmental aspects -- Illinois -- Chicago Metropolitan Area -- Costs -- Mathematical models.

HC108.C4 R37 1999
Rast, Joel,
Remaking Chicago: the political origins of urban industrial change/ Joel Rast. DeKalb, Ill.: Northern Illinois University Press, 1999. xiii, 201 p.
98-033177   338.9773/11 21   0875802486
Manufacturing industries -- Illinois -- Chicago -- History -- 20th century. Urban economics -- Case studies.

HC108.C5.R67 1985
Ross, Steven Joseph.
Workers on the edge: work, leisure, and politics in industrializing Cincinnati, 1788-1890/ Steven J. Ross. New York: Columbia University Press, 1985. xx, 406 p.
84-021376   331/.09771/78   023105520X
Working class -- Ohio -- Cincinnati -- History -- 19th century. Working class -- Ohio -- Cincinnati - - History -- 18th century. Industrial relations -- Ohio -- Cincinnati -- History. Cincinnati (Ohio) -- History.

HC108.D6.F37 2000
Farley, Reynolds, 1938-
Detroit divided/ Reynolds Farley, Harry J. Holzer, Sheldon Danziger. New York: Russell Sage Foundation, 2000. 309 p.
99-087514   306/.09774/34   0871542439
Detroit (Mich.) -- Economic conditions. Detroit (Mich.) -- Social conditions. Detroit (Mich.) -- Race relations.

HC108.D6.Z86 1982
Zunz, Olivier.
The changing face of inequality: urbanization, industrial development, and immigrants in Detroit, 1880-1920/ by Olivier Zunz. Chicago: University of Chicago Press, 1982. xix, 481 p.
82-006986   307.7/64/0977434   0226994570
Industries -- Michigan -- Detroit -- History. Alien labor -- Michigan -- Detroit -- History. Social classes -- Michigan -- Detroit -- History.

HC108.G3.H87 1995
Hurley, Andrew, 1961-
Environmental inequalities: class, race, and industrial pollution in Gary, Indiana, 1945-1980/ Andrew Hurley. Chapel Hill: University of North Carolina Press, c1995. xviii, 246 p.
94-017992   363.7/009772/99   0807821748
Environmental policy -- Social aspects -- Indiana -- Gary. NIMBY syndrome -- Indiana -- Gary. Pollution -- Social aspects -- Indiana -- Gary. Gary (Ind.) -- Environmental conditions. Gary (Ind.) -- Race relations. Gary (Ind.) -- Social conditions.

HC108.K2 G68 2002
Gotham, Kevin Fox.
Race, real estate, and uneven development: the Kansas City experience, 1900-2000/ Kevin Fox Gotham. Albany: State University of New York Press, c2002. xii, 204 p.
2002-017745   363.5/1 21   0791453782
Housing--Missouri--Kansas City -- History -- 20th century.

HC108.N7.B343 2001
Beckert, Sven, 1965-
The monied metropolis: New York City and the consolidation of the American bourgeoisie, 1850-1896/ Sven Beckert. Cambridge, UK; Cambridge University Press, 2001. xvii, 492 p.
00-058605   305.5/5/09747109034   0521790395
Middle class -- New York (State) -- New York -- History -- 19th century. Elite (Social sciences) -- New York (State) -- New York -- History -- 19th century. New York (N.Y.) -- Economic conditions. New York (N.Y.) -- Social conditions.

HC108.N7.O86 1995
The other city: people and politics in New York and London/ edited by Susanne MacGregor and Arthur Lipow. Atlantic Highlands, N.J.: Humanities Press, 1995. xvi, 237 p.
94-024212   307.76/09421   0391038524
Urban policy -- New York (State) -- New York. Urban policy -- England -- London. New York (N.Y.) -- Social conditions. London (England) -- Social conditions. New York (N.Y.) -- Economic conditions.

HC108.P7.K64 1989
Kleinberg, S. J.
The shadow of the mills: working-class families in Pittsburgh, 1870-1907/ S.J. Kleinberg. Pittsburgh, Pa.: University of Pittsburgh Press, c1989. xxv, 414 p.
88-023627   305.5/62/0974886   0822935996
Working class families -- Pennsylvania -- Pittsburgh -- History. Women -- Employment -- Pennsylvania -- Pittsburgh -- History. Pittsburgh (Pa.) -- Economic conditions.

HC108.S2.A64 1991
Adler, Jeffrey S.
Yankee merchants and the making of the urban West: the rise and fall of Antebellum St. Louis/ Jeffrey S. Adler. Cambridge; Cambridge University Press, 1991. vii, 274 p.
91-009106   381/.09778/66   0521412846
Sectionalism (United States) -- History. Saint Louis (Mo.) -- Commerce -- History. Saint Louis (Mo.) -- Economic conditions.

HC108.S725F3
Fallows, James M.
The water lords; Ralph Nader's study group report on industry and environmental crisis in Savannah, Georgia, by James M. Fallows. New York, Grossman Publishers, 1971. xxi, 294 p.
70-149318   333.7   067075160X
Pollution -- Savannah. Water -- Pollution -- Savannah River (Ga. and S.C.) Environmental policy -- Savannah.

HC108.W3.H68 1973
Howell, Joseph T.
Hard living on Clay Street; portraits of blue collar families [by] Joseph T. Howell. Garden City, N.Y., Anchor Press, 1973. xvi, 381 p.
73-079736   301.44/1   0385053177
Poor -- Washington (D.C.) -- Case studies. Working class -- Washington (D.C.) -- Case studies.

HC110.A4.M37 2000
Markets for clean air: the U.S. acid rain program/ A. Denny Ellerman ... [et al.]. Cambridge, UK; Cambridge University Press, 2000. xxi, 362 p.
99-016913   363.738/7   0521660831
Emissions trading -- United States. Air quality management -- Government policy -- United States. Acid rain -- Environmental aspects -- Government policy -- United States.

HC110.C3.M37 1996
The market revolution in America: social, political, and religious expressions, 1800-1880/ edited by Melvyn Stokes and Stephen Conway. Charlottesville: University Press of Virginia, 1996. viii, 351 p.
95-042346   330.973/05   0813916496
Capitalism -- United States -- History. Capitalism -- Political aspects -- United States -- History. Capitalism -- Religious aspects -- History.

HC110.C3.S58 1988
Sklar, Martin J., 1935-
The corporate reconstruction of American capitalism, 1890-1916: the market, the law, and politics/ Martin J. Sklar. Cambridge [Cambridgeshire]; Cambridge University Press, 1988. xiv, 484 p.
87-009408   338.8/0973   0521309212
Capital -- United States -- History. Progressivism (United States politics) Antitrust law -- United States -- History.

HC110.C6.C53 2000
Clements, Kendrick A., 1939-
Hoover, conservation, and consumerism: engineering the good life/ Kendrick A. Clements. Lawrence: University Press of Kansas, c2000. xiii, 332 p.
00-028316   333.7/0973 21   0700610332
Hoover, Herbert, -- 1874-1964.   Conservation of natural resources -- United States. Environmental economics -- United States. Environmental policy -- United States.

HC110.C6 C537 2003
Cohen, Lizabeth.
A consumer's republic: the politics of mass consumption in postwar America/ by Lizabeth Cohen. New York: Knopf, 2003.
2002-141599   339.4/7/0973 21   0375407502
Consumption (Economics) -- United States. Consumer behavior -- United States.

HC110.C6 C586 1999
Consuming desires: consumption, culture, and the pursuit of happiness / edited by Roger Rosenblatt. Washington, D.C.: Island Press, c1999. viii, 230 p.
99-021667   306.3/0973 21   1559635355
Consumption (Economics) -- United States. Consumer behavior -- United States. Individualism -- United States.

HC110.C6 C76 2000
Cross, Gary S.
An all-consuming century: why commercialism won in modern America/ Gary Cross. New York: Columbia University Press, 2000. ix, 320 p.
99-087282   306.3/0973/0904 21   0231113129
Consumers -- United States.

HC110.C6.G48 1998
Getting and spending: European and American consumer societies in the twentieth century/ edited by Susan Strasser, Charles McGovern, Matthias Judt. Cambridge, England; Cambridge University Press, 1998. xiv, 477 p.
98-003707   339.4/7/09409049   0521622379
Consumption (Economics) -- United States -- History -- 20th century. Consumption (Economics) -- Europe -- History -- 20th century. Consumption (Economics) -- Germany -- History -- 20th century.

HC110.C6.H58 1985
Horowitz, Daniel, 1938-
The morality of spending: attitudes toward the consumer society in America, 1875-1940/ Daniel Horowitz. Baltimore: Johns Hopkins University Press, c1985. xxxi, 254 p.
84-027851   339.4/7/0973   080182530X
Consumption (Economics) -- United States -- History. Consumers -- United States -- History. Consumption (Economics) -- Moral and ethical aspects -- History.

HC110.C6.H6 1970
Houthakker, Hendrik S.
Consumer demand in the United States; analyses and projections [by] H. S. Houthakker [and] Lester D. Taylor. Cambridge, Mass., Harvard University Press, 1970. xii, 321 p.
79-095915   339.4/7/0973   0674166019
Consumption (Economics) -- United States. Economic forecasting -- United States.

HC110.C6.H87 2001
Hurley, Andrew, 1961-
Diners, bowling alleys, and trailer parks: chasing the American dream in the postwar consumer culture/ Andrew Hurley. New York: Basic Books, 2001.
00-058530   306.3/0973/09045   0465031862
Consumption (Economics) -- United States -- History -- 20th century. Diners -- United States -- History -- 20th century. Bowling alleys -- United States -- History -- 20th century.

HC110.C6.L393 1993
Lebergott, Stanley.
Pursuing happiness: American consumers in the twentieth century/ Stanley Lebergott. Princeton, N.J.: Princeton University Press, c1993. xiii, 188 p.
92-040491   339.4/7/09730904   0691043221
Consumption (Economics) -- United States -- History -- 20th century.   United States -- Economic conditions -- 1918-1945. United States -- Economic conditions -- 1945-

HC110.C6 M544 2001
Mitchell, Susan,
Generation X: Americans aged 18 to 34/ by Susan Mitchell. 3rd ed. Ithaca, N.Y.: New Strategist Publications, c2001. xvi, 384 p.
2003-267368   658.8/34/08420973   21
1885070365
Young adult consumers -- United States -- Statistics. Young consumers -- United States -- Statistics. Young adults -- United States -- Statistics.

HC110.C6 M545 2003
Mitchell, Susan,
American generations: who they are, how they live, what they think/ by Susan Mitchell. 4th ed. Ithaca, N.Y.: New Strategist Publications, c2000. xx, 487 p.
2003-511433   1885070462
Consumers -- United States -- Statistics.

HC110.C6 O34
Household spending: who spends how much on what. Ithaca, N.Y.: New Strategist Publications, <c1997- >
98-658564   658 13
Consumers -- United States -- Statistics.-- Periodicals. Consumption (Economics) -- United States -- Statistics -- Periodicals. Finance, Personal -- United States -- Statistics -- Periodicals.

HC110.C6 S27 1995
Scanlon, Jennifer,
Inarticulate longings: The ladies' home journal, gender, and the promises of consumer culture/ by Jennifer Scanlon. New York: Routledge, 1995. x, 278 p.
95-000699   659.13/2 20   0415911575
Women consumers -- United States -- History. Advertising, Magazine -- United States -- History. Popular literature -- United States -- History and criticism.

HC110.C6.S35 1994
Schwartz, Barry, 1946-
The costs of living: how market freedom erodes the best things in life/ Barry Schwartz. New York: W.W. Norton, c1994. 393 p.
93-037328   339.4/2/0973   0393036464
Consumers -- United States. Materialism -- United States. Values -- United States.

HC110.C6.S73 1999
Statistical handbook on consumption and wealth in the United States/ edited by Chandrika Kaul and Valerie Tomaselli-Moschovitis. Phoenix, Ariz.: Oryx Press, 1999. xviii, 290 p.
99-038530   339.4/1/0973021   1573562513
Consumption (Economics) -- United States -- Statistics. Wealth -- United States -- Statistics.

HC110.C6.T89 1999
Twitchell, James B., 1943-
Lead us into temptation: the triumph of American materialism / James B. Twitchell. New York: Columbia University Press, c1999. 310 p.
98-045385   339.4/7/0973 21   0231115180
Consumption (Economics) -- United States. Materialism -- Social aspects -- United States.

HC110.C6.W44 1998
Weems, Robert E., 1951-
Desegregating the dollar: African American consumerism in the twentieth century/ Robert E. Weems, Jr. New York: New York University Press, c1998. x, 195 p.
97-033866   381.3/089/96073 21   0814792901
Afro-American consumers -- History -- 20th century. Racism -- United States -- History -- 20th century.

HC110.D4.A58 2000
Accordino, John J.
Captives of the Cold War economy: the struggle for defense conversion in American communities/ John J. Accordino. Westport, Conn.: Praeger, c2000. xvi, 205 p.
99-088486   338.4/76233/0973 21   0275965619
Military base conversion -- United States. Economic conversion -- United States. Defense industries -- United States.

HC110.D4.B716 1997
Brandes, Stuart D. 1940-
Warhogs: a history of war profits in America/ Stuart D. Brandes. Lexington, Ky.: University Press of Kentucky, c1997. 371 p.
96-053139   355.02 21   0813120209
War -- Economic aspects -- United States -- History. Profiteering -- United States -- History.

HC110.D4.K638 1996
Koistinen, Paul A. C.
Beating plowshares into swords/ Paul A.C. Koistinen. Lawrence, Kan.: University Press of Kansas, c1996. xv, 376 p.
96-026399   338.4/76233/0973 20   0700607919
War -- Economic aspects -- United States -- History. United States -- Defenses -- History.

HC110.D4.K643 1997
Koistinen, Paul A. C.
Mobilizing for modern war: the political economy of American warfare, 1865-1919/ Paul A.C. Koistinen. Lawrence, Kan.: University Press of Kansas, c1997. xiii, 391 p.
97-019148   338.4/76233/0973 21   0700608605
War -- Economic aspects -- United States -- History. Industrial mobilization -- United States -- History. United States -- Defenses -- History.

HC110.D5.E58 1990
Enterprise zones: new directions in economic development/ edited by Roy E. Green. Newbury Park, Calif.: Sage Publications, c1991. ix, 270 p.
90-020104 382.7/1/0973 0803936907
Enterprise zones -- United States.

HC110.E5.A66163 2001
Anderson, Terry Lee,
Free market environmentalism today/ Terry L. Anderson and Donald R. Leal. New York, N.Y.: Palgrave, 2001. viii, 241 p.
00-062696 333.7/0973 21 0312235038
Environmental policy -- United States. Free enterprise -- United States. Natural resources -- United States -- Management.

HC110.E5.A6663 1997
Anderson, Terry Lee, 1946-
Enviro-capitalists: doing good while doing well/ Terry L. Anderson and Donald R. Leal. Lanham, Md.: Rowman & Littlefield Publishers, c1997. vii, 189 p.
96-040115 363.7/00973 21 0847683818
Environmental protection -- Economic aspects -- United States. Sustainable development -- United States. Capitalism -- Environmental aspects -- United States.

HC110.E5.B58 1989
Blueprint for the environment: a plan for federal action/ edited by T. Allan Comp. Salt Lake City: Howe Brothers, 1989. xiv, 335 p.
89-080293 333.7/0973 0935704507
Environmental policy -- United States. Administrative agencies -- United States.

HC110.E5.C665 1993
Confronting environmental racism: voices from the grassroots/ edited by Robert D. Bullard; foreword by Benjamin F. Chavis, Jr. Boston, Mass.: South End Press, c1993. 259 p.
92-028125 363.7/008/693 0896084477
Environmental policy -- United States. Hazardous waste sites -- United States. Afro-Americans -- Politics and government.

HC110.E5.C87
Current issues in U.S. environmental policy/ Paul R. Portney, editor; A. Myrick Freeman III ... [et al.]. Baltimore: Published for Resources for the Future by the Jo c1978. xv, 207 p.
78-004328 301.31/0973 0801821185
Environmental policy -- United States -- Addresses, essays, lectures. Pollution -- Economic aspects -- United States -- Addresses, essays, lectures.

HC110.E5 D74 2003
Driesen, David M.
The economic dynamics of environmental law/ David M. Driesen. Cambridge, Mass.: MIT Press, c2003. viii, 268 p.
2002-071764 333.7/0973 21 0262541394
Environmental policy -- United States. Environmental law -- United States.

HC110.E5.E26 1970b
Ecotactics: the Sierra Club handbook for environment activists. Edited by John G. Mitchell with Constance L. Stallings. And with an introd. by Ralph Nader. New York, Simon and Schuster [1970] 288 p.
73-124171 301.3 0671207792
Environmental policy -- United States.

HC110.E5.E49879 1989
Environmental politics and policy: theories and evidence/ edited by James P. Lester. Durham: Duke University Press, 1989. x, 405 p.
89-035743 363.7/05/0973 0822309386
Environmental policy -- United States.

HC110.E5.G7345 1992
The Greening of American business: making bottom-line sense of environmental responsibility/ editor, Thomas F.P. Sullivan. Rockville, Md.: Government Institutes, 1992. xix, 358 p.
92-071551 658.4/08 0865872953
Industries -- Environmental aspects -- United States. Business enterprises -- Environmental aspects -- United States. Green movement -- United States.

HC110.E5.G86 1995
Gundersen, Adolf G., 1958-
The environmental promise of democratic deliberation/ Adolf G. Gundersen. Madison, Wis.: University of Wisconsin Press, c1995. xiv, 265 p.
94-036212 363.7/058/0973 0299144801
Environmental policy -- United States -- Citizen participation. Democracy -- United States.

HC110.E5.I52 1992
Innovation in environmental policy: economic and legal aspects of recent developments in environmental enforcement and liability/ edited by T.H. Tietenberg. Aldershot, Hants, England: E. Elgar; c1992. xiii, 269 p.
91-039435 363.7/056/0973 1852785888
Environmental policy -- United States. Environmental law -- United States.

HC110.E5.M33
McHarg, Ian L.
Design with nature [by] Ian L. McHarg. Garden City, N.Y., Published for the American Museum of Natural His 1969. viii, 197 p.
76-077344 304.2
Environmental policy -- United States. Human ecology. Nature -- Effect of human beings on.

HC110.E5.N67 1991
Norton, Bryan G.
Toward unity among environmentalists/ Bryan G. Norton. New York: Oxford University Press, 1991. xvi, 287 p.
91-016719 363.7/058/0973 0195061128
Environmental policy -- United States -- Citizen participation -- History.

HC110.E5 R665 2002
Rosenbaum, Walter A.
Environmental politics and policy/ Walter A. Rosenbaum. 5th ed. Washington, D.C.: CQ Press, c2002. xii, 404 p.
2001-003863 363.7/056/0973 21 1568026455
Environmental policy -- United States.

HC110.E5.S385 1990
Scarce, Rik, 1958-
Eco-warriors: understanding the radical environmental movement/ Rik Scarce; foreword by David Brower. Chicago: Noble Press, c1990. xvii, 291 p.
90-060017 363.7/0574/0973 096226833X
Environmental policy -- United States -- Citizen participation. Human ecology -- United States.

HC110.E5 S49 1998
Shuman, Michael.
Going local: creating self-reliant communities in a global age/ Michael H. Shuman. New York: Free Press, c1998. xiv, 306 p.
97-027339 338.973 21 0684830124
Sustainable development -- United States -- Case studies. Free enterprise -- United States -- Case studies. Community development -- United States -- Case studies.

HC110.H53 R64 2001
Rohlfs, Jeffrey H.
Bandwagon effects in high-technology industries/ Jeffrey H. Rohlfs. Cambridge, Mass.: MIT Press, c2001. xiv, 256 p.
2001-030659 338.4/762/000973 21 0262182173
High technology industries -- United States -- Case studies.

HC110.H53.T94 1993
Tyson, Laura D'Andrea, 1947-
Who's bashing whom?: trade conflicts in high-technology industries/ Laura D'Andrea Tyson. Washington, DC: Institute for International Economics, c1993. xviii, 324 p.
92-015646 382/.3/0973 0881321516
High technology industries -- United States. Competition, International. United States -- Commercial policy.

HC110.I5.B539 2000
Bluestone, Barry.
Growing prosperity: the battle for growth with equity in the twenty-first century/ Barry Bluestone and Bennett Harrison. Boston: Houghton Mifflin, 2000. xv, 345 p.
99-046647 339.2/0973 0395822866
Income distribution -- United States. United States -- Economic conditions -- 1981- United States -- Economic policy.

HC110.I5 C38 2001
The causes and consequences of increasing inequality/ edited by Finis Welch. Chicago: University of Chicago Press, 2001. vi, 379 p.
00-051220 339.2/0973 21 0226893014
Income distribution -- United States.

HC110.I5.E27 1991
Economic inequality and poverty: international perspectives/ editor, Lars Osberg. Armonk, N.Y.: M.E. Sharpe, c1991. xiv, 258 p.
90-031795 339.2/0973 0873325281
Income distribution -- United States.

HC110.I5.H27 1997
Hacker, Andrew.
Money: who has how much and why/ Andrew Hacker. New York: Scribner, c1997. 254 p.
97-009038 339.2/2/0973 21 0684196468
Income -- United States. Income distribution -- United States.

HC110.I5.H87 1998
Huston, James L., 1947-
Securing the fruits of labor: the American concept of wealth distribution, 1765-1900/ James L. Huston. Baton Rouge: Louisiana State University Press, c1998. xxiv, 482 p.
97-044939 339.2/0973 21 0807122068
Income distribution -- United States -- History. Distributive justice -- United States -- History. Wealth -- Moral and ethical aspects -- United States -- History.

HC110.I5.K38 2000
Keister, Lisa A., 1968-
Wealth in America: trends in wealth inequality/ Lisa A. Keister. Cambridge; Cambridge University Press, 2000. x, 307 p.
99-040250 339.2/0973 0521621682
Income distribution -- United States. Equality -- United States. Wealth -- United States.

HC110.I5.K76 1993
Kuenne, Robert E.
Economic justice in American society/ Robert E. Kuenne. Princeton, N.J.: Princeton University Press, 1993. xxiii, 435 p.
93-016273 330.1 069103219X
Income distribution -- United States. Social justice. United States -- Economic conditions.

HC110.I5.L47 1998
Levy, Frank, 1941-
The new dollars and dreams: American incomes and economic change/ Frank Levy. New York: Russell Sage Foundation, c1998. xiii, 248 p.
98-020635 339.2/0973 21 0871545144
Income distribution -- United States. Income -- United States. United States -- Economic conditions -- 1981-

HC110.I5.R95 1998
Ryscavage, Paul.
Income inequality in America: an analysis of trends/ Paul Ryscavage. Armonk, N.Y.: M.E. Sharpe, 1998. xvi, 229 p.
98-023186 339.2/2/0973 0765602334
Income distribution -- United States.

HC110.I5.S616 2001
Slesnick, Daniel T.
Consumption and social welfare: living standards and their distribution in the United States/ Daniel T. Slesnick. Cambridge; Cambridge University Press, 2001. vi, 236 p.
99-047766 339.4/7/097309049 0521497205
Income distribution -- United States. Cost and standard of living -- United States. Consumption (Economics) -- United States. United States -- Economic conditions -- 1945-

HC110.I5.U47 1993
Uneven tides: rising inequality in America/ edited by Sheldon Danziger and Peter Gottschalk. New York: Russell Sage Foundation, c1993. x, 287 p.
92-014233 339.2/0973 0871542226
Income -- United States. Income distribution -- United States. Wages -- United States. United States -- Economic conditions -- 1981-

HC110.I52.J668 1995
Jorgenson, Dale Weldeau, 1933-
Productivity/ Dale W. Jorgenson. Cambridge, Mass.: MIT Press, c1995. 2 v.
94-022733 338.9 0262100495
Industrial productivity -- United States. Capital investments -- United States. Industrial productivity -- Japan. United States -- Economic conditions -- 1945- Japan -- Economic conditions -- 1945- Germany (West) -- Economic conditions.

HC110.I52.L47 1998
Lester, Richard K. 1954-
The productive edge: how U.S. industries are pointing the way to a new era of economic growth/ Richard K. Lester. New York: W.W. Norton, c1998. 368 p.
97-035029 338.0973 21 0393045749
Industrial productivity -- United States.

HC110.I52.M34 1989
Made in America: regaining the productive edge/ Michael L. Dertouzos ... [et al.]. Cambridge, Mass.: MIT Press, c1989. x, 344 p.
89-002251 338/.06/0973 0262041006
Industrial productivity -- United States. Technological innovations -- Economic aspects -- United States. Research, Industrial -- United States.

HC110.I53.E25 1995
Economic development in local government: a handbook for public officials and citizens/ edited by Roger L. Kemp. Jefferson, N.C.: McFarland & Co., c1995. xi, 346 p.
95-000800 338.973/009173/2 0786400951
Industrial promotion -- United States. Local government -- United States. Community development -- United States.

HC110.I53.E56 1988
Eisinger, Peter K.
The rise of the entrepreneurial state: state and local economic development policy in the United States/ Peter K. Eisinger. Madison, Wis.: University of Wisconsin Press, c1988. xvii, 382 p.
88-040184 338.973 0299118703
Industrial promotion -- United States -- States. Regional planning -- United States. Federal government -- United States. United States -- Economic policy -- 1981-1993.

HC110.I53.T48 1993
Theories of local economic development: perspectives from across the disciplines/ edited by Richard D. Bingham, Robert Mier. Newbury Park: Sage Publications, c1993. xvi, 319 p.
93-017611 338.973 0803948670
Industrial promotion -- United States. Local government -- United States. United States -- Economic policy -- 1981-

HC110.I55.G65 1994
Golden, James Reed.
Economics and national strategy in the information age: global networks, technology policy, and cooperative competition/ James R. Golden. Westport, Conn.: Praeger, 1994. xix, 301 p.
93-048208 337.73 0275948137
Information technology -- Government policy -- United States. National security -- United States. International economic relations.

HC110.I55.N37 2000
A nation transformed by information: how information has shaped the United States from Colonial times to the present/ editors, Alfred D. Chandler, Jr., James W. Cortada. Oxford [England]; Oxford University Press, 2000. xii, 380 p.
99-014438 338.973/06 0195127013
Information technology -- United States -- History.

HC110.L3.B38 1989
Baumol, William J.
Productivity and American leadership: the long view/ William J. Baumol, Sue Anne Batey Blackman, and Edward N. Wolff. Cambridge, MA: MIT Press, c1989. x, 395 p.
88-037204 331.11/8/0973 0262022931
Labor productivity -- United States.

HC110.P55.B37 1994
Barnett, Harold C.
Toxic debts and the superfund dilemma/ Harold C. Barnett. Chapel Hill: University of North Carolina Press, c1994. xiv, 334 p.
93-032059 363.73/84/0973 0807821241
Environmental policy -- United States. Hazardous waste sites -- Cleaning -- Finance -- Government policy -- United States.

HC110.P55.C48 1993
Church, Thomas W., 1945-
Cleaning up the mess: implementation strategies in Superfund/ Thomas W. Church and Robert T. Nakamura. Washington, D.C.: Brookings Institution, c1993. xii, 209 p.
92-039493 363.72/876/0973 0815714149
Hazardous wastes -- United States -- Management -- Finance -- Case studies. Liability for hazardous substances pollution damages -- United States -- Cases. Hazardous waste sites -- United States -- Case studies.

HC110.P55.L68 1991
Lowry, William R.
The dimensions of federalism: state governments and pollution control policies/ William R. Lowry. Durham: Duke University Press, c1991. xiv, 168 p.
91-013582 363.7/06/0973 0822311623
Pollution -- Government policy -- United States -- States. Federal government -- United States.

HC110.P55.R56 1993
Ringquist, Evan J., 1962-
Environmental protection at the state level: politics and progress in controlling pollution/ Evan J. Ringquist. Armonk, N.Y.: Sharpe, c1993. xvi, 243 p.
93-012298 363.7/056/0973 1563242036
Pollution -- Government policy -- United States -- States. Environmental policy -- United States -- States. Environmental protection -- United States -- States.

HC110.P6 A85 2001
Assets for the poor: the benefits of spreading asset ownership/ Thomas M. Shapiro and Edward N. Wolff, editors. New York: Russell Sage Foundation, c2001. xiv, 389 p.
00-069807 332.024/06942 21 0871549492
Poverty -- Government policy -- United States. Saving and investment -- Government policy -- United States. Poor -- United States -- Finance, Personal.

HC110.P6.B87 1992
Burton, C. Emory.
The poverty debate: politics and the poor in America/ C. Emory Burton. New York: Greenwood Press, 1992. x, 203 p.
92-014353 362.5/8/0973 0313285942
Poor -- United States. Welfare recipients -- Employment -- United States. Poor -- United States -- Social conditions.

HC110.P6.D86 1999
Duncan, Cynthia M.
Worlds apart: why poverty persists in rural America/ Cynthia M. Duncan; with a foreward by Robert Coles. New Haven: Yale University Press, c1999. xvii, 235 p.
98-044964 305.569/0973 21 0300076282
Poverty -- United States. Rural poor -- United States -- Interviews. United States -- Rural conditions. United States -- Social conditions -- 1980-

HC110.P6.G36 1995
Gans, Herbert J.
The war against the poor: the underclass and antipoverty policy/ Herbert J. Gans. New York, NY: BasicBooks, c1995. xii, 195 p.
95-013180   362.5/8/0973   0465019900
Poor -- United States. Public welfare -- United States. Economic assistance, Domestic -- United States.

HC110.P6.H37 1984
Harrington, Michael, 1928-
The new American poverty/ Michael Harrington. New York: Holt, Rinehart, and Winston, c1984. xii, 271 p.
84-003746   305.5/69/0973   0030621577
Poor -- United States. Economic assistance, Domestic -- United States.

HC110.P6.I45 1996
Imig, Douglas R., 1962-
Poverty and power: the political representation of poor Americans/ Douglas R. Imig. Lincoln: University of Nebraska Press, c1996. xvi, 159 p.
95-017949   322.4/4/0973 20   0803225008
Poor -- United States -- Political activity. Economic assistance, Domestic -- United States. Public welfare -- United States. United States -- Politics and government -- 1981-1989.

HC110.P6.O33 2001
O'Connor, Alice, 1958-
Poverty knowledge: social science, social policy, and the poor in twentieth-century U.S. history/ Alice O'Connor. Princeton, N.J.: Princeton University Press, c2001. xi, 373 p.
00-034682   362.5/0973/0904 21   0691009171
Poverty -- United States -- History -- 20th century. Poor -- United States -- History -- 20th century. Economic assistance, Domestic -- United States -- History -- 20th century.

HC110.P6.P328 2000
Page, Benjamin I.
What government can do: dealing with poverty and inequality/ Benjamin I. Page, James R. Simmons. Chicago: University of Chicago Press, 2000. xiii, 409 p.
00-008807   362.5/8/0973   0226644812
Poverty -- United States. Income distribution -- United States. Economic assistance, Domestic -- United States. United States -- Social policy.

HC110.P6.R43 1996
Reducing poverty in America: views and approaches/ edited by Michael R. Darby. Thousand Oaks, [Calif.]: Sage Publications, c1996. x, 390 p.
95-035748   362.5/0973 20   0761900063
Poverty -- United States. Poor -- United States. Public welfare -- United States. United States -- Social policy -- 1993- United States -- Economic policy -- 1993-

HC110.P6.R89 1992
Rural poverty in America/ edited by Cynthia M. Duncan; foreword by Susan E. Sechler. New York: Auburn House, 1992 xxvii, 300 p.
91-018655   362.5/0973/091734   0865690146
Rural poor -- United States. Economic assistance, Domestic -- United States.

HC110.P6 S327 2002
Schwartz-Nobel, Loretta.
Growing up empty: the hunger epidemic in America/ by Loretta Schwartz-Nobel. New York: HarperCollins, 2002.
2002-020737   363.8/2/0973 21   0060195630
Poverty -- United States. Hunger -- United States. Malnutrition -- United States.

HC110.P6.T76 1998
Tropman, John E.
Does America hate the poor?: the other American dilemma: lessons for the 21st century from the 1960s and the 1970s/ John E. Tropman. Westport, Conn.: Praeger, 1998. xii, 172 p.
98-011135   305.569/0973   027596132X
Poor -- United States. Poverty -- United States. Discrimination -- United States.

HC110.P63.D42 1977
A Decade of Federal antipoverty programs: achievements, failures, and lessons/ edited by Robert H. Haveman. New York: Academic Press, c1977. x, 381 p.
76-042969   362.5/0973   0123332508
Economic assistance, Domestic -- United States -- Congresses.

HC110.P63.G69
Government assistance almanac.   Washington, D.C.: Foggy Bottom Publications, [c1985-]
86-658073   353.0082/025
Economic assistance, Domestic -- United States -- Handbooks, manuals, etc. Grants-in-aid -- United States -- Handbooks, manuals, etc. Administrative agencies -- United States -- Handbooks, manuals, etc.

HC110.P63.M6
Moynihan, Daniel P. 1927-
Maximum feasible misunderstanding; community action in the war on poverty [by] Daniel P. Moynihan. New York, Free Press [1969] xxi, 218 p.
69-018005   362.5/0973
Community Action Program (U.S.)

HC110.P63.R49 1988
Riemer, David R.
The prisoners of welfare: liberating America's poor from unemployment and low wages/ David Raphael Riemer. New York: Praeger, 1988. xix, 200 p.
88-003926   362.5/8/0973   0275927059
Economic assistance, Domestic -- United States. Poor -- Government policy -- United States. Public welfare -- United States.

HC110.P63.S34 1988
Schwartz, Marvin, 1948-
In service to America: a history of VISTA in Arkansas, 1965-1985/ by Marvin Schwartz; preface by Governor Bill Clinton. Fayetteville: University of Arkansas Press, 1988. xiv, 491 p.
87-019440   361.6/09767   1557280053
Volunteer workers in social service -- Arkansas. Volunteer workers in community development -- Arkansas.

HC110.R4.L84 1991
Luger, Michael I.
Technology in the garden: research parks and regional economic development/ Michael I. Luger & Harvey A. Goldstein. Chapel Hill: University of North Carolina Press, c1991. ix, 242 p.
91-050255   607/.2   0807820008
Research parks -- United States -- Case studies.

HC110.R4.T43 1991
The Technology pork barrel/ [edited by] Linda R. Cohen & Roger G. Noll, with Jeffrey S. Banks, Susan A. Edelman, and William M. Pegram. Washington, D.C.: Brookings Institution, c1991. xiii, 400 p.
91-008832   338/.064   0815715080
Research, Industrial -- Government policy -- United States. Technology and state -- United States. Research and development contracts, Government -- United States.

HC110.S3.B67 1992
Bosworth, Barry, 1942-
Saving and investment in a global economy/ Barry P. Bosworth. Washington, D.C.: The Brookings Institution, c1993. xi, 188 p.
92-035664   339.4/3/0973   0815710445
Saving and investment -- United States. Saving and investment. Competition, International. United States -- Economic conditions -- 1981-

HC110.S3.D8 1989
Du Boff, Richard B.
Accumulation & power: an economic history of the United States/ Richard B. DuBoff. Armonk, N.Y.: M.E. Sharpe, c1989. xii, 223 p.
88-039542   339/.0973   0873325168
Saving and investment -- United States -- History. Capital investments -- United States -- History. Monopolies -- United States -- History.

HC110.S8.L47 1989
Lesser, Ian O., 1957-
Resources and strategy/ Ian O. Lesser. New York: St. Martin's Press, 1989. x, 240 p.
88-033331   333.7/0973   0312023723
Strategic materials -- United States. Strategic materials. War -- Economic aspects -- United States.

HC110.T4.M68 1989
Mowery, David C.
Technology and the pursuit of economic growth/ David C. Mowery, Nathan Rosenberg. Cambridge [England]; Cambridge University Press, 1989. viii, 330 p.
89-017294   338/.064/0973   0521380332
Technological innovations -- Economic aspects -- United States -- History. Technological innovations -- Economic aspects -- Great Britain -- History. Science and industry -- United States -- History.

HC110.T4.S82 2000
Suarez-Villa, Luis.
Invention and the rise of technocapitalism/ Luis Suarez-Villa. Lanham, [Md.]: Rowman & Littlefield Publishers, c2000. xv, 265 p.
99-089709   338/.064/0973 21   074250204X
Technological innovations -- United States -- History. Capitalism -- United States -- History. Creative ability in business -- United States -- History.

HC110.T4.T65 1992
Tolchin, Martin.
Selling our security: the erosion of America's assets/ Martin and Susan J. Tolchin. New York: Knopf, 1992. xiii, 427 p.
92-004499   332.6/73/0973   0394583094
Technology transfer -- Economic aspects -- United States. Investments, Foreign -- United States. National security -- United States.

HC110.W24.R6 1984
Rockoff, Hugh.
Drastic measures: a history of wage and price controls in the United States/ Hugh Rockoff. Cambridge [Cambridgeshire]; Cambridge University Press, 1984. xi, 289 p.
83-021019   331.2/973   052124496X
Wage-price policy -- United States -- History.

HC110.W3.U54 1995
Footing the bill for superfund cleanups: who pays and how?/ Katherine N. Probst ... [et al.]. Washington, D.C.: Brookings Institution: c1995. xiv, 176 p.
94-037702   338.4/736337384/0973   0815729944
Hazardous waste sites -- Cleaning -- United States -- Finance.

HC110.W4.B73 1991
Braun, Dennis Duane.
The rich get richer: the rise of income inequality in the United States and the world/ Denny Braun. Chicago: Nelson-Hall Publishers, c1991. xi, 383 p.
90-035294   339.2/0973   0830412646
Wealth -- United States. Income distribution -- United States. Wealth -- Brazil.

HC110.W4.C65 2000
Collins, Robert M.
More: the politics of economic growth in postwar America/ Robert M. Collins. Oxford; Oxford University Press, c2000. xi, 299 p.
99-022524   338.973 21   0195046463
Wealth -- United States -- History -- 20th century. Liberalism -- United States -- History -- 20th century. National characteristics, American. United States -- Economic policy. United States -- Economic conditions -- 1945-

HC110.W4.G58 1999
Goff, Brian L.
Spoiled rotten: affluence, anxiety, and social decay in America/ Brian Goff, Arthur A. Fleisher III. Boulder, Colo.: Westview Press, 1999. xii, 254 p.
99-017259   339.2/0973   081333618X
Wealth -- United States. Income distribution -- United States. United States -- Economic conditions. United States -- Social conditions.

HC110.W4.S64
Soltow, Lee.
Men and wealth in the United States, 1850-1870/ Lee Soltow. New Haven: Yale University Press, 1975. xx, 206 p.
74-029738   330.1/6   0300018142
Wealth -- United States -- History.

HC113.H68 1999
Howlett, Michael,
The political economy of Canada: an introduction/ Michael Howlett, Alex Netherton, M. Ramesh. 2nd. ed. Don Mill, Ont.: Oxford University Press, c1999. 384 p.
00-551883   330.971 21   0195413482
Economics -- Canada -- History.

HC115.E2757 1989
Economic decline and political change: Canada, Great Britain, the United States/ Harold D. Clarke, Marianne C. Stewart, and Gary Zuk, editors. Pittsburgh, PA: University of Pittsburgh Press, c1989. xii, 290 p.
88-019812   338.9   0822936054
Canada -- Economic policy. Canada -- Economic conditions -- 1945- Great Britain -- Economic policy -- 1945-1964.

HC117.O6.M28 1993
McCalla, Douglas, 1942-
Planting the province: the economic history of Upper Canada, 1784-1870/ Douglas McCalla. Toronto; University of Toronto Press, c1993. xviii, 446 p.
93-244536   330.9713   0802034071
Ontario -- Economic conditions.

HC118.M6.L49 2000
Lewis, Robert, 1954-
Manufacturing Montreal: the making of an industrial landscape, 1850 to 1930/ Robert Lewis. Baltimore: The Johns Hopkins University Press, c2000. xvii, 336 p.
99-050708   338.4/767/0971428 21   080186349X
Industries -- Quebec (Province) -- Montreal. Manufacturing industries -- Quebec (Province) -- Montreal. Industrial productivity -- Quebec (Province) -- Montreal. Montreal (Quebec) -- Economic conditions.

HC120.I5.B36 1982
Banting, Keith G.
The welfare state and Canadian federalism/ Keith G. Banting. Kingston: McGill-Queen's University Press: 1982. xii, 226 p.
82-203732   354.710082/56   0773503803
Income maintenance programs -- Canada. Social security -- Canada. Federal government -- Canada.

HC123-232 By region or country — America. Western Hemisphere — Latin America

HC123.B85 1994
Bulmer-Thomas, V.
The economic history of Latin America since independence/ Victor Bulmer-Thomas. Cambridge; Cambridge University Press, 1994. xv, 485 p.
93-036441   330.98 20   0521368723
Latin America -- Economic conditions. Latin America -- Economic policy.

HC123.S83 2000
Stallings, Barbara.
Growth, employment, and equity: the impact of the economic reforms in Latin America and the Caribbean/ Barbara Stallings, Wilson Peres. Washington, D.C.: Brookings Institution Press; xiv, 252 p.
00-008633   338.98 21   0815780877
Free enterprise -- Latin America. Free enterprise -- Caribbean Area.

HC125.B455 1998
Beyond tradeoffs: market reforms and equitable growth in Latin America/ Nancy Birdsall, Carol Graham, and Richard H. Sabot, editors. Washington, D.C.: Inter-American Development Bank: 1998. 367 p.
98-072692   0815709218
Economic development -- Congresses. Income distribution -- Latin America -- Congresses. Equality -- Latin America -- Congresses. Latin America -- Economic policy -- Congresses.

HC125.C34153
Cardoso, Fernando Henrique.
Dependency and development in Latin America/ Fernando Henrique Cardoso and Enzo Faletto; translated by Marjory Mattingly Urquidi. Berkeley: University of California Press, c1979. xxv, 227 p.
75-046033   309.1/8/003   0520031938
Latin America -- Economic conditions -- 1945- Latin America -- Social conditions -- 1945-1982. Latin America -- Politics and government -- 1948-

HC125.D488 1993
Development from within: toward a neostructuralist approach for Latin America/ edited by Osvaldo Sunkel. Boulder, CO: L. Rienner, 1993. ix, 441 p.
92-023922   338.98   155587326X
Latin America -- Economic policy. Latin America -- Economic conditions -- 1945-

HC125.E37365 2000
An economic history of twentieth-century Latin America/ edited by Enrique Cardenas, Jose Antonio Ocampo, and Rosemary Thorp. Houdsmills, Basingstoke, Hampshire; Palgrave; [2000-] v. 1-2.
00-040449   330.98/0033   0333913043
Latin America -- Economic conditions. Latin America -- Economic conditions -- 1918-

HC125.F682 1999
Franko, Patrice M., 1958-
The puzzle of Latin American economic development/ Patrice M. Franko. Lanham, MD: Rowman & Littlefield Publishers, 1999. xv, 527 p.
99-023761   338.98   0847695247
Latin America -- Economic conditions -- 1982- Latin America -- Economic policy.

HC125.F78
Furtado, Celso.
Economic development of Latin America; a survey from colonial times to the Cuban revolution. Translated by Suzette Macedo. Cambridge [Eng.] University Press, 1970. xvi, 271 p.
74-121365   330.98   0521078288
Latin America -- Economic conditions. Latin America -- Social conditions.

HC125.H645 1999
Hofman, Andre A., 1953-
The economic development of Latin America in the twentieth century/ Andre A. Hofman. Northampton, MA: Edward Elgar Pub., 1999. xvi, 322 p.
98-027904   338.98   1858988527
Latin America -- Economic conditions -- 20th century.

HC125.L3435 1998
Latin America and the world economy since 1800/ edited by John H. Coatsworth and Alan M. Taylor. Cambridge, Mass.: Harvard University/David Rockefeller center for 1998.
98-040390   330.98/03   0674512804
Latin America -- Economic conditions -- 19th century. Latin America -- Economic conditions -- 1918- Latin America -- Foreign economic relations.

HC125.M23 1997
MacDonald, Scott B.
Fast forward: Latin America on the edge of the 21st century/ Scott B. MacDonald and Georges A. Fauriol. New Brunswick, N.J., U.S.A: Transaction Publishers, 1997. viii, 318 p.
96-054513   1560002077
Latin America -- Economic conditions -- 1982- Latin America -- Economic policy. Latin America -- Politics and government -- 1980-

HC125.O33 1978
Odell, Peter R.
Economies and societies in Latin America: a geographical interpretation/ Peter R. Odell and David A. Preston. Chichester, Eng.; Wiley, c1978. vii, 289 p.
77-012400   330.9/8   0471995886
Latin America -- Economic conditions. Latin America -- Social conditions.

HC125.P4379 1996
Pereira, Luiz Carlos Bresser.
Economic crisis and state reform in Brazil: toward a new interpretation of Latin America/ Luiz Carlos Bresser Pereira. Boulder, Colo.: L. Rienner, 1996. vi, 258 p.
94-028296   338.98   1555875327
Latin America -- Economic policy. Latin America -- Economic conditions -- 1982- Brazil -- Economic policy.

HC125.P775 1990
Progress toward development in Latin America: from Prebisch to technological autonomy/ edited by James L. Dietz and Dilmus D. James. Boulder, Colo.: L. Rienner Publishers, 1990. viii, 232 p.
89-077636 338.98 1555871798
Technology transfer -- Economic aspects -- Latin America. Debts, External -- Latin America. Capitalism -- Latin America. Latin America -- Economic policy.

HC125.R4127 1995
Reform, recovery, and growth: Latin America and the Middle East/ edited by Rudiger Dornbusch and Sebastian Edwards. Chicago: University of Chicago Press, 1995. ix, 426 p.
94-027934 338.956 0226158454
Structural adjustment (Economic policy) -- Latin America. Structural adjustment (Economic policy) -- Turkey. Structural adjustment (Economic policy) -- Israel. Latin America -- Economic conditions -- 1982-

HC125.S76
Stein, Stanley J.
The colonial heritage of Latin America; essays on economic dependence in perspective [by] Stanley J. and Barbara H. Stein. New York, Oxford University Press, 1970. viii, 222 p.
73-083053 330.98
Latin America -- Economic conditions.

HC125.T4 1997
Technopols: freeing politics and markets in Latin America in the 1990s/ [edited by] Jorge I. Dominguez. University Park: Pennsylvania State University Press, c1997. xiv, 287 p.
96-012003 338.98 20 0271016132
Finance ministers -- Latin America. Latin America -- Politics and government -- 1948- Latin America -- Economic policy.

HC125.T523 1998
Thorp, Rosemary.
Progress, poverty and exclusion: an economic history of Latin America in the 20th century/ Rosemary Thorp. Washington, D.C.: Inter-American Development Bank; c1998. xii, 369 p.
98-073731 330.98/0033 21 1886938350
Economic history -- 20th century. Economic development -- History -- 20th century. Poverty -- Latin America -- History -- 20th century. Latin America -- Economic conditions -- 20th century.

HC125.T7 1992
Towards a new development strategy for Latin America: pathways from Hirschman's thought/ Simon Teitel, editor. Washington, D.C.: Inter-American Development Bank; 1992. xii, 403 p.
93-117502 338.98 094060244X
Hirschman, Albert O. Economic development. Latin America -- Economic conditions -- 1982- Latin America -- Economic policy.

HC125.W46 1998
What kind of democracy? What kind of market?: Latin America in the age of neoliberalism/ edited by Philip D. Oxhorn and Graciela Ducatenzeiler. University Park, Pa.: Pennsylvania State University Press, c1998. viii, 270 p.
97-049899 338.98 21 0271017996
Democracy -- Latin America. Latin America -- Politics and government -- 1980- Latin America -- Economic conditions -- 1982- Latin America -- Economic policy.

HC130.I5.P67 1998
Poverty, economic reform, and income distribution in Latin America/ edited by Albert Berry. Boulder: L. Rienner Publishers, 1998. x, 273 p.
97-022276 339.2/098 155587746X
Income distribution -- Latin America. Poverty -- Latin America. Structural adjustment (Economic policy) -- Latin America. Latin America -- Economic policy.

HC130.P6.C67 1995
Coping with austerity: poverty and inequality in Latin America/ Nora Lustig, editor. Washington, D.C.: Brookings Institution, c1995. xviii, 460 p.
94-028839 339.4/6/098 0815753187
Poverty -- Latin America. Income distribution -- Latin America. Structural adjustment (Economic policy) -- Latin America. Latin America -- Economic conditions -- 1982-

HC130.P6.P69 1998
Poverty and inequality in Latin America: issues and new challenges/ edited by Victor E. Tokman and Guillermo O'Donnell. Notre Dame, Ind.: University of Notre Dame Press, c1998. xiv, 245 p.
97-046841 339.4/6/098 21 0268038244
Poverty -- Latin America -- Congresses. Latin America -- Social policy -- Congresses.

HC133.C6 1983
Cockcroft, James D.
Mexico: class formation, capital accumulation, and the state/ James D. Cockcroft. New York: Monthly Review Press, c1983. viii, 384 p.
81-084748 330.972 0853455600
Social classes -- Mexico -- History. Mexico -- Economic conditions. Mexico -- Politics and government. Mexico -- Social conditions.

HC134.G37 1993
Garner, Richard L.
Economic growth and change in Bourbon Mexico/ Richard L. Garner with Spiro E. Stefanou. Gainesville: University Press of Florida, c1993. xiii, 354 p.
92-027064 338.972 0813011833
Agriculture -- Economic aspects -- Mexico -- History -- 18th century. Mexico -- Economic conditions -- 1540-1810.

HC135.A856
Avila, Manuel, 1921-
Tradition and growth; a study of four Mexican villages. Chicago, University of Chicago Press [1969] xv, 219 p.
73-086134 309.1/72 0226032450
Villages -- Mexico -- Case studies. Mexico -- Economic conditions -- 1918- -- Case studies. Mexico -- Rural conditions -- Case studies.

HC135.B875 2001
Butler, Edgar W.
Mexico and Mexico City in the world economy/ Edgar W. Butler, James B. Pick, W. James Hettrick. Boulder, CO: Westview Press, 2001. xvi, 388 p.
2001-017749 330.972 0813335426
Mexico -- Economic conditions -- 1994- Mexico City (Mexico) -- Economic conditions

HC135.C212 1989
Camp, Roderic Ai.
Entrepreneurs and politics in twentieth-century Mexico/ Roderic A. Camp. New York: Oxford University Press, 1989. xiv, 306 p.
88-028745 338/.04/0922 0195057198
Businesspeople -- Mexico -- History -- 20th century. Elite (Social sciences) -- Mexico -- History -- 20th century. Business and politics -- Mexico -- History -- 20th century. Mexico -- Politics and government -- 20th century.

HC135.C44 1996
Changing structure of Mexico: political, social, and economic prospects/ Laura Randall, editor. Armonk, N.Y.: M.E. Sharpe, c1996. xv, 413 p.
95-025404 972.08/35 20 1563246414
Mexico -- Economic conditions -- 1994- Mexico -- Social conditions -- 1970- Mexico -- Politics and government -- 1988-

HC135.L87 1998
Lustig, Nora.
Mexico: the remaking of an economy/ Nora Lustig. 2nd ed. Washington, DC: Brookings Institution Press, c1998. xviii, 287 p.
98-026072 338.972 21 0815773013
Mexico -- Economic policy -- 1970- Mexico -- Economic conditions -- 1982-

HC135.M569 1998
Mexico's private sector: recent history, future challenges/ edited by Riordan Roett. Boulder: Lynne Rienner, 1998. xi, 241 p.
98-025921 330.972/0836 1555877133
Free enterprise -- Mexico. Mexico -- Economic policy -- 1994- Mexico -- Economic conditions -- 1994-

HC135.P715 1998
The post-NAFTA political economy: Mexico and the Western Hemisphere/ edited by Carol Wise. University Park, Penn.: The Pennsylvania State University Press, ix, 382 p.
98-016941 330.972/0836 21 0271018232
Mexico -- Economic conditions -- 1994- North America -- Economic integration. America -- Economic integration. Canada. Treaties, etc. 1992 Oct. 7.

HC137.C47 B46 1996
Benjamin, Thomas,
A rich land, a poor people: politics and society in modern Chiapas/ Thomas Benjamin. Rev. ed./ with a foreword by Lorenzo Meyer. Albuqueque: University of New Mexico Press, c1996. xxiii, 376 p.
95-041262 338.972/75 20 0826317138
Elite (Social sciences) -- Mexico -- Chiapas -- Political activity -- History. Peasantry -- Mexico -- Chiapas -- History. Agricultural industries -- Mexico -- Chiapas -- History.

HC137.M46.B47 1994
Betts, Dianne C.
Crisis on the Rio Grande: poverty, unemployment, and economic development on the Texas-Mexico border/ Dianne C. Betts and Daniel J. Slottje, with Jesus Vargas-Garza. Boulder: Westview Press, 1994. xi, 195 p.
93-038472 330.972/1 0813388120
Mexican-American Border Region -- Social conditions. Mexican-American Border Region -- Economic conditions.

HC137.Y8.L36 1991
Land, labor & capital in modern Yucatan: essays in regional history and political economy/ edited by Jeffery T. Brannon and Gilbert M. Joseph. Tuscaloosa: University of Alabama Press, c1991. x, 322 p.
90-046746   330.972/65   0817305556
Land tenure -- Mexico -- Yucatan (State) -- History. Haciendas -- Mexico -- Yucatan (State) -- History. Plantations -- Mexico -- Yucatan (State) -- History. Yucatan (Mexico: State) -- Economic conditions. Yucatan (Mexico: State) -- Social conditions.

HC141.B78 1987
Bulmer-Thomas, V.
The political economy of Central America since 1920/ Victor Bulmer-Thomas. Cambridge; Cambridge University Press, 1987. xxiii, 416 p.
87-011779   338.9728   0521342848
Central America -- Economic policy.

HC141.T6713 1993
Torres-Rivas, Edelberto.
History and society in Central America/ by Edelberto Torres Rivas; translated by Douglass Sullivan-Gonzalez. Austin: University of Texas Press, 1993. xix, 193 p.
93-005974   330.9728/052   0292781288
Central America -- Economic conditions. Central America -- Social conditions. Central America -- Economic integration.

HC141.Z9.E54 1993
Faber, Daniel J.
Environment under fire: imperialism and the ecological crisis in Central America/ Daniel Faber. New York: Monthly Review Press, c1993. x, 301 p.
92-041825   363.5/06/098   0853458391
Environmental policy -- Central America. Economic development -- Environmental aspects. Central America -- Foreign economic relations -- United States. United States -- Foreign economic relations -- Central America. Central America -- Economic conditions -- 1979-

HC145.Z9.E57 1993
Stonich, Susan C.
"I am destroying the land!": the political ecology of poverty and environmental destruction in Honduras/ Susan C. Stonich. Boulder, CO: Westview Press, 1993. xvi, 191 p.
93-002258   363.7/0097283   0813386497
Agriculture -- Environmental aspects -- Honduras. Rural poor -- Honduras. Environmental degradation -- Honduras. Honduras -- Economic conditions.

HC146.L83 1995
Luciak, Ilja A.
The Sandinista legacy: lessons from a political economy in transition/ Ilja A. Luciak. Gainesville: University Press of Florida, c1995. xx, 238 p.
95-006520   338.97285   0813013690
Agriculture -- Economic aspects -- Nicaragua. Cooperative societies -- Nicaragua. Nicaragua -- Rural conditions. Nicaragua -- Economic conditions -- 1979- Nicaragua -- Politics and government -- 1979-1990.

HC147.Z44 1991
Zimbalist, Andrew S.
Panama at the crossroads: economic development and political change in the twentieth century/ Andrew Zimbalist and John Weeks. Berkeley: University of California Press, c1991. xi, 219 p.
90-050923   338.97287/009/04   0520073118
Panama -- Economic conditions. Panama -- Politics and government.

HC148.E283 1996
Economic policy for building peace: the lessons of El Salvador/ edited by James K. Boyce. Boulder, Colo.: Lynne Reinner Publishers, 1996. xvii, 359 p.
96-012269   338.97284   1555875262
El Salvador -- Economic policy. El Salvador -- Economic conditions -- 1945- El Salvador -- Politics and government -- 1979-1992.

HC151.C312 2002
Caribbean economies in the twenty-first century/ edited by Irma T. Alonso. Gainesville: University Press of Florida, c2002. 232 p.
2002-018074   330.9729 21   0813025389
Caribbean Area -- Economic conditions -- 1945- United States -- Foreign economic relations -- Caribbean Area. Caribbean Area -- Foreign economic relations -- United States.

HC151.G58 1998
Globalization and neoliberalism: the Caribbean context/ edited by Thomas Klak. Lanham: Rowman & Littlefield, c1998. xxiv, 319 p.
97-030698   338.9729 21   0847685365
Caribbean Area -- Economic conditions -- 1945- Caribbean Area -- Economic policy.

HC151.W375 1987
Watts, David, 1935-
The West Indies: patterns of development, culture, and environmental change since 1492/ David Watts. Cambridge [Cambridgeshire]; Cambridge University Press, 1987. xxii, 609 p.
87-005156   330.9729   0521245559
Sugar trade -- West Indies -- History. West Indies -- Economic conditions. West Indies -- Social conditions.

HC152.5.C7984 2000
Cuba: the contours of change/ edited by Susan Kaufman Purcell, David J. Rothkopf. Boulder: L. Rienner Publishers, 2000. xi, 157 p.
00-031093   330.97291   1555879330
Cuba -- Economic conditions -- 1990- Cuba -- Politics and government -- 1959- Cuba -- Foreign economic relations -- United States.

HC152.5.M47
Mesa-Lago, Carmelo, 1934-
The economy of socialist Cuba: a two-decade appraisal/ Carmelo Mesa-Lago. Albuquerque: University of New Mexico Press, c1981. xvi, 235 p.
80-054570   330.97291/064   0826305784
Cuba -- Economic conditions -- 1959-1990.

HC152.5.P47 1987
Perez-Lopez, Jorge F.
Measuring Cuban economic performance/ by Jorge F. Perez-Lopez. Austin: University of Texas Press, 1987. xii, 202 p.
86-024907   339.37291   0292750927
National income -- Cuba -- Accounting. Gross national product -- Cuba. Cuba -- Economic conditions -- 1959-1990.

HC153.F37 1988
Fass, Simon M.
Political economy in Haiti: the drama of survival/ Simon M. Fass. New Brunswick, N.J., U.S.A.: Transaction Books, c1988. xxxi, 369 p.
87-025532   338.97294   0887381588
Haiti -- Economic policy. Haiti -- Economic conditions -- 1971-

HC154.E34 1990
Edie, Carlene J.
Democracy by default: dependency and clientelism in Jamaica/ Carlene J. Edie. Boulder, Colo.: L. Rienner; 1991. xiv, 170 p.
90-047119   338.97292   1555872255
Democracy. Jamaica -- Economic policy. Jamaica -- Commerce. Jamaica -- Politics and government.

HC154.K45 1992
Keith, Nelson W.
The social origins of democratic socialism in Jamaica/ Nelson W. Keith, Novella Z. Keith. Philadelphia: Temple University Press, 1992. xxiv, 320 p.
91-021325   338.97292   0877229066
Social classes -- Jamaica. Socialism -- Jamaica. Capitalism -- Jamaica. Jamaica -- Economic conditions. Jamaica -- Economic policy. Jamaica -- Politics and government -- 1962-

HC154.5.P36 1990
Pantojas-Garcia, Emilio.
Development strategies as ideology: Puerto Rico's export-led industrialization experience/ Emilio Pantojas-Garcia. Boulder: Lynne Rienner; 1990. xiv, 205 p.
90-033397   338.97291   1555871984
Exports -- Puerto Rico. Foreign trade promotion -- Puerto Rico. Puerto Rico -- Economic policy.

HC154.5.Z7.S343 1996
Berman Santana, Deborah, 1952-
Kicking off the bootstraps: environment, development, and community power in Puerto Rico/ Deborah Berman Santana. Tucson: University of Arizona Press, c1996. xii, 211 p.
96-010096   338.97295 20   0816515905
Economic development -- Environmental aspects -- Puerto Rico -- Salinas. Environmental degradation -- Puerto Rico -- Salinas. Community organization -- Puerto Rico -- Salinas.

HC157.B8.G74
Green, William A., 1935-
British slave emancipation: the sugar colonies and the great experiment 1830-1865/ William A. Green. Oxford [Eng.]: Clarendon Press, 1976. x, 449 p.
76-361326   301.44/93/09729   0198224362
Slaves -- Emancipation -- West Indies, British. West Indies, British -- Economic conditions. West Indies, British -- Social conditions. Great Britain -- Colonies -- Administration.

HC157.B8.R3 1963
Ragatz, Lowell J. 1897-
The fall of the planter class in the British Caribbean, 1763-1833; a study in social and economic history. New York, Octagon Books, 1963 [c1928] xiv, 520 p.
63-020894   330.97297
West Indies, British -- Social conditions. West Indies, British -- Economic conditions. West Indies, British -- Commerce.

HC165.F675 1983
Foxley, Alejandro.
Latin American experiments in neoconservative economics/ Alejandro Foxley. Berkeley: University of California Press, c1983. xv, 213 p.
82-020252   338.98   0520048075
Economic stabilization -- Southern Cone of South America. Monetary policy -- Southern Cone of South America. Chicago school of economics. Southern Cone of South America -- Economic policy. Chile -- Economic policy.

HC165.M4569 1999
Mercosur: regional integration, world markets/ edited by Riordan Roett. Boulder, Colo.: Lynne Rienner, 1999. xi, 139 p.
98-037779 337.1/8 1555878377
South America -- Economic integration. South America -- Commerce.

HC165.N62 1973
Normano, J. F. 1890-1945.
The struggle for South America: economy and ideology. With an introd. by Clarence H. Haring. Westport, Conn., Greenwood Press [1973] 294 p.
71-136542 330.9/8/003 0837154634
South America -- Economic conditions -- 1918- Latin America -- Relations -- Spain. Spain -- Relations -- Latin America.

HC165.P46 1993
Pereira, Luiz Carlos Bresser.
Economic reforms in new democracies: a social-democratic approach/ Luiz Carlos Bresser Pereira, Jose Maria Maravall, Adam Przeworski. Cambridge [England]; Cambridge University Press, 1993. vii, 227 p.
92-017342 338.98 0521432596
Mixed economy -- Latin America. Democracy -- Latin America. Mixed economy -- Europe, Southern. Europe, Eastern -- Economic policy. Latin America -- Economic policy. Europe, Southern -- Economic policy.

HC165.P89 1982
Puyana de Palacios, Alicia, 1941-
Economic integration among unequal partners: the case of the Andean group/ Alicia Puyana de Palacios. New York: Pergamon Press, c1982. xxvi, 405 p.
81-021005 337.1/8 0080288227
Andes region -- Economic integration.

HC165.W46 2002
Weyland, Kurt Gerhard.
The politics of market reform in fragile democracies: Argentina, Brazil, Peru, and Venezuela/ Kurt Weyland. Princeton: Princeton University Press, c2002.
2002-016903 338.98 21 0691096430
Public opinion -- South America. Democracy -- South America.

HC175.B77
Brown, Jonathan C. 1942-
A socioeconomic history of Argentina, 1776-1860/ Jonathan C. Brown. Cambridge [Eng.]; Cambridge University Press, 1979. xiv, 302 p.
78-006800 330.9/82 0521222192
Argentina -- Economic conditions. Argentina -- Social conditions.

HC175.C6684 2002
Corrales, Javier,
Presidents without parties: the politics of economic reform in Argentina and Venezuela in the 1990s/ Javier Corrales. University Park, Pa.: Pennsylvania State University Press, c2002. xvi, 364 p.
2001-055951 338.982 21 0271021942
Executive power -- Argentina. Executive power -- Venezuela. Political parties -- Argentina.

HC175.K44 1997
Keeling, David J.
Contemporary Argentina: a geographical perspective/ David J. Keeling. Boulder, Colo.: WestviewPress, 1997. xxiv, 349 p.
97-004465 330.982 0813386802
Economic forecasting -- Argentina. Social prediction -- Argentina. Regional planning -- Argentina. Argentina -- Social conditions -- 1983- Argentina -- Social policy. Argentina -- Economic policy.

HC175.P42 1991
Peralta-Ramos, Monica.
The political economy of Argentina: power and class since 1930/ Monica Peralta-Ramos. Boulder: Westview Press, 1992. viii, 191 p.
91-022385 338.982 0813375568
Social conflict -- Argentina -- History -- 20th century. Peronism -- History. Argentina -- Economic conditions -- 1918- Argentina -- Politics and government -- 20th century.

HC175.S54 1989
Smith, William C., 1946-
Authoritarianism and the crisis of the Argentine political economy/ William C. Smith. Stanford, Calif.: Stanford University Press, 1989. xv, 395 p.
89-031681 338.982 0804716722
Authoritarianism -- Argentina. Argentina -- Economic conditions -- 1945- Argentina -- Economic policy. Argentina -- Politics and government -- 1955-

HC177.B82
Auyero, Javier.
Poor people's politics: Peronist survival networks and the legacy of Evita/ Javier Auyero. Durham: Duke University Press, 2001. xxiv, 257 p.
00-037115 322.4/4/0982 0822326213
Poor -- Argentina -- Buenos Aires -- Political activity. Patronage, Political -- Argentina -- Buenos Aires. Peronism.

HC183.C48.L36 1989
Langer, Erick Detlef.
Economic change and rural resistance in southern Bolivia, 1880-1930/ Erick D. Langer. Stanford, Calif.: Stanford University Press, 1989. ix, 269 p.
88-031117 303.4/0984/24 0804714916
Economic development -- Social aspects -- Case studies. Chuquisaca (Bolivia: Dept.) -- Rural conditions. Chuquisaca (Bolivia: Dept.) -- Social conditions. Chuquisaca (Bolivia: Dept.) -- Economic conditions.

HC183.E4 G54 2000
Gill, Lesley.
Teetering on the rim: global restructuring, daily life, and the armed retreat of the Bolivian state/ Lesley Gill. New York: Columbia University Press, c2000. x, 222 p.
99-055581 338.984/12 21 0231118058
El Alto (Bolivia) -- Economic conditions. El Alto (Bolivia) -- Social conditions. Bolivia -- Economic policy.

HC187.B147 2001
Baer, Werner,
The Brazilian economy: growth and development/ Werner Baer. 5th ed. Westport, Conn.: Praeger, 2001. xix, 498 p.
00-058017 330 981 21 0275966798
Brazil -- Economic conditions.

HC187.C219 2001
Cardoso, Fernando Henrique.
Charting a new course: the politics of globalization and social transformation/ Fernando Cardoso; edited and introduced by Mauricio A. Font. Lanham, MD: Rowman & Littlefield Publishers, c2001. viii, 334 p.
00-066468 338.98 21 0742508927
Dependency. Latin America -- Economic policy. Brazil -- Politics and government. Latin America -- Politics and government.

HC187.D865 1999
Duquette, Michel, 1947-
Building new democracies: economic and social reform in Brazil, Chile, and Mexico/ Michel Duquette. Toronto; University of Toronto Press, c1999. x, 287 p.
00-550530 338.98 21 0802044026
Democracy -- Brazil. Democracy -- Chile. Democracy -- Mexico. Chile -- Social policy. Mexico -- Economic policy -- 1970-1994. Mexico -- Social policy.

HC187.F733 1971
Frank, Andre Gunder, 1929-
Capitalism and underdevelopment in Latin America: historical studies of Chile and Brazil. Harmondsworth, Penguin, 1971. 368 p.
73-174622 330.9/81/06 0140213341
Brazil -- Economic conditions. Chile -- Economic conditions.

HC187.H68 1997
How Latin America fell behind: essays on the economic histories of Brazil and Mexico, 1800-1914/ edited by Stephen Haber. Stanford, Calif.: Stanford Unviversity Press, 1997. xi, 315 p.
96-012673 330.972 0804727376
Brazil -- Economic conditions -- 19th century. Mexico -- Economic conditions -- 19th century.

HC187.M2823 1992
Maddison, Angus.
Brazil and Mexico/ Angus Maddison and associates. Oxford, England; Published for the World Bank [by] Oxford Univers c1992. xiv, 248 p.
92-015645   0195208749
Income distribution -- Brazil. Income distribution -- Mexico. Mexico -- Economic policy. Brazil -- Economic policy.

HC187.P392213 1984
Pereira, Luiz Carlos Bresser.
Development and crisis in Brazil, 1930-1983/ Luiz Bresser Pereira; with a foreword by Thomas C Bruneau; translated from the Portuguese by Marcia Van Dyke. Boulder, Colo.: Westview Press, 1984. xiv, 241 p.
83-010232 338.981 0865315590
Industrial policy -- Brazil -- History -- 20th century. Brazil -- Economic policy. Brazil -- Economic conditions -- 1918- Brazil -- Politics and government -- 20th century.

HC187.T558 1987
Topik, Steven.
The political economy of the Brazilian State, 1889-1930/ by Steven Topik. Austin: University of Texas Press, 1987. xii, 241 p.
87-005835 338.981 0292765002
Finance -- Brazil -- History. Coffee Industry -- Brazil -- History. Railroads -- Brazil -- History. Brazil -- Economic policy. Brazil -- History -- 1889-1930.

HC188.A5.H35 1997
Hall, Anthony L., 1947-
Sustaining Amazonia: grassroots action for productive conservation/ Anthony Hall. Manchester, UK; Manchester University Press; 1997.
 97-005366 333.7/0981/1 071904698X
Sustainable development -- Amazon River Region. Natural resources -- Amazon River Region -- Management. Sustainable development -- Brazil.

HC188.S3.D4
Dean, Warren.
The industrialization of Sao Paulo, 1880-1945. Austin, Published for the Institute of Latin American St [1969] x, 263 p.
73-096435 338/.0981/6 0292700040
Industrialization -- Brazil -- Sao Paulo (State) -- History.

HC189.R4.P56 1997
Pino, Julio Cesar.
Family and favela: the reproduction of poverty in Rio de Janeiro/ Julio Cesar Pino. Westport, Conn.: Greenwood Press, 1997. x, 199 p.
96-047433 330.981/53064 0313303622
Poverty -- Brazil -- Rio de Janeiro -- History -- 20th century. Poor -- Brazil -- Rio de Janeiro -- History -- 20th century. Family -- Economic aspects -- Brazil -- Rio de Janeiro -- History -- 20th century.

HC192.C575 1995
Collins, Joseph, 1945-
Chile's free-market miracle: a second look/ Joseph Collins and John Lear; [foreword by Walden Bello; epilogue by Stephanie Rosenfeld. Oakland, Calif.: Food First, c1995. xi, 320 p.
94-030596 338.983 0935028633
Free enterprise -- Chile. Chile -- Economic policy. Chile -- Economic conditions -- 1973-1988. Chile -- Economic conditions -- 1988-

HC192.M29
Mamalakis, Markos.
The growth and structure of the Chilean economy: from independence to Allende/ Markos J. Mamalakis. New Haven: Yale University Press, 1976. xx, 390 p.
74-029729 330.9/83/064 0300018606
Chile -- Economic conditions.

HC192.M34 1996
Martinez Bengoa, Javier.
Chile, the great transformation/ Javier Martinez, Alvaro Diaz. Washington, D.C.: Brookings Institution; c1996. xii, 156 p.
95-052628 338.983 20 0815754787
Chile -- Politics and government -- 1973- Chile -- Economic conditions -- 1973-1988. Chile -- Economic conditions -- 1988-

HC192.M4553 2000
Meller, Patricio.
The Unidad Popular and the Pinochet dictatorship: a political economy analysis/ Patricio Meller; translated by Tim Ennis. New York, N.Y.: St. Martin's Press, 2000. xiii, 222 p.
00-033294 330.981/0646 0333800532
Chile -- Economic conditions -- 1970-1973. Chile -- Economic conditions -- 1973-1988. Chile -- Politics and government -- 1970-1973.

HC192.M47 2000
Mesa-Lago, Carmelo, 1934-
Market, socialist, and mixed economies: comparative policy and performance: Chile, Cuba, and Costa Rica/ Carmelo Mesa-Lago; with Alberto Arenas de Mesa ... [et al]. Baltimore: Johns Hopkins University Press, 2000. xxiv, 707 p.
99-042559 338.9 0801861721
Chile -- Economic policy. Cuba -- Economic policy. Costa Rica -- Economic policy.

HC192.P48 1994
Petras, James F., 1937-
Democracy and poverty in Chile: the limits to electoral politics/ James Petras and Fernando Ignacio Leiva, with Henry Veltmeyer. Boulder, Colo.: Westview Press, 1994. xv, 215 p.
93-043013 338.983 0813382173
Democracy -- Chile. Chile -- Economic conditions -- 1973-1988. Chile -- Economic policy. Chile -- Economic conditions -- 1988-

HC192.V18 1995
Valdes, Juan Gabriel.
Pinochet's economists: the Chicago school in Chile/ Juan Gabriel Valdes. Cambridge, England; Cambridge University Press, 1995. xiii, 334 p.
94-028011 338.983 0521451469
Chicago school of economics. Chile -- Economic policy. Chile -- Economic conditions -- 1973-1988.

HC197.C634 1992
The Colombian economy: issues of trade and development/ edited by Alvin Cohen and Frank R. Gunter; foreword by Rodolfo Segovia S. Boulder, Colo.: Westview Press, 1992. xvi, 399 p.
92-020194 330.9861/0632 0813316324
Colombia -- Economic conditions -- 1970- Colombia -- Economic policy.

HC202.A65 1995
Andrien, Kenneth J., 1951-
The kingdom of Quito, 1690-1830: the state and regional development/ Kenneth J. Andrien. Cambridge; Cambridge University Press, 1995. xi, 255 p.
94-044080 338.9866/00903 0521481252
Quito (Kingdom) -- Economic conditions. Quito (Kingdom) -- Politics and government.

HC227.S435 1999
Sheahan, John, 1923-
Searching for a better society: the Peruvian economy from 1950/ John Sheahan. University Park, Pa.: Pennsylvania State University Press, c1999. xi, 211 p.
98-039335 338.985 21 0271018720
Peru -- Economic policy. Peru -- Economic conditions -- 1918- Peru -- Economic conditions -- 1968-

HC227.S55 1989
Slater, David, 1946-
Territory and state power in Latin America: the Peruvian case/ David Slater. New York: St. Martin's Press, 1989. xiii, 273 p.
89-030608 338.985 0312030738
Economic development -- Case studies. Capitalism -- Developing countries -- Case studies. Peru -- Economic conditions -- 1918-1968. Peru -- Economic conditions -- 1968-

HC228.L6.S26 2000
Santos-Granero, Fernando, 1955-
Tamed frontiers: economy, society, and civil rights in upper Amazonia/ Fernando Santos-Granero, Frederica Barclay. Boulder, Colo.: Westview Press, 2000. xiv, 386 p.
99-016846 330.985/440633 0813337178
Civil society -- Peru -- Loreto (Dept.) Civil rights -- Peru -- Loreto (Dept.) Loreto (Peru: Dept.) -- Economic conditions. Loreto (Peru: Dept.) -- Social conditions.

HC232.F56 1982
Finch, M. H. J.
A political economy of Uruguay since 1870/ M. H. J. Finch. New York: St. Martin's Press, 1982, c1981. xiii, 339 p.
80-021047 330.9895/06 0312622449
Uruguay -- Economic policy. Uruguay -- Economic conditions.

HC240.A1 By region or country — Europe — Societies. Serials

HC240.A1 O187
OECD economic surveys. Paris: OECD, <2001->
 2001-238197
European Union countries -- Economic conditions -- Periodicals. European Union countries -- Economic policy -- Periodicals.

HC240.A1.U477
Economic survey of Europe in .../ prepared by the Research and Planning Division, Economic Commission for Europe. Geneva, Switzerland: [United Nations], [1954-]
48-010193 330.94/005
Europe -- Economic conditions -- 1945- Periodicals.

HC240.A5944-Z9 By region or country — Europe — General works

HC240.A5944 1990
Ahnstrom, Leif, 1934-
Economic growth, stagnation, and the working population in Western Europe/ Leif Ahnstrom. London; Belhaven Press, 1990. xii, 198 p.
90-033775 338.94 1852931256
Industries -- Europe. Occupations -- Europe. Labor supply -- Europe. Europe -- Economic conditions -- 1945-

HC240.A832
Arkes, Hadley.
Bureaucracy, the Marshall Plan, and the national interest. Princeton, N.J., Princeton University Press [1973, c1972] xiv, 395 p.
78-166360 338.91/73 0691046077
Economic assistance, American.

HC240.B297 1987
Barriers to European growth: a transatlantic view/ Robert Z. Lawrence, Charles L. Schultze, editors. Washington, D.C.: Brookings Institution, c1987. xvii, 619 p.
87-026900 338.94 0815777701
Europe -- Economic conditions -- 1945- -- Congresses. Europe -- Economic policy -- Congresses.

HC240.B84 1993 vol. 1
The Single market and monetary unification/ edited by Mario Baldassarri and Robert Mundell. New York: St. Martin's Press in association with Rivista d 1993. 679 p.
92-189371 338.94 s 0312089775
Monetary unions -- European Economic Community countries. Monetary policy -- European Economic Community countries. Europe 1992.

HC240.C312
The Cambridge economic history of Europe; general editors, M.M. Postan and H.J. Habakkuk. Cambridge, Cambridge U.P., 1966-1989.
66-066029 330.94
Europe -- Economic conditions. Europe -- History.

HC240.C49513 1993
Cipolla, Carlo M.
Before the industrial revolution: European society and economy, 1000-1700/ Carlo M. Cipolla. 3rd ed. London; Routledge, 1993. xiv, 333 p.
93-006919 330.94 20 0415090059
Europe -- Economic conditions.

HC240.C68 2000
Craig, Lee A.
The European macroeconomy: growth and integration and cycles 1500-1913/ Lee A. Craig, Douglas Fisher. Cheltenham, UK; Edward Elgar, c2000. xii, 389 p.
99-031597 330.94 21 1852786434
Industries -- Europe -- History. Capitalism -- Europe -- History. Europe -- Economic conditions. Europe -- Economic integration -- History.

HC240.C763 2001
Crouzet, Francois, 1922-
A history of the European economy, 1000-2000/ Francois Crouzet. Charlottesville: University Press of Virginia, 2001. xx, 329 p.
00-051297 330.94 0813920248
Europe -- Economic conditions.

HC240.D32
Davis, Ralph, 1915-
The rise of the Atlantic economies. Ithaca, N.Y., Cornell University Press [1973] xiv, 352 p.
73-077683 330.9/4 0801408016
Europe -- Economic conditions. America -- Economic conditions.

HC240.D48 1976
De Vries, Jan, 1943 Nov. 14-
Economy of Europe in an age of crisis, 1600-1750/ Jan de Vries. Cambridge, [Eng.]; Cambridge University Press, 1976. xi, 284 p.
75-030438 330.9/4/055 0521211239
Europe -- Economic conditions -- 17th century. Europe -- History -- 17th century. Europe -- History -- 18th century.

HC240.E274 1996
Economic growth in Europe since 1945/ edited by Nicholas Crafts and Gianni Toniolo. Cambridge; Cambridge University Press, 1996. xxii, 600 p.
96-178431 338.94/009/045 0521496276
Europe -- Economic conditions -- 1945-

HC240.E748 2000
Eurojargon: a dictionary of European Union acronyms, abbreviations, and sobriquets/ edited by Anne Ramsay. 6th ed. Chicago: Fitzroy Dearborn Publishers, c2000. ix, 376 p.
2002-276081 341.242/2/03 21 1579582745
European Union -- Dictionaries. European Union -- Terminology. European communities -- Terminology.

HC240.E8362 1994
The European economy, 1750-1914: a thematic approach/ edited by Derek H. Aldcroft and Simon P. Ville. Manchester; Manchester University Press; c1994. x, 323 p.
93-027921 330.94 0719035988
Europe -- Economic conditions -- 18th century. Europe -- Economic conditions -- 19th century. Europe -- Economic conditions -- 20th century.

HC240.G465
Gerschenkron, Alexander.
Continuity in history, and other essays. Cambridge, Mass., Belknap Press of Harvard University Press, 1968. x, 545 p.
68-014257 330.9
Industries -- Europe -- History. Economic history. Europe -- Economic conditions.

HC240.G564 1988
Goodman, Jordan.
Gainful pursuits: the making of industrial Europe, 1600-1914/ Jordan Goodman and Katrina Honeyman. London: E. Arnold; 1988. 262 p.
89-133518 0713165456
Industrialization -- Europe -- History. Europe -- Economic conditions -- History.

HC240.H314 1983
Hamerow, Theodore S.
The birth of a new Europe: state and society in the nineteenth century/ Theodore S. Hamerow. Chapel Hill: University of North Carolina Press, c1983. xii, 447 p.
82-020162 940.2/8 0807815489
Europe -- Economic conditions -- 1789-1900. Europe -- Social conditions -- 1789-1900. Europe - - Politics and government -- 1789-1900.

HC240.H3516 2000
Harrop, Jeffrey.
The political economy of integration in the European Union/ Jeffrey Harrop. Cheltenham, UK: E. Elgar Pub., c2000. xiii, 339 p.
99-049222 337.1/42 21 1840640995
European Union. Europe -- Economic integration.

HC240.H614 1987
Hogan, Michael J., 1943-
The Marshall Plan: America, Britain, and the reconstruction of Western Europe, 1947-1952/ Michael J. Hogan. Cambridge [Cambridgeshire]; Cambridge University Press, 1987. xiv, 482 p.
86-031773 338.91/73/04 0521251400
Reconstruction (1939-1951) United States -- Foreign economic relations -- Europe. Europe -- Foreign economic relations -- United States. Great Britain -- Foreign economic relations -- Europe.

HC240.K53 1998
Klausen, Jytte.
War and welfare: Europe and the United States, 1945 to the present/ Jytte Klausen. New York: St. Martin's Press, 1998. 341 p.
98-003792 338.94/009/045 0312210337
Europe -- Economic conditions -- 1945- Capitalism -- Europe -- History. Welfare state -- Europe -- History.

HC240.M27317 2001
The Marshall plan: fifty years after/ edited by Martin Schain. 1st ed. New York: Palgrave, 2001. xiii, 297 p.
00-045808 338.91/7304/09044 21 0312229623
Reconstruction (1939-1951)

HC240.M645 1977b
Milward, Alan S.
The development of the economies of continental Europe, 1850-1914/ Alan S. Milward and S. B. Saul. Cambridge, Mass.: Harvard University Press, 1977. 555 p.
76-055137 330.9/4/028 0674200233
Europe -- Economic conditions.

HC240.M754 1995
Moussis, Nicolas.
Handbook of European Union: institutions and policies/ by Nicholas Moussis. Rixensart [Belgium]: EDIT-EUR, 1995. 354 p.
96-175034 337.1/42 2930119071
European Union. Law -- European Union countries. European Union countries -- Economic policy. European Union countries -- Social policy.

HC240.M793 1999
Musgrave, Peter, 1947-
The early modern European economy/ Peter Musgrave. New York: St. Martin's Press, 1999. vii, 236 p.
99-012189 330.94 0312223315
Europe -- Economic conditions.

HC240.N66
North, Douglass Cecil.
The rise of the Western world; a new economic history [by] Douglass C. North and Robert Paul Thomas. Cambridge [Eng.] University Press, 1973. viii, 170 p.
73-077258 330.9/4 0521201713
Europe -- Economic conditions.

HC240.P596
Pollard, Sidney.
Peaceful conquest: the industrialization of Europe, 1760-1970/ by Sidney Pollard. Oxford; Oxford University Press, 1981. xii, 451 p.
80-041061 338.094 0198770936
Industrialization -- Europe -- History.

HC240.R334 1995
Regini, Marino, 1943-
Uncertain boundaries: the social and political construction of European economies/ Marino Regini. Cambridge; Cambridge University Press, 1995. x, 164 p.
94-021946 330.12/6/094 0521473713
Europe -- Economic policy. Europe -- Economic conditions -- 1945- Europe -- Politics and government -- 1945-

HC240.R4355 1992
Reshaping Europe in the twenty-first century/ edited by Patrick Robertson; foreword by Margaret Thatcher. New York: St. Martin's Press, 1992. xvi, 269 p.
91-024191 338.94 0312068891
European federation. Europe -- Politics and government -- 1945- Europe -- Economic integration. Europe -- Economic policy.

HC240.T56 1987
Tipton, Frank B., 1943-
An economic and social history of Europe, 1890-1939/ Frank B. Tipton and Robert Aldrich. Baltimore: Johns Hopkins University Press, 1987. vii, 323 p.
87-003869 330.94/028 0801835372
Europe -- Economic conditions -- 19th century. Europe -- Economic conditions -- 20th century. Europe -- Social conditions -- 1789-1900.

HC240.V258 2002
Vanthoor, W. F. V.
A chronological history of the European Union, 1946-2001/ Wim F.V. Vanthoor. Cheltenham, UK; Edward Elgar, c2002. xxii, 331 p.
2002-072170 330.94/055 21 1843761017
European Union countries -- Economic conditions -- Chronology. Monetary policy -- European Union countries -- History -- Chronology.

HC240.Z9.W45 1998
Landes, David S.
The wealth and poverty of nations: why some are so rich and some so poor/ David S. Landes. New York: W.W. Norton, c1998. xxi, 650 p.
97-027508 330.1/6 21 0393040178
Wealth -- Europe -- History. Wealth -- History. Poverty -- Europe -- History.

HC240.25 By region or country — Europe — European Union in relation to individual regions or countries, A-Z

HC240.25.H9
Andor, Laszlo.
Hungary on the road to the European Union: transition in blue/ Laszlo Andor. Westport, Conn.: Praeger, 2000. 199 p.
99-043101 337.43904 0275963942
European Union -- Hungary. Hungary -- Economic integration. Hungary -- Economic conditions -- 1989- Hungary -- Social conditions -- 1989-

HC240.9 By region or country — Europe — Special topics, A-Z

HC240.9.C3.T43 1988
Technology and the rise of the networked city in Europe and America/ edited by Joel A. Tarr and Gabriel Dupuy. Philadelphia: Temple University Press, c1988. xvii, 339 p.
87-027787 363/.09173/2 0877225400
Infrastructure (Economics) -- Europe -- History -- Case studies. Urban policy -- Europe -- History -- Case studies. Technological innovations -- Economic aspects -- Europe -- History -- Case studies.

HC240.9.C6.H34 1992
Hallsworth, A. G. 1947-
The new geography of consumer spending: a political economy approach/ Alan G. Hallsworth. London: Belhaven Press; c1992. viii, 199 p.
92-024767 339.4/7/094 1852932007
Consumption (Economics) -- Europe. Finance -- Europe. Retail trade -- Europe. Japan -- Economic conditions -- 1945-

HC240.9.I5.P685 1995
Poverty, inequality, and the future of social policy: Western states and the new world order/ Katherine McFate, Roger Lawson, William Julius Wilson, editors. New York: Russell Sage Foundation, c1995. xii, 756 p.
94-021887 362.5/094 0871545101
Income distribution -- Europe. Income distribution -- United States. Poor -- Europe. Europe -- Social policy. United States -- Social policy -- 1993-

HC240.9.L3.C37x 1987
Carew, Anthony, 1943-
Labour under the Marshall plan: the politics of productivity and the marketing of management science/ Anthony Carew. Manchester, U.K.: Manchester University Press, c1987. 293 p.
88-199327 0719019869
Labor productivity -- Europe -- History. Economic assistance, American -- Europe -- History. Europe -- Economic conditions -- 1945-

HC240.9.P6.G4713 1994
Geremek, Bronislaw.
Poverty: a history/ Bronislaw Geremek; translated by Agnieszka Kolakowska. Oxford; Blackwell, 1994. xi, 273 p.
94-008783 362.5/094 0631154256
Poor -- Europe -- History. Poverty -- Religious aspects -- Christianity. Church work with the poor -- Europe -- History. Europe -- Social conditions.

HC240.9.T4.T4 1990
The technical challenges and opportunities of a united Europe/ edited by Michael S. Steinberg. Savage, Md.: Barnes & Noble, c1990. 195 p.
89-077848 338/.064/094 0389209007
Technology transfer -- Government policy -- European Economic Community countries -- Congresses. Technology and state -- Economic aspects -- European Economic Community countries -- Congresses. European federation -- Congresses.

HC241-241.25 By region or country — Europe — European economic integration

HC241.C73 1997
Craig, Lee A. 1960-
The integration of the European economy 1850-1913/ Lee A. Craig and Douglas Fisher. New York: St. Martin's Press, c1997. xviii, 327 p.
96-001268 337.4 20 0312129637
Europe -- Economic integration -- History. European Economic Community countries -- Economic policy.

HC241.M5313 1992
Minc, Alain.
The great European illusion: business in the wider community/ Alain Minc; with a foreword by Ronnie Lessem; translated by Lindsey Jones. Oxford, UK; Blackwell Publishers, 1992. 257 p.
91-023290 337.1/4 0631176950
European federation. Europe 1992. Europe -- Economic integration.

HC241.N4 1998
Neal, Larry, 1941-
The economics of the European Union and the economies of Europe/ Larry Neal, Daniel Barbezat. New York: Oxford University Press, 1998. xvii, 396 p.
97-004221 330.94/0559 0195110676
European Union. European Union countries -- Economic conditions.

HC241.O765 1998
The origins and development of European integration: a reader and commentary/ edited by Peter M.R. Stirk and David Weigall. New York: Pinter, 1998. xvi, 336 p.
98-020773 337.1/4 1855675161
Europe -- Economic integration -- History.

HC241.S515 1991
The Shape of the new Europe/ edited by Gregory F. Treverton. New York: Council on Foreign Relations Press, c1992. vi, 232 p.
91-023295 337.1/4 0876091079
Europe -- Economic integration. European federation. International economic relations. Europe -- Politics and government -- 1989-

HC241.U52 1979
Underdeveloped Europe: studies in core-periphery relations/ edited by Dudley Seers, Bernard Schaffer, Marja-Liisa Kiljunen. Atlantic Highlands, N.J.: Humanities Press, 1979. xxi, 325 p.
78-026518 338.91/4 0391009621
Industries -- Europe -- Case studies. Regional economics -- Case studies. Europe -- Economic integration -- Case studies. Europe -- Economic conditions -- Regional disparities -- Case studies.

HC241.U78 1995
Urwin, Derek W.
The community of Europe: a history of European integration since 1945 / Derek W. Urwin. 2nd ed. London; Longman, 1995. xi, 292 p.
94-015314 337.1/4/09045 20 058223199X
Europe -- Economic integration -- History. European Economic Community -- History. Europe -- Economic conditions -- 1945-

HC241.2.C63448 2001
Competitiveness and cohesion in EU policies/ edited by Ronald Hall, Alasdair Smith, Loukas Tsoukalis. Oxford; Oxford University Press, 2001. xix, 366 p.
00-046956 338.94 21 0198295227
Competition -- European Union countries.

HC241.2.D476 1999
Dinan, Desmond, 1957-
Ever closer union: an introduction to European integration/ Desmond Dinan. Boulder, Colo.: L. Rienner Publishers, 1999. xiii, 597 p.
99-011101 337.1/42 1555877397
European federation.

HC241.2.E77 1991
Euro-politics: institutions and policymaking in the new European community/ Alberta M. Sbragia, editor. Washington, D.C.: Brookings Institution, c1991. xi, 303 p.
91-040355 341.24/22 0815777248
Europe 1992. European communities.

HC241.2.E81285 1990
Europe 1992: an American perspective/ Gary Clyde Hufbauer, editor. Washington, D.C.: Brookings Institution, c1990. xxiii, 406 p.
90-035041 337.4 0815738102
Europe 1992. European Economic Community countries -- Commercial policy. United States -- Commercial policy. European Economic Community countries -- Foreign economic relations -- United States.

HC241.2.G52 1994
Gianaris, Nicholas V.
The European Community, Eastern Europe, and Russia: economic and political changes/ Nicholas V. Gianaris. Westport, Conn.: Praeger, 1994. x, 202 p.
93-040198　330.94　0275947084
　European Economic Community countries -- Economic conditions. European Economic Community countries -- Politics and government. Europe, Eastern -- Economic conditions -- 1989-

HC241.2.M487 2000
Milward, Alan S.
The European rescue of the nation-state/ Alan S. Milward with the assistance of George Brennan and Federico Romero. London; Routledge, 2000. xv, 466 p.
99-044300　337.1/42　0415216281
　European Economic Community -- Economic policy. Great Britain -- Economic policy -- 1945-1964.

HC241.2.M49 1978
Minshull, G. N.
The new Europe, an economic geography of the EEC/ G. N. Minshull. New York: Holmes & Meier, 1978. 281 p.
78-006581　330.94/0557　0841903913
　European Economic Community countries.

HC241.2.M58 2001
Molle, Willem.
The economics of European integration: theory, practice, policy/ Willem Molle. 4th ed. Aldershot; Ashgate, c2001. xiii, 548 p.
00-053601　337.1/42 21　0754621952
　Monetary policy -- European Economic Community countries.

HC241.2.S743 2000
Archer, Clive.
The European Union: structure and process/ Clive Archer. 3rd ed. London; Continuum, 2000. xiii, 242 p.
00-055477　341.24/22 21　0826451098
　European Union.

HC241.2.T74 1991
Tsoukalis, Loukas.
The new European economy: the politics and economics of integration/ Loukas Tsoukalis. Oxford [England]; Oxford University Press, 1991. xvii, 333 p.
91-004311　337.1/42　019828750X
　Europe 1992. European Economic Community countries -- Economic policy.

HC241.25.G7.G675 1999
Gowland, D. A.
Reluctant Europeans: Britain and European integration, 1945-1998/ David Gowland and Arthur Turner. New York: Addison Wesley Longman, 1999.
 99-020912　337.4041　0582369576
　European Union -- Great Britain. Great Britain -- Politics and government -- 1945-

HC241.25.G7.K5
King, Anthony Stephen.
Britain says yes: the 1975 referendum on the Common Market/ Anthony King. Washington: American Enterprise Institute for Public Policy c1977. 153 p.
77-083257　382/.9142/0941　0844732605
European Economic Community -- Great Britain.

HC241.25.G8.L39 1997
Lavdas, Kostas A., 1964-
The Europeanization of Greece: interest politics and the crises of integration/ Kostas A. Lavdas. New York: St. Martin's Press, c1997. xiv, 337 p.
97-005318　337.40495 21　0312174632
　European Union -- Greece. Corporate state -- Greece. Greece -- Politics and government.

HC241.25.I748 1991
Ireland and EC membership evaluated/ edited by Patrick Keatinge. New York: St. Martin's Press, 1991. xxi, 298 p.
90-024899　341.24/22　0312060947
European Economic Community -- Ireland.

HC241.25.S6.T68 1990
Tovias, Alfred.
Foreign economic relations of the European Community: the impact of Spain and Portugal/ Alfred Tovias. Boulder: L. Rienner, c1990. xii, 137 p.
89-038557　337.4/0049　1555871755
　European Economic Community countries -- Foreign economic relations.

HC241.25.U5.C56 1993
Coffey, Peter.
The EC and the United States/ Peter Coffey. New York: St. Martin's Press, 1993. viii, 295 p.
92-028470　341.24/22　0312085680
European Economic Community -- United States.

HC243 By region or country — Europe — Northern Europe. Baltic states

HC243.E36 1992
Economic survey of the Baltic states/ Brian Van Arkadie and Mats Karlsson. Washington Square, N.Y.: New York University Press, 1992. xix, 344 p.
91-036162　330.947/40854　0814787681
　Baltic States -- Economic conditions. Baltic States -- Economic policy.

HC243.5 By region or country — Europe — Sovet ekonomicheskoi vzaimopomoshshchi. Counsil for Mutual Economic Assistance. COMECON

HC243.5.C7513 1990
Csaba, Laszlo, 1954-
Eastern Europe in the world economy/ by Laszlo Csaba. Cambridge [England]; Cambridge University Press, c1990. 403 p.
89-077362　337.1/47　0521334268
　Europe, Eastern -- Foreign economic relations.

HC244 By region or country — Europe — Central Europe. Eastern Europe

HC244.A622 1995
Aldcroft, Derek Howard.
Economic change in Eastern Europe since 1918/ Derek H. Aldcroft and Steven Morewood. Aldershot, Hants, England; E. Elgar, c1995. xiii, 277 p.
94-016370　330.947/084　1852788194
　Europe, Eastern -- Economic conditions -- 1945-1989. Europe, Eastern -- Economic conditions -- 1989- Europe -- Economic conditions -- 20th century.

HC244.A813 2002
Åslund, Anders,
Building capitalism: the transformation of the former Soviet bloc/ Anders Åslund. Cambridge, UK; Cambridge University Press, 2002. xvii, 508 p.
00-065989　338.947 21　0521805252
　Post-communism -- Europe, Eastern. Privatization -- Europe, Eastern. Privatization -- Russia (Federation)

HC244.B695 1993
Bookman, Milica Zarkovic.
The economics of secession/ Milica Zarkovic Bookman. New York: St. Martin's Press, 1993. 262 p.
92-024999　338.947　0312084439
　Europe, Eastern -- Economic policy -- 1989- Europe, Eastern -- Politics and government -- 1989-

HC244.B699 1995
Bosworth, Barry, 1942-
Reforming planned economies in an integrating world economy/ Barry P. Bosworth and Gur Ofer. Washington, D.C.: Brookings Institution, c1995. xxvi, 186 p.
95-003848　338.947　0815710488
　Post-communism -- Economic aspects -- Europe, Eastern. Post-communism -- Economic aspects -- Europe, Central. Europe, Eastern -- Economic policy -- 1989- Europe, Central -- Economic policy. China -- Economic policy -- 1976-

HC244.B7273 1993
Brabant, Jozef M. van.
The New Eastern Europe and the world economy/ edited by Jozef M. van Brabant. Boulder, Colo.: Westview Press, 1993. xii, 219 p.
93-006600　337.47　0813315239
　Europe, Eastern -- Economic conditions -- 1989- Europe, Eastern -- Foreign economic relations. Europe, Eastern -- Economic integration.

HC244.B7274
Brabant, Jozef M. van.
The planned economies and international economic organizations/ Jozef M. van Brabant. Cambridge [England]; Cambridge University Press, 1991. xv, 318 p.
90-001470　338.947　0521383501
　Central planning -- Europe, Eastern. International finance. International economic relations. Europe, Eastern -- Economic policy -- 1989-

HC244.B72743 1998
Brabant, Jozef M. van.
The political economy of transition: coming to grips with history and methodology/ Josef M. van Brabant. London; Routledge, 1998. xvi, 559 p.
97-031300   338.947   0415169461
Post-communism -- Europe, Eastern. Free enterprise -- Europe, Eastern. Communism -- Europe, Eastern. Europe, Eastern -- Economic policy -- 1989-

HC244.C35 1991
Campbell, Robert Wellington.
The socialist economies in transition: a primer on semi-reformed systems/ Robert W. Campbell. Bloomington: Indiana University Press, c1991. x, 241 p.
91-008653   338.947   0253313015
Europe, Eastern -- Economic conditions -- 1989- Europe, Eastern -- Economic conditions -- 1945-1989. Soviet Union -- Economic conditions -- 1985-1991.

HC244.E22
East European integration and East-West trade/ edited by Paul Marer, John Michael Montias. Bloomington: Indiana University Press, c1980. xvi, 432 p.
79-003181   337.47   0253168651
East-West trade (1945-) -- Congresses. Europe, Eastern -- Economic integration -- Congresses.

HC244.E484 1998
Emerging from Communism: lessons from Russia, China, and Eastern Europe/ edited by Peter Boone, Stanislaw Gomulka, and Richard Layard. Cambridge, Mass.: MIT Press, c1998. vii, 244 p.
98-023560   338.947 21   0262024470
Structural adjustment (Economic policy) -- Europe, Eastern. Post-communism -- Europe, Eastern. Structural adjustment (Economic policy) -- Russia (Federation) Russia (Federation) -- Economic policy -- 1991- Europe, Eastern -- Economic policy -- 1976-

HC244.H344 1991
Handbook of reconstruction in Eastern Europe and the Soviet Union/ edited by Stephen White; contributors John B. Allcock ... [et al.]. Harlow, Essex, U.K.: Longman Group; c1991. viii, 407 p.
91-191740   338.947   0582085020
Communism -- Europe, Eastern. Post-communism -- Europe, Eastern. Communism -- Soviet Union. Europe, Eastern -- Politics and government -- 1989- Soviet Union -- Economic conditions -- 1985-1991. Soviet Union -- Politics and government -- 1985-1991.

HC244.H565 1998
Hoen, Herman Willem, 1960-
The transformation of economic systems in Central Europe/ Herman W. Hoen. Cheltenham, UK; E. Elgar Pub., 1998. xi, 203 p.
97-047522   338.943   1858982715
Europe, Central -- Economic policy. Europe, Central -- Economic conditions.

HC244.I24 2002
Iankova, Elena A.
Eastern European capitalism in the making/ Elena A. Iankova. New York: Cambridge University Press, c2002. xiv, 223 p.
2002-066514   330.9438 21   052181314X
Capitalism -- Europe, Eastern. Post-communism -- Europe, Eastern. Social conflict -- Europe, Eastern.

HC244.K485 2001
King, Lawrence P.
The basic features of postcommunist capitalism in Eastern Europe: firms in Hungary, the Czech Republic, and Slovakia/ Lawrence Peter King. Westport, Conn.: Praeger, c2001. x, 150 p.
00-023310   330.12/2/0947 21   0275968391
Capitalism -- Europe, Eastern. Post-communism -- Europe, Eastern. Europe, Eastern -- Economic policy -- 1989-

HC244.K6315 2000
Kolodko, Grzegorz W.
From shock to therapy: the political economy of postsocialist transformation/ Grzegorz W. Kolodko. Oxford; Oxford University Press, 2000. xi, 457 p.
00-033981   338.9/009171/7   0198297432
Post-communism -- Case studies. Privatization -- Case studies. Mixey economy -- Case studies. Vietnam -- Economic policy. Europe, Eastern -- Economic policy -- 1989- Poland -- Economic policy -- 1990-

HC244.K66913 1995
Kornai, Janos.
Highway and byways: studies on reform and post-communist transition/ Janos Kornai. Cambridge, Mass.: MIT Press, c1995. xv, 241 p.
94-021566   338.947   0262111985
Mixed economy -- Europe, Eastern. Post-communism -- Europe, Eastern. Europe, Eastern -- Economic policy -- 1989- Europe, Eastern -- Economic conditions -- 1989-

HC244.L3749 1995
Lavigne, Marie, 1935-
The economics of transition: from socialist economy to market economy/ Marie Lavigne. New York: St. Martin's Press, 1995. xvi, 295 p.
95-008199   338.947   0312127200
Free enterprise -- Europe, Eastern. Post-communism -- Europe, Eastern. Democracy -- Europe, Eastern. Europe, Eastern -- Economic policy -- 1989-

HC244.M224 1991
Macesich, George, 1927-
Reform and market democracy/ George Macesich. New York: Praeger, 1991. xi, 145 p.
91-010179   338.947   0275939898
Mixed economy -- Europe, Eastern. Capitalism -- Europe, Eastern. Democracy. Europe, Eastern -- Economic conditions -- 1989-

HC244.M226 1993
The Macroeconomics of transition: developments in East Central Europe/ edited by Jan Winiecki and Andrzej Kondratowicz. London; Routledge, 1993. ix, 154 p.
92-032041   330.947/0009/049   0415091675
Mixed economy -- Europe, Eastern. Europe, Eastern -- Economic policy -- 1989- Europe, Eastern -- Economic conditions -- 1989-

HC244.M256 1993
Making markets: economic transformation in Eastern Europe and the post-Soviet states/ edited by Shafiqul Islam and Michael Mandelbaum. New York: Council on Foreign Relations Press, c1993. ix, 238 p.
92-040676   338.947   087609129X
Mixed economy -- Europe, Eastern. Mixed economy -- Former Soviet republics. Europe, Eastern -- Economic conditions -- 1989- Former Soviet republics -- Economic conditions. Europe, Eastern -- Economic policy -- 1989-

HC244.P8 1991
Przeworski, Adam.
Democracy and the market: political and economic reforms in Eastern Europe and Latin America/ Adam Przeworski. Cambridge; Cambridge University Press, 1991. xii, 210 p.
91-007524   338.947   0521412250
Mixed economy -- Europe, Eastern. Mixed economy -- Latin America. Democracy -- Europe, Eastern. Latin America -- Economic policy. Latin America -- Politics and government -- 1980- Europe, Eastern -- Economic policy -- 1989-

HC244.S555 2000
Smith, Alan, 1944-
The return to Europe: the reintegration of Eastern Europe into the European economy/ Alan Smith. New York: St. Martin's Press, in association with School o 2000. xiv, 215 p.
99-087195   337.4704   0312232624
European Union. Europe -- Economic integration. Europe, Eastern -- Economic conditions -- 1989-

HC244.S743 2002
Stone, Randall W.,
Lending credibility: the International Monetary Fund and the post-communist transition/ Randall W. Stone. Princeton, N.J. Princeton University Press, c2002. xxii, 286 p.
2002-023662   332.1/52 21   0691095299
Post-communism -- Europe, Eastern.

HC244.T69897 2002
Transition, the first ten years: analysis and lessons for Eastern Europe and the former Soviet Union Washington, D.C.: World Bank, c2002. xxxii, 128 p.
2001-056873   338.947 21   0821350382
Europe, Eastern -- Economic conditions -- 1989- Former Soviet republics -- Economic conditions. Europe, Eastern -- Politics and government -- 1989- Former Soviet republics -- Politics and government.

HC244.W364 1998
Wedel, Janine R., 1957-
Collision and collusion: the strange case of western aid to Eastern Europe, 1989-1998/ Janine R. Wedel. New York: St. Martin's Press, 1998. xii, 286 p.
98-038646   338.91/0947   0312212151
Economic assistance -- Europe, Eastern -- Evaluation. Economic assistance -- Former Soviet republics -- Evaluation. Former Soviet republics -- Economic conditions. Europe, Eastern -- Economic conditions -- 1989-

HC244.W667 2000
World Bank.
Making transition work for everyone: poverty and inequality in Europe and Central Asia. Washington, D.C.: World Bank, c2000. x, 524 p.
00-043950   362.5/7/0947 21   0821347209
Post-communism -- Europe, Eastern. Poverty -- Europe, Eastern. Income distribution -- Europe, Eastern. Former Soviet republics -- Economic policy. Europe, Eastern -- Economic policy -- 1989- Europe, Eastern -- Economic conditions -- 1989-

HC244.Z57 1994
Zloch-Christy, Iliana, 1953-
Eastern Europe in a time of change: economic and political dimensions/ Iliana Zloch-Christy. Westport, Conn.: Praeger, 1994. xviii, 143 p.
93-026469   338.947   0275947076
Europe, Eastern -- Economic conditions -- 1989- Former Soviet republics -- Economic conditions. Europe, Eastern -- Social conditions.

HC244.Z9.E52 1993
Environmental action in Eastern Europe: responses to crisis/ edited by Barbara Jancar-Webster. Armonk, N.Y.: M.E. Sharpe, c1993. 238 p.
92-037852　363.7/056/0947　156324036X
Environmental policy -- Europe, Eastern -- Congresses. Europe, Eastern -- Economic policy -- 1989- -- Congresses.

HC244.Z9.I514 1992
Atkinson, A. B.
Economic transformation in Eastern Europe and the distribution of income/ Anthony B. Atkinson and John Micklewright. Cambridge [England]; Cambridge University Press, 1992. xvi, 448 p.
92-017601　339.2/0947　0521433290
Income distribution -- Europe, Eastern. Income distribution -- Europe, Central. Europe, Eastern -- Economic conditions -- 1945-1989. Europe, Central -- Economic conditions.

HC251-260 By region or country — Europe — Great Britain. England

HC251.T3 1963
Tawney, R. H. 1880-1962.
Tudor economic documents: being select documents illustrating the economic and social history of Tudor England/ Edited by R. H. Tawney and Eileen Power. -- New York: Barnes & Noble, [1963, c1961] 3 v.
64-055563
Great Britain -- Economic conditions. Great Britain -- Industries -- History. Great Britain -- History -- Tudors, 1485-1603 -- Sources.

HC253.R46 1989
Regions and industries: a perspective on the industrial revolution in Britain/ edited by Pat Hudson. Cambridge [England]; Cambridge University Press, 1989. xiii, 277 p.
89-000501　338.0941　052134106X
Industrial revolution -- Great Britain.

HC253.U55 1997
Understanding decline: perceptions and realities of British economic performance/ edited by Peter Clarke and Clive Trebilcock. Cambridge; Cambridge University Press, 1997. xv, 313 p.
97-008905　338.941
Great Britain -- Economic conditions. Great Britain -- Economic policy.

HC254.H55 1968
Hill, Christopher, 1912-
Reformation to Industrial Revolution; the making of modern English society, 1530-1780 [by] Christopher Hill. New York, Pantheon Books [1968, c1967] 256 p.
68-010698　309.142
Great Britain -- Economic conditions. Great Britain -- Politics and government. Great Britain -- Social conditions.

HC254.V48 1968b
Vinogradoff, Paul, 1854-1925.
English society in the eleventh century; essays in English mediaeval history. Oxford, Clarendon P., 1968. xii, 599 p.
71-429427　309.1/42　0198213808
Land tenure -- Great Britain -- History. England -- Social conditions -- 1066-1485. Great Britain -- Economic conditions. Great Britain -- History -- Medieval period, 1066-1485.

HC254.4.C64
Coleman, D. C. 1920-
The economy of England, 1450-1750/ D. C. Coleman. London; Oxford University Press, 1977. viii, 223 p.
77-364391　330.9/42　0192153552
Great Britain -- Economic conditions.

HC254.4.W74 2000
Wrightson, Keith.
Earthly necessities: economic lives in early modern Britain/ Keith Wrightson. New Haven, CT: Yale University Press, c2000. xii, 372 p.
00-033557　330.942 21　0300083912
Households -- Great Britain -- History. Markets -- Great Britain -- History. Great Britain -- Economic conditions. Great Britain -- Social conditions.

HC254.5.B64 1990
Boyer, George R.
An economic history of the English poor law, 1750-1850/ George R. Boyer. Cambridge; Cambridge University Press, 1990. xiii, 297 p.
89-022365　362.5/85/0942　0521434795
Poor -- Great Britain -- History. Poor laws -- Great Britain -- History. Great Britain -- Economic conditions -- 18th century. Great Britain -- Economic conditions -- 19th century.

HC254.5.B88 1999
The British industrial revolution: an economic perspective/ edited by Joel Mokyr. 2nd ed. Boulder, CO: Westview Press, c1999. 354 p.
98-045108　338.0941 21　081333389X
Industrial revolution -- Great Britain.

HC254.5.C73 1985
Crafts, N. F. R.
British economic growth during the industrial revolution/ N.F.R. Crafts. Oxford [Oxfordshire]: Clarendon Press; 1985. 193 p.
85-002926　338.941　0198730667
Industrial revolution -- Great Britain. Great Britain -- Economic conditions -- 1760-1860.

HC254.5.D23 1995
Daunton, M. J.
Progress and poverty: an economic and social history of Britain, 1700-1850/ M.J. Daunton. Oxford, England; Oxford University Press, 1995. xv, 620 p.
94-046403　330.941　0198222823
Great Britain -- Economic conditions -- 18th century. Great Britain -- Economic conditions -- 19th century. Great Britain -- Social conditions -- 18th century.

HC254.5.D3 1979
Deane, Phyllis.
The first industrial revolution/ Phyllis Deane. Cambridge [Eng.]; Cambridge University Press, 1979. ix, 318 p.
78-026388　338/.0941　0521226678
Industrial revolution -- Great Britain. Great Britain -- Economic conditions -- 1760-1860.

HC254.5.E27 1994
The Economic history of Britain since 1700/ edited by Roderick Floud and Donald McCloskey. Cambridge [England]; Cambridge University Press, 1994. 3 v.
93-020093　330.941/07　0521414989
Great Britain -- Economic conditions.

HC254.5.I38 1990
The Industrial Revolution: a compendium/ edited for the Economic History Society by L.A. Clarkson. Atlantic Highlands, NJ: Humanities Press International, 1990. xi, 308 p.
89-001967　338.0941　0391036483
Industrial revolution -- Great Britain. Great Britain -- Economic conditions -- 1760-1860.

HC254.5.K535 2001
King, Steven.
Making sense of the Industrial Revolution/ Steven King and Geoffrey Timmins. New York: Manchester University Press, 2001. xiii, 402 p.
2001-030104　338.0941　0719050227
Industrial revolution -- Great Britain. Great Britain -- Economic conditions -- 1760-1860.

HC254.5.K87 1989
Kussmaul, Ann.
A general view of the rural economy of England, 1538-1840/ Ann Kussmaul. Cambridge [England]; Cambridge University Press, 1990. xiv, 216 p.
89-007240　330.942/009173/4　0521306345
Marriage -- England -- Statistics. England -- Rural conditions. England -- Economic conditions.

HC254.5.L72 1990
Lines, Clifford John.
Companion to the Industrial Revolution/ Clifford Lines; foreword by Asa Briggs; consultant editor, Barrie Trinder. New York: Facts on File, c1990. x, 262 p.
89-029633　338.0941/09/033　0816021570
Industrial revolution -- Great Britain. Great Britain -- Economic conditions -- 1760-1860.

HC254.5.W5 1961
Williams, Eric Eustace, 1911-
Capitalism & slavery. New York, Russell & Russell, 1961 [c1944] 285 p.
61-013088　338.0942
Industries -- Great Britain -- History. Slave-trade -- Great Britain.

HC254.5.W52
Wilson, C. H.
England's apprenticeship, 1603-1763 [by] Charles Wilson. New York, St. Martin's Press [1965] xvi, 413 p.
65-010814　330.942
Great Britain -- Economic conditions. Great Britain -- Social conditions.

HC255.A8 1964
Ashton, Thomas Southcliffe.
The industrial revolution, 1760-1830. New York, Oxford University Press, 1964. 119 p.
64-001714
Industrial revolution -- Great Britain. Great Britain -- Economic conditions -- 1760-1860.

HC255.B59 1998
Blackford, Mansel G.,
The rise of modern business in Great Britain, the United States, and Japan/ Mansel G. Blackford. 2nd ed., revised and updated. Chapel Hill: University of North Carolina Press, c1998. 249 p.
97-032867　338.09 21　0807847321
Industries -- Great Britain -- History. Industries -- United States -- History. Industries -- Japan -- History.

HC255.C53 1975
Church, Roy A.
The great Victorian boom, 1850-1873/ prepared for the Economic History Society by R. A. Church. London: Macmillan, 1975. 95 p.
76-352972   330.9/41/081   0333143507
Great Britain -- Economic conditions -- 19th century. Great Britain -- Social conditions -- 19th century.

HC255.C623 1992
Coleman, D. C. 1920-
Myth, history, and the Industrial Revolution/ D.C. Coleman. London; Hambledon Press, 1992. xii, 225 p.
92-009138   330.941/07   1852850744
Industrial revolution -- Great Britain. Businesspeople -- Great Britain -- History. Great Britain -- Economic conditions -- 1760-1860. Great Britain -- Historiography.

HC255.C7313 1982
Crouzet, Francois, 1922-
The Victorian economy/ Francois Crouzet; translated by Anthony Forster. New York: Columbia University Press, 1982. xiii, 430 p.
82-001292   330.941/081   0231055420
Great Britain -- Economic conditions -- 19th century.

HC255.E89 2001
Evans, Eric J.,
The forging of the modern state: early industrial Britain, 1783-1870 / Eric J. Evans. 3rd ed. Harlow, England; New York: Pearson Education 2001. xl, 585 p.
2003-428859   330.941/07 21   0582472679
Industrial revolution -- Great Britain.

HC255.J69 1980b
Joyce, Patrick.
Work, society, and politics: the culture of the factory in later Victorian England/ Patrick Joyce. New Brunswick. N.J.: Rutgers University Press, c1980. xxv, 356 p.
79-093087   306/.3   0813508991
Industries -- England -- History. Social classes -- England. Great Britain -- Politics and government.

HC255.K45 1987
Kennedy, William P. 1944-
Industrial structure, capital markets, and the origins of British economic decline/ William P. Kennedy. Cambridge [Cambridgeshire]; Cambridge University Press, 1987. xii, 230 p.
87-024411   0521230187
Capital market -- Great Britain -- History. Great Britain -- Economic conditions -- 19th century. Great Britain -- Economic conditions -- 20th century. Great Britain -- Industries -- History.

HC255.R53 1990
Richards, Thomas, 1956-
The commodity culture of Victorian England: advertising and spectacle, 1851-1914/ Thomas Richards. Stanford, Calif.: Stanford University Press, 1990. xiv, 306 p.
89-037035   659.1/0941   0804716528
Capitalism -- Great Britain -- History. Commercial products -- Great Britain -- History. Advertising -- Great Britain -- History.

HC255.S43 1998
Searle, G. R.
Morality and the market in Victorian Britain/ G.R. Searle. Oxford: Clarendon Press; 1998. xi, 300 p.
97-048954   330.12/2/094109034   0198206984
Capitalism -- Great Britain -- History -- 19th century. Great Britain -- Moral conditions.

HC256.B68 2001
Booth, Alan.
The British economy in the twentieth century/ Alan Booth. New York: Palgrave, 2001. x, 244 p.
2001-027370   330.941/082   033369841X
Great Britain -- Economic conditions -- 20th century. Great Britain -- Economic policy -- 20th century.

HC256.C65 1997
Cox, Andrew W.
The political economy of modern Britain/ Andrew Cox, Simon Lee, Joe Sanderson. Cheltenham, UK, US; E. Elgar, c1997. viii, 276 p.
96-048952   338.941 21   1852784113
Industrial policy -- Great Britain. Great Britain -- Economic conditions -- 20th century.

HC256.P62 1983
Pollard, Sidney.
The development of the British economy, 1914-1980/ Sidney Pollard. London; E. Arnold, 1983. vi, 440 p.
85-128828   330.941   071316395X
Great Britain -- Economic conditions -- 20th century.

HC256.3.M418 1985
Middleton, Roger, 1955-
Towards the managed economy: Keynes, the Treasury, and the fiscal policy debate of the 1930s/ Roger Middleton. London; Methuen, 1985. ix, 244 p.
84-029607   339.5/2/0941   0416358306
Keynesian economics -- History. Fiscal policy -- Great Britain -- History. Great Britain -- Economic policy -- 1918-1945.

HC256.4.Z94 2000
Zweiniger-Bargielowska, Ina.
Austerity in Britain: rationing, controls, and consumption, 1939-1955 / Ina Zweiniger-Bargielowska. Oxford; Oxford University Press, 2000. xiii, 286 p.
00-709384   0198204531
Rationing -- Great Britain -- History -- 20th century. Consumption (Economics) -- Great Britain -- History -- 20th century. World War, 1939-1945 -- Economic aspects -- Great Britain.

HC256.5.B56
Bogdanor, Vernon, 1943-
The age of affluence, 1951-1964; edited by Vernon Bogdanor and Robert Skidelsky. London, Macmillan, 1970. 352 p.
78-535294   309.1/42   0333092678
Great Britain -- Economic conditions -- 1945-1993. Great Britain -- Politics and government -- 1945- Great Britain -- Social conditions -- 1945-

HC256.5.C257 1995
Cairncross, Alec,
The British economy since 1945: economic policy and performance, 1945-1995/ Alec Cairncross. 2nd ed. Cambridge, MA: Blackwell Publishers, 1995. xv, 356 p.
95-017554   338.94/009/045 20   0631199616
Great Britain -- Economic conditions -- 1945-1964. Great Britain -- Economic conditions -- 1964-1979. Great Britain -- Economic conditions -- 1979-1997. Great Britain -- Economic policy -- 1945-1964. Great Britain -- Economic policy -- 1964-1979. Great Britain -- Economic policy -- 1979-1997.

HC256.5.G68
Gough, Ian.
The political economy of the welfare state/ Ian Gough. London: Macmillan, 1979. xii, 196 p.
79-315902   330.9/41/0857   0333215826
Welfare state. Great Britain -- Economic policy -- 1964-1979. Great Britain -- Economic policy -- 1945-1964.

HC256.5.G73 1969
Gregg, Pauline.
The welfare state; an economic and social history of Great Britain from 1945 to the present day. Amherst, University of Massachusetts Press, 1969. xii, 388 p.
69-013109   309.1/42
Great Britain -- Economic policy -- 1945-1964. Great Britain -- Economic policy -- 1964-1979. Great Britain -- Social policy.

HC256.5.R644 1967
Robinson, Joan, 1903-
Economics: an awkward corner. With an introd. to the American ed. by Robert Lekachman. New York, Pantheon Books [1967] xiii, 86 p.
67-025427   330
Economic history -- 1945-1971. Great Britain -- Economic conditions -- 1945-

HC256.5.R69
Royal Institute of International Affairs.
Documents on European recovery and defence, March 1947-April 1949. London, [1949] vii, 150 p.
49-049256   338.94
Reconstruction (1939-1951) -- Europe. Europe -- Economic policy. Europe -- History -- 1945- -- Sources.

HC256.6.D448 1995
Dellheim, Charles, 1952-
The disenchanted isle: Mrs. Thatcher's capitalist revolution/ Charles Dellheim. New York: W.W. Norton, c1995. 416 p.
94-041712   338.941/009/048   0393038122
Thatcher, Margaret -- Views on economic policy. Capitalism -- Great Britain -- History -- 20th century. Great Britain -- Economic policy -- 1945- Great Britain -- Economic conditions -- 1945-1993.

HC256.6.G35 1994
Gamble, Andrew.
Britain in decline: economic policy, political strategy, and the British state/ Andrew Gamble. 4th ed. New York, N.Y.: St. Martin's Press, 1994. xxi, 263 p.
94-016020   338.941 20   031212239X
Great Britain -- Economic policy -- 1979-1997. Great Britain -- Economic policy -- 1964-1979. Great Britain -- Politics and government -- 1964-1979. Great Britain -- Politics and government -- 1979-1997.

HC256.6.H545 1989
Holmes, Martin.
Thatcherism: scope and limits, 1983-87/ Martin Holmes. New York: St. Martin's Press, 1989. viii, 174 p.
88-007812   338.941   0312027672
Thatcher, Margaret. Conservatism -- Great Britain. Great Britain -- Economic policy -- 1979-1997. Great Britain -- Politics and government -- 1979-1997.

HC256.6.J63 1993
Johnson, Christopher, 1931-
The grand experiment: Mrs. Thatcher's economy and how it spread/ Christopher Johnson. Boulder: Westview Press, 1993. xiv, 341 p.
93-009937 338.941/009/048 0813319137
Great Britain -- Economic policy -- 1979-1997.

HC256.6.R53 1985
Riddell, Peter.
The Thatcher government/ Peter Riddell. Oxford, OX, UK; B. Blackwell, 1985. viii, 296 p.
85-015678 338.941 0631145192
Thatcher, Margaret -- Views on economic policy. Great Britain -- Social policy -- 1979- Great Britain -- Politics and government -- 1979-1997. Great Britain -- Economic policy -- 1979-1997.

HC257.E5.M37 1982
McKendrick, Neil.
The birth of a consumer society: the commercialization of eighteenth-century England/ Neil McKendrick, John Brewer, and J.H. Plumb. Bloomington: Indiana University Press, c1982. viii, 345 p.
82-047953 306/.3/0942 0253312051
Consumers -- England -- History -- 18th century. Consumption (Economics) -- England -- History -- 18th century. Leisure -- England -- History -- 18th century. England -- Economic conditions -- 18th century.

HC257.I6.K39 1975
Kennedy, Kieran Anthony.
Economic growth in Ireland: the experience since 1947/ Kieran A. Kennedy and Brendan R. Dowling. Dublin: Gill and Macmillan [for] the Economic and Social 1975. xix, 345 p.
76-357776 338/.09417 0717107442
Economic development. Ireland -- Economic conditions -- 1949-

HC257.K45.E25 1995
The economy of Kent, 1640-1914/ edited by Alan Armstrong. Woodbridge, Suffolk, UK; Boydell Press; 1995. xiv, 318 p.
95-038023 330.9422/3 0851155820
Kent (England) -- Economic conditions.

HC257.S4 C3 1985
Campbell, R. H.
Scotland since 1707: the rise of an industrial society/ R.H. Campbell. 2nd ed. Edinburgh: J. Donald Publishers; ix, 272 p.
86-113684 330.9411 19 0859761223
Industrialization -- Scotland.

HC257.S4.G7 1976
Grant, I. F.
The economic history of Scotland/ by I. F. Grant. New York: AMS Press, 1976. xvi, 295 p.
75-041120 330.9/411 0404147992
Industries -- Scotland -- History. Scotland -- Social conditions. Scotland -- Economic conditions.

HC257.W3.D6 1971
Dodd, A. H.
The Industrial Revolution in North Wales, [by] A. H. Dodd. Cardiff, University of Wales Press, 1971. xlv, 439 p.
78-872048 338/.09429 0900768924
Industrial revolution -- Wales, North. Wales, North -- Economic conditions. Wales, North -- Social conditions.

HC258.B76.S23 1991
Sacks, David Harris, 1942-
The widening gate: Bristol and the Atlantic economy, 1450-1700/ David Harris Sacks. Berkeley: University of California Press, c1991. xxvi, 464 p.
90-019878 330.9423/93 0520071484
Capitalism -- England -- Bristol -- History. Bristol (England) -- Economic conditions. Bristol (England) -- Commerce -- History.

HC258.C85.P7
Prest, John M.
The industrial revolution in Coventry. [London] Oxford University Press, 1960. 152 p.
61-000509 330.94248
Coventry (England) -- Economic conditions.

HC258.L6.B76
Brooke, Christopher Nugent Lawrence.
London, 800-1216: the shaping of a city/ Christopher N. L. Brooke, assisted by Gillian Keir. Berkeley: University of California Press, 1975. xxi, 424 p.
73-092620 330.9/421/2 0520026861
London (England) -- History -- To 1500.

HC258.L6.G73 1995
Green, David R., 1954-
From artisans to paupers: economic change and poverty in London, 1790-1870/ David R. Green. Aldershot, Hants, England: Scolar Press; c1995. xvii, 298 p.
95-002702 339.4/6/09421 1859280331
Poverty -- England -- London -- History. Poor -- England -- London -- History. London (England) -- Economic conditions.

HC258.L6.S5 1971
Sheppard, F. H. W. 1921-
London, 1808-1870: the infernal wen [by] Francis Sheppard. Berkeley, University of California Press, 1971. xx, 427 p.
71-142067 309.1/421/07 0520018478
London (England) -- Economic conditions. London (England) -- Social conditions. London (England) -- History -- 1800-1950.

HC258.W47.L48 1991
Levine, David, 1946-
The making of an industrial society: Whickham, 1560-1765/ David Levine and Keith Wrightson. Oxford [England]: Clarendon Press; 1991. xviii, 456 p.
90-039320 330.9428/73 0198200668
Industries -- England -- Whickham -- History. Whickham (England) -- Social conditions. Whickham (England) -- Economic conditions.

HC259.C73 1984
Constantine, Stephen.
The making of British colonial development policy, 1914-1940/ Stephen Constantine. London, England; F. Cass, 1984. xii, 326 p.
85-122006 338.91/41/01724 071463204X
Great Britain -- Colonies -- Economic policy.

HC260.C6.G86 1998
Gunter, Barrie.
Understanding the older consumer: the grey market/ Barrie Gunter. London; Routledge, 1998. vi, 182 p.
99-158006 658.8/34/0846 0415186439
Aged consumers -- Great Britain. Marketing -- Great Britain. Consumer behavior -- Great Britain.

HC260.C6.K69 1997
Kowaleski-Wallace, Elizabeth, 1954-
Consuming subjects: women, shopping, and business in the eighteenth century/ Elizabeth Kowaleski-Wallace. New York: Columbia University Press, 1997. 185 p.
96-022778 381/.1/082 0231105789
Women consumers -- Great Britain -- History -- 18th century. Women consumers -- Great Britain -- History -- 19th century. Consumer behavior -- Great Britain -- History -- 18th century.

HC260.C6.S5 1990
Shammas, Carole.
The pre-industrial consumer in England and America/ Carole Shammas. Oxford [England]: Clarendon Press; 1990. xi, 319 p.
90-031433 339.4/7/094209034 0198283024
Consumption (Economics) -- England -- History -- 18th century. Consumption (Economics) -- United States -- History -- 18th century. Home-based businesses -- Great Britain -- History -- 18th century.

HC260.C6 S873 2000
Sussman, Charlotte.
Consuming anxieties: consumer protest, gender, and British slavery, 1713-1833/ Charlotte Sussman. Stanford, Calif.: Stanford University Press, c2000. v, 267 p.
00-022872 322.4/4/094109033 21 0804731039
Consumption (Economics) -- Great Britain -- History. Women abolitionists -- Great Britain -- History. Slavery -- Great Britain -- History.

HC260.F3.F36 1989
Famine, disease, and the social order in early modern society/ edited by John Walter and Roger Schofield. Cambridge; Cambridge University Press, 1989. xiv, 335 p.
88-030181 363.8/0942 0521259061
Appleby, Andrew B. Famines -- England -- History. Famines -- France -- History. England -- Economic conditions. England -- Population -- History. France -- Economic conditions.

HC260.I53.T48
Thirsk, Joan.
Economic policy and projects: the development of a consumer society in early modern England/ by Joan Thirsk. Oxford: Clarendon Press, 1978. vi, 199 p.
78-315763 338/.0941 0198282745
Industrial promotion -- England -- History. England -- Economic policy -- History. England -- Economic conditions.

HC260.W24.P35
Panitch, Leo.
Social democracy & industrial militancy: the Labour Party, the trade unions, and incomes policy, 1945-1974/ Leo Panitch. Cambridge [Eng.]; Cambridge University Press, 1976. x, 318 p.
75-016869 330.9/41/0854 0521207797
Wage-price policy -- Great Britain -- History. Labor policy -- Great Britain -- History.

HC260.5 By region or country — Europe — Ireland. Irish Republic

HC260.5.K564 1994
Kinealy, Christine.
This great calamity: the Irish famine, 1845-52/ Christine Kinealy. Dublin: Gill & Macmillan, c1994. xxi, 450 p.
94-241713   0717118819
Famines -- Ireland -- History -- 19th century. Ireland -- Economic conditions. Ireland -- Population -- History -- 19th century. Ireland -- History -- Famine, 1845-1852.

HC260.5.M64 1983
Mokyr, Joel.
Why Ireland starved: a quantitative and analytical history of the Irish economy, 1800-1850/ Joel Mokyr. London; Allen & Unwin, 1983. x, 330 p.
82-024508   330.9415/081   0049410105
Poor -- Ireland -- History. Famines -- Ireland. Ireland -- Economic conditions. Ireland -- Rural conditions.

HC260.5.O435 1994
O Grada, Cormac.
Ireland: a new economic history, 1780-1939/ Cormac O Grada. Oxford: Clarendon Press; 1994. xii, 536 p.
93-049444   330.9415   0198202105
Ireland -- Economic conditions.

HC260.5.W477 2000
Whelan, Bernadette.
Ireland and the Marshall Plan, 1947-57/ Bernadette Whelan. Dublin: Four Courts Press, 2000. 426 p.
00-699945   338.91/730417/09044   1851825177
Economic assistance, American -- Ireland.

HC260.5.Z7.U474 1985
An Economic history of Ulster, 1820-1940/ edited by Liam Kennedy and Philip Ollerenshaw. Manchester [Greater Manchester]; Manchester University Press, c1985. 248 p.
84-026079   330.9416   0719017505
Ulster (Northern Ireland and Ireland) -- Economic conditions -- Addresses, essays, lectures. Northern Ireland -- Economic conditions -- Addresses, essays, lectures.

HC267 By region or country — Europe — Austria

HC267.A2.B3823 1974
Berend, T. Ivan 1930-
Hungary; a century of economic development [by] I.T. [i.e. T.I.] Berend and G. Ranki. Newton Abbot, David & Charles; [1974] 263 p.
74-158570   330.9/439/04   0064903710
Hungary -- Economic conditions.

HC270.28 By region or country — Europe — Czechoslovakia. Czech Republic

HC270.28.B37 1988
Batt, Judy.
Economic reform and political change in eastern Europe: a comparison of the Czechoslovak and Hungarian experiences/ Judy Batt. New York: St. Martin's Press, , 1988. x, 353 p.
87-024065   338.9437   0312011962
Czechoslovakia -- Economic policy -- 1945-1992. Czechoslovakia -- Economic conditions -- 1945-1992. Czechoslovakia -- Politics and government -- 1945-1992.

HC270.28.T45 1988
Teichova, Alice.
The Czechoslovak economy, 1918-1980/ Alice Teichova. London; Routledge, 1988. xxiii, 178 p.
88-011404   330.9437/03   0415003768
Czechoslovakia -- Economic conditions -- 1945-1992. Czechoslovakia -- Economic conditions -- 1918-1945.

HC272.5-280 By region or country — Europe — France

HC272.5.L68.C37 1993
Carls, Stephen Douglas.
Louis Loucheur and the shaping of modern France, 1916-1931/ Stephen D. Carls. Baton Rouge: Louisiana State University Press, c1993. xv, 330 p.
92-040840   338.944/0092   0807117870
Loucheur, Louis, -- 1872-1931. Politicians -- France -- Biography. Industrialists -- France -- Biography. France -- Economic conditions -- 1918-1945. France -- Politics and government -- 1914-1940.

HC273.C28 1979
Caron, Francois, 1931-
An economic history of modern France/ Francois Caron; translated from the French by Barbara Bray. New York: Columbia University Press, 1979. 384 p.
78-015353   330.9/44   0231038607
France -- Economic conditions.

HC275.A6613 1990
Aftalion, Florin.
The French Revolution, an economic interpretation/ Florin Aftalion; translated by Martin Thom. Cambridge [England]; Cambridge University Press; 1990. xviii, 226 p.
89-036121   330.944/04   0521362415
France -- Economic conditions -- 18th century. France -- History -- Revolution, 1789-1799.

HC275.C64
Cole, Charles Woolsey, 1906-
French mercantilism, 1683-1700, by Charles Woolsey Cole. New York, Columbia University Press, 1943. viii, 354 p.
43-011223   330.151
Mercantile system -- France. France -- Economic policy.

HC276.K55 1964
Kindleberger, Charles Poor, 1910-
Economic growth in France and Britain, 1851-1950. Cambridge, Mass., Harvard University Press, 1964. viii, 378 p.
64-013424
France -- Economic conditions. Great Britain -- Economic conditions.

HC276.K94
Kuisel, Richard F.
Capitalism and the state in modern France: renovation and economic management in the twentieth century/ Richard F. Kuisel. Cambridge [Eng.]; Cambridge University Press, 1981. xiv, 344 p.
81-000616   338.944   0521234743
France -- Economic policy -- 20th century. France -- Economic conditions -- 20th century.

HC276.L46 1999
Levy, Jonah D.
Tocqueville's revenge: state, society, and economy in contemporary France/ Jonah D. Levy. Cambridge, Mass.: Harvard University Press, 1999. xi, 386 p.
98-045015   338.944   0674894324
Civil society -- France. Central planning -- France. Liberalism -- France. Economic policy -- 1945- Besancon (France) -- Economic policy. Saint-Etienne (Loire, France) -- Economic policy.

HC276.2.A72 1982
Ardagh, John, 1928-
France in the 1980s/ John Ardagh. London: Secker & Warburg, 1982. 672 p.
82-148666   944.083   0436017474
France -- Economic conditions -- 1945- France -- Social conditions -- 1945- France -- Civilization -- 20th century.

HC276.2.A73 1968b
Ardagh, John, 1928-
The new French Revolution. New York, Harper & Row [1968, c1969] xvi, 501 p.
68-028187   914.4/03/83
France -- Economic conditions -- 1945- France -- Social conditions -- 1945- France -- Civilization -- 20th century.

HC276.2.C59813 1995
Cohen, Daniel, 1953-
The misfortunes of prosperity: an introduction to modern political economy/ Daniel Cohen; translated by Jacqueline Lindenfeld. Cambridge, Mass.: The MIT Press, c1995. xiii, 170 p.
94-047022   338.9   0262032309
Economic history -- 1945- Keynesian economics. Economics. France -- Economic conditions -- 1945-

HC276.2.F44 1999
Fenby, Jonathan.
France on the brink/ Jonathan Fenby. New York: Arcade, 1999. xii, 449 p.
98-049658   944.083/9 21   1559704888
Social values -- France.

HC276.2.F699 1987
The French socialists in power, 1981-1986/ edited by Patrick McCarthy with essays by D.S. Bell ... [et al.]. New York: Greenwood Press, c1987. xii, 212 p.
86-033569   338.944   0313254079
Socialism -- France. France -- Politics and government -- 1981-1995. France -- Economic policy -- 1945- France -- Social policy.

HC276.2.T5
Thompson, Ian Bentley.
Modern France: a social and economic geography, by I. B. Thompson. London, Butterworths, 1970. 465 p.
77-532632   309.1/44   0408700165
France -- Economic conditions -- 1945- France -- Social conditions -- 1945-

HC276.3.T86 1988
Tuppen, John N.
France under recession, 1981-1986/ John Tuppen. Albany: State University of New York Press, c1988. xiv, 280 p.
87-001980 338.944 0887065805
Socialism -- France. Privatization -- France. Local government -- France. France -- Politics and government -- 1981-1995. France -- Economic conditions -- 1981- France -- Economic policy -- 1981-

HC277.B8.B67 1991
Bouchard, Constance Brittain.
Holy entrepreneurs: Cistercians, knights, and economic exchange in twelfth-century Burgundy/ Constance Brittain Bouchard. Ithaca, N.Y.: Cornell University Press, 1991. xiv, 242 p.
91-008929 330.944/4022 0801425271
Nobility -- France -- Burgundy -- Economic conditions -- History. Commerce -- History -- Medieval, 500-1500. Burgundy (France) -- Economic conditions. Burgundy (France) -- Commerce -- History.

HC278.B3.H8
Hufton, Olwen H.
Bayeux in the late eighteenth century: a social study, by Olwen H. Hufton. Oxford, Clarendon P., 1967. iii-xi, 317 p.
67-109452 309.1/44/22
Bayeux (France) -- Social conditions. Bayeux (France) -- Economic conditions.

HC280.C6 T54 2001
Tiersten, Lisa,
Marianne in the market: envisioning consumer society in fin-de-siècle France/ Lisa Tiersten. Berkeley: University of California Press, c2001. xiii, 321 p.
00-066629 339.4/7/0820944 21 0520225295
Women consumers -- France -- History -- 19th century. Consumption (Economics) -- France -- History -- 19th century. Middle class -- France -- History -- 19th century.

HC280.C6 W35 1992
Walton, Whitney.
France at the Crystal Palace: bourgeois taste and artisan manufacture in the nineteenth century/ Whitney Walton. Berkeley: University of California Press, c1992. xii, 240 p.
91-041181 338.4/767/094409034 20 0520076923
Consumption (Economics) -- France -- History -- 19th century. Middle class -- France -- History -- 19th century. Manufactures -- France -- History -- 19th century.

HC280.T4.H45 1996
Heller, Henry.
Labour, science, and technology in France, 1500-1620/ Henry Heller. Cambridge; Cambridge University Press, 1996. xii, 258 p.
95-006125 338/.064/094409031 0521550319
Technological innovations -- Economic aspects -- France -- History -- 16th century. Technology and state -- France -- History -- 16th century. Industrialization -- France -- History -- 16th century. France -- Economic policy. France -- History -- 16th century.

HC285-290.782 By region or country — Europe — Germany

HC285.B395 1994
Berghahn, Volker Rolf.
Imperial Germany, 1871-1914: economy, society, culture, and politics/ V.R. Berghahn. Providence: Berghahn Books, 1994. xvii, 362 p.
94-020683 943.08/3 1571810137
Germany -- Economic conditions -- 1888-1918. Germany -- Politics and government -- 1871-1918. Germany -- Social conditions -- 1871-1918.

HC285.H442
Henderson, W. O. 1904-
The rise of German industrial power, 1834-1914/ W. O. Henderson. Berkeley: University of California Press, c1975. 264 p.
75-017293 338/.0943 0520030737
Industries -- Germany -- History.

HC285.K659 1999
Kocka, Jürgen.
Industrial culture and bourgeois society: business, labor, and bureaucracy in modern Germany/ Jürgen Kocka. New York: Berghahn Books, 1999. xviii, 325 p.
98-026015 305.5/62/094309034 21 1571811982
Businesspeople -- Germany -- History. Entrepreneurship -- Germany -- History. Working class -- Germany -- History.

HC286.B74 1990
Braun, Hans-Joachim.
The German economy in the twentieth century/ Hans-Joachim Braun. London; Routledge, 1990. xi, 279 p.
89-010480 330.943/08 0415021014
Germany -- Economic conditions -- 20th century. Germany (West) -- Economic conditions.

HC286.G54 1992
Giersch, Herbert.
The fading miracle: four decades of market economy in Germany/ Herbert Giersch, Karl-Heinz Paque, Holger Schmieding. Cambridge [England]; Cambridge University Press, 1992. xiv, 302 p.
91-022347 338.943/009/045 0521353513
Germany (West) -- Economic policy.

HC286.H3613
Hardach, Karl.
The political economy of Germany in the twentieth century/ Karl Hardach. Berkeley: University of California Press, c1980. xii, 235 p.
78-064754 330.943/08 0520038096
Germany -- Economic conditions -- 20th century.

HC286.2.F4
Feldman, Gerald D.
Army, industry, and labor in Germany, 1914-1918, by Gerald D. Feldman. Princeton, N.J., Princeton University Press, 1966. xvi, 572 p.
66-010553 940.31
Manpower -- Germany. World War, 1914-1918 -- Economic aspects -- Germany.

HC286.3.B32513 1990
Barkai, Avraham.
Nazi economics: ideology, theory, and policy/ Avraham Barkai; translated from the German by Ruth Hadass-Vashitz. New Haven: Yale University Press, 1990. xii, 291 p.
89-052113 338.943/009/043 0300044666
National socialism -- Economic aspects. Germany -- Economic policy -- 1933-1945.

HC286.4.M45 1988
Mierzejewski, Alfred C.
The collapse of the German war economy, 1944-1945: Allied air power and the German National Railway/ Alfred C. Mierzejewski. Chapel Hill: University of North Carolina Press, c1988. xx, 285 p.
88-004777 330.943/087 0807817929
Bombing, Aerial -- Germany -- History. Transportation -- Germany -- History -- 20th century. Railroads and state -- Germany -- History -- 20th century. Germany -- Economic conditions -- 1918-1945. Germany -- Strategic aspects.

HC286.5.N474 1994
Nicholls, Anthony James, 1934-
Freedom with responsibility: the social market economy in Germany, 1918-1963/ A.J. Nicholls. Oxford: Clarendon Press; 1994. xiii, 422 p.
93-032122 338.43/009/04 0198204256
Germany -- Economic policy. Germany -- Economic conditions.

HC286.5.R39 1990
Reich, Simon, 1959-
The fruits of fascism: postwar prosperity in historical perspective/ Simon Reich. Ithaca: Cornell University Press, 1990. xii, 341 p.
90-055136 330.94/086 0801424402
Economic history -- 20th century. World politics -- 20th century. Germany (West) -- Politics and government. Germany -- Politics and government -- 1933-1945. Great Britain -- Economic conditions -- 20th century.

HC286.8.L33 1998
Lange, Thomas, 1967-
The economics of German unification: an introduction/ Thomas Lange, Geoffrey Pugh. Cheltenham, UK; Edward Elgar Pub., 1998. xxiii, 209 p.
97-038249 330.943/09/049 1858980909
Germany -- History -- Unification, 1990 -- Economic aspects. Germany (East) -- Economic conditions -- 1990-

HC286.8.S69 1992
Smyser, W. R., 1931-
The economy of United Germany: colossus at the crossroads/ W.R. Smyser. New York: St. Martin's, 1992. x, 273 p.
91-035709 330.943/0879 0312047886
Germany -- Economic conditions -- 1990- Germany -- Economic policy -- 1990- Germany -- Foreign economic relations.

HC290.5.C6.C37 1997
Carter, Erica.
How German is she?: postwar West German reconstruction and the consuming woman/ Erica Carter. Ann Arbor: University of Michigan Press, c1997. xiv, 272 p.
96-035067 306.3 20 0472107550
Women consumers -- Germany -- History. Consumer behavior -- Germany -- History.

HC290.5.E5.D66 1992
Dominick, Raymond H., 1945-
The environmental movement in Germany: prophets and pioneers, 1871-1971/ Raymond H. Dominick III. Bloomington: Indiana University Press, c1992. xiii, 290 p.
91-028558 363.7/058/0943 025331819X
Green movement -- Germany -- History. Environmental protection -- Germany -- History. Nature conservation -- Germany -- History.

HC290.5.P6 Z4513 1999
Time and poverty in western welfare states: United Germany in perspective/ Lutz Leisering and Stephan Leibfried; with contributions by Petra Buhr, Monika Ludwig, and others; translation by John Veit-Wilson and Lutz Leisering. Cambridge; Cambridge University Press, c1999. xvi, 379 p.
98-039070   362.5/8/0943 21   0521590132
Poverty -- Germany. Poor -- Germany. Public welfare -- Germany.

HC290.78.B8 1991
Bryson, Phillip J.
The end of the East German economy: from Honecker to reunification/ Phillip J. Bryson, Manfred Melzer. New York: St. Martin's Press, 1991. xiii, 148 p.
90-045275   338.943/009/048   0312055560
Central planning -- Germany (East)   Germany (East) -- Economic conditions. Germany (East) -- Economic policy. Germany (East) -- Commerce.

HC290.78.K66 1997
Kopstein, Jeffrey.
The politics of economic decline in East Germany, 1945-1989/ Jeffrey Kopstein. Chapel Hill: University of North Carolina Press, c1997. xii, 246 p.
96-011614   338.9431/00945 20   0807823031
Germany (East) -- Economic policy. Germany (East) -- Economic conditions.

HC290.782.P53 1997
Pickel, Andreas.
The grand experiment: debating shock therapy, transition theory, and the East German experience/ Andreas Pickel and Helmut Wiesenthal. Boulder, Colo.: Westview Press, 1997. x, 262 p.
97-006440   338.9431   0813329809
Post-communism -- Germany (East)   Germany (East) -- Economic policy. Germany (East) -- Economic conditions.

HC290.782.S82 1997
Successful transformations?: the creation of market economies in Eastern Germany and the Czech Republic/ Martin Myant ... [et al.]. Cheltenham, UK; E. Elgar, 1997. xiii, 267 p.
96-023168   338.9431   1858984955
Germany (East) -- Economic conditions. Czech Republic -- Economic conditions. Germany (East) -- Economic policy.

HC294-295 By region or country — Europe — Greece

HC294.E25 2002
The economic history of Byzantium: from the seventh through the fifteenth century/ Angeliki E. Laiou, editor-in-chief; scholarly committee, Charalambos Bouras ... [et al.]. Washington, D.C.: Dumbarton Oaks Research Library and Collection 3 v.
2001-032597   330.9495/02 21   0884022889
Byzantine Empire -- Economic conditions.

HC295.G5 1988
Gianaris, Nicholas V.
Greece & Turkey: economic and geopolitical perspectives/ Nicholas V. Gianaris. New York: Praeger, 1988. xii, 204 p.
88-002396   330.9495/076   0275930254
Greece -- Economic conditions -- 1974- Turkey -- Economic conditions -- 1960- Greece -- Foreign economic relations.

HC295.G52 1984
Gianaris, Nicholas V.
Greece and Yugoslavia: an economic comparison/ Nicholas V. Gianaris. New York: Praeger, 1984. xiv, 258 p.
83-027010   330.9495/076   0275911691
Yugoslavia -- Economic conditions -- 1945-1992. Greece -- Economic conditions -- 1974- Yugoslavia -- Economic conditions -- 1945-

HC295.M2
McNeill, William Hardy, 1917-
Greece: American aid in action, 1947-1956. New York, Twentieth Century Fund, 1957. 240 p.
57-012382   338.9495
Technical assistance, American -- Greece. Economic assistance, American -- Greece. Greece, Modern -- Economic conditions -- 1918-

HC295.P55 1997
Pirounakis, Nicholas G., 1955-
The Greek economy: past, present and future/ Nicholas G.Pirounakis. New York: St. Martin's Press, 1997.
97-009653   330.9495   0312175175
Economic forecasting -- Greece.   Greece -- Economic policy. Greece -- Economic conditions.

HC300.24-300.282 By region or country — Europe — Hungary

HC300.24.B44 1985
Berend, T. Ivan 1930-
The Hungarian economy in the twentieth century/ Ivan T. Berend and Gyorgy Ranki. New York: St. Martin's Press, 1985. 316 p.
84-017773   330.9439/05   0312401183
Hungary -- Economic conditions.

HC300.24.R66 1997
Rona-Tas, Akos.
The great surprise of the small transformation: the demise of communism and the rise of the private sector in Hungary/ Akos Rona-Tas. Ann Arbor, Mich.: University of Michigan Press, c1997. xv, 289 p.
96-054238   338.9439 21   047210795X
Post-communism -- Hungary.   Hungary -- Economic policy -- 1945- Hungary -- Politics and government -- 1945- Hungary -- Politics and government -- 1945-1989.

HC300.28.R48 1990
Revesz, G.
Perestroika in Eastern Europe: Hungary's economic transformation, 1945-1988/ Gabor Revesz; with a foreword by Paul Marer. Boulder: Westview Press, 1990. xv, 182 p.
89-037019   338.9439/009/045   0813377528
Central planning -- Hungary. Perestroika. Hungary -- Economic policy -- 1945-

HC300.282.B37 1997
Bartlett, David L., 1956-
The political economy of dual transformations: market reform and democratization in Hungary/ David L. Bartlett. Ann Arbor, Mich.: University of Michigan Press, c1997. xv, 299 p.
96-036553   338.9439 21   0472107941
Hungary -- Politics and government -- 1989- Post-communism -- Hungary. Democracy -- Hungary. Hungary -- Economic conditions -- 1989- Hungary -- Economic policy -- 1989-

HC300.282.H86 1993
Hungary: an economy in transition/ edited by Istvan P. Szekely and David M.G. Newbery. Cambridge [England]; Cambridge University Press, 1993. xxvii, 360 p.
92-029669   338.9439   0521440181
Hungary -- Economic conditions -- 1989- Hungary -- Economic policy -- 1989-

HC300.282.K6713 1990
Kornai, Janos.
The road to a free economy: shifting from a socialist system: the example of Hungary/ Janos Kornai. New York: Norton, c1990. 224 p.
90-006865   338.9439   0393028879
Capitalism -- Hungary.   Hungary -- Economic conditions -- 1989- Hungary -- Economic policy -- 1989-

HC300.282.S74 1999
Stephan, Johannes.
Economic transition in Hungary and East Germany: gradualism and shock therapy in catch-up development/ Johannes Stephan. New York, N.Y.: St. Martin's Press, 1999. xv, 293 p.
98-044286   338.9431 21   0312219911
Hungary -- Economic policy -- 1989- Hungary -- Economic conditions -- 1989- Germany -- Economic policy -- 1990- Germany -- Economic conditions -- 1990-

HC305-308 By region or country — Europe — Italy

HC305.H47
Hildebrand, George Herbert.
Growth and structure in the economy of modern Italy [by] George H. Hildebrand. Cambridge, Harvard University Press, 1965. xx, 475 p.
65-024450   330.945
Italy -- Economic conditions -- 1945-

HC305.L64 1995
Locke, Richard M., 1959-
Remaking the Italian economy/ Richard M. Locke. Ithaca: Cornell University Press, 1995. xiii, 232 p.
94-038366   338.954   0801428912
Industrial relations -- Italy. Competition, International.   Italy -- Economic policy. Italy -- Economic conditions -- 1994-

HC305.N35913 1993
Negri Zamagni, Vera.
The economic history of Italy, 1860-1990/ Vera Zamagni. Oxford: Clarendon Press; 1993. xv, 413 p.
93-010775   330.945   0198287739
Italy -- Economic conditions.

HC305.T357
Templeman, Donald C.
The Italian economy/ Donald C. Templeman. New York, N.Y.: Praeger, 1981. xxiv, 360 p.
80-023478   330.945/0927   0030576121
Italy -- Economic conditions -- 1976-1994. Italy -- Economic policy.

HC307.S69.C374 1989
Carello, Adrian Nicola, 1957-
The northern question: Italy's participation in the European Economic Community and the Mezzogiorno's underdevelopment/ Adrian Nicola Carello. Newark: University of Delaware Press; c1989. 213 p.
87-040642   330.945/7092   0874133424
Italy, Southern -- Economic conditions -- 1945-

HC308.F6.H4713 1985
Herlihy, David.
Tuscans and their families: a study of the
Florentine catasto of 1427/ David Herlihy and
Christiane Klapisch-Zuber. New Haven: Yale
University Press, c1985. xxiv, 404 p.
84-040195 945/.51 0300030568
  *Florence (Italy) -- Economic conditions --
Sources. Florence (Italy) -- Social conditions --
Sources. Florence (Italy) -- History -- 1421-1737 --
Sources.*

HC308.V4.R36
Rapp, Richard T.
Industry and economic decline in seventeenth-
century Venice/ Richard Tilden Rapp. Cambridge,
Mass.: Harvard University Press, 1976. ix, 195 p.
75-016149 330.9/45/31 0674445457
  *City and town life -- Italy -- Venice -- History --
17th century. Venice (Italy) -- Economic
conditions.*

HC323-324 By region or country — Europe — Benelux countries. Low countries

HC323.H643 2000
Wintle, Michael J.
An economic and social history of the Netherlands,
1800-1920: demographic, economic, and social
transition/ Michael Wintle. Cambridge, UK;
Cambridge University Press, 2000. xv, 399 p.
99-086453 306/.09492 0521782953
  *Netherlands -- Social conditions. Demography --
Netherlands -- History. Netherlands -- Economic
conditions. Netherlands -- Population -- History.
Netherlands -- Statistics, Vital.*

HC324.V72 1997
Vries, J. de
The first modern economy: success, failure, and
perseverance of the Dutch economy, 1500-1815/
Jan de Vries, Ad van der Woude. New York:
Cambridge University Press, 1997. xx, 767 p.
96-003298 330.9492 0521570611
  *Economic history -- 1750-1918. Industries --
Netherlands -- History. Economic history -- 16th
century. Netherlands -- Economic conditions.
Netherlands -- Commerce -- History.*

HC333-340 By region or country — Europe — Russia. Soviet Union. Former Soviet republics

HC333.B543
Blackwell, William L.,
[Russian economic development from Peter the
Great to] Stalin. Edited, with an introd., by
William L. Blackwell. New York, New
Viewpoints, 1974. xxxiv, 459 p.
73-011162 330.9/47 0531063631
  *Industrialization -- Soviet Union -- History.
Soviet Union -- Economic policy. Soviet Union --
Economic conditions.*

HC334.5.G74 1994
Gregory, Paul R.
Before command: an economic history of Russia
from emancipation to the first five-year plan/ Paul
R. Gregory. Princeton, N.J.: Princeton University
Press, c1994. viii, 188 p.
93-039139 330.947 0691042659
  *Russia -- Economic conditions -- 1861-1917.
Soviet Union -- Economic conditions -- 1917-1945.*

HC334.5.K34 1989
Kahan, Arcadius.
Russian economic history: the nineteenth century/
Arcadius Kahan; edited by Roger Weiss. Chicago:
University of Chicago Press, 1989. xii, 244 p.
88-026093 330.947 0226422429
  *Russia -- Economic conditions -- 1861-1917.
Russia -- Social conditions -- 1801-1917. Russia --
Economic conditions -- To 1861.*

HC335.D63 1966a
Dobb, Maurice Herbert, 1900-
Soviet economic development since 1917, by
Maurice Dobb. New York, International Publishers
[1967, c1966] viii, 515 p.
67-000911 330.947
  *Soviet Union -- Economic conditions -- 1917-
1945. Soviet Union -- Economic conditions --
1945-1955.*

HC335.G565
Goldman, Marshall I.
The Soviet economy: myth and reality [by]
Marshall I. Goldman. Englewood Cliffs, N.J.,
Prentice-Hall [1968] xiii, 176 p.
68-014467 330.947
  Soviet Union -- Economic conditions.

HC335.G723 1998
Gregory, Paul R.
Russian and Soviet economic performance and
structure/ Paul R. Gregory, Robert C. Stuart. 6th
ed. Reading, Mass.: Addison-Wesley, c1998. xii,
484 p.
97-025648 330.947/0854 21 0321014278
  *Soviet Union -- Economic conditions. Soviet Union
-- Economic policy. Former Soviet republics --
Economic conditions. Former Soviet republics --
Economic policy.*

HC335.M495 1990
Millar, James R., 1936-
The Soviet economic experiment/ James R. Millar;
edited and with an introduction by Susan J. Linz.
Urbana: University of Illinois Press, c1990. xv,
297 p.
89-031777 330.947/084 0252016572
  *Soviet Union -- Economic conditions. Soviet
Union -- Economic policy.*

HC335.N68 1992
Nove, Alec.
An economic history of the USSR, 1917-1991/
Alec Nove. 3rd ed. London, England; Penguin
Books, 1992. 473 p.
93-219035 330.947/084 20 0140157743
  *Soviet Union -- Economic conditions. Soviet Union
-- Economic policy.*

HC335.O83 1995
Owen, Thomas C.
Russian corporate capitalism from Peter the Great
to perestroika/ Thomas C. Owen. New York:
Oxford University Press, 1995. xii, 259 p.
94-049317 338.7/0947 0195096770
  *Capitalism -- Russia. Capitalism -- Soviet Union.
Corporations -- Russia. Russia -- Economic
conditions. Soviet Union -- Economic conditions --
1985-1991.*

HC335.2.B33 1987
Ball, Alan M.
Russia's last capitalists: the Nepmen, 1921-1929/
Alan M. Ball. Berkeley: University of California
Press, c1987. xvii, 226 p.
86-014662 338.947 0520057171
  Soviet Union -- Economic policy -- 1917-1928.

HC335.3.H86 1992
Hunter, Holland.
Faulty foundations: Soviet economic policies,
1928-1940/ Holland Hunter and Janusz M.
Szyrmer. Princeton, N.J.: Princeton University
Press, c1992. xvi, 339 p.
91-024018 338.947/009/043 0691042810
  *Soviet Union -- Economic policy -- 1928-1932.
Soviet Union -- Economic policy -- 1933-1937.
Soviet Union -- Economic policy -- 1938-1942.*

HC335.4.K87 1988
Kuromiya, Hiroaki.
Stalin's industrial revolution: politics and workers,
1928-1932/ Hiroaki Kuromiya. Cambridge
[England]; Cambridge University Press, 1988.
xviii, 364 p.
87-025010 338.947 052135157X
  *Stalin, Joseph, -- 1879-1953. Industrialization --
Soviet Union. Working class -- Soviet Union --
History -- 20th century. Central planning -- Soviet
Union. Soviet Union -- Politics and government --
1917-1936. Soviet Union -- Economic policy --
1928-1932.*

HC335.6.H36 1996
Harrison, Mark,
Accounting for war: Soviet production,
employment, and the defence burden, 1940-1945/
Mark Harrison. New York: Cambridge University
Press, 1996. xxxiv, 338 p.
95-040147 0521482658
  *World War, 1939-1945 -- Economic aspects --
Soviet Union.*

HC336.L29 1985
Lane, David Stuart.
Soviet economy and society/ David Lane. New
York: New York University Press, 1985. xiii,
342 p.
84-016523 306/.0947 081475015X
  *Soviet Union -- Economic conditions. Soviet
Union -- Social conditions.*

HC336.2.B43
Bergson, Abram, 1914-
The economics of Soviet planning. New Haven,
Yale University Press, 1964. xvii, 394 p.
64-020910 338.947
  *Industrial management -- Soviet Union. Soviet
Union -- Economic policy -- 1959-1965.*

HC336.23.B64 1970
Bornstein, Morris, 1927-
The Soviet economy; a book of readings. Edited by
Morris Bornstein and Daniel R. Fusfeld.
Homewood, Ill., R. D. Irwin, 1970. x, 467 p.
73-098247 330.947
  *Soviet Union -- Economic conditions -- 1955-
1965. Soviet Union -- Economic conditions --
1965-1975.*

HC336.25.H48 1988
Hewett, Edward A.
Reforming the Soviet economy: equality versus
efficiency/ Ed A. Hewett. Washington, D.C.:
Brookings Institution, c1988. xi, 404 p.
87-029500 338.947 0815736045
  *Soviet Union -- Economic policy -- 1986-1991.
Soviet Union -- Economic conditions -- 1985-1991.*

HC336.25.S6834 1983
The Soviet economy: toward the year 2000/ edited
by Abram Bergson and Herbert S. Levine. London;
G. Allen & Unwin, 1983. xvi, 452 p.
82-015611 338.5/443/0947 0043350453
  *Economic forecasting -- Soviet Union. Soviet
Union -- Economic conditions -- 1975-1985.*

HC336.26.A42 1988
Aganbegian, Abel Gezevich.
The economic challenge of perestroika/ Abel
Aganbegyan; edited by Michael Barratt Brown;
introduced by Alec Nove; translated by Pauline M.
Tiffen. Bloomington: Indiana University Press,
c1988. xxvii, 248 p.
88-003000   338.947   0253320933
*Perestroika. Soviet Union -- Economic policy --
1986-1991.*

HC336.26.A84 1991
Aslund, Anders, 1952-
Gorbachev's struggle for economic reform/ Anders
Aslund. Ithaca, N.Y.: Cornell University Press,
1991. xi, 262 p.
91-009268   338.947/09/048   0801426391
*Gorbachev, Mikhail Sergeevich, -- 1931-   Soviet
Union -- Politics and government -- 1985-1991.
Soviet Union -- Economic policy -- 1986-1991.
Soviet Union -- Commercial policy.*

HC336.26.D47 1989
Desai, Padma.
Perestroika in perspective: the design and
dilemmas of Soviet reform/ Padma Desai.
Princeton, N.J.: Princeton University Press, c1989.
viii, 138 p.
88-032477   338.947   0691042438
*Perestroika.   Soviet Union -- Politics and
government -- 1985-1991. Soviet Union --
Economic policy -- 1986-1991.*

HC336.26.D48 1998
The destruction of the Soviet economic system: an
insiders' history/ edited by Michael Ellman and
Vladimir Kontorovich. Armonk, N.Y.: M.E.
Sharpe, 1998. xxiv, 326 p.
97-052682   338.947/009/048   0765602636
*Perestroika. Soviet Union -- Economic policy --
1986-1991.*

HC336.26.F45 1990
Feinberg, Richard E.
Economic reform in three giants: U.S. foreign
policy and the USSR, China, and India/ Richard E.
Feinberg, John Echeverri-Gent, Friedemann Muller
and contributors, Rensselaer W. Lee III, Richard P.
Suttmeier, Elena B. Arefieva. New Brunswick,
USA: Transaction Books, c1990. viii, 248 p.
90-010739   338.9   0887388205
*Soviet Union -- Economic policy -- 1986-1991.
China -- Economic policy -- 1976- India --
Economic policy -- 1980-*

HC336.26.K668 1997
Kotz, David M.
Revolution from above: the demise of the Soviet
system/ David M. Kotz and Fred Weir. London;
Routledge, 1997. xi, 302 p.
96-007570   338.947 20   0415143179
*Soviet Union -- Economic conditions -- 1985-1991.
Soviet Union -- Politics and government -- 1985-
1991. Former Soviet republics -- Economic
conditions.*

HC336.26.M555 1991
Milestones in glasnost and perestroyka/ Ed A.
Hewett and Victor H. Winston, editors.
Washington, D.C.: Brookings Institution, [c1991-
] v. 1-2.
91-015304   338.947/009/048   0815736223
*Glasnost. Perestroika. Soviet Union -- Economic
policy -- 1986-1991. Soviet Union -- Economic
conditions -- 1985-1991.*

HC336.26.M69 1993
Moskoff, William.
Hard times: impoverishment and protest in the
Perestroika years: the Soviet Union 1985-1991/
William Moskoff. Armonk, N.Y.: M.E. Sharpe,
c1993. xi, 243 p.
93-020098   330.947/0854   1563242133
*Cost and standard of living -- Soviet Union.
Perestroika -- Social aspects. Protest movements --
Soviet Union. Soviet Union -- Economic conditions
-- 1985-1991.*

HC336.26.P464 1989
Perestroika and the economy: new thinking in
Soviet economics/ edited by Anthony Jones and
William Moskoff. Armonk, N.Y.: M.E. Sharpe,
c1989. xxi, 277 p.
89-006147   338.947/09/048   0873325699
Soviet Union -- Economic policy -- 1986-1991.

HC336.26.R46 1988
Reorganization and reform in the Soviet economy/
edited by Susan J. Linz and William Moskoff.
Armonk, N.Y.: M.E. Sharpe, c1988. x, 147 p.
87-035630   338.947   0873324722
*Soviet Union -- Economic policy -- 1986-1991.
Soviet Union -- Economic policy.*

HC336.27.E28 1996
Economic transition in Russia and the new states of
Eurasia/ editor, Bartlomiej Kaminski. Armonk,
N.Y.: M.E. Sharpe, c1996. xviii, 430 p.
96-007284   338.947 20   1563243660
*Former Soviet republics -- Economic
conditions. Former Soviet republics -- Economic
policy.*

HC336.27.F744 2000
Freeland, Chrystia, 1968-
Sale of the century: Russia's wild ride from
communism to capitalism/ Chrystia Freeland. New
York, N.Y: Crown Business, c2000. xxvi, 389 p.
2001-274629   338.947/009/049 21   0812932153
*Capitalism -- Russia (Federation) Industries --
Russia (Federation)   Russia (Federation) --
Economic conditions -- 1991-*

HC337.R852.S52697 1987
Siberia: problems and prospects for regional
development/ edited by Alan Wood. London;
Croom Helm, c1987. 233 p.
87-015437   330.957/0854   0709936559
*Industries -- Russia (Federation) -- Siberia.
Industries -- Russia (Federation) -- Russian Far
East. Siberia (Russia) -- Economic conditions.
Russian Far East (Russia) -- Economic conditions.*

HC337.U5.M28 1991
Marples, David R.
Ukraine under perestroika: ecology, economics,
and the workers' revolt/ David R. Marples. New
York: St. Martin's Press, 1991. xi, 243 p.
91-008110   330.947/710854   031206196X
*Perestroika -- Ukraine. Pollution -- Economic
aspects -- Ukraine. Chernobyl Nuclear Accident,
Chornobyl, Ukraine, 1986 -- Social aspects.
Ukraine -- Economic conditions -- 1945-1991.
Ukraine -- Social conditions -- 1945-1991.*

HC340.E5.P79 1991
Pryde, Philip R.
Environmental management in the Soviet Union/
Philip R. Pryde. Cambridge [England]; Cambridge
University Press, 1991. xx, 314 p.
90-001855   363.7/056/0947   052136079X
*Environmental policy -- Soviet Union.
Environmental management -- Soviet Union.*

HC340.I5.M2
McAuley, Alastair, 1938-
Economic welfare in the Soviet Union: poverty,
living standards, and inequality/ Alastair McAuley.
Madison: University of Wisconsin Press, c1979.
xix, 389 p.
78-053290   339.2/0947   0299076407:
*Income distribution -- Soviet Union. Poor --
Soviet Union.*

HC340.P55.P47 1993
Peterson, D. J.
Troubled lands: the legacy of Soviet environmental
destruction/ D.J. Peterson. Boulder: Westview
Press, c1993. xviii, 276 p.
92-030796   363.7/00947   0813316731
*Pollution -- Environmental aspects -- Soviet
Union. Environmental policy -- Soviet Union --
Citizen participation. Environmental degradation -
- Soviet Union.*

HC340.S6.S515 1988
Siegelbaum, Lewis H.
Stakhanovism and the politics of productivity in
the USSR, 1935-1941/ Lewis H. Siegelbaum.
Cambridge; Cambridge University Press, 1988. xv,
326 p.
87-025605   331.11/8/0947   0521345480
*Stakhanov movement -- History. Industrial
productivity -- Soviet Union. Industrial relations --
Soviet Union -- History. Soviet Union -- Economic
policy -- 1938-1942.*

HC340.T4.I52 1982
Industrial innovation in the Soviet Union/ edited by
Ronald Amann and Julian Cooper. New Haven:
Yale University Press, 1982. xxix, 526 p.
81-070484   338/.06   0300027729
*Technological innovations -- Soviet Union --
Case studies. Industries -- Soviet Union -- Case
studies.*

HC340.T4.P29 1983
Parrott, Bruce, 1945-
Politics and technology in the Soviet Union/ Bruce
Parrott. Cambridge, Mass.: MIT Press, c1983.
428 p.
82-022953   338/.06   0262160927
*Technological innovations -- Soviet Union.
Technology and state -- Soviet Union.*

HC340.12 By region or country — Europe — Russia (Federation)

HC340.12.A84 1995
Aslund, Anders, 1952-
How Russia became a market economy/ Anders
Aslund. Washington, D.C.: Brookings Institution,
c1995. xviii, 378 p.
95-000786   338.947   0815704267
*Soviet Union -- Economic conditions -- 1985-
1991. Soviet Union -- Economic policy -- 1986-
1991. Russia (Federation) -- Economic conditions -
- 1991-*

HC340.12.B7 1999
Brady, Rose, 1956-
Kapitalizm: Russia's struggle to free its economy/
Rose Brady. New Haven, Conn.: Yale University
Press, c1999. xxvii, 289 p.
98-038353   338.947 21   0300077939
*Capitalism -- Russia (Federation)   Russia
(Federation) -- Social conditions -- 1991- Russia
(Federation) -- Economic conditions -- 1991-*

HC340.12.B72 2000
Braginskiæi, S. V.
Incentives and institutions: the transition to a market economy in Russia/ Serguey Braguinsky and Grigory Yavlinsky. Princeton, N.J.: Princeton University Press, c2000. xi, 282 p.
99-041742   339.5/0947/09049 21   0691009937
   Economic stabilization -- Russia (Federation) Privatization -- Russia (Federation)

HC340.12.G87 1999
Gustafson, Thane.
Capitalism Russian-style/ Thane Gustafson. Cambridge, England; Cambridge University Press, 1999. xvi, 264 p.
98-040307   330.12/2/0947 21   0521645956
   Capitalism -- Russia (Federation) Post-communism -- Russia (Federation)

HC340.12.H68 2001
Hough, Jerry F., 1935-
The logic of economic reform in Russia/ Jerry F. Hough. Washington, D.C.: Brookings Institution Press, c2001. xvi, 318 p.
00-012817   338.947 21   0815737548
   Privatization -- Russia (Federation) Russia (Federation) -- Economic conditions -- 1991- Russia (Federation) -- Economic policy -- 1991- Russia (Federation) -- Politics and government -- 1991-

HC340.12.H86 2002
Humphrey, Caroline.
The unmaking of Soviet life: everyday economies after socialism/ Caroline Humphrey. Ithaca: Cornell University Press, 2002. xxvii, 265 p.
2001-005841   330.947 21   0801487730
   Post-communism -- Russia (Federation) Post-communism -- Mongolia.

HC340.12.N48 2001
The new Russia: transition gone awry/ edited by Lawrence R. Klein and Marshall Pomer. Stanford, Calif.: Stanford University Press, c2001. xxiii, 454 p.
00-034443   338.947 21   0804741271
   Russia (Federation) -- Economic policy -- 1991- Russia (Federation) -- Economic conditions -- 1991-

HC340.12.S494 2000
Shleifer, Andrei.
Without a map: political tactics and economic reform in Russia/ Andrei Shleifer, Daniel Treisman. Cambridge, Mass.: MIT Press, c2000. ix, 223 p.
99-045036   338.947 21   0262194341
Russia (Federation) -- Economic conditions -- 1991- Russia (Federation) -- Politics and government -- 1991-

HC340.12.S55 2000
Silverman, Bertram.
New rich, new poor, new Russia: winners and losers on the Russian road to capitalism/ Bertram Silverman and Murray Yanowitch. Expanded ed. Armonk, NY: M.E. Sharpe, c2000. xxv, 187 p.
99-462036   330.947/086 21   0765605236
   Wealth -- Russia (Federation) Poverty -- Russia (Federation) Capitalism -- Russia (Federation)

HC340.12.Z9.A445 1997
Hill, Malcolm R.
Environment and technology in the former USSR: the case of 'acid rain' and power generation/ by Malcolm R. Hill. Lyme, N.H.: Edward Elgar Pub., [1997]. xii, 261 p.
97-016473   363.739/2/0947   1858985838
   Air -- Pollution -- Former Soviet republics. Fossil fuel power plants -- Environmental aspects -- Former Soviet republics. Acid rain -- Former Soviet republics.

HC340.19 By region or country — Europe — Ukraine

HC340.19.S54 1996
Shen, Raphael.
Ukraine's economic reform: obstacles, errors, lessons/ Raphael Shen. Westport, Conn.: Praeger, 1996. xii, 214 p.
95-050468   338.947/71   0275952401
   Ukraine -- Economic policy -- 1991- Ukraine -- Economic conditions -- 1991-

HC340.3 By region or country — Europe — Poland

HC340.3.A56 1999
Adam, Jan,
Social costs of transformation to a market economy in post-socialist countries: the case of Poland, the Czech Republic, and Hungary/ Jan Adam. New York: St. Martin's Press, 1999.
98-055364   338.943 21   0312221606
   Post-communism -- Poland. Post-communism -- Czech Republic. Post-communism -- Hungary.

HC340.3.B45 2001
Bell, Janice,
The political economy of reform in post-communist Poland/ Janice Bell. Cheltenham, UK; E. Elgar, 2001. xiv, 243 p.
2001-023164   338.9438 21   1840641231
   Public opinion -- Poland.

HC340.3.H86 1998
Hunter, Richard J.
From autarchy to market: Polish economics and politics, 1945-1995/ Richard J. Hunter, Jr. and Leo V. Ryan. Westport, Conn.: Praeger, 1998. xii, 287 p.
98-011123   338.9438   0275962199
   Poland -- Economic policy -- 1990- Poland -- Economic policy -- 1981-1990. Poland -- Economic policy -- 1945-1981.

HC340.3.K656363 2000
Kolodko, Grzegorz W.
Post-Communist transition: the thorny road/ Grzegorz W. Kolodko. Rochester, NY: University of Rochester Press, 2000. 199 p.
00-056389   338.9438   1580460577
   Privatization -- Poland. Post-communism -- Poland. Poland -- Economic policy -- 1990-

HC340.3.O73 2001
Orenstein, Mitchell A.
Out of the red: building capitalism and democracy in postcommunist Europe/ Mitchell A. Orenstein. Ann Arbor, Mich.: University of Michigan Press, c2001. xiv, 166 p.
00-012902   338.947 21   047206746X
   Post-communism -- Poland. Post-communism -- Czech Republic. Post-communism -- Czechoslovakia.

HC340.3.P699 1996
Poznanski, Kazimierz.
Poland's protracted transition: institutional change and economic growth 1970-1994/ Kazimierz Z. Poznanski. Cambridge; Cambridge University Press, 1996. 337 p.
97-160980   338.9438   0521553962
   Communism -- Economic aspects -- Poland. Post-communism -- Economic aspects -- Poland. Poland -- Economic conditions. Poland -- Economic policy.

HC340.3.S213 1993
Sachs, Jeffrey.
Poland's jump to the market economy/ Jeffrey Sachs. Cambridge, Mass.: MIT Press, c1993. xv, 126 p.
93-001738   338.9438   0262193124
   Capitalism -- Poland. Poland -- Economic conditions -- 1981-1990. Poland -- Economic policy -- 1990- Poland -- Economic conditions -- 1990-

HC340.3.S59 1994
Slay, Ben, 1958-
The Polish economy: crisis, reform, and transformation/ Ben Slay. Princeton, N.J.: Princeton University Press, c1994. xvi, 229 p.
93-044823   338.9438   0691036160
   Post-communism -- Poland. Poland -- Economic conditions -- 1981-1990. Poland -- Economic policy -- 1990- Poland -- Economic policy -- 1981-1990.

HC375 By region or country — Europe — Scandinavia

HC375.M25 2000
Magnusson, Lars, 1952-
An economic history of Sweden/ Lars Magnusson. New York: Routledge, 2000. xvii, 305 p.
99-039725   330.9485   0415181674
   Sweden -- Economic conditions.

HC385-388 By region or country — Europe — Spain

HC385.L463 1995
Lieberman, Sima, 1927-
Growth and crisis in the Spanish economy, 1940-93/ Sima Lieberman. London; Routledge, 1995. xv, 377 p.
95-002227   330.946/082   041512428X
   Spain -- Economic conditions -- 1918-1975. Spain -- Economic conditions -- 1975-

HC385.M27213 1999
Martin, Carmela.
The Spanish economy in the new Europe/ Carmela Martin; translated from the Spanish by Philip Hill and Sarah Nicholson. New York: St. Martin's Press, 1999. xix, 307 p.
99-049727   330.946/083   0312230060
   Spain -- Economic conditions -- 1975- Spain -- Economic policy. Spain -- Foreign economic relations.

HC385.M62313 1987
The economic modernization of Spain, 1830-1930/ edited by Nicolas Sanchez-Albornoz; translated by Karen Powers and Manuel Sanudo. New York: New York University Press, c1987. xv, 295 p.
87-005535   330.946/07   0814778615
   Spain -- Economic conditions -- 19th century. Spain -- Economic conditions -- 20th century. Spain -- History -- 19th century.

HC385.R514 1996
Ringrose, David R.
Spain, Europe, and the "Spanish miracle", 1700-1900/ David R. Ringrose. Cambridge; Cambridge University Press, 1996. xv, 439 p.
96-158113   0521434866
    Spain -- Economic conditions -- 18th century. Spain -- Economic conditions -- 19th century. Spain -- History -- 18th century.

HC385.T64313 2000
Tortella Casares, Gabriel.
The development of modern Spain: an economic history of the nineteenth and twentieth centuries/ Gabriel Tortella; translated by Valerie J. Herr. Cambridge, Mass.: Harvard University Press, 2000. xvi, 528 p.
99-056711   330.946/07   0674000943
    Spain -- Economic conditions -- 19th century. Spain -- Economic conditions -- 20th century.

HC388.B3.B3 1995
Bensch, Stephen P.
Barcelona and its rulers, 1096-1291/ Stephen P. Bensch. Cambridge [England]; Cambridge University Press, 1995. xviii, 457 p.
93-004251   946/.7202   0521435110
    Nobility -- Spain -- Barcelona -- History -- To 1500. Barcelona (Spain) -- Commerce -- History. Barcelona (Spain) -- History. Barcelona (Spain) -- Economic conditions.

HC388.M3.R56 1983
Ringrose, David R.
Madrid and the Spanish economy, 1560-1850/ David R. Ringrose. Berkeley: University of California Press, c1983. xviii, 405 p.
82-001971   330.946/41   0520043111
    Madrid (Spain) -- Economic conditions. Spain -- Economic conditions.

HC401-407 By region or country — Europe — Balkan States

HC401.P76 1996
Problems of economic and political transformation in the Balkans/ edited by Ian Jeffries. New York: Pinter, 1996. vi, 199 p.
95-026834   330.9496   1855673193
    Balkan Peninsula -- Economic conditions. Balkan Peninsula -- Politics and government -- 1989-

HC403.B75 1996
Bristow, J. A.
The Bulgarian economy in transition/ John A. Bristow. Cheltenham, UK; Edward Elgar, c1996. xiii, 248 p.
95-036671   338.94977 20   1852789948
    Post-communism -- Economic aspects -- Bulgaria. Bulgaria -- Economic conditions -- 1989- Bulgaria -- Economic policy -- 1989-

HC405.L68 1996
Love, Joseph LeRoy.
Crafting the third world: theorizing underdevelopment in Rumania and Brazil/ Joseph L. Love. Stanford, Calif.: Stanford University Press, 1996. xiv, 348 p.
95-022991   338.9498   0804725462
    Socialism -- Romania. Socialism -- Brazil. Romania -- Dependency on foreign countries. Brazil -- Dependency on foreign countries. Brazil -- Economic policy.

HC407.B39 1995
Beyond Yugoslavia: politics, economics, and culture in a shattered community/ edited by Sabrina Petra Ramet and Ljubisa Adamovich. Boulder: Westview Press, 1995. x, 502 p.
94-035987   338.9497   0813379539
    Yugoslavia -- Economic conditions -- 1945-1992. Yugoslavia -- Politics and government -- 1980-1992. Yugoslavia -- Social conditions.

HC407.L95 1989
Lydall, Harold.
Yugoslavia in crisis/ Harold Lydall. Oxford: Clarendon Press; 1989. xii, 255 p.
88-007633   338.9497   0198286953
    Management -- Employee participation -- Yugoslavia. Yugoslavia -- Politics and government -- 1980-1992. Yugoslavia -- Economic conditions.

HC407.Y822 1992
Yugoslavia in the age of democracy: essays on economic and political reform/ edited by George Macesich; with the assistance of Rikard Lang, Ljubisav Markovic, and Dragomir Vojnic; foreword by Bernard F. Sliger. Westport, Conn.: Praeger, 1992. xii, 237 p.
91-034495   338.9497   0275941752
    Yugoslavia -- Economic conditions -- 1945-1992. Yugoslavia -- Economic policy -- 1945-1992. Yugoslavia -- Politics and government -- 1945-1980.

HC412 By region or country — Asia

HC412.A756 2002
The Asian economies in the twentieth century/ edited by Angus Maddison, D.S. Prasada Rao, and William F. Shepherd. Cheltenham; E. Elgar, c2002. xi, 250 p.
2001-055509   330.95/043 21   1840640456
Asia -- Economic conditions -- 20th century.

HC412.E246 1997
Economies in transition: comparing Asia and Eastern Europe/ edited by Wing Thye Woo, Stephen Parker, and Jeffrey D. Sachs. Cambridge, Mass.: MIT Press, c1997. xiv, 412 p.
96-045192   338.947 21   0262231913
    Post-communism -- Asia. Post-communism -- Europe, Eastern. Asia -- Economic policy. Europe, Eastern -- Economic policy -- 1989-

HC412.G34 1999
Gapinski, James H.
Economic growth in the Asia Pacific region/ James H. Gapinski. New York: St. Martin's Press, 1999. xviii, 253 p.
99-020612   338.95   031221619X
    Labor productivity -- Asia. Labor productivity -- Pacific Area. Asia -- Economic policy. Pacific Area -- Economic policy. Asia -- Economic conditions.

HC412.H55 1972
Hla Myint, U.
Southeast Asia's economy: development policies in the 1970s; a study sponsored by the Asian Development Bank, (by) H. Myint. Harmondsworth, Penguin, 1972. 189 p.
73-330833   330.9/59   0140806563
    Asia, Southeastern -- Economic conditions.

HC412.I523185 2003
International business risk: a handbook for the Asia Pacific Region/ edited by D.S.L. Jarvis. Cambridge; Cambridge University Press, 2003. xxi, 474 p.
2002-031469   330.95 21   0521821940
    Risk assessment -- Asia. Risk assessment -- Pacific Area.

HC412.K895 2001
Kwan, C. H.,
Yen bloc: toward economic integration in Asia/ C. H. Kwan. Washington, D.C.: Brookings Institution Press, c2001. xviii, 214 p.
2001-001712   337.1/5 21   0815700830
    Monetary policy -- Asia.

HC412.L44 1989
Lessons in development: a comparative study of Asia and Latin America/ edited by Seiji Naya ... [et al.]. San Francisco, Calif.: International Center for Economic Growth; c1989. xvii, 361 p.
89-019996   338.95   1558150528
    Asia -- Economic policy -- Congresses. Latin America -- Economic policy -- Congresses. Asia -- Commercial policy -- Congresses.

HC412.M9 1968b
Myrdal, Gunnar, 1898-
Asian drama; an inquiry into the poverty of nations. New York, Twentieth Century Fund, 1968. 3 v.
67-027845   330.95
    South Asia -- Economic conditions. Asia, Southeastern -- Economic conditions.

HC412.N2433 1996
Naisbitt, John.
Megatrends Asia: eight Asian megatrends that are reshaping our world/ John Naisbitt. New York: Simon & Schuster, c1996. 298 p.
95-050102   330.95 20   0684815427
    Economic forecasting -- Asia. Asia -- Economic conditions -- 1945-

HC412.R365 2001
Ravenhill, John.
APEC and the construction of Pacific Rim regionalism/ John Ravenhill. Cambridge, UK; Cambridge University Press, 2001. xii, 294 p.
2001-043601   337.1/5 21   0521667976
    Pacific Area cooperation. Regionalism -- Pacific Area.

HC415 By region or country — Asia — Special topics (not otherwise provided for), A-Z

HC415.W4 T47 2002
Terry, Edith.
How Asia got rich: Japan, China and the Asian miracle/ Edith Terry foreword by Chalmers Johnson. Armonk, N.Y.: M.E. Sharpe, c2002. xxix, 688 p.
2001-034217   330.95 21   076560356X
    Wealth -- Asia.

HC415.15-415.33 By region or country — Asia — Middle East. Near East

HC415.15.C37 1998
Carkoglu, Ali, 1963-
The political economy of regional cooperation in the Middle East/ Ali Carkoglu, Mine Eder and Kemal Kirisci. London; Routledge, 1998. x, 268 p.
98-017666   337.56   0415194458
Arab cooperation. Middle East — Economic integration. Middle East — Economic conditions — 1979- Middle East — Foreign economic relations.

HC415.15.D36 2000
Dana, Leo Paul.
Economies of the eastern Mediterranean region: economic miracles in the making/ Leo Paul Dana. Singapore; World Scientific, 2000. 245 p.
00-054545   330.956   9810244746
Middle East — Economic conditions — 1979-

HC415.15.G58 2001
Glasser, Bradley Louis, 1966-
Economic development and political reform: impact of external capital on the Middle East/ by Bradley Louis Glasser. Northampton, Mass.: E. Elgar, 2001. vi, 147 p.
00-056006   338.956/009/048   1858989272
Middle East — Economic conditions — 1979- Middle East — Politics and government — 1979-

HC415.15.I83
The Islamic Middle East, 700-1900: studies in economic and social history/ edited by A. L. Udovitch. Princeton, N.J.: Darwin Press, c1981. 838 p.
79-052703   330.956/01   0878500308
Middle East — Economic conditions. Islamic Empire — Economic conditions. Africa, North — Economic conditions.

HC415.15.I84 1982
Issawi, Charles Philip.
An economic history of the Middle East and North Africa/ Charles Issawi. New York: Columbia University Press, 1982. xiii, 304 p.
81-019518   330.956   0231034431
Middle East — Economic conditions. Africa, North — Economic conditions.

HC415.15.O935 1998
Owen, Roger, 1935-
A history of Middle East economies in the twentieth century/ Roger Owen & Sevket Pamuk. Cambridge, Mass: Harvard University Press, c1998. xviii, 310 p.
98-029099   330.956/04 21   0674398300
Middle East — Economic conditions — 20th century.

HC415.15.R53 1996
Richards, Alan, 1946-
A political economy of the Middle East/ Alan Richards, John Waterbury. Boulder, Colo.: Westview Press, 1996. xviii, 445 p.
96-024374   338.956   0813324106
Working class — Middle East. Middle East — Economic policy. Middle East — Economic conditions — 1979- Middle East — Politics and government — 1979-

HC415.15.Z9.D43 1993
The Economics of Middle East peace: views from the region/ edited by Stanley Fischer, Dani Rodrik, Elias Tuma. Cambridge, Mass.: MIT Press, c1993. xii, 370 p.
92-021503   330.956/053   0262061538
War — Economic aspects — Middle East — Congresses. Peace — Economic aspects — Congresses. Economic stabilization — Middle East — Congresses. Middle East — Foreign economic relations — Congresses. Middle East — Defenses — Economic aspects — Congresses.

HC415.24.W55 1995
Wilson, Rodney.
Economic development in the Middle East/ Rodney Wilson. London; Routledge, 1995. vii, 218 p.
95-021623   338.956   0415125537
Economic development — Religious aspects — Islam. Middle East — Economic conditions — 1979-

HC415.25.D48 1999
Development under adversity: the Palestinian economy in transition/ edited by Ishac Diwan and Radwan A. Shaban. Washington, DC: World Bank, 1999. xvi, 240 p.
99-012532   338.95694   0821344188
Palestine — Economic conditions. Palestine — Economic policy.

HC415.25.E26 1989
Economic and social policy in Israel: the first generation/ Moshe Sanbar, editor ... [et al.]. Lanham: University Press of America; c1990. 297 p.
89-030483   338.95694   081917498X
Israel — Economic policy. Israel — Social policy.

HC415.25.L48 1993
Lewin-Epstein, Noah.
The Arab minority in Israel's economy: patterns of ethnic inequality/ Noah Lewin-Epstein and Moshe Semyonov. Boulder: Westview Press, 1993. xvii, 169 p.
92-047403   330.95694/054/0899274 0813315255
Palestinian Arabs — Employment — Israel. Palestinian Arabs — Government policy — Israel. Palestinian Arabs — Israel — Economic conditions. Israel — Ethnic relations.

HC415.25.P25 1997
The Palestinian economy: between imposed integration and voluntary separation/ by Arie Arnon ... [et al.]. Leiden; Brill, 1997. xiv, 278 p.
97-026555   330.95694   9004105387
Palestine — Economic conditions. West Bank — Economic conditions. Gaza Strip — Economic conditions.

HC415.25.R33 1988
Rabi`, Muhammad, 1940-
The politics of foreign aid: U.S. foreign assistance and aid to Israel/ Mohamed Rabie. New York: Praeger, 1988. x, 187 p.
88-003096   338.91/73/05694   0275930009
Economic assistance, American — Israel.

HC415.25.R58 1992
Rivlin, Paul.
The Israeli economy/ Paul Rivlin. Boulder: Westview Press, 1992. xv, 183 p.
91-038465   330.95694   081337653X
Israel — Economic conditions.

HC415.25.Z7.W4725 1992
Drury, Richard Toshiyuki.
Plowshares and swords: the economics of occupation in the West Bank/ Richard Toshiyuki Drury and Robert C. Winn with Michael O'Connor; with a foreword by Drew S. Days III. Boston: Beacon Press, c1992. xi, 222 p.
91-041457   330.95695/3   0807069043
Human rights — West Bank. Intifada, 1987- West Bank — Economic conditions. West Bank — Economic policy.

HC415.25.Z7.W47915 1994
Securing peace in the Middle East: project on economic transition/ edited by Stanley Fischer ... [et al.]. Cambridge, Mass.: MIT Press, c1994. xxxv, 166 p.
93-041541   338.953/1   0262061686
West Bank — Economic policy. Gaza Strip — Economic policy. Israel — Foreign economic relations — Jordan.

HC415.26.P57 1998
Piro, Timothy J., 1960-
The political economy of market reform in Jordan/ Timothy J. Piro. Lanham, Md.: Rowman & Littlefield, c1998. xvi, 131 p.
98-024370   330.95695 21   084768881X
Jordan — Economic conditions. Jordan — Economic policy. Jordan — Politics and government.

HC415.3.C48 1999
Change and development in the Gulf/ edited by Abbas Abdelkarim. New York: St. Martin's Press, 1999. ix, 270 p.
98-034976   338.9536   0312216580
Persian Gulf Region — Economic conditions. Persian Gulf Region — Economic policy. Persian Gulf Region — Social conditions.

HC415.33.C49 1997
Chaudhry, Kiren Aziz.
The price of wealth: economies and institutions in the Middle East/ Kiren Aziz Chaudhry. Ithaca: Cornell University Press, 1997. xiii, 330 p.
97-001536   338.953   0801431646
Saudi Arabia — Economic policy. Yemen — Economic policy. Middle East — Economic conditions.

HC420.3 By region or country — Asia — Central Asia

HC420.3.C44 2000
Central Asia and the new global economy/ edited by Boris Rumer. Armonk, N.Y.: M.E. Sharpe, c2000. xiii, 288 p.
00-026579   338.958 21   0765606291
Post-communism — Asia, Central. Asia, Central — Politics and government — 1991- Asia, Central -- Economic conditions — 1991- Asia, Central — Foreign relations.

HC420.3.C455 1996
Central Asia in transition: dilemmas of political and economic development/ edited by Boris Rumer. Armonk, N.Y.: M.E. Sharpe, c1996. xx, 286 p.
96-008137   338.958 20   1563247666
Asia, Central — Economic conditions. Asia, Central — Economic policy.

HC420.3.P76 1995
Pomfret, Richard W. T.
The economies of Central Asia/ Richard Pomfret. Princeton, N.J.: Princeton University Press, c1995. xii, 216 p.
95-006829 330.958 0691043752
Asia, Central -- Economic conditions. Former Soviet Republics -- Economic conditions.

HC422 By region or country — Asia — Burma

HC422.M382 1998
Maung, Mya, 1933-
The Burma road to capitalism: economic growth versus democracy/ Mya Maung. Westport, CT: Praeger, 1998. xvi, 302 p.
97-043959 338.9591 0275962164
Burma -- Economic conditions -- 1948- Burma -- Foreign economic relations. Burma -- Politics and government -- 1948-

HC424 By region or country — Asia — Sri Lanka. Ceylon

HC424.B78 1992
Bruton, Henry J.
Sri Lanka and Malaysia/ Henry J. Bruton in collaboration with Gamini Abeysekera, Nimal Sanderatne, and Zainal Aznam Yusof. Oxford [England]; Published for the World Bank [by] Oxford Univers c1992. xiv, 422 p.
92-001243 330.95493 0195208242
Income distribution -- Sri Lanka. Poor -- Sri Lanka. Malaysia -- Economic conditions. Malaysia -- Economic policy. Sri Lanka -- Economic policy. Sri Lanka -- Economic conditions.

HC426-430 By region or country — Asia — China

HC426.C482
China economic review. Greenwich, Conn.: JAI Press, [1989-]
90-656610 330.951/005
China -- Economic conditions -- 1949- -- Periodicals. China -- Economic policy -- 1949- -- Periodicals.

HC427.C5598
China's modern economy in historical perspective: sponsored by the Social Science Research Council/ contributors, Kang Chao ... [et al.]; edited by Dwight H. Perkins. Stanford, Calif.: Stanford University Press, 1975. xiv, 344 p.
74-082779 330.9/52 0804708711
Economic development. China -- Economic conditions. China -- Economic policy.

HC427.L486 1987
Lippit, Victor D.
The economic development of China/ Victor D. Lippit. Armonk, N.Y.: M.E. Sharpe, c1987. ix, 269 p.
86-020410 338.951 087332403X
Social classes -- China -- History. Elite (Social sciences) -- China -- History. Saving and investment -- China -- History. China -- Economic policy. China -- Economic conditions.

HC427.R45 1999
Richardson, Philip.
Economic change in China, c. 1800-1950/ prepared for the Economic History Society by Philip Richardson. New York: Cambridge University Press, c1999. xii, 117 p.
99-012835 330.951 21 0521583969
China -- Economic conditions. China -- Economic policy.

HC427.8.T36 1966
Tawney, R. H. 1880-1962.
Land and labor in China. With an introd. by Barrington Moore, Jr. Boston, Beacon Press [1966] 207 p.
67-002097 330.951
Peasantry -- China. China -- Economic conditions -- 1912-1949.

HC427.9.C52178
Cheng, Chu-yuan.
China's economic development: growth and structural change/ Chu-yuan Cheng. Boulder, Colo.: Westview Press, 1982. xxiii, 535 p.
81-011671 338.951 0891587888
China -- Economic conditions -- 1949-1976. China -- Economic conditions -- 1976-

HC427.9.E28
Eckstein, Alexander, 1915-
China's economic revolution/ Alexander Eckstein. Cambridge; Cambridge University Press, 1977. xii, 340 p.
76-009176 330.9/51/05 0521212839
China -- Economic policy. China -- Economic conditions -- 1949-1976.

HC427.9.H868 2002
Hughes, Neil C.,
China's economic challenge: smashing the iron rice bowl/ Neil C. Hughes. Armonk, N.Y.: M.E. Sharpe, c2002. xv, 235 p.
2001-049909 338.951 21 0765608081
China -- Economic policy -- 1976-2000. China -- Economic policy -- 2000- China -- Economic conditions -- 1976-2000.

HC427.9.L599 1965
Liu, Ta-chung.
The economy of the Chinese mainland: national income and economic development, 1933-1959 [by] Ta-chung Liu [and] Kung-chia Yeh. Princeton, N.J., Princeton University Press, 1965. xvi, 771 p.
64-012223 330.951
China (People's Republic of China, 1949-) -- Economic conditions.

HC427.9.L599213 1988
Liu, Tsai-hsing.
The economic geography of China/ [Liu Zaixing, Wu Yuwen, and Lian Yitong]; editor, Sun Jingzhi. Hong Kong; Oxford University Press, 1988. xvii, 404 p.
87-034713 330.951/05 0195840798
China -- Economic conditions -- 1949-

HC427.9.P95 1997
Pyle, David J.
China's economy: from revolution to reform/ David J. Pyle. New York: St. Martin's Press, 1997. ix, 189 p.
97-000205 338.951/009/045 0312174608
China -- Economic policy -- 1949-1976. China -- Economic policy -- 1976- China -- Economic conditions -- 1949-1976.

HC427.9.R39 1989
Remaking the economic institutions of socialism: China and Eastern Europe/ edited by Victor Nee and David Stark with Mark Selden. Stanford, Calif.: Stanford University Press, 1989. xi, 405 p.
88-038223 338.947 0804714940
Socialism -- China. Socialism -- Europe, Eastern. China -- Economic policy -- 1949- Europe, Eastern -- Economic policy.

HC427.92.B736 2000
Bramall, Chris.
Sources of Chinese economic growth, 1978-1996/ Chris Bramall. Oxford [England]; Oxford University Press, 2000. 558 p.
00-032700 338.951 0198296975
China -- Economic conditions -- 1976- China -- Economic policy -- 1976- China -- Politics and government -- 1976-

HC427.92.C3375 2001
Chang, Gordon G.
The coming collapse of China/ Gordon G. Chang. 1st ed. New York: Random House, c2001. xxii, 344 p.
00-054782 951 21 037550477X
China -- Economic conditions -- 1976-2000. China -- Social conditions -- 1976-2000. China -- Politics and government -- 1976-

HC427.92.C3533 1995
Chen, Feng, 1955-
Economic transition and political legitimacy in post-Mao China: ideology and reform/ Feng Chen. Albany, NY: State University of New York Press, c1995. xvi, 246 p.
95-008783 338.951/009/049 0791426572
Capitalism -- China. Communism -- China. China -- Economic policy -- 1976- China -- Politics and government -- 1976-

HC427.92.C3544 2001
Chen, Ming-Jer.
Inside Chinese business: a guide for managers worldwide/ Ming-Jer Chen. Boston, Mass.: Harvard Business School Press, c2001. xix, 234 p.
00-047115 306/.0951 21 1578512328
Investments, Foreign -- China. China -- Economic conditions -- 1976- China -- Civilization. China -- Social and customs.

HC427.92.C45145648 1993
China's provincial statistics, 1949-1989/ edited by Hseh Tien-tung, LI Qiang, Liu Shucheng. Boulder: Westview Press, 1993. xxiii, 595 p.
93-014244 330.951/05/021 0813387329
China -- Economic conditions -- 1976- -- Statistics. China -- Social conditions -- 1976- -- Statistics.

HC427.92.C46553 1990
China's rural industry = [Hsiang chen kung yeh]: structure, development, and reform/ edited by William A. Byrd and Lin Qingsong. Oxford [England]; Published for the World Bank [by] Oxford Univers c1990. xiv, 445 p.
89-026665 338.951/009173/4 20 0195208226
Rural industries -- China. Industrial policy -- China. China -- Economic policy -- 1976-

HC427.92.E58 1999
Enterprise reform in China: ownership, transition, and performance/ edited by Gary H. Jefferson and Inderjit Singh. Oxford; Oxford University Press, c1999. xi, 298 p.
97-036569 338.0951 21 0195211200
Industries -- China -- 1976- Industrial productivity -- China. Government ownership -- China.

HC427.92.G86 1998
Guo, Rongxing.
How the Chinese economy works: a multiregional overview/ Rongxing Guo. New York: St. Martin's Press, 1998. xvi, 204 p.
98-017296 330.951 0312215703
China -- Economic conditions. China -- Economic policy -- 1976-

HC427.92.H37 1987
Harding, Harry, 1946-
China's second revolution: reform after Mao/ Harry Harding. Washington, D.C.: Brookings Institution, c1987. xx, 369 p.
87-027235 330.951 081573462X
China -- Economic policy -- 1976- China -- Foreign economic relations. China -- Politics and government -- 1976-

HC427.92.K383 1996
Kao, Shang-chuan.
China's economic reform/ Shangquan Gao; forewords by Sir Alec Cairncross and Sir Edward Heath. Houndmills, Basingstoke, Hampshire: Macmillan Press; 1996. xiii, 251 p.
93-038043 338.951 0333611225
China -- Economic policy -- 1976-

HC427.92.K55 1990
Kleinberg, Robert.
China's "opening" to the outside world: the experiment with foreign capitalism/ Robert Kleinberg. Boulder: Westview Press, 1990. xiv, 277 p.
90-012477 338.951/27 0813379040
Investments, Foreign -- China. China -- Economic policy -- 1976- China -- Commercial policy. China -- Foreign economic relations.

HC427.92.L37 1994
Lardy, Nicholas R.
China in the world economy/ Nicholas R. Lardy. Washington, D.C.: Institute for International Economics, 1994. xi, 158 p.
94-000491 337.51 0881322008
China -- Economic policy -- 1976- China -- Foreign economic relations.

HC427.92.L524 1991
Lichtenstein, Peter M., 1944-
China at the brink: the political economy of reform and retrenchment in the post-Mao era/ Peter M. Lichtenstein. New York: Praeger, 1991. xiv, 159 p.
91-009594 338.951 0275940527
Communism -- China. China -- Economic policy -- 1976-

HC427.92.L55 2001
Lin, Yi-min.
Between politics and markets: firms, competition, and institutional change in post-Mao China/ Yi-min Lin. Cambridge; Cambridge University Press, 2001. xiv, 255 p.
00-027206 338.0951 21 0521771307
Mixed economy -- China.

HC427.92.M635 1999
Mok, Ka-Ho, 1964-
Social and political development in post-reform China/ Ka-Ho Mok; foreward by Andrew Nathan; preface by Paul Wilding. New York: St. Martin's Press, 1999. xxii, 244 p.
99-016306 338.951 0312224885
China -- Economic policy -- 1976- China -- Economic conditions -- 1976- China -- Social conditions -- 1976-

HC427.92.M665 2002
Moore, Thomas Geoffrey,
China in the world market: Chinese industry and international sources of reform in the post-Mao era/ Thomas G. Moore. Cambridge, UK; Cambridge University Press, 2002. xviii, 344 p.
2001-025634 337.51 21 052166442X
Industries -- China. Economic history -- 1945-

HC427.92.M87 1998
Murray, Geoffrey, 1942-
China: the next superpower: dilemmas in change and continuity/ Geoffrey Murray. New York: St. Martin's Press, 1998. x, 260 p.
98-006004 306/.0951 0312215339
China -- Economic conditions -- 1976- China -- Social conditions -- 1976- China -- Politics and government -- 1976-

HC427.92.N64 2001
Nolan, Peter,
China and the global economy: national champions, industrial policy, and the big business revolution/ Peter Nolan. Houndmills, Basingstoke, Hampshire; Palgrave, 2001. xi, 244 p.
2001-021736 337.51 21 0333945654
International economic relations.

HC427.92.O35 1999
Oi, Jean Chun
Rural China takes off: institutional foundations of economic reform/ Jean C. Oi. Berkeley: University of California Press, 1999. xv, 253 p.
98-026762 330.951/058 0520200063
Rural industries -- China. Rural development -- China. Entrepreneurship -- China. China -- Politics and government -- 1976- China -- Economic conditions -- 1976-

HC427.92.P39 1997
Pearson, Margaret M., 1959-
China's new business elite: the political consequences of economic reform/ Margaret M. Pearson. Berkeley: University of California Press, c1997. x, 207 p.
96-026088 338.951 20 0520207181
Businesspeople -- China -- History. Entrepreneurship -- China -- History. Elite (Social sciences) -- China -- History. China -- Politics and government -- 1976-

HC427.92.S63 1993
Solinger, Dorothy J.
China's transition from socialism: statist legacies and market reforms, 1980-1990/ Dorothy J. Solinger. Armonk, N.Y.: M.E. Sharpe, c1993. vii, 292 p.
92-043250 338.951 156324067X
Central planning -- China. Socialism -- China. China -- Economic policy -- 1976-

HC427.92.W494 1996
White, Gordon, 1942-
In search of civil society: market reform and social change in contemporary China/ Gordon White, Jude Howell, and Shang Xiaoyuan. Oxford: Clarendon Press; 1996. x, 241 p.
95-046909 338.951 0198289561
China -- Economic conditions -- 1976- China -- Social conditions -- 1976- China -- Economic policy -- 1976-

HC427.92.W514 1998
White, Lynn T.
Unstately power/ Lynn T. White, III. Armonk, N.Y.: M.E. Sharpe, c1998. 2 v.
97-026804 338.951 21 0765600447
Local government -- China. Entrepreneurship -- China. Political planning -- China. China -- Economic policy -- 1976-

HC427.92.W52 2001
Whiting, Susan H., 1964-
Power and wealth in rural China: the political economy of institutional change/ Susan H. Whiting. New York: Cambridge University Press, 2001. xix, 348 p.
99-054879 338.951/0091734 0521623227
Rural industries -- China.

HC427.92.W655 1991
Woo, Henry K. H., 1946-
Effective reform in China: an agenda/ Henry K.H. Woo. New York: Praeger, 1991. viii, 260 p.
90-045197 338.951 0275937402
Socialism -- China. China -- Economic conditions -- 1976- China -- Economic policy -- 1976-

HC427.92.W853 1994
Wu, Yu-Shan.
Comparative economic transformations: mainland China, Hungary, the Soviet Union, and Taiwan/ Yu-Shan Wu. Stanford, Calif.: Stanford University Press, 1994. xii, 282 p.
94-020504 338.9 0804723885
Right of property -- China. Mixed economy -- China. Comparative economics. China -- Economic conditions -- 1976- Hungary -- Economic policy. Soviet Union -- Economic policy -- 1917-1928.

HC428.C34.I38 1996
Ikels, Charlotte.
The return of the god of wealth: the transition to a market economy in urban China/ Charlotte Ikels. Stanford, Calif.: Stanford University Press, c1996. viii, 311 p.
95-034237 0804725802
Mixed economy -- China -- Guangzhou. Guangzhou (China) -- Economic conditions. Guangzhou (China) -- Economic policy.

HC428.N6.B37 1993
Barnett, A. Doak.
China's far West: four decades of change/ A. Doak Barnett. Boulder: Westview Press, 1993. xiii, 688 p.
93-004194 330.951/405 0813317738
China, Northwest -- Economic conditions. China, Southwest -- Economic conditions. China -- Politics and government -- 1949-

HC428.S52.P66 1993
Pomeranz, Kenneth.
The making of a hinterland: state, society, and economy in inland North China, 1853-1937/ Kenneth Pomeranz. Berkeley: University of California Press, c1993. xxiii, 336 p.
92-017008 338.951/14 0520080513
Shandong Sheng (China) -- Economic policy. Shandong Sheng (China) -- Economic conditions.

HC428.T23
Gilley, Bruce, 1966-
Model rebels: the rise and fall of China's richest village/ Bruce Gilley. Berkeley: University of California Press, c2001. xvi, 219 p.
00-022321 330.951/154 21 0520225325
Yu, Zuomin -- Political activity. Crime -- China -- Daqiuzhuang. Peasantry -- China -- Daqiuzhuang. Daqiuzhuang (China) -- Economic conditions.

HC430.C6.G56 2000
Gillette, Maris Boyd.
Between Mecca and Beijing: modernization and consumption among urban Chinese Muslims/ Maris Boyd Gillette. Stanford, Calif.: Stanford University Press, c2000. xii, 279 p.
00-027259 306.3/0951/43 21 0804736944
Consumption (Economics) -- China -- Xi'an (Shaanxi Sheng) Muslims -- China -- Xi'an (Shaanxi Sheng) Xi'an (Shaanxi Sheng, China) -- Social conditions.

HC430.C6.L48 1999
Li, CongHua.
China: the consumer revolution/ by CongHua Li, Deloitte & Touche Consulting Group. Singapore; J. Wiley & Sons, c1999. xx, 247 p.
97-035917 381.3/0951 21 0471248622
Consumers -- China. Consumption (Economics) -- China.

HC430.I5 C484 2001
China's retreat from equality: income distribution and economic transition/ Carl Riskin, Zhao Renwei, Li Shi, editors. Armonk, N.Y.: M.E. Sharpe, c2001. xvi, 358 p.
00-052214 339.2/0951 21 0765606917
Income distribution -- China.

HC430.Z6.P35 1997
Pak, Chong-dong.
The special economic zones of China and their impact on its economic development/ Jung-Dong Park. Westport, Conn: Praeger, 1997. xvii, 219 p.
96-026875 338.951 027595613X
Economic zoning -- China. Investments, Foreign -- China. China -- Economic policy -- 1976-

HC430.25 By region or country — Asia — Outer Mongolia. Mongolian People's Republic

HC430.25.M65 1991
The Mongolian People's Republic: toward a market economy/ by Elizabeth Milne ... [et al.]. Washington, D.C.: International Monetary Fund, c1991. viii, 81 p.
91-004710 338.951/7 1557752079
Mixed economy -- Mongolia. Mongolia -- Economic policy. Mongolia -- Economic conditions.

HC430.5 By region or country — Asia — Taiwan. Formosa

HC430.5.C67 1989
Clark, Cal, 1945-
Taiwan's development: implications for contending political economy paradigms/ Cal Clark. New York: Greenwood Press, 1989. xvi, 269 p.
89-007494 338.95124/9 0313254486
Taiwan -- Economic policy -- 1945- Taiwan -- Economic conditions -- 1945- Taiwan -- Politics and government -- 1945-

HC430.5.H6
Ho, Sam P. S.
Economic development of Taiwan, 1860-1970/ Samuel P. S. Ho. New Haven: Yale University Press, 1978. xx, 461 p.
77-005555 330.951/249 0300020872
Taiwan -- Economic conditions -- To 1945. Taiwan -- Economic conditions -- 1945-1975.

HC430.5.K57 1995
Klintworth, Gary,
New Taiwan, New China: Taiwan's changing role in the Asia-Pacific region/ Gary Klintworth. 1st ed. Melbourne: Longman; 1995. viii, 328 p.
95-017233 337.5124/9 20 031212550X
Taiwan -- Economic conditions -- 1975- Taiwan -- Politics and government -- 1988- Taiwan -- Foreign economic relations -- Pacific Area. Pacific Area -- Foreign economic relations -- Taiwan. China -- Economic conditions -- 1976-

HC430.5.M38 1998
McBeath, Gerald A.
Wealth and freedom: Taiwan's new political economy/ Gerald A. McBeath. Aldershot; Ashgate, c1998. viii, 288 p.
97-039118 338.95124/9 21 1840140410
Taiwan -- Economic conditions -- 1945- Taiwan -- Social conditions -- 1945- Taiwan -- Politics and government -- 1945-

HC430.5.T296 2002
Taiwan in the global economy: from an agrarian economy to an exporter of high-tech products/ edited by Peter C.Y. Chow; foreword by Robert E. Lipsey. Westport, Conn.: Praeger, 2002. xxx, 284 p.
2001-036679 337.5124/9 21 0275970795
Globalization.

HC430.5.T88 1991
Two societies in opposition: the Republic of China and the People's Republic of China after forty years/ edited by Ramon H. Myers. Stanford, Calif.: Hoover Institution Press, 1991. liii, 370 p.
90-049364 951.05/9 0817990917
Taiwan -- Economic conditions -- 1945- Taiwan -- Social conditions -- 1945- Taiwan -- Politics and government -- 1945-

HC430.6-440.8 By region or country — Asia — South Asia

HC430.6.R67 1985
Rosen, George, 1920-
Western economists and Eastern societies: agents of change in South Asia, 1950-1970/ George Rosen. Baltimore: Johns Hopkins University Press, c1985. xxii, 270 p.
84-004370 338.91/0954 0801831873
Technical assistance -- South Asia -- History. Economic development projects -- India -- History. Economic development projects -- Pakistan -- History.

HC430.6.S59 1990
Singh, Inderjit, 1941-
The great ascent: the rural poor in South Asia/ Inderjit Singh. Baltimore: Published for the World Bank, the Johns Hopkins c1990. xxvii, 444 p.
90-005122 338.954/09173/4 0801839548
Rural poor -- South Asia. Agricultural productivity -- South Asia -- Regional disparities. South Asia -- Economic conditions -- Regional disparities.

HC433.B47 1993
Bhagwati, Jagdish N.,
India in transition: freeing the economy/ Jagdish Bhagwati. Oxford [England]: Clarendon Press; viii, 108 p.
93-016303 338.954 20 0198288476
India -- Economic policy -- 1947- India -- Politics and government -- 1947-

HC433.C35 1982
The Cambridge economic history of India/ edited by Tapan Raychaudhuri and Irfan Habib. Cambridge [Eng.]; Cambridge University Press, [1982-] v. 1.
80-040454 330.954 0521226929
India -- Economic conditions.

HC434.L35 1988
Lal, Deepak.
Cultural stability and economic stagnation: India, c. 1500 BC - AD 1980/ Deepak Lal. Oxford: Clarendon Press; 1988. xxvii, 345 p.
88-017916 330.954 0198284985
India -- Economic conditions. India -- Social conditions. India -- History.

HC435.I8328 2000
Institutions, incentives, and economic reforms in India/ edited by Satu Kähkönen, Anthony Lanyi. New Delhi; Sage, 2000. 516 p.
00-024741 338.954 21 8170368944
Privatization -- India. Tax incentives -- India. Finance -- India.

HC435.R77 1987
Rudolph, Lloyd I.
In pursuit of Lakshmi: the political economy of the Indian state/ Lloyd I. Rudolph and Susanne Hoeber Rudolph. Chicago: University of Chicago Press, 1987. xvii, 529 p.
86-024903 338.954 0226731383
India -- Economic policy -- 1947- India -- Economic conditions -- 1947- India -- Politics and government -- 1947-

HC435.2.B383 1992
Becker, Charles M., 1954-
Indian urbanization and economic growth since 1960/ Charles M. Becker, Jeffrey G. Williamson, and Edwin S. Mills. Baltimore: Johns Hopkins University Press, c1992. xiv, 328 p.
90-028392 307.76/0954 0801841798
Urbanization -- India. Rural-urban migration -- India. Cities and towns -- India -- Growth. India -- Economic conditions -- 1947-

HC435.2.B449 1992
Bhalla, A. S.
Uneven development in the Third World: a study of China and India/ A.S. Bhalla. New York: St. Martin's Press, 1992. xix, 353 p.
91-024074 338.951 0312068212
India -- Economic policy -- 1947- India -- Economic conditions -- 1947- China -- Economic policy -- 1949-

HC435.2.C467 1987
Chakravarty, Sukhamoy.
Development planning: the Indian experience/ Sukhamoy Chakravarty. Oxford [Oxfordshire]: Clarendon Press; 1987. viii, 137 p.
87-001554 338.954 0198285558
India -- Economic policy -- 1947- India -- Social policy.

HC435.2.D2927 1994
Dandekar, Vinayak Mahadev, 1920-
The Indian economy, 1947-92/ V.M. Dandekar. New Delhi; Sage Publications, 1994-1996 v. 1-2.
94-031777 330.954/04 0803991851
India -- Economic conditions -- 1947-

HC435.2.I5327 1997
The India handbook/ edited by C. Steven LaRue ... [et al.]. Chicago: Fitzroy Dearborn Publishers, c1997. viii, 335 p.
98-122585 1884964893
Economic forecasting -- India.

HC435.2.I55464 1998
The Indian economy: major debates since independence/ edited by Terence J. Byres. Delhi; Oxford University Press, 1998. 424 p.
98-902982   0195644603
India -- Economic policy -- 1980- India -- Economic conditions -- 1947-

HC435.2.M825 1984
Mukherjee, Pranab, 1935-
Beyond survival: emerging dimensions of Indian economy/ Pranab Mukherjee. New Delhi: Vikas, c1984. vii, 257 p.
84-901728   338.954   0706926587
India -- Economic policy -- 1947- India -- Economic conditions -- 1947-

HC435.2.R67 2000
Roy, Tirthankar.
The economic history of India, 1857-1947/ Tirthankar Roy. New Delhi; Oxford University Press, 2000. xvi, 318 p.
00-411997   0195651545
India economic conditions -- 19th century. India economic conditions -- 20th century.

HC435.2.S494 1999
Sharma, Shalendra D., 1958-
Development and democracy in India/ Shalendra D. Sharma. Boulder, Colo.: Lynne Rienner Publishers, 1999. ix, 281 p.
99-026091   338.954   1555878105
Rural development -- India. Democracy -- India. India -- Economic conditions -- 1947- India -- Economic policy -- 1980- India -- Politics and government -- 1977-

HC435.2.U64 1984
Uppal, J. S., 1927-
Indian economic planning: three decades of development/ J.S. Uppal. Delhi: Macmillan India Ltd., 1984. 140 p.
84-901162   338.954   0333904516
India -- Economic policy -- 1947-

HC437.W44.M35 1993
Mallick, Ross.
Development policy of a communist government: West Bengal since 1977/ Ross Mallick. Cambridge [England]; Cambridge University Press, 1993. xiv, 236 p.
92-020010   338.954/14/009047   0521432928
Communism -- India -- West Bengal. West Bengal (India) -- Economic policy.

HC438.T47.G68 1989
Gough, Kathleen, 1925-
Rural change in southeast India, 1950s to 1980s/ Kathleen Gough. Delhi: Oxford University Press, 1989. xix, 578 p.
89-207631
Rural development -- India -- Thanjavur (District) Thanjavur (India: District) -- Politics and government. Thanjavur (India: District) -- Economic conditions.

HC438.V57.N34
Nafziger, E. Wayne.
Class, caste and entrepreneurship: a study of Indian industrialists/ E. Wayne Nafziger. Honolulu: Published for the East-West Center by the Univer c1978. x, 188 p.
78-016889   301.44/47/0954   0824805755
Businesspeople -- India -- Visakhapatnam. Businesspeople -- India. Entrepreneurship -- Case studies.

HC439.M35 1996
Maharatna, Arup.
The demography of famines: an Indian historical perspective/ Arup Maharatna. Delhi: Oxford University Press, 1996. xviii, 317 p.
96-900514   0195637119
Famines -- India -- History. Demography -- India. Population -- India.

HC440.E44.P37 1999
Parasuraman, S.
The development dilemma: displacement in India/ S. Parasuraman; with an introductory study by Michael M. Cernea. New York: St. Martin's Press in association with Institute 1999. xxi, 299 p.
98-030659   338.954   0312220103
Economic development projects -- Social aspects -- India. Socially handicapped -- India. Land settlement -- India.

HC440.I5.S58 2000
Sivasubramonian, S.
The national income of India in the twentieth century/ S. Sivasubramonian. New Delhi; Oxford University Press, 2000. xxx, 665 p.
00-410447   0195650506
National income -- India. Savings and investment -- India.

HC440.P6.C87 2000
Currie, Bob, 1965-
The politics of hunger in India: a study of democracy, governance, and Kalahandi's poverty/ Bob Currie. Houndmills, Basingstoke, Hampshire: Macmillan Press; 2000. xxv, 275 p.
99-053055   363.8/8/095413   0333735285
Poverty -- India -- Kalahandi (District) Hunger - India -- Kalahandi (District) Hunger -- Government policy -- India -- Kalahandi (District) Kalahandi (India: District) -- Politics and government.

HC440.P6.E243 1993
Echeverri-Gent, John.
The state and the poor: public policy and political development in India and the United States/ John Echeverri-Gent. Berkeley: University of California Press, c1993. xi, 312 p.
92-028991   362.5/8/0954   0520080823
Rural poor -- Government policy -- India. Rural poor -- Government policy -- United States. Rural development -- Government policy -- India. India -- Social conditions -- 1947- United States -- Social conditions -- 1933-1945.

HC440.T4 K56 2002
The knowledge economy in India/ edited by Frank-Jürgen Richter & Parthasarathi Banerjee; with a foreword by Narayana Murthy. New York: Palgrave Macmillan, 2002.
2002-025816   338.954/06 21   1403901104
Technological innovations -- Economic aspects -- India.

HC440.5.A723 1984
Ahmed, Viqar.
The management of Pakistan's economy, 1947-82/ Viqar Ahmed and Rashid Amjad. Karachi; Oxford University Press, 1984. xi, 315 p.
85-159341   338.9549/1   0195773160
Pakistan -- Economic policy.

HC440.5.H747 1999
Husain, Ishrat,
Pakistan: the economy of an elitist state/ Ishrat Husain. Karachi; Oxford University Press, 1999. xvi, 451 p.
99-210405   330.95491 21   0195790146
Pakistan -- Economic conditions.

HC440.5.L66 1997
Looney, Robert E.
The Pakistani economy: economic growth and structural reform/ Robert E. Looney. Westport, Conn: Praeger, 1997. xii, 199 p.
96-037731   338.95491   0275947378
Pakistan -- Economic policy. Pakistan -- Economic conditions.

HC440.5.P35 1983
Pakistan, the roots of dictatorship: the political economy of a praetorian state/ Hassan Gardezi and Jamil Rashid, editors. London: Zed Press; 1983. xvii, 394 p.
83-225418   338.9549/2   0862320461
Debts, External -- Pakistan. Islam and politics -- Pakistan. Pakistan -- Economic policy. Pakistan -- Social policy.

HC440.5.P3638 1999
Pal, Izzud-Din.
Pakistan, Islam, and economics: failure of modernity/ Izzud-Din Pal. Karachi: Oxford University Press, 1999. xxiii, 195 p.
99-921971   330.95491 21   0195790685
Islam and state -- Pakistan. Economics -- Religious aspects -- Islam.

HC440.8.Z9.P6155 1995
Holcombe, Susan.
Managing to empower: the Grameen Bank's experience of poverty alleviation/ Susan Higinbotham Holcombe; with a foreword by James Gustave Speth. [Atlantic Highlands], NJ: Zed Books, 1995. 203 p.
95-013955   332.2/8/095492   1856493156
Poverty -- Bangladesh. Economic assistance, Domestic -- Bangladesh. Bank management -- Bangladesh.

HC441-455 By region or country — Asia — Southeastern Asia. Indochina

HC441.B69 1997
Bowie, Alasdair.
The politics of open economies: Indonesia, Malaysia, the Philippines, and Thailand/ Alasdair Bowie and Danny Unger. Cambridge, U.K.; Cambridge University Press, xi, 245 p.
96-049358   330.959 21   0521586836
Asia, Southeastern -- Economic policy. Asia, Southeastern -- Economic conditions.

HC441.B75 1997
Brown, Ian, 1947-
Economic change in South-East Asia, c.1830-1980/ Ian Brown. Kuala Lumpur; Oxford University Press, 1997. xvii, 300 p.
96-043168   330.959   9835600147
Asia, Southeastern -- Economic conditions. Asia, Southeastern -- History -- 19th century. Asia, Southeastern -- History -- 20th century.

HC441.P645 2001
The political economy of South-East Asia: conflicts, crises and change/ edited by Garry Rodan, Kevin Hewison and Richard Robison. 2nd ed. Melbourne: Oxford University Press, 2001. xx, 316 p.
2001-536286   330.959 21   0195513495
Asia, Southeastern -- Economic conditions. Asia, Southeastern -- Politics and government -- 1945-

HC441.T663 2002
Tongzon, Jose L.,
The economies of Southeast Asia: before and after the crisis/ Jose L. Tongzon. 2nd ed. Cheltenham, UK; Edward Elgar Pub., c2002. xiv, 308 p.
2002-022846   330.959 21   1840643188
Asia, Southeastern -- Economic conditions. Asia, Southeastern -- Economic integration.

HC441.Z9 E538 2003
Fahn, James.
A land on fire: the environmental consequences of the Southeast Asian boom/ James Fahn. Boulder, Colo.: Westview Press, c2003.
2002-153121   333.7/0959 21   0813340535
Environmental policy -- Asia, Southeastern. Pollution -- Asia, Southeastern.

HC442.M87
Murray, Martin J.
The development of capitalism in colonial Indochina (1870-1940)/ Martin J. Murray. Berkeley: University of California Press, c1980. xii, 685 p.
80-016472   330.9597/03   0520040007
Capitalism. Indochina -- Economic conditions.

HC443.L365 1997
Laos' dilemmas and options: the challenge of economic transition in the 1990s/ edited by Mya Than & Joseph L.H. Tan. New York: St. Martin's Press; 1997. xiv, 319 p.
96-049102   320.9594   0312173105
Laos -- Economic policy. Laos -- Economic conditions.

HC444.F458 1996
Fforde, Adam.
From plan to market: the economic transition in Vietnam/ Adam Fforde and Stefan de Vylder. Boulder, Colo.: Westview Press, 1996. xiii, 358 p.
96-001080   338.9597   0813326842
Vietnam -- Economic policy. Vietnam -- Economic conditions.

HC444.H37 1997
Harvie, Charles, 1954-
Vietnam's reforms and economic growth/ Charles Harvie and Tran Van Hoa. Houndmills, Basingstoke, Hampshire: MacMillan Press Ltd; 1997. xiv, 232 p.
96-030026   338.9597   0333689488
Economic forecasting -- Vietnam. Vietnam -- Economic policy. Vietnam -- Economic conditions.

HC444.T732 2002
Tran-Nam, Binh,
The Vietnamese economy: awakening the dormant dragon/ Binh Tran-Nam, Chi Do Pham. New York: Routledge, 2002.
2002-068228   330.9597 21   041529651X
Vietnam -- Economic conditions -- 1975-

HC444.V593 1990
Vo, Nhan Tri.
Vietnam's economic policy since 1975/ Vo Nhan Tri. Singapore: ASEAN Economic Research Unit, Institute of South c1990. xii, 253 p.
90-944752   338.9597   9813035609
Vietnam -- Economic policy.

HC445.B45 1998
Bello, Walden F.
A Siamese tragedy: development and disintegration in modern Thailand / Walden Bello, Shea Cunningham, and Li Kheng Poh. Oakland Calif.: Food First; xiv, 267 p.
98-030887   338.9593 21   0935028749
Environmental degradation -- Thailand. Rural development -- Thailand. Human rights -- Thailand.

HC445.D59 1999
Dixon, C. J.
The Thai economy: uneven development and internationalisation/ Chris Dixon. London; Routledge, 1999. xx, 316 p.
98-004882   330.9593/044   0415024420
Thailand -- Economic conditions.

HC445.P39 2002
Pasuk Phongpaichit.
Thailand, economy and politics/ Pasuk Phongpaichit, Chris Baker. 2nd ed. Oxford; Oxford University Press, c2002. xvii, 509 p.
2002-022021   330.9593 21   983560066X
Thailand -- Economic conditions. Thailand -- Politics and government.

HC445.5.C52 1990
Cho, George, 1946-
The Malaysian economy: spatial perspectives/ George Cho. London; Routledge, 1990. xv, 314 p.
89-024185   330.9595/054   0415020964
Malaysia -- Economic conditions. Malaysia -- Social conditions. Malaysia -- Rural conditions.

HC445.5.F66 1989
Fong, Chan Onn.
The Malaysian economic challenge in the 1990s: transformation for growth/ Fong Chan Onn. Singapore: Longman, c1989. xxi, 346 p.
90-942330   338.9595   9971899663
Malaysia -- Economic policy. Malaysia -- Economic conditions. Malaysia -- Social conditions.

HC445.5.G65 1999
Gomez, Edmund Terence.
Malaysia's political economy: politics, patronage and profits/ Edmund Terence Gomez and Jomo K.S. 2nd ed. Cambridge; Cambridge University Press, 1999. xix, 228 p.
99-030801   338.9595 21   0521663687
Malaysia -- Economic conditions. Malaysia -- Economic policy. Malaysia -- Politics and government.

HC445.5.J65 1990
Jomo K. S.
Growth and structural change in the Malaysian economy/ Jomo K.S. New York: St. Martin's Press, 1990. xxii, 262 p.
90-032159   338.9595 20   0312047401
Malaysia -- Economic conditions. Malaysia -- Economic policy.

HC445.5.Y68
Young, Kevin, 1945-
Malaysia, growth and equity in a multiracial society/ Kevin Young, Willem C.F. Bussink, Parvez Hasan, coordinating authors. Baltimore: Published for the World Bank [by] Johns Hopkins c1980. xix, 345 p.
79-003677   330.9595/053   0801823846
Malaysia -- Economic conditions. Malaysia -- Economic policy.

HC445.5.Z9 I51834 1986
Mehmet, Ozay.
Development in Malaysia: poverty, wealth, and trusteeship/ Ozay Mehmet. London; Croom Helm, c1986. 183 p.
85-029079   338.9595 19   0709935250
Income distribution -- Malaysia. Elite (Social sciences) -- Malaysia.

HC445.8.H84 1994
Huff, W. G.
The economic growth of Singapore: trade and development in the twentieth century/ W.G. Huff. Cambridge; Cambridge University Press, 1994. xxi, 472 p.
93-003977   338.95957/009/04 20   052137037X
Singapore -- Economic conditions. Singapore -- Economic policy. Singapore -- Commerce. Singapore -- Strategic aspects. Singapore -- Emigration and immigration -- Economic aspects.

HC445.8.P44 1996
Peebles, Gavin, 1947-
The Singapore economy/ Gavin Peebles and Peter Wilson. Cheltenham; Edward Elgar, c1996. xii, 286 p.
95-036676   330.95957 20   1858982863
Singapore -- Economic conditions. Singapore -- Economic policy.

HC447.E495 2002
The emergence of a national economy: an economic history of Indonesia, 1800-2000/ Howard Dick ... [et al.]. Crows Nest, Australia: Asian Studies Association of Australia in xvii, 286 p.
2001-052255   330.9598 21   0824825527
Indonesia -- Economic conditions.

HC447.H55 2000
Hill, Hal,
The Indonesian economy/ Hal Hill. 2nd ed. Cambridge, UK; Cambridge University Press, 2000. xviii, 366 p.
99-054121   338.9598 21   0521663679
Indonesia -- Economic policy. Indonesia -- Economic conditions -- 1945-

HC447.I55635 1999
Indonesia: the challenge of change/ edited by Richard W. Baker ... [et al.]. New York: St. Martin's Press, 1999. xx, 305 p.
98-050388   338.9598 21   0312222610
Indonesia -- Economic conditions -- 1945- Indonesia -- Politics and government -- 1998- Indonesia -- Social conditions.

HC447.O45 1992
The Oil boom and after: Indonesian economic policy and performance in the Soeharto era/ edited by Anne Booth. Singapore; Oxford University Press, 1992. xxvi, 448 p.
91-023712   338.9598/009/047   019588969X
Petroleum industry and trade -- Indonesia. Indonesia -- Economic conditions -- 1945- Indonesia -- Economic policy.

HC453.D67 1992
Doronila, Amando, 1928-
The state, economic transformation, and political change in the Philippines, 1946-1972/ Amando Doronila. Singapore; Oxford University Press, 1992. xii, 199 p.
91-036771   338.9599/009/04   0195885775
Philippines -- Economic policy. Philippines -- Economic conditions -- 1946-1986. Philippines -- Politics and government -- 1946-1973.

HC455.H53
Hicks, George L.
Trade and growth in the Philippines; an open dual economy [by] George L. Hicks and Geoffrey McNicoll. Ithaca, Cornell University Press [1971] xi, 244 p.
73-139507   330.9599/04   0801406129
Dual economy -- Philippines.

HC455.P469 2003
The Philippine economy: development, policies, and challenges/ edited by Arsenio M. Balisacan, Hal Hill. Oxford; Oxford University Press, 2003. xxv, 466 p.
2002-031180   330.9599 21   0195158970
Philippines -- Economic conditions -- 1986-Philippines -- Economic policy. Philippines -- Social conditions.

HC455.Y67 1985
Yoshihara, Kunio, 1939-
Philippine industrialization: foreign and domestic capital/ Yoshihara Kunio. Quezon City, Metro Manila: Ateneo de Manila University Press; 1985. x, 180 p.
86-149596   338.6/041/09599   9711130432
Industrialization -- Philippines. Investments -- Philippines. Investments, Foreign -- Philippines.

HC460.5-470.3 By region or country — Asia — East Asia. Far East

HC460.5.A516 1994
Abegglen, James C.
Sea change: Pacific Asia as the new world industrial center/ James C. Abegglen. New York: Free Press; xiv, 290 p.
93-036426   338.095 20   0029001552
Competition, International.

HC460.5.C258 2000
Camilleri, Joseph A., 1944-
States, markets and civil society in Asia-Pacific/ Joseph A. Camilleri. Northampton, MA: Edward Elgar Pub., [2000-] v. <1 >
00-034816   338.95   1858988381
National security -- East Asia. National security -- Pacific Area. East Asia -- Politics and government. Pacific Area -- Politics and government. East Asia -- Economic policy.

HC460.5.C66 1989
Confucianism and economic development: an oriental alternative?/ edited by Hung-chao Tai. Washington, D.C.: Washington Institute Press, c1989. x, 233 p.
89-005483   338.95   0887020488
Confucianism -- Economic aspects. East Asia -- Economic policy. Singapore -- Economic policy.

HC460.5.E275 1993
The East Asian miracle: economic growth and public policy. New York, N.Y.: Oxford University Press, c1993. xvii, 389 p.
93-030466   338.95   0195209931
East Asia -- Economic policy. East Asia -- Economic conditions. Asia, Southeastern -- Economic policy.

HC460.5.F683 1998
The four Asian tigers: economic development and the global political economy/ edited by Eun Mee Kim. San Diego, CA: Academic Press, 1998. xxi, 234 p.
98-084346   337.5   0124074405
Finance -- East Asia. East Asia -- Foreign economic relations. East Asia -- Economic conditions. Korea (South) -- Economic conditions.

HC460.5.L47 1997
Lessons from East Asia/ edited by Danny M. Leipziger. Ann Arbor: University of Michigan Press, c1997. xi, 590 p.
96-035267   338.95 20   0472106791
Economic development.

HC460.5.N63 1998
Noble, Gregory W.
Collective action in East Asia: how ruling parties shape industrial policy/ Gregory W. Noble. Ithaca: Cornell University Press, 1998. xi, 249 p.
98-036834   338.954   0801431778
Industrial policy -- East Asia. Industrialization -- East Asia. East Asia -- Economic policy.

HC460.5.R38 2000
Ravich, Samantha Fay.
Marketization and democracy: East Asian experiences/ Samantha F. Ravich. Cambridge; Cambridge University Press, 2000. xv, 277 p.
99-040315   320.45/09/045   052166165X
Free trade -- East Asia -- Econometric models. Democracy -- East Asia. East Asia -- Economic policy. East Asia -- Economic conditions -- Econometric models. East Asia -- Politics and government.

HC460.5.R48 2001
Rethinking the East Asia miracle/ Joseph E. Stiglitz and Shahid Yusuf, editors. Washington, D.C.: World Bank; x, 526 p.
00-051329   330.95/0429 21   0195216008
Finance -- East Asia.

HC460.5.S63 1995
So, Alvin Y., 1953-
East Asia and the world economy/ Alvin Y. So, Stephen W.K. Chiu. Thousand Oaks, CA: Sage Publications, c1995. xii, 307 p.
95-010325   337.5   0803948999
International economic relations. International trade. East Asia -- Economic conditions. East Asia -- Commercial policy.

HC460.5.T56 1998
Tipton, Frank B.,
The rise of Asia: economy, society, and politics in the industrial age/ Frank B. Tipton. Honolulu, Hi.: University of Hawaii Press, c1998. xiv, 527 p.
97-047687   330.95 21   0824820568
East Asia -- Economic conditions. Asia, Southeastern -- Economic conditions. East Asia -- Social conditions. Asia, Southeastern -- Social conditions. East Asia -- Politics and government. Asia, Southeastern -- Politics and government.

HC460.5.V64 1991
Vogel, Ezra F.
The four little dragons: the spread of industrialization in East Asia/ Ezra F. Vogel. Cambridge, Mass.: Harvard University Press, 1991. x, 138 p.
91-016051   338.095   0674315251
Industrialization -- East Asia. East Asia -- Economic conditions.

HC462.K63 1990
Komiya, Ryutaro, 1928-
The Japanese economy: trade, industry, and government/ Ryutaro Komiya. [Tokyo]: University of Tokyo Press, c1990. xiii, 396 p.
91-152986   338.952   4130470485
Industries -- Japan. Industrial policy -- Japan. Japan -- Economic policy. Japan -- Commercial policy.

HC462.S36
Schumpeter, Elizabeth Boody,
The industrialization of Japan and Manchuko, 1930-1940: population, raw materials and industry, edited by E. B. Schumpeter. Contributors: G. C. Allen, E. F. Penrose, M. S. Gordon [and] E. B. Schumpeter. New York, The Macmillan Company, 1940. xxviii, 944 p.
40-035446   338.0952/09/043
Japan -- Economic conditions -- 1918- Japan -- Industries. Japan -- Population. Manchuria (China) -- Economic conditions.

HC462.S47 1993
Sheridan, Kyoko.
Governing the Japanese economy/ Kyoko Sheridan. Cambridge, UK: Polity Press; 1993. ix, 331 p.
92-046616   338.952   0745610609
Industrial policy -- Japan -- History. Japan -- Economic policy.

HC462.5.I86 2000
Ito, Makoto, 1936-
The Japanese economy reconsidered/ Makoto Itoh. Houndmills, Basingstoke, Hampshire; PALGRAVE, 2000. xiv, 153 p.
00-041488   330.952   0333665198
Japan -- Economic conditions -- 1945-

HC462.7.H25 1975
Halliday, Jon.
A political history of Japanese capitalism/ Jon Halliday. 1st ed. New York: Pantheon Books, [1975] xxxiii, 466 p.
74-004774   330.9/52/03   039448391X
Japan -- Economic conditions -- 1868- Japan -- Economic policy. Japan -- Politics and government -- 1868-

HC462.9.D663 1987
Dore, Ronald Philip.
Taking Japan seriously: a Confucian perspective on leading economic issues/ Ronald Dore. Stanford, Calif.: Stanford University Press, 1987. ix, 264 p.
86-061030   338.952   0804713502
Industries -- Japan. Industrial policy -- Japan. Industries -- Great Britain.

HC462.9.G74 2001
Grimes, William W.
Unmaking the Japanese miracle: macroeconomic politics, 1985-2000/ William W. Grimes. Ithaca, N.Y.: Cornell University Press, 2001. xix, 254 p.
00-012396   339.5/0952   0801438497
Structural adjustment (Economic policy) -- Japan. Japan -- Economic policy -- 1989-

HC462.9.I587 1988
Inside the Japanese system: readings on contemporary society and political economy/ edited by Daniel I. Okimoto and Thomas P. Rohlen. Stanford, Calif.: Stanford University Press, c1988. xiii, 286 p.
87-018820   330.952/04   0804714258
Japan -- Economic conditions -- 1945-1989. Japan -- Social conditions -- 1945- Japan -- Politics and government -- 1945-

HC462.9.N397 1990
Nester, William R., 1956-
Japan's growing predominance over East Asia and the world economy/ William R. Nester. New York: St. Martin's Press, 1990. xiv, 282 p.
89-035713   382/.0952   0312035306
Japan -- Economic policy -- 1989- Japan -- Foreign economic relations -- East Asia. East Asia -- Foreign economic relations -- Japan.

HC462.9.P4 1982
Pempel, T. J., 1942-
Policy and politics in Japan: creative conservatism/ T.J. Pempel. Philadelphia: Temple University Press, 1982. xix, 330 p.
81-014464   338.952   0877222495
Public administration -- Decision making. Japan -- Economic policy -- 1945- Japan -- Social policy. Japan -- Politics and government -- 1945-

HC462.9.P57 1987
The Political economy of Japan. Stanford, Calif.: Stanford University Press, 1987-1992. 3 v.
86-030037   338.952   0804713804
Japan -- Economic conditions -- 1945- Japan -- Economic policy -- 1945-1989. Japan -- Foreign economic relations.

HC462.9.U2613 1983
Uchino, Tatsuro, 1925-
Japan's postwar economy: an insider's view of its history and its future/ by Tatsuro Uchino; translated by Mark A. Harbison. Tokyo; Kodansha International, 1983. 286 p.
83-047621   330.952/04   0870115952
Japan -- Economic conditions -- 1945-1989. Japan -- Economic policy -- 1945-1989.

HC462.95.H84 1994
Huber, Thomas M.
Strategic economy in Japan/ Thomas M. Huber. Boulder: Westview Press, 1994. ix, 173 p.
93-043012   338.952   0813320925
Industrial policy -- Japan.   Japan -- Economic policy -- 1989-

HC462.95.K388 2003
Katz, Richard,
Japanese Phoenix: the long road to economic revival/ Richard Katz. Armonk, N.Y.: M.E. Sharpe, c2003. xvi, 351 p.
2002-029408   338.952 21   0765610736
Structural adjustment (Economic policy) -- Japan. Economic stabilization -- Japan. Globalization.

HC462.95.T34 1991
Takenaka, Heizo.
Contemporary Japanese economy and economic policy/ Heizo Takenaka. Ann Arbor: University of Michigan Press, c1991. viii, 208 p.
91-029530   338.952/009/048   0472101978
Japan -- Economic conditions -- 1989- Japan -- Economic policy -- 1989-

HC463.K346 M66 1989
Moon, Okpyo,
From paddy field to ski slope: the revitalisation of tradition in Japanese village life/ Okpyo Moon. Manchester; Manchester University Press; vii, 191 p.
89-012679   307.76/2/0952133 20   0719029570
Rural families -- Japan -- Katashina-mura. Country life -- Japan -- Katashina-mura. Villages -- Japan.

HC465.H53.O35 1989
Okimoto, Daniel I., 1942-
Between MITI and the market: Japanese industrial policy for high technology/ Daniel I. Okimoto. Stanford, Calif.: Stanford University Press, 1989. xv, 267 p.
88-039837   338.4/762/000952   0804712980
High technology industries -- Government policy -- Japan.

HC465.T4.H47 1995
Herbig, Paul A.
Innovation Japanese style: a cultural and historical perspective/ Paul Herbig. Westport, Conn.: Quorum Books, 1995. x, 275 p.
94-039343   338/.064/0952   0899309682
Technological   innovations   --   Japan. Organizational change -- Japan. Research, Industrial -- Japan. Japan -- Economic conditions -- 1945- Japan -- Civilization -- 20th century.

HC467.C41564 1994
Cho, Sun, 1928-
The dynamics of Korean economic development/ Cho Soon. Washington, DC: Institute for Internationsl Economics, 1994. xiv, 216 p.
93-042822   338.95195   0881321621
Industrial promotion -- Korea (South)   Korea (South) -- Economic policy -- 1960- Korea (South) -- Economic conditions -- 1960-

HC467.C6486 1998
Clifford, Mark, 1957-
Troubled tiger: businessmen, bureaucrats, and generals in South Korea/ Mark L. Clifford. Armonk, N.Y.: M.E. Sharpe, c1998. xiii, 373 p.
97-035048   338.95195 21   0765601400
Korea (South) -- Economic policy. Korea (South) -- Economic conditions -- 1948-1960. Korea (South) -- Economic conditions -- 1960-

HC467.H3675 2002
Harvie, Charles,
Korea's economic miracle: fading or reviving?/ Charles Harvie,   Hyun-Hoon Lee. New York: Palgrave, 2002.
2002-022418   330.95195/043 21   0333924991
Korea (South) -- Economic conditions -- 1960- Korea (South) -- Economic policy -- 1960-

HC467.H76 1989
Huer, Jon.
Marching orders: the role of the military in South Korea's "economic miracle," 1961-1971/ Jon Huer. New York: Greenwood Press, 1989. xvi, 219 p.
88-038381   338.9519/5   0313266484
Civil-military relations -- Korea (South)   Korea (South) -- Politics and government -- 1960-1988. Korea (South) -- Economic policy -- 1960-

HC467.K45 1992
Kim, Byoung-lo Philo.
Two Koreas in development: a comparative study of principles and strategies of capitalist and communist Third World development/ Byoung-lo Philo Kim. New Brunswick, N.J., U.S.A.: Transaction Publishers, c1992. xix, 240 p.
91-008160   338.9519   0887384374
Economic development. Capitalism. Communism. Korea (South) -- Social conditions. Korea (North) -- Economic conditions. Korea (North) -- Social conditions.

HC467.N658 2000
Noland, Marcus, 1959-
Avoiding the Apocalypse: the future of the two Koreas/ Marcus Noland. Washington, DC: Institute for International Economics, 2000. xvi, 431 p.
00-038314   338.9519   0881322784
Korea (South) -- Economic policy -- 1960- Korea (North) -- Foreign economic relations. Korea -- Economic conditions -- 1945-

HC467.P22 1992
Pae, Sung M.
Korea leading developing nations: economy, democracy & welfare/ Sung Moon Pae. Lanham, Md.: University Press of America, c1992. xvii, 518 p.
92-016787   330.95195/043   0819187429
Democracy -- Korea (South) Public welfare -- Korea (South)   Korea (South) -- Economic conditions.

HC467.S77 1997
The strains of economic growth: labor unrest and social dissatisfaction in Korea/ David L. Lindauer ... [et al.]. [Cambridge, MA]: Harvard Institute for International Development; xiii, 194 p.
97-005513   338.95193 21   0674839811
Labor disputes -- Korea (South) Social conflict -- Korea (South)

HC467.Y51395 1996
Yi, Hyong-gu, 1940-
The Korean economy: perspectives for the twenty-first century/ Hyung-Koo Lee. Albany: State University of New York Press, c1996. xv, 254 p.
95-039691   330.95195 20   0791428877
Korea (South) -- Economic conditions. Korea (South) -- Economic policy.

HC470.2.E25 1999
Eberstadt, Nick,
The end of North Korea/ Nicholas Eberstadt. Washington, D.C.: AEI Press, 1999. x, 191 p.
99-012628   330.95193 21   0844740888
Korean reunification question (1945-)

HC470.2.Z9 F36 2001
Natsios, Andrew S.
The great North Korean famine/ Andrew S. Natsios. Washington, D.C.: United States Institute of Peace Press, 2001. xxi, 295 p.
2001-039667   363.8/095193 21   1929223331
Famines -- Korea (North) Food supply -- Korea (North)

HC470.3.M87 1990
Mushkat, Miron.
The economic future of Hong Kong/ Miron Mushkat. Boulder: L. Rienner Publishers; 1990. xii, 171 p.
89-070067   330.95125/001/12   1555871976
Economic forecasting -- Hong Kong.   Hong Kong (China) -- Economic conditions.

HC473-480 By region or country — Asia — Iran. Persia

HC473.A48 1990
Amirahmadi, Hooshang, 1947-
Revolution and economic transition: the Iranian experience/ Hooshang Amirahmadi. Albany: State University of New York Press, c1990. xx, 420 p.
90-033035   330.955/054   0791405095
Iran -- Economic conditions -- 1979- Iran -- Economic policy.

HC475.A644 1993
Amuzegar, Jahangir.
Iran's economy under the Islamic Republic/ Jahangir Amuzegar. London; I.B. Tauris; 1993. xi, 398 p.
94-138288   330.955/054   1850436037
Iran -- Economic conditions -- 1979- Iran -- Economic policy.

HC475.B5
Bharier, Julian.
Economic development in Iran, 1900-1970. London, Oxford University Press, 1971. xviii, 314 p.
73-875594   330.955/05   0192153420
Iran -- Economic conditions.

HC480.D4.M64 1990
Mofid, Kamran.
The Economic consequences of the Gulf war./ Kamran Mofid. London; Routledge, 1990. xxiv, 177 p.
90-031657   955.05/4   0415052955
Iran-Iraq War, 1980-1988 -- Economic aspects. Iraq -- defenses -- Economic aspects. Iran -- Defenses -- Economic aspects.

HC491-495 By region or country — Asia — Turkey

HC491.E26
The Economic history of Turkey, 1800-1914/ [edited by] Charles Issawi. Chicago: University of Chicago Press, 1980. xvi, 390 p.
80-000444   330.9561/01   0226386031
Turkey -- Economic conditions.

HC492.E295 1994
An economic and social history of the Ottoman Empire, 1300-1914/ edited by Halil çInalc,k with Donald Quataert. Cambridge; Cambridge University Press, 1994. xxxi, 1026 p.
93-014763   330.9561/015 20   0521343151
Turkey -- Economic conditions -- 1288-1918. Turkey -- Social conditions -- 1288-1918.

HC492.K37 1988
Kasaba, Resat, 1954-
The Ottoman empire and the world economy: the nineteenth century/ Resat Kasaba. Albany: State University of New York Press, c1988. xii, 191 p.
88-003039   330.9561/038   0887068049
Turkey -- Economic conditions. Turkey -- Commerce -- History -- 19th century. Turkey -- Foreign economic relations -- Europe.

HC492.K497 1987
Keyder, Caglar.
State and class in Turkey: a study in capitalist development/ Caglar Keyder. London; Verso, 1987. 252 p.
87-014992   338.9561   0860918777
Capitalism -- Turkey -- History -- 19th century. Capitalism -- Turkey -- History -- 20th century. Social classes -- Turkey -- History -- 19th century. Turkey -- Economic conditions.

HC495.C3.T87 1985
Turkey in the world capitalist system: a study of industrialisation, power, and class/ edited by Huseyin Ramazanoglu. Aldershots, Hants, England; Gower, c1985. xi, 260 p.
85-017587   338.9561   0566050498
Capitalism -- Turkey. Industrial policy -- Turkey. Turkey -- Economic policy.

HC498.A667-R58 By region or country — Arab countries — General works

HC498.A667 1991
Alnasrawi, Abbas.
Arab nationalism, oil, and the political economy of dependency/ Abbas Alnasrawi. New York: Greenwood Press, 1991. x, 221 p.
90-025225   337/.0917/4927   0313276102
Petroleum industry and trade -- Political aspects -- Arab countries. Panarabism. Arab countries -- Economic conditions. Arab countries -- Economic integration. Arab countries -- Dependency on foreign countries.

HC498.A7195 2003
The Arab world competitiveness report 2002-2003. New York: Oxford University Press, 2003. xiii, 394 p.
2003-266572   330.917/4927 21   019516170X
Economic development -- Arab countries. Competition -- Arab countries.

HC498.M75
Musrey, Alfred G.
An Arab common market; a study in inter-Arab trade relations, 1920-67 [by] Alfred G. Musrey. New York, Praeger [1969] xiii, 274 p.
69-014573   382
Arab countries -- Economic integration. Arab countries -- Commerce.

HC498.R5 1982
Rich and poor states in the Middle East: Egypt and the new Arab order/ edited by Malcolm H. Kerr and El Sayed Yassin. Boulder, Colo.: Westview Press; 1982. x, 482 p.
82-153936   338.9/00917/4927   0865312753
Arab countries -- Economic policy.

HC498.R58 2001
Rivlin, Paul.
Economic policy and performance in the Arab world/ Paul Rivlin. Boulder: Lynne Rienner Publishers, 2001. x, 237 p.
00-046001   338.9/00917/4927   1555879322
Arab countries -- Economic policy. Arab countries -- Economic conditions.

HC498.9 By region or country — Arab countries — Special topics, not otherwise provided for, A-Z

HC498.9.D4 S23 1993
Sadowski, Yahya M.
Scuds or butter?: the political economy of arms control in the Middle East/ Yahya M. Sadowski. Washington, D.C.: Brookings Institution, c1993. xii, 116 p.
92-028969   338.4/76234/09174927 20   0815776632
Arms control -- Arab countries. National security -- Arab countries. Military assistance, American -- Arab countries.

HC498.9.P6 E18 2000
Earnings inequality, unemployment, and poverty in the Middle East and North Africa/ edited by Wassim Shahin and Ghassan Dibeh. Westport, Conn.: Greenwood Press, 2000. xiv, 233 p.
99-046153   330.917/49270828 21   0313309779
Poverty -- Arab countries -- Congresses. Wages -- Arab countries -- Congresses. Income distribution -- Arab countries -- Congresses.

HC499 By region or country — Islamic countries

HC499.Z65 P76 2002
Production and the exploitation of resources/ edited by Michael G. Morony. Aldershot, Hampshire, Great Britain; xxxiii, 364 p.
2001-022364   333.7/013/0917671 21   0860787060
Natural resources -- Islamic countries -- History. Industries -- Islamic countries -- History. Labor -- Islamic countries -- History.

HC502-591 By region or country — Africa (General) *See* HC800-1065

HC502.D8413 1966
Dumont, René,
False start in Africa. Translated by Phyllis Nauts Ott. Introd. by Thomas Balogh. With an additional chapter by John Hatch. New York, Praeger [1966] 320 p.
66-016593   338.0967
Africa, Sub-Saharan -- Economic conditions -- 1918-

HC502.H33 1967
Hance, William Adams,
African economic development [by] William A. Hance. Rev. ed. New York, Published for the Council on Foreign Relations [by] Praeger xiv, 326 p.
67-020480   330.96
Africa -- Economic conditions.

HC502.W6 1968b
Woolf, Leonard, 1880-1969.
Empire & commerce in Africa: a study in economic imperialism by Leonard Woolf. London, Allen & Unwin, 1968. viii, 374 p.
79-355226   382
Economic policy. Competition, International. Africa -- Economic conditions -- To 1918. Africa -- Politics and government.

HC503.W4 C87
Curtin, Philip D.
Economic change in precolonial Africa; Senegambia in the era of the slave trade [by] Philip D. Curtin. [Madison] University of Wisconsin Press [1975] xxix, 363 p.
74-005899   330.9/66/301   0299066401
Slave-trade -- Africa, West -- History.

HC517.K4.L49
Leys, Colin.
Underdevelopment in Kenya: the political economy of neo-colonialism, 1964-1971/ Colin Leys. Berkeley: University of California Press, 1974 xv, 284 p.
74-076387   330.9/676/204   0520027310
Kenya -- Economic conditions. Kenya -- Politics and government. Kenya -- Social conditions -- 1963-

HC535.M17
Mabro, Robert.
The Egyptian economy, 1952-1972/ by Robert Mabro. Oxford: Clarendon Press, 1974. xii, 254 p.
74-188342   330.9/62/05   0198770308
Egypt -- Economic conditions -- 1952- Egypt -- Economic policy.

HC591.A3.P24
Pankhurst, Richard.
Economic history of Ethiopia, 1800-1935 [by]
Richard Pankhurst. Addis Ababa, Haile Sellassie I
University Press, 1968. 772 p.
78-009298   330.963
Ethiopia -- Economic conditions.

HC591.C6 Z37
Zaire, the political economy of underdevelopment/
edited by Guy Gran with the assistance of Galen
Hull. New York: Praeger, 1979. xviii, 331 p.
79-019512   330.9/675/103   0030489164
*Congo (Democratic Republic) -- Economic policy.
Congo (Democratic Republic) -- Politics and
government. Congo (Democratic Republic) --
Social conditions. Congo (Democratic Republic) --
Rural conditions. Congo (Democratic Republic) --
Foreign relations -- 1960-1997.*

HC603-605 By region or country — Australia

HC603.D97 1999
Meredith, David,
Australia in the global economy: continuity and
change/ David Meredith, Barrie Dyster.
Cambridge; Cambridge University Press, 1999. xii,
388 p.
99-037270   330.994/066 21   0521637309
*Australia -- Economic conditions. Australia --
Foreign economic relations.*

HC604.B883 1994
Butlin, N. G.
Forming a colonial economy, Australia 1810-1850/
N.G. Butlin. Cambridge; Cambridge University
Press, 1994. viii, 263 p.
94-016623   330.994/02   0521440068
*Australia -- Economic conditions. Australia --
Population. Great Britain -- Colonies -- Economic
policy.*

HC605.W459 1996
Walter, James, 1949-
Tunnel vision: the failure of political imagination/
James Walter. St. Leonards, NSW: Allen & Unwin,
1996. xvii, 152 p.
96-205411   1863737456
*Political parties -- Australia.   Australia --
Politics and government -- 1945- Australia --
Economic policy.*

HC665 By region or country — New Zealand

HC665.M38 1995
Massey, Patrick.
New Zealand: market liberalization in a developed
economy/ Patrick Massey. New York: St. Martin's
Press, 1995. xvi, 245 p.
94-034878   338.993   0333633482
*New Zealand -- Economic policy. New Zealand
-- Economic conditions -- 1945-*

HC681 By region or country — Pacific Area. Pacific Ocean islands. Oceania — General

HC681.J66 1993
Jones, E. L.
Coming full circle: an economic history of the
Pacific Rim/ Eric Jones, Lionel Frost & Colin
White. Boulder: Westview Press, 1993. xv, 188 p.
93-004130   330.9182/3   081331240X
*Pacific Area -- Economic conditions. East Asia
-- Economic conditions.*

HC681.W48 1998
What is in a rim?: critical perspectives on the
Pacific Region idea/ edited by Arif Dirlik. Lanham,
Md: Rowman and Littlefield, c1998. vi, 384 p.
97-028861   330.99 21   0847684687
*Pacific Area -- Economic conditions. Pacific
Area -- Foreign economic relations. Pacific Area --
Politics and government.*

HC681.W54 2000
Wiegersma, Nancy.
US economic development policies towards the
Pacific Rim: successes and failures of US aid/ Nan
Wiegersma and Joseph E. Medley. New York: St.
Martin's Press, 2000. xii, 177 p.
99-054920   338.91/7301823 21   031223130X
*Economic assistance, American -- Pacific Area.
Economic assistance, American -- Asia.*

HC681.3 By region or country — Pacific Area. Pacific Ocean islands. Oceania — Special topics, A-Z

HC681.3.I55.C67 1988
The Cost of thinking: information economies of ten
Pacific countries/ edited by Meheroo Jussawalla,
Donald M. Lamberton, and Neil D. Karunaratne.
Norwood, N.J.: Ablex Pub. Corp., c1988. xii,
249 p.
87-022937   338.4/7004/099   0893914193
*Information technology -- Economic aspects --
Pacific Area.*

HC687 By region or country — Pacific Area. Pacific Ocean islands. Oceania — Samoan Islands

HC687.F5.B4
Belshaw, Cyril S.
Under the ivi tree; society and economic growth in
rural Fiji, by Cyril S. Belshaw. Berkeley,
University of California Press, 1964. xiii, 336 p.
65-007165   330.99611
Fiji -- Economic conditions.

HC687.F5 F72
France, Peter.
The charter of the land; custom and colonization in
Fiji. Melbourne, Oxford University Press, 1969.
xiv, 229 p.
78-428374   333.3/0996/11   0195503058
Land tenure -- Fiji.

HC695 By region or country — Tropics

HC695.K25
Kamarck, Andrew M.
The tropics and economic development: a
provocative inquiry into the poverty of nations/
Andrew M. Kamarck. Baltimore: Published for the
World Bank [by] Johns Hopkins c1976. xiv, 113 p.
76-017242   338.1/09172/4   0801818915
*Tropics -- Economic conditions. Developing
countries -- Economic conditions.*

HC695.Z65 M33 1993
MacKerron, Conrad B.
Business in the rain forests: corporations,
deforestation, and sustainability/ Conrad B.
MacKerron; Douglas G. Cogan, editor.
Washington, D.C.: Investor Responsibility
Research Center, c1993. xiii, 239 p.
94-112489   1879775085
*Natural resources -- Tropics -- Management.
Sustainable development -- Tropics. Rain forests.*

HC704 By region or country — Communist countries

HC704.E258 1990
Economic planning in transition: socio economic
development and planning in post-socialist and
capitalist societies/ edited by Janos Kovacs and
Bruno Dallago. Aldershot, Hants., England;
Dartmouth, c1990. 232 p.
90-045399   338.9/009171/7   1855211130
*Central planning -- Communist countries --
Congresses. Economic policy -- Congresses. Social
policy -- Congresses. Communist countries --
Economic policy -- Congresses. Communist
countries -- Social policy -- Congresses.*

HC704.J34 1990
Jeffries, Ian.
A guide to the socialist economies/ Ian Jeffries.
London; Routledge, 1990. xxii, 322 p.
89-010387   338.9/009171/7   0415007461
*Central planning -- Communist countries.
Central planning -- Soviet Union. Communist
countries -- Economic policy. Soviet Union --
Economic policy.*

HC710 By region or country — Communist countries — Special topics, A-Z

HC710.P6 E24 1988
Eberstadt, Nick,
The poverty of communism/ Nick Eberstadt. New
Brunswick, N.J., USA: Transaction Books, c1988.
x, 317 p.
87-019097   362.5/09171/7 19   088738188X
Poor -- Communist countries. Communism.

HC735 By region or country — Arctic regions

HC735.Y68 1992
Young, Oran R.
Arctic politics: conflict and cooperation in the circumpolar North/ Oran R. Young. Hanover: University Press of New England [for] Dartmouth c1992. xv, 287 p.
92-053869   333.7/0998   0874516056
Natural resources -- Arctic regions. Arctic regions -- Social conditions. Arctic regions -- Economic conditions.

HC800 By region or country — Africa — General

HC800.A5265 2000
Abrahamsen, Rita, 1966-
Disciplining democracy: development discourse and good governance in Africa/ Rita Abrahmsen. London; Zed Books, c2000. xv, 168 p.
00-043430   338.96 21   1856498581
Africa -- Economic policy. Democracy -- Africa. Economic development.

HC800.A53 1989
Abubakar, Ahmad.
Africa and the challenge of development: acquiescence and dependency versus freedom and development/ Ahmad Abubakar. New York: Praeger, 1989. viii, 152 p.
88-032290   338.96   0275932214
Economic assistance -- Africa. Africa -- Economic policy. Africa -- Economic conditions -- 1960- Africa -- Dependency on foreign countries.

HC800 .A55257 1994
Adjusting to policy failure in African economies/ edited by David E. Sahn. Ithaca [N.Y.]: Cornell University Press, c1994. xiv, 421 p.
93-029987   338.967 20   0801481368
Structural adjustment (Economic policy) -- Africa, Sub-Saharan -- Case

HC800.A55258 1994
Adjustment in Africa: reforms, results, and the road ahead. New York, N.Y.: Oxford University Press, c1994. xix, 284 p.
93-047887   338.967 20   019520994X
Structural adjustment (Economic policy) -- Africa, Sub-Saharan.

HC800.A557 1986
Africa in economic crisis/ edited by John Ravenhill. New York: Columbia University Press, 1986. xiii, 359 p.
85-026972   330.967 19   0231063830
Africa, Sub-Saharan -- Economic conditions. World Bank -- Africa, Sub-Saharan.

HC800.A628 2001
Aid and reform in Africa: lessons from ten case studies/ edited by Shantayanan Devarajan, David R. Dollar, Torgny Holmgren. Washington, D.C.: World Bank, c2001. xiii, 696 p.
00-050359   338.96 21   0821346695
Economic assistance -- Africa. Africa -- Economic policy.

HC800.A98 1998
Ayittey, George B. N.,
Africa in chaos/ George B.N. Ayittey. 1st St. Martin's ed. New York: St. Martin's Press, 1998. xvi, 399 p.
97-011236   330.967/032 21   0312164009
Africa -- Economic conditions -- 1960- Africa -- Economic policy. Africa -- Social conditions -- 1960- Africa -- Politics and government -- 1960-

HC800.B42 1994
Becker, Charles M.
Beyond urban bias in Africa: urbanization in an era of structural adjustment/ Charles M. Becker, Andrew M. Hamer, Andrew R. Morrison. Portsmouth, NH: Heinemann; 1994. ix, 294 p.
93-032405   307.76/0973   0435080911
Structural adjustment (Economic policy) -- Africa, Sub-Saharan. Urbanization -- Africa, Sub-Saharan. Africa, Sub-Saharan -- Economic conditions.

HC800.C27 1992
Case-studies in economic development.   New York: St. Martin's Press, c1992-1993. v. 1-2.
91-033541   338.96   0312074921
Structural adjustment (Economic policy) -- Africa -- Case studies. Africa -- Economic policy -- Case studies. Developing countries -- Economic policy -- Case studies.

HC800.C628 1996
Leys, Colin.
The rise & fall of development theory/ Colin Leys. Nairobi: EAEP; c1996. viii, 205 p.
95-039293   338.9 20   025321016X
Development economics. Economic development. Africa, Sub-Saharan -- Economic conditions -- 1960-

HC800.C6663 2001
Contending issues in African development: advances, challenges, and the future/ edited by Obioma M. Iheduru. Westport, CT: Greenwood Press, 2001. viii, 342 p.
00-032797   338.96 21   0313309612
Africa -- Economic policy. Africa -- Social policy.

HC800.C745 1988
The Crisis and challenge of African development/ edited by Harvey Glickman. New York: Greenwood Press, 1988. xii, 257 p.
87-031792   338.96   0313259887
Africa -- Economic policy. Africa -- Economic conditions -- 1960-

HC800.E2768 1996
Economic reform and the poor in Africa/ edited by David E. Sahn. Oxford: Clarendon Press;   xv, 488 p.
96-002137   338.96 20   0198290357
Foreign exchange administration -- Africa. Fiscal policy -- Africa. Agriculture and state -- Africa.

HC800.E543 2000
Englebert, Pierre,
State legitimacy and development in Africa/ Pierre Englebert. Boulder, Colo.: Lynne Rienner Publishers, 2000. xii, 244 p.
00-032857   338.96 21   1555878644
Structural adjustment (Economic policy) -- Africa. Legitimacy of governments -- Africa.

HC800.F543 1994
Fieldhouse, D. K. 1925-
Merchant capital and economic decolonization: the United Africa Company, 1929-1987/ D.K. Fieldhouse. Oxford: Clarendon Press; 1994. xxviii, 832 p.
94-009679   382/.06/067   019822625X
Capital -- Africa -- History. Africa -- Colonial influence. Africa -- Dependency on foreign countries. Africa -- Economic conditions.

HC800.H633 1991
Hodd, Michael.
The economies of Africa: geography, population, history, stability, structure, performance, forecasts/ Michael Hodd. Boston, MA: G.K. Hall, c1991. viii, 263 p.
91-006376   330.96 20   0816173575
Economic forecasting -- Africa.

HC800.I53 1981
Indigenization of African economies/ edited by Adebayo Adedeji. New York: Africana Pub. Co., 1981. 413 p.
81-007112   330.96/032   0841907080
Africanization. Africa -- Economic conditions -- 1945- Africa -- Colonial influence.

HC800.K46 1988
Kennedy, Paul T., 1941-
African capitalism: the struggle for ascendency/ Paul Kennedy. Cambridge; Cambridge University Press, 1988. x, 233 p.
88-002563   332/.041/096   0521265991
Capitalism -- Africa. Africa -- Economic conditions -- 1960-

HC800.L465 2003
Leonard, David K.
Africa's stalled development: international causes and cures/ David K. Leonard, Scott Straus. Boulder, Colo.: Lynne Rienner Publishers, 2003. xi, 159 p.
2002-031839   338.967 21   1588261166
Debts, External -- Africa. Technical assistance -- Africa.

HC800.M86 1990
Mwereria, G. K.
The root causes of debt crisis in Africa: an agenda for continental collective self-reliance/ Godfrey K. M'Mwereria. Nairobi, Kenya: Southern Network for Development, Africa Region, 1990. 43 p.
93-850153
Community development -- Africa. Debts, External -- Africa. Africa -- Economic policy.

HC800.O55 1988
Onimode, Bade.
A political economy of the African crisis/ Bade Onimode. London; Zed Books with the Institute for African Alterna 1988. 333 p.
88-014268   330.96/0328   0862323738
Africa -- Economic conditions -- 1960- Africa -- Social conditions -- 1960-

HC800.R44 1997
Regional integration and trade liberalization in subsaharan Africa. New York: St. Martin's Press, <1997- >
96-049387   337.67 21   0312173210
Africa, Sub-Saharan -- Economic integration. Africa, Sub-Saharan -- Economic policy. Africa, Sub-Saharan -- Foreign economic relations.

HC800.R62 1981
Rodney, Walter.
How Europe underdeveloped Africa/ by Walter Rodney with a postscript by A.M. Babu. Washington, D.C.: Howard University Press, 1981. xxiv, 312 p.
81-006240   330.96   0882580965
Africa -- Economic conditions. Africa -- Colonial influence. Europe -- Foreign economic relations -- Africa.

HC800.S23 1997
Sahn, David E.
Structural adjustment reconsidered: economic policy and poverty in Africa/ David E. Sahn, Paul A. Dorosh, Stephen D. Younger. Cambridge [England]; Cambridge University Press, xiv, 304 p.
96-040018   338.96 21   0521584515
Structural adjustment (Economic policy) -- Africa, Sub-Saharan. Poverty -- Africa, Sub-Saharan.

HC800.S26 1985
Sandbrook, Richard.
The politics of Africa's economic stagnation/ Richard Sandbrook with Judith Barker. Cambridge [Cambridgeshire]; Cambridge University Press, 1985. xiii, 180 p.
84-028588   960/.328   0521265878
Africa -- Economic conditions -- 1960- Africa -- Politics and government -- 1960- Africa -- Social conditions -- 1960-

HC800.S389 2001
Schwab, Peter,
Africa, a continent self-destructs/ Peter Schwab. 1st ed. New York: Palgrave for St. Martin's Press, 2001. x, 212 p.
2001-021864   967.04 21   031224018X
Africa -- Economic conditions -- 1960- Africa -- Social conditions -- 1960- Africa -- Politics and government -- 1960-

HC800.T52 1998
Tignor, Robert L.
Capitalism and nationalism at the end of empire: state and business in decolonizing Egypt, Nigeria, and Kenya, 1945-1963/ Robert L. Tignor. Princeton, N.J.: Princeton University Press, c1998. viii, 419 p.
97-013796   330.96/032 21   0691015848
Capital -- Africa -- History. Industrial policy -- Africa -- History. Nationalism -- Africa. Africa -- Economic conditions -- 1945-1960. Africa -- Colonial influence.

HC800.T72 1990
Towards economic recovery in sub-Saharan Africa: essays in honour of Robert Gardiner/ edited by James Pickett and Hans Singer. London; Routledge, 1990. xv, 273 p.
90-032100   338.967   0415054095
Gardiner, Robert K. A. -- (Robert Kweku Atta) Africa, Sub-Saharan -- Economic conditions -- 1960- Africa, Sub-Saharan -- Social conditions -- 1960- Africa, Sub-Saharan -- Economic policy.

HC800.W518 1986
Wickins, P. L., 1925-
Africa, 1880-1980: an economic history/ Peter Lionel Wickins. Cape Town: Oxford University Press, 1986. x, 321 p.
87-119035   330.96   0195704169
Africa -- Economic conditions. Africa -- Politics and government.

HC800.Z65.J35 1991
James, Valentine Udoh, 1952-
Resource management in developing countries: Africa's ecological and economic problems/ Valentine U. James. New York: Praeger, 1991. x, 158 p.
90-049217   333.7/096   0897892240
Natural resources -- Africa -- Management.

HC800.Z9.F315 1989
Africa beyond famine: a report to the Club of Rome/ edited by Aklilu Lemma and Pentti Malaska. London; Published for the Club of Rome by Tycooly Pub.,b 1989. xxiv, 347 p.
89-005076   363.8/096   1851480390
Famines -- Africa.

HC800.Z9.F37 1990
The Political economy of hunger/ edited by Jean Dreze and Amartya Sen. Oxford [England]: Clarendon Press; 1990-1991. 3 v.
90-007663   363.8/83/0967   019828635X
Famines -- Africa, Sub-Saharan -- Case studies. Food relief -- Africa, Sub-Saharan -- Case studies. Famines -- South Asia -- Case studies.

HC800.Z9 F388 1999
Von Braun, Joachim,
Famine in Africa: causes, responses, and prevention/ Joachim von Braun, Tesfaye Teklu, and Patrick Webb. Baltimore, Md.: Johns Hopkins University Press, 1999. xvii, 219 p.
98-008734   363.8/096 21   0801861217
Famines -- Africa. Food supply -- Africa -- Case studies. Famines -- Prevention -- Government policy -- Africa.

HC800.Z9 I5136 1988
Nafziger, E. Wayne.
Inequality in Africa: political elites, proletariat, peasants, and the poor/ E. Wayne Nafziger. Cambridge [Cambridgeshire]; Cambridge University Press, xii, 204 p.
87-024263   339.2/096 19   0521317037
Income distribution -- Africa. Poor -- Africa. Peasantry -- Africa.

HC800.Z9.P625 1987
Iliffe, John.
The African poor: a history/ John Iliffe. Cambridge [Cambridgeshire]; Cambridge University Press, 1987. ix, 387 p.
87-014622   305.5/62/096   0521344158
Poor -- Africa -- History.

HC805-835 By region or country — Africa — North Africa

HC805.N67 1996
North Africa: development and reform in a changing global economy/ Dirk Vandewalle, editor. New York: St. Martin's Press, c1996. xviii, 286 p.
95-053211   338.961/009/045 20   031215853X
Africa, North -- Economic policy. Africa, North -- Economic conditions.

HC815.B48 1988
Bennoune, Mahfoud.
The making of contemporary Algeria, 1830-1987: colonial upheavals and post-independence development/ Mahfoud Bennoune. Cambridge [England]; Cambridge University Press, 1988. xii, 323 p.
87-033814   338.965   0521301505
Algeria -- Economic conditions -- 1962- Algeria -- Economic policy. Algeria -- History -- 1830-1962.

HC820.M87 1999
Murphy, Emma.
Economic and political change in Tunisia: from Bourguiba to Ben Ali/ Emma C. Murphy. New York, N.Y.: St. Martin's Press in association with Universit 1999. xii, 285 p.
98-033304   330.9611/05   0312221428
Tunisia -- Economic conditions -- 1956-1987. Tunisia -- Economic policy. Tunisia -- Politics and government -- 1956-1987.

HC830.H36 1991
Hansen, Bent,
Egypt and Turkey/ Bent Hansen. Oxford [England]; Published for the World Bank [by] xvii, 572 p.
91-027935   330.9561 20   0195208250
Income distribution -- Egypt -- History. Poor -- Egypt -- History. Income distribution -- Turkey -- History.

HC830.H37 1997
Harik, Iliya F.
Economic policy reform in Egypt/ Iliya Harik. Gainesville, FL: University Press of Florida, c1997. 258 p.
96-038520   338.962 20   0813014832
Egypt -- Economic policy. Egypt -- Social policy.

HC830.T54 1984
Tignor, Robert L.
State, private enterprise, and economic change in Egypt, 1918-1952/ Robert L. Tignor. Princeton, N.J.: Princeton University Press, c1984. xvi, 317 p.
83-043097   338.962   0691054169
Corporations -- Egypt -- Finance -- History -- 20th century. Investments -- Egypt -- History -- 20th century. Middle class -- Egypt -- History -- 20th century. Egypt -- Economic conditions -- 1918-

HC830.W37 1983
Waterbury, John.
The Egypt of Nasser and Sadat: the political economy of two regimes/ John Waterbury. Princeton, N.J.: Princeton University Press, c1983. xxiv, 475 p.
82-061393   338.962   0691076502
Egypt -- Economic policy -- 1952- Egypt -- Politics and government -- 1952-

HC830.Z9 P625 2000
Sabra, Adam Abdelhamid,
Poverty and charity in medieval Islam: Mamluk Egypt, 1250-1517/ Adam Sabra. Cambridge, UK; Cambridge University Press, 2000. xiii, 192 p.
00-023607   362.5/57/0962 21   0521772915
Poverty -- Egypt -- History -- 1250-1517. Charities -- Egypt -- History -- 1250-1517. Mamelukes -- Economic conditions -- Attitudes.

HC835.D38 1996
Davidson, Andrew Parks
In the shadow of history: the passing of lineage society/ Andrew P. Davidson. New Brunswick, N.J.: Transaction Publishers, c1996. xvi, 328 p.
95-025160   306/.09628 20   1560002301
Households -- Sudan -- Nuba Mountains -- Cases studies. Kinship -- Sudan -- Nuba Mountains -- Case studies. Economic anthropology -- Sudan -- Nuba Mountains -- Case studies.

HC835.Z7.D377 1988
Tully, Dennis.
Culture and context in Sudan: the process of market incorporation in Dar Masalit/ Dennis Tully. Albany, N.Y.: State University of New York Press, c1988. xiii, 306 p.
86-023180 338.1/09627 0887065023
Agriculture -- Sudan -- Dar Masalit. Economic anthropology -- Sudan -- Dar Masalit. Dar Masalit (Sudan) -- Economic conditions.

HC835.Z9.F3476 1994
Keen, David, 1958-
The benefits of famine: a political economy of famine and relief in southwestern Sudan, 1983-1989/ David Keen. Princeton, N.J.: Princeton University Press, c1994. xvi, 289 p.
93-034900 363.8/09624 0691034230
Famines -- Political aspects -- Sudan. Sudan -- Politics and government -- 1985-

HC845-850 By region or country — Africa — Northeast Africa

HC845.A7 1995
Araia, Ghelawdewos.
Ethiopia: the political economy of transition/ Ghelawdewos Araia. Lanham, Md.: University Press of America, c1995. iii, 229 p.
94-024368 338.963 20 081919770X
Ethiopia -- Economic policy. Ethiopia -- Economic conditions -- 1974- Ethiopian Peoples' Revolutionary Party. Ethiopia -- History -- Revolution, 1974.

HC845.E26 1992
The Economy of Ethiopia/ edited by Keith Griffin. Houndmills, Basingstoke, Hampshire: Macmillan; 1992. xiii, 312 p.
91-047751 338.963 0333565789
Ethiopia -- Economic conditions -- 1974- Ethiopia -- Economic policy.

HC845.K43 1992
Kebbede, Girma.
The state and development in Ethiopia/ Girma Kebbede. Atlantic Highlands, N.J.: Humanities Press, 1992. viii, 177 p.
91-018846 330.963 0391037315
Ethiopia -- Economic conditions -- 1974- Ethiopia -- Dependency on foreign countries. Ethiopia -- Politics and government -- 1974-

HC845.Z9.F33 1985
Clay, Jason W.
Politics and the Ethiopian famine, 1984-1985/ by Jason W. Clay and Bonnie K. Holcomb. Cambridge, MA (11 Divinity Ave., Cambridge 02138 Cultural Survival, 1985. xi, 250 p.
86-153948 363.8/56/0963
Famines -- Ethiopia. Refugees -- Ethiopia. Agriculture and state -- Ethiopia. Ethiopia -- Politics and government -- 1974-

HC845.Z9.F343 1985
Hancock, Graham.
Ethiopia: the challenge of hunger/ by Graham Hancock. London: V. Gollancz, 1985. 127 p.
85-170257 363.8/83/0963 057503680X
Famines -- Ethiopia. Food supply -- Ethiopia.

HC850.M83 1996
Mubarak, Jamil Abdalla.
From bad policy to chaos in Somalia: how an economy fell apart/ Jamil Abdalla Mubarak. Westport, Conn.: Praeger, 1996. xiv, 181 p.
95-051426 338.96773 0275954862
Somalia -- Economic conditions -- 1960- Somalia -- Economic policy.

HC865-890 By region or country — Africa — Southeast Africa

HC865.H56 1994
Himbara, David, 1950-
Kenyan capitalists, the state, and development/ by David Himbara. Boulder: L. Rienner Publishers, 1994. xvi, 192 p.
93-014453 338.96762 1555874304
Capitalism -- Kenya. East Indians -- Kenya. Businesspeople -- Kenya. Kenya -- Economic policy.

HC870.D53 1998
Dicklitch, Susan, 1966-
The elusive promise of NGOs in Africa: lessons from Uganda/ Susan Dicklitch. New York: St. Martin's Press, 1998. xiv, 294 p.
97-053273 338.96761 031221412X
Non-governmental organizations -- Uganda. Non-governmental organizations -- Africa. Democracy -- Uganda. Uganda -- Politics and government. Africa -- Politics and government. Uganda -- Economic policy.

HC885.C68 1982
Coulson, Andrew.
Tanzania: a political economy/ by Andrew Coulson. Oxford [Oxfordshire]: Clarendon Press; 1982. xiv, 394 p.
81-014034 330.9678 0198282923
Tanzania -- Economic conditions.

HC885.Z7.D377 1997
Tripp, Aili Mari.
Changing the rules: the politics of liberalization and the urban informal economy in Tanzania/ Aili Mari Tripp. Berkeley: University of California Press, c1997. xxii, 260 p.
95-053702 330.9678 20 0520202783
Informal sector (Economics) -- Tanzania -- Dar es Salaam. Government, Resistance to -- Tanzania. Tanzania -- Economic policy. Dar es Salaam (Tanzania) -- Economic conditions.

HC890.A57 1995
Abrahamsson, Hans, 1949-
Mozambique, the troubled transition: from socialist construction to free market capitalism/ Hans Abrahamsson and Anders Nilsson; translated by Mary Dally. London; Zed Books, 1995. xvii, 285 p.
95-021717 330.9679/05 1856493237
Mozambique -- Economic conditions -- 1975-

HC905-930 By region or country — Africa — Southern Africa

HC905.J66 1992
Jones, Stuart.
The South African economy, 1910-90/ Stuart Jones and Andre Muller. New York: St. Martin's Press, 1992. ix, 384 p.
91-033633 330.968/05 0312075073
South Africa -- Economic conditions. South Africa -- Economic policy.

HC905.L49 1990
Lewis, Stephen R.
The economics of apartheid/ Stephen R. Lewis, Jr. New York: Council on Foreign Relations Press, c1990. xi, 195 p.
89-001451 330.968/063 0876090560
Apartheid -- Economic aspects -- South Africa -- History. South Africa -- Economic conditions. South Africa -- Economic policy.

HC905.M39 1991
Mbeki, Govan, 1910-
Learning from Robben Island: the prison writings of Govan Mbeki. London: J. Currey; 1991. xxx, 202 p.
91-003198 330.968/06 0821410067
Apartheid -- South Africa. South Africa -- Politics and government. South Africa -- Economic conditions.

HC905.Z7 K8343 2002
Hart, Gillian Patricia.
Disabling globalization: places of power in post-apartheid South Africa/ Gillian Hart. Berkeley: University of California Press, c2002. xi, 358 p.
2002-074223 330.9684 21 0520237560
Globalization -- Economic aspects -- South Africa -- KwaZulu-Natal. Globalization -- Social aspects -- South Africa -- KwaZulu-Natal. Investments, Taiwan -- South Africa -- KwaZulu-Natal.

HC905.Z9 P619 1999
Poverty and inequality in South Africa: meeting the challenge/ edited by Julian May. New York: Zed Books, 1999.
99-054460 339.4/6/0968 21 1856498085
Poverty -- South Africa. Income distribution -- South Africa.

HC910.M357 1998
Dashwood, Hevina S. 1960-
Zimbabwe: the political economy of transformation/ Hevina S. Dashwood. Toronto; University of Toronto Press, c2000. xii, 252 p.
00-455213 0802044239
Structural adjustment (Economic policy) -- Zimbabwe. Zimbabwe -- Economic policy.

HC910.S58 1995
Skalnes, Tor.
The politics of economic reform in Zimbabwe: continuity and change in development/ Tor Skalnes. New York, N.Y.: St. Martin's Press, 1995. ix, 217 p.
94-043719 338.96891 0312125747
Zimbabwe -- Economic policy. Zimbabwe -- Politics and government.

HC930.H37 1990
Harvey, Charles,
Policy choice and development performance in Botswana/ Charles Harvey and Stephen R. Lewis, Jr.; foreword by Keith Griffin. New York: St. Martin's Press, 1990. xxii, 341 p.
89-029689 338.96883 0312040466
Botswana -- Economic policy. Botswana -- Economic conditions -- 1966-

HC930.H67 1997
Hope, Kempe R.
African political economy: contemporary issues in development/ Kempe Ronald Hope, Sr. Armonk, N.Y.: M.E. Sharpe, c1997. xiii, 230 p.
96-024893 338.96 20 1563249421
Botswana -- Economic conditions -- 1966- Botswana -- Economic policy. Africa -- Economic conditions -- 1960- Africa -- Economic policy.

HC1000-1065 By region or country — Africa — West Africa. West Coast

HC1000.A86 1986
Asante, S. K. B.
The political economy of regionalism in Africa: a decade of the Economic Community of West African States (ECOWAS)/ S.K.B. Asante. New York: Praeger, 1986. xvii, 267 p.
85-016740   337.1/66   003005902X
Africa, West -- Economic integration -- History.

HC1000.R56 1984
Rimmer, Douglas.
The economies of West Africa/ Douglas Rimmer. New York: St. Martin's Press, 1984. xii, 308 p.
83-040604   330.966   0312236743
Africa, West -- Economic conditions -- 1960- Africa, West -- Economic policy.

HC1035.R63 1987
Roberts, Richard L.,
Warriors, merchants, and slaves: the state and the economy in the Middle Niger Valley, 1700-1914/ Richard L. Roberts. Stanford, Calif.: Stanford University Press, 1987. xii, 293 p.
86-023138   330.966/23 19   0804713782
Mali -- Economic conditions. Niger River Valley -- Economic conditions. Mali -- History.

HC1045.B65 1992
Boone, Catherine.
Merchant capital and the roots of state power in Senegal, 1930-1985/ Catherine Boone. Cambridge [England]; Cambridge University Press, 1992. xv, 299 p.
91-046536   338.9663 20   0521410789
Industrial policy -- Senegal. Textile industry -- Senegal.

HC1055.A7 1992
Anunobi, Fredoline O.
The implications of conditionality: the International Monetary Fund and Africa/ Fredoline O. Anunobi. Lanham, Md.: University Press of America, c1992. 338 p.
92-024477   338.9669   0819187941
Conditionality (International relations) Nigeria -- Economic policy. Africa -- Economic policy.

HC1055.F57 1981
First things first: meeting the basic needs of the people of Nigeria: report to the Government of Nigeria/ by a JASPA basic needs mission. Addis Ababa: International Labour Office, Jobs and Skills Programme x, 256 p.
82-980553   338.9669 19   9221026825
Nigeria -- Economic conditions -- 1970- Nigeria -- Social conditions -- 1960- Nigeria -- Economic policy. Nigeria -- Social policy.

HC1055.W75 1998
Wright, Stephen, 1954-
Nigeria: struggle for stability and status/ Stephen Wright. Boulder, Colo.: Westview Press, 1998. xiii, 188 p.
98-013964   338.9669   0813321409
Economic stabilization -- Nigeria. Nigeria -- Economic conditions -- 1970-

HC1060.G46 1993
Ghana under PNDC rule/ E. Gyimah-Boadi, editor. Senegal: Codesria, 1993. 221 p.
94-194400   2869780192
Provisional National Defense Council (Ghana) Ghana -- Economic policy. Ghana -- Economic conditions -- 1979- Ghana -- Politics and government -- 1979-

HC1060.H47 1993
Herbst, Jeffrey Ira.
The politics of reform in Ghana, 1982-1991/ Jeffrey Herbst. Berkeley: University of California Press, c1993. xii, 180 p.
92-003297   338.9667   0520077520
Ghana -- Economic policy. Ghana -- Politics and government -- 1979- Africa -- Politics and government -- 1960-

HC1060.H87 1989
Huq, M. M.
The economy of Ghana: the first 25 years since independence/ M.M. Huq. New York: St. Martin's Press, 1989. xxix, 355 p.
88-018158   330.9667/05   0312021070
Ghana -- Economic conditions -- 1957-1979. Ghana -- Economic conditions -- 1979-

HC1065.W44 1992
Weeks, John, 1941-
Development strategy and the economy of Sierra Leone/ John Weeks. New York: St. Martin's Press, 1992. xi, 191 p.
91-039069   338.9664   0312072120
Structural adjustment (Economic policy) -- Sierra Leone. Sierra Leone -- Economic conditions -- 1961-

---

HD Industries. Land Use. Labor

HD20.4-21 Management. Industrial management

HD20.4.M33 1964
Marris, Robin Lapthorn, 1924-
The economic theory of 'managerial' capitalism/ by Robin Marris. New York: Free Press of Glencoe, c1964. xviii, 346 p.
64-010371   658/.001/82
Industrial management -- Mathematical models. Industrial organization -- Mathematical models. Managerial economics -- Mathematical models.

HD20.5.K313 1968
Kaufmann, A. 1911-
Introduction to operations research [by] A. Kaufmann [and] R. Faure. Translated by Henry C. Sneyd. New York, Academic Press, 1968. xi, 300 p.
67-023162   658.4
Operations research. Industrial management -- Research.

HD20.5.W34 1975
Wagner, Harvey M.
Principles of operations research: with applications to managerial decisions/ Harvey M. Wagner. 2d ed. Englewood Cliffs, N.J.: Prentice-Hall, [1975] xii, 1039 p.
74-029418   001.4/24   0137095929
Operations research.

HD21.C64
Classics in scientific management: a book of readings/ [edited by] Donald Del Mar, Rodger D. Collons. University: University of Alabama Press, c1976. xiii, 443 p.
75-020471   658.4   0817387013
Industrial management -- Addresses, essays, lectures. Industrial management -- United States -- Addresses, essays, lectures.

HD21.K45 1964
Kerr, Clark,
Industrialism and industrial man: the problems of labor and management in economic growth, by Clark Kerr [and others. 2d ed.] New York, Oxford University Press, 1964. 263 p.
64-010063   338.9
Industrialization. Industrial relations.

HD21.S815
Stigler, George Joseph, 1911-
The organization of industry [by] George J. Stigler. Homewood, Ill., R. D. Irwin, 1968. viii, 328 p.
68-030846   338.7
Industrial organization (Economic theory) Industries. Anti-trust law -- Economic aspects.

HD28 Management. Industrial management — Periodicals. Societies. Serials

HD28.J62
Journal of managerial issues: JMI. Pittsburg, KS: Gladys A. Kelce School of Business and Economics,
90-640805   658 11
Management -- Periodicals.

HD30.15 Management. Industrial management — Dictionaries. Encyclopedias

HD30.15.E49 2000
Encyclopedia of management/ edited by Marilyn M. Helms; foreword by David A. Whetten. 4th ed. Detroit, [Mich.]: Gale Group, 2000. xxviii, 1020 p.
99-047817   658/.003 21   0787630659
Industrial management -- Dictionaries.

HD30.19 Management. Industrial management — Theory. Method. Relation to other subjects — Relation to the social sciences

HD30.19.A45 1996
Alvesson, Mats, 1956-
Making sense of management: a critical introduction/ Mats Alvesson and Hugh Willmott. London; Sage Publications, 1996. x, 246 p.
96-068525   658   0803983883
Management. Critical theory.

HD30.2 Management. Industrial management — Theory. Method. Relation to other subjects — Electronic data processing. Information technology

HD30.2.C347 2002
Cairncross, Frances.
The company of the future: how the communications revolution is changing management/ Frances Cairncross. Boston, Mass.: Harvard Business School Press, c2002. xv, 229 p.
2001-051486   658.4/5 21   1578516579
Information technology -- Management. Communication in management. Industrial management.

HD30.2.C66 1991
The Corporation of the 1990s: information technology and organizational transformation/ edited by Michael S. Scott Morton. New York: Oxford University Press, 1991. xii, 331 p.
90-037886   658.4/038   0195063589
Management -- Data processing. Information technology -- Management. Organizational change.

HD30.2.D68 1998
Downes, Larry, 1959-
Unleashing the killer app: digital strategies for market dominance/ Larry Downes and Chunka Mui. Boston, Mass.: Harvard Business School Press, c1998. xix, 243 p.
98-011311   658.4/038 21   087584801X
Information technology -- United States -- Management. Digital communications -- United States -- Management. Organizational change -- United States.

HD30.2.K6363 2001
Knowledge emergence: social, technical, and evolutionary dimensions of knowledge creation/ edited by Ikujiro Nonaka, Toshihiro Nishiguchi. Oxford; Oxford University Press, 2001. ix, 303 p.
00-042795   658.4/038 21   0195130634
Knowledge management. Information society.

HD30.2.K63686 2000
Knowledge management: classic and contemporary works/ edited by Daryl Morey, Mark Maybury, Bhavani Thuraisingham. Cambridge, Mass.: MIT Press, c2000. xiv, 435 p.
00-046042   658.4/038 21   0262133849
Knowledge management.

HD30.2.K6377 2002
Knowledge management strategy and technology/ Richard Bellaver, John Lusa, editors. Boston: Artech House, 2002. xxii, 243 p.
2001-053530   658.4/038 21   1580531059
Knowledge management. Information technology -- Management. Information networks -- Management.

HD30.2.R48 1990
Revolution in real time: managing information technology in the 1990s/ with a preface by William G. McGowan. Boston, MA: Harvard Business School Pub., c1991. xii, 276 p.
90-046351   658.4/038 20   0875842429
Management -- Data processing. Information technology -- Management.

HD30.2122 Management. Industrial management — Theory. Method. Relation to other subjects — Virtual reality in management

HD30.2122.M37 1996
Martin, James, 1938-
Cybercorp: the new business revolution/ James Martin. New York: Amacom, c1996. x, 326 p.
96-033074   658/.00285/467 20   0814403514
Virtual reality in management. Industrial management. Organizational change.

HD30.213 Management. Industrial management — Theory. Method. Relation to other subjects — Management information systems. Decision support systems

HD30.213.C476 2001
Choo, Chun Wei.
Information management for the intelligent organization: the art of scanning the environment/ Chun Wei Choo. 3rd ed. Medford, NJ: Information Today, 2002. xix, 325 p.
2001-039406   658.4/038 21   1573871257
Management information systems. Information resources management. Information technology -- Management.

HD30.213.D38 2000
Davenport, Thomas H.,
Mission critical: realizing the promise of enterprise systems/ Thomas H. Davenport. Boston, MA: Harvard Business School Press, 2000. x, 335 p.
99-051644   658.4/038/011 21   0875849067
Management information systems.

HD30.213.J64 1996
Johnson, J. David.
Information seeking: an organizational dilemma/ J. David Johnson. Westport, Conn.: Quorum, 1996. xiii, 179 p.
95-050745   658.4/038   0899309992
Management information systems. Information resources management. Office information systems.

HD30.213.R689 1996
Rowe, Alan J.
Intelligent information systems: meeting the challenge of the knowledge era/ Alan J. Rowe, Sue Anne Davis in collaboration with Sushmita Vij. Westport, Conn.: Quorum Books, 1996. xii, 183 p.
95-046277   658.4/038/011   0899309127
Management information systems. Decision support systems. Information storage and retrieval systems -- Business.

HD30.22 Management. Industrial management — Theory. Method. Relation to other subjects — Managerial economics

HD30.22.C358 2000
Cappels, Thomas M.,
Financially focused quality/ Thomas M. Cappels. Boca Raton, FL: St. Lucie Press, c2000. xviii, 294 p.
99-028173   658.4/013 21   1574442481
Managerial economics. Quality control.

HD30.22.N45 1997
Nellis, J. G.
The essence of business economics/ Joseph G. Nellis and David Parker. New York: Prentice Hall, c1997.
97-012766   338.5/024/658 21   0135731305
Managerial economics.

HD30.23 Management. Industrial management — Theory. Method. Relation to other subjects — Decision making

HD30.23.B875 1991
Butler, Richard, 1938-
Designing organizations: a decision-making perspective/ Richard Butler. London; Routledge, 1991. xv, 281 p.
90-008905   658.4/02   0415053315
Decision making. Organization.

HD30.23.C469 2000
Choices, values, and frames/ edited by Daniel Kahneman, Amos Tversky. New York: Russell sage Foundation; xx, 840 p.
99-059883   658.4/03 21   0521627494
Decision-making. Uncertainty. Risk-taking (Psychology)

HD30.23.C73 1999
Crainer, Stuart.
The 75 greatest management decisions ever made/ Stuart Crainer. New York: AMACOM c1999. xixx, 239 p.
99-030611   658.4/03 21   081440491X
Decision making -- Case studies. Decision making -- History. Management -- Case studies.

HD30.23.K35
Keen, Peter G. W.
Decision support systems: an organizational perspective/ Peter G. W. Keen, Michael S. Scott Morton. Reading, Mass.: Addison-Wesley Pub. Co., c1978. xv, 264 p.
77-090176   658.4/03   0201036673
Decision support systems.

HD30.23.N883 2002
Nutt, Paul C.
Why decisions fail: avoiding the blunders and traps that lead to debacles/ Paul C. Nutt. 1st ed. San Francisco, CA: Berrett-Koehler Publishers, 2002. xv, 332 p.
2001-043678   658.4/03 21   1576751503
Decision making.

HD30.23.S556 2001
Simon, Julian Lincoln, 1932-
Developing decision-making skills for business/ Julian L. Simon. Armonk, N.Y.: M.E. Sharpe, 2001. xiv, 229 p.
00-030118   158.7   0765606763
Decision making. Corporate culture. Psychology, Industrial.

HD30.255 Management. Industrial management — Theory. Method. Relation to other subjects — Environmental aspects

HD30.255.E67 1996
Epstein, Marc J.
Measuring corporate environmental performance: best practices for costing and managing an effective environmental strategy/ Marc J. Epstein. Chicago: Irwin Professional Pub., 1996. xxxix, 319 p.
95-020807   658.4/08   0786302305
Industrial management -- Environmental aspects. Strategic planning -- Environmental aspects -- Cost effectiveness.

HD30.255.H638 2000
Hoffman, Andrew J.,
Competitive environmental strategy: a guide to the changing business landscape/ Andrew J. Hoffman. Washington, D.C.: Island Press, c2000. xviii, 301 p.
00-008012   658.4/08 21   1559637722
Industrial management -- Environmental aspects -- United States. Strategic planning -- Environmental aspects -- United States. Environmental policy -- United States.

HD30.255.N388 1999
Nattrass, Brian F.
The natural step for business: wealth, ecology, and the evolutionary corporation/ Brian Nattrass and Mary Altomare; foreword by Karl-Henrik Robèrt; afterword by Paul Hawken. Gabriola Island, BC: New Society Publishers, c1999. xvi, 222 p.
00-361744   658.4/08 21   0865713847
Industrial management -- Environmental aspects Business enterprises -- Environmental aspects. Environmental protection -- Economic aspects.

HD30.27 Management. Industrial management — Theory. Method. Relation to other subjects — Forecasting

HD30.27.D78 1999
Drucker, Peter Ferdinand, 1909-
Management challenges for the 21st century/ Peter F. Drucker. New York: HarperBusiness, c1999. xi, 207 p.
99-017087   658 21   0887309984
Management -- Forecasting. Twenty-first century -- Forecasts.

HD30.27.M355 1993
Maynard, Herman Bryant, 1946-
The fourth wave: business in the 21st century/ Herman Bryant Maynard, Jr., Susan E. Mehrtens. San Francisco: Berrett-Koehler, c1993. xviii, 217 p.
93-002705   338.5/44   188105215X
Business forecasting. Twenty-first century -- Forecasts.

HD30.28 Management. Industrial management — Theory. Method. Relation to other subjects — Planning. Business planning. Strategic planning

HD30.28.A75 1995
Arkebauer, James B., 1939-
The McGraw-Hill guide to writing a high-impact business plan: a proven blueprint for entrepreneurs/ James B. Arkebauer. New York: McGraw-Hill, c1995.
94-021739   0070030596
Strategic planning -- Handbooks, manuals, etc. Proposal writing in business -- Handbooks, manuals, etc.

HD30.28.B592 2001
The Blackwell handbook of strategic management/ edited by Michael A. Hitt, R. Edward Freeman, Jeffrey S. Harrison. Oxford, UK; Blackwell, 2001. xx, 716 p.
2001-000957   658.4/012 21   0631218602
Teams in the workplace.

HD30.28.B7822 1998
Brown, Shona L.
Competing on the edge: strategy as structured chaos/ Shona L. Brown and Kathleen M. Eisenhardt. Boston, Mass.: Harvard Business School Press, c1998. xii, 299 p.
97-041459   658.4/012 21   0875847544
Strategic planning. Organizational change. Competition.

HD30.28.B79 1995
Bryson, John M. 1947-
Strategic planning for public and nonprofit organizations: a guide to strengthening and sustaining organizational achievement/ John M. Bryson. San Francisco: Jossey-Bass Publishers, c1995. xxi, 325 p.
95-022313   658.4/012   0787901415
Strategic planning. Nonprofit organizations -- Management. Public administration.

HD30.28.D59 1991
Dixit, Avinash K.
Thinking strategically: the competitive edge in business, politics, and everyday life/ by Avinash K. Dixit and Barry J. Nalebuff. New York: Norton, c1991. xi, 393 p.
90-033760   658.4/012   0393029239
Strategic planning.

HD30.28.G697 1994
Graham, John W.
Mission statements: a guide to the corporate and nonprofit sectors/ John W. Graham and Wendy C. Havlick; with a foreword by John A. Pearce II. New York: Garland, 1994. xx, 551 p.
94-000540   658.4/012   0815312970
Mission statements.

HD30.28.G716 2003
Grant, Robert M.,
Cases in contemporary strategy analysis/ Robert M. Grant, Kent E. Neupert. 3rd ed. Malden, Mass.: Blackwell, c2003.
2002-151887   658.4/012 21   1405111801
Strategic planning -- Case studies. Decision making -- Case studies.

HD30.28.H36656 2002
Handbook of strategy and management/ edited by Andrew Pettigrew, Howard Thomas and Richard Whittington. London; Sage Publications, 2002. xviii, 519 p.
2001-132892   658.4/012 21   0761958932
Strategic planning. Industrial management.

HD30.28.H69 1990
Houlden, Brian Thomas.
Understanding company strategy: an introduction to thinking and acting strategically/ Brian Houlden. Oxford, UK; B. Blackwell, 1990.
89-018608   658.4/012   0631170332
Strategic planning.

HD30.28.K3544 2001
Kaplan, Robert S.
The strategy-focused organization: how balanced scorecard companies thrive in the new business environment/ Robert S. Kaplan, David P. Norton. Boston, Mass.: Harvard Business School Press, c2001. x, 400 p.
00-033515   658.4/012 21   1578512506
Strategic planning.

HD30.28.M56 1994
Mintzberg, Henry.
The rise and fall of strategic planning: reconceiving roles for planning, plans, planners/ Henry Mintzberg. New York: Free Press; c1994. xix, 458 p.
93-027323   658.4/012   0029216052
Strategic planning.

HD30.28.M6479 1996
Morris, David, 1944-
Market power and business strategy: in search of the unified organization/ David Joseph Morris, Jr. Westport, Conn.: Quorum Books, 1996. xiii, 210 p.
95-050742   658.4/012   1567200451
Strategic planning. Organizational effectiveness.

HD30.28.O35 1995
O'Hara, Patrick D.
The total business plan: how to write, rewrite, and revise/ Patrick D. O'Hara. 2nd ed. New York: J. Wiley, c1995. xiii, 316 p.
94-017935   658.4/012 20   0471078298
Business planning -- Handbooks, manuals, etc. Business enterprises -- Finance -- Handbooks, manuals, etc.

HD30.28.P674 2001
The portable MBA in strategy/ edited by Liam Fahey and Robert M. Randall. 2nd ed. New York: Wiley, c2001. xvii, 414 p.
00-033003   658.4/012 21   0471197084
Strategic planning. Business planning.

HD30.28.V43 2000
Vega, Gina.
A passion for planning: financials, operations, marketing, management, and ethics/ Gina Vega. Lanham, MD: University Press of America, 2000.
00-048854   658.4/012   0761818537
Business planning.

HD30.28.W46 1993
Whittington, Richard.
What is strategy, and does it matter?/ Richard Whittington. London; Routledge, 1993. viii, 165 p.
92-042818   658.4/012   0415073855
Strategic planning.

HD30.3 Management. Industrial management — Communication in management. Communication in organizations. Communication of information — General works

HD30.3.B364 1994
Baker, Wayne E.
Networking smart: how to build relationships for personal and organizational success/ Wayne E. Baker. New York: McGraw-Hill, c1994. xxii, 374 p.
93-022704   658.4/5   0070050929
Communication in management. Communication in organizations. Public relations.

HD30.3.C725 1998
Crainer, Stuart.
The ultimate book of business gurus: 110 thinkers who really made a difference/ Stuart Crainer. New York: AMACOM, c1998. xxviii, 314 p.
98-007432   658 21   0814404480
Management. Business. Executives.

HD30.3.H3575 2001
The new handbook of organizational communication: advances in theory, research, and methods/ Fredric M. Jablin, Linda L. Putnam, editors. Thousand Oaks, Calif.: Sage Publications, c2001. xxxi, 911 p.
00-010051   658.4/5 21   0803955030
Communication in organizations.

HD30.3.H4 1994
Heath, Robert L. 1941-
Management of corporate communication: from interpersonal contacts to external affairs/ Robert L. Heath. Hillsdale, N.J.: Erlbaum, 1994. ix, 306 p.
93-048157   658.4/5   0805815511
Communication in management. Communication in organizations. Corporations -- Public relations.

HD30.3.K49 1993
Keyes, Jessica, 1950-
Infotrends: the competitive use of information/ Jessica Keyes. New York: McGraw-Hill, c1993. xiv, 221 p.
92-029939   658.4/038   0070344647
Management -- United States -- Communication systems -- Technological innovations -- Case studies. Corporations -- United States -- Communication systems -- Technological innovations -- Case studies. Information resources management -- Case studies.

HD30.3.M86 1988
Mumby, Dennis K.
Communication and power in organizations: discourse, ideology, and domination/ Dennis K. Mumby. Norwood, N.J.: Ablex Pub. Corp., c1988. xvi, 194 p.
88-003356   302.3/5 19   0893914800
Communication in organizations. Corporate culture. Organizational behavior.

HD30.3.P46 2000
Perspectives on organizational communication: finding common ground/ Steven R. Corman, Marshall Scott Poole, editors. New York: Guilford Press, c2000. vi, 265 p.
00-061695   302.2 21   1572306025
Communication in organizations. Telecommunication. Communication.

HD30.3.Q35 2001
Qualitative research: applications in organizational life/ edited by Sandra L. Herndon, Gary L. Kreps. 2nd ed. Cresskill, N.J.: Hampton Press, c2001. xiii, 302 p.
00-054154   302.3/5 21   1572733713
Communication in organizations. Communication -- Methodology.

HD30.3.R823 1989
Ruch, William V.
International handbook of corporate communication/ by William V. Ruch. Jefferson, N.C.: McFarland, c1989. x, 486 p.
88-043481   658.4/5   0899503861
Communication in management. Communication in organizations.

HD30.3.S373 2002
Schwarz, Roger M.,
The skilled facilitator: a comprehensive resource for consultants, facilitators, managers, trainers, and coaches/ Roger Schwarz. 2nd ed. San Francisco: Jossey-Bass, c2002 xxi, 407 p.
2002-007934   658.4/036 21   0787947237
Communication in management. Communication in personnel management. Group facilitation.

HD30.3.Y38 1989
Yates, JoAnne, 1951-
Control through communication: the rise of system in American management/ JoAnne Yates. Baltimore: Johns Hopkins University Press, c1989. xx, 339 p.
88-013745   658.4/5   080183757X
Communication in management. Communication in management -- United States -- History -- Case studies.

HD30.335 Management. Industrial management — Communication in management. Communication in organizations. Communication of information — Communication systems

HD30.335.H67 1997
Hope, Jeremy.
Competing in the third wave: the ten key management issues of the information age/ Jeremy Hope, Tony Hope. Boston, Mass.: Harvard Business School Press, c1997. vii, 253 p.
97-005197   303.48/33 21   0875848079
Industrial management -- Communication systems. Information technology. Social history -- 1945-

HD30.37 Management. Industrial management — Communication in management. Communication in organizations. Communication of information — Computer networks. Computer network resources

HD30.37.G38 1999
Gates, Bill, 1955-
Business @ the speed of thought: using a digital nervous system/ Bill Gates with Collins Hemingway. New York, NY: Warner Books, c1999. xxii, 470 p.
99-060040   658 21   0446525685
Business enterprises -- Computer networks. Business enterprises -- Communication systems.

HD30.4 Management. Industrial management — Study and teaching. Research — General works

HD30.4.C63 2000
Coaching for leadership: how the world's greatest coaches help leaders learn/ edited by Marshall Goldsmith, Laurence Lyons, Alyssa Freas. 1st ed. San Francisco: Jossey Bass/Pfeiffer, c2000. xxxvi, 392 p.
00-035209   658.4/07124 21   0787955175
Executives -- Training of. Leadership -- Study and teaching. Mentoring in business.

HD30.4.F84 2001
Fulmer, Robert M.
The leadership investment: how the world's best organizations gain strategic advantage through leadership development/ Robert M. Fulmer, Marshall Goldsmith. New York: AMACOM, c2001. xvi, 334 p.
00-033157   658.4/07124 21   0814405584
Executives -- Training of -- Case studies. Leadership -- Study and teaching -- Case studies.

HD30.4.L63 2001
Locke, Karen D.
Grounded theory in management research/ Karen Locke. London; Sage Publications, 2001. xi, 148 p.
2001-266628   658/.007/2 21   0761964282
Management -- Research. Grounded theory.

HD30.42 Management. Industrial management — Study and teaching. Research — By region or country, A-Z

HD30.42.U5.G55 1991
Gillespie, Richard, 1952-
Manufacturing knowledge: a history of the Hawthorne experiments/ Richard Gillespie. Cambridge [England]; Cambridge University Press, 1991. x, 282 p.
90-025639   658   0521403588
Industrial management -- Research -- United States -- Case studies.

HD30.5 Management. Industrial management — History — General works

HD30.5.B4 1998
Beatty, Jack.
The world according to Peter Drucker/ Jack Beatty. New York: Free Press, c1998. xii, 204 p.
97-036988   658.4/0092.aB 21   068483801X
Drucker Peter Ferdinand, 1909- Managemen t-- History.

HD30.5.G85 1993
Guillet de Monthoux, Pierre, 1946-
The moral philosophy of management: from Quesnay to Keynes/ Pierre Guillet de Monthoux. Armonk, N.Y.: M.E. Sharpe, c1993. xv, 304 p.
93-016576   658/.001   1563240815
Industrial management — History. Industrial management -- Philosophy -- History. Managerial economics -- History.

HD30.5.W37 1991
Waring, Stephen P.
Taylorism transformed: scientific management theory since 1945/ Stephen P. Waring. Chapel Hill: University of North Carolina Press, c1991. xi, 288 p.
91-011027   658/.001   0807819727
Industrial management -- History.

HD30.55 Management. Industrial management — History — Special schools

HD30.55.M35 1997
Managing across cultures: issues and perspectives/ edited by Pat Joynt and Malcolm Warner. London; International Thomson Business Press, 1997. xvi, 408 p.
96-038877   658   1861523505
Comparative management.

HD31 Management. Industrial management — General works — English

HD31.B3682 1997
Barnatt, Christopher, 1967-
Challenging reality: in search of the future organization/ Christopher Barnatt. Chichester, England; John Wiley & Sons, 1997. x, 306 p.
96-039899   658   0471970727
Organization. Management.

HD31.B3734 1997
Begin, James P.
Dynamic human resource systems: cross-national comparisons/ James P. Begin. Berlin; Walter de Gruyter, 1997 xx, 377 p.
97-019625   658.3   3110155141
Industrial management. Comparative management. Human capital.

HD31.B6135 2003
Bolman, Lee G.
Reframing organizations: artistry, choice, and leadership/ Lee G. Bolman, Terrence E. Deal. 3rd ed. San Francisco: Jossey-Bass, c2003.
2003-006453   658.4/063 21   0787964271
Management. Organizational behavior. Leadership.

HD31.B7235 2003
Walker, Danielle Medina.
Doing business internationally: the guide to cross-cultural success/ Danielle Medina Walker, Thomas Walker, Joerg Schmitz. 2nd ed. New York: McGraw-Hill, 2003. xvii, 330 p.
2001-054412   658/.049 21   0071378324
Industrial management -- Cross-cultural studies. Intercultural communication. Negotiation in business -- Cross-cultural studies.

HD31.B7417 2001
Brindle, Margaret.
Facing up to management faddism: a new look at an old force/ Margaret C. Brindle and Peter N. Stearns. Westport, Conn.: Quorum Books, 2001. 211 p.
00-045846   658   1567203965
Industrial management. Fads.

HD31.C3433 1999
Cappelli, Peter.
The new deal at work: managing the market-driven workforce/ Peter Cappelli. Boston: Harvard Business School Press, 1999. x, 307 p.
98-042221   658.3   0875846688
Industrial management. Organizational change. Corporate reorganizations.

HD31.C56 2001
Classics of organization theory/ [edited by] Jay M. Shafritz, J.   Steven Ott. 5th ed. Fort Worth: Harcourt College Publishers, c2001. xiv, 542 p.
00-103359   658 21   0155068695
Organization. Management.

HD31.C586 1993
Cohen, Allan R.
The portable MBA in management/ Allan R. Cohen. New York: J. Wiley, c1993. vi, 392 p.
92-041917   658.4   0471573795
Industrial management. Personnel management. Teams in the workplace.

HD31.C6134 1990
The Portable MBA/ [edited by] Eliza G.C. Collins, Mary Anne Devanna. New York: Wiley, c1990. xii, 386 p.
89-027382   658   0471619973
Industrial management. Marketing. Accounting.

HD31.D77337 1995
Drucker, Peter Ferdinand, 1909-
Managing in a time of great change/ Peter F. Drucker. New York: Truman Talley Books/Dutton, 1995. xi, 371 p.
95-013316   658   0525940537
Management. Organization.

HD31.D77339 2002
Drucker, Peter Ferdinand,
Managing in the next society/ Peter F. Drucker. 1st ed. New York: St. Martin's Press, 2002. xiii, 321 p.
2001-054096   658 21   0312289774
Management. Industrial management.

HD31.D7742 1998
Drucker, Peter Ferdinand, 1909-
Peter Drucker on the profession of management/ Peter F. Drucker. Boston, Mass.: Harvard Business School Press, c1998. xv, 201 p.
97-039984   658 21   0875848362
Industrial management.

HD31.E477 1997
Eitington, Julius E.
The winning manager: leadership skills for greater innovation, quality, and employee commitment/ Julius E. Eitington. Houston, Tex.: Gulf Pub. Co., c1997. x, 662 p.
96-048028   658.4/092 21   0884159027
Management. Leadership.

HD31.E654 1993
Enteman, Willard F.
Managerialism: the emergence of a new ideology/ Willard F. Enteman. Madison, Wis.: University of Wisconsin Press, c1993. xiv, 258 p.
93-007444   658.4   0299139204
Management. Ideology. Right and left (Political science)

HD31.H229 1990
Hall, Edward Twitchell, 1914-
Understanding cultural differences/ Edward T. Hall and Mildred Reed Hall. Yarmouth, Me.: Intercultural Press, c1990. xxi, 196 p.
89-084388   306   093366284X
Industrial management -- Cross-cultural studies. Industrial management -- United States. Industrial management -- France.

HD31.H31257 1996
Handbook of organization studies/ edited by Stewart R. Clegg, Cynthia Hardy, and Walter R. Nord. London; Sage Publications, 1996. xxix, 730 p.
96-069122   658   0761951326
Organization. Management.

HD31.M293948 1993
Managers and national culture: a global perspective/ edited by Richard B. Peterson. Westport, Conn.; Quorum Books, 1993. xiv, 460 p.
92-001747   658/.049   0899306020
Industrial management -- Cross-cultural studies. Personnel management -- Cross-cultural studies. International business enterprises -- Personnel management.

HD31.M435 1995
Milakovich, Michael E.
Improving service quality: achieving high performance in the public and private sectors/ Michael E. Milakovich. Delray Beach, Fla.: St. Lucie Press, c1995. xx, 258 p.
94-046379   658.5/62   188401545X
Industrial management. Quality control.

HD31.M628 1997
Morgan, Gareth, 1943-
Images of organization/ Gareth Morgan. Thousand Oaks, Calif.: Sage Publications, c1997. 485 p.
96-035682   658.4 20   0761906312
Organization. Organizational behavior. Management.

HD31.N86 1997
Nurmi, Raimo.
International management leadership: the primary competitive advantage/ Raimo W. Nurmi, John R. Darling. New York: International Business Press, c1997. xiv, 221 p.
97-002108   658.4/092 21   0789000903
Industrial management. Leadership.

HD31.P394 1999
Petzinger, Thomas.
The new pioneers: the men and women who are transforming the workplace and marketplace/ Thomas Petzinger, Jr. New York: Simon & Schuster, c1999. 302 p.
98-050132   658 21   0684846365
Industrial management. Corporate culture. Creative ability in business.

HD31.R787 1991
Rozen, Marvin E.
The economics of organizational choice: workers, jobs, labor markets, and implicit contracting/ Marvin E. Rozen. Ann Arbor: University of Michigan Press, c1991. ix, 202 p.
91-028042   302.3/5   0472102788
Industrial organization. Industrial management - - Employee participation. Employee motivation.

HD31.S322 1990
Savage, Charles M.
Fifth generation management: integrating enterprises through human networking/ Charles M. Savage. [Bedford, Mass.]: Digital Press, c1990. xvi, 267 p.
89-025889   658.4/02   1555580378
Industrial management. Organization. Computer integrated manufacturing systems.

HD31.S55 1976
Simon, Herbert Alexander, 1916-
Administrative behavior: a study of decision-making processes in administrative organization/ Herbert A Simon; with a foreword by Chester I. Barnard. New York: Free Press, c1976. l, 364 p.
75-018009   658.4   0029289718
Management. Decision making.

HD31.W5136
Whyte, William Foote, 1914-
Organizational behavior: theory and application. Homewood, Ill., R. D. Irwin, 1969. xiv, 807 p.
72-078391   658
Organizational behavior. Management.

HD31.W559 1994
Winslow, Charles D.
FutureWork: putting knowledge to work in the knowledge economy/ Charles D. Winslow, William L. Bramer. New York: Free Press; c1994. ix, 384 p.
94-015202   658.4/03   0029354153
Industrial management. Information technology.

HD38 Management. Industrial management — General special

HD38.B258 1993
Barsoux, Jean-Louis.
Funny business: humour, management and business culture/ Jean-Louis Barsoux. London; Cassell, 1993. 200 p.
94-139301   158.26   0304326771
Humor in business. Management -- Humor. Corporate culture -- Humor.

HD38.N42 1990
Newstrom, John W.
Windows into organizations/ John W. Newstrom and Jon L. Pierce. New York, NY: AMACOM, American Management Association, c1990. xiv, 400 p.
89-046216   658.4/02   0814459552
Management -- Charts, diagrams. etc.

HD38.O738 2000
Organization charts: structures of 230 businesses, government agencies, and non-profit organizations/ edited by Nick Sternberg and Scott Heil. 3rd ed. Detroit: Gale Research, c2000. xi, 353 p.
00-702790   658.4/02 21   0787624527
Industrial organization -- Charts, diagrams, etc. Organization charts. Business enterprises -- Charts, diagrams, etc.

HD38.2 Management. Industrial management — Executives. Executive ability — General works

HD38.2.B74 1996
Broken ladders: managerial careers in the new economy/ edited by Paul Osterman. New York: Oxford University Press, 1996. xii, 259 p.
96-025776   658   0195093534
Executives -- Job descriptions. Career development.

HD38.2.B83 1999
Buckingham, Marcus.
First, break all the rules: what the world's greatest managers do differently/ Marcus Buckingham and Curt Coffman. New York, NY.: Simon & Schuster, c1999. 271 p.
99-019452   658.4/09 21   0684852861
Executive ability. Management. Executives -- Attitudes.

HD38.2.G58 2000
Global literacies: lessons on business leadership and national cultures: a landmark study of CEOs from 28 countries/ Robert Rosen ... [et al.]. New York: Simon & Schuster, c2000. 409 p.
99-054914   658.4/092 B 21   0684859025
Chief executive officers. Leadership.

HD38.2.M53 2001
Michaels, Ed,
The war for talent/ Ed Michaels, Helen Handfield-Jones, Beth Axelrod. Boston, Mass.: Harvard Business School Press, c2001. xxiii, 200 p.
2001-024864   658.4/07 21   1578514592
Executive ability. Leadership. Employee motivation.

HD38.2.M67 1992
Morrison, Ann M.
The new leaders: guidelines on leadership diversity in America/ Ann M. Morrison. San Francisco, Calif.: Jossey-Bass, c1992. xxiii, 317 p.
92-020107   658.4/092   1555424597
Executives -- United States. Women executives -- United States. Minority executives -- United States.

HD38.4 Management. Industrial management — Bureaucracy

HD38.4.J32 1983
Jackson, P. M.
The political economy of bureaucracy/ P.M. Jackson. Totowa, N.J.: Barnes & Noble Books, 1983. viii, 295 p.
82-022674   350/.001   0389203521
Bureaucracy.

HD38.4.P56 1993
Pinchot, Gifford.
The end of bureaucracy & the rise of the intelligent organization/ Gifford & Elizabeth Pinchot. San Francisco: Berrett-Koehler Publishers, c1993. xxi, 399 p.
93-040302   350   1881052346
Bureaucracy. Management. Organizational sociology.

HD38.5 Management. Industrial management — Business logistics

HD38.5.F738 2001
Fredendall, Lawrence D.
Basics of supply chain management/ by Lawrence D. Fredendall, Ed Hill. Boca Raton, Fla.: St. Lucie Press; c2001. xx, 237 p.
00-011246   658.7 21   1574441205
Business logistics. Materials management.

HD38.5.G67 1992
Gopal, Christopher.
Logistics in manufacturing/ Christopher Gopal, Gerard Cahill. Homewood, IL: Business One Irwin, c1992. xi, 312 p.
91-025189   658.5   1556233892
Business logistics -- United States. Competition -- United States.

HD38.7 Management. Industrial management — Business intelligence. Trade secrets

HD38.7.F5 1997
Fialka, John J.
War by other means: economic espionage in America/ John J. Fialka. New York: Norton, c1997. xiv, 242 p.
96-016699   364.1/68 20   0393040143
Business intelligence -- United States. Trade secrets -- United States.

HD38.7.M55 2000
Miller, Jerry,
Millennium intelligence: understanding and conducting competitive intelligence in the digital age/ Jerry Miller and the Business Intelligence Braintrust. Medford, N.J.: CyberAge Books, 2000. xiii, 276 p.
00-021342   658.4/7 21   0910965285
Business intelligence. Business information services. Business -- Databases.

HD38.7.S48 1999
Shaker, Steven M.
War room guide to competitive intelligence/ Steven M. Shaker, Mark P. Gembicki. New York: McGraw-Hill, 1999.
98-049540   658.4/7   007058057X
Business intelligence. Competition.

HD39.5 Management. Industrial management — Capital. Capital investments — Industrial procurement

HD39.5.B875 2003
Burt, David N.
World class supply management: the key to supply chain management/ David N. Burt, Donald W. Dobler, Stephen L. Starling. 7th ed. Boston: McGraw-Hill/Irwin, c2003. xlvi, 689 p.
2002-021920   658.7 21   0071123105
Industrial procurement. Purchasing. Materials management.

HD39.5.S873 2001
Supply chain management/ John T. Mentzer, editor. Thousand Oaks, Calif.: Sage Publications, c2001. xii, 512 p.
00-010197   658.7 21   0761921117
Business logistics. Industrial procurement -- Management. Materials management.

HD41 Management. Industrial management — Competition

HD41.A84 1988
Auerbach, Paul.
Competition: the economics of industrial change/ Paul Auerbach. Oxford, UK; B. Blackwell, 1988. viii, 339 p.
87-029384   338.6/048   0631159665
Competition. Capitalism.

HD41.P668 1985
Porter, Michael E., 1947-
Competitive advantage: creating and sustaining superior performance/ Michael E. Porter. New York: Free Press; c1985. xviii, 557 p.
83-049518   658   0029250900
Competition. Industrial management.

HD41.P67 1980
Porter, Michael E., 1947-
Competitive strategy: techniques for analyzing industries and competitors/ Michael E. Porter. New York: Free Press, c1980. xx, 396 p.
80-065200   658   0029253608
Competition. Industrial management.

HD41.W494 1997
Wharton on dynamic competitive strategy/ editors, George S. Day and David J. Reibstein, with Robert E. Gunther. New York: John Wiley, c1997. xi, 465 p.
96-053177   658.4/012 21   0471172073
Competition. Industrial management. Strategic planning.

HD42 Management. Industrial management — Conflict management

HD42.M38 2002
Masters, Marick Francis,
The complete guide to conflict resolution in the workplace/ Marick F. Masters and Robert R. Albright. New York: AMACOM, c2002 vii, 343 p
2001-055987   658.4/053 21   0814406297
Conflict management. Dispute resolution (Law)

HD45 Management. Industrial management — Technological innovations

HD45.G36 1990
Gattiker, Urs E.
Technology management in organizations/ Urs E. Gattiker. Newbury Park, Calif.: Sage Publications, c1990. 339 p.
90-008227   658.5/14   0803936079
Technological innovations -- Management. Manpower planning. Organizational behavior.

HD45.G58 1990
Goodman, Paul S.
Technology and organizations/ Paul S. Goodman, Lee S. Sproull, and associates. San Francisco: Jossey-Bass, 1990. xxi, 281 p.
89-026993   658.5/14   1555422098
Technological innovations -- Management. Technology -- Management. Organizational behavior.

HD45.H84 1997
The Human side of managing technological innovation: a collection of readings/ edited by Ralph Katz. New York: Oxford University Press, 1997. xvii, 618 p.
96-038714   658.5/14   0195096932
Technological innovations -- Management.

HD45.R77 1989
Rubenstein, Albert Harold, 1923-
Managing technology in the decentralized firm/ Albert H. Rubenstein. New York: Wiley, c1989. xxiv, 476 p.
88-020875   658.5/14   0471610240
Technological innovations -- Management. Technology -- Management. Research, Industrial -- Management.

HD45.S627 1999
Sources of industrial leadership: studies of seven industries/ edited by David C. Mowery, Richard R. Nelson. Cambridge, UK; Cambridge University Press, 1999. viii, 401 p.
98-044552   658.5/14   052164254X
Technological innovations -- Management. Industries -- Technolgical innovations -- Case studies. Comparative advantage (International trade)

HD47.3 Management. Industrial management — Costs. Industrial costs — Cost control

HD47.3.M37 2000
Martin, John D., 1945-
Value based management: the corporate response to the shareholder revolution/ John D. Martin, J. William Petty. Boston, Mass.: Harvard Business School Press, c2000. xvi, 249 p.
00-031910   658 21   0875848001
Value analysis (Cost control) Industrial management.

HD47.4 Management. Industrial management — Costs. Industrial costs — Cost effectiveness

HD47.4.K56 2001
Kingma, Bruce R.
The economics of information: a guide to economic and cost-benefit analysis for information professionals/ Bruce R. Kingma. 2nd ed. Englewood, CO: Libraries Unlimited, 2001. xii, 180 p.
00-050701   658.15/54 21   1563088169
Cost effectiveness. Information science -- Economic aspects.

HD49 Management. Industrial management — Crisis management. Emergency management — General works

HD49.W45 2001
Weick, Karl E.
Managing the unexpected: assuring high performance in an age of complexity/ Karl E. Weick, Kathleen M. Sutcliffe. 1st ed. San Francisco: Jossey-Bass, c2001. xvi, 200 p.
2001-001341   658.4/056 21   0787956279
Crisis management. Leadership. Industrial management.

HD51 Management. Industrial management — Division of labor. Specialization

HD51.D57 2002
Distributed work/ edited by Pamela Hinds and Sara Kiesler. Cambridge, Mass.: MIT Press, c2002. xviii, 475 p.
2001-056237   658.4/036 21   0262083051
Division of labor. International division of labor. Teams in the workplace.

HD53 Management. Industrial management — Intellectual work. Intellectual capital

HD53.B76 1997
Brooking, Annie.
Intellectual capital/ Annie Brooking. London; International Thomson Business Press, 1997. vii, 204 p.
96-038887   650.1/3   1861520239
Intellectual capital.

HD53.H356 1988
Handbook for creative and innovative managers/ Robert Lawrence Kuhn, editor in chief. New York: McGraw-Hill, c1988. xx, 652 p.
87-003189   658.4/094   0070356076
Creative ability in business.

HD53.S893 1997
Sveiby, Karl Erik.
The new organizational wealth: managing & measuring knowledge-based assets/ Karl Erik Sveiby. San Francisco: Berrett-Koehler Publishers, c1997. xii, 220 p.
97-001964   658 21   1576750140
Intangible property -- Management. Intangible property -- Valuation. Organization.

HD56 Management. Industrial management — Industrial productivity — General works

HD56.K46
Kendrick, John W.
Understanding productivity: an introduction to the dynamics of productivity change/ John W. Kendrick. Baltimore: Johns Hopkins University Press, c1977. vii, 141 p.
77-004786   338/.0973   0801819962
Industrial productivity. Industrial productivity -- United States.

HD57 Management. Industrial management — Industrial productivity — Labor productivity

HD57.G88 1983
Guzzo, Richard A.
A guide to worker productivity experiments in the United States, 1976-81/ Richard A. Guzzo, Jeffrey S. Bondy. New York: Pergamon Press, c1983. xi, 161 p.
82-013248   331.11/8/0973   0080295487
Labor productivity -- United States.

HD57.7 Management. Industrial management — Leadership

HD57.7.B454 1992
Bellman, Geoffrey M., 1938-
Getting things done when you are not in charge/ by Geoffrey M. Bellman. San Francisco: Berrett-Koehler Publishers, c1992. xx, 278 p.
92-070094   658.4/092   1881052028
Leadership. Executive ability. Organizational effectiveness.

HD57.7.B4578 2002
Bennis, Warren G.
Geeks & geezers: how era, values, and defining moments shape leaders / Warren G. Bennis, Robert J. Thomas. Boston: Harvard Business School Press, c2002. xxvii, 224 p.
2002-004910   303.3/4 21   1578515823
Leadership. Executive ability. Executives -- Biography.

HD57.7.B66 1998
The book of leadership wisdom: classic writings by legendary business leaders/ edited by Peter Krass. New York: Wiley, c1998. xiv, 493 p.
98-033921   658.4/092 21   0471294551
Leadership.

HD57.7.C546 2003
Clawson, James G.
Practical problems in organizations: cases in leadership, organizational behavior, and human resources/ James G. Clawson. Upper Saddle River, N.J.: Prentice Hall, c2003. xi, 468 p.
2001-055415   658 21   0130083895
Leadership -- Case studies. Organizational behavior -- Case studies. Personnel management -- Case studies.

HD57.7.C765 2002
Cross-cultural approaches to leadership development/ edited by C. Brooklyn Derr, Sylvie Roussillon, and Frank Bournois. Westport, Conn.: Quorum Books, 2002. xx, 321 p.
2001-019587   658.4/07124 21   156720466X
Leadership -- Cross-cultural studies.

HD57.7.F348 1997
Fairholm, Gilbert W.
Capturing the heart of leadership: spirituality and community in the new American workplace/ Gilbert W. Fairholm. Westport, Conn.: Praeger, 1997. xi, 235 p.
96-026282   658.4/092   0275957438
Leadership -- Moral and ethical aspects. Corporate culture -- United States.

HD57.7.F76 1992
Frontiers of leadership: an essential reader/ edited by Michel Syrett and Clare Hogg. Oxford, UK; Blackwell, 1992. xxii, 585 p.
91-030908   658.4/092   0631168656
Leadership. Management.

HD57.7.H525 2001
Hiebert, Murray, 1943-
The encyclopedia of leadership: a practical guide to popular leadership theories and techniques/ Murray Hiebert, Bruce Klatt. New York: McGraw-Hill, c2001. xxxi, 479 p.
2001-268718   658.4/092 B 21   0071363084
Leadership -- Handbooks, manuals, etc.

HD57.7.K67 1988
Kotter, John P., 1947-
The leadership factor/ John P. Kotter. New York: Free Press; c1988. ix, 161 p.
87-019805   658.4/092   0029183316
Leadership. Industrial management.

HD57.7.K68 2002
Kouzes, James M.,
The leadership challenge/ by James M. Kouzes and Barry Z. Posner. 3rd ed. San Francisco: Jossey-Bass, c2002. xxviii, 458 p.
2002-009871   658.4/092 21   0787956783
Leadership. Executive ability. Management.

HD57.7.K733 1999
Multiple intelligences and leadership/ edited by Ronald E. Riggio, Susan E. Murphy, Francis J. Pirozzolo. Mahwah, N.J.: Lawrence Erlbaum Associates, c2002. xv, 264 p.
2001-023919   658.4/092 21   0805834664
Leadership -- Congresses. Multiple intelligences -- Congresses.

HD57.7.L423 1999
The leaders change handbook: an essential guide to setting direction and taking action/ Jay A. Conger, Gretchen M. Spreitzer, Edward E. Lawler III, editors. San Francisco: Jossey-Bass, c1999. xlvi, 375 p.
98-040101   658.4/092 B 21   0787943517
Leadership. Organizational change.

HD57.7.M396 1992
McLean, J. W.
Leadership--magic, myth, or method?/ J.W. McLean and William Weitzel. New York, NY: AMACOM, American Management Association, c1992. xiv, 249 p.
91-034595   303.3/4   0814450547
Leadership. Management.

HD57.7.U45 1999
Ulrich, David, 1953-
Results-based leadership/ Dave Ulrich, Jack Zenger, Norm Smallwood. Boston: Harvard Business School Press, 1999. xiv, 234 p.
98-042243   658.4/092   0875848710
Leadership. Executive ability.

HD58 Management. Industrial management — Location of industry

HD58.S674
Spatial analysis, industry, and the industrial environment: progress in research and applications/ edited by F.E. Ian Hamilton and G.J.R. Linge. Chichester, Eng.; Wiley, c1979-c1983 v. 1-3.
78-010298   338.6/042   0471997382
Industrial location. Manufactures.

HD58.6 Management. Industrial management — Negotiation. Negotiation in business

HD58.6.A93 1997
Aubuchon, Norbert.
The anatomy of persuasion/ Norbert Aubuchon. New York: Amacom, c1997. xii, 193 p.
96-051050   658.4/052 21   0814479529
Negotiation in business. Persuasion (Psychology) Persuasion (Rhetoric)

HD58.6.B74 2001
Brett, Jeanne M.
Negotiating globally: how to negotiate deals, resolve disputes, and make decisions across cultural boundaries/ Jeanne M. Brett. 1st ed. San Francisco: Jossey-Bass, c2001. xxxi, 246 p.
00-011770   658.4/052 21   0787955868
Negotiation in business -- Cross-cultural studies. Negotiation -- Cross-cultural studies. Decision making -- Cross-cultural studies.

HD58.6.H63 2000
Hodgson, James D., 1915-
Doing business with the new Japan/ James Day Hodgson, Yoshihiro Sano, John L. Graham. Lanham: Rowman & Littlefield Publishers, c2000. xiii, 230 p.
99-057658   658.4/052 21   0847699285
Negotiation in business -- United States. Negotiation in business -- Japan. Intercultural communication -- United States. United States -- Commerce -- Japan. Japan -- Commerce -- United States

HD58.6.R342 2002
Raiffa, Howard,
Negotiation analysis: the science and art of collaborative decision making/ Howard Raiffa with John Richardson, David Metcalfe. Cambridge, MA: Belknap Press of Harvard University Press, 2002. xiv, 548 p.
2002-074688　658.4/052 21　0674008901
Negotiation in business. Negotiation. Decision making.

HD58.7 Management. Industrial management — Organizational behavior. Corporate culture

HD58.7.C37 1991
Casson, Mark, 1945-
The economics of business culture: game theory, transaction costs, and economic performance/ Mark Casson. Oxford: Clarendon Press; 1991. xi, 286 p.
91-002067　338.5/14　019823875X
Corporate culture. Business ethics. Game theory.

HD58.7.C6214 2001
Cohen, Don,
In good company: how social capital makes organizations work/ Don Cohen, Laurence Prusak. Boston: Harvard Business School Press, c2001. xii, 214 p.
00-059739　302.3/5 21　087584913X
Organizational behavior. Corporate culture. Quality of work life.

HD58.7.D46 1990
Denison, Daniel R.
Corporate culture and organizational effectiveness/ Daniel R. Denison. New York: Wiley, c1990. xvii, 267 p.
89-027938　302.3/5　047180021X
Corporate culture. Organizational effectiveness.

HD58.7.F735 1995
Frederick, William Crittenden, 1925-
Values, nature, and culture in the American corporation/ William C. Frederick. New York: Oxford University Press, 1995. xviii, 313 p.
94-038396　302.3/5　0195094115
Corporate culture -- United States. Business ethics -- United States. Social responsibility of business -- United States.

HD58.7.G334 2000
Gabriel, Yiannis,
Storytelling in organizations: facts, fictions, and fantasies/ Yiannis Gabriel. Oxford; Oxford University Press, 2000. vii, 266 p.
99-059052　302.3/5 21　0198297068
Organizational behavior. Management. Storytelling.

HD58.7.H355 2001
Handbook of organizational behavior/ edited by Robert T. Golembiewski. 2nd ed., rev. and expanded. New York: Marcel Dekker, c2001. xv, 805 p.
00-060195　302.3/5 21　0824703936
Organizational behavior.

HD58.7.H363 2000
Handbook of organizational culture & climate/ Neal M. Ashkanasy, Celeste P.M. Wilderom, Mark F. Peterson, editors. Thousand Oaks, Calif.: Sage Publications, c2000. xxxiii, 629 p.
00-008367　658.4 21　0761916024
Organizational behavior. Corporate culture.

HD58.7.H376 1988
Harvey, Jerry B.
The Abilene paradox and other meditations on management/ Jerry B. Harvey. Lexington, Mass.: Lexington Books; c1988. viii, 150 p.
88-045176　658/.00207　0669191795
Organizational behavior -- Moral and ethical aspects -- Humor. Management -- Moral and ethical aspects -- Humor.

HD58.7.H385 2000
Haslam, S. Alexander.
Psychology in organizations: the social identity approach/ S. Alexander Haslam. London; SAGE, 2001. xvi, 411 p.
2001-267824　158.7 21　0761961585
Organizational behavior. Social psychology. Group identity.

HD58.7.H4 1997
Hatch, Mary Jo
Organization theory: modern, symbolic, and postmodern perspectives/ Mary Jo Hatch. Oxford; Oxford University Press, 1997. xxviii, 387 p.
97-170130　302.3/5　0198774907
Organizational behavior. Organizational sociology. Organization.

HD58.7.L4 1998
Leading organizations: perspectives for a new era/ Gill Robinson Hickman, editor. Thousand Oaks, Calif.: Sage Publications, c1998. xv, 613 p.
98-025335　658.4/06 21　0761914226
Organizational behavior. Organizational effectiveness. Leadership.

HD58.7.M3747 1999
Marx, Elisabeth.
Breaking through culture shock: what you need to succeed in international business/ Elisabeth Marx. London; Nicholas Brealey, 1999. xv, 233 p.
98-046502　658　1857882202
Corporate culture. Business etiquette. Culture shock.

HD58.7.O324 1997
Oden, Howard W.
Managing corporate culture, innovation, and intrapreneurship/ Howard W. Oden. Westport, Conn.: Quorum Books, 1997. xiv, 279 p.
96-054283　658.4　1567200478
Corporate culture. Organizational behavior. Organizational change.

HD58.7.O717 2003
Organizational behavior: the state of the science/ edited by Jerald Greenberg. 2nd ed. Mahwah, NJ: Lawrence Erlbaum, 2003. xxv, 470 p.
2002-033869　302.3/5 21　0805845410
Organizational behavior.

HD58.7.S33 1992
Schein, Edgar H.
Organizational culture and leadership/ Edgar H. Schein. 2nd ed. San Francisco: Jossey-Bass, c1992. xix, 418 p.
92-023849　302.3/5 20　1555424872
Corporate culture. Culture. Leadership.

HD58.7.S584 1986
Sims, Henry P., 1939-
The thinking organization/ Henry P. Sims, Jr., Dennis A. Gioia, and associates. San Francisco: Jossey-Bass, 1986. xxvii, 375 p.
85-045913　302.3/5　0875896901
Organizational behavior. Cognition. Social perception.

HD58.7.T73 1989
Tracy, Lane, 1934-
The living organization: systems of behavior/ Lane Tracy. New York: Praeger, 1989. xii, 216 p.
88-039746　302.3/5　027593084X
Organizational behavior.

HD58.7.T74 1993
Trice, Harrison Miller, 1920-
The cultures of work orgranizations/ Harrison M. Trice, Janice M. Beyer. Englewood Cliffs, N.J.: Prentice Hall, c1993. xvii, 510 p.
92-009291　302.2/5　0131914383
Corporate culture.

HD58.8 Management. Industrial management — Organizational change. Organizational development

HD58.8.A38 1990
Advances in organization development/ edited by Fred Massarik. Norwood, NJ: Ablex Pub. Corp., [c1990-] v. 1.
89-017852　658.4/06　0893912425
Organizational change.

HD58.8.B675 2002
The boundaryless organization: breaking the chains of organizational structure/ Ron Ashkenas ... [et al.]; forewords by C. K. Prahalad and Lawrence A. Bossidy. 2nd ed. San Francisco, CA: Jossey-Bass, c2002. xxxviii, 346 p.
2001-006128　658.4/063 21　078795943X
Organizational change. Industrial organization. Interorganizational relations.

HD58.8.B784 1993
Brunsson, Nils, 1946-
The reforming organization/ Nils Brunsson and Johan P. Olsen. London; Routledge, 1993. vi, 216 p.
93-018708　658.4/063　0415082870
Organizational change. Organizational behavior.

HD58.8.B876 2002
Burke, W. Warner
Organization change: theory and practice/ W. Warner Burke. Thousand Oaks, Calif.: Sage Publications, c2002. xviii, 325 p.
2002-003624　658.4/06 21　0761914838
Organizational change. Leadership.

HD58.8.C452 1997
Change at work/ Peter Cappelli ... [et al.]. New York: Oxford University Press, 1997. viii, 276 p.
96-023911　658.4/06　0195103270
Organizational change -- United States. Corporate reorganizations -- United States. Downsizing of organizations -- United States.

HD58.8.C646 1996
Competing in the information age: strategic alignment in practice/ edited by Jerry N. Luftman. New York: Oxford University Press, 1996. xvii, 414 p.
95-009343　658.4/038　0195090160
Organizational change. Strategic planning. Information technology -- Management.

HD58.8.H3618 1994
Handy, Charles B.
The age of paradox/ Charles Handy. Boston, Mass.: Harvard Business School Press, 1994. xiii, 303 p.
93-036586   302.3/5   0875844251
Organizational change. Organizational behavior. Social prediction.

HD58.8.H363 1989
Hannan, Michael T.
Organizational ecology/ Michael T. Hannan, John Freeman. Cambridge, Mass.: Harvard University Press, 1989. xvi, 366 p.
88-015470   302.3/5   0674643488
Organizational change. Organizational behavior.

HD58.8.I577 1993
Institutional change: theory and empirical findings/ editor, Sven-Erik Sjostrand. Armonk, N.Y.: M.E. Sharpe, c1993. xi, 428 p.
92-040744   302.3/5   1563240807
Organizational change. Organizational change -- Case studies. Economic conversion -- Europe -- Case studies.

HD58.8.K645 2002
Kotter, John P.,
The heart of change: real-life stories of how people change their organizations/ John P. Kotter, Dan S. Cohen. Boston, Mass.: Harvard Business School Press, c2002. xiv, 190 p.
2002-001475   658.4/06 21   1578512549
Organizational change.

HD58.8.M257 1994
Manganelli, Raymond L.
The reengineering handbook: a step-by-step guide to business transformation/ Raymond L. Manganelli, Mark M. Klein. New York: AMACOM, c1994. xvi, 318 p.
94-026609   658.4/063   0814402364
Organizational change -- Management. Corporate reorganizations. Reengineering (Management)

HD58.8.M43 2002
Measuring and analyzing behavior in organizations: advances in measurement and data analysis/ Fritz Drasgow, Neal Schmitt, editors; foreword by Neal Schmitt. San Francisco, CA: Jossey-Bass, c2002. xxvi, 591 p.
2001-001763   158.7 21   0787953016
Organizational behavior -- Evaluation. Organizational change -- Evaluation.

HD58.8.O47 2001
Olson, Edwin E.
Facilitating organization change: lessons from complexity science/ Edwin E. Olson, Glenda H. Eoyang; forewords by Richard Bekhard and Peter Vaill. San Francisco, Calif.: Jossey-Bass/Pfeiffer, c2001. xlvii, 191 p.
00-011521   658.4/092 21   078795330X
Organizational change.

HD58.8.O7284 1997
The organization of the future/ Frances Hesselbein, Marshall Goldsmith, Richard Beckhard, editors. San Francisco, Calif.: Jossey-Bass Publishers, c1997. xvi, 397 p.
96-045826   658.4/06 21   0787903035
Organizational change.

HD58.8.O7289 2000
Organizational change & gender equity: international perspectives on fathers and mothers at the workplace/ editors, Linda L. Haas, Philip Hwang, Graeme Russell. Thousand Oaks, Calif.: Sage Publications, c2000. xii, 291 p.
99-006398   331.25 21   076191045X
Organizational change. Work and family. Parents -- Employment.

HD58.8.P35 1996
Papadakis, Elim.
Environmental politics and institutional change/ Elim Papadakis. Cambridge [England]; Cambridge University Press, 1996. xiii, 240 p.
96-015629   658.4/06   0521554071
Organizational change. Environmental policy -- Political aspects. Political science.

HD58.8.T7 1992
Transforming organizations/ Thomas A. Kochan, Michael Useem, editors. New York: Oxford University Press, 1992. xi, 420 p.
91-016837   658.4/06   0195065042
Organizational change -- Congresses.

HD58.8.Z55 1991
Zimmerman, Frederick Michael.
The turnaround experience: real-world lessons in revitalizing corporations/ Frederick M. Zimmerman. New York: McGraw-Hill, c1991. xii, 335 p.
91-003509   658.1/6   0070728992
Industrial management. Quality of products. Corporate turnarounds.

HD58.82 Management. Industrial management — Organizational learning

HD58.82.A37 1997
Allee, Verna, 1949-
The knowledge evolution: expanding organizational intelligence/ Verna Allee. Boston, Mass.: Butterworth-Heinemann, c1997. xvii, 274 p.
96-048561   658.4/038 21   075069842X
Organizational learning.

HD58.82.G37 2000
Garvin, David A.
Learning in action: a guide to putting the learning organization to work/ David A. Garvin. Boston, Mass.: Harvard Business School Press, c2000. xvi, 256 p.
99-048911   658.4/06 21   1578512514
Organizational learning. Organizational learning -- Case studies.

HD58.82.H36 2001
Handbook of organizational learning and knowledge/ edited by Meinolf Dierkes ... [et al.]. Oxford; Oxford University Press, 2001. xxv, 979 p.
2001-021816   658.4/038 21   0198295839
Organizational learning -- Handbooks, manuals, etc. Knowledge management -- Handbooks, manuals, etc.

HD58.9 Management. Industrial management — Organizational effectiveness — General works

HD58.9.B43 2001
Becker, Brian E.
The HR scorecard: linking people, strategy, and performance/ Brian E. Becker, Mark A. Huselid, Dave Ulrich. Boston, MA: Harvard Business School Press, c2001. xiii, 235 p.
00-053945   658.3 21   1578511364
Organizational effectiveness -- Evaluation. Industrial management. Human capital.

HD58.9.B875 2002
Business performance measurement: theory and practice/ edited by Andy Neely. Cambridge: Cambridge University Press, 2002. xiii, 366 p.
2002-283000   658.4/01 21   052180342X
Organizational effectiveness -- Measurement. Performance -- Measurement. Total quality management.

HD58.9.L48 2002
Levinson, Harry.
Organizational assessment: a step-by-step guide to effective consulting/ Harry Levinson. 1st ed. Washington, DC: American Psychological Association, c2002. xii, 317 p.
2002-018251   001 21   1557989214
Organizational effectiveness -- Evaluation. Business consultants.

HD58.9.S36 1990
Schonberger, Richard.
Building a chain of customers: linking business functions to create the world class company/ Richard J. Schonberger. New York: Free Press; c1990. ix, 349 p.
89-077552   658.8   0029279917
Organizational effectiveness. Industrial management.

HD59 Management. Industrial management — Public relations. Industrial publicity — General works

HD59.F37 2002
Fearn-Banks, Kathleen.
Crisis communications: a casebook approach/ Kathleen Fearn-Banks. 2nd ed. Mahwah, N.J.: Lawrence Erlbaum Associates, 2002. xiv, 354 p.
2001-280102   659.2 21   0805836039
Public relations -- Management -- Case studies. Crisis management -- Case studies. Advertising -- Case studies.

HD59.G78 2001
Grunig, Larissa A.
Women in public relations: how gender influences practice/ Larissa A Grunig, Elizabeth Lance Toth, Linda Childers Hon; foreword by Kathleen Larey Lewton. New York: Guilford Press, 2001. xxi, 424 p.
00-052088   331.4/816592 21   1572306262
Public relations. Sex role in the work environment.

HD59.H267 2001
Handbook of public relations/ Robert L. Heath, editor; Gabriel Vasquez, contributing editor. Thousand Oaks, Calif.: Sage Publications, c2001. xiv, 802 p.
00-008736   659.2 21   076191286X
Public relations.

HD59.2 Management. Industrial management — Public relations. Industrial publicity — Corporate image

HD59.2.B87 1999
Burke, Edmund M.
Corporate community relations: the principle of the neighbor of choice/ Edmund M. Burke; foreword by Raymond V. Gilmartin. Westport, Conn.: Quorum Books, 1999. xviii, 185 p.
98-027837   658.4/08   156720192X
Corporate image. Social responsibility of business. Public relations.

HD59.2.M33 1993
Mackiewicz, Andrea.
The economist intelligence unit guide to building a global image/ Andrea Mackiewicz. New York: McGraw-Hill, c1993. xvi, 184 p.
93-006485   659.2   0070093504
Corporate image. Strategic planning. Competition, International.

HD59.2.O39 1990
Olins, Wally.
Corporate identity: making business strategy visible through design/ Wally Olins. Boston, Mass.: Harvard Business School Press, 1990. 224 p.
90-004526   658.4/012   087584250X
Corporate image. Organizational behavior.

HD59.5 Management. Industrial management — Public relations. Industrial publicity — Issues management

HD59.5.H4 1988
Heath, Robert L. 1941-
Strategic issues management: how organizations influence and respond to public interests and policies/ Robert L. Heath and associates. San Francisco: Jossey-Bass Publishers, 1988. xxi, 415 p.
87-046335   658.4/012   1555420834
Issues management. Business planning. Strategic planning.

HD59.6 Management. Industrial management — Public relations. Industrial publicity — By region or country, A-Z

HD59.6.U6 R35 2001
Rampton, Sheldon,
Trust us, we're experts!: how industry manipulates science and gambles with your future/ Sheldon Rampton and John Stauber. New York: Jeremy P. Tarcher/Putnam, c2001. 360 p.
00-062920   659.2 21   158542059X
Industrial publicity -- Corrupt practices -- United States. Corporations -- Public relations -- Corrupt practices -- United States. Public relations consultants -- Corrupt practices -- United States.

HD60 Management. Industrial management — Social responsibility of business — General works

HD60.D26 1994
Danley, John R., 1948-
The role of the modern corporation in a free society/ by John R. Danley. Notre Dame: University of Notre Dame Press, c1994. xiv, 345 p.
93-002103   658.4/08   026801647X
Social responsibility of business. Business ethics. Corporations -- Philosophy.

HD60.F74 1984
French, Peter A.
Collective and corporate responsibility/ Peter A. French. New York: Columbia University Press, 1984. xiv, 215 p.
84-003226   658.4/08   0231058365
Industries -- Social aspects. Social responsibility of business. Corporations -- Corrupt practices.

HD60.H393 1993
Hawken, Paul.
The ecology of commerce: a declaration of sustainability/ Paul Hawken. New York, NY: HarperBusiness, c1993. xvi, 250 p.
93-031111   658.4/08   0887306551
Social responsibility of business. Sustainable development. Economic development -- Environmental aspects.

HD60.H47 2001
Hertz, Noreena.
The silent takeover: global capitalism and the death of democracy/ Noreena Hertz. New York: Free Press, c2001. 247 p.
2002-021452   338.8/8 21   0743234782
Social responsibility of business. Corporations -- Social aspects. Globalization.

HD60.P33 1995
Pava, Moses L.
Corporate responsibility and financial performance: the paradox of social cost/ Moses L. Pava, Joshua Krausz. Westport, Conn.: Quorum Books, 1995. xii, 176 p.
94-045284   658.4/08   0899309216
Social responsibility of business. Social responsibility of business -- Costs. Corporations -- Finance.

HD60.P73
Preston, Lee E.
Private management and public policy: the principle of public responsibility/ Lee E. Preston, James E. Post. Englewood Cliffs, N.J.: Prentice-Hall, [1975] xv, 157 p.
74-026551   658.4/08   0137109881
Industries -- Social aspects. Industries -- Social aspects -- United States.

HD60.S39 1999
Schwartz, Peter, 1946-
When good companies do bad things: responsibility and risk in an age of globalization/ Peter Schwartz and Blair Gibb. New York: John Wiley, 1999. xiv, 194 p.
98-031700   658.4/08   0471323322
Social responsibility of business. International business enterprises.

HD60.5 Management. Industrial management — Social responsibility of business — By region or country, A-Z

HD60.5.U5.C66
Committee for Economic Development.
Social responsibilities of business corporations; a statement on national policy by the Research and Policy Committee of the Committee for Economic Development, June 1971. [New York, [1971] 74 p.
76-168378   658.4/08/0973
Industries -- Social aspects -- United States.

HD60.5.U5.H4
Heald, Morrell.
The social responsibilities of business, company, and community, 1900-1960. Cleveland, Press of Case Western Reserve University, 1970. xix, 339 p.
75-084490   301.2/4   0829501762
Social responsibility of business -- United States -- History.

HD60.5.U5 J664 2003
Johnson, Roberta Ann.
Whistleblowing: when it works--and why/ Roberta Ann Johnson. Boulder: L. Rienner Publishers, c2003. xi, 171 p.
2002-073940   174/.4 21   1588261395
Whistle blowing -- United States. Business ethics -- United States. Administrative agencies -- Corrupt practices -- United States.

HD61 Management. Industrial management — Social responsibility of business — Risk management. Risk in industry

HD61.A24
Acceptable risk/ Baruch Fischhoff ... [et al.]. Cambridge; Cambridge University Press, 1981. xv, 185 p.
81-009957   658   0521241642
Risk. Risk management -- Decision making.

HD61.B466 1996
Bernstein, Peter L.
Against the gods: the remarkable story of risk/ Peter L. Bernstein. New York: John Wiley & Sons, c1996. xi, 383 p.
96-033861   368 20   0471121045
Risk management. Decision making.

HD61.S45 2003
Shiller, Robert J.
The new financial order: risk in the 21st century/ Robert J. Shiller. Princeton, NJ: Princeton University Press, c2003. xvi, 366 p.
2002-042563   368 21   0691091722
Risk management. Information technology.

HD62.15 Management. Industrial management — Social responsibility of business — Total quality management. Benchmarking

HD62.15.C3639 1999
Cartin, T. J. 1924-
Principles and practices of organizational performance excellence/ T. J. Cartin. Milwaukee, Wis.: ASQ Quality Press, c1999. xiv, 334 p.
98-042726   658.4/013 21   0873894286
Total quality management. Industrial management. Industrial productivity -- Management.

HD62.15.C668 1995
Cortada, James W.
The McGraw-Hill encyclopedia of quality terms & concepts/ James W. Cortada, John A. Woods. New York; McGraw-Hill, c1995. vi, 392 p.
95-015695   658.5/62/03   007024099X
Total quality management -- Encyclopedias. Quality control -- Encyclopedias.

HD62.15.F35 2001
Fairfield-Sonn, James W., 1948-
Corporate culture and the quality organization/ James W. Fairfield-Sonn; foreword by Lawrence K. Williams. Westport, Conn.: Quorum Books , 2001. xxii, 217 p.
00-032809   658.4/013   0899309038
Total quality management. Corporate culture.

HD62.15.G463 1994
George, Stephen, 1948-
Total quality management: strategies and techniques proven at today's most successful companies/ Stephen George, Arnold Weimerskirch. New York: Wiley, c1994. xv, 286 p.
93-024465   658.4/013   0471595381
Total quality management -- United States -- Case studies. Malcolm Baldrige National Quality Award.

HD62.15.H37 1992
Hart, Christopher W. L.
The Baldrige: what it is, how it's won, how to use it to improve quality in your company/ Christopher W.L. Hart, Christopher E. Bogan. New York: McGraw-Hill, c1992. xxii, 281 p.
92-012344   658.4/013/07973   0070269122
Malcolm Baldrige National Quality Award. Total quality management -- United States.

HD62.15.H38 1999
Hatry, Harry P.
Performance measurement: getting results/ Harry P. Hatry; with a chapter by Joseph S. Wholey. Washington, D.C.: Urban Institute Press, c1999. xx, 286 p.
99-041582   658.4/013 21   087766692X
Benchmarking (Management). Performance -- Evaluation.

HD62.15.H623 1998
Hodgetts, Richard M.
Measures of quality and high performance: simple tools and lessons learned from America's most successful corporations/ Richard M. Hodgetts. New York: AMACOM, c1998. xiii, 224 p.
97-035583   658.5/62 21   0814403778
Total quality management -- Case studies. Organizational effectiveness -- Case studies.

HD62.15.J65 1994
Joiner, Brian L.
Fourth generation management: the new business consciousness/ Brian L. Joiner in collaboration with Sue Reynard; with contributions from Yukihiro Ando ... [et al.]. New York: McGraw-Hill, c1994. xiii, 289 p.
93-040042   658.4   0070327157
Total quality management. Organizational change. Strategic planning.

HD62.15.M47 1997
Merrill, Peter.
Do it right the second time: benchmarking best practices in the quality change process/ Peter Merrill. Portland, Or.: Productivity Press, c1997. xx, 268 p.
97-000783   658.5/62 21   1563271753
Benchmarking (Management) Total quality management.

HD62.15.S363 1993
Schmidt, Warren H.
TQManager: a practical guide for managing in a total quality organization/ Warren H. Schmidt, Jerome P. Finnigan. San Fransisco: Jossey-Bass, c1993. xv, 196 p.
93-004588   658.5/62   1555425593
Total quality management.

HD62.15.S55 2001
Shiba, Shoji, 1933-
Four practical revolutions in management: systems for creating unique organizational capability/ Shoji Shiba, David Walden. Portland, Or.: Productivity Press, 2001.
00-068424   658.4/013   1563272172
Total quality management. Total quality management -- Case studies. Organizational change.

HD62.25 Management. Industrial management — Management of special enterprises — Family-owned business enterprises. Family corporations. Close corporations

HD62.25.G46 1997
Generation to generation: life cycles of the family business/ Kelin E. Gersick ... [et al.]. Boston, Mass.: Harvard Business School Press, 1997. x, 302 p.
96-012529   658/.041   087584555X
Family-owned business enterprises -- Management. Family-owned business enterprises -- Succession.

HD62.37 Management. Industrial management — Management of special enterprises — High technology industries

HD62.37.A76 2002
Arora, Ashish.
Markets for technology: the economics of innovation and corporate strategy/ Ashish Arora, Andrea Fosfuri, Alfonso Gambardella. Cambridge, Mass.: MIT Press, 2002. xi, 338 p.
2001-044324   338/.064 21   0262011905
High technology industries -- Management. Technology -- Marketing. License agreements.

HD62.37.M355 1990
Managing complexity in high technology organizations/ edited by Mary Ann Von Glinow, Susan Albers Mohrman. New York: Oxford University Press, 1990. xvi, 327 p.
89-003030   620/.0068   0195057201
High technology industries -- Management. Organizational behavior.

HD62.4 Management. Industrial management — Management of special enterprises — International business enterprises

HD62.4.A88 1990
Austin, James E.
Managing in developing countries: strategic analysis and operating techniques/ James E. Austin. New York: Free Press; c1990. xiii, 465 p.
89-023734   658/.049 20   0029011027
International business enterprises -- Developing countries -- Management. Business and politics -- Developing countries. Industrial policy -- Developing countries.

HD62.4.B36 1998
Bartlett, Christopher A.,
Managing across borders: the transnational solution/ Christopher A. Bartlett and Sumantra Ghoshal. 2nd ed. Boston, Mass: Harvard Business School Press, c1998. xxiii, 391 p.
98-026004   658/.049 21   0875848494
International business enterprises -- Management.

HD62.4.B58 2002
The Blackwell handbook of cross-cultural management/ edited by Martin J. Gannon and Karen L. Newman. Oxford, UK; Malden, MA: Blackwell Business, c2002. xxiii, 509 p.
00-011796   658/.049 21   0631214305
International business enterprises -- Management -- Social aspects. Management -- Cross-cultural studies. Corporate culture -- Cross-cultural studies.

HD62.4.C365 1997
Carroll, Stephen J., 1930-
Ethical dimensions of international management/ Stephen J. Carroll, Martin J. Gannon. Thousand Oaks, Calif.: Sage Publications, c1997. xii, 224 p.
96-025308   658/.049 20   080395543X
International business enterprises -- Management -- Moral and ethical aspects. Business ethics.

HD62.4.E423 2001
Elashmawi, Farid.
Competing globally: mastering multicultural management and negotiation/ Farid Elashmawi. Boston: Butterworth-Heinemann, c2001. xviii, 262 p.
2001-018458   658/.049 21   0877193711
International business enterprises -- Management. International business enterprises -- Management -- Cross-cultural Intercultural communication.

HD62.4.H37 2000
Harris, Philip R.
Managing cultural differences/ Philip R. Harris, Robert T. Moran. 5th ed. Houston, TX: Gulf Pub., 2000. xvii, 454 p.
00-032488   658.1/8 21   0877193452
International business enterprises -- Management. Acculturation. Cross-cultural studies.

HD62.4.I52 2000
Innovations in international and cross-cultural management/ edited by P. Christopher Earley, Harbir Singh. Thousand Oaks: Sage Publications, c2000. viii, 374 p.
00-008094   658/.049 21   0761912355
International business enterprises -- Management -- Research. Management -- Cross-cultural studies.

HD62.4.L49 2000
Lewis, Richard D.
When cultures collide: managing successfully across cultures/ Richard D. Lewis. 2nd ed. rev. London; Nicholas Brealey, 2000. iv, 462 p.
99-051394   658/.049 21   1857880870
International business enterprises -- Management -- Social aspects. Management -- Social aspects. Intercultural communication.

HD62.4.R48 1996
Rhinesmith, Stephen H.
A manager's guide to globalization: six skills for success in a changing world/ Stephen H. Rhinesmith. Chicago: Irwin Professional Pub., c1996. xxix, 256 p.
95-045171   658/.049 20   0786305452
International business enterprises -- Management. Executive ability. Success in business.

HD62.4.R53 1999
Ricks, David A.
Blunders in international business/ David A. Ricks. 3rd ed. Oxford, UK; Blackwell Publishers, 1999. ix, 172 p.
99-033931   658/.049 21   0631217762
International business enterprises -- Management -- Case studies. Business failures -- Case studies.

HD62.47 Management. Industrial management — Management of special enterprises — Joint ventures

HD62.47.B33 1991
Badaracco, Joseph.
The knowledge link: how firms compete through strategic alliances/ Joseph L. Badaracco, Jr. Boston, Mass.: Harvard Business School Press, c1991. xiv, 189 p.
90-044763   658.1/8   0875842267
Joint ventures -- Management. Competition. Information resources management.

HD62.5 Management. Industrial management — Management of special enterprises — New business enterprises. Starting a new business. Business incubators

HD62.5.E559 2001
Start your own business: the only start-up book you'll ever need/ Rieva Lesonsky, editorial director, and the staff of Entrepreneur magazine. 2nd ed. Irvine, CA: Entrepreneur Press, c2001. xiv, 771 p.
00-052814   658/.041 21   1891984217
New business enterprises -- Management. Small business -- Management.

HD62.5.H37374 1999
Harris, Wendy
The Black enterprise guide to starting your own business/ Wendy Beech. New York: Wiley, c1999. xi, 465 p.
98-055275   658.1/141/08996073   21
047132454X
New business enterprises. Black business enterprises.

HD62.5.H3738 1999
Harvard business review on entrepreneurship. Boston, Mass.: Harvard Business School Press, 1999. v, 217 p.
98-031399   658.4/21 21   0875849105
New business enterprises -- Management. Entrepreneurship.

HD62.5.L63 2001
Lodish, Leonard M.
Entrepreneurial marketing: lessons from wharton's pioneering MBA course/ Leonard M. Lodish, Howard Lee Morgan, Amy Kallianpur. New York: Wiley, c2001. xvi, 272 p.
00-049644   658.8 21   0471382442
New business enterprises -- Management. Marketing -- Management.

HD62.5.T76 1989
Tropman, John E.
Entrepreneurial systems for the 1990s: their creation, structure, and management/ John E. Tropman & Gersh Morningstar; foreword by Sam Zell. New York: Quorum Books, 1989. xvi, 260 p.
88-015424   658.4/2   0899302882
New business enterprises. Entrepreneurship -- United States.

HD62.6 Management. Industrial management — Management of special enterprises — Nonprofit organizations

HD62.6.B66 1999
Bonk, Kathy,
The Jossey-Bass guide to strategic communications for nonprofits: a step-by-step guide to working with the media to generate publicity, enhance fundraising, build membership, change public policy, handle crises, and more/ Kathy Bonk, Henry Griggs, Emily Tynes. 1st ed. San Francisco, Calif.: Jossey-Bass, c1999. xviii, 188 p.
98-040285   659.2/88 21   0787943738
Nonprofit organizations -- Management. Corporations -- Public relations.

HD62.6.C66 2000
The complete guide to nonprofit management/ Smith, Bucklin & Associates; edited by Robert H. Wilbur. 2nd ed. New York: Wiley, 2000. xxi, 374 p.
00-025513   658/.048 21   0471380628
Nonprofit organizations -- Management.

HD62.6.D78 1990
Drucker, Peter Ferdinand, 1909-
Managing the non-profit organization: practices and principles/ Peter F. Drucker. New York, N.Y.: HarperCollins, 1990. xix, 235 p.
89-046525   658/.048   0060165073
Nonprofit organizations -- Management. Associations, institutions, etc. -- Management.

HD62.6.J67 1994
The Jossey-Bass handbook of nonprofit leadership and management/ Robert D. Herman and associates. San Francisco: Jossey-Bass, c1994. xxvi, 653 p.
93-047556   658/.048   1555426514
Nonprofit organizations -- Management.

HD62.6.L49 2001
Lewis, David.
The management of non-governmental development organizations: an introduction/ David Lewis. New York: Routledge, 2001.
00-045936   338.9/0068 21   0415207592
Non-governmental organizations -- Management.

HD62.6.L543 2002
Light, Paul Charles.
Pathways to nonprofit excellence/ Paul C. Light. Washington, D.C.: Brookings Institution Press, c2002. ix, 188 p.
2002-001313   658/.048 21   0815706251
Nonprofit organizations -- Management. Organizational effectiveness. Leadership.

HD62.6.N662 2001b
The nonprofit handbook. edited by Tracy Daniel Connors. 3rd ed. New York: Wiley, c2001. xxviii, 932 p.
00-061960   658/.048 21   0471415251
Nonprofit organizations -- Management -- Handbooks, manuals, etc. Nonprofit organizations -- Finance -- Handbooks, manuals, etc. Total quality management -- Handbooks, manuals, etc.

HD62.7 Management. Industrial management — Management of special enterprises — Small business

HD62.7.B865
Business plans handbook: a compilation of actual business plans developed by small businesses throughout North America.   Detroit, MI: Gale Research, Inc., <c1995- >
96-640794   658.4/012/05 20
Small business -- United States -- Planning -- Handbooks, manuals, etc. Small business -- Canada -- Planning -- Handbooks, manuals, etc. Business planning -- United States -- Handbooks, manuals, etc.

HD62.7.E568 1999
The Entrepreneur magazine small business advisor/ Entrepreneur Media, Inc. 2nd ed. New York: J. Wiley, 1999. xviii, 648 p.
98-055378   658.02/2 21   0471332224
Small business -- Management -- Handbooks, manuals, etc. Entrepreneurship -- Handbooks, manuals, etc.

HD62.7.H553 2002
Hillstrom, Kevin,
Encyclopedia of small business/ Kevin Hillstrom,
Laurie Collier Hillstrom. 2nd ed. Detroit, MI: Gale
Group, c2002. 2 v.
2001-033781   658.02/2 21   0787649082
Small business -- Managemen -- Encyclopedias.
Small business -- Finance -- Encyclopedias.

HD66 Management.
Industrial management —
Work groups.
Teams in the workplace —
General works

HD66.G758 2001
Groups at work: theory and research/ edited by
Marlene E. Turner. Mahwah, N.J.: L. Erlbaum,
2001. xiv, 552 p.
99-049323   658.4/02 21   0805820795
Teams in the workplace.

HD66.K384 1993
Katzenbach, Jon R., 1932-
The wisdom of teams: creating the high-
performance organization/ Jon R. Katzenbach,
Douglas K. Smith. Boston, Mass.: Harvard
Business School Press, c1993. xii, 291 p.
92-020395   658.3/128   0875843670
Teams in the workplace.

HD66.L468 2001
Levi, Daniel,
Group dynamics for teams/ Daniel Levi. Thousand
Oaks, Calif.: Sage Publications, c2001. xiv, 362 p.
00-011857   658.4/036 21   0761922547
Teams in the workplace.

HD66.M3946 2002
McKenna, Patrick J.
F1rst among equals: how to manage a group of
professionals/ Patrick J. McKenna, David H.
Maister. New York: Free Press, c2002. xxix, 290 p.
2002-283385   658.4/02 21   0743225511
*Teams in the workplace. Leadership. Executives -
- Training of.*

HD66.P348 2001
Parker, Glenn M.,
Team workout: a trainer's sourcebook of 50 team-
building games and activities/ Glenn Parker,
Richard Kropp. New York: AMACOM, c2001. v,
346 p.
2001-018924   658.4/02 21   081447120X
Teams in the workplace -- Problems, exercises,
etc. Group games. Group relations training.

HD66.T48 1982
Thompson, Philip C.
Quality circles: how to make them work in
America/ Philip C. Thompson. New York, N.Y.:
AMACOM, c1982. viii, 198 p.
82-004072   658.4/036   0814457312
Quality circles -- United States.

HD66.2 Management.
Industrial management —
Work groups.
Teams in the workplace —
Data processing. Groupware

HD66.2.L56 2000
Lipnack, Jessica.
Virtual teams: people working across boundaries
with technology/ Jessica Lipnack and Jeffrey
Stamps. 2nd ed. New York: Wiley, c2000. xxxi,
317 p.
00-702920   658.4/02/0285 21   0471388254
Teams in the workplace -- Computer networks.
Business enterprises -- Computer networks.

HD69.B7 Management.
Industrial management —
Other, A-Z —
Brand name products.
Business names

HD69.B7.M373 2000
Marconi, Joe.
The brand marketing book: creating, managing,
and extending the value of your brand/ Joe
Marconi. Lincolnwood, IL: NTC Business Books,
c2000. xv, 247 p.
99-023371   658.8/27 21   0844222577
Brand name products -- Marketing.

HD69.C6 Management.
Industrial management —
Other, A-Z — Business consultants

HD69.C6 B537 2002
Biswas, Sugata,
Management consulting: a complete guide to the
industry/ Sugata Biswas and Daryl Twitchell. 2nd
ed. New York: John Wiley, c2002. xii, 336 p.
2001-040147   001/.023/73 21   0471444014
Business consultants. Business consultants --
Vocational guidance.

HD69.D4 Management.
Industrial management —
Other, A-Z — Decision making

HD69.D4.F3
Fabrycky, W. J. 1932-
Economic decision analysis [by] W. J. Fabrycky
[and] G. J. Thuesen. Englewood Cliffs, N.J.,
Prentice-Hall [1974] x, 390 p.
73-013900   658.4/03   0132232715
Decision making. Decision making --
Mathematical models. Capital investments.

HD69.D4.S49 1977
Simon, Herbert Alexander, 1916-
The new science of management decision/ Herbert
A. Simon. Englewood Cliffs, N.J.: Prentice-Hall,
c1977. xi, 175 p.
76-040414   658.4/03   0136161448
Decision making -- Data processing. Industrial
management -- Data processing. Automation --
Economic aspects.

HD69.I7 Management.
Industrial management —
Other, A-Z —
International business enterprises

HD69.I7.G54
Gladwin, Thomas N.
Multinationals under fire: lessons in the
management of conflict/ Thomas N. Gladwin, Ingo
Walter. New York: Wiley, c1980. xiv, 689 p.
79-021741   658.1/8   0471019690
International business enterprises --
Management. International business enterprises --
Social aspects. Conflict management.

HD69.P6 Management.
Industrial management —
Other, A-Z —
Pollution control policy

HD69.P6.B87 1993
Business and the environment: implications of the
new environmentalism/ edited by Denis Smith.
New York: St. Martin's Press, 1993. x, 194 p.
92-041552   363.7/057   031209518X
Industrial management -- Environmental aspects.
Green movement. Social responsibility of business.

HD69.P75 Management.
Industrial management —
Other, A-Z — Project management

HD69.P75.G564 1996
Keeling, Ralph.
Project management: an international perspective/
Ralph Keeling. New York: St. Martin's Press,
2000. xxiv, 215 p.
99-088129   658.4/04   0312232918
Project management.

HD69.P75 G845 2000
A guide to the project management body of
knowledge (PMBOK guide). 2000 ed. Newtown
Square, Penn., USA: Project Management Institute,
c2000. x, 216 p.
00-051727   658.4/04 21   1880410230
Project management.

HD69.P75 L488 2002
Lewis, James P.,
Fundamentals of project management: developing
core competencies to help outperform the
competition/ James P. Lewis. 2nd ed. New York:
AMACOM, c2002. xii, 148 p.
2001-045210   658.4/04 21   0814471323
Project management.

HD69.P75.R36 1988
Randolph, W. Alan.
Effective project planning and management:
getting the job done/ W. Alan Randolph, Barry Z.
Posner. Englewood Cliffs, N.J.: Prentice-Hall,
[1987], c1988 x, 163 p.
87-011399   658.4/04   0132448157
Industrial project management.

HD69.P75.W38 1996
Watson, Charles S.
Managing projects for personal success/ Charles S.
Watson with Dawid J. Williams. Boston:
International Thomson Business Press, 1996.
96-039625   658.4/04   0412717409
Industrial project management.

HD69.S5 Management. Industrial management — Other, A-Z — Size of industries

HD69.S5 A77 1994
Arthur, W. Brian.
Increasing returns and path dependence in the economy/ W. Brian Arthur; with a foreword by Kenneth J. Arrow. Ann Arbor: c1994. xx, 201 p.
94-009127   330/.01/51 20   0472064967
Economies of scale -- Mathematical models. Economic development -- Mathematical models. Economics, Mathematical.

HD69.S5.T59 1990
Tomasko, Robert M.
Downsizing: reshaping the corporation for the future/ Robert M. Tomasko. New York, NY: AMACOM, c1990. xix, 311 p.
87-047709   338.6/4   0814477348
Industries -- Size -- United States. Middle managers -- United States. Industrial organization -- United States.

HD69.S8 Management. Industrial management — Other, A-Z — Strategic alliances. Business networks

HD69.S8 A94 2000
Austin, James E.
The collaboration challenge: how nonprofits and businesses succeed through strategic alliances/ James E. Austin; foreword by Frances Hesselbein and John C. Whitehead. 1st ed. San Francisco, Calif.: Jossey-Bass Publishers, c2000. xiii, 203 p.
99-088237   658/.044 21   0787952206
Strategic alliances (Business) Strategic planning. Industrial management.

HD69.S8.G47 1992
Gerlach, Michael L.
Alliance capitalism: the social organization of Japanese business/ Michael L. Gerlach. Berkeley: University of California Press, c1992. xxii, 351 p.
92-016619   338.8/0952   0520076885
Strategic alliances (Business) -- Japan. Industrial organization -- Japan.

HD69.S8.G66 1996
Gomes-Casseres, Benjamin.
The alliance revolution: the new shape of business rivalry/ Benjamin Gomes-Casseres. Cambridge, Mass.: Harvard University Press, 1996. xii, 305 p.
95-044555   338.8   0674016475
Strategic alliances (Business) Competition. Interorganizational relations.

HD69.S8 K58 2001
Knoke, David.
Changing organizations: business networks in the new political economy/ David Knoke. Boulder, Colo.: Westview Press, 2001. xxi, 474 p.
00-063302   658/.044 21   0813334535
Business networks -- United States. Strategic alliances (Business) -- United States.

HD69.S8.S54 2001
Shuman, Jeffrey C., 1945-
Collaborative communities: partnering for profit in the networked economy/ Jeffrey Shuman and Janice Twombly with David Rottenberg. Chicago: Dearborn Trade, 2001. xv, 224 p.
2001-000506   658/.044   0793144353
Business networks. Information technology -- Economic aspects. Computer networks -- Economic aspects.

HD69.T46 Management. Industrial management — Other, A-Z — Theory of constraints

HD69.T46 S65 2000
Smith, Debra,
The measurement nightmare: how the theory of constraints can resolve conflicting strategies, policies, and measures/ Debra Smith. Boca Raton, Fla.: St. Lucie Press, c2000. xxii, 184 p.
99-053106   658.15/11 21   1574442465
Theory of constraints (Management) Managerial accounting.

HD70 Management. Industrial management — By region or country, A-Z

HD70.A34 M35 1999
Management of organizations in Africa: a handbook and reference/ edited by J. Muruku Waiguchu, Edward Tiagha and Muroki Mwaura. Westport, Conn.: Quorum, 1999. x, 417 p.
98-004975   658/.0096 21   1567201881
Management -- Africa.

HD70.C2.C67 1995
Corporate decision-making in Canada/ general editors, Ronald J. Daniels & Randall Morck. Calgary, Alta., Canada: University of Calgary Press, c1995. xiv, 705 p.
96-171844   658.4/03/0971   189517676X
Industrial management -- Canada -- Decision making -- Congresses. Corporate governance -- Canada -- Congresses. Decision making -- Canada -- Congresses.

HD70.C5 M334 2000
Management and organizations in the Chinese context/ edited by J.T. Li, Anne S. Tsui and Elizabeth Weldon. New York: St. Martin's Press, 2000. xv, 359 p.
99-041116   658/.00951 21   0312228414
Management -- China. Organization -- China.

HD70.E8 L39 2000
Lawrence, Peter A.
Management in Western Europe/ Peter Lawrence and Vincent Edwards. Houndmills, Basingstoke, Hampshire: Macmillan Business, 2000. ix, 251 p.
99-045121   658/.0094 21   0333733045
Management -- Europe, Western.

HD70.E8.M36 1993
Management in Western Europe: society, culture and organization in twelve nations/ editor, David J. Hickson. Berlin; Walter de Gruyter, 1993. xiv, 288 p.
92-042234   658/.0094   0899257690
Management -- Europe -- Cross-cultural studies. Industrial management -- Europe -- Cross-cultural studies.

HD70.I4.N43 1975
Negandhi, Anant R.
The frightening angels: a study of U.S. multinationals in developing nations/ Anant R. Negandhi, S. Benjamin Prasad. [Kent, Ohio]: Kent State University Press, [1975] xix, 249 p.
74-030491   658.1/8   0873381696
Industrial management. Corporations, Foreign -- Developing countries. Subsidiary corporations -- United States.

HD70.J3 D67 2000
Dore, Ronald Philip.
Stock market capitalism: welfare capitalism: Japan and Germany versus the Anglo-Saxons/ Ronald Dore. Oxford [UK];a New York: Oxford University Press, 2000. xiv, 264 p.
00-025534   330.12/2 21   0199240612
Management -- Japan. Management -- Germany. Management -- United States.

HD70.J3.L67 1994
Lorriman, John.
Japan's winning margins: management, training, and education/ John Lorriman and Takashi Kenjo. Oxford; Oxford University Press, 1994. xvii, 214 p.
93-037586   658/.00952   0198563744
Management -- Japan. Vocational education -- Japan. Occupational training -- Japan.

HD70.K6.F54 1995
Fields, Karl J.
Enterprise and the state in Korea and Taiwan/ Karl J. Fields. Ithaca: Cornell University Press, 1995. xiv, 269 p.
94-046142   338.95124/9   0801430097
Industrial organization -- Korea (South) Industrial organization -- Taiwan. Conglomerate corporations -- Korea (South)

HD70.U5.G33 1999
Gabor, Andrea.
The capitalist philosophers/ Andrea Gabor. New York: Times Business, 1999. xvi, 384 p.
99-026324   658/.00973   0812928202
Taylor, Frederick Winslow, -- 1853-1929 -- Influence. Scientific management -- United States -- History. Corporations -- United States -- History -- 20th century. Industrial sociologists -- United States -- Biography.

HD70.U5.K36 1989
Kanter, Donald L. 1925-
The cynical Americans: living and working in an age of discontent and disillusion/ Donald L. Kanter, Philip H. Mirvis. San Francisco: Jossey-Bass, 1989. xxii, 329 p.
88-046087   306/.36/0973   1555421504
Industrial management -- United States. Work environment -- United States. Work ethic -- United States.

HD70.U5.O69 2000
O'Reilly, Charles A.
Hidden value: how great companies achieve extraordinary results with ordinary people/ Charles A. O'Reilly III, Jeffrey Pfeffer. Boston, Mass.: Harvard Business School Press, c2000. xvii, 286 p.
00-025016   658 21   0875848982
Industrial management -- United States -- Case studies. Human capital -- United States -- Case studies.

HD70.U5.P425 1985
Peters, Thomas J.
A passion for excellence: the leadership difference/ Tom Peters, Nancy Austin. New York: Random House, c1985. xxv, 437 p.
84-045767   658.4/092/0973   0394544846
Industrial management -- United States.

HD73 Economic development. Development economics. Economic growth — Congresses

HD73.B36 1999
Governance, equity, and global markets: the Annual Bank Conference on Development Economics, Europe/ edited by Joseph E. Stiglitz, Pierre-Alain Muet. New York, N.Y.: Oxford University Press, 2001. xxviii, 324 p.
2001-018552   338.9 21   0199241554
Economic development -- Congresses.

HD74-74.5 Economic development. Development economics. Economic growth — Collected works (nonserial)

HD74.P56 1987
Pioneers in development. Theodore W. Schultz ... [et al.]; Gerald M. Meier, editor. New York: Published for the World Bank [by] Oxford Univers c1987. viii, 244 p.
86-023511   338.9   0195205421
Economic development.

HD74.5.K35 1986
Kalecki, Michal.
Selected essays on economic planning/ Michal Kalecki; edited, translated and introduced by Jan Toporowski. Cambridge [England]; Cambridge University Press, 1986. vi, 123 p.
86-011790   338.9   0521308372
Economic policy.

HD75 Economic development. Development economics. Economic growth — Theory. Method. Relation to other subjects — General works

HD75.B365 1997
Barro, Robert J.
Determinants of economic growth: a cross-country empirical study/ Robert J. Barro. Cambridge, Mass.: The MIT Press, c1997. xii, 145 p.
96-050235   338.9 21   0262024217
Economic development -- Cross-cultural studies. Economic policy -- Cross-cultural studies.

HD75.B367 1991
Bartik, Timothy J.
Who benefits from state and local economic development policies?/ Timothy J. Bartik. Kalamazoo, Mich.: W.E. Upjohn Institute for Employment Research, 1991. xi, 354 p.
91-027375   338.9   0880991143
Economic development. Economic policy.

HD75.B54 1999
Black, Jan Knippers,
Development in theory and practice: paradigms and paradoxes/ Jan Knippers Black. 2nd ed. Boulder, Colo: Westview Press, 1999. xv, 302 p.
99-033823   338.9 21
Economic development. Economic assistance, American -- Developing countries. Economic assistance -- Developing countries.

HD75.C848 2000
Cultural factors in economic growth/ Mark Casson, Andrew Godley, editors. New York: Springer, 2000.
00-055638   306.3 21   3540662936
Economic development -- Social aspects. Entrepreneurship -- Social aspects. Technological innovations -- Social aspects.

HD75.D498 2002
Development theory and practice: critical perspectives/ edited by Uma Kothari and Martin Minogue. Houndmills, Basinstoke, Hampshire; Palgrave, 2002. x, 222 p.
2001-036096   338.9 21   0333800710
Economic development.

HD75.E73 1994
Escobar, Arturo, 1952-
Encountering development: the making and unmaking of the Third World/ Arturo Escobar. Princeton, N.J.: Princeton University Press, c1995. ix, 290 p.
94-021025   338.9   0691034095
Economic development. Economic history -- 1945- Developing countries -- Economic conditions. Developing countries -- Social conditions.

HD75.G74 2000
Griffin, Keith B.
Studies in development strategy and systemic transformation/ Keith Griffin. New York, N.Y.: St. Martin's Press, 2000. xiii, 335 p.
99-087198   338.9   0312232578
Economic development.

HD75.H86 1989
Hunt, Diana, 1942-
Economic theories of development: an analysis of competing paradigms/ Diana Hunt. Savage, Md.: Barnes & Noble Books, 1989. xv, 363 p.
89-032733   338.9/009172/4   0389207403
Economic development. Developing countries -- Economic policy.

HD75.K697 1997
Kotler, Philip.
The marketing of nations: a strategic approach to building national wealth/ Philip Kotler, Somkid Jatusripitak, Suvit Maesincee. New York: Free Press, c1997. xi, 451 p.
97-001285   338.9 21   068483488X
Economic development. Economic policy. Industrial policy.

HD75.L824 2002
Lucas, Robert E.
Lectures on economic growth/ Robert E. Lucas, Jr. Cambridge, Mass.: Harvard University Press, 2002. xi, 204 p.
2001-045263   338.9 21   0674006275
Economic development.

HD75.M25 1999
Malizia, Emil E.
Understanding local economic development/ Emil E. Malizia, Edward J. Feser. New Brunswick, N.J.: Center for Urban Policy Research, c1999. xvi, 298 p.
98-044999   338.9 21   0882851632
Economic development. Economic policy. Regional development -- United States.

HD75.M44 1984
Meier, Gerald M.
Emerging from poverty: the economics that really matters/ Gerald M. Meier. New York: Oxford University Press, 1984. ix, 258 p.
84-004441   338.9/009172/4   0195033744
Economic development. Economic assistance. Developing countries.

HD75.Q35 2000
The quality of growth/ Vinod Thomas ... [et al.]. Oxford; World Bank, 2000. xxxiv, 262 p.
00-028324   338.9   0195215931
Economic development. Sustainable development.

HD75.S65 1990
Somjee, A. H.
Development theory: critiques and explorations/ A.H. Somjee. New York: St. Martin's Press, 1991. xx, 185 p.
90-008552   338.9/001   0312048866
Economic development. Developing countries -- Economic policy.

HD75.S95 1984
Sylos Labini, Paolo.
The forces of economic growth and decline/ Paolo Sylos-Labini. Cambridge, Mass.: MIT Press, c1984. xiv, 253 p.
84-009699   338.9   0262192241
Economic development. Technological innovations. Industrial organization (Economic theory)

HD75.6 Economic development. Development economics. Economic growth — Theory. Method. Relation to other subjects — Environmental aspects

HD75.6.C368 2000
Carley, Michael.
Managing sustainable development/ Michael Carley and Ian Christie. 2nd ed. London; Earthscan, 2000. xiv, 322 p.
2002-728239   338.9/27 21   1853834408
Sustainable development. Sustainable development -- Case studies.

HD75.6.C376 1996
The case against the global economy: and for a turn toward the local/ edited by Jerry Mander and Edward Goldsmith. San Francisco: Sierra Club Books, c1996. x, 550 p.
96-020149   363.7 20   0871563525
Economic development -- Environmental aspects. Environmental policy -- International cooperation. Sustainable development.

HD75.6.C6454 1995
Common, Michael S.
Sustainability and policy: limits to economics/ Michael Common. Cambridge; Cambridge University Press, 1995. xii, 348 p.
94-034142 333.7 0521430011
Sustainable development. Economic development -- Environmental aspects.

HD75.6.D35 1994
Daly, Herman E.
For the common good: redirecting the economy toward community, the environment, and a sustainable future/ Herman E. Daly and John B. Cobb, Jr.; with contributions by Clifford W. Cobb. 2nd ed., updated and expanded. Boston: Beacon Press, c1994. viii, 534 p.
93-024460 338.9 20 0807047058
Economic development -- Environmental aspects. Environmental policy. Sustainable development.

HD75.6.D367 2001
Dasgupta, Partha.
Human well-being and the natural environment/ Partha Dasgupta. Oxford [England]; Oxford University Press, 2001. xxii, 305 p.
2001-036597 306 21 0199247889
Sustainable development. Natural resources -- Management. Human ecology.

HD75.6.E57 1989
Environmental management and economic development/ Gunter Schramm and Jeremy J. Warford, editors. Baltimore: Published for the World Bank [by] Johns Hopkins c1989. x, 208 p.
89-008001 363.7 0801839505
Economic development -- Environmental aspects. Environmental management.

HD75.6.H95 1988
Hyman, Eric.
Combining facts and values in environmental impact assessment: theories and techniques/ Eric L. Hyman and Bruce Stiftel, with David H. Moreau and Robert C. Nichols. Boulder: Westview Press, 1988. xvi, 304 p.
85-026630 333.7/1 0813371627
Economic development -- Environmental aspects -- Cost effectiveness. Natural resources -- Cost effectiveness. Environmental impact analysis -- Cost effectiveness.

HD75.6.I82 1994
Is capitalism sustainable?: political economy and the politics of ecology/ edited by Martin O'Connor. New York: Guilford Press, c1994. xiv, 283 p.
94-011689 363.7 0898621275
Economic development -- Environmental aspects. Sustainable development. Environmental policy.

HD75.6.J33 1991
Jacobs, Michael, 1960-
The green economy: environment, sustainable development, and the politics of the future/ Michael Jacobs. London; Pluto Press, 1991. xxii, 312 p.
91-002824 363.7/058 0745303129
Economic development -- Environmental aspects. Environmental protection. Green movement.

HD75.6.M33 1991
MacNeill, Jim.
Beyond interdependence: the meshing of the world's economy and the earth's ecology/ Jim MacNeill, Pieter Winsemius, Taizo Yakushiji. New York: Oxford University Press, 1991. xx, 159 p.
91-007348 363.7 0195071263
Economic development -- Environmental aspects. Environmental policy. Economic history -- 1971-

HD75.6.P375 1998
Park, Se Hark, 1935-
Industrial development and environmental degradation: a source book on the origins of global pollution/ Se Hark Park, Walter C. Labys. Cheltenham, UK; Edward Elgar, c1998. xiii, 187 p.
98-005815 363.73/1 21 1858988837
Industrialization -- Environmental aspects. Pollution. Industries -- Environmental aspects.

HD75.6.P67 1992
Population, technology, and lifestyle: the transition to sustainability/ edited by Robert Goodland, Herman E. Daly, and Salah El Serafy. Washington, D.C.: Island Press, c1992. xvi, 154 p.
92-014403 304.2 1559631996
Economic development -- Environmental aspects. Population -- Economic aspects. Sustainable development.

HD75.6.S35 1992
Schmidheiny, Stephan, 1947-
Changing course: a global business perspective on development and the environment/ Stephan Schmidheiny with the Business Council for Sustainable Development. Cambridge, Mass.: MIT Press, c1992. xxiii, 374 p.
92-006457 363.7/05765 0262193183
Economic development -- Environmental aspects -- Case studies. Environmental policy -- Costs -- Case studies. International business enterprises -- Case studies.

HD75.6.S74 1996
Stead, W. Edward.
Management for a small planet: strategic decision making and the environment/ W. Edward Stead, Jean Garner Stead. Thousand Oaks: Sage Publications, c1996. xiv, 282 p.
95-050214 333.7 20 0761902937
Economic development -- Environmental aspects. Natural resources -- Management. Strategic planning.

HD75.6.T565 1990
Tisdell, C. A.
Natural resources, growth, and development: economics, ecology and resource-scarcity/ Clement A. Tisdell. New York: Praeger, 1990. xiii, 186 p.
90-042118 333.7/09172/4 0275934799
Economic development -- Environmental aspects. Natural resources -- Management. Natural resources -- Developing countries -- Management. Developing countries -- Economic policy.

HD75.7 Economic development. Development economics. Economic growth — Theory. Method. Relation to other subjects — Educational influence on economic development

HD75.7.E38 1984
Education and economic productivity/ edited by Edwin Dean. Cambridge, Mass.: Ballinger Pub. Co., c1984. xiv, 223 p.
84-003046 338.9 0884109437
Economic development -- Effect of education on.

HD76 Economic development. Development economics. Economic growth — Communication of information — General works

HD76.R54 2002
The right to tell: the role of mass media in economic development. Washington, D.C.: World Bank, c2002. ix, 322 p.
2002-031121 338.9 21 0821352032
Communication in economic development. Mass media -- Economic aspects. Economic development -- Information services.

HD78 Economic development. Development economics. Economic growth — History

HD78.M38 1994
McPherson, Natalie.
Machines and economic growth: the implications for growth theory of the history of the industrial revolution/ Natalie McPherson. Westport, Conn.: Greewood Press, 1994. x, 264 p.
93-044509 338.9/009 0313292558
Economic development -- History. Industrial revolution. Capitalism -- History.

HD78.W64 1996
Wolfe, Marshall.
Elusive development/ Marshall Wolfe. London; Zed Books, 1996. vi, 198 p.
95-036346 338.9 1856493792
Economic development. Economic development -- Social aspects. Developing countries.

HD82 Economic development. Development economics. Economic growth — General works — English

HD82.A657 1987
Apter, David Ernest, 1924-
Rethinking development: modernization, dependency, and postmodern politics/ David E. Apter. Newbury Park, Calif.: Sage Publications, c1987. 326 p.
86-029642 338.9 0803929714
Economic development. Dependency. Developing countries -- Politics and government.

HD82.B3257 2001
Bates, Robert H.
Prosperity and violence: the political economy of development/ Robert H. Bates. New York: W. W. Norton, c2001. 144 p.
00-056608 338.9 21 0393050386
Economic development. Social policy. Violence.

HD82.B5543 1995
Blair, John P., 1947-
Local economic development: analysis and practice/ John P. Blair. Thousand Oaks: SAGE Publications, c1995. x, 345 p.
95-003023 338.9 0803953763
Economic development. Economic policy. Local government.

HD82.C5714
Cole, J. P. 1928-
The development gap: a spatial analysis of world poverty and inequality/ by J. P. Cole. Chichester [Eng.]; J. Wiley, c1981. x, 454 p.
80-040284 338.9 0471277967
Economic development. Developing countries -- Economic conditions.

HD82.D3874 2003
Development and democracy: new perspectives on an old debate/ Sunder Ramaswamy and Jeffrey W. Cason, editors. Hanover, [N.H.]: Middlebury College Press, published by University xv, 306 p.
2002-015335 338.9 21 1584652756
Economic development -- Political aspects. Democracy. Economic history.

HD82.D45 1988
Devine, P. J.
Democracy and economic planning: the political economy of a self-governing society/ Pat Devine. Boulder, Colo.: Westview Press, 1988. ix, 306 p.
88-020708 338.9 0813307996
Economic policy. Central planning. Capitalism.

HD82.D7
Drucker, Peter Ferdinand, 1909-
The future of industrial man, a conservative approach, by Peter F. Drucker. New York, The John Day Co. [1942] 298 p.
42-021925 330.1
Industrial policy. Sociology. Economic policy.

HD82.G2 1964a
Galbraith, John Kenneth, 1908-
Economic development. Cambridge, Harvard University Press, 1964. xiii, 109 p.
64-018762
Economic development.

HD82.H388
Heilbroner, Robert L.
Between capitalism and socialism: essays in political economics, by Robert L. Heilbroner. New York, Random House [1970] xviii, 294 p.
79-117700 330.1 0394416651
Comparative economics.

HD82.H489 1995
Hirschman, Albert O.
A propensity to self-subversion/ Albert O. Hirschman. Cambridge, Mass.: Harvard University Press, 1995. viii, 262 p.
94-046737 338.9 0674715578
Hirschman, Albert O. Economic history -- 1990- Economic development.

HD82.H618
Horowitz, Irving Louis.
Three worlds of development; the theory and practice of international stratification. New York, Oxford University Press, 1966. xiv, 475 p.
66-015421 309
Economic development. Economic history -- 1945-1971. Social history -- 1945-

HD82.L3273 2000
Leading issues in economic development/ [edited by] Gerald M. Meier, James E. Rauch. New York: Oxford University Press, 2000. xviii, 578 p.
99-059308 338.9 0195115899
Economic development.

HD82.T33 1993
Tausch, Arno, 1951-
Towards a socio-liberal theory of world development/ Arno Tausch in collaboration with Fred Prager. New York: St. Martin's Press, 1993. xvi, 265 p.
91-027475 338.9 0312062109
Economic development. Capitalism.

HD82.V62 1995
Von Tunzelmann, G. N.
Technology and industrial progress: the foundations of economic growth/ G.N. von Tunzelmann. Aldershot, Hants, England; E. Elgar, c1995. xiv, 532 p.
95-010745 338/.064 1858981743
Economic development. Technological innovations -- Economic aspects. Industrialization.

HD87 Economic development. Development economics. Economic growth — Public policy (General). Economic policy — General works

HD87.F715 2002
Franzese, Robert J.,
Macroeconomic policies of developed democracies/ Robert J. Franzese, Jr. Cambridge, UK; Cambridge University Press, 2002. xxiv, 306 p.
2001-035033 339.5 21 0521004411
Economic policy. Comparative economics. Democracy.

HD87.L374 2002
Lane, Jan-Erik.
Government and the economy: a global perspective/ Jan-Erik Lane and Svante Ersson. London; Continuum, 2002. xii, 338 p.
2001-037099 338.9 21 0826454925
Economic policy -- Case studies. Economic development -- Case studies. Mixed economy -- Case studies.

HD87.L44 1993
Lee, Dwight R.
Failure and progress: the bright side of the dismal science/ Dwight R. Lee and Richard B. McKenzie. Washington, D.C.: Cato Institute, c1993. xiv, 163 p.
93-016921 338.9 1882577035
Economic policy. Economic security.

HD87.L53 1991
Liberalization in the process of economic development/ edited by Lawrence B. Krause and Kim Kihwan. Berkeley: University of California Press, c1991. xxiv, 413 p.
90-041127 338.9 0520063570
Economic policy. Economic development.

HD87.M273 1995
Managing the global economy/ edited by Jonathan Michie and John Grieve Smith. Oxford; Oxford University Press, 1995. xxvii, 343 p.
94-036912 338.9 0198289693
Economic policy. Keynesian economics. International finance.

HD87.O47 2000
Olson, Mancur.
Power and prosperity: outgrowing communist and capitalist dictatorships/ Mancur Olson. New York: Basic Books, 2000. xxvii, 233 p.
99-052774 338.9 0465051952
Economic policy. Comparative economics. Free enterprise.

HD87.P637 1996
Political and economic liberalization: dynamics and linkages in comparative perspective/ edited by Gerd Nonneman. Boulder, Colo.: Lynne Rienner Publishers, 1996. xi, 329 p.
96-001320 338.9 1555876390
Economic policy. Comparative economics. Democracy.

HD87.S38 1992
Scully, Gerald W.
Constitutional environments and economic growth/ Gerald W. Scully. Princeton, N.J.: Princeton University Press, c1992. xv, 241 p.
91-042650 338.9 0691042616
Economic development -- Political aspects. Civil rights -- Economic aspects. State, The.

HD87.T376 2000
Tanzi, Vito.
Policies, institutions and the dark side of economics/ Vito Tanzi. Cheltenham, UK; E. Elgar, c2000. xi, 282 p.
99-044605 338.9 21 1858987296
Economic policy -- Decision making. Institutional economics. Political corruption.

HD87.W45 1998
Weiss, Linda, 1952-
The myth of the powerless state/ Linda Weiss. Ithaca, NY: Cornell University Press, 1998. xvii, 260 p.
97-048666 338.9 0801435471
Economic policy. Industrial policy. East Asia -- Economic policy. Sweden -- Economic policy. Japan -- Economic policy -- 1989-

HD108.15 Land use — Theory. Method. Relation to other subjects — Data processing

HD108.15.P46 2003
People and the environment: approaches for linking household and community surveys to remote sensing and GIS/ edited by Jefferson Fox ... [et al.]. Boston: Kluwer Academic Publishers, c2003. xvii, 319 p.
2002-035709 333.73/13/0285 21 1402073224
Land use -- Data processing. Land use -- Remote sensing. Land use -- Environmental aspects -- Data processing.

HD111 Land use — General works

HD111.U7 1983
Urban land policy, issues and opportunities/ Harold B. Dunkerley, coordinating editor; with the assistance of Christine M.E. Whitehead. New York: Published for the World Bank [by] Oxford Univers c1983. viii, 214 p.
82-020247 333.77/17 0195204034
Land use, Urban. Urban policy. Land tenure.

HD133-139 Land use — History — Ancient

HD133.H36 1995
Hanson, Victor Davis.
The other Greeks: the family farm and the agrarian roots of western civilization/ Victor Davis Hanson. New York: Free Press, c1995. xvi, 541 p.
94-043551   338.1/6   0029137519
Land use, Rural -- Greece -- History. Agriculture -- Economic aspects -- Greece -- History. Family farms -- Greece -- History. Greece -- Rural conditions.

HD139.A36.K439 1997
Kehoe, Dennis P.
Investment, profit, and tenancy: the jurists and the Roman agrarian economy/ Dennis P. Kehoe. Ann Arbor: University of Michigan Press, c1997. xiv, 269 p.
97-024345   338.1/0937 21   0472108026
Agricultural laws and legislation (Roman law) Agriculture -- Rome -- Finance. Farm management -- Economic aspects -- Rome.

HD141 Land use — History — Medieval

HD141.S57 1983
Social relations and ideas: essays in honour of R.H. Hilton/ edited by T.H. Aston ... [et al.]. Cambridge [Cambridgeshire]; Cambridge University Press, xiii, 337 p.
82-009727   306/.094 19   052125132X
Hilton, R. H. (Rodney Howard), 1916- Land tenure -- History. Serfdom -- History. Feudalism -- History.

HD156 Land use — History — Modern

HD156.A34 1994
Adger, W. Neil.
Land use and the causes of global warming/ W. Neil Adger and Katrina Brown. Chichester [England]; Wiley, c1994. x, 271 p.
94-015145   333.73/13   0471948853
Land use -- Environmental aspects. Global warming. Greenhouse effect, Atmospheric.

HD181-257.5 Land use — By region or country — America

HD181.G8.C57
Clawson, Marion, 1905-
The Bureau of Land Management. New York, Praeger Publishers [1971] xiii, 209 p.
71-101656   353/.008/232
United States. Bureau of Land Management.

HD194.H3 1970
Harris, Marshall Dees, 1903-
Origin of the land tenure system in the United States, by Marshall Harris. Westport, Conn., Greenwood Press [1970, c1953] xiv, 445 p.
70-130038   333.3/0973   0837137314
Land tenure -- United States -- History.

HD201.B8 1963
Buck, Solon J. 1884-1962.
The Granger movement; a study of agricultural organization and its political, economic, and social manifestations, 1870-1880. Lincoln, University of Nebraska Press [1963, c1913] 384 p.
63-009713   338.10973
Agriculture -- United States. Agriculture -- Economic aspects -- United States. Railroads and state -- United States.

HD205.B43 1994
Beatley, Timothy, 1957-
Ethical land use: principles of policy and planning/ Timothy Beatley. Baltimore: Johns Hopkins University Press, c1994. xvi, 302 p.
93-040870   333.73/13/0973   0801846986
Land use -- Government policy -- United States. Land use -- Moral and ethical aspects -- United States -- Planning. Land use -- Environmental aspects -- United States.

HD205.L336 1993
Land conservation through public/private partnerships/ edited by Eve Endicott; foreword by John H. Chafee. Washington, D.C.: Island Press, c1993. xvi, 364 p.
92-035638   333.73/16/0973   1559631775
Land use -- Government policy -- United States. Conservation Operations Program. Land trusts -- United States.

HD205.N49 2001
The new agrarianism: land, culture, and the community of life/ Eric T. Freyfogle [editor]. Washington, DC: Island Press: c2001. xli, 291 p.
2001-004025   333.73 21   1559639210
Land tenure -- Environmental aspects -- United States. Land use -- Environmental aspects -- United States. Sustainable agriculture -- United States.

HD205.P84 1989
Public interest in the use of private lands/ edited by Benjamin C. Dysart III and Marion Clawson. New York: Praeger, 1989. xii, 187 p.
89-003913   333.73/15/0973   0275929914
Land use -- Government policy -- United States. Land use -- Environmental aspects -- United States. Right of property -- United States.

HD205.W66 1988
Wondolleck, Julia Marie.
Public lands conflict and resolution: managing national forest disputes/ Julia M. Wondolleck. New York: Plenum Press, c1988. xv, 263 p.
88-013991   333.1/0973   030642861X
Public lands -- United States. Forest reserves -- United States. Forest policy -- United States.

HD210.M55.H64
Holley, Donald, 1940-
Uncle Sam's farmers: the New Deal communities in the Lower Mississippi Valley/ Donald Holley. Urbana: University of Illinois Press, [1975] xv, 312 p.
75-020091   333.1/0976   0252005104
Land settlement -- Mississippi River Valley. Farmers -- Mississippi River Valley -- History. New Deal, 1933-1939. Mississippi River Valley -- Rural conditions.

HD211.K2G3
Gates, Paul Wallace,
Fifty million acres: conflicts over Kansas land policy, 1854-1890. Ithaca, N.Y., Cornell University Press [1954] xiii, 311 p.
54-007385   333.1
Land use -- Kansas. Public lands -- Kansas.

HD211.N2.H87 2000
Huston, Reeve, 1960-
Land and freedom: rural society, popular protest, and party politics in antebellum New York/ Reeve Huston. New York: Oxford University Press, 2000. ix, 291 p.
99-088532   333.3/09747   0195136004
Land tenure -- New York (State) Antirent War, N.Y., 1839-1846. Agriculture -- Economic aspects -- New York (State) New York (State) -- Politics and government -- 19th century.

HD211.T2M35 1982
McDonald, Michael J.,
TVA and the dispossessed: the resettlement of population in the Norris Dam area/ Michael J. McDonald, John Muldowny. 1st ed. Knoxville: University of Tennessee Press, c1982. xv, 334 p.
81-016333   307/.2   0870493450
Land settlement -- Tennessee -- Norris Lake region. Water resources development -- Social aspects -- Tennessee -- Norris Lake

HD216.C529 1983
Clawson, Marion, 1905-
The federal lands revisited/ Marion Clawson. Washington, D.C.: Resources for the Future; c1983. xix, 302 p.
83-042904   333.1/0973   0801830982
Public lands -- United States.

HD216.C53
Clawson, Marion, 1905-
The Federal lands since 1956; recent trends in use and management. Washington, Resources for the Future; Distributed by the Joh [1967] xi, 113 p.
67-016034   333.1/0973
Public lands -- United States.

HD216.D5
Dick, Everett Newfon, 1898-
The lure of the land; a social history of the public lands from the Articles of Confederation to the New Deal [by] Everett Dick. Lincoln, University of Nebraska Press [1970] xii, 413 p.
66-013015   333.1/0973   0803207255
Public lands -- United States -- History.

HD216.L44 1995
Lehmann, Scott.
Privatizing public lands/ Scott Lehmann. New York: Oxford University Press, 1995. xi, 248 p.
94-012012   333.1/6   0195089723
Public lands -- United States -- Management. Privatization -- United States.

HD216.V35 1984
Valuation of wildland resource benefits/ edited by George L. Peterson and Alan Randall. Boulder: Westview Press, 1984. xiii, 258 p.
84-051044   333.78/2   0813300185
Public lands -- United States. Natural areas -- Economic aspects -- United States. Wilderness areas -- Economic aspects -- United States.

HD221.L66 2002
Loomis, John B.
Integrated public lands management: principles and applications to national forests, parks, wildlife refuges, and BLM lands/ John B. Loomis. 2nd ed. New York: Columbia University Press, c2002. xxiv, 594 p.
2001-042390   333.1/0973 21   0231124457
Public lands -- United States -- Planning. Public lands -- United States -- Management.

HD241.F6 1969
Foss, Phillip O.
Politics and grass; the administration of grazing on the public domain, Phillip O. Foss. New York, Greenwood Press [1969, c1960] ix, 236 p.
75-090508   333.7/4   0837121361
Grazing -- United States. Public lands -- United States.

HD243.N5.D87 1992
Durant, Robert F., 1949-
The administrative presidency revisited: public lands, the BLM, and the Reagan revolution/ Robert F. Durant. Albany, NY: State University of New York Press, c1992. xvii, 401 p.
91-014098   333.1/0973   0791409597
Reagan, Ronald.   Public lands -- New Mexico. Natural resources -- Government policy -- New Mexico. Natural resources -- Government policy -- United States.

HD243.N5.L36 1987
Land, water, and culture: new perspectives on Hispanic land grants/ edited by Charles L. Briggs & John R. Van Ness. Albuquerque: University of New Mexico, c1987. ix, 422 p.
87-010957   333.1/6/09788   0826309895
Land grants -- New Mexico -- History. Land grants -- Colorado -- History. Pueblo Indians -- Land tenure -- History.

HD243.W38.P83 1997
Public lands management in the West: citizens, interest groups, and values/ edited by Brent S. Steel. Westport, Conn.: Praeger, 1997. xv, 208 p.
96-026878   333.1/0978   0275956954
Public lands -- West (U.S.) -- Management. Public lands -- Management -- Public opinion. Public opinion -- West (U.S.)

HD255.R47 1999
Reshaping the built environment: ecology, ethics, and economics/ edited by Charles J. Kibert; foreword by Alex Wilson. Washington, D.C.: Island Press, c1999. xvi, 362 p.
99-012892   333.73/15 21   1559637021
Real estate development -- Environmental aspects -- United States. Construction industry -- Environmental aspects -- United States.

HD257.5.B75 2002
Brownfields: a comprehensive guide to redeveloping contaminated property/ Todd S. Davis, [editor]. 2nd ed. Chicago, Ill.: Section of Environment, Energy, and Resources, liii, 1077 p.
2001-041379   363.739/66/0973 21   1570739617
Brownfields -- United States. Hazardous waste site remediation -- United States. Liability for hazardous substances pollution damages -- United States.

HD257.5.M67 2000
Mossberger, Karen.
The politics of ideas and the spread of enterprise zones/ Karen Mossberger. Washington, DC: Georgetown University Press, c2000. xvi, 269 p.
00-026360   307.3/33/0973 21   0878408002
Enterprise zones -- United States -- Case studies. Local government -- United States -- Decision-making -- Case studies.

HD319-1035 Land use — By region or country — Other regions or countries

HD319.O5.G37
Gates, Lillian F.
Land policies of Upper Canada, by Lillian F. Gates. [Toronto] University of Toronto P. [1968] 378 p.
68-097201   333/.009713
Land use -- Ontario. Land tenure -- Ontario.

HD320.5.L3
Landsberger, Henry A.
Latin American peasant movements. Edited by Henry A. Landsberger. Ithaca, Cornell University Press [1969] xi, 476 p.
74-087020   301.2/4   0801405246
Peasantry -- Latin America.

HD325.L45 1997
Liberals, the Church, and Indian peasants: corporate lands and the challenge of reform in nineteenth-century Spanish America/ edited by Robert H. Jackson. Albuquerque: University of New Mexico Press, c1997. 228 p.
96-025225   333.3/0972/09034 20   0826317626
Land tenure -- Mexico -- History -- 19th century. Land tenure -- Andes Region -- History -- 19th century. Liberalism -- Mexico -- History -- 19th century.

HD489.L3.K57 1993
Klein, Herbert S.
Haciendas and ayllus: rural society in the Bolivian Andes in the eighteenth and nineteenth centuries/ Herbert S. Klein. Stanford, Calif.: Stanford University Press, 1993. xvi, 230 p.
92-019596   305.5/0984/12   0804720576
Land tenure -- Bolivia -- La Paz (Dept.) -- History -- 18th century. Land tenure -- Bolivia -- La Paz (Dept.) -- History -- 19th century. Haciendas -- Bolivia -- La Paz (Dept.) -- History -- 18th century.

HD499.A44.A457 1995
Almeida, Anna Luiza Ozorio de.
Sustainable settlement in the Brazilian Amazon/ Anna Luiza Ozorio de Almeida and Joao S. Campari. Oxford; Oxford University Press, c1995. ix, 189 p.
95-010600   333.3/1811   0195211049
Land settlement -- Amazon River Region. Land settlement -- Brazil. Sustainable agriculture -- Amazon River Region.

HD505.L68 1975
Loveman, Brian.
Struggle in the countryside; politics and rural labor in Chile, 1919-1973. Bloomington, Indiana University Press [c1976] xxxvi, 439 p.
74-006521   333.1/0983   0253355656
Land tenure -- Chile. Land reform -- Chile. Chile -- Rural conditions.

HD556.B5513
Blanco, Hugo.
Land or death; the peasant struggle in Peru. New York, Pathfinder Press, 1972. 178 p.
73-186689   333.3/2/0985
Land reform -- Peru. Peasant uprisings -- Peru. Peasantry -- Peru.

HD585.J29
Jackson, George D.
Comintern and peasant in East Europe, 1919-1930 [by] George D. Jackson, Jr. New York, Columbia University Press, 1966. ix, 339 p.
66-015489   335.44
Agriculture and state -- Europe, Eastern. Peasantry -- Europe, Eastern.

HD594.H54
Hilton, R. H. 1916-
The English peasantry in the later Middle Ages: the Ford lectures for 1973 and related studies/ by R. H. Hilton. Oxford: Clarendon Press, 1975. 256 p.
75-316774   301.44/43/0942   019822432X
Peasantry -- England.   Great Britain -- Economic conditions. Great Britain -- Social conditions.

HD594.T3
Tawney, R. H. 1880-1962.
The agrarian problem in the sixteenth century, by R. H. Tawney, with six maps in colour. London, Longmans, Green, 1912. xii, 464 p.
13-000154
Land tenure -- Great Britain -- History. Agriculture -- England -- History. Peasantry -- England.

HD603.A36
The Agrarian history of England and Wales; general editor, H. P. R. Finberg. London, Cambridge U.P., 1967-<2000 >
66-019763   333.7/6/0942
Land use -- England -- History. Land use -- Wales -- History. Agriculture -- England -- History.

HD643.B613
Bloch, Marc Leopold Benjamin, 1886-1944.
French rural history; an essay on its basic characteristics [by] Marc Bloch. Foreword by Bryce Lyon. Translated from the French by Janet Sondheimer. Berkeley, University of California Press, 1966. xxxiii, 258 p.
66-015483   630.1144
Land tenure -- France -- History. Peasantry -- France. Feudalism -- France.

HD779.J34.H47 1989
Herr, Richard.
Rural change and royal finances in Spain at the end of the old regime/ Richard Herr. Berkeley: University of California Press, c1989. xxx, 879 p.
86-025027   333.3/0946/25   0520059484
Church lands -- Spain -- Jaen (Province) -- History -- 18th century. Secularization -- Spain -- Jaen (Province) -- History -- 18th century. Agriculture -- Economic aspects -- Spain -- Jaen (Province) -- History -- 18th century. Jaen (Spain: Province) -- History. Salamanca (Spain: Province) -- History.

HD855.W3
Warriner, Doreen, 1904-
Land and poverty in the Middle East. London & New York, Royal Institute of International Affairs [1948] vii, 148 p.
48-003636
Land tenure -- Middle East.   Middle East -- Social conditions.

HD868.B8 1964
Buck, John Lossing, 1890-
Land utilization in China; a study of 16,786 farms in 168 localities, and 38,256 farm families in twenty-two provinces in China, 1929-1933. New York, Paragon Book Reprint Corp., 1964. xxxii, 494 p.
64-018448 333.76
Agriculture -- China. Agriculture -- Economic aspects -- China. Food supply -- China.

HD997.Z63.B35 1993
Baker, C. A.
Seeds of trouble: government policy and land rights in Nyasaland, 1946-1964/ Colin Baker. London; British Academic Press; 1993. viii, 215 p.
93-247584 1850436150
Land tenure -- Government policy -- Malawi. Land tenure -- Malawi -- History -- 20th century. Land settlement -- Malawi -- History -- 20th century.

HD1018.Z63.M33 1995
McMillan, Della E.
Sahel visions: planned settlement and river blindness control in Burkina Faso/ Della E. McMillan. Tucson: University of Arizona Press, c1995. xxxi, 223 p.
94-021940 338.9/1/096625 0816514879
Land use -- Burkina Faso -- Planning. Land settlement -- Burkina Faso. Rural development projects -- Burkina Faso.

HD1035.R6 1964
Roberts, Stephen Henry, 1901-
The squatting age in Australia, 1835-1847 [by] Stephen H. Roberts. [Melbourne] Melbourne University Press; [1964] ix, 378 p.
65-002443
Land tenure -- Australia -- History. Squatters -- Australia. Australia -- Emigration and immigration.

HD1131 Land use — By region or country — Developing countries

HD1131.A25 2001
Access to land, rural poverty, and public action/ edited by Alain de Janvry ... [et al.]. Oxford; Oxford University Press, 2001. xiii, 451 p.
00-050426 333.3/09172/4 21 0199242178
Land use, Rural -- Developing countries. Land reform -- Developing countries. Land tenure -- Developing countries.

HD1251 Land use — Land tenure — General works

HD1251.B85 1996
Bull, Philip.
Land, politics and nationalism: a study of the Irish land question/ Philip Bull. New York: St. Martin's Press, 1996. x, 242 p.
96-028749 333.3/09415 0312164424
Land tenure -- Ireland -- History. Nationalism -- Ireland -- History. Ireland -- Politics and government.

HD1331 Land use — Land tenure — Landlord peasant

HD1331.L29.A39 1995
Agrarian structure & political power: landlord & peasant in the making of Latin America/ Evelyne Huber and Frank Safford, editors. Pittsburgh: University of Pittsburgh Press, c1995. viii, 242 p.
95-016082 333.33/554/098 0822938804
Landowners -- Latin America -- History -- Congresses. Peasantry -- Latin America -- History -- Congresses. Agriculture -- Economic aspects -- Latin America -- Congresses.

HD1332-1333 Land use — Land tenure — Land reform. Agrarian reform

HD1332.C47 1990
Christodoulou, Demetrios.
The unpromised land: agrarian reform and conflict worldwide/ Demetrios Christodoulou. London, UK; Zed Books, 1990. xvii, 236 p.
88-031885 333.3/1 0862327784
Land reform. Land tenure. Farm tenancy.

HD1333.E8.K53 1990
Kidane Mengisteab
Ethiopia: failure of land reform and agricultural crisis/ Kidane Mengisteab. New York: Greenwood Press, 1990. xviii, 216 p.
90-032335 338.1/0963 0313274231
Land reform -- Ethiopia. Famines -- Ethiopia. Agriculture -- Economic aspects -- Ethiopia.

HD1333.E85 H66 1999
Hopcroft, Rosemary L.
Regions, institutions, and agrarian change in European history/ Rosemary L. Hopcroft. Ann Arbor: University of Michigan Press, c1999. xiv, 272 p.
99-006089 338.1/094 21 0472110233
Land reform -- Europe -- History. Agriculture -- Economic aspects -- Europe -- History. Land tenure -- Europe -- History.

HD1333.G7.B76 1999
Bronstein, Jamie L., 1968-
Land reform and working-class experience in Britain and the Unied States, 1800-1862/ Jamie L. Bronstein. Stanford, Calif.: Stanford University Press, c1999. viii, 372 p.
98-028068 333.3/142 21 0804734518
Land reform -- Great Britain -- History -- 19th century. Land reform -- United States -- History -- 19th century. Working class -- Great Britain -- History -- 19th century.

HD1333.I4.J36 1994
Jannuzi, F. Tomasson, 1934-
India's persistent dilemma: the political economy of agrarian reform/ F. Tomasson Jannuzi. Boulder: Westview, 1994. xiv, 241 p.
94-000538 333.3/154 081338835X
Land reform -- India.

HD1333.I7.N34 1987
Najmabadi, Afsaneh, 1946-
Land reform and social change in Iran/ Afsaneh Najmabadi. Salt Lake City: University of Utah Press, 1987. x, 246 p.
87-031630 333.3/1/55 0874802857
Land reform -- Iran. Peasantry -- Iran. Agriculture -- Economic aspects -- Iran. Iran -- Rural conditions.

HD1333.M6.R445 1996
Reforming Mexico's agrarian reform/ Laura Randall, editor. Armonk, N.Y.: M.E. Sharpe, c1996. xiv, 343 p.
95-025771 333.3/172 20 1563246430
Land reform -- Mexico -- Congresses.

HD1333.N5 E569 1997
Enríquez, Laura J.
Agrarian reform and class consciousness in Nicaragua/ Laura J. Enríquez. Gainesville: University Press of Florida, c1997. viii, 206 p.
96-039604 322.4/4/097285 21 0813014891
Land reform -- Political aspects -- Nicaragua. Peasantry -- Nicaragua -- Political activity.

HD1333.S2.P45 1997
Pelupessy, Wim.
The limits of economic reform in El Salvador/ Wim Pelupessy. New York: St. Martin's Press, 1997. xi, 218 p.
96-049057 338.1/87284 0312173237
Land reform -- El Salvador. Agriculture and state -- El Salvador. Agriculture -- Economic aspects -- El Salvador. El Salvador -- Economic conditions. El Salvador -- Politics and government.

HD1339 Land use — Land tenure — Small holdings. Peasant proprietors. Parcellation

HD1339.C8.E33 1999
Edelman, Marc.
Peasants against globalization: rural social movements in Costa Rica/ Marc Edelman. Stanford, Calif.: Stanford University Press, 1999. xxii, 308 p.
99-031301 322.4/4/097286 0804734011
Peasantry -- Costa Rica -- Political activity. Social movements -- Costa Rica. Costa Rica -- Economic policy.

HD1365 Land use — Real estate business — Dictionaries. Encyclopedias

HD1365.S48 1996
Shim, Jae K.
Dictionary of real estate/ Jae K. Shim, Joel G. Siegel, Stephen W. Hartman. New York: J. Wiley, c1996. xi, 307 p.
95-016514 333.33/03 20 0471013366
Real estate business -- Dictionaries. Real property -- Dictionaries.

HD1393.5 Land use — Real estate business — Industrial real estate

HD1393.5.P484 2002
Peters, Alan H.
State enterprise zone programs: have they worked?/ Alan H. Peters and Peter S. Fisher. Kalamazoo, Mich.: W.E. Upjohn Institute for Employment Research, xiii, 345 p.
2002-013032 307.3/42 21 0880992506
Enterprise zones.

HD1415 Agricultural economics — General works — 1945-

HD1415.D68 1988
Dovring, Folke.
Progress for food or food for progress?: the political economy of agricultural growth and development/ Folke Dovring. New York: Praeger, 1988. vi, 324 p.
87-028874   338.1/9   0275929043
Agriculture -- Economic aspects. Food industry and trade. Economic development.

HD1415.F636 1989
Food, policy, and politics: a perspective on agriculture and development/ edited by George Horwich and Gerald J. Lynch. Boulder, Colo.: Westview Press, 1989. 292 p.
88-037521   338.1/8/091724   0813377250
Agriculture and state. Agriculture and state -- Developing countries. Agriculture -- Economic aspects.

HD1415.G684 1992
Grigg, David B.
The transformation of agriculture in the West/ David Grigg. Oxford, UK; Blackwell, 1992. xiv, 141 p.
92-130360   338.1   0631170944
Agriculture -- Economic aspects -- History -- 20th century. Agriculture -- Economic aspects -- Europe -- History -- 20th century. Agriculture -- Economic aspects -- America -- History -- 20th century.

HD1415.J6 1990
Johnson, D. Gale 1916-
World agriculture in disarray/ D. Gale Johnson. New York: St. Martin's Press, 1991. xx, 365 p.
90-019211   338.1/8/091722   0312057997
Agriculture -- Economic aspects. Agriculture and state.

HD1415.O47 1991
Olsen, Wallace C.
Agricultural economics and rural sociology: the contemporary core literature/ Wallace C. Olsen; with contributions by Margot A. Bellamy and Bernard F. Stanton. Ithaca, N.Y.: Cornell University Press, 1991. xi, 346 p.
91-055261   338.1   0801426774
Agriculture -- Economic aspects. Sociology, Rural. Agriculture -- Economic aspects -- Developing countries. Developing countries -- Rural conditions.

HD1417 Agricultural economics — Developing countries

HD1417.A475 1991
Agriculture and the state: growth, employment, and poverty in developing countries/ edited by C. Peter Timmer. Ithaca: Cornell University Press, 1991. xiii, 311 p.
90-027706   338.1/8/091724   0801426014
Agriculture and state -- Developing countries -- Congresses. Agricultural laborers -- Developing countries -- Congresses. Rural poor -- Developing countries -- Congresses.

HD1417.C63 1989
Colman, David.
Principles of agricultural economics: markets and prices in less developed countries/ David Colman and Trevor Young. Cambridge; Cambridge University Press, 1989. x, 323 p.
88-010297   338.1/09172/4   0521334306
Agriculture -- Economic aspects -- Developing countries. Agricultural prices -- Developing countries.

HD1417.E45 1992
Ellis, Frank, 1947-
Agricultural policies in developing countries/ Frank Ellis. Cambridge; Cambridge University Press, 1992. xv, 357 p.
91-018837   338.1/8/091724   052140004X
Agriculture and state -- Developing countries.

HD1417.M68 1978
Morgan, W. B.
Agriculture in the Third World: a spatial analysis/ W. B. Morgan. Boulder, Colo.: Westview Press, 1978. xiii, 290 p.
77-024064   338.1/09172/4   0891588205
Agriculture -- Developing countries. Agricultural geography.

HD1417.T83 2000
Tucker, Richard P., 1938-
Insatiable appetite: the United States and the ecological degradation of the tropical world/ Richard P. Tucker. Berkeley: University of California Press, c2000. xiii, 551 p.
00-037774   333.7/0913 21   0520220870
Tropical crops -- Economic aspects -- History -- 20th century. Tropical crops -- Environmental aspects -- History -- 20th century. Investments, American -- Tropics -- History -- 20th century.

HD1421 Agricultural economics — Developing countries — Collections of statistics

HD1421.P76
Food and Agriculture Organization of the United Nations.
FAO production yearbook. Annuaire FAO de la production. Anuario FAO de produccion. Rome, Food and Agriculture Organization of the United 11 v.
79-649153   338.1/0212
Agriculture -- Statistics -- Periodicals.

HD1437 Agricultural economics — Theory. Method. Relation to other subjects — Agricultural finance

HD1437.R57 2003
Risk management and the environment: agriculture in perspective/ edited by Bruce A. Babcock, Robert W. Fraser, and Joseph N. Lekakis. Dordrecht; Kluwer Academic, c2003. xi, 204 p.
2002-034362   368.1/21 21   140200981X
Agriculture -- Finance. Risk management. Agricultural prices.

HD1471 Agricultural economics — Size of farms — Large farms. Plantations

HD1471.C82.G84 1992
Edelman, Marc.
The logic of the latifundio: the large estates of northwestern Costa Rica since the late nineteenth century/ Marc Edelman. Stanford, Calif.: Stanford University Press, 1992. xv, 478 p.
91-045600   333.3/097286/6   0804720444
Latifundio -- Costa Rica -- Guanacaste -- History -- 20th century. Haciendas -- Costa Rica -- Guanacaste -- History -- 20th century. Agriculture -- Economic aspects -- Costa Rica -- Guanacaste -- History -- 20th century.

HD1471.U5.P68
Powell, Lawrence N.
New masters: northern planters during the Civil War and Reconstruction/ Lawrence N. Powell. New Haven: Yale University Press, 1980. xiv, 253 p.
79-064226   338.1/0975   0300022174
Plantations -- Southern States -- History. Cotton growing -- Southern States -- History. Afro-American agricultural laborers -- Southern States -- History. Southern States -- History -- 1865-1877.

HD1476 Agricultural economics — Size of farms — Small farms. Family farms

HD1476.U5 G7 2002
Grant, Michael Johnston,
Down and out on the family farm: rural rehabilitation in the Great Plains, 1929-1945/ Michael Johnston Grant. Lincoln, [Neb.]: University of Nebraska Press, c2002. ix, 232 p.
2002-022850   38.1/878/09043 21   0803271050
Family farms -- Great Plains. Farms, Small -- Government policy -- Great Plains. Rural development -- Great Plains.

HD1476.U5 H28 1996
Hanson, Victor Davis.
Fields without dreams: defending the agrarian idea/ Victor Davis Hanson. New York: Free Press, c1996. xxiii, 289 p.
95-040875   338.1/6 20   0684822997
Family farms -- United States. Agriculture -- Economic aspects -- United States.

HD1476.U5.M32 1984
MacFadyen, J. Tevere.
Gaining ground: the renewal of America's small farms/ J. Tevere MacFadyen. New York: Holt, Rinehart, and Winston, c1984. xi, 242 p.
83-013003   338.1/0973   0030695635
Farms, Small -- United States.

HD1478.U6 Agricultural economics — Sharecropping — By region or country, A-Z

HD1478.U6.C6
Conrad, David Eugene.
The forgotten farmers; the story of sharecroppers in the New Deal. Urbana, University of Illinois Press, 1965. 223 p.
65-011734   338.173351
Sharecropping. Agriculture -- Economic aspects -- Southern States.

HD1485-1486 Agricultural economics — Agricultural associations, societies, etc. — By region or country

HD1485.A45.K5
Kile, Orville Merton, 1886-
The Farm Bureau through three decades. Baltimore, Waverly Press [1948] ix, 416 p.
48-004550   338.106273
Aurella gens. Art, Roman. Rome (City) -- Description.

HD1485.N35.M58 1987
Mitchell, Theodore R.
Political education in the Southern Farmers' Alliance, 1887-1900/ Theodore R. Mitchell. Madison, Wis.: University of Wisconsin Press, 1987. xiv, 242 p.
87-040141   338.1/06/075   0299114708
Farmers -- Southern States -- Political activity -- History -- 19th century. Farmers -- Education -- Southern States -- History -- 19th century. Civics -- Study and teaching -- Southern States -- History -- 19th century.

HD1485.N39 M37 1991
Marti, Donald B.,
Women of the Grange: mutuality and sisterhood in rural America, 1866-1920/ Donald B. Marti. New York: Greenwood Press, 1991. viii, 157 p.
91-011328   338.1/06/073 20   031325723X
Rural women -- United States -- History. Women in agriculture -- United States -- History. Women farmers -- United States -- History.

HD1485.P5.W66 1991
Woods, Thomas A.
Knights of the plow: Oliver H. Kelley and the origins of the Grange in Republican ideology/ Thomas A. Woods. Ames: Iowa State University Press, 1991. xxii, 254 p.
90-004442   338.1/06073   0813802393
Kelley, Oliver H. -- (Oliver Hudson), -- 1826-1913.

HD1486.F8.B47
Berger, Suzanne.
Peasants against politics; rural organization in Brittany, 1911-1967. Cambridge, Mass., Harvard University Press, 1972. xi, 298 p.
73-174541   322/.094411   0674659252
Agriculture -- France -- Cotes-d'Armor -- Societies, etc. Agriculture -- France -- Finistere (Dept.) -- Societies, etc. Cotes-d'Armor (France) -- Politics and government. Finistere (France) -- Politics and government.

HD1491 Agricultural economics — Cooperative agriculture

HD1491.P3.W38
Weintraub, Dov.
Moshava, kibbutz, and moshav; patterns of Jewish rural settlement and development in Palestine [by] D. Weintraub, M. Lissak, and Y. Azmon. Foreword by S. N. Eisenstadt. Ithaca [N.Y.] Cornell University Press [1969] xxiii, 360 p.
69-018362   335/.9/5694   0801405203
Moshavim. Agricultural colonies -- Israel. Kibbutzim.

HD1491.P4.K67 1990
Korovkin, Tanya.
Politics of agricultural co-operativism: Peru, 1969-1983/ Tanya Korovkin. Vancouver: University of British Columbia Press, c1990. x, 186 p.
91-154073   334/.683/0985   0774803495
Agriculture, Cooperative -- Peru -- History -- 20th century. Cotton growing -- Peru -- History -- 20th century. Agriculture and state -- Peru -- History -- 20th century.

HD1491.U5.M37 1986
McBride, Glynn.
Agricultural cooperatives: their why and their how/ Glynn McBride. Westport, CT: AVI Pub. Co., c1986. xvii, 352 p.
86-017324   334/.683/0973   0870555340
Agriculture, Cooperative -- United States. Agriculture, Cooperative -- Law and legislation -- United States.

HD1492 Agricultural economics — Collective farms

HD1492.C5.N65 1988
Nolan, Peter.
The political economy of collective farms: an analysis of China's post-Mao rural reforms/ Peter Nolan. Boulder, Colo.: Westview Press, 1988. viii, 259 p.
88-015371   338.7/63/0951   0813307457
Collective farms -- China -- History -- 20th century. Rural development -- China -- History -- 20th century.

HD1492.R9.S74
Stuart, Robert C., 1938-
The collective farm in Soviet agriculture [by] Robert C. Stuart. Lexington, Mass., Lexington Books [1972] xx, 254 p.
77-175164   338.1   066981265X
Collective farms -- Soviet Union. Collective farms -- Management.

HD1492.S65 F58 1994
Fitzpatrick, Sheila.
Stalin's peasants: resistance and survival in the Russian village after collectivization/ Sheila Fitzpatrick. New York: Oxford University Press, 1994. xx, 386 p.
93-004786   306.3/64/0947 20   019506982X
Collectivization of agriculture -- Soviet Union. Agriculture and state -- Soviet Union.

HD1492.V5.F47 1989
Fforde, Adam.
The agrarian question in North Vietnam, 1974-1979: a study of cooperator resistance to state policy/ Adam Fforde. Armonk, N.Y.: M.E. Sharpe, c1989. xxii, 265 p.
88-006726   338.7/63/09597   0873324862
Collectivization of agriculture -- Vietnam -- History -- 20th century. Collective farms -- Vietnam -- History -- 20th century.

HD1510 Agricultural economics — Farm tenancy — General works

HD1510.C87
Currie, J. M.
The economic theory of agricultural land tenure/ J.M. Currie. Cambridge; Cambridge University Press, 1981. vii, 194 p.
80-041114   333.3   0521236347
Farm tenancy -- Economic aspects. Agriculture -- Economic aspects.

HD1511 Agricultural economics — Farm tenancy — By region or country, A-Z

HD1511.G7.R53 1982
Richards, Eric.
A history of the Highland clearances: Agrarian transformation and the evictions 1746-1886/ Eric Richards. London: Croom Helm, c1982. 532 p.
81-208122   333.33/5   085664496X
Crofters -- History. Farm tenancy -- Scotland -- Highlands -- History. Eviction -- Scotland -- Highlands -- History. Highlands (Scotland) -- Economic conditions.

HD1513 Agricultural economics — Peasant proprietors

HD1513.A755.S36
Scott, James C.
The moral economy of the peasant: rebellion and subsistence in Southeast Asia/ James C. Scott. New Haven: Yale University Press, 1976. ix, 246 p.
75-043334   301.44/43/0959   0300018622
Peasantry -- Asia, Southeastern.

HD1513.V5.P66
Popkin, Samuel L.
The rational peasant: the political economy of rural society in Vietnam/ Samuel L. Popkin. Berkeley: University of California Press, c1979. xxi, 306 p.
77-083105   301.44/43/09597   0520035615
Peasantry -- Vietnam -- History. Peasantry. Vietnam -- Rural conditions.

HD1525-1538 Agricultural economics — Agricultural laborers. Peasantry — By region or country

HD1525.S63
Sosnick, Stephen H.
Hired hands: seasonal farm workers in the United States/ by Stephen H. Sosnick. Santa Barbara: McNally & Loftin, West, c1978. xi, 453 p.
78-013908   331.5/44/0973
Agricultural laborers -- United States. Seasonal labor -- United States. Migrant agricultural laborers -- United States.

HD1527.A14.B37 1994
Barger, W. K. 1941-
The farm labor movement in the midwest: social change and adaptation among migrant farmworkers/ W.K. Barger and Ernesto M. Reza; foreword by Baldemar Velasquez. Austin: University of Texas Press, 1994. xix, 235 p.
93-003962 331.5/44/0977 0292707967
Migrant agricultural laborers -- Middle West. Mexican American migrant agricultural laborers -- Middle West.

HD1527.A19.G36 1990
Gamboa, Erasmo.
Mexican labor and World War II: braceros in the Pacific Northwest, 1942-1947/ Erasmo Gamboa. Austin: University of Texas Press, 1990. xiv, 178 p.
89-037605 331.5/44/08968720795 0292751176
Migrant agricultural laborers -- Northwest, Pacific -- History -- 20th century. Alien labor, Mexican -- Northwest, Pacific -- History -- 20th century. World War, 1939-1945 -- Manpower -- Northwest, Pacific.

HD1527.A9.H34 1997
Hahamovitch, Cindy.
The fruits of their labor: Atlantic coast farmworkers and the making of migrant poverty, 1870-1945/ Cindy Hahamovitch. Chapel Hill: University of North Carolina Press, c1997. xiii, 287 p.
96-041762 331.5/44/0975 20 0807823309
Migrant agricultural laborers -- Atlantic States -- History.

HD1527.C2.G84 1994
Guerin-Gonzales, Camille.
Mexican workers and American dreams: immigration, repatriation, and California farm labor, 1900-1939/ Camille Guerin-Gonzales. New Brunswick, N.J.: Rutgers University Press, c1994. xi, 197 p.
93-024223 331.54/4/0979409041 0813520479
Agricultural laborers, Mexican -- California -- History -- 20th century. Mexican American agricultural laborers -- California -- History -- 20th century. Repatriation -- Mexico -- History -- 20th century. Mexico -- Emigration and immigration -- History -- 20th century. California -- Emigration and immigration -- History -- 20th century.

HD1531.C9.P47 1989
Perez, Louis A., 1943-
Lords of the mountain: social banditry and peasant protest in Cuba, 1878-1918/ Louis A. Perez, Jr. Pittsburgh, PA: University of Pittsburgh Press, c1989. xvii, 267 p.
88-019815 322.4/4/097291 0822936011
Peasant uprisings -- Cuba -- History -- 19th century. Peasant uprisings -- Cuba -- History -- 20th century. Land tenure -- Cuba -- History. Cuba -- Rural conditions.

HD1531.M6.P87 1999
Purnell, Jennie, 1957-
Popular movements and state formation in revolutionary Mexico: the agraristas and cristeros of Michoacan/ Jennie Purnell. Durham, NC: Duke University Press, 1999. x, 271 p.
98-046237 972/.37 082232282X
Peasantry -- Mexico -- Michoacan de Ocampo -- Political activity. Cristero Rebellion, 1926-1929. Land reform -- Mexico -- Michoacan de Ocampo -- History -- 20th century.

HD1531.N5.G68 1990
Gould, Jeffrey L.
To lead as equals: rural protest and political consciousness in Chinandega, Nicaragua, 1912-1979/ Jeffrey L. Gould. Chapel Hill: University of North Carolina Press, c1990. xi, 377 p.
89-029790 322.4/4/09728511 0807819042
Peasantry -- Nicaragua -- Chinandega -- Political activity. Peasantry -- Nicaragua -- Chinandega -- History -- 20th century. Agricultural laborers -- Nicaragua -- Chinandega -- History -- 20th century. Chinandega (Nicaragua) -- History. Nicaragua -- Politics and government -- 20th century.

HD1531.5.R6713 1992
Rosener, Werner.
Peasants in the Middle Ages/ Werner Rosener; translated and with foreword and glossary by Alexander Stutzer. Urbana: University of Illinois Press, 1992. xi, 338 p.
92-158902 305.5/633/0940902 0252062892
Peasantry -- Europe -- History. Agriculture -- Economic aspects -- Europe -- History. Farm buildings -- Europe -- History.

HD1534.H59
Horn, Pamela.
Labouring life in the Victorian countryside/ Pamela Horn. Dublin: Gill and Macmillan, 1976. 292 p.
76-377375 301.44/42/0942 0717107280
Agricultural laborers -- Great Britain -- History -- 19th century. Great Britain -- History -- Victoria, 1837-1901. Great Britain -- Rural conditions -- 19th century.

HD1536.F8.F66 1991
Frader, Laura Levine, 1945-
Peasants and protest: agricultural workers, politics, and unions in the Aude, 1850-1914/ Laura Levine Frader. Berkeley: University of California Press, c1991. xiv, 260 p.
90-031951 331.88/1348/094487 0520068092
Peasantry -- France -- Aude -- History. Vinyard laborers -- France -- Aude -- History. Agricultural laborers -- Labor unions -- France -- Aude -- Political activity -- History.

HD1536.F8.M6813 1991
Moulin, Annie.
Peasantry and society in France since 1789/ Annie Moulin; translated from the French by M.C. and M.F. Cleary. Cambridge; Cambridge University Press; 1991. xxiii, 247 p.
90-022363 305.5/633/0944 0521395348
Peasantry -- France -- History. France -- Rural conditions.

HD1537.C5.P73 1999
Prazniak, Roxann.
Of camel kings and other things: rural rebels against modernity in late imperial China/ Roxann Prazniak. Lanham, Md.: Rowman & Littlefield, c1999. xi, 305 p.
98-023323 951/.034 21 0847690067
Peasant uprisings -- China -- History. China -- History -- Taiping Rebellion, 1850-1864. China -- History -- 1861-1912.

HD1537.V5.W54 1988
Wiegersma, Nancy.
Vietnam--peasant land, peasant revolution: patriarchy and collectivity in the rural economy/ Nancy Wiegersma. New York: St. Martin's Press, 1988. xix, 281 p.
87-027352 305.5/63 0312013582
Peasantry -- Vietnam -- History. Farm tenancy -- Vietnam -- History. Socialism -- Vietnam -- History. Vietnam -- Rural conditions.

HD1538.E3.B76 1990
Brown, Nathan J.
Peasant politics in modern Egypt: the struggle against the state/ Nathan J. Brown. New Haven: Yale University Press, c1990. x, 280 p.
89-016725 323.3/224 0300045387
Peasantry -- Egypt -- Political activity -- History. Peasantry -- Egypt -- History.

HD1538.S6.K75 1993
Krikler, Jeremy.
Revolution from above, rebellion from below: the agrarian Transvaal at the turn of the century/ Jeremy Krikler. Oxford: Clarendon Press; 1993. xi, 261 p.
92-039144 968.2/048 0198203802
Agricultural laborers -- South Africa -- Transvaal -- History. Land reform -- South Africa -- Transvaal -- History. South African War, 1899-1902. Transvaal (South Africa) -- Politics and government.

HD1641 Agricultural economics — Utilization and culture of special classes of lands — Pastures

HD1641.I73.J66 1995
Jones, David Seth, 1947-
Graziers, land reform, and political conflict in Ireland/ David Seth Jones. Washington, D.C.: Catholic University of America Press, c1995. xv, 287 p.
94-012475 333.76/09415 0813208157
Pastures -- Ireland -- History. Rangelands -- Ireland -- History. Grazing districts -- Ireland -- History. Ireland -- Politics and government.

HD1691 Agricultural economics — Water resources development. Water supply — General works

HD1691.M47 1997
Merrett, Stephen.
Introduction to the economics of water resources: an international perspective/ Stephen Merrett. London; UCL Press, 1997. xv, 211 p.
97-199057 1857286367
Water resources development -- Economic aspects. Water resources development -- International cooperation.

HD1694-1698 Agricultural economics — Water resources development. Water supply — By region or country

HD1694.A3 1998
Rivera, Jose A., 1944-
Acequia culture: water, land, and community in the Southwest/ Jose A. Rivera. Albuquerque: University of New Mexico Press, c1998. xxvi, 243 p.
98-023877 333.91/15/097644 21 0826318584
Water resources development -- Economic aspects -- Rio Grande Watershed -- History. Watershed management -- Rio Grande Watershed -- History. Land use -- Rio Grande Watershed -- History. Rio Grande Watershed -- Economic conditions. Rio Grande Watershed -- Social conditions. Rio Grande Watershed -- Environmental conditions -- History.

HD1694.A5.A75 1997
Anderson, Terry Lee, 1946-
Water markets: priming the invisible pump/ Terry L. Anderson & Pamela Snyder. Washington, DC: Cato Institute, 1997. vii, 228 p.
97-014369 333.91/16/0973 1882577434
Water-supply -- Economic aspects -- United States.

HD1694.A5.H76
Hunter, Louis C.
A history of industrial power in the United States, 1780-1930/ Louis C. Hunter. Charlottesville: Published for the Eleutherian Mills-Hagley Found 1979-1985. v. 1-2.
78-017538 338.4/0973 0813907829
Water-power -- Economic aspects -- United States -- History. Water rights -- United States -- History. Industries -- Power supply -- United States -- History.

HD1694.C2.B55 1992
Blomquist, William A. 1957-
Dividing the waters: governing groundwater in Southern California/ William A. Blomquist. San Francisco, Calif.: ICS Press; c1992. xix, 415 p.
92-024878 333.91/04/097949 1558152008
Water-supply -- Government policy -- California, Southern. Groundwater -- Government policy -- California, Southern.

HD1694.C2.H83 1992
Hundley, Norris.
The great thirst: Californians and water, 1770s-1990s/ Norris Hundley, Jr. Berkeley: University of California Press, c1992. xix, 551 p.
91-040995 333.91/009794 0520077865
Water-supply -- California -- History. California -- History.

HD1695.A165.S25 1987
Saliba, Bonnie.
Water markets in theory and practice: market transfers, water values, and public policy/ by Bonnie Colby Saliba and David B. Bush. Boulder: Westview Press, 1987. viii, 273 p.
87-021687 333.91/0979 0813374650
Water transfer -- Southwestern States. Water transfer -- Government policy -- Southwestern States. Water-supply -- Southwestern States.

HD1695.W4.P57 1996
Pisani, Donald J.
Water, land, and law in the West: the limits of public policy, 1850-1920/ Donald J. Pisani; foreword by Hal K. Rothman. Lawrence: University Press of Kansas, 1996. xii, 273 p.
96-014093 333.91/00978 0700607951
Water-supply -- Government policy -- West (U.S.) -- History. Water rights -- West (U.S.) -- History. Riparian rights -- West (U.S.) -- History.

HD1697.I8.S6 1998
Squatriti, Paolo, 1963-
Water and society in early medieval Italy: AD 400-1000/ Paolo Squatriti. Cambridge, UK; Cambridge University Press, 1998. xii, 195 p.
97-038745 306./0945/0902 0521621925
Water-supply -- Italy -- History. Social history -- Medieval, 500-1500.

HD1698.M53.D65 1999
Dolatyar, Mostafa.
Water politics in the Middle East: a context for conflict or cooperation?/ Mostafa Dolatyar and Tim S. Gray. New York: St. Martin's Press, 1999. xiv, 255 p.
99-022104 333.91/00956 031222382X
Water-supply -- Middle East. Water-supply -- Political aspects -- Middle East. Water resources development -- Middle East. Middle East -- Strategic aspects.

HD1698.M53.H55 1994
Hillel, Daniel.
Rivers of Eden: the struggle for water and the quest for peace in the Middle East/ Daniel Hillel. New York: Oxford University Press, 1994. x, 355 p.
94-019092 333.91/00956 0195080688
Water resources development -- Middle East. Water-supply -- Political aspects -- Middle East. Riparian rights -- Middle East.

HD1739 Agricultural economics — Irrigation — By region or country

HD1739.A17.R45 1986
Reisner, Marc.
Cadillac desert: the American West and its disappearing water/ Marc Reisner. New York, N.Y., U.S.A.: Viking, 1986. viii, 582 p.
85-040814 333.91/00978 0670199273
Irrigation -- Government policy -- West (U.S.) -- History. Water resources development -- Government policy -- West (U.S.) -- History. Political corruption -- West (U.S.) -- History.

HD1739.C2.P57 1984
Pisani, Donald J.
From the family farm to agribusiness: the irrigation crusade in California and the West, 1850-1931/ Donald J. Pisani. Berkeley: University of California Press, c1984. xiii, 521 p.
83-017928 338.1/62 0520051270
Irrigation -- Economic aspects -- California -- History. Agriculture -- Economic aspects -- California -- History.

HD1761-1775 Agricultural economics — By region or country — America

HD1761.B37 1966
Benedict, Murray R. b. 1892.
Farm policies of the United States, 1790-1950: a study of their origins and development, by Murray R. Benedict. New York, Octagon Books, 1966 [c1953] xv, 548 p.
66-028382 338.1/0973
Agriculture and state -- United States.

HD1761.C3
Capper, Arthur,
The agricultural bloc, by Arthur Capper. New York, Harcourt, Brace [c1922] vii, 171 p.
22-021173
Agriculture -- Economic aspects. Agriculture -- United States.

HD1761.H355 1991
Hamilton, David E., 1954-
From new day to New Deal: American farm policy from Hoover to Roosevelt, 1928-1933/ David E. Hamilton. Chapel Hill: University of North Carolina Press, c1991. xi, 333 p.
90-012950 338.1/873/09042 0807819611
Agriculture and state -- United States -- History -- 20th century. New Deal, 1933-1939.

HD1761.K5
Kirkendall, Richard Stewart, 1928-
Social scientists and farm politics in the age of Roosevelt. Columbia, University of Missouri Press [1966] ix, 358 p.
66-014032 338.120973
Agriculture and state -- United States.

HD1761.M27
McGovern, George S. 1922-
Agricultural thought in the twentieth century/ edited by George McGovern. Indianapolis: Bobbs-Merrill, c1967. lv, 570 p.
67-029211 630/.973
Agriculture and state -- United States.

HD1761.M68 1990
Moyer, Wayne.
The politics of agricultural reform in the United States and the European Community/ by Wayne Moyer and Tim Josling. Ames, Iowa: Iowa State University Press, 1990, c1989.
89-048550 338.1/873 0813813719
Agriculture and state -- United States. Agricultural price supports -- United States. Agriculture and state -- European Economic Community countries.

HD1761.S556
Shover, John L.
First majority, last minority: the transforming of rural life in America/ John L. Shover. DeKalb: Northern Illinois University Press, c1976. xix, 338 p.
75-026473 307.7/2/0973 0875800564
Agriculture -- Economic aspects -- United States -- History. United States -- Rural conditions.

HD1761.T25 1971
Taylor, Carl Cleveland, 1884-
The farmers' movement, 1620-1920 [by] Carl C. Taylor. Westport, Conn., Greenwood Press [1971, c1953] vi, 519 p.
78-136087 331.7/63/06373 0837152372
Agriculture -- United States -- History. Agriculture and state -- United States. Agriculture -- Economic aspects -- United States.

HD1765 1935.B3
Baldwin, Sidney, 1922-
Poverty and politics; the rise and decline of the Farm Security Administration. [Chapel Hill, University of North Carolina Press, [1968] xvi, 438 p.
68-018052 353.81
Agricultural administration -- United States.

HD1765 1976.C6 1976
Cochrane, Willard Wesley, 1914-
American farm policy, 1948-1973/ by Willard W. Cochrane and Mary E. Ryan. Minneapolis: University of Minnesota Press, c1976. xiv, 431 p.
75-032671 338.1/873 0816607834
Agriculture and state -- United States.

HD1765.A43 1990
Albrecht, Don E.
The sociology of U.S. agriculture: an ecological perspective/ Don E. Albrecht, Steve H. Murdock. Ames: Iowa State University Press, 1990. vii, 249 p.
89-077423   306.3/49/0973   0813801923
Agriculture -- United States -- Sociological aspects. Agricultural ecology -- United States. Human ecology -- United States. United States -- Rural conditions.

HD1773.A3.L38 2000
Lauck, Jon, 1971-
American agriculture and the problem of monopoly: the political economy of grain belt farming, 1953-1980/ Jon Lauck. Lincoln: University of Nebraska Press, c2000. xiv, 259 p.
99-038710   338.1/0977/09045 21   0803229321
Agriculture -- Economic aspects -- Middle West -- History -- 20th century. Agriculture and state -- Middle West -- History -- 20th century. Agricultural industries -- Mergers -- Middle West -- History -- 20th century.

HD1773.A5.G73 1973
Gray, L. C.
History of agriculture in the southern United States to 1860. Clifton [N.J.] A. M. Kelley, 1973. 2 v.
72-013878   338.1/0975   0678009570
Agriculture -- Economic aspects -- Southern States. Agriculture -- Southern States.

HD1775.G4.B74 1970
Brooks, Robert Preston, 1881-
The agrarian revolution in Georgia, 1865-1912. Westport, Conn., Negro Universities Press [1970] 129 p.
73-129939   338.1/09758   0837116031
Agriculture -- Economic aspects -- Georgia. Farm tenancy -- Georgia -- History. Land tenure -- Georgia -- History.

HD1775.N2B73
Bremer, Richard G.
Agricultural change in an urban age: the Loup country of Nebraska, 1910-1970/ Richard G. Bremer. Lincoln: University of Nebraska, 1976. xii, 239 p.
75-044808   338.1/09782/4
Agriculture -- Economic aspects -- Nebraska -- Loup River Valley -- History.

HD1790.5-2132 Agricultural economics — By region or country — Other regions or countries

HD1790.5.Z8.D4 1981
De Janvry, Alain.
The agrarian question and reformism in Latin America/ Alain de Janvry. Baltimore: The Johns Hopkins University Press, c1981. xvi, 311 p.
81-004147   338.1/88   0801825318
Agriculture and state -- Latin America. Land reform -- Latin America.

HD1792.U19 1987
U.S.-Mexico relations: agriculture and rural development/ edited by Bruce F. Johnston ... [et al.]. Stanford, Calif.: Stanford University Press, c1987. xii, 401 p.
86-023103   338.1/872   0804713197
Agriculture -- Economic aspects -- Mexico -- Congresses. Agriculture -- Economic aspects -- United States -- Congresses. Rural development -- Mexico -- Congresses. Mexico -- Commerce -- United States -- Congresses. United States -- Commerce -- Mexico -- Congresses.

HD1817.C64 1982
Collins, Joseph, 1945-
What difference could a revolution make?: food and farming in the new Nicaragua/ by Joseph Collins, with Frances Moore Lappe and Nick Allen. San Francisco, CA: Institute for Food and Development Policy, c1982. x, 185 p.
82-021032   338.1/097285   0935028102
Agriculture -- Economic aspects -- Nicaragua. Land tenure -- Nicaragua. Land reform -- Nicaragua.

HD1825.L67.G8
Gudeman, Stephen.
The demise of a rural economy: from subsistence to capitalism in a Latin American village/ Stephen Gudeman. London; Routledge & K. Paul, 1978. 176 p.
79-307023   330.9/8/003   0710088353
Agriculture -- Economic aspects -- Panama -- Los Boquerones region. Sugar growing -- Panama -- Los Boquerones region. Los Boquerones region, Panama -- Rural conditions.

HD1870.C62.L37 1988
Larson, Brooke.
Colonialism and agrarian transformation in Bolivia: Cochabamba, 1550-1900/ Brooke Larson. Princeton, N.J.: Princeton University Press, c1988. xv, 375 p.
87-034463   305.5/63   069107738X
Agriculture -- Economic aspects -- Bolivia -- Cochabamba Region -- History. Peasantry -- Bolivia -- Cochabamba Region -- History. Mercantile system -- Bolivia -- Cochabamba Region -- History. Cochabamba Region (Bolivia) -- Rural conditions. Cochabamba Region (Bolivia) -- Politics and government.

HD1870.S25.G54 1987
Gill, Lesley.
Peasants, entrepreneurs, and social change: frontier development in lowland Bolivia/ Lesley Gill. Boulder: Westview Press, 1987. xiv, 246 p.
86-028207   303.4/0984/3   0813373395
Agriculture -- Economic aspects -- Bolivia -- Santa Cruz (Dept.) Sugarcane industry -- Bolivia -- Santa Cruz (Dept.) Land settlement -- Bolivia -- Santa Cruz (Dept.) Santa Cruz (Bolivia: Dept.) -- Commerce.

HD1917.D813
Duby, Georges.
Rural economy and country life in the medieval West. Translated by Cynthia Postan. Columbia, University of South Carolina Press [1968] xv, 600 p.
68-020530   338.1/094
Agriculture -- Economic aspects -- Europe. Country life -- Europe -- History. Agriculture -- History. Europe -- Rural conditions.

HD1918.I53 1999
Ingersent, K. A.
Agricultural policy in Western Europe and the United States/ K.A. Ingersent, A.J. Rayner. Northampton, MA: Edward Elgar Pub., 1999. xii, 450 p.
98-056514   338.1/84   1852780207
Agriculture and state -- Europe, Western. Agriculture and state -- United States.

HD1927.C66 1989
Cooper, Andrew Fenton, 1950-
British agricultural policy, 1912-36: a study in Conservative politics/ Andrew Fenton Cooper. Manchester, UK; Manchester University Press; c1989. viii, 240 p.
88-013758   338.1/841   0719028868
Agriculture and state -- Great Britain -- History -- 20th century.

HD1930.E17.P76 1978
Property, paternalism, and power: class and control in rural England/ Howard Newby ... [et al.]. Madison: University of Wisconsin Press, c1978. 432 p.
78-020301   307.7/2/09426   0229078701
Farmers -- England -- East Anglia. Land tenure -- England -- East Anglia. Paternalism -- England -- East Anglia. East Anglia (England) -- Rural conditions.

HD1930.E5.O93 1996
Overton, Mark.
Agricultural revolution in England: the transformation of the agrarian economy, 1500-1850/ Mark Overton. Cambridge; Cambridge University Press, 1996. xiv, 258 p.
95-033963   338.1/61/0942   0521246822
Agriculture -- Economic aspects -- England -- History. England -- Economic conditions.

HD1943.H64 1996
Hoffman, Philip T., 1947-
Growth in a traditional society: the French countryside, 1450-1815/ Philip T. Hoffman. Princeton, N.J.: Princeton University Press, c1996. xiv, 361 p.
95-031936   338.1/0944 20   0691029830
Agriculture -- Economic aspects -- France -- History. Agricultural productivity -- France -- History. France -- Rural conditions. France -- Economic conditions.

HD1945.C58 1989
Cleary, M. C.
Peasants, politicians, and producers: the organisation of agriculture in France since 1918/ M.C. Cleary. Cambridge; Cambridge University Press, 1989. ix, 209 p.
88-039764   306.34   0521333474
Agriculture -- France -- Societies, etc. -- History -- 20th century. Agriculture, Cooperative -- France -- History -- 20th century. Peasantry -- France -- History -- 20th century.

HD1992.M19 1987
Macey, David A. J., 1942-
Government and peasant in Russia, 1861-1906: the prehistory of the Stolypin reforms/ David A.J. Macey. Dekalb, Ill.: Northern Illinois University Press, 1987. xviii, 380 p.
87-007684   338.1/847   0875801226
Agriculture -- Economic aspects -- Russia -- History -- 19th century. Agriculture and state -- Russia -- History -- 19th century. Peasantry -- Russia -- History -- 19th century. Russia -- Economic conditions -- 1861-1917.

HD1992.S5944 1984
The Soviet rural economy/ edited by Robert C. Stuart. Totowa, N.J.: Rowman & Allanheld, 1984, c1983. viii, 326 p.
83-009668   338.1/0947   0865980926
Agriculture -- Economic aspects -- Soviet Union -- Congresses. Agriculture and state -- Soviet Union -- Congresses. Rural development -- Government policy -- Soviet Union -- Congresses. Soviet Union -- Economic policy -- Congresses. Soviet Union -- Rural conditions -- Congresses.

HD1993.H43 1984
Hedlund, Stefan, 1953-
Crisis in Soviet agriculture/ Stefan Hedlund. London: Croom Helm; 1984. 228 p.
83-042998   338.1/847   0312174012
Agriculture and state -- Soviet Union. Agriculture -- Economic aspects -- Soviet Union. Agriculture -- Soviet Union.

HD2025.C325.R85 1994
Ruiz, Teofilo F., 1943-
Crisis and continuity: land and town in late medieval Castile/ Teofilo F. Ruiz. Philadelphia: University of Pennsylvania Press, c1994. xvi, 351 p.
93-035573   330.946/3   0812232283
Agriculture -- Economic aspects -- Spain -- Castile -- History. Cities and towns, Medieval -- Spain -- Castile. Castile (Spain) -- Economic conditions. Castile (Spain) -- Social conditions.

HD2027.P67 1987
Portuguese agriculture in transition/ Scott R. Pearson ... [et al.]. Ithaca: Cornell University Press, 1987. 283 p.
86-029198   338.1/09469   0801419549
Agriculture -- Economic aspects -- Portugal. Agriculture and state -- Portugal. Agriculture -- Portugal.

HD2056.5.A64 1985
Agricultural development in the Middle East/ edited by Peter Beaumont and Keith McLachlan. Chichester [Sussex]; Wiley, c1985. xiv, 349 p.
85-006414   338.1/0956   0471907626
Agriculture -- Economic aspects -- Middle East. Agriculture -- Middle East.

HD2058.5.K36 1991
Kamen, Charles Samuel, 1939-
Little common ground: Arab agriculture and Jewish settlement in Palestine, 1920-1948/ Charles S. Kamen. Pittsburgh, Pa.: University of Pittsburgh Press, c1991. xi, 327 p.
90-049090   338.1/089/92705694   0822936682
Agriculture -- Economic aspects -- Palestine -- History. Land settlement -- Palestine -- History. Jews -- Palestine -- History.

HD2072.F68
Franda, Marcus F.
India's rural development: an assessment of alternatives/ Marcus Franda. Bloomington: Published in association with the American Unive c1979. xi, 306 p.
79-002177   338.1/0954   025319315X
Rural development -- India. Agriculture and state -- India. India -- Politics and government -- 1947-

HD2075.N56.H39 1991
Hazell, P. B. R.
The Green Revolution reconsidered: the impact of high-yielding rice varieties in South India/ Peter B.R. Hazell, C. Ramasamy; with contributions by P.K. Aiyasamy ... [et al.]. Baltimore: Johns Hopkins University Press, c1991. xiv, 286 p.
90-026234   330.954/8205   0801841852
Green Revolution -- India -- North Arcot. Rice -- India -- North Arcot. Farmers -- India -- North Arcot.

HD2080.V5.S35
Sansom, Robert L.
The economics of insurgency in the Mekong Delta of Vietnam [by] Robert L. Sansom. Cambridge, Mass., M.I.T. Press [1970] xviii, 283 p.
70-090753   330.9597   0262190648
Agriculture -- Economic aspects -- Vietnam -- Mekong River Valley. Land tenure -- Mekong River Valley. Vietnamese Conflict, 1961-1975 -- Economic aspects -- Mekong River Valley.

HD2098.L37 1983
Lardy, Nicholas R.
Agriculture in China's modern economic development/ Nicholas R. Lardy. Cambridge [Cambridgeshire]; Cambridge University Press, 1983. xiii, 285 p.
82-023555   338.1/0951   0521252466
Agriculture and state -- China. Agriculture -- Economic aspects -- China. Food supply -- China. China -- Economic policy -- 1976-

HD2117.A37 1992
Aid to African agriculture: lessons from two decades of donors' experience/ Uma Lele, editor. Baltimore: Johns Hopkins University Press, c1991 xix, 627 p.
91-038842   338.1/8   0801843669
Agricultural assistance -- Africa, Sub-Saharan. Economic assistance -- Africa, Sub-Saharan. Agriculture -- Economic aspects -- Africa, Sub-Saharan.

HD2118 1981.B37
Bates, Robert H.
Markets and states in tropical Africa: the political basis of agricultural policies/ Robert H. Bates. Berkeley: University of California Press, c1981. xi, 178 p.
80-039732   338.1/867   0520042530
Agriculture and state -- Africa, Sub-Saharan. Agriculture -- Economic aspects -- Africa, Sub-Saharan.

HD2118.A34 1983
Agrarian policies and rural poverty in Africa/ edited by Dharam Ghai and Samir Radwan. Geneva: International Labour Office, 1983. ix, 311 p.
83-140896   338.1/86   9221031004
Agriculture and state -- Africa. Rural development -- Government policy -- Africa. Rural poor -- Africa. Africa -- Rural conditions.

HD2123.R5 1982
Richards, Alan, 1946-
Egypt's agricultural development, 1800-1980: technical and social change/ Alan Richards. Boulder, Colo.: Westview Press, 1982. xvi, 296 p.
81-012919   338.1/0962   0865310998
Agriculture -- Economic aspects -- Egypt -- History.

HD2125.A63 1989
Abdi Ismail Samatar.
The state and rural transformation in Northern Somalia, 1884-1986/ Abdi Ismail Samatar. Madison, Wis.: University of Wisconsin Press, c1989. xix, 204 p.
88-040443   338.1/86773   0299119904
Agriculture and state -- Somalia -- History. Rural development -- Government policy -- Somalia. Somalia -- Economic policy. Somalia -- Social conditions. Somalia -- Colonial influence.

HD2126.L86 1990
Lundahl, Mats, 1946-
Incentives and agriculture in East Africa/ Mats Lundahl. London; Routledge, 1990. xi, 223 p.
90-008156   338.1/8676   0415037360
Agriculture -- Economic aspects -- Africa, Eastern. Incentives in industry -- Africa, Eastern. Communism -- Africa, Eastern.

HD2128.5.G5 1992
Giblin, James Leonard.
The politics of environmental control in northeastern Tanzania, 1840-1940/ James L. Giblin. Philadelphia: University of Pennsylvania Press, c1992. xiv, 209 p.
92-028388   338.1/09678/27   0812231775
Agriculture -- Economic aspects -- Tanzania -- History. Famines -- Tanzania -- History. Environmental policy -- Tanzania -- History. Tanzania -- Economic conditions -- To 1964. Tanzania -- Politics and government.

HD2131.Z8.D75 1991
Drinkwater, Michael.
The state and agrarian change in Zimbabwe's communal areas/ Michael Drinkwater. New York: St. Martin's Press, 1991. xv, 348 p.
90-008934   338.1/86891   0312053509
Agriculture and state -- Zimbabwe.

HD2132.Z8.F47 1990
Ferguson, James, 1959-
The anti-politics machine: "development," depoliticization, and bureaucratic power in Lesotho/ James Ferguson. Cambridge [England]; Cambridge University Press, 1990. xvi, 320 p.
89-036130   338.1/86885   0521373824
Rural development projects -- Lesotho -- Case studies. Bureaucracy -- Lesotho. Decentralization in government -- Lesotho. Lesotho -- Economic conditions -- 1966- Lesotho -- Politics and government -- 1966-

HD2321 Industry — History

HD2321.I58 1987
International capitalism and industrial restructuring: a critical analysis/ edited by Richard Peet. Boston: Allen & Unwin, 1987. xvi, 315 p.
86-028870   338.7   0043381324
Industries -- History. Industrial organization. Economic history -- 1945-

HD2321.S74 1993
Stearns, Peter N.
The industrial revolution in world history/ Peter N. Stearns. Boulder, Colo.: Westview Press, 1993. xiii, 254 p.
93-018719   338.09   0813385962
Industrial revolution. Economic history.

HD2326 Industry — Theory. Relation to other subjects

HD2326.B38 1982
Baumol, William J.
Contestable markets and the theory of industry structure/ William J. Baumol, John C. Panzar, Robert D. Willig, with contributions by Elizabeth E. Bailey, Dietrich Fischer, Herman C. Quirmbach. New York: Harcourt Brace Jovanovich, c1982. xxix, 510 p.
81-084084   338.6   015513910X
Industrial organization (Economic theory) Microeconomics.

HD2326.F55 1991
Fisher, Franklin M.
Industrial organization, economics, and the law: collected papers of Franklin M. Fisher/ edited by John Monz. Cambridge, Mass.: MIT Press, 1991. xx, 490 p.
90-044282   338.8/0973   0262061392
Industrial organization (Economic theory) Monopolies. Equilibrium (Economics)

HD2326.H28 1989
Handbook of industrial organization/ edited by Richard Schmalensee and Robert D. Willig. Amsterdam; North-Holland; 1989. 2 v.
88-025138   338.6   0444704345
Industrial organization (Economic theory) -- Handbooks, manuals, etc.

HD2326.L45 1987
Leibenstein, Harvey.
Inside the firm: the inefficiencies of hierarchy/ Harvey Leibenstein. Cambridge, Mass.: Harvard University Press, 1987. xiv, 276 p.
87-008426   302.3/5   0674455150
Industrial organization (Economic theory) Competition, Imperfect. Industrial management -- Japan.

HD2326.M3 1970
Marshall, Alfred, 1842-1924.
Industry & trade; a study of industrial technique and business organization, and of their influences on the conditions of various classes and nations. New York, A. M. Kelley, 1970. xxiv, 874 p.
72-104007   338/.09   0678006024
Industries. Commerce. Economic history -- 1750-1918.

HD2326.S88 1991
Sutton, John, 1948-
Sunk costs and market structure: price competition, advertising, and the evolution of concentration/ John Sutton. Cambridge, Mass.: MIT Press, c1991. 577 p.
90-022722   338.6   0262193051
Industrial organization (Economic theory) Game theory. Advertising -- Costs -- Mathematical models.

HD2336 Industry — Home labor. Home-based businesses — By region or country, A-Z

HD2336.U5.H66 1989
Homework: historical and contemporary perspectives on paid labor at home/ edited by Eileen Boris and Cynthia R. Daniels. Urbana: University of Illinois Press, c1989. x, 299 p.
88-023232   331.4/0973   0252016017
Home labor -- United States -- History. Women -- Employment -- United States -- History.

HD2336.U5.L69 1989
Lozano, Beverly.
The invisible work force: transforming American business with outside and home-based workers/ Beverly Lozano. New York: Free Press; c1989. x, 218 p.
89-011696   331.25   0029194423
Home labor -- California -- San Francisco Bay Area. Home labor -- United States.

HD2336.3 Industry — Home labor. Home-based businesses — Telecommuting

HD2336.3.N55 1998
Nilles, Jack M.
Managing telework: strategies for managing the virtual workforce/ Jack M. Nilles. New York: Wiley, c1998. xxii, 330 p.
98-013509   658.3 21   0471293164
Telecommuting centers -- Management.

HD2339 Industry — Sweatshops — By region or country, A-Z

HD2339.G7.B9 1978
Bythell, Duncan.
The sweated trades: outwork in nineteenth century Britain/ Duncan Bythell. New York: St. Martin's Press, 1978. 287 p.
78-000451   338.6/34/0941   0312779992
Sweat shops -- Great Britain -- History. Home labor -- Great Britain -- History.

HD2341 Industry — Small business. Medium-sized business — General works

HD2341.I534 1989
The Informal economy: studies in advanced and less developed countries/ edited by Alejandro Portes, Manuel Castells, Lauren A. Benton. Baltimore, Md.: Johns Hopkins University Press, c1989. viii, 327 p.
88-023004   331.12/09172/4   0801837359
Informal sector (Economics) -- Case studies. Informal sector (Economics) -- Government policy -- Case studies.

HD2341.T52 1992
Thomas, J. J.
Informal economic activity/ J.J. Thomas. Ann Arbor: University of Michigan Press, c1992. xii, 371 p.
92-028162   330   0472104209
Informal sector (Economics) Informal sector (Economics) -- Developing countries.

HD2341.U47 1989
The Underground economies: tax evasion and information distortion/ edited by Edgar L. Feige. Cambridge [England]; Cambridge University Press, 1989. xi, 378 p.
88-004252   330   0521262305
Informal sector (Economics)

HD2344.5 Industry — Small business. Medium-sized business — Minority business enterprises

HD2344.5.U6.E53 1999
Encyclopedia of African American business history/ edited by Juliet E.K. Walker. Westport, Conn.: Greenwood Press, 1999. xxxi, 721 p.
98-044218   338.6/422/08996073   0313295492
Afro-American business enterprises -- History. Afro-American business enterprises -- Encyclopedias. Slavery -- United States -- Chronology.

HD2344.5.U6.W35 1998
Walker, Juliet E. K., 1940-
The history of Black business in America: capitalism, race, entrepreneurship/ Juliet E.K. Walker. New York: Twayne Publishers, 1998. xxv, 482 p.
98-023170   338.6/422/08996073   0805716505
Afro-American business enterprises -- History.

HD2344.5.U62.A853 1999
Boston, Thomas D.
Affirmative action and black entrepreneurship/ Thomas D. Boston. London; Routledge, 1999. xiv, 114 p.
99-183108   0415095948
Afro-American business enterprises -- Georgia -- Atlanta. Afro-American businesspeople -- Georgia -- Atlanta. Afro-American business enterprises.

HD2346 Industry — Small business. Medium-sized business — By region or country, A-Z

HD2346.A58.I54 1996
The informal sector and microfinance institutions in West Africa/ edited by Leila Webster, Peter Fidler. Washington, D.C.: World Bank, c1996. xv, 365 p.
96-022495   330 20   0821335979
Informal sector (Economics) -- Africa, French-speaking West. Informal sector (Economics) -- Africa, West. Banks and banking, Cooperative -- Africa, West.

HD2346.C72.B657 1992
Sowell, David, 1952-
The early Colombian labor movement: artisans and politics in Bogota, 1832-1919/ David Sowell. Philadelphia: Temple University Press, 1992. xvi, 269 p.
91-045958   322/.2/0986148   0877229651
Artisans -- Colombia -- Bogota -- Political activity -- History -- 19th century. Labor movement -- Colombia -- Bogota -- History -- 19th century.

HD2346.C8.I89 2000
Itzigsohn, Jose, 1960-
Developing poverty: the state, labor market deregulation, and the informal economy in Costa Rica and the Dominican Republic/ Jose Itzigsohn. University Park: Pennsylvania State University Press, c2000. xiii, 197 p.
99-055443   338.98 21   027102027X
Informal sector (Economics) -- Costa Rica. Informal sector (Economics) -- Dominican Republic. Labor market -- Costa Rica.

HD2346.C84.P47 1995
Perez-Lopez, Jorge F.
Cuba's second economy: from behind the scenes to center stage/ Jorge F. Perez-Lopez. New Brunswick, N.J., U.S.A.: Transaction Publishers, c1995. 221 p.
94-030755   330   1560001895
Informal sector (Economics) -- Cuba. Cuba -- Economic conditions -- 1990- Cuba -- Economic policy.

HD2346.F8.Z38 1990
Zdatny, Steven M.
The politics of survival: artisans in twentieth-century France/ Steven M. Zdatny. New York: Oxford University Press, 1990. x, 257 p.
89-036983   322/.2/09440904   0195059409
Artisans -- France -- Political activity -- History -- 20th century. Middle class -- France -- Political activity -- History -- 20th century. Fascism -- France -- History -- 20th century. France -- Politics and government -- 20th century.

HD2346.I5.S547 1988
Small scale enterprises in industrial development: the Indian experience/ edited by K.B. Suri. New Delhi; Sage Publications, 1988. 348 p.
87-023221   338.6/42/0954   0803995393
Small business -- India -- Congresses.

HD2346.I75.S56 1995
Schnell, Izhak.
Arab industrialization in Israel: ethnic entrepreneurship in the periphery/ Izhak Schnell, Michael Sofer, and Israel Drori. Westport, Conn.: Praeger, 1995. xiv, 204 p.
95-013916   338/.04/089927405694   0275948560
Business enterprises, Palestinian Arab. Factories -- Location -- Israel. Minority business enterprises -- Government policy -- Israel.

HD2346.L38.B49 1992
Beyond regulation: the informal economy in Latin America/ edited by Victor E. Tokman. Boulder: Lynne Rienner, 1992. viii, 295 p.
92-014361   330   1555873189
Informal sector (Economics) -- Latin America. Informal sector (Economics) -- Law and legislation -- Latin America.

HD2346.P7.A85 1985
Aslund, Anders, 1952-
Private enterprise in Eastern Europe: the non-agricultural private sector in Poland and the GDR, 1945-1983/ Anders Aslund; foreword by Wlodzimierz Brus. New York: St. Martin's Press, 1985. xv, 294 p.
84-040388   338.6/42/09438   0312647069
Small business -- Germany (East) Informal sector (Economics) -- Poland. Informal sector (Economics) -- Germany (East) Germany (East) -- Economic policy. Poland -- Economic policy -- 1945-1955.

HD2346.S7.B46 1990
Benton, Lauren A.
Invisible factories: the informal economy and industrial development in Spain/ Lauren A. Benton. Albany: State University of New York Press, c1990. xii, 231 p.
89-004543   338.0946   0791402231
Informal sector (Economics) -- Spain. Industrialization -- Spain.

HD2346.U5.B343 1996
Bean, Jonathan J.
Beyond the broker state: federal policies toward small business, 1936-1961/ Jonathan J. Bean. Chapel Hill: University of North Carolina Press, c1996. xiv, 281 p.
96-010868   338.6/42/0973 20   0807822965
Small business -- Government policy -- United States -- History -- 20th century. Small business -- Law and legislation -- United States.

HD2346.U5.B56 1991
Blackford, Mansel G., 1944-
A history of small business in America/ Mansel G. Blackford. New York: Twayne Publishers; c1991. xx, 176 p.
91-041983   338.6/42/0973   0805798242
Small business -- United States -- History. Small business -- Government policy -- United States -- History.

HD2346.U5.D78 1985
Drucker, Peter Ferdinand, 1909-
Innovation and entrepreneurship: practice and principles/ Peter F. Drucker. New York: Harper & Row, c1985. ix, 277 p.
84-048593   658.4/2   0060154284
Small business -- United States. New business enterprises -- United States. Entrepreneurship.

HD2346.U52G44 2000
Gillespie, Michele.
Free labor in an unfree world: white artisans in slaveholding Georgia, 1789-1860/ Michele Gillespie. Athens: University of Georgia Press, c2000. xxii, 236 p.
99-028866   331.7/94/0975809034   21   0820319686
Artisans -- Georgia -- History. Slavery -- Georgia -- History. Working class -- Georgia -- History.

HD2346.U52.M497 1998
Staudt, Kathleen A.
Free trade?: informal economies at the U.S.-Mexico border/ Kathleen Staudt. Philadelphia: Temple University Press, 1998. xii, 211 p.
97-012414   338.0972/1   1566395674
Informal sector (Economics) -- Mexican-American Border Region. Industries -- Mexico, North. Industries -- Texas.

HD2346.U52.N5524
Rock, Howard B., 1944-
Artisans of the New Republic: the tradesmen of New York City in the age of Jefferson/ Howard B. Rock. New York: New York University Press, 1979. xviii, 340 p.
78-055570   301.44/42   0814773796
Artisans -- New York (State) -- New York -- History. New York (N.Y.) -- Social conditions.

HD2356 Industry — Large industry. Factory system. Big business — By region or country, A-Z

HD2356.U5.N44 1995
Nelson, Daniel, 1941-
Managers and workers: origins of the twentieth-century factory system in the United States, 1880-1920/ Daniel Nelson. Madison, Wis.: University of Wisconsin Press, c1995. xi, 250 p.
95-006356   658.3/009073   0299148807
Factory system -- United States -- History. Personnel management -- United States -- History. Industrial sociology -- United States -- History.

HD2356.U5.P73 2000
Prechel, Harland N.
Big business and the state: historical transitions and corporate transformation, 1880s-1990s/ Harland Prechel. Albany: State University of New York Press, c2000. xvi, 317 p.
99-054293   338.973/009/04 21   0791445933
Big business -- Government policy -- United States -- History. Industrial policy -- United States -- History. Corporation law -- United States -- History.

HD2385 Industry — Contracting. Letting of contracts. Contracting out — Subcontracting

HD2385.J3.N57 1994
Nishiguchi, Toshihiro.
Strategic industrial sourcing: the Japanese advantage/ Toshihiro Nishiguchi. New York: Oxford University Press, 1994. xxi, 318 p.
92-013254   658.7/2/0952   0195071093
Subcontracting -- Japan. Industrial procurement -- Japan.

HD2731 Industry — Corporations — General works

HD2731.B27 1967
Baumol, William J.
Business behavior, value and growth [by] William J. Baumol. New York, Harcourt, Brace & World [1967] xiii, 159 p.
67-014320   330/.01/8
Oligopolies. Economic development.

HD2731.D7 1972
Drucker, Peter Ferdinand, 1909-
Concept of the corporation [by] Peter F. Drucker. 1972 ed. with a new pref. and new epilogue by the author. New York, John Day Co. [1972] xxv, 319 p.
72-000074   338.7/4/0973
Corporations. Corporations -- United States.

HD2731.J69 1988
Joyce, Joseph P.
The economic activities of business: an analysis of the modern corporation/ Joseph P. Joyce. New York: Praeger, 1988. x, 140 p.
88-014106   658   0275923169
Corporations. Business enterprises. Industrial management.

HD2741-2746.5 Industry — Corporations — Corporate organization. Corporate governance

HD2741.B39
Benston, George J.
Conglomerate mergers: causes, consequences, and remedies/ George J. Benston. Washington, D.C.: American Enterprise Institute for Public Policy c1980. 76 p.
80-012017   338.8/3/0973   0844733733
Consolidation and merger of corporations -- United States. Conglomerate corporations -- United States.

HD2741.I585 1987
Intercorporate relations: the structural analysis of business/ edited by Mark S. Mizruchi, Michael Schwartz. Cambridge [Cambridgeshire]; Cambridge University Press, 1987. x, 330 p.
87-006388   338.7   0521335035
Corporations. Directors of corporations. Capitalists and financiers.

HD2745.D45 1992
Demb, Ada.
The corporate board: confronting the paradoxes/ Ada Demb, F.-Friedrich Neubauer. New York: Oxford University Press, 1992. xiv, 208 p.
91-031116   658.4/22   0195070399
Directors of corporations.

HD2746.5.A38 1990
Alkhafaji, Abbass F.
Restructuring American corporations: causes, effects, and implications/ Abbass F. Alkhafaji. New York: Quorum Books, 1990. xii, 194 p.
90-032699   338.8/3/0973   0899305733
Consolidation and merger of corporations -- United States. Corporate reorganizations -- United States.

HD2746.5.C675 1988
Corporate takeovers: causes and consequences/ edited by Alan J. Auerbach. Chicago: University of Chicago Press, 1988. ix, 343 p.
87-037497   338.8/3/0973   0226032116
Consolidation and merger of corporations -- Congresses. Consolidation and merger of corporations -- United States -- Congresses.

HD2746.5.H357 1992
Halperin, Michael, 1940-
Research guide to corporate acquisitions, mergers, and other restructuring/ Michael Halperin and Steven J. Bell. New York: Greenwood Press, 1992. xv, 208 p.
91-024199   016.6581/6   0313272204
Consolidation and merger of corporations -- Information services.

HD2746.5.W65 1988
Wojahn, Ellen.
Playing by different rules/ Ellen Wojahn. New York, NY: AMACOM, c1988. xiv, 306 p.
88-011684   338.8/3/0973   0814458610
Consolidation and merger of corporations -- United States -- Case studies. Corporate divestiture -- United States -- Case studies.

HD2755.5 Industry — Corporations — International business enterprises. Multinational

HD2755.5.C392 1987
Casson, Mark, 1945-
The firm and the market: studies on multinational enterprise and the scope of the firm/ Mark Casson. Cambridge, Mass.: MIT Press, 1987. xii, 283 p.
86-027199   658/.049   0262031299
International business enterprises.

HD2755.5.D65 1989
Donaldson, Thomas, 1945-
The ethics of international business/ Thomas Donaldson. New York: Oxford University Press, 1989. xvi, 196 p.
89-009471   174/.4   0195058747
International business enterprises -- Moral and ethical aspects. Business ethics.

HD2755.5.F734
Frank, Isaiah, 1917-
Foreign enterprise in developing countries/ Isaiah Frank. Baltimore: Johns Hopkins University Press, c1980. xv, 199 p.
79-003722   338.8/881724   0801823439
International business enterprises -- Developing countries.

HD2755.5.G66 1987
Goodman, Louis Wolf.
Small nations, giant firms/ Louis W. Goodman. New York: Holmes & Meier, c1987. xiii, 181 p.
87-000042   338.8/888   0841909962
International business enterprises. International business enterprises -- Latin America. States, Small.

HD2755.5.G73 1990
Gray, S. J.
Handbook of international business and management/ S.J. Gray, M.C. McDermott, and E.J. Walsh. Oxford [England]; B. Blackwell, 1990. xviii, 222 p.
89-077224   658/.049/03   0631150242
International business enterprises -- Dictionaries.

HD2755.5.I38 1992
Ietto-Gillies, Grazia.
International production: trends, theories, effects/ Grazia Ietto-Gillies. Cambridge, UK: Polity Press; 1992. x, 242 p.
92-013155   338.8/8   0745605761
International business enterprises. International trade.

HD2755.5.L59 1989
Livingstone, J. M., 1925-
The internationalization of business/ J.M. Livingstone. New York: St. Martin's Press, 1989. viii, 280 p.
88-029702   338.8/8   0312024185
International business enterprises.

HD2755.5.L67 1992
Lorange, Peter.
Strategic alliances: formation, implementation, and evolution/ Peter Lorange and Johan Roos. Cambridge, Mass., USA: Blackwell Business, 1992. vii, 295 p.
91-023298   658/.044   1557861021
International business enterprises -- Case studies. Joint ventures -- Case studies. Strategic alliances (Business) -- Case studies.

HD2755.5.M8345 1982
Multinational managers and poverty in the Third World/ Lee A. Tavis, editor. Notre Dame, Ind.: University of Notre Dame Press, c1982. xii, 269 p.
82-050288   658.4/08/091724   0268013535
International business enterprises -- Social aspects -- Developing countries -- Congresses. Poor -- Developing countries -- Congresses.

HD2755.5.M96 1998
The myth of the global corporation/ Paul N. Doremus ... [et al.] Princeton, N.J.: Princeton University Press, c1998. xiii, 193 p.
97-018349   338.8/8 21   0691036365
International business enterprises. Competition, International.

HD2755.5.P635 1985
Political risks in international business: new directions for research, management, and public policy/ edited by Thomas L. Brewer. New York: Praeger, 1985. x, 374 p.
84-024801   658.1/8   0030637589
International business enterprises -- Political aspects -- Addresses, essays, lectures. Investments, Foreign -- Political aspects -- Addresses, essays, lectures. Political stability -- Evaluation -- Addresses, essays, lectures.

HD2755.5.S565 1991
Sklair, Leslie.
Sociology of the global system/ Leslie Sklair. Baltimore: Johns Hopkins University Press, 1991. xii, 269 p.
90-021658   338.8/8   0801841860
International business enterprises. Capitalism. Consumption (Economics)

HD2755.5.W3213 1982
Wagner, Gerrit A.
Business in the public eye/ by G.A. Wagner; translated by Theodore Plantinga. Grand Rapids, MI.: W.B. Eerdmans Pub. Co., c1982. 125 p.
81-019486   338.8/8   0802835678
International business enterprises. Industries -- Social aspects. Petroleum industry and trade.

HD2756 Industry — Corporations — Diversification. Conglomerate corporations

HD2756.U5.B53
Biggadike, E. Ralph, 1937-
Corporate diversification: entry, strategy, and performance/ E. Ralph Biggadike. Boston: Division of Research, Graduate School of Busines c1979. xvi, 220 p.
79-084159   338.8   087584118X
Diversification in industry -- United States. New products. Conglomerate corporations -- United States.

HD2757-2763 Industry — Corporation — Industrial concentration

HD2757.B76 1982
Brozen, Yale, 1917-
Concentration, mergers, and public policy/ Yale Brozen with the assistance of George Bittlingmayer. New York: Macmillan Pub. Co.; c1982. xxiii, 427 p.
82-070080   338.8/0973   0029042704
Industrial concentration -- Government policy. Industrial concentration -- Government policy -- United States. Trusts, Industrial -- Government policy -- United States.

HD2757.C66 1989
Concentration and price/ edited by Leonard W. Weiss. Cambridge, Mass.: MIT Press, c1989. xiii, 290 p.
89-031997   338.6/44   0262231433
Industrial concentration. Prices. Pricing.

HD2757.2.S48 1989
Sherman, Roger, 1930-
The regulation of monopoly/ Roger Sherman. Cambridge; Cambridge University Press, 1989. xi, 315 p.
88-014185   338.8/2   0521368626
Monopolies -- Government policy. Welfare economics.

HD2757.5.L43 2000
LeClair, Mark S.
International commodity markets and the role of cartels/ Mark S. LeClair. Armonk, N.Y.: M.E. Sharpe, c2000. xx, 176 p.
00-025510   338.8/7 21   0765605163
Cartels. Raw materials. International economic relations.

HD2763.N45 1999
Newbery, David M. G.
Privatization, restructuring, and regulation of network utilities/ David M. Newbery. Cambridge, Mass.: MIT Press, c1999. xvi, 466 p.
99-052764   363.6 21   0262140683
Public utilities. Privatization. Public utilities -- Government policy.

HD2769.2 Industry — Corporation — Nonprofit organizations

HD2769.2.U6.N37 2001
The nature of the nonprofit sector/ edited by J. Steven Ott. Boulder, CO: Westview Press, 2001. xiii, 434 p.
00-043996 061/.3 0813367859
Nonprofit organizations -- United States.

HD2769.2.U6.W45 1988
Weisbrod, Burton Allen, 1931-
The nonprofit economy/ Burton A. Weisbrod. Cambridge, Mass.: Harvard University Press, 1988. ix, 251 p.
87-023718 338.7/4 0674626257
Nonprofit organizations -- United States.

HD2785-2932 Industry — Corporation — By region or country

HD2785.C4732 1988
Chandler, Alfred Dupont.
The essential Alfred Chandler: essays toward a historical theory of big business/ edited and with an introduction by Thomas K. McCraw. Boston, Mass.: Harvard Business School Press, c1988. vi, 538 p.
87-029754 338.6/44/0973 0875841767
Big business -- United States -- History. Industrial management -- United States -- History.

HD2785.L36 1985
Lamoreaux, Naomi R.
The great merger movement in American business, 1895-1904/ Naomi R. Lamoreaux. Cambridge [Cambridgeshire]; Cambridge University Press, 1985. xii, 208 p.
84-016983 338.8/3/0973 0521267552
Consolidation and merger of corporations -- United States -- History.

HD2785.M64 1968
Moody, John, 1868-1958.
The truth about the trusts; a description and analysis of the American trust movement. New York, Greenwood Press, 1968 [c1904] xxii, 514 p.
68-028643 338.8/5/0973
Trusts, Industrial -- United States.

HD2785.R43 1992
Reardon, John J.
America and the multinational corporation: the history of a troubled partnership/ John J. Reardon. Westport, Conn.: Praeger, 1992. viii, 185 p.
92-012211 338.8/8973 0275939189
International business enterprises -- United States -- History.

HD2785.W46 1999
Whitman, Marina von Neumann.
New world, new rules: the changing role of the American corporation/ Marina v.N. Whitman. Boston, Mass.: Harvard Business School Press, c1999. 261 p.
98-045835 338.7/0973 21 0875848583
Corporations -- United States

HD2785.Z86 1990
Zunz, Olivier.
Making America corporate, 1870-1920/ Olivier Zunz. Chicago: University of Chicago Press, 1990. x, 267 p.
90-031028 338.7/4/097309034 0226994597
Big business -- United States -- History. Corporations -- United States -- History.

HD2795.A23 1991
Adams, Walter, 1922 Aug. 27-
Antitrust economics on trial: a dialogue on the new laissez-faire/ Walter Adams and James W. Brock. Princeton, N.J.: Princeton University Press, c1991. xiv, 132 p.
91-017176 338.8 20 0691003912
Trusts, Industrial -- United States. Consolidation and merger of corporations -- United States. Trade regulation -- United States.

HD2795.D485 1990
Dewey, Donald
The antitrust experiment in America/ Donald Dewey. New York: Columbia University Press, c1990. xi, 160 p.
90-030658 338.8/5/0973 0231067100
Trusts, Industrial -- Government policy -- United States -- History. Antitrust law -- United States -- History.

HD2795.W68 1995
Williamson, James R., 1935-
Federal antitrust policy during the Kennedy-Johnson years/ James R. Williamson. Westport, Conn.: Greenwood Press, 1995. xii, 180 p.
95-007908 338.8/0973/09046 0313296413
Trusts, Industrial -- Government policy -- United States -- History. Antitrust law -- Economic aspects -- United States -- History. Public interest -- United States -- History.

HD2810.5.O18 1996
O'Brien, Thomas F., 1947-
The revolutionary mission: American enterprise in Latin America, 1900-1945/ Thomas F. O'Brien. New York: Cambridge University Press, 1996. xiv, 356 p.
95-008391 338.8/897308 0521550157
Corporations, American -- Social aspects -- Latin America -- History. Corporate culture -- United States -- History. Corporate culture -- Latin America -- History.

HD2859.L4 1966
Levy, Hermann, 1881-1949.
Industrial Germany; a study of its monopoly organisations and their control by the State. New York, A. M. Kelley, 1966. x, 245 p.
66-031836 338.820943
Trusts, Industrial -- Germany. Industrial policy -- Germany. Monopolies -- Germany.

HD2907.J347 1994
The Japanese firm: the sources of competitive strength/ edited by Masahiko Aoki and Ronald Dore. Oxford [England]; Oxford University Press, 1994. xi, 410 p.
93-037583 338.7/0952 0198288158
Corporations -- Japan. Industrial organization -- Japan.

HD2908.M36 1990
McNamara, Dennis L.
The colonial origins of Korean enterprise, 1910-1945/ Dennis L. McNamara. Cambridge [England]; Cambridge University Press, 1990. xiv, 208 p.
90-001376 338.7/4/09519509041 0521385652
Corporations -- Korea (South) -- History -- 20th century. Korea -- Economic conditions -- 1910-1945. Korea -- History -- Japanese occupation, 1910-1945.

HD2928.F67 1994
Forrest, Tom
The advance of African capital: the growth of Nigerian private enterprise/ Tom Forrest. Charlottesville: University Press of Virginia, 1994. xv, 300 p.
94-012171 338.6/1/09669 0813915627
Business enterprises -- Nigeria -- History -- 20th century. Saving and investment -- Nigeria -- History -- 20th century. Free enterprise -- Nigeria -- History -- 20th century.

HD2932.R45 1988
Rekindling development: multinational firms and world debt/ Lee A. Tavis, editor. Notre Dame, Ind.: University of Notre Dame Press, c1988. xii, 369 p.
87-040619 338.8/881724 0268016348
International business enterprises -- Developing countries -- Congresses. Debts, External -- Developing countries -- Congresses. Economic development -- Congresses.

HD3134 Industry — Cooperation. Cooperative societies — Producer cooperatives

HD3134.W67 1984
Worker cooperatives in America/ edited by Robert Jackall, Henry M. Levin. Berkeley: University of California Press, c1984. x, 311 p.
84-000061 334/.6/0973 0520051173
Producer cooperatives -- United States. Producer cooperatives -- United States -- History. Employee ownership -- United States.

HD3325-3334 Industry — Cooperation. Cooperative societies — Cooperative distribution

HD3325.A4.G87 1996
Gurney, Peter.
Co-operative culture and the politics of consumption in England, 1870-1930/ Peter Gurney. Manchester; Manchester University Press; 1996. ix, 350 p.
96-016160 334/.5/0941 0719049504
Consumer cooperatives -- Great Britain -- History.

HD3334.F87 1991
Furlough, Ellen, 1953-
Consumer cooperation in France: the politics of consumption, 1834-1930/ Ellen Furlough. Ithaca: Cornell University Press, c1991. ix, 311 p.
90-055726 334/.5/09440903 0801425123
Consumer cooperatives -- France -- History. Consumption (Economics) -- France -- History.

HD3538 Industry — Cooperation. Cooperative societies — By region or country

HD3538.B375 1995
Baviskar, B. S. 1931-
Finding the middle path: the political economy of cooperation in rural India/ B.S. Baviskar and Donald W. Attwood; with D.P. Apte ... [et al.]. Boulder, Colo.: Westview Press, 1995. ix, 437 p.
94-035986   334/.0954   0813389038
Cooperative societies -- India.   India -- Economic conditions -- 1947- -- Regional disparities.

HD3611 Industry — Industrial policy. The state and industrial organization — General works

HD3611.A83 1989
Audretsch, David B.
The Market and the state: government policy towards business in Europe, Japan, and the United States/ David B. Audretsch. New York: New York University Press, 1989. xiv, 325 p.
89-012307   338.9   0814714323
Industrial policy. Competition, International. United States -- Commercial policy. Japan -- Commercial policy. European Economic Community countries -- Commercial policy.

HD3611.B93 1997
Business and democracy: cohabitation or contradiction?/ edited by Ann Bernstein and Peter L. Berger. London; Pinter, 1998. ix, 179 p.
97-011792   338.9   185567498X
Industrial policy. Business and politics -- Cross-cultural studies. Democracy.

HD3611.P654 1990
Porter, Michael E., 1947-
The competitive advantage of nations/ Michael E. Porter. New York: Free Press, c1990. xx, 855 p.
89-025632   382/.1042   0029253616
Industrial policy. Competition, International. International business enterprises.

HD3612 Industry — Industrial policy. The state and industrial organization — Trade regulation

HD3612.D48 1990
Deregulation or re-regulation?: regulatory reform in Europe and the United States/ edited by Giandomenico Majone. London: Pinter; 1990. 262 p.
89-029482   338.94   0861878345
Deregulation.   Deregulation   --   Europe. Deregulation -- United States.

HD3616 Industry — Industrial policy. The state and industrial organization — By region or country, A-Z

HD3616.D44.K57 1984
Kirkpatrick, C. H. 1944-
Industrial structure and policy in less developed countries/ C.H. Kirkpatrick, N. Lee, and F.I. Nixson. London; Allen & Unwin, 1984. xii, 263 p.
84-014493   338.9/009172/4   0043381154
Industrial policy -- Developing countries. Industries -- Developing countries. Economic development.

HD3616.E23.C65 1988
Conaghan, Catherine M.
Restructuring domination: industrialists and the state in Ecuador/ Catherine M. Conaghan. Pittsburgh, Pa.: University of Pittsburgh Press, c1988. xiii, 197 p.
88-001335   338.9866   082293826X
Industrial policy -- Ecuador. Industrialists -- Ecuador -- Political activity. Elite (Social sciences) -- Ecuador -- Political activity. Ecuador -- Politics and government -- 1944-

HD3616.E32.B53 1989
Bianchi, Robert, 1945-
Unruly corporatism: associational life in twentieth-century Egypt/ Robert Bianchi. New York: Oxford University Press, 1989. ix, 268 p.
89-002862   338.962   0195060318
Corporate state -- Egypt.   Egypt -- Politics and government -- 1919-1952. Egypt -- Politics and government -- 1952-

HD3616.E83.I53
Industrial policies in Western Europe/ edited by Steven J. Warnecke, Ezra N. Suleiman. New York: Praeger, 1975. x, 249 p.
75-023998   338.94   0275016706
Industrial policy -- European Economic Community countries -- Addresses, essays, lectures. Trade and professional associations -- European Economic Community countries -- Addresses, essays, lectures. European Economic Community countries -- Economic policy -- Addresses, essays, lectures.

HD3616.G72.M47 1995
Mercer, H.
Constructing a competitive order: the hidden history of British antitrust policies/ Helen Mercer. Cambridge; Cambridge University Press, 1995. xi, 274 p.
94-009622   338.8/0941   0521412927
Trade regulation -- Great Britain -- History -- 20th century. Competition -- Great Britain -- History -- 20th century. Monopolies -- Great Britain -- History -- 20th century.

HD3616.G72.T66 1994
Tomlinson, Jim.
Government and the enterprise since 1900: the changing problem of efficiency/ Jim Tomlinson. Oxford: Clarendon Press; 1994. xv, 455 p.
93-032725   338.941/009/04   0198287496
Industrial policy -- Great Britain -- History -- 20th century.   Great Britain -- Economic conditions -- 20th century.

HD3616.G73.F67 1992
Foster, Christopher D.
Privatization, public ownership, and the regulation of natural monopoly/ C.D. Foster. Oxford, UK; Blackwell, 1992. ix, 458 p.
91-047004   338.941   0631184864
Trade regulation -- Great Britain. Privatization -- Great Britain. Government ownership -- Great Britain.

HD3616.J33.F73 1992
Francks, Penelope, 1949-
Japanese economic development: theory and practice/ Penelope Francks. London; Routledge, 1992. x, 288 p.
91-012622   338.952   0415041007
Industrial policy -- Japan. Agriculture -- Economic aspects -- Japan. Industries -- Japan.

HD3616.J33.J643 1982
Johnson, Chalmers A.
MITI and the Japanese miracle: the growth of industrial policy, 1925-1975/ Chalmers Johnson. Stanford, Calif.: Stanford University Press, 1982. xvi, 393 p.
81-051330   354.520082/06   0804711283
Industrial policy -- Japan -- History.

HD3616.J33.U74 1996
Uriu, Robert M., 1959-
Troubled industries: confronting economic change in Japan/ Robert M. Uriu. Ithaca, N.Y.: Cornell University Press, 1996. xiii, 285 p.
96-003229   338.952   0801430291
Industrial policy -- Japan. Industries -- Japan.

HD3616.P92.B38 1993
Baver, Sherrie L.
The political economy of colonialism: the state and industrialization in Puerto Rico/ Sherrie L. Baver. Westport, Conn.: Praeger, 1993. xvi, 153 p.
92-046553   338.97295   0275945030
Industrial policy -- Puerto Rico -- History -- 20th century. Industrial promotion -- Government policy -- Puerto Rico -- History -- 20th century. Industrialization -- Puerto Rico -- History -- 20th century.

HD3616.R92.B87 2001
Business and state in contemporary Russia/ edited by Peter Rutland. Boulder, Colo.: Westview Press, c2001. xii, 191 p.
00-043987   330.947 21   0813336562
Industrial policy -- Russia (Federation) Business and politics -- Russia (Federation)

HD3616.S472.S5 1996
Shearer, David R., 1952-
Industry, state, and society in Stalin's Russia, 1926-1934/ David R. Shearer. Ithaca, N.Y.: Cornell University Press, 1996. xiv, 263 p.
96-008178   338.947/009/042   0801432073
Industrial policy -- Soviet Union. Soviet Union -- Economic policy -- 1917-1928. Soviet Union -- Economic policy -- 1928-1932.

HD3616.U46.N38 1998
Nester, William R., 1956-
A short history of American industrial policies/ William R. Nester. New York: St. Martin's Press, 1998. v, 329 p.
97-036090   338.973   0312211023
Industrial policy -- United States -- History.

HD3616.U46.V53 1994
Vietor, Richard H. K., 1945-
Contrived competition: regulation and deregulation in America/ Richard H.K. Vietor. Cambridge, Mass.: Belknap Press of Harvard University Press, 1994. 439 p.
93-028975   338.973   067416962X
Trade regulation -- United States -- Case studies. Deregulation -- United States -- Case studies.

HD3616.U47.G67 1987
Goodman, Marshall R.
Managing regulatory reform: the Reagan strategy and its impact/ Marshall R. Goodman, Margaret T. Wrightson. New York: Praeger, 1987. xvi, 236 p.
87-002436   338.973
Trade regulation -- United States.   United States -- Politics and government -- 1981-1989.

HD3616.U48.A137 1992
Rosenfeld, Stuart A.
Competitive manufacturing: new strategies for regional development/ Stuart A. Rosenfeld; with a foreword by Ray Marshall. New Brunswick, N.J.: Center for Urban Policy Research, c1992. xviii, 400 p.
91-039699   338.4/767/0975   0882851373
Industrial policy -- Southern States. Manufacturing industries -- Southern States. Rural development -- Southern States.

HD3850-4420.8 Industry — Industrial policy. The state and industrial organization — State industries. Public works. Government ownership

HD3850.D66 1989
Donahue, John D.
The privatization decision: public ends, private means/ John D. Donahue. New York: Basic Books, c1989. viii, 264 p.
89-042511   353.0071/2   0465063586
Privatization. Privatization -- Case studies. Privatization -- United States -- Case studies.

HD3850.P62 1990
The Political economy of public sector reform and privatization/ edited by Ezra N. Suleiman and John Waterbury. Boulder: Westview Press, 1990. ix, 388 p.
90-044537   338.9   0813379962
Government ownership. Government business enterprises -- Case studies. Privatization.

HD3850.P745 1991
Privatization and economic efficiency: a comparative analysis of developed and developing countries/ edited by Attiat F. Ott and Keith Hartley. Aldershot, Hants, England; E. Elgar Pub., c1991. xii, 277 p.
91-008132   338.9   1852784148
Privatization. Privatization -- Case studies. Industrial efficiency.

HD3850.P75 1988
The promise of privatization: a challenge for U.S. policy/ Raymond Vernon. New York, N.Y.: Council on Foreign Relations, c1988. vii, 295 p.
88-010948   338.973   087609034X
Privatization.   United States -- Foreign economic relations.

HD3861.J3.W66 1996
Woodall, Brian.
Japan under construction: corruption, politics, and public works/ Brian Woodall. Berkeley, Calif.: University of California Press, c1996. xiii, 214 p.
95-033484   364.1/323/0952 20   0520088158
Public contracts -- Japan. Public works -- Japan. Letting of contracts -- Japan -- Corrupt practices.

HD3888.K48 1993
Kettl, Donald F.
Sharing power: public governance and private markets/ Donald F. Kettl. Washington, D.C.: The Brookings Institution, c1993. xi, 219 p.
92-041705   338.973   0815749066
Privatization -- United States. Public contracts -- United States. Contracting out -- United States.

HD3888.S35 2000
Sclar, Elliott.
You don't always get what you pay for: the economics of privatization/ Elliott D. Sclar. Ithaca: Cornell University Press, 2000. xiii, 184 p.
99-055904   338.973/05   0801437334
Privatization -- United States. Privatization -- United States -- Case studies.

HD4005.L38 1988
Laux, Jeanne Kirk, 1942-
State capitalism: public enterprise in Canada/ Jeanne Kirk Laux and Maureen Appel Molot. Ithaca: Cornell University Press, 1988. ix, 250 p.
87-047600   338.6/2/0971   0801420792
Government business enterprises -- Canada.

HD4010.5.P765 1996
Privatizing monopolies: lessons from the telecommunications and transport sectors in Latin America/ edited by Ravi Ramamurti. Baltimore: Johns Hopkins University Press, c1996. vi, 401 p.
95-018040   388/.049 20   0801851351
Privatization -- Latin America. Telephone companies -- Latin America. Airlines -- Latin America.

HD4014.T44 1995
Teichman, Judith A., 1947-
Privatization and political change in Mexico/ Judith A. Teichman. Pittsburgh: University of Pittsburgh Press, c1995. xiv, 291 p.
95-025839   338.972   0822939282
Privatization -- Mexico. Government business enterprises -- Mexico. Mexico -- Economic policy -- 1994-

HD4093.T727 1983
Trebat, Thomas J.
Brazil's state-owned enterprises: a case study of the state as entrepreneur/ Thomas J. Trebat. Cambridge [Cambridgeshire]; Cambridge University Press, 1983. xviii, 294 p.
82-009564   354.8109/2   0521237165
Government business enterprises -- Brazil. Corporations, Government -- Brazil.

HD4098.H3313 1993
Hachette, Dominique.
Privatization in Chile: an economic appraisal/ by Dominique Hachette and Rolf Luders. San Francisco, Calif.: ICS Press, 1993. xiv, 284 p.
92-022670   338.983   1558152083
Privatization -- Chile. Government business enterprises -- Chile.

HD4140.7.S73 1998
Stark, David Charles.
Postsocialist pathways: transforming politics and property in East Central Europe/ David Stark, Laszlo Bruszt. Cambridge [England]; Cambridge University Press, 1998. xi, 284 p.
97-021299   338.943   0521580358
Privatization -- Europe, Central. Right of property -- Europe, Central. Post-communism -- Europe, Central. Europe, Central -- Economic conditions. Europe, Central -- Politics and government -- 1989-

HD4145.B3
Barry, E. Eldon.
Nationalisation in British politics: the historical background [by] E. Eldon Barry. Stanford, Calif., Stanford University Press, 1965. 397 p.
64-008704   338.942
Government ownership -- Great Britain. Socialism -- Great Britain.

HD4145.P69 1994
Privatization and economic performance/ edited by Matthew Bishop, John Kay, Colin Mayer. Oxford; Oxford University Press, 1994. xii, 378 p.
94-010326   338.941   0198773439
Privatization -- Great Britain. Great Britain -- Economic conditions -- 1979-1994.

HD4145.R39 1995
The regulatory challenge/ edited by Matthew Bishop, John Kay, Colin Mayer. Oxford [England]; Oxford University Press, 1995. xiii, 455 p.
94-029639   338.941   0198773412
Privatization -- Great Britain. Deregulation -- Great Britain.

HD4215.7.M93 1993
Myant, M. R.
Transforming socialist economies: the case of Poland and Czechoslovakia/ Martin Myant. Aldershot, England; E. Elgar, c1993. xii, 297 p.
93-002692   338.9438   1852787864
Privatization -- Poland -- Case studies. Privatization -- Czechoslovakia -- Case studies. Central planning -- Poland -- Case studies. Poland -- Economic policy -- 1981-1990 -- Case studies. Czechoslovakia -- Economic policy -- 1989-1992 -- Case studies.

HD4276.5.P75 1992
Privatization and liberalization in the Middle East/ edited by Iliya Harik and Denis J. Sullivan. Bloomington: Indiana University Press, c1992. vi, 242 p.
92-005174   338.956   0253326974
Privatization -- Middle East -- Congresses. Free enterprise -- Middle East -- Congresses.

HD4420.8.A33 1992
Adam, Christopher.
Adjusting privatization: case studies from Developing countries/ Christopher Adam, William Cavendish, Percy S. Mistry. London: J. Currey; 1992. xiii, 400 p.
92-004079   338.9   0852551320
Privatization -- Developing countries -- Case studies. Privatization.

HD4420.8.P74 1988
Privatisation in less developed countries/ edited by Paul Cook, Colin Kirkpatrick. [Brighton] Sussex: Wheatsheaf Books; 1988. xix, 315 p.
87-036937   338.9/009172/4   0312019556
Privatization -- Developing countries.

HD4464-4482 Industry — Industrial policy. The state and industrial organization — Municipal services. Municipal public works

HD4464.L7K33 1982
Kahrl, William L.,
Water and power:the conflict over Los Angeles' water supply in the Owens Valley/ William L. Kahrl. Berkeley: University of California Press, c1982. xii, 583 p.
81-007428 333.91/009794/9 0520044312
Water-supply -- California -- Los Angeles. Water-supply -- California -- Owens Valley.

HD4482.K47 1990
Kharbanda, Om Prakash.
Waste management: towards a sustainable society/ O.P. Kharbanda and E.A. Stallworthy. New York: Auburn House, 1990. xix, 268 p.
89-018496 363.72/8
Refuse and refuse disposal.

HD4813 Labor. Work. Working class — Congresses

HD4813.B49 1996
Beyond survival: wage labor in the late twentieth century/ Cyrus Bina, Laurie Clements, Chuck Davis, editors. Armonk, N.Y.: M.E. Sharpe, 1996. x, 261 p.
95-042401 331 1563245159
Labor -- Congresses. Labor market -- Congresses. Industrial relations -- Congresses.

HD4813.S78
Studies in labor markets/ edited by Sherwin Rosen. Chicago: University of Chicago Press, 1981. ix, 395 p.
81-007488 331 0226726282
Labor economics -- Congresses. Labor market -- United States -- Congresses.

HD4839 Labor. Work. Working class — Dictionaries. Encyclopedias

HD4839.D58 1996
Docherty, J. C.
Historical dictionary of organized labor/ James C. Docherty. Lanham, Md.: Scarecrow Press, 1996. xviii, 357 p.
96-011417 331.88/03 0810831813
Labor movement -- History -- Encyclopedias. Labor unions -- History -- Encyclopedias.

HD4841 Labor. Work. Working class — History — General works

HD4841.P4
Perlman, Selig, 1888-
A theory of the labor movement, by Selig Perlman ... New York, The Macmillan Company, 1928. xii, 321 p.
28-014392
Labor and laboring classes. Labor unions. Labor and laboring classes -- Europe.

HD4854 Labor. Work. Working class — History — Modern

HD4854.C6
Correa, Hector.
The economics of human resources. Amsterdam, North-Holland Pub. Co., 1963. 262 p.
64-002216
Labor and laboring classes -- 1914- Education -- Economic aspects.

HD4875 Labor. Work. Working class — Labor systems — Contract labor. Peonage. Forced labor. Indentured servants

HD4875.G4.W67 2000
Working for the enemy: Ford, General Motors, and forced labor in Germany during the Second World War/ Reinhold Billstein ... [et al.]. New York: Berghahn Books, 2000. xii, 309 p.
00-026126 331.11/732 1571812245
World War, 1939-1945 -- Prisoners and prisons, German. Forced labor -- Germany -- History -- 20th century. World War, 1939-1945 -- Conscript labor -- Germany.

HD4875.N7.P43 2000
Peck, Gunther.
Reinventing free labor: padrones and immigrant workers in the North American West, 1880-1930/ Gunther Peck. Cambridge; Cambridge University Press, 2000. xiii, 293 p.
99-026123 331.6/2/0978 0521641608
Padrone system -- North America -- History. Right to labor -- North America -- History. Alien labor, Greek -- North America -- History. North America -- Emigration and immigration -- History.

HD4875.S75.H64 1998
Hoefte, Rosemarijn, 1959-
In place of slavery: a social history of British Indian and Javanese laborers in Suriname/ Rosemarijn Hoefte. Gainesville: University Press of Florida, c1998. xii, 275 p.
98-039085 331.5/42/09883 21 0813016258
Contract labor -- Surinam -- History. East Indians -- Surinam -- History. Javanese (Indonesian people) -- Surinam -- History. Surinam -- Social conditions. Surinam -- Economic conditions.

HD4901 Labor. Work. Working class — General works

HD4901.D49 1991
Devine, Theresa J.
Empirical labor economics: the search approach/ Theresa J. Devine, Nicholas M. Kiefer. New York: Oxford University Press, 1991. x, 343 p.
90-006852 331 0195059360
Labor economics.

HD4901.M22
McNulty, Paul J.
The origins and development of labor economics: a chapter in the history of social thought/ Paul J. McNulty. Cambridge, Mass.: MIT Press, c1980. viii, 248 p.
80-015320 331/.09 0262131625
Labor economics -- History. Economics -- History.

HD4903 Labor. Work. Working class — Free choice of employment. Freedom of labor. Discrimination in employment — General works

HD4903.M36 2000
Mangan, John.
Workers without traditional employment: an international study of non-standard work/ John Mangan. Cheltenham, UK; Edward Elgar, c2000. xvii, 205 p.
00-044258 331.2 21 184064267X
Labor. Work -- Forecasting. Employment forecasting.

HD4903.S47 1994
Siegel, Richard L.
Employment and human rights: the international dimension/ Richard Lewis Siegel. Philadelphia: University of Pennsylvania Press, c1994. x, 272 p.
93-032175 331.01/1 0812232119
Right to labor. Human rights. Unemployment.

HD4903.5 Labor. Work. Working class — Free choice of employment. Freedom of labor. Discrimination in employment — By region or country, A-Z

HD4903.5.U58.B4 1971
Becker, Gary Stanley, 1930-
The economics of discrimination [by] Gary S. Becker. Chicago, University of Chicago Press [1971] x, 167 p.
73-157422 331.1/33/0973 0226041158
Discrimination in employment -- United States. Afro-Americans -- Employment. Afro-Americans -- Economic conditions.

HD4903.5.U58.D37 1998
Darity, William A., 1953-
Persistent disparity: race and economic inequality in the United States since 1945/ William A. Darity Jr, Samuel L. Myers Jr. Cheltenham, UK; E. Elgar Pub., c1998. xiii, 191 p.
97-030626 331.13/3/097309045 21 1858986583
Discrimination in employment -- United States. Race discrimination -- Economic aspects -- United States. Afro-Americans -- Economic conditions. United States -- Economic conditions -- 1945-

HD4903.5.U58.Q47 1989
The Question of discrimination: racial inequality in the U.S. labor market/ edited by Steven Shulman and William Darity, Jr.; essays by Robert Higgs ... [et al.]. Middletown, Conn.: Wesleyan University Press, 1989. xii, 394 p.
89-005481   331.13/3/0973   0819552143
Discrimination in employment -- United States. Affirmative action programs -- United States. Race discrimination -- United States. United States -- Race relations.

HD4904 Labor. Work. Working class — Theory. Method. Relation to other subjects — General works

HD4904.H54 1987
The Historical meanings of work/ edited by Patrick Joyce. Cambridge [Cambridgeshire]; Cambridge University Press, 1987. v, 320 p.
87-000788   306/.36   0521308976
Work. Leisure. Work ethic.

HD4904.N347 1990
The Nature of work: sociological perspectives/ edited by Kai Erikson and Steven Peter Vallas. New Haven: Yale University Press, c1990. viii, 378 p.
90-030425   306.3/6   0300045204
Work. Industrial sociology.

HD4904.25 Labor. Work. Working class — Work and family

HD4904.25.D66 1990
Domestic strategies: work and family in France and Italy, 1600-1800/ edited by Stuart Woolf. Cambridge [England]; Cambridge University Press; 1991. viii, 207 p.
89-013997   306.3/6   0521391644
Work and family -- France -- History. Work and family -- Italy -- History. Guilds -- Italy -- History.

HD4904.25.W67 1984
Work & family: changing roles of men and women/ edited by Patricia Voydanoff. Palo Alto, Calif.: Mayfield Pub. Co., c1984. viii, 383 p.
83-061534   306/.36   0874845769
Work and family.

HD4904.6 Labor. Work. Working class — Leisure and work

HD4904.6.S36 1991
Schor, Juliet.
The overworked American: the unexpected decline of leisure/ Juliet B. Schor. [New York, N.Y.]: Basic Books, c1991. xvii, 247 p.
91-070057   306.4/812/0973 20   0465054331
Leisure -- United States. Hours of labor -- United States.

HD4904.7 Labor. Work. Working class — Human capital

HD4904.7.I58 1995
Investment in women's human capital/ edited by T. Paul Schultz. Chicago: University of Chicago Press, 1995. vi, 461 p.
94-040577   331.4   0226740870
Human capital -- Developing countries. Sex discrimination in education -- Developing countries. Women -- Employment -- Developing countries.

HD4905 Labor. Work. Working class — Ethics. Dignity of labor. Work ethic — General works

HD4905.F87 1990
Furnham, Adrian.
The Protestant work ethic: the psychology of work-related beliefs and behaviours/ Adrian Furnham. London [England]; Routledge, 1990. xv, 305 p.
89-033213   306.3/613   0415017041
Protestant work ethic -- Psychological aspects.

HD4906-4909 Labor. Work. Working class — Wages — General works

HD4906.M43 1987
Michie, Jonathan.
Wages in the business cycle: an empirical and methodological analysis/ Jonathan Michie. London: F. Pinter, 1987. vii, 194 p.
87-148946   331.2/1   0861876865
Wages -- Econometric models. Business cycles -- Econometric models.

HD4906.W343 1997
Wage differentials: an international comparison/ edited by Toshiaki Tachibanaki. New York: St. Martin's Press, 1998. x, 378 p.
97-006280   331.2/2   0312174829
Wages -- Case studies. Wage differentials -- Case studies.

HD4909.H5 1963
Hicks, John Richard, 1904-
The theory of wages. London, Macmillan, 1963. xix, 388 p.
64-035917
Wages. Labor economics. Unemployed.

HD4909.R67 1967
Rothschild, Kurt W. 1914-
The theory of wages, by K. W. Rothschild. New York, A. M. Kelley, 1967. viii, 180 p.
67-005911   331.2/1
Wages.

HD4909.S7513 1994
Stirati, Antonella.
The theory of wages in classical economics: a study of Adam Smith, David Ricardo, and their contemporaries/ Antonella Stirati; translated by Joan Hall. Aldershot, England; E. Elgar, c1994. xviii, 221 p.
93-042452   331.2/101   1852787104
Wages. Classical school of economics. Economics -- History.

HD4918 Labor. Work. Working class — Wages — Minimum wage

HD4918.E375 2001
Ehrenreich, Barbara.
Nickel and dimed: on (not) getting by in America/ Barbara Ehrenreich. 1st ed. New York: Metropolitan Books, 2001. 221 p.
00-052514   305.569/092.B 21   0805063889
Minimum wage -- United States. Working poor -- United States. Unskilled labor -- United States.

HD4918.L447 2001
Levin-Waldman, Oren M.
The case of the minimum wage: competing policy models/ Oren M. Levin-Waldman. Albany: State University of New York Press, c2001. xiii, 236 p.
00-038770   331.2/3 21   079144855X
Minimum wage -- United States. Minimum wage -- Law and legislation -- United States -- History. Labor policy -- United States -- History.

HD4928 Labor. Work. Working class — Wages — Methods of remuneration. Wage payment systems

HD4928.N6.H37 1984
Hart, Robert A.
The economics of non-wage labour costs/ Robert A. Hart. London; Allen & Unwin, 1984. xii, 173 p.
83-022328   331.25/5   0043310966
Employee fringe benefits. Labor costs.

HD4975 Labor. Work. Working class — Wages — By region or country, A-Z

HD4975.G28 1998
Galbraith, James K.
Created unequal: the crisis in American pay/ James K. Galbraith. New York: Free Press, c1998. xviii, 350 p.
98-013573   331.2/973 21   0684849887
Wages -- United States. Income distribution -- United States. Labor market -- United States. United States -- Economic policy -- 1981-1993. United States -- Economic policy -- 1993-

HD4975.H929 2000
Hyclak, Thomas.
Rising wage inequality: the 1980s experience in urban labor markets/ Thomas Hyclak. Kalamazoo, Mich.: W.E. Upjohn Institute for Employment Research, c2000. x, 159 p.
00-031996   331.2/973 21   0880992077
Wages -- United States. Wages -- United States -- Regional disparities. Wages -- Effect of education on -- United States.

HD5106 Labor. Work.
Working class — Hours of labor —
General works

HD5106.W65 1991
Working time in transition: the political economy of working hours in industrial nations/ edited by Karl Hinrichs, William Roche, and Carmen Sirianni. Philadelphia: Temple University Press, 1991. vi, 277 p.
90-042337   331.25/7   0877227578
Hours of labor. Hours of labor, Flexible.

HD5109.2 Labor. Work.
Working class — Hours of labor —
Flexible work hours

HD5109.2.U5.O46 1994
Olmsted, Barney.
Creating a flexible workplace: how to select & manage alternative work options/ Barney Olmsted, Suzanne Smith. New York: AMACOM, c1994. xiii, 402 p.
94-028096   331.25/72/0973   0814402143
Hours of labor, Flexible -- United States. Compressed work week -- United States. Part-time employment -- United States.

HD5110.2 Labor. Work.
Working class — Hours of labor —
Part-time employment

HD5110.2.U5.N44 1993
Negrey, Cynthia, 1953-
Gender, time, and reduced work/ Cynthia Negrey. Albany: State University of New York Press, c1993. xiv, 148 p.
92-011955   331.4/0973   0791414078
Part-time employment -- United States. Work sharing -- United States. Temporary employment -- United States.

HD5110.2.U5.T548 1996
Tilly, Chris.
Half a job: bad and good part-time jobs in a changing labor market/ Chris Tilly. Philadelphia: Temple University Press, 1996. xii, 228 p.
95-020654   331.25/72   1566393817
Part-time employment -- United States.

HD5115 Labor. Work.
Working class — Hours of labor —
Attendance. Punctuality.
Absenteeism

HD5115.C47 1982
Chadwick-Jones, J. K.
Social psychology of absenteeism/ J.K. Chadwick-Jones, Nigel Nicholson, and Colin Brown. New York, N.Y.: Praeger, 1982. xiv, 161 p.
81-023395   331.25/98   0030566525
Absenteeism (Labor)

HD5124-5166 Labor. Work.
Working class — Hours of labor —
By region or country

HD5124.O94 1989
Owen, John D.
Reduced working hours: cure for unemployment or economic burden?/ John D. Owen. Baltimore: Johns Hopkins University Press, c1989. vi, 181 p.
88-030352   331.25/72/0973   0801837847
Hours of labor -- United States. Hours of labor -- Europe. Work sharing -- United States.

HD5166.L35
Langenfelt, Gosta, 1888-
The historic origin of the eight hours day; studies in English traditionalism.   Westport, Conn., Greenwood Press [1974] 151 p.
73-019224   331.2/572   0837173140
Alfred, -- King of England, -- 849-899.   Eight-hour movement -- History.   England -- Economic conditions.

HD5324-5395 Labor. Work.
Working class — Labor disputes.
Strikes and lockouts —
By region or country

HD5324.B53
Blackman, John L.
Presidential seizure in labor disputes [by] John L. Blackman, Jr. Cambridge, Harvard University Press, 1967. xvi, 351 p.
67-020871   331.89/8/0973
Labor disputes -- United States. Executive power -- United States.

HD5324.B7 1997
Brecher, Jeremy.
Strike!/ Jeremy Brecher. Boston, MA: South End Press, c1997. ii, 421 p.
97-033289   331.892/973   0896085708
Strikes and lockouts -- United States -- History.

HD5324.G7 1968
Griffin, John Ignatius, 1916-
Strikes; a study in quantitative economics.   New York, AMS Press [1968] 319 p.
68-058585   331.89/2973
Strikes and lockouts -- United States.

HD5324.L32 1990
Labor conflict in the United States: an encyclopedia/ edited by Ronald L. Filippelli; editorial assistant, Carol Reilly. New York: Garland Pub., 1990. xlviii, 609 p
90-003534   331.89/2973   082407968X
Strikes and lockouts -- United States -- Encyclopedias.

HD5325.P152 1985.A877 1993
Rachleff, Peter J.
Hard-pressed in the heartland: the Hormel strike and the future of the labor movement/ Peter Rachleff. Boston, Mass.: South End Press, c1993. 135 p.
92-026022   331.89/28649/00977617
0896084507
Geo. A Hormel & Company Strike, Austin, Minn., 1985-1986. Strikes and lockouts -- Packing-house workers -- Minnesota -- Austin.

HD5325.R2 1877.S76 1999
Stowell, David O.
Streets, railroads, and the Great Strike of 1877/ David O. Stowell. Chicago: University of Chicago Press, 1999. xii, 181 p.
98-050941   331.89/281385/097309034
0226776689
Railroad Strike, U.S., 1877. Strikes and lockouts -- Railroads -- United States -- History -- 19th century. Railroads -- United States -- Employees -- History -- 19th century.

HD5325.T252 1883
Gabler, Edwin, 1949-
The American telegrapher: a social history, 1860-1900/ Edwin Gabler. New Brunswick, N.J.: Rutgers University Press, c1988. viii, 264 p.
87-019878   331.89/2813841/0973   0813512859
Western Union Telegraph Company Strike, 1883. Telegraphers -- Labor unions -- United States -- History -- 19th century. Telegraphers -- United States -- History -- 19th century.

HD5325.T42 1913.P387 1987
Tripp, Anne Huber, 1934-
The I.W.W. and the Paterson silk strike of 1913/ Anne Huber Tripp. Urbana: University of Illinois Press, c1987. xiv, 317 p.
86-024989   331.89/287739/0974924
0252013824
Silk Workers' Strike, Paterson, N.J., 1913 -- History.   Paterson (N.J.) -- Economic conditions.

HD5325.T42 1934.I76 2000
Irons, Janet Christine.
Testing the New Deal: the general textile strike of 1934 in the American South/ Janet Irons. Urbana: University of Illinois Press, c2000. ix, 266 p.
99-006498   331.892/877/00975 21   025202527X
Textile workers -- Southern States -- History. Textile workers -- Labor unions -- Southern States -- History. Textile Workers' Strike, Southern States, 1934.

HD5331.A6.S75
Stevens, Evelyn P.
Protest and response in Mexico [by] Evelyn P. Stevens. Cambridge, Mass., MIT Press [1974] viii, 372 p.
74-002232   301.6/3/0972   0262191288
Strikes and lockouts -- Mexico. Communication and traffic -- Mexico. Violence -- Mexico.

HD5353.S26 1993
Sandoval, Salvador A. M.
Social change and labor unrest in Brazil since 1945/ Salvador A.M. Sandoval. Boulder, Colo.: Westview Press, 1993. xv, 245 p.
93-016955   331.89/2981/09045   0813382467
Strikes and lockouts -- Brazil -- History -- 20th century. Industrial relations -- Brazil -- History -- 20th century.

HD5364.5.A6.W34 1983
Walsh, Kenneth.
Strikes in Europe and the United States: measurement and incidence/ Kenneth Walsh. New York: St. Martin's Press, 1983. xiv, 230 p.
83-040055   331.89/2   0312766416
Strikes and lockouts -- European Economic Community countries -- Statistical methods. Strikes and lockouts -- United States -- Statistical methods.

HD5365.M615.C48 1998
Church, Roy A.
Strikes and solidarity: coalfield conflict in Britain 1889-1966/ Roy Church and Quentin Outram. Cambridge [England]; Cambridge University Press, 1998. xx, 314 p.
97-012821 331.892/822334/0941 0521554608
Strikes and lockouts -- Coal mining -- Great Britain -- History. Coal miners -- Labor unions -- Great Britain -- History. Solidarity.

HD5374.S55
Shorter, Edward.
Strikes in France, 1830-1968 [by] Edward Shorter [and] Charles Tilly. [London, Cambridge University Press [1974] xxiii, 428 p.
73-080475 331.89/2944 0521202930
Strikes and lockouts -- France -- History.

HD5395.K64 1989
Koenker, Diane, 1947-
Strikes and revolution in Russia, 1917/ Diane P. Koenker, William G. Rosenberg. Princeton, N.J.: Princeton University Press, c1989. xix, 393 p.
89-003891 331.89/2947/09041 0691055785
Strikes and lockouts -- Russia -- History -- 20th century. Soviet Union -- History -- Revolution, 1917-1921.

HD5504 Labor. Work. Working class — Industrial arbitration. Mediation and conciliation — By region or country

HD5504.A3.L283 1997
Labor arbitration under fire/ edited by James L. Stern and Joyce M. Najita. Ithaca: Cornell University Press, 1997. xii, 265 p.
96-034096 331.89/143/0973 0801433053
Arbitration, Industrial -- United States. Grievance arbitration -- United states. Mediation and conciliation, Industrial -- United States.

HD5650 Labor. Work. Working class — Employee participation in management. Employee ownership. Industrial democracy. Works councils — General works

HD5650.L354 1992
Lawler, Edward E.
The ultimate advantage: creating the high-involvement organization/ Edward E. Lawler III. San Francisco, Calif.: Jossey-Bass, c1992. xvii, 371 p.
91-041095 658.3/152 1555424147
Management -- Employee participation. Quality of work life. Organizational effectiveness.

HD5650.S4
Self-management: economic liberation of man: selected readings/ Jaroslav Vanek. Harmondsworth, Eng.; Penguin Books, 1975. 478 p.
76-355352 658.31/52 0140808787
Management -- Employee participation.

HD5650.V33
Vanek, Jaroslav.
The general theory of labor-managed market economies. Ithaca, Cornell University Press [1970] xiv, 409 p.
78-106355 658.31/5 0801405572
Management -- Employee participation. Profit-sharing. Welfare economics.

HD5650.V332
Vanek, Jaroslav.
The participatory economy; an evolutionary hypothesis and a strategy for development. Ithaca, Cornell University Press [1971] viii, 181 p.
77-148024 338.6 0801406390
Management -- Employee participation. Employee ownership.

HD5660 Labor. Work. Working class — Employee participation in management. Employee ownership. Industrial democracy. Works councils — By region or country, A-Z

HD5660.C9.F85 1992
Fuller, Linda, 1944-
Work and democracy in socialist Cuba/ Linda Fuller. Philadelphia: Temple University Press, 1992. xx, 274 p.
91-017102 331/.097291 0877228930
Management -- Employee participation -- Cuba. Industrial relations -- Cuba. Labor unions -- Cuba.

HD5660.J3.O95 1991
Ozaki, Robert S.
Human capitalism: the Japanese enterprise system as world model/ Robert S. Ozaki. New York, N.Y. U.S.A.: Penguin, 1992. ix, 211 p.
91-008095 331/.01/12 4770015496
Management -- Employee participation -- Japan. Management -- Employee participation. Industrial management -- Japan.

HD5660.U5.D44
Derber, Milton.
The American idea of industrial democracy, 1865-1965. Urbana, University of Illinois Press [1970] xv, 553 p.
70-100376 331.15/2 0252000854
Industrial management -- Employee participation -- United States -- History. Industrial relations -- United States -- History.

HD5660.U5.P53 1996
Plas, Jeanne M.
Person-centered leadership: an American approach to participatory management/ Jeanne M. Plas. Thousand Oaks, Calif.: Sage Publications, c1996. x, 251 p.
95-050204 658.3 20 0803955987
Management -- Employee participation -- United States. Interpersonal relations -- United States. Leadership -- United States -- Case studies.

HD5660.U5.W57
Witte, John F.
Democracy, authority, and alienation in work: workers' participation in an American corporation/ John F. Witte. Chicago: University of Chicago Press, 1980. xii, 216 p.
80-016241 658.3/152/0973 0226904202
Management -- Employee participation -- United States.

HD5706 Labor. Work. Working class — Labor market. Labor supply. Labor demand — General works

HD5706.G33 1978
Garraty, John Arthur, 1920-
Unemployment in history: economic thought and public policy/ by John A. Garraty. New York: Harper & Row, c1978. xii, 273 p.
76-026227 331.1/379 0060114576
Unemployed -- History.

HD5706.H36 1993
Hamermesh, Daniel S.
Labor demand/ Daniel S. Hamermesh. Princton, N.J.: Princeton University Press, c1993. xvii, 444 p.
92-023775 331.12/3 0691042543
Labor demand. Labor market.

HD5706.P47 1968
Pigou, A. C. 1877-1959.
The theory of unemployment. New York, A. M. Kelley, 1968. xxv, 319 p.
67-024752 331.1/37/01
Unemployment.

HD5707 Labor. Work. Working class — Labor market. Labor supply. Labor demand — General special

HD5707.P425 1996
Peck, Jamie.
Work-place: the social regulation of labor markets/ Jamie Peck. New York: Guilford Press, c1996. xvi, 320 p.
96-001005 331.12 20 1572300434
Labor supply -- Social aspects. Industrial sociology. Labor policy.

HD5707.S624 1990
Solow, Robert M.
The labor market as a social institution/ Robert M. Solow. Cambridge, MA: B. Blackwell, 1990. xviii, 116 p.
89-018648 306.3/6 1557860866
Labor market. Social institutions.

HD5707.5-5708.75 Labor. Work. Working class — Labor market. Labor supply. Labor demand — Unemployment. Unemployed

HD5707.5.U545 1987
Unemployment and the structure of labor markets/ edited by Kevin Lang and Jonathan S. Leonard. New York, NY, USA: B. Blackwell, 1987. vi, 253 p.
86-024478 331.13/7 0631153780
Unemployment. Wage-price policy.

HD5708.C68 2001
Cottle, Thomas J.
Hardest times: the trauma of long term unemployment/ Thomas J. Cottle. Westport, Conn.: Praeger, 2001. xiv, 311 p.
00-032373 331.13/7/019 0275969843
Unemployed -- United States -- Psychology -- Case studies. Hard-core unemployed -- United States -- Psychology -- Case studies. Unemployed -- United States -- Interviews.

HD5708.45.U6.W67 1984
Work in America Institute.
Employment security in a free economy/ directed
by Jerome M. Rosow and Robert Zager. New York:
Pergamon Press, c1984. xi, 180 p.
84-019067   658.3/142   0080309755
Job security -- United States.

HD5708.5.G67 1981
Gordus, Jeanne P.
Plant closings and economic dislocation/ Jeanne
Prial Gordus, Paul Jarley, Louis A. Ferman.
Kalamazoo, Mich.: W.E. Upjohn Institute for
Employment Research, c1981. xiii, 173 p.
81-016188   338.6/042   091155890X
Plant shutdowns. Unemployed. Labor mobility.

HD5708.55.U6.B58 1982
Bluestone, Barry.
The deindustrialization of America: plant closings,
community abandonment, and the dismantling of
basic industry/ Barry Bluestone, Bennett Harrison.
New York: Basic Books, c1982. x, 323 p.
82-070844   338.6/042   0465015905
*Deindustrialization -- United States. Plant
shutdowns -- United States. Industries -- United
States.*

HD5708.55.U6.J63 1991
Job displacement: consequences and implications
for policy/ edited by John T. Addison. Detroit:
Wayne State University Press, c1991. 306 p.
90-022623   331.13/704   0814322859
*Displaced workers -- United States. Displaced
workers -- Government policy -- United States.*

HD5708.55.U6.P67 1990
Portz, John, 1953-
The politics of plant closings/ John Portz.
Lawrence, Kan.: University Press of Kansas,
c1990. ix, 214 p.
90-032817   338.6/042   0700604723
*Plant shutdowns -- Political aspects -- United
States -- Case studies. Municipal government --
United States -- Case studies.*

HD5708.75.U6.B87 1988
Buss, Terry F.
Hidden unemployment: discouraged workers and
public policy/ Terry F. Buss and F. Stevens
Redburn. New York: Praeger, 1988. xvi, 143 p.
88-011760   331.13/704   0275926125
*Disguised unemployment -- United States.
Disguised unemployment -- Government policy --
United States.*

HD5710.7 Labor. Work.
Working class — Labor market.
Labor supply. Labor demand —
Foreign trade and employment.
Foreign investments

HD5710.7.G68 1990
Goto, Junichi.
Labor in international trade theory: a new
perspective on Japanese-American issues/ Junichi
Goto. Baltimore: Johns Hopkins University Press,
c1990. viii, 203 p.
89-013880   331.12/0973   0801840058
*Foreign trade and employment -- Mathematical
models.   United States -- Commerce -- Japan.
Japan -- Commerce -- United States.*

HD5713.2-5713.6 Labor. Work.
Working class — Labor market.
Labor supply. Labor demand —
Manpower policy

HD5713.2.D75 1987
Driver, Ciaran.
Towards full employment: a policy appraisal/
Ciaran Driver. London; Routledge & Kegan Paul,
1987. xii, 238 p.
87-009814   339.5   0710209185
*Employment stabilization. Full employment
policies. Unemployment.*

HD5713.6.U54.R67 1994
Rose, Nancy Ellen.
Put to work: relief programs in the Great
Depression/ Nancy E. Rose. New York: Monthly
Review Press, c1994. 144 p.
93-026617   331.13/77/0973   0853458715
*Public service employment -- United States --
History. Depressions -- 1929 -- United States.
Public works -- United States -- Employees --
History.*

HD5715.2 Labor. Work.
Working class — Labor market.
Labor supply. Labor demand —
Occupational training.
Occupational retraining

HD5715.2.K45 1993
Kemple, James J.
The National JTPA Study: site characteristics and
participation patterns/ James J. Kemple, Fred
Doolittle, John W. Wallace. New York: Manpower
Demonstration Research Corporation, c1993. xii,
247 p.
92-045223   331.25/92/0973
*Occupational training -- Government policy --
United States.*

HD5717-5717.5 Labor. Work.
Working class — Labor market.
Labor supply. Labor demand —
Labor and occupational mobility.
Labor turnover

HD5717.M83
Mueller, Charles F.
The economics of labor migration: a behavioral
analysis/ Charles F. Mueller. New York: Academic
Press, c1982. xii, 199 p.
81-019046   331.12/79   0125095805
*Labor mobility. Emigration and immigration.
Migration, Internal.*

HD5717.5.U6.D38 1996
Davis, Steven J.
Job creation and destruction/ Steven J. Davis, John
C. Haltiwanger, Scott Schuh. Cambridge, Mass.:
MIT Press, c1996. xxii, 260 p.
95-046260   331.12/0973 20   0262041529
*Job creation -- United States. Business cycles --
United States. Occupational mobility -- United
States.*

HD5724-5812.2 Labor. Work.
Working class — Labor market.
Labor supply. Labor demand —
By region or country

HD5724.B63
Bowen, William G.
The economics of labor force participation, by
William G. Bowen and T. Aldrich Finegan.
Princeton, N.J., Princeton University Press, 1969.
xxvi, 897 p.
69-017396   331.1/1/0973
*Labor supply -- United States. Unemployed --
United States.*

HD5724.C485 1994
The Changing U.S. labor market/ edited by Eli
Ginzberg. Boulder: Westview Press, 1994. vii,
215 p.
94-003994   331.12/0973   0813321638
*Labor market -- United States. Human capital --
United States.*

HD5724.H43 1998
Herzenberg, Stephen.
New rules for a new economy: employment and
opportunity in postindustrial America/ Stephen A.
Herzenberg, John A. Alic & Howard Wial. Ithaca:
ILR Press, 1998. xiii, 216 p.
98-018220   331.12/0973   0801435242
*Employment forecasting -- United States. Labor
market -- United States. Service industries workers
-- Supply and demand -- United States --
Forecasting.*

HD5724.J36 1990
Janoski, Thomas.
The political economy of unemployment: active
labor market policy in West Germany and the
United States/ Thomas Janoski. Berkeley:
University of California Press, c1990. xxvi, 351 p.
89-049053   331.12/042/0943   0520068858
*Manpower policy -- United States. Manpower
policy -- Germany (West)*

HD5724.K64 1990
Korver, Ton.
The fictitious commodity: a study of the U.S. labor
market, 1880-1940/ Ton Korver. New York:
Greenwood Press, 1990. 196 p.
90-002717   331.12/0973   0313273383
Labor market -- United States -- History.

HD5724.L215 1991
Labor in a global economy: perspectives from the
U.S. and Canada/ Steven Hecker, Margaret
Hallock, editors. Eugene, OR: Labor Education and
Research Center, University c1991. v, 305 p.
91-024239   331/.0973   0871141531
*Labor supply -- United States -- Congresses.
Labor supply -- Canada -- Congresses. Labor
mobility -- United States -- Congresses.*

HD5724.M78 1990
Mucciaroni, Gary.
The political failure of employment policy, 1945-
1982/ Gary Mucciaroni. Pittsburgh, Pa.: University
of Pittsburgh Press, c1990. xi, 317 p.
90-031987   331.11/0973   0822936488
*Manpower policy -- United States.   United
States -- Politics and government -- 1945-1989.*

HD5724.P58 1995
Potter, Edward E.
Keeping America competitive: employment policy for the twenty-first century/ Edward E. Potter, Judith A. Youngman. Lakewood, CO: Glenbridge Pub., c1995. xii, 434 p.
94-077235   331.2/0973 20   0944435289
Manpower policy -- United States. Employees -- Training of -- United States. Management -- Employee participation -- United States.

HD5724.W38 1991
Weir, Margaret, 1952-
Politics and jobs: the boundaries of employment policy in the United States/ Margaret Weir. Princeton, N.J.: Princeton University Press, c1992. xvi, 238 p.
91-018287   339.5/0973   069107853X
Full employment policies -- United States. Manpower policy -- United States. Public service employment -- United States.

HD5728.S54 1993
Small differences that matter: labor markets and income maintenance in Canada and the United States/ edited by David Card and Richard B. Freeman. Chicago: University of Chicago Press, 1993. ix, 277 p.
93-010513   362.5/82/0971   0226092836
Labor market -- Canada. Labor market -- United States. Income maintenance programs -- Canada.

HD5730.5.A6.G56 1997
Global restructuring, employment, and social inequality in urban Latin America/ edited by Richard Tardanico and Rafael Menjivar Larin. Coral Gables, Fla.: North-South Center Press: c1997. ii, 295 p.
97-030442   338.98 21   157454019X
Labor supply -- Latin America. Structural adjustment (Economic policy) -- Latin America. Latin America -- Economic policy.

HD5731.A6.S47 1994
Sernau, Scott.
Economies of exclusion: underclass poverty and labor market change in Mexico/ Scott Sernau. Westport, Conn.: Praeger, 1994. xv, 156 p.
94-006374   331.12/0972   0275949354
Poor -- Employment -- Mexico. Labor market -- Mexico. Mexico -- Economic conditions -- 1994-

HD5764.A6.E49 1988
Employment forecasting: the employment problem in industrialised countries/ edited by M.J.D. Hopkins. London; Pinter Publishers, 1988. xvii, 257 p.
87-021882   331.12/094   0861879384
Employment forecasting -- Europe -- Congresses. Unemployment -- Europe -- Congresses.

HD5764.A6.L27 1994
Labor market institutions in Europe: a socioeconomic evaluation of performance/ Gunther Schmid, editor. Armonk, N.Y.: M.E. Sharpe, c1994. xii, 291 p.
93-047020   331.12/042/094   156324411X
Full employment policies -- Europe -- Evaluation. Labor policy -- Europe -- Evaluation.

HD5764.A6.R48
Reubens, Beatrice G.
The hard-to-employ: European programs [by] Beatrice G. Reubens. Foreword by Eli Ginzberg. New York, Columbia University Press, 1970. xxii, 420 p.
78-117018   331.1/12/094   0231033885
Hard-core unemployed -- Europe. Manpower policy -- Europe.

HD5765.A6.G367 1990
Garside, W. R.
British unemployment, 1919-1939: a study in public policy/ W.R. Garside. Cambridge [England]; Cambridge University Press, 1990. xvi, 414 p.
89-033212   331.13/7941   0521364434
Unemployment -- Great Britain -- History -- 20th century. Full employment policies -- Great Britain -- History -- 20th century. Depressions -- 1929 -- Great Britain. Great Britain -- Economic policy -- 1918-1945.

HD5765.A6.W69 1991
Worswick, G. D. N.
Unemployment: a problem of policy: analysis of British experience and prospects/ by G.D.N. Worswick. Cambridge; Cambridge University Press, 1991. xiv, 280 p.
90-044287   331.13/7941   0521400341
Unemployed -- Great Britain. Unemployment -- Great Britain. Wages -- Great Britain. Great Britain -- Economic policy -- 1964-1979. Great Britain -- Economic policy -- 1979-1997.

HD5792.Z36 1993
Zanden, J. L. van.
The rise and decline of Holland's economy: merchant capitalism and the labour market/ J.L. van Zanden. Manchester, UK; Manchester University Press: c1993. xii, 186 p.
93-002708   330.9492   0719038065
Labor market -- Netherlands -- History. Netherlands -- Economic conditions. Netherlands -- Commerce -- History.

HD5796.M67 1984
Moskoff, William.
Labour and leisure in the Soviet Union: the conflict between public and private decision-making in a planned economy/ William Moskoff. New York: St. Martin's Press, 1984. xv, 225 p.
83-024701   331.13/6/0947   0312462417
Labor supply -- Soviet Union. Leisure -- Soviet Union. Labor policy -- Soviet Union.

HD5796.S23 1982
Sacks, Michael Paul.
Work and equality in Soviet society: the division of labor by age, gender, and nationality/ Michael Paul Sacks. New York, N.Y.: Praeger, 1982. xv, 206 p.
82-000278   306/.3   0030461413
Labor supply -- Soviet Union. Women -- Employment -- Soviet Union. Minorities -- Employment -- Soviet Union.

HD5811.85.A6.U73 1989
Urban poverty and the labour market: access to jobs and incomes in Asian and Latin American cities/ edited by Gerry Rodgers. Geneva: International Labour Office, 1989. xv, 257 p.
90-133036   331.12/095   9221065006
Labor market -- Asia. Labor market -- Latin America. Urban poor -- Asia.

HD5812.2.A7.H35 2000
Bernstein, Deborah.
Constructing boundaries: Jewish and Arab workers in mandatory Palestine/ Deborah S. Bernstein. Albany, N.Y.: State University of New York Press, c2000. xvi, 277 p.
99-037759   331.12/095694/6 21   0791445399
Labor market -- Israel -- Haifa -- History -- 20th century. Jews -- Israel -- Haifa -- Economic conditions. Palestinian Arabs -- Employment -- Israel -- Haifa. Haifa (Israel) -- Economic conditions. Haifa (Israel) -- Ethnic relations.

HD5852 Labor. Work. Working class — Labor market. Labor supply. Labor demand — Developing countries

HD5852.G87 1989
Gupta, Kanhaya L. 1935-
Industrialization and employment in developing countries: a comparative study/ Kanhaya L. Gupta. London; Routledge, 1989. xv, 205 p.
89-148292   331.12/3/091724   0415006228
Labor demand -- Developing countries -- Mathematical models. Manufacturing industries -- Employees -- Supply and demand -- Developing countries -- Mathematical models. Industrialization -- Developing countries -- Mathematical models.

HD5854.2 Labor. Work. Working class — Temporary employment — By region or country, A-Z

HD5854.2.U6.C66 1998
Contingent work: American employment relations in transition/ edited by Kathleen Barker and Kathleen Christensen. Ithaca: ILR Press, 1998. viii, 350 p.
98-011445   331.25/72   080143369X
Temporary employment -- United States. Part-time employment -- United States. Seasonal labor -- United States.

HD5856 Labor. Work. Working class — Seasonal labor. Migrant labor — By region or country, A-Z

HD5856.D44.S73 1990
Stark, Oded.
The migration of labor/ Oded Stark. Cambridge, Mass., USA; B. Blackwell, 1991. x, 406 p.
90-030980   331.12/791   1557860300
Migrant labor -- Developing countries. Migrant remittances -- Developing countries.

HD5875 Labor. Work. Working class — Employment agencies. State — By region or country

HD5875.B55
Blau, Peter Michael.
The structure of organizations [by] Peter M. Blau [and] Richard A. Schoenherr. New York, Basic Books [1971] xix, 445 p.
74-126956   301.18/32   0465082408
Employment agencies -- United States. Organization.

HD6052-6220 Labor. Work. Working class — Classes of labor — Women

HD6052.E6
Equal employment policy for women: strategies for implementation in the United States, Canada, and Western Europe/ edited by Ronnie Steinberg Ratner. Philadelphia: Temple University Press, 1980. xxii, 520 p.
79-019509   331.4   0877221561
Women -- Employment -- Congresses. Sex discrimination in employment -- Congresses.

HD6052.W566 1987
Women, work, and technology: transformations/ edited by Barbara Drygulski Wright ... [et al.]. Ann Arbor: University of Michigan Press, c1987. viii, 387 p.
87-016236   331.4   0472063731
Women -- Employment -- Effect of technological innovations on -- Congresses.

HD6053.E26 1980
The Economics of women and work/ edited by Alice H. Amsden. New York, NY: St. Martin's Press, 1980. 409 p.
80-015970   331.4   0312236700
Women -- Employment -- Addresses, essays, lectures.

HD6053.F43 1988
Feminization of the labor force: paradoxes and promises/ edited by Jane Jenson, Elisabeth Hagen, and Ceallaigh Reddy. New York: Oxford University Press, 1988. xii, 295 p.
88-009958   331.4   0195206266
Women -- Employment.

HD6053.W66
Women working: theories and facts in perspective/ edited by Ann H. Stromberg and Shirley Harkess. Palo Alto, Calif.: Mayfield Pub. Co., 1978. xxvii, 458 p.
77-089921   331.4   0874843014
Women -- Employment. Pay equity. Women -- Employment -- United States.

HD6054.H37 1991
Haslett, Beth.
The organizational woman: power and paradox/ Beth J. Haslett, Florence L. Geis, Mae R. Carter. Norwood, N.J.: Ablex Pub., c1992. xv, 270 p.
91-035889   658.4/09/082   0893918377
Women executives. Success in business.

HD6054.2.U6.S65 1992
Sokoloff, Natalie J.
Black women and white women in the professions: occupational segregation by race and gender, 1960-1980/ Natalie J. Sokoloff. New York: Routledge, 1992. xix, 175 p.
92-003988   331.4/133/0973   0415906083
Afro-American women in the professions. Women in the professions. Professional employees -- United States.

HD6054.3.W35 1998
Wajcman, Judy.
Managing like a man: women and men in corporate management/ Judy Wajcman. University Park, PA: Pennsylvania State University Press, 1998. vii, 180 p.
98-022627   658.4/09/082   0271018402
Women executives -- Attitudes. Executives -- Attitudes. Executive ability.

HD6054.4.U6.G355 1997
Gamber, Wendy, 1958-
The female economy: the millinery and dressmaking trades, 1860-1930/ Wendy Gamber. Urbana: University of Illinois Press, c1997. xiii, 300 p.
96-025211   331.4/887/0973   025202298X
Businesswomen -- United States -- History. Women consumers -- United States -- History. Women's clothing industry -- United States -- History.

HD6055.A3
Adams, Carolyn Teich.
Mothers at work: public policies in the United States, Sweden, and China/ Carolyn Teich Adams, Kathryn Teich Winston. New York: Longman, c1980. vi, 312 p.
79-018670   331.4   0582280648
Mothers -- Employment -- United States. Mothers -- Employment -- Sweden. Mothers -- Employment -- China.

HD6056.B66 2000
Bookman, Milica Zarkovic.
The third career: revisiting the home vs. work choice in middle age/ Milica Z. Bookman. Westport, Conn.: Praeger, 2000. xviii, 217 p.
99-045992   331.3/94/082   0275968111
Middle aged women -- Employment. Age and employment. Home economics -- Social aspects.

HD6056.2.U6.U56 1983
Unplanned careers: the working lives of middle-aged women/ edited by Lois Banfill Shaw. Lexington, Mass.: LexingtonBooks, c1983. viii, 149 p.
82-047925   331.3/94/088042   0669057010
Middle aged women -- United States -- Longitudinal studies.

HD6057.5.U5.L37 1999
Latinas and African American women at work: race, gender, and economic inequality/ Irene Browne, editor. New York: Russell Sage Foundation, 1999. x, 441 p.
98-019536   331.4/089/96073   0871541475
Afro-American women -- Employment. Hispanic American women -- Employment.

HD6057.5.U5.W66 1992
Woody, Bette.
Black women in the workplace: impacts of structural change in the economy/ Bette Woody. New York: Greenwood Press, 1992. xii, 211 p.
91-028745   331.4/089/96073   0313255911
Afro-American women -- Employment -- United States.

HD6058.B67 1985
Bose, Christine E.
Jobs and gender: a study of occupational prestige/ Christine E. Bose. New York: Praeger, 1985. xiv, 206 p.
85-006305   305.4/3/00973   0030716926
Women -- Employment -- United States. Occupational prestige -- United States.

HD6059.5.E85.W65 1986
Women and work in preindustrial Europe/ edited by Barbara A. Hanawalt. Bloomington: Indiana University Press, c1986. xviii, 233 p.
85-042829   331.4/094   0253366100
Women -- Employment -- Europe -- History. Women -- Europe -- Economic conditions. Occupations -- Europe -- History.

HD6060.J33 1989
Jacobs, Jerry A., 1955-
Revolving doors: sex segregation and women's careers/ Jerry A. Jacobs. Stanford, Calif.: Stanford University Press, 1989. xi, 230 p.
88-024986   331.4/133   0804714894
Sex discrimination in employment. Sex role in the work environment. Sexual division of labor.

HD6060.5.U5.H53 1987
Hidden aspects of women's work/ edited by Christine Bose, Roslyn Feldberg, and Natalie Sokoloff; with the Women and Work Research Group. New York: Praeger, 1987. x, 380 p.
87-002449   331.4/133/0973   0275924157
Sex discrimination in employment -- United States -- History. Sex role in the work environment -- United States -- History. Sex discrimination against women -- United States -- History.

HD6060.5.U5.W55 1989
Williams, Christine L., 1959-
Gender differences at work: women and men in nontraditional occupations/ Christine L. Williams. Berkeley: University of California Press, c1989. xviii, 191 p.
88-010778   305.3   0520063732
Sex role in the work environment -- United States. Women and the military -- United States. Male nurses -- United States.

HD6060.5.U52.A65 1991
Kelly, Rita Mae.
The gendered economy: work, careers, and success/ Rita Mae Kelly. Newbury Park, CA: Sage Publications, 1991. xv, 262 p.
91-014938   331.4/133/09791   080394215X
Sex discrimination in employment -- Arizona. Sexual division of labor -- Arizona. Sex role -- Arizona.

HD6060.65.B6.H86 1987
Humphrey, John, 1950-
Gender and work in the Third World: sexual divisions in Brazilian industry/ John Humphrey. London; Tavistock Publications, 1987. x, 229 p.
87-012416   305.4/3/00981   0422619000
Sexual division of labor -- Brazil.

HD6060.65.P6.E95 1992
Eviota, Elizabeth U.
The political economy of gender: women and the sexual division of labour in the Philippines/ Elizabeth Uy Eviota. London; Zed Books, c1992. viii, 212 p.
93-110498   1856491099
Sexual division of labor -- Philippines. Women -- Employment -- Philippines.

HD6061.P47 1994
Perlman, Richard.
Sex discrimination in the labour market: the case for comparable worth/ Richard Perlman and Maureen Pike. Manchester [England]; Manchester University Press; c1994. viii, 170 p.
93-040664   331.2/153   0719033365
Pay equity. Sex discrimination in employment.

HD6061.2.U6.E54 1992
England, Paula.
Comparable worth: theories and evidence/ Paula England. New York: Aldine de Gruyter, c1992. xii, 346 p.
92-000900   331.2/153   0202303489
Pay equity -- United States. Pay equity.

HD6061.2.U6.K56 1990
Killingsworth, Mark R., 1946-
The economics of comparable worth/ Mark R. Killingsworth. Kalamazoo, Mich.: W.E. Upjohn Institute for Employment Research, 1990. xi, 306 p.
89-025044   331.2/153   0880990864
Pay equity -- United States.

HD6061.2.U62.O72 1989
Acker, Joan.
Doing comparable worth: gender, class, and pay equity/ Joan Acker. Philadelphia: Temple University Press, 1989. ix, 254 p.
88-026845   331.2/1   0877226210
Pay equity -- Oregon -- Case studies. Sex discrimination against women -- Oregon -- Case studies. Working class women -- Oregon -- Case studies.

HD6065.5.U6.D54 1993
Vogel, Lise.
Mothers on the job: maternity policy in the U.S. workplace/ Lise Vogel. New Brunswick, N.J.: Rutgers University Press, c1993. viii, 202 p.
92-021874   331.4/4   0813519187
Maternity leave -- United States. Maternity leave -- Government policy -- United States. Pregnant women -- Employment -- United States.

HD6065.5.U6.K35 1983
Kamerman, Sheila B.
Maternity policies and working women/ Sheila B. Kamerman, Alfred J. Kahn, and Paul Kingston. New York: Columbia University Press, 1983. 183 p.
83-007624   331.4/25763   0231057504
Maternity leave -- United States. Insurance, Maternity -- United States.

HD6066.U5.W57 2001
Wisensale, Steven K., 1945-
Family leave policy: the political economy of work and family in America/ Steven K. Wisensale. Armonk, N.Y.: M.E. Sharpe, c2001. xii, 297 p.
00-046387   331.25/763 21   0765604965
Parental leave -- United States. Family policy -- United States.

HD6072.W67 1990
Work without wages: comparative studies of domestic labor and self-employment/ edited by Jane L. Collins and Martha Gimenez. Albany: State University of New York Press, c1990. x, 264 p.
88-037031   331.4/8164046   0791401065
Domestics. Housewives. Informal sector (Economics)

HD6072.2.U5.D82 1983
Dudden, Faye E.
Serving women: household service in nineteenth-century America/ Faye E. Dudden. Middletown, Conn.: Wesleyan University Press; c1983. viii, 344 p.
83-001263   305.4/364   0819550728
Domestics -- United States -- History -- 19th century.

HD6072.2.U5.K37
Katzman, David M.
Seven days a week: women and domestic service in industrializing America/ David M. Katzman. New York: Oxford University Press, 1978. xviii, 374 p.
77-013714   331.7/61/640460973   0195023684
Domestics -- United States -- History. Women -- United States -- History. United States -- Social conditions -- 1865-1918.

HD6072.6.U5.A76 1991
Aronson, Robert Louis, 1917-
Self-employment: a labor market perspective/ Robert L. Aronson. Ithaca, N.Y.: ILR Press, c1991. xiii, 156 p.
91-010487   331.12   0875461751
Self-employed -- United States. Self-employed.

HD6073.A292.A353 1988
Agriculture, women, and land: the African experience/ edited by Jean Davison. Boulder: Westview Press, 1988. vii, 278 p.
88-016924   331.4/83/096   0813374219
Women in agriculture -- Africa. Land use -- Africa. Land tenure -- Africa.

HD6073.E32.I818 1993
Willson, Perry R.
The clockwork factory: women and work in Fascist Italy/ Perry R. Willson. Oxford: Clarendon Press; 1993. 291 p.
93-014160   331.4/8213/094521   0198227329
Women electric industry workers -- Italy -- Milan -- History -- 20th century.

HD6073.E372.U653 1994
Dangler, Jamie Faricellia, 1958-
Hidden in the home: the role of waged homework in the modern world-economy/ Jamie Faricellia Dangler. Albany, N.Y.: State University of New York Press, c1994. xvi, 225 p.
94-000282   331.4/4/0973   0791421295
Women electronic industry workers -- New York (State) Cottage industries -- New York (State) Sexual division of labor -- New York (State)

HD6073.H842.U625 1990
Boydston, Jeanne.
Home and work: housework, wages, and the ideology of labor in the early republic/ Jeanne Boydston. New York: Oxford University Press, 1990. xx, 222 p.
90-031349   331.4/8164046/0973   0195060091
Housewives -- United States -- History. Wages -- Housewives -- United States -- History. Home economics -- United States -- History. United States -- Economic conditions -- To 1865.

HD6073.L62.G723 1996
Bennett, Judith M.
Ale, beer and brewsters in England: women's work in a changing world, 1300-1600/ Judith M. Bennett. New York: Oxford University Press, 1996. xiv, 260 p.
96-001271   331.4/86342/0942   0195073908
Women brewers -- England -- History. Women -- England -- History -- Middle Ages, 500-1500.

HD6073.O332.M4954 1998
Cravey, Altha J., 1952-
Women and work in Mexico's maquiladoras/ Altha J. Cravey. Lanham, Md: Rowman & Littlefield, c1998. xii, 176 p.
98-036864   331.4/87/0972 21   0847688852
Women offshore assembly industry workers -- Mexico. Industrial policy -- Mexico. Work and family -- Mexico.

HD6079.S3
Schneiderman, Rose, 1882-
All for one, by Rose Schneiderman with Lucy Goldthwaite. New York, P. S. Eriksson [1967] viii, 264 p.
67-027015   331.88/0924
Trade-unions -- United States. Women -- Employment -- United States.

HD6079.2.U5.F65 1979
Foner, Philip Sheldon, 1910-
Women and the American labor movement/ Philip S. Foner. New York: Free Press, c1979-1980. 2 v.
79-063035   331.4   0029103703
Women labor union members -- United States -- History. Women -- Employment -- United States -- History. Women in the labor movement -- United States -- History.

HD6079.2.U5.G33 1990
Gabin, Nancy Felice.
Feminism in the labor movement: women and the United Auto Workers, 1935-1975/ Nancy F. Gabin. Ithaca: Cornell University Press, 1990. xi, 257 p.
90-001571   331.4/8292/0973   0801424356
Women labor union members -- United States -- Case studies.

HD6079.2.U5.K57 1991
Kirby, Diane Elizabeth.
Alice Henry: the power of pen and voice: the life of an Australian-American labor reformer/ Diane Kirkby. Cambridge; Cambridge University Press, 1991. xxvi, 254 p.
90-044367   331.4/78/092   0521391024
Henry, Alice, -- 1857-1943. Women labor union members -- United States -- Biography. Feminists -- United States -- Biography.

HD6079.2.U5.P38 1988
Payne, Elizabeth Anne, 1943-
Reform, labor, and feminism: Margaret Dreier Robins and the Women's Trade Union League/ Elizabeth Anne Payne. Urbana: University of Illinois Press, c1988. xiv, 218 p.
87-010794   331.88/092/4   0252014456
Robins, Margaret Dreier. Women labor union members -- United States -- Biography. Feminism -- United States -- History.

HD6079.2.U5.W66 1987
Women, work, and protest: a century of US women's labor history/ edited by Ruth Milkman. London; Routledge & Kegan Paul, 1987, c1985. xiv, 333 p.
84-027732   331.4/0973   0710099401
Women labor union members -- United States -- History -- 20th century. Sex discrimination against women -- United States -- History -- 20th century.

HD6095.A6 1969
Abbott, Edith, 1876-1957.
Women in industry; a study in American economic history. New York, Arno, 1969. xxii, 408 p.
70-089714   331.4/0973
Women -- Employment -- United States -- History. United States -- Economic conditions.

HD6095.A662 1976
America's working women/ compiled and edited by Rosalyn Baxandall, Linda Gordon and Susan Reverby. New York: Random House, c1976. xxii, 408 p.
76-010574   331.4/0973   0394491505
Women -- Employment -- United States -- History -- Sources. Women -- Employment -- United States -- History.

HD6095.B57 1997
Blackwelder, Julia Kirk, 1943-
Now hiring: the feminization of work in the United States, 1900-1995/ Julia Kirk Blackwelder. College Station: Texas A&M University Press, c1997. xv, 308 p.
97-015922   331.4/0973/0904 21   0890967768
Women -- Employment -- United States -- History -- 20th century.

HD6095.G65 1990
Goldin, Claudia Dale.
Understanding the gender gap: an economic history of American women/ Claudia Goldin. New York: Oxford University Press, 1990. xviii, 287 p.
89-033502 331.4/0973 0195050770
  Women -- Employment -- United States -- History. Sex discrimination in employment -- United States -- History.

HD6095.K449 1982
Kessler-Harris, Alice.
Out to work: a history of wage-earning women in the United States/ Alice Kessler-Harris. New York: Oxford University Press, 1982. xvi, 400 p.
81-011237 331.4/0973 0195030249
  Women -- Employment -- United States -- History. Working class women -- United States -- History.

HD6095.K45
Kessler-Harris, Alice.
Women have always worked: a historical overview/ Alice Kessler-Harris; [photo research by Flavia Rando]. Old Westbury, N.Y.: Feminist Press; c1981. xiii, 193 p.
80-013400 331.4/0973 091267086X
  Women -- Employment -- United States -- History.

HD6095.L558
Lloyd, Cynthia B., 1943-
The economics of sex differentials/ Cynthia B. Lloyd and Beth T. Niemi. New York: Columbia University Press, 1979. xvi, 355 p.
79-009569 331.4/0973 0231040385
  Women -- Employment -- United States. Sex discrimination in employment -- United States. Sex discrimination against women -- United States.

HD6095.S3
Scharf, Lois.
To work and to wed: female employment, feminism, and the Great Depression/ Lois Scharf. Westport, Conn.: Greenwood Press, c1980. xiii, 240 p.
79-052325 331.4/3/0973 031321445X
  Married women -- Employment -- United States -- History. Feminism -- United States -- History. Sex discrimination in employment -- United States -- History.

HD6095.S34 1993
Schneider, Dorothy.
The ABC-CLIO companion to women in the workplace/ Dorothy Schneider and Carl J. Schneider. Santa Barbara, Calif.: ABC-CLIO, c1993. xxix, 371 p.
93-023533 331.4/0973 0874366941
  Women -- Employment -- United States -- History -- Dictionaries.

HD6095.T44
Tentler, Leslie Woodcock.
Wage-earning women: industrial work and family life in the United States, 1900-1930/ Leslie Woodcock Tentler. New York: Oxford University Press, 1979. 266 p.
79-012802 331.4/0973 0195026276
  Women -- Employment -- United States -- History. Women -- United States -- History. Sex role.

HD6095.W47 1977
Wertheimer, Barbara M.
We were there: the story of working women in America/ Barbara Mayer Wertheimer, with the research assistance of Ida Goshkin and Ellen Wertheimer. New York: Pantheon Books, c1977. xx, 427 p.
76-009597 331.4/0973 039449590X
  Women -- Employment -- United States -- History. Women labor union members -- United States -- History.

HD6100.5.G46 1997
The gendered worlds of Latin American women workers: from household and factory to the union hall and ballot box/ John D. French and Daniel James, editors. Durham, N.C.: Duke University Press, 1997. viii, 320 p.
97-020053 331.4/098 0822320002
  Women -- Latin America -- Economic conditions. Working class women -- Latin America -- Economic conditions. Women -- Identity -- Latin America.

HD6113.Z6.K553 1996
Bolles, Augusta Lynn.
Sister Jamaica: a study of women, work, and households in Kingston/ A. Lynn Bolles. Lanham: University Press of America, c1996. xix, 129 p.
95-046006 331.4/097292 20 0761802118
  Women -- Employment -- Jamaica -- Kingston. Women -- Jamaica -- Kingston -- Economic conditions. Women -- Jamaica -- Kingston -- Social conditions.

HD6114.S24 1995
Safa, Helen Icken.
The myth of the male breadwinner: women and industrialization in the Caribbean/ Helen Safa. Boulder: Westview Press, 1995. xvi, 208 p.
94-047478 305.43/09729 0813312116
  Women -- Employment -- Puerto Rico. Women -- Employment -- Dominican Republic. Women -- Employment -- Cuba.

HD6134.S54 1998
Simonton, Deborah, 1948-
A history of European women's work: 1700 to the present/ Deborah Simonton. London; Routledge, 1998. xii, 337 p.
98-009480 331.4/094 0415055318
  Women -- Employment -- Europe -- History. Rural women -- Employment -- Europe -- History. Women domestics -- Europe -- History.

HD6135.H377 1997
Hatt, Sue, 1946-
Gender, work, and labour markets/ Sue Hatt. Houndmills, Basingstoke, Hampshire: Macmillan Press; 1997. xi, 200 p.
96-043973 331.4/0941 0333657780
  Women -- Employment -- Great Britain. Men -- Employment -- Great Britain. Work and family -- Great Britain.

HD6135.S86 1984
Summerfield, Penny.
Women workers in the Second World War: production and patriarchy in conflict/ Penny Summerfield. London; Croom Helm, c1984. 214 p.
85-127263 331.4/0941 0709923171
  Women -- Employment -- Great Britain -- History -- 20th century. Women -- Employment -- Public opinion -- History -- 20th century. Public opinion -- Great Britain -- History -- 20th century.

HD6138.P95 1990
Pyle, Jean Larson, 1944-
The state and women in the economy: lessons from sex discrimination in the Republic of Ireland/ Jean Larson Pyle. Albany: State University of New York Press, c1990. xviii, 202 p.
89-026160 331.4/09415 0791403793
  Women -- Employment -- Ireland. Labor policy -- Ireland. Family policy -- Ireland.

HD6162.P68 1993
Pott-Buter, Hettie.
Facts and fairy tales about female labor, family, and fertility: a seven-country comparison, 1850-1990/ Hettie A. Pott-Buter. Amsterdam: Amsterdam University Press, c1993. xiii, 370 p.
93-247341 331.4/094 9053560459
  Women -- Employment -- Netherlands -- History. Women -- Employment -- Europe -- History. Family -- Netherlands -- History.

HD6181.9.M644 1998
Moghadam, Valentine M., 1952-
Women, work, and economic reform in the Middle East and North Africa/ Valentine M. Moghadam. Boulder, Colo.: Lynne Rienner Publishers, 1998. xi, 259 p.
97-026798 331.4/0956 1555877850
  Women -- Employment -- Middle East. Women -- Employment -- Africa, North. Women -- Africa, North -- Social conditions.

HD6194.Z6.J388 1992
Wolf, Diane L.
Factory daughters: gender, household dynamics, and rural industrialization in Java/ Diane Lauren Wolf. Berkeley: University of California Press, c1992. xv, 323 p.
91-041844 331.4/09598/2 0520070720
  Women -- Employment -- Indonesia -- Java. Households -- Indonesia -- Java. Work and family -- Indonesia -- Java.

HD6197.C66
Cook, Alice Hanson.
Working women in Japan: discrimination, resistance, and reform/ Alice H. Cook and Hiroko Hayashi. Ithaca, N.Y.: New York State School of Industrial and Labor Re c1980. 124 p.
80-017706 331.4/133/0952 087546078X
  Women -- Employment -- Japan. Sex discrimination in employment -- Japan. Sex discrimination against women -- Japan.

HD6206.M53 1998
Middle Eastern women and the invisible economy/ edited by Richard A. Lobban with a foreword by Elizabeth W. Fernea. Gainesville, Fla.: University Press of Florida, c1998. xviii, 302 p.
98-012588 331.4/0917/4927 21 0813015774
  Women -- Employment -- Arab countries. Informal sector (Economics) -- Arab countries.

HD6220.P56 1993
Pink collar blues: work, gender & technology/ edited by Belinda Probert, Bruce W. Wilson. [Carlton, Vic.]: Melbourne University Press; 1993. xiii, 173 p.
94-107811 331.4/0994 0522845207
  Women -- Employment -- Australia. Employees -- Effect of technological innovations on -- Australia.

HD6231-6250 Labor. Work. Working class — Classes of labor — Children

HD6231.H63 1999
Hobbs, Sandy.
Child labor: a world history companion/ Sandy Hobbs, Jim McKechnie, and Michael Lavalette. Santa Barbara, Calif.: ABC-CLIO, c1999. xx, 292 p.
99-029203 331.3/1 21 0874369568
Child labor -- History.

HD6231.S27 1988
Sawyer, Roger, 1931-
Children enslaved/ Roger Sawyer. London; Routledge, 1988. xviii, 238 p.
87-031659 306/.362/088054 0415002737
Child slaves -- Cross-cultural studies. Slavery -- History -- 20th century. Child prostitution -- Cross-cultural studies.

HD6250.G7.N28 1990
Nardinelli, Clark.
Child labor and the Industrial Revolution/ Clark Nardinelli. Bloomington: Indiana University Press, c1990. x, 194 p.
89-046001 331.3/4/0941 0253339715
Child labor -- Great Britain -- History. Child labor -- History. Child welfare -- Great Britain -- History.

HD6250.G7 T88 1999
Tuttle, Carolyn.
Hard at work in factories and mines: the economics of child labor during the British Industrial Revolution/ Carolyn Tuttle. Boulder, Colo.: Westview Press, 1999. 308 p.
99-016847 331.3/1/094109034 21 0813336988
Child labor -- Great Britain -- History -- 19th century. Labor economics -- Great Britain -- History -- 19th century. Industrial revolution -- Great Britain.

HD6250.I42.W45 1991
Weiner, Myron.
The child and the state in India: child labor and education policy in comparative perspective/ Myron Weiner. Princeton, N.J.: Princeton University Press, c1991. xiv, 213 p.
90-037869 331.3/4/0954 0691078688
Child labor -- Government policy -- India. Child labor -- Government policy. Education, Compulsory -- India.

HD6250.U3.T7
Trattner, Walter I.
Crusade for the children; a history of the National Child Labor Committee and child labor reform in America, by Walter I. Trattner. Chicago, Quadrangle Books, 1970. 319 p.
76-116090 331.3/1/0973 081290141X
Children -- Employment -- United States.

HD6278 Labor. Work. Working class — Classes of labor — College graduates

HD6278.U5.F73 1976
Freeman, Richard B. 1943-
The overeducated American/ Richard B. Freeman. New York: Academic Press, c1976. xi, 218 p.
75-036646 331.7/1 012267250X
College graduates -- Employment -- United States. Labor supply -- United States.

HD6278.U5.R85
Rumberger, Russell W.
Overeducation in the U.S. labor market/ Russell W. Rumberger; foreword by Henry M. Levin. New York: Praeger, 1981. x, 148 p.
80-024648 331.11/423 0030579643
College graduates -- Employment -- United States. Education, Higher -- Economic aspects -- United States. Labor supply -- United States.

HD6279-6280 Labor. Work. Working class — Classes of labor — Middle-aged workers. Aged workers

HD6279.L48 1988
Levine, Martin.
Age discrimination and the mandatory retirement controversy/ Martin Lyon Levine. Baltimore: Johns Hopkins University Press, c1988. xvii, 231 p.
88-009280 331.3/94 0801833574
Aged -- Employment. Age discrimination in employment. Retirement, Mandatory.

HD6280.A447 1990
The Aging of the American work force: problems, programs, policies/ edited by Irving Bluestone, Rhonda J.V. Montgomery, and John D. Owen; with a foreword by Ann McLaughlin. Detroit: Wayne State University Press, c1990. 429 p.
89-005572 331.3/94/0973 0814321747
Age and employment -- United States.

HD6300 Labor. Work. Working class — Classes of labor — Immigrant labor. Alien labor

HD6300.P6813 1990
Potts, Lydia, 1957-
The world labour market: a history of migration/ Lydia Potts; translated by Terry Bond. London; Zed Books, 1990. 247 p.
89-025041 331.12/791 0862328829
Alien labor -- History. Forced labor -- History.

HD6300.S734 2000
Stalker, Peter.
Workers without frontiers: the impact of globalization on international migration/ Peter Stalker. Boulder, Colo.: Lynne Rienner Publishers; c2000. xii, 163 p.
99-037487 331.6/2 21 1555878563
Alien labor. Emigration and immigration -- Economic aspects. International economic relations.

HD6331-6331.2 Labor. Work. Working class — Machinery in the workplace. Technological unemployment. Effect of technological innovations on employees — General works

HD6331.C279 2000
Carnoy, Martin.
Sustaining the new economy: work, family, and community in the information age/ Martin Carnoy. New York, N.Y.: Russell Sage Foundation; 2000. xi, 238 p.
00-027030 306.3/6 067400373X
Employees -- Effect of technological innovations on. Work and family.

HD6331.T419 1992
Technology and the future of work/ Paul S. Adler, editor. New York: Oxford University Press, 1992. xiv, 336 p.
91-017526 331.25 0195071719
Employees -- Effect of technological innovations on.

HD6331.2.A8.J66 1982
Jones, Barry O.
Sleepers, wake!: technology and the future of work/ Barry Jones. Melbourne; Oxford University Press, 1982. 285 p.
83-125170 303.4/83/0994 0195543432
Machinery in the workplace -- Australia. Technological innovations -- Social aspects -- Australia. Technological unemployment -- Australia.

HD6338.2 Labor. Work. Working class — Church and labor — By region or country, A-Z

HD6338.2.U5.L39 1995
Lazerow, Jama.
Religion and the working class in antebellum America/ Jama Lazerow. Washington: Smithsonian Institution Press, c1995. xxi, 353 p.
95-008600 261.8/34562/097309034 1560985445
Church and labor -- United States -- History -- 19th century. Labor movement -- United States -- Religious aspects -- Protestant churches -- History -- 19th century. Working class -- Religious life -- United States -- History -- 19th century.

HD6338.2.U5.L55 1984
Link, Eugene P., 1907-
Labor-religion prophet: the times and life of Harry F. Ward/ Eugene P. Link; with a foreword by Corliss Lamont and illustrations by Lynd Ward. Boulder, Colo.: Westview Press, 1984. xxiii, 351 p.
83-017108 261.8/34562/0924 086531621X
Ward, Harry Fredrick, -- 1873-1966. Church and labor -- United States -- History. Church and social problems -- United States -- History. Sociology, Christian -- United States -- History.

HD6476-6477 Labor. Work. Working class — Trade unions. Labor unions. Workers' associations — History

HD6476.T47 1987
Theories of the labor movement/ edited by Simeon Larson and Bruce Nissen. Detroit, Mich.: Wayne State University Press, 1987. xi, 395 p.
86-032414 331.88/09 0814318150
Labor unions -- History.

HD6477.S523 1941
Sorel, Georges, 1847-1922.
Reflections on violence, by Georges Sorel. Authorised translation, by T. E. Hulme. New York, P. Smith, 1941. x, 299 p.
41-003199 331.8862
Strikes and lockouts. Syndicalism.

HD6483 Labor. Work. Working class — Trade unions. Labor unions. Workers' associations — General works

HD6483.A26 1984
Addison, John T.
Trade unions and society: some lessons of the British experience/ John T. Addison and John Burton. Vancouver, B.C., Canada: Fraser Institute, 1984. xxviii, 190 p.
84-184353   331.88   0889750564
Labor unions. Labor unions -- Great Britain.

HD6483.F74
Frontiers of collective bargaining. John T. Dunlop and Neil W. Chamberlain, editors. New York, Harper & Row [1967] ix, 318 p.
67-022525   331.1/16
Collective bargaining -- Addresses, essays, lectures.

HD6483.M78
Mulvey, Charles.
The economic analysis of trade unions/ Charles Mulvey. New York: St. Martin's Press, 1978. viii, 159 p.
78-009094   331.88   0312226845
Labor unions. Labor economics.

HD6483.T673 1981
Trade unions in the developed economies/ edited by E. Owen Smith. New York: St. Martin's, 1981. 218 p.
81-051469   331.88/09172/2   0312812221
Labor unions -- Case studies.

HD6483.T87 1991
Turner, Lowell.
Democracy at work: changing world markets and the future of labor unions/ Lowell Turner. Ithaca, N.Y.: Cornell University Press, 1991. xvi, 279 p.
91-055049   331   0801426278
Industrial relations. Labor unions. Industrial management -- Employee participation.

HD6490 Labor. Work. Working class — Trade unions. Labor unions. Workers' associations — Special topics

HD6490.C612.U65 1988
Gitelman, Howard M.
Legacy of the Ludlow Massacre: a chapter in American industrial relations/ H.M. Gitelman. Philadelphia: University of Pennsylvania Press, c1988. xv, 355 p.
87-035843   331.89/2822334/0978851
0812280997
King, William Lyon Mackenzie, -- 1874-1950. Rockefeller, John D. -- (John Davison), -- 1874-1960. Company unions -- United States -- History -- 20th century. Coal Strike, Colo., 1913-1914.

HD6490.F582.G78 1988
Weiler, Peter, 1942-
British Labour and the cold war/ Peter Weiler. Stanford, Calif.: Stanford University Press, 1988. ix, 431 p.
88-002299   322/.2/0941   0804714649
World politics -- 1945- Labor unions and international relations -- Great Britain. Cold War. Great Britain -- Politics and government -- 1945-1964.

HD6490.O72.U64 1982
Fulmer, William E.
Union organizing: management and labor conflict/ William E. Fulmer. New York, N.Y.: Praeger, 1982. 228 p.
82-016172   331.89/12   003062603X
Labor unions -- Organizing -- United States.

HD6490.R22.U647 1995
Griffler, Keith P.
What price alliance?: Black radicals confront White labor, 1918-1938/ Keith P. Griffler. New York: Garland, 1995. v, 266 p.
94-032944   331.6/396073   0815319215
Afro-American labor union members -- History -- 20th century. Afro-American communists -- History -- 20th century.

HD6490.S6.V313
Vall, Mark van de.
Labor organizations; a macro-and micro-sociological analysis on a comparative basis. [London] Cambridge, University Press, 1970. xi, 257 p.
75-100030   301.5/5   0521076374
Labor unions -- Social aspects.

HD6508-6857 Labor. Work. Working class — Trade unions. Labor unions. Workers' associations — By region or country

HD6508.B59
Bok, Derek Curtis.
Labor and the American community, by Derek C. Bok and John T. Dunlop. New York, Simon and Schuster [1970] 542 p.
78-092184   331/.0973   0671203665
Labor unions -- United States. Collective bargaining -- United States.

HD6508.B8113
Brody, David, 1930-
Workers in industrial America: essays on the twentieth century struggle/ David Brody. New York: Oxford University Press, 1980. ix, 257 p.
78-027157   331.88/0973   0195024907
Labor unions -- United States -- History. Working class -- United States -- History -- 20th century.

HD6508.D44 1972
Derber, Milton.
Labor and the New Deal, edited by Milton Derber and Edwin Young. New York, Da Capo Press, 1972 [c1957] xi, 392 p.
70-169656   331.88/0973   0306703645
Labor unions -- United States. Labor movement -- United States. New Deal, 1933-1939.

HD6508.F57 1975
Foner, Philip Sheldon, 1910-
History of the labor movement in the United States/ by Philip S. Foner. New York: International Publishers, [1975-c1988]
75-315606   331.88/0973   071780092X
Labor unions -- United States -- History. Labor movement -- United States -- History.

HD6508.G275 1996
Galenson, Walter, 1914-
The American labor movement, 1955-1995/ Walter Galenson. Westport, Conn.: Greenwood Press, 1996. x, 171 p.
95-035686   331.88/0973/09045   0313296774
Labor unions -- United States -- History -- 20th century. Labor unions -- United States.

HD6508.M583 1971
Mills, C. Wright 1916-1962.
The new men of power; America's labor leaders, by C. Wright Mills with the assistance of Helen Schneider. New York, A. M. Kelley [1971, c1948] 323 p.
68-056261   331.873/0973   0678007152
Labors unions -- United States -- History. Labor leaders -- United States -- History.

HD6508.T25
Taft, Philip, 1902-
Organized labor in American history. New York, Harper & Row [1964] xxi, 818 p.
64-012712   331.880973
Labor unions -- United States -- History.

HD6508.U43 1993
Union voices: labor's responses to crisis/ edited by Glenn Adler and Doris Suarez. Albany, N.Y.: State University of New York Press, c1993. vi, 321 p.
91-038444   331.88/0973   0791412474
Labor unions -- United States.

HD6508.5.O36 1997
O'Donnell, L. A., 1925-
Irish voice and organized labor in America: a biographical study/ L.A. O'Donnell. Westport, Conn.: Greenwood Press, 1997. xiv, 227 p.
95-048358   331.88/089/9162073   0313299447
Labor unions -- United States -- Officials and employees -- Biography. Labor unions -- United States -- History. Labor leaders -- United States -- Biography.

HD6509.C48.G75 1995
Griswold del Castillo, Richard.
Cesar Chavez: a triumph of spirit/ by Richard Griswold del Castillo and Richard A. Garcia. Norman, Okla: University of Oklahoma Press, c1995. xvii, 206 p.
95-015230   331.88/13/092 B 20   0806127589
Chavez, Cesar, -- 1927- Migrant agricultural laborers -- Labor unions -- United States -- Officials and employees -- Biography. Labor leaders -- United States -- Biography. Mexican American migrant agricultural laborers -- Biography.

HD6509.D8.A33
Dubinsky, David, 1892-
David Dubinsky: a life with labor/ David Dubinsky and A. H. Raskin. New York: Simon and Schuster, c1977. 351 p.
76-052414   331.88/18/7120924   0671224379
Dubinsky, David, -- 1892- Clothing workers -- Labor unions -- United States -- History. Trade-unions -- United States -- Officials and employees -- Biography.

HD6509.M37.A33
Marquart, Frank, 1898-
An auto worker's journal: the UAW from crusade to one-party union/ Frank Marquart. University Park: Pennsylvania State University Press, c1975 161 p.
75-011993   331.88/12/920924   0271011963
Marquart, Frank, -- 1898-

HD6509.M375.S25 1988
Salmond, John A.
Miss Lucy of the CIO: the life and times of Lucy Randolph Mason, 1882-1959/ John A. Salmond. Athens: University of Georgia Press, c1988. xiii, 227 p.
87-005822   331.88/33/0924   0820309567
Mason, Lucy Randolph, -- 1882-1959.   Labor unions -- United States -- Officials and employees -- Biography. Feminists -- United States -- Biography.

HD6509.R4.L53 1995
Lichtenstein, Nelson.
The most dangerous man in Detroit: Walter Reuther and the fate of American labor/ Nelson Lichtenstein. New York, NY: Basic Books, c1995. xiii, 575 p.
95-016874   331.88/1292/092 B 20   046509080X
Reuther, Walter, -- 1907-1970.   Labor leaders -- United States -- Biography. Trade-unions -- Automobile industry workers -- United States -- History. Labor unions -- United States -- Officials and employees -- Biography.

HD6510.A46 2001
American labor unions in the electoral arena/ Herbert B. Asher ... [et al.]. Lanham, Md.: Rowman & Littlefield, c2001. xiii, 207 p.
00-051762   322/.2/0973 21   0847688658
Labor unions -- United States -- Political activity -- History. Presidents -- United States -- Election -- History. Elections -- United States -- History.

HD6510.F67 1991
Forbath, William E., 1952-
Law and the shaping of the American labor movement/ William E. Forbath. Cambridge, Mass.: Harvard University Press, 1991. xvi, 211 p.
90-049662   322/.2/0973   0674517814
Labor unions -- United States -- Political activity -- History. Working class -- United States -- Political activity -- History. Labor disputes -- United States -- History.

HD6515.A29.M44
Meister, Dick.
A long time coming: the struggle to unionize America's farm workers/ Dick Meister and Anne Loftis. New York: Macmillan, c1977. xi, 241 p.
76-054510   331.88/13/0973   0025839209
Agricultural laborers -- Labor unions -- United States -- History.

HD6515.A292.C33
Galarza, Ernesto, 1905-
Farm workers and agri-business in California, 1947-1960/ Ernesto Galarza. Notre Dame: University of Notre Dame Press, c1977. xvii, 405 p.
76-051615   331.88/13/09794   0268009414
Agricultural laborers -- Labor unions -- California -- History.

HD6515.A292.C38 1975
Taylor, Ronald B.
Chavez and the farm workers/ Ronald B. Taylor. Boston: Beacon Press, [1975] ix, 342 p.
74-016671   331.88/13/0924   0807004987
Chavez, Cesar, -- 1927- Agricultural laborers -- Labor unions -- California.

HD6515.A8.H6
Howe, Irving.
The UAW and Walter Reuther, by Irving Howe and B.J. Widick. New York, Random House [1949] x, 309 p.
49-005873   331.881292
Reuther, Walter, -- 1907-1970.

HD6515.A82.I574 1988
Halpern, Martin, 1945-
UAW politics in the cold war era/ Martin Halpern. Albany, N.Y.: State University of New York Press, c1988. 361 p.
87-013890   322/.2/0973   0887066712
Trade-unions and communism -- United States -- History -- Case studies.

HD6515.C27.F75 1994
Friday, Chris, 1959-
Organizing Asian American labor: the Pacific Coast canned-salmon industry, 1870-1942/ Chris Friday. Philadelphia: Temple University Press, 1994. viii, 276 p.
93-029471   331.6/25079   1566391393
Cannery workers -- Labor unions -- Pacific Coast (U.S.) Salmon canning industry -- Pacific Coast (U.S.) -- Employees. Asian Americans -- Employment -- Pacific Coast (U.S.)

HD6515.C5.C33
Carpenter, Jesse T. 1899-1986.
Competition and collective bargaining in the needle trades, 1910-1967. Ithaca, New York State School of Industrial and Labor Re 1972. xx, 910 p.
79-630987   331.89/048/70973   0875460356
Collective bargaining -- Clothing industry -- United States. Clothing trade -- United States.

HD6515.C62.I558 1995
Tyler, Gus.
Look for the union label: a history of the International Ladies' Garment Workers' Union/ Gus Tyler. Armonk, N.Y.: M.E. Sharpe, c1995. xxiii, 336 p.
94-025223   331.4/78187/0973 20   1563244098
Clothing workers -- Labor unions -- United States -- History. Women clothing workers -- United States -- History.

HD6515.F72.U547 1987
Ruiz, Vicki.
Cannery women, cannery lives: Mexican women, unionization, and the California food processing industry, 1930-1950/ Vicki L. Ruiz. Albuquerque: University of New Mexico Press, c1987. xviii, 194 p.
87-013878   331.88/1640282/09794   0826310060
Women labor union members -- California -- History -- Case studies. Mexican American women -- California -- History -- Case studies. Women cannery workers -- California -- History -- Case studies.

HD6515.L92.H853 1987
Cornford, Daniel A., 1947-
Workers and dissent in the redwood empire/ Daniel A. Cornford. Philadelphia: Temple University Press, 1987. x, 276 p.
87-006526   322/.2/0979412   0877224994
Lumbermen -- Labor unions -- California -- Humboldt County -- History. Lumbermen -- California -- Humboldt County -- History. Humboldt County (Calif.) -- Politics and government. Humboldt County (Calif.) -- Economic conditions. Humboldt County (Calif.) -- Social conditions.

HD6515.M615.P47 1984
Perry, Charles R.
Collective bargaining and the decline of the United Mine Workers/ by Charles R. Perry. Philadelphia, Pa., U.S.A.: Industrial Research Unit, the Wharton School, Un c1984. xi, 273 p.
84-047503   331.88/122/0973   0895460432
Collective bargaining -- Coal mining industry -- United States. Coal miners -- Labor unions -- United States.

HD6515.R36.S26 1989
Santino, Jack.
Miles of smiles, years of struggle: stories of Black Pullman porters/ Jack Santino. Urbana: University of Illinois Press, c1989. x, 160 p.
88-020981   331.88/1138522/0973   0252015916
Afro-American labor union members -- History. Discrimination in employment -- United States -- History. Race discrimination -- United States -- History.

HD6515.S4.N45 1988
Nelson, Bruce, 1940-
Workers on the waterfront: seamen, longshoremen, and unionism in the 1930s/ Bruce Nelson. Urbana: University of Illinois Press, c1988. xiii, 352 p.
87-028749   331.88/113875/0973   0252014871
Merchant mariners -- Labor unions -- United States -- History -- 20th century. Stevedores -- Labor unions -- United States -- History -- 20th century. Strikes and lockouts -- Merchant marine -- United States -- History -- 20th century.

HD6515.T3.H6
Hoffa, James R. 1913-
The trials of Jimmy Hoffa, an autobiography [by] James R. Hoffa. As told to Donald I. Rogers. Chicago, H. Regnery Co. [1970] 308 p.
72-095364   331.881/1/3883240924
Hoffa, James R. -- (James Riddle), -- 1913- Hoffa, James R. -- (James Riddle), -- 1913- Trade-unions -- United States -- Officials and employees -- Biography.

HD6517.A13.O74 1991
Organized labor in the twentieth-century South/ edited by Robert H. Zieger. Knoxville: University of Tennessee Press, c1991. 289 p.
90-022448   331.88/0975/0904   0870496972
Labor unions -- Southern States -- History -- Sources.   Southern States -- Race relations -- Sources.

HD6517.T4.Z363 1993
Zamora, Emilio.
The world of the Mexican worker in Texas / Emilio Zamora. College Station: Texas A&M University Press, c1993. xii, 285 p.
92-024813   331.6/2720764/09041   0890965145
Labor unions -- Texas -- History -- 20th century. Labor unions -- Mexico -- History -- 20th century. Mexicans -- Employment -- Texas -- History -- 20th century.

HD6519.M45.H66 1993
Honey, Michael K.
Southern labor and Black civil rights: organizing Memphis workers/ Michael K. Honey. Urbana: University of Illinois Press, c1993. xiii, 364 p.
92-028735   331.6/396073076819   0252020006
Labor unions -- Tennessee -- Memphis -- History -- 20th century. Afro-American labor union members -- Tennessee -- Memphis. Labor movement -- Tennessee -- Memphis -- History -- 20th century.

HD6524.W56 1989
Winch, David M., 1933-
Collective bargaining and the public interest: a welfare economics assessment/ David M. Winch. Kingston: McGill-Queen's University Press, c1989. viii, 184 p.
90-127356   331.89/0971   0773506969
Collective bargaining -- Canada. Labor unions -- Canada. Welfare economics

HD6528.P42.E537 1990
Rankin, Thomas Donald.
New forms of work organization: the challenge for
North American unions/ Tom Rankin. Toronto;
University of Toronto Press, c1990. xvi, 191 p.
92-121266   331.88/166/00971327   0802026982
*Chemical workers -- Labor unions -- Ontario --
Sarnia. Petroleum industry and trade -- Ontario --
Sarnia. Petroleum workers -- Labor unions --
Ontario -- Sarnia.*

HD6530.5.A7213
Alba, Victor.
Politics and the labor movement in Latin America.
Stanford, Calif.: Stanford University Press, 1968.
404 p.
66-015298   331.88/098
*Trade-unions -- Latin America. Labor movement
-- Latin America -- History. Latin America --
Politics and government.*

HD6530.5.L38 1987
Latin American labor organizations/ edited by
Gerald Michael Greenfield and Sheldon L. Maram.
New York: Greenwood Press, 1987. xiv, 929 p.
86-033613   331.88/098   0313228345
*Labor unions -- Latin America -- History. Labor
movement -- Latin America -- History.*

HD6602.B3
Baily, Samuel L.
Labor, nationalism, and politics in Argentina [by]
Samuel L. Baily. New Brunswick, N.J., Rutgers
University Press [1967] ix, 241 p.
67-023508   322/.4/0982
*Labor unions -- Argentina. Nationalism --
Argentina. Argentina -- Politics and government --
1943-1955.*

HD6614.A29.P47 1997
Pereira, Anthony W.
The end of the peasantry: the rural labor movement
in northeast Brazil, 1961-1988/ Anthony W.
Pereira. Pittsburgh, Pa.: University of Pittsburgh
Press, c1997. xxi, 232 p.
96-045889   331.88/13/09813 21   0822939649
*Agricultural laborers -- Labor unions -- Brazil,
Northeast -- History. Peasantry -- Brazil,
Northeast -- History. Land reform -- Brazil,
Northeast -- History.*

HD6657.E946 1992
European labor unions/ edited by Joan Campbell.
Westport, Conn.: Greenwood Press, 1992. xvii,
648 p.
92-012281   331.88/094   031326371X
Labor unions -- Europe -- Encyclopedias.

HD6657.T69 2000
Trade unions, immigration, and immigrants in
Europe, 1960-1993: a comparative study of the
attitudes and actions of trade unions in seven West
European countries/ edited by Rinus Penninx and
Judith Roosblad. New York: Berghahn Books,
2000. viii, 248 p.
99-045029   331.88/094   1571817646
*Labor unions -- Europe, Western -- Case studies.
Alien labor -- Europe, Western -- Case studies.
Emigration and immigration -- Government policy
-- Europe, Western -- Case studies.*

HD6658.5.S59 1996
Slomp, Hans, 1945-
Between bargaining and politics: an introduction to
European labor relations/ Hans Slomp. Westport,
Conn.: Praeger, 1996. xvi, 165 p.
96-002205   322/.2/094   0275956083
*Labor unions -- Europe -- Political activity.
Collective bargaining -- Europe. Industrial
relations -- Europe.*

HD6664.B598 1995
Booth, Alison L.
The economics of the trade union/ Alison L. Booth.
Cambridge; Cambridge University Press, 1995.
xvi, 295 p.
93-050224   331.88/0941   0521464676
*Labor unions -- Economic aspects -- Great
Britain. Labor unions -- Economic aspects --
United States. Labor market -- Great Britain.*

HD6664.M37 1988
McIlroy, John.
Trade unions in Britain today/ John McIlroy.
Manchester; Manchester University Press; c1988.
x, 261 p.
88-011781   331.88/0941   0719026547
Labor unions -- Great Britain.

HD6664.T4 1978
Taylor, Robert, 1943-
The Fifth estate: Britain's unions in the seventies/
Robert Taylor. London; Routledge & K. Paul,
1978. xvi, 368 p.
77-030402   331.88/0941   0710087519
Labor unions -- Great Britain.

HD6667.B76 1983
Brown, Henry Phelps, 1906-
The origins of trade union power/ by Henry Phelps
Brown. Oxford: Clarendon Press; 1983. vi, 320 p.
83-001920   322/.2/0941   0198771150
*Labor unions -- Great Britain -- Political activity
-- History. Labor policy -- Great Britain -- History.
Trade-unions -- Political activity.*

HD6670.3.B69 1988
Boyle, John William, 1914-
The Irish labor movement in the nineteenth
century/ John W. Boyle. Washington, D.C.:
Catholic University of America Press, c1988. xvi,
384 p.
87-027983   331.88/09415   0813206375
*Labor unions -- Ireland -- History -- 19th
century. Working class -- Ireland -- History -- 19th
century.*

HD6684.J46 1990
Jennings, Jeremy, 1952-
Syndicalism in France: a study of ideas/ Jeremy
Jennings. New York: St. Martin's Press, 1990. viii,
276 p.
89-024114   335/.82/0944   031204027X
Syndicalism -- France -- History.

HD6687.H67 1990
Horne, John N.
Labour at war: France and Britain, 1914-1918/
John N. Horne. Oxford [England]: Clarendon
Press; 1991. xix, 463 p.
90-037796   322/.2/094109044   019820180X
*Labor unions -- France -- Political activity.
Labor unions -- Great Britain -- Political activity.
World War, 1914-1918 -- Social aspects -- France.*

HD6709.B36 1995
Bedani, Gino, 1940-
Politics and ideology in the Italian workers'
movement: union development and the changing
role of the Catholic and communist subcultures in
postwar Italy/ Gino Bedani. Oxford, UK; Berg,
1995. xiii, 365 p.
95-145333   085496827X
*Labors unions -- Italy -- History -- 20th century.
Labors unions -- Italy -- Political activity. Church
and labor -- Italy. Italy -- Politics and government
-- 20th century.*

HD6732.B7
Brown, Emily Clark, 1895-
Soviet trade unions and labor relations.
Cambridge, Harvard University Press, 1966. ix,
394 p.
66-021332   331.1947
*Trade-unions -- Soviet Union. Industrial
relations -- Soviet Union.*

HD6763.5.F57 1990
Fishman, Robert M., 1955-
Working-class organization and the return to
democracy in Spain/ Robert M. Fishman. Ithaca,
N.Y.: Cornell University Press, 1990. xiii, 277 p.
89-042887   322/.2/094609048   080142061X
*Labor unions -- Spain -- Political activity --
History -- 20th century. Working class -- Spain --
History -- 20th century. Representative government
and representation -- Spain -- History -- 20th
century. Spain -- Politics and government -- 1975-*

HD6796.L3 1988
Labour and unions in Asia and Africa:
contemporary issues/ edited by Roger Southall.
New York: St. Martin's Press, 1988. x, 258 p.
87-021475   331.88/095   0312013620
Labor unions -- Asia. Labor unions -- Africa.

HD6812.S56 1984
Sinha, Ramesh P.
Social dimension of trade unionism in India/ R.P.
Sinha. New Delhi: Uppal Pub. House, c1984. xiii,
193 p.
84-900975   331.88/0954
Labor unions -- India.

HD6832.A97
Ayusawa, Iwao Frederick, 1894-
A history of labor in modern Japan, by Iwao F.
Ayusawa. Honolulu, East-West Center Press
[c1966] xvi, 406 p.
66-030068   331.88/0952
Labor unions -- Japan. -- Japan -- History.

HD6857.D3
Davies, Ioan, 1936-
African trade unions. Harmondsworth, Penguin,
1966. 256 p.
66-073537   331.88096
Labor unions -- Africa.

HD6955 Labor. Work.
Working class —
Industrial sociology.
Social conditions of labor —
General works

HD6955.B73 1995
Braun, Jerome.
The humanized workplace: a psychological,
historical, and practical perspective/ Jerome
Braun. Westport, Conn.: Praeger, 1995. xiii, 179 p.
94-031694   306.3/6   027594915X
*Quality of work life. Industrial sociology. Work
environment.*

HD6955.R47 1999
Rethinking the labor process/ edited by Mark
Wardell, Thomas L. Steiger, and Peter Meiksins.
Albany, N.Y.: State University of New York Press,
c1999. ix, 279 p.
98-051013   331 21   0791442810
*Braverman, Harry. Industrial sociology. Division
of labor. Employees -- Effect of technological
innovations on.*

HD6957 Labor. Work.
Working class —
Industrial sociology.
Social conditions of labor —
By region or country, A-Z

HD6957.U6.B55 1992
Bluestone, Barry.
Negotiating the future: a labor perspective on American business/ Barry Bluestone and Irving Bluestone. New York, NY: Basic Books, c1992. xv, 335 p.
91-059007   331/.0973   0465049176
Industrial relations -- United States. Management -- Employee participation -- United States.

HD6957.U6.N48 1995
The new modern times: factors reshaping the world of work/ edited by David B. Bills. Albany: State University of New York Press, c1995. ix, 319 p.
94-001044   306.3/6/0973 20   0791422275
Work -- Social aspects -- United States. Industrial sociology -- United States. Technological innovations -- United States.

HD6971 Labor. Work.
Working class —
Industrial relations —
General works

HD6971.B368 1985
Bean, R. 1938-
Comparative industrial relations: an introduction to cross-national perspectives/ R. Bean. New York: St. Martin's Press, 1985. 261 p.
84-022889   331   031215335X
Industrial relations. Comparative industrial relations.

HD6971.M39 1977
Mayo, Elton, 1880-1949.
The human problems of an industrial civilization/ Elton Mayo. New York: Arno Press, 1977, c1933. 194 p.
77-070515   658.3   0405101848
Industrial relations. Personnel management. Industrial sociology.

HD6971.M79
Multinationals, unions, and labor relations in industrialized countries/ Robert F. Banks and Jack Stieber, editors. Ithaca: New York State School of Industrial & Labor Rela 1977. viii, 200 p.
77-004463   331   087546064X
Industrial relations -- Congresses. International business enterprises -- Congresses. Collective bargaining -- International business enterprises -- Congresses.

HD6971.S82 1999
The state and globalization: comparative studies of labour and capital in national economies/ edited by Martin Upchurch. New York: Mansell, 1999.
98-052856   331   0720123674
Industrial relations. International division of labor. International economic integration.

HD6971.W856 1994
Workplace industrial relations and the global challenge/ edited by Jacques Belanger, P.K. Edwards, and Larry Haiven, editors. Ithaca, N.Y.: ILR Press, c1994. ix, 325 p.
94-001668   331   0875463274
Comparative industrial relations. Comparative management. Industrial management -- Case studies.

HD6971.5 Labor. Work.
Working class —
Industrial relations —
Collective bargaining

HD6971.5.F75 1994
Friedman, Raymond A. 1958-
Front stage, backstage: the dramatic structure of labor negotiations/ Raymond A. Friedman. Cambridge, Mass.: MIT Press, c1994. xi, 257 p.
93-044591   331.89   0262061678
Collective bargaining.

HD6971.8 Labor. Work.
Working class —
Industrial relations —
Employee rights

HD6971.8.E38 1993
Edwards, Richard, 1944-
Rights at work: employment relations in the post-union era/ Richard Edwards. Washington, D.C.: Brookings Institution, c1993. xii, 265 p.
92-043228   331.01/1/0973   0815721048
Employee rights -- United States.

HD7023 Labor. Work.
Working class —
Cost and standard of living —
By region or country

HD7023.B78 1981
Brown, Henry Phelps, 1906-
A perspective of wages and prices/ Henry Phelps Brown and Sheila V. Hopkins. London; Methuen, 1981. xvii, 214 p.
81-188230   331.2/941   0416319505
Cost and standard of living -- Great Britain -- History. Wages -- Great Britain -- History. Income distribution -- Great Britain -- History.

HD7091 Labor. Work.
Working class — Social insurance.
Social security. Pensions —
General works

HD7091.R48
Rimlinger, Gaston V., 1926-
Welfare policy and industrialization in Europe, America, and Russia [by] Gaston V. Rimlinger. New York, Wiley [1971] xi, 362 p.
74-132856   368.4   0471722200
Social security -- History -- Case studies. Public welfare -- History -- Case studies.

HD7096 Labor. Work.
Working class — Social insurance.
Social security. Pensions —
Unemployment insurance

HD7096.C2.S87 1983
Struthers, James, 1950-
No fault of their own: unemployment and the Canadian welfare state, 1914-1941/ James Struthers. Toronto; University of Toronto Press, c1983. x, 268 p.
83-177072   368.4/4/00971   0802024807
Insurance, Unemployment -- Canada -- History -- 20th century. Unemployment -- Canada -- History -- 20th century. Welfare state -- History -- 20th century.

HD7096.U5.B5397 1993
Blaustein, Saul J., 1924-
Unemployment insurance in the United States: the first half century/ Saul J. Blaustein; with Wilbur J. Cohen and William Haber. Kalamazoo, Mich.: W.E. Upjohn Insitute for Employment Research, 1993. xi, 367 p.
93-013480   368.4/4/00973   0880991364
Insurance, Unemployment -- United States -- History.

HD7096.U5.H275
Hamermesh, Daniel S.
Jobless pay and the economy/ Daniel S. Hamermesh. Baltimore: Johns Hopkins University Press, c1977. viii, 114 p.
76-047369   368.4/4/00973   080181927X
Insurance, Unemployment -- United States.

HD7101-7102 Labor. Work.
Working class — Social insurance.
Social security. Pensions —
State medical plans

HD7101.G54 1991
Glaser, William A.
Health insurance in practice: international variations in financing, benefits, and problems/ William A. Glaser. San Francisco: Jossey-Bass Publishers, 1991. xxi, 542 p.
91-007035   368.3   1555423736
Insurance, Health. Medicine, State. Financing, Organized -- economics.

HD7102.U4.C638 1994
Coughlin, Teresa A.
Medicaid since 1980: costs, coverage, and the shifting alliance between the federal government and the states/ Teresa A. Coughlin, Leighton Ku, and John Holahan. Washington, D.C.: Urban Institute Press; c1994. xvi, 181 p.
93-041868   368.4/2/00973   0877666172
Medicaid.

HD7105.3-7105.35 Labor. Work. Working class — Social insurance. Social security. Pensions — Old age pensions

HD7105.3.E58 1997
Enterprise and the welfare state/ edited by Martin Rein, Eskil Wadensjo. Cheltenham, UK; E. Elgar, c1997. xix, 385 p.
97-024228   331.25/2/0973 21   1858986648
Old age pensions -- Cross-cultural studies. Pension trusts -- Cross-cultural studies. Retirement income -- Cross-cultural studies.

HD7105.3.W67 1989
Workers versus pensioners: intergenerational justice in an ageing world/ edited by Paul Johnson, Christoph Conrad, and David Thomson. Manchester; Manchester University Press; c1989. xvi, 204 p.
89-031029   331.25/2   0719030382
Old age pensions -- Congresses. Old age pensions -- Finance -- Congresses. Intergenerational relations -- Congresses.

HD7105.35.U6.G45 1992
Ghilarducci, Teresa.
Labor's capital: the economics and politics of private pensions/ Teresa Ghilarducci. Cambridge, Mass.: MIT Press, c1992. xi, 213 p.
91-038544   331.25/2/0973   0262071398
Old age pensions -- United States. Pensions -- United States.

HD7125-7165 Labor. Work. Working class — Social insurance. Social security. Pensions — By region or country

HD7125.A178 1982
Aaron, Henry J.
Economic effects of social security/ Henry J. Aaron. Washington, D.C.: Brookings Institution, c1982. xii, 84 p.
82-073654   368.4/3/00973   081570030X
Social security -- United States.

HD7125.B38 1991
Berkowitz, Edward D.
America's welfare state: from Roosevelt to Reagan/ Edward D. Berkowitz. Baltimore: Johns Hopkins University Press, c1991. xxii, 216 p.
90-046424   361.973   0801841275
Social security -- United States. Public welfare -- United States. Medical care -- United States.

HD7125.B55 2000
Blahous, Charles P., 1963-
Reforming social security for ourselves and our posterity/ Charles P. Blahous III. Westport, Conn.: Praeger; 2000. xviii, 262 p.
00-035968   368.4/3/00973   0275970442
Social security -- United States. Social security -- United States -- Finance.

HD7125.C476 1982
A Challenge to social security: the changing roles of women and men in American society/ edited by Richard V. Burkhauser, Karen C. Holden. New York: Academic Press, c1982. xxii, 272 p.
82-001596   368.4/3/00973   0121446808
Social security -- United States. Survivors' benefits -- United States. Family policy -- United States.

HD7125.E267 1994
Economic security and intergenerational justice: a look at North America/ Theodore R. Marmor, Timothy M. Smeeding, Vernon L. Greene, editors. Washington, D.C.: Urban Institute Press; c1994. xvi, 355 p.
94-007382   368.4/3/00973   0877666199
Social security -- United States. Economic security -- United States. Social security -- Canada.

HD7125.S526 2000
Shaviro, Daniel N.
Making sense of Social Security reform/ Daniel Shaviro. Chicago: University of Chicago Press, c2000. xi, 177 p.
00-021709   368.4/3/00973 21   0226751163
Social security -- United States. Social security -- Finance -- Government policy -- United States.

HD7125.S5992 1988
Social security: beyond the rhetoric of crisis/ edited by Theodore R. Marmor, Jerry L. Mashaw. Princeton, N.J.: Princeton University Press, c1988. xvi, 249 p.
88-010238   368.4/3/00973   0691077762
Social security -- United States.

HD7125.S5994 1988
Social Security, the first half-century/ edited by Gerald D. Nash, Noel H. Pugach, Richard F. Tomasson. Albuquerque: University of New Mexico Press, c1988. xiii, 344 p.
87-036853   368.4/3/00973   0826310680
Social security -- United States -- History.

HD7130.5.M44 1989
Mesa-Lago, Carmelo, 1934-
Ascent to bankruptcy: financing social security in Latin America/ Carmelo Mesa-Lago. Pittsburgh, Pa.: University of Pittsburgh Press, c1989. xviii, 290 p.
89-035475   368.4/01/098   0822936003
Social security -- Latin America -- Finance -- Case studies. Social security -- Latin America -- Finance.

HD7130.5.M445 1994
Mesa-Lago, Carmelo, 1934-
Changing social security in Latin America: toward alleviating the social costs of economic reform/ Carmelo Mesa-Lago. Boulder, Colo.: Lynne Rienner, 1994. xii, 213 p.
93-038662   368.4/0098   155587486X
Social security -- Latin America. Structural adjustment (Economic policy) -- Latin America.

HD7165.H55 1990
Hill, Michael J. 1937-
Social security policy in Britain/ Michael Hill. Aldershot, Hants, England; E. Elgar, c1990. ix, 184 p.
90-038633   368.4/00941   1852783001
Social security -- Great Britain -- History. Social security -- Great Britain.

HD7256 Labor. Work. Working class — Vocational rehabilitation. Employment of people with disabilities — By region or country

HD7256.U5.B87 1982
Burkhauser, Richard V.
Disability and work: the economics of American policy/ Richard V. Burkhauser and Robert H. Haveman with the assistance of George Parsons. Baltimore: Johns Hopkins University Press, c1982. vii, 131 p.
82-000113   331.5/9/0973   0801828341
Handicapped -- Employment -- United States. Handicapped -- Government policy -- United States.

HD7256.U5.H39 1984
Haveman, Robert H.
Public policy toward disabled workers: cross-national analyses of economic impacts/ Robert H. Haveman, Victor Halberstadt, Richard V. Burkhauser. Ithaca: Cornell University Press, 1984. xi, 583 p.
83-073115   362.8/5/0973   0801416264
Vocational rehabilitation -- Government policy -- United States. Insurance, Disability -- Government policy -- United States. Vocational rehabilitation -- Government policy.

HD7262 Labor. Work. Working class — Industrial hygiene. Industrial welfare — Hazardous occupations. Industrial accidents

HD7262.D58 1996
Dorman, Peter.
Markets and mortality: economics, dangerous work, and the value of human life/ Peter Dorman. Cambridge [England]; Cambridge University Press, 1996. xi, 274 p.
95-009287   331.2   0521553067
Hazardous occupations -- Economic aspects. Industrial safety -- Economic aspects. Life -- Valuation.

HD7287-7361 Labor. Work. Working class — Industrial hygiene. Industrial welfare — Housing

HD7287.E53 1998
The encyclopedia of housing/ Willem Van Vliet--, editor. Thousand Oaks, Calif.: Sage, c1998. xxiv, 712 p.
98-008949   363.5/03 21   0761913327
Housing -- Encyclopedias. Housing -- United States -- Encyclopedias.

HD7287.R68 1993
Rowe, Peter G.
Modernity and housing/ Peter G. Rowe. Cambridge, Mass.: MIT Press, c1993. 408 p.
92-045140   363.5/09/04   0262181517
Housing -- History -- 20th century -- Case studies. Housing development -- History -- 20th century -- Case studies. Architecture, Domestic -- History -- 20th century -- Case studies.

HD7287.5.H46 1982
Housing and identity: cross-cultural perspectives/ edited by James S. Duncan. New York: Holmes & Meier, 1982. 250 p.
81-004837   363.5   0841907013
Housing. Housing -- Psychological aspects. Architecture, Domestic.

HD7287.82.M62.M494 1993
Gilbert, Alan, 1944-
In search of a home: rental and shared housing in Latin America/ Alan Gilbert, in association with Oscar Olinto Carnacho, Rene Coulomb, Andres Necochea. Tucson: University of Arizona Press, 1993. xii, 177 p.
92-045800   333.3/098   0816513880
Home ownership -- Mexico -- Mexico City. Home ownership -- Venezuela -- Caracas. Home ownership -- Chile -- Santiago.

HD7287.92.U54.G63 1992
Golant, Stephen M.
Housing America's elderly: many possibilities/few choices/ Stephen M. Golant. Newbury Park, Calif.: Sage Publications, c1992. xi, 354 p.
92-019949   363.5/946/0973   0803947631
Aged -- Housing -- United States.

HD7288.72.U5.E45 2000
Ellen, Ingrid Gould, 1965-
Sharing America's neighborhoods: the prospects for stable racial integration/ Ingrid Gould Ellen. Cambridge, Mass.: Harvard University Press, 2000. viii, 228 p.
00-038929   305.8/00973   0674003012
Afro-Americans -- Housing. Race discrimination -- United States. Neighborhood -- United States. United States -- Race relations.

HD7288.78.U52.C476 2000
Venkatesh, Sudhir Alladi.
American project: the rise and fall of a modern ghetto/ Sudhir Alladi Venkatesh. Cambridge, Mass.: Harvard University Press, 2000. xvi, 332 p.
00-039621   363.5/85/0977311   0674003217
Public housing -- Illinois -- Chicago. Afro-Americans -- Housing -- Illinois -- Chicago. Low-income housing -- Illinois -- Chicago.

HD7288.78.U52.C54 1988
Fairbanks, Robert B. 1950-
Making better citizens: housing reform and the community development strategy in Cincinnati, 1890-1960/ Robert B. Fairbanks. Urbana: University of Illinois Press, c1988. xii, 243 p.
88-001584   363.5/8   0252015541
Public housing -- Ohio -- Cincinnati -- History -- 20th century. Housing policy -- Ohio -- Cincinnati -- History -- 20th century. Community development -- Ohio -- Cincinnati -- History -- 20th century.

HD7288.78.U52.M48 2000
Vale, Lawrence J., 1959-
From the Puritans to the projects: public housing and public neighbors/ Lawrence J. Vale. Cambridge, MA: Harvard University Press, 2000. 460 p.
00-035084   363.5/85/0974461   0674002865
Public housing -- Massachusetts -- Boston -- History. Housing policy -- Massachusetts -- Boston -- History. Poor -- Massachusetts -- Boston -- History.

HD7288.92.U6.H68 1993
Housing markets and residential mobility/ G. Thomas Kingsley and Margery Austin Turner, editors. Washington, D.C.: Urban Institute Press; c1993. xxii, 315 p.
92-042594   304.8/0973   0877665826
Residential mobility -- United States. Discrimination in housing -- United States. Housing -- Resident satisfaction -- United States.

HD7289.62.U6.W35 1991
Wallis, Allan D.
Wheel estate: the rise and decline of mobile homes/ Allan D. Wallis. New York: Oxford University Press, 1991. x, 283 p.
90-031275   338.4/7690879/0973   0195061837
Mobile homes -- United States -- Psychological aspects. Mobile homes -- United States -- Sociological aspects. Mobile home industry -- United States.

HD7293.C583 1996
Clark, W. A. V.
Households and housing: choice and outcomes in the housing market/ William A.V. Clark, Frans M. Dieleman. New Brunswick, N.J.: Center for Urban Policy Research, c1996. xxiii, 252 p.
95-052803   333.33/822/09492 20   088285156X
Housing -- United States. Housing -- Netherlands. Households -- United States.

HD7293.H7822 1997
Housing statistics of the United States/ Patrick A. Simmons, editor. Lanham, Md., USA: Bernan Press, 1997. xxiv, 418 p.
97-214122   0890590656
Housing -- United States -- Statistics.

HD7293.H826 1987
Hughes, James W.
The dynamics of America's housing/ James W. Hughes, George Sternlieb. New Brunswick, N.J.: Center for Urban Policy Research, c1987. xiv, 224 p.
87-004515   363.5/0973   0882851225
Housing -- United States.

HD7293.L27 1989
Lang, Michael H.
Homelessness amid affluence: structure and paradox in the American political economy/ Michael H. Lang. New York: Praeger, 1989. xi, 236 p.
89-032271   363.5/1/0973   0275931676
Housing policy -- United States. Homelessness -- United States. Poor -- Housing -- United States.

HD7293.T77 1990
Tucker, William, 1942-
The excluded Americans: homelessness and housing policies/ William Tucker. Washington, D.C.: Regnery Gateway; c1990. xxiii, 389 p.
89-010769   363.5/8/0973   0895265516
Housing policy -- United States. Homelessness -- United States. Rent control -- United States.

HD7305.A3.S38 1987
Sayegh, Kamal S.
Housing: a Canadian perspective/ Kamal S. Sayegh. Ottawa: ABCD Academy Book, 1987. xi, 626 p.
88-129130   363.5/0971   0921139004
Housing -- Canada. Housing policy -- Canada.

HD7334.A3.B87
Burnett, John, 1925-
A social history of housing, 1815-1970/ John Burnett; illustrated by Christopher Powell. Newton Abbot [Eng.]; David and Charles, 1978. viii, 344 p.
77-091461   363.5/0941   0715375245
Housing -- England -- History.

HD7345.A3.A68 1984
Andrusz, Gregory D.
Housing and urban development in the USSR/ Gregory D. Andrusz. Albany: State University of New York Press, c1984. xix, 354 p.
83-024258   363.5/0947   0873959116
Housing -- Soviet Union. Housing policy -- Soviet Union. City planning -- Soviet Union.

HD7361.A3.W53
Wiebe, Paul D.
Social life in an Indian slum/ Paul D. Wiebe. Durham, N.C.: Carolina Academic Press, c1975. vi, 179 p.
75-005480   301.36/3   089089051X
Slums -- India. City and town life -- India. India -- Social conditions -- 1947-

HD7654 Labor. Work.
Working class —
Industrial hygiene.
Industrial welfare —
By region or country

HD7654.K63 1996
Kohn, James P.
Fundamentals of occupational safety and health/ James P. Kohn, Mark A. Friend, Celeste A. Winterberger. Rockville, Md.: Government Institutes, c1996. xxiii, 429 p.
96-207211   0865875391
Industrial safety -- United States. Industrial hygiene -- United States.

HD7801 Labor. Work.
Working class —
Labor policy. Labor and the state
— International bureaus

HD7801.A53 1971b
Alcock, Antony Evelyn.
History of the International Labor Organization, by Antony Alcock. New York, Octagon Books, 1971. x, 384 p.
78-144821   331/.061/1   0374901279
International Labour Organisation -- History.

HD8005.2-8005.6 Labor. Work.
Working class — Labor policy.
Labor and the state —
Trade unions for government
employees. Employee-management

HD8005.2.U5.R53 1990
Riccucci, Norma.
Women, minorities, and unions in the public sector/ Norma M. Riccucci. New York: Greenwood Press, 1990. xii, 189 p.
89-007481   331.4/781135/0000973   0313260435
Government employee unions -- United States. Women in the civil service -- United States. Civil service -- Minority employment -- United States.

HD8005.6.U5.P57 1992
Piskulich, John Patrick.
Collective bargaining in state and local government/ John Patrick Piskulich. New York: Praeger, 1992. xi, 127 p.
91-028142   331.89/04135/0000973   0275940438
Collective bargaining -- State government employees -- United States. Collective bargaining -- Government employees -- United States. Employee-management relations in government -- United States.

HD8008 Labor. Work. Working class — Labor policy. Labor and the state — Government business enterprise employees

HD8008.M6
Moskow, Michael H.
Collective bargaining in public employment [by] Michael H. Moskow, J. Joseph Loewenberg [and] Edward Clifford Koziara. New York, Random House [1970] xiv, 336 p.
78-101742   353.001/74
Collective bargaining -- Government employees -- United States.

HD8008.S36
Schick, Richard P.
The public interest in government labor relations/ Richard P. Schick, Jean J. Couturier. Cambridge, Mass.: Ballinger Pub. Co., c1977. xvi, 264 p.
76-046642   331.89/041/35   0884102459
Collective bargaining -- Government employees -- United States -- Case studies. Public interest.

HD8038 Labor. Work. Working class — Professions (General). Professional employees

HD8038.A1.C63 1993
Coalitions and competition: the globalization of professional business services/ edited by Yair Aharoni. London; Routledge, 1993. xii, 320 p.
93-006937   658.8   0415082285
Professions -- Marketing. Service industries -- Management.

HD8039 Labor. Work. Working class — By industry or trade, A-Z

HD8039.A82.U643 1988
End of the line: autoworkers and the American dream/ edited by Richard Feldman and Michael Betzold. New York: Weidenfeld & Nicolson, c1988. xvii, 297 p.
88-004108   338.7/6292/0973   1555841708
Automobile industry workers -- United States -- Interviews.

HD8039.A82.U653 1997
Milkman, Ruth, 1954-
Farewell to the factory: auto workers in the late twentieth century/ Ruth Milkman. Berkeley: University of California Press, c1997. xiii, 234 p.
96-022684   331.7/6292/0974936   20   0520206770
Automobile industry and trade -- New Jersey -- Linden. Automobile industry workers -- New Jersey -- Linden.

HD8039.B232.C83 1989
Bourgois, Philippe I., 1956-
Ethnicity at work: divided labor on a Central American banana plantation/ Philippe I. Bourgois. Baltimore: Johns Hopkins University Press, c1989. xviii, 311 p.
88-011778   331.6/097286   080183693X
Banana trade -- Costa Rica -- Employees -- Case studies. Banana trade -- Panama -- Employees -- Case studies. Discrimination in employment -- Costa Rica -- Case studies.

HD8039.B72.U63 1988
Blewett, Mary H.
Men, women, and work: class, gender, and protest in the New England shoe industry, 1780-1910/ Mary H. Blewett. Urbana: University of Illinois Press, c1988. xxii, 444 p.
87-019039   338.4/768531/00974   0252014847
Shoe industry -- New England -- Employees -- History -- 19th century. Shoe industry -- New England -- History -- 19th century. Working class -- New England -- History. New England -- Economic conditions.

HD8039.C6382.B67 1988
Stolcke, Verena.
Coffee planters, workers, and wives: class conflict and gender relations on Sao Paulo plantations, 1850-1980/ Verena Stolcke. New York: St. Martin's Press, 1988. xviii, 344 p.
87-030767   305.5/63   031201693X
Coffee plantation workers -- Brazil -- Sao Paulo (State) -- History. Women coffee plantation workers -- Brazil -- Sao Paulo (State) -- History. Coffee plantation workers' spouses -- Brazil -- Sao Paulo (State) -- History.

HD8039.C662.U68 1994
Weber, Devra, 1946-9
Dark sweat, white gold: California farm workers, cotton, and the New Deal/ Devra Weber. Berkeley: University of California Press, c1994. xv, 338 p.
93-036933   331.6/2720794   0520084896
Cotton farmers -- California -- History. Migrant agricultural laborers -- California -- History. Alien labor, Mexican -- California -- History.

HD8039.C662.Z285 1997
Likaka, Osumaka, 1953-
Rural society and cotton in colonial Zaire/ Osumaka Likaka. Madison, Wis.: University of Wisconsin Press, c1997. xvi, 189 p.
96-036690   338.1/7351/0967510941   20   0299153304
Cotton farmers -- Congo (Democratic Republic) -- History. Cotton trade -- Congo (Democratic Republic) -- History. Peasantry -- Congo (Democratic Republic) -- History. Congo (Democratic Republic) -- Rural conditions.

HD8039.D52.F85 1983
Maza, Sarah C., 1953-
Servants and masters in eighteenth-century France: the uses of loyalty/ Sarah C. Maza. Princeton, N.J.: Princeton University Press, c1983. xiv, 368 p.
83-042566   305.4/364   0691053944
Domestics -- France -- History -- 18th century. Master and servant -- France -- History -- 18th century.

HD8039.F32.U64
Fite, Gilbert Courtland, 1918-
American farmers: the new minority/ Gilbert C. Fite. Bloomington: Indiana University Press, c1981. ix, 265 p.
80-008843   306/.3   0253301823
Farmers -- United States. Farmers -- United States -- Political activity. Agriculture -- Economic aspects -- United States. United States -- Rural conditions.

HD8039.I52.U56
Kornblum, William.
Blue collar community/ William Kornblum; with a foreword by Morris Janowitz. Chicago: University of Chicago Press, 1974. xvii, 260 p.
74-005733   301.44/42/0977311   0226450376
Iron and steel workers -- Illinois -- Chicago. Iron and steel workers -- Labor unions -- Illinois -- Chicago. Iron and steel workers -- Illinois -- Chicago -- Political activity. Chicago (Ill.) -- Social conditions.

HD8039.L32.U675 1987
Siu, Paul C. P. 1906-
The Chinese laundryman: a study of social isolation/ Paul C.P. Siu; edited by John Kuo Wei Tchen. New York: New York University Press, c1987. xlii, 311 p.
87-005609   331.6/2/51073   0814778593
Laundry workers -- United States. Chinese Americans -- Social conditions.

HD8039.L452.U67 1985
Thomas, Robert J.
Citizenship, gender, and work: the social organization of industrial agriculture/ Robert J. Thomas. Berkeley: University of California Press, c1985. xiii, 247 p.
84-008626   305/.9633   0520053109
Lettuce industry -- Southwestern States -- Employees.

HD8039.M62.S68 1987
Shubert, Adrian, 1953-
The road to revolution in Spain: the coal miners of Asturias, 1860-1934/ Adrian Shubert. Urbana: University of Illinois Press, c1987. 183 p.
86-024998   331.7/622334/094615   0252013689
Coal miners -- Spain -- Asturias -- History -- 20th century. Strikes and lockouts -- Coal mining -- Spain -- Asturias -- History -- 20th century. Coal miners -- Labor unions -- Spain -- Asturias -- History -- 20th century.

HD8039.M62.U6444 1989
Long, Priscilla.
Where the sun never shines: a history of America's bloody coal industry/ Priscilla Long. New York: Paragon House, 1989. xxv, 420 p.
89-003157   338.2/724/0973   1557782245
Coal miners -- United States -- History. Coal miners -- Labor unions -- United States -- History. Strikes and lockouts -- Coal mining -- United States -- History.

HD8039.M62.U66943 1990
Trotter, Joe William, 1945-
Coal, class, and color: Blacks in southern West Virginia, 1915-32/ Joe William Trotter, Jr. Urbana: University of Illinois Press, c1990. xvi, 290 p.
89-020501   331.6/3960730754   0252061195
Afro-American coal miners -- West Virginia -- History -- 20th century. Afro-Americans -- West Virginia -- Social conditions.

HD8039.M732.S646 1992
James, Wilmot Godfrey, 1953-
Our precious metal: African labour in South Africa's gold industry, 1970-1990/ Wilmot G. James. Cape Town: D. Philip; 1992. ix, 188 p.
91-028479   331.7/6223422/0968   0864861656
Gold miners -- South Africa. Gold industry -- South Africa.

HD8039.M732.S655 1994
Moodie, T. Dunbar.
Going for gold: men, mines, and migration/ T. Dunbar Moodie with Vivienne Ndatshe. Berkeley: University of California Press, c1994. xxi, 337 p.
93-038187   305.9/622   0520081307
Gold miners -- South Africa -- Social conditions. Blacks -- South Africa -- Social conditions.

HD8039.R12.U612 2001
Arnesen, Eric.
Brotherhoods of color: black railroad workers and the struggle for equality/ Eric Arnesen. Cambridge, Mass.: Harvard University Press, 2001. 332 p.
00-057515   331.6/396073   0674003195
Railroads -- United States -- Employees -- History. African-Americans -- Employment -- History. Discrimination in employment -- United States -- History.

HD8039.S4.O67 1989
Sager, Eric W., 1946-
Seafaring labour: the merchant marine of Atlantic Canada, 1820-1914/ Eric W. Sager. Kingston, Ont.: McGill-Queen's University Press, 1989. xviii, 321 p.
89-199831   305/.93875/09715   0773506705
Merchant mariners -- Maritime Provinces -- History -- 19th century. Merchant mariners -- Newfoundland -- History -- 19th century. Merchant mariners -- Maritime Provinces -- History -- 19th century.

HD8039.S86.D647 1991
Murphy, Martin F. 1949-
Dominican sugar plantations: production and foreign labor integration/ Martin F. Murphy. New York: Praeger, 1991. xii, 186 p.
90-044147   331.6/21729407293   0275931137
Sugar workers -- Dominican Republic. Sugarcane industry -- Dominican Republic. Alien labor, Haitian -- Dominican Republic.

HD8039.S86.W475 1993
Look Lai, Walton.
Indentured labor, Caribbean sugar: Chinese and Indian migrants to the British West Indies, 1838-1918/ Walton Look Lai; introd. by Sidney W. Mintz. Baltimore: Johns Hopkins University Press, c1993. xxviii, 370 p.
92-033812   306.3/63   0801844657
Sugar workers -- West Indies, British -- History -- 19th century. Indentured servants -- West Indies, British -- History -- 19th century. Alien labor, Chinese -- West Indies, British -- History -- 19th century. West Indies, British -- Emigration and immigration -- History -- 19th century.

HD8039.T42.G72
Bythell, Duncan.
The handloom weavers: a study in the English cotton industry during the Industrial Revolution. London, Cambridge U.P., 1969. xiv, 302 p.
69-010487   338.4/7/67721   0521075807
Weavers -- Great Britain. Industrial revolution -- Great Britain.

HD8055-8085 Labor. Work. Working class — By region or country — America

HD8055.A5.L6 1972
Lorwin, Lewis Levitzki, 1883-1970.
The American Federation of Labor; history, policies, and prospects.   Clifton [N.J.] A. M. Kelley, 1972. xix, 573 p.
70-174559   331.88/32/0973   0678008809
American Federation of Labor.

HD8055.A5.T3 1970
Taft, Philip, 1902-
The A.F. of L. in the time of Gompers. New York, Octagon Books, 1970 [c1957] xx, 508 p.
71-096192   331.88/0973
American Federation of Labor.

HD8055.C75.G75 1988
Griffith, Barbara S.
The crisis of American labor: Operation Dixie and the defeat of the CIO/ Barbara S. Griffith. Philadelphia: Temple University Press, 1988. xvi, 239 p.
87-009998   331.88/33/0975   0877225036
Labor unions -- Organizing -- Southern States -- History.

HD8055.C75.K32 1971
Kampelman, Max M., 1920-
The Communist Party vs. the C.I.O. [by] Max M. Kampelman. New York, Arno, 1971 [c1957] xv, 299 p.
78-156445   331.88/33/0973   0405029292
Labor unions -- United States.

HD8055.C75.S7
Stolberg, Benjamin, 1891-1951.
The story of the CIO [by] Benjamin Stolberg. New York, The Viking press, 1938. 294 p.
38-031214
Congress of Industrial Organizations (U.S.)

HD8066.B45 1997
Bernstein, Paul, 1927-
American work values: their origin and development/ Paul Bernstein. Albany: State University of New York Press, c1997. viii, 368 p.
96-021982   306.3/613/0973 20   0791432157
Work ethic -- United States -- History. Industrialization -- United States -- History. Public welfare -- United States -- History.

HD8066.D76 2000
Dubofsky, Melvyn, 1934-
Hard work: the making of labor history/ Melvyn Dubofsky. Urbana: University of Illinois Press, 2000. ix, 249 p.
99-006862   331.88/0973/0904   0252025512
Labor -- United States -- History. Working class -- United States -- History. Labors unions -- United States -- History.

HD8066.J33 1998
Jacoby, Daniel, 1951-
Laboring for freedom: a new look at the history of labor in America/ Daniel Jacoby. Armonk, NY: M.E. Sharpe, c1998. ix, 209 p.
97-031985   331/.0973 21   0765602512
Labor -- United States -- History. Labor movement -- United States -- History. Labor policy -- United States -- History.

HD8066.K38 1993
Kaufman, Bruce E.
The origins & evolution of the field of industrial relations in the United States/ Bruce E. Kaufman. Ithaca, N.Y.: ILR Press, c1993. xv, 286 p.
92-019055   331/.0973   0875461913
Industrial relations -- United States -- History.

HD8070.G58 1991
Glickstein, Jonathan A., 1948-
Concepts of free labor in Antebellum America/ Jonathan A. Glickstein. New Haven: Yale University Press, c1991. 514 p.
91-012224   331.11/72/09034   0300047894
Manual work -- United States -- History -- 19th century -- Public opinion. Public opinion -- United States -- History -- 19th century. Manual work -- Great Britain -- History -- 19th century -- Public opinion.

HD8070.W67 1988
Work and labor in early America/ edited by Stephen Innes. Chapel Hill: Published for the Institute of Early American Hi c1988. 297 p.
87-038088   331/.0973   0807817988
Labor -- United States -- History. United States -- Economic conditions -- To 1865. United States -- Social conditions -- To 1865.

HD8072.A5136 1995
American labor in the era of World War II/ edited by Sally M. Miller and Daniel A. Cornford. Westport, Conn.: Praeger, 1995. x, 228 p.
94-024570   331/.0973/09046   0275951855
Labor -- United States -- History -- 20th century. Working class -- United States -- History -- 20th century. Industrial relations -- United States -- History -- 20th century.

HD8072.B365 1985
Bernstein, Irving, 1916-
A caring society: the New Deal, the worker, and the Great Depression: a history of the American worker, 1933-1941/ Irving Bernstein. Boston: Houghton Mifflin, 1985. 338 p.
84-025129   362.8/5/0973   0395331161
Working class -- United States -- History -- 20th century. Labor policy -- United States -- History -- 20th century. Unemployment -- United States -- History -- 20th century.

HD8072.D846 1985
Dubofsky, Melvyn, 1934-
Industrialism and the American worker, 1865-1920/ Melvyn Dubofsky. Arlington Heights, Ill.: H. Davidson, c1985. xiii, 167 p.
84-027407   331/.0973   0882958313
Working class -- United States -- History -- 19th century. Working class -- United States -- History -- 20th century. Labor unions -- United States -- History.

HD8072.G97 1987
Gutman, Herbert George, 1928-
Power & culture: essays on the American working class/ Herbert G. Gutman; edited by Ira Berlin. New York, N.Y.: Pantheon Books, c1987. xi, 452 p.
87-043018   305.5/62/0973   0394561716
Working class -- United States -- History. Afro-Americans -- History. Slavery -- United States -- History.

HD8072.G98 1976
Gutman, Herbert George, 1928-
Work, culture, and society in industrializing America: essays in American working-class and social history/ Herbert G. Gutman. New York: Knopf: distributed by Random House, c1976. xiv, 343 p.
75-035733   301.44/42/0973   0394496949
Working class -- United States -- History. Industrial relations -- United States -- History. United States -- Social conditions -- 1865-1918. United States -- Social conditions -- To 1865.

HD8072.M189 1997
McCartin, Joseph Anthony.
Labor's great war: the struggle for industrial democracy and the origins of modern American labor relations, 1912-1921/ Joseph A. McCartin. Chapel Hill: University of North Carolina Press, c1997. xvi, 303 p.
97-009364   331/.01/120973 21   0807823724
Labor movement -- United States -- History -- 20th century. Industrial relations -- United States -- History -- 20thcentury. Labor unions -- United States -- History -- 20th century.

HD8072.M328 1991
Meltzer, Milton, 1915-
Bread--and roses: the struggle of American labor, 1865-1915/ Milton Meltzer. New York: Facts on File, 1991. viii, 167 p.
90-039759   331.88/0973   0816023719
Labor movement -- United States -- History. Labors unions -- United States -- History. Labor movement -- History. United States -- Social conditions -- 1865-1918.

HD8072.M74
Montgomery, David, 1927-
Workers' control in America: studies in the history of work, technology, and labor struggles/ David Montgomery. Cambridge [Eng.]; Cambridge University Press, 1979. x, 189 p.
78-032001   331.8/0973   0521225809
Working class -- United States -- History. Labors unions -- United States -- History. Industrial relations -- United States -- History.

HD8072.R34
Ramirez, Bruno.
When workers fight: the politics of industrial relations in the progressive era, 1898-1916/ Bruno Ramirez. Westport, Conn.: Greenwood Press, 1978. viii, 241 p.
77-083895   331/.0973   0837198267
Industrial relations -- United States -- History. Labor unions -- United States -- History.

HD8072.R76
Rodgers, Daniel T.
The work ethic in industrial America, 1850-1920/ Daniel T. Rodgers. Chicago: University of Chicago Press, 1978. xv, 300 p.
77-081737   301.5/5   0226723518
Labor -- United States -- History. Working Class -- United States -- History. Work ethic -- United States.

HD8072.5.A66 1994
Appelbaum, Eileen, 1940-
The new American workplace: transforming work systems in the United States/ Eileen Appelbaum and Rosemary Batt. Ithaca, N.Y.: ILR Press, 1994. ix, 287 p.
93-031201   331.25/0973   0875463185
Work -- United States. Work environment -- United States. Industrial organization -- United States.

HD8072.5.H42 1988
Heckscher, Charles C., 1949-
The new unionism: employee involvement in the changing corporation/ Charles C. Heckscher. New York: Basic Books, c1988. xi, 302 p.
87-047769   331.88/0973   0465050980
Industrial relations -- United States. Labor unions -- United States. Industrial management -- Employee participation -- United States.

HD8072.5.L56 1994
Lipsitz, George.
Rainbow at midnight: labor and culture in the 1940s/ George Lipsitz. Urbana: University of Illinois Press, c1994. vi, 359 p.
93-036425   305.5/0973   0252020944
Working class -- United States -- History -- 20th century. Labor -- United States -- History -- 20th century. Industrial relations -- United States -- History -- 20th century. United States -- Economic policy -- 1933-1945. United States -- Social conditions -- 1945- United States -- Social conditions -- 1933-1945.

HD8072.5.R45 2000
Reich, Robert B.
The future of success/ Robert B. Reich. New York: A. Knopf, c2000. 289 p.
00-040552   306.3/61 21   0375411127
Work. Information society -- United States. Quality of work life -- United States.

HD8072.5.S39 1997
Schwarz, John E.
Illusions of opportunity: the American dream in question/ John E. Schwarz. New York: W.W. Norton, c1997. 237 p.
97-002282   306/.0973 21   039304534X
Work ethic -- United States. Labor policy -- United States. Labor market -- United States. United States -- Moral conditions. United States -- Social policy.

HD8072.5.S84 1989
Sweeney, John J., 1934-
Solutions for the new work force: policies for a new social contract/ John J. Sweeney and Karen Nussbaum; preface by Eli Ginzberg. Cabin John, MD: Seven Locks Press, c1989. xviii, 220 p.
89-004252   331.1/0973   0932020623
Labor policy -- United States. Economic security -- United States. Wages -- United States.

HD8073.B8A3 1971
Buchanan, Joseph Ray, 1851-1924.
The story of a labor agitator.   Freeport, N.Y., Books for Libraries Press [1971] xi, 460 p.
75-148873   331.88/0924   0836956443
Buchanan, Joseph Ray, -- 1851-1924.   Working class -- United States. Strikes and lockouts -- United States.

HD8073.C67.G37 1994
Garcia, Mario T.
Memories of Chicano history: the life and narrative of Bert Corona/ Mario T. Garcia. Berkeley: University of California Press, c1994. xviii, 369 p.
92-041578   323.1/16872   0520082192
Corona, Bert N. Labor leaders -- United States -- Biography. Alien labor, Mexican -- United States -- History. Mexican Americans -- Politics and government.

HD8073.E33.A3
Edelman, John W., 1893-1971.
Labor lobbyist; the autobiography of John W. Edelman. Edited by Joseph Carter. Indianapolis, Bobbs-Merrill [1974] 231 p.
73-001729   331.88/092/4   0672516772
Edelman, John W., -- 1893-1971.   Labor leaders -- United States -- Biography.

HD8073.G6.A3 1984
Gompers, Samuel, 1850-1924.
Seventy years of life and labor: an autobiography/ Samuel Gompers; edited with an introduction by Nick Salvatore. Ithaca, NY: ILR Press, New York State School of Industrial a c1984. xli, 236 p.
84-010765   331.88/32/0924   0875461123
Gompers, Samuel, -- 1850-1924.   Labor unions -- United States -- Officials and employees -- Biography. Labor movement -- United States.

HD8073.G7.P54 1989
Phelan, Craig, 1958-
William Green: biography of a labor leader/ Craig Phelan. Albany, NY: State University of New York Press, 1989. x, 223 p.
88-012356   331.88/32/0924   0887068707
Green, William, -- 1872-1952.   Labor unions -- United States -- Officials and employees -- Biography. Labor leaders -- United States -- Biography.

HD8073.J6A3 1990
Jones, Mother
The autobiography of Mother Jones/ Mary Harris Jones; edited by Mary Field Parton; foreword by Meridel LeSueur; introduction by Clarence Darrow; a tribute by Eugene V. Debs; afterword by Fred Thompson. Pittston Strike commemorative ed. Chicago: C.H. Kerr Pub. Co., 1990. xii, 302 p.
90-030701   331.88/092   0882861662
Jones, Mother, 1843?-1930.   Women labor union members -- United States -- Biography. Working class women -- United States -- Biography. Women labor leaders -- United States -- Biography.

HD8073.J6.G67 2001
Gorn, Elliott J., 1951-
Mother Jones: the most dangerous woman in America/ Elliott J. Gorn. New York: Hill and Wang, 2001. xiii, 408 p.
00-044997   331.88/092   0809070936
Jones, -- Mother, -- 1843?-1930.   Women labor union members -- United States -- Biography. Working class women -- United States -- Biography. Women labor leaders -- United States -- Biography.

HD8073.M2.A3
McDonald, David J. 1902-1979.
Union man, by David J. McDonald. New York, Dutton, 1969. 352 p.
77-078947   331.881/72/0924
Strikes and lockouts -- Steel industry -- United States.

HD8073.M5.P48 1994
Phelan, Craig, 1958-
Divided loyalties: the public and private life of labor leader John Mitchell/ Craig Phelan. Albany, N.Y.: State University of New York Press, c1994. xii, 438 p.
93-042744   331.88/12233/092   0791420876
Mitchell, John, -- 1870-1919.   Labor leaders -- United States -- Biography. Coal miners -- Labor unions -- United States -- History. Anthracite coal industry -- United States -- History.

HD8073.P38.M63
Mohr, Lillian Holmen, 1926-
Frances Perkins, that woman in FDR's cabinet!/ By Lillian Holmen Mohr. [Croton-on-Hudson, N.Y.]: North River Press, c1979. viii, 328 p.
78-023597   973.917/092/4   088427019X
Perkins, Frances, -- 1880-1965.   Women in Politics -- United States -- Biography. Labor policy -- United States -- History.

HD8073.S34.A37
Schrank, Robert.
Ten thousand working days/ Robert Schrank. Cambridge, Mass.: MIT Press, c1978. xiv, 243 p.
77-014521   301.44/42/0973   0262191695
Schrank, Robert.   Working class -- United States -- Biography.

HD8073.S64
Richards, Yevette.
Maida Springer: Pan-Africanist and international labor leader/ Yevette Richards. [Pittsburgh]: University of Pittsburgh Press, c2000. xv, 366 p.
00-009652   331.88/092 B 21   0822941392
Springer, Maida.   Women labor leaders -- United States -- Biography. Women labor union members -- United States -- Biography. Afro-American women -- Biography.

HD8079.C4.H57 1990
Hirsch, Eric L., 1952-
Urban revolt: ethnic politics in the nineteenth-century Chicago labor movement/ Eric L. Hirsch. Berkeley: University of California Press, c1990. xvii, 253 p.
89-004885   322/.2/0977311   0520065859
Working class -- Illinois -- Chicago -- History -- 19th century. Labor movement -- Illinois -- Chicago -- History -- 19th century.

HD8081.A5.B75 2001
Briggs, Vernon M.
Immigration and American unionism/ Vernon M. Briggs, Jr. Ithaca: Cornell University Press, 2001. 213 p.
00-011871   331.88/0973   0801438705
Alien labor -- United States. Labor unions -- United States. United States -- Emigration and immigration.

HD8081.A5.C473 1988
Chiswick, Barry R.
Illegal aliens: their employment and employers/ Barry R. Chiswick. Kalamazoo, Mich.: W.E. Upjohn Institute for Employment Research, 1988. ix, 160 p.
88-010062   331.6/2/0973   0880990589
Illegal aliens -- Employment -- United States.

HD8081.A5.L33 1990
Labor divided: race and ethnicity in United States labor struggles, 1835-1960/ Robert Asher and Charles Stephenson, editors. Albany: State University of New York Press, c1990. xi, 378 p.
88-026334   305.5/62/0973   0887069703
Labor movement -- United States -- History. Labor unions -- United States -- History. Minorities -- United States -- History.

HD8081.A5.P37
Parmet, Robert D., 1938-
Labor and immigration in industrial America/ by Robert D. Parmet. Boston, Mass.: Twayne, 1981. 268 p.
81-001438   331.6/2/0973   0805784187
Alien labor -- United States -- History. Labor unions -- United States -- History. Working class -- United States -- History. United States -- Emigration and immigration -- History.

HD8081.A65.H66 1999
Honey, Michael K.
Black workers remember: an oral history of segregation, unionism, and the freedom struggle/ Michael Keith Honey. Berkeley, Calif.: University of California Press, c1999. xxi, 402 p.
99-016357   331.6/396073 21   0520217748
Afro-Americans -- Employment -- History -- Sources. Labor movement -- United States -- History -- Sources. Afro-American labor union members -- History -- Sources.

HD8081.A65.N45 2001
Nelson, Bruce, 1940-
Divided we stand: American workers and the struggle for Black equality/ Bruce Nelson. Princeton: Princeton University Press, c2001. xliv, 388 p.
00-040094   331.6/396073 21   0691017328
African Americans -- Employment -- History. Minorities -- Employment -- United States -- History. Alien labor -- United States -- History.

HD8081.A8.W66 2000
Woo, Deborah, 1951-
Glass ceilings and Asian Americans: the new face of workplace barriers/ Deborah Woo. Walnut Creek, Calif.: AltaMira Press, c2000. 241 p.
99-006106   331.6/395/073 21   0761989765
Asian Americans -- Employment. Discrimination in employment -- United States.

HD8081.H7.D44 1991
DeFreitas, Gregory.
Inequality at work: Hispanics in the U.S. labor force/ Gregory DeFreitas. New York: Oxford University Press, 1991. xvi, 284 p.
91-007283   331.6/368073   0195064216
Hispanic Americans -- Employment. United States -- Emigration and immigration -- Economic aspects.

HD8081.H7.H59 1992
Hispanics in the workplace/ Stephen B. Knouse, Paul Rosenfeld, Amy Culbertson, editors. Newbury Park, Calif.: Sage Publications, c1992. viii, 292 p.
92-002709   331.6/368073   0803939434
Hispanic Americans -- Employment.

HD8081.M6.D38 1981
Davidson, John, 1947-
The long road north/ by John Davidson. Austin, Tex.: Texas Monthly Press, c1981. 145 p.
81-008742   331.6/2/72073   0932012159
Alien labor, Mexican -- Texas. Mexicans -- Texas.

HD8081.M6.R44 1976
Reisler, Mark.
By the sweat of their brow: Mexican immigrant labor in the United States, 1900-1940/ Mark Reisler. Westport, Conn.: Greenwood, Press, 1976. xi, 298 p.
76-005329   331.6/2/72073   0837188946
Alien labor, Mexican -- United States -- History. United States -- Emigration and immigration -- History.

HD8081.M6.V37 1993
Vargas, Zaragosa.
Proletarians of the North: a history of Mexican industrial workers in Detroit and the Midwest, 1917-1933/ Zaragosa Vargas. Berkeley: University of California Press, c1993. xv, 277 p.
92-009122   331.6/2172075   0520071565
Mexican Americans -- Employment -- Middle West -- History. Mexican Americans -- Employment -- Michigan -- Detroit -- History.

HD8083.A11.M87 1992
Murphy, Teresa Anne.
Ten hours' labor: religion, reform, and gender in early New England/ Teresa Anne Murphy. Ithaca: Cornell University Press, 1992. xii, 231 p.
91-055534   331/.0974/09034   0801426839
Labor movement -- New England -- History -- 19th century. Labor leaders -- New England -- History -- 19th century. Hours of labor -- New England -- History -- 19th century.

HD8083.M53.N45 1995
Nelson, Daniel, 1941-
Farm and factory: workers in the Midwest, 1880-1990/ Daniel Nelson. Bloomington: Indiana University Press, c1995. ix, 258 p.
94-045185   305.5/62/0975   0253328837
Working class -- Middle West -- History -- 19th century. Working class -- Middle West -- History -- 20th century. Farmers -- Middle West -- History -- 19th century. Middle West -- Economic conditions.

HD8083.N7.Y4
Yellowitz, Irwin.
Labor and the progressive movement in New York State, 1897-1916. Ithaca, Cornell University Press [1965] ix, 288 p.
65-016500   331.8809747
Labor and laboring classes -- New York (State) -- History. Labor laws and legislation -- New York (State) Labor unions -- New York (State) -- History.

HD8085.B63.F75
Fried, Marc.
The world of the urban working class, by Marc Fried with Ellen Fitzgerald [and others] Cambridge, Harvard University Press, 1973. ix, 410 p.
73-081673   301.44/42/0942   0674961951
Working class -- Massachusetts -- Boston. Slums -- Massachusetts -- Boston. Boston (Mass.) -- Social conditions.

HD8085.L963.C85
Cumbler, John T.
Working-class community in industrial America: work, leisure, and struggle in two industrial cities, 1880-1930/ John T. Cumbler. Westport, Conn.: Greenwood Press, 1979. xiv, 283 p.
78-057768   301.44/42/0973   0313206155
Working class -- Massachusetts -- Lynn -- History. Working class -- Massachusetts -- Fall River -- History. Lynn (Mass.) -- Social conditions. Fall River (Mass.) -- Social conditions.

HD8085.N53.W54 1984
Wilentz, Sean.
Chants democratic: New York City & the rise of the American working class, 1788-1850/ Sean Wilentz. New York: Oxford University Press, 1984. xii, 446 p.
83-002352   305.5/62/097471   0195033426
Working class -- New York (State) -- New York -- History. New York (N.Y.) -- History.

HD8085.P53.L38
Laurie, Bruce.
Working people of Philadelphia, 1800-1850/ Bruce Laurie. Philadelphia: Temple University Press, 1980. xiii, 273 p.
79-028679 305.5/6 0877221685
Working class -- Pennsylvania -- Philadelphia -- History -- 19th century. Philadelphia (Pa.) -- Social conditions.

HD8085.S433.C37 1989
Cassity, Michael J.
Defending a way of life: an American community in the nineteenth century/ Michael Cassity. Albany: State University of New York Press, c1989. xv, 259 p.
88-012324 307.7/4/0977845 0887068685
Working class -- Missouri -- Sedalia -- History -- 19th century. Working class -- Missouri -- Pettis County -- History -- 19th century. Sedalia (Mo.) -- Social conditions. Sedalia (Mo.) -- Economic conditions. Pettis County (Mo.) -- Economic conditions.

HD8109-8848 Labor. Work. Working class — By region or country — Other regions or countries

HD8109.N672.M67 1994
Morrison, William R. 1942-
Working the North: labor and the Northwest defense projects, 1942-1946/ William R. Morrison, Kenneth A. Coates. [Fairbanks]: University of Alaska Press, 1994. xiv, 270 p.
93-041687 305.5/62/097192 0912006722
Working class -- Northwest, Canadian -- History -- 20th century. World War, 1939-1945.

HD8119.M49.P46 1997
Pena, Devon Gerardo.
The terror of the machine: technology, work, gender, and ecology on the U.S.-Mexico border/ Devon G.Pena. Austin: CMAS Books, c1997. xi, 460 p.
96-002352 331.4/87042/09721 0292765614
Labor -- Mexican-American Border Region. Quality of work life -- Mexican-American Border Region. Industrial hygiene -- Mexican-American Border Region. Mexican-American Border Region -- Social conditions. Mexican-American Border Region -- Economic conditions.

HD8138.5.B55.C48 1996
Chomsky, Aviva, 1957-
West Indian workers and the United Fruit Company in Costa Rica, 1870-1940/ Aviva Chomsky. Baton Rouge: Louisiana State University Press, c1996. xiii, 302 p.
95-021958 331.6/2729207286 20 0807119792
Agricultural laborers -- Costa Rica -- History. Banana trade -- Costa Rica -- History. Alien labor, West Indian -- Costa Rica -- History.

HD8146.5.R44 1996
Reed, Thomas F.
The sky never changes: testimonies from the Guatemalan labor movement/ Thomas F. Reed and Karen Brandow. Ithaca, N.Y.: ILR Press, 1996. xvi, 192 p.
95-052508 331.88/097281 0875463541
Labor movement -- Guatemala.

HD8259.S65.D7 1996
Drake, Paul W., 1944-
Labor movements and dictatorships: the Southern Cone in comparative perspective/ Paul W. Drake. Baltimore; Johns Hopkins University Press, 1996. 253 p.
96-000790 322/.2/098 0801853265
Labor movement -- Southern Cone of South America -- History -- 20th century. Labor unions -- Southern Cone of South America -- Political activity -- History -- 20th century. Authoritarianism -- Southern Cone of South America -- History -- 20th century. Southern Cone of South America -- Politics and government.

HD8290.R43.B37 1999
Barros, Mauricio Rands, 1961-
Labour relations and the new unionism in contemporary Brazil/ Mauricio Rands Barros. New York, N.Y.: St. Martin's Press, 1999. xx, 321 p.
98-044284 331/.0981/34 031221846X
Labor unions -- Brazil -- Recife. Political participation -- Brazil -- Recife. Industrial relations -- Brazil -- Recife.

HD8368.D38 1989
Davis, Charles L., 1943-
Working-class mobilization and political control: Venezuela and Mexico/ Charles L. Davis. Lexington: University Press of Kentucky, c1989. xii, 211 p.
88-023314 322/.2/0987 0813116708
Working class -- Venezuela -- Political activity. Working class -- Mexico -- Political activity. Political participation -- Venezuela.

HD8374.S57 1990
Slomp, Hans, 1945-
Labor relations in Europe: a history of issues and developments/ Hans Slomp. New York: Greenwood Press, c1990. xi, 230 p.
89-023262 331/.094 0313267561
Industrial relations -- Europe -- History.

HD8376.G4 1981
Geary, Dick.
European labour protest, 1848-1939/ Dick Geary. New York, NY: St. Martin's Press, 1981. 195 p.
81-004474 331.89/294 0312269749
Working class -- Europe -- History. Labor disputes -- Europe -- History.

HD8376.L23 1989
Labour and socialist movements in Europe before 1914/ edited by Dick Geary. Oxford; Berg; 1989. v, 278 p.
88-021418 322/.2/094 085496200X
Labor movement -- Europe -- History. Labor unions -- Europe -- History.

HD8376.5.S42 1988
The search for labour market flexibility: the European economies in transition/ edited by Robert Boyer. Oxford [Oxfordshire]: Clarendon Press; 1988. xiv, 309 p.
87-034802 331/.094 0198285604
Industrial relations -- Europe. Industrial relations -- Government policy -- Europe. Social security -- Europe.

HD8378.5.A2.E85 1992
Ethnic minorities and industrial change in Europe and North America/ edited by Malcolm Cross. Cambridge, England; Cambridge University Press, 1992. xvii, 341 p.
91-032091 331.6 0521372445
Minorities -- Employment -- Europe. Minorities -- Employment -- North America. Europe -- Race relations. North America -- Race relations.

HD8383.D67 1983
Dorfman, Gerald Allen, 1939-
British trade unionism against the Trades Union Congress/ Gerald A. Dorfman. Stanford, Calif.: Hoover Institution Press, Stanford University, c1983. vii, 158 p.
82-083300 331.88/0941 0817978119
Labor unions -- Great Britain -- Political activity.

HD8383.T74.D66
Dorfman, Gerald Allen, 1939-
Government versus trade unionism in British politics since 1968/ Gerald A. Dorfman. Stanford, Calif.: Hoover Institution Press, Stanford University, 1979. vii, 179 p.
78-070886 322/.2/0941 0817972412
Labor unions -- Great Britain -- Political activity. Wage-price policy -- Great Britain. Great Britain -- Politics and government -- 1964-1979.

HD8388.K57 1994
Kirk, Neville, 1947-
Labour and society in Britain and the USA/ Neville Kirk. Aldershot, Hants, England: Scolar Press; c1994. 2 v.
93-047283 305.5/62/094 1859280218
Labor movement -- Great Britain -- History. Labor movement -- United States -- History. Working class -- Great Britain -- History. Great Britain -- Social conditions. United States -- Social conditions.

HD8388.P76 1984
Proletarianization and family history/ edited by David Levine. Orlando: Academic Press, 1984. xii, 315 p.
84-006301 305.5/62/0941 0124449808
Working class -- Great Britain -- History. Family -- Great Britain -- History. Proletariat -- History.

HD8388.T47
Thompson, E. P. 1924-
The making of the English working class. New York, Pantheon Books [1964, c1963] 848 p.
64-010769 331.44
Working class -- England -- History. England -- Social conditions.

HD8390.L68 1986
Lowe, Rodney.
Adjusting to democracy: the role of the Ministry of Labour in British politics, 1916-1939/ Rodney Lowe. Oxford [Oxfordshire]: Clarendon Press; 1986. xii, 284 p.
86-000733 354.410083 0198200943
Labor policy -- Great Britain -- History -- 20th century. Great Britain -- Economic policy -- 1918-1945. Great Britain -- Politics and government -- 20th century.

HD8390.M175 2000
MacRaild, Donald M.
Labour in British society, 1830-1914/ Donald M. MacRaild and David E. Martin. New York: St. Martin's Press, 2000. xi, 214 p.
99-045253 331.88/0941/09034 0312233132
Labor movement -- Great Britain -- History. Labor unions -- Great Britain -- History. Social conflict -- Great Britain -- History. Great Britain -- Social conditions.

HD8390.M365 2001
McIvor, Arthur.
A history of work in Britain, 1880-1950/ Arthur J. McIvor. Houndmills, Basingstoke, Hampshire; Palgrave, 2001. xii, 276 p.
00-031114   331/.0941   0333596161
Labor -- Great Britain -- History. Industrial sociology -- Great Britain -- History. Labor movement -- Great Britain -- History.

HD8390.P79 1992
Powell, David, 1930-
British politics and the labour question, 1868-1990/ David Powell. New York: St. Martin's Press, 1992. vii, 180 p.
92-018697   322/.2/0941   0312083742
Labor movement -- Great Britain -- History. Labor policy -- Great Britain -- History. Industrial relations -- Great Britain -- History. Great Britain -- Politics and government -- 19th century. Great Britain -- Politics and government -- 20th century.

HD8391.D3535 1987
Daniel, W. W. 1938-
Workplace industrial relations and technical change/ W.W. Daniel. London: F. Pinter in association with Policy Studies Ins c1987. 312 p.
87-154801   331/.0941   0861879171
Industrial relations -- Effect of technological innovations on -- Great Britain.

HD8391.M33 1992
Marsh, David, 1946-
The new politics of British trade unionism: union power and the Thatcher legacy/ David Marsh. Ithaca, N.Y.: ILR Press, c1992. xx, 268 p.
91-027146   322/.2/094109048   0875467040
Labor policy -- Great Britain. Labor unions -- Great Britain -- Political activity. Industrial relations -- Great Britain.

HD8393.C57.W74
Wright, A. W.
G. D. H. Cole and socialist democracy/ A. W. Wright. Oxford: Clarendon Press; 1979. 301 p.
78-040644   335/.1   0198274211
Cole, G. D. H. -- (George Douglas Howard), -- 1889-1959. Guild socialism.

HD8393.L3.L3
Larkin, Emmet J., 1927-
James Larkin. Irish labour leader, 1876-1947, by Emmet Larkin. Cambridge, M.I.T. Press [1965] xviii, 334 p.
64-022134   923.31415
Larkin, James, -- 1876-1947. Trade-unions -- Ireland. Labor and laboring classes -- Ireland.

HD8399.E52.S73 1999
Steinberg, Marc W. 1956-
Fighting words: working-class formation, collective action, and discourse in early nineteenth-century England/ Marc W. Steinberg. Ithaca, N.Y.: Cornell University Press, 1999. xviii, 286 p.
99-017936   305.5/62/094209034   080143582X
Working class -- England -- History -- 19th century. Social conflict -- England -- History -- 19th century.

HD8400.B42.M86 1987
Munck, Ronaldo.
Belfast in the thirties: an oral history/ Ronnie Munck & Bill Rolston. New York: St. Martin's Press, 1987. 209 p.
85-018395   305.5/62/094167   0312074247
Working class -- Northern Ireland -- Belfast -- History -- 20th century. Socialism -- Northern Ireland -- Belfast -- History -- 20th century. Unemployment -- Northern Ireland -- Belfast -- History -- 20th century. Belfast (Northern Ireland) -- Politics and government.

HD8410.K57 1996
Kirk, Tim, 1958-
Nazism and the working class in Austria: industrial unrest and political dissent in the "national community"/ Tim Kirk. Cambridge; Cambridge University Press, 1996. xiv, 190 p.
95-048269   305.5/62/0943609043   0521475015
Working class -- Austria -- History -- 20th century. National socialism -- Austria. Austria -- Economic conditions -- 1918-1945. Austria -- History -- 20th century.

HD8419.S82.L49 1991
Lewis, Jill.
Fascism and the working class in Austria, 1918-1934: the failure of labour in the first republic/ Jill Lewis. New York: Berg: 1991. x, 236 p.
90-041438   335.6/09436/509041   0854965815
Working class -- Austria -- Styria -- History. Industrial relations -- Austria -- Styria -- History. Fascism -- Austria -- History.

HD8433.A1.F74 1993
The French worker: autobiographies from the early industrial era/ edited, translated, and with an introduction by Mark Traugott. Berkeley: University of California Press, c1993. xi, 382 p.
92-006310   331.7/00944   0520079310
Working class -- France -- Biography. Working class -- France -- History -- 19th century. Occupations -- France -- History -- 19th century.

HD8435.H3
Hamilton, Richard F.
Affluence and the French worker in the Fourth Republic [by] Richard F. Hamilton. Princeton, N.J., Princeton University Press, 1967. 323 p.
67-011033   331/.0944
Working class -- France. Political psychology.

HD8450.H43213 1997
Herbert, Ulrich, 1951-
Hitler's foreign workers: enforced foreign labor in Germany under the Third Reich/ Ulrich Herbert; translated by William Templer. Cambridge; Cambridge University Press, 1997. xxi, 510 p.
97-145431   0521470005
Alien labor -- Germany -- History. Alien labor, Polish -- Germany -- History. World War, 1939-1945 -- Economic aspects -- Germany.

HD8450.S55 1998
Silverman, Dan P., 1935-
Hitler's economy: Nazi work creation programs, 1933-1936/ Dan P. Silverman. Cambridge, Mass.: Harvard University Press, 1998. x, 372 p.
97-044972   331.12/042/094309043   0674740718
Labor policy -- Germany -- History -- 20th century. National socialism. Germany -- Economic conditions -- 1918-1945. Germany -- Politics and government -- 1933-1945. Germany -- Economic policy -- 1933-1945.

HD8455.F85 1999
Fuller, Linda, 1944-
Where was the working class?: revolution in Eastern Germany/ Linda Fuller. Urbana: University of Illinois Press, c1999. x, 242 p.
98-019766   322.2/09431 21   0252024427
Working class -- Germany (East) -- Political activity -- History -- 20th century. Labor movement -- Germany (East) -- History -- 20th century. Socialism -- Germany (East) -- History -- 20th century.

HD8526.M385 1988
McDaniel, Tim.
Autocracy, capitalism, and revolution in Russia/ Tim McDaniel. Berkeley: University of California Press, c1988. xi, 500 p.
86-030790   322.4/2/0947   0520055322
Working class -- Russia -- History. Labor policy -- Russia -- History. Russia -- Economic conditions -- 1861-1917.

HD8526.5.C594 1991
Connor, Walter.
The accidental proletariat: workers, politics, and crisis in Gorbachev's Russia/ Walter D. Connor. Princeton, N.J.: Princeton University Press, c1991. xv, 374 p.
91-008557   322/.2/0947   0691077878
Labor -- Soviet Union. Working class -- Soviet Union. Working class -- Soviet Union -- Political activity.

HD8537.N783.G66 1991
Goodwyn, Lawrence.
Breaking the barrier: the rise of Solidarity in Poland/ Lawrence Goodwyn. New York: Oxford University Press, 1991. xxx, 466 p.
90-039898   322/.2/09438   0195061225
Poland -- Politics and government -- 1945-

HD8537.N783.K83 1994
Kubik, Jan, 1953-
The power of symbols against the symbols of power: the rise of Solidarity and the fall of state socialism in Poland/ Jan Kubik. University Park, Pa.: Pennsylvania State University Press, c1994. xiv, 322 p.
93-009895   322/.2/09438   0271010835
Socialism -- Poland -- History -- 20th century. Poland -- Politics and government -- 1945-

HD8537.N783.L33 1991
Laba, Roman, 1944-
The roots of Solidarity: a political sociology of Poland's working-class democratization/ Roman Laba. Princeton, N.J.: Princeton University Press, c1991. xii, 247 p.
90-042595   322/.2/09438   0691078629
Working class -- Poland -- Political activity. Labor unions -- Poland -- Political activity. Social classes -- Poland. Poland -- Politics and government -- 1980-1989.

HD8541.T87 1998
Turner, Lowell.
Fighting for partnership: labor and politics in unified Germany/ Lowell Turner. Ithaca: Cornell University Press, 1998. x, 195 p.
97-048683   331/.0943   0801434866
Labor -- Germany. Industrial relations -- Germany.

HD8584.M28 1990
Martin, Benjamin, 1917-
The agony of modernization: labor and industrialization in Spain/ Benjamin Martin. Ithaca, NY: ILR Press, School of Industrial and Labor Relati c1990. xvii, 570 p.
89-077909   331/.0946   0875461654
Labor movement -- Spain -- History -- 20th century. Labor unions -- Spain -- History -- 20th century. Industrialization -- Spain -- History -- 20th century.

HD8588.R69 2000
Royo, Sebastian, 1966-
From social democracy to neoliberalism: the consequences of party hegemony in Spain, 1982-1996/ Sebastian Royo. New York: St. Martin's Press, c2000. xviii, 318 p.
99-041530   331.1/0946 21   0312223900
Labor policy -- Spain.

HD8653.5.L48 1997
Levine, Marvin J., 1930-
Worker rights and labor standards in Asia's four new tigers: a comparative perspective/ Marvin J. Levine. New York: Plenum Press, c1997. xv, 476 p.
97-008964   331/.01/1095 21   0306454777
Employee rights -- Asia. Industrial relations -- Asia. Labor laws and legislation -- Asia.

HD8656.W67 1994
Workers and working classes in the Middle East: struggles, histories, historiographies/ edited by Zachary Lockman. Albany: State University of New York Press, c1994. xxxi, 341 p.
92-042701   305.5/62/0956   0791416658
Working class -- Middle East -- History -- 19th century. Labor movement -- Middle East -- History -- 19th century. Working class -- Middle East -- Historiography.

HD8660.A5.H584 1992
Shalev, Michael.
Labour and the political economy in Israel/ Michael Shalev. Oxford; Oxford University Press, 1992. x, 400 p.
91-025159   338.95694   0198285132
Labor unions -- Israel -- History. Industrial relations -- Israel -- History. Israel -- Economic policy.

HD8724.H39 1997
Hazama, Hiroshi, 1929-
The history of labour management in Japan/ Hiroshi Hazama; translated by Mari Sako and Eri Sako; foreword by Mari Sako and Michio Morishima. New York: St. Martin's Press, 1997. xl, 222 p.
96-043241   331/.0952   0333575318
Industrial relations -- Japan -- History.

HD8728.G65 1990
Gordon, Andrew, 1952-
Labor and imperial democracy in prewar Japan/ Andrew Gordon. Berkeley: University of California Press, c1991. xvi, 364 p.
90-010872   322/.2/095209041   0520067835
Working class -- Japan -- Political activity -- History -- 20th century. Labor disputes -- Japan -- History -- 20th century. Labor movement -- Japan - - History -- 20th century. Japan -- Politics and government -- 20th century.

HD8728.5.S45 2001
Sellek, Yoko, 1956-
Migrant labour in Japan/ Yoko Sellek. New York: Palgrave, 2001. x, 261 p.
00-034488   331.6/2/0952   0333804325
Alien labor -- Japan. Social integration -- Japan.

HD8736.5.S465 1998
Sheehan, Jackie, 1966-
Chinese workers: a new history/ Jackie Sheehan. London; Routledge, 1998. x, 269 p.
98-020170   305.5/62//0951   0415172063
Working class -- China -- History. Labor movement -- China -- History.

HD8736.5.W34 1986
Walder, Andrew G. 1953-
Communist neo-traditionalism: work and authority in Chinese industry/ Andrew G. Walder. Berkeley: University of California Press, c1986. xxi, 302 p.
85-027093   306/.36/0951   0520054393
Industrial relations -- China. Communism -- China. Working class -- China.

HD8776.C66 1996
Cooper, Frederick, 1947-
Decolonization and African society: the labor question in French and British Africa/ Frederick Cooper. Cambridge, [England]; Cambridge University Press, 1996. xvii, 677 p.
95-046203   331/.06   0521562511
Labor -- Africa -- History -- 20th century. Labor movement -- Africa -- History -- 20th century. Labor unions -- Africa -- History -- 20th century. France -- Colonies -- Africa. Great Britain -- Colonies -- Africa. Africa -- Colonial influence.

HD8786.P67 1997
Posusney, Marsha Pripstein.
Labor and the state in Egypt: workers, unions, and economic restructuring/ Marsha Pripstein Posusney. New York: Columbia University Press, c1997. xii, 327 p.
97-003929   331/.0962/09045 21   0231106920
Working class -- Egypt -- History -- 20th century. Industrial relations -- Egypt -- History -- 20th century. Labor unions -- Egypt -- History -- 20th century.

HD8798.Z8.M325 1995
Penvenne, Jeanne.
African workers and colonial racism: Mozambican strategies and struggles in Lourenco Marques, 1877-1962/ Jeanne Marie Penvenne. Portsmouth, NH: Heinemann; c1995. xvii, 229 p.
94-010574   331/.09679/1   0435089528
Labor -- Mozambique -- Maputo -- History. Working class -- Mozambique -- Maputo -- History. Labor disputes -- Mozambique -- Maputo -- History. Maputo (Mozambique) -- Colonial influence. Maputo (Mozambique) -- Race relations.

HD8808.B38 1998
Bauer, Gretchen, 1959-
Labor and democracy in Namibia, 1971-1996/ Gretchen Bauer. Athens: Ohio University Press: c1998. x, 229 p.
97-049202   331.88/096881 21   0821412167
Labor unions -- Namibia -- History -- 20th century. Democracy -- Namibia -- History -- 20th century. Namibia -- Politics and government -- 1946-1990. Namibia -- Politics and government -- 1990-

HD8811.Z8.K586 1988
Northrup, David.
Beyond the bend in the river: African labor in eastern Zaire, 1865-1940/ by David Northrup. Athens, Ohio: Ohio University Center for International Studies 1988. xvii, 264 p.
88-004701   331.11/73/0967517   0896801519
Working class -- Congo (Democratic Republic) -- Kivu (Zaire) -- History. Working class -- Congo (Democratic Republic) -- Province orientale -- History. Slavery -- Congo (Democratic Republic) -- History.

HD8848.G6 1967
Gollan, Robin.
Radical and working class politics; a study of eastern Australia, 1850-1910. [Carlton, Melbourne University Press in association with t [1967] xi, 226 p.
68-106936   322/.2/0994
Working class -- Australia -- Political activity. Labor unions -- Australia -- Political activity -- History. Australia -- Politics and government -- To 1900.

HD8943 Labor. Work. Working class — By region or country — Developing countries

HD8943.P42
Peasants and proletarians: the struggles of Third World workers/ edited by Robin Cohen, Peter C. W. Gutkind, and Phyllis Brazier. New York: Monthly Review Press, c1979. 505 p.
79-010020   331/.09172/4   0853454213
Working class -- Developing countries. Labor unions -- Developing countries. Peasantry -- Developing countries.

HD9000.1-9018 Special industries and trades — Agricultural industries — Food supply. Produce trade

HD9000.1.F587.A23 1991
Abbott, John Cave, 1919-
Politics and poverty: a critique of the Food and Agriculture Organization of the United Nations/ John Abbott. London; Routledge, 1992. xi, 206 p.
90-026679   630/.6/01   0415066506
Agricultural assistance. Economic assistance. World politics -- 1945-

HD9000.5.K883 1991
Kutzner, Patricia L.
World hunger: a reference handbook/ Patricia L. Kutzner. Santa Barbara, Calif.: ABC-Clio, c1991. xii, 359 p.
90-025185   363.8   0874365589
Food supply. Poor -- Nutrition. Malnutrition.

HD9000.5.W587 1986
World food marketing systems/ edited by Erdener Kaynak. London; Butterworths, 1986. xviii, 333 p.
85-028371   380.1/456413   0407003584
Produce trade. Food industry and trade. Farm produce -- Marketing -- Case studies.

HD9000.9.A1.B63 1986
Boardman, Robert, 1945-
Pesticides in world agriculture: the politics of international regulation/ Robert Boardman. New York, NY: St. Martin's Press, 1986. x, 221 p.
85-027742   363.1/79   0312602855
Pesticide residues in food -- International cooperation. Pesticides -- Environmental aspects. Environmental policy -- International cooperation.

HD9005.U19 1990
U.S. agricultural groups: institutional profiles/ edited by William P. Browne and Allan J. Cigler. New York: Greenwood Press, 1990. xxxi, 274 p.
89-025786   338.1/06/073   031325088X
Agricultural industries -- United States -- Societies, etc. Agriculture -- United States -- Societies, etc. Produce trade -- United States -- Societies, etc.

HD9006.D65 1985
Doyle, Jack, 1947-
Altered harvest: agriculture, genetics, and the fate of the world's food supply/ by Jack Doyle. New York, N.Y., U.S.A.: Viking, 1985. xix, 502 p.
84-040458   338.1/9/73   067011524X
Food industry and trade -- Technological innovations -- Government policy -- United States. Agricultural innovations -- Government policy -- United States. Genetic engineering industry -- Government policy -- United States.

HD9006.T49 1992
Thompson, Paul B., 1951-
The ethics of aid and trade: U.S. food policy, foreign competition, and the social contract/ Paul B. Thompson. Cambridge [England]; Cambridge University Press, 1992. x, 233 p.
92-001036   363.8/83/091724   0521414687
Produce trade -- Government policy -- Moral and ethical aspects -- United States. Food relief -- Government policy -- Moral and ethical aspects -- United States. Agricultural assistance, American -- Government policy -- Moral and ethical aspects.

HD9014.M62.F69 1993
Fox, Jonathan, 1958-
The politics of food in Mexico: state power and social mobilization/ Jonathan Fox. Ithaca, N.Y.: Cornell University Press, 1993. x, 280 p.
92-025948   363.8/56/0972   0801427169
Food supply -- Government policy -- Mexico. Mexico -- Politics and government -- 20th century.

HD9014.M62.O24 2000
Ochoa, Enrique.
Feeding Mexico: the political uses of food since 1910/ Enrique C. Ochoa. Wilmington, Del.: Scholarly Resources, 2000. xiii, 267 p.
99-087310   363.8/0972   0842028129
Food supply -- Government policy -- Mexico -- 20th century. Nutrition policy -- Mexico -- History -- 20th century. Agriculture and state -- Mexico -- History -- 20th century.

HD9015.S652.M67 1990
Moskoff, William.
The bread of affliction: the food supply in the USSR during World War II/ William Moskoff. Cambridge [England]; Cambridge University Press, 1990. xvi, 256 p.
90-001365   363.8/0947/09044   0521374995
Food supply -- Soviet Union -- History -- 20th century. World War, 1939-1945 -- Food supply -- Soviet Union.

HD9017.A2.F44 1987
Feeding African cities: studies in regional social history: edited by Jane I. Guyer. Bloomington: Indiana University Press in association with the c1987. x, 249 p.
86-046323   338.1/9/6   0253321026
Food supply -- Africa. Cities and towns -- Africa -- Growth. Households -- Africa.

HD9017.A26.P68 1988
Poverty, policy, and food security in southern Africa/ edited by Coralie Bryant. Boulder, Colo.: L. Rienner; 1988. xii, 291 p.
87-032243   363.8/56/0968   1555870929
Food supply -- Africa, Southern. Poor -- Africa, Southern. Apartheid -- South Africa. Africa, Southern -- Economic policy. South Africa -- Foreign relations -- Africa, Southern. Africa, Southern -- Foreign relations -- South Africa.

HD9018.D44.A367 1988
Agricultural price policy for developing countries/ edited by John W. Mellor and Raisuddin Ahmed. Baltimore: Johns Hopkins University Press, c1988. xiii, 327 p.
87-026862   338.1/8/091724   0801835860
Food prices -- Government policy -- Developing countries. Agricultural prices -- Government policy -- Developing countries.

HD9018.D44.B5 1993
The bias against agriculture: trade and macroeconomic policies in developing countries/ edited by Romeo M. Bautista and Alberto Valdes. San Francisco, Calif.: International Center for Economic Growth; c1993. xxii, 339 p.
92-036105   338.1/8/091724   1558152458
Produce trade -- Government policy -- Developing countries -- Case studies. Agriculture and state -- Developing countries -- Case studies. Developing countries -- Commercial policy -- Case studies.

HD9018.D44.F666 1988
Food subsidies in developing countries: costs, benefits, and policy options/ edited by Per Pinstrup-Andersen. Baltimore: Published for the International Food Policy Rese c1988. xvii, 374 p.
88-001709   338.1/8   0801836328
Agricultural subsidies -- Developing countries. Food relief -- Developing countries.

HD9018.D44.U88 1992
Utting, Peter.
Economic reform and third-world socialism: a political economy of food policy in post-revolutionary societies/ Peter Utting. New York: St. Martin's Press, 1992. xvi, 320 p.
91-024939   338.1/91724   0312068077
Food supply -- Government policy -- Developing countries. Agriculture and state -- Developing countries. Land reform -- Developing countries. Developing countries -- Economic policy.

HD9018.D44.W37 1987
Warnock, John W., 1933-
The politics of hunger: the global food system/ John W. Warnock. Toronto; Methuen, c1987. xv, 334 p.
87-001659   363.8/09172/4   0458806307
Food supply -- Developing countries. Agriculture -- Economic aspects -- Developing countries. Hunger.

HD9036-9066 Special industries and trades — Agricultural industries — Grain trade. Hay trade

HD9036.L53 1992
Libby, Ronald T.
Protecting markets: U.S. policy and the world grain trade/ Ronald T. Libby. Ithaca: Cornell University Press, 1992. xvii, 152 p.
91-055536   382/.4131/0973   0801426170
Grain trade -- Government policy -- United States.

HD9042.7.N67.M64 1998
Miller, Judith A., 1956-
Mastering the market: the State and the grain trade in Northern France, 1700-1860/ Judith A. Miller. Cambridge; Cambridge University Press, 1998. xviii, 334 p.
98-020682   0521621291
Grain trade -- France, Northern -- History -- 18th century. Grain trade -- France, Northern -- History -- 19th century.

HD9046.C62.W335 1984
Walker, Kenneth R.
Food grain procurement and consumption in China/ Kenneth R. Walker. Cambridge [Cambridgeshire]; Cambridge University Press, 1984. xxi, 329 p.
83-007820   381/.4131/0951   0521256496
Grain trade -- China. Food consumption -- China. Grain trade -- Government policy -- China.

HD9058.B743.F85 1996
Kaplan, Steven L.
The bakers of Paris and the bread question, 1700-1775/ by Steven Laurence Kaplan. Durham: Duke University Press, 1996. xviii, 761 p.
95-023182   664/.7523/0944361   0822317060
Bread industry -- France -- Paris Region -- History -- 18th century. Bakers and bakeries -- France -- Paris Region -- History -- 18th century. Food supply -- France -- Paris Region -- History -- 18th century.

HD9066.U45.D48 1988
Dethloff, Henry C.
A history of the American rice industry, 1685-1985/ Henry C. Dethloff. College Station: Texas A & M University Press, c1988. xiii, 215 p.
88-001316   338.1/7318/0973   089096338X
Rice trade -- United States -- History.

HD9075-9093 Special industries and trades — Agricultural industries — Cotton

HD9075.W58
Woodman, Harold D.
King cotton & his retainers; financing & marketing the cotton crop of the South, 1800-1925 [by] Harold D. Woodman. Lexington, University of Kentucky Press, 1968. xiv, 386 p.
67-029337   338.1/7/3510973
Cotton trade -- Southern States -- History. Cotton trade -- United States -- History.

HD9093.U6.S688 1995
Wrenn, Lynette Boney, 1928-
Cinderella of the new South: a history of the cottonseed industry, 1855-1955/ Lynette Boney Wrenn. Knoxville: University of Tennessee Press, c1995. xxiv, 280 p.
94-018733   338.1/735121/0975   0870498827
Cottonseed -- Southern States -- History -- 19th century. Cottonseed -- Southern States -- History -- 20th century. Cottonseed oil -- Southern States -- History -- 19th century.

HD9100.5-9116 Special industries and trades — Agricultural industries — Sugar

HD9100.5.G29 1989
Galloway, J. H.
The sugar cane industry: an historical geography from its origins to 1914/ J.H. Galloway. Cambridge [England]; Cambridge University Press, 1989. xiii, 266 p.
88-022823   338.4/763361/09   0521248531
Sugarcane industry -- History.

HD9100.6.E27 1993
The Economics and politics of world sugar policies/ edited by Stephen V. Marks and Keith E. Maskus. Ann Arbor: University of Michigan Press, c1993. viii, 176 p.
92-042179   382/.4136   0472104284
Sugar trade -- Government policy.

HD9105.E4
Eichner, Alfred S.
The emergence of oligopoly; sugar refining as a case study [by] Alfred S. Eichner. Baltimore, Johns Hopkins Press [1969] xi, 388 p.
74-079300   338.4/7/6641   080181068X
Sugar -- Manufacture and refining -- United States.

HD9114.C89.D79 1998
Dye, Alan, 1958-
Cuban sugar in the age of mass production: technology and the economics of the sugar central, 1899-1929/ Alan Dye. Stanford, Calif.: Stanford University Press, 1998. xiii, 343 p.
97-006657   338.1/7361/097291   0804728194
Sugar trade -- Cuba -- History -- 20th century. Sugar trade -- Cuba -- Technological innovations -- History -- 20th century. Sugar factories -- Cuba -- History -- 20th century.

HD9115.F82.S74 1988
Stein, Robert Louis.
The French sugar business in the eighteenth century/ Robert Louis Stein. Baton Rouge: Louisiana State University Press, c1988. xi, 185 p.
87-026957   338.4/76641/0944   0807114340
Sugar trade -- France -- History -- 18th century. Sugar trade -- West Indies, French -- History -- 18th century. Slave labor -- West Indies, French -- History -- 18th century.

HD9116.P61.L37 1993
Larkin, John A.
Sugar and the origins of modern Philippine society/ John A. Larkin. Berkeley: University of California Press, c1993. xvi, 337 p.
92-006325   338.1/7361/09599   0520079566
Sugar trade -- Philippines -- History. Philippines -- Economic conditions. Philippines -- Social conditions. Philippines -- History.

HD9135-9149 Special industries and trades — Agricultural industries — Tobacco

HD9135.C5 1996
The cigarette papers/ Stanton A. Glantz ... [et al.]; foreword by C. Everett Koop. Berkeley: University of California Press, c1996. xix, 539 p.
95-044169   362.29/6 20   0520205723
Tobacco industry -- United States. Tobacco -- Health aspects. Smoking -- Health aspects.

HD9136.T65 1988
Tollison, Robert D.
Smoking and the state: social costs, rent seeking, and public policy/ Robert D. Tollison, Richard E. Wagner. Lexington, Mass.: Lexington Books, c1988. x, 123 p.
87-045981   362.2   066917100X
Tobacco industry -- Government policy -- United States. Tobacco -- Taxation -- United States. Smoking -- United States.

HD9149.C42U68. 1971
Tennant, Richard B.
The American cigarette industry; a study in economic analysis and public policy, by Richard B. Tennant. [Hamden, Conn.] Archon Books, 1971 [c1950] xxvi, 411 p.
79-019733   338.4/7/679730973   0208010254
Cigarette industry -- United States.

HD9161 Special industries and trades — Agricultural industries — Rubber

HD9161.A2.B32 1994
Barlow, Colin.
The world rubber industry/ Colin Barlow, Sisira Jayasuriya, and C. Suan Tan. London; Routledge, 1994. xiii, 364 p.
93-034912   338.4/76782   0415023696
Rubber industry and trade.

HD9161.U54.B143 1996
Blackford, Mansel G., 1944-
BFGoodrich: tradition and transformation, 1870-1995/ Mansel G. Blackford, K. Austin Kerr. Columbus: Ohio State University Press, c1996. x, 507 p.
96-013482   338.7/6782/0973 20   0814206964
Rubber industry and trade -- United States -- History. Tire industry -- United States -- History.

HD9198-9199 Special industries and trades — Agricultural industries — Tea and coffee

HD9198.C5.E85 1993
Etherington, Dan M.
Green gold: the political economy of China's post-1949 tea industry/ Dan M. Etherington and Keith Forster. Hong Kong; Oxford University Press, 1993. xvii, 270 p.
93-020844   338.1/7372/095109045   0195857542
Tea trade -- China.

HD9198.C52.F854 1994
Gardella, Robert Paul.
Harvesting mountains: Fujian and the China tea trade, 1757-1937/ Robert Gardella. Berkeley: University of California Press, c1994. xiv, 259 p.
93-005404   382/.41372/0951245   0520084144
Tea trade -- China -- Fujian Sheng -- History.

HD9198.I42.G75
Griffiths, Percival Joseph, 1899-
The history of the Indian tea industry, by Sir Percival Griffiths. London, Weidenfeld & Nicolson [1967] xii, 730 p.
67-099180   338.1/7/372/0954
Tea trade -- India -- History.

HD9199.A2.B27 1997
Bates, Robert H.
Open-economy politics: the political economy of the world coffee trade/ Robert H. Bates. Princeton, N.J.: Princeton University Press, c1997. xvii, 221 p.
96-020694   382/.41373 20   0691026556
Coffee industry.

HD9199.B8.S217 1990
Font, Mauricio.
Coffee, contention, and change in the making of modern Brazil/ Mauricio A. Font. Cambridge, Mass., USA: B. Blackwell, 1990. xii, 351 p.
89-035990   338.1/7373/098161   1557860424
Coffee industry -- Brazil -- Sao Paulo (State) -- History. Coffee growers -- Brazil -- Sao Paulo (State) -- History. Industrialization -- Brazil -- Sao Paulo (State) -- History. Sao Paulo (Brazil: State) -- Politics and government.

HD9199.L382.S4 1998
The second conquest of Latin America: coffee, henequen, and oil during the export boom, 1850-1930/ edited by Steven C. Topik and Allen Wells. Austin: Institute of Latin American Studies, University 1998. viii, 271 p.
97-032607   382/.6/098   0292781571
Coffee industry -- Latin America -- History. Henequen industry -- Latin America -- History. Petroleum industry and trade -- Latin America -- History.

HD9259 Special industries and trades — Agricultural industries — Fruit trade. Nuts industry

HD9259.B3.G834 1993
Dosal, Paul J. 1960-
Doing business with the dictators: a political history of United Fruit in Guatemala, 1899-1944/ Paul J. Dosal. Wilmington, Del.: SR Books, 1993. xi, 256 p.
93-010118   338.7/634772/097281   0842024751
Banana trade -- Guatemala -- History. Banana trade -- Guatemala -- Political activity. Guatemala -- Politics and government -- 1821-1945.

HD9259.S83.U648 1996
Wells, Miriam J., 1945-
Strawberry fields: politics, class, and work in California agriculture/ Miriam J. Wells. Ithaca, N.Y.: Cornell University Press, 1996. xxv, 339 p.
96-002613   338.1/7475/09794   0801431727
Strawberry industry -- California. Strawberry industry -- California -- Employees. Agricultural laborers -- California.

HD9282 Special industries and trades — Agricultural industries — Dairy products

HD9282.U4.M25
McMenamin, Michael.
Milking the public: political scandals of the dairy lobby from L. B. J. to Jimmy Carter/ Michael McMenamin and Walter McNamara. Chicago: Nelson-Hall, c1980. xvi, 300 p.
80-011546   328.73/078   0882295527
Milk trade -- Political aspects -- United States. Milk -- Prices -- Political aspects -- United States. Political corruption -- United States.

HD9349-9394.7 Special industries and trades — Agricultural industries — Beverages. Beverage containers

HD9349.S633.U67 1991
Tollison, Robert D.
Competition and concentration: the economics of the carbonated soft drink industry/ by Robert D. Tollison, David P. Kaplan, Richard S. Higgins. Lexington, Mass.: Lexington Books, [1991] x, 212 p.
90-044544   338.4/766362/0973   066927139X
Soft drink industry -- United States. Industrial concentration -- United States. Competition -- United States.

HD9394.7.C48 1990
Christian, David, 1946-
Living water: vodka and Russian society on the eve of emancipation/ David Christian. Oxford [England]: Clarendon Press; 1990. x, 447 p.
89-026446   338.4/76635   0198222866
Vodka industry -- Russia -- History -- 19th century. Vodka -- Social aspects -- Russia. Drinking of alcoholic beverages -- Russia -- History -- 19th century. Russia -- Social conditions -- 1801-1917.

HD9415-9433 Special industries and trades — Agricultural industries — Animal industry

HD9415.A68 1995
Any way you cut it: meat processing and small-town America/ edited by Donald D. Stull, Michael J. Broadway, David Griffith. Lawrence, Kan.: University Press of Kansas, c1995. xiv, 269 p.
95-000259   338.4/76649/00973   0700607218
Meat industry and trade -- United States -- Case studies. Rural development -- United States -- Case studies. United States -- Rural conditions -- Case studies.

HD9433.U4.G7
Gray, James R.
Ranch economics [by] James R. Gray. Ames, Iowa State University Press [1968] viii, 534 p.
68-012022   338.1/7/6
Cattle -- United States. Sheep -- Economic aspects -- United States. Ranches -- United States -- Management.

HD9433.U5.K215
Dykstra, Robert R., 1930-
The cattle towns [by] Robert R. Dykstra. New York, Knopf, 1968. x, 386 p.
68-012677   978.1/03
Cattle trade -- Kansas. Frontier and pioneer life -- Kansas.

HD9450.5 Special industries and trades — Agricultural industries — Fishery product industry. Fish trade. Aquaculture industry. Seafood industry

HD9450.5.L38 1984
Lawson, Rowena M.
Economics of fisheries development/ Rowena M. Lawson. New York: Praeger, 1984. xi, 283 p.
84-015074   338.3/72709172/4   0030012430
Fisheries -- Economic aspects. Fishery management. Fisheries -- Economic aspects -- Developing countries.

HD9490.5 Special industries and trades — Agricultural industries — Agricultural supply industries. Farm supply industries. Accessory industries

HD9490.5.P343.A3585 1997
Lynn, Martin, 1931-
Commerce and economic change in West Africa: the palm oil trade in the nineteenth century/ Martin Lynn. Cambridge; Cambridge University Press, 1997. xvi, 270 p.
97-007352   380.1/413851/0967   0521590744
Palm oil industry -- Africa, West -- History -- 19th century.

HD9502 Special industries and trades — Energy industries. Energy policy. Fuel trade — General works

HD9502.A2.A574 1993
Anderson, Victor, 1952-
Energy efficiency policies/ Victor Anderson. London; Routledge, 1993. xi, 93 p.
92-023582   333.79   0415086965
Energy policy. Global warming -- Economic aspects.

HD9502.A2.C643 1976
Commoner, Barry, 1917-
The poverty of power: energy and the economic crisis/ Barry Commoner. New York: Knopf; distributed by Random House, 1976. 314 p.
75-036798   333.7   0394403711
Power resources. Power (Mechanics) Energy policy -- United States. United States -- Economic policy -- 1971-1981.

HD9502.A2.G67
Gordon, Richard L., 1934-
An economic analysis of world energy problems/ Richard L. Gordon. Cambridge, Mass.: MIT Press, c1981. xvii, 282 p.
80-028663   333.79   0262070804
Energy policy. Power resources.

HD9502.A2.W4 1980
Webb, Michael Gordon.
The economics of energy/ Michael G. Webb and Martin J. Ricketts. New York: Wiley, c1980. xiii, 315 p.
79-018708   333.7   0470268417
Energy policy. Economic policy. Power resources.

HD9502.D442.F83 2000
Fuel for change: World Bank energy policy - rhetoric and reality/ edited by Ian Tellam. London; Zed Books, c2000. xvi, 208 p.
00-027614   333.79 21   185649781X
Energy development -- Europe, Eastern -- Finance -- Case studies. Renewable energy sources -- Developing countries. Renewable energy sources -- Europe, Eastern.

HD9502.S652.G87 1989
Gustafson, Thane.
Crisis amid plenty: the politics of Soviet energy under Brezhnev and Gorbachev/ Thane Gustafson. Princeton, N.J.: Princeton University Press, c1989. xxv, 362 p.
89-031519   333.79/15/094709048   0691078351
Energy policy -- Soviet Union. Petroleum industry and trade -- Government policy -- Soviet Union. Gas industry -- Government policy -- Soviet Union.

HD9502.U52.E4914 1983
Energy future: report of the energy project at the Harvard Business School/ Robert Stobaugh, Daniel Yergin, editors; I.C. Bupp ... [et al.]. New York: Vintage Books, 1983, c1980. xii, 459 p.
81-040078   333.79/0973   039474750X
Energy policy -- United States. Power resources -- United States.

HD9502.U52.M347 1993
Making national energy policy/ edited by Hans H. Landsberg. Washington, D.C.: Resources for the Future, c1993. vi, 151 p.
93-025320   333.79/0973   0915707705
Energy policy -- United States -- Congresses.

HD9502.U53.C36 1991
Regulatory choices: a perspective on developments in energy policy/ edited by Richard J. Gilbert. Berkeley: University of California Press, c1991. vii, 399 p.
90-046760   333.79/0973   0520070569
Energy policy -- California. Energy policy -- United States. Public utilities -- California.

HD9506 Special industries and trades — Mineral industries. Metal trade — General works

HD9506.A2.V36 1986
Van Rensburg, W. C. J.
Strategic minerals/ W.C.J. van Rensburg. Englewood Cliffs, N.J.: Prentice-Hall, c1986. 2 v.
85-006569   333.8   0138513872
Mineral industries -- Government policy -- Case studies. Metal trade -- Government policy -- Case studies. Strategic materials -- Government policy -- Case studies.

HD9506.A59.K48 1990
Khawlie, M. R.
Beyond the oil era?: Arab mineral resources and future development/ M.R. Khawlie. London; Mansell, 1990. x, 132 p.
89-049352   333.8/5/09174927   0720120403
Mineral industries -- Arab countries -- Forecasting. Petroleum industry and trade -- Arab countries -- Forecasting.

HD9506.U63C64 1986
Dempsey, Stanley,
Mining the summit: Colorado's Ten Mile District, 1860-1960/ by Stanley Dempsey and James E. Fell, Jr. 1st ed. Norman: University of Oklahoma Press, c1986. xiv, 306 p.
86-040071   338.2/09788/44   0806120053
Mineral industries -- Colorado -- History.

HD9510.5-9539 Special industries and trades — Mineral industries. Metal trade — Particular metals

HD9510.5.B25 1992
Bain, Trevor.
Banking the furnace: restructuring of the steel industry in eight countries/ Trevor Bain. Kalamazoo, Mich.: W.E. Upjohn Institute for Employment Research, 1992. x, 191 p.
92-018358   338.4/7669142   0880991275
Steel industry and trade. Collective bargaining -- Steel industry and trade. Corporate reorganizations.

HD9515.S734 1998
Stein, Judith, 1940-
Running steel, running America: race, economic policy and the decline of Liberalism/ Judith Stein. Chapel Hill: University of North Carolina Press, c1998. xvi, 410 p.
97-032600   338.4/7669142/097309045   21
0807824143
Steel industry and trade -- United States -- History. United States -- Economic conditions -- 1945- United States -- Social conditions -- 1945- United States -- Race relations.

HD9519.S68.L49 1994
Lewis, W. David 1931-
Sloss Furnaces and the rise of the Birmingham district: an industrial epic/ W. David Lewis. Tuscaloosa: University of Alabama Press, c1994. xxiv, 645 p.
93-048178   338.7/6722/09761781   0817307087
Iron foundries -- Alabama -- Birmingham -- History. Iron founding -- Alabama -- Birmingham -- History. Iron -- Metallurgy. Birmingham (Ala.) -- Social conditions. Birmingham (Ala.) -- Economic conditions.

HD9525.E8.H68 1991
Houseman, Susan N., 1956-
Industrial restructuring with job security: the case of European steel/ Susan N. Houseman. Cambridge, Mass.: Harvard University Press, 1991. ix, 164 p.
90-044471   331.12/9691/094   0674451759
Steel industry and trade -- European Economic Community countries. Iron and steel workers -- Supply and demand -- European Economic Community countries. Job security -- European Economic Community countries -- Case studies.

HD9536.B63.P68513 1993
Tandeter, Enrique.
Coercion and market: silver mining in colonial Potosí, 1692-1826/ Enrique Tandeter. Albuquerque: University of New Mexico Press, c1993. xiv, 332 p.
93-014687   338.2/7421/098414   0826314309
Silver mines and mining -- Bolivia -- Potosí (Dept.) -- History. Forced labor -- Bolivia -- Potosí (Dept.) -- History.

HD9536.G5.D86 1998
Dumett, Raymond E.
El Dorado in West Africa: the gold-mining frontier, African labor, and colonial capitalism in the Gold Coast, 1875-1900/ Raymond E. Dumett. Athens: Ohio University Press; c1998. xviii, 396 p.
97-046494   338.2/741/09667 21   0821411977
Gold mines and mining -- Ghana -- History -- 19th century. Gold miners -- Ghana -- History -- 19th century. Capitalism -- Ghana -- History -- 19th century.

HD9539.B8.U538 1982
Brecher, Jeremy.
Brass Valley: the story of working people's lives and struggles in an American industrial region/ the Brass Workers History Project; compiled and edited by Jeremy Brecher, Jerry Lombardi, and Jan Stackhouse. Philadelphia: Temple University Press, 1982. xvi, 284 p.
82-005770   331.7/6733/097467   0877222711
Brass industry and trade -- Employees -- Labor unions -- Connecticut -- Naugatuck River Valley -- History. Brass industry and trade -- Connecticut -- Naugatuck River Valley -- Employees -- Interviews. Ethnology -- Connecticut -- Naugatuck River Valley. Naugatuck River Valley (Conn.) -- Social conditions. Naugatuck River Valley (Conn.) -- Biography. Naugatuck River Valley (Conn.) -- Economic conditions.

HD9539.C7.U539 1998
Finn, Janet L., 1956-
Tracing the veins: of copper, culture, and community from Butte to Chuquicamata/ Janet L. Finn. Berkeley: University of California Press, c1998. xviii, 309 p.
97-045120   338.2/743/0978668 21   0520211367
Anaconda Company. Copper industry and trade -- Social aspects -- Montana -- Butte. Copper industry and trade -- Social aspects -- Chile -- Chuquicamata.

HD9539.C7.U548 1991
Lankton, Larry D.
Cradle to grave: life, work, and death at the Lake Superior copper mines/ Larry Lankton. New York: Oxford University Press, 1991. xi, 319 p.
90-040520   338.7/622343/0977499   0195062639
Copper industry and trade -- Michigan -- Keweenaw Peninsula -- History. Copper miners -- Michigan -- Keweenaw Peninsula -- History.

HD9545-9551.5 Special industries and trades — Mineral industries. Metal trade — Coal

HD9545.V54
Vietor, Richard H. K., 1945-
Environmental politics and the coal coalition/ by Richard H. K. Vietor. College Station: Texas A&M University Press, c1980. xiv, 285 p.
79-005277   363.7/392   0890960941
Coal mines and mining -- Environmental aspects -- United States. Industrial policy -- United States.

HD9545.Z55
Zimmerman, Martin B.
The U.S. coal industry: the economics of policy choice/ Martin B. Zimmerman. Cambridge, Mass.: MIT Press, c1981. xiv, 205 p.
81-001124   338.2/724/0973
Coal trade -- United States. Coal trade -- United States -- Mathematical models.

HD9551.5.H57 1984
The History of the British coal industry. Oxford [England]: Clarendon Press; 1984-1993. 5 v.
83-004194   338.2/724/0941   0198282834
Coal trade -- Great Britain -- History. Coal mines and mining -- Great Britain -- History. Coal trade -- Government ownership -- Great Britain -- History.

HD9560.1-9579 Special industries and trades — Mineral industries. Metal trade — Petroleum

HD9560.4.P37 1987
Pereira, A.
Socio-economic and policy implications of energy price increases/ Armand Pereira, Alistair Ulph, and Wouter Tims. Aldershot, Hants, England; Gower, c1987. xxiv, 317 p.
87-011955   338.2/3   0566055201
Petroleum products -- Prices. Energy policy. Economic policy.

HD9560.5.A5153 1985
Alnasrawi, Abbas.
OPEC in a changing world economy/ Abbas Alnasrawi. Baltimore: Johns Hopkins University Press, c1985. xi, 188 p.
84-007196   341.7/5472282   0801832160
Petroleum industry and trade.

HD9560.5.H26 1998
Hannesson, Rognvaldur.
Petroleum economics: issues and strategies of oil and natural gas production/ Rognvaldur Hannesson. Westport, Conn.: Quorum, 1998. x, 163 p.
98-006837   338.2/7282   1567202209
Petroleum industry and trade.

HD9560.5.K685 1989
Koopmann, Georg.
Oil and the international economy: lessons from two price shocks/ Georg Koopmann, Klaus Matthies, and Beate Reszat. New Brunswick, N.J., U.S.A.: Transaction Publishers, c1989. 451 p.
88-027133   332/.042   0887386164
Petroleum industry and trade. International economic relations. International finance.

HD9560.5.N67 1994
Nowell, Gregory P. 1954-
Mercantile states and the world oil cartel, 1900-1939/ Gregory P. Nowell. Ithaca, N.Y.: Cornell University Press, 1994. x, 326 p.
93-038020   338.8/7   0801428785
Petroleum industry and trade -- History -- 20th century. Petroleum industry and trade -- France -- History -- 20th century. Cartels -- History -- 20th century.

HD9560.5.O3658 1995
Oil in the new world order/ edited by Kate Gillespie and Clement Moore Henry. Gainesville, Fla.: University Press of Florida, c1995. xi, 339 p.
95-005517   338.2/7282   0813013674
Petroleum industry and trade. Petroleum industry and trade -- Government policy.

HD9560.5.S755 1988
Stevens, Paul, 1947-
Oil and gas dictionary/ editor, Paul Stevens. New York: Nichols Pub., c1988. x, 270 p.
88-019626   333.8/23/0321   0893973254
Petroleum industry and trade -- Dictionaries. Gas industry -- Dictionaries.

HD9560.6.C53 2001
Claes, Dag Harald.
The politics of oil-producer cooperation/ Dag Harald Claes. Boulder, Colo.: Westview Press, 2001. xvii, 407 p.
00-044774   338.2/7282   081336843X
Petroleum industry and trade -- International cooperation -- Political aspects.

HD9560.6.C68 1985
Cowhey, Peter F., 1948-
The problems of plenty: energy policy and international politics/ Peter F. Cowhey. Berkeley: University of California Press, c1985. xiii, 447 p.
83-009275   333.79   0520046935
Petroleum industry and trade -- Political aspects. Energy industries -- Political aspects. International economic relations. United States -- Foreign relations -- 1945-1989.

HD9565.O647 1990
Olien, Roger M., 1938-
Easy money: oil promoters and investors in the Jazz Age/ Roger M. Olien and Diana Davids Olien. Chapel Hill: University of North Carolina Press, c1990. xi, 216 p.
90-050017   364.1/68   080781928X
Petroleum industry and trade -- Finance -- Corrupt practices -- United States -- History -- 20th century. Speculation -- United States -- History -- 20th century. Fraud -- United States -- History -- 20th century. United States -- Economic conditions -- 1918-1945.

HD9566.B62 1996
Bradley, Robert L., 1955-
Oil, gas & government: the U.S. experience/ Robert L. Bradley, Jr. Lanham, MD: Rowman & Littlefield Publishers, c1996. 2 v.
95-021325   338.2/728/0973 20   0847681106
Petroleum industry and trade -- Government policy -- United States -- History. Gas industry -- Government policy -- United States -- History. Petroleum law and legislation -- United States -- History.

HD9566.I525 1988
Ikenberry, G. John.
Reasons of state: oil politics and the capacities of American government/ G. John Ikenberry. Ithaca: Cornell University Press, 1988. xii, 213 p.
88-003660   333.79/0973   0801494885
Petroleum industry and trade -- Government policy -- United States. Energy policy -- United States.

HD9566.R36 1985
Randall, Stephen J., 1944-
United States foreign oil policy, 1919-1948: for profits and security/ Stephen J. Randall. Kingston: McGill-Queen's University Press, c1985. viii, 328 p.
85-211907   338.2/7282/0973   0773504494
Petroleum industry and trade -- Government policy -- United States -- History -- 20th century. Petroleum industry and trade -- Political aspects -- United States. United States -- Foreign relations -- 20th century.

HD9566.T85 1988
Tugwell, Franklin, 1942-
The energy crisis and the American political economy: politics and markets in the management of natural resources/ Franklin Tugwell. Stanford, Calif.: Stanford University Press, 1988. ix, 294 p.
88-012175   333.79/0973   0804715009
Petroleum industry and trade -- Government policy -- United States. Energy policy -- United States.

HD9570.M3M3 1992
Mathews, John Joseph,
Life and death of an oilman: the career of E.W. Marland/ by John Joseph Mathews; with drawings by J. Craig Sheppard. Norman: University of Oklahoma Press, [1989], c1951. xi, 259 p.
89-070455   338.4/76223382/092   0806112387
Marland, Ernest Whitworth, 1874-1941. Industrialists -- United States -- Biography. Petroleum industry and trade -- United States -- History.

HD9574.B82.R36 1993
Randall, Laura.
The political economy of Brazilian oil/ Laura Randall. Westport, Conn.: Praeger, 1993. xii, 315 p.
92-015781   338.2/7282/0981   0275940918
Petroleum industry and trade -- Government policy -- Brazil -- History. Petroleum industry and trade -- Brazil -- History.

HD9574.M6.T45 1988
Teichman, Judith A., 1947-
Policymaking in Mexico: from boom to crisis/ Judith A. Teichman. Boston: Allen & Unwin, c1988. 178 p.
87-018704   338.2/7282/0972   0044450338
Petroleum industry and trade -- Government policy -- Mexico. Banks and banking -- Government ownership -- Mexico. Mexico -- Economic policy -- 1970-

HD9574.V42.S357 1994
Salazar-Carrillo, Jorge.
Oil and development in Venezuela during the twentieth century/ Jorge Salazar-Carrillo; with the assistance of Robert D. Cruz. Westport, Conn.: Praeger, 1994. 280 p.
93-037882   338.987/009/04   0275928497
Petroleum industry and trade -- Venezuela -- History -- 20th century.

HD9575.N57.C5
Chapman, Keith.
North Sea oil and gas: a geographical perspective/ [by] Keith Chapman. Newton Abbot; David and Charles, 1976. 240 p.
76-004369   333.8/2   0715371835
Petroleum in submerged lands -- North Sea. Petroleum industry and trade -- North Sea.

HD9575.R82.K57
Klinghoffer, Arthur Jay, 1941-
The Soviet Union & international oil politics/ Arthur Jay Klinghoffer. New York: Columbia University Press, 1977. ix, 389 p.
76-052411   338.2/7/2820947   0231041047
Petroleum industry and trade -- Soviet Union. World politics -- 1975-1985. Soviet Union -- Foreign economic relations.

HD9576.C372.E53 2000
Energy and conflict in Central Asia and the Caucasus/ edited by Robert Ebel and Rajan Menon. Lanham, MD: Rowman & Littlefield Publishers, c2000. viii, 267 p.
00-040302   333.8/23/09475 21   0742500624
Petroleum industry and trade -- Caspian Sea Region. Petroleum industry and trade -- Political aspects -- Caspian Sea Region. Gas industry -- Caspian Sea Region.

HD9576.C372.G65 2001
The politics of Caspian oil/ edited by Bulent Gokay. Houndmills, Basingstoke, Hampshire; St. Martin's Press, 2001. ix, 232 p.
00-059175   333.8/23/09475   0333739736
Petroleum industry and trade -- Political aspects -- Caspian Sea Region. Geopolitics -- Caspian Sea Region. Caspian Sea Region -- Politics and government.

HD9576.I52.B37 1995
Barnes, Philip, 1934-
Indonesia, the political economy of energy/ Philip Barnes. Oxford; Oxford University Press for the Oxford Institute 1995. xiv, 193 p.
96-118860   0197300162
Petroleum industry and trade -- Indonesia. Gas industry -- Indonesia. Power resources -- Indonesia. Indonesia -- Economic conditions -- 1945-.

HD9576.I62.E46 1992
Elm, Mostafa.
Oil, power, and principle: Iran's oil nationalization and its aftermath/ Mostafa Elm. Syracuse, N.Y.: Syracuse University Press, 1992. xvii, 413 p.
91-012390   338.2/7282/0955   0815625510
Mosaddeq, Mohammad, -- 1880-1967. Anglo-Iranian Oil Dispute, 1951-1954. Petroleum industry and trade -- Government ownership -- Iran. Iran -- Politics and government -- 1941-1979.

HD9576.I72.A647 1994
Alnasrawi, Abbas.
The economy of Iraq: oil, wars, destruction of development and prospects, 1950-2010/ Abbas Alnasrawi. Westport, Conn.: Greenwood Press, 1994. xvi, 186 p.
93-037510   330.9567/0442   0313291861
Petroleum industry and trade -- Iraq -- History -- 20th century. Petroleum industry and trade -- Iraq -- Forecasting. Iran-Iraq War, 1980-1988 -- Economic aspects -- Iraq. Iraq -- Economic conditions.

HD9576.P52.G85 1990
The Gulf, energy, and global security: political and economic issues/ edited by Charles F. Doran, Stephen W. Buck. Boulder, Colo.: L. Rienner Publishers, 1991. xii, 234 p.
90-009100   338.2/7282/09536   1555872549
Petroleum industry and trade -- Political aspects -- Persian Gulf Region. World politics -- 1985-1995. Persian Gulf Region -- Politics and government.

HD9576.S35.A72
Anderson, Irvine H., 1928-
Aramco, the United States, and Saudi Arabia: a study of the dynamics of foreign oil policy, 1933-1950/ Irvine H. Anderson. Princeton, N.J.: Princeton University Press, c1981. xiii, 259 p.
80-008535   338.7/6223382/09538   0691046794
Petroleum industry and trade -- Saudi Arabia. Petroleum industry and trade -- United States. United States -- Foreign economic relations -- Saudi Arabia. United States -- Foreign relations -- Saudi Arabia.

HD9577.N52.A334 1994
Ahmad Khan, Sarah.
Nigeria: the political economy of oil/ Sarah Ahmad Khan. Oxford: Oxford University Press for the Oxford Institute 1994. xiv, 234 p.
95-114629   338.2728209669   0197300146
Petroleum industry and trade -- Nigeria.

HD9579.C32.C45 1991
Chapman, Keith.
The international petrochemical industry: evolution and location/ Keith Chapman. Oxford, UK; B. Blackwell, 1991. xiv, 322 p.
91-010435   338.4/7661804   0631160981
Petroleum chemicals industry.

HD9581 Special industries and trades — Mineral industries. Metal trade — Natural gas

HD9581.D442.N38 1990
Natural gas: its role and potential in economic development/ edited by Walter Vergara, Nelson E. Hay, and Carl W. Hall. Boulder: Westview Press, 1990. xiii, 319 p.
89-033756   338.2/7285/091724   0813378125
Gas industry -- Developing countries. Natural gas. Economic development.

HD9581.U5.D43 1995
De Vany, Arthur S.
The emerging new order in natural gas: markets versus regulation/ Arthur S. De Vany, W. David Walls. Westport, Conn.: Quorum Books, 1995. xii, 136 p.
94-046198   338.2/7285/0973   0899309445
Gas industry -- United States. Natural gas -- United States -- Marketing.

HD9581.U5.G23 1993
Gallick, Edward C.
Competition in the natural gas pipeline industry: an economic policy analysis/ Edward C. Gallick. Westport, Conn.: Praeger, 1993. xvi, 284 p.
92-014536   388.5/6/0973   0275943461
Gas industry -- Government policy -- United States. Natural gas pipelines -- Government policy -- United States. Competition -- Government policy -- United States.

HD9581.U52.A1153 1993
Castaneda, Christopher James, 1959-
Regulated enterprise: natural gas pipelines and northeastern markets, 1938-1954/ Christopher James Castaneda. Columbus: Ohio State University Press, c1993. xiv, 203 p.
92-023827   388.5/6/0974   0814205909
Gas industry -- Government policy -- Northeastern States -- History -- 20th century. Natural gas pipelines -- Northeastern States -- History -- 20th century.

HD9581.U53.P363 1996
Castaneda, Christopher James, 1959-
Gas pipelines and the emergence of America's regulatory state: a history of Panhandle Eastern Corporation, 1928-1993/ Christopher J. Castaneda, Clarance M. Smith. New York, NY: Cambridge University Press, 1996. xx, 296 p.
96-197025   0521561663
Gas industry -- Government policy -- United States -- History -- 20th century. Natural gas pipelines -- United States -- History -- 20th century.

HD9650.5-9660 Special industries and trades — Chemical industries — Special products, A-Z

HD9650.5.C535 1998
Chemicals and long-term economic growth: insights from the chemical industry/ edited by Ashish Arora, Ralph Landau, Nathan Rosenberg. New York: Wiley, c1998. ix, 564 p.
97-028674   338.4/766 21   0471182478
Chemical industry -- Case studies. Chemical industry -- History. Chemical industry -- Technological innovations -- History.

HD9651.9.D6.B73 1997
Brandt, E. N.
Growth company: Dow Chemical's first century/ E.N. Brandt. East Lansing: Michigan State University Press, c1997. xxi, 649 p.
97-000749   338.7/66/00973 21   0870134264
Dow, Herbert Henry, -- 1866-1930. Industrialists -- United States -- Biography. Chemical industry -- United States -- History.

HD9651.9.D8.T39 1984
Taylor, Graham D., 1944-
Du Pont and the international chemical industry/ Graham D. Taylor and Patricia E. Sudnik. Boston, Mass.: Twayne, c1984. xxi, 251 p.
84-008933   338.8/87   0805798056
Chemical industry -- United States -- History. Chemical industry -- History.

HD9651.95.C37.C48 1995
Cheape, Charles W., 1945-
Strictly business: Walter Carpenter at Du Pont and General Motors/ Charles W. Cheape. Baltimore: Johns Hopkins University Press, 1995. xix, 309 p.
94-022652   658.4/0092   0801849411
Carpenter, Walter Samuel, -- 1888-1976. Chemical industry -- United States -- Management -- History. Executives -- United States -- Biography. Automobile industry and trade -- United States -- Management -- History.

HD9654.9.I5.S76 1988
Stokes, Raymond G.
Divide and prosper: the heirs of I.G. Farben under Allied authority, 1945-1951/ Raymond G. Stokes. Berkeley: University of California Press, c1988. xiv, 290 p.
88-001326   338.7/66/00943   0520062485
Chemical industry -- Political aspects -- Germany (West) -- History -- 20th century. United States -- Foreign economic relations -- Germany (West) Germany (West) -- Foreign economic relations -- United States.

HD9660.D843.E858 1993
Travis, A. S.
The rainbow makers: the origins of the synthetic dyestuffs industry in western Europe/ Anthony S. Travis. Bethlehem: Lehigh University Press; c1993. 335 p.
91-060412   338.4/76672/094   0934223181
Dye industry -- Europe -- History.

HD9665.6-9674 Special industries and trades — Pharmaceutical industry — Special products, A-Z

HD9665.6.C47 1989
Chetley, Andrew.
A healthy business?: world health and the pharmaceutical industry/ Andrew Chetley. London; Zed Books, 1990. xv, 206 p.
89-035871   338.4/76151   0862327342
Pharmaceutical industry -- Government policy.

HD9666.5.S79 1983
Statman, Meir.
Competition in the pharmaceutical industry: the declining profitability of drug innovation/ Meir Statman. Washington: American Enterprise Institute for Public Policy c1983. 84 p.
83-003880   338.4/36151/0973   0844735140
Pharmaceutical industry -- United States. Drugs -- Research -- United States -- Costs. Generic drugs -- United States.

HD9667.9.G53.D38 1992
Davenport-Hines, R. P. T. 1953-
Glaxo: a history to 1962/ R.P.T. Devenport-Hines and Judy Slinn. Cambridge [England]; Cambridge University Press, 1992. xiv, 406 p.
91-042204   338.4/76151/0941   052141539X
Pharmaceutical industry -- Great Britain -- History.

HD9674.D44.S54 1992
Silverman, Milton, 1910-
Bad medicine: the prescription drug industry in the Third World/ Milton Silverman, Mia Lydecker, Philip R. Lee. Stanford, Calif.: Stanford University Press, 1992. xvii, 358 p.
91-005085   338.4/76151/091724   0804716692
Pharmaceutical industry -- Corrupt practices -- Developing countries. Pharmaceutical policy -- Developing countries. Drug Industry -- standards. Developing Countries.

HD9680 Special industries and trades — Mechanical industries — General works

HD9680.U52.E25 1991
Eckley, Robert S.
Global competition in capital goods: an American perspective/ Robert S. Eckley. New York: Quorum Books, 1991. xiii, 180 p.
90-026489   338.4/76218/0973   0899305598
Industrial equipment industry -- United States -- Case studies. Competition, International.

HD9685-9688 Special industries and trades — Mechanical industries — Electric utilities. Electrification

HD9685.A2.E46 1996
Electric power industry outlook and atlas, 1997 to 2001/ PennWell power group magazine editors and contributors. Tulsa, Okla.: PennWell Books, 1996. xxi, 330 p.
96-047644   333.793/2   0878146520
Electric utilities. Electric utilities -- Forecasting. Electric power consumption -- Forecasting.

HD9685.C3.J363 1985
Bourassa, Robert, 1933-
Power from the North/ Robert Bourassa; with a foreword by James Schlesinger. Scarborough, Ont.: Prentice-Hall Canada, c1985. x, 181 p.
85-158461   333.79/3215/097141   0136883672
Water resources development -- James Bay Region (Ont. and Quebec) Electric power production -- Economic aspects -- James Bay Region (Ont. and Quebec)

HD9685.F84.E52 1991
Frost, Robert L., 1952-
Alternating currents: nationalized power in France, 1946-1970/ Robert L. Frost. Ithaca, N.Y.: Cornell University Press, 1991. xii, 285 p.
90-055727   333.79/32/0944   0801423511
Electric utilities -- France. Electric utilities -- Government ownership. Electric utilities -- Technological innovations.

HD9685.U5 B74 2002
Brennan, Timothy J.
Alternating currents: electricity markets and public policy/ Timothy J. Brennan, Karen L. Palmer, and Salvador A. Martinez. Washington, DC: Resources for the Future, c2002. xi, 210 p.
2002-017328   333.793/2/0973 21   1891853074
Electric utilities -- United States. Electric utilities -- Government policy -- United States. Electric utilities -- United States -- Management.

HD9685.U5.F59 1998
Flowers, Edward B., 1939-
U.S. utility mergers and the restructuring of the new global power industry/ Edward B. Flowers. Westport, Conn.: Quorum Books, 1998. viii, 261 p.
97-046575   333.793/2/0973   1567201636
Electric utilities -- Mergers -- United States. Gas industry -- Mergers -- United States. Electric utilities -- United States -- Finance.

HD9685.U5.H568 1999
Hirsh, Richard F.
Power loss: the origins of deregulation and restructuring in the American electric utility system/ Richard F. Hirsh. Cambridge, Mass.: MIT Press, c1999. x, 406 p.
99-015443   333.793/2/0973 21   026208273X
Electric utilities -- Deregulation -- United States. Electric utilities -- Government policy -- United States -- History. Electric utilities -- Law and legislation -- United States -- History.

HD9685.U5.H57 1989
Hirsh, Richard F.
Technology and transformation in the American electric utility industry/ Richard F. Hirsh. Cambridge [England]; Cambridge University Press, 1989. xiv, 274 p.
89-032978   333.79/32/0973   0521364787
Electric utilities -- United States -- Technological innovations.

HD9685.U5.N94 1990
Nye, David E., 1946-
Electrifying America: social meanings of a new technology, 1880-1940/ David E. Nye. Cambridge, Mass.: MIT Press, c1990. xv, 479 p.
90-036689   333.79/32/0973   0262140489
Electrification -- United States -- History. Electrification -- Social aspects -- United States.

HD9685.U5.T63 1996
Tobey, Ronald C.
Technology as freedom: the New Deal and the electrical modernization of the American home/ Ronald C. Tobey. Berkeley: University of California Press, c1996. xviii, 316 p.
96-023123   333.79/32/097309043   20   0520204212
Electrification -- United States -- History -- 20th century. Electrification -- Social aspects -- United States. Rural electrification -- United States -- History -- 20th century.

HD9685.U7.T333 1997
Colignon, Richard A., 1951-
Power plays: critical events in the institutionalization of the Tennessee Valley Authority/ Richard A. Colignon. Albany: State University of New York Press, c1997. xii, 367 p.
95-039702   353.0082/3/09768 20   0791430111
Electric utilities -- Tennessee River Valley -- History. Corporations, Government -- United States -- History.

HD9688.U52.B76
Brown, D. Clayton 1941-
Electricity for rural America: the fight for the REA/ D. Clayton Brown. Westport, Conn.: Greenwood Press, 1980. xvi, 178 p.
79-008287   353.008/72208/09   0313214786
Rural electrification -- United States -- History.

HD9696 Special industries and trades — Mechanical industries — Electronic industries

HD9696.A3.D446 1988
Katz, Raul Luciano.
The information society: an international perspective/ Raul Luciano Katz. New York: Praeger, 1988. xvii, 168 p.
87-025884   338.4/7004/091724   0275926591
Information technology -- Economic aspects -- Developing countries. Information society -- Developing countries.

HD9696.A3.J39317 1999
Partner, Simon.
Assembled in Japan: electrical goods and the making of the Japanese consumer/ Simon Partner. Berkeley: University of California Press, c1999. xiv, 303 p.
98-037375   338.4/7621381/0952   21   0520217926
Electronic industries -- Japan. Consumers -- Japan.

HD9696.A3.U5334 1999
Cowie, Jefferson R.
Capital moves: RCA's seventy-year quest for cheap labor/ Jefferson Cowie. Ithaca, N.Y.: Cornell University Press, 1999. x, 272 p.
98-049784   338.7/621381/0973   0801435250
Electronics industry workers -- United States -- History. Business relocation.

HD9696.C62.C47 1987
Cortada, James W.
Historical dictionary of data processing--organizations/ James W. Cortada. New York: Greenwood Press, 1987. x, 309 p.
86-019394   338.7/61004/09   0313233039
Computer industry -- History. Computer service industry -- History. Electronic data processing -- Societies, etc. -- History.

HD9696.C63.U52628 1997
Moschella, David C.
Waves of power: dynamics of global technology leadership, 1964-2010/ David C. Moschella. New York: AMACOM, c1997. xx, 300 p.
96-049652   338.4/7004/09045 21   0814403794
Computer industry -- United States. Computer software industry -- United States. Computer industry.

HD9696.C63.U58339 1997
Sichel, Daniel E.
The computer revolution: an economic perspective/ Daniel E. Sichel. Washington, D.C.: Brookings Institution Press, c1997. xii, 152 p.
97-007425   338.4/7004/0973 21   0815778961
Computer industry -- United States. Computer service industry -- United States. Computer software industry -- United States. United States -- Economic conditions.

HD9696.C64.I4858 1988
Mills, Daniel Quinn.
The IBM lesson: the profitable art of full employment/ D. Quinn Mills. New York: Times Books, c1988. 216 p.
87-040593   331.7/61004/0973   0812916905
Computer industry -- United States -- Employees.

HD9696.C772.B87 1994
Burke, Colin B., 1936-
Information and secrecy: Vannevar Bush, Ultra, and the other Memex/ by Colin Burke; with a foreword by Michael Buckland. Metuchen, N.J.: Scarecrow Press, 1994. xxvi, 466 p.
93-039656   338.4/70058/0973   0810827832
Bush, Vannevar, -- 1890-1974. Electronic analog computers -- History. World War, 1939-1945 -- Cryptography. Cryptography equipment industry -- History.

HD9696.R363.G747 1988
Pocock, Rowland F.
The early British radio industry/ by Rowland F. Pocock. Manchester, UK; Manchester University Press; c1988. viii, 184 p.
88-008816   384.54/0941   0719026210
Radio supplies industry -- Great Britain -- History. Radio supplies industry -- History. Radio broadcasting -- Great Britain -- History.

HD9696.S43.U466 1996
Flamm, Kenneth, 1951-
Mismanaged trade?: strategic policy and the semiconductor industry/ Kenneth Flamm. Washington, D.C.: Brookings Institution Press, c1996. xvii, 472 p.
94-021324   382/.4562138152/0973   20   0815728468
Semiconductor industry -- Government policy -- United States. Semiconductor industry -- Government policy -- Japan. United States -- Foreign economic relations -- Japan. Japan -- Foreign economic relations -- United States.

HD9696.T444.C57 2000
Bunnell, David.
Making the Cisco connection: the story behind the real Internet superpower/ David Bunnell, with Adam Brate. New York: John Wiley & Sons, c2000. xxi, 218 p.
2001-269143   0471357111
Routers (Computer networks) Telecommunication. Telecommunication -- Equipment and supplies.

HD9696.2-9696.63 Special industries and trades — Mechanical industries — Computer industry

HD9696.2.E182.D43 1998
Dedrick, Jason.
Asia's computer challenge: threat or opportunity for the United States & the world?/ Jason Dedrick, Kenneth L. Kraemer. New York: Oxford University Press, 1998. xviii, 364 p.
98-019114   338.4/7004/095   0195122011
Computer industry -- East Asia. Computer industry -- Japan. Computer industry -- United States.

HD9696.63.U64.M5364 1999
Liebowitz, S. J., 1950-
Winners, losers & Microsoft: competition and antitrust in high technology/ Stan J. Leibowitz, Stephen E. Margolis; foreword by Jack Hirshleifer. Oakland, Calif.: Independent Institute, c1999. xiv, 288 p.
99-073414   338.8/2610053/0973   21
0945999801
Computer software industry -- United States. Competition -- Government policy -- United States. Antitrust investigations -- United States.

HD9696.63.U64.M538 2000
Tsang, Cheryl D., 1947-
Microsoft first generation: the success secrets of the visionaries who launched a technology empire/ Cheryl D. Tsang. New York: J. Wiley & Sons, 2000. xvii, 253 p.
99-027007   338.7/610053/0973   0471332062
Microsoft Corporation -- History. Businessmen -- United States -- Biography. Computer software industry -- United States -- History.

HD9697 Special industries and trades — Mechanical industries — Electric industries

HD9697.A3.U588 2001
Lowe, Janet.
Welch: an American icon/ Janet Lowe. New York: Wiley, 2001. 304 p.
00-054564   338.7/62138/092   0471413356
Welch, Jack -- (John Francis), -- 1935-   Electric industries -- United States. Chief executive officers -- United States -- Biography. Leadership -- United States.

HD9697.T454.W473 1999
Adams, Stephen B., 1955-
Manufacturing the future: a history of Western Electric/ Stephen B. Adams, Orville R. Butler. Cambridge; Cambridge University Press, 1999. xi, 270 p.
98-034294   338.7/6213/0973   0521651182
Telephone supplies industry -- United States -- History. Electronic industries -- United States -- History.

HD9698 Special industries and trades — Mechanical industries — Nuclear industry

HD9698.U5.D76 1997
Duffy, Robert J.
Nuclear politics in America: a history and theory of government regulation/ Robert J. Duffy. Lawrence, Kan.: University Press of Kansas, c1997. vii, 304 p.
97-019146   333.792/4/0973 21   0700608524
Nuclear industry -- Government policy -- United States. Nuclear power plants -- Law and legislation -- United States.

HD9698.U52.E25 1997
Eckstein, Rick, 1960-
Nuclear power and social power/ Rick Eckstein. Philadelphia: Temple University Press, 1997. xiii, 191 p.
96-023908   333.792/4   1566394856
Nuclear industry -- Government policy -- United States -- Citizen participation.

HD9698.U52.H55 1989 vol. 3
Hewlett, Richard G.
Atoms for peace and war, 1953-1961: Eisenhower and the Atomic Energy Commission/ Richard G. Hewlett and Jack M. Holl; with a foreword by Richard S. Kirkendall and an essay on sources by Roger M. Anders. Berkeley: University of California Press, 1989. xxix, 696 p.
88-029578   333.79/24/0973   0520060180
Eisenhower, Dwight D. -- (Dwight David), -- 1890-1969.   Nuclear energy -- United States -- History. United States -- Politics and government -- 1953-1961.

HD9698.U52.R46 1993
Rhodes, Richard.
Nuclear renewal: common sense about energy/ Richard Rhodes. New York, N.Y., U.S.A.: Whittle Books in association with Viking, 1993. ix, 127 p.
93-022021   333.792/4/0973   0670852074
Nuclear industry -- United States.

HD9698.U54.S543 1997
Aron, Joan B.
Licensed to kill?: the Nuclear Regulatory Commission and the Shoreham Power Plant/ Joan Aron. Pittsburgh: University of Pittsburgh Press, c1997. xv, 184 p.
97-021163   333.792/4/0979727 21   0822940442
Nuclear industry -- Government policy -- United States. Nuclear power plants -- Licenses -- New York (State)

HD9706.6 Special industries and trades — Mechanical industries — Instrument industry

HD9706.6.G74
Wood, Audrey,
Magnetic venture: the story of Oxford Instruments/ Audrey Wood. Oxford; Oxford University Press, 2001. xx, 387 p.
00-040059   338.7/681/0941
Scientific apparatus and instruments industry -- Great Britain -- History. Medical instruments and apparatus industry -- Great Britain -- History. Nuclear magnetic resonance -- Industrial applications -- History.

HD9710-9711.75 Special industries and trades — Mechanical industries — Transportation equipment. Vehicles

HD9710.A2.W65 1990
Womack, James P.
The machine that changed the world: based on the Massachusetts Institute of Technology 5-million dollar 5-year study on the future of the automobile/ James P. Womack, Daniel T. Jones, Daniel Roos. New York: Rawson Associates, c1990. viii, 323 p.
89-063284   338.4/7629222/0112   0892563508
Automobile industry and trade -- Forecasting.

HD9710.A7852.D66 1991
Doner, Richard F.
Driving a bargain: automobile industrialization and Japanese firms in Southeast Asia/ Richard F. Doner. Berkeley: University of California Press, c1991. xv, 371 p.
90-040198   338.8/8952059   0520069382
Automobile industry and trade -- Asia, Southeastern -- Foreign ownership. Corporations, Japanese -- Asia, Southeastern.

HD9710.J32.B49 1996
Beyond Japanese management: the end of modern times?/ edited by Paul Stewart. London; Frank Cass, 1996. 206 p.
96-044871   658/.00951   0714647616
Automobile industry and trade -- Japan -- Management. Automobile industry and trade -- Management -- Case studies. Comparative management.

HD9710.U52.A787 1990
The Automobile industry, 1896-1920/ edited by George S. May. New York: Facts on File, c1990. xxiv, 485 p.
89-011672   338.4/76292/097309034
0816020841
Automobile industry and trade -- United States -- History. Automobile industry and trade -- United States -- Biography. Industrialists -- United States -- Biography.

HD9710.U52.D858
Weisberger, Bernard A., 1922-
The dream maker: William C. Durant, founder of General Motors/ by Bernard A. Weisberger. Boston: Little, Brown, c1979. xix, 396 p.
79-090456   338.7/6292/0924   0316928747
Durant, William Crapo, 1861-1947. Businesspeople -- United States -- Biography.

HD9710.U52.Q56 1988
Quinn, Dennis Patrick, 1955-
Restructuring the automobile industry: a study of firms and states in modern capitalism/ Dennis Patrick Quinn, Jr. New York: Columbia University Press, 1988. xv, 395 p.
87-015919   338.4/76292/0941   0231065248
Automobile industry and trade -- United States. Automobile industry and trade -- Great Britain. Industrial policy -- United States.

HD9710.U52.R83 1992
Rubenstein, James M., 1949-
The changing US auto industry: a geographical analysis/ James M. Rubenstein. London [England]; Routledge, 1992. vi, 318 p.
91-016821   338.4/76292/0973   041505544X
Automobile industry and trade -- United States.

HD9710.U54.G397 2001
Freeland, Robert F., 1957-
The struggle for control of the modern corporation: organizational change at General Motors, 1924-1970/ Robert F. Freeland. Cambridge, UK; Cambridge University Press, 2001. xvii, 364 p.
00-036302   338.7/6292/0973   0521630347
Organizational change. Industrial management.

HD9710.U54.S834 1996
Critchlow, Donald T., 1948-
Studebaker: the life and death of an American corporation/ Donald T. Critchlow. Bloomington: Indiana University Press, c1996. x, 273 p.
95-052639   338.7/6292222 20   0253330653
Automobile industry and trade -- United States -- History.

HD9711.F72.C53 1990
Chapman, Herrick.
State capitalism and working-class radicalism in the French aircraft industry/ Herrick Chapman. Berkeley: University of California Press, c1991. xvii, 412 p.
90-010790   338.4/762913/0944   0520059530
Aircraft industry -- Government ownership -- France. Aircraft industry workers -- France -- Political activity.

HD9711.U63.B6364 2001
Sell, T. M.
Wings of power: Boeing and the politics of growth in the Northwest/ T.M. Sell. Seattle: University of Washington Press, c2001. xxx, 162 p.
00-060702   338.7/629133/0973 21   0295980494
Aircraft industry -- United States -- History. Aircraft industry -- United States -- Employees. Aeronautics, Commercial -- United States -- History. Seattle Metropolitan Area (Wash.) -- Economic conditions.

HD9711.75.U62.G66 1989
Goodrich, Jonathan N.
The commercialization of outer space: opportunities and obstacles for American business/ Jonathan N. Goodrich. New York: Quorum Books, 1989. xxviii, 211 p.
88-023665   338.0919   0899303420
Space industrialization -- United States.

HD9715 Special industries and trades — Construction industry and materials — General works

HD9715.G73.L63 1991
Clarke, Linda, 1947-
Building capitalism: historical change and the labour process in the production of the built environment/ Linda Clarke. London; Routledge, 1992. xv, 316 p.
91-003200   338.4/769/009421   0415015529
Construction industry -- England -- London -- History. Wages -- Construction workers -- England -- London -- History. Urbanization -- England -- London -- History. London (England) -- Economic conditions.

HD9718 Special industries and trades — Environmental engineering industries. Pollution control industry — General works

HD9718.A2 R46 2000
Renner, Michael,
Working for the environment: a growing source of jobs/ Michael Renner. Washington, DC: Worldwatch Institute, 2000. 85 p.
00-108015   1878071548
Pollution control industry. Environmental policy. Job creation.

HD9720.1-9734 Special industries and trades — Manufacturing industries

HD9720.1.M33
Manufacturing worldwide: industry analyses, statistics, products, and leading companies and countries. New York: Gale Research, [c1995-]
98-657674   338.4/767/05
Manufacturing industries -- Statistics -- Periodicals. Industrial statistics -- Periodicals.

HD9720.5.M38 1991
Manufacturing systems: foundations of world-class practice/ Joseph A. Heim and W. Dale Compton, editors. Washington, D.C.: National Academy Press, 1992. viii, 273 p.
91-036171   658.5   0309046785
Manufacturing industries -- Management. Industrial management.

HD9725.C38 1990
Caves, Richard E.
Efficiency in U.S. manufacturing industries/ Richard E. Caves and David R. Barton. Cambridge, Mass.: MIT Press, c1990. viii, 194 p.
89-028832   338/.06/0973   0262031574
Manufacturing industries -- Labor productivity -- United States. Industrial productivity -- United States.

HD9725.H38 1988
Hayes, Robert H.
Dynamic manufacturing: creating the learning organization/ Robert H. Hayes, Steven C. Wheelwright, Kim B. Clark. New York: Free Press; c1988. x, 429 p.
88-000367   658.5   0029142113
Manufacturing industries -- United States -- Management.

HD9725.M367 1991
Maskell, Brian H.
Performance measurement for world class manufacturing: a model for American companies/ Brian H. Maskell. Cambridge, Mass.: Productivity Press, c1991. xxi, 408 p.
91-006855   658.5/036 20   0915299992
Manufacturing industries -- United States -- Management. Manufacturing industries -- Labor productivity -- United States -- Measurement.

HD9734.M42.K67 1996
Kopinak, Kathryn.
Desert capitalism: maquiladoras in North America's western industrial corridor/ Kathryn Kopinak. Tucson: University of Arizona Press, c1996. xvi, 232 p.
95-032506   338.4/7/0009721 20   0816515980
Offshore assembly industry -- Mexico. Offshore assembly industry -- Employees -- Mexico. Mexico -- Social conditions -- 1970-

HD9734.M43.M497 1989
Sklair, Leslie.
Assembling for development: the maquila industry in Mexico and the United States/ Leslie Sklair. Boston: Unwin Hyman, 1989. xvi, 256 p.
88-037613   338.4/767/09721   0044452780
Offshore assembly industry -- Mexican-American Border Region. Investments, Foreign -- Mexican-American Border Region. Mexico -- Economic policy -- 1970-

HD9743 Special industries and trades — Manufacturing industries — Defense industries. Weapons industry

HD9743.A2.K45 1995
Keller, William W. 1950-
Arm in arm: the political economy of the global arms trade/ William W. Keller. New York: Basic Books, c1995. xvi, 222 p.
95-023152   338.4/76234   0465026672
Defense industries. Arms transfers. Arms race.

HD9743.B682.M35 1994
Maldifassi, Jose O.
Defense industries in Latin American countries: Argentina, Brazil, and Chile/ Jose O. Maldifassi and Pier A. Abetti. Westport, Conn.: Praeger, 1994. xiii, 260 p.
93-043070   338.4/76233/0981   0275947297
Defense industries -- Brazil. Defense industries -- Argentina. Defense industries -- Chile. Argentina -- Defenses. Brazil -- Defenses. Chile -- Defenses.

HD9743.R92.R87 1998
Russia and the arms trade/ edited by Ian Anthony. Solna, Sweden: SIPRI; 1998. xiv, 304 p.
97-046862   382/.456233/0947   0198292783
Arms transfers -- Russia (Federation) Defense industries -- Russia (Federation)

HD9743.S62.L36 1989
Landgren, Signe.
Embargo disimplemented: South Africa's military industry/ Signe Landgren. Oxford; Oxford University Press, 1989. xv, 276 p.
88-025255   382/.456234/0968   0198291272
Munitions -- South Africa.

HD9743.U6.S64 1995
Spear, Joanna, 1961-
Carter and arms sales: implementing the Carter administration's arms transfer restraint policy/ Joanna Spear. New York, N.Y.: St. Martin's Press, 1995. xiv, 246 p.
95-004168   327.1/74/0973   0312126816
Arms transfers -- Government policy -- United States. United States -- Foreign relations -- 1977-1981. United States -- Politics and government -- 1977-1981.

HD9743.U7.C25 1992
Lotchin, Roger W.
Fortress California, 1910-1961: from warfare to welfare/ Roger W. Lotchin. New York: Oxford University Press, 1992. xviii, 420 p.
91-021408   338.4/76233/09796   0195047796
Defense industries -- California -- History -- 20th century. Military bases -- Economic aspects -- California -- History -- 20th century. Military-industrial complex -- California -- History -- 20th century. United States -- Armed Forces -- California -- History -- 20th century. California -- Economic conditions.

HD9750.5-9769 Special industries and trades — Manufacturing industries — Forest products. Lumber

HD9750.5.T55 1985
Tillman, David A.
Forest products: advanced technologies and economic analyses/ David A. Tillman. Orlando: Academic Press, 1985. xii, 283 p.
85-070363   338.1/7498   012691270X
Forest products industry. Forest products industry -- Technological innovations.

HD9757.W2R443
Ficken, Robert E.
Lumber and politics: the career of Mark E. Reed/ Robert E. Ficken. Santa Cruz, Calif.: Forest History Society, c1979. xi, 264 p.
78-021756   338.7/63/49820924   0295956550
Reed, Mark E. (Mark Edward), 1866-1933. Lumber trade -- Washington (State) -- History. Businesspeople -- United States -- Biography.

HD9759.B37M54 1983
Milliken, Roger.
Forest for the trees: a history of the Baskahegan Company/ Roger Milliken, Jr. [Augusta, Me.]: R. Milliken, c1983. 140 p.
83-146610   338.7/674/09741
Lumber trade -- Maine -- History.

HD9760.B83.M39 1988
Mayor, Archer H.
Southern timberman: the legacy of William Buchanan/ Archer H. Mayor. Athens: University of Georgia Press, c1988. xvii, 263 p.
87-022897   338.7/63498/0975   0820309990
Buchanan, William, -- 1849-1923. Businesspeople -- Southern States -- Biography. Lumber trade -- Southern States -- History. Family corporations -- Southern States -- History.

HD9766.C52.R53 1990
Richardson, S. D. 1925-
Forests and forestry in China: changing patterns of resource development/ S.D. Richardson; foreword by Jeff Romm. Washington, D.C.: Island Press, 1990. xxii, 352 p.
89-024514   333.75/0951   155963023X
Forests and forestry -- Economic aspects -- China. Forest policy -- China. Forest management -- China.

HD9769.B323.A453 1991
Anderson, Anthony B. 1950-
The subsidy from nature: palm forests, peasantry, and development on an Amazon frontier/ Anthony B. Anderson, Peter H. May, and Michael J. Balick. New York: Columbia University Press, c1991. xxv, 233 p.
91-014347   338.1/73851   0231072228
Babassu products industry -- Amazon River Region. Peasantry -- Amazon River Region. Amazon River Region -- Economic conditions.

HD9801 Special industries and trades — Manufacturing industries — Office equipment and supplies

HD9801.U542.C67 1993
Cortada, James W.
Before the computer: IBM, NCR, Burroughs, and Remington Rand and the industry they created, 1865-1956/ James W. Cortada. Princeton, N.J.: Princeton University Press, c1993. xx, 344 p.
92-025399   338.4/768   069104807X
Office equipment and supplies industry -- United States -- History. Electronic office machine industry -- United States -- History.

HD9826-9827 Special industries and trades — Manufacturing industries — Paper. Paper products

HD9826.S65 1997
Smith, Maureen, 1956-
The U.S. paper industry and sustainable production: an argument for restructuring/ Maureen Smith. Cambridge, Mass.: MIT Press, 1997. xii, 303 p.
96-041991   338.4/5676/0973   0262193779
Paper industry -- Government policy -- United States. Wood-pulp industry -- Government policy -- United States.

HD9827.M2O8
Osborn, William C.
The paper plantation; Ralph Nader's study group report on the pulp and paper industry in Maine [by] William C. Osborn. Introd. by Ralph Nader. New York, Grossman Publishers, 1974. xx, 300 p.
73-019107   338.4/7/67609741   0670538078
Paper industry -- Maine. Wood-pulp industry -- Maine.

HD9855-9926 Special industries and trades — Manufacturing industries — Textile industries. Textile fibers

HD9855.J47
Jeremy, David J.
Transatlantic industrial revolution: the diffusion of textile technologies between Britain and America, 1790-1830s/ David J. Jeremy. North Andover, Mass.: Merrimack Valley Textile Museum; c1981. xvii, 384 p.
81-000517   338.4/5677/00941   0262100223
Textile industry -- Technological innovations -- United States -- History. Textile industry -- Technological innovations -- Great Britain -- History. Diffusion of innovations -- United States -- History.

HD9857.A11.N48 1982
The New England mill village, 1790-1860/ edited by Gary Kulik, Roger Parks, Theodore Z. Penn. Cambridge, Mass.: MIT Press, c1982. xxxv, 520 p.
81-023665   307.7/6   0262110849
Textile industry -- New England -- History -- Sources. Textile factories -- New England -- History -- Sources. Textile workers -- New England -- History -- Sources. New England -- Social conditions -- Sources.

HD9858.L9.D35 1987
Dalzell, Robert F.
Enterprising elite: the Boston Associates and the world they made/ Robert F. Dalzell, Jr. Cambridge, Mass.: Harvard University Press, 1987. xviii, 298 p.
86-033649   338.4/7677/0097444   0674257650
Textile industry -- Massachusetts -- Waltham -- History -- 19th century. Textile industry -- Massachusetts -- Lowell -- History -- 19th century. Boston Region (Mass.) -- History.

HD9860.S5.T83 1984
Tucker, Barbara M.
Samuel Slater and the origins of the American textile industry, 1790-1860/ Barbara M. Tucker. Ithaca: Cornell University Press, 1984. 268 p.
84-045145   338.7/67721/092   0801415942
Slater, Samuel, -- 1768-1835. Textile industry -- United States -- Biography. Textile industry -- United States -- History.

HD9875.C63 1990
Cohen, Isaac, 1946-
American management and British labor: a comparative study of the cotton spinning industry/ Isaac Cohen. New York: Greenwood Press, 1990. vi, 250 p.
90-002753   338.4/76772122/0973   0313267804
Cotton textile industry -- United States -- History. Cotton textile industry -- Great Britain -- History.

HD9884.U64.C764 1992
Flamming, Douglas.
Creating the modern South: millhands and managers in Dalton, Georgia, 1884-1984/ Douglas Flamming. Chapel Hill: University of North Carolina Press, c1992. xxxi, 433 p.
92-053624   338.7/67721/09758324   0807820563
Cotton textile industry -- Georgia -- Dalton -- History. Industries -- Southern States -- Case studies. Dalton (Ga.) -- Economic conditions.

HD9901.5.J46 1982
Jenkins, D. T.
The British wool textile industry, 1770-1914/ D.T. Jenkins and K.G. Ponting. London: Heinemann Educational Books: 1982. xii, 388 p.
82-125943   338.4/767731/0941   0435324691
Woolen goods industry -- Great Britain -- History.

HD9901.7.E54.S6 1999
Smail, John.
Merchants, markets and manufacture: the English wool textile industry in the eighteenth century/ John Smail. New York, N.Y.: St. Martin's Press, 1999. x, 198 p.
98-055577   338.4/767731/094209033   0312221622
Wool industry -- England -- History -- 18th century. Textile industry -- England -- History -- 18th century. England -- Economic conditions -- 18th century.

HD9926.E92.L85 1996
Lui, Hsin-ju.
Silk and religion: an exploration of material life and the thought of people, AD 600-1200/ Xinru Liu. Delhi: Oxford University Press, 1996. viii, 235 p.
96-900522   0195636554
Silk industry -- Eurasia. Silk -- Religious aspects.

HD9940-9944 Special industries and trades — Manufacturing industries — Clothing. Apparel

HD9940.G82.E545 1997
Lemire, Beverly, 1950-
Dress, culture, and commerce: the English clothing trade before the factory, 1660-1800/ Beverly Lemire. New York, N.Y.: St. Martin's Press, 1997. xv, 224 p.
96-026645   338.4/7687/0942   0312164041
Clothing trade -- England -- History. Clothing and dress -- England -- History. England -- Social life and customs.

HD9940.U4.J3 1987
Jarnow, Jeannette A.
Inside the fashion business: text and readings/ Jeannette A. Jarnow, Miriam Guerreiro, Beatrice Judelle. New York: Macmillan, c1987. xvii, 525 p.
86-016359   338.4/7687/0973   0023600004
Fashion merchandising -- United States. Clothing trade -- United States.

HD9940.U6.L457 2000
Schoenberger, Karl.
Levi's children: coming to terms with human rights in the global marketplace/ Karl Schoenberger. New York: Atlantic Monthly Press, c2000. ix, 290 p.
99-055104   338.7/687/092 21   0871138093
Clothing trade -- United States -- History. Human rights -- Case studies. Labor policy -- United States -- Case studies.

HD9944.U46.A193 1983
Karamanski, Theodore J., 1953-
Fur trade and exploration: opening the Far Northwest, 1821-1852/ by Theodore J. Karamanski. Norman: University of Oklahoma Press, c1983. xxii, 330 p.
82-040453   380.1/456753/09795   0806118334
Fur trade -- Northwest, Pacific -- History -- 19th century. Northwest, Pacific -- Discovery and exploration.

HD9980.5-9981.1 Special industries and trades — Service industries (General)

HD9980.5.G776 1990
Gronroos, Christian, 1947-
Service management and marketing: managing the moments of truth in service competition/ Christian Gronroos. Lexington, Mass.: Lexington Books, c1990. xxii, 298 p.
89-029201   658.8   0669200352
Service industries -- Marketing. Customer service.

HD9980.5.H36 2000
Handbook of services marketing & management/ Teresa A. Swartz, Dawn Iacobucci, editors. Thousand Oaks: Sage Publications, c2000. ix, 521 p.
99-006902   658 21   0761916113
Service industries -- Marketing. Service industries -- Management. Customer services -- Marketing.

HD9981.1.S47
Service industries USA: industry analyses, statistics, and leading organizations. Detroit: Gale Research Inc., [c1992-]
92-645930   338.4
Service industries -- United States -- States -- Statistics -- Periodicals.

HD9995 Special industries and trades — Medical instruments and apparatus industry. Medical supplies industry — Special industries, A-Z

HD9995.C64.A234 1992
Grant, Nicole J., 1952-
The selling of contraception: the Dalkon Shield case, sexuality, and women's autonomy/ Nicole J. Grant. Columbus: Ohio State University Press, c1992. xii, 223 p.
91-041227   363.9/6/0973   0814205720
Dalkon Shield (Intrauterine contraceptive) -- Marketing. Intrauterine contraceptives -- Complications. Intrauterine contraceptives industry -- United States.

HD9995.C64.A2344 1994
Hicks, Karen M., 1947-
Surviving the Dalkon shield IUD: women v. the pharmaceutical industry/ Karen M. Hicks; foreword by Diana Scully. New York: Teachers College Press, c1994. ix, 197 p.
93-036105   338.7/616139435   0807762717
Dalkon Shield (Intrauterine contraceptive) Intrauterine contraceptives -- Complications. Intrauterine contraceptives industry -- United States.

HD9999 Special industries and trades — Miscellaneous industries and trades, A-Z

HD9999.B443.U647 1995
Kornberg, Arthur, 1918-
The golden helix: inside biotech ventures/ Arthur Kornberg. Sausalito, Calif.: University Science Books, c1995. xi, 287 p.
94-043482   338.7/6606/0973   0935702326
Biotechnology industries -- United States -- Case studies. New business enterprises -- United States - - Case studies. Biotechnology -- United States -- Industrial applications -- Case studies.

HD9999.L383.U634 1999
Mohun, Arwen, 1961-
Steam laundries: gender, technology, and work in the United States and Great Britain, 1880-1940/ Arwen P. Mohun. Baltimore: Johns Hopkins University Press, 1999. x, 348 p.
98-038245   338.7/6166713/0973   0801860024
Laundry industry -- United States -- History. Laundry industry -- Great Britain -- History.

HD9999.S74.P7674 1993
Swasy, Alecia.
Soap opera: the inside story of Procter & Gamble/ Alecia Swasy. New York: Times Books, c1993. xvi, 378 p.
93-012793   338.7/67   0812920600
Soap trade -- United States.

HE Transportation and Communications

HE193 Government policy (General)

HE193.F75
Fromm, Gary.
Transport investment and economic development. Washington, Brookings Institution, Transport Research Progra [1965] x, 314 p.
65-015416   385.082
Transportation.

HE199.9 Passenger traffic (General)

HE199.9.M34
Manheim, Marvin L.
Fundamentals of transportation systems analysis/ Marvin L. Manheim. Cambridge, Mass.: MIT Press, [c1979-]
78-011535   380.5   0262131293
Transportation -- Planning. Transportation -- Mathematical models. System analysis.

HE202.5-206.3 By region or country — America — North America

HE202.5.T72
Transportation and public utilities USA: industry analyses, statistics, and leading companies. Detroit, Mich.: Gale, [c1998-]
98-641092   388/0973/021
Transportation -- United States -- Statistics -- Periodicals. Public utilities -- United States -- Statistics -- Periodicals.

HE203.R54 1995
Richter, William L. 1942-
The ABC-CLIO companion to transportation in America/ William L. Richter. Santa Barbara, Calif.: ABC-CLIO, c1995. xxxvi, 653 p.
95-013170   388/.0973   0874367891
Transportation -- United States -- History.

HE206.2.D46 1989
Dempsey, Paul Stephen.
The social and economic consequences of deregulation: the transportation industry in transition/ Paul Stephen Dempsey. New York: Quorum Books, 1989. xii, 277 p.
89-003168   380.5/9   0899303803
Transportation -- Deregulation -- United States. Transportation and state -- United States.

HE206.2.G37 1996
Garrett, Mark.
Transportation planning on trial: the Clean Air Act and travel forecasting/ Mark Garrett, Martin Wachs. Thousand Oaks, Calif.: Sage Publications, c1996. vii, 232 p.
95-050228　388/.041 20　0803973527
Transportation and state -- United States. Transportation -- United States -- Planning. Transportation, Automotive -- Law and legislation -- United States.

HE206.3.W48 1998
Whitnah, Donald Robert, 1925-
U.S. Department of Transportation: a reference history/ Donald R. Whitnah. Westport, Conn: Greenwood Press, 1998. xv, 228 p.
97-021992　354.76/0973　0313283400
Transportation and state -- United States -- History.

HE242 By region or country — Other regions or countries

HE242.V54 1990
Ville, Simon P.
Transport and the development of the European economy, 1750-1918/ Simon P. Ville. New York: St. Martin's Press, 1990. xiii, 252 p.
89-070303　388/.094　0312044887
Transportation -- Europe -- History. Europe -- Economic conditions -- 1789-1900.

HE305 Urban transportation — General works

HE305.M49 1984
Meyer, Michael D.
Urban transportation planning: a decision-oriented approach/ Michael D. Meyer, Eric J. Miller. New York: McGraw-Hill, c1984. xvii, 524 p.
83-025573　388.4/068　0070417520
Urban transportation -- Planning.

HE305.O9
Owen, Wilfred.
The accessible city [by] Wilfred Owen with the assistance of Inai Bradfield. Washington, D.C., Brookings Institution [1972] viii, 150 p.
76-039698　388.4　0815767706
Urban transportation.

HE305.P87 1977
Pushkarev, Boris.
Public transportation and land use policy/ Boris S. Pushkarev, Jeffrey M. Zupan. Bloomington: Indiana University Press, c1977. ix, 242 p.
76-029299　388.4　0253346827
Urban transportation policy. Choice of transportation. Land use, Urban.

HE305.S84
Stopher, Peter R.
Urban transportation modeling and planning/ Peter R. Stopher, Arnim H. Meyburg. Lexington, Mass.: Lexington Books, [1975] xix, 345 p.
74-021876　388.4/01/84　0669969419
Urban transportation -- Mathematical models. Traffic estimation -- Mathematical models.

HE305.W67 2002
Cities on the move: a World Bank urban transport strategy review. Washington, DC: World Bank, 2002. xxi, 206 p.
2002-025882　388.4 21　0821351486
Urban transportation. Urbanization.

HE308-310 Urban transportation — By region or country

HE308.A63
Altshuler, Alan A., 1936-
The urban transportation system: politics and policy innovation/ Alan Altshuler, with James P. Womack, John R. Pucher. Cambridge, Mass.: MIT Press, c1979. xii, 558 p.
78-025805　388.4/0973　0262010550
Urban transportation policy -- United States. Local transit -- United States.

HE308.J65 1977
Jones, Ian Shore.
Urban transport appraisal/ Ian S. Jones. New York: Wiley, c1977. x, 144 p.
76-054811　388.4/0973　0470990325
Urban transportation policy -- United States. Urban transportation -- United States -- Costs.

HE308.P44
Pikarsky, Milton.
Urban transportation policy and management/ Milton Pikarsky, Daphne Christensen. Lexington, Mass.: Lexington Books, c1976. xiv, 255 p.
76-021933　388.4/0973　0669009555
Urban transportation policy -- United States. Transportation -- United States -- Passenger traffic.

HE308.W45 1999
Weiner, Edward.
Urban transportation planning in the United States: an historical overview/ Edward Weiner. Westport, Conn.: Praeger, 1999. xx, 247 p.
98-038286　388.4/0973　0275963292
Urban transportation policy -- United States -- History.

HE310.B6.C45
Cheape, Charles W., 1945-
Moving the masses: urban public transit in New York, Boston, and Philadelphia, 1880-1912/ Charles W. Cheape. Cambridge, Mass.: Harvard University Press, 1980. vii, 285 p.
79-015875　388.4/0974　0674588274
Transportation -- Massachusetts -- Boston -- History. Transportation -- New York (State) -- New York -- History. Transportation -- Pennsylvania -- Philadelphia -- History.

HE333 Traffic engineering — General works

HE333.M28 1994
Manual of transportation engineering studies/ H. Douglas Robertson, editor, Joseph E. Hummer, assistant editor, Donna C. Nelson, assistant editor. Englewood Cliffs, N.J.: Prentice Hall, c1994. xii, 514 p.
93-013519　629.04　0130975699
Traffic engineering. Transportation engineering.

HE333.T68 1965
Traffic engineering handbook. Editor, John E. Baerwald. Washington, Institute of Traffic Engineers, 1965. 770 p.
65-017560
Traffic engineering.

HE336 Traffic engineering — By subject, A-Z

HE336.C5.U52 1997
Understanding travel behaviour in an era of change/ edited by Peter Stopher and Martin Lee-Gosselin. Oxford, OX, UK; Pergamon, 1997. xv, 583 p.
96-011486　388　0080423906
Choice of transportationn -- Forecasting -- Congresses. Urban transportationn -- Forecasting -- Congresses.

HE336.R68.B68 1990
Bovy, Piet H. L., 1943-
Route choice: wayfinding in transport networks/ by Piet H.L. Bovy and Eliahu Stern. Dordrecht; Kluwer Academic Publishers, c1990. xiv, 309 p.
90-004912　388.3/143　0792308123
Route choice.

HE355-356 Traffic engineering — History — Modern

HE355.H94 1998
Human factors in intelligent transportation systems/ edited by Woodrow Barfield, Thomas A. Dingus. Mahwah, N.J.: Lawrence Erlbaum Associates, 1998. xxi, 458 p.
97-014434　388.1/0973　0805814337
Roads -- Social aspects -- United States. Intelligent Vehicle Highway Systems.

HE355.O848 1966
Owen, Wilfred.
The metropolitan transportation problem. Garden City, N.Y., Anchor Books [1966] xiii, 266 p.
66-021151　380.5091732
Traffic engineering -- United States.

HE355.R675
Rose, Mark H., 1942-
Interstate: express highway politics, 1941-1956/ Mark H. Rose. Lawrence: Regents Press of Kansas, c1979. xii, 169 p.
78-014940　388.1/2　0700601864
Express highways -- United States -- History. Express highways -- Government policy -- United States -- History. Transportation and state -- United States -- History.

HE355.3.C64.D69 1992
Downs, Anthony.
Stuck in traffic: coping with peak-hour traffic congestion/ Anthony Downs. Washington, D.C.: Brookings Institution; c1992. xi, 210 p.
92-012692　388.4/13142/0973　0815719248
Traffic congestion -- United States. Traffic flow -- United States. Land use, Urban -- United States.

HE356.C2.H68 1998
Howard, Thomas Frederick, 1946-
Sierra crossing: first roads to California/ Thomas Frederick Howard. Berkeley: University of California Press, c1998. ix, 218 p.
97-028012   388.1/09794/4 21   0520206703
Roads -- Sierra Nevada (Calif. and Nev.) -- History -- 19th century. Overland journeys to the Pacific. Sierra Nevada (Calif. and Nev.) -- Description and travel.

HE395-443 Water transportation — Waterways — By region or country

HE395.O34S34 1987
Scheiber, Harry N.
Ohio canal era: a case study of government and the economy, 1820-1861 / Harry N. Scheiber. Athens: Ohio University Press, 1987. xxvi, 430 p.
86-023800   386/.48/09771   0821408666
Canals -- Ohio -- History -- 19th century. Canals -- Government policy -- Ohio -- History -- 19th century. Railroads -- Ohio -- History -- 19th century.

HE443.G45 1994
Geiger, Reed G.
Planning the French canals: bureaucracy, politics, and enterprise under the Restoration/ Reed G. Geiger. Newark: University of Delaware Press; c1994. 338 p.
94-007829   386/.48/0944   0874135273
Canals -- France -- History -- 19th century. Canals -- France -- Planning -- History -- 19th century. Business enterprises -- France -- History -- 19th century.

HE526-554 Water transportation — Waterways — By type of waterway

HE526.H33 1986
Hadfield, Charles, 1909-
World canals: inland navigation past and present/ Charles Hadfield. New York, N.Y.: Facts on File, c1986. 432 p.
85-029272   387.4/09   0816013764
Canals -- History. Inland navigation -- History.

HE537.D5 2001
Diaz Espino, Ovidio.
How Wall Street created a nation: J.P. Morgan, Teddy Roosevelt, and the Panama Canal/ Ovidio Diaz Espino. New York: Four Walls Eight Windows, 2001. xviii, 254 p.
2001-023187   972.87/503   1568581963
Roosevelt, Theodore, -- 1858-1919. Cromwell, William Nelson, -- 1854-1948. Morgan, J. Pierpont -- (John Pierpont), -- 1837-1913. Wall Street. Panama -- History -- 20th century. Panama Canal (Panama) -- Finance -- History.

HE551.B52 1986
Branch, Alan E.
Elements of port operation and management/ Alan E. Branch. London; Chapman and Hall, 1986. xiv, 265 p.
85-024301   387.1/068   0412252503
Harbors -- Management.

HE554.H65S5 1968
Sibley, Marilyn McAdams.
The port of Houston; a history. Austin, University of Texas Press [1968] xvi, 246 p.
68-021251   387.1/09764/235
Harbors -- Texas -- Houston.

HE566 Water transportation — Shipping — Special classes of vessels, A-Z

HE566.P3.O84 1990
Owens, Harry P.
Steamboats and the cotton economy: river trade in the Yazoo-Mississippi delta/ Harry P. Owens. Jackson: University Press of Mississippi, c1990. xiii, 255 p.
90-033067   386/.22436   0878054367
Steamboats -- Mississippi -- Delta (Region) -- History. Inland water transportation -- Mississippi -- Delta (Region) -- History. Cotton trade -- Mississippi -- Delta (Region) -- History. Delta (Miss.: Region) -- Commerce -- History.

HE567 Water transportation — Shipping — Dictionaries. Encyclopedias

HE567.B65
Branch, Alan E.
Dictionary of shipping/international trade terms and abbreviations/ by Alan E. Branch. London: Witherby, 1976. ix, 117 p.
77-361617   387.5/44/03   0900886161
Shipping -- Dictionaries. Shipping -- Abbreviations. Commerce -- Dictionaries.

HE571 Water transportation — Shipping — General works

HE571.A36
Advances in maritime economics/ edited by R. O. Goss; contributors, B. M. Gardner ... [et al.] Cambridge; Cambridge University Press, 1977. 294 p.
76-001135   387.5/1   0521212324
Shipping -- Addresses, essays, lectures. Merchant marine -- Addresses, essays, lectures.

HE571.G67
Goss, R. O.
Studies in maritime economics [by] R. O. Goss. London, Cambridge U.P., 1968. viii, 194 p.
68-029328   387   0521073294
Shipping.

HE630 Water transportation — Shipping — Inland navigation. Inland water transportation

HE630.C4.H65 1991
Holly, David C.
Tidewater by steamboat: a saga of the Chesapeake: the Weems line on the Patuxent, Potomac, and Rappahannock/ David C. Holly. Baltimore, Md.: Johns Hopkins University Press in association wi c1991. xix, 314 p.
90-027826   387/.009163/47   0801841682
Steamboats -- Chesapeake Bay (Md. and Va.) -- History. Steamboat lines -- Chesapeake Bay (Md. and Va.) -- History.

HE736-894 Water transportation — Shipping — Merchant marine. Ocean shipping. Coastwise shipping

HE736.C37
Carlisle, Rodney P.
Sovereignty for sale: the origins and evolution of the Panamanian and Liberian flags of convenience/ Rodney Carlisle. Annapolis, Md.: Naval Institute Press, c1981. xvii, 278 p.
81-607020   387.2/45   0870216686
Flags of convenience -- Panama -- History. Flags of convenience -- Liberia -- History. Ships -- Registration and transfer -- Panama -- History.

HE745.D39 1994
De La Pedraja Toman, Rene.
A historical dictionary of the U.S. merchant marine and shipping industry: since the introduction of steam/ Rene de La Pedraja. Westport, Conn.: Greenwood Press, 1994. xiii, 754 p.
93-039354   387.5/03   0313272255
Merchant marine -- United States -- History -- Dictionaries. Shipping -- United States -- History -- Dictionaries.

HE745.W495 1983
Whitehurst, Clinton H., 1927-
The U.S. merchant marine: in search of an enduring maritime policy/ by Clinton H. Whitehurst, Jr. Annapolis, Md.: Naval Institute Press, c1983. xviii, 314 p.
83-013467   387.5/068   0870217372
Merchant marine -- United States. Shipping -- United States.

HE823.B63 1995
Boyce, Gordon, 1954-
Information, mediation, and institutional development: the rise of large-scale enterprise in British shipping, 1870-1919/ Gordon Boyce. Manchester; Manchester University Press; c1995. xi, 346 p.
94-029773   387.5/1   0719038472
Shipping -- Great Britain -- History.

HE894.H45 1989
Heine, Irwin M.
China's rise to commercial maritime power/ Irwin Millard Heine. New York: Greenwood Press, 1989. xv, 175 p.
88-025095   387.5/0951   0313264546
Merchant marine -- China -- History -- 20th century.

HE1021 Railroads — History

HE1021.W47 1981
Westwood, J. N.
Railways at war/ John Westwood. San Diego, Calif.: Howell-North Books, 1980. 224 p.
80-025429   385/.09/04   0831071389
Railroads -- History -- 20th century. World politics -- 20th century.

HE1041 Railroads —
Relation to other subjects —
Railways and civilization

HE1041.R35 1991
Railway imperialism/ edited by Clarence B. Davis and Kenneth E. Wilburn, Jr., with Ronald E. Robinson. New York: Greenwood Press, 1991. xix, 225 p.
89-026025   385/.09   0313259666
Railroads -- History. Railroads -- Political aspects -- History. Imperialism -- History.

HE2236 Railroads — Location —
Traffic

HE2236.G73
Greenberg, Dolores.
Financiers and railroads, 1869-1889: a study of Morton, Bliss & Company/ Dolores Greenberg. Newark: University of Delaware Press; c1980. 286 p.
78-066830   385/.1   0874131480
Railroads -- United States -- Finance -- History.

HE2741-2791 Railroads —
By region or country — America

HE2741.A5 1972
The American railway: its construction, development, management, and appliances, by Thomas Curtis Clarke [and others] With an introd. by Thomas M. Cooley. New York, B. Blom, 1972. xxviii, 456 p.
74-189048   385/.0973
Railroads -- United States.

HE2751.C45
Chandler, Alfred Dupont,
The railroads, the Nation's first big business; sources and readings. Compiled and edited by Alfred D. Chandler, Jr. New York, Harcourt, Brace & World [1965] ix, 213 p.
65-012850   385.0973
Railroads -- United States -- History -- Addresses, essays, lectures.

HE2751.K47
Kerr, K. Austin
American railroad politics, 1914-1920; rates, wages, and efficiency [by] K. Austin Kerr. [Pittsburgh] University of Pittsburgh Press [1968] viii, 250 p.
68-021628   385/.0973
Railroads -- United States. Railroads and state -- United States.

HE2751.M35 1992
Martin, Albro.
Railroads triumphant: the growth, rejection, and rebirth of a vital American force/ Albro Martin. New York: Oxford University Press, 1992. xiv, 428 p.
90-007845   385/.0973   0195038533
Railroads -- United States -- History.

HE2751.R143 1988
Encyclopedia of American business history and biography:Railroads in the age of regulation, 1900-1980/ edited by Keith L. Bryant, Jr. New York: Facts On File, c1988. xxix, 518 p.
87-036493   385/.0973   0816013713
Railroads -- United States -- Biography. Railroads -- United States -- History -- 20th century. Railroads and state -- United States -- History -- 20th century.

HE2751.S74
Stover, John F.
The life and decline of the American railroad [by] John F. Stover. New York, Oxford University Press, 1970. xi, 324 p.
77-083054   385/.0973
Railroads -- United States -- History.

HE2752.L48 1981
Lewis, Oscar,
The big four: the story of Huntington, Stanford, Hopkins, and Crocker, and of the building of the Central Pacific/ Oscar Lewis. New York: Arno Press, 1981, c1938. xi, 418 p.
80-001324   385/.092/2   0405137990
Huntington, Collis Potter, 1821-1900. Stanford, Leland, 1824-1893. Hopkins, Mark 1813-1878. Capitalists and financiers -- United States -- Biography.

HE2754.B5.W56 1991
Winks, Robin W.
Frederick Billings: a life/ Robin W. Winks. New York: Oxford University Press, 1991. x, 398 p.
90-022367   385/.092   0195068149
Billings, Frederick, -- 1823-1890. Businesspeople -- United States -- Biography.

HE2757.B47 1994
Berk, Gerald.
Alternative tracks: the constitution of American industrial order, 1865-1917/ Gerald Berk. Baltimore: Johns Hopkins University Press, c1994. xi, 243 p.
93-001753   385/.0973   0801846560
Railroads and state -- United States -- History. Railroads -- Political aspects -- United States -- History. Railroad law -- United States -- History.

HE2771.C2.D48 1994
Deverell, William Francis.
Railroad crossing: Californians and the railroad, 1850-1910/ William Deverell. Berkeley: University of California Press, c1994. xiii, 278 p.
92-040128   385/.09794   0520082141
Railroads -- Social aspects -- California -- History. Railroads -- California -- History.

HE2771.M5.P37
Parks, Robert J.
Democracy's railroads; public enterprise in Jacksonian Michigan [by] Robert J. Parks. Port Washington, N.Y., Kennikat Press, 1972. 261 p.
79-189557   385/.09774   0804690278
Railroads and state -- Michigan.

HE2771.P4
Majewski, John D., 1965-
A house dividing: economic development in Pennsylvania and Virginia before the Civil War/ John Majewski. Cambridge, UK; Cambridge University Press, 2000. xvii, 214 p.
99-028146   330.9748/03   052159023X
Railroads -- Pennsylvania -- History -- 19th century. Railroads -- Virginia -- History -- 19th century. Free enterprise -- Pennsylvania -- History -- 19th century. Pennsylvania -- Economic conditions. Virginia -- Economic conditions.

HE2791.A563.N53 1998
Nice, David C., 1952-
Amtrak: the history and politics of a national railroad/ David C. Nice. Boulder, Colo: Lynne Rienner, 1998. x, 119 p.
97-037756   385/.22/0973   1555877346
Railroads -- United States -- Passenger traffic -- History. Railroads -- Government policy -- United States -- History.

HE2791.C643.O79
Overton, Richard Cleghorn, 1907-
Burlington route; a history of the Burlington lines [by] Richard C. Overton. New York, Knopf, 1965. xxviii, 623 p.
64-019106   385.0973
Chicago, Burlington & Quincy Railroad Company.

HE2791.U55.A4
Ames, Charles Edgar, b. 1895.
Pioneering the Union Pacific; a reappraisal of the builders of the railroad.   New York, Appleton-Century-Crofts [1969] xvii, 591 p.
69-013448   338.4/7/6251
Union Pacific Railroad Company.

HE2818-3138 Railroads —
By region or country —
Other regions or countries

HE2818.P59 1972
Pletcher, David M.
Rails, mines, and progress: seven American promoters in Mexico, 1867-1911, by David M. Pletcher. Port Washington, N.Y., Kennikat Press [1972, c1958] x, 321 p.
79-153237   385/.0972   0804615470
Railroads -- Mexico -- History. Mineral industries -- Mexico. Investments, American -- Mexico -- Case studies.

HE2960.C65.C54 1998
Clark, A. Kim, 1964-
The redemptive work: railway and nation in Ecuador, 1895-1930/ A. Kim Clark. Wilmington, Del.: SR Books, 1998. 244 p.
97-014679   385/.09866   0842026746
Railroads -- Social aspects -- Ecuador. Nationalism -- Ecuador. Liberalism -- Ecuador. Ecuador -- Economic conditions. Ecuador -- Social conditions.

HE3005.S86 1993
Strohl, Mitchell P.
Europe's high speed trains: a study in geo-economics/ Mitchell P. Strohl; foreword by Michel Walrave. Westport, Conn.: Praeger, 1993. xix, 306 p.
93-006768   385/.2   027594252X
High speed trains -- Europe.

HE3018.S58 1991
Simmons, Jack, 1915-
The Victorian railway/ Jack Simmons. New York, N.Y.: Thames and Hudson, 1991. 416 p.
90-070200   385/.0941/09034   050025110X
Railroads -- Great Britain -- History. Railroads -- Social aspects -- Great Britain -- History.

HE3080.D4.M535 1999
Mierzejewski, Alfred C.
The most valuable asset of the Reich: a history of the German National Railway/ by Alfred C. Mierzejewski. Chapel Hill: University of North Carolina Press, [1999-] 2 v.
98-053440   385/.06/543   0807824968
Railroads and state -- Germany -- History -- 20th century.

HE3138.H385 1998
Haywood, Richard Mowbray.
Russia enters the railway age, 1842-1855/ Richard Mowbray Haywood. Boulder: East European Monographs; 1998. xxvi, 635 p.
98-070323 385/.0947 0880333901
Railroads -- Russia -- History. Railroad travel -- Russia -- History. Russia -- History -- Nicholas I, 1825-1855.

HE4211 Railroads — Local transit. Street railways. Subways — General works

HE4211.V83
Vuchic, Vukan R.
Urban public transportation: systems and technology/ Vukan R. Vuchic. Englewood Cliffs, N.J.: Prentice-Hall, c1981. xiv, 673 p.
80-021081 388.4 0139394966
Local transit.

HE4441-4491 Railroads — Local transit. Street railways. Subways — By region or country

HE4441.U735 1985
Urban transit: the private challenge to public transportation/ edited by Charles A. Lave; foreword by John Meyer. San Francisco, Calif.: Pacific Institute for Public Policy Research; 1985. xxii, 372 p.
84-021529 388.4/0973 0884109690
Local transit -- United States -- Addresses, essays, lectures. Paratransit services -- United States -- Addresses, essays, lectures.

HE4451.U72
Urban mass transit planning. Edited by Wolfgang S. Homburger. Berkeley, Calif., 1967. v, 212 p.
68-064018 711/.7/0973
Local transit -- United States -- Addresses, essays, lectures.

HE4491.C5.C8788 1998
Young, David, 1940 Sept. 22
Chicago Transit: an illustrated history/ David M. Young. DeKalb, Ill.: Northern Illinois University Press, 1998. viii, 213 p.
98-023655 388.4/09773/11 0875802419
Local transit -- Illinois -- Chicago -- History,.

HE5611 Automotive transportation — General works

HE5611.B43 1975
Bendixson, Terence.
Without wheels: alternatives to the private car/ Terence Bendixson. Bloomington: Indiana University Press, 1975, c1974. 256 p.
74-021680 338.4 0253365600
Transportation, Automotive. Transportation, Automotive -- Great Britain. Urban transportation policy.

HE5611.P67 1999
Porter, Richard C.
Economics at the wheel: the costs of cars and drivers/ Richard C. Porter. San Diego: Academic Press, c1999. xiii, 258 p.
98-088417 388.3 21 0125623607
Transportation, Automotive -- Economic aspects. Automobiles -- Economic aspects. Automobiles -- Environmental aspects.

HE5620 Automotive transportation — Special, A-Z

HE5620.D7.R668 1992
Ross, H. Laurence
Confronting drunk driving: social policy for saving lives/ H. Laurence Ross; foreword by Joseph R. Gusfield. New Haven: Yale University Press, c1992. xv, 220 p.
91-037598 363.12/51 0300054564
Drinking and traffic accidents -- Government policy. Drunk driving -- Government policy.

HE5623 Automotive transportation — By region or country — United States

HE5623.B45
Berger, Michael L., 1943-
The devil wagon in God's country: the automobile and social change in rural America, 1893-1929/ Michael L. Berger. Hamden, Conn.: Archon Books, 1979. 269 p.
79-017185 301.24/3 0208017046
Automobiles -- Social aspects -- United States -- History. United States -- Rural conditions.

HE5623.K36 1997
Kay, Jane Holtz.
Asphalt nation: how the automobile took over America, and how we can take it back/ Jane Holtz Kay. New York: Crown Publishers, c1997. xii, 418 p.
97-001605 303.48/32 21 0517587025
Automobiles -- Social aspects -- United States. City and town life -- United States. Sociology, Urban -- United States.

HE5623.M35 1994
McShane, Clay.
Down the asphalt path: the automobile and the American city/ Clay McShane. New York: Columbia University Press, c1994. xvii, 288 p.
93-017219 307.76/0973 0231083904
Automobiles -- Social aspects -- United States. City and town life -- United States. Sociology, Urban -- United States.

HE5623.T3 1986
Taff, Charles Albert, 1916-
Commercial motor transportation/ Charles A. Taff. Centreville, Md.: Cornell Maritime Press, 1986. xi, 434 p.
85-047905 388.3/0973 0870333453
Transportation, Automotive -- United States.

HE5623.W35 2000
Walsh, Margaret.
Making connections: the long-distance bus industry in the United States/ Margaret Walsh. Aldershot, Hants, England; Ashgate, c2000. xvii, 245 p.
00-029982 388.3/22/0973 21 0754602079
Bus lines -- United States -- History. Transportation, Automotive -- United States -- History.

HE5736 Bicycles — General works

HE5736.F67 1983
Forester, John, 1929-
Bicycle transportation/ John Forester. Cambridge, Mass.: MIT Press, c1983. xiii, 394 p.
83-007932 388.4/132 026206085X
Bicycle commuting. Bicycle commuting -- United States.

HE5784 Ferries — By region or country — North America

HE5784.N5.C84 1990
Cudahy, Brian J.
Over and back: the history of ferryboats in New York Harbor/ Brian J. Cudahy. New York: Fordham University Press, c1990. 472 p.
89-084357 0823212459
Ferries -- New York Harbor (N.Y and N.J.) -- History.

HE5903 Express service — By region or country — United States

HE5903.A55.G76 1987
Grossman, Peter Z., 1948-
American Express: the unofficial history of the people who built the great financial empire/ Peter Z. Grossman. New York: Crown Publishers, c1987. x, 389 p.
86-019925 380.5/2 0517562383
American Express Company -- History.

HE6182-6239 Postal service — Special topics — Stamps. Postmarks

HE6182.H34 1998
Harding, Les, 1950-
Dead countries of the nineteenth and the twentieth centuries: Aden to Zululand/ by Les Harding. Lanham, Md.: Scarecrow Press, 1998. xi, 393 p.
97-039850 909 0810834456
Postage stamps -- History. Stamp collecting.

HE6185.U5.J634 1995
John, Richard R., 1959-
Spreading the news: the American postal system from Franklin to Morse/ Richard R. John. Cambridge, Mass.: Harvard University Press, 1995. xiii, 369 p.
95-020067 383/.4973 0674833384
Postal service -- United States -- History.

HE6239.E54.U55 1995
Universal access to E-mail: feasibility and societal implications/ Robert H. Anderson ... [et al.]. Santa Monica, CA: RAND, 1995. xxviii, 267 p.
95-053853   384.3/4   0833023314
Electronic mail systems.

HE6371-6499 Postal service — By region or country — United States

HE6371.F84
Fuller, Wayne Edison, 1919-
The American mail; enlarger of the common life [by] Wayne E. Fuller. Chicago, University of Chicago Press [1972] xi, 378 p.
72-078254   383/.49/73   0226268845
Postal service -- United States -- History.

HE6375.B8 1960
Bradley, Glenn Danford,
The story of the pony express. [2d ed.]Edited by Waddell F. Smith. San Francisco, Hesperian House [c1960] 195 p.
76-011126   383.4973
Pony express.

HE6376.A1T417 1985
Austerman, Wayne R.
Sharps rifles and Spanish mules: the San Antonio--El Paso mail, 1851-1881/ by Wayne R. Austerman. 1st ed. College Station: Texas A&M University Press, c1985. x, 367 p.
84-040557   383/.49764   0890962200
Postal service -- Texas -- History -- 19th century. Coaching (Transportation) -- Texas -- History -- 19th century.

HE6499.D18 2000
Damp, Dennis V.
Post Office jobs: how to get a job with the U.S. Postal Service/ Dennis V. Damp. Moon Township, PA: Bookhaven Press, c2000. viii, 224 p.
99-032727   383/.145/02373 21   0943641195
Postal service -- Vocational guidance -- United States. Postal service -- United States -- Employees. Postal service -- United States -- Examinations, questions, etc.

HE7572 Information superhighway — By region or country, A-Z

HE7572.U6.B87 1995
Burstein, Daniel.
Road warriors: dreams and nightmares along the information highway/ Daniel Burstein and David Kline. New York: Dutton, 1995. viii, 466 p.
95-032859   004.6/7   0525937269
Information superhighway -- United States. Telecommunication policy -- United States. Telecommunication -- United States.

HE7631 Telecommunication industry. Telegraph — General works

HE7631.B785 1990
Collapsing space and time: geographic aspects of communications and information/ edited by Stanley D. Brunn, Thomas R. Leinbach. London; HarperCollinsAcademic, 1991. xxvi, 404 p.
90-012815   384/.041   0049101196
Telecommunication. Space in economics. Economic development.

HE7631.C34 2001
Cairncross, Frances.
The death of distance: how the communications revolution is changing our lives/ Frances Cairncross. Completely new ed. Boston: Harvard Business School Press, c2001. xvii, 317 p.
2001-016551   303.48/33 21   157851438X
Telecommunication. Telecommunication -- Social aspects. Telecommunication -- Forecasting.

HE7631.H453 1994
Heldman, Robert K.
Information telecommunications: networks, products, & services/ Robert K. Heldman. New York: McGraw-Hill, c1994. xiv, 393 p.
93-008259   384   0070280401
Telecommunication -- Social aspects. Information networks -- Social aspects. Information science -- Social aspects.

HE7631.S613 1997
Culture of the internet/ edited by Sara Kiesler. Mahwah, N.J.: Lawrence Erlbaum Associates, Publishers, 1997. xvi, 463 p.
96-031388   302.23   0805816356
Telecommunication -- Social aspects. Computer networks -- Social aspects.

HE7631.T443 1984
Telecommunications: an interdisciplinary text/ edited by Leonard Lewin. Dedham, MA: Artech House, c1984. xxii, 687 p.
84-070225   384   0890061408
Telecommunication. Telecommunication policy. Telecommunication systems.

HE7645 Telecommunication industry. Telegraph — Government policy. Telecommunication policy

HE7645.D38 1994
Davies, Andrew, 1962-
Telecommunications and politics: the decentralised alternative/ Andrew Davies. London; Pinter Publishers; 1994. xi, 265 p.
93-039414   384/.068   1855671441
Telecommunication policy.

HE7775-7781 Telecommunication industry. Telegraph — By region or country — United States

HE7775.H39 2000
Having all the right connections: telecommunications and rural viability/ edited by Peter F. Korsching, Patricia C. Hipple, and Eric A. Abbott. Westport, CT: Praeger, 2000. xvi, 348 p.
99-086113   384/.0973/091734   0275965821
Rural telecommunication -- United States. Rural development -- United States.

HE7781.A94 1999
Aufderheide, Patricia.
Communications policy and the public interest: the telecommunications act of 1996/ Patricia Aufderheide. New York: Guilford Press, 1999. ix, 323 p.
98-054130   384/.0973   1572304189
Public interest -- United States. Telecommunication policy -- United States.

HE7781.B75 1994
Brock, Gerald W.
Telecommunication policy for the information age: from monopoly to competition/ Gerald W. Brock. Cambridge, Mass.: Harvard University Press, 1994. xii, 324 p.
94-003911   384/.041   0674872770
Telecommunication policy -- United States.

HE7781.I694 1989
Irwin, Manley Rutherford.
Competitive freedom versus national security regulation/ Manley Rutherford Irwin. New York: Quorum Books, 1989. xii, 199 p.
88-018254   343.73/08   0899302335
Telecommunication policy -- United States. Foreign trade regulation -- United States. National security -- United States.

HE7781.T444 1990
Teske, Paul Eric.
After divestiture: the political economy of state telecommunications regulation/ Paul Eric Teske. Albany: State University of New York Press, c1990. xv, 162 p.
89-021851   384/.068   0791403238
Telecommunication policy -- United States -- States. Telephone -- Government policy -- United States -- States. Telecommunication policy -- United States -- States -- Case studies.

HE8675 Telecommunication industry. Telegraph — Wireless telegraph. Radiotelegraphy — General works

HE8675.L49 1990
Lewis, Peter M.
The invisible medium: public, commercial, and community radio/ Peter M. Lewis and Jerry Booth. Washington, D.C.: Howard University Press, 1990. xv, 245 p.
90-004357   384.54   0882580329
Radio broadcasting.

HE8689.4 Telecommunication industry. Telegraph — Broadcasting. Radio and television broadcasting — General works

HE8689.4.B76 1989
Browne, Donald R.
Comparing broadcast systems: the experiences of six industrialized nations/ Donald R. Browne. Ames: Iowa State University Press, 1989. xv, 447 p.
88-034693   384.54   0813801133
Radio broadcasting. Television broadcasting.

HE8689.7 Telecommunication industry. Telegraph — Broadcasting. Radio and television broadcasting — Special topics, A-Z

HE8689.7.A8.B46 1985
Beville, Hugh Malcolm.
Audience ratings: radio, television, and cable/ Hugh Malcolm Beville, Jr. Hillsdale, N.J.: L. Erlbaum Associates, 1985. xvi, 362 p.
85-001529   384.54/3   0898595355
Radio programs -- Rating. Television programs - - Rating.

HE8689.7.P6.P35 1998
Paletz, David L., 1934-
The media in American politics: contents and consequences/ David L. Paletz. New York: Longman, 1998.
98-035082   302.23/0973   0321044967
Mass media -- Political aspects. United States - - Politics and government -- 20th century.

HE8689.8-8689.95 Telecommunication industry. Telegraph — Broadcasting. Radio and television broadcasting — By region or country

HE8689.8.E53 1996
Engelman, Ralph.
Public radio and television in America: a political history/ Ralph Engelman. Thousand Oaks, Calif.: Sage Publications, c1996. x, 342 p.
95-050232   0803954069
Public broadcasting -- Political aspects -- United States -- History. Radio broadcasting -- Political aspects -- United States -- History. Television broadcasting -- Political aspects -- United States -- History.

HE8689.8.P34
Paley, William S. 1901-
As it happened: a memoir/ William S. Paley. Garden City, N.Y.: Doubleday, 1979. 418 p.
78-073191   384.54/092/4   0385146396
Paley, William S. -- (William Samuel), -- 1901- Broadcasting -- United States. Businesspeople -- United States -- Biography.

HE8689.8.S7295 1984
Sterling, Christopher H., 1943-
Electronic media: a guide to trends in broadcasting and newer technologies, 1920-1983/ by Christopher H. Sterling. New York: Praeger, 1984. xxix, 337 p.
83-027019   384.54/0973   003054341X
Broadcasting -- United States -- Statistics.

HE8689.95.K37
Katz, Elihu, 1926-
Broadcasting in the Third World: promise and performance/ Elihu Katz and George Wedell, with Michael Pilsworth and Dov Shinar. Cambridge: Harvard University Press, 1977. xvi, 305 p.
77-008282   384.55/4/091724   0674083415
Broadcasting -- Developing countries.

HE8697-8698 Telecommunication industry. Telegraph — Broadcasting. Radio and television broadcasting — Radio broadcasting

HE8697.P6.M3
MacNeil, Robert, 1931-
The people machine; the influence of television on American politics. New York, Harper & Row [1968] xx, 362 p.
68-028209   329/.01
Television in politics -- United States. United States -- Politics and government -- 1945-1989.

HE8697.4.W66 1992
Wood, James, 1920-
History of international broadcasting/ James Wood. London: P. Peregrinus Ltd. in association with the Scien c1992. xvix, 258 p.
93-171088   384.54   0863412815
International broadcasting.

HE8697.45.A8.H63 1995
Hodge, Errol, 1936-
Radio wars: truth, propaganda, and the struggle for radio Australia/ Errol Hodge. Cambridge [England]; Cambridge University Press, 1995. xii, 324 p.
94-035093   384.54/06/594   0521473802
International broadcasting -- Australia -- History.

HE8697.45.G7.R39 1996
Rawnsley, Gary D.
Radio diplomacy and propaganda: the BBC and VOA in international politics, 1956-64/ Gary D. Rawnsley. New York: St. Martin's Press, 1996. x, 224 p.
95-052176   384.54/0941   0333649435
International broadcasting -- Great Britain. International broadcasting -- United States. Radio in propaganda -- Great Britain -- History -- 20th century.

HE8697.8.N45 1997
Nelson, Michael, 1929 April 30
War of the black heavens: the battles of Western broadcasting in the Cold War/ Michael Nelson; with a foreword by Lech Walesa. [Syracuse, N.Y.]: Syracuse University Press, 1997. xx, 277 p.
97-013789   384.54/09171/3   0815604793
International broadcasting -- History -- 20th century. Cold War -- History. Radio in propaganda -- History -- 20th century.

HE8698.F68 2000
Foust, James C.
Big voices of the air: the battle over clear channel radio/ James C. Foust. Ames, Iowa: Iowa State University Press, 2000. ix, 249 p.
99-055027   384.54/524/0973   081382804X
Radio frequency allocation -- United States -- History -- 20th century. Radio broadcasting policy -- United States -- History -- 20th century.

HE8698.S6 1994
Smulyan, Susan.
Selling radio: the commercialization of American broadcasting, 1920-1934/ Susan Smulyan. Washington: Smithsonian Institution Press, c1994. viii, 223 p.
93-012833   384.54/3/0973   1560983124
Radio broadcasting -- Economic aspects -- United States -- History. Radio advertising -- United States -- History. Corporate sponsorship -- United States -- History.

HE8700.4-8700.8 Telecommunication industry. Telegraph — Broadcasting. Radio and television broadcasting — Television broadcasting

HE8700.4.C65 1990
Collins, Richard, 1914-
Television: policy and culture/ Richard Collins. London; Unwin Hyman, 1990. xii, 276 p.
90-039825   384.55/068   0044457650
Television broadcasting policy.

HE8700.4.D86 1990
Dunnett, Peter J. S.
The world television industry: an economic analysis/ Peter Dunnett. London; Routledge, 1990. xiii, 246 p.
89-027591   384.55/1   0415001625
Television broadcasting. Television broadcasting -- United States. Television broadcasting -- Government policy.

HE8700.6.Q47 1990
Quester, George H.
The international politics of television/ George H. Quester. Lexington, Mass.: Lexington Books, c1990. xiv, 288 p.
90-030474   384.55   0669209929
Television broadcasting -- Government policy. Television broadcasting -- Social aspects. Television and politics.

HE8700.7.A8.F69 1982
Frank, Ronald Edward, 1933-
Audiences for public television/ Ronald E. Frank and Marshall G. Greenberg. Beverly Hills, Calif.: Sage Publications, c1982. 230 p.
82-016754   384.55/44   0803907648
Television viewers -- United States. Public television -- United States.

HE8700.76.I4
Rajagopal, Arvind.
Politics after television: religious nationalism and the reshaping of the Indian public/ Arvind Rajagopal. Cambridge, UK; Cambridge University Press, c2001. viii, 393 p.
00-028954   306.2/0954 21   0521640539
Television in politics -- India. Elections -- India. Mass media -- Political aspects -- India.

HE8700.76.L29.T45 1993
Television, politics, and the transition to democracy in Latin America/ edited by Thomas E. Skidmore. Washington, D.C.: Woodrow Wilson Center Press; c1993. xii, 188 p.
92-037345 324.7/3/098 0943875447
Television in politics -- Latin America -- Congresses. Presidents -- Latin America -- Election -- Congresses. Elections -- Latin America -- Congresses. Latin America -- Politics and government -- 1980- -- Congresses.

HE8700.76.U6.F66 1990
Foote, Joe S.
Television access and political power: the networks, the presidency, and the "loyal opposition"/ Joe S. Foote; foreword by Newton N. Minow. New York: Praeger, 1990. xxviii, 212 p.
89-029763 324.7/3/0973 0275934381
Television in politics -- United States.

HE8700.76.U6.M54 1989
Mickelson, Sig.
From whistle stop to sound bite: four decades of politics and television/ Sig Mickelson. New York: Praeger, 1989. x, 186 p.
89-003554 324.7/3/0973 0275923517
Television in politics -- United States. United States -- Politics and government -- 1945-1989.

HE8700.79.U6.B85 1997
Bullert, B. J., 1955-
Public television: politics and the battle over documentary film/ B.J. Bullert. New Brunswick, N.J.: Rutgers University press, c1997. xix, 242 p.
97-017633 384.55/4/0973 21 0813524695
Public television -- United States. Documentary films -- United States. Documentary television programs -- United States.

HE8700.79.U6.F73 1996
Frantzich, Stephen E.
The C-span revolution/ by Stephen Frantzich and John Sullivan. Norman: University of Oklahoma Press, c1996. xiv, 433 p.
96-018189 384.55/532 20 0806128704
Television programs, Public service -- United States.

HE8700.8.L48
Levin, Harvey Joshua, 1924-
Fact and fancy in television regulation: an economic study of policy alternatives/ Harvey J. Levin. New York: Russell Sage Foundation, c1980. xvii, 505 p.
79-090148 384.55/443 0871545314
Television broadcasting policy -- United States. Television broadcasting -- United States.

HE8700.8.M36 1978
Mankiewicz, Frank, 1924-
Remote control: television and the manipulation of American life/ Frank Mankiewicz and Joel Swerdlow. New York: Times Books, c1978. viii, 308 p.
76-009726 301.24/3 0812906497
Television broadcasting -- Social aspects -- United States.

HE8815-8846 Telephone industry — By region or country — America

HE8815.A34 1991
After the breakup: assessing the new post-AT&T divestiture era/ edited by Barry G. Cole. New York: Columbia University Press, c1991. xxvi, 480 p.
90-040710 384/.06/573 0231073224
Telecommunication policy -- United States. Competition -- United States. Telephone -- United States.

HE8819.M84 1993
Mueller, Milton.
Telephone companies in paradise: a case study in telecommunications deregulation/ Milton L. Mueller. New Brunswick, N.J., U.S.A.: Transaction Publishers, c1993. xii, 185 p.
93-003741 384.6/3 1560001038
Telephone -- United States -- Deregulation -- Case studies. Telephone companies -- United States -- Case studies. Telephone -- Deregulation -- Nebraska.

HE8846.A55.F38 1987
Faulhaber, Gerald R.
Telecommunications in turmoil: technology and public policy/ Gerald R. Faulhaber. Cambridge, Mass.: Ballinger Pub. Co., c1987. xviii, 186 p.
87-001377 384/.068 0887301576
Telephone -- United States. Telecommunication -- United States.

HE8846.A55.H46 1988
Henck, Fred W., 1921-
A slippery slope: the long road to the breakup of AT&T/ Fred W. Henck and Bernard Strassburg. New York: Greenwood Press, 1988. xiii, 277 p.
87-028043 384.6/065/73 0313260257
Telephone companies -- United States. Telecommunication -- United States. Corporate divestiture -- United States.

HE8846.A55.T44 1987
Temin, Peter.
The fall of the Bell system: a study in prices and politics/ Peter Temin with Louis Galambos. Cambridge; Cambridge University Press, 1987. xviii, 378 p.
87-010293 384.6/065/73 052134557X
Telephone companies -- United States -- History.

HE9777.7 Air transportation. Airlines — Government policy. Aeronautics and state

HE9777.7.D4 1989
De Murias, Ramon, 1916-
The economic regulation of international air transport/ Ramon de Murias. Jefferson, N.C.: McFarland, c1989. v, 266 p.
88-042534 387.7/1 0899503438
Aeronautics, Commercial -- Government policy. Aeronautics, Commercial -- Deregulation.

HE9785 Air transportation. Airlines — Management of airlines — Local service airlines

HE9785.D38 1995
Davies, R. E. G.
Commuter airlines of the United States/ R.E.G. Davies and I.E. Quastler; foreword by George Haddaway. Washington: Smithsonian Institution Press, c1995. xxiv, 480 p.
94-019849 387.7/42/0973 156098404X
Local service airlines -- United States -- History. Local service airlines -- Government policy -- United States.

HE9786 Air transportation. Airlines — Management of airlines — Transoceanic traffic

HE9786.S7
Straszheim, Mahlon R., 1939-
The international airline industry [by] Mahlon R. Straszheim. Washington, Brookings Institution, Transport Research Progra [1969] viii, 297 p.
67-030604 338.4/7/3877
Aeronautics, Commercial.

HE9797.5 Air transportation. Airlines — Airports. Heliports. Seaplane bases — By region or country, A-Z

HE9797.5.U52 B66
Nelkin, Dorothy.
Jetport: the Boston airport controversy/ by Dorothy Nelkin. New Brunswick, N.J.: Transaction Books, [1974] 197 p.
74-078793 387.7/36/0974461 0878551115
Airports -- Massachusetts -- Boston.

HE9803 Air transportation. Airlines — By region or country — North America

HE9803.A3.A36
Airline deregulation: the early experience/ John R. Meyer and Clinton V. Oster, Jr., editors; [authors] John R. Meyer ... [et. al.]. Boston, Mass.: Auburn House Pub. Co., c1981. xx, 287 p.
81-003620 387.7/0973 0865690782
Aeronautics, Commercial -- Deregulation -- United States -- History. Aeronautics, Commercial -- Law and legislation -- United States -- History. Airlines -- Deregulation -- United States -- History.

HE9803.A3.H47 1995
Heppenheimer, T. A., 1947-
Turbulent skies: the history of commercial aviation/ T.A. Heppenheimer. New York: J. Wiley & Sons, c1995. xii, 388 p.
95-021508 387.7/0973 0471109614
Airlines -- United States -- History. Aeronautics, Commercial -- United States -- History.

HE9803.A35.B5 1982
Biederman, Paul.
The U.S. airline industry: end of an era/ Paul Biederman. New York, N.Y.: Praeger, 1982. xxiii, 198 p.
81-017845 387.7/065/73 0030603242
Aeronautics, Commercial -- United States.

HE9803.A4.B32 1985
Bailey, Elizabeth E.
Deregulating the airlines/ Elizabeth E. Bailey, David R. Graham, Daniel P. Kaplan. Cambridge, Mass.: MIT Press, c1985. xiv, 243 p.
84-021816 387.7/068 0262022133
Aeronautics, Commercial -- Government policy -- United States. Aeronautics, Commercial -- Law and legislation -- United States.

HE9803.A4.W53 1994
Williams, George, 1948-
The airline industry and the impact of deregulation/ George Williams. Aldershot, Hants, England: Avebury Aviation; c1994. xii, 206 p.
94-027724 387.7/1 0291398243
Aeronautics, Commercial -- Deregulation -- United States. Airlines -- Deregulation -- United States. Aeronautics, Commercial -- Deregulation.

HE9803.T7.R86 1991
Rummel, Robert W.
Howard Hughes and TWA/ Robert W. Rummel. Washington: Smithsonian Institution Press, c1991. x, 431 p.
90-039534 387.7/06/573 1560980176
Hughes, Howard, -- 1905-1976.

HE9882 Air transportation. Airlines — By region or country — Other regions or countries

HE9882.A35.G88 1998
Guttery, Ben R.
Encyclopedia of African airlines/ Ben R. Guttery. Jefferson, N.C.: McFarland, c1998. xvi, 291 p.
98-020087 387.7/06/56 21 0786404957
Aeronautics, Commercial -- Africa -- Encyclopedias.

HF Commerce

HF54.5 Information services. Business information services — General works

HF54.5.P33 1994
Pagell, Ruth A.
International business information: how to find it, how to use it/ by Ruth A. Pagell and Michael Halperin. Phoenix, Ariz.: Oryx Press, 1994. xiv, 371 p.
93-049000 016.33 0897747364
Business information services -- Handbooks, manuals, etc. Business -- Bibliography -- Handbooks, manuals, etc.

HF54.52 Information services. Business information services — By region or country, A-Z

HF54.52.C36
Konn, Tania
Guide to business information on Central and Eastern Europe/ Tania Konn. -- Chicago: Fitzroy Dearborn, c2000. ii, 235 p.
2001-279281 157958263X
Affaires -- Documentation, Services de -- Europe centrale -- Repertoires. Affaires -- Documentation, Services de -- Europe de l'Est -- Repertoires. Affaires -- Ouvrages de reference -- Bibliographie

HF54.52.E85.E53 1993
Encyclopedia of business information sources. edited by M. Balachandran. Detroit: Gale Research, 1993. lxxxiv, 877 p.
92-010924 016.33 0810384590
Business information services -- Europe -- Directories. Business -- Reference books -- Bibliography. Business -- Periodicals -- Bibliography.

HF54.56 Information services. Business information services — Electronic information resources

HF54.56.L364 2001
Lanza, Sheri R.,
International business information on the web: Searcher magazine's guide to sites and strategies for global business research/ Sheri R. Lanza; edited and with a foreword by Barbara Quint. Medford, N.J.: CyberAge Books, c2001. xxiii, 396 p.
2001-028735 025.06/65 21 0910965463
Business information services -- Computer network resources Web sites -- Directories.

HF54.56.L58 1998
Liu, Lewis-Guodo
Internet resources and services for international business: a global guide/ Lewis-Guodo Liu. Phoenix, Ariz.: Oryx Press, c1998. xv, 389 p.
98-021251 025.04 21 1573561193
Business information services -- Computer network resources -- Directories. International trade -- Computer network resources -- Directories. Economic history -- 1990- -- Computer network resources -- Directories.

HF81 Theory. Method

HF81.O5 1967
Ohlin, Bertil Gotthard, 1899-
Interregional and international trade. Cambridge, Harvard University Press, 1967. xv, 324p.
67-017317 382
Commerce. Foreign exchange. Prices.

HF373-377 History — By period — Ancient

HF373.M45 1992
Meijer, Fik.
Trade, transport, and society in the ancient world: a sourcebok/ Fik Meijer and Onno van Nijf. London; Routledge, 1992. xxii, 201 p.
91-046010 380/.093 041500344X
Transportation -- Greece -- History -- Sources. Transportation -- Rome -- History -- Sources. Rome -- Commerce -- History -- Sources. Greece -- Commerce -- History -- Sources.

HF375.T73 1983
Trade in the ancient economy/ edited by Peter Garnsey, Keith Hopkins, and C.R. Whittaker. Berkeley: University of California Press, 1983. xxv, 230 p.
82-013652 382/.093 0520048032
Greece -- Commerce -- History. Rome -- Commerce -- History.

HF377.C86 1988
Cunliffe, Barry W.
Greeks, Romans, and barbarians: spheres of interaction/ Barry Cunliffe. New York: Methuen, 1988. xii, 243 p.
87-034167 306/.094 0416019919
Civilization, Greco-Roman. Rome -- Commerce -- Europe -- History. Europe -- Commerce -- Rome -- History.

HF377.R66 1991
Rome and India: the ancient sea trade/ edited by Vimala Begley and Richard Daniel De Puma. Madison, Wis.: University of Wisconsin Press, c1991. xix, 226 p.
91-006579 382/.0934037 0299126404
Rome -- Commerce -- India. India -- Commerce -- Rome.

HF416-442 History — By period — Middle Ages

HF416.H86 1994
Hunt, Edwin S.
The medieval super-companies: a study of the Peruzzi Company of Florence/ Edwin S. Hunt. Cambridge [England]; Cambridge University Press, 1994. x, 291 p.
93-040289 380.1/06/04551 0521461561
Merchants -- Italy -- Florence -- History. Florence (Italy) -- Commerce -- History.

HF442.F7.S745
Strieder, Jacob, 1877-
Jacob Fugger the rich, merchant and banker of Augsburg, 1459-1525, by Jacob Strieder. Translated by Mildred L. Hartsough. Edited by N. S. B. Gras. New York, The Adelphi company [c1931] xxvi, 227 p.
32-010409 923.343
Fugger, Jakob, -- 1459-1525.

HF493 History — By period — Modern

HF493.J413
Jeannin, Pierre.
Merchants of the sixteenth century. Translated by Paul Fittingoff. New York, Harper & Row [1972] vi, 146 p.
75-161638 380.1 0061388785
Merchants.

HF499 History — By period — 1789-

HF499.B26 1996
Baker, Geoffrey L. 1924-
Trade winds on the Niger: the saga of the Royal Niger Company, 1930[i.e. 1830]-1971/ Geoffrey L. Baker. London; Radcliffe Press; 1996. xvii, 333 p.
95-062306 1860640141
Colonial companies -- Nigeria -- History. Nigeria -- Commerce -- History.

HF1001 Dictionaries. Encyclopedias — General

HF1001.C68 1995
Cross, Wilbur.
Prentice Hall encyclopedic dictionary of business terms/ Wilbur Cross. Englewood Cliff, N.J.: Prentice Hall, c1995. viii, 472 p.
95-023813 650/.03 0130262218
Business -- Dictionaries. Management -- Dictionaries.

HF1001.E466 1995
Encyclopedia of business/ John G. Maurer ... [et al.], editors. Detroit, MI: Gale Research, 1995. 2 v.
95-033676 650/.103 0810391872
Finance -- Encyclopedias. Finance -- North America -- Encyclopedias. Business -- Encyclopedias. North America -- Commerce -- Encyclopedias.

HF1001.S525 1989
Shim, Jae K.
Encyclopedic dictionary of accounting and finance/ Jae K. Shim and Joel G. Siegel. Englewood Cliffs, N.J.: Prentice Hall, c1989. viii, 504 p.
89-003628 657/.03 0132758016
Accounting -- Dictionaries. Finance -- Dictionaries.

HF1002 Dictionaries. Encyclopedias — Bilingual and polyglot

HF1002.C59 1990
Collin, P. H.
Dictionary of business: English-French, French-English/ P.H. Collin and Nicole Marin ... [et al.]. Teddington, Middlesex: P. Collin Pub., 1990. 336 p.
91-190926 650/.03 0948549106
Business -- Dictionaries. English language -- Dictionaries -- French. Business -- Dictionaries -- French.

HF1002.F43 1993
Ferber, Gene.
Cassell English-Japanese business dictionary/ Gene Ferber. New York, NY: Cassell, 1993. 632 p.
93-033900 330/.03 030432552X
Business -- Dictionaries. English language -- Dictionaries -- Japanese. Business -- Dictionaries -- Japanese.

HF1002.Z25 1996
Zagorskaia, A. P.
Russian-English, English-Russian business dictionary/ Aleksandra Zagorskaya with Nina Petrochenko. Chichester, U.K.; Wiley, c1996. ix, 650 p.
95-022028 650/.03 20 0471957852
Business -- Dictionaries -- Russian. Russian language -- Dictionaries -- English. Business -- Dictionaries.

HF1008 General works — 1979-

HF1008.E83 1989
Evans, H. David
Comparative advantage and growth: trade and development in theory and practice/ H.D. Evans. New York: St. Martin's Press, 1989. xvii, 363 p.
87-016370 382 0312009550
Commerce. Economic development. Comparative advantage (International trade)

HF1008.G65 1987
Gomes, Leonard.
Foreign trade and the national economy: mercantilist and classical perspectives/ Leonard Gomes. New York: St. Martin's Press, 1987. viii, 323 p.
87-004674 382 0312007655
International trade. Mercantile system. Classical school of economics.

HF1009.5 Export and international marketing

HF1009.5.K39 1984
Keegan, Warren J.
Multinational marketing management/ Warren J. Keegan. Englewood Cliffs, N.J.: Prentice-Hall, c1984. xxii, 698 p.
83-024751 658.8/48 0136050492
Export marketing -- Management. Export marketing -- Management -- Case studies.

HF1025 Commercial geography. Economic geography — General works

HF1025.B333 1996
Barnes, Trevor J.
Logics of dislocation: models, metaphors, and meanings of economic space/ Trevor J. Barnes. New York: Guilford Press, c1996. xii, 292 p.
95-042463 330 20 1572300337
Economic geography.

HF1025.G38 1997
Geographies of economies/ edited by Roger Lee and Jane Wills. London; Arnold, 1997. xviii, 406 p.
96-029757 330.9
Economic geography. Regional economic disparities. Industrial location.

HF1025.K75 1991
Krugman, Paul R.
Geography and trade/ Paul Krugman. Leuven, Belgium: Leuven University Press; c1991. xi, 142 p.
91-011984 338.6/042 0262111594
Commercial geography -- Mathematical models. Economic geography -- Mathematical models. Regional economic disparities -- Mathematical models..

HF1025.L584 1977
Lloyd, Peter E.
Location in space: a theoretical approach to economic geography/ Peter E. Lloyd & Peter Dicken. London; Harper & Row, c1977. xii, 474 p.
77-023256 330.9 0060440481
Economic geography. Space in economics. Industrial location.

HF1025.S69 1973
Stamp, L. Dudley 1898-1966.
A commercial geography [by] Sir Dudley Stamp. London] Longman [1973] viii, 824 p.
74-155452 330.9 0582310431
Commercial geography.

HF1040.7 Commodities. Commercial products — General works

HF1040.7.R33 1990
Radetzki, Marian.
A guide to primary commodities in the world economy/ Marian Radetzki. Oxford, OX, UK; B. Blackwell, 1990.
89-034520 382/.4 0631171126
Primary commodities. Commercial policy. Primary commodities -- Prices.

HF1041.5 Commodities. Commercial products — Commodity and commercial products classification. Industrial classification — General works

HF1041.5.N35 2000
NAICS desk reference: The North American Industry Classification System desk reference. Indianapolis, IN: JIST, 2000. xlvi, 569 p.
00-023827 338/.02/0127 1563706946
Industries -- North America -- Classification. Commercial products -- North America -- Classification.

HF1052 Commodities. Commercial products — Raw materials

HF1052.P33
Page, Talbot.
Conservation and economic efficiency: an approach to materials policy/ Talbot Page. Baltimore: Published for Resources for the Future by the Jo c1977. xvii, 266 p.
76-022846 338/.0973 0801819040
Raw materials -- United States. Conservation of natural resources -- United States. Recycling (Waste, etc.)

HF1131 Business education. Commercial education — By region or country — United States and Canada

HF1131.M58 1993
Mitroff, Ian I.
The unbounded mind: breaking the chains of traditional business thinking/ Ian I. Mitroff and Harold A. Linstone. New York: Oxford University Press, 1993. viii, 177 p.
92-015708 650/.071/173 0195077830
Business education -- United States. Critical thinking -- Study and teaching (Higher) -- United States.

HF1359 International economic relations — General works

HF1359.A96 1995
Axford, Barrie.
The global system: economics, politics, and culture/ Barrie Axford. New York: St. Martin's Press, 1995. x, 250 p.
95-034537 337 0312158289
International economic relations. International cooperation.

HF1359.C64 1990
Cohen, Benjamin J.
Crossing frontiers: explorations in international political economy/ Benjamin J. Cohen. Boulder: Westview Press, 1991. x, 336 p.
90-043899 337.73 0813379903
International economic relations. Monetary policy -- United States. United States -- Economic policy. United States -- Foreign economic relations. European Economic Community countries -- Foreign economic relations.

HF1359.D46 2000
Democratizing the global economy: the battle against the Work Bank and the IMF/ edited by Kevin Danaher. Monroe, ME: Common Courage Press, 2000.
00-064532 332.1/52 1567512097
International economic relations. Structural adjustment (Economic policy) Economic assistance -- Developing countries.

HF1359.F54 1988
Fieleke, Norman S.
The international economy under stress/ Norman S. Fieleke. Cambridge, Mass.: Ballinger Pub. Co., c1988. xxv, 253 p.
88-019248 337 0887302246
International economic relations. Protectionism. Balance of payments.

HF1359.G5515 2000
Gilpin, Robert.
The challenge of global capitalism: the world economy in the 21st century/ Robert Gilpin; with the assistance of Jean Millis Gilpin. Princeton, NJ: Princeton University Press, c2000. xii, 373 p.
99-044906 337 21 0691049351
International economic relations. International relations. Structural adjustment (Economic policy)

HF1359.G5516 2001
Gilpin, Robert.
Global political economy: understanding the international economic order/ Robert Gilpin with the assistance of Jean M. Gilpin. Princeton, N.J.: Princeton University Press, c2001. xii, 423 p.
00-051684 337 21 069108677X
International economic relations. Free trade. International finance.

HF1359.G55 1988
Gill, Stephen, 1950-
The global political economy: perspectives, problems, and policies/ Stephen Gill and David Law. Baltimore: Johns Hopkins University Press, c1988. xxvi, 394 p.
88-045409 337 0801837634
International economic relations. International trade. International finance.

HF1359.H575 1999
Hirst, Paul Q.
Globalization in question: the international economy and the possibilities of governance/ Paul Hirst and Grahame Thompson. 2nd ed. Cambridge, UK; Polity, 1999. xviii, 318 p.
99-031062 337 21 0745621643
International economic relations. International business enterprises. Investments, Foreign.

HF1359.J36 2001
James, Harold.
The end of globalization: lessons from the Great Depression/ Harold James. Cambridge, Mass.: Harvard University Press, 2001. vi, 260 p.
00-054157 337 0674004744
International economic relations. International trade. International finance.

HF1359.P338 1996
Palan, Ronen, 1957-
State strategies in the global political economy/ Ronen Palan and Jason Abbott, with Phil Deans. London; Pinter, 1996. 234 p.
95-048394 337 1855673428
International economic relations. Economic policy. Competition, International.

HF1359.P65 1994
Political economy and the changing global order/ editors, Richard Stubbs and Geoffrey R.D. Underhill. New York: St. Martin's Press, 1994. 553 p.
94-186727 337 0312121962
International economic relations. World politics -- 1989- Economic history -- 1990-

HF1359.P74 1991
Presner, Lewis A., 1945-
The international business dictionary and reference/ Lewis A. Presner. New York: Wiley, c1991. xviii, 486 p.
91-009328 658/.049/03 0471545945
International economic relations -- Encyclopedias. International finance -- Encyclopedias. International relations -- Encyclopedias.

HF1359.W46 2000
Went, Robert, 1955-
Globalization: neoliberal challenge, radical responses/ Robert Went; translated by Peter Drucker, foreword by Tony Smith. London; Pluto Press with the International Institute for 2000. xii, 170 p.
00-008824 337 0745314279
International economic relations. International business enterprises. Capitalism.

HF1379 International economic relations — International trade — General works

HF1379.C74 1989
Cohen, Richard, 1946-
World trade and payments cycles: the advance and retreat of the post war order/ Richard Cohen; foreword by Norman A. Bailey. New York: Praeger, 1989. xxiii, 299 p.
89-003856 382.1/7 0275932516
International trade -- History. East-West trade (1945-) Balance of payments -- History.

HF1379.E27 1988
Economic development and international trade/ edited by David Greenaway. New York: St. Martin's Press, 1988. xi, 211 p.
87-025629 382 0312015887
International trade. Economic development. Developing countries -- Economic policy.

HF1379.G75 1989
Grimwade, Nigel, 1949-
International trade: new patterns of trade, production, and investment/ Nigel Grimwade. London; Routledge, c1989. xv, 459 p.
88-023957 382 0415003962
International trade. International economic relations. Investments, Foreign.

HF1379.H45 1989
Helpman, Elhanan.
Trade policy and market structure/ Elhanan Helpman and Paul R. Krugman. Cambridge, Mass.: MIT Press, c1989. xii, 191 p.
88-032609 382/.3 0262081822
International trade. Commercial policy

HF1379.M36 1994
Mansfield, Edward D., 1962-
Power, trade, and war/ Edward D. Mansfield. Princeton, N.J.: Princeton University Press, 1994. xvii, 278 p.
93-013700 382 0691032882
International trade. War -- Economic aspects. Power (Social sciences)

HF1379.O996 2001
The Oxford handbook of international business/ edited by Alan M. Rugman and Thomas L. Brewer. New York: Oxford University Press, 2001. xviii, 877 p.
2001-016400 658.8/48 21 0199241821
International trade.

HF1379.P653 1991
The Political economy of merchant empires/ James D. Tracy, editor. Cambridge; Cambridge University Press, 1991. vi, 504 p.
91-007444 382/.09 0521410460
International trade -- History -- Congresses. Shipping -- History -- Congresses. Merchants -- History -- Congresses. Europe -- Commerce -- History -- Congresses.

HF1379.Z45 1999
Zeiler, Thomas W.
Free trade, free world: the advent of GATT/ Thomas W. Zeiler. Chapel Hill: University of North Carolina Press, c1999. xii, 267 p.
98-022832 382 21 0807824585
International trade -- History. Cold War.

HF1385 International economic relations — International trade — International trade agencies

HF1385.W778 2000
The WTO after Seattle/ edited by Jeffrey J. Schott. Washington, DC: Institute for International Economics, 2000. xix, 292 p.
00-039668   382/.92   0881322903
Foreign trade regulation. International trade.

HF1410 International economic relations — Foreign commercial policy — Societies. Serials

HF1410.I579 vol. 4
Markets, politics, and change in the global political economy/ edited by William P. Avery & David P. Rapkin. Boulder: L. Rienner, 1989. xii, 227 p.
89-003626   337/.05 s   1555871488
Debts, External — Developing countries. Capitalism — Developing countries. Investments, Foreign — Developing countries. Developing countries — Economic policy. Developing countries — Politics and government.

HF1410.N4835
The New international economic order: the North-South debate/ Jagdish N. Bhagwati, editor. Cambridge, Mass.: MIT Press, c1977. xiv, 390 p.
77-007062   382.1   0262021269
International economic relations — Congresses. Developing countries — Foreign economic relations — Congresses.

HF1411 International economic relations — Foreign commercial policy — General works

HF1411.A28
Adler-Karlsson, Gunnar, 1933-
Western economic warfare 1947-1967. A case study in foreign economic policy. With a foreword by Gunnar Myrdal. Stockholm, Almqvist & Wiksell (distr.), 1968. xv, 319 p.
68-141874   338.91
International economic relations. East-West trade (1945-) United States — Foreign economic relations.

HF1411.H5 1980
Hirschman, Albert O.
National power and the structure of foreign trade/ by Albert O. Hirschman. Berkeley: University of California Press, c1980. xxii, 172 p.
81-161425   382.1/04   0520040848
International trade. International economic relations. World politics.

HF1411.I368 1980
Independent Commission on International Development Issues
North-South, a programme for survival: report of the Independent Commission on International Development Issues.   Cambridge, Mass.: MIT Press, 1980. 304 p.
80-050086   337/.09/04   0262520591
International economic relations. Economic development. Developing countries — Foreign economic relations.

HF1411.K5 1968
Kindleberger, Charles Poor, 1910-
International economics [by] Charles P. Kindleberger. Homewood, Ill., R. D. Irwin, 1968. xix, 611 p.
67-030239   382
International economic relations.

HF1411.L533 1988
Lieberman, Sima, 1927-
The economic and political roots of the new protectionism/ Sima Lieberman. Totowa, N.J.: Rowman & Littlefield, 1988. xv, 184 p.
87-023329   382.7/3/09048   0847675955
International economic relations — History — 20th century. Protectionism — History — 20th century. Economic history — 20th century.

HF1411.L536 2000
Pugel, Thomas A.
International economics/ Thomas A. Pugel, Peter H. Lindert. 11th ed. Boston: McGraw-Hill, c2000. xxiii, 709 p.
99-056092   337 21   0072903872
International economic relations. Commercial policy. Foreign exchange.

HF1411.P5915 1988
Pomfret, Richard W. T.
Unequal trade: the economics of discriminatory international trade policies/ Richard Pomfret. Oxford, OX, UK; B. Blackwell, 1988. x, 227 p.
87-034006   382/.3   0631153411
International trade. Commercial policy. Protectionism.

HF1411.S454 1994
Simmons, Beth A., 1958-
Who adjusts?: domestic sources of foreign economic policy during the interwar years/ Beth A. Simmons. Princeton, N.J.: Princeton University Press, c1994. xii, 330 p.
93-002272   337/.09/04   0691086419
International economic relations — History — 20th century. Gold standard — History — 20th century.

HF1411.S8866 1989
Suzuki, Yoshio, 1931-
Japan's economic performance and international role/ Yoshio Suzuki. [Tokyo]: University of Tokyo Press, c1989. x, 177 p.
89-187885   337.52   4130470434
International economic relations. Monetary policy — Japan. International finance. Japan — Foreign economic relations.

HF1411.W66
World politics and international economics/ C. Fred Bergsten and Lawrence B. Krause, editors; contributions by C. Fred Bergsten ... [et al.]. Washington: Brookings Institution, [1975] xi, 359 p.
75-015684   338.91   0815709161
International economic relations — Addresses, essays, lectures. International finance — Addresses, essays, lectures. World politics — 1965-1975 — Addresses, essays, lectures.

HF1412 International economic relations — General special

HF1412.R53 1982
Rich country interests and Third World development/ edited by Robert Cassen ... [et al.]. New York: St. Martins Press, 1982. 369 p.
82-042561   337/.09/048   0312681011
International economic relations. Developing countries — Economic conditions.

HF1412.S3 1994
Scherer, F. M.
Competition policies for an integrated world economy/ F.M. Scherer. Washington, D.C.: Brookings Institution, c1994. xxii, 133 p.
94-011819   337   0815777981
Commercial policy. Competition, International. International economic integration.

HF1413 International economic relations — Developing countries

HF1413.A4513 1990
Amin, Samir.
Delinking: towards a polycentric world/ Samir Amin; translated by Michael Wolfers. London; Zed Books, 1990. xvi, 194 p.
89-028953   337/.09172/4   0862328020
International economic relations. Income distribution. Capitalism. Developing countries — Dependency on foreign countries.

HF1413.H45 1990
Helleiner, Gerald K.
The new global economy and the developing countries: essays in international economics and development/ G.K. Helleiner. Aldershot, Hants, England: E. Elgar, c1990. xiii, 290 p.
90-038600   337/.09172/4   185278329X
International economic relations. International finance. Developing countries — Foreign economic relations.

HF1413.K73 1995
Krueger, Anne O.
Trade policies and developing nations/ Anne O. Krueger. Washington, D.C.: Brookings Institution, c1995. xxvi, 124 p.
95-014295   382/.3/091724   0815750560
Import substitution — Developing countries. Developing countries — Foreign economic relations. Developing countries — Commerce. Developing countries — Commercial policy.

HF1413.N495 1982
The New Communist Third World: an essay in political economy/ edited by Peter Wiles. New York: St. Martin's Press, 1982. 392 p.
81-013620   337/.09172/4   0312566077
Developing countries — Commerce — Addresses, essays, lectures. Communist countries — Commerce — Addresses, essays, lectures.

HF1413.R34 1995
Rahnama-Moghadam, Mashaalah.
Doing business in less developed countries: financial opportunities and risks/ Mashaalah Rahnama-Moghadam, Hedayeh Samavati, and David A. Dilts. Westport, Conn.: Quorum Books, 1995. vi, 209 p.
94-024986 332.6/73/091724 0899308546
Investments, Foreign -- Developing countries. Developing countries -- Commerce. Developing countries -- Foreign economic relations.

HF1413.W54 1991
Williams, Marc.
Third World cooperation: the group of 77 in UNCTAD/ Marc Williams. London: Pinter Publishers; 1991. ix, 182 p.
90-022680 337/.09172/4 0861871545
International economic relations -- Developing countries. Developing countries -- Commercial policy.

HF1413.5 International economic relations — Economic sanctions. Boycotts

HF1413.5.B47 1994
Bergeijk, Peter A. G. van, 1959-
Economic diplomacy, trade, and commercial policy: positive and negative sanctions in a new world order/ Peter A.G. van Bergeijk. Aldershot, England; E. Elgar, c1994. xiv, 224 p.
94-006035 337 1852188933
Economic sanctions. Commercial policy. International economic relations.

HF1413.5.C67 2000
Cortright, David, 1946-
The sanctions decade: assessing UN strategies in the 1990s/ David Cortright, George A. Lopez, with Richard W. Conroy, Jaleh Dashti-Gibson & Julia Wagler. Boulder, Colo.: Lynne Rienner Publishers, 2000. xiv, 274 p.
99-089665 337 1555878911
Economic sanctions -- Case studies. Economic sanctions.

HF1413.5.E27 1995
Economic sanctions: panacea or peacebuilding in a post-cold war world?/ edited by David Cortright and George A. Lopez; with a foreword by Ronald V. Dellums. Boulder: Westview Press, 1995. xvii, 231 p.
95-002899 337 0813389089
Economic sanctions. Economic sanctions -- Case studies.

HF1413.5.F86 1988
Funigiello, Philip J.
American-Soviet trade in the Cold War/ Philip J. Funigiello. Chapel Hill: University of North Carolina Press, c1988. xii, 289 p.
87-035836 382/.0973/047 0807817848
Economic sanctions, American -- Soviet Union -- History -- 20th century. East-West trade (1945-) United States -- Foreign economic relations -- Soviet Union. Soviet Union -- Foreign economic relations -- United States.

HF1413.5.K34 1992
Kaempfer, William H.
International economic sanctions: a public choice perspective/ William H. Kaempfer and Anton D. Lowenberg. Boulder: Westview, 1992. xiv, 189 p.
92-004444 337 0813380456
Economic sanctions.

HF1413.5.M37 1992
Martin, Lisa L., 1961-
Coercive cooperation: explaining multilateral economic sanctions/ Lisa L. Martin. Princeton, N.J.: Princeton University Press, c1992. xiii, 299 p.
91-040190 337 0691086249
Economic sanctions. Economic sanctions -- Case studies. International economic relations.

HF1413.5.M59 1992
Miyagawa, Makio, 1951-
Do economic sanctions work?/ Makio Miyagawa. Houndmills, Basingstoke, Hampshire: Macmillan; 1992. xi, 240 p.
92-014516 337 0312085443
Economic sanctions.

HF1413.5.S258 2000
Sanctions as economic statecraft: theory and practice/ edited by Steve Chan and A. Cooper Drury. New York: St. Martin's Press , 2000. xii, 258 p.
00-035259 337.73 0312231970
Economic sanctions, American -- History. United States -- Commercial policy -- History.

HF1414 International economic relations — Competition. International competition

HF1414.C456 2001
Cho, Tong-song.
From Adam Smith to Michael Porter: evolution of competitiveness theory/ Dong-Sung Cho, Hwy-Chang Moon. Singapore; World Scientific Pub., 2001. xvii, 223 p.
00-054087 338.6/048 9810244312
Competition, International.

HF1414.D65 1993
Dollar, David.
Competitiveness, convergence, and international specialization/ David Dollar, Edward N. Wolff. Cambridge, Mass.: MIT Press, c1993. 228 p.
92-027958 338.6/048 0262041359
Competition, International. Competition -- United States. Industrial productivity.

HF1414.I575 1988
International competitiveness/ edited by A. Michael Spence and Heather A. Hazard. Cambridge, Mass.: Ballinger Pub. Co., c1988. xxiii, 451 p.
87-030792 382/.3 0887302505
Competition, International. Industrial policy. Trade regulation.

HF1414.N37 1996
National diversity and global capitalism/ edited by Suzanne Berger and Ronald Dore. Ithaca, [N.Y.]: Cornell University Press, 1996. viii, 387 p.
95-048267 337 0801432340
Competition, International. International economic relations.

HF1414.P67 1998
Porter, Michael E., 1947-
On competition/ Michael E. Porter. Boston, MA: Harvard Businesss School Publishing, c1998. vi, 485 p.
98-007643 382/.1042 21 0875847951
Competition, International. Comparative advantage (International trade) Industrial policy.

HF1414.4 International economic relations — Exports — General works

HF1414.4.S49 2000
Seyoum, Belay, 1953-
Export-import theory, practices, and procedures/ Belay Seyoum. New York: International Business Press, c2000. xiv, 485 p.
99-036499 382 21 0789005670
Exports. Imports. Export marketing.

HF1414.5 International economic relations — Exports — Export controls

HF1414.5.J66 1994
Jones, Kent Albert.
Export restraint and the new protectionism: the political economy of discriminatory trade restrictions/ Kent Albert Jones. Ann Arbor: University of Michigan Press, c1994. xi, 227 p.
94-031943 382/.64 0472105272
Export controls. Restraint of trade. Protectionism.

HF1414.5.M27 1992
Mastanduno, Michael.
Economic containment: CoCom and the politics of East-West trade/ Michael Mastanduno. Ithaca, N.Y.: Cornell University Press, 1992. xiv, 353 p.
92-052766 382/.09171/301717 0801499968
Export controls -- International cooperation. National security -- International cooperation. East-West trade (1945-)

HF1416 International economic relations — Exports — Export marketing. International marketing

HF1416.G55 1993
The Global business: four key marketing strategies/ Erdener Kaynak, editor. New York: International Business Press, c1993. xxv, 432 p.
91-034596 658.8/48 1560242485
Export marketing -- Management. Intercultural communication.

HF1416.G58 1994
Globalization of consumer markets: structures and strategies/ Salah S. Hassan, Erdener Kaynak, editors. New York: International Business Press, c1994. xxi, 333 p.
93-010607 658.8/48 1560244291
Export marketing -- Management. Advertising -- Standards. Consumer behavior.

HF1416.M55 1995
Miller, Richard 1929-
Multinational direct marketing: the methods and the markets/ Richard Miller. New York: McGraw-Hill, c1995. xii, 354 p.
95-018495 658.8/4 0070423563
Export marketing -- Management. Direct marketing -- Management.

HF1416.M78 1997
Morrison, Terri.
Dun & Bradstreet's guide to doing business around the world/ Terri Morrison, Wayne A. Conaway, Joseph J. Douress. Englewood Cliffs, NJ: Prentice Hall, 1997.
　96-040929　658.8/48　0135314844
　Export marketing -- Cross-cultural studies -- Handbooks, manuals, etc. International trade -- Cross-cultural studies -- Handbooks, manuals, etc. International business enterprises -- Cross-cultural studies -- Handbooks, manuals, etc.

HF1418.5 International economic relations — International economic integration

HF1418.5.B44 1984
Behrman, Jack N.
Industrial policies: international restructuring and transnationals/ Jack N. Behrman. Lexington, Mass.: Lexington Books, c1984. xiv, 254 p.
　83-049533　337.1　0669082759
　International economic integration. International business enterprises. Industrial policy.

HF1418.5.B68 1988
Bourdet, Yves.
International integration, market structure, and prices/ Yves Bourdet. London; Routledge, 1988. 241 p.
　89-101625　337.1/4　0415003938
　International economic integration. Automobile industry and trade -- Europe. Europe -- Economic integration.

HF1418.5.E4 1989
El-Agraa, A. M.
The theory and measurement of international integration/ Ali M. El-Agraa. New York: St. Martin's Press, 1989.
　88-023370　337.1　031202519X
　International economic integration.

HF1418.5.J68 1992
Jovanovic, Miroslav N., 1957-
International economic integration/ Miroslav N. Jovanovic; foreword by Richard G. Lipsey. London; Routledge, 1992. xxiv, 302 p.
　91-010671　337.1　0415038197
　International economic integration.

HF1418.5.O46 1990
Omae, Kenichi, 1943-
The borderless world: power and strategy in the interlinked economy/ Kenichi Ohmae. New York: HarperBusiness, c1990. 223 p.
　90-033770　337　0887304737
　International economic integration. International business enterprises. International trade.

HF1418.7 International economic relations — Trade blocs

HF1418.7.B47 1997
Bhalla, A. S.
Regional blocs: building blocks or stumbling blocks/ A.S. Bhalla, P. Bhalla. New York: St. Martin's Press, 1997. xv, 242 p.
　97-009155　382/.91　0312175280
　Trade blocs. Regionalism. International economic integration.

HF1418.7.O45 1995
Ohmae, Kenichi, 1943-
The end of the nation state: the rise of regional economies/ Kenichi Ohmae. New York: Free Press, c1995. x, 214 p.
　95-013613　337.1　0029233410
　International economic integration Trade blocs Regionalism

HF1418.7.P66 1997
Pomfret, Richard W. T.
The economics of regional trading arrangements/ Richard Pomfret. Oxford: Clarendon Press; 1997. xiv, 440 p.
　97-026763　382/.9　0198233353
　Trade blocs. Commercial policy.

HF1421 International economic relations — Trade adjustment assistance

HF1421.S76 1996
Stone, Randall W., 1966-
Satellites and commissars: strategy and conflict in the politics of Soviet-Bloc trade/ Randall W. Stone. Princeton, N.J.: Princeton University Press, c1996. xviii, 283 p.
　95-017510　337.47 20　0691044147
　Trade adjustment assistance -- Soviet Union. Europe, Eastern -- Foreign economic relations -- Soviet Union. Europe, Eastern -- Foreign relations -- Soviet Union.

HF1425 International economic relations — Dumping — General works

HF1425.A58 1993
Antidumping: how it works and who gets hurt/ edited by J. Michael Finger with the assistance of Nellie T. Artis. Ann Arbor: University of Michigan Press, c1993. xiv, 267 p.
　92-038988　382/.7　0472104063
　Antidumping duties. Protectionism. Dumping (International trade)

HF1428 International economic relations — International commodity control

HF1428.N485
Newbery, David M. G.
The theory of commodity price stabilization: a study in the economics of risk/ David M.G. Newbery and Joseph E. Stiglitz. Oxford: Clarendon Press; 1981. xv, 462 p.
　81-201605　338.5/2　0198284179
　Commodity control. Risk.

HF1430 International economic relations — Nontariff trade barriers

HF1430.L34 1990
Laird, Sam.
Quantitative methods for trade-barrier analysis/ Sam Laird and Alexander Yeats. New York: New York University Press, 1990. xiv, 307 p.
　89-049635　382/.5/015195　0814750494
　Nontariff trade barriers -- Econometric models.

HF1452.5-1456.5 International economic relations — North America

HF1452.5.J3.N47 1993
Nester, William R., 1956-
American power, the new world order, and the Japanese challenge/ William R. Nester. New York, N.Y.: St. Martin's Press, 1993. vi, 492 p.
　92-028897　337.73052　0312089910
　International economic relations. Japan -- Foreign economic relations -- United States. United States -- Commercial policy. Japan -- Commercial policy.

HF1452.5.M6.U15 1988
U.S.-Mexican economic relations: prospects and problems/ edited by Khosrow Fatemi. New York: Praeger, 1988. xvi, 223 p.
　88-000311　337.73072　0275929558
　United States -- Foreign economic relations -- Mexico. Mexico -- Foreign economic relations -- United States.

HF1455.A72 1990
An American trade strategy: options for the 1990s/ Robert Z. Lawrence, Charles L. Schultze, editors. Washington, D.C.: Brookings Institution, c1990. ix, 234 p.
　90-042576　382/.3/0973　081575180X
　Free trade -- United States. Protectionism -- United States. United States -- Commercial policy.

HF1455.B328 1993
Batra, Raveendra N.
The myth of free trade: a plan for America's economic revival/ Ravi Batra. New York: C. Scribner's Sons; c1993. 274 p.
　92-040683　382/.71　0684195925
　Free trade -- United States. United States -- Foreign economic relations.

HF1455.B48 2000
Bhagwati, Jagdish N., 1934-
The wind of the hundred days: how Washington mismanaged globalization/ Jagdish Bhagwati. Cambridge, Mass.: MIT Press, c2000. xxiii, 383 p.
　00-064596　337.73 21　0262024950
　Free trade. Capital movements. Globalization -- Economic aspects. United States -- Foreign economic relations. United States -- Commercial policy.

HF1455.C724 1993
Competitiveness and American society/ edited by Steven L. Goldman. Bethlehem: Lehigh University Press; c1993. 299 p.
　92-054262　336.6/048　0934223289
　Competition -- United States. Competition, International. International economic relations. United States -- Foreign economic relations.

HF1455.G5
Gilpin, Robert.
U.S. power and the multinational corporation: the political economy of foreign direct investment/ Robert Gilpin. New York: Basic Books, [1975] xii, 291 p.
75-007265   382.1/0973   0465089518
International business enterprises. International economic relations. United States -- Foreign economic relations. United States -- Foreign relations.

HF1455.G65 1993
Goldstein, Judith.
Ideas, interests, and American trade policy/ Judith Goldstein. Ithaca: Cornell University Press, 1993. xiii, 268 p.
93-029481   382/.73/0973   0801426952
Protectionism -- United States -- History. Tariff -- United States -- History. Pressure groups -- United States -- History. United States -- Commercial policy -- History. United States -- Foreign relations.

HF1455.K282 1982
Kaufman, Burton Ira.
Trade and aid: Eisenhower's foreign economic policy, 1953-1961/ Burton I. Kaufman. Baltimore: Johns Hopkins University Press, c1982. xiv, 279 p.
81-015594   337.73   0801826233
Eisenhower, Dwight D. -- (Dwight David), -- 1890-1969.   United States -- Foreign economic relations.

HF1455.L88 1993
Luttwak, Edward.
The endangered American dream: how to stop the United States from becoming a Third World country and how to win the geo-economic struggle for industrial supremacy/ Edward N. Luttwak. New York: Simon & Schuster, c1993. 365 p.
93-005715   338.973   0671869639
Industries -- United States. Competition, International. United States -- Foreign economic relations. United States -- Economic conditions -- 1981- United States -- Commerce.

HF1455.N58 1993
Nivola, Pietro S.
Regulating unfair trade/ Pietro S. Nivola. Washington, D.C.: Brookings Institution, c1993. xviii, 190 p.
92-036232   382/.3/0973   0815760906
Foreign trade regulation -- United States. Competition, Unfair. United States -- Commercial policy.

HF1455.O37 1994
O'Halloran, Sharyn, 1963-
Politics, process, and American trade policy/ Sharyn O'Halloran. Ann Arbor: University of Michigan Press, c1994. xi, 202 p.
94-019986   382/.3/0973   0472105167
United States -- Commercial policy.

HF1455.R615 1999
Rosenberg, Emily S., 1944-
Financial missionaries to the world: the politics and culture of dollar diplomacy, 1900-1930/ Emily S. Rosenberg. Cambridge, Mass.: Harvard University Press, 1999. x, 334 p.
99-022995   337.73   0674000595
International finance -- History -- 20th century. United States -- Economic policy -- To 1933. United States -- Foreign economic relations -- 20th century.

HF1455.S813 1993
States and provinces in the international economy/ edited by Douglas M. Brown, Earl H. Fry. Berkeley: Institute of Governmental Studies Press, Univers 1993. xiii, 248 p.
92-044595   337.73   0877723354
Foreign trade promotion -- United States -- States. Foreign trade promotion -- Canada -- Provinces. Canada -- Foreign economic relations. United States -- Foreign economic relations.

HF1455.Z45 1992
Zeiler, Thomas W.
American trade and power in the 1960's/ Thomas W. Zeiler. New York: Columbia University Press, c1992. xiv, 371 p.
92-015550   382/.0973/009046   0231079303
United States -- Commercial policy -- History -- 20th century. United States -- Commerce -- History -- 20th century. United States -- Economic conditions -- 1961-1971.

HF1456.5.A64.G67 1990
Gordon, Bernard K., 1932-
New directions for American policy in Asia/ Bernard K. Gordon. London; Routledge, 1990. xiii, 170 p.
90-034966   337.7305   0415022894
United States -- Foreign economic relations -- Asia. Asia -- Foreign economic relations -- United States. United States -- Foreign relations -- Asia.

HF1456.5.C2.E36 1991
Economic opportunities in freer U.S. trade with Canada/ edited by Fredric C. Menz and Sarah A. Stevens. Albany: State University of New York Press, c1991. x, 206 p.
90-034663   382/.0973071   0791405303
International business enterprises -- Canada. International business enterprises -- United States. Canada -- Foreign economic relations -- United States. United States -- Foreign economic relations -- Canada.

HF1456.5.C4.C69 1994
Cox, Ronald W., 1962-
Power and profits: U.S. policy in Central America/ Ronald W. Cox. Lexington, Ky.: University Press of Kentucky, c1994. 189 p.
93-041718   337.730728   0813118654
Industrial concentration -- Central America. Central America -- Foreign economic relations -- United States. United States -- Economic policy. Central America -- Economic policy.

HF1456.5.C6.B49 1994
Beyond MFN: trade with China and American interests/ edited by James R. Lilley and Wendell L. Willkie II. Washington, D.C.: AEI Press, 1994. xv, 171 p.
94-008228   337.51073   0844738565
Favored nation clause -- United States. Human rights -- China. United States -- Commerce -- China. China -- Commerce -- United States. United States -- Foreign economic relations -- China.

HF1456.5.D44.A44 1988
America's new competitors: the challenge of the newly industrializing countries/ edited by Thornton F. Bradshaw ... [et al.]. Cambridge, Mass.: Ballinger Pub. Co., c1988. xiv, 290 p.
87-019295   337.730172/4   0887301355
Competition, International. United States -- Foreign economic relations -- Developing countries. Developing countries -- Foreign economic relations -- United States.

HF1456.5.D44.K78 1993
Krueger, Anne O.
Economic policies at cross-purposes: the United States and developing countries/ Anne O. Krueger. Washington, D.C.: Brookings Institution, c1993. xii, 253 p.
92-035941   337.730172/4   0815750544
Economic assistance, American -- Developing countries. Developing countries -- Foreign economic relations -- United States. United States -- Foreign economic relations -- Developing countries.

HF1456.5.J3.R43 1993
Bergsten, C. Fred, 1941-
Reconcilable differences?: United States-Japan economic conflict/ C. Fred Bergsten, Marcus Noland. Washington, DC: Institute for International Economics, 1993. ix, 271 p.
93-013689   382/.0973052   088132129X
United States -- Commerce -- Japan. Japan -- Commerce -- United States. United States -- Commercial policy.

HF1456.5.L3.K74 1990
Krenn, Michael L., 1957-
U.S. policy toward economic nationalism in Latin America, 1917-1929/ Michael L. Krenn. Wilmington, Del.: SR Books, 1990. xxi, 169 p.
89-024122   337.7308   0842023461
Investments, American -- Latin America -- History -- 20th century. Nationalism -- Latin America -- History -- 20th century. United States -- Foreign economic relations -- Latin America. Latin America -- Foreign economic relations -- United States. Latin America -- Economic policy.

HF1456.5.M6.W45 1990
Weintraub, Sidney, 1922-
A marriage of convenience: relations between Mexico and the United States/ Sidney Weintraub. New York: Oxford University Press, 1990. xi, 270 p.
89-039386   337.73072   019506125X
United States -- Foreign economic relations -- Mexico. Mexico -- Foreign economic relations -- United States.

HF1456.5.S624.L53 1989
Libbey, James K.
American-Russian economic relations: a survey of issues and references/ James K. Libbey. Claremont, CA: Regina Books, c1989. xiii, 202 p.
89-032604   337.73047   0941690350
United States -- Foreign economic relations -- Soviet Union. Soviet Union -- Foreign economic relations -- United States. United States -- Foreign economic relations -- Soviet Union -- Sources.

HF1456.5.Z4.E855 1991
Kunz, Diane B., 1952-
The economic diplomacy of the Suez crisis/ Diane B. Kunz. Chapel Hill: University of North Carolina Press, c1991. xii, 295 p.
90-024882   327.73/009045   0807819670
Europe -- Foreign economic relations -- United States -- History -- 20th century. United States -- Foreign economic relations -- Egypt -- History -- 20th century. Egypt -- Foreign economic relations -- United States -- History -- 20th century.

HF1480.5-1613.4
International economic relations —
Other regions or countries

HF1480.5.S33 1992
Sanderson, Steven E.
The politics of trade in Latin American development/ Steven E. Sanderson. Stanford, Calif.: Stanford University Press, 1992. xii, 292 p.
91-039863 382/.3/098 0804719837
Latin America -- Commercial policy. Latin America -- Economic policy.

HF1480.5.W43 2000
Weaver, Frederick Stirton, 1939-
Latin America in the world economy: mercantile colonialism to global capitalism/ Frederick Stirton Weaver. Boulder, CO: Westview Press, 2000. xvii, 252 p.
00-039879 337.8 081333747X
Latin America -- Foreign economic relations. Latin America -- Economic conditions. Latin America -- Economic policy.

HF1500.5.U5.K36 1998
Kaplowitz, Donna Rich, 1962-
Anatomy of a failed embargo: U.S. sanctions against Cuba/ Donna Rich Kaplowitz. Boulder: Lynne Rienner Publishers, 1998. x, 247 p.
97-032754 337.7291073 1555876161
Economic sanctions, American -- Cuba. Embargo. Cuba -- Foreign economic relations -- United States. United States -- Commerce -- Cuba. Cuba -- Commerce -- United States.

HF1500.5.U5.S38 1999
Schwab, Peter, 1940-
Cuba: confronting the U.S. embargo/ Peter Schwab. New York: St. Martin's Press, 1999. xiii, 226 p.
98-044271 337.7291073 0312216203
Economic sanctions, American -- Cuba. Embargo. United States -- Foreign economic relations -- Cuba. Cuba -- Foreign economic relations -- United States. Cuba -- Economic conditions -- 1990-

HF1532.7.L25 1994
Winters, L. Alan.
Eastern Europe's international trade/ L. Alan Winters and Zhen Kun Wang. Manchester; Manchester University Press; c1994. xvi, 189 p.
93-040662 382/.0947 0719042763
Europe, Eastern -- Commercial policy. Europe, Eastern -- Foreign economic relations.

HF1533.B64 1987
Boyce, Robert W. D., 1943-
British capitalism at the crossroads, 1919-1932: a study in politics, economics, and international relations/ Robert W.D. Boyce. Cambridge [Cambridgeshire]; Cambridge University Press, 1987. xv, 504 p.
86-023243 337.41 0521325358
Industries -- Great Britain -- History. Great Britain -- Economic conditions -- 1918-1945. Great Britain -- Foreign economic relations.

HF1533.P58
Platt, D. C. M. 1934-
Finance, trade, and politics in British foreign policy 1815-1914 [by] D. C. M. Platt. Oxford, Clarendon P., 1968. xl, 454 p.
68-093648 327.42 0198213778
Great Britain -- Foreign economic relations -- History. Great Britain -- Foreign relations -- 19th century. Great Britain -- Foreign relations -- 1901-1910.

HF1533.R59 1993
Rooth, Tim.
British protectionism and the international economy: overseas commercial policy in the 1930s/ Tim Rooth. Cambridge; Cambridge University Press, 1993. xv, 357 p.
92-008965 382/.3/094109043 0521416086
Protectionism -- Great Britain -- History. Great Britain -- Commercial policy -- History. Great Britain -- Foreign economic relations.

HF1533.Z4
Forbes, Neil.
Doing business with the Nazis: Britain's economic and financial relations with Germany, 1931-1939/ Neil Forbes. London; Frank Cass, 2000. xviii, 250 p.
00-057004 337.41043/09/043 071465082X
Nazis. Germany -- Foreign economic relations -- Great Britain. Great Britain -- Commercial policy. Great Britain -- Foreign economic relations -- Germany.

HF1534.5.J3.B76 1998
Brown, Kenneth Douglas.
Britain and Japan: a comparative economic and social history since 1900/ Kenneth D. Brown. Manchester; Manchester University Press; 1998. xi, 269 p.
0719052904
Great Britain -- Foreign relations -- Japan. Japan -- Foreign relations -- Great Britain. Great Britain -- Foreign relations -- 20th century.

HF1557.P46 1990
Perestroika and East-West economic relations: prospects for the 1990's/ edited by Michael Kraus and Ronald D. Liebowitz. New York: New York University Press, c1990. x, 356 p.
90-005446 337.470171/3 0814746047
Perestroika -- Congresses. East-West trade -- Congresses. Soviet Union -- Foreign economic relations -- Congresses.

HF1583.D79 1988
Drysdale, Peter.
International economic pluralism: economic policy in East Asia and the Pacific/ Peter Drysdale. New York: Columbia University Press, c1988. 294 p.
88-025597 338.95 0231069367
International economic relations. Pacific Area -- Commercial policy. Australia -- Commercial policy. Japan -- Commercial policy.

HF1583.4.P65 1998
The political economy of Turkey in the post-Soviet era: going West and looking East?/ edited by Libby Rittenberg. Westport, Conn.: Praeger, 1998. xi, 221 p.
97-026174 337.561 0275955966
Turkey -- Foreign economic relations. Turkey -- Economic conditions -- 1960- Turkey -- Foreign relations -- 1980-

HF1586.3.I73 2000
Iraq under siege: the deadly impact of sanctions and war/ edited by Anthony Arnove; with essays by Ali Abunimah ... [et al.]. Cambridge, Mass.: South End Press, c2000. 216 p.
00-021052 330.9567/0443 21 0896086194
Economic sanctions -- Iraq. Persian Gulf War, 1991 -- Economic aspects. Iraq -- Economic conditions.

HF1590.5.I84
Islam, Nurul, 1929-
Foreign trade and economic controls in development: the case of United Pakistan/ Nurul Islam. New Haven [Conn.]: Yale University Press, c1981. xv, 271 p.
81-001122 382/.095491 0300025351
Pakistan -- Commercial policy -- History. Pakistan -- Economic policy. Pakistan -- Economic conditions.

HF1601.C35 1993
Calder, Kent E.
Strategic capitalism: private business and public purpose in Japanese industrial finance/ Kent E. Calder. Princeton, N.J.: Princeton University Press, c1993. xxii, 373 p.
92-039043 338.7/0952 0691043183
Industrial policy -- Japan. Industrial organization -- Japan. Corporations -- Japan -- Finance. Japan -- Commercial policy. Japan -- Foreign economic relations.

HF1601.H6
Hollerman, Leon.
Japan's dependence on the world economy; the approach toward economic liberalization. Princeton, N.J., Princeton University Press, 1967. xv, 291 p.
66-026586 382/.0952
Japan -- Foreign economic relations. Japan -- Commercial policy.

HF1601.K29 1998
Katz, Richard, 1951-
Japan, the system that soured: the rise and fall of the Japanese economic miracle/ Richard Katz. Armonk, N.Y.: M. E. Sharpe, c1998. xvi, 463 p.
98-011091 338.952 21 0765603098
Japan -- Commercial policy. Industrial policy -- Japan. Japan -- Economic conditions -- 1989-

HF1601.L55 1993
Lincoln, Edward J.
Japan's new global role/ Edward J. Lincoln. Washington, D.C.: Brookings Institution, c1993. xi, 320 p.
93-025951 337.52 081575258X
Japan -- Foreign economic relations.

HF1602.15.A74.H38 1996
Hatch, Walter.
Asia in Japan's embrace: building a regional production alliance/ Walter Hatch and Kozo Yamamura. Cambridge; Cambridge University Press, 1996. xv, 281 p.
96-000282 337.5052 0521561760
Strategic alliances (Business) -- Japan. Strategic alliances (Business) -- Asia. Trading blocs -- Asia. Asia -- Foreign economic relations -- Japan. Japan -- Foreign economic relations -- Asia.

HF1602.15.J3.U56 1991
Uno, Kimio.
Technology, investment, and trade/ Kimio Uno. New York: Elsevier, c1991. xxii, 426 p.
91-016517 337.52 0444016155
Investments, Japanese. Technological innovations -- Japan. International trade. Japan -- Foreign economic relations.

HF1604.H78 1990
Hsu, John C.
China's foreign trade reforms: impact on growth and stability/ John C. Hsu. Cambridge [England]; Cambridge University Press, 1990. xii, 221 p.
89-032581   382/.3/0951 052137197X
China -- Commercial policy. China -- Commerce. China -- Economic policy -- 1976-

HF1604.Z4
Where China meets Southeast Asia: social & cultural change in the border regions/ edited by Grant Evans, Chris Hutton, Kuah Khun Eng. New York: St. Martin's Press , 2000. viii, 346 p.
00-035258   303.4/8251059 0312236344
China -- Foreign economic relations -- Indochina. Indochina -- Foreign economic relations -- China. China -- Foreign economic relations -- Burma.

HF1610.Z4.I825 1998
Feiler, Gil, 1959-
From boycott to economic cooperation: the political economy of the Arab boycott of Israel/ Gil Feiler. London; Frank Cass, 1998. xv, 335 p.
98-024519   327.1/17 0714648663
Economic sanctions, Arab countries -- Israel. Boycotts -- Arab countries. Boycotts -- Israel. Arab countries -- Foreign economic relations -- Israel. Israel -- Foreign economic relations -- Arab countries.

HF1613.4.Z4.A4352 1991
Blumenfeld, Jesmond.
Economic interdependence in southern Africa: from conflict to cooperation?/ Jesmond Blumenfeld. London: Pinter Publishers; 1991. viii, 187 p.
91-036331   337.68 0861870441
Economic sanctions -- South Africa. Africa, Southern -- Foreign economic relations -- South Africa. South Africa -- Foreign economic relations -- Africa, Southern. Africa, Southern -- Economic integration.

HF1711 Tariff. Free trade. Protectionism — History

HF1711.B45 1991
Bhagwati, Jagdish N., 1934-
The world trading system at risk/ Jagdish Bhagwati. Princeton, N.J.: Princeton University Press, c1991. viii, 156 p.
90-021389   382/.92 0691042845
International trade.

HF1713 Tariff. Free trade. Protectionism — General works

HF1713.A528 1988
Anderson, James E. 1943-
The relative inefficiency of quotas/ James E. Anderson. Cambridge, Mass.: MIT Press, c1988. x, 225 p.
87-029712   382/.52 0262011034
Import quotas -- Mathematical models. Tariff -- Mathematical models.

HF1713.I78 1996
Irwin, Douglas A., 1962-
Against the tide: an intellectual history of free trade/ Douglas A. Irwin. Princeton, N.J.: Princeton University Press, c1996. viii, 265 p.
95-025447   382/.71 20 0691011389
Free trade.

HF1713.M37 1994
McGee, Robert W.
A trade policy for free societies: the case against protectionism/ Robert W. McGee. Westport, Conn.: Quorum Books, 1994. ix, 197 p.
93-042760   382/.71 0899308988
Protectionism. Dumping (International trade) Free trade.

HF1713.M56 1988
Milner, Helen V., 1958-
Resisting protectionism: global industries and the politics of international trade/ Helen V. Milner. Princeton, N.J.: Princeton University Press, c1988. xiii, 329 p.
88-009945   382.7 0691056706
Free trade -- United States -- Case studies. Free trade -- France -- Case studies. Protectionism -- United States -- Case studies.

HF1713.N35 1990
Neff, Stephen C.
Friends but no allies: economic liberalism and the law of nations/ Stephen C. Neff. New York: Columbia University Press, c1990. xii, 345 p.
90-002119   380/.3 0231071426
Free trade. Free enterprise. Commerce.

HF1713.T686 2000
Tonelson, Alan, 1953-
The race to the bottom: why a worldwide worker surplus and uncontrolled free trade are sinking American living standards/ Alan Tonelson. Boulder, CO: Westview Press, 2000. xviii, 222 p.
00-043706   382/.71 0813368170
Free trade. Globalization. Labor supply. United States -- Economic policy -- 1993-2001.

HF1721 Tariff. Free trade. Protectionism — Tariff preferences. Reciprocity. Favored nation clause — General works

HF1721.H347 1991
Haus, Leah A., 1960-
Globalizing the GATT: the Soviet Union's successor states, Eastern Europe, and the international trading system/ Leah A. Haus. Washington, D.C.: Brookings Institution, c1992. x, 141 p.
91-045868   382/.92 0815735049
International economic integration. International trade. East-West trade. Europe, Eastern -- Foreign economic relations. Soviet Union -- Foreign economic relations.

HF1721.P7324 1995
Preeg, Ernest H.
Traders in a brave new world: the Uruguay Round and the future of the international trading system/ Ernest H. Preeg. Chicago: University of Chicago Press, 1995. xiv, 298 p.
95-018585   382/.92 0226679594
International trade.

HF1731 Tariff. Free trade. Protectionism — Tariff preferences. Reciprocity. Favored nation clause — By region or country

HF1731.E25 1996
The economics of preferential trade agreements/ edited by Jagdish Bhagwati and Arvind Panagariya. Washington, D.C.: AEI Press; 1996. xx, 168 p.
96-041434   382/.973 0844739685
Tariff preferences -- United States -- Congresses. Trade blocs -- United States -- Congresses. United States -- Commercial policy -- Congresses.

HF1745-1756 Tariff. Free trade. Protectionism — By region or country — America. Western Hemisphere

HF1745.E57 1993
The Enterprise for the Americas initiative: issues and prospects for a free trade agreement in the Western Hemisphere/ edited by Roy E. Green. Westport, Conn.: Praeger, 1993. xxv, 209 p.
93-020299   382/.917 027594266X
Free trade -- America. Free ports and zones -- America. United States -- Foreign economic relations -- Latin America. Latin America -- Foreign economic relations -- United States. North America -- Commercial policy.

HF1746.A85 1993
Assessing NAFTA: a trinational analysis/ edited by Steven Globerman and Michael Walker. Vancouver: Fraser Institute, c1993. xxxv, 314 p.
93-200727   382/.917 0889751560
Free trade -- North America. North America -- Economic integration.

HF1746.B49 1993
Beyond NAFTA: an economic, political, and sociological perspective/ edited by A.R. Riggs and Tom Velk. Vancouver: Fraser Institute, c1993. xxi, 272 p.
94-136475   382/.917 0889751625
Free trade -- North America -- Congresses. Foreign trade regulation -- North America -- Congresses.

HF1746.C33 2000
Cameron, Maxwell A.
The making of NAFTA: how the deal was done/ Maxwell A. Cameron and Brian W. Tomlin. Ithaca, N.Y.: Cornell University Press, 2000. xiv, 264 p.
00-008915   382/.917 0801438004
Free trade -- United States. Free trade -- Canada. Free trade -- Mexico. North America -- Commercial treaties -- History.

HF1746.G53 1998
Gianaris, Nicholas V.
The North American Free Trade Agreement and the European Union/ Nicholas V. Gianaris. Westport, Conn.: Praeger, 1998. xii, 275 p.
97-034757   382/.09407 0275961672
Free trade -- North America. European Union -- North America. Free trade -- European Union countries. North America -- Foreign economic relations -- European Union countries. European Union countries -- Foreign economic relations -- North America.

HF1746.M338 1998
Mayer, Frederick.
Interpreting NAFTA: the science and art of political analysis/ Frederick W. Mayer. New York: Columbia University Press, c1998. xiv, 374 p.
98-003019   382/.917 21   0231109806
Free trade -- North America. North America -- Commercial treaties. United States -- Commercial policy. United States -- Politics and government -- 20th century.

HF1746.N333 1994
The NAFTA debate: grappling with unconventional trade issues/ edited by M. Delal Baer, Sidney Weintraub. Boulder, Colo.: Lynne Rienner Publishers, 1994. xi, 211 p.
93-038663   382/.917 1555874649
Free trade -- North America. Free trade -- Political aspects -- North America. North America -- Economic integration.

HF1746.O75 1993
Orme, William A.
Continental shift: free trade & the new North America/ William A. Orme, Jr. Washington, D.C.: Washington Post Co., c1993. x, 235 p.
93-242220   382/.917   0962597120
Free trade -- North America. Public opinion -- North America. Mexico -- Economic policy -- 1982- United States -- Commercial policy.

HF1755.R38 1994
Reitano, Joanne R.
The tariff question in the Gilded Age: the great debate of 1888/ Joanne Reitano. University Park, Pa.: Pennsylvania State University Press, c1994. xxiii, 190 p.
93-005313   382/.7/0973   0271010355
Tariff -- United States -- History -- 19th century. Protectionism -- United States -- History -- 19th century. United States -- Commercial policy -- History -- 19th century.

HF1756.I68 2002
Irwin, Douglas A.,
Free trade under fire/ Douglas A. Irwin. Princeton, N.J.: Princeton University Press, c2002. x, 257 p.
2001-043159   382/.71 21   0691088438
Free trade -- United States. Globalization.

HF1756.M49 1993
The Mexico-U.S. free trade agreement/ edited by Peter M. Garber. Cambridge, Mass.: MIT Press, c1993. vi, 317 p.
93-008946   382/.917 0262071525
Free trade -- United States -- Congresses. Free trade -- Mexico -- Congresses. Wages -- United States -- Congresses. United States -- Foreign economic relations -- Mexico -- Congresses. Mexico -- Foreign economic relations -- United States -- Congresses.

HF1756.P68 1998
Preeg, Ernest H.
From here to free trade: essays in post-Uruguay round trade strategy/ Ernest H. Preeg. Washington [D.C.]: Center for Strategic and International Studies; 1998. xi, 154 p.
97-035616   382/.71/0973   0226679616
Free trade -- United States. International trade. United States -- Commercial policy. United States - - Foreign economic relations.

HF1756.W65 1992
Wolman, Paul.
Most favored nation: the Republican revisionists and U.S. tariff policy, 1897-1912/ Paul Wolman. Chapel Hill: University of North Carolina Press, c1992. xxv, 328 p.
91-050792   382/.7/0973   0807820229
Tariff -- United States -- History. United States -- Commercial policy -- History

HF1766-2046 Tariff. Free trade. Protectionism — By region or country — Other regions or countries

HF1766.H388 1994
Hart, Michael, 1944-
Decision at midnight: inside the Canada-US free trade negotiations/ Michael Hart, with Bill Dymond and Colin Robertson; foreword by Donald Macdonald; with cartoons by Alan King of the Ottawa Citizen. Vancouver: UBC Press, c1994. xvi, 456 p.
95-166209   382/.971073   0774805145
Free trade -- United States. Free trade -- Canada. Libre-echange -- Canada. United States -- Commerce -- Canada. Canada -- Commerce -- United States. Canada -- Accords commerciaux.

HF1766.W29 1988
Warnock, John W., 1933-
Free trade and the new right agenda/ John W. Warnock. Vancouver: New Star Books, c1988. 324 p.
89-109383   382/.0973071   0919573800
Free trade -- Canada. Free trade -- United States. Conservatism -- Canada. Canada -- Commerce -- United States. United States -- Commerce -- Canada. Canada -- Commercial policy.

HF2036.B78 1997
Brusse, Wendy Asbeek, 1965-
Tariffs, trade, and European integration, 1947-1957: from study group to Common Market/ Wendy Asbeek Brusse. New York: St. Martin's Press, 1997. 318 p.
96-039531   382/.7/094   0312165188
Tariff -- Europe -- History. Europe -- Economic integration -- History -- 20th century. Europe -- Commercial policy -- History.

HF2046.P65 1968
Pigou, A. C. 1877-1959.
Protective and preferential import duties. New York, A. M. Kelley, 1968. xiv, 117 p.
67-024751   382.7/0942
Tariff -- Great Britain. Imperial preference.

HF3004 By region or country — United States — Statistics (Monographs)

HF3004. 1992
Lenz, Allen J.
Narrowing the U.S. current account deficit: a sectoral assessment/ Allen J. Lenz; assisted by Hunter K. Monroe, Bruce Parsell. Washington, DC: Institute for International Economics, c1992. xviii, 607 p.
92-008778   382/.17/0973   0881321486
Exports -- United States. Balance of trade -- United States. Manufacturing industries -- United States.

HF3021-3031 By region or country — United States — History

HF3021.C55
Cochran, Thomas Childs, 1902-
Business in American life: a history, by Thomas C. Cochran. New York, McGraw-Hill [1972] x, 402 p.
78-038740   917.3/03   0070115206
United States -- Commerce -- History.

HF3025.S717
Shepherd, James F.
Shipping, maritime trade, and the economic development of colonial North America, by James F. Shepherd and Gary M. Walton. Cambridge [Eng.] University Press, 1972. ix, 255 p.
76-176256   382/.0973   0521084091
Shipping -- United States -- History United States -- Commerce -- History. United States -- History -- Colonial period, ca. 1600-1775.

HF3031.A83 1987
Arndt, Sven W.
Competitiveness: the United States in world trade/ Sven W. Arndt and Lawrence Bouton. Washington, D.C.: American Enterprise Institute for Public Policy c1987. 120 p.
87-001250   382/.0973   0844736252
Foreign exchange -- United States. Competition, International. United States -- Economic policy -- 1981-1993. United States -- Commerce.

HF3031.B54 1992
Blecker, Robert A., 1956-
Beyond the twin deficits: a trade strategy for the 1990s/ Robert A. Blecker. Armonk, N.Y.: M.E. Sharpe, c1992. 177 p.
92-009033   382/.17/0973   1563240904
Balance of trade -- United States. Budget deficits -- United States. Industrial policy -- United States. United States -- Commercial policy.

HF3043-3130 By region or country — United States — Foreign commerce

HF3043.P48 1994
Perry, John Curtis.
Facing West: Americans and the opening of the Pacific/ John Curtis Perry. Westport, Conn.: Praeger, 1994. xxi, 367 p.
94-011302   382/.097309   0275949206
Merchant marine -- United States -- History. Pacific Area -- Commerce -- United States -- History. United States -- Commerce -- Pacific Area -- History. United States -- Foreign economic relations -- Pacific Area.

HF3127.C64 1985
Cohen, Stephen D.
Uneasy partnership: competition and conflict in U.S.-Japanese trade relations/ Stephen D. Cohen. Cambridge, Mass.: Ballinger Pub. Co., c1985. xvi, 228 p.
84-016924   382/.0952/073   0887300200
United States -- Commerce -- Japan. Japan -- Commerce -- United States.

HF3130.B35 1995
Baldwin, Robert E.
Political economy of U.S.-Taiwan trade/ Robert E. Baldwin, Tain-Jy Chen, Douglas Nelson. Ann Arbor: University of Michigan Press, c1995. xi, 218 p.
95-013471   382/.0973051249   0472105515
Protectionism. Taiwan -- Commerce -- United States. United States -- Commerce -- Taiwan.

HF3211 By region or country — America (General) — General works

HF3211.H83 1993
Hufbauer, Gary Clyde.
NAFTA: an assessment/ Gary Clyde Hufbauer and Jeffrey J. Schott; assisted by Robin Dunnigan and Diana Clark. Washington, DC: Institute for International Economics, c1993. xiii, 164 p.
92-038904   382/.71/097   0881321982
Free trade -- North America. North America -- Commercial policy. North America -- Commerce.

HF3211.L57 1983
Liss, Peggy K.
Atlantic empires: the network of trade and revolution, 1713-1826/ Peggy K. Liss. Baltimore: Johns Hopkins University Press, c1983. xiii, 348 p.
82-013099   382/.094/08   0801827426
America -- Commerce -- History. Europe -- Commerce -- History. United States -- History -- Revolution, 1775-1783 -- Influence.

HF3211.N666 1993
North American Free Trade Agreement: opportunities and challenges/ edited by Khosrow Fatemi. New York: St. Martin's Press, 1993. xx, 301 p.
93-018906   382/.911812   0312099762
Free trade -- North America. North America -- Commercial policy. North America -- Commerce.

HF3211.N667 1992
North American free trade: assessing the impact/ Nora Lustig, Barry P. Bosworth, and Robert Z. Lawrence, editors. Washington, D.C.: Brookings Institution, c1992. xii, 274 p.
92-026402   382/.71/097   0815753160
Free trade -- North America. North America -- Commerce. North America -- Commercial policy.

HF3230.5-4055 By region or country — Other regions or countries

HF3230.5.B3
Baerresen, Donald W.
Latin American trade patterns, by Donald W. Baerresen, Martin Carnoy [and] Joseph Grunwald. Washington, Brookings Institution [1965] xiv, 329 p.
65-027966   382.918
Commercial statistics. Latin America -- Commerce.

HF3230.5.Z7.U55 1996
Nevaer, Louis E. V.
New business opportunities in Latin America: trade and investment after the Mexican meltdown/ Louis E.V. Nevaer. Westport, Conn.: Quorum, 1996. xiv, 222 p.
95-038752   382/.098073   1567200230
Free trade -- Latin America. United States -- Commerce -- Latin America. Latin America -- Commerce -- United States. Latin America -- Economic integration.

HF3235.H63 1991
Hoberman, Louisa Schell, 1942-
Mexico's merchant elite, 1590-1660: silver, state, and society/ Louisa Schell Hoberman. Durham: Duke University Press, 1991. xiv, 352 p.
90-020659   305.5/56   0822311348
Merchants -- Mexico -- History -- 17th century. Elite (Social sciences) -- Mexico -- History -- 17th century. Mexico -- Economic conditions -- 1540-1810.

HF3239.O3.H35 1971
Hamnett, Brian R.
Politics and trade in southern Mexico, 1750-1821, by Brian R. Hamnett. Cambridge [Eng.] University Press, 1971. viii, 214 p.
70-116839   382/.0972/7
Oaxaca Valley (Mexico) -- Commerce -- History. Oaxaca Valley (Mexico) -- Commercial policy.

HF3495.F3813 1998
Favier, Jean, 1932-
Gold & spices: the rise of commerce in the Middle Ages/ Jean Favier; translated from the French by Caroline Higgitt. New York: Holmes & Meier, 1998. 390 p.
98-014166   382/.094/00902   0841912327
Middle Ages -- History. Merchants -- Europe -- History. Europe -- Commerce -- History. Europe -- Economic conditions -- To 1492.

HF3496.5.H62 1987
Holzman, Franklyn D.
The economics of Soviet bloc trade and finance/ Franklyn D. Holzman. Boulder: Westview Press, 1987. xi, 215 p.
86-032598   382/.0947   0813372747
Finance -- Europe, Eastern. Balance of payments -- Europe, Eastern. Europe, Eastern -- Commerce.

HF3505.B75 1993
Britnell, R. H.
The commercialisation of English society, 1000-1500/ R.H. Britnell. Cambridge; Cambridge University Press, 1993. xiv, 273 p.
92-005868   380.1/0942   0521418232
Commerce -- History -- Medieval, 500-1500. Feudalism -- Great Britain. Great Britain -- History -- Medieval period, 1066-1485. Great Britain -- Commerce -- History.

HF3508.G3.C8
Cullen, L. M.
Anglo-Irish trade, 1660-1800, by L. M. Cullen. New York, A. M. Kelley, 1968. vi, 252 p.
68-056548   382/.09415/042
Great Britain -- Commerce -- Ireland. Ireland -- Commerce -- Great Britain.

HF3510.L8.T4
Thrupp, Sylvia L. 1903-
The merchant class of medieval London, 1300-1500. [Chicago] Univ. of Chicago Press [1948] xix, 401 p.
48-003697   323.32
Merchants, British. London -- Social life and customs. London -- Commerce.

HF3515.M37 1997
Masschaele, James, 1961-
Peasants, merchants, and markets: inland trade in medieval England, 1150-1350/ James Masschaele. New York: St. Martin's Press, 1997. xii, 275 p.
96-052279   381/.1/0942   0312160356
Markets -- England -- History. Peasantry -- England -- History. Commerce -- History -- Medieval, 500-1500. England -- Commerce -- History. England -- Economic conditions -- 1066-1485. Huntingdonshire (England) -- Commerce -- History.

HF3520.L65.H36 1995
Hancock, David.
Citizens of the world: London merchants and the integration of the British Atlantic community, 1735-1785/ David Hancock. Cambridge; Cambridge University Press, 1995. xxiii, 477 p.
94-041566   382/.092/241   0521474302
Merchants -- England -- London -- History -- 18th century. London (England) -- Commerce -- United States -- History -- 18th century. United States -- Commerce -- England -- London -- History -- 18th century. London (England) -- History -- 18th century.

HF3614.I87 1989
Israel, Jonathan Irvine.
Dutch primacy in world trade, 1585-1740/ Jonathan I. Israel. Oxford [England]: Clarendon Press; 1989. xxi, 462 p.
88-025356   382/.09492   0198227299
Netherlands -- Commerce -- History. Netherlands -- History -- Wars of Independence, 1556-1648. Netherlands -- History -- 1648-1795.

HF3626.B254 1997
Banerji, Arup.
Merchants and markets in revolutionary Russia, 1917-30/ Arup Banerji. New York: St. Martin's Press in association with the Centr 1997. xxiii, 237 p.
96-021858   381/.0947/09041   0333668936
Soviet Union -- Commerce -- History. Soviet Union -- Economic policy -- 1917-1928.

HF3628.A4.S7
Stokke, Baard Richard.
Soviet and Eastern European trade and aid in Africa. New York, F. A. Praeger [1967] xx, 326 p.
67-025250   338.91/47/06
Economic assistance, Soviet -- Africa. Economic assistance, East European -- Africa. Soviet Union -- Commerce -- Africa. Africa -- Commerce -- Soviet Union. Europe, Eastern -- Commerce -- Africa.

HF3628.G7.W46 1993
White, Christine A.
British and American commercial relations with Soviet Russia, 1918-1924/ by Christine A. White. Chapel Hill: University of North Carolina Press, c1992. x, 345 p.
92-000301   382/.0941047   0807820334
Soviet Union -- Commerce -- Great Britain -- History. Great Britain -- Commerce -- Soviet Union -- History. Soviet Union -- Commerce -- United States -- History.

HF3685.S74 2000
Stein, Stanley J.
Silver, trade, and war: Spain and America in the making of early modern Europe/ Stanley J. Stein & Barbara H. Stein. Baltimore: Johns Hopkins University Press, 2000. ix, 351 p.
99-038574 382/.0946/07 0801861357
Silver industry -- America -- History. Spain -- Commerce -- America -- History. America -- Commerce -- Spain -- History. Spain -- Colonies -- America -- Commerce -- History.

HF3698.A78.B69 1993
Boyajian, James C., 1949-
Portuguese trade in Asia under the Habsburgs, 1580-1640/ James C. Boyajian. Baltimore: Johns Hopkins University Press, c1993. xvii, 356 p.
92-012042 382/.0946905 0801844053
Marranos -- Portugal -- History -- 16th century. Marranos -- Portugal -- History -- 17th century. Asia -- Commerce -- Portugal -- History -- 16th century. Asia -- Commerce -- Portugal -- History -- 17th century. Portugal -- Commerce -- Asia -- History -- 16th century.

HF3756.5.Z7.M6284 1990
Goffman, Daniel, 1954-
Izmir and the Levantine World, 1550-1650/ Daniel Goffman. Seattle: University of Washington Press, c1990. xv, 236 p.
89-039759 382.09562 0295969326
Izmir (Turkey) -- Commerce -- Middle East -- History -- 17th century. Middle East -- Commerce -- Turkey -- Izmir -- History -- 17th century. Izmir (Turkey) -- Economic conditions.

HF3765.B43 1992
Bhacker, M. Reda 1955-
Trade and empire in Muscat and Zanzibar: roots of British domination/ M. Reda Bhacker. London; Routledge, 1992. xxix, 278 p.
91-047666 337.4105353 0415079977
Oman -- Commerce -- History. Oman -- Foreign economic relations -- Great Britain. Great Britain -- Foreign economic relations -- Oman.

HF3788.C6.L58 1988
Liu, Hsin-ju.
Ancient India and ancient China: trade and religious exchanges, AD 1-600/ Xinru Liu. Delhi; Oxford University Press, 1988. xxi, 231 p.
88-900004 019562050X
Buddhism -- India -- History. Buddhism -- China -- History -- To 581. India -- Commerce -- China -- History. China -- Commerce -- India -- History.

HF3788.E83.D35 1994
Dale, Stephen Frederic.
Indian merchants and Eurasian trade, 1600-1750/ Stephen Frederic Dale. Cambridge [England]; Cambridge University Press, 1994. xiv, 162 p.
93-031404 382/.095405 0521454603
India -- Commerce -- Eurasia -- History. Eurasia -- Commerce -- India -- History.

HF3790.8.Z7.S556 1991
Regnier, Philippe.
Singapore, city-state in South-East Asia/ Philippe Regnier; translated from the French by Christopher Hurst. Honolulu: University of Hawaii Press, c1991. xiv, 301 p.
91-013257 337.5905957 0824814061
Singapore -- Foreign economic relations -- Asia, Southeastern. Asia, Southeastern -- Foreign relations -- Singapore. Singapore -- Foreign relations -- Asia, Southeastern.

HF3820.5.Z5.C7 1993
Cragg, Claudia.
Hunting with the tigers: doing business with Hong Kong, Indonesia, South Korea, Malaysia, the Philippines, Singapore, Taiwan, Thailand, and Vietnam/ Claudia Cragg. Amsterdam; Pfeiffer, c1993. xii, 451 p.
92-050996 382/.095 0893842044
East Asia -- Commerce. Asia, Southeastern -- Commerce.

HF3824.H68 1996
Howe, Christopher.
The origins of Japanese trade supremacy: development and technology in Asia from 1540 to the Pacific War/ Christopher Howe. Chicago: University of Chicago Press, 1996. xxvii, 471 p.
95-003400 382/.0952 0226354857
Industrial promotion -- Japan -- History. Technology -- Japan -- History. Foreign trade promotion -- Japan -- History. Japan -- Foreign economic relations. Japan -- Commerce -- History.

HF3826.S77 1988
Sugiyama, Shinya, 1949-
Japan's industrialization in the world economy, 1859-1899: export trade and overseas competition/ Shinya Sugiyama. London; Athlone Press, 1988. 304 p.
88-003352 382/.6/0952 0485112671
Exports -- Japan -- History. Industrialization -- Japan -- History -- 19th century. Japan -- Commerce -- History. Japan -- Economic conditions -- 1868-1918.

HF3826.5.M37 1989
Maswood, Syed Javed.
Japan and protection: the growth of protectionist sentiment and the Japanese response/ Syed Javed Maswood. London; Routledge; 1989. xiii, 242 p.
88-018286 382.7/3 0415010306
Protectionism -- Japan. International trade. Japan -- Commercial policy.

HF3828.S64.H8
Huh, Kyung Mo.
Japan's trade in Asia: developments since 1926, prospects for 1970. New York, F.A. Praeger [1966] xx, 283 p.
66-015449 382.0952059
Japan -- Commerce -- Asia, Southeastern. Asia, Southeastern -- Commerce -- Japan.

HF3830.5.M39 1996
McNamara, Dennis L.
Trade and transformation in Korea, 1876-1945/ Dennis L. McNamara. Boulder, Colo.: Westview Press, 1996. xvi, 228 p.
96-016626 382/.09519 0813389941
Grain trade -- Korea -- History. Korea -- Commerce -- History -- 20th century. Korea -- Commerce -- History -- 19th century. Korea -- Economic conditions.

HF3834.L84 1997
Lufrano, Richard John, 1952-
Honorable merchants: commerce and self-cultivation in late imperial China/ Richard John Lufrano. Honolulu: University of Hawai'i Press, c1997. xii, 241 p.
96-034019 380.1/0951 20 0824817400
Merchants -- China -- History. Business ethics -- China -- History. China -- Commerce -- History. China -- Economic conditions -- 1644-1912.

HF3840.C36.D69 1997
Downs, Jacques M., 1926-
The golden ghetto: the American commercial community at Canton and the shaping of American China policy, 1784-1844/ Jacques M. Downs. Bethlehem: Lehigh University Press, c1997. 495 p.
96-004167 337.51/275 20 0934223351
Americans -- China -- Guangzhou -- History. Merchants -- China -- Guangzhou -- History. Guangzhou (China) -- Commerce -- History. United States -- Foreign economic relations -- China. China -- Foreign economic relations -- United States.

HF3868.Z7.E854 1999
Fleet, Kate.
European and Islamic trade in the early Ottoman state: the merchants of Genoa and Turkey/ Kate Fleet. Cambridge; Cambridge University Press, 1999. x, 204 p.
98-038430 382/.094017671 0521642213
Islamic countries -- Commerce -- Europe. Europe -- Commerce -- Islamic countries. Turkey -- History -- Ottoman Empire, 1288-1918.

HF3876.5.B37 1992
Barratt Brown, Michael.
Short changed: Africa and world trade/ Michael Barratt Brown and Pauline Tiffen; foreword by Susan George. London; Pluto Press; 1992. xix, 220 p.
92-034001 382/.0967 0745306942
Foreign trade promotion -- Africa, Sub-Saharan. Structural adjustment (Economic policy) -- Africa, Sub-Saharan. Natural resources -- Africa, Sub-Saharan.

HF3882.K37 1996
Kapchan, Deborah A.
Gender on the market: Moroccan women and the revoicing of tradition/ Deborah A. Kapchan. Philadelphia: University of Pennsylvania Press, c1996. xvii, 325 p.
95-051427 381/.18/082 20 0812231554
Women merchants -- Morocco. Markets -- Morocco. Women -- Morocco -- Economic conditions.

HF3899.E3.A46 1975
Alpers, Edward A.
Ivory and slaves: changing pattern of international trade in East Central Africa to the later nineteenth century/ Edward A. Alpers. Berkeley: University of California Press, 1975. xviii, 296 p.
73-093046 382/.0967 0520026896
Ivory industry -- Africa. Slave-trade -- Africa, Eastern -- History. Africa, Eastern -- Commerce -- History.

HF3932.B69 1999
Bowditch, Nathaniel H., 1944-
The last emerging market: from Asian tigers to African lions?: the Ghana file/ Nathaniel H. Bowditch. Westport, Conn.: Praeger, 1999. xviii, 201 p.
99-018011 338.7/09667 0275965880
Business enterprises -- Ghana. Businesspeople -- Ghana. Business enterprises, Foreign -- Ghana. Ghana -- Civilization. Ghana -- Social conditions.

HF4055.M33 1993
Madeley, John
Trade and the poor: the impact of international trade on developing countries/ John Madeley. New York: St. Martin's Press, 1993. xiii, 209 p.
92-039846 330.9172/4 0312092369
Commercial products -- Developing countries. Competition, Unfair. International trade. Developing countries -- Economic conditions. Developing countries -- Commerce.

HF5035 Business — Directories — By region or country

HF5035.H66
Hoover's billion dollar directory: the complete guide to U.S. public companies. Austin, Tex.: Hoover's Business Press, [c1997-]
97-038133
Corporations, American -- Directories. Business enterprises -- United States -- Directories.

HF5343 Business — History

HF5343.C584
Chandler, Alfred Dupont.
The visible hand: the managerial revolution in American business/ Alfred D. Chandler, Jr. Cambridge, Mass.: Belknap Press, 1977. xvi, 608 p.
77-001529 658.4/00973 0674940512
Industrial management -- United States -- History. Industrial organization -- United States -- History. Industries -- United States.

HF5351 Business — General works, treatises, and textbooks

HF5351.K584 1987
Koestenbaum, Peter, 1928-
The heart of business: ethics, power, and philosophy/ by Peter Koestenbaum. San Francisco: Saybrook Pub. Co.; c1987. xiii, 368 p.
87-013665 658.4/09 0933071159
Business. Philosophy. Intellect.

HF5351.L352 1968
Lasser, J. K. 1896-1954,
Business management handbook. Bernard Greisman, editor. New York, McGraw-Hill [1968] xiii, 770 p.
68-011929 658/.002/02
Business. Industrial management.

HF5351.V38 1935
Veblen, Thorstein, 1857-1929.
The theory of business enterprise, by Thorstein Veblen ... New York, C. Scribner's, 1935. 1 v.
39-001058 658
Business. Capital.

HF5381 Business — Vocational guidance. Career development — Societies. Serials

HF5381.E516 1992
The Encyclopedia of career change and work issues/ edited by Lawrence K. Jones. Phoenix, Ariz.: Oryx Press, 1992. xxvii, 379 p.
91-033913 650.1 0897746104
Vocational guidance -- Encyclopedias. Career changes -- Encyclopedias. Labor -- Encyclopedias.

HF5381.L6558 1998
London, Manuel.
Career barriers: how people experience, overcome, and avoid failure/ Manuel London. Mahwah, N.J.: Lawrence Erlbaum Associates, 1998. xxiv, 215 p.
97-022282 650.14 0805825797
Career development. Employee motivation. Alienation (Social psychology)

HF5381.M39625 1989
McDaniels, Carl.
The changing workplace: career counseling strategies for the 1990s and beyond/ Carl McDaniels. San Francisco: Jossey-Bass Publishers, 1989. xx, 255 p.
88-046081 331.7/02 1555421466
Vocational guidance. Professions -- Forecasting. Occupations -- Forecasting.

HF5382.6 Business — Vocational guidance for women — General works

HF5382.6.S53 2001
Skarbek, Janet L.
Planning your future: a guide for professional women/ Janet L. Skarbek. Cinnaminson, NJ: Professional Women's Institute, 2001. xiv, 270 p.
00-134096 0970234473
Vocational guidance for women. Women in the professions.

HF5382.7 Business — Job hunting — General works

HF5382.7.B64
Bolles, Richard Nelson.
What color is your parachute?/ Richard Nelson Bolles. Berkeley, Calif.: Ten Speed Press, [1971-]
84-649334 650.1/4/05
Job hunting -- Periodicals. Career changes -- Periodicals. Vocational guidance -- Periodicals.

HF5383 Business — Applications for positions. Resumes. Employment portfolios

HF5383.D47 1981
Dickhut, Harold W., 1911-
The professional resume & job search guide/ Harold W. Dickhut. Englewood Cliffs, N.J.: Prentice-Hall, c1981. 218 p.
80-015824 650.1/4 0137257058
Resumes (Employment) Applications for positions. Employment interviewing.

HF5383.F37
Lauber, Daniel.
Non-profits' job finder by Daniel Lauber. Forest, Ill: Planning Communications 1992 306 p.
91-092910 650.14
Job hunting.

HF5386 Business — Success in business

HF5386.A513 1979
Adams, Jane,
Women on top: success patterns and personal growth/ Jane Adams. New York: Hawthorn Books, c1979. ix, 227 p.
79-084666 650.1/02/4042 0801587883
Success in business. Businesswomen -- United States.

HF5386.B279
Baumhart, Raymond.
An honest profit; what businessmen say about ethics in business. New York, Holt, Rinehart and Winston [1968] xiv, 248 p.
67-012907 174/.4/0973
Businesspeople -- United States. Business ethics -- United States.

HF5386.S6363 1997
Slywotzky, Adrian J.
The profit zone: how strategic business design will lead you to tomorrow's profits/ Adrian J. Slywotzky and David J. Morrison, with Bob Andelman. New York: Times Business, c1997. x, 342 p.
97-027496 658.15/5 21 0812929004
Success in business. Corporate profits. Competition.

HF5386.S7548 1998
Spulber, Daniel F.
The market makers: how leading companies create and win markets/ Daniel F. Spulber. New York: McGraw-Hill, c1998. x, 314 p.
98-006168 658.8 21 007060584X
Success in business. Market share.

HF5387 Business — Business ethics — General works

HF5387.A4 1994
Aguilar, Francis J.
Managing corporate ethics: learning from America's ethical companies how to supercharge business performance/ Francis J. Aguilar. New York: Oxford University Press, 1994. viii, 177 p.
93-005803 174/.4 0195085345
Business ethics -- United States. Business ethics -- United States -- Case studies.

HF5387.B32 1997
Badaracco, Joseph.
Defining moments: when managers must choose between right and right/ Joseph L. Badaracco, Jr. Boston, Mass.: Harvard Business School Press, c1997. xi, 147 p.
97-017613 174/.4 21 0875848036
Business ethics. Executives -- Professional ethics.

HF5387.B537 1996
Bird, Frederick B. 1938-
The muted conscience: moral silence and the practice of ethics in business/ Frederick Bruce Bird. Westport, Conn: Quorum Books, 1996. ix, 268 p.
96-000591 174/.4 0899306527
Business ethics. Ethics.

HF5387.B63 1999
Boatright, John Raymond, 1941-
Ethics in finance/ John R. Boatright. Malden, Mass.: Blackwell Publishers, 1999. ix, 209 p.
98-033146 174/.4 0631214267
Business ethics. Finance -- Moral and ethical aspects.

HF5387.B876 1991
Business ethics: the state of the art/ edited by R. Edward Freeman. New York: Oxford University Press, 1991. x, 225 p.
90-007372 174/.4 019506478X
Business ethics. Industries -- Social aspects.

HF5387.C33 1999
Calhoun, Charles H.
Ethics and the CPA: building trust and value-added services/ Charles H. Calhoun, Mary Ellen Oliverio, Philip Wolitzer. New York: John Wiley, c1999. xiv, 257 p.
98-017658   174/.4 21   0471184888
Business ethics. Accounting -- Moral and ethical aspects. Finance -- Moral and ethical aspects.

HF5387.C55 1993b
Clark, Ralph W.
Workplace ethics: winning the integrity revolution/ Ralph W. Clark, Alice Darnell Lattal. Lanham, Md.: Rowman & Littlefield Publishers, c1993. xi, 135 p.
92-021386   174/.4   0847677893
Business ethics.

HF5387.E8 1999
Ethical issues in business: a philosophical approach/ edited by Thomas Donaldson, Patricia H. Werhane. Upper Saddle River, N.J.: Prentice Hall, c1999. xii, 611 p.
98-031341   174/.4 21   0132906287
Business ethics -- Case studies. Social responsibility of business -- Case studies.

HF5387.F67 1994
The Ford Pinto case: a study in applied ethics, business, and technology/ edited by Douglas Birsch and John H. Fielder. Albany, NY: State University of New York Press, c1994. xxvi, 312 p.
94-000838   338.4/76292222   079142233X
Social responsibility of business -- Case studies. Business ethics -- Case studies. Pinto automobile.

HF5387.G55 1996
Gilbert, Daniel R., 1952-
Ethics through corporate strategy/ Daniel R. Gilbert, Jr. New York: Oxford University Press, c1996. xv, 165 p.
96-020932   174/.4 20   019509624X
Business ethics. Strategic planning -- Moral and ethical aspects.

HF5387.L54 1990
Liebig, James E.
Business ethics: profiles in civic virtue/ James E. Liebig. Golden, Colo.: Fulcrum Pub., c1990. xxii, 237 p.
89-029522   338.092/273   1555910599
Business ethics. Businesspeople -- United States -- Biography.

HF5387.L56 1995
Lippke, Richard L., 1954-
Radical business ethics/ Richard L. Lippke. Lanham, Md.: Rowman & Littlefield, c1995. ix, 203 p.
95-018514   174/.4   084768069X
Business ethics. Social responsibility of business.

HF5387.M335 1990
Manley, Walter W.
Critical issues in business conduct: legal, ethical, and social challenges for the 1990s/ Walter W. Manley II with William A. Shrode; forewords by Robert H. Stovall and LeRoy Collins. New York: Quorum Books, 1990. xxii, 309 p.
90-030009   658.4/06   0899305709
Business ethics. Industries -- Social aspects.

HF5387.M648 1998
The moral imagination: how literature and films can stimulate ethical reflection in the business world/ edited by Oliver F. Williams. Notre Dame, Ind.: University of Notre Dame Press, c1997. viii, 210 p.
97-046844   174/.4 21   0268014329
Business ethics. Business ethics in literature. Business ethics in motion pictures.

HF5387.S57 1994
Sims, Ronald R.
Ethics and organizational decision making: a call for renewal/ Ronald R. Sims. Westport, Conn.: Quorum Books, 1994. viii, 214 p.
93-050071   174/.4   0899308600
Business ethics. Decision making -- Moral and ethical aspects. Organizational behavior.

HF5387.S612 1999
Solomon, Robert C.
A better way to think about business: how personal integrity leads to corporate success/ Robert C. Solomon. New York: Oxford University Press, 1999. xxiv, 145 p.
98-034297   174/.4   0195112385
Business ethics.

HF5387.S614 1992
Solomon, Robert C.
Ethics and excellence: cooperation and integrity in business/ Robert C. Solomon. New York: Oxford University Press, 1992. xiv, 288 p.
91-032363   174/.4   0195064305
Business ethics.

HF5387.S655 2001
Spiritual goods: faith traditions and the practice of business/ Stewart W. Herman, editor; with Arthur Gross Schaefer. [S.l.]: Philosophy Documentation Center, c2001. vii, 407 p.
00-111022   1889680214
Business ethics. Business -- Religious aspects.

HF5389 Business — Business etiquette. Office etiquette — General works

HF5389.E53 1991
Engholm, Christopher.
When business East meets business West: the guide to practice and protocol in the Pacific Rim/ Christopher Engholm. New York: Wiley, c1991. x, 354 p.
91-012204   395/.52/099   0471530336
Business etiquette -- Pacific Area. Intercultural communication -- United States. Cross-cultural orientation -- United States.

HF5414 Business — Marketing — Social aspects. Social marketing

HF5414.H36 2001
Handbook of marketing and society/ Paul N. Bloom, Gregory T. Gundlach, editors. Thousand Oaks, Calif.: Sage, c2001. xxii, 543 p.
00-009055   658.8/02 21   0761916261
Social marketing.

HF5415 Business — Marketing — General works

HF5415.A46 1995
AMA marketing encyclopedia: issues and trends shaping the future/ American Marketing Association; Jeffrey Heilbrunn, editor. Lincolnwood, Ill., USA: NTC Business Books, 1995. x, 348 p.
94-017747   658/.003   0844235938
Marketing -- Encyclopedias.

HF5415.B277 1989
Baker, Michael John.
Marketing and competitive success/ Michael J. Baker and Susan J. Hart. New York: P. Allan, 1989. vii, 200 p.
88-038568   658.8   0860035662
Marketing. Success in business.

HF5415.C52717 1991
Christopher, Martin.
Relationship marketing: bringing quality, customer service, and marketing together/ Martin Christopher, Adrian Payne, and David Ballantyne. Oxford; Butterworth-Heinemann, 1991. viii, 204 p.
92-164121   658.8   0750602589
Relationship marketing. Customer services. Quality control.

HF5415.D38
Dawson, John A.
The marketing environment/ John A. Dawson. New York: St. Martin's Press, 1979. 379 p.
78-031580   381   0312515308
Marketing.

HF5415.D4874 1995
Dictionary of marketing terms/ Peter D. Bennett, editor. Lincolnwood, Ill., USA: NTC Business Books, c1995. xiv, 316 p.
94-039784   658.8/003 20   0844235989
Marketing -- Dictionaries.

HF5415.E65 1983
Engel, James F.
Promotional strategy: managing the marketing communications process/ James F. Engel, Martin R. Warshaw, Thomas C. Kinnear. Homewood, Ill.: R.D. Irwin, 1983. xv, 655 p.
82-084060   658.8/2   025602846X
Marketing. Advertising. Marketing -- Management.

HF5415.H178
Halbert, Michael.
The meaning and sources of marketing theory. New York, McGraw-Hill [1965] 330 p.
64-066043   658.801
Marketing.

HF5415.H1867 1986
Handbook of modern marketing/ Victor P. Buell, editor. New York: McGraw-Hill, c1986. 1 v.
85-014903   658.8   0070088543
Marketing.

HF5415.M2583 1987
McIver, Colin, 1914-
The marketing mirage: how to make it a reality/ Colin McIver. New York: Nichols Pub. Co., 1987. viii, 215 p.
87-014048   658.8   0893972851
Marketing.

HF5415.O76 1988
Ostrow, Rona.
The dictionary of marketing/ Rona Ostrow, Sweetman R. Smith. New York: Fairchild Publications, c1988. 258 p.
87-082654   380.1/03/21   0870055739
Marketing -- Dictionaries.

HF5415.P233
Palda, Kristian S.
Pricing decisions and marketing policy [by] Kristian S. Palda. Englewood Cliffs, N.J., Prentice-Hall [1971] x, 116 p.
78-139413   658.8/16   0136996604
Pricing. Marketing.

HF5415.R237 1996
Rados, David L., 1933-
Marketing for nonprofit organizations/ David L. Rados. Westport, Conn.; Auburn House, 1996. xiv, 463 p.
95-013609   658.8   0865692548
Nonprofit organizations -- Marketing.

HF5415.R3245 1994
Rapp, Stan.
Beyond MaxiMarketing: the new power of caring and daring/ Stan Rapp, Thomas L. Collins. New York: McGraw-Hill, c1994. xxvii, 319 p.
93-023545   658.8   0070513430
Marketing -- Case studies. Sales promotion -- Case studies.

HF5415.S859
Stone, Merlin, 1948-
Marketing and economics/ by Merlin Stone. New York: St. Martin's Press, 1980. vii, 181 p.
79-022206   658.8   0312515278
Marketing. Economics.

HF5415.1-5415.12 Business — Marketing — By region or country

HF5415.1.B42 1973
Beckman, Theodore N., 1894-
Marketing [by] Theodore N. Beckman, William R. Davidson [and] W. Wayne Talarzyk. New York, Ronald Press Co. [1973] xii, 642 p.
72-096965   658.8
Marketing -- United States.

HF5415.1.B79 1988
Brown, Paul B.
Marketing masters: lessons in the art of marketing from those who do it best/ Paul B. Brown. New York: Harper & Row, c1988. 216 p.
87-045601   658.8   0060158689
Marketing -- United States -- Case studies. Success in business -- United States -- Case studies.

HF5415.1.K5
King, William Richard, 1938-
Quantitative analysis for marketing management [by] William R. King. New York, McGraw-Hill [1967] xviii, 574 p.
67-021595   658.8/001/82
Marketing -- Mathematical models. Marketing -- Management -- Mathematical models. Decision making -- Mathematical models.

HF5415.1.O87 1989
Ostroff, Jeff.
Successful marketing to the 50+ consumer: How to capture one of the biggest and fastest-growing markets in America/ Jeff Ostroff. Englewood Cliffs, N.J.: Prentice Hall, c1989. xxiii, 371 p.
89-031324   658.8/00880564   0138602719
Marketing -- United States. Advertising -- United States. Aged consumers -- United States.

HF5415.1.P55
Porter, Glenn.
Merchants and manufacturers; studies in the changing structure of nineteenth-century marketing [by] Glenn Porter and Harold C. Livesay. Baltimore, Johns Hopkins Press [1971] x, 257 p.
72-156071   380.1/0973/09034   0801812518
Marketing -- Management -- United States -- History -- 19th century.   United States -- Commerce -- History -- 19th century.

HF5415.1.T44 1990
Tedlow, Richard S.
New and improved: the story of mass marketing in America/ Richard S. Tedlow. New York: Basic Books, c1990. xi, 481 p.
89-018331   381/.0973   0465050239
Marketing -- United States -- History. Marketing -- United States -- Case studies.

HF5415.12.R9
Frye, Timothy.
Brokers and bureaucrats: building market institutions in Russia/ Timothy Frye. Ann Arbor: University of Michigan Press, c2000. xv, 272 p.
99-006810   332.63/2 21   047209713X
Marketing -- Russia (Federation) Capitalism -- Russia (Federation) Post-communism -- Russia (Federation) Russia (Federation) -- Economic conditions -- 1991-

HF5415.122 Business — Marketing — General special

HF5415.122.K68 1989
Kotler, Philip.
Social marketing: strategies for changing public behavior/ Philip Kotler, Eduardo L. Roberto. New York: Free Press; c1989. xii, 401 p.
89-045735   658.8   0029184614
Social marketing. Behavior modification.

HF5415.122.M367 1997
Marconi, Joe.
Crisis marketing: when bad things happen to good companies/ Joe Marconi. Chicago, Ill.: NTC Business Books, c1997. x, 246 p.
97-030304   658.8 21   0844232378
Marketing. Marketing -- Case studies. Crisis management.

HF5415.124 Business — Marketing — Communication of information. Communication in marketing

HF5415.124.F7 1994
Ganly, John.
Data sources for business and market analysis/ by John Ganly. Metuchen, N.J.: Scarecrow Press, 1994. xvii, 458 p.
93-023453   016.6588/3973   0810827581
Marketing -- United States -- Information services. Marketing -- Bibliography. Commerce -- Bibliography. United States -- Commerce -- Information services.

HF5415.125 Business — Marketing — Data processing

HF5415.125.C58 1994
Clancy, Kevin J., 1942-
Simulated test marketing: technology for launching successful new products/ Kevin J. Clancy, Robert S. Shulman, Marianne M. Wolf. New York: Lexington Books; c1994. xiii, 306 p.
94-017718   658.8/00285   0029055059
Marketing -- Computer simulation. New products -- Marketing. Test marketing.

HF5415.1265 Business — Marketing — Telemarketing. Internet marketing

HF5415.1265.E395 1997
Electronic marketing and the consumer/ editor, Robert A. Peterson. Thousand Oaks, Calif.: Sage Publications, c1997. xiii, 193 p.
97-004753   658.8/4 21   0761910697
Internet marketing. Broadcast advertising. Twenty-first century -- Forecasts.

HF5415.1265.N495 2000
Newell, Frederick, 1926-
Loyalty.com: customer relationship management in the new era of Internet marketing/ Frederick Newell. New York: McGraw-Hill, c2000. xx, 325 p.
99-058215   658.8/4 21   0071357750
Internet marketing. Customer relations.

HF5415.1265.S735 2000
Steinbock, Dan.
The birth of Internet marketing communications/ Dan Steinbock. Westport, Conn.: Quorum, 2000. xvi, 308 p.
99-013713   658.8/00285/4678   1567203035
Internet marketing. Communication in marketing. World Wide Web.

HF5415.127 Business — Marketing — Market segmentation. Target marketing

HF5415.127.H65 1992
Hollander, Stanley C., 1919-
Was there a Pepsi Generation before Pepsi discovered it?: youth-based segmentation in marketing/ Stanley C. Hollander, Richard Germain; foreword by Richard S. Tedlow. Chicago, Ill.: American Marketing Associaton; c1992. xiv, 144 p.
92-013905   658.8/348   0844234567
Market segmentation -- United States -- History. Young consumers -- United States -- History. Marketing -- United States -- History.

HF5415.127.M66 1998
Mooij, Marieke K. de, 1943-
Global marketing and advertising: understanding cultural paradoxes/ Marieke de Mooij. Thousand Oaks, Calif.: Sage Publications, c1998. xx, 316 p.
97-004800   658.8/02 21   0803959699
Target marketing -- Cross-cultural studies. Advertising -- Cross-cultural studies. Consumer behavior -- Cross-cultural studies.

HF5415.127.S94 1990
Swenson, Chester A.
Selling to a segmented market: the lifestyle approach/ Chester A. Swenson. New York: Quorum Books, c1990. xix, 177 p.
89-049432   658.8/35   089930446X
Market segmentation -- United States. Consumers' preferences -- United States. Consumer behavior -- United States.

HF5415.129 Business — Marketing — Marketing channels

HF5415.129.M38 1992
McCalley, Russell W.
Marketing channel development and management/ Russell W. McCalley; foreword by Ray A. Goldberg. Westport, Conn.: Quorum Books, 1992. xiv, 280 p.
92-015768   658.8/4   0899307809
Marketing channels. Marketing -- Management.

HF5415.13-5415.157 Business — Marketing — Marketing management

HF5415.13.D367 1999
Day, George S.
The market driven organization: understanding, attracting, and keeping valuable customers/ George S. Day. New York: Free Press, c1999. xii, 285 p.
99-016155   658.8 21   0684864673
Marketing -- Management. Sales management. Consumer satisfaction.

HF5415.13.H47 1992
Hiam, Alexander.
The portable MBA in marketing/ Alexander Hiam, Charles D. Schewe. New York: J. Wiley, c1992. xiv, 464 p.
91-037515   658.8   047154728X
Marketing -- Management.

HF5415.13.J587 1996
Johnson, William C. 1954-
Total quality in marketing/ by William C. Johnson, Richard J. Chvala. Delray Beach, Fla.: St. Lucie Press, c1996. xix, 276 p.
95-206662   658.8 20   1884015131
Marketing -- Management. Total quality management.

HF5415.13.L538 1995
Linneman, Robert E., 1928-
Marketing planning in a total quality environment/ Robert E. Linneman, John L. Stanton. New York: Haworth Press, c1995. xvi, 464 p.
94-048363   658.8/02   1560249382
Marketing -- Planning. Total quality management.

HF5415.13.M3691832 1997
McDonald, Malcolm.
Marketing plans that work: targeting growth and profitability/ Malcolm H. B. McDonald, Warren J. Keegan. Boston: Butterworth-Heinemann, c1997. viii, 236 p.
97-007401   658.8/02 21   0750698284
Marketing -- Planning.

HF5415.13.M677 1994
Moschis, George P., 1944-
Marketing strategies for the mature market/ George P. Moschis. Westport, Conn.: Quorum Books, 1994. xiv, 198 p.
94-008542   658.8/02   0899308872
Marketing -- Management. Market segmentation. New products -- Marketing.

HF5415.13.S24 1992
Samli, A. Coskun.
Social responsibility in marketing: a proactive and profitable marketing management strategy/ A. Coskun Samli. Westport, Conn.: Quorum Books, 1992. 198 p.
92-009810   658.8/02   0899306284
Marketing -- Management. Marketing -- Social aspects. Green marketing -- Management.

HF5415.13.S345 1991
Schnaars, Steven P.
Marketing strategy: a customer-driven approach/ Steven P. Schnaars. New York: Free Press; c1991. xvi, 319 p.
90-043633   658.8/02   0029279534
Marketing -- Management. Strategic planning. Competition.

HF5415.13.W547 1992
Wilson, R. M. S.
Strategic marketing management: planning, implementation, and control/ Richard M.S. Wilson and Colin Gilligan, with David J. Pearson. Oxford; Butterworth-Heinemann, 1992. xx, 644 p.
91-029728   658.8/02   0750603291
Marketing -- Management.

HF5415.135.S26 1996
Samli, A. Coskun.
Information-driven marketing decisions: development of strategic information systems/ A. Coskun Samli. Westport, Conn.: Quorum Books, 1996. xx, 196 p.
95-024086   658.8/02   0899309763
Marketing -- Decision making. Marketing research. Management information systems.

HF5415.15.M334 2001
Mark, Margaret.
The hero and the outlaw: building extraordinary brands through the power of archetypes/ Margaret Mark and Carol S. Pearson. New York: McGraw-Hill, c2001. xii, 384 p.
2001-274378   658.8/27 21   0071364153
Product management. Brand name products. Brand name products -- Marketing.

HF5415.153.H36 1991
Hall, John A. 1932-
Bringing new products to market: the art and science of creating winners/ John A. Hall. New York: AMACOM, c1991. xvi, 248 p.
90-056188   658.5/75   0814450172
New products.

HF5415.153.S58 1993
Slade, Bernard N.
Compressing the product development cycle: from research to marketplace/ Bernard N. Slade. New York: American Management Association, c1993. ix, 214 p.
92-027375   658.5/75   0814450067
New products -- United States. Product management.

HF5415.155.O55 1989
Onkvisit, Sak.
Product life cycles and product management/ Sak Onkvisit & John J. Shaw. New York: Quorum Books, c1989. x, 162 p.
88-026509   658.5/038   0899303196
Product life cycle. Product management.

HF5415.157.G34 1994
Gale, Bradley T.
Managing customer value: creating quality and service that customers can see/ Bradley T. Gale with Robert Chapman Wood. New York: Free Press; c1994. xxii, 424 p.
93-041905   658.8/12   0029110459
Quality of products -- Evaluation. Consumer satisfaction -- Evaluation. Marketing -- Management.

HF5415.157.P39 1994
Payson, Steven, 1957-
Quality measurement in economics: new perspectives on the evolution of goods and services/ Steven Payson. Aldershot, England; Elgar, 1994. xii, 242 p.
93-028612   658.5/62   1852789263
Quality of products -- United States -- Cost effectiveness -- Econometric models. Technological innovations -- United States -- Econometric models.

HF5415.2-5415.33 Business — Marketing — Marketing research. Marketing research companies

HF5415.2.B333 1995
Barabba, Vincent P., 1934-
Meeting of the minds: creating the market-based enterprise/ Vincent P. Barabba. Boston, Mass.: Harvard Business School Press, c1995. xv, 247 p.
95-013342   658.8/3   0875845770
Marketing research. Marketing -- Decision making. New products.

HF5415.2.B555 1998
Blankenship, Albert Breneman, 1914-
State of the art marketing research/ A.B. Blankenship, George Edward Breen, Alan Dutka. Lincolnwood, Ill.: NTC Business Books, c1998. x, 454 p.
97-029370   658.8/3 21   0844234435
Marketing research.

HF5415.2.K748 1994
Kress, George.
Forecasting and market analysis techniques: a practical approach/ George J. Kress & John Snyder. Westport, Conn: Quorum Books, 1994. xiv, 286 p.
93-011890   658.8/35   089930835X
Sales forecasting. Marketing research.

HF5415.2.M35585 1997
The marketing research guide/ Robert E. Stevens ... [et al.]. New York: Haworth Press, c1997. xv, 488 p.
96-019070   658.8/3 20   1560243392
Marketing research.

HF5415.2.M945
Myers, John G.
Marketing research and knowledge development: an assessment for marketing management/ John G. Myers, William F. Massy, Stephen A. Greyser. Englewood Cliffs, N.J.: Prentice-Hall, c1980. xiv, 306 p.
80-013929   658.8/3973   0135576865
Marketing research -- United States.

HF5415.2.S29 2001
Sayre, Shay.
Qualitative methods for marketplace research/
Shay Sayre. Thousand Oaks, Calif.: Sage, c2001.
xv, 255 p.
00-012352   658.8/3 21   0761922695
Marketing research -- Methodology.

HF5415.3.B323 1993
Bearden, William O., 1945-
Handbook of marketing scales: multi-item
measures for marketing and consumer behavior
research/ William O. Bearden, Richard G.
Netemeyer, Mary F. Mobley. Newbury Park,
Calif.: Sage Publications, c1993. xii, 352 p.
92-045241   658.8/3   0803951558
*Marketing research. Consumer behavior --
Research.*

HF5415.3.E527 1994
Encyclopedia of consumer brands/ editor, Janice
Jorgensen. Detroit: St. James Press, c1994. 3 v.
93-037940   658.8/343   1558623353
*Brand choice -- United States. Brand name
products -- United States. Consumers' preferences
-- United States.*

HF5415.3.M278 1984
Marketing to the changing household: management
and research perspectives/ edited by Mary Lou
Roberts and Lawrence H. Wortzel. Cambridge,
Mass.: Ballinger Pub. Co., c1984. xxv, 349 p.
84-012288   658.8   0884109860
*Households -- United States. Marketing research.
Marketing -- Management.*

HF5415.32.E48 1999
The Elgar companion to consumer research and
economic psychology/ edited by Peter E. Earl and
Simon Kemp. Northampton, Mass.: Edward Elgar
Pub., c1999. xxii, 649 p.
98-038240   658.8/342 21   1858985544
*Consumers -- Research. Consumer behavior.
Economics -- Psychological aspects.*

HF5415.32.H36 1991
Handbook of consumer behavior/ [edited by]
Thomas S. Robertson, Harold H. Kassarjian.
Englewood Cliffs, N.J.: Prentice-Hall, c1991. x,
614 p.
90-040459   658.8/342   0133727491
*Consumer behavior. Motivation research
(Marketing)*

HF5415.32.L33 1994
Laaksonen, Pirjo, 1943-
Consumer involvement: concepts and research/
Pirjo Laarksonen [sic]. London; Routledge, 1994.
viii, 220 p.
93-045989   658.8/343   0415097606
Consumer behavior. Marketing.

HF5415.32.O74 1992
O'Shaughnessy, John.
Explaining buyer behavior: central concepts and
philosophy of science issues/ John O'Shaughnessy.
New York: Oxford University Press, 1992. 385 p.
91-022140   658.8/342   0195071085
Consumer behavior -- Methodology.

HF5415.32.S56 1990
Smith, N. Craig, 1958-
Morality and the market: consumer pressure for
corporate accountability/ N. Craig Smith. London;
Routledge, 1990. x, 351 p.
89-010239   381.3/2   0415004373
*Consumer behavior. Boycotts. Social
responsibility of business.*

HF5415.33.E542.L667 2000
Rappaport, Erika Diane, 1963-
Shopping for pleasure: women in the making of
London's West End/ Erika Diane Rappaport.
Princeton, NJ: Princeton University Press, 2000.
xiii, 323 p.
99-028152   658.8/342   0691044775
*Consumer behavior -- England -- London -- Sex
differences -- History. Consumption (Economics) --
England -- London -- Sex differences -- History.
Women consumers -- England -- London -- History.
West End (London, England) -- Economic
conditions.*

HF5415.33.G7.M67 1996
Mort, Frank.
Cultures of consumption: masculinities and social
space in late twentieth-century Britain/ Frank Mort.
London; Routledge, 1996. viii, 280 p.
95-021633   306.3   041503051X
*Consumer behavior -- Great Britain -- Sex
differences -- History -- 20th century. Consumption
(Economics) -- Great Britain -- History -- 20th
century. Great Britain -- Economic conditions --
20th century.*

HF5415.33.U6.C66 1997
The consumer society/ edited by Neva R.
Goodwin, Frank Ackerman, and David Kiron.
Washington, D.C.: Island Press, c1997. xxxviii,
385 p.
96-022627   306.3/4 20   1559634855
*Consumer behavior -- Social aspects -- United
States. Consumption (Economics) -- Social aspects
-- United States.*

HF5415.5-5415.55 Business — Marketing — Customer services. Customer relations

HF5415.5.B3673 2000
Barlow, Janelle, 1943-
Emotional value: creating strong bonds with your
customers/ Janelle Barlow and Dianna Maul;
foreword by Michael Edwardson. San Francisco:
Berrett-Koehler Publishers, c2000. xviii, 310 p.
99-086124   658.8/12 21   1576750795
Customer services.

HF5415.5.R438 1996
Reichheld, Frederick F.
The loyalty effect: the hidden force behind growth,
profits, and lasting value/ Frederick F. Reichheld
with Thomas Teal. Boston, Mass.: Harvard
Business School Press, c1996. xii, 323 p.
95-039972   658.4 20   0875844480
*Customer relations. Consumer satisfaction. Job
satisfaction.*

HF5415.5.V357 1999
Vandermerwe, Sandra.
Customer capitalism: the new business model of
increasing returns in new market spaces/ Sandra
Vandermerwe. Naperville, Ill.: Nicholas Brealey
Publishing, 1999. xvi, 296 p.
98-056043   658.8/12   1857882415
*Customer services. Target marketing.
Capitalism.*

HF5415.5.W39 1997
Wayland, Robert E. 1946-
Customer connections: new strategies for growth/
Robert E. Wayland, Paul M. Cole. Boston, Mass:
Harvard Business School Press, c1997. xi, 265 p.
97-010783   658.8/12 21   0875847994
Customer relations.

HF5415.55.H36 2000
Handbook of relationship marketing/ Jagdish N.
Sheth, Atul Parvatiyar, editors. Thousand Oaks:
Sage Publications, c2000. xvi, 660 p.
99-050408   658.8 21   0761918108
Relationship marketing.

HF5422 Business — Wholesale trade — Jobbers. Brokers

HF5422.S54 1988
Silliphant, Leigh.
Making Leigh and Sureleigh Silliphant. Berkeley,
Calif.: Ten Speed Press, c1988. iv, 190 p.
88-002103   658.8/5   0898152410
*Manufacturers' agents -- United States. Self-
employed -- United States.*

HF5429.23-5429.235 Business — Retail trade — Franchises

HF5429.23.F673 1989
Foster, Dennis L.
The encyclopedia of franchises and franchising/ by
Dennis L. Foster. New York: Facts on File, c1989.
465 p.
89-011774   381/.13/03   0816020817
Franchises (Retail trade) -- Dictionaries.

HF5429.235.U5.L88 1985
Luxenberg, Stan.
Roadside empires: how the chains franchised
America/ by Stan Luxenberg. New York, N.Y.,
U.S.A.: Viking, 1985. viii, 313 p.
83-040231   381/.13/0973   0670326585
Franchises (Retail trade) -- United States.

HF5429.5-5429.6 Business — Retail trade — By region or country

HF5429.5.L7.L663 1999
Longstreth, Richard W.
The drive-in, the supermarket, and the
transformation of commercial space in Los
Angeles, 1914-1941/ Richard Longstreth.
Cambridge, Mass.: MIT Press, c1999. xviii, 248 p.
98-039140   381/.1 21   0262122146
*Retail trade -- California -- Los Angeles
Metropolitan Area -- History. Drive-in facilities --
California -- Los Angeles Metropolitan Area --
History. Supermarkets -- California -- Los Angeles
Metropolitan Area -- History.*

HF5429.6.E9.F58 1992
Fitzell, Philip B.
Private label marketing in the 1990s: the evolution
of price labels into global brands/ by Philip Fitzell.
New York: Global Book Productions, c1992. xv,
294 p.
92-097124   0963292013
*Retail trade -- Europe. House brands -- Europe -
- Marketing.*

HF5438.25 Business — Selling — General works

HF5438.25.B243 1997
Baber, Michael.
How champions sell/ Michael Baber. New York:
AMACOM, c1997. xvi, 279 p.
96-023715   658.85 21   0814403719
Selling.

HF5438.25.B52 1989
Biggart, Nicole Woolsey.
Charismatic capitalism: direct selling organizations in America/ Nicole Woolsey Biggart. Chicago: University of Chicago Press, 1989. xii, 223 p.
88-019833 658.8/4 0226047857
Direct selling -- United States. Sales personnel -- United States. Commercial agents -- United States.

HF5438.25.K546 1994
Kimball, Bob.
AMA handbook for successful selling/ Bob Kimball. Chicago, Ill.: American Marketing Association; c1994. ix, 197 p.
93-002784 658.8/5 0844235881
Selling.

HF5465 Business — Department stores — By region or country, A-Z

HF5465.G73.L36 1995
Lancaster, William, 1938-
The department store: a social history/ Bill Lancaster. London; Leicester University Press, 1995. vii, 212 p.
95-018851 381/.141/0941 0718513746
Department stores -- Great Britain -- History. Industrial relations -- Great Britain -- History. Department stores -- Social aspects -- Great Britain -- History.

HF5465.U6.M27
Hower, Ralph Merle, 1903-
History of Macy's of New York, 1858-1919; chapters in the evolution of the department store, by Ralph M. Hower ... Cambridge, Mass., Harvard University Press, 1943. xxvii, 500 p.
43-001889 658.871
Macy's (Firm)

HF5500.2-5500.3 Business — Business organization and administration

HF5500.2.L37
Lessons of leadership; 21 top executives speak out on creating, developing, and managing success. Presented by the editors of Nation's business. Garden City, N.Y., Doubleday, 1968. xvi, 271 p.
68-011795 650/.1/0922
Executives -- United States -- Case studies. Success -- Case studies.

HF5500.2.M248 1984
Marshall, Judi.
Women managers: travellers in a male world/ Judi Marshall. Chichester [Sussex]; Wiley, c1984. vii, 251 p.
83-023579 658.4/09/088042 0471904198
Women executives.

HF5500.3.U54.D38 1982
Davis, George, 1939-
Black life in corporate America: swimming in the mainstream/ George Davis and Glegg Watson. Garden City, N.Y.: Anchor Press/Doubleday, 1982. 204 p.
81-022760 658.4/09/08996073 0385147015
Afro-American executives. Afro-American businesspeople.

HF5500.3.U54.F474 1981
Fernandez, John P., 1941-
Racism and sexism in corporate life: changing values in American business/ John P. Fernandez. Lexington, Mass.: Lexington Books, c1981. xxiii, 359 p.
80-008945 658.3/041 0669044776
Minority executives -- United States. Women executives -- United States. Discrimination in employment -- United States.

HF5547.5 Business — Office management — Office practice. Secretarial practice

HF5547.5.N5 1998
The New York Public Library business desk reference. New York: J. Wiley, c1998. xiv, 494 p.
97-007408 651 21 0471144428
Office practice -- United States -- Handbooks, manuals, etc.

HF5548.2 Business — Data processing — General works

HF5548.2.C675 1996
Cortada, James W.
Information technology as business history: issues in the history and management of computers/ James W. Cortada. Westport, Conn.: Greenwood Press, 1996. xi, 263 p.
96-003644 658/.05 0313299501
Business -- Data processing -- History. Information technology -- Management -- History. Electronic data processing -- History.

HF5548.2.K395 1991
Keen, Peter G. W.
Shaping the future: business design through information technology/ Peter G.W. Keen. [Boston, Mass.]: Harvard Business School Press, c1991. xi, 264 p.
90-049732 658.4/038
Business -- Data processing -- Management. Business -- Communication systems -- Management. Management information systems.

HF5548.32 Business — Data processing — Electronic commerce

HF5548.32.F57 2001
Fitz-enz, Jac.
The e-aligned enterprise: how to map and measure your company's course in the new economy/ Jac Fitz-enz. New York: AMACOM, 2001. xvi, 265 p.
2001-016041 658.8/4 0814406254
Electronic commerce.

HF5548.32.M36 2000
Mann, Catherine L.
Global electronic commerce: a policy primer/ Catherine L. Mann, Sue E. Eckert, Sarah Cleeland Knight. Washington, DC: Institute for International Economics, 2000. xv, 213 p.
00-044898 382/.3 0881322741
Electronic commerce. Electronic commerce -- Government policy. Electronic commerce -- Law and legislation.

HF5548.32.W56 2000
Windham, Laurie.
The soul of the new consumer: the attitudes, behaviors, and preferences of E-customers/ Laurie Windham with Ken Orton. New York: Allworth Press, c2000. x, 307 p.
00-040611 658.8/34 21 1581150660
Electronic commerce. Consumer behavior. Brand choice.

HF5548.8 Business — Industrial psychology — General works

HF5548.8.B686 1988
Brockner, Joel.
Self-esteem at work: research, theory, and practice/ Joel Brockner. Lexington, Mass.: Lexington Books, c1988. xii, 258 p.
84-048747 158.7 0669097551
Work -- Psychological aspects. Self-esteem. Psychology, Industrial.

HF5548.8.H265 1990
Handbook of industrial and organizational psychology/ Marvin D. Dunnette and Leaetta M. Hough, editors. Palo Alto, Calif.: Consulting Psychologists Press, c1990-c1994. 4 v.
90-002294 158.7 20 0891060413
Psychology, Industrial. Organizational behavior.

HF5548.8.M3754 1998
Maslow, Abraham H.
Maslow on management/ Abraham H. Maslow with Deborah C. Stephens and Gary Heil. New York: John Wiley, 1998. xxiii, 312 p.
98-021068 158.7 0471247804
Maslow, Abraham H. -- (Abraham Harold) -- Contributions in management. Maslow, Abraham H. -- (Abraham Harold) -- Diaries. Psychology, Industrial. Self-actualization (Psychology)

HF5549.A23 Business — Personnel management. Employment management — Dictionaries. Encyclopedias

HF5549.A23.T73 1991
Tracey, William R.
The human resources glossary: a complete desk reference for HR professionals/ William R. Tracey. New York, N.Y.: American Management Association, 1991.
90-056195 658.3/003 0814450113
Personnel management -- Dictionaries.

HF5549.H2975-V75 Business — Personnel management. Employment management — General works

HF5549.H2975 1991
A Handbook of psychological assessment in business/ edited by Curtiss P. Hansen and Kelley A. Conrad. New York: Quorum Books, 1991. xiii, 352 p.
91-006822 658.3/001/9 0899305652
Personnel management -- Psychological aspects. Psychology, Industrial. Prediction of occupational success.

HF5549.H78424 1990
Human resource management: an international comparison/ editor, Rudiger Pieper. Berlin; W. de Gruyter, c1990. xii, 283 p.
90-040428   658.3   0899257208
Personnel management -- Congresses. Personnel management -- Cross-cultural studies -- Congresses.

HF5549.N376 2000
The new relationship: human capital in the American corporation/ Margaret M. Blair, Thomas A. Kochan, eds. Washington, D.C.: Brookings Institution Press, c2000. x, 395 p.
99-050476   658.3/00973 21   0815709021
Personnel management. Human capital. Corporations.

HF5549.V75 1988
Von Glinow, Mary Ann Young, 1949-
The new professionals: managing today's high-tech employees/ Mary Ann Von Glinow. Cambridge, Mass.: Ballinger Pub. Co., c1988. xvi, 199 p.
88-018737   658.3   0887302718
High technology industries -- Personnel management. High technology industries -- Employees. Professional employees.

HF5549.2 Business — Personnel management. Employment management — By region or country, A-Z

HF5549.2.U5.B865 1993
Building the competitive workforce: investing in human capital for corporate success/ Philip H. Mirvis, editor. New York: Wiley, c1993. xv, 256 p.
92-042165   658.3   0471592579
Personnel management -- United States. Human capital -- United States. Competition -- United States.

HF5549.2.U5.O77 1988
Osterman, Paul.
Employment futures: reorganization, dislocation, and public policy/ Paul Osterman. New York: Oxford University Press, 1988. ix, 207 p.
87-031459   331.11/0973   019505279X
Manpower planning -- United States. Manpower policy -- United States. Industrial relations -- United States.

HF5549.5 Business — Personnel management. Employment management — By topic, A-Z

HF5549.5.A34.C484 1998
Chavez, Lydia, 1951-
The color bind: California's battle to end affirmative action/ Lydia Chavez. Berkeley: University of California Press, 1998. xiv, 305 p.
97-013397   331.13/3/09794   0520206878
Affirmative action programs -- California.

HF5549.5.A34.D68 1999
Doverspike, Dennis.
Affirmative action: a psychological perspective/ Dennis Doverspike, Mary Anne Taylor, Winfred Arthur. Commack, N.Y.: Nova Science, 1999.
99-055099   331.13/3   1560727624
Affirmative action programs.

HF5549.5.A34.D73 1996
Drake, Willie Avon, 1946-
Affirmative action and the stalled quest for Black progress/ W. Avon Drake and Robert D. Holsworth. Urbana: University of Illinois Press, c1996. 214 p.
95-041799   331.13/3/0973 20   0252022386
Affirmative action programs -- United States. Afro-Americans -- Employment. Public contracts -- United States.

HF5549.5.A34.E39 1999
Eisaguirre, Lynne, 1951-
Affirmative action: a reference handbook/ Lynne Eisaguirre. Santa Barbara, Calif.: ABC-CLIO, c1999. xii, 222 p.
99-035720   331.13/3/0973 21   0874368545
Affirmative action programs -- United States -- History. Affirmative action programs -- Law and legislation -- United States.

HF5549.5.A34.M38 1996
McWhirter, Darien A.
The end of affirmative action: where do we go from here?/ Darien A. McWhirter. New York: Carol Pub. Group, c1996. xix, 188 p.
95-050095   331.13/3/0973 20   1559723394
Affirmative action programs -- United States. Discrimination in employment -- United States. Reverse discrimination in employment -- United States.

HF5549.5.A34.S57 1996
Skrentny, John David.
The ironies of affirmative action: politics, culture, and justice in America/ John David Skrentny. Chicago: University of Chicago Press, 1996. xiii, 312 p.
95-036820   331.13/3/0973   0226761770
Affirmative action programs -- United States.

HF5549.5.A4.A4
Alcoholism and its treatment in industry/ Carl J. Schramm, editor. Baltimore: Johns Hopkins University Press, c1977. xii, 191 p.
77-004783   658.38/2   0801819733
Alcoholism and employment -- Addresses, essays, lectures. Alcoholism -- Treatment -- Addresses, essays, lectures.

HF5549.5.C35.G88 1993
Gutteridge, Thomas G.
Organizational career development: benchmarks for building a world-class workforce/ Thomas G. Gutteridge, Zandy B. Leibowitz, Jane E. Shore; foreword by Stephen K. Merman. San Francisco: Jossey-Bass, c1993. xxxi, 266 p.
93-000029   658.3/12   1555425267
Career development. Personnel management.

HF5549.5.C35.H36 1989
Handbook of career theory/ edited by Michael B. Arthur, Douglas T. Hall, Barbara S. Lawrence. Cambridge, England; Cambridge University Press, 1989. xix, 549 p.
88-028563   650.1/4   0521330157
Career development.

HF5549.5.C6.T49 1991
Thiederman, Sondra B.
Bridging cultural barriers for corporate success: how to manage the multicultural work force/ Sondra Thiederman. Lexington, Mass.: Lexington Books, c1991. xxiii, 256 p.
90-040664   658.3/041   0669219304
Communication in personnel management -- United States -- Cross-cultural studies. Personnel management -- United States -- Cross-cultural studies. Intercultural communication -- United States.

HF5549.5.D39.F47 1990
Fernandez, John P., 1941-
The politics and reality of family care in corporate America/ John P. Fernandez. Lexington, Mass.: Lexington Books, c1990. xxv, 276 p.
89-029170   331.25   0669215627
Employer-supported day care -- United States. Day care centers -- United States. Day care centers for the aged -- United States.

HF5549.5.D39.V36 1991
Vanderkolk, Barbara Schwarz.
The work and family revolution: how companies can keep employees happy and business profitable/ Barbara Schwarz Vanderkolk and Ardis Armstrong Young. New York: Facts on File, c1991. xii, 212 p.
91-010785   331.25   0816023646
Employer-supported day care -- United States. Employee fringe benefits -- United States. Parental leave -- United States.

HF5549.5.D7.M37 1999
Marijuana and the workplace: interpreting research on complex social issues/ edited by Charles R. Schwenk, and Susan L. Rhodes. Westport, Conn.: Quorum, 1999. viii, 197 p.
99-027819   331.25   1567202918
Drugs and employment -- United States. Drugs and employment -- Research -- United States. Employees -- Drug testing -- United States.

HF5549.5.D7.U53 1994
Under the influence?: drugs and the American work force/ Jacques Normand, Richard O. Lempert, and Charles P. O'Brien, editors. Washington, D.C.: National Academy Press, 1994. ix, 321 p.
93-044292   658.3/822   0309048850
Drugs and employment -- United States. Alcoholism and employment -- United States. Employee assistance programs -- United States.

HF5549.5.E43.B65 1996
Bologna, Jack.
Corporate crime investigation/ Jack Bologna and Paul Shaw. Boston: Butterworth-Heinemann, c1997. vi, 250 p.
96-042951   363.2/5968 20   0750696591
Commercial crimes -- United States. Employee theft -- Investigation -- United States. Employee crimes -- United States.

HF5549.5.E45.H86 1990
Human resource management in international firms: change, globalization, innovation/ edited by Paul Evans, Yves Doz, Andre Laurent. New York: St. Martin's Press, 1990. xvi, 258 p.
89-024340   658.3   0312041322
International business enterprises -- Personnel management.

HF5549.5.J63.B74 1992
Bruce, Willa M.
Balancing job satisfaction & performance: a guide for human resource professionals/ Willa M. Bruce and J. Walton Blackburn. Westport, Conn.: Quorum Books, 1992. ix, 245 p.
92-015989   658.3/14   0899306586
Job satisfaction. Quality of work life. Performance.

HF5549.5.J63.R62 1989
Roth, William F.
Work and rewards: redefining our work-life reality/ William F. Roth, Jr. New York: Praeger, 1989. x, 196 p.
88-025572   306/.36   0275931668
Job satisfaction. Job enrichment. Work and family.

HF5549.5.M3.H66 1991
Hopkins, Kevin R.
Help wanted: how companies can survive and thrive in the coming worker shortage/ Kevin R. Hopkins, Susan L. Nestleroth, Clint Bolick. New York: McGraw-Hill, c1991. xii, 244 p.
90-031479   658.3/01   007030341X
Manpower planning -- United States. Employment forecasting -- United States.

HF5549.5.M5.C383 1995
Carnevale, Anthony Patrick.
The American mosaic: an in-depth report on the future of diversity at work/ Anthony Patrick Carnevale, Susan Carol Stone. New York: McGraw-Hill, c1995. xi, 528 p.
95-012618   331.11/43   0070113777
Diversity in the workplace -- United States. Affirmative action programs -- United States. Manpower policy -- United States.

HF5549.5.M5.D567 1996
The diversity factor: capturing the competitive advantage of a changing workforce/ Elsie Y. Cross, Margaret Blackburn White, editors. Chicago: Irwin Professional Pub., c1996. xviii, 266 p.
96-003208   658.3/041 20   0786308583
Diversity in the workplace. Organizational change. Corporate culture.

HF5549.5.M5.H46 1994
Henderson, George, 1932-
Cultural diversity in the workplace: issues and strategies/ George Henderson. Westport, Conn.: Quorum Books, 1994. xii, 268 p.
94-002991   658.3/041   0899308880
Minorities -- Employment -- United States. Multiculturalism -- United States. Personnel management -- United States.

HF5549.5.M5.M365 1997
Managing the organizational melting pot: dilemmas of workplace diversity/ Pushkala Prasad ... [et al.], editors. Thousand Oaks, Calif.: Sage Publications, c1997. vii, 395 p.
96-035610   658.3/041 20   0803974108
Diversity in the workplace. Multiculturalism.

HF5549.5.M5.T39 1996
Tayeb, Monir H.
The management of a multicultural workforce/ Monir H. Tayeb. Chichester; Wiley, c1996. xiii, 222 p.
96-000933   658.3/041 20   0471958050
Diversity in the workplace. Personnel management. Intercultural communication.

HF5549.5.M63.M49 1997
Meyer, John P., 1950-
Commitment in the workplace: theory, research, and application/ John P. Meyer and Natalie J. Allen. Thousand Oaks, Calif.: Sage Publications, c1997. x, 150 p.
96-045780   658.3/14 20   0761901043
Employee motivation. Employee morale. Work ethic.

HF5549.5.M63.U45 1997
Ultimate rewards: what really motivates people to achieve/ edited with an introduction by Steven Kerr. [Boston, MA: Harvard Business School Press], c1997. xxi, 238 p.
97-019265   658.3/14 21   0875848087
Employee motivation. Awards. Incentive awards.

HF5549.5.R3.M863 1995
Murphy, Kevin R., 1952-
Understanding performance appraisal: social, organizational, and goal-based perspectives/ Kevin R. Murphy, Jeanette N. Cleveland. Thousand Oaks, Calif.: Sage Publications, c1995. xvii, 502 p.
94-023537   658.3/125   0803954743
Employees -- Rating of. Performance standards.

HF5549.5.S38.M67 1996
Morgan, Ronald B., 1952-
Staffing the new workplace: selecting and promoting for quality improvement/ Ronald B. Morgan and Jack E. Smith. Milwaukee, Wis.: ASQC Quality Press; c1996. xiv, 577 p.
95-004512   658.3/11 20   0873893611
Employee selection. Employees -- Recruiting. Manpower planning.

HF5549.5.T7.B2917 1997
Barron, John M.
On-the-job training/ John M. Barron, Mark C. Berger, Dan A. Black. Kalamazoo, Mich.: W.E. Upjohn Institute for Employment Research, 1997. viii, 207 p.
97-010295   658.3/12404   088099178X
Employees -- Training of -- Evaluation. Organizational learning.

HF5549.5.T7.G547 1994
Gordon, Edward E.
Futurework: the revolution reshaping American business/ Edward E. Gordon, Ronald R. Morgan, Judith A. Ponticell. Westport, Conn.: Praeger, 1994. xviii, 265 p.
93-039380   658.3/124   027594848X
Employees -- Training of -- United States. Employer-supported education -- United States.

HF5549.5.T7.M423 1994
Meister, Jeanne C.
Corporate quality universities: lessons in building a world-class work force/ Jeanne C. Meister. Alexandria, Va.: American Society for Training and Development;h c1994. xix, 255 p.
93-001268   658.3/124   1556237901
Employees -- Training of -- United States.

HF5549.5.T7.S83 2001
Sustaining distance training: integrating learning technologies into the fabric of the enterprise/ Zane L. Berge, editor. San Francisco: Jossey-Bass, c2001. xxxiv, 413 p.
00-009882   658.3/124 21   0787953318
Employees -- Training of. Distance education. Employees -- Training of -- United States -- Case studies.

HF5601 Business — Accounting. Bookkeeping — Societies. Serials

HF5601.A872.W4 1978
Webster, Norman Edward, 1869-
The American Association of Public Accountants: its first twenty years, 1886-1906/ compiled by Norman E. Webster. New York: Arno Press, 1978, c1954. vi, 402 p.
77-087292   657/.06/273   0405109199
Accountants -- United States -- Biography.

HF5605 Business — Accounting. Bookkeeping — History

HF5605.A23 1996
Accounting history from the Renaissance to the present: a remembrance of Luca Pacioli/ edited by T.A. Lee, A. Bishop, and R.H. Parker. New York: Garland Pub., 1996. xxiv, 290 p.
95-051120   657/.09   0815322712
Pacioli, Luca, -- d. ca. 1514. Accounting -- History. Accountants -- Biography. Information technology.

HF5605.H573 1996
The History of accounting: an international encyclopedia/ edited by Michael Chatfield, Richard Vangermeersch. New York: Garland, 1996. xxv, 649 p.
95-020710   657/.09   0815308094
Accounting -- History.

HF5605.L5 1981
Littleton, A. C. 1886-
Accounting evolution to 1900/ by A. C. Littleton. University, Ala.: University of Alabama Press, 1981. ix, 373 p.
80-022353   657/.09   0817300651
Accounting -- History.

HF5616 Business — Accounting. Bookkeeping — By region or country, A-Z

HF5616.E8.O43 1987
Oldham, K. Michael
Accounting systems and practice in Europe/ K. Michael Oldham. Aldershot, Hants, England; Gower Pub. Co., c1987. xiii, 333 p.
86-019570   657/.094   0566026120
Accounting -- Europe.

HF5616.U5.M54 1990
Miranti, Paul J.
Accountancy comes of age: the development of an American profession, 1886-1940/ Paul J. Miranti, Jr. Chapel Hill: University of North Carolina Press, c1990. xi, 275 p.
89-027925   657/.0973/09034   0807818933
Accounting -- United States -- History.

HF5616.U5.P72
Previts, Gary John.
A history of accounting in America: an historical interpretation of the cultural significance of accounting/ Gary John Previts, Barbara Dubis Merino. New York: Wiley, c1979. xii, 378 p.
79-000616   657/.0973   0471051721
Accounting -- United States -- History.

HF5616.U7.P752 1993
Allen, David Grayson, 1943-
Accounting for success: a history of Price Waterhouse in America, 1890-1990/ David Grayson Allen, Kathleen McDermott. Boston: Harvard Business School Press, c1993. xx, 373 p.
92-015492   338.7/61657/0973   087584328X
Accounting -- United States -- History.

HF5621 Business — Accounting. Bookkeeping — Dictionaries. Encyclopedias

HF5621.K6 1983
Kohler, Eric Louis, 1892-1976.
Kohler's Dictionary for accountants/ edited by W.W. Cooper, Yuji Ijiri. Englewood Cliffs, N.J.: Prentice-Hall, c1983. xi, 574 p.
82-013354   657/.03/21   0135166586
Accounting -- Dictionaries.

HF5626 Business — Accounting. Bookkeeping — Standards

HF5626.G67 1992
Gore, Pelham.
The FASB conceptual framework project, 1973-1985: an analysis/ Pelham Gore. Manchester, UK; Manchester University Press; c1992. viii, 189 p.
92-005508   657/.0218   071903633X
Accounting -- Standards.

HF5630 Business — Accounting. Bookkeeping — Study and teaching. Research

HF5630.A428 1994
Accounting education for the 21st century: the global challenges/ edited by Jane O. Burns and Belverd E. Needles, Jr. [Elmsford, N.Y.]: Pergamon in association with the International A 1994. iii, 499 p.
94-009175   657/.071/073   0080424058
Accounting -- Study and teaching. Comparative accounting. Curriculum planning.

HF5630.R53 1997
Riahi-Belkaoui, Ahmed, 1943-
Research perspectives in accounting/ Ahmed Riahi-Belkaoui. Westport, Conn.: Quorum, 1997. x, 156 p.
97-001697   657/.072   1567201008
Accounting -- Research -- Methodology.

HF5635 Business — Accounting. Bookkeeping — General works

HF5635.B4167
Belkaoui, Ahmed, 1943-
Accounting theory/ Ahmed Belkaoui. New York: Harcourt Brace Jovanovich, c1981. xii, 318 p.
80-082704   657/.01   0155004700
Accounting.

HF5657 Business — Accounting. Bookkeeping — General special

HF5657.C687 1990
Cottell, Philip G.
Accounting ethics: a practical guide for professionals/ Philip G. Cottell, Jr., and Terry M. Perlin. New York: Quorum Books, 1990. xii, 171 p.
89-024366   174/.9657   089930401X
Accountants -- Professional ethics.

HF5657.L394 1992
Lehman, Cheryl R.
Accounting's changing role in social conflict/ Cheryl R. Lehman. New York: Markus Wiener Pub.; c1992. xi, 174 p.
91-047864   657   155876030X
Accounting -- Social aspects. Social conflict.

HF5657.M34 1993
McCabe, R. K.
The accountant's guide to peer and quality review/ R.K. McCabe. Westport, Conn.: Quorum Books, 1993. xix, 226 p.
92-034946   657/.068/5   0899306853
Accounting -- Quality control. Peer review.

HF5657.R49 1995
Riahi-Belkaoui, Ahmed, 1943-
The cultural shaping of accounting/ Ahmed Riahi-Belkaoui. Westport, Conn.: Quorum Books, 1995. 157 p.
94-045274   657   0899309534
Accounting -- Social aspects. Comparative accounting. Cultural relativism.

HF5657.4 Business — Accounting. Bookkeeping — Managerial accounting

HF5657.4.D46 1994
Demski, Joel S.
Managerial uses of accounting information/ by Joel S. Demski. Boston, Mass.: Kluwer Academic Pub., c1994. x, 654 p.
93-034340   658.15/11   0792394062
Managerial accounting.

HF5657.4.M38 1992
McKinnon, Sharon M.
The information mosaic/ Sharon M. McKinnon, William J. Bruns, Jr.; foreword by William E. Langdon. Boston: Harvard Business School Press, c1992. x, 265 p.
91-046758   658.4/038   0875843174
Managerial accounting. Management information systems.

HF5657.4.R526 1992
Riahi-Belkaoui, Ahmed, 1943-
The new foundations of management accounting/ Ahmed Riahi-Belkaoui. New York: Quorum Books, 1992. xii, 175 p.
91-036667   658.15/11   0899307000
Managerial accounting.

HF5667-5668.25 Business — Accounting. Bookkeeping — Auditing

HF5667.S765 1983
Spronck, Lambert H., 1916-
Managing coordinated external and internal audits/ Lambert H. Spronck. New York: Wiley, c1983. ix, 254 p.
82-016150   657/.45   0471861405
Auditing. Auditing, Internal.

HF5668.25.M36 2000
Accountant's guide to fraud detection and control/ Howard R. Davia ... [et al.]. New York: Wiley, c2000. xv, 368 p.
99-088273   657/.458 21   0471353787
Auditing, Internal. Managerial accounting. Fraud.

HF5668.25.S93 1991
Swanson, G. A.
Internal auditing theory: a systems view/ G.A. Swanson and Hugh L. Marsh. New York: Quorum Books, 1991. xiii, 217 p.
90-026409   657/.458   089930608X
Internal auditing.

HF5679 Business — Accounting. Bookkeeping — Data processing

HF5679.N445 1994
Nelson, Glen.
The computer-ready CPA, selected readings/ compiled by Glen Nelson. New York: American Institute of Certified Public Accountan c1994. 1 v.
95-152288   657/.0285
Accounting -- Data processing. Business -- Data processing.

HF5681 Business — Accounting. Bookkeeping — Accounts and books

HF5681.B2.F64 1986
Foster, George, 1948-
Financial statement analysis/ George Foster. Englewood Cliffs, N.J.: Prentice-Hall, c1986. xii, 625 p.
85-028112   657/.3   0133163172
Financial statements.

HF5681.B2.P59 1993
Understanding the bottom line: finance for nonfinancial managers and business owners. Hawthorne, NJ: Career Press, c1993. 123 p.
93-017887   658.15   156414108X
Financial statements -- Handbooks, manuals, etc. Corporations -- Finance -- Handbooks, manuals, etc.

HF5681.B2.S3243 1993
Schilit, Howard Mark, 1952-
Financial shenanigans: how to detect accounting gimmicks and fraud in financial reports/ Howard M. Schilit. New York: McGraw-Hill, c1993. xv, 191 p.
93-006481   657/.3   0070561311
Financial statements, Misleading. Fraud.

HF5681.B2.S69 1997
Stittle, John.
Company financial reporting for business students: an introduction for non-accountants/ John Stittle. Malden, Mass.: Blackwell Business, 1997. v, 234 p.
97-010148   658.15/12   0631201661
Financial statements. Corporation reports. Financial statements -- United States.

HF5681.P8.M85 1996
Mulford, Charles W.
Financial warnings/ Charles W. Mulford, Eugene E. Comiskey. New York: John Wiley & Sons, c1996. xvii, 478 p.
95-048809   657/.48 20   0471120448
Corporate profits -- Accounting. Financial statements. Assets (Accounting)

HF5681.R25.I53
Industry norms and key business ratios. [New York]: Dun & Bradstreet Credit Services,
84-647330   338.0973
Ratio analysis -- Periodicals. Line of business reporting -- United States -- Statistics -- Periodicals. United States -- Industries -- Statistics -- Periodicals.

HF5686 Business — Accounting. Bookkeeping — By business or activity, A-Z

HF5686.C7.E34 1987
Edwards, J. S. S.
The economic analysis of accounting profitability/ Jeremy Edwards, John Kay, Colin Mayer. Oxford: Clarendon Press; 1987. 133 p.
87-005575   657/.95   0198772416
Corporations -- Accounting. Accounting -- Effect of inflation on. Deferred tax.

HF5686.C7.G568 1993
Gray, Rob.
Accounting for the environment/ Rob Gray with Jan Bebbington & Diane Walters; editorial adviser, Martin Houldin. New York, NY: M. Wiener Pub.; 1993. xix, 348 p.
93-006808   657   155876075X
Corporations -- Accounting -- Case studies. Industries -- Environmental aspects -- Accounting -- Case studies. Environmental protection -- Economic aspects -- Accounting -- Case studies.

HF5686.C8.B674 1991
Brimson, James A., 1947-
Activity accounting: an activity-based costing approach/ James A. Brimson. New York: J. Wiley, c1991. x, 214 p.
90-021506   657/.42   0471539856
Activity-based costing. Computer integrated manufacturing systems -- Evaluation.

HF5686.C8.B6743 1999
Brimson, James A., 1947-
Driving value using activity-based budgeting/ James A. Brimson, John Antos; with contributions by Jay Collins. New York: Wiley, c1999. xii, 276 p.
98-028231   658.15/4 21   0471086312
Activity-based costing. Managerial accounting. Cost accounting.

HF5686.C8.H48 1990
Heymann, H. G.
Opportunity cost in finance and accounting/ H.G. Heymann and Robert Bloom. New York: Quorum Books, 1990. xv, 199 p.
90-036025   658.15   0899304001
Cost accounting. Finance. Opportunity costs.

HF5686.C8.R457 1993
Riahi-Belkaoui, Ahmed, 1943-
Quality and control: an accounting perspective/ Ahmed Riahi-Belkaoui. Westport, Conn.: Quorum, 1993. x, 219 p.
92-034942   657/.42   0899307671
Quality control -- Costs -- Accounting. Quality of products -- Cost effectiveness.

HF5686.C8.W4476 1995
Wiersema, William H.
Activity-based management: today's powerful new tool for controlling costs and creating profits/ William H. Wiersema. New York: Amacom, c1995. xxi, 234 p.
94-023628   658.15/11   0814402518
Activity-based costing. Managerial accounting.

HF5686.I56.B443 1991
Riahi-Belkaoui, Ahmed, 1943-
Multinational financial accounting/ Ahmed R. Belkaoui. New York: Quorum Books, 1991. xi, 222 p.
91-008400   657/.96   0899306144
International business enterprises -- Accounting.

HF5686.I56.B445 1991
Belkaoui, Ahmed, 1943-
Multinational management accounting/ Ahmed Belkaoui. New York: Quorum Books, 1991. xii, 292 p.
90-008896   657/.96   0899305296
International business enterprises -- Accounting.

HF5686.I56.H36 1997
International accounting and finance handbook/ edited by Frederick D.S. Choi. New York: Wiley, c1997. 1 v.
96-053593   657/.96 21   0471152811
International business enterprises -- Accounting. International business enterprises -- Accounting -- Standards. Comparative accounting.

HF5686.M3.B68 1996
Bragg, Steven M.
Just-in-time accounting: how to decrease costs and increase efficiency/ Steven M. Bragg. New York: Wiley, c1996. xiii, 398 p.
96-011201   657/.068/5 20   0471137685
Just-in-time systems -- Accounting.

HF5686.N3.R8 1994
Rubenstein, Daniel Blake.
Environmental accounting for the sustainable corporation: strategies and techniques/ Daniel Blake Rubenstein. Westport, Conn.: Quorum Books, 1994. xiv, 207 p.
93-050066   651   089930866X
Natural resources -- Accounting. Sustainable development. Corporations -- Accounting.

HF5691 Business — Business mathematics. Commercial arithmetic — General works. By language

HF5691.M562 1967
Minrath, William R
Handbook of business mathematics [by] William R. Minrath. Princeton, N. J., Van Nostrand [1967] xii, 658 p.
67-018055   511.8
Business mathematics.

HF5694 Business — Business mathematics. Commercial arithmetic — Problems, exercises, etc.

HF5694.L36 1988
Lange, Walter Henry.
Mathematics for business and consumers/ Walter H. Lange, Temeleon G. Rousos, Robert D. Mason. Plano, Tex.: Business Publications, Inc., 1988. xvi, 550 p.
87-071676   510   0256059209
Business mathematics -- Problems, exercises, etc.

HF5695 Business — Business mathematics. Commercial arithmetic — General special

HF5695.S83 1993
Stutely, Richard, 1955-
The Economist guide to business numeracy/ [Richard Stutely]; The Economist Books. New York: Wiley, c1993. 237 p.
93-013998   650/.01/513   0471305553
Business mathematics. Numeracy. Problem solving -- Statistical methods.

HF5718 Business — Business communication — General works

HF5718.M83 1993
Munger, Susan H.
The international business communications desk reference/ Susan H. Munger. New York: AMACOM, c1993. iv, 252 p.
93-006944   651.7   0814477860
Business communication -- Handbooks, manuals, etc. Communication in international trade -- Handbooks, manuals, etc.

HF5718.W467 1996
Whalen, D. Joel.
I see what you mean: persuasive business communication/ D. Joel Whalen. Thousand Oaks, Calif.: Sage Publications, c1996. xix, 251 p.
95-032533   650.1/3 20   0761900306
Business communication.

HF5805 Business — Advertising — Directories of advertisers and advertising agents

HF5805.F69 1996
Fowles, Jib.
Advertising and popular culture/ Jib Fowles. Thousand Oaks, Calif.: Sage Publications, c1996. xviii, 278 p.
95-041754   659.1/042/0973 20   0803954824
Advertising -- Social aspects -- United States. Popular culture -- United States.

HF5810 Business — Advertising — Biography

HF5810.A2.A3 1994
The Ad men and women: a biographical dictionary of advertising/ edited by Edd Applegate. Westport, Conn.: Greenwood Press, 1994. xvii, 401 p.
93-028040   659.1/092/273   0313278016
Advertising -- United States -- Biography -- Dictionaries.

HF5813 Business — Advertising — By region or country, A-Z

HF5813.U6.A6177 1996
Advertising and culture: theoretical perspectives/ edited by Mary Cross. Westport, Conn.: Praeger, 1996. xiii, 136 p.
95-026518   659.1/042/0973   0275953513
Advertising -- United States. Popular culture -- United States. Communication in marketing -- United States.

HF5813.U6.A635 1999
The advertising business: operations, creativity, media planning, integrated communications/ edited by John Philip Jones. Thousand Oaks, Calif.: Sage Publications, c1999. 548 p.
98-040120   659.1 21   076191238X
Advertising -- United States. Advertising.

HF5813.U6.G64 1990
Goodrum, Charles A.
Advertising in America: the first 200 years/ Charles Goodrum and Helen Dalrymple. New York: Harry N. Abrams, 1990. 288 p.
90-000130   659.1/0973   0810911876
Advertising -- United States -- History.

HF5813.U6.J33 2000
Jackall, Robert.
Image makers: advertising, public relations, and the ethos of advocacy/ Robert Jackall and Janice M. Hirota. Chicago, IL: University of Chicago Press, c2000. xii, 333 p.
99-050270   659/.0973 21   0226389162
Advertising -- United States. Public relations -- United States.

HF5813.U6.K47 1994
Kern-Foxworth, Marilyn.
Aunt Jemima, Uncle Ben, and Rastus: Blacks in advertising, yesterday, today, and tomorrow/ Marilyn Kern-Foxworth; foreword by Alex Haley. Westport, Conn.: Greenwood Press, 1994. xxi, 205 p.
93-037507   659.1/089/96073   0313267987
Afro-Americans in advertising -- United States -- History.

HF5813.U6.M26 1985
Marchand, Roland.
Advertising the American dream: making way for modernity, 1920-1940/ Roland Marchand. Berkeley: University of California Press, c1985. xxii, 448 p.
84-028082   659.1/0973   0520052536
Advertising -- United States -- History.

HF5813.U6.N67 1990
Norris, James D.
Advertising and the transformation of American society, 1865-1920/ James D. Norris. New York: Greenwood Press, 1990. xviii, 206 p.
90-002760   659.1/042/097309034   0313268010
Advertising -- United States -- History -- 19th century. Advertising -- United States -- History -- 20th century.

HF5813.U6.T85 1997
Turow, Joseph.
Breaking up America: advertisers and the new media world/ Joseph Turow. Chicago: University of Chicago Press, 1997. xiv, 242 p.
96-009853   659.1/042   0226817490
Advertising -- Social aspects -- United States. Target marketing -- United States.

HF5821-5822 Business — Advertising — Theory. Relation to other subjects

HF5821.B53 1996
Bogart, Leo.
Strategy in advertising: matching media and messages to markets and motivations/ Leo Bogart. Lincolnwood, IL: NTC Business Books, c1996. xxi, 374 p.
95-011297   659.1 20   0844230146
Advertising.

HF5821.P64 1983
Pope, Daniel, 1946-
The making of modern advertising/ Daniel Pope. New York: Basic Books, c1983. x, 340 p.
82-072404   338.4/76591   0465043259
Advertising.

HF5821.W46 1991
Wernick, Andrew.
Promotional culture: advertising, ideology, and symbolic expression/ Andrew Wernick. London; Sage Publications, 1991. ix, 208 p.
91-050676   659.1/042   0803983905
Advertising -- Social aspects. Symbolism in advertising. Imagery (Psychology)

HF5822.M33 1996
Maddock, Richard C.
Marketing to the mind: right brain strategies for advertising and marketing/ Richard C. Maddock and Richard L. Fulton. Westport, Conn.: Quorum Books, 1996. xvii, 280 p.
95-050743   659.1/01/9   1567200311
Advertising -- Psychological aspects. Motivation research (Marketing) Marketing.

HF5822.N66 1988
Nonverbal communication in advertising/ edited by Sidney Hecker, David W. Stewart. Lexington, Mass.: Lexington Books, c1988. viii, 296 p.
87-017143   659.1/01/9   0669141720
Advertising -- Psychological aspects. Body language.

HF5822.P78 1985
Psychological processes and advertising effects: theory, research, and applications/ edited by Linda F. Alwitt and Andrew A. Mitchell. Hillsdale, N.J.: L. Erlbaum Associates, 1985. ix, 305 p.
84-028773   659.1/01/9   0898595150
Advertising -- Psychological aspects.

HF5823 Business — Advertising — General works

HF5823.B7157 1994
Brand power/ edited by Paul Stobart. Washington Square, N.Y.: New York University Press, c1994. xvi, 255 p.
94-022778   658.8/27   0814779654
Advertising -- Brand name products. Brand name products -- Marketing.

HF5823.H58 1998
How advertising works: the role of research/ edited by John Philip Jones. Thousand Oaks, Calif.: Sage Publications, c1998. 358 p.
98-008871   659.1 21   0761912401
Advertising. Advertising -- Research.

HF5823.K363 1999
Kilbourne, Jean.
Deadly persuasion: why women and girls must fight the addictive power of advertising/ Jean Kilbourne. New York, NY: Free Press, c1999. 366 p.
99-038496   658.8/34/082 21   0684865998
Women in advertising. Women consumers.

HF5823.M93 1998
Myers, Greg, 1954-
Ad worlds: brands, media, audiences/ Greg Myers. New York: Arnold, 1998.
98-020774   659.1   0340700068
Advertising.

HF5823.P3528 1991
Patti, Charles H.
Business-to-business advertising: a marketing management approach/ Charles H. Patti, Steven W. Hartley, and Susan L. Kennedy. Lincolnwood, Ill., USA: NTC Business Books, c1991. xii, 286 p.
90-047970   659.1/315   0844234710
Advertising, Industrial. Industrial marketing -- Management.

HF5827 Business — Advertising — General special

HF5827.B37 1988
Barthel, Diane L., 1949-
Putting on appearances: gender and advertising/ Diane Barthel. Philadelphia: Temple University Press, 1988. ix, 219 p.
87-020010   659.1/042   0877225281
Sex role in advertising -- United States. Visual communication -- United States -- Psychological aspects. Imagery (Psychology)

HF5837-5843 Business — Advertising — Methods

HF5837.E53 2000
Encyclopedia of major marketing campaigns/ Thomas Riggs, editor. Detroit: Gale Group, 2000. xxii, 2063 p.
99-031858   659.1/0973   078763042X
Advertising campaigns -- United States -- History -- 20th century.

HF5843.F73 1991
Fraser, James Howard, 1934-
The American billboard: 100 years/ by James Fraser. New York: H.N. Abrams, 1991. 192 p.
91-008450   659.13/42   0810931168
Billboards -- United States -- History.

HF6161 Business — Advertising — By products, profession, service, or industry, A-Z

HF6161.B4.W67 1996
Woodside, Arch G.
Measuring the effectiveness of image and linkage advertising: the nitty-gritty of maxi-marketing/ Arch G. Woodside. Westport, Conn.: Quorum Books, 1996. xxiv, 251 p.
95-050739   658.8/343   0899309844
Advertising -- Brand name products. Brand choice. Corporate image.

HF6161.C33.P43 1998
Pecora, Norma Odom.
The business of children's entertainment/ Norma Odom Pecora. New York: Guilford Press, c1998. vii, 190 p.
97-040876   658.8/34/083 21   1572302801
Advertising -- Children's paraphernalia. Child consumers. Television advertising and children.

HG Finance

HG11 Societies. Serials — Europe — Great Britain

HG11.E22.E2 1944
The Economist, 1843-1943, a centenary volume. [London] Oxford University Press [1944] 178 p.
45-001431　330.5

HG151 Dictionaries. Encyclopedias

HG151.C54 1999
Clark, John Owen Edward.
International dictionary of banking and finance/ John Clark. Chicago: Glenlake Pub. Co.: c1999. 352 p.
99-482832　332/.03 21　1579581609
Finance -- Dictionaries. Banks and banking -- Dictionaries. International finance -- Dictionaries.

HG151.N48 1992
The new Palgrave dictionary of money & finance/ edited by Peter Newman, Murray Milgate, John Eatwell. London: Macmillan Press Ltd.; 1992. 3 v.
92-028016　332/.03　156159041X
Finance -- Dictionaries.

HG172 Biography

HG172.A2
Train, John.
Money masters of our time/ John Train. New York, N.Y.: HarperBusiness, c2000. xi, 388 p.
00-712870　332.6/092/2 21　0887307914
Capitalists and financiers -- United States -- Biography. Investments -- United States.

HG172.B84.L69 1995
Lowenstein, Roger.
Buffett: the making of an American capitalist/ Roger Lowenstein. New York: Random House, c1995. xvii, 473 p.
95-008494　332.6/092　067941584X
Buffett, Warren. Capitalists and financiers -- United States -- Biography. Stockbrokers -- United States -- Biography.

HG172.S63.S58 1996
Slater, Robert, 1943-
Soros: the life, times & trading secrets of the world's greatest investor/ Robert Slater. Burr Ridge, Ill.: Irwin Professional Pub., c1996. xii, 269 p.
95-006557　332.6/092 B 20　0786303611
Soros, George. Capitalists and financiers -- Biography. Investments.

HG173 General works — English

HG173.C665 1996
Coleman, William D. 1950-
Financial services, globalization and domestic policy change/ William D. Coleman. New York: St. Martin's Press, 1996. xv, 297 p.
96-005595　332.1　0312129793
Financial services industry. Financial services industry -- Government policy. Banks and banking, Central.

HG173.F76 1990
Frontiers of finance: the Batterymarch Fellowship papers/ edited by Deborah H. Miller and Stewart C. Myers. Cambridge, Mass., USA: Blackwell, 1990. xix, 747 p.
89-018620　332　1557860858
Finance.

HG173.H33 1987
Handbook of financial markets and institutions/ edited by Edward I. Altman; associate editor Mary Jane McKinney. New York: Wiley, c1987. 1197 p.
86-011125　658.1/5　0471819549
Finance -- Handbooks, manuals, etc. Finance -- United States -- Handbooks, manuals, etc. Corporations -- Finance -- Handbooks, manuals, etc.

HG179 Personal finance

HG179.R76 1997
Rubin, Rose M.
Expenditures of older Americans/ Rose M. Rubin and Michael L. Nieswiadomy. Westport, Conn.: Praeger, 1997. xvi, 153 p.
97-019755　332.024/0565　0275958744
Aged -- United States -- Finance, Personal. Retirement income -- United States. Aged -- United States -- Economic conditions.

HG181 By region or country — United States — General works

HG181.C6515 1998
Coggins, Bruce, 1958-
Does financial deregulation work?: a critique of free market approaches/ Bruce Coggins. Cheltenham, UK; Edward Elgar, c1998. viii, 230 p.
97-030627　332.1 21　1858986389
Financial services industry -- Deregulation -- United States.

HG181.G358 1989
Gart, Alan.
An analysis of the new financial institutions: changing technologies, financial structures, distribution systems, and deregulation/ Alan Gart. New York: Quorum Books, 1989. xx, 376 p.
88-004933　332.1/0973　0899302718
Financial services industry -- United States. Financial institutions -- United States. Financial services industry.

HG181.G367 1988
Gart, Alan.
Handbook of the money and capital markets/ Alan Gart. New York: Quorum Books, 1988. xx, 306 p.
87-024938　332.63/2/0973　089930270X
Money market -- United States. Capital market -- United States. Financial institutions -- United States.

HG181.S792 1996
Stability in the financial system/ edited by Dimitri B. Papadimitriou. London: MacMillan Press Ltd; 1996. xviii, 441 p.
96-010557　332.1/0973　0312159358
Finance -- United States. Financial institutions -- United States. Banks and banking -- United States.

HG181.T7 1993
Transforming the U.S. financial system: equity and efficiency for the 21st century/ Gary A. Dymski, Gerald Epstein, Robert Pollin, editors. Armonk, N.Y.: M.E. Sharpe, c1993. xi, 364 p.
93-023796　332.1/0973　1563242680
Finance -- United States. Monetary policy -- United States.

HG185 By region or country — Other regions or countries — America

HG185.M6.S27 1988
Saragoza, Alex.
The Monterrey elite and the Mexican State, 1880-1940/ by Alex M. Saragoza. Austin: University of Texas Press, 1988. x, 258 p.
87-023779　305.5/234/097213　0292711131
Garza-Sada family. Capitalism -- Mexico -- Monterrey -- History. Elite (Social sciences) -- Mexico -- Monterrey -- History. Capitalists and financiers -- Mexico -- Monterrey -- History. Monterrey (Mexico) -- Economic conditions.

HG186 By region or country — Other regions or countries — Europe

HG186.E8.S76 1997
Story, Jonathan.
Political economy of financial integration in Europe: the battle of the systems/ Jonathan Story and Ingo Walter. Cambridge, Mass.: MIT Press, c1997. xiv, 337 p.
97-072739　332.1/094 21　0262193965
Financial services industry -- European Union countries. European Union countries -- Economic integration.

HG186.E82.D48 1994
The development and reform of financial systems in Central and Eastern Europe/ edited by John P. Bonin and Istvan P. Szekely. Aldershot, Hants, England; E. Elgar, c1994. xi, 364 p.
94-025519　332.1/0947　1858980240
Financial institutions -- Europe, Eastern. Financial institutions -- Europe, Central. Europe, Eastern -- Economic policy -- 1989- Europe, Central -- Economic policy. Europe, Eastern -- Economic conditions -- 1989-

HG186.G7.C36 1990
Capitalism in a mature economy: financial institutions, capital exports and British industry, 1870-1939/ edited by J.J. Van Helten and Y. Cassis. Aldershot, Hants, England: E. Elgar; 1990. xi, 226 p.
90-003535　332/.0941　1852783184
Finance -- Great Britain -- History. Investments, British -- History. Capital -- Great Britain -- History.

HG187 By region or country — Other regions or countries — Asia

HG187.C6.D56 1994
Dipchand, Cecil R.
The Chinese financial system/ Cecil R. Dipchand, Zhang Yichun, and Ma Mingjia. Westport, Conn.: Greenwood Press, 1994. viii, 223 p.
93-050539   332.1/0951   0313292825
Financial institutions -- China.

HG187.H85.F74 1991
Freris, Andrew F., 1945-
The financial markets of Hong Kong/ Andrew F. Freris. London; Routledge, 1991. xvi, 264 p.
90-035380   332.1/095125   0415020794
Financial institutions -- Hong Kong.

HG187.I5.C65 1996
Cole, David Chamberlin, 1928-
Building a modern financial system: the Indonesian experience/ David C. Cole, Betty F. Slade. New York: Cambridge University Press, 1996. xxvii, 379 p.
95-051786   332.1/09598   0521570921
Finance -- Indonesia. Banks and banking -- Indonesia -- State supervision. Financial services industry -- Indonesia.

HG205 Money — Congresses — Individual congresses

HG205 1944.D67 1978
Dormael, Armand van, 1916-
Bretton Woods: birth of a monetary system/ Armand van Dormael. New York: Holmes & Meier Publishers, c1978. xi, 322 p.
77-010651   332.4/5/09   0841903263
International finance -- History.

HG205. 1984
Exchange rate theory and practice/ edited by John F. O. Bilson and Richard C. Marston. Chicago: University of Chicago Press, 1984. ix, 528 p.
84-002441   332.4/5   0226050963
Foreign exchange -- Congresses.

HG216 Money — Dictionaries. Encyclopedias

HG216.A43 1999
Allen, Larry.
Encyclopedia of money/ Larry Allen. Santa Barbara, CA: ABC-CLIO, c1999. xiii, 328 p.
99-038048   332.4/03 21   1576070379
Money -- Encyclopedias.

HG220 Money — Theory. Method. Relation to other subjects

HG220.A2.G68 1992
Green, Roy, 1951-
Classical theories of money, output and inflation: a study in historical economics/ Roy Green. New York: St. Martin's Press, 1992. xii, 271 p.
92-020308   332.4   0312085567
Money. Inflation (Finance) Credit.

HG220.A2.M583 1998
Money and the nation state: the financial revolution, government, and the world monetary system/ edited by Kevin Dowd & Richard H. Timberlake, Jr.; foreword by Merton H. Miller. New Brunswick, NJ: Transaction Publishers, c1998. viii, 453 p.
97-040091   332.4 21   1560009306
Money -- History. International finance -- History. National state.

HG220.E85.V36 1997
Van Dormael, Armand, 1916-
The power of money/ Armand Van Dormael. Washington, Square, N.Y.: New York University Press, 1997. vii, 184 p.
96-035577   332.4/9   0814787916
Economic history -- 20th century. Money -- Europe -- History -- 20th century. Money -- United States -- History -- 20th century.

HG221 Money — General works

HG221.E254 1994
The economics of F.A. Hayek. Aldershot, Hants, England; E. Elgar, c1994. 2 v.
93-042575   330.1   1852785454
Hayek, Friedrich A. von -- (Friedrich August), -- 1899- Business cycles. Capitalism. Socialism.

HG221.H346 1984
Hayek, Friedrich A. von 1899-
Money, capital, and fluctuations: early essays/ F.A. Hayek; edited by Roy McCloughry. Chicago, IL: University of Chicago Press; 1984. xi, 196 p.
84-000227   332.4   0226320928
Money. Capital. Business cycles.

HG221.H633 1989
Hicks, John Richard, 1904-
A market theory of money/ John Hicks. Oxford: Clarendon Press; 1989. viii, 142 p.
89-003364   332.4/01   0198287240
Money.

HG221.J46 1964
Jevons, William Stanley, 1835-1882.
Investigations in currency & finance [by] W. Stanley Jevons. New York, A.M. Kelley, bookseller, 1964. xliv, 428 p.
64-022238   332.41
Money. Finance. Prices.

HG221.J663
Johnson, Harry G. 1923-1977.
Essays in monetary economics [by] Harry G. Johnson. London, Allen & Unwin, 1967. 332 p.
67-088230   332.4/01
Money. Monetary policy. Fiscal policy.

HG221.K45
Keynes, John Maynard, 1883-1946.
A treatise on money, by John Maynard Keynes. New York, Harcourt, Brace [1930] 2 v.
31-000311   332.4
Money. Banks and banking.

HG221.L243 1990
Laidler, David E. W.
Taking money seriously and other essays/ David Laidler. Cambridge, Mass.: MIT Press, c1990. xiv, 226 p.
89-013609   332.4   0262121484
Money. Monetary policy.

HG221.M655
Milton Friedman's monetary framework: a debate with his critics/ edited by Robert J. Gordon; Milton Friedman ... [et al.]. Chicago: University of Chicago Press, 1974. xii, 192 p.
73-092599   332.4/01   0226264076
Friedman, Milton, -- 1912- -- Theoretical framework for monetary analysis. Quantity theory of money. Money.

HG221.N66
Niehans, Jurg.
The theory of money/ Jurg Niehans. Baltimore: Johns Hopkins University Press, c1978. xi, 312 p.
77-017247   332.4/01   0801820553
Money.

HG221.V5415 1991
Visser, H. 1943-
Modern monetary theory: a critical survey of recent developments/ Hans Visser. Aldershot, Hants, England; Elgar, c1991. x, 199 p.
91-022155   332.4   1852780924
Money.

HG226.3 Money — Money supply

HG226.3.D56 1991
Dimitrijevic, Dimitrije.
The money supply process: a comparative analysis/ Dimtrije Dimitrijevic and George Macesich. New York: Praeger, 1991. xii, 181 p.
90-039155   332.4/14   0275935973
Money supply. Money supply -- Mathematical models.

HG226.3.G72 1987
Graziano, Loretta.
Interpreting the money supply: human and institutional factors/ Loretta Graziano. New York: Quorum Books, 1987. xiii, 245 p.
87-002539   332.4/14   0899301517
Money supply.

HG229 Money — Money and prices. Inflation. Deflation. Purchasing power — General works

HG229.B379 1992
Beckerman, Paul Ely.
The economics of high inflation/ Paul Beckerman. New York: St. Martin's Press, 1992. viii, 228 p.
91-021534   332.4/1   0312055552
Inflation (Finance) Economic stabilization.

HG229.B595 1996
Bootle, R. P.
The death of inflation: surviving and thriving in the zero era/ Roger Bootle. London; Nicholas Brealey Pub., 1996.
96-007874   332.4/1   1857881451
Inflation (Finance) Cost and standard of living. Interest rates.

HG229.F624
Flemming, John Stanton, 1941-
Inflation/ by J. S. Flemming. London: Oxford University Press, 1976. 136 p.
76-377976   332.4/1   0198770855
Inflation (Finance) Inflation (Finance) -- Great Britain.

HG229.H3 1967
Hayek, Friedrich A. von 1899-
Prices and production, by Friedrich A. Hayek. New York, A.M. Kelley [1967] xiv, 162 p.
67-019586 338.52/2
Money. Prices. Currency question.

HG229.H49 1995
Heymann, Daniel.
High inflation: the Arne Ryde memorial lectures/ Daniel Heymann and Axel Leijonhufvud. Oxford: Clarendon Press; 1995. xii, 233 p.
94-048638 332.4/1 0198288441
Inflation (Finance) Economic stabilization. Monetary policy.

HG229.I4512 1982
Inflation, causes and effects/ edited by Robert E. Hall. Chicago: University of Chicago Press, c1982. ix, 290 p.
82-010932 332.4/1 0226313239
Inflation (Finance) Inflation (Finance) -- United States.

HG229.L2
Laidler, David E. W.
Essays on money and inflation/ D. E. W. Laidler. Chicago: University of Chicago Press, 1975. xiii, 246 p.
75-022170 332.4/1 0226467937
Inflation (Finance) Monetary policy -- Mathematical models.

HG229.5 Money — Money and prices. Inflation. Deflation. Purchasing power — Indexation

HG229.5.W43 1988
Weaver, R. Kent, 1953-
Automatic government: the politics of indexation/ R. Kent Weaver. Washington, D.C.: Brookings Institution, c1988. xii, 276 p.
88-010562 331.2/15 0815792581
Indexation (Economics) -- Government policy -- United States. Indexation (Economics) -- United States.

HG230.3 Money — Monetary policy — General works

HG230.3.B37 1990
Barro, Robert J.
Macroeconomic policy/ Robert J. Barro. Cambridge, Mass.: Harvard University Press, 1990. 379 p.
89-071679 339.5 0674540808
Monetary policy. Fiscal policy. Economic policy.

HG230.3.L34 1982
Laidler, David E. W.
Monetarist perspectives/ David Laidler. Cambridge, Mass.: Harvard University Press, 1982. xii, 218 p.
82-015406 332.4/1 0674582403
Monetary policy. Macroeconomics.

HG230.3.M32 1992
Macesich, George, 1927-
Monetary policy and politics: rules versus discretion/ George Macesich. Westport, Conn.: Praeger, 1992. 161 p.
92-003379 332.4/6 0275943356
Monetary policy.

HG230.3.M6375 1993
Monetary policy in developed economies/ edited by Michele U. Fratianni and Dominick Salvatore. Westport, Conn.: Greenwood Press, 1993. xiv, 575 p.
92-004886 332.4/91722 031326869X
Monetary policy.

HG231 Money — History — General works

HG231.M585 1997
Money: a history/ edited by Jonathan Williams, with Joe Cribb and Elizabeth Errington. New York: St. Martin's Press, 1997. 256 p.
96-035188 332.4/09 0312166028
Money -- History.

HG237 Money — History — Ancient

HG237.C65 1992
Cohen, Edward E.
Athenian economy and society: a banking perspective/ Edward E. Cohen. Princeton, N.J.: Princeton University Press, c1992. xviii, 288 p.
92-005685 332.1/0938/5 0691036098
Banks and banking -- Greece -- Athens -- History. Greece -- History -- Spartan and Theban Supremacies, 404-362 B.C.

HG243 Money — History — Medieval

HG243.C5 1967
Cipolla, Carlo M.
Money, prices, and civilization in the Mediterranean world, fifth to seventhteenth century, by Carlo M. Cipolla. New York, Gordian Press, 1967. x, 75 p.
67-018440 332.4/9/4
Money -- Europe -- History. Prices -- Europe -- History.

HG255 Money — History — 20th century

HG255.S2885 1995
Schild, Georg.
Bretton Woods and Dumbarton Oaks: American economic and political postwar planning in the summer of 1944/ Georg Schild. New York: St. Martin's Press, 1995. xiii, 254 p.
94-034125 337.73 0312122160
International finance -- History -- 20th century. World War, 1939-1945 -- Diplomatic history. Reconstruction (1939-1951)

HG297 Money — Precious metals. Bullion — Gold

HG297.O35 1996
Officer, Lawrence H.
Between the dollar-sterling gold points: exchange rates, parity, and market behavior/ Lawrence H. Officer. Cambridge [England]; Cambridge University Press, 1996. xxi, 342 p.
95-034575 332.4/56/0941 052145462X
Gold standard -- History. Foreign exchange rates -- United States -- History. Foreign exchange rates -- Great Britain -- History.

HG307 Money — Precious metals. Bullion — Silver

HG307.E5.J37
Jastram, Roy W., 1915-
Silver: the restless metal/ Roy W. Jastram. New York: Wiley, c1981. xvii, 224 p.
80-028361 332.4/223/09 0471039128
Silver -- England -- History. Silver -- United States -- History.

HG501-604 Money — By region or country — United States

HG501.B75 1989
Brunner, Karl, 1916-
Monetary economics/ Karl Brunner and Allan H. Meltzer. Oxford, UK; B. Blackwell, c1989 388 p.
88-024341 332.4/973 0631163352
Money -- United States. Monetary policy -- United States. Fiscal policy -- United States.

HG501.D44 1987
Degen, Robert A.
The American monetary system: a concise survey of its evolution since 1896/ Robert A. Degen. Lexington, Mass.: Lexington Books, c1987. x, 242 p.
86-046363 332.4/973 0669158275
Money -- United States -- History. Monetary policy -- United States -- History. Banks and banking -- United States -- History.

HG501.H53 1993
Hixson, William F.
Triumph of the bankers: money and banking in the eighteenth and nineteenth centuries/ William F. Hixson. Westport, Conn.: Praeger, 1993. x, 193 p.
93-000296 332.1/0973 027594607X
Money supply -- United States -- History -- 18th century. Money supply -- Great Britain -- History -- 18th century. Money supply -- United States -- History -- 19th century.

HG501.T59 1993
Timberlake, Richard H.
Monetary policy in the United States: an intellectual and institutional history/ Richard H. Timberlake. Chicago: University of Chicago Press, c1993. xxv, 502 p.
92-044937 332.4/973 0226803821
Monetary policy -- United States -- History.

HG538.F866
Friedman, Milton, 1912-
The optimum quantity of money, and other essays. Chicago, Aldine Pub. Co. [1969] vi, 296 p.
68-008148 332.4/9/73
Money supply -- United States. Monetary policy -- United States. Money.

HG538.O5
Okun, Arthur M.
Inflation: the problems it creates and the policies it requires [by] Arthur M. Okun, Henry M. Fowler [and] Milton Gilbert. New York, New York University Press, 1970. xxviii, 232 p.
75-114759 332.4/14
Inflation (Finance) -- United States. Fiscal policy -- United States. International finance.

HG539.M44 1997
Mehrling, Perry.
The money interest and the public interest: American monetary thought, 1920-1970/ Perry G. Mehrling. Cambridge, Mass.: Harvard University Press, 1997. xiv, 283 p.
97-017051   332.4/973   0674584309
Monetary policy -- United States -- History.

HG540.M39 1981
Mayer, Thomas, 1927-
Money, banking, and the economy/ Thomas Mayer, James S. Duesenberry, Robert Z. Aliber. New York: Norton, c1981. xii, 755 p.
80-029109   332.1/0973   0393951219
Money -- United States. Banks and banking -- United States. Monetary policy -- United States.

HG540.M655 1989
Monetary policy for a volatile global economy/ edited by William S. Haraf and Thomas D. Willett. Washington, D.C.: AEI Press; c1990. xiii, 198 p.
89-018486   332.4/973   0844737135
Monetary policy -- United States. International finance.

HG540.S65 1996
Solomon, Lewis D.
Rethinking our centralized monetary system: the case for a system of local currencies/ Lewis D. Solomon; foreword by Bob Swann. Westport, Conn.: Praeger, 1996. x, 167 p.
95-034441   332.4/973   0275953769
Money -- United States. Currency question -- United States. Banks and banking -- United States.

HG555.W44
Weinstein, Allen.
Prelude to Populism: origins of the silver issue, 1867-1878.   New Haven, Yale University Press, 1970. x, 433 p.
70-099846   332.4/22   0300012292
Silver question.

HG604.M68 1960
Mitchell, Wesley Clair, 1874-1948.
A history of the greenbacks: with special reference to the economic consequences of their issue, 1862-65/ by Wesley Clair Mitchell. Chicago: University of Chicago Press, 1960, c1903. 577 p.
60-051189   332.53
Greenbacks -- History.

HG660.5-1282 Money —
By region or country —
Other regions or countries

HG660.5.I54 1988
Inflation stabilization: the experience of Israel, Argentina, Brazil, Bolivia, and Mexico/ edited by Michael Bruno ... [et al.]. Cambridge, Mass.: MIT Press, c1988. xi, 419 p.
88-002768   332.4/1/098   0262022796
Inflation (Finance) -- Latin America -- Case studies -- Congresses. Inflation (Finance) -- Israel -- Congresses. Latin America -- Economic policy -- Case studies -- Congresses. Israel -- Economic policy -- Congresses.

HG835.P4413 1987
Pereira, Luiz Carlos Bresser.
The theory of inertial inflation: the foundation of economic reform in Brazil & Argentina/ Luiz Bresser Pereira, Yoshiaki Nakano; foreword by Rudiger Dornbusch; [translated from the Portuguese by Colleen Reeks]. Boulder, Colo.: L. Rienner Publishers, 1987. xiii, 206 p.
86-029832   332.4/1/0981   1555870074
Inflation (Finance) -- Brazil. Monetary policy -- Brazil. Monetary policy -- Argentina.

HG925.C655 1994
Collignon, Stefan, 1951-
Europe's monetary future/ Stefan Collignon with Peter Bofinger, Christopher Johnson and Bertrand de Maigret. Rutherford: Fairleigh Dickinson University Press; 1994. xxx, 238 p.
94-012181   332.4/566/094   0838636063
Monetary policy -- European Union countries.

HG925.V3613 1997
Vanthoor, W. F. V.
European Monetary Union since 1848/ Wim F.V. Vanthoor. Brookfield, VT: Edward Elgar Pub. Co., 1997. xvi, 207 p.
96-031270   332.4/94   1858984610
Monetary policy -- Europe -- History.   Europe -- Economic integration.

HG930.5.U47 1997
Ungerer, Horst.
A concise history of European monetary integration: from EPU to EMU/ Horst Ungerer. Westport, Conn.: Quorum Books, 1997. xii, 338 p.
96-050079   332.4/94   089930981X
Monetary policy -- European Economic Community countries. Monetary policy -- European Union countries. Money -- European Economic Community countries.

HG939.C29 1985
Capie, Forrest.
A monetary history of the United Kingdom, 1870-1982/ Forrest Capie, Alan Webber. London; Allen & Unwin, [1985-] v. 1.
84-020431   332.4/941   004332097X
Money -- Great Britain -- History. Money -- Great Britain -- Statistics -- History.

HG939.5.D68 1988
Dow, J. C. R.
A critique of monetary policy: theory and British experience/ J.C.R. Dow and I.D. Saville. Oxford: Clarendon Press; 1988. x, 259 p.
87-031540   332.4/941   019828599X
Monetary policy -- Great Britain. Interest rates -- Government policy -- Great Britain. Monetary policy.

HG939.5.H648 1993
Howson, Susan, 1945-
British monetary policy, 1945-51/ Susan Howson. Oxford: Clarendon Press; 1993. xiii, 369 p.
93-018831   332.4/941   0198286562
Monetary policy -- Great Britain -- History.

HG939.5.H65
Howson, Susan, 1945-
Domestic monetary management in Britain, 1919-38/ Susan Howson. Cambridge; Cambridge University Press, 1975. ix, 213 p.
75-021032   332.4/941   0521210593
Monetary policy -- Great Britain.

HG950.I8.S8 1935
Swift, Jonathan, 1667-1745.
The Drapier's letters to the people of Ireland against receiving Wood's halfpence, by Jonathan Swift; edited by Herbert Davis. Oxford, Clarendon Press, 1965. 400 p.
35-015568   332.409415
Wood, William, -- 1671-1730.   Money -- Ireland -- History. Coinage -- Ireland.

HG976.M49 1984
Miskimin, Harry A.
Money and power in fifteenth-century France/ Harry A. Miskimin. New Haven: Yale University Press, c1984. x, 303 p.
83-021754   332.4/944   0300031327
Money -- France -- History. Monetary policy -- France -- History. Fiscal policy -- France -- History. France -- Politics and government -- 1328-1589.

HG1040.V46.M84 1997
Mueller, Reinhold C.
The Venetian money market: banks, panics, and the public debt, 1200-1500/ Reinhold C. Mueller. Baltimore: John Hopkins University Press, 1997. xxvi, 711 p.
96-036921   332.1/0945/31   0801854377
Money -- Italy -- Venice -- History. Banks and banking -- Italy -- Venice -- History. Money market -- Italy -- Venice -- History.

HG1210.L46 1993
Leiderman, Leonardo, 1951-
Inflation and disinflation: the Israeli experiment/ Leonardo Leiderman. Chicago: University of Chicago Press, 1993. xv, 333 p.
92-037436   332.4/1/095694   0226471101
Inflation (Finance) -- Israel. Inflation (Finance) -- Israel -- Econometric models. Fiscal policy -- Israel.

HG1270.5.E47 1991
Emery, Robert F. 1927-
The money markets of developing East Asia/ Robert F. Emery. New York: Praeger, 1991. xvii, 340 p.
90-023784   332/.0412/095   0275934101
Money market -- East Asia.

HG1282.V66 1996
Von Glahn, Richard.
Fountain of fortune: money and monetary policy in China, 1000-1700/ Richard von Glahn. Berkeley, Calif.: University of California Press, c1996. xii, 338 p.
96-005579   332.4/951 20   0520204085
Money -- China -- History. Monetary policy -- China -- History.

HG1496 Money —
By region or country —
Developing countries

HG1496.C56
Cline, William R.
World inflation and the developing countries/ William R. Cline and associates; William R. Cline ... [et al.]. Washington, D.C.: Brookings Institution, c1981. xiv, 266 p.
80-025426   332.4/1/091724   0815714688
Inflation (Finance) -- Developing countries.

HG1552 Banking — History — Biography

HG1552.A1.F46 1998
Ferguson, Niall, 1947-
The house of Rothschild: money's prophets 1798-1848/ by Niall Ferguson. New York: Viking, 1998.
98-044706   332.1/092/24   0670857688
Rothschild family.   Bankers -- Europe -- Biography. Banks and banking -- Europe -- History -- 19th century. Jews -- Europe -- Biography.

HG1552.R8.W56 1988
Wilson, Derek A.
Rothschild: the wealth and power of a dynasty/ Derek Wilson. New York: Scribner, 1988. ix, 490 p.
88-019736   332.1/092/2   0684190184
Rothschild family.   Bankers -- Europe -- Biography. Businesspeople -- Europe -- Biography. Europe -- Politics and government -- 1789-1900.

HG1586 Banking — Theory. Method. Relations to other subjects

HG1586.S38 1988
Selgin, George A., 1957-
The theory of free banking: money supply under competitive note issue/ George A. Selgin. [Washington, D.C.]: Cato Institute; 1988. xiv, 218 p.
87-020012   332.4   0847675785
Banks and banking. Money supply. Monetary policy.

HG1615.7 Banking — Bank management — Personnel management

HG1615.7.M5.I76 1985
Irons, Edward D.
Black managers: the case of the banking industry/ Edward D. Irons and Gilbert W. Moore; foreword by Phyllis Wallace. New York: Praeger, 1985. xviii, 184 p.
84-018304   332.1/023/73   0030719380
Afro-American bankers. Banks and banking -- United States -- Vocational guidance.

HG1685 Banking — Drafts — General works

HG1685.D68 1996
Dowd, Kevin.
Competition and finance: a reinterpretation of financial and monetary economics/ Kevin Dowd. New York: St. Martin's Press, 1996. xii, 572 p.
96-013141   332.1   0312162189
Free banking. Free enterprise. Monetary policy.

HG1722 Banking — Bank mergers

HG1722.S585 2001
Shull, Bernard, 1931-
Bank mergers in a deregulated environment: promise and peril/ Bernard Shull, Gerald A. Hanweck. Westport, Conn.: Quorum Books, 2001. xv, 217 p.
00-042557   332.1/6   1567203795
Bank mergers -- United States. Bank mergers -- Europe, Western. Banks and banking -- Deregulation -- United States.

HG1811 Banking — Special classes of banks and financial institutions — Central banks. Banks and the treasury

HG1811.D423 1994
Deane, Marjorie.
The central banks/ Marjorie Deane and Robert Pringle; with a foreword by Paul Volcker. New York, N.Y., U.S.A.: Viking, 1995. ix, 369 p.
94-023017   332.1/1   0670848239
Banks and banking, Central.

HG1811.D68 1989
Dowd, Kevin.
The state and the monetary system/ Kevin Dowd. New York: St. Martin's Press, 1989. ix, 213 p.
89-034681   332.1   0312035098
Banks and banking, Central. Free banking. Banks and banking -- State supervision.

HG2040.5 Banking — Special classes of banks and financial institutions — Mortgage credit agencies. Mortgage loans. Mortgage banks

HG2040.5.U5.B35 1990
Ball, Michael.
Under one roof: retail banking and the international mortgage finance revolution/ Michael Ball. New York: St. Martin's Press, 1990. xi, 227 p.
90-046816   332.7/2   0312055668
Mortgage banks -- United States. Mortgages -- United States. Mortgage loans -- United States.

HG2151 Banking — Special classes of banks and financial institutions — Savings and loan associations. Building and loan associations. Thrift

HG2151.E34 1989
Eichler, Ned.
The thrift debacle/ Ned Eichler. Berkeley: University of California Press, c1989. ix, 163 p.
88-040554   332.3/2/09730904   0520066316
Thrift institutions -- United States -- History -- 20th century. Banks and banking -- United States -- State supervision -- History -- 20th century.

HG2151.K4 1977
Kendall, Leon T.
The savings and loan business: its purposes, functions, and economic justification/ Leon T. Kendall for the United States Savings and Loan League. Westport, Conn.: Greenwood Press, 1977, c1962. xvii, 170 p.
77-014207   332.3/2/0973   0837198437
Savings and loan associations -- United States.

HG2461-2613 Banking — By region or country — America. Western Hemisphere

HG2461.B46 1990
Benston, George J.
The separation of commercial and investment banking: the Glass-Steagall Act revisited and reconsidered/ George J. Benston. New York: Oxford University Press, 1990. x, 263 p.
90-006946   332.1/0973   0195208307
Investment banking -- United States -- History. Banks and banking -- United States -- History. Banking law -- United States.

HG2463.L28.L3
Lamont, Thomas Stilwell, 1899-1967.
Thomas Stilwell Lamont. Edited by Edward M. Lamont. New York, Horizon Press, 1969. 221 p.
70-083174   332.1/0924
Lamont, Thomas Stilwell, -- 1899-1967.

HG2471.M3
McFaul, John M.
The politics of Jacksonian finance [by] John M. McFaul. Ithaca [N.Y.] Cornell University Press [1972] xv, 230 p.
72-004635   332.1/0973   0801407389
Banks and banking -- United States -- History. Currency question -- United States -- History. United States -- Politics and government -- 1815-1861.

HG2481.W493 1996
Wicker, Elmus.
The banking panics of the Great Depression/ Elmus Wicker. Cambridge; Cambridge University Press, 1996. xviii, 174 p.
95-049436   332.1/0973/09043   0521562619
Banks and banking -- United States -- History -- 20th century. Bank failures -- United States -- History -- 20th century. Financial crises -- United States -- History -- 20th century. United States -- Economic conditions -- 1918-1945.

HG2491.B275 1992
Barth, James R.
The future of American banking/ James R. Barth, R. Dan Brumbaugh, Jr., Robert E. Litan. Armonk, N.Y.: M.E. Sharpe, c1992. xxiii, 207 p.
91-042825   332.1/0973   1563240343
Banks and banking -- United States. Bank failures -- United States. Banking law -- United States.

HG2491.D36 1990
Damanpour, Faramarz.
The evolution of foreign banking institutions in the United States: developments in international finance/ Faramarz Damanpour; foreword by Terri Sohrab. New York: Quorum Books, 1990. xxii, 243 p.
89-010692   332.1/5/0973   0899303714
Banks and banking, Foreign -- United States.

HG2491.E39 1996
Edwards, Franklin R., 1937-
The new finance: regulation and financial stability/ Franklin R. Edwards. Washington, DC: AEI Press, 1996. xiv, 221 p.
96-014226 332.1/0973 084473988X
 Banks and banking -- Deregulation -- United States. Banking law -- United States. Financial institutions -- United States.

HG2491.M342 1997
Mayer, Martin, 1928-
The bankers: the next generation/ Martin Mayer. New York: Truman Talley Books, c1997. x, 514 p.
96-034801 332.1/0973 20 0525938656
 Banks and banking -- United States. Financial services industry -- United States.

HG2491.R428 1995
Reinicke, Wolfgang H.
Banking, politics, and global finance: American commercial banks and regulatory change, 1980-1990/ Wolfgang H. Reinicke. Aldershot, England; Edward Elgar, c1995. ix, 242 p.
94-034103 332.1/0973 185898176X
 Banks and banking -- Deregulation -- United States. Investment banking -- Deregulation -- United States. Banking law -- United States.

HG2491.R648 1997
Rose, Peter S.
Banking across state lines: public and private consequences/ Peter S. Rose. Westport, Conn.: Quorum, 1997. xv, 173 p.
96-046085 332.1/6 1567200079
 Interstate banking -- United States -- State supervision. Interstate banking -- Law and legislation -- United States.

HG2491.R664 1991
Rose, Peter S.
Japanese banking and investment in the United States: an assessment of their impact upon U.S. markets and institutions/ Peter S. Rose. New York: Quorum Books, 1991. xiv, 203 p.
91-002275 332.6/7352073 0899306225
 Banks and banking, Japanese -- United States. Investments,Japanese -- United States.

HG2491.T38 1989
Taylor, Jeremy F.
The banking system in troubled times: new issues of stability and continuity/ Jeremy F. Taylor. New York: Quorum Books, 1989. xvi, 187 p.
88-035683 332.1/0973 0899304265
 Banks and banking -- United States.

HG2525.K36 1999
Kaplan, Edward S.
The Bank of the United States and the American economy/ Edward S. Kaplan. Westport, Conn.: Greenwood Press, 1999. x, 172 p.
99-015390 332.1/1/0973 0313308667
 United States -- Economic conditions -- To 1865.

HG2562.F8.W54 1972
Willis, Parker B. 1907-
The Federal funds market, its origin and development/ by Parker B. Willis. [Boston]: Federal Reserve Bank of Boston, 1970 vii, 128 p.
77-601197 332.1/13
 Federal funds market (United States)

HG2562.L6.G37 1988
Garcia, G. G.
The Federal Reserve: lender of last resort/ Gillian Garcia and Elizabeth Plautz. Cambridge, Mass.: Ballinger, c1988. xvii, 310 p.
88-019261 332.1/1/0973 0887303242
 Federal Reserve banks. Lenders of last resort -- United States.

HG2563.B46 1992
Biographical dictionary of the Board of Governors of the Federal Reserve/ edited by Bernard S. Katz. New York: Greenwood Press, 1992. xvii, 385 p.
91-011329 332.1/1/092273 0313266581
Board of Governors of the Federal Reserve System (U.S.) -- Biography -- Dictionaries.

HG2563.P65 1990
The Political economy of American monetary policy/ edited by Thomas Mayer. Cambridge [England]; Cambridge University Press, 1990. x, 314 p.
89-023900 332.1/12/0973 0521363160
 Monetary policy -- United States.

HG2563.W44 1991
Wheelock, David C.
The strategy and consistency of Federal Reserve monetary policy, 1924-1933/ David C. Wheelock. Cambridge [England]; Cambridge University Press, 1991. xiv, 126 p.
91-008869 332.4/973/09042 0521391555
 Federal Reserve banks. Monetary policy -- United States -- History -- 20th century.

HG2565.W654 2001
Woodward, Bob.
Maestro: Greenspan's Fed and the American boom/ Bob Woodward. New York: Simon & Schuster, 2000. 270 p.
00-052627 332.1/12/0973 0743204123
 Greenspan, Alan, -- 1926- Monetary policy -- United States -- History -- 20th century.

HG2569.D65 1996
Dombrowski, Peter.
Policy responses to the globalization of American banking/ Peter Dombrowski. Pittsburgh: University of Pittsburgh Press, c1996. vii, 247 p.
95-032769 332.1/0973 20 0822939010
 Banks and banking, American -- Government policy. Monetary policy. International finance.

HG2604.S39 1987
Schweikart, Larry.
Banking in the American South from the age of Jackson to Reconstruction/ Larry Schweikart. Baton Rouge: Louisiana State University Press, c1987. xiv, 367 p.
87-012784 332.1/0975 0807114030
 Banks and banking -- Southern States -- History. Monetary policy -- Southern States -- History. Southern States -- History -- 1775-1865. United States -- History -- Civil War, 1861-1865 -- Finance.

HG2613.P54.B45 1996
Rappaport, George David.
Stability and change in Revolutionary Pennsylvania: banking, politics, and social structure/ George David Rappaport. University Park, Pa.: Pennsylvania State University Press, c1996. xix, 276 p.
95-035472 332.1/09748/09033 20 0271015314
 Banks and banking -- Pennsylvania -- History -- 18th century. Social structure -- Pennsylvania -- History -- 18th century. Pennsylvania -- History -- Revolution, 1775-1783 -- Influence. Pennsylvania -- Social conditions.

HG2974-3368 Banking — By region or country — Other regions or countries

HG2974.F56 1992
Finance and financiers in European history, 1880-1960/ edited by Youssef Cassis. Cambridge; Cambridge University Press; 1992. xiv, 445 p.
90-019525 332/.094 0521400244
 Banks and banking -- Europe -- History -- 19th century -- Congresses. Banks and banking -- Europe -- History -- 20th century -- Congresses. Capitalists and financiers -- Europe -- History -- 19th century -- Congresses.

HG2980.5.A7.G66 1992
Goodman, John B. 1957-
Monetary sovereignty: the politics of central banking in western Europe/ John B. Goodman. Ithaca, N.Y.: Cornell University Press, 1992. xii, 239 p.
91-057897 331.11/094 0801480132
 Banks and banking, Central -- European Economic Community countries.

HG2980.7.A6.B362 1998
Banking in transition economies: developing market oriented banking sectors in Eastern Europe/ John Bonin ... [et al.]. Cheltenham; Edward Elgar Pub., c1998. xii, 195 p.
97-041480 332.1/0947 21 1858986044
 Banks and banking -- Europe, Eastern. Banks and banking -- Europe, Central. Post-communism -- Europe, Eastern. Europe, Eastern -- Economic policy -- 1989- Europe, Central -- Economic policy.

HG2986.M5
Mints, Lloyd W. 1888-
A history of banking theory in Great Britain and the United States, by Lloyd W. Mints. Chicago, Ill., University of Chicago Press [1945] 319 p.
45-004815 332.1
 Banks and banking -- Great Britain. Banks and banking -- United States.

HG2994.F46 1991
Fforde, John.
The Bank of England and public policy, 1941-1958/ John Fforde. Cambridge [England]; Cambridge University Press, 1992. xix, 861 p.
90-033131 332.1/1/094109045 0521391393
 Monetary policy -- Great Britain -- History -- 20th century. Banks and banking, Central -- Great Britain -- History -- 20th century.

HG3058.D4
James, Harold.
The Deutsche Bank and the Nazi economic war against the Jews: the expropriation of Jewish-owned property/ Harold James. Oxford, UK; Cambridge University Press, 2001. xi, 268 p.
00-048651 940.53/1 0521803292
 World War, 1939-1945 -- Economic aspects -- Germany. World War, 1939-1945 -- Jews -- Germany.

HG3204.B38 1998
Bauer, Hans, 1901-
Swiss banking: an analytical history/ Hans Bauer and Warren J. Blackman. New York: St. Martin's Press, 1998. x, 264 p.
97-041759 332.1/09494 0312212836
 Banks and banking -- Switzerland -- History.

HG3204.R53 1999
Rickman, Gregg J.
Swiss banks and Jewish souls/ Gregg J. Rickman. New Brunswick, NJ: Transaction, c1999. xvii, 294 p.
99-017332   940.53/494 21   1560004266
Banks and banking -- Corrupt practices -- Switzerland -- History -- 20th century. Foreign bank accounts -- Switzerland -- History -- 20th century. Holocaust, Jewish (1939-1945)

HG3324.P74 1981
Prindl, Andreas R.
Japanese finance: a guide to banking in Japan/ Andreas R. Prindl. Chichester; Wiley, c1981. xii, 137 p.
81-212198   332.1/0952   0471099821
Banks and banking -- Japan. Finance -- Japan.

HG3366.A6.W53 1983
Wilson, Rodney.
Banking and finance in the Arab Middle East/ Rodney Wilson. New York: St. Martin's Press, 1983. xii, 208 p.
81-021432   332.1/0917/5927   0312066309
Banks and banking -- Arab countries. Finance -- Arab countries.

HG3368.A6.E4 1987
El-Ashker, Ahmed Abdel-Fattah, 1943-
The Islamic business enterprise/ Ahmed Abdel-Fattah El-Ashker. London; Croom Helm, c1987. xi, 242 p.
86-024271   332.1/0917/671   0709909853
Banks and banking -- Islamic countries -- Case studies. Business enterprises -- Islamic countries -- Case studies. Banks and banking -- Religious aspects -- Islam.

HG3701 Credit. Debt. Loans — General works

HG3701.C575 2000
Clayton, James L.
The global debt bomb/ James L. Clayton. Armonk, N.Y.: M.E. Sharpe, c2000. xii, 194 p.
99-022986   336.3/4 21   0765604752
Debt. Debts, Public.

HG3755.8-3756 Credit. Debt. Loans — Commercial credit. Commercial loans. Credit management — Consumer credit. Personal loans

HG3755.8.U6.M36 2000
Manning, Robert D., 1957-
Credit card nation: the consequences of America's addiction to credit/ Robert D. Manning. New York: Basic Books, 2000. x, 406 p.
00-063101   332.7/65//0973   0465043666
Credit cards -- United States. Consumer credit -- United States.

HG3755.8.U6.E94 1999
Evans, David S.
Paying with plastic: the digital revolution in buying and borrowing/ David S. Evans, Richard Schmalensee. Cambridge, Mass.: MIT Press, c1999. xii, 373 p.
99-023902   332.7/65/0973 21   0262050625
Credit cards -- United States. Bank credit cards -- United States. Electronic funds transfers -- United States.

HG3756.U54.C35 1999
Calder, Lendol Glen.
Financing the American dream: a cultural history of consumer credit/ Lendol Calder. Princeton, N.J.: Princeton University Press, 1999. xv, 377 p.
98-034875   332.7/0973   069105827X
Consumer credit -- United States -- History. Consumption (Economics) -- United States -- History. Consumers -- United States -- History.

HG3769 Credit. Debt. Loans — Commercial credit. Commercial loans. Credit management — Bankruptcy. Insolvency

HG3769.G73.E54 1987
Hoppit, Julian.
Risk and failure in English business, 1700-1800/ Julian Hoppit. Cambridge [Cambridgeshire]; Cambridge University Press, 1987. vii, 228 p.
87-000743   332.7/5/0942   0521326249
Bankruptcy -- England -- History -- 18th century. Business enterprises -- England -- History -- 18th century. Business cycles -- England -- History -- 18th century.

HG3811-3815 Foreign exchange. International finance — Foreign exchange — History

HG3811.E35 1970
Einzig, Paul, 1897-
The history of foreign exchange. London, Macmillan; 1970. xxi, 362 p.
74-124951   332.4/5/09   0333064925
Foreign exchange -- History.

HG3815.G72 1989
Grauwe, Paul de.
International money: post-war trends and theories/ Paul De Grauwe. Oxford [England]: Clarendon Press; 1989. xi, 257 p.
88-025254   332.4/5   0198285981
Foreign exchange. Economic history -- 1945-

HG3821-3823 Foreign exchange. International finance — Foreign exchange — Theory. Method. Relation to other subjects

HG3821.D69 1988
Dornbusch, Rudiger.
Exchange rates and inflation/ Rudiger Dornbusch. Cambridge, Mass.: MIT Press, c1988. x, 475 p.
88-005367   332.4/56   0262040964
Foreign exchange rates. Inflation (Finance)

HG3821.E3
The Economics of exchange rates: selected studies/ edited by Jacob A. Frenkel, Harry G. Johnson. Reading, Mass.: Addison-Wesley Pub. Co., c1978. xvii, 218 p.
77-088058   332.4/5   0201023741
Foreign exchange rates.

HG3821.H63 1989
Honeygold, Derek.
International financial markets/ Derek Honeygold. New York: Nichols Pub. Co., 1989. 230 p.
89-002896   332.6/5   0893973432
International finance. Financial institutions, International. Securities.

HG3821.N595 1984
Niehans, Jurg.
International monetary economics/ Jurg Niehans. Baltimore: Johns Hopkins University Press, 1984. xii, 340 p.
83-014960   332/.042   0801830214
Foreign exchange. International finance. Monetary policy.

HG3823.R667 1996
Rosenberg, Michael Roy, 1947-
Currency forecasting: a guide to fundamental and technical models of exchange rate determination/ Michael R. Rosenberg. Chicago, Ill.: Irwin Professional Publishing, c1996. xii, 388 p.
95-024868   332.4/5 20   1557389187
Foreign exchange rates -- Mathematical models. Foreign exchange -- Forecasting -- Mathematical models.

HG3851 Foreign exchange. International finance — Foreign exchange — General works

HG3851.B427 2001
Ben-Ami, Daniel.
Cowardly capitalism: the myth of the global financial casino/ Daniel Ben-Ami. Chichester, England; J. Wiley, c2001. x, 196 p.
00-069699   332 21   0471899631
International finance. Capitalism. Investments, Foreign.

HG3851.C77 1991
**Currency convertibility in Eastern Europe/ John Williamson, editor. Washington: Institute for International Economics, c1991. x, 461 p.
91-029947   332.4/56/0947   0881321443
Currency convertibility -- Europe, Eastern -- Case studies. Money -- Europe, Eastern -- Case studies. Monetary policy -- Europe, Eastern -- Case studies.

HG3851.I49 1990
International financial markets and agricultural trade/ edited by Thomas Grennes. Boulder: Westview Press, 1990. 306 p.
89-009062   382/.41   0813378117
Foreign exchange. International finance. Produce trade.

HG3877 Foreign exchange. International finance — Foreign exchange — Developing countries

HG3877.D47 2001
DeRosa, David F.
In defense of free capital markets: the case against a new international financial architecture/ David F. DeRosa. Princeton, NJ: Bloomberg Press, 2001. xv, 230 p.
00-062090   332/.042/091724   157660036X
Foreign exchange -- Developing countries -- Case studies. Capital market -- Developing countries -- Case studies. Free enterprise -- Developing countries -- Case studies.

HG3881 Foreign exchange. International finance — International finance. International monetary system. International banking — General works

HG3881.C648 1966aa
Monetary problems of the international economy; [papers and discussions] Edited by Robert A. Mundell and Alexander K. Swoboda. Chicago, University of Chicago Press [1969] x, 405 p.
68-016710   332.1/5   0226550656
International finance -- Congresses.

HG3881.C674 1986
Corden, W. M.
Inflation, exchange rates, and the world economy: lectures on international monetary economics/ W.M. Corden. Chicago: University of Chicago Press, 1986. viii, 195 p.
85-051490   332.4/5   0226115828
International finance. Balance of payments. Inflation (Finance)

HG3881.D43 1988
Development aid: a guide to national and international agencies/ researched and compiled by Eurofi (UK) Limited. London; Butterworths; 1988, c1987. 587 p.
87-035543   332.1/53/025   0408009918
Banks and banking, International -- Directories. Development banks -- Directories. Economic assistance -- Directories.

HG3881.E346 1990
Eichengreen, Barry J.
Elusive stability: essays in the history of international finance, 1919-1939/ Barry Eichengreen. Cambridge [England]; Cambridge University Press, 1990. xi, 335 p.
89-007189   332/.042/0904   0521365384
International finance -- History -- 20th century.

HG3881.I575124 1991
International banking, 1870-1914/ edited by Rondo Cameron and V.I. Bovykin with the assistance of Boris Ananich ... [et al.]. New York: Oxford University Press, 1991. xiv, 655 p.
89-026656   332.1/5/09034   019506271X
Banks and banking, International -- History.

HG3881.K28 1989
Kaplan, Jacob J. 1920-
The European Payments Union: financial diplomacy in the 1950s/ by Jacob J. Kaplan and Gunther Schleiminger. Oxford [England]: Clarendon Press; 1989. xx, 396 p.
89-033657   341.7/54   0198286759
International finance -- History.

HG3881.M575 1983
Moffitt, Michael, 1951-
The world's money: international banking, from Bretton Woods to the brink of insolvency/ Michael Moffitt. New York: Simon and Schuster, c1983. 284 p.
83-000402   332/.042   0671446827
International finance.

HG3881.O27 1982
Odell, John S., 1945-
U.S. international monetary policy: markets, power, and ideas as sources of change/ John S. Odell. Princeton, N.J.: Princeton University Press, c1982. xvi, 385 p.
82-047607   332.4/5/0973   0691076421
International finance. Monetary policy -- United States. Devaluation of currency -- United States. United States -- Foreign economic relations.

HG3881.O772 1992
Orr, Bill.
The global economy in the 90s: a user's guide/ Bill Orr. New York: New York University Press, c1992. xxiii, 330 p.
91-036551   330.9/049   0814761763
International finance. International trade.

HG3881.P34 1997
Pauly, Louis W.
Who elected the bankers?: surveillance and control in the world economy/ Louis W. Pauly. Ithaca: Cornell University Press, 1997. xiv, 184 p.
96-045087   332.1/5   0801433223
Financial institutions, International -- History -- 20th century. International Monetary Fund -- History -- 20th century.

HG3881.S5372 2000
Singh, Kavaljit.
Taming global financial flows: challenges and alternatives in the era of financial globalization: a citizen's guide/ Kavaljit Singh. London; Zed Books, c2000. xvii, 237 p.
00-025711   332.4/6 21   1856497836
International finance. Monetary policy. Capital movements -- Law and legislation.

HG3881.S5568 1999
Solomon, Robert.
Money on the move: the revolution in international finance since 1980/ Robert Solomon. Princeton, NJ: Princeton University Press, 1999. xiii, 210 p.
98-026714   332/.042   0691004447
International finance.

HG3881.S5574 1977
Solomon, Robert.
The international monetary system, 1945-1976: an insider's view/ Robert Solomon. New York: Harper & Row, c1977. xiii, 381 p.
76-010094   332.4/5   006013898X
International finance.

HG3881.T495 1987
Threats to international financial stability/ edited by Richard Portes and Alexander K. Swoboda. Cambridge; Cambridge University Press, 1987. xviii, 307 p.
87-010310   332/.042   0521345561
International finance.

HG3881.V65 1992
Volcker, Paul A.
Changing fortunes: the world's money and the threat to American leadership/ Paul A. Volcker, Toyoo Gyohten. New York: Times Books, c1992. xix, 394 p.
91-051035   332/.042   081292018X
International finance.

HG3881.W268 1991
Walter, Andrew, 1961-
World power and world money: the role of hegemony and international monetary order/ Andrew Walter. New York: St. Martin's Press, 1991. xiv, 273 p.
91-024314   332/.042   0312067860
International finance. World politics. International economic relations.

HG3881.5 Foreign exchange. International finance — International finance. International monetary system. International banking — Individual international financial institutions, A-Z

HG3881.5.I58.G867 1998
Gup, Benton E.
Bank failures in the major trading countries of the world: causes and remedies/ Benton E. Gup. Westport, CT: Quorum, 1998. ix, 174 p.
98-004976   332.1   156720208X
Bank failures -- Europe. Bank failures -- Japan. Bank failures -- United States.

HG3881.5.I58.I39 1984
The IMF and stabilization: developing country experiences/ directed and edited by Tony Killick; contributors, Graham Bird ... [et al.]. New York: St. Martin's Press, 1984. viii, 216 p.
83-040190   332.1/52   0312402295
Economic stabilization -- Developing countries. Balance of payments -- Developing countries. Developing countries -- Economic policy.

HG3881.5.W57.D4 1987
De Vries, Barend A.
Remaking the World Bank/ Barend A. de Vries; foreword by I.G. Patel. Washington, DC: Seven Locks Press; c1987. xvi, 184 p.
87-023406   332.1/532   0932020496
World Bank.

HG3881.5.W57.K48 1999
Khan, Shahrukh Rafi.
Do World Bank and IMF policies work?/ Shahrukh Rafi Khan. New York, N.Y.: St. Martin's Press, 1999. x, 197 p.
98-027631   332.1/5   0312217048
Banks and banking, International.

HG3881.5.W57.L4 1989
Le Prestre, Philippe G.
The World Bank and the environmental challenge/ Philippe Le Prestre. Selinsgrove: Susquehanna University Press; c1989. 263 p.
88-042825   332.1/532   0941664988
Development banks -- Developing countries. Environmental policy -- Developing countries. Economic development projects -- Environmental aspects -- Developing countries.

HG3881.5.W57.M68 1991
Mosley, Paul.
Aid and power: the World Bank and policy-based lending / Paul Mosley, Jane Harrigan, and John Toye. London; Routledge, [1991-] v. 2.
90-009153   332.1/532   041506077X
Loans, Foreign -- Developing countries -- Case studies. Developing countries -- Economic policy -- Case studies.

HG3881.5.W57.R47 1991
Restructuring economies in distress: policy reform and the World Bank/ edited by Vinod Thomas ... [et al.]. Oxford, England; Published for the World Bank [by] Oxford Univers c1991. xiv, 566 p.
90-025999   339.5/09172/4   0195208706
Balance of payments -- Developing countries. Economic stabilization -- Developing countries. Developing countries -- Economic policy.

HG3881.5.W57.R53 1994
Rich, Bruce.
Mortgaging the earth: the World Bank, environmental impoverishment, and the crisis of development/ Bruce Rich. Boston: Beacon Press, c1994. xiv, 376 p.
93-003848   332.1/532/091724   080704704X
Environmental policy -- Developing countries. Economic assistance -- Developing countries.

HG3882-3890 Foreign exchange. International finance — International finance. International monetary system. International banking — Balance of payments

HG3882.D58 1996
Dluhosch, Barbara.
International competitiveness and the balance of payments: do current account deficits and surpluses matter?/ Barbara Dluhosch, Andreas Freytag, and Malte Kruger. Cheltenham, UK; E. Elgar Pub., c1996. ix, 235 p.
95-040197   382/.17 20   1858982103
Balance of payments. Competition, International. Balance of payments -- Case studies.

HG3890.D4 1987
De Vries, Margaret Garritsen, 1922-
Balance of payments adjustment, 1945 to 1986: the IMF experience/ Margaret Garritsen de Vries. Washington, D.C.: International Monetary Fund, 1987. xi, 336 p.
87-017242   332.1/52   0939934930
Balance of payments -- Developing countries. International finance.

HG3891 Foreign exchange. International finance — International finance. International monetary system. International banking — Capital movements

HG3891.G67 1995
Gordon, Sara L.
The United States and global capital shortages: the problem and possible solutions/ Sara L. Gordon. Westport, Conn.: Quorum Books, 1995. xi, 228 p.
95-003264   332/.041/0973   0899307728
Capital movements. Capital movements -- United States. Saving and investment -- United States.

HG3891.M34 1996
Mahon, James E., 1955-
Mobile capital and Latin American development/ James E. Mahon, Jr. University Park, Pa.: Pennsylvania State University Press, c1996. xii, 212 p.
95-017440   332/.042 20   027101525X
Capital movements -- Latin America. Foreign exchange -- Latin America. Debts, External -- Latin America. Latin America -- Economic policy.

HG3891.5 Foreign exchange. International finance — International finance. International monetary system. International banking — Foreign loans. International lending. External debts

HG3891.5.B57 1989
Bird, Graham R.
Commercial bank lending and Third World debt/ Graham Bird. New York: St. Martin's Press, c1989.
88-028194   332.1/53/091724   0312027257
Commercial loans -- Developing countries. Bank loans -- Developing countries. Country risk -- Developing countries.

HG3891.5.M34 1984
Makin, John H.
The global debt crisis: America's growing involvement/ John H. Makin. New York: Basic Books, c1984. xiv, 281 p.
84-045075   336.3/435/091724   0465026818
Loans, Foreign -- Developing countries. Debts, External -- Developing countries. Loans, American -- Developing countries.

HG3897 Foreign exchange. International finance — International finance. International monetary system. International banking — Monetary unions. Currency areas

HG3897.H63 1982
Hogan, W. P. 1929-
The incredible Eurodollar/ W.P. Hogan and I.F. Pearce. London; G. Allen & Unwin, 1982. viii, 144 p.
81-019154   332.4/5   0043320813
Euro-dollar market. International finance.

HG3903-3915.5 Foreign exchange. International finance — By region or country

HG3903.G68 1983
Gowa, Joanne S.
Closing the gold window: domestic politics and the end of Bretton Woods/ Joanne Gowa. Ithaca: Cornell University Press, 1983. 208 p.
83-007184   332.4/560973   0801416221
Foreign exchange -- United States. Devaluation of currency -- United States. International finance. United States -- Politics and government -- 1969-1974. United States -- Foreign economic relations -- Case studies.

HG3915.5.G76 1994
Grosse, Robert E.
Foreign exchange black markets in Latin America/ Robert E. Grosse with Clarice Pechman. Westport, Conn.: Praeger, 1994. xiv, 224 p.
93-041628   332.4/56   0275947580
Foreign exchange -- Latin America -- Case studies. Informal sector (Economics) -- Latin America -- Case studies.

HG4012 Financial management. Business finance. Corporation finance — Theory. Method. Relation to other subjects — Mathematical models

HG4012.C47 1995
Chorafas, Dimitris N.
Financial models and simulation/ Dimitris N. Chorafas. New York, N.Y.: St. Martins, 1995. xvii, 359 p.
95-002012   658.15   0312126301
Corporations -- Finance -- Mathematical models. Financial services industry -- Technological innovations. Fuzzy systems.

HG4017 Financial management. Business finance. Corporation finance — History

HG4017.B37 1997
Baskin, Jonathan Barron.
A history of corporate finance/ Jonathan Barron Baskin, Paul J. Miranti, Jr. Cambridge [England]; Cambridge University Press, 1997. x, 350 p.
96-019598   658.15   0521555140
Corporations -- Finance -- History.

HG4026 Financial management. Business finance. Corporation finance — General works

HG4026.G37 1988
Garrison, Sharon Hatten.
Financial forecasting and planning: a guide for accounting, marketing, and planning managers/ Sharon Hatten Garrison, Wallace N. Davidson, and Michael A. Garrison. New York: Quorum, c1988. 160 p.
87-036097   658.1/5/   0899302653
Business enterprises -- Finance. Business forecasting.

HG4026.H43 1981
Willson, James D.
Controllership, the work of the managerial accountant/ James D. Willson and John B. Campbell. New York: Wiley, c1981. ix, 889 p.
80-039552   658.1/51   0471057118
Controllership. Managerial accounting.

HG4027.35 Financial management. Business finance. Corporation finance — Chief financial officers

HG4027.35.C43 1997
The CFO handbook/ [edited by] Mark E. Haskins, Benjamin R. Makela. Chicago: Irwin Professional Publishing, c1997. xxvi, 429 p.
96-022774   658.15 20   1556238517
Chief financial officers -- Handbooks, manuals, etc. Corporations -- United States -- Finance -- Handbooks, manuals, etc.

HG4027.5 Financial management. Business finance. Corporation finance — International business enterprises

HG4027.5.K47 1981
Kettell, Brian.
The finance of international business/ Brian Kettell; foreword by Andreas R. Prindl; with a new introd. by the author. Westport, Conn.: Quorum Books, 1981. xviii, 275 p.
80-028878   658.1/599   0899300111
International business enterprises -- Finance. International finance.

HG4027.7 Financial management. Business finance. Corporation finance — Small business finance

HG4027.7.H356 1998
Hankin, Jo Ann.
Financial management for nonprofit organizations/ Jo Ann Hankin, Alan G. Seidner, John T. Zietlow. New York: John Wiley, c1998. xii, 610 p.
97-008604   658.15 21   0471168424
Nonprofit organizations -- Finance.

HG4028 Financial management. Business finance. Corporation finance — Other topics, A-Z

HG4028.B2.L87 1984
Lurie, Adolph G.
How to read annual reports intelligently: a stockholder's guide/ Adolph Lurie. Englewood Cliffs, N.J.: Prentice-Hall, c1984. viii, 168 p.
84-011719   338.7/4   0134305620
Corporation reports.

HG4028.B8.U46 1987
Umapathy, Srinivasan.
Current budgeting practices in U.S. industry: the state of the art/ Srinivasan Umapathy; foreword by John Leslie Livingstone. New York: Quorum Books, 1987. xxxix, 176 p.
87-005969   658.1/54   0899302505
Budget in business. Corporations -- United States -- Finance -- Planning.

HG4028.C45.C58 1985
Corporate cash management: techniques and analysis/ edited by Frank J. Fabozzi and Leslie N. Masonson. Homewood, Ill.: Dow Jones-Irwin, c1985. xv, 373 p.
84-071295   658.1/5244   0870944770
Cash management -- United States. Cash management.

HG4028.M4.B335 1998
Baker, George P.
The new financial capitalists: Kohlberg Kravis Roberts and the creation of corporate value/ George P. Baker, George David Smith. Cambridge, UK; Cambridge University Press, 1998. xiv, 257 p.
98-028007   338.8/3/0973   0521642604
Leveraged buyouts -- United States. Consolidation and merger of corporations -- United States -- Finance.

HG4028.W65.H54 1995
Hill, Ned C.
Short-term financial management: text and cases/ Ned C. Hill, William L. Sartoris. New York: Macmillan College Pub. Co.; c1995.
94-008771   658.15/244   0023548320
Working capital. Corporations -- Finance.

HG4057-4061 Financial management. Business finance. Corporation finance — By region or country — United States

HG4057.A28616
Hoover's guide to private companies. Austin, Tex.: Reference Press, Inc., c1994. 1 v.
95-648110   338.7/4/02573
Private companies -- United States -- Rankings -- Directories. Private companies -- United States -- Finance -- Directories. Business enterprises -- United States -- Finance -- Directories.

HG4057.A28617
Hoover's handbook of American business. Austin, Tex.: Reference Press, Inc., [c1991-]
92-641835   338.7/4/02573
Corporations -- United States -- Directories. Business enterprises -- United States -- Directories.

HG4061.R48 1988
Rhyne, Elisabeth.
Small business, banks, and SBA loan guarantees: subsidizing the weak or bridging a credit gap?/ Elisabeth Holmes Rhyne. New York: Quorum Books, 1988. x, 178 p.
87-036098   338.6/42/0973   0899302564
Small business -- United States -- Finance. Loans -- United States -- Government guaranty.

HG4513 Investment, capital formation, speculation — Dictionaries. Encyclopedias

HG4513.R67 1993
Rosenberg, Jerry Martin.
Dictionary of investing/ Jerry M. Rosenberg. New York: Wiley, c1993. xiii, 368 p.
92-006357   332.6/03   0471574333
Investments -- Dictionaries.

HG4513.S37 1997
Scott, David Logan, 1942-
Wall Street words: an essential A to Z guide for today's investor/ David L. Scott. Boston, Mass.: Houghton Mifflin Co., c1997. xii, 433 p.
97-010608   332.6/03 21   0395853923
Investments -- Dictionaries. Securities -- Dictionaries. Stock exchanges -- Dictionaries.

HG4515.15 Investment, capital formation, speculation — Theory. Method. Relation to other subjects — Psychological aspects

HG4515.15.S53 2000
Shefrin, Hersh, 1948-
Beyond greed and fear: understanding behavioral finance and the psychology of investing/ Hersh Shefrin. Boston, Mass.: Harvard Business School Press, c2000. x, 368 p.
99-028153   332.6/01/9 21   0875848729
Investments -- Psychological aspects. Stock exchanges -- Psychological aspects. Finance -- Psychological aspects.

HG4521 Investment, capital formation, speculation — General works

HG4521.H227 2001
Hagstrom, Robert G., 1956-
The essential Buffett: timeless principles for the new economy/ Robert G. Hagstrom. New York: Wiley, c2001. xix, 283 p.
2001-026075   332.6 21   047138979X
Buffett, Warren. Investments. Portfolio management.

HG4521.M284 1996
Malkiel, Burton Gordon.
A random walk down Wall Street: including a life-cycle guide to personal investing/ Burton G. Malkiel. New York: Norton, c1996. 522 p.
95-008148   332.6 20   0393038882
Investments. Stocks. Random walks (Mathematics)

HG4521.S71148 1994
Sobel, Andrew Carl, 1953-
Domestic choices, international markets: dismantling national barriers and liberalizing securities markets/ Andrew C. Sobel. Ann Arbor: University of Michigan Press, c1994. x, 211 p.
94-017691   332.64   047210506X
Securities industry. Stock exchanges. Securities industry -- United States.

HG4521.S89 1996
Suutari, Raymond K.
Business strategy and security analysis: the key to long-term investment profits/ Raymond K. Suutari. Chicago: Irwin Professional Pub., c1996. xxvi, 384 p.
96-003565 658.15/2 20 078630409X
Investments. Corporations -- Finance. Rate of return.

HG4523 Investment, capital formation, speculation — Capital market

HG4523.J365 1990
Japanese capital markets: analysis and characteristics of equity, debt, and financial futures markets/ [edited by] Edwin J. Elton, Martin J. Gruber. New York: Harper & Row, Ballenger Division, c1990. xvii, 371 p.
89-036967 332.63/2/0952 0887303390
Capital market -- Japan. Securities -- Japan.

HG4523.M35 1997
McLindon, Michael P.
Privatization and capital market development: strategies to promote economic growth/ Michael P. McLindon; foreword by Ceslav Ciobanu. Westport, Conn.: Praeger, 1996. 176 p.
96-021320 332/.0414 0275950662
Capital market. Privatization.

HG4527 Investment, capital formation, speculation — Handbooks, manuals, etc.

HG4527.K525 1992
The Social investment almanac: a comprehensive guide to socially responsible investing/ edited by Peter D. Kinder, Steven D. Lydenberg, Amy L. Domini. New York: H. Holt and Co., 1992. xvii, 904 p.
91-036732 332.6/78 0805017690
Investments — Social aspects — Handbooks, manuals, etc. Investments — Social aspects — Directories. Investments — Social aspects — Bibliography.

HG4528 Investment, capital formation, speculation — General special

HG4528.G35 1993
Galbraith, John Kenneth, 1908-
A short history of financial euphoria/ John Kenneth Galbraith. New York, N.Y.: Whittle Books in association with Viking, 1993. xii, 113 p.
92-050765 332.64/5 0670850284
Speculation -- Case studies.

HG4529 Investment, capital formation, speculation — Investment analysis. Technical analysis

HG4529.B66 1999
The book of investing wisdom: classic writings by great stock-pickers and legends of Wall Street/ edited by Peter Krass. New York: Wiley, 1999. xiv, 498 p.
98-054153 332.6 0471294543
Investment analysis. Securities.

HG4529.T34 1993
Tainer, Evelina M., 1958-
Using economic indicators to improve investment analysis/ Evelina M. Tainer. New York: Wiley, c1993. xi, 270 p.
93-000429 332.6 047158049X
Investment analysis -- Statistical methods. Economic indicators -- United States.

HG4529.5 Investment, capital formation, speculation — Portfolio management. Asset allocation

HG4529.5.I58 1998
Investment management/ Peter L. Bernstein, ed., Aswath Damodaran, ed. New York: J. Wiley, 1998. xi, 466 p.
97-043844 332.6 0471197165
Portfolio management. Investment analysis.

HG4538 Investment, capital formation, speculation — Foreign investments

HG4538.A567 1993
Aliber, Robert Z.
The multinational paradigm/ Robert Z. Aliber. Cambridge, Mass.: MIT Press, c1993. 282 p.
92-039490 332.6/73 0262011271
Investments, Foreign. International business enterprises. Economic development.

HG4538.D823 1987
Dunning, John H.
IRM directory of statistics of international investment and production/ John Dunning and John Cantwell; with the assistance of Paz E. Tolentino and Faith Province. New York: New York University Press, c1987. xix, 820 p.
86-012610 338.8/8/021 0814717837
Investments, Foreign -- Statistics. International business enterprises -- Statistics.

HG4538.R82
Rugman, Alan M.
International diversification and the multinational enterprise/ Alan M. Rugman. Lexington, Mass.: Lexington Books, c1979. xviii, 137 p.
78-020603 338.8/8 0669027723
Investments, Foreign. International business enterprises -- Finance.

HG4551 Investment, capital formation, speculation — Stock exchanges — General works

HG4551.B465 1989
Black Monday and the future of financial markets/ Robert J. Barro ... [et al.]; edited by Robert W. Kamphuis, Jr., Roger C. Kormendi, and J.W. Henry Watson. Homewood, Ill.: Dow Jones-Irwin; c1989. xiii, 396 p.
88-025749 332.64/2 1556231385
Stock Market Crash, 1987. Stocks -- Prices.

HG4551.B485 2000
Bolten, Steven E.
Stock market cycles: a practical explanation/ Steven E. Bolten. Westport, Conn.: Quorum Books, 2000. viii, 174 p.
99-046054 332.64/2 1567203205
Stock exchanges.

HG4551.D29 1993
How the stock market works/ edited by John M. Dalton. New York: New York Institute of Finance, c1993. xii, 325 p.
93-036063 332.64/273 0130978663
Stock exchanges. Stocks.

HG4572-4575.2 Investment, capital formation, speculation — Stock exchanges — Major exchanges

HG4572.B46 2000
Benn, Alec, 1918-
The unseen Wall Street of 1969-1975: and its significance for today/ Alec Benn. Westport, Conn.: Quorum Books, 2000. xxii, 216 p.
99-462243 332.64/273 1567203337
Wall Street -- History -- 20th century. Stock exchanges -- United States -- History -- 20th century.

HG4572.B67 1993
Blume, Marshall.
Revolution on Wall Street: the rise and decline of the New York Stock Exchange/ Marshall E. Blume, Jeremy J. Siegel, and Dan Rottenberg. New York: W.W. Norton, c1993. 320 p.
93-009238 332.64/273 0393035263
Stock exchanges. International finance.

HG4572.P33 1998
Parks, Robert H.
Unlocking the secrets of Wall street: a noted expert guides you through today's financial markets/ Robert H. Parks. Amherst, New York: Prometheus Books, 1998. 490 p.
98-020698 332.6/0973 1573922315
Wall Street. Stocks -- Valuation -- United States. Monetary policy -- United States.

HG4575.2.B78 1991
Bruchey, Stuart Weems.
Modernization of the American Stock Exchange, 1971-1989/ by Stuart Bruchey. New York: Garland Pub., 1991. xiii, 211 p.
91-035983 332.64/273 0815307225
Stock exchanges -- United States.

HG4636 Investment, capital formation, speculation — Prices. Values. Stock quotations

HG4636.B49 1990
Berlin, Howard M.
The handbook of financial market indexes, averages, and indicators/ Howard M. Berlin. Homewood, Ill.: Dow Jones-Irwin, c1990. xxv, 262 p.
89-017197   332.63/222   1556231253
Stock price indexes -- Handbooks, manuals, etc. Stock exchanges -- Handbooks, manuals, etc.

HG4636.J37 1989
Jarrell, Howard R.
Common stock newspaper abbreviations and trading symbols/ by Howard R. Jarrell. Metuchen, N.J.: Scarecrow Press, 1989. x, 413 p.
89-010653   332.63/22/0973   0810822555
Securities -- United States -- Abbreviations. Ticker symbols -- United States.

HG4638 Investment, capital formation, speculation — Charts, diagrams, etc.

HG4638.P57 1989
Pistolese, Clifford.
Using technical analysis/ Clifford Pistolese. Chicago, Ill.: Probus Pub. Co., c1989. xi, 228 p.
89-010837   332.63/222   1557380767
Stocks -- Prices -- Charts, diagrams, etc.

HG4651 Investment, capital formation, speculation — Securities. By form — Fixed-income securities

HG4651.F28 1989
Fabozzi, Frank J.
Bond markets, analysis and strategies/ Frank J. Fabozzi & T. Dessa Fabozzi. Englewood Cliffs, N.J.: Prentice Hall, c1989. xix, 347 p.
88-022446   332.63/23   013079922X
Bonds. Investment analysis. Portfolio management.

HG4907-4963 Investment, capital formation, speculation — By region or country — America. Western Hemisphere

HG4907.S46 1995
Silver, A. David 1941-
Quantum companies: 100 companies that will change the face of tomorrow's business/ A. David Silver. Princeton, N.J.: Peterson's/Pacesetter Books, c1995. 342 p.
94-033198   338.7/4/02573   1560793732
Corporations -- United States -- Finance -- Directories. Market share -- United States.

HG4910.B77 1987
Bruyn, Severyn Ten Haut, 1927-
The field of social investment/ Severyn T. Bruyn. Cambridge; Cambridge University Press, 1987. xi, 304 p.
86-026393   332.6   0521332923
Investments -- Social aspects -- United States. Investments, American -- Social aspects. Industries -- Social aspects -- United States.

HG4910.C66
Cowing, Cedric B.
Populists, plungers, and progressives; a social history of stock and commodity speculation, 1890-1936, by Cedric B. Cowing. Princeton, N.J., Princeton University Press, 1965. vi, 299 p.
65-012988   332.6450973
Stock exchanges -- United States. Investments -- United States. Speculation.

HG4910.G44 1992
Geisst, Charles R.
Entrepot capitalism: foreign investment and the American dream in the twentieth century/ Charles R. Geisst. New York: Praeger, 1992. xxi, 154 p.
91-034168   332.6/73/0973   0275938948
Capital market -- United States -- History -- 20th century. Investments, Foreign -- United States -- History -- 20th century. Capitalism -- United States -- History -- 20th century. United States -- Economic conditions -- 1918-1945. United States -- Economic conditions -- 1945-

HG4910.G74 1991
Graham, Edward M. 1944-
Foreign direct investment in the United States/ Edward M. Graham, Paul R. Krugman. Washington, DC: Institute for International Economics, 1991. xv, 195 p.
90-023526   332.6/73/0973   0881321397
Investments, Foreign -- United States.

HG4910.J84 1990
Judd, Elizabeth, 1963-
Investing with a social conscience/ Elizabeth Judd. New York: Pharos Books, 1990. 272 p.
89-078436   332.6/78   0886874718
Investments -- Social aspects -- United States. Corporations -- United States -- Evaluation. Industries -- Social aspects -- United States.

HG4910.R69 1982
Rosenberg, Jerry Martin.
Inside the Wall Street journal: the history and the power of Dow Jones & Company and America's most influential newspaper/ Jerry M. Rosenberg. New York: Macmillan; c1982. xi, 335 p.
82-013005   071/.47/1   0026048604
Dow Jones & Co. -- History. Wall Street journal -- History.

HG4910.S5633 2001
Smith, B. Mark, 1953-
Toward rational exuberance: the evolution of the modern stock market/ B. Mark Smith. New York: Farrar, Straus and Giroux, 2001. ix, 342 p.
00-049477   332.64/273   0374281777
Stock exchanges -- United States. Stocks -- United States.

HG4910.U83 1996
Useem, Michael.
Investor capitalism: how money managers are changing the face of corporate America/ Michael Useem. New York: Basic Books, c1996. viii, 332 p.
96-007847   658.15 20   046505031X
Institutional investments -- United States. Investment advisors.

HG4928.5.M39 1992
Mayer, Martin, 1928-
Stealing the market: how the giant brokerage firms, with help from the SEC, stole the stock market from investors/ Martin Mayer. New York, NY: Basic Books, c1992. xi, 208 p.
91-055600   364.1/68   0465053629
Stockbrokers -- Corrupt practices -- United States. Securities industry -- Corrupt practices -- United States. Stock exchanges -- Corrupt practices -- United States.

HG4930.L69 2000
Lowenstein, Roger.
When genius failed: the rise and fall of Long-Term Capital Management/ Roger Lowenstein. New York: Random House, c2000. xxi, 264 p.
00-028091   332.6 21   037550317X
Hedge funds -- United States.

HG4930.5.D46 1985
Deregulating Wall Street: commercial bank penetration of the corporate securities market/ Ingo Walter, editor. New York: Wiley, c1985. xii, 315 p.
85-005321   332.1/754/0973   0471817139
Investment banking -- United States. Banks and banking -- United States. Wall Street.

HG4963.C37
Carosso, Vincent P.
Investment banking in America, a history [by] Vincent P. Carosso. Research associates: Marian V. Sears [and] Irving Katz. Cambridge, Mass., Harvard University Press, 1970. xiii, 569 p.
70-099515   332.6/6/0973   0674465741
Investment banking -- United States.

HG5152-5851 Investment, capital formation, speculation — By region or country — Other regions or countries

HG5152.L39 1989
Laxer, Gordon, 1944-
Open for business: the roots of foreign ownership in Canada/ Gordon Laxer. Toronto: Oxford University Press, 1989. viii, 247 p.
89-203151   332.6/73/0971   0195407342
Investments, Foreign -- Canada -- History. Canada -- Economic policy.

HG5160.5.A3.A76 1988
Armstrong, Christopher, 1942-
Southern exposure: Canadian promoters in Latin America and the Caribbean, 1896-1930/ Christopher Armstrong and H.V. Nelles. Toronto; University of Toronto Press, c1988. xv, 375 p.
89-168028   332.6/737108   0802026605
Investments, Canadian -- Latin America -- History -- 19th century. Investments, Canadian -- Latin America -- History -- 20th century. Public utilities -- Latin America -- Finance -- History -- 19th century.

HG5160.5.A3.F675 1988
Foreign investment, debt, and economic growth in Latin America/ edited by Antonio Jorge and Jorge Salazar-Carrillo. New York: St. Martin's Press, 1988. xix, 250 p.
87-018808   332.6/73/098   0312009364
Investments, Foreign -- Latin America -- Congresses. Debts, External -- Latin America -- Congresses. Latin America -- Economic conditions -- 1982- -- Congresses.

HG5160.5.A3.O27 1999
O'Brien, Thomas F., 1947-
The century of U.S. capitalism in Latin America/ Thomas O'Brien. Albuquerque: University of New Mexico Press, c1999. xiii, 199 p.
98-033361   332.67/37308 21   0826319955
Investments, American -- Latin America -- History. Business enterprises, Foreign -- Latin America -- History. United States -- Commerce -- Latin America -- History. Latin America -- Commerce -- United States -- History. United States -- Foreign economic relations -- Latin America.

HG5160.5.A3.S73 1987
Stallings, Barbara.
Banker to the Third World: U.S. portfolio investment in Latin America, 1900-1986/ Barbara Stallings. Berkeley: University of California Press, c1987. xvii, 434 p.
86-024988   332.6/7373/08   0520057260
Investments, American -- Latin America -- History. Loans, American -- Latin America -- History.

HG5162.W48 1992
Whiting, Van R.
The political economy of foreign investment in Mexico: nationalism, liberalism, and constraints on choice/ Van R. Whiting, Jr. Baltimore: Johns Hopkins University Press, c1992. xii, 313 p.
91-017669   332.6/73/0972   0801842271
Investments, Foreign -- Government policy -- Mexico. Industrial policy -- Mexico.

HG5422.P56 1984
Platt, D. C. M. 1934-
Foreign finance in continental Europe and the United States, 1815-1870: quantities, origins, functions, and distribution/ D.C.M. Platt. London; G. Allen & Unwin, 1984. viii, 216 p.
83-072851   332.6/73/094   0043303366
Investments, Foreign -- Europe -- History -- 19th century. Investments, Foreign -- United States -- History -- 19th century. Railroads -- Europe -- Finance -- History -- 19th century.

HG5422.W35 2000
Walter, Ingo.
High finance in the Euro-zone: competing in the new European capital market/ Ingo Walter and Roy C. Smith. London; Financial Times/Prentice Hall, 2000. xix, 344 p.
332.66094   0273637371
Capital market -- Europe. Free enterprise -- Europe. Investment banking -- Europe. Europe -- Economic conditions -- 20th century.

HG5432.C37 1996
Carruthers, Bruce G.
City of capital: politics and markets in the English financial revolution/ Bruce G. Carruthers. Princeton, N.J.: Princeton University Press, c1996. xiv, 303 p.
95-053190   332/.0414 20   0691044554
Capital market -- History -- 18th century. Capital market -- History -- 17th century. Great Britain -- Politics and government -- 18th century. Great Britain -- Politics and government -- 1689-1702.

HG5432.N43 1990
Neal, Larry, 1941-
The rise of financial capitalism: international capital markets in the Age of Reason/ Larry Neal. Cambridge; Cambridge University Press, 1990. x, 278 p.
90-001424   332.63/2/0941   052138205X
Capital market -- Great Britain -- History. Capital market -- Netherlands -- History. International finance -- History.

HG5770.5.A3.C43 1995
The changing capital markets of East Asia/ edited by Ky Cao. London; Routledge, 1995. x, 343 p.
94-047337   332/.041   0415122856
Capital market -- East Asia.

HG5782.P43 1991
Pearson, Margaret M., 1959-
Joint ventures in the People's Republic of China: the control of foreign direct investment under socialism/ Margaret M. Pearson. Princeton, N.J.: Princeton University Press, c1991. xiv, 335 p.
90-019955   338.8/8851   0691078823
Joint ventures -- China. Investments, Foreign -- China.

HG5836.A3.V58 1995
Vitalis, Robert, 1955-
When capitalists collide: business conflict and the end of empire in Egypt/ Robert Vitalis. Berkeley: University of California Press, c1995. xxi, 282 p.
94-016550   332.6/0962   0520085930
Investments -- Egypt -- History. Industrial policy -- Egypt -- History. Egypt -- Economic conditions -- 1918-

HG5851.A3.H85 1990
Hull, Richard W., 1940-
American enterprise in South Africa: historical dimensions of engagement and disengagement/ Richard W. Hull. New York: New York University Press, c1990. xviii, 419 p.
89-012548   338.8/8973/068   0814734626
Investments, American -- South Africa -- History. Corporations, American -- South Africa -- History. International business enterprises -- South Africa -- History.

HG5993 Investment, capital formation, speculation — By region or country — Developing countries

HG5993.B56 1993
Billet, Bret L.
Modernization theory and economic development: discontent in the developing world/ Bret L. Billet. Westport, Conn.: Praeger, 1993. xiii, 143 p.
93-019115   338.9/009172/4   0275944468
Investments, Foreign -- Developing countries. International business enterprises -- Developing countries. Economic development.

HG5993.K46 1997
Keppler, Michael.
Emerging markets: research, strategies and benchmarks/ Michael Keppler and Martin Lechner. Chicago: Irwin Professional Pub., c1997. x, 374 p.
96-017950   332.6/73/091724 20   0786308818
Investments, Foreign -- Developing countries. Capital movements -- Developing countries.

HG6008 Investment, capital formation, speculation — Speculation — History

HG6008.R4 1933
Reading, Gerald Rufus Isaacs, 1889-
The South sea bubble, by Viscount Erleigh. New York, G. P. Putnam's sons, 1933. 176 p.
33-029382   332.630942
South sea company.

HG6024-6046 Investment, capital formation, speculation — Speculation — Futures. Futures market

HG6024.A3.F58 1988
Fitzgerald, M. Desmond.
Directory of financial futures exchanges/ M. Desmond Fitzgerald. New York: Stockton Press, 1988. xxv, 251 p.
86-030138   332.6/44   0935859039
Financial futures -- Directories. Options (Finance) -- Directories. Commodity exchanges -- Directories.

HG6024.U6.A73 1996
Arditti, Fred D.
Derivatives: a comprehensive resource for options, futures, interest rate swaps, and mortgage securities/ Fred D. Arditti. Boston: Harvard Business School Press, c1996. xxi, 394 p.
95-031894   332.64/5 20   0875845606
Derivative securities -- United States.

HG6024.3.A26 1996
Abolafia, Mitchel.
Making markets: opportunism and restraint on Wall Street/ Mitchel Y. Abolafia. Cambridge, Mass.: Harvard University Press, 1996. ix, 216 p.
96-020665   332.64   0674543246
Financial futures. Bond market. Stock exchanges.

HG6046.H36 1984
Handbook of futures markets: commodity, financial, stock index, and options/ Perry J. Kaufman. New York: Wiley, c1984. 1 v.
84-003504   332.63/28   0471087149
Commodity exchanges -- Handbooks, manuals, etc.

HG6126 Lotteries — By region or country — United States

HG6126.C55 1989
Clotfelter, Charles T.
Selling hope: state lotteries in America/ Charles T. Clotfelter and Philip J. Cook. Cambridge, Mass.: Harvard University Press, c1989. xii, 323 p.
89-032398   336.1/7/0973   0674800974
Lotteries -- United States -- States. Lotteries -- Government policy -- United States -- States.

HG8053 Insurance — General special

HG8053.M86 1995
Munro, Roderick H.
International insurance/ Roderick H. Munro, coordinating author, Lowell S. Young. Malvern, PA: American Institute for CPCU, 1995. ix, 60 p.
95-077154   0894630733
Insurance. International business enterprises.

HG8535 Insurance —
By region or country —
United States

HG8535.M44 1988
Meier, Kenneth J., 1950-
The political economy of regulation: the case of insurance/ Kenneth J. Meier. Albany: State University of New York Press, c1988. xviii, 230 p.
87-033769   368/.973   088706731X
Insurance -- United States -- State supervision. Insurance law -- Economic aspects -- United States.

HG8782 Insurance —
Life insurance — Actuarial science

HG8782.G4713 1995
Gerber, Hans U.
Life insurance mathematics/ Hans U. Gerber; with exercises contributed by Samuel H. Cox. Berlin; Springer, c1995. xv, 217 p.
95-039148   368.3/2/01   3540588582
Insurance, Life -- Mathematics.

HG8951-8963 Insurance —
Life insurance —
By region or country

HG8951.I44 1990
Individual and family markets.   Chicago, Ill.: Dearborn/R&R Newkirk, c1990. ix, 245 p.
90-030339   368.3/2/00688   0793100445
Insurance, Life -- United States -- Marketing. Homeowner's insurance -- United States -- Marketing.

HG8963.N9553W4 1993
Weare, Walter B.
Black business in the new south: a social history of the North Carolina Mutual Life Insurance Company/ Walter B. Weare. Durham: Duke University Press, 1993. xv, 312 p.
92-037508   368.3/2/0065756563   0822313383
North Carolina Mutual Life Insurance Company.

HG9390 Insurance —
Health insurance —
Long-term care insurance

HG9390.A27 1999
Abromovitz, Les.
Long-term care insurance made simple/ Les Abromovitz. Los Angeles, Calif.: Health Information Press, c1999. vi, 220 p.
99-012994   368.38/2 21   1885987145
Insurance, Long-term care -- United States. Aged -- Long-term care -- United States.

HG9396 Insurance —
Health insurance —
By region or country

HG9396.H322 1994
Hall, Mark A., 1955-
Reforming private health insurance/ Mark A. Hall. Washington, D.C.: AEI Press, 1994. v, 111 p.
94-014779   368.3/82/00973   084473862X
Insurance, Health -- United States.

HG9396.H638 2001
Hoffman, Beatrix Rebecca.
The wages of sickness: the politics of health insurance in progressive America/ Beatrix Hoffman. Chapel Hill: University of North Carolina Press, c2001. xii, 261 p.
00-044735   368.38/2/00973 21   0807825883
Insurance, Health -- United States -- History -- 20th century. Progressivism (United States politics)

HG9396.M55 1996
Miller, Irwin.
American health care blues: Blue Cross, HMOs, and pragmatic reform since 1960/ Irwin Miller. New Brunswick, N.J.: Transaction Publishers, c1996. 148 p.
96-017334   368.3/82/00973 20   1560002654
Insurance, Health -- United States. Insurance, Hospitalization -- United States. Health maintenance organizations -- United States.

HG9396.P38 1997
Pauly, Mark V., 1941-
Health benefits at work: an economic and political analysis of employment-based health insurance/ Mark V. Pauly. Ann Arbor: University of Michigan press, c1997. vi, 187 p.
97-018341   658.38/201 21   0472108573
Insurance, Health -- United States -- Costs. Employee fringe benefits -- United States -- Costs.

HJ Public Finance

HJ141 General works —
1701-

HJ141.I58 1988
International aspects of fiscal policies/ edited by Jacob A. Frenkel. Chicago: University of Chicago Press, 1988. x, 408 p.
87-025549   332/.042   0226262510
Fiscal policy. International economic relations.

HJ141.M79
Musgrave, Richard Abel, 1910-
Fiscal systems, by Richard A. Musgrave. New Haven, Yale University Press, 1969. xix, 397 p.
69-015455   336
Finance, Public.

HJ141.M796 1986
Musgrave, Richard Abel, 1910-
Public finance in a democratic society: collected papers of Richard A. Musgrave. New York: New York University Press, 1986. 2 v.
85-032053   336   0814754287
Finance, Public.

HJ192-192.5 General works
— Fiscal policy

HJ192.O18
Oates, Wallace E.
Fiscal federalism [by] Wallace E. Oates. New York, Harcourt Brace Jovanovich [1972] xvi, 256 p.
78-185772   336.1/85   015527452X
Intergovernmental fiscal relations. Grants-in-aid. Finance, Public.

HJ192.5.F573 1997
Fiscal policy: lessons from economic research/ edited by Alan J. Auerbach. Cambridge, Mass.: MIT Press, c1997. xii, 475 p.
96-053456   336.3/0973 21   0262011603
Fiscal policy -- Congresses. Fiscal policy -- United States -- Congresses.

HJ219 History — Ancient —
Greece

HJ219.F4
Ferguson, William Scott, 1875-1954.
The treasurers of Athena, by William Scott Ferguson. Cambridge, Mass., Harvard university press, 1932. ix, 108 p.
32-003703   336.09385
Finance, Public -- Athens. Chronology, Greek. Inscriptions, Greek -- Athens. Athens (Greece) -- Politics and government.

HJ241 By region or country —
United States — General works

HJ241.M36 1994
Makin, John H.
Debt and taxes/ John H. Makin and Norman J. Ornstein. New York: Times Books, c1994. x, 337 p.
93-030517   336.3/0973   081292312X
Fiscal policy -- United States -- History.

HJ241.M93
Myers, Margaret G. 1899-
A financial history of the United States, by Margaret G. Myers. New York, Columbia University Press, 1970. viii, 451 p.
70-104900   332/.0973   0231024428
Finance, Public -- United States -- History. Finance -- United States -- History.

HJ257-257.2 By region or country
— United States — 20th century

HJ257.B62
Blum, John Morton, 1921-
Roosevelt and Morgenthau.   Boston, Houghton Mifflin, 1970. xvi, 686 p.
75-096063   336.73
Morgenthau, Henry, -- 1891-1967.   Finance, Public -- United States -- 1933- Currency question -- United States.

HJ257.G54
Gilbert, Charles, 1913-
American financing of World War I. Westport, Conn., Greenwood, [1970] xix, 259 p.
73-079060   336.73   0837114969
World War, 1914-1918 -- Finance -- United States. Finance, Public -- United States -- History.

HJ257.H33
Harris, Seymour Edwin, 1897-
Economics of social security; the relation of the American program to consumption, savings, output and finance [by] Seymour E. Harris. New York, McGraw-Hill, 1941. xxvi, 455 p.
41-018846   368.4/00973   837136857
Social security -- United States. Finance, Public -- United States. Finance, Public -- United States -- 1933- United States -- Economic policy -- 1933-1945.

HJ257.P45 1965
Phelps, Edmund S.,
Private wants and public needs; issues surrounding the size and scope of Government expenditure. Edited with an introd. by Edmund S. Phelps. New York, W. W. Norton [1965] xiii, 178 p.
65-012517   350
Fiscal policy -- United States.

HJ257.S78 1996
Stein, Herbert, 1916-
The fiscal revolution in America: policy in pursuit of reality/ Herbert Stein. Washington, D.C.: AEI Press, 1996. xiii, 623 p.
95-051843   336.73   0844739367
Fiscal policy -- United States. Monetary policy -- United States.

HJ257.2.B82 1970
Buchanan, James M.
The public finances; an introductory textbook [by] James M. Buchanan. Homewood, Ill., R. D. Irwin, 1970. xvii, 492 p.
79-105910   336.73
Finance, Public -- United States -- 1933-

HJ257.2.F75 1988
Friedman, Benjamin M.
Day of reckoning: the consequences of American economic policy under Reagan and after/ Benjamin Friedman. New York: Random House, c1988. ix, 323 p.
88-011693   336.3/4/0973   0394565533
Fiscal policy -- United States. Debts, Public -- United States. Loans, Foreign -- United States. United States -- Economic conditions -- 1981-

HJ257.2.P4 1983
Pechman, Joseph A., 1918-
Federal tax policy/ Joseph A. Pechman. Washington, D.C.: Brookings Institution, c1983. xix, 410 p.
83-023126   336.2/00973   0815769644
Fiscal policy -- United States. Taxation -- United States.

HJ275 By region or country — United States — States collectively. Intergovernmental fiscal relations

HJ275.B29
Barfield, Claude E.
Rethinking federalism: block grants and federal, state, and local responsibilities/ Claude E. Barfield. Washington: American Enterprise Institute for Public Policy c1981. ix, 99 p.
81-017602   336.1/85   0844734799
Block grants -- United States. Intergovernmental fiscal relations -- United States. Federal government -- United States.

HJ275.B47 1991
Bickers, Kenneth N., 1960-
Federal domestic outlays, 1983-1990: a data book/ Kenneth N. Bickers and Robert M. Stein. Armonk, N.Y.: M.E. Sharpe, c1991. vi, 294 p.
91-000651   336.1/85   087332840X
Grants-in-aid -- United States -- Statistics. Economic assistance, Domestic -- United States -- Statistics.

HJ275.D47
Derthick, Martha.
The influence of federal grants; public assistance in Massachusetts. Cambridge, Mass., Harvard University Press, 1970. vii, 285 p.
73-095919   338.4/7/361609744   0674454251
Grants-in-aid -- United States. Public welfare -- Massachusetts.

HJ275.F552 1995
The fiscal crisis of the states: lessons for the future/ edited by Steven D. Gold. Washington, D.C.: Georgetown University Press, c1995. xiii, 396 p.
94-032275   336/.01373   0878405747
Finance, Public -- United States -- States. Fiscal policy -- United States -- States. Intergovernmental fiscal relations -- United States.

HJ275.F558 1988
Fiscal federalism: quantitative studies/ edited by Harvey S. Rosen. Chicago: University of Chicago Press, 1988. ix, 262 p.
87-028726   336.1/85   0226726193
Intergovernmental fiscal relations -- United States -- Congresses.

HJ275.M8
Musgrave, Richard Abel, 1910-
Essays in fiscal federalism [by] Richard A. Musgrave. Washington, Brookings Institution [1965] xvi, 301 p.
65-028605   336.73
Intergovernmental fiscal relations -- United States. Intergovernmental tax relations -- United States.

HJ275.S728 1995
Stein, Robert M.
Perpetuating the pork barrel: policy subsystems and American democracy/ Robert M. Stein, Kenneth N. Bickers. Cambridge; Cambridge University Press, c1995. xiv, 232 p.
95-000858   336.3/9/0973   0521482984
Economic assistance, Domestic -- United States. Budget deficits -- United States. Campaign funds -- United States.

HJ384-605 By region or country — United States — By state

HJ384.W34 1987
Wallenstein, Peter.
From slave South to New South: public policy in nineteenth-century Georgia/ Peter Wallenstein. Chapel Hill: University of North Carolina Press, c1987. xii, 284 p.
86-019359   336.758   0807817171
Fiscal policy -- Georgia -- History -- 19th century. Finance, Public -- Georgia -- History -- 19th century. Reconstruction -- Georgia.

HJ605.T86 1988
The Two New Yorks: state-city relations in the changing federal system/ Gerald Benjamin and Charles Brecher, editors. New York: Russell Sage Foundation, c1988. xviii, 557 p.
88-015778   336.747   0871541076
Intergovernmental fiscal relations -- New York (State) State-local relations -- New York (State)

HJ915-971 By region or country — Latin America — South America

HJ915.G35 1991
Gallo, Carmenza.
Taxes and state power: political instability in Bolivia, 1900-1950/ Carmenza Gallo. Philadelphia: Temple University Press, 1991. x, 174 p.
90-042055   336.2/00984   0877228000
Finance, Public -- Bolivia. Taxation -- Bolivia. Exports -- Bolivia. Bolivia -- Economic policy. Bolivia -- Politics and government -- 1879-1938. Bolivia -- Politics and government -- 1938-1952.

HJ971.A53 1985
Andrien, Kenneth J., 1951-
Crisis and decline: the Viceroyalty of Peru in the seventeenth century/ Kenneth J. Andrien. Albuquerque: University of New Mexico Press, c1985. x, 287 p.
84-023436   336.85   0826307914
Finance, Public -- Peru (Viceroyalty) Finance, Public -- Spain -- Colonies -- History -- 17th century. Spain -- Colonies -- America -- Economic policy.

HJ1000.7 By region or country — Europe — Eastern Europe. Central Europe

HJ1000.7.D48 1993
Developing public finance in emerging market economies/ edited by Kalman Mizsei. New York: Institute for EastWest Studies; 1993. vii, 208 p.
93-023606   336.47   0913449369
Finance, Public -- Central Europe. Budget -- Central Europe. Economic stabilization -- Central Europe.

HJ1005-1023.7 By region or country — Europe — Great Britain. England

HJ1005.H37
Harriss, G. L.
King, Parliament, and public finance in medieval England to 1369/ G. L. Harriss. Oxford: Clarendon Press, 1975. xii, 554 p.
75-328267   336.42   0198224354
Finance, Public -- England -- History. Taxation -- England -- History. Constitutional history, Medieval. Great Britain -- Politics and government -- 1066-1485. England -- Economic conditions -- 1066-1485.

HJ1012.C87 1987
Cust, Richard.
The forced loan and English politics, 1626-1628/ Richard Cust. Oxford [Oxfordshire]: Clarendon Press; 1987. x, 358 p.
87-007977   336.42   0198229518
Finance, Public -- Great Britain -- To 1688. Intergovernmental fiscal relations -- Great Britain -- History -- 17th century. Great Britain -- Politics and government -- 1625-1649.

HJ1023.7.T73 1993
Transition to market: studies in fiscal reform/ edited by Vito Tanzi. Washington, D.C.: International Monetary Fund, 1993. ix, 387 p.
93-019120   336.3/0947   1557752753
Fiscal policy -- Europe, Eastern. Capitalism -- Europe, Eastern. Fiscal policy -- Former Soviet republics.

HJ1068 By region or country — Europe — Hungary

HJ1068.P83 1998
Public finance reform during the transition: the experience of Hungary/ edited by Lajos Bokros, Jean-Jacques Dethier. Washington, D.C.: World Bank, c1998. xv, 580 p.
98-042499 336.439 21 0821342525
Finance, Public -- Hungary.

HJ1199 By region or country — Europe — Other European regions or countries

HJ1199.F55.K58 1991
Kittell, Ellen E.
From ad hoc to routine: a case study in medieval bureaucracy/ Ellen E. Kittell. Philadelphia: University of Pennsylvania Press, c1991. x, 265 p.
90-047800 336.493/1 0812230795
Finance, Public -- Belgium -- Flanders -- History. Bureaucracy -- Belgium -- Flanders -- History. Belgium -- History -- To 1555.

HJ1620 By region or country — Developing countries

HJ1620.F57 1989
Fiscal policy, stabilization, and growth in developing countries/ edited by Mario I. Blejer and Ke-young Chu. Washington, D.C.: International Monetary Fund, 1989. ix, 387 p.
89-015237 339.5/09172/4 1557750343
Fiscal policy -- Developing countries. Economic stabilization -- Developing countries.

HJ1620.G66 1984
Goode, Richard B.
Government finance in developing countries/ Richard Goode. Washington, D.C.: Brookings Institution, c1984. xii, 334 p.
83-020989 336/.09172/4 0815731965
Finance, Public -- Developing Countries.

HJ2005 Budget. Income and expenditure — General works

HJ2005.B797 1999
Budget deficits and debt: a global perspective/ edited by Siamack Shojai. Westport, Conn.: Praeger, 1999. xiii, 194 p.
98-015653 339.5/23 0275957128
Budget deficits. Debts, Public.

HJ2005.N48 1988
New directions in budget theory/ Irene S. Rubin, editor. Albany, N.Y.: State University of New York Press, c1988. viii, 207 p.
87-009977 350.72/2 0887066240
Budget.

HJ2005.O88 1993
Ott, Attiat F.
Public sector budgets: a comparative study/ Attiat F. Ott. Hants, Eng.; E. Elgar Pub. Co., 1993. xv, 285 p.
93-022654 350.72/2 1852786183
Budget. Budget -- United States. Budget -- Case studies.

HJ2051-2053 Budget. Income and expenditure — By region or country — United States

HJ2051.E93 1997
Evans, Gary R., 1946-
Red ink: the budget, deficit, and debt of the U.S. government/ by Gary R. Evans. San Diego: Academic Press, c1997. xix, 297 p.
97-009581 336.3/4/0973 21 012244079X
Budget -- United States. Budget deficits -- United States. Debts, Public -- United States.

HJ2051.F73 1993
Franklin, Daniel P.
Making ends meet: congressional budgeting in the age of deficits/ Daniel P. Franklin. Washington, D.C.: CQ Press, c1993. xi, 254 p.
92-033123 353.0072/2 0871877171
Budget -- United States. Budget deficits -- United States.

HJ2051.H325 1997
Hager, George.
Mirage: why neither Democrats nor Republicans can balance the budget, end the deficit, and satisfy the public/ George Hager and Eric Pianin. New York: Times Books, c1997. xi, 337 p.
96-041859 336.3/0973 20 0812924525
Budget deficits -- United States. Government spending policy -- United States. Fiscal policy -- United States.

HJ2051.I66 1990
Ippolito, Dennis S.
Uncertain legacies: federal budget policy from Roosevelt through Reagan/ Dennis S. Ippolito. Charlottesville: University Press of Virginia, 1990. xiv, 297 p.
90-036590 353.0072/2/09043 0813912873
Budget -- United States -- History -- 20th century. Government spending policy -- United States -- History -- 20th century.

HJ2051.K34 1997
Kahn, Jonathan, 1958-
Budgeting democracy: state building and citizenship in America, 1890-1928/ Jonathan Kahn. Ithaca, NY: Cornell University Press, 1997. xi, 222 p.
97-003847 352.4/973/009 0801429501
Budget -- United States -- History. Budget -- United States -- States -- History. Municipal budgets -- United States -- History -- 20th century. United States -- Politics and government -- 20th century.

HJ2051.M49 1989
Meyer, Annette E.
Evolution of United States budgeting: changing fiscal and financial concepts/ Annette E. Meyer. New York: Greenwood Press, 1989. xiv, 179 p.
89-001890 353.0072/2 0313258686
Budget -- United States.

HJ2051.M52 1994
Miller, James Clifford.
Fix the U.S. budget!: urgings of an abominable no-man/ James C. Miller III. Stanford, Calif.: Hoover Institution Press, Stanford University, c1994. xvi, 176 p.
93-040600 336.73 0817992111
Budget -- United States. Tax and expenditure limitations -- United States. Government spending policy -- United States.

HJ2051.N167 1987
Nathan, Richard P.
Reagan and the States/ Richard P. Nathan, Fred C. Doolittle, and associates. Princeton, N.J.: Princeton University Press, c1987. xv, 375 p.
87-045529 353.0072/5 0691077487
Budget -- United States. Grants-in-aid -- United States. Intergovernmental fiscal relations -- United States. United States -- Economic policy -- 1981-1993.

HJ2051.S33 1990
Schick, Allen.
The capacity to budget/ Allen Schick. Washington, D.C.: Urban Institute Press; c1990. xviii, 225 p.
89-025003 336.73 0877664382
Budget -- United States. Government spending policy -- United States.

HJ2051.S3424 2000
Schick, Allen.
The federal budget: politics, policy, process/ by Allen Schick, with the assistance of Felix LoStracco. Washington, D.C.: Brookings Institution Press, c2000. x, 307 p.
99-050857 352.4/8/0973 21 0815777264
Budget -- United States. Budget process -- United States.

HJ2051.S74 1989
Stein, Herbert, 1916-
Governing the Herbert Stein. New York: Oxford University Press, 1989. viii, 145 p.
88-034531 339.5/2/0973 0195060385
Budget -- United States. Fiscal policy -- United States.

HJ2051.T63 1998
Tomkin, Shelley Lynne, 1950-
Inside OMB: politics and process in the President's Budget Office/ Shelley Lynne Tomkin. Armonk, N.Y.: M.E. Sharpe, c1998. xxii, 365 p.
97-046969 352.4/0973 21 1563244543
Budget -- United States.

HJ2051.W485 1984
Wildavsky, Aaron B.
The politics of the budgetary process/ Aaron Wildavsky. Boston: Little, Brown, c1984. xxxvi, 323 p.
83-013588 353.0072/221 0316940410
Budget -- United States.

HJ2052.C35 1992
Calleo, David P., 1934-
The bankrupting of America: how the federal budget is impoverishing the nation/ David P. Calleo. New York: W. Morrow, c1992. 301 p.
91-030373 339.5/23/0973 0688051626
Budget deficits -- United States. Fiscal policy -- United States.

HJ2052.I77
Ippolito, Dennis S.
Congressional spending/ Dennis S. Ippolito. Ithaca, N.Y.: Cornell University Press, 1981. 286 p.
81-067971   336.3/9/0973   0801492300
Government spending policy -- United States. United States -- Appropriations and expenditures.

HJ2052.P48 1988
Peterson, Peter G.
On borrowed time: how the growth in entitlement spending threatens America's future/ Peter G. Peterson and Neil Howe. San Francisco, Calif.: ICS Press; c1988. xii, 430 p.
88-023798   353.0084   155815003X
Entitlement spending -- United States. Budget deficits -- United States. Economic forecasting -- United States. United States -- Economic policy -- 1981-1993.

HJ2052.S337 1992
Schier, Steven E.
A decade of deficits: congressional thought and fiscal action/ Steven E. Schier. Albany, N.Y.: State University of New York Press, c1992. xi, 195 p.
91-013464   339.5/23/0973   0791409554
Fiscal policy -- United States. Budget deficits -- United States.

HJ2053.A1.F88 1998
The future of state taxation/ David Brunori, editor. Washington, D.C.: Urban Institute Press; c1998. xii, 235 p.
98-016507   336.2/00973 21   0877666806
Taxation -- United States -- States. Local taxation -- United States.

HJ2053.A1.S35
Schick, Allen.
Budget innovation in the States.   Washington, Brookings Institution [1971] x, 223 p.
76-161594   353.9/3/722   0815777302
Budget -- United States -- States. Program budgeting -- United States -- States.

HJ2250 Revenue. Taxation. Internal revenue — History — General works

HJ2250.L48 1988
Levi, Margaret.
Of rule and revenue/ Margaret Levi. Berkeley: University of California Press, c1988. x, 253 p.
87-028397   336.02   0520060911
Income tax -- History -- Case studies. State, The -- History -- Case studies. Revenue -- History -- Case studies.

HJ2305 Revenue. Taxation. Internal revenue — General works — 1801-

HJ2305.B87 1993
Burgess, Ronald.
Public revenue without taxation/ Ronald Burgess. London: Shepheard-Walwyn, 1993. vii, 120 p.
94-148823   336.02   0856831352
Taxation. Revenue. Inflation (Finance)

HJ2305.E27
The Economics of taxation/ Henry J. Aaron and Michael J. Boskin, editors. Washington, D.C.: Brookings Institution, c1980. xviii, 418 p.
79-003774   336.2/00973   0815700148
Taxation -- Addresses, essays, lectures. Taxation -- United States -- Addresses, essays, lectures. Fiscal policy -- Addresses, essays, lectures.

HJ2305.E53 1999
The encyclopedia of taxation and tax policy/ Joseph J. Cordes, Robert D. Ebel, and Jane G. Gravelle, editors. Washington, D.C.: Urban Institute Press; c1999. xi, 452 p.
98-040996   336.2/003 21   0877666822
Taxation -- Encyclopedias.

HJ2305.J328 1998
James, Simon R.
A dictionary of taxation/ Simon James. Cheltenham, UK; E. Elgar, c1998. vi, 173 p.
97-035421   336.2/003 21   1852780169
Taxation -- Dictionaries.

HJ2305.T179 1998
Tax policy in the real world/ edited by Joel Slemrod. Cambridge; Cambridge University Press, 1999. x, 515 p.
98-031981   336.2   0521641373
Taxation. Fiscal policy.

HJ2305.W68 1990
World tax reform: case studies of developed and developing countries/ edited by Michael J. Boskin and Charles E. McLure, Jr. San Francisco, Calif.: ICS Press; c1990. xiv, 332 p.
89-026902   336.2/05   1558150927
Taxation -- Case studies.

HJ2322 Revenue. Taxation. Internal revenue — Tax incidence. Tax shifting. Tax equity — By region or country

HJ2322.A3.D57 1995
Distributional analysis of tax policy/ edited by David F. Bradford. Washington, D.C.: AEI Press, 1995. xvii, 312 p.
95-018681   336.2/94/0973   0844738913
Tax incidence -- United States. Taxation -- United States. Income distribution -- United States.

HJ2322.A3.P42 1985
Pechman, Joseph A., 1918-
Who paid the taxes, 1966-85?/ Joseph A. Pechman. -- Washington, D.C.: Brookings Institution, c1985. xi, 84 p.
83-045845   336.2/94/0973   0815769970
Tax incidence -- United States. Taxation -- United States.

HJ2348.6 Revenue. Taxation. Internal revenue — Tax evasion

HJ2348.6.C68 1990
Cowell, Frank A.
Cheating the government: the economics of evasion/ Frank A. Cowell. Cambridge, Mass.: MIT Press, c1990. xii, 267 p.
89-012921   336.2   0262031531
Tax evasion -- United States. Informal sector (Economics) -- United States.

HJ2351 Revenue. Taxation. Internal revenue — Inflation and taxation

HJ2351.B5 1975
Bird, Richard Miller, 1938-
Readings on taxation in developing countries/ edited by Richard M. Bird and Oliver Oldman. Baltimore: Johns Hopkins University Press, 1975. ix, 555 p.
74-024385   336.2/009172/4   0801816939
Taxation -- Developing countries.

HJ2362-2425 Revenue. Taxation. Internal revenue — By region or country — United States

HJ2362.P65 1996
Pollack, Sheldon David.
The failure of U.S. tax policy: revenue and politics/ Sheldon D. Pollack. University Park, Pa.: Pennsylvania State University Press, 1996. xi, 321 p.
95-026110   336.2/00973   0271015829
Taxation -- United States -- History. Revenue -- United States -- History.

HJ2368.B76 1993
Brown, Roger H.
Redeeming the Republic: Federalists, taxation, and the origins of the Constitution/ Roger H. Brown. Baltimore: Johns Hopkins University Press, c1993. 337 p.
92-028958   336.2/00973/09033   0801844975
Taxation -- United States -- States -- History -- 18th century. Taxation -- United States -- History -- 18th century. Constitutional history -- United States. United States -- Politics and government -- 1783-1789.

HJ2381.H684 1997
Howard, Christopher, 1961-
The hidden welfare state: tax expenditures and social policy in the United States/ Christopher Howard. Princeton, N.J.: Princeton University Press, c1997. xi, 250 p.
96-050044   336.2/06/0973 21   0691026467
Taxation -- United States. Tax expenditures -- United States. United States -- Social policy.

HJ2381.K77 2001
Krugman, Paul R.
Fuzzy math: the essential guide to the Bush tax plan/ Paul Krugman New York: Norton, 2001. 128 p.
2001-031477   336.2/00973   0393050629
Taxation -- United States. Budget -- United States. United States -- Appropriations and expenditures.

HJ2381.P39 1993
Payne, James L.
Costly returns: the burdens of the U.S. tax system/ James L. Payne. San Francisco, Calif.: ICS Press; c1993. x, 264 p.
92-019854   336.2/00973   1558152024
Taxation -- United States -- Costs.

HJ2381.T396 1996
Taxing America/ edited by Karen B. Brown and Mary Louise Fellows. New York: New York University Press, c1996. ix, 363 p.
96-025302   336.2/00973 20   0814726615
Taxation -- United States -- Congresses. Taxation -- Law and legislation -- United States -- Congresses. Income tax -- United States -- Congresses. United States -- Economic policy -- 1993- -- Congresses.

HJ2381.T53
Thurow, Lester C.
The impact of taxes on the American economy [by] Lester C. Thurow. New York, Praeger [1971] xiv, 171 p.
70-141363   330.973
Taxation -- United States. Fiscal policy -- United States. United States -- Economic conditions -- 1971-1981.

HJ2381.Z45 1998
Zelizer, Julian E.
Taxing America: Wilbur D. Mills, Congress, and the state, 1945-1975/ Julian E. Zelizer. Cambridge, UK; Cambridge University Press, 1998. xv, 384 p.
98-021974   336.2/00973   0521621666
Mills, Wilbur D. -- (Wilbur Daigh), -- 1909- Taxation -- United States -- History.

HJ2425.A2P3 1928a
Parker, Coralie,
The history of taxation in North Carolina during the colonial period, 1663-1776, by Coralie Parker. New York, Columbia University Press, 1928. x, 178 p.
28-025845
Taxation -- North Carolina.

HJ2479 Revenue. Taxation. Internal revenue — By region or country — Latin America

HJ2479.E26 1985
The Economics of the Caribbean Basin/ edited by Michael B. Connolly and John McDermott. New York: Praeger, 1985. xxiii, 355 p.
85-003419   330.9182/1   0030016746
Taxation -- Caribbean Area. Tariff -- Caribbean Area. Debts, External -- Latin America.

HJ2610-2646 Revenue. Taxation. Internal revenue — By region or country — Europe

HJ2610.K4
Kennedy, W.
English taxation, 1640-1799; an essay on policy and opinion. London, G. Bell & sons ltd., 1913. 199 p.
13-022315
Taxation -- Great Britain -- History.

HJ2646.S75 1972
Strayer, Joseph Reese, 1904-
Studies in early French taxation, by Joseph R. Strayer and Charles H. Taylor. Westport, Conn., Greenwood Press [1972, c1939] xiii, 200 p.
78-138187   336.2/00944   0837156440
Taxation -- France -- History.

HJ3252 Revenue. Taxation. Internal revenue — Taxation. Administration and procedure

HJ3252.B45 1989
Beito, David T.
Taxpayers in revolt: tax resistance during the Great Depression/ David T. Beito. Chapel Hill: University of North Carolina Press, c1989. xv, 216 p.
88-026032   336.2/91   0807818364
Tax collection -- United States -- History. Taxpayer compliance -- United States -- History. Depressions -- 1929 -- United States.

HJ3833 Revenue. Taxation. Internal revenue — Revenue from sources other than taxation — By region or country

HJ3833.S26 1996
Sbragia, Alberta M.
Debt wish: entrepreneurial cities, U.S. federalism, and economic development/ Alberta M. Sbragia. Pittsburgh, PA: University of Pittsburgh Press, c1996. ix, 296 p.
95-051285   336.73 20   0822939428
Investment of public funds -- United States. Intergovernmental fiscal relations -- United States. Municipal finance -- United States.

HJ4120 Revenue. Taxation. Internal revenue — Property tax — By region or country

HJ4120.A62
Aaron, Henry J.
Who pays the property tax?: A new view/ Henry J. Aaron. Washington: Brookings Institution, [1975] xii, 110 p.
75-019270   336.2/2/0973   0815700229
Property tax -- United States.

HJ4120.P673
Property taxes, housing and the cities [by] George E. Peterson [and others] Lexington, Mass., Lexington Books [1973] xv, 203 p.
73-011673   336.2/2/0973   0669910252
Property tax -- United States. Cities and towns -- United States.

HJ4132 Revenue. Taxation. Internal revenue — Property tax — Capital levy. Capital taxes

HJ4132.T39 1993
Tax reform and the cost of capital: an international comparison/ Dale W. Jorgenson, Ralph Landau, editors. Washington, D.C.: Brookings Institution, c1993. xix, 420 p.
93-018812   336.2/05   0815747160
Capital levy. Income tax. Capital gains tax.

HJ4153-4191 Revenue. Taxation. Internal revenue — Property tax — Land tax. Real property tax. Land value taxation

HJ4153.B57
Bird, Richard Miller, 1938-
Taxing agricultural land in developing countries [by] Richard M. Bird. Cambridge, Harvard University Press, 1974. xvi, 361 p.
73-077991   336.2/091724   0674868552
Land value taxation -- Developing countries. Agriculture -- Taxation -- Developing countries.

HJ4191.O85 1995
O'Sullivan, Arthur.
Property taxes and tax revolts: the legacy of Proposition 13/ Arthur O'Sullivan, Terri A. Sexton, Steven M. Sheffrin. Cambridge [England]; Cambridge University Press, 1995. x, 159 p.
94-006770   336.22/09794   0521461596
Real property tax -- California. Real property tax -- United States. Tax and expenditure limitations -- California.

HJ4629 Revenue. Taxation. Internal revenue — Income tax — General works

HJ4629.A8 1995
Atkinson, A. B.
Public economics in action: the basic income/flat tax proposal/ A.B. Atkinson. Oxford: Clarendon Press; c1995. xiii, 169 p.
94-036055   336.24   0198283369
Income tax. Flat-rate income tax. Social security -- Finance.

HJ4651-4655 Revenue. Taxation. Internal revenue — Income tax — By region or country

HJ4651.S73 1993
Stanley, Robert, 1953-
Dimensions of law in the service of order: origins of the federal income tax, 1861-1913/ Robert Stanley. New York: Oxford University Press, 1993. xiv, 331 p.
92-024107   336.24/0973   0195058488
Income tax -- United States -- History.

HJ4652.D6 1991
Do taxes matter?: the impact of the Tax Reform Act of 1986/ edited by Joel Slemrod. Cambridge, Mass.: MIT Press, c1990. x, 349 p.
90-042398   336.2/00973   0262193027
Income tax -- United States -- Congresses. Taxation -- Law and legislation -- United States -- Congresses. United States -- Economic conditions -- 1981- -- Congresses.

HJ4652.G6 1976
Goode, Richard B.
The individual income tax/ Richard Goode. Washington: Brookings Institution, c1976. xiv, 346 p.
75-038735   336.2/42/0973   0815731981
Income tax -- United States.

HJ4652.S475
Simons, Henry Calvert, 1849-1946.
Personal income taxation: the definition of income as a problem of fiscal policy/ by Henry C. Simons. Chicago, Ill.: University of Chicago Press, c1938. xi, 238 p.
38-027193   336.240973
Income tax -- United States.

HJ4652.T396 1989
Taxpayer compliance/ Jeffrey A. Roth, John T. Scholz, and Ann Dryden Witte, editors. Philadelphia: University of Pennsylvania Press, c1989. 2 v.
88-036250   336.2/91   081228187X
Taxpayer compliance -- United States. Taxation -- Law and legislation -- United States.

HJ4653.C3.D33
David, Martin Heidenhain.
Alternative approaches to capital gains taxation [by] Martin David. Washington, Brookings Institution [1968] xvi, 280 p.
67-030592   336.2/4
Capital gains tax -- United States.

HJ4653.C7.M334 1991
Martin, Cathie J.
Shifting the burden: the struggle over growth and corporate taxation/ Cathie J. Martin. Chicago: University of Chicago Press, 1991. viii, 251 p.
90-024497   336.24/3/0973   0226508323
Income tax -- United States. Corporations -- Taxation -- United States. Corporations -- Taxation -- Law and legislation -- United States.

HJ4655.A1.P43
Penniman, Clara.
State income taxation/ Clara Penniman. Baltimore: Johns Hopkins University Press, c1980. xiii, 292 p.
79-020081   353.9/3/724   0801822904
Income tax -- United States -- States. Tax administration and procedure -- United States -- States.

HJ5018 Revenue. Taxation. Internal revenue — Internal Revenue Service

HJ5018.B87 1989
Burnham, David, 1933-
A law unto itself: power, politics, and the IRS/ David Burnham. New York: Random House, c1989. 419 p.
89-042778   353.0072/4   0394560973
Tax administration and procedure -- Corrupt practices -- United States.

HJ5021 Revenue. Taxation. Internal revenue — Illicit distilling and taxation. Moonshining

HJ5021.M55 1991
Miller, Wilbur R., 1944-
Revenuers & moonshiners: enforcing federal liquor law in the mountain south, 1865-1900/ Wilbur R. Miller. Chapel Hill: University of North Carolina Press, c1991. xii, 251 p.
90-049549   364.1/33   080781959X
Distilling, Illicit -- Appalachian Region -- History -- 19th century. Liquor laws -- Appalachian Region -- History -- 19th century. Southern States -- History -- 1865-1951.

HJ5707 Revenue. Taxation. Internal revenue — Excise tax — By region or country, A-Z

HJ5707.U5.T39 1997
Taxing choice: the predatory politics of fiscal discrimination/ William F. Shughart II, editor; with a foreword by Paul W. McCracken. New Brunswick, N.J., U.S.A.: Transaction Publishers, c1997. xv, 396 p.
97-013662   336.2/00973 21   1560003030
Excise tax -- United States. Taxation -- Political aspects -- United States.

HJ5711 Revenue. Taxation. Internal revenue — Sales tax. Spending tax. Turnover tax. Value-added tax — General works

HJ5711.T36 1988
Tait, Alan A.
Value-added tax: international practice and problems/ Alan A. Tait. Washington, D.C.: International Monetary Fund, 1988. xii, 450 p.
88-013135   336.2/714   1557750122
Value-added tax.

HJ5715 Revenue. Taxation. Internal revenue — Sales tax. Spending tax. Turnover tax. Value-added tax — By region or country, A-Z

HJ5715.E9.V29
The Value-added tax: lessons from Europe/ Henry J. Aaron, editor. Washington, D.C.: Brookings Institution, c1981. xi, 107 p.
81-038475   336.2/714/094   0815700288
Value-added tax -- Europe. Value-added tax -- United States.

HJ5715.U6.S45 1997
Seidman, Laurence S.
The USA tax: a progressive consumption tax/ Laurence S. Seidman. Cambridge, Mass.: MIT Press, c1997. x, 160 p.
96-041990   336.2/7 21   0262193833
Spendings tax -- United States. Value-added tax -- United States. Taxation of articles of consumption -- United States.

HJ6645 Customs administration — By region or country — United States

HJ6645.E8
Evans, Stephen Hadley, 1905-
The United States Coast Guard, 1790-1915; a definitive history (with a postscript: 1915-1949) Annapolis, Md., United States Naval Institute, 1949. xiii, 228 p.
50-000375   351.792
United States. Coast Guard.

HJ6645.R2
Rachlis, Eugene.
The story of the U.S. Coast Guard/ illus. with official U.S. Coast Guard photographs. Random House, 1961. 176 p.
91-111269   351.792
United States. Coast Guard.

HJ6891 Customs administration — By region or country — Other regions or countries

HJ6891.H65
Hoon, Elizabeth Evelynola.
The organization of the English customs system, 1696-1786, by Elizabeth Evelynola Hoon. New York and London, D. Appleton-Century Company, inc. [c1938] ix, 322 p.
38-011118   336.260942
Customs administration -- Great Britain -- History.

HJ7390 Customs administration — By region or country — Developing countries

HJ7390.P74 2000
Premchand, A., 1933-
Control of public money: the fiscal machinery in developing countries/ A. Premchand. New Delhi; Oxford University Press, 2000. xxvi, 494 p.
00-410450   0195653688
Expenditure, Public. Finance, Public -- Developing countries -- Accounting. Government spending policy -- Developing countries.

HJ7461 Expenditures. Government spending — General works

HJ7461.P7 1968b
Pryor, Frederic L.
Public expenditures in communist and capitalist nations [by] Frederic L. Pryor. Homewood, Ill., R. D. Irwin, 1968. 543 p.
68-014872   336.3/9
Expenditures, Public.

HJ7537 Expenditures. Government spending — By region or country — United States

HJ7537.P39 1991
Payne, James L.
The culture of spending: why Congress lives beyond our means/ James L. Payne. San Francisco, Calif.: ICS Press, c1991. ix, 225 p.
91-018994   336.3/9/0973   1558151346
Government spending policy -- United States.

HJ7755 Expenditures. Government spending — By region or country — Other regions or countries

HJ7755.S38 1995
The scope of government/ edited by Ole Borre and Elinor Scarbrough. Oxford; Oxford University Press, 1995. xviii, 437 p.
95-010793   336.3/9/094   019827954X
Government spending policy -- Europe -- Public opinion. Welfare state -- Public opinion. Taxation -- Europe -- Public opinion.

HJ8003 Public debts — History

HJ8003.V47 1990
Veseth, Michael.
Mountains of debt: crisis and change in Renaissance Florence, Victorian Britain, and postwar America/ Michael Veseth. New York: Oxford University Press, 1990. vii, 246 p.
89-049029   336.3/4/09   0195064208
Debts, Public -- History -- Case studies. Debt -- History -- Case studies. Debts, External -- Italy -- Florence -- History.

HJ8119 Public debts — By region or country — United States

HJ8119.F4
Ferguson, James Milton.
Public debt and future generations, edited by James M. Ferguson. Chapel Hill, University of North Carolina Press [1964] 234 p.
64-022528   336.3433
Debts, Public -- United States. Fiscal policy -- United States.

HJ8119.H43 1989
Heilbroner, Robert L.
The debt and the deficit: false alarms/real possibilities/ Robert Heilbroner and Peter Bernstein. New York: Norton, c1989. 144 p.
89-003260   336.3/4/0973   039302752X
Debts, Public -- United States. Budget deficits -- United States.

HJ8514.5-8519 Public debts — By region or country — Latin America

HJ8514.5.L393 1989
Latin American debt and adjustment: external shocks and macroeconomic policies/ edited by Philip L. Brock, Michael B. Connolly, and Claudio Gonzalez-Vega. New York: Praeger, 1989. xxii, 261 p.
88-025021   336.3/435/098   0275931234
Debts, External -- Latin America -- Case studies. Economic stabilization -- Latin America -- Case studies. Latin America -- Economic conditions -- 1982- -- Case studies.

HJ8514.5.L395 1987
Latin America's debt crisis: adjusting to the past or planning for the future?/ edited by Robert A. Pastor. Boulder, Colo.: L. Rienner, 1987. xiii, 176 p.
87-004956   336.3/435/098   1555870538
Debts, External -- Latin America -- Congresses. Loans, Foreign -- Latin America -- Congresses.

HJ8514.5.M357 1989
Marichal, Carlos.
A century of debt crises in Latin America: from independence to the Great Depression, 1820-1930/ Carlos Marichal. Princeton, N.J.: Princeton University Press, c1989. xiv, 283 p.
88-017843   336.3/435/098   0691077924
Debts, External -- Latin America -- History.

HJ8519.O42 1992
Oliveri, Ernest J.
Latin American debt and the politics of international finance/ Ernest J. Oliveri. Westport, Conn.: Praeger, 1992. 235 p.
91-030394   336.3/435/098   027594123X
Debts, External -- Mexico. Debts, External -- Brazil. Debts, External -- Argentina.

HJ8615 Public debts — By region or country — Europe

HJ8615.Z57 1987
Zloch-Christy, Iliana, 1953-
Debt problems of Eastern Europe/ Iliana Zloch-Christy. Cambridge [Cambridgeshire]; Cambridge University Press, 1987. xix, 220 p.
87-011634   336.3/435/0947   0521335426
Debts, External -- Europe, Eastern. Foreign exchange -- Europe, Eastern.

HJ8615.Z573 1991
Zloch-Christy, Iliana, 1953-
East-West financial relations: current problems and future prospects/ Iliana Zloch-Christy. Cambridge; Cambridge University Press, 1991. xiii, 126 p.
90-001898   336.3/435/0947   0521395305
Debts, External -- Europe, Eastern. East-West trade. Foreign exchange -- Europe, Eastern.

HJ8826 Public debts — By region or country — Other regions or countries

HJ8826.A36 1986
African debt and financing/ edited by Carol Lancaster and John Williamson. Washington, DC: Institute for International Economics, 1986. 223 p.
86-007421   336.3/435/096   0881320447
Debts, External -- Africa -- Congresses. Loans, Foreign -- Africa -- Congresses.

HJ8826.I54 1989
The IMF, the World Bank, and the African debt/ edited by Bade Onimode. London; Zed Books, 1989. 2 v.
89-008871   336.3/435/090   0862328284
Debts, External -- Africa. Loans, Foreign -- Africa.

HJ8826.N34 1993
Nafziger, E. Wayne.
The debt crisis in Africa/ E. Wayne Nafziger. Baltimore: Johns Hopkins University Press, c1993. xxiv, 287 p.
92-023735   336.3/435/0967   0801844762
Debts, External -- Africa, Sub-Saharan.

HJ8899 Public debts — By region or country — Developing countries

HJ8899.C37 1984
Carvounis, Chris C.
The debt dilemma of developing nations: issues and cases/ Chris C. Carvounis. Westport, Conn.: Quorum Books, 1984. xvi, 189 p.
84-001981   336.3/435/091724   0899300626
Debts, External -- Developing countries. Debts, External -- Developing countries -- Case studies.

HJ8899.D434 1989
Debt disaster?: banks, governments, and multilaterals confront the crisis/ edited by John F. Weeks. New York: New York University Press, c1989. xxii, 289 p.
89-009207   336.3/435/09172409048   0814792332
Debts, External -- Developing countries. Debt relief -- Developing countries. Developing countries -- Economic policy.

HJ8899.D4815 1989
Developing country debt and economic performance/ edited by Jeffrey D. Sachs. Chicago: University of Chicago Press, 1989. 3 v.
88-020866   336.3/435/091724   0226733327
Debts, External -- Developing countries -- Congresses. International finance -- Congresses. Developing countries -- Economic conditions -- Congresses.

HJ8899.D482 1989
Developing country debt and the world economy/ edited by Jeffrey D. Sachs. Chicago: University of Chicago Press, c1989. xi, 335 p.
88-020798   336.3/435/091724   0226733386
Debts, External -- Developing countries. International finance.

HJ8899.D67 1989
Dornbusch, Rudiger.
The road to economic recovery: report of the Twentieth Century Fund Task Force on International Debt: background paper/ by Rudiger Dornbusch. New York,: Priority Press Publications, 1989. ix, 123 p.
89-040031   336.3/435/091724   0870782282
Debts, External -- Developing countries. Debt relief -- Developing countries.

HJ8899.G56 1990
The Global debt crisis: forecasting for the future/ edited by Scott MacDonald, Margie Lindsay, and David L. Crum. London; Pinter Publishers, 1990. vii, 256 p.
90-034581   336.3/435/091724   086187742X
Debts, External -- Developing countries.

HJ8899.M33 1990
MacEwan, Arthur.
Debt and disorder: international economic instability and U.S. imperial decline/ Arthur MacEwan. New York: Monthly Review Press, c1990. 147 p.
89-013416   336.3/435/091724   0853457956
Debts, External -- Developing countries. Debts, External -- Latin America. Debts, External -- United States.

HJ8899.T6813 1999
Toussaint, Eric.
Your money or your life!: the tyranny of global finance/ Eric Toussaint; translated by Raghu Krishnan with the collaboration of Vicki Briault Manus. Sterling, VA: Pluto Press, 1999. xxviii, 322 p.
99-013344   336.3/435/091724   0745314171
Debts, External -- Developing countries.

HJ9145-9157 Local finance. Municipal finance — By region or country — United States

HJ9145.B73 1993
Brace, Paul, 1954-
State government and economic performance/ Paul Brace. Baltimore: Johns Hopkins University Press, c1993. xv, 152 p.
92-024177   336/.01473   0801844940
Local finance -- United States. Finance, Public -- United States -- States. Intergovernmental fiscal relations -- United States.

HJ9145.L32 1989
Ladd, Helen F.
America's ailing cities: fiscal health and the design of urban policy/ Helen F. Ladd and John Yinger. Baltimore: Johns Hopkins University Press, c1989. xiii, 334 p.
88-013653   336/.014/73   0801837677
Municipal finance -- United States. Intergovernmental fiscal relations -- United States. Municipal services -- United States.

HJ9145.L35
Lamb, Robert, 1941-
Municipal bonds: the comprehensive review of tax-exempt securities and public finance/ by Robert Lamb & Stephen P. Rappaport. New York: McGraw-Hill, c1980. xiv, 379 p.
79-027105   336.3/1   0070360820
Municipal finance -- United States. Municipal bonds -- United States. Securities, Tax-exempt -- United States.

HJ9145.P35 1990
Pammer, William J.
Managing fiscal strain in major American cities: understanding retrenchment in the public sector/ William J. Pammer, Jr. New York: Greenwood Press, 1990. xviii, 133 p.
89-017073   352.1/0973   0313266565
Municipal finance -- United States. Local budgets -- United States. Municipal services -- United States -- Finance.

HJ9145.S36 1989
Schneider, Mark, 1946-
The competitive city: the political economy of suburbia/ Mark Schneider. Pittsburgh, Pa.: University of Pittsburgh Press, c1989. xii, 249 p.
89-030015   363/.0973   0822936100
Metropolitan finance -- United States. Metropolitan government -- United States. Municipal services -- United States.

HJ9147.F7 1993
Frank, Howard A.
Budgetary forecasting in local government: new tools and techniques/ Howard A. Frank. Westport, Conn.: Quorum Books, 1993. xiv, 213 p.
93-006765   352.1/22042/0973   0899307256
Local budgets -- United States -- Forecasting. Program budgeting -- United States.

HJ9156.A64 1993
Altshuler, Alan A., 1936-
Regulation for revenue: the political economy of land use exactions/ Alan A. Altshuler and Jose A. Gomez-Ibanez, with Arnold M. Howitt. Washington, D.C.: Brookings Institution; c1993. xiii, 175 p.
92-035660   336.1/6   0815703562
Impact fees -- United States. Infrastructure (Economics) -- Finance. Local finance -- United States.

HJ9157.M47 1987
Merriman, David.
The control of municipal budgets: toward the effective design of tax and expenditure limitations/ David Merriman. New York: Quorum Books, c1987. x, 170 p.
87-002495   352.1/2/0973   0899302173
Tax and expenditure limitations -- United States. Municipal budgets -- United States.

HJ9745 Public accounting. Auditing — Data processing

HJ9745.S92 1989
Swanson, G. A.
Measurement and interpretation in accounting: a living systems theory approach/ G.A. Swanson and James Grier Miller. New York: Quorum Books, 1989. xvi, 219 p.
89-003857   657/.835   0899304222
Finance, Public -- Accounting. Information measurement. System analysis.

HJ9777 Public accounting. Auditing — Local finance accounting. Municipal accounting — United States

HJ9777.A3.L95 1983
Lynn, Edward S.
Fund accounting: theory and practice/ Edward S. Lynn, Robert J. Freeman. Englewood Cliffs, N.J.: Prentice-Hall, c1983. xiv, 930 p.
82-021587   657/.835/00973   0133324117
Municipal finance -- United States -- Accounting. Local finance -- United States -- Accounting. Finance, Public -- United States -- Accounting.

HJ9801 Public accounting. Auditing — By region or country — United States

HJ9801.L54 1993
Light, Paul Charles.
Monitoring government: inspectors general and the search for accountability/ Paul C. Light. Washington, D.C.: Brookings Institution: c1993. xiii, 274 p.
92-032451   353.0072/32   0815752563
Finance, Public -- United States -- Auditing. Administrative agencies -- United States -- Auditing. Governmental investigations -- United States.

HM Sociology

HM13 Congresses

HM13.S49 1988
Social change and the life course/ editor, Matilda White Riley. Newbury Park, Calif.: Sage Publications, c1988 v. 2.
87-037658   301   0803932855
Sociology -- Congresses. Aging -- Social aspects -- Congresses. Life cycle, Human -- Social aspects -- Congresses.

HM17 Dictionaries. Encyclopedias

HM17.I53 1995
International encyclopedia of sociology/ editor, Frank N. Magill; consulting editor, Héctor L. Delgado; general bibliography, Alan Sica. London; Fitzroy Dearborn, 1995. 2 v.
97-136095   301/.03 21   1884964451
Sociology -- Encyclopedias.

HM17.J37 1991
Jary, David.
The HarperCollins dictionary of sociology/ David Jary and Julia Jary. New York: HarperPerennial, c1991. v, 601 p.
91-055446   301/.03   0062715437
Sociology -- Dictionaries.

HM19 History — General works

HM19.F35 1997
Feminist sociology: life histories of a movement/ Barbara Laslett and Barrie Thorne, editors. New Brunswick, N.J.: Rutgers University Press, c1997. vi, 286 p.
97-001778   301/.0823 21   0813524288
Women sociologists -- Biography. Feminists -- Biography. Feminist theory.

HM19.G532
Giddens, Anthony.
New rules of sociological method: a positive critique of interpretative sociologies/ Anthony Giddens. New York: Basic Books, c1976. 192 p.
76-009672   301/.09   0465050832
Sociology -- History. Sociology -- Methodology.

HM19.I59 1994
International handbook of contemporary developments in sociology/ edited by Raj P. Mohan & Arthur S. Wilke. Westport, Conn.: Greenwood Press, 1994. xviii, 837 p.
93-037504   301/.09   0313267197
Sociology -- History -- Handbooks, manuals, etc. Sociology -- Study and teaching -- Handbooks, manuals, etc. Sociology -- Research -- Handbooks, manuals, etc.

HM19.K48 1998
Kilminster, Richard, 1942-
The sociological revolution: from the Enlightenment to the global age/ Richard Kilminster. London; Routledge, 1998. xiv, 221 p.
98-023813   301/.09   0415029201
Sociology -- History. Sociology -- Philosophy. Knowledge, Sociology of.

HM19.M39 1989
Mazlish, Bruce, 1923-
A new science: the breakdown of connections and the birth of sociology/ Bruce Mazlish. New York: Oxford University Press, 1989. xiv, 333 p.
88-031952   301/.09   0195058461
Sociology -- History. Community -- History -- 19th century. Individualism -- History -- 19th century.

HM19.N53
Nisbet, Robert A.
Sociology as an art form/ Robert Nisbet. New York: Oxford University Press, 1976. 145 p.
76-009278   301/.01   0195021029
Sociology -- History -- 19th century. Intellectual life. Art and society.

HM22 History — By region or country, A-Z

HM22.F8.B383 1991
Gane, Mike.
Baudrillard: critical and fatal theory/ Mike Gane. London; Routledge, 1991. 243 p.
90-049946   301/.0944   0415037743
Baudrillard, Jean. Sociology -- France -- History. Postmodernism.

HM22.F8.D774 1992
Cladis, Mark Sydney.
A communitarian defense of liberalism: Emile Durkheim and contemporary social theory/ Mark S. Cladis. Stanford, Calif.: Stanford Univerisyty Press, c1992. viii, 339 p.
92-010125   301/.01   0804720428
Durkheim, Emile, -- 1858-1917. Liberalism. Social ethics. Sociology -- France -- History.

HM22.F8.D845 1972
Lukes, Steven.
Emile Durkheim; his life and work, a historical and critical study. New York, Harper & Row [c1972] xi, 676 p.
75-156534   301/.092/4   0060127279
Durkheim, Emile, -- 1858-1917. Sociology -- History. France -- Social conditions -- 19th century.

HM22.F8.D869 1989
Pearce, Frank.
The radical Durkheim/ Frank Pearce. London; Unwin Hyman, 1989. xvi, 232 p.
88-031366   301/.092/4   0044452691
Durkheim, Emile, -- 1858-1917. Sociology -- France -- History.

HM22.F8.S93 1997
Swartz, David, 1945-
Culture & power: the sociology of Pierre Bourdieu/ David Swartz. Chicago: University of Chicago Press, 1997. viii, 333 p.
97-007479   301/.0944   0226785947
Bourdieu, Pierre. Sociology -- France -- History. Sociology -- Methodology.

HM22.G2.L53 1988
Liebersohn, Harry.
Fate and utopia in German sociology, 1870-1923/ Harry Liebersohn. Cambridge, Mass.: MIT Press, c1988. x, 282 p.
87-026048   301/.0943   0262121336
Sociology -- Germany -- History -- 19th century. Sociology -- Germany -- History -- 20th century.

HM22.G3.F458 1987
Muller, Jerry Z., 1954-
The other god that failed: Hans Freyer and the deradicalization of German conservatism/ Jerry Z. Muller. Princeton, N.J.: Princeton University Press, 1987. xv, 449 p.
87-018781   301/.0943   0691055084
Freyer, Hans, -- 1887-1969. Sociologists -- Germany -- Biography. Sociology -- Germany -- History -- 20th century. Intellectuals -- Germany -- History -- 20th century. Germany -- Intellectual life -- 20th century.

HM22.G3.H333 1991
Braaten, Jane, 1956-
Habermas's critical theory of society/ Jane Braaten. Albany, N.Y.: State University of New York Press, c1991. x, 191 p.
90-047708   301/.01   0791407594
Habermas, Jurgen. Critical theory.

HM22.G3.H348 1988
White, Stephen K.
The recent work of Jurgen Habermas: reason, justice, and modernity/ Stephen K. White. Cambridge [Cambridgeshire]; Cambridge University Press, 1988. xi, 190 p.
87-003005   301/.0943   0521343607
Habermas, Jurgen. Sociology -- Germany. Frankfurt school of sociology.

HM22.G3.M3253 1995
Kettler, David.
Karl Mannheim and the crisis of liberalism: the secret of these new times/ David Kettler, Volker Meja. New Brunswick, N.J.: Transaction Publishers, c1995. x, 350 p.
94-047504   301/.092   1560001887
Mannheim, Karl, -- 1893-1947. Sociologists -- Germany -- Biography. Sociology -- Germany -- History. Knowledge, Sociology of.

HM22.G3.S493 1994
Sellerberg, Ann-Mari, 1943-
A blend of contradictions: Georg Simmel in theory and practice/ Ann-Mari Sellerberg. New Brunswick, N.J., U.S.A.: Transaction Publishers, c1994. xviii, 128 p.
93-019449   301/.092   1560001208
Simmel, Georg, -- 1858-1918 Sociology -- Germany -- History.

HM22.G3.W446813 1988
Kasler, Dirk, 1944-
Max Weber: an introduction to his life and work/ Dirk Kasler; translated by Philippa Hurd. Chicago: University of Chicago Press; 1988. x, 287 p.
88-019618   301/.092   0226425592
Weber, Max, -- 1864-1920. Sociology -- Germany -- History.

HM22.G3.W4587 1992
Turner, Charles, 1962-
Modernity and politics in the work of Max Weber/ Charles Turner. London; Routledge, 1992. x, 219 p.
92-000289   301/.0943   0415064902
Weber, Max, -- 1864-1920 -- Contributions in political science. Sociology -- Germany -- History. Sociology -- Methodology -- History.

HM22.G8.G5434 1991
Craib, Ian, 1945-
Anthony Giddens/ Ian Craib. London; Routledge, 1992. 209 p.
91-012147   301/.01   0415070724
Giddens, Anthony. Sociology -- Methodology. Social structure. Sociology -- Great Britain.

HM22.G8.M334 1994
Hundert, E. J.
The enlightenment's fable: Bernard Mandeville and the discovery of society/ E.J. Hundert. Cambridge [England]; Cambridge University Press, 1994. xii, 284 p.
93-036440   301/.092   0521460824
Mandeville, Bernard, -- 1670-1733 -- Contributions in sociology. Mandeville, Bernard, -- 1670-1733 -- Contributions in economics. Mandeville, Bernard, -- 1670-1733. -- Fable of the bees. Self-interest. Economic man. Enlightenment.

HM22.G8.M344 1992
Hoecker-Drysdale, Susan.
Harriet Martineau, first woman sociologist/ Susan Hoecker-Drysdale. Oxford [England]; Berg; 1992. x, 190 p.
91-033223   301/.092   0854966455
Martineau, Harriet, -- 1802-1876. Women sociologists -- Great Britain -- Biography. Sociology -- Great Britain -- History -- 19th century.

HM22.U5.G76 1997
Grimes, Michael D.
Caught in the middle: contradictions in the lives of sociologists from working-class backgrounds/ Michael D. Grimes and Joan M. Morris. Westport, Conn.: Praeger, 1997. xii, 234 p.
97-005586   301/.092/2   027595711X
Sociologists -- United States -- Attitudes. Sociologists -- Education -- United States. Sociologists -- United States -- Economic conditions.

HM22.U5.K44 1999
Keen, Mike Forrest.
Stalking the sociological imagination: J. Edgar Hoover's FBI surveillance of American sociology/ Mike Forrest Keen. Westport, Conn: Greenwood Press, 1999. x, 235 p.
98-047819   301/.0973/0904   0313298130
Sociology -- United States -- History -- 20th century. United States. -- Federal Bureau of Investigation.

HM22.U5.T87 1990
Turner, Stephen P., 1951-
The impossible science: an institutional analysis of American sociology/ Stephen Park Turner, Jonathan H. Turner. Newbury Park, Calif.: Sage Publications, c1990. 222 p.
90-008553   301/.0973   0803938381
Sociology -- United States -- History.

HM22.U5.W66 1991
Women in sociology: a bio-bibliographical sourcebook/ edited by Mary Jo Deegan. New York: Greenwood Press, 1991. xv, 468 p.
90-043376   016.301/092/2   0313260850
Women sociologists -- United States -- Biography. Sociology -- United States -- Bio-bibliography.

HM22.U6.A34 1988
Deegan, Mary Jo, 1946-
Jane Addams and the men of the Chicago school, 1892-1918/ Mary Jo Deegan. New Brunswick (U.S.A.): Transaction Books, c1988. xv, 352 p.
86-006964   301/.092/4   0887380778
Addams, Jane, -- 1860-1935 -- Contributions in sociology. Chicago school of sociology.

HM22.U6.B448 1996
Waters, Malcolm, 1946-
Daniel Bell/ Malcolm Waters. London; Routledge, 1996. 198 p.
95-019336   301/.092   0415105773
Bell, Daniel. Sociologists -- United States -- Biography. Sociology -- United States -- History. Conservatism -- United States -- History.

HM22.U6.B4717 1991
Bannister, Robert C.
Jessie Bernard: the making of a feminist/ Robert C. Bannister. New Brunswick: Rutgers University Press, c1991. xii, 276 p.
90-034390   301/.092   0813516145
Bernard, Jessie Shirley, -- 1903- Sociologists -- United States -- Biography. Feminists -- United States -- Biography.

HM22.U6.F736 1991
Platt, Anthony M.
E. Franklin Frazier reconsidered/ Anthony M. Platt. New Brunswick [N.J.]: Rutgers University Press, [c1991] xi, 278 p.
90-036223   301/.092   0813516315
Frazier, Edward Franklin, -- 1894-1962. Sociologists -- United States -- Biography. Sociology -- United States -- History.

HM22.U6.G642 1991
Burns, Tom, 1913-
Erving Goffman/ Tom Burns. London; Routledge, 1992. viii, 386 p.
90-028958   301/.092   0415064929
Goffman, Erving. Sociologists -- United States -- Biography. Social interaction.

HM22.U6.L698 1987
Lowenthal, Leo.
An unmastered past: the autobiographical reflections of Leo Lowenthal/ edited with an introduction by Martin Jay. Berkeley: University of California Press, c1987. x, 281 p.
86-024942   301/.092/4   0520056388
Lowenthal, Leo -- Interviews. Sociologists -- United States -- Interviews. Frankfurt school of sociology.

HM22.U6.P274 1994
Horowitz, Daniel, 1938-
Vance Packard & American social criticism/ Daniel Horowitz. Chapel Hill: University of North Carolina Press, c1994. xviii, 375 p.
93-035608   301/.092   0807821411
Packard, Vance Oakley, -- 1914- Journalists -- United States -- Biography. United States -- Social conditions -- 1945-

HM22.U6.W48 1994
Whyte, William Foote, 1914-
Participant observer: an autobiography/ William Foote Whyte. Ithaca, New York: ILR Press, c1994. 346 p.
93-047550   301/.092   087546324X
Whyte, William Foote, -- 1914- Sociologists -- United States -- Biography.

HM24 Theory. Method. Relation to other subjects — General works

HM24.A38 1989
Agger, Ben.
Socio(onto)logy, a disciplinary reading/ Ben Agger. Urbana: University of Illinois Press, c1989. 426 p.
88-010697   301   0252060199
Sociology. Positivism. Marxian school of sociology.

HM24.A4647 1988
Alexander, Jeffrey C.
Action and its environments: toward a new synthesis/ Jeffrey C. Alexander. New York: Columbia University Press, 1988. xii, 342 p.
87-023910   305   0231062087
Social structure. Social action. Social structure -- United States.

HM24.A4649 1989
Alexander, Jeffrey C.
Structure and meaning: relinking classical sociology/ Jeffrey C. Alexander. New York: Columbia University Press, c1989. viii, 258 p.
88-022019   301   0231066880
Sociology. Civilization, Modern.

HM24.A73 1988
Aronowitz, Stanley.
Science as power: discourse and ideology in modern society/ Stanley Aronowitz. Minneapolis: University of Minnesota Press, c1988. xii, 384 p.
88-004782   301/.01   0816616582
Sociology -- Philosophy. Ideology. Science -- Philosophy.

HM24.A88 1990
Authors of their own lives: intellectual autobiographies / by twenty American sociologists; edited and with an introduction by Bennett M. Berger; essays by Reinhard Bendix ... [et al.]. Berkeley: University of California Press, c1990. xxviii, 503 p.
89-005117   301/.092/2   0520065557
Sociology -- Biographical methods. Sociologists -- United States -- Biography. Sociology -- United States -- History.

HM24.B386
Bell, Daniel.
The winding passage: essays and sociological journeys, 1960-1980/ Daniel Bell. Cambridge, Mass.: Abt Books, c1980. xxiv, 370 p.
79-057350   301   0890115451
Sociology. Social history -- 1960-1970. Social history -- 1970-

HM24.B619 1984
Bottomore, T. B.
Sociology and socialism/ Tom Bottomore. New York: St. Martin's Press, 1984. 212 p.
83-022930   301   0312740042
Sociology. Paradigms (Social sciences) Socialism.

HM24.C37 1988
Center: ideas and institutions/ edited by Liah Greenfeld and Michel Martin. Chicago: University of Chicago Press, 1988. xxii, 282 p.
88-017094   306   0226306860
Shils, Edward, -- 1910-1995. Pluralism (Social sciences) Social values. Religion and sociology.

HM24.D962 1938
Durkheim, Emile, 1858-1917.
The rules of sociological method/ by Emile Durkheim. [New York]: Free Press of Glencoe, 1964, c1938. lx, 146 p.
64-057427   301.8
Sociology -- Methodology.

HM24.G284 1991
Game, Ann.
Undoing the social: towards a deconstructive sociology/ Ann Game. Milton Keynes: Open University Press, 1991. xiv, 210 p.
92-139512   0335093841
Sociology -- Philosophy. Deconstruction.

HM24.G425 1992
Gellner, Ernest.
Reason and culture: the historic role of rationality and rationalism/ Ernest Gellner. Oxford, UK; Basil Blackwell, 1992. xi, 193 p.
91-027067   301/.01   0631134794
Sociology -- Philosophy. Reason. Rationalism.

HM24.G446
Giddens, Anthony.
Central problems in social theory: action, structure, and contradiction in social analysis/ Anthony Giddens. Berkeley: University of California Press, 1979. 294 p.
79-064667   301   0520039726
Sociology. Structuralism. Functionalism (Social sciences)

HM24.G479 1989
Gilbert, Margaret.
On social facts/ Margaret Gilbert. London; Routledge, 1989. x, 521 p.
88-031640   301/.01   0415024447
Sociology -- Methodology. Social groups. Social action.

HM24.G65
Gouldner, Alvin Ward, 1920-
The coming crisis of Western sociology [by] Alvin W. Gouldner. New York, Basic Books [1970] xv, 528 p.
77-110771   301/.09   0465012787
Sociology. Sociology -- History.

HM24.H2713 1989
Habermas, Jurgen.
The structural transformation of the public sphere: an inquiry into a category of bourgeois society/ Jurgen Habermas; translated by Thomas Burger with the assistance of Frederick Lawrence. Cambridge, Mass.: MIT Press, c1989. xix, 301 p.
88-013456   305   0262081806
Sociology -- Methodology. Social structure. Public interest.

HM24.H322 1992
Habermas and the public sphere/ edited by Craig Calhoun. Cambridge, Mass.: MIT Press, c1992. x, 498 p.
91-016736   305   0262031833
Habermas, Jurgen. -- Strukturwandel der Offentlichkeit -- Congresses. Sociology -- Methodology -- Congresses. Political sociology -- Congresses. Social structure -- Congresses.

HM24.H457
Held, David.
Introduction to critical theory: Horkheimer to Habermas/ David Held. Berkeley: University of California Press, c1980. 511 p.
80-010535   301/.01   0520041216
Habermas, Jurgen. Horkheimer, Max, -- 1895-1973. Frankfurt school of sociology. Social institutions. Critical theory.

HM24.I799 1996
Itzkowitz, Gary.
Contingency theory: rethinking the boundaries of social thought/ Gary Itzkowitz. Lanham: University Press of America, c1996. 268 p.
96-020844   301/.01 20   0761804420
Sociology -- Philosophy.

HM24.K5893 1995
Knowledge, experience, and ruling relations: studies in the social organization of knowledge/ edited by Marie Campbell and Ann Manicom. Toronto; University of Toronto Press, c1995. xix, 288 p.
96-134516   301/.01   0802007201
Sociology -- Methodology. Knowledge, Sociology of, Feminist theory.

HM24.L447 1990
Leonard, Stephen T., 1954-
Critical theory in political practice/ Stephen T. Leonard. Princeton, N.J.: Princeton University Press, c1990. xxiv, 295 p.
90-033736   306.2   0691078408
Critical theory. Political sociology.

HM24.M472
Merton, Robert King, 1910-
Sociological ambivalence and other essays/ Robert K. Merton. New York: Free Press, c1976. xii, 287 p.
76-001033   301   0029211204
Sociology. Social structure. Ethnic attitudes.

HM24.M622 1994
Morrow, Raymond Allen.
Critical theory and methodology/ Raymond A. Morrow, with David D. Brown. Thousand Oaks, Calif.: Sage Publications, c1994. xvii, 381 p.
94-010888   301/.01   0803946821
Critical theory. Social sciences -- Philosophy. Sociology -- Methodology.

HM24.M685 1995
Mouzelis, Nicos P.
Sociological theory: what went wrong?: diagnosis and remedies/ Nicos Mouzelis. London; Routledge, 1995 xi, 220 p.
94-044296   301/.01   0415127203
Sociology -- Philosophy.

HM24.P6642 1994
Postmodernism and social inquiry/ edited by David R. Dickens, Andrea Fontana; foreword by Fred Dallmayr. New York: Guilford Press, c1994. xi, 259 p.
93-050860   301/.01   0898624150
Sociology -- Methodology. Postmodernism -- Social aspects.

HM24.R92 1983
Runciman, W. G. 1934-
A treatise on social theory/ W.G. Runciman. Cambridge [Cambridgeshire]; Cambridge University Press, 1983-1997. 3 v.
82-004490   301/.01   0521249066
Sociology -- Methodology. Sociology -- Philosophy. Social sciences -- Methodology. England -- Social conditions -- 20th century.

HM24.S356 1994
Scheuerman, William E., 1965-
Between the norm and the exception: the Frankfurt school and the rule of law/ William E. Scheuerman. Cambridge, Mass.: MIT Press, c1994. 331 p.
94-008309   301/.01   0262193515
Frankfurt school of sociology. Welfare state. Rule of law.

HM24.S53923 1990
Smith, Dorothy E., 1926-
Texts, facts, and femininity: exploring the relations of ruling/ Dorothy E. Smith. London; Routledge, 1990. vii, 247 p.
89-010961   301/.01   0415032318
Sociology -- Methodology. Social history -- Methodology. Discourse analysis.

HM24.S5444 1989
Social theory of modern societies: Anthony Giddens and his critics/ edited by David Held and John B. Thompson. Cambridge [England]; Cambridge University Press, 1989. viii, 311 p.
89-031431   301/.01   052126197X
Giddens, Anthony. Sociology -- Methodology.

HM24.S773 1993
Strauss, Anselm L.
Continual permutations of action/ Anselm L. Strauss. New York: Aldine de Gruyter, c1993. xv, 280 p.
93-004075   302   020230471X
Action theory. Social interaction.

HM24.W48613 1994
Wiggershaus, Rolf, 1944-
The Frankfurt School: its history, theories, and political significance/ Rolf Wiggershaus; translated by Michael Robertson. Cambridge, Mass.: MIT Press, c1994. ix, 787 p.
93-014039   301/.01   0262231743
Frankfurt school of sociology. Critical theory. Marxian school of sociology.

HM24.W64 1993
Wolfe, Alan, 1942-
The Human difference: animals, computers, and the necessity of social science/ Alan Wolfe. Berkeley: University of California Press, c1993. xvii, 243 p.
92-008355   301/.01   0520080130
Sociology -- Methodology. Social sciences -- Methodology. Sociobiology.

HM26 Theory. Method. Relation to other subjects — Relation to philosophy

HM26.E43 1998
Elias, Norbert.
Norbert Elias on civilization, power, and knowledge: selected writings/ edited and with an introduction by Stephen Mennell and Johan Goudsblom. Chicago: University of Chicago Press, c1998. ix, 302 p.
97-020799   301/.01 21   0226204316
Elias, Norbert -- Influence. Elias, Norbert. Power (Social sciences) Knowledge, Sociology of. Power (Social sciences)

HM26.M87 1989
Murphy, John W.
Postmodern social analysis and criticism/ John W. Murphy. New York: Greenwood Press, 1989. viii, 177 p.
88-035774   301/.01   0313266832
Sociology -- Philosophy. Postmodernism. Philosophy and social sciences.

HM27 Theory. Method. Relation to other subjects — Relation to psychology

HM27.M5 1964
Mills, C. Wright 1916-1962.
Sociology and pragmatism: the higher learning in America [by] C. Wright Mills. Edited with an introd. by Irving Louis Horowitz. New York, Paine-Whitman Publishers [1964] 475 p.
64-019448   191
Sociology. Pragmatism.

HM35 Theory. Method. Relation to other subjects — Relation to economics

HM35.E89 1988
Etzioni, Amitai.
The moral dimension: toward a new economics/ Amitai Etzioni. New York: Free Press; c1988. xvi, 314 p.
88-000368   174/.4   0029099005
Economics -- Sociological aspects. Economics -- Moral and ethical aspects. Social choice.

HM35.S625 1991
Socio-economics: toward a new synthesis/ editors, Amitai Etzioni, Paul R. Lawrence. Armonk, N.Y.: M.E. Sharpe, c1991. xv, 359 p.
90-040462   306.3   0873326857
Economics -- Sociological aspects -- Congresses.

HM36 Theory. Method. Relation to other subjects — Relation to history and geography

HM36.B85 1993
Burke, Peter.
History and social theory/ Peter Burke. Ithaca, N.Y.: Cornell University Press, 1993. ix, 198 p.
92-054434   301   0801428610
Sociology. History.

HM36.5 Theory. Method. Relation to other subjects — Relation to war

HM36.5.L8 1987
Luard, Evan, 1926-
War in international society: a study in international sociology/ Evan Luard. New Haven: Yale University Press, 1987, c1986. 468 p.
87-008175   303.6/6   0300040164
War and society. International relations.

HM47 Study and teaching — By region or country, A-Z

HM47.E852.E27 1994
Eastern Europe in transformation: the impact on sociology/ edited by Mike Forrest Keen and Janusz Mucha. Westport, Conn.: Greenwood Press, 1994. xii, 208 p.
93-044515   301/.0947   0313283753
Sociology -- Study and teaching -- Europe, Eastern. Sociology -- Study and teaching -- Europe, Central. Sociology -- Europe, Eastern -- History.

HM48 Research

HM48.C37 1991
A Case for the case study/ edited by Joe R. Feagin, Anthony M. Orum, and Gideon Sjoberg. Chapel Hill: University of North Carolina Press, c1991. viii, 290 p.
90-027036   301/.01   0807819735
Sociology -- Research -- Methodology. Social sciences -- Research -- Methodology. Case method.

HM48.R47 1982
The Research craft: an introduction to social research methods/ John B. Williamson ... [et al.]; in collaboration with Stephen T. Barry, Richard S. Dorr. Boston: Little, Brown, c1982. xi, 434 p.
81-081757   300/.72   0316943649
Sociology -- Research. Social sciences -- Research.

HM51 General works — English

HM51.B364 2001
Bauman, Zygmunt.
Thinking sociologically/ Zygmunt Bauman and Tim May. 2nd ed. Malden, MA: Blackwell Publishers, 2001.
00-069768   301 21   0631219293
Sociology.

HM51.B394 1970
Bendix, Reinhard.
Embattled reason; essays on social knowledge. New York, Oxford University Press, 1970. xi, 395 p.
79-111644   301
Sociology -- Addresses, essays, lectures. Social change -- Addresses, essays, lectures.

HM51.D25
Dahrendorf, Ralf.
Essays in the theory of society. Stanford, Calif., Stanford University Press, 1968. x, 300 p.
67-026526   301
Sociology -- Addresses, essays, lectures.

HM51.H249 1988
Handbook of sociology/ Neil J. Smelser, editor. Newbury Park, Calif.: Sage Publications, c1988. 824 p.
87-036762   301   0803926650
Sociology.

HM51.L352 1988
Lee, Alfred McClung, 1906-
Sociology for people: toward a caring profession/ Alfred McClung Lee. Syracuse, N.Y.: Syracuse University Press, 1988. xviii, 257 p.
88-009672   301   0815624425
Sociology.

HM51.P312
Park, Robert Ezra, 1864-1944.
On social control and collective behavior. Selected papers, edited and with an introd. by Ralph H. Turner. Chicago, University of Chicago Press [1967] xlvi, 274 p.
67-025084   301
Sociology.

HM51.P37
Parsons, Talcott, 1902-
Sociological theory and modern society. New York, Free Press [1967] xii, 564 p.
67-012517   301
Sociology.

HM51.R42 1991
Restivo, Sal P.
The sociological worldview/ Sal Restivo. Cambridge, Mass., USA: B. Blackwell, 1991. x, 211 p.
90-034916   301   0631177795
Sociology.

HM51.S638 1987
Smith, Dorothy E., 1926-
The everyday world as problematic: a feminist sociology/ Dorothy E. Smith. Boston: Northeastern University Press, c1987. vi, 244 p.
87-015295   301   155553015X
Sociology. Feminist theory.

HM51.S8112
Spencer, Herbert, 1820-1903.
The evolution of society; selections from Herbert Spencer's Principles of sociology. Edited and with an introd. by Robert L. Carneiro. Chicago, University of Chicago Press [1967] lvii, 241 p.
67-020581   301
Sociology.

HM57 General works — German

HM57.M33 1964
Marx, Karl, 1818-1883.
Selected writings in sociology & social philosophy. Newly translated by T. B. Bottomore. Edited, with an introd. and notes, by Mr. Bottomore and Maximilien Rubel, and with a foreword by Erich Fromm. New York, McGraw-Hill [1964] xviii, 268 p.
64-005474   301
Sociology. Capitalism.

HM59 General works — Italian

HM59.P1813
Pareto, Vilfredo, 1848-1923.
Sociological writings. Selected and introduced by S. E. Finer. Translated by Derick Mirfin. New York, Praeger [1966] viii, 335 p.
66-012277   301
Sociology.

HM61 General works — Other European languages

HM61.S673 1998
Sorokin, Pitirim Aleksandrovich, 1889-1968.
On the practice of sociology/ Pitirim A. Sorokin; edited and with an introduction by Barry V. Johnston. Chicago: University of Chicago Press, 1998. vii, 328 p.
97-032778   301   0226768287
Sociology.

HM73 General special

HM73.B29 1991
Bauman, Zygmunt.
Intimations of postmodernity/ Zygmunt Bauman. London; Routledge, 1992. xxviii, 232 p.
91-003115   303.3/72   0415067499
Postmodernism -- Social aspects. Social values.

HM73.B468 1997
Best, Steven.
The postmodern turn/ Steven Best, Douglas Kellner. New York: Guilford Press, 1997. xiv, 306 p.
97-015234   301/.01   1572302208
Postmodernism -- Social aspects. Sociology -- Philosophy.

HM73.H38 1990
Heller, Agnes.
Can modernity survive?/ Agnes Heller. Berkeley: University of California Press, c1990. 177 p.
90-010996   303.4   0520072545
Postmodernism -- Social aspects. Civilization, Modern -- 20th century. Political ethics.

HM73.I48 1995
The impact of values/ edited by Jan W. van Deth and Elinor Scarbrough. Oxford; Oxford University Press, 1995. xvii, 588 p.
95-020297   303.4/094   0198279574
Social values -- Europe. Social change -- Europe.

HM73.I544 1998
Inglehart, Ronald.
Human values and beliefs: a cross-cultural sourcebook: political, religious, sexual, and economic norms in 43 societies; findings from the 1990-1993 world value survey/ Ronald Inglehart, Miguel Basanez, and Alejandro Moreno. Ann Arbor: University of Michigan Press, c1998. xxi, 534 p.
97-020731   303.3/72 21   0472108336
Social values -- Cross-cultural studies.

HM73.L35 1990
Lash, Scott.
Sociology of postmodernism/ Scott Lash. London; Routledge, 1990. xi, 300 p.
89-024184   301   0415047846
Sociology. Postmodernism -- Social aspects.

HM73.L95 1997
Lyman, Stanford M.
Postmodernism and a sociology of the absurd and other essays on the "nouvelle vague" in American social science/ Stanford M. Lyman. Fayetteville: University of Arkansas Press, 1997. xiv, 392 p.
96-050984   301/.01   1557284539
Postmodernism -- Social aspects. Sociology -- Philosophy. Structuralism.

HM73.M478 1994
Mestrovic, Stjepan Gabriel.
The Balkanization of the West: the confluence of postmodernism and postcommunism/ Stjepan G. Mestrovic. London; Routledge, c1994. xiv, 226 p.
94-016377   940.55/9   0415087546
Yugoslav War, 1991- Postmodernism -- Social aspects. Post-communism.

HM73.M479 1993
Mestrovic, Stjepan Gabriel.
The barbarian temperament: toward a postmodern critical theory/ Stjepan Mestrovic. London; Routledge, 1993. xviii, 326 p.
92-045836   303.4   0415102413
Regression (Civilization) Postmodernism -- Social aspects. Civilization, Modern -- 1950-

HM73.O55 1994
O'Neill, John, 1933-
The poverty of postmodernism/ John O'Neill. London; Routledge, 1994. 205 p.
94-007260   303.4   0415116864
Postmodernism -- Social aspects.

HM73.R59 1991
Rosenau, Pauline Marie, 1943-
Post-modernism and the social sciences: insights, inroads, and intrusions/ Pauline Marie Rosenau. Princeton, N.J.: Princeton University Press, c1992. xiv, 229 p.
91-019258   300/.1   0691023476
Social sciences -- Philosophy. Social movements. Postmodernism -- Social aspects.

HM73.S89 1990
Swaan, A. de.
The management of normality: critical essays in health and welfare/ Abram de Swaan. London; Routledge, 1990. vi, 234 p.
89-010352   303.3/2   0415032008
Social norms. Conformity. Helping behavior.

HM73.V35 1993
Value, welfare, and morality/ edited by R.G. Frey and Christopher W. Morris. Cambridge, England; Cambridge University Press, 1993. x, 324 p.
92-036143   303.3/72   0521416965
Social values. Values.

HM101 Culture. Progress — General works

HM101.A654 1988
Archer, Margaret Scotford.
Culture and agency: the place of culture in social theory/ Margaret S. Archer. Cambridge [Cambridgeshire]; Cambridge University Press, 1988. xxvi, 343 p.
87-019722   306   0521346231
Culture. Social structure. Social interaction.

HM101.A715
Aron, Raymond, 1905-
Progress and disillusion; the dialectics of modern society. New York, F. A. Praeger [1968] xvii, 230 p.
67-022287   309.1/04
Social history -- 20th century. Progress. Equality.

HM101.B4717 1995
Berger, Bennett M.
An essay on culture: symbolic structure and social structure/ Bennett M. Berger. Berkeley: University of California Press, c1995. xiii, 192 p.
94-033086   306   0520200160
Culture. Social structure.

HM101.B74 1987
Brenkman, John.
Culture and domination/ John Brenkman. Ithaca: Cornell University Press, 1987. xi, 239 p.
87-047543   306   0801414571
Culture. Sociology -- Philosophy. Hermeneutics.

HM101.B775 1999
Brooker, Peter.
Cultural theory: a glossary/ Peter Brooker. London; Arnold, c1999. xiii, 285 p.
98-020411   306/.014 21   0340691468
Culture -- Terminology.

HM101.D527 1996
A dictionary of cultural and critical theory/ editor, Michael Payne; associate editor, Meenakshi Ponnuswami; assistant editor, Jennifer Payne; advisory board, Simon Frith ... [et al.]. Oxford, OX, UK; Blackwell Reference, 1996. xii, 644 p.
95-008003   306/.03   0631171975
Culture -- Dictionaries. Critical theory -- Dictionaries.

HM101.F35 1995
Featherstone, Mike.
Undoing culture: globalization, postmoderism and identity/ Mike Featherstone. London; Sage Publications, 1995. x, 178 p.
95-074766   306   0803976054
Culture. Popular culture -- History -- 20th century. Postmodernism.

HM101.I28935 1998
Identity and agency in cultural worlds/ Dorothy Holland ... [et al.]. Cambridge, Mass.: Harvard University Press, 1998. ix, 349 p.
98-019269   306   0674815661
Culture. Identity (Psychology) Agent (Philosophy)

HM101.M268
Marcuse, Herbert, 1898-
One dimensional man; studies in the ideology of advanced industrial society. Boston, Beacon Press [c1964] xvii, 260 p.
64-010088   301.243
Civilization, Modern -- 20th century.

HM101.N574 1980
Nisbet, Robert A.
History of the idea of progress/ Robert Nisbet. New York: Basic Books, c1980. xi, 370 p.
79-001979   303.4   0465030254
Progress.

HM101.R56 1998
Rochon, Thomas R., 1952-
Culture moves: ideas, activism, and changing values/ Thomas R. Rochon. Princeton, N.J.: Princeton University Press, c1998. xviii, 282 p.
97-027020   306 21
Culture. Social change. Social values.

HM101.R63 1996
Rosen, Michael.
On voluntary servitude: false consciousness and the theory of ideology/ Michael Rosen. Cambridge, Mass.: Harvard University Press, 1996. xi, 289 p.
95-051510   306.4   0674637798
Ideology.

HM101.S54 1989
Silka, Linda.
Intuitive judgments of change/ Linda Silka. New York: Springer-Verlag, c1989. viii, 214 p.
88-016006   303.4
Social change -- Psychological aspects. Personality change. Judgment.

HM101.S947 1998
Surber, Jere Paul.
Culture and critique: an introduction to the critical discourses of cultural studies/ Jere Paul Surber. Boulder, Colo.: Westview Press, 1998. ix, 294 p.
97-029379   306/.071   0813320461
Culture -- Study and teaching. Culture -- Philosophy. Critical theory.

HM101.T44 1994
Tester, Keith, 1960-
Media, culture, and morality/ Keith Tester. London; Routledge, 1994. 138 p.
93-039858   306   0415098351
Culture. Mass media. Ethics.

HM101.T6513 1988
Touraine, Alain.
Return of the actor: social theory in postindustrial society/ Alain Touraine; foreword by Stanley Aronowitz; translation by Myrna Godzich. Minneapolis: University of Minnesota Press, c1988. xxvi, 171 p.
87-013558   303.4   0816615934
Social change. Social action. Social movements.

HM101.W225 1995
Walters, Suzanna Danuta.
Material girls: making sense of feminist cultural theory/ Suzanna Danuta Walters. Berkeley: University of California Press, c1995. x, 221 p.
94-029007   305.42/01   0520089774
Culture. Feminist criticism. Women in popular culture.

HM101.W278 1993
Watkins, Evan, 1946-
Throwaways: work culture and consumer education/ Evan Watkins. Stanford, Calif.: Stanford University Press, c1993. 230 p.
93-019270   303.4   0804722498
Social change. Social status. Consumption (Economics)

HM104 Culture. Progress — Historical sociology

HM104.M55 1998
Miller, Pavla, 1950-
Transformations of patriarchy in the west: 1500-1900/ Pavla Miller. Bloomington: Indiana University Press, c1998. xviii, 397 p.
98-035746   306.83 21   0253334691
Historical sociology. Patriarchy. Social institutions.

HM106 Culture. Progress — Evolution. Biological sociology — General works

HM106.D37 1991
Degler, Carl N.
In search of human nature: the decline and revival of Darwinism in American social thought/ Carl N. Degler. New York: Oxford University Press, 1991. x, 400 p.
90-039903   304.5   0195063805
Social Darwinism -- United States -- History. Sociobiology -- History. Eugenics -- History.

HM106.H38 1997
Hawkins, Mike, 1946-
Social Darwinism in European and American thought, 1860-1945: nature as model and nature as threat/ Mike Hawkins. Cambridge; Cambridge University Press, 1997. x, 344 p.
96-020946   304/.09   0521574005
Social Darwinism -- History.

HM110 Culture. Progress — Human body

HM110.S55 1993
Shilling, Chris.
The body and social theory/ Chris Shilling. London; Sage Publications, 1993. 232 p.
93-083675   306.4   0803985851
Body, Human -- Social aspects.

HM126 Unity. Solidarity

HM126.M57 1996
Misztal, Barbara A.
Trust in modern societies: the search for the bases of social order/ Barbara A. Misztal. Cambridge, U.K.: Polity Press; 1996. vi, 296 p.
95-047706   301   0745612482
Solidarity. Trust. Civil society.

HM131 Association. Mutuality. Social groups — General works

HM131.B3754 1997
Baum, Howell S.
The organization of hope: communities planning themselves/ Howell S. Baum. Albany, NY: State University of New York Press, c1997. xii, 318 p.
96-005109   0791431932
Community -- Case studies. Community organization -- Case studies. Community organization -- Maryland -- Baltimore.

HM131.C2525 1996
Carbaugh, Donal A.
Situating selves: the communication of social identities in American scenes/ Donal Carbaugh. Albany, N.Y.: State University of New York Press, c1996. xix, 238 p.
95-016183   302.2/0973 20   0791428273
Group identity -- United States. Communication and culture -- United States. Ethnicity -- United States.

HM131.C7393 1990
Clegg, Stewart.
Modern organizations: organization studies in the postmodern world/ Stewart R. Clegg. London; Sage Publications, 1990. ix, 261 p.
90-061987   302.3/5   0803983298
Organizational sociology. Organization. Postmodernism -- Social aspects.

HM131.C74543 1991
Conflict resolution: cross-cultural perspectives/ edited by Kevin Avruch, Peter W. Black, and Joseph A. Scimecca. New York: Greenwood Press, 1991. x, 244 p.
91-015991   303.6/9   0313257965
Intergroup relations -- Cross-cultural studies. Conflict management -- Cross-cultural studies.

HM131.C74775 1991
Coser, Rose Laub, 1916-
In defense of modernity: role complexity and individual autonomy/ Rose Laub Coser. Stanford, Calif.: Stanford University Press, 1991. ix, 199 p.
91-006374   302.5/44   0804718717
Social role. Autonomy (Psychology) Alienation (Social psychology)

HM131.E97 1990
Extending families: the social networks of parents and their children/ Moncrieff Cochran ... [et al.]. Cambridge [England]; Cambridge University Press, 1990. xix, 444 p.
89-028147   306.87   0521375304
Family -- United States. Social networks -- United States. Parents -- Social networks -- United States.

HM131.F388 1995
Feldman, Martha S., 1953-
Strategies for interpreting qualitative data/ Martha S. Feldman. Thousand Oaks: Sage Publications, c1995. vii, 71 p.
94-023071   300/.72   080395915X
Organizational sociology -- Research -- Case studies. Social sciences -- Research -- Case studies. Student housing -- Michigan -- Management -- Case studies.

HM131.G397 1990
Giddens, Anthony.
The consequences of modernity/ Anthony Giddens. Stanford, Calif.: Stanford University Press, 1990. ix, 186 p.
89-062426   303.44   0804717621
Social structure. Civilization, Modern. Postmodernism.

HM131.G55
Goffman, Erving.
Relations in public; microstudies of the public order. New York, Basic Books [1971] xvii, 396 p.
76-167764   301.11   0465068952
Social interaction. Human behavior.

HM131.H399 1991
Heskin, Allan David.
The struggle for community/ Allan David Heskin. Boulder: Westview Press, 1991. vi, 195 p.
91-015786   307   0813383382
Community. Community development -- California -- Los Angeles -- Case studies. Urban homesteading -- California -- Los Angeles -- Case studies.

HM131.J44 1997
Jervis, Robert, 1940-
System effects: complexity in political and social life/ Robert Jervis. Princeton, N.J.: Princeton University Press, c1997. ix, 309 p.
97-001108   301 21   0691026246
Social systems. International relations. Complexity (Philosophy)

HM131.K92 1972c
Kropotkin, Petr Alekseevich, 1842-1921.
Mutual aid, a factor of evolution, [by] Peter Kropotkin; edited and with an introd. by Paul Avrich. New York, New York University Press, 1972. vi, 278 p.
79-188872   335/.83   0814745555
Cooperation. Social groups. Social institutions.

HM131.M3767 1998
McClure, Bud A.
Putting a new spin on groups: the science of chaos/ Bud A. McClure. Mahwah, NJ: Lawrence Erlbaum, 1998. xii, 248 p.
98-013600   305   0805829040
Social groups. Social interaction. Leadership.

HM131.N453 1998
Networks in the global village: life in contemporary communities/ [edited] by Barry Wellman. Boulder, Colo: Westview Press, 1998.
98-029479   307   0813311500
Social networks. Community. Community life.

HM131.N47 1991
The New institutionalism in organizational analysis/ edited by Walter W. Powell and Paul J. DiMaggio. Chicago: University of Chicago Press, c1991. vii, 478 p.
91-009999   302.3/5   0226677087
Organization. Social institutions. Social change.

HM131.S3845 1995
Scott, W. Richard.
Institutions and organizations/ W. Richard Scott. Thousand Oaks: SAGE c1995. xv, 178 p.
95-010016   302.3/5   0803956525
Organizational sociology. Social institutions.

HM131.S5832 1999
Sidanius, Jim.
Social dominance: an intergroup theory of social hierarchy and oppression/ Jim Sidanius, Felicia Pratto. Cambridge, UK; Cambridge University Press, 1999. x, 403 p.
98-044356   305   0521622905
Social groups. Social conflict. Social psychology.

HM132 Association. Mutuality. Social groups — Interpersonal relations

HM132.A695 1991
Argyle, Michael.
Cooperation, the basis of sociability/ Michael Argyle. London; Routledge, 1991. xi, 276 p.
90-008299   302/.14   0415035457
Interpersonal relations. Cooperativeness. Social groups.

HM132.C86 1994
Cupach, William R.
Facework/ William R. Cupach, Sandra Metts. Thousand Oaks, Calif.: Sage Publications, c1994. xiv, 122 p.
94-004600   302   0803947119
Interpersonal relations. Interpersonal communication. Interpersonal conflict.

HM132.D828 1991
Duck, Steve.
Understanding relationships/ Steve Duck. New York: Guilford Press, 1991. vii, 222 p.
91-006658   158/.2   0898627583
Interpersonal relations. Friendship. Interpersonal Relations.

HM132.H3325 1988
Handbook of personal relationships: theory, research, and interventions/ edited by Steve Duck; sections edited by Steve Duck ... [et al.]. Chichester [England]; Wiley, c1988. xvii, 702 p.
87-022168   302.3/4   0471914916
Interpersonal relations.

HM132.J675 1992
Josselson, Ruthellen.
The space between us: exploring the dimensions of human relationships/ Ruthellen Josselson. San Francisco: Jossey-Bass Publishers, c1992. xix, 292 p.
91-039213   158/.2   1555424104
Interpersonal relations.

HM132.K4 1995
Kellenberger, James.
Relationship morality/ J. Kellenberger. University Park, Pa.: Pennsylvania State University Press, c1995. x, 450 p.
94-015347   177   0271014040
Interpersonal relations -- Moral and ethical aspects. Ethics.

HM132.T83 1996
Turner, Jeffrey S.
Encyclopedia of relationships across the lifespan/ Jeffrey S. Turner. Westport, Conn.: Greenwood Press, 1996. xii, 495 p.
95-000573   302/.03   031329576X
Interpersonal relations -- Encyclopedias. Social interaction -- Encyclopedias. Developmental psychology -- Encyclopedias.

HM132.5 Association. Mutuality. Social groups — Sociology of friendship

HM132.5.R38 1991
Rawlins, William K., 1952-
Friendship matters: communication, dialectics, and the life course/ William K. Rawlins. New York: Aldine de Gruyter, c1992. xii, 307 p.
91-030676   302.3/4   0202304035
Friendship -- United States -- Sociological aspects. Interpersonal relations. Life cycle, Human.

HM136 Individualism. Differentiation. Struggle — General works

HM136.A324 1994
Aho, James Alfred, 1942-
This thing of darkness: a sociology of the enemy/ James A. Aho. Seattle: University of Washington Press, c1994. viii, 224 p.
94-012015   303.6   0295973552
Social conflict. Hate -- Political aspects. Enemies (Persons)

HM136.A85 1998
Autonomy and community: readings in contemporary Kantian social philosophy/ edited by Jane Kneller, Sidney Axinn. Albany: State University of New York Press, 1998. xi, 334 p.
97-035898   301/.01   0791437434
Kant, Immanuel, -- 1724-1804 -- Ethics. Kant, Immanuel, -- 1724-1804 -- Political and social views. Kant, Immanuel, -- 1724-1804 -- Influence. Social problems. Social conflict.

HM136.B783 1997
Burgess, Heidi.
Encyclopedia of conflict resolution/ Heidi Burgess and Guy M. Burgess. Santa Barbara, Calif.: ABC-CLIO, c1997. x, 356 p.
97-008637   303.6/9/03 21   0874368391
Conflict management -- Encyclopedias. Dispute resolution (Law) -- Encyclopedias.

HM136.E4613 1991
Elias, Norbert.
The society of individuals/ Norbert Elias; edited by Michael Schroter; translated by Edmund Jephcott. Oxford, UK; Basil Blackwell, 1991. x, 247 p.
90-048373   302.5/4   0631164197
Individualism. Human beings. Self-consciousness.

HM136.H59813 1995
Honneth, Axel, 1949-
The struggle for recognition: the moral grammar of social conflicts/ Axel Honneth; translated by Joel Anderson. Cambridge, Mass.: Polity Press, 1995.
95-002732   303.6   0745611605
Social conflict. Social sciences -- Philosophy. Recognition (Psychology)

HM136.M52 1993
Milner, Murray.
Status and sacredness: a general theory of status relations and an analysis of Indian culture/ Murray Milner, Jr. New York: Oxford University Press, 1994. xiii, 336 p.
93-020052   305.5/122/0954   0195084896
Social status. Social structure. Sociology -- Philosophy.

HM136.M59 1991
Miyanaga, Kuniko, 1945-
The creative edge: emerging individualism in Japan/ Kuniko Miyanaga; with a foreword by Peter L. Berger. New Brunswick (U.S.A.): Transaction Publishers, c1991. xx, 137 p.
90-049774   302.5/4/0952   0887384072
Individualism -- Japan. Technology -- Social aspects -- Japan.

HM136.S282 1996
Schellenberg, James A., 1932-
Conflict resolution: theory, research, and practice/ James A. Schellenberg. Albany, NY: State University of New York Press, c1996. ix, 247 p.
95-052851   303.6/9 20   0791431010
Conflict management.

HM136.W345 1990
Wartenberg, Thomas E.
The forms of power: from domination to transformation/ Thomas E. Wartenberg. Philadelphia: Temple University Press, 1990. x, 253 p.
89-037385   303.3   0877226482
Power (Social sciences)

HM141 Individualism. Differentiation. Struggle — The great man. Leadership. Prestige

HM141.B847 1978
Burns, James MacGregor.
Leadership/ James MacGregor Burns. New York: Harper & Row, c1978. ix, 530 p.
76-005117   301.15/53   0060105887
Leadership.

HM141.C275 1996
Carlton, Eric.
The few and the many: a typology of elites/ Eric Carlton. Aldershot, England: Scolar Press; c1996. 225 p.
95-025475   305.5/2 20   185928194X
Elite (Social sciences) Elite (Social sciences) -- Case studies.

HM141.G687 1998
Greenleaf, Robert K.
The power of servant-leadership: essays/ by Robert K. Greenleaf; edited and introduction by Larry C. Spears; foreword by Peter B. Valli; afterword by James P. Shannon. San Francisco, Calif.: Berrett-Koehler Publishers, 1998. xxvi, 313 p.
98-024143   303.3/4   1576750353
Leadership. Associations, institutions, etc. Christian leadership.

HM141.H385 1994
Heifetz, Ronald A. 1951-
Leadership without easy answers/ Ronald A. Heifetz. Cambridge, Mass.: Belknap Press of Harvard University Press, 1994. xi, 348 p.
94-015184   303.3/4   0674518586
Leadership.

HM141.L553 1990
Lindholm, Charles, 1946-
Charisma/ Charles Lindholm. Cambridge, Mass., USA: B. Blackwell, 1990. 238 p.
90-032760   303.3/4   1557860211
Leadership. Charisma (Personality trait) Cults -- Psychology.

HM141.W525 1994
Wills, Garry, 1934-
Certain trumpets: the call of leaders/ Garry Wills. New York: Simon & Schuster, c1994. 336 p.
94-006526   303.3/4   067165702X
Leadership -- Case studies. Power (Social sciences) -- Case studies. Social participation -- Case studies.

HM146 Individualism. Differentiation. Struggle — Equality

HM146.K64 1998
Koggel, Christine M., 1955-
Perspectives on equality: constructing a relational theory/ Christine M. Koggel. Lanham, MD: Rowman & Littlefield Publishers, c1998. xiii, 313 p.
97-035810   305 21   0847688054
Equality.

HM146.T45 1993
Temkin, Larry S.
Inequality/ Larry S. Temkin. New York: Oxford University Press, 1993. xiii, 352 p.
92-009497   305   0195078608
Equality.

HM206 Social elements, forces, laws — Environment. Regional sociology — General works

HM206.D48 1997
Diamond, Jared M.
Guns, germs, and steel: the fates of human societies/ Jared Diamond. New York: W.W. Norton & Co., c1997. 480 p.
96-037068   303.4 21   0393038912
Social evolution. Civilization -- History. Ethnology.

HM206.D87
Dubos, Rene J. 1901-
So human an animal [by] Rene Dubos. New York, Scribner [1968] xiv, 267 p.
68-027794   301.3
Human ecology. Human beings -- Effect of environment on. Technology and civilization.

HM206.M95 1997
Murphy, Raymond, 1943-
Sociology and nature: social action in context/ Raymond Murphy. Boulder, Colo.: Westview Press, 1997. xiii, 321 p.
97-003286   304.2   0813328659
Human ecology. Sociology -- Philosophy. Environmentalism.

HM206.P54 1992
Piel, Gerard.
Only one world: our own to make and to keep/ Gerard Piel. New York: W.H. Freeman and Co., c1992. xii, 367 p.
92-002867   304.2   0716723166
Human ecology. Economic development -- Social aspects. Environmental policy.

HM206.S53
Shepard, Paul, 1925-
The subversive science; essays toward an ecology of man, edited by Paul Shepard and Daniel McKinley. Boston, Houghton Mifflin [1969] x, 453 p.
69-015029   301.3/2/08
Human ecology -- Addresses, essays, lectures.

HM211 Social elements, forces, laws — Economic

HM211.D58 1992
Dittmar, Helga.
The social psychology of material possessions: to have is to be/ Helga Dittmar. Hemel Hempstead, Hertfordshire: Harvester Wheatsheaf; 1992. xi, 250 p.
92-013443   302.5   0745009557
Property -- Social aspects. Property -- Psychological aspects. Acquisitiveness.

HM213 Social elements, forces, laws — Intellectual

HM213.S22 1992
Sadri, Ahmad.
Max Weber's sociology of intellectuals/ Ahmad Sadri; with a foreword by Arthur J. Vidich. New York: Oxford University Press, 1992. xiv, 167 p.
92-004395   305.5/52   0195065565
Weber, Max, -- 1864-1920. Intellectuals.

HM216 Social elements, forces, laws — Moral

HM216.E85 1996
Etzioni, Amitai.
The new golden rule: community and morality in a democratic society/ Amitai Etzioni. New York: BasicBooks, c1996. xxii, 314 p.
96-021192   303.3/72 20   0465052975
Social ethics. Social values. Communitarianism.

HM216.F38 1997
Fein, Melvyn L.
Hardball without an umpire: the sociology of morality/ Melvyn L. Fein. Westport, Conn.: Praeger, 1997. xi, 254 p.
97-005585   301   0275959244
Sociology -- Moral and ethical aspects. Sociology -- Philosophy. Ethics.

HM216.G564 1988
Goodin, Robert E.
Reasons for welfare: the political theory of the welfare state/ Robert E. Goodin. Princeton, N.J.: Princeton University Press, c1988. xiii, 423 p.
88-005822   303.3/72   0691077665
Social justice. Welfare state -- Moral and ethical aspects.

HM216.H26 1996
Harvey, David, 1935-
Justice, nature, and the geography of difference/ David Harvey. Cambridge, Mass.: Blackwell Publishers, 1996. vi, 468 p.
96-000961   303.3/72   1557866805
Social justice. Social change. Social values.

HM216.J58
John Rawls' theory of social justice: an introduction/ H. Gene Blocker, Elizabeth H. Smith, editors. Athens: Ohio University Press, c1980. xxiii, 520 p.
80-011272   320/.01/1   0821404458
Rawls, John, -- 1921- -- Congresses. Social justice -- Congresses.

HM216.R62 1992
Roche, Maurice.
Rethinking citizenship: welfare, ideology, and change in modern society/ Maurice Roche. Cambridge, UK: Polity Press; 1992. vi, 280 p.
92-020497   323.6   0745603068
Social ethics -- United States. Social policy. United States -- Social policy -- 1980-1993.

HM216.R68 1989
Rowe, Stephen C., 1945-
Leaving and returning: on America's contribution to a world ethic/ Stephen C. Rowe. Lewisburg [Pa.]: Bucknell University Press; c1989. 165 p.
88-047944   306/.0973   0838751636
Social ethics. United States -- Social conditions -- 1960-1980. United States -- Social conditions -- 1980-

HM216.S553 1997
Social justice in a diverse society/ Tom R. Tyler ... [et al.]. Boulder, CO: Westview Press, 1997. xi, 305 p.
96-049150   303.3/72   0813332141
Social justice. Equality -- United States. United States -- Social conditions.

HM216.T24 1998
Tam, Henry Benedict.
Communitarianism: a new agenda for politics and citizenship/ Henry Tam. New York: New York University Press, c1998. x, 288 p.
97-045738   303.3/72 21   0814782353
Communitarianism. Community -- Moral and ethical aspects. Social ethics.

HM216.V47 1994
Values and public policy/ Henry J. Aaron, Thomas E. Mann, Timothy Taylor, editors. Washington, D.C.: Brookings Institution, c1994. xiv, 216 p.
93-038466   303.3/72   0815700563
Social values -- United States. Social ethics -- United States. United States -- Social policy.

HM216.W65 1989
Wolfe, Alan, 1942-
Whose keeper?: social science and moral obligation/ Alan Wolfe. Berkeley: University of California Press, c1989. xvii, 371 p.
88-037389   300   0520065514
Social ethics. Political ethics. Social sciences and state.

HM221 Social elements, forces, laws — Technological

HM221.B83 1994
Buchanan, R. A. 1930-
The power of the machine: the impact of technology from 1700 to the present day/ R.A. Buchanan. London; Penguin, 1994. xvii, 299 p.
94-209957   303.48/3   0140170634
Technology and civilization.

HM221.F384 1995
Feenberg, Andrew.
Alternative modernity: the technical turn in philosophy and social theory/ Andrew Feenberg. Berkeley: University of California Press, c1995. xi, 251 p.
95-008666   303.48/3   0520089855
Technology -- Social aspects. Culture. Democracy.

HM221.H395 1995
Haywood, Trevor, 1943-
Info-rich--info-poor: access and exchange in the global information society/ Trevor Haywood. London; Bowker-Saur, c1995. xiv, 274 p.
95-003993   303.48/33   0862916313
Information society. Information resources management. Information technology -- Economic aspects.

HM221.P44 1998
Perelman, Michael.
Class warfare in the information age/ Michael Perelman. New York, N.Y.: St. Martin's Press, 1998. 154 p.
97-053280   303.6   0312177585
Information society. Information technology -- Social aspects. Social classes.

HM221.R47 1995
Resisting the virtual life: the culture and politics of information/ edited by James Brook and Iain A. Boal. San Francisco: City Lights; c1995. xv, 278 p.
95-007962   303.48/33   0872862992
Information society. Computers and civilization. Computer networks -- Social aspects.

HM221.R644 1998
Rosen, Bernard Carl.
Winners and losers of the information revolution: psychosocial change and its discontents/ Bernard Carl Rosen. Westport, Conn.: Praeger, 1998. x, 320 p.
98-015652   303.48/33   0275962776
Information society. Elite (Social sciences) Social classes.

HM221.W35 1991
Wajcman, Judy.
Feminism confronts technology/ Judy Wajcman. University Park, Pa.: Pennsylvania State University Press, 1991. x, 184 p.
91-018539   306.4/6   0271008016
Technology -- Social aspects. Feminist criticism.

HM251 Social psychology — General works

HM251.A782 1991
Argyle, Michael.
The social psychology of everyday life/ Michael Argyle. London; Routledge, 1992. x, 319 p.
91-017444   302   0415010713
Social psychology. Social interaction. Social groups.

HM251.B476 1995
The Blackwell encyclopedia of social psychology/ edited by Antony S.R. Manstead and Miles Hewstone; advisory editors, Susan T. Fiske ... [et al.]. Oxford, UK; Blackwell, 1995. xvi, 694 p.
93-051074   302/.03   0631181466
Social psychology -- Encyclopedias.

HM251.H72 1997
Howard, Judith A.
Gendered situations, gendered selves: a gender lens on social psychology/ Judith A. Howard, Jocelyn A. Hollander. Thousand Oaks, Calif.: Sage Publications, c1997. xiv, 209 p.
96-010130   302 20   0803956045
Social psychology. Sex role. Personality and situation.

HM251.L242 1991
Lana, Robert E., 1932-
Assumptions of social psychology: a reexamination/ Robert E. Lana. Hillsdale, N.J.: L. Erlbaum, 1991. viii, 145 p.
91-006637   302   0805810226
Social psychology.

HM251.S2623 1991
Sampson, Edward E.
Social worlds, personal lives: an introduction to social psychology/ Edward E. Sampson. San Diego: Harcourt Brace Jovanovich, c1991. xi, 369 p.
90-084204   302   0155818058
Social psychology.

HM251.S459 1991
Shapiro, Edward R., 1941-
Lost in familiar places: creating new connections between the individual and society/ Edward R. Shapiro and A. Wesley Carr. New Haven: Yale University Press, c1991. xiii, 193 p.
90-019662   302   0300049471
Social psychology. Organizational behavior. Family psychotherapy.

HM251.S6743 1996
Social psychology: handbook of basic principles/ edited by E. Tory Higgins, Arie W. Kruglanski. New York: Guilford Press, 1996. x, 947 p.
96-022623   302   1572301007
Social psychology.

HM254 Social psychology — Sociodrama

HM254.S74 1989
Sternberg, Patricia.
Sociodrama: who's in your shoes?/ Patricia Sternberg & Antonina Garcia; foreword by Zerka T. Moreno. New York: Praeger, 1989. xvi, 201 p.
89-033970   302/.15   027593053X
Sociodrama.

HM256 Social psychology — Risk perception. Risk assessment

HM256.L8413 1993
Luhmann, Niklas.
Risk: a sociological theory/ Niklas Luhmann; translated by Rhodes Barrett. New York: A. de Gruyter, c1993. xiii, 236 p.
92-031317   302.1/2   0202304434
Risk -- Sociological aspects.

HM256.U53 1996
Understanding risk: informing decisions in a democratic society/ Paul C. Stern and Harvey V. Fineberg, editors. Washington, D.C.: National Academy Press, 1996. xii, 249 p.
96-016152   302/.12   030905396X
Risk assessment. Policy sciences.

HM258 Social psychology — Communication

HM258.C678 1996
Couch, Carl J.
Information technologies and social orders/ Carl J. Couch; edited with an introduction by David R. Maines and Shing-Ling Chen. New York: Aldine de Gruyter, c1996. xviii, 272 p.
96-014824   302 20   0202305155
Communication -- Social aspects. Information technology -- Social aspects. Information society.

HM258.H574 1991
Hofstede, Geert H.
Cultures and organizations: software of the mind/ Geert Hofstede. London; McGraw-Hill, c1991. xii, 279 p.
91-000205   306   0077074742
Intercultural communication. Organization -- Research. International cooperation.

HM258.L674 1994
Lorimer, Rowland, 1944-
Mass communications: a comparative introduction/ Rowland Lorimer with Paddy Scannell. Manchester; Manchester University Press; c1994. xvi, 318 p.
94-019057   302.2   0719039460
Communication -- Social aspects. Mass media -- Social aspects.

HM258.M49 1985
Meyrowitz, Joshua.
No sense of place: the impact of electronic media on social behavior/ Joshua Meyrowitz. New York: Oxford University Press, 1985. xv, 416 p.
84-003950   302.2/34   0195034740
Mass media -- Social aspects. Communication -- Social aspects. Social change. United States -- Social conditions.

HM258.S586 1994
Social scientists meet the media/ edited by Cheryl Haslam and Alan Bryman. London; Routledge, 1994. xii, 227 p.
93-024572   302.23   0415081904
Mass media -- Social aspects. Communication in the social sciences. Social sciences -- Research.

HM258.W37 1994
Wark, McKenzie, 1961-
Virtual geography: living with global media events/ McKenzie Wark. Bloomington: Indiana University Press, c1994. xvii, 252 p.
93-048986   302.23   0253208947
Mass media -- Social aspects.

HM259 Social psychology — Social influence

HM259.K87 1995
Kuran, Timur.
Private truths, public lies: the social consequences of preference falsification/ Timur Kuran. Cambridge, Mass.: Harvard University Press, 1995. xv, 423 p.
94-047969   303.3/4   0674707575
Social influence. Truthfulness and falsehood -- Social aspects. Knowledge, Theory of.

HM261 Social psychology — Public opinion

HM261.B69 1988
Bradburn, Norman M.
Polls & surveys: understanding what they tell us/ Norman M. Bradburn, Seymour Sudman. San Francisco: Jossey-Bass, 1988. xx, 249 p.
88-042778   303.3/8   1555420982
Public opinion polls.

HM261.B694 1993
Brehm, John, 1960-
The phantom respondents: opinion surveys and political representation/ John Brehm. Ann Arbor: University of Michigan Press, c1993. x, 266 p.
92-040475   303.3/8   0472095234
Public opinion polls. Representative government and representation.

HM261.C695 1997
Crespi, Irving.
The public opinion process: how the people speak/ Irving Crespi. Mahwah, N.J.: Erlbaum, 1997. xvi, 190 p.
97-001381   303.3/8   0805826645
Public opinion.

HM261.I68
International journal of public opinion research. Oxford: Oxford University Press, [1989-]
91-642201   303.3/8/05
Public opinion -- Periodicals. Public opinion polls -- Periodicals.

HM261.Y684 1991
Young, Michael L.
Dictionary of polling: the language of contemporary opinion research/ Michael L. Young. New York: Greenwood Press, 1992. xii, 266 p.
91-024198   303.3/8/03   031327598X
Public opinion polls -- Dictionaries.

HM261.Z35 1992
Zaller, John, 1949-
The nature and origins of mass opinion/ John R. Zaller. Cambridge [England]; Cambridge University Press, 1992. xiii, 367 p.
91-043032   303.3/8   0521404495
Public opinion. Attitude (Psychology) Political psychology.

HM263 Social psychology — Public relations. Publicity. Propaganda

HM263.B323 1995
Banks, Stephen P.
Multicultural public relations: a social-interpretive approach/ Stephen P. Banks. Thousand Oaks: Sage Publications, c1995. x, 141 p.
94-049583   659.2   0803948409
Public relations. Intercultural communication. Multiculturalism.

HM263.B394 1965
Bernays, Edward L., 1891-
Biography of an idea: memoirs of public relations counsel Edward L. Bernays. New York, Simon and Schuster [1965] 849 p.
65-015030   659.20924

HM263.E413
Ellul, Jacques.
Propaganda; the formation of men's attitudes. Translated from the French by Konrad Kellen and Jean Lerner. With an introd. by Konrad Kellen. New York, Knopf, 1965. xxii, 320 p.
64-017708   301.1523
Propaganda.

HM263.E849 1996
Ewen, Stuart.
PR!: a social history of spin/ Stuart Ewen. New York: Basic Books, c1996. xv, 480 p.
96-002243   659.2 20   0465061680
Public relations. Public relations -- United States.

HM263.N44 1996
Nelson, Richard Alan, 1947-
A chronology and glossary of propaganda in the United States/ Richard Alan Nelson. Westport, Conn.: Greenwood Press, 1996. xvi, 340 p.
94-047427   303.3/75/0973   0313292612
Propaganda -- United States -- History -- Chronology.

HM271 Social psychology — Authority and freedom — General works

HM271.A457 1988
Altemeyer, Bob, 1940-
Enemies of freedom: understanding right-wing authoritarianism/ Bob Altemeyer; foreword by M. Brewster Smith. San Francisco: Jossey-Bass Publishers, 1988. xxix, 378 p.
88-042774   303.3/6   1555420974
Authoritarianism. Right and left (Political science) Conservatism.

HM271.F74
Fromm, Erich, 1900-
Escape from freedom, by Erich Fromm. New York [etc.] Farrar & Rinehart, inc. [1941] ix, 305 p.
41-014128   323.44
Liberty. Democracy. Totalitarianism.

HM271.H297 1998
Harle, Vilho.
Ideas of social order in the ancient world/ Vilho Harle. Westport, Conn.: Greenwood Press, 1998. xvii, 252 p.
97-033962   303.3/3/09   031330582X
Social control -- History. Social institutions -- History. International organization -- History.

HM271.M39 1994
McMahon, Christopher, 1945-
Authority and democracy: a general theory of government and management/ Christopher McMahon. Princeton, N.J.: Princeton University Press, c1994. xiv, 307 p.
94-001366   350   0691036624
Authority. Democracy. Management -- Employee participation.

HM276 Social psychology — Authority and freedom — Liberalism. Toleration

HM276.B39 1992
Bellamy, Richard
Liberalism and modern society: a historical argument/ Richard Bellamy. University Park, Pa.: Pennsylvania State University Press, c1992. x, 310 p.
92-007406   320.5/1   0271008792
Liberalism. Liberalism -- Europe -- History.

HM276.C625 1998
Communicating prejudice/ Michael L. Hecht, editor. Thousand Oaks, Calif.: Sage Publications, c1998. ix, 404 p.
97-033906   303.3/85 21   0761901248
Toleration. Prejudices. Prejudices -- United States.

HM276.D4
Dewey, John, 1859-1952.
Liberalism and social action, by John Dewey. New York, G. P. Putnam's Sons [c1935] viii, 93p.
35-015252   301.15
Liberalism. Economic policy.

HM276.H7 1980
Hobhouse, L. T. 1864-1929.
Liberalism/ L. T. Hobhouse; introd. by Alan P. Grimes. Westport, Conn.: Greenwood Press, 1980, c1964. 130 p.
80-010822   320.5/1   0313223327
Liberalism -- Great Britain. Great Britain -- Politics and government -- 1837-1901.

HM276.K96 1989
Kymlicka, Will.
Liberalism, community, and culture/ Will Kymlicka. Oxford [England]: Clarendon Press; 1989. 280 p.
88-029649   302.5   0198275994
Liberalism. Community. Minorities -- Civil rights.

HM276.L57 1979
Lowi, Theodore J.
The end of liberalism: the second republic of the United States/ Theodore J. Lowi. New York: Norton, c1979. xviii, 331 p.
78-027093   320.5/1/0973   0393057100
Liberalism -- United States.

HM276.M56 1993
Moon, J. Donald.
Constructing community: moral pluralism and tragic conflicts/ J. Donald Moon. Princeton, N.J.: Princeton University Press, c1993. xi, 235 p.
93-012930   320.5/1   0691086427
Liberalism. Pluralism (Social sciences) Community.

HM276.W497 1997
Wilkinson, J. Harvie, 1944-
One nation indivisible: how ethnic separatism threatens America/ J. Harvie Wilkinson, III. Reading, Mass.: Addison-Wesley Pub. Co., c1997. ix, 294 p.
96-039225   305.8/00973   0201180723
Pluralism (Social sciences) -- United States. Multiculturalism -- United States. United States -- Ethnic relations.

HM278 Social psychology — Passive resistance

HM278.P76 1997
Protest, power, and change: an encyclopedia of nonviolent action from ACT-UP to women's suffrage/ editors, Roger S. Powers, William B. Vogele; associate editors, Christopher Kruegler, Ronald M. McCarthy. New York: Garland Pub., 1997. xxv, 610 p.
96-026869   303.61/03   0815309139
Nonviolence -- Encyclopedias.

HM278.S37 1990
Scott, James C.
Domination and the arts of resistance: hidden transcripts/ James C. Scott. New Haven: Yale University Press, c1990. xviii, 251 p.
90-035207   303.6/1   0300047053
Passive resistance. Power (Social sciences) Dominance (Psychology)

HM278.T73 1996
Tracy, James.
Direct action: radical pacifism from the Union Eight to the Chicago Seven/ James Tracy. Chicago, Ill.; The University of Chicago Press, 1996. xv, 196 p.
96-012278   303.6/1   0226811271
Passive resistance -- United States -- History. Pacifists -- United States -- History. Direct action -- History.

HM281 Social psychology — Crowds. Tumults. Revolutions. Violence — Theory

HM281.C3513 1956
Camus, Albert, 1913-1960.
The rebel; an essay on man in revolt. With a foreword by Sir Herbert Read. A rev. and complete translation of L'homme revolte by Anthony Bower. New York, Vintage Books, 1956. 306 p.
56-013684   301.6/333
Revolutions.

HM281.G82
Gurr, Ted Robert, 1936-
Why men rebel. Princeton, N.J., Published for the Center of International Studie 1970. xi, 421 p.
74-084865   301.2/4   069107528X
Revolutions. Violence.

HM281.K47 1990
Kimmel, Michael S.
Revolution, a sociological interpretation/ Michael S. Kimmel. Philadelphia: Temple University Press, 1990. ix, 252 p.
90-010869   303.6/4   0877227365
Revolutions.

HM281.M39 1991
McPhail, Clark, 1936-
The myth of the madding crowd/ Clark McPhail. New York: A. de Gruyter, c1991. xxx, 265 p.
90-042787   302.3/3   0202304248
Collective behavior. Crowds.

HM281.R8
Rude, George F. E.
Ideology and popular protest/ by George Rude. New York: Pantheon Books, c1980. 176 p.
80-008030   303.6/4/09   039451372X
Ideology. Revolutions -- History. Social movements -- History.

HM281.S635 1997
Spinosa, Charles.
Disclosing new worlds: entrepreneurship, democratic action, and the cultivation of solidarity/ Charles Spinosa, Fernando Flores, and Hubert L. Dreyfus. Cambridge, Mass.: MIT Press, c1997. x, 222 p.
96-029295 306 0262193817
Social action. Collective behavior. Entrepreneurship.

HM283 Social psychology — Crowds. Tumults. Revolutions. Violence — History

HM283.B68 1993
Bouton, Cynthia A.
The flour war: gender, class, and community in late Ancien Regime French society/ Cynthia A. Bouton. University Park, Pa.: Pennsylvania State University Press, c1993. xxvi, 307 p.
93-020349 306/.0944/09033 0271010533
Crowds -- France -- History -- 18th century. Riots -- France -- History -- 18th century. Food prices -- France -- History -- 18th century. France -- History -- Revolution, 1789-1799 -- Causes. France -- History -- Revolution, 1789-1799 -- Economic aspects.

HM283.R38 1989
Revolution in the world-system/ edited by Terry Boswell. New York: Greenwood Press, 1989. xiv, 239 p.
88-037518 303.6/4 031326726X
Revolutions -- Congresses. Revolutions -- Developing countries -- Congresses. Social change -- Congresses.

HM291 Social psychology — Other special

HM291.B269 1998
Barbalet, J. M., 1946-
Emotion, social theory, and social structure: a macrosociological approach/ J.M. Barbalet. Cambridge; Cambridge University Press, 1998. ix, 210 p.
97-025639 302 0521621909
Emotions -- Sociological aspects. Social structure. Social interaction.

HM291.B3413 1993
Baudrillard, Jean.
Symbolic exchange and death/ Jean Baudrillard; translated by Iain Hamilton Grant; with an introduction by Mike Gane. London; Sage Publications, 1993. xiv, 254 p.
93-085813 301/.01 0803983980
Social psychology. Value. Death.

HM291.B535 1999
Blackmore, Susan J., 1951-
The meme machine/ Susan Blackmore. New York: Oxford University Press, 1999. xx, 264 p.
98-049180 304.5 0198503652
Memetics. Imitation. Behavior evolution.

HM291.C652 1998
Cooney, Mark, 1955-
Warriors and peacemakers: how third parties shape violence/ Mark Cooney. New York: New York University Press, c1998. xi, 210 p.
97-045350 303.6 21 0814715141
Violence. Interpersonal conflict. Homicide.

HM291.D467 1993
Deutscher, Irwin, 1923-
Sentiments and acts/ Irwin Deutscher, Fred P. Pestello, and H. Frances G. Pestello. New York: Aldine de Gruyter, c1993. xi, 268 p.
92-027887 302/.072 0202304442
Social psychology -- Research. Attitude (Psychology) Personality and situation.

HM291.D4962 1993
Dijk, Teun Adrianus van, 1943-
Elite discourse and racism/ Teun A. van Dijk. Newbury Park, Calif.: Sage Publications, c1993. xii, 320 p.
92-039455 305.8 0803950705
Racism. Elite (Social sciences) Communication.

HM291.E78 1988
Erving Goffman: exploring the interaction order/ edited by Paul Drew and Anthony Wootton. Boston: Northeastern University Press, 1988. iv, 298 p.
88-002665 302 1555530370
Goffman, Erving -- Congresses. Social interaction -- Congresses.

HM291.G659 1987
Graebner, William.
The engineering of consent: democracy and authority in twentieth-century America/ William Graebner. Madison, Wis.: University of Wisconsin Press, 1987. xi, 262 p.
87-008266 303.3/6 0299111709
Social engineering -- United States -- History -- 20th century. Authority -- History -- 20th century. Democracy -- History -- 20th century. United States -- Social conditions.

HM291.L235 1996
Lamb, Sharon.
The trouble with blame: victims, perpetrators, and responsibility/ Sharon Lamb. Cambridge, MA: Harvard University Press, 1996. 244 p.
95-047457 302/.12 0674910109
Attribution (Social psychology) Blame -- Moral and ethical aspects. Victims -- Psychology.

HM291.M49 1986
Miller, Arthur G., 1940-
The obedience experiments: a case study of controversy in social science/ Arthur G. Miller. New York: Praeger, 1986. ix, 295 p.
85-025738 303.3/6 0030617979
Obedience. Obedience -- Research. Authority.

HM291.M772513 1991
Mugny, Gabriel.
The social psychology of minority influence/ Gabriel Mugny and Juan A. Perez; translated by Vivian Waltz Lamongie. Cambridge; Cambridge University Press; 1991. xiv, 190 p.
90-002658 303.3/2 0521390540
Social integration. Minorities. Influence (Psychology)

HM291.P727 1996
Prus, Robert C.
Symbolic interaction and ethnographic research: intersubjectivity and the study of human lived experience/ Robert Prus. Albany: State University of New York Press, c1996. xxiv, 301 p.
94-049571 302.20 0791427013
Symbolic interactionism. Sociology -- Methodology. Social sciences -- Philosophy.

HM291.S58837 1990
Social influence processes and prevention/ edited by John Edwards ... [et al.]. New York: Plenum Press, c1990. xxi, 345 p.
89-023236 362/.0424 0306432935
Deviant behavior -- Prevention. Health promotion. Social influence.

HM291.Y68 1990
Young, T. R.
The drama of social life: essays in post-modern social psychology/ T.R. Young. New Brunswick, U.S.A.: Transaction Publishers, c1990. xiii, 367 p.
89-004594 302 0887382029
Social interaction. Social psychology. Drama -- Psychological aspects.

HM291.Z64 1994
Zohar, Danah, 1945-
The quantum society: mind, physics and a new social vision/ Danah Zohar & Ian Marshall. New York: Morrow, 1994. 362 p.
93-034348 302 068810603X
Social psychology. Quantum theory. Physics -- Philosophy.

HM299 Miscellaneous special

HM299.S585 1988
The Social psychology of time: new perspectives/ edited by Joseph E. McGrath. Newbury Park, Calif.: Sage Publications, c1988. 271 p.
87-037700 302 0803927665
Time -- Social aspects. Time -- Psychological aspects. Time perception.

HM299.S6 1968
Sorokin, Pitirim Aleksandrovich, 1889-1968.
Man and society in calamity; the effects of war, revolution, famine, pestilence upon human mind, behavior, social organization, and cultural life. New York, Greenwood Press, 1968 [c1942] 352 p.
69-010157 301.2/4
Disasters. Social psychology. Social problems.

HM425 Dictionaries. Encyclopedias

HM425.E5 2000
Encyclopedia of sociology/ Edgar F. Borgatta, editor-in-chief, Rhonda Montgomery, managing editor. New York: Macmillan Reference USA, c2000. 5 v.
00-028402 301/.03 21 0028648536
Sociology -- Encyclopedias.

HM449 History of sociology. History of sociological theory — By period — 20th century

HM449.P67 2000
Postmodern times: a critical guide to the contemporary/ edited by Thomas Carmichael and Alison Lee. DeKalb, Ill.: Northern Illinois University Press, 2000. 272 p.
99-028171 306 0875802516
Postmodernism -- Social aspects.

HM479 Biography — Individual, A-Z

HM479.M55.A3 2000
Mills, C. Wright 1916-1962.
Letters and autobiographical writings/ C. Wright Mills; edited by Kathryn Mills with Pamela Mills; introduction by Dan Wakefield. Berkeley: University of California Press, c2000. xxviii, 378 p.
99-029106   301/.092 B 21   0520211065
Mills, C. Wright -- (Charles Wright), -- 1916-1962 -- Correspondence. Mills, C. Wright -- (Charles Wright), -- 1916-1962. Sociologists -- United States -- Biography.

HM479.W42.C36 2000
The Cambridge companion to Weber/ edited by Stephen Turner. New York: Cambridge University Press, 2000. xx, 288 p.
99-015846   301/.09   0521561493
Weber, Max, -- 1864-1920. Sociology -- History.

HM511 By region or country — Islamic countries

HM511.E45 2002
Eliæson, Sven,
Max Weber's methodologies: interpretation and critique/ Sven Eliaeson. Cambridge, UK: Polity Press in association with Blackwell Publishers   x, 230 p.
2002-001669   301/.01 21   0745618138
Weber, Max, 1864-1920. Sociology -- Methodology.

HM535 Theory. Method. Relations to other subjects — Methodology — Mathematical sociology. Quantitative methods

HM535.B47 2001
Best, Joel.
Damned lies and statistics: untangling numbers from the media, politicians, and activists/ Joel Best. Berkeley: University of California Press, c2001. ix, 190 p.
00-064910   303.3/8 21   0520219783
Sociology -- Statistical methods. Social problems -- Statistical methods. Social indicators.

HM548 Theory. Method. Relations to other subjects — Relation to economics

HM548.G47 2000
Gershuny, Jonathan.
Changing times: work and leisure in postindustrial society/ Jonathan Gershuny. Oxford [England]; Oxford University Press, 2000. viii, 304 p.
00-032362   306.3/6   0198287879
Economics -- Sociological aspects. Work -- Sociological aspects. Leisure -- Sociological aspects.

HM548.S55 2001
Slater, Don.
Market society: markets and modern social theory/ Don Slater and Fran Tonkiss. Cambridge, U.K.: Polity Press; c2001. 233 p.
00-040088   306.3 21   0745620264
Economics -- Sociological aspects. Markets -- Sociological aspects. Sociology -- Economic aspects.

HM606 General works — Other languages, A-Z

HM606.D36
Classical and modern social theory/ edited by Heine Andersen and Lars Bo Kaspersen. Malden, Mass.: Blackwell, 2000. xi, 524 p.
99-058779   301/.01   0631212876
Sociology -- Philosophy. Sociology -- Philosophy -- History.

HM621 Culture — General works

HM621.S57 2001
Smith, Philip 1964-
Cultural theory: an introduction/ Philip Smith. Malden, Mass.: Blackwell, 2001. viii, 268 p.
00-057906   306   0631211756
Culture.

HM621.W67 2000
The World Wide Web and contemporary cultural theory/ edited by Andrew Herman & Thomas Swiss. New York: Routledge, 2000. 312 p.
00-044643   306.4/6   0415925010
Culture. World Wide Web -- Social aspects. Internet -- Social aspects.

HM646 Culture — Subculture

HM646.P35 2000
Palmer, Bryan D.
Cultures of darkness: night travels in the histories of transgression/ Bryan D. Palmer. New York: Monthly Review Press, c2000. xiii, 609 p.
00-045086   306/.1 21   1583670262
Subculture -- History. Marginality, Social -- History. Deviant behavior -- History.

HM665 Social control — Social ethics

HM665.C64 1999
Coffin, William Sloane.
The heart is a little to the left: essays on public morality/ William Sloane Coffin. Hanover, NH: University Press of New England [for] Dartmouth c1999. x, 81 p.
99-034297   303.3/72 21   0874519586
Social ethics. Social values. Moral conditions.

HM676 Social control — Social norms

HM676.S63 2001
Social norms/ Michael Hechter and Karl-Dieter Opp, editors. New York: Russell Sage Foundation, c2001. xx, 429 p.
00-051000   306 21   0871543540
Social norms.

HM726 Groups and organizations — Social groups. Group dynamics — Age groups. Peer groups

HM726.W56 2001
Williams, Angie.
Intergenerational communication across the life span/ Angie Williams, Jon F. Nussbaum. Mahwah, NJ: Lawrence Erlbaum Associates, 2000. xvi, 342 p.
99-056785   306.87   0805822488
Intergenerational communication. Intergenerational relations. Communication in the family.

HM756 Groups and organizations — Community — General works

HM756.M36 2000
Mandelbaum, Seymour J.
Open moral communities/ Seymour J. Mandelbaum. Cambridge, Mass.: MIT Press, c2000. xiv, 242 p.
99-043445   307 21   0262133652
Community. Community -- Moral and ethical aspects. Pluralism (Social sciences)

HM776 Groups and organizations — Community — Community power

HM776.M39 2000
Mayo, Marjorie.
Cultures, communities, identities: cultural strategies for participation and empowerment/ Marjorie Mayo; consultant editor, Jo Campling. Houndmills, Basingstoke, Hampshire; Palgrave, 2000. viii, 217 p.
00-033295   307.1/4/091724   0333716620
Community power -- Developing countries. Community organization -- Developing countries. Community development -- Developing countries.

HM846-851 Social change — Causes — Technological innovations. Technology

HM846.H663 2000
Homer-Dixon, Thomas F.
The ingenuity gap/ Thomas Homer-Dixon. New York: Knopf, 2000. 480 p.
00-064904   303.48/33   0375401865
Technology -- Social aspects. Creative ability. Social change.

HM851.B76 2000
Brown, John Seely.
The social life of information/ John Seely Brown and Paul Duguid. Boston: Harvard Business School Press, c2000. x, 320 p.
99-049068   303.48/33 21   08775847625
Information society. Information technology -- Social aspects.

HM851.M37 2000
Margolis, Michael.
Politics as usual: the cyberspace "revolution"/ Michael Margolis, David Resnick. Thousand Oaks: Sage Publications, c2000. viii, 246 p.
99-050650   303.48/33 21   0761913300
Internet -- Political aspects. Internet -- Political aspects -- United States. Cyberspace -- Political aspects.

HM851.S87 2001
Sunstein, Cass R.
Republic.com/ Cass Sunstein. Princeton, N.J.: Princeton University Press, c2001. 224 p.
00-045331   303.48/33 21   0691070253
Information society. Information society -- Political aspects. Internet -- Social aspects.

HM881-886 Social change — Causes — Collective behavior. Mass behavior

HM881.K45 2001
Kelly, Christine A., 1961-
Tangled up in red, white, and blue: new social movements in America/ Christine A. Kelly. Lanham, Md.: Rowman & Littlefield, c2001. xv, 195 p.
00-057587   303.48/4/0973 21   0742508129
Social movements -- United States. Ideology -- United States. Radicalism -- United States.

HM886.E53 1999
Encyclopedia of violence, peace & conflict/ editor-in-chief, Lester Kurtz; associate editor, Jennifer Turpin. San Diego: Academic Press, c1999. 3 v.
99-060408   303.6/03 21   012227010X
Violence -- Encyclopedias. Conflict (Psychology) -- Encyclopedias. Social conflict -- Encyclopedias.

HM1033 Social psychology — General works

HM1033.C95 2000
Cziko, Gary.
The things we do: using the lessons of Bernard and Darwin to understand the what, how, and why of our behavior/ Gary Cziko. Cambridge, Mass.: MIT Press, c2000. xi, 290 p.
99-051843   304 21   0262032775
Social psychology. Sociobiology. Behavior evolution.

HM1206-1236 Social psychology — Social influence. Social pressure — Attitude

HM1206.M67 2000
Morley, David, 1949-
Home territories: media, mobility, and identity/ David Morley. New York: Routledge, 2000.
00-035316   306   0415157641
Mass media -- Social aspects. Population geography. Group identity.

HM1236.L48 2001
Lewis, Justin, 1958-
Constructing public opinion: how political elites do what they like and why we seem to go along with it/ Justin Lewis. New York: Columbia University Press, c2001. xiv, 250 p.
00-063924   303.3/8 21   0231117663
Public opinion. Public opinion -- United States. Mass media and public opinion -- United States.

HM1251 Social psychology — Social influence. Social pressure — Authority

HM1251.S45 2000
Seligman, A.
Modernity's wager: authority, the self, and transcendence/ Adam B. Seligman. Princeton: Princeton University Press, c2000. xii, 177 p.
00-027418   303.3/6 21   0691050619
Authority. Self. Transcendence (Philosophy)

HM1271 Social psychology — Social influence. Social pressure — Multiculturalism. Pluralism. Toleration

HM1271.G35 2002
Galeotti, Anna E.
Toleration as recognition/ Anna Elisabetta Galeotti. Cambridge, UK; Cambridge University Press, 2002. viii, 242 p.
2001-043624   303.3/85 21   0521806763
Toleration. Pluralism (Social sciences) Equality.

HM1271.N44 1999
Nederman, Cary J.
Worlds of difference: European discourses of toleration, c. 1100-c. 1550/ Cary J. Nederman. University Park: Pennsylvania State University Press, c2000. x, 157 p.
99-042596   179/.9 21   0271020164
Toleration -- History -- To 1500. Religious tolerance -- History -- To 1500. Toleration in literature.

HM1271.P37 2000
Parekh, Bhikhu C.
Rethinking multiculturalism: cultural diversity and political theory/ Bhikhu Parekh. Cambridge, Mass.: Harvard University Press, 2000. xii, 379 p.
00-036975   306   0674004361
Multiculturalism. Pluralism (Social sciences)

HM1281 Social psychology — Social influence. Social pressure — Hybridity

HM1281.S74 2000
Steger, Manfred B., 1961-
Gandhi's dilemma: nonviolent principles and nationalist power/ Manfred B. Steger. New York: St. Martin's Press, 2000. xii, 232 p.
00-038239   303.6/1   0312221770
Gandhi, -- Mahatma, -- 1869-1948.   Passive resistance. Nonviolence. Nationalism -- India.

HN Social History and Conditions. Social Problems. Social Reform

HN3 Congresses

HN3.G57 1988
Global crisis and social movements: artisans, peasants, populists and the world economy/ edited by Edmund Burke, III. Boulder, Colo.: Westview Press, 1988. xi, 276 p.
87-020138   303.4/84   0813306094
Social movements -- History -- 19th century -- Congresses. Social movements -- History -- 20th century -- Congresses. Business cycles -- History -- 19th century -- Congresses.

HN10 History — Ancient — Special, A-Z

HN10.G7.G73 1992
Grant, Michael, 1914-
A social history of Greece and Rome/ Michael Grant. New York: Scribner; c1992. ix, 197 p.
92-032690   937   0684193094
Greece -- Social conditions -- To 146. Rome -- Social conditions.

HN10.R7.C43 1991
Champlin, Edward, 1948-
Final judgments: duty and emotion in Roman wills, 200 B.C.-A.D. 250/ Edward Champlin. Berkeley: University of California Press, c1991. xi, 217 p.
90-038795   306/.0945/632   0520071034
Social structure -- Rome. Wills (Roman law) Rome -- Social conditions.

HN10.R7 S45 1998
Shelton, Jo-Ann.
As the Romans did: a sourcebook in Roman social history/ Jo-Ann Shelton. 2nd ed. New York: Oxford University Press, 1998. xxv, 483 p.
96-035257   306/.0945/632 20   019508974X
Social structure -- Rome. Social history -- To 500.

HN11 History — Medieval

HN11.D78 1977b
Duby, Georges.
The chivalrous society/ Georges Duby; translated by Cynthia Postan. Berkeley: University of California Press, c1977. viii, 246 p.
74-081431   309.1/4/01   0520028139
Social classes -- Europe -- History.

HN11.R49 1990
Richards, Jeffrey.
Sex, dissidence, and damnation: minority groups in the Middle Ages/ Jeffrey Richards. London; Routledge, 1990 xii, 179 p.
90-008338   306.7/09   041503342X
Social history -- Medieval, 500-1500. Minorities -- History. Dissenters -- History.

HN13 History — Modern — General and early modern

HN13.B84 2000
Buechler, Steven M., 1951-
Social movements in advanced capitalism: the political economy and cultural construction of social activism/ Steven M. Buechler. New York: Oxford University Press, 2000. xiii, 240 p.
98-042230   303.48/4   0195126033
Social movements. Collective behavior.

HN13.T54
Tilly, Charles.
As sociology meets history/ Charles Tilly. New York: Academic Press, c1981. xiii, 237 p.
81-012728   907/.2   0126912807
Social history. Sociology — Methodology. History — Methodology.

HN13.W88 1989
Wuthnow, Robert.
Communities of discourse: ideology and social structure in the Reformation, the Enlightenment, and European socialism/ Robert Wuthnow. Cambridge, Mass.: Harvard University Press, 1989. viii, 739 p.
88-035792   303.3/72   067415164X
Social history. Ideology. Reformation.

HN15-15.5 History — Modern — 19th century

HN15.M263 1967
Mannheim, Karl, 1893-1947.
Man and society in an age of reconstruction; studies in modern social structure. With a bibliographical guide to the study of modern society. New York, Harcourt, Brace & World [1967] xxii, 469 p.
67-005016   301
Civilization. Sociology. Social psychology.

HN15.M775 1993
Moore, Barrington,
Social origins of dictatorship and democracy: lord and peasant in the making of the modern world/ Barrington Moore; with a new foreword by Edward Friedman and James C. Scott. Boston: Beacon Press, 1993. xxv, 559 p.
93-017802   301 20   0807050733
Social history. Economic history. Revolutions.

HN15.5.L37
Lasch, Christopher.
The world of nations; reflections on American history, politics, and culture. New York, Knopf; [distributed by Random House] 1973. xii, 348 p.
73-004309   309.1/04   0394483944
Social history — Modern.

HN16-18 History — Modern — 20th century

HN16.A3313 1998
Adorno, Theodor W., 1903-1969.
Critical models: interventions and catchwords/ Theodor W. Adorno; translated and with a preface by Henry W. Pickford. New York: Columbia University Press, c1998. xii, 404 p.
97-039500   301/.01 21   0231076347
Social history — 20th century. Social sciences — Philosophy.

HN16.B59913 1996
Bornschier, Volker, 1944-
Western society in transition/ Volker Bornschier. New Brunswick, N.J.: Transaction Publishers, c1996. vii, 453 p.
96-000389   306/.09/04 20   1560002271
Social history — 20th century. Economic history — 20th century. Social change.

HN16.F765 1992
Frontiers in social movement theory/ edited by Aldon D. Morris and Carol McClurg Mueller. New Haven, Conn.: Yale University Press, c1992. xii, 382 p.
92-003393   303.48/4   0300054858
Social movements. Social movements — United States. Social action.

HN16.G65 1996
Goldthorpe, J. E.
The sociology of post-colonial societies: economic disparity, cultural diversity, and development/ J.E. Goldthorpe. Cambridge; Cambridge University Press, 1996. xi, 279 p.
95-026762   306/.09172/4 20   0521578000
Social history — 20th century.

HN16.R63
Roszak, Theodore, 1933-
Person/planet: the creative disintegration of industrial society/ Theodore Roszak. Garden City, N.Y.: Anchor Press/Doubleday, 1978. xxx, 347 p.
75-006165   301.1   0385000634
Social history — 20th century. Social psychology. Human ecology.

HN17.T69 2000
Tourish, Dennis.
On the edge: political cults right and left/ Dennis Tourish, Tim Wohlforth. Armonk, N.Y.: M.E. Sharpe , c2000. xvi, 246 p.
00-024818   303.48/4 21   0765606399
Radicalism. Social movements. Politics and culture.

HN17.5.C354 2000
Castells, Manuel.
End of millennium/ Manuel Castells. Malden, MA: Blackwell Publishers, 2000. xv, 448 p.
00-037873   306/.09   0631221395
Social history — 1970- Economic history — 1990- Technology and civilization.

HN17.5.C575 1994
Clement, Wallace.
Relations of ruling: class and gender in postindustrial societies/ Wallace Clement and John Myles. Montreal; McGill-Queen's University Press, c1994. xiii, 303 p.
94-237450   305.5   0773511644
Social classes. Sex role. Power (Social sciences)

HN17.5.D48
The Development of welfare states in Europe and America/ edited by Peter Flora and Arnold J. Heidenheimer. New Brunswick, U.S.A.: Transaction Books, c1981. 417 p.
79-065227   361.6/5   0878553576
Welfare state — Addresses, essays, lectures.

HN17.5.E82 1988
Estes, Richard J.
Trends in world social development: the social progress of nations, 1970-1987/ Richard J. Estes. New York: Praeger, 1988. xx, 218 p.
87-036132   303.4/4   0275926133
Social history — 1970- Progress. Social indicators.

HN17.5.E99 1991
Eyerman, Ron.
Social movements: a cognitive approach/ Ron Eyerman and Andrew Jamison. University Park, Pa.: Pennsylvania State University Press, c1991. 184 p.
90-021197   303.48/4   0271007524
Social movements. Social movements — United States — Case studies.

HN17.5.N4855 1994
New social movements: from ideology to identity/ edited by Enrique Larana, Hank Johnston, and Joseph R. Gusfield. Philadelphia: Temple University Press, 1994. 368 p.
93-037495   303.48/4   1566391865
Social movements. Social history — 1945- Social psychology.

HN17.5.O24 1992
Oberschall, Anthony.
Social movements: ideologies, interests, and identities/ Anthony Oberschall. New Brunswick (U.S.A.): Transaction, c1993. x, 402 p.
91-047657   303.48/4   1560000112
Social movements. Social conflict. Social movements — United States — History — 20th century. United States — Social conditions — 1960-1980. United States — Social conditions — 1980-

HN17.5.R356 1995
The radicalism handbook: radical activists, groups, and movements of the twentieth century/ [compiled by] John Button. Santa Barbara, Calif.: ABC-CLIO, c1995. xx, 460 p.
95-015213   303.48/4   0874368383
Radicalism — Handbooks, manuals, etc. Radicals — Biography.

HN17.5.T64
Toffler, Alvin.
Future shock. New York, Random House [1970] xii, 505 p.
67-012744   301.2/4
Social history — 1945- Social change. Civilization, Modern — 1950-

HN17.5.W42
Weitz, Raanan, 1913-
From peasant to farmer; a revolutionary strategy for development. With the assistance of Levia Applebaum. New York, Columbia University Press, 1971. xvi, 292 p.
76-170926   301.3/5   0231035926
Rural development. Economic development — Social aspects. Agriculture — Economic aspects.

HN17.5.W55 1975
Wilensky, Harold L.
The welfare state and equality: structural and ideological roots of public expenditures/ by Harold L. Wilensky. Berkeley: University of California Press, [1974] c1975. xvii, 151 p.
74-079146   361.6   0520028007
Welfare state. Equality.

HN17.5.W665 1994
World social situation in the 1990s. New York: United Nations, 1994. ix, 319 p.
95-161342   306/.09   9211301610
Social history — 1970- Social indicators.

HN17.5.Z57 1997
Zirakzadeh, Cyrus Ernesto, 1951-
Social movements in politics: a comparative study/ Cyrus Ernesto Zirakzadeh. London; Longman, 1997. xiv, 269 p.
96-053294 306.2 0582209463
Political participation -- Case studies. Social movements -- Political aspects -- Case studies.

HN18.B635 1990
Bookchin, Murray, 1921-
Remaking society: pathways to a green future/ Murray Bookchin. Boston, MA: South End Press, c1990. 222 p.
89-021990 361.6/1 089608373X
Social policy. Social structure. Radicalism.

HN18.H395 1999
Herman, A. L.
Community, violence, and peace: Aldo Leopold, Mohandas K. Gandhi, Martin Luther King, Jr., and Gautama the Buddha in the twenty-first century/ A. L. Herman. Albany, N.Y.: State University of New York Press, c1999. xi, 245 p.
97-047500 306/.09 21 0791439836
Social history. Community. Violence -- History.

HN18.K22
Kahn, Alfred J., 1919-
Studies in social policy and planning [by] Alfred J. Kahn. New York, Russell Sage Foundation, 1969. x, 326 p.
70-083536 309.1/73
Social policy. United States -- Social policy.

HN18.K23
Kahn, Alfred J., 1919-
Theory and practice of social planning [by] Alfred J. Kahn. New York, Russell Sage Foundation, 1969. xii, 348 p.
79-081406 309
Social planning. Social planning -- United States.

HN25 Statistics. Social indicators. Quality of life

HN25.P65 2000
The political economy of social inequalities: consequences for health and quality of life/ edited by Vicente Navarro. Amityville, NY: Baywood Pub. Co., 2000. v, 530 p.
00-044494 306 0895032201
Quality of life. Poverty. Equality.

HN25.P67 1998
Postrel, Virginia I., 1960-
The future and its enemies: the growing conflict over creativity, enterprise, and progress/ Virginia Postrel. New York: Free Press, 1998. xviii, 265 p.
98-034090 303.49 0684827603
Social prediction. Quality of life -- Forecasting. Technological forecasting.

HN25.Q33 1993
The Quality of life/ edited by Martha Nussbaum and Amartya Sen. Oxford [England]: Clarendon Press; 1993. xi, 453 p.
91-042030 306 0198283954
Quality of life -- Congresses. Public welfare -- Congresses. Human services -- Congresses.

HN25.T39 1983
Taylor, Charles Lewis.
World handbook of political and social indicators/ Charles Lewis Taylor and David A. Jodice. 3rd ed. New Haven: Yale University Press, c1983. 2 v.
82-040447 301./07/2 19 0300030282
Social indicators. Political indicators.

HN28 Theory. Method. Relation to other subjects — General works

HN28.C85 1995
Cultural politics and social movements/ edited by Marcy Darnovsky, Barbara Epstein, and Richard Flacks. Philadelphia: Temple University Press, 1995. xxiii, 360 p.
94-037908 303.48/4 1566393221
Social movements -- Congresses. Group identity -- Political aspects -- Congresses.

HN28.E53 1994
Encyclopedia of social history/ edited by Peter N. Stearns. New York: Garland, 1994. xxxvi, 856 p.
93-029230 306/.09 0815303424
Social history -- Encyclopedias.

HN28.I46 1995
Images of issues: typifying contemporary social problems/ Joel Best, editor. 2nd ed. New York: A. De Gruyter, c1995. ix, 362 p.
94-047575 361.1 20 0202305392
Social problems. Sociology.

HN28.L56 1990
Lindblom, Charles Edward, 1917-
Inquiry and change: the troubled attempt to understand and shape society/ Charles E. Lindblom. New Haven [Conn.]: Yale University Press, c1990. xii, 314 p.
90-037655 361.1 0300047940
Social problems. Social sciences -- Methodology. Social scientists.

HN28.M69 1996
Moynihan, Daniel P. 1927-
Miles to go: a personal history of social policy/ Daniel Patrick Moynihan. Cambridge, Mass.: Harvard University Press, 1996. 245 p.
96-008291 361.6/1 0674574400
Social policy. United States -- Social policy. United States -- Social conditions -- 1980-

HN29 Study and teaching. Research

HN29.S645 1992
The Social survey in historical perspective, 1880-1940/ edited by Martin Bulmer, Kevin Bales, and Kathryn Kish Sklar. Cambridge; Cambridge University Press, 1991. xix, 383 p.
90-038520 300/.723 0521363349
Social surveys -- United States -- History. Social surveys -- Great Britain -- History.

HN37 The church and social problems — Religious denominations — Special denominations, A-Z

HN37.A6.E45 1940
Eliot, T. S. 1888-1965.
The idea of a Christian society [by] T.S. Eliot. New York, Harcourt, Brace and Company [c1940] vii, 104 p.
40-003912 261
Sociology, Christian.

HN37.C3 D358 1992
Day, Dorothy,
Dorothy Day, selected writings: By little and by little/ edited and with an introduction by Robert Ellsberg. Maryknoll, N.Y.: Orbis Books, c1992. xli, 371 p.
92-025801 261.8/3 20 0883448025
Church and social problems -- Catholic Church.

HN37.C3.G66
The Gospel of peace and justice: Catholic social teaching since Pope John/ presented by Joseph Gremillion. Maryknoll, N.Y.: Orbis Books, c1976. xiv, 623 p.
75-039892 261.8/3 0883441659
John -- XXIII, -- Pope, -- 1881-1963. Paul -- VI, -- Pope, -- 1897-1978. Church and social problems -- Catholic Church -- Papal documents. Social justice.

HN39 The church and social problems — Religious denominations — Special regions or countries, A-Z

HN39.L3.G8413 1983
Gutierrez, Gustavo, 1928-
The power of the poor in history: selected writings/ Gustavo Gutierrez; translated from the Spanish by Robert R. Barr. Maryknoll, NY: Orbis Books, 1983. xvi, 240 p.
82-022252 261.8/3/098 0883443880
Church and social problems -- Latin America. Poor -- Latin America. Liberation theology.

HN49 Special topics (not otherwise provided for), A-Z

HN49.C6.C573 1998
Clarke, Susan E., 1945-
The work of cities/ Susan E. Clarke and Gary L. Gaile. Minneapolis: University of Minnesota Press, c1998. xvi, 282 p.
98-010858 307.1/416/0973 21 0816628920
Community development, Urban. Urban economics. Community development, Urban -- Case studies.

HN49.C6.C635 1996
Community development around the world: practice, theory, research, training/ edited by Hubert Campfens. Toronto; University of Toronto Press, c1997. xxiii, 481 p.
97-133084 307.1/4 21 0802009034
Community development -- Cross-cultural studies. Community development -- Research. Community development -- Philosophy.

HN49.C6.L43 1995
Lean, Mary.
Bread, bricks, and belief: communities in charge of their future/ Mary Lean. West Hartford, Conn., USA: Kumarian Press, 1995. ix, 182 p.
95-014670   307.1/4   1565490460
Community development -- Case studies. Sustainable development -- Case studies.

HN49.C6.P84 1998
Public-private partnerships for local economic development/ edited by Norman Walzer and Brian D. Jacobs. Westport, Conn.: Praeger, 1998. viii, 251 p.
97-027923   307.1/416   0275961532
Community development, Urban. Urban renewal. Public-private sector cooperation.

HN49.C6.W437 2000
Weinberg, Adam S.
Urban recycling and the search for sustainable community development/ Adam S. Weinberg, David N. Pellow, and Allan Schnaiberg. Princeton, N.J.: Princeton University Press, c2000. x, 225 p.
00-021055   307.1/4 21   0691050147
Community development. Sustainable development. Recycling (Waste, etc.)

HN49.P6.D36 1990
Dandeker, Christopher.
Surveillance, power, and modernity: bureaucracy and discipline from 1700 to the present day/ Christopher Dandeker. New York: St. Martin's Press, 1990, c1989. ix, 243 p.
89-070085   303.3   0312042221
Power (Social sciences) -- History. Bureaucracy -- History. Abuse of administrative power -- History.

HN50 By region or country — America

HN50.G74 1988
Greene, Jack P.
Pursuits of happiness: the social development of early modern British colonies and the formation of American culture/ Jack P. Greene. Chapel Hill: University of North Carolina Press, c1988. xv, 284 p.
88-005908   306/.0973   0807818046
Great Britain -- Colonies -- America -- Social conditions. United States -- Social conditions -- To 1865. United States -- Civilization -- To 1783.

HN57-59.2 By region or country — United States — History and description

HN57.A55 1976
Adamic, Louis, 1899-1951.
My America, 1928-1938/ by Louis Adamic. New York: Da Capo Press, 1976, c1938. xiii, 669 p.
76-002050   309.1/73/0917   0306708019
Adamic, Louis, -- 1899-1951.   Labor -- United States -- 1914- Working Class -- United States -- 1914- New Deal, 1933-1939. United States -- Social conditions -- 1933-1945.

HN57.A57
Allen, Robert L., 1942-
Reluctant reformers; racism and social reform movements in the United States, by Robert L. Allen with the collaboration of Pamela P. Allen. Washington, Howard University Press, 1974. 324 p.
73-085495   301.24/2/0973   0882580027
Social movements.   United States -- Social conditions. United States -- Race relations.

HN57.A584 1998
Amenta, Edwin, 1957-
Bold relief: institutional politics and the origins of modern American social policy/ Edwin Amenta. Princeton, NJ: Princeton University Press, c1998. xiii, 343 p.
97-024509   361.6/1/0973 21   0691017123
Public welfare -- United States -- History. United States -- Social policy. United States -- Politics and government -- 1933-1945.

HN57.A67
Anonymous Americans; explorations in nineteenth-century social history. Edited by Tamara K. Hareven. Englewood Cliffs, N.J., Prentice-Hall [1971] xxii, 314 p.
77-143813   309.1/73   0130383988
United States -- History -- Addresses, essays, lectures. United States -- Social conditions -- Addresses, essays, lectures.

HN57.B26
Baltzell, E. Digby 1915-
The Protestant establishment: aristocracy & caste in America, by E. Digby Baltzell. New York, Random House [1964] xviii, 429 p.
64-014840   301.440973
Social classes -- United States. WASPs (Persons) -- United States. Social status -- United States. United States -- Social conditions.

HN57.B334 1997
Barron, Hal S.
Mixed harvest: the second great transformation in the rural North, 1870-1930/ Hal S. Barron. Chapel Hill, N.C.: University of North Carolina Press, 1997. xiv, 301 p.
96-051451   307.72/0973   0807823546
Social change -- United States -- History. United States -- Rural conditions.

HN57.B659 1999
Brown, Michael K.
Race, money, and the American welfare state/ Michael K. Brown. Ithaca: Cornell University Press, 1999. xxii, 381 p.
98-031999   361.6/1/0973   0801435102
Social classes -- United States.   United States -- Politics and government -- 1933-1945. United States -- Politics and government -- 1945-1989. United States -- Social policy.

HN57.B87 1993
Burnham, John C. 1929-
Bad habits: drinking, smoking, taking drugs, gambling, sexual misbehavior, and swearing in American history/ John C. Burnham. New York: New York University Press, c1993. xviii, 385 p.
92-034840   306/.0973   0814711871
Vices -- Public opinion. Deviant behavior -- Public opinion. Public opinion -- United States. United States -- Moral conditions. United States -- Social conditions.

HN57.E58 1993
Encyclopedia of American social history/ Mary Kupiec Cayton, Elliott J. Gorn, Peter W. Williams, editors. New York: Scribner; c1993. 3 v.
92-010577   301/.0973   0684192462
Social history -- Encyclopedias. United States -- Social life and customs -- Encyclopedias. United States -- Social conditions -- Encyclopedias.

HN57.G6
Gordon, Milton Myron, 1918-
Assimilation in American life: the role of race, religion, and national origins. New York, Oxford University Press, 1964. 276 p.
64-015010   301.23
Assimilation (Sociology) Social groups. United States -- Social conditions.

HN57.G64 1995
Graff, Harvey J.
Conflicting paths: growing up in America/ Harvey J. Graff. Cambridge, Mass.: Harvard University Press, 1995. xiii, 426 p.
94-028404   305.2/35/0973   0674160665
Adolescence -- History. Children -- United States -- History. United States -- Social conditions.

HN57.G695 1999
Greenberg, Michael R.
Restoring America's neighborhoods: how local people make a difference/ Michael R. Greenberg. New Brunswick, N.J.: Rutgers University Press, c1999. xi, 212 p.
99-014063   307.3/362/0973 21   0813527112
Neighborhood -- United States. Inner cities -- United States. Community organization -- United States.

HN57.J246 1990
Jackson, Walter A.
Gunnar Myrdal and America's conscience: social engineering and racial liberalism, 1938-1987/ Walter A. Jackson. Chapel Hill: University of North Carolina Press, c1990. xxi, 447 p.
90-012015   306/.0973/0904   0807819115
Myrdal, Gunnar, -- 1898- -- American dilemma. Race discrimination -- United States -- History -- 20th century.   United States -- Social conditions -- 1933-1945. United States -- Social conditions -- 1945-

HN57.K38 1994
Keller, Morton.
Regulating a new society: public policy and social change in America, 1900-1933/ Morton Keller. Cambridge, Mass.: Harvard University Press, 1994. xi, 396 p.
93-047567   303.4/0973/0904   0674753666
Social change -- United States. Progressivism (United States politics) United States -- History -- 20th century. United States -- Social policy.

HN57.K55 1993
Klein, Maury, 1939-
The flowering of the third America: the making of an organizational society, 1850-1920/ Maury Klein. Chicago: Ivan R. Dee, c1993. 217 p.
93-013869   306/.0973/09034   1566630290
Corporate culture -- United States -- History. United States -- Economic conditions -- 1865-1918. United States -- Social conditions -- 1865-1918.

HN57.L8 1929
Lynd, Robert Staughton, 1892-
Middletown, a study in contemporary American culture, by Robert S. Lynd and Helen Merrell Lynd; foreword by Clark Wissler. New York, Harcourt, Brace and Company [c1929] x, 550 p.
29-026177   309.173
Cities and towns -- United States. Cost and standard of living -- United States. Social surveys. United States -- Social conditions. United States -- Religion.

HN57.L84
Lynd, Robert Staughton, 1892-
Middletown in transition; a study in cultural conflicts, by Robert S. Lynd & Helen Merrell Lynd. New York, Harcourt, Brace and company [c1937] xviii, 604 p.
37-027243   309.173
Cities and towns -- United States. Community life. United States -- Social conditions. United States -- Economic conditions -- 1918-1945. United States -- Religion -- 1901-1945.

HN57.M56 1995
Mintz, Steven, 1953-
Moralists and modernizers: America's pre-Civil War reformers/ Steven Mintz. Baltimore: Johns Hopkins University Press, 1995. xxii, 179 p.
94-043690   306/.0973   0801850800
Social reformers -- United States -- History. United States -- Economic conditions -- To 1865. United States -- Social conditions -- To 1865.

HN57.S49 1999
Sharp, Elaine B.
The sometime connection: public opinion and social policy/ Elaine B. Sharp. Albany, N.Y.: State University of New York Press, c1999. viii, 289 p.
98-053599   361.6/1/0973 21   0791442950
Public opinion -- United States.   United States -- Social policy -- Public opinion.

HN57.S525 1995
Skocpol, Theda.
Social policy in the United States: future possibilities in historical perspective/ Theda Skocpol. Princeton, N.J.: Princeton University Press, c1995. 326 p.
94-013215   361.6/1/0973   0691037868
Welfare state.   United States -- Social policy.

HN57.S68 1990
Staples, William G.
Castles of our conscience: social control and the American state, 1800-1985/ William G. Staples. New Brunswick, N.J.: Rutgers University Press, 1990. xii, 197 p.
90-037620   361.6/1/0973   0813516269
Prison administration -- United States -- History. Social service -- United States -- History. Social control -- History. United States -- Social policy.

HN57.S7 1968
Steffens, Lincoln, 1866-1936.
Upbuilders. Introd. by Earl Pomeroy. Seattle, University of Washington Press [1968, c1909] xxxvii, 334 p.
68-019419   301.15/3
Fagan, Mark, -- 1869- Colby, Everett, -- 1874- Lindsey, Ben B. -- (Ben Barr), -- 1869-1943.

HN57.T77 1998
Tucker, David M., 1937-
Mugwumps: public moralists of the gilded age/ David M. Tucker. Columbia: University of Missouri Press, c1998. x, 139 p.
98-020718   303.48/4/0973 21   0826211879
Social reformers -- United States -- History. Ethicists -- United States -- History. Social justice.

HN57.V47 1995
Vergara, Camilo J.
The new American ghetto/ Camilo Jose Vergara. New Brunswick, N.J.: Rutgers University Press, c1995. xvii, 235 p.
94-045707   307.3/362   0813522099
Inner cities -- United States -- Pictorial works.

HN57.W27 1990
Wall, Helena M.
Fierce communion: family and community in early America/ Helena M. Wall. Cambridge, Mass.: Harvard University Press, 1990. x, 243 p.
89-026806   306.85/0973   0674299582
Family -- United States -- History. Community -- History. Interpersonal relations -- History. United States -- Social conditions -- To 1865. United States -- History -- Colonial period, ca. 1600-1775.

HN57.W45 1988
Weiss, Richard,
The American myth of success: from Horatio Alger to Norman Vincent Peale/ Richard Weiss. Illini Books ed. Urbana: University of Illinois Press, 1988, c1969. 276 p.
88-018720   306/.0973 19   0252060431
Success -- United States. Success in literature.

HN57.Z83 1998
Zunz, Olivier.
Why the American century?/ Olivier Zunz. Chicago: University of Chicago Press, 1998. xvi, 254 p.
98-018972   306/.0973   0226994619
Social change -- United States -- History -- 20th century. Social history -- 20th century. Great powers. United States -- History -- 20th century. United States -- Foreign relations -- 20th century. United States -- Civilization -- 20th century.

HN58.B427 1996
Bennett, Michael J., 1936-
When dreams came true: the GI Bill and the making of modern America/ Michael J. Bennett. Washington, D.C.: Brassey's, c1996. xvi, 336 p.
96-027804   306/.0973 20   1574880411
Social change -- United States -- History -- 20th century. Veterans -- Education -- United States -- History. Veterans -- Education -- Law and legislation -- United States -- History. United States -- Social conditions -- 1945-

HN58.D575
Domhoff, G. William.
The higher circles; the governing class in America, by G. William Domhoff. New York, Random House [1970] xii, 367 p.
79-102332   301.44
Upper class -- United States.   United States -- Social conditions -- 1945- United States -- Foreign relations -- 1945-1989. United States -- Politics and government -- 1945-1989.

HN58.D58
Domhoff, G. William.
Who rules America? [By] G. William Domhoff. Englewood Cliffs, N.J., Prentice-Hall [1967] 184 p.
67-025926   301.44/0973
Upper class -- U.S.   United States -- Social conditions -- 1945- United States -- Economic conditions -- 1945- United States -- Politics and government -- 1945-1989.

HN58.F37 1996
Farley, Reynolds, 1938-
The new American reality: who we are, how we got here, where we are going/ Reynolds Farley. New York: Russell Sage Foundation, c1996. x, 385 p.
96-020404   306/.0973 20   0871542374
Social indicators -- United States. Economic indicators -- United States. Social change -- United States. United States -- Social conditions -- 1945- United States -- Economic conditions -- 1945- United States -- Census.

HN58.H245 1981
Harrington, Michael, 1928-
The next America: the decline and rise of the United States/ Michael Harrington; photographs by Bob Adelman; designed by Neil Shakery. New York: Holt, Rinehart, and Winston, c1981. vi, 154 p.
81-001086   973.92   0030574684
Radicalism -- United States.   United States -- Politics and government -- 1945-1989. United States -- Social conditions -- 1945-

HN59.C26
Califano, Joseph A., 1931-
Governing America: an insider's report from the White House and the Cabinet/ Joseph A. Califano, Jr. New York: Simon and Schuster, c1981. 474 p.
81-000652   361.6/1/0973   0671254286
Califano, Joseph A., -- 1931- Social legislation -- United States.   United States -- Social policy.

HN59.G57 1988
Glazer, Nathan.
The limits of social policy/ Nathan Glazer. Cambridge, Mass.: Harvard University Press, 1988. 215 p.
88-004029   361.6/1/0973   0674534433
Public welfare -- United States. Welfare state. United States -- Social policy.

HN59.H27
Harris, Marvin, 1927-
America now: the anthropology of a changing culture/ Marvin Harris. New York: Simon and Schuster, c1981. 208 p.
81-009132   973.92   067143148X
United States -- Social conditions -- 1980- United States -- Economic conditions -- 1981-

HN59.L96 1996
Lyons, Paul, 1942-
New Left, new right, and the legacy of the sixties/ Paul Lyons. Philadelphia, Pa.: Temple University Press, 1996. xii, 242 p.
96-013397   306/.0973   1566394775
Baby boom generation -- United States. United States -- Social conditions -- 1960-1980. United States -- Politics and government -- 1945-1989.

HN59.P39 2000
Patterson, James T.
America's struggle against poverty in the twentieth century/ James T. Patterson. Cambridge, Mass.: Harvard University Press, 2000. xiv, 312 p.
00-038277   361.6/1/0973   0674004345
Public welfare -- United States -- History -- 20th century. Poverty -- Government policy -- United States -- History -- 20th century. United States -- Social policy. United States -- Economic conditions.

HN59.Q28 1994
Quadagno, Jill S.
The color of welfare: how racism undermined the war on poverty/ Jill Quadagno. New York: Oxford University Press, 1994. viii, 254 p.
93-041892   305.5/69/0973   0195079191
Economic assistance, Domestic -- United States. Poor -- United States. United States -- Social policy. United States -- Race relations -- Economic aspects.

HN59.U7
Urban America (Organization)
One year later; an assessment of the Nation's response to the crisis described by the National Advisory Commission on Civil Disorders [by] Urban America, and the Urban Coalition. Forewords by John W. Gardner and Terry Sanford. New York, Praeger [1969] xi, 122 p.
71-082148   309.1/73
Afro-Americans -- Economic conditions. Afro-Americans -- Social conditions. United States -- Social conditions -- 1960-1980.

HN59.Y33 1981
Yankelovich, Daniel.
New rules, searching for self-fulfillment in a world turned upside down/ Daniel Yankelovich. New York: Random House, c1981. xxi, 278 p.
80-006011   973   0394502035
Self-realization.   United States -- Social conditions -- 1960- United States -- Moral conditions.

HN59.2.A34 1994
Age and structural lag: society's failure to provide meaningful opportunities in work, family, and leisure / edited by Matilda White Riley, Robert L. Kahn, Anne Foner; editorial associate, Karin A. Mack. New York: Wiley, c1994. xiv, 290 p.
93-046344   303.4/0973   0471016780
Social change -- United States. Social structure -- United States. Aging -- Social aspects -- United States.

HN59.2.A67 1996
Apraku, Kofi Konadu, 1954-
Outside looking in: an African perspective on American pluralistic society/ Kofi K. Apraku. Westport, Conn.: Praeger, 1996. xxii, 120 p.
94-012349   306/.0973   0275942074
United States -- Social conditions -- 1980- United States -- Politics and government -- 20th century. United States -- Ethnic relations.

HN59.2.B68 1996
Bork, Robert H.
Slouching towards Gomorrah: modern liberalism and American decline/ Robert H. Bork. New York: Regan Books, c1996. xiv, 382 p.
96-031277   306/.0973 20   0060391634
Liberalism -- United States. Social values -- United States. United States -- Social conditions -- 1980-

HN59.2.C437 1995
The changing American countryside: rural people and places/ edited by Emery N. Castle; foreword by Clifton Wharton, Jr. Lawrence: University Press of Kansas, c1995. xx, 563 p.
95-008076   307.72/0973   0700607242
Rural poor -- United States.   United States -- Rural conditions.

HN59.2.C68 1999
Couto, Richard A., 1941-
Making democracy work better: mediating structures, social capital, and the democratic prospect/ Richard A. Couto with Catherine S. Guthrie. Chapel Hill: University of North Carolina Press, 1999. xx, 336 p.
98-053439   302/.14   0807824887
Social participation -- United States. Democracy -- United States. Social capital (Sociology) -- United States.

HN59.2.D35 1996
Davidson, Osha Gray.
Broken heartland: the rise of America's rural ghetto/ Osha Gray Davidson. Expanded ed. Iowa City: University of Iowa Press, c1996. xiii, 220 p.
96-012117   307.3/366/0973 20   0877455546
Rural poor -- United States. Farmers -- United States -- Social conditions.

HN59.2.D44 1989
Deegan, Mary Jo, 1946-
American ritual dramas: social rules and cultural meanings/ Mary Jo Deegan. New York: Greenwood Press, 1989. xii, 188 p.
88-017772   306/.0973   031326337X
Social interaction -- United States. Symbolic interactionism. United States -- Social conditions -- 1980- United States -- Social life and customs -- 1971-

HN59.2.H34 1999
Hall, John A., 1949-
Is America breaking apart?/ John A. Hall and Charles Lindholm. Princeton, NJ: Princeton University Press, c1999. xi, 162 p.
98-027793   306/.0973 21   0691004102
Social values -- United States. National characteristics, American. Sociology -- United States. United States -- Social conditions -- 1980- United States -- Politics and government -- Philosophy.

HN59.2.H56 1995
Himmelfarb, Gertrude.
The de-moralization of society: from Victorian virtues to modern values/ Gertrude Himmelfarb. New York: A.A. Knopf: 1995. x, 314 p.
94-012365   303.3/72   0679438173
Social values -- United States. Social values -- England.   United States -- Moral conditions. England -- Moral conditions. United States -- Social conditions.

HN59.2.M374 1990
Marmor, Theodore R.
America's misunderstood welfare state: persistent myths, enduring realities/ Theodore R. Marmor, Jerry L. Mashaw, and Philip L. Harvey. New York: Basic Books, c1990. xvii, 268 p.
90-080240   361.6/1/0973   0465059694
Public welfare -- United States. Social security -- United States. Medicare. United States -- Social policy.

HN59.2.O72 1983
Ordinary people and everyday life: perspectives on the new social history/ edited by James B. Gardner and George Rollie Adams. Nashville, Tenn.: American Association for State and Local History c1983. viii, 215 p.
83-003707   973   091005066X
United States -- Social conditions -- 1960- United States -- Historiography.

HN59.2.P52 1994
Pierson, Paul.
Dismantling the welfare state?: Reagan, Thatcher, and the politics of retrenchment/ Paul Pierson. Cambridge, England; Cambridge University Press, 1994. viii, 213 p.
93-040381   361.6/1/0973   0521403820
Welfare state.   Great Britain -- Social policy -- 1979- United States -- Social policy -- 1980-1993.

HN59.2.W37 1999
Warnke, Georgia.
Legitimate differences: interpretation in the abortion controversy and other public debates/ Georgia Warnke. Berkeley, Calif.: University of California Press, c1999. xi, 214 p.
98-041409   303.3/72/0973 21   0520216334
Social ethics -- United States. Social values -- United States. Hermeneutics. United States -- Social policy -- Moral and ethical aspects.

HN59.2.W38 1995
Wattenberg, Ben J.
Values matter most: how Republicans or Democrats or a third party can win and renew the American way of life/ Ben J. Wattenberg. New York: Free Press, c1995. vi, 426 p.
95-034915   303.3/72   002933795X
Social values -- United States. Public opinion -- United States. Political parties -- United States. United States -- Politics and government -- 1993-

HN59.2.W525 1991
Wilkinson, Kenneth P.
The community in rural America/ Kenneth P. Wilkinson; under the auspices of the Rural Sociological Society. New York: Greenwood Press, 1991. x, 141 p.
90-047534   307.72/0973   0313264678
Rural development -- United States. Sociology, Rural. Community. United States -- Rural conditions.

HN59.2.Z85 1991
Zukin, Sharon.
Landscapes of power: from Detroit to Disney World/ Sharon Zukin. Berkeley: University of California Press, c1991. xii, 326 p.
90-011167   307.1/2/0973   0520072219
Cities and towns -- United States. Industrial location -- United States. Regional planning -- United States.   United States -- Economic conditions -- 1981- -- Regional disparities. United States -- Social conditions -- 1980-

HN60 By region or country — United States — Statistics. Social indicators. Quality of life

HN60.A5 1995
Andrews, Alice C.
The atlas of American society/ Alice C. Andrews and James W. Fonseca; cartography and graphic design by Daniel F. Van Dorn. New York: New York University Press, c1995. ix, 303 p.
95-005648   301/.0973/021   0814726267
United States -- Social conditions -- 1980- -- Statistics. United States -- Population -- Statistics.

HN60.B65 1996
Bok, Derek Curtis.
The state of the nation: government and the quest for a better society/ Derek Bok. Cambridge, Mass.: Harvard University Press, 1996. vii, 483 p.
96-022881 306./0973 0674292103
Quality of life -- United States. United States -- Social conditions -- 1945- United States -- Economic conditions -- 1945- United States -- Politics and government -- 1945-1989.

HN60.W55 1998
Williams, Walter.
Honest numbers and democracy: Walter Williams. Washington, DC: Georgetown University Press, c1998. xvii, 292 p.
97-037972 306./0973 21 0878406700
Social indicators -- United States. United States -- Social conditions -- 1945- -- Statistics. United States -- Statistical services -- Methodology. United States -- Social policy -- Decision making.

HN64-65 By region or country — United States — Social reform literature

HN64.A2 1907a
Addams, Jane, 1860-1935.
Democracy and social ethics. Edited by Anne Firor Scott. Cambridge, Belknap Press of Harvard University Press, 1964. lxxvii, 281 p.
64-025050 309.73
Social sciences. Social ethics. United States -- Social conditions.

HN64.C89 1965
Croly, Herbert David, 1869-1930.
The promise of American life. Edited by Arthur M. Schlesinger. Jr. Cambridge, Belknap Press of Harvard University Press, 1965. xxvii, 468 p.
65-013851 320.973
United States -- Politics and government. United States -- Social conditions.

HN64.L29
Lasch, Christopher.
The new radicalism in America, 1889-1963: the intellectual as a social type. New York, Knopf, 1965. xviii, 349 p.
65-011126 301.153
Intellectuals -- United States. Progressivism (United States politics) United States -- Social conditions. United States -- Civilization -- 20th century.

HN64.L53 1985
Lippmann, Walter,
Drift and mastery: an attempt to diagnose the current unrest/ Walter Lippmann; with a revised introduction and note by William E. Leuchtenburg. Madison, Wis.: University of Wisconsin Press, 1985. viii, 177 p.
85-040764 306./0973 19 0299106047
Progressivism (United States politics)

HN64.M393 1974
Woodhull, Victoria C. 1838-1927.
The Victoria Woodhull reader/ edited by Madeleine B. Stern. Weston, Mass.: M&S Press, 1974. 640 p.
74-193236 309.1/73/08 0877300097
United States -- Social conditions -- 1865-1918 -- Addresses, essays, lectures.

HN64.M872 2001
Moskowitz, Eva S.
In therapy we trust: America's obsession with self-fulfillment/ Eva S. Moskowitz. Baltimore: Johns Hopkins University Press, c2001. x, 342 p.
00-008987 361.1/0973 21 0801864038
Social problems -- United States -- History -- 19th century. Social problems -- United States -- History -- 20th century. Psychotherapy -- Popular works. United States -- Social conditions.

HN64.W2136 1978
Walters, Ronald G.
American reformers, 1815-1860/ Ronald G. Walters; consulting editor, Eric Foner. New York: Hill and Wang, 1978. xiv, 235 p.
78-007545 301.24/2/0973 0809025574
Social reformers -- United States -- History.

HN65.B47 1990
Betten, Neil.
The roots of community organizing, 1917-1939/ Neil Betten and Michael J. Austin with contributions by Robert Fisher ... [et al.]. Philadelphia: Temple University Press, 1990. viii, 230 p.
89-032536 361.2/5/097309042 0877226628
Community organization -- United States -- History -- 20th century. Social service -- United States -- History -- 20th century. Social action -- United States -- History -- 20th century.

HN65.C46 1990
Change in societal institutions/ edited by Maureen T. Hallinan, David M. Klein, and Jennifer Glass. New York: Plenum Press, c1990. xv, 277 p.
90-007464 306./0973 0306435411
Social institutions -- United States. Social structure -- United States. United States -- Social conditions -- 1980-

HN65.D339 1988
De Leon, David.
Everything is changing: contemporary U.S. movements in historical perspective/ David De Leon. New York: Praeger, c1988. xvii, 285 p.
87-007323 303.4/0973 0275928926
Social movements -- United States. Minorities -- United States -- Social conditions. United States -- Social conditions -- 1980-

HN65.D37 1994
Delgado, Richard.
Failed revolutions: social reform and the limits of legal imagination/ Richard Delgado and Jean Stefancic. Boulder, Colo.: Westview Press, 1994. xix, 207 p.
94-011403 303.48/4 0813318068
Social movements -- United States. Sociological jurisprudence. Law reform -- Social aspects -- United States.

HN65.H4 1990
Heidenheimer, Arnold J.
Comparative public policy: the politics of social choice in America, Europe, and Japan/ Arnold J. Heidenheimer, Hugo Heclo, Carolyn Teich Adams. 3rd ed. New York, NY: St. Martin's Press; xv, 416 p.
88-063047 361.6/1 20 0333524853
United States -- Social policy. Europe -- Social policy. Japan -- Social policy.

HN65.L33 1978
Lasch, Christopher.
The culture of narcissism: American life in an age of diminishing expectations/ Christopher Lasch. New York: Norton, 1978, c1979. xviii, 268 p.
78-016233 309.1/73/092 0393011771
Social values. United States -- Social conditions -- 1960-1980. United States -- Moral conditions.

HN65.M38 1993
McGuire, William, 1917-
American social leaders/ William McGuire and Leslie Wheeler; editors, Amy Lewis, Paula McGuire, consulting editors, Gary Gerstle, James M. McPherson. Santa Barbara, Calif.: ABC-CLIO, c1993. xv, 500 p.
93-003991 303.48/4/092273 087436633X
Social reformers -- United States -- Biography -- Dictionaries.

HN65.P635 1988
The Politics of social policy in the United States/ edited by Margaret Weir, Ann Shola Orloff, and Theda Skocpol. Princeton, N.J.: Princeton University Press, c1988. xiii, 465 p.
87-025702 361.6/1/0973 0691094365
Public welfare -- United States -- Congresses. Welfare state -- Congresses. United States -- Social policy -- Congresses. United States -- Politics and government -- 1945-1989 -- Congresses. United States -- Social conditions -- 1945- -- Congresses.

HN65.R9 1976
Ryan, William, 1923-
Blaming the victim/ by William Ryan. New York: Vintage Books, 1976. xv, 351 p.
76-378867 309.1/73/092 0394717627
Blame -- Social aspects -- United States. United States -- Social conditions -- 1960-1980.

HN65.S32 1979
Savitch, H. V.
Urban policy and the exterior city: Federal, State, and corporate impacts upon major cities/ H. V. Savitch. New York: Pergamon Press, c1979. xv, 359 p.
79-011552 301.36/3 0080233902
Urban policy -- United States. Power (Social sciences)

HN65.S48 1996
Shaw, Randy, 1956-
The activist's handbook: a primer for the 1990s and beyond/ Randy Shaw. Berkeley: University of California Press, c1996. x, 299 p.
95-033113 361.2 20 0520203151
Social action -- United States. Community organization -- United States. Political activists -- United States.

HN65.S5635 2000
Skocpol, Theda.
The missing middle: working families and the future of American social policy/ Theda Skocpol. New York: W.W. Norton, c2000. xii, 207 p.
99-037842 361.6/1/0973 21 0393048225
Working class families -- Government policy -- United States. Middle class families -- Government policy -- United States. United States -- Social policy -- 1993- United States -- Politics and government -- 1993-

HN65.S5649 1991
Slater, Philip Elliot.
A dream deferred: America's discontent and the search for a new democratic ideal/ Philip Slater. Boston: Beacon Press, c1991. ix, 224 p.
90-022592 306/.0973 0807043044
Authoritarianism -- United States. Democracy. United States -- Politics and government -- 1945-1989. United States -- Social conditions -- 1945-

HN65.T36
Taylor, William L., 1931-
Hanging together; equality in an urban nation, by William L. Taylor. New York, Simon and Schuster [1971] 348 p.
76-132772 309.1/73/09 0671207113
Civil rights -- United States. United States -- Social conditions -- 1945- United States -- Social policy.

HN65.T45
Thernstrom, Stephan.
Poverty and progress; social mobility in a nineteenth century city. Cambridge, Harvard University Press, 1964. xii, 286 p.
64-021793 309.17445
City and town life -- United States -- History -- 19th century. Social mobility -- United States -- History -- 19th century. Newburyport (Mass.) -- Social conditions.

HN65.T7 1997
Trend, David.
Cultural democracy: politics, media, new technology/ David Trend. Albany, NY: State University of New York Press, c1997. 216 p.
97-000629 306/.0973 21 0791433196
Democracy -- United States. Politics and culture -- United States. United States -- Social conditions -- 1980-

HN65.Z36 1990
Zander, Alvin Frederick, 1913-
Effective social action by community groups/ Alvin Zander. San Francisco: Jossey-Bass, 1990. xviii, 245 p.
89-078373 361.8/0973 1555422233
Community organization -- United States. Social action -- United States.

HN65.Z57 1993
Zito, George V.
The death of meaning/ George V. Zito. Wesport, Conn.: Praeger, c1993. xi, 162 p.
93-015351 306/.0973 0275946746
Social change -- United States. Meaning (Philosophy) United States -- Social conditions -- 1980-

HN79-80 By region or country — United States — Local

HN79.A11.H47 2001
Herndon, Ruth Wallis.
Unwelcome Americans: living on the margin in early New England/ Ruth Wallis Herndon. Philadelphia: University of Pennsylvania Press, c2001. xi, 243 p.
00-047975 305.5/6/0974 21 0812217659
Marginality, Social -- New England -- History -- 18th century. Poor -- New England -- Biography. Poor laws -- New England -- History -- 18th century. New England -- Social conditions -- 18th century.

HN79.A127.F54 1993
Fighting back in Appalachia: traditions of resistance and change/ edited by Stephen L. Fisher. Philadelphia: Temple University Press, 1993. x, 365 p.
92-017683 307.72/0974 0877229767
Community organization -- Appalachian Region. Dissenters -- Appalachian Region. Appalachian Region -- Rural conditions.

HN79.A127.P83 2000
Puckett, Anita, 1949-
Seldom ask, never tell: labor and discourse in Appalachia/ Anita Puckett. Oxford; Oxford University Press, 2000. xv, 309 p.
99-040241 306/.0974 0195102770
Sociology, Urban -- United States. Appalachian Region -- Economic conditions. Appalachian Region -- Social conditions.

HN79.A13.F67 1997
Fossett, Mark Alan.
Long time coming: racial inequality in the nonmetropolitan South, 1940-1990/ Mark A. Fossett and M. Therese Seibert. Boulder, Colo.: Westview Press, c1997. xvii, 284 p.
96-029842 305/.0975 21 0813389321
Sociology, Rural -- Southern States. Equality -- Southern States -- Statistics. Afro-Americans -- Southern States -- Economic conditions -- Statistics. Southern States -- Race relations.

HN79.A13.I58
The Invisible minority, urban Appalachians/ William W. Philliber & Clyde B. McCoy, editors, with Harry C. Dillingham. Lexington, Ky.: University Press of Kentucky, c1981. 192 p.
79-004008 974 0813113954
Rural-urban migration -- United States -- Congresses. Mountain whites (Southern States) -- Congresses. Appalachian Region -- Social conditions -- Congresses.

HN79.A13.N48 1989
Newby, I. A. 1931-
Plain folk in the new South: social change and cultural persistence, 1880-1915/ I.A. Newby. Baton Rouge: Louisiana State University Press, c1989. xiv, 588 p.
88-017439 307.7/2/0975 0807114561
Rural development -- Southern States -- History. Rural poor -- Southern States -- History. Southern States -- Rural conditions.

HN79.A13.S82
Stephenson, John B.
Shiloh: a mountain community [by] John B. Stephenson. Lexington, University of Kentucky Press, 1968. xi, 232 p.
68-055044 309.1/75
Family -- Appalachian Region, Southern. Appalachian Region, Southern -- Social conditions -- Case studies.

HN79.A133.C64 1989
Flynt, J. Wayne, 1940-
Poor but proud: Alabama's poor whites/ Wayne Flynt. Tuscaloosa: University of Alabama Press, c1989. xiii, 469 p.
88-020859 305.5/69/09761 081730424X
Rural development -- Alabama. Rural poor -- Alabama. Alabama -- Rural conditions.

HN79.A14.H37 1993
Harvey, David L., 1936-
Potter addition: poverty, family, and kinship in a heartland community/ David L. Harvey. New York: Aldine de Gruyter, c1993. x, 326 p.
92-022422 305.5/69/0977 0202304418
Rural families -- Middle West -- Case studies. Rural poor -- Middle West -- Case studies. Kinship -- Middle West -- Case studies. Middle West -- Rural conditions -- Case studies.

HN79.A165.H35 1989
Hall, Thomas D., 1946-
Social change in the Southwest, 1350-1880/ Thomas D. Hall. Lawrence, Kan.: University Press of Kansas, c1989. xvi, 287 p.
88-014250 306/.0979 0700603743
Indians of North America -- Cultural assimilation -- Southwest, New. Social change. Southwest, New -- Social conditions. Southwest, New -- Ethnic relations -- History. Southwest, New -- Economic conditions.

HN79.C22.L677 2000
Prismatic metropolis: inequality in Los Angeles/ Lawrence D. Bobo ... [et al.], editors. New York: Russell Sage Foundation, c2000. xiii, 611 p.
00-027029 305.8/009794/94 21 0871541297
Discrimination in employment -- California -- Los Angeles County. Minorities -- California -- Los Angeles County -- Social conditions. Minorities -- California -- Los Angeles County -- Economic conditions. Los Angeles County (Calif.) -- Race relations. Los Angeles County (Calif.) -- Social conditions. Los Angeles County (Calif.) -- Economic conditions.

HN79.C22.O949 1991
Walton, John, 1937-
Western times and water wars: state, culture, and rebellion in California/ John Walton. Berkeley: University of California Press, c1992. xx, 378 p.
91-012889 303.48/4/0979494 0520072456
Social movements -- California -- Owens River Valley -- History. Water rights -- California -- Owens River Valley -- History. Water rights -- California -- Los Angeles -- History. Owens River Valley (Calif.) -- Social conditions.

HN79.C23.P83 2000
Baldassare, Mark.
California in the New Millennium: the changing social and political landscape/ Mark Baldassare. Berkeley: University of California Press, c2000. xviii, 265 p.
99-055785 306/.09794 21 0520225120
Public opinion -- California. California -- Politics and government -- 1951- California -- Social conditions.

HN79.C6.H64 1990
Hogan, Richard.
Class and community in frontier Colorado/ Richard Hogan. Lawrence, Kan.: University Press of Kansas, c1990. xii, 250 p.
89-028317 306/.09788 0700604626
Social classes -- Colorado -- History -- 19th century. Cities and towns -- Colorado -- History -- 19th century. Frontier and pioneer life -- Colorado. Colorado -- Economic conditions. Colorado -- Social conditions.

HN79.G42.M354 1991
Greene, Melissa Fay.
Praying for sheetrock: a work of nonfiction/ Melissa Fay Greene. Reading, Mass.: Addison-Wesley, c1991. x, 335 p.
91-000547 306/.09758/737 0201550482
Poppell, Thomas Hardwick.   Criminal justice, Administration of -- Georgia -- McIntosh County -- History -- 20th century. Police corruption -- Georgia -- McIntosh County -- History -- 20th century. Political corruption -- Georgia -- McIntosh County -- History -- 20th century. McIntosh County (Ga.) -- Social conditions. McIntosh County (Ga.) -- Race relations. McIntosh County (Ga.) -- Politics and government.

HN79.I3K44
Keiser, John H.,
Building for the centuries: Illinois, 1865 to 1898/ John H. Keiser. Urbana: University of Illinois Press, c1977. xvi, 386 p.
77-001764 977.3/04 0252006178
Urbanization -- Illinois.

HN79.K42.H377 1995
Scott, Shaunna L., 1960-
Two sides to everything: the cultural construction of class consciousness in Harlan County, Kentucky/ by Shaunna L. Scott. Albany: State University of New York Press, c1995. xxvii, 259 p.
94-013464 305.5/09769/154 0791423433
Class consciousness -- Kentucky -- Harlan County. Coal miners -- Kentucky -- Harlan County -- Social conditions. Harlan County (Ky.) -- Social conditions.

HN79.M32.C37 1991
Carr, Lois Green.
Robert Cole's world: agriculture and society in early Maryland/ Lois Green Carr, Russell R. Menard, Lorena S. Walsh. Chapel Hill: Published for the Institute of Early American Hi c1991. xxi, 362 p.
90-026168 306/.09752/09032 0807819859
Cole, Robert, -- fl. 1652-1660.   Cole family. Plantations -- Chesapeake Bay Region (Md. and Va.) -- History -- 17th century. Plantation life -- Chesapeake Bay Region (Md. and Va.) -- History -- 17th century. Virginia -- Social life and customs -- To 1775. Chesapeake Bay Region (Md. and Va.) -- Rural conditions. Maryland -- Social life and customs -- To 1775.

HN79.N4.F58 1991
Fitchen, Janet M.
Endangered spaces, enduring places: change, identity, and survival in rural America/ Janet M. Fitchen; with illustrations by Sandra Rosenzweig Gittelman. Boulder: Westview Press, 1991. xvi, 314 p.
90-019908 307.72/0973 0813311144
Farm life -- New York (State) Rural poor -- New York (State) Community organization -- New York (State) New York (State) -- Rural conditions.

HN79.N8E83 1985
Escott, Paul D.,
Many excellent people: power and privilege in North Carolina,   1850-1900/ by Paul D. Escott. Chapel Hill: University of North Carolina Press, c1985. xxii, 344 p.
84-028107 306/.09756 0807816515
Social classes -- North Carolina -- History -- 19th century. Power (Social sciences) Elite (Social sciences) -- North Carolina -- History -- 19th century.

HN79.O3.M45 1994
Melko, Matthew.
Millfield on Saturday: searching for community in a metropolitan village/ Matthew Melko, Thomas E. Koebernick, David Michael Orenstein. Dayton, Ohio: Wright State University Press, c1994. v, 154 p.
93-040796 307.76/2 1882090098
Villages -- Ohio -- Case studies. Community -- Case studies. Social surveys -- Ohio.

HN79.O72.R633 1995
Brown, Beverly A., 1951 Feb. 21-
In timber country: working people's stories of environmental conflict and urban flight/ Beverly A. Brown. Philadelphia: Temple University Press, 1995. xx, 300 p.
94-021274 306/.09795/27 1566392721
Working class -- Oregon -- Rogue River Valley (Klamath County-Curry County) -- Interviews. Urban-rural migration -- Oregon -- Rogue River Valley (Klamath County-Curry County) Forests and forestry -- Environmental aspects -- Oregon -- Rogue River Valley (Klamath County-Curry County) Rogue River Valley (Klamath Country-Curry County, Or.) -- Rural conditions.

HN79.S83.S76 1992
Stock, Catherine McNicol.
Main street in crisis: the great depression and the old middle class on the northern plains/ Catherine McNicol Stock. Chapel Hill: University of North Carolina Press, c1992. xiii, 305 p.
91-032613 305.5/5/09783 0807820113
Middle class -- South Dakota -- History -- 20th century. Middle class -- North Dakota -- History -- 20th century. Depressions -- 1929 -- South Dakota. South Dakota -- Social conditions. North Dakota -- Social conditions.

HN79.T22.E35 1997
Hsiung, David C., 1961-
Two worlds in the Tennessee mountains: exploring the origins of Appalachian stereotypes/ David C. Hsiung. Lexington: University Press of Kentucky, c1997. xv, 239 p.
96-042954 306/.09768 20 0813120012
Social isolation -- Tennessee, East -- History. Stereotype (Psychology) -- Tennessee, East -- History. Tennessee, East -- Economic conditions. Tennessee, East -- Social conditions. Tennessee, East -- Geography.

HN79.V82.L687 1996
Stevenson, Brenda E.
Life in black and white: family and community in the slave South/ Brenda E. Stevenson. New York: Oxford University Press, 1996. xv, 457 p.
95-017359 306.8/09755/28 0195095367
Family -- Virginia -- Loudon County -- History -- 19th century. Slavery -- Virginia -- Loudon County -- History -- 19th century. Loudoun County (Va.) -- Social conditions.

HN79.W2.A43 1994
Allen, John C. 1954-
Against all odds: rural community in the information age/ John C. Allen, Don A. Dillman. Boulder, Colo.: Westview Press, 1994. xviii, 238 p.
94-027434 307.72/09797 081338821X
Washington (State) -- Rural conditions.

HN79.W6.P43 1992
Pederson, Jane Marie.
Between memory and reality: family and community in rural Wisconsin, 1870-1970/ Jane Marie Pederson. Madison, Wis.: University of Wisconsin Press, c1992. xvi, 314 p.
91-045787 307.72/09775 0299132803
Wisconsin -- Rural conditions. Pigeon (Wis.) -- Rural conditions. Lincoln (Wis.) -- Rural conditions.

HN80.A33.R33 1996
Rabrenovic, Gordana, 1957-
Community builders: a tale of neighborhood mobilization in two cities/ Gordana Rabrenovic. Philadelphia, PA: Temple University Press, 1996. xii, 233 p.
95-033292 307.3/362 1566394090
Community organization -- New York (State) -- Albany. Community organization -- New York (State) -- Schenectady. Homeowners' associations -- New York (State) -- Albany. Albany (N.Y.) -- Social conditions. Schenectady (N.Y.) -- Social conditions.

HN80.A8.A86 2000
The Atlanta paradox/ David L. Sjoquist, editor. New York: Russell Sage Foundation, c2000. 300 p.
00-020793 305.8/009758/231 21 0871548089
Equality -- Georgia -- Atlanta. Atlanta (Ga.) -- Economic conditions. Atlanta (Ga.) -- Race relations. Atlanta (Ga.) -- Social conditions.

HN80.B7.B67 2000
The Boston renaissance: race, space, and economic change in an American metropolis/ Barry Bluestone and Mary Huff Stevenson, [editors]; with contributions from Michael Massaagli, Philip Moss, and Chris Tilly. New York: Russell Sage Foundation, 2000. xiii, 461 p.
99-462260 306/.09744/61 0871541254
Boston (Mass.) -- Social conditions. Boston (Mass.) -- Economic conditions. Boston (Mass.) -- Ethnic relations.

HN80.B7.S76
Story, Ronald.
The forging of an aristocracy: Harvard & the Boston upper class, 1800-1870/ Ronald Story. Middletown, Conn.: Wesleyan University Press; c1980. xv, 256 p.
80-000460 305.5/2/09 0819550442
Elite (Social sciences) -- Massachusetts -- Boston -- History -- 19th century. Elite (Social sciences) -- New England -- History -- 19th century. Boston (Mass.) -- Social conditions.

HN80.B7.T45
Thernstrom, Stephan.
The other Bostonians; poverty and progress in the American metropolis, 1880-1970. Cambridge, Mass., Harvard University Press, 1973. xvi, 345 p.
73-077469 301.44/0973 0674644956
Social mobility -- United States. Social classes -- United States. Occupational mobility. Boston (Mass.) -- Social conditions.

HN80.C36.H84 1995
Hugill, Peter J.
Upstate Arcadia: landscape, aesthetics, and the triumph of social differentiation in America/ Peter J. Hugill. Lanham, Md.: Rowman & Littlefield, c1995. xviii, 255 p.
93-046142 305.5/0973 0847678555
Social classes -- New York (State) -- Cazenovia. Elite (Social sciences) -- New York (State) -- Cazenovia. City planning -- New York (State) -- Cazenovia. Cazenovia (N.Y.) -- History. Cazenovia (N.Y.) -- Social conditions.

HN80.C5.C54 1987
Chicago: race, class, and the response to urban decline/ Gregory D. Squires ... [et al.]. Philadelphia: Temple University Press, 1987. xii, 230 p.
87-001876 306/.09773/11 0877224870
Community organization -- Illinois -- Chicago. Urban renewal -- Illinois -- Chicago. Chicago (Ill.) -- Social conditions. Chicago (Ill.) -- Economic conditions. Chicago (Ill.) -- Race relations.

HN80.C5.D85 1998
Duis, Perry, 1943-
Challenging Chicago: coping with everyday life, 1837-1920/ Perry R. Duis. Urbana: University of Illinois Press, c1998. xiii, 430 p.
97-045252 307.76/09773/11 21 0252023943
Sociology, Urban -- Illinois -- Chicago. City and town life -- Illinois -- Chicago. Social mobility -- Illinois -- Chicago. Chicago (Ill.) -- Social life and customs. Chicago (Ill.) -- Social conditions. Chicago (Ill.) -- Economic conditions.

HN80.C5.S97
Suttles, Gerald D.
The social order of the slum; ethnicity and territory in the inner city [by] Gerald D. Suttles. Pref. by Morris Janowitz. Chicago, University of Chicago Press [1968] xxii, 243 p.
68-026762 309.1/773/11
Inner cities -- Illinois -- Chicago. Slums -- Illinois -- Chicago. Poor -- Illinois -- Chicago. Chicago (Ill.) -- Social conditions.

HN80.C55.H35 1998
Halperin, Rhoda H.
Practicing community: class culture and power in an urban neighborhood/ Rhoda H. Halperin. Austin: University of Texas Press, 1998. xv, 352 p.
97-033917 306/.09771/78 0292731183
Community life -- Ohio -- Cincinnati. Community development -- Ohio -- Cincinnati -- Citizen participation. Working class -- Ohio -- Cincinnati. Cincinnati (Ohio) -- Social conditions. East End (Cincinnati, Ohio) -- Social conditions.

HN80.G46.W6
Wolf, Stephanie Grauman.
Urban village: population, community, and family structure in Germantown, Pennsylvania, 1683-1800/ Stephanie Grauman Wolf. Princeton, N.J.: Princeton University Press, c1976. xi, 361 p.
76-003025 301.36/1/0974811 0691046328
Family -- Pennsylvania -- Germantown. Urbanization -- Pennsylvania -- Germantown. Community organization -- Pennsylvania -- Germantown. Germantown (Philadelphia, Pa.) -- Social conditions.

HN80.G65.G65 1991
Goldsteen, Raymond L.
Demanding democracy after Three Mile Island/ Raymond L. Goldsteen and John K. Schorr. Gainesville: University of Florida Press, c1991. xxi, 246 p.
91-009806 363.17/9 081301073X
Community organization -- Pennsylvania -- Newberry (Township) Environmental policy -- Pennsylvania -- Goldsboro -- Citizen participation. Environmental policy -- Pennsylvania -- Newberry (Township) -- Citizen participation.

HN80.J44.M67 1988
Morain, Thomas J., 1947-
Prairie grass roots: an Iowa small town in the early twentieth century/ Thomas J. Morain. Ames: Iowa State University Press, 1988. xviii, 287 p.
88-000652 306/.09777/466 0813800684
Social change -- Case studies. Jefferson (Iowa) -- Social conditions. Jefferson (Iowa) -- Rural conditions. Middle West -- Social conditions -- Case studies.

HN80.K5.B55 1976
Blumin, Stuart M.
The urban threshold: growth and change in a nineteenth-century American community/ Stuart M. Blumin. Chicago: University of Chicago Press, c1976. 298 p.
75-027891 309.1/747/34 0226061698
Cities and towns -- United States -- History -- 19th century -- Case studies. Urbanization -- United States -- History -- 19th century -- Case studies. Kingston (N.Y.) -- Social conditions. Kingston (N.Y.) -- Economic conditions.

HN80.L4.G3
Gans, Herbert J.
The Levittowners; ways of life and politics in a new suburban community, by Herbert J. Gans. New York, Pantheon Books [1967] xxix, 474 p.
66-017359 301.3/62/0974961
Suburban life -- Case studies. Willingboro.

HN80.L7.C57 1996
The city: Los Angeles and urban theory at the end of the twentieth century/ edited by Allen J. Scott, Edward W. Soja. Berkeley: University of California Press, c1996. xii, 483 p.
96-005512 307.76/09794/94 20 0520204247
City planning -- California -- Los Angeles. Sociology, Urban -- California -- Los Angeles. Los Angeles (Calif.) Los Angeles (Calif.) -- Social conditions.

HN80.L7.R47 1996
Rethinking Los Angeles/ edited by Michael J. Dear, H. Eric Schockman, Greg Hise. Thousand Oaks, Calif.: Sage Publications, c1996. xvi, 278 p.
96-010037 306/.0979/494 20 0803972865
Urban policy -- California -- Los Angeles Metropolitan Area. Los Angeles Metropolitan Area (Calif.) -- Politics and government. Los Angeles Metropolitan Area (Calif.) -- Social conditions.

HN80.M66.P37 1998
Pardo, Mary S., 1946-
Mexican American women activists: identity and resistance in two Los Angeles communities/ Mary S. Pardo. Philadelphia: Temple University Press, 1998. x, 322 p.
97-013960 305.48/86872079493 1566395720
Women in community organization -- California -- Monterey Park. Women in community organization -- California -- Boyle Heights. Community power -- California -- Monterey Park. Monterey Park (Calif.) -- Politics and government. Boyle Heights (Calif.) -- Politics and government.

HN80.M85.C313 2000
Caccamo De Luca, Rita.
Back to Middletown: three generations of sociological reflections/ Rita Caccamo. Stanford, Calif.: Stanford University Press, 2000. xxiii, 149 p.
99-016822 306/.09772/65 0804734933
Lynd, Robert Staughton, -- 1892- -- Middletown. Lynd, Helen Merrell, -- 1896- Muncie (Ind.) -- Social conditions. Muncie (Ind.) -- Social life and customs.

HN80.N5.F76 1994
From urban village to east village: the battle for New York's Lower East Side/ Janet L. Abu-Lughod and others. Oxford, UK; Blackwell, 1994. xvi, 386 p.
93-031977 307.3/362/097471 155786523X
East Village (New York, N.Y.) -- Social conditions. Neighborhood -- New York (State) -- New York. Gentrification -- New York (State) -- New York New York (N.Y.) -- Social conditions.

HN80.N5.R66 1995
Rooney, Jim, 1948-
Organizing the South Bronx/ Jim Rooney; foreword by Nathan Glazer. Albany: State University of New York Press, c1995. xii, 283 p.
93-049671 307.1/416/097471 0791422097
Community organization -- New York (State) -- New York -- Case studies. Housing policy -- New York (State) -- New York -- Citizen participation -- Case studies. Church and social problems -- New York (State) -- New York -- Case studies. Bronx (New York, N.Y.) -- Social conditions -- Case studies.

HN80.N5.S27 1992
Scherzer, Kenneth A., 1953-
The unbounded community: neighborhood life and social structure in New York City, 1830-1875/ Kenneth A. Scherzer. Durham: Duke University Press, 1992. xviii, 356 p.
91-040452 307.3/362/097471 082231228X
Neighborhood -- New York (State) -- New York -- History -- 19th century. Community life -- New York (State) -- New York -- History -- 19th century. Social structure -- New York (State) -- New York -- History -- 19th century. New York (N.Y.) -- Social conditions.

HN80.N5.S54 1997
Siegel, Frederick F., 1945-
The future once happened here: New York, D.C., L.A., and the fate of America's big cities/ Fred Siegel. New York: Free Press, c1997. xii, 260 p.
97-023050 307.76/0973 21 0684827476
Urban policy -- New York (State) -- New York. Urban policy -- Washington (D.C.) Urban policy -- California -- Los Angeles.

HN80.P5.P477 1991
Philadelphia: neighborhoods, division, and conflict in a postindustrial city/ Carolyn Adams ... [et al.]. Philadelphia: Temple University Press, 1991. xiv, 210 p.
91-007571 307.1/416/0974811 0877228426
Community development -- Pennsylvania -- Philadelphia Metropolitan Area. Inner cities -- Pennsylvania -- Philadelphia Metropolitan Area. Neighborhood -- Pennsylvania -- Philadelphia Metropolitan Area. Philadelphia Metropolitan Area (Pa.) -- Race relations. Philadelphia Metropolitan Area (Pa.) -- Economic conditions.

HN80.S4.L34 1994
Laguerre, Michel S.
The informal city/ Michel S. Laguerre. New York: St. Martin's Press, 1994. xvi, 180 p.
94-016010 307.76/09794/6 0312122098
Sociology, Urban -- California -- San Francisco Metropolitan Area. Sociology, Urban -- California -- Oakland Metropolitan Area. City and town life -- California -- San Francisco Metropolitan Area.

HN80.S78.B6
Bodnar, John E., 1944-
Immigration and industrialization: ethnicity in an American mill town, 1870-1940/ John Bodnar. Pittsburgh: University of Pittsburgh Press, c1977. xix, 213 p.
77-074549   306/.09748/18   0822933489
Social classes -- Pennsylvania -- Steelton -- History. Immigrants -- Pennsylvania -- Steelton -- History. Minorities -- Employment -- Pennsylvania -- Steelton -- History. Steelton (Pa.) -- Social conditions.

HN80.W3.G55 1995
Gillette, Howard.
Between justice and beauty: race, planning, and the failure of urban policy in Washington, D.C./ Howard Gillette, Jr. Baltimore: Johns Hopkins University Press, c1995. xiii, 297 p.
94-045938   307.76/09753   080185069X
Urban policy -- Washington (D.C.) City planning -- Washington (D.C.) Washington (D.C.) -- Politics and government. Washington (D.C.) -- Social conditions. Washington (D.C.) -- Race relations.

HN90 By region or country — United States — Special topics (not otherwise provided for), A-Z

HN90.C6.D68
Downs, Anthony.
Neighborhoods and urban development/ Anthony Downs. Washington, D.C.: Brookings Institution, c1981. xii, 189 p.
81-066190   307.7/6/0973   0815719205
Community development, Urban -- United States. Urbanization -- United States.

HN90.C6.E88 1993
Etzioni, Amitai.
The spirit of community: rights, responsibilities, and the communitarian agenda/ Amitai Etzioni. New York: Crown Publishers, c1993. viii, 323 p.
92-031527   307.1/4/0973   0517592770
Community development -- United States. Social action -- United States. Public interest -- United States. United States -- Moral conditions.

HN90.C6.J37 1996
Jargowsky, Paul A.
Poverty and place: ghettos, barrios, and the American city/ Paul A. Jargowsky. New York: Russell Sage Foundation, c1997. xiv, 288 p.
96-002109   307.3/366/0973 21   0871544059
Urban poor -- United States. Pluralism (Social sciences) -- United States. Community development, Urban -- United States. United States -- Race relations.

HN90.C6.M45 1987
Melvin, Patricia Mooney.
The organic city: urban definition & community organization, 1880-1920/ Patricia Mooney Melvin. Lexington, KY: University Press of Kentucky, c1987. xii, 227 p.
87-013322   307.7/6/0973   081311585X
Phillips, Wilbur C., -- b. 1880.   Community organization -- United States -- History -- 20th century. Community development, Urban -- United States -- History -- 20th century. Neighborhood -- United States.

HN90.C6.R735 2000
Rubin, Herbert J.
Renewing hope within neighborhoods of despair: the community-based development model/ Herbert J. Rubin. Albany: State University of New York Press, c2000. xvi, 304 p.
99-039478   307.1/416/0973   0791445534
Community development, Urban -- United States. Community organization -- United States. Economic development projects -- United States.

HN90.C6.R815 1991
Rural policies for the 1990s/ edited by Cornelia B. Flora and James A. Christenson. Boulder, Colo.: Westview Press, 1991. xi, 361 p.
90-022323   307.72/0973   081337815X
Rural development -- Government policy -- United States. Agriculture -- Social aspects -- United States. Agriculture and state -- United States. United States -- Rural conditions. United States -- Social conditions -- 1980-

HN90.E4.D648 1990
Domhoff, G. William.
The power elite and the state: how policy is made in America/ G. William Domhoff. New York: A. de Gruyter, c1990. xix, 315 p.
90-000393   305.5/2/0973   0202303721
Elite (Social sciences) -- United States. Power (Social sciences) United States -- Politics and government -- 20th century.

HN90.E4 D652 1998
Domhoff, G. William.
Who rules America?: power and politics in the year 2000/ G. William Domhoff. 3rd ed. Mountain View, Calif.: Mayfield Pub. Co., c1998. xi, 335 p.
97-031049   305.5/2/0973 21   1559349735
Elite (Social sciences) -- United States. Power (Social sciences) -- United States. Social classes -- United States.

HN90.E4 D93 2002
Dye, Thomas R.
Who's running America?: the Bush restoration/ Thomas R. Dye. 7th ed. Upper Saddle River, N.J.: Prentice Hall, c2002. xi, 220 p.
2001-054896   305.5/2/0973 21   0130974625
Elite (Social sciences) -- United States. Power (Social sciences) Leadership.

HN90.E4.L47 1996
Lerner, Robert, 1953-
American elites/ Robert Lerner, Althea K. Nagai, Stanley Rothman. New Haven: Yale University Press, c1996. xii, 176 p.
96-016343   305.5/2/0973 20   0300065345
Elite (Social sciences) -- United States. Social surveys -- United States. United States -- Social conditions -- 1980-

HN90.E4.Z94 1998
Zweigenhaft, Richard L.
Diversity in the power elite: have women and minorities reached the top?/ Richard L. Zweigenhaft and G. William Domhoff. New Haven: Yale University Press, c1998. viii, 215 p.
97-017541   305.5/2/0973 21   0300072368
Elite (Social sciences) -- United States. Power (Social sciences) -- United States. Pluralism (Social sciences) -- United States.

HN90.I58.W35 1997
Wallach, Glenn, 1959-
Obedient sons: the discourse of youth and generations in American culture, 1630-1860/ Glenn Wallach. Amherst: University of Massachusetts Press, c1997. ix, 265 p.
96-018193   305.2/35 20   1558490574
Intergenerational relations -- United States -- History. Youth -- United States -- Public opinion -- History. Young men -- United States -- Public opinion -- History.

HN90.M26.M34 1995
Mahler, Sarah J., 1959-
American dreaming: immigrant life on the margins/ Sarah J. Mahler. Princeton, N.J.: Princeton University Press, c1995. xiv, 268 p.
95-013473   305.5/6   0691037833
Marginality, Social -- United States. Immigrants -- United States.

HN90.M3.C96 1982
Czitrom, Daniel J., 1951-
Media and the American mind: from Morse to McLuhan/ by Daniel J. Czitrom. Chapel Hill: University of North Carolina Press, c1982. xiv, 254 p.
81-014810   302.2/3   0807815004
Mass media -- Social aspects -- United States. Popular culture -- United States.

HN90.M3 M43 2000
Media power in politics/ [edited by] Doris A. Graber. 4th ed. Washington, D.C.: CQ Press, c2000. xii, 436 p.
99-088687   302.23 21   1568024169
Mass media -- Political aspects -- United States. Mass media -- Social aspects -- United States.

HN90.M3.W63 1996
Wood, Donald N., 1934-
Post-intellectualism and the decline of democracy: the failure of reason and responsibility in the twentieth century/ Donald N. Wood; foreword by Neil Postman. Westport, Conn.: Praeger, 1996. xvii, 302 p.
96-010420   301   0275954218
Mass media -- Social aspects -- United States. Social problems -- United States. Democracy -- United States.

HN90.M6.H38 1997
Hearn, Frank.
Moral order and social disorder: the American search for civil society/ Frank Hearn. New York: Aldine de Gruyter, c1997. xv, 206 p.
97-018771   306/.0973 21   0202306038
Social problems -- United States. Social values -- United States. Civil society -- United States. United States -- Social conditions -- 1980- United States -- Moral conditions.

HN90.M6.L35 1996
Lakoff, George.
Moral politics: what conservatives know that liberals don't/ George Lakoff. Chicago: University of Chicago Press, 1996. xi, 413 p.
95-047690   172   0226467961
Political ethics -- United States. Social ethics -- United States. Social values -- United States. United States -- Moral conditions.

HN90.M6.M94 2000
Myers, David G.
The American paradox: spiritual hunger in an age of plenty/ David G. Myers; foreword by Martin E. Marty. New Haven: Yale University Press, c2000. xv, 414 p.
99-088870   306/.0973 21   0300081111
Social ethics -- United States. Communitarianism -- United States.   United States -- Moral conditions.

HN90.M6.W34 1997
Wagner, David.
The new temperance: the American obsession with sin and vice/ David Wagner. Boulder, Colo.: Westview Press, 1997. x, 226 p.
96-051514   306/.0973   0813325684
Temperance -- United States.   Behavior modification -- United States. Political correctness -- United States. United States -- Moral conditions.

HN90.M6.W87 1996
Wuthnow, Robert.
Poor Richard's principle: recovering the American dream through the moral dimension of work, business, and money/ Robert Wuthnow. Princeton, N.J.: Princeton University Press, c1996. xii, 429 p.
96-006799   306/.0973 20   0691028923
Work -- Moral and ethical aspects -- United States. Money -- Moral and ethical aspects -- United States. Business ethics -- United States. United States -- Moral conditions.

HN90.P57.L37 1995
Lasch, Christopher.
The revolt of the elites: and the betrayal of democracy/ Christopher Lasch. New York: W.W. Norton, c1995. x, 276 p.
94-037270   306/.0973   0393036995
Polarization (Social sciences) Democracy -- United States. Elite (Social sciences) -- United States. United States -- Social conditions -- 1945- United States -- Politics and government -- 20th century.

HN90.P8.B46
Bennett, W. Lance.
Public opinion in American politics/ W. Lance Bennett; under the general editorship of James David Barber. New York: Harcourt Brace Jovanovich, c1980. xi, 420 p.
79-092686   303.3/8   0155738100
Public opinion -- United States. Public opinion. Political socialization -- United States.

HN90.P8.E76 1993
Erikson, Robert S.
Statehouse democracy: public opinion and policy in the American states/ Robert S. Erikson, Gerald C. Wright, John P. McIver. Cambridge; Cambridge University Press, 1993. ix, 269 p.
93-007076   303.3/8   0521413494
Public opinion -- United States -- States. State governments -- United States.

HN90.P8.G29 1999
Gallup, Alec.
The Gallup poll cumulative index: public opinion, 1935-1997/ Alec Gallup. Wilmington, Del.: Scholarly Resources, 1999.
98-045927   303.3/8/0973   0842025871
Public opinion -- United States -- Indexes. Social surveys -- United States -- Indexes. Public opinion polls -- Indexes.

HN90.P8.G36 1992
Gamson, William A.
Talking politics/ William A. Gamson. Cambridge [England]; Cambridge University Press, 1992. xiv, 272 p.
92-000766   303.3/8   0521430623
Public opinion -- United States. Working class -- United States -- Attitudes. Political participation -- United States.

HN90.P8.H47 1993
Herbst, Susan.
Numbered voices: how opinion polling has shaped American politics/ Susan Herbst. Chicago: University of Chicago Press, 1993. xi, 227 p.
92-014256   303.3/8/0973   0226327426
Public opinion -- United States. Public opinion -- United states -- History. Public opinion polls.

HN90.P8.M4 1984
McClosky, Herbert.
The American ethos: public attitudes toward capitalism and democracy/ Herbert McClosky, John Zaller. Cambridge, Mass.: Harvard University Press, 1984. xviii, 342 p.
84-012793   330.12/2   0674023307
Public opinion -- United States. Capitalism -- Public opinion. Democracy -- Public opinion.

HN90.P8.M43 1991
McCombs, Maxwell E.
Contemporary public opinion: issues and the news/ Maxwell McCombs, Edna Einsiedel, David Weaver. Hillsdale, N.J.: L. Erlbaum, 1991. viii, 114 p.
91-016323   303.3/8/0973   0805805370
Public opinion -- United States. Mass media -- Social aspects -- United States.

HN90.P8.M58 1998
Mitchell, Susan, 1958-
American attitudes: who thinks what about the issues that shape our lives/ by Susan Mitchell. Ithaca, N.Y.: New Strategist Publications, c1998. xviii, 446 p.
99-217496   303.3/8/0973 21   1885070179
Public opinion -- United States. Social surveys -- United States.   United States -- Politics and government -- 1993- United States -- Social conditions -- 1980-

HN90.P8.P34 1991
Page, Benjamin I.
The rational public: fifty years of trends in Americans' policy preferences/ Benjamin I. Page and Robert Y. Shapiro. Chicago: University of Chicago Press, 1992. xvi, 489 p.
91-015590   303.3/8/0973   0226644774
Public opinion -- United States -- History -- 20th century.

HN90.P8.P74 1995
Presidential polls and the news media/ edited by Paul J. Lavrakas, Michael W. Traugott, and Peter V. Miller. Boulder: Westview Press, 1995. xvi, 279 p.
95-012277   303.3/8/0973   0813389437
Public opinion -- United States. Public opinion polls. Presidents -- United States -- Election.

HN90.P8 S84 1998
Stimson, James A.
Public opinion in America: moods, cycles, and swings/ James A. Stimson. 2nd ed. Boulder, Colo: Westview Press, 1998.
98-036784   303.3/8/0973 21   0813368901
Public opinion -- United States.

HN90.P8.S88 1988
Sussman, Barry.
What Americans really think: and why our politicians pay no attention/ Barry Sussman. New York: Pantheon Books, c1988. x, 278 p.
87-046069   306/.0973   0394563034
Public opinion -- United States. Public opinion polls.   United States -- Economic conditions -- 1981- -- Public opinion. United States -- Social conditions -- 1980- -- Public opinion. United States -- Politics and government -- 1981-1989 -- Public opinion.

HN90.R3 A66 1990
Alpert, Jane.
Growing up underground/ by Jane Alpert; [introductions by Susan Brownmiller and Martha Plimpton]. 1st Citadel Underground ed. New York: Citadel Underground, 1990. 374 p.
91-195008   322.4/2/092 20   0806511966
Alpert, Jane.   Radicals -- United States -- Biography. Radicals -- United States.

HN90.R3.D47
Dellinger, David T., 1915-
More power than we know: the people's movement toward democracy/ Dave Dellinger. Garden City, N.Y.: Anchor Press, 1975. viii, 326 p.
73-173272   322.4/4/0973   0385001622
Radicalism -- United States.   United States -- Social conditions -- 1960-1980.

HN90.R3.E55 1998
Ellis, Richard
The dark side of the Left: illiberal Egalitarianism in America/ Richard J. Ellis. Lawrence, Kan.: University Press of Kansas, c1998. xiii, 426 p.
97-027340   303.48/4 21   0700608753
Radicalism -- United States. Authoritarianism -- United States. Authoritarianism (Personality trait) -- United States.

HN90.R3.E67 1991
Epstein, Barbara Leslie, 1944-
Political protest and cultural revolution: nonviolent direct action in the 1970s and 1980s/ Barbara Epstein. Berkeley: University of California Press, c1991. xiii, 327 p.
90-044230   303.6/1   0520070100
Radicalism -- United States -- Case studies. Social movements -- United States -- Case studies. Direct action -- Case studies.

HN90.R3.H355 1996
Hamilton, Neil A., 1949-
Militias in America: a reference handbook/ Neil A. Hamilton. Santa Barbara, Calif.: ABC-CLIO, c1996. xiv, 235 p.
96-026538   303.48/4 20   0874368596
Militia movements -- United States. Right-wing extremists -- United States. Government, Resistance to -- United States.

HN90.R3.J33 1997
Jacobs, Ron.
The way the wind blew: a history of the Weather Underground/ Ron Jacobs. London; Verso, 1997. viii, 216 p.
97-028084   322.4/2/097309045   1859841678
New Left -- United States.

HN90.R3.J49 1992
Jezer, Marty.
Abbie Hoffman, American rebel/ Marty Jezer. New Brunswick, N.J.: Rutgers University Press, c1992. xviii, 345 p.
92-007766   303.48/4   0813518504
Hoffman, Abbie.   Radicals -- United States -- Biography. Radicalism -- United States. Popular culture -- United States. United States -- Civilization -- 1970-

HN90.R3.L495 1994
Levy, Peter B.
The new left and labor in the 1960s/ Peter B. Levy. Urbana: University of Illinois Press, c1994. xvii, 291 p.
93-030844   303.48/4   0252063678
New Left -- United States. Labor unions -- United States -- Political activity. Working class -- United States -- Political activity.

HN90.R3.L93 1997
Lynd, Staughton.
Living inside our hope: a steadfast radical's thoughts on rebuilding the movement/ Staughton Lynd. Ithaca, NY: ILR press, 1997. xii, 281 p.
96-039270   320.53   0801433630
New Left -- United States. Radicalism -- United States.

HN90.R3.R64 1998
Rossinow, Douglas C.
The politics of authenticity: liberalism, Christianity, and the New Left in America/ Doug Rossinow. New York: Columbia University Press, c1998. x, 500 p.
97-042950   306.2/0973 21   0231110561
New Left -- United States. Christianity and politics -- United States.

HN90.R3.R88
Rubin, Jerry.
Growing up at thirty-seven/ Jerry Rubin. New York: M. Evans; c1976. 208 p.
75-031572   322.4/2/0924   0871311895
Rubin, Jerry.   Radicalism -- United States.

HN90.R3.S67 1996
Stock, Catherine McNicol.
Rural radicals: righteous rage in the American grain/ Catherine McNicol Stock. Ithaca: Cornell University Press, 1996. xi, 219 p.
96-003023   303.48/4   0801432944
Radicalism -- United States -- History. Political violence -- United States -- History. Farmers -- United States -- Political activity -- History. United States -- Rural conditions.

HN90.R3.W36 1992
Walter, Edward, 1932-
The rise and fall of leftist radicalism in America/ Edward Walter. Westport, Conn.: Praeger, 1992. viii, 194 p.
92-013241   303.48/4   0275942767
Radicalism -- United States. United States -- Politics and government -- 20th century. Right and left (Political science)

HN90.S6.B67 1988
Boston, Thomas D.
Race, class, and conservatism/ Thomas D. Boston. Boston: Unwin Hyman, 1988. xix, 172 p.
88-000982   305.5/0973   0043303684
Social classes -- United States. Afro-Americans -- Social conditions. Afro-Americans -- Employment. United States -- Race relations.

HN90.S6.D46 1990
DeMott, Benjamin, 1924-
The imperial middle: why Americans can't think straight about class/ Benjamin DeMott. New York: Morrow, c1990. 264 p.
90-034634   305.5/0973   1557100233
Social classes -- United States. Equality -- United States. Social conflict -- United States.

HN90.S6.G75 1991
Grimes, Michael D.
Class in twentieth-century American sociology: an analysis of theories and measurement strategies/ Michael D. Grimes. New York: Praeger, 1991. xiv, 228 p.
90-027840   305.5/0973/0904   0275938778
Social classes -- United States. Social classes. Sociology -- United States -- History.

HN90.S6.H66 2000
Hooks, Bell
Where we stand: class matters/ Bell Hooks. New York: Routledge, 2000.
00-034470   305.5/0973   0415929113
Social classes -- United States.

HN90.S6.J3 1983
Jackman, Mary R.
Class awareness in the United States/ Mary R. Jackman and Robert W. Jackman. Berkeley: University of California Press, 1983. x, 231 p.
82-002766   305.5/0973   0520046749
Social classes -- United States.

HN90.S6.K56 2000
Kingston, Paul W.
The classless society/ Paul W. Kingston. Stanford, Calif.: Stanford University Press, 2000. xviii, 258 p.
00-023556   305.5   0804738041
Social classes -- United States. Social mobility -- United States.

HN90.S6.N47 1993
Newman, Katherine S., 1953-
Declining fortunes: the withering of the American dream/ Katherine S. Newman. New York: BasicBooks, c1993. xiii, 257 p.
92-053246   305.5/13   046501593X:
Social mobility -- United States. Middle class -- United States.   United States -- Economic conditions -- 1981- United States -- Social conditions -- 1980-

HN90.S6.R67 2000
Rose, Fred, 1960-
Coalitions across the class divide: lessons from the labor, peace, and environmental movements/ Fred Rose. Ithaca, NY: Cornell University Press, c2000. xi, 253 p.
99-041669   305.5/0973 21   0801436052
Social classes -- United States. Social reformers -- United States. Labor movement -- United States.

HN90.S6.W66 2000
Wood, Mark David, 1959-
Cornel West and the politics of prophetic pragmatism/ Mark David Wood. Urbana: University of Illinois Press, 2000. 239 p.
99-050749   305.5/0973   0252025784
West, Cornel.   Racism -- United States. Communism and Christianity. Liberation theology. United States -- Race relations.

HN90.S65 N48 1989
Newman, Katherine S.,
Falling from grace: the experience of downward mobility in the American middle class/ Katherine S. Newman. 1st Vintage Books ed. New York: Vintage Books, 1989, c1988. xiv, 320 p.
89-040151   305.5/13/0973 20   0679723978
Social mobility -- United States. Middle class -- United States.

HN90.S65.Z94 1991
Zweigenhaft, Richard L.
Blacks in the white establishment?: a study of race and class in America/ Richard L. Zweigenhaft and G. William Domhoff. New Haven: Yale University Press, c1991. ix, 198 p.
90-038640   370.19/34   0300047886
Social mobility -- United States -- Case studies. Afro-American college graduates -- Case studies. Private schools -- United States -- Case studies.

HN90.V5.C56 1998
Clarke, James W., 1937-
The lineaments of wrath: race, violent crime, and American culture/ James W. Clarke. New Brunswick, N.J., U.S.A.: Transaction Publishers, c1998. xvii, 339 p.
97-051699   305.8/00973 21   1560003588
Violence -- United States -- History. Violent crimes -- United States -- History. Racism -- United States -- History. United States -- Race relations -- History.

HN90.V5.K56 1991
Kleck, Gary, 1951-
Point blank: guns and violence in America/ Gary Kleck. New York: A. de Gruyter, c1991. xv, 512 p.
91-016780   303.6/0973   0202304191
Violence -- United States. Firearms -- Social aspects -- United States. Gun control -- United States.

HN90.V5.L55 1995
Linsky, Arnold S.
Stress, culture, & aggression/ Arnold S. Linsky, Ronet Bachman, Murray A. Straus. New Haven: Yale University Press, c1995. viii, 200 p.
94-048643   303.6   0300057067
Violence -- United States. Self-destructive behavior -- United States. Stress (Psychology) -- United States.

HN90.V5.S833 1996
Statistical handbook on violence in America/ Adam Dobrin ... [et al.]. Phoenix, Ariz.: Oryx Press, 1996. xxiv, 394 p.
95-042437   303.6/0973/021   0897749456
Violence -- United States -- Statistics. Criminal statistics -- United States. United States -- Social conditions -- 1980- -- Statistics.

HN90.V5.U53 1993
Understanding and preventing violence/ Albert J. Reiss, Jr., and Jeffrey A. Roth, editors. Washington, D.C.: National Academy Press, 1993-1994. 4 v.
92-032137   303.6   0309045940
Violence -- United States. Violence -- United States -- Prevention. Violent crimes -- United States.

HN90.V64.W88 1991
Wuthnow, Robert.
Acts of compassion: caring for others and helping ourselves/ Robert Wuthnow. Princeton, N.J.: Princeton University Press, c1991. viii, 334 p.
91-002128   302/.14   0691073902
Voluntarism -- United States. Helping behavior. Caring.

HN103.5-110 By region or country — Other regions or countries — Canada

HN103.5.O93 1996
Owram, Doug, 1947-
Born at the right time: a history of the baby-boom generation/ Doug Owram. Toronto; University of Toronto Press, c1996. xiv, 392 p.
96-223106 306/.0971 20 0802059570
Baby boom generation -- Canada. Canada -- Social conditions -- 1945- Canada -- Economic conditions -- 1945- Canada -- Politics and government -- 1980-

HN110.C35.P63 1991
Pocius, Gerald L.
A place to belong: community order and everyday space in Calvert, Newfoundland/ Gerald L. Pocius. Athens: University of Georgia Press; c1991. xx, 350 p.
91-007334 306/.09718 0820313300
Human ecology -- Newfoundland -- Calvert. Spatial behavior -- Newfoundland -- Calvert. Sociology, Rural -- Newfoundland -- Calvert. Calvert (Nfld.) -- Social life and customs. Calvert (Nfld.) -- Social conditions.

HN110.E4.C53
Clement, Wallace.
The Canadian corporate elite: an analysis of economic power/ Wallace Clement; with a foreword by John Porter. Toronto: McClelland and Stewart, [1975] xvii, 479 p.
75-319029 301.44/92/0971 0771097891
Elite (Social sciences) -- Canada. Capitalists and financiers -- Canada. Social mobility -- Canada.

HN110.L3.K45 1995
Kennedy, John Charles.
People of the bays and headlands: anthropological history and the fate of the communities in the unknown Labrador/ John C. Kennedy. Toronto; University of Toronto Press, c1995. xii, 296 p.
96-107611 971.8/2 0802006469
Fishing villages -- Newfoundland -- Labrador. Labrador (Nfld.) -- Economic conditions. Labrador (Nfld.) -- Social conditions. Labrador (Nfld.) -- History.

HN110.O5.B37 1994
Barrett, Stanley R.
Paradise: class, commuters, and ethnicity in rural Ontario/ Stanley R. Barrett. Toronto; University of Toronto Press, c1994. xiv, 315 p.
94-204033 307.72/09713 0802004423
Urban-rural migration -- Ontario. Sociology, Rural -- Ontario. Social classes -- Ontario. Ontario -- Rural conditions. Ontario -- Race relations. Ontario -- Ethnic relations.

HN110.Q4.M32
McRoberts, Kenneth.
Quebec: social change and political crisis/ Kenneth McRoberts, Dale Posgate. Toronto: McClelland and Stewart, c1976. vi, 216 p.
76-373940 309.1/714 0771071752
Quebec (Province) -- Social conditions. Quebec (Province) -- Economic conditions. Quebec (Province) -- Politics and government.

HN110.W5.A74
Artibise, Alan F. J.
Winnipeg: a social history of urban growth, 1874-1914/ Alan F. J. Artibise. Montreal: McGill-Queen's University Press, 1975. xiv, 382 p.
75-325419 309.1/7127/4 0773502025
Urbanization -- Winnipeg, Man. Winnipeg (Man.) -- Social conditions.

HN110.5-170 By region or country — Other regions or countries — Latin America

HN110.5.A8.C845 1998
Cultures of politics/politics of cultures: re-visioning Latin American social movements/ edited by Sonia E. Alvarez, Evelina Dagnino, Arturo Escobar. Boulder, Colo.: Westview Press, 1998. xiii, 459 p.
97-043513 303.48/4/098 0813330718
Social movements -- Latin America. Civil society -- Latin America. Political participation -- Latin America.

HN110.5.A8.V42 1999
Veltmeyer, Henry.
The dynamics of social change in Latin America/ Henry Veltmeyer, James Petras. New York: St. Martin's Press, 1999.
99-021890 303.4/098 0312222777
Social change -- Latin America. Free enterprise -- Latin America. Social movements -- Latin America. Latin America -- Social conditions -- 1982- Latin America -- Economic conditions -- 1982-

HN110.5.A8.W486 1997
Williamson, Robert Clifford, 1916-
Latin American societies in transition/ Robert C. Williamson. Westport, Conn.: Praeger, 1997. xi, 272 p.
96-026879 306/.098 0275957500
Social change -- Latin America. Social conflict -- Latin America. Latin America -- Social conditions -- 1982-

HN110.5.Z9.V58 1991
Vigilantism and the state in modern Latin America: essays on extralegal violence/ edited by Martha K. Huggins. New York: Praeger, 1991. xii, 266 p.
90-028185 364.4/045763/098 0275934764
Violence -- Latin America. Vigilance committees -- Latin America. Death squads -- Latin America.

HN120.C46.W39 1993
Wasserman, Mark, 1946-
Persistent oligarchs: elites and politics in Chihuahua, Mexico, 1910-1940/ Mark Wasserman. Durham: Duke University Press, 1993. x, 265 p.
92-039296 305.5/2/097216 0822313294
Elite (Social sciences) -- Mexico -- Chihuahua (State) -- History -- 20th century. Chihuahua (Mexico: State) -- Politics and government. Mexico -- Politics and government -- 1910-1946.

HN120.M53.G58 1995
Gledhill, John.
Neoliberalism, transnationalization, and rural poverty: a case study of Michoacan, Mexico/ John Gledhill. Boulder: Westview Press, 1995. xi, 243 p.
95-017420 306/.0972/37 0813324351
Michoacan de Ocampo (Mexico) -- Social conditions. Michoacan de Ocampo (Mexico) -- Rural conditions. Michoacan de Ocampo (Mexico) -- Economic conditions.

HN120.N64
Davidson, Miriam.
Lives on the line: dispatches from the U.S.-Mexico border/ Miriam Davidson; photographs by Jeffry Scott. Tucson: University of Arizona Press, c2000. 211 p.
00-008566 306/.0972/62 21 0816519978
Nogales (Nogales, Mexico) -- Social conditions. Nogales (Ariz.) -- Social conditions. Mexican-American Border Region -- Social conditions.

HN120.O29.M87 1991
Murphy, Arthur D.
Social inequality in Oaxaca: a history of resistance and change/ Arthur D. Murphy, Alex Stepick; foreword by Henry A. Selby. Philadelphia: Temple University Press, 1991. xix, 282 p.
91-007453 305.5/0972/74 087722868X
Social classes -- Mexico -- Oaxaca de Juarez. Neighborhood -- Mexico -- Oaxaca de Juarez. Community development -- Mexico -- Oaxaca de Juarez. Oaxaca de Juarez (Mexico) -- Social conditions.

HN120.S6.F74 1996
French, William E., 1956-
A peaceful and working people: manners, morals, and class formation in northern Mexico/ William E. French. Albuquerque: University of New Mexico Press, c1996. ix, 262 p.
95-032446 305.5/0972/16 20 0826316832
Social classes -- Mexico -- Chihuahua (State) -- History. Working class -- Mexico -- Chihuahua (State) -- History. Middle class -- Mexico -- Chihuahua (State) -- History.

HN120.Z9.E47
Smith, Peter H.
Labyrinths of power: political recruitment in twentieth-century Mexico/ Peter H. Smith. Princeton, N.J.: Princeton University Press, c1979. xvi, 384 p.
78-051191 301.44/92/0972 0691075921
Elite (Social sciences) -- Mexico. Power (Social sciences) Mexico -- Politics and government.

HN120.Z9.P86 1996
Polling for democracy: public opinion and political liberalization in Mexico/ edited by Roderic Ai Camp. Wilmington, Del.: SR Books, 1996. viii, 186 p.
96-012036 303.3/8/0972 0842025839
Public opinion -- Mexico. Elections -- Mexico. Mexico -- Politics and government -- 1988-

HN143.5.A63
Adams, Richard Newbold, 1924-
Crucifixion by power; essays on Guatemalan national social structure, 1944-1966. With chapters by Brian Murphy and Bryan Roberts. Austin, University of Texas Press [1970] xiv, 553 p.
79-121125 309.1/7281 0292700350
Social classes -- Guatemala. Guatemala -- Social conditions.

HN150.Z9.V545 2001
Moser, Caroline O. N.
Violence in a post-conflict context: urban poor perceptions from Guatemala/ Caroline Moser, Cathy McIlwaine. Washington, D.C.: World Bank, c2001. xi, 163 p.
00-043981 303.6/097281 21 0821348361
Violence -- Guatemala -- Public opinion. Urban poor -- Guatemala -- Attitudes. Public opinion -- Guatemala.

HN170.B37.H54 1992
Higgins, Michael James.
Oigame! Oigame!: struggle and social change in a Nicaraguan urban community/ Michael James Higgins and Tanya Leigh Coen. Boulder: Westview Press, 1992. xiv, 184 p.
90-025258 303.4/097285/13 0813380839
Political participation -- Nicaragua -- Barrio William Diaz Romero (Managua) Barrio William Diaz Romero (Managua, Nicaragua) -- Social conditions.

HN203-370 By region or country — Other regions or countries — South America

HN203.I23 1998
Ibarra, Jorge.
Prologue to revolution: Cuba, 1898-1958/ Jorge Ibarra; translated by Marjorie Moore. Boulder: Lynne Rienner Publishers, 1998. viii, 231 p.
97-049324 306/.097291 1555877915
Social structure -- Cuba -- History -- 20th century. Cuba -- Social conditions. Cuba -- Social conditions -- 1918-1959. Cuba -- Economic conditions.

HN203.5.L48 1977
Lewis, Oscar, 1914-1970.
Living the revolution: an oral history of contemporary Cuba/ Oscar Lewis, Ruth M. Lewis, Susan M. Rigdon. Urbana: University of Illinois Press, c1977-1978. 3 v.
76-054878 309.1/7291/064 0252006283
Poor -- Cuba. Family -- Cuba -- Case studies. Cuba -- Politics and government -- 1959- Cuba -- Social conditions.

HN223.C8 1968
Curtin, Philip D.
Two Jamaicas; the role of ideas in a tropical colony, 1830-1865 [by] Philip D. Curtin. New York, Greenwood Press, 1968 [c1955] xii, 270 p.
69-010082 309.1/7292
Jamaica -- Social conditions.

HN270.B8.S3
Scobie, James R., 1929-1981.
Buenos Aires: plaza to suburb, 1870-1910/ James R. Scobie. New York: Oxford University Press, 1974. xvii, 323 p.
74-079629 309.1/82/1 0195018214
Buenos Aires (Argentina) -- Social conditions. Buenos Aires (Argentina) -- Economic conditions. Buenos Aires (Argentina) -- History.

HN270.B8.S97 1988
Szuchman, Mark D., 1948-
Order, family, and community in Buenos Aires, 1810-1860/ Mark D. Szuchman. Stanford, Calif.: Stanford University Press, c1988. xiii, 307 p.
87-034479 306/.0982/12 0804714614
Neighborhood -- Argentina -- Buenos Aires -- History -- 19th century. Family -- Argentina -- Buenos Aires -- History -- 19th century. Community organization -- Argentina -- Buenos Aires -- History -- 19th century. Buenos Aires (Argentina) -- Social conditions.

HN270.C67.S36 1988
Scobie, James R., 1929-1981.
Secondary cities of Argentina: the social history of Corrientes, Salta, and Mendoza, 1850-1910/ James R. Scobie; completed and edited by Samuel L. Baily; with a foreword by Ingrid Winther Scobie. Stanford, Calif.: Stanford University Press, c1988. xvi, 276 p.
87-018093 306/.0982/22 0804714193
Urbanization -- Argentina -- History. Corrientes (Argentina) -- Social conditions. Salta (Argentina) -- Social conditions. Mendoza (Argentina) -- Social conditions.

HN290.J83.C48 1990
Chilcote, Ronald H.
Power and the ruling classes in northeast Brazil: Juazeiro and Petrolina in transition/ Ronald H. Chilcote. Cambridge; Cambridge University Press, 1990.
89-015797 305.5/2/098142 0521373840
Elite (Social sciences) -- Brazil -- Juazeiro (Bahia) Capitalism -- Brazil -- Juazeiro (Bahia) Elite (Social sciences) -- Brazil -- Petrolina (Pernambuco) Juazeiro (Bahia, Brazil) -- Economic conditions. Petrolina (Pernambuco, Brazil) -- Economic conditions.

HN290.R47.P47
Perlman, Janice E.
The myth of marginality: urban poverty and politics in Rio de Janeiro/ Janice E. Perlman. Berkeley: University of California Press, c1976. xxi, 341 p.
73-087246 301.44/94/09815 0520025962
Marginality, Social -- Brazil -- Rio de Janeiro. Poor -- Brazil -- Rio de Janeiro. Rio de Janeiro (Brazil) -- Politics and government.

HN290.S32.L56 1992
Linger, Daniel Touro.
Dangerous encounters: meanings of violence in a Brazilian city/ Daniel Touro Linger. Stanford, Calif.: Stanford University Press, c1992. x, 289 p.
91-028599 303.6/0981/21 0804719268
Violence -- Brazil -- Sao Luis do Maranhao. Carnival -- Brazil -- Sao Luis do Maranhao.

HN290.Z9.C647 1988
Lang, James, 1944-
Inside development in Latin America: a report from the Dominican Republic, Colombia, and Brazil/ by James Lang. Chapel Hill: University of North Carolina Press, c1988. xx, 307 p.
87-005950 307.1/4/0981 0807817538
Rural development projects -- Brazil. Rural development projects -- Dominican Republic. Rural development projects -- Colombia.

HN290.Z9.S643 1989
Modern Brazil: elites and masses in historical perspective/ edited by Michael L. Conniff and Frank D. McCann. Lincoln: University of Nebraska Press, c1989. xxiv, 305 p.
88-019088 305.5/2/0981 0803231318
Social classes -- Brazil -- History. Elite (Social sciences) -- Brazil -- History. Brazil -- Social conditions.

HN293.B38
Bauer, Arnold J.
Chilean rural society from the Spanish conquest to 1930/ Arnold J. Bauer. Cambridge [Eng.]; Cambridge University Press, 1975. xviii, 265 p.
75-002724 309.1/83 0521207274
Chile -- Rural conditions.

HN293.5.P34 2001
Paley, Julia, 1964-
Marketing democracy: power and social movements in post-dictatorship Chile/ Julia Paley. Berkeley: University of California Press, c2001. xviii, 255 p.
00-037405 303.48/4/0983 21 0520225139
Social movements -- Chile. Power (Social sciences) -- Chile. Democracy -- Chile. Chile -- Politics and government -- 1988-

HN310.Z9
Violence in Colombia, 1990-2000: waging war and negotiating peace/ edited by Charles Bergquist, Ricardo Penaranda, and Gonzalo Sanchez G. Wilmington, Del.: SR Books, c2001. xxv, 300 p.
00-063559 303.6/09861 21 0842028692
Violence -- Colombia -- History -- 20th century. War and society -- Colombia -- History -- 20th century. Colombia -- Social conditions -- 1970-

HN317.C8
Cultural transformations and ethnicity in modern Ecuador/ edited by Norman E. Whitten, Jr. Urbana: University of Illinois Press, c1981. xvii, 811 p.
81-004402 986.6 0252008324
Indians of South America -- Ecuador -- Social conditions. Minorities -- Ecuador. Ecuador -- Social conditions.

HN320.Q57.M56 1994
Minchom, Martin.
The people of Quito, 1690-1810: change and unrest in the underclass/ Martin Minchom. Boulder: Westview Press, c1994. xvii, 297 p.
94-006022 306/.09866/13 0813388317
Poor -- Ecuador -- Quito -- History. Socially handicapped -- Ecuador -- Quito -- History. Social conflict -- Ecuador -- Quito -- History. Quito (Ecuador) -- Social conditions.

HN350.L5.D54 1998
Dietz, Henry A.
Urban poverty, political participation, and the state: Lima, 1970-1990/ Henry Dietz. Pittsburgh: University of Pittsburgh Press, c1998. x, 307 p.
98-009054 306.2/0985/25 21 0822940639
Urban poor -- Peru -- Lima -- Political activity. Political participation -- Peru -- Lima.

HN363.5.G87 2000
Guss, David M.
The festive state: race, ethnicity, and nationalism as cultural performance/ David M. Guss. Berkeley, Calif.: University of California Press, 2000. xiii, 239 p.
99-056890 306/.0987 0520202899
Popular culture -- Venezuela. Festivals -- Venezuela. Folklore -- Performance -- Venezuela. Venezuela -- Social conditions -- 1958-

HN370.C5.P4
Peattie, Lisa Redfield.
The view from the barrio. Ann Arbor, University of Michigan Press [1968] 147 p.
68-016441 309.1/87/6
Ciudad Guayana (Venezuela) -- Social conditions.

HN372-650.7 By region or country — Other regions or countries — Europe

HN372.E74
Ethnic diversity and conflict in Eastern Europe/ Peter F. Sugar, editor. Santa Barbara, Calif.: ABC-Clio, c1980. xii, 553 p.
80-012032 305.8/00947 0874362970
Nationalism -- Europe, Eastern -- Congresses. Ethnicity -- Europe, Eastern -- Congresses. Anthropological linguistics -- Europe, Eastern -- Congresses. Europe, Eastern -- Ethnic relations -- Congresses.

HN373.B55
Blum, Jerome, 1913-
The end of the old order in rural Europe/ Jerome Blum. Princeton, N.J.: Princeton University Press, c1978. xiii, 505 p.
77-085530 309.2/63/094 0691052662
Peasantry -- Europe -- History. Feudalism -- Europe -- History. Social classes -- Europe -- History. Europe -- Rural conditions.

HN373.E63 2001
Encyclopedia of European social history from 1350 to 2000/ Peter N. Stearns, editor-in-chief. New York: Scribner, c2001. 6 v.
00-046376 306/.094/03 21 0684806452
Social history -- Encyclopedias.

HN373.K293 2000
Kamen, Henry Arthur Francis.
Early modern European society/ Henry Kamen. New York: Routledge, 2000. x, 281 p.
99-037008 306/.094 21 0415158656
Europe -- Social conditions -- 16th century. Europe -- Social conditions -- 17th century. Europe -- Social conditions -- 18th century.

HN373.T33
Tannenbaum, Edward R.
1900, the generation before the Great War/ Edward R. Tannenbaum. Garden City, N.Y.: Anchor Press, 1976, c1977. xii, 463 p.
76-018369 309.1/4/0288 0385004311
Europe -- Social conditions -- 20th century.

HN373.W37 1984
Watts, S. J.
A social history of Western Europe, 1450-1720: tensions and solidarities among rural people/ Sheldon J. Watts. London; Hutchinson University Library, 1984. 275 p.
84-159439 306/.094 0091560810
Social history. Europe -- Rural conditions.

HN373.5.C78 1999
Crouch, Colin, 1944-
Social change in Western Europe/ Colin Crouch. New York: Oxford University Press, 1999. xx, 543 p.
99-032731 303.4/094 0198780680
Social change -- Europe, Western. Europe, Western -- Social conditions -- 20th century.

HN373.5.F35 1998
Falkner, Gerda.
EU social policy in the 1990s: towards a corporatist policy community/ Gerda Falkner. London; Routledge, 1998. xii, 254 p.
98-013694 361.6/1/094 0415157773
European Union countries -- Social policy.

HN373.5.K47 1995
Kersbergen, Kees van, 1958-
Social capitalism: a study of Christian democracy and the welfare state/ Kees van Kersbergen. London; Routledge, 1995. xii, 289 p.
95-007804 361.2/5/094 0415116708
Christian democracy -- Europe. Welfare state. Europe -- Social policy.

HN373.5.R36 1991
Ramet, Sabrina P., 1949-
Social currents in Eastern Europe: the sources and meaning of the great transformation/ Sabrina P. Ramet. Durham: Duke University Press, 1991. xii, 434 p.
90-024049 306/.0947 0822311488
Europe, Eastern -- Social conditions. Europe, Eastern -- Politics and government -- 1945-1989.

HN373.5.S37 1990
Scott, Alan.
Ideology and the new social movements/ Alan Scott. London [England]; Unwin Hyman, 1990. 174 p.
90-031122 303.48/4 0043012752
Social movements -- Europe. Social movements -- North America. Ideology.

HN380.M4.P5
Pitt-Rivers, Julian Alfred.
Mediterranean countrymen; essays in the social anthropology of the Mediterranean. Edited by Julian Pitt-Rivers. Contributors: A.M. Abou Zeid [and others] Paris, Mouton, 1963. 236 p.
64-006680 309.14
Mediterranean Region -- Social conditions.

HN380.P6.M66 1987
Moore, R. I. 1941-
The formation of a persecuting society: power and deviance in Western Europe, 950-1250/ R.I. Moore. Oxford, UK; B. Blackwell, 1987. viii, 168 p.
86-028402 323.1/4 0631137467
Power (Social sciences) -- History. Social history -- Medieval, 500-1500. Persecution -- Europe -- History. Europe -- Social conditions -- To 1492.

HN380.Z9.I585 2000
The myth of generational conflict: the family and state in ageing societies/ edited by Sara Arber and Claudine Attias-Donfut. London; Routledge, 2000. xii, 232 p.
99-028669 306.87/094 0415207703
Intergenerational relations -- Europe. Conflict of generations -- Europe.

HN380.Z9.S638
Connor, Walter D.
Socialism, politics, and equality: hierarchy and change in Eastern Europe and the USSR/ Walter D. Connor. New York: Columbia University Press, 1979. x, 389 p.
78-014780 301.44/0947 023104318X
Social classes -- Europe, Eastern. Social classes -- Soviet Union. Social mobility -- Europe, Eastern.

HN380.Z9.S6385
Consciousness and class experience in nineteenth-century Europe/ edited by John M. Merriman. New York: Holmes & Meier Publishers, 1979. vii, 261 p.
79-016032 0841904448
Labor and laboring classes -- Europe -- Case studies. Social classes -- Europe -- Case studies.

HN380.Z9.S6434 1989
Gella, Aleksander.
Development of class structure in Eastern Europe: Poland and her southern neighbors/ Aleksander Gella. Albany: State University of New York Press, c1989. xvii, 326 p.
87-037498 305.5/0947 0887068332
Social classes -- Europe, Eastern -- History. Social classes -- Europe, Central -- History. Europe, Eastern -- Social conditions. Europe, Central -- Social conditions.

HN380.Z9.S64365 1991
Hamilton, Richard F.
The bourgeois epoch: Marx and Engels on Britain, France, and Germany/ Richard F. Hamilton. Chapel Hill: University of North Carolina Press, c1991. xii, 293 p.
91-050252 305.5/094 080781976X
Marx, Karl, -- 1818-1883. Engels, Friedrich, -- 1820-1895. Social classes -- Europe -- History -- 19th century. Europe -- Social conditions -- 1789-1900.

HN380.7.A8.L448 1999
Left parties and social policy in postcommunist Europe/ edited by Linda J. Cook, Mitchell A. Orenstein, and Marilyn Rueschemeyer. Boulder, Colo.: Westview Press, 1999. vii, 270 p.
00-551444 361.6/1/0943 081333568X
Socialism -- Europe, Eastern. Socialism -- Russia (Federation) Post-communism -- Europe, Eastern. Europe, Eastern -- Politics and government -- 1989- Russia (Federation) -- Politics and government -- 1991- Europe, Eastern -- Social policy.

HN380.7.A8.M47 1993
Mestrovic, Stjepan Gabriel.
The Road from paradise: prospects for democracy in Eastern Europe/ Stjepan G. Mestrovic, with Miroslav Goreta and Slaven Letica. Lexington, Ky.: University Press of Kentucky, c1993. xx, 204 p.
92-032442 306/.0947 0813118271
Post-communism -- Europe, Eastern. Europe, Eastern -- Social conditions -- 1989- Europe, Eastern -- Politics and government -- 1989-

HN380.7.A8.O38 1997
Offe, Claus.
Varieties of transition: the East European and East German experience/ Claus Offe. Cambridge, Mass.: MIT Press, 1997. viii, 249 p.
96-009046 306/.0947 0262150484
Post-communism -- Europe, Eastern. Europe, Eastern -- Social policy. Democracy -- Europe, Eastern. Europe, Eastern -- Politics and government -- 1989- Europe, Eastern -- Social conditions -- 1989-

HN380.7.A8.Q56 1998
Quinn, Frederick.
Democracy at dawn: notes from Poland and points East/ Frederick Quinn. College Station, Tex.: Texas A&M University Press, c1998. xxi, 250 p.
97-029954 306/.0947 21 0890967865
Post-communism -- Europe, Eastern. Post-communism -- Former Soviet republics. Europe, Eastern -- Social life and customs. Europe, Eastern -- Social conditions -- 1989- Former Soviet republics -- Social conditions.

HN380.7.A8.T74 1994
Transition to capitalism?: the communist legacy in Eastern Europe/ Janos Matyas Kovacs, editor. New Brunswick, N.J.: Transaction Publishers, c1994. xxiii, 323 p.
93-050827   306/.0947   1560001674
Privatization -- Europe, Eastern. Mixed economy -- Europe, Eastern. Post-communism -- Europe, Eastern. Europe, Eastern -- Economic conditions -- 1989- Europe, Eastern -- Social conditions -- 1989-

HN383.5.J66 1991
Jones, Kathleen, 1922-
The making of social policy in Britain, 1830-1990/ Kathleen Jones. London; Athlone, 1991. xii, 268 p.
90-047008   361.6/1/0941   0485113929
Great Britain -- Social policy. Great Britain -- Social conditions -- 19th century. Great Britain -- Social conditions -- 20th century.

HN383.5.L69 1999
Lowe, Rodney.
The welfare state in Britain since 1945/ Rodney Lowe. 2nd ed. New York: St. Martin's Press, 1999. xi, 406 p.
98-018577   361.6/1/0941 21   0312216335
Welfare state.

HN385.C14 1990
The Cambridge social history of Britain, 1750-1950/ edited by F.M.L. Thompson. Cambridge [England]; Cambridge University Press, 1990. 3 v.
89-009840   306/.0941   0521257883
Social institutions -- Great Britain -- History. Associations, institutions, etc. -- Great Britain -- History. Great Britain -- Social conditions.

HN385.G7 1982
Gregg, Pauline.
A social and economic history of Britain, 1760-1980/ by Pauline Gregg. London: Harrap, 1982. 636 p.
83-174304   306/.0941   0245539387
Great Britain -- Social conditions. Great Britain -- Economic conditions.

HN385.H33 1993
Harris, Jose.
Private lives, public spirit: a social history of Britain, 1870-1914/ Jose Harris. Oxford; Oxford University Press, 1993. xi, 283 p.
92-046507   306/.0941/09034   0198204124
Great Britain -- Social conditions -- 19th century. Great Britain -- Social conditions -- 20th century.

HN385.R57
Roberts, David, 1923-
Paternalism in early Victorian England/ David Roberts. New Brunswick, N.J.: Rutgers University Press, c1979. x, 337 p.
79-014669   301.44/92/0942   0813508681
Paternalism -- England -- History -- 19th century. Great Britain -- History -- Victoria, 1837-1901.

HN385.S73 1990
Spadafora, David, 1951-
The idea of progress in eighteenth-century Britain/ David Spadafora. New Haven: Yale University Press, c1990. xv, 464 p.
89-029303   306/.0941/09033   0300046715
Progress. Great Britain -- Social conditions -- 18th century. Great Britain -- Intellectual life -- 18th century.

HN385.5.A43 1996
Alcock, Peter, 1951-
Social policy in Britain: themes and issues/ Pete Alcock; consultant editor: Jo Campling. New York, N.Y.: St. Martin's Press, 1996. xix, 319 p.
96-007687   361.6/1/0941   0312162014
Great Britain -- Social policy.

HN385.5.J6 1979
Johns, Edward Alistair.
The social structure of modern Britain/ by E. A. Johns. Oxford; Pergamon Press, 1979. xiv, 284 p.
78-040531   309.1/41/0857   0080233422
Great Britain -- Social conditions -- 1945-

HN385.5.P58 1992
Policy and change in Thatcher's Britain/ edited by Paul Cloke. Oxford [England]; Pergamon Press, 1992. xii, 381 p.
91-033813   361.6/1/0941   0080406475
Critical theory. Great Britain -- Social conditions -- 1945- Great Britain -- Economic policy -- 1945- Great Britain -- Economic conditions -- 1945-1993.

HN385.5.W515 1990
Williamson, Bill, 1944-
The temper of the times: British society since World War II/ Bill Williamson. Oxford, UK; B. Blackwell, 1990. ix, 308 p.
89-077330   306/.0941   0631159193
Great Britain -- Social conditions -- 1945- Great Britain -- Politics and government -- 1945-

HN388.E53.J69 1990
Joyce, Patrick.
Visions of the people: industrial England and the question of class, 1848-1914/ Patrick Joyce. Cambridge; Cambridge University Press, 1991. 449 p.
89-077387   305.5/0942/09034   052137152X
Social classes -- England -- History -- 19th century. England -- Social life and customs -- 19th century.

HN389.T43 1992
Thompson, Paul Richard,
The Edwardians: the remaking of British society/ Paul Thompson. 2nd ed. London; Routledge, 1992. xx, 342 p.
91-045628   306/.0941/09041 20   0415061148
Social classes -- Great Britain -- History -- 20th century.

HN389.T58 1969
Titmuss, Richard Morris, 1907-1973.
Essays on "the welfare state" [by] Richard M. Titmuss. Boston, Beacon Press [1969] 262 p.
77-088219   309.1/41/08
National Health Service (Great Britain) Welfare state. Great Britain -- Social policy.

HN398.E3.A73 1990
Archer, John E.
By a flash and a scare: incendiarism, animal maiming, and poaching in East Anglia, 1815-1870/ John E. Archer. Oxford: Clarendon Press; 1990. viii, 282 p.
90-033322   303.6/09426   019820177X
Social conflict -- England -- East Anglia -- History -- 19th century. Terrorism -- England -- East Anglia -- History -- 19th century. Arson -- England -- East Anglia -- History -- 19th century. East Anglia (England) -- Rural conditions.

HN398.E45.G54 1990
Gies, Frances.
Life in a medieval village/ Frances and Joseph Gies. New York: Harper & Row, c1990. ix, 257 p.
89-033759   306/.09426/5   0060162155
Peasantry -- England -- Elton (Cambridgeshire) -- History. Villages -- England -- Elton (Cambridgeshire) -- History. Social history -- Medieval, 500-1500. Elton (Cambridgeshire, England) -- Rural conditions. England -- Social life and customs -- 1066-1485. Elton (Cambridgeshire, England) -- Social conditions.

HN398.E5.H68 1987
Horn, Pamela.
Life and labour in rural England, 1760-1850/ Pamela Horn. Houndmills, Basingstoke, Hampshire: Macmillan Education, 1987. x, 184 p.
88-100117   942/.009734   033337584X
England -- Rural conditions. England -- Social conditions -- 18th century. England -- Social conditions -- 19th century.

HN398.E5.M38 1998
McIntosh, Marjorie Keniston.
Controlling misbehavior in England, 1370-1600/ Marjorie Keniston McIntosh. Cambridge, U.K.; Cambridge University Press, 1998. xviii, 289 p.
98-141859   361.1/0942   0521557011
Social control -- England -- History. Deviant behavior -- England -- History. Justice, Administration of -- England -- History. England -- Moral conditions -- History. England -- Social conditions.

HN398.E5.M57 1990
Mingay, G. E.
A social history of the English countryside/ G.E. Mingay. London; Routledge, 1990. xiv, 246 p.
89-070221   307.72/0942   0415034086
England -- Rural conditions.

HN398.E5.P47 1981
Perkin, Harold James.
The structured crowd: essays in English social history/ Harold Perkin. Brighton, Sussex: Harvester Press; 1981. xi, 238 p.
81-215098   306/.0942   0855274131
Social history. England -- Social conditions -- 20th century. England -- Social conditions -- 19th century.

HN398.E5.R54 1995
Rigby, S. H. 1955-
English society in the later middle ages: class, status, and gender/ S.H. Rigby. New York: St. Martin's Press, 1995. xii, 408 p.
94-043981   305.5/0942   0312125445
Social classes -- England -- History. Social status -- England -- History. Middle Ages -- Historiography. England -- Social conditions -- 1066-1485.

HN398.E5.V56 2000
Violence in medieval society/ edited by Richard W. Kaeuper. Rochester, NY: Boydell Press, 2000. xiii, 226 p.
00-020946   303.6/0942   0851157742
Violence -- England -- History. Violence -- History -- To 1500. Middle Ages.

HN398.L38.B37 1990
Barnard, Sylvia M., 1942-
To prove I'm not forgot: living and dying in a Victorian city/ Sylvia M. Barnard. Manchester; Manchester University Press; c1990. xi, 212 p.
89-013262   306.9/09428/19   0719025222
Death -- Social aspects -- England -- Leeds -- History -- 19th century. Leeds (England) -- Social life and customs. Leeds (England) -- Social conditions.

HN398.L7 G4 1985
George, M. Dorothy
London life in the eighteenth century/ M. Dorothy George. Chicago, IL: Academy Chicago, 1984. 457 p.
85-018486   306/.0942 19   0897331478
Poor -- England -- London -- History -- 18th century. Working class -- England -- London -- History -- 18th century.

HN398.L7.R37 1989
Rappaport, Steve Lee.
Worlds within worlds: structures of life in sixteenth-century London/ Steve Rappaport. Cambridge; Cambridge University Press, 1989. xv, 449 p.
88-010205   306/.09421   0521350654
Social structure -- England -- London -- History -- 16th century. London (England) -- Social conditions. London (England) -- Economic conditions.

HN398.M27.H48 1996
Hewitt, Martin.
The emergence of stability in the industrial city: Manchester, 1832-67/ Martin Hewitt. Aldershot, England: Scolar Press; c1996. xii, 335 p.
95-047155   306/.09427/33 20   1859282768
Industries -- England -- Manchester -- History -- 19th century. Working class -- England -- Manchester -- History -- 19th century. Manchester (England) -- Social conditions. Manchester (England) -- Politics and government.

HN398.M27.T39 1996
Taylor, Ian R.
A tale of two cities: global change, local feeling, and everyday life in the North of England: a study in Manchester and Sheffield/ Ian Taylor, Karen Evans and Penny Fraser. London; Routledge, c1996. xviii, 391 p.
95-037938   306/.09427/33 20   0415138280
Manchester (England) -- Social conditions. Sheffield (England) -- Social conditions. Manchester (England) -- Social life and customs.

HN398.N6.S65 1991
Smith, David John, 1941-
Inequality in Northern Ireland/ David J. Smith and Gerald Chambers. Oxford [England]: Clarendon Press; 1991. xvi, 401 p.
90-007741   305/.09416   0198275544
Equality -- Northern Ireland. Protestants -- Northern Ireland. Catholics -- Northern Ireland. Northern Ireland -- Social conditions. Northern Ireland -- Economic conditions.

HN398.S2.R6
Roberts, Robert, 1905-
The classic slum: Salford life in the first quarter of the century. Manchester, Manchester University Press, 1971. xiii, 219 p.
74-855642   942.7/32   0719004535
Poor -- England -- Salford (Greater Manchester) Salford (Greater Manchester, England) -- Social conditions.

HN398.S3.C35 1983
Camic, Charles.
Experience and enlightenment: socialization for cultural change in eighteenth-century Scotland/ Charles Camic. Chicago: University of Chicago Press, 1983. x, 301 p.
83-004992   306/.09411   0226092380
Enlightenment -- Scotland. Socialization. Scotland -- Intellectual life. Scotland -- Social conditions. Scotland -- History -- 18th century.

HN398.S3 M38 2001
McCrone, David.
Understanding Scotland: the sociology of a nation/ David McCrone. 2nd ed. London; Routledge, 2001. x, 222 p.
00-051738   306/.09411 21   0415251648
Nationalism -- Scotland. Regionalism -- Great Britain.

HN398.W26.J624 1989
Jones, David J. V.
Rebecca's children: a study of rural society, crime, and protest/ David J.V. Jones. Oxford: Clarendon Press; 1989. ix, 423 p.
89-023966   942.9081   0198200994
Rebecca Riots, 1839-1844. Wales -- Rural conditions.

HN398.W45.R87 1997
Cloke, Paul J.
Rural Wales: community and marginalization/ Paul Cloke, Mark Goodwin, Paul Milbourne. Cardiff: University of Wales Press, 1997. 189 p.
97-176359   307.720942909045   0708313655
Wales -- Rural conditions.

HN400.M6.J46 1992
Jenkins, Philip, 1952-
Intimate enemies: moral panics in contemporary Great Britain/ Philip Jenkins. New York: Aldine de Gruyter, c1992. xiii, 262 p.
92-007171   306/.0941   0202304353
Crime -- England -- Public opinion. Cults -- England -- Public opinion. Sex customs -- England -- Public opinion. England -- Moral conditions -- Public opinion.

HN400.R3.B45 1996
Belchem, John.
Popular radicalism in nineteenth-century Britain/ John Belchem. New York: St. Martin's Press, 1996. vi, 222 p.
95-031061   303.48/4   0312157991
Radicalism -- Great Britain -- History -- 19th century. Popular culture -- Great Britain -- History -- 19th century.

HN400.R3.C48 1988
Chase, Malcolm.
"The people's farm": English radical agrarianism, 1775-1840/ Malcolm Chase. Oxford [England]: Clarendon Press; 1988. vi, 221 p.
88-001680   322.4/4/094212   0198201052
Spence, Thomas, -- 1750-1814. Radicalism -- Great Britain -- History -- 18th century. Radicalism -- Great Britain -- History -- 19th century. Land reform -- Great Britain -- History -- 18th century.

HN400.R3.M34 1988
McCalman, Iain.
Radical underworld: prophets, revolutionaries, and pornographers in London, 1795-1840/ Iain McCalman. Cambridge [Cambridgeshire]; Cambridge University Press, 1988. xvi, 338 p.
87-011770   322.4/4/094212   0521307554
Spence, Thomas, -- 1750-1814. Radicalism -- England -- London -- History -- 19th century.

HN400.S6.C356 1999
Cannadine, David, 1950-
The rise and fall of class in Britain/ David Cannadine. New York: Columbia University Press, 1999. xv, 293 p.
98-028611   305.5/0941   0231096666
Social classes -- Great Britain. Social mobility -- Great Britain.

HN400.S6 G64 1987
Goldthorpe, John H.
Social mobility and class structure in modern Britain/ John H. Goldthorpe, in collaboration with Catriona Llewellyn and Clive Payne. [2nd ed.]. Oxford [Oxfordshire]: Clarendon Press; ix, 377 p.
87-007916   305.5/0941 19   0198272855
Social classes -- Great Britain. Social mobility -- Great Britain.

HN400.S6.K63 1990
Koditschek, Theodore.
Class formation and urban-industrial society: Bradford, 1750-1850/ Theodore Koditschek. Cambridge [England]; Cambridge University Press, 1990. xi, 611 p.
89-017484   305.5/09428/17   0521327717
Social classes -- England -- Bradford -- History. Middle class -- England -- Bradford -- History. Working class -- England -- Bradford -- History. Bradford (England) -- Social conditions.

HN400.S6.M39 1998
McKibbin, Ross.
Classes and cultures: England 1918-1951/ Ross McKibbin. Oxford; Oxford University Press, 1998. x, 562 p.
97-033044   305.5/0942/0904   0198206720
Social classes -- England -- History -- 20th century. Social structure -- England -- History -- 20th century. Class consciousness -- England -- History -- 20th century. England -- Social conditions -- 20th century. England -- Social life and customs -- 20th century.

HN400.S6.P47 1989
Perkin, Harold James.
The rise of professional society: England since 1880/ Harold Perkin. London; Routledge, 1989. xvi, 604 p.
88-010113   305.5/0942   0415008905
Social classes -- England -- History -- 19th century. Social classes -- England -- History -- 20th century. Professions -- England -- Sociological aspects -- History -- 19th century. England -- Social conditions -- 19th century. England -- Social conditions -- 20th century.

HN400.V5.F45 1991
Feldman, Allen.
Formations of violence: the narrative of the body and political terror in Northern Ireland/ Allen Feldman. Chicago: University of Chicago Press, 1991. vii, 319 p.
90-047977   303.6/09416   0226240703
Political violence -- Northern Ireland. Counterinsurgency -- Northern Ireland. Political prisoners -- Northern Ireland -- Case studies.

HN400.Z9.V56 1992
Maddern, Philippa C.
Violence and social order: East Anglia 1422-1442/ Philippa C. Maddern. Oxford: Clarendon Press; 1992. 270 p.
92-249590   303.6/09426/09024   0198202350
Violence -- England -- East Anglia -- History. East Anglia (England) -- Social conditions.

HN400.3.A8.B69 1983
Bowen, Kurt Derek.
Protestants in a Catholic state: Ireland's privileged minority/ Kurt Bowen. Kingston: McGill-Queen's University Press; c1983. x, 237 p.
84-192877   305.6/30417   0773504125
Protestants -- Ireland -- History -- 20th century. Ireland -- Social conditions.

HN400.3.Z9.S654 1989
Hout, Michael.
Following in father's footsteps: social mobility in Ireland/ Michael Hout. Cambridge, Mass.: Harvard University Press, 1989. viii, 394 p.
89-032790   305.5/13/09415   0674307283
Social mobility -- Ireland. Social mobility -- Northern Ireland. Occupational mobility -- Ireland. Ireland -- Economic conditions -- 1949- Northern Ireland -- Economic conditions.

HN418.V5.G78 1991
Gruber, Helmut, 1928-
Red Vienna: experiment in working-class culture, 1919-1934/ Helmut Gruber. New York: Oxford University Press, 1991. x, 270 p.
90-024065   306/.09436/13   0195069145
Working class -- Austria -- Vienna -- History -- 20th century. Popular culture -- Austria -- Vienna -- History -- 20th century. Austro-Marxist school -- History -- 20th century. Vienna (Austria) -- Social policy. Vienna (Austria) -- Social conditions. Vienna (Austria) -- History -- 1918-

HN418.V5.R68 1992
Rotenberg, Robert Louis, 1949-
Time and order in metropolitan Vienna: a seizure of schedules/ Robert Rotenberg. Washington: Smithsonian Institution Press, 1992. x, 262 p.
91-032894   306/.09436/13   1560981032
Time -- Social aspects -- Austria -- Vienna Metropolitan Area. Vienna Matropolitan Area (Austria) -- Social life and customs. Vienna Metropolitan Area (Austria) -- Social conditions.

HN420.5.K56.B44 1984
Bell, Peter D.
Peasants in Socialist transition: life in a collectivized Hungarian village/ Peter D. Bell. Berkeley: University of California Press, c1984. ix, 322 p.
80-025126   307.7/2/09439   0520041577
Villages -- Hungary -- Case studies. Collective farms -- Hungary -- Case studies. Kislapos (Hungary) -- Social conditions. Hungary -- Rural conditions -- Case studies.

HN425.B6313 1992
Bois, Guy.
The transformation of the year one thousand: the village of Lournand from antiquity to feudalism/ Guy Bois; translated by Jean Birrell. Manchester, UK; Manchester University Press; c1992. x, 177 p.
92-001488   306/.0944   0719035651
Feudalism -- France -- Case studies. Peasantry -- France -- History -- Case studies. Lournand (France) -- Social conditions -- Case studies. France -- Social conditions -- To 987 -- Case studies. France -- Social conditions -- 987-1515 -- Case studies.

HN425.C6713 1995
Corbin, Alain.
Time, desire, and horror: towards a history of the senses/ Alain Corbin; translated by Jean Birrell. Cambridge, UK: Polity Press; 1995. x, 212 p.
95-033038   306/.0944   0745611311
Prostitution -- France -- History -- 19th century. France -- Social conditions -- 19th century.

HN425.D78313
Duby, Georges.
The three orders: feudal society imagined/ Georges Duby; translated by Arthur Goldhammer; with a foreword by Thomas N. Bisson. Chicago: University of Chicago Press, 1980. x, 382 p.
80-013158   321.3/0944   0226167712
Feudalism -- France. Social history -- Medieval, 500-1500. France -- Social conditions.

HN425.P75 1987
Price, Roger, 1944 Jan. 7-
A social history of nineteenth-century France/ Roger Price. New York: Holmes & Meier, 1987. xii, 403 p.
87-022684   306/.0944   0841911665
France -- Social conditions -- 19th century.

HN425.T54
Tilly, Charles.
The rebellious century, 1830-1930/ Charles Tilly, Louise Tilly, and Richard Tilly. Cambridge: Harvard University Press, 1975. xi, 354 p.
74-016802   309.1/4/028   0674749553
Violence. France -- Social conditions -- 19th century. Italy -- Social conditions. Germany -- Social conditions.

HN425.5.D89 1995
Duyvendak, Jan Willem.
The power of politics: new social movements in France/ Jan Willem Duyvendak. Boulder, Colo.: Westview Press, c1995. xii, 251 p.
95-023074   303.48/4/0944   0813387221
Social movements -- France. France -- Social conditions -- 1945- France -- Politics and government -- 1981-1995.

HN426.W4 1976
Weber, Eugen Joseph, 1925-
Peasants into Frenchmen: the modernization of rural France, 1870-1914/ Eugen Weber. Stanford, Calif.: Stanford University Press, 1976. xv, 615 p.
75-007486   309.2/63/0944   0804708983
Peasantry -- France -- History. France -- Rural conditions. France -- Social conditions -- 19th century.

HN438.B73.D38 1988
Davies, Wendy.
Small worlds: the village community in early medieval Brittany/ Wendy Davies. Berkeley: University of California Press, c1988. x, 226 p.
88-050829   307.72/0944/1   0520064836
Villages -- France -- Brittany -- History. Social history -- Medieval, 500-1500. Brittany (France) -- Rural conditions.

HN438.P3.R8 1971
Rude, George F. E.
Paris and London in the eighteenth century; studies in popular protest [by] George Rude. New York, Viking Press [1970] 350 p.
73-148267   301.6/332/09421   0670538329
Riots -- England -- London. Riots -- France -- Paris. London (England) -- Social conditions. Paris (France) -- Social conditions.

HN440.E4.E43 1981
Elites in France: origins, reproduction, and power/ edited by Jolyon Howorth, Philip G. Cerny. New York: St. Martin's Press, 1981. vi, 253 p.
81-009147   305.5/2   0312242425
Elite (Social sciences) -- France -- History. France -- Politics and government.

HN440.M26.G4713 1987
Geremek, Bronislaw.
The margins of society in late medieval Paris/ Bronislaw Geremek; translated from the French by Jean Birrell. Cambridge; Cambridge University Press; 1987. xi, 319 p.
86-032651   306/.0944/361   0521301564
Marginality, Social -- France -- Paris. Social history -- Medieval, 500-1500. Prostitution -- France -- Paris. Paris (France) -- Moral conditions.

HN445.B47 1993
Bessel, Richard.
Germany after the First World War/ Richard Bessel. Oxford: Clarendon Press; 1993. xv, 325 p.
92-040025   306/.0943/09042   0198219385
Germany -- Social conditions -- 1918-1933. Germany -- History -- 1918-1933.

HN445.G472 1996
Germany: a new social and economic history. London; Arnold; [1996-] v. 1-2.
95-017543   306/.0943   0340513322
Germany -- Social conditions. Germany -- Economic conditions.

HN445.G85 1971
Guillebaud, C. W.
The social policy of Nazi Germany, by C. W. Guillebaud. New York, H. Fertig, 1971. viii, 134 p.
71-080553   309.1/43/085
Working class -- Germany.

HN445.5.A73 1995
Ardagh, John,
Germany and the Germans/ John Ardagh; consultant and research assistant, Katharina Ardagh. 3rd ed. London; Penguin Books, 1995. xvi, 604 p.
96-159148   943.08/7 20   0140252665
Germany (West) -- Social conditions. Germany (East) -- Social conditions. Germany -- Civilization -- 20th century.

HN458.H3.E95 1987
Evans, Richard J.
Death in Hamburg: society and politics in the cholera years, 1830-1910/ Richard J. Evans. Oxford [Oxfordshire]: Clarendon Press; 1987. xxii, 676 p.
87-005556   304.2/7/0943515   0198228643
Cholera -- Germany -- Hamburg -- History -- 19th century. Hamburg (Germany) -- Social conditions.

HN458.L3.R63 1989
Robisheaux, Thomas Willard.
Rural society and the search for order in early modern Germany/ Thomas Robisheaux. Cambridge [England]; Cambridge University Press, 1989. xvi, 297 p.
88-027450   307.7/2/094347   0521356261
Langenburg Region (Germany) -- Social conditions. Langenburg Region (Germany) -- Rural conditions.

HN460.P8.K47 1983
Kershaw, Ian.
Popular opinion and political dissent in the Third Reich, Bavaria 1933-1945/ Ian Kershaw. Oxford, [Oxfordshire]; Clarendon Press; 1983. xii, 425 p.
82-012617   303.3/8/09433   0198219229
Public opinion -- Germany (West) Public opinion -- Germany -- Bavaria. National socialism -- Public opinion. Bavaria (Germany) -- Politics and government -- 1918-1945. Germany -- Politics and government -- 1933-1945.

HN460.S6.K613 1984
Kocka, Jurgen.
Facing total war: German society, 1914-1918/
Jurgen Kocka; translated from the German by
Barbara Weinberger. Cambridge, Mass.: Harvard
University Press, 1984. 278 p.
84-019269   306/.0943   0674290313
*Social classes -- Germany. World War, 1914-
1918 -- Economic aspects -- Germany.*

HN460.5.A8.D46 1993
Dennis, Mike, 1940-
Social and economic modernization in eastern
Germany from Honecker to Kohl/ Mike Dennis.
London: Pinter Publishers; 1993. viii, 252 p.
93-008747   306/.09431   0861871669
*Germany (East) -- Social conditions. Germany
(East) -- Economic conditions.*

HN460.5.A8.M36 1991
Marxist historiography in transformation: East
German social history in the 1980s/ edited by
Georg Iggers; translated by Bruce Little. New
York: Berg: 1991. ix, 263 p.
90-020251   306/.09431   085496228X
*Marxian historiography -- Germany (East).
Germany (East) -- Social conditions.*

HN460.5.Z9.P82 1999
Allinson, Mark.
Politics and popular opinion in East Germany
1945-1968/ Mark Allinson. New York, N.Y.:
Manchester University Press, 1999. xi, 178 p.
99-043348   306/.09431   0719055547
*Public opinion -- Germany (East) -- History --
20th century. Political culture -- Germany (East) --
History -- 20th century. Germany (East) -- Politics
and government.*

HN475.C59 1992
Cohn, Samuel Kline.
The cult of remembrance and the Black Death: six
Renaissance cities in central Italy/ Samuel K.
Cohn, Jr. Baltimore: Johns Hopkins University
Press, c1992. xiii, 429 p.
91-045267   306/.0945   0801843030
*Lifestyles -- Italy -- History. Black death --
Social aspects -- Italy -- History. Charitable
bequests -- Italy -- History. Italy -- Social
conditions -- 1268-1559.*

HN488.L82.W5313 1998
Wickham, Chris, 1950-
Community and clientele in twelfth-century
Tuscany: the origins of the rural commune in the
plain of Lucca/ Chris Wickham. Oxford; Clarendon
Press, 1998. vii, 276 p.
97-050496   307.72/0945/53   0198207042
*Rural population -- Italy -- Lucca (Province) --
History. Villages -- Italy -- Lucca (Province) --
History. Lucca (Italy: Province) -- Rural
conditions.*

HN490.V5.M67 1989
Moss, David, 1946-
The politics of left-wing violence in Italy, 1969-85/
David Moss. New York: St. Martin's Press, 1989.
xv, 317 p.
89-030611   303.6/2/0945   0312028148
*Violence -- Italy. Terrorism -- Italy. Radicalism -
- Italy. Italy -- Social conditions -- 1976-1994.*

HN490.V5.V56
Violence and civil disorder in Italian cities, 1200-
1500. Edited by Lauro Martines. Berkeley,
University of California Press, 1972. viii, 353 p.
71-145791   309.1/45   0520019067
*Violence -- Italy -- History -- Congresses. Cities
and towns, Medieval -- Italy -- History --
Congresses. Social history -- Medieval, 500-1500 -
- Congresses.*

HN513.D4813 1991
Deursen, Arie Theodorus van.
Plain lives in a golden age: popular culture,
religion, and society in seventeenth-century
Holland/ A.T. Van Deursen; translated by Maarten
Ultee. Cambridge [England]; Cambridge
University Press, 1991. viii, 408 p.
90-001684   306/.09492/09032   0521366062
*Immigrants -- Netherlands -- History -- 17th
century. Working class -- Netherlands -- History --
17th century. Netherlands -- Social conditions.
Netherlands -- Economic conditions.*

HN513.5.V8513 2000
Vuijsje, Herman.
The politically correct Netherlands: since the
1960s/ Herman Vuijsje; translated and annotated
by Mark T. Hooker. Westport, CT: Greenwood
Press, 2000. vi, 244 p.
99-462061   306/.09492   0313315094
*Social problems -- Netherlands. Netherlands --
Social conditions -- 1945- Netherlands -- Social
policy.*

HN523.F57 1999
Fitzpatrick, Sheila.
Everyday Stalinism: ordinary life in extraordinary
times: Soviet Russia in the 1930s/ Sheila
Fitzpatrick. New York: Oxford University Press,
1999. x, 288 p.
98-015421   306/.0947   0195050002
*City and town life -- Soviet Union. Communism --
Soviet Union. Soviet Union -- Social conditions.
Soviet Union -- History -- 1925-1953.*

HN523.S46 1993
Semyonova Tian-Shanskaia, Olga, 1863-1906.
Village life in late tsarist Russia/ by Olga
Semyonova Tian-Shanskaia; edited by David L.
Ransel; translated by David L. Ransel, with
Michael Levine. Bloomington: Indiana University
Press, c1993. xxx, 175 p.
92-028558   307.72/0947   0253347971
*Villages -- Russia -- History -- 19th century. Sex
customs -- Russia -- History -- 19th century.
Russia -- Rural conditions. Russia -- Social
conditions -- 1801-1917.*

HN523.5.P44 1991
Perestroika from below: social movements in the
Soviet Union/ edited by Judith B. Sedaitis and Jim
Butterfield. Boulder: Westview, 1991. xii, 220 p.
91-013389   303.48/4/0947   0813380685
*Social movements -- Soviet Union. Perestroika.
Pressure groups -- Soviet Union. Soviet Union --
Politics and government -- 1985-1991.*

HN523.5.P63 1987
Politics, work, and daily life in the USSR: a survey
of former Soviet citizens/ edited by James R.
Millar. Cambridge [Cambridgeshire]; Cambridge
University Press, 1987. xiv, 423 p.
87-010855   306/.0947   0521334764
*Quality of life -- Soviet Union. Soviet Union --
Politics and government -- 1953-1985. Soviet
Union -- Economic conditions -- 1975-1985. Soviet
Union -- Social conditions -- 1970-1991.*

HN523.5.S434 1989
Shlapentokh, Vladimir.
Public and private life of the Soviet people:
changing values in post-Stalin Russia/ by Vladimir
Shlapentokh. New York: Oxford University Press,
1989. 281 p.
87-034962   306/.0947   0195042662
*Privacy -- Soviet Union. Quality of life -- Soviet
Union. Soviet Union -- Moral conditions. Soviet
Union -- Social conditions -- 1970-1991.*

HN523.5.S69 1988
The Soviet Union and the challenge of the future/
edited by Alexander Shtromas and Morton A.
Kaplan. New York: Paragon House, c1988-1989. v.
1, 3.
87-006904   306/.0947   0943852293
*Soviet Union -- Social conditions -- 1945-1991
-- Congresses. Soviet Union -- Politics and
government -- 1945-1991 -- Congresses. Soviet
Union -- Economic policy -- 1986-1991 --
Congresses.*

HN523.5.Z8 1998
Zubkova, E. IU.
Russia after the war: hopes, illusions, and
disappointments, 1945-1957/ by Elena Zubkova;
translated and edited by Hugh Ragsdale. Armonk,
N.Y.: M. E. Sharpe, 1998. x, 238 p.
98-017042   306/.0947   076560227X
*Reconstruction (1939-1951) -- Soviet Union.
Soviet Union -- Economic conditions -- 1945-1955.
Soviet Union -- Social conditions -- 1945-1991.*

HN527.A4713 1985
Alekseeva, Liudmila, 1927-
Soviet dissent: contemporary movements for
national, religious, and human rights/ by Ludmilla
Alexeyeva; translated by Carol Pearce and John
Glad. Middletown, Conn.: Wesleyan University
Press, c1985. xii, 521 p.
84-011811   303.4/84   0819551244
*Social movements -- Soviet Union -- History.
Dissenters -- Soviet Union -- History. Civil rights -
- Soviet Union -- History. Soviet Union -- Social
conditions -- 1945-1991.*

HN530.R87.W67 1991
Worobec, Christine.
Peasant Russia: family and community in the post-
emancipation period/ Christine D. Worobec.
Princeton, N.J.: Princeton University Press, c1991.
xiv, 257 p.
90-041811   305.5/633/0947   0691031517
*Rural families -- Russia (Federation) -- History -
- 19th century. Peasantry -- Russia (Federation) --
History -- 19th century. Russia (Federation) --
Rural conditions.*

HN530.U5.E34 1987
Edelman, Robert, 1945-
Proletarian peasants: the revolution of 1905 in
Russia's southwest/ Robert Edelman. Ithaca:
Cornell University Press, 1987. xv, 195 p.
87-047544   306/.0947/71   0801494737
*Peasantry -- Ukraine -- History -- 20th century.
Strikes and lockouts -- Ukraine -- History -- 20th
century. Ukraine -- Rural conditions. Ukraine --
History -- Revolution, 1905-1907.*

HN530.Z9.E43 1988
Elites and political power in the USSR/ edited by
David Lane. Aldershot, Hants, England: Elgar;
c1988. xii, 299 p.
88-003856   305.5/2/0947   1852780444
*Elite (Social sciences) -- Soviet Union. Soviet
Union -- Politics and government -- 1985-1991.*

HN530.Z9.E434 1992
Farmer, Kenneth C.
The Soviet administrative elite/ Kenneth C. Farmer. New York: Praeger, 1992. xii, 296 p.
91-033599   305.5/2/0947   0275941396
Elite (Social sciences) -- Soviet Union. Political leadership -- Soviet Union. Government executives -- Soviet Union.

HN530.Z9.E45
Matthews, Mervyn.
Privilege in the Soviet Union: a study of elite life-styles under communism/ Mervyn Matthews. London; G. Allen & Unwin, 1978. 197 p.
78-315486   301.44/92/0947   0043230202
Elite (Social sciences) -- Soviet Union. Social mobility -- Soviet Union. Equality.

HN530.2.A8.B83 1993
Buckley, Mary
Redefining Russian society and polity/ Mary Buckley. Boulder, Colo.: Westview Press, 1993. xviii, 346 p.
93-015755   306/.0947   0813315808
Glasnost. Perestroika. Social change -- Russia (Federation) Soviet Union -- Politics and government -- 1985-1991. Russia (Federation) -- Social conditions -- 1991- Russia (Federation) -- Politics and government.

HN530.2.Z9.E454 1999
Lane, David Stuart.
The transition from communism to capitalism: ruling elites from Gorbachev to Yeltsin/ David Lane and Cameron Ross. New York: St. Martin's Press, 1999. xii, 259 p.
98-045020   305.5/2/0947   0312216122
Elite (Social sciences) -- Russia (Federation) Elite (Social sciences) -- Soviet Union. Political leadership -- Russia (Federation) Russia (Federation) -- Politics and government -- 1991- Russia (Federation) -- Economic conditions -- 1991- Russia (Federation) -- Social conditions -- 1991-

HN537.5.L67 2000
Los, Maria.
Privatizing the police-state: the case of Poland/ Maria Los and Andrzej Zybertowicz; foreword by Gary T. Marx. New York: St. Martin's Press, 2000. xx, 270 p.
99-088982   306/.09438   0312231504
Social change -- Poland. Secret service -- Poland. Democratization -- Poland. Poland -- Social conditions -- 1980-

HN537.5.P532 1994
Podgorecki, Adam.
Polish society/ Adam Podgorecki. Westport, Conn.: Praeger, c1994. 189 p.
93-025056   301/.09438   0275947289
Post-communism -- Poland. Social structure -- Poland. Poland -- Social conditions -- 1980-

HN537.5.P5379 1987
The Polish dilemma: views from within/ edited by Lawrence S. Graham, Maria K. Ciechocinska. Boulder, Colo.: Westview Press, 1987. xiv, 258 p.
86-001638   306/.09438   0813371600
Poland -- Social conditions -- 1980- Poland -- Social conditions -- 1945-

HN553.B96 1988
Byock, Jesse L.
Medieval Iceland: society, sagas, and power/ Jesse L. Byock. Berkeley: University of California Press, c1988. xi, 264 p.
87-038078   949.1/2   0520054202
Civilization, Medieval, in literature. Sagas -- History and criticism. Ethnology -- Iceland. Iceland -- History -- To 1262. Iceland -- Social conditions.

HN577.V3313 1987
Welfare in transition: a survey of living conditions in Sweden, 1968-1981/ edited by Robert Erikson and Rune Aberg. Oxford [Oxfordshire]: Clarendon Press; 1987. xv, 297 p.
86-016485   361.6/1/09485   0198285167
Welfare state. Sweden -- Economic policy. Sweden -- Social conditions -- 1945- Sweden -- Social policy.

HN583.R85 2001
Ruiz, Teofilo F., 1943-
Spanish society, 1400-1600/ Teofilo F. Ruiz. Harlow, England; Longman 2001. xv, 286 p.
00-046139   306/.0946   0582286921
Spain -- History -- 16th century. Social classes -- Spain. Spain -- History -- 711-1516. Spain -- Social conditions -- to 1800. Spain -- Social life and customs.

HN590.B3.K37 1992
Kaplan, Temma, 1942-
Red city, blue period: social movements in Picasso's Barcelona/ Temma Kaplan. Berkeley: University of California Press, c1992. xiv, 266 p.
91-004686   303.48/4/094672   0520075072
Picasso, Pablo, -- 1881-1973. Arts and society -- Spain -- Barcelona. Social movements -- Spain -- Barcelona -- History. Barcelona (Spain) -- Intellectual life. Barcelona (Spain) -- Social life and customs. Spain -- History -- Alfonso XIII, 1886-1931.

HN590.C36
Kosto, Adam J.
Making agreements in medieval Catalonia: power, order, and the written word, 1000-1200/ Adam J. Kosto. Cambridge, UK; Cambridge University Press, 2001. xix, 366 p.
00-062162   303.3   0521792398
Power (Social sciences) -- Spain -- Catalonia -- History -- To 1500. Juristic acts -- Spain -- Catalonia -- History -- To 1500. Oaths -- Spain -- Catalonia -- History -- To 1500.

HN590.S4.P54
Pike, Ruth, 1931-
Aristocrats and traders; Sevillian society in the sixteenth century. Ithaca [N.Y.] Cornell University Press [1972] xiii, 243 p.
76-037756   309.1/46/86   0801406994
Social classes -- Spain -- Seville -- History. Seville (Spain) -- Social conditions.

HN590.Z9.V59 1988
Zulaika, Joseba.
Basque violence: metaphor and sacrament/ Joseba Zulaika. Reno: University of Nevada Press, c1988. xxxi, 423 p.
87-035432   303.6/2/0946   0874171326
Violence -- Spain -- Case studies. Basques -- Social conditions -- Case studies. Basques -- Rites and ceremonies -- Case studies.

HN600.F66.O5413 1987
O'Neill, Brian Juan, 1950-
Social inequality in a Portuguese hamlet: land, late marriage, and bastardy, 1870-1978/ Brian Juan O'Neill. Cambridge [Cambridgeshire]; Cambridge University Press, 1987. xix, 431 p.
86-024433   305/.09469/2   0521322847
Fontelas (Vila Real, Portugal) -- Rural conditions. Fontelas (Vila Real, Portugal) -- Economic conditions.

HN603.S35
Schmid, Carol L.
Conflict and consensus in Switzerland/ Carol L. Schmid. Berkeley: University of California Press; c1981. vii, 198 p.
80-018458   305.8/009494   0520040791
Pluralism (Social sciences) Minorities -- Switzerland. Religion and state -- Switzerland. Switzerland -- Politics and government. Switzerland -- Ethnic relations.

HN613.5.M47 1993
Mestrovic, Stjepan Gabriel.
Habits of the Balkan heart: social character and the fall of Communism/ by Stjepan G. Mestrovic with Slaven Letica and Miroslav Goreta. College Station: Texas A&M University Press, c1993. xiv, 181 p.
93-011072   306/.09496   0890965560
Political culture -- Balkan Peninsula. Post-communism -- Balkan Peninsula. Balkan Peninsula -- Social conditions.

HN650.O48.K53 1993
Kideckel, David A., 1948-
The solitude of collectivism: Romanian villagers to the revolution and beyond/ David A. Kideckel. Ithaca: Cornell University Press, 1993. xix, 255 p.
92-031985   306/.09498/2   0801427460
Collectivism -- Romania -- Olt Region. Socialism and society. Post-communism -- Romania -- Olt Region. Olt Region (Romania) -- Social conditions. Romania -- Social conditions -- 1945-1989.

HN650.5.A8.M33
McNeill, William Hardy, 1917-
The metamorphosis of Greece since World War II/ William H. McNeill. Chicago: University of Chicago Press, 1978. viii, 264 p.
77-026105   309.1/495/07   0226561569
Greece -- Social conditions. Greece -- Economic conditions -- 1918-1974. Greece -- Politics and government -- 20th century.

HN650.5.Z9.V58 2000
Tritle, Lawrence A., 1946-
From Melos to My Lai: war and survival/ Lawrence A. Tritle. London; Routledge, 2000. xv, 220 p.
99-055816   303.6/09495   0415171601
Violence -- Greece -- History. Violence -- United States -- History. Violence -- Cross-cultural studies.

HN650.7.A8.S68 1997
Southern European welfare states: between crisis and reform/ edited by Martin Rhodes. London; Frank Cass, 1997. 278 p.
97-010305   361.6/5/094   0714647888
Europe, Southern -- Social policy.

HN655.2-766 By region or country — Other regions or countries — Asia

HN655.2.C6.C67 2000
Rosegrant, Mark W.
Transforming the rural Asian economy: the unfinished revolution/ by Mark W. Rosegrant and Peter B.R. Hazell. New York: Oxford University Press, 2000. xxi, 512 p.
00-068153 307.1/412/095 0195924479
Rural development -- Asia. Agriculture -- Economic aspects -- Asia. Agricultural development projects -- Asia. Asia -- Economic conditions -- 1945-

HN656.G47 1987
Gerber, Haim.
The social origins of the modern Middle East/ Haim Gerber. Boulder, Colo.: L. Rienner; 1987. vii, 221 p.
86-021925 306/.0956 0931477638
Agriculture and state -- Turkey -- History. Agriculture -- Social aspects -- Middle East -- History. Land tenure -- Middle East -- History. Middle East -- Social conditions. Middle East -- History -- 1517- Middle East -- Politics and government.

HN656.5.A8.G63 1996
Gocek, Fatma Muge.
Rise of the bourgeoisie, demise of empire: Ottoman westernization and social change/ Fatma Muge Gocek. New York: Oxford University Press, 1996. vi, 220 p.
95-010331 306/.09561 0195099257
Social change -- Turkey. Middle class -- Turkey - - History. Turkey -- History -- Ottoman Empire, 1288-1918.

HN660.A8.G65 1996
Goldscheider, Calvin.
Israel's changing society: population, ethnicity, and development/ Calvin Goldscheider. Boulder, Colo.: Westview Press, c1996. xix, 271 p.
95-022944 306/.095694 20 0813377935
Israel -- Social conditions. Israel -- Population. Israel -- Ethnic relations.

HN660.A8.S63 1980
The Sociology of the Palestinians/ edited by Khalil Nakhleh and Elia Zureik. New York: St. Martin's Press, 1980. 238 p.
79-012706 301.45/19/275694 0312740735
Palestinian Arabs -- Social conditions.

HN660.A8.S83
Studies of Israeli society/ editor, Ernest Krausz. New Brunswick: Transaction Books, c1980-c1990 v. 1-5.
79-093045 306/.095694 087855369X
Kibbutzim. Israel -- Social conditions. Israel -- Emigration and immigration. Israel -- Ethnic relations.

HN660.Z9.E46 1997
Robinson, Glenn E., 1959-
Building a Palestinian state: the incomplete revolution/ Glenn E. Robinson. Bloomington: Indiana University Press, c1997. xiii, 228 p.
96-024708 305.52/095694 20 0253332176
Elite (Social sciences) -- Palestine. Intifada, 1987- Palestinian Arabs -- Politics and government. Palestine -- Politics and government.

HN660.Z9.S63 1989
Ben-Porat, Amir.
Divided we stand: class structure in Israel from 1948 to the 1980s/ Amir Ben-Porat. New York: Greenwood Press, 1989. xiv, 143 p.
89-007493 305.5/095694 0313264023
Social classes -- Israel. Social classes -- Israel -- Statistics. Israel -- Social conditions.

HN660.Z9.V57 1999
Sprinzak, Ehud.
Brother against brother: violence and extremism in Israeli politics from Altalena to the Rabin assassination/ Ehud Sprinzak. New York, NY: Free Press, c1999. xii, 366 p.
98-034983 303.6/09594/09045 21 0684853442
Rabin, Yitzhak, -- 1922- -- Assassination. Right-wing extremists -- Israel -- History. Orthodox Judaism -- Political aspects -- Israel. Political violence -- Israel -- History. Israel -- Politics and government.

HN664.Z9.C678 1988
Swagman, Charles F., 1952-
Development and change in highland Yemen/ Charles F. Swagman. Salt Lake City: University of Utah Press, 1988. xviii, 200 p.
88-020603 307.1/4/095332 0874802954
Rural development -- Yemen -- Case studies. Villages -- Yemen -- Case studies.

HN669.A8.I82
Ismael, Jacqueline S.
Kuwait: social change in historical perspective/ Jacqueline S. Ismael. Syracuse, N.Y.: Syracuse University Press, c1982. xii, 202 p.
81-021244 953/.67 0815622546
Kuwait -- Social conditions. Kuwait -- Economic conditions.

HN670.2.A8.F67 1993
Foran, John.
Fragile resistance: social transformation in Iran from 1500 to the revolution/ John Foran. Boulder: Westview Press, 1993. xiv, 452 p.
92-036456 306/.0955 0813384788
Social change. Iran -- Social conditions.

HN670.7.A8.M38 1991
Maung, Mya, 1933-
The Burma road to poverty/ Mya Maung; foreword by Everett E. Hagen. New York: Praeger, 1991. xxv, 333 p.
90-027555 306/.09591 0275936139
Socialism -- Burma. Burma -- Economic conditions -- 1948- Burma -- Social conditions. Burma -- Politics and government -- 1948-

HN670.8.A8.P454 1998
Perera, Nihal.
Society and space: colonialism, nationalism, and postcolonial identity in Sri Lanka/ Nihal Perera. Boulder, Colo.: Westview Press, 1998. 217 p.
97-050122 306/.095493 0813329795
Space (Architecture) -- Social aspects -- Sri Lanka. Spatial systems. Postcolonialism -- Sri Lanka. Sri Lanka -- Social conditions.

HN673.H75
Hsu, Cho-yun, 1930-
Ancient China in transition; an analysis of social mobility, 722-222 B.C. Stanford, Calif., Stanford University Press, 1965. viii, 238 p.
65-013110 301.440951
Social mobility -- China. China -- Social conditions.

HN680.C55.F7 1969
Fried, Morton H. 1923-1986.
Fabric of Chinese society; a study of the social life of a Chinese county seat, by Morton H. Fried. New York, Octagon Books, 1969 [c1953] xi, 243 p.
76-075993 309.1/51/225
Chu-hsien, China (Anhwei Province) -- Social conditions.

HN683.F69 1989
Fox, Richard Gabriel, 1939-
Gandhian Utopia: experiments with culture/ Richard G. Fox. Boston: Beacon Press, c1989. x, 330 p.
88-043315 303.4/84 0807041009
Gandhi, -- Mahatma, -- 1869-1948 -- Political and social views. Social movements -- India -- History -- 20th century. Utopias. India -- Civilization.

HN683.S5 1990
Shah, Ghanshyam.
Social movements in India: a review of the literature/ Ghanshyam Shah. New Delhi; Sage Publications, 1990. 222 p.
90-020102 303.48/4/0954 817036213X
Social movements -- India -- History.

HN683.5.B58 1990
Bonner, Arthur.
Averting the Apocalypse: social movements in India today/ Arthur Bonner. Durham: Duke University Press, 1990. vi, 467 p.
89-028006 303.48/4/0954 0822310481
Social movements -- India -- Case studies. Social action -- India -- Case studies. Social problems -- Case studies. India -- Social conditions -- 1947- -- Case studies.

HN683.5.C59 1990
Oommen, T. K., 1937-
Protest and change: studies in social movements/ T.K. Oommen. New Delhi: Sage Publications, 1990. 309 p.
90-036608 303.48/4/0954 8170361982
Social structure -- India. Social movements -- India.

HN687.S34.B37 1996
Basu, Aparna.
Mridula Sarabhai: rebel with a cause/ Aparna Basu. Delhi: Oxford University Press, 1996. ix, 275 p.
96-130172 303.48/4/092 0195631102
Sarabhai, Mrdula, -- 1911-1974. Social reformers -- India -- Biography.

HN690.R35.S74
Srinivas, Mysore Narasimhachar.
The remembered village/ M. N. Srinivas. Berkeley: University of California Press, c1976. xvi, 356 p.
75-007203 301.35/2/095487 0520029976
Villages -- India -- Rampura (Karnataka) Rampura, India (Karnataka) -- Rural conditions.

HN690.S97.H38 1991
Haynes, Douglas E.
Rhetoric and ritual in colonial India: the shaping of a public culture in Surat City, 1852-1928/ Douglas E. Haynes. Berkeley: University of California Press, c1991. xi, 363 p.
90-024309 306/.0954/75 0520067258
Elite (Social sciences) -- India -- Surat -- History. Surat (India) -- Social conditions. Surat (India) -- Politics and government.

HN690.Z9.C6846 1995
Varshney, Ashutosh, 1957-
Democracy, development, and the countryside: urban-rural struggles in India/ Ashutosh Varshney. Cambridge [England]; Cambridge University Press, 1995. x, 214 p.
94-027665 338.954 0521441536
Rural development -- India. Urbanization -- India. India -- Politics and government -- 1947-

HN690.Z9.C685376 1998
Village voices: forty years of rural transformation in South India/ [edited by] T. Scarlett Epstein, A.P. Suryanarayana, T. Thimmegowda. Thousand Oaks, CA: Sage Publications, 1998.
98-024646 303.4/0954 0761992650
Rural development -- India. Social change -- India. Villages -- India. India -- Rural conditions.

HN690.Z9.E464 1992
Mitra, Subrata Kumar, 1949-
Power, protest, and participation: local elites and the politics of development in India/ Subrata K. Mitra. London; Routledge, 1992. xvii, 315 p.
92-004000 305.5/2/0954 0415078407
Elite (Social sciences) -- India. Rural development -- India. Political participation -- India. India -- Politics and government -- 1947-

HN690.Z9.E466 1989
Navlakha, Suren, 1934-
Elite and social change: a study of elite formation in India/ Suren Navlakha. New Delhi; Sage Publications, 1989. 190 p.
89-039056 305.5/52/0954 0803996276
Elite (Social sciences) -- India. Social classes -- India.

HN690.Z9.M325 1989
Hartmann, Paul, 1938-
The mass media and village life: an Indian study/ Paul Hartmann, B.R. Patil, Anita Dighe. New Delhi; Sage Publications, 1989. 286 p.
88-018458 302.2/34/0954 0803995814
Mass media -- India -- Influence. Mass media in community development -- India. Communication in rural development -- India.

HN690.Z9.S6438 1997
Sharma, Kanhaiyalal.
Social stratification in India: issues and themes/ K.L. Sharma. Thousand Oaks, Calif.: Sage Publications, 1997.
97-003382 305.5/0954 0803993625
Social classes -- India. Caste -- India.

HN690.6.A8.G37 1995
Gardner, Katy.
Global migrants, local lives: travel and transformation in rural Bangladesh/ Katy Gardner. Oxford [England]: Clarendon Press; 1995. x, 301 p.
94-029636 304.8/095492 0198279191
Return migration -- Bangladesh. Bangladesh -- Emigration and immigration. Bangladesh -- Rural conditions.

HN700.C32.H54
Hildebrand, George C.
Cambodia: starvation and revolution/ George C. Hildebrand, Gareth Porter. New York: Monthly Review Press, c1976. 124 p.
76-001646 320.9/596/04 0853453829
Starvation. Food supply -- Cambodia. Cambodia -- Rural conditions. Cambodia -- History -- Civil War, 1970-1975.

HN700.4.A8.E9 1990
Evans, Grant, 1948-
Lao peasants under Socialism/ Grant Evans. New Haven: Yale University Press, c1990. xv, 268 p.
89-070466 307.72/09594 0300045980
Peasantry -- Laos -- History. Collectivization of agriculture -- Laos -- History. Socialism -- Laos -- History. Laos -- Rural conditions.

HN700.5.A8.V55 1995
Vietnam's rural transformation/ edited by Benedict J. Tria Kerkvliet and Doug J. Porter. Boulder, Colo.: Westview Press; c1995. xiv, 251 p.
95-015855 307.1/412/09597 20 081338950X
Rural development -- Vietnam. Vietnam -- Rural conditions.

HN700.55.Z9.C634 1990
Hirsch, Philip, 1957-
Development dilemmas in rural Thailand/ Philip Hirsch. Singapore; Oxford University Press, 1990. xvii, 244 p.
90-035056 307.1/412/09593 0195889681
Rural development -- Thailand. Rural development -- Lan Sak (Thailand: Amphoe) -- Case studies.

HN700.67.A8.T76 1990
Trocki, Carl A.
Opium and empire: Chinese society in Colonial Singapore, 1800-1910/ Carl Trocki. Ithaca, N.Y.: Cornell University Press, c1990. xiv, 260 p.
90-055123 306/.095957 0801423902
Chinese -- Singapore -- History -- 19th century. Opium trade -- Singapore -- History -- 19th century. Alien labor, Chinese -- Singapore -- History -- 19th century. Singapore -- Social conditions.

HN703.5.I494 2000
Indonesia in transition: social aspects of reformasi and crisis/ edited by Chris Manning & Peter Van Diermen. New York: Zed Books, 2000.
00-043592 306/.09598 1856499235
Indonesia -- Social policy. Indonesia -- Social conditions. Indonesia -- Economic policy.

HN710.M6.G4 1975
Geertz, Clifford.
The social history of an Indonesian town/ Clifford Geertz. Westport, Conn.: Greenwood Press, 1975, c1965. v, 217 p.
75-029282 309.1/598/2 0837184312
Java (Indonesia) -- Social conditions -- Case studies. Modjokerto, Indonesia -- Social conditions.

HN713.P45 1982
Philippine social history: global trade and local transformations/ edited by Alfred W. McCoy & Ed. C. de Jesus. Quezon City, Metro Manila: Ateneo de Manila University Press, 1982. vi, 479 p.
82-244917 306/.09599 9710200062
Philippines -- Social conditions. Philippines -- Commerce.

HN720.Z9.C66417 1995
Nazarea, Virginia D. 1954-
Local knowledge and agricultural decision making in the Philippines: class, gender, and resistance/ Virginia D. Nazarea-Sandoval. Ithaca: Cornell University Press, 1995. xiii, 226 p.
94-003500 338.9599/1 0801428017
Rural development -- Philippines -- Kabaritan. Traditional farming -- Philippines -- Kabaritan. Agriculture -- Philippines -- Kabaritan -- Decision making. Kabaritan (Philippines) -- Social life and customs.

HN720.5.A8
Tang, Kwong-Leung.
Social welfare development in East Asia/ Kwong-leung Tang. Houndmills, Basingstoke, Hampshire [England]; Palgrave, 2000. viii, 214 p.
00-027538 361.6/1/095 0312234864
Public welfare -- East Asia. East Asia -- Social policy.

HN723.S7 1997
Sugimoto, Yoshio, 1939-
An introduction to Japanese society/ Yoshio Sugimoto. Cambridge; Cambridge University Press, 1997. x, 285 p.
96-028229 306/.0952 0521416922
National characteristics, Japanese. Japan -- Social life and customs. Japan -- Social conditions.

HN723.W56 1995
White, James W. 1941-
Ikki: social conflict and political protest in early modern Japan/ James W. White. Ithaca: Cornell University Press, 1995. xiii, 348 p.
95-016279 303.6/0952 0801431549
Social conflict -- Japan -- History. Peasant uprisings -- Japan -- History. Japan -- Social conditions -- 1600-1868. Japan -- Politics and government -- 1600-1868.

HN723.W673 1997
Woronoff, Jon.
The Japanese social crisis/ Jon Woronoff. Houndmills, Basingstoke, Hampshire: Macmillan Press LTD; 1997. viii, 287 p.
96-046623 301/.0952 0312172613
National characteristics, Japanese. Japan -- Social conditions -- 1945-

HN723.5.K756 1996
Kumagai, Fumie.
Unmasking Japan today: the impact of traditional values on modern Japanese society/ Fumie Kumagai with the assistance of Donna J. Keyser. Westport, Conn.: Praeger, 1996. xi, 192 p.
95-023224 306/.0952 0275951448
Social values -- Japan -- History -- 20th century. Japan -- Social life and customs -- 20th century. Japan -- Social conditions -- 1945-

HN723.5.S578 2000
Social attitudes in Japan: trends and cross-national perspectives/ by Masamichi Sasaki & Tatsuzo Suzuki; [with a preface by Alex Inkeles]. Leiden; Boston: Brill, 2000. xix, 298 p.
00-039801 303.3/8/0952 9004118535
Attitude (Psychology) Public opinion -- Japan. Japan -- Social conditions -- 1945- -- Public opinion.

HN723.5.V63
Vogel, Ezra F.
Japan as number one: lessons for America/ Ezra F. Vogel. Cambridge, Mass.: Harvard University Press, 1979. xi, 272 p.
78-024059 309.1/52/04 0674472152
Japan -- Social conditions -- 1945- Japan -- Economic conditions -- 1945-1989. Japan -- Politics and government -- 1945-

HN726.R44 1988
Reflections on the way to the gallows: rebel women in prewar Japan/ translated and edited with an introduction by Mikiso Hane. Berkeley: University of California Press, c1988. viii, 275 p.
87-036649 303.4/84 0520062590
Women social reformers -- Japan -- Biography. Radicalism -- Japan -- History -- 20th century. Japan -- Social conditions -- 1912-1945.

HN727.F813 1972
Fukutake, Tadashi, 1917-
Japanese rural society. Translated by R. P. Dore. Ithaca, Cornell University Press [1972, c1967] xiv, 230 p.
72-004314 309.1/52/04 0801491274
Villages -- Japan. Japan -- Rural conditions.

HN730.T65.B47 1989
Bestor, Theodore C.
Neighborhood Tokyo/ Theodore C. Bestor. Stanford, Calif.: Stanford University Press, 1989. xvi, 347 p.
88-012383 307.3/362/0952135 0804714398
Neighborhood -- Japan -- Tokyo. Tokyo (Japan) -- Social conditions -- 1945-

HN730.Z9.E45 1993
Rothacher, Albrecht.
The Japanese power elite/ Albrecht Rothacher. New York: St. Martin's Press, 1993. xix, 311 p.
93-014245 305.5/2/0952 0312102917
Elite (Social sciences) -- Japan.

HN730.Z9.E49 1987
Verba, Sidney.
Elites and the idea of equality: a comparison of Japan, Sweden, and the United States/ Sidney Verba and Steven Kelman ... [et al.]. Cambridge, Mass.: Harvard University Press, 1987. x, 331 p.
87-007432 305.5/2 0674246853
Elite (Social sciences) -- Japan. Elite (Social sciences) -- Sweden. Elite (Social sciences) -- United States.

HN730.Z9.S654 1992
Ishida, Hiroshi.
Social mobility in contemporary Japan: educational credentials, class and the labour market in a cross-national perspective/ Hiroshi Ishida. Stanford, CA: Stanford University Press, 1993. xxi, 310 p.
91-068446 305.5/13/0952 0804720878
Social mobility -- Japan. Social classes -- Japan. Japan -- Social conditions -- 1945-

HN730.5.A8.A24 1996
Abelmann, Nancy.
Echoes of the past, epics of dissent: a South Korean social movement/ Nancy Abelmann. Berkeley: University of California Press, c1996. xviii, 306 p.
95-035055 303.48/4 20 0520085906
Social movements -- Korea (South) -- Case studies. Tenant farmers -- Korea (South) -- Political activity. Land tenure -- Korea (South)

HN730.5.Z9.C6674 1993
Villages astir: community development, tradition, and change in Korea/ John E. Turner ... [et al.]. Westport, Conn.: Praeger, 1993. viii, 350 p.
92-028549 307.76/2/09519 0275943720
Community development -- Korea. Villages -- Korea. Social change. Korea -- Social policy.

HN733.E25 1988
Eastman, Lloyd E.
Family, fields, and ancestors: constancy and change in China's social and economic history, 1550-1949/ Lloyd E. Eastman. New York: Oxford University Press, 1988. x, 267 p.
87-012320 306/.0951 0195052692
China -- Social conditions. China -- Economic conditions.

HN733.R85 1998
Ruf, Gregory A.
Cadres and kin: making a socialist village in West China, 1921-1991/ Gregory A. Ruf. Stanford, Calif.: Stanford University Press, 1998. xvii, 249 p.
98-016522 307.76/2/0951 0804733775
Villages -- China -- Case studies. Villages -- China -- History -- 20th century. Communism -- China -- History -- 20th century.

HN733.5.F75 1991
Friedman, Edward, 1934-
Chinese village, socialist state/ Edward Friedman, Paul G. Pickowicz, Mark Selden with Kay Ann Johnson. New Haven: Yale University Press, c1991. xxiv, 336 p.
90-071877 307.72/0951/15 0300046553
China -- Rural conditions.

HN733.5.P68 1990
Potter, Sulamith Heins.
China's peasants: the anthropology of a revolution/ by Sulamith Heins Potter and Jack M. Potter. Cambridge [England]; Cambridge University Press, 1990. xiv, 358 p.
89-031420 305.5/633/0951 0521355214
Communism -- China -- History. China -- Social conditions -- 1949- China -- Rural conditions.

HN733.5.S598 2000
Smith, Christopher J.
China in the post-Utopian age/ Christopher J. Smith. Boulder, CO: Westview Press, 2000. xviii, 629 p.
99-057687 306/.0951 0813319862
China -- Social conditions -- 1976- China -- Economic conditions -- 1976- China -- Social life and customs -- 1976-

HN733.5.Z94 1997
Zweig, David.
Freeing China's farmers: rural restructuring in the reform era/ David Zweig. Armonk, NY: M.E. Sharpe, c1997. xvii, 365 p.
97-016303 307.72/0951 1563248379
Rural development -- China. Land reform -- China. China -- Rural conditions.

HN740.H36.R69 1989
Rowe, William T.
Hankow: conflict and community in a Chinese city, 1796-1895/ William T. Rowe. Stanford, Calif.: Stanford University Press, 1989. x, 440 p.
89-031183 306/.0951 0804715416
Community organization -- China -- Hankou (Wuhan) Social conflict -- China -- Hankou (Wuhan) -- History -- 19th century. Working class -- China -- Hankou (Wuhan) -- History -- 19th century. Hankou (Wuhan, China) -- Social conditions.

HN740.H78.M3613 1990
Mao, Tse-tung, 1893-1976.
Report from Xunwu/ Mao Zedong; translated, and with an introduction and notes by Roger R. Thompson. Stanford, Calif.: Stanford University Press, 1990. ix, 278 p.
89-021776 324.251/075/09 0804716781
Hsun-wu hsien (China) -- Rural conditions.

HN740.K365.J56 1996
Jing, Jun, 1957-
The temple of memories: history, power, and morality in a Chinese village/ Jun Jing. Stanford, Calif.: Stanford University Press, 1996. viii, 217 p.
96-015406 306/.095145 0804727562
Kung family. Memory -- Social aspects -- China -- Gansu Sheng. Gansu Sheng (China) -- Social conditions.

HN740.S54
Liu, Xin, 1957-
In one's own shadow: an ethnographic account of the condition of post-reform rural China/ Xin Liu. Berkeley: University of California Press, c2000. xvi, 245 p.
99-031248 306/.0951/43 21 0520219937
Rural development -- China -- Shaanxi Sheng. Social change -- China -- Shaanxi Sheng. Shaanxi Sheng (China) -- Rural conditions. Shaanxi Sheng (China) -- Social life and customs.

HN740.T34
Goodman, David S. G.
Social and political change in revolutionary China: the Taihang Base area in the War of Resistance to Japan, 1937-1945/ David S.G. Goodman. Lanham: Rowman & Littlefield Publishers, c2000. xxxii, 345 p.
00-031109 303.4/0951 21 0742508641
Social change -- China -- Tai-hang Mountains Region. Sino-Japanese Conflict, 1937-1945. Tai-hang Mountains Region (China) -- Politics and government. Tai-hang Mountains Region (China) -- Social conditions.

HN740.T55.D37 1996
Dardess, John W., 1937-
A Ming society: Tai-ho County, Kiangsi, fourteenth to seventeenth centuries/ John W. Dardess. Berkeley: University of California Press, c1996. xi, 316 p.
96-003631 306/.0951/222 20 0520204255
Tai-ho hsien (Jiangxi Sheng, China) -- xSocial conditions. China -- History -- Ming dynasty, 1368-1644.

HN740.Z9.C633 1988
Duara, Prasenjit.
Culture, power, and the state: rural North China, 1900-1942/ Prasenjit Duara. Stanford, Calif.: Stanford University Press, 1988. viii, 326 p.
87-018173 307.7/2/09514 0804714452
Rural development -- China, Northwest -- History -- 20th century. Power (Social sciences) Local government -- China, North -- History -- 20th century. China -- Social conditions -- 1912-1949.

HN740.Z9.C6388 1992
Kelliher, Daniel Roy.
Peasant power in China: the era of rural reform, 1979-1989/ Daniel Kelliher. New Haven: Yale University Press, c1992. xx, 264 p.
92-014883 307.1/412/0951 0300054653
Rural development -- China -- History -- 20th century. Rural development -- Government policy -- China -- History -- 20th century. Private plot agriculture -- China -- History -- 20th century. China -- Rural conditions. China -- Politics and government -- 1976-

HN740.Z9.C668 1993
Putterman, Louis G.
Continuity and change in China's rural development: collective and reform eras in perspective/ Louis Putterman. New York: Oxford University Press, 1993. ix, 379 p.
92-018541 307.1/412/0951 0195078721
Rural development -- China.

HN740.Z9.C685 1996
Yang, Dali L.
Calamity and reform in China: state, rural society, and institutional change since the great leap famine/ Dali L. Yang. Stanford, Calif.: Stanford University Press, 1996. xv, 351 p.
95-030871   307.1/412/0951   0804725578
Rural development -- China. Agriculture and state -- China. Famines -- China. China -- Politics and government -- 1949-

HN740.Z9.E48
Zonis, Marvin, 1936-
The political elite of Iran. [Princeton] Princeton University Press, 1971. xvi, 389 p.
74-090966   301.44/92   0691030839
Elite (Social sciences) -- Iran. Iran -- Politics and government -- 1941-1979.

HN740.Z9.P65 1996
Lupher, Mark.
Power restructuring in China and Russia/ Mark Lupher. Boulder, Colo.: Westview Press, 1996. xv, 335 p.
96-005370   303.3/0951   0813325463
Power (Social sciences) -- China -- History. Power (Social sciences) -- Russia (Federation) -- History. Power (Social sciences) -- Soviet Union -- History. China -- Politics and government. Russia (Federation) -- Politics and government -- 1991- Soviet Union -- Politics and government.

HN740.Z9.V55 1990
Lewis, Mark Edward, 1954-
Sanctioned violence in early China/ Mark Edward Lewis. Albany: State University of New York Press, c1990. viii, 374 p.
88-037052   303.6/2/0951   079140076X
Violence -- China -- History. China -- Social conditions -- To 221 B.C. China -- History -- Warring States, 403-221 B.C.

HN749.L8.D44 1995
DeGlopper, Donald R. 1942-
Lukang: commerce and community in a Chinese city/ Donald R. DeGlopper. Albany: State University of New York Press, c1995. xi, 296 p.
95-002525   306/.095124/9 20   0791426890
Ethnology -- Taiwan -- Lu-kang chen. City and town life -- Taiwan -- Lu-kang chen. Lu-kang chen (Taiwan) -- Social conditions. Lu-kang chen (Taiwan) -- Economic conditions. Lu-kang chen (Taiwan) -- Social life and customs.

HN749.T35.M37 1996
Marsh, Robert Mortimer.
The great transformation: social change in Taipei, Taiwan since the 1960s/ Robert M. Marsh. Armonk, N.Y.: M.E. Sharpe, c1996. vii, 409 p.
96-006317   303.4/095124/9 20   1563247879
Social change -- Taiwan -- Taipei. Taipei (Taiwan) -- Social conditions.

HN766.A8.C86 1993
Cunningham, Robert, 1937-
Wasta: the hidden force in Middle Eastern society/ Robert B. Cunningham, Yasin K. Sarayrah. Westport, Conn.: Praeger, 1993. viii, 209 p.
92-036274   303.6/9   0275944026
Wasitah. Social exchange. Conflict management -- Arab countries. Arab countries -- Social life and customs.

HN773.5-803 By region or country — Other regions or countries — Africa

HN773.5.R53 1997
Richburg, Keith B.
Out of America: a black man confronts Africa/ Keith B. Richburg. New York: BasicBooks, c1997. xiv, 257 p.
96-043260   306/.0967 20   0465001874
Richburg, Keith B. -- Journeys -- Africa, Sub-Saharan. Human rights -- Africa, Sub-Saharan. Africa, Sub-Saharan -- Description and travel. Africa, Sub-Saharan -- Social conditions -- 1960-

HN777.S63 1991
Social development in Africa: strategies, policies, and programmes after the Lagos Plan/ editor, Duri Mohammed. London; published for the African Centre for Applied Res 1991. vi, 257 p.
90-042843   361.6/1/096   0905450280
Africa -- Social conditions -- 1960- Africa -- Social policy.

HN780.Z9.C6722 1991
Rural households in emerging societies: technology and change in sub-Saharan Africa/ edited by Margaret Haswell and Diana Hunt. Oxford; Berg; 1991. xiv, 261 p.
90-026657   307.1/412/0967   0854967303
Rural development -- Africa, Sub-Saharan. Rural development -- Africa, Sub-Saharan -- Case studies. Family farms -- Africa, Sub-Saharan.

HN781.A8.N67 1998S
North Africa in transition: state, society, and economic transformation in the 1990s/ Yahia H. Zoubir, editor; foreword by William B. Quandt. Gainesville, FL: University Press of Florida, 1998. xvi, 299 p.
98-039084   306/.0961   081301655X
Islam -- Africa, North. Africa, North -- Economic conditions. Africa, North -- Politics and government. Africa, North -- Social conditions.

HN784.A8.A53 1986
Anderson, Lisa, 1950-
The state and social transformation in Tunisia and Libya, 1830-1980/ Lisa Anderson. Princeton, N.J.: Princeton University Press, c1986. xxiv, 325 p.
85-043266   305/.0961/1   0691054622
Social structure -- Tunisia. Social structure -- Libya. Tunisia -- Rural conditions. Libya -- Rural conditions. Tunisia -- Politics and government.

HN786.A8.T65 1990
Toledano, Ehud R.
State and society in mid-nineteenth-century Egypt/ Ehud R. Toledano. Cambridge [England]; Cambridge University Press, 1990. xiv, 320 p.
89-009755   306/.0962/09034   0521371945
Social classes -- Egypt -- History -- 19th century. Egypt -- Social conditions. Egypt -- Rural conditions. Egypt -- Politics and government -- 640-1882.

HN786.C3.W55 1996
Wikan, Unni, 1944-
Tomorrow, God willing: self-made destinies in Cairo/ Unni Wikan. Chicago: University of Chicago Press, 1996. xvii, 333 p.
95-026658   306/.096216   0226898342
Poor -- Egypt -- Cairo. Cairo (Egypt) -- Social conditions.

HN787.Z9.C625 1997
Cole, David Chamberlin, 1928-
Between a swamp and a hard place: developmental challenges in remote rural Africa/ David C. Cole, Richard Huntington; with an afterword by Francis Mading Deng. [Cambridge, MA]: Harvard Institute for International Development c1997. xii, 297 p.
97-012483   307.1/412/09624 21   0674068602
Rural development -- Sudan -- Abyei District -- Case studies.

HN789.Z9.C643 1990
Ethiopia: options for rural development/ edited by Siegfried Pausewang ... [et al.]. London; Zed Books Ltd., 1990. 256 p.
90-039967   307.1/412/0963   0862329582
Rural development -- Ethiopia. Agriculture -- Economic aspects -- Ethiopia.

HN793.C63.P67 1991
Porter, Doug.
Development in practice: paved with good intentions/ Doug Porter, Bryant Allen, and Gaye Thompson. London; Routledge, 1991. xxi, 247 p.
90-039002   307.1/412/0967623   0415066263
Rural development -- Kenya -- Coast Province. Rural development projects -- Kenya -- Coast Province. Economic assistance -- Kenya -- Coast Province. Coast Province (Kenya) -- Economic policy.

HN793.K58.H37 1991
Hill, Martin J. D.
The harambee movement in Kenya: self-help, development, and education among the Kamba of Kitui district/ Martin J.D. Hill. London; Athlone Press, 1991. viii, 329 p.
90-032450   307.1/4/0967624   048519564X
Community development -- Kenya -- Kitui (District) Kamba (African people) -- Social conditions.

HN793.Z9.E44 1987
Harris, Joseph E., 1929-
Repatriates and refugees in a colonial society: the case of Kenya/ Joseph E. Harris. Washington, D.C.: Howard University Press, 1987. ix, 201 p.
87-003176   304.8/676/2   0882581481
Elite (Social sciences) -- Kenya -- History -- Case studies. Freedmen -- Kenya -- History -- Case studies. Return migration -- Kenya -- History -- Case studies. Kenya -- Colonization -- History.

HN797.Z9.S645 1990
Sender, John.
Poverty, class, and gender in rural Africa: a Tanzanian case study/ John Sender and Sheila Smith. London; Routledge, 1990. xii, 194 p.
90-032349   305.5/09678   0415052467
Social classes -- Tanzania -- Case studies. Women in development -- Tanzania -- Case studies. Rural development -- Tanzania -- Case studies. Tanzania -- Rural conditions -- Case studies.

HN800.A8.M86 1989
Mungazi, Dickson A.
The struggle for social change in southern Africa: visions of liberty/ Dickson A. Mungazi. New York: Crane Russak, 1989. xii, 144 p.
88-039163   306/.0968   0844815942
Apartheid. Africa, Southern -- Social conditions -- 1975- Africa, Southern -- Colonial influence.

HN801.A8.K44 1988
Keegan, Timothy J.
Facing the storm: portraits of Black lives in rural South Africa/ Tim Keegan. London: Zed Books; 1988. vi, 169 p.
88-025585   305.8/96068   0821409247
Blacks -- South Africa -- Social conditions -- Case studies.   South Africa -- Rural conditions -- Case studies.

HN801.A95.M39 1996
Mayekiso, Mzwanele.
Township politics: civic struggles for a new South Africa/ Mzwanele Mayekiso; edited by Patrick Bond; foreword by Mel King. New York: Monthly Review Press, 1996. 288 p.
95-033985   303.6/09682/1   0853459665
Social conflict -- South Africa -- Alexandra. Social movements -- South Africa -- Alexandra. Alexandra (South Africa) -- Politics and government.

HN801.Z9.E436 1989
Dreyer, Lynette, 1949-
The modern African elite of South Africa/ Lynette Dreyer. New York: St. Martin's Press, 1989. xii, 186 p.
88-007048   305.5/2/0968   0312016751
Elite (Social sciences) -- South Africa.   South Africa -- Social conditions -- 1961-

HN801.Z9.V53 1991
Chidester, David.
Shots in the streets: violence and religion in South Africa/ David Chidester. Boston: Beacon Press, c1991. xix, 220 p.
91-012834   303.6/0968   0807002186
Violence -- South Africa. Violence -- Religious aspects.

HN802.Z9.C648 1995
Mararike, C. G.
Grassroots leadership: the process of rural development in Zimbabwe/ C.G. Mararike. Harare: University of Zimbabwe Publications, c1995. xiv, 114 p.
95-981787   307.1/412/096891 20   090830739X
Rural development -- Zimbabwe. Political leadership -- Zimbabwe.

HN803.Z9.V54 1981
Kaunda, Kenneth D. 1924-
The riddle of violence/ Kenneth Kaunda; edited by Colin M. Morris. San Francisco: Harper & Row, [1981] c1980. 184 p.
80-008348   303.6/2/096894   0062504509
Violence -- Zambia. Nonviolence.

HN833-930.9 By region or country — Other regions or countries — Australia

HN833.Z9.S66 1991
Mukonoweshuro, Eliphas G., 1953-
Colonialism, class formation, and underdevelopment in Sierra Leone/ Eliphas G. Mukonoweshuro. Lanham, Md.: University Press of America, 1991. x, 257 p.
91-014706   305.5/5/09664   0819182826
Middle class -- Sierra Leone -- History. Capitalism -- Sierra Leone -- History. Decolonization -- Sierra Leone -- History. Sierra Leone -- Social conditions -- To 1961. Sierra Leone -- Economic conditions -- To 1896. Sierra Leone -- Economic conditions -- 1896-1961.

HN835.Z9.S65
Hlophe, Stephen S.
Class, ethnicity, and politics in Liberia: a class analysis of power struggles in the Tubman and Tolbert administrations, from 1944-1975/ Stephen S. Hlophe. Washington, D.C.: University Press of America, c1979. 317 p.
79-063261   306/.2/096662   0819107212
Social classes -- Liberia. Social conflict -- Liberia.   Liberia -- Ethnic relations. Liberia -- Politics and government -- 1944-1971. Liberia -- Politics and government -- 1971-1980.

HN850.N49.C68 1988
Cowlishaw, Gillian.
Black, white, or brindle: race in rural Australia/ Gillian Cowlishaw. Cambridge [England]; Cambridge University Press, c1988. iv, 297 p.
88-015027   307.7/2/0994   0521346606
Australian aborigines -- Australia -- New South Wales -- Social conditions.   New South Wales -- Rural conditions. New South Wales -- Race relations.

HN850.Z9.S6446 1991
Jamrozik, Adam.
Class, inequality, and the state: social change, social policy, and the new middle class/ Adam Jamrozik. South Melbourne: Macmillan, 1991. xx, 348 p.
91-185712   305.5/0994   0732902444
Social classes -- Australia. Equality -- Australia. Middle class -- Australia. Australia -- Social policy.

HN930.5.C36.H38 1991
Hatch, Elvin.
Respectable lives: social standing in rural New Zealand/ Elvin Hatch. Berkeley: University of California Press, c1992. vii, 214 p.
91-014963   307.72/099315/5   0520074726
Social structure -- New Zealand -- Canterbury. Occupational prestige -- New Zealand -- Canterbury.   Canterbury (N.Z.) -- Rural conditions.

HN930.9.A8S55 2000
Sillitoe, Paul.
Social change in Melanesia: development and history/ Paul Sillitoe. Cambridge; Cambridge University Press, 2000. xx, 264 p.
99-015845   306/.0995   0521778069
Melanesia -- Social conditions. Melanesia -- History.

HN939.5 By region or country — Other regions or countries — Pacific area. Pacific Ocean Islands

HN939.5.T34.L625 1992
Lockwood, Victoria S., 1953-
Tahitian transformation: gender and capitalist development in a rural society/ Victoria S. Lockwood. Boulder: Lynne Rienner Publishers, 1993. xii, 180 p.
92-024045   307.1/412/0996211   1555873170
Women in development -- French Polynesia -- Tahiti.   Tahiti -- Rural conditions. Rural development -- French Polynesia -- Tahiti.

HN980 By region or country — Developing countries — General works

HN980.A29 1987
Adjustment with a human face/ edited by Giovanni Andrea Cornia, Richard Jolly, and Frances Stewart. Oxford [Oxfordshire]: Clarendon Press; c1987-1988. 2 v.
87-011137   362.7/042   0198286090
Developing countries -- Social policy. Developing countries -- Economic policy. Child welfare -- Developing countries.

HN980.I59 1982
Introduction to the sociology of "developing societies"/ edited by Hamza Alavi and Teodor Shanin. New York: Monthly Review Press, c1982. xii, 474 p.
81-016892   909/.09724   0853455953
Developing countries -- Social conditions -- Addresses, essays, lectures.

HN980.W65 1982
Women and development: the sexual division of labor in rural societies: a study/ prepared for the International Labour Office within the framework of the World Employment Programme: edited by Lourdes Beneria. New York, N.Y.: Praeger, 1982. xxiii, 257 p.
82-000606   306/.36   0030618029
Women in rural development. Sexual division of labor. Rural development.

HN981 By region or country — Developing countries — Special topics, A-Z

HN981.C6.B47 1992
Berger, Guy.
Social structure and rural development in the Third World/ Guy Berger. Cambridge; Cambridge University Press, 1992. 186 p.
91-031982   307.1/412/091724   0521392586
Rural development -- Developing countries. Social structure -- Developing countries.

HN981.C6.M66 1988
Montgomery, John Dickey, 1920-
Bureaucrats and people: grassroots participation in Third World development/ John D. Montgomery. Baltimore: Johns Hopkins University Press, c1988. xviii, 140 p.
87-015344   307.1/4/091724   0801835410
Community development -- Developing countries. Bureaucracy -- Developing countries.

HN981.C6.R86 1990
Rural development and population: institutions and policy/ edited by Geoffrey McNicoll, Mead Cain; based on the Expert Consultation on Population and Agricultural and Rural Development convened by the Food and Agriculture Organization, Rome. New York: Population Council; 1990. vii, 366 p.
90-043047   307.1/412/091724   0195068475
Rural development -- Developing countries -- Congresses. Rural population -- Developing countries -- Congresses. Developing countries -- Rural conditions -- Congresses. Developing countries -- Social conditions -- Congresses.

HN981.C6.S63 1997
Smith, Alan G.
Human rights and choice in poverty: food insecurity, dependency, and human rights-based development aid for the Third World rural poor/ Alan G. Smith. Westport, Conn.: Praeger, 1997. viii, 182 p.
96-047616   307.1/412/091722   0275958264
Rural development -- Developing countries. Rural development projects -- Developing countries. Agricultural assistance -- Developing countries.

HN981.C6.S73 1992
Jazairy, Idriss.
The State of world rural poverty: an inquiry into its causes and consequences/ Idriss Jazairy, Mohiuddin Alamgir, Theresa Panuccio. New York, NY: Published for the International Fund for Agricul c1992. xxiii, 514 p.
92-000211   307.1/412/091724   0814737536
Rural development -- Developing countries. Agricultural development projects -- Developing countries. Rural poor -- Developing countries.

HN981.C6.U66 1998
Uphoff, Norman Thomas.
Reasons for success: learning from instructive experiences in rural development/ Norman Uphoff, Milton J. Esman, Anirudh Krishna. West Hartford, Conn: Kumarian Press, 1998. x, 233 p.
97-038550   307.1/412/091724   1565490770
Rural development -- Developing countries. Agricultural development projects -- Developing countries. Human services -- Developing countries.

HQ The Family. Marriage. Women

HQ7 Congresses

HQ7.H68 1984
Households: comparative and historical studies of the domestic group/ edited by Robert McC. Netting, Richard R. Wilk, Eric J. Arnould. Berkeley: University of California Press, c1984. xxxviii, 480 p.
83-017975   306.8/5   0520049969
Households -- Congresses. Family -- Congresses. Social change -- Congresses.

HQ9 Dictionaries. Encyclopedias

HQ9.E52 1995
Encyclopedia of marriage and the family/ David Levinson, editor in chief. New York: Macmillan Library Reference USA; c1995. 2 v.
95-018682   306.8/03   002897235X
Marriage -- Encyclopedias. Family -- Encyclopedias.

HQ9.H846 1994
Human sexuality: an encyclopedia/ edited by Vern L. Bullough and Bonnie Bullough. New York: Garland Pub., 1994. xvii, 643 p.
93-032686   306.7/03   0824079728
Sex -- Dictionaries.

HQ10.5 Study and teaching. Research — By region or country, A-Z

HQ10.5.U6.H36 1993
Handbook of family life education/ edited by Margaret E. Arcus, Jay D. Schvaneveldt, J. Joel Moss. Newbury Park, Calif.: Sage Publications, c1993. 2 v.
93-026637   306.85/07   080394294X
Family life education -- United States -- Handbooks, manuals, etc.

HQ12 Sexual life — History. Sex customs — General

HQ12.B84
Bullough, Vern L.
Sexual variance in society and history/ Vern L. Bullough. New York: Wiley, c1976. xvi, 715 p.
75-038911   301.41/79   0471120804
Sex customs -- History. Sexual deviation -- History. Sex behavior -- History.

HQ12.M35 1991
Margulis, Lynn, 1938-
Mystery dance: on the evolution of human sexuality/ Lynn Margulis and Dorion Sagan. New York: Summit Books, c1991. 224 p.
91-018450   306.7/09   0671633414
Sex -- History. Sex (Biology) -- History.

HQ12.M57
Montagu, Ashley, 1905-
Sex, man, and society. New York, Putnam [1969] 287 p.
70-081653   392
Sex customs -- History.

HQ13-16 Sexual life — History. Sex customs — By period

HQ13.B44 1990
Before sexuality: the construction of erotic experience in the ancient Greek world/ David M. Halperin, John J. Winkler, and Froma I. Zeitlin, editors. Princeton, N.J.: Princeton University Press, c1990. xix, 526 p.
89-010548   306.7/0938   0691035385
Sex customs -- Greece -- History. Sex (Psychology) Sex role -- Greece -- History.

HQ14.B84 1982
Bullough, Vern L.
Sexual practices & the medieval church/ Vern L. Bullough & James Brundage. Buffalo, N.Y.: Prometheus Books, 1982. xii, 289 p.
80-085227   261.8/357   087975141X
Sex customs -- History. Sex (Theology) -- History of doctrines -- Middle Ages -- 600-1500.

HQ16.A38 2001
Altman, Dennis.
Global sex/ Dennis Altman. Chicago: University of Chicago Press, 2001. xii, 216 p.
00-036884   306.7   0226016064
Sex customs. Globalization.

HQ16.H85
Human sexual behavior; variations in the ethnographic spectrum. Edited by Donald S. Marshall and Robert C. Suggs. New York, Basic Books [1971] xviii, 302 p.
78-135552   392/.6   0465031579
Sex customs -- Case studies.

HQ16.P67 1992
Posner, Richard A.
Sex and reason/ Richard A. Posner. Cambridge, Mass.: Harvard University Press, 1992. vii, 458 p.
91-030700   306.7   0674802799
Sex -- Economic aspects. Sex customs. Sex and law.

HQ18 Sexual life — History. Sex customs — By region or country, A-Z

HQ18.B7.C38 1999
Caulfield, Sueann.
In defense of honor: sexual morality, modernity, and nation in early twentieth century Brazil/ by Sueann Caulfield. Durham, N.C.: Duke University Press, 1999. xiv, 311 p.
99-028323   306.7/0981/0904   082232377X
Sex customs -- Brazil -- History -- 20th century. Sexual ethics -- Brazil -- History -- 20th century. Virginity -- Brazil -- History -- 20th century.

HQ18.C6.C53813 1997
Sexual behavior in modern China: report on the nationwide survey of 20,000 men and women = [Chung-kuo tang tai hsing wen hua]/ Dalin Liu ... [et al.]; English-language edition by Man lun Ng and Erwin J. Haeberle. New York: Continuum, 1997. 569 p.
96-001072   306.7/0951   0826408869
Chinese -- Sexual behavior. Sexual ethics -- China. Sexual behavior surveys -- China.

HQ18.E8.M67 1985
Mosse, George L. 1918-
Nationalism and sexuality: respectability and abnormal sexuality in modern Europe/ George L. Mosse. New York: H. Fertig, 1985. viii, 232 p.
84-006082   306.7/094   0865273502
Sex customs -- Europe -- History. Sexual ethics -- Europe -- History. Middle class -- Europe -- Conduct of life.

HQ18.G7.A7 1995
Anderson, Patricia
When passion reigned: sex and the Victorians/ by Patricia Anderson. New York: BasicBooks, c1995. x, 209 p.
95-004108   306.7/0941 20   0465089917
Sex customs -- Great Britain -- History -- 19th century. Great Britain -- Social life and customs -- 19th century.

HQ18.G7.M28 1994
Mason, Michael, 1941-
The making of Victorian sexuality/ Michael Mason. Oxford; Oxford University Press, 1994. 338 p.
93-028824   306.7/0942   0198122470
Sex customs -- Great Britain -- History -- 19th century. Sexual ethics -- Great Britain -- History -- 19th century.

HQ18.G7.P67 1995
Porter, Roy, 1946-
The facts of life: the creation of sexual knowledge in Britain, 1650-1950/ Roy Porter and Lesley Hall. New Haven: Yale University Press, 1995. xii, 415 p.
94-021091 306.7/0941 0300062214
Sexology -- Great Britain -- History. Sex instruction literature -- Great Britain -- History.

HQ18.M53.B35 1999
Bailey, Beth L., 1957-
Sex in the heartland/ Beth Bailey. Cambridge, Mass.: Harvard University Press, 1999. vii, 265 p.
99-021754 306.7/0977 0674802780
Sex customs -- Middle West -- History -- 20th century. Sexual ethics -- Middle West -- History -- 20th century.

HQ18.U5.A38 2000
Allyn, David
Make love, not war: the sexual revolution, an unfettered history/ David Allyn. Boston, Mass: Little, Brown, c2000. xi, 381 p.
99-033784 306.7/0973 21 0316039306
Sex customs -- United States -- History -- 20th century. Sexual ethics -- United States -- History -- 20th century. Sex in popular culture -- United States -- History -- 20th century. United States -- Moral conditions -- History -- 20th century. United States -- Social life and customs -- 20th century.

HQ18.U5.D45 1988
D'Emilio, John.
Intimate matters: a history of sexuality in America/ John D'Emilio and Estelle B. Freedman. New York: Harper & Row, c1988. xx, 428 p.
87-045608 306.7/0973 0060158557
Sex customs -- United States -- History.

HQ18.U5.K5
Kinsey, Alfred C. 1894-1956.
Sexual behavior in the human male [by] Alfred C. Kinsey. Wardell B. Pomeroy [and] Clyde E. Martin. Philadelphia, W. B. Saunders Co., 1948. xv, 804 p.
48-005195 392.6
Sexual behavior surveys -- United States.

HQ18.U5.R45 2000
God forbid religion and sex in American public life/ edited by Kathleen M. Sands. Oxford; Oxford University Press, 2000. x, 269 p.
99-046265 291.1/78357/0973 0195121627
Sexual ethics -- United States. Sex -- United States -- Religious aspects. Sex and law -- United States.

HQ18.U5.S59 1994
The social organization of sexuality: sexual practices in the United States/ Edward O. Laumann ... [et al.]. Chicago: University of Chicago Press, 1994. xxxii, 718 p.
94-003736 306.7/0973 0226469573
Sex customs -- United States. Sexual behavior surveys -- United States.

HQ18.3 Sexual life — Biography of sexologists — Collective

HQ18.3.R6
Robinson, Paul A., 1940-
The modernization of sex: Havelock Ellis, Alfred Kinsey, William Masters, and Virginia Johnson/ Paul Robinson. New York: Harper & Row, c1976. viii, 200 p.
75-024500 301.41/792/2 0060135832
Ellis, Havelock, -- 1859-1939. Kinsey, Alfred C. -- (Alfred Charles), -- 1894-1956. Masters, William H. Sexologists -- Biography. Sex -- Research -- History.

HQ18.32 Sexual life — Biography of sexologists — Individual, A-Z

HQ18.32.K56.J65 1997
Jones, James H. 1943-
Alfred C. Kinsey: a public/private life/ James H. Jones. New York: W.W. Norton, c1997. xx, 937 p.
97-027506 306.7/0973 21 0393040860
Kinsey, Alfred C. -- (Alfred Charles), -- 1894-1956. Sexologists -- United States -- Biography. Sexology -- United States.

HQ21-23 Sexual life — Sexual behavior and attitudes. Sexuality — General

HQ21.B95 1994
Buss, David M.
The evolution of desire: strategies of human mating/ David M. Buss. New York: BasicBooks, 1994. x, 262 p.
93-021113 306.7 0465077501
Sex. Sex (Psychology) Sexual attraction.

HQ21.C449 1984
Chafetz, Janet Saltzman.
Sex and advantage: a comparative, macro-structural theory of sex stratification/ Janet Saltzman Chafetz. Totowa, N.J.: Rowman & Allanheld, 1984. x, 134 p.
83-019077 305.4/2 0865981590
Sex discrimination against women. Social structure. Discrimination in employment.

HQ21.I68 1997
The International encyclopedia of sexuality/ edited by Robert T. Francoeur; preface by Timothy Perper; introduction by Ira L. Reiss. New York: Continuum, 1997-2001. 4 v.
95-016481 306.7/03 0826408419
Sex - Encyclopedias. Sex customs -- Encyclopedias.

HQ21.M46157 1985
Masters, William H.
Human sexuality/ William H. Masters, Virginia E. Johnson, Robert C. Kolodny. Boston: Little, Brown, c1985. xxi, 698 p.
84-017171 612/.6 0316549959
Sex. Sex (Psychology) Sex (Biology)

HQ21.M464
Mead, Margaret, 1901-1978.
Male and female, a study of the sexes in a changing world. New York, W. Morrow, 1949. xii, 477 p.
49-010784 392
Sex. Women. Men.

HQ21.P68 1983
Powers of desire: the politics of sexuality/ edited by Ann Snitow, Christine Stansell, and Sharon Thompson. New York: Monthly Review Press, c1983. 489 p.
82-048037 306.7 0853456097
Sex -- History -- 19th century. Sex -- History -- 20th century. Power (Social sciences)

HQ21.R415 1990
Reinisch, June Machover.
The Kinsey Institute new report on sex: what you must know to be sexually literate/ June M. Reinisch with Ruth Beasley; edited and compiled by Debra Kent. New York: St. Martin's Press, c1990. xx, 540 p.
90-041444 306.7/0973 0312052685
Sex. Hygiene, Sexual. Sex customs -- United states.

HQ21.S478 2000
Sexuality, society, and feminism/ edited by Cheryl B. Travis and Jacquelyn W. White. Washington, DC: American Psychological Assoc., c2000. viii, 432 p.
99-044905 306.7 21 1557986177
Sex. Sexual ethics. Sex (Psychology)

HQ23.A25 1995
Abramson, Paul R., 1949-
With pleasure: thoughts on the nature of human sexuality/ Paul R. Abramson, Steven D. Pinkerton. New York: Oxford University Press, 1995. xi, 308 p.
94-044883 306.7 0195093585
Sex. Sexual excitement. Pleasure.

HQ27.5-29 Sexual life — Sexual behavior and attitudes. Sexuality — By sex, age, or other special groups

HQ27.5.O34 1995
Odem, Mary E.
Delinquent daughters: protecting and policing adolescent female sexuality in the United States, 1885-1920/ Mary E. Odem. Chapel Hill: University of North Carolina Press, c1995. xiv, 265 p.
95-013185 306.7/0835 0807822159
Teenage girls -- United States -- Sexual behavior -- History. Sexual ethics -- United States -- History. Social problems -- United States -- History.

HQ27.5.W65 1997
Wolf, Naomi.
Promiscuities: the secret struggle for womanhood/ Naomi Wolf. New York: Random House, c1997. xxx, 286 p.
96-046724 306.7/0835/2 21 067941603X
Teenage girls -- United States -- Sexual behavior. Women -- United States -- Sexual behavior. United States -- Social conditions -- 1960-1980.

HQ29.M35 1998
Maines, Rachel P.
The technology of orgasm: "hysteria," the vibrator, and women's sexual satisfaction/ Rachel P. Maines. Baltimore, Md: The Johns Hopkins University Press, 1998. xviii, 181 p.
98-020213   306.7/082/09   0801859417
Women -- Sexual behavior -- History. Female orgasm -- History. Anorgasmy -- History.

HQ29.M46 1994
McCormick, Naomi B.
Sexual salvation: affirming women's sexual rights and pleasures/ Naomi B. McCormick; forewords by Elizabeth Rice Allgeier and Albert Ellis. Westport, Conn.: Praeger, 1994. xiv, 284 p.
94-006378   306.7/082   0275943593
Women -- Sexual behavior. Sexual ethics for women.

HQ31 Sexual life — Sex instruction and sexual ethics — Practical works. Popular manuals. Scientific treatises

HQ31.F65413 1991
Flandrin, Jean Louis.
Sex in the Western world: the development of attitudes and behaviour/ by Jean-Louis Flandrin; translated from the French by Sue Collins. Chur, Switzerland; Harwood Academic Publishers, c1991. vi, 368 p.
91-007646   306.7/094   3718652013
Sexual ethics -- Europe -- History. Sex customs -- Europe -- History.

HQ32 Sexual life — Sex instruction and sexual ethics — Sexual ethics

HQ32.H3 1999
Haag, Pamela.
Consent: sexual rights and the transformation of American liberalism/ Pamela Haag. Ithaca [N.Y.]: Cornell University Press, 1999. xx, 232 p.
99-013288   176   080142142X
Sexual ethics -- United States. Sexual consent -- United States. Women's rights -- United States.

HQ32.H822
Human sexuality, new directions in American Catholic thought: a study/ commissioned by the Catholic Theological Society of America; Anthony Kosnik, chairperson ... [et al.]. New York: Paulist Press, c1977. xvi, 322 p.
77-074586   261.8/343   0809102234
Sexual ethics -- United States. Sex -- Religious aspects -- Christianity.

HQ32.W367 1999
Warner, Michael, 1958-
The trouble with normal: sex, politics, and the ethics of queer life/ Michael Warner. New York: Free Press, 1999. ix, 227 p.
99-044356   306.76/6   0684865297
Sexual ethics. Homosexuality. Gays.

HQ57.5 Sexual life — Sex instruction and sexual ethics — Sex teaching

HQ57.5.A3.M66 2000
Moran, Jeffrey P.
Teaching sex: the shaping of adolescence in the 20th century/ Jeffrey P. Moran. Cambridge, Mass.: Harvard University Press, 2000. x, 281 p.
99-054303   613.9/071
Sex instruction -- United States -- History. Sex instruction for teenagers -- United States -- History. Sexual ethics for teenagers -- United States -- History.

HQ57.5.A3.S489 1992
Sexuality and the curriculum: the politics and practices of sexuality education/ edited by James T. Sears. New York: Teachers College Press, c1992. xv, 366 p.
91-043984   305.3/07/073   0807731536
Sex instruction -- United States. Sex instruction -- United States -- Curricula.

HQ60 Sexual life — Sex instruction and sexual ethics — Sex research

HQ60.I79 1990
Irvine, Janice M.
Disorders of desire: sex and gender in modern American sexology/ Janice M. Irvine. Philadelphia: Temple University Press, 1990. xii, 345 p.
89-036961   306.7/0973   087722689X
Sex -- Research -- United States. Sexology -- United States.

HQ71 Sexual life — Sexual deviations — General works

HQ71.A4
Allen, Charlotte Vale, 1941-
Daddy's girl/ by Charlotte Vale Allen. New York: Wyndham Books, c1980. 255 p.
80-013778   306.7   0671610244
Allen, Charlotte Vale, -- 1941-   Incest -- Biography.

HQ71.J58 1992
Johnson, Janis Tyler.
Mothers of incest survivors: another side of the story/ Janis Tyler Johnson. Bloomington: Indiana University Press, c1992. xi, 162 p.
91-046253   306.877   0253330963
Incest victims -- Family relationships -- Case studies. Mothers and daughters -- Case studies.

HQ71.L24 1990
La Fontaine, J. S. 1931-
Child sexual abuse/ Jean La Fontaine. Cambridge, UK; Polity Press, c1990. viii, 248 p.
89-078236   362.7/6   0745605613
Child sexual abuse.

HQ71.S424 1981
Sexually abused children and their families/ edited by Patricia Beezley Mrazek and C. Henry Kempe. Oxford; Pergamon Press, 1981. xii, 271 p.
80-042146   306.7   0080267963
Sexually abused children -- Family relationships. Incest victims -- Family relationships. Child sexual abuse.

HQ72 Sexual life — Sexual deviations — By region or country, A-Z

HQ72.C3.B34 1990
Bagley, Christopher.
Child sexual abuse: the search for healing/ Christopher Bagley and Kathleen King. London; Tavistock/Routledge, 1990. ix, 276 p.
88-036431   362.7/044   0415006058
Child sexual abuse -- Canada. Sexually abused children -- Services for -- Canada. Child sexual abuse -- United States.

HQ72.U53.W87 1992
Wurtele, Sandy K. 1955-
Preventing child sexual abuse: sharing the responsibility/ Sandy K. Wurtele and Cindy L. Miller-Perrin. Lincoln: University of Nebraska Press, c1992. xiii, 285 p.
92-003600   362.7/6   0803247532
Child sexual abuse -- United States. Child sexual abuse -- United States -- Prevention.

HQ75 Sexual life — Homosexuality. Lesbianism — Serials

HQ75.H63 1998
Hogan, Steve.
Completely queer: the Gay and Lesbian encyclopedia/ Steve Hogan and Lee Hudson. New York: Henry Holt, 1998. xiii, 704 p.
96-022676   305.9/0664   0805036296
Gays -- Encyclopedias. Gay men -- Encyclopedias. Lesbians -- Encyclopedias.

HQ75.15 Sexual life — Homosexuality. Lesbianism — Gay and lesbian studies

HQ75.15.L47 1996
The new lesbian studies: into the twenty-first century/ edited by Bonnie Zimmerman and Toni A. H. McNaron; foreword by Margaret Cruikshank. New York: Feminist Press at the City University of New Yor 1996. xix, 295 p.
95-050927   306.76/07   1558611363
Gay and lesbian studies. Women's studies.

HQ75.2 Sexual life — Homosexuality. Lesbianism — Biography (Collective)

HQ75.2.R63 1999
Robinson, Paul A., 1940-
Gay lives: homosexual autobiography from John Addington Symonds to Paul Monette/ Paul Robinson. Chicago: University of Chicago Press, 1999. xxiii, 428 p.
98-024460   306.76/62/0922   0226721809
Gays -- Biography.

HQ75.5-75.6 Sexual life — Homosexuality. Lesbianism — Lesbians

HQ75.5.C36 1995
Card, Claudia.
Lesbian choices/ Claudia Card. New York: Columbia University Press, c1995. xv, 310 p.
94-012527 305.48/9664 0231080085
Lesbianism. Choice (Psychology)

HQ75.5.F33 1981b
Faderman, Lillian.
Surpassing the love of men: romantic friendship and love between women from the Renaissance to the present/ Lillian Faderman. New York: Morrow, 1981. 496 p.
80-024482 306.7/6/09 068803733X
Lesbianism -- History. Lesbians -- Psychology. Love.

HQ75.5.L4395 2000
Lesbian histories and cultures: an encyclopedia/ Bonnie Zimmerman, editor. New York: Garland Pub., 2000. lvi, 862 p.
99-045010 306.76/6/03 0815319207
Lesbianism -- Encyclopedias. Lesbians -- Encyclopedias.

HQ75.53.B87 1993
Burke, Phyllis, 1951-
Family values: two moms and their son/ Phyllis Burke. New York: Random House, c1993. xvi, 233 p.
92-053818 306.874 0679421882
Lesbian mothers -- California -- San Francisco. Lesbian couples -- California -- San Francisco. Children of gay parents -- California -- San Francisco.

HQ75.53.L49 1993
Lewin, Ellen.
Lesbian mothers: accounts of gender in American culture/ Ellen Lewin. Ithaca, N.Y.: Cornell University Press, 1993. xviii, 233 p.
92-054977 306.874/3/086643 0801428572
Lesbian mothers -- United States. Single mothers -- United States.

HQ75.6.E5 T73 2002
Traub, Valerie,
The renaissance of lesbianism in early modern England/ Valerie Traub. Cambridge; Cambridge University Press, 2002. xvi, 492 p.
2001-037954 306.76/63/0942 21 0521448859
Lesbianism -- England -- History -- 16th century. Lesbianism -- England -- History -- 17th century. Lesbianism in literature.

HQ75.6.U5.F35 1999
Faderman, Lillian.
To believe in women: what lesbians have done for America--a history/ Lillian Faderman. Boston: Houghton Mifflin, 1999. xii, 434 p.
99-026209 305.48/9664/0973 039585010X
Lesbian feminism -- United States -- History. Lesbians -- United States -- History.

HQ75.6.U5.F73 1996
Franzen, Trisha, 1951-
Spinsters and lesbians: independent womanhood in the United States/ Trisha Franzen. New York: New York University Press, c1996. xxvii, 229 p.
95-032464 306.76/63 20 0814726410
Lesbianism -- United States. Single women -- United States. Feminism -- United States.

HQ75.8-76.2 Sexual life — Homosexuality. Lesbianism — Gay men

HQ75.8.H39.T56 1990
Timmons, Stuart, 1957-
The trouble with Harry Hay: founder of the modern gay movement/ by Stuart Timmons. Boston: Alyson, 1990. xvii, 317 p.
90-045443 306.76/62/092 1555831753
Hay, Harry. Gay liberation movement -- United States -- History -- 20th century. Actors -- United States -- Biography. Communists -- United States -- Biography.

HQ76.B438 1981
Bell, Alan P., 1932-
Sexual preference, its development in men and women/ Alan P. Bell, Martin S. Weinberg, Sue Kiefer Hammersmith. Bloomington: Indiana University Press, c1981. xii, 242 p.
81-047006 306.7/6 0253166721
Homosexuality. Homosexuality -- Social aspects. Homosexuality -- Psychological aspects.

HQ76.2.U5.B45
Bell, Alan P., 1932-
Homosexualities: a study of diversity among men and women/ Alan P. Bell, Martin S. Weinberg. New York: Simon and Schuster, c1978. 505 p.
78-007398 301.41/57/0973 0671242121
Homosexuality -- United States.

HQ76.2.U5.G37 1991
Gay culture in America: essays from the field/ edited by Gilbert Herdt. Boston: Beacon Press, c1992. x, 255 p.
91-012819 306/.1 0807079146
Gay men -- United States. Subculture -- United States. Gay communities -- United States.

HQ76.2.U5.H47 1993
Herdt, Gilbert H., 1949-
Children of Horizons: how gay and lesbian teens are leading a new way out of the closet/ Gilbert Herdt, Andrew Boxer. Boston: Beacon Press, c1993. xxi, 290 p.
92-041793 305.9/0664 0807079286
Gay teenagers -- United States. Coming out (Sexual orientation) -- United States. Closeted gays -- United States.

HQ76.2.U5.K39 1993
Kayal, Philip M., 1943-
Bearing witness: Gay Men's Health Crisis and the politics of AIDS/ Philip M. Kayal. Boulder: Westview Press, c1993. xxii, 275 p.
92-040293 305.38/9664 0813317282
Gay men -- New York (State) -- New York -- Social conditions. Gay men -- New York (State) -- New York -- Attitudes. Volunteer workers in community health services -- New York (State) -- New York.

HQ76.2.U5.L46 1995
LeVay, Simon.
City of friends: a portrait of the gay and lesbian community in America/ Simon LeVay and Elisabeth Nonas. Cambridge, Mass.: MIT Press, c1995. xi, 456 p.
95-034824 306.76/0973 20 0262121948
Gay communities -- United States. Lesbian communities -- United States. Gay men -- United States -- Social conditions.

HQ76.2.U5.L68 1998
Loughery, John.
The other side of silence: men's lives and gay identities: a twentieth century history/ John Loughery. New York: H. Holt, 1998. xviii, 509 p.
97-042575 305.38/9664 0805038965
Gay men -- United States -- History -- 20th century. Gay men -- United States -- Social conditions. Gays -- United States -- Identity.

HQ76.25 Sexual life — Homosexuality. Lesbianism — General works

HQ76.25.E53 1990
Encyclopedia of homosexuality/ edited by Wayne Dynes; associate editors, Warren Johansson, William A. Percy; with the assistance of Stephen Donaldson. New York: Garland Pub., 1990. 2 v.
89-028128 306.76/6/03 0824065441
Homosexuality -- Dictionaries.

HQ76.25.F7 2001
Fone, Byrne R. S.
Homophobia: a history/ Byrne Fone. New York: Metropolitan Books, 2000. xi, 480 p.
99-087004 306.76/6/09 0805045597
Homophobia. Homosexuality -- History.

HQ76.25.H54 1997
Highwater, Jamake.
The mythology of transgression: homosexuality as metaphor/ Jamake Highwater. New York: Oxford University Press, 1997. 261 p.
96-020576 306.76/6/01 0195101804
Homosexuality -- Philosophy. Homosexuality -- Mythology. Homosexuality -- Religious aspects.

HQ76.25.L497 1996
LeVay, Simon.
Queer science: the use and abuse of research into homosexuality/ Simon LeVay. Cambridge, Mass.: MIT Press, c1996. x, 364 p.
96-012906 306.76/0723 20 0262121999
Homosexuality -- Research -- Social aspects. Sexual orientation -- Research -- Social aspects.

HQ76.25.M55 1992
Miller, Neil, 1945-
Out in the world: gay and lesbian life from Buenos Aires to Bangkok/ Neil Miller. New York: Random House, c1992. xviii, 365 p.
92-006309 305.9/0664 0679402411
Homosexuality. Gays. Lesbians.

HQ76.25.R87 1988
Ruse, Michael.
Homosexuality: a philosophical inquiry/ Michael Ruse. New York, NY: Blackwell, 1990. xi, 299 p.
87-030924 306.7/66 0631175539
Homosexuality -- Psychological aspects.

HQ76.25.S39 2001
Savin-Williams, Ritch C.
Mom, Dad. I'm gay: how families negotiate coming out/ by Ritch C. Savin-Williams. Washington, DC: American Psychological Association, c2001. xii, 276 p.
00-056910 306.874 21 1557987416
Gay youth -- Family relationships. Coming out (Sexual orientation) Parents of gays.

HQ76.3 Sexual life — Homosexuality. Lesbianism — By region or country, A-Z

HQ76.3.E8.B67
Boswell, John, 1947-1994.
Christianity, social tolerance, and homosexuality: gay people in Western Europe from the beginning of the Christian era to the fourteenth century/ John Boswell. Chicago: University of Chicago Press, c1980. xviii, 424 p.
79-011171   306.7/66/094   0226067106
Homosexuality -- Europe -- History -- To 1500. Homosexuality -- Religious aspects -- Christianity -- History.

HQ76.3.G8.D68 1978
Dover, Kenneth James.
Greek homosexuality/ K. J. Dover. Cambridge, Mass.: Harvard University Press, 1978. x, 244 p.
77-022423   301.41/57/0938   0674362616
Homosexuality -- Greece -- History. Homosexuality -- Law and legislation -- Greece -- History. Homosexuality and art -- Greece. Greece -- Civilization -- To 146 B.C.

HQ76.3.N67.M87 1996
Murray, Stephen O.
American gay/ Stephen O. Murray. Chicago: University of Chicago Press, 1996. ix, 337 p.
95-049388   306.76/6/097   0226551911
Gays -- North America. Homosexuality -- North America.

HQ76.3.U5.A4 1982
Altman, Dennis.
The homosexualization of America: the Americanization of the homosexual/ Dennis Altman. New York: St. Martin's Press, c1982. xiv, 242 p.
81-023193   306.7/66/0973   0312388888
Homosexuality -- United States.

HQ76.3.U5.H49 1996
Hertzog, Mark, 1960-
The lavender vote: lesbians, gay men, and bisexuals in American electoral politics/ Mark Hertzog. New York: New York University Press, c1996. x, 278 p.
96-004520   306.76/0973 20   0814735290
Gays -- United States -- Political activity. Bisexuals -- United States -- Political activity.

HQ76.3.U5.H644 1993
Homosexual issues in the workplace/ edited by Louis Diamant. Washington, DC: Taylor & Francis, c1993. xxii, 268 p.
93-000399   305.9/0664   1560320389
Homosexuality -- United States. Gays -- Employment -- United States.

HQ76.3.U5.K37 1976
Katz, Jonathan, 1938-
Gay American history: lesbians and gay men in the U.S.A.: A documentary/ by Jonathan Katz. New York: Crowell, 1976. xiv, 690 p.
76-002039   301.41/57/0973   0690011652
Homosexuality -- United States -- History. Lesbianism -- United States -- History.

HQ76.3.U5.R86 1999
Rupp, Leila J., 1950-
A desired past: a short history of same-sex love in America/ Leila J. Rupp. Chicago: University of Chicago Press, 1999. xii, 232 p.
98-056542   306.76/6/0973   0226731553
Gays -- United States -- History. Homosexuality -- United States -- History.

HQ76.3.U5.W48 1991
Weston, Kath, 1958-
Families we choose: lesbians, gays, kinship/ Kath Weston. New York: Columbia University Press, c1991. xi, 261 p.
90-049349   306.87   0231072880
Gay couples -- United States. Gay parents -- United States. Kinship -- United States.

HQ76.3.U52.N486 1997
Kaiser, Charles.
The gay metropolis: 1940-1996/ Charles Kaiser. Boston: Houghton Mifflin, 1997. xii, 404 p.
97-025297   305.9/0664/09747   0395657814
Gays -- New York (State) -- New York -- History. Homosexuality -- New York (State) -- New York -- History.

HQ76.8 Sexual life — Homosexuality. Lesbianism — Gay rights movement. Gay liberation movement. Homophile movement

HQ76.8.U5.C78 1992
Cruikshank, Margaret.
The gay and lesbian liberation movement/ Margaret Cruikshank. New York, NY: Routledge, 1992. xvii, 225 p.
92-008622   305.9/0664   0415906474
Gay liberation movement -- United States.

HQ76.8.U5.D45 1983
D'Emilio, John.
Sexual politics, sexual communities: the making of a homosexual minority in the United States, 1940-1970/ John D'Emilio. Chicago: University of Chicago Press, 1983. x, 257 p.
82-016000   306.7/66/0973   0226142655
Gay liberation movement -- United States -- History.

HQ76.8.U5.G355 1996
Gallagher, John, 1937 July 31-
Perfect enemies: the religious right, the gay movement, and the politics of the 1990s/ John Gallagher and Chris Bull. New York: Crown Publishers, c1996. xv, 300 p.
96-213163   305.9/0664 21   0517701987
Gay rights -- United States. Gay liberation movement -- United States. Homophobia -- United States. United States -- Politics and government -- 1989-

HQ76.8.U5.K73 2000
Kranz, Rachel.
Gay rights/ Rachel Kranz and Tim Cusick. New York: Facts on File, 2000. 298 p.
00-035348   305.9/0664   0816042357
Gay rights -- United States.

HQ76.95 Sexual life — Homosexuality. Lesbianism — Gay press publications

HQ76.95.U5.S77 1995
Streitmatter, Rodger.
Unspeakable: the rise of the gay and lesbian press in America/ Rodger Streitmatter. Boston: Faber and Faber, 1995. xvi, 424 p.
95-021803   305.9/0664/0973   0571198732
Gay press publications -- United States -- History. Gay press -- United States -- History.

HQ77 Sexual life — Transvestism — General works

HQ77.B785 1993
Bullough, Vern L.
Cross dressing, sex, and gender/ Vern L. Bullough and Bonnie Bullough. Philadelphia: University of Pennsylvania Press, c1993. xi, 382 p.
92-032030   306.77   0812231635
Transvestism. Transvestites.

HQ77.D63 1988
Docter, Richard F.
Transvestites and transsexuals: toward a theory of cross-gender behavior/ Richard F. Docter. New York: Plenum Press, c1988. xiii, 251 p.
88-019586   305.3   0306428784
Transvestism -- United States -- Psychological aspects. Transsexuals -- United States -- Psychology. Sexual behavior surveys -- United States.

HQ77.8 Sexual life — Transsexualism — Biography

HQ77.8.M39.A3 1999
McCloskey, Deirdre N.
Crossing: a memoir/ Deirdre McCloskey. Chicago, Ill.: University of Chicago Press, 1999. xvi, 266 p.
99-019450   305.9/066   0226556689
McCloskey, Deirdre N. Transsexuals -- United States -- Biography. Transsexuals -- United States -- Psychology. Gender identity -- United States -- Psychological aspects.

HQ77.9 Sexual life — Transsexualism — General works

HQ77.9.F45 1996
Feinberg, Leslie, 1949-
Transgender warriors: making history from Joan of Arc to RuPaul/ Leslie Feinberg. Boston: Beacon Press, c1996. xvii, 212 p.
95-033421   305.3 20   0807079405
Transsexualism -- History. Transvestism -- History. Gender identity -- History.

HQ79 Sexual life — Sadism. Masochism. Fetishism, etc.

HQ79.C43 1992
Chancer, Lynn S., 1954-
Sadomasochism in everyday life: the dynamics of power and powerlessness/ Lynn S. Chancer. New Brunswick, NJ: Rutgers University Press, c1992. ix, 238 p.
91-032362   303.3   0813518075
Sadomasochism -- United States. Power (Social sciences) Interpersonal relations.

HQ79.H36 1998
Hart, Lynda, 1953-
Between the body and the flesh: performing sadomasochism/ Lynda Hart. New York: Columbia University Press, c1998. xiii, 269 p.
97-026544   306.77/5 21   0231084021
Sadomasochism. Lesbians -- Sexual behavior. Lesbianism.

HQ117 Sexual life — Prostitution — General works. History

HQ117.B37 1995
Barry, Kathleen.
The prostitution of sexuality/ Kathleen Barry. New York: New York University Press, c1995. v, 381 p.
94-027897   306.74   0814712177
Prostitution -- Moral and ethical aspects. Sex-oriented businesses. Sex crimes.

HQ117.W57 1992
West, D. J. 1924-
Male prostitution/ Donald J. West in association with Buz de Villiers. New York: Haworth Press, c1993. xix, 358 p.
92-040327   306.74/3   1560243686
Male prostitution.

HQ125 Sexual life — Prostitution — Regulation

HQ125.U6.J46 1993
Jenness, Valerie, 1963-
Making it work: the Prostitute's Rights Movement in perspective/ Valerie Jenness. New York: Aldine de Gruyter, c1993. xiv, 150 p.
92-043845   306.74/0973   0202304639
Prostitution -- Moral and ethical aspects -- United States. Prostitutes -- Legal status, laws, etc. -- United States. Sex and law -- United States.

HQ144-250 Sexual life — Prostitution — By region or country

HQ144.C35 1988
Campagna, Daniel S.
The sexual trafficking in children: an investigation of the child sex trade/ Daniel S. Campagna, Donald L. Poffenberger. Dover, Mass.: Auburn House Pub. Co., c1988. xiv, 250 p.
87-001242   306.7/4/088054   0865691541
Child prostitution -- United States. Child prostitution -- United States -- Prevention. Children in pornography -- United States.

HQ144.R76 1982
Rosen, Ruth.
The lost sisterhood: prostitution in America, 1900-1918/ Ruth Rosen. Baltimore: Johns Hopkins University Press, c1982. xvii, 245 p.
81-023678   306.7/4/0973   0801826640
Prostitution -- United States.

HQ145.A17.B88 1985
Butler, Anne M., 1938-
Daughters of joy, sisters of misery: prostitutes in the American West, 1865-90/ Anne M. Butler. Urbana: University of Illinois Press, c1985. xx, 179 p.
84-000195   306.7/42/0978   0252011392
Prostitutes -- West (U.S.) -- History -- 19th century. Prostitution -- West (U.S.) -- History -- 19th century.

HQ146.N7.G55 1992
Gilfoyle, Timothy J.
City of Eros: New York City, prostitution, and the commercialization of sex, 1790-1920/ Timothy J. Gilfoyle. New York, N.Y.: W.W. Norton, c1992. 462 p.
91-045024   306.74/09747/1   0393028003
Prostitution -- New York (State) -- New York -- History. Sex-oriented businesses -- New York (State) -- New York -- History.

HQ185.A5.W34
Walkowitz, Judith R.
Prostitution and Victorian society: women, class, and the state/ Judith R. Walkowitz. Cambridge; Cambridge University Press, 1980. ix, 347 p.
79-021050   301.41/54/0941   0521223342
Prostitution -- Great Britain -- History -- 19th century. Sexually transmitted diseases -- Great Britain -- History -- 19th century. Sexually transmitted diseases -- Law and legislation -- Great Britain -- History -- 19th century.

HQ194.C6513 1990
Corbin, Alain.
Women for hire: prostitution and sexuality in France after 1850/ Alain Corbin; translated by Alan Sheridan. Cambridge, Mass.: Harvard University Press, 1990. xvii, 478 p.
89-015320   306.74/2/09034   0674955439
Prostitution -- France -- History -- 19th century. Prostitution -- France -- History -- 20th century.

HQ250.S52.H4613 2001
Henriot, Christian.
Prostitution and sexuality in Shanghai: a social history 1849-1949/ Christian Henriot; translated by Noel Castelino. Cambridge, UK; Cambridge University Press, 2001. xviii, 467 p.
00-020001   306.74/0951/132   0521571650
Prostitution -- China -- Shanghai -- History. Prostitutes -- China -- Shanghai -- History.

HQ281 Sexual life — Prostitution — Traffic in women

HQ281.J37 1988
Jaschok, Maria.
Concubines and bondservants: a social history/ Maria Jaschok. London; Zed Books, 1988. 156 p.
88-029347   306.7/42/0951   0862327822
Prostitution -- China -- History. Concubinage -- China -- History. China -- Social life and customs. China -- Rural conditions.

HQ449 Sexual life — Emasculation. Eunuchs, etc.

HQ449.N36 1989
Nanda, Serena.
Neither man nor woman: the Hijras of India/ Serena Nanda. Belmont, Calif.: Wadsworth Pub. Co., c1990. xxv, 170 p.
89-036901   305.3   0534122043
Eunuchs -- India.

HQ449.S364 2000
Scholz, Piotr O.
Eunuchs and castrati: a cultural history/ Piotr O. Scholz; translated from the German by John A. Broadwin and Shelley L. Frisch. Princeton, NJ: Markus Wiener Publishers, 2000.
00-063415   306.76/2   1558762000
Eunuchs.

HQ461 Erotica — Literature — Early to 1800

HQ461.A55 1959
Andre le Chapelain.
The art of courtly love/ New York: Ungar, 1959. xi, 218 p.
59-009148
Love.

HQ470 Erotica — Literature — 1801-

HQ470.S3.V3 1962
Vatsyayana.
The Kama sutra: the classic Hindu treatise on love and social conduct/ translated by Richard F. Burton. Forward by Santha Rama Rau. Intro. by John W. Spellman. New York, Dutton, 1962. 252 p.
62-014720   392   014019360X
Love.

HQ471 Erotica — Pornography. Obscene literature

HQ471.B47 1991
Berger, Ronald J.
Feminism and pornography/ Ronald J. Berger, Patricia Searles, and Charles E. Cottle. New York: Praeger, 1991. x, 178 p.
90-024125   363.4/7   0275938190
Pornography -- Social aspects -- United States. Feminism -- United States. Obscenity (Law) -- United States.

HQ471.C47 1990
Christensen, F. M.
Pornography: the other side/ F.M. Christensen. New York: Praeger, 1990. viii, 188 p.
89-026543   363.4/7   027593537X
Pornography -- Social aspects.

HQ471.H387 1988
Hawkins, Gordon, 1919-
Pornography in a free society/ Gordon Hawkins, Franklin E. Zimring. Cambridge [England]; Cambridge University Press, 1988. xiii, 236 p.
88-017058   363.4/7   0521363179
Pornography -- Government policy. Pornography -- Social aspects. Obscenity (Law)

HQ471.M32 1993
Making violence sexy: feminist views on pornography/ Diana E.H. Russell, editor. New York: Teachers College Press, c1993. xii, 302 p.
92-041999   363.4/7   0807762695
Pornography -- Social aspects. Violent crimes. Women -- Crimes against.

HQ471.S59 2000
Slade, Joseph W.
Pornography in America: a reference handbook/ Joseph W. Slade. Santa Barbara, Calif.: ABC-CLIO, c2000. xiii, 349 p.
00-035548   363.4/7 21   1576070859
Pornography.

HQ471.T27 1980b

Take back the night: women on pornography/ edited by Laura Lederer. New York: Morrow, 1980. 359 p.

80-017084   363.4/7   0688037283

Pornography -- Addresses, essays, lectures. Pornography -- Social aspects -- United States. Pornography -- Religious aspects.

HQ471.W66 1985

Women against censorship/ edited by Varda Burstyn; essays by Varda Burstyn ... [et al.]. Vancouver: Douglas & McIntyre, c1985. 210 p.

85-146745   363.4/7   0888944551

Pornography -- Social aspects. Censorship. Feminism.

HQ472 Erotica — Pornography. Obscene literature — By region or country, A-Z

HQ472.U6.C36 1994

Caputi, Mary, 1957-

Voluptuous yearnings: a feminist theory of the obscene/ Mary Caputi. Lanham, Md.: Rowman & Littlefield, c1994. 115 p.

93-026056   363.4/7/0973   0847678857

Pornography -- Social aspects -- United States. Obscenity (Law) Women -- Crimes against -- United States.

HQ472.U6.S86 1991

Stoller, Robert J.

Porn: myths for the twentieth century/ Robert J. Stoller. New Haven: Yale University Press, c1991. ix, 228 p.

91-013623   363.4/7/0973   0300050925

Pornography -- United States. Sex-oriented businesses -- United States. Sex in motion pictures.

HQ472.U6.S87 1995

Strossen, Nadine.

Defending pornography: free speech, sex, and the fight for women's rights/ Nadine Strossen. New York: Scribner, c1995. 320 p.

94-040372   363.4/7   0684197499

Pornography -- Social aspects -- United States. Feminism -- United States. Feminist criticism -- United States.

HQ503 The family. Marriage. Home — History — General works

HQ503.C65 1996

Coltrane, Scott.

Family man: fatherhood, housework, and gender equity/ Scott Coltrane. New York: Oxford University Press, 1996. x, 293 p.

95-014414   306.85   0195082168

Family. Fatherhood. Sex role.

HQ503.Q35 1988

Quale, G. Robina 1931-

A history of marriage systems/ G. Robina Quale. New York: Greenwood Press, 1988. xii, 399 p.

87-024957   306.8/1/09   0313260109

Marriage -- History. Family -- History. Marriage -- Cross-cultural studies.

HQ511 The family. Marriage. Home — History — Ancient

HQ511.D59 1991

Dixon, Suzanne.

The Roman family/ Suzanne Dixon. Baltimore: Johns Hopkins University Press, c1992. xiv, 279 p.

91-025876   306.85/0945/632   0801841992

Family -- Rome -- History.

HQ513 The family. Marriage. Home — History — Medieval

HQ513.G53 1987

Gies, Frances.

Marriage and the family in the Middle ages/ Frances and Joseph Gies. New York: Harper & Row, c1987. viii, 372 p.

87-045048   306.8/09/02   0060157917

Marriage -- History. Family -- History. Social history -- Medieval, 500-1500.

HQ518 The family. Marriage. Home — History — Modern

HQ518.B47 1972

Bernard, Jessie Shirley, 1903-

The future of marriage [by] Jessie Bernard. New York, World Pub. [1972] xvi, 367 p.

77-183085   301.42   0529045214

Marriage. Sex role.

HQ518.L27

Lasch, Christopher.

Haven in a heartless world: the family besieged/ Christopher Lasch. New York: Basic Books, c1977. xviii, 230 p.

77-075246   301.42   0465028837

Family -- History. Marriage -- History. Socialization.

HQ518.S56 1971

Skolnick, Arlene S., 1933-

Family in transition; rethinking marriage, sexuality, child rearing, and family organization [compiled by] Arlene S. Skolnick [and] Jerome H. Skolnick. Boston, Little, Brown [1971] xiii, 542 p.

76-154524   301.42/08

Family -- Addresses, essays, lectures.

HQ520 The family. Marriage. Home — Television and family

HQ520.S75 1992

Spigel, Lynn.

Make room for TV: television and the family ideal in postwar America/ Lynn Spigel. Chicago: University of Chicago Press, 1992. x, 236 p.

91-032770   306.87   0226769666

Television and family -- United States.

HQ520.T53 1991

Tichi, Cecelia, 1942-

Electronic hearth: creating an American television culture/ Cecelia Tichi. New York: Oxford University Press, 1991. x, 249 p.

91-010640   302.23/45   0195065492

Television and family -- United States. Television and children -- United States. Television broadcasting -- Social aspects -- United States.

HQ534-557 The family. Marriage. Home — By region or country — North America

HQ534.E53 1999

Encyclopedia of family life/ editor, Carl L. Bankston III; project editor, R. Kent Rasmussen. Pasadena, Calif.: Salem Press, c1999. 5 v.

98-042491   306.85/097/03 21   0893569402

Family -- North America -- Encyclopedias. Domestic relations -- North America -- Encyclopedias. Family services -- North America -- Encyclopedias.

HQ535.A585 1991

American families: a research guide and historical handbook/ edited by Joseph M. Hawes and Elizabeth I. Nybakken. New York: Greenwood Press, 1991. viii, 435 p.

90-025221   306.85/0973   0313262330

Family -- United States -- History. Family research literature -- United States.

HQ535.C415

Cherlin, Andrew J., 1948-

Marriage, divorce, remarriage/ Andrew J. Cherlin. Cambridge, Mass.: Harvard University Press, c1981. xiv, 142 p.

81-002901   306.8/0973   0674550803

Marriage -- United States. Divorce -- United States. Remarriage -- United States.

HQ535.C643 1992

Coontz, Stephanie.

The way we never were: American families and the nostalgia trap/ Stephanie Coontz. New York, NY: BasicBooks, c1992. viii, 391 p.

91-059009   306.85/0973   0465001351

Family -- United States -- History -- 20th century. Nostalgia. United States -- Social conditions.

HQ535.D42 1986

Demos, John.

Past, present, and personal: the family and the life course in American history/ John Demos. New York: Oxford University Press, 1986. xiii, 215 p.

85-030996   306.8/5/0973 19   0195037774

Family -- United States -- History. Family -- United States -- Historiography. Public history -- United States.

HQ535.H58

Holmstrom, Lynda Lytle.

The two-career family. Cambridge, Mass., Schenkman Pub. Co.; distributed by General Learn 1972. vii, 203 p.

70-189095   301.42/7

Dual-career families -- United States -- Case studies. Professions. Husband and wife.

HQ535.M386 1995

May, Elaine Tyler.

Barren in the promised land: childless Americans and the pursuit of happiness/ Elaine Tyler May. New York: BasicBooks, c1995. xii, 318 p.

94-041427   306.87   0465006094

Childlessness -- United States -- History.

HQ535.S44
Seward, Rudy Ray.
The American family: a demographic history/ Rudy Ray Seward; foreword by Herman R. Lantz. Beverly Hills, Calif.: Sage Publications, c1978. 223 p.
78-019609 301.42/0973 0803911122
Family -- United States -- History. Family -- Research -- United States. Urbanization -- United States.

HQ535.S56 1991
Skolnick, Arlene S., 1933-
Embattled paradise: the American family in an age of uncertainty/ Arlene Skolnick. [New York]: Basic Books, c1991. xx, 284 p.
91-070056 306.85/0973/09045 0465019234
Family -- United States -- History -- 20th century. United States -- Social conditions -- 1945-

HQ535.W435 2000
Weiss, Jessica.
To have and to hold: marriage, the baby boom, and social change/ Jessica Weiss. Chicago: University of Chicago Press, 2000. viii, 299 p.
99-040312 306.8/0973 0226886700
Marriage -- United States. Family -- United States. Baby boom generation -- United States.

HQ536.B3
Bane, Mary Jo.
Here to stay: American families in the twentieth century/ Mary Jo Bane. New York: Basic Books, c1976. xvi, 195 p.
76-044877 301.42/0973 0465029272
Family -- United States.

HQ536.B63
Bohen, Halcyone H., 1937-
Balancing jobs and family life: do flexible work schedules help?/ Halcyone H. Bohen, Anamaria Viveros-Long. Philadelphia: Temple University Press, 1981. xxiv, 336 p.
80-025165 306.8/7 0877221995
Work and family -- United States -- Case studies. Hours of labor, Flexible -- United States. United States -- Officials and employees -- Family relationships.

HQ536.C39 1988
The changing American family and public policy/ Andrew J. Cherlin, editor. Washington, D.C.: Urban Institute Press; c1988. xii, 261 p.
88-020484 306.8/5/0973 0877664226
Family policy -- United States. Family -- United States. Social change.

HQ536.C757 2000
Cott, Nancy F.
Public vows: a history of marriage and the nation/ Nancy F. Cott. Cambridge, Mass.: Harvard University Press, 2000. 297 p.
00-031898 306.85/0973 0674003209
Marriage -- United States -- History. United States -- Social life and customs.

HQ536.G44 1974
Gelles, Richard J.
The violent home: a study of physical aggression between husbands and wives/ Richard J. Gelles. Beverly Hills, Calif.: Sage Publications, [1974] c1972. 230 p.
73-094288 301.42/7 0803903812
Conjugal violence. Child abuse. Wife abuse.

HQ536.G65 1991
Goldscheider, Frances K.
New families, no families?: the transformation of the American home/ Frances K. Goldscheider and Linda J. Waite. Berkeley: University of California Press, c1991. xvi, 303 p.
91-015452 306.85/0973 0520072227
Family -- United States. Marriage -- United States. Home -- United States.

HQ536.H318 1992
Hamburg, David A., 1925-
Today's children: creating a future for a generation in crisis/ David A. Hamburg. New York: Times Books, c1992. viii, 376 p.
91-050188 305.23/0973 0812919149
Family -- United States. Children -- United States. Child development -- United States.

HQ536.P59 1985
Pleck, Joseph H.
Working wives, working husbands/ Joseph H. Pleck. Beverly Hills, Calif.: Published in cooperation with the National Counc c1985. 167 p.
85-011974 306.8/7 0803924895
Dual-career families -- United States. Sexual division of labor -- United States. Sex role -- United States.

HQ536.P76 1996
Promises to keep: decline and renewal of marriage in America/ edited by David Popenoe, Jean Bethke Elshtain, and David Blankenhorn. Lanham, Md.: Rowman & Littlefield Publishers, 1996. xii, 337 p.
96-007003 306.8/0973 0847682307
Marriage -- United States. Divorce -- United States. Single-parent families -- United States. United States -- Social conditions.

HQ536.R66
Ross, Heather L.
Time of transition: the growth of families headed by women/ Heather L. Ross and Isabel V. Sawhill; with the assistance of Anita R. MacIntosh. Washington, D.C.: Urban Institute, c1975. xii, 223 p.
75-038209 306.8
Single-parent families -- United States. Paternal deprivation.

HQ536.R8
Rubin, Lillian B.
Worlds of pain: life in the working-class family/ Lillian Breslow Rubin. New York: Basic Books, c1976. xii, 268 p.
76-021648 301.42/0973 0465092454
Working class families -- United States. United States -- Social conditions -- 1960-1980.

HQ536.S727 1999
Statistical handbook on the American family/ edited by Bruce A. Chadwick and Tim B. Heaton. Phoenix, Ariz.: Oryx Press, 1999. xvi, 326 p.
98-042669 306.85/0973/021 157356169X
Family -- United States -- Statistics. United States -- Statistics, Vital.

HQ536.S735 1997
Steil, Janice M. Ingham, 1941-
Marital equality: its relationship to the well-being of husbands and wives/ Janice M. Steil. Thousand Oaks, Calif.: Sage Publications, c1997. xxii, 145 p.
97-004797 306.81 21 0803952503
Marriage -- United States -- Psychological aspects. Married people -- United States -- Psychology. Equality -- United States -- Psychological aspects.

HQ536.S74
Steiner, Gilbert Yale, 1924-
The futility of family policy/ Gilbert Y. Steiner. Washington, D.C.: Brookings Institution, c1981. viii, 221 p.
80-026448 306.8/0973 0815781245
Family -- United States. Family policy -- United States.

HQ536.T85 1982
Two paychecks: life in dual-earner families/ edited by Joan Aldous. Beverly Hills: Sage Publications, c1982. 247 p.
82-010538 306.8/7 0803918828
Dual-career families -- United States. Married people -- Employment -- United States.

HQ536.V37 1989
Vannoy, Dana.
Equal partners: successful women in marriage/ Dana Vannoy-Hiller, William W. Philliber. Newbury Park, Calif.: Sage Publications, c1989. 168 p.
89-033175 306.872/0973 0803928130
Dual-career families -- United States. Marriage -- United States. Work and family -- United States.

HQ536.W33 2000
Waite, Linda J.
The case for marriage: why married people are happier, healthier, and better off financially/ Linda J. Waite, Maggie Gallagher. New York: Doubleday, 2000. 260 p.
00-022672 306.81/0973 0385500858
Married couples -- United States -- Psychology. Man-woman relationships -- United States. Single people -- United States -- Psychology.

HQ536.15.S26.S73 1990
Stacey, Judith.
Brave new families: stories of domestic upheaval in late twentieth century America/ Judith Stacey. [New York]: Basic Books, c1990. xiv, 328 p.
90-080244 306.85/0973 0465007465
Family -- California -- Santa Clara County -- Case studies. Working class families -- California -- Santa Clara County -- Case studies.

HQ553.F37
Faragher, John Mack, 1945-
Women and men on the overland trail/ John Mack Faragher. New Haven: Yale University Press, 1979. xiii, 281 p.
78-010290 301.42/0978 0300022670
Family -- West (U.S.) -- History -- 19th century. Women -- West (U.S.) -- History -- 19th century. Frontier and pioneer life -- West (U.S.) -- History -- 19th century.

HQ557.C5.S45
Sennett, Richard, 1943-
Families against the city; middle class homes of industrial Chicago, 1872-1890. Cambridge, Mass., Harvard University Press, 1970. x, 258 p.
73-115190 301.44/1 0674292251
Middle class families -- Illinois -- Chicago. Chicago (Ill.) -- Social conditions.

HQ560.5-684 The family. Marriage. Home — By region or country — Other regions or countries

HQ560.5.S48 1989
Sexuality and marriage in colonial Latin America/ edited by Asuncion Lavrin. Lincoln: University of Nebraska Press, c1989. viii, 349 p.
88-033980   306.8/1/098   0803228856
Marriage -- Latin America -- History. Sex customs -- Latin America -- History. Latin America -- History -- To 1830.

HQ562.L39
Lewis, Oscar, 1914-
A death in the Sanchez family.   New York, Random House [1969] xxxii, 119 p.
75-085569   301.29/72
Family -- Mexico -- Case studies. Poor -- Mexico -- Mexico City. Funeral rites and ceremonies -- Mexico.

HQ562.L43
Lewis, Oscar, 1914-
Pedro Martinez; a Mexican peasant and his family. Drawings by Alberto Beltran. New York, Random House [1964] lvii, 507 p.
64-010530   309.172
Family -- Mexico -- Case studies. Peasantry -- Mexico -- Case studies. Mexico -- Social conditions.

HQ611.O968 2001
Ozment, Steven E.
Ancestors: the loving family in old Europe/ Steven Ozment. Cambridge, Mass.: Harvard University Press, 2001. 162 p.
00-063447   306.85/094   0674004833
Family -- Europe -- History. Family -- Europe -- Historiography.

HQ611.O97 1983
Ozment, Steven E.
When fathers ruled: family life in Reformation Europe/ Steven Ozment. Cambridge, Mass.: Harvard University Press, 1983. viii, 238 p.
83-006098   306.8/094   0674951204
Marriage -- Europe -- History. Family -- Europe -- History. Husbands -- Europe -- History.

HQ611.S43 1992
Seccombe, Wally.
A millennium of family change: feudalism to capitalism in Northwestern Europe/ Wally Seccombe. London; Verso, 1992. vii, 343 p.
91-032062   306.85/094   0860913325
Family -- Europe -- History. Family -- Economic aspects -- Europe -- History. Sex role -- Europe -- History.

HQ613.G55 1985
Gillis, John R.
For better, for worse: British marriages, 1600 to the present/ John R. Gillis. New York: Oxford University Press, 1985. x, 417 p.
85-013701   306.8/0941   019503614X
Marriage -- Great Britain -- History. Courtship -- Great Britain -- History.

HQ613.R67 1983
Rose, Phyllis, 1942-
Parallel lives: five Victorian marriages/ Phyllis Rose; drawings by David Schorr. New York: Knopf, 1983. 318 p.
83-047785   306.8/1/0941   0394524322
Marriage -- Great Britain -- History -- 19th century -- Case studies. Married people -- Great Britain -- Biography. Authors, English -- 19th century -- Biography.

HQ615.B45 1998
Behlmer, George K.
Friends of the family: the English home and its guardians, 1850-1940/ George K. Behlmer. Stanford, Calif.: Stanford University Press, 1998. x, 455 p.
98-011235   306.85/0942   0804733139
Family -- England -- History -- 19th century. Family -- England -- History -- 20th century. England -- Social conditions -- 19th century. England -- Social conditions -- 20th century.

HQ615.F64 2001
Fleming, Peter, 1958-
Family and household in medieval England/ Peter Fleming. New York: St. Martin's Press, 2000. viii, 162 p.
00-059127   306.85/0942   0333610784
Family -- England -- History -- To 1500. Households -- England -- History -- To 1500. England -- Social life and customs -- 1066-1485.

HQ615.M33 1986
Macfarlane, Alan.
Marriage and love in England: modes of reproduction, 1300-1840/ Alan Macfarlane. Oxford, UK; B. Blackwell, 1986. xi, 380 p.
85-013351   306.8/1/0942   0631139923
Marriage -- England -- History. Family -- England -- History. Malthusianism.

HQ623.D8313 1983
Duby, Georges.
The knight, the lady, and the priest: the making of modern marriage in medieval France/ Georges Duby; translated by Barbara Bray. New York: Pantheon Books, [1983] xx, 311 p.
83-004000   306.8/1/0944   0394524454
Marriage -- France -- History. Marriage -- Religious aspects -- Catholic Church. Marriage customs and rites, Medieval.

HQ623.F5513
Flandrin, Jean Louis.
Families in former times: kinship, household, and sexuality/ by Jean-Louis Flandrin; translated by Richard Southern. Cambridge [Eng.]; Cambridge University Press, 1979. xi, 265 p.
78-018095   301.42/0944   0521223237
Family -- France -- History.

HQ629.F36 1991
The Family in Italy from antiquity to the present/ edited by David I. Kertzer and Richard P. Saller. New Haven: Yale University Press, c1991. xiii, 399 p.
91-012478   306.85/0945   0300050372
Family -- Italy -- History -- Congresses.

HQ637.F35
The Family in Imperial Russia: new lines of historical research/ edited by David L. Ransel. Urbana: University of Illinois Press, c1978. 342 p.
78-017579   301.42/0947   0252007018
Family -- Soviet Union -- History -- Congresses. Social classes -- Soviet Union -- History -- Congresses.

HQ637.G37
Geiger, H. Kent.
The family in Soviet Russia, by H. Kent Geiger. Cambridge, Mass., Harvard University Press, 1968. xii, 381 p.
68-015637   301.42/0947
Family -- Soviet Union.

HQ649.R44 1997
Reher, David Sven.
Perspectives on the family in Spain, past and present/ David S. Reher. Oxford: Clarendon Press; 1997. xv, 356 p.
96-034857   306.85/0946   0198233140
Family -- Spain -- History.

HQ662.5.A25 1998
Patterson, Cynthia.
The family in Greek history/ Cynthia B. Patterson. Cambridge, Mass.: Harvard University Press, 1998. 286 p.
98-009295   306.85/09495   0674292707
Family -- Greece -- History. Domestic relations -- Greece -- History. Family in literature.

HQ667.F3
Family and kinship in Chinese society. Contributors: Ai-li S. Chin [and others] Edited by Maurice Freedman. Stanford, Calif., Stanford University Press, 1970. xv, 269 p.
69-018493   301.44/2/0951   0804707138
Family -- China -- Addresses, essays, lectures. Kinship -- Addresses, essays, lectures.

HQ668.95.W63
Wolf, Margery.
The house of Lim; a study of a Chinese farm family.   New York, Appleton-Century-Crofts [1968] xx, 147 p.
68-011211   301.42/0951/249
Family -- Taiwan.

HQ684.A15 1979
Baker, Hugh D. R.
Chinese family and kinship/ Hugh D. R. Baker. New York: Columbia University Press, 1979. xii, 243 p.
78-026724   301.42/0951   0231047681
Family -- China -- History. Kinship -- China -- History.

HQ684.A25 1993
Ebrey, Patricia Buckley, 1947-
The inner quarters: marriage and the lives of Chinese women in the Sung period/ Patricia Buckley Ebrey. Berkeley: University of California Press, c1993. xviii, 332 p.
92-031376   306.872/0951/09021   0520081560
Marriage -- China -- History. Women -- China -- Social conditions. China -- Social conditions -- 960-1644.

HQ684.P37
Parish, William L.
Village and family in contemporary China/ William L. Parish, Martin King Whyte. Chicago: University of Chicago Press, 1978. xiii, 419 p.
78-003411   301.42/0951   0226645908
Rural families -- China. Villages -- China -- Case studies. China -- Rural conditions.

HQ728 The family. Marriage. Home — Treatises — Scientific

HQ728.E3
Economics of the family: marriage, children, and human capital:a conference report of the National Bureau of Economic Research/ edited by Theodore W. Schultz. Chicago: Published for the National Bureau of Economic Re 1974. 584 p.
73-081484   301.42   0226740854
Family -- Congresses. Marriage -- Congresses. Family size -- Economic aspects -- Congresses.

HQ728.F454 1992
Fisher, Helen E.
Anatomy of love: the natural history of monogamy, adultery, and divorce/ Helen E. Fisher. New York: Norton, c1992. 431 p.
92-004809   306.7   0393034232
Marriage. Adultery. Divorce.

HQ728.H395
Henry, Jules, 1904-1969.
Pathways to madness. New York, Random House [1971] xxii, 477 p.
77-159349   616.8/9/071   039447323X
Family -- United States -- Case studies. Interpersonal relations. Psychology, Pathological.

HQ728.K64
Komarovsky, Mirra, 1906-
Blue-collar marriage. With the collaboration of Jane H. Philips. New York, Random House [1964] xv, 395 p.
64-020031   301.426
Marriage -- Case studies.

HQ728.T68 1990
Handbook of family measurement techniques/ John Touliatos, Barry F. Perlmutter, Murray A. Straus, editors. Newbury Park, Calif.: Sage, c1990. 797 p.
89-010542   306.85   0803931212
Family -- Testing -- Abstracts. Psychological tests -- Abstracts.

HQ728.W526 1990
Whyte, Martin King.
Dating, mating, and marriage/ Martin King Whyte. New York: Aldine de Gruyter, c1990. x, 325 p.
89-017996   306.81/0973   0202304159
Marriage -- United States. Dating (Social customs) -- United States. Mate selection -- United States.

HQ734 The family. Marriage. Home — Treatises — Other. Popular, the home, etc.

HQ734.B56 1983
Berger, Brigitte.
The war over the family: capturing the middle ground/ by Brigitte Berger and Peter L. Berger. Garden City, N.Y.: Anchor Press/Doubleday, 1983. ix, 252 p.
82-045237   306.8/5   0385180012
Family. Middle class families. Family policy.

HQ734.F228 1982
Families that work: children in a changing world/ Sheila B. Kamerman and Cheryl D. Hayes, editors; Panel on Work, Family, and Community, Committee on Child Development Research and Public Policy, Commission on Behavioral and Social Sciences and Education, National Research Council. Washington, D.C.: National Academy Press, 1982. xi, 341 p.
82-081829   306.8/7   0309032822
Work and family. Children of working parents. Child development.

HQ734.G7137 1994
Gottman, John Mordechai.
What predicts divorce?: the relationship between marital processes and marital outcomes/ John Mordechai Gottman. Hillsdale, N.J.: Lawrence Erlbaum Associates, 1994. xvi, 521 p.
93-012547   306.81   0805812857
Marriage -- Psychological aspects. Married people -- Psychology. Divorce -- Psychological aspects.

HQ734.G743 1991
Greil, Arthur L.
Not yet pregnant: infertile couples in contemporary America/ Arthur L. Greil. New Brunswick [N.J.]: Rutgers University Press, c1991. viii, 243 p.
90-021142   306.872   081351682X
Marriage -- United States. Childlessness -- United States. Infertility -- Social aspects -- United States.

HQ734.K353 1993
Kayser, Karen.
When love dies: the process of marital disaffection/ Karen Kayser. New York: Guilford Press, c1993. xv, 191 p.
93-010227   306.81   0898620864
Marriage. Love.

HQ751 The family. Marriage. Home — Eugenics — General works

HQ751.W37 1985
Warren, Mary Anne.
Gendercide: the implications of sex selection/ Mary Anne Warren. Totowa, N.J.: Rowman & Allanheld, 1985. viii, 209 p.
85-014452   305.3   0847673308
Eugenics. Sex preselection. Sex of children, Parental preferences for.

HQ755.5 The family. Marriage. Home — Eugenics — By region or country, A-Z

HQ755.5.U5.K84 1994
Kuhl, Stefan.
The Nazi connection: eugenics, American racism, and German national socialism/ Stefan Kuhl. New York: Oxford University Press, 1994. xviii, 166 p
93-017283
Political Systems -- history -- Germany Prejudice -- history -- Germany Prejudice -- history -- United States

HQ755.5.U5.L37 1995
Larson, Edward J.
Sex, race, and science: eugenics in the deep South/ by Edward J. Larson. Baltimore: Johns Hopkins University Press, 1995. ix, 251 p.
94-028124   363.9/2/0975   0801849381
Eugenics -- Southern States -- History -- 20th century.

HQ755.5.U5.R45 1991
Reilly, Philip, 1947-
The surgical solution: a history of involuntary sterilization in the United States/ Philip R. Reilly. Baltimore: Johns Hopkins University Press, c1991. xvi, 190 p.
90-005090   363.9/7   0801840961
Eugenics -- United States -- History. Mentally handicapped -- Surgery -- United States -- History. Eugenics -- history -- United States.

HQ755.8 The family. Marriage. Home — Parents. Parenthood — General works

HQ755.8.D489 1999
Deutsch, Francine, 1948-
Halving it all: how equally shared parenting works/ Francine M. Deutsch. Cambridge, MA: Harvard University Press, 1999. 327 p.
98-030738   649/.1   0674368002
Parenting. Sex role. Dual-career families.

HQ755.8.M34 1995
Mahony, Rhona.
Kidding ourselves: breadwinning, babies, and bargaining power/ Rhona Mahony. New York, NY: BasicBooks, c1995. ix, 277 p.
95-005761   306.872   0465085946
Parenting. Dual-career families. Sexual division of labor.

HQ755.83 The family. Marriage. Home — Parents. Parenthood — Parental attitudes

HQ755.83.D36 1982
Daniels, Pamela, 1937-
Sooner or later: the timing of parenthood in adult lives/ Pamela Daniels, Kathy Weingarten. New York: Norton, c1982. xi, 366 p.
81-011006   306.8   0393014843
Parenthood -- Psychological aspects. Life cycle, Human.

HQ755.85 The family. Marriage. Home — Parents. Parenthood — Relationship between parent and child

HQ755.85.D38 1989
Daughters and fathers/ edited by Lynda E. Boose and Betty S. Flowers. Baltimore: Johns Hopkins University Press, c1989. vii, 453 p.
88-045407   306.8/742   0801836654
Fathers and daughters.

HQ755.85.R67 1990
Rossi, Alice S., 1922-
Of human bonding: parent-child relations across the life course/ Alice S. Rossi and Peter H. Rossi. New York: A. de Gruyter, c1990. xviii, 542 p.
89-071418   306.874   0202303608
Parent and child. Intergenerational relations. Kinship.

HQ755.86 The family. Marriage. Home — Parents. Parenthood — Relationship between parent and adult child

HQ755.86.C55 1992
Climo, Jacob, 1945-
Distant parents/ Jacob Climo. New Brunswick, N.J.: Rutgers University Press, c1992. xi, 279 p.
91-032605   306.874   0813517966
Parent and adult child -- United States. Aging parents -- United States -- Family relationships. Autonomy (Psychology) in old age -- United States.

HQ755.86.L64 1996
Logan, John R., 1946-
Family ties: enduring relations between parents and their grown children/ John R. Logan, Glenna D. Spitze. Philadelphia: Temple University Press, 1996. xxix, 265 p.
96-013008   306.874   1566394716
Parent and adult child. Intergenerational relations.

HQ756 The family. Marriage. Home — Parents. Parenthood — Husbands. Fathers

HQ756.A8 1995
Arendell, Terry.
Fathers & divorce/ Terry Arendell. Thousand Oaks: Sage Publications, c1995. xii, 303 p.
94-042213   306.89   0803971885
Divorced fathers -- New York (State)

HQ756.F382 1988
Fatherhood today: men's changing role in the family/ edited by Phyllis Bronstein, Carolyn Pape Cowan. New York: J. Wiley, c1988. xix, 364 p.
88-144615   306.8/742   0471836273
Fathers -- United States. Father and child -- United States.

HQ756.G78 1993
Griswold, Robert L., 1950-
Fatherhood in America: a history/ Robert L. Griswold. New York: BasicBooks, c1993. xi, 356 p.
92-054516   306.874/2/0973   0465001408
Fatherhood -- United States -- History.

HQ756.P65 1996
Popenoe, David, 1932-
Life without father: compelling new evidence that fatherhood and marriage are indispensable for the good of children and society/ David Popenoe. New York: Martin Kessler Books, c1996. viii, 275 p.
95-046233   306.874/2 20   0684822970
Fatherless families -- United States. Fatherhood -- United States. Fathers -- United States. United States -- Social conditions.

HQ756.R635 1988
Robinson, Bryan E.
Teenage fathers/ Bryan E. Robinson; foreword by Harriette McAdoo. Lexington, Mass.: Lexington Books, c1988. xvi, 173 p.
86-045896   362.7/96   0669145866
Teenage fathers -- United States. Teenage fathers -- United States -- Psychology. Teenage fathers -- Services for -- United States.

HQ759-759.5 The family. Marriage. Home — Parents. Parenthood — Wives. Mothers

HQ759.A5
Andre, Rae.
Homemakers, the forgotten workers/ Rae Andr_e. Chicago: University of Chicago Press, c1981. xi, 299 p.
80-021258   305.4/3   0226019934
Housewives -- United States. Displaced homemakers -- United States.

HQ759.B53 1983
Between ourselves: letters between mothers and daughters, 1750-1982/ edited by Karen Payne. Boston: Houghton Mifflin, 1983. xvi, 416 p.
83-010803   306.8/743   0395339693
Mothers -- Correspondence. Daughters -- Correspondence. Mothers and daughters -- History.

HQ759.D248 1983
Dally, Ann G.
Inventing motherhood: the consequences of an ideal/ Ann Dally. New York: Schocken Books, 1983, c1982. 360 p.
82-010517   649/.1   0805238301
Motherhood.

HQ759.G3 1995
Gabor, Andrea.
Einstein's wife: work and marriage in the lives of five great twentieth-century women/ Andrea Gabor. New York, N.Y., U.S.A.: Viking, 1995. xxiv, 341 p.
95-002998   920.72   0670842109
Wives -- Biography. Spouses -- Biography. Celebrities -- Biography.

HQ759.G75 1998
Grant, Julia, 1953-
Raising baby by the book: the education of American mothers/ Julia Grant. New Haven: Yale University Press, c1998. ix, 309 p.
97-037286   649/.1 21   0300072147
Mothers -- United States. Motherhood -- United States. Child rearing -- United States.

HQ759.G76 1988
Greif, Geoffrey L.
Mothers without custody/ by Geoffrey L. Greif, Mary S. Pabst. Lexington, Mass.: Lexington Books, c1988. x, 292 p.
86-045006   306.8/9   0669130249
Absentee mothers -- United States. Custody of children -- United States.

HQ759.H37 1996
Hays, Sharon, 1956-
The cultural contradictions of motherhood/ Sharon Hays. New Haven: Yale University Press, c1996. xv, 252 p.
96-010262   306.874/3 20   0300066821
Motherhood. Mothers -- United States.

HQ759.J645 1988
Johnson, Miriam M.
Strong mothers, weak wives: the search for gender equality/ Miriam M. Johnson. Berkeley: University of California Press, c1988. xii, 347 p.
87-030896   305.4/890655   0520061616
Wives -- Psychology. Mothers -- Psychology. Sex role.

HQ759.M88 1984
Mothering: essays in feminist theory/ edited by Joyce Trebilcot. Totowa, N.J.: Rowman & Allanheld, 1984, c1983. viii, 336 p.
83-004517   306.8/58   0847671151
Motherhood. Mothers. Feminism.

HQ759.R53 1976
Rich, Adrienne Cecile.
Of woman born: motherhood as experience and institution/ Adrienne Rich. New York: Norton, c1976. 318 p.
76-018744   301.42/7   0393087506
Motherhood. Mother and child. Feminism.

HQ759.R68 1989
Rothman, Barbara Katz.
Recreating motherhood: ideology and technology in a patriarchal society/ Barbara Katz Rothman. New York: Norton, c1989. 282 p.
88-014182   306.8/743   0393026450
Motherhood. Patriarchy. Feminism.

HQ759.4.H387 1997
Harris, Kathleen Mullan, 1950-
Teen mothers and the revolving welfare door/ Kathleen Mullan Harris; foreword by Frank F. Furstenberg, Jr. Philadelphia: Temple University Press, 1997. xv, 195 p.
96-036157   306.874/3   1566394996
Teenage mothers -- United States. Unmarried mothers -- United States. Maternal and infant welfare -- United States.

HQ759.4.M87 1993
Musick, Judith S.
Young, poor, and pregnant: the psychology of teenage motherhood/ Judith S. Musick. New Haven: Yale University Press, c1993. xi, 271 p.
92-034612   306.7/0835   0300053533
Teenage mothers -- United States.

HQ759.4.V55 1988
Vinovskis, Maris.
An "epidemic" of adolescent pregnancy?: some historical and policy considerations/ Maris A. Vinovskis. New York: Oxford University Press, 1988. xix, 284 p.
87-011075   362.7/96   0195049977
Teenage mothers -- United States. Teenage pregnancy -- United States -- History. Teenage pregnancy -- Government policy -- United States.

HQ759.45.L83 1997
Ludtke, Melissa.
On our own: unmarried motherhood in America/ Melissa Ludtke. New York: Random House, c1997. xii, 465 p.
96-052233   306.874/3/0973 21   0679424148
Ludtke, Melissa. Unmarried mothers -- United States -- Biography. Single mothers -- United States. Unmarried mothers -- United States.

HQ759.45.P66 1993
Polakow, Valerie.
Lives on the edge: single mothers and their children in the other America/ Valerie Polakow. Chicago: University of Chicago Press, 1993. ix, 222 p.
92-021977   306.85/6/0973   0226671836
Single mothers -- United States. Poor women -- United States. Poor children -- United States.

HQ759.48.E94 1996
Eyer, Diane E., 1944-
Motherguilt: how our culture blames mothers for what's wrong with society/ Diane Eyer. New York: Times Books/Random House, c1996. xviii, 317 p.
95-007692 306.874/3 20 0812924169
Working mothers -- United States -- Psychology. Motherhood -- United States -- Psychological aspects. Attachment behavior.

HQ759.48.L47 1991
Lerner, Jacqueline V.
Employed mothers and their children/ Jacqueline V. Lerner, Nancy L. Galambos. New York: Garland, 1991. xiv, 295 p.
90-025897 306.874/3 0824063449
Working mothers -- United States. Children of working mothers -- United States. Work and family -- United States.

HQ759.5.S53 1988
Shannon, Thomas A. 1940-
Surrogate motherhood: the ethics of using human beings/ Thomas A. Shannon. New York: Crossroad, 1988. xi, 191 p.
88-025671 306.8/743 0824508998
Surrogate motherhood -- Moral and ethical aspects. Surrogate mothers -- Legal status, laws, etc. -- United States.

HQ759.64 The family. Marriage. Home — Parents. Parenthood — Teenage parents. Adolescent parents

HQ759.64.C65 1997
Coles, Robert.
The youngest parents: teenage pregnancy as it shapes lives/ Robert Coles; with Robert E. Coles, Daniel A. Coles, and Michael H. Coles; photographs by Jocelyn Lee and John Moses. New York: Published by the Center for Documentary Studies c1997. 223 p.
96-047258 305.235 21 0393040828
Teenage parents -- United States -- Case studies. Teenage pregnancy -- United States -- Case studies.

HQ759.9 The family. Marriage. Home — Parents. Parenthood — Grandparents

HQ759.9.G7364 2000
Grandparents raising grandchildren: theoretical, empirical, and clinical perspectives/ Bert Hayslip, Jr., Robin Goldberg-Glen, editors. New York: Springer Pub. Co., 2000. xxi, 410 p.
00-021540 306.874/5 0826113362
Grandparents as parents -- United States. Grandparenting -- United States. Grandparents -- United States -- Psychology.

HQ759.915 The family. Marriage. Home — Parents. Parenthood — Single parents. Divorced parents

HQ759.915.D69 1997
Dowd, Nancy E., 1949-
In defense of single-parent families/ Nancy E. Dowd. New York: New York University Press, c1997. viii, 200 p.
96-025268 306.85/6 20 0814718698
Single-parent families -- United States. Single mothers -- United States. Single fathers -- United States.

HQ759.915.E34 1997
Edin, Kathryn, 1962-
Making ends meet: how single mothers survive welfare and low-wage work/ Kathryn Edin and Laura Lein. New York: Russell Sage Foundation, c1997. xxxi, 305 p.
96-040379 306.85/6 21 0871542293
Single mothers -- United States -- Social conditions. Single mothers -- Employment -- United States. Maternal and infant welfare -- United States.

HQ759.96 The family. Marriage. Home — Brothers. Sisters

HQ759.96.A75 2000
Atkins, Annette, 1950-
We grew up together: brothers and sisters in nineteenth-century America/ Annette Atkins. Urbana: University of Illinois Press, c2001. xviii, 194 p.
00-008453 306.875/3 21 0252026055
Brothers and sisters -- United States -- History -- 19th century. Brothers and sisters -- United States -- History -- 20th century.

HQ759.98 The family. Marriage. Home — Family demography

HQ759.98.L38 1989
Later phases of the family cycle: demographic aspects/ edited by E. Grebenik, C. Hohn, R. Mackensen. Oxford [England]: Clarendon Press; 1989. 249 p.
88-019622 306.8/5 0198286570
Family demography -- Cross-cultural studies. Life cycle, Human -- Cross-cultural studies.

HQ764-767.5 The family. Marriage. Home — Family size — Family planning. Birth control

HQ764.S3.D66
Douglas, Emily (Taft) 1899-
Margaret Sanger; pioneer of the future. New York, Holt, Rinehart and Winston [1969, c1970] viii, 274 p.
72-080339 613.94/3/0924 0030818443
Sanger, Margaret, -- 1879-1966. Women social reformers -- United States -- Biography. Birth control -- Biography.

HQ764.S3.K45
Kennedy, David M.
Birth control in America; the career of Margaret Sanger [by] David M. Kennedy. New Haven, Yale University Press, 1970. xi, 320 p.
79-099827 613.94/3/0924 0300012020
Sanger, Margaret, -- 1879-1966. Birth control -- United States -- History. Birth control -- Biography.

HQ766.B143 1989
Back, Kurt W.
Family planning and population control: the challenges of a successful movement/ Kurt W. Back. Boston: Twayne, c1989. viii, 177 p.
88-021768 303.4/84 0805797114
Birth control. Social movements. Population policy.

HQ766.E52 2001
Encyclopedia of birth control/ Vern L. Bullough, editor; Brenda Appleby ... [et al.], associate editors; with James A. Brundage ... [et al.]. Santa Barbara, Calif.: ABC-CLIO, c2001. xv, 349 p.
2001-001345 363.9/6/03 21 1576071812
Birth control -- Encyclopedias. Contraception -- Encyclopedias. Contraception -- Encyclopedias -- English.

HQ766.M35 1991
McLaren, Angus.
A history of contraception: from antiquity to the present day/ Angus McLaren. Oxford, UK; B. Blackwell, 1990. viii, 275 p.
90-034917 363.9/6/09 0631167110
Birth control -- History. Contraception -- History.

HQ766.P542 1999
Pillai, Vijayan K.
Women's reproductive rights in developing countries/ Vijayan K. Pillai, Guang-zhen Wang. Aldershot, Hants, England; Ashgate, c1999. xiii, 194 p.
99-072243 363.9/6/091724 21 1840149086
Birth control -- Developing countries. Women's rights -- Developing countries. Human reproduction -- Developing coutnries.

HQ766.R445 1997
Reproductive rights in practice: a feminist report on quality of care/ edited by Anita Hardon and Elizabeth Hayes. New York: Zed Books, 1997. xii, 235 p.
97-028038 363.9/6 1856494519
Birth control. Birth control clinics. Family size.

HQ766.3.N6
Noonan, John Thomas, 1926-
Contraception; a history of its treatment by the Catholic theologians and canonists [by] John T. Noonan, Jr. Cambridge, Belknap Press of Harvard University Press, 1965. x, 561 p.
65-016687 261.83
Birth control -- Religious aspects -- Catholic Church -- History of doctrines. Contraception -- Religious aspects -- Catholic Church -- History of doctrines.

HQ766.5.U5.F3455 2001
Family planning sourcebook/ edited by Amy Marcaccio Keyzer. Detroit, MI: Omnigraphics, c2001. xv, 520 p.
00-053029 363.9/6/0973 21 0780803795
Birth control -- United States. Contraception -- United States.

HQ766.5.U5.G67
Gordon, Linda.
Woman's body, woman's right: a social history of birth control in America/ Linda Gordon. New York: Grossman, 1976. xviii, 479 p.
76-022691   301.32/1   0670778176
Birth control -- United States -- History.

HQ766.5.U5.M436 2001
McFarlane, Deborah R., 1951-
The politics of fertility control: family planning and abortion policies in the American states/ Deborah R. McFarlane, Kenneth J. Meier. New York: Chatham House Publishers, c2001. xv, 197 p.
99-050685   363.46/0973 21   1889119393
Birth control -- Government policy -- United States. Abortion -- Government policy -- United States.

HQ766.5.U5.R44
Reed, James, 1944-
From private vice to public virtue: the birth control movement and American society since 1830/ James Reed. New York: Basic Books, c1978. xvi, 456 p.
77-074571   363.9/6/0973   046502582X
Birth control -- United States -- History. Contraception -- United States -- History.

HQ766.5.U5.W325 1998
Watkins, Elizabeth Siegel.
On the pill: a social history of oral contraceptives, 1950-1970/ Elizabeth Siegel Watkins. Baltimore: Johns Hopkins University Press, c1998. viii, 183 p.
98-005003   363.9/6/0973 21   0801858763
Birth control -- United States -- Social aspects. Oral contraceptives -- United States -- History. Sex customs -- United States -- History -- 20th century.

HQ766.7.H35 1993
Hardin, Garrett James, 1915-
Living within limits: ecology, economics, and population taboos/ Garrett Hardin. New York: Oxford University Press, 1993. x, 339 p.
92-024250   304.6/66   019507811X
Birth control. Population.

HQ767.I668 1988
International handbook on abortion/ edited by Paul Sachdev. New York: Greenwood Press, 1988. xii, 520 p.
87-011994   363.4/6   0313234639
Abortion -- Cross-cultural studies -- Handbooks, manuals, etc. Abortion -- Government policy -- Handbooks, manuals, etc. Abortion -- Law and legislation -- Handbooks, manuals, etc.

HQ767.15.C38 2000
Cannold, Leslie.
The abortion myth: feminism, morality, and the hard choices women make/ Leslie Cannold. Hanover: University Press of New England, 2000. xxxix, 169 p.
99-034374   363.46   0819563773
Abortion -- Moral and ethical aspects. Abortion -- Public opinion. Women -- Attitudes.

HQ767.15.K36 1992
Kamm, F. M.
Creation and abortion: a study in moral and legal philosophy/ F.M. Kamm. New York: Oxford University Press, 1992. viii, 227 p.
91-022932   363.4/6   0195072839
Abortion -- Moral and ethical aspects. Abortion -- Law and legislation. Abortion -- Law and legislation -- United States.

HQ767.15.R83 1996
Rudy, Kathy.
Beyond pro-life and pro-choice: moral diversity in the abortion debate/ Kathy Rudy. Boston: Beacon Press, c1996. xxvii, 185 p.
95-047648   363.4/6 20   080700426X
Abortion -- Moral and ethical aspects. Abortion -- Religious aspects -- Christianity.

HQ767.25.B53 1993
Blanchard, Dallas A.
Religious violence and abortion: the Gideon Project/ Dallas A. Blanchard and Terry J. Prewitt. Gainesville: University Press of Florida, c1993. xvi, 347 p.
92-039693   363.4/6/0975999   0813011930
Abortion -- Religious aspects -- Christianity. Pro-life movement -- United States. Bombings -- Florida -- Pensacola -- Case studies.

HQ767.3.H37 1983
Harrison, Beverly Wildung, 1932-
Our right to choose: toward a new ethic of abortion/ Beverly Wildung Harrison. Boston: Beacon Press, c1983. xi, 334 p.
81-070488   179/.76   0807015083
Abortion -- Moral and ethical aspects. Abortion -- Religious aspects -- Christianity. Abortion -- Political aspects -- United States.

HQ767.3.T66 1983
Tooley, Michael, 1941-
Abortion and infanticide/ Michael Tooley. Oxford: Clarendon Press; c1983. ix, 441 p.
83-006261   363.4/6   0198246749
Abortion -- Moral and ethical aspects. Infanticide -- Moral and ethical aspects. Abortion, Induced -- Psychology.

HQ767.5.U5.B58 1994
Blanchard, Dallas A.
The anti-abortion movement and the rise of the religious right: from polite to fiery protest/ Dallas A. Blanchard. New York: Twayne Publishers; c1994. xiii, 177 p.
93-038457   363.4/6/0973   080573872X
Pro-life movement -- United States -- History. Abortion -- United States -- History.

HQ767.5.U5.C67 1991
Costa, Marie, 1951-
Abortion: a reference handbook/ Marie Costa. Santa Barbara, Calif.: ABC-Clio, c1991. xvii, 258 p.
91-015231   363.4/6   087436602X
Abortion -- United States -- Handbooks, manuals, etc.

HQ767.5.U5.C73 1993
Craig, Barbara Hinkson, 1942-
Abortion and American politics/ Barbara Hinkson Craig and David M. O'Brien. Chatham, N.J.: Chatham House, c1993. xvi, 382 p.
92-041395   363.4/6/0973   0934540888
Abortion -- Political aspects -- United States. Abortion -- Government policy -- United States. Abortion -- Law and legislation -- United States.

HQ767.5.U5.F38 1990
Faux, Marian.
Crusaders: voices from the abortion front/ by Marian Faux. Secaucus, N.J.: Carol Pub. Group, c1990. xvi, 289 p.
90-002228   363.4/6   1559720204
Pro-choice movement -- United States -- Case studies. Pro-life movement -- United States -- Case studies. Social reformers -- United States -- Case studies.

HQ767.5.U5.J33
Jaffe, Frederick S.
Abortion politics: private morality and public policy/ by Frederick S. Jaffe, Barbara L. Lindheim, Philip R. Lee. New York: McGraw-Hill, c1981. viii, 216 p.
80-017035   363.4/6/0973   0070321892
Abortion -- United States.

HQ767.5.U5.L84 1984
Luker, Kristin.
Abortion and the politics of motherhood/ Kristin Luker. Berkeley: University of California Press, c1984. xvi, 324 p.
83-047849   363.4/6/0973   0520043146
Abortion -- United States. Abortion -- Political aspects -- United States. Pro-life movement -- United States.

HQ767.5.U5.N45 1998
The new civil war: the psychology, culture, and politics of abortion/ edited by Linda J. Beckman, S. Marie Harvey. Washington, D.C.: American Psychological Association, c1998. xxix, 406 p.
98-003553   363.46/0973 21   1557985170
Abortion -- United States. Pregnancy, Unwanted -- United States. Abortion services -- United States.

HQ767.5.U5.R378 1997
Reagan, Leslie J.
When abortion was a crime: women, medicine, and law in the United States, 1867-1973/ Leslie J. Reagan. Berkeley: University of California Press, c1997. xiii, 387 p.
96-022568   363.4/6/0973 20   0520088484
Abortion -- United States -- History. Abortion services -- United States -- History. Abortion -- Law and legislation -- United States -- History.

HQ767.5.U5.S734 1991
Staggenborg, Suzanne.
The pro-choice movement: organization and activism in the abortion conflict/ Suzanne Staggenborg. New York: Oxford University Press, 1991. xiv, 229 p.
90-023877   363.4/6/0973   0195065964
Pro-choice movement -- United States. Abortion -- United States.

HQ767.5.U5.T73 1990
Tribe, Laurence H.
Abortion: the clash of absolutes/ Laurence H. Tribe. New York: Norton, c1990. xvi, 270 p.
90-032205   363.4/6   0393028453
Abortion -- Political aspects -- United States. Abortion -- Government policy -- United States. Abortion -- Moral and ethical aspects.

HQ767.84 The family. Marriage. Home — Children. Child development — Dictionaries. Encyclopedias

HQ767.84.B76 1995
Broude, Gwen J.
Growing up: a cross-cultural encyclopedia/ Gwen J. Broude. Santa Barbara, Calif.: ABC-CLIO, c1995. xvi, 376 p.
95-044079   305.23/1/03   0874367670
Child development -- Cross-cultural studies -- Encyclopedias. Child rearing -- Cross-cultural studies -- Encyclopedias. Socialization -- Cross-cultural studies -- Encyclopedias.

HQ767.87 The family. Marriage. Home — Children. Child development — History

HQ767.87.P64 1983
Pollock, Linda A.
Forgotten children: parent-child relations from 1500 to 1900/ Linda A. Pollock. Cambridge [Cambridgeshire]; Cambridge University Press, 1983. xi, 334 p.
83-005315 305.2/3/09 0521250099
Children -- History. Children -- Public opinion -- History. Parent and child -- History.

HQ767.9 The family. Marriage. Home — Children. Child development — General works

HQ767.9.T76 1994
Troubling children: studies of children and social problems/ Joel Best, editor. New York: Aldine de Gruyter, c1994. vi, 253 p.
93-050052 305.23 0202304914
Children -- Social conditions. Social problems.

HQ767.9.Z67 2000
Zornado, Joseph L.
Inventing the child: culture, ideology, and the story of childhood/ by Joseph L. Zornado. New York: Garland Pub., 2000. xviii, 234 p.
00-039338 305.23 0815335245
Children -- Social conditions. Children and adults. Parent and child.

HQ769-778.7 The family. Marriage. Home — Children. Child development — Child rearing

HQ769.C437
Chess, Stella.
Your child is a person; a psychological approach to parenthood without guilt [by] Stella Chess, Alexander Thomas [and] Herbert G. Birch. New York, Viking Press [1965] ix, 213 p.
65-024005 649.122
Child rearing.

HQ769.F717 1996
Franck, Irene M.
Parenting A to Z/ Irene Franck, David M. Brownstone. New York: HarperCollins Publishers, 1996. viii, 728 p.
96-006311 649/.1 0062715984
Child rearing -- United States -- Handbooks, manuals, etc. Parenting -- United States -- Handbooks, manuals, etc. Children -- United States -- Handbooks, manuals, etc.

HQ769.R466 1994
Ribbens, Jane.
Mothers and their children: a feminist sociology of childrearing/ Jane Ribbens. London; Sage, 1994. 236 p.
94-068659 649/.1 0803988346
Child rearing. Mother and infant. Feminist theory.

HQ769.R7647
Rubin, Zick.
Children's friendships/ Zick Rubin. Cambridge, Mass.: Harvard University Press, 1980. 165 p.
79-025644 305.2/3 0674116186
Friendship in children. Child development.

HQ770.4.G74 1990
Greven, Philip J.
Spare the child: the religious roots of punishment and the psychological impact of physical abuse/ Philip Greven. New York: Knopf: 1991. xiv, 263 p.
90-053171 649/.1 0394578600
Corporal punishment -- United States -- History. Corporal punishment -- Psychological aspects. Corporal punishment -- Religious aspects -- Christianity -- History of doctrines.

HQ770.4.S77 1994
Straus, Murray A. 1926-
Beating the devil out of them: corporal punishment in American families/ Murray A. Straus, with Denise A. Donnelly. New York: Lexington Books; c1994. xvii, 297 p.
93-048219 306.874 0029317304
Corporal punishment -- United States. Child abuse -- United States. Discipline of children -- United States.

HQ772.G24 1990
Gabriel, H. Paul.
The inner child: understanding your child's emotional growth in the first six years of life/ H. Paul Gabriel & Robert Wool. New York: Times Books, c1990. x, 230 p.
89-049560 649/.1 0812917936
Child psychology. Child rearing.

HQ773.5.W55 1996
Winner, Ellen.
Gifted children: myths and realities/ Ellen Winner. New York: Basic Books, c1996. xi, 449 p.
95-049279 155.45/5 20 0465017606
Gifted children.

HQ775.K56 1999
Kindlon, Daniel J. 1953-
Raising Cain: protecting the emotional life of boys/ Dan Kindlon and Michael Thompson with Teresa Barker. New York: Ballantine Books, 1999. xv, 287 p.
98-054182 305.23 0345424573
Boys -- Psychology. Emotions in children. Emotions in adolescence.

HQ777.G5745 2001
Girlhood in America: an encyclopedia/ Miriam Forman-Brunell, editor; foreword by Susan Douglas. Santa Barbara, Calif.: ABC-CLIO, c2001. 2 v.
2001-001346 305.23/0973/03 21 1576072061
Girls -- United States -- Encyclopedias.

HQ777.4.M39 1994
McLanahan, Sara.
Growing up with a single parent: what hurts, what helps/ Sara McLanahan, Gary Sandefur. Cambridge, Mass.: Harvard University Press, 1994. viii, 196 p.
94-019995 306.85/6 0674364074
Children of single parents -- United States. Single-parent families -- United States.

HQ777.4.W44
Weiss, Robert Stuart, 1925-
Going it alone: the family life and social situation of the single parent/ Robert S. Weiss. New York: Basic Books, c1979. xvi, 303 p.
78-019936 301.42/7 0465026885
Single-parent families -- United States.

HQ777.5.B796 1996
Buchanan, Christy M.
Adolescents after divorce/ Christy M. Buchanan, Eleanor E. Maccoby, Sanford M. Dornbusch. Cambridge, Mass.: Harvard University Press, 1996. 331 p.
96-011882 306.874 0674005171
Children of divorced parents -- United States -- Attitudes. Teenagers -- United States -- Attitudes. Divorce -- United States.

HQ777.5.F87 1991
Furstenberg, Frank F., 1940-
Divided families: what happens to children when parents part/ Frank F. Furstenberg, Jr., Andrew J. Cherlin. Cambridge, Mass.: Harvard University Press, 1991. vi, 142 p.
90-048171 306.89 0674655761
Children of divorced parents -- United States. Divorce -- Economic aspects -- United States.

HQ777.7.V57
Visher, Emily B., 1918-
Stepfamilies: a guide to working with stepparents and stepchildren/ Emily B. Visher and John S. Visher. New York: Brunner/Mazel, c1979. xx, 280 p.
78-025857 301.42/7 0876301901
Stepfamilies -- United States. Stepparents -- United States. Stepchildren -- United States.

HQ778.63.M52 1999
Michel, Sonya, 1942-
Children's interests/mothers' rights: the shaping of America's child care policy/ Sonya Michel. New Haven, CT: Yale University Press, 1999. xii, 410 p.
98-034830 362.71/2/0973 0300059515
Child care -- Government policy -- United States -- History. Child care services -- United States -- History.

HQ778.7.U6.B49 1993
Berry, Mary Frances.
The politics of parenthood: child care, women's rights, and the myth of the good mother/ Mary Frances Berry. New York: Viking, 1993. xiii, 303 p.
92-050388 362.7/12/0973 0670837059:
Child care -- Government policy -- United States. Child care services -- Government policy -- United States. Women -- Employment -- United States.

HQ778.7.U6.B76 1990
Browne Miller, Angela, 1952-
The day care dilemma: critical concerns for American families/ Angela Browne Miller. New York: Insight Books, c1990. xii, 316 p.
89-026664 362.7/12/0973 0306434350
Child care services -- United States. Day care centers -- United States.

HQ778.7.U6.R44 1992
Reeves, Diane Lindsey, 1959-
Child care crisis: a reference handbook/ Diane Lindsey Reeves. Santa Barbara, Calif.: ABC-CLIO, c1992. xiii, 173 p.
92-038144 362.7/12 0874366453
Child care services -- United States. Child care services -- Government policy -- United States.

HQ778.7.U6.W53 1990
Who cares for America's children?: child care policy for the 1990s/ Cheryl D. Hayes, John L. Palmer, and Martha J. Zaslow, editors; Panel on Child Care Policy, Committee on Child Development Research and Public Policy, Commission on Behavioral and Social Sciences and Education, National Research Council. Washington, D.C.: National Academy Press, 1990. xvii, 362 p.
90-005813 362.7 0309040329
Child care -- United States. Child care -- Government policy -- United States. Child care services -- Government policy -- United States.

HQ782-784 The family. Marriage. Home — Children. Child development — Child life (Descriptive). Activities of childhood

HQ782.M47 1982
Mergen, Bernard.
Play and playthings: a reference guide/ Bernard Mergen. Westport, Conn.: Greenwood Press, 1982. xi, 281 p.
82-006139 790.1/922 0313221367
Play -- United States -- History. Children -- United States. Play -- United States -- Bibliography.

HQ783.D44 1991
Delgado-Gaitan, Concha.
Crossing cultural borders: education for immigrant families in America/ Concha Delgado-Gaitan and Henry Trueba. London; Falmer Press, 1991. viii, 203 p.
90-040815 305.2/3/08968073 185000885X
Socialization. Hispanic American children. Hispanic Americans -- Cultural assimilation.

HQ783.M83
Mussen, Paul Henry.
Roots of caring, sharing, and helping: the development of prosocial behavior in children/ Paul Mussen, Nancy Eisenberg-Berg. San Francisco: W. H. Freeman, c1977. ix, 212 p.
77-022750 301.15/72 071670045X
Socialization. Child development. Sharing in children.

HQ784.M3.L48 1996
Levine, Madeline.
Viewing violence: how media violence affects your child's and adolescent's development/ Madeline Levine. New York: Doubleday, 1996. xvi, 256 p.
95-048266 302.23/083 0385476868
Mass media and children. Mass media and teenagers. Violence in mass media.

HQ784.S56.V36 2001
Van Ausdale, Debra, 1954-
The first R: how children learn race and racism/ Debra Van Ausdale and Joe R. Feagin. Lanham, Md.: Rowman & Littlefield, c2001. vii, 231 p.
00-042563 305.8/0083 21 0847688615
Social interaction in children. Racism. Prejudices in children.

HQ784.T4.K57 1993
Kline, Stephen.
Out of the garden: toys, TV, and children's culture in the age of marketing/ Stephen Kline. London; Verso, 1993. x, 406 p.
93-034292 305.23/083 086091397X
Television advertising and children. Child consumers. Mass media and children.

HQ784.T4.S533 2001
Handbook of children and the media/ Dorothy G. Singer, Jerome L. Singer, editors. Thousand Oaks, Calif.: Sage Publications, c2001. xvii, 765 p.
00-009006 302.23/45/083 21 0761919546
Television and children -- United States. Mass media and children -- United States. Video games -- Psychological aspects.

HQ784.T4.S56
Singer, Jerome L.
Television, imagination, and aggression: a study of preschoolers/ Jerome L. Singer, Dorothy G. Singer. Hillsdale, N.J.: L. Erlbaum Associates, 1981. x, 213 p.
80-036810 791.45/01/3 0898590604
Television and children -- Longitudinal studies. Imagination in children. Aggressiveness in children.

HQ784.T4.V333 1990
Van Evra, Judith Page.
Television and child development/ Judith Van Evra. Hillsdale, N.J.: L. Erlbaum Associates, 1990. xviii, 239 p.
90-035064 302.23/45/083 0805805753
Television and children. Child development.

HQ784.T68.S45 1993
Seiter, Ellen, 1957-
Sold separately: children and parents in consumer culture/ Ellen Seiter. New Brunswick, N.J.: Rutgers University Press, c1993. xii, 257 p.
92-044227 305.23 0813519888
Television advertising and children -- United States. Child consumers -- United States.

HQ784.V55.D65 2001
Domestic violence in the lives of children: the future of research, intervention, and social policy/ edited by Sandra A. Graham-Bermann and Jeffrey L. Edleson. Washington, DC: American Psychological Association, c2001. xi, 332 p.
00-069972 362.82/923 21 1557987793
Children and violence -- Congresses. Children and violence -- Research -- Congresses. Children of abused wives -- Congresses.

HQ784.W3.S54 2000
Sherrow, Victoria.
Encyclopedia of youth and war: young people as participants and victims/ Victoria Sherrow. Phoenix, AZ: Oryx Press, 2000. xvi, 366 p.
99-043452 305.235 1573562874
Children and war. Youth.

HQ789 The family. Marriage. Home — Children. Child development — Children's rights. The child and state

HQ789.E35 1996
Edmonds, Beverly C.
Children's rights: a reference handbook/ Beverly C. Edmonds, William R. Fernekes. Santa Barbara, Calif.: ABC-CLIO, c1996. xvii, 364 p.
96-043167 305.23 20 0874367646
Children's rights -- Juvenile literature. Children's rights -- United States -- Juvenile literature. Children's rights.

HQ792 The family. Marriage. Home — Children. Child development — Social conditions of children. By region or country, A-Z

HQ792.E8.S53 1990
Shahar, Shulamith.
Childhood in the Middle Ages/ Shulamith Shahar. London; Routledge, 1990. x, 342 p.
89-006227 305.2/3/0940902 0415026245
Children -- Europe -- History. Social history -- Medieval, 500-1500. Education, Medieval -- Europe.

HQ792.G7.H27 1993
Hanawalt, Barbara.
Growing up in medieval London: the experience of childhood in history/ Barbara A. Hanawalt. New York: Oxford University Press, 1993. xvii, 300 p.
92-045682 305.23/09421/2 0195084055
Children -- England -- London -- History. City and town life -- England -- London. Social history -- Medieval, 500-1500.

HQ792.G7.J67 1987
Jordan, Thomas Edward.
Victorian childhood: themes and variations/ Thomas E. Jordan. Albany: State University of New York Press, c1987. xv, 391 p.
86-030184 305.2/3/0941 0887065449
Children -- Great Britain -- Social conditions. Great Britain -- Social conditions -- 19th century.

HQ792.G7.S65 1992
Sommerville, C. John 1938-
The discovery of childhood in Puritan England/ C. John Sommerville. Athens: University of Georgia Press, c1992. x, 211 p.
90-023436 305.23/0942/09032 082031353X
Children -- Great Britain -- History -- 17th century. Great Britain -- Social conditions -- 17th century.

HQ792.G73.G65 1990
Golden, Mark, 1948-
Children and childhood in classical Athens/ Mark Golden. Baltimore: Johns Hopkins University Press, c1990. xix, 268 p.
89-024748 305.23/0938/5 0801839807
Children -- Greece -- Athens -- History. Family -- Greece -- Athens -- History. Athens (Greece) -- Social conditions. Greece -- Social conditions -- To 146 B.C.

HQ792.P3.B47
Bettelheim, Bruno.
The children of the dream. [New York] Macmillan [1969] xiii, 363 p.
69-010505 301.43/1/095694
Children -- Israel. Kibbutzim.

HQ792.U5.C35 1992
Calvert, Karin Lee Fishbeck.
Children in the house: the material culture of early childhood, 1600-1900/ Karin Calvert. Boston: Northeastern University Press, c1992. xi, 189 p.
92-014142 305.23/09 1555531385
Children -- United States -- History. Material culture -- United States. United States -- Social life and customs.

HQ792.U5.C565 1997
Clement, Priscilla Ferguson, 1942-
Growing pains: children in the industrial age, 1850-1890/ Priscilla Ferguson Clement. New York: Twayne Publishers; c1997. xii, 287 p.
96-041085   305.23 20   0805741097
Children -- United States -- History -- 19th century.

HQ792.U5.C66 2000
Conley, Dalton, 1969-
Honky/ Dalton Conley. Berkeley: University of California Press, c2000. xii, 231 p.
00-023774   305.23/09747 21   0520215869
White children -- New York (State) -- New York -- Social conditions. Whites -- Race identity -- New York (State) -- New York. Whites -- New York (State) -- New York -- Biography. Lower East Side (New York, N.Y.) -- Social conditions.

HQ792.U5.K69 2000
Kozol, Jonathan.
Ordinary resurrections: children in the years of hope/ Jonathan Kozol. New York: Crown Publishers, c2000. ix, 388 p.
99-059808   305.23/0974/1 21   051770000X
Children -- New York (State) -- New York -- Social conditions. Socially handicapped children -- New York (State) -- New York. Mott Haven (New York, N.Y.) -- Social conditions.

HQ792.U5.M39 1997
Mayer, Susan E.
What money can't buy: family income and children's life chances/ Susan E. Mayer. Cambridge, Mass.: Harvard University Press, 1997. viii, 230 p.
96-034429   305.23/0973   0674587332
Children -- United States -- Social conditions. Children -- United States -- Economic conditions. Social mobility -- United States.

HQ792.U5.R37 1996
Reinier, Jacqueline S.
From virtue to character: American childhood, 1775-1850/ Jacqueline S. Reinier. New York: Twayne Publishers; c1996. xii, 258 p.
96-025091   305.23/0973 20   080574102X
Children -- United States -- History. Child rearing -- United States -- History.

HQ792.U5.S534 1999
Shirk, Martha.
Lives on the line: American families and the struggle to make ends meet/ Martha Shirk, Neil G. Bennett, and J. Lawrence Aber. Boulder, Colo.: Westview Press, 1999. ix, 294 p.
99-023948   306.85/0973   0813366534
Poor children -- United States -- Case studies. Poor -- United States -- Case studies. Family -- United States -- Case studies.

HQ792.U5.W5
Wishy, Bernard W., 1925-
The child and the Republic; the dawn of modern American child nurture, by Bernard Wishy. Philadelphia, University of Pennsylvania Press [1967, c1968] x, 205 p.
67-026223   649/.09
Child rearing -- History. Child psychology -- United States -- History.

HQ792.U5.Z45 1985
Zelizer, Viviana A. Rotman.
Pricing the priceless child: the changing social value of children/ Viviana A. Zelizer. New York: Basic Books, c1985. x, 277 p.
84-045302   305.2/0973   046506325X
Children -- Economic aspects -- United States -- History. Child rearing -- United States -- Costs. Child labor -- United States.

HQ796-798 The family. Marriage. Home — Youth. Adolescents. Teenagers — General, and United States

HQ796.C635
Cole, Larry.
Street kids, by Larry Cole, with Ralph Romero [and others] New York, Grossman, 1970. 180 p.
78-121374   301.43/15/097471   0670678171
Youth -- New York (State) -- New York. Social work with youth.

HQ796.D335 1999
Davis, Nanette J.
Youth crisis: growing up in the high-risk society/ Nanette J. Davis; foreword by David Matza. Westport, Conn.: Praeger, 1999. xiv, 373 p.
98-024558   305.235   0275959392
Youth -- Social conditions. Juvenile delinquency -- Prevention.

HQ796.E58 1990
Encyclopedia of adolescence/ edited by Richard Lerner, Anne C. Petersen, Jeanne Brooks-Gunn. New York: Garland Pub., 1991. 2 v.
90-014033   305.23/5   0824043782
Adolescence -- Encyclopedias.

HQ796.H256
Handlin, Oscar, 1915-
Facing life; youth and the family in American history, by Oscar Handlin and Mary F. Handlin. Boston, Little, Brown [1971] ix, 326 p.
74-161852   301.43/15/0973
Youth -- United States -- History. Young adults -- United States -- History. United States -- Social conditions.

HQ796.I235 1993
Identity and inner-city youth: beyond ethnicity and gender/ edited by Shirley Brice Heath and Milbrey W. McLaughlin. New York: Teachers College Press, c1993. vi, 250 p.
92-045696   305.23/5/0973   0807732532
Urban youth -- United States -- Attitudes. Youth -- United States -- Societies and clubs. Social work with youth -- United States.

HQ796.L444 1997
Lightfoot, Cynthia.
The culture of adolescent risk-taking/ Cynthia Lightfoot; foreword by Jaan Valsiner. New York: Guilford Press, c1997. xviii, 187 p.
96-047250   305.235 21   1572301899
Adolescence. Risk-taking (Psychology) in adolescence.

HQ796.S4139 1991
Schlegel, Alice.
Adolescence: an anthropological inquiry/ Alice Schlegel, Herbert Barry III. New York: Free Press; c1991. viii, 263 p.
90-025216   305.23/5   0029278953
Adolescence -- Cross-cultural studies.

HQ796.S8237 1996
Statistical handbook on adolescents in America/ edited by Bruce A. Chadwick and Tim B. Heaton. Phoenix, Ariz.: Oryx Press, 1996. xviii, 323 p.
96-010514   305.23/5   0897749227
Teenagers -- United States -- Statistics.

HQ796.Y583 1985
Youniss, James.
Adolescent relations with mothers, fathers, and friends/ James Youniss and Jacqueline Smollar. Chicago: University of Chicago Press, 1985. viii, 201 p.
84-028067   305.2/35   0226964876
Youth. Interpersonal relations in adolescence. Parent and teenager.

HQ798.B724 1997
Brumberg, Joan Jacobs.
The body project: an intimate history of American girls/ Joan Jacobs Brumberg. New York: Random House, c1997. xxxiii, 267 p.
96-021885   305.23/5 20   0679402977
Teenage girls -- United States -- History. Young women -- United States -- History. Body, Human -- Social aspects -- United States -- History.

HQ798.T39 1995
Taylor, Jill McLean, 1944-
Between voice and silence: women and girls, race and relationship/ Jill McLean Taylor, Carol Gilligan, Amy M. Sullivan. Cambridge, Mass: Harvard University Press, 1995. xii, 253 p.
95-036209   305.23/5   0674068793
Teenage girls -- United States -- Psychology -- Longitudinal studies. Socially handicapped teenagers -- United States -- Psychology -- Longitudinal studies. Minority teenagers -- United States -- Psychology -- Longitudinal studies.

HQ799 The family. Marriage. Home — Youth. Adolescents. Teenagers — Other regions or countries, A-Z

HQ799.G72.E53 1994
Ben-Amos, Ilana Krausman.
Adolescence and youth in early modern England/ Ilana Krausman Ben-Amos. New Haven: Yale University Press, 1994. xi, 335 p.
93-038314   305.23/5/0942   0300055978
Youth -- England -- History.

HQ799.J3.W37 1995
Wardell, Steven, 1971-
Rising sons and daughters: life among Japan's new young/ Steven Wardell; foreword by Haru Matsukata Reischauer. Cambridge, Mass.: Plympton Press International, 1995. xxv, 291 p.
94-000181   305.23/5/0952   0963923080
Wardell, Steven -- 1971- Teenagers -- Japan -- Social life and customs. Teenagers -- Japan -- Social conditions. Students, Foreign -- Japan -- Biography. Japan -- Social conditions -- 1945- Japan -- Social life and customs -- 1945-

HQ799.R9.P495 1994
Pilkington, Hilary, 1964-
Russia's youth and its culture: a nation's constructors and constructed/ Hilary Pilkington. London; Routledge, 1994. xiv, 358 p.
93-026766   305.23/5/0947   0415090431
Youth -- Russia (Federation) Youth -- Soviet Union. Russia (Federation) -- Social conditions -- 1991- Soviet Union -- Social conditions -- 1970-1991.

HQ799.U65.W45 1993
White, Merry I., 1941-
The material child: coming of age in Japan and America/ Merry White. New York: Free Press; c1993. v, 256 p.
92-034730 305.23/5/0952 0029350352
Teenagers -- United States -- Social conditions. Teenagers -- Japan -- Social conditions. Adolescence.

HQ799.15 The family. Marriage. Home — Youth. Adolescents. Teenagers — Parent and teenager

HQ799.15.L37 1994
Larson, Reed, 1950-
Divergent realities: the emotional lives of mothers, fathers, and adolescents/ Reed Larson and Maryse H. Richards. New York: BasicBooks, c1994. x, 333 p.
93-046394 306.874 0465016626
Parent and teenager -- United States. Adolescent psychology -- United States. Family -- United States -- Psychological aspects.

HQ799.2 The family. Marriage. Home — Youth. Adolescents. Teenagers — Special topics, A-Z

HQ799.2.M35.S87 1995
Strasburger, Victor C., 1949-
Adolescents and the media: medical and psychological impact/ Victor C. Strasburger. Thousand Oaks: Sage Publications, c1995. xi, 137 p.
94-045245 302.23/0935 0803954999
Mass media and teenagers.

HQ799.2.T4
Bodroghkozy, Aniko, 1960-
Groove tube: sixies television and the youth rebellion/ Aniko Bodroghkozy. Durham, NC: Duke University Press, 2001. xii, 320 p.
00-061748 302.23/45/08350973 0822326566
Television and youth -- United States. New Left -- United States. United States -- Social conditions -- 1960-1980.

HQ799.7 The family. Marriage. Home — Young men and women — By region or country

HQ799.7.C66 1971
Cook, Bruce, 1932-
The beat generation. New York, Scribner [1971] 248 p.
73-143950 301.44/94 0684123711
Bohemianism -- United States. Beat generation.

HQ799.7.K45
Keniston, Kenneth.
Young radicals; notes on committed youth. New York, Harcourt, Brace & World [1968] xi, 368 p.
68-023578 301.43/15/0973
Young adults -- United States -- Political activity. Youth -- United States -- Political activity. Radicalism -- United States.

HQ799.7.K46
Keniston, Kenneth.
Youth and dissent; the rise of a new opposition. New York, Harcourt Brace Jovanovich [1971] xii, 403 p.
71-160404 301.6/3 0151998906
Young adults -- United States -- Political activity. Alienation (Social psychology) Radicalism -- United States.

HQ800.15 The family. Marriage. Home — Single people — Celibacy

HQ800.15.K58 1989
Kitch, Sally.
Chaste liberation: celibacy and female cultural status/ Sally L. Kitch. Urbana: University of Illinois Press, c1989. 225 p.
88-027928 306.7/32 0252016084
Celibacy.

HQ800.2 The family. Marriage. Home — Single people — Single women

HQ800.2.C43 1984
Chambers-Schiller, Lee Virginia, 1948-
Liberty, a better husband: single women in America: the generations of 1780-1840/ Lee Virginia Chambers-Schiller. New Haven: Yale University Press, c1984. x, 285 p.
84-003524 305.4/890652 0300031645
Single women -- United States -- History. United States -- Social life and customs -- 1783-1865.

HQ800.2.V53 1985
Vicinus, Martha.
Independent women: work and community for single women, 1850-1920/ Martha Vicinus. Chicago: University of Chicago Press, c1985. xv, 396 p.
84-016158 305.4/890652 0226855678
Single women -- England -- Social conditions. Middle class -- England -- History -- 19th century. Single women -- Employment -- England -- History -- 19th century.

HQ800.3 The family. Marriage. Home — Single people — Single men. Bachelors

HQ800.3.C58 1999
Chudacoff, Howard P.
The age of the bachelor: creating an American subculture/ Howard P. Chudacoff. Princeton, N.J.: Princeton University Press, c1999. x, 341 p.
98-035154 305.38/9652 21 069102796X
Bachelors -- United States.

HQ800.4 The family. Marriage. Home — Single people — By region or country, A-Z

HQ800.4.U6.P47 1981
Peterson, Nancy L.
Our lives for ourselves: women who have never married/ Nancy L. Peterson. New York: Putnam, c1981. 264 p.
80-023101 305.4/8 0399124764
Single women -- United States.

HQ801 The family. Marriage. Home — Man-woman relationship. Courtship. Dating — Historic courtships. "Great lovers"

HQ801.R85 1984
Rothman, Ellen K., 1950-
Hands and hearts: a history of courtship in America/ Ellen K. Rothman. New York: Basic Books, Inc., c1984. xi, 370 p.
83-045261 306.7/34/0973 0465028802
Courtship -- United States -- History. United States -- Social life and customs.

HQ801.S5244 1998
Shem, Samuel.
We have to talk: healing dialogues between women and men/ Samuel Shem and Janet Surrey. New York, NY: Basic Books, c1998. 225 p.
98-020014 306.7 21 0465080634
Man-woman relationships. Interpersonal communication. Communication -- Sex differences.

HQ806 The family. Marriage. Home — Adultery

HQ806.B367 2001
Barash, David P.
The myth of monogamy: fidelity and infidelity in animals and people/ David P. Barash & Judith Eve Lipton. New York: W.H. Freeman and Co., c2001. ix, 227 p.
2001-023209
Adultery. Sex customs. Sexual behavior in animals.

HQ809.3 The family. Marriage. Home — Family violence

HQ809.3.G7.L39 1988
Lawson, Annette, 1936-
Adultery: an analysis of love and betrayal/ Annette Lawson. New York: Basic Books, c1988. xv, 440 p.
88-047685 306.7/36 0465000754
Adultery -- Great Britain. Adultery.

HQ809.3.U5.D37 1983
The Dark side of families: current family violence research/ edited by David Finkelhor ... [et al.]. Beverly Hills: Sage Publications, c1983. 384 p.
82-021496 306.8/7 0803919344
Family violence -- United States. Wife abuse -- United States. Child abuse -- United States.

HQ809.3.U5.H35 1988
Handbook of family violence/ edited by Vincent B. Van Hasselt ... [et al.]. New York: Plenum Press, c1988. xviii, 500 p.
87-007204 362.8/2 030642648X
Family violence -- United States. Family. Violence.

HQ809.3.U5.M385 1995
McCue, Margi Laird.
Domestic violence: a reference handbook/ Margi Laird McCue. Santa Barbara, Calif.: ABC-CLIO, c1995. xiii, 273 p.
95-044080 362.82/92 087436762X
Family violence -- United States. Family violence -- United States -- Prevention. Victims of family violence -- Service for -- United States.

HQ809.3.U5.S77 1983
Stacey, William A.
The family secret: domestic violence in America/
William Stacey, Anson Shupe. Boston: Beacon
Press, c1983. xxi, 237 p.
82-073965   306.8/7/0973   0807041440
*Family violence -- United States. Family violence
-- Texas.*

HQ809.3.U5.S777 1983
Star, Barbara.
Helping the abuser: intervening effectively in
family violence/ Barbara Star. New York: Family
Service Association of America, c1983. xvii,
262 p.
83-048129   362.8/2   0873042026
*Family violence -- United States. Family social
work -- United States.*

HQ809.3.U5.S87
Straus, Murray A. 1926-
Behind closed doors: violence in the American
family/ Murray A. Straus, Richard J. Gelles,
Suzanne K. Steinmetz. Garden City, N.Y.: Anchor
Press/Doubleday, 1980. viii, 301 p.
78-022741   301.42   0385142595
Family violence -- United States.

HQ814 The family. Marriage.
Home — Divorce — General works

HQ814.G62 1993
Goode, William Josiah.
World changes in divorce patterns/ William J.
Goode New Haven: Yale University Press, c1993.
xiii, 354 p.
92-044530   306.89   0300055374
Divorce -- Cross-cultural studies.

HQ814.S38 1997
Schwartz, Lita Linzer.
Painful partings: divorce and its aftermath/ Lita
Linzer Schwartz, Florence W. Kaslow. New York:
J. Wiley, c1997. x, 310 p.
96-019118   306.89 20   0471110094
*Divorce. Divorce -- Psychological aspects.
Divorced people -- Family relationships.*

HQ834-835 The family. Marriage.
Home — Divorce —
By region or country

HQ834.H33
Halem, Lynne Carol.
Separated and divorced women/ Lynne Carol
Halem. Westport, Conn.: Greenwood Press, 1982.
xiv, 335 p.
81-013178   306.8/9   0313231605
Divorced women -- United States.

HQ834.R55 1991
Riley, Glenda, 1938-
Divorce an American tradition/ Glenda Riley. New
York: Oxford University Press, 1991. xi, 262 p.
90-047746   306.89/0973   0195061233
Divorce -- United States -- History.

HQ834.W356 2000
Wallerstein, Judith S.
The unexpected legacy of divorce: a 25 year
landmark study/ Judith Wallerstein, Julia Lewis
and Sandra Blakeslee. New York: Hyperion,
c2000. xxxv, 347 p.
00-035071   306.89/0973 21   0786863943
*Children of divorced parents -- United States --
Longitudinal studies. Divorce -- United States --
Longitudinal studies.*

HQ834.W358 1989
Wallerstein, Judith S.
Second chances: men, women, and children a
decade after divorce/ Judith S. Wallerstein and
Sandra Blakeslee. New York: Ticknor & Fields,
1989. xxi, 329 p.
88-023320   306.8/9   0899196489
*Divorced people -- United States -- Longitudinal
studies. Children of divorced parents -- United
States -- Longitudinal studies.*

HQ834.W68 1975
Women in Transition Inc.
Women in transition: a feminist handbook on
separation and divorce/ Women in Transition, inc.
New York: Scribner, [1975] xiv, 538 p.
75-015728   301.42/8   0684142589
*Divorce -- United States. Divorced women -- Life
skills guides. Women -- Employment.*

HQ835.C2.M33 1992
Maccoby, Eleanor E., 1917-
Dividing the child: social and legal dilemmas of
custody/ Eleanor E. Maccoby and Robert H.
Mnookin; with Charlene E. Depner and H.
Elizabeth Peters. Cambridge, Mass.: Harvard
University Press, 1992. xi, 369 p.
92-000096   306.89   0674212940
*Divorce -- California -- Longitudinal studies.
Custody of children -- California -- Longitudinal
studies. Divorce -- United States.*

HQ967 The family. Marriage.
Home — Free love —
Particular communities.
By region or country, A-Z

HQ967.U6.S68 1988
Spurlock, John C., 1954-
Free love: marriage and middle-class radicalism in
America, 1825-1860/ John C. Spurlock. New York:
New York University Press, 1988. xiv, 277 p.
88-019916   306.7/35   0814778836
*Free love -- United States -- History -- 19th
century Middle class -- United States -- History --
19th century. Radicalism -- United States --
History -- 19th century.*

HQ971 The family. Marriage.
Home — Communal living.
Communes —
By region or country

HQ971.M55 1999
Miller, Timothy, 1944-
The 60s communes: hippies and beyond/ Timothy
Miller. Syracuse, NY: Syracuse University Press,
1999. xxvi, 329 p.
99-037768   307.77/4/0973   0815628110
*Communal living -- United States. United States
-- Social conditions -- 1960-1980.*

HQ971.Z3
Zablocki, Benjamin David, 1941-
Alienation and charisma: a study of contemporary
American communes/ Benjamin Zablocki. New
York: Free Press, c1980. xxiv, 455 p.
79-055938   307.7   0029357802
*Communal living -- United States -- History.
Collective settlements -- United States -- History.
Communal living -- History.*

HQ981-994 The family. Marriage.
Home —
Non-monogamous relationships —
Polygamy

HQ981.A45 1996
Altman, Irwin.
Polygamous families in contemporary society/
Irwin Altman, Joseph Ginat. Cambridge;
Cambridge Unversity Press, 1996. xv, 512 p.
95-046687   306.84/23   0521561698
*Polygamy -- United States -- History. Mormon
Church -- United States -- History. Mormon
families -- United States -- History.*

HQ994.E52 1987
Embry, Jessie L.
Mormon polygamous families: life in the principle/
by Jessie L. Embry; foreword by Linda King
Newell. Salt Lake City: University of Utah Press,
1987. xvii, 238 p.
87-018991   306.8/423   0874802776
*Polygamy -- United States -- History. Mormon
Church -- United States -- History. Mormon
families -- United States -- History.*

HQ998 The family. Marriage.
Home — Illegitimacy.
Unmarried mothers —
General works

HQ998.B3
Bastardy and its comparative history: studies in the
history of illegitimacy and marital nonconformism
in Britain, France, Germany, Sweden, North
America, Jamaica, and Japan/ edited by Peter
Laslett, Karla Oosterveen, and Richard M. Smith.
Cambridge, Mass.: Harvard University Press, 1980.
xv, 431 p.
79-027692   306.7   0674063384
Illegitimate children -- History.

HQ999 The family. Marriage.
Home — Illegitimacy.
Unmarried mothers —
By region or country, A-Z

HQ999.U6.S65 1992
Solinger, Rickie, 1947-
Wake up little Susie: single pregnancy and race
before Roe v. Wade/ Rickie Solinger. New York:
Routledge, 1992. xi, 324 p.
91-025068   306.85/6/097309045   041590448X
*Illegitimacy -- United States -- History.
Unmarried mothers -- United States -- History.*

HQ1031 The family. Marriage. Home — Mixed marriages. Intermarriage. Interfaith marriage

HQ1031.D34 2000
Dalmage, Heather M., 1965-
Tripping on the color line: Black-white multiracial families in a racially divided world/ c Heather M. Dalmage. New Brunswick, N.J.: Rutgers University Press , c2000. x, 200 p.
00-032350   306.84/6 21   0813528437
Interracial marriage -- United States. Racially mixed children -- United States. United States -- Social conditions. United States -- Race relations.

HQ1031.G6
Gordon, Albert Isaac, 1903-
Intermarriage: interfaith, interracial, interethnic. Boston, Beacon Press [1964] xiii, 420 p.
64-013534   301.422
Intermarriage. Interfaith marriage. Interracial marriage.

HQ1031.R69 1995
Rosenblatt, Paul C.
Multiracial couples: Black and white voices/ Paul C. Rosenblatt, Terri A. Karis, Richard D. Powell. Thousand Oaks: Sage Publications, c1995. xiv, 305 p.
95-016778   306.84/6/09776579   080397258X
Interracial marriage -- Minnesota -- Minneapolis Metropolitan Area. Interracial marriage -- Minnesota -- Saint Paul Metropolitan Area. Married people -- Minnesota -- Minneapolis Metropolitan Area -- Interviews.

HQ1031.S75 1989
Spickard, Paul R., 1950-
Mixed blood: intermarriage and ethnic identity in twentieth-century America/ Paul R. Spickard. Madison, Wis.: University of Wisconsin Press, c1989. xii, 532 p.
89-031235   306.8/46   0299121100
Intermarriage -- United States -- History -- 20th century. Ethnicity -- United States -- History -- 20th century.

HQ1058 The family. Marriage. Home — Widows and widowers. Widowhood — General works

HQ1058.L64 1996
Lopata, Helena Znaniecka, 1925-
Current widowhood: myths & realities/ Helena Znaniecka Lopata. Thousand Oaks, Calif.: Sage Publications, c1996. xv, 251 p.
95-035750   305.48/9654 20   0803973950
Widows -- United States -- Psychology. Widows -- United States -- Social conditions. Widows -- Services for -- United States.

HQ1058.5 The family. Marriage. Home — Widows and widowers. Widowhood — By region or country, A-Z

HQ1058.5.U5.H95 1983
Hyman, Herbert Hiram, 1918-
Of time and widowhood: nationwide studies of enduring effects/ Herbert H. Hyman. Durham, N.C.: Duke University Press, 1983. 118 p.
82-025138   306.8/8   0822305046
Widows -- United States -- Longitudinal studies. Widowers -- United States -- Longitudinal studies. Family life surveys -- United States.

HQ1059.4-1059.5 The family. Marriage. Home — Middle age

HQ1059.4.A68 1995
Apter, T. E.
Secret paths: women in the new midlife/ Terri Apter. New York: W.W. Norton, c1995. 347 p.
95-002151   305.4   0393037665
Middle aged women -- Psychology. Middle age -- Psychological aspects.

HQ1059.5.U5.F37 1981
Farrell, Michael P., 1942-
Men at midlife/ Michael P. Farrell, Stanley D. Rosenberg. Boston: Auburn House, c1981. xiv, 242 p.
81-003624   305.2/4   0865690731
Middle aged men -- United States. Middle aged men -- United States -- Case studies. Middle age -- United States.

HQ1059.5.U5.H36 1997
Handbook on women and aging/ edited by Jean M. Coyle. Westport, Conn.: Greenwood Press, 1997. xix, 484 p.
96-032414   305.24/4   0313288577
Middle aged women -- United States. Aged women -- United States.

HQ1061 The family. Marriage. Home — Aged. Gerontology (Social aspects). Retirement — General works

HQ1061.A4555 1991
Aging and ethics: philosophical problems in gerontology/ edited by Nancy S. Jecker. Clifton, N.J.: Humana Press, c1991. xi, 394 p.
91-010792   305.26   0896032019
Gerontology -- Moral and ethical aspects. Aging -- Moral and ethical aspects. Death -- Moral and ethical aspects.

HQ1061.B4123 1989
Becoming and being old: sociological approaches to later life/ edited by Bill Bytheway ... [et al.]. London; Sage, 1989. 184 p.
88-062124   305.2/6   0803981708
Old age.

HQ1061.C663 1980
Cowley, Malcolm, 1898-
The view from 80/ Malcolm Cowley. New York: Viking Press, 1980. xv, 74 p.
79-056286   305.2/6/0924   0670746142
Cowley, Malcolm, -- 1898-   Aged -- United States -- Biography.

HQ1061.E53 2001
The encyclopedia of aging: a comprehensive resource in gerontology and geriatrics/ George L. Maddox, editor-in-chief. New York: Springer Pub., c2001. 2 v.
00-049663   305.26/03 21   0826148425
Gerontology -- Encyclopedias. Aged -- Encyclopedias.

HQ1061.F59
Fontana, Andrea.
The last frontier: the social meaning of growing old/ Andrea Fontana; preface by Fred Davis. Beverly Hills, Calif.: Sage Publications, c1977. 215 p.
77-023186   301.43/5   0803908326
Aged.

HQ1061.H3353 1995
Handbook of aging and the family/ edited by Rosemary Blieszner and Victoria Hilkevitch Bedford; foreword by Lillian E. Troll. Westport, Conn.: Greenwood Press, 1995. xxiii, 509 p.
94-017988   305.26   0313283958
Aging. Aged -- Family relationships.

HQ1061.H338 1988
Harris, Diana K.
Dictionary of gerontology/ Diana K. Harris. New York: Greenwood Press, 1988. xii, 201 p.
87-025142   016.3052/6/03   0313252874
Gerontology -- Dictionaries. Gerontology -- Bibliography.

HQ1061.I535
International handbook on aging: contemporary developments and research/ edited by Erdman Palmore. Westport, Conn.: Greenwood Press, 1980. xviii, 529 p.
78-073802   301.43/5   0313208905
Gerontology -- Cross-cultural studies.

HQ1061.N65
Neugarten, Bernice Levin, 1916-
Middle age and aging: a reader in social psychology. Edited by Bernice L. Neugarten. Chicago, University of Chicago Press [1968] xiii, 596 p.
68-055150   301.43/4/08   0226573826
Middle age. Old age. Aging

HQ1061.P388 1999
Peterson, Peter G.
Gray dawn/ Peter G. Peterson. New York: Times Books, 1999. viii, 280 p.
98-047749   305.26   0812931955
Aging -- Government policy. Aging -- Economic aspects. Aging -- Social aspects.

HQ1061.S844 1994
Studies in the economics of aging/ edited by David A. Wise. Chicago: University of Chicago Press, c1994. xi, 456 p.
94-016196   305.26   0226902943
Old age -- Economic aspects -- Congresses. Aging -- Economic aspects -- Congresses. Retirement -- Economic aspects -- Congresses.

HQ1061.T47
Themes of work and love in adulthood/ edited by Neil J. Smelser and Erik H. Erikson. Cambridge, Mass.: Harvard University Press, 1980. x, 297 p.
79-026130   301.43/4   0674877500
Adulthood — Congresses. Work — Congresses. Love — Congresses.

HQ1063.2 The family. Marriage. Home — Aged. Gerontology (Social aspects). Retirement — Retirement

HQ1063.2.U6.D35 1998
Dailey, Nancy, 1953-
When baby boom women retire/ Nancy Dailey. Westport, Conn.: Praeger, 1998. x, 150 p.
97-027003   306.3/8/082   0275960706
Women — United States — Retirement. Baby boom generation — United States — Retirement. Retirement income — United States.

HQ1063.2.U6.S39 2000
Savishinsky, Joel S.
Breaking the watch: the meanings of retirement in America/ Joel S. Savishinsky. Ithaca: Cornell University Press, c2000. x, 281 p.
00-009092   306.3/8/0973 21   0801437717
Retirement — United States. Retirees — Recreation — United States.

HQ1063.6 The family. Marriage. Home — Aged. Gerontology (Social aspects). Retirement — Aged parents

HQ1063.6.M47 1997
Merrill, Deborah M., 1962-
Caring for elderly parents: juggling work, family, and caregiving in middle and working class families/ Deborah M. Merrill. Westport, Conn.: Auburn House, 1997. x, 232 p.
96-045347   306.874   0865692696
Aging parents — Care.

HQ1063.6.S74 1988
Steinmetz, Suzanne K.
Duty bound: elder abuse and family care/ Suzanne K. Steinmetz. Newbury Park, Calif.: Sage Publications, c1988. 288 p.
87-030770   362.6/042   0803929188
Aging parents — Home care — United States. Abused aged — United States. Caregivers — United States — Psychology.

HQ1064 The family. Marriage. Home — Aged. Gerontology (Social aspects). Retirement — By region or country, A-Z

HQ1064.A88.S38 1990
Schulz, James H.
Economics of population aging: the "graying" of Australia, Japan, and the United States/ James H. Schulz, Allan Borowski, and William H. Crown with the assistance of Shinya Hoshino ... [et al.]. New York: Auburn House, 1991. xiv, 364 p.
90-000437   362.6   0865690081
Aged — Government policy — Australia. Aged — Government policy — Japan. Aged — Government policy — United States.

HQ1064.F7.T76 1989
Troyansky, David G.
Old age in the old regime: image and experience in eighteenth-century France/ David G. Troyansky. Ithaca: Cornell University Press, 1989. xiv, 260 p.
88-043286   305.2/6/0944   080142299X
Aged — France — History — 18th century. Old age — France — Public opinion — History — 18th century. Public opinion — France — History — 18th century.

HQ1064.G7.T44 2000
Thane, Pat.
Old age in English history: past experiences, present issues/ Pat Thane. Oxford [UK]; Oxford University Press, 2000. 536 p.
99-054442   305.26/0941   0198203829
Aged — Great Britain — History. Old age — Great Britain — History.

HQ1064.J3.C36 1992
Campbell, John Creighton.
How policies change: the Japanese government and the aging society/ John Creighton Campbell. Princeton, N.J.: Princeton University Press, c1992. xv, 418 p.
91-023482   305.26/0952   069107884X
Aged — Government policy — Japan. Aged — Services for — Japan. Aged — Japan — Social conditions.

HQ1064.U5.A26
Achenbaum, W. Andrew.
Old age in the new land: the American experience since 1790/ W. Andrew Achenbaum. Baltimore: Johns Hopkins University Press, c1978. xii, 237 p.
77-028666   301.43/5/0973   080182107X
Aged — United States — History. Aged — United States — Public opinion. Public opinion — United States.

HQ1064.U5.A6342 1993
Aging in Black America/ edited by James S. Jackson, Linda M. Chatters, Robert Joseph Taylor. Newbury Park, Calif.: Sage Publications, c1993. xvi, 338 p.
92-030719   305.26/08996073   0803935358
Afro-American aged — Social conditions.

HQ1064.U5.A63457 1993
Aging in rural America/ C. Neil Bull, editor. Newbury Park, Calif.: Sage Publications, c1993. xvi, 279 p.
93-025528   305.26/0973   0803948859
Aged — United States — Social conditions. Aged - - Services for — United States. United States — Rural conditions.

HQ1064.U5.B379 2001
Bettelheim, Adriel.
Aging in America A to Z/ Adriel Bettelheim. Washington, DC: CQ Press, 2001. xv, 280 p.
2001-035484   305.26/0973/03   156802584X
Aged — United States — Encyclopedias. Aging — United States — Encyclopedias. Gerontology — United States — Encyclopedias.

HQ1064.U5.C526 1991
Cole, Thomas R., 1949-
The journey of life: a cultural history of aging in America/ Thomas R. Cole. Cambridge [England]; Cambridge University Press, 1992. xxxv, 260 p.
91-008867   305.26/0973   0521410207
Old Age — United States — History. Aged — United States — Social conditions. Aging — Social aspects — United States.

HQ1064.U5.F84 1997
Furman, Frida Kerner, 1948-
Facing the mirror: older women and beauty shop culture/ Frida Kerner Furman. New York: Routledge, 1997. x, 218 p.
97-012407   305.26   0415915236
Aged women — United States — Psychology — Case studies. Aged women — Social networks — United States — Case studies. Jewish women — Social networks — United States — Case studies.

HQ1064.U5.H183 1993
Haber, Carole, 1951-
Old age and the search for security: an American social history/ Carole Haber and Brian Gratton. Bloomington: Indiana University Press, c1993. xv, 230 p.
93-012258   305.26/0973   0253326915
Old age — United States — History. Aged — United States — Economic conditions. Aged — United States — Social conditions.

HQ1064.U5.J64
Johnson, Elizabeth S.
Growing old: the social problems of aging/ Elizabeth S. Johnson, John B. Williamson. New York: Holt, Rinehart, and Winston, c1980. viii, 196 p.
78-067459   301.43/5/0973   0030403162
Aged — United States — Social conditions. Aging. Age discrimination — United States.

HQ1064.U5.K39 2001
Kausler, Donald H.
The graying of America: an encyclopedia of aging, health, mind, and behavior/ Donald H. Kausler and Barry C. Kausler. Urbana: University of Illinois Press, c2001. xiv, 479 p.
00-011202   305.26/03 21   0252026357
Aged — United States — Encyclopedias. Aging — United States — Encyclopedias. Old age — United States — Encyclopedias.

HQ1064.U5.L29 1983
Lammers, William W.
Public policy and the aging/ William W. Lammers. Washington, D.C.: CQ Press, c1983. xv, 265 p.
82-022138   362.6/0973   0871872463
Aged — Government policy — United States.

HQ1064.U5.P26
Palmore, Erdman Ballagh, 1930-
Social patterns in normal aging: findings from the Duke longitudinal study/ Erdman Palmore. Durham, N.C.: Duke University Press, 1981. xii, 135 p.
81-009800   305.2/6   0822304589
Aging — Social aspects — United States — Longitudinal studies.

HQ1064.U5.R512 1984
Rich, Bennett Milton, 1909-
The aging, a guide to public policy/ Bennett M. Rich and Martha Baum. Pittsburgh, Pa.: University of Pittsburgh Press, c1984. xiii, 275 p.
84-040228   362.6/0973   0822953641
Aged — Government policy — United States. Aged — Legal status, laws, etc. — United States. Old age assistance — United States.

HQ1064.U5.S467 1990
Serow, William J.
Population aging in the United States/ William J. Serow, David F. Sly, and J. Michael Wrigley. New York: Greenwood Press, 1990. xvii, 220 p.
89-025699   305.26/0973   0313273111
Aged — United States. Age distribution (Demography) — United States. United States — Population.

HQ1064.U5.S695 1994
Statistical handbook on aging Americans/ Frank L. Schick and Renee Schick, editors. Phoenix, Ariz.: Oryx Press, 1994. xxii, 335 p.
93-036711   305.26/0973/021   0897747216
Aged -- United States -- Statistics. Aging -- United States -- Handbooks, manuals, etc.

HQ1064.U5.V494 1990
Vierck, Elizabeth, 1945-
Fact book on aging/ Elizabeth Vierck. Santa Barbara, Calif.: ABC-CLIO, c1990. xxii, 199 p.
90-034667   305.26/0973   0874362849
Aged -- United States -- Handbooks, manuals, etc. Old age -- United States -- Handbooks, manuals, etc. Aging -- United States -- Handbooks, manuals, etc.

HQ1064.U5.W5923 1985
Williamson, John B.
Aging and public policy: social control or social justice?/ by John B. Williamson, Judith A. Shindul, Linda Evans. Springfield, Ill., U.S.A.: C.C. Thomas, c1985. xvii, 332 p.
84-026735   362.6/0973   0398051046
Aged -- Government policy -- United States. Pensions -- Government policy -- United States. Medical policy -- United States.

HQ1064.U6.I28 1984
Golant, Stephen M.
A place to grow old: the meaning of environment in old age/ Stephen M. Golant. New York: Columbia University Press, 1984. xi, 421 p.
84-005042   305.2/6   0231048408
Aged -- Illinois -- Evanston -- Social conditions. Human ecology -- Illinois -- Evanston. Aged -- Housing -- Illinois -- Evanston.

HQ1073 Thanatology. Death. Dying — General works

HQ1073.E54 1989
Encyclopedia of death/ edited by Robert Kastenbaum and Beatrice Kastenbaum. Phoenix, Ariz.: Oryx Press, 1989. xix, 295 p.
89-009401   306.9/03   089774263X
Death -- Encyclopedias.

HQ1073.Q54 1994
Quigley, Christine, 1963-
Death dictionary: over 5,500 clinical, legal, literary, and vernacular terms/ compiled and edited by Christine Quigley. Jefferson, N.C.: McFarland, c1994. xi, 195 p.
93-028817   306.9/03   0899508693
Death -- Dictionaries.

HQ1073.5 Thanatology. Death. Dying — By region or country, A-Z

HQ1073.5.R66.K95 1998
Kyle, Donald G.
Spectacles of death in ancient Rome/ Donald G. Kyle. London; Routledge, 1998. xii, 288 p.
97-043475   306.9   0415096782
Death -- Social aspects -- Rome. Funeral rites and ceremonies -- Rome. Violence -- Rome -- History. Rome -- Social life and customs.

HQ1075 Sex role — General works

HQ1075.A435 2002
Alsop, Rachel.
Theorizing gender/ Rachel Alsop, Annette Fitzsimons, and Kathleen Lennon; with a guest chapter on psychoanalysis by Ros Minsky. Malden, MA: Blackwell, c2002. 282 p.
2001-006332   305.3 21   0745619444
Sex role.

HQ1075.B44 1990
Beere, Carole A., 1944-
Gender roles: a handbook of tests and measures/ Carole A. Beere. New York: Greenwood Press, 1990. xiv, 575 p.
89-017033   305.3/072   0313262780
Sociometry -- Methodology -- Handbooks, manuals, etc. Scale analysis (Psychology) -- Handbooks, manuals, etc. Sex role -- Research -- Methodology -- Handbooks, manuals, etc.

HQ1075.B45 1993
Bem, Sandra L.
The lenses of gender: transforming the debate on sexual inequality/ Sandra Lipsitz Bem. New Haven: Yale University Press, c1993. xii, 244 p.
92-026345   305.3   0300056761
Sex role. Sex differences (Psychology) Sexism.

HQ1075.D52 1984
A Dictionary of sexist quotations/ [compiled by] Simon James. Brighton, Sussex: Harvester Press; 1984. xii, 206 p.
84-011108   305.3/03/21   038920501X
Sex role -- Dictionaries. Sex role -- Anecdotes. Sexism -- Dictionaries.

HQ1075.F39 2000
Fausto-Sterling, Anne, 1944-
Sexing the body: gender politics and the construction of sexuality/ Anne Fausto-Sterling. New York, NY: Basic Books, c2000. xii, 473 p.
00-703212   0465077137
Sex differences. Gender identity. Sex differentiation.

HQ1075.I58 1993
International handbook on gender roles/ edited by Leonore Loeb Adler; foreword by Nancy Felipe Russo. Westport, Conn.: Greenwood Press, 1993. xxii, 525 p.
92-045080   305.3   0313283362
Sex role -- Cross-cultural studies.

HQ1075.J64 1997
Johnson, Allan G.
The gender knot: unraveling our patriarchal legacy/ Allan G. Johnson. Philadelphia: Temple University Press, 1997. x, 294 p.
96-041982   305.3   1566395186
Sex role. Patriarchy. Feminism.

HQ1075.M34 1990
Making a difference: psychology and the construction of gender/ edited by Rachel T. Hare-Mustin & Jeanne Marecek. New Haven: Yale University Press, c1990. xiv, 212 p.
89-038800   305.3   0300047150
Sex role. Sex differences (Psychology) Women -- Psychology.

HQ1075.M386 2001
McElvaine, Robert S., 1947-
Eve's seed: biology, the sexes, and the course of history/ Robert S. McElvaine. New York: McGraw-Hill, c2001. viii, 453 p.
00-056634   305.3/09 21   0071355286
Sex role -- History.

HQ1075.S26
Sanday, Peggy Reeves.
Female power and male dominance: on the origins of sexual inequality/ Peggy Reeves Sanday. Cambridge; Cambridge University Press, 1981. xvii, 295 p.
80-018461   305.3   0521236185
Sex role. Sexism. Power (Social sciences)

HQ1075.W526 2001
Wiesner, Merry E.,
Gender in history/ Merry E. Wiesner-Hanks. Malden, Mass.: Blackwell, 2001. ix, 246 p.
00-013063   305.3/09 21   0631210369
Sex role -- History. Social history.

HQ1075.W67 1985
Women, gender, and social psychology/ edited by Virginia E. O'Leary, Rhoda Kesler Unger, Barbara Strudler Wallston. Hillsdale, NJ: L. Erlbaum, 1985. xii, 381 p.
84-023114   305.3   0898594472
Sex role. Women -- Psychology. Social psychology.

HQ1075.5 Sex role — By region or country, A-Z

HQ1075.5.A8.G66 1994
Goodnow, Jacqueline J.
Men, women, and household work/ Jacqueline J. Goodnow & Jennifer M. Bowes. Melbourne; Oxford University Press, 1994. vii, 224 p.
94-123076   306.3/615/0994   0195535723
Sex role -- Australia. Sexual division of labor -- Australia. Home economics -- Social aspects -- Australia.

HQ1075.5.E5.F54 1995
Fletcher, Anthony.
Gender, sex, and subordination in England, 1500-1800/ Anthony Fletcher. New Haven: Yale University Press, 1995. xxii, 442 p.
95-021565   305.3/0942   0300065310
Sex role -- England -- History. Patriarchy -- England -- History -- 16th century. Patriarchy -- England -- History -- 17th century. England -- Social conditions -- History.

HQ1075.5.G7.K46 1993
Kent, Susan Kingsley.
Making peace: the reconstruction of gender in interwar Britain/ Susan Kingsley Kent. Princeton, N.J.: Princeton University Press, c1993. x, 182 p.
93-018776   305.3/0941/0904   0691031401
Sex role -- Great Britain -- History -- 20th century. Feminism -- Great Britain -- History -- 20th century. War and society.

HQ1075.5.G7.P66 1988
Poovey, Mary.
Uneven developments: the ideological work of gender in mid-Victorian England/ Mary Poovey. Chicago: University of Chicago Press, 1988. xi, 282 p.
88-004783   305.3/0942   0226675297
Sex role -- Great Britain -- History -- 19th century. Anesthesia in obstetrics -- History -- 19th century. Divorce -- Great Britain -- History -- 19th century.

HQ1075.5.I4.M36 1988
Mandelbaum, David Goodman, 1911-
Women's seclusion and men's honor: sex roles in north India, Bangladesh, and Pakistan/ David G. Mandelbaum. Tucson: University of Arizona Press, c1988. xvi, 153 p.
87-036547   305.3/0954   0816510431
Sex role -- India. Sex role -- Bangladesh. Sex role -- Pakistan.

HQ1075.5.U6.C36 1987
Cancian, Francesca M.
Love in America: gender and self-development/ Francesca M. Cancian. Cambridge [Cambridgeshire]; Cambridge University Press, 1987. ix, 210 p.
87-010277   305.3/0973   0521342023
Sex role -- United States. Androgyny (Psychology) Love.

HQ1075.5.U6.E67 1988
Epstein, Cynthia Fuchs.
Deceptive distinctions: sex, gender, and the social order/ Cynthia Fuchs Epstein. New Haven: Yale University Press; c1988. xv, 300 p.
88-005717   305.3   0300041756
Sex role -- United States. Sex differences (Psychology) Social structure -- United States.

HQ1075.5.U6.H63 1997
Hodes, Martha Elizabeth.
White women, Black men: illicit sex in the nineteenth-century South/ Martha Hodes. New Haven, CT: Yale University Press, c1997. xii, 338 p.
97-009320   306.7/0975/09034 21   0300069707
Sex role -- United States -- History -- 19th century. Sex customs -- United States -- History -- 19th century. White women -- United States -- Sexual behavior. United States -- History -- Civil War, 1861-1865. United States -- Social conditions -- To 1865.

HQ1075.5.U6.N67 1996
Norton, Mary Beth.
Founding mothers & fathers: gendered power and the forming of American society/ Mary Beth Norton. New York: A.A. Knopf: 1996. x, 496 p.
95-043791   306/.0973   0679429654
Sex role -- United States -- History -- 17th century. Family -- United States -- History -- 17th century. United States -- Social conditions -- To 1865. United States -- Politics and government -- To 1775.

HQ1088 Men — Study and teaching. Men's studies. Research

HQ1088.M35 1987
The Making of masculinities: the new men's studies/ edited by Harry Brod. Boston: Allen & Unwin, c1987. xvi, 346 p.
86-028796   305.3/1   0044970358
Men's studies -- United States. Men -- United States. Masculinity -- United States.

HQ1090 Men — General works

HQ1090.A45 1993
Allen, Marvin, 1944-
In the company of men: a new approach to healing for husbands, fathers, and friends/ Marvin Allen with Jo Robinson. New York: Random House, c1993. xix, 235 p.
92-056801   305.32   0679422870
Men's movement. Masculinity. Men -- Psychology.

HQ1090.H67 1995
Horrocks, Roger, 1946-
Male myths and icons: masculinity in popular culture/ Roger Horrocks. New York: St. Martin's Press, c1995. viii, 203 p.
95-007737   305.32   0312126220
Men in popular culture. Masculinity.

HQ1090.H68 1994
Horrocks, Roger, 1946-
Masculinity in crisis: myths, fantasies, and realities/ Roger Horrocks; consultant editor, Jo Campling. New York: St. Martin's Press, 1994. viii, 210 p.
93-037500   155.3/32   0333593227
Men. Masculinity. Sex role.

HQ1090.K57 1991
Kipnis, Aaron R.
Knights without armor: a practical guide for men in quest of masculine soul/ Aaron R. Kipnis; foreword by Robert A. Johnson. Los Angeles: Tarcher; c1991. xv, 293 p.
91-014820   305.31   0874776589
Men -- Psychology. Masculinity (Psychology)

HQ1090.M47 1992
Men's friendships/ edited by Peter M. Nardi. Newbury Park: Sage Publications, c1992. viii, 246 p.
91-045060   302.3/4/081   0803937733
Men -- Psychology. Masculinity. Male friendship -- Sociological aspects.

HQ1090.R7 1994
Ross, John Munder.
What men want: mothers, fathers, and manhood/ John Munder Ross. Cambridge, Mass.: Harvard University Press, 1994. 242 p.
93-046057   155.3/32   0674950801
Men -- Psychology. Fatherhood -- Psychological aspects. Masculinity.

HQ1090.S43 1990
Segal, Lynne.
Slow motion: changing masculinities, changing men/ Lynne Segal. New Brunswick, N.J.: Rutgers University Press, 1990. xiii, 396 p.
90-041862   305.31   0813516196:
Men -- Psychology. Masculinity. Sex role.

HQ1090.3 Men — By region or country — United States

HQ1090.3.B59 1990
Bly, Robert W.
Iron John: a book about men/ Robert Bly. Reading, Mass.: Addison-Wesley, 1990. xi, 268 p.
90-037877   305.31   0201517205
Men -- United States. Masculinity. Men -- United States -- Psychology.

HQ1090.3.K55 1995
Kimbrell, Andrew.
The masculine mystique: the politics of masculinity/ Andrew Kimbrell. New York: Ballantine Books, 1995. xvi, 367 p.
95-013408   305.32   0345386582
Men -- United States -- Identity. Masculinity -- United States. Sex role -- United States.

HQ1090.3.M475 1997
Messner, Michael A.
Politics of masculinities: men in movements/ Michael A. Messner. Thousand Oaks, Calif.: Sage Publications, c1997. xviii, 137 p.
96-035667   305.32 20   0803955766
Men's movement -- United States. Men -- United States. Sex role -- United States.

HQ1090.3.R69 1993
Rotundo, E. Anthony.
American manhood: transformations in masculinity from the Revolution to the modern era/ E. Anthony Rotundo. New York: BasicBooks, c1993. xii, 382 p.
92-053247   305.32/0973   0465014097
Men -- United States -- History -- 19th century. Masculinity -- United States -- History -- 19th century.

HQ1090.3.W45 1990
Weiss, Robert Stuart, 1925-
Staying the course: the emotional and social lives of men who do well at work/ Robert S. Weiss. New York: Free Press; c1990. xvii, 314 p.
89-071506   305.33   002934090X
Men -- United States -- Psychology. Executives -- United States -- Psychology. Success in business -- United States -- Psychological aspects.

HQ1090.7 Men — By region or country — Other regions or countries, A-Z

HQ1090.7.G7.M35 1991
Manful assertions: masculinities in Britain since 1800/ edited by Michael Roper and John Tosh. London; Routledge, 1991. x, 221 p.
90-049417   305.31/0941   0415053226
Men -- Great Britain -- History. Masculinity -- Great Britain -- History.

HQ1101 Women. Feminism — Serials — English

HQ1101.C64 1998
Cornell, Drucilla.
At the heart of freedom: feminism, sex, and equality/ Drucilla Cornell. Princton, N.J.: Princeton University Press, c1998. xvi, 254 p.
98-003548   305.42 21   0691028974
Feminism. Women's rights.

HQ1106 Women. Feminism — Congresses

HQ1106.B49 1984
Beyond domination: new perspectives on women and philosophy/ edited by Carol C. Gould. Totowa, N.J.: Rowman & Allanheld, 1984, c1983. xii, 321 p.
83-010894   305.4/2   0847672026
Feminist theory -- Congresses.

HQ1115 Women. Feminism — Dictionaries. Encyclopedias

HQ1115.B65 1996
Boles, Janet K., 1944-
Historical dictionary of feminism/ by Janet K. Boles, Diane Long Hoeveler, Rebecca Bardwell. Lanham, Md.: Scarecrow Press, c1996. xv, 429 p.
95-018558 305.42/03 20 0810830426
Feminism -- Dictionaries.

HQ1115.H86 1995
Humm, Maggie.
The dictionary of feminist theory/ Maggie Humm. Columbus: Ohio State University Press, c1995. xix, 354 p.
94-048253 305.42/01 0814206662
Feminist theory -- Dictionaries.

HQ1115.R68 2000
The Routledge critical dictionary of feminism and postfeminism/ edited by Sarah Gamble. New York: Routledge, 2000. xii, 370 p.
99-054689 305.42/03 0415925185
Feminism -- Dictionaries.

HQ1115.R69 2000
Routledge international encyclopedia of women: global women's issues and knowledge/ general editors, Cheris Kramarae, Dale Spender. New York: Routledge, 2000. 4 v.
00-045792 305.4/03 0415920884
Women -- Encyclopedias. Feminism -- Encyclopedias.

HQ1115.S25 1991
Salmonson, Jessica Amanda.
The encyclopedia of Amazons: women warriors from antiquity to the modern era/ Jessica Amanda Salmonson. New York: Paragon House, 1991. xiii, 290 p.
90-046258 355/.0082 1557784205
Women -- History. Women -- Biography -- Dictionaries. Women soldiers -- Biography -- Dictionaries.

HQ1115.W6425 1997
Women's issues/ consulting editor, Margaret McFadden. Pasadena, Calif.: Salem Press, c1997. 3 v.
96-048989 305.4/03 21 0893567655
Women -- Encyclopedias. Feminism -- Encyclopedias. Women -- United States -- Encyclopedias.

HQ1115.W645 1999
Women's studies encyclopedia/ edited by Helen Tierney. Rev. and expanded ed. Westport, Conn.: Greenwood Press, 1999. 3 v.
98-014236 305.4/03 21 0313310734
Women -- United States -- Encyclopedias. Women -- Encyclopedias. Feminism -- Encyclopedias.

HQ1121 Women. Feminism — History — General works

HQ1121.C45 1986
Chafetz, Janet Saltzman.
Female revolt: women's movements in world and historical perspective/ Janet Saltzman Chafetz, Anthony Gary Dworkin with the assistance of Stephanie Swanson. Totowa, N.J.: Rowman & Allanheld, 1986. x, 260 p.
85-022141 305.4/2/09 0847673596
Feminism -- History. Feminism -- Cross-cultural studies. Women's rights -- History.

HQ1121.L47 1986 vol. 2
Lerner, Gerda, 1920-
The creation of feminist consciousness: from the Middle Ages to eighteen-seventy/ Gerda Lerner. New York: Oxford University Press, 1993. xii, 395 p.
92-020411 305.42 0195066049
Women -- History. Feminist theory -- History. Women intellectuals -- History.

HQ1121.O47 1994
Olsen, Kirstin.
Chronology of women's history/ Kirstin Olsen. Westport, Conn.: Greenwood Press, 1994. xiv, 506 p.
93-050542 305.4/09 0313288038
Women -- History -- Chronology.

HQ1121.S79513 1992
A history of women in the West/ Georges Duby and Michelle Perrot, general editors. Cambridge, Mass.: Belknap Press of Harvard University Press, 1992-1994. 5 v.
91-034134 305.4/094 0674403703
Women -- History. Women -- Europe -- History.

HQ1121.W88
Woman in Western thought/ edited by Martha Lee Osborne. New York: Random House, c1979. xx, 341 p.
78-016116 301.41/2 039432112X
Women. Women -- Social conditions. Women -- History.

HQ1122 Women. Feminism — History — General special

HQ1122.B4 1968
Beard, Mary Ritter, 1876-1958.
On understanding women. New York, Greenwood Press, 1968 [c1931] viii, 541 p.
68-054773 301.41/2
Women. Women -- History. Civilization.

HQ1122.D55 1996
Dijkstra, Bram.
Evil sisters: the threat of female sexuality and the cult of manhood/ Bram Dijkstra. New York: Alfred A. Knopf, 1996. x, 480 p.
96-007448 305.42/09
Women in popular culture -- History. Femmes fatales -- History. Sexism -- History.

HQ1122.M62 1999
Moane, Geraldine, 1956-
Gender and colonialism: a psychological analysis of oppression and liberation/ Geraldine Moane; foreword by Mary Daly; consultant editor, Jo Campling. New York: St. Martin's Press, 1999. xiii, 228 p.
98-035652 305.42 0312220081
Women -- Social conditions -- Psychological aspects. Sex discrimination against women -- Psychological aspects. Oppression (Psychology)

HQ1122.T73 1994
Trager, James.
The women's chronology: a year-by-year record from prehistory to the present/ James Trager. New York: H. Holt, 1994. ix, 787 p.
93-041513 305.4/09
Women -- History -- Chronology. Chronology, Historical.

HQ1127-1137 Women. Feminism — History — Ancient

HQ1127.C53 1993
Clark, Gillian.
Women in late antiquity: pagan and Christian life-styles/ Gillian Clark. Oxford: Clarendon Press; 1993. xix, 158 p.
92-021513 305.4/09/01 0198146752
Women -- History -- To 500.

HQ1127.S25 2001
Salisbury, Joyce E.
Encyclopedia of women in the ancient world/ Joyce E. Salisbury; foreword by Mary Lefkowitz. Santa Barbara, Calif.: ABC-CLIO, c2001. xxiii, 385 p.
00-013117 305.4/09/0103 21 1576070921
Women -- History -- To 500 -- Encyclopedias. Women -- Biography -- To 500 -- Encyclopedias. Civilization, Ancient -- Encyclopedias.

HQ1127.W6525 1991
Women's history and ancient history/ edited by Sarah B. Pomeroy. Chapel Hill: University of North Carolina Press, c1991. xvi, 317 p.
90-024488 305.4/09 0807819492
Women -- History -- To 500. Women -- Greece -- History. Women -- Rome -- History.

HQ1127.W653 1993
Women's life in Greece & Rome: a source book in translation/ [compiled by] Mary R. Lefkowitz & Maureen B. Fant. 2nd ed. Baltimore: Johns Hopkins University Press, 1992. xxv, 387 p.
92-006845 305.4/0945/632 20 0801844754
Women -- History -- To 500 -- Sources. Women -- Rome -- History -- Sources. Women -- Greece -- History -- Sources.

HQ1134.B58 1995
Blundell, Sue.
Women in ancient Greece/ Sue Blundell. Cambridge, Mass.: Harvard University Press, 1995. 224 p.
93-036217 305.4/0938 0674954734
Women -- Greece -- History.

HQ1134.P64
Pomeroy, Sarah B.
Goddesses, whores, wives, and slaves: women in classical antiquity/ Sarah B. Pomeroy. New York: Schocken Books, 1975. xiii, 265 p.
74-008782 301.41/2/0938 0805235620
Women -- History -- To 500. Greece -- Social conditions -- To 146 B.C. Rome -- Social conditions.

HQ1134.W63 1984
Women in the ancient world: the Arethusa papers/
John Peradotto and J.P. Sullivan, editors. Albany:
State University of New York Press, c1984. 377 p.
83-004975 305.4/0938 0873957725
*Women -- Greece. Women -- Rome. Civilization,
Classical.*

HQ1136.L54 2000
Lightman, Marjorie.
Biographical dictionary of ancient Greek and
Roman women: notable women from Sappho to
Helena/ Marjorie Lightman and Benjamin
Lightman. New York: Facts On File, c2000. xix,
298 p.
99-020682 305.42/092/2376 21 0816031126
*Women -- Rome -- Biography -- Dictionaries.
Women -- Greece -- Biography -- Dictionaries.
Women -- Biography -- To 500 -- Dictionaries.*

HQ1137.E3.P65 1984
Pomeroy, Sarah B.
Women in Hellenistic Egypt: from Alexander to
Cleopatra/ Sarah B. Pomeroy. New York:
Schocken Books, 1984. xxii, 241 p.
84-003122 305.4/0932 0805239111
*Women -- Egypt -- History. Greeks -- Egypt --
History. Egypt -- History -- 332-30 B.C.*

HQ1143-1147 Women. Feminism — History — Medieval

HQ1143.B56 1991
Bloch, R. Howard.
Medieval misogyny and the invention of Western
romantic love/ R. Howard Bloch. Chicago:
University of Chicago Press, 1991. ix, 298 p.
91-012699 305.4/09/02 0226059723
*Women -- History -- Middle Ages, 500-1500.
Social history -- Medieval, 500-1500. Misogyny --
Europe -- History.*

HQ1143.G53 1978
Gies, Frances.
Women in the Middle Ages/ Frances and Joseph
Gies. New York: Crowell, c1978. 264 p.
77-025832 301.41/2/0902 0690017243
*Women -- History -- Middle Ages, 500-1500.
Social history -- Medieval, 500-1500. Women --
Europe -- Social conditions.*

HQ1143.M43
Medieval women/ edited by Derek Baker;
dedicated and presented to Professor Rosalind
M.T. Hill on the occasion of her seventieth
birthday. Oxford: Published for the Ecclesiastical
History Society 1978. xii, 399 p.
80-499721 305.4/2/094 0631192603
*Hill, Rosalind M. T. Women -- History -- Middle
Ages, 500-1500. Social history -- Medieval, 500-
1500. Women and religion -- History.*

HQ1143.P68 1997
Power, Eileen Edna,
Medieval women/ Eileen Power; edited by M. M.
Postan; [with a foreword by Maxine Berg]. Canto
ed. Cambridge; Cambridge University Press, 1997.
xxviii, 104 p.
97-219610 305.4/09/02 21 0521595568
*Women -- History -- Middle Ages, 500-1500.
Social history -- Medieval, 500-1500. Women --
Europe -- Social conditions.*

HQ1143.W64
Women in medieval society/ Brenda M. Bolton ...
[et al.]; edited, with an introd., by Susan Mosher
Stuard. [Philadelphia]: University of Pennsylvania
Press, 1976. 219 p.
75-041617 301.41/2/0902 0812277082
*Women -- History -- Middle ages, 500-1500.
Social history -- Medieval, 500-1500.*

HQ1147.E85 S73 1998
Stafford, Pauline.
Queens, concubines, and dowagers: the king's wife
in the early Middle Ages/ Pauline Stafford.
London; Leicester University Press, c1998. xxiii,
248 p.
97-052934 305.4/09/02 21 0718501748
*Women -- History -- Middle Ages, 500-1500.
Queens -- Europe -- History. Princesses -- Europe
-- History.*

HQ1147.F7.G65 1985
Gold, Penny Schine.
The lady & the Virgin: image, attitude, and
experience in twelfth-century France/ Penny
Schine Gold. Chicago: University of Chicago
Press, 1985. xxiv, 182 p.
84-023701 305.4/0944 0226300870
*Mary, -- Blessed Virgin, Saint -- Symbolism.
Social history -- Medieval, 500-1500. Women --
France -- History -- Middle ages, 500-1500.*

HQ1147.G7.L49 1995
Leyser, Henrietta.
Medieval women: a social history of women in
England, 450-1500/ Henrietta Leyser. New York:
St. Martin's Press, 1995. xi, 337 p.
95-221665 305.4/0942/0902 0312129343
*Women -- England -- History -- Middle Ages,
500-1500.*

HQ1147.G7.L82 1983
Lucas, Angela M.
Women in the Middle Ages: religion, marriage,
and letters/ Angela M. Lucas. New York: St.
Martin's Press, c1983. xvi, 214 p.
82-042578 305.4/2/0942 0312887434
*Women -- England -- History -- Middle Ages,
500-1500. Women -- History.*

HQ1147.I8.S58 2001
Skinner, Patricia, 1965-
Women in Medieval Italian society 500-1200/
Patricia Skinner. Harlow, England; Pearson
Education, 2001. x, 230 p.
00-051492 305.4/0945/0902 0582273684
*Women -- Italy -- History -- Middle Ages, 500-
1500. Family -- Italy -- History. Italy -- Social life
and customs.*

HQ1148-1149 Women. Feminism — History — Renaissance

HQ1148.K56 1991
King, Margaret L., 1947-
Women of the Renaissance/ Margaret L. King.
Chicago: University of Chicago Press, c1991. xv,
333 p.
91-019960 305.4/094 0226436179
*Women -- History -- Renaissance, 1450-1600.
Women -- Europe -- History.*

HQ1149.F8.F73 1984
French women and the Age of Enlightenment/
edited by Samia I. Spencer. Bloomington: Indiana
University Press, c1984. xv, 429 p.
83-048403 305.4/0944 0253324815
*Women -- France -- History -- 18th century.
Women -- France -- Social conditions.*

HQ1149.G3.W54 1986
Wiesner, Merry E., 1952-
Working women in Renaissance Germany/ Merry
E. Wiesner. New Brunswick, N.J.: Rutgers
University Press, c1986. xiii, 263 p.
85-014451 305.4/3/00943 0813511380
*Women -- Germany -- History -- Renaissance,
1450-1600. Women -- Germany -- Economic
conditions. Women -- Employment -- Germany --
History.*

HQ1150-1154 Women. Feminism — History — Modern

HQ1150.B63 2000
Boxer, Marilyn J.
Connecting spheres: European women in a
globalizing world, 1500 to the present/ Marilyn J.
Boxer, Jean H. Quataert, with Barbara Franzoi Bari
... [et al.]; foreword by Joan W. Scott. 2nd ed. New
York: Oxford University Press, 2000. xiv, 338 p.
99-019863 305.4/094 21 0195109511
*Women -- History -- Cross-cultural studies.
Women -- Europe -- History. Feminism -- History -
- Cross-cultural studies.*

HQ1150.F46 1983
Feminist theorists: three centuries of key women
thinkers/ edited by Dale Spender; introduction by
Ellen Carol DuBois. New York; Pantheon Books,
c1983. xiii, 402 p.
83-047747 305.4/2/0922 0394534387
Feminists -- Biography.

HQ1150.S68 1992
Spain, Daphne.
Gendered spaces/ Daphne Spain. Chapel Hill:
University of North Carolina Press, c1992. xviii,
294 p.
91-025057 305.3 0807820121
*Sex discrimination against women -- History.
Space (Architecture) -- History. Sex role -- History.*

HQ1150.S73 1995
Statistical record of women worldwide/ Linda
Schmittroth, editor. 2nd ed. New York: Gale
Research, c1995. xxxv, 1047 p.
95-037853 305.4/021 20 0810388723
*Women -- Statistics. Women -- United States --
Statistics.*

HQ1154.A685 1987
Analyzing gender: a handbook of social science
research/ editors, Beth B. Hess and Myra Marx
Ferree. Newbury Park, Calif.: Sage Publications,
c1987. 580 p.
87-023439 305.4/09 0803927193
Women -- History. Sex role. Feminism.

HQ1154.A745 1989
Aptheker, Bettina.
Tapestries of life: women's work, women's
consciousness, and the meaning of daily
experience/ Bettina Aptheker. Amherst: University
of Massachusetts Press, c1989. x, 298 p.
88-026715 305.4/2 087023658X
*Women -- Social conditions. Feminism.
Lesbianism.*

HQ1154.B268 1981
Banks, Olive.
Faces of feminism: a study of feminism as a social
movement/ Olive Banks. New York: St. Martin's
Press, 1981. 285 p.
81-013582 305.4/2/09 0312279523
Feminism -- History.

HQ1154.B88 1990
Butler, Judith P.
Gender trouble: feminism and the subversion of identity/ Judith Butler. New York: Routledge, 1990. xiv, 172 p.
89-006438 305.3 0415900425
Feminist theory. Sex role. Sex differences (Psychology)

HQ1154.C25 2000
The Cambridge companion to Feminism in philosophy/ edited by Miranda Fricker and Jennifer Hornsby. Cambridge, U.K.; Cambridge University Press, 2000. xiii, 280 p.
99-021117 305.42/01 0521624517
Feminist theory.

HQ1154.D314 1984
Daly, Mary, 1928-
Pure lust: elemental feminist philosophy/ Mary Daly. Boston: Beacon Press, c1984. xiv, 471 p.
83-071944 305.4/2/01 0807015040
Feminism. Social ethics.

HQ1154.D3 1985
Daly, Mary, 1928-
Beyond God the Father: toward a philosophy of women's liberation/ by Mary Daly. Boston: Beacon Press, 1985, c1973. xxxiv, 225 p.
84-045067 305.4/2 0807015024
Feminism. Women in Christianity.

HQ1154.E8 1977
Evans, Richard J.
The feminists: women's emancipation movements in Europe, America, and Australasia, 1840-1920/ Richard J. Evans. London: Croom Helm; 1977. 266 p.
77-077490 322.4/4 0064920372
Feminism -- History.

HQ1154.F4457 1988
The Feminist papers: from Adams to de Beauvoir/ edited, with introductory essays and a new preface, by Alice S. Rossi. 1st Northeastern University Press ed. Boston: Northeastern University Press, 1988, c1973. xxiv, 716 p.
88-005257 305.4/2/09 19 1555530281
Women -- History -- Modern period, 1600- -- Sources. Women's rights -- History -- Sources. Feminism -- History -- Sources.

HQ1154.F4458 1988
Feminist perspectives in philosophy/ edited by Morwenna Griffiths and Margaret Whitford. Bloomington: Indiana University Press, c1988. x, 234 p.
87-045774 305.4/2 0253321727
Feminist theory. Feminism.

HQ1154.F446 1979
Feminist quotations: voices of rebels, reformers, and visionaries/ compiled by Carol McPhee, Ann FitzGerald. New York: Crowell, c1979. xiv, 271 p.
78-003308 301.41/2/08 0690017707
Feminism -- Quotations, maxims, etc.

HQ1154.F448 1988
Feminist thought and the structure of knowledge/ edited by Mary McCanney Gergen. New York: New York University Press, c1988. xix, 200 p.
87-033980 305.4/2/01 0814730132
Feminist theory. Women scholars. Knowledge, Theory of.

HQ1154.F744 1992
French, Marilyn, 1929-
The war against women/ Marilyn French. New York: Summit Books, c1992. 223 p.
92-000705 305.42 0671778293
Sex discrimination against women. Women -- Social conditions. Sexism.

HQ1154.G56 2000
Global feminisms since 1945: a survey of issues and controversies/ edited by Bonnie G. Smith. London; Routledge, 2000. xii, 319 p.
99-089441 305.42 0415184908
Feminism -- Cross-cultural studies. Women's rights -- Cross-cultural studies. Women in politics -- Cross-cultural studies.

HQ1154.G63
Gornick, Vivian,
Woman in sexist society; studies in power and powerlessness. Edited by Vivian Gornick and Barbara K. Moran. New York, Basic Books [1971] xxv, 515 p.
70-157125 301.41/2/08 0465091997
Women -- History -- Modern period, 1600- Power (Social sciences) Sex discrimination.

HQ1154.J3
Janeway, Elizabeth.
Man's world, woman's place: a study in social mythology. New York, Morrow, 1971. 319 p.
73-142405 301.41/2
Women -- Social conditions. Social role.

HQ1154.K38 1984
Kelly, Joan, 1928-1982.
Women, history & theory: the essays of Joan Kelly/ Joan Kelly. Chicago: University of Chicago Press, 1984. xxvi, 163 p.
84-002558 305.4/09 0226430278
Feminism. Women -- History.

HQ1154.M3965 1999
McFadden, Margaret.
Golden cables of sympathy: the transatlantic sources of nineteenth-century feminism/ Margaret H. McFadden. Lexington, Ky.: University Press of Kentucy, c1999. xiv, 270 p.
98-049993 305.42/09/034 21 0813121175
Feminism -- History -- 19th century. Women's rights -- History -- 19th century. Feminism -- International cooperation -- History -- 19th century. United States -- Civilization -- European influences. Europe -- Civilization -- American influences.

HQ1154.M5
Millett, Kate.
Sexual politics. Garden City, N.Y., Doubleday, 1970. xii, 393 p.
70-103769 301.41/2
Women -- History -- Modern period, 1600- Power (Social sciences) Sex role.

HQ1154.M53 1972
Mitchell, Juliet, 1940-
Woman's estate. New York] Pantheon Books [1972, c1971] 182 p.
77-164419 323.4 0394473426
Feminism. Women -- History -- Modern period, 1600-

HQ1154.O18 1981
Oakley, Ann.
Subject women/ Ann Oakley. New York: Pantheon Books, c1981. x, 406 p.
81-047208 305.4/2 0394749049
Women's rights -- History -- 20th century. Feminism -- History -- 20th century.

HQ1154.R744 1992
Rosser, Sue Vilhauer.
Biology & feminism: a dynamic interaction/ Sue V. Rosser. New York: Twayne Publishers; c1992. xvii, 191 p.
92-036338 305.42 080579770X
Feminism. Human biology -- Social aspects. Sexism in sociobiology.

HQ1154.R745
Rossi, Alice S., 1922-
Essays on sex equality [by] John Stuart Mill & Harriet Taylor Mill. Edited and with an introductory essay by Alice S. Rossi. Chicago, University of Chicago Press [1970] ix, 242 p.
78-133381 301.41/2/08 0226525457
Women -- History -- Modern period, 1600- -- Addresses, essays, lectures.

HQ1154.R746
Rossi, Alice S., 1922-
The feminist papers: from Adams to de Beauvoir. Edited and with introductory essays by Alice S. Rossi. New York, Columbia University Press, 1973. xix, 716 p.
73-008828 301.41/2/08 0231037953
Women -- History -- Modern period, 1600- -- Sources. Women's rights -- History -- Sources. Feminism -- History -- Sources.

HQ1154.R75
Roszak, Betty,
Masculine/ feminine: readings in sexual mythology and the liberation of women. Edited by Betty Roszak and Theodore Roszak. New York, Harper & Row [c1969] xii, 316 p.
74-133277 301.41
Women's rights. Women -- Sexual behavior. Men -- Sexual behavior.

HQ1154.S54 1996
Sisterhood is global: the international women's movement anthology/ compiled, edited, introduced, and with a new preface by Robin Morgan. New York: Feminist Press, c1996. xxiii, 821 p.
96-038456 305.42 20 1558611606
Feminism. Women's rights.

HQ1154.T38 1983
The Technological woman: interfacing with tomorrow/ edited by Jan Zimmerman. New York: Praeger, c1983. viii, 296 p.
82-014033 305.4 0030628296
Women. Technology. Home economics.

HQ1154.T53 2001
Tickner, J. Ann.
Gendering world politics: issues and approaches in the post-Cold War era/ J. Ann Tickner. New York: Columbia University Press, 2001. xii, 200 p.
00-047503 305.42 0231113668
Feminism. World politics -- 1945- Sex role -- Political aspects.

HQ1154.W37 1991
Ware, Vron.
Beyond the pale: white women, racism, and history/ Vron Ware. London; Verso, 1992. xviii, 263 p.
91-035739 305.42 0860913368
Feminism -- History. White women -- History. Racism -- History.

HQ1154.W49 1995
Whittier, Nancy, 1966-
Feminist generations: the persistence of the radical women's movement/ Nancy Whittier. Philadelphia: Temple University Press, 1995. ix, 309 p.
94-026260   305.42/0973   1566392810
Feminism -- United States. Radicalism -- United States.

HQ1154.W878 1976
Women and philosophy: toward a theory of liberation/ edited by Carol C. Gould and Marx W. Wartofsky. New York: Putnam, c1976. viii, 364 p.
75-033604   301.41/2/09   0399116524
Feminism -- History.

HQ1166 Women. Feminism — Women from various cultures, races, ethnic and minority groups, etc. — Latin

HQ1166.P47 1976
Pescatello, Ann M.
Power and pawn: the female in Iberian families, societies, and cultures/ Ann M. Pescatello. Westport, Conn.: Greenwood Press, 1976. xix, 281 p.
75-035352   301.41/2/0946   0837185831
Women -- History. Women -- Social conditions. National characteristics, Spanish.

HQ1170 Women. Feminism — Women from various cultures, races, ethnic and minority groups, etc. — Muslim

HQ1170.C75 2001
Cooke, Miriam.
Women claim Islam: creating Islamic feminism through literature/ Miriam Cooke. New York: Routledge , 2001. xxix, 175 p.
00-035315   0415925533
Muslim women -- Arab countries -- History -- 20th century. Muslim women -- Arab countries -- Intellectual life -- 20th century. Feminism -- Arab countries -- History -- 20th century.

HQ1170.G45 1996
Gerami, Shahin.
Women and fundamentalism: Islam and Christianity/ Shahin Gerami. New York: Garland Pub., 1996. xiii, 178 p.
95-004925   305.48/6971   0815306636
Muslim women. Women in fundamentalist churches. Women in Islam.

HQ1170.M46 1987
Mernissi, Fatima.
Beyond the veil: male-female dynamics in modern Muslim society/ Fatima Mernissi. Bloomington: Indiana University Press, 1987. xxix, 200 p.
86-046034   305.4/862971   0253311624
Muslim women. Women -- Morocco.

HQ1170.W588 1998
Women in the medieval Islamic world: power, patronage, and piety/ edited by Gavin R.G. Hambly. New York: St. Martin's Press, 1998. 566 p.
97-045665   305.48/6971   0312210574
Muslim women -- History.

HQ1170.W59
Women in the Muslim world/ edited by Lois Beck and Nikki Keddie. Cambridge, Mass.: Harvard University Press, 1978. xi, 698 p.
78-003633   301.41/2/0917671   0674954807
Muslim women.

HQ1170.W595 1991
Women, Islam, and the state/ edited by Deniz Kandiyoti. Philadelphia: Temple University Press, 1991. viii, 276 p.
90-040855   305.48/6971   0877227853
Muslim women. Women -- Government policy -- Middle East. Women -- Government policy -- South Asia.

HQ1172 Women. Feminism — Women from various cultures, races, ethnic and minority groups, etc. — Jewish

HQ1172.B3 1993
Baker, Adrienne, 1936-
The Jewish woman in contemporary society: transitions and traditions/ Adrienne Baker; preface by Susie Orbach; Jo Campling, consultant editor. New York: New York University Press, 1993. xii, 234 p.
93-016206   305.48/696   081471210X
Jewish women -- Great Britain. Jewish women -- United States. Women in Judaism.

HQ1172.D85 2000
Dworkin, Andrea.
Scapegoat: the Jews, Israel, and women's liberation/ Andrea Dworkin. New York: Free Press, c2000. xi, 436 p.
99-053819   305.42/01 21   0684836122
Jewish women. Feminist theory. Women -- Israel.

HQ1172.F57 1993
Fishman, Sylvia Barack, 1942-
A breath of life: feminism in the American Jewish community/ Sylvia Barack Fishman. New York, N.Y.: Free Press; c1993. xii, 308 p.
92-047003   305.48/8924073   0029103428
Jewish women -- United States. Feminism -- United States. Women in Judaism -- United States.

HQ1172.J48
The Jewish woman: new perspectives/ edited by Elizabeth Koltun. New York: Schocken Books, 1976. xx, 294 p.
75-035445   301.41/2   0805236147
Jewish women. Women in Judaism.

HQ1172.M37
Marcus, Jacob Rader, 1896-
The American Jewish woman, 1654-1980/ by Jacob R. Marcus. New York: Ktav Pub. House; 1981. xiv, 231 p.
81-001720   305.4/8   0870687514
Jewish women -- United States -- History. Jews -- United States -- History. Women -- United States -- History. United States -- Ethnic relations.

HQ1180 Women. Feminism — Women's studies. Study and teaching. Research — General works

HQ1180.F465 1990
Feminist research methods: exemplary readings in the social sciences / edited by Joyce McCarl Nielsen. Boulder: Westview Press, 1990. ix, 262 p.
89-029019   305.42/072 20   0813305772
Women's studies -- Methodology. Feminism -- Research -- Methodology.

HQ1180.K67 1997
Korenman, Joan Smolin.
Internet resources on women: using electronic media in curriculum transformation/ Joan Korenman. Baltimore, MD: National Center for Curriculum Transformation Re 1997. xii, 111 p.
98-191027   025.063054   1885303084
Women -- United States -- Computer network resources. Women's studies -- United State -- Computer network resources. Internet (Computer network)

HQ1180.R448 1992
Reinharz, Shulamit.
Feminist methods in social research/ Shulamit Reinharz with the assistance of Lynn Davidman. New York: Oxford University Press, 1992. viii, 413 p.
91-027838   301/.072   0195073851
Women's studies -- Methodology. Feminism -- Research -- Methodology. Social sciences -- Research -- Methodology.

HQ1180.T35 1996
Talking gender: public images, personal journeys, and political critiques/ edited by Nancy Hewitt, Jean O'Barr, and Nancy Rosebaugh. Chapel Hill: University of North Carolina Press, 1996. 205 p.
95-051645   305.4/07   0807822884
Women's studies.

HQ1180.T48 1983
Theories of women's studies/ edited by Gloria Bowles and Renate Duelli Klein. London; Routledge & Kegan Paul, 1983. xiv, 277 p.
82-019512   305.4/2/072   0710094884
Women's studies.

HQ1180.W68
Women's studies international. [Old Westbury, N.Y.: Feminist Press, c1982-
86-643277   305.4/05
Women's studies -- Periodicals. Feminism -- Periodicals. Women -- Periodicals.

HQ1180.W6876 2002
Women's studies on its own: a next wave reader in institutional change/ edited by Robyn Wiegman. Durham: Duke University Press, 2002. vii, 502 p.
2002-004596   305.4/071 21   0822329867
Women's studies. Women's studies -- United States.

HQ1181 Women. Feminism — Women's studies. Study and teaching. Research — By region or country, A-Z

HQ1181.U5.B69 1998
Boxer, Marilyn J.
When women ask the questions: creating women's studies in America/ Marilyn Jacoby Boxer; foreward by Catherine R. Stimpson. Baltimore: Johns Hopkins University Press, c1998. xxiii, 360 p.
97-048491 305.4/07 21 0801858348
Women's studies -- United States -- History. Women's studies -- United States -- Philosophy.

HQ1181.U5.M37 2000
Mandle, Joan D.
Can we wear our pearls and still be feminists?: memoirs of a campus struggle/ Joan D. Mandle. Columbia: University of Missouri Press, c2000. x, 210 p.
00-029923 305.42/07 21 0826212891
Women's studies -- New York (State)

HQ1181.U5.T73 1991
Transforming the curriculum: ethnic studies and women's studies/ edited by Johnnella E. Butler and John C. Walter. Albany: State University of New York Press, c1991. xxii, 341 p.
90-037670 305.4/071/173 0791405869
Women's studies -- United States. Ethnology -- Study and teaching (Graduate) -- United States.

HQ1181.U5.Z56 1992
Zinsser, Judith P.
History & feminism: a glass half full/ Judith P. Zinsser. New York: Twayne Publishers, c1993. x, 204 p.
92-028707 305.4/07/073 0805797513
Women's studies -- United States. Women -- United States -- Historiography. Education, Higher -- United States.

HQ1185-1186 Women. Feminism — Women's studies. Study and teaching. Research — Biographical methods

HQ1185.I58 1989
Interpreting women's lives: feminist theory and personal narratives/ edited by The Personal Narratives Group, Joy Webster Barbre ... [et al.]. Bloomington: Indiana University Press, c1989. viii, 277 p.
88-045445 305.4/2 025333070X
Women's studies -- Biographical methods. Autobiography -- Women authors. Feminist criticism.

HQ1185.L54 1988
Life/lines: theorizing women's autobiography/ edited by Bella Brodzki and Celeste Schenck. -- Ithaca: Cornell University Press, 1988. xiii, 363 p.
88-047718 305.4/092/4 0801495202
Women's studies -- Biographical methods.

HQ1185.U57 1996
Unrelated kin: race and gender in women's personal narratives/ edited by Gwendolyn Etter-Lewis and Michele Foster. New York: Routledge, 1996. viii, 228 p.
95-010653 305.4/08/693 0415911389
Women's studies -- Biographical methods. Autobiography -- Women authors. Minority women -- Social conditions.

HQ1186.U6.G65 1996
Goldman, Anne E., 1960-
Take my word: autobiographical innovations of ethnic American working women/ Anne E. Goldman. Berkeley: University of California Press, c1996. xxxv, 237 p.
95-006078 331.4/08/693 20 0520200969
Women's studies -- United States -- Biographical methods. Working class women -- United States -- Biography. Minority women -- United States -- Biography.

HQ1190-1190.5 Women. Feminism — Feminist theory

HQ1190.A87 1996
Assiter, Alison.
Enlightened women: modernist feminism in a postmodern age/ Alison Assiter. London; Routledge, 1996. ix, 164 p.
95-016865 305.42/01 0415083389
Feminist theory. Postmodernism. Feminism.

HQ1190.B48 1993
Beyond economic man: feminist theory and economics/ edited by Marianne A. Ferber and Julie A. Nelson. Chicago: The University of Chicago Press, 1993. 178 p.
92-040149 305.42/01 0226242005
Feminist economics. Economics.

HQ1190.C64 1991
Code, Lorraine.
What can she know?: feminist theory and the construction of knowledge/ Lorraine Code. Ithaca: Cornell University Press, 1991. xiv, 349 p.
90-055755 305.42/01 0801424763
Feminist theory. Knowledge, Theory of.

HQ1190.D87 1991
Duran, Jane.
Toward a feminist epistemology/ Jane Duran. Savage, Md.: Rowman & Littlefield, c1991. xiii, 275 p.
90-046615 305.42 20 0847676358
Feminist theory. Knowledge, Theory of.

HQ1190.E24 1996
Ebert, Teresa L., 1951-
Ludic feminism and after: postmodernism, desire, and labor in late capitalism/ Teresa L. Ebert. Ann Arbor: University of Michigan Press, c1996. xiii, 338 p.
95-004333 305.42/01 20 0472095765
Feminist theory. Postmodernism.

HQ1190.E63 2000
Encyclopedia of feminist theories/ edited by Lorraine Code. London; Routledge, 2000. xxvi, 530 p.
99-087342 305.42/03 0415132746
Feminist theory -- Encyclopedias.

HQ1190.E92 1997
Evans, Mary, 1946-
Introducing contemporary feminist thought/ Mary Evans. Malden, MA: Polity Press, 1997. vi, 170 p.
97-000559 305.42/01 0745614752
Feminist theory.

HQ1190.F444 2001
Feminist consequences: theory for the new century/ edited by Elisabeth Bronfen and Misha Kavka. New York: Columbia University Press, c2001. xxvi, 468 p.
00-060141 305.42/01 21 0231117043
Feminist theory. Feminism.

HQ1190.F453 2000
Feminist interpretations of Mary Daly/ edited by Sarah Lucia Hoagland and Marilyn Frye. University Park, Pa.: Pennsylvania State University c2000. xi, 452 p.
99-058656 305.42/01 21 0271020180
Daly, Mary, -- 1928- Feminist theory. Feminist theology.

HQ1190.F4613 1996
Feminist interpretations of Michel Foucault/ edited by Susan J. Hekman. University Park, Pa.: Pennsylvania State University Press, c1996. ix, 320 p.
95-047060 305.42/01 20 0271015845
Foucault, Michel. Sex role. Power (Social sciences) Feminist theory.

HQ1190.F77 1998
Friedman, Susan Stanford.
Mappings: feminism and the cultural geographies of encounter/ Susan Stanford Friedman. Princeton, N.J.: Princeton University Press, c1998. xii, 314 p.
98-011525 305.42/01 21 0691058032
Feminist theory. Women's studies. Feminism and education.

HQ1190.G7 1993
Grant, Judith, 1956-
Fundamental feminism: contesting the core concepts of feminist theory/ Judith Grant. New York: Routledge, 1993. xi, 226 p.
93-017451 305.42/01 0415908264
Feminist theory.

HQ1190.H37 1997
Haraway, Donna Jeanne.
Modest-Witness@Second-Millennium.FemaleMan-Meets-OncoMouse: feminism and technoscience/ Donna J. Haraway; with paintings by Lynn M. Randolph. New York: Routledge, 1997. xi, 361 p.
96-012174 305.42/01 041591244X
Feminist theory. Feminist criticism. Technology -- Social aspects.

HQ1190.J356 1998
Jakobsen, Janet R., 1960-
Working alliances and the politics of difference: diversity and feminist ethics/ Janet R. Jakobsen. Bloomington: Indiana University Press, c1998. xi, 230 p.
97-022852 305.42 21 0253333571
Feminist theory. Social movements. Feminist ethics.

HQ1190.J64 1994
Johnson, Pauline, 1953-
Feminism as radical humanism/ Pauline Johnson. Boulder, Colo.: Westview Press, 1994. xv, 168 p.
94-016160 305.42/01 0813323576
Feminist theory. Humanism.

HQ1190.M376 2000
Mascia-Lees, Frances E., 1953-
Taking a stand in a postfeminist world: toward an engaged cultural criticism/ Frances E. Mascia-Lees and Patricia Sharpe. Albany: State University of New York Press, 2000. xi, 243 p.
99-059783 305.42/01 0791447154
Feminist theory. Feminist criticism. Feminist anthropology.

HQ1190.N93 1995
Nye, Andrea, 1939-
Philosophy & feminism: at the border/ Andrea Nye. New York: Twayne Publishers; c1995. xxvii, 232 p.
95-013828 305.42/01 0805797637
Feminist theory. Feminist ethics. Women philosophers.

HQ1190.P46 1993
Phillips, Anne.
Democracy and difference/ Anne Phillips. University Park, Pa.: Pennsylvania State University Press, 1993. vii, 175 p.
93-019490 305.42 0271010967
Feminist theory. Women and democracy. Equality.

HQ1190.R483 1998
Revisioning gender/ editors, Myra Marx Ferree, Judith Lorber, Beth B. Hess. Thousand Oaks, Calif.: Sage Publications, c1999. xxxvi, 500 p.
98-025488 305.3 21 0761906169
Feminist theory. Women -- Social conditions. Sex role.

HQ1190.S34 1993
Scheman, Naomi.
Engenderings: constructions of knowledge, authority, and privilege/ Naomi Scheman. New York: Routledge, 1993. xxii, 254 p.
93-007337 305.42/01 041590739X
Feminist theory.

HQ1190.S95 1994
Sylvester, Christine, 1949-
Feminist theory and international relations in a postmodern era/ Christine Sylvester. Cambridge [England]; Cambridge University Press, 1994. xi, 265 p.
93-010251 305.42/01 0521393051
Feminist theory. Women in politics. International relations.

HQ1190.T48 1993
Theory on gender/feminism on theory/ Paula England, editor. New York: A. de Gruyter, c1993. xii, 377 p.
92-027886 305.42/01 020230437X
Feminist theory.

HQ1190.W47 1995
Whelehan, Imelda, 1960-
Modern feminist thought: from the second wave to "post-feminism"/ Imelda Whelehan. New York: New York University Press, 1995. 270 p.
95-011225 305.42/01 0814792995
Feminist theory. Feminism -- History -- 20th century.

HQ1190.W56 1991
Winders, James A., 1949-
Gender, theory, and the canon/ James A. Winders. Madison, Wis.: University of Wisconsin Press, c1991. xi, 195 p.
90-050655 305.42/01 0299129209
Feminist criticism. Feminist literary criticism. Authorship -- Sex differences.

HQ1190.W685 1994
Women, gender, and world politics: perspectives, policies, and prospects/ edited by Peter R. Beckman and Francine D'Amico. Westport, Conn.: Bergin & Garvey, 1994. xi, 250 p.
94-015857 305.42 0897893050
Feminist theory. World politics. International relations.

HQ1190.W688 1996
Women, knowledge, and reality: explorations in feminist philosophy/ Edited by Ann Garry, Marilyn Pearsall. 2nd ed. New York: Routledge, 1996. x, 500 p.
96-025166 305.42/01 20 0415917972
Feminist theory. Philosophy. Knowledge, Theory of.

HQ1190.5.U6.S58 1995
Shugar, Dana R., 1961-
Separatism and women's community/ Dana R. Shugar. Lincoln: University of Nebraska Press, c1995. xvii, 216 p.
94-032900 305.42 0803242441
Feminist theory -- United States. Feminism -- United States. Radicalism -- United States.

HQ1201 Women. Feminism — General works — Early to 1800

HQ1201.H67 1977
History of ideas on woman: a source book/ Rosemary Agonito. New York: Putnam, c1977. 414 p.
77-005061 301.41/2 0399119647
Women -- Addresses, essays, lectures.

HQ1206-1229 Women. Feminism — General works — 1800-

HQ1206.B23
Bardwick, Judith M., 1933-
Psychology of women; a study of bio-cultural conflicts [by] Judith M. Bardwick. New York, Harper & Row [1971] vii, 242 p.
70-137799 155.6/33 0060404973
Women -- Psychology.

HQ1206.B34
Becoming female: perspectives on development/ edited by Claire B. Kopp, in collaboration with Martha Kirkpatrick. New York: Plenum Press, c1979. xviii, 469 p.
79-009970 301.41/2 0306402297
Women -- Psychology. Developmental psychology. Child development.

HQ1206.B345 1997
Belenky, Mary Field.
A tradition that has no name: nurturing the development of people, families, and communities/ Mary Field Belenky, Lynne A. Bond, and Jacqueline S. Weinstock. New York: BasicBooks, c1997. xi, 367 p.
96-053583 155.6/33 0465026052
Women -- United States -- Psychology. Women -- United States -- Attitudes. Self-actualization (Psychology)

HQ1206.B374
Bernard, Jessie Shirley, 1903-
The female world/ Jessie Bernard. New York: Free Press, c1981. x, 614 p.
80-069880 305.4/2 0029030005
Women -- Psychology. Women -- Social conditions.

HQ1206.C52 1989
Chodorow, Nancy.
Feminism and psychoanalytic theory/ Nancy J. Chodorow. New Haven [Conn.]: Yale University Press, 1989. x, 286 p.
89-051037 155.6/33 0300044178
Women -- Psychology. Psychoanalysis and feminism.

HQ1206.C69 1987
Competition, a feminist taboo?/ edited by Valerie Miner and Helen E. Longino; foreword by Nell Irvin Painter. New York: The Feminist Press at the City University of New 1987. xvi, 260 p.
87-008515 305.4/2 0935312749
Women -- Psychology. Competition (Psychology) Feminism -- Psychological aspects.

HQ1206.D357 1996
Dean, Jodi, 1962-
Solidarity of strangers: feminism after identity politics/ Jodi Dean. Berkeley: University of California Press, c1996. x, 219 p.
95-013906 305.42 20 0520202309
Feminism. Feminist theory. Identity (Psychology)

HQ1206.D683 2000
Dowling, Colette.
The frailty myth: women approaching physical equality/ Colette Dowling. New York: Random House, c2000. xxvii, 319 p.
00-028093 305.4/072 21 0375502351
Women -- Psychology. Sex differences. Women -- Physiology.

HQ1206.E43 1988
Eichenbaum, Luise.
Between women: love, envy, and competition in women's friendships/ Luise Eichenbaum and Susie Orbach. New York, N.Y., U.S.A.: Viking, 1988, c1987. xiii, 223 p.
87-040293 155.6/33 0670811416
Women -- United States -- Psychology. Female friendship. Interpersonal relations.

HQ1206.F44 1982b
"Femininity," "masculinity," and "androgyny": a modern philosophical discussion/ edited by Mary Vetterling-Braggin. Totowa, N.J.: Rowman and Littlefield, c1982. x, 326 p.
82-000529 305.3 0847670708
Women -- Psychology. Men -- Psychology. Sex differences (Psychology)

HQ1206.F45 1987
Feminism as critique: on the politics of gender/ edited by Seyla Benhabib and Drucilla Cornell. Minneapolis: University of Minnesota Press, c1987. 193 p.
87-010939 305.4/2 0816616353
Feminist criticism. Marxian school of sociology.

HQ1206.F72 1997
Friday, Nancy.
My mother/my self: the daughter's search for identity/ Nancy Friday. 20th anniversary ed. New York: Delta Trade Paperbacks, c1997. xviii, 425 p.
98-115632 158.2/4 21 0385320159
Women -- Psychology. Mothers and daughters. Love, Maternal.

HQ1206.F74 1995
From Nairobi to Beijing: second review and appraisal of the implementation of the Nairobi forward-looking strategies for the advancement of women/ report of the Secretary General. New York: United Nations 1995. xxi, 366 p.
95-210322   305.42
Women in development. Women's rights. Women -- Social conditions.

HQ1206.G58 1993
Gilligan, Carol,
In a different voice: psychological theory and women's development/ Carol Gilligan. Cambridge, Mass.: Harvard University Press, 1993. xxvii, 184 p.
93-243596   305.42 20   0674445449
Women -- Psychology -- Longitudinal studies. Developmental psychology -- Longitudinal studies. Moral development -- Longitudinal studies.

HQ1206.H43 1979
Heilbrun, Carolyn G., 1926-
Reinventing womanhood/ Carolyn G. Heilbrun. New York: Norton, c1979. 244 p.
78-025607   301.41/2   0393012107
Women -- Psychology. Sex role. Women in literature.

HQ1206.H45 1990
Hekman, Susan J.
Gender and knowledge: elements of a postmodern feminism/ by Susan J. Hekman. Boston: Northeastern University Press, 1990. vi, 212 p.
90-007091   305.42/01   1555530877
Feminist theory. Postmodernism.

HQ1206.J33 1983
Jaggar, Alison M.
Feminist politics and human nature/ Alison M. Jaggar. Totowa, N.J.: Rowman & Allanheld, 1983. vi, 408 p.
83-003402   305.4/2   084767181X
Feminist theory. Women in politics. Women and socialism.

HQ1206.J67 1987
Josselson, Ruthellen.
Finding herself: pathways to identity development in women/ Ruthellen Josselson. San Francisco: Jossey-Bass, 1987. xvii, 225 p.
87-045414   155.6/33   1555420494
Women -- United States -- Psychology -- Longitudinal studies. Women -- United States -- Identity -- Longitudinal studies. Identity (Psychology) -- United States -- Longitudinal studies.

HQ1206.J673 1996
Josselson, Ruthellen.
Revising herself: the story of women's identity from college to midlife/ Ruthellen Josselson. New York: Oxford University Press, 1996. xii, 298 p.
96-010380   155.6/33   0195108396
Women -- United States -- Psychology -- Longitudinal studies. Women -- United States -- Identity -- Longitudinal studies. Identity (Psychology) -- United States -- Longitudinal studies.

HQ1206.K37 1992
Kaschak, Ellyn, 1943-
Engendered lives: a new psychology of women's experience/ Ellyn Kaschak. New York, NY: Basic Books, c1992. x, 265 p.
91-058602   155.6/33   0465013473
Women -- Psychology. Feminist psychology. Feminist therapy.

HQ1206.M37 1982
McMillan, Carol, 1954-
Women, reason, and nature: some philosophical problems with feminism/ Carol McMillan. Princeton, N.J.: Princeton University Press, c1982. x, 165 p.
82-012207   305.4/2   0691072744
Feminist theory. Woman (Philosophy) Women's studies -- Philosophy.

HQ1206.M83 1992
Mulqueen, Maggie, 1955-
On our own terms: redefining competence and femininity/ Maggie Mulqueen. Albany: State University of New York Press, c1992. ix, 221 p.
91-012245   305.42   0791409511
Women -- United States -- Psychology -- Longitudinal studies. Self-esteem in women -- United States -- Longitudinal studies. Self-perception in women -- United States -- Longitudinal studies.

HQ1206.O24
O'Brien, Mary, 1926-
The politics of reproduction/ Mary O'Brien. Boston: Routledge & Kegan Paul, 1981. x, 240 p.
81-203741   320/.01/1   0710008104
Feminism. Reproduction.

HQ1206.O38 1992
Okin, Susan Moller.
Women in Western political thought: [with new afterword]/ Susan Moller Okin. [1992 ed.]. Princeton, N.J.: Princeton University Press, [1992] 413 p.
91-047547   305.42 20   0691021910
Plato -- Political science. Rousseau, Jean-Jacques, 1712-1778 -- Political science. Mill, John Stuart, 1806-1873 -- Contributions in political science. Women. Sex role. Feminism.

HQ1206.P35 1988
Pateman, Carole.
The sexual contract/ Carole Pateman. Stanford, Calif.: Stanford University Press, 1988. xi, 264 p.
87-063007   305.3   0804714762
Feminist theory. Social contract. Patriarchy.

HQ1206.P58 1992
Polster, Miriam.
Eve's daughters: the forbidden heroism of women/ Miriam F. Polster. San Francisco: Jossey-Bass, c1992. xix, 206 p.
92-008806   305.42   1555424643
Women heroes -- Psychology. Women -- Socialization.

HQ1206.P745 1993
Probyn, Elspeth, 1958-
Sexing the self: gendered positions in cultural studies/ Elspeth Probyn. London; Routledge, 1993. x, 189 p.
92-022143   155.3/33   0415073553
Women -- Psychology. Feminist theory. Self.

HQ1206.P747 1993
Psychology of women: a handbook of issues and theories/ edited by Florence L. Denmark and Michele A. Paludi; foreword by Leonore Loeb Adler. Westport, Conn.: Greenwood Press, 1993. xix, 760 p.
92-008642   155.3/33   0313262950
Women -- Psychology. Feminist psychology.

HQ1206.R65
Rosaldo, Michelle Zimbalist.
Woman, culture, and society. Edited by Michelle Zimbalist Rosaldo and Louise Lamphere. Contributors: Joan Bamberger [and others] Stanford, Calif., Stanford University Press, 1974. xi, 352 p.
73-089861   301.41/2   0804708509
Women -- History -- Modern period, 1600- -- Addresses, essays, lectures.

HQ1206.S443 1983
Schur, Edwin M.
Labeling women deviant: gender, stigma, and social control/ Edwin M. Schur. Philadelphia: Temple University Press, 1983. x, 286 p.
83-010942   305.4/2   0877223327
Women -- Social conditions. Deviant behavior -- Labeling theory. Sex discrimination against women.

HQ1206.S666 1988
Spelman, Elizabeth V.
Inessential woman: problems of exclusion in feminist thought/ Elizabeth V. Spelman. Boston: Beacon Press, c1988. xiii, 221 p.
87-047878   305.4/2/01   080706744X
Feminist theory.

HQ1206.S68 1982
Spender, Dale.
Women of ideas and what men have done to them: from Aphra Behn to Adrienne Rich/ Dale Spender. London; Routledge & Kegan Paul, 1982. xii, 586 p.
82-012208   305.4   0710093535
Women intellectuals. Women intellectuals -- Case studies. Sex discrimination against women.

HQ1206.S86 1974
Strouse, Jean,
Women & analysis; dialogues on psychoanalytic views of femininity. New York, Grossman Publishers, 1974. viii, 375 p.
73-007313   155.6/33   0670778419
Women -- Psychology. Femininity.

HQ1206.T33 1983
Taylor, Barbara, 1950-
Eve and the New Jerusalem: socialism and feminism in the nineteenth century/ Barbara Taylor. New York: Pantheon Books, c1983. xviii, 394 p.
82-019007   305.4/2/09034   0394527666
Feminism -- History -- 19th century. Women and socialism -- History -- 19th century.

HQ1206.T45 1990
Theoretical perspectives on sexual difference/ edited by Deborah L. Rhode. New Haven: Yale University Press, c1990. xi, 315 p.
89-025083   305.42/01   0300044275
Feminist theory. Sex differences. Sex role.

HQ1206.U47
Ulanov, Ann Belford.
The feminine in Jungian psychology and in Christian theology. Evanston [Ill.] Northwestern University Press, 1971. xi, 347 p.
74-149922   0810103516
Femininity. Jungian psychology -- Religious aspects -- Christianity. Psychology, Religious.

HQ1206.U49 2000
Crawford, Mary
Women and gender: a feminist psychology/ Mary Crawford, Rhoda Unger. 3rd ed. Boston: McGraw-Hill, 2000. xxii, 666 p.
99-032603   305.42 21   0070392137
Women -- Psychology. Feminist psychology.

HQ1206.V24 1995
VanEvery, Jo.
Heterosexual women changing the family: refusing to be a 'wife'!/ Jo VanEvery. Bristol, PA: Taylor & Francis, 1995 x, 165 p.
95-006647 305.42 0748402837
Women -- United States -- Psychology. Marriage -- United States. Unmarried couples -- United States.

HQ1206.W865 1983
Woman's nature: rationalizations of inequality/ [edited by] Marian Lowe, Ruth Hubbard. New York: Pergamon Press, c1983. xii, 155 p.
83-004066 305.4 0080301436
Women -- Social conditions. Equality. Feminism.

HQ1206.W879 1991
Women's growth in connection: writings from the Stone Center/ Judith V. Jordan ... [et al.]. New York: Guilford Press, c1991. x, 310 p.
91-012093 305.42 0898625629
Women -- Psychology. Self-actualization. Self.

HQ1208.S7713 1986
Women in culture and politics: a century of change/ edited by Judith Friedlander ... [et al.]. Bloomington: Indiana University Press, c1986. xvii, 394 p.
85-045098 305.4/094 0253313287
Women -- Europe -- Congresses. Women -- United States -- Congresses. Feminism -- Europe -- Congresses.

HQ1219.A38 1993
Aesthetics in feminist perspective/ edited by Hilde Hein and Carolyn Korsmeyer. Bloomington: Indiana University Press, c1993. xv, 252 p.
92-023948 305.42/01 0253328616
Aesthetics. Feminist theory. Feminism and the arts.

HQ1219.B35 1996
Beauty queens on the global stage: gender, contests, and power/ edited by Colleen Ballerino Cohen, Richard Wilk, and Beverly Stoeltje. New York: Routledge, 1996. vii, 256 p.
95-008994 305.42/079 0415911524
Beauty contests -- Cross-cultural studies.

HQ1219.T74 1995
Tseelon, Efrat.
The masque of femininity: the presentation of woman in everyday life/ Efrat Tseelon. London: Sage Publications, 1995. 152 p.
95-069789 0803988060
Feminine beauty (Aesthetics) Femininity. Women -- Sociological aspects.

HQ1219.W65 1991
Wolf, Naomi.
The beauty myth: how images of beauty are used against women/ Naomi Wolf. New York: W. Morrow, c1991. 348 p.
90-049983 305.42 0688085105
Feminine beauty (Aesthetics) Femininity. Sex role.

HQ1220.U5.B36 1999
Banet-Weiser, Sarah, 1966-
The most beautiful girl in the world: beauty pageants and national identity/ Sarah Banet-Weiser. Berkeley: University of California Press, c1999. xiii, 277 p.
99-019922 791.6/2 21 0520217896
Beauty contests -- United States. National characteristics. Racism in popular culture.

HQ1221.H27 1985
Harrison, Beverly Wildung, 1932-
Making the connections: essays in feminist social ethics/ Beverly Wildung Harrison; edited by Carol S. Robb. Boston: Beacon Press, c1985. xxii, 312 p.
84-045718 305.4/2 0807015245
Feminism -- Moral and ethical aspects -- Addresses, essays, lectures. Social ethics -- Addresses, essays, lectures. Christian ethics -- Addresses, essays, lectures.

HQ1221.M25 1931
Mencken, H. L. 1880-1956.
In defense of women, by H. L. Mencken. Garden City, N.Y., Garden City Pub. Co. [1931] xvi, 210 p.
32-011723
Women -- Social and moral questions.

HQ1221.W893 1985
Women's consciousness, women's conscience: a reader in feminist ethics/ edited by Barbara Hilkert Andolsen, Christine E. Gudorf, Mary D. Pellauer Minneapolis: Winston Press, c1985. xxvi, 310 p.
85-050124 305.4/2 0866839585
Feminism -- Moral and ethical aspects. Feminism -- Religious aspects. Social ethics -- United States.

HQ1229.G66 1997
Gomersall, Meg.
Working-class girls in nineteenth-century England: life, work, and schooling/ Meg Gomersall; consultant editor, Jo Campling. New York: St. Martin's Press, 1997. ix, 187 p.
95-051280 305.4/0942 0333622006
Girls -- England -- History -- 19th century. Women -- Education -- England -- History -- 19th century. Working class families -- England -- History -- 19th century.

HQ1233 Women. Feminism — General special (Special aspects of the subject as a whole)

HQ1233.B25 1991
Bacon-Smith, Camille.
Enterprising women: television fandom and the creation of popular myth/ Camille Bacon-Smith; photographs by Stephanie A. Hall. Philadelphia: University of Pennsylvania Press, c1992. x, 338 p.
91-029875 306.4/85/082 0812230981
Television and women -- United States. Television viewers -- United States. Fans (Persons) -- United States -- Societies and clubs.

HQ1233.D5 1994
Diamond, Irene, 1947-
Fertile ground: women, earth, and the limits of control/ Irene Diamond. Boston: Beacon Press, c1994. xi, 202 p.
93-039064 304.6/32 0807067725
Ecofeminism. Birth control -- Social aspects. Fertility, Human -- Social aspects.

HQ1233.E26 1993
Ecofeminism: women, animals, nature/ edited by Greta Gaard. Philadelphia: Temple University Press, 1993. viii, 331 p.
92-006598 304.2 0877229880
Ecofeminism. Human ecology. Nature -- Effect of human beings on.

HQ1233.E55 1993
Enloe, Cynthia H., 1938-
The morning after: sexual politics at the end of the Cold War/ Cynthia Enloe. Berkeley: University of California Press, c1993. 326 p.
92-043416 305.3 0520083350
Sex role. Man-woman relationships. Feminist theory.

HQ1233.I34 1993
Identity politics and women: cultural reassertions and feminisms in international perspective/ edited by Valentine M. Moghadam. Boulder: Westview Press, 1994. xiv, 458 p.
93-028018 305.42 0813386918
Women -- Social conditions -- Cross-cultural studies. Women -- Middle East -- Social conditions. Muslim women -- Social conditions.

HQ1233.P74 1991
Press, Andrea Lee.
Women watching television: gender, class, and generation in the American television experience/ Andrea L. Press. Philadelphia: University of Pennsylvania Press, c1991. x, 238 p.
90-021274 302.23/082 081221286X
Television and women -- United States. Women on television. Television viewers -- United States.

HQ1233.T415 1990
Television and women's culture: the politics of the popular/ edited by Mary Ellen Brown. London; Sage Publications, 1990. 244 p.
89-063638 302.23/45/082 0803982283
Television and women. Television viewers. Television criticism.

HQ1233.W297 2000
Warren, Karen, 1947-
Ecofeminist philosophy: a western perspective on what it is and why it matters/ Karen J. Warren. Lanham, Md.: Rowman & Littlefield, 2000. xviii, 253 p.
99-087025 305.42/01 0847692981
Ecofeminism.

HQ1233.W75 1994
Writing women and space: colonial and postcolonial geographies/ edited by Alison Blunt, Gillian Rose. New York: Guilford Press, c1994. ix, 256 p.
94-011691 305.42 0898624975
Feminism and literature. Space perception -- Social aspects. Women and literature.

HQ1236 Women. Feminism — Women and the state. Women's rights. Women's political activity — General works

HQ1236.A76 1999
Arneil, Barbara.
Politics and feminism: an introduction/ by Barbara Arneil. Oxford, UK; Blackwell, 1999. vi, 284 p.
98-029203 305.42 0631198121
Women in politics. Feminism -- Political aspects. Women's rights.

HQ1236.B27 1998
Bashevkin, Sylvia B.
Women on the defensive: living through conservative times/ Sylvia Bashevkin. Toronto: University of Toronto Press; c1998. viii, 318 p.
97-035168   305.42/09/04 21   0802081878
Women's rights -- History -- 20th century -- Cross-cultural studies. Women in politics -- History -- 20th century -- Cross-cultural studies. Feminism -- History -- 20th century -- Cross-cultural studies.

HQ1236.C47 1993
Chapman, Jenny, 1941-
Politics, feminism, and the reformation of gender/ Jenny Chapman. London; Routledge, 1993. xx, 315 p.
92-009372   305.42   0415016983
Women in politics. Women political activists. Feminism.

HQ1236.E47 1993
Elshtain, Jean Bethke,
Public man, private woman: women in social and political thought/ Jean Bethke Elshtain. 2nd ed. Princeton, N.J.: Princeton University Press, 1993. xviii, 390 p.
92-029726   305.42 20   0691024766
Women in politics. Political science -- History. Knowledge, Theory of.

HQ1236.G45 1989
Gelb, Joyce, 1940-
Feminism and politics: a comparative perspective/ Joyce Gelb. Berkeley: University of California Press, c1989. 267 p.
88-010773   305.4/2   0520063074
Women in politics -- Cross-cultural studies. Women's rights -- Cross-cultural studies. Feminism -- Cross-cultural studies.

HQ1236.G4617 1998
Gender politics in global governance/ edited by Mary K. Meyer and Elisabeth Prugl. Lanham, MD: Rowman & Littlefield Publishers, 1998. xii, 315 p.
98-039357   305.42   0847691608
Women in politics. International relations. International agencies.

HQ1236.H87 1995
The Human Rights Watch global report on women's human rights/ Human Rights Watch, Women's Rights Project. New York: Human Rights Watch, c1995. xxi, 458 p.
95-079554   305.42   0300065469
Women's rights. Women -- Crimes against. Human rights.

HQ1236.J33 1998
Jackson, Robert Max.
Destined for equality: the inevitable rise of women's status/ Robert Max Jackson. Cambridge, Mass.: Harvard University Press, 1998. 316 p.
97-052359   305.42/09   067405511X
Women's rights -- History. Women -- Economic conditions. Women -- Social conditions.

HQ1236.K45
Kelly, Rita Mae.
The making of political women: a study of socialization and role conflict/ Rita Mae Kelly & Mary Boutilier. Chicago: Nelson-Hall, c1978. x, 368 p.
77-017081   301.41/2/0973   0882292900
Women in politics -- United States. Sex role. Statesmen's spouses -- Biography.

HQ1236.M34 1989
MacKinnon, Catharine A.
Toward a feminist theory of the state/ Catharine A. MacKinnon. Cambridge, Mass.: Harvard University Press, 1989. xvii, 330 p.
89-007540   305.42   0674896459
Women's rights. Feminism -- Political aspects. Women in politics.

HQ1236.M343 1996
Makus, Ingrid.
Women, politics, and reproduction: the liberal legacy/ Ingrid Makus. Toronto; University of Toronto Press, c1996. vi, 274 p.
96-223098   305.4 21   0802007163
Hobbes, Thomas, -- 1588-1679 -- Views on women. Locke, John, -- 1632-1704 -- Views on women. Mill, John Stuart, -- 1806-1873 -- Views on women. Feminist theory.

HQ1236.M347 2000
Martin, Mart, 1944-
The almanac of women and minorities in world politics/ Mart Martin. Boulder, Colo.: Westview Press, 2000. xxxiii, 466 p.
99-057270   305.43/329/0973   0813368057
Women in politics -- Handbooks, manuals, etc. Women politicians -- Handbooks, manuals, etc. Minorities -- Political activity -- Handbooks, manuals, etc.

HQ1236.P49 1991
Phillips, Anne.
Engendering democracy/ Anne Phillips. University Park, Pa.: Pennsylvania State University Press, 1991. 183 p.
90-027912   305.42   0271007834
Feminism. Women and democracy. Women in politics.

HQ1236.S27 1983
Sapiro, Virginia.
The political integration of women: roles, socialization, and politics/ Virginia Sapiro. Urbana: University of Illinois Press, c1983. 205 p.
82-002672   306/.2   0252009207
Women in politics -- United States. Political socialization -- United States. Sex role -- United States.

HQ1236.W586 1998
Women and democracy: Latin America and Central and Eastern Europe/ edited by Jane S. Jaquette and Sharon L. Wolchik. Baltimore, Md.: Johns Hopkins University Press, 1998. ix, 250 p.
98-005120   305.42/098   0801858372
Women in politics -- Latin America. Women in politics -- Europe, Central. Women in politics -- Europe, Eastern.

HQ1236.W6363 1994
Women and politics worldwide/ edited by Barbara J. Nelson and Najma Chowdhury. New Haven: Yale University Press, c1994. xi, 818 p.
93-028668   320/.082   0300054076
Women in politics -- Cross-cultural studies. Women's rights -- Cross-cultural studies.

HQ1236.W6364 1994
Women and revolution in Africa, Asia, and the New World/ edited by Mary Ann Tetreault. Columbia, S.C.: University of South Carolina Press, c1994. viii, 456 p.
94-018706   305.42   1570030162
Women in politics -- History. Revolutions -- History.

HQ1236.W65 1979
Women, war, and revolution/ edited by Carol R. Berkin and Clara M. Lovett. New York: Holmes & Meier, 1980. xiii, 310 p.
79-026450   301.41/2   0841905029
Women in politics -- History -- Congresses. War -- Congresses. Revolutions -- Congresses.

HQ1236.W6523 1998
Women's movements and public policy in Europe, Latin America, and the Caribbean/ edited by Geertje Lycklama a Nijeholt, Virginia Vargas, and Saskia Wieringa. New York: Garland Pub., 1998. xvi, 189 p.
97-013518   305.42   0815324790
Women in politics -- Cross-cultural studies. Women in politics -- Case studies. Feminism -- Cross-cultural studies.

HQ1236.W6524 2000
Women's political participation and good governance: 21st century challenges/ United Nations Development Programme. New York: UNDP, 2000. v, 99 p.
00-690563   9211261287
Women in politics.

HQ1236.W6527 2001
Women's rights: a global view/ edited by Lynn Walter. Westport, CT: Greenwood Press, 2000. xxviii, 257 p.
00-027632   305.42   031330890X
Women's rights. Women -- Social conditions.

HQ1236.5 Women. Feminism — Women and the state. Women's rights. Women's political activity — By region or country, A-Z

HQ1236.5.A357.W65 1989
Women and the state in Africa/ edited by Jane L. Parpart & Kathleen A. Staudt. Boulder, Col.: L. Rienner Publishers, 1989. ix, 229 p.
88-023974   305.4/2/096   1555870821
Women in politics -- Africa, Sub-Saharan. Sex role -- Africa, Sub-Saharan. Women -- Africa, Sub-Saharan -- Social conditions.

HQ1236.5.B6.A44 1990
Alvarez, Sonia E., 1956-
Engendering democracy in Brazil: women's movements in transition politics/ Sonia E. Alvarez. Princeton, N.J.: Princeton University Press, c1990. x, 304 p.
90-033837   305.42/0981   0691078564
Women in politics -- Brazil. Feminism -- Brazil. Democracy -- Brazil. Brazil -- Politics and government -- 1964-1985. Brazil -- Politics and government -- 1985-

HQ1236.5.C2.G46 1995
Gender and politics in contemporary Canada/ edited by Francois-Pierre Gingras. Toronto; Oxford University Press, 1995. xii, 273 p.
96-129069   305.42/0971   0195410114
Women in politics -- Canada. Sexism -- Canada. Women -- Government policy -- Canada.

HQ1236.5.C2.V53 1993
Vickers, Jill, 1942-
Politics as if women mattered: a political analysis of the National Action Committee on the Status of Women/ Jill Vickers, Pauline Rankin, and Christine Appelle. Toronto; University of Toronto Press, c1993. xvi, 347 p.
93-184367   305.42/06/071   0802058507
Women's rights -- Canada. Women -- Canada -- Social conditions.

HQ1236.5.C2.Y68 2001
Young, Lisa.
Feminists and party politics/ Lisa Young. Ann Arbor: University of Michigan Press, 2001. xiv, 246 p.
00-068270   324.2/082/0971   0472087827
Women in politics -- Canada. Women in politics -- United States. Political parties -- Canada.

HQ1236.5.C9.S76 1991
Stoner, K. Lynn.
From the house to the streets: the Cuban woman's movement for legal reform, 1898-1940/ K. Lynn Stoner. Durham: Duke University Press, 1991. xi, 242 p.
90-048182   305.42/097291   0822311496
Women's rights -- Cuba -- History. Women -- Legal status, laws, etc. -- Cuba -- History. Feminism -- Cuba -- History.

HQ1236.5.E25.D45 2000
Democracy and the status of women in East Asia/ edited by Rose J. Lee, Cal Clark. Boulder, Colo.: L. Rienner, c2000. ix, 213 p.
99-048191   305.42/095 21   1555878881
Women and democracy -- East Asia. Women in politics -- East Asia. Women -- Government policy -- East Asia.

HQ1236.5.E82.W65 1985
Women and politics in Western Europe/ edited by Sylvia Bashevkin. London: Cass, 1985. 160 p.
85-038379   323.3/4/094   0714632759
Women in politics -- Europe.

HQ1236.5.E85.E82 1987
Evans, Richard J.
Comrades and sisters: feminism, socialism, and pacifism in Europe, 1870-1945/ Richard J. Evans. Brighton, Sussex: Wheatsheaf Books; 1987. xii, 203 p.
87-009475   305.4/2/094   0312009631
Women's rights -- Europe -- History -- 20th century. Women and socialism -- Europe -- History -- 20th century. Women in politics -- Europe -- History -- 20th century.

HQ1236.5.E85.W65 1985
Women, state, and party in Eastern Europe/ edited by Sharon L. Wolchik and Alfred G. Meyer. Durham: Duke University Press, 1985. xiv, 453 p.
85-016262   305.4/0947   0822306603
Women -- Europe, Eastern -- Congresses. Women in politics -- Europe, Eastern -- Congresses. Women and socialism -- Europe, Eastern -- Congresses.

HQ1236.5.E852.W66 1998
Women in the politics of postcommunist Eastern Europe/ edited by Marilyn Rueschemeyer. Armonk, New York: M.E. Sharpe, c1998. xii, 308 p.
98-015195   320/.082 21   0765602954
Women in politics -- Europe, Eastern. Europe, Eastern -- Politics and government -- 1989-

HQ1236.5.F8.F3813 1991
Faure, Christine.
Democracy without women: feminism and the rise of liberal individualism in France/ by Christine Faure; translated by Claudia Gorbman and John Berks. Bloomington: Indiana University Press, c1991. viii, 196 p.
90-045845   305.4/2/0944   0253321557
Political science -- France -- History. Women in public life -- France -- History. Feminism -- France -- History.

HQ1236.5.G3.S55 1998
Smith, Harold L.
The British women's suffrage compaign, 1866-1928/ Harold L. Smith. London; Longman, 1998.
98-004025   305.42/0941   0582298113
Women's movement -- Great Britain -- History. Women -- Suffrage -- Great Britain -- History. Women in politics -- Great Britain -- History.

HQ1236.5.G7.A44 1989
Alberti, Johanna, 1940-
Beyond suffrage: feminists in war and peace, 1914-28/ Johanna Alberti. New York: St. Martin's Press, 1989. vi, 249 p.
89-033425   305.42/0941/09042   031203265X
Women in politics -- Great Britain -- History -- 20th century. Suffragists -- Great Britain -- Biography. Feminism -- Great Britain -- History -- 20th century.

HQ1236.5.G7.L68 1993
Lovenduski, Joni.
Contemporary feminist politics: women and power in Britain/ by Joni Lovenduski and Vicky Randall. Oxford; Oxford University Press, 1993. xiv, 388 p.
92-041371   305.42/0941   0198277385
Women in politics -- Great Britain. Feminism -- Great Britain.

HQ1236.5.I4.B37 1992
Basu, Amrita, 1953-
Two faces of protest: contrasting modes of women's activism in India/ Amrita Basu. Berkeley: University of California Press, c1992. xii, 308 p.
91-044884   320.954/082   0520065069
Women in politics -- India. Women political activists -- India. Right and left (Political science) India -- Politics and government -- 1947-

HQ1236.5.I4.B375 1999
Basu, Srimati.
She comes to take her rights: Indian women, property, and propriety/ Srimati Basu. Albany, NY: State University of New York Press, c1999. xiv, 305 p.
98-025982   305.42/0954 21   0791440958
Women's rights -- India. Women -- Legal status, laws, etc. (Hindu law) Sex role -- India.

HQ1236.5.I7.P35 1995
Paidar, Parvin.
Women and the political process in twentieth-century Iran/ Parvin Paidar. Cambridge [England]; Cambridge University Press, 1995. xvi, 401 p.
94-016062   305.42/0955   0521473403
Women in politics -- Iran. Women -- Iran -- History. Feminism -- Iran.

HQ1236.5.I75.H46 1999
Hertsog, Hanah.
Gendering politics: women in Israel/ Hanna Herzog. Ann Arbor: University of Michigan Press, c1999. xvi, 292 p.
98-053596   320/.082/095694 21   0472109456
Women in politics -- Israel. Local government -- Israel.

HQ1236.5.J3.L43 1999
LeBlanc, Robin M., 1966-
Bicycle citizens: the political world of the Japanese housewife/ Robin M. LeBlanc; with a foreword by Saskia Sassen. Berkeley, Calif.: University of California Press, c1999. xvii, 243 p.
98-046632   305.42/0952 21   0520212908
Women in politics -- Japan. Housewives -- Japan -- Political activity. Housewives -- Japan -- Social conditions.

HQ1236.5.M6.W65 1998
Women's participation in Mexican political life/ edited by Victoria E. Rodriguez. Boulder, Colo.: Westview Press, 1998. xix, 260 p.
98-020771   320/.082/0972   0813335299
Women in politics -- Mexico -- Congresses.

HQ1236.5.M8.B73 1998
Brand, Laurie A.
Women, the state, and political liberalization: Middle Eastern and North African experiences/ Laurie A. Brand. New York: Columbia University Press, 1998. xviii, 320 p
98-004431   305.42/095695   0231112661
Women in politics -- Morocco. Women -- Morocco -- Social conditions. Women in politics -- Jordan.

HQ1236.5.P18.M86 1987
Mumtaz, Khawar.
Women of Pakistan: two steps forward, one step back?/ Khawar Mumtaz and Farida Shaheed (eds.). London; Zed Books, c1987. xi, 196 p.
87-013319   305.4/2/095491   0862322804
Women's rights -- Pakistan -- History -- 20th century. Feminism -- Pakistan -- History -- 20th century.

HQ1236.5.S6.R87 1989
Russell, Diana E. H.
Lives of courage: women for a new South Africa/ Diana E.H. Russell. New York: Basic Books, c1989. xiv, 375 p.
89-042525   305.4/0968   0465041396
Women in politics -- South Africa -- Biography. Women, Black -- South Africa -- Biography. Women in public life -- South Africa -- Biography.

HQ1236.5.S63.F57 1993
Fisher, Jo 1954-
Out of the shadows: women, resistance and politics in South America/ Jo Fisher. London: Latin America Bureau; 1993. 228 p.
93-172850   305.42/098   0906156777
Women in politics -- South America. Feminism -- South America. South America -- Politics and government -- 20th century.

HQ1236.5.S63.W66 1989
The Women's movement in Latin America: feminism and the transition to democracy/ edited by Jane S. Jaquette. Boston: Unwin Hyman, 1989. viii, 215 p.
89-005509   305.4/2/098   0044451865
Women in politics -- South America -- Case studies. Feminism -- South America -- Case studies. Women and democracy. South America -- Politics and government.

HQ1236.5.S68.B76 1987
Browning, Genia K.
Women and politics in the USSR: consciousness raising and Soviet women's groups/ Genia K. Browning. Sussex: Wheatsheaf Books; 1987. ix, 178 p.
87-009604   320/.088042   0312009534
Women in politics -- Soviet Union. Women -- Soviet Union -- Societies and clubs. Soviet Union -- Politics and government.

HQ1236.5.S73.H35 1996
Hale, Sondra.
Gender politics in Sudan: Islamism, socialism, and the state/ Sondra Hale. Boulder, Colo.: Westview Press, 1996. xv, 294 p.
96-016438   305.42/09624   0813324319
Women in politics -- Sudan. Women and socialism -- Sudan. Women in Islam -- Sudan.

HQ1236.5.U6.A45 2000
Allgor, Catherine, 1958-
Parlor politics: in which the ladies of Washington help build a city and a government/ Catherine Allgor. Charlottesville: University Press of Virginia, 2000. 299 p.
00-033415   305.42/09753/09034   0813919983
Women in politics -- Washington (D.C.) -- History -- 19th century. Upper class women -- Washington (D.C.) -- History -- 19th century. Entertaining -- Washington (D.C.) -- History -- 19th century. Washington (D.C.) -- History -- 19th century. Washington (D.C.) -- Politics and government -- 19th century. Washington (D.C.) -- Social life and customs -- 19th century.

HQ1236.5.U6.B45 2001
Behling, Laura L., 1967-
The masculine woman in America, 1890-1935/ Laura L. Behling. Urbana: University of Illinois Press, c2001. 215 p.
00-009894   305.42/0973 21   0252026276
Women's rights -- United States -- History. Women -- Suffrage -- United States -- History. Women -- United States -- Public opinion.

HQ1236.5.U6.B69 1988
Boydston, Jeanne.
The limits of sisterhood: the Beecher sisters on women's rights and woman's sphere/ Jeanne Boydston, Mary Kelley, Anne Margolis. Chapel Hill: University of North Carolina Press, c1988. xxiv, 369 p.
87-019771   305.4/2/0973   0807817686
Beecher, Catharine Esther, -- 1800-1878. Stowe, Harriet Beecher, -- 1811-1896. Hooker, Isabella Beecher, -- 1822-1907. Women's rights -- United States -- History -- 19th century -- Sources. Feminism -- United States -- History -- 19th century -- Sources. Women -- United States -- History -- 19th century -- Sources.

HQ1236.5.U6.B87 1994
Burrell, Barbara C., 1947-
A woman's place is in the House: campaigning for Congress in the feminist era/ Barbara C. Burrell. Ann Arbor: University of Michigan Press, c1994. 211 p.
94-007641   320/.082   0472104799
Women legislators -- United States. Electioneering -- United States. Women in politics -- United States. United States -- Politics and government -- 1945-1989. United States -- Politics and government -- 1989-

HQ1236.5.U6.C67 1992
Costain, Anne N., 1948-
Inviting women's rebellion: a political process interpretation of the women's movement/ Anne N. Costain. Baltimore: Johns Hopkins University Press, c1992. xx, 188 p.
91-039293   305.42   0801843332
Women -- Government policy -- United States. Feminism -- Political aspects -- United States. Women in politics -- United States.

HQ1236.5.U6.E53 1999
Encyclopedia of women in American politics/ edited by Jeffrey D. Schultz and Laura van Assendelft; foreword by Helen Thomas. Phoenix, Ariz.: Oryx Press, 1999. xxviii, 354 p.
98-036327   320/.082   1573561312
Women in politics -- United States -- History -- Encyclopedias.

HQ1236.5.U6.H37 1988
Harrison, Cynthia Ellen.
On account of sex: the politics of women's issues, 1945-1968/ Cynthia Harrison. Berkeley: University of California Press, c1988. xxii, 337 p.
87-025550   305.4/2/0973   0520061217
Women's rights -- United States -- History -- 20th century. Women -- Legal status, laws, etc. -- United States -- History -- 20th century. Sex discrimination against women -- United States -- History -- 20th century.

HQ1236.5.U6.H38 1989
Hartmann, Susan M.
From margin to mainstream: American women and politics since 1960/ Susan M. Hartmann. New York: Knopf, c1989. xi, 218 p.
88-013645   320/.088042   0394356101
Women in politics -- United States -- History -- 20th century.

HQ1236.5.U6.H64 1995
Hoffert, Sylvia D.
When hens crow: the woman's rights movement in antebellum America/ Sylvia D. Hoffert. Bloomington: Indiana University Press, c1995. x, 153 p.
94-044083   305.42/0973/09034   0253328802
Women's rights -- United States -- History -- 19th century. Women in politics -- United States -- History -- 19th century. Feminism -- United States -- History -- 19th century.

HQ1236.5.U6.I83 1998
Isenberg, Nancy
Sex and citizenship in antebellum America/ Nancy Isenberg. Chapel Hill, N.C.: The University of North Carolina Press, c1998. xviii, 319 p.
98-013349   305.42/0973 21   0807824429
Women -- Suffrage -- United States -- History. Women's rights -- United States -- History. Feminism -- United States -- History.

HQ1236.5.U6.K47 1998
Kerber, Linda K.
No constitutional right to be ladies: women and the obligations of citizenship/ Linda K. Kerber. New York: Hill and Wang, 1998. xxiv, 405 p.
98-021393   305.42/0973   0809073838
Women and democracy -- United States -- History. Women -- Legal status, laws, etc. -- United States -- History. Citizenship -- United States.

HQ1236.5.U6.L96 1992
Lynn, Susan, 1945-
Progressive women in conservative times: racial justice, peace, and feminism, 1945 to the 1960s/ Susan Lynn. New Brunswick, N.J.: Rutgers University Press, c1992. xi, 218 p.
92-007978   305.42/0973   0813518679
Women political activists -- United States -- History -- 20th century. Women social reformers -- United States -- History -- 20th century. Feminists -- United States -- History -- 20th century. United States -- Race relations. United States -- Social conditions -- 1945-

HQ1236.5.U6.M37 1986
Mansbridge, Jane J.
Why we lost the ERA/ Jane J. Mansbridge. Chicago: University of Chicago Press, 1986. xii, 327 p.
86-006954   305.4/2/0973   0226503577
Women's rights -- United States. Equal rights amendments -- United States. Feminism -- United States.

HQ1236.5.U6.M3778 1999
Martin, Mart, 1944-
The almanac of women and minorities in American politics/ Mart Martin; foreword by Paula D. McCain. Boulder, Colo.: Westview Press, 1998.
98-015202   306.2/082/0973   0813368707
Women in politics -- United States -- Handbooks, manuals, etc. Women politicians -- United States -- Handbooks, manuals, etc. Minorities -- United States -- Political activity -- Handbooks, manuals, etc.

HQ1236.5.U6.M38 1990
Mathews, Donald G.
Sex, gender, and the politics of ERA: a state and the nation/ Donald G. Mathews, Jane Sherron De Hart. New York: Oxford University Press, 1990. xv, 283 p.
90-007174   305.42/09756   0195038584
Women's rights -- North Carolina. Equal rights amendments -- North Carolina. Feminism -- North Carolina.

HQ1236.5.U6.M3845 1997
Matthews, Jean V., 1937-
Women's struggle for equality: the first phase, 1828-1876/ Jean V. Matthews. Chicago: Ivan R. Dee, c1997. x, 212 p.
96-047500   305.42/0973 21   1566631459
Women's rights -- United States -- History. Feminism -- United States -- History.

HQ1236.5.U6.S32 1999
Schenken, Suzanne O'Dea.
From suffrage to the Senate: an encyclopedia of American women in politics/ Suzanne O'Dea Schenken; foreword by Ann W. Richards. Santa Barbara: ABC-CLIO, c1999. 2 v.
99-048951   320/.082/0973 21   0874369606
Women in politics -- United States -- Encyclopedias.

HQ1236.5.U6.W4 1999
We have come to stay: American women and political parties, 1880-1960/ edited by Melanie Gustafson, Kristie Miller, and Elisabeth I. Perry. Albuquerque: University of New Mexico Press, c1999. xiv, 205 p.
98-037401   320/.082 21   0826319696
Women in politics -- United States -- History. Women political activists -- United States -- History.

HQ1236.5.U6.W63 2000
Wolbrecht, Christina.
The politics of women's rights: parties, positions, and change/ Christina Wolbrecht. Princeton, N.J.: Princeton University Press, c2000. xvi, 266 p.
99-048918   305.42/0973 21   0691048568
Women's rights -- United States. Political parties -- United States. United States -- Politics and government -- 1945-1989. United States -- Politics and government -- 1989-1993.

HQ1236.5.U6.W65 1988
Women and the politics of empowerment/ edited by Ann Bookman and Sandra Morgen. Philadelphia: Temple University Press, 1988. xi, 324 p.
87-006504   320/.088042   0877225044
Women in politics -- United States -- Case studies. Working class women -- United States -- Case studies. Feminism -- United States -- Case studies.

HQ1236.5.U6.W6665 1997
Women, media, and politics/ edited by Pippa Norris. New York: Oxford University Press, 1997. xvi, 269 p.
95-052162   305.4   0195105664
Women in politics -- United States. Mass media and women -- United States.

HQ1236.5.U6.W69 1999
Woods, Harriett.
Stepping up to power: the political journey of American women/ Harriett Woods. Boulder, Colo.: Westview Press, 1999. ix, 252 p.
99-056832   320/.082/0973   0813368154
Women in politics -- United States.

HQ1237 Women. Feminism — Sex discrimination against women. Sexual harassment — General works

HQ1237.C76 2001
Crouch, Margaret A., 1956-
Thinking about sexual harassment: a guide for the perplexed/ Margaret A. Crouch. Oxford; New York: Oxford University Press, c2001. 315 p.
00-035965   305.3 21   0195140303
Sexual harassment.

HQ1237.R83 1995
Ruether, Rosemary Radford.
New woman, new earth: sexist ideologies and human liberation/ Rosemary Radford Ruether. Boston: Beacon Press, c1995. xxiv, 221 p.
95-016969   261.8/344 20   080706503X
Sexism. Women in Christianity. Race discrimination.

HQ1237.V35 1998
Valian, Virginia.
Why so slow?: the advancement of women/ Virginia Valian. Cambridge, Mass.: MIT Press, c1998. xvii, 401 p.
96-037029   305.42 21   0262220547
Sex discrimination against women -- Psychological aspects. Sexism. Women in the professions.

HQ1237.5 Women. Feminism — Sex discrimination against women. Sexual harassment — By region or country, A-Z

HQ1237.5.U6.G37 1995
Gardner, Carol Brooks.
Passing by: gender and public harassment/ Carol Brooks Gardner. Berkeley: University of California Press, c1995. xiii, 256 p.
95-003208   305.42   0520081870
Sexual harassment of women -- Indiana -- Indianapolis. Invective -- Indiana -- Indianapolis. Etiquette -- Indiana -- Indianapolis.

HQ1237.5.U6.M67 1994
Morris, Celia, 1935-
Bearing witness: sexual harassment and beyond--everywoman's story/ Celia Morris. Boston: Little, Brown and Co., c1994. 326 p.
93-029383   305.42   0316584223
Sexual harassment of women -- United States.

HQ1240 Women. Feminism — Women in development — General works

HQ1240.G46 1987
Geography of gender in the Third World/ edited by Janet Henshall Momsen and Janet G. Townsend. Albany, N.Y.: State University of New York Press, c1987. 424 p.
86-014564   305.4/2/091724   0887064418
Women in development. Sexual division of labor -- Developing countries. Sex role -- Developing countries.

HQ1240.N87 2000
Nussbaum, Martha Craven, 1947-
Women and human development: the capabilities approach/ Martha C. Nussbaum. Cambridge; Cambridge University Press, 2000. xxi, 312 p.
99-015850   305.42/09172/4   0521660866
Women in development Women -- Developing countries.

HQ1240.P54 1994
Pietilä, Hilkka.
Making women matter: the role of the United Nations/ Hilkka Pietilä and Jeanne Vickers; foreword by Gertrude Mongella. Updated and expanded ed. London; Zed Books, 1994. x, 198 p.
95-100581   305.42 20   1856492702
Women in development. International Women's Decade, 1976-1985. Women's rights.

HQ1240.S28 1996
Sachs, Carolyn E., 1950-
Gendered fields: rural women, agriculture, and environment/ Carolyn E. Sachs. Boulder: WestviewPress, 1996. xiv, 205 p.
95-043943   338.9/0082   0813325196
Women in rural development. Rural women. Women in agriculture.

HQ1240.W662 1997
Women, international development, and politics: the bureaucratic mire / edited by Kathleen Staudt. Updated and expanded ed. Philadelphia: Temple University Press, 1997. xii, 356 p.
97-003227   305.42 21   1566395461
Women in development. Women -- Government policy. Women in politics.

HQ1240.W6627 1994
Women, the environment and sustainable development: towards a theoretical synthesis/ Rosi Braidotti ... [et al.]. London; Zed Books in association with INSTRAW, 1994. xiii, 220 p.
94-001964   305.42   1856491838
Women in development -- Environmental aspects. Sustainable development. Human ecology.

HQ1240.Y68 1993
Young, Kate.
Planning development with women: making a world of difference/ Kate Young. New York: St. Martin's Press, 1993. vii, 187 p.
92-029477   305.42   0312090900
Women in development.

HQ1240.5 Women. Feminism — Women in development — By region or country, A-Z

HQ1240.5.A35.F45 1999
The feminization of development processes in Africa: current and future perspectives/ edited by Valentine Udoh James and James S. Etim. Westport, Conn.: Praeger, 1999. xvi, 240 p.
98-019300   305.42/096   0275959465
Women in development -- Africa. Women in public life -- Africa. Feminism -- Africa.

HQ1240.5.A35.G67 1996
Gordon, April A.
Transforming capitalism and patriarchy: gender and development in Africa/ April A. Gordon. Boulder, Col.: Lynne Rienner, 1996. ix, 219 p.
95-041235   305.42/096   1555874029
Women in development -- Africa. Capitalism -- Africa. Patriarchy -- Africa.

HQ1240.5.A35.S69 1995
Snyder, Margaret C., 1929-
African women and development: a history/ Margaret C. Snyder, Mary Tadesse. Johannesburg: Witwatersrand University Press; 1995. xiii, 239 p.
94-040205   305.42/096   1856492990
Women in development -- Africa -- History.

HQ1240.5.A357.A34 1994
Gender, work & population in sub-Saharan Africa/ edited by Aderanti Adepoju, Christine Oppong. London: Published on behalf of International Labour Offi 1994. x, 245 p.
93-050628   305.42/0967   0852554079
Women in rural development -- Africa, Sub-Saharan. Women -- Employment -- Africa, Sub-Saharan. Work and family -- Africa, Sub-Saharan.

HQ1240.5.A357.A36 1997
African feminism: the politics of survival in sub-Saharan Africa/ edited by Gwendolyn Mikell. Philadelphia: University of Pennsylvania Press, c1997. xv, 361 p.
97-006260   305.42/0967 21   0812233492
Women in development -- Africa, Sub-Saharan. Feminism -- Africa, Sub-Saharan. Women -- Africa, Sub-Saharan -- Social conditions.

HQ1240.5.A78.W63 2000
Women in Asia: tradition, modernity, and globalisation/ edited by Louise Edwards & Mina Roces. Ann Arbor: University of Michigan Press, c2000. 327 p.
00-033804   305.42/095 21   0472087517
Women in development -- Asia. Women -- Asia -- Social conditions. Women -- Asia -- Economic conditions.

HQ1240.5.D44.W662 1993
Women in developing economies: making visible the invisible/ [edited by Joycelin Massiah]. Providence, RI, U.S.A.: Berg; 1993. 300 p.
92-024168   305.42/09172/4   0854963456
Women in development -- Developing countries. Informal sector (Economics) -- Developing countries.

HQ1240.5.L29.S74 1997
Stephen, Lynn.
Women and social movements in Latin America: power from below/ Lynn Stephen. Austin: University of Texas Press, 1997. xviii, 332 p.
96-045788   305.42/098   0292777159
Women in development -- Latin America -- Case studies. Social movements -- Latin America -- Case studies. Feminism -- Latin America -- Case studies.

HQ1240.5.S63.T68 1995
Townsend, Janet G., 1944-
Women's voices from the rainforest/ Janet Gabriel Townsend; in collaboration with Ursula Arrevillaga ... [et al.]. London; Routledge, 1995. 212 p.
94-012466 305.42/098 0415105315
Women in development -- Environmental aspects -- South America. Women in development -- Environmental aspects -- Tropics. Rain forests -- South America.

HQ1240.5.S65.B75 1987
Bridger, Susan.
Women in the Soviet countryside: women's roles in rural development in the Soviet Union/ Susan Bridger. Cambridge [Cambridgeshire]; Cambridge University Press, 1987. xv, 259 p.
87-011723 305.4/2/0947 0521328624
Women in rural development -- Soviet Union. Rural women -- Soviet Union. Rural families -- Soviet Union. Soviet Union -- Rural conditions.

HQ1240.5.Z55
Sylvester, Christine, 1949-
Producing women and progress in Zimbabwe: narratives of identity and work from the 1980s/ Christine Sylvester. Portsmouth, NH: Heinemann, c2000. xii, 277 p.
99-028369 305.42/096891 21 0325000700
Women in development -- Zimbabwe. Women -- Employment -- Zimbabwe. Women -- Zimbabwe -- Economic conditions.

HQ1381 Women. Feminism — Women and economics

HQ1381.E24 1994
The Economic status of women under capitalism: institutional economics and feminist theory/ edited by Janice Peterson and Doug Brown. Aldershot, Hants, England; Edward Elgar, c1994. xvii, 187 p.
93-008713 305.42 1852788941
Women -- Economic conditions. Feminist theory -- Economic aspects. Institutional economics.

HQ1381.E44 1999
The Elgar companion to feminist economics/ edited by Janice Peterson, Margaret Lewis. Cheltenham, UK Edward Elgar, c1999. xvii, 811 p.
99-033956 330/.082 21 185989453X
Feminist economics. Women -- Economic conditions.

HQ1381.H48 1999
Hewitson, Gillian J., 1961-
Feminist economics: interrogating the masculinity of rational economic man/ Gillian J. Hewiston. Northampton, Mass.: Edward Elgar Pub., 1999. vii, 277 p.
98-038336 330/.082 1858989469
Feminist economics. Neoclassical school of economics. Economic man.

HQ1381.R63 1995
Robb, Carol S.
Equal value: an ethical approach to economics and sex/ Carol S. Robb. Boston, Mass.: Beacon Press, c1995. viii, 198 p.
95-015090 305.42 0807065048
Women -- Economic conditions. Sex role -- Economic aspects. Social justice.

HQ1391 Women. Feminism — Women in public services. Women in public life — General works

HQ1391.E85.W66 1987
Women, state and revolution: essays on power and gender in Europe since 1789/ edited by Sian Reynolds. Amherst: University of Massachusetts Press, 1987. xvi, 190 p.
86-016074 320/.088042 0870235524
Women in politics -- Europe -- History. Women -- Europe -- History. Feminism -- Europe -- History.

HQ1391.F7.L36 1988
Landes, Joan B., 1946-
Women and the public sphere in the age of the French Revolution/ Joan B. Landes. Ithaca: Cornell University Press, 1988. xi, 276 p.
88-003723 305.4/0944 0801421411
Women in public life -- France -- History -- 18th century. Women -- France -- History -- 18th century. Women's rights -- France -- History -- 18th century. France -- History -- Revolution, 1789-1799 -- Women.

HQ1391.G7.J66 2000
Jones, Helen, 1926-
Women in British public life, 1914-1950: gender, power, and social policy/ Helen Jones. New York: Pearson Education, 2000.
00-035686 305.42/0941 0582277310
Women in public life -- Great Britain -- History -- 20th century. Great Britain -- Social policy.

HQ1391.J3.H47 1991
Heroic with grace: legendary women of Japan/ edited by Chieko Irie Mulhern. Armonk, N.Y.: M.E. Sharpe, c1991. xvii, 326 p.
90-028750 305.4/0952 0873325273
Women in public life -- Japan -- Biography. Women -- Japan -- Biography. Women -- Japan -- History.

HQ1391.U5 C37 1994
Carroll, Susan J.,
Women as candidates in American politics/ Susan J. Carroll. 2nd ed. Bloomington: Indiana University Press, c1994. xv, 240 p.
93-041856 305.4/3329 20 0253208777
Women in politics -- United States. Elections -- United States.

HQ1391.U5.F64 1996
Foerstel, Karen.
Climbing the Hill: gender conflict in Congress/ Karen Foerstel and Herbert N. Foerstel. Westport, CT: Praeger, 1996. 201 p.
95-037651 320/.082 0275949141
Women legislators -- United States. Women in politics -- United States. Sex discrimination against women -- United States.

HQ1391.U5.K55 1998
Kierner, Cynthia A., 1958-
Beyond the household: women's place in the early South, 1700-1835/ Cynthia A. Kierner. Ithaca, NY: Cornell University Press, 1998. xii, 295 p.
98-022999 305.42/0975 080143453X
Women in public life -- Southern States -- History. Women -- Southern States -- History.

HQ1391.U5.K57
Kirkpatrick, Jeane J.
Political woman/ Jeane J. Kirkpatrick. New York: Basic Books, [1974] xiii, 274 p.
73-090130 329 0465059708
Women in politics -- United States. Political participation -- United States. Power (Social sciences)

HQ1391.U5.M38 1992
Matthews, Glenna.
The rise of public woman: woman's power and woman's place in the United States, 1630-1970/ Glenna Matthews. New York: Oxford University Press, 1992. x, 297 p.
91-047518 305.4/0973 0195054601
Women in public life -- United States -- History. Women -- United States -- Social conditions. Feminism -- United States -- History.

HQ1391.U5.R67 1982
Rossi, Alice S., 1922-
Feminists in politics: a panel analysis of the First National Women's Conference/ Alice S. Rossi. New York: Academic Press, c1982. xxvii, 411 p.
82-008807 320/.088/042 0125982801
Women in politics -- United States -- Congresses -- Evaluation. Feminism -- United States -- Congresses -- Evaluation.

HQ1391.U5.R9 1990
Ryan, Mary P.
Women in public: between banners and ballots, 1825-1880/ Mary P. Ryan. Baltimore: Johns Hopkins University Press, c1990. xii, 202 p.
89-032863 305.4/2/0973 0801839084
Women in public life -- Louisiana -- New Orleans -- History -- 19th century. Women in public life -- California -- San Francisco -- History -- 19th century. Women in public life -- New York (State) -- New York -- History -- 19th century.

HQ1391.U5.S85 1996
Sullivan, Patricia Ann.
From the margins to the center: contemporary women and political communication/ Patricia A. Sullivan and Lynn H. Turner. Westport, Conn.: Praeger, 1996. xxii, 151 p.
96-020707 320/.082 0275949931
Women in public life -- United States. Communication in politics -- United States. Communication -- Sex differences.

HQ1391.U5.W63 1998
Women and elective office: past, present, and future/ edited by Sue Thomas and Clyde Wilcox. New York: Oxford University Press, 1998. xiii, 241 p.
97-027331 320/.082 019511230X
Women in public life -- United States. Women in politics -- United States. Women political candidates -- United States.

HQ1393-1394 Women. Feminism — Women and religion

HQ1393.F44 1982
The Feminist mystic, and other essays on women and spirituality/ edited by Mary E. Giles. New York: Crossroad, 1982. vii, 159 p.
81-022130 305.4 0824504321
Women and religion.

HQ1394.D28 1985
Daly, Mary, 1928-
The church and the second sex/ Mary Daly, with the feminist postChristian introduction and new archaic afterwords by the author. Boston: Beacon Press, c1985. xxx, 231 p.
85-047519   261.8/344   0807011010
Feminism -- Religious aspects -- Catholic Church. Sexism in religion. Women in Christianity.

HQ1397 Women. Feminism — Women in science and the arts

HQ1397.K63 1992
The Knowledge explosion: generations of feminist scholarship/ edited by Cheris Kramarae and Dale Spender. New York: Teachers College Press, c1992. x, 533 p.
91-014334   305.42/0973   080776258X
Women scholars -- United States. Women's studies -- United States. Feminism -- United States.

HQ1410-1439 Women. Feminism — By region or country — America

HQ1410.A2525 1997
Stanton, Elizabeth Cady, 1815-1902.
The selected papers of Elizabeth Cady Stanton and Susan B. Anthony/ Ann D. Gordon, editor. New Brunswick, N.J.: Rutgers University Press, [c1997-] v. 1.
97-005666   016.30542   0813523176
Stanton, Elizabeth Cady, -- 1815-1902 -- Archives. Anthony, Susan B. -- (Susan Brownell), -- 1820-1906 -- Archives. Feminists -- United States -- Archives. Suffragists -- United States -- Archives. Feminism -- United States -- History -- 19th century -- Sources.

HQ1410.A46 1991
Amott, Teresa L.
Race, gender, and work: a multicultural economic history of women in the United States/ Teresa Amott and Julie Matthaei. Boston, MA: South End Press, c1991. xiii, 433 p.
90-048222   305.4/0973   0896083764
Women -- United States -- Economic conditions. Women -- United States -- History. Women -- Employment -- United States.

HQ1410.C3813 1990
Castro, Ginette.
American feminism: a contemporary history/ Ginette Castro; translated from the French by Elizabeth Loverde-Bagwell. New York: New York University Press, c1990. xii, 302 p.
90-030323   305.42/0973   0814714358
Feminism -- United States. Feminism -- United States -- History.

HQ1410.C44 1984
Clinton, Catherine, 1952-
The other civil war: American women in the nineteenth century/ Catherine Clinton; consulting editor, Eric Foner. New York: Hill and Wang, c1984. xiii, 242 p.
84-000525   305.4/0973   0809074605
Women -- United States -- History -- 19th century. Feminism -- United States -- History -- 19th century.

HQ1410.C85 2000
Cullen-DuPont, Kathryn.
Encyclopedia of women's history in America/ Kathryn Cullen-DuPont. New York: Facts On File, c2000. xiii, 418 p.
99-087498   305.4/0973/03 21   0816041008
Women -- United States -- History -- Encyclopedias. Feminism -- United States -- History -- Encyclopedias.

HQ1410.E83 1989
Evans, Sara M. 1943-
Born for liberty: a history of women in America/ Sara M. Evans. New York: Free Press; c1989. xii, 386 p.
88-033544   305.4/0973   0029029902
Women -- United States -- History. Women -- United States -- Social conditions. Women in politics -- United States -- History.

HQ1410.F76 1994
Frost-Knappman, Elizabeth.
The ABC-CLIO companion to women's progress in America/ Elizabeth Frost-Knappman, with the assistance of Sarah Kurian. Santa Barbara, Calif.: ABC-CLIO, c1994. xi, 389 p.
94-009355   305.4/0973   0874366674
Women -- United States -- History -- Encyclopedias. Women's rights -- United States -- Encyclopedias.

HQ1410.H365 1998
Harlan, Judith.
Feminism: a reference handbook/ Judith Harlan. Santa Barbara, Calif.: ABC-CLIO, c1998. xvi, 308 p.
98-002970   305.42 21   0874368626
Feminism -- United States -- History -- Handbooks, manuals, etc. Feminist theory -- United States -- Handbooks, manuals, etc.

HQ1410.K45
Kennedy, Susan Estabrook.
If all we did was to weep at home: a history of white working-class women in America/ Susan Estabrook Kennedy. Bloomington: Indiana University Press, c1979. xx, 331 p.
78-020431   301.41/2/0973   0253191548
Women -- United States -- Social conditions. Working class -- United States -- History. Working class whites -- United States.

HQ1410.M355 1999
Manton, Catherine, 1942-
Fed up: women and food in America/ Catherine Manton. Westport, Conn.: Bergin & Garvey, 1999. xiv, 170 p.
98-019215   305.4/0973   0897896297
Women -- United States -- Social conditions. Women -- United States -- Psychology. Food -- Social aspects -- United States.

HQ1410.M38 1987
Matthews, Glenna.
"Just a housewife": the rise and fall of domesticity in America/ Glenna Matthews. New York: Oxford University Press, 1987. xvii, 281 p.
86-033318   305.4/2/0973   0195038592
Women -- United States -- Social conditions. Housewives -- United States -- History -- 19th century. Housewives -- United States -- History -- 20th century.

HQ1410.M96 1982
Myres, Sandra L.
Westering women and the frontier experience, 1800-1915/ Sandra L. Myres. Albuquerque: University of New Mexico Press, c1982. xxii, 365 p.
82-006956   305.4/2/0978   082630625X
Women -- West (U.S.) -- History -- 19th century. Frontier and pioneer life -- West (U.S.)

HQ1410.N475 1998
Newman, Louise Michele.
White women's rights: the racial origins of feminism in the United States/ Lousie Michele Newman. New York: Oxford University Press, 1998. vii, 261 p.
97-053286   0195086929
Feminism -- United States -- History. Women's rights -- United States -- History. Racism -- United States -- History.

HQ1410.N6 2000
No small courage: a history of women in the United States/ edited by Nancy F. Cott. Oxford; Oxford University Press, 2000. ix, 646 p.
00-021130   305.4/0973   0195139461
Women -- United States -- History.

HQ1410.R43 1998
The reader's companion to U.S. women's history/ editors, Wilma Mankiller ... [et al.]. Boston, Mass.: Houghton Mifflin Co., c1998. xxii, 696 p.
97-039923   305.4/0973 21   0395671736
Women -- United States -- History -- Sources. Women -- United States -- Social conditions. Feminism -- United States -- History.

HQ1410.R67 1982
Rosenberg, Rosalind, 1946-
Beyond separate spheres: intellectual roots of modern feminism/ Rosalind Rosenberg. New Haven: Yale University Press, c1982. xxii, 288 p.
81-015967   305.4/2/0973   0300026951
Feminist theory. Women social scientists -- United States -- Attitudes -- History. Women college graduates -- United States -- Attitudes -- History.

HQ1410.V36 1988
Van Horn, Susan Householder, 1934-
Women, work, and fertility, 1900-1986/ Susan Householder Van Horn. New York: New York University Press, c1988. xiv, 232 p.
87-024018   305.4/0973   0814787592
Women -- United States -- History -- 20th century. Women -- Employment -- United States -- History -- 20th century. Family -- United States -- History -- 20th century.

HQ1410.W73 1997
Writing the range: race, class, and culture in the women's West/ edited and with introductions by Elizabeth Jameson and Susan Armitage. Norman: University of Oklahoma Press, c1997. xiii, 656 p.
96-039163   305.4/0978 21   0806129522
Women -- West (U.S.) -- History. Minority women -- West (U.S.) -- History. Frontier and pioneer life -- West (U.S.) -- History.

HQ1412.C638 1980
Coles, Robert.
Women of crisis II: lives of work and dreams/ Robert Coles and Jane Hallowell Coles. New York: Delacorte Press/S. Lawrence, c1980. xii, 237 p.
79-025210   301.41/2/0973   0440096359
Women -- United States -- Biography. Minority women -- United States -- Biography. Working class women -- United States -- Biography. United States -- Social conditions.

HQ1412.C64 1978
Coles, Robert.
Women of crisis: lives of struggle and hope/ Robert Coles and Jane Hallowell Coles. New York: Delacorte Press/S. Lawrence, c1978. vi, 291 p.
78-005068   301.41/2/0973   0440095360
Women -- United States -- Biography. Minority women -- United States -- Biography. Working class women -- United States -- Biography.

HQ1412.C7
Cross, Barbara M.
The educated woman in America; selected writings of Catharine [sic] Beecher, Margaret Fuller, and M. Carey Thomas. Edited, with an introd. and notes, by Barbara M. Cross. New York, Teachers College Press [1965] viii, 175 p.
65-023578   301.4120973
Women in the United States.

HQ1412.S25
St. Johns, Adela Rogers.
Some are born great.   Garden City, N.Y., Doubleday, 1974. vi, 297 p.
74-007636   301.41/2/0922   0385087691
Women -- United States -- Biography.

HQ1412.S36 1984
Scott, Anne Firor, 1921-
Making the invisible woman visible/ Anne Firor Scott. Urbana: University of Illinois Press, c1984. xxvii, 387 p.
83-017962   305.4/0973   0252011104
Women -- United States -- Biography. Women -- United States -- History. Women -- Southern States -- History.

HQ1412.S72 1981
Stanton, Elizabeth Cady, 1815-1902.
Elizabeth Cady Stanton, Susan B. Anthony, correspondence, writings, speeches/ edited and with a critical commentary by Ellen Carol DuBois; foreword by Gerda Lerner. New York: Schocken Books, 1981. xv, 272 p.
80-027603   305.4/092/2   0805237593
Stanton, Elizabeth Cady, -- 1815-1902. Anthony, Susan B. -- (Susan Brownell), -- 1820-1906. Feminists -- United States -- Correspondence. Feminism -- United States -- History -- 19th century -- Addresses, essays, lectures.

HQ1413.A55.B36 1988
Barry, Kathleen.
Susan B. Anthony: a biography of a singular feminist/ Kathleen Barry. New York: New York University Press, c1988. xi, 426 p.
88-001228   305.4/2/0924   0814711057
Anthony, Susan B. -- (Susan Brownell), -- 1820-1906. Feminists -- United States -- Biography. Biography as a literary form.

HQ1413.A55.S48 1995
Sherr, Lynn.
Failure is impossible: Susan B. Anthony in her own words/ Lynn Sherr. New York: Times Books, c1995. xxviii, 382 p.
94-029913   324.6/23/092   0812924304
Anthony, Susan B. -- (Susan Brownell), -- 1820-1906. Feminists -- United States -- Biography. Suffragists -- United States -- Biography.

HQ1413.B36.A3 1998
Banner, Lois W.
Finding Fran: history and memory in the lives of two women/ Lois W. Banner. New York: Columbia University Press, c1998. xiii, 243 p.
98-023608   305.4/092/2 21   0231112165
Banner, Lois W. Durkee, Noura. Women in Islam. Feminists -- California -- Biography.

HQ1413.B4.S54
Sklar, Kathryn Kish.
Catharine Beecher; a study in American domesticity.   New Haven, Yale University Press, 1973. xv, 356 p.
73-077166   301.41/2/0924   0300015801
Beecher, Catharine Esther, -- 1800-1878.

HQ1413.B76.C68 1988
Cote, Charlotte.
Olympia Brown: the battle for equality/ by Charlotte Cote. Racine, WI: Mother Courage Press, c1988. 216 p.
88-060777   305.42/092   0941300099
Brown, Olympia, -- 1835-1926. Feminists -- United States -- Biography. Suffragists -- United States -- Biography. Universalist churches -- United States -- Clergy -- Biography.

HQ1413.C45.K37 1994
Karcher, Carolyn L., 1945-
The first woman in the republic: a cultural biography of Lydia Maria Child/ by Carolyn L. Karcher. Durham: Duke University Press, 1994. xxv, 804 p.
94-009151   303.48/4/092
Child, Lydia Maria Francis, -- 1802-1880. Women social reformers -- United States -- Biography. Authors, American -- 19th century -- Biography.

HQ1413.D2.E25 1984
Eckhardt, Celia Morris, 1935-
Fanny Wright: rebel in America/ Celia Morris Eckhardt. Cambridge, Mass.: Harvard University Press, 1984. xii, 337 p.
83-008571   303.4/84
Wright, Frances, -- 1795-1852. Women -- Biography. Feminists -- United States -- Biography.

HQ1413.D86.M69 1983
Moynihan, Ruth Barnes.
Rebel for rights, Abigail Scott Duniway/ Ruth Barnes Moynihan. New Haven: Yale University Press, c1983. xv, 273 p.
83-001142   324.6/23/0924   0300029527
Duniway, Abigail Scott, -- 1834-1915. Suffragists -- United States -- Biography. Women's rights -- United States -- History -- 19th century. Women -- Suffrage -- United States -- History -- 19th century.

HQ1413.F75.A34 1976
Friedan, Betty.
It changed my life: writings on the women's movement/ Betty Friedan. New York: Random House, c1976. xix, 388 p.
75-010305   301.41/2/0973   0394463986
Friedan, Betty. Feminism -- United States -- History.

HQ1413.F75.H456 1999
Hennessee, Judith Adler.
Betty Friedan: a biography/ Judith Adler Hennessee. New York: Random House, 1999. xvii, 330 p.
98-024876   305.42/092   0679432035
Friedan, Betty. Feminists -- United States -- Biography. Feminism -- United States.

HQ1413.G54.H54
Hill, Mary Armfield.
Charlotte Perkins Gilman: the making of a radical feminist, 1860-1896/ Mary A. Hill. Philadelphia: Temple University Press, 1980. xi, 362 p.
79-022395   301.41/2/0924   087722160X
Gilman, Charlotte Perkins, -- 1860-1935. Feminism -- United States -- History -- 19th century. Authors, American -- 19th century -- Biography. Feminists -- United States -- Biography.

HQ1413.G74.A3 1987
Greer, Germaine, 1939-
The madwoman's underclothes: essays and occasional writings/ Germaine Greer. New York: Atlantic Monthly Press, 1987, c1986. xxvii, 305 p.
87-011475   305.4/2/0973   0871131609
Greer, Germaine, -- 1939- Feminists -- Biography. Feminism. Social history -- 1945-

HQ1413.K45.S58 1995
Sklar, Kathryn Kish.
Florence Kelley and the nation's work/ Kathryn Kish Sklar. New Haven: Yale University Press, [c1995-] v. 1.
94-022725   305.42/092   0300059124
Kelley, Florence, -- 1859-1932. Women social reformers -- United States -- Biography. Feminists -- United States -- Biography.

HQ1413.M54.M55 1995
Millett, Kate.
A.D., a memoir/ Kate Millett. New York: W.W. Norton, c1995. 325 p.
95-001727   306.87   0393035247
Millett, Kate -- Family. Feminists -- United States -- Family relationships. Lesbians -- United States -- Family relationships. Aunts -- United States -- Case studies.

HQ1413.M68.B33
Bacon, Margaret Hope.
Valiant friend: the life of Lucretia Mott/ by Margaret Hope Bacon. New York, N.Y.: Walker, 1980. x, 265 p.
79-091253   361.2/092/4   0802706452
Mott, Lucretia, -- 1793-1880. Feminists -- United States -- Biography. Abolitionists -- United States -- Biography.

HQ1413.S67.G74 1984
Griffith, Elisabeth.
In her own right: the life of Elizabeth Cady Stanton/ Elisabeth Griffith. New York: Oxford University Press, 1984. xx, 268 p.
83-025120   324.6/23/0924   0195034406
Stanton, Elizabeth Cady, -- 1815-1902. Feminists -- United States -- Biography. Suffragists -- United States -- Biography. Women's rights -- United States -- History.

HQ1413.S67K47 2001
Kern, Kathi,
Mrs. Stanton's Bible/ Kathi Kern. Ithaca, N.Y.: Cornell University Press, 2001. xi, 288 p.
00-010756   305.42/092   0801482887
Stanton, Elizabeth Cady, 1815-1902. Stanton, Elizabeth Cady, 1815-1902 Woman's Bible. Feminists -- United States -- Biography. Feminism -- Religious aspects -- Christianity. Women's rights -- United States -- History -- 19th century.

HQ1413.S73.K47 1992
Kerr, Andrea Moore, 1940-
Lucy Stone: speaking out for equality/ Andrea Moore Kerr. New Brunswick, N.J.: Rutgers University Press, c1992. 301 p.
92-006159   305.42/092   0813518598
Stone, Lucy, -- 1818-1893.   Feminists -- United States -- Biography. Suffragists -- United States -- Biography. Abolitionists -- United States -- Biography.

HQ1413.W66.U53 1995
Underhill, Lois Beachy, 1935-
The woman who ran for president: the many lives of Victoria Woodhull/ Lois Beachy Underhill. Bridgehampton, N.Y.: Bridge Works Pub.; 1995. xvii, 347 p.
94-049519   973.8/092   1882593103
Woodhull, Victoria C. -- (Victoria Claflin), -- 1838-1927.   Women -- United States -- Biography. Feminists -- United States -- Biography. Women in politics -- United States -- Biography.

HQ1416.S65 1972
Spruill, Julia Cherry.
Women's life and work in the Southern colonies. With an introd. to the Norton library ed. by Anne Firor Scott. New York, Norton [1972] x, 426 p.
72-006149   301.41/2/0975   039300662X
Women -- Southern States -- History.

HQ1416.T74 1996
Treckel, Paula A.
To comfort the heart: women in seventeenth-century America/ Paula A. Treckel. New York, N.Y.: Twayne Publishers; c1996. xvi, 267 p.
95-039990   305.4/0973/09032 20   0805799176
Women -- United States -- History -- 17th century.

HQ1418.A87 1999
Attwood, Lynne.
Creating the new Soviet woman: women's magazines as engineers of female identity, 1922-53/ Lynne Attwood. New York: St. Martin's Press, 1999.
99-025942   305.4/0947   031222544X
Women -- Soviet Union -- Identity. Women's periodicals, Russian. Women -- Soviet Union -- History.

HQ1418.B5
Berg, Barbara J.
The remembered gate: origins of American feminism: the woman and the city, 1800-1860/ Barbara J. Berg. New York: Oxford University Press, 1978. xvi, 334 p.
76-051709   301.41/2/0973   0195022807
Women -- United States -- History. Women -- United States -- Social conditions. Feminism -- United States -- History.

HQ1418.C58 2000
Clinton, Catherine, 1952-
The Columbia guide to American women in the Nineteenth Century/ Catherine Clinton, Christine Lunardini. New York: Columbia University Press, c2000. xv, 331 p.
98-050373   0231109202
Women -- United States -- History -- 19th century.

HQ1418.C67 1997
Cott, Nancy F.
The bonds of womanhood: "woman's sphere" in New England, 1780-1835/ Nancy F. Cott. 2nd ed. with a new preface New Haven: Yale University Press, 1997. xxx, 225 p.
97-060429   305.42/0974 21   0300072988
Women -- New England -- Social conditions. Women -- New England -- History.

HQ1418.G56 1990
Ginzberg, Lori D.
Women and the work of benevolence: morality, politics, and class in the nineteenth-century United States/ Lori D. Ginzberg. New Haven: Yale University Press, c1990. xii, 230 p.
89-024930   305.4/0973   0300047045
Women social reformers -- United States -- History -- 19th century. Women in charitable work -- United States -- History -- 19th century. Middle class women -- United States -- History -- 19th century. United States -- Moral conditions.

HQ1418.K47 1986
Kerber, Linda K.
Women of the Republic: intellect and ideology in revolutionary America/ Linda K. Kerber. New York: Norton, c1986. xiv, 304 p.
86-008716   305.4/2/0973 19   0393303454
Women -- United States -- History.

HQ1418.N67 1996
Norton, Mary Beth.
Liberty's daughters: the revolutionary experience of American women, 1750-1800: with a new preface/ Mary Beth Norton. Ithaca, N.Y.: Cornell University Press, 1996. xxii, 384 p.
96-012247   305.42/0973 20   0801483476
Women -- United States -- History -- Sources. Women in politics -- United States -- History -- Sources.

HQ1418.S38
Scott, Anne Firor, 1921-
The Southern lady: from pedestal to politics, 1830-1930.   Chicago, University of Chicago Press [1970] xv, 247 p.
73-123750   301.41/2/0975   0226743462
Women -- Southern States -- History.

HQ1418.T53 1996
Theriot, Nancy M.
Mothers and daughters in nineteenth-century America: the biosocial construction of femininity/ Nancy M. Theriot. [Rev. ed.]. Lexington, Ky.: University Press of Kentucky, c1996. 226 p.
95-014672   305.42/0973 20   0813108586
Middle class women -- United States -- History -- 19th century. Women -- Health and hygiene -- United States -- Sociological aspects. Mothers and daughters -- United States -- History -- 19th century.

HQ1419.G46 1991
Gender, class, race, and reform in the progressive era/ Noralee Frankel, Nancy S. Dye, editors. Lexington, Ky.: University Press of Kentucky, c1991. 202 p.
91-016843   0813117631
Women -- United States -- History -- 19th century -- Congresses. Women -- United States -- History -- 20th century -- Congresses. Progressivism (United States politics) -- Congresses.

HQ1419.I75 2000
Irving, Katrina.
Immigrant mothers: narratives of race and maternity, 1890-1925/ Katrina Irving. Urbana: University of Illinois Press, 2000. x, 148 p.
99-006616   305.48/9691   0252025342
Women immigrants -- United States -- Public opinion -- History. Mothers -- United States -- Public opinion -- History. Xenophobia -- United States -- History. United States -- Emigration and immigration -- Public opinion -- History. United States -- Ethnic relations -- History.

HQ1420.A65
Anderson, Karen, 1947-
Wartime women: sex roles, family relations, and the status of women during World War II/ Karen Anderson. Westport, Conn.: Greenwood Press, 1981. 198 p.
80-001703   305.4/2/0973   0313208840
Women -- United States -- History -- 20th century. World War, 1939-1945 -- Women -- United States. World War, 1939-1945 -- Social aspects -- United States.

HQ1420.B5 1970
Bird, Caroline.
Born female; the high cost of keeping women down, by Caroline Bird with Sara Welles Briller. New York, McKay [1970] xiv, 302 p.
71-134801   301.41/2/0973
Women -- United States. Women -- Employment -- United States.

HQ1420.C67 1987
Cott, Nancy F.
The grounding of modern feminism/ Nancy F. Cott. New Haven: Yale University Press, c1987. xiii, 372 p.
87-010642   305.4/2/0973   0300038925
Feminism -- United States -- History. Women's rights -- United States -- History. Women -- Suffrage -- United States -- History.

HQ1420.G4 1985
Gerson, Kathleen.
Hard choices: how women decide about work, career, and motherhood/ Kathleen Gerson. Berkeley: University of California Press, c1985. xix, 312 p.
84-008602   305.4/0973   0520051742
Women -- United States -- Social conditions. Mothers -- United States -- Social conditions. Women -- Employment -- United States -- History.

HQ1420.L66
Lopata, Helena Znaniecka, 1925-
Occupation: housewife.   New York, Oxford University Press, 1971. xvi, 387 p.
77-083046   305.4/3   0195014685
Housewives. Women -- United States.

HQ1420.N68 1994
Not June Cleaver: women and gender in postwar America, 1945-1960/ edited by Joanne Meyerowitz. Phliadelphia: Temple University Press, 1994. vi, 411 p.
93-026987   305.42/0973/09045   1566391709
Women -- United States -- History -- 20th century. Women -- Employment -- United States -- History -- 20th century.

HQ1420.S68 1998
Spurlock, John C., 1954-
New and improved: the transformation of American women's emotional culture/ John C. Spurlock and Cynthia A. Magistro. New York: New York University Press, c1998. xiii, 213 p.
98-009050 305.4/0973/0904 21 0814780458
Women -- United States -- History -- 20th century. Women -- United States -- Psychology -- History -- 20th century. Emotions -- Social aspects -- United States -- History -- 20th century. United States -- Social life and customs -- 20th century -- Psychological aspects.

HQ1420.T34 1996
Statistical handbook on women in America/ compiled and edited by Cynthia M. Taeuber; forewords by Gail Sheehy, Wilma Vaught, Sheila Wellington. Phoenix, Ariz.: Oryx Press, 1996. xxvi, 354 p.
96-001521 305.4/0973/021 1573560057
Women -- United States -- Statistics.

HQ1420.W66 1998
Women's magazines, 1940-1960: gender roles and the popular press/ edited with an introduction by Nancy A. Walker. Boston: Bedford/St. Martin's, c1998. xii, 274 p.
97-074972 0312163827
Women -- United States -- History -- 20th century -- Sources. Sex role -- United States -- History -- 20th century -- Sources. Women's periodicals, American.

HQ1421.B47 1999
Berkeley, Kathleen C.
The women's liberation movement in America/ Kathleen C. Berkeley. Westport, Conn.: Greenwood Press, 1999. xxvi, 225 p.
99-025007 305.42/0973 0313298750
Feminism -- United States -- History -- 20th century. Women's rights -- United States -- History -- 20th century.

HQ1421.B56 2002
Blau, Francine D.
The economics of women, men, and work/ Francine D. Blau, Marianne A. Ferber, Anne E. Winkler. 4th ed. Upper Saddle River, N.J.: Prentice Hall, c2002. xviii, 446 p.
2001-018559 305.42/0973 21 013090922X
Women -- United States -- Economic conditions. Feminist economics -- United States. Women -- Employment -- United States.

HQ1421.E25 1989
Echols, Alice.
Daring to be bad: radical feminism in America, 1967-1975/ Alice Echols; foreword by Ellen Willis. Minneapolis: University of Minnesota Press, c1989. xix, 416 p.
89-005058 305.4/2/097309047 0816617864
Feminism -- United States -- History -- 20th century. Women's rights -- United States -- History -- 20th century.

HQ1421.G47 2001
Gerhard, Jane F.
Desiring revolution: second-wave feminism and the rewriting of American sexual thought, 1920 to 1982/ Jane Gerhard. New York: Columbia University Press, c2001. ix, 232 p.
00-063863 305.42/0973/0904 21 0231112041
Feminism -- United States -- History -- 20th century. Women -- United States -- Sexual behavior -- History -- 20th century. Sex (Psychology)

HQ1421.H87 1996
Hurtado, Aida.
The color of privilege: three blasphemies on race and feminism/ Aida Hurtado. Ann Arbor: University of Michigan Press, c1996. xii, 203 p.
96-021187 305.42/0973 20 0472095315
Minority women -- United States. Feminism -- United States. Marginality, Social -- United States. United States -- Ethnic relations. United States -- Race relations.

HQ1421.S675 1996
Spain, Daphne.
Balancing act: motherhood, marriage, and employment among American women/ Daphne Spain and Suzanne M. Bianchi. New York: Russell Sage Foundation, c1996. xv, 240 p.
96-005087 305.4/0973 20 0871548151
Women -- United States -- Social conditions. Women -- Employment -- United States. Mothers -- Employment -- United States.

HQ1421.U43 1996
Umansky, Lauri, 1959-
Motherhood reconceived: feminism and the legacies of the sixties/ Lauri Umansky. New York: New York University Press, c1996. x, 262 p.
96-008798 305.42 20 0814785611
Feminism -- United States. Motherhood -- United States. Sex role -- United States.

HQ1423.D8 1999
DuBois, Ellen Carol,
Feminism and suffrage: the emergence of an independent women's movement in America, 1848-1869/ Ellen Carol DuBois. Ithaca: Cornell University Press, [1999] 220 p.
00-268307 305.42/0973 21 0801486416
Feminism -- United States -- History. Women's rights -- United States -- History.

HQ1423.G79 1988
Grimke, Sarah Moore, 1792-1873.
Letters on the equality of the sexes, and other essays/ Sarah Grimke; edited and with an introduction by Elizabeth Ann Bartlett. New Haven: Yale University Press, c1988. xii, 174 p.
87-023940 305.4/2/0973 0300041136
Women -- United States -- Social conditions. Women's rights -- United States.

HQ1423.H47
Hersh, Blanche Glassman, 1928-
The slavery of sex: feminist-abolitionists in America/ Blanche Glassman Hersh. Urbana: University of Illinois Press, c1978. xi, 280 p.
78-014591 301.41/2/0973 025200695X
Feminism -- United States -- History. Women's rights -- United States -- History. Feminists -- United States -- History.

HQ1423.L39 1984
Lebsock, Suzanne.
The free women of Petersburg: status and culture in a southern town, 1784-1860/ Suzanne Lebsock. New York: Norton, c1984. xx, 326 p.
83-008065 305.4/2/09755581 0393017389
Women -- Virginia -- Petersburg -- History -- 19th century. Women -- Virginia -- Petersburg -- Social conditions. Women -- Virginia -- Petersburg -- Economic conditions. Petersburg (Va.) -- History.

HQ1423.Y45 1989
Yellin, Jean Fagan.
Women & sisters: the antislavery feminists in American culture/ Jean Fagan Yellin. New Haven: Yale University Press, c1989. xxi, 226 p.
89-016540 305.42/0973 0300045158
Feminism -- United States -- History -- 19th century. Antislavery movements -- United States.

HQ1426.B685 1983
Borenstein, Audrey, 1930-
Chimes of change and hours: views of older women in twentieth-century America/ Audrey Borenstein. Rutherford [N.J.]: Fairleigh Dickinson University Press; c1983. 518 p.
82-048159 305.2/44/0973 0838631703
Middle aged women -- United States -- Social conditions. Aged women -- United States -- Social conditions.

HQ1426.B82
Buhle, Mari Jo, 1943-
Women and American socialism, 1870-1920/ Mari Jo Buhle. Urbana: University of Illinois Press, c1981. xix, 344 p.
80-000719 305.4/2/0973 0252008731
Women and socialism -- United States -- History. Feminism -- United States -- History. United States -- History -- 1865-1921.

HQ1426.C45 1991
Chafe, William Henry.
The paradox of change: American women in the 20th century/ William H. Chafe. New York: Oxford University Press, 1991. x, 256 p.
90-043457 305.42/0973/0904 0195044185
Women -- United States -- History -- 20th century. Women's rights -- United States -- History -- 20th century.

HQ1426.C453
Chafe, William Henry.
Women and equality: changing patterns in American culture/ William H. Chafe. New York: Oxford University Press, 1977. xiii, 207 p.
76-042639 301.41/2/0973 0195021584
Women -- Social conditions. Feminism -- United States. Sex role.

HQ1426.C634 1990
Conflicts in feminism/ edited by Marianne Hirsch & Evelyn Fox Keller. New York: Routledge, 1990. ix, 397 p.
90-034999 305.42/0973 0415901774
Feminism -- United States. Feminist criticism -- United States.

HQ1426.D54 1985
Dignity: lower income women tell of their lives and struggles: oral histories/ compiled by Fran Leeper Buss; introduction by Susan Contratto. Ann Arbor: University of Michigan Press, c1985. 290 p.
85-000990 305.4/3 047206357X
Working class women -- United States -- Case studies. Urban women -- United States -- Case studies. Poor women -- United States -- Case studies.

HQ1426.E38
Ehrenreich, Barbara.
For her own good: 150 years of the experts' advice to women/ Barbara Ehrenreich, Deirdre English. Garden City, N.Y.: Anchor Press, 1978. x, 325 p.
77-076234 305.4/2/0973 0385126506
Women -- United States -- Social conditions. Maternal and infant welfare -- United States -- History. Women's health services -- Social aspects -- United States -- History.

HQ1426.E9 1979
Evans, Sara.
Personal politics: the roots of women's liberation in the civil rights movement and the new left/ by Sara Evans. New York: Knopf: distributed by Random House, 1979. xii, 274 p.
78-054929   301.41/2/0973   0394419111
Women -- United States -- Social conditions. Radicalism -- United States. Feminism -- United States.

HQ1426.F4727 1995
Feminist organizations: harvest of the new women's movement/ edited by Myra Marx Ferree and Patricia Yancey Martin. Philadelphia: Temple University Press, 1995. xi, 474 p.
94-002718   305.42/06/073   1566392284
Feminism -- United States -- Societies, etc. Women -- United States -- Societies and clubs.

HQ1426.F475 1994
Ferree, Myra Marx.
Controversy and coalition: the new feminist movement across three decades of change/ Myra Marx Ferree and Beth B. Hess. Rev. ed. New York: Twayne; 1994. xi, 278 p.
94-014318   305.42/0973 20   0805738827
Feminism -- United States.

HQ1426.G45 1970
Gilman, Charlotte Perkins, 1860-1935.
Women and economics. [New York] Source Book Press [1970, c1898] vii, 340 p.
78-134188   301.41/2   0876810814
Women -- Economic conditions.

HQ1426.G657 1991
Gordon, Suzanne, 1945-
Prisoners of men's dreams: striking out for a new feminine future/ Suzanne Gordon. Boston: Little, Brown, c1991. xii, 324 p.
90-013309   305.42/0973   0316321060
Feminism -- United States. Women -- United States -- Social conditions.

HQ1426.H33
Hayden, Dolores.
The grand domestic revolution: a history of feminist designs for American homes, neighborhoods, and cities/ Dolores Hayden. Cambridge, Mass.: MIT Press, c1981. 367 p.
80-018917   305.4/2   0262081083
Feminism -- United States -- Addresses, essays, lectures. Division of labor -- Addresses, essays, lectures. Housewives -- United States -- Addresses, essays, lectures.

HQ1426.J67 1986
Joseph, Gloria I.
Common differences: conflicts in black and white feminist perspectives/ by Gloria I. Joseph and Jill Lewis. Boston, MA: South End Press, 1986, c1981. xii, 306 p.
86-013864   305.4/2/0973 19   0896083179
Feminism -- United States. Afro-American women.

HQ1426.K58 1984
Klein, Ethel, 1952-
Gender politics: from consciousness to mass politics/ Ethel Klein. Cambridge, Mass.: Harvard University Press, 1984. x, 209 p.
84-008992   305.4/2/0973   0674341961
Women in politics -- United States -- History -- 20th century. Feminism -- United States -- History -- 20th century. Women's rights -- United States -- History -- 20th century.

HQ1426.L45
Lemons, J. Stanley.
The woman citizen; social feminism in the 1920's [by] J. Stanley Lemons. Urbana, University of Illinois Press [1973] xiii, 266 p.
72-075488   301.41/2/0973   0252002679
Feminism -- United States -- History -- 20th century. Women -- United States -- Social conditions. Women in politics -- United States.

HQ1426.L47
Lerner, Gerda,
The majority finds its past: placing women in history/ Gerda Lerner. New York: Oxford University Press, 1979. xxxii, 217 p.
79-014048   301.41/2/0973   0195025970
Women -- United States -- History. Afro-American women -- History. Feminism -- United States -- History.

HQ1426.M46 1985
Men's ideas/women's realities: Popular science, 1870-1915/ edited by Louise Michele Newman. New York: Pergamon Press, c1985. xxviii, 337 p.
84-001072   305.4/2/0973   0080319300
Feminism -- United States -- History. Women's rights -- United States -- History. Women -- United States -- Social conditions.

HQ1426.O85 1989
Okin, Susan Moller.
Justice, gender, and the family/ Susan Moller Okin. New York: Basic Books, c1989. viii, 216 p.
89-042519   305.42/0973   046503702X
Sex discrimination against women -- United States. Women's rights -- United States. Sex role -- United States.

HQ1426.P67
Porterfield, Amanda, 1947-
Feminine spirituality in America: from Sarah Edwards to Martha Graham/ Amanda Porterfield. Philadelphia: Temple University Press, 1980. 238 p.
80-012116   305.4/2/0973   0877221758
Women -- United States -- Attitudes. Feminism -- United States. Sex role in literature.

HQ1426.R72 1986
Robinson, Lillian S.
Sex, class, and culture/ Lillian S. Robinson. New York: Methuen, 1986, c1978. xxxiii, 349 p.
85-029838   305.4/0973   0416012418
Feminism -- United States. Culture. Criticism (Philosophy)

HQ1426.R93 1992
Ryan, Barbara, 1942-
Feminism and the women's movement: dynamics of change in social movement ideology, and activism/ Barbara Ryan. New York: Routledge, 1992. xii, 203 p.
92-000091   305.42/0973   0415905982
Feminism -- United States -- History -- 19th century. Feminism -- United States -- History -- 20th century.

HQ1426.S65 1989
Solomon, Irvin D.
Feminism and Black activism in contemporary America: an ideological assessment/ Irvin D. Solomon. New York: Greenwood Press, 1989. xiv, 186 p.
89-001980   305.42/0973   0313262047
Feminism -- United States. Women's rights -- United States. Afro-Americans -- Civil rights.

HQ1426.T48 1988
Theriot, Nancy M.
The biosocial construction of femininity: mothers and daughters in nineteenth-century America/ Nancy M. Theriot. New York: Greenwood Press, 1988. 168 p.
87-029545   305.4/2/0973   0313254834
Middle class women -- United States -- History -- 19th century. Mothers and daughters -- United States -- History -- 19th century. Sex role -- United States -- History -- 19th century.

HQ1426.T64 1997
Tobias, Sheila.
Faces of feminism: an activist's reflections on the women's movement/ Sheila Tobias. Boulder, Colo.: Westview Press, 1997. xvi, 332 p.
96-040894   305.42   081332842X
Feminism -- United States. Feminist theory.

HQ1426.W35 1988
Wandersee, Winifred D.
On the move: American women in the 1970s/ Winifred D. Wandersee. Boston: Twayne Publishers, c1988. xvii, 259 p.
87-029050   305.4/2/0973   0805799095
Feminism -- United States -- History. Women -- United States -- Social conditions. United States -- Social conditions -- 1960-1980.

HQ1426.W645 1982
Women, power, and policy/ edited by Ellen Boneparth. New York: Pergamon Press, c1982. xii, 319 p.
81-013825   305.4/2/0973   008028048X
Feminism -- United States. Women in politics -- United States. Women -- Employment -- United States.

HQ1438.A13.C58 1982
Clinton, Catherine, 1952-
The plantation mistress: woman's world in the old South/ Catherine Clinton. New York: Pantheon Books, c1982. xix, 331 p.
82-003549   305.4/2/0975   0394516869
Plantation owners' spouses -- Southern States. Women plantation owners -- Southern States. Slaveholders -- Southern States. Southern States -- Social life and customs -- 1775-1865.

HQ1438.A13.F69 1988
Fox-Genovese, Elizabeth, 1941-
Within the plantation household: Black and White women of the Old South/ Elizabeth Fox-Genovese. Chapel Hill: University of North Carolina Press, c1988. xvii, 544 p.
88-040139   305.4/0975   0807818089
Afro-American women -- Southern States -- History. White women -- Southern States -- History. Plantation life -- Southern States -- History. Southern States -- Race relations -- History.

HQ1438.A17.W45 1988
Western women: their land, their lives/ edited by Lillian Schlissel, Vicki L. Ruiz, and Janice Monk. Albuquerqe: University of New Mexico Press, c1988. vi, 354 p.
88-010717   305.4/0978   0826310907
Women -- West (U.S.) -- History -- Congresses. Indian women -- West (U.S.) -- History -- Congresses. Mexican American women -- West (U.S.) -- History -- Congresses.

HQ1438.A19 W65 2001
Women in Pacific Northwest history/ edited by Karen J. Blair. Rev. ed. Seattle: University of Washington Press, c2001. ix, 324 p.
00-049755 305.4/09795 21 029598046X
Women -- Northwest, Pacific -- History -- 19th century. Women -- Northwest, Pacific -- History -- 20th century.

HQ1438.G4.N37 2000
Nasstrom, Kathryn L.
Everybody's grandmother and nobody's fool: Frances Freeborn Pauley and the struggle for social justice/ Kathryn L. Nasstrom; foreword by Julian Bond. Ithaca, N.Y.: Cornell University Press, 2000. xi, 221 p.
99-059993 303.48/4/092 0801437822
Pauley, Frances Freeborn, -- 1905- Women social reformers -- Georgia -- Biography. Women civil rights workers -- Georgia -- Biography.

HQ1438.G75.R55 1988
Riley, Glenda, 1938-
The female frontier: a comparative view of women on the prairie and the plains/ Glenda Riley. Lawrence, Kan.: University Press of Kansas, c1988. x, 299 p.
87-032447 305.4/2/0978 0700603549
Women pioneers -- Great Plains -- History. Women pioneers -- Middle West -- History. Frontier and pioneer life -- Great Plains -- History.

HQ1438.K2.S77
Stratton, Joanna L.
Pioneer women: voices from the Kansas frontier/ Joanna L. Stratton; introd. by Arthur M. Schlesinger, Jr. New York: Simon and Schuster, c1981. 319 p.
80-015960 305.4/2/09781 0671226118
Women pioneers -- Kansas -- History. Frontier and pioneer life -- Kansas.

HQ1438.N35.C73 1998
Crane, Elaine Forman.
Ebb tide in New England: women, seaports, and social change, 1630-1800/ Elaine Forman Crane. Boston: Northeastern University Press, c1998. x, 333 p.
97-043479 305.4/0974 21 155553337X
Women -- New England -- History. Women -- New England -- Social conditions. Women -- New England -- Economic conditions.

HQ1438.N35.R45 1997
Reis, Elizabeth 1958-
Damned women: sinners and witches in Puritan New England/ Elizabeth Reis. Ithaca: Cornell University Press, 1997. xix, 212 p.
96-053411 305.4/0974/09032 0801428343
Women -- New England -- History -- 17th century. Women -- New England -- Social conditions. Women -- Religious life -- New England.

HQ1438.N57.O88 1991
Osterud, Nancy Grey, 1948-
Bonds of community: the lives of farm women in nineteenth-century New York/ Nancy Grey Osterud. Ithaca: Cornell University Press, 1991. ix, 303 p.
90-041814 305.4 0801425107
Rural women -- New York (State) -- History -- 19th century. New York (State) -- Rural conditions.

HQ1438.N6.B96 1992
Bynum, Victoria E.
Unruly women: the politics of social and sexual control in the old South/ Victoria E. Bynum. Chapel Hill: University of North Carolina Press, c1992. xiv, 233 p.
91-033851 305.4/09756 0807820164
Women -- North Carolina -- History -- 19th century. Deviant behavior -- History -- 19th century. Female offenders -- North Carolina -- History -- 19th century. North Carolina -- Race relations.

HQ1438.S63.E35 1997
Edwards, Laura F.
Gendered strife & confusion: the political culture of Reconstruction/ Laura Edwards. Urbana: University of Illinois Press, c1997. xvi, 378 p.
96-025317 305.3/0973/09034 0252022971
Women -- Southern States -- History -- 19th century. Sex role -- Southern States -- History -- 19th century. Reconstruction.

HQ1438.S63.T34 1998
Taking off the white gloves: Southern women and women historians/ edited by Michele Gillespie and Catherine Clinton. Columbia: University of Missouri Press, c1998. x, 187 p.
98-027670 305.4/0975 21 0826212093
Women -- Southern States -- History. Women historians -- Southern States.

HQ1438.S63.W65 1995
Wolfe, Margaret Ripley, 1947-
Daughters of Canaan: a saga of southern women/ Margaret Ripley Wolfe. Lexington: University Press of Kentucky, c1995. xii, 281 p.
94-030150 305.4/0975 0813119022
Women -- Southern States -- History. Sex role -- Southern States -- History.

HQ1438.V5L43 1987
Lebsock, Suzanne.
Virginia women, 1600-1945: "A share of honour"/ by Suzanne Lebsock. Richmond: Virginia State Library, 1987. x, 174 p.
86-023410 305.4/074/0155451 0884901394
Women -- Virginia -- History. Women -- Virginia -- Social conditions.

HQ1438.W45.J43 1979
Jeffrey, Julie Roy.
Frontier women: the trans-Mississippi West, 1840-1880/ Julie Roy Jeffrey. New York: Hill and Wang, 1979. xvi, 240 p.
79-012279 301.41/2/0978 0809048035
Women -- West (U.S.) -- History. Frontier and pioneer life -- West (U.S.)

HQ1439.B7.D48 2000
Deutsch, Sarah.
Women and the city: gender, space, and power in Boston, 1870-1940/ Sarah Deutsch. New York: Oxford University Press, 2000. xi, 387 p.
99-034659 305.4/09744/61 0195057058
Women -- Massachusetts -- Boston -- History. Women in community organization -- Massachusetts -- Boston -- History. Women in public life -- Massachusetts -- Boston -- History.

HQ1439.N6.A35 1997
Adickes, Sandra, 1933-
To be young was very heaven: women in New York before the First World War/ Sandra Adickes. New York: St. Martin's Press, 1997. x, 294 p.
97-009799 305.4/09747 0312162499
Women -- New York (State) -- New York -- History -- 20th century. Women social reformers -- New York (State) -- New York -- History -- 20th century. Greenwich Village (New York, N.Y.) -- History -- 20th century.

HQ1439.P58.K73 1991
Krause, Corinne Azen.
Grandmothers, mothers, and daughters: oral histories of three generations of ethnic American women/ Corinne Azen Krause. Boston: Twayne Publishers, 1991. xiv, 231 p.
90-046014 305.48/8/0973 0805791051
Minority women -- Pennsylvania -- Pittsburgh. Mothers and daughters -- Pennsylvania -- Pittsburgh. Intergenerational relations -- Pennsylvania -- Pittsburgh.

HQ1439.R62 H48 2001
Hewitt, Nancy A.,
Women's activism and social change: Rochester, New York, 1822-1872/ Nancy A. Hewitt. Lanham, MD: Lexington Books, c2001. 283 p.
2001-037700 305.42/09747/89 21 0739102974
Feminism -- New York (State) -- Rochester -- History -- 19th century.

HQ1453-1823 Women. Feminism
— By region or country
— Other regions or countries

HQ1453.A54 1988
Adamson, Nancy.
Feminist organizing for change: the contemporary women's movement in Canada/ Nancy Adamson, Linda Briskin, Margaret McPhail. Toronto: Oxford University Press, 1988. iv, 332 p.
89-136669 305.42/0971 0195406583
Feminism -- Canada.

HQ1453.B55 1995
Billson, Janet Mancini.
Keepers of the culture: the power of tradition in women's lives/ Janet Mancini Billson. New York: Lexington Books, c1995. xix, 476 p.
95-003611 305.42/0971 0029035120
Women -- Canada -- Social conditions. Minority women -- Canada -- Social conditions. Minority women -- Canada -- Social life and customs.

HQ1459.A4.S55 1984
Silverman, Eliane Leslau.
The last best West: women on the Alberta frontier, 1880-1930/ by Eliane Leslau Silverman. Montreal: Eden Press, c1984. xiii, 183 p.
84-178150 305.4/097123 0920792294
Women -- Alberta -- History. Women -- Alberta -- Social conditions. Frontier and pioneer life -- Alberta.

HQ1459.O57.E77 1995
Errington, Jane, 1951-
Wives and mothers, schoolmistresses, and scullery maids: working women in Upper Canada, 1790-1840/ Elizabeth Jane Errington. Montreal; McGill-Queen's University Press, 1995. xix, 375 p.
96-154381 305.42/009713/09034 0773513094
Women -- Ontario -- Social conditions. Women -- Ontario -- History -- 19th century. Women -- Employment -- Ontario -- History -- 19th century.

HQ1459.P7.C37 1997
Carter, Sarah.
Capturing women: the manipulation of cultural imagery in Canada's prairie west/ Sarah Carter. Montreal; McGill-Queen's University Press, c1997. xviii, 247 p.
00-551037   0773516557
White women -- Prairie Provinces -- History -- 19th century. Indian women -- Prairie Provinces -- History -- 19th century. Indian captivities -- Prairie Provinces -- History -- 19th century. Prairie Provinces -- Social conditions -- 19th century. Prairie Provinces -- Race relations -- History -- 19th century.

HQ1459.W47
Telling tales: essays in western women's history/ edited by Catherine A. Cavanaugh and Randi R. Warne. Vancouver: UBC Press, c2000. xii, 359 p.
2001-430832   305.4/09712/09034   21
0774807946
Women -- Canada, Western -- History -- 19th century. Women -- Canada, Western -- History -- 20th century. Women pioneers -- Canada -- History -- 19th century. Canada, Western -- History -- 19th century. Canada, Western -- History -- 20th century. Canada (Ouest) -- Histoire.

HQ1460.5.L37
Latin American women: historical perspectives/ edited by Asuncion Lavrin. Westport, Conn.: Greenwood Press, 1978. xiv, 343 p.
77-094758   301.41/2/098   0313203091
Women -- Latin America -- History. Women -- Latin America -- Social conditions.

HQ1460.5.M64 2001
Molyneux, Maxine.
Women's movements in international perspective: Latin America and beyond/ Maxine Molyneux. New York: Palgrave, c2001. ix, 244 p.
00-062707   305.42/098 21   0333786777
Feminism -- Latin America -- History -- 19th century. Feminism -- Latin America -- History -- 20th century. Women -- Latin America -- Social conditions -- 19th century.

HQ1460.5.S64 2000
Socolow, Susan Migden, 1941-
The women of colonial Latin America/ Susan Migden Socolow. Cambridge, UK: Cambridge University Press, 2000. xiii, 237 p.
99-029134   305.4/098   0521470528
Women -- Latin America -- History. Women -- Latin America -- Social conditions. Sex role -- Latin America -- History.

HQ1460.5.W6 1986
Women and change in Latin America/ June Nash, Helen Safa, and contributors. South Hadley, Mass.: Bergin & Garvey Publishers, 1986, c1985. 372 p.
85-018563   305.4/098   0897890698
Women -- Latin America -- Economic conditions. Women -- Latin America -- Social conditions. Women -- Employment -- Latin America.

HQ1460.5.W624 1990
Women, culture, and politics in Latin America/ Seminar on Feminism and Culture in Latin America; Emilie Bergmann ...[et al.]. Berkeley: University of California Press, c1990. xi, 269 p.
89-077866   305.42/098   0520065522
Feminism -- Latin America -- Congresses. Women in politics -- Latin America -- Congresses. Women -- Latin America -- Intellectual life -- Congresses.

HQ1465.C5.E45 1976
Elmendorf, Mary L.
Nine Mayan women: a village faces change. Cambridge, Mass., Schenkman Pub. Co. [c1976] xxiv, 159 p.
74-012464   301.41/2/09726   0470238623
Women -- Mexico -- Chan Kom -- Case studies. Mayas -- Social life and customs. Mayas -- Religion and mythology.

HQ1465.M63.B44 1993
Behar, Ruth, 1956-
Translated woman: crossing the border with Esperanza's story/ Ruth Behar. Boston: Beacon Press, c1993. xiv, 372 p.
92-005588   305.42/0972/44   0807070521
Hernandez, Esperanza. Rural women -- Mexico -- Mexquitic -- Social conditions -- Case studies. Ethnology -- Mexico -- Mexquitic. Mexquitic (Mexico) -- Rural conditions.

HQ1470.5.M33 1996
McClaurin, Irma.
Women of Belize: gender and change in Central America/ Irma McClaurin. New Brunswick, N.J.: Rutgers University Press, c1996. x, 218 p.
95-052269   305.4/097282 20   0813523079
Women -- Belize -- Social conditions.

HQ1487.M48 2000
Metoyer, Cynthia Chavez, 1965-
Women and the state in post-Sandinista Nicaragua/ Cynthia Chavez Metoyer. Boulder: Lynne Rienner, 2000. v, 149 p.
99-034284   305.42/097285   1555877516
Women -- Nicaragua -- Social conditions. Nicaragua -- Social conditions -- 1979- Nicaragua -- Social policy.

HQ1501.S46 1991
Senior, Olive.
Working miracles: women's lives in the English-speaking Caribbean/ Olive Senior. London: J. Currey; 1991. xiii, 210 p.
91-004013   305.4/09729   0253351367
Women -- Caribbean, English-speaking -- Economic conditions. Women -- Caribbean, English-speaking -- Social life and customs. Women -- Socialization -- Caribbean, English-speaking.

HQ1507.R37 1981
Randall, Margaret, 1936-
Women in Cuba, twenty years later/ by Margaret Randall; with photographs by Judy Janda. New York, N.Y.: Smyrna Press, c1981. 167 p.
80-054055   305.4/2/097291   0918266149
Women -- Cuba -- History -- 20th century. Women and socialism -- Cuba -- History -- 20th century.

HQ1507.S63 1996
Smith, Lois M.
Sex and revolution: women in socialist Cuba/ Lois M. Smith and Alfred Padula. New York: Oxford University Press, 1996. xiv, 247 p.
95-011827   305.42/097291   0195094905
Women -- Cuba -- Social conditions. Sex role -- Cuba. Women's rights -- Cuba.

HQ1532.L38 1995
Lavrin, Asuncion.
Women, feminism, and social change in Argentina, Chile, and Uruguay, 1890-1940/ Asuncion Lavrin. Lincoln, Neb.: University of Nebraska Press, c1995. x, 480 p.
95-002729   305.4/0982   080322897X
Women -- Argentina. Women -- Chile. Women -- Uruguay.

HQ1533.C28 1988
Carlson, Marifran, 1942-
Feminismo!: the woman's movement in Argentina from its beginnings to Eva Peron/ by Marifran Carlson; introduction by George I. Blanksten. Chicago, Ill.: Academy Chicago, 1988. vii, 224 p.
85-018567   305.4/2/0982   0897331524
Feminism -- Argentina -- History. Women social reformers -- Argentina -- History -- 19th century. Feminists -- Argentina -- History.

HQ1587.A53 2000
Anderson, Bonnie S.
A history of their own: women in Europe from prehistory to the present/ Bonnie S. Anderson, Judith P. Zinsser. Rev. ed. New York: Oxford University Press, 2000. 2 v.
98-046743   305.4/094 21   0195128397
Women -- Europe -- History. Feminism -- Europe -- History.

HQ1587.S69 1992
Snyder, Paula, 1954-
The European women's almanac/ Paula Snyder. New York: Columbia University Press, c1992. 399 p.
92-013451   305.4/094   0231080646
Women -- Europe -- Handbooks, manuals, etc.

HQ1587.W54 2000
Wiesner, Merry E.,
Women and gender in early modern Europe/ Merry E. Wiesner. 2nd ed. New York: Cambridge University Press, 2000. xiii, 325 p.
00-022070   305.4/094 21   0521771056
Women -- Europe -- History.

HQ1588.R6 1982
Robertson, Priscilla Smith.
An experience of women: pattern and change in nineteenth-century Europe/ Priscilla Robertson; with an appendix by Steve Hochstadt. Philadelphia: Temple University Press, 1982. xii, 673 p.
81-009315   305.4/2/094   0877222347
Women -- Europe -- History -- 19th century. Feminism -- Europe -- History -- 19th century.

HQ1588.W645 1983
Women, the family, and freedom: the debate in documents/ edited by Susan Groag Bell & Karen M. Offen. Stanford, Calif.: Stanford University Press, 1983. 2 v.
82-061081   305.4/09   0804711704
Feminism -- Europe -- History -- Sources. Feminism -- United States -- History -- Sources. Women's rights -- Europe -- History -- Sources.

HQ1593.B33 1993
Banks, Olive.
The politics of British feminism, 1918-1970/ Olive Banks. Aldershot, England; E. Elgar, c1993. v, 149 p.
93-018896   305.42/0941   1852781084
Feminism -- Great Britain -- History -- 20th century. Women -- Great Britain -- Social conditions.

HQ1593.B43 1989
Beddoe, Deirdre.
Back to home and duty: women between the wars, 1918-1939/ Deirdre Beddoe. London; Pandora, 1989. 175 p.
98-211632   305.42/0941   0044405154
Women -- Great Britain -- History -- 20th century. Women -- Great Britain -- Social conditions.

HQ1593.G55 1995
Giles, Judy.
Women, identity, and private life in Britain, 1900-50/ Judy Giles. New York: St. Martin's Press, 1995. viii, 189 p.
95-002958   305.4/0941   0312126247
Women -- Great Britain -- Social conditions. Women -- Great Britain -- History -- 20th century. Great Britain -- Social conditions -- 20th century.

HQ1593.K73 1999
Kranidis, Rita S.
The Victorian spinster and colonial emigration: contested subjects/ Rita S. Kranidis. New York: St. Martin's Press, 1999. x, 228 p.
98-042901   305.48/9691   031221605X
Single women -- Great Britain -- Colonies -- History -- 19th century. White women -- Great Britain -- Colonies -- History -- 19th century. Women immigrants -- Great Britain -- Colonies -- History -- 19th century. Great Britain -- Emigration and immigration -- History -- 19th century.

HQ1593.P65 1990
Women in twentieth-century Britain/ edited by Ina Zweiniger-Bargielowska. Harlow: Longman, 2001. x, 378 p.
305.420941   0582404800
Women -- Great Britain -- Social conditions. Great Britain -- Social conditions -- 20th century.

HQ1593.P84 1992
Pugh, Martin.
Women and the women's movement in Britain, 1914-1959/ Martin Pugh. New York: Paragon House, 1993. 347 p.
92-024099   305.42/0941   1557785929
Feminism -- Great Britain -- History. Women -- Great Britain -- Social conditions.

HQ1593.S85 1991
Strobel, Margaret, 1946-
European women and the second British Empire/ Margaret Strobel. Bloomington: Indiana University Press, c1991. xiii, 108 p.
90-043509   305.4/0941   0253355516
White women -- Great Britain -- Colonies -- History -- 19th century. White women -- Great Britain -- Colonies -- History -- 20th century. Great Britain -- Colonies -- Social conditions.

HQ1593.W54 1980
Wilson, Elizabeth, 1936-
Only halfway to paradise: women in postwar Britain, 1945-1968/ Elizabeth Wilson. London; Tavistock Publications, 1980. 233 p.
80-142364   305.4/2/0941   0422768707
Women -- Great Britain -- Social conditions. Women -- Great Britain -- History -- 20th century. Great Britain -- Social conditions -- 1945-

HQ1595.A3.C34 1992
Caine, Barbara.
Victorian feminists/ Barbara Caine. New York: Oxford University Press, 1992. xii, 284 p.
91-024220   305.42/0941   0198201702
Feminists -- Great Britain -- Biography. Feminism -- Great Britain -- History -- 19th century.

HQ1595.F27.S76 1994
Stone, James S. 1919-
Emily Faithfull, Victorian champion of women's rights/ James S. Stone. Toronto: P.D. Meany Publishers, c1994. iii, 336 p.
95-188264   305.42/092   0888350406
Faithfull, Emily, -- 1836?-1895. Women social reformers -- Great Britain -- Biography. Feminists -- Great Britain -- Biography. Women's rights -- Great Britain -- History -- 19th century.

HQ1595.P34.W56 1996
Winslow, Barbara, 1945-
Sylvia Pankhurst: sexual politics and political activism/ Barbara Winslow; foreword by Sheila Rowbotham. New York: St. Martin's Press, 1996. xxvii, 236 p.
96-019740   324.6/23/092   0312162685
Pankhurst, E. Sylvia -- (Estelle Sylvia), -- 1882-1960. Suffragists -- England -- Biography. Feminists -- England -- Biography.

HQ1596.V5 1972
Vicinus, Martha.
Suffer and be still; women in the Victorian age. Edited by Martha Vicinus. Bloomington, Indiana University Press [1972] xv, 239 p.
71-184524   301.41/2/0942   0253355729
Women -- Great Britain -- History -- 19th century. Women -- Great Britain -- Social conditions.

HQ1596.W37 1983
Warnicke, Retha M.
Women of the English Renaissance and Reformation/ Retha M. Warnicke. Westport, Conn.: Greenwood Press, 1983. viii, 228 p.
82-024180   305.4/0942   0313236119
Women -- England -- History -- Renaissance, 1450-1600. Humanists -- England -- History -- 16th century. Women -- Education -- England -- History -- 16th century. Great Britain -- History -- Tudors, 1485-1603. Great Britain -- Social life and customs -- 16th century.

HQ1596.W44 1977
A Widening sphere: changing roles of Victorian women/ edited by Martha Vicinus. Bloomington: Indiana University Press, c1977. xix, 326 p.
76-026433   301.41/2/0941   0253365406
Women -- Great Britain -- History -- 19th century. Women -- Great Britain -- Social conditions. Feminism -- Great Britain -- History -- 19th century. Great Britain -- Social conditions -- 19th century. Great Britain -- History -- Victoria, 1837-1901.

HQ1596.W6 1975b
Wollstonecraft, Mary, 1759-1797.
A vindication of the rights of woman: an authoritative text, backgrounds, criticism/ Mary Wollstonecraft; edited by Carol H. Poston. New York: Norton, c1975. ix, 240 p.
75-037775   301.41/2   0393044270
Women -- Social and moral questions. Women's rights.

HQ1597.B78 1990
British feminism in the twentieth century/ edited by Harold L. Smith. Amherst: University of Massachusetts Press, 1990. x, 214 p.
89-020249   305.42/0941/0904   0870237055
Feminism -- Great Britain -- History -- 20th century. Women -- Great Britain -- Social conditions.

HQ1597.O15 1975
Oakley, Ann.
The sociology of housework/ Ann Oakley. New York: Pantheon Books, [1975] c1974. x, 242 p.
75-004668   301.41/2   0394497740
Women -- Great Britain -- Social conditions. Feminism. Home economics.

HQ1599.E5.B57 1989
Black, Naomi, 1935-
Social feminism/ Naomi Black. Ithaca: Cornell University Press, 1989. x, 390 p.
88-047937   305.4/2   0801495733
Feminism -- England. Feminism -- France. Feminism -- United States.

HQ1599.E5.C47 1988
Chinn, Carl.
They worked all their lives: women of the urban poor in England, 1880-1939/ Carl Chinn. Manchester [England]; Manchester University Press; c1988. xii, 187 p.
87-036701   305.4/2/0942   0719024366
Poor women -- England -- History. Urban women -- England -- History. Urban poor -- England -- History.

HQ1599.E5.G36 1988
George, Margaret.
Women in the first capitalist society: experiences in seventeenth-century England/ Margaret George. Urbana: University of Illinois Press, c1988. 260 p.
87-035691   305.4/0942   0252015347
Middle class women -- England -- History -- 17th century. Middle class women -- England -- Biography. Middle class -- England -- History -- 17th century.

HQ1599.E5.K37 2000
Honeyman, Katrina.
Women, gender, and industrialisation in England, 1700-1870/ Katrina Honeyman. New York: St. Martin's Press, 2000. vii, 204 p.
99-055824   306.3/615/0942   0312231784
Women -- England -- History. Women -- Employment -- England -- History. Sexual division of labor -- England -- History.

HQ1599.E5.L49 1984
Lewis, Jane
Women in England, 1870-1950: sexual divisions and social change/ Jane Lewis. Brighton, Sussex: Wheatsheaf Books; 1984. xv, 240 p.
84-048437   305.4/0942   0253366089
Working class women -- England -- History. Middle class women -- England -- History. Mothers -- England -- History.

HQ1599.E5.P47 1995
Perkin, Joan.
Victorian women/ Joan Perkin. New York: New York University Press, 1995. vii, 264 p.
94-042382   305.42/0942   0814766242
Women -- England -- History -- 19th century. Women -- England -- Social conditions.

HQ1599.E5.S54 1992
Shiman, Lilian Lewis.
Women and leadership in nineteenth-century England/ Lilian Lewis Shiman. New York: St. Martin's Press, 1992. xiii, 263 p.
91-043786   305.42/0942   0312079125
Women -- England -- History -- 19th century. Women social reformers -- England -- History -- 19th century. Women -- England -- Social conditions.

HQ1599.E5.S62 1982
Smith, Hilda L., 1941-
Reason's disciples: seventeenth-century English feminists/ Hilda L. Smith. Urbana: University of Illinois Press, c1982. xx, 237 p.
81-014834   305.4/2/0942   0252009126
Feminism -- England -- History -- 17th century. Women authors.

HQ1599.E5.V47 1998
Vickery, Amanda.
The gentleman's daughter: women's lives in Georgian England/ Amanda Vickery. New Haven, Conn.: Yale University Press, c1998. ix, 436 p.
97-045792   305.42/0942 21   0300075316
Women -- England -- History -- 18th century. England -- Social conditions -- 18th century. Gentry -- England -- History -- 18th century.

HQ1599.E5.W64 1985
Women in English society, 1500-1800/ edited by Mary Prior. London; Methuen, 1985. xvi, 294 p.
84-020547   305.4/0942   0416357008
Women -- England -- History -- 16th century. Women -- England -- History -- 17th century. Women -- England -- History -- 18th century.

HQ1599.E5.W65
The Women of England: from Anglo-Saxon times to the present: interpretive bibliographical essays/ edited with an introd. by Barbara Kanner. Hamden, Conn.: Archon Books, 1979. 429 p.
78-032166   301.41/2/0942   0208016392
Women -- England -- History -- Sources. Women -- England -- History -- Bibliography.

HQ1600.3.W65
Women in Irish society: the historical dimension/ edited by Margaret MacCurtain and Donncha O Corrain. Westport, Conn.: Greenwood Press, 1979. 125 p.
79-000964   301.41/2/09415   0313212546
Women -- Ireland -- History. Women -- Ireland -- Social conditions. Women -- Ireland -- Economic conditions.

HQ1610.5.C67 1994
Corrin, Chris, 1956-
Magyar women: Hungarian women's lives, 1960s-1990s/ Chris Corrin; consultant editor, Jo Campling. New York: St. Martin's Press, 1994. xiii, 312 p.
93-004301   305.42/09439   0312106890
Women -- Hungary -- Social conditions. Feminism -- Hungary -- History. Hungary -- Social conditions -- 1945-1989. Hungary -- Social conditions -- 1989-

HQ1613.B5 1982
Bidelman, Patrick Kay.
Pariahs stand up!: the founding of the liberal feminist movement in France, 1858-1889/ Patrick Kay Bidelman. Westport, Conn.: Greenwood Press, 1982. xxviii, 285 p.
81-004222   305.4/2/0944   0313230064
Women -- France -- History -- 19th century. Men -- France -- History -- 19th century. Feminism -- France -- History -- 19th century.

HQ1613.D8 1986
Duchen, Claire.
Feminism in France: from May '68 to Mitterrand/ Claire Duchen. London; Routledge & Kegan Paul, 1986. x, 165 p.
85-010705   305.4/2/0944   0710204558
Feminism -- France -- History -- 20th century. Women in politics -- France -- History -- 20th century.

HQ1613.G53 1989
Gibson, Wendy, 1944-
Women in seventeenth-century France/ Wendy Gibson. New York: St. Martin's Press, 1989. vii, 440 p.
88-018176   305.4/0944/09032   0312023472
Women -- France -- History -- 17th century.

HQ1613.S54
Smith, Bonnie G., 1940-
Ladies of the leisure class: the bourgeoises of northern France in the nineteenth century/ Bonnie G. Smith. Princeton, N.J.: Princeton University Press, c1981. x, 303 p.
81-047157   305.4/0944   0691053308
Middle class women -- France, Northern -- History -- 19th century. Middle class -- France, Northern -- History -- 19th century.

HQ1615.A3.G67 1996
Gordon, Felicia.
Early French feminisms, 1830-1940: a passion for liberty/ by Felicia Gordon and Maire Cross. Cheltenham, U.K.; Edward Elgar, c1996. vii, 287 p.
95-042408   305.42/092/244 20   1852789697
Feminists -- France -- Biography. Feminism -- France -- History. Women socialists -- France -- Biography.

HQ1615.M67 1984
Moses, Claire Goldberg, 1941-
French feminism in the nineteenth century/ Claire Goldberg Moses. Albany: State University of New York Press, c1984. xiii, 311 p.
83-018040   305.4/2/0944   0873958594
Feminism -- France -- History -- 19th century.

HQ1616.L68
Lougee, Carolyn C., 1942-
Le paradis des femmes: women, salons, and social stratification in seventeenth-century France/ by Carolyn C. Lougee. Princeton, N.J.: Princeton University Press, 1976. ix, 252 p.
76-003266   301.41/2/0944   0691052395
Women -- France -- History -- Modern period, 1600- Social classes -- France -- History -- 17th century. Feminism -- France -- History -- 17th century.

HQ1616.S38 1996
Scott, Joan Wallach.
Only paradoxes to offer: French feminists and the rights of man/ Joan Wallach Scott. Cambridge, Mass.: Harvard University Press, 1996. xiii, 229 p.
95-031953   305.42/0944   0674639308
Feminism -- France -- History. Feminism -- France -- Case studies. Feminists -- France -- History.

HQ1623.R43 1995
Reagin, Nancy Ruth, 1960-
A German women's movement: class and gender in Hanover, 1880-1933/ Nancy R. Reagin. Chapel Hill: University of North Carolina Press, c1995. xii, 322 p.
94-039348   305.42/0943   0807822108
Feminism -- Germany -- Hannover -- History -- 19th century. Feminism -- Germany -- Hannover -- History -- 20th century. Women -- Germany -- Hannover -- History -- 19th century.

HQ1623.S73 1975
Stephenson, Jill.
Women in Nazi society/ Jill Stephenson. New York: Barnes & Noble Books, 1975. 223 p.
76-355728   301.41/2/0943   0064965287
Women -- Germany -- Social conditions. Germany -- Politics and government -- 1933-1945.

HQ1623.W475 1984
When biology became destiny: women in Weimar and Nazi Germany/ edited by Renate Bridenthal, Atina Grossmann, and Marion Kaplan. New York: Monthly Review Press, 1984. xiv, 364 p.
84-018969   305.4/0943   0853456429
Women -- Germany -- History -- 20th century. Right and left (Political science) Germany -- Politics and government -- 1918-1933. Germany -- Politics and government -- 1933-1945.

HQ1623.W8513 1998
Wunder, Heide.
He is the sun, she is the moon: women in early modern Germany/ Heide Wunder; translated by Thomas Dunlap. Cambridge, Mass.: Harvard University Press, 1998. x, 310 p.
97-038959   305.4/0943   0674383214
Women -- Germany -- History. Women -- Germany -- Social conditions.

HQ1625.G467 1984
German women in the nineteenth century: a social history/ edited by John C. Fout. New York: Holmes & Meier, 1984. xi, 439 p.
83-018596   305.4/0943   0841908435
Women -- Germany -- History -- 19th century.

HQ1627.F69713 1989
Frevert, Ute.
Women in German history: from bourgeois emancipation to sexual liberation/ Ute Frevert; translated by Stuart McKinnon-Evans in association with Terry Bond and Barbara Norden. Oxford; Berg, 1989, c1988. 346 p.
88-013123   305.4/2/0943   0854962336
Feminism -- Germany -- History. Women's rights -- Germany -- History. Women -- Germany -- Social conditions.

HQ1638.D4 1991
De Grazia, Victoria.
How fascism ruled women: Italy, 1922-1945/ Victoria de Grazia. Berkeley: University of California Press, c1992. xiii, 350 p.
91-008901   305.42/0945   0520074564
Women -- Italy -- History -- 20th century. Women -- Government policy -- Italy -- History -- 20th century. Fascism -- Italy -- History -- 20th century. Italy -- Politics and government -- 1922-1945.

HQ1638.H45x 1987
Hellman, Judith Adler.
Journeys among women: feminism in five Italian cities/ Judith Adler Hellman. Cambridge [Cambridgeshire]: Polity; 1987. 275 p.
88-672183   0745603556
Feminism -- Italy. Women -- Italy -- Social conditions.

HQ1655.V47.A47 1988
Alter, George.
Family and the female life course: the women of Verviers, Belgium, 1849-1880/ George Alter. Madison, Wis.: University of Wisconsin Press, 1988. xiv, 226 p.
87-040360   305.4/09493/4   0299112004
Women -- Belgium -- Verviers -- History -- 19th century. Working class women -- Belgium -- Verviers -- History -- 19th century. Family -- Belgium -- Verviers -- History -- 19th century.

HQ1662.E54 1994
Engel, Barbara Alpern.
Between the fields and the city: women, work, and family in Russia, 1861-1914/ Barbara Alpern Engel. Cambridge [England]; Cambridge University Press, 1994. xi, 254 p.
93-031191 305.4/0947 0521442362
Women -- Russia -- History -- 19th century. Women -- Russia -- History -- 20th century. Women -- Employment -- Russia -- History -- 19th century.

HQ1662.K6.C55
Clements, Barbara Evans, 1945-
Bolshevik feminist: the life of Aleksandra Kollontai/ Barbara Evans Clements. Bloomington: Indiana University Press, c1979. xiii, 352 p.
78-003240 335.43/092/4 0253312094
Kollontai, A. -- (Aleksandra), -- 1872-1952. Socialists -- Soviet Union -- Biography.

HQ1662.M367 2002
Marrese, Michelle Lamarche,
A woman's kingdom: noblewomen and the control of property in Russia, 1700-1861/ Michelle Lamarche Marrese. Ithaca; Cornell University Press, c2002. xiv, 276 p.
2001-007531 305.4/0947 21 0801439116
Women landowners -- Russia -- History. Inheritance and succession -- Russia -- History. Women -- Russia -- History.

HQ1662.R88 1990
Russia's women: accommodation, resistance, transformation/ edited by Barbara Evans Clements, Barbara Alpern Engel, Christine D. Worobec. Berkeley: University of California Press, c1990. xi, 300 p.
90-037203 305.4/0947 0520070232
Women -- Soviet Union -- History. Women -- Soviet Union -- Social conditions.

HQ1662.S735
Stites, Richard.
The women's liberation movement in Russia: feminism, nihilism, and bolshevism, 1860-1930/ Richard Stites. Princeton, N.J.: Princeton University Press, c1978. xx, 464 p.
77-072137 301.41/2/0947 0691052549
Feminism -- Soviet Union -- History. Nihilism. Women -- Soviet Union -- History.

HQ1663.E53 1983
Engel, Barbara Alpern.
Mothers and daughters: women of the intelligentsia in nineteenth century Russia/ Barbara Alpern Engel. Cambridge; Cambridge University Press, 1983. x, 230 p.
82-014611 305.4/2/0947 0521251257
Women in politics -- Russia -- History -- 19th century. Mothers -- Russia -- History -- 19th century. Daughters -- Russia -- History -- 19th century. Russia -- Social conditions -- 1801-1917.

HQ1663.L33
Lapidus, Gail Warshofsky.
Women in Soviet society: equality, development, and social change/ Gail Warshofsky Lapidus. Berkeley: University of California Press, c1978. x, 381 p.
74-016710 305.4/0947 0520028686
Women -- Soviet Union -- Social conditions. Women's rights -- Soviet Union. Sex role.

HQ1663.W63 1984
Women and Russia: feminist writings from the Soviet Union/ Tatyana Mamonova, editor; with the assistance of Sarah Matilsky; foreword by Robin Morgan; translated by Rebecca Park and Catherine A. Fitzpatrick. Boston: Beacon Press, c1984. xxiii, 273 p.
82-073963 305.4/2/0947 0807067083
Feminism -- Soviet Union.

HQ1665.15.A6.W66 1994
Women's glasnost vs. naglost: stopping Russian backlash/ Tatyana Mamonova, with the assistance of Chandra Niles Folsom. Westport, Conn.: Bergin & Garvey, 1994. xx, 184 p.
93-015181 305.42/0947 0897893395
Women -- Russia (Federation) -- Social conditions. Glasnost. Soviet Union -- Social conditions -- 1970-1991. Russia (Federation) -- Social conditions -- 1991-

HQ1665.15.S685 1999
Sperling, Valerie.
Organizing women in contemporary Russia: engendering transition/ Valerie Sperling. Cambridge; Cambridge University Press, 1999. x, 303 p.
98-043642 305.42/0947 0521660173
Feminism -- Russia (Federation) Women -- Russia (Federation) -- Social conditions. Russia (Federation) -- Social conditions -- 1991-

HQ1687.B65 1991
Bok, Sissela.
Alva Myrdal: a daughter's memoir/ Sissela Bok. Reading, Mass.: Addison-Wesley Pub. Co., c1991. xvi, 375 p.
90-026144 305.42/092 0201570866
Myrdal, Alva Reimer, -- 1902- Feminists -- Sweden -- Biography. Social reformers -- Sweden -- Biography.

HQ1715.5.J36 1990
Jancar-Webster, Barbara, 1935-
Women & revolution in Yugoslavia, 1941-1945/ by Barbara Jancar-Webster. Denver, Colo.: Arden Press, 1990. xvi, 245 p.
89-032120 305.4/2/0949709044 0912869097
Women -- Yugoslavia -- Social conditions. Women and the military -- Yugoslavia -- History. World War, 1939-1945 -- Underground movements -- Yugoslavia. Yugoslavia -- History -- Axis occupation, 1941-1945.

HQ1726.5.G73 1988
Graham-Brown, Sarah.
Images of women: the portrayal of women in photography of the Middle East, 1860-1950/ Sarah Graham-Brown. New York: Columbia University Press, 1988. xi, 274 p.
88-002852 305.4/2/0956 0231068263
Women -- Middle East -- Social conditions. Women -- Middle East -- Social conditions -- Pictorial works. Family -- Middle East -- Pictorial works. Middle East -- Social life and customs -- Pictorial works.

HQ1726.5.M64 1993
Moghadam, Valentine M., 1952-
Modernizing women: gender and social change in the Middle East/ Valentine M. Moghadam. Boulder, CO: L. Rienner, 1993. xvi, 311 p.
92-037454 305.42/0956 1555873464
Women -- Middle East -- Social conditions. Muslim women -- Middle East -- Social conditions. Women -- Middle East -- Economic conditions.

HQ1726.5.R45 1998
Remaking women: feminism and modernity in the Middle East/ edited by Lila Abu-Lughod. Princeton, N.J.: Princeton University Press, c1998. ix, 300 p.
97-046125 305.42/0956 21 0691057915
Women -- Middle East -- Social conditions. Women in Islam -- Middle East. Feminism -- Middle East.

HQ1726.5.W66 1992
Women in Middle Eastern history: shifting boundaries in sex and gender/ edited by Nikki R. Keddie, Beth Baron. New Haven: Yale University Press, c1991. xii, 343 p.
91-019665 305.42/0956 0300050062
Women -- Middle East -- History.

HQ1726.7.G65 1996
Gole, Nilufer, 1953-
The forbidden modern: civilization and veiling/ Nilufer Gole. Ann Arbor: University of Michigan Press, c1996. 173 p.
96-018179 305.42/09561 20 0472096303
Women -- Turkey -- Social conditions. Muslim women -- Turkey. Women in Islam -- Turkey.

HQ1728.5.G67 1996
Gorkin, Michael.
Three mothers, three daughters: Palestinian women's stories/ Michael Gorkin, Rafiqa Othman. Berkeley: University of California Press, c1996. xviii, 234 p.
95-043324 305.48/89274 20 0520203291
Women, Palestinian Arab -- West Bank -- Social conditions. Women, Palestinian Arab -- West Bank -- Interviews. Jewish-Arab relations.

HQ1728.5.Z8.W4773 1995
Sharoni, Simona.
Gender and the Israeli-Palestinian conflict: the politics of women's resistance/ Simona Sharoni. Syracuse: Syracuse University Press, 1995. xiii, 199 p.
94-032264 305.42/095695/3 0815626436
Women, Palestinian Arab -- West Bank -- Political activity. Women, Palestinian Arab -- Gaza Strip -- Political activity. Jewish women -- Israel -- Political activity.

HQ1728.5.Z8.W4775 1992
Strum, Philippa.
The women are marching: the second sex and the Palestinian revolution/ Philippa Strum. Chicago, Ill.: Lawrence Hill Books, c1992. xi, 345 p.
91-042410 305.42/5695/3 1556521227
Women, Palestinian Arab -- West Bank -- Political activity. Women, Palestinian Arab -- Gaza Strip -- Political activity. Intifada, 1987- -- Participation, Female.

HQ1728.7.R8 2001
Rubenberg, Cheryl.
Palestinian women: patriarchy and resistance in the West Bank/ Cheryl A. Rubenberg. Boulder, Co.: Lynne Rienner Publishers, 2001. ix, 318 p.
00-046002 305.38/89274056953 155587956X
Women, Palestinian Arab -- West Bank -- Social conditions. Patriarchy -- West Bank.

HQ1728.8.P35 1998
Palestinian women of Gaza and the West Bank/ edited by Suha Sabbagh. Bloomington: Indiana University Press, c1998. 262 p.
97-040148 305.48/892740531 21 0253333776
Women, Palestinian Arab -- Gaza Strip. Women, Palestinian Arab -- West Bank. Women, Palestinian Arab -- Gaza Strip -- Social conditions.

HQ1730.D68 2000
Doumato, Eleanor Abdella.
Getting God's ear: women, Islam, and healing in Saudi Arabia and the Gulf/ Eleanor Abdella Doumato. New York: Columbia University Press, c2000. xii, 312 p.
99-035113 305.42/09538 21 0231116667
Women -- Saudi Arabia -- Social conditions -- 20th century. Women -- Religious life -- Saudi Arabia -- History -- 20th century. Women healers -- Saudi Arabia -- History -- 20th century.

HQ1731.Z8.S838 1982
Wikan, Unni, 1944-
Behind the veil in Arabia: women in Oman/ Unni Wikan. Baltimore: Johns Hopkins University Press, c1982. xiii, 314 p.
81-018622 305.4/2/09538 0801827299
Women -- Oman -- Suhar. Sex customs -- Oman -- Suhar. Marriage -- Oman -- Suhar. Suhar (Oman) -- Social life and customs.

HQ1734.M84
Mughni, Haya.
Women in Kuwait: the politics of gender/ Haya al-Mughni. London: Saqi, 2001. 220 p.
305.42095367 0863563589
Women -- Kuwait -- Social conditions. Women -- Arab countries -- Social conditions. Women -- Societies and clans. Kuwait -- Social conditions.

HQ1735.2.I75 1997
Isfandiyari, Halah.
Reconstructed lives: women and Iran's Islamic revolution/ Haleh Esfandiari. Washington, D.C.: Woodrow Wilson Center Press; c1997. 234 p.
97-003080 305.48/6971055 21 0801856191
Muslim women -- Iran -- Social conditions. Muslim women -- Iran -- Civil rights. Iran -- History -- Revolution, 1979. Iran -- Social conditions -- 1979-1997. Iran -- Politics and government -- 1979-1997.

HQ1735.2.M55 1999
Mir-Hosseini, Ziba.
Islam and gender: the religious debate in contemporary Iran/ Ziba Mir-Hosseini. Princeton, NJ: Princeton University Press, 1999. xx, 305 p.
99-022786 305.4/0955 0691058156
Women -- Iran. Muslim women -- Iran. Women in Islam -- Iran.

HQ1737.S56 1976
Smedley, Agnes, 1892-1950.
Portraits of Chinese women in revolution/ by Agnes Smedley; edited with an introd. by Jan MacKinnon and Steve MacKinnon; with an afterword by Florence Howe. Old Westbury, N.Y.: Feminist Press, 1976. xxxv, 203 p.
76-018896 301.41/2/0951 0912670444
Smedley, Agnes, -- 1892-1950. Women -- China -- History.

HQ1737.W65
Women in Chinese society/ edited by Margery Wolf and Roxane Witke; contributors, Emily M. Ahern ... [et al.]. Stanford, Calif.: Stanford University Press, 1975. x, 315 p.
74-082782 301.41/2/0951 0804708746
Women -- China -- Social conditions.

HQ1742.A43 2000
Ali, Azra Asghar.
The emergence of feminism among Indian Muslim women, 1920-1947/ Azra Asghar Ali. Oxford; Oxford University Press, 2000. xxi, 291 p.
00-708439 0195791525
Muslim women -- India -- History. Women in Islam -- India -- History. Feminism -- India -- History.

HQ1742.J44 1989
Jeffery, Patricia, 1947-
Labour pains and labour power: women and childbearing in India/ Patricia Jeffery, Roger Jeffery, Andrew Lyon. London; Zed Books, 1989, c1988. xi, 292 p.
88-029346 305.4/2/0954 0862324858
Rural women -- India. Childbirth -- India. Sex role -- India.

HQ1742.S235 1994
Sahgal, Manmohini Zutshi, 1909-
An Indian freedom fighter recalls her life/ Manmohini Zutshi Sahgal; edited by Geraldine Forbes; with a foreword by B.K. Nehru. Armonk, N.Y.: M.E. Sharpe, c1994. xxvii, 167 p.
94-027345 305.42/092 1563243393
Sahgal, Manmohini Zutshi, -- 1909- Women social reformers -- India -- Biography. Women political activists -- India -- Biography. Kashmiri Pandits -- Social life and customs.

HQ1743.C35 1992
Calman, Leslie J.
Toward empowerment: women and movement politics in India/ Leslie J. Calman. Boulder: Westview Press, 1992. xxiii, 230 p.
92-006420 305.42/0954 0813381037
Feminism -- India. Women in politics -- India. Women -- India -- Social conditions.

HQ1743.D38 1989
Dhruvarajan, Vanaja.
Hindu women and the power of ideology/ Vanaja Dhruvarajan. [Granby], Mass.: Bergin & Garvey, 1989. viii, 168 p.
88-028692 305.4/0882945 0897891457
Hindu women -- India -- Social conditions. Sex role -- India. Women in Hinduism.

HQ1743.S63 1989
Somjee, Geeta, 1930-
Narrowing the gender gap/ Geeta Somjee. New York: St. Martin's Press, 1989. xvi, 155 p.
88-003087 305.4/2/0954 0312012071
Women -- India -- Social conditions. Women -- Socialization -- India. Sex role -- India. India -- Social conditions -- 1947-

HQ1744.B4.E64 1996
Engels, Dagmar.
Beyond purdah?: women in Bengal 1890-1939/ Dagmar Engels. Delhi: Oxford University Press, 1996. x, 282 p.
96-902119 305.4/0954/14 0195637208
Women -- India -- Bengal -- History -- 19th century. Women -- India -- Bengal -- Economic conditions. Bengal (India) -- Social conditions.

HQ1744.B4.R68
Roy, Manisha, 1936-
Bengali women/ Manisha Roy. Chicago: University of Chicago Press, 1975. xvii, 205 p.
74-033521 301.41/2/095414 0226730417
Women -- India -- West Bengal. Hindu women -- India -- West Bengal. Upper class -- India -- West Bengal.

HQ1745.B65.M58 1991
Mitter, Sara S., 1938-
Dharma's daughters: contemporary Indian women and Hindu culture/ Sara S. Mitter. New Brunswick, N.J.: Rutgers University Press, c1991. xi, 198 p.
90-019387 305.42/0954/7923 0813516773
Women -- India -- Bombay -- Social conditions. Hindu women -- India -- Bombay. Feminism -- India -- Bombay. Bombay (India) -- Social conditions.

HQ1745.M37.B34 1995
Bagwe, Anjali Narottam.
Of woman caste: the experience of gender in rural India/ Anjali Bagwe. London; Zed Books, c1995. xi, 245 p.
95-031267 305.4/0954/792 1856493210
Women, Maratha -- India -- Masure -- Social conditions -- Case studies. Women, Maratha -- India -- Masure -- Economic conditions -- Case studies. Women farmers -- India -- Masure -- Case studies. Masure (India) -- Social life and customs -- Case studies. Masure (India) -- Religious life and customs -- Case studies.

HQ1745.6.H375 2000
Hashmi, Taj ul-Islam, 1948-
Women and Islam in Bangladesh: beyond subjection and tyranny/ Taj. I. Hashmi. New York: St. Martin's Press, 2000. xi, 254 p.
99-044913 305.48/697105492 031222219X
Women -- Bangladesh -- Social conditions. Muslim women -- Bangladesh -- Social conditions. Women in Islam -- Bangladesh.

HQ1745.6.I59 1987
The Invisible resource: women and work in rural Bangladesh/ Ben J. Wallace ... [et al.]. Boulder: Westview Press, 1987. xiii, 161 p.
86-032614 305.4/2/095492 0813372798
Rural women -- Bangladesh -- Social conditions.

HQ1745.6.W54 1992
White, Sarah C.
Arguing with the crocodile: gender and class in Bangladesh/ Sarah C. White. London; Zed Books, c1992. 186 p.
92-017852 305.42/095492 1856490858
Rural women -- Bangladesh. Rural women -- Bangladesh -- Kumirpur. Social classes -- Bangladesh.

HQ1752.S43 1996
Fantasizing the feminine in Indonesia/ Laurie J. Sears, editor. Durham: Duke University Press, 1996. xvi, 349 p.
95-009320 305.42/09598 0822316846
Women -- Indonesia -- Social conditions. Women in popular culture -- Indonesia. Sex role -- Indonesia.

HQ1757.L55 1997
Lindio-McGovern, Ligaya.
Filipino peasant women: exploitation and resistance/ Ligaya Lindio-McGovern. Philadelphia: University of Pennsylvania Press, c1997. xiv, 225 p.
97-019617 305.48/9624 21 0812234103
Women peasants -- Philippines. Women peasants -- Philippines -- Political activity. Women agricultural laborers -- Philippines.

HQ1762.B76 1997
Broken silence: voices of Japanese feminism/ [edited by] Sandra Buckley. Berkeley: University of California Press, c1997. xix, 382 p.
95-051306 305.42/0952 20 0520085132
Feminists -- Japan -- Interviews. Feminism -- Japan. Feminist theory -- Japan.

HQ1762.I925 1993
Iwao, Sumiko, 1935-
The Japanese woman: traditional image and changing reality/ Sumiko Iwao. New York: Free Press; c1993. xii, 304 p.
92-024871 305.4/2/0952 0029323150
Women -- Japan -- Social conditions. Sex role -- Japan. Japan -- Social conditions -- 1945-

HQ1762.R43 1991
Recreating Japanese women, 1600-1945/ edited with an introduction by Gail Lee Bernstein. Berkeley: University of California Press, c1991. xi, 340 p.
90-011194   305.42/0952   0520070151
Women -- Japan -- History. Feminism -- Japan -- History. Women -- Employment -- Japan -- History.

HQ1762.R6 1983
Robins-Mowry, Dorothy, 1921-
The hidden sun: women of modern Japan/ Dorothy Robins-Mowry; with a foreword by Edwin O. Reischauer. Boulder, Colo.: Westview Press, 1983. xxii, 394 p.
82-020230   305.4/0952   0865314217
Women -- Japan -- Social conditions.

HQ1762.V65 1996
Voices from the Japanese women's movement/ edited by AMPO, Japan Asia quarterly review. Armonk, N.Y.: M.E. Sharpe, c1996. xxi, 207 p.
95-043512   305.42/0952 20   1563247259
Feminism -- Japan. Women -- Japan.

HQ1763.L4 1984
Lebra, Takie Sugiyama, 1930-
Japanese women: constraint and fulfillment/ Takie Sugiyama Lebra. Honolulu: University of Hawaii Press, c1984. xi, 345 p.
83-018029   305.4/0952   0824808681
Women -- Japan -- Social conditions -- Case studies. Life cycle, Human -- Case studies. Sex role -- Japan -- Case studies.

HQ1764.O44
Keyso, Ruth Ann, 1968-
Women of Okinawa: nine voices from a garrison island/ Ruth Ann Keyso; afterword by Masahide Ota. Ithaca: Cornell University Press, 2000. xv, 166 p.
00-008916   305.4/0952/294   0801437881
Women -- Japan -- Okinawa Island -- Interviews. Women and war -- Japan -- Okinawa Island -- History -- 20th century. World War, 1939-1945 -- Campaigns -- Japan -- Okinawa Island.

HQ1767.H65 1988
Honig, Emily.
Personal voices: Chinese women in the 1980's/ Emily Honig & Gail Hershatter. Stanford, Calif.: Stanford University Press, 1988. vi, 387 p.
87-018013   305.4/0951   0804714169
Women -- China -- Social conditions. Women -- China -- Conduct of life.

HQ1767.J33 1997
Jacka, Tamara, 1965-
Women's work in rural China: change and continuity in an era of reform/ Tamara Jacka. Cambridge; Cambridge University Press, 1997. viii, 264 p.
96-041501   306.3/615/0951   0521562252
Rural women -- China -- Social conditions. Women -- Employment -- China. China -- Social conditions -- 1976-

HQ1767.S63 1978
Spence, Jonathan D.
The death of woman Wang/ Jonathan D. Spence. New York: Viking Press, 1978. xvii, 169 p.
77-029134   951   0670262323
Women -- China -- History. Runaway wives -- China.

HQ1767.T43 1996
Thakur, Ravni, 1962-
Rewriting gender: reading contemporary Chinese women/ Ravni Thakur. London; Zed Books, 1996. 224 p.
96-017966   305.4/0951   1856494098
Women -- China -- Social conditions. Women and literature -- China. Chinese literature -- Women authors -- History and criticism.

HQ1784.A67 1992
Ahmed, Leila.
Women and gender in Islam: historical roots of a modern debate/ Leila Ahmed. New Haven: Yale University Press, c1992. viii, 296 p.
91-026901   305.48/6971   0300049420
Women -- Arab countries -- Social conditions. Sexism -- Arab countries -- History. Muslim women -- Attitudes.

HQ1784.A72 1993
Arab women: old boundaries, new frontiers/ edited by Judith E. Tucker. Bloomington: Indiana University Press, c1993. xviii, 264 p.
92-033583   305.42/0917/4927   025336096X
Women -- Arab countries -- Social conditions. Women -- Arab countries -- Economic conditions. Feminism -- Arab countries.

HQ1784.H54 1988
Hijab, Nadia.
Womanpower: the Arab debate on women at work/ Nadia Hijab. Cambridge [Cambridgeshire]; Cambridge University Press, 1988. xiv, 176 p.
87-021217   305.4/0917/4927   052126443X
Women -- Arab countries. Family -- Arab countries. Women -- Employment -- Arab countries -- Public opinion.

HQ1784.W65 1985
Women and the family in the Middle East: new voices of change/ edited by Elizabeth Warnock Fernea. Austin: University of Texas Press, c1985. xii, 356 p.
84-011944   305.4/2/09174927   0292755287
Women -- Arab countries. Family -- Arab countries. Women -- Iran. Arab countries -- Social life and customs.

HQ1787.A3.L54 1988
Life histories of African women/ edited by Patricia W. Romero. London; Ashfield Press, 1988. 200 p.
87-001441   305.4/0967   094866004X
Women -- Africa, Sub-Saharan -- Biography. Women -- Africa, Sub-Saharan -- Social conditions -- Case studies. Muslim women -- Africa, Sub-Saharan -- Social conditions -- Case studies.

HQ1787.C6613 1997
Coquery-Vidrovitch, Catherine.
African women: a modern history/ Catherine Coquery-Vidrovitch; translated by Beth Gillian Raps. Boulder, Colo.: WestviewPress, 1997. xviii, 308 p.
96-047847   305.4/0967   0813323606
Women -- Africa, Sub-Saharan -- History -- 19th century. Women -- Africa, Sub-Saharan -- History -- 20th century.

HQ1787.C68 1996
Courtyards, markets, city streets: urban women in Africa/ edited by Kathleen Sheldon. Boulder, Colo.: WestviewPress, c1996. viii, 342 p.
96-026118   305.4/096 20   0813386853
Urban women -- Africa.

HQ1787.W53 2001
"Wicked" women and the reconfiguration of gender in Africa/ edited by Dorothy L. Hodgson and Sheryl A. McCurdy. Portsmouth, NH: Heinemann, c2001. xv, 325 p.
00-040882   305.4/096 21   0325070059
Women -- Africa -- Social conditions. Sex role -- Africa.

HQ1788.A57 1995
African women south of the Sahara/ edited by Margaret Jean Hay and Sharon Stichter. 2nd ed. Harlow, Essex, England; Longman Scienctific & Technical; xvii, 308 p.
95-016886   305.4/0967 20   0582212413
Women -- Africa, Sub-Saharan -- Economic conditions. Women -- Africa, Sub-Saharan -- Social conditions. Women in politics -- Africa, Sub-Saharan.

HQ1793.A67 1987
Abdel Kader, Soha.
Egyptian women in a changing society, 1899-1987/ Soha Abdel Kader. Boulder: Lynne Rienner Publishers, 1987. x, 163 p.
87-013234   305.4/2/0962   0931477476
Women -- Egypt -- Social conditions. Muslim women -- Egypt -- Social conditions. Feminism -- Egypt -- History -- 20th century.

HQ1793.A68 1993
Abu-Lughod, Lila.
Writing women's worlds: Bedouin stories/ Lila Abu-Lughod. Berkeley: University of California Press, c1993. xxiii, 266 p.
91-039685   305.48/6971/0962   0520079469
Muslim women -- Egypt -- Social conditions. Women, Bedouin -- Egypt. Ethnology -- Egypt -- Biographical methods.

HQ1793.A75 2000
Al-Ali, Nadje Sadig.
Secularism, gender and the state in the Middle East: the Egyptian women's movement/ Nadje Al-Ali. Cambridge, U.K.; Cambridge University Press, 2000. xv, 264 p.
99-053434   305.420962   0521780225
Feminism -- Egypt.

HQ1793.B33 1995
Badran, Margot.
Feminists, Islam, and nation: gender and the making of modern Egypt/ Margot Badran. Princeton, N.J.: Princeton University Press, c1995. xi, 352 p.
94-019055   305.42/0962   069103706X
Feminism -- Egypt -- History. Women -- Egypt -- History. Muslim women -- Egypt -- History.

HQ1793.K37 1998
Karam, Azza M.
Women, Islamisms, and the state: contemporary feminisms in Egypt/ Azza M. Karam. New York: St. Martin's Press, 1998. xvii, 284 p.
97-007123   305.4/0962   0312175019
Women -- Egypt. Women in politics -- Egypt. Feminism -- Egypt.

HQ1793.Z75.A55 1999
Ahmed, Leila.
A border passage: from Cairo to America--a woman's journey/ Leila Ahmed. New York: Farrar, Straus and Giroux, 1999. viii, 307 p.
98-039027   305.42/092   0374115184
Ahmed, Leila. Women -- Egypt -- Biography. Muslim women -- Egypt -- Biography. Women in Islam -- Egypt.

HQ1796.5.W3613 1989
Three Swahili women: life histories from Mombasa, Kenya/ edited and translated by Sarah Mirza and Margaret Strobel. Bloomington: Indiana University Press, c1989. xii, 157 p.
88-045093 305.4/2/0967623 0253288541
Women -- Kenya -- Mombasa -- History. Muslim women -- Kenya -- Mombasa -- Biography. Sociology -- Biographical methods.

HQ1799.U73 1989
Urdang, Stephanie.
And still they dance: women, war, and the struggle for change in Mozambique/ Stephanie Urdang. New York: Monthly Review Press, c1989. 256 p.
88-029068 305.4/0967/9 0853457727
Women -- Mozambique. Women in development -- Mozambique. Mozambique -- Social conditions -- 1975-

HQ1800.W65 1990
Women and gender in southern Africa to 1945/ edited by Cherryl Walker. Cape Town: D. Philip; 1990. 390 p.
91-139998 305.4/0968 0864860900
Women -- Africa, Southern -- History. Women, Black -- Africa, Southern -- History.

HQ1800.5.R67 1998
Romero, Patricia W.
Profiles in diversity: women in the new South Africa/ Patricia W. Romero. East Lansing, Mich: Michigan State University Press, c1998. x, 231 p.
98-020674 305.42/0968 21 0870134477
Women -- South Africa -- Social conditions. Women -- South Africa -- Interviews. Apartheid -- South Africa. South Africa -- Politics and government -- 20th century.

HQ1810.C35 1994
Callaway, Barbara.
The heritage of Islam: women, religion, and politics in West Africa/ Barbara Callaway, Lucy Creevey. Boulder, Colo.: Lynne Rienner, 1994. x, 221 p.
93-035396 305.42/0966 1555872530
Women -- Africa, West -- Social conditions. Women -- Legal status, laws, etc. (Islamic law) -- Africa, West. Muslim women -- Nigeria.

HQ1815.5.Z75.R355 1997
Johnson-Odim, Cheryl, 1948-
For women and the nation: Funmilayo Ransome-Kuti of Nigeria/ Cheryl Johnson-Odim and Nina Emma Mba. Urbana: University of Illinois Press, c1997. xvi, 198 p.
96-025390 305.42/092 B 20 0252023137
Ransome-Kuti, Funmilayo, -- 1900-1978. Ransome-Kuti, Israel Oludotun, -- 1891-1955. Women political activists -- Nigeria -- Biography. Political activists -- Nigeria -- Biography.

HQ1816.M62.M3
Maher, Vanessa.
Women and property in Morocco: their changing relation to the process of social stratification in the Middle Atlas/ Vanessa Maher. London; Cambridge University Press, 1974. xii, 238 p.
74-080351 301.41/2/0964 0521205484
Women -- Morocco -- Social conditions. Marriage -- Morocco. Morocco -- Social conditions.

HQ1822.D58 1999
Dixson, Miriam.
The real Matilda: woman and identity in Australia, 1788 to the present/ Miriam Dixson. 4th ed. Sydney: UNSW Press, 1999. 318 p.
00-340418 305.4/0994 21 0868407372
Women -- Australia -- History. Women's rights.

HQ1823.B85 1997
Bulbeck, Chilla, 1951-
Living feminism: the impact of the women's movement on three generations of Australian women/ Chilla Bulbeck. Cambridge; Cambridge University Press, 1997. xxiii, 279 p.
97-026347 305.42/0994 0521460425
Feminism -- Australia -- History -- 20th century. Women -- Australia -- History -- 20th century. Women -- Australia -- Social conditions.

HQ1823.E47 1991
Eisenstein, Hester.
Gender shock: practicing feminism on two continents/ Hester Eisenstein. Boston: Beacon Press, c1991. vi, 138 p.
91-016225 305.4/2/0973 0807067628
Feminism -- Australia. Feminism -- United States.

HQ1870.9 Women. Feminism — By region or country — Developing countries

HQ1870.9.B79 1989
Brydon, Lynne.
Women in the Third World: gender issues in rural and urban areas/ Lynne Brydon, Sylvia Chant. New Brunswick, N.J.: Rutgers University Press, 1989. 327 p.
89-006119 305.4/09172/4 0813514703
Women -- Developing countries -- Social conditions. Women in development -- Developing countries. Sex role -- Developing countries.

HQ1870.9.H65 1988
A Home divided: women and income in the Third World/ Daisy Dwyer and Judith Bruce, editors; contributors, Mead Cain ... [et al.]. Stanford, Calif.: Stanford University Press, 1988. xi, 289 p.
88-004938 305.4/3/091724 0804714851
Women -- Developing countries -- Economic conditions. Wages -- Women -- Developing countries. Women -- Employment -- Developing countries.

HQ1870.9.M64 2003
Mohanty, Chandra Talpade,
Feminism without borders: decolonizing theory, practicing solidarity / Chandra Talpade Mohanty. Durham; Duke University Press, c2003.
2002-013266 305.42 21 0822330210
Feminism -- Developing countries. Women -- Developing countries -- Social conditions.

HQ1870.9.T49 1991
Third World women and the politics of feminism/ edited by Chandra Talpade Mohanty, Ann Russo, Lourdes Torres. Bloomington: Indiana University Press, c1991. xi, 338 p.
90-043510 305.42/09172/4 0253338735
Feminism -- Developing countries. Women -- Developing countries -- Social conditions.

HQ1870.9.W6548 1998
Women in the Third World: an encyclopedia of contemporary issues/ editor, Nelly P. Stromquist; assistant editor, Karen Monkman. New York: Garland Pub., 1998. xxxiv, 683 p.
98-014689 305.42/09172/4 0815301502
Women -- Developing countries -- Social conditions. Women -- Developing countries -- Economic conditions. Women -- Legal status, laws, etc. -- Developing countries.

HQ1883 Women. Feminism — Women's clubs, societies, etc. — Directories

HQ1883.E53 1993
Encyclopedia of women's associations worldwide: a guide to over 3,400 national and multinational nonprofit women's and women-related organizations/ Jacqueline K. Barrett, editor; Jane A. Malonis, associate editor. London; Gale Research, c1993. lxvi, 471 p.
93-013702 305.4/06 1873477252
Women -- Societies and clubs -- Directories. Women -- Societies and clubs -- Encyclopedias. Women's rights -- Societies, etc. -- Directories.

HQ1904-1977.2 Women. Feminism — Women's clubs, societies, etc. — By region or country

HQ1904.B56
Blair, Karen J.
The clubwoman as feminist: true womanhood redefined, 1868-1914/ Karen J. Blair; pref. by Annette K. Baxter. New York: Holmes & Meier Publishers, 1980. xv, 199 p.
79-026390 301.41/2/0973 084190538X
Women -- United States -- Societies and clubs -- History. Women in public life -- United States -- History. Feminism -- United States -- History.

HQ1904.J43 1996
Jeansonne, Glen, 1946-
Women of the far right: the mothers' movement and World War II/ Glen Jeansonne. Chicago, Ill.: University of Chicago Press, 1996. xix, 264 p.
95-035974 305.4/06/073 0226395871
Women -- United States -- Societies and clubs -- History -- 20th century. Neutrality -- United States -- Societies, etc. Neutrality -- United States -- History -- 20th century. United States -- Politics and government -- 1933-1945.

HQ1904.S28 1991
Scott, Anne Firor, 1921-
Natural allies: women's associations in American history/ Anne Firor Scott. Urbana: University of Illinois Press, c1991. xii, 242 p.
91-010979 305.4/06/073 025201846X
Women -- United States -- Societies and clubs -- History. Women -- United States -- Social conditions. Women volunteers in social service -- United States -- History.

HQ1904.U2 1995
U.S. women's interest groups: institutional profiles/ edited by Sarah Slavin. Westport, Conn.: Greenwood Press, 1995. xl, 645 p.
94-038500 305.4/06/073 0313250731
Women -- United States -- Societies and clubs -- Directories. Pressure groups -- United States -- Directories. Women's rights -- United States -- Societies, etc. -- Directories.

HQ1945.G67 2001
Gordon, Peter, 1927-
Dictionary of British women's organisations, 1825-1960/ Peter Gordon and David Doughan; with a foreword by Sheila Rowbotham. London; Woburn Press, 2001. viii, 218 p.
00-012399 305.4/06/041 0713002239
Women -- Great Britain -- Societies and clubs -- Dictionaries.

HQ1977.2.R33 1997
Racioppi, Linda.
Women's activism in contemporary Russia/ Linda Racioppi and Katherine O'Sullivan See. Philadelphia: Temple University Press, 1997. xiii, 277 p.
96-036093   305.42/0947   1566395208
Women -- Russia (Federation) -- Societies and clubs. Feminism -- Russia (Federation) Feminists -- Russia (Federation) -- Interviews.

HQ2042-2044 Life style

HQ2042.S36 2001
Sandall, Roger.
The culture cult: designer tribalism and other essays/ Roger Sandall. Boulder, CO: Westview Press, 2000. x, 214 p.
00-043704   306/.1   0813338638
Ethnopsychology. Ethnophilosophy. Alternative lifestyles.

HQ2044.U62.N674 1996
Durning, Alan Thein.
This place on earth: home and the practice of permanence/ Alan Thein Durning. Seattle: Sasquatch Books, c1996. 326 p.
96-020592   306 20   1570610401
Lifestyles -- Northwest, Pacific. Simplicity. Home.

HS Societies: Secret, Benevolent, etc.

HS61 Societies — By region or country — United States

HS61.A17 2000
Beito, David T.
From mutual aid to the welfare state: fraternal societies and social services, 1890-1967/ David Beito. Chapel Hill: University of North Carolina Press, c2000. xiv, 320 p.
99-041895   334/.7/0973 21   080782531X
Friendly societies -- United States -- History. Insurance, Fraternal -- United States -- History. Mutualism -- United States -- History.

HS310 Secret societies — By region or country

HS310.O86 1996
Ownby, David, 1958-
Brotherhoods and secret societies in early and mid-Qing China: the formation of a tradition/ David Ownby. Stanford, Calif.: Standford University Press, 1996. xii, 235 p.
95-031759   368/.0951   0804726515
Secret societies -- China -- History.   China -- History -- Ching dynasty, 1644-1912.

HS523 Freemasons — By region or country — North America

HS523.B85 1996
Bullock, Steven C.
Revolutionary brotherhood: Freemasonry and the transformation of the American social order, 1730-1840/ Steven C. Bullock. Chapel Hill: University of North Carolina Press, c1996. xviii, 421 p.
95-039554   366/.1/0973 20   0807822825
Freemasonry -- United States -- History -- 18th century. Freemasonry -- United States -- History -- 19th century.

HS765 Freemasons — Other Masonic bodies and rites — Scottish rite

HS765.F69 1997
Fox, William L., 1953-
Lodge of the Double-Headed Eagle: two centuries of Scottish Rite Freemasonry in America's Southern Jurisdiction/ William L. Fox. [Fayetteville]: University of Arkansas Press, 1997. xvi, 491 p.
97-014064   366/.1/0975   1557284776
Scottish Rite (Masonic order). Southern Masonic Jurisdiction -- History. Scottish Rite (Masonic order). Southern Masonic Jurisdiction -- Biography.

HS1538 Other societies. By classes — Religious societies — By church

HS1538.K65
Kauffman, Christopher J., 1936-
Patriotism and fraternalism in the Knights of Columbus: a history of the fourth degree/ Christopher J. Kauffman. New York: Crossroad, c2001. xix, 174 p.
00-011652   267/.242 21   0824518853
Anti-Catholicism -- United States -- History.

HS2330 Other societies. By classes — Political and "patriotic" societies — By region or country

HS2330.K63.B44 1991
Blee, Kathleen M.
Women of the Klan: racism and gender in the 1920s/ Kathleen M. Blee. Berkeley: University of California Press, c1991. viii, 228 p.
90-011287   322.4/2/082   0520072634
Ku Klux Klan (1915-) -- History. Women of the Ku Klux Klan -- Indiana -- History.

HS2330.K63.F44 1999
Feldman, Glenn.
Politics, society, and the Klan in Alabama, 1915-1949/ Glenn Feldman. Tuscaloosa: University of Alabama Press, c1999. xii, 457 p.
99-006123   322.4/2/09761/0904 21   0817309837
Alabama -- Race relations -- History -- 20th century. Alabama -- Social conditions -- 20th century. Alabama -- Politics and government -- 1865-1950.

HS2330.K63.I58 1991
The Invisible empire in the West: toward a new historical appraisal of the Ku Klux Klan of the 1920s/ edited by Shawn Lay. Urbana: University of Illinois Press, c1992. 230 p.
91-002081   322.4/2/0978   025201832X
Ku Klux Klan (1915-) -- West (U.S.) -- History.

HS2330.K63.J44 1990
Jenkins, William D., 1941-
Steel Valley Klan: the Ku Klux Klan in Ohio's Mahoning Valley/ William D. Jenkins. Kent, Ohio: Kent State University Press, c1990. xii, 222 p.
90-034701   322.4/2/0977139   0873384156
Mahoning River Valley (Ohio and Pa.) -- History.

HS2330.K63.L33 1995
Lay, Shawn.
Hooded knights on the Niagara: the Ku Klux Klan in Buffalo, New York/ Shawn Lay. New York: New York University Press, c1995. xiv, 198 p.
95-004285   322.4/2/0974797   0814751016
Ku Klux Klan (1915-) -- New York (State) -- Buffalo -- History.

HS2330.K63.L87 1991
Lutholtz, M. William, 1954-
Grand dragon: D.C. Stephenson and the Ku Klux Klan in Indiana/ M. William Lutholtz. West Lafayette, Ind.: Purdue University Press, c1991. xix, 362 p.
90-020132   322.4/2/092   1557530106
Stephenson, David Curtis, -- 1891-1966.   Murder -- Indiana -- Case studies.

HS2330.K63.M225 1994
MacLean, Nancy.
Behind the mask of chivalry: the making of the second Ku Klux Klan/ Nancy MacLean. New York: Oxford University Press, 1994. xvii, 292 p.
93-027548   322.4/2/0975818   0195072340
Athens (Ga.) -- Race relations. Athens (Ga.) -- Social conditions.

HS2330.K63 M66 1991
Moore, Leonard Joseph,
Citizen klansmen: the Ku Klux Klan in Indiana, 1921-1928/ Leonard J. Moore. Chapel Hill: University of North Carolina Press, c1991. xlv, 259 p.
91-002602   322.4/2/0977209042   0807819816
Ku Klux Klan (1915-) -- Indiana -- History.

HS2723 Clubs — By region or country — United States

HS2723.C48 1993
Charles, Jeffrey A., 1958-
Service clubs in American society: Rotary, Kiwanis, and Lions/ Jeffrey A. Charles. Urbana: University of Illinois Press, c1993. x, 226 p.
93-009803   369.5/0973   0252020154
Clubs -- United States -- Case studies.

HT Communities. Classes. Races

HT65 Human settlements. Communities — General works

HT65.U73 1996
An urbanizing world: global report on human settlements, 1996/ United Nations Centre for Human Settlements (HABITAT). Oxford; Oxford University Press for the United Nations C 1996. xxxiv, 559 p.
96-001388   307.76   0198233469
Human settlements. Human settlements -- Developing countries. Regional planning -- Developing countries.

HT108.5 Urban groups. The city. Urban sociology — Dictionaries. Encyclopedias

HT108.5.E53 2002
Encyclopedia of urban cultures: cities and cultures around the world / edited by Melvin Ember and Carol R. Ember. Danbury, Conn.: Grolier, 2002.
2002-070034   307.76/03 21   0717256987
Cities and towns -- Encyclopedias. Sociology, Urban -- Encyclopedias.

HT108.5.K87 1994
Kurian, George Thomas.
World encyclopedia of cities/ George Thomas Kurian. Santa Barbara, Calif.: ABC-CLIO, [c1994-] v. 1-2.
93-043133   307.76/03   0874366496
Cities and towns -- Encyclopedias.

HT111 Urban groups. The city. Urban sociology — History — General

HT111.C65 2000
A companion to the city/ edited by Gary Bridge and Sophie Watson. Oxford, UK; Blackwell, 2000. xiv, 640 p.
00-024885   307.76   0631210520
Cities and towns. Cities and towns -- Cross-cultural studies.

HT111.S63 1998
Southall, Aidan William.
The city in time and space/ Aidan Southall. Cambridge [England]; Cambridge University Press, 1998. x, 473 p.
97-008671   307.76/09   0521462118
Cities and towns -- History.

HT114-119 Urban groups. The city. Urban sociology — History — By period

HT114.H35
Hammond, Mason, 1903-
The city in the ancient world, by Mason Hammond, assisted by Lester J. Bartson. Cambridge, Mass., Harvard University Press, 1972. xiv, 617 p.
73-180153   301.36/093
Cities and towns, Ancient. Cities and towns, Ancient -- Bibliography.

HT114.S7 1988
Stambaugh, John E.
The ancient Roman city/ John E. Stambaugh. Baltimore: Johns Hopkins University Press, c1988. xviii, 395 p.
87-026861   307.7/64/0937   0801835747
Cities and towns, Ancient -- Rome. City and town life -- Rome. Rome -- Social conditions.

HT115.H55 1992
Hilton, R. H. 1916-
English and French towns in feudal society: a comparative study/ R.H. Hilton. Cambridge [England]; Cambridge University Press, 1992. xi, 174 p.
91-012206   307.76/0942/0902   0521413524
Cities and towns, Medieval -- England. Cities and towns, Medieval -- France. Feudalism -- England.

HT115.N53 1997
Nicholas, David, 1939-
The growth of the medieval city: from late antiquity to the early fourteenth century/ David Nicholas. London; Longman, 1997. xviii, 413 p.
96-027185   307.76/09/02   0582299071
Cities and towns, Medieval. Cities and towns, Ancient.

HT119.B96 2001
Byrne, D. S. 1947-
Understanding the urban/ David Byrne. Houndmills, Basingstoke [England]; Palgrave, 2001. ix, 220 p.
00-062599   307.76   0333724283
Cities and towns. Metropolitan areas. City and town life.

HT119.S62 2000
Smith, Michael P.
Transnational urbanism: locating globalization/ Michael Peter Smith. Malden: Blackwell Publishers, 2000.
00-025866   307.76   0631184236
Cities and towns. Urbanization. Urban policy.

HT121-149.5 Urban groups. The city. Urban sociology — History — By region or country

HT121.U72 1993
Urban policy in twentieth-century America/ edited by Arnold R. Hirsch and Raymond A. Mohl. New Brunswick, N.J.: Rutgers University Press, c1993. xiii, 238 p.
92-009429   307.76/0973   0813519055
Urban policy -- United States.

HT123.D39 1991
Davis, John Emmeus, 1949-
Contested ground: collective action and the urban neighborhood/ John Emmeus Davis. Ithaca, N.Y.: Cornell University Press, 1991. x, 356 p.
90-042034   307.3/36216/0973   0801422159
Neighborhood -- United States. Neighborhood -- Ohio -- Cincinnati -- Case studies. Community power -- United States.

HT123.E5 1998
Encyclopedia of urban America: the cities and suburbs/ Neil Larry Shumsky, editor. Santa Barbara, Calif.: ABC-CLIO, c1998. 2 v.
98-011698   307.76/0973/03 21   0874368464
Cities and towns -- United States -- Encyclopedias. Suburbs -- United States -- Encyclopedias. Cities and towns -- United States -- History.

HT123.F887 1990
The Future of national urban policy/ Marshall Kaplan and Franklin James, editors. Durham [N.C.]: Duke University Press, 1990. vii, 405 p.
88-033545   307.7/6/0973   0822309084
Urban policy -- United States.

HT123.K67 2000
Kotkin, Joel.
The new geography: how the digital revolution is reshaping the American landscape/ Joel Kotkin. New York: Random House, c2000. 242 p.
00-028096   307.76 21   0375501991
Cities and towns -- Effect of technological innovations on -- United States.

HT123.N36 1996
Nenno, Mary K., 1923-
Ending the stalemate: moving housing and urban development into the mainstream of America's future/ Mary K. Nenno. Lanham, Md.: University Press of America, c1996. xv, 335 p.
95-047283   307.76/0973 20   0761802169
Housing policy -- United States. Community development, Urban -- United States. Urban renewal -- United States.

HT123.O87 1991
Our changing cities/ edited by John Fraser Hart; cartographic design by Gregory Chu. Baltimore: Johns Hopkins University Press, c1991. xv, 261 p.
91-009226   307.76/0973   0801840872
Cities and towns -- Effect of technological innovations on -- United States. Cities and towns -- United States -- Growth.

HT123.W555 1990
Wong, Kenneth K., 1955-
City choices: education and housing/ Kenneth K. Wong. Albany: State University of New York Press, c1990. x, 218 p.
89-004587   307.76/0973   0791402258
Urban policy -- United States. Education, Urban -- United States. Housing policy -- United States.

HT123.5.M53.M34 1989
Mahoney, Timothy R., 1953-
River towns in the Great West: the structure of provincial urbanization in the American Midwest, 1820-1870/ Timothy R. Mahoney. Cambridge [England]; Cambridge University Press, 1990. xi, 319 p.
89-032208   307.76/0977   0521361303
Cities and towns -- Middle West -- History -- 19th century. Urbanization -- Middle West -- History -- 19th century. Land settlement -- Middle West -- History -- 19th century.

HT123.5.S6.D69 1990
Doyle, Don Harrison, 1946-
New men, new cities, new South: Atlanta, Nashville, Charleston, Mobile, 1860-1910/ Don H. Doyle. Chapel Hill: University of North Carolina Press, c1990. xix, 369 p.
89-034924   307.76/0975   0807818836
Urbanization -- Southern States -- History -- 19th century. Cities and towns -- Southern States -- History -- 19th century. Southern States -- Social conditions -- 1865-1945. Southern States -- Economic conditions.

HT127.C59 1996
City lives and city forms: critical research and Canadian urbanism/ edited by Jon Caulfield and Linda Peake. Toronto; University of Toronto Press, c1996. x, 347 p.
97-123137   307.76/0971 20   0802005144
Cities and towns -- Canada. Sociology, Urban -- Canada.

HT127.5.A85 1990
Atlantic port cities: economy, culture, and society in the Atlantic world, 1650-1850/ edited by Franklin W. Knight and Peggy K. Liss. Knoxville: University of Tennessee Press, c1991. xvii, 302 p.
90-037698   307.76/09729   0870496573
Cities and towns -- Latin America -- History -- Case studies -- Congresses. Urbanization -- Latin America -- History -- Case studies -- Congresses. Cities and towns -- Caribbean Area -- History -- Case studies -- Congresses. Latin America -- Economic conditions -- Case studies -- Congresses. Latin America -- Commerce -- History -- Case studies -- Congresses. Caribbean Area -- Economic conditions -- Case studies -- Congresses.

HT127.5.K34 2000
Kagan, Richard L., 1943-
Urban images of the Hispanic world, 1493-1793/ Richard L. Kagan, with the collaboration of Fernando Marias. New Haven: Yale University Press, c2000. x, 235 p.
99-058713   307.76/09171/246 21   0300083149
Cities and towns -- Latin America -- History -- Pictorial works. Cities and towns -- Spain -- History -- Pictorial works.

HT127.7.A77 1993
Arreola, Daniel D. 1950-
The Mexican border cities: landscape anatomy and place personality/ Daniel D. Arreola, James R. Curtis. Tucson: University of Arizona Press, c1993. xix, 258 p.
92-022777   307.76/0972/1   0816512876
Cities and towns -- Mexico, North. Urbanization -- Mexico, North. Urban geography -- Mexico, North. Mexico, North -- Geography.

HT133.G57 1990
Girouard, Mark, 1931-
The English town: a history of urban life/ Mark Girouard. New Haven: Yale University Press, 1990. 330 p.
90-070101   307.76/0941   0300046359
Cities and towns -- England -- History. City and town life -- England -- History.

HT133.T58 2001
Tittler, Robert.
Townspeople and nation: English urban experiences, 1540-1640/ Robert Tittler. Stanford: Stanford University Press, 2001. xi, 251 p.
00-063733   307.76/0942/09031   0804738688
Cities and towns -- England -- History.

HT147.C48.S76 2000
Stapleton, Kristin Eileen.
Civilizing Chengdu: Chinese urban reform, 1895-1937/ Kristin Stapleton. Cambridge, Mass.: Published by the Harvard University Asia Center c2000. xii, 341 p.
99-059751   307.1/216/095138 21   0674002466
Urbanization -- China -- Chengdu. City planning -- China -- Chengdu. China -- History -- 20th century.

HT149.5.U7337 1996
The Urban transformation of the developing world/ edited by Josef Gugler. Oxford; Oxford University Press, 1996. xviii, 327 p.
95-034814   307.76/09172/4   0198741596
Urbanization -- Developing countries. Cities and towns -- Developing countries.

HT151 Urban groups. The city. Urban sociology — General works. "The city problem"

HT151.F52 1993
Flanagan, William G.
Contemporary urban sociology/ William G. Flanagan. Cambridge; Cambridge University Press, 1993. vi, 185 p.
93-006588   307.76   0521365198
Sociology, Urban.

HT153 Urban groups. The city. Urban sociology — General special

HT153.T27 2000
Tajbakhsh, Kian, 1962-
The promise of the city: space, identity, and politics in contemporary social thought/ Kian Tajbakhsh. Berkeley: University of California Press, c2001. xv, 229 p.
99-056668   307.76 21   0520222776
Sociology, Urban. Marxian school of sociology.

HT161 Urban groups. The city. Urban sociology — Garden cities. "The city beautiful" — General works

HT161.B84 1990
Buder, Stanley.
Visionaries and planners: the garden city movement and the modern community/ Stanley Buder. New York: Oxford University Press, 1990. xii, 260 p.
89-026507   307.76/8   0195061748
Garden cities. Garden cities -- United States.

HT166 Urban groups. The city. Urban sociology — City planning — General works

HT166.E33 1993
Ecology of greenways: design and function of linear conservation areas/ Daniel S. Smith & Paul Cawood Hellmund, editors; foreword by Richard T.T. Forman. Minneapolis: University of Minnesota Press, c1993. xvi, 222 p.
92-043261   304.2   0816621578
Greenways. Urban ecology (Biology)

HT166.M259 2000
Marshall, Alex, 1959-
How cities work: suburbs, sprawl, and the roads not taken/ Alex Marshall. Austin: University of Texas Press, 2000. xxiii, 243 p.
00-026691   307.76   0292752393
City planning. Cities and towns -- Growth. Suburbs.

HT167-169 Urban groups. The city. Urban sociology — City planning — By region or country

HT167.C44 1991
Challenging uneven development: an urban agenda for the 1990s/ edited by Philip W. Nyden and Wim Wiewel. New Brunswick, N.J.: Rutgers University Press, c1991. xii, 233 p.
90-045521   307.1/176/0973   0813516587
City planning -- Illinois -- Chicago Metropolitan Area -- Citizen participation. Community development -- Illinois -- Chicago Metropolitan Area. Gentrification -- Illinois -- Chicago Metropolitan Area.

HT167.F73 1996
Francaviglia, Richard V.
Main street revisited: time, space, and image building in small-town America/ Richard V. Francaviglia; foreword by Wayne Franklin. Iowa City: University of Iowa Press, c1996. xxiv, 224 p.
95-047773   307.76/2/0973 20   0877455422
City planning -- United States. City planning -- United States -- Maps. City planning -- United States -- Pictorial works.

HT167.F78 1999
Frug, Gerald E., 1939-
City making: building communities without building walls/ Gerald E. Frug. Princeton, N.J.: Princeton University Press, c1999. 256 p.
99-012209   307.1/216/0973 21   0691007411
City planning -- United States. Urban policy -- United States. Zoning law -- United States. United States -- Social conditions. United States -- Race relations.

HT167.G75 1995
Greenberg, Mike, 1947-
The poetics of cities: designing neighborhoods that work/ Mike Greenberg. Columbus: Ohio State University Press, c1995. xiv, 288 p.
94-026658   307.3/36216/0973   0814206565
City planning -- United States. Neighborhood -- United States -- Planning. Community development, Urban -- United States.

HT167.I57 1983
Introduction to planning history in the United States/ edited by Donald A. Krueckeberg. New Brunswick, N.J.: Center for Urban Policy Research, c1983. xiii, 302 p.
82-014572   307./12/0973   0882850830
City planning -- United States -- History.

HT167.5.C2.L68 1998
Loukaitou-Sideris, Anastasia, 1958-
Urban design downtown: poetics and politics of form/ Anastasia Loukaitou-Sideris and Tridib Banerjee. Berkeley: University of California Press, c1998. xxix, 350 p.
97-010758   307.1/216/09794 21   0520209303
City planning -- California -- Case studies. Central business districts -- California -- Case studies. Urban policy -- California -- Case studies.

HT168.G37.C38 1993
Catlin, Robert A.
Racial politics and urban planning: Gary, Indiana, 1980-1989/ Robert A. Catlin. Lexington: University Press of Kentucky, c1993. viii, 241 p.
92-043016   307.1/216/0977299   0813117984
Hatcher, Richard G., -- 1933-   City planning -- Indiana -- Gary.   Gary (Ind.) -- Race relations -- Political aspects.   Gary (Ind.) -- Politics and government.

HT168.N5.D66 1996
Domosh, Mona, 1957-
Invented cities: the creation of landscape in nineteenth-century New York & Boston/ Mona Domosh. New Haven: Yale University Press, c1996. x, 185 p.
95-006740   307.1/216/09747109034   20
0300062370
City planning -- New York (State) -- New York -- History -- 19th century. City planning -- Massachusetts -- Boston -- History -- 19th century. Landscape -- New York (State) -- New York -- History -- 19th century.

HT168.N5.P34 1999
Page, Max.
The creative destruction of Manhattan, 1900-1940/ Max Page. Chicago: University of Chicago Press, 1999. xiv, 303 p.
99-022544   307.1/216/09747109041
0226644685
City planning -- New York (State) -- New York -- History -- 20th century.   New York (N.Y.) -- Social conditions.   New York (N.Y.) -- Economic conditions.

HT168.N5.R45 1999
Reichl, Alexander J., 1960-
Reconstructing Times Square: politics and culture in urban development/ Alexander J. Reichl. Lawrence, Kan.: University Press of Kansas, c1999. xii, 239 p.
98-055259   307.1/216/097471 21   0700609490
City planning -- New York (State) -- Times Square (New York) Urban renewal -- New York (State) -- Times Square (New York) Special districts -- New York (State) -- Times Square (New York) New York (N.Y.) -- Politics and government. New York (N.Y.) -- Race relations.

HT168.S174.S74 1997
Stephenson, R. Bruce 1955-
Visions of Eden: environmentalism, urban planning, and city building in St. Petersburg, Florida, 1900-1995/ R. Bruce Stephenson. Columbus, OH: Ohio State University Press, 1997. ix, 234 p.
96-039627   307.1/216/0975963   0814207251
City planning -- Florida -- Saint Petersburg -- History. City planning -- Environmental aspects -- Florida -- Saint Petersburg -- History.

HT169.A5.B76 1997
Browder, John O.
Rainforest cities: urbanization, development, and globalization of the Brazilian Amazon/ John O. Browder and Brian J. Godfrey. New York: Columbia University Press, c1997. xxvi, 429 p.
96-033481   307.1/216/09811 20   0231106548
City planning -- Amazon River Region. Regional planning -- Amazon River Region. Land use, Rural -- Amazon River Region. Amazon River Region -- Social conditions. Amazon River Region -- Economic conditions.

HT169.C62.S999 2000
Xu, Yinong, 1961-
The Chinese city in space and time: the development of urban form in Suzhou/ Yinong Xu. Honolulu: University of Hawai'i Press, c2000. xi, 361 p.
99-037240   307.1/216/0951136 21   0824820762
City planning -- China -- Suzhou (Jiangsu Sheng) -- History. Urbanization -- China -- Suzhou (Jiangsu Sheng) -- History. Suzhou (Jiangsu Sheng, China) -- History.

HT169.F72.T68 1997
Wakeman, Rosemary.
Modernizing the provincial city: Toulouse, 1945-1975/ Rosemary Wakeman. Cambridge, Mass.: Harvard University Press, 1997. xii, 323 p.
97-023077   307.1/216/094862   0674580729
City planning -- France -- Toulouse -- History -- 20th century.   Toulouse (France) -- Economic conditions.

HT169.I82.J473 2000
Bollens, Scott A.
On narrow ground: urban policy and ethnic conflict in Jerusalem and Belfast/ Scott A. Bollens. Albany: State University of New York Press, c2000. xx, 415 p.
99-039693   307.76/0956952 21   0791444139
Urban policy -- Jerusalem. Urban policy -- Northern Ireland -- Belfast. Jerusalem -- Ethnic relations. Belfast (Northern Ireland) -- Ethnic relations.

HT169.57 Urban groups. The city. Urban sociology — City planning — Planned communities. New towns

HT169.57.U62.S45 1997
Kelbaugh, Doug.
Common place: toward neighborhood and regional design/ Douglas Kelbaugh. Seattle: University of Washington Press, c1997. x, 334 p.
96-042311   307.76/8/0979772 20   0295975903
Planned communities -- Washington (State) -- Seattle Region.

HT169.57.U62.S63 1995
Danielson, Michael N.
Profits and politics in paradise: the development of Hilton Head Island/ by Michael N. Danielson; with the assistance of Patricia R.F. Danielson. Columbia, S.C.: University of South Carolina Press, c1995. xv, 323 p.
95-004364   333.7/15/0975799   1570030391
Planned communities -- South Carolina -- Sea Pines Plantation -- History. Planned communities -- South Carolina -- Hilton Head Island -- History. City planning -- South Carolina -- Sea Pines Plantation -- History. Hilton Head Island (S.C.) -- History. Sea Pines Plantation (Hilton Head, S.C.) -- History.

HT175-178 Urban groups. The city. Urban sociology — Urban renewal. Urban redevelopment — By region or country

HT175.F75 1989
Frieden, Bernard J.
Downtown, Inc.: how America rebuilds cities/ Bernard J. Frieden, Lynne B. Sagalyn. Cambridge, Mass.: MIT Press, c1989. xiv, 382 p.
89-036211   307.3/4216/0973   0262061287
Urban renewal -- United States. Central business districts -- United States.

HT175.G56 1992
Gittell, Ross J., 1957-
Renewing cities/ Ross J. Gittell. Princeton, N.J.: Princeton University Press, 1992. x, 232 p.
92-010020   307.3/416/0973   0691042934
Urban renewal -- United States -- Case studies. Urban renewal -- Economic aspects -- United States -- Case studies. Community development, Urban -- United states -- Case studies.

HT175.K76 2000
Kromer, John, 1948-
Neighborhood recovery: reinvestment policy for the new hometown/ John Kromer. New Brunswick, N.J.: Rutgers University Press, c2000. x, 262 p.
99-028161   307.3/416/0973 21   0813527163
Urban renewal -- United States. Urban policy -- United States. Community development, Urban -- United States.

HT175.P32 1995
Pagano, Michael A.
Cityscapes and capital: the politics of urban development/ Michael A. Pagano and Ann O'M. Bowman. Baltimore: Johns Hopkins University Press, 1995. xvi, 190 p.
94-040582   307.3/416   0801850347
Urban renewal -- United States -- Case studies. Urban policy -- United States -- Case studies. Metropolitan government -- United States -- Case studies.

HT175.R48 1996
Revitalizing urban neighborhoods/ edited by W. Dennis Keating, Norman Krumholz, and Philip Star. Lawrence: University Press of Kansas, c1996. xv, 287 p.
96-018180   307.3/416/0973 20   0700607897
Urban renewal -- United States.

HT175.T38 2001
Tax increment financing and economic development: uses, structures, and impacts/ edited by Craig L. Johnson and Joyce Y. Man. Albany, NY: State University of New York Press, c2001. xi, 276 p.
00-057392   336.22/0973 21   0791449750
Tax increment financing -- United States. Urban renewal -- United States -- Finance.

HT177.B6R64 2000
Roessner, Jane.
A decent place to live: from Columbia Point to Harbor Point: a community history/ Jane Roessner. Boston: Northeastern University Press, c2000. x, 314 p.
99-086659   307.76/09744/61 21   1555534368
Urban renewal -- Massachusetts -- Boston -- History -- Case studies. City planning -- Massachusetts -- Boston -- History -- Case studies. Public housing -- Massachusetts -- Boston -- History -- Case studies.

HT177.C53.M55 1998
Miller, Zane L.
Changing plans for America's inner cities: Cincinnati's Over-The-Rhine and twentieth-century urbanism/ Zane L. Miller and Bruce Tucker. Columbus: Ohio State University Press, c1998. xxi, 227 p.
97-026206   307.3/416/0977178 21   0814207626
Urban renewal -- Ohio -- Cincinnati -- History. Over-the-Rhine (Cincinnati, Ohio) -- History.

HT177.D4.T56 1997
Thomas, June Manning.
Redevelopment and race: planning a finer city in postwar Detroit/ June Manning Thomas. Baltimore: Johns Hopkins University Press, c1997. xx, 274 p.
96-029370   307.1/216/0977434 20   080185444X
Urban renewal -- Michigan -- Detroit -- History. City planning -- Michigan -- Detroit -- History. Afro-Americans -- Michigan -- Detroit -- History. Detroit (Mich.) -- Race relations -- History.

HT177.S38.M34 1998
McGovern, Stephen J., 1959-
The politics of downtown development: dynamic political cultures in San Francisco and Washington, D.C./ Stephen J. McGovern. Lexington, Ky.: University Press of Kentucky, c1998. xiv, 342 p.
97-053074   307.3/42176/09753 21   0813120527
Urban renewal -- California -- San Francisco. Urban renewal -- Washington (D.C.) Central business districts -- California -- San Francisco.

HT178.C2.L49 1996
Ley, David.
The new middle class and the remaking of the central city/ David Ley. Oxford; Oxford University Press, 1996. xvi, 383 p.
96-011424   305.5/5/0971   0198232926
Gentrification -- Canada. Urban renewal -- Canada. Middle class -- Canada.

HT178.J3.G55 2001
Gilman, Theodore J., 1965-
No miracles here: fighting urban decline in Japan and the United States/ Theodore J. Gilman. Albany: State University of New York Press, c2001. xi, 208 p.
00-038771   307.3/416/0952 21   079144791X
Urban renewal -- Japan. Urban renewal -- United States. Urban policy -- Japan. Japan -- Social conditions. United States -- Social conditions.

HT206 Urban groups. The city. Urban sociology — City population — Children in cities

HT206.D327 1990
Dargan, Amanda, 1950-
City play/ by Amanda Dargan and Steven Zeitlin; photographs by Martha Cooper, Arthur Leipzig, and other great photographers of urban play; with an afterword by Barbara Kirshenblatt-Gimblett. New Brunswick: Rutgers University Press, c1990. xi, 212 p.
90-030667   305.23/09747/1   0813515777
Children -- New York (State) -- New York. Children -- New York (State) -- New York -- Pictorial works. Play -- New York (State) -- New York.

HT221 Urban groups. The city. Urban sociology — City population — Race relations in cities. Ethnic relations in cities

HT221.K46 2000
Kennedy, Liam, 1961-
Race and urban space in contemporary American culture/ Liam Kennedy. Edinburgh: Edinburgh University Press, c2000. xii, 178 p.
0748609520
Sociology, Urban -- United States. Cities and towns in literature. Cities and towns in mass media. United States -- Race relations.

HT243 Urban groups. The city. Urban sociology — Urban ecology

HT243.M62.M487 1998
Pezzoli, Keith.
Human settlements and planning for ecological sustainability: the case of Mexico City/ Keith Pezzoli. Cambridge, Mass.: MIT Press, c1998. xxi, 437 p.
97-039497   363.7/07/097253 21   0262161737
Land use -- Mexico -- Mexico City. Sustainable development -- Mexico -- Mexico City. Land use -- Mexico -- Mexico City -- Planning -- Citizen participation. Mexico City -- Environmental conditions. Ajusco (Mexico)

HT243.U6.E26 1994
The Ecological city: preserving and restoring urban biodiversity/ edited by Rutherford H. Platt, Rowan A. Rowntree, and Pamela C. Muick. Amherst: University of Massachusetts Press, c1994. x, 291 p.
93-026506   307.76   0870238833
Urban ecology -- United States. Urban geography -- United States. Urban forestry -- United States.

HT321 Urban groups. The city. Urban sociology — The city as an economic factor. Urban economics

HT321.H388 2000
Heikkila, Eric John.
The economics of planning/ Eric J. Heikkila. New Brunswick, N.J.: Center for Urban Policy Research, c2000. xxvii, 228 p.
99-031560   330.9173/2 21   0882851624
Urban economics. City planning -- Economic aspects. Regional planning -- Economic aspects.

HT321.M23 2000
Maki, Wilbur R.
Urban regional economics: concepts, tools, applications/ Wilbur R. Maki and Richard W. Lichty. Ames: Iowa State University Press, c2000. xviii, 496 p.
99-059767   330.9173/2 21   0813826799
Urban economics. Regional economics.

HT330 Urban groups. The city. Urban sociology — Metropolitan areas — General works

HT330.J66 1989
Jones, Emrys.
Metropolis/ Emrys Jones. Oxford; Oxford University Press, 1990. viii, 228 p.
89-022863   307.76/4   0192192353
Metropolitan areas. Cities and towns -- History.

HT334 Urban groups. The city. Urban sociology — Metropolitan areas — By region or country, A-Z

HT334.U5.S67 1992
Sources of metropolitan growth/ edited by Edwin S. Mills and John F. McDonald; Mary L. McLean, associate editor. New Brunswick, N.J.: Center for Urban Policy Research, c1992. xxvii, 307 p.
91-008650   307.1/416/0973   0882851357
Metropolitan areas -- United States -- Congresses. Cities and towns -- United States -- Growth -- Congresses. Industrial location -- United States -- Congresses.

HT352 Urban groups. The city. Urban sociology — Suburban cities and towns

HT352.C22.T674 1996
Harris, Richard, 1952-
Unplanned suburbs: Toronto's American tragedy, 1900 to 1950/ Richard Harris. Baltimore: Johns Hopkins University Press, 1996. xvi, 356 p.
95-031010   307.76/09713/541   0801851424
Suburbs -- Ontario -- Toronto -- History. Toronto Suburban Area (Ont.) -- History.

HT352.U6.L36 1994
Langdon, Philip.
A better place to live: reshaping the American suburb/ Philip Langdon. Amherst: University of Massachusetts Press, c1994. xvi, 270 p.
93-042348   307.1/216/0973   0870239147
Suburbs -- United States -- Planning.

HT352.U6.L83 2000
Lucy, William H.
Confronting suburban decline: strategic planning for metropolitan renewal/ William H. Lucy, David L. Phillips. Washington, D.C.; Covelo, Calif.: Island Press, c2000. xxi, 321 p.
99-050952   307.1/216/0973 21   1559637706
Suburbs -- United States. Suburbs -- United States -- Case studies. Urban policy -- United States. United States -- Social conditions -- 1960-

HT352.U6.R68 1991
Rowe, Peter G.
Making a middle landscape/ Peter G. Rowe. Cambridge, Mass.: MIT Press, c1991. 325 p.
90-006674   307.76/0973   026218138X
Suburbs -- United States. City planning -- United States. Public spaces -- United States -- Planning.

HT352.U6.S75 1988
Stilgoe, John R., 1949-
Borderland: origins of the American suburb, 1820-1939/ John R. Stilgoe. New Haven: Yale University Press, c1988. xiv, 353 p.
88-013981   307.7/4/0973   0300042574
Suburbs -- United States -- History -- 19th century. Suburbs -- United States -- History -- 20th century. Landscape -- United States -- History -- 19th century.

HT361 Urban groups. The city. Urban sociology — Urbanization. City and country — General works

HT361.H35 1990
Hamer, D. A.
New towns in the New World: images and perceptions of the nineteenth-century urban frontier/ David Hamer. New York: Columbia University Press, c1990. ix, 328 p.
89-027777   307.76/09   0231066201
Urbanization -- History -- 19th century. Urbanization -- United States -- History -- 19th century. Urbanization -- Australia -- History -- 19th century.

HT371 Urban groups. The city. Urban sociology — Urbanization. City and country — Growth of cities

HT371.L64 1995
Logan, Michael F., 1950-
Fighting sprawl and City Hall: resistance to urban growth in the Southwest/ Michael F. Logan. Tucson: University of Arizona Press, c1995. viii, 223 p.
95-005590   307.1/716/09791776   0816515123
Cities and towns -- Growth. Opposition (Political science) Albuquerque (N.M.) -- Politics and government. Tucson (Ariz.) -- Politics and government.

HT381 Urban groups. The city. Urban sociology — Urbanization. City and country — Movement to the country

HT381.J33 1997
Jacob, Jeffrey, 1942-
New pioneers: the back-to-the-land movement and the search for a sustainable future/ Jeffrey Jacob. University Park, Penn.: Pennsylvania State University Press, c1997. xvi, 262 p.
96-012913   307.2/6/0973 20   0271016213
Urban-rural migration -- United States. Country life -- United States.

HT381.W65 1999
Wolf, Peter M.
Hot towns: the future of the fastest growing communities in America/ Peter Wolf. New Brunswick, N.J.: Rutgers University Press, c1999. xi, 283 p.
99-011942   307.2/4/0973 21   0813526965
Urban-rural migration -- United States. Cities and towns -- United States -- Ratings. United States -- Rural conditions.

HT384 Urban groups. The city. Urban sociology — Urbanization. City and country — By region or country, A-Z

HT384.C37.U695 1997
The Urban Caribbean: transition to the new global economy/ edited by Alejandro Portes, Carlos Dore-Cabral, and Patricia Landolt. Baltimore, Md.: Johns Hopkins University, [1997] xvii, 260 p.
96-035184   307.76/09729   0801855179
Urbanization -- Caribbean Area. Caribbean Area -- Economic conditions. Caribbean Area -- Social conditions.

HT384.C6.G38 1996
Gaubatz, Piper Rae, 1962-
Beyond the Great Wall: urban form and transformation on the Chinese frontiers/ Piper Rae Gaubatz. Stanford, Calif.: Stanford University Press, 1996. xvii, 378 p.
95-002555   307.76/0973   0804723990
Urbanization -- China -- History. Cities and towns -- China -- Growth -- History. City planning -- China -- History.

HT384.C6.Y87 1997
Yusuf, Shahid, 1949-
The dynamics of urban growth in three Chinese cities/ Shahid Yusuf, Weiping Wu. New York: Oxford University Press, c1997. xi, 229 p.
97-002013   307.76/0951 21   0195211138
Urbanization -- China -- Case studies. Industrialization -- China -- Case studies. Shanghai (China) -- Economic conditions. Tianjin (China) -- Economic conditions. Guangzhou (China) -- Economic conditions.

HT384.G7.W54 1990
Williamson, Jeffrey G., 1935-
Coping with city growth during the British Industrial Revolution/ Jeffrey G. Williamson. Cambridge [England]; Cambridge University Press, 1990. xxi, 344 p.
89-027453   307.76/0941/09033   0521364809
Cities and towns -- Great Britain -- Growth -- History -- 19th century. Industrial revolution -- Great Britain. Great Britain -- Economic conditions -- 1760-1860.

HT384.G8.L46 1990
Leontidou, Lila.
The Mediterranean city in transition: social change and urban development/ Lila Leontidou. Cambridge; Cambridge University Press, 1990. xviii, 296 p.
89-007346   307.76/09495/0904   0521344670
Urbanization -- Greece -- History -- 20th century -- Case studies. Cities and towns -- Greece -- Growth -- History -- 20th century -- Case studies. Urbanization -- Mediterranean Region -- History -- 20th century.

HT384.I66.P76 1995
Proudfoot, L. J.
Urban patronage and social authority: the management of the Duke of Devonshire's towns in Ireland, 1764-1891/ Lindsay J. Proudfoot. Washington, D.C.: Catholic University of America Press, c1995. xiv, 398 p.
94-022416   307.76/09415   081320819X
Devonshire, Dukes of. City planning -- Ireland -- History. Administration of estates -- Ireland -- History. Urbanization -- Ireland -- History.

HT384.I67.W48 2001
Wheatley, Paul.
The places where men pray together: cities in Islamic lands, seventh through the tenth centuries/ Paul Wheatley. Chicago: University of Chicago Press, c2001. xviii, 572 p.
99-049896   307.76/0917/671 21   0226894282
Urbanization -- Islamic countries. Cities and towns -- Islamic countries.

HT384.M62.M483 1994
Davis, Diane E., 1953-
Urban leviathan: Mexico City in the twentieth century/ Diane E. Davis. Philadelphia: Temple University Press, 1994. xiii, 391 p.
93-023069   307.76/0972/53   1566391504
Urbanization -- Mexico -- Mexico City -- History -- 20th century. Mexico City (Mexico) -- Politics and government. Mexico City (Mexico) -- Economic conditions.

HT384.T34.L84 1995
Lugalla, Joe.
Crisis, urbanization, and urban poverty in Tanzania: a study of urban poverty and survival politics/ Joe Lugalla. Lanham, MD: University Press of America, c1995. xxi, 223 p.
94-032954   307.76/09678   0819197416
Urbanization -- Tanzania. Urban poor -- Tanzania. Tanzania -- Economic conditions.

HT384.U5.W55 2000
Williams, Donald C.
Urban sprawl: a reference handbook/ Donald C. Williams. Santa Barbara, Calif.: ABC-CLIO, c2000. xiii, 264 p.
00-011033   307.76/0973 21   1576072258
Cities and towns -- United States -- Growth. City planning -- United States -- History. Land use -- United States -- History.

HT384.U52.A135 1990
Larsen, Lawrence Harold, 1931-
The urban South: a history/ Lawrence H. Larsen. Lexington, KY: University Press of Kentucky, c1990. xiii, 199 p.
89-034162   307.76/0975   0813103096
Urbanization -- Southern States -- History. Cities and towns -- Southern States -- History.

HT391 Urban groups. The city. Urban sociology — Regional planning — General works

HT391.B83 1996
Bush, David M.
Living by the rules of the sea/ David M. Bush, Orrin H. Pilkey, and William J. Neal. Durham, N.C.: Duke University Press, 1996. xiii, 179 p.
95-050855   333.91/7   0822318016
Coastal zone management. Hurricane protection. Barrier islands.

HT391.C494 1996
Clark, John R., 1927-
Coastal zone management handbook/ John R. Clark. Boca Raton, FL: Lewis Publishers, c1996. 694 p.
95-010219   333.78/4 20   1566700922
Coastal zone management. Coastal zone management -- Case studies.

HT391.N58 2000
Nordstrom, Karl F.
Beaches and dunes of developed coasts/ Karl F. Nordstrom. New York: Cambridge University Press, 2000. xiii, 338 p.
99-013766   333.91/7   0521470137
Coastal zone management. Coastal ecology. Coasts.

HT392-395 Urban groups. The city. Urban sociology — Regional planning — By region or country

HT392.H35
Hansen, Niles M.
Rural poverty and the urban crisis; a strategy for regional development [by] Niles M. Hansen. Bloomington, Indiana University Press [1970] xv, 352 p.
72-108207   309.2/5/0973   0253190020
Regional planning -- United States. Economic assistance, Domestic -- United States. Rural poor -- United States.

HT394.L67E34 2000
Eden by design: the 1930 Olmsted-Bartholomew plan for the Los Angeles region/ Greg Hise and William Deverell; afterword by Laurie Olin. Berkeley: University of California Press, 2000. ix, 314 p.
99-045101   711/.4/0979494   0520224159
Regional planning -- California -- Los Angeles Metropolitan Area -- History.

HT394.L67.H57 1997
Hise, Greg.
Magnetic Los Angeles: planning the twentieth-century metropolis/ Greg Hise. Baltimore: Johns Hopkins University Press, 1997. xiii, 294 p.
96-050423   307.1/216/0979494   0801855438
Regional planning -- California -- Los Angeles Metropolitan Area. Land use -- California -- Los Angeles Metropolitan Area -- Planning.

HT395.S62.E375 1999
Nel, Etienne Louis.
Regional and local economic development in South Africa: the experience of the Eastern Cape/ Etienne Louis Nel. Aldershot, Hants, England; Ashgate, c1999. xi, 359 p.
99-072648   1840149418
Regional planning -- South Africa -- Eastern Cape. Eastern Cape (South Africa) -- Economic policy.

HT609 Classes — General works

HT609.S57 1996
Sitton, John F., 1952-
Recent Marxian theory: class formation and social conflict in contemporary capitalism/ by John F. Sitton. Albany: State University of New York Press, c1996. xiii, 358 p.
95-031700   305.5 20   0791429415
Social classes. Social conflict. Proletariat.

HT609.W698 1997
Wright, Erik Olin.
Class counts: comparative studies in class analysis/ Erik Olin Wright. Cambridge; Cambridge University Press; 1997. xxxv, 576 p.
96-011871   305.5   0521553873
Social classes. Social mobility. Class consciousness.

HT653 Classes — Classes arising from birth — Nobility. Aristocracy

HT653.I8.C35 1997
Cardoza, Anthony L., 1947-
Aristocrats in bourgeois Italy: the Piedmontese nobility, 1861-1930/ Anthony L. Cardoza. Cambridge, UK; Cambridge University Press, 1997. xiv, 248 p.
97-001848   305.5/223/09451   0521593034
Nobility -- Italy -- Piemonte -- History. Nobility -- Italy -- Piemonte -- Political activity. Nobility -- Italy -- Piemonte -- Economic conditions. Piemonte (Italy) -- History.

HT653.I8.S59 1995
Skinner, Patricia, 1965-
Family power in southern Italy: the duchy of Gaeta and its neighbours, 850-1139/ Patricia Skinner. Cambridge; Cambridge University Press, 1995. xii, 322 p.
94-009512   305.5/223/0945623   052146479X
Nobility -- Italy -- Gaeta -- History. Nobility -- Italy -- Amalfi -- History. Nobility -- Italy -- Naples -- History. Italy, Southern -- Social conditions. Italy, Southern -- History -- 535-1268.

HT653.M6.N88 1995
Nutini, Hugo G.
The wages of conquest: the Mexican aristocracy in the context of Western aristocracies/ Hugo G. Nutini. Ann Arbor: University of Michigan Press, c1995. xviii, 444 p.
94-024553   305.5/2/0972   0472104845
Aristocracy (Social class) -- Mexico -- History.

HT687-690 Classes — Classes arising from occupation — Middle class

HT687.B75 1994
Brint, Steven G.
In an age of experts: the changing role of professionals in politics and public life/ Steven Brint. Princeton, N.J.: Princeton University Press, c1994. x, 278 p.
93-050578   305.5/53   0691033994
Professions -- Social aspects -- United States. Middle class -- United States. Intellectuals -- United States.

HT687.H26 1991
Haber, Samuel.
The quest for authority and honor in the American professions, 1750-1900/ Samuel Haber. Chicago: University of Chicago Press, 1991. xiv, 478 p.
90-046752   305.5/53/0973   0226311732
Professions -- Social aspects -- United States -- History. Social status -- United States -- History. Occupational prestige -- United States -- History.

HT687.H5 1992
Hidden technocrats: the new class and new capitalism/ [edited by] Hansfried Kellner, Frank W. Heuberger. New Brunswick, U.S.A.: Transaction Publishers, c1992. xi, 246 p.
91-012907   305.5/5   0887384439
Middle class. Technocracy. Professions.

HT687.K68 1996
Krause, Elliott A.
Death of the guilds: professions, states, and the advance of capitalism, 1930 to the present/ Elliott A. Krause. New Haven, Conn.: Yale University Press, c1996. xi, 305 p.
96-001040   305.5/53 20   0300067585
Professions -- Sociological aspects. Power (Social sciences)

HT690.B7.O95 1999
Owensby, Brian Philip, 1959-
Intimate ironies: modernity and the making of middle-class lives in Brazil/ Brian P. Owensby. Stanford, Calif.: Stanford University Press, 1999. xiii, 332 p
98-046129   305.5/5/0981   0804733600
Middle class -- Brazil -- History. Social change -- Brazil.

HT690.E73.C7613 1995
Crossick, Geoffrey.
The petite bourgeoisie in Europe, 1780-1914: enterprise, family, and independence/ Geoffrey Crossick and Heinz-Gerhard Haupt. London; Routledge, 1995.
95-013871   305.5/5/094   0415118824
Middle class -- Europe -- History -- 19th century. Europe -- Social conditions -- 1789-1900.

HT690.G7.H85 1996
Hunt, Margaret R., 1953-
The middling sort: commerce, gender, and the family in England, 1680-1780/ Margaret R. Hunt. Berkeley: University of California Press, c1996. xiii, 343 p.
96-018063   305.5/0942 20   0520202600
Middle class -- Great Britain -- History -- 17th century. Middle class -- Great Britain -- History -- 18th century. Middle class families -- Great Britain -- History -- 17th century.

HT690.K8.L48 1998
Lett, Denise Potrzeba, 1956-
In pursuit of status: the making of South Korea's "new" urban middle class/ Denise Potrzeba Lett. Cambridge, (Mass.): Harvard University Asia Center; distributed by 1998. ix, 256 p.
97-037532 305.5/5/095195 0674445953
Middle class -- Korea (South) Social status -- Korea (South) Korea (South) -- Social conditions.

HT690.P4.P37 1998
Parker, D. S. 1960-
The idea of the middle class: white-collar workers and Peruvian society, 1900-1950/ D.S. Parker. University Park, Pa.: Pennsylvania State University Press, c1998. xii, 266 p.
97-016294 305.5/5/0985 21 0271017430
Middle class -- Peru. White collar workers -- Peru. Peru -- Social conditions.

HT855 Classes — Slavery — Congresses

HT855.S58 1991
Slavery and the rise of the Atlantic system/ edited by Barbara L. Solow. Cambridge: Cambridge University Press; 1991. viii, 355 p.
90-044953 380.1/44/091821 0521400902
Slave-trade -- Africa -- Congresses. Slave-trade -- Europe -- Congresses. Slave-trade -- America -- Congresses.

HT861 Slavery — History — General

HT861.H57 1997
The Historical encyclopedia of world slavery/ Junius P. Rodriguez, general editor. Santa Barbara, Calif.: ABC-CLIO, 1997. 2 v.
97-042839 306.3/62/03 0874368855
Slavery -- Encyclopedias.

HT861.H59 1998
A historical guide to world slavery/ edited by Seymour Drescher and Stanley L. Engerman. New York: Oxford University press, 1998. xxiv, 429 p.
97-047659 306.3/62 0195120914
Slavery -- History. Slavery -- Cross-cultural studies. Antislavery movements -- History.

HT867 Classes — Slavery — History

HT867.B35 1999
Bales, Kevin.
Disposable people: new slavery in the global economy/ Kevin Bales. Berkeley, Calif.: University of California Press, c1999. 298 p.
98-047869 306.3/62 21 0520217977
Slavery. Slave labor. Poor -- Employment.

HT867.B37 2000
Bales, Kevin.
New slavery: a reference handbook/ Kevin Bales. Santa Barbara, CA: ABC-CLIO, Inc., 2000. xvii, 225 p.
00-010873 306.3/62/0904 1576072398
Slavery -- History -- 20th century.

HT867.B87 2000
Bush, M. L.
Servitude in modern times/ M.L. Bush. Cambridge; Polity Press, 2000. xii, 292 p.
00-035645 331.11/73/09 0745617298
Slavery -- History. Forced labor -- History. Serfdom -- History.

HT985 Classes — Slavery — The slave trade

HT985.T47 1997
Thomas, Hugh, 1931-
The slave trade: the story of the Atlantic slave trade, 1440-1870/ Hugh Thomas. New York, NY: Simon & Schuster, c1997. 908 p.
97-017234 382/.44 21 0684810638
Slave-trade -- History.

HT1048-1394 Classes — Slavery — By region or country

HT1048.E47 2000
Eltis, David, 1940-
The rise of African slavery in the Americas/ David Eltis. Cambridge, UK; Cambridge University Press, 2000. xvii, 353 p.
99-013352 306.3/62/097 0521652316
Slavery -- America -- History. Slave trade -- America -- History. Colonies -- America -- History. Great Britain -- Colonies -- America -- History.

HT1049.M62 1996
More than chattel: Black women and slavery in the Americas/ edited by David Barry Gaspar and Darlene Clark Hine. Bloomington: Indiana University Press, c1996. xi, 341 p.
95-036096 306.3/62/082 20 0253330173
Slavery -- America. Women slaves -- America -- Social conditions. Women, Black -- America -- Social conditions.

HT1071.B44 1999
Beckles, Hilary, 1955-
Centering woman: gender discourses in Caribbean slave society/ Hilary McD. Beckles. Kingston: I. Randle; 1999. xxv, 211 p.
98-043652 305.42/09729 9768123796
Women slaves -- Caribbean Area -- Social conditions. Women -- Caribbean Area -- History -- 17th century. Women -- Caribbean Area -- History -- 18th century.

HT1072.S75 1995
Stinchcombe, Arthur L.
Sugar island slavery in the age of enlightenment: the political economy of the Caribbean world/ Arthur L. Stinchcombe. Princeton, N.J.: Princeton University Press, c1995. xiv, 361 p.
95-009227 306.3/62/09729 0691029954
Slavery -- Caribbean Area -- History. Slave-trade -- Caribbean Area -- History. Sugar workers -- Caribbean Area -- History.

HT1078.S38 1999
Schmidt-Nowara, Christopher.
Empire and antislavery: Spain, Cuba, and Puerto Rico, 1833-1874/ Christopher Schmidt-Nowara. Pittsburgh: University of Pittsburgh Press, c1999. xiii, 239 p.
99-006423 326/.8/09171246 21 0822940892
Antislavery movements -- Puerto Rico. Antislavery movements -- Spain. Antislavery movements -- Cuba. Spain -- Colonies -- America.

HT1079.E4
Diaz, Maria Elena, 1955-
The Virgin, the king, and the royal slaves of El Cobre: negotiating freedom in colonial Cuba, 1670-1780/ Maria Elena Diaz. Stanford, Calif.: Stanford University Press, 2000. xviii, 440 p.
00-032197 306.3/62/09729165 0804737185
Slavery -- Cuba -- El Cobre -- History. Caridad, Virgen de la. El Cobre (Cuba) -- Social conditions.

HT1096.M4 1993
McDonald, Roderick A. 1947-
The economy and material culture of slaves: goods and chattels on the sugar plantations of Jamaica and Louisiana/ Roderick A. McDonald. Baton Rouge: Louisiana State University Press, c1993. xiv, 339 p.
93-000392 306.3/62/097292 0807117943
Slavery -- Jamaica -- History. Slavery -- Louisiana -- History. Sugar trade -- Jamaica -- History.

HT1107.S58 2000
Slavery in the Caribbean Francophone world: distant voices, forgotten acts, forged identities/ edited by Doris Y. Kadish. Athens: University of Georgia Press, c2000. xxiii, 247 p.
99-037913 306.3/62/0972976 21 0820321664
Slavery -- West Indies, French -- History -- Congresses. Slave insurrections -- West Indies, French -- History -- Congresses. Slaves -- West Indies, French -- Social conditions -- Congresses.

HT1108.M3.T66 1990
Tomich, Dale W., 1946-
Slavery in the circuit of sugar: Martinique and the world economy, 1830-1848/ Dale W. Tomich. Baltimore: Johns Hopkins University Press, c1990. xiv, 353 p.
89-026678 306.3/62/0972982 0801839181
Slavery -- Martinique -- History -- 19th century. Slave labor -- Martinique -- History -- 19th century. Sugarcane industry -- Martinique -- History -- 19th century. Martinique -- Economic conditions.

HT1119.V6.H36 1992
Hall, N. A. T.
Slave society in the Danish West Indies: St. Thomas, St. John, and St. Croix/ Neville A.T. Hall; edited by B.W. Higman. Baltimore: Johns Hopkins University Press, c1992. xxiv, 287 p.
92-006844 306.3/62/09729722 0801844738
Slavery -- Virgin Islands of the United States -- History. Slaves -- Virgin Islands of the United States -- Social conditions.

HT1126.S39 1992
Schwartz, Stuart B.
Slaves, peasants, and rebels: reconsidering Brazilian slavery/ Stuart B. Schwartz. Urbana; University of Illinois Press, c1992. xiv, 174 p.
91-021938 306.3/62/0981 0252018745
Slavery -- Brazil.

HT1148.L56.H87 1994
Hunefeldt, Christine.
Paying the price of freedom: family and labor among Lima's slaves, 1800-1854/ Christine Hunefeldt; translated by Alexandra Stern. Berkeley: University of California Press, c1994. xi, 269 p.
94-004507 306.3/62/098525 0520082354
Slavery -- Peru -- Lima -- History -- 19th century. Slaves -- Peru -- Lima -- Family relationships -- History -- 19th century.

HT1178.J46 2000
Jennings, Lawrence C.
French anti-slavery: the movement for the abolition of slavery in France, 1802-1848/ Lawrence C. Jennings. Cambridge, UK; Cambridge University Press, 2000. x, 320 p.
99-045555   326/.8/094409034   0521772494
Slaves -- Emancipation -- France -- History -- 19th century -- Sources. Slavery -- France -- History -- 19th century -- Sources.

HT1191.E67 2001
Epstein, Steven, 1952-
Speaking of slavery: color, ethnicity, and human bondage in Italy/ Steven A. Epstein. Ithaca: Cornell University Press, 2001. xiv, 215 p.
00-010868   306.3/62/0945   0801438489
Slavery -- Italy -- History. Ethnicity -- Italy -- History.

HT1211.K37 1988
Karras, Ruth Mazo, 1957-
Slavery and society in medieval Scandinavia/ Ruth Mazo Karras. New Haven [Conn.]: Yale University Press, c1988. x, 309 p.
87-032167   306/.362/0948   0300041217
Slavery -- Scandinavia -- History. Social history -- Medieval, 500-1500. Slavery -- Europe -- History. Scandinavia -- Social conditions. Europe -- Social conditions -- To 1492.

HT1238.E73 1996
Erdem, Y. Hakan.
Slavery in the Ottoman Empire and its demise, 1800-1909/ Y. Hakan Erdem. Houndmills, Basingstoke, Hampshire: Macmillan Press; 1996. xxii, 229 p.
96-007125   306.3/62/0956/09034   0333643232
Slavery -- Turkey -- History -- 19th century. Slave-trade -- Turkey -- History -- 19th century. Antislavery movements -- History. Turkey -- History -- Ottoman Empire, 1288-1918.

HT1316.T65 1998
Toledano, Ehud R.
Slavery and abolition in the Ottoman Middle East/ Ehud R. Toledano. Seattle: University of Washington Press, c1998. xii, 185 p.
97-009571   306.3/62/0956 21   029597642X
Slavery -- Middle East -- History. Slave-trade -- Middle East -- History. Slavery and Islam -- History. Turkey -- History -- Ottoman Empire, 1288-1918.

HT1322.K54 1999
Klein, Herbert S.
The Atlantic slave trade/ Herbert S. Klein. Cambridge, U.K.; Cambridge University Press, 1999. xxi, 234 p.
98-034549   382/.44   0521460204
Slave trade -- Africa. Slave trade -- Europe. Slave trade -- America.

HT1381.J65 2001
Jok, Jok Madut.
War and slavery in Sudan/ Jok Madut Jok. Philadelphia: University of Pennsylvania Press, c2001. xv, 211 p.
00-052774   305.8/009624 21   0812235959
Slavery -- Sudan. Racism -- Sudan. Sudan -- History -- Civil War, 1983-

HT1394.I43.O34 1997
O'Hear, Ann.
Power relations in Nigeria: Ilorin slaves and their successors/ Ann O'Hear. Rochester, NY, USA: University of Rochester Press, 1997. x, 338 p.
97-020263   305.5/67/0966957   1878822861
Slavery -- Nigeria -- Ilorin -- History -- 19th century. Elite (Social sciences) -- Nigeria -- Ilorin -- History -- 20th century. Great Britain -- Colonies -- Africa -- Administration. Ilorin (Nigeria) -- Social conditions. Ilorin (Nigeria) -- History. Ilorin (Nigeria) -- Politics and government.

HT1521 Races — General works

HT1521.F84 1998
Furedi, Frank, 1947-
The silent war: imperialism and the changing perception of race/ Frank Furedi. New Brunswick, N.J.: Rutgers University Press, 1998. 282 p.
98-036640   305.8/009/04   0813526116
Race relations -- History -- 20th century. Racism -- History -- 20th century. World politics -- 20th century.

HT1521.G54 1997
Global convulsions: race, ethnicity, and nationalism at the end of the twentieth century/ edited by Winston A. Van Horne. Albany: State University of New York Press, c1997. xx, 364 p.
96-015321   305.8 20   0791432351
Race relations. Racism. Ethnicity.

HT1521.M283 1998
Marx, Anthony W.
Making race and nation: a comparison of South Africa, the United States, and Brazil/ Anthony W. Marx. Cambridge, U.K.; Cambridge University Press, 1998. xviii, 390 p.
97-020437   305.8   0521584558
Race discrimination -- Case studies. Race relations -- Case studies. Brazil -- Race relations. South Africa -- Race relations. United States -- Race relations.

HT1523 Races — General special

HT1523.N63 2000
Nobles, Melissa.
Shades of citizenship: race and the census in modern politics/ Melissa Nobles. Stanford, CA: Stanford University Press, 2000. xiv, 248 p.
00-026707   305.8/007/2   0804740135
Race. Group identity. Census. United States -- Census. Brazil -- Census.

HT1523.P27 1997
Parikh, Sunita, 1959-
The politics of preference: democratic institutions and affirmative action in the United States and India/ Sunita Parikh. Ann Arbor: University of Michigan Press, c1997. ix, 230 p.
96-025176   305.8/00973 20   0472107453
Race discrimination -- Government policy -- United States -- History. Minorities -- Government policy -- United States -- History. Affirmative action programs -- Government policy -- United States -- History. United States -- Politics and government -- 1989- United States -- Politics and government -- 1945-1989. India -- Politics and government -- 1857-1919.

HT1581 Races — By race — Black. Hamitic

HT1581.G694 1997
Globalization and survival in the Black diaspora: the new urban challenge/ edited by Charles Green. Albany: State University of New York Press, c1997. 396 p.
96-041495   305.8/96 20   079143415X
Blacks -- Social conditions. Blacks -- Economic conditions. Poverty.

HT1581.M35 1993
McKee, James B., 1919-
Sociology and the race problem: the failure of a perspective/ James B. McKee. Urbana, Ill.: University of Illinois Press, c1993. 376 p.
92-042293   305.8/00973   0252020227
Blacks. Afro-Americans. United States -- Race relations.

HV Social pathology. Social and public welfare. Criminology

HV10.5 Social work as a profession

HV10.5.R42 1990
Reamer, Frederic G.,
Ethical dilemmas in social service/ Frederic G. Reamer. 2nd ed. New York: Columbia University Press, c1990. xvii, 266 p.
89-022124   174/.9362 20   0231069685
Social service -- Moral and ethical aspects. Social workers -- Professional ethics. Social service -- United States.

HV11 Study and teaching. Research. Schools. Social work education — General works

HV11.H342 2001
The handbook of social work research methods/ edited by Bruce A. Thyer. Thousand Oaks, Calif.: Sage Publications, c2001. xiv, 546 p.
00-010587   361/.007/2 21   0761919058
Social service -- Research.

HV11.I565 1995
International handbook on social work education/ edited by Thomas D. Watts, Doreen Elliott, and Nazneen S. Mayadas; foreword by Katherine A. Kendall. Westport, Conn.: Greenwood Press, 1995. xvii, 453 p.
95-006674   361.3/2/07   0313279152
Social work education -- Handbooks, manuals, etc.

HV11.I93 1994
Ivanoff, Andre Marie.
Involuntary clients in social work practice: a research-based approach/ Andre Ivanoff, Betty J. Blythe, and Tony Tripodi. New York: Aldine de Gruyter, c1994. xiii, 239 p.
93-036647　361.3/2 20　0202360873
Social service -- Research -- Methodology. Social service.

HV11.S493 1999
Shulman, Lawrence.
The skills of helping individuals, families, groups and communities/ Lawrence Shulman. 4th ed. Itasca, Ill.: F.E. Peacock, c1999. xxiii, 884 p.
97-076294　361.3 21　087581414X
Social work education.

HV11.T75
Tripodi, Tony.
Uses & abuses of social research in social work. New York, Columbia University Press, 1974. xii, 222 p.
73-017280　361/.007/2　0231036620
Social service -- Research. Social service -- Sociological aspects. Sociology -- Research.

HV12 Dictionaries. Encyclopedias

HV12.B53 2000
The Blackwell encyclopaedia of social work/ edited by Martin Davies; assistant editor Rose Barton. Oxford; Blackwell, 2000. xviii, 412 p.
00-037953　361.3/2/03　063121450X
Social service -- Encyclopedias.

HV12.I58 1990
International encyclopedia of foundations/ Joseph C. Kiger, editor-in-chief; foreword by Thomas R. Buckman. New York: Greenwood Press, 1990. xxi, 355 p.
89-023246　361.7/632/03　0313259836
Endowments -- Handbooks, manuals, etc.

HV12.T54 1982
Timms, Noel.
Dictionary of social welfare/ Noel and Rita Timms. London; Routledge & K. Paul, 1982. vi, 217 p.
82-005385　361/.003/21　0710090846
Social service -- Dictionaries. Social policy -- Dictionaries.

HV16 History of philanthropy — General

HV16.B74 1996
Bremner, Robert Hamlett, 1917-
Giving: charity and philanthropy in history/ Robert H. Bremner; with a new afterword by the author. New Brunswick, N.J., U.S.A.: Transaction Publishers, 1996. xiii, 241 p.
93-014165　361.7/09　1560001372
Charities -- History.

HV16.P46 1998
Philanthropy in the world's traditions/ edited by Warren F. Ilchman, Stanley N. Katz, and Edward L. Queen, II. Bloomington: Indiana University Press, c1998. xv, 382 p.
97-051241　361.7/632/09 21　025333392X
Charities -- Cross-cultural studies. Charities -- History -- Cross-cultural studies. Social service -- Cross-cultural studies.

HV28 Biography — Individual, A-Z

HV28.A35.L47
Levine, Daniel, 1934-
Jane Addams and the liberal tradition. Madison, State Historical Society of Wisconsin, 1971. xviii, 277 p.
70-634145　361/.924　0870201093
Addams, Jane, -- 1860-1935.

HV28.A35.L5
Linn, James Weber, 1876-1939.
Jane Addams; a biography, by James Weber Linn ... New York, Appleton-Century Company, Incorporated, 1935. 457 p.
35-018354　923.673
Addams, Jane, -- 1860-1935. Women social reformers -- United States -- Biography. Women social workers -- United States -- Biography.

HV28.D6.B75 1998
Brown, Thomas J., 1960-
Dorothea Dix: New England reformer/ Thomas J. Brown. Cambridge, Mass.: Harvard University Press, 1998. xv, 422 p.
97-044207　362.2/1/092　0674214889
Dix, Dorothea Lynde, -- 1802-1887. Women social reformers -- United States -- Biography. Unitarians -- United States -- Biography. Mentally ill -- Care -- United States -- History.

HV28.D6.G65 1995
Gollaher, David, 1949-
Voice for the mad: the life of Dorothea Dix/ David Gollaher. New York: Free Press, c1995. xi, 538 p.
95-004134　362.2/1/092 B 20　0029123992
Dix, Dorothea Lynde, -- 1802-1887. Women social reformers -- United States -- Biography. Mentally ill -- Care -- United States -- History.

HV28.H66.H66 1999
Hopkins, June, 1940-
Harry Hopkins: sudden hero, brash reformer/ June Hopkins. New York: St. Martin's Press, 1999. x, 271 p.
98-037963　361.2/4/092　0312212062
Hopkins, Harry Lloyd, -- 1890-1946. Social reformers -- United States -- Biography. Public welfare -- United States -- History -- 20th century. New Deal, 1933-1939. United States -- Social policy.

HV28.L66.W38 1997
Waugh, Joan.
Unsentimental reformer: the life of Josephine Shaw Lowell/ Joan Waugh. Cambridge, Mass.: Harvard University Press, 1997. 296 p.
97-015647　361.92　0674930363
Lowell, Josephine Shaw, -- 1843-1905. Women social reformers -- New York (State) -- Biography. Women philanthropists -- New York (State) -- Biography.

HV28.M3 W5
Wilson, Howard Eugene,
Mary McDowell, neighbor, by Howard E. Wilson. Chicago, Ill., The University of Chicago Press [1928] 235 p.
29-003139
McDowell, Mary E., 1854-

HV28.P4 P29 1995
Parker, Franklin,
George Peabody, a biography/ Franklin Parker; foreword by Merle Curti. Rev. ed. Nashville: Vanderbilt University Press, 1995. xv, 278 p.
94-024306　361.7/4/092.aB 20　0826512569
Peabody, George 1795-1869. Philanthropists -- United States -- Biography. Capitalists and financiers -- United States -- Biography.

HV28.P67
Hall, Randal L., 1971-
William Louis Poteat: a leader of the progressive-era South/ Randal L. Hall. Lexington, Ky.: University Press of Kentucky, c2000. 262 p.
99-049444　378.756/55 21　0813121558
Poteat, William Louis, -- 1856-1938. Biology teachers -- North Carolina -- Biography. College teachers -- North Carolina -- Biography. Baptists -- North Carolina -- Biography.

HV28.R48 A3 1991
Reynolds, Bertha Capen,
An uncharted journey: fifty years of growth in social work/ Bertha C. Reynolds. 3rd ed. Silver Spring, MD: NASW Press, 1991. 352 p.
90-028265　361.3/2/092.aB 20　087101193X
Reynolds, Bertha Capen, 1885- Social workers -- United States -- Biography.

HV29.2 Data processing — General works

HV29.2.M87 1991
Murphy, John W.
The computerization of human service agencies: a critical appraisal/ John W. Murphy and John T. Pardeck. New York: Auburn House, 1991. viii, 180 p.
90-022750　361/.00285　0865690235
Human services -- Data processing -- Social aspects. Electronic data processing -- Philosophy.

HV31 Treatises — 1871-

HV31.B75 1992
Bryson, Lois.
Welfare and the state: who benefits?/ Lois Bryson. New York: St. Martin's Press, 1992. x, 270 p.
92-006861　361　0312080549
Public welfare. Social security. Welfare state.

HV31.C85 1992
Culpitt, Ian.
Welfare and citizenship: beyond the crisis of the welfare state?/ Ian Culpitt. London; Sage, 1992. 222 p.
92-056381　　0803986173
Social policy. Welfare state. Public welfare.

HV31.H9 1965
Hunter, Robert, 1874-1942.
Poverty; social conscience in the progressive era. Edited by Peter d'A. Jones. New York, Harper & Row [1965] xxix, 382 p.
65-002717　301.441
Poverty. Poor -- United States.

HV31.M55 1994
Milner, Henry.
Social democracy and rational choice: the Scandinavian experience and beyond/ Henry Milner. London; Routledge, 1994. xii, 304 p.
94-015094　361.6/5/0948　0415116996
Welfare state. Socialism -- Scandinavia. Scandinavia -- Social policy.

HV31.N47 1996
Neugeboren, Bernard.
Environmental practice in the human services: integration of micro and macro roles, skills, and contexts/ Bernard Neugeboren. New York: Haworth Press, c1996. xxiv, 384 p.
95-025071   361 20   1560249447
Human services. Social service. Social ecology.

HV31.N67
Northen, Helen.
Clinical social work/ by Helen Northen. New York: Columbia University Press, 1982. xii, 369 p.
81-010235   361.3/2   0231038003
Social service. Social case work. Medical social work.

HV31.T39 1991
Taylor-Gooby, Peter.
Social change, social welfare, and social science/ Peter Taylor-Gooby. Toronto; University of Toronto Press, 1991. xii, 244 p.
92-211733   080202680X
Welfare state. Public welfare. Social change.

HV35 Handbooks, manuals, etc.

HV35.S6
Encyclopedia of social work. New York, National Association of Social Workers.
30-030948   361/.003
Social service -- Periodicals.

HV37 Addresses, essays, lectures

HV37.C62 1999
Compton, Beulah Roberts.
Social work processes/ Beulah R. Compton, Burt Galaway. 6th ed. Pacific Grove: Brooks/Cole Publishing, c1999. xxviii, 560 p.
98-021140   362.3/2/0973 21   0534358705
Social service. Social case work. Social service -- United States.

HV37.P28 1989
Pampel, Fred C.
Age, class, politics, and the welfare state/ Fred C. Pampel, John B. Williamson. Cambridge [England]; Cambridge University Press, 1989. xvi, 199 p.
88-027028   361
Public welfare. Welfare state. Income distribution.

HV37.T44 1988
Testing the limits of social welfare: international perspectives on policy changes in nine countries/ edited by Robert Morris. Hanover, NH: Published for Brandeis University Press by Unive c1988. xiv, 311 p.
88-005559   361.6   087451455X
Public welfare -- Cross-cultural studies. Welfare state -- Cross-cultural studies. Social policy -- Cross-cultural studies.

HV37.T465 1985
Theory and practice of community social work/ edited by Samuel H. Taylor and Robert W. Roberts. New York: Columbia University Press, 1985. xiii, 442 p.
84-015628   361.8   0231053681
Social service. Community organization.

HV40 Social service. Social work. Charity organization and practice — General works

HV40.F5 1968
Fink, Arthur E. 1903-
The field of social work [by] Arthur E. Fink, C. Wilson Anderson [and] Merrill B. Conover. New York, Holt, Rinehart and Winston [1968] viii, 534 p.
68-009141   361.3
Social service. Social service -- United States.

HV40.R35 1993
Reamer, Frederic G., 1953-
The philosophical foundations of social work/ Frederic G. Reamer. New York: Columbia University Press, c1993. xv, 219 p.
92-028971   361/.001 20   0231071264
Social service -- Philosophy.

HV40.S617 1983
Social support networks: informal helping in the human services/ [edited by] James K. Whittaker, James Garbarino, and associates. Hawthorne, N.Y.: Aldine Pub. Co., 1983. xx, 479 p.
83-011761   362   0202360318
Social service. Helping behavior. Friendship.

HV40.W435 1983
Weissman, Harold H.
Agency-based social work: neglected aspects of clinical practice/ Harold Weissman, Irwin Epstein, and Andrea Savage. Philadelphia: Temple University Press, 1983. xviii, 344 p.
83-009314   361/.0068   087722322X
Social work administration.

HV40.42 Social service. Social work. Charity organization and practice — Social workers — Volunteers in social work

HV40.42.D36 1988
Daniels, Arlene Kaplan, 1930-
Invisible careers: women civic leaders from the volunteer world/ Arlene Kaplan Daniels. Chicago: University of Chicago Press, c1988. xxviii, 303 p.
87-025515   361.3/7/088042   0226136108
Women volunteers in social service -- United States. Women civic leaders -- United States. Voluntarism -- United States.

HV40.8 Social service. Social work. Charity organization and practice — Social workers — By region or country, A-Z

HV40.8.U6.R44 1990
Reeser, Linda Cherrey.
Professionalization and activism in social work: the sixties, the eighties, and the future/ Linda Cherrey Reeser and Irwin Epstein. New York: Columbia University Press, c1990. xvi, 165 p.
89-017470   361.3/2 20   0231067887
Social workers -- United States -- Attitudes. Social service -- United States.

HV41 Social service. Social work. Charity organization and practice — General special

HV41.C4428 1992
Cherny, Julius.
Accounting--a social institution: a unified theory for the measurement of the profit and nonprofit sectors/ Julius Cherny, Arlene R. Gordon, and Richard J.L. Herson; foreword by Joshua Ronen. New York: Quorum Books, 1992. xxvi, 211 p.
91-025524   657/.98   089930690X
Human services -- Evaluation. Social accounting.

HV41.K22
Kadushin, Alfred.
Consultation in social work/ Alfred Kadushin. New York: Columbia University Press, 1977. xi, 236 p.
77-024345   361/.06   0231041241
Social service. Social service -- Teamwork. Medical consultation.

HV41.L53
Lipsky, Michael.
Street-level bureaucracy: dilemmas of the individual in public services/ Michael Lipsky. New York: Russell Sage Foundation, c1980. xviii, 244 p.
79-007350   361.3/01   0871545241
Social workers. Social policy.

HV41.W368 1990
Weiner, Myron E.
Human services management: analysis and applications/ Myron E. Weiner. 2nd ed. Belmont, Calif.: Wadsworth Pub. Co., c1990. xiv, 498 p.
89-039406   361/.0068 20   053412528X
Human services -- Management.

HV41.2 Social service. Social work. Charity organization and practice — Fund raising — General works

HV41.2.U6O64
Operating grants for nonprofit organizations 2000. Phoenix, AZ: Oryx Press, c2000. xi, 273 p.
00-697797   361 13   157356396X
Fund raising. Nonprofit organizations -- Finance -- Directories.

HV41.9 Social service. Social work. Charity organization and practice — Fund raising — By region or country, A-Z

HV41.9.U5.B58 1996
Blum, Laurie.
The complete guide to getting a grant: how to turn your ideas into dollars/ Laurie Blum. New York: John Wiley & Sons, 1996. 368 p.
96-016543   658.15/224   0471155098
Fund raising -- United States -- Handbooks, manuals, etc. Proposal writing for grants -- United States -- Handbooks, manuals, etc.

HV43 Social service. Social work. Charity organization and practice — Social case work. Friendly visiting — General works

HV43.C534 1983
Clinical social work in the eco-systems perspective/ Carol H. Meyer, editor. New York: Columbia University Press, 1983. xii, 262 p.
83-002124 361.3/2 0231051948
Social case work.

HV43.D56 1995
Differential diagnosis and treatment in social work/ edited by Francis J. Turner; with a foreword by Florence Hollis. 4th ed. New York: Free Press, c1995. xlix, 1387 p.
95-016212 361.3 20 0028740076
Social case work. Psychiatric social work. Medical social work.

HV43.G47 1996
Germain, Carel B.
The life model of social work practice: advances in theory & practice / Carel B. Germain, Alex Gitterman. 2nd ed. New York: Columbia University Press, c1996. xii, 490 p.
95-041023 361.3/2 20 0231064160
Social case work. Human beings -- Effect of environment on.

HV43.K26 1997
Kadushin, Alfred.
The social work interview: a guide for human service professionals/ Alfred Kadushin, Goldie Kadushin. 4th ed. New York: Columbia University Press, c1997. xvii, 458 p.
96-038296 361.3/22 20 0231096593
Interviewing. Social service.

HV43.K64
Koos, Earl Lomon.
...Families in trouble. With a preface by Robert S. Lynd. New York: King's crown press, 1946. xvi, 134 p.
46-002902 392
New York (City) -- Poor. Family. Social case work.

HV43.M285 1998
Maple, Frank F.
Goal-focused interviewing/ Frank F. Maple. Thousand Oaks, Calif.: Sage Publications, c1998. vii, 143 p.
97-021126 361.3/22 21 0761901809
Social case work. Interviewing. Solution-focused therapy.

HV43.R383 1992
Reid, William James, 1928-
Task strategies: an empirical approach to clinical social work/ William J. Reid; with contributions by Julie S. Abramson, Anne E. Fortune, Norma Wasko. New York: Columbia University Press, 1992. viii, 329 p.
91-040553 361.3/2/0973 0231075502
Social case work -- United States. Problem solving.

HV43.S34
Schwartz, Arthur.
Social casework: a behavioral approach/ Arthur Schwartz and Israel Goldiamond, with Michael W. Howe. New York: Columbia University Press, 1975. xiii, 315 p.
75-002298 361.3 0231037783
Social case work. Behavior. Social service.

HV43.T43 1998
Tice, Karen Whitney, 1955-
Tales of wayward girls and immoral women: case records and the professionalization of social work/ Karen W. Tice. Urbana: University of Illinois Press, c1998. x, 260 p.
97-033863 361.3/2 21 0252023978
Social case work -- United States -- History. Social case work reporting -- United States -- History. Social service -- United States -- Records and correspondence -- History.

HV43.W518 1978
Wilson, Suanna J., 1943-
Confidentiality in social work: issues and principles/ Suanna J. Wilson. New York: Free Press, c1978. xiii, 274 p.
77-018475 361.3/2 0029347505
Confidential communications -- Social case work. Privacy, Right of.

HV43.W64 2000
Woods, Mary E.,
Casework: a psychosocial therapy/ Mary E. Woods and Florence Hollis. 5th ed. Boston: McGraw-Hill, c2000. xxviii, 667 p.
99-028076 361.3/2 21 0072901799
Social case work. Psychotherapy -- Social aspects.

HV45 Social service. Social work. Charity organization and practice — Social group work

HV45.P46 1980
Perspectives on social group work practice: a book of readings/ edited by Albert S. Alissi. New York: Free Press, c1980. x, 405 p.
79-007633 361.4 0029004802
Social group work -- Addresses, essays, lectures.

HV45.T48
Theories of social work with groups/ Robert W. Roberts and Helen Northen, editors. New York: Columbia University Press, 1976. xviii, 401 p.
76-004967 361.4 0231038852
Social group work.

HV57 Social service. Social work. Charity organization and practice — Public relief — Elberfeld system

HV57.G56 2000
Gillon, Steven M.
That's not what we meant to do: reform and its unintended consequences in twentieth-century America/ Steven M. Gillon. New York: W.W. Norton, c2000. 288 p.
99-059626 361.6/1/0973 21 0393048845
Social legislation -- United States. Campaign funds -- United States. United States -- Social policy. United States -- Politics and government -- 20th century.

HV63 Social service. Social work. Charity organization and practice — Institutional care. Indoor relief — By region or country, A-Z

HV63.M6
Arrom, Silvia Marina, 1949-
Containing the poor: the Mexico City Poor House, 1774-1871/ Silvia Marina Arrom. Durham, NC: Duke University Press, 2000. xii, 398 p.
00-029396 362.5/85/097253 21 0822325276
Almshouses -- Mexico -- Mexico City -- History. Mexico City (Mexico) -- Social policy. Mexico City (Mexico) -- Economic conditions.

HV88 By region or country — United States — Societies. Associations

HV88.S59
Social service organizations/ editor-in-chief Peter Romanofsky, advisory editor Clarke A. Chambers. Westport, Conn.: Greenwood Press, 1978. 2 v.
77-084754 361.7/0973 0837198291
Charities -- United States -- History. Charities, Medical -- United States -- History. Social service -- Societies, etc. -- History.

HV91 By region or country — United States — General works. History

HV91.B696 1988
Brock, William Ranulf.
Welfare, democracy, and the New Deal/ William R. Brock. Cambridge [England]; Cambridge University Press, 1988. viii, 376 p.
87-020926 361.6/0973 0521333792
Public welfare -- United States -- History -- 20th century. New Deal, 1933-1939. United States -- Social policy. United States -- Social conditions -- 1933-1945.

HV91.C35 1994
Caplow, Theodore.
Perverse incentives: the neglect of social technology in the public sector/ Theodore Caplow. Westport, Conn.: Praeger, 1994. 164 p.
94-002981 361.973 0275949117
Social service -- United States. Human services -- United States. Criminal justice, Administration of -- United States.

HV91.C62 1993
Coles, Robert.
The call of service: a witness to idealism/ Robert Coles. Boston: Houghton Mifflin Co., 1993. xxviii, 306 p.
93-002317 361.973 0395636477
Social service -- United States. Volunteer workers in social service -- United States. Voluntarism -- United States.

HV91.C75 1990
Critical issues in American philanthropy: strengthening theory and practice/ Jon Van Til and associates. San Francisco: Jossey-Bass, 1990. xxviii, 298 p.
90-004877 361.7/0973 1555422780
Charities -- United States. Voluntarism -- United States. Fund raising -- United States.

HV91.D3524 1996
Davies, Gareth, 1965-
From opportunity to entitlement: the transformation and decline of Great Society liberalism/ Gareth Davies. Lawrence: University Press of Kansas, c1996. xii, 320 p.
95-046919   361.973 20   0700607579
Public welfare -- United States -- History. Liberalism -- United States -- History. Individualism -- United States -- History. United States -- Social policy.

HV91.E26 1999
Economic conditions and welfare reform/ Sheldon H. Danziger, editor. Kalamazoo, Mich.: W.E. Upjohn Institute for Employment Research, 1999. vii, 321 p.
99-049277   361.973   088099200X
Public welfare -- Economic aspects -- United States -- Congresses. Welfare recipients -- United States -- Economic conditions -- Congresses. United States -- Economic conditions -- 1981- -- Congresses.

HV91.E38 1985
Ehrenreich, John, 1943-
The altruistic imagination: a history of social work and social policy in the United States/ John H. Ehrenreich. Ithaca: Cornell University Press, 1985. 271 p.
84-045807   361.3/0973   0801417643
Social service -- United States -- History. United States -- Social policy -- History.

HV91.F3 1992
Fabricant, Michael.
The welfare state crisis and the transformation of social service work/ Michael B. Fabricant, Steve Burghardt. Armonk, N.Y.: M.E. Sharpe, c1992. xvii, 258 p.
91-021549   361.973 20   0873326423
Social service -- United States. Public welfare -- United States. Poor -- United States.

HV91.G47 1983
Ginsberg, Leon H.
The practice of social work in public welfare/ Leon H. Ginsberg. New York: Free Press; c1983. xiii, 226 p.
82-071888   361.3/0973   0029117607
Public welfare -- United States. Social service -- United States. Social case work -- United States.

HV91.H265 1990
Handbook of social work practice with vulnerable populations/ edited by Alex Gitterman. New York: Columbia University Press, c1991. xiii, 804 p.
90-039815   361.3/2 20   0231070489
Social service -- United States. Social work with the socially handicapped -- United States.

HV91.H6
Hopkins, Harry Lloyd, 1890-1946.
Spending to save: the complete story of relief/ Harry L. Hopkins. New York: W.W. Norton, c1936. 197 p.
36-027473
Unemployed -- United States. Public welfare -- United States.

HV91.K349 1986
Katz, Michael B., 1939-
In the shadow of the poorhouse: a social history of welfare in America/ Michael B. Katz. New York: Basic Books, c1986. xiv, 338 p.
85-073875   362.5/8/0973   0465032257
Public welfare -- United States -- History. Social service -- United States -- History. United States -- Social policy.

HV91.L35 1987
Lauffer, Armand.
Working in social work: growing and thriving in human services practice/ Armand Lauffer. Newbury Park, Calif.: Sage Publications, c1987. 339 p.
86-029700   361.3/0973   0803920415
Social service -- United States. Social work administration -- United States. Social workers -- Professional ethics -- United States.

HV91.L37
Leiby, James.
A history of social welfare and social work in the United States/ James Leiby. New York: Columbia University Press, 1978. viii, 426 p.
78-003774   361/.973   0231033524
Public welfare -- United States -- History. Social service -- United States -- History.

HV91.L8
Lubove, Roy.
The professional altruist; the emergence of social work as a career, 1880-1930. Cambridge, Harvard University Press, 1965. viii, 291 p.
65-012786   361.973
Social workers -- United States. Charities -- United States.

HV91.N23 1994
Nagai, Althea K., 1954-
Giving for social change: foundations, public policy, and the American political agenda/ Althea K. Nagai, Robert Lerner, and Stanley Rothman. Westport, Conn.: Praeger, 1994. xiv, 218 p.
93-025060   361.7/632/0973   0275946975
Endowments -- Political aspects -- United States. Charities -- Political aspects -- United States. Elite (Social sciences) -- United States. United States -- Social policy.

HV91.P38 1998
Payne, James L.
Overcoming welfare: expecting more from the poor--and from ourselves/ James L. Payne. New York: Basic Books, c1998. xii, 243 p.
98-005360   362.5/8/0973 21   046506924X
Public welfare -- United States. Poor -- Government policy -- United States. Welfare recipients -- United States. United States -- Social policy -- 1993-

HV91.P694 1999
Poverty: opposing viewpoints/ Laura K. Egendorf, book editor. San Diego, Calif.: Greenhaven Press, c1999. 224 p.
98-017866   362.5/0973 21   1565109473
Poor -- United States. Poverty -- United States. Public welfare -- United States.

HV91.R33 1990
Rabinowitz, Alan.
Social change philanthropy in America/ Alan Rabinowitz; foreword by David R. Hunter. New York: Quorum Books, 1990. xix, 227 p.
89-024362   361.7/0973   0899305369
Charities -- United States. Endowments -- United States. Social change.

HV91.R36 1994
Rank, Mark R.
Living on the edge: the realities of welfare in America/ Mark Robert Rank. New York: Columbia University Press, c1994. xiii, 266 p.
93-022818   362.5/0973 20   0231084242
Welfare recipients -- United States -- Interviews. Public welfare -- United States.

HV91.R445 1995
Reinventing human services: community- and family-centered practice/ Paul Adams and Kristine Nelson, editors. New York: Aldine de Gruyter, c1995. ix, 286 p.
95-008047   361.8/0973 20   0202360970
Human services -- United States. Social service -- United States. Community organization -- United States.

HV91.R772 1989
Rural poverty: special causes and policy reforms/ edited by Harrell R. Rodgers, Jr., and Gregory Weiher; prepared under the auspices of the Policy Studies Organization. New York: Greenwood Press, 1989. xix, 171 p.
88-035817   362.5/8/0973   0313266301
Social service, Rural -- United States. Public welfare -- United States. Rural poor -- United States -- Social conditions. United States -- Rural conditions.

HV91.S2945 1997
Schorr, Lisbeth B.
Common purpose: strengthening families and neighborhoods to rebuild America/ Lisbeth B. Schorr. New York: Anchor Books, Doubleday, 1997. xxviii, 482 p.
97-011595   361.973   0385475322
Human services -- United States. Public welfare -- United States. Community development -- United States. United States -- Social policy -- 1993-

HV91.S3 1997
Sealander, Judith.
Private wealth & public life: foundation philanthropy and the reshaping of American social policy from the Progressive Era to the New Deal/ Judith Sealander. Baltimore: Johns Hopkins University Press, c1997. xii, 349 p.
96-041649   361.7/0973 20   0801854601
Endowments -- United States -- History -- 20th century. United States -- Social policy.

HV91.S555 2000
Singleton, Jeff, 1947-
The American dole: unemployment relief and the welfare state in the Great Depression/ Jeff Singleton. Westport, Conn.: Greenwood Press, 2000. viii, 243 p.
99-462054   362.5/82/097309043   0313314004
Public welfare -- United States -- History -- 20th century. Insurance, Unemployment -- United States -- History -- 20th century. Social security -- United States -- History -- 20th century.

HV91.S56 1992
Skocpol, Theda.
Protecting soldiers and mothers: the political origins of social policy in the United States/ Theda Skocpol. Cambridge, Mass.: Belknap Press of Harvard University Press, 1992. xiv, 714 p.
92-008062   361.973   0674717651
Public welfare -- United States -- History -- 19th century. Public welfare -- United States -- History -- 20th century. United States -- Social policy.

HV91.S6275 2000
Soss, Joe, 1967-
Unwanted claims: the politics of participation in the U.S. welfare system/ Joe Soss. Ann Arbor: University of Michigan Press, c2000. viii, 247 p.
00-008551   362.5/0973 21   047211168X
Public welfare -- United States. Welfare recipients -- United States -- Interviews.

HV91.S6292 1994
Specht, Harry.
Unfaithful angels: how social work has abandoned its mission/ Harry Specht, Mark E. Courtney. New York: Free Press; c1994. xii, 209 p.
93-023934   361.973 20   0029303559
Social service -- United States. Psychotherapy -- Social aspects -- United States. Social workers -- United States.

HV91.T7 1984
Trattner, Walter I.
From poor law to welfare state: a history of social welfare in America/ Walter I. Trattner. New York: Free Press; c1984. xx, 362 p.
83-048725   361/.973   0029330106
Public welfare -- United States -- History. Social service -- United States -- History.

HV91.W466 1999
Weissberg, Robert.
The politics of empowerment/ Robert Weissberg. Westport, Conn.: Praeger, 1999. x, 255 p.
98-038285   361.8/0973 21   0275964264
Social service -- United States -- Citizen participation. Community organization -- United States -- Citizen participation. Community power -- United States.

HV91.W49 1989
Wenocur, Stanley, 1938-
From charity to enterprise: the development of American social work in a market economy/ Stanley Wenocur and Michael Reisch. Urbana: University of Illinois Press, c1989. xiii, 327 p.
88-018836   361/.973 19   0252015568
Social service -- United States -- History.

HV91.W497 2000
Who will provide?: the changing role of religion in American social welfare/ edited by Mary Jo Bane, Brent Coffin, Ronald Thiemann.. Boulder, Colo.: Westview Press, 2000. xiv, 322 p.
00-063303   361.7/5/0973 20   081333876X
Social service -- United States. Church charities -- United States. Public welfare -- United States.

HV95 By region or country — United States — Policy, etc.

HV95.A5988 1997
Albelda, Randy Pearl.
Glass ceilings and bottomless pits: women's work, women's poverty/ by Randy Albelda and Chris Tilly. Boston, Ma.: South End Press, 1997. xv, 221 p.
97-017419   362.83/086/942   089608566X
Public welfare -- United States. Poor women -- United States. Welfare recipients -- United States. United States -- Social policy -- 1993-

HV95.C32 1998
Cammisa, Anne Marie.
From rhetoric to reform?: welfare policy in American politics/ Anne Marie Cammisa. Boulder, Colo.: Westview Press, 1998. xviii, 169 p.
97-049311   362.5/8/0973   0813329957
Public welfare -- United States. United States -- Social policy -- 1993-

HV95.F48 2000
Finding jobs: work and welfare reform/ David E. Card and Rebecca M. Blank, editors. New York: Russell Sage Foundation, c2000. viii, 549 p.
00-020794   362.5/8/0973 21   0871541165
Welfare recipients -- Employment -- United States. Unskilled labor -- United States.

HV95.G32 2000
Gaffaney, Timothy J.
Freedom for the poor: welfare and the foundations of democratic citizenship/ Timothy J. Gaffaney. Boulder, Colo.: Westview Press, 2000. viii, 200 p.
99-059999   362.5/0973   0813367816
Public welfare -- United States. Conservatism -- United States. Liberalism -- United States.

HV95.G54 2000
Glenn, Charles Leslie, 1938-
The ambiguous embrace: government and faith-based schools and social agencies/ Charles L. Glenn; with a foreword by Peter L. Berger. Princeton, N.J.: Princeton University Press, c2000. xii, 315 p.
99-035074   361.7/5/0973 21   0691048525
Human services -- Contracting out -- United States. Human services -- Contracting out -- Europe. Civil society -- United States.

HV95.H259 1991
Handler, Joel F.
The moral construction of poverty: welfare reform in America/ Joel F. Handler, Yeheskel Hasenfeld. Newbury Park: Sage Publications, c1991. vii, 269 p.
91-006939   361.6/8/0973 20   0803941978
Public welfare -- Moral and ethical aspects -- United States. Poor -- Government policy -- United States.

HV95.H264 1997
Handler, Joel F.
We the poor people: work, poverty, and welfare/ Joel F. Handler and Yeheskel Hasenfeld. New Haven, Conn.: Yale University Press, c1997. xii, 281 p.
97-017475   362.5/0973 21   0300072481
Public welfare -- United States. Welfare recipients -- Employment -- United States. Poverty -- United States.

HV95.H554 1996
Hombs, Mary Ellen.
Welfare reform: a reference handbook/ Mary Ellen Hombs. Santa Barbara, Calif.: ABC-CLIO, c1996. xv, 165 p.
96-047515   361.973 21   0874368448
Public welfare -- United States -- Handbooks, manuals, etc.

HV95.H6 1943
Howard, Donald S. 1912-
The WPA and federal relief policy/ by Donald S. Howard. New York: Russell Sage Foundation, 1943. 879 p.
43-014619   331.1377
Public service employment -- United States. Unemployed -- United States. Public welfare -- United States.

HV95.J355 2001
Jansson, Bruce S.
The sixteen-trillion-dollar mistake: how the U.S. bungled its national priorities from the New Deal to the present/ Bruce S. Jansson. New York: Columbia University Press, c2001. xi, 492 p.
00-060323   361.973 21   023111432X
Human services -- United States -- Finance. Government spending policy -- United States. United States -- Appropriations and expenditures. United States -- Politics and government -- 20th century.

HV95.K278 1993
Kagan, Sharon Lynn.
Integrating services for children and families: understanding the past to shape the future/ Sharon Lynn Kagan with Peter R. Neville. New Haven: Yale University Press, c1993. xi, 226 p.
93-031023   361.973 20   0300058713
Social service -- United States. Social work administration -- United States.

HV95.M49 1990
Miller, Dorothy C.
Women and social welfare: a feminist analysis/ Dorothy C. Miller. New York: Praeger, 1990. x, 181 p.
89-016207   362.83/0973   0275929736
Public welfare administration -- United States. Poor women -- United States. Social security -- United States. United States -- Social policy.

HV95.M87 1997
Murray, Michael L., 1937-
--and economic justice for all: welfare reform for the 21st century/ Michael L. Murray. Armonk, N.Y.: M.E. Sharpe, 1997. xi, 234 p.
96-048442   362.5/82   156324988X
Public welfare -- United States. Guaranteed annual income -- United States. Distributive justice.

HV95.N53 1997
Noble, Charles, 1948-
Welfare as we knew it: a political history of the American welfare state/ Charles Noble. New York: Oxford University Press, 1997. 210 p.
97-023704   361.973   0195113365
Public welfare -- United States -- History. United States -- Social policy.

HV95.O44 1996
O'Looney, John.
Redesigning the work of human services/ John O'Looney. Westport, Conn.: Quorum, 1996. 333 p.
95-024915   362.973   0899309410
Human services -- United States. Human services -- Government policy -- United States. Public welfare -- United States.

HV95.P43 2001
Peck, Jamie.
Workfare states/ Jamie Peck; foreword by Frances Fox Piven and Richard Cloward. New York: Guilford Press, c2001. xviii, 414 p.
00-067764   362.5 21   1572306351
Public welfare -- United States. Public welfare -- Canada. Public welfare -- Great Britain. United States -- Social policy -- 1993- Canada -- Social policy. Great Britain -- Social policy -- 1979-

HV95.P736 1989
Privatization and the welfare state/ edited by Sheila B. Kamerman, Alfred J. Kahn. Princeton, N.J.: Princeton University Press, c1989. ix, 283 p.
88-039316   361/.973 19   0691078114
Human services -- United States. Human services -- Contracting out -- United States. Privatization -- United States.

HV95.R59 1992
Rooney, Ronald H., 1945-
Strategies for work with involuntary clients/ Ronald H. Rooney. New York: Columbia University Press, c1992. xvi, 405 p.
92-007393   361.3/2/0973 20   0231067682
Social service -- United States.

HV95.S585 1993
Smith, Steven Rathgeb, 1951-
Nonprofits for hire: the welfare state in the age of contracting/ Steven Rathgeb Smith and Michael Lipsky. Cambridge, Mass.: Harvard University Press, 1993. xii, 292 p.
92-026625   361.6   0674626389
Social service -- Contracting out -- United States.

HV95.S64 1998
Solow, Robert M.
Work and welfare/ Robert M. Solow; [comments by] Gertrude Himmelfarb ... [et al.]; edited by Amy Gutmann. Princeton, N.J.: Princeton University Press, c1998. xix, 100 p.
98-006478   362.5/0973 21   0691058830
Public welfare -- United States. Welfare recipients -- Employment -- United States. Poor -- Employment -- United States.

HV95.S824 2000
Stoesz, David.
A poverty of imagination: bootstrap capitalism, sequel to welfare reform/ David Stoesz. Madison, Wis.: University of Wisconsin Press, c2000. xxi, 203 p.
00-008036   362.5/0973 21   0299169502
Public welfare -- United States. Welfare recipients -- Employment -- United States. Poor -- Government policy -- United States.

HV95.T36 1996
Tanner, Michael, 1956-
The end of welfare: fighting poverty in the civil society/ Michael Tanner. Washington, D.C.: Cato Institute, c1996. vii, 226 p.
96-036010   362.5/8/0973 20   188257737X
Public welfare -- United States. Welfare recipients -- Employment -- United States. Welfare state.

HV95.W32 1997
Waddan, Alex, 1964-
The politics of social welfare and the rise of the right/ Alex Waddan. Brookfield, Vt.: Edward Elgar Pub. Co., 1997. vii, 204 p.
96-038187   361.973   1858983665
Public welfare -- United States. Liberalism -- United States. Welfare state. United States -- Social policy.

HV95.W38 2000
Weaver, R. Kent, 1953-
Ending welfare as we know it/ R. Kent Weaver. Washington, D.C.: Brookings Institution Press, c2000. xiv, 482 p.
99-050856   361.973 21   0815792484
Public welfare -- United States. Poor -- Government policy -- United States. Welfare recipients -- Government policy -- United States. United States -- Social policy -- 1993- United States -- Politics and government -- 1993-

HV95.W453 1997
Welfare: opposing viewpoints/ Charles P. Cozic, Paul A. Winters, book editors. San Diego, CA: Greenhaven Press, c1997. 208 p.
96-031261   362.5/8/0973 20   1565105192
Public welfare -- United States -- Philosophy. Public welfare -- Law and legislation -- United States. United States -- Social policy. United States -- Economic policy.

HV97 By region or country — United States — National institutions

HV97.A64.S26 1996
Samson, Gloria Garrett.
The American Fund for Public Service: Charles Garland and radical philanthropy, 1922-1941/ Gloria Garrett Samson. Westport, Conn.: Greenwood Press, 1996. xiv, 263 p.
95-035689   361.7/632/0973   0313298734
Garland, Charles. Baldwin, Roger Nash, -- 1884- Social movements -- United States -- Finance. Charities -- United States -- History -- 20th century. Social change -- United States -- Finance.

HV97.C3.L34 1989
Lagemann, Ellen Condliffe, 1945-
The politics of knowledge: the Carnegie Corporation, philanthropy, and public policy/ Ellen Condliffe Lagemann. Middletown, Conn.: Wesleyan University Press, c1989. xv, 347 p.
89-016634   361.7/632/0973   0819552046
Endowments -- United States.   United States -- Social policy.

HV97.N34.W47
West, Guida.
The national welfare rights movement: the social protest of poor women/ Guida West. New York, N.Y.: Praeger, 1981. xxi, 451 p.
80-039554   362.5/82/06073   0030521661
Welfare rights movement -- United States. Poor women -- United States.

HV98 By region or country — United States — By region or state, A-Z

HV98.H3.M37 1996
Mast, Robert H., 1928-
Autobiography of protest in Hawai'i/ Robert H. Mast and Anne B. Mast. Honolulu: University of Hawaii Press, c1996. vi, 450 p.
96-031153   303.48/4/092 B 20   0824817842
Social reformers -- Hawaii -- Biography. Political activists -- Hawaii -- Biography. Working class -- Hawaii. Hawaii -- Social conditions. Hawaii -- Economic conditions. Hawaii -- Politics aand government.

HV98.M39 K4 1969
Kelso, Robert Wilson,
The history of public poor relief in Massachusetts, 1620-1920, by Robert W. Kelso. Montclair, N.J., Patterson Smith, 1969 [c1922] 200 p.
69-014936   362.5/09744   0875850316
Poor -- Massachusetts. Public welfare -- Massachusetts. Domicile in public welfare -- Massachusetts.

HV98.N82.D853 1998
Durden, Robert Franklin.
Lasting legacy to the Carolinas: the Duke Endowment, 1924-1994/ Robert F. Durden. Durham, NC: Duke University Press, 1998. xiv, 386 p.
97-031427   361.7/632/09756 21   0822321513
Endowments -- North Carolina -- History. Endowments -- South Carolina -- History.

HV99 By region or country — United States — By city, A-Z

HV99.N59.P66 1989
Pope, Jacqueline.
Biting the hand that feeds them: organizing women on welfare at the grass roots level/ Jacqueline Pope. New York: Praeger, 1989. ix, 161 p.
88-027505   362.8/3/097471   0275929221
Welfare rights movement -- New York (State) -- New York -- History. Poor women -- New York (State) -- New York -- History. Welfare recipients -- New York (State) -- New York -- History. Brooklyn (New York, N.Y.)

HV108 By region or country — Other regions or countries — Canada

HV108.C48 2000
Christie, Nancy, 1958-
Engendering the state: family, work, and welfare in Canada/ Nancy Christie. Toronto; University of Toronto Press, 2000. xiv, 459 p.
00-708602   0802047688
Family policy -- Canada -- History -- 20th century. Public welfare -- Canada -- History -- 20th century. Social security -- Canada -- History -- 20th century.

HV238-344 By region or country — Other regions or countries — Europe

HV238.B66 2000
Bonoli, Giuliano.
European welfare futures: towards a theory of retrenchment/ Giuliano Bonoli, Vic George, and Peter Taylor-Gooby. Cambridge, U.K.: Polity Press; 2000. ix, 190 p.
99-039727   361.94 21   0745618103
Social service -- European Union countries. European Union countries -- Social policy.

HV238.G56 2001
Globalization and European welfare states: challenges and change/ edited by M. Robert Sykes, Bruno Palier, and Pauline M. Prior; consultant editor, Jo Campling. New York: Palgrave, 2000. xix, 236 p.
00-048302   361.6/5/094 21   0333790189
Public welfare -- Europe. Welfare state. International cooperation. Europe -- Social policy.

HV245.F56 1994
Finlayson, Geoffrey B. A. M.
Citizen, state, and social welfare in Britain 1830-1990/ Geoffrey Finlayson. Oxford [England]: Clarendon Press; 1994. 467 p.
93-028926   361.941   0198227604
Public welfare -- Great Britain -- History. Welfare state -- History. Great Britain -- Social policy.

HV245.H88 1995
Humphreys, Robert, 1928-
Sin, organized charity, and the poor law in Victorian England/ Robert Humphreys. New York, N.Y.: St. Martin's Press, 1995. xii, 226 p.
95-014318   361.7/63/0942109034   0312127553
Charities -- Great Britain -- History -- 19th century. Poor laws -- Great Britain -- History -- 19th century.

HV245.S72 1990
The State of welfare: the welfare state in Britain since 1974/ Nicholas Barr ... [et al.]; John Hills, editor. Oxford: Clarendon Press; 1990. xvi, 395 p.
90-007648   361.6/5/094109047   0198233051
Public welfare -- Great Britain. Welfare state. Great Britain -- Social policy.

HV248.W35 1991
Waine, Barbara.
The rhetoric of independence: the ideology and practice of social policy in Thatcher's Britain/ Barbara Waine. New York: Berg: 1991. ix, 172 p.
90-028480   361.6/1/0941   0854963111
Human services -- Great Britain.   Great Britain -- Social policy -- 1979-

HV249.E89.L48 1991
Lewis, Jane
Women and social action in Victorian and Edwardian England/ Jane Lewis. Stanford, Calif.: Stanford University Press, 1991. vii, 338 p.
90-071680   0804719055
Women social workers -- England -- Biography. Women volunteers in social service -- England -- History.

HV249.S5.L48 1988
Levitt, Ian.
Poverty and welfare in Scotland, 1890-1948/ Ian Levitt. Edinburgh: Edinburgh University Press, c1988. 241 p.
89-122022   361/.9411   0852245580
Public welfare -- Scotland -- History.

HV265.F64 1981
Forrest, Alan I.
The French Revolution and the poor/ Alan Forrest. New York: St. Martin's Press, 1981. x, 198 p.
80-029105   362.5/8/0944   0312305249
Charities -- France -- History -- 18th century. Poor -- France -- History -- 18th century. France -- History -- Revolution, 1789-1799.

HV275.C74 1998
Crew, David F., 1946-
Germans on welfare: from Weimar to Hitler/ David F. Crew. New York: Oxford University Press, 1998. xiii, 287 p.
97-008445   362.5/8/094309041   0195053117
Public welfare -- Germany -- History -- 20th century. Poor -- Germany -- History -- 20th century. Germany -- Social policy. Germany -- Social conditions -- 1918-1933.

HV280.E45.F44 1999
Fehler, Timothy G.
Poor relief and Protestantism: the evolution of social welfare in sixteenth-century Emden/ Timothy G. Fehler. Aldershot, England; Ashgate, c1999. xii, 332 p.
98-052490   362.5/8/09435917 21   1859283780
Public welfare -- Germany -- Emden (Lower Saxony) -- History -- 16th century.

HV280.H3.L56 1990
Lindemann, Mary.
Patriots and paupers: Hamburg, 1712-1830/ Mary Lindemann. New York: Oxford University Press, 1990. vii, 339 p.
89-016302   361.6/0943/51509033   0195061403
Public welfare -- Germany -- Hamburg -- History -- 18th century. Charities -- Germany -- Hamburg -- History -- 18th century. Middle class -- Germany -- Hamburg -- Political activity -- History -- 18th century.

HV295.T82.C38 1995
Cavallo, Sandra.
Charity and power in early modern Italy: benefactors and their motives in Turin, 1541-1789/ Sandra Cavallo. Cambridge; Cambridge University Press, 1995. xv, 280 p.
94-017672   361.8/0945/12   0521460913
Charities -- Italy -- Turin -- History. Public welfare -- Italy -- Turin -- History. Charities, Medical -- Italy -- Turin -- History. Italy -- History -- 1492-1870.

HV313.L55 1996
Lindenmeyr, Adele.
Poverty is not a vice: charity, society, and the state in imperial Russia/ Adele Lindenmeyr. Princeton, NJ: Princeton University Press, c1996. xiv, 335 p.
95-037961   362.5/8/09747 20   0691044899
Poor -- Government policy -- Russia -- History. Charities -- Russia -- History. Poverty -- Russia -- History. Russia -- History -- 1613-1917.

HV344.C37.B76 1998
Brodman, James.
Charity and welfare: hospitals and the poor in medieval Catalonia/ James William Brodman. Philadelphia, PA: University of Pennsylvania Press, c1998. xv, 229 p.
97-045102   362.1/0946/70902 21   0812234367
Charities -- Spain -- Catalonia -- History. Hospitals, Medieval -- Spain -- Catalonia -- History. Social history -- Medieval, 500-1500.

HV393-413 By region or country — Other regions or countries — Asia

HV393.G87 1989
Gupta, Sumitra.
Social welfare in India/ Sumitra Gupta. Allahabad, India: Chugh Publications, 1989. viii, 262 p.
88-905872   362.954   818507660X
Public welfare -- India.

HV413.A69 1993
Anderson, Stephen J.   1957-
Welfare policy and politics in Japan: beyond the developmental state/ Stephen J. Anderson. New York: Paragon House, 1993. viii, 194 p.
92-016699   361.952   1557785716
Public welfare -- Japan. Social security -- Japan. Human services -- Japan. Japan -- Social policy.

HV470.5 By region or country — Other regions or countries — Indian Ocean islands

HV470.5.L56 1996
Lingayah, Sam.
Social welfare in Mauritius: a critical analysis of social service provisions/ by Sam Lingayah. Faversham, Kent [England]: Sankris Pub. Ltd.; 1996. 315 p.
97-983030   0952915812
Public welfare -- Mauritius. Human services -- Mauritius. Evaluation research (Social action programs) -- Mauritius.

HV525 By region or country — Other regions or countries — Developing countries

HV525.J66 1989
Jones, Howard, 1918-
Social welfare in Third World development/ Howard Jones. New York: St. Martin's Press, 1989. xiii, 324 p.
89-010782   361.9172/4   031203749X
Human services -- Developing countries. Developing countries -- Social conditions.

HV530 The church and charity

HV530.L6 1988
Loewenberg, Frank M.
Religion and social work practice in contemporary American society/ Frank M. Loewenberg. New York: Columbia University Press, 1988. xii, 176 p.
87-027043   361.3/2   0231064527
Social service -- Religious aspects. Social workers -- United States -- Religious life.

HV530.W56 2001
Wineburg, Robert J.
A limited partnership: the politics of religion, welfare, and social service/ Bob Wineburg. New York: Columbia University Press, c2001. xi, 229 p.
00-064507   361.7/5 21   0231120842
Church charities -- United States. Social service -- United States.

HV541 Women and charity

HV541.L83 1995
Luddy, Maria.
Women and philanthropy in nineteenth-century Ireland/ Maria Luddy. Cambridge, England; Cambridge University Press, 1995. xiv, 251 p.
94-030052   361.7/4/082   0521474337
Women philanthropists -- Ireland -- History -- 19th century. Women social reformers -- Ireland -- History -- 19th century.

HV541.P37 1989
Parker, Julia
Women and welfare: ten Victorian women in public social service/ Julia Parker. New York: St. Martin's Press, 1989. vii, 220 p.
89-030666   361/.0088042   0312031130
Women in charitable work -- Great Britain -- History -- 19th century. Women in charitable work -- Great Britain -- Biography. Women social workers -- Great Britain -- History -- 19th century.

HV544 Charity fairs, bazaars, etc.

HV544.G67 1998
Gordon, Beverly.
Bazaars and fair ladies: the history of the American fundraising fair/ Beverly Gordon. Knoxville: University of Tennessee Press, 1998. xxvii, 285 p.
97-045425   361.7/0973   1572330147
Bazaars (Charities) -- United States -- History. Women in charitable work -- United States -- History.

HV551.2 Emergency management

HV551.2.T63 1997
Tobin, Patrick D.
Emergency planning and management on the Internet/ by Patrick D. Tobin, Ryan P. Tobin. Rockville, Md.: Government Institutes, 1997.
97-044667   025.06/658477   0865876002
Emergency management -- Computer network resources. Internet (Computer network)

HV551.5 Emergency management — By region or country — Other regions or countries, A-Z

HV551.5.S83.P74 1997
Prendergast, John, 1963-
Crisis response: humanitarian band-aids in Sudan and Somalia/ John Prendergast. London; Pluto Press, 1997. ix, 172 p.
96-034393   363.3/4/09624   0745311563
Emergency management -- Sudan. Emergency management -- Somalia. Humanitarian assistance -- Sudan.

HV553 Emergency management — Relief in case of disasters — General works

HV553.B47 1993
Benthall, Jonathan.
Disasters, relief and the media/ Jonathan Benthall. London; I.B. Tauris, 1993. xiii, 267 p.
94-060187   1850437378
Disaster relief. Disasters -- Press coverage. Mass media.

HV553.D572 1994
Disasters, collective behavior, and social organization/ edited by Russell R. Dynes snd Kathleen J. Tierney. Newark: University of Delaware Press; c1994. 378 p.
93-046766   363.3/4 20   0874134986
Disaster relief -- Social aspects. Disasters -- Research. Emergency management -- Research.

HV553.F76 1996
From massacres to genocide: the media, public policy, and humanitarian crises/ Robert I. Rotberg, Thomas G. Weiss, editors. Washington, D.C.: Brookings Institution, c1996. x, 203 p.
95-050159   363.3/4526 20   0815775903
Disaster relief. International relief. Disasters -- Press coverage.

HV553.L38 2000
Larabee, Ann, 1957-
Decade of disaster/ Ann Larabee. Urbana: University of Illinois Press, c2000. xii, 194 p.
99-006114   363.34 21   0252024834
Disasters -- Social aspects. Technology -- Social aspects. System failures (Engineering) -- Social aspects.

HV553.M39 1999
Maynard, Kimberly A.
Healing communities in conflict: international assistance in complex emergencies/ Kimberly A. Maynard. New York: Columbia University Press, c1999. xxii, 245 p.
98-046125   362.8/7526 21   0231112785
International relief. Humanitarian assistance. Refugees.

HV553.N37 1997
Natsios, Andrew S.
U.S. foreign policy and the Four Horsemen of the Apocalypse: humanitarian relief in complex emergencies/ Andrew S. Natsios; foreword by George Bush. Westport, Conn.: Praeger, 1997. xxii, 192 p.
96-052721   361.6/0973   0275959201
Humanitarian assistance. Humanitarian assistance, American. United States -- Foreign relations -- 1989-

HV555 Emergency management — Relief in case of disasters — By region or country, A-Z

HV555.U6.C64 1998
Comerio, Mary C.
Disaster hits home: new policy for urban housing recovery/ Mary Comerio. Berkeley: University of California Press, c1998. xix, 300 p.
98-006245   363.34/8/0973 21   0520207807
Disaster relief -- United States. Housing policy -- United States. Buildings -- Natural disaster effects -- United States.

HV555.U6.H35 1990
Handbook of emergency management: programs and policies dealing with major hazards and disasters/ edited by William L. Waugh, Jr. and Ronald John Hy. New York: Greenwood Press, 1990. x, 336 p.
90-002744   363.3/48/068   0313256918
Disaster relief -- United States -- Management.

HV568-580 Emergency management — Relief in case of disasters — Red Cross. Red Crescent

HV568.B47 1997
Berry, Nicholas O.
War and the Red Cross: the unspoken mission/ Nicholas O. Berry. New York: St. Martin's Press, 1997. x, 159 p.
96-048926   361.7/7   031216517X
Red Cross. Humanitarian assistance. Pacific settlement of international disputes.

HV568.H87 1996
Hutchinson, John F.
Champions of charity: war and the rise of the Red Cross/ John F. Hutchinson. Boulder: Westview Press, 1996. xxii, 448 p.
95-026628   361.7/634   0813325269
Red Cross -- History. War -- Relief of sick and wounded -- History.

HV568.J86 1996
Junod, Dominique-D., 1945-
The imperiled Red Cross and the Palestine-Eretz-Yisrael conflict, 1945-1952: the influence of institutional concerns on a humanitarian operation/ Dominique-D. Junod. London; K. Paul International; 1996. xvi, 344 p.
95-008732   361.7/634/095694   0710305192
Jewish-Arab relations -- 1917-1949. Jewish-Arab relations -- 1949-1967. Israel-Arab conflicts.

HV569.B3.B4
Barton, William Eleazar, 1861-1930.
The life of Clara Barton, founder of the American Red cross, by William E. Barton. Boston; Houghton Mifflin company, 1922. 2 v.
22-004689
Barton, Clara, -- 1821-1912. Red Cross.

HV580.S9.M66 1999
Moorehead, Caroline.
Dunant's dream: war, Switzerland, and the history of the Red Cross/ Caroline Moorehead. New York: Carroll & Graf Pub., 1999. xxxi, 780 p.
00-267219   361.7/634/09494   0786706090
Dunant, Henry, -- 1828-1910. Red Cross -- Switzerland -- History. Voluntary Health Agencies -- history.

HV600-639 Emergency management — Relief in case of disasters — Special types of disasters

HV600 1994.C2B65 1998
Bolin, Robert C.
The Northridge earthquake: vulnerability and disaster/ Robert Bolin with Lois Stanford. London; Routledge, 1998. xiii, 272 p.
98-011099   363.34/95/0979494   0415178975
Earthquakes -- California -- Los Angeles Region. Disaster relief -- California -- Los Angeles Region. Northridge (Los Angeles, Calif.)

HV609.P45 1996
Philippi, Nancy S., 1935-
Floodplain management: ecologic and economic perspectives/ by Nancy S. Philippi. Georgetown, TX: R.G. Landes, 1996. 225 p.
96-020763   363.3/4936   1570593647
Floods -- United States. Emergency management -- United States. Floodplain management -- United States.

HV639.H37 1998
Hard choices: moral dilemmas in humanitarian intervention / edited by Jonathan Moore. Lanham, Md.: Rowman & Littlefield, c1998. xiii, 322 p.
98-019157   363.34/988 21   084769030X
Humanitarian assistance. War victims -- Services for.

HV640 Refugee problems — Refugee relief — General works

HV640.D57 1990
Displaced peoples and refugee studies: a resource guide/ edited by the Refugee Studies Programme, University of Oxford; compiled by Julian Davies. London; H. Zell, c1990. xii, 219 p.
90-004296   362.87 20   0905450760
Refugees -- Research -- Handbooks, manuals, etc.

HV640.G66 1994
Gorman, Robert F.
Historical dictionary of refugee and disaster relief organizations/ Robert F. Gorman. Lanham, Md.: Scarecrow Press , 2000. xxxvi, 356 p.
00-024789 362.87/8/025 0810837749
Refugees -- Services for -- Directories. Disaster relief -- Directories.

HV640.L62 1993
Loescher, Gil.
Beyond charity: international cooperation and the global refugee crisis/ Gil Loescher. New York: Oxford University Press, 1993. x, 260 p.
92-039365 362.87/8 0195081838
Refugees. Refugees -- Services for.

HV640.R35 2000
Risks and reconstruction: experiences of resettlers and refugees/ edited by Michael M. Cernea, Christopher McDowell. Washington, DC: World Bank, 2000. xv, 487 p.
99-059266 362.87/09172/4 0821344447
Refugees -- Developing countries. Forced migration -- Developing countries. Land settlement -- Developing countries.

HV640.R432 1985
Refugees and world politics/ edited by Elizabeth G. Ferris. New York: Praeger, 1985. xiv, 224 p.
85-000495 362.8/7 0030720435
World politics. Refugees.

HV640.S675 1993
The state of the world's refugees, 1993: the challenge of protection/ UNHCR, United Nations High Commission for Refugees. New York: Penguin Books, 1993. ix, 191 p.
93-028920 362.87 014023487X
Refugees.

HV640.W335 2001
Waters, Tony.
Bureaucratizing the good samaritan: the limitations to humanitarian relief operation/ Tony Waters. Boulder, CO: Westview Press, 2001. xiv, 314 p.
00-043988 362.87/526 0813367905
Refugees -- International cooperation. Humanitarian assistance. Bureaucracy.

HV640.4 Refugee problems — Refugee relief — By region or country providing relief, A-Z

HV640.4.E8.S57 1995
Skran, Claudena M.
Refugees in inter-war Europe: the emergence of a regime/ Claudena M. Skran. Oxford [England]: Clarendon Press; 1995. viii, 324 p.
94-025052 362.87/094/0904 0198273924
Refugees -- Europe -- History -- 20th century. Refugees -- Government policy -- Europe -- History -- 20th century. Europe -- Emigration and immigration -- History -- 20th century.

HV640.4.U54.R425 1996
Refugees in America in the 1990s: a reference handbook/ edited by David W. Haines. Westport, Conn.: Greenwood Press, 1996. x, 467 p.
95-050902 362.87/0973 0313293449
Refugees -- United States.

HV640.5 Refugee problems — Refugee relief — By ethnic or national group receiving relief, A-Z

HV640.5.A6.M67 1987
Morris, Benny, 1948-
The birth of the Palestinian refugee problem, 1947-1949/ Benny Morris. Cambridge [Cambridgeshire]; Cambridge University Press, 1987. xx, 380 p.
87-014295 362.8/7/0899275694 0521330289
Refugees, Arab. Palestinian Arabs. Israel-Arab War, 1948-1949 -- Refugees.

HV640.5.C9.T74 1998
Triay, Victor Andres, 1966-
Fleeing Castro: Operation Pedro Pan and the Cuban Children's Program/ Victor Andres Triay. Gainesville: University Press of Florida, c1998. xiv, 126 p.
98-005942 362.87/083 21 0813016126
Refugee children -- Cuba. Refugee children -- United States. Refugee children -- Services for -- United States.

HV640.5.I5.H44 1995
Hein, Jeremy.
From Vietnam, Laos, and Cambodia: a refugee experience in the United States/ Jeremy Hein. New York: Twayne Publishers; c1995. xi, 193 p.
94-041960 362.87/089/959 20 0805784322
Refugees -- Indochina. Refugees -- United States.

HV640.5.I5.H46 1993
Hein, Jeremy.
States and international migrants: the incorporation of Indochinese refugees in the United States and France/ Jeremy Hein. Boulder: Westview Press, 1993. xv, 214 p.
92-032777 362.87 0813385415
Refugees -- Indochina. Refugees -- France. Refugees -- United States.

HV640.5.I5.R42 1987
Refugees as immigrants: Cambodians, Laotians, and Vietnamese in America/ edited by David W. Haines. Totowa, N.J.: Rowman & Littlefield, 1989. xii, 198 p.
87-026637 362.8/7/089959 084767553X
Refugees -- Indochina. Refugees -- United States. Indochinese -- Cultural assimilation -- United States.

HV640.5.I5.R63 1998
Robinson, W. Courtland 1955-
Terms of refuge: the Indochinese exodus & the international response/ W. Courtland Robinson. London; Zed Books; 1998. xi, 322 p.
98-027305 325/.21/09597 1856496090
Refugees -- Indochina.

HV640.5.V5.D38 1991
Davis, Leonard.
Hong Kong and the asylum-seekers from Vietnam/ Leonard Davis. New York: St. Martin's Press, 1991. xii, 255 p.
91-021409 362.87/089/959205125 0312067631
Refugees -- Vietnam. Refugees -- Hong Kong. Refugee camps -- Hong Kong.

HV645 Refugee problems — Church work with refugees, including the sanctuary movement

HV645.T65 1987
Tomsho, Robert, 1953-
The American sanctuary movement/ by Robert Tomsho. Austin, Tex.: Texas Monthly Press, c1987. xii, 214 p.
87-010228 261.8/32 0877190674
Sanctuary movement. Political refugees -- Central America. Church work with refugees -- United States.

HV675.72 Accidents. Prevention of accidents — Special classes of persons — Children

HV675.72.S28 1991
Saving children: a guide to injury prevention/ Modena Hoover Wilson ... [et al.]. New York: Oxford University Press, 1991. xiv, 247 p.
90-007279 363.1/0083 0195061152
Children's accidents -- United States -- Prevention. Traffic safety and children -- United States. Home accidents -- United States -- Prevention.

HV687 Free professional services — Medical charities — Social service to the sick

HV687.C68 2000
Cowles, Lois A. Fort.
Social work in the health field: a care perspective/ Lois A. Fort Cowles. New York: Haworth Press, c2000. xi, 349 p.
99-016078 362.1/0425 21 0789060337
Medical social work.

HV687.W34 1984
Wallace, Stephen R.
Clinical social work in health care: new biopsychosocial approaches/ Stephen R. Wallace, Richard J. Goldberg, Andrew E. Slaby. New York, NY: Praeger, 1984. ix, 242 p.
83-013744 362.1/0425 0030641837
Medical social work. Psychiatric social work. Social work.

HV689 Free professional services — Medical charities — Psychiatric social work

HV689.F7
French, Lois Angelina (Meredith) 1897-
Psychiatric social work [by] Lois Meredith French ... New York, The Commonwealth fund; 1940. xvi, 344 p.
41-001261 361.1
Psychology, Pathological. Social service.

HV689.W62
Wodarski, John S.
Behavioral social work/ John S. Wodarski, Dennis A. Bagarozzi. New York: Human Sciences Press, c1979 335 p.
78-026356   362.2/04/25   0877053758
Psychiatric social work. Behavior modification.

HV696 Free professional services — Other, A-Z

HV696.F6.B53 1992
Black, Maggie, 1945-
A cause for our times: Oxfam: the first 50 years/ Maggie Black. Oxford [England]: Oxfam; 1992. ix, 325 p.
92-029021   361.7/7   0192852833
Food relief -- Great Britain -- Societies, etc. -- History.

HV696.F6.E47 1998
Eisinger, Peter K.
Toward an end to hunger in America/ Peter K. Eisinger. Washington, D.C.: Brookings Institution, c1998. xi, 177 p.
98-025392   363.8/83 21   0815722826
Food relief -- United States. Hunger -- United States.

HV696.F6.F6256 1991
Food aid reconsidered: assessing the impact on Third World countries/ edited by Edward Clay and Olav Stokke. London; F. Cass, c1991. xv, 209 p.
92-144987   363.8/83/091724 20   071463414X
Food relief -- Developing countries. Agricultural assistance -- Developing countries.

HV696.F6.G3813 1995
Geier, Gabriele.
Food security policy in Africa between disaster relief and structural adjustment: reflections on the conception and effectiveness of policies: the case of Tanzania/ Gabriele Geier. London; F. Cass, 1995. 242 p.
95-003885   363.8/83/096   0714641839
Food relief -- International cooperation. Food relief -- Economic aspects -- Africa. Food relief -- Economic aspects -- Tanzania -- Case studies.

HV696.F6.K56 2000
King, Ronald Frederick, 1949-
Budgeting entitlements: the politics of food stamps/ Ronald F. King. Washington, D.C.: Georgetown University Press, c2000. ix, 256 p.
00-026374   363.8/83/0973 21   0878407979
Food stamps -- Political aspects -- United States. Food relief -- United States -- Finance. Budget -- United States.

HV696.F6.M35 1989
Maney, Ardith.
Still hungry after all these years: food assistance policy from Kennedy to Reagan/ Ardith L. Maney. New York: Greenwood Press, 1989. x, 192 p.
88-007711   363.8/83/0973   0313263272
Food relief -- Government policy -- United States.

HV697-700.7 Protection, assistance and relief — Special classes — Families. Mothers. Widow's pensions

HV697.F353 2001
Family-centered policies and practices: international implications/ Katharine Briar-Lawson ... [et al.]. New York: Columbia University Press, c2001. xvi, 462 p.
00-060257   362.82 21   0231121067
Family policy. Family services.

HV699.A424 1988
Abramovitz, Mimi.
Regulating the lives of women: social welfare policy from colonial times to the present/ by Mimi Abramovitz. Boston, MA: South End Press, c1988. x, 406 p.
87-036907   362.8/3/0973   0896083306
Poor women -- United States -- History. Public welfare -- United States -- History. Family social work -- United States -- History.

HV699.B49 1997
Berry, Marianne, 1960-
The family at risk: issues and trends in family preservation services/ Marianne Berry. Columbia: University of South Carolina Press, c1997. xv, 197 p.
97-004722   362.82/8/0973 21   1570031630
Family social work -- United States. Home-based family services. Problem families -- United States.

HV699.C535 1990
Combs-Orme, Terri.
Social work practice in maternal and child health/ Terri Combs-Orme. New York: Springer Pub. Co., c1990. xix, 311 p.
89-026218   362.1/9892 20   082616370X
Maternal and infant welfare -- United States. Child health services -- United States. Teenage pregnancy -- United States.

HV699.G64 1992
Golden, Olivia Ann.
Poor children and welfare reform/ Olivia Golden; foreword by Lisbeth Schorr. Westport, Conn.: Auburn House, 1992. xiv, 193 p.
92-000886   362.7/1/0973   0865690456
Family services -- United States. Child welfare -- United States. Poor children -- United States.

HV699.H35 1983
Hartman, Ann.
Family-centered social work practice/ Ann Hartman, Joan Laird. New York: Free Press; c1983. xii, 419 p.
83-047656   362.8/2   0029141001
Family social work -- United States.

HV699.K35 1996
Kagan, Richard.
Turmoil to turning points: building hope for children in crisis placements/ Richard Kagan. New York: W.W. Norton & Co., c1996. xviii, 270 p.
96-011005   362.7 20   0393702189
Family social work -- United States. Family counseling -- United States. Problem families -- United States.

HV699.K58 1993
Kissman, Kris.
Single-parent families/ Kris Kissman, Jo Ann Allen. Newbury Park, Calif.: Sage Publications, c1993. viii, 160 p.
92-035502   362.82/94/0973 20   0803943229
Family social work -- United States. Single-parent families -- United States.

HV699.M525 1995
Mink, Gwendolyn, 1952-
The wages of motherhood: inequality in the welfare state, 1917-1942/ Gwendolyn Mink. Ithaca, NY: Cornell University Press, 1995. xi, 198 p.
94-039190   362.83/0973   0801422345
Maternal and infant welfare -- Government policy -- United States. Motherhood -- Government policy -- United States. Poor women -- Government policy -- United States. United States -- Economic conditions -- 1918-1945.

HV699.P88 1994
Putting families first: America's family support movement and the challenge of change/ Sharon L. Kagan and Bernice Weissbourd, editors. San Francisco: Jossey-Bass, c1994. xli, 514 p.
94-009713   362.82/0973 20   1555426670
Family social work -- United States. Family policy -- United States.

HV699.T45 1996
Teles, Steven Michael.
Whose welfare?: AFDC and elite politics/ Steven Michael Teles. Lawrence: University Press of Kansas, c1996. x, 226 p.
96-012351   362.7/13/0973 20   070060801X
Aid to families with dependent children programs -- United States. Public welfare -- United States. Elite (Social sciences) -- United States.

HV699.3.W2.K56 1991
Kinney, Jill, 1944-
Keeping families together: the homebuilders model/ Jill Kinney, David Haapala, and Charlotte Booth. New York: Aldine de Gruyter, 1991. xi, 235 p.
90-019973   362.82/8/09797 20   0202360679
Family services -- Washington (State) Family social work -- Washington (State)

HV699.4.C48.G66 1997
Goodwin, Joanne L.
Gender and the politics of welfare reform: mothers' pensions in Chicago, 1911-1929/ Joanne L. Goodwin. Chicago: University of Chicago Press, 1997. xii, 284 p.
96-047158   362.83/82/0977311   0226303926
Mothers' pensions -- Illinois -- Chicago -- History. Women heads of households -- Government policy -- Illinois -- Chicago -- History.

HV700.C64.F35 1997
Family change and family policies in Great Britain, Canada, New Zealand, and the United States/ edited by Sheila B. Kamerman and Alfred J. Kahn. Oxford [England]: Clarendon Press; 1997. xi, 463 p.
98-156452   306.85   019829025X
Family policy -- Commonwealth countries. Family policy -- United States. Family -- Economic aspects -- Commonwealth countries.

HV700.5.A27 1998
Abrahamson, Mark.
Out-of-wedlock births: the United States in comparative perspective/ Mark Abrahamson. Westport, Conn.: Praeger, 1998. viii, 172 p.
97-043954 306.874/3/09 0275956628
Unmarried mothers -- United States. Unmarried mothers -- History. Illegitimate births -- United States.

HV700.5.K86 1993
Kunzel, Regina G., 1959-
Fallen women, problem girls: unmarried mothers and the professionalization of social work, 1890-1945/ Regina G. Kunzel. New Haven: Yale University Press, c1993. xi, 264 p.
93-010013 362.83/92/0973 20 0300050909
Unmarried mothers -- United States -- History. Maternity homes -- United States -- History. Unmarried mothers -- Services for -- United States -- History.

HV700.5.M56 1998
Mink, Gwendolyn, 1952-
Welfare's end/ Gwendolyn Mink. Ithaca, N.Y.: Cornell University Press, 1998. xii, 180 p.
97-038838 362.83/928/0973 0801433479
Unmarried mothers -- Government policy -- United States. Poor women -- Government policy -- United States. Welfare recipients -- United States. United States -- Social policy.

HV700.7.Y68 1993
Young unwed fathers: changing roles and emerging policies/ edited by Robert I. Lerman and Theodora J. Ooms. Philadelpha: Temple University Press, c1993. vi, 348 p.
92-039617 362.8 20 1566390486
Unmarried fathers -- United States. Unmarried fathers -- Government policy -- United States.

HV703-1210 Protection, assistance and relief — Special classes — Children

HV703.B53 1996
Black, Maggie, 1945-
Children first: the story of UNICEF, past and present/ Maggie Black. Oxford; Oxford University Press, 1996. xvii, 361 p.
96-008167 341.7/6 0198280947
Child welfare -- History. Child welfare -- Developing countries -- History.

HV713.C3826 1997
Child poverty and deprivation in the industrialized countries, 1945-1995/ edited by Giovanni Andrea Cornia and Sheldon Danziger. Oxford: Clarendon Press; 1997. xiv, 430 p.
96-036784 362.7/09172/2 0198290756
Poor children -- History -- 20th century. Poverty -- History -- 20th century.

HV713.S32 2002
Savicki, Victor.
Burnout across thirteen cultures: stress and coping in child and youth care workers/ Victor Savicki. Westport, Conn.: Praeger, 2002. xvi, 229 p.
2001-036707 362.7 21 0275974537
Social work with children -- Cross-cultural studies. Social work with youth -- Cross-cultural studies. Burn out (Psychology) -- Cross-cultural studies.

HV713.T94 1991
Tzeng, Oliver C. S.
Theories of child abuse and neglect: differential perspectives, summaries, and evaluations/ Oliver C.S. Tzeng, Jay W. Jackson, and Henry C. Karlson. New York: Praeger, 1991. xxi, 355 p.
90-046516 362.7/6 0275938328
Child abuse. Child sexual abuse.

HV713.W27 1998
Waldfogel, Jane.
The future of child protection: how to break the cycle of abuse and neglect/ Jane Waldfogel. Cambridge, Mass.: Harvard University Press, 1998. viii, 285 p.
98-020429 362.76/8/0973 0674338111
Child welfare. Child welfare -- United States. Child abuse -- Prevention.

HV713.Z5 1969
Zietz, Dorothy.
Child welfare: services and perspectives.   New York, Wiley [1969] xi, 346 p.
79-081335 362.7/0973 047198275X
Child welfare. Child welfare -- United States.

HV715.E34 1991
The Effects of child abuse and neglect: issues and research/ edited by Raymond H. Starr, Jr., David A. Wolfe. London; Guilford, 1991. xiv, 304 p.
91-020247 362.7/6 0898627591
Child abuse -- Research -- Methodology. Child abuse -- Research -- United States -- Methodology. Child abuse -- Longitudinal studies.

HV741.A53
Abbott, Grace, 1878-1939.
The child and the state ..., select documents, with introductory notes of Grace Abbott ... Chicago, Ill., The University of Chicago Press [1938] 2 v.
38-035004 331.30973
Children -- Law -- United States. Children -- Law -- Great Britain. Apprentices -- United States.

HV741.B77
Bremner, Robert Hamlett, 1917-
Children and youth in America: a documentary history. Editor, Robert H. Bremner; associate editors, John Barnard, Tamara K. Hareven [and] Robert M. Mennel. Cambridge, Mass., Harvard University Press, 1970-74. 3 v. in 5.
74-115473 362.7/0973 0674116100
Child welfare -- United States -- History. Children -- United States -- History. Youth -- United States -- History.

HV741.C536145 1991
Children in poverty: child development and public policy/ edited by Aletha C. Huston. Cambridge; Cambridge University Press, 1991. x, 331 p.
91-009814 362.7/08/6942 0521391628
Poor children -- United States -- Congresses. Poor children -- Government policy -- United States -- Congresses. Child welfare -- United States -- Congresses.

HV741.C5377 1994
Children's Defense Fund (U.S.)
Wasting America's future: the Children's Defense Fund report on the costs of child poverty/ by Arloc Sherman; introduction by Marian Wright Edelman; foreword by Robert M. Solow. Boston: Beacon Press, c1994. xxix, 154 p.
94-028889 362.5/083 20 0807041068
Poor children -- United States.

HV741.C665 1996
Costin, Lela B.
The politics of child abuse in America/ Lela B. Costin, Howard Jacob Karger, David Stoesz. New York: Oxford University Press, 1996. xi, 194 p.
94-049130 362.76/8/0973 0195089308
Abused children -- Services for -- United States -- History. Child abuse -- United States -- Prevention -- History. Social work with children -- United States -- History.

HV741.D35
Damaged parents, an anatomy of child neglect/ Norman A. Polansky ... [et al.]. Chicago: University of Chicago Press, 1981. xii, 271 p.
80-022793 362.7/044 0226672212
Child abuse -- United States -- Addresses, essays, lectures. Socially handicapped children -- United States -- Addresses, essays, lectures. Social work with the socially handicapped -- United States -- Addresses, essays, lectures.

HV741.H338 1996
Harris, Irving B. 1910-
Children in jeopardy: can we break the cycle of poverty?/ Irving B. Harris. New Haven: Yale Child Study Center: c1996. xxxi, 236 p.
96-010329 362.7/0973 20 0300068921
Child welfare -- United States. Socially handicapped children -- Services for -- United States. Poor children -- Services for -- United States.

HV741.H4
Helfer, Ray E.
The battered child, edited by Ray E. Helfer and C. Henry Kempe. With a foreword by Katherine B. Oettinger. Chicago, University of Chicago Press [1968] xv, 268 p.
68-016695 364.15
Child abuse -- United States -- Addresses, essays, lectures.

HV741.I537 1997
Indicators of children's well-being/ Robert M. Hauser, Brett V. Brown, and William R. Prosser, editors. New York: Russell Sage Foundation, c1997. xxiv, 508 p.
97-013242 362.7/0973 21 0871543869
Child welfare -- United States. Children -- United States -- Social conditions. Children -- United States -- Economic conditions.

HV741.I7 1998
Invisible children in the society and its schools/ edited by Sue Books. Mahwah, N.J.: Lawrence Erlbaum Associates, 1998. xxxii, 214 p.
98-033966 362.7 0805823689
Socially handicapped teenagers -- United States. Socially handicapped teenagers -- Education -- United States. Educational sociology -- United States.

HV741.I94 1990
Iverson, Timothy J., 1959-
Child abuse and neglect: an information and reference guide/ Timothy J. Iverson, Marilyn Segal. New York: Garland Pub. 1990. x, 220 p.
89-071495 362.7/6/0973 0824077768
Child abuse -- United States. Abused children -- Services for -- United States. Child abuse -- United States -- Prevention.

HV741.J63 1999
Johnson, Earl
Fathers' fair share: helping poor men manage child support and fatherhood/ Earl S. Johnson, Ann Levine, and Fred C. Doolittle. New York: Russell Sage Foundation, c1999. xiv, 241 p.
98-047551   362.7/1 21   0871544113
Child welfare -- Government policy -- United States. Child support -- Government policy -- United States. Fathers -- Services for -- United States.

HV741.K26 1980
Kadushin, Alfred.
Child welfare services/ Alfred Kadushin. New York: Macmillan, c1980. xi, 718 p.
79-013416   362.7/0973   0033618108
Child welfare -- United States.

HV741.L525 1997
Lindenmeyer, Kriste, 1955-
A right to childhood: the U.S. Children's Bureau and child welfare, 1912-46/ Kriste Lindenmeyer. Urbana: University of Illinois Press, c1997. xi, 368 p.
96-010031   362.7/1/0973 20   0252022750
Child welfare -- United States -- History.

HV741.L527 1994
Lindsey, Duncan.
The welfare of children/ Duncan Lindsey. New York: Oxford University Press, 1994. ix, 404 p.
93-040132   362.7/0973   0195085183
Child welfare -- United States -- History. Child welfare -- North America -- History. Child abuse -- United States -- Prevention -- Finance.

HV741.M344 1986
Maluccio, Anthony N.
Permanency planning for children: concepts and methods/ Anthony N. Maluccio, Edith Fein, and Kathleen A. Olmstead. New York: Tavistock Publications, 1986. xiii, 328 p.
85-017333   362.7/95   0422788406
Social work with children -- United States. Child welfare -- United States. Custody of children -- United States.

HV741.M4
Meyer, Henry Joseph, 1913-
Girls at vocational high: an experiment in social work intervention [by] Henry J. Meyer, Edgar F. Borgatta [and] Wyatt C. Jones. In collaboration with Elizabeth P. Anderson, Hanna Grunwald [and] Dorothy Headley. New York, Russell Sage Foundation, 1965. 225 p.
65-016221   364.4
Social work with youth. Delinquent girls. Juvenile Delinquency

HV741.M82 1991
Muncy, Robyn.
Creating a female dominion in American reform, 1890-1935/ Robyn Muncy. New York: Oxford University Press, 1991. xvii, 221 p.
90-038389   331.4/8136132/0973   0195057023
Child welfare -- United States -- History. Women social reformers -- United States -- History. Women social workers -- United States -- History.

HV741.N3157
National directory of children & youth services. Denver, Colo., American Association for Protecting Children (Am
80-644422   362.7/025/73
Youth -- Services for -- United States -- Directories. Child welfare -- United States -- Directories. Adolescence -- United States -- directories.

HV741.N383 1997
Neighborhood poverty/ Jeanne Brooks-Gunn, Greg J. Duncan, and J. Lawrence Aber, editors. New York: Russell Sage Foundation, c1997. 2 v.
97-007864   362.5/0973 21   0871541459
Poor children -- United States -- Case Studies. Urban poor -- United States -- Case studies. Family -- United States -- Case studies. Urban policy -- United States -- Case studies. United States -- Social policy -- Case studies.

HV741.P445 1989
Pelton, Leroy H.
For reasons of poverty: a critical analysis of the public child welfare system in the United States/ Leroy H. Pelton. New York: Praeger, 1989. xvii, 203 p.
89-033968   362.7/0973   0275930734
Child welfare -- United States. Social work with children -- United States. Foster home care -- United States.

HV741.R54 1997
Rickel, Annette U., 1941-
Keeping children from harm's way: how national policy affects psychological development/ Annette U. Rickel, Evvie Becker. Washington, DC: American Psychological Association, 1997. x, 234 p.
97-020445   362.7/0973   1557984433
Socially handicapped children -- United States. Socially handicapped teenagers -- United States. Problem children -- United States.

HV741.R62 2002
Roberts, Dorothy E.,
Shattered bonds: the color of child welfare/ Dorothy Roberts. New York: Basic Books, c2002. x, 341 p.
2001-043139   362.7/089/96073 21   0465070590
Child welfare -- United States. Racism in social services -- United States. Social work with African American children.

HV741.S367 1999
Schwartz, Ira M.
Kids raised by the government/ Ira M. Schwartz and Gideon Fishman; Simon Hakim, advisory editor. Westport, Conn.: Praeger, 1999. 150 p.
98-021667   362.7/0973   0275962644
Child welfare -- United States. Child welfare -- Michigan. Foster children -- United States.

HV741.S385 2000
Securing the future: investing in children from birth to college/ Sheldon Danziger and Jane Waldfogel, editors. New York: Russell Sage Foundation, 2000. xv, 330 p.
00-028004   362.7/0973   0871548992
Child welfare -- United States. Children -- United States -- Social conditions. Children -- Government policy -- United States.

HV741.S432 1999
Shapiro, Michael, 1952-
Solomon's sword: two families and the children the state took away/ Michael Shapiro. New York: Times Books, c1999. xv, 331 p.
98-048830   362.7/0973 21   0812923944
Child welfare -- United States -- Case studies. Family services -- United States -- Case studies.

HV741.W32 1996
Weissbourd, Rick.
The vulnerable child: what really hurts America's children and what we can do about it/ Richard Weissbourd. Reading, Mass.: Addison-Wesley Pub., c1996. xv, 280 p.
95-036789   362.7/6/0973 20   0201483955
Child welfare -- United States. Problem children -- United States. Problem families -- United States.

HV742.W5.H34 1995
Hagedorn, John, 1947-
Forsaking our children: bureaucracy and reform in the child welfare system/ by John M. Hagedorn. Chicago: Lake View Press, 1995. xvii, 245 p.
95-031317   362.7/09775   0941702413
Child welfare -- Wisconsin -- Milwaukee County.

HV743.C5
Reynolds, Arthur J.
Success in early intervention: the Chicago child parent centers/ by Arthur J. Reynolds; foreword by Edward Zigler. Lincoln, Neb.: University of Nebraska Press, c2000. xxviii, 261 p.
99-045985   362.7/086/940977311 21   080323936X
Socially handicapped children -- Services for -- Illinois -- Chicago. Socially handicapped children -- Education (Early childhood) -- Illinois -- Chicago. Socially handicapped children -- Illinois -- Chicago -- Longitudinal studies.

HV743.N49.L694 1992
Fanshel, David.
Serving the urban poor/ David Fanshel, Stephen J. Finch, and John F. Grundy. Westport, Conn.: Praeger, 1992. viii, 348 p.
91-044572   362.82/8/097471   0275940756
Child welfare -- New York (State) -- New York -- Case studies. Family social work -- New York (State) -- New York -- Case studies.

HV752.L7.D39 1996
Davin, Anna.
Growing up poor: home, school, and street in London, 1870-1914/ Anna Davin. London: Rivers Oram Press; 1996. xiv, 289 p.
95-219623   185489062X
Poor children -- England -- London -- History -- 19th century. Poor children -- England -- London -- History -- 20th century. London (England) -- Social conditions.

HV763.D53 1996
Dickinson, Edward Ross.
The politics of German child welfare from the empire to the Federal Republic/ Edward Ross Dickinson. Cambridge, Mass.: Harvard University Press, 1996. xiv, 365 p.
95-038644   262.7/0943   0674688627
Child welfare -- Germany -- History. Child welfare -- Government policy -- Germany -- History.

HV800.I8.J33 1982
Jaffe, Eliezer David, 1933-
Child welfare in Israel/ Eliezer David Jaffe. New York, N.Y.: Praeger, 1982. xiii, 319 p.
81-015422   362.7/95/095694   0030577527
Child welfare -- Israel.

HV804.M94 1992
Myers, Robert G.
The twelve who survive: strengthening programmes of early childhood development in the Third World/ Robert Myers. London; Routledge in co-operation with UNESCO for the Co 1992. xxvii, 468 p.
91-032497   362.7/1/091724   0415073073
Child welfare -- Developing countries. Child development -- Developing countries. Children -- Health and hygiene -- Developing countries.

HV804.W65 1989
Women, work, and child welfare in the Third World/ edited by Joanne Leslie, and Michael Paolisso. Boulder, Colo.: Published by Westview Press for the American Ass 1989. xii, 265 p.
89-014683   362.7/09172/4   0813378052
Child welfare -- Developing countries. Children of working mothers -- Developing countries. Women -- Employment -- Developing countries.

HV854.D39 1982
Day care: scientific and social policy issues/ edited by Edward F. Zigler, Edmund W. Gordon; under the auspices of the American Orthopsychiatric Association. Boston, Mass.: Auburn House Pub. Co., c1982. xix, 515 p.
81-012838   362.7/12/0973   0865690987
Day care centers -- United States. Child care services -- Government policy -- United States.

HV866.G7.R47 2000
Residential child care: links with families and peers/ edited by Mono Chakrabarti and Malcolm Hill. London; Philadelphia: Jessica Kingsley Publishers, 2000. 176 p.
99-041647   362.73/0941 21   1853026875
Children -- Institutional care -- Great Britain. Foster home care -- Great Britain. Foster children -- Great Britain -- Family relationships. Foster children -- Social networks -- Great Britain. Child welfare -- Great Britain.

HV873.R54 1988
Ressler, Everett M.
Unaccompanied children: care and protection in wars, natural disasters, and refugee movements/ Everett M. Ressler, Neil Boothby, and Daniel J. Steinbock. New York: Oxford University Press, 1988. x, 421 p.
86-031289   362.7/044   0195040910
Abandoned children. Child welfare. Abandoned children -- Legal status, laws, etc.

HV873.S88 1995
Swift, Karen.
Manufacturing "bad mothers": a critical perspective on child neglect/ Karen J. Swift. Toronto; University of Toronto Press, c1995. x, 218 p.
95-171073   362.7/68 20   0802029787
Abandoned children -- Services for. Abused children -- Services for. Child abuse -- Prevention.

HV875.B467 2000
Berebitsky, Julie.
Like our very own: adoption and the changing culture of motherhood, 1851-1950/ Julie Berebitsky. Lawrence, Kan.: University Press of Kansas, c2000. viii, 248 p.
00-034952   362.73/4 21   0700610510
Adoption. Motherhood. Adoptive parents.

HV875.P38 1998
Pavao, Joyce Maguire.
The family of adoption/ Joyce Maguire Pavao. Boston: Beacon Press, c1998. xv, 138 p.
97-052346   362.73/4 21   0807028002
Adoption. Family. Adopted children -- Family relationships.

HV875.55.A28 2000
Adamec, Christine A., 1949-
The encyclopedia of adoption/ Christine Adamec, William L. Pierce. New York: Facts on File, c2000. xxix, 368 p.
99-040340   362.73/4/0973 21   0816040419
Adoption -- United States -- Encyclopedias.

HV875.55.B38 1993
Bartholet, Elizabeth.
Family bonds: adoption and the politics of parenting/ Elizabeth Bartholet. Boston: Houghton Mifflin, 1993. xxii, 276 p.
92-043666   362.7/34/0973   0395510856
Adoption -- United States. Adoption -- Law and legislation -- United States. Intercountry adoption -- United States.

HV875.55.C38 1998
Carp, E. Wayne, 1946-
Family matters: secrecy and disclosure in the history of adoption/ E. Wayne Carp. Cambridge, Mass.: Harvard University Press, 1998. xii, 304 p.
97-040023   362.73/4/0973   0674796683
Adoption -- United States -- History. Open adoption -- United States -- History. Adoptees -- United States -- Identification.

HV875.55.G76 1996
Groze, Victor K.
Successful adoptive families: a longitudinal study of special needs adoption/ Victor Groze; foreword by James A. Rosenthal. Westport, Conn.: Praeger, 1996. xviii, 161 p.
95-011264   362.7/34   0275953432
Special needs adoption -- United States -- Longitudinal studies.

HV875.55.L68 1997
Loux, Ann Kimble.
The Limits of hope: an adoptive mother's story/ Ann Kimble Loux. Charlottesville: University Press of Virginia, 1997. xiii, 266 p.
96-046372   362.73/4/092   0813917107
Loux, Ann Kimble. Special needs adoption -- United States. Older child adoption -- United States. Adoptive parents -- United States -- Biography.

HV875.55.M39 1988
McRoy, Ruth G.
Openness in adoption: new practices, new issues/ Ruth G. McRoy, Harold D. Grotevant, Kerry L. White. New York: Praeger, 1988. viii, 163 p.
88-002471   362.7/34/0973   0275929337
Adoption -- United States -- Case studies.

HV875.55.P47 2000
Pertman, Adam.
Adoption nation: how the adoption revolution is transforming America/ Adam Pertman. New York: Basic Books, c2000. xiii, 349 p.
00-034297   362.73/4/0973 21   0465056512
Adoption -- United States.

HV875.55.R45 1992
Reitz, Miriam, 1935-
Adoption and the family system: strategies for treatment/ Miriam Reitz, Kenneth W. Watson. New York: Guilford Press, c1992. xii, 340 p.
91-044266   362.82/98/0973 20   0898627974
Adoption -- United States. Family social work -- United States. Family psychotherapy -- United States.

HV875.55.R68 1992
Rosenthal, James Aaron.
Special-needs adoption: a study of intact families/ James A. Rosenthal, Victor K. Groze; foreword by Drenda S. Lakin and Kathryn S. Donley. New York: Praeger, 1992. xx, 240 p.
91-030278   362.7/34/0973   0275937909
Special needs adoption -- United States. Older child adoption -- United States. Handicapped children -- United States.

HV875.55.S66 1992
Solnit, Albert J.
When home is no haven: child placement issues/ Albert J. Solnit, Barbara F. Nordhaus, Ruth Lord. New Haven: Yale University Press, c1992. xiii, 184 p.
91-004904   362.7/6 20   0300050917
Foster home care -- United States -- Case studies. Adoption -- United States -- Case studies. Abused children -- United States -- Family relationships -- Case studies.

HV875.55.W44 1997
Wegar, Katarina.
Adoption, identity, and kinship: the debate over sealed birth records/ Katarina Wegar. New Haven, Conn.: Yale University Press, c1997. xv, 169 p.
96-008145   362.7/34 20   0300067593
Adoption -- United States. Birthparents -- United States -- Identification. Adoptees -- United States -- Identification.

HV875.64.R87 2000
Rush, Sharon.
Loving across the color line: a white adoptive mother learns about race/ Sharon E. Rush. Lanham, Md.: Rowman & Littlefield Publishers, c2000. x, 190 p.
99-089362   305.8/00973 21   0847699129
Rush, Sharon. Interracial adoption -- United States. Racism -- United States. United States -- Race relations.

HV881.A78 1997
Ashby, LeRoy.
Endangered children: dependency, neglect, and abuse in American history/ LeRoy Ashby. New York: Twayne Pub., c1997. xiii, 258 p.
96-036013   362.7/6/0973 20   0805741003
Abandoned children -- United States -- History. Orphans -- United States -- History. Abused children -- United States -- History.

HV881.F36
Fanshel, David.
Children in foster care: a longitudinal investigation/ David Fanshel and Eugene B. Shinn. New York: Columbia University Press, 1978. xiv, 520 p.
77-002872   362.7/33/0973   0231035764
Foster children -- United States -- Longitudinal studies.

HV881.P74 1990
Preparing adolescents for life after foster care: the central role of foster parents/ edited by Anthony N. Maluccio, Robin Krieger, Barbara A. Pine. Washington, DC: Child Welfare League of America, c1990. xv, 225 p.
90-035033   362.7/33/0835 20   0878684336
Foster home care -- United States. Foster parents -- United States. Adolescence.

HV885.B7.H65 1989
Holloran, Peter C., 1947-
Boston's wayward children: social services for homeless children, 1830-1930/ Peter C. Holloran. Rutherford [N.J.]: Fairleigh Dickinson University Press; c1989. 330 p.
87-046425   362.7/32/0974461   0838632971
Children -- Institutional care -- Massachusetts -- Boston -- History. Social work with children -- Massachusetts -- Boston -- History. Abandoned children -- Services for -- Massachusetts -- Boston -- History.

HV885.B7.S74 1994
Stein, Edith Sarah, 1921-
A time for every purpose: life stories of foster grandparents/ Edith Sarah Stein. Manchester, CT: Knowledge, Ideas, and Trends, 1994. xv, 289 p.
93-032167   362.7/33/092   1879198118
Foster grandparents -- Massachusetts -- Boston -- Biography.

HV887.B82.N674 1998
Hecht, Tobias, 1964-
At home in the street: street children of Northeast Brazil/ Tobias Hecht. Cambridge, U.K.: Press Syndicate of the University of Cambridge 1998. xi, 267 p.
97-034145   362.76/0981/3   0521591325
Street children -- Brazil, Northeast -- Social conditions. Street children -- Abuse of -- Brazil, Northeast. Children and violence -- Brazil, Northeast.

HV887.G5.S47 1998
Sherington, Geoffrey.
Fairbridge: empire and child migration/ Geoffrey Sherington and Chris Jeffery. London; Woburn Press, 1998. xiii, 289 p.
98-024334   362.73   0713002069
Fairbridge, Kingsley Ogilvie, -- 1885-1924. Socially handicapped children -- Great Britain -- Colonies -- History -- 20th century. Great Britain -- Colonies -- Emigration and immigration -- History -- 20th century.

HV887.K4.K55 2000
Kilbride, Philip Leroy.
Street children in Kenya: voices of children in search of a childhood/ Philip Kilbride, Collette Suda, and Enos Njeru. Westport, Conn.: Bergin & Garvey, 2000. xvi, 162 p.
99-046150   305.9/06/945096762
Street children -- Kenya.

HV888.5.S45 1989
Seligman, Milton, 1937-
Ordinary families, special children: a systems approach to childhood disability/ Milton Seligman, Rosalyn Benjamin Darling. New York: Guilford Press, c1989. xii, 272 p.
88-024460   362.4/088054 19   0898627427
Handicapped children -- United States -- Family relationships. Parents of handicapped children -- United States. Family social work -- United States.

HV891.C63 1999
Coleman, Jeanine G.
The early intervention dictionary: a multidisciplinary guide to terminology/ Jeanine G. Coleman. Bethesda, Md.: Woodbine House, 1999. xiii, 410 p.
99-029729   362.1/968   1890627054
Developmentally disabled children -- Terminology. Early childhood education -- Terminology.

HV891.K58 1976
Koch, Richard, 1921-
The mentally retarded child and his family: a multidisciplinary handbook/ edited by Richard Koch and James C. Dobson. New York: Brunner/Mazel, c1976. xiii, 546 p.
75-042133   362.7/8/3   0876301219
Mentally handicapped children. Mentally handicapped children -- Family relationships. Mental retardation.

HV983.F75 1994
Friedman, Reena Sigman.
These are our children: Jewish orphanages in the United States, 1880-1925/ Reena Sigman Friedman. Hanover, N.H.: University Press of New England [for] Brandeis U c1994. xiv, 298 p.
93-036809   362.7/32/089924 20   087451665X
Jewish orphanages -- United States -- History. Jewish children -- Institutional care -- United States -- History.

HV983.H33 1997
Hacsi, Timothy A.
Second home: orphan asylums and poor families in America/ Timothy A. Hacsi. Cambridge, Mass.: Harvard University Press, 1997. x, 297 p.
97-017063   362.73/2/0973   0674796446
Orphanages -- United States -- History.

HV985.H65 1992
Holt, Marilyn Irvin, 1949-
The orphan trains: placing out in America/ Marilyn Irvin Holt. Lincoln: University of Nebraska Press, c1992. 248 p.
91-029155   362.7/34/0973 20   0803223609
Orphan trains.

HV995.A32.A533 1996
Dulberger, Judith A.
"Mother donit fore the best": correspondence of a nineteenth-century orphan asylum/ Judith A. Dulberger. Syracuse, N.Y.: Syracuse University Press, 1996. xiii, 206 p.
95-040038   362.7/32/0974743   0815626967
Orphanages -- New York (State) -- Albany -- History -- 19th century. Orphans -- New York (State) -- Albany -- Correspondence. Foster children -- New York (State) -- Albany -- Correspondence

HV995.B2.Z46 1994
Zmora, Nurith, 1950-
Orphanages reconsidered: child care institutions in progressive era Baltimore/ Nurith Zmora. Philadelphia: Temple University Press, 1994. xvi, 240 p.
93-014640   362.7/32/097526   1566390710
Orphanages -- Maryland -- Baltimore -- History -- Case studies.

HV995.C42.C553 1995
Cmiel, Kenneth.
A home of another kind: one Chicago orphanage and the tangle of child welfare/ Kenneth Cmiel. Chicago: University of Chicago Press, 1995. viii, 243 p.
95-014573   362.7/32/0977311   0226110842
Orphanages -- Illinois -- Chicago -- History. Problem children -- Institutional care -- Illinois -- Chicago -- History.

HV995.M5.L33 1949
Burmeister, Eva E.
Forty-five in the family; the story of a home for children. New York, Columbia Univ. Press, 1949. xii, 247 p.
49-007896   362.73
Children -- Institutional care.

HV1150.L8.C486 1995
Manzione, Carol Kazmierczak, 1952-
Christ's Hospital of London, 1552-1598: a passing deed of pity/ Carol Kazmierczak Manzione. Selinsgrove, Pa.: Susquehanna University Press; 1995. 232 p.
94-016865   362.7/32/094212   0945636717
Orphanages -- England -- London -- History.

HV1210.A52.B86 1997
McCants, Anne E. C. 1962-
Civic charity in a golden age: orphan care in early modern Amsterdam/ Anne E.C. McCants. Urbana: University of Illinois Press, c1997. viii, 281 p.
96-051239   362.73/2 21   0252023331
Orphanages -- Netherlands -- Amsterdam -- History -- 17th century. Orphanages -- Netherlands -- Amsterdam -- History -- 18th century. Poor -- Services for -- Netherlands -- Amsterdam -- History.

HV1421-1441 Protection, assistance and relief — Special classes — Young adults. Youth. Teenagers

HV1421.L67 1993
Losing generations: adolescents in high-risk settings/ Panel on High-Risk Youth, Commission on Behavioral and Social Sciences and Education, National Research Council. Washington, D.C.: National Academy Press, 1993. ix, 276 p.
93-004358   362.7/4/0973   0309048281
Socially handicapped youth -- United States.

HV1431.B37 1990
Barth, Richard P., 1952-
Preventing adolescent abuse: effective intervention strategies and techniques/ by Richard P. Barth and David S. Derezotes. Lexington, Mass.: Lexington Books, c1990. xv, 222 p.
90-030978   362.7/67/0835 20   0669209031
Teenagers -- Abuse of -- United States -- Prevention. Teenagers -- Abuse of -- California -- Prevention -- Case studies.

HV1431.C88 1994
Cutler, Evan Karl, 1968-
Runaway me: a survivor's story, a book/ written and lived by Evan Karl Cutler. Fort Collins, Colo.: Blooming Press Co., 1994. 381 p.
93-074729   362.7/4   1884607152
Cutler, Evan Karl, -- 1968- Runaway teenagers -- United States. Runaway children -- United States. Abused children -- United States.

HV1431.D79 1990
Dryfoos, Joy G.
Adolescents at risk: prevalence and prevention/ Joy
G. Dryfoos. New York: Oxford University Press,
1990. vi, 280 p.
89-070975   362.7/96/0973   0195057716
*Socially handicapped teenagers -- United States.
Teenagers -- Counseling of -- United States.
Juvenile delinquency -- United States --
Prevention.*

HV1431.F56 1998
Finnegan, William.
Cold new world: growing up in a harder country/
William Finnegan. New York: Random House,
c1998. xxiii, 421 p.
97-045927   305.235/0973 21   0679448705
*Teenagers -- United States -- Social conditions.
Subculture -- United States. Poverty -- United
States. United States -- Social conditions -- 1980-*

HV1431.R44 1992
Reiman, Richard A.
The New Deal & American youth: ideas & ideals
in a depression decade/ Richard A. Reiman.
Athens: University of Georgia Press, c1992. viii,
253 p.
91-022124   362.7/0973 20   0820314072
*Youth -- United States -- History. New Deal,
1933-1939. United States -- Social conditions --
1933-1945.*

HV1441.G3.H37 1993
Harvey, Elizabeth.
Youth and the welfare state in Weimar Germany/
Elizabeth Harvey. Oxford: Clarendon Press; 1993.
x, 352 p.
93-018199   362.7/1/094309042   0198204140
*Youth -- Services for -- Germany. Youth --
Government policy -- Germany. Welfare state.
Germany -- Social policy.*

HV1441.4 Protection, assistance and relief — Special classes — Men

HV1441.4.A28 2001
The abuse of men: trauma begets trauma/ Barbara
Jo Brothers, editor. New York: Haworth Press,
2001. 119 p.
2001-024317   362.8 21   0789013797
*Abused men. Adult child abuse victims. Husband
abuse.*

HV1441.4.M44 2002
Men as caregivers: theory, research, and service
implications/ Betty J. Kramer, Edward H.
Thompson, editors. New York: Springer Pub.,
2002. xii, 394 p.
2001-042874   362/.0425 21   0826114725
Male caregivers. Social work with men.

HV1444-1448 Protection, assistance and relief — Special classes — Women

HV1444.B88 1991
Butler, Sandra, 1938-
Feminist groupwork/ Sandra Butler and Claire
Wintram. London; Sage Publications, 1991. 200 p.
91-053085   0803982097
*Social work with women. Social group work.
Feminist psychology.*

HV1444.F46 1990
The Feminization of poverty: only in America?/
edited by Gertrude Schaffner Goldberg & Eleanor
Kremen. New York: Greenwood Press, 1990. xii,
231 p.
90-036628   362.83/08/6942   031326421X
*Poor women -- Cross-cultural studies. Poor
women -- United States. Women heads of
households -- Cross-cultural studies.*

HV1444.S35 1996
Sainsbury, Diane.
Gender, equality, and welfare states/ Diane
Sainsbury. Cambridge [England]; Cambridge
University Press, 1996. xiv, 258 p.
95-050672   362.83   0521562775
*Women -- Government policy. Women --
Economic conditions. Public welfare.*

HV1445.B47 1995
Berrick, Jill Duerr.
Faces of poverty: portraits of women and children
on welfare/ Jill Duerr Berrick. New York: Oxford
University Press, 1995. x, 214 p.
94-043371   362.5/0973   0195097548
*Poor women -- United States -- Case studies.
Poor children -- United States -- Case studies.
Welfare recipients -- United States -- Case studies.*

HV1445.K57 1996
Kingfisher, Catherine Pelissier.
Women in the American welfare trap/ Catherine
Pelissier Kingfisher. Philadelphia: University of
Pennsylvania Press, c1996. x, 206 p.
96-019862   362.83/8/093 20   0812232879
*Poor women -- United States. Welfare recipients
-- United States. Human services personnel --
United States.*

HV1445.S47 2001
Shostack, Albert L.
Shelters for battered women and their children: a
comprehensive guide to planning and operating
safe and caring residential programs/ by Albert L.
Shostack. Springfield, Ill.: Charles C Thomas,
c2001. xxi, 236 p.
00-046683   362.82/9285/068 21   0398071446
*Women's shelters -- United States -- Handbooks,
manuals, etc. Abused women -- Services for --
United States -- Handbooks, manuals, etc.*

HV1445.W43 1996
Whalen, Mollie.
Counseling to end violence against women: a
subversive model/ Mollie Whalen. Thousand Oaks,
Calif.: Sage Publications, c1996. xviii, 166 p.
95-050177   362.82/9286/0973 20   0803973799
*Abused women -- Counseling of -- United States.
Feminist therapy -- United States.*

HV1446.A17.P37 1990
Pascoe, Peggy.
Relations of rescue: the search for female moral
authority in the American west, 1874-1939/ Peggy
Pascoe. New York: Oxford University Press, 1990.
xxiii, 301 p.
89-036475   362.8/292/0973   0195060083
*Abused women -- West (U.S.) -- History -- 19th
century. Women volunteers in social service --
West (U.S.) -- History -- 19th century. Women's
shelters -- West (U.S.) -- History -- 19th century.
West (U.S.) -- Moral conditions.*

HV1446.N5.A54 1997
Ames, Lynda J.
Women reformed, women empowered: poor
mothers and the endangered promise of Head Start/
Lynda J. Ames with Jeanne Ellsworth.
Philadelphia: Temple University Press, 1997. x,
251 p.
96-020537   362.83/8   1566394929
*Head Start programs -- New York (State) Poor
women -- Services for -- New York (State)*

HV1448.B72.S26413 1995
Dias, Maria Odila Leite da Silva.
Power and everyday life: the lives of working
women in nineteenth-century Brazil/ Maria Odila
Silva Dias; translated by Ann Frost. New
Brunswick, N.J.: Rutgers University Press, 1995. x,
221 p.
94-047497   305.5/69/082   0813522048
*Poor women -- Brazil -- Sao Paulo -- History --
19th century. Women -- Brazil -- Sao Paulo --
Social conditions. Poor women -- Brazil -- Sao
Paulo -- Social conditions.*

HV1448.I8.C65 1992
Cohen, Sherrill.
The evolution of women's asylums since 1500:
from refuges for ex-prostitutes to shelters for
battered women/ Sherrill Cohen. New York:
Oxford University Press, 1992. viii, 262 p.
91-036251   362.83/85/0945   0195051645
*Women's shelters -- Italy -- History -- 16th
century. Women's shelters -- Italy -- History -- 17th
century. Women -- Italy -- Social conditions.*

HV1448.S2.G65 1991
Golden, Renny.
The hour of the poor, the hour of women:
Salvadoran women speak/ Renny Golden. New
York: Crossroad, 1991. 207 p.
91-015140   362.83/08/6942   0824510887
*Poor women -- El Salvador -- Interviews.
Feminists -- El Salvador -- Interviews. Women and
war -- El Salvador.*

HV1449 Protection, assistance and relief — Special classes — Gay men. Lesbians

HV1449.M35 1998
Mallon, Gerald P.
We don't exactly get the Welcome Wagon: the
experiences of gay and lesbian adolescents in child
welfare systems/ Gerald P. Mallon. New York:
Columbia University Press, c1998. xii, 193 p.
97-045545   362.7/083 21   0231104545
*Gay teenagers -- Institutional care -- North
America. Child welfare -- North America.
Homophobia -- North America.*

HV1451-1468 Protection, assistance and relief — Special classes — Aged

HV1451.A38 1997
The aging family: new visions in theory, practice,
and reality/ edited by Terry D. Hargrave and
Suzanne Midori Hanna. New York:
Brunner/Mazel, c1997. xi, 321 p.
96-045236   362.6 21   0876308418
*Social work with the aged. Family social work.
Aged -- Care.*

HV1451.I547 1994
International handbook on services for the elderly/ edited by Jordan I. Kosberg; foreword by Alfred Grech. Westport, Conn.: Greenwood Press, 1994. xxvi, 501 p.
93-044507   361.6   0313283389
Aged -- Services for -- Handbooks, manuals, etc.

HV1451.R4
Reaching the aged: social services in forty-four countries/ editors, Morton I. Teicher, Daniel Thursz, Joseph L. Vigilante. Beverly Hills: Sage Publications, c1979. 256 p.
79-018525   362.6   0803913656
Aged -- Services for. Social work with the aged. Aged -- Family relationships.

HV1451.W359 2001
Working with older people and their families: key issues in policy and practice/ Mike Nolan, Sue Davies, Gordon Grant (editors) Phildelphia, Pa.: Open University, 2001. xi, 228 p.
00-045271   362.6 21   0335205607
Social work with the aged. Aged -- Care. Aged -- Family relationships.

HV1454.2.U6.S36 1990
Schmidt, Mary Gwynne.
Negotiating a good old age: challenges of residential living in late life/ Mary Gwynne Schmidt. San Francisco: Jossey-Bass, 1990. xxiii, 299 p.
90-038688   362.6/1/0973   1555422934
Old age homes -- United States -- Case studies. Long-term care facilities -- United States -- Case studies. Aged -- Institutional care -- United States -- Case studies.

HV1457.O42
Older Americans information directory.   Detroit, MI: Gale Research Inc., [c1994-]
94-660686   362.6/025/73
Aged -- Services for -- United States -- Directories. Aged -- United States -- Information services -- Directories.

HV1461.A28 1984
Abuse of the elderly: a guide to resources and services/ [edited by] Joseph J. Costa. Lexington, Mass.: Lexington Books, c1984. xiii, 289 p.
82-048472   362.8/8/0880565   0669061425
Aged -- Abuse of -- United States. Abused aged -- Services for -- United States.

HV1461.C36 1992
Care for frail elders: developing community solutions/ Walter N. Leutz ... [et al.]; foreword by James J. Callahan, Jr. Westport, Conn.: Auburn House, 1992. xiii, 300 p.
92-011506   362.6   0865690294
Frail elderly -- Home care -- United States. Frail elderly -- Services for -- United States.

HV1461.C37 1989
The Care of tomorrow's elderly/ Marion Ein Lewin & Sean Sullivan, editors. Washington, D.C.: American Enterprise Institute for Public Policy 1989. xii, 189 p.
88-035120   362.6/0973   0844736813
Aged -- Care -- United States. Retirement income -- United States. Aged -- Government policy -- United States.

HV1461.C388 2001
Cason, Ann.
Circles of care: how to set up quality home care for our elders/ Ann Cason; foreword by Reeve Lindbergh. 1st ed. Boston: Shambhala, 2001. xxiv, 168 p.
00-049655   362.6 21   1570624712
Aged -- Home care -- United States.

HV1461.C53 1988
Clark, William F.
Old and poor: a critical assessment of the low-income elderly/ William F. Clark, Anabel O. Pelham, Marleen L. Clark. Lexington, Mass.: Lexington Books, 1988. x, 222 p.
88-000858   362.6/0973   0669110787
Old age assistance -- United States -- Case studies. Aged -- Care -- United States -- Case studies. Cost and standard of living -- United States -- Case studies.

HV1461.C666 1999
Conner, Karen Ann, 1946-
Continuing to care: older Americans and their families / Karen A. Conner. New York: Falmer Press, 1999.
99-037922   362.6/0973   0815328893
Aged -- Home care -- United States -- Forecasting. Aged -- United States -- Family relationships -- Forecasting. Caregivers -- United States -- Social conditions -- Forecasting.

HV1461.C74 1993
Cox, Carole B.
The frail elderly: problems, needs, and community responses/ Carole Cox. Westport, Conn.: Auburn House, 1993. x, 208 p.
92-038000   362.6   0865690316
Frail elderly -- Services for -- United States.

HV1461.E464 2001
Empowering frail elderly people: opportunities and impediments in housing, health, and support service delivery/ edited by Leonard F. Heumann, Mary E. McCall, and Duncan P. Boldy. Westport, CT: Praeger , 2001. xiii, 282 p.
00-025465   362.6   0275966518
Frail elderly -- Services for -- United States.

HV1461.E5 1995
Encyclopedia of home care for the elderly/ edited by Ada Romaine-Davis, Jennifer Boondas, and Ayeliffe Lenihan; foreword by Robert N. Butler. Westport, Conn.: Greenwood Press, 1995. xv, 436 p.
94-017989   362.6   0313285322
Aged -- Home care -- United States. Aged -- United States.

HV1461.H39 1997
Harris, Phyllis Braudy.
Men giving care: reflections of husbands and sons/ Phyllis Braudy Harris, Joyce Bichler. New York: Garland Pub., 1997. xiv, 223 p.
96-048449   362.1/96831   0815317921
Aged -- Care -- United States -- Case studies. Alzheimer's disease -- Patients -- Care -- United States -- Case studies. Caregivers -- United States -- Case studies.

HV1461.H57 1988
Hispanic elderly in transition: theory, research, policy, and practice/ edited by Steven R. Applewhite. New York: Greenwood Press, 1988. xii, 238 p.
87-037563   362.6/0896873   0313244782
Hispanic American aged -- Services for. Hispanic American aged -- Social conditions.

HV1461.K39 1990
Kaye, Lenard W.
Men as caregivers to the elderly: understanding and aiding unrecognized family support/ by Lenard W. Kaye and Jeffrey S. Applegate. Lexington, Mass.: Lexington Books, c1990. xx, 202 p.
90-006149   362.6 20   0669197726
Aged -- Care -- United States. Caregivers -- United States -- Psychology. Men -- United States -- Psychology.

HV1461.K63 1993
Koch, Tom, 1949-
A place in time: care givers for their elderly/ Tom Koch. Westport, Conn.: Praeger, 1993. 236 p.
92-001754   362.6   0275944832
Aged -- Care -- United States -- Case studies. Frail elderly -- Home care -- United States -- Case studies. Caregivers -- United States -- Case studies.

HV1461.K68 1991
Kramer, Jane S. 1956-
Who cares for the elderly: formal and informal support/ Jane Susan Kramer. New York: Garland Publishing, 1991. 188 p.
91-037869   362.6   081530529X
Aged -- Care -- United States -- Case studies. Caregivers -- United States -- Case studies. Arthritis -- Patients -- United States -- Case studies.

HV1461.M36 1990
Margolis, Richard J.
Risking old age in America/ Richard J. Margolis. Boulder, Colo.: Westview Press, 1990. xi, 202 p.
89-022620   305.26/0973   0813309395
Aged -- United States. Aged -- Housing -- United States. Aged -- Care -- United States.

HV1461.M66 1996
Moon, Marilyn.
Entitlements and the elderly: protecting promises, recognizing reality/ Marilyn Moon and Janemarie Mulvey. Washington, D.C.: Urban Institute Press; c1996. xiv, 177 p.
95-038696   362.6/3/0973 20   0877666369
Old age assistance -- United States. Aged -- Government policy -- United States. Aged -- Medical care -- Government policy -- United States.

HV1461.O44 1992
The Oldest old/ edited by Richard M. Suzman, David P. Willis, Kenneth G. Manton. New York: Oxford University Press, 1992. xi, 444 p.
90-014340   305.26/0973   0195050606
Aged -- Services for -- United States. Aged -- United States -- Social conditions. Social work with the aged -- United States.

HV1461.S83 1983
Steinberg, Raymond M.
Case management and the elderly: a handbook for planning and administering programs/ Raymond M. Steinberg, Genevieve W. Carter. Lexington, Mass.: LexingtonBooks, c1983. xii, 211 p.
82-017127   362.6/042   0669060895
Social work with the aged -- United States -- Handbooks, manuals, etc. Social work administration -- United States -- Handbooks, manuals, etc. Health services for the aged -- Organization and administration -- Handbooks.

HV1461.V56 1995
Vincent, John A., 1947-
Inequality and old age/ John A. Vincent. New York, N.Y.: St. Martin's Press, 1995. vi, 218 p.
95-000555 305.26/0973 0312159897
Aged -- United States. Equality -- United States. Aging -- Social aspects -- United States.

HV1465.G36 1994
Gallagher, Sally K.
Older people giving care: helping family and community/ Sally K. Gallagher. Westport, Conn.: Auburn House, 1994. xiv, 182 p.
93-009017 361.3/7/0846 0865692335
Aged volunteers in social service -- United States. Caregivers -- United States.

HV1465.M84 1998
Mui, Ada C., 1949-
Long-term care and ethnicity/ Ada C. Mui, Namkee G. Choi, and Abraham Monk. Westport, Conn: Auburn House, 1998. xii, 216 p.
98-011157 362.1/6/08900973 0865692327
Afro-American aged -- Long-term care -- United States. Hispanic American aged -- Long-term care -- United States. Frail elderly -- Long-term care -- United States.

HV1468.M6.H38 1995
Havir, Linda Marie.
But will they use it?: social service utilization by rural elderly/ Linda M. Havir. New York: Garland Pub., 1995. xxiii, 217 p.
95-013768 362.6/3/09776 0815319649
Rural aged -- Services for -- Minnesota.

HV1553-3021 Protection, assistance and relief — Special classes — People with disabilities

HV1553.D544 2000
Disabilities sourcebook: basic consumer health information about physical and psychiatric disabilities .../ edited by Dawn D. Matthews. Detroit: Omnigraphics, c2000. xii, 616 p.
99-056930 362.4/048/0973 21 0780803892
Handicapped -- United States -- Handbooks, manuals, etc. Physically handicapped -- United States -- Handbooks, manuals, etc. Mentally handicapped -- United States -- Handbooks, manuals,etc.

HV1553.D564 1994
The Disabled, the media, and the information age/ edited by Jack A. Nelson. Westport, Conn.: Greenwood Press, 1994. x, 249 p.
93-007700 302.23/087 0313284725
Handicapped in mass media. Handicapped -- United States -- Social conditions. Mass media -- United States.

HV1553.F58 2001
Fleischer, Doris Zames.
The disability rights movement: from charity to confrontation/ Doris Zames Fleischer and Frieda Zames. Philadelphia: Temple University Press, 2001. xxix, 278 p.
00-039282 323.3 1566398118
Handicapped -- Civil rights -- United States. Discrimination against the handicapped -- United States.

HV1553.P46 1989
Percy, Stephen L.
Disability, civil rights, and public policy: the politics of implementation/ Stephen L. Percy. Tuscaloosa: University of Alabama Press, c1989. xii, 309 p.
89-030317 362.4/0973 0817304444
Handicapped -- Government policy -- United States. Handicapped -- Civil rights -- United States.

HV1553.R48 1998
Resources for people with disabilities: a national directory/ edited by Elizabeth H. Oakes, John Bradford. Chicago: Ferguson Pub. Co., c1998. 2 v.
98-009663 362.4/048/02573 21 0894342428
Handicapped -- Services for -- United States -- Directories. Handicapped -- Services for -- United States -- Finance -- Directories. Self-help devices for the disabled -- United States -- Directories.

HV1555.M6.W55 1996
Williams, Marie Sheppard, 1931-
The worldwide church of the handicapped: and other stories/ by Marie Sheppard Williams. Minneapolis, Minn.: Coffee House Press, c1996. 220 p.
96-002578 362.4/09776 20 1566890470
Williams, Marie Sheppard, -- 1931- Social work with the handicapped -- Minnesota -- Anecdotes. Handicapped -- Minnesota -- Anecdotes.

HV1568.E53 1995
Encyclopedia of disability and rehabilitation/ Arthur E. Dell Orto, Robert P. Marinelli, editors. New York: Macmillan Library Reference USA; c1995. xxiv, 820 p.
95-024454 362.4/03 20 002897297X
Handicapped -- Rehabilitation -- Encyclopedias.

HV1568.M277 1999
Marshak, Laura E.
Disability and the family life cycle/ Laura E. Marshak, Milton Seligman, Fran Prezant. New York, NY: Basic Books, c1999. xiii, 318 p. 0465016324
Handicapped -- Home care. Handicapped -- Family relationships.

HV1568.R435 1997
Rehabilitation counseling: profession and practice/ Dennis R. Maki, T.F. Riggar, editors. New York: Springer Pub. Co., c1997. xiii, 377 p.
96-046426 362.4/0486 21 0826195105
Handicapped -- Counseling of. Handicapped -- Rehabilitation.

HV1568.R45 2000
Reinders, Hans S.
The future of the disabled in liberal society: an ethical analysis/ Hans S. Reinders. Notre Dame, IN: University of Notre Dame Press, c2000. xii, 280 p.
00-029891 305.9/0816 21 0268028567
Sociology of disability. Handicapped -- Social conditions. Handicapped -- Government policy.

HV1568.S38 1997
Schwartz, David B., 1948-
Who cares?: rediscovering community/ David B. Schwartz. Boulder: WestviewPress, 1997. xiii, 169 p.
96-034625 362.4 0813332079
Handicapped -- Care. Caregivers. Community.

HV1568.S63 2001
Smart, Julie.
Disability, society, and the individual/ Julie Smart. Gaithersburg, MD: Aspen, 2001. xv, 357 p.
00-058285 305.9/0816 21 0834216019
Handicapped -- Social conditions. Discrimination against people with disabilities. Sociology of disability.

HV1568.2.M37 1999
Marks, Deborah, 1964-
Disability: controversial debates and psychosocial perspectives/ Deborah Marks. London; Routledge, 1999. xiv, 217 p.
99-014620 362.4 0415162025
Disability studies. Sociology of disability. Handicapped.

HV1569.5.A45 2000
Alliance for Technology Access.
Computer and web resources for people with disabilities: a guide to exploring today's assistive technology/ Alliance for Technology Access. Alameda, CA: Hunter House Publishers, c2000. xvi, 364 p.
99-059323 004/.087 21 0897933001
Computers and the handicapped. Computers and the handicapped -- Equipment and supplies. Web site development.

HV1569.5.S57 1991
Shrout, R. N.
Resource directory for the disabled/ Richard Neil Shrout. New York: Facts on File, c1991. viii, 392 p.
91-010244 681/.76 20 081602216X
Self-help devices for the disabled -- United States -- Information services -- Directories.

HV1624.B7.F74 2001
Freeberg, Ernest.
The education of Laura Bridgman: first deaf and blind person to learn language/ Ernest Freeberg. Cambridge, Mass.: Harvard University Press, 2001. 264 p.
00-054219 362.4/1/092 0674005899
Bridgman, Laura Dewey, -- 1829-1889. Blind-deaf women -- United States -- Biography. Blind-deaf women -- Education -- United States.

HV1624.B7G57 2001
Gitter, Elisabeth, 1945-
The imprisoned guest: Samuel Howe and Laura Bridgman, the original deaf-blind girl/ Elisabeth Gitter. New York: Farrar, Straus and Giroux: 2001. x, 341 p.
00-047642 362.4/1/092 0374117381
Bridgman, Laura Dewey, -- 1829-1889. Howe, S. G. -- (Samuel Gridley), -- 1801-1876. Blind-deaf women -- United States -- Biography. Teachers of the blind-deaf -- United States -- Biography.

HV1624.K4.H47 1998
Herrmann, Dorothy.
Helen Keller: a life/ Dorothy Herrmann. New York: A. Knopf, 1998. xvi, 394 p.
98-014556 362.4/1/092 0679443541
Keller, Helen, -- 1880-1968. Blind-deaf women -- United States -- Biography. Blind-deaf women -- Education -- United sTates.

HV1788.M52 1990
Matson, Floyd W.
Walking alone and marching together: a history of the organized blind movement in the United States, 1940-1990/ by Floyd Matson. Baltimore, Md.: National Federation of the Blind, c1990. v, 1116 p.
90-006476 362.4/15763/0973 20 096241221X
Blind -- United States -- Societies, etc. -- History.

HV2042.M37 1999
Metzger, Melanie.
Sign language interpreting: deconstructing the myth of neutrality/ Melanie Metzger. Washington, D.C.: Gallaudet University Press, 1999. x, 234 p.
98-049308   419   1563680742
Interpreters for the deaf -- United States -- Psychology. American Sign Language -- Translating. Translating and interpreting -- United States -- Psychological aspects.

HV2367.L36 1984
Lane, Harlan L.
When the mind hears: a history of the deaf/ Harlan Lane. New York: Random House, c1984. xvii, 537 p.
83-043201   305/.908162/0973   0394508785
Clerc, Laurent, -- 1785-1869. Deaf -- History. Deaf -- Biography. Deaf -- Education -- History.

HV2373.L36 1995
Lang, Harry G.
Deaf persons in the arts and sciences: a biographical dictionary/ Harry G. Lang and Bonnie Meath-Lang. Westport, Conn.: Greenwood Press, 1995. xvii, 424 p.
94-024206   920/.0087/1   0313291705
Deaf -- Biography.

HV2380.L27 1996
Lane, Harlan L.
A journey into the deaf-world/ Harlan Lane, Robert Hoffmeister, Ben Bahan. San Diego, Calif.: DawnSignPress, c1996. x, 510 p.
96-019522   305.9/08162/0973 20   0915035626
Deaf -- Social conditions. Deaf -- United States -- Social conditions. Deaf -- Means of communication -- United States.

HV2390.D42
Deaf children: developmental perspectives/ edited by Lynn S. Liben. New York: Academic Press, 1978. xv, 246 p.
77-077237   155.4/5/12   0124479502
Deaf children. Deafness -- In infancy and childhood. Deafness -- Rehabilitation.

HV2391.M26 1997
Marschark, Marc.
Raising and educating a deaf child/ Marc Marschark. New York: Oxford University Press, 1997. xx, 235 p.
96-005504   362.4/2/083   0195094670
Deaf children. Deaf children -- Language. Parents of deaf children.

HV2395.H53
Higgins, Paul C.
Outsiders in a hearing world: a sociology of deafness/ Paul C. Higgins; foreword by Robert A. Scott. Beverly Hills, Calif.: Sage Publications, c1980. 205 p.
80-012150   305   0803914210
Deaf. Deafness -- Social aspects.

HV2430.A38 1991
Advances in cognition, education, and deafness/ David S. Martin, editor. Washington, D.C.: Gallaudet University Press, 1991. xvii, 447 p.
91-010693   371.91/2   0930323793
Deaf -- Education -- Congresses. Cognition -- Congresses.

HV2430.E383 1990
Educational and developmental aspects of deafness/ Donald F. Moores, Kathryn P. Meadow-Orlans, editors. Washington, D.C.: Gallaudet University Press, 1990. x, 451 p.
90-014014   371.91/2   0930323521
Deaf -- United States -- Education. Deaf children -- Psychology.

HV2430.I77 1998
Issues unresolved: new perspectives on language and deaf education/ Amatzia Weisel, editor. Washington, D.C.: Gallaudet University Press, c1998. xxii, 250 p.
98-023762   371.91/2 21   156368067X
Deaf -- Education -- Congresses. Deaf children -- Education -- Congresses. Deaf -- Means of communication -- Congresses.

HV2469.S63.G74 1993
Greenberg, Mark T.
Promoting social and emotional development in deaf children: the PATHS project/ Mark T. Greenberg and Carol A. Kusche. Seattle: University of Washington Press, c1993. xvi, 248 p.
93-015605   371.91/2 20   0295972270
Deaf children -- Education. Deaf -- Education. Social skills -- Study and teaching.

HV2471.A63 1998
American sign language: shattering the myth/ essays by Frances M. Parsons, Larry G. Stewart; with additional contributions from Otto J. Menzel ... [et al.]; edited by Tom Bertling. Wilsonville, Or.: Kodiak Media Group, 1998. 112 p.
98-066201   419
American Sign Language. Deaf -- Education -- United States. Deaf -- Means of communication -- United States.

HV2471.B39 1996
Baynton, Douglas C.
Forbidden signs: American culture and the campaign against sign language/ Douglas C. Baynton. Chicago: University of Chicago Press, 1996. xi, 228 p.
96-012889   419   0226039633
Deaf -- Means of communication -- United States -- History. Sign language -- Study and teaching -- United States -- History. Deaf -- United States -- Social conditions.

HV2471.P38 2000
Peters, Cynthia.
Deaf American literature: from carnival to the canon/ Cynthia Peters. Washington, D.C.: Gallaudet University Press, 2000. vii, 217 p.
00-031523   419   1563680947
American Sign Language. Interpreters for the deaf.

HV2474.D25 2001
Daniels, Marilyn.
Dancing with words: signing for hearing children's literacy/ Marilyn Daniels. Westport: Bergin & Garvey, 2001. xi, 183 p.
00-027239   419/.0973   0897897234
Sign language. American Sign Language. Literacy.

HV2475.C66 1997
Costello, Elaine.
Random House Webster's American sign language dictionary/ by Elaine Costello; illustrated by Lois Lenderman, Paul M. Setzer, Linda C. Tom. New York: Random House, 1997.
97-021538   419/.03   0679780114
American Sign Language -- Dictionaries.

HV2475.S77 1998
Sternberg, Martin L. A.
American Sign Language/ Martin L.A. Sternberg; illustrated by Herbert Rogoff. New York: HarperCollins Publishers, c1998. xxi, 983 p.
98-026649   419 21   0062716085
American Sign Language -- Dictionaries.

HV2475.T46 1998
Tennant, Richard A.
The American Sign Language handshape dictionary/ Richard A. Tennant, Marianne Gluszak Brown; illustrated by Valerie Nelson-Metlay. Washington, D.C.: Clerc Books, Gallaudet University Press, c1998. 407 p.
97-048389   419 21   1563680432
American Sign Language -- Dictionaries.

HV2508.B35 1993
Baldwin, Stephen C., 1944-
Pictures in the air: the story of the National Theatre of the Deaf/ Stephen C. Baldwin. Washington, D.C.: Gallaudet University Press, c1993. xvi, 142 p.
93-037250   792/.087/2 20   1563680254
Deaf, Theater for the -- History.

HV2530.B83 1999
Buchanan, Robert
Illusions of equality: deaf Americans in school and factory, 1850-1950/ Robert M. Buchanan. Washington, D.C.: Gallaudet University Press, c1999. xvii, 214 p.
99-040421   305.9/08162 21   156368084X
Deaf -- Education -- United States -- History. Deaf -- Employment -- United States -- History.

HV2530.J35 1997
Jankowski, Katherine A.
Deaf empowerment: emergence, struggle, and rhetoric/ Katherine A. Jankowski. Washington, D.C.: Gallaudet University Press, 1997. viii, 197 p.
97-011897   362.4/2/0973   1563680610
Deaf -- United States -- History. Deaf -- Civil rights -- United States -- History. Deaf -- Means of communication -- United States -- History.

HV2534.S76.M35 1996
Maher, Jane, 1947-
Seeing language in sign: the work of William C. Stokoe/ by Jane Maher; foreword by Oliver Sacks. Washington, D.C.: Gallaudet University Press, 1996. xviii, 195 p.
95-046906   419/.092   156368053X
Stokoe, William C. Teachers of the deaf -- United States -- Biography. Linguists -- United States -- Biography. American Sign Language.

HV2551.T68 1992
Toward effective public school programs for deaf students: context, process, and outcomes/ edited by Thomas N. Kluwin, Donald F. Moores, Martha Gonter Gaustad. New York: Teachers College Press, c1992. viii, 264 p.
92-002932   371.91/2/0973 20   0807731609
Deaf children -- Education -- United States. Mainstreaming in education -- United States. Public schools -- United States.

HV2561.I483.C43 1994
Banks, Jeri.
All of us together: the story of inclusion at the Kinzie School/ Jeri Banks. Washington, D.C.: Gallaudet University Press, 1994. ix, 199 p.
94-007508   371.91/2/0977311   1563680289
Deaf -- Education -- Illinois -- Chicago -- Case studies. Mainstreaming in education -- Illinois -- Chicago -- Case studies.

HV2748.B5413 1999
Biesold, Horst, 1939-
Crying hands: eugenics and deaf people in Nazi Germany/ Horst Biesold; translation by William Sayers; introduction by Henry Friedlander. Washington, D.C.: Gallaudet University Press, 1999. xix, 230 p.
99-027291 362.4/2094309043 1563680777
Deaf -- Government policy -- Germany. Deafness -- Germany. History of medicine, 20th century -- Germany.

HV3004.B95 2000
Byrne, Peter, 1950-
Philosophical and ethical problems in mental handicap/ Peter Byrne. New York: St. Martin's Press, 2000. xiii, 175 p.
00-027830 362.3 0312234600
Mentally handicapped. Mental retardation -- Moral and ethical aspects.

HV3006.A4.A48 1998
Angrosino, Michael V.
Opportunity house: ethnographic stories of mental retardation/ Michael V. Angrosino. Walnut Creek, CA: AltaMira Press, c1998. 287 p.
97-033813 362.3/0973 21 0761989161
Mental retardation -- United States. Ethnology -- United States.

HV3006.A4.F33
Farber, Bernard.
Mental retardation: its social context and social consequences. Boston, Houghton Mifflin [1968] xi, 287 p.
68-004800 301.47/685/88
Mentally handicapped -- United States. Mental retardation.

HV3006.A4.T74 1994
Trent, James W.
Inventing the feeble mind: a history of mental retardation in the United States/ James W. Trent, Jr. Berkeley: University of California Press, c1994. xii, 356 p.
93-032239 362.3/0973 20 0520082435
Mentally handicapped -- United States -- History. Mental retardation -- United States -- History. Mentally handicapped -- Institutional care -- United States -- History.

HV3009.5.A35 A355 2000
Aging and developmental disability: current research, programming, and practice implications/ Joy Hammel, Susan M. Nochajski, editors. New York: Haworth Press, c2000. 100 p.
00-049890 362.1/968 21 0789010402
Developmentally disabled aged. Developmentally disabled aged -- Services for. Physical therapy for the aged.

HV3021.W66.W68 1988
Women with disabilities: essays in psychology, culture, and politics/ edited by Michelle Fine and Adrienne Asch. Philadelphia: Temple University Press, 1988. xv, 347 p.
87-010099 362.4/088042 0877224749
Physically handicapped women. Sex discrimination against women. Physically handicapped women -- Psychology.

HV3176 Protection, assistance and relief — Special classes. By race or ethnic group — General works

HV3176.D46 1996
Devore, Wynetta.
Ethnic-sensitive social work practice/ Wynetta Devore, Elfriede G. Schlesinger. 4th ed. Boston: Allyn and Bacon, c1996. xiii, 338 p.
95-018932 361.3 20 0205189806
Social work with minorities. Social work with minorities -- United States.

HV3176.H46 1994
Henderson, George, 1932-
Social work interventions: helping people of color/ George Henderson. Westport, Conn.: Bergin & Garvey, 1994. xii, 245 p.
93-040164 362.84/00973 0897893824
Social work with minorities -- United States.

HV3181-3193 Protection, assistance and relief — Special classes. By race or ethnic group — Special race or ethnic group

HV3181.B55
Black heritage in social welfare, 1860-1930/ compiled and edited by Edyth L. Ross. Metuchen, N.J.: Scarecrow Press, 1978. xviii, 488 p.
78-008403 362.8/4 0810811456
Social work with Afro-Americans -- History. Afro-Americans -- Charities -- History. Social service -- United States -- History.

HV3181.C48 1991
Child welfare: an Africentric perspective/ edited by Joyce E. Everett, Sandra S. Chipungu, and Bogart R. Leashore. New Brunswick, N.J.: Rutgers University Press, c1991. xiii, 325 p.
90-028752 362.7/9796073 20 0813517125
Social work with Afro-American children. Social work with Afro-Americans. Child welfare -- United States.

HV3181.N88 1994
Nurturing young Black males: challenges to agencies, programs, and social policy/ Ronald B. Mincy, editor. Washington, D.C.: Urban Institute Press; c1994. xvi, 243 p.
93-032879 362.7/9796073 20 0877665982
Afro-American teenage boys -- Services for. Afro-American men -- Services for. Afro-American juvenile delinquents -- Services for -- United States.

HV3181.P85 1995
Pullman, Wesley E.
African American men in crisis: proactive strategies for urban youth/ Wesley E. Pullman. New York: Garland Pub., 1995. 277 p.
95-009660 362.84/96073 0815311125
Social work with Afro-Americans -- Case studies. Afro-American boys -- Services for -- Case studies. Social work with youth -- United States -- Case studies.

HV3193.G7.R69 1999
Rozin, Mordechai.
The rich and the poor: Jewish philanthropy and social control in nineteenth-century London/ Mordechai Rozin. Brighton; Sussex Academic Press, 1999. xi, 268 p.
98-043070 361.7/089/924 1898723796
Jews -- England -- London -- Charities -- History -- 19th century. Working class Jews -- Services for -- England -- London -- History -- 19th century. Immigrants -- Services for -- England -- London -- History -- 19th century. London (England) -- Emigration and immigration -- Social aspects.

HV4010 Protection, assistance and relief — Immigrants — By region or country

HV4010.J46 1989
Jensen, Leif, 1957-
The new immigration: implications for poverty and public assistance utilization/ Leif Jensen. New York: Greenwood Press, 1989. xiv, 205 p.
88-025096 362.8/4/00973 0313264554
Social work with immigrants -- United States. Social work with minorities -- United States. Poor -- United States. United States -- Emigration and immigration -- Social aspects.

HV4010.S629 2000
Social work practice with immigrants and refugees/ edited by Pallassana R. Balgopal. New York: Columbia University Press, c2000. xiv, 265 p.
00-020725 362.87/0973 21 0231108567
Social work with immigrants -- United States. Immigrants -- United States. Refugees -- United States. United States -- Emigration and immigration -- Social aspects.

HV4028 Protection, assistance and relief — Poor in cities. Slums — General works

HV4028.D43 1987
Dear, M. J.
Landscapes of despair: from deinstitutionalization to homelessness/ Michael J. Dear and Jennifer R. Wolch. Princeton, N.J.: Princeton University Press, 1987. 306 p.
87-003435 362.5 0691077541
Urban poor. Public welfare. Institutional care.

HV4028.M38 1993
Mayne, A. J. C. 1955-
The imagined slum: newspaper representation in three cities, 1870-1914/ Alan Mayne. Leicester; Leicester University Press; 1993. 228 p.
93-020477 307.3/364 0718513894
Slums -- Case studies. Slums -- California -- San Francisco. Press -- California -- San Francisco.

HV4028.M68 1996
Moser, Caroline O. N.
Confronting crisis: a summary of household responses to poverty and vulnerability in four, poor urban communities/ Caroline O.N. Moser. Washington, D.C.: World Bank, c1996. ix, 19 p.
96-000009 362.5/09173/2 20 0821335618
Urban poor -- Case studies. Urban poor -- Housing -- Case studies. Informal sector (Economics) -- Case studies.

HV4044-4140 Protection, assistance and relief — Poor in cities. Slums — By region or country

HV4044.S33 2000
Schwartz, Joel, 1950-
Fighting poverty with virtue: moral reform and America's urban poor, 1825-2000/ Joel Schwartz. Bloomington: Indiana University Press, c2000. xxii, 353 p.
00-027603 362.5/8/0973091732 21 0253337712
Urban poor -- United States -- History. Poverty -- Moral and ethical aspects -- United States.

HV4044.U56 1993
The "Underclass" debate: views from history/ Michael B. Katz, editor. Princeton, N.J.: Princeton University Press, c1993. viii, 507 p.
92-024994 362.5/0973 20 069104810X
Urban poor -- United States -- History. Afro-Americans -- Social conditions. Afro-Americans -- Economic conditions.

HV4044.W37 1989
Ward, David, 1938-
Poverty, ethnicity, and the American city, 1840-1925: changing conceptions of the slum and the ghetto/ David Ward. Cambridge [England]; Cambridge University Press, 1989. xiv, 263 p.
88-028250 362.5/0973 0521257832
Urban poor -- United States -- History -- 19th century. Immigrants -- United States -- History -- 19th century. Minorities -- United States -- History -- 19th century. United States -- Social conditions -- 1865-1918.

HV4045.A9 1999
Auletta, Ken.
The underclass/ Ken Auletta. Rev. and updated ed. Woodstock, NY: Overlook Press, 1999. 416 p.
98-047781 362.5/0973 21 0879519290
People with social disabilities -- United States. Poor -- United States.

HV4045.G65 1992
Goldsmith, William W.
Separate societies: poverty and inequality in U.S. cities/ William W. Goldsmith and Edward J. Blakely; foreword by Harvey Gantt. Philadelphia: Temple University Press, 1992. xviii, 247 p.
91-033128 362.5/0973/091734 0877229325
Urban poor -- United States. Inner cities -- United States. Urban renewal -- United States. United States -- Social policy -- 1980-1993.

HV4045.H63 1989
Hoch, Charles, 1948-
New homeless and old: community and the skid row hotel/ Charles Hoch and Robert A. Slayton. Philadelphia: Temple University Press, 1989. ix, 299 p.
88-021669 362.5/0973 0877226008
Urban poor -- United States. Single-room occupancy hotels -- United States. Homelessness -- United States.

HV4045.I56 1990
Inner-city poverty in the United States/ Laurence E. Lynn, Jr., and Michael G.H. McGeary, editors; Committee on National Urban Policy, Commission on Behavioral and Social Sciences and Education, National Research Council. Washington, D.C.: National Academy Press, 1990. viii, 280 p.
90-045776 362.5/0973/091732 0309042798
Urban poor -- United States. Urban poor -- Government policy -- United States. Inner cities -- United States.

HV4045.J46 1994
Jennings, James, 1949-
Understanding the nature of poverty in urban America/ James Jennings. Westport, Conn.: Praeger, 1994. x, 209 p.
94-016111 362.5/0973 0275949532
Urban poor -- United States. Public welfare -- United States.

HV4045.N48 1999
Newman, Katherine S., 1953-
No shame in my game: the working poor in the inner city/ Katherine S. Newman. New York: Knopf and the Russell Sage Foundation, 1999. xix, 388 p.
98-038244 362.5/0973/091732 0375402543
Urban poor -- United States. Urban poor -- Employment -- United States. Inner cities -- United States.

HV4045.S54 1997
Slessarev, Helene.
The betrayal of the urban poor/ Helene Slessarev. Philadelphia: Temple University Press, 1997. 208 p.
96-052817 362.5/0973 1566395429
Urban poor -- United States. Manpower policy -- United States. Social mobility -- United States. United States -- Economic policy -- 1981-1993. United States -- Economic policy -- 1993-

HV4045.W55 1987
Wilson, William J., 1935-
The truly disadvantaged: the inner city, the underclass, and public policy/ William Julius Wilson. Chicago: University of Chicago Press, 1987. xi, 254 p.
87-010822 362.5/0973 0226901300
Urban poor -- United States. Inner cities -- United States. Urban policy -- United States. United States -- Race relations.

HV4045.W553 1996
Wilson, William J., 1935-
When work disappears: the world of the new urban poor/ William Julius Wilson. New York: Knopf, 1996. xxiii, 322 p.
96-011803 362.5/0973/091732 0394579356
Urban poor -- United States. Afro-Americans -- Employment. Inner cities -- United States.

HV4045.5.T4.W37 1999
Ward, Peter M., 1951-
Colonias and public policy in Texas and Mexico: urbanization by stealth/ Peter M. Ward. Austin: University of Texas Press, c1999. xviii, 287 p.
98-025402 307.3/36416/09721 21 0292791240
Urban poor -- Texas. Slums -- Texas. Urban poor -- Mexican-American Border Region.

HV4046.N6.R5 1969
Riis, Jacob A. 1849-1914.
The battle with the slum. Montclair, N.J.: Patterson Smith, 1969 [c1902] xi, 465 p.
69-016245 301.44/1 0875850774
Poor. Poor -- New York (State) -- New York. Tenement houses -- New York (State) -- New York.

HV4076.S26.S36 1995
Schneider, Cathy Lisa, 1955-
Shantytown protest in Pinochet's Chile/ Cathy Lisa Schneider. Philadelphia: Temple University Press, 1995. xxiv, 269 p.
95-002098 322.4/4/098331509047 1566393051
Urban poor -- Chile -- Santiago -- Political activity. Urban poor -- Chile -- Santiago -- Political activity -- Interviews. Social movements -- Chile -- Santiago. Chile -- Politics and government -- 1973-1988. Chile -- History -- 1973-1988.

HV4086.A3.H54 1991
Himmelfarb, Gertrude.
Poverty and compassion: the moral imagination of the late Victorians/ Gertrude Himmelfarb. New York: Knopf, 1991. xii, 475 p.
90-053416 362.5/0942/09034 0679401199
Poor -- England -- History -- 19th century. Charities -- England -- History -- 19th century. Great Britain -- Economic conditions -- 19th century.

HV4086.A3.H55 1985
Himmelfarb, Gertrude.
The idea of poverty: England in the early Industrial Age/ Gertrude Himmelfarb. New York: Vintage Books, 1985, c1983. x, 595 p.
84-040005 362.5/0942 0394726073
Poor -- England -- History -- 19th century. Poor -- England -- History -- 18th century. Great Britain -- Economic conditions -- 1760-1860.

HV4086.A3.Y45 1993
Yelling, J. A. 1940-
Slums and redevelopment: policy and practice in England, 1918-45, with particular reference to London/ J.A. Yelling. New York: St. Martin's Press, 1992. x, 210 p.
92-027872 307.3/36416/09420904 0312090781
Slums -- England -- History -- 20th century. Housing policy -- England -- History -- 20th century. Urban renewal -- England -- History -- 20th century.

HV4088.D8.P78 1998
Prunty, Jacinta.
Dublin slums, 1800-1925: a study in urban geography/ Jacinta Prunty. Dublin; Irish Academic Press, 1998. xvii, 366 p.
96-152346 307.3/36416/0941835 0716525380
Slums -- Ireland -- Dublin -- History. Poor -- Ireland -- Dublin -- History. Dublin (Ireland) -- Social conditions. Dublin (Ireland) -- Geography.

HV4132.56.A5.B39 1997
Bayat, Assef.
Street politics: poor people's movements in Iran/ Asef Bayat. New York: Columbia University Press, c1997. xxiii, 232 p.
97-018986 322.4/4 21 0231108583
Squatter settlements -- Iran. Squatters -- Iran. Vending stands -- Iran. Iran -- Politics and government -- 1979-1997.

HV4140.C34.T45 1997
Thomas, Frederic C.
Calcutta poor: elegies on a city above pretense/ Frederic C. Thomas. Armonk, N.Y.: M.E. Sharpe, c1997. ix, 189 p.
96-035877 362.5/0954/147 20 1563249812
Poor -- India -- Calcutta. Economic assistance, Domestic -- India -- Calcutta.

HV4194-4196 Protection, assistance and relief — Poor in cities. Slums — Social settlements. College settlements, etc.

HV4194.A3.D3 1967
Davis, Allen Freeman, 1931-
Spearheads for reform; the social settlements and the progressive movement, 1890-1914 [by] Allen F. Davis. New York, Oxford University Press, 1967. xviii, 322 p.
67-025457   362/.9/73
Social settlements -- United States -- History. Progressivism (United States politics) Cities and towns -- United States -- History.

HV4194.T74 1987
Trolander, Judith Ann, 1942-
Professionalism and social change: from the settlement house movement to neighborhood centers, 1886 to the present/ Judith Ann Trolander. New York: Columbia University Press, 1987. x, 300 p.
87-006414   362.5/57/0973   0231064721
Social settlements -- United States -- History -- 19th century. Social settlements -- United States -- History -- 20th century.

HV4196.C4.H7 1911
Addams, Jane, 1860-1935.
Twenty years at Hull-house, with autobiographical notes, by Jane Addams ... with illustrations by Norah Hamilton ... New York, The Macmillan company, 1911. xvii, 462 p.
13-007309
Chicago (Ill.) -- Social conditions.

HV4196.C4.H72
Addams, Jane, 1860-1935.
The second twenty years at Hull-House, September 1909 to September 1929: with a record of a growing world consciousness/ by Jane Addams. New York; The Macmillan Company, 1930. xiii, 413 p.
30-031867   331.852
Social history. Peace. Hull House, Chicago.

HV4196.C4S74 1997
Stebner, Eleanor J.,
The women of Hull House: a study in spirituality, vocation, and friendship/ Eleanor J. Stebner. Albany, NY: State University of New York Press, c1997. x, 246 p.
97-004960   361.3/092/277311   B   21
0791434885
Addams, Jane, 1860-1935.   Social settlements -- Illinois -- Chicago -- History. Women social reformers -- Illinois -- Chicago -- Biography. Women social workers -- Illinois -- Chicago -- Biography.

HV4493 Protection, assistance and relief — Mendicancy. Vagabondism. Tramps. Homelessness — General works

HV4493.G53 1994
Glasser, Irene.
Homelessness in global perspective/ Irene Glasser. New York: G.K. Hall; c1994. x, 154 p.
93-025087   362.5 20   0816173796
Homelessness.

HV4493.H37 1991
Harris, Maxine.
Sisters of the shadow/ by Maxine Harris. Norman: University of Oklahoma Press, c1991. xii, 252 p.
90-049624   362.83/086942 20   0806123249
Homeless women -- Psychology. Shadow (Psychoanalysis) Women -- Mythology.

HV4493.R35 1996
Ralston, Meredith L.
Nobody wants to hear our truth: homeless women and theories of the welfare state/ Meredith L. Ralston. Westport, Conn.: Greenwood Press, 1996. xiii, 202 p.
95-019319   362.83/08/6942   0313292922
Homeless women -- Interviews. Addicts -- Interviews. Welfare state.

HV4504-4545 Protection, assistance and relief — Mendicancy. Vagabondism. Tramps. Homelessness — By region or country

HV4504.R67 1989
Rossi, Peter Henry, 1921-
Down and out in America: the origins of homelessness/ Peter H. Rossi. Chicago: University of Chicago Press, 1989. xi, 247 p.
89-031598   362.5/1/0973   0226728285
Homelessness -- United States -- History. Urban poor -- United States -- History.

HV4505.B37 1991
Barak, Gregg.
Gimme shelter: a social history of homelessness in contemporary America/ Gregg Barak. New York: Praeger, 1991. xiv, 212 p.
90-024567   363.5/8/0973   0275933202
Homelessness -- United States. Homeless persons -- Services for -- United States.

HV4505.B378 1993
Baum, Alice S.
A nation in denial: the truth about homelessness/ Alice S. Baum and Donald W. Burnes. Boulder: Westview Press, 1993. xiv, 247 p.
92-042265   362.5/0973   0813382440
Homelessness -- United States. Homeless persons -- United States.

HV4505.B52 1992
Blau, Joel.
The visible poor: homelessness in the United States/ Joel Blau. New York: Oxford University Press, 1992. xi, 235 p.
91-029828   362.5/0973   0195057430
Homelessness -- United States. Homeless persons -- United States.

HV4505.B88 1992
Burt, Martha R.
Over the edge: the growth of homelessness in the 1980s/ Martha R. Burt. New York: Russell Sage Foundation; c1992. xi, 267 p.
91-018000   362.5/0973 20   0871541777
Homelessness -- United States.   United States -- Social conditions -- 1980-

HV4505.C37 1990
Caton, Carol L. M.
Homeless in America/ Carol L.M. Caton. New York: Oxford University Press, 1990. xvi, 236 p.
89-016259   362.5/8/0973   0195039181
Homelessness -- United States. Homeless persons -- Services for -- United States.

HV4505.H647 1990
Hombs, Mary Ellen.
American homelessness: a reference handbook/ Mary Ellen Hombs. Santa Barbara, Calif.: ABC-CLIO, c1990. xiii, 193 p.
90-030936   362.5/0973 20   0874365473
Homelessness -- United States -- Handbooks, manuals, etc.

HV4505.H6515 1990
Homeless children and youth: a new American dilemma/ edited by Julee H. Kryder-Coe, Lester M. Salamon, and Janice M. Molnar; with a foreword by George Miller. New Brunswick, N.J., U.S.A.: Transaction Publishers, c1991. xviii, 323 p.
90-042495   362.7/08/6942 20   0887383866
Homeless children -- United States. Homeless youth -- United States.

HV4505.H656 1989
Homelessness in the United States/ edited by Jamshid A. Momeni; foreword by Bruce Wiegand. New York: Greenwood Press, 1989-1990. 2 v.
88-010964   362.5/0973   0313255660
Homelessness -- United States. Homeless persons -- Services for -- United States.

HV4505.H854 1998
Hudson, Christopher G.
An interdependency model of homelessness: the dynamics of social disintegration/ Christopher G. Hudson. Lewiston, NY: E. Mellen Press, c1998. xxi, 409 p.
98-020712   362.5 21   0773482881
Homelessness -- United States. Homeless persons -- United States.   United States -- Social conditions.

HV4505.J46 1994
Jencks, Christopher.
The homeless/ Christopher Jencks. Cambridge, Mass.: Harvard University Press, 1994. viii, 161 p.
93-046424   362.5/8/0973   0674405951
Homelessness -- United States. Homelessness -- Government policy -- United States.

HV4505.R67 1989
Rossi, Peter Henry, 1921-
Without shelter: homelessness in the 1980's/ by Peter Rossi. New York: Priority Press Publications, 1989. vi, 79 p.
88-031811   362.5/0973   0870782355
Homelessness -- United States. Homelessness -- Government policy -- United States.

HV4505.S53 1996
Shane, Paul G., 1935-
What about America's homeless children?: hide and seek/ Paul G. Shane. Thousand Oaks: Sage Publications, c1996. xiv, 247 p.
96-010042   362.7/08/6942 20   0803949820
Homeless children -- United States. Homeless youth -- United States. Homelessness -- United States -- Prevention.

HV4505.V57 1996
Vissing, Yvonne Marie.
Out of sight, out of Mind: homeless children and families in small-town America/ Yvonne M. Vissing. Lexington, Ky.: University Press of Kentucky, c1996. xii, 271 p.
96-003749   362.5/0973 20   081311943X
Homelessness -- United States. Homeless children -- United States. Homeless persons -- United States. United States -- Rural conditions.

HV4505.W23 1993
Wagner, David.
Checkerboard Square: culture and resistance in a homeless community/ David Wagner. Boulder: Westview Press, 1993. xii, 200 p.
93-003744 362.5/0973 0813315859
Homeless persons -- United States -- Case studies. Homeless persons -- Services for -- United States -- Case studies. Homeless persons -- United States -- Attitudes -- Case studies.

HV4505.W75 1989
Wright, James D.
Address unknown: the homeless in America/ James D. Wright. New York: A. de Gruyter, c1989. xix, 170 p.
89-033254 362.5/0973 0202303640
Homelessness -- United States.

HV4505.W76 1998
Wright, James D.
Beside the golden door: policy, politics, and the homeless/ James D. Wright, Beth A. Rubin, and Joel A. Devine. New York: Aldine de Gruyter, c1998. xix, 238 p.
97-052031 363.5/96942/0973 21 0202306135
Homelessness -- Government policy -- United States. Homelessness -- United States -- Public opinion. Poor -- Housing -- United States. United States -- Economic policy. United States -- Politics and government.

HV4505.W77 1997
Wright, Talmadge.
Out of place: homeless mobilizations, subcities, and contested landscapes/ Talmadge Wright. Albany: State University of New York Press, c1997. xiv, 408 p.
96-048447 362.5/8/0973 21 0791433692
Homelessness -- United States. Homeless persons -- United States -- Political activity. Public spaces -- United States.

HV4506.N6.D67 1997
Dordick, Gwendolyn A., 1961-
Something left to lose: personal relations and survival among New York's homeless/ Gwendolyn A. Dordick. Philadelphia: Temple University Press, 1997. xi, 220 p.
96-025094 305.5/69 1566395135
Homeless persons -- New York (State) -- New York -- Case studies. Interpersonal relations -- New York (State) -- New York -- Case studies.

HV4506.O76.C66 2000
Connolly, Deborah R., 1969-
Homeless mothers: face to face with women and poverty/ Deborah R. Connolly. Minneapolis: University of Minnesota Press, c2000. xxiii, 218 p.
99-050683 362.83/086/942 21 0816632812
Homeless women -- Oregon -- Case studies. Homeless families -- Oregon -- Case studies. Social services -- Oregon -- Case studies.

HV4506.S36.R67 1994
Rosenthal, Rob, 1951-
Homeless in Paradise: a map of the terrain/ Rob Rosenthal. Philadelphia: Temple University Press, 1994. x, 265 p.
93-017275 362.5/09794/91 1566391296
Homelessness -- California -- Santa Barbara. Homeless persons -- California -- Santa Barbara. Santa Barbara (Calif.) -- Social conditions.

HV4506.W2.L54 1993
Liebow, Elliot.
Tell them who I am: the lives of homeless women/ Elliot Liebow. New York: Free Press; c1993. xxi, 339 p.
92-039453 362.83/08/6942 20 0029190959
Homeless women -- Washington Region -- Case studies. Shelters for the homeless -- Washington Region -- Case studies. Homelessness -- Washington Region -- Case studies.

HV4545.A3.H85 1999
Humphreys, Robert, 1928-
No fixed abode: a history of responses to the roofless and the rootless in Britain/ Robert Humphreys. New York: Palgrave, c1999. xiii, 222 p.
99-026120 362.5/8/0941 21 0312225636
Homelessness -- Government policy -- Great Britain -- History. Homeless persons -- Government policy -- Great Britain -- History. Vagrancy -- Government policy -- Great Britain -- History.

HV4708 Protection, assistance and relief — Protection of animals. Animal rights. Animal welfare — General works

HV4708.A248 1994
Adams, Carol J.
Neither man nor beast: feminism and the defense of animals/ Carol J. Adams. New York: Continuum, 1994. 271 p.
94-021360 179/.3 082640670X
Animal welfare. Animal rights. Feminist theory.

HV4708.A25 1990
Adams, Carol J.
The sexual politics of meat: a feminist-vegetarian critical theory/ Carol J. Adams. New York: Continuum, 1990. 256 p.
89-022338 179/.3 0826404553
Animal welfare. Vegetarianism -- Social aspects. Patriarchy.

HV4708.C38 1992
Carruthers, Peter, 1952-
The animals issue: moral theory in practice/ Peter Carruthers. Cambridge [England]; Cambridge University Press, 1992. xiii, 206 p.
92-009338 179/.3 0521430925
Animal rights.

HV4708.D44 1996
DeGrazia, David.
Taking animals seriously: mental life and moral status/ David DeGrazia. Cambridge; Cambridge University Press, 1996. x, 302 p.
95-046689 179/.3 052156140X
Animal welfare -- Moral and ethical aspects. Animal psychology.

HV4708.D63 1999
Attitudes to animals: views in animal welfare/ edited by Francine L. Dolins. Cambridge, U.K.; Cambridge University Press, 1999. x, 262 p.
97-032155 179/.3 052147342X
Animal welfare -- Moral and ethical aspects. Human-animal relationships -- Moral and ethical aspects.

HV4708.D86 2001
Dunayer, Joan.
Animal equality: language and liberation/ Joan Dunayer; foreword by Carol J. Adams. Derwood, Md.: Ryce Pub., c2001. xviii, 265 p.
00-192984 179/.3 21 0970647557
Animal rights. Animal welfare. Language and ethics.

HV4708.E53 1998
Encyclopedia of animal rights and animal welfare/ edited by Marc Bekoff with Carron A. Meaney; foreword by Jane Goodall. Westport, Conn.: Greenwood Press, 1998. xxi, 446 p.
97-035098 179/.3 0313299773
Animal rights -- Encyclopedias. Animal welfare -- Encyclopedias.

HV4708.L43 1991
Leahy, Michael P. T., 1934-
Against liberation: putting animals in perspective/ Michael P.T. Leahy. London; Routledge, 1991. xi, 273 p.
90-023775 179/.3 0415035848
Animal rights. Animal welfare -- Moral and ethical aspects.

HV4708.L57 1999
The lives of animals/ J.M. Coetzee ... [et al.]; edited and introduced by Amy Gutmann. Princeton, NJ: Princeton University Press, 1999. 127 p.
98-039591 179/.3 21 0691004439
Animal rights -- Philosophy. Animal welfare -- Moral and ethical aspects.

HV4708.P48 1999
Petrinovich, Lewis F.
Darwinian dominion: animal welfare and human interests/ Lewis Petrinovich. Cambridge, Mass.: MIT Press, c1999. ix, 431 p.
98-005036 179/.3 21 0262161788
Animal welfare. Animal rights.

HV4708.P67 1995
Pluhar, Evelyn B.
Beyond prejudice: the moral significance of human and nonhuman animals/ Evelyn B. Pluhar; foreword by Bernard E. Rollin. Durham: Duke University Press, 1995. xix, 370 p.
95-000865 179/.3 082231634X
Animal rights. Human rights. Philosophical anthropology.

HV4708.R43 1983
Regan, Tom.
The case for animal rights/ Tom Regan. Berkeley: University of California Press, c1983. xv, 425 p.
83-001087 179/.3 0520049047
Animal rights -- Philosophy.

HV4708.R45 2000
Reichmann, James B., 1923-
Evolution, animal 'rights' & the environment/ James B. Reichmann. Washington, D.C.: Catholic University of America Press, c2000. xiii, 399 p.
98-047146 179/.3 21 0813209315
Animal rights -- Philosophy. Human-animal relationships. Evolution (Biology)

HV4708.R63 1990
Rodd, Rosemary.
Biology, ethics, and animals/ Rosemary Rodd. Oxford [England]: Clarendon Press; 1990. 272 p.
89-070902 179/.3 0198242239
Animal welfare -- Moral and ethical aspects. Animal rights. Bioethics.

HV4708.R69 1998
Rowlands, Mark.
Animal rights: a philosophical defence/ Mark Rowlands; consultant editor, J Campling. New York: St. Martin's Press, 1998. vii, 192 p.
98-023544   179/.3   031221720X
Animal rights -- Philosophy.

HV4708.T39 1999
Taylor, Angus, 1945-
Magpies, monkeys, and morals: what philosophers say about animal liberation/ Angus Taylor. Peterborough, Ont.; Broadview Press, c1999. 167 p.
99-460603
Animal rights -- Philosophy. Animal welfare -- Moral and ethical aspects. Livestock factories -- Moral and ethical aspects.

HV4711 Protection, assistance and relief — Protection of animals. Animal rights. Animal welfare — Addresses, essays, lectures

HV4711.A55 1989
Animal experimentation: the consensus changes/ edited by Gill Langley. New York: Chapman and Hall, 1989. xii, 268 p.
89-017379   619   0412024012
Animal experimentation. Animal welfare.

HV4711.R366 2001
Regan, Tom.
Defending animal rights/ Tom Regan. Urbana: University of Illinois Press, c2001. xii, 179 p.
00-008708   179.3 21   025202611X
Animal rights -- Philosophy. Animal welfare -- Moral and ethical aspects.

HV4712 Protection, assistance and relief — Protection of animals. Animal rights. Animal welfare — Study and teaching. Humane education

HV4712.C32 1999
Child abuse, domestic violence, and animal abuse: linking the circles of compassion for prevention and intervention/ edited by Frank R. Ascione and Phil Arkow. West Lafayette, Ind.: Purdue University Press, c1999. xx, 479 p.
98-048878   362.82/927/0973 21   1557531420
Animal welfare -- Moral and ethical aspects. Violence. Cruelty.

HV4757 Protection, assistance and relief — Protection of animals. Animal rights. Animal welfare — Classes

HV4757.K86 2000
Kunkel, H. O.
Human issues in animal agriculture/ H.O. Kunkel with contributions by William P. Browne, Stanley E. Curtis, and Paul B. Thompson. College Station, TX: Texas A&M University Press, 2000. xiv, 334 p.
99-053235   338.1/76   0890969272
Livestock industry -- Moral and ethical aspects. Animal welfare.

HV4764 Protection, assistance and relief — Protection of animals. Animal rights. Animal welfare — By region or country

HV4764.A24 1996
Achor, Amy Blount.
Animal rights: a beginner's guide: a handbook of issues, organizations, actions, and resources/ Amy Blount Achor. Yellow Springs, Ohio: WriteWare, c1996. 452 p.
96-090093   179/.3 20   0963186515
Animal rights -- United States. Animal welfare -- United States. Vegetarianism.

HV4764.F73 1996
Francione, Gary L. 1954-
Rain without thunder: the ideology of the animal rights movement/ Gary L. Francione. Philadelphia, Pa.: Temple University Press, 1996. xii, 269 p.
95-049676   179/.3   1566394600
Animal rights movement -- United States. Animal welfare -- United States -- Philosophy.

HV4764.S5 1994
Sherry, Clifford J.
Animal rights: a reference handbook/ Clifford J. Sherry. Santa Barbara, Calif.: ABC-CLIO, c1994. xvii, 240 p.
94-007168   179/.3 20   0874367336
Animal rights -- United States -- Handbooks, manuals, etc. Animal welfare -- Law and legislation -- United States -- Handbooks, manuals, etc.

HV4764.T62 1999
Tobias, Michael.
Voices from the underground: for the love of animals/ Michael Tobias. Pasadena, Calif.: New Paradigm Books, c1999. 166 p.
99-027389   179/.3 21   0932727484
Animal welfare -- United States. Animal rights -- United States. Animal rights activists -- United States.

HV4915 Protection, assistance and relief — Animal experimentation. Anti-vivisection — General works. History

HV4915.A64 1991
Animal experimentation: the moral issues/ edited by Robert M. Baird & Stuart E. Rosenbaum. Buffalo, N.Y.: Prometheus Books, 1991. 182 p.
90-028879   179/.4   0879756675
Animal experimentation -- Moral and ethical aspects. Animal rights. Animal experimentation -- Moral and ethical aspects.

HV4915.G73 2000
Greek, C. Ray.
Sacred cows and golden geese: the human cost of experiments on animals/ C. Ray Greek and Jean Swingle Greek; foreword by Jane Goodall. New York: Continuum, 2000. 256 p.
99-057157   179/.4   0826392262
Animal experimentation.

HV4915.M65 2000
Monamy, Vaughan, 1958-
Animal experimentation: a guide to the issues/ Vaughan Monamy. Cambridge, United Kingdom; Cambridge University Press, 2000. xi, 110 p.
00-027642   179/.4   0521660939
Animal experimentation. Laboratory animals.

HV4915.O75 1993
Orlans, F. Barbara.
In the name of science: issues in responsible animal experimentation/ F. Barbara Orlans. New York: Oxford University Press, 1993. ix, 297 p.
92-039344   179/.4   0195070437
Animal experimentation -- Moral and ethical aspects.

HV4915.R8 2000
Rudacille, Deborah.
The scalpel and the butterfly: the war between animal research and animal protection/ Deborah Rudacille. New York: Farrar, Straus, and Giroux, 2000. vii, 389 p.
00-028758   174/.4   0374254206
Animal experimentation -- Moral and ethical aspects. Animal welfare -- Moral and ethical aspects.

HV4943 Protection, assistance and relief — Animal experimentation. Anti-vivisection — By region or country

HV4943.G3 S38 2000
Sax, Boria.
Animals in the Third Reich: pets, scapegoats, and the Holocaust/ Boria Sax; foreword by Klaus P. Fischer. New York: Continuum, 2000. 206 p.
00-034038   179/.3/094309043 21   0826412890
Animal experimentation -- Germany -- History -- 20th century. Animal welfare -- Government policy -- Germany -- History -- 20th century. Eugenics -- Germany -- History -- 20th century.

HV4997 Substance abuse — Societies. Serials

HV4997.C68 2001
Courtwright, David T., 1952-
Forces of habit: drugs and the making of the modern world/ David T. Courtwright. Cambridge, Mass.: Harvard University Press, 2001. viii, 277 p.
00-061466   362.29   0674004582
Substance abuse -- History. Psychotropic drugs -- History. Substance abuse -- Economic aspects.

HV5006 Alcoholism. Intemperance. Temperance reform — Societies (International)

HV5006.F33 1996
Fahey, David M.
Temperance and racism: John Bull, Johnny Reb, and the Good Templars/ David M. Fahey. Lexington: University Press of Kentucky, 1996. xii, 209 p.
96-012156   363.4/1/09   0813119847
Race discrimination.

HV5020 Alcoholism. Intemperance. Temperance reform — History — General works

HV5020.S6813 1990
Sournia, Jean-Charles.
A history of alcoholism/ Jean-Charles Sournia; with an introduction by Roy Porter; translated by Nick Hindley and Gareth Stanton. Oxford, UK; B. Blackwell, 1990. xix, 232 p.
89-015138 394.1/3/09 0631160264
Alcoholism -- History. Drinking of alcoholic beverages -- History.

HV5025 Alcoholism. Intemperance. Temperance reform — History — 19th-20th centuries

HV5025.D75 1990
Drinking: behavior and belief in modern history/ edited with an introduction by Susanna Barrows and Robin Room. Berkeley: University of California Press, c1991. vi, 454 p.
89-020616 394.1/3/09 20 0520056531
Drinking of alcoholic beverages -- History. Alcoholism -- History. Temperance -- History.

HV5032 Alcoholism. Intemperance. Temperance reform — Biography of reformers — Individual, A-Z

HV5032.W19.R36 2000
Raphael, Matthew J.
Bill W. and Mr. Wilson: the legend and life of A.A.'s cofounder/ Matthew J. Raphael. Amherst: University of Massachusetts Press, c2000. xiv, 206 p.
99-086304 362.292/86/092 21 1558492453
W., Bill. Alcoholics -- Biography.

HV5035 Alcoholism. Intemperance. Temperance reform — General works — Scientific

HV5035.A465 2000
The alcohol report/ edited by Martin Plant and Douglas Cameron. London; Free Association, 2000. xii, 290 p.
2001-273053 362.292 1853435252
Drinking of alcoholic beverages. Alcoholism.

HV5035.C63 1983
Cohen, Sidney, 1910-
The alcoholism problems: selected issues/ Sidney Cohen. New York: Haworth Press, c1983. ix, 193 p.
83-000179 616.86/1 0866562095
Alcoholism.

HV5035.H25 1995
Hanson, David J., 1941-
Preventing alcohol abuse: alcohol, culture, and control/ David J. Hanson. Westport, Conn.: Praeger, 1995. xiv, 140 p.
94-037889 362.29/27 0275949265
Alcoholism. Alcoholism -- Prevention. Drinking of alcoholic beverages.

HV5035.H65 1998
Holder, Harold D.
Alcohol and the community: a systems approach to prevention/ Harold D. Holder. Cambridge, UK; Cambridge University Press, 1998. xiii, 183 p.
97-020455 362.292/7 0521591872
Alcoholism -- Social aspects. Alcoholism -- Prevention.

HV5035.I57 1995
International handbook on alcohol and culture/ edited by Dwight B. Heath. Westport, Conn.: Greenwood Press, 1995. xxiv, 391 p.
95-007184 394.1/3 0313252343
Drinking of alcoholic beverages -- Cross-cultural studies. Drinking customs -- Cross-cultural studies. Alcoholism -- Cross-cultural studies.

HV5045 Alcoholism. Intemperance. Temperance reform — Psychology of alcoholism

HV5045.W55 1998
Wilcox, Danny M., 1950-
Alcoholic thinking: language, culture, and belief in Alcoholics Anonymous/ Danny M. Wilcox. Westport, CT: Praeger, 1998. xiii, 141 p.
97-034740 362.292/86 0275960498
Alcoholism -- Psychological aspects. Recovering alcoholics -- Psychology.

HV5047 Alcoholism. Intemperance. Temperance reform — Addresses, essays, lectures

HV5047.C65 1987
Constructive drinking: perspectives on drink from anthropology/ edited by Mary Douglas. Cambridge; Cambridge University Press; 1987. ix, 291 p.
86-033388 394.1/3 0521335043
Drinking of alcoholic beverages -- Cross-cultural studies. Drinking customs -- Cross-cultural studies. Alcoholism -- Cross-cultural studies.

HV5053 Alcoholism. Intemperance. Temperance reform — Social degeneration and alcoholism — Alcoholism and crime

HV5053.P45 1991
Pernanen, Kai.
Alcohol in human violence/ Kai Pernanen; foreword by Dwight B. Heath. New York: Guilford, 1991. xiii, 280 p.
91-016338 364.2/4 0898621712
Alcoholism and crime. Violence. Alcoholism -- Psychological aspects.

HV5068 Alcoholism. Intemperance. Temperance reform — Miscellany. Stories, dialogues, etc. — Narratives. Tales. Allegories

HV5068.D78 1999
Drunkard's progress: narratives of addiction, despair, and recovery/ edited by John W. Crowley. Baltimore, Md.: Johns Hopkins University Press, 1999. xiv, 202 p.
98-008732 362.292 0801860083
Temperance. Alcoholism.

HV5088-5090 Alcoholism. Intemperance. Temperance reform — Alcoholism and the state. Regulation, control — Practice. Methods of regulation and control

HV5088.T48 1991
Thornton, Mark.
The economics of prohibition/ Mark Thornton. Salt Lake City: University of Utah Press, c1991. x, 184 p.
91-050333 338.4/336341/0973 20 0874803756
Prohibition -- Economic aspects. Prohibition -- Economic aspects -- United States. Narcotics, Control of -- Economic aspects -- United States.

HV5089.R67 1996
Rose, Kenneth D. 1946-
American women and the repeal of Prohibition/ Kenneth D. Rose. New York: New York University Press, c1996. xix, 215 p.
95-004396 363.4/1 20 0814774644
Prohibition -- United States -- History. Women in politics -- United States -- History. Women social reformers -- United States -- History.

HV5089.R84 1989
Rumbarger, John J., 1938-
Profits, power, and prohibition: alcohol reform and the industrializing of America, 1800-1930/ John J. Rumbarger. Albany: State University of New York Press, c1989. xxv, 272 p.
88-001884 363.4/1/0973 0887067824
Prohibition -- United States -- History. Temperance -- United States -- History. Industrialization -- United States -- History.

HV5090.I3.H35 1998
Hallwas, John E.
The bootlegger: a story of small-town America/ John E. Hallwas. Urbana: University of Illinois Press, c1998. xi, 274 p.
97-045253 364.1/33 21 0252023951
Wagle, Thomas Henry, -- 1886-1929. Prohibition -- Illinois -- Colchester -- History. Liquor industry -- Illinois -- Colchester -- History. Colchester (Ill.) -- History.

HV5128 Alcoholism. Intemperance. Temperance reform — Alcoholism and education — By region or country, A-Z

HV5128.U5.A43 1994
Alcohol use and misuse by young adults/ George S. Howard and Peter E. Nathan, editors. Notre Dame, Ind.: University of Notre Dame Press, c1994. vi, 198 p.
93-043478   362.29/22/0835 20   0268006415
College students -- United States -- Alcohol use. Young adults -- United States -- Alcohol use. Alcoholism -- United States -- Prevention.

HV5128.U5.Z55 1999
Zimmerman, Jonathan, 1961-
Distilling democracy: alcohol education in America's public schools, 1880-1925/ Jonathan Zimmerman. Lawrence: University Press of Kansas, c1999. xvii, 208 p.
98-044935   362.292/071/073 21   0700609458
Alcoholism -- Study and teaching -- United States -- History. Temperance -- United States -- History.

HV5132 Alcoholism. Intemperance. Temperance reform — Alcohol and the family. Children of alcoholics

HV5132.A43 1982
Alcohol and the family/ edited by Jim Orford and Judith Harwin. New York: St. Martin's Press, 1982. 295 p.
82-050090   362.8/2   0312017065
Alcoholics -- Family relationships.

HV5132.B748 1999
Brown, Stephanie, 1944-
The alcoholic family in recovery: a developmental model/ Stephanie Brown, Virginia Lewis. New York: Guilford Press, c1999. xviii, 318 p.
98-036077   362.292/3 21   1572304022
Recovering alcoholics -- Family relationships. Alcoholics -- Rehabilitation. Temperance -- Psychological aspects.

HV5132.D43
Deutsch, Charles, 1947-
Broken bottles, broken dreams: understanding and helping the children of alcoholics/ Charles Deutsch. New York: Teachers College, Columbia University, c1982. xiv, 213 p.
81-005729   362.8/28   0807726648
Children of alcoholics. Alcoholism. Child health services.

HV5132.W57 1991
Wiseman, Jacqueline P.
The other half: wives of alcoholics and their social-psychological situation/ Jacqueline P. Wiseman; with a foreword by Robin Room. New York: A. de Gruyter, c1991. xx, 297 p.
91-011740   362.29/23 20   0202303829
Alcoholics -- United States -- Family relationships. Wives -- United States -- Psychology. Codependency -- United States.

HV5133 Alcoholism. Intemperance. Temperance reform — Alcoholism and the child

HV5133.M37 1987
Marlin, Emily.
Hope: new choices and recovery strategies for adult children of alcoholics/ Emily Marlin; produced by the Philip Lief Group. New York: Harper & Row, c1987. xv, 287 p.
86-046158   362.2/92   0060157690
Adult children of alcoholics -- United States. Alcoholics -- United States -- Family relationships. Alcoholism -- Treatment -- United States.

HV5135 Alcoholism. Intemperance. Temperance reform — Alcohol and youth

HV5135.Y68 1978
Youth, alcohol, and social policy/ edited by Howard T. Blane and Morris E. Chafetz. New York: Plenum Press, c1979. xxvi, 424 p.
79-009094   362.2/92/0973   030640253X
Youth -- Alcohol use -- United States -- Congresses. Alcoholism -- United States -- Prevention -- Congresses. Alcoholism -- United States -- Congresses.

HV5137 Alcoholism. Intemperance. Temperance reform — Alcohol and women

HV5137.W38 2000
Waterson, Jan, 1949-
Women and alcohol in social context: mother's ruin revisited/ Jan Waterson; foreword by Elizabeth Ettorre; consultant editor, Jo Campling. Houndmills, Basingstoke, Hampshire [England]; Palgrave, 2000. xiii, 223 p.
00-034785   362.292/082/094   0333665899
Women -- Alcohol use -- Great Britain.

HV5198 Alcoholism. Intemperance. Temperance reform — Alcoholism and indigenous peoples — General works

HV5198.S34 1998
Saggers, Sherry.
Dealing with alcohol: indigenous usage in Australia, New Zealand and Canada/ Sherry Saggers and Dennis Gray. Cambridge, UK; Cambridge University Press, 1998. vii, 240 p.
98-007278   362.292/089   0521620325
Indigenous peoples -- Alcohol use. Australian aborigines -- Alcohol use. Maori (New Zealand people) -- Alcohol use.

HV5227-5247 Alcoholism. Intemperance. Temperance reform — Women and temperance reform — By region or country

HV5227.T97 1991
Tyrrell, Ian R.
Woman's world/Woman's empire: the Woman's Christian Temperance Union in international perspective, 1880-1930/ Ian Tyrrell. Chapel Hill: University of North Carolina Press, c1991. xiii, 381 p.
90-043246   322.4/4/0973 20   0807819506
Temperance -- United States -- Societies, etc. -- History. Reformers -- United States -- Biography. Feminists -- United States -- Biography.

HV5229.M37 1998
Mattingly, Carol, 1945-
Well-tempered women: nineteenth-century temperance rhetoric/ Carol Mattingly. Carbondale: Southern Illinois University Press, c1998. xv, 213 p.
98-016297   363.4/1/097309034 21   0809322099
Temperance -- United States -- History -- 19th century. Women social reformers -- United States -- History -- 19th century. Women social reformers -- United States -- Language.

HV5232.N3 A7
Asbury, Herbert,
Carry Nation, by Herbert Asbury. New York, A. A. Knopf, 1929. xxii, 307 p.
29-021266
Nation, Carry Amelia, 1846-1911. Prohibition.

HV5247.G4.A49 1996
Akyeampong, Emmanuel Kwaku.
Drink, power, and cultural change: a social history of alcohol in Ghana, c. 1800 to recent times/ Emmanuel Kwaku Akyeampong. Portsmouth, NH: Heinemann; c1996. xxiii, 189 p.
96-032887   394.1/3/09667 20   043508996X
Drinking of alcoholic beverages -- Ghana -- History. Drinking of alcoholic beverages -- Social aspects -- Ghana. Social change -- Ghana. Ghana -- Social conditions.

HV5278 Alcoholism. Intemperance. Temperance reform — Care and rehabilitation of alcoholics — Practice. Methods of treatment

HV5278.A756 1996
Alcoholics Anonymous as a mutual-help movement: a study in eight societies/ Klaus Makela ... [et al.]. Madison, Wis.: University of Wisconsin Press, c1996. xii, 310 p.
95-042146   362.29/286 20   0299150003
Alcoholics -- Rehabilitation -- Cross-cultural studies. Twelve-step programs -- Cross-cultural studies. Self-help groups -- Cross-cultural studies.

HV5279 Alcoholism. Intemperance. Temperance reform — Care and rehabilitation of alcoholics — By region or country

HV5279.D38 1998
Daugherty, Ray.
Reducing the risks for substance abuse: a lifespan approach/ Raymond P. Daugherty, Carl Leukefeld. New York: Plenum Press, c1998. xiii, 178 p.
98-029801　362.29/17/0973 21　0306458985
Alcoholism -- United States -- Prevention. Drug abuse -- United States -- Prevention. Behavior modification -- United States.

HV5279.D43 1993
Denzin, Norman K.
The alcoholic society: addiction and recovery of the self/ Norman K. Denzin; with a new introduction by the author and a foreword by John M. Johnson. New Brunswick, N.J., U.S.A.: Transaction Publishers, c1993. xxxii, 412 p.
92-035675　616.86/1/0019 20　1560006692
Alcoholics -- Rehabilitation -- United States. Alcoholism -- Treatment -- United States. Alcoholism -- Psychological aspects.

HV5289-5292 Alcoholism. Intemperance. Temperance reform — By region or country — United States

HV5289.A75 1991
Alcohol in America: drinking practices and problems/ Walter B. Clark and Michael E. Hilton, editors; with contributions by Raul Caetano ... [et al.]. Albany: State University of New York Press, 1991. xi, 380 p.
90-045048　362.29/2/0973　0791406954
Alcoholism -- United States. Drinking of alcoholic beverages -- United States.

HV5292.B35 1999
Barr, Andrew.
Drink: a social history of America/ Andrew Barr. New York: Carroll & Graf, 1999. xii, 466 p.
00-503361　394.1/3/0973　0786705590
Drinking of alcoholic beverages -- United States -- History.

HV5292.G77 1996
Gusfield, Joseph R., 1923-
Contested meanings: the construction of alcohol problems/ Joseph R. Gusfield. Madison, Wis.: University of Wisconsin Press, c1996. ix, 374 p.
95-043786　391.1/3/0973 20　0299149307
Alcoholism -- Social aspects -- United States. Drinking of alcoholic beverages -- Social aspects -- United States.

HV5292.L4 1982
Lender, Mark Edward, 1947-
Drinking in America: a history/ by Mark Edward Lender, James Kirby Martin. New York: Free Press; c1982. xv, 222 p.
82-070076　394.1/3/0973　0029185300
Alcoholism -- United States -- History.

HV5292.M4 1985
Mendelson, Jack H. 1929-
Alcohol, use and abuse in America/ Jack H. Mendelson, Nancy K. Mello. Boston: Little, Brown, c1985. xii, 395 p.
85-006959　362.2/92/0973　0316566632
Alcoholism -- United States -- History. Alcohol -- Physiological effect.

HV5292.P44 1998
Pegram, Thomas R., 1955-
Battling demon rum: the struggle for a dry America, 1800-1933/ Thomas R. Pegram. Chicago: Ivan R. Dee, c1998. xv, 207 p.
98-015875　363.4/1/0973 21　1566632080
Temperance -- United States -- History. Alcoholism -- United States -- Prevention -- History. Prohibition -- United States -- History.

HV5438-5515.15 Alcoholism. Intemperance. Temperance reform — By region or country — Other regions or countries

HV5438.M37 2001
Martin, A. Lynn.
Alcohol, sex, and gender in late medieval and early modern Europe/ A. Lynn Martin. Houndmills, Basingstoke, Hampshire; Palgrave, 2001. x, 200 p.
00-023343　394.1/3/094　0312234147
Drinking of alcoholic beverages -- Europe -- History. Women -- Alcohol use -- Europe -- History. Men -- Alcohol use -- Europe -- History.

HV5515.15.W48 1996
White, Stephen, 1945-
Russia goes dry: alcohol, state and society/ Stephen White. Cambridge; Cambridge University Press, 1996. xiii, 250 p.
95-013221　362.29/2/0947　0521552117
Alcoholism -- Russia (Federation) -- History. Alcoholism -- Soviet Union -- History. Temperance -- Russia (Federation) -- History.

HV5735 Tobacco habit — Other general (not A-Z)

HV5735.T65 1991
Tollison, Robert D.
The economics of smoking/ by Robert D. Tollison, Richard E. Wagner. Boston: Kluwer Academic, c1992. xi, 253 p.
91-031510　338.4/36797 20　0792392248
Smoking -- Economic aspects. Tobacco habit -- Economic aspects. Tobacco industry -- Government policy.

HV5745.G75 1994
Growing up tobacco free: preventing nicotine addiction in children and youths/ Barbara S. Lynch and Richard J. Bonnie, editors; Committee on Preventing Nicotine Addiction in Children and Youths, Institute of Medicine. Washington, D.C.: National Academy Press, 1994. xiii, 306 p.
94-031455　362.29/67/083　0309051290
Children -- Tobacco use -- United States -- Prevention. Youth -- Tobacco use -- United States -- Prevention.

HV5745.M85 1997
Mullen, Laura, 1960-
Tobacco-free youth: an activity guide!/ [developed by Laura Mullen and Denise Victory]. Springfield, MA: STAT (Stop Teenage Addiction to Tobacco), c1997. iii, 46 p.
98-135308
Teenagers -- Tobacco use -- Prevention -- Study and teaching -- Activity programs -- United States. Tobacco habit -- Prevention -- Study and teaching -- Activity programs -- United States.

HV5760-5765 Tobacco habit — By region or country — United States

HV5760.H57 1999
Hirschfelder, Arlene B.
Encyclopedia of smoking and tobacco/ Arlene B. Hirschfelder. Phoenix, AZ: Oryx Press, 1999. xviii, 411 p.
99-043450　362.29/6/097303　1573562025
Tobacco habit -- United States -- Encyclopedias. Smoking -- United States -- Encyclopedias. Tobacco industry -- United States -- Encyclopedias.

HV5763.R43 2000
Reducing tobacco use: a report of the Surgeon General: executive summary. [Washington, D.C.]: Dept. of Health and Human Services, U.S. Public 2000. iii, 22 p.
00-328196　016050418X
Smoking -- United States -- Prevention. Smoking cessation programs -- United States. Tobacco habit -- Treatment -- United States.

HV5765.D66 1991
D'Onofrio, Carol.
Tobacco talk: educating young children about tobacco/ Carol N. D'Onofrio. Santa Cruz, CA: Network Publications, 1991. viii, 163 p.
91-000007　372.3/7　1560710527
Tobacco habit -- Prevention -- Study and teaching (Primary) -- United States. Smoking -- Prevention -- Study and teaching (Primary) -- United States.

HV5765.V57 1992
Viscusi, W. Kip.
Smoking: making the risky decision/ W. Kip Viscusi. New York: Oxford University Press, 1992. x, 170 p.
91-047138　616.86/5　0195074866
Smoking -- United States -- Psychological aspects. Tobacco habit -- United States -- Psychological aspects. Smoking -- Economic aspects -- United States.

HV5770 Tobacco habit — By region or country — Other regions or countries, A-Z

HV5770.G8.U4 1991
UK smoking statistics/ edited by Nicholas Wald and Ans Nicolaides-Bouman. London: Wolfson Institute of Preventive Medicine; 1991. xxxiv, 243 p.
91-017732　362.29/621/0941021　0192616803
Cigarette habit -- Great Britain -- Statistics. Smoking -- Great Britain -- Statistics. Cigarette industry -- Great Britain -- Statistics.

HV5801 Drug habits. Drug abuse — General works

HV5801.C583 1998
The control of drugs and drug users: reason or reaction?/ edited by Ross Coomber. Amsterdam, The Netherlands: Harwood Academic Publishers, c1998. xxv, 265 p.
99-521801   9057021889
Narcotics, Control of. Narcotics, Control of -- Great Britain. Narcotics, Control of -- United States.

HV5801.D724 2000
Drug abuse sourcebook: basic consumer health information about illicit substances of abuse and the diversion of prescription medications .../ edited by Karen Bellenir. New York: Omnigraphics, c2000. xii, 629 p.
00-055071   362.29 21   078080242X
Drug abuse -- Prevention -- Handbooks, manuals, etc. Drug abuse -- Treatment -- Handbooks, manuals, etc. Narcotic habit -- Treatment -- Handbooks, manuals, etc.

HV5801.F75 1996
Friman, H. Richard.
NarcoDiplomacy: exporting the U.S. war on drugs/ H. Richard Friman. Ithaca, N.Y.: Cornell University Press, 1996. xiii 170 p.
96-018387   363.4/5/0973   080143274X
Narcotics, Control of. Drug traffic.

HV5801.I575 1992
International handbook on drug control/ edited by Scott B. MacDonald and Bruce Zagaris. Westport, Conn.: Greenwood Press, 1992. vii, 454 p.
91-035118   363.4/5   0313273758
Narcotics, Control of. Drug traffic. Narcotics, Control of -- International cooperation.

HV5801.P595 2000
Plant, Sadie, 1964-
Writing on drugs/ Sadie Plant. New York: Farrar, Straus, and Giroux, 2000. x, 294 p.
00-020822   394.1/4   0374293341
Drug abuse -- Social aspects. Drugs and literature.

HV5801.S75 1996
Stares, Paul B.
Global habit: the drug problem in a borderless world/ Paul B. Stares. Washington, D.C.: Brookings Institution, c1996. xii, 171 p.
95-041815   362.29/17 20   0815781407
Drug abuse. Drug abuse -- Prevention. Substance abuse.

HV5801.T78 1991
Tullis, F. LaMond, 1935-
Handbook of research on the illicit drug traffic: socioeconomic and political consequences/ LaMond Tullis in cooperation with the United Nations Research Institute for Social Development; foreword by Keith Griffin. New York: Greenwood, 1991. xxviii, 641 p.
90-025218   363.4/5   0313278466
Drug traffic. Narcotics, Control of.

HV5804 Drug habits. Drug abuse — Dictionaries. Encyclopedias

HV5804.A23 1984
Abel, Ernest L., 1943-
A dictionary of drug abuse terms and terminology/ Ernest L. Abel. Westport, Conn.: Greenwood Press, 1984. xi, 187 p.
83-022867   362.2/93/0321   0313240957
Drug abuse -- Dictionaries.

HV5804.C47 1999
Chepesiuk, Ronald.
The war on drugs: an international encyclopedia/ Ron Chepesiuk. Santa Barbara, Calif.: ABC-CLIO, c1999. xxxiv, 317 p.
99-054389   363.45/03 21   0874369851
Narcotics, Control of -- Encyclopedias. Drug traffic -- Encyclopedias. Drug abuse -- Prevention -- Encyclopedias.

HV5804.E53 2001
Encyclopedia of drugs, alcohol & addictive behavior/ Rosalyn Carson-DeWitt, editor-in-chief. New York: Macmillan Reference USA, c2001. 4 v.
00-046068   362.29/03 21   0028655419
Drug abuse -- Encyclopedias. Substance abuse -- Encyclopedias. Alcoholism -- Encyclopedias.

HV5810 Drug habits. Drug abuse — Special — Cocaine. Crack

HV5810.B45 1993
Belenko, Steven R.
Crack and the evolution of anti-drug policy/ Steven R. Belenko. Westport, Conn.: Greenwood Press, 1993. xii, 199 p.
93-009312   362.29/87/0973   0313280304
Crack (Drug) Drug abuse -- Government policy -- United States.

HV5810.B68 1995
Bourgois, Philippe I., 1956-
In search of respect: selling crack in El Barrio/ Philippe Bourgois. Cambridge; Cambridge University Press, 1995 [1996] xii, 392 p.
95-005929   363.4/5/097471   0521435188
Crack (Drug) -- New York (State) -- New York. Drug trafficking -- New York (State) -- New York. Afro-Americans -- Drug use -- New York (State) -- New York. New York (N.Y.) -- Economic conditions. New York (N.Y.) -- Social conditions.

HV5816 Drug habits. Drug abuse — Special — Opium

HV5816.R87 1990
Rush, James R. 1944-
Opium to Java: revenue farming and Chinese enterprise in colonial Indonesia, 1860-1910/ James R. Rush. Ithaca: Cornell University Press, 1990. x, 281 p.
89-045974   363.4/5/095982   0801422183
Opium trade -- Indonesia -- Java -- History -- 19th century.

HV5822 Drug habits. Drug abuse — Special — Other, A-Z

HV5822.C3
Matthews, Patrick.
Cannabis culture: a journey through disputed territory/ Patrick Matthews. London: Bloomsbury, 1999. 256 p.
99-494722   615.7827   0747542813
Cannabis.

HV5822.H4.B35 2000
Baldino, Rachel Greene, 1967-
Welcome to methadonia: a social worker's candid account of life in a methadone clinic/ Rachel Greene Baldino. Harrisburg, PA: White Hat Communications, c2000. 210 p.
00-009137   362.29/36/0973 21   1929109024
Heroin habit -- Treatment -- United States. Methadone maintenance -- United States. Social work with narcotic addicts -- United States.

HV5822.H4.K36 1983
Kaplan, John, 1929-1989.
The hardest drug: heroin and public policy/ John Kaplan. Chicago: University of Chicago Press, c1983. x, 247 p.
82-017514   362.2/93   0226424278
Heroin. Narcotics, Control of -- United States.

HV5822.M3.K53 1989
Kleiman, Mark.
Marijuana: costs of abuse, costs of control/ Mark A.R. Kleiman. New York: Greenwood Press, 1989. xx, 197 p.
88-007712   362.2/9   0313258538
Marijuana -- United States. Narcotics, Control of -- United States.

HV5823.5 Drug habits. Drug abuse — Special — Drug testing

HV5823.5.U5.D77 1991
Drug testing: issues and options/ edited by Robert H. Coombs and Louis Jolyon West. New York: Oxford University Press, 1991. xxiii, 245 p.
90-007848   362.29/364/0973   0195054148
Drug testing -- United States. Civil Rights -- United States. Substance Abuse Detection.

HV5824 Drug habits. Drug abuse — Drugs and special classes of persons, A-Z

HV5824.A33.L56 1988
Lipton, Helene L.
Drugs and the elderly: clinical, social, and policy perspectives/ Helene Levens Lipton, Philip R. Lee, with contributions by Mark S. Freeland. Stanford, Calif.: Stanford University Press, 1988. xv, 263 p.
87-033574   362.2/9   0804712956
Aged -- Drug use -- United States. Medication abuse -- United States. Drug abuse -- United States -- Prevention.

HV5824.E85.J36 1996
James, William H. 1940-
Doin' drugs: patterns of African American addiction/ William H. James and Stephen L. Johnson. Austin: University of Texas Press, c1996. xiv, 173 p.
96-016400 362.29/12/08996073 20 0292740409
Afro-Americans -- Drug use. Afro-Americans -- Alcohol use. Afro-Americans -- Social conditions.

HV5824.W6.K35 1996
Kandall, Stephen R.
Substance and shadow: women and addiction in the United States/ Stephen R. Kandall; with the assistance of Jennifer Petrillo. Cambridge, Mass.: Harvard University Press, 1996. iii, 353 p.
96-010207 362.29/082 0674853601
Women -- Drug use -- United States -- History. Drug abuse -- United States -- History. Narcotic addicts -- United States -- History.

HV5824.W6.M345 1997
Maher, Lisa.
Sexed work: gender, race, and resistance in a Brooklyn drug market/ Lisa Maher. Oxford; New York: 1997. xiii, 279 p.
97-008002 305.48/9694 019826495X
Minority women -- Drug use -- New York (State) -- New York. Women -- Drug use -- new York (State) -- New York. Women -- New York (State) -- New York -- Economic conditions.

HV5824.W6.T39 1993
Taylor, Avril.
Women drug users: an ethnography of a female injecting community/ Avril Taylor. Oxford [England]: Clarendon Press; 1993. 182 p.
93-213810 362.29/082 0198257961
Women -- Drug use -- Scotland -- Glasgow. Drug abuse -- Scotland -- Glasgow.

HV5824.W6.W55 1998
Williams, Kimberly M., 1968-
Learning limits: college women, drugs, and relationships/ Kimberly M. Williams. Westport, Conn.: Bergin & Garvey, 1998. xxvii, 191 p.
97-031520 362.29/082/0973 0897895568
Women college students -- Drug use -- United States. Interpersonal relations -- United States. Man-woman relationships -- United States.

HV5824.Y68.G55 1987
Glassner, Barry.
Drugs in adolescent worlds: burnouts to straights/ Barry Glassner and Julia Loughlin. New York: St. Martin's Press, c1987. x, 301 p.
86-001278 362.2/93/088055 031221992X
Teenagers -- Drug use -- United States. Drug abuse -- United States. Drug abuse surveys -- United States.

HV5824.Y68.N49 1988
Newcomb, Michael D.
Consequences of adolescent drug use: impact on the lives of young adults/ by Michael D. Newcomb and Peter M. Bentler. Newbury Park, Calif.: Sage Publications, c1988. 285 p.
87-024061 362.2/9 0803928475
Teenagers -- Drug use -- United States -- Longitudinal studies. Drug abuse -- United States -- Psychological aspects -- Longitudinal studies. Drug abuse -- Social aspects -- United States -- Longitudinal studies.

HV5824.Y68.V45 1998
Vega, William.
Drug use and ethnicity in early adolescence/ William A. Vega, Andres G. Gil, and associates. New York: Plenum Press, c1998. xviii, 234 p.
98-014620 362.29/12/089009759381 21 0306457377
Teenagers -- Drug use -- Florida -- Miami -- Longitudinal studies. Minority teenagers -- Drug use -- Florida -- Miami -- Longitudinal studies. Drug abuse -- Social aspects -- Florida -- Miami -- Longitudinal studies.

HV5824.Y68.Y68
Youth drug abuse: problems, issues, and treatment/ edited by George M. Beschner, Alfred S. Friedman. Lexington, Mass.: Lexington Books, c1979. xxxi, 681 p.
78-021197 362.7/8/2930973 0669028045
Youth -- Drug use -- United States. Drug abuse -- United States. Drug abuse -- United States -- Prevention.

HV5825-5833 Drug habits. Drug abuse — By region or country — United States

HV5825.C619 1989
Communication campaigns about drugs: government, media, and the public/ edited by Pamela J. Shoemaker. Hillsdale, N.J.: L. Erlbaum Associates, 1989. x, 127 p.
88-022760 362.2/93 0805802304
Drugs and mass media -- United States -- Congresses. Drug abuse -- United States -- Prevention -- Congresses. Narcotics, Control of -- United States -- Congresses.

HV5825.C74
Criminal justice and drugs: the unresolved connection/ edited by James C. Weissman and Robert L. DuPont. Port Washington, N.Y.: Kennikat Press, 1982. xii, 204 p.
81-003701 363.4/5 0804692912
Drug abuse -- United States -- Addresses, essays, lectures. Drug abuse -- Treatment -- United States -- Addresses, essays, lectures. Drug abuse and crime -- United States -- Addresses, essays, lectures.

HV5825.D772 1980
Drug Abuse Council (Washington, D.C.)
The facts about "drug abuse"/ The Drug Abuse Council. New York: Free Press, c1980. xi, 291 p.
79-054668 362.2/93/0973 0029077206
Drug abuse -- United States -- Addresses, essays, lectures. Narcotics, Control of -- United States -- Addresses, essays, lectures.

HV5825.D77736 1999
Drug use in metropolitan America/ Robert M. Bray, Mary Ellen Marsden, editors. Thousand Oaks, Calif.: Sage Publications, c1999. xxii, 344 p.
98-019675 362.29/12/0973 21 0761903747
Drug abuse -- United States.

HV5825.D7778 1996
Drug war politics: the price of denial/ Eva Bertram ... [et al.]. Berkeley: University of California Press, c1996. xiv, 347 p.
95-019168 363.4/5/0973 20 0520203097
Narcotics, Control of -- United States. Drug traffic -- Government policy -- United States. Drug abuse -- Government policy -- United States.

HV5825.G6954 2001
Gray, James P., 1945-
Why our drug laws have failed and what we can do about it: a judicial indictment of the War on Drugs/ James P. Gray. Philadelphia, [Pa.]: Temple University Press, 2001. x, 272 p.
00-047677 362.29/16/0973 1566398592
Drug abuse -- Government policy -- United States. Narcotics, Control of -- United States.

HV5825.H43
Helmer, John.
Drugs and minority oppression/ John Helmer. New York: Seabury Press, [1975] xi, 192 p.
75-002114 362.8/4 0816492166
Drug abuse -- United States. Minorities -- United States. United States -- Social conditions.

HV5825.H69 1998
How to legalize drugs/ edited by Jefferson M. Fish. Northvale, N.J.: Jason Aronson, c1998. xxiv, 675 p.
97-040745 362.29/0973 21 0765701510
Drug legalization -- United States. Drug abuse -- United States. Narcotics, Control of -- United States.

HV5825.I85 1998
Isralowitz, Richard.
Drug use, policy, and management/ Richard E. Isralowitz and Darwin Telias. Westport, Conn.: Praeger, 1998. xii, 157 p.
98-014908 363.4/5/0973 0275961281
Drug abuse -- United States. Drug abuse -- United States -- Prevention.

HV5825.J46 1999
Jenkins, Philip, 1952-
Synthetic panics: the symbolic politics of designer drugs/ by Philip Jenkins. New York: New York University Press, 1999. xi, 247 p.
99-006057 363.45/0973 21 0814742432
Narcotics, Control of -- United States. Designer drugs -- Government policy -- United States. Drug abuse -- United States.

HV5825.L37 1989
The Latin American narcotics trade and U.S. national security/ edited by Donald J. Mabry; foreword by Janos Radvanyi. New York: Greenwood Press, 1989. x, 206 p.
89-012030 363.4/5/0973 0313267863
Narcotics, Control of -- United States. Drug traffic -- Latin America. National security -- United States. United States -- Foreign relations -- Latin America. Latin America -- Foreign relations -- United States.

HV5825.L38 2001
Lawson, Gary.
Essentials of chemical dependency counseling/ Gary W. Lawson, Ann W. Lawson, P. Clayton Rivers. 3rd ed. Gaithersburg, Md.: Aspen Publishers, 2001. xii, 504 p.
00-033161 362.29/186 21 0834218240
Drug abuse counseling -- United States. Alcoholism counseling -- United States.

HV5825.M377 1996
Menzel, Sewall H. 1942-
Fire in the Andes: U.S. foreign policy and cocaine politics in Bolivia and Peru/ Sewall H. Menzel. Lanham, Md.: University Press of America, c1996. xvi, 281 p.
96-034246 363.4/5/098 20 0761805079
Narcotics, Control of -- United States. Narcotics, Control of -- Bolivia. Narcotics, Control of -- Peru. United States -- Foreign relations -- Bolivia. United States -- Foreign relations -- Peru.

HV5825.M58 1993
Minkler, Meredith.
Grandmothers as caregivers: raising children of the crack cocaine epidemic/ Meredith Minkler, Kathleen M. Roe. Newbury Park, Calif.: Sage, c1993. xvi, 240 p.
92-038077   362.29/83/0973 20   0803948468
Narcotic addicts -- United States -- Family relationships. Children of narcotic addicts -- United States -- Family relationships. Grandparenting -- United States.

HV5825.P375 1991
Persuasive communication and drug abuse prevention/ edited by Lewis Donohew, Howard E. Sypher, William J. Bukoski. Hillsdale, N.J.: L. Erlbaum Associates, 1991. xxi, 349 p.
90-014017   362.29/17/0973   0805806938
Drug abuse -- United States -- Prevention -- Congresses. Drugs and mass media -- United States -- Congresses. Narcotics, Control of -- United States -- Congresses.

HV5825.R44 1996
Rengert, George F.
The geography of illegal drugs/ George F. Rengert. Boulder, Colo.: Westview Press, 1996. xi, 147 p.
96-012154   363.4/5/0973   0813389860
Drug traffic -- United States.

HV5825.S36 1991
Schilit, Rebecca.
Drugs and behavior: a sourcebook for the helping professions/ Rebecca Schilit, Edith S. Lisansky Gomberg. Newbury Park, Calif.: Sage Publications, c1991. viii, 355 p.
91-017558   362.29/18/0973 20   0803934610
Drug abuse -- United States. Drug abuse -- Treatment -- United States. Psychotropic Drugs.

HV5825.S393 1992
Scriven, Paul.
The medicine society/ Paul Scriven. East Lansing: Michigan State University Press, 1992. xiii, 217 p.
92-053724   363.4/5/0973   0870133152
Drug abuse -- United States. Drug traffic -- United States. Narcotics, Control of -- United States.

HV5825.S396 1991
Searching for alternatives: drug-control policy in the United States/ edited and with an introduction by Melvyn B. Krauss and Edward P. Lazear. Stanford, Calif.: Hoover Institution Press, Stanford University, c1991. xxxvii, 454 p.
91-020103   363.4/5/0973 20   0817991417
Narcotics, Control of -- United States. Drug legalization -- United States.

HV5825.S597 2000
Spillane, Joseph.
Cocaine: from medical marvel to modern menace in the United States, 1884-1920/ Joseph F. Spillane. Baltimore, MD: Johns Hopkins University Press, 2000. x, 214 p.
99-032725   362.29/8/0973   0801862302
Cocaine habit -- United States -- History. Cocaine -- United States -- History. Cocaine industry -- United States -- History.

HV5831.K4.C53 1995
Clayton, Richard R.
Marijuana in the "Third World": Appalachia, U.S.A./ by Richard R. Clayton. Boulder: L. Rienner Publishers, 1995. xii, 123 p.
95-017942   338.1/7379/09769   155587553X
Marijuana -- Government policy -- Kentucky. Marijuana industry -- Government policy -- Kentucky. Marijuana -- Law and legislation -- Kentucky. Kentucky -- Economic conditions. Kentucky -- Social conditions.

HV5833.N45
Sommers, Ira Brant.
Workin' hard for the money: the social and economic lives of women drug sellers/ Ira Sommers, Deborah Baskin, and Jeffrey Fagan. Huntington, N.Y.: Nova Science Publishers, c2000. 182 p.
00-033955   364.1/77/082097471   21 1560728205
Women narcotics dealers -- New York (State) -- New York -- Social conditions. Women narcotics dealers -- New York (State) -- New York -- Economic conditions. Narcotics and crime -- New York (State) -- New York.

HV5840 Drug habits. Drug abuse
— By region or country
— Other regions or countries, A-Z

HV5840.A5.C58 1996
Clawson, Patrick, 1951-
The Andean cocaine industry/ Patrick L. Clawson and Rensselaer W. Lee III. New York: St. Martin's Press, 1996. xii, 276 p.
95-052824   363.4/5/098   0312124007
Cocaine industry -- Andes Region. Medellin Cartel. Narcotics, Control of -- Andes Region.

HV5840.A5.M33 1989
MacDonald, Scott B.
Mountain high, white avalanche: cocaine and power in the Andean states and Panama/ Scott B. MacDonald; foreword by Norman A. Bailey. New York: Praeger, 1989. xiii, 153 p.
88-039214   363.4/5/098   0275932346
Drug traffic -- Andes Region. Drug traffic -- Panama. Cocaine industry -- Andes Region.

HV5840.A74.J45 1997
Jennings, John M., 1962-
The opium empire: Japanese imperialism and drug trafficking in Asia, 1895-1945/ John M. Jennings. Westport, Conn.: Praeger, 1997. x, 161 p.
96-027454   363/.45/095   0275957594
Opium trade -- Asia -- History. Drug traffic -- Political aspects -- Asia -- History. Japan -- Foreign relations -- History.

HV5840.B6.M35 1992
Malamud Goti, Jaime E.
Smoke and mirrors: the paradox of the drug wars/ Jaime Malamud-Goti. Boulder: Westview Press, 1992. xxi, 117 p.
91-017076   363.4/5/0984   0813313600
Narcotics, Control of -- United States -- International cooperation. Coca industry -- Bolivia -- Chapare. Drug traffic -- Bolivia -- Chapare.

HV5840.B93.R45 1996
Renard, Ronald D.
The Burmese connection: illegal drugs and the making of the Golden Triangle/ Ronald D. Renard. Boulder: L. Rienner Publishers, 1996. xix, 147 p.
95-021261   363.4/5/09591   1555876188
Drug traffic -- Burma -- History. Drug traffic -- Golden Triangle (Southeastern Asia) -- History. Drug abuse -- Burma -- History. Burma -- Economic conditions. Burma -- Politics and government.

HV5840.C315.G75 1997
Griffith, Ivelaw L.
Drugs and security in the Caribbean: sovereignty under siege/ Ivelaw Lloyd Griffith. University Park, Pa.: Pennsylvannia State University Press, c1997. xix, 295 p.
96-040024   363.45/09729 21   027101718X
Narcotics, Control of -- Caribbean Area. Narcotics, Control of -- International cooperation. National security -- Caribbean Area.

HV5840.C37.P64 2000
The political economy of drugs in the Caribbean/ edited by Ivelaw L. Griffith. New York, N.Y.: St. Martin's Press, 2000. xxii, 273 p.
99-087197   363.45/09729   0312232586
Drug traffic -- Caribbean Area. Narcotics, Control of -- Caribbean Area.

HV5840.C6.S54 2001
Slack, Edward R., 1963-
Opium, state, and society: China's narco-economy and the Guomindang, 1924-1937/ Edward R. Slack, Jr. Honolulu: University of Hawai'i Press, 2001. xiii, 240 p.
00-042315   363.45/0951   0824822781
Opium habit -- China. Opium trade -- Government policy -- China. China -- Politics and government -- 1928-1937.

HV5840.C7.T48 1995
Thoumi, Francisco E.
Political economy and illegal drugs in Colombia/ Francisco E. Thoumi. Boulder: L. Rienner, 1995. xvi, 320 p.
94-191659   363.4/5/09861   155587536X
Drug traffic -- Colombia. Drug traffic -- Government policy -- Colombia. Narcotics, Control of -- Colombia. Colombia -- Economic conditions -- 1918-

HV5840.S64.E45 2000
Emdad-ul Haq, M.
Drugs in South Asia: from the opium trade to the present day/ M. Emdad-ul Haq. Houndmills, Basingstoke, Hampshire; St. Martin's Press, 2000. xiv, 319 p.
99-059428   363.45/095   031222379X
Drug traffic -- South Asia. Drug traffic -- South Asia -- History -- 20th century.

HV6001 Criminology —
Periodicals. Serials — English

HV6001.C67
Criminal justice abstracts. Monsey, N.Y. [etc.] Willow Tree Press [etc.]
77-647645   364
Criminal justice, Administration of -- Periodicals. Criminal justice, Administration of -- Abstracts -- Periodicals. Crime -- Abstracts -- Periodicals.

HV6017 Criminology — Encyclopedias. Dictionaries

HV6017.C97 1996
Cyriax, Oliver.
Crime: an encyclopedia/ Oliver Cyriax. North Pomfret, Vermont: Trafalgar Square, 1996, c1993. xi, 468 p.
96-060232   364/.03   1570760640
Crime -- Encyclopedias. Criminals -- Biography -- Dictionaries. Crime -- Dictionaries.

HV6017.E52 1983
Encyclopedia of crime and justice/ Sanford H. Kadish, editor in chief. New York: Free Press, c1983. 4 v.
83-007156   364/.03/21   0029181100
Criminology -- Encyclopedias. Criminal justice, Administration of -- Encyclopedias.

HV6017.E5425 1992
Dictionary of crime: criminal justice, criminology & law enforcement/ [edited by] Jay Robert Nash. New York: Paragon House, 1992. iii, 433 p.
91-038107   364/.03   1557785090
Crime -- Dictionaries. Criminal justice, Administration of -- Dictionaries. Law enforcement -- Dictionaries.

HV6018 Criminology — Theory and methodology

HV6018.G68 1990
Gottfredson, Michael R.
A general theory of crime/ Michael R. Gottfredson and Travis Hirschi. Stanford, Calif.: Stanford University Press, 1990. xvi, 297 p.
89-022027   364   0804717737
Criminology -- Methodology.

HV6018.M54 1994
Miethe, Terance D.
Crime and its social context: toward an integrated theory of offenders, victims, and situations/ Terance D. Miethe, Robert F. Meier. Albany: State University of New York Press, c1994. xiv, 209 p.
93-024503   364 20   0791419010
Criminology. Criminal behavior. Victims of crimes.

HV6022 Criminology — History of the science — By region or country, A-Z

HV6022.G3
Wetzell, Richard F.
Inventing the criminal: a history of German criminology, 1880-1945/ Richard F. Wetzell. Chapel Hill: University of North Carolina Press, c2000. xiv, 348 p.
99-042798   364.943 21   0807825352
Criminology -- Germany -- History.

HV6022.G7.W54 1990
Wiener, Martin J.
Reconstructing the criminal: culture, law, and policy in England, 1830-1914/ Martin J. Wiener. Cambridge [England]; Cambridge University Press, 1990. ix, 381 p.
90-001593   364.942/09/034   052135045X
Criminology -- England -- History -- 19th century. Criminal justice, Administration of -- England -- History -- 19th century.

HV6023 Criminology — History of the science — Biography. Criminologists

HV6023.G74 2000
Greene, Helen Taylor, 1949-
African American criminological thought/ Helen Taylor Greene and Shaun L. Gabbidon; with a foreword by Julius Debro. Albany: State University of New York Press, c2000. xvii, 192 p.
00-032930   364/.089/96073 21   0791446956
African American criminologists -- Biography. Criminology -- United States -- History.

HV6024.5 Criminology — Research

HV6024.5.D65 2000
Doing research on crime and justice/ edited by Roy D. King and Emma Wincup. New York: Oxford University Press, 2000. xxi, 441 p.
00-026723   364/.072   0198765401
Crime -- Research -- Great Britain. Criminal justice, Administration of -- Research -- Great Britain.

HV6024.5.J87 1989
Jupp, Victor.
Methods of criminological research/ Victor Jupp. London; Unwin Hyman, 1989. xiv, 192 p.
88-036279   364/.072   0044450664
Criminology -- Research. Criminal justice, Administration of -- Research.

HV6025 Criminology — General works — English

HV6025.C582 2000
Coleman, Clive.
Introducing criminology/ Clive Coleman, Clive Norris. Cullompton, Devon, UK; Willan, c2000. ix, 202 p.
2001-267814   364 21   1903240107
Criminology.

HV6025.C65
Cortes, Juan B.
Delinquency and crime: a biopsychosocial approach; empirical, theoretical, and practical aspects of criminal behavior [by] Juan B. Cortes, with Florence M. Gatti. New York, Seminar Press, 1972. x, 468 p.
76-154390   364.2   0128169508
Criminal psychology. Crime. Criminal anthropology.

HV6025.D43 1988
De Sola, Ralph, 1908-
Crime dictionary/ Ralph De Sola. New York, N.Y.: Facts on File, c1988. xiii, 222 p.
87-020133   364/.03/21   0816018723
Crime -- Dictionaries. Criminology -- Dictionaries.

HV6025.F46 1998
Findlay, Mark.
The globalization of crime/ Mark Findlay. Cambridge; Cambridge University Press, 1998. x, 243 p.
98-024884   364   0521621259
Criminology. Social change.

HV6025.H274 1989
Hagan, John, 1946-
Structural criminology/ John Hagan in collaboration with Celesta Albonetti ... [et al.]. New Brunswick, N.J.: Rutgers University Press, 1989. viii, 294 p.
88-042887   364   0813513758
Criminology. Social structure. Structuralism.

HV6025.H36 1989
Heidensohn, Frances.
Crime and society/ Frances Heidensohn. New York: New York University Press, 1989. x, 214 p.
88-025904   364   0814734553
Criminology. Crime -- Great Britain.

HV6030 Criminology — General special (Special aspects of the subject as a whole)

HV6030.A73 1984
Archer, Dane, 1946-
Violence and crime in cross-national perspective/ Dane Archer and Rosemary Gartner. New Haven: Yale University Press, c1984. ix, 341 p.
83-021700   364/.042   0300031491
Crime -- History -- 20th century -- Cross-cultural studies. Violent crimes -- History -- 20th century -- Cross-cultural studies.

HV6030.N33 1996
Naffine, Ngaire.
Feminism and criminology/ Ngaire Naffine. Cambridge, MA: Polity Press, 1996.
96-009483   364/.082 20   1566395070
Feminist criminology.

HV6030.T69 1995
Cultural criminology/ Jeff Ferrell & Clinton R. Sanders [editors]. Boston: Northeastern University Press, c1995. x, 365 p.
95-011501   364.973 20   1555532357
Crime -- United States. Popular culture -- United States. Crime in mass media. United States -- Social conditions.

HV6035 Criminology — Criminal anthropology — General works

HV6035.C65 2000
Colvin, Mark, 1947-
Crime and coercion: an integrated theory of chronic criminality/ by Mark Colvin. New York: St. Martin's Press , 2000. xxx, 361 p.
00-038237   364   0312233892
Criminal anthropology. Criminal behavior.

HV6035.E74 1998
Ethnography at the edge: crime, deviance, and field research/ Jeff Ferrell and Mark S. Hamm, editors. Boston: Northeastern University Press, c1998. xviii, 309 p.
97-036683   364.2/4 21   1555533418
Criminal anthropology -- Research. Criminal anthropology -- Field work. Criminal behavior -- Research.

HV6035.H65 1969
Hooton, Earnest Albert, 1887-1954.
The American criminal; an anthropological study.
[1] The native white criminal of native parentage.
With the collaboration of the Statistical Laboratory
of the Division of Anthropology, Harvard
University. New York, Greenwood Press [1969,
c1939] 1 v.
69-013935   364.3
*Criminal anthropology. Criminology -- United
States.*

HV6035.V6 1986
Vold, George B. 1896-1967.
Theoretical criminology/ by George B. Vold and
Thomas J. Bernard. New York: Oxford University
Press, 1986. xiv, 374 p.
85-011558   364.2   0195036166
*Criminal anthropology. Criminology. Deviant
behavior.*

HV6046-6049 Criminology — Criminal anthropology — Criminal types

HV6046.C54 1997
Chesney-Lind, Meda.
The female offender: girls, women, and crime/
Meda Chesney-Lind. Thousand Oaks: Sage
Publications, c1997. xii, 220 p.
96-045845   364.3/74/0973 21   0803950993
*Female offenders -- United States. Female
juvenile delinquents -- United States.
Discrimination in criminal justice administration --
United States.*

HV6046.E56 2000
Encyclopedia of women and crime/ Nicole Hahn
Rafter, editor-in-chief. Phoenix, AZ: Oryx Press,
2000.
00-033625   364/.082 21   1573562149
*Female offenders -- Dictionaries. Women,
Crimes against -- Dictionaries.*

HV6046.M36 1984
Mann, Coramae Richey, 1931-
Female crime and delinquency/ Coramae Richey
Mann. University, Ala.: University of Alabama
Press, c1984. xv, 331 p.
82-016052   364.3/74/0973   0817301445
*Female offenders. Female offenders -- United
States. Female juvenile delinquents.*

HV6046.S46 1996
Shapiro, Ann-Louise, 1944-
Breaking the codes: female criminality in fin-de-
siecle Paris/ Ann-Louise Shapiro. Stanford, Calif.:
Stanford University Press, 1996. vi, 265 p.
95-037867   364.3/74/094436109041
0804716633
Female offenders -- France -- Paris -- History.

HV6046.W67 1990
Worrall, Anne.
Offending women: female lawbreakers and the
criminal justice system/ Anne Worrall. London;
Routledge, 1990. ix, 189 p.
89-010475   364.3/74/0941   0415037247
*Female offenders -- Great Britain. Deviant
behavior -- Labeling theory. Sex discrimination in
criminal justice administration -- Great Britain.*

HV6047.R33 1997
Rafter, Nicole Hahn, 1939-
Creating born criminals/ Nicole Hahn Rafter.
Urbana: University of Illinois Press, c1997. xi,
284 p.
96-035672   364.2/4 20   0252022378
*Criminal behavior -- United States -- Genetic
aspects. Eugenics -- United States.*

HV6049.S47 2000
Serial offenders: current thought, recent findings/
edited by Louis B. Schlesinger. Boca Raton: CRC
Press, c2000. 349 p.
00-040350   364.3 21   0849322367
Recidivism. Recidivists.

HV6074 Criminology — Criminal anthropology — Criminal anthropometry

HV6074.B34 2001
Beavan, Colin.
Fingerprints: the origins of crime detection and the
murder case that launched forensic science/ Colin
Beavan. New York: Hyperion, c2001. xvi, 232 p.
00-066365   363.25/8 21   0786866071
*Fingerprints. Fingerprints -- Identification.
Criminal investigation.*

HV6074.C557 2001
Cole, Simon A., 1967-
Suspect identities: a history of fingerprinting and
criminal identification/ Simon A. Cole. Cambridge,
MA: Harvard University Press, 2001. 369 p.
00-054054   363.25/8   0674004558
*Fingerprints -- Identification. Fingerprints --
Classification. Criminals -- Identification.*

HV6080-6089 Criminology — Criminal anthropology — Criminal psychology

HV6080.G28 1994
Gabor, Thomas.
"Everybody does it!": crime by the public/ Thomas
Gabor. Toronto; University of Toronto Press,
c1994. xv, 378 p.
94-214154   0802068286
*Criminal behavior. Criminal behavior -- Canada.
Criminal behavior -- United States.*

HV6080.R46 1999
Rhodes, Richard.
Why they kill: the discoveries of a maverick
criminologist/ Richard Rhodes. New York: Alfred
A. Knopf, 1999. x, 371 p.
99-018920   364.3   0375402497
*Athens, Lonnie H.   Violent crimes -- Case studies.
Criminal behavior -- Research -- Methodology.
Criminal psychology -- Case studies.*

HV6080.S83 1992
Stephenson, G. M.
The psychology of criminal justice/ Geoffrey M.
Stephenson. Oxford, UK; Blackwell, 1992. x,
286 p.
92-015564   364.3/01/9   063114546X
*Criminal psychology. Criminal justice,
Administration of -- Psychological aspects.*

HV6089.D47 1998
DeRosia, Victoria R. 1957-
Living inside prison walls: adjustment behavior/
Victoria R. DeRosia. Westport, Conn.: Praeger,
1998. x, 206 p.
98-015659   365/.6 0275958957
*Prison psychology. Adjustment (Psychology)
Criminals -- Rehabilitation.*

HV6089.Z36 1988
Zamble, Edward.
Coping, behavior, and adaptation in prison
inmates/ Edward Zamble, Frank J. Porporino. New
York: Springer-Verlag, c1988. xiii, 204 p.
87-033097   365/.6/019   0387966137
*Prison psychology -- Case studies. Adjustment
(Psychology) -- Case studies.*

HV6115 Criminology — Criminal anthropology — Causes of crime. Criminal etiology

HV6115.W35 1990
Walters, Glenn D.
The criminal lifestyle: patterns of serious criminal
conduct/ Glenn D. Walters. Newbury Park, Calif.:
Sage Publications, c1990. 224 p.
90-037509   364.3 20   0803938403
*Criminal behavior. Criminal behavior -- United
States -- Cases studies.*

HV6245-6248 Criminology — Criminal classes — Biography

HV6245.F74 1996
Frasier, David K., 1951-
Murder cases of the twentieth century: biographies
and bibliographies of 280 convicted or accused
killers/ by David K. Frasier. Jefferson, N.C.:
McFarland & Co., 1996. xviii, 552 p.
96-014984   364.1/523/0922   0786401842
*Murderers -- Biography -- Encyclopedias.
Murder -- History -- 20th century -- Encyclopedias.*

HV6245.N49 2000
Newton, Michael, 1951-
The encyclopedia of serial killers/ Michael
Newton. New York: Facts on File, c2000. vii,
391 p.
99-014384   364.15/23/03 21   081603978X
Serial murderers -- Encyclopedias.

HV6248.S3.A4 1971
Sacco, Nicola, 1891-1927.
The letters of Sacco and Vanzetti. Edited by
Marion Denman Frankfurter and Gardner Jackson.
New York, Octagon Books, 1971 [c1928] xi,
414 p.
76-159224   364.15/23/0922   0374970033
Sacco-Vanzetti Trial, Dedham, Mass., 1921.

HV6250.25 Criminology — Victims of crimes. Victimology — General works

HV6250.25.M38 1994
Mawby, R. I.
Critical victimology: international perspectives/
R.I. Mawby and S. Walklate. London; Sage, 1994.
224 p.
93-086519   362.88   0803985118
Victims of crimes.

HV6250.25.S42 1996
Sebba, Leslie.
Third parties: victims and the criminal justice system/ Leslie Sebba. Columbus: Ohio State University Press, c1996. x, 446 p.
95-050577   362.88 20   0814206646
Victims of crimes. Victims of crimes -- Legal status, laws, etc. Criminal justice, Administration of.

HV6250.25.W47 1998
Westervelt, Saundra Davis, 1968-
Shifting the blame: how victimization became a criminal defense/ Saundra Davis Westervelt. New Brunswick, NJ: Rutgers University Press, c1998. xi, 193 p.
98-015629   362.88 21   0813525837
Victims of crimes. Abused women -- Psychology. Crime -- Sociological aspects.

HV6250.3 Criminology — Victims of crimes. Victimology — By region or country, A-Z

HV6250.3.U5.E46 1993
Elias, Robert, 1950-
Victims still: the political manipulation of crime victims/ Robert Elias. Newbury Park, Calif.: Sage Publications, c1993. ix, 177 p.
93-006511   362.88 20   0803950527
Victims of crimes -- United States. Criminal justice, Administration of -- United States. Reparation -- United States.

HV6250.3.U5.J45 1997
Jenness, Valerie, 1963-
Hate crimes: new social movements and the politics of violence/ Valerie Jenness and Kendal Broad. New York: Aldine de Gruyter, c1997. xi, 215 p.
97-008950   364.1 21   0202306011
Hate crimes -- United States. Social movements -- United States. Gays -- Crimes against -- United States.

HV6250.3.U5.W44 1995
Weed, Frank, 1942-
Certainty of justice: reform in the crime victim movement/ Frank J. Weed. New York: Aldine de Gruyter, c1995. x, 158 p.
95-005658   362.88 20   0202305171
Victims of crimes -- Services for -- United States. Victims of crimes -- Legal status, laws, etc. -- United States. Social movements -- United States.

HV6250.4 Criminology — Victims of crimes. Victimology — Special classes of persons as victims, A-Z

HV6250.4.H66.C66 1991
Comstock, Gary David, 1945-
Violence against lesbians and gay men/ Gary David Comstock. New York: Columbia University Press, c1991. xiv, 319 p.
90-047126   362.88 20   0231073305
Gay men -- Crimes against -- United States. Lesbians -- Crimes against -- United States.

HV6250.4.W65.B46 1997
Benedict, Jeff.
Public heroes, private felons: athletes and crimes against women/ Jeff Benedict. Boston: Northeastern University Press, 1997. xvii, 254 p.
97-006528   364.15/3   1555533167
Women -- Crimes against. Athletes -- Psychology. College athletes -- Psychology.

HV6250.4.W65.B87 1992
Burstow, Bonnie, 1945-
Radical feminist therapy: working in the context of violence/ Bonnie Burstow. Newbury Park: Sage Publications, c1992. xviii, 302 p.
92-030005   155.6/33 20   0803947879
Abused women -- North America. Feminist therapy -- North America. Women -- Crimes against -- North America.

HV6250.4.W65.D4 1998
D'Cruze, Shani.
Crimes of outrage: sex, violence and Victorian working women/ Shani D'Cruze. DeKalb: Northern Illinois University Press, c1998. viii, 263 p.
98-014886   364.15/3/0820941 21   0875802427
Women -- Crimes against -- Great Britain -- History -- 19th century. Sex discrimination against women -- Great Britain -- History -- 19th century. Sexual abuse victims -- Great Britain -- History -- 19th century.

HV6250.4.W65.F55 1994
Flowers, Ronald B.
The victimization and exploitation of women and children: a study of physical, mental, and sexual maltreatment in the United States/ by R. Barri Flowers. Jefferson, N.C.: McFarland & Co., c1994. xiv, 240 p.
94-016362   362.82/92 20   0899509789
Women -- Crimes against -- United States. Children -- Crimes against -- United States. Abused women -- United States.

HV6250.4.W65.G74 1999
Green, December.
Gender violence in Africa: African women's responses/ December Green. New York: St. Martin's Press, 1999. 298 p.
99-017320   362.88/082/096   0312219431
Women -- Crimes against -- Africa. Violence -- Africa. Abused women -- Africa.

HV6250.4.W65.M325 1997
Madriz, Esther, 1943-
Nothing bad happens to good girls: fear of crime in women's lives/ Esther Madriz. Berkeley: University of California Press, c1997. xv, 187 p.
96-037659   362.88/082 21   0520202910
Women -- Crimes against -- United States. Fear of crime -- United States. Women -- United States -- Psychology.

HV6250.4.W65.S33 1982
Schechter, Susan.
Women and male violence: the visions and struggles of the battered women's movement/ Susan Schechter. Boston: South End Press, c1982. ii, 367 p.
82-061150   0896081591
Abused women -- United States. Abused wives -- United States. Abused wives -- Services for -- United States.

HV6250.4.W65.S54 1996
Singh, Priyam, 1933-
Victims or criminals?: a study of women in colonial North-Western Provinces and Oudh, India, 1870-1910/ Priyam Singh. Middletown, N.J.: Caslon, 1996. xii, 143 p.
96-003782   364.954/2   0391039717
Women -- Crimes against -- India -- United Provinces of Agra and Oudh. Female offenders -- India -- United Provinces of Agra and Oudh. Women -- India -- United Provinces of Agra and Oudh -- Social conditions. India -- History -- British occupation, 1765-1947.

HV6250.4.W65.S68 2001
The sourcebook on violence against women/ editors Claire M. Renzetti, Jeffrey L. Edleson, Raquel Kennedy Bergen. Thousand Oaks, Calif.: Sage Publications, c2001. xii, 539 p.
00-010215   362.82/92 21   0761920048
Women -- Crimes against. Abused women. Family violence.

HV6250.4.W65.U53 1996
Understanding violence against women/ Nancy A. Crowell and Ann W. Burgess, editors. Washington, D.C.: National Academy Press, 1996. x, 225 p.
96-017335   362.82/92   0309054257
Women -- Crimes against -- United States. Women -- Crimes against -- Research -- United States. Wife abuse -- United States.

HV6250.4.W65.V565 1998
Violence against women: philosophical perspectives/ edited by Stanley G. French, Wanda Teays, Laura M. Purdy. Ithaca: Cornell University Press, 1998. ix, 260 p.
97-046848   362.88/082   0801434416
Women -- Crimes against. Sexual harassment of women. Sexual abuse victims.

HV6250.4.W65.W453 1998
Websdale, Neil.
Rural woman battering and the justice system: an ethnography/ Neil Websdale. Thousand Oaks, Calif.: Sage Publications, c1998. xxxii, 263 p.
97-033760   364.15/553/09769 21   076190851X
Abused women -- Kentucky. Rural women -- Kentucky -- Social conditions. Criminal justice, Administration of -- Kentucky.

HV6250.4.W65.W467 1998
What women do in wartime: gender and conflict in Africa/ edited by Meredeth Turshen & Clotilde Twagiramariya. London; Zed Books, 1998. xi, 180 p.
99-187635   185649537X
Women -- Crimes against -- Africa, Sub-Saharan. Women and war -- Africa, Sub-Saharan. Women in war -- Africa, Sub-Saharan.

HV6278-6322.7 Criminology — Crimes and offenses — Political crimes

HV6278.L45 1988
Lentz, Harris M.
Assassinations and executions: an encyclopedia of political violence, 1865-1986/ by Harris M. Lentz III. Jefferson, N.C.: McFarland, c1988. xviii, 275 p.
87-046383   909.8   0899503128
Assassination -- History -- Chronology. Executions and executioners -- History -- Chronology.

HV6278.S54 2001
Sifakis, Carl.
Encyclopedia of assassinations/ Carl Sifakis. New York, NY: Facts on File, c2001. xi, 258 p.
2001-017465　364.15/24/0922 21　0816043329
Assassination -- History -- Encyclopedias. Murder victims -- Biography -- Dictionaries.

HV6285.D53 1992
Diamond, Sigmund.
Compromised campus: the collaboration of universities with the intelligence community, 1945-1955/ Sigmund Diamond. New York: Oxford University Press, 1992. ix, 371 p.
91-015668　364.1/31　0195053826
Political crimes and offenses -- Investigation -- United States -- History -- 20th century. Higher education and state -- United States -- History -- 20th century. Academic freedom -- United States -- History -- 20th century.

HV6301.M33 1997
McChesney, Fred S., 1948-
Money for nothing: politicians, rent extraction, and political extortion/ Fred S. McChesney. Cambridge, Mass.: Harvard University Press, 1997. xi, 216 p.
96-047873　364.1/323　0674583302
Bribery -- Economic aspects. Extortion -- Economic aspects. Lobbying -- Economic aspects.

HV6321.I693.P48 1997
Phythian, Mark.
Arming Iraq: how the U.S. and Britain secretly built Saddam's war machine/ Mark Phythian. Boston: Northeastern University Press, c1997. xxvii, 325 p.
96-018166　382/.456234/09567 20　1555532853
Illegal arms transfers -- Iraq. Illegal arms transfers -- United States. Illegal arms transfers -- Great Britain.

HV6321.J3.M57 1996
Mitchell, Richard H.
Political bribery in Japan/ Richard H. Mitchell. Honolulu, Hawaii: University of Hawaii Press, c1996. xvii, 206 p.
96-025662　364.1/323 20　0824818199
Bribery -- Japan -- History. Political corruption -- Japan -- History.

HV6322.3.A7.A74 1999
Arditti, Rita, 1934-
Searching for life: the grandmothers of the Plaza de Mayo and the disappeared children of Argentina/ Rita Arditti. Berkeley: University of California Press, c1999. xvi, 235 p.
98-046637　362.7 21　0520211138
Children of disappeared persons -- Argentina -- Family relationships. Missing children -- Argentina -- Family relationships. Civil rights -- Argentina.

HV6322.3.S2.H87 1998
Hutchinson, Bill, 1947-
When the dogs ate candles: a time in El Salvador/ by Bill Hutchinson. Niwot, Colo: University Press of Colorado, c1998. xxi, 229 p.
97-048727　972.8405/3/092 B 21　0870814753
State-sponsored terrorism -- El Salvador. Human rights workers -- El Salvador. El Salvador -- Politics and government -- 1979-1992.

HV6322.7.A58 2001
Alvarez, Alex.
Governments, citizens, and genocide: a comparative and interdisciplinary approach/ Alex Alvarez. Bloomington: Indiana University Press, c2001. x, 224 p.
00-057501　304.6/63 21　0253338492
Genocide.

HV6322.7.C44 1990
Chalk, Frank Robert, 1937-
The history and sociology of genocide: analyses and case studies/ Frank Chalk & Kurt Jonassohn. New Haven: Yale University Press, c1990. xviii, 461 p.
89-027381　304.6/63 20　0300044461
Genocide -- History. Genocide -- Case studies.

HV6322.7.E53 1999
Encyclopedia of genocide/ Israel W. Charny, editor in chief; forewords by Desmond M. Tutu and Simon Wiesenthal. Santa Barbara, Calif.: ABC-CLIO, 1999. 2 v.
99-052695　364.15/1/03　0874369282
Genocide -- Encyclopedias. Genocide -- Encyclopedias.

HV6322.7.M37 1995
Markusen, Eric.
The Holocaust and strategic bombing: genocide and total war in the twentieth century/ Eric Markusen, David Kopf. Boulder: Westview Press, 1995. xvi, 354 p.
94-032807　304.6/63　0813375320
Genocide -- History -- 20th century. World War, 1939-1945 -- Aerial operations. Bombing, Aerial -- History.

HV6322.7.M39 1990
Mazian, Florence, 1942-
Why genocide?: the Armenian and Jewish experiences in perspective/ Florence Mazian. Ames: Iowa State University Press, 1990. xiii, 291 p.
89-015268　304.6/63/095662　0813801435
Genocide. Armenian massacres, 1915-1923. Holocaust, Jewish (1939-1945) -- Causes.

HV6401 Criminology — Crimes and offenses — Offenses against the environment

HV6401.R45 1991
Reich, Michael, 1950-
Toxic politics: responding to chemical disasters/ Michael R. Reich. Ithaca: Cornell University Press, 1991. xi, 317 p.
91-055054　363.73/84　0801424348
Offenses against the environment -- Political aspects. Hazardous substances -- Accidents -- Political aspects.

HV6431-6433 Criminology — Crimes and offenses — Offenses against public safety

HV6431.A537 1995
Anderson, Sean,
Historical dictionary of terrorism/ by Sean Anderson and Stephen Sloan. Metuchen, N.J.: Scarecrow Press, 1995. xli, 452 p.
94-017408　909 20　0810829142
Terrorism -- History -- Dictionaries. Terrorists -- History -- Dictionaries.

HV6431.A87 1992
Atkins, Stephen E.
Terrorism: a reference handbook/ Stephen E. Atkins. Santa Barbara. Calif.: ABC-CLIO, c1992. ix, 199 p.
92-028530　909.82 20　0874366704
Terrorism -- Handbooks, manuals, etc. Terrorism -- Bibliography. Terrorists -- Directories.

HV6431.B24 1998
Babkina, A. M.
Terrorism: an annotated bibliography/ A.M. Babkina. Commack, N.Y.: Nova Science Publishers, c1998. 327 p.
2003-615759　1560726237
Terrorism -- Bibliography.

HV6431.B495 2002
Beyond September 11th: an anthology of dissent/ edited by Phil Scraton. London; Pluto Press, 2002. xiii, 251 p.
2002-005037　973.931 21　0745319629
Terrorism. War on Terrorism, 2001- Government, Resistance to.

HV6431.C554 1990
Clutterbuck, Richard L.
Terrorism and guerrilla warfare: forecasts and remedies/ Richard Clutterbuck. London; Routledge, 1990. xx, 235 p.
89-032955　303.6/25　0415024404
Terrorism. Guerrilla warfare. Drug traffic.

HV6431.C6472 1997
Combs, Cindy C.
Terrorism in the twenty-first century/ Cindy C. Combs. Upper Saddle River, N.J.: Prentice Hall, c1997. x, 243 p.
96-028270　303.6/25/0112 21　0134907310
Terrorism. Terrorism -- Forecasting.

HV6431.C6473 1991
Common ground on terrorism: Soviet-American cooperation against the politics of terror/ edited by Igor Beliaev and John Marks. New York: W.W. Norton, 1991. 183 p.
90-021173　363.3/2/0947　0393029867
Terrorism -- United States. Terrorism -- Soviet Union. Terrorism -- Prevention -- International cooperation. Soviet Union -- Foreign relations -- UnitedStates. Soviet Union -- Foreign relations -- United States.

HV6431.D43 1994
The deadly sin of terrorism: its effect on democracy and civil liberty in six countries/ edited by David A. Charters. Westport, Conn.: Greenwood Press, 1994. 246 p.
93-031604　303.6/25　0313289646
Terrorism. Terrorism -- Prevention. Civil rights.

HV6431.D473 2002
Dershowitz, Alan M.
Why terrorism works: understanding the threat, responding to the challenge/ Alan M. Dershowitz. New Haven: Yale University Press, c2002. 271 p.
2002-006387　303.6/25 21　0300097662
Terrorism. Terrorism -- Prevention.

HV6431.D73 1998
Drake, C. J. M., 1962-
Terrorists' target selection/ C.J.M. Drake. Houndmills, Basingstoke, Hampshire: Macmillan Press; 1998. xiii, 272 p.
97-038269　303.6/25　031221197X
Terrorism -- Philosophy. Terrorism -- Psychological aspects. Victims of terrorism.

HV6431.E53 1997
Encyclopedia of world terrorism/ [Martha Crenshaw, John Pimlott, editors]. Armonk, N.Y.: Sharpe Reference, c1997. 3 v.
96-009913   303.6/25/0904 20   1563248069
Terrorism. Terrorism -- History -- 20th century.

HV6431.G79 1995
Guelke, Adrian.
The age of terrorism and the international political system/ Adrian Guelke. London; Tauris Academic Studies, I.B. Tauris Publishers 1995. ix, 230 p.
95-060217   1850439524
Terrorism.

HV6431.G87 2000
Gurr, Nadine.
The new face of terrorism: threats from weapons of mass destruction/ Nadine Gurr and Benjamin Cole. London; I.B. Tauris; 2000. viii, 308 p.
2001-267799   322.4/2   1860644600
Terrorism. Weapons of mass destruction.

HV6431.H363 2000
Harclerode, Peter, 1947-
Secret soldiers: special forces in the war against terrorism/ Peter Harclerode. London: Cassell, 2000. 620 p.
2001-326915   0304355070
Terrorism -- Prevention. Special forces (Military science)

HV6431.H365 2000
Harmon, Christopher C.
Terrorism today/ Christopher C. Harmon. London; Frank Cass, 2000. xix, 316 p.
99-037193   303.6/25   0714649988
Terrorism. Terrorism -- Prevention.

HV6431.H43 2001
Henderson, Harry, 1951-
Terrorism/ Harry Henderson. New York: Facts on File, 2001. 300 p.
00-059315   303.6/25 21   0816042594
Terrorism -- Research.

HV6431.H626 1998
Hoffman, Bruce, 1954-
Inside terrorism/ Bruce Hoffman. New York: Columbia University Press, c1998. 288 p.
98-023789   303.6/25 21   0231114680
Terrorism.

HV6431.H95 1991
Hyland, Francis P.
Armenian terrorism: the past, the present, the prospects/ Francis P. Hyland. Boulder: Westview Press, 1991. xi, 248 p.
91-016076   303.6/25/08991992   081338124X
Terrorism. Armenians -- Politics and government. Terrorism -- History -- Chronology.

HV6431.I48 1988
Inside terrorist organizations/ edited by David C. Rapoport. New York: Columbia University Press, 1988. 259 p.
87-027734   303.6/25   0231067208
Terrorism. Terrorists -- Psychology.

HV6431.I5568 1990
International terrorism: characteristics, causes, controls/ edited by Charles W. Kegley, Jr. New York, NY: St. Martin's, c1990. vi, 280 p.
89-010440   363.3/2 20   0312007345
Terrorism. Terrorism -- Prevention.

HV6431.K43 1998
Khatchadourian, Haig.
The morality of terrorism/ Haig Khatchadourian. New York: P. Lang, c1998. xv, 180 p.
97-008540   179.7 21   0820437905
Terrorism -- Moral and ethical aspects.

HV6431.L578 1994
Livingston, Steven.
The terrorism spectacle/ Steven Livingston. Boulder: Westview Press, 1994. xvi, 220 p.
93-032042   070.4/49303625/0973   0813387760
Terrorism -- Political aspects. Terrorism in the mass media -- United States.   United States -- Foreign relations.

HV6431.M335 1991
MacWillson, Alastair C., 1953-
Hostage-taking   terrorism: incident-response strategy/ Alastair C. MacWillson. New York: St. Martin's Press, 1992. xii, 263 p.
91-025749   363.3/2   0312067844
Terrorism -- Prevention. Hostage negotiations.

HV6431.M367 2003
Martin, Gus.
Understanding terrorism: challenges, perspectives, and issues/ Gus Martin. Thousand Oaks: Sage Publications, c2003. 1 v.
2002-155355   303.6/25 21   076192616X
Terrorism.

HV6431.M499 1997
Mickolus, Edward F.
Terrorism, 1992-1995: a chronology of events and a selectively annotated bibliography/ Edward F. Mickolus with Susan L. Simmons. Westport, Conn.: Greenwood Press, 1997. xiii, 958 p.
97-009149   303.6/25/09   0313304688
Terrorism -- History -- Chronology. Terrorism -- Bibliography.

HV6431.M87 1989
Murphy, John Francis, 1937-
State support of international terrorism: legal, political, and economic dimensions/ John F. Murphy. Boulder, Colo.: Westview Press; 1989. vii, 128 p.
89-036171   363.3/2   0813308615
Terrorism -- Government policy.

HV6431.N48 1995
Netanyahu, Binyamin.
Fighting terrorism: how democracies can defeat domestic and international terrorists/ Benjamin Netanyahu. New York: Farrar Straus Giroux, 1995. vi, 151 p.
95-004849   363.3/2   0374154929
Terrorism.   Terrorism   --   Prevention   -- Government policy.

HV6431.O55 1998
Oliverio, Annamarie, 1961-
The state of terror/ Annamarie Oliverio. Albany, NY: State University of New York Press, c1998. xix, 189 p.
97-017274   303.6/25 21   0791437078
Terrorism. International relations. Terrorism in mass media.

HV6431.O74 1990
Origins of terrorism: psychologies, ideologies, theologies, states of mind/ edited by Walter Reich. [Washington,   D.C.]:   Woodrow   Wilson International Center for Scholars 1990. xi, 289 p.
89-070815   303.6/25   0521385636
Terrorism -- Psychological aspects. Terrorists -- Psychology.

HV6431.P43 1991
Pearlstein, Richard M.   1953-
The mind of the political terrorist/ Richard M. Pearlstein. Wilmington, Del.: SR Books, 1991. xii, 237 p.
90-009134   303.6/25   0842023453
Terrorists -- Psychology. Narcissism. Terrorists -- Case studies.

HV6431.P56 2001
Pillar, Paul R., 1947-
Terrorism and U.S. foreign policy/ Paul R. Pillar. Washington, D.C.: Brookings Institution Press, c2001. xii, 272 p.
00-013070   327.73 21   0815700040
Terrorism. Terrorism -- Prevention.   United States -- Foreign relations.

HV6431.S375 1998
Schweitzer, Glenn E., 1930-
Superterrorism: assassins, mobsters, and weapons of mass destruction/ Glenn E. Schweitzer with Carole C. Dorsch. New York: Plenum Trade, c1998. 363 p.
98-028476   303.6/25 21   0306459906
Terrorism.

HV6431.S74 1999
Stern, Jessica,
The ultimate terrorists/ Jessica Stern. Cambridge, MA: Harvard University Press, 1999. 214 p.
98-042453   303.6/25   0674617908
Terrorism.   Terrorism   --   Technological innovations. Weapons of mass destruction.

HV6431.T39 1998
Tanter, Raymond.
Rogue regimes: terrorism and proliferation/ Raymond Tanter. New York: St. Martin's Press, 1998. xiv, 331 p.
97-021494   327.1/17   0312173008
State-sponsored   terrorism.   International relations. Nuclear nonproliferation. United States -- Foreign relations -- 20th century.

HV6431.T433 1993
Technology   and   terrorism/   edited   by   Paul Wilkinson. London, England; F. Cass, 1993. 153 p.
93-028481   363.3/2   0714645524
Terrorism   --   Prevention.   Terrorism   -- Technological innovations. Terrorism -- Security measures.

HV6431.T4613 1992
Terrorism and democracy: some contemporary cases: report of a study group of the David Davies Memorial Institute of International Studies/ edited by Peter Janke; introduction by Sir Anthony Parsons. New York: St. Martin's Press, 1992. xvii, 232 p.
91-031619   363.3/2   0312068220
Terrorism -- Case studies.

HV6431.T4618 1991
Terrorism and politics/ edited by Barry Rubin. New York: St. Martin's Press in association with the Johns 1991. xi, 174 p.
91-008116   363.3/2   0312060688
Terrorism -- Political aspects. Terrorism -- Prevention.

HV6431.T4665 1995
Terrorism in context/ edited by Martha Crenshaw. University Park, Pa.: Pennsylvania State University Press, c1995. xvi, 633 p.
93-013785   363.3/2 20   0271010142
Terrorism -- Congresses. Terrorism -- History -- Congresses.

HV6431.T495 1991
Terrorism research and public policy/ edited by Clark McCauley. London, England; F. Cass, 1991. 162 p.
91-012424 363.4/5 0714634298
Terrorism -- Psychological aspects. Terrorists -- Psychology. Terrorism -- Government policy.

HV6431.T83 1997
Tucker, David, 1951-
Skirmishes at the edge of empire: the United States and international terrorism/ David Tucker. Westport, Conn.: Praeger, c1997. xv, 224 p.
96-041391 303.6/25 20 0275957624
Terrorism. Terrorism -- Prevention -- Government policy -- United States.

HV6431.W47 1991
Western state terrorism/ edited by Alexander George. New York: Routledge, 1991. 264 p.
91-002715 363.4/5 0415904722
Terrorism -- Government policy. Terrorism -- Government policy -- United States. State-sponsored terrorism.

HV6431.W564 2001
Wilkinson, Paul, 1937-
Terrorism versus democracy: the liberal state response/ Paul Wilkinson. London; Frank Cass, 2001. xvi, 255 p.
00-047530 363.3/2 0714651397
Terrorism -- Prevention. Democracy. Liberalism.

HV6431.W75 1991
Wright, Joanne, 1960-
Terrorist propaganda: the Red Army Faction and the Provisional IRA, 1968-86/ Joanne Wright. New York: St. Martin's Press, 1991. xiv, 281 p.
90-044352 364.1 0312047614
Propaganda -- Case studies. Baader-Meinhof gang. Terrorism -- Case studies. Germany (West) -- Politics and government. Northern Ireland -- Politics and government -- 1969-1994.

HV6431.Z85 1996
Zulaika, Joseba.
Terror and taboo: the follies, fables, and faces of terrorism/ Joseba Zulaika and William A. Douglass. New York: Routledge, 1996. xi, 292 p.
95-046989 303.6/25 0415917581
Terrorism. Terrorism -- Government policy. Terrorism in mass media.

HV6432.H365 1997
Hamm, Mark S.
Apocalypse in Oklahoma: Waco and Ruby Ridge revenged/ Mark S. Hamm. Boston: Northeastern University Press, c1997. x, 283 p.
96-052897 320.55/3 21 1555533000
McVeigh, Timothy -- Political and social views. Nichols, Terry, -- 1955- -- Political and social views. Oklahoma City Federal Building Bombing, Oklahoma City, Okla., 1995. Waco Branch Davidian Disaster, Tex., 1993. Political persecution -- United States -- Case studies.

HV6432.H49 1998
Heymann, Philip B.
Terrorism and America: a commonsense strategy for a democratic society/ Philip B. Heymann. Cambridge, Mass.: MIT Press, c1998. xxiv, 179 p.
98-004073 363.3/2/0973 21 0262082721
Terrorism -- United States. Terrorism -- United States -- Prevention.

HV6432.K87 1998
Kushner, Harvey W.
Terrorism in America: a structured approach to understanding the terrorist threat/ by Harvey W. Kushner. Springfield, Ill.: Charles C. Thomas, c1998. xiii, 218 p.
98-027285 364.1 21 0398068941
Terrorism -- United States.

HV6432.R42 1999
Reeve, Simon.
The new jackals: Ramzi Yousef, Osama Bin Laden and the future of terrorism/ Simon Reeve. Boston: Northeastern University Press, c1999. 294 p.
99-037245 364.1/09747/1 21 1555534074
Yousef, Ramzi Ahmed. Bin Laden, Osama, -- 1957- World Trade Center Bombing, New York, N.Y., 1993. Terrorism -- New York (State) -- New York.

HV6433.E85.E87 1992
Europe's red terrorists: the fighting communist organizations/ [edited by] Yonah Alexander and Dennis A. Pluchinsky. London; F. Cass, 1992. x, 258 p.
92-026147 303.6/25/094 0714634883
Terrorism -- Europe -- Case studies. Terrorists -- Europe -- Case studies. Communism -- Europe -- Case studies.

HV6433.E85.T65 1991
Tolerating terrorism in the West: an international survey/ edited by Noemi Gal-Or. London; Routledge, 1991. xx, 172 p.
91-003399 363.3/2/094 0415024412
Terrorism -- Europe -- Public opinion. Terrorism -- Israel -- Public opinion. Terrorism -- Government policy -- Europe.

HV6433.F6.L44 1998
Lee, Rensselaer W., 1937-
Smuggling Armageddon: the nuclear black market in the Former Soviet Union and Europe/ Rensselaer W. Lee. New York: St. Martin's Press, 1998. xvii, 200 p.
98-003793 363.3/2 0312211562
Nuclear terrorism -- Former Soviet republics -- Prevention. Nuclear nonproliferation. Illegal arms transfers -- Former Soviet republics.

HV6433.I82.R436 1990
Meade, Robert C., 1949-
The Red Brigades: the story of Italian terrorism/ Robert C. Meade, Jr.; foreword by Richard N. Gardner. New York: St. Martin's Press, 1990. xxviii, 301 p.
89-034719 364.1/0945 0312035934
Red brigades -- History. Terrorism -- Italy -- History.

HV6433.M5.C53 1999
Chasdi, Richard J., 1958-
Serenade of suffering: a portrait of Middle East terrorism, 1968-1993/ Richard J. Chasdi. Lanham, Md.: Lexington Books, c1999. xv, 265 p.
98-052753 303.6/25/0956 21 0739100572
Terrorism -- Middle East.

HV6433.P4.T37 1990
Tarazona-Sevillano, Gabriela.
Sendero Luminoso and the threat of narcoterrorism/ Gabriela Tarazona-Sevillano with John B. Reuter; foreword by David E. Long. New York: Praeger, 1990. xvi, 168 p.
90-037058 322.4/2/0985 0275936422
Terrorism -- Peru. Coca industry -- Peru.

HV6433.S2.S73 1996
Stanley, William Deane, 1958-
The protection racket state: elite politics, military extortion, and civil war in El Salvador/ William Stanley. Philadelphia: Temple University Press, 1996. x, 328 p.
95-020998 972.8405 1566393914
State-sponsored terrorism -- El Salvador -- History -- 20th century. Death squads -- El Salvador -- History -- 20th century. Political persecution -- El Salvador -- History -- 20th century. El Salvador -- Politics and government -- 20th century.

HV6439-6491 Criminology — Crimes and offenses — Offenses against the public order

HV6439.G7
Alexander, Claire E.
The Asian gang: ethnicity, identity, masculinity/ Claire E. Alexander. Oxford; Berg, 2000. xv, 262 p.
305.2350899141260421 185973314X
Gangs -- England -- London. Bangladeshis -- England -- London. Minority youth -- England -- London.

HV6439.S62
Glaser, Clive, 1964-
Bo-tsotsi: the youth gangs of Soweto, 1935-1976/ Clive Glaser. Portsmouth, NH: Heinemann, c2000. xvi, 214 p.
99-049242 364.1/06/60968 21 0325002193
Gangs -- South Africa -- Soweto. Juvenile delinquency -- South Africa -- Soweto. Urban youth -- South Africa -- Soweto. Soweto (South Africa) -- Social conditions.

HV6439.U5.D8 1996
Du, Phuoc Long.
The dream shattered: Vietnamese gangs in America/ Patrick Du Phuoc Long with Laura Ricard. Boston: Northeastern University Press, c1996. xii, 250 p.
95-020446 364.1/066/0899592073 20 1555532322
Gangs -- United States. Juvenile delinquents -- United States. Vietnamese Americans.

HV6439.U5.G36 1990
Gangs in America/ edited by C. Ronald Huff. Newbury Park, Calif.: Sage Publications, c1990. 351 p.
90-039608 364.1/06/0973 20 0803938284
Gangs -- United States.

HV6439.U5.H34 1993
Hamm, Mark S.
American skinheads: the criminology and control of hate crime/ Mark S. Hamm; foreword by William J. Chambliss. Westport, Conn.: Praeger, 1993. xvii, 243 p.
92-023061 364.1 0275943550
Skinheads -- United States -- Case studies. Subculture -- United States -- Case studies. White supremacy movements -- United States -- Case studies.

HV6439.U5.K663 1994
Knox, George W., 1950-
National gangs resource handbook: an encyclopedic reference .../ George W. Knox. Bristol, IN: Wyndham Hall Press, c1994. 240 p.
95-137840 364.1/06/60973 20 1556052561
Gangs -- United States -- Handbooks, manuals, etc.

HV6439.U5.S64 1995
Spergel, Irving A.
The youth gang problem: a community approach/ Irving A. Spergel. New York: Oxford University Press, 1995. xvi, 346 p.
94-008227   364.1/06/0973   0195092031
Gangs -- United States. Juvenile delinquency -- United States. Juvenile delinquents -- United States. United States -- Social conditions -- 1980- United States -- Social policy -- 1993-

HV6439.U5.Y3 1997
Yablonsky, Lewis.
Gangsters: fifty years of madness, drugs, and death on the streets of America/ Lewis Yablonsky. New York: New York University Press, c1997. xx, 237 p.
96-035713   302.3/4 20   0814796796
Gangs -- United States. Gangs -- United States -- Prevention.

HV6439.U7.C4 1936
Thrasher, Frederic Milton, 1892-1962.
The gang; a study of 1,313 gangs in Chicago, by Frederic M. Thrasher. Chicago, University of Chicago Press [c1936] xxi, 605 p.
36-035233   [159.92277]   136.77
Gangs. Chicago (Ill.) -- Social conditions.

HV6439.U7.D68 1993
Taylor, Carl S.
Girls, gangs, women and drugs/ Carl S. Taylor. East Lansing, Mich.: Michigan State University Press, 1993. v, 217 p.
93-024037   364.1/06/0977434   0870133209
Gangs -- Michigan -- Detroit -- Case studies. Afro-American women -- Michigan -- Detroit -- Case studies. Drug abuse -- Michigan -- Detroit -- Case studies.

HV6439.U7.K55 1996
Kinnear, Karen L.
Gangs: a reference handbook/ Karen L. Kinnear. Santa Barbara, Calif.: ABC-CLIO, 1996. xiv, 237 p.
96-009076   364.1/06/60973   0874368219
Gangs -- United States -- Handbooks, manuals, etc.

HV6439.U7.L77 1993
Rodriguez, Luis J., 1954-
Always running: la vida loca, gang days in L.A./ by Luis J. Rodriguez. Willimantic, CT: Curbstone Press; 1993. 260 p.
92-039002   364.1/092   1880684063
Rodriguez, Luis J., -- 1954- Gangs -- California - - Los Angeles -- Biography. Mexican American youth -- California -- Los Angeles -- Biography.

HV6439.U7.S723 1996
Decker, Scott H.
Life in the gang: family, friends and violence/ Scott H. Decker, Barrik Van Winkle. Cambridge, England; Cambridge University Press, 1996. xi, 303 p.
96-007896   364.1/06/60977866   0521562929
Gang members -- Missouri -- St. Louis -- Case studies. Gangs -- Missouri -- St. Louis -- Case studies. Group identity -- Missouri -- St. Louis -- Case studies.

HV6441.S53 1999
Sifakis, Carl.
The mafia encyclopedia/ Carl Sifakis. New York: Facts on File, c1999. xvii, 414 p.
98-042297   364.1/06/03 21   0816038562
Mafia -- Dictionaries. Criminals -- Biography -- Dictionaries.

HV6446.F56 1998
Finckenauer, James O.
Russian mafia in America: immigration, culture, and crime/ James O. Finckenauer, Elin J. Waring. Boston: Northeastern University Press, c1998. xvi, 303 p.
98-023540   364.1/06/0899171073   21   1555533744
Russian American criminals -- United States. Organized crime -- United States.

HV6446.K43 2000
Kelly, Robert J.
Encyclopedia of organized crime in the United States: from Capone's Chicago to the new urban underworld/ Robert J. Kelly. Westport, Conn: Greenwood Press, 2000. xxx, 358 p.
99-033801   364.1/06/0973   0313306532
Organized crime -- United States -- Encyclopedias.

HV6452.A128.W35 1988
Waller, Altina L.   1940-
Feud: Hatfields, McCoys, and social change in Appalachia, 1860-1900/ Altina L. Waller. Chapel Hill: University of North Carolina Press, c1988. xiii, 313 p.
87-026567   975.4/404   0807817708
Hatfield-McCoy feud.   Appalachian Region, Southern -- Social conditions.

HV6452.P4.M64 1998
Kenny, Kevin, 1960-
Making sense of the Molly Maguires/ Kevin Kenny. New York: Oxford University Press, 1998. xii, 336 p.
96-053599   364.1/06/09748   0195106644
Molly Maguires. Coal miners -- Pennsylvania -- History. Irish Americans -- Pennsylvania -- History.

HV6453.C75
Sanchez G., Gonzalo.
Bandits, peasants, and politics: the case of "La Violencia" in Colombia/ by Gonzalo Sanchez and Donny Meertens; translated by Alan Hynds. Austin: University of Texas Press, 2001. xviii, 229 p.
00-053517   364.9861   0292777582
Outlaws -- Colombia -- History. Brigands and robbers -- Colombia -- History. Political violence - - Colombia -- History. Colombia -- Politics and government -- 1946-1974.

HV6453.E9.R84 1996
Ruggiero, Vincenzo.
Organized and corporate crime in Europe: offers that can't be refused/ Vincenzo Ruggiero. Aldershot; Dartmouth Pub. Co., c1996. xi, 186 p.
95-022887   364.1/06/094 20   1855215225
Organized crime -- Europe. Commercial crimes - - Europe. Corporations -- Corrupt practices -- Europe.

HV6453.I83.M327 1989
Duggan, Christopher.
Fascism and the Mafia/ Christopher Duggan. New Haven: Yale University Press, 1989. xiii, 322 p.
88-011110   364.1/06/0458   0300043724
Mafia -- Italy -- Sicily -- History. Fascism -- Italy -- Sicily -- History. Sicily (Italy) -- History -- 1870-1945.

HV6453.I83.M3415 2000
Fentress, James.
Rebels & mafiosi: death in a Sicilian landscape/ James Fentress. Ithaca: Cornell University Press, 2000. 197 p.
99-055041   364.1/06/09458   0801435390
Mafia -- Italy -- Sicily -- History. Revolutions -- Italy -- Sicily -- History -- 19th century. Government, Resistence to -- Italy -- Sicily -- History -- 19th century. Sicily (Italy) -- Social conditions.

HV6453.T8.B37 1994
Barkey, Karen, 1958-
Bandits and bureaucrats: the Ottoman route to state centralization/ Karen Barkey. Ithaca, N.Y.: Cornell University Press, 1994.
94-006099   364.1/09561 20   0801429447
Brigands and robbers -- Turkey -- History -- 17th century. Outlaws -- Turkey -- History -- 17th century. Peasantry -- Turkey -- History -- 17th century. Turkey -- History -- Ottoman Empire, 1288-1918.

HV6457.B76 2000
Brown, Mary Jane, 1939-
Eradicating this evil: women in the American anti-lynching movement, 1892-1940/ Mary Jane Brown. New York: Garland Pub., 2000. ix, 357 p.
99-054623   364.1/34   0815336322
Lynching -- United States -- History. Women in politics -- United States -- History. Women political activists -- United States -- History.

HV6464.U49 1997
Under sentence of death: lynching in the South/ edited by W. Fitzhugh Brundage. Chapel Hill: University of North Carolina Press, c1997. ix, 330 p.
96-030204   364.1/34 20   0807823260
Lynching -- Southern States -- History. Afro-Americans -- Crimes against -- History. Racism -- Southern States -- History. Southern States -- Race relations -- History.

HV6474.H67 2001
Horowitz, Donald L.
The deadly ethnic riot/ Donald L. Horowitz. Berkeley: University of California Press, c2001. xvii, 588 p.
99-086512   303.6/23 21   0520224477
Riots. Violence. Ethnic relations.

HV6477.B87
Button, James W., 1942-
Black violence: political impact of the 1960s riots/ James W. Button. Princeton, N.J.: Princeton University Press, c1978. xii, 248 p.
78-051158   301.5/92/0973   069107531X
Riots -- United States. Afro-Americans -- Social conditions -- 1964-1975. Economic assistance, Domestic -- United States. United States -- Politics and government -- 1963-1969. United States -- Politics and government -- 1969-1974.

HV6477.L63 1998
Locked in the poorhouse: cities, race, and poverty in the United States/ edited by Fred R. Harris and Lynn A. Curtis. Lanham: Rowman & Littlefield, c1998. vii, 188 p.
98-029542   305.569/089/00973 21   0847691357
Riots -- United States. Urban poor -- United States. Afro-Americans. United States -- Race relations.

HV6483.B6
Tager, Jack.
Boston riots: three centuries of social violence/ Jack Tager; picture researcher, Ruth Owen Jones. Boston: Northeastern University Press, c2001. xi, 289 p.
00-041816   303.6/23/0974461 21   1555534619
Riots -- Massachusetts -- Boston -- History. Violence -- Massachusetts -- Boston -- History. Boston (Mass.) -- History. Boston (Mass.) -- Social conditions. Boston (Mass.) -- Race relations.

HV6485.S64.T35 1996
Tambiah, Stanley Jeyaraja, 1929-
Leveling crowds: ethnonationalist conflicts and collective violence in South Asia/ Stanley J. Tambiah. Berkeley: University of California Press, c1996. x, 395 p.
95-048114   303.6/23/0954 20   0520200020
Riots -- South Asia. Crowds -- South Asia. Communalism -- South Asia. South Asia -- Ethnic relations.

HV6491.J3.S29 1991
Sato, Ikuya, 1955-
Kamikaze biker: parody and anomy in affluent Japan/ Ikuya Sato; with a foreword by Gerald D. Suttles. Chicago: University of Chicago Press, 1991. xviii, 277 p.
90-048610   364.1/06/0952   0226735257
Subculture. Motorcycle gangs -- Japan. Juvenile delinquency -- Japan.

HV6515-6626.54 Criminology — Crimes and offenses — Crimes against the person

HV6515.E5325 1992
World encyclopedia of 20th century murder/ [edited by] Jay Robert Nash. New York, N.Y.: Paragon House, 1992. vi, 693 p.
91-040492   364/.03   1557785066
Murder -- Encyclopedias. Murder -- Biography -- Encyclopedias. Murder victims -- Biography -- Encyclopedias.

HV6515.S44 1992
Segrave, Kerry, 1944-
Women serial and mass murderers: a worldwide reference, 1580 through 1990/ by Kerry Segrave. Jefferson, N.C.: McFarland & Co., c1992. vi, 327 p.
91-050949   364.1/523/092 B 20   0899506801
Women serial murderers -- Biography -- Dictionaries. Serial murders -- History -- Dictionaries. Mass murder -- History -- Dictionaries.

HV6529.H644 1994
Holmes, Ronald M.
Murder in America/ Ronald M. Holmes, Stephen T. Holmes. Thousand Oaks: Sage Publications, c1994. x, 205 p.
93-011775   364.1/523/0973 20   0803950543
Murder -- United States. Homicide -- United States.

HV6529.S45 1998
Seltzer, Mark, 1951-
Serial killers: death and life in America's wound culture/ Mark Seltzer. New York: Routledge, 1998. 302 p.
97-026176   364.15/23/0973   0415914809
Serial murderers -- United States -- Psychology. Homicide in popular culture -- United States. Violence in popular culture -- United States.

HV6533.K3.C3
Capote, Truman, 1924-
In cold blood; a true account of a multiple murder and its consequences. New York, Random House [1966, c1965] 343 p.
65-011257   364.15/23/0978144
Hickock, Richard Eugene, -- 1931-1965. Smith, Perry Edward, -- 1928-1965. Murder -- Kansas.

HV6534.A7.H43 1998
Headley, Bernard D.
The Atlanta youth murders and the politics of race/ Bernard Headley. Carbondale: Southern Illinois University Press, c1998. xviii, 241 p.
97-052169   364.15/23/09758231   21
0809322145
Williams, Wayne Bertram. Afro-American youth -- Crimes against -- Georgia -- Atlanta. Murder -- Investigation -- Georgia -- Atlanta. Trials (Murder) -- Georgia -- Atlanta. Atlanta (Ga.) -- Race relations.

HV6535.A82.V536 1994
Polk, Kenneth.
When men kill: scenarios of masculine violence/ Kenneth Polk. Cambridge, UK; Cambridge University Press, 1994. vii, 222 p.
94-008969   364.1/523/081   0521462673
Homicide -- Australia -- Victoria -- Sex differences. Violence -- Australia -- Victoria -- Sex differences. Masculinity -- Australia -- Victoria.

HV6542.H45 1992
Heide, Kathleen M., 1954-
Why kids kill parents: child abuse and adolescent homicide/ Kathleen M. Heide. Columbus: Ohio State University Press, c1992. xix, 197 p.
91-032256   364.1/523/0835 20   0814205631
Parricide -- United States. Problem families -- United States. Family violence -- United States.

HV6543.D76 1991
Droge, Arthur J., 1953-
A noble death: suicide and martyrdom among Christians and Jews in antiquity/ Arthur J. Droge, James D. Tabor. San Francisco: HarperSanFrancisco, c1992. xii, 203 p.
91-055280   394/.8 20   0060620951
Suicide -- Moral and ethical aspects -- History. Suicide -- Mediterranean Region -- History. Social history -- To 500.

HV6545.B26 1995
Battin, M. Pabst.
Ethical issues in suicide/ Margaret Pabst Battin. Englewood Cliffs, N.J.: Prentice-Hall, c1995. xiv, 240 p.
94-038363   179/.7 20   0133046680
Suicide -- Moral and ethical aspects. Suicide -- Religious aspects.

HV6545.C67 1995
Cosculluela, Victor.
The ethics of suicide/ Victor Cosculluela. New York: Garland, 1995. xi, 170 p.
94-045150   179/.7 0815320310
Suicide -- Moral and ethical aspects.

HV6545.D6
Douglas, Jack D.
The social meanings of suicide, by Jack D. Douglas. Princeton, N.J., Princeton University Press, 1967. xiv, 398 p.
67-014408   301.1
Durkheim, Emile, -- 1858-1917. -- Suicide. Suicide -- Sociological aspects.

HV6546.C87 1987
Curran, David K., 1951-
Adolescent suicidal behavior/ David K. Curran. Washington: Hemisphere Pub. Corp., c1987. xiii, 208 p.
87-008650   362.2   0891166181
Youth -- Suicidal behavior -- United States. Suicide -- in adolescence.

HV6546.J645 1999
Johnson, Wanda Yvonne, 1936-
Youth suicide: the school's role in prevention and response/ [Wanda Y. Johnson]. Bloomington, Ind.: Phi Delta Kappa Educational Foundation, c1999. 89 p.
98-068592   0873678125
Youth -- Suicidal behavior -- Prevention. Suicide -- Prevention. Counseling in secondary education.

HV6548.G7.B35 1998
Bailey, Victor, 1948-
This rash act: suicide across the life cycle in the Victorian city/ Victor Bailey. Standford, Calif.: Stanford University Press, 1998. xvi, 349 p.
97-032785   362.28/09428/3709034   0804731233
Suicide -- Sociological aspects -- England -- Hull. Suicide -- England -- Hull -- History -- 19th century.

HV6548.G8.E55 1990
MacDonald, Michael, 1945-
Sleepless souls: suicide in early modern England/ Michael MacDonald, Terence R. Murphy. Oxford [England]: Clarendon Press; 1990. xvi, 383 p.
90-033323   362.2/8/0941   0198229194
Suicide -- England -- History. England -- Social conditions.

HV6548.R9.P36 1997
Paperno, Irina.
Suicide as a cultural institution in Dostoevsky's Russia/ Irina Paperno. Ithaca: Cornell University Press, 1997. ix, 319 p.
97-022593   362.28/0947   0801433975
Suicide -- Russia -- History -- 19th century. Suicide -- Social aspects. Dostoyevsky, Fyodor, -- 1821-1881 -- Criticism and interpretation. Russia -- Civilization -- 1801-1917.

HV6548.U5.K87 1989
Kushner, Howard I.
Self-destruction in the promised land: a psychocultural biology of American suicide/ Howard I. Kushner. New Brunswick [N.J.]: Rutgers University Press, c1989. xvii, 284 p.
88-018351   362.2 19   0813513774
Suicide -- United States -- History. Suicide -- United States -- Psychological aspects. Suicide -- Physiological aspects.

HV6556.T73 1993
Transforming a rape culture/ edited by Emilie Buchwald, Pamela R. Fletcher, Martha Roth. Minneapolis, MN: Milkweed Editions, 1993. xiv, 467 p.
93-005693   306.7 0915943069
Sexual harassment of women. Rape. Women -- Crimes against.

HV6558.C34 2001
Cahill, Ann J.
Rethinking rape/ Ann J. Cahill. Ithaca: Cornell University Press, c2001. x, 230 p.
00-011504   364.15/32 21   0801437946
Rape. Feminist theory.

HV6558.E45 1989
Ellis, Lee, 1942-
Theories of rape: inquiries into the causes of sexual aggression/ Lee Ellis. New York: Hemisphere Pub. Corp., c1989. xiii, 185 p.
89-001997   364.1/532/019 19   0891161724
Rape. Rape -- Psychological aspects. Criminal behavior -- Genetic aspects.

HV6558.G55 1994
Gilmartin, Pat, 1950-
Rape, incest, and child sexual abuse: consequences and recovery/ Pat Gilmartin. New York: Garland Publishing, 1994. xxi, 367 p.
93-033582   362.7/6   0815313268
Rape. Incest. Child sexual abuse.

HV6558.G76
Groth, A. Nicholas.
Men who rape: the psychology of the offender/ A. Nicholas Groth, with H. Jean Birnbaum. New York: Plenum Press, c1979. xviii, 227 p.
79-018624   364.1/53   0306402688
Rape. Criminal psychology.

HV6558.J64 1997
Johnson, Ida M.
Forced sexual intercourse in intimate relationships/ Ida M. Johnson and Robert T. Sigler. Aldershot, England; Ashgate/Dartmouth, c1997. ix, 189 p.
96-048559   362.883 21   1855219174
Rape in marriage. Acquaintance rape.

HV6558.T48 2000
Thornhill, Randy.
A natural history of rape: biological bases of sexual coercion/ Randy Thornhill, Craig T. Palmer. Cambridge, Mass.: MIT Press, c2000. xvi, 251 p.
99-031685   364.15/32 21   0262201259
Rape. Men -- Sexual behavior. Human evolution.

HV6561.B34 1989
Baron, Larry.
Four theories of rape in American society: a state-level analysis/ Larry Baron and Murray A. Straus. New Haven: Yale University Press, c1989. xiv, 250 p.
89-005716   364.1/532   0300045190
Rape -- United States -- States. Rape -- Research -- United States -- Statistical methods. Criminal behavior, Prediction of -- Statistical methods.

HV6561.B48 1996
Bergen, Raquel Kennedy.
Wife rape: understanding the response of survivors and service providers/ Raquel Kennedy Bergen. Thousand Oaks: Sage Publications, c1996. x, 179 p.
96-004426   0803972407
Rape in marriage -- United States. Rape in marriage -- United States -- Case studies. Abused wives -- United States -- Case studies.

HV6561.B49 2000
Bevacqua, Maria, 1968-
Rape on the public agenda: feminism and the politics of sexual assault/ Maria Bevacqua. Boston: Northeastern University Press, c2000. xiii, 280 p.
00-020542   364.15/32/0973 21   1555534473
Rape -- United States. Feminism -- United States. Feminists -- United States -- Political activity.

HV6561.K45 1988
Kelly, Liz.
Surviving sexual violence/ Liz Kelly. Minneapolis: University of Minnesota Press, c1988. xi, 273 p.
88-022033   362.8/8   0816617511
Rape victims -- United States -- Psychology. Rape -- United States. Sex crimes -- United States.

HV6561.R37 1985
Rape and sexual assault: a research handbook/ Ann Wolbert Burgess, editor. New York: Garland Pub., 1985. xvi, 433 p.
83-048217   362.8/83/0973   0824090497
Rape -- United States -- Prevention. Rape victims -- United States. Rapists -- United States.

HV6561.R86 2000
Russell, Diana E. H.
The epidemic of rape and child abuse in the United States/ Diana E.H. Russell, Rebecca M. Bolen. Thousand Oaks, Calif.: Sage Publications, c2000. xvii, 318 p.
00-008111   364.15/32/072073 21   0761903011
Rape -- Research -- United States -- Evaluation. Child sexual abuse -- Research -- United States -- Evaluation. Victims of crimes surveys -- United States -- Evaluation.

HV6561.S25 1990
Sanday, Peggy Reeves.
Fraternity gang rape: sex, brotherhood, and privilege on campus/ Peggy Reeves Sanday. New York: New York University Press, c1990. xxv, 203 p.
90-005865   306.77 20   0814779026
Gang rape -- United States -- Case studies. Greek letter societies -- Case studies. College students -- United States -- Sexual behavior -- Case studies.

HV6561.W45 1989
Webster, Linda, 1947-
Sexual assault and child sexual abuse: a national directory of victim/survivor services and prevention programs/ compiled and edited by Linda Webster. Phoenix, Ariz.: Oryx Press, 1989. xxi, 353 p.
89-008549   362.88/3   0897744454
Rape victims -- Services for -- United States -- Directories. Sexually abused children -- Services for -- United States -- Directories. Adult child sexual abuse victims -- Services for -- United States -- Directories.

HV6565.C2.R87 1984
Russell, Diana E. H.
Sexual exploitation: rape, child sexual abuse, and workplace harassment/ Diana E.H. Russell. Beverly Hills, Calif.: Sage Publications, c1984. 319 p.
84-006950   364.1/532/09794   0803923546
Rape -- California. Child sexual abuse -- California. Sexual harassment -- California.

HV6568.G54.L43 1997
Lefkowitz, Bernard.
Our guys: the Glen Ridge rape and the secret life of the perfect suburb/ Bernard Lefkowitz. Berkeley, Calif.: University of California Press, c1997. xi, 443 p.
96-048276   364.15/32/0974931 21   0520205960
Gang rape -- New Jersey -- Glen Ridge. Mentally handicapped women -- Crimes against -- New Jersey -- Glen Ridge. Sexism -- United States. United States -- Moral conditions.

HV6569.F8
Vigarello, Georges.
A history of rape: sexual violence in France from the 16th to the 20th century/ by Georges Vigarello; translated by Jean Birrell. Malden, Mass.: Polity Press, 2001. vi, 306 p.
00-033620   364.15/32/09   0745621694
Rape -- France -- History. Rape -- Psychological aspects.

HV6570.K545 1998
Kincaid, James R.
Erotic innocence: the culture of child molesting/ by James R. Kincaid. Durham, NC: Duke University Press, 1998. xii, 352 p.
97-041074   362.76   0822321777
Child sexual abuse.

HV6570.K55 1995
Kinnear, Karen L.
Childhood sexual abuse: a reference handbook/ Karen L. Kinnear. Santa Barbara, Calif.: ABC-CLIO, c1995. xii, 333 p.
95-040065   362.7/6 20   0874366917
Child sexual abuse. Child sexual abuse -- Prevention. Sexually abused children.

HV6570.2.L42 1997
Leberg, Eric.
Understanding child molesters: taking charge/ Eric Leberg; foreword by Lucy Berliner. Thousand Oaks, Calif.: Sage Publications, c1997. xvi, 264 p.
97-004754   364.15/554/019 21   0761901868
Child molesters -- United States -- Psychology. Child molesters -- Legal status, laws, etc. -- United States. Child molesters -- Rehabilitation -- United States.

HV6570.2.P77 1996
Pryor, Douglas W.
Unspeakable acts: why men sexually abuse children/ Douglas W. Pryor. New York: New York University Press, c1996. xi, 351 p.
96-009938   364.1/536 20   0814766374
Child molesters -- United States -- Interviews. Child sexual abuse -- United States -- Case studies.

HV6570.4.G7.J32 2000
Jackson, Louise A. 1967-
Child sexual abuse in Victorian England/ Louise A. Jackson. London; Routledge, 2000. 209 p.
00-266537   041522649X
Child sexual abuse -- England -- History -- 19th century. Sexually abused children -- England -- History -- 19th century.

HV6570.7.J33 1994
Jacobs, Janet Liebman.
Victimized daughters: incest and the development of the female self/ Janet Liebman Jacobs. New York: Routledge, 1994. xiii, 209 p.
93-039239   362.7/64   0415906261
Incest victims -- United States -- Psychology. Personality development -- United States. Fathers and daughters -- United States.

HV6570.7.R67 1996
Rosen, Leora N.
The hostage child: sex abuse allegations in custody disputes/ Leora N. Rosen, Michelle Etlin. Bloomington: Indiana University Press, c1996. xiv, 225 p.
95-047113   347.30617 20   0253330459
Incest -- United States -- Case studies. Custody of children -- United States -- Case studies.

HV6594.M85 2000
Mullen, Paul E.
Stalkers and their victims/ Paul E. Mullen, Michele Pathe, and Rosemary Purcell. Cambridge, U.K.; Cambridge University Press, 2000. x, 310 p.
99-044607   362.88   0521669502
Stalking. Stalkers. Women -- Crimes against -- Prevention.

HV6626.E28 1989
Edwards, Susan S. M.
Policing "domestic" violence: women, the law, and the state/ Susan S.M. Edwards. London; Sage Publications, 1989. viii, 259 p.
89-060526 363.2/3 0803980329
Wife abuse. Law enforcement. Wife abuse -- England.

HV6626.G54 1983
Giles-Sims, Jean.
Wife battering, a systems theory approach/ Jean Giles-Sims; foreword by Murray A. Straus. New York: Guilford Press, c1983. xiv, 193 p.
82-015555 362.8/3 0898620759
Wife abuse -- United States. System analysis. Spouse abuse.

HV6626.L677 2001
Loue, Sana.
Intimate partner violence: societal, medical, legal, and individual responses/ Sana Loue. New York: Kluwer Academic/Plenum Publishers, c2001. xv, 199 p.
00-049772 362.82/92 21 0306465191
Conjugal violence. Conjugal violence -- United States. Conjugal violence -- United States -- Prevention.

HV6626.M665 2000
Mooney, Jayne, 1964-
Gender, violence, and the social order/ Jayne Mooney. Houndmills, Basingstoke, Hampshire: Macmillan Press; 2000. xi, 260 p.
99-088131 362.88/082 0333734807
Women -- Crimes against. Family violence. Feminist theory.

HV6626.W345 1984
Walker, Lenore E.
The battered woman syndrome/ Lenore E. Walker. New York: Springer Pub. Co., c1984. xiv, 256 p.
84-001324 362.8/3 0826143202
Wife abuse -- United States. Abused wives -- United States -- Psychology.

HV6626.2.A27 2000
Abraham, Margaret, 1960-
Speaking the unspeakable: marital violence among South Asian immigrants in the United States/ Margaret Abraham. New Brunswick, NJ: Rutgers University Press, c2000. xvii, 234 p.
99-045632 362.84/914073 21 0813527929
Conjugal violence -- United States. Family violence -- United States. South Asians -- United States -- Social conditions.

HV6626.2.A29 1991
Abused and battered: social and legal responses to family violence/ Dean D. Knudsen and JoAnn L. Miller (editors). New York: A. de Gruyter, c1991. xvi, 232 p.
90-022716 362.82/92 20 0202304132
Wife abuse -- United States. Child abuse -- United States. Family violence -- United States.

HV6626.2.D39 1998
Davis, Richard L., 1941-
Domestic violence: facts and fallacies/ Richard L. Davis. Westport, CT: Praeger, 1998. 202 p.
97-027924 362.82/92/0973 0275961265
Family violence -- Government policy -- United States. Family violence -- United States -- Prevention.

HV6626.2.D66 2000
Domestic violence and child abuse sourcebook: basic consumer health information about spousal/partner, child, sibling, parent, and elder abuse .../ edited by Helene Henderson. Detroit, MI: Omnigraphics, c2000. xx, 1064 p.
00-058436 362.82/927/0973 21 0780802357
Family violence -- United States. Child abuse -- United States. Family violence -- United States -- Prevention.

HV6626.2.F56 2000
Flowers, Ronald B.
Domestic crimes, family violence and child abuse: a study of contemporary American society/ by R. Barri Flowers. Jefferson, N.C.: McFarland, c2000. xii, 300 p.
00-030483 362.82/92/0973 21 0786408235
Family violence -- United States.

HV6626.2.G34 1998
Gagne, Patricia.
Battered women's justice: the movement for clemency and the politics of self-defense/ Patricia Gagne. New York: Twayne Publishers; c1998. xi, 245 p.
98-017893 362.82/92/0973 21 0805791507
Abused women -- United States. Abused women -- Legal status, laws, etc. -- United States. Women murderers -- United States.

HV6626.2.K35 1998
Kakar, Suman, 1953-
Domestic abuse: public policy/criminal justice approaches towards child, spousal, and elderly abuse/ Suman Kakar. San Francisco: Austin & Winfield, 1998. 526 p.
97-032801 362.82/92/0973 1572920610
Family violence -- United States. Family violence -- Government policy -- United States. Family violence -- United States -- Prevention.

HV6626.2.R37 2000
Raphael, Jody.
Saving Bernice: battered women, welfare, and poverty/ Jody Raphael. Boston: Northeastern University Press, c2000. viii, 184 p.
99-088074 362.82/928/0973 21 1555534392
Abused women -- United States. Welfare recipients -- Abuse -- United States. Public welfare -- United States.

HV6626.2.S54 1992
Sherman, Lawrence W.
Policing domestic violence: experiments and dilemmas/ Lawrence W. Sherman with Janell D. Schmidt and Dennis P. Rogan. New York: Free Press; c1992. xvi, 443 p.
92-017545 363.2/595553/0973 20 0029287316
Wife abuse -- United States. Family violence -- United States. Police -- United States.

HV6626.2.T54 1993
Tifft, Larry.
Battering of women: the failure of intervention and the case for prevention/ Larry L. Tifft. Boulder: Westview Press, 1993. xiv, 230 p.
93-018313 362.82/927/0973 0813313902
Abused women -- United States. Wife abuse -- United States -- Prevention. Abusive men -- Counseling of -- United States.

HV6626.2.U5.S37 2000
Sattler, Cheryl L.
Teaching to transcend: educating women against violence/ Cheryl L. Sattler. Albany: State University of New York Press, c2000. xxii, 152 p.
99-046214 362.82/927/0973 21 079144595X
Wife abuse -- United States -- Prevention. Family violence -- United States -- Prevention. Women -- Crimes against -- United States -- Prevention.

HV6626.22.K4
Beattie, L. Elisabeth, 1953-
Sisters in pain: battered women fight back/ L. Elisabeth Beattie, Mary Angela Shaughnessy. Lexington, KY: University Press of Kentucky, c2000. xxix, 214 p.
99-047706 362.82/92/0922769 21 0813121515
Abused women -- Kentucky -- Interviews. Wife abuse -- Kentucky. Abusive men -- Kentucky -- Mortality.

HV6626.22.U6.C48 1996
Chang, Valerie Nash.
I just lost myself: psychological abuse of women in marriage/ Valerie Nash Chang. Westport, Conn.: Praeger, 1996. xi, 166 p.
95-030660 362.82/92 0275952096
Wife abuse -- United States. Wife abuse -- United States -- Psychological aspects. Women -- United States -- Psychology.

HV6626.3.B73 2000
Brogden, Michael.
Crime, abuse and the elderly/ Michael Brogden, Preet Nijhar. Devon: Willan, 2000. 191 p.
00-710679 1903240034
Aged -- Abuse of. Aged offenders. Aged -- Crimes against.

HV6626.5.C472 2001
Child abuse: a global view/ edited by Beth M. Schwartz-Kenney, Michelle McCauley, and Michelle A. Epstein; foreword by David Finkelhor. Westport, Conn: Greenwood Press, 2001. xvi, 273 p.
00-035364 362.76 0313307458
Child abuse.

HV6626.5.C475 1996
Child abuse: abstracts of the psychological and behavioral literature, 1990-1995/ editors, Seth C. Kalichman, Anthony T. Gary. Washington, DC: American Psychological Association, c1996. x, 403 p.
96-030460 364.1/536 20 1557983941
Child abuse -- Abstracts.

HV6626.5.C57 2001
Clark, Robin E.
The encyclopedia of child abuse/ Robin E. Clark and Judith Freeman Clark with Christine Adamec; introduction by Richard J. Gelles. New York: Facts on File, c2001. xxiv, 344 p.
00-035384 362.76/0973/03 21 0816040605
Child abuse -- United States -- Dictionaries. Child abuse -- Dictionaries.

HV6626.52.B38 1995
Baumrind, Diana, 1927-
Child maltreatment and optimal caregiving in social contexts/ Diana Baumrind. New York: Garland Pub., 1995. xix, 175 p.
95-017454 362.7/61/0973 0815319185
Child abuse -- United States. Abusive parents -- United States.

HV6626.52.J36 1994
Janko, Susan.
Vulnerable children, vulnerable families: the social construction of child abuse/ Susan Janko. New York: Teachers College Press, c1994. vii, 168 p.
93-033595   362.7/68/0973 20   0807733164
Abused children -- Services for -- United States -- Case studies. Abusive parents -- Behavior modification -- United States -- Case studies. Family social work -- United States -- Case studies.

HV6626.52.M54 1998
Michener, Anna J., 1977-
Becoming Anna: the autobiography of a sixteen-year-old/ Anna J. Michener. Chicago: University of Chicago Press, c1998. 256 p.
98-011049   362.76/092 B 21   0226524019
Michener, Anna J., -- 1977-   Abused children -- United States -- Biography. Psychologically abused children -- United States -- Biography.

HV6626.52.N38 1993
National Research Council (U.S.).
Understanding child abuse and neglect/ Panel on Research on Child Abuse and Neglect, Commission on Behavioral and Social Sciences and Education, National Research Council. Washington, D.C.: National Academy Press, 1993. xiii, 393 p.
93-029640   362.76/0973   0309048893
Child abuse -- United States -- Prevention. Abused children -- United States -- Psychology.

HV6626.52.T693 2002
Tower, Cynthia Crosson.
When children are abused: an educator's guide to intervention/ Cynthia Crosson-Tower. Boston: Allyn and Bacon, c2002. viii, 200 p.
2001-022872   371.7/8 21   0205319629
Child abuse -- United States -- Prevention. Child abuse -- Reporting -- United States. School social work -- United States.

HV6626.54.G7.L3 1998
La Fontaine, J. S. 1931-
Speak of the devil: tales of satanic abuse in contemporary England/ J.S. La Fontaine. Cambridge; Cambridge University Press, 1998. xi, 224 p.
97-009822   364.15/554/0941   0521620821
Ritual abuse -- Great Britain. Satanism -- Great Britain. Occult crime -- Great Britain.

HV6626.54.G7.R43 1993
Reder, Peter, 1946-
Beyond blame: child abuse tragedies revisited/ Peter Reder, Sylvia Duncan, and Moira Gray. London; Routledge, 1993. xi, 191 p.
93-168470   362.7/68/0941   0415066786
Child abuse -- Great Britain. Child abuse -- Great Britain -- Case studies. Child Abuse -- prevention & control.

HV6635-6695 Criminology — Crimes and offenses — Crimes against property

HV6635.G35 1977
Geis, Gilbert,
White-collar crime: offenses in business, politics, and the professions/ edited, with introd. and notes by Gilbert Geis and Robert F. Meier. New York: Free Press, c1977. xii, 356 p.
76-027223   364/.1   0029115906
White collar crimes -- United States.

HV6651.S44 2001
Segrave, Kerry, 1944-
Shoplifting: a social history/ by Kerry Segrave. Jefferson, N.C.: McFarland, c2001. v, 182 p.
00-053707   364.16/2 21   0786409088
Shoplifting -- History.

HV6658.A24 1989
Abelson, Elaine S.
When ladies go a-thieving: middle-class shoplifters in the Victorian department store/ Elaine S. Abelson. New York: Oxford University Press, 1989. ix, 292 p.
89-009379   364.1/62   0195051254
Shoplifting -- United States -- History -- 19th century. Female offenders -- United States -- History -- 19th century. Middle class women -- United States -- History -- 19th century.

HV6658.K54 1992
Klemke, Lloyd W.
The sociology of shoplifting: boosters and snitches today/ Lloyd W. Klemke. Westport, Conn.: Praeger, 1992. xvi, 159 p.
91-045609   364.1/62   0275941086
Shoplifting -- United States.

HV6658.S54 1996
Shover, Neal.
Great pretenders: pursuits and careers of persistent thieves/ Neal Shover. Boulder, Colo.: Westview Press, 1996. xvi, 219 p.
96-000464   364.1/62   0813387302
Burglary -- United States -- Case studies. Thieves -- United States.

HV6695.N67 1998
Norrgard, Lee E.
Consumer fraud/ Santa Barbara, CA: ABC-CLIO, Inc., c1998 338 p.
94-042276   364.16/3 21   0874369916
Fraud--United States. -- Consumer protection-- United States. -- sears

HV6707-6715 Criminology — Crimes and offenses — Offenses against public morals

HV6707.U5.W66 1988
Woodiwiss, Michael.
Crime, crusades, and corruption: prohibitions in the United States, 1900-1987/ Michael Woodiwiss. Totowa, N.J.: Barnes & Noble Books, 1988. ix, 260 p.
88-014451   364.1   0389207969
Crimes without victims -- United States -- History -- 20th century. Police corruption -- United States -- History -- 20th century. Political corruption -- United States -- History -- 20th century. United States -- Moral conditions.

HV6710.B74 1990
Brenner, Reuven.
Gambling and speculation: a theory, a history, and a future of some human decisions/ Reuven Brenner with Gabrielle A. Brenner. Cambridge [England]; Cambridge University Press, 1990. xi, 286 p.
89-017378   363.4/2/09   0521381800
Gambling. Gambling -- History.

HV6710.T48 1994
Thompson, William Norman.
Legalized gambling: a reference handbook/ William N. Thompson. Santa Barbara, Calif.: ABC-CLIO, c1994. xviii, 209 p.
94-021258   795 20   0874367298
Gambling -- Handbooks, manuals, etc. Gambling -- United States -- Handbooks, manuals, etc. Gambling -- Canada -- Handbooks, manuals, etc.

HV6711.L44 1999
Legalized casino gaming in the United States: the economic and social impact/ Cathy H.C. Hsu, editor. Binghamton, N.Y.: Haworth Hospitality Press, c1999. xx, 264 p.
98-037326   338.4/3795/0973 21   0789006405
Casinos -- Economic aspects -- United States. Casinos -- Social aspects -- United States. Gambling -- Economic aspects -- United States.

HV6715.B37 2000
Barker, Thomas.
Jokers wild: legalized gambling in the twenty-first century/ Thomas Barker and Marjie Britz. Westport, Conn.: Praeger, 2000. vii, 224 p.
99-059852   795/.0973   0275965872
Gambling -- United States.

HV6715.F33 1990
Fabian, Ann.
Card sharps, dream books, & bucket shops: gambling in 19th-century America/ Ann Fabian. Ithaca: Cornell University Press, 1990. xi, 250 p.
90-055121   394/.3   0801425018
Gambling -- Social aspects -- United States -- History -- 19th century.

HV6715.M4 1994
McGowan, Richard, 1952-
State lotteries and legalized gambling: painless revenue or painful mirage / Richard McGowan. Westport, Conn.: Praeger, 1994. xiv, 171 p.
94-015884   336.1/7/0973   0899308597
Gambling -- Government policy -- United States. Lotteries -- Government policy -- United States.

HV6768-6771 Criminology — Crimes and offenses — Commercial crimes. Financial crimes

HV6768.C76 1992
Croall, Hazel, 1947-
White collar crime: criminal justice and criminology/ Hazel Croall. Buckingham; Open University Press, 1992. vii, 195 p.
91-044926   364.1/68   0335096573
White collar crimes. White collar crimes -- Great Britain. White collar crimes -- United States.

HV6768.F75 1996
Friedrichs, David O.
Trusted criminals: white collar crime in contemporary society/ David O. Friedrichs. Belmont: Wadsworth Pub. Co., c1996. xxi, 441 p.
95-022353   0534505171
White collar crimes. White collar crimes -- United States.

HV6768.P85 1996
Punch, Maurice.
Dirty business: exploring corporate misconduct: analysis and cases/ Maurice Punch. London; Sage Publications, 1996. xiii, 299 p.
96-070156   364.16/8   0803976038
White collar crimes -- Case studies. Corporation law -- Criminal provisions -- Case studies. Corporations -- Corrupt practices -- Case studies.

HV6769.C558 1990
Clinard, Marshall Barron, 1911-
Corporate corruption: the abuse of power/ Marshall B. Clinard. New York: Praeger, 1990. xi, 215 p.
89-023088   364.1/68   0275934853
Corporations -- Corrupt practices -- United States.

HV6769.C56 1980
Clinard, Marshall Barron, 1911-
Corporate crime/ Marshall B. Clinard and Peter C. Yeager, with the collaboration of Ruth Blackburn Clinard. New York: Free Press; c1980. xiii, 386 p.
80-002156   364.1/68/0973   0029057108
Corporations -- Corrupt practices -- United States. Commercial crimes -- United States.

HV6769.P67 1994
Poveda, Tony G.
Rethinking white-collar crime/ Tony G. Poveda. Westport, Conn.: Praeger, 1994. xii, 171 p.
94-001143   364.1/68/0973   0275945863
White collar crimes -- United States.

HV6769.T55 1998
Tillman, Robert.
Broken promises: fraud by small business health insurers/ Robert Tillman. Boston: Northeastern University Press, c1998. viii, 216 p.
98-023539   364.16/3 21   1555533760
Insurance crimes -- United States. Insurance, Health -- Corrupt practices -- United States. Self-employed -- Crimes against -- United States.

HV6771.G8.R63 1992
Robb, George.
White-collar crime in modern England: financial fraud and business morality, 1845-1929/ George Robb. Cambridge [England]; Cambridge University Press, 1992. 250 p.
91-046847   364.1/68/0941   052141234X
Commercial crimes -- Great Britain -- History -- 19th century. Commercial crimes -- Great Britain -- History -- 20th century. Securities fraud -- Great Britain -- History -- 19th century.

HV6773-6773.3 Criminology — Crimes and offenses — Computer crimes

HV6773.C65.P37 1983
Parker, Donn B.
Fighting computer crime/ Donn B. Parker. New York: Scribner, c1983. xiii, 352 p.
83-003217   364.1/68   068417796X
Computer crimes -- Prevention.

HV6773.M86 1992
Mungo, Paul.
Approaching zero: the extraordinary underworld of hackers, phreakers, virus writers, and keyboard criminals/ Paul Mungo and Bryan Clough. New York: Random House, 1992. xix, 247 p.
91-053159   364.1/68   0679409386
Computer crimes. Computer viruses. Computer hackers.

HV6773.3.U5
Cybercrime: law enforcement, security and surveillance in the information age/ edited by Douglas Thomas and Brian D. Loader. London; Routledge, 2000. xiv, 300 p.
99-049215   364.16/8   0415213258
Computer crimes -- United States -- Prevention. Computer crimes -- Prevention. Privacy, Right of.

HV6773.52 Criminology — Crimes and offenses — Hate crimes

HV6773.52.A47 1999
Altschiller, Donald.
Hate crimes: a reference handbook/ Donald Altschiller. Denver, Colo.: ABC-CLIO, 1999. xi, 204 p.
98-050275   364.1   0874369371
Hate crimes -- United States.

HV6773.52.P47 2001
Perry, Barbara, 1962-
In the name of hate: understanding hate crimes/ Barbara Perry. New York: Routledge, 2001. xii, 276 p.
00-062739   364.1   0415927722
Hate crimes -- United States.

HV6783-7015.15 Criminology — Crimes and criminal classes — By region or country

HV6783.A85 2000
Atlas of crime: mapping the criminal landscape/ [edited by] Linda S. Turnbull, Elaine Hallisey Hendrix, and Borden D. Dent. Phoenix, AZ: Oryx Press, 2000. xxiii, 270 p.
00-009772   364.973/09/04 21   1573562416
Crime -- United States -- History -- 20th century. Crime analysis -- United States. Applied human geography -- United States.

HV6787.D87 1996
Durham, Jennifer L.
Crime in America: a reference handbook/ Jennifer L. Durham. Santa Barbara, Calif.: ABC-CLIO, c1996. xi, 318 p.
96-009077   364.973 20   0874368413
Crime -- United States -- Handbooks, manuals, etc. Criminology -- Handbooks, manuals, etc.

HV6787.S73 1996
Statistics on crime & punishment: a selection of statistical charts, graphs, and tables about crime and punishment from a variety of published sources with explanatory comments/ Timothy L. Gall and Daniel M. Lucas, editors; Peter C. Kratcoski and Lucille Dunn Kratcoski, contributing editors. Detroit: Gale, c1996. xxvi, 235 p.
98-131564   078760528X
Criminal statistics -- United States. Punishment -- United States -- Statistics.

HV6789.A82 1997
Athens, Lonnie H.
Violent criminal acts and actors revisited/ Lonnie Athens; foreword by Herbert Blumer. Urbana: University of Illinois Press, c1997. x, 175 p.
96-025235   364.1/5 20   0252023064
Violent crimes. Criminals. Violence.

HV6789.B47 1999
Best, Joel.
Random violence: how we talk about new crimes and new victims/ Joel Best. Berkeley: University of California Press, c1999. xv, 242 p.
98-006234   364.973 21   0520215710
Fear of crime -- United States. Crime -- United States -- Public opinion. Violence -- United States -- Public opinion.

HV6789.F58 1989
Flowers, Ronald B.
Demographics and criminality: the characteristics of crime in America/ Ronald Barri Flowers. New York: Greenwood Press, 1989. xvi, 207 p.
89-001897   364/.042/0973   0313253676
Crime -- United States. Criminal statistics -- United States.

HV6789.L34 1998
LaFree, Gary D.
Losing legitimacy: street crime and the decline of social institutions in America/ Gary LaFree. Boulder, Colo: Westview Press, 1998. xvi, 240 p.
98-013957   364.973   0813334500
Crime -- United States. Crime prevention -- United States. Social control. United States -- Social conditions -- 1980-

HV6789.R63 1997
Roberts, Julian V.
Public opinion, crime, and criminal justice/ Julian V. Roberts and Loretta J. Stalans. Boulder, Colo.: Westview Press, 1997. x, 337 p.
97-015795   364.973   0813323185
Crime -- United States -- Public opinion. Crime -- Great Britain -- Public opinion. Criminal justice, Administration of -- United States -- Public opinion.

HV6789.S537 2001
Sifakis, Carl.
The encyclopedia of American crime/ Carl Sifakis. New York: Facts on File, 2001. 2 v.
99-058740   364.973/03   0816040400
Crime -- United States -- Encyclopedias.

HV6789.W53 1983
Wilson, James Q.
Thinking about crime/ James Q. Wilson. New York: Basic Books, c1983. x, 293 p.
83-070752   364/.973   0465085504
Crime -- United States. Criminal justice, Administration of -- United States.

HV6791.B42 1997
Beckett, Katherine, 1964-
Making crime pay: law and order in contemporary American politics/ Katherine Beckett. New York: Oxford University Press, 1997. vi, 158 p.
96-031521   364.973   019511289X
Crime -- Political aspects -- United States. Criminal justice, Administration of -- Political aspects -- United States. Crime prevention -- Political aspects -- United States. United States -- Politics and government -- 1989-

HV6791.S57 1990
Skogan, Wesley G.
Disorder and decline: crime and the spiral of decay in American neighborhoods/ Wesley G. Skogan. New York: Free Press; c1990. ix, 218 p.
90-003094   364.2/56 20   0029291518
Crime prevention -- United States -- Case studies. Inner cities -- United States -- Case studies. Quality of life -- United States -- Case studies.

HV6793.F6.D46 1997
Denham, James M.
A rogue's paradise: crime and punishment in Antebellum Florida, 1821-1861/ James M. Denham. Tuscaloosa: University of Alabama Press, c1997. xii, 385 p.
96-024837 364.9759/09/034 20 0817308474
Crime -- Florida -- History -- 19th century. Criminal justice, Administration of -- Florida -- History -- 19th century. Florida -- History -- 1821-1865.

HV6795.R33.S5 1991
Shannon, Lyle W.
Changing patterns of delinquency and crime: a longitudinal study in Racine/ Lyle W. Shannon, with the assistance of Judith L. McKim, Kathleen R. Anderson, William E. Murph. Boulder: Westview Press, 1991. xi, 174 p.
90-025337 364.3/6/0977596 0813382882
Crime -- Wisconsin -- Racine -- Longitudinal studies. Juvenile delinquency -- Wisconsin -- Racine -- Longitudinal studies.

HV6806.H35 2001
Haggerty, Kevin D.
Making crime count/ Kevin D. Haggerty. Toronto; Buffalo: c2001. viii, 222 p.
2001-270303 364.971 21 0802048099
Criminal statistics -- Canada. Statistiques criminelles -- Canada.

HV6815.M4.H37 1999
Haslip-Viera, Gabriel.
Crime and punishment in late colonial Mexico City, 1692-1810/ Gabriel Haslip-Viera. Albuquerque: University of New Mexico Press, c1999. xii, 193 p.
98-058106 364.972/53 21 0826318754
Crime -- Mexico -- Mexico City -- History. Punishment -- Mexico -- Mexico City -- History. Criminal justice, Administration of -- Mexico -- Mexico City -- History. Mexico City (Mexico) -- Social conditions.

HV6872.S26 1994
Santiago-Valles, Kelvin A., 1951-
"Subject people" and colonial discourses: economic transformation and social disorder in Puerto Rico, 1898-1947/ Kelvin A. Santiago-Valles. Albany: State University of New York Press, c1994. xiii, 304 p.
92-030542 364.97295/09/04 20 0791415899
Crime -- Puerto Rico -- History -- 20th century. Social conflict -- Puerto Rico -- History -- 20th century. Puerto Rico -- Economic conditions. Puerto Rico -- Social conditions.

HV6895.S3
Caldeira, Teresa Pires do Rio.
City of walls: crime, segregation, and citizenship in Sao Paulo/ Teresa P.R. Caldeira. Berkeley: University of California Press, c2000. xvii, 487 p.
00-028713 364.981/61 21 0520221427
Crime -- Brazil -- Sao Paulo. Segregation -- Brazil -- Sao Paulo. Social classes -- Brazil -- Sao Paulo. Sao Paulo (Brazil) -- Social conditions.

HV6949.E5.G37 2000
Gaskill, Malcolm.
Crime and mentalities in early modern England/ Malcolm Gaskill. Cambridge, UK; Cambridge University Press, 2000. xiii, 377 p.
99-036622 364.942 0521572754
Crime -- England -- History.

HV6949.E5.M35 1989
McLynn, F. J.
Crime and punishment in eighteenth-century England/ Frank McLynn. London; Routledge, 1989. xviii, 392 p.
88-036411 364/.942 0415010144
Crime -- England -- History -- 18th century. Criminal justice, Administration of -- England -- History -- 18th century.

HV6949.E5.T48 1998
Thomas, Donald Serrell.
The Victorian underworld/ Donald Thomas. New York: New York University Press, 1998. 346 p.
98-014866 364.942 0814782388
Crime -- Sociological aspects -- England. Criminals -- England -- Social conditions. Crime -- England -- History -- 19th century. England -- Social conditions -- 19th century.

HV6950.L56.D38 1994
Davey, B. J.
Rural crime in the eighteenth century: North Lincolnshire, 1740-80/ B.J. Davey. [Hull?]: University of Hull Press, 1994. xv, 167 p.
94-220945 367.9625/3/09033 0859586189
Rural crimes -- England -- Lincolnshire -- History -- 18th century.

HV6973.J64 1995
Johnson, Eric A. 1948-
Urbanization and crime: Germany, 1871-1914/ Eric A. Johnson. New York: Cambridge University Press, 1995. x, 246 p.
94-045503 364.943 052147017X
Crime -- Germany -- History -- 19th century. Crime prevention -- Germany -- History -- 19th century. Criminal justice, Administration of -- Germany -- History -- 19th century.

HV6973.R84 1999
Rublack, Ulinka.
The crimes of women in early modern Germany/ Ulinka Rublack. Oxford; Clarendon Press, 1999. ix, 292 p.
98-003196 364.3/74/0943 0198206372
Female offenders -- Germany -- History. Crime -- Germany -- History. Women -- Germany -- Social conditions.

HV6974.E95 1998
Evans, Richard J.
Tales from the German underworld: crime and punishment in the nineteenth century/ Richard J. Evans. New Haven: Yale University Press, c1998. x, 278 p.
97-044612 364.6/0943/09034 21 0300072244
Crime -- Germany -- History -- 19th century. Criminals -- Germany -- History -- 19th century. Detective and mystery stories, German.

HV6979.O24.S3813 1994
Schulte, Regina, 1949-
The village in court: arson, infanticide, and poaching in the court records of Upper Bavaria, 1848-1910/ Regina Schulte; translated by Barrie Selman. Cambridge; Cambridge University Press, 1994. vii, 199 p.
93-014229 364.1/0943/36 0521431867
Rural crimes -- Germany -- Oberbayern -- History -- 19th century. Village communities -- Germany -- Oberbayern -- History -- 19th century. Criminal registers -- Germany -- Oberbayern. Oberbayern (Germany) -- Rural conditions.

HV7015.15.S47 1998
Sergeyev, Victor M., 1944-
The wild East: crime and lawlessness in post-communist Russia/ Victor M. Sergeyev. Armonk, N.Y.: M.E. Sharpe, c1998. xvi, 191 p.
97-026607 364.947 21 0765602318
Crime -- Russia (Federation) Social change -- Russia (Federation) Russia (Federation) -- Social conditions -- 1991-

HV7245 Criminal justice administration — Documents — United States

HV7245.N37b
Sourcebook of criminal justice statistics. Washington, D.C.: U.S. Dept. of Justice, Bureau of Justice Statist
74-601963 364/.973
Criminal statistics -- United States. Corrections -- United States -- Statistics.

HV7419.5 Criminal justice administration — Research

HV7419.5.C75 1998
Criminal justice information: how to find it, how to use it/ by Dennis C. Benamati ... [et al.]. Phoenix, Ariz.: Oryx Press, 1998. x, 237 p.
97-039576 364/.07/2 089774957X
Criminal justice, Administration of -- Research. Criminal justice, Administration of -- Information services. Information storage and retrieval systems -- Criminal justice, Administration of.

HV7431 Criminal justice administration — Prevention of crime, methods, etc.

HV7431.E38 1996
Elikann, Peter T.
The tough-on-crime myth: real solutions to cut crime/ Peter T. Elikann. New York: Insight Books, c1996. xvi, 323 p.
96-032712 364.4/0973 20 0306454033
Crime prevention -- United States. Crime -- United States. Law enforcement -- United States.

HV7436 Criminal justice administration — Gun control — By region or country

HV7436.B54 1999
Bijlefeld, Marjolijn, 1960-
People for and against gun control: a biographical reference/ Marjolijn Bijlefeld. Westport, Conn.: Greenwood Press, 1999. xii, 324 p.
98-053383 363.3/3/0973 0313306907
Gun control -- United States.

HV7436.C37 1997
Carter, Gregg Lee, 1951-
The gun control movement/ Gregg Lee Carter. New York: Twayne Publishers; c1997. xiii, 166 p.
97-006371 363.3/3/0973 21 0805738851
Gun control -- United States -- History. Firearms -- Law and legislation -- United States -- History. Firearms -- Social aspects -- United States.

HV7436.D43 2001
DeConde, Alexander.
Gun violence in America: the struggle for control/ Alexander DeConde. Boston: Northeastern University Press, c2001. 394 p.
00-054821   363.3/3/0973 21   1555534864
Gun control -- United States. Violent crimes -- United States. Firearms ownership -- United States. United States -- Politics and government.

HV7436.H65 2001
Homsher, Deborah, 1952-
Women & guns: politics and the culture of firearms in America/ Deborah Homsher. Armonk, N.Y.: M.E. Sharpe, c2001. ix, 246 p.
00-041018   363.3/3/0973 21   076560678X
Gun control -- United States -- Public opinion. Women -- United States -- Attitudes. Firearms and crime -- United States -- Public opinion.

HV7436.S68 1995
Spitzer, Robert J., 1953-
The politics of gun control/ Robert J. Spitzer. Chatham, N.J.: Chatham House, c1995. xiii, 210 p.
94-046138   363.3/3/0973 20   1566430224
Gun control -- United States.

HV7436.V59 2000
Vizzard, William J., 1944-
Shots in the dark: the policy, politics, and symbolism of gun control/ William J. Vizzard. Lanham, Md.: Rowman & Littlefield Publishers, c2000. xviii, 257 p.
00-038739   363.3/3/0973 21   084769559X
Gun control -- Government policy -- United States. Gun control -- Political aspects -- United States. Gun control -- Law and legislation -- United States. United States -- Social policy. United States -- Politics and government.

HV7901 Criminal justice administration — Police. Detectives. Constabulary — Dictionaries. Encyclopedias

HV7901.E53 1995
The encyclopedia of police science/ editor, William G. Bailey; editorial board members, Victor G. Strecher, Larry T. Hoover, Jerry L. Dowling. New York: Garland Pub., 1995. xvii, 865 p.
94-046828   363.2/03   0815313314
Police -- United States -- Encyclopedias.

HV7903 Criminal justice administration — Police. Detectives. Constabulary — History

HV7903.R67 2001
Roth, Mitchel P., 1953-
Historical dictionary of law enforcement/ Mitchel P. Roth. Westport, CT: Greenwood Press, 2001. xi, 480 p.
00-024646   363.2/03   0313305609
Police -- History -- Dictionaries. Police -- Biography -- Dictionaries. Law enforcement -- History -- Dictionaries.

HV7911 Criminal justice administration — Police. Detectives. Constabulary — Biography

HV7911.B72.A3 1998
Bratton, William J.
Turnaround: how America's top cop reversed the crime epidemic/ William Bratton with Peter Knobler. New York: Random House, c1998. xxxiii, 329 p.
97-028105   363.2/092 B 21   0679452516
Bratton, William J.   Police chiefs -- New York (State) -- New York -- Biography. Police administration -- New York (State) -- New York. Police-community relations -- New York (State) -- New York.

HV7911.E37.S76 1998
Stolberg, Mary M.
Bridging the river of hatred: the pioneering efforts of Detroit Police Commissioner George Edwards/ Mary M. Stolberg. Detroit: Wayne State University Press, c1998. 347 p.
97-015023   363.2/092 B 21   0814325726
Edwards, George C. -- (George Clifton), -- 1914- Police chiefs -- Michigan -- Detroit -- Biography. Police administration -- Michigan -- Detroit -- History -- 20th century.

HV7911.H6.G46 1991
Gentry, Curt, 1931-
J. Edgar Hoover: the man and the secrets/ Curt Gentry. New York: Norton, c1991. 846 p.
90-030576   353.0074/09 20   0393024040
Hoover, J. Edgar -- (John Edgar), -- 1895-1972. Police -- United States -- Biography. Government executives -- United States -- Biography.

HV7911.H6.T54 1988
Theoharis, Athan G.
The boss: J. Edgar Hoover and the Great American Inquisition/ Athan G. Theoharis and John Stuart Cox. Philadelphia: Temple University Press, 1988. xiv, 489 p.
87-018105   353.0074/092/4   087722532X
Hoover, J. Edgar -- (John Edgar), -- 1895-1972. Police -- United States -- Biography. Government executives -- United States -- Biography. Subversive activities -- United States.

HV7911.H6.T545 1995
Theoharis, Athan G.
J. Edgar Hoover, sex, and crime: an historical antidote/ Athan Theoharis. Chicago: Ivan R. Dee, 1995. 175 p.
94-036630   353.0074/092   1566630711
Hoover, J. Edgar -- (John Edgar) -- 1895-1972. Hoover, J. Edgar -- (John Edgar) -- 1895-1972 -- Sexual behavior. Organized crime -- United States -- Prevention.

HV7911.S75.A3 1998
Starnes, John.
Closely guarded: a life in Canadian security and intelligence/ John Starnes. Toronto; University of Toronto Press, c1998. xii, 258 p.
99-217713   0802009751
Starnes, John.   Intelligence officers -- Canada -- Biography.

HV7921 Criminal justice administration — Police. Detectives. Constabulary — General works

HV7921.B36 1994
Bayley, David H.
Police for the future/ David H. Bayley. New York: Oxford University Press, 1994. x, 187 p.
93-046099   363.2   0195091167
Police -- Cross-cultural studies. Law enforcement -- Cross-cultural studies.

HV7921.B6
Bordua, David Joseph,
The police: six sociological essays. Edited by David J. Bordua. New York, Wiley [1967] xv, 258 p.
66-029624   363.2
Police -- Addresses, essays, lectures.

HV7921.E75 1997
Ericson, Richard Victor.
Policing the risk society/ Richard V. Ericson, Kevin D. Haggerty. Toronto; University of Toronto Press, c1997. xiv, 487 p.
97-160534   0802041213
Police. Police -- Canada. Risk communication.

HV7921.M37 1994
Marion, Nancy E.
A history of federal crime control initiatives, 1960-1993/ Nancy E. Marion. Westport, Conn.: Praeger, 1994. vi, 278 p.
93-048214   364.973   0275946495
Criminal justice, Administration of -- United States -- History -- 20th century. United States -- Politics and government -- 20th century.

HV7921.P5715 1994
Police practices: an international review/ edited by Dilip K. Das. Metuchen, N.J.: Scarecrow Press, 1994. xxvi, 448 p.
94-018256   363.2   0810829088
Police -- Cross-cultural studies. Law enforcement -- Cross-cultural studies.

HV7924 Criminal justice administration — Police. Detectives. Constabulary — Ethics

HV7924.C64 1991
Cohen, Howard, 1944-
Power and restraint: the moral dimension of police work/ Howard S. Cohen and Michael Feldberg. New York: Praeger, 1991. xvii, 166 p.
90-028100   174/.93632/0973   0275938565
Police ethics. Law enforcement -- Moral and ethical aspects -- United States. Police ethics -- Case studies.

HV7935-8023 Criminal justice administration — Police. Detectives. Constabulary — Administration and organization

HV7935.S69 1994
Sparrow, Malcolm K.
Imposing duties: government's changing approach to compliance/ Malcolm K. Sparrow. Westport, Conn.: Praeger, 1994. xxxiii, 181 p.
93-011895 350.74 0275947807
Police administration -- United States. Environmental policy -- United States. Tax administration and procedure -- United States.

HV7936.C83.L86 1999
Lyons, William, 1960-
The politics of community policing: rearranging the power to punish/ William Lyons. Ann Arbor: University of Michigan Press, c1999. xiv, 241 p.
98-040135 363.2/3/0973 21 0472109537
Community policing -- Washington (State) -- Seattle. Law enforcement -- Washington (State) -- Seattle. Seattle (Wash.) -- Social conditions. Seattle (Wash.) -- Politics and government.

HV7936.C83.M6 1999
Miller, Susan L.
Gender and community policing: walking the talk/ Susan L. Miller. Boston: Northeastern University Press, c1999. xiv, 255 p.
99-025017 363.2/082/0977 21 1555534147
Community policing -- Middle West. Police -- Middle West -- Social conditions. Policewomen -- Middle West -- Social conditions.

HV7936.C83.S56 1997
Skogan, Wesley G.
Community policing, Chicago style/ Wesley G. Skogan, Susan M. Hartnett. New York: Oxford University Press, 1997. x, 258 p.
96-027841 363.2/3 0195105605
Crime prevention -- Illinois -- Chicago -- Citizen participation. Police administration -- Illinois -- Chicago. Community policing -- Illinois -- Chicago.

HV7936.D54.B76 1981
Brown, Michael K.
Working the street: police discretion and the dilemmas of reform/ Michael K. Brown. New York: Russell Sage Foundation, c1981. xvi, 349 p.
80-069175 363.2/32 0871541904
Police discretion -- California. Police patrol -- California. Police professionalization -- California.

HV7965.B43 1995
Bechtel, H. Kenneth, 1946-
State police in the United States: a socio-historical analysis/ H. Kenneth Bechtel. Westport, Conn.: Greenwood Press, 1995. xii, 179 p.
94-030929 363.2/0973 0313263809
Police, State -- United States -- History.

HV7965.T67 1987
Torres, Donald A.
Handbook of state police, highway patrols, and investigative agencies/ Donald A. Torres. New York: Greenwood Press, 1987. xv, 375 p.
86-027142 363.2/0973 0313249334
Police, State -- United States -- Handbooks, manuals, etc.

HV8023.A66 1998
Appier, Janis, 1952-
Policing women: the sexual politics of law enforcement and the LAPD/ Janis Appier. Philadelphia: Temple University Press, 1998. x, 227 p.
97-009965 363.2/082 1566395593
Policewomen -- United States -- History -- 20th century. Police administration -- United States -- History -- 20th century. Police professionalization -- United States -- History -- 20th century.

HV8023.B76 2000
Brown, Jennifer, 1948-
Gender and policing: comparative perspectives/ Jennifer Brown and Frances Heidensohn. New York, N.Y.: St. Martin's Press, 2000. x, 203 p.
99-086555 363.2/082 0312233086
Policewomen. Sex role in the work environment. Law enforcement.

HV8023.D68 1999
Douglas, R. M., 1963-
Feminist freikorps: the British voluntary women police, 1914-1940/ R.M. Douglas. Westport, Conn.: Praeger, 1999. xiv, 171 p.
98-015648 363.2/082/094109041 0275962490
Policewomen -- Great Britain -- History. Volunteer workers in law enforcement -- Great Britain -- History. Women radicals -- Great Britain -- History.

HV8023.H48 1992
Heidensohn, Frances.
Women in control?: the role of women in law enforcement/ Frances Heidensohn. Oxford [England]: Clarendon Press; 1992. ix, 283 p.
92-025902 363.2/2/082 0198252552
Policewomen -- Great Britain. Policewomen -- United States.

HV8023.S28 1995
Schulz, Dorothy Moses.
From social worker to crimefighter: women in United States municipal policing/ Dorothy Moses Schulz. Westport, Conn.: Praeger, 1995. x, 175 p.
94-042841 363.2/082 0275949966
Policewomen -- United States -- History.

HV8059-8079.2 Criminal justice administration — Police. Detectives. Constabulary — Police duty. Methods of protection

HV8059.B395 2000
Bellesiles, Michael A.
Arming America: the origins of a national gun culture/ Michael A. Bellesiles. New York: Alfred A. Knopf, 2000. 603 p.
00-106191 683.4/00973 0375402101
Firearms ownership -- United States -- History.

HV8059.S47
Sherrill, Robert.
The Saturday night special, and other guns with which Americans won the West, protected bootleg franchises, slew wildlife, robbed countless banks, shot husbands purposely and by mistake, and killed Illustrated by Julio Fernandez. New York, Charterhouse [1973] xiii, 338 p.
73-084076 363.3/3 0883270161
Gun control -- United States. Firearms -- Law and legislation -- United States.

HV8073.E517 2000
Encyclopedia of forensic sciences/ editor-in- chief, Jay A. Siegel; editors, Pekka J. Saukko, Geoffrey C. Knupfer. San Diego: Academic Press, c2000. 3 v.
99-067362 363.25/03 21 0122272153
Forensic sciences -- Encyclopedias. Criminal laboratories -- Encyclopedias. Criminals -- Identification -- Encyclopedias.

HV8073.I57 1997
Introduction to forensic sciences/ edited by William G. Eckert. Boca Raton, Fla.: CRC Press, 1997. xi, 390 p.
96-054316 363.25 0849381010
Forensic sciences. Medical jurisprudence. Criminal investigation.

HV8077.5.C6.F67 1992
Forensic examination of fibres/ editor, James Robertson. New York: E. Horwood, 1992. 268 p.
92-020700 363.2/562 0133253090
Criminal investigation. Textile fibers -- Identification.

HV8078.M36 1996
Matte, James Allan.
Forensic psychophysiology using the polygraph: scientific truth verification, lie detection/ by James Allan Matte. Williamsville, New York, U.S.A.: J.A.M. Publications, c1996. xxiii, 773 p.
96-095246 363.25/4 21 0965579409
Lie detectors and detection -- United States. Psychophysiology -- United States. Psychology, Forensic -- United States.

HV8079.2.R76 1990
Romano, Anne T.
Taking charge: crisis intervention in criminal justice/ Anne T. Romano. New York: Greenwood Press, 1990. xxi, 183 p.
89-037995 362 0313268908
Police social work. Assistance in emergencies. Crisis intervention (Mental health services)

HV8138-8272 Criminal justice administration — Police. Detectives. Constabulary — Police

HV8138.D66 1990
Donner, Frank J.
Protectors of privilege: red squads and police repression in urban America/ Frank Donner. Berkeley: University of California Press, c1990. xiv, 503 p.
89-020292 363.2/32 20 0520059514
Police misconduct -- United States -- History -- 20th century. Political crimes and offenses -- Investigation -- United States -- History -- 20th century. Political persecution -- United States -- History -- 20th century.

HV8138.D85 1996
Dulaney, W. Marvin, 1950-
Black police in America/ W. Marvin Dulaney. Bloomington: Indiana University Press, c1996. xviii, 193 p.
95-019359 363.2/089/96073 20 0253330068
Afro-American police -- History. Police -- United States -- History. United States -- Race relations.

HV8138.J33 1989
Jackson, Pamela Irving.
Minority group threat, crime, and policing: social context and social control/ Pamela Irving Jackson. New York: Praeger, 1989. xiii, 153 p.
88-031927   363.2/32/0973   0275929833
Police -- United States. Police-community relations -- United States. Minorities -- United States -- Social conditions. United States -- Race relations.

HV8138.L353 1993
Leinen, Stephen H.
Gay cops/ Stephen Leinen. New Brunswick, N.J.: Rutgers University Press, c1993. xii, 245 p.
93-009216   363.2/08/664 20   0813520002
Gay police -- United States -- Social conditions. Gay police -- United States -- Attitudes. Homosexuality -- United States.

HV8138.R42
Reiman, Jeffrey H.
The rich get richer and the poor get prison: ideology, class and criminal justice/ Jeffrey H. Reiman. New York: Wiley, c1979. xii, 214 p.
78-023986   364/.973   0471047260
Criminal justice, Administration of -- United States.

HV8138.W627 2000
Wilson, Christopher P. 1952-
Cop knowledge: police power and cultural narrative in twentieth-century America/ Christopher P. Wilson. Chicago: University of Chicago Press, 2000. xii, 281 p.
99-049209   363.2/0973   0226901327
Police -- United States -- History. Police in popular culture -- United States -- History. Police power -- United States -- History.

HV8141.B49 1995
Beyond the Rodney King story: an investigation of police conduct in minority communities/ prepared by Charles J. Ogletree, Jr. ... et al.; Criminal Justice Institute at Harvard Law School for the National Association for the Advancement of Colored People. Boston: Northeastern University Press, c1995. xxiii, 197 p.
94-030409   363.2/32/0973 20   1555532020
Police misconduct -- United States. Discrimination in law enforcement -- United States. Police-community relations -- United States.

HV8141.C46 1988
Churchill, Ward.
Agents of repression: the FBI's secret wars against the Black Panther Party and the American Indian Movement/ by Ward Churchill and Jim Vander Wall. Boston, MA: South End Press, c1988. xvi, 509 p.
88-016844   363.2/32   0896082946
United States. Federal Bureau of Investigation. Black Panther Party. American Indian Movement.

HV8141.G89 1991
Guyot, Dorothy.
Policing as though people matter/ Dorothy Guyot. Philadelphia: Temple University Press, 1991. xvii, 357 p.
90-034691   363.2/09747/41   0877227551
Police administration -- United States -- Case studies. Police administration -- New York (State) -- Troy.

HV8141.H298 2002
Harris, David A.,
Profiles in injustice: why racial profiling cannot work/ David A. Harris. New York: New Press, c2002. xi, 276 p.
2001-044177   363.2/3/08900973   21
1565846966
Racial profiling in law enforcement -- United States. Law enforcement -- United States.

HV8141.K45 1996
Kelling, George L.
Fixing broken windows: restoring order and reducing crime in our communities/ George L. Kelling, Catherine M. Coles. New York: Martin Kessler Books, 1996. xvi, 319 p.
96-027232   364.4/0973   0684824469
Law enforcement -- United States. Crime prevention -- United States. Police administration -- United States.

HV8141.P36 1994
Perez, Douglas Werner.
Common sense about police review/ Douglas W. Perez. Philadelphia, Penn.: Temple University Press, 1994. xi, 322 p.
93-011192   363.2/3   1566391326
Police -- Complaints against -- United States. Police administration -- United States.

HV8141.P567 2000
Police brutality: an anthology/ edited by Jill Nelson. 1st ed. New York: W.W. Norton & Co., c2000. 265 p.
00-020532   363.2/32 21   0393048837
Police brutality -- United States. Discrimination in law enforcement -- United States.

HV8141.P595 1996
Police violence: understanding and controlling police abuse of force/ edited by William A. Geller, Hans Toch. New Haven, CT: Yale University Press, c1996. x, 379 p.
96-033939   363.2/3 20   0300064292
Police misconduct -- United States. Police psychology -- United States. Police training -- United States.

HV8141.R67 2000
Ross, Jeffrey Ian.
Making news of police violence: a comparative study of Toronto and New York City/ Jeffrey Ian Ross; foreword by Donna C. Hale. Westport, Conn.: Praeger, 2000. xviii, 174 p.
99-054878   363.2/32   0275968251
Police brutality -- Public opinion -- Case studies. Police in mass media -- Case studies.

HV8141.S53 1998
Shielded from justice: police brutality and accountability in the United States. New York: Human Rights Watch, c1998. 440 p.
98-086155   1564321835
Police brutality -- United States. Police misconduct -- United States. Police administration -- United States -- Citizen participation.

HV8141.S56 1993
Skolnick, Jerome H.
Above the law: police and the excessive use of force/ Jerome H. Skolnick, James J. Fyfe. New York: Free Press, c1993. xviii, 313 p.
92-038815   363.2/2 20   002929312X
Police misconduct -- United States. Tort liability of police -- United States.

HV8144.B87.V59 1997
Vizzard, William J., 1944-
In the cross fire: a political history of the Bureau of Alcohol, Tobacco, and Firearms/ William J. Vizzard. Boulder: Lynne Rienner Publishers, 1997. xi, 228 p.
96-048456   363.3/3/0973   1555876714
Law enforcement -- United States -- History. Law enforcement -- Political aspects -- United States -- History.

HV8144.F43.C48 1990
Churchill, Ward.
The COINTELPRO papers: documents from the FBI's secret wars against domestic dissent/ by Ward Churchill and Jim Vander Wall; foreword by John Trudell; preface by Brian Glick. Boston, MA: South End Press, c1990. xxii, 467 p.
90-040185   363.2/32 20   0896083594
Political crimes and offenses -- Investigation -- United States -- History -- 20th century -- Sources. Political persecution -- United States -- History -- 20th century -- Sources.

HV8144.F43.H35 1993
Haines, Gerald K., 1943-
Unlocking the files of the FBI: a guide to its records and classification system/ Gerald K. Haines and David A. Langbart. Wilmington, Del.: Scholarly Resources, 1993. xviii, 348 p.
92-016728   026/.3530074   0842023380
Law enforcement -- United States -- Archival resources.

HV8144.F43.P67 1998
Potter, Claire Bond, 1958-
War on crime: bandits, G-men, and the politics of mass culture/ Claire Bond Potter. New Brunswick, N.J.: Rutgers University Press, c1998. xi, 250 p.
97-022311   364.973 21   0813524865
Hoover, J. Edgar -- (John Edgar), -- 1895-1972. Criminal investigation -- United States -- History -- 20th century. Crime -- United States -- History -- 20th century. Crime -- Government policy -- United States -- History -- 20th century.

HV8144.F43.T48 1999
Theoharis, Athan G.
The FBI: a comprehensive reference guide/ [written and] edited by Athan G. Theoharis with Tony G. Poveda, Susan Rosenfeld, Richard Gid Powers. Phoenix, Ariz.: Oryx Press, 1999. xi, 409 p.
98-026642   363.25/0973   089774991X
United States. Federal Bureau of Investigation. United States. Federal Bureau of Investigation -- History.

HV8148.C4.L55 1991
Lindberg, Richard, 1953-
To serve and collect: Chicago politics and police corruption from the Lager Beer Riot to the Summerdale Scandal/ Richard C. Lindberg. New York: Praeger, 1991. xi, 366 p.
90-038713   364.1/323/0977311   0275934152
Police -- Illinois -- Chicago -- History. Police corruption -- Illinois -- Chicago -- History. Chicago (Ill.) -- Politics and government.

HV8148.C42.C65 1973
Commission of Inquiry into the Black Panthers and the Police.
Search and destroy; a report. Roy Wilkins and Ramsey Clark, chairmen. New York, Metropolitan Applied Research Center [1973] xii, 284 p.
73-007068   363.2/34   0060108282
Police -- Illinois -- Chicago. Police-community relations.

HV8148.D4.B392
Bayley, David H.
Minorities and the police; confrontation in America, by David H. Bayley and Harold Mendelsohn. New York, Free Press [1968, c1969] xii, 209 p.
69-012119   363.2/09788/83
Police -- Colorado -- Denver. Minorities -- Colorado -- Denver. Police-community relations.

HV8148.L55.E73 1999
Escobar, Edward J., 1946-
Race, police, and the making of a political identity: Mexican Americans and the Los Angeles Police Department, 1900-1945/ Edward J. Escobar. Berkeley: University of California Press, 1999. xiv, 358 p.
98-023322   365/.9794/93   0520213343
Police -- California -- Los Angeles -- History -- 20th century. Police-community relations -- California -- Los Angeles -- History -- 20th century. Mexican Americans -- California -- Los Angeles -- History -- 20th century.

HV8148.S452.M35 1992
McLaughlin, Vance.
Police and the use of force: the Savannah study/ Vance McLaughlin; foreword by Richard R.E. Kania. Westport, Conn.: Praeger, 1992. xvi, 154 p.
92-010154   363.2/32   0275943445
Police misconduct -- Georgia -- Savannah -- Case studies. Police shootings -- Georgia -- Savannah -- Case studies. Nonlethal weapons -- Georgia -- Savannah -- Case studies.

HV8160.A2.H84 998
Huggins, Martha Knisely, 1944-
Political policing: the United States and Latin America/ Martha K. Huggins. Durham, NC: Duke University Press, 1998. xxi, 247 p.
97-052378   363.2/0973   0822321599
Police -- Latin America -- International cooperation. Police training -- Latin America -- International cooperation. Technical assistance, American -- Latin America. United States -- Foreign relations -- Latin America. Latin America -- Foreign relations -- United States.

HV8185.R5.H65 1993
Holloway, Thomas H., 1944-
Policing Rio de Janeiro: repression and resistance in a 19th-century city/ Thomas H. Holloway. Stanford, Calif.: Stanford University Press, 1993. xvii, 369 p.
92-045685   363.2/0981/53   0804720568
Police -- Brazil -- Rio de Janeiro -- History -- 19th century.

HV8194.A2.L53 1992
Liang, Hsi-huey, 1929-
The rise of modern police and the European state system from Metternich to the Second World War/ Hsi-huey Liang. Cambridge, [England]; Cambridge University Press, 1992. xiii, 345 p.
92-017111   363.2/096   0521430224
Police -- Europe -- History -- 19th century. Police -- Europe -- History -- 20th century. Europe -- Politics and government -- 1815-1871. Europe -- Politics and government -- 1871-1918. Europe -- Politics and government -- 1918-1945.

HV8195.A2.H65 1996
Holdaway, Simon.
The racialisation of British policing/ Simon Holdaway. Houndmills, Basingstoke, Hampshire: Macmillan Press; 1996. ix, 226 p.
95-042139   363.2/0941   0333563948
Police -- Great Britain. Discrimination in law enforcement -- Great Britain. Great Britain -- Race relations.

HV8195.A2.R44
Reiner, Robert, 1946-
The blue-coated worker: a sociological study of police unionism/ Robert Reiner. Cambridge [Eng.]; Cambridge University Press, 1978. 295 p.
77-085695   331.88/11/36320941   0521218896
Police -- Labor unions -- Great Britain. Police -- Great Britain -- Attitudes. Police -- Great Britain.

HV8195.A2.T68 1993
Townshend, Charles.
Making the peace: public order and public security in modern Britain/ Charles Townshend. Oxford; Oxford University Press, 1993. 264 p.
93-026964   363.2/0941   019822978X
Law enforcement -- Great Britain. Public policy (Law) -- Great Britain.

HV8195.A2.W44 1990
Weinberger, Barbara.
Keeping the peace?: policing strikes in Britain, 1906-1926/ Barbara Weinberger. New York: Berg, 1991. ix, 229 p.
90-031202   363.2/33   0854966757
Police -- Great Britain -- History -- 20th century. Strikes and lockouts -- Great Britain -- History -- 20th century.

HV8195.A3.O97 1991
Out of order?: policing black people/ edited by Ellis Cashmore and Eugene McLaughlin. London; Routledge, 1991. viii, 243 p.
90-027272   363.2/32   0415037263
Police -- Great Britain. Police -- United States. Discrimination in law enforcement -- Great Britain. Great Britain -- Race relations. United States -- Race relations.

HV8195.T39 1997
Taylor, David, 1946 May 10-
The new police in nineteenth-century England: crime, conflict, and control/ David Taylor. Manchester; Manchester University Press; 1997. xi, 180 p.
96-032187   363.2/0942/09034   0719047285
Police -- England -- History -- 19th century. Law enforcment -- England -- History -- 19th century. Great Britain -- History -- 19th century.

HV8196.A2.E47 1991
Emsley, Clive.
The English police: a political and social history/ Clive Emsley. Hemel Hempstead, Herts.: Harvester Wheatsheaf; 1991. xiii, 253 p.
91-018946   363.2/0942   0312067224
Police -- England -- History.

HV8197.5.A3.W75 2000
Wright, Joanne, 1960-
Policing and conflict in Northern Ireland/ Joanne Wright and Keith Bryett. Houndsmills, Basingstoke, Hampshire: Macmillan Press; 2000. xx, 155 p.
00-022340   363.2/09416   0312233558
Police -- Northern Ireland.

HV8203.E47 1999
Emsley, Clive.
Gendarmes and the state in nineteenth-century Europe/ Clive Emsley. Oxford; Oxford University Press, 1999. x, 288 p.
99-023234   363.2/0944/09034   0198207980
Police -- France -- History. Police -- Europe -- History.

HV8209.D87.S64 1992
Spencer, Elaine Glovka, 1939-
Police and the social order in German cities: the Dusseldorf District, 1848-1914/ Elaine Glovka Spencer. DeKalb: Northern Illinois University Press, 1992. xvi, 245 p.
92-001279   363.2/3/094355   0875801706
Law enforcement -- Germany -- Dusseldorf (Regierungsbezirk) -- History. Police -- Germany -- Dusseldorf (Regierungsbezirk) -- History. Dusseldorf (Regierungsbezirk) -- Social conditions. Dusseldorf (Regierungsbezirk) -- Politics and government. Germany -- History -- 1848-1870.

HV8212.N56 1995
Nippel, Wilfried.
Public order in ancient Rome/ Wilfried Nippel. Cambridge; Cambridge University Press, 1995. ix, 163 p.
94-045107   363.2/0937   0521383277
Law enforcement -- Rome.

HV8215.B65.D86 1997
Dunnage, Jonathan, 1963-
The Italian police and the rise of Fascism: a case study of the Province of Bologna, 1897-1925/ Jonathan Dunnage. Westport, Conn.: Praeger, 1997. xvi, 198 p.
97-005457   363.2/0945   0275952681
Police -- Italy -- Bologna (Province) -- History -- 20th century. Police administration -- Italy -- Bologna (Province) -- History -- 20th century. Socialism -- Italy -- Bologna (Province) -- History -- 20th century.

HV8224.D29 1998
Daly, Jonathan W.
Autocracy under siege: security police and opposition in Russia, 1866-1905/ Jonathan W. Daly. DeKalb: Northern Illinois University Press, 1998. xi, 260 p.
98-025021   363.2//3/094709034   0875802435
Secret service -- Russia. Police -- Russia. Internal security -- Russia.

HV8224.K57 1988
Knight, Amy W., 1946-
The KGB: police and politics in the Soviet Union/ Amy W. Knight. Boston: Unwin Hyman, c1988. xx, 348 p.
87-019533   363.2/83/0947   0044450354
Police -- Soviet Union -- History. Soviet Union -- Politics and government -- 1945-1991.

HV8224.S376 1996
Shelley, Louise I.
Policing Soviet society: the evolution of state control/ Louise I. Shelley. New York: Routledge, 1996. xx, 269 p.
95-034020   363.2/0947   0415104696
Police -- Soviet Union -- History. Law enforcement -- Soviet Union -- History.

HV8225.7.O54.Z83 1996
Zuckerman, Fredric Scott, 1944-
The tsarist secret police in Russian society, 1880-1917/ Fredric S. Zuckerman. New York: New York University Press, 1996. xvii, 345 p.
95-016138   363.2/83/0947   0814796737
Police -- Russia. Secret service -- Russia. Russia -- History -- Alexander III, 1881-1894. Russia -- History -- Nicholas II, 1894-1917.

HV8227.2.A3.K59 1996
Knight, Amy W. 1946-
Spies without cloaks: the KGB's successors/ Amy Knight. Princeton, N.J.: Princeton University Press, c1996. 318 p.
95-026281   363.2/83/0947 20   0691025770
Secret service -- Russia (Federation)

HV8260.A2.D87 1992
Dutton, Michael Robert.
Policing and punishment in China: from patriarchy to "the people"/ Michael R. Dutton. Cambridge; Cambridge University Press, 1992. xii, 391 p.
91-022888 364.6/0951 052140097X
Law enforcement -- China -- History. Corrections -- China -- History. Family -- China -- History.

HV8260.A2.M35 1992
McKnight, Brian E.
Law and order in Sung China/ Brian E. McKnight. Cambridge [England]; Cambridge University Press, 1992. xiv, 557 p.
91-034373 363.2/0951/09021 0521411211
Law enforcement -- China -- History. Corrections -- China -- History. China -- History -- Sung dynasty, 960-1279.

HV8272.A2.B74 1994
Brewer, John D.
Black and blue: policing in South Africa/ John D. Brewer. Oxford; Clarendon Press, 1994. xi, 378 p.
93-040020 363.2/0968 0198273827
Police -- South Africa -- History.

HV8272.A3.C39 1997
Cawthra, Gavin.
Securing South Africa's democracy: defense, development, and security in transition/ Gavin Cawthra. Houndmills, Basingstoke, Hampshire: Macmillan Press; 1997. xiii, 230 p.
96-046508 363.2/0968 0312174195
Police -- South Africa. Internal security -- South Africa. Democracy -- South Africa. South Africa -- Armed Forces. South Africa -- Politics and government -- 1994-

HV8497-8613 Criminal justice administration — Penology. Prisons. Corrections — History and antiquities

HV8497.R85 1968
Rusche, Georg.
Punishment and social structure, by Georg Rusche and Otto Kirchheimer. With a foreword by Thorsten Sellin. New York, Russell & Russell [1968, c1939] xiv, 268 p.
68-015157 364.6
Punishment. Prisons. Crime and criminals.

HV8501.O94 1995
The Oxford history of the prison: the practice of punishment in western society/ edited by Norval Morris and David J. Rothman. New York: Oxford University Press, 1995. xiv, 489 p.
95-006280 365/.9 0195061535
Prisons -- History.

HV8523.S28 1991
Saunders, Trevor J., 1934-
Plato's penal code: tradition, controversy, and reform in Greek penology/ Trevor J. Saunders. Oxford: Clarendon Press; 1991. xvii, 414 p.
90-049681 364.6/0938 0198148933
Plato -- Views on punishment. Plato -- Views on criminal law. Punishment -- Greece -- History. Criminal law (Greek law)

HV8599.B7.C3813 1998
Catholic Church.
Torture in Brazil: a shocking report on the pervasive use of torture by Brazilian military governments, 1964-1979/ secretly prepared by the Archdiocese of Sao Paulo; translated by Jaime Wright; edited with a new preface by Joan Dassin. Austin, Tex: Institute of Latin American Studies, University 1998. xxviii, 238 p.
98-013511 365/.644 0292704844
Torture -- Brazil. Political persecution -- Brazil. Brazil -- Politics and government -- 1964-1985.

HV8599.C16.C48 1999
Chandler, David P.
Voices from S-21: terror and history in Pol Pot's secret prison/ David Chandler. Berkeley: University of California Press, c1999. xiii, 238 p.
99-013924 303.6/09596 21 0520220056
Torture -- Cambodia. Political prisoners -- Cambodia. Political persecution -- Cambodia. Cambodia -- Politics and government -- 1975-1979.

HV8599.F7
Silverman, Lisa.
Tortured subjects: pain, truth, and the body in early modern France/ Lisa Silverman. Chicago: University of Chicago Press, 2001. xv, 264 p.
00-009586 364.6/7 0226757536
Torture -- France -- History. Criminal justice, Administration of -- France -- History.

HV8599.I7.R45 1994
Rejali, Darius M.
Torture & modernity: self, society, and state in modern Iran/ Darius M. Rejali. Boulder: Westview Press, 1994. xviii, 289 p.
93-008524 365/.645 081331660X
Torture -- Iran. Punishment -- Iran. Power (Social sciences) Iran -- Politics and government -- 1979-1997.

HV8599.S6.F67 1987
Foster, Don H.
Detention & torture in South Africa: psychological, legal & historical studies/ Don Foster; with contributions by Dennis Davis & research assistance from Diane Sandler. New York: St. Martin's Press, 1987. vi, 250 p.
86-033918 363.2/32 031200785X
Torture -- South Africa. Detention of persons -- South Africa. South Africa -- Social conditions -- 1961-

HV8613.S43
Scott, George Ryley, 1886-
The history of corporal punishment; a survey of flagellation in its historical, anthropological, and sociological aspects. London, T. W. Laurie ltd. [1938] xxiii, 261 p.
38-024534 343.2
Corporal punishment. Flagellants and flagellation.

HV8657 Criminal justice administration — Penology. Prisons. Corrections — Biography of famous prisoners, famous escapes, etc.

HV8657.J35 1989
Jail journeys: the English prison experience since 1918: modern prison writings/ selected and edited by Philip Priestley. London; Routledge, 1989. 197 p.
88-030666 365/.941 0415034582
Prisoners -- England -- Biography. Prisons -- England -- History -- 20th century. Prisons in literature.

HV8657.W35 1997
Walens, Susann.
War stories: an oral history of life behind bars/ Susann Walens. Westport, Conn.: Praeger, 1997. viii, 184 p.
96-021322 365/.4/092273 0275955753
Prisoners -- United States -- Biography.

HV8665-8666 Criminal justice administration — Penology. Prisons. Corrections — General works. Treatises

HV8665.B68
Bowker, Lee H.
Prisoner subcultures/ Lee H. Bowker. Lexington, Mass.: Lexington Books, c1977. xii, 173 p.
77-006182 365/.6 066901429X
Prisoners. Subculture.

HV8666.F6813 1977
Foucault, Michel.
Discipline and punish: the birth of the prison/ Michel Foucault; translated from the French by Alan Sheridan. New York: Pantheon Books, c1977. 333 p.
77-005301 365 0394499425
Prisons. Prison discipline. Punishment.

HV8675 Criminal justice administration — Penology. Prisons. Corrections — Theory of punishment

HV8675.A35 1991
Adler, Jacob, 1953-
The urgings of conscience: a theory of punishment/ Jacob Adler. Philadelphia: Temple University Press, 1992. ix, 316 p.
90-024041 364.6 0877228264
Punishment -- Philosophy.

HV8675.P75 1989
Primorac, Igor.
Justifying legal punishment/ Igor Primoratz. Atlantic Highlands, N.J.: Humanities Press International, 1989. x, 196 p.
88-009198 364.6 0391035746
Punishment -- Moral and ethical aspects. Punishment -- Philosophy.

HV8675.T44 1987
Ten, C. L.
Crime, guilt, and punishment: a philosophical introduction/ C.L. Ten. Oxford: Clarendon Press; 1987. 175 p.
87-005571   364.6   019875082X
Punishment. Criminal law. Criminal justice, Administration of.

HV8693-8749 Criminal justice administration — Penology. Prisons. Corrections — Forms of punishment (Modern)

HV8693.D85 2001
Duff, Antony.
Punishment, communication, and community/ R.A. Duff. Oxford; Oxford University Press, 2001. xx, 245 p.
99-049374   364.6   0195104293
Punishment -- Philosophy. Criminal justice, Administration of -- Philosophy. Sentences (Criminal procedure) -- Philosophy.

HV8694.G76 1998
Grossman, Mark.
Encyclopedia of capital punishment/ Mark Grossman. Santa Barbara, Calif.: ABC-CLIO, c1998. xii, 330 p.
98-021248   364.66/03 21   0874368715
Capital punishment -- Encyclopedias. Capital punishment -- History -- Encyclopedias. Executions and executioners -- Encyclopedias.

HV8694.P35 2001
Palmer, Louis J.
Encyclopedia of capital punishment in the United States/ by Louis J. Palmer, Jr. Jefferson, N.C.: McFarland, c2001. vii, 606 p.
00-058396   364.66/0973/03 21   0786409444
Capital punishment -- United States -- Encyclopedias.

HV8698.B47 1981
Black, Charles Lund, 1915-
Capital punishment: the inevitability of caprice and mistake/ Charles L. Black, Jr. New York: Norton, c1981. 174 p.
81-002824   364.6/6   0393013332
Capital punishment.

HV8698.S74 1998
Steffen, Lloyd H., 1951-
Executing justice: the moral meaning of the death penalty/ Lloyd Steffen. Cleveland, Ohio: Pilgrim Press, 1998. vi, 185 p.
98-036236   364.66/0973   0829812199
Capital punishment. Capital punishment -- United States.

HV8699.G3.E93 1996
Evans, Richard J.
Rituals of retribution: capital punishment in Germany, 1600-1987/ Richard J. Evans. Oxford; Oxford University Press, 1996. xxxii, 1014 p.
95-036714   364.6/6/0943   0198219687
Capital punishment -- Germany -- History.

HV8699.G8.G38 1994
Gatrell, V. A. C., 1941-
The hanging tree: execution and the English people, 1770-1868/ V.A.C. Gatrell. Oxford; Oxford University Press, 1994. xix, 634 p.
94-004108   364.6/6/0941   0198204132
Capital punishment -- Great Britain -- History. Executions and executioners -- Great Britain -- History. Hanging -- Great Britain -- History.

HV8699.G8.P67 1993
Potter, Harry.
Hanging in judgment: religion and the death penalty in England/ Harry Potter. New York: Continuum, 1993. 292 p.
93-036539   261.8/3366/0941   0826406262
Church and social problems -- Church of England -- History. Capital punishment -- England -- History.

HV8699.U5.B39 1987
Bedau, Hugo Adam.
Death is different: studies in the morality, law, and politics of capital punishment/ Hugo Adam Bedau. Boston: Northeastern University Press, c1987. xii, 307 p.
86-031266   364.6/6/0973   1555530087
Capital punishment -- United States. Capital punishment -- Moral and ethical aspects -- United States. Capital punishment -- Political aspects -- United States.

HV8699.U5.B47 1997
Bessler, John D.
Death in the dark: midnight executions in America/ John D. Bessler. Boston: Northeastern University Press, c1997. x, 319 p.
97-008110   364.66/0973 21   1555533221
Capital punishment -- United States. Executions and executioners -- United States.

HV8699.U5 C3 1997
Capital punishment in the United States: a documentary history/ edited by Bryan Vila and Cynthia Morris. Westport, Conn.: Greenwood Press, 1997. xl, 337 p.
96-051137   364.66/0973 21   0313299420
Capital punishment -- United States -- History -- Sources. Capital punishment -- Law and legislation -- United States -- History. Capital punishment -- Moral and ethical aspects -- United States.

HV8699.U5 D37 1997
The death penalty in America: current controversies/ edited by Hugo Adam Bedau. New York: Oxford University Press, 1997. xvii, 524 p.
96-007028   364.6/6/0973 20   0195104382
Capital punishment -- United States.

HV8699.U5.G76 1989
Gross, Samuel R.
Death & discrimination: racial disparities in capital sentencing/ Samuel R. Gross & Robert Mauro. Boston: Northeastern University Press, c1989. xvi, 268 p.
88-025269   364.6/6/0973   1555530400
Discrimination in capital punishment -- United States. Discrimination in criminal justice administration -- United States. Afro-American criminals -- Civil rights. United States -- Race relations.

HV8699.U5.M35 1994
Marquart, James W. 1954-
The rope, the chair, and the needle: capital punishment in Texas, 1923-1990/ James W. Marquart, Sheldon Ekland-Olson, Jonathan R. Sorensen. Austin: University of Texas Press, 1994. xii, 275 p.
93-015717   364.6/6/097640904   0292751583
Capital punishment -- Texas -- History -- 20th century.

HV8699.U5.M36 1989
Masur, Louis P.
Rites of execution: capital punishment and the transformation of American culture, 1776-1865/ Louis P. Masur. New York: Oxford University Press, 1989. viii, 208 p.
88-022719   364.6/6/0973   0195048997
Capital punishment -- United States -- History. Executions and executioners -- United States -- History.

HV8705.M38 1990
Mathiesen, Thomas.
Prison on trial: a critical assessment/ Thomas Mathiesen. London; Sage Publications, 1990. 184 p.
90-060966   365   0803982240
Imprisonment. Punishment -- Philosophy.

HV8749.G7.C76 1997
Crompton, Frank.
Workhouse children/ Frank Crompton. Thrupp, Stroud, Gloucestershire: Sutton, 1997. xvi, 271 p.
97-158877   0750912812
Workhouses -- England -- Worcestershire -- History -- 19th century. Poor children -- Institutional care -- England -- Worcestershire -- History -- 19th century. Children of prisoners -- England -- Worcestershire -- History -- 19th century.

HV8886-8929 Criminal justice administration — Penology. Prisons. Corrections — Prison methods and practice

HV8886.U5.C37 1992
Carlson, Bonnie E.
Inmates and their wives: incarceration and family life/ Bonnie E. Carlson and Neil Cervera. Westport, Conn.: Greenwood Press, 1992. 163 p.
92-019428   365/.6/019   0313274819
Prisoners -- United States -- Family relationships. Prisoners' spouses -- United States. Prisoners' families -- United States.

HV8929.A22.C87 2000
Curtin, Mary Ellen, 1961-
Black prisoners and their world, Alabama, 1865-1900/ Mary Ellen Curtin. Charlottesville: University Press of Virginia, c2000. xi, 261 p.
00-028214   365/.65 21   0813919819
Convict labor -- Alabama -- History. Afro-American prisoners -- Alabama -- Social conditions. Coal mines and mining -- Alabama -- Birmingham Region -- History.

HV8929.S92.M36 1996
Mancini, Matthew J.
One dies, get another: convict leasing in the American South, 1866-1928/ Matthew J. Mancini. Columbia, S.C.: University of South Carolina Press, c1996. xi, 283 p.
95-050208   365/.65 20   1570030839
Convict labor -- Southern States -- History. Prisoners -- Southern States -- History.

HV8950 Criminal justice administration — Penology. Prisons. Corrections — Penal colonies. Transportation

HV8950.A8.O95 1996
Oxley, Deborah, 1963-
Convict maids: the forced migration of women to Australia/ Deborah Oxley. Cambridge [England]; Cambridge University Press, 1996. xi, 339 p.
95-036710   364.6/8   0521441315
Convict labor -- Australia -- History. Penal colonies -- Australia -- History. Women prisoners -- Australia -- History.

HV8978 Criminal justice administration — Penology. Prisons. Corrections — Prison reform

HV8978.F7.W5 1972
Whitney, Janet, 1894-
Elizabeth Fry, Quaker heroine, by Janet Whitney. New York, B. Blom, 1972. 327 p.
72-083752   365/.924
Fry, Elizabeth (Gurney) -- 1780-1845. Prison reformers -- Biography.

HV8978.G38.B33 2000
Bacon, Margaret Hope.
Abby Hopper Gibbons: prison reformer and social activist/ Margaret Hope Bacon. Albany: State University of New York Press, c2000. xvii, 217 p.
99-039701   365/.7/092 21   079144497X
Gibbons, Abby Hopper, -- 1801-1893. Prison reformers -- United States -- Biography. Women social reformers -- United States -- Biography. Quaker women -- United States -- Biography.

HV8978.M34.G53 1995
Glaser, Daniel.
Preparing convicts for law-abiding lives: the pioneering penology of Richard A. McGee/ Daniel Glaser. Albany: State University of New York Press, c1995. xii, 224 p.
95-008938   365/.66 B 20   0791426955
McGee, Richard A. Prison reformers -- United States -- Biography. Criminals -- Rehabilitation -- United States. Prison administration -- United States -- Philosophy.

HV8978.V35.F74 1996
Freedman, Estelle B., 1947-
Maternal justice: Miriam Van Waters and the female reform tradition/ Estelle B. Freedman. Chicago: University of Chicago Press, c1996. xvii, 458 p.
95-049171   365/.43/0973 20   0226261492
Van Waters, Miriam. Prison reformers -- United States -- Biography. Women correctional personnel -- United States -- Biography. Women social reformers -- United States -- Biography.

HV9067-9147 Criminal justice administration — Penology. Prisons. Corrections — The Juvenile offender. Juvenile delinquency. Reform schools, etc.

HV9067.H6.E95 1990
Ewing, Charles Patrick, 1949-
When children kill: the dynamics of juvenile homicide/ Charles Patrick Ewing. Lexington, Mass.: Lexington Books, c1990. xvi, 171 p.
89-048514   364.1/523/083 20   0669218839
Juvenile homicide -- United States.

HV9067.H6.H44 1999
Heide, Kathleen M., 1954-
Young killers: the challenge of juvenile homicide/ Kathleen M. Heide. Thousand Oaks, Calif.: Sage Publications, c1999. xix, 299 p.
98-025341   364.15/23/083 21   0761900624
Juvenile homicide. Juvenile homicide -- Case studies.

HV9069.C514
Cicourel, Aaron Victor, 1928-
The social organization of juvenile justice [by] Aaron V. Cicourel. New York, Wiley [1967, c1968] xi, 345 p.
67-029850   364.36
Juvenile justice, Administration of. Juvenile delinquency. Social control.

HV9069.H312 2001
Handbook of youth and justice/ edited by Susan O. White. New York: Kluwer Academic/Plenum Publishers, c2001. xi, 442 p.
00-023857   364.36/0973 21   0306463393
Juvenile justice, Administration of. Juvenile courts. Criminal justice, Administration of.

HV9069.J57
Johnson, Richard E., 1949-
Juvenile delinquency and its origins: an integrated theoretical approach/ Richard E. Johnson. Cambridge [Eng.]; Cambridge University Press, 1979. x, 182 p.
78-067263   364.3/6   0521224772
Juvenile delinquency. Criminal behavior, Prediction of.

HV9069.J79 1982
Juvenile delinquency: a book of readings/ [edited by] Rose Giallombardo. New York: Wiley, 1982. viii, 591 p.
81-006927   364.3/6   0471083445
Juvenile delinquency. Juvenile justice, Administration of. Juvenile delinquency -- Prevention.

HV9069.R92 1998
Rutter, Michael, 1962-
Antisocial behavior by young people/ Michael Rutter, Henri Giller, Ann Hagell. Cambridge, UK; Cambridge University Press, 1998. xi, 478 p.
98-036581   364.36   0521641578
Juvenile delinquency. Conduct disorders in children.

HV9069.S246 1993
Sampson, Robert J.
Crime in the making: pathways and turning points through life/ Robert J. Sampson and John H. Laub. Cambridge, Mass.: Harvard University Press, 1993. ix, 309 p.
92-035723   364.3/6   0674176049
Glueck, Sheldon, -- 1896-- Unraveling juvenile delinquency. Juvenile delinquents -- Longitudinal studies. Criminals -- Longitudinal studies. Juvenile delinquency -- Longitudinal studies.

HV9069.S764 1982
Stott, D. H. 1909-
Delinquency: the problem and its prevention/ by Denis Stott. New York: SP Medical & Scientific Books, c1982. 345 p.
80-025928   364.3/6   0893351458
Juvenile delinquency. Juvenile delinquency -- Prevention. Juvenile delinquency -- United States.

HV9094.B7.G6
Glueck, Sheldon, 1896-
One thousand juvenile delinquents; their treatment by court and clinic, by Sheldon Glueck and Eleanor T. Glueck; with an introduction by Felix Frankfurter. Cambridge, Harvard University Press, 1934. xxix, 341 p.
34-005870   364
Criminal statistics -- Massachusetts -- Boston. Juvenile delinquency -- Boston. Judicial statistics -- Massachusetts -- Boston.

HV9094.B7.G63
Glueck, Sheldon, 1896-
Juvenile delinquents grown up [by] Sheldon and Eleanor Glueck. New York, Commonwealth Fund, 1940. viii, 330 p.
40-009761
Criminal statistics -- Massachusetts -- Boston. Juvenile delinquency -- Boston. Boston (Mass.) -- Juvenile courts.

HV9103.A545 1968
United States.
Juvenile delinquency (national, Federal, and youth-serving agencies). Hearings before the Subcommittee to Investigate Juvenile Delinquency of the Committee on the Judiciary, United States Senate, Ei New York, Greenwood Press [1968] iv, 734 p.
68-055115   364.36/0973
Juvenile delinquency -- United States.

HV9104.A77 1990
Alternative treatments for troubled youth: the case of diversion from the justice system/ William S. Davidson II ... [et al.]. New York: Plenum Press, c1990. xiv, 293 p.
89-071154   364.3/6/0973 20   0306434210
Juvenile delinquents -- Rehabilitation -- United States. Juvenile corrections -- United States. Social work with juvenile delinquents -- United States.

HV9104.B335 1991
Baker, Falcon O.
Saving our kids from delinquency, drugs, and despair/ Falcon Baker. New York, NY: Cornelia & Michael Bessie Books, 1991. xviii, 348 p.
89-046516   364.3/6/0973   0060391154
Juvenile delinquency -- United States -- Prevention. Youth -- Government policy -- United States.

HV9104.B58 1997
Bortner, M. A., 1948-
Youth in prison: we the people of Unit Four/ M.A.
Bortner and Linda M. Williams. New York:
Routledge, 1997. xvii, 245 p.
97-017823 364.36/0973 0415914388
*Juvenile corrections -- Government policy --
United States. Juvenile delinquents -- United States
-- Public opinion. Juvenile justice, Administration
of -- United States.*

HV9104.C59 1977
Cottle, Thomas J.
Children in jail: seven lessons in American justice/
Thomas J. Cottle. Boston: Beacon Press, c1977.
xiii, 178 p.
75-077440 365/.42/0973 0807004928
*Juvenile delinquency -- United States -- Case
studies. Juvenile corrections -- United States --
Case studies.*

HV9104.C85 1992
Currie, Elliott.
Dope and trouble: portraits of delinquent youth/
Elliott Currie. New York: Pantheon Books, c1991.
xxvi, 290 p.
90-052577 364.3/6/0973 20 0394561511
*Juvenile delinquents -- United States --
Interviews.*

HV9104.E438 1999
Elikann, Peter T.
Superpredators: the demonization of our children
by the law/ Peter Elikann. New York: Insight
Books, 1999.
99-012713 364.36/0973 0306460076
*Juvenile corrections -- United States. Juvenile
delinquency -- United States -- Prevention.
Problem youth -- Services for -- United States.*

HV9104.F44 1993
Feld, Barry C.
Justice for children: the right to counsel and the
juvenile courts/ Barry C. Feld. Boston:
Northeastern University Press, c1993. xvii, 329 p.
92-038429 364.3/6/0973 20 1555531571
*Juvenile justice, Administration of -- United
States. Juvenile courts -- United States.*

HV9104.G83 1996
Guarino-Ghezzi, Susan.
Balancing juvenile justice/ Susan Guarino-Ghezzi
and Edward J. Loughran. New Brunswick, N.J.:
Transaction Publishers, c1996. ix, 213 p.
95-018852 364.3/6/0973 20 1560002131
*Juvenile justice, Administration of -- United
States. Juvenile corrections -- United States.*

HV9104.J67 1995
Joseph, Janice.
Black youths, delinquency, and juvenile justice/
Janice Joseph. Westport, Conn.: Praeger, 1995. ix,
213 p.
95-007987 364.3/6/08996073 0275949095
*Afro-American juvenile delinquents -- United
States. Afro-American youth. Discrimination in
criminal justice administration -- United States.*

HV9104.K68 1988
Kramer, Rita.
At a tender age: violent youth and juvenile justice/
Rita Kramer. New York: Holt, c1988. viii, 309 p.
87-025202 364.3/6/0973 080500419X
*Juvenile justice, Administration of -- United
States -- Case studies. Juvenile delinquency -- Age
factors -- United States -- Case studies. Violent
crimes -- United States -- Case studies.*

HV9104.M28 1997
Maxson, Cheryl Lee.
Responding to troubled youth/ Cheryl L. Maxson
& Malcolm W. Klein. New York: Oxford
University Press, 1997. xi, 207 p.
96-023946 364.3/6/0973 0195098536
*Status offenders -- United States. Juvenile
delinquency -- United States -- Prevention.
Juvenile justice, Administration of -- United States.*

HV9104.M33 1988
McGarrell, Edmund F., 1956-
Juvenile correctional reform: two decades of policy
and procedural change/ Edmund F. McGarrell.
Albany, N.Y.: State University of New York Press,
c1988. xvi, 219 p.
87-024499 364.3/0973 088706759X
*Juvenile corrections -- United States. Juvenile
justice, Administration of -- United States. Juvenile
delinquents -- Deinstitutionalization -- United
States.*

HV9104.S323 1990
Schneider, Anne L.
Deterrence and juvenile crime: results from a
national policy experiment/ Anne L. Schneider.
New York: Springer-Verlag, c1990. x, 127 p.
89-011600 364.3/6/0973 20 0387970576
*Juvenile corrections -- United States --
Evaluation. Juvenile delinquency -- United States -
- Prevention.*

HV9104.S3286 1989
Schwartz, Ira M.
(In)justice for juveniles: rethinking the best
interests of the child/ by Ira M. Schwartz;
[foreword by Birch Bayh]. Lexington, Mass.:
Lexington Books, c1989. xviii, 184 p.
88-015049 364.3/6/0973 0669149640
*Juvenile justice, Administration of -- United
States.*

HV9104.S42 1998
Serious & violent juvenile offenders: risk factors
and successful interventions/ Rolf Loeber, David P.
Farrington, editors. Thousand Oaks, Calif.: Sage
Publications, c1998. xxv, 507 p.
97-033930 364.40973 21 0761912754
*Juvenile delinquency -- United States --
Prevention. Deviant behavior -- United States --
Prevention. Violent crimes -- United States --
Prevention.*

HV9104.T68 1996
Tracy, Paul E.
Continuity and discontinuity in criminal careers/
Paul E. Tracy and Kimberly Kempf-Leonard. New
York: Plenum Press, c1996. xvii, 263 p.
96-043659 364.3/6/0973 20 0306453479
*Juvenile delinquents -- United States --
Longitudinal studies. Criminals -- United States --
Longitudinal studies. Crime analysis -- United
States.*

HV9105.M5.G65 1992
Gold, Martin, 1931-
Personality and peer influence in juvenile
corrections/ Martin Gold and D. Wayne Osgood.
Westport, Conn.: Greenwood Press, 1992. xvii,
230 p.
92-009328 364.3/6/019 0313279705
*Juvenile delinquents -- Michigan -- Psychology --
Case studies. Juvenile corrections -- Michigan --
Psychological aspects -- Case studies. Peer
pressure in adolescence -- Michigan -- Case
studies.*

HV9105.N7.A67 1995
Alexander, Ruth M., 1954-
The girl problem: female sexual delinquency in
New York, 1900-1930/ Ruth M. Alexander. Ithaca:
Cornell University Press, 1995. x, 200 p.
94-047525 364.36/082 0801428211
*Female juvenile delinquents -- New York (State) -
- Case studies. Female juvenile delinquents -- New
York (State) -- Rehabilitation. Juvenile delinquency
-- New York (State) -- Case studies.*

HV9106.K2.F58 1998
Fleisher, Mark S.
Dead end kids: gang girls and the boys they know/
Mark S. Fleisher. Madison, Wis.: University of
Wisconsin Press, c1998. xii, 278 p.
98-015537   364.36/082/09778411   21
0299158802
*Female juvenile delinquents -- Missouri --
Kansas City -- Case studies. Gang members --
Missouri -- Kansas City -- Case studies. Problem
youth -- Missouri -- Kansas City -- Case studies.*

HV9106.N6.P56 1997
Pinderhughes, Howard.
Race in the hood: conflict and violence among
urban youth/ Howard Pinderhughes. Minneapolis,
Minn.: University of Minnesota Press, c1997. xi,
200 p.
97-013526 305.8/009747/1 21 0816629188
*Juvenile delinquency -- New York (State) -- New
York -- Case studies. Youth -- Crimes against --
New York (State) -- New York -- Case studies. Hate
crimes -- New York (State) -- New York -- Case
studies. New York (N.Y.) -- Race relations -- Case
studies.*

HV9106.N6.S85 1989
Sullivan, Mercer L., 1950-
"Getting paid": youth crime and work in the inner
city/ Mercer L. Sullivan. Ithaca: Cornell University
Press, 1989. viii, 275 p.
89-042882 364.3/6/097471 0801423708
*Juvenile delinquency -- New York (State) -- New
York -- Case studies. Urban youth -- Employment -
- New York (State) -- New York -- Case studies.
Brooklyn (New York, N.Y.)*

HV9145.A5.J35 1995
James, Oliver.
Juvenile violence in a winner-loser culture: socio-
economic and familial origins of the rise in
violence against the person/ Oliver James. London;
Free Association Books, 1995. ix, 171 p.
97-191467 1853433098
*Juvenile delinquency -- Great Britain. Violent
crimes -- Great Britain. Teenage boys -- Great
Britain -- Conduct of life.*

HV9145.E45 1995
Emler, Nicholas.
Adolescence and delinquency: the collective
management of reputation/ Nicholas Emler and
Stephen Reicher. Cambridge, Mass.: Blackwell,
c1995. xiv, 267 p.
95-015293 364.3/6/0941 20 0631138021
*Juvenile delinquency -- Great Britain --
Psychological aspects. Juvenile delinquents --
Great Britain -- Psychology. Adolescent
psychology -- Great Britain.*

HV9146.L65.S48 1999
Shore, Heather, 1964-
Artful dodgers: youth and crime in early nineteenth-century London/ Heather Shore. Rochester, NY: Royal Historical Society/Boydell Press, 1999. xiii, 193 p.
99-018224   364.36/09421/09034   0861932420
Juvenile delinquency -- England -- London -- History -- 19th century. Juvenile delinquency -- England -- London -- History -- 19th century -- Sources. Juvenile delinquents -- England -- London -- History -- 19th century.

HV9147.S4.M34 1995
Mahood, Linda, 1960-
Policing gender, class, and family: Britain, 1850-1940/ Linda Mahood. London: UCL Press, 1995. viii, 215 p.
96-158007   1857281888
Reformatories -- Scotland -- History. Juvenile delinquency -- Scotland -- History. Family policy -- Scotland -- History.

HV9275-9306 Criminal justice administration — Penology. Prisons. Corrections — Reformation and reclamation of adult prisoners

HV9275.B73 1989
Braithwaite, John.
Crime, shame, and reintegration/ John Braithwaite. Cambridge [Cambridgeshire]; Cambridge University Press, 1989. viii, 226 p.
88-007294   364.6/8   0521356687
Criminals -- Rehabilitation. Shame.

HV9276.5.B66 1994
Bondeson, Ulla, 1937-
Alternatives to imprisonment: intentions and reality/ Ulla V. Bondeson. Boulder: Westview Press, 1994. xv, 279 p.
94-002285   364.6   0813320119
Alternatives to imprisonment. Sentences (Criminal procedure)

HV9304.C365 1998
Carroll, Leo.
Lawful order: a case study of correctional crisis and reform/ Leo Carroll. New York: Garland Pub., 1998. xx, 348 p.
97-039224   365/.7/0973   0815316178
Prisons -- Government policy -- United States. Prisoners -- United States -- Social conditions. Prison administration -- United States.

HV9304.H57 1992
Hirsch, Adam Jay.
The rise of the penitentiary: prisons and punishment in early America/ Adam Jay Hirsch. New Haven: Yale University Press, c1992. xvi, 243 p.
91-037294   365/.974 20   0300042973
Corrections -- United States -- History. Corrections -- Massachusetts -- History. Prisons -- United States -- History.

HV9304.L56 2000
Lin, Ann Chih.
Reform in the making: the implementation of social policy in prison/ Ann Chih Lin. Princeton, N.J.: Princeton University Press, c2000. xiii, 213 p.
99-045173   365/.7/09573 21   0691009848
Prisons -- Government policy -- United States. Criminals -- Rehabilitation -- United States. Prisoners -- United States -- Social conditions.

HV9304.M67 1990
Morris, Norval.
Between prison and probation: intermediate punishments in a rational sentencing system/ Norval Morris, Michael Tonry. New York: Oxford University Press, 1990. 283 p.
89-023230   364.6/5/0973   019506108X
Corrections -- United States. Sentences (Criminal procedure) -- United States.

HV9304.O145 2001
O'Brien, Patricia, 1955-
Making it in the "free world": women in transition from prison/ Patricia O'Brien. Albany: State University of New York Press, c2001. xvi, 201 p.
00-036566   364.3/74 21   0791448614
Women ex-convicts -- Services for -- United States. Women ex-convicsts -- Rehabilitation -- United States. Prison psychology -- United States.

HV9304.P57 1994
Pisciotta, Alexander W.
Benevolent repression: social control and the American reformatory-prison movement/ Alexander W. Pisciotta. New York: New York University Press, c1994. xii, 197 p.
93-041515   365/.7/0973 20   0814766234
Criminals -- Rehabilitation -- United States -- History. Corrections -- United States -- History. Prisons -- United States -- History.

HV9304.W54 1996
Williams, Vergil L.
Dictionary of American penology/ Vergil L. Williams. Westport, Conn.: Greenwood Press, 1996. xii, 488 p.
96-003640   365/.973   0313266891
Corrections -- United States -- Dictionaries. Prisons -- United States -- Dictionaries. Criminal justice, Administration of -- United States -- Dictionaries.

HV9306.B7.S36 1991
Schneider, Eric C., 1951-
In the web of class: delinquents and reformers in Boston, 1810s-1930s/ Eric C. Schneider. New York: New York University Press, 1992. xiii, 260 p.
91-027617   364.3/6/0974461   0814779336
Social work with juvenile delinquents -- Massachusetts -- Boston -- History. Juvenile corrections -- Massachusetts -- Boston -- History. Child welfare -- Massachusetts -- Boston -- History.

HV9306.J472.P383 1989
Carney, Francis L.
Criminality and its treatment--the Patuxent experience/ Francis L. Carney. Malabar, Fla.: R.E. Krieger Pub. Co., 1989. viii, 159 p.
88-008444   364.3/01/9   0894643487
Criminals -- Rehabilitation -- Maryland -- Jessup. Criminal psychology. Social work with criminals -- Maryland -- Jessup.

HV9466-9813 Criminal justice administration — Penology. Prisons. Corrections — By region or country

HV9466.B55 2000
Blomberg, Thomas G.
American penology: a history of control/ Thomas G. Blomberg, Karol Lucken. Hawthorne, N.Y.: Aldine de Gruyter, c2000. xi, 259 p.
00-043031   365/.973 21   0202306372
Prisons -- United States -- History. Punishment -- United States -- History.

HV9466.C47 1998
Christianson, Scott.
With liberty for some: 500 years of imprisonment in America/ Scott Christianson. Boston, MA: Northeastern University Press, 1998. xix, 394 p.
98-023541   365/.973   1555533647
Prisoners -- United States -- History. Imprisonment -- United States -- History. Prisons -- United States -- History.

HV9466.F73
Freedman, Estelle B., 1947-
Their sisters' keepers: women's prison reform in America, 1830-1930/ Estelle B. Freedman. Ann Arbor: University of Michigan Press, c1981. viii, 248 p.
80-024918   365/.43/0973   0472100084
Reformatories for women -- United States -- History. Prison reformers -- United States -- History.

HV9466.K48 1991
Keve, Paul W.
Prisons and the American conscience: a history of U.S. federal corrections/ Paul W. Keve, with a foreword by Myrl E. Alexander. Carbondale: Southern Illinois University Press, 1991. xvi, 276 p.
91-002833   365/.32/0973   0809317109
Corrections -- United States -- History. Prisons -- United States -- History.

HV9466.O74 1999
O'Shea, Kathleen A.
Women and the death penalty in the United States, 1900-1998/ Kathleen A. O'Shea; foreword by Ann Patrick Conrad. Westport, Conn.: Praeger, 1999. xxiii, 404 p.
98-023550   364.66/082/0973   027595952X
Women prisoners -- United States -- History -- 20th century -- Case studies. Death row inmates -- United States -- History -- 20th century -- Case studies. Capital punishment -- United States -- History -- 20th century -- Case studies.

HV9466.W85 1994
Wright, Richard A. 1953-
In defense of prisons/ Richard A. Wright. Westport, Conn.: Greenwood Press, 1994. xi, 202 p.
93-015839   365/.973   0313279268
Prisons -- United States. Punishment -- United States.

HV9468.T57.A3 1997
Timilty, Joseph F., 1938-
Prison journal: an irreverent look at life on the inside/ Joseph Timilty with Jack Thomas. Boston: Northeastern University Press, c1997. ix, 253 p.
97-010280   365/.6/092 B 21   1555533124
Timilty, Joseph F., -- 1938- -- Diaries. Politicians -- Massachusetts -- Boston -- Diaries. Prisoners -- Pennsylvania -- Schuylkill County -- Diaries.

HV9469.A774 1991
American jails: public policy issues/ edited by Joel A. Thompson and G. Larry Mays. Chicago: Nelson-Hall, c1991. xv, 288 p.
90-013486   365/.973 20   083041262X
Prisons -- Government policy -- United States. Prison administration -- United States. Prisoners -- Health and hygiene -- United States.

HV9469.C65 1997
Collins, Catherine Fisher.
The imprisonment of African American women: causes, conditions, and future implications/ by Catherine Fisher Collins. Jefferson, N.C.: McFarland, c1997. xiv, 152 p.
96-039937 364.3/74/08996073 21 0786402366
Afro-American prisoners -- United States. Women prisoners -- United States. Prisons -- Government policy -- United States.

HV9469.H25 2001
Hallinan, Joseph T.
Going up the river: travels in a prison nation/ Joseph T. Hallinan. New York: Random House, c2001. xvii, 262 p.
00-062552 365/.973 21 0375502637
Imprisonment -- United States. Prisons -- United States.

HV9469.R93 1989
Ryan, Mick.
Privatization and the penal system: the American experience and the debate in Britain/ Mick Ryan and Tony Ward. New York: St. Martin's Press, 1989. xiv, 120 p.
89-006316 365/.973 0312032145
Prisons -- United States. Prisons -- Great Britain. Privatization -- United States.

HV9469.S86 1990
Sullivan, Larry E.
The prison reform movement: forlorn hope/ Larry E. Sullivan. Boston: Twayne Publishers, 1990. xi, 164 p.
89-027488 365/.7/0973 0805797394
Prisons -- United States -- History.

HV9469.U84 1996
Useem, Bert.
Resolution of prison riots: strategies and policies/ Bert Useem, Camille Graham Camp, George M. Camp. New York: Oxford University Press, 1996. vi, 223 p.
95-032607 365/.641 0195093240
Prison riots -- United States -- Case studies. Prison administration -- United States -- Case studies. Prison riots -- Prevention.

HV9469.Z56 1991
Zimring, Franklin E.
The scale of imprisonment/ Franklin E. Zimring & Gordon Hawkins. Chicago: University of Chicago Press, c1991. xiv, 244 p.
90-044613 365/.973 20 0226983536
Imprisonment -- United States. Prisons -- United States.

HV9471.E425 1996
Encyclopedia of American prisons/ editors, Marilyn D. McShane, Frank P. Williams III. New York: Garland Pub., 1996. xxv, 532 p.
95-041593 365/.973 0815313500
Prisons -- United States -- History -- Encyclopedias. Prison administration -- United States -- History -- Encyclopedias.

HV9471.E5 2001
Enos, Sandra, 1949-
Mothering from the inside: parenting in a women's prison/ Sandra Enos. Albany, NY: State University of New York Press, c2001. viii, 176 p.
00-032952 362.7 21 0791448495
Women prisoners -- United States. Absentee mothers -- United States. Motherhood.

HV9471.H29 1995
Hamm, Mark S.
The abandoned ones: the imprisonment and uprising of the Mariel boat people/ Mark S. Hamm. Boston: Northeastern University Press, c1995. xv, 235 p.
94-025285 365/.641 20 1555532306
Prisoners -- Cuba. Cubans -- United States. Prison riots -- Louisiana -- Oakdale.

HV9471.J32 1999
Jacobson-Hardy, Michael, 1951-
Behind the razor wire: portrait of a contemporary American prison system/ photographs and text by Michael Jacobson-Hardy; foreword by Angela Y. Davis; essays by John Edgar Wideman, Marc Mauer, and James Gilligan. New York: New York University Press, c1999. xviii, 134 p.
98-024771 365/.973 21 0814742408
Prisons -- United States. Prisons -- United States -- Pictorial works. Criminal justice, Administration of -- United States.

HV9471.S59 2000
Skotnicki, Andrew.
Religion and the development of the American penal system/ Andrew Skotnicki. Lanham, Md.: University Press of America, c2000. 188 p.
00-060712 365/.973 21 0761818103
Prisons -- United States -- History. Imprisonment -- United States -- History. Imprisonment -- Religious aspects -- Protestantism.

HV9471.U84 1989
Useem, Bert.
States of siege: U.S. prison riots, 1971-1986/ Bert Useem and Peter Kimball. New York: Oxford University Press, 1989. vi, 278 p.
88-018792 365/.641 0195057112
Prison riots -- United States -- Case studies.

HV9471.Z55 1995
Zimring, Franklin E.
Incapacitation: penal confinement and the restraint of crime/ Franklin E. Zimring, Gordon Hawkins. New York: Oxford University Press, 1995. ix, 188 p.
94-008630 365/.973 0195092333
Imprisonment -- United States.

HV9475.C3.C83 1994
Cummins, Eric, 1949-
The rise and fall of California's radical prison movement/ Eric Cummins. Stanford, Calif.: Stanford University Press, 1994. xi, 319 p.
93-017831 365/.9794 0804722315
Prisoners -- California. Prisoners' writings, American -- California. Prison riots -- California.

HV9475.C82.N537 1997
Rierden, Andi, 1953-
The farm: life inside a women's prison/ Andi Rierden. Amherst: University of Massachusetts Press, c1997. xviii, 193 p.
96-051511 365/.43/097465 21 1558490795
Reformatories for women -- Connecticut.

HV9475.F6.M55 2000
Miller, Vivien M. L.
Crime, sexual violence, and clemency: Florida's pardon board and penal system in the Progressive Era/ Vivien M.L. Miller; foreword by John David Smith. Gainesville: University Press of Florida, c2000. xiv, 366 p.
00-034413 365/.9759 21 0813018080
Prisons -- Florida -- History. Prisoners -- Government policy -- Florida -- History. Prison administration -- Florida -- History. Florida -- Race relations. Florida -- Social policy.

HV9475.M52.M533 1996
Bright, Charles, 1943-
The powers that punish: prison and politics in the era of the "Big house," 1920-1955/ Charles Bright. Ann Arbor: University of Michigan Press, c1996. 326 p.
96-009954 365/.9774 20 0472107321
Prisons -- Michigan -- Jackson -- History. Corrections -- Political aspects -- Michigan -- History. Michigan -- Politics and government.

HV9475.M72.M576 1996
Oshinsky, David M., 1944-
Worse than slavery: Parchman Farm and the ordeal of Jim Crow justice/ David M. Oshinsky. New York: Free Press, c1996. xiv, 306 p.
95-052880 365/.9762 20 0684822989
Criminal justice, Administration of -- Mississippi -- History. Prisoners -- Mississippi -- History.

HV9475.N6.D53 1996
Diaz-Cotto, Juanita, 1953-
Gender, ethnicity, and the state: Latina and Latino prison politics/ Juanita Diaz-Cotto. Albany: State University of New York Press, c1996. xvii, 480 p.
95-016255 365/.6/089680747 20 079142815X
Corrections -- New York (State) Discrimination in criminal justice administration -- New York (State) Hispanic American prisoners -- New York (State)

HV9475.N72.S563 2000
Conover, Ted.
Newjack: guarding Sing Sing/ Ted Conover. New York: Random House, c2000. 321 p.
99-087895 365/.9/2 21 0375501770
Conover, Ted. Prisons -- New York (State) -- Ossining. Correctional personnel -- New York (State) -- Ossining -- Biography. Prisons -- New York (State) -- Ossining -- Officials and employees -- Biography.

HV9475.N82.B534 1999
Girshick, Lori B.
No safe haven: stories of women in prison/ Lori B. Girshick. Boston: Northeastern University Press, c1999. x, 201 p.
98-048852 365/.975688 21 1555533736
Women prisoners -- North Carolina -- Interviews. Women prisoners -- North Carolina -- Social conditions.

HV9475.S65.M94 1998
Myers, Martha A.
Race, labor, and punishment in the new South/ Martha A. Myers. Columbus: Ohio State University Press, c1998. ix, 326 p.
98-020124 364.6/0975 21 0814207979
Criminal justice, Administration of -- Southern States -- History. Convict labor -- Southern States -- History. Prisoners -- Southern States -- History.

HV9475.T4.C76 1989
Crouch, Ben M.
An appeal to justice: litigated reform of Texas prisons/ Ben M. Crouch and James W. Marquart; foreword by John Irwin. Austin: University of Texas Press, 1989. xiii, 280 p.
88-029476 364/.973 0292704070
Prisons -- Texas. Prison administration -- Texas. Prisons -- Law and legislation -- Texas.

HV9509.O5.O54 1998
Oliver, Peter, 1939-
'Terror to evil-doers': prisons and punishment in
nineteenth-century Ontario/ Peter Oliver. Toronto;
Published for the Osgoode Society for Canadian L
c1998. xxvi, 575 p.
98-197057   365/.9713/09024 21   0802043453
Prisons -- Ontario -- History -- 19th century.
Punishment -- Ontario -- History -- 19th century.

HV9649.E5.Z43 1991
Zedner, Lucia.
Women, crime, and custody in Victorian England/
Lucia Zedner. Oxford: Clarendon Press; 1991.
364 p.
92-136980   364.3/74/082   0198202644
*Women prisoners -- England -- History -- 19th
century. Female offenders -- England -- History --
19th century.*

HV9650.L72.F533 1996
Brown, Roger Lee.
A history of the Fleet Prison, London: the anatomy
of the Fleet/ Roger Lee Brown. Lewiston: Edwin
Mellen Press, c1996. xviii, 353 p.
96-020614   365/.94212 20   077348762X
Fleet Prison (London, England) -- History.

HV9650.3.C377 2000
Carroll-Burke, Patrick.
Colonial discipline: the making of the Irish convict
system/ Patrick Carroll-Burke. Dublin; Four Courts
Press, c2000. 256 p.
2001-265203   1851824588
Prisoners -- Ireland -- History -- 18th century.
Prisoners -- Ireland -- History -- 19th century.
Prisoners -- Ireland -- History -- 18th century.

HV9712.A63 1996
Adams, Bruce Friend.
The politics of punishment: prison reform in
Russia, 1863-1917/ Bruce F. Adams. DeKalb, Ill.:
Northern Illinois University Press, 1996. viii,
237 p.
96-010422   365/.7/0947   087580215X
Prisons -- Russia -- History -- 19th century.
*Prison administration -- Russia -- History -- 19th
century. Prisons -- Government policy -- Russia --
History -- 19th century.*

HV9713.S59 1996
Smith, Theresa C., 1951-
No asylum: state psychiatric repression in the
former USSR/ Theresa C. Smith; in collaboration
with Thomas A. Oleszczuk. New York: New York
University Press, 1996. xi, 290 p.
96-016533   365/.46/0947   081478061X
*Political prisoners -- Soviet Union. Psychiatric
hospitals -- Soviet Union. Dissenters -- Soviet
Union.*

HV9742.5.C84.A313 1998
Cuevas, Tomasa, 1917-
Prison of women: testimonies of war and resistance
in Spain, 1939-1975/ Tomasa Cuevas; translated
and edited by Mary E. Giles. Albany: State
University of New York Press, 1998. xxii, 247 p.
97-033352   365/.45/0820946   0791438570
*Cuevas, Tomasa, -- 1917-   Women political
prisoners -- Spain -- Biography. Francoism.
Reformatories for women -- Spain. Spain -- Politics
and government -- 1939-1975.*

HV9800.5.Z55 2001
Zinoman, Peter, 1965-
The colonial Bastille: a history of imprisonment in
Vietnam, 1862-1940/ Peter Zinoman Berkeley:
University of California Press, c2001 xix, 351 p.
00-031690   365/.9597 21   0520224124
*Prisons -- Vietnam -- History. National
liberation movements -- Vietnam -- History.
Nationalism -- Vietnam -- History.*

HV9813.J64 1996
Johnson, Elmer Hubert.
Japanese corrections: managing convicted
offenders in an orderly society/ Elmer H. Johnson.
Carbondale: Southern Illinois University Press,
c1996. xviii, 336 p.
95-020808   364.6/0952 20   0809317362
*Corrections -- Japan. Correctional institutions --
Japan. Prisons -- Japan.*

HV9950-9956 Criminal justice administration — By region or country — United States

HV9950.B49 1998
Benson, Bruce, 1949-
To serve and protect: privatization and community
in criminal justice/ Bruce L. Benson; foreword by
Marvin E. Wolfgang. New York: New YorK
University Press, c1998. xxviii, 372 p.
98-019688   364.973 21   0814713270
*Criminal justice, Administration of -- United
States. Privatization -- United States. Police --
Contracting out -- United States.*

HV9950.C34 1993
Calder, James D.
The origins and development of federal crime
control policy: Herbert Hoover's initiatives/ James
D. Calder; foreword by George H. Nash. Westport,
Conn.: Praeger, 1993. xiv, 311 p.
93-020298   363.2/0973   0275942848
*Hoover, Herbert, -- 1874-1964.   Criminal justice,
Administration of -- United States -- History --
20th century.   United States -- Politics and
government -- 1929-1933.*

HV9950.C58 1999
Cole, David, 1958-
No equal justice: race and class in the American
criminal justice system/ David Cole. New York:
New Press: c1999. 218 p.
00-276744   1565844734
*Discrimination in criminal justice administration
-- United States. Criminal justice, Administration
of -- United States. Race discrimination -- United
States.*

HV9950.D94 2000
Dyer, Joel.
The perpetual prisoner machine: how America
profits from crime/ by Joel Dyer. Boulder, Colo:
Westview Press, 2000. x, 318 p.
99-045576   364.973   0813335078
*Criminal justice, Administration of -- Economic
aspects -- United States. Crime -- Economic
aspects -- United States. Fear of crime -- United
States.*

HV9950.G38 1995
Gaubatz, Kathlyn Taylor.
Crime in the public mind/ Kathlyn Taylor Gaubatz.
Ann Arbor: University of Michigan Press, c1995.
246 p.
94-025221   364.973 20   0472105825
*Criminal justice, Administration of -- United
States -- Public opinion. Crime -- United States --
Public opinion. Public opinion -- California --
Oakland.*

HV9950.G47 1999
Gerber, Rudolph Joseph, 1938-
Cruel and usual: our criminal injustice system/
Rudolph J. Gerber; foreword by Patrick M.
Brennan. Westport, Conn.: Praeger, 1999.
99-014853   364.973   0275964752
*Criminal justice, Administration of -- Moral and
ethical aspects -- United States. Imprisonment --
Moral and ethical aspects -- United States.
Criminal law -- United States.*

HV9950.G65 1990b
Goldstein, Herman, 1931-
Problem-oriented policing/ Herman Goldstein.
Philadelphia: Temple University Press, 1990. xv,
206 p.
89-020577   363.2/0973   0877227195
*Criminal justice, Administration of -- United
States. Police -- United States. Crime prevention --
United States -- Citizen participation.*

HV9950.H87 1996
Hutchinson, Earl Ofari.
Betrayed: a history of presidential failure to protect
Black lives/ Earl Ofari Hutchinson. Boulder, Colo.:
Westview Press, 1996. x, 262 p.
95-052170   364.973/089/96073   0813324653
*Discrimination in criminal justice administration
-- United States -- History -- 20th century. Afro-
Americans -- Crimes against -- History -- 20th
century. Presidents -- United States -- History --
20th century.*

HV9950.L63 1999
Lock, Shmuel, 1969-
Crime, public opinion, and civil liberties: the
tolerant public/ Shmuel Lock. Westport, Conn.:
Praeger, 1999. 267 p.
98-033606   364.973   0275964329
*Criminal justice, Administration of -- Public
opinion. Crime -- Public opinion. Criminal law --
Public opinion.*

HV9950.M26 1993
Mann, Coramae Richey, 1931-
Unequal justice: a question of color/ Coramae
Richey Mann. Bloomington: Indiana University
Press, c1993. xiv, 301 p.
92-025110   364/.089/96073 20   0253336767
*Discrimination in criminal justice administration
-- United States. Minorities -- United States.
United States -- Race relations.*

HV9950.M3 1996
Martin, Susan Ehrlich.
Doing justice, doing gender/ Susan Ehrlich Martin,
Nancy C. Jurik. Thousand Oaks, Calif.: Sage
Publications, c1996. ix, 270 p.
95-041817   364/.082 20   0803951973
*Sex discrimination in criminal justice
administration -- United States. Policewomen --
United States. Women correctional personnel --
United States.*

HV9950.M55 1996
Miller, Jerome G., 1931-
Search and destroy: African-American males in the criminal justice system/ Jerome G. Miller. Cambridge; Cambridge University Press, 1996. xiv, 304 p.
95-026128   364/.08996073   0521460212
Discrimination in criminal justice administration -- United States. Criminal justice, Administration of -- United States. Afro-American criminals.

HV9950.R87 1998
Russell, Katheryn K., 1961-
The color of crime: racial hoaxes, white fear, black protectionism, police harassment, and other macroaggressions/ Katheryn K. Russell. New York: New York University Press, c1998. xvi, 203 p.
97-033806   305.8 21   0814774717
Discrimination in criminal justice administration -- United States. Crime and race -- United States. Afro-American criminals.

HV9950.U85 1999
Uviller, H. Richard.
The tilted playing field: is criminal justice unfair?/ H. Richard Uviller. New Haven: Yale University Press, c1999. ix, 314 p.
98-046459   364/.089/00973 21   0300075847
Discrimination in criminal justice administration -- United States. Criminal justice, Administration of -- Moral and ethical aspects -- United States.

HV9950.W56 1998
Windlesham, David James George Hennessy, 1932-
Politics, punishment, and populism/ Lord Windlesham. New York: Oxford University Press, 1998. vi, 278 p.
97-051415   364.973   0195115309
Criminal justice, Administration of -- United States. Crime prevention -- United States. Gun control -- United States.

HV9956.N48.D35 1994
Daly, Kathleen, 1948-
Gender, crime, and punishment/ Kathleen Daly. New Haven: Yale University Press, c1994. xi, 337 p.
94-001582   364/.082 20   0300059558
Sex discrimination in criminal justice administration -- Connecticut -- New Haven. Female offenders -- Connecticut -- New Haven. Women prisoners -- Connecticut -- New Haven.

HV9960 Criminal justice administration — By region or country — Other regions or countries, A-Z

HV9960.E86.C58 1990
Clutterbuck, Richard L.
Terrorism, drugs, and crime in Europe: after 1992/ Richard Clutterbuck. London; Routledge, 1990. xx, 231 p.
90-008279   364.94   0415054435
Criminal justice, Administration of -- European Economic Community countries. Terrorism -- European Economic Community countries. Drug traffic -- European Economic Community countries.

HV9960.G7.R87 1993
Rutherford, Andrew, 1940-
Criminal justice and the pursuit of decency/ Andrew Rutherford; foreword by Lord Scarman. Oxford; Oxford University Press, 1993. xii, 199 p.
92-001686   364.941   0192158961
Criminal justice, Administration of -- Moral and ethical aspects -- Great Britain. Criminal justice personnel -- Great Britain -- Interviews.

HV9960.G72.E544 2001
Follett, Richard R., 1963-
Evangelicalism, penal theory, and the politics of criminal law reform in England, 1808-30/ Richard R. Follett. Houndsmills, England: Palgrave c2001. xi, 231 p.
00-059151   364.942/09/034 21   0333803884
Criminal justice, Administration of -- England -- History -- 19th century. Criminal law -- England -- History -- 19th century. Social reformers -- England -- History -- 19th century. Great Britain -- Politics and government -- 1800-1837.

HV9960.G72.K463 1991
Conley, Carolyn, 1953-
The unwritten law: criminal justice in Victorian Kent/ Carolyn A. Conley. New York: Oxford University Press, 1991. ix, 244 p.
90-032733   364.9422/3/09034   0195063384
Criminal justice, Administration of -- England -- Kent -- History -- 19th century.

HV9960.R9.F7 1999
Frank, Stephen, 1955-
Crime, cultural conflict, and justice in rural Russia, 1856-1914/ Stephen P. Frank. Berkeley, Calif.: University of California Press, 1999. xxii, 352 p.
98-041218   364.947/09034   0520213416
Criminal justice, Administration of -- Russia -- History -- 19th century. Criminal justice, Administration of -- Russia -- History -- 20th century. Rural crimes -- Russia. Russia -- Rural conditions. Russia -- Social conditions -- 1801-1917.

HX Socialism. Communism. Anarchism

HX11 Societies. Associations

HX11.I5.M43 1998
Messer-Kruse, Timothy.
The Yankee International: Marxism and the American reform tradition, 1848-1876/ Timothy Messer-Kruse. Chapel Hill: University of North Carolina Press, c1998. xi, 319 p.
97-036875   324.1/7 21   0807824038
Socialism -- United States -- History -- 19th century. Radicalism -- United States -- History -- 19th century. Social reformers -- United States -- History -- 19th century.

HX17 Dictionaries. Encyclopedias

HX17.D63 1997
Docherty, J. C.
Historical dictionary of socialism/ James C. Docherty. Lanham, Md.: Scarecrow Press, 1997. xvi, 395 p.
97-015782   335/.003   0810833581
Socialism -- History -- 19th century -- Dictionaries. Socialism -- History -- 20th century -- Dictionaries.

HX21 History — General works

HX21.C35 2000
Callaghan, John
The retreat of social democracy/ John Callaghan. New York: Manchester University Press, 2000. xiv, 255 p.
00-021788   335/.009   0719050316
Socialism -- History.

HX39-44 History — By period — Modern

HX39.W17 1995
Walicki, Andrzej.
Marxism and the leap to the kingdom of freedom: the rise and fall of the Communist utopia/ Andrzej Walicki. Stanford, Calif.: Stanford University Press, 1995. xii, 641 p.
94-032893   320.5/31/09   0804723842
Socialism -- History. Communism -- History. Freedom -- History.

HX39.5.K388 1995
Kemple, Thomas M., 1962-
Reading Marx writing: melodrama, the market, and the "Grundrisse"/ Thomas M. Kemple. Stanford, Calif.: Stanford University Press, 1995. xviii, 274 p.
94-042468   335.4/12   0804724083
Marx, Karl, -- 1818-1883. Marx, Karl, -- 1818-1883. -- Grundrisse der Kritik der politischen Okonomie.

HX40.F86513 1999
Furet, Francois, 1927-
The passing of an illusion: the idea of communism in the twentieth century/ Francois Furet; translated by Deborah Furet. Chicago: University of Chicago Press, c1999. xiii, 596 p.
98-042109   335.4/09/04 21   0226273407
Communism -- History -- 20th century. Communism -- Soviet Union -- History.

HX40.H5673 1998
Hoberman, J.
The Red Atlantis: communist culture in the absence of communism/ J. Hoberman. Philadelphia: Temple University Press, 1998. 315 p.
98-016178   335.43/097   1566396433
Communism -- History -- 20th century. Communist aesthetics -- History -- 20th century.

HX40.L248 1996
Lane, David Stuart.
The rise and fall of state socialism: industrial society and the socialist state/ David Lane. Cambridge, UK: Polity Press; c1996. viii, 233 p.
96-042467 320.5/32 20 074560742X
Communism. Communism -- History -- 20th century. Post-communism.

HX40.L7913 1991
Lukacs, Gyorgy, 1885-1971.
The process of democratization/ Georg Lukacs; translated by Susanne Bernhardt and Norman Levine; with an introduction by Norman Levine. Albany: State University of New York Press, c1991. x, 179 p.
90-047554 320.5/31/09 0791407616
Socialism -- History -- 20th century. Capitalism -- History -- 20th century. Democracy -- History -- 20th century.

HX44.B346 1991
Barnard, F. M.
Pluralism, socialism, and political legitimacy: reflections on opening up communism/ F.M. Barnard. Cambridge [England]; Cambridge University Press, 1991. xii, 189 p.
91-008143 320.5 0521402522
Communism. Socialism. Pluralism. Soviet Union -- Politics and government -- 1985- Europe, Eastern -- Politics and government -- 1989-

HX51 History — Special systems and movements — Christian socialism

HX51.L494 1999
Latham, J. E. M., 1928-
Search for a new Eden: James Pierrepont Greaves (1777-1842), the sacred socialist and his followers/ J.E.M. Latham. Madison: Fairleigh Dickinson University Press; London; c1999. 292 p.
99-024087 335/.7/092 B 21 0838638090
Greaves, James Pierrepont, -- 1777-1842. Socialism, Christian.

HX73 General works — 1981-

HX73.K6715 1992
Kornai, Janos.
The socialist system: the political economy of communism/ Janos Kornai. Princeton, N.J.: Princeton University Press, c1992. xxviii, 644 p.
91-037866 335.43 0691042985
Communism.

HX73.P54 1995
Pierson, Christopher.
Socialism after communism: the new market socialism/ Christopher Pierson. University Park, Pa.: Pennsylvania State University Press, c1995. x, 249 p.
94-047518 335 0271014784
Socialism. Post-communism. Mixed economy.

HX73.S385 1995
Schwartz, Joseph M., 1954-
The permanence of the political: a democratic critique of the radical impulse to transcend politics/ Joseph M. Schwartz. Princeton, N.J.: Princeton University Press, c1995. xii, 336 p.
95-003045 335 0691033579
Socialism. Social conflict. Social justice.

HX73.S499 1995
Sherman, Howard J.
Reinventing marxism/ Howard J. Sherman. Baltimore: Johns Hopkins University Press, 1995. xviii, 366 p.
95-011951 335.4 0801850762
Socialism. Post-communism. Communism.

HX81-86 By region or country — America — United States

HX81.M57 1999
Mishler, Paul C.
Raising reds: the young pioneers, radical summer camps, and Communist political culture in the United States/ Paul C. Mishler. New York: Columbia University Press, c1999. x, 172 p.
98-039593 324.273/75/09 21 0231110448
Communism and youth -- United States -- History. Children -- United States -- Social conditions. Children and politics -- United States -- History.

HX83.B44 1992
Berry, Brian Joe Lobley, 1934-
America's utopian experiments: communal havens from long-wave crises/ Brian J.L. Berry. Hanover, NH: Dartmouth College: c1992. xviii, 271 p.
92-0001 335/.973 0874515890
Utopias -- History. Collective settlements -- United States -- History. Sects -- United states -- History.

HX83.L54 2000
Lieberman, Robbie, 1954-
The strangest dream: communism, anticommunism and the U.S. peace movement 1945-1963/ Robbie Lieberman. New York: Syracuse University Press, 2000. xvii, 244 p.
99-086248 335.43/0973 0815628412
Communism -- United States -- History. Peace movements -- United States -- History -- 20th century. War and socialism -- United States -- History.

HX83.L56 1997
Lloyd, Brian, 1954-
Left out: pragmatism, exceptionalism, and the poverty of American Marxism, 1890-1922/ Brian Lloyd. Baltimore, MD: Johns Hopkins University Press, c1997. x, 472 p.
96-047995 335.43/4/0973 21 0801855411
Communism -- United States -- History. Socialism -- United States -- History. Radicalism -- United States -- History.

HX83.R44 1998
Red diapers: growing up in the communist left/ edited by Judy Kaplan and Linn Shapiro. Urbana: University of Illinois Press, c1998. xi, 320 p.
98-008905 335.4/092/273 21 0252021614
Communism -- United States -- History -- 20th century -- Sources. Children and politics -- History -- 20th century -- Sources.

HX83.S665 1998
Solomon, Mark I.
The cry was unity: communists and African Americans, 1917-36/ Mark Solomon. Jackson: University Press of Mississippi, c1998. xxviii, 403 p.
98-016013 335.43/089/96073 21 157806094X
Communism -- United States -- History. Afro-American communists -- History. Afro-Americans -- Politics and government. United States -- Race relations.

HX84.B69.R93 1997
Ryan, James G., 1947-
Earl Browder: the failure of American communism/ James G. Ryan. Tuscaloosa, Ala.: University of Alabama Press, c1997. xi, 332 p.
96-025763 335.43/092 B 20 0817308431
Browder, Earl, -- 1891-1973. Communists -- United States -- Biography. Communism -- United States -- History -- 20th century.

HX84.D28.H67 1993
Horne, Gerald.
Black liberation/red scare: Ben Davis and the Communist Party/ Gerald Horne. Newark, Del.: University of Delaware Press, 1993. 455 p.
92-053778 324.273/75/08996073 0874134722
Davis, Benjamin J. -- (Benjamin Jefferson), -- 1903-1964. Afro-American communists -- United States -- Biography. Communism -- United States -- History.

HX84.D3.A4 1995
Debs, Eugene V. 1855-1926.
Gentle rebel: letters of Eugene V. Debs/ edited by J. Robert Constantine. Urbana: University of Illinois Press, c1995. xxxviii, 312 p.
93-048601 335/.3/092 0252020189
Debs, Eugene V. -- (Eugene Victor), -- 1855-1926 -- Correspondence. Socialists -- United States -- Correspondence. Socialism -- United States -- History -- Sources. United States -- Politics and government -- 1865-1933 -- Sources.

HX84.F5.C36 1995
Camp, Helen C.
Iron in her soul: Elizabeth Gurley Flynn and the American Left/ Helen C. Camp. Pullman, Wash.: WSU Press, c1995. xxviii, 396 p.
94-043829 335/.0092 0874221056
Flynn, Elizabeth Gurley. Women labor leaders -- United States -- Biography. Communists -- United States -- Biography.

HX84.F6.B37 1999
Barrett, James R., 1950-
William Z. Foster and the tragedy of American radicalism/ James R. Barrett . Urbana: University of Illinois Press, c1999. xiii, 352 p.
99-006192 331.88/092 B 21 0252020464
Foster, William Z., -- 1881-1961. Communists -- United States -- Biography. Labor leaders -- United States -- Biography. Radicalism -- United States -- History -- 20th century.

HX84.F6.J65 1994
Johanningsmeier, Edward P., 1956-
Forging American communism: the life of William Z. Foster/ Edward P. Johanningsmeier. Princeton, N.J.: Princeton University Press, c1994. xiv, 433 p.
93-027539 324.273/75/092 0691033315
Foster, William Z., -- 1881-1961. Communists -- United States -- Biography.

HX84.H43.A3 1990
Healey, Dorothy.
Dorothy Healey remembers a life in the American communist party/ Dorothy Healey, Maurice Isserman. New York: Oxford University Press, 1990. viii, 263 p.
89-028394 335.43/092 0195038193
Healey, Dorothy. Communists -- United States -- Biography.

HX84.O39.B83 1996
Buckingham, Peter H., 1948-
Rebel against injustice: the life of Frank P. O'Hare/ Peter H. Buckingham. Columbia: University of Missouri Press, c1996. xii, 276 p.
95-053146   335/.0092 B 20   0826210554
O'Hare, Frank P., -- d. 1960. Socialists -- United States -- Biography.

HX84.R4.H66 1990
Homberger, Eric.
John Reed/ Eric Homberger. Manchester; Manchester University Press; c1990. 248 p.
90-038282   070/.92   0719021944
Reed, John, -- 1887-1920. Communists -- United States -- Biography.

HX84.R43.D45 1997
Denton, James A. 1936-
Rocky Mountain radical: Myron W. Reed, Christian Socialist/ James A. Denton. Albuquerque: University of New Mexico Press, c1997. x, 206 p.
97-004846   335/.0092 21   0826318142
Reed, Myron W., -- 1836-1899. Socialists -- United States -- Biography. Socialism, Christian -- United States -- History -- 19th century.

HX84.S42.A3 1998
Schrank, Robert.
Wasn't that a time?: growing up radical and red in America/ Robert Schrank. Cambridge, Mass.: MIT Press, c1998. xvi, 452 p.
98-009714   335/.0092 B 21   0262193892
Schrank, Robert. Socialists -- United States -- Biography. Radicals -- United States -- Biography. Labor movement -- United States -- History -- 20th century.

HX86.E58 1998
Encyclopedia of the American left/ edited by Mari Jo Buhle, Paul Buhle, and Dan Georgakas. New York: Oxford University Press, 1998. xxv, 988 p.
98-030423   335/.00973   0195120884
Socialism -- United States -- Dictionaries. Communism -- United States -- Dictionaries. New Left -- United States -- Dictionaries.

HX86.O35 1995
Hutchinson, Earl Ofari.
Blacks and reds: race and class in conflict, 1919-1990/ Earl Ofari Hutchinson. East Lansing: Michigan State University Press, 1995. 338 p.
94-045031   335.43/089/96073   0870133616
Communism -- United States -- History. Afro-American communists -- History. Afro-Americans -- Politics and government.

HX113-198 By region or country — Other regions or countries — Latin America

HX113.C37 1992
Carr, Barry.
Marxism & communism in twentieth-century Mexico/ Barry Carr. Lincoln: University of Nebraska Press, c1992. xiii, 437 p.
92-005890   335.4/3/0972   0803214588
Socialism -- Mexico -- History -- 20th century. Communism -- Mexico -- History -- 20th century. Mexico -- Politics and government -- 20th century.

HX158.5.B45 1994
Bengelsdorf, Carollee.
The problem of democracy in Cuba: between vision and reality/ Carollee Bengelsdorf. New York: Oxford University Press, 1994. viii, 229 p.
93-008052   335.43/097291   0195058267
Communism -- Cuba -- History. Democracy -- Cuba -- History.

HX158.5.E35 1994
Eckstein, Susan, 1942-
Back from the future: Cuba under Castro/ Susan Eva Eckstein. Princeton, N.J.: Princeton University Press, c1994. xix, 286 p.
93-045884   338.97291   0691034451
Communism -- Cuba. Cuba -- Social policy. Cuba -- Economic policy. Cuba -- Politics and government -- 1959-

HX160.P35.R67 1997
Rosendahl, Mona.
Inside the revolution: everyday life in socialist Cuba/ Mona Rosendahl. Ithaca: Cornell University Press, 1997. x, 197 p.
97-016517   335.43/47   0801433819
Socialism -- Cuba -- Palmera. Political culture -- Cuba -- Palmera. Palmera (Cuba) -- Social conditions. Cuba -- History -- Revolution, 1959 -- Social aspects.

HX198.F38 1988
Faúndez, Julio.
Marxism and democracy in Chile: from 1932 to the fall of Allende/ Julio Faúndez. New Haven: Yale University Press, 1988. xi, 305 p.
88-009646   324.283/07/09 19   0300040245
Socialism -- Chile -- History -- 20th century.

HX238-373.5 By region or country — Other regions or countries — Europe

HX238.H67 1996
Horn, Gerd-Rainer.
European socialists respond to fascism: ideology, activism, and contingency in the 1930s/ Gerd-Rainer Horn. New York: Oxford University Press, 1996. xii, 211 p.
95-046426   335/.0094   0195093747
Socialism -- Europe -- History -- 20th century. National socialism. Europe -- Politics and government -- 1918-1945.

HX240.7.A6.E44 1996
Ekiert, Grzegorz, 1956-
The state against society: political crises and their aftermath in East Central Europe/ Grzegorz Ekiert. Princeton, N.J.: Princeton University Press, c1996. xvi, 435 p.
96-011807   306.2/0943 20   0691011141
Communism -- Europe, Eastern. Hungary -- History -- Revolution, 1956. Communism -- Hungary. Europe, Eastern -- Politics and government -- 1945-1989. Czechoslovakia -- History -- Intervention, 1968. Poland -- Politics and government -- 1980-1989.

HX240.7.A6.L44 1995
The legacies of communism in Eastern Europe/ edited by Zoltan Barany and Ivan Volgyes. Baltimore: Johns Hopkins University Press, 1995. xiv, 338 p.
94-043245   335.43   0801849977
Communism -- Europe, Eastern. Communism -- Former Soviet republics. Post-communism -- Europe, Eastern. Europe, Eastern -- Social conditions -- 1989- Former Soviet republics -- Social conditions.

HX240.7.A6.L4713 1991
Lesourne, Jacques, 1928-
After Communism: from the Atlantic to the Urals/ Jacques Lesourne, Bernard Lecomte; translated from the French by Chris Miller. Chur, Switzerland; Harwood Academic Publishers, c1991. 271 p.
91-036893   335.43/0947   3718652110
Communism -- Europe, Eastern. European Economic Community countries -- Economic conditions.

HX240.7.A6 S29
Saxonberg, Steven.
The fall: a comparative study of the end of communism in Czechoslovakia, East Germany, Hungary and Poland/ Steven Saxonberg. Amsterdam: Harwood Academic, c2001. xvii, 434 p.
905823097X
Communism -- Europe, Eastern -- History -- 20th century. Europe, Eastern -- History -- 1945-Europe, Eastern -- Politics and government -- 1945-

HX243.W38 1990
Waters, Chris.
British socialists and the politics of popular culture, 1884-1914/ Chris Waters. Stanford, Calif.: Stanford University Press, 1990. 252 p.
89-062182   335.00941   0804717583
Socialism -- Great Britain -- History. Popular culture. Socialism and culture -- Great Britain.

HX243.W45 1996
Weinroth, Michelle, 1959-
Reclaiming William Morris: Englishness, sublimity, and the rhetoric of dissent/ Michelle Weinroth. Montreal; McGill-Queen's University Press, c1996. xii, 302 p.
97-182551   0773514392
Morris, William, -- 1834-1896 -- Influence. Arnot, Robert Page, -- 1890- -- William Morris. Communism -- Great Britain -- History -- 20th century. Socialism -- England -- History -- 19th century. National characteristics, English.

HX249.K64 1991
Koelble, Thomas A., 1957-
The left unraveled: social democracy and the new left challenge in Britain and West Germany/ Thomas A. Koelble. Durham: Duke University Press, c1991. xii, 162 p.
90-045573   324.1/7   0822311089
Socialist parties -- Great Britain. Socialist parties -- Germany (West) New Left -- Great Britain. Great Britain -- Politics and government -- 1945- Germany (West) -- Politics and government.

HX260.5.A6.W36 1995
The waning of the communist state: economic origins of political decline in China and Hungary/ edited by Andrew G. Walder. Berkeley: University of California Press, c1995. xiv, 280 p.
94-026931   335.43/09439   0520088514
Communism -- Hungary. Communism -- China. Hungary -- Economic policy -- 1968-1989. Hungary -- Politics and government -- 1945-1989. China -- Politics and government -- 1976-

HX273.J66 1999
Jones, William David, 1953-
The lost debate: German socialist intellectuals and totalitarianism/ William David Jones. Urbana: University of Illinois Press, c1999. xx, 358 p.
98-058029   335/.00943/0904 21   025202480X
Socialism -- Germany -- History -- 20th century. Socialists -- Germany -- History -- 20th century. Intellectuals -- Germany -- History -- 20th century. Germany -- Politics and government -- 20th century.

HX280.5.A6.M4 1995
McFalls, Laurence H.
Communism's collapse, democracy's demise?: the cultural context and consequences of the East German revolution/ Laurence H. McFalls. New York: New York University Press, 1995. xi, 218 p.
94-020535   306.2/09431   0814755216
Communism -- Germany (East) -- History. Germany (East) -- Politics and government. Germany (East) -- Politics and government -- 1989-1990.

HX280.5.A6.R67 2000
Ross, Corey, 1969-
Constructing socialism at the grass-roots: the transformation of East Germany, 1945-65/ Corey Ross. New York: St. Martin's Press, 2000. xii, 262 p.
99-049746   335.43/0943/109045   0312230419
Socialism -- Germany (East) -- History -- 20th century. Germany (East) -- Social conditions.

HX280.5.A6.W385 1997
Weitz, Eric D.
Creating German communism, 1890-1990: from popular protests to socialist state/ Eric D. Weitz. Princeton, N.J.: Princeton University Press, c1997. xviii, 445 p.
96-020678   335.43/0943 20   0691025940
Communism -- Germany -- History. Communism -- Germany (East) -- History. Germany -- Politics and government -- 1871- Germany (East) -- Politics and government.

HX311.5.H37 1996
Harding, Neil.
Leninism/ Neil Harding. Durham, N.C.: Duke University Press, 1996. ix, 346 p.
96-003874   335.43   0822318679
Lenin, Vladimir Ilich, -- 1870-1924. Communism. Communism -- Soviet Union.

HX313.G666 2000
Gorsuch, Anne E.
Youth in revolutionary Russia: enthusiasts, bohemians, delinquents/ Anne E. Gorsuch. Bloomington: Indiana University Press, 2000. x, 274 p.
00-024181   305.235/0947/09041   0253337666
Socialism and youth -- Soviet Union. Propaganda, Communist -- Soviet Union. Communist education -- Soviet Union.

HX313.7.C64 1997
Clements, Barbara Evans, 1945-
Bolshevik women / Barbara Evans Clements. Cambridge, UK; Cambridge University Press, 1997. xiv, 338 p.
96-050036   335.43/082/092247   0521454034
Women communists -- Soviet Union -- Biography. Women revolutionaries -- Soviet Union -- Biography. Women and communism -- Soviet Union -- History.

HX313.8.L46.A54 1995
Anderson, Kevin, 1948-
Lenin, Hegel, and Western Marxism: a critical study/ Kevin Anderson. Urbana: University of Illinois Press, c1995. xvii, 311 p.
94-045414   335.43   0252021673
Lenin, Vladimir Ilich, -- 1870-1924. Hegel, Georg Wilhelm Friedrich, -- 1770-1831. Communism. Philosophy, Marxist.

HX315.L77.S22 1990
Sabaliunas, Leonas.
Lithuanian social democracy in perspective, 1893-1914/ Leonas Sabaliunas. Durham: Duke University Press, 1990. viii, 205 p.
89-027306   335.5/0947/5   0822310155
Socialism -- Lithuania -- History. Socialists -- Lithuania -- History. Lithuania -- Politics and government.

HX373.5.V47 1996
Verdery, Katherine.
What was socialism, and what comes next?/ Katherine Verdery. Princeton, N.J.: Princeton University Press, c1996. 298 p.
95-032123   338.9498 20   0691011338
Socialism -- Romania. Communism -- Romania. Post-communism -- Romania.

HX392.5-418.5 By region or country —
Other regions or countries — Asia

HX392.5.M35 1994
Mallick, Ross.
Indian communism: opposition, collaboration, and institutionalization/ Ross Mallick. Delhi; Oxford University Press, 1994. xi, 277 p.
93-911541   392.5   0195632354
Communism -- India -- History.

HX417.5.T48 1997
Thaxton, Ralph, 1944-
Salt of the earth: the political origins of peasant protest and communist revolution in China/ Ralph A. Thaxton, Jr. Berkeley: University of California Press, c1997. xix, 425 p.
96-020359   322.4/4/095109041 20   0520203186
Communism -- China -- History -- 20th century. Peasant uprisings -- China -- History -- 20th century. China -- Politics and government -- 20th century.

HX418.5.S87 1995
Sun, Yan, 1959-
The Chinese reassessment of socialism 1976-1992/ by Yan Sun. Princeton, N.J.: Princeton University Press, 1995 xii, 352 p.
95-006349   335.43/45   0691029997
Communism -- China. Socialism -- China. China -- Economic policy -- 1976- China -- Politics and government -- 1976-

HX443 By region or country —
Other regions or countries —
Africa

HX443.A6.G56 1997
Ginat, Rami.
Egypt's incomplete revolution: Lutfi al-Khuli and Nasser's socialism in the 1960s/ Rami Ginat. London; Frank Cass, 1997. xiv, 223 p.
96-044955   335.4/0962/09045   0714647381
Khuli, Lutfi. Socialism -- Egypt -- History. Egypt -- Politics and government -- 1952-

HX518 Special topics, A-Z

HX518.L4
Li, Cheng, 1956-
China's leaders: the new generation/ Cheng Li. Lanham, [Md.]: Rowman & Littlefield Publishers, c2001. xviii, 285 p.
00-062539   320.951 21   0847694968
Communist leadership -- China. Political leadership -- China. China -- Politics and government -- 1976-

HX536 Communism and religion.
Socialism and religion

HX536.J28 1998
Janz, Denis.
World Christianity and Marxism/ Denis R. Janz. New York: Oxford University Press, 1998. viii, 188 p.
97-022760   261.2/1   0195119444
Communism and Christianity -- History.

HX541 Communism/socialism and science

HX541.K54 1994
Kitching, G. N.
Marxism and science: analysis of an obsession/ Gavin Kitching. University Park, Pa.: Pennsylvania State University Press, c1994. xii, 258 p.
93-002304   335.4/11   0271010266
Communism and science. Socialism.

HX542 Communism and society.
Socialism and society

HX542.M31785 1996
Martin, Bill, 1956-
Politics in the impasse: explorations in postsecular social theory/ Bill Martin. New York: State University of New York Press, c1996. x, 300 p.
95-013739   306.2 20   0791427935
Communism and society. Post-communism. Cynicism.

HX546 Communism and women.
Socialism and women.
Communism/socialism and the family

HX546.G54 1995
Gilmartin, Christina K.
Engendering the Chinese revolution: radical women, communist politics, and mass movements in the 1920s/ Christina Kelley Gilmartin. Berkeley: University of California Press, c1995. xiii, 303 p.
94-024723   335.43/082   0520089812
Women and socialism -- China. Communism -- China -- History. China -- History -- 1912-1928.

HX546.R35 1994
Randall, Margaret, 1936-
Sandino's daughters revisited: feminism in Nicaragua/ Margaret Randall. New Brunswick, N.J.: Rutgers University Press, c1994. xvi, 311 p.
93-010819   324.27285/075/082   081352024X
Women -- Nicaragua -- Interviews. Feminism -- Nicaragua. Women and socialism -- Nicaragua. Nicaragua -- History -- 1979-1990.

HX546.W35 2001
Weigand, Kate, 1965-
Red feminism: American communism and the making of women's liberation/ Kate Weigand. Baltimore, Md.: Johns Hopkins University Press, 2001. xiv, 220 p.
00-008874   324.273/75/082   0801864895
Women and communism -- United States -- History -- 20th century. Women in politics -- United States -- History -- 20th century. Women's rights -- United States -- History -- 20th century. United States -- Politics and government -- 20th century. United States -- Social conditions -- 20th century.

HX550
Communism/socialism in relation to other topics, A-Z

HX550.A37.B65 1998
Bokovoy, Melissa K. 1961-
Peasants and communists: politics and ideology in the Yugoslav countryside, 1941-1953/ Melissa K. Bokovoy. Pittsburgh, Pa.: University of Pittsburgh Press, c1998. xvii, 211 p.
97-033877   305.5/633/0949709045   21
0822940612
Communism and agriculture -- Yugoslavia -- History. Peasantry -- Yugoslavia -- History. Yugoslavia -- Politics and government -- 1945-1980.

HX550.A37.P79 1992
Pryor, Frederic L.
The red and the green: the rise and fall of collectivized agriculture in Marxist regimes/ Frederic L. Pryor. Princeton, N.J.: Princeton University Press, c1992. x, 550 p.
91-032459   306.3/45   0691042993
Communism and agriculture. Collectivization of agriculture -- Communist countries. Agriculture and state -- Communist countries.

HX550.J4.F57 1991
Fischman, Dennis K., 1958-
Political discourse in exile: Karl Marx and the Jewish question/ Dennis K. Fischman. Amherst: University of Massachusetts Press, c1991. viii, 145 p.
90-024603   335.4   0870237462
Marx, Karl, -- 1818-1883.   Communism and Judaism. Judaism -- Influence.

HX550.J4.J33 1991
Jacobs, Jack Lester, 1953-
On socialists and "the Jewish question" after Marx/ Jack Jacobs. New York: New York University Press, c1992. xi, 300 p.
91-016630   335/.0089/924   0814741789
Jewish socialists. Socialism and antisemitism. Jews -- Europe -- Public opinion.

HX550.N3.C38 2001
Chang, Maria Hsia.
Return of the dragon: China's wounded nationalism/ Maria Hsia Chang. Boulder, Colo.: Westview Press, 2001. x, 257 p.
00-053182   320.54/0951   0813338565
Nationalism and communism -- China. Nationalism -- China. China -- Politics and government -- 1976- China -- Economic policy -- 1976-

HX550.N3.G53 1990
Gilberg, Trond, 1940-
Nationalism and communism in Romania: the rise and fall of Ceausescu's personal dictatorship/ Trond Gilberg. Boulder: Westview Press, 1990. x, 289 p.
89-025056   306.2/09498   0813374979
Nationalism and communism -- Romania -- History. Romania -- Politics and government.

HX626 Communism: Utopian socialism, collective settlements — History — General works

HX626.O95 1995
Ozinga, James R.
The recurring dream of equality: communal sharing and communism throughout history/ James R. Ozinga. Lanham, MD: University Press of America, 1995. xvi, 293 p.
95-042407   335/.9   076180188X
Collective settlements -- History. Communism -- History.

HX626.T73 1999
Trahair, R. C. S.
Utopias and Utopians: an historical dictionary/ Richard C.S. Trahair. Westport, Conn.: Greenwood Press, 1999. xvi, 480 p.
98-028286   321/.07/09   0313294658
Utopias -- History -- Dictionaries. Utopian socialism -- History -- Dictionaries. Socialists -- Biography -- Dictionaries.

HX632 Communism: Utopian socialism, collective settlements — History — Modern

HX632.S87 1994
Sutton, Robert P.
Les Icariens: the utopian dream in Europe and America/ Robert P. Sutton. Urbana: University of Illinois Press, c1994. xiv, 199 p.
93-008609   335/.02   0252020677
Icarian movement -- History.

HX653-704 Communism: Utopian socialism, collective settlements — General works. By region or country — North America

HX653.A63 1997
America's communal utopias/ edited by Donald E. Pitzer; foreword by Paul S. Boyer. Chapel Hill: University of North Carolina Press, c1997. xxi, 537 p.
96-010889   335/.9/0973 20   080782299X
Collective settlements -- United States -- History. Communitarianism -- United States.

HX654.K46 1993
Kesten, Seymour R.
Utopian episodes: daily life in experimental colonies dedicated to changing the world/ Seymour R. Kesten. Syracuse, N.Y.: Syracuse University Press, 1993. xii, 344 p.
92-040186   335/.12   0815625936
Collective settlements -- United States.

HX655.S68.B78 1996
Brundage, W. Fitzhugh 1959-
A socialist utopia in the new South: the Ruskin colonies in Tennessee and Georgia, 1894-1901/ W. Fitzhugh Brundage. Urbana: University of Illinois Press, c1996. xi, 263 p.
95-041805   335/.0768 20   0252022440
Ruskin, John, -- 1819-1900 -- Contributions in communitarianism. Ruskin, John, -- 1819-1900 -- Disciples. Utopias -- Southern States -- Case studies. Collective settlements -- Southern States -- Case studies. Communitarianism -- Southern States -- Case studies. United States -- Social conditions -- 1865-1918.

HX656.N75.C53 1995
Clark, Christopher, 1953-
The communitarian moment: the radical challenge of the Northampton Association/ Christopher Clark. Ithaca: Cornell University Press, 1995. xiv, 269 p.
94-046310   335/.974423   0801427304
Collective settlements -- United States -- History -- 19th century. Utopian socialism -- United States -- History -- 19th century. Abolitionists -- United States -- History -- 19th century.

HX704.C7.B44 2001
Beecher, Jonathan.
Victor Considerant and the rise and fall of French romantic socialism/ Jonathan Beecher. Berkeley: University of California Press, c2001. xvi, 584 p.
00-028717   335/.0092 21   0520222970
Considerant, Victor, -- 1808-1893.   Socialists -- France -- Biography. Utopian socialism -- France -- History -- 19th century.

HX806 Utopias.
The ideal state — General works. History

HX806.D66 1998
Donnelly, Dorothy F., 1937-
Patterns of order and Utopia/ Dorothy F. Donnelly. New York: St. Martin's Press, 1998. x, 150 p.
98-003794   321/.07/09   0312164963
Utopias -- History. Order (Philosophy) -- History.

HX806.L47 1998
Leslie, Marina.
Renaissance utopias and the problem of history/
Marina Leslie. Ithaca, N.Y.: Cornell University
Press, 1998 viii, 200 p.
98-017865   321/.07   0801434009
*Utopias -- History. Utopias in literature.
Literature and history.*

HX806.S34 1995
Sciabarra, Chris Matthew, 1960-
Marx, Hayek, and utopia/ Chris Matthew
Sciabarra. Albany: State University of New York
Press, c1995. x, 178 p.
94-039676   335/.02/0922   0791426157
*Marx, Karl, -- 1818-1883. Hayek, Friedrich A. von
-- (Friedrich August), -- 1899- Radicalism. Social
sciences -- Philosophy. Utopias.*

HX810.5 Utopias. The ideal state
— Particular works
— Individual utopias

HX810.5.E54 2001
More, Thomas, 1478-1535.
Utopia/ Thomas More; translated and with an
introduction by Clarence Miller. New Haven, CT:
Yale University Press, c2001. xxviii, 173 p.
00-044917   335/.02 21   0300084285
Utopias -- Early works to 1800.

HX830 Anarchism —
Biography (Collective)

HX830.G39 1999
Gay, Kathlyn.
Encyclopedia of political anarchy/ Kathlyn Gay
and Martin K. Gay. Santa Barbara, Calif.: ABC-
CLIO, c1999. xiv, 242 p.
99-017551   320.5/7/0922 21   0874369827
*Anarchists -- Biography. Anarchism --
Encyclopedias.*

HX843.7 Anarchism —
By region or country —
North America

HX843.7.L33.A53 1998
Anderson, Carlotta R., 1929-
All-American anarchist: Joseph A. Labadie and the
labor movement/ Carlotta R. Anderson. Detroit,
Mich.: Wayne State University Press, c1998.
324 p.
97-042353   335/.83/092 21   0814327079
*Labadie, Jo, -- 1850-1933. Anarchists -- United
States -- Biography. Labor movement -- Michigan -
- History.*

HX843.7.S23.A97 1991
Avrich, Paul.
Sacco and Vanzetti: the anarchist background/ Paul
Avrich. Princeton, N.J.: Princeton University
Press, c1991. x, 265 p.
90-040838   364.1/523/09227447   B   20
0691047898
*Sacco, Nicola, -- 1891-1927. Vanzetti, Bartolomeo,
-- 1888-1927. Anarchists -- United States --
Biography. Anarchism -- United States -- History.
Sacco-Vanzetti Trial, Dedham, Mass., 1921.*

HX851 Anarchism —
By region or country —
Latin America

HX851.H63 1995
Hodges, Donald Clark, 1923-
Mexican anarchism after the revolution/ Donald C.
Hodges. Austin: University of Texas Press, 1995.
xiv, 251 p.
94-020488   335/.83/09720904   0292730934
*Anarchism -- Mexico -- History -- 20th century.
Mexico -- Politics and government -- 1910-1946.*

HX896-914.7 Anarchism —
By region or country — Europe

HX896.P3.V37 1996
Varias, Alexander, 1953-
Paris and the anarchists: aesthetes and subversives
during the fin-de-siecle/ Alexander Varias. New
York: St. Martin's Press, c1996. viii, 208 p.
96-030670   320.5/7/094436109034   20
0312160615
*Anarchism -- France -- Paris -- History -- 19th
century. Politics and culture -- France -- Paris --
History -- 19th century.*

HX914.A9
Avrich, Paul.
The Russian anarchists. Princeton, N.J., Princeton
University Press, 1967. vii, 303 p.
66-025418   335/.83/0947
Anarchists -- Soviet Union.

HX914.7.K7.C34 1989
Cahm, Caroline.
Kropotkin and the rise of revolutionary anarchism,
1872-1886/   Caroline   Cahm.   Cambridge;
Cambridge University Press, 1989. xii, 372 p.
89-007195   335/.83/092   0521364450
*Kropotkin, Petr Alekseevich, -- kniaz, -- 1842-
1921. Anarchists -- Soviet Union -- Biography.
Anarchism -- History -- 19th century.*

<u>INDEXES</u>

Author Index

"Epidemic" of adolescent pregnancy?: some historical and policy considerations, An/ HQ759.4.V55 1988

"Everybody does it!": crime by the public/ HV6080.G28 1994

"Femininity," "masculinity," and "androgyny": a modern philosophical discussion/ HQ1206.F44 1982b

"Getting paid": youth crime and work in the inner city/ HV9106.N6.S85 1989

"I am destroying the land!": the political ecology of poverty and environmental destruction in Honduras/ HC145.Z9.E57 1993

"Just a housewife": the rise and fall of domesticity in America/ HQ1410.M38 1987

"Mother donit fore the best": correspondence of a nineteenth-century orphan asylum/ HV995.A32.A533 1996

"Poor Carolina": politics and society in colonial North Carolina, 1729-1776/ HC107.N8.E37

"Subject people" and colonial discourses: economic transformation and social disorder in Puerto Rico, 1898-1947/ HV6872.S26 1994

"The people's farm": English radical agrarianism, 1775-1840/ HN400.R3.C48 1988

"Torrey Canyon" pollution and marine life: a report by the Plymouth Laboratory of the Marine Biological Association of the United Kingdom, GC1311.M37

"Underclass" debate: views from history, The/ HV4044.U56 1993

"Wicked" women and the reconfiguration of gender in Africa/ HQ1787.W53 2001

(In) justice for juveniles: rethinking the best interests of the child/ HV9104.S3286 1989

...Families in trouble. HV43.K64

[Russian economic development from Peter the Great to] Stalin. HC333.B543

1900, the generation before the Great War/ HN373.T33

20,000 years of fashion: the history of costume and personal adornment/ GT510.B6713 1987

21st century capitalism/ HB501.H395 1993

21st century leisure: current issues/ GV14.45.K447 2000

60s communes: hippies and beyond, The/ HQ971.M55 1999

75 greatest management decisions ever made, The/ HD30.23.C73 1999

A to Z of American women in sports/ GV697.A1 E28 2002

A.D., a memoir/ HQ1413.M54.M55 1995

A.F. of L. in the time of Gompers, The/ HD8055.A5.T3 1970

AAAS atlas of population & environment/ HB849.415.H374 2000

Abandoned ones: the imprisonment and uprising of the Mariel boat people, The/ HV9471.H29 1995

Abbie Hoffman, American rebel/ HN90.R3.J49 1992

Abby Hopper Gibbons: prison reformer and social activist/ HV8978.G38.B33 2000

ABC-CLIO companion to the environmental movement, The/ GE197.G76 1994

ABC-CLIO companion to transportation in America, The/ HE203.R54 1995

ABC-CLIO companion to women in the workplace, The/ HD6095.S34 1993

ABC-CLIO companion to women's progress in America, The/ HQ1410.F76 1994

ABC-CLIO world history companion to capitalism, The/ HC79.C3.A45 1998

Abilene paradox and other meditations on management, The/ HD58.7.H376 1988

Aboriginal adolescence: maidenhood in an Australian community/ GN663.B88 1988

Aboriginal Australians: black response to white dominance, 1788-1980/ GN665.B76 1982

Aboriginal autonomy: issues and strategies/ GN666.C657 1994

Aboriginal environmental impacts/ GF801.K65 1995

Abortion: a reference handbook/ HQ767.5.U5.C67 1991

Abortion: the clash of absolutes/ HQ767.5.U5.T73 1990

Abortion and American politics/ HQ767.5.U5.C73 1993

Abortion and infanticide/ HQ767.3.T66 1983

Abortion and the politics of motherhood/ HQ767.5.U5.L84 1984

Abortion myth: feminism, morality, and the hard choices women make, The/ HQ767.15.C38 2000

Abortion politics: private morality and public policy/ HQ767.5.U5.J33

Above the law: police and the excessive use of force/ HV8141.S56 1993

Absentee ownership and business enterprise in recent times; the case of America. HC106.V4 1964

Abuse of men: trauma begets trauma, The/ HV1441.4.A28 2001

Abuse of the elderly: a guide to resources and services/ HV1461.A28 1984

Abused and battered: social and legal responses to family violence/ HV6626.2.A29 1991

Academic mind and reform; the influence of Richard T. Ely in American life, The/ HB119.E5.R3

Acceptable risk/ HD61.A24

Access to land, rural poverty, and public action/ HD1131.A25 2001

Accessible city, The/ HE305.O9

Accidental proletariat: workers, politics, and crisis in Gorbachev's Russia, The/ HD8526.5.C594 1991

Accountancy comes of age: the development of an American profession, 1886-1940/ HF5616.U5.M54 1990

Accountant's guide to fraud detection and control/ HF5668.25.M36 2000

Accountant's guide to peer and quality review, The/ HF5657.M34 1993

Accounting education for the 21st century: the global challenges/ HF5630.A428 1994

Accounting ethics: a practical guide for professionals/ HF5657.C687 1990

Accounting evolution to 1900/ HF5605.L5 1981

Accounting for success: a history of Price Waterhouse in America, 1890-1990/ HF5616.U7.P752 1993

Accounting for the environment/ HF5686.C7.G568 1993

Accounting for United States economic growth, 1929-1969 HC106.3.D3667

Accounting for war: Soviet production, employment, and the defence burden, 1940-1945/ HC335.6.H36 1996

Accounting history from the Renaissance to the present: a remembrance of Luca Pacioli/ HF5605.A23 1996

Accounting systems and practice in Europe/ HF5616.E8.O43 1987

Accounting theory/ HF5635.B4167

Accounting--a social institution: a unified theory for the measurement of the profit and nonprofit sectors/ HV41.C4428 1992

Accounting's changing role in social conflict/ HF5657.L394 1992

Accumulation & power: an economic history of the United States/ HC110.S3.D8 1989

Acequia culture: water, land, and community in the Southwest/ HD1694.A3 1998

Achieving broad-based sustainable development: governance, environment, and growth with equity/ HC79.E5.W43 1997

Acquisitive society, The/ HB199.T35

Across fortune's tracks: a biography of William Rand Kenan, Jr./ HC102.5.K457.C35 1996

Across the top of the world: the quest for the Northwest Passage/ G640.D45 1999

ACSM fitness book/ GV481.A322 2002

ACSM's health/fitness facility standards and guidelines/ GV429.A45 1997

Action and its environments: toward a new synthesis/ HM24.A4647 1988

Action research and organizational development/ H62.C813 1993

Active youth: ideas for implementing CDC physical activity promotion guidelines/ GV443.A27 1998

Activist's handbook: a primer for the 1990s and beyond, The/ HN65.S48 1996

Activity accounting: an activity-based costing approach/ HF5686.C8.B674 1991

Activity-based management: today's powerful new tool for controlling costs and creating profits/ HF5686.C8.W4476 1995

Acts of compassion: caring for others and helping ourselves/ HN90.V64.W88 1991

Ad men and women: a biographical dictionary of advertising, The/ HF5810.A2.A3 1994

Ad worlds: brands, media, audiences/ HF5823.M93 1998

Adam Smith and his legacy for modern capitalism/ HB103.S6.W38 1991

Adam Smith in his time and ours: designing the decent society/ HB103.S6 M83 1995

Adam Smith's marketplace of life/ HB501.O824 2002

Adam Smith's system of liberty, wealth, and virtue: the moral and political foundations of The wealth of nations/ HB103.S6.F58 1995

Adapted aquatics programming: a professional guide/ GV837.4.L47 1998

Adapted physical education and sport/ GV445.A3 2000

Adapted physical education national standards/ GV445.N38 1995

Address unknown: the homeless in America/ HV4505.W75 1989

Adjusting privatization: case studies from Developing countries/ HD4420.8.A33 1992

Adjusting to democracy: the role of the Ministry of Labour in British politics, 1916-1939/ HD8390.L68 1986

Adjusting to policy failure in African economies/ HC800 .A55257 1994

Adjustment in Africa: reforms, results, and the road ahead. HC800.A55258 1994

Adjustment with a human face/ HN980.A29 1987

Administrative behavior: a study of decision-making processes in administrative organization/ HD31.S55 1976

Administrative presidency revisited: public lands, the BLM, and the Reagan revolution, The/ HD243.N5.D87 1992

Adolescence: an anthropological inquiry/ HQ796.S4139 1991

Adolescence and delinquency: the collective management of reputation/ HV9145.E45 1995

Adolescence and youth in early modern England/ HQ799.G72.E53 1994

Adolescent relations with mothers, fathers, and friends/ HQ796.Y583 1985

Adolescent suicidal behavior/ HV6546.C87 1987

Adolescents after divorce/ HQ777.5.B796 1996

Adolescents and the media: medical and psychological impact/ HQ799.2.M35.S87 1995

Adolescents at risk: prevalence and prevention/ HV1431.D79 1990

Title Index

Agriculture in the Third World: a spatial analysis/ HD1417.M68 1978

Agriculture, women, and land: the African experience/ HD6073.A292.A353 1988

Aid and power: the World Bank and policy-based lending / HG3881.5.W57.M68 1991

Aid and reform in Africa: lessons from ten case studies/ HC800.A628 2001

Aid to African agriculture: lessons from two decades of donors' experience/ HD2117.A37 1992

Airline deregulation: the early experience/ HE9803.A3.A36

Airline industry and the impact of deregulation, The/ HE9803.A4.W53 1994

Alan shrugged: the life and times of Alan Greenspan, the world's most powerful banker/ HB119.G74 T83 2002

Alcohol and the community: a systems approach to prevention/ HV5035.H65 1998

Alcohol and the family/ HV5132.A43 1982

Alcohol in America: drinking practices and problems/ HV5289.A75 1991

Alcohol in human violence/ HV5053.P45 1991

Alcohol report, The/ HV5035.A465 2000

Alcohol use and misuse by young adults/ HV5128.U5.A43 1994

Alcohol, sex, and gender in late medieval and early modern Europe/ HV5438.M37 2001

Alcohol, use and abuse in America/ HV5292.M4 1985

Alcoholic family in recovery: a developmental model, The/ HV5132.B748 1999

Alcoholic society: addiction and recovery of the self, The/ HV5279.D43 1993

Alcoholic thinking: language, culture, and belief in Alcoholics Anonymous/ HV5045.W55 1998

Alcoholics Anonymous as a mutual-help movement: a study in eight societies/ HV5278.A756 1996

Alcoholism and its treatment in industry/ HF5549.5.A4.A4

Alcoholism problems: selected issues, The/ HV5035.C63 1983

Ale, beer and brewsters in England: women's work in a changing world, 1300-1600/ HD6073.L62.G723 1996

Alfred C. Kinsey: a public/private life/ HQ18.32.K56.J65 1997

Alfred Marshall in retrospect/ HB103.M3.A67 1990

Alfred Vincent Kidder and the development of Americanist archaeology/ GN21.K5.G58 1992

Alice Henry: the power of pen and voice: the life of an Australian-American labor reformer/ HD6079.2.U5.K57 1991

Alien in Antarctica: reflections upon forty years of exploration and research on the frozen continent, An/ G875.S95.A3 1997

Alienation and charisma: a study of contemporary American communes/ HQ971.Z3

All for one, HD6079.S3

All of us together: the story of inclusion at the Kinzie School/ HV2561.I483.C43 1994

All on a Mardi Gras day: episodes in the history of New Orleans Carnival/ GT4211.N4.M57 1995

All possible worlds: a history of geographical ideas/ G80.J34 1981

All the world and her husband: women in twentieth-century consumer culture/ HC79.C6.A43 2000

All-American anarchist: Joseph A. Labadie and the labor movement/ HX843.7.L33.A53 1998

All-consuming century: why commercialism won in modern America, An/ HC110.C6 C76 2000

Alliance capitalism: the social organization of Japanese business/ HD69.S8.G47 1992

Alliance revolution: the new shape of business rivalry, The/ HD69.S8.G66 1996

Allocation of income within the household/ HB523.L39 1988

Alluvial fans: a field approach/ GB591.A45 1990

Almanac of state legislatures: changing patterns 1990-1997, The/ G1201.F7 .L5 1998

Almanac of women and minorities in American politics, The/ HQ1236.5.U6.M3778 1999

Almanac of women and minorities in world politics, The/ HQ1236.M347 2000

Alone G585.B8.A33 1938

Alone across the Atlantic/ GV822.G5.C5 1961a

Altered harvest: agriculture, genetics, and the fate of the world's food supply/ HD9006.D65 1985

Alternating currents: electricity markets and public policy/ HD9685.U5 B74 2002

Alternating currents: nationalized power in France, 1946-1970/ HD9685.F84.E52 1991

Alternative approaches to capital gains taxation HJ4653.C3.D33

Alternative modernity: the technical turn in philosophy and social theory/ HM221.F384 1995

Alternative strategies for economic development/ HC59.7.G747 1999

Alternative tracks: the constitution of American industrial order, 1865-1917/ HE2757.B47 1994

Alternative treatments for troubled youth: the case of diversion from the justice system/ HV9104.A77 1990

Alternatives to capitalism/ HB501.A558 1989

Alternatives to imprisonment: intentions and reality/ HV9276.5.B66 1994

Altruistic imagination: a history of social work and social policy in the United States, The/ HV91.E38 1985

Alva Myrdal: a daughter's memoir/ HQ1687.B65 1991

Alvin Ailey: a life in dance/ GV1785.A38 D85 1996

Always running: la vida loca, gang days in L.A./ HV6439.U7.L77 1993

AMA handbook for successful selling/ HF5438.25.K546 1994

AMA marketing encyclopedia: issues and trends shaping the future/ HF5415.A46 1995

Amazonian ethnobotanical dictionary/ GN564.P4.D85 1994

Ambiguous embrace: government and faith-based schools and social agencies, The/ HV95.G54 2000

America and the multinational corporation: the history of a troubled partnership/ HD2785.R43 1992

America challenged: population change and the future of the United States, An/ HB3505.M868 1995

America now: the anthropology of a changing culture/ HN59.H27

American agriculture and the problem of monopoly: the political economy of grain belt farming, 1953-1980/ HD1773.A3.L38 2000

American Association of Public Accountants: its first twenty years, 1886-1906, The/ HF5601.A872.W4 1978

American attitudes: who thinks what about the issues that shape our lives/ HN90.P8.M58 1998

American baseball/ GV863.A1.V65 1983

American beginnings: the prehistory and palaeoecology of Beringia/ GN885.A44 1996

American billboard: 100 years, The/ HF5843.F73 1991

American book of days, The/ GT4803.D6

American business and its environment HC106.5.W32

American business in the twentieth century HC106.C6315

American business leaders: a biographical dictionary/ HC102.5.A2.H36 1999

American business, 1920-2000: how it worked/ HC106.82.M39 2000

American capitalism and the changing role of government/ HC106.82.S5 1999

American census: a social history, The/ HA37.U55.A53 1988

American cigarette industry; a study in economic analysis and public policy, The/ HD9149.C42U68. 1971

American circus: an illustrated history, The/ GV1803.C85 1990

American criminal; an anthropological study. [1] The native white criminal of native parentage, The/ HV6035.H65 1969

American dole: unemployment relief and the welfare state in the Great Depression, The/ HV91.S555 2000

American dreaming: immigrant life on the margins/ HN90.M26.M34 1995

American economic history: a comprehensive revision of the earlier work by Harold Underwood Faulkner/ HC103.F3 1976

American economic policy in the 1990s/ HC106.82.A456 2002

American economists of the late twentieth century/ HB119.A3.A42 1996

American economy: the struggle for supremacy in the 21st century, The/ HC106.5.S696 1995

American economy in transition, The/ HC106.5.A5948

American elites/ HN90.E4.L47 1996

American enterprise in South Africa: historical dimensions of engagement and disengagement/ HG5851.A3.H85 1990

American environmental history/ HC103.7.P48 1988

American environmental leaders: from colonial times to the present/ GE55.B43 2000

American ethos: public attitudes toward capitalism and democracy, The/ HN90.P8.M4 1984

American exodus: the Dust Bowl migration and Okie culture in California/ HB1985.C2G74 1989

American Express: the unofficial history of the people who built the great financial empire/ HE5903.A55.G76 1987

American families: a research guide and historical handbook/ HQ535.A585 1991

American family: a demographic history, The/ HQ535.S44

American farm policy, 1948-1973/ HD1765 1976.C6 1976

American farmers: the new minority/ HD8039.F32.U64

American Federation of Labor; history, policies, and prospects, The/ HD8055.A5.L6 1972

American feminism: a contemporary history/ HQ1410.C3813 1990

American financing of World War I. HJ257.G54

American folklore: an encyclopedia/ GR101.A54 1996

American folklore and the mass media/ GR105.D44 1994

American food habits in historical perspective/ GT2853.U5.M39 1995

American foreign aid and global power projection: the geopolitics of resource allocation/ HC60.C6534 1990

American Fund for Public Service: Charles Garland and radical philanthropy, 1922-1941, The/ HV97.A64.S26 1996

American gay/ HQ76.3.N67.M87 1996

American generations: who they are, how they live, what they think/ HC110.C6 M545 2003

American health care blues: Blue Cross, HMOs, and pragmatic reform since 1960/ HG9396.M55 1996

American homelessness: a reference handbook/ HV4505.H647 1990

American idea of industrial democracy, 1865-1965. HD5660.U5.D44

505

Debt disaster?: banks, governments, and multilaterals confront the crisis/ HJ8899.D434 1989

Debt problems of Eastern Europe/ HJ8615.Z57 1987

Debt wish: entrepreneurial cities, U.S. federalism, and economic development/ HJ3833.S26 1996

Decade of deficits: congressional thought and fiscal action, A/ HJ2052.S337 1992

Decade of disaster/ HV553.L38 2000

Decade of Federal antipoverty programs: achievements, failures, and lessons, A/ HC110.P63.D42 1977

Decathlon: a colorful history of track and field's most challenging event, The/ GV1060.7.Z36 1989

Decent place to live: from Columbia Point to Harbor Point: a community history, A/ HT177.B6R64 2000

Deceptive distinctions: sex, gender, and the social order/ HQ1075.5.U6.E67 1988

Decision at midnight: inside the Canada-US free trade negotiations/ HF1766.H388 1994

Decision support systems: an organizational perspective/ HD30.23.K35

Declining fortunes: the withering of the American dream/ HN90.S6.N47 1993

Decolonization and African society: the labor question in French and British Africa/ HD8776.C66 1996

Deep Atlantic: life, death, and exploration in the abyss/ GC87.2.A86.E45 1996

Deep ecology and world religions: new essays on sacred grounds/ GE195.D437 2001

Deeper shades of green: the rise of blue-collar and minority environmentalism in America/ GE197.S3 1994

Defenders of the race: Jewish doctors and race science in fin-de-siecle Europe/ GN547.E34 1994

Defending a way of life: an American community in the nineteenth century/ HD8085.S433.C37 1989

Defending animal rights/ HV4711.R366 2001

Defending pornography: free speech, sex, and the fight for women's rights/ HQ472.U6.S87 1995

Defense industries in Latin American countries: Argentina, Brazil, and Chile/ HD9743.B682.M35 1994

Defensive football strategies/ GV951.18.D44 2000

Defining moments: when managers must choose between right and right/ HF5387.B32 1997

Deindustrialization of America: plant closings, community abandonment, and the dismantling of basic industry, The/ HD5708.55.U6.B58 1982

Delinking: towards a polycentric world/ HF1413.A4513 1990

Delinquency: the problem and its prevention/ HV9069.S764 1982

Delinquency and crime: a biopsychosocial approach; empirical, theoretical, and practical aspects of criminal behavior HV6025.C65

Delinquent daughters: protecting and policing adolescent female sexuality in the United States, 1885-1920/ HQ27.5.O34 1995

Demanding democracy after Three Mile Island/ HN80.G65.G65 1991

Demise of a rural economy: from subsistence to capitalism in a Latin American village, The/ HD1825.L67.G8

Democracy and difference/ HQ1190.P46 1993

Democracy and economic planning: the political economy of a self-governing society/ HD82.D45 1988

Democracy and poverty in Chile: the limits to electoral politics/ HC192.P48 1994

Democracy and social ethics/ HN64.A2 1907a

Democracy and the market: political and economic reforms in Eastern Europe and Latin America/ HC244.P8 1991

Democracy and the status of women in East Asia/ HQ1236.5.E25.D45 2000

Democracy at dawn: notes from Poland and points East/ HN380.7.A8.Q56 1998

Democracy at work: changing world markets and the future of labor unions/ HD6483.T87 1991

Democracy by default: dependency and clientelism in Jamaica/ HC154.E34 1990

Democracy without women: feminism and the rise of liberal individualism in France/ HQ1236.5.F8.F3813 1991

Democracy, authority, and alienation in work: workers' participation in an American corporation/ HD5660.U5.W57

Democracy, development, and the countryside: urban-rural struggles in India/ HN690.Z9.C6846 1995

Democracy, dialogue, and environmental disputes: the contested languages of social regulation/ H97.W544 1995

Democracy's railroads; public enterprise in Jacksonian Michigan HE2771.M5.P37

Democratizing the global economy: the battle against the Work Bank and the IMF/ HF1359.D46 2000

Demographic transition: stages, patterns, and economic implications: a longitudinal study of sixty-seven countries covering the period 1720-1984, The/ HB887.C4813 1992

Demographic yearbook. Annuaire demographique. HA17.D45

Demographics and criminality: the characteristics of crime in America/ HV6789.F58 1989

Demographics of the U.S.: trends and projections/ HB849.49.R875 2000

Demography and Roman society/ HB853.R66.P37 1992

Demography for business decision making/ HB849.41.P633 1997

Demography of famines: an Indian historical perspective, The/ HC439.M35 1996

Demography of Roman Egypt, The/ HB3661.7.A3.B33 1994

Demon slayers and other stories: Bengali folk tales, The/ GR305.5.B4.D27 1995

Demons and development: the struggle for community in a Sri Lankan village/ GN635.S72.B76 1996

De-moralization of society: from Victorian virtues to modern values, The/ HN59.2.H56 1995

Dental anthropology: fundamentals, limits, and prospects/ GN209.D48 1998

Department store: a social history, The/ HF5465.G73.L36 1995

Dependency and development: an introduction to the Third World/ HC59.7.L4172 1995

Dependency and development in Latin America/ HC125.C34153

Depression of the nineties; an economic history, The/ HC105.H8 1970

Deregulating the airlines/ HE9803.A4.B32 1985

Deregulating Wall Street: commercial bank penetration of the corporate securities market/ HG4930.5.D46 1985

Deregulation or re-regulation?: regulatory reform in Europe and the United States/ HD3612.D48 1990

Derivatives: a comprehensive resource for options, futures, interest rate swaps, and mortgage securities/ HG6024.U6.A73 1996

Desegregating the dollar: African American consumerism in the twentieth century/ HC110.C6.W44 1998

Desert capitalism: maquiladoras in North America's western industrial corridor/ HD9734.M42.K67 1996

Desert geomorphology/ GB611.C66 1993

Desertification: exploding the myth/ GB611.T48 1994

Deserts: the encroaching wilderness: a world conservation atlas/ GB611.D48 1993

Design with nature HC110.E5.M33

Designing a new America: the origins of New Deal planning, 1890-1943/ HC106.3.R36 1999

Designing for play/ GV425.H46 2001

Designing organizations: a decision-making perspective/ HD30.23.B875 1991

Designing qualitative research/ H62.M277 1989

Designing resistance training programs/ GV505.F58 1987

Designing social inquiry: scientific inference in qualitative research/ H61.K5437 1994

Designing the physical education curriculum/ GV365.M45 1996

Designs within disorder: Franklin D. Roosevelt, the economists, and the shaping of American economic policy, 1933-1945/ HC106.3.B269 1996

Desired past: a short history of same-sex love in America, A/ HQ76.3.U5.R86 1999

Desiring revolution: second-wave feminism and the rewriting of American sexual thought, 1920 to 1982/ HQ1421.G47 2001

Destined for equality: the inevitable rise of women's status/ HQ1236.J33 1998

Destruction of the Soviet economic system: an insiders' history, The/ HC336.26.D48 1998

Detention & torture in South Africa: psychological, legal & historical studies/ HV8599.S6.F67 1987

Determinants of economic growth: a cross-country empirical study/ HD75.B365 1997

Determinants of fertility in developing countries/ HB901.D48 1983

Deterrence and juvenile crime: results from a national policy experiment/ HV9104.S323 1990

Detroit divided/ HC108.D6.F37 2000

Deutsche Bank and the Nazi economic war against the Jews: the expropriation of Jewish-owned property, The/ HG3058.D4

Developing countries and regional economic cooperation/ HC59.7.B6893 1994

Developing country debt and economic performance/ HJ8899.D4815 1989

Developing country debt and the world economy/ HJ8899.D482 1989

Developing decision-making skills for business/ HD30.23.S556 2001

Developing poverty: the state, labor market deregulation, and the informal economy in Costa Rica and the Dominican Republic/ HD2346.C8.I89 2000

Developing public finance in emerging market economies/ HJ1000.7.D48 1993

Development aid: a guide to national and international agencies/ HG3881.D43 1988

Development and change in highland Yemen/ HN664.Z9.C678 1988

Development and crisis in Brazil, 1930-1983/ HC187.P392213 1984

Development and democracy: new perspectives on an old debate/ HD82.D3874 2003

Development and democracy in India/ HC435.2.S494 1999

Development and democratization in the Third World: myths, hopes, and realities/ HC59.69.D45 1992

Development and reform of financial systems in Central and Eastern Europe, The/ HG186.E82.D48 1994

Development and underdevelopment: the political economy of global inequality/ HC59.7.D4453 1998

Development dilemma: displacement in India, The/ HC440.E44.P37 1999

Evolution of highland Papua New Guinea societies, The/ GN671.N5.F45 1987

Evolution of Homo Erectus: comparative anatomical studies of an extinct human species, The/ GN284.R54 1990

Evolution of political systems: sociopolitics in small-scale sedentary societies, The/ GN492.E96 1990

Evolution of society; selections from Herbert Spencer's Principles of sociology, The/ HM51.S8112

Evolution of the Polynesian chiefdoms, The/ GN670.K56 1984

Evolution of United States budgeting: changing fiscal and financial concepts/ HJ2051.M49 1989

Evolution of women's asylums since 1500: from refuges for ex-prostitutes to shelters for battered women, The/ HV1448.I8.C65 1992

Evolution, animal 'rights' & the environment/ HV4708.R45 2000

Evolutionary biology and human social behavior: an anthropological perspective/ GN365.9.E96

Evolutionary theory of economic change, An/ HB71.N44 1982

Evolve!: succeeding in the digital culture of tomorrow/ HC79.I55.K358 2001

Evolving coast, The/ GB451.2.D39 1994

Evolving female: a life-history perspective, The/ GN281.E93 1997

Exchange rate theory and practice/ HG205. 1984

Exchange rates and inflation/ HG3821.D69 1988

Excluded Americans: homelessness and housing policies, The/ HD7293.T77 1990

Executing justice: the moral meaning of the death penalty/ HV8698.S74 1998

Exemplary economists: introducing economics of the 20th century/ HB76.E96 2000

Exercise psychology/ GV481.2.W55 1992

Exotics at home: anthropologies, others, American modernity/ GN33.D5 1998

Expenditures of older Americans/ HG179.R76 1997

Experience and enlightenment: socialization for cultural change in eighteenth-century Scotland/ HN398.S3.C35 1983

Experience of women: pattern and change in nineteenth-century Europe, An/ HQ1588.R6 1982

Experiencing the new genetics: family and kinship on the medical frontier/ GN480.2.F56 2000

Experimental methods: a primer for economists/ HB131.F75 1994

Explaining buyer behavior: central concepts and philosophy of science issues/ HF5415.32.O74 1992

Explorations into constitutional economics/ HB846.8.B79 1989

Explorers and discoverers of the world/ G200.E88 1993

Exploring sport and exercise psychology/ GV706.4.E96 2002

Export restraint and the new protectionism: the political economy of discriminatory trade restrictions/ HF1414.5.J66 1994

Export-import theory, practices, and procedures/ HF1414.4.S49 2000

Extending families: the social networks of parents and their children/ HM131.E97 1990

Extinct humans/ GN281.4.T39 2000

Eye on the flesh: fashions of masculinity in the early twentieth century/ GT720.B67 1996

F1rst among equals: how to manage a group of professionals/ HD66.M3946 2002

Fabric of Chinese society; a study of the social life of a Chinese county seat, HN680.C55.F7 1969

Fabulous kingdom: the exploration of the Arctic, A/ G608.O33 2001

Faces of feminism: a study of feminism as a social movement/ HQ1154.B268 1981

Faces of feminism: an activist's reflections on the women's movement/ HQ1426.T64 1997

Faces of poverty: portraits of women and children on welfare/ HV1445.B47 1995

Facework/ HM132.C86 1994

Facilitating organization change: lessons from complexity science/ HD58.8.O47 2001

Facing life; youth and the family in American history, HQ796.H256

Facing the mirror: older women and beauty shop culture/ HQ1064.U5.F84 1997

Facing the storm: portraits of Black lives in rural South Africa/ HN801.A8.K44 1988

Facing total war: German society, 1914-1918/ HN460.S6.K613 1984

Facing up to management faddism: a new look at an old force/ HD31.B7417 2001

Facing West: Americans and the opening of the Pacific/ HF3043.P48 1994

Facing zero population growth: reactions and interpretations, past and present/ HB871.S6514

Fact and fancy in television regulation: an economic study of policy alternatives/ HE8700.8.L48

Fact book on aging/ HQ1064.U5.V494 1990

Factory daughters: gender, household dynamics, and rural industrialization in Java/ HD6194.Z6.J388 1992

Facts about "drug abuse", The/ HV5825.D772 1980

Facts and fairy tales about female labor, family, and fertility: a seven-country comparison, 1850-1990/ HD6162.P68 1993

Facts of life: the creation of sexual knowledge in Britain, 1650-1950, The/ HQ18.G7.P67 1995

Facts on File dictionary of marine science, The/ GC9.F28 2001

Fading miracle: four decades of market economy in Germany, The/ HC286.G54 1992

Failed revolutions: social reform and the limits of legal imagination/ HN65.D37 1994

Failure and progress: the bright side of the dismal science/ HD87.L44 1993

Failure is impossible: Susan B. Anthony in her own words/ HQ1413.A55.S48 1995

Failure of U.S. tax policy: revenue and politics, The/ HJ2362.P65 1996

Fair play: sports, values, and society/ GV706.5.S56 1991

Fair sex, family size and structure in Britain, 1900-39/ HB995.G55 1982

Fairbridge: empire and child migration/ HV887.G5.S47 1998

Fairy tale as myth/myth as fairy tale/ GR550.Z56 1994

Fall: a comparative study of the end of communism in Czechoslovakia, East Germany, Hungary and Poland, The/ HX240.7.A6 S29

Fall of the Bell system: a study in prices and politics, The/ HE8846.A55.T44 1987

Fall of the planter class in the British Caribbean, 1763-1833; a study in social and economic history, The/ HC157.B8.R3 1963

Fallen women, problem girls: unmarried mothers and the professionalization of social work, 1890-1945/ HV700.5.K86 1993

Falling from grace: the experience of downward mobility in the American middle class/ HN90.S65 N48 1989

False spring, A/ GV865.J67.A34

False start in Africa. HC502.D8413 1966

Families against the city: middle class homes of industrial Chicago, 1872-1890. HQ557.C5.S45

Families in former times: kinship, household, and sexuality/ HQ623.F5513

Families that work: children in a changing world/ HQ734.F228 1982

Families we choose: lesbians, gays, kinship/ HQ76.3.U5.W48 1991

Family and favela: the reproduction of poverty in Rio de Janeiro/ HC189.R4.P56 1997

Family and gender in the Pacific: domestic contradictions and the colonial impact/ GN663.F36 1989

Family and household in medieval England/ HQ615.F64 2001

Family and kinship in Chinese society. HQ667.F3

Family and the female life course: the women of Verviers, Belgium, 1849-1880/ HQ1655.V47.A47 1988

Family at risk: issues and trends in family preservation services, The/ HV699.B49 1997

Family bonds: adoption and the politics of parenting/ HV875.55.B38 1993

Family change and family policies in Great Britain, Canada, New Zealand, and the United States/ HV700.C64.F35 1997

Family in Greek history, The/ HQ662.5.A25 1998

Family in Imperial Russia: new lines of historical research, The/ HQ637.F35

Family in Italy from antiquity to the present, The/ HQ629.F36 1991

Family in Soviet Russia, The/ HQ637.G37

Family in transition; rethinking marriage, sexuality, child rearing, and family organization HQ518.S56 1971

Family leave policy: the political economy of work and family in America/ HD6066.U5.W57 2001

Family man: fatherhood, housework, and gender equity/ HQ503.C65 1996

Family matters: secrecy and disclosure in the history of adoption/ HV875.55.C38 1998

Family of adoption, The/ HV875.P38 1998

Family planning and population control: the challenges of a successful movement/ HQ766.B143 1989

Family planning on a crowded planet. HB875.Y35

Family planning sourcebook/ HQ766.5.U5.F3455 2001

Family power in southern Italy: the duchy of Gaeta and its neighbours, 850-1139/ HT653.I8.S59 1995

Family secret: domestic violence in America, The/ HQ809.3.U5.S77 1983

Family ties: enduring relations between parents and their grown children/ HQ755.86.L64 1996

Family values: two moms and their son/ HQ75.53.B87 1993

Family, fields, and ancestors: constancy and change in China's social and economic history, 1550-1949/ HN733.E25 1988

Family, population and development in Africa/ HB3661.A3.F365 1997

Family-centered policies and practices: international implications/ HV697.F353 2001

Family-centered social work practice/ HV699.H35 1983

Famine in Africa: causes, responses, and prevention/ HC800.Z9 F388 1999

Famine, disease, and the social order in early modern society/ HC260.F3.F36 1989

Famous first facts about sports/ GV571.F73 2001

Fanny Wright: rebel in America/ HQ1413.D2.E25 1984

Fantasizing the feminine in Indonesia/ HQ1752.S43 1996

FAO production yearbook. Annuaire FAO de la production. Anuario FAO de produccion. HD1421.P76

Farewell to the factory: auto workers in the late twentieth century/ HD8039.A82.U653 1997

Farm: life inside a women's prison, The/ HV9475.C82.N537 1997

Farm and factory: workers in the Midwest, 1880-1990/ HD8083.M53.N45 1995

Marshall Plan: America, Britain, and the reconstruction of Western Europe, 1947-1952, The/ HC240.H614 1987

Marshall plan: fifty years after, The/ HC240.M27317 2001

Marshall's tendencies: what can economists know?/ HB135.S825 2000

Martha: the life and work of Martha Graham/ GV1785.G7.D4 1992

Marx and Engels on the population bomb; selections from the writings of Marx and Engels dealing with the theories of Thomas Robert Malthus. HB863.M253 1971

Marx and modern economic analysis/ HB97.5.M334194 1991

Marx, Hayek, and utopia/ HX806.S34 1995

Marxian political economy: theory, history, and contemporary relevance/ HB97.5.M5525 2000

Marxism & communism in twentieth-century Mexico/ HX113.C37 1992

Marxism and democracy in Chile: from 1932 to the fall of Allende/ HX198.F38 1988

Marxism and science: analysis of an obsession/ HX541.K54 1994

Marxism and the leap to the kingdom of freedom: the rise and fall of the Communist utopia/ HX39.W17 1995

Marxist economic theory. HB97.5.M2713 1969

Marxist historiography in transformation: East German social history in the 1980s/ HN460.5.A8.M36 1991

Marx's theory of crisis/ HB3714.C57 1994

Mary Douglas: an intellectual biography/ GN21.D68.F37 1999

Mary McDowell, neighbor, HV28.M3 W5

Masculine/ feminine: readings in sexual mythology and the liberation of women. HQ1154.R75

Masculine mystique: the politics of masculinity, The/ HQ1090.3.K55 1995

Masculine woman in America, 1890-1935, The/ HQ1236.5.U6.B45 2001

Masculinities, gender relations, and sport/ GV706.5.M365 2000

Masculinity in crisis: myths, fantasies, and realities/ HQ1090.H68 1994

Masks: faces of culture/ GN419.5.N85 1999

Maslow on management/ HF5548.8.M3754 1998

Masque of femininity: the presentation of woman in everyday life, The/ HQ1219.T74 1995

Mass communications: a comparative introduction/ HM258.L674 1994

Mass media and village life: an Indian study, The/ HN690.Z9.M325 1989

Massine: a biography/ GV1785.M35.G37 1995

Mastering karate/ GV1114.3.B44 2003

Mastering the market: the State and the grain trade in Northern France, 1700-1860/ HD9042.7.N67.M64 1998

Masters of illusion: the World Bank and the poverty of nations/ HC60.C345 1996

Material anthropology: contemporary approaches to material culture/ GN406.M349 1987

Material child: coming of age in Japan and America, The/ HQ799.U65.W45 1993

Material culture/ GN406.G53 1999

Material girls: making sense of feminist cultural theory/ HM101.W225 1995

Maternal justice: Miriam Van Waters and the female reform tradition/ HV8978.V35.F74 1996

Maternity policies and working women/ HD6065.5.U6.K35 1983

Mathematical formulas for economists/ HB135.L83 2002

Mathematical methods and models for economists/ HB137.F83 2000

Mathematical theory of sampling, The/ HA33.H4

Mathematics for business and consumers/ HF5694.L36 1988

Mathematics for economics and finance: methods and modelling/ HB135.A62 1996

Mathematics for innumerate economists/ HB135.K47 1982

Mating and marriage/ GN484.3.M38 1990

Matter of interest: reexamining money, debt, and real economic growth, A/ HC106.3.H544 1991

Matter, materiality, and modern culture/ GN406.G73 2000

Mawson's will: the greatest polar survival story ever written/ G875.M33.B53 2000

Max Weber: an introduction to his life and work/ HM22.G3.W446813 1988

Max Weber: politics and the spirit of tragedy/ H59.W4.D54 1996

Max Weber on the methodology of the social sciences; H61.W4

Max Weber's methodologies: interpretation and critique/ HM511.E45 2002

Max Weber's sociology of intellectuals/ HM213.S22 1992

Maximum feasible misunderstanding; community action in the war on poverty HC110.P63.M6

Maximum fitness :the complete guide to cross training/ Smith, contributions by M. Laurel Cutlip and James C. Villepigue. GV481.S6443 2001

Maynard Keynes: an economist's biography/ HB103.K47.M563 1992

McGraw-Hill encyclopedia of economics, The/ HB61.E55 1994

McGraw-Hill encyclopedia of quality terms & concepts, The/ HD62.15.C668 1995

McGraw-Hill guide to writing a high-impact business plan: a proven blueprint for entrepreneurs, The/ HD30.28.A75 1995

Meaning and power in a Southeast Asian realm/ GN635.I65.E76 1989

Meaning and sources of marketing theory, The/ HF5415.H178

Measurement and interpretation in accounting: a living systems theory approach/ HJ9745.S92 1989

Measurement concepts in physical education and exercise science/ GV436.M42 1989

Measurement in physical education/ GV436.M37 1978

Measurement nightmare: how the theory of constraints can resolve conflicting strategies, policies, and measures, The/ HD69.T46 S65 2000

Measurement of labor cost, The/ HC106.3.C714 vol. 48

Measures of quality and high performance: simple tools and lessons learned from America's most successful corporations/ HD62.15.H623 1998

Measuring and analyzing behavior in organizations: advances in measurement and data analysis/ HD58.8.M43 2002

Measuring corporate environmental performance: best practices for costing and managing an effective environmental strategy/ HD30.255.E67 1996

Measuring Cuban economic performance/ HC152.5.P47 1987

Measuring the benefits of clean air and water/ HC79.E5.K578 1984

Measuring the condition of the world's poor: the physical quality of life index/ HC59.7.M592 1979

Measuring the effectiveness of image and linkage advertising: the nitty-gritty of maxi-marketing/ HF6161.B4.W67 1996

Meat on the hoof; the hidden world of Texas football. GV939.S43.A35

Media and the American mind: from Morse to McLuhan/ HN90.M3.C96 1982

Media in American politics: contents and consequences, The/ HE8689.7.P6.P35 1998

Media power in politics/ HN90.M3 M43 2000

Media, culture, and morality/ HM101.T44 1994

Media, sports & society/ GV742.M33 1989

Medicaid since 1980: costs, coverage, and the shifting alliance between the federal government and the states/ HD7102.U4.C638 1994

Medicine society, The/ HV5825.S393 1992

Medieval expansion of Europe, The/ G89.P48 1988

Medieval games: sports and recreations in feudal society/ GV575.C372 1992

Medieval Iceland: society, sagas, and power/ HN553.B96 1988

Medieval maps/ GA221.H37 1991

Medieval misogyny and the invention of Western romantic love/ HQ1143.B56 1991

Medieval super-companies: a study of the Peruzzi Company of Florence, The/ HF416.H86 1994

Medieval women/ HQ1143.M43, HQ1143.P68 1997

Medieval women: a social history of women in England, 450-1500/ HQ1147.G7.L49 1995

Mediterranean city in transition: social change and urban development, The/ HT384.G8.L46 1990

Mediterranean countrymen; essays in the social anthropology of the Mediterranean. HN380.M4.P5

Medium of the video game, The/ GV1469.3.M43 2002

Meeting of the minds: creating the market-based enterprise/ HF5415.2.B333 1995

Megatrends Asia: eight Asian megatrends that are reshaping our world/ HC412.N2433 1996

Meme machine, The/ HM291.B535 1999

Memories of Chicano history: the life and narrative of Bert Corona/ HD8073.C67.G37 1994

Memory and the postcolony: African anthropology and the critique of power/ GN645.M47 1998

Memory in oral traditions: the cognitive psychology of epic, ballads, and counting-out rhymes/ GR67.R83 1995

Memos to the president: a guide through macroeconomics for the busy policymaker/ HB172.5.S365 1992

Men and wealth in the United States, 1850-1870/ HC110.W4.S64

Men as caregivers: theory, research, and service implications/ HV1441.4.M44 2002

Men as caregivers to the elderly: understanding and aiding unrecognized family support/ HV1461.K39 1990

Men at midlife/ HQ1059.5.U5.F37 1981

Men giving care: reflections of husbands and sons/ HV1461.H39 1997

Men who rape: the psychology of the offender/ HV6558.G76

Men, ships, and the sea, G540.V646

Men, women, and household work/ HQ1075.5.A8.G66 1994

Men, women, and work: class, gender, and protest in the New England shoe industry, 1780-1910/ HD8039.B72.U63 1988

Men's friendships/ HQ1090.M47 1992

Men's ideas/women's realities: Popular science, 1870-1915/ HQ1426.M46 1985

Mental retardation: its social context and social consequences. HV3006.A4.F33

Mentally retarded child and his family: a multidisciplinary handbook, The/ HV891.K58 1976

Mercantile states and the world oil cartel, 1900-1939/ HD9560.5.N67 1994

Merce Cunningham: dancing in space and time/ GV1785.C85 M48 1998

Merchant capital and economic decolonization: the United Africa Company, 1929-1987/ HC800.F543 1994

Merchant capital and the roots of state power in Senegal, 1930-1985/ HC1045.B65 1992

Sea has many voices: oceans policy for a complex world, The/ GC1023.15.S43 1994

Sea level rise: history and consequences/ GC89.S429 2000

Sea levels, land levels, and tide gauges/ GC89.E54 1991

Seafaring labour: the merchant marine of Atlantic Canada, 1820-1914/ HD8039.S4.O67 1989

Sea-level change/ GC89.S413 1990

Search and destroy: African-American males in the criminal justice system/ HV9950.M55 1996

Search and destroy; a report. HV8148.C42.C65 1973

Search for a new Eden: James Pierrepont Greaves (1777-1842), the sacred socialist and his followers/ HX51.L494 1999

Search for Eve, The/ GN281.4.B76 1990

Search for labour market flexibility: the European economies in transition, The/ HD8376.5.S42 1988

Searching for a better society: the Peruvian economy from 1950/ HC227.S435 1999

Searching for alternatives: drug-control policy in the United States/ HV5825.S396 1991

Searching for life: the grandmothers of the Plaza de Mayo and the disappeared children of Argentina/ HV6322.3.A7.A74 1999

Searching for safety/ H91.W56 1988

Searching for the Franklin expedition: the Arctic journal of Robert Randolph Carter/ G665 1850 .C36 1998

Season on the brink: a year with Bob Knight and the Indiana Hoosiers, A/ GV884.K58 F44 1986

Second chances: men, women, and children a decade after divorce/ HQ834.W358 1989

Second conquest of Latin America: coffee, henequen, and oil during the export boom, 1850-1930, The/ HD9199.L382.S4 1998

Second home: orphan asylums and poor families in America/ HV983.H33 1997

Second nature: the history and implications of Australia as Aboriginal landscape/ GF801.H36 2000

Second thoughts: myths and morals of U.S. economic history/ HC103.S43 1993

Second twenty years at Hull-House, September 1909 to September 1929: with a record of a growing world consciousness, The/ HV4196.C4.H72

Second wind: the memoirs of an opinionated man/ GV884.R86.A35

Secondary cities of Argentina: the social history of Corrientes, Salta, and Mendoza, 1850-1910/ HN270.C67.S36 1988

Secret paths: women in the new midlife/ HQ1059.4.A68 1995

Secret soldiers: special forces in the war against terrorism/ HV6431.H363 2000

Secularism, gender and the state in the Middle East: the Egyptian women's movement/ HQ1793.A75 2000

Secure from rash assault: sustaining the Victorian environment/ GF551.W56 1999

Securing peace in the Middle East: project on economic transition/ HC415.25.Z7.W47915 1994

Securing South Africa's democracy: defense, development, and security in transition/ HV8272.A3.C39 1997

Securing the fruits of labor: the American concept of wealth distribution, 1765-1900/ HC110.I5.H87 1998

Securing the future: investing in children from birth to college/ HV741.S385 2000

Security and economy in the Third World/ HC59.72.D4.B35 1988

Seed and the soil: gender and cosmology in Turkish village society, The/ GR450.D45 1992

Seeds of trouble: government policy and land rights in Nyasaland, 1946-1964/ HD997.Z63.B35 1993

Seeing language in sign: the work of William C. Stokoe/ HV2534.S76.M35 1996

Seldom ask, never tell: labor and discourse in Appalachia/ HN79.A127.P83 2000

Selected essays on economic planning/ HD74.5.K35 1986

Selected papers of Elizabeth Cady Stanton and Susan B. Anthony, The/ HQ1410.A2525 1997

Selected writings in sociology & social philosophy. HM57.M33 1964

Self-destruction in the promised land: a psychocultural biology of American suicide/ HV6548.U5.K87 1989

Self-employment: a labor market perspective/ HD6072.6.U5.A76 1991

Self-esteem at work: research, theory, and practice/ HF5548.8.B686 1988

Self-inflicted wounds: from LBJ's guns and butter to Reagan's voodoo economics/ HC106.6.R69 1994

Self-made map: cartographic writing in early modern France, The/ GA863.5.A1.C66 1996

Self-management: economic liberation of man: selected readings/ HD5650.S4

Self-organizing economy, The/ HB199.K75 1996

Selling free enterprise: the business assault on labor and liberalism, 1945-60/ HB95.F66 1994

Selling hope: state lotteries in America/ HG6126.C55 1989

Selling of contraception: the Dalkon Shield case, sexuality, and women's autonomy, The/ HD9995.C64.A234 1992

Selling of the South: the Southern crusade for industrial development, 1936-1980, The/ HC107.A13.C65 1982

Selling our security: the erosion of America's assets/ HC110.T4.T65 1992

Selling radio: the commercialization of American broadcasting, 1920-1934/ HE8698.S6 1994

Selling to a segmented market: the lifestyle approach/ HF5415.127.S94 1990

Sendero Luminoso and the threat of narcoterrorism/ HV6433.P4.T37 1990

Sentiments and acts/ HM291.D467 1993

Separate societies: poverty and inequality in U.S. cities/ HV4045.G65 1992

Separated and divorced women/ HQ834.H33

Separation of commercial and investment banking: the Glass-Steagall Act revisited and reconsidered, The/ HG2461.B46 1990

Separatism and women's community/ HQ1190.5.U6.S58 1995

Serenade of suffering: a portrait of Middle East terrorism, 1968-1993/ HV6433.M5.C53 1999

Serial killers: death and life in America's wound culture/ HV6529.S45 1998

Serial offenders: current thought, recent findings/ HV6049.S47 2000

Serious & violent juvenile offenders: risk factors and successful interventions/ HV9104.S42 1998

Serious fun: a history of spectator sports in the USSR/ GV623.E27 1993

Servants and masters in eighteenth-century France: the uses of loyalty/ HD8039.D52.F85 1983

Service clubs in American society: Rotary, Kiwanis, and Lions/ HS2723.C48 1993

Service industries USA: industry analyses, statistics, and leading organizations. HD9981.1.S47

Service management and marketing: managing the moments of truth in service competition/ HD9980.5.G776 1990

Serving the urban poor/ HV743.N49.L694 1992

Serving women: household service in nineteenth-century America/ HD6072.2.U5.D82 1983

Servitude in modern times/ HT867.B87 2000

Seven daughters of Eve, The/ GN289.S94 2001

Seven days a week: women and domestic service in industrializing America/ HD6072.2.U5.K37

Seventy years of life and labor: an autobiography/ HD8073.G6.A3 1984

Sex and advantage: a comparative, macro-structural theory of sex stratification/ HQ21.C449 1984

Sex and citizenship in antebellum America/ HQ1236.5.U6.I83 1998

Sex and reason/ HQ16.P67 1992

Sex and revolution: women in socialist Cuba/ HQ1507.S63 1996

Sex discrimination in the labour market: the case for comparable worth/ HD6061.P47 1994

Sex in the heartland/ HQ18.M53.B35 1999

Sex in the Western world: the development of attitudes and behaviour/ HQ31.F65413 1991

Sex roles, population, and development in West Africa: policy-related studies on work and demographic issues/ HB3665.5.A3.S49 1987

Sex, class, and culture/ HQ1426.R72 1986

Sex, dissidence, and damnation: minority groups in the Middle Ages/ HN11.R49 1990

Sex, gender, and the politics of ERA: a state and the nation/ HQ1236.5.U6.M38 1990

Sex, man, and society. HQ12.M57

Sex, race, and science: eugenics in the deep South/ HQ755.5.U5.L37 1995

Sex, violence & power in sports: rethinking masculinity/ GV706.5.M47 1994

Sexed work: gender, race, and resistance in a Brooklyn drug market/ HV5824.W6.M345 1997

Sexing the body: gender politics and the construction of sexuality/ HQ1075.F39 2000

Sexing the self: gendered positions in cultural studies/ HQ1206.P745 1993

Sexual assault and child sexual abuse: a national directory of victim/survivor services and prevention programs/ HV6561.W45 1989

Sexual attraction and childhood association: a Chinese brief for Edward Westermarck/ GT2783.5.W65 1995

Sexual behavior in modern China: report on the nationwide survey of 20,000 men and women = [Chung-kuo tang tai hsing wen hua]/ HQ18.C6.C53813 1997

Sexual behavior in the human male HQ18.U5.K5

Sexual contract, The/ HQ1206.P35 1988

Sexual exploitation: rape, child sexual abuse, and workplace harassment/ HV6565.C2.R87 1984

Sexual meanings, the cultural construction of gender and sexuality/ GN479.65.S49

Sexual politics of meat: a feminist-vegetarian critical theory, The/ HV4708.A25 1990

Sexual politics, sexual communities: the making of a homosexual minority in the United States, 1940-1970/ HQ76.8.U5.D45 1983

Sexual politics. HQ1154.M5

Sexual practices & the medieval church/ HQ14.B84 1982

Sexual preference, its development in men and women/ HQ76.B438 1981

Sexual salvation: affirming women's sexual rights and pleasures/ HQ29.M46 1994

Sexual trafficking in children: an investigation of the child sex trade, The/ HQ144.C35 1988

Sexual variance in society and history/ HQ12.B84

Sexuality and marriage in colonial Latin America/ HQ560.5.S48 1989

Sexuality and the curriculum: the politics and practices of sexuality education/ HQ57.5.A3.S489 1992

Sexuality, society, and feminism/ HQ21.S478 2000

Social and economic history of Britain, 1760-1980, A/ HN385.G7 1982

Social and economic modernization in eastern Germany from Honecker to Kohl/ HN460.5.A8.D46 1993

Social and political change in revolutionary China: the Taihang Base area in the War of Resistance to Japan, 1937-1945/ HN740.T34

Social and political development in post-reform China/ HC427.92.M635 1999

Social anthropology/ GN316.L4 1982

Social anthropology in Polynesia: a review of research/ GN670.K43 1980

Social attitudes in Japan: trends and cross-national perspectives/ HN723.5.S578 2000

Social capitalism: a study of Christian democracy and thewelfare state/ HN373.5.K47 1995

Social casework: a behavioral approach/ HV43.S34

Social change and applied anthropology: essays in honor of David W. Brokensha/ GN397.5.S67 1990

Social change and labor unrest in Brazil since 1945/ HD5353.S26 1993

Social change and the life course/ HM13.S49 1988

Social change in Melanesia: development and history/ HN930.9.A8S55 2000

Social change in the Southwest, 1350-1880/ HN79.A165.H35 1989

Social change in Western Europe/ HN373.5.C78 1999

Social change philanthropy in America/ HV91.R33 1990

Social change, social welfare, and social science/ HV31.T39 1991

Social costs of transformation to a market economy in post-socialist countries: the case of Poland, the Czech Republic, and Hungary/ HC340.3.A56 1999

Social currents in Eastern Europe: the sources and meaning of the great transformation/ HN373.5.R36 1991

Social Darwinism in European and American thought, 1860-1945: nature as model and nature as threat/ HM106.H38 1997

Social democracy & industrial militancy: the Labour Party, the trade unions, and incomes policy, 1945-1974/ HC260.W24.P35

Social democracy and rational choice: the Scandinavian experience and beyond/ HV31.M55 1994

Social demography/ HB849.S62

Social demography. HB885.F58

Social development in Africa: strategies, policies, and programmes after the Lagos Plan/ HN777.S63 1991

Social dimension of trade unionism in India/ HD6812.S56 1984

Social dominance: an intergroup theory of social hierarchy and oppression/ HM131.S5832 1999

Social evolutionism: a critical history/ GN360.S25 1990

Social fabric and spatial structure in colonial Latin America/ GF514.S63

Social feminism/ HQ1599.E5.B57 1989

Social history of an Indonesian town, The/ HN710.M6.G4 1975

Social history of Greece and Rome, A/ HN10.G7.G73 1992

Social history of housing, 1815-1970, A/ HD7334.A3.B87

Social history of leisure since 1600, A/ GV14.45.C76 1990

Social history of nineteenth-century France, A/ HN425.P75 1987

Social history of the English countryside, A/ HN398.E5.M57 1990

Social history of the fool, A/ GT3670.B45 1984

Social history of Western Europe, 1450-1720: tensions and solidarities among rural people, A/ HN373.W37 1984

Social indicators of development. HC59.69.S63

Social inequality in a Portuguese hamlet: land, late marriage, and bastardy, 1870-1978/ HN600.F66.O5413 1987

Social inequality in Oaxaca: a history of resistance and change/ HN120.O29.M87 1991

Social influence processes and prevention/ HM291.S58837 1990

Social investment almanac: a comprehensive guide to socially responsible investing, The/ HG4527.K525 1992

Social issues in sport/ Mike Sleap. GV706.5.S59 1998

Social justice in a diverse society/ HM216.S553 1997

Social life in an Indian slum/ HD7361.A3.W53

Social life of information, The/ HM851.B76 2000

Social marketing: strategies for changing public behavior/ HF5415.122.K68 1989

Social meanings of suicide, The/ HV6545.D6

Social mobility and class structure in modern Britain/ HN400.S6 G64 1987

Social mobility in contemporary Japan: educational credentials, class and the labour market in a cross-national perspective/ HN730.Z9.S654 1992

Social movements: a cognitive approach/ HN17.5.E99 1991

Social movements: ideologies, interests, and identities/ HN17.5.O24 1992

Social movements in advanced capitalism: the political economy and cultural construction of social activism/ HN13.B84 2000

Social movements in India: a review of the literature/ HN683.S5 1990

Social movements in politics: a comparative study/ HN17.5.Z57 1997

Social norms/ HM676.S63 2001

Social order of the slum; ethnicity and territory in the inner city, The/ HN80.C5.S97

Social organization of juvenile justice, The/ HV9069.C514

Social organization of leisure in human society, The/ GV14.C47

Social organization of sexuality: sexual practices in the United States, The/ HQ18.U5.S59 1994

Social origins of democratic socialism in Jamaica, The/ HC154.K45 1992

Social origins of dictatorship and democracy: lord and peasant in the making of the modern world/ HN15.M775 1993

Social origins of the modern Middle East, The/ HN656.G47 1987

Social patterns in normal aging: findings from the Duke longitudinal study/ HQ1064.U5.P26

Social policy in Britain: themes and issues/ HN385.5.A43 1996

Social policy in the United States: future possibilities in historical perspective/ HN57.S525 1995

Social policy of Nazi Germany, The/ HN445.G85 1971

Social psychology: handbook of basic principles/ HM251.S6743 1996

Social psychology of absenteeism/ HD5115.C47 1982

Social psychology of consumer behaviour, The/ HB801.B267 2002

Social psychology of everyday life, The/ HM251.A782 1991

Social psychology of material possessions: to have is to be, The/ HM211.D58 1992

Social psychology of minority influence, The/ HM291.M772513 1991

Social psychology of time: new perspectives, The/ HM299.S585 1988

Social relations and ideas: essays in honour of R.H. Hilton/ HD141.S57 1983

Social responsibilities of business corporations; HD60.5.U5.C66

Social responsibilities of business, company, and community, 1900-1960, The/ HD60.5.U5.H4

Social responsibility in marketing: a proactive and profitable marketing management strategy/ HF5415.13.S24 1992

Social rules: origin, character, logic, change/ GN493.3.S68 1996

Social science and the self: personal essays on an art form/ H35.K68 1991

Social science encyclopedia, The/ H41.S63 1996

Social scientists and farm politics in the age of Roosevelt. HD1761.K5

Social scientists meet the media/ HM258.S586 1994

Social security: beyond the rhetoric of crisis/ HD7125.S5992 1988

Social security policy in Britain/ HD7165.H55 1990

Social Security, the first half-century/ HD7125.S5994 1988

Social service organizations/ HV88.S59

Social significance of sport: an introduction to the sociology of sport, The/ GV706.5.M37 1989

Social statistics HA29.B59 1972

Social stratification in India: issues and themes/ HN690.Z9.S6438 1997

Social structure and rural development in the Third World/ HN981.C6.B47 1992

Social structure of modern Britain, The/ HN385.5.J6 1979

Social support networks: informal helping in the human services/ HV40.S617 1983

Social survey in historical perspective, 1880-1940, The/ HN29.S645 1992

Social theory for action: how individuals and organizations learn to change/ H62.W457 1991

Social theory in a changing world: conceptions of modernity/ H61.D3377 1999

Social theory of modern societies: Anthony Giddens and his critics/ HM24.S5444 1989

Social welfare development in East Asia/ HN720.5.A8

Social welfare in India/ HV393.G87 1989

Social welfare in Mauritius: a critical analysis of social service provisions/ HV470.5.L56 1996

Social welfare in Third World development/ HV525.J66 1989

Social work in the health field: a care perspective/ HV687.C68 2000

Social work interventions: helping people of color/ HV3176.H46 1994

Social work interview: a guide for human service professionals, The/ HV43.K26 1997

Social work practice in maternal and child health/ HV699.C535 1990

Social work practice with immigrants and refugees/ HV4010.S629 2000

Social work processes/ HV37.C62 1999

Social worlds, personal lives: an introduction to social psychology/ HM251.S2623 1991

Socialism after communism: the new market socialism/ HX73.P54 1995

Socialism, politics, and equality: hierarchy and change in Eastern Europe and the USSR/ HN380.Z9.S638

Socialist economies in transition: a primer on semi-reformed systems, The/ HC244.C35 1991

Socialist system: the political economy of communism, The/ HX73.K6715 1992

Socialist utopia in the new South: the Ruskin colonies in Tennessee and Georgia, 1894-1901, A/ HX655.S68.B78 1996